PSYCHIATRY

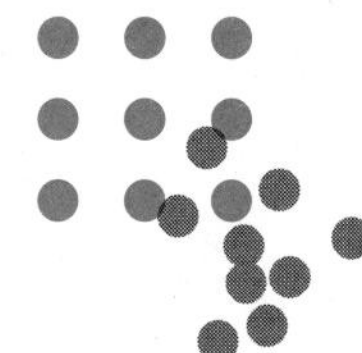

Section Editors

Special Clinical Settings and Problems

Stephen M. Goldfinger, MD
Assistant Professor of Psychiatry
Harvard Medical School
Senior Psychiatrist
Massachusetts Department of Mental Health
Boston, Massachusetts

Therapeutics

Samuel J. Keith, MD
Professor of Psychiatry and Psychology
Chairman, Department of Psychiatry
University of New Mexico
School of Medicine
Albuquerque, New Mexico

A Developmental Perspective on Normal Domains of Mental and Behavioral Function

David A. Mrazek, MD, FRC Psych
Professor of Psychiatry, Behavioral Sciences, and Pediatrics
The George Washington University School of Medicine
Chairman of Psychiatry and Behavioral Sciences
Director, Neuroscience Center
Children's Research Institute
Children's National Medical Center
Washington, DC

Scientific Foundations of Psychiatry

Charles B. Nemeroff, MD, PhD
Reunette W. Harris Professor and Chairman
Department of Psychiatry and Behavioral Sciences
Emory University School of Medicine
Chief of Psychiatry
Emory University Hospital
Atlanta, Georgia

Disorders

Harold Alan Pincus, MD
Deputy Medical Director
Director, Office of Research
American Psychiatric Association
Clinical Professor
Department of Psychiatry and Behavioral Sciences
The George Washington University
Washington, DC
Clinical Professor of Psychiatry
Uniformed Services University of the Health Sciences
Bethesda, Maryland

Manifestations of Psychiatric Illness

Andrew E. Skodol, MD
Professor of Clinical Psychiatry
Columbia University College of Physicians and Surgeons
Research Psychiatrist
New York State Psychiatric Institute
New York, New York

Approaches to the Patient

Robert J. Ursano, MD
Professor and Chairman
Department of Psychiatry
Uniformed Services University of the Health Sciences
F. Edward Hebert School of Medicine
Bethesda, Maryland

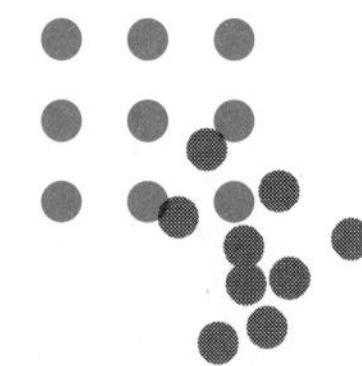

Associate Section Editors

Childhood Disorders

Harold S. Koplewicz, MD
Vice-Chairman for Child and Adolescent Psychiatry
New York University Medical Center
New York, New York

Substance Use Disorders

Thomas R. Kosten, MD
Professor of Psychiatry
Director, Division of Substance Abuse
Yale University
New Haven, Connecticut

Therapeutics

Gregory Franchini, MD
Assistant Professor
Director of Medical Student Education in Psychiatry
Department of Psychiatry
University of New Mexico
School of Medicine
Albuquerque, New Mexico

Alison Reeve, MD
Assistant Professor
Department of Psychiatry
University of New Mexico
School of Medicine
Neuropsychiatric Consultant to Continuum of Care Project
University of New Mexico
Albuquerque, New Mexico

•TASMAN
•KAY
•LIEBERMAN

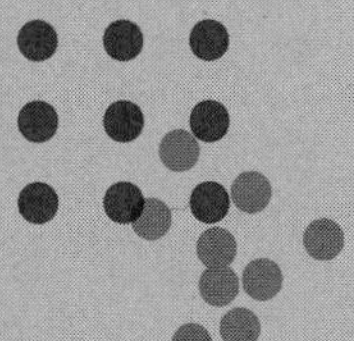

PSYCHIATRY

VOLUME 1

Allan Tasman, MD
Professor and Chair, Department of Psychiatry
and Behavioral Sciences
School of Medicine
University of Louisville
Louisville, Kentucky

Jerald Kay, MD
Professor and Chair
Department of Psychiatry
Wright State University School of Medicine
Dayton, Ohio

Jeffrey A. Lieberman, MD
Vice-Chairman of Psychiatry
Professor of Psychiatry, Pharmacology, and Radiology
University of North Carolina School of Medicine
Chapel Hill, North Carolina

W.B. SAUNDERS COMPANY
Harcourt Brace & Company
Philadelphia London Toronto Montreal Sydney Tokyo

W.B. SAUNDERS COMPANY
A Division of Harcourt Brace & Company

The Curtis Center
Independence Square West
Philadelphia, Pennsylvania 19106

Library of Congress Cataloging-in-Publication Data

Psychiatry / [edited by] Allan Tasman, Jerald Kay, Jeffrey A. Lieberman.—1st ed.

p. cm.

ISBN 0–7216–5255–7 (set)

I. Tasman, Allan. II. Kay, Jerald. III. Lieberman, Jeffrey A.
[DNLM: 1. Mental Disorders. 2. Psychotherapy. 3. Human Development. 4. Physician-Patient Relations. 5. Psychiatry. WM 140 P975 1997]

RC454.P7816 1997 616.89—dc20

DNLM/DLC 95-46938

Psychiatry

ISBN 0–7216–5256–5 Volume 1
0–7216–5257–3 Volume 2
0–7216–5255–7 Set

Printed in United States of America.

Last digit is the print number: 9 8 7 6 5 4 3 2 1

With love and thanks to Cathy, Joshua, David, and Sarah, and to my parents, Goodie and Zelda.

A. T.

To my wife Rena, to my children Sarah, Rachel, and Jonathan, and to my parents, Max and Miriam Kay for their extraordinary support and their love.

J. K.

To my father (Howard RIP) and mother (Ruth) who inspired me; and to my wife (Rosemarie) and sons (Jonathan and Jeremy) who supported me then and now.

J. A. L.

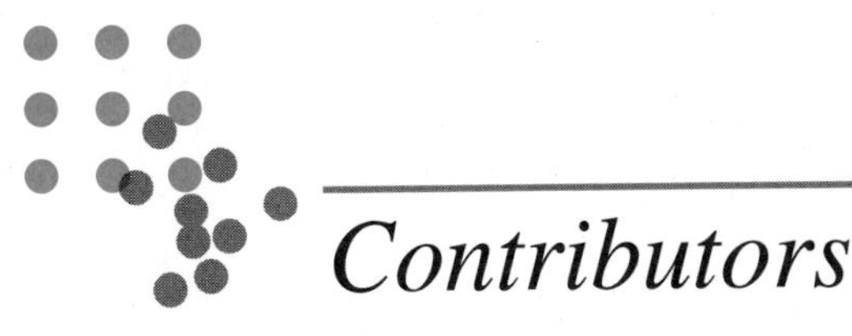

Contributors

Sonia Ancoli-Israel, PhD
Professor, Department of Psychiatry, University of California, San Diego, School of Medicine, La Jolla, CA; Director, Sleep Disorders Clinic, Veterans Affairs Medical Center, San Diego, CA

Martin M. Antony, PhD
Assistant Professor, Department of Psychiatry, University of Toronto; Psychologist, Anxiety Disorders Clinic, Clarke Institute of Psychiatry, Toronto, Ontario, Canada

Thomas F. Babor, PhD, MPH
Professor, Department of Psychiatry, University of Connecticut, Farmington, CT

David H. Barlow, PhD
Professor and Director of Clinical Programs, Center for Anxiety and Related Disorders, Boston University, Boston, MA

Mark S. Bauer, MD
Associate Professor, Department of Psychiatry and Human Behavior, Brown University Program in Medicine; Chief, Mental Health and Behavioral Sciences Service, Veterans Affairs Medical Center, Providence, RI

William R. Beardslee, MD
George P. Gardner/Olga M. Monks Professor of Child Psychiatry, Harvard Medical School; Psychiatrist-in-Chief and Chairman, Department of Psychiatry, Children's Hospital, Boston, MA

David Bienenfeld, MD
Associate Professor, Vice Chair, and Director of Residency Training, Department of Psychiatry, Wright State University, Dayton, OH

Robert J. Boland, MD
Assistant Professor, Department of Psychiatry and Human Behavior, Brown University, Providence, RI

Neil W. Boris, MD
Assistant Professor, Division of Infant, Child and Adolescent Psychiatry, Louisiana State University School of Medicine, New Orleans, LA; Clinical Assistant Professor, Departments of Pediatrics and Psychiatry and Human Behavior, Brown University School of Medicine, Providence, RI

Olga Brawman-Mintzer, MD
Assistant Professor, Department of Psychiatry and Behavioral Sciences, Medical University of South Carolina, Charleston, SC

Alan Breier, MD
Chief, Section on Clinical Studies, Experimental Therapeutics Branch, National Institute of Mental Health, National Institutes of Health, Bethesda, MD

Evelyn Bromet, PhD
Professor of Psychiatry and Behavioral Science, School of Medicine, State University of New York at Stony Brook, Stony Brook, NY

Deborah L. Cabaniss, MD
Assistant Clinical Professor of Psychiatry, Columbia University College of Physicians and Surgeons, New York, NY

Kenneth Certa, MD
Clinical Assistant Professor of Psychiatry, Jefferson Medical College; Director, Psychiatric Emergency Services, Thomas Jefferson University Hospital, Philadelphia, PA

Linda Chafetz, RN, DNSc
Associate Professor and Vice-Chair, Department of Mental Health, Community, and Administrative Nursing, University of California, San Francisco, San Francisco, CA

Irene Chatoor, MD
Professor of Psychiatry and Behavioral Sciences, The George Washington University School of Medicine; Director of Infant Psychiatry, Children's Hospital National Medical Center, Washington, DC

John F. Clarkin, PhD
Professor of Clinical Psychology and Psychiatry, Cornell University Medical College, New York, NY; Director of Psychology, New York Hospital–Cornell Medical Center, Westchester Division, White Plains, NY

Keith H. Claypoole, PhD
Assistant Professor, Department of Psychiatry and Behavioral Science, University of Washington School of Medicine; Director, Neuropsychological Assessment Service, University of Washington Hospital, Seattle, WA

Robert B. Clyman, MD
Assistant Professor, Departments of Psychiatry, Behavioral Sciences, and Pediatrics, The George Washington University Medical Center; Research Scientist and Director, Developmental Psychiatry, Children's Hospital National Medical Center, Washington, DC

Edwin H. Cook, MD
Associate Professor of Psychiatry and Pediatrics and Director, Laboratory of Developmental Neurosciences, The University of Chicago, Pritzker School of Medicine, Chicago, IL

Patrick W. Corrigan, PsyD
Associate Professor of Psychiatry, The University of Chicago, Pritzker School of Medicine; Director, University of Chicago Center for Psychiatric Rehabilitation, Chicago, IL

Francine Cournos, MD
Professor of Clinical Psychiatry, Columbia University College of Physicians and Surgeons; Director, Washington Heights Community Service, New York State Psychiatric Institute, New York, NY

Linda W. Craighead, PhD
Associate Professor, Department of Psychology, University of Colorado, Boulder, Boulder, CO

W. Edward Craighead, PhD
Professor, Department of Psychology, University of Colorado, Boulder, Boulder, CO

Martha E. Crotts, MD
Fellow, Section of Child and Adolescent Psychiatry, The University of Chicago, Pritzker School of Medicine, Chicago, IL

Jonathan R. T. Davidson, MD
Professor, Department of Psychiatry and Behavioral Sciences, Duke University Medical Center, Durham, NC

Pedro L. Delgado, MD
Associate Professor of Psychiatry, Director of Research, and Associate Head, Department of Psychiatry, University of Arizona College of Medicine, Tucson, AZ

Joel E. Dimsdale, MD
Professor of Psychiatry and Director, Program in Consultation Psychiatry and Behavioral Medicine, University of California, San Diego, School of Medicine, La Jolla, CA

Ken Duckworth, MD
Instructor in Psychiatry, Harvard Medical School; Medical Director, Continuing Care Service, Massachusetts Mental Health Center, Boston, MA

Jonathan E. Dunn, PhD
Faculty, Department of Psychiatry, California Pacific Medical Center; Member, San Francisco Psychoanalytic Institute, San Francisco, CA

Jane L. Eisen, MD
Assistant Professor, Department of Psychiatry and Human Behavior, Brown University Program in Medicine; Director, Obsessive-Compulsive Disorder Clinic, Butler Hospital, Providence, RI

Richard S. Epstein, MD
Clinical Professor, Uniformed Services University of the Health Sciences, F. Edward Hébert School of Medicine, Bethesda, MD; Clinical Professor, Georgetown University School of Medicine, Washington, DC

Milton Erman, MD
Clinical Professor of Psychiatry, University of California, San Diego, School of Medicine; Scripps Clinic and Research Foundation, La Jolla, CA

Eugene W. Farber, PhD
Assistant Professor, Department of Psychiatry and Behavioral Sciences, Emory University School of Medicine; Clinical Psychologist, Grady Health System, Atlanta, GA

Susan J. Fiester, MD
Private practice, Chevy Chase, MD

Michael B. First, MD
Assistant Professor of Clinical Psychiatry, Columbia University, New York, NY; Editor, DSM-IV Text and Criteria, American Psychiatric Association, Washington, DC

Allen Frances, MD
Chairman, Department of Psychiatry and Behavioral Sciences, Duke University Medical Center, Durham, NC

Gregory Franchini, MD
Assistant Professor, Director of Medical Student Education in Psychiatry, Department of Psychiatry, University of New Mexico School of Medicine, Albuquerque, NM

Robert L. Frierson, MD
Professor of Psychiatry and Director of Consultation/Liaison Psychiatry, University of Louisville School of Medicine; Psychiatrist, Jefferson Alcohol and Drug Abuse Center, Louisville, KY

Robert M. Galatzer-Levy, MD
Lecturer, University of Chicago, Pritzker School of Medicine; Training and Supervising Analyst, Child and Adolescent Supervising Analyst, Institute for Psychoanalysis, Chicago, IL

Alan J. Gelenberg, MD
Professor and Head, Department of Psychiatry, University of Arizona College of Medicine, Tucson, AZ

J. Christian Gillin, MD
Professor of Psychiatry, University of California, San Diego, School of Medicine, La Jolla, CA; Director of Mental Health Clinical Research Center, Veterans Affairs Medical Center, San Diego, CA

Sybil A. Ginsburg, MD
Associate Professor, Department of Psychiatry and Behavioral Science, Emory University School of Medicine; Training and Supervising Psychoanalyst, Emory University Psychoanalytic Institute, Atlanta, GA

Stephen M. Goldfinger, MD
Assistant Professor of Psychiatry, Harvard Medical School; Senior Psychiatrist, Massachusetts Department of Mental Health, Boston, MA

Robert S. Goldman, PhD
Staff, Albert Einstein College of Medicine, Bronx, NY; Chief, Neuropsychology Laboratory, Hillside Hospital, Glen Oaks, NY

Reed D. Goldstein, PhD
Clinical Associate, Department of Psychiatry, University of Pennsylvania School of Medicine; Research Associate, Dave Garroway Laboratory for the Study of Depression, Pennsylvania Hospital; Clinical Consultant, Psychology Department, Institute of Pennsylvania Hospital, Philadelphia, PA

Jackie Gollan, MS
Graduate Student, Department of Psychiatry, Center for Clinical Research, University of Washington, Seattle, WA

Eric Gortner, PhD
Graduate Student, Department of Psychiatry, Center for Clinical Research, University of Washington, Seattle, WA

Michael D. Greenberg, MA
Graduate Student, Department of Psychology, Duke University, Durham, NC

Laurence L. Greenhill, MD
Associate Professor of Clinical Psychiatry, Columbia University College of Physicians and Surgeons; Research Psychiatrist II and Medical Director, Disruptive Behavior Disorders Clinic, New York State Psychiatric Institute, New York, NY

Stanley I. Greenspan, MD
Clinical Professor of Psychiatry, Behavioral Sciences, and Pediatrics, The George Washington University School of Medicine; Faculty, Children's Hospital National Medical Center, Washington, DC

Roland R. Griffiths, PhD
Professor, Department of Psychiatry and Behavioral Sciences and Neuroscience, Johns Hopkins University School of Medicine, Baltimore, MD

Amanda J. Gruber, MD
Instructor, Department of Psychiatry, Harvard Medical School, Boston, MA; Assistant Psychiatrist, McLean Hospital, Belmont, MA

Alan M. Gruenberg, MD
Professor, Jefferson Medical College; Director, Dave Garroway Laboratory for the Study of Depression, Pennsylvania Hospital; Senior Attending Psychiatrist, Institute of Pennsylvania Hospital, Philadelphia, PA; Lecturer, Yale University School of Medicine, New Haven, CT

Barry Gurland, FRCP, FRC Psych
Sidney Katz Professor of Psychiatry, Columbia University College of Physicians and Surgeons; Director, Stroud Center, New York State Psychiatric Institute, New York, NY

Jeffrey M. Halperin, PhD
Professor, Department of Psychology, Queens College of the City University of New York, Flushing, NY; Professorial Lecturer, Department of Psychiatry, Mt. Sinai School of Medicine, New York, NY

Alexis D. Henry, ScD, OTR
Assistant Professor, Occupational Therapy Department, Worcester State College, Worcester, MA

Michael E. Henry, MD
Clinical Instructor, Department of Psychiatry, Harvard Medical School, Boston, MA; Director of Electroconvulsive Therapy, McLean Hospital, Belmont, MA

Ralph E. Hoffman, MD
Associate Professor of Psychiatry, Yale University School of Medicine; Attending Psychiatrist and Director, Center for Biocognitive Studies, Yale Psychiatric Institute, New Haven, CT

Michael F. Hogan, PhD
Associate Clinical Professor, Department of Psychiatry, Ohio State University College of Medicine, Columbus, OH

Heather Stone Hopkins, MD
Associate Editor, Department of Psychiatry, University of Arizona Health Science Center, Tucson, AZ

Stephen S. Ilardi, PhD
Instructor, Department of Psychology, University of Colorado, Boulder, Boulder, CO

Lawrence B. Inderbitzin, MD
Professor of Psychiatry and Behavioral Sciences, Emory University School of Medicine; Training and Supervising Analyst, Emory University Psychoanalytic Institute; Director of Clinical Psychiatric Services, Grady Health System, Atlanta, GA

Neil Jacobson, PhD
Professor of Psychology, University of Washington, Seattle, WA

Mark E. James, MD
Clinical Assistant Professor, Emory University School of Medicine, Atlanta, GA

Michael A. Jenike, MD
Professor of Psychiatry, Harvard Medical School; Associate Chief of Psychiatry, Massachusetts General Hospital, Boston, MA

Steven M. Jenkusky, MD
Clinical Instructor, Department of Psychiatry, University of New Mexico School of Medicine, Albuquerque, NM; Staff Psychiatrist, Charter Brookside Behavioral Health Services of New England, Nashua, NH

Dilip V. Jeste, MD
Professor of Psychiatry and Neurosciences, University of California, San Diego; Director, Geriatric Psychiatry, Clinical Research Center, San Diego VA Medical Center, San Diego, CA

Michael Kahn, MD
Instructor, Department of Psychiatry, Harvard Medical School; Medical Director, Deaconess/DMH Inpatient Unit, New England Deaconess Hospital, Massachusetts Department of Mental Health, Boston, MA

Marshall B. Kapp, JD, MPH
Professor, Departments of Psychiatry and Community Health, and Director, Office of Geriatric Medicine and Gerontology, Wright State University School of Medicine, Dayton, OH

Nadine J. Kaslow, PhD
Associate Professor, Department of Psychiatry and Behavioral Sciences, Emory University School of Medicine; Chief Psychologist, Department of Psychiatry, Grady Health System, Atlanta, GA

Jerald Kay, MD
Professor and Chair, Department of Psychiatry, Wright State University School of Medicine, Dayton, OH

Rena L. Kay, MD
Clinical Associate Professor of Psychiatry, University of Cincinnati College of Medicine; Training and Supervising Analyst, Cincinnati Psychoanalytic Institute, Cincinnati, OH

Samuel J. Keith, MD
Professor of Psychiatry and Psychology and Chairman, Department of Psychiatry, University of New Mexico School of Medicine, Albuquerque, NM

Martin B. Keller, MD
Mary E. Zucker Professor and Chairman, Department of Psychiatry and Human Behavior, Brown University Program in Medicine; Psychiatrist-in-Chief, Butler Hospital and Women and Infants Hospital; Executive Psychiatrist-in-Chief, Veterans Administration Medical Center, Emma Pendleton Bradley Hospital, Miriam Hospital, Rhode Island Hospital, and Roger Williams General Hospital, Providence, RI; Executive Psychiatrist-in-Chief, Memorial Hospital (Pawtucket), Pawtucket, RI

Otto F. Kernberg, MD
Professor of Psychiatry, Cornell University Medical College; Training and Supervising Analyst, Columbia University Center for Psychoanalytic Training and Research, New York, NY; Director, Personality Disorders Institute, The New York Hospital–Cornell Medical Center, Westchester Division, White Plains, NY

Clinton D. Kilts, PhD
Associate Professor, Department of Psychiatry and Behavioral Sciences, and Assistant Professor, Department of Pathology and Laboratory Medicine, Emory University School of Medicine, Atlanta, GA

Joel E. Kleinman, MD, PhD
Chief, Neuropathology Section, and Deputy Chief, Clinical Brain Disorders Branch, National Institute of Mental Health, DIRP, National Institutes of Health Neuroscience Center at St. Elizabeth's, Washington, DC

William M. Klykylo, MD
Asssociate Professor and Director, Division of Child and Adolescent Psychiatry, Wright State University School of Medicine, Dayton, OH

Michael B. Knable, DO
Clinical Research Associate, Clinical Brain Disorders Branch, National Institute of Mental Health, National Institutes of Health Neuroscience Center at St. Elizabeth's, Washington, D.C.

Robert Kohn, MD
Assistant Professor, Department of Psychiatry and Human Behavior, Brown University School of Medicine, and Butler Hospital, Providence, RI

Alex Kopelowicz, MD
Assistant Professor of Psychiatry, UCLA Neuropsychiatric Institute and Hospital, Los Angeles, CA;
Medical Director, San Fernando Mental Health Center, Mission Hills, CA

Harold S. Koplewicz, MD
Professor, New York University;
Vice Chairman for Child and Adolescent Psychiatry, New York University Medical Center, New York, NY

Thomas R. Kosten, MD
Professor of Psychiatry and Director, Division of Substance Abuse, Yale University School of Medicine, New Haven, CT

Henry R. Kranzler, MD
Associate Professor of Psychiatry, University of Connecticut School of Medicine, Farmington, CT

Stanley Kutcher, MD
Professor and Head, Department of Psychiatry, Dalhousie University;
Psychiatrist-in-Chief, Queen Elizabeth II Health Sciences Center, Halifax, Nova Scotia, Canada

Lucy LaFarge, MD
Assistant Clinical Professor of Psychiatry, Columbia University College of Physicians and Surgeons, and Training and Supervising Analyst, Columbia University Psychoanalytic Center, New York, NY

Harriet P. Lefley, PhD
Professor of Psychiatry and Behavioral Sciences, University of Miami School of Medicine, Miami, FL

James L. Levenson, MD
Professor of Psychiatry, Medicine, and Surgery, Chairman, Division of Consultation/Liaison Psychiatry, Vice Chairman, Department of Psychiatry, Virginia Commonwealth University Medical College of Virginia, Richmond, VA

Bennett L. Leventhal, MD
Professor of Psychiatry and Pediatrics, Director of Child and Adolescent Psychiatry, and Chairman, Department of Psychiatry, The University of Chicago, Pritzker School of Medicine, Chicago, IL

Stephen B. Levine, MD
Clinical Professor of Psychiatry, Case Western Reserve University School of Medicine, Cleveland, OH;
Co-Director, Center for Marital and Sexual Health, Inc., Beachwood, OH

Steven T. Levy, MD
Bernard C. Holland Professor and Vice Chairman, Department of Psychiatry and Behavioral Sciences, Emory University School of Medicine;
Director, Emory University Psychoanalytic Institute;
Chief of Psychiatry, Grady Health System, Atlanta, GA

Roberto Lewis-Fernández, MD
Lecturer, Department of Social Medicine, Harvard Medical School, Boston, MA; Investigator, Behavioral Science Research Institute, University of Puerto Rico, San Juan, Puerto Rico

Robert Paul Liberman, MD
Professor of Psychiatry, UCLA School of Medicine, UCLA Neuropsychiatric Institute, and UCLA Hospital;
Director, Clinical Research Center for Schizophrenia and Psychiatric Rehabilitation, West Los Angeles Veterans Administration Medical Center, Los Angeles, CA, and Camarillo State Hospital, Camarillo, CA

Walter Ling, MD
Professor and Chief of Substance Abuse Program, Department of Psychiatry and Biobehavioral Sciences, UCLA School of Medicine; Associate Chief of Psychiatry for Substance Abuse, West Los Angeles Veterans Administration Medical Center; Director, Los Angeles Addiction Treatment Research Center; Medical Director, The Matrix Center, Inc., Health Care Delivery Services, Friends Medical Science Research, Los Angeles, CA

Joyce H. Lowinson, MD
Professor of Epidemiology and Social Medicine and Special Assistant (for Substance Abuse) to the Dean, Albert Einstein College of Medicine of Yeshiva University, Bronx, NY

Christopher P. Lucas, MB ChB, MRC Psych, M Med Sc
Assistant Professor of Child Psychiatry, Columbia University College of Physicians and Surgeons; Director, Suicide Disorders Clinic, Department of Pediatric Psychiatry, Columbia Presbyterian Medical Center, New York, NY

R. Bruce Lydiard, PhD, MD
Professor of Psychiatry, Department of Psychiatry and Behavioral Sciences, Medical University of South Carolina, Charleston, SC

José R. Maldonado, MD
Assistant Professor of Psychiatry and Behavioral Sciences, Stanford University School of Medicine;
Section Chief, Medical Psychiatry, Medical Director, Consultation/Liaison Psychiatry, and Chief, Medical Psychotherapy Clinic, Stanford University Medical Center, Stanford, CA

John S. March, MD, MPH
Director, Pediatric Anxiety Disorders Program, Duke University Medical Center, Durham, NC

Stephen R. Marder, MD
Professor and Vice Chair, Department of Psychiatry, UCLA School of Medicine; Chief, Psychiatry Service, West Los Angeles Veterans Administration Medical Center, Los Angeles, CA

John C. Markowitz, MD,
Associate Professor of Clinical Psychiatry, Cornell University Medical College; Associate Attending Psychiatrist, The New York Hospital, New York, NY

Ronald L. Martin, MD
Professor and Chair, Department of Psychiatry and Behavioral Sciences, University of Kansas School of Medicine—Wichita, Wichita, KS

Kristin Matler-Sharma, PhD
Staff Psychologist, Rusk Institute of Rehabilitation Medicine, New York University Medical Center, New York, NY

Elinore F. McCance, MD, PhD
Assistant Professor, Division of Substance Abuse, Department of Psychiatry, Yale University School of Medicine, New Haven, CT

Thomas H. McGlashan, MD,
Professor of Psychiatry, Yale University School of Medicine; Chief Executive Officer, Yale Psychiatric Institute, New Haven, CT

G. Darlene Warrick McLaughlin, MD
Assistant Professor of Clinical Psychiatry, University of Texas Southwestern Medical School at Dallas;
Director of Clinical Program Development and Attending Psychiatrist, Mental Health Connections, Dallas, TX

Laura F. McNicholas, MD, PhD
Assistant Professor, Department of Psychiatry, University of Pennsylvania School of Medicine, and Veterans Administration Medical Center, Philadelphia, PA

Arthur T. Meyerson, MD
Professor and Vice Chair, Department of Psychiatry, University of Medicine and Dentistry of New Jersey; Clinical Director, UMDNJ Behavioral Health Care Programs of Newark, Newark, NJ

Juan E. Mezzich, MD, PhD
Professor of Psychiatry and Head, Division of Psychiatric Epidemiology, Mount Sinai School of Medicine of the City University of New York, New York, NY

David J. Miklowitz, PhD
Associate Professor of Psychology, University of Colorado, Boulder, Boulder, CO

Paul C. Mohl, MD
Professor of Psychiatry and Director of Residency Training, University of Texas Southwestern Medical Center at Dallas, Dallas, TX

Pamela Moore, MD
Assistant Professor, University of Connecticut Health Center School of Medicine; Assistant Professor, Inpatient Unit Attending, John Dempsey Hospital, Farmington, CT

Richard F. Morrissey, PhD
Assistant Professor of Psychiatry, Albert Einstein College of Medicine, Bronx, NY; Coordinator of Psychological Services, Division of Child and Adolescent Psychiatry, Long Island Jewish Medical Center, New Hyde Park, NY

Loren R. Mosher, MD
Clinical Professor of Psychiatry, Uniformed Services University of the Health Sciences, Bethesda, MD; Chief Medical Director, Psychiatry, Montgomery County Department of Human Services, Rockville, MD

David A. Mrazek, MD, FRC Psych
Professor of Psychiatry, Behavioral Sciences, and Pediatrics, The George Washington University School of Medicine;
Professor and Chairman of Psychiatry and Behavioral Sciences and Director, Neuroscience Center, Children's Research Institute, Children's Hospital National Medical Center, Washington, DC

Jeff J. Mulchahey, MBA, PhD
Assistant Professor, Department of Psychiatry and Behavioral Sciences, Emory University School of Medicine, Atlanta, GA

Philip R. Muskin, MD
Associate Professor of Clinical Psychiatry and Collaborating Psychoanalyst, Psychiatric Center for Training and Research, Columbia University; Associate Chief of Service, Consultation/Liaison Psychiatry, Columbia-Presbyterian Medical Center, New York, NY

Dominique L. Musselman, MD
Research Fellow in Neuroendocrinology, Department of Psychiatry and Behavioral Sciences, Emory University School of Medicine; Assistant Professor, Adult Psychiatry Consultation/Liaison Service, Emory University Hospital, Atlanta, GA

David Naimark, MD
Geriatric Psychiatry Fellow, San Diego Veterans Administration Medical Center, University of California, San Diego, School of Medicine, La Jolla, CA

Kalpana I. Nathan, MD
Assistant Clinical Professor, Department of Psychiatry, University of California, San Francisco, School of Medicine; Unit Chief, Multidiagnosis Unit, San Francisco General Hospital, San Francisco, CA

Charles B. Nemeroff, MD, PhD
Reunette W. Harris Professor and Chairman, Department of Psychiatry and Behavioral Sciences, Emory University School of Medicine; Chief of Psychiatry, Emory University Hospital, Atlanta, GA

Jeffrey H. Newcorn, MD
Associate Professor of Psychiatry and Pediatrics and Director, Division of Child and Adolescent Psychiatry, Mount Sinai School of Medicine of the City University of New York, New York, NY

John M. Oldham, MD
Professor and Vice Chairman, Department of Psychiatry, Columbia University College of Physicians and Surgeons; Director, New York State Psychiatric Institute, New York, NY

Michael J. Owens, PhD
Assistant Professor, Department of Psychiatry and Behavioral Sciences, Laboratory of Neuropsychopharmacology, Emory University School of Medicine, Atlanta, GA

Michele T. Pato, MD
Associate Professor and Director of Residency Training in Psychiatry, State University of New York at Buffalo; Medical Director, Outpatient Services, Department of Psychiatry, Buffalo General Hospital/Community Mental Health Center, Buffalo, NY

Robert A. Paul, PhD
Charles Howard Candler Professor of Anthropology, Emory University; Associate Professor, Department of Psychiatry and Behavioral Sciences, Emory University, Atlanta, GA

Katharine A. Phillips, MD
Assistant Professor, Department of Psychiatry and Human Behavior, Brown University School of Medicine; Chief of Outpatient Service and Director, Body Dysmorphic Disorder Program, Butler Hospital, Providence, RI

Debra A. Pinals, MD
Clinical Instructor, Harvard Medical School, Boston, MA; Charles C. Gaughan Fellow in Forensic Psychiatry, Bridgewater State Hospital, Bridgewater, MA

Harold Alan Pincus, MD
Deputy Medical Director and Director, Office of Research, American Psychiatric Association, Washington, DC; Clinical Professor, Department of Psychiatry and Behavioral Sciences, George Washington University School of Medicine, Washington, DC; Adjunct Professor of Psychiatry and Behavioral Sciences, Duke University Medical Center, Durham, NC; Clinical Professor of Psychiatry, Uniformed Services University of the Health Sciences, Bethesda, MD

Paul M. Plotsky, PhD
Professor, and Director, Stress Neurobiology Laboratory, Emory University School of Medicine, Atlanta, GA

Harrison G. Pope, Jr., MD
Associate Professor of Psychiatry, Harvard Medical School, Boston MA; Psychiatrist, McLean Hospital, Belmont, MA

Alison Reeve, MD
Assistant Professor, Department of Psychiatry, and Neuropsychiatric Consultant to Continuum of Care Project, University of New Mexico School of Medicine, Albuquerque, NM

Arnold D. Richards, MD
Clinical Assistant Professor, Department of Psychiatry, New York University School of Medicine;
Training and Supervising Analyst, New York Psychoanalytic Institute, New York, NY

Mark A. Riddle, MD
Director, Division of Child and Adolescent Psychiatry, Johns Hopkins University School of Medicine, Baltimore, MD

Priscilla Ridgway, MSW
Research Associate, Office of Social Policy Analysis, University of Kansas School of Social Welfare, Lawrence, KS

Arthur Rifkin, MD
Professor of Psychiatry, Albert Einstein College of Medicine, Bronx, NY; Attending Psychiatrist, Hillside Hospital, Long Island Jewish Medical Center, Glen Oaks, NY

Ellen A. Rosenblatt, MD
Clinical Assistant Professor of Psychiatry, Case Western Reserve University School of Medicine, Cleveland, OH; Director, The Program for Women, Center for Marital and Sexual Health, Inc., Beachwood, OH

Neil Rosenberg, MD
Colorado Neurological Institute, Englewood, CO

Mark Rosenfeld, PhD, OTR
Assistant Professor, Occupational Therapy Department, Worcester State College, Worcester, MA

Ralph E. Roughton, MD
Clinical Professor of Psychiatry, Department of Psychiatry and Behavioral Science, Emory University School of Medicine; Training and Supervising Psychoanalyst, Emory University Psychoanalytic Institute, Atlanta, GA

Matthew V. Rudorfer, MD
Assistant Chief, Clinical Treatment Research Branch, Division of Clinical and Treatment Research, National Institute of Mental Health, National Institutes of Health, Rockville, MD

Harold A. Sackeim, PhD
Professor of Clinical Psychology in Psychiatry, Columbia University College of Physicians and Surgeons; Chief, Department of Biological Psychiatry, New York State Psychiatric Institute, New York, NY

Cynthia J. Sanderson, PhD
Director, Personality Disorders Program, Department of Psychiatry, New York Hospital–Cornell Medical Center, Westchester, Division, White Plains, NY

Alan F. Schatzberg, MD
Kenneth T. Norris, Jr., Professor and Chairman, Department of Psychiatry and Behavioral Sciences, Stanford University School of Medicine;
Chief of Psychiatry, Stanford University Hospital, Stanford, CA

Michael S. Scheeringa, MD
Department of Psychiatry, Kennedy-Kreiger Institute, Baltimore, MD

Lon S. Schneider, MD
Associate Professor of Psychiatry, Neurology, and Gerontology, Department of Psychiatry and the Behavioral Sciences, University of Southern California School of Medicine, Los Angeles, CA

John E. Schowalter, MD
Albert Solnit Professor of Child Psychiatry and Pediatrics, Yale University Child Study Center; Associate Chief, Department of Child Psychiatry, Yale–New Haven Medical Center, New Haven, CT

Judith L. Schreiber, MSW
Private practice, San Diego, CA

Beth Seelig, MD
Assistant Professor of Psychiatry, Training and Supervising Analyst, and Director, Outpatient Psychoanalytic Training Program, Department of Psychiatry and Behavioral Science, Emory University School of Medicine; Assistant Director, Division of Consultation/Liaison Psychiatry, Grady Memorial Hospital, Atlanta, GA

Larry J. Seidman, PhD
Assistant Professor of Psychology, Department of Psychiatry, Harvard Medical School;
Director, Neuropsychology Laboratory, Massachusetts Mental Health Center, Boston, MA

Richard I. Shader, MD
Professor of Pharmacology and Experimental Therapeutics and Psychiatry, Tufts University School of Medicine, Boston, MA

David Shaffer, FRCP, FRC Psych
Irving Philips Professor of Child Psychiatry, Columbia University, College of Physicians and Surgeons; Director, Division of Child and Adolescent Psychiatry, Columbia Presbyterian Medical Center, New York, NY

Theodore Shapiro, MD
Professor of Psychiatry and Psychiatry in Pediatrics, Cornell University Medical College; Director, Child and Adolescent Psychiatry, Payne Whitney Clinic, New York Hospital, New York, NY

Vanshdeep Sharma, MD
Department of Psychiatry, Mt. Sinai Medical Center, New York, NY

Charles W. Sharp, PhD
Associate Director, Special Programs, National Institute on Drug Abuse, National Institutes of Health, Rockville, MD

M. Katherine Shear, MD
Associate Professor of Psychiatry, University of Pittsburgh School of Medicine; Director, Anxiety Disorders Prevention Program, Western Psychiatric Institute and Clinic, Pittsburgh, PA

Edward K. Silberman, MD
Clinical Professor of Psychiatry and Director of Residency Education, Jefferson Medical College, Philadelphia, PA

J. Arturo Silva, MD
Associate Professor of Psychiatry, University of Texas Health Care Center at San Antonio; Staff Psychiatrist, Audie Murphy Veterans Administration Medical Center, San Antonio, TX

Larry B. Silver, MD
Clinical Professor of Psychiatry and Director of Training in Child and Adolescent Psychiatry, Georgetown University School of Medicine, Washington, DC

Daphne Simeon, MD
Assistant Professor of Clinical Psychiatry, Mount Sinai School of Medicine of the City University of New York, New York, NY

Malini Singh, PhD
Staff Psychologist, St. Vincent's Hospital and Medical Center, New York, NY

Andrew E. Skodol, MD
Professor of Clinical Psychiatry, Columbia University College of Physicians and Surgeons;
Research Psychiatrist, New York State Psychiatric Institute, New York, NY

Mark A. Slater, PhD
Assistant Clinical Professor of Psychiatry, University of California, San Diego, School of Medicine, La Jolla, CA; Vice President, Research, Sharp Healthcare, San Diego, CA

Irma C. Smet, PhD
Staff Neuropsychologist, University of Michigan Medical Center, Ann Arbor, MI

David E. Smith, MD
Associate Clinical Professor, Clinical Toxicology and Occupational Health, University of California, San Francisco Medical Center; Founder, President, and Medical Director, Haight-Ashbury Free Clinics, Inc., San Francisco;
President, American Society of Addiction Medicine, Chevy Chase, MD;
Research Director, MPI Treatment Services, Inc., Oakland, CA

Henry F. Smith, MD
Assistant Clinical Professor of Psychiatry, Harvard Medical School;
Faculty, Psychoanalytic Institute of New England, Boston, MA

Janet L. Sobell, PhD
Assistant Professor of Epidemiology and Psychiatry, Mayo Clinic/Foundation, Rochester, MN

Phyllis Solomon, PhD
Professor of Social Work and Social Work in Psychiatry, University of Pennsylvania School of Social Work, Philadelphia, PA

Steve S. Sommer, MD, PhD
Professor of Molecular Biology, Mayo Clinic/Foundation, Rochester, MN

Stephen M. Sonnenberg, MD
Clinical Professor of Psychiatry, Uniformed Sciences University of the Health Sciences, F. Edward Hebert School of Medicine, Bethesda, MD, and Baylor College of Medicine, Houston, TX; Training and Supervising Analyst, Houston-Galveston Psychoanalytic Institute, Houston and Austin, TX

David Spiegel, MD
Professor of Psychiatry and Behavioral Sciences, Stanford University School of Medicine; Attending Psychiatrist, Stanford University Hospital, Stanford, CA

Michael H. Stone, MD
Professor of Clinical Psychiatry, Columbia University College of Physicians and Surgeons;
Lecturer, New York State Psychiatric Institute, New York, NY

Walter N. Stone, MD
Professor of Psychiatry, University of Cincinnati College of Medicine, Cincinnati, OH

Steven C. Stout, BA
Medical Scientist Training Program, Emory University School of Medicine, Atlanta, GA

Eric C. Strain, MD
Associate Professor, Department of Psychiatry and Behavioral Sciences, Johns Hopkins University School of Medicine, Baltimore, MD

James J. Strain, MD
Professor of Psychiatry and Director, Division of Behavioral Medicine and Consultation Psychiatry, Mount Sinai School of Medicine of the City University of New York, New York, NY

Gordon Strauss, MD
Professor and Director, Residency Education Department of Psychiatry and Behavioral Science, University of Louisville School of Medicine;
Staff Psychiatrist, Louisville Veterans Administration Medical Center, Louisville, KY

Loree Sutton, MD
Assistant Professor, Department of Psychiatry, Uniformed Services University of the Health Sciences, F. Edward Hébert School of Medicine, Bethesda, MD

Holly A. Swartz, MD
Instructor, Department of Psychiatry, Cornell University Medical College;
Clinical Affiliate in Psychiatry, The New York Hospital, New York, NY

Ludwik S. Szymanski, MD
Assistant Professor of Psychiatry, Harvard Medical School;
Director of Psychiatry, Institute for Community Inclusion, Children's Hospital, Boston, MA

Pierre N. Tariot, MD
Department of Psychiatry, University of Rochester School of Medicine, Monroe Community Hospital, Rochester, NY

Michael E. Thase, MD
Professor of Psychiatry, University of Pittsburgh School of Medicine;
Director, Mood Disorders Module, and Associate Director, Clinical Research Center, University of Pittsburgh Medical Center, Western Psychiatric Institute and Clinic, Pittsburgh, PA

Mauricio Tohen, MD, DrPH
Associate Professor of Psychiatry, Harvard Medical School;
Associate Professor of Epidemiology, Harvard School of Public Health, Boston, MA

Kenneth E. Towbin, MD
Associate Professor of Psychiatry and Behavioral Science and Director of Residency Training in Psychiatry, Children's Hospital National Medical Center, The George Washington University School of Medicine, Washington, DC

Gary J. Tucker, MD
Professor and Chairman, Department of Psychiatry and Behavioral Sciences, University of Washington School of Medicine, Seattle, WA

E. H. Uhlenhuth, MD
Professor of Psychiatry, University of New Mexico School of Medicine, Albuquerque, NM

Robert J. Ursano, MD
Professor and Chairman, Department of Psychiatry, Uniformed Services University of the Health Sciences, F. Edward Hébert School of Medicine, Bethesda, MD

George Vaillant, MD
Professor of Psychiatry, Harvard Medical School; Director of Research, Division of Psychiatry, Brigham and Women's Hospital, Boston, MA

Susan C. Vaughan, MD
Instructor in Clinical Psychiatry, Columbia University College of Physicians and Surgeons;
Research Fellow in Affective and Anxiety Disorders, New York State Psychiatric Institute, New York, NY

John T. Walkup, MD
Associate Professor, Johns Hopkins University School of Medicine, Baltimore, MD

Charles J. Wallace, PhD, MBA
Associate Research Psychologist, UCLA Neuropsychiatric Institute and UCLA Hospital, Los Angeles, CA;
Chief, Behavioral Analysis and Social Skills Laboratory, Clinical Research Center for the Study of Schizophrenia and Psychiatric Rehabilitation, Camarillo State Hospital, Camarillo, CA

B. Timothy Walsh, MD
William & Joy Ruane Professor of Clinical Psychiatry, Columbia University College of Physicians and Surgeons; Director, Eating Disorders Research Program, New York State Psychiatric Institute, New York, NY

Margaret Watson, DSW, LCSW
Director, Missoula Emergency Services, Western Montana Mental Health Center, Missoula, MT

Anne L. Weickgenant, PhD
Research Assistant, Veterans Administration Medical Center, San Diego, CA

Daniel R. Weinberger, MD
Chief, Clinical Brain Disorders Branch, National Institute of Mental Health, DIRP, National Institutes of Health Neuroscience Center at St. Elizabeth's, Washington, DC

Daniel S. Weiss, PhD
Professor of Medical Psychology, Department of Psychiatry, University of California, San Francisco, School of Medicine; Director of Research, Post-Traumatic Stress Disorder Program, Veterans Administration Medical Center, San Francisco, CA

Jay M. Weiss, PhD
Professor, Department of Psychiatry and Behavioral Sciences, Emory University School of Medicine, Atlanta, GA

Donald R. Wesson, MD
Associate Clinical Professor, Department of Psychiatry, University of California, San Francisco, School of Medicine, San Francisco, CA; Medical Director and Scientific Director, MPI Treatment Services, Summit Medical Center, Oakland, CA

Thomas A. Widiger, PhD
Professor, Department of Psychology, University of Kentucky, Lexington, KY

Serena Wieder, PhD
Washington School of Psychiatry, Washington, DC; Co-chair, Diagnostic Classification Task Force, Zero to Three National Center for Clinical Infant Programs, Washington, DC

Maija Wilska, MD
Developmental Pediatrician and Chief Physician (Retired), Rinnekoti Central Institution for Mental Retardation Espoo, Finland

Ronald M. Winchel, MD
Assistant Professor of Clinical Psychiatry, Columbia University College of Physicians and Surgeons; Psychiatrist, New York State Psychiatric Institute, New York, NY

June Grant Wolf, PhD
Instructor in Psychology, Department of Psychiatry, Harvard Medical School; Director of Psychology, Massachusetts Mental Health Center, Boston, MA

George E. Woody, MD
Clinical Professor, Department of Psychiatry, University of Pennsylvania; Chief, Substance Abuse Treatment Unit, Veterans Administration Medical Center, Philadelphia, PA

Jesse H. Wright, MD, PhD
Professor of Psychiatry, Department of Psychiatry and Behavioral Sciences, University of Louisville School of Medicine; Medical Director, Norton Psychiatric Clinic, Louisville, KY

Yoram Yovell, MD
Assistant Professor of Clinical Psychiatry, Columbia University College of Physicians and Surgeons; Psychiatrist, New York State Psychiatric Institute, New York, NY

Sean H. Yutzy, MD
Assistant Professor of Psychiatry and Director of Forensic Services, Washington University Medical School; Assistant Professor of Psychiatry, Barnes Hospital, St. Louis, MO

Richard B. Zimmer, MD
Assistant Clinical Professor of Psychiatry, Columbia University College of Physicians and Surgeons; Faculty, Columbia University Center for Psychoanalytic Training and Research, New York, NY

Charles H. Zeanah, MD
Professor, Division of Infant, Child, and Adolescent Psychiatry, Louisiana State University School of Medicine, New Orleans, Louisiana

Stephen R. Zukin, MD
Director, Division of Clinical and Services Research, National Institute on Drug Abuse, National Institutes of Health, Rockville, MD; Professor of Psychiatry and Neuroscience, Albert Einstein College of Medicine of Yeshiva University, Bronx, NY

Ilana Zylberman, MD
Assistant Professor of Psychiatry, Mount Sinai School of Medicine of the City University of New York; Attending Psychiatrist, Mount Sinai Medical Center, New York, NY

Preface

This is an exciting time in the field of psychiatry. Scientific progress has expanded the diagnostic and therapeutic capabilities of psychiatry at the same time that psychiatry has begun to play a larger role in the delivery of care to a wider population, both in mental health and in primary care settings. Psychiatry at the end of the 20th century plays an important role among the medical specialties.

The physician-patient relationship provides the framework for quality psychiatric practice. The skilled clinician must acquire a breadth and depth of knowledge and skills in the conduct of the clinical interaction with the patient. To succeed in this relationship, the psychiatrist must have an understanding of normal developmental processes across the life cycle (physiological, psychological, and social) and how these processes are manifested in behavior and mental functions. The psychiatrist must also be expert in the identification and evaluation of the signs and symptoms of abnormal behavior and mental processes and be able to classify them among the defined clinical syndromes that constitute the psychiatric nosology.

To arrive at a meaningful clinical assessment, one must understand the etiology and pathophysiology of the illness along with the contributions of the patient's individual environmental and sociocultural experiences. Furthermore, the psychiatrist must have a command of the range of therapeutic options for any given condition, including comparative benefits and risks, and must weigh the special factors that can influence the course of treatment such as medical comorbidity and constitutional, sociocultural, and situational factors.

The view of psychiatric practice just described forms the framework for *Psychiatry.* Section I, Approaches to the Patient, describes the importance of therapeutic listening and the development of the skills and knowledge necessary to assess and manage the interpersonal context in which psychiatric treatment occurs. Section II, A Developmental Perspective on Normal Domains of Mental and Behavioral Function, provides a review of normal development from a variety of perspectives across the life cycle. Section III, Scientific Foundations of Psychiatry, follows with a review of the scientific knowledge on which our understanding of behavior and mental functions, as well as psychopathology, is based.

Because we believe that good clinical practice must be based on comprehensive and sophisticated clinical assessment, Section IV, Manifestations of Psychiatric Illness, provides a detailed review of clinical assessment. What logically follows in Section V, which constitutes the heart of *Psychiatry,* is the discussion of psychiatric disorders. This section, which follows the nosology of the *Diagnostic and Statistical Manual of Mental Disorders,* Fourth Edition, differs from that found in other textbooks by the depth of the discussion of the clinical management of patients with each of these disorders. Unlike other texts, we have included substantial information on practical management; descriptions of common problems in management, including the treatment of refractory conditions; and discussions of typical issues that arise in the physician-patient relationship as treatment progresses.

The chapters in Section VI, Therapeutics, reflect our view that psychiatrists must be knowledgeable about a wide range of treatment options that include both somatic and psychotherapeutic interventions. The final section of the book, Section VII, Special Clinical Settings and Problems, reflects our belief that the sociocultural context within which the patient lives is a central aspect of the treatment process. Thus, we have included discussions of legal issues, reimbursement systems, ethical standards, the role of peer support and consumer advocacy, and the development of innovative non–hospital-based treatment programs.

Because no one should practice psychiatry without an appreciation of how the current knowledge base and treatment modalities have evolved historically, Appendix I, A Brief History of Psychiatry, provides a highly readable and scholarly review of the history of modern psychiatry. Because lifelong learning and the acquisition of new knowledge and skills are essential to optimal clinical practice, Appendix II, Research Methodology and Statistics, and Appendix III, Continued Professional Development, provide valuable information needed to assess the scientific worth of newly published literature in the field.

In a book with the depth and breadth of *Psychiatry,* a number of editorial decisions had to be made regarding the inclusion or omission of specific material and how information should be organized and presented. To make *Psychiatry* "user friendly," we have liberally used tables, charts, and illustrations to highlight key information. For example, clinical vignettes throughout the text are highlighted by a standard graphic element. Thus, an individual wishing to focus on the clinical aspects of psychiatry can do so by searching for the clinical vignettes located throughout the book. Whenever possible, we have used diagnostic and treatment decision trees to help both the novice and the experienced clinician arrive at a more rational method for making these clinical decisions. This reinforces the emphasis on clinical management issues in the section on disorders

(Section V). Also, each chapter is extensively referenced so that the interested reader can use the information from any chapter for further exploration of a topic.

For hundreds of years, modern medicine has struggled to understand the interactions of the mind and body. A review of medical history of the last several centuries reveals that this problem was resolved in Western cultures by splitting the functions of the mind and the body. In recent decades, as a result of substantial research advances, this approach has begun to change. We come down clearly on the side of those who believe that such a split not only is undesirable but also does not reflect the true state of human life. Thus, we have made every possible attempt to integrate the information in this book within a biopsychosocial framework. Along with the emergence of neurobiology as a discipline, social psychiatry has evolved in recent decades as we have become more aware that the unique social and cultural background of each individual patient can influence the development and manifestations of illness, the physician-patient relationship, the response to treatment, and long-term management. Rather than relegate these issues to a specific chapter, we have chosen to integrate them throughout the entire book.

We envision that *Psychiatry* will have multiple uses. Clinicians at all levels of experience, from the medical student who wishes a quick review to the experienced clinician who wishes to delve into a particular psychiatric topic, will find that the structure and format of *Psychiatry* are conducive to meeting a variety of needs. Health care professionals in other fields of medicine who must recognize or treat psychiatric illness will also find much useful information here.

Psychiatry is the centerpiece of a series of works that will provide a comprehensive program for psychiatric learning. Companion texts will include a review and self-assessment referenced to *Psychiatry,* a behavioral sciences text for medical students that offers a distillation of key information that every physician in training must have, a pocket guide for ready reference in the clinical setting, and a book that focuses on the pharmacological aspects of psychiatric practice.

Psychiatry has been enriched by the contributions of literally hundreds of individuals. Our section editors did an outstanding job both in helping to select chapter authors and in developing the specific format and content of each section. Although editing a multiple-authored text such as *Psychiatry* is a complex and challenging task, our work was made considerably easier by the uniform excellence of our authors' chapters and the diligence of our section editors in helping to mold first drafts into final products.

In addition to the scholarly aspects of the text, a work of this magnitude cannot be produced without the strong and ongoing support of a large number of individuals responsible for its production. Each of us has had experience in editing other books, but never have we received such sustained and outstanding editorial support. Particular thanks go to Judy Fletcher, who approached Allan Tasman with her original idea for this book. Judy's accomplishments include not only successfully nurturing *Psychiatry* to fruition but also nurturing a baby daughter in the process. Judy was unfailingly available and helpful to us. Once the material reached the production stage, Les Hoeltzel, our developmental editor, did yeoman's work. A master of persuasion, Les shepherded the manuscripts through the production process into a finished textbook. Joanie Milnes, in Les' office, was consistently helpful and available.

Joan Lucas, in Allan Tasman's office, deserves our everlasting gratitude for her ability to keep track of hundreds of details and thousands of pages of manuscript and to maintain contact among three editors, seven section editors, and more than 100 chapter authors. Her level of organizational skill is matched only by her diplomatic skill in teasing delayed material from reluctant authors. Judy Yanko, in Jerry Kay's office, was also invaluable in sustaining our efforts. Maureen Ward, in Jeff Lieberman's office in New York (before he moved to North Carolina), efficiently and patiently coaxed, catalogued, and transferred dozens of chapters during the course of this project.

Most important, this work could not have been accomplished without strong support and encouragement from our families. With understanding and good humor, our spouses and children endured many hours of evening and weekend time devoted to work on *Psychiatry* that in other circumstances would have been devoted to them.

ALLAN TASMAN, MD

JERALD KAY, MD

JEFFREY A. LIEBERMAN, MD

Contents

Volume 1

Color Plates Follow the Table of Contents

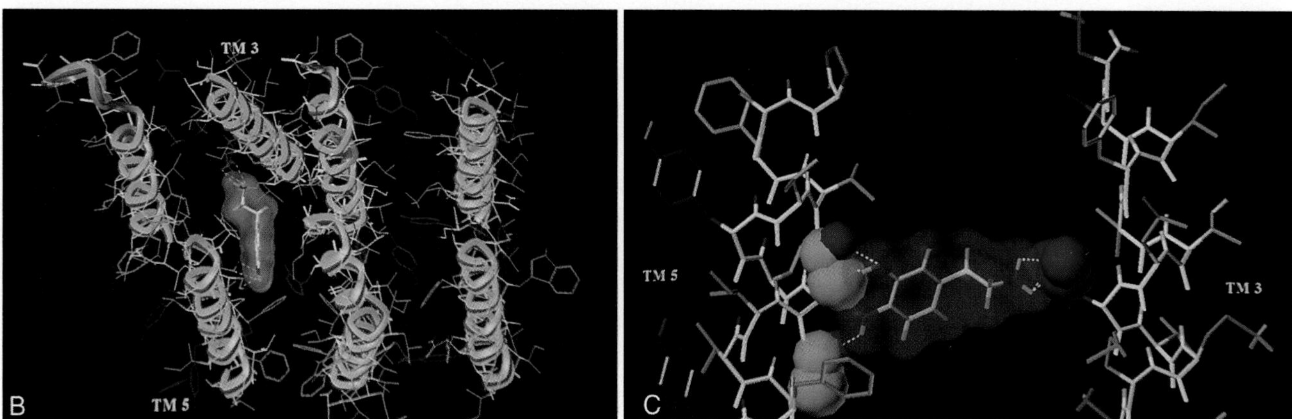

Figure 14–5 *Continued* (B) *Computer model of dopamine bound to the D_2 receptor. Shown is an oblique view of dopamine resting within the ligand binding domain formed by the transmembrane segments of the human D_2 receptor. Only the transmembrane portion of the receptor is shown; the intracellular region is below the plane of the illustration. The color scheme for the elemental structure of dopamine is as follows: C, white; N, dark blue; O, red; H, light blue. Dopamine is shown surrounded by a transparent green surface that approximates its molecular volume. The yellow dotted lines between the dopamine molecule and the receptor represent putative interactions between the ligand and the receptor. The receptor side chains are color coded for the following properties and amino acids: hydrophobic, green; acidic, red; basic, blue; neutral or polar, orange; Ser, green-blue; Pro, red-orange; Cys, magenta. The putative receptor helices are highlighted light blue–magenta ribbon. Transmembrane domains 3 and 5 (TM3 and TM5) are labeled for orientation. The figure was produced using the molecular modeling software SYBYL on a Silicon Graphics Indigo Elan. The illustration is not intended to reflect a quantitative reality. Distances between the transmembrane segments are intentionally large to facilitate visual examination.* (C) *Critical residues involved in dopamine binding to the ligand recognition site. This illustration highlights the interaction between dopamine (shown within its blue volume contour) and the aspartic acid (red) in TM3 and the two serine residues (green-blue) in TM5. The portions of the aspartic acid and serine residues that interact with dopamine are rendered in space-filling mode; the hydrogen atoms are shown as dark red. The figure was produced using the molecular modeling software SYBYL on a Silicon Graphics Indigo Elan.* (B *and* C *courtesy of L. Taylor, PhD, and H. Akil, PhD, Mental Health Research Institute, University of Michigan, Ann Arbor, MI.)*

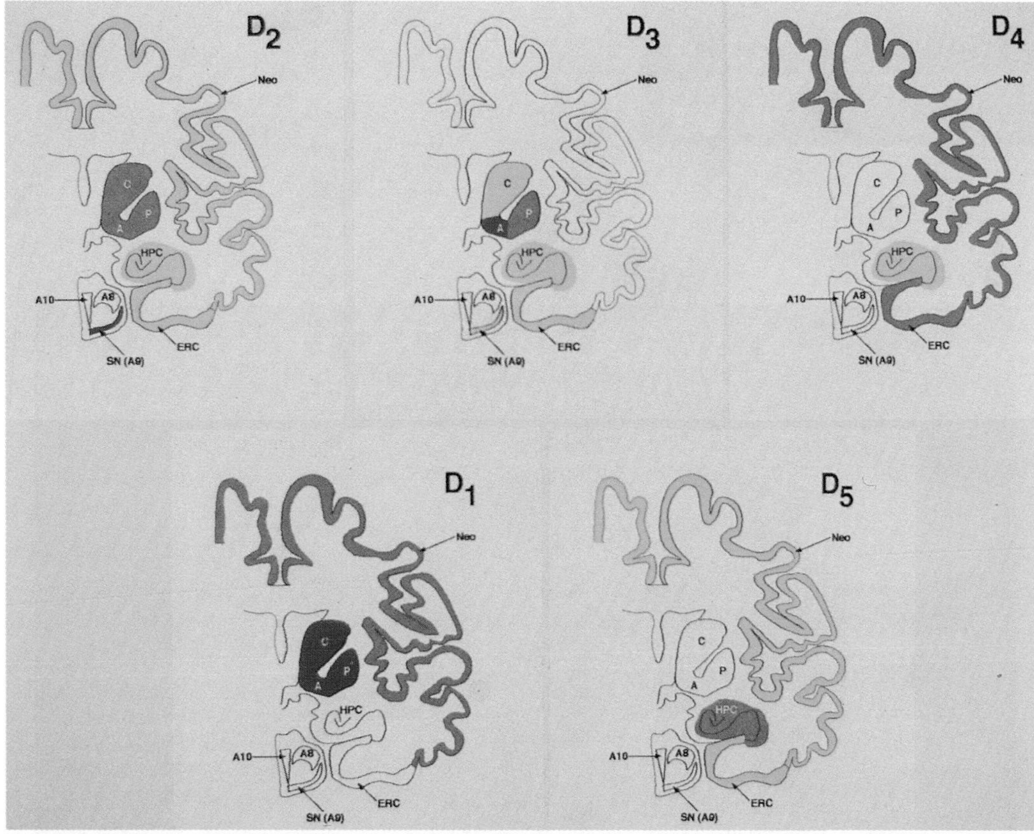

Figure 14–12 *Brain region location of mRNA for human dopamine receptors. Cx, Cerebral cortex; L, lateral ventricle; 3, third ventricle; C, caudate nucleus; P, putamen; G, globus pallidus; AC, nucleus accumbens; ICJ, islands of Calleja; H, hypothalamus; O, olfactory tubercle; AM, amygdala; Hipp, hippocampus; VTA, ventral tegmental area; SN, substantia nigra. (Courtesy of James Meador-Woodruff, MD, University of Michigan, Ann Arbor, MI. Modified by permission of Elsevier Science Inc. from Dopamine receptor sequences: Therapeutic levels of neuroleptics occupy D_2 receptors, clozapine occupies D_4, by Seeman P, Neuropsychopharmacology 7:261–284. Copyright 1992 by the American College of Neuropsychopharmacology.)*

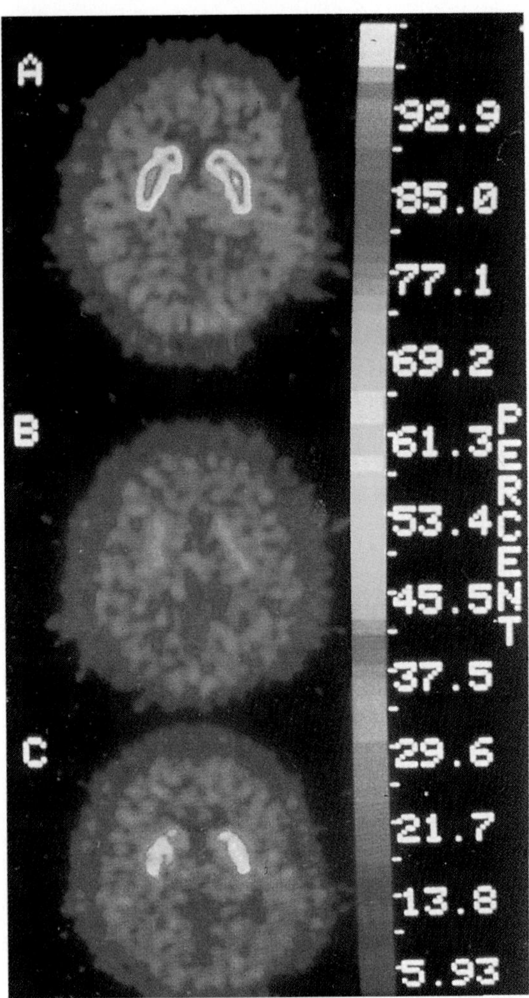

Figure 52–3 *[^{11}C]Raclopride labeling of D_2 receptors in the striatum.* (A) *Medication-free healthy control subject.* (B) *Patient treated with 4 mg of haloperidol.* (C) *Patient treated with 500 mg of clozapine. (From Farde L, Wiesel FA, Halldin C, Sedvall G: Central D_2-dopamine receptor occupancy in schizophrenic patients treated with antipsychotic drugs. Arch Gen Psychiatry 1988; 45:71–76. Copyright 1988, American Medical Association.)*

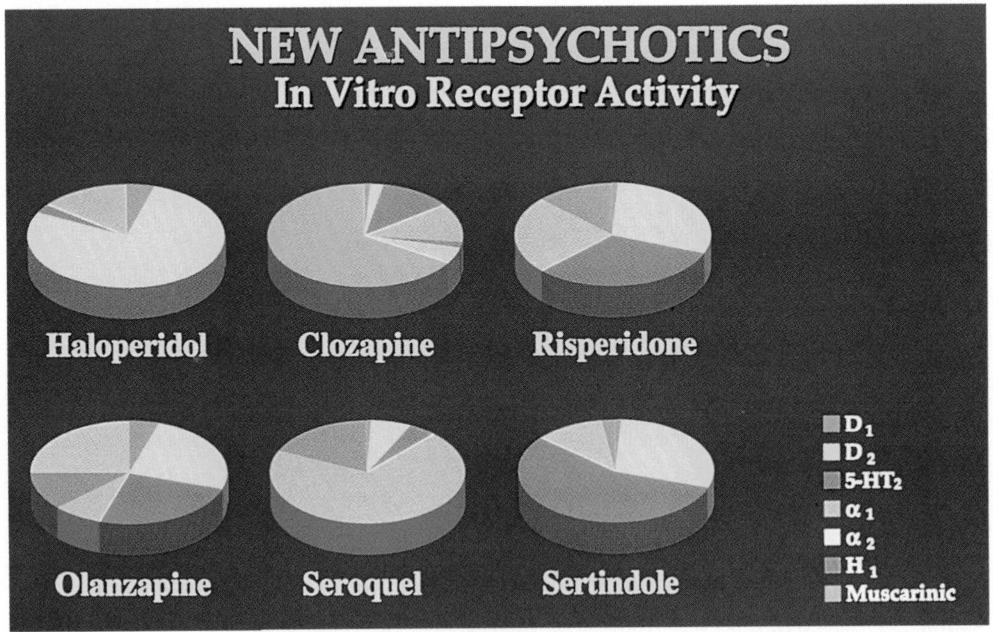

Figure 52-7 *In vitro receptor affinity of new antipsychotic agents.*

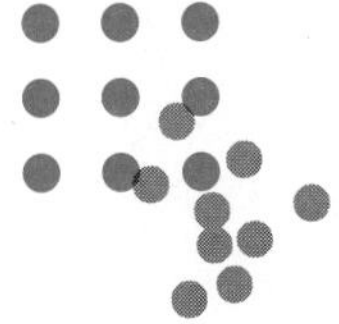

SECTION I

Robert J. Ursano, Section Editor

Approaches to the Patient

CHAPTER

1 Listening to the Patient

Paul C. Mohl
G. Darlene Warrick McLaughlin

Middle English	*listnen, lustnen, listen*
Anglo-Saxon	*hlyst,* hearing *hlystan,* to listen, to list
Definition	To harken, to give ear, to attend closely with a view to heed

Listening: The Key Skill in Psychiatry

It was Freud who raised the psychiatric technique of examination—listening—to a level of expertise unexplored in the prefreudian era. As Binswanger[1] has said of the period before freudian influence, psychiatric "auscultation" and "percussion" were performed as if through the patient's shirt, so much of the patient's essence remaining covered or muffled, layers of meaning unpeeled away or unexamined. Many writers have tried to find words that describe the special qualities of psychiatric listening: listening with the third ear, the interpretive stance, interpersonal sensitivity, a narrative attitude. All psychiatrists, regardless of theoretical stance, must learn this skill and struggle with how it is to be defined and taught. The psychodynamic psychiatrist listens for the unconscious conflicts; the cognitive psychiatrist listens for the patient's hidden distortions and assumptions about the world; the behaviorist listens for hidden associations and patterns; and the interpersonal psychiatrist listens for stereotypical role definitions, interpersonal conflicts, and repertoire deficits.

An attitude of inquiry addresses the questions

- Who is the patient?
- What is the patient saying?
- What is the patient's perception of what he or she is saying?
- Does the patient suffer from a psychiatric disorder?
- If so, what differential diagnoses does the presentation call to mind?
- What diagnosis does the patient have?

Havens[2] might say that psychiatric listening is more like listening *ear to ear.* Listening to the patient requires a sensitivity to who the storyteller is, an orientation to the patient rather than to the disease.[3, 4] If the attitude of inquiry is pointed at the patient, how do you make a possible diagnosis jump to mind? The listener's intent is to uncover something "wrong" and to put a label on it. At the same time, the listener is on a journey to discover who the patient *is,* not just what condition is present. The listener employs tools of asking, looking, testing, and clarifying and invites the patient to collaborate as an active informer. Listening work takes time, concentration, imagination, an attitude that places the patient as the hero of his or her own life story, and a sense of humor. Key listening skills are listed in Table 1–1.

One might question the trustworthiness of listening in a way that objectifies the patient. The training of listening, for example, is one of guiding the depressed patient to tell a story of loss in addition to having the patient name, describe, and quantify symptoms of depression. The listener, in hearing the story, experiences the world and the patient from the patient's point of view and helps carry the burden of loss, lightening and transforming the load. In hearing the sufferer, the depression itself is lifted and relieved; and yet, if hearing is done well, the listener becomes a better disease diagnostician. The best listeners hear both the patient and the disease clearly.

The Primary Tools: Words, Analogies, Metaphors, and Similes

To listen and understand require that the language used between the speaker and the listener be shared—the meanings of words and phrases are commonly held.[5] Common language is the predominant factor in the social organization of humanity and is probably the single most important key to the establishment of an active listener–engaged storyteller dyad, which the helping alliance represents.

Patients are *storytellers* who have the hope of being heard and understood.[6, 7] Their hearers are physicians who expect to listen actively and be with the patient in a new level of understanding. Because we listen to so many different people every day, we tend to think of it as an automatic ongoing process, yet this sort of listening remains one of the central skills in clinical psychiatry. It underpins all other skills in diagnosis, alliance building, and communication. In all medical examinations, the

Table 1–1 Key Listening Skills

Hearing	Connotative meanings of words Idiosyncratic uses of language Figures of speech that tell a deeper story Voice tones and modulation (e.g., hard edge, voice cracking) Stream of associations
Seeing	Posture Gestures Facial expressions (e.g., eyes watering, jaw clenched) Other outward expressions of emotion
Comparing	Noting what is omitted Dissonances between modes of expression
Intuiting	Attending to one's own internal reactions
Reflecting	Thinking it all through outside the immediate pressure to respond during the interview

patient is telling a story that only she or he has experienced. The physician must glean the salient information and then use it in appropriate ways.

Inevitably, even when language is common, there are subtle differences in meanings based on differences in gender, age, religion, socioeconomic class, race, and region of upbringing as well as idiosyncrasies of individual history. These differences are particularly important to keep in mind in the use of analogies, similes, and metaphors. These figures of speech, in which one thing is held representational of another by comparison, are important windows to the inner world of the patient.

All language is symbolic, a word standing for an object, event, memory, experience, or state of mind. Differences in meanings attached can complicate their use. In assessment for psychotherapeutic treatment, the need to regard these subtleties of language becomes the self-conscious focus of the psychiatrist, yet failure to harken and heed can affect simple medical diagnosis.

Clinical Vignette 1

A psychiatric consultant was asked to see a 48-year-old man in the coronary care unit for chest pain deemed "functional" by the cardiologist, who had asked the patient if his chest pain was "crushing." The patient said no. The results of a variety of other routine tests were also negative. The psychiatrist asked the patient to describe his pain. He said, "It's like a truck sitting on my chest, squeezing it down." The psychiatrist promptly recommended additional tests, which confirmed the diagnosis of myocardial infarction. The cardiologist may have been tempted to label the patient a "bad historian," but the most likely culprit of this potentially fatal misunderstanding lies in the connotative meanings each ascribed to the word crushing or to other variances in metaphorical communication.

In psychotherapy, the special meanings of words become the central focus of the treatment.

Clinical Vignette 2

A psychiatrist had been treating a 35-year-old man with narcissistic personality and dysthymic disorders for 2 years. Given the brutality and deprivation of the patient's childhood, the psychiatrist was persistently puzzled by the remarkable strength the patient had. It was not at all clear whence his capacities for empathy, self-observation, idealistic values, and modulation of intense rage had developed. During a session, in telling a childhood story, the patient began, "When I was a little fella . . . ." It struck the therapist that the patient always said "little fella" when referring to himself as a boy and that this was fairly distinctive phraseology. Almost all other patients will say "when I was young/a kid/a girl (boy)/in school," designate an age, or the like. On inquiry about this, the patient immediately identified the Andy Griffith Show as the source. This revealed a secret identification with the characters of the warmly humorous 1960s television show and a model that said to a young boy, "There are other ways to be a man than what you see around you."

How Does One Hear Words in This Way?

The preceding clinical vignettes, once described, sound straightforward and easy. Yet, to listen in this way requires the presence of specific yet difficult to learn skills and attitudes. It is extremely difficult to put into words the listening processes embodied in these examples and those to follow, yet that is what this chapter must attempt to do.

Students, when observing experienced psychiatrists interviewing patients, often experience a sense of wonder: How did she know to ask that? Why did the patient open up with him but not with me? What made the diagnosis so clear in that interview and not in all the others? The student may respond with a sense of awe, a feeling of ineptitude and doubt at ever achieving such facility, or even a reaction of disparagement that the process seems so indefinable and inexact. The key is the psychiatrist's ability to listen. Without a refined capacity to hear deeply, the chapters on other aspects of interviewing in this textbook are of no use. However, it is not mystical, magical, or indefinable (although it is difficult to articulate); such skills are the product of hard work, much thought, intense supervision, and extensive exposure to many different kinds of patients, in depth.

Psychiatrists, more than any other physician, must constantly listen in multiple ways: symptomatically, narratively and experientially,[8] behaviorally, interpersonally, cognitively, cross-culturally, and from a systems perspective. Symptomatic listening is what we think of as traditional medical history taking in which the focus is on the presence or absence of a particular symptom, the most overt content level of an interview. Narrative-experiential listening is based on the idea that all humans are constantly interpreting their experiences, attributing meaning to them, and weaving a story of their lives with themselves as the central character. This process goes on continuously, both consciously and unconsciously. All humans, in addition to whatever immediate external focus they have, within themselves participate in a running reaction and commentary on their lives. This commentary includes personal history, repetitive behaviors, learned assumptions about the world, and interpersonal roles. These are, in turn, the products of individual background, cultural norms and values, and family system forces.

Clinical Vignette 3

A 46-year-old man was referred to a psychiatrist from a drug study. The patient had both major depressive disorder and dysthymic disorder since a business failure 2 years earlier. His primary symptoms were increased sleep and decreased mood, libido, energy, and interests. After no improvement during the "blinded" portion of the study, he had continued to show little response once the code was broken on two different active drugs. He was referred for psychotherapy and further antidepressant trials. The therapy progressed slowly with only episodic improvement. One day, the patient reported that his wife had been teasing him about how, during his afternoon nap, his snoring could be heard above the noise of a vacuum cleaner. The psychiatrist immediately asked additional questions and eventually obtained sleep electroencephalographic studies. After appropriate treatment for sleep apnea, the patient's depression improved dramatically.

It seems that three factors were present that enabled this psychiatrist to listen well and identify an unusual diagnosis that had been missed by at least three other excellent clinicians who had all been using detailed structured interviews that are extremely inclusive in their symptom reviews. First, the psychiatrist had to have all sorts of symptoms and syndromes readily available in mind. Second, he had to be in a curious mode. In fact, this psychiatrist had a gnawing sense that something was missing in his understanding of the patient. His mind was open to seeing a "zebra" despite the ongoing assumption that the weekly "hoofbeats" he heard represented the everyday "horse" of clinical depression. Finally, he had to hear the patient's story in multiple, flexible ways, including the possibility that a symptom might be embedded in it, so that a match could be noticed between a detail of the story and a symptom. Eureka! The zebra could then be seen, although it had been standing there weekly for months.

Looking back at clinical vignette 2, we see the same phenomenon of a detail's leaping out as a significant piece of missing information that dramatically influences the treatment process. To accomplish this requires a cognitive template (symptoms and syndromes, developmental and personality theories), a searching curious stance, and flexible processing of the data presented. If one keeps in mind Figure 1–1, the listener begins to hear the meanings in the words.

Listening as More Than Hearing

The ear has been clearly identified as the organ of receptivity for hearing. As stated previously, words must have a shared or common meaning for expression and listening in a way that connects the psychiatrist and patient. When we think of listening, we tend to associate it with hearing. We have spoken of hearing not only words but also inflection, metaphor, and stream of associations. This mode of listening also requires much in the way of seeing—movement, gestures, facial expressions, subtle changes in all of these, and dissonances between what is heard and what is seen.

It was Darwin who first observed that there appears to be a biogrammar of primary emotions that all humans possess and express in predictable fixed action patterns.[9] This insight was lost until the late 1960s, when Sylvan Tomkins[10] returned to it and demonstrated the cross-cultural consistency of emotional expression in all human beings. Leslie Brothers,[11] using this work and her own experiments with primates, developed a hypothesis about the biology of empathy based on seeing as well as hearing. Andrew Schwartz (unpublished data, 1988) took this a step further as he hypothesized that our brains are programmed to hear not only the symbols but all of the tonal and inflective qualities, *and* to observe the subtle facial and gestural signals, *and* to integrate this not only cognitively and consciously but also in the form of an inner felt reaction within the listener. The point here is that listening is far more than hearing and that our brains are programmed to "see" another in this way.

Clinical Vignette 4

A 38-year-old Hispanic construction worker presented to a small-town emergency department in the Southwest complaining of pain on walking, actually described in a Spanish-accented English as "a little pain." His voice was tight, his face was drawn, and his physical demeanor was burdened and hesitant. His response to the invitation to walk was met by a labored attempt to walk without favor to his painful limb. A physician could have discharged him from the emergency department with a small prescription of ibuprofen. The careful physician in the emergency department responded to the powerful visual message that he was in pain, was beaten down by it, and had suffered long before coming in. This recognition came first to the physician as an intuition that this man was somehow sicker than he made himself sound. A radiograph of the femur revealed a lytic lesion that later proved to be metastatic renal cell carcinoma. To hear the unspoken, one had to be keenly aware of the patient's tone and of how he looked and to keep in mind, too, the cultural taboos forbidding him to give in to pain or to appear to need help.[12]

In addition to hearing words as symbols and metaphors—having the cognitive template, curiosity, flexibility, and "seeing"—attitudes that enable effective listening and awareness of potential blocks to it are essential.

Common Blocks to Effective Listening

Many factors influence the ability to listen. Psychiatrists come to the patient as the product of their own life experiences. Does the listener tune into what he or she hears in a more attentive way if the listener and the patient share characteristics? What blocks to listening (Table 1–2) are posed by differences in sex, age, religion, socioeconomic class, race, or culture?[13–15] What blind spots may be induced by superficial similarities in but different personal meanings attributed to the same cultural symbol? Separate and apart from the differences in the development of empathy when

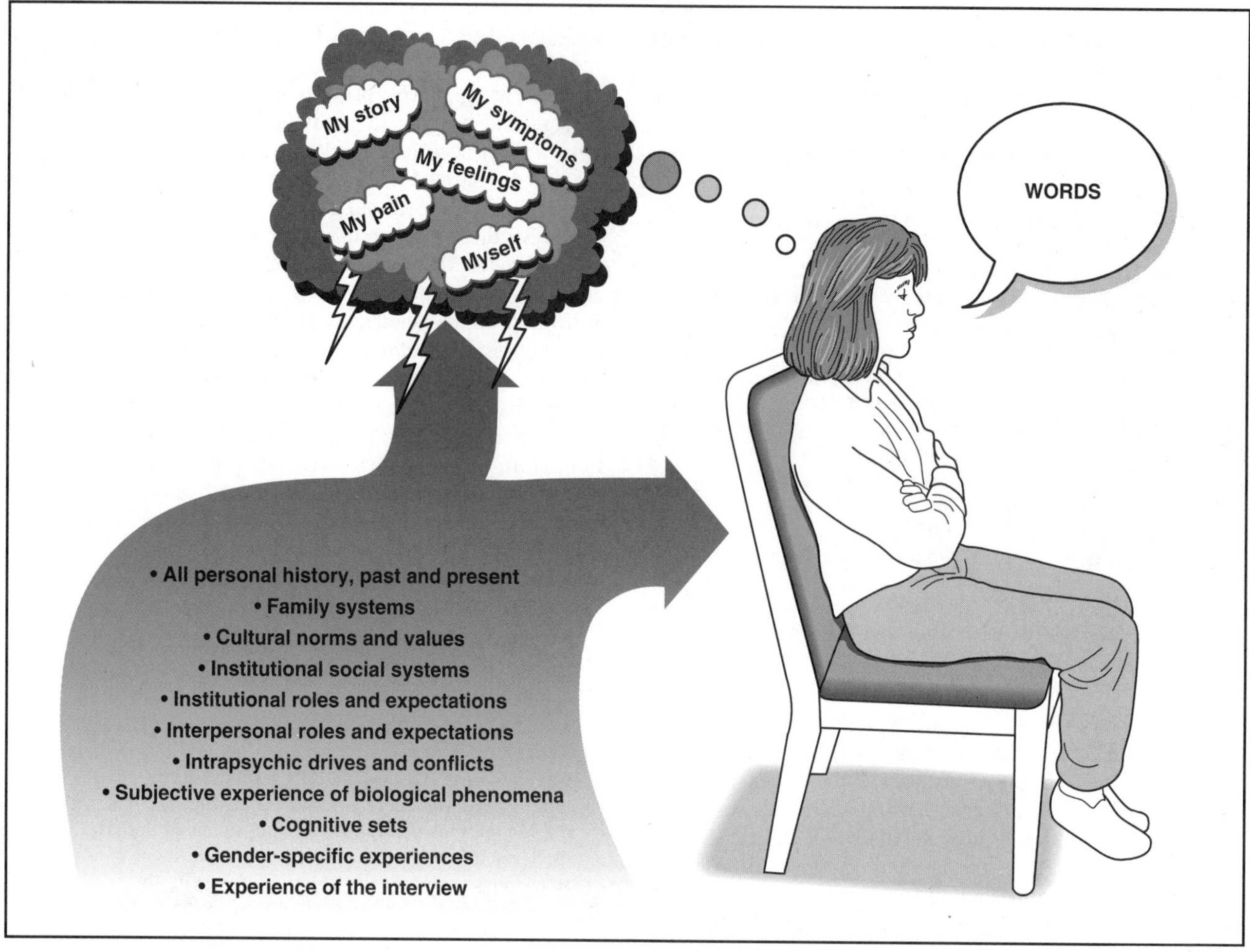

Figure 1–1 *Finding the patient.*

the dyad hold in common certain features, the act of listening is inevitably influenced by similarities and differences between the psychiatrist and the patient.

Would a woman have reported the snoring in clinical vignette 3, or would she have been too embarrassed? Would she have reported it more readily to a woman physician? How comfortable are most physicians in asking women about snoring? What about the image in clinical vignette 1 of a truck sitting on someone's chest? How gender- and culture-bound is it? Would the Andy Griffith Show have had the impact on a young African-American boy that it did on a white one? Consider these additional examples.

Table 1–2 Blocks to Effective Listening

Patient-psychiatrist dissimilarities	Race Sex Culture Religion Regional dialect Individual differences Socioeconomic class
Superficial similarities	May lead to incorrect assumptions of shared meanings
Countertransference	Psychiatrist fails to hear or reacts inappropriately to content reminiscent of own unresolved conflicts
External forces	Managed care setting Emergency department Control-oriented inpatient unit
Attitudes	Need for control Psychiatrist having a bad day

Clinical Vignette 5

A female patient came to see her male psychiatrist for their biweekly session. She, having just been given new duties on her job, came in excitedly and began sharing with her psychiatrist how happy she was to have been chosen by her male supervisor to help him with an important project at their office. The session continued with the theme of the patient's pride in having been recognized for her attributes, talents, and hard work. At the next session, she said that she had become embarrassed after the previous session at the thought that she had been "strutting her stuff." The psychiatrist reflected back to her the thought that she sounded like a rooster strutting his stuff, connecting her embarrassment with having revealed that she strove for the recognition and power of men in her company and that she in fact envied the position of her supervisor. The patient objected to the comparison of a rooster and likened it more to feeling like a woman of the streets strutting her stuff. She stated that she felt like a prostitute being used by her supervisor. The psychiatrist was off the mark by missing the opportunity to point out in the analogous way that the patient's source of embarrassment was in being used, not so much in being envious of the male position.

It is likely that different life experiences based on gender fostered this misunderstanding. How many women easily identify with the stereotyped role of the barnyard rooster? How many men readily identify with the role of a prostitute? These are but two examples of the myriad different meanings our specific sex many incline us toward. Although metaphor is a powerful tool in listening to the patient, cross-cultural barriers pose potentially unheeded blocks to understanding.

Clinical Vignette 6

A 36-year-old black woman complained to her psychiatrist of like language, race, and socioeconomic class that her husband was a snake, meaning that he was no good, treacherous, and a hidden danger. The psychiatrist, understanding this commonly held definition of a snake, reflected back to the patient pertinent supportive feedback concerning the care and caution the patient was exercising in divorce dealings with the husband.

In contrast, a 36-year-old Chinese woman fluent in English, living in this country for 15 years and assimilated in Western culture, represented her husband to her white native-born psychiatrist as being like a dragon. The psychiatrist, without checking on the meaning of the word dragon with her patient, assumed it connoted an implication of evil, one of malicious intent and oppression. The patient, however, was using dragon as a metaphor of her husband, the fierce, watchful guardian of the family, in keeping with the ancient Chinese folklore in which the dragon is stationed at the gates of the lord's castle to guard and protect from evil and danger.

Even more subtle regional variations may produce similar problems in listening and understanding.

Clinical Vignette 7

In a family session, a southern native psychiatrist referred to the mother of her patient as "your mama," intending a meaning of warmth and respect. The patient instantly became enraged at the use of such an offensive term toward her mother.

Although being seen in Texas, the patient and her family had recently moved from a large city in New Jersey. The use of the term *mama* among working-class Italians in that area was looked on with derision by people of Irish descent, the group to which the patient was ethnically connected. The patient had used the term *mother* to refer to her mother, a term the psychiatrist had heard with a degree of coolness attached. What she knew of her patient's relationship with her mother did not fit the aloof, distant connotations mother has to most southerners; hence, almost out of awareness, she switched terms, leading to a response of indignation and outrage from the patient.

Psychiatrists discern meaning in that which they hear through filters of their own—cultural backgrounds, life experiences, feelings, the day's events, their own physical sense of themselves, sex roles, religious meanings systems, and intrapsychic conflicts. The filters can serve as blocks or as magnifiers if certain elements of what is being said resonate with something within the psychiatrist. When the filters block, we call it countertransference or insensitivity. When they magnify, we call it empathy or sensitivity. One may observe a theme for a long time repeated with a different tone, embellishment, inflection, or context before the idea of what is happening comes to mind. Once again, the little fella example of clinical vignette 2 illustrates a message that had been communicated many ways and times in exactly the same language before the psychiatrist "got it." On discovering a significant meaning that has been signaled before in many ways, the psychiatrist often has the experience, How could I have been so stupid? It's been staring me in the face for months!

Managed care can alter our attitudes toward the patient and our abilities to be transforming listeners. The requirements for authorization for minimal visits or time spent on the phone with utilization review nurses attempting to justify continuing therapy can be blocks to listening to the patient. With these time limits and other managed care considerations (i.e., need for a billable diagnostic code from the *Diagnostic and Statistical Manual of Mental Disorders,* Fourth Edition [DSM-IV]), the psychiatrist, as careful listener, must heed the external pressures influencing the approach to the patient. Many benefits packages provide coverage in any therapeutic setting only for relief of symptoms, restoration of minimal function, acute problem solving, and shoring up of defenses. Unless these pressures are attended to, listening will be accomplished with a different purpose in mind, more closely approximating the crisis intervention model of the emergency department or the medical model for either inpatient or outpatient care. In these settings, thoughtful psychiatrists will arm themselves with check lists, inventories, and scales for objectifying severity of illness and response to treatment: The ear is tuned to measurable and observable signs of responses to therapy and biological intervention.

With emphasis on learning here-and-now symptoms that can bombard the dyad with foreground static and noise, the worry is that the patient will not be found in the encounter. The same approach to listening occurs in the setting of the emergency department for crisis intervention. Emphasis is on symptom relief, assurance of capacities to keep oneself safe, restoration of minimal function, acute problem solving, and shoring up of defenses. Special attention is paid to identifying particular stressors. What can be done quickly to change stressors that threw the patient's world into a state of disequilibrium? The difference in the emergency department is that the careful listener may have

3 to 6 hours as opposed to three to six sessions for the patient with a health maintenance organization or preferred provider organization contract. In meeting with the support system, friends, family, and lovers (often harboring the source of distress), one listens for the shift necessary to set about a return to equilibrium. If one is lucky, and good at being an active listener-bargainer, seeds of change can be planted in the hope of allowing them time to grow between visits to the emergency department for the borderline patient. If one could hope for another change, it would be for a decrease in chaos in the patient's inner world and outer world.

Clinical Vignette 8

An army private was brought to the emergency department in Germany by his friends, having threatened to commit suicide while holding a gun to his head. He was desperate, disorganized, impulsive, enraged, pacing, and talking almost incoherently. Gradually, primarily through his friends, the story emerged that his first sergeant had recently made a decision for the entire unit that had a particularly adverse effect on the patient. He was a fairly primitive character who relied on his wife for a sense of stability and coherence in his life. The sergeant's decision was to send the entire unit into the field for more than a month, just at the time the patient's wife was about to arrive from the United States, after a long delay.

After piecing together this story, the psychiatrist said to the patient, "It's not yourself you want to kill, it's your first sergeant!" The patient at first giggled a little, then gradually broke out into a belly laugh that echoed throughout the emergency department. It was clear that when he recognized the true object of his anger, a coherence was restored that enabled him to feel his rage without the impulse to act on it. The psychiatrist then enlisted the friends in a plan to support the patient through the month and to establish regular phone contact with his wife as she set up their new home in Germany. No medication was necessary. Hospitalization was averted, and a request for humanitarian dispensation that would have compromised the patient in the eyes of both his peers and superiors was avoided as well. With luck, the young man had an opportunity to grow as well.

This psychiatrist refused to allow the external context of a military emergency department to interfere with good clinical listening.

Crucial Attitudes That Enable Effective Listening

The first step in developing good listening skills involves coming to grips with the importance of inner experience (Table 1–3) in psychiatric treatment and diagnosis. The third revised edition of the *Diagnostic and Statistical Manual of Mental Disorders* (DSM-III-R) and DSM-IV have made enormous advances in reliability and accuracy of diagnosis, but their emphasis on seemingly observable phenomena has allowed the willing user to forget the importance of inner experience, even in such basic diagnoses as major depressive disorder. Consider the symptom "depressed mood most of the day" or "markedly diminished interest or pleasure" or even "decrease or increase in appetite." These are entirely subjective symptoms. Simply reporting depression is not usually sufficient to convince a psychiatrist that a diagnosis of depression is warranted. In fact, the majority of psychiatric patients are so demoralized by their illnesses that they often announce depression as their first complaint. Further, a significant number of patients do not acknowledge depression, yet they are so diagnosed. The psychiatrist might well comment, "Sitting with him makes me feel very sad." Perspectives of Brothers[11] are important to remember in these instances.

The psychiatrist must "listen to" much more than the patient's overt behavior. There are qualities in the communication, including the inner experiences induced in the listener, that are being harkened to. The experienced psychiatrist listens to the words, watches the behavior, engages in and notices the ongoing interaction, allows himself or herself to experience his or her own inner reactions to the process, and *never forgets that depression and almost all other psychiatric symptoms are exclusively private experiences.* The behavior and interactions are useful insofar as they assist the psychiatrist to infer the patient's inner experience.

Therefore, for a good psychiatrist to be convinced that a patient is depressed, not only must the patient say that she or he is depressed but the observable behavior must convey it (sad-looking face, sighing, unexpressive intonations), and the interaction with the interviewer must convey depressive qualities (e.g., sense of neediness, sadness induced in interviewer, beseeching qualities expressed). In the absence of both of these, other diagnoses should be considered. In the absence of other symptoms of depression, but in the presence of such qualities, depression needs to remain in the differential diagnosis.

Even when we make statements about brain function related to a particular patient, we use this kind of listening, generally by making at least two inferences. We first listen to and observe the patient and then *infer* some aspect of the patient's private experience. Then, if we possess sufficient scientific knowledge, we make a second inference to a disturbance in neurochemistry, neurophysiology, or neuroanatomy.

As one moves toward treatment from diagnosis, the content of inner experience inferred may change to more varied states of feelings, needs, and conflicts. However, the fundamental process of listening remains the same. One "listens" to all behavior, to the ongoing interpersonal relationship the patient attempts to establish, and to the inner experiences of the psychiatrist.

Table 1–3 Attitudes Important to Listening
The centrality of *inner experience*
There are no bad historians
The answer is always inside the patient
Control and power are shared in the interview
It is OK to feel confused and uncertain
Objective truth is never as simple as it seems
Listen to yourself, too
Everything you hear is modified by the patient's filters
Everything you hear is modified by your own filters
There will always be another opportunity to hear more clearly

Despite all of the technological advances in medicine in general and their growing presence in psychiatry, history taking remains the first and central skill for all physicians. Even in the most basic of medical situations, the patient is trying to communicate a set of private experiences (How does one describe the qualities of pain or discomfort?) that the physician may infer and sort into possible syndromes and diagnoses. In psychiatry, this process is multiplied as indicated in Figure 1–1. William Styron,[16] a prize-winning novelist, had to go to extraordinary lengths in his eloquent attempt in *Darkness Visible* to convey the "searing internal mental pain" that he experienced when suffering from a major depression.

Silvano Arieti[17] hypothesized that cognitive development produces changes over time in the experience of various affects. Does a person with borderline personality disorder experience anxiety in the same qualitative and quantitative manner in which a neurotic person does? What is the relationship between feelings of sadness and guilt and empty experiences of depression? This perspective underlies the principle articulated in text after text on interviewing that emphasizes the importance of establishing rapport in the process of history taking. The sense in the narrator that the listener is truly present, connected and with the patient, enormously enhances the accuracy of the story reported.

Words that have been used to describe this process in the listener include interest, empathy, attentiveness, and noncontingent positive regard. However, these are words that may say less than they seem to. It is the constant curious awareness on the listener's part that she or he is trying to grasp the private inner experience of the patient, and the storyteller's sense of this, that impels the ever more revealing process of history taking. This quality of listening by facilitating a growing sense of closeness between psychiatrist and patient produces what we call rapport, without which psychiatric histories become spotty, superficial, and even suspect. There are no bad historians, only patients who have not yet found the right listener.

In treatment, we even find empirical data to support this perspective. The two most powerful predictors of outcome in *any* form of psychotherapy are empathy and the therapeutic alliance.[18] This has been shown again and again in study after study for dynamic therapy, cognitive therapy, behavior therapy, and even medication management. This even led some researchers and theorists to propose that psychotherapy's power can be understood solely as a remoralization phenomenon based on support and empathy. The power of this can be seen in the remarkable therapeutic success of the "clinical management" cell of the National Institute of Mental Health Collaborative Study on the Treatment of Major Depression.[19] Although the clinical management cell was not as effective as the cells that included specific drugs or specific psychotherapeutic interventions, 35% of patients with moderate to severe major depressive disorder improved significantly with carefully structured supportive clinical management alone.

Good psychiatric listening requires a complicated attitude toward control and power in the interview (see Table 1–3). The psychiatrist invites the patient-storyteller to collaborate as an active informer. Patients are invited, too, to question and observe themselves. This method of history taking remains the principal tool of general clinical medicine. However, as Freud pointed out, these methods of active uncovering are more complex in the psychic realm.[20] The use of the patient as a voluntary reporter requires that the investigator keep in mind the unconscious and its power over the patient and listener. Can patients be reliable objective witnesses to themselves or their symptoms? Can the listeners hold in mind their own set of filters, meanings, and distortions as they hear? Listeners translate for themselves and their patients the patients' articulation of their own experience and inner world into our definition of symptoms, syndromes, and differential diagnoses that make up the concept of the medical model.

Objective-descriptive examiners are like detectives closing in on disease. The psychiatric detective enters the inquiry with an attitude of unknowing and suspends prior opinion. The techniques of listening invoke a wondering and a wandering with the patient. Periods of head scratching and exclamations of "I'm confused" or "I don't understand" or "That's awful!" or "Tell me more" allow the listener to follow or to point the way for the dyad.[21] So, finally, clear and precise descriptions can be held up for scrutiny by the two, and it is to be hoped that a diagnostic label or new information about who the patient is comes to mind.

It is embarking on the history-taking journey together, free of judgments, opinions, criticisms, or preconceived notions, that underpins rapport. Good listening requires a complex understanding of what objective truth is and how it may be found. The effective psychiatrist must eschew the traditional medical role in interviewing and tolerate a collaborative, at times meandering, direction in which control is at best shared and at times wholly with the patient. The psychiatrist constantly asks, What is being said? What is the meaning of what is being said? In what context is this all emerging, and what does that tell me about the meanings?

Theoretical Perspectives on Listening

Listening is the effort or work of placing the psychiatrist where the patient is (lives). Greenson,[22] a psychoanalyst, would call it "going along with"; Rogers,[23] a humanistic psychologist, "centering on the client." The ear of the empathic listener is the organ of receptivity, gratifying and at times indulging the patient. Greenson would say that it is better to be deceived going along with the patient than to reject the patient prematurely and have the door slammed to the patient's inner world. That is what is meant by the suspension of beliefs for the discovery of the true self. Harry Stack Sullivan,[24] the father of interpersonal psychiatry, would remind us to heed those shrewd, small questions, What is the patient up to? Where is the patient taking us? Every human being has a preferred interpersonal stance, a set of relationships, and transactions with which she or he is most comfortable and feels most gratified. The problem is that for most psychiatric patients, they do not work well. This is the wisdom that Sullivan was articulating.

Beyond attitudes that enable or prevent listening, there is a role for specific knowledge. It is important to achieve the cognitive structure to use these attitudes with rigor and discipline in the service of patients so that psychiatrists use more than global "feelings" or "hunches." In striving to grasp the inner experience of any other human being, one must know what it is to be human; one must have an idea of what is inside any person that this particular one will not, cannot, knows not how to communicate or communicates in some distinctive idiosyncratic pattern. Personality theory is absolutely crucial to this process.

Whether we acknowledge it, every one of us has a theory of human personality (in this day of porous boundaries between psychology and biology, we should really speak of a psychobiological theory of human experience) that we apply in various situations, social or clinical. These theories become part of the template alluded to earlier that allows certain words, stories, actions, and cues from the patient to jump out with profound meaning to the psychiatrist for what the inner experience must be. There is no substitute for a thorough knowledge of many theories of human functioning and a well-disciplined synthesis and internal set of rules for which theories to use in what situations.

Different theoretical positions offer slightly different perspectives on listening (Table 1–4). The basic tools of therapeutic power and diagnostic acumen spring from the following:

1. Freud's associative methods and ego psychology,[25] in which one listens for the associative trends and conflicts.
2. Melanie Klein's and Harry Stack Sullivan's object relations theory and practice, which in the United States they are often called the mother and father of. She discovered the story through inner world exploration and recognizing the introjected persons of the past who live in the patient's head; he, the knowing through the interpersonal experience of the therapeutic dyad.[26]
3. Binswanger's understanding of the condition of empathy, in which the listener gives up his or her own position for that of the storyteller.[27]
4. Kohut's self psychology, which places the listener in a mirroring position, reflecting back to the storyteller assurances of being known and found.[28]

Table 1–4 Theoretical Perspectives on Listening

Theory	Focus of Attention	Listening Stance
Ego psychology	Stream of associations	Neutral, hovering attention
Object relations	Introjects (internalized images of others within the patient)	Neutral, hovering attention
Interpersonal	What relationship is the patient attempting to construct?	Participant observer
Existential	Feelings, affect	Empathic identification with the patient
Self psychology	Sense of self from others	Empathic mirroring and affirmation
Patient centered	Content control by patient	Noncontingent positive regard, empathy
Cognitive	Hidden assumptions and distortions	Benign expert
Behavioral	Behavioral contingencies	Benign expert
Family systems	Complex forces maneuvering each member	Neutral intruder who forces imbalance in the system

Each of the great schools of psychotherapy places the psychiatrist at a particular position physically and psychologically in relation to the patient. In a psychoanalytic stance, the psychiatrist, traditionally unseen behind the patient, assumes an active, hovering attention. In existential listening, the psychiatrist seeks the patient's position and places herself or himself close and facing. Interpersonal psychiatry suggests a position beside, stressing a collaborative dialogue with shared control. It requires that the listener sense what the storyteller is doing to and with the listener. It stresses the need for each participant to act within that interpersonal social field. In the object relations stance, the ego has learned roles. It is not such an executive presiding over itself, the id, and the superego. It is not presiding in executive fashion over the relationship between the psychiatrist and patient, because it is made up at least partly of introjects, parts, fragments, and pieces of significant others. So the listener keeps in mind the "other people in the room" with him or her and the storyteller.

In connecting with the patient, the listener is also tuned in to the fact that parts and fragments of himself or herself are taken in by the patient. The listener is digested and changed within the head of the patient and represents an internalized object. The listener becomes another person in the room of the patient's life experience within and outside the therapeutic hour. The cognitive and behavioral psychiatrists are kindly experts listening for hidden assumptions and connections. The family systems psychiatrist sits midway among the pressures and forces emanating from each individual, seeking to manipulate the system so that all must adapt differently.

Referring again to clinical vignette 2, we can see the different theoretical models of the listening process in the discovery of the meaning of little fella. Freud's model is that the psychiatrist had listened repeatedly to a specific association and inquired of its meaning. The object relations theorists would note that the psychiatrist had discovered a previously unidentified, powerful introject in the room with the therapeutic dyad. The interpersonal psychiatrists would see the shared exploration of this idiosyncratic manner of describing one's youth; the patient had been continually trying to take the psychiatrist to the Andy Griffith Show.

Existentialists would note how the psychiatrist was changed dramatically by the patient's repeated use of this phrase and then altered even more profoundly by the memory of Andy Griffith, the consummate good father in the patient's words; the psychiatrist could never see the patient in the same way again, and the patient sensed it immediately. Kohut would note the mirroring quality of the psychiatrist's echoing of how important a memory and discovery this meaning was: mirroring at its most powerful, affirming the patient's important differences from his family and consolidating them. The behavioral psychiatrist would note the reciprocal inhibition that had gone on, with Andy Griffith soothing the phobic anxieties in a brutal family.

A cognitive psychiatrist would wonder whether the patient's depression resulted from a hidden assumption that anything less than television's idyllic images was not good enough. The family systems psychiatrist would help the patient see that he had manipulated the forces at work on him and actually changed the definition of his family.

The ways and tools of listening also change according to the purpose and the nature of the therapeutic dyad. The ways of listening also change depending on whether the psychiatrist happens to be having a good or bad day! The medical model psychiatrist listens for signs and symptoms. The analyst listens for the truth often clothed in fantasy and metaphor. The existentialist listens for feeling, and the interpersonal theorist listens for facts placed on a screen before the patient and the psychiatrist. Regardless of the theoretical stance and regardless of the mental tension between the medical model's need to know symptoms and signs and the humanistic psychiatrist's listening to know the sufferer, the essence of therapeutic listening is the suspension of belief before any presentation of the story and the storyteller. The listener is asked to clarify and classify the inner world of the storyteller at the same time he or she is experiencing it—no small feat!

Using One's Personhood in Listening

In knowing what it is to be a person, perhaps even more important than theory is listening to oneself. Understanding transference and countertransference is crucial to effective listening. Tomkins[10] and Brothers[11] have given us a basic science, biological perspective on this process. However one defines these terms, whatever one's theoretical stance about these issues, Sullivan[29] had it right when he said that individuals with schizophrenia are more human than anything else. He was saying that in our wish to distance ourselves from a frightening disease, we may forget the person who has the illness. To know ourselves is to begin to know our patients more deeply. There are many routes to this point. Personal therapy is one. Ongoing life experience is another. Supervision that emphasizes one's emotional reactions to patients is still a third.

To know oneself is to be aware that there are certain common human needs, drives, feelings, and reactions. Every person must deal in some way with attachment, dependence, authority, autonomy, selfhood, values and ideals, remembered others, work, love, and hate. To know these things about oneself is to be in a position to hear them, wonder about them, and note what may be unspoken in one's patients. Thus, Figure 1–1 should really look like Figure 1–2. The most psychotic patient in the world is still struggling with these universal human functions.

Clinical Vignette 9

A young man with paranoid schizophrenia had been admitted to the hospital for a near-lethal attack on his father. When asked about this incident, he became frankly delusional, speaking of the Arab-Israeli conflict, the preciousness of Jerusalem, and how the Israelis must defend it at all costs. Unspoken was his conviction that he was like the Israelis, with the entire world attacking and threatening him. He believed that his father had threatened and attacked him when in fact his father had done little more than seek to be a bit closer, more comforting, and somewhat directive toward the patient. The year was 1979. The psychiatrist understood him to be speaking of that core of selfhood that we all possess, which, when threatened, creates a sense of vulnerability and panic unlike any other. The psychiatrist spoke to the patient of Anwar Sadat's visit to Jerusalem and engaged him in a discussion of how that had gone: What had the outcome been? Had the threat been lessened or increased? The patient, although still delusional, visibly relaxed and began to speak much more directly of his own sense of vulnerability and uncertainty about any inner sense of personal integrity that might withstand any closeness. He still needed neuroleptic medication for his illness; however, his violence was reduced dramatically, he was able to begin interacting with his father, and his behavior on the ward changed as well.

In this case, the psychiatrist was able to connect with a patient's inner experience in a manner that had a fairly dramatic impact on the clinical course. That is the goal of listening. The art is in hearing the patient's inner experience and then addressing it in some fashion that enables the patient to feel found and heard. There are no rules about this, and at any given point in a clinical encounter there are many ways to accomplish this. The skilled psychiatrist, just as she or he never forgets that it is the patient's inner experience that is to be heard, also never stops struggling to find just the right words, gestures, expressions, and inflections that say to a patient, "You have been understood." The most clever diagnostician or insightful interpreter who cannot connect with the patient in this manner will miss valuable information. This issue has been addressed by writers who have pointed out how little understood the concepts of support and empathy truly are.

Being human is also to be a creature of habit and pattern in linguistic, interpersonal, and emotional realms. The skilled psychiatrist listens with this ever in mind. What we see in the interview, what we hear in interactions may be presumed to be repetitions of many other events. The content may vary, but the form, motive, process, and evolution are generally universal for any given individual. This, too, is part of listening. To know what is fundamentally human, to have a well-synthesized rigorous theory, and to hear the person's unique but repetitive ways of being fundamentally human are the essence of listening. These skills "find" the patient in all his or her humanity, but then the psychiatrist must find the right communication that allows the patient to feel found.

To Be Found: The Psychological Product of Being Heard

Psychiatric patients are lonely, isolated, demoralized, and desperate, regardless of the specific diagnosis. They have lost themselves and their primary relationships, if they ever had any. Jackson[4] made the point that before anything else can happen, patients must be found and feel found. They can be found only within the context of their own specific histories, cultures, religions, genders, and social contexts. There is nothing more healing than that experience of being found by another. In childhood, we call it attachment. Sullivan,[29] in latency, spoke of the importance of the chum, pal, or buddy. In adulthood, we call it love. Psychiatric patients, deep inside, have lost or never had that experience. However obnoxious, destructive, or desperate the overt

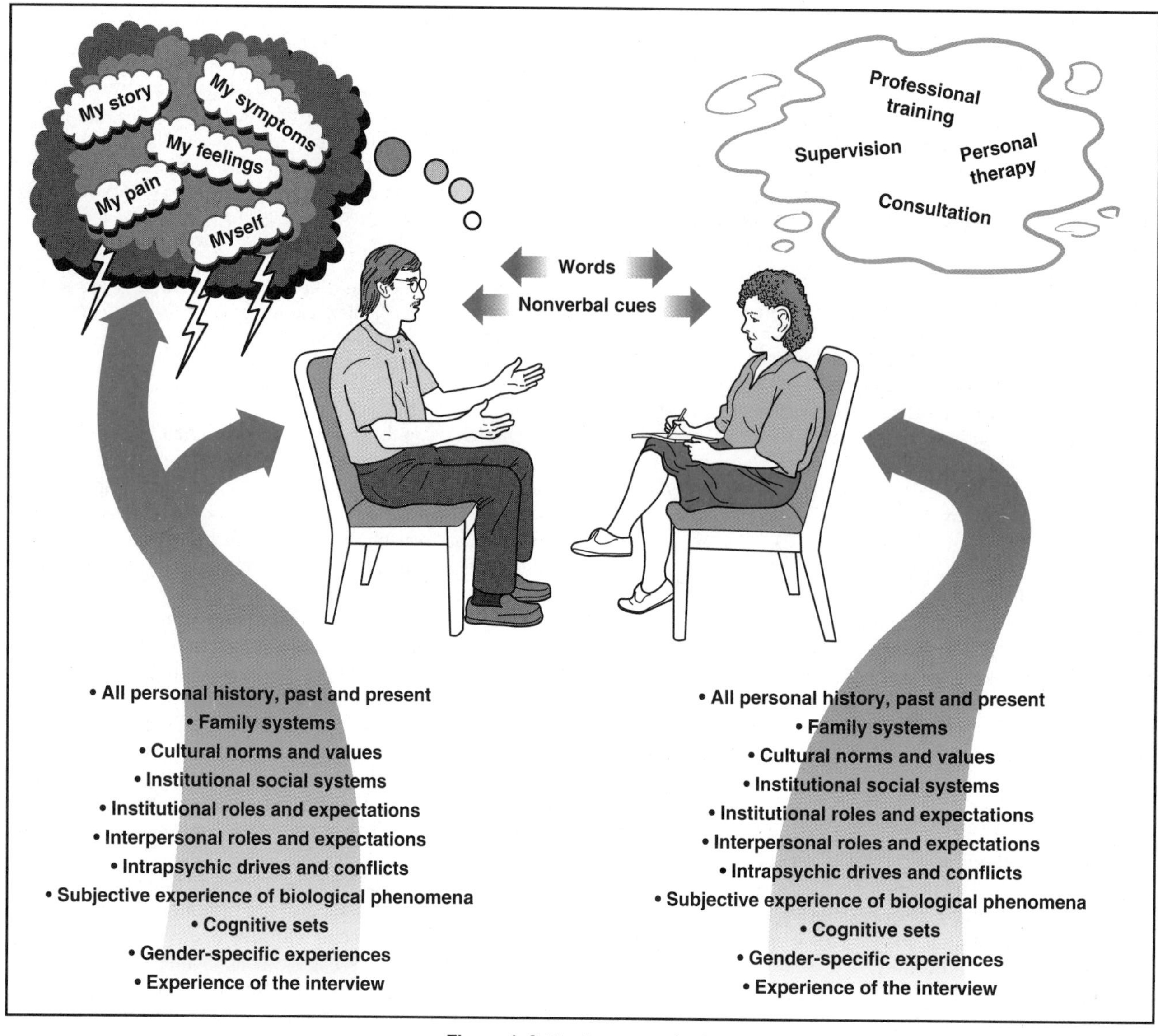

Figure 1–2 *The therapeutic dyad.*

behavior, it is the psychiatrist's job to seek and find the patient. That is the purpose of listening.

If we look at clinical vignette 2, wherein the phrase little fella bespoke such deep and important unverbalized meaning, the patient's reaction to the memory and recognition by the psychiatrist was dramatic. He had always known that he was different in some indefinable ways from his family. That difference had been a source of both pride and pain to him at various developmental stages. However, the recognition of the specific source, its meaning, and its constant presence in his life created a whole new sense of himself. He had been found by his psychiatrist, who echoed the discovery, and he had found an entire piece of himself that he had enacted for years yet which had been disconnected from any integrated sense of himself.

Sometimes objectifying and defining the disease or disorder enable the person to be seen and feel found. One of the most challenging patients to hear and experience is the acting-out, self-destructive, demanding person with borderline personality disorder. Even as the prior sentence conveys, psychiatrists often experience the diagnosis as who the patient is rather than what the patient suffers. The following vignette conveys how one third-year resident was able to hear such a patient and, in his listening to her, introduce the idea that the symptoms were not her but her disorder.

Clinical Vignette 10

He was working the midnight Friday to 11 AM Saturday shift in a psychiatric emergency department. The patient was a 26-year-old woman brought in by ambulance for overdosing on sertraline after an argument with her boyfriend. She had been partying with him and became enraged at the attention he was paying to the date of a friend who was accompanying them. After being cleared medically, the patient was transferred to the psychiatric service for crisis intervention. It was about 4 AM when she arrived. She was crying and screaming for the technicians to release her. She had grabbed a suture scissors attached to the uniform of the charge nurse in the medicine emergency department as she was escorted to the psychiatric ward. The report was given to the psychiatric resident that she had been a "management problem" in the medicine emergency department.

The psychiatrist sat wearily and listened to the patient tell her story with tears, shouts, and expletives sputtered through clenched teeth. She stated that she did not remember ever being happy and that she had frequently thought of suicide. She had overdosed twice before, after a divorce from her first husband at the age of 19 years and then 8 months before this episode when she had been fired from a job for arguing with her supervisor. Her parents had kept her 6-year-old and 7-year-old sons since her divorce. She was currently working as a file clerk and living with her boyfriend of 2 months. She felt as if there was a cold ice cube stuck in her chest as she watched her boyfriend flirting with the other woman. She felt empty and utterly alone even in the crowded bar. She had raised a scene and they continued to argue until they got home. Then he had laughed at her and left, stating that he would come back when she had cooled down.

The resident sat quietly and listened. He looked dreary. The night had been a busy one. She looked at him and complained, "Don't let me and my problems bore you!" He looked at her and said, "Quite the contrary. I've been thinking as you speak that I know what disorder you suffer." With that statement, he pulled out the DSM-III-R and read with her the description of the symptoms and signs of borderline personality disorder. She had been in therapy off and on since she was 16 years old. No one had ever shared with her the name of the diagnosis, but instead, therapists had responded to her as if the disorder was the definition of who she was. In his listening, the psychiatrist was able to hear her symptoms as a disorder and not as the person. In his ability to separate the two, he was able to allow her to distance herself from the symptoms, too, and see herself in a new light with her first inkling of her own personhood.

Gender can play an enormous role in the experience of feeling found. Some individuals feel that it is easier to connect with a person of the same sex, others with someone of the opposite sex. Clinical vignette 5 is an excellent example of this. In these days of significant change in and sensitivity to sex roles, a misinterpretation such as that early in treatment could result in a permanent rupture in the alliance. Psychiatrists vary in their sensitivity to the different sexes. Some may do better with those who have chosen more traditional roles; others may be more sensitive to those who are at the cutting edge of changing sex roles.

Table 1–5 The Basic Sciences of Listening

Neurobiology of primary affects
Universality of certain affective expressions
Neurobiology of empathy
Biological need for interpersonal regulation
Psychobiology of attachment
Biological impact of social support
Environmental impact on central nervous system structure and function

We now know that just as there is a neurobiological basis for empathy and countertransference, there is a similar biological basis for the power of listening to heal, to lift psychological burdens, to remoralize, and to provide emotional regulation to patients who feel out of control of their rage, despair, terror, or other feelings (Table 1–5). Attachment and social support are psychobiological processes that provide necessary physiological regulation to human beings. This has been shown by the work of Hofer, Cobb, House and colleagues, Kraemer, and many others.[30] Additional work of Paul Ekman supports the notion of the patient's capacity to perceive empathy through the powerful nonverbal, universally understood communication of facial expressions. His research in basic human emotions sets forth the idea of their understanding across cultures and ages. It further supports the provocative idea that facial expressions of the listener may generate autonomic and central nervous system changes not only within the listener but within the one being heard, and vice versa.[31] When we listen in this way, we are intervening not only in a psychological manner to connect, heal, and share burdens but also in a neurobiological fashion to regulate, modulate, and restore functioning. When patients feel found, they are responding to this psychobiological process.

Listening to Oneself to Listen Better

To hold in mind what has been said and heard after and between sessions is the most powerful and active tool of listening. It is a crucial step often overlooked by students and those new at listening. It is necessary to hear our patients in our thoughts during the in-between times to pull together repetitive patterns of thinking, behaving, and feeling, giving us the closest idea of how patients experience themselves and their world.

Clinical Vignette 11

A second-year resident, treating a number of severely psychotic patients with histories of multiple admissions, dual diagnoses, homelessness, criminal records, and significant histories of medical noncompliance, was particularly struggling with a 33-year-old woman admitted for the 11th time since the age of 19 years. The patient invariably stopped medications shortly after discharge, never kept follow-up appointments, and ended up living on the streets, psychotic and high on crack. She would then be involuntarily committed for medical stabilization, and so the cycle would repeat itself. The resident saw the patient daily, hearing the same litany: "I'm not sick. I don't need to be here. I don't need medicines." She regularly refused doses.

The resident spoke often of her patient to other residents and found herself ruminating about her abject lostness. The resident came in for supervision either frustrated or feeling hopeless that anything would change. Shortly after a particularly difficult encounter with the patient concerning her refusal to take an evening dose of haloperidol, the resident reported that she had awakened terrorized by dreaming the night before that she had been diagnosed with schizophrenia. She had been intensely affected by overwhelming pain, confusion, and despair as she heard the diagnosis in her dream. "It can't be!" she screamed, waking herself with a shaking start. "I'm not sick! I don't need to be here! I don't need medicine!" The words of her patient echoed in her mind as her own echoed in her ears. She had taken the patient's story and words home with her, keeping them in mind at an unconscious level to be brought up in her dream. The patient and resident continued to struggle, but after the dream, the resident was able to approach the patient and her story from a position of understanding the meaning of a lack of awareness or absence of insight. To acknowledge the presence of the disorder was more than the patient's already fragmented ego could bear, and now the resident heard it.

As verbal interaction with the patient occurs, psychiatrists may find themselves expressing thoughts and feeling ways that may be different from their usual repertoire. This is another situation in which listening to oneself becomes crucial. The following vignette is an example.

Clinical Vignette 12

A 45-year-old divorced woman being observed for bipolar disorder and borderline personality traits who had been stable for several years with lithium came in for weekly psychotherapy. She had been moving into another apartment closer to her work the weekend before. She had overslept on Saturday, the day of the move, and woke up with a start. The admonition to herself as she awoke was, "You lazy bitch! You can never manage on your own." In growing up, she had experienced a mother who was at once needy, engulfing, punishing, hostile, critical, and dependent on the patient. Her psychiatrist, having some knowledge of the patient and her background, said, "Your mother is still with you. It was she in your head continuing to bombard you with derogatory statements."

The same patient was often 10 or 15 minutes late for sessions. Her psychiatrist, being fairly rigid concerning time management, found herself irritated at the patient's habitual tardiness. To the psychiatrist's surprise and enlightenment, she found herself thinking, "What a chaotic woman! She'll never manage to be here on time." She, too, had heard the voice of her patient's mother. In the next session, she wondered with her patient whether she found herself wishing to place her psychiatrist in the position of her mother, wanting at once to be engulfed and punished.

Listening in Special Clinical Situations

Children

Listening to children involves inviting them to play, then engaging them in describing what is happening to the play action. The psychiatrist pays careful attention to the child's feelings. These feelings are usually attributed to a doll, puppet, or other humanized toy. If a child describes Raggedy Andy as being scared, the psychiatrist may say, "I wonder if you, too, are scared when . . ." or "That sounds like you when . . . ." The following vignette is an example.

Clinical Vignette 13

A 4-year-old boy was brought in for psychiatric evaluation. He and his dad had come upon the scene of a serious automobile accident. One person had been thrown from the car and was lying clearly visible on the pavement, with arms and legs positioned at grotesque angles and a gaping head wound, obviously dead. The child's dad was an off-duty police officer who stopped to assist in the extraction of two other people trapped in the car as he kept a careful eye on the youngster who was left in the car. The child observed the scene for about 30 minutes until others arrived on the scene and his dad was able to leave. That night and for days to come, the child preoccupied himself with his toy cars, which he repetitiously rammed into each other. He was awakened by nightmares three times in the next couple of weeks.

When he was brought in, he was evaluated in the play therapy room, where he also engaged in ramming toy cars together. In addition, with the availability of dolls, he tossed the dolls about and arranged limbs haphazardly. As he was encouraged to put some words to his action, he spoke of being frightened of the dead body and of being afraid to be left alone. He was afraid of the possibility of being hurt himself. He came in for three more play sessions, which went much the same way. His preoccupation with ramming cars at home diminished and disappeared, as did the nightmares. The play represented his story, which could be used to help him put words and labels on his scare.

For a child to be heard and the child's inner experience understood, the language of play and fantasy is used. Healing occurs in being listened to and understood. To hear the voice of a child telling her or his story, one listens in on the child's play. At the same time, one must be with the child in play to observe, guide, and provide labels for the emotional experience of the child. With the help of imagination, one is free to explore what this child's world is like, and that imagination is aided by having been a child once before.

Geriatric Patients

A difference is seen in listening to an octogenarian man when the psychiatrist is a woman in her 40s.

Clinical Vignette 14

A psychiatrist was asked to examine an 87-year-old man whom the family believed to be depressed. He was becoming increasingly detached and disinterested. When seen, he was cooperative and compliant but stated that he did not believe he needed to see anyone. He had faced multiple losses in the past few years. After retiring, he acquired the habit of meeting male friends each morning at 7 AM. Now, all but he and one other were dead, and the other was in a nursing home unable to recognize the patient. The patient's wife had died 15 years before. He had missed her terribly at first but then, after a year, got on about his life.

Several years later, he suffered a retinal detachment and was no longer able to drive. What he missed most was the independence of going places when it suited him rather than relying on his son or grandson to get him around. He had taken to watching televised church services rather than trouble his son. His mind remained sharp, he said, but his body was wearing out, and all the people with whom he had shared a common history had died. His answers were "fine" and "all right" when questions of quality of sleep and mood were asked. He retorted "Would you be?" when questioned about his ability to experience joy. His youngest sister had died a year earlier at the age of 76 years. He had been particularly close to her because she had been only 3 years old when their mother died. He had been her caretaker all her life.

Although he denied feelings of guilt, he said that it "wasn't right" that he had outlived the youngest member of his family. His family said that he had taken her death especially hard. After her death, it fell to him to dispose of her possessions. At first he said that he could not face the task. Finally, some 2 months later, he was able to close her estate. During that time, he had significant sleep disturbance and reduced energy, and his family often experienced him as crotchety and complaining. They and he marked it down to mourning her loss. Now they were particularly alarmed that he had said to his son that he was "ready to die." Together, he and the psychiatrist decided that he was indeed grieving. This time, however, he was grieving for his own decline and death. He was in fact in the final acceptance phase of that process. This determination was made only after he was coaxed into having an organic work-up. A family meeting facilitated discussions that he was facing the end of life and that there were thoughts for them to share, including the pain.

It is difficult to pull the elements of a story together, especially when they span years that compose a generation or more. The elderly are often stoic and noncomplaining. In the face of losses that mark the closing years of life, denial often becomes a healthy tool allowing one to proceed in the time of decline for oneself and loss through death and debilitation of one's circle of friends and loved ones. The psychiatrist must keep in mind the processes of grief and how these processes differ from and are similar to depression. Careful listening requires tracking the story, keeping in mind the person represented as one is also differentiating among and between diagnoses that sometimes overlap in characteristics. He had been a young man in his 20s and early 30s during the depression. How did that experience influence his outlook on life in general and his approach to dealing with the inevitable losses accompanying the last years of a long life? How can the psychiatrist connect with the patient? How can the psychiatrist help the elderly connect with the important people in their present world as they enter that transition marking life's end, when it is an important developmental step to detach and transcend this physical life and the social and physical losses that are part of it?

Chronically Mentally Ill

Listening to the chronically mentally ill can be especially challenging, too. The unique choice of words characteristic of many who have a thought disorder requires that the psychiatrist search for the meanings of certain words and phrases that may be peculiar to that particular person. Clinical vignettes 9 and 11 are examples of this important challenge for the psychiatric listener.

Clinical Vignette 15

A young man with schizotypal personality disorder and obsessive-compulsive disorder presented for weeks and months with adjectives describing himself as "broken" and "fragmented." Only after listening carefully, not aided by the expected or normal affect of a depressed person, was the psychiatrist able to pick up the truth in his story—he was clinically depressed but did not have the usual words and affect to say it.

Clinical Vignette 16

A 32-year-old woman who had multiple hospitalizations for schizophrenia and lived with her mother recently came into the community psychiatric center for routine medication follow-up. Her psychiatrist found her to have an increase in the frequency of auditory hallucinations, especially ones of a derogatory nature. The voices were tormenting her with the ideas that she was not good, that she should die, that she was worthless and not loved.
On exploring what was going on with her, her psychiatrist heard her say that she had wrecked her mom's car 2 weeks previously. The streets had been wet and the tires worn. She had slid into the rear of a car that had come to an abrupt stop ahead of her on a freeway. Her mom had not been critical or judgmental. However, the patient felt overwhelming guilt as she watched her mom struggle to arrange transportation for herself each day to and from work.

As this case illustrates, the chronically psychiatrically disabled patient has a unique way of presenting the inner world experience. Sometimes the link to outer world experience is not so apparent. However, increases in psychotic symptoms are often linked in a reality-based way to patients' experience of themselves, persons close to them, and their world. The psychiatrist is regularly challenged with making sense of the meanings of the content and changes in intensity or frequency of the hallucinations, and the patient has the opportunity to be heard and understood as a person with schizophrenia, not as a schizophrenic.

Physically Ill Patients

In the work of psychiatry, one is often listening to a patient who has a physical illness, either chronic or acute. The invitation to listen to these persons often comes in the form of a request for consultation from a colleague in a medical or surgical specialty. If the patient is hospitalized, the communication from the primary physician may lend some degree of preconceived notion to how the psychiatrist will experience the patient and what the psychiatrist will hear from the patient. It falls to the psychiatrist, then, not only to listen to the story of the patient but also to keep in mind the story as reflected in the hospital records, the nursing staff's notes, and the medical or surgical team's findings. Then the psychiatrist truly serves as the liaison not only between psychiatry and the rest of the medical profession but also between the patient (who may not have been adequately heard) and the medical or surgical team that is providing primary care.

Clinical Vignette 17

A 35-year-old woman was hospitalized for complications of a pancreas-kidney transplant performed 20 months previously. Before surgery, she had been undergoing dialysis for more than a year, having been forced to take a leave of absence from her job as a social worker. Her life had been on hold while she awaited the possibility of the transplant. At the time of this hospitalization, she had been back at work for 8 months. A urinary tract infection then developed that did not respond to several rounds of antibiotics. She was discharged after finally responding and went back to work. Now, once again, she was hospitalized. Her creatinine level was 12 mg/dL and climbing. Her physicians found her to be paranoid, hostile, and labile. They dreaded going into her room each morning. They were treating her with multiple antibiotics, steroids, and antirejection drugs. They found themselves limiting their interactions with her. Why should they allow themselves to be exposed to the hostility and blaming of this patient? Besides, they, too, were struggling with the idea that they had failed her.

Psychiatric consultation was sought after a particularly difficult interaction among the charge nurse, the leader of the transplant team, and the infectious disease expert who was participating in her care. The patient had become pressured, hostile, blaming, agitated, and circumstantial; she ended the morning rounds by refusing any further medications and pulling out her intravenous lines. The consultation requested assistance in hospital management.

When interviewed, the patient was lying quietly in bed but visibly stiffened when the psychiatrist introduced herself. She quickly exhibited the symptoms described in the consultation request. Certainly the primary physicians were astute in their description, but once again, where is the patient in the description? She did indeed respond to a medical approach to some of her symptoms. Low doses of haloperidol relieved her of much of the hostile labile projection.

Follow-up revealed a patient whose story was one of having struggled with juvenile-onset diabetes since the age of 9 years. Despite the fact that she had always been compliant with her diet and insulin regimen, control of blood glucose levels had always been brittle. As complication after complication occurred, she often had the belief that her physicians thought she was a "bad" patient. Now, the hope that her life would normalize to the point that she could carry on with her career was dashed. She felt misunderstood and alone in her struggle with a long-term, chronic illness, whose conclusion would likely be early death. The patient herself was found only after the psychiatrist combined hearing her story as a medical physician, listening for ways to address symptoms from the medical standpoint, with approaching her as one human being to another. Someone was there to worry with her over the tragic turn that her life had taken.

Integrating All of This and Growing as a Listener

The example of clinical vignette 17 also demonstrates feelings of the patient toward her medical staff and her ideas of how they perceived her. Transference and countertransference influence not only relationships in traditional psychotherapy but also interactions between physicians and patient, no matter what the specialty or purpose of the encounter. The impact of countertransference stems from its ubiquitous, ever-present quality. It is always present as a filter or reverberator to that which is heard. However, not even the most experienced of listeners is always aware of the ways in which the patient's stories are affected by countertransference. Psychiatry is a listening profession. It is one that requires those who choose to make listening their life's work to not work in isolation. To seek consultation, collaboration, and supervision of cases is a matter of course for psychiatrists. To do so allows one to step outside oneself and the therapeutic dyad and to gain insight from another as the story of the patient is shared.

Patients come, too, with tendencies and predispositions to experience the listener, the other person in the therapeutic dyad, in certain ways: with dependency needs, so that the patient may idealize and adapt to whatever insight is given back; with hostility and distrust, so that the psychiatrist is identified in an unconscious way with one who has been rejecting in the past; with shame and guilt, so that the story is always vague, the patient hiding from one who is expected to judge and criticize.

All of these facts come together as the psychiatrist listens to the "stream of consciousness."[32] Eventually, the psychiatrist comes in touch with a thread of continuity and purposefulness. A continuous theme emerges over time, a continuity of flow as one thread is dropped and another picked up, then in another hour, a loop back to a thread long dropped. So the fabric of meaning is woven. In becoming more familiar with the patient, the psychiatrist may hear a tapestry for a long time before the idea or notion of what is happening becomes clear. That awareness may come through a sign or symptom, or a fantasy, feeling, or fact. It can be reflected back as a hunch or idea, the words of the psychiatrist like notes to be played on the mind of the patient.

There is an increasing recognition that to be a healing listener, one must be able to bear the burden of hearing what is told. There is often a fear of what might be heard. The story may be one of rage in response to early childhood attachment ruptures, sadness as personal losses are remembered, or terror in response to disorganization during the experience of perceptual abnormalities accompanying psychotic breaks. The hearing may invoke anger, shame, guilt, abject helplessness, or sexual feelings within the listener. These feelings, unless attended to, appreciated, and understood, will block the listening that is essential for healing to take place.

Every insight is colored by what the listener has known. It is impossible to know that which is not experienced. The psychiatrist comes with his or her own experiences and the experiences he or she has had with others. To listen in the manner we are describing here is another way of truly experiencing the world. The experiences include the imaginings of how it must be to be

87 years old as a patient when one is a 32-year-old physician just finishing residency; to be female when one is male; to be a child again; to grow up African-American in a small white suburb of a large city. One comes to know by listening with imagination, allowing the words of the patient to resonate with one's own experiences or with what one has come to know through hearing with imagination the stories of other patients, or by listening to the thoughts or insights of supervisors.

The best psychiatrists continue all their professional lives to learn how to listen better. This may be thought of as a matter not only of mastering countertransference but of self-education. One must learn to recognize when one has a patient one is not listening well to and seek education, from a colleague or perhaps even from the patient. Consider these two examples.

Clinical Vignette 18

A Jewish resident was treating an 8-year-old Catholic boy who came in one day and mentioned offhandedly that he was about to go to his first confession. The psychiatric resident made no particular note of the issue and kept on listening to the boy's story and its themes. He noted that guilt, which had been an ongoing theme, was prominent again. When he presented the session in supervision, the supervisor wondered about the connection. It emerged that there was a large gulf between the therapist and the boy. Jewish concepts of sin and atonement are different from Christian ones, and the rituals surrounding them have different intentions and ideas of resolution. The resident had missed the opportunity to explore the young boy's first introduction to the belief in a forgiving God, a potentially important step in helping the child to resolve his ongoing struggles with guilt over his own greedy impulses.

Clinical Vignette 19

A psychiatrist began treating a Nigerian who was suffering from posttraumatic stress disorder after being assaulted in his work as a clerk in a convenience store. After several sessions, the psychiatrist felt a sense of being at a loss in terms of what the patient was expecting out of work, how the therapist was being seen by the patient, and the train of meanings in their transactions. He took several sessions to inquire of the patient about his tribe, its structure, family roles, definitions of healing, who took on such roles, and ideas of illness and wellness. After this exploration, the psychiatrist adopted a different stance with the patient and heard the communications differently. The therapy proceeded much more smoothly and comfortably to a successful conclusion.

Invitations to the teller of the story are many. Even if a patient is coming of her or his own choosing to the presence of the listener, how can the psychiatrist's demeanor convey to patients that they are safe to tell their story, that the listener is one who can be trusted to be with them, to worry with them, and to serve as a helper? Much is written about the demeanor of the psychiatrist. The air, deportment, manner, or bearing is one of quiet anticipation, to receive that which the patient has come to tell and share in the telling. Signals of anticipation and curiosity may be conveyed by such statements as "Catch me up," "I've thought about what you said last time," "How do you feel about . . . ?" "What if . . . ?"

These efforts for clarification give feedback throughout the sessions and often serve as bridges between sessions, to affirm the listener's investment of energy in the process of listening and coming to fuller understanding of the patient. Patients have the need to experience the psychiatrist as empathic. Empathy describes the feeling one has in hearing a story that causes one to conjure up or imagine how it would be to actually have had the experience. How does one integrate all this so that it is automatic but not deadened by automaticity? How does the psychiatrist continue to hear the "same old thing" with freshness and renewal? How does one encourage the patient with consistency, clarity, and assurance in the face of the uncertainty and occasional confusion? Not by assurance that everything will be all right when things will most assuredly not be. Not by attempting to talk the patient into seeing things the psychiatrist's way. Rather, it is by the psychiatrist's capacity to hear things the patient's way and from the patient's perspective, to ultimately cup an ear in the direction of the patient to hear the world from the patient's point of view.

Psychiatry is one of those rare disciplines in life in which the experience of listening over and over again allows the listener to grow in the capacity to hear. The practice allows one to get better and better with advancing years; to become smoother, seamless, and natural, with a style that blends one's own personality and training with one's unique view of the patients and their world. It is the philosophical approach of allowing renewal of oneself in shared experiences with those being heard. When the therapist listens to a patient's history, change occurs in the patient because he or she has been heard and in the therapist because he or she has listened.

To hear stories of the human condition reminds psychiatrists that they, too, are human, with good and bad days. Patients are forgiving over the long haul. There is always time to make discoveries that may have been there for the discovering in a previous time, and maybe in a previous patient. So the good listener must have the capacities to ease up; to be attentive and alert to his or her own particular moods, thoughts, and energies and to seek ways of renewal even in the midst of a bad day or a bad time in one's own life; and to hone and sharpen the tools for listening. The patients will always be there one way or another to tell their stories. The psychiatrist continues to grow by being the perpetual student, always with an ear for the lesson, the remarkable life stories of the patients.

References

1. Binswanger L: Being in the World. New York: Basic Books, 1963.
2. Havens L: A Safe Place. Cambridge, MA: Harvard University Press, 1989.
3. Binswanger L: The case of Ellen West. In May R, Angel E, Ellenberger HF (eds): Existence: A New Dimension in Psychiatry and Psychology. New York: Basic Books, 1958:237–365.

4. Jackson S: The listening healer in the history of psychological healing. Am J Psychiatry 1992; 149:(12): 1623–1632.
5. Chomsky N: Language and Mind. New York: Harcourt Brace Jovanovich, 1972.
6. Andresen JJ, Andresen AI: Psychoanalysis and autobiography: Tell me my story. Presented at the Texas Society of Psychiatric Physicians Annual Meeting and Scientific Program; November 1993; Fort Worth TX.
7. Edelson M: Telling and enacting stories in psychoanalysis and psychotherapy. Psychoanal Study Child 1993; 48:293–325.
8. McHugh PR, Slavney PR: Perspectives of Psychiatry. Baltimore: The Johns Hopkins University Press, 1986.
9. Darwin C: Expressions of the Emotions in Man and Animals. New York: Philosophical Library, 1955.
10. Tomkins S: Affect, Imagery, Consciousness, Volumes 1 and 2. New York: Springer Publishing, 1962–63.
11. Brothers L: A biological perspective on empathy. Am J Psychiatry 1989; 146:10–19.
12. Kleinman A: Clinical relevance of anthropological and cross-cultural research: Concepts and strategies. Am J Psychiatry 1978; 135(4): 427–431.
13. Comas-Diaz L, Jacobsen F: Ethnocultural transference and counter-transference in the therapeutic dyad. Am J Orthopsychiatry 1991; 61:392–402.
14. Bauman R: Ethnographic Framework for Investigation of Communicative Behaviors, Language and Cultural Diversity in American Education. Engelwood Cliffs, NJ: Prentice-Hall, 1972.
15. Kochman T: Black and White: Styles in Conflict. Chicago: University of Chicago Press, 1991.
16. Styron W: Darkness Visible. New York: Random House Books, 1990.
17. Arieti S: The Intrapsychic Self: Feelings, Cognitions, and Creativity in Health and Mental Illness. New York: Basic Books, 1967.
18. Gabbard GO: Psychodynamic Psychiatry in Clinical Practice, 2nd ed. Washington, DC: American Psychiatric Press, 1994.
19. Elkin I, Shea MT, Watkins JT, et al: National Institute of Mental Health Treatment of Depression Collaborative Research Program: General effectiveness of treatments. Arch Gen Psychiatry 1989; 46:971–982.
20. Brill AA (ed): The Basic Writings of Sigmund Freud. New York: Random House Modern Library, 1938.
21. Havens L: Making Contact. Cambridge, MA: Harvard University Press, 1986.
22. Greenson RR: Explorations in Psychoanalysis. New York: International Universities Press, 1978.
23. Rogers CR: Client-Centered Therapy: Its Current Practice, Implications, and Theory. Boston: Houghton Mifflin, 1951.
24. Sullivan HS: Conceptions of Modern Psychiatry. New York: WW Norton, 1953.
25. Freud S: A General Introduction to Psychoanalysis. New York: Garden City Publishing, 1938.
26. Havens L: Participant Observation. New York: Aronson, 1976.
27. May R, Angel E, Ellenberger HF (eds): Existence: A New Dimension in Psychiatry and Psychology. New York: Basic Books, 1958.
28. Kohut H: The Search for the Self: Selected Writings of Heinz Kohut, 1978–1981. Madison, CT: International Universities Press, 1991.
29. Sullivan HS: Schizophrenia as a Human Process. New York: WW Norton, 1969.
30. Ursano RJ, Fullerton SC: Psychotherapy: Medical intervention and the concept of normality. In Daniel O, Sabshin M (eds): The Diversity of Normal Behavior. New York: Basic Books, 1991.
31. Ekman P: Facial expressions of emotion: An old controversy and new findings. Philos Trans R Soc Lond Biol 1992; 335:63–69.
32. James W: The Principles of Psychology. New York: H Holt, 1890.

CHAPTER

2 Psychiatric Interview: Settings and Techniques

Edward K. Silberman
Kenneth Certa

The interview is the principal means of assessment in clinical psychiatry. Despite major advances in neuroimaging and neurochemistry, no laboratory procedures are as informative as observing, listening to, and interacting with the patient, and none as yet is more than supplementary to the information gathered by the psychiatric interview. This chapter deals with the interview as a means of assessing the patient and developing an initial treatment plan in clinical situations.

Psychiatric interviews are analogous to the history and physical examination in a general medical assessment, and they share the major features of other types of medical interviews[1]; they systematically survey subjective and objective aspects of illness and generate a differential diagnosis and plan for further evaluation and treatment. They differ from other medical interviews in the wide range of biological and psychosocial data that they must take into account and in their attention to the emotional reactions of the patient and the process of interaction between the patient and the interviewer. The nature of the interaction is informative diagnostically as well as being a means of building rapport and eliciting the patient's cooperation, which is especially important in psychiatry.[2]

The style and content of a psychiatric interview are necessarily shaped by the interviewer's theory of psychopathology.[3] Thus, a biological theory of illness leads to an emphasis on signs, symptoms, and course of illness; a psychodynamic theory dictates a focus on motivations, attitudes, feelings, and personal interactions; a behavioral viewpoint looks at antecedents and consequences of symptoms or maladaptive behaviors. In past times, when these and other theories competed for theoretical primacy, an interviewer might view exploration from a particular single perspective as adequate. However, modern psychiatry views these perspectives as complementary rather than mutually exclusive and recognizes the contributions of biological, intrapsychic, social, and environmental factors to human behavior and its disorders.[4] The interviewer, therefore, faces the task of understanding each of these dimensions, adequately surveying them in the interview, and making informed judgments about their relative importance and treatment implications.[5]

The written psychiatric database, the mental organization that the interviewer maintains during the interview, and the structure of the interview itself may differ considerably from one another. The written psychiatric database is an orderly exposition of information gathered in the interview, presented in a relatively fixed format. The mental organization of the interviewer consists of questions and tentative hypotheses. It evolves flexibly over the course of the interview and is determined by the goals of the interview and emerging information that indicates needed areas of focus.[6]

The third structure is that of the interview itself. Although guided by general principles of interviewing, this structure is the most flexible of the three, being determined not only by the purpose of the interview and the type of problem that the patient presents but also by the patient's mode of communication and style of interaction with the interviewer. Thus, the interviewer must hold her or his own structure in mind while responding flexibly to the patient.

Goals of the Psychiatric Interview

The interview may be thought of as seeking the answers to several basic questions about the patient and the presenting problems. These questions provide the mental framework of the interview (although not its explicit form). They begin with the triage of patients into broad categories of type and severity and progress to inquiry about details in each salient area. Table 2–1 lists the questions that the interview addresses and the implications of each for understanding and treating the patient. The questions are as follows.

Does the Patient Have a Psychiatric Disorder?

This is the most basic question that the psychiatrist is called on to answer. It determines whether there is any need for further psychiatric assessment or treatment.

How Severe Is the Disorder?

The answer to this question determines the necessary level of treatment, ranging from hospitalization with close observation to infrequent outpatient visits. The main determinants of severity are dangerousness to self and others,

Table 2–1 Issues to Be Addressed in a Psychiatric Assessment

Question	Implications
Does the patient have a psychiatric disorder?	Need for treatment
How severe is the disorder?	Need for hospitalization Need for structure or assistance in daily life Ability to function in major life roles
What is the diagnosis?	Description of the illness Prognosis and treatment response
Are there abnormalities of brain function?	Degree of dysfunction of major mental processes, such as perception, cognition, communication, regulation of mood and affect Responsivity of symptoms to environmental and motivational factors Responsivity of symptoms to biological treatment
What is the patient's baseline level of functioning?	Determination of onset of illness State versus trait pathology Goals for treatment Capacity for treatment
What environmental factors contribute to the disorder?	Prediction of conditions that may trigger future episodes of illness Need for focus on precipitating stressors Prevention of future episodes through amelioration of environmental stressors or increased environmental and social support
What biological factors contribute to the disorder?	Need for biological therapy Place of biological factors in explanation of illness presented to the patient Focus on biological factors as part of ongoing therapy
What psychological factors contribute to the disorder?	Responsivity of symptoms to motivational, interpersonal, and reinforcement factors Need to deal with psychological or interpersonal issues in therapy
What is the patient's motivation and capacity for treatment?	Decision to treat Choice of treatment

impairment in ability to care for oneself, and ability to function in social and occupational roles.

What Is the Diagnosis?

In psychiatry, as in the rest of medicine, descriptive information about signs, symptoms, and course over time is used to assign a diagnosis to the presenting problem. Not all psychiatric diagnoses have well-established validity, but most convey knowledge of prognosis, comorbidity, treatment response, occurrence in family members, or associated biological or psychological findings.[7] Even in the case of poorly understood entities, our present system of diagnosis using specific criteria maximizes uniformity in the description and naming of psychiatric disorders.

Are There Abnormalities of Brain Function?

One important implication of diagnosis is whether there may be reduced plasticity of brain functioning due to anatomical or physiological abnormalities. Symptoms, deficits, and behaviors that stem from such abnormalities vary less in response to environmental and motivational factors than do those that arise in the context of normal brain function. For example, mood swings in a patient with bipolar disorder, a condition for which there is strong evidence of a biological-genetic cause, typically recur at regular time intervals, often independently of the patient's life situation. By contrast, mood swings in a patient with narcissistic personality disorder are much more likely to be triggered by interactions with other people. Furthermore, when brain function is impaired, biological treatments are more likely to be necessary, and verbal, interpersonal, or environmental interventions are less likely to be sufficient. Thus, the likelihood of altered brain function has major implications for understanding and treating the patient's problems.

Although the question of brain abnormalities is basic to psychiatric triage, we do not yet have a clear-cut biological cause for any disorder outside of those historically classified as organic. Standard laboratory studies (such as brain imaging or electroencephalography) are not generally diagnostic of psychopathological processes; however, there is research-based evidence for altered brain function in many psychiatric disorders. Table 2–2 presents an overview of the current state of knowledge of brain abnormalities in psychiatric disorders along with known responses to biological and psychosocial treatments.

What Is the Patient's Baseline Level of Functioning?

Determining what the patient has been like in his or her best or most usual state is a vital part of the assessment. This information allows the interviewer to gauge when the patient became ill and how he or she is different when ill versus well. Environmental, biological, and psychological factors that contribute to low baseline levels of functioning may also predispose to the development of psychiatric disorders. Thus, information about baseline functioning provides clues about the patient's areas of vulnerability to future illness as well as his or her capacity to benefit from treatment. It is also an important guide to realistic goals and expectations for such treatment. Table 2–3 lists major components of functioning with examples of elements of each.

What Environmental Factors Contribute to the Disorder?

Environmental contributions to the presenting problem are factors external to the patient. They may be acute events that precipitate illness or long-standing factors that increase general vulnerability. Loss, change, and traumatic events are common acute precipitants.[63] Long-standing environmental stressors may predispose to the development of illness and may also worsen the outlook for recovery.

It is important to identify adverse environmental influences that can be modified and to help the patient or

Table 2–2 Brain Dysfunction in Psychiatric Disorders

Disorder	Evidence for Brain Dysfunction	Response to Biological Treatments	Response to Psychosocial Treatments
Delirium, dementia, amnestic and cognitive disorders[8–11]	Well established	Reversible causes respond to appropriate treatment; neuroleptics, anxiolytics, antidepressants, lithium, anticonvulsants, and β-blockers may help.	Environmental support and supportive psychotherapy may help.
Schizophrenia[12–15]	Strong evidence	Most respond to antipsychotics; antidepressants, lithium, and anxiolytics may be helpful adjunctively.	Environmental support, supportive psychotherapy, family therapy, and social skills training may help.
Delusional disorder[16, 17]	Little evidence—few studies	Response to antipsychotics is poor to fair.	Response to psychotherapy is poor.
Schizoaffective disorder[18–20]	Evidence for relationship to schizophrenia and mood disorders	Most respond to combinations of antipsychotics, antidepressants, lithium, carbamazepine, and electroconvulsive therapy.	Not well established; similar range of treatments as for schizophrenia may help.
Brief psychotic disorder[21, 22]	Little evidence—few studies	Not well established.	Environmental support and supportive psychotherapy may be helpful.
Bipolar disorder[23–25]	Strong evidence	Most respond to lithium, antidepressants, anticonvulsants, or electroconvulsive therapy.	Supportive and educative psychotherapy and family therapy may be helpful.
Major depressive disorder[26–28]	Evidence suggestive; considerable heterogeneity	Often respond to antidepressants or electroconvulsive therapy.	Less severe cases respond to cognitive, interpersonal, and psychodynamic psychotherapy.
Panic disorder[29, 30]	Evidence suggestive	Most respond to anxiolytics or antidepressants.	Variable; cognitive-behavioral therapy is more effective than psychodynamic therapy.
Generalized anxiety disorder[31]	Little evidence	Variable; anxiolytics may help.	Variable; psychodynamic or cognitive-behavioral psychotherapies often help.
Specific phobia[32, 33]	Little evidence	Medications are not usually helpful.	Most respond to behavioral therapy.
Posttraumatic stress disorder[34, 35]	Little evidence	Variable; antidepressants and anxiolytics may help.	Psychotherapy with exploratory, supportive, and behavioral features usually helps.
Obsessive-compulsive disorder[36–38]	Evidence suggestive	Most respond to selective serotonin reuptake inhibitor antidepressants.	Rituals but not obsessive thoughts respond to behavioral therapy.
Somatization disorder[39, 40]	None known	Poor; medication for comorbid depression or anxiety may help.	Poor; supportive psychotherapy may help.
Conversion disorder[41, 42]	None known	Amobarbital (Amytal) interview may help, otherwise not indicated.	Most respond to psychotherapy with exploratory, expressive, and behavioral features; may remit spontaneously.
Hypochondriasis[43, 44]	None known	No direct response; medications may help for treatment of comorbid depression or anxiety.	Variable; supportive-educative psychotherapy may help.
Dissociative disorders[45, 46]	None known	No direct response; medications may help for treatment of comorbid depression and anxiety.	Variable; many respond to expressive-exploratory psychotherapy.
Alcohol use disorders[47, 48]	Strong evidence in subgroups	There are no well-demonstrated direct effects.	Group and individual psychotherapies are the most common treatment modalities; response is variable, relapse rate is high.
Psychoactive substance use disorders[49, 50]	Little evidence; some substances may induce long-lasting brain changes	There are no well-demonstrated direct effects.	Group and individual psychotherapies are the most common treatment modalities; response is variable, relapse rate is high.

Table continued on following page

Table 2–2 Brain Dysfunction in Psychiatric Disorders *Continued*

Disorder	Evidence for Brain Dysfunction	Response to Biological Treatments	Response to Psychosocial Treatments
Sexual disorders[51, 52]	May be due to metabolic disorders; otherwise little evidence	Medications for underlying medical conditions may be necessary; antiandrogens or serotoninergic antidepressants may help for paraphilias.	Sexual dysfunctions often respond to behaviorial therapy; couples therapy or exploratory therapy may also help.
Eating disorders[53, 54]	Evidence suggestive	Antidepressants may help ameliorate symptoms.	Expressive exploration, family, and behavioral therapies often help.
Adjustment disorders[55, 56]	None known	Medications may alleviate symptoms of anxiety or depression.	Supportive psychotherapy often helps.
Personality disorders Cluster A[57, 58]	Evidence for relationship of schizotypal personality to schizophrenia; otherwise none known	Schizotypal patients may improve with antipsychotic medication; otherwise it is not indicated.	Poor; supportive psychotherapy may help.
Cluster B[59, 60]	Evidence suggestive for antisocial and borderline personalities; otherwise none known	Antidepressants, antipsychotics, and mood stabilizers may help for borderline personality; otherwise they are not indicated.	Response is poor in antisocial personality, variable in borderline, narcissistic, and histrionic personalities.
Cluster C[61, 62]	None known	No direct response; medications may help with comorbid anxiety or depression.	Most common treatment for these disorders; response is variable.

family make necessary changes. For example, a patient with recurrent paranoid psychoses needed yearly hospitalization as long as she worked in an office with many other people. However, she no longer suffered severe relapses when she was helped to find work that she could do in her home. Even irreversible precipitants, however, such as death of a loved one, must be identified and dealt with in the treatment plan.

Table 2–3 Assessment of Baseline Functioning

Component	Examples
Level of symptoms	Depression Anxiety Obsessions and compulsions Delusions Hallucinations Impulsive behaviors
Interpersonal relations	Sexual relationships and marriage Quality and longevity of friendships Capacity for intimacy and commitment
Work adjustment	Employment history Level of responsibility Functioning in nonpaid roles (e.g., homemaker, parent) Satisfaction with work life
Leisure activities	Hobbies and interests Group and social activities Travel Ability to take pleasure in nonwork activities
Ego functions	Talents, skills, intelligence Ability to cope Reality testing Control over affects and behaviors Ability to formulate and carry through plans Stable sense of self and others Capacity for self-observation

What Biological Factors Contribute to the Disorder?

Biological factors may contribute to psychiatric disorders directly by their effects on the central nervous system and indirectly through the effects of pain, disability, or social stigma. Thus, biological factors must be assessed both through the psychiatric history and diagnosis and through the general medical history.

Biological factors affecting the central nervous system may be genetic, prenatal, perinatal, or postnatal. There is strong evidence for genetic contributions to schizophrenia, bipolar disorder, and alcoholism, among others[12, 22, 46]; conditions such as maternal substance abuse or intrauterine infections may affect fetal brain development; birth complications may cause cerebral hypoxia with resultant brain damage. In postnatal life, the entire range of diseases that affect the brain may alter mental function and behavior, as may exposure to toxins at work, in the environment, and through substance abuse. In addition, medical conditions that do not directly affect brain functioning may have profound effects on patients' state of mind and behavior.

Biological factors may both predispose to and precipitate episodes of illness. Thus, a patient with a genetic vulnerability to schizophrenic illness may have an episode of acute psychosis precipitated by heavy cocaine use. Similarly, a patient with borderline low intellectual capacity due to hypoxia at birth may have marginal ability for self-care. An accident resulting in a fractured arm might overwhelm this person's coping capacity and precipitate a severe adjustment disorder.

What Psychological Factors Contribute to the Disorder?

Psychological factors are mental traits that the patient brings to life situations. Although they interact with social and environmental factors, they are intrinsic to the individual and not readily changed by outside influences.

Psychological factors predisposing to illness include both general and focal deficits in coping and adaptability. General deficits encompass the entire range of ego functioning, including poor reality testing; rigid or maladaptive psychological defense mechanisms; low ability to tolerate and contain affects; impulsivity; poorly formed or unstable sense of self; low self-esteem; and hostile, distant, or dependent relationships with others.[64] Patients with such deficits generally meet diagnostic criteria for one or more personality disorders and are at increased risk for episodes of acute psychiatric illness. General deficits in psychological functioning are illustrated by the following example.

Clinical Vignette 1

A 30-year-old married woman suffers from chronic low mood and lack of enjoyment of life. She is highly dependent on her husband for practical and emotional support, although she frequently flies into rages at him, feeling that he is cold and uncaring. She has had a series of secretarial jobs, which she begins enthusiastically, but soon, she comes to feel that her employers are highly critical and belittling, whereupon she resigns. Her friendships are limited to people with whom she can have special, exclusive friendships. She deals poorly with change and loss, which frequently trigger episodes of acute dysfunction. When a friend is not sufficiently available to her, she feels betrayed and worthless; her mood plummets and she becomes lethargic, has eating binges, and is unable to work or pursue her usual routine for weeks at a time.

Focal psychological issues may also contribute to mental disorders. These issues, which typically involve conflicts between opposing motivations, may affect the patient in certain specific areas of function or life situations, leaving other broad areas of function intact.[65] Such conflicts are most likely to cause maladaptive behaviors or symptoms when the patient is not clearly aware of them. The following is an example.

Clinical Vignette 2

A patient functions well in a responsible job and has had a long-standing, stable marriage. However, he is driven by the need to be liked and accepted by all who know him and has a deep-seated, but not conscious, belief that he must continually fulfill the wishes of others to accomplish this. At the same time, he has a chronic feeling of powerlessness and an unarticulated wish to be able to say no. At times of increased demands by family members or coworkers, he develops influenza-like symptoms and stays home from work "recuperating," relieved of responsibility for fulfilling the expectations of others.

The meaning of an event in the context of the patient's life course is another focal issue that may contribute to illness.

Clinical Vignette 3

A young woman became acutely depressed on receiving her acceptance to medical school. She was the oldest of four children and had been expected to assume a major caretaking role with her younger siblings. Her mother, a busy physician, wished for her daughter to have a similar career. To the patient, entering medical school meant accepting a lifelong role as a caretaker and forever relinquishing her own wishes to be taken care of.

What Is the Patient's Motivation and Capacity for Treatment?

Whatever the psychiatrist's view of the presenting problem, the patient's wishes and capacities are a major determinant of treatment choice.[66] Some patients seek relief of symptoms; some wish to change their behavior or the nature of their relationships; some want to understand themselves better. Patients may wish to talk or to receive medication or instructions.

The patient's capacity for treatment must also be considered in the treatment plan. For example, a patient with schizophrenia may agree to medication but be too disorganized to take it reliably without help. Suitability for exploratory psychotherapy depends on such factors as the ability to observe oneself, tolerate unpleasant affects, and establish and maintain a working relationship with the treater.[67] Such factors must be evaluated in the interview.

The Psychiatric Database

The body of information to be gathered from the interview may be termed the psychiatric database (Table 2–4). It is a variable set of data: either specific or general, mainly limited to the present state or focused on early life, dominated by neurological questions or inquiry into relationships. To avoid setting the impossible task of learning everything about every patient, one must consider certain factors that modify the required database.

Whose questions are to be answered—the patient's concern about himself or herself, a family's or friend's concern about the patient, another physician's diagnostic dilemma, a civil authority's need to safeguard the public safety, or a research protocol's requirement? Who will have access to the data gathered and under what circumstances? Is the interview to be the first session of a psychotherapy regimen, or is it a one-time-only evaluation? What is the nature of the disorder? For example, negative responses regarding the presence of major psychotic symptoms, coupled with a history of good occupational function, generally preclude a detailed inventory of psychotic features. A missed orientation or memory question requires careful cognitive testing. Patients with personality disorder symptoms warrant careful attention to their history of significant relationships,[68] to their work history, and to the feelings evoked in the interviewer during the evaluation process. The database should be expanded in areas of diagnostic concern, to support or rule out particular syndromes. The amount and

Table 2–4 Core Database

Identifying Data	Chief Complaint	History of Present Illness
Name Age/date of birth Next of kin	Reason for consultation	Major symptoms Time course Stressors Change in functioning Current medical problems and treatment
Psychiatric History	**Medical History**	**Family History**
Any previous psychiatric treatment History of suicide attempts Functioning problems secondary to psychiatric symptoms Alcohol or drug abuse	Ever hospitalized Surgery Medications	Psychiatric illness
Personal History	**Mental Status**	
Educational level Ever married or in a committed relationship Work history Means of support Living situation	Appearance Attitude Affect Behavior Speech Thought process Thought content Perception Cognition Insight Judgment	

nature of the data obtained are also limited, of necessity, by the patient's ability to communicate and her or his cooperativeness.

Database Components

Identifying Data

This information establishes the patient's identity, especially for the purpose of obtaining past history from other contacts, when necessary, as well as to fix the patient's position in society. The patient's name should be recorded, along with any nickname or alternative names he or she may have been known by in the past. This is important for women who might have been treated previously under a maiden name or for a patient who has had legal entanglements and so has adopted aliases.

Date of birth, or at least age, and race are other essential parts of every person's database. A number of different classifications for race exist as well as different terms and controversies.[69] In the United States and Canada, the categories of white, black (or African-American), Asian, Native American, and Other are generally accepted. Additional modifiers of ethnicity, especially Hispanic or non-Hispanic, are becoming more widely used. If a patient is a member of a particular subculture on the basis of ethnicity, country of origin, or religious affiliation, it may be noted here.

A traditional part of the identifying data is a reference to the patient's civil status—single, married, separated, divorced, or widowed. The evolution of relationship patterns in the past two decades, with less frequent formalization of relationships, has made classification more difficult,[70] especially in the case of homosexual patients, whose relationships are not legally recognized in most jurisdictions.

The patient's Social Security number (or other national identification number) can be a useful bit of data in seeking information from other institutions.

In most cases, it is assumed that the informant (supplier of the history) is the patient. If other sources are used, and especially if the patient is not the primary informant, this should be noted at the beginning of the database.

Chief Complaint

The chief complaint is the patient's response to the question, What brings you to see me/to the hospital today? or some variant. It is usually quoted verbatim, placed within quotation marks, and should be no more than one or two sentences.

Even if the patient is disorganized or hostile, quoting his or her response can give an immediate sense of where the patient is as the interview begins. If the patient responds with an expletive or a totally irrelevant remark, the reader of the database is immediately informed about how the rest of the information may be distorted. In such cases, or if the patient gives no response, a brief statement of how the patient came to be evaluated should be made, enclosed in parentheses.

History of the Present Illness

Minimal Essential Database. The present illness history should begin with a brief description of the major symptoms that brought the patient to psychiatric attention. The most troubling symptoms should be detailed initially; later, a more thorough review will be stated. At a minimum, the approximate time since the patient was last at her or his baseline level of functioning, and in what way she or he is different from that now, should be described, along with any known stressors, the sequence of symptom development, and the beneficial or deleterious effects of interventions.

How far back in a patient's history to go, especially when the patient has chronic psychiatric illness, is sometimes a problem. In patients who have required repeated hospitalization, a summary of events since last discharge (if within 6 months) or last stable baseline level is indicated. It is rare for more than 6 months of history to be included in the history of the present illness, and detailed history is more commonly given for the past month.

Expanded Database. A more expanded description of the history of the present illness would include events in a patient's life at the onset of symptoms as well as exactly how the symptoms have affected the patient's occupational functioning and important relationships. Any concurrent medical illness symptoms, medication use (and particularly changes), alterations in sleep-wake cycle, appetite disturbances, and eating patterns should be noted; significant negative findings should also be remarked on.

Psychiatric History

Minimal Essential Database. Most of the major psychiatric illnesses are chronic in nature. For this reason, patients have often had previous episodes of illness with or without treatment. New onset of symptoms without any previous psychiatric history becomes increasingly important with advancing age in terms of diagnostic categories to be considered. At a minimum, the presence or absence of past psychiatric symptoms and diagnoses should be recorded, along with psychiatric interventions taken as well as the result of such interventions. An explicit statement about past suicide attempts should be included.

Expanded Database. A more detailed history would include names and places of psychiatric treatment, dosages of medications used, and time course of response. The type of psychotherapy, the patient's feelings about former therapists, the patient's compliance with treatment, and circumstances of termination are also important. Note what the patient has learned about his or her biological and psychological predisposing factors to illness and whether there were precipitating events.

Medical History

Minimal Essential Database. In any clinical assessment, it is important to know how a patient's general health status has been. In particular, any current medical illness and treatment should be noted,[71] along with any major past illness requiring hospitalization. Previous endocrine or neurological illness is of particular pertinence.[72]

Expanded Database. An expanded database could include significant childhood illnesses, how these were handled by the patient and the family, and therefore the degree to which the patient was able to develop a sense of comfort and security about his or her physical well-being. Illnesses later in life should be assessed for the degree of regression produced. The amount of time a patient has had to take off work, how well the patient has been able to follow a regimen of medical care, and the patient's relationship with the family physician or treating specialist can all be useful in predicting future response to treatment. A careful medical history can also at times bring to light a suicide attempt, substance abuse, or dangerously careless behavior that might not be obtained any other way.

Family History

Minimal Essential Database. Given the evidence for familial, genetic factors in so many psychiatric conditions, noting the presence and type of mental illness in biological relatives of the patient is a necessary part of any database.[73] It is important to specify during questioning the degree of family to be considered, usually to the second degree: aunts, uncles, cousins, and grandparents as well as parents, siblings, and children.

Expanded Database. A history of familial medical illness is a useful part of an expanded database. A genogram (pedigree), including known family members with dates and causes of death, as well as other known chronic illnesses, is helpful. Questioning about causes of death also occasionally brings out hidden psychiatric illness—sudden, unexpected deaths that were likely suicides, or illness secondary to substance abuse, for example.

Personal History

Minimal Essential Database. Recording the story of a person's life can be a daunting undertaking, and this is often where a database can expand dramatically. At a minimum, this part of the history should include where a patient was born and raised, and in what circumstances (whether there was an intact family; number of siblings; degree of material comfort). Note how far the patient went in school, how she or he did there, and what her or his occupational functioning has been. If the patient is not working, why not? Has the patient ever been involved in criminal activity, and with what consequences? Has the patient ever married or been involved in a committed relationship? Are there any children? What is the patient's current source of support? Does he or she live alone or with someone? Has he or she ever used alcohol or other drugs to excess, and is there current use? Has the patient ever been physically or sexually abused or the victim of some other trauma?

Expanded Database. An expanded database can include a great deal of material beginning even before the patient's conception. What follows is an outline of the kind of data that may be gathered, along with an organizational framework.

Family of Origin

- Were parents married or in a committed relationship?
- What were the personality and significant events in life of mother, father, or other significant caregiver?
- Siblings: the number, ages, significant life events, personality, and relationship to patient
- Who else shared the household with the family?

Prenatal and Perinatal

- Was the pregnancy planned? What was the quality of prenatal care and the mother's and father's response to pregnancy?
- Was there illness, medication or substance abuse, smoking, or trauma during pregnancy? Was labor induced or spontaneous?
- How many weeks of gestation? What was the difficulty of delivery (vaginal or cesarean section)? What was the Apgar score?
- Did the patient go home with mother or stay in hospital? Was there jaundice? What was the birth weight?

Early Childhood

- Developmental milestones: smiling, sitting, standing, walking, talking; type of feeding; food allergies or intolerance
- Consistency of caregiving; interruptions by illness, birth of siblings
- Reaction to weaning, toilet training, maternal separation
- Earliest memories; problem behavior (tantrums, bed-wetting, hair-pulling, or nail-biting)
- Temperament (shy, overactive, outgoing, fussy)

Later Childhood

- Early school experiences; evidence of separation anxiety
- Behavioral problems at home or school: fire-setting, bed-wetting, aggression toward others, cruelty to animals, nightmares
- Developmental milestones: learning to read, write
- Relationships with other children and family, any loss or trauma
- Reaction to illness

Adolescence

- School performance; ever in special classes?
- Athletic abilities and participation in sportsEvidence of gender identity concerns; overly feminine or masculine in appearance and behavior or perception by peers?
- Ever run away? Able to be left alone and assume responsibility?
- Age at onset of puberty (menarche or nocturnal emissions); reaction to puberty

Identity

- Sexual preference and gender identity; religious affiliation (same as parents?)
- Career goals; ethnic identification

Sexual History

- Early sexual teaching; earliest sexual experiences; experience of being sexually abused; attitudes toward sexual behavior
- Dating history; precautions taken to prevent sexually transmitted diseases and pregnancy
- Episodes of impotence with what reaction
- Masturbating patterns and fantasies
- Preoccupation with particular sexual practices; current sexual functioning; duration of significant relationships, ages of partners

Adulthood

- Age at which left home; level of educational attainments; employment history, relationships with supervisors and peers at work; reason for job change
- History of significant relationships, including duration, typical roles in relationships, patterns of conflict; marital history
- Legal entanglements and criminal history, both covert and detected; ever victim or perpetrator of violence?
- Major medical illness as adult
- Participation in community affairs
- Financial status; own or rent home, stability of living situation
- Ever on disability or public assistance?
- Current family structure, reaction to losses of missing members (parents, siblings), if applicable
- Substance abuse history

Mental Status Examination

It can be helpful to conceptualize the recording of the Mental Status Examination as a progression. One begins with a snapshot, what can be gained from a cursory visual examination, without any movement or interaction—appearance and affect. Next, motion is added—behavior. Then comes sound—the patient's speech, although initially only as sound. The ideas being expressed come next—the thought process and content, perception, cognition, insight, and judgment. Table 2–5 gives a summary of areas to be commented on, along with common terms.

At every level of the Mental Status Examination, preference should be given to explicit description over jargon. Stating that a patient is delusional is less helpful than describing the patient as believing that the neighbors are pumping poisonous gases into the bedroom while he or she sleeps. A complete discussion of the mental status examination and its terminology can be found in Chapter 21.

Table 2–5 Mental Status Examination

Appearance
Level of consciousness (alert, hypervigilant, somnolent, stuporous) Dress (casual, appropriate for weather, eccentric, careless, disheveled) Grooming (style of hair, degree of make-up, shaven or unshaven, clean, malodorous) Idiosyncrasies (tattoos, professional or amateur; prominent scars; religious emblems)
Attitude
Cooperative, hostile, evasive, threatening, obsequious
Affect
Range (restricted, expansive, blunted, flat) Appropriateness to items discussed Stability (labile, shallow) Quality (silly, anxious)
Mood
Response to question, How are you feeling/How's your mood been?
Behavior
Psychomotor agitation or retardation
Speech
Rate (rapid, slowed, pressured, hard to interrupt) Volume (loud, soft, monotone, highly inflected or dramatic) Quality (neologisms, fluent, idiosyncratic)
Thought Process
Goal directed, disorganized, loose associations, tangential, circumstantial, flight of ideas
Thought Content
Major preoccupations, ideas of reference, delusions (grandiose, paranoid, bizarre; state exactly what it is the patient appears to believe) Thought broadcasting, insertion, or withdrawal Suicidal or homicidal ideation; plan and intent to carry out ideas

Conduct of the Interview

Factors That Affect the Interview

A skillful interview will not necessarily yield all the relevant information but will make the most of the opportunities in a clinical situation, given the limitations that both the patient and the interviewer bring. Factors that influence the development of an alliance and the amount that can be learned in the interview include the following.

Patient's Physical or Emotional Distress

Patients who are in acute distress either from physical discomfort or from emotional factors, such as severe depression or anxiety, will be limited in their motivation and ability to interact with the interviewer. The interviewer may be able to enhance communication by addressing the patient's discomfort in a supportive manner. However, the interviewer must also recognize times when the patient's discomfort necessitates a more limited interview.

Table 2–5 Mental Status Examination *Continued*

Perception
Illusions and hallucinations: type (auditory, visual, olfactory, tactile, gustatory); evidence (patient's spontaneous report, answer to interviewer's question, observation of patient attending or responding to nonexistent external stimuli)
Patient's beliefs about hallucinatory phenomena (Do they seem to originate from outside or inside? How many voices? What gender? Are they talking to the patient or to other voices? Are they keeping up constant commentary on the patient?)
Cognition
Orientation to time, place, person, and situation
Memory: number of remembered objects, digit span, naming of presidents from the present backward, recent events
Concentration: serial sevens, *world* spelled backward
Abstraction: proverb interpretation (What would someone mean by "The grass is always greener on the other side of the fence"? "Get off my back"?)
Similarities (How are these things alike: apple-orange, table-chair, eye-ear, praise-punishment?)
Computation: number of digits successfully added or subtracted, ability to calculate change (How many quarters are in $1.50? If you bought a loaf of bread for 89 cents and gave the cashier a dollar, what change would you get back?)
Insight
Knows something is wrong, that he or she is ill, that illness is psychiatric; understands ways in which illness disrupts function
Judgment
Response to standard questions (If you found a sealed, addressed, stamped letter, what would you do? What would you do if you smelled smoke in a crowded theater?)
Evidence from behavior before and during interview (Was the patient caring for himself or herself properly, handling business affairs well? Does the behavior during the interview match his or her stated goals, e.g., if he or she wishes to be thought in control, is he or she keeping voice down and movement in check?)

Cognitive Capacities of the Patient

Patients who are demented, retarded, disorganized, thought disordered, amnesic, aphasic, or otherwise impaired in intellectual or cognitive capacity have biologically based deficits that limit the amount of information they can convey.

Emotionally Based Biases of the Patient

Patients bring to the interview a wide variety of preconceptions, expectations, and tendencies toward distortion that influence how they view and relate to the interviewer. Such biases are commonly referred to as *transference* because they can frequently be understood as arising from interactions with important figures in childhood, such as parents, which then color perceptions of others during adult life.[74] Transferential biases may be positive or negative. Thus, even before the start of the interview, one patient may be primed to view the psychiatrist as a wise and kindly healer, whereas another may be predisposed to see the psychiatrist as an exploitative charlatan. Clearly, such biases affect the amount of openness and trust that the patient brings to the interview and the quality of information provided.

Emotionally Based Biases of the Interviewer

The interviewer, like the patient, may have feelings stirred up by the interaction. The interviewer's emotional reactions to the patient can be an invaluable asset in assessment if the interviewer can be conscious of them and reflect on their causes. For example, an interviewer is becoming increasingly annoyed at a highly polite patient. On reflection, the interviewer realizes that the politeness serves to rebuff the interviewer's attempts to establish a warmer, more spontaneous relationship and is a manifestation of the patient's underlying hostile attitude.

When interviewers are unable to monitor and examine their emotional reactions, those reactions are more likely to impede than enhance understanding of the patient. This is likely to happen when emotional reactions are driven by the interviewer's own biases more than by the patient's behaviors. Such reactions are referred to as the interviewer's *countertransference.*[75] In the preceding example, the interviewer might inaccurately perceive a polite patient as rigid and hostile because of unconscious biases (countertransference) based on the interviewer's relationship with her or his own rigidly polite parent. The entire range of countertransferential interviewer attitudes toward the patient, from aversion to infatuation, might similarly bias judgment.

Situational Factors

Patients' attitudes toward the interview are strongly influenced by the situation in which the consultation arises. Some patients decide for themselves that they need treatment, whereas others come reluctantly, under pressure from others. Patients who are being evaluated for disability or in connection with a lawsuit may feel a need to prove that they are ill; those being evaluated for civil commitment or at the insistence of family members may need to prove that they are well. Similarly, a patient's history of relationships with psychiatrists, or with health professionals in general, is likely to color his or her attitude toward the interviewer.

The interviewer may also be affected by situational factors. Press of time in a busy emergency service, for example, may influence the interviewer to omit important areas of inquiry and reach premature closure; the recent experience of a patient's suicide may bias the interviewer toward overestimation of risk in someone with suicidal thoughts. As with countertransference reactions, it is important for the interviewer to minimize distortions due to situational factors by being as aware of them as possible.

Racial, Ethnic, and Cultural Factors

The degree of racial, ethnic, cultural, and socioeconomic similarity between the patient and the interviewer can influence the course and outcome of the interview in many ways. It may affect the level of rapport between patient and interviewer, the way both view the demands of the situation, the way they interpret each other's verbal and nonverbal communications, and the meaning that the interviewer assigns to the patient's statements and behaviors.[76] Not only racial or cultural prejudice but also well-intentioned ignorance can interfere with communication and accurate assessment.

Some cultures, for example, place a higher value on politeness and respect for authority than does Western culture. A patient from such a background might be reluctant to correct or disagree with the interviewer's statements, even when they are erroneous. The interviewer might not suspect that the information provided was distorted, or, conversely, might see the patient as pathologically inhibited or unemotional. Many non-Western cultures place a higher value on family solidarity than on individuality. Pressing a patient from such a culture to report angry feelings toward family members might raise the anxiety level, decrease rapport with the interviewer, and produce defensive distortions in the material.

General Features of Psychiatric Interviews

Setting

The ideal interview setting is one that provides a pleasant atmosphere and is reasonably comfortable, private, and free from outside distractions. Such a setting not only provides the physical necessities for an interview but conveys that the patient will be well cared for and safe. Providing such a setting may pose special problems in certain interviewing situations. For example, it may be necessary to interview highly agitated patients in the presence of security personnel; interviewers on medical-surgical units in a hospital must pay special attention to the patient's comfort and privacy.

Verbal Communication

Verbal communication may be straightforward imparting of information: "Every year around November, I begin to lose interest in everything and my energy gets very low." However, patients may convey information indirectly through metaphor or use words for noninformational purposes, such as to express or contain emotions or create an impact on the interviewer.

In metaphorical language, one idea is represented by another with which it shares some features. For example, when asked how she gets along with her daughter-in-law, a woman replies, "I can never visit their house because she always likes to keep the thermostat down. It's never as warm as I need." Such a reply suggests that the woman may not feel "warmly" accepted and welcomed by her son's wife. Metaphor may also use the body to represent ideas or feelings. A man who proved to meet the diagnostic criteria for major depressive disorder described his mood as "OK" but complained that his life was being ruined by constant aching in his chest for which the doctors could find no cause. In this instance, the pain of depression was experienced and described metaphorically as a somatic symptom.

Language may be used to express emotions directly ("I'm afraid of you and I don't want to talk to you") but more often is used indirectly by influencing the process of the interview.[77] Patients may shift topics, make offhand remarks or jokes, ask questions, and compliment or belittle the interviewer as a way of expressing feelings. The process of the interview frequently expresses the patient's feelings about her or his immediate situation or interaction with the interviewer.[78] For example, a woman being evaluated for depression and anxiety suddenly said, "I was just wondering, doctor, do you have any children?" The further course of the interview revealed that she was terrified of being committed to a hospital and abandoned. The question was an attempt to establish whether the interviewer was a good parent and therefore safe as a caretaker for her.

Language may also be used in the service of psychological defense mechanisms to contain rather than express emotions.[79] For example, a young man with generalized anxiety was asked whether he was sexually active. He replied by talking at length about how all the women he knew at college were either unappealing or attached to other men. Further discussion revealed that he had severe symptoms of anxiety whenever he was with a woman to whom he felt sexually attracted. His initial reply represented an automatic, verbal mechanism (in this case, a rationalization) for keeping the anxiety out of awareness.

Another form of process communication is the use of language to make an impact on the interviewer.[80] A statement such as "If you can't help me I'm going to kill myself" might convey suicidal intent, but it may also serve to stir up feelings of concern and involvement in the interviewer. Similarly, the patient who says "Dr. X really understood me, but he was much older and more experienced than you are" may be feeling vulnerable and ashamed and unconsciously trying to induce similar feelings in the interviewer. When language is used in this way, the interviewer's subjective reaction may be the best clue to the underlying feelings and motivations of the patient.

Nonverbal Communication

Emotions and attitudes are communicated nonverbally through facial expressions; gestures; body position; movements of the hands, arms, legs, and feet; interpersonal distance; dress and grooming; and speech prosody.[81] Some nonverbal communications, such as gestures, are almost always conscious and deliberate; others often occur automatically outside one's awareness. The latter type are particularly important to observe during an interview because they may convey entirely separate or even contradictory messages to what is being said.

Facial expression, body position, tone of voice, and speech emphasis are universal in the way they convey meaning.[82] The interviewer will automatically decode these signals but may ignore the message because of countertransference or social pressure from the patient. For example, a patient may say "I feel very comfortable with you, doctor" but sit stiffly upright and maintain a rigidly fixed smile, conveying a strong nonverbal message of tension and mistrust. The nonverbal message may be missed if, for example, the interviewer has a strong need to be liked by the patient. Another patient denies angry feelings while sitting with a tightly clenched fist. By ignoring the body language, the interviewer may unconsciously collude with the patient's need to avoid anger.

As with any medical examination, observation of nonverbal behavior may provide important diagnostic information. For example, a leaden body posture may indicate depression, movements of the foot may arise from anxiety or tardive dyskinesia, and sudden turning of the head or eyes may suggest hallucinations.

Nonverbal communication proceeds in both directions, and the nonverbal messages of the interviewer are likely to have a considerable effect on the patient. Thus, the interviewer who sits back in the chair and looks down at notes communicates less interest and involvement than one who sits upright and makes eye contact. Similarly, an interviewer who gives a weak handshake and sits behind a desk or far across the room from the patient communicates a sense of distance that may interfere with establishing rapport. It is important that the interviewer be aware of his or her own nonverbal messages and adapt them to the needs of the patient.

Listening and Observation

The complexity of communication in the psychiatric interview is mirrored by the complexity of listening.[83] The interviewer must remain open to literal and metaphorical messages from the patient, to the impact the patient is trying to make, and to the degree to which nonverbal communication complements or contradicts what is being said. Doing this optimally requires that the interviewer also be able to listen to her or his own mental processes throughout the interview, including both thoughts and emotional reactions. Listening of this kind depends on having a certain level of comfort, confidence, and space to reflect and may be difficult when the patient is hostile, agitated, demanding, or putting pressure on the interviewer in any other way. With such patients, it may take many interviews to do enough good listening to gain an adequate understanding of the case.

Another important issue in listening is maintaining a proper balance between forming judgments and remaining open to new information and new hypotheses. On the one hand, one approaches the interview with knowledge of diagnostic classifications, psychological mechanisms, behavioral patterns, social forces, and other factors that shape one's understanding of the patient. The interviewer hears the material with an ear to fitting the information into these preformed patterns and categories. On the other hand, the interviewer must remain open to hearing and seeing things that extend or modify judgments about the patient. At times, the interviewer may listen narrowly to confirm a hypothesis; at others, the interviewer may listen more openly, with relatively little preconception. Thus, listening must be structured enough to generate a formulation but open enough to avoid premature judgments.

Attitude and Behavior of the Interviewer

The optimal attitude of the interviewer is one encompassing interest, concern, and intention to help the patient. Although the interviewer must be tactful and thoughtful about what he or she says, this should not preclude behaving with natural warmth and spontaneity. Indeed, these qualities may be needed to support patients through a stressful interview process. Similarly, the interviewer must try to use natural, commonly understood language and avoid jargon or technical terms. The interviewer must communicate an intention to keep the patient as safe as possible, whatever the circumstances. Thus, although one must at times set limits on the behavior of an agitated, threatening, or abusive patient, one should never be attacking or rejecting.

Empathy is an important quality in psychiatric interviewing. Whereas sympathy is an expression of agreement or support for another, empathy entails putting oneself in another's place and experiencing her or his state of mind. Empathy comprises both one's experiencing of another person's mental state and the expression of that understanding to the other person.[84] For example, in listening to a man talk about the death of his wife, the interviewer may allow himself or herself to resonate empathically with the patient's feelings of loneliness and desolation. On the basis of this resonance, the interviewer might respond, "After a loss like that, it feels as if the world is completely empty."

As a mode of listening, empathy is an important way of understanding the patient; as a mode of response, it is important in building rapport and alliance. Patients who feel great emotional distance from the interviewer may make empathic understanding difficult or impossible. Thus, the interviewer's inability to empathize may itself be a clue to the patient's state of mind.

Structure of the Interview

The overall structure of the psychiatric interview is generally one of reconnaissance and detailed inquiry.[85] In reconnaissance phases, the interviewer inquires about broad areas of symptoms, functioning, or life course: Have you ever had long periods when you felt low in mood? How have you been getting along at work? What did you do between high school and when you got married? In responding to such questions, patients give the interviewer leads that must then be pursued with more detailed questioning. Leads may include references to symptoms, difficulty functioning, interpersonal problems, ideas, states of feeling, or stressful life events. Each such lead raises questions about the nature of the underlying problem, and the interviewer must attempt to gather enough detailed information to answer these questions.

In general, the initial reconnaissance consists of asking how the patient comes to treatment at this particular time. This is done by asking an open-ended question, such as What brings you to see me today? or How did you come to be in the hospital right now? A well-organized and cooperative patient may spontaneously provide most of the needed information, with little intervention from the interviewer. However, the patient may reveal deficits in thought process, memory, or ability to communicate, which dictate more structured and narrowly focused questioning.

The patient's emotional state and attitude may also impede a smooth flow of information. If the patient shows evidence, for example, of anxiety, hostility, suspiciousness, or indifference, the interviewer must first build a working alliance before trying to collect information. This usually requires acknowledging the emotions that the patient presents, helping the patient to express his or her feelings and related thoughts, and discussing these concerns in an accepting and empathic manner.[86] As new areas of content open up, the interviewer must continue to attend to the patient's reactions, both verbal and nonverbal, and to identify and address resistance to open communication.

Setting an appropriate level of structure is an important aspect of psychiatric interviewing. In the past two decades, a variety of structured interview formats have been developed for psychiatric assessment.[87, 88] In these interviews, the organization, content areas, and, to varying degrees, wording of the questions are standardized; vague, overly complex, leading or biased, and judgmental questions are eliminated, as is variability in the attention given to different areas of content. The major benefits of such interviews are that they ensure complete coverage of the specified areas and greatly increase the reliability of information gathered and diagnostic judgments. In addition, formats that completely specify the wording of questions can be administered by less highly trained interviewers or even administered as patients' self-reports.

The disadvantages of highly structured interviews are that they diminish ability to respond flexibly to the patient and preclude exploration of any areas not specified in the format.[89] Therefore, they are used to best advantage for interviews with focused goals. For example, such interviews may aim to survey certain Axis I disorders (*Diagnostic and Statistical Manual of Mental Disorders,* Fourth Edition), to assess the type and degree of substance abuse, or to delineate the psychological and behavioral consequences of a traumatic event. They are less useful in a general psychiatric assessment when the scope and focus of the interview cannot be preordained.

In the usual clinical situation, although the interviewer may have a standardized general plan of approach, she or he must adapt the degree of structure to the individual patient. Open-ended, nondirective questions derive from the psychoanalytic tradition. They are most useful for opening up and following emotionally salient themes in the patient's life story and interpersonal history. Focused, highly structured questioning derives from the medical-descriptive tradition and is most useful for delineating the scope and evolution of pathological signs and symptoms. In general, one uses the least amount of structure needed to maintain a good flow of communication and cover the necessary topic areas.

Phases of the Interview

The typical interview comprises opening, middle, and closing phases. In the opening phase,[1] the interviewer and patient are introduced, and the purposes and procedures of the interview are set. It is generally useful for the interviewer to begin by summarizing what he or she already knows about the patient and proceeding to the patient's own account of the situation. For example, the interviewer may say, "Dr. Smith has told me that you have had several episodes of depression in the past, and now you may be going into another one," or "I understand that you were brought in by the police because you were threatening people on the street. What do you think is happening with you?" or "When we spoke on the phone you said you thought your marriage was in trouble. What has been going wrong?" Such an approach orients the patient and sets a collaborative tone.

The opening phase may also include clarification of what the patient hopes to get from the consultation. Patients may sometimes state this explicitly but often do not, and the interviewer should not assume that her or his goals are the same as the patient's.[66] A question such as "How were you hoping I could help you with the problem you have told me about?" invites the patient to formulate and express his or her request and avoids situations in which the patient and interviewer work at cross-purposes. The interviewer must also be explicit about her or his own goals and the extent to which they fit with the patient's expectations. This is especially important when the interests of a third party, such as an employer, a family member, or a court of law, are involved.

The middle phase of the interview consists of assessing the major issues in the case and filling in enough detail to answer the salient questions and construct a working formulation. Most of the work of determining the relative importance of biological, psychological, environmental, and sociocultural contributions to the problem is done during this phase. The patient's attitudes and transferential perceptions are also monitored during this phase so that the interviewer can recognize and address barriers to communication and collaboration.

When appropriate, formal aspects of the mental status examination are performed during the middle phase of the interview. Whereas most of the mental status evaluation is accomplished simply by observing the patient, certain components, such as cognitive testing and review of psychotic symptoms, may not fit smoothly into the rest of the interview. These are generally best covered toward the end of the interview, after the issues of greatest importance to the patient have been discussed and rapport has been established. A brief explanation that the interviewer has a few standard questions that need to be answered before the end of the interview serves as a bridge and minimizes the awkwardness of asking questions that may seem incongruous or pejorative.

In general, note taking during an assessment interview is helpful to the interviewer and not disruptive of rapport with the patient.[1] Notes should be limited to brief recording of factual material, such as dates, durations, symptom lists, important events, and past treatments, which might be difficult to keep in memory accurately. The interviewer must take care not to become so involved in taking notes as to lose touch with the patient. It is especially important to maintain a posture of attentive listening when the patient is talking about emotionally intense or meaningful issues. When done with interpersonal sensitivity, note taking during an assessment interview may actually enhance rapport by communicating that what the patient says is important and worth remembering. This is to be distinguished from note taking during psychotherapy sessions, which is more likely to diminish the treater's ability to listen and respond flexibly.

In the third or closing phase of the interview, the interviewer shares his or her conclusions with the patient, makes treatment recommendations, and elicits reactions. In situations when the assessment runs longer than one session, the interviewer may sum up what has been covered in the interview and what needs to be done in subsequent sessions. Communications of this kind serve several purposes. They allow the patient to correct or add to the salient facts as understood by the interviewer. They contribute to the patient's feeling of having gotten something from the interview. They are also the first step in initiating the treatment process, because they present a provisional understanding of the problem and a plan for dealing with it. All treatment plans must be negotiated with the patient, including discussion of mutual goals, expected benefits, liabilities, limitations, and alternatives, if any. In many cases, such negotiations extend beyond the initial interview and may constitute the first phase of treatment.

Dimensions of Interviewing Technique

Although many systems have been suggested for classifying interviewing techniques,[90] it is convenient to think about four major dimensions of interviewing style: degree of directiveness, degree of emotional support, degree of fact versus feeling orientation, and degree of feedback to the patient. The interviewer must seek a balance among these dimensions to best cover the needed topics, build rapport, and arrive at a plan of treatment.

Directiveness

Directiveness in the interview ensures that the necessary areas of information are covered and supplies whatever cognitive support the patient needs in discussing them. Table 2–6 lists interventions that are low, moderate, and high in directiveness.

Low-directive interventions request information in the broadest, most open ended way and do not go beyond the material supplied by the patient. Moderately directive interventions are narrower in focus and may extend beyond what the patient himself or herself has said. For example, confrontation makes the patient aware of paradoxes or inconsistencies in the material and requests the patient to resolve them; interpretation requests the patient to consider explanations or connections that had not previously occurred to him or her. Highly directive interventions aim to focus and restrict the patient's content or behavior. Such interventions include yes or no and symptom checklist–type questions and requests for the patient to modify behaviors that impede progress of the interview.

Supportiveness

Patients vary considerably in the degree of emotional as well as cognitive support they need in the interview. Table 2–7 lists examples of emotionally supportive interventions.

Table 2–6 Degrees of Directiveness in the Interview

Directiveness	Intervention	Examples
Low	Open-ended questions	What brings you to the hospital? Tell me about your current situation in life.
Low	Repetition	*Patient:* Last night I suddenly started to feel so terrible I was afraid I was going to die. *Interviewer:* You were afraid you were going to die.
Low	Restatement	*P:* Nobody is on my side anymore—even my family is out to get me. *I:* So it seems as if everyone has turned against you.
Low	Summarization	To review what we have been discussing, over the last month you've been very low in mood, you've felt overwhelmed even by small chores, and you no longer want to see any of your friends.
Low	Clarification	You told me that it "upsets" you to have to say no. It seems that when you say no to your boss your feeling is fear, but when you say no to your children you feel guilty.
Low	Nonverbal acknowledgment	"Uh-huh"; nodding of head
Low	Attentive listening	In talking about the recent death of his wife, the patient becomes tearful and hesitant in speech. The interviewer remains silent, but attentive, allowing the patient time to express himself.
Moderate	Broad-focus questions	What do you notice about yourself lately that is different from usual? What is it about your job that you find stressful?
Moderate	Use of examples	Sometimes illness seems to be triggered by something that happens, like a change in finances or living situation, or losing someone who's close to you. Has anything like that been happening to you?
Moderate	Confrontation	You told me you got a "terrible" evaluation at work, but in 9 of 10 categories your rating was actually excellent. You don't feel the medicine does you any good, but whenever you've stopped it you've had to go back into the hospital. How do you account for that?
Moderate	Interpretation	Part of the tension between you and your wife is that you forget things she tells you. Perhaps this is what you do when you are angry at her.
High	Narrow-focus questions	Do you have trouble getting to sleep or staying asleep? How much alcohol do you drink in a week?
High	Question repetition	*I:* How has your daily routine changed in the last month? *P:* I used to like to read, but now I don't anymore. My husband thinks I would feel better if I pushed myself to keep busy, but I tell him that this dizziness makes it impossible for me to do anything. I don't know what to think anymore. *I:* How else has your routine changed lately?
High	Redirection	*P:* I've always thought that my father's personality caused a lot of my trouble in life. *I:* I'd like to hear more of your thoughts about that, but first I need to get a clearer picture of what's been happening with you lately. When did you decide to make the appointment with me?
High	Change of topics	You mentioned before that your brother had problems similar to yours. Can you tell me how many brothers and sisters you have, and if they've had any emotional problems? We've been talking about your marriage, but now I'd like to know something about your work.
High	Limit setting	I'm going to have to interrupt you because there are a few more things we need to cover in the time left. I know you feel restless, but I have to ask you to try to stay in your chair and concentrate on what we're talking about.

Table 2–7 Supportive Interventions

Intervention	Examples
Encouragement	*Patient:* I'm not sure I'm making any sense today, doctor. *Interviewer:* You're doing very well at describing the troubles you've been having.
Approval	You did the right thing by coming in for an appointment. You've been doing your best to keep going under very difficult circumstances.
Reassurance	What you are telling me about may seem very strange to you, but many people have had similar experiences. You feel like you will be sick forever, but with treatment you have a very good chance of feeling better soon.
Acknowledgment of affect	You look very sad when you talk about your brother. I have the impression that my question made you angry. I can see that you don't feel very safe here.
Empathic statements	When your boyfriend doesn't call you, you feel completely helpless and unloved. It seems unfair for you to get sick so many times while others remain well.
Nonverbal communication	Smiling, firm handshake, attentive body posture, gentle touch on shoulder.
Avoidance of affect-laden material	Interviewer elects to defer discussion or probing of topics that arouse intense feelings of anxiety, shame, or anger.

Each such intervention supports the patient's sense of security and self-esteem. Some patients may come to the interview feeling safe and confident; others have considerable anxiety about being criticized, ridiculed, rejected, taken advantage of, or attacked (literally so, in the case of some psychotic patients). Overt manifestations of insecurity range widely, from fearful demeanor and tremulousness, to requests for reassurance, to haughty contemptuousness. The interviewer's task is to identify such anxiety when it arises and respond in a manner that conveys empathic understanding, acceptance, and positive regard.

Obstructive interventions are ones that (usually unintentionally) impede the flow of information and diminish rapport. Table 2–8 lists common examples of such interventions. Compound or vague questions are often confusing to the patient and may produce ambiguous or unclear answers. Biased or judgmental questions suggest what answer the interviewer wants to hear or that the interviewer does not approve of what the patient is saying. *Why* questions often sound critical or invite rationalizations. *How* questions better serve the purposes of the interview ("How did you come to change jobs?" rather than "Why did you change jobs?"). Other interventions are obstructive because they disregard the patient's feeling state or what the patient is trying to say. Paradoxically, this may include premature reassurance or advice. When reassurance or advice is given before the interviewer has explored and understood the issue, it has

Table 2–8 Obstructive Interventions

Intervention	Examples
Suggestive or biased questions	You haven't been feeling suicidal, have you? You've had six jobs in the last 2 years. I guess none of them held your interest?
Judgmental questions or statements	How long have you been behaving so selfishly? What you've told me is typical of delusional thinking.
Why questions	Why can't you sit still? Why do you keep choosing men who can't make a commitment to you?
Ignoring the patient's leads	*Patient:* I'm afraid I'm going to fall apart. *Interviewer:* Have you had any odd experiences, such as hearing voices? *P:* No, but I just feel as though I can't cope and I wanted to talk to someone about it. *I:* Has your sleep pattern or appetite changed? *P:* Well, I don't sleep as well as I used to, but it's getting through the days that's the hardest. *I:* Have you had any suicidal thoughts?
Crowding the patient with questions	*P:* I just can't get it out of my mind that this cancer of mine is a punishment of some kind because I. . . . *I:* Have you been in a low mood or been tearful?
Compound questions	Have you ever heard voices or thought that other people were out to harm you?
Vague questions	Do you feel socially self-conscious a lot? How much trouble do you have with your memory?
Minimization or dismissal	*P:* I don't seem to be able to enjoy my life as much as I think I should. *I:* You're doing well at your job and have a family—you're probably just feeling some minor stress.
Premature advice or reassurance	*P:* I've been having terrible headaches and I forget a lot of things. There's nothing wrong with my brain, is there? *I:* Headaches and forgetfulness are common and are probably due to some minor cause in your case. *P:* I've started to have thoughts that I married the wrong man and I should leave my husband. *I:* Maybe the two of you ought to take some time away together.
Nonverbal communication	Sitting at a distance, yawning, looking at watch, fidgeting, frowning, rolling of eyes.

Table 2–9 Fact-Oriented Interventions in the Psychiatric Interview

Intervention	Examples
Questions about symptoms	Do the voices seem to come from within your own head or from outside? When did you first begin to check your door lock many times before going out?
Questions about behavior	What do you do when you fly into a rage—do you yell, hit the furniture, or hit people? Since you've had your pain, how is your daily routine different from what it used to be?
Questions about events	What was the next thing you did after you took the overdose of medication? What led up to your decision to move out of your parents' home?
Requests for biographical data	Who lived with you when you were growing up? How many times have you been in a psychiatric hospital? Tell me about your close relationships with women.
Requests for medical data	What medicines do you take? What conditions do you see a doctor for?

the effect of cutting off feelings and coming to premature closure.

Fact Versus Feeling Orientation

Interviews differ in the degree to which they focus on factual-objective versus feeling- and meaning-oriented material. Tables 2–9 and 2–10 provide examples of interventions of both types. The interviewer must determine what the salient issues are in a given case and develop the focus accordingly. For example, at one extreme, the principal task in assessing a cyclically occurring mood disorder might be to delineate precisely the symptoms, time course, and treatment response of the illness. At the other end of the spectrum might be a patient with a circumscribed difficulty in living, such as inability to achieve an intimate, lasting love relationship. In such a case, the interviewer may focus not only on the facts of the patient's interactions with others but also on the feelings, fantasies, and thoughts associated with such relationships.

Feedback

Interviews differ in how much the interviewer conveys to the patient of her or his own thoughts, feelings, conclusions, and recommendations. Table 2–11 presents common types of feedback from the interviewer. Judicious statements about the interviewer's ongoing thoughts and feelings can be used to pose questions or make clarifications or interpretations while enhancing rapport and trust. Communication of factual information, formulations of the problem, and recommendations for treatment are the foundation of joint treatment planning with the patient. Responding to questions and giving advice may serve an educational purpose as well as enhance the alliance. When responding to requests for advice or information, the interviewer must take care first to be sure what is being asked, and for what reason.

There are few systematic data on the superiority of one clinical interviewing style over another, but what there is suggests that many styles can be used effectively. Rutter and colleagues[91–93] have investigated this question in a series of naturalistic and experimental studies of interviews of parents in a child psychiatry clinic. The major findings of these studies are

1. Active, structured techniques are no better than nondirective styles in eliciting positive findings (i.e., areas of disease). However, active techniques are better in eliciting more detailed and thorough information in areas where disease is found and are also better at delineating areas without disease.
2. An active, fact-gathering style does not prevent the interviewer from effectively eliciting emotional reactions from informants.
3. Use of open questions, direct requests for feelings, interpretations of feelings, and expressions of sympathy are associated with greater expression of emotions by informants.

Table 2–10 Feeling-Oriented Interventions in the Psychiatric Interview

Intervention	Examples
Questions about feelings in specific situations	Some people might have been angry in the situation you told me about. Did you feel that way? How did you feel when your doctor told you that you had had a heart attack? I noticed your voice got much quieter when you answered my last question. What were you feeling just then?
Questions or comments about emotional themes or patterns	Growing up, you never felt like you measured up to your mother's expectations. Do you feel that same way in your marriage? You've had a very competitive relationship with your brother. When you were asking about my qualifications just now, I wonder if you were feeling competitive with me also.
Questions or comments about the personal meaning of events	You are concerned about becoming enraged at your daughter. When she disregards your wishes, what do you feel it means about you as a parent? From what you have said, I think your becoming ill means to you that you will no longer have the respect of the people who depend on you.

Table 2–11 Feedback in the Psychiatric Interview

Intervention	Examples
Sharing of ongoing thoughts	As you were talking I began to wonder whether you had ever lost anyone very close to you. As I hear your story, it occurs to me that you've been an outsider every place you've lived in.
Sharing of subjective reactions	What you are saying makes me feel quite sad. You've told me how you left treatment with your last psychiatrist, but I still feel a bit confused about what happened. I notice I'm feeling somewhat tense right now and I wonder if you might be feeling it too.
Imparting of information	About 75% of people with your condition respond well to medication. The tendency to have the kind of symptoms you described runs in families and is probably inherited.
Proposing a formulation	I think the immediate cause of your depression and insomnia is your heavy drinking. When you are under stress, you tend not to think clearly and to have unrealistic fears. It seems as though your present stress comes from the way you and your family are getting along at home.
Making treatment recommendations	For you to keep safe and begin treatment, I think it would be best to go into the hospital for a while. Medication should help you get out of your depression much faster. When you are feeling better, it would be a good idea for us to try to understand how you got so isolated from your friends and family.
Advice	It might be better not to decide about changing jobs until you're feeling back to your regular self.
Response to questions	*Patient:* What type of psychiatrist are you, doctor? *Interviewer:* I'm a general psychiatrist who uses medication and psychotherapy. I also have a special interest in anxiety disorders. *P:* Have you ever seen another patient like me? *I:* I can answer your question better if you tell me what there is about you that I might never have seen before. *P:* Do you think I'm a terrible person? *I:* I don't think you're terrible, but I wonder what you think about yourself that you would ask me that.

4. Less activity on the interviewer's part is associated with more informant talkativeness and spontaneous emotional expression. Less directive techniques also tend to produce more emotional responses at times when they are not specifically requested. Conversely, more active styles of asking about feelings may be more effective for informants who are low in spontaneous emotional expression.[5]
5. In summary, techniques that actively elicit both facts and emotions are likely to produce the richest, most detailed database. When skillfully used, these do not impair the psychiatrist-patient relationship.

Special Problems in Interviewing

The Delusional Patient

Clinical Vignette 4

A 26-year-old man presented to the emergency department seeking a safe haven from "the mob." He was convinced that he was being set up to be killed, as evidenced by the sequence of license plate numbers of the cars that had passed him on the way to work. He had initially gone to a police station, which had referred him to the hospital.

Psychotic patients often present with a variety of delusions—fixed, false beliefs that are not consistent with their cultural milieu. Delusions may be persecutory, grandiose, or a variety of other types. Conducting an interview with a patient who is not in touch with reality can be unsettling; such patients are often aware that what they are saying is odd and may seek reassurances that they are believed.

The interviewer must walk a fine line between giving reassurance and at the same time not validating the delusions. Often the question Do you believe me? can be interpreted as Will you help me? The psychiatrist should not simply agree with a patient's bizarre belief system. Instead, the psychiatrist might express genuine surprise at the ideas presented (a surprise that the patient probably shares and that is likely to enhance a sense of common purpose) and question whether the patient is sure of this or how it is known for certain. If pressed, a reasonable response could be "it seems unlikely," with an offer to work with the patient to discover the truth. It may also be helpful to agree with the affect but not with the facts. Thus, one might say, "You don't feel safe out there right now."

It is also important to keep in mind that delusions are by definition unresponsive to logical argument. Whatever psychological or neurobiological purpose they serve will not be easily abandoned. The interviewer risks any chance of alliance, with almost no chance of benefit, by trying to persuade a patient that he or she is mistaken. In clinical vignette 4, if the interviewer sought to convince the patient that he was not the object of a potential murder, it is possible that the patient would begin to suspect that the interviewer was a part of the conspiracy.

The Violent, Agitated Patient

Clinical Vignette 5

A 48-year-old woman with a history of alcohol dependence is in her second postoperative day. Her physician was called after she assaulted the nurse who came to check her vital signs. The patient was being restrained by security personnel when the physician arrived. She was screaming, "They're coming to kill me. I have to get out." She was trying to bite the hands of those restraining her.

The clinical interview with such a patient requires first of all that a safe environment be established. No helpful intervention can be made in an atmosphere of fear and uncertainty. Adequate resources, such as additional people, physical restraint, seclusion, or distance, must be used to obtain an appropriate assessment.

In conducting an interview with an unpredictable or potentially violent person, it is appropriate to make the patient aware of one's concern that he or she might be unable to control himself or herself and find out whether the patient agrees. If the patient does agree, then the patient and interviewer together must ensure a safe environment. Most potentially violent people fear the violence as much as anyone and are relieved by efforts to help them maintain control—even the use of four-point leather restraints.

If a patient is unable to agree with needed measures, and the potential for violence mandates their use, the intervention should proceed in an orderly manner. Explanation should be given to the patient concurrently, including exactly what will be done, the reason for it, assurance of the patient's safety, and what behavioral requirements there are for the cessation of the intervention.

Sometimes patients refuse to conduct an interview after safety measures have been instituted. They will insist that the interview room door not be left open, that security personnel leave, that they be permitted out of a seclusion room, or that restraints be removed. Assuming that the initial decision for such intervention was appropriate, it is useful to remind the patient that a valid assessment is the quickest way to achieve what he or she and you wish. No one should accept an unsafe situation as part of a bargain to get questions answered.

The Hostile Patient

Clinical Vignette 6

A 15-year-old girl is brought to the office by her mother because of illicit drugs found in her room. The patient slouches in a chair and tells the interviewer, "I don't like you and I don't like this place. My mother's the one with the problem. Talk to her."

A therapeutic alliance is the sine qua non of most interviews. Without an agreed basis on which to work, anything an interviewer says can be interpreted as intrusive and provoke an angry response. Overt hostility must be acknowledged right at the outset, or else the patient may perceive further things to feel hostile about. Pointing out the incongruity of the anger, once it is acknowledged, can be the next step; after all, the psychiatrist is presumably conducting an evaluation in the service of the patient.

An understanding of the true object of the patient's anger, such as her mother in clinical vignette 6 (or more precisely, what the mother represents), can be helpful, especially if the psychiatrist can define a boundary between this object and herself or himself. "I'd like to be of help to you; your mother will have to wait."

Clearly, responding to hostile provocation with hostility has no place in an interview. Ignoring it or being too accommodating to provocative acts can have deleterious effects as well, by breaking the usual interview frame of two people working together to solve the problems of one of them.

The Depressed Patient

Clinical Vignette 7

A 70-year-old man is brought for evaluation by his children. Since his wife's death 8 months ago, he has lost 30 pounds. The children report that he leaves his home only when they strongly encourage him and that he has stopped joining in conversation.

Talking to a profoundly depressed patient can sap the energy of the interviewer. The patient often has the classic symptom of prolonged latency of response; it can be difficult to avoid repeating the question, suggesting responses, or simply changing the line of inquiry. An occasional rephrasing or seeking to find out whether the patient understands the question is all the interviewer can do. A great deal of patience is required in conducting an evaluation of someone who is extremely depressed.

Another difficult aspect of dealing with a depressed person is the emotional drain. The pessimism, hopelessness, and helplessness of these patients can be somewhat infectious. Those who express existential despair (lamenting the human condition) or who have suffered a painful loss with which the interviewer might tend to identify (e.g., the death of a child) can evoke an empathic response of shared pain or futility. It is important to recognize this as another element of the diagnosis, reflect a bit of it back to the patient to aid in rapport building, but keep oneself well centered.

Crying is a frequently encountered affect in the interview of a depressed patient, which is sometimes a problem. Especially when the patient's first priority is expressing the depth of his or her emotion, it may be difficult to get needed information. At times, the patient must be told of this difficulty and the importance of completing the assessment in a timely manner to reduce the pain.

When the widower insists that life is meaningless now that he is old and alone, the interviewer must be careful to detect the nihilism of depression and to educate the patient about this process.

The Confused Patient

Clinical Vignette 8

A 76-year-old woman is brought by her family for evaluation after she was found wandering in the streets surrounding her home. She has had a progressive decline in her memory and ability to care for herself, and her family is concerned that she might need to be placed in a nursing home. The patient has become combative at times when caretakers are brought into the home to assist her, because she believes they are trying to rob her.

Assessing a patient with cognitive loss requires a lowering of expectations for historical data and the realization that the going will be slow. Most patients who are confused will not be able to respond to open-ended questions reliably; the unstructured stimulus requires too much secondary processing on the patient's part. Instead, simple yes or no questions, of no more than about 10 words, are likely to yield the most reliable responses.

Patients with memory problems also need to be frequently reoriented to their surroundings as well as to the task at hand. It is helpful to query these patients about their current situation at times and provide the reassurance of their being in a treatment situation dedicated to their welfare.

The mental status examination of the confused patient deserves special attention. It is important that the patient's performance be characterized precisely; both the requested task as well as the patient's response should be included. The format of most standard tests (serial sevens, remembering three objects, naming of presidents from the present backward, digit span, spelling *world* backward) does not require explication; it is important, however, to describe exactly how the patient responded to which test, rather than just to note poor memory or concentration.

With confused patients, more than any other, the setting of the interview can markedly affect the results. Patients with impaired cognitive processing are susceptible to extraneous distractions—the capacity to focus attention is often lost. As much as possible, stimuli other than the interviewer should be at a minimum. When outside forces interfere, they should be noted as part of the database; this includes physical aspects of the patient's comfort, such as uncomfortable positioning in restraints or pain from underlying medical illness.

The Seductive Patient

Clinical Vignette 9

A woman in her 30s is referred by another patient for an evaluation for anxiety and work inhibition. She describes a series of unhappy relationships and then begins to discuss what she knows of the interviewer's personal life, by way of comparison. She announces, "Jill was right—you are very easy to talk to. What am I going to do when I fall in love with you? I guess that's easy—the real question is, what are *you* going to do?"

Psychiatric assessment requires that the interviewer display a degree of emotional openness and support that can stimulate a powerful longing in some patients. Few aphrodisiacs can compare in potency with the sincere, nonjudgmental interest from another person, especially one in a position of relative power. In particular, patients who have been sexually abused as children, or those who have been unable to achieve close relationships, sometimes find the interview an invitation to greater intimacy.

At one level, the management of this problem is straightforward. The patient is reminded of the limits of the situation, what role he or she and the interviewer have, and the inviolable boundaries that apply. However, it is important to set limits in a way that does not imply reproach. A good psychiatrist will try to foster an atmosphere wherein the patient can feel comfortable sharing anything, including such deeply personal things as sexual attraction. Therefore, the interviewer must maintain the boundary between expression of sexual feelings and acting on them.

The interviewer's emotional reaction to the patient, including at times sexual attraction (or repulsion), can play a part in how she or he responds to seductiveness. An awareness that the patient is usually responding more to what he or she needs to see or hear (that is, to transferential perceptions) rather than to the actual person of the interviewer can help keep the interaction in perspective.

Seductiveness in an initial interview, such as described in clinical vignette 9, is rare. It may signify a frontal lobe dysfunction or hypomania, or a misunderstanding of the clinical situation. Pointing out this misunderstanding is an effective way of management. "My understanding is that you're here for help with some things that are troubling you. Helping as a doctor is something I can do, but that is a specifically limited relationship."

Cultural Disparity

Clinical Vignette 10

A man in his 20s is brought to the emergency department by his male lover-partner for treatment of self-inflicted wrist cuts. These had occurred during a violent fight between the two. The patient refused to be evaluated by a male psychiatric resident unless he first answered a long list of questions about his attitudes toward gays.

Significant cultural, religious, ethnic, racial, language, and other differences between the patient and the interviewer create at least three major problems, which are closely related: the basic problem of obtaining information, the interpretation of information in the appropriate cultural context, and finally the establishment of necessary rapport. The information-gathering problem is obvious when the patient literally speaks a different language, but it can be just as much of a problem, or even more so, when the patient belongs to a subculture with idiosyncratic word use, nuances, values, and styles of interaction.

The use of an interpreter deserves special mention. Whenever possible, an unbiased third party should be used, rather than a family member. The interpreter must be explicitly instructed to interpret verbatim, as much as possible, except perhaps in the fortuitous circumstance when the interpreter is also a psychiatrist. The purpose of the interview, how long it will last, and of course the need to respect confidentiality should all be explained. Confidentiality is especially important in dealing with members of small minority groups because the likelihood of common business or social ties is high.

Membership in subcultures creates problems for understanding "peculiarities" of word choice and concept. Assessment for delusional beliefs in particular must take the patient's background into account; a delusion cannot be diagnosed if the belief is shared by a significant percentage of the patient's peers. The degree of emotional expressiveness, guardedness in the presence of others, the amount of eye contact, and the rate and tone of speech are all cultural variables. Consultation with other members of the culture helps set the norm against which the patient must be evaluated.

The final issue, and the one described in clinical vignette 10, is the degree of comfort a patient can have with an "outsider." The wish to be understood, to be accepted, and to be valued is part of the human condition and is at work in nearly every interview. When there are cultural discrepancies between the patient and the psychiatrist, the fears of being misunderstood can be overwhelming. It is the interviewer's responsibility to give reassurance of a commitment to understanding the patient as best as possible and to take steps to minimize the chance of distortion.

The Deceitful Patient

Clinical Vignette 11

A man in his 50s presents to a hospital emergency department complaining of memory loss after having fallen. A work-up for mental status change is begun, until the patient is recognized by a resident who had seen him while moonlighting in another hospital. His complaint of memory loss had mysteriously vanished after he spent the night and ate breakfast in the emergency department.

One of the basic expectations of the physician-patient relationship is honesty. Patients come in asking for help and are expected to give whatever information is required honestly. One of the formative events of any physician's professional development is the dawn of awareness that sometimes patients lie, either by omitting important parts of the history or by actually fabricating symptoms.

There are many different reasons for the deception. Most commonly, the patient has a different agenda, which he or she feels must be kept hidden from the interviewer and which is often directed toward achieving the secondary gains of illness. At times, the patient hides symptoms, because of fear of them or because of fear of what treatment might be required. Patients who mistrust the medical establishment may be unwilling to share important information, believing themselves to be the best judge of what care they need, and will couch their replies in the way they think will best achieve their own ends.

In addition to consciously lying to achieve secondary gain (known as malingering), there is another scenario in which patients speak falsely. Factitious disorder or Munchausen's syndrome is an example of a patient's making false statements about himself or herself and a disease. These are usually elaborate tales of illness, often accompanied by hidden actions to bolster the story and even to induce sometimes life-threatening symptoms. In this circumstance, there is no secondary gain; the motivation appears to be simply to attain the role of patient, and fool medical caregivers, to satisfy deeper psychological conflicts.

Both of these types of deceit, malingering and factitious disorder, must be distinguished from the patient who is unaware that she or he is giving misinformation. Patients with conversion disorder experience neurological symptoms purely on a psychological basis and may be unable to speak, or walk, or see but have no organic defect. These patients are not being deceitful; they truly cannot function and will not until their illness is treated.

References

1. Mackinnon RA, Yudofsky SC: The psychiatric interview. In Mackinnon RA, Yudofsky SC: The Psychiatric Interview in Clinical Practice. Philadelphia: JB Lippincott, 1986.
2. Reiser D, Schroder A: The interview process. In Patient Interviewing. The Human Dimension. Baltimore: Williams & Wilkins, 1980:111–136.
3. Lazare A: Hidden conceptual models in psychiatry. N Engl J Med 1973; 288:345–351.
4. Leigh M, Reiser M: Approach to a patient: The patient evaluation grid. In The Patient: Biological, Psychological, and Social Dimensions of Medical Practice, 3rd ed. New York: Plenum Publishing, 1992.
5. Shea S: Contemporary psychiatric interviewing: Integration of DSM III R, psychodynamic concerns, and mental status. In Goldstein G, Hersen M (eds): Handbook of Psychological Assessment, 2nd ed. New York: Pergamon Press, 1990:283–307.
6. Lazare A: The psychiatric examination in the walk-in clinic. Hypothesis generation and hypothesis testing. Arch Gen Psychiatry 1976; 33:96–102.
7. Tischler GL (ed): Diagnosis and Classification in Psychiatry: A Critical Appraisal of DSM III. Cambridge, UK: Cambridge University Press, 1987.
8. Popkin MK: Syndromes of brain dysfunction presenting with cognitive impairment or behavioral disturbance: Delirium, dementia, and mental disorders due to a general medical condition. In Winokur G, Clayton PJ (eds): The Medical Basis of Psychiatry, 2nd ed. Philadelphia: WB Saunders, 1994:17–37.
9. Lipowski ZJ: Organic mental disorders—an American perspective. Br J Psychiatry 1984; 144:542–546.
10. Lishman WA: Organic Psychiatry. Oxford: Blackwell Scientific Publications, 1978.
11. Leigh H, Reiser M: Confusion, delirium, and dementia: Organic brain syndromes and the elderly patient. In The Patient: Biological, Psychological, and Social Dimensions of Medical Practice, 3rd ed. New York: Plenum Publishing, 1992.
12. Cohen RM, Semple WE, Gross M, Nordahl TE: From syndrome to illness: Delineating the pathophysiology of schizophrenia with PET. Schizophr Bull 1988; 14:169–176.
13. Weinberger DR, Wagner RL, Wyatt RJ: Neuropathological studies of schizophrenia: A selective review. Schizophr Bull 1983; 9:193–212.
14. Davis JM: Overview: Maintenance therapy in psychiatry: I. Schizophrenia. Am J Psychiatry 1975; 132:1237–1245.
15. Falloon IRH, Boyd JL, McGill CW, et al: Family management in the prevention of morbidity of schizophrenia: Clinical outcome of a two-year longitudinal style. Arch Gen Psychiatry 1985; 42:887–896.

16. Kendler KS: Demography of paranoid psychosis (delusional disorder): A review and comparison with schizophrenia and affective illness. Arch Gen Psychiatry 1982; 39:890–902.
17. Munro A: Delusional (paranoid) disorders: Etiologic and taxonomic considerations: II. A possible relationship between delusional and affective disorders. Can J Psychiatry 1988; 33:175–178.
18. Kendler KS: Mood-incongruent psychotic affective illness. A historical empirical review. Arch Gen Psychiatry 1991; 48:362–369.
19. Glassman AH, Kantor SJ, Shostak M: Depression, delusions, and drug response. Am J Psychiatry 1975; 132:716–718.
20. Post RM, Leverich GS, Rosoff AS, Altshuler LL: Carbamazepine prophylaxis in refractory affective disorders: A focus on long-term follow-up. J Clin Psychopharmacol 1990; 10:318–327.
21. Stephens JH, Shaffer JW, Carpenter WT: Reactive psychoses. J Nerv Ment Dis 1982; 170:657–663.
22. Retterstll N: The Scandinavian concept of reactive psychosis, schizophreniform psychosis, and schizophrenia. Psychiatr Clin 1978; 11:180–187.
23. Goodwin FK, Jamison KR: Manic-Depressive Illness. New York: Oxford University Press, 1990.
24. Janowsky DS, El-Yousef MK, Davis JM: Interpersonal maneuvers of manic patients. Am J Psychiatry 1974; 131:250–255.
25. Jamison KR, Goodwin FK: Psychotherapeutic issues in bipolar illness. In Grinspoon L (ed): Psychiatric Update, Volume 2. Washington, DC: American Psychiatric Press, 1983.
26. Siever LJ, Davis KL: Overview: Toward a dysregulation hypothesis of depression. Am J Psychiatry 1985; 142:1017–1033.
27. Nurnberger JI, Gershon ES: Genetics of affective disorders. In Post RM, Ballenger JC (eds): Neurobiology of Mood Disorders. Baltimore: Williams & Wilkins, 1984:76–101.
28. Elkin I, Shea T, Watkins J, et al: National Institute of Mental Health Treatment of Depression Collaborative Research Program. General effectiveness of treatments. Arch Gen Psychiatry 1989; 46:971–982.
29. Barlow DH: Anxiety and Its Disorders—The Nature and Treatment of Anxiety and Panic. New York: Guilford Press, 1988.
30. Klein DF: False suffocation alarms, spontaneous panics, and related conditions. An integrative hypothesis. Arch Gen Psychiatry 1993; 50:306–317.
31. Blazer DC, Hughes D, George LK: Generalized anxiety disorder. In Robins LN (ed): Psychiatric Disorders in America: The Epidemiologic Catchment Area Study. New York: Free Press, 1991:180–203.
32. Fyer AJ, Munnuzza S, Gallops MS, et al: Familial transmission of simple phobias and fears: A preliminary report. Arch Gen Psychiatry 1990; 47:252–256.
33. Marks IM: Fears, Phobias and Rituals: Panic, Anxiety and Their Disorders. New York: Oxford University Press, 1987.
34. Van der Kolk BA: Psychological Trauma. Washington, DC: American Psychiatric Press, 1987.
35. Figley CR (ed): Trauma and Its Wake: The Study and Treatment of Post-Traumatic Stress Disorder. New York: Brunner/Mazel, 1985.
36. Lieberman J: Evidence for a biological hypothesis of obsessive-compulsive disorder. Neuropsychobiology 1984; 11:14–21.
37. Insel TR: Toward a neuroanatomy of obsessive-compulsive disorder. Arch Gen Psychiatry 1992; 49:739–744.
38. Steketee G, Foa EB, Grayson JB: Recent advances in the behavioral treatment of obsessive-compulsives. Arch Gen Psychiatry 1982; 39:1365–1376.
39. Cloninger R, Martin RL, Guze SB, Clayton PJ: A prospective follow-up and family study of somatization in men and women. Am J Psychiatry 1986; 143:873–878.
40. Morrison JR: Management of Beriquet's syndrome (hysteria). West J Med 1978; 128:482–487.
41. Lazare A: Current concepts in psychiatry: Conversion symptoms. N Engl J Med 1981; 305:745–748.
42. Dickes RA: Brief therapy of conversion reactors: An in-hospital technique. Am J Psychiatry 1974; 131:584–586.
43. Kellner R: Hypochondriasis and somatization. JAMA 1987; 258:2718–2722.
44. Barsky AJ, Klerman GL: Overview: Hypochondriasis, bodily complaints, and somatic styles. Am J Psychiatry 1983; 140:273–283.
45. Kluft RP: An update on multiple personality disorders. Hosp Community Psychiatry 1987; 38:365–373.
46. Meller YL: Depersonalization—symptoms, meaning, therapy. Acta Psychiatr Scand 1982; 66:451–458.
47. Schukit MA: Biological vulnerability to alcoholism. J Consult Clin Psychol 1987; 55:301–309.
48. Merlett GA: Addictive behaviors: Etiology and treatment. Annu Rev Psychol 1988; 39:223–252.
49. Millman RB (section editor): Drug abuse and dependence. In Frances AJ, Hales RF (eds): Psychiatric Update: American Psychiatric Association Annual Review, Volume 5. Washington, DC: American Psychiatric Press, 1986:120–227.
50. McClellan AT, Luborsky L, O'Brien CP, et al: Is treatment for substance abuse effective? JAMA 1982; 247:1423–1428.
51. LoPiccolo J: Diagnosis and treatment of male sexual dysfunction. J Sex Marital Ther 1985; 2:215–232.
52. Marshall WL, Barbaree HE: An integrated theory of the etiology of sexual offending. In Marshall WL, Laws DN, Barbaree HE (eds): Handbook of Sexual Assault: Issues, Theories, and Treatment of the Offender. New York: Plenum Publishing, 1990:257–275.
53. Johnson C, Connors ME: The Etiology and Treatment of Bulimia Nervosa. New York: Basic Books, 1987.
54. Blinder BJ, Chaitin B, Goldstein R (eds): The Eating Disorders. New York: Pergamon Press, 1987.
55. Andreasen N, Hoeuk PR: The predictive value of adjustment disorders: A follow-up study. Am J Psychiatry 1982; 139:584–590.
56. Looney JG, Gunderson EK: Transient situational disturbances: Course and outcome. Am J Psychiatry 1978; 135:660–663.
57. Kendler KS, Masterson CL, Ungaro R, Davis KL: A family history study of schizophrenia-related personality disorders. Am J Psychiatry 1984; 143:424–427.
58. Slever LJ, Coccaro ER, Zemishlany Z, et al: Psychobiology of personality disorders: Pharmacologic implications. Psychopharmacol Bull 1987; 23:333–336.
59. Tarnepolsky A, Berlowitz M: Borderline personality—a review of recent research. Br J Psychiatry 1987; 151:724–734.
60. Grove W, Eckert E, Heston L: Heritability of substance abuse and antisocial behavior: A study of monozygotic twins reared apart. Biol Psychiatry 1990; 27:1293–1304.
61. Cloninger CR: A systematic model for clinical description and classification of personality variants. Arch Gen Psychiatry 1987; 44:573–588.
62. Liebowitz M, Stone M, Turkat I: Treatment of personality disorders. In Frances AJ, Hales RE (eds): Psychiatric Update: American Psychiatric Association Annual Review, Volume 5. Washington, DC: American Psychiatric Press, 1986:329–334.
63. Paykel ES: Contribution of life events to causation of psychiatric illness. Psychol Med 1978; 8:245–253.
64. Valliant GE: Adaptation to Life. Boston: Little, Brown, 1977.
65. Nemiah J: Psychological conflict. In Nemiah J: Foundations of Psychopathology. New York: Oxford University Press, 1961:35–55.
66. Lazare A, Eisenthal S, Wasserman L: The customer approach to patienthood: Attending to patient requests in a walk-in clinic. Arch Gen Psychiatry 1975; 32:553–558.
67. Strupp H, Binder J: Assessment. In Strupp H, Binder J: Psychotherapy in a New Key. New York: Basic Books, 1984:51–64.
68. Nurnberg HG, Raskin M, Levine PE, et al: Hierarchy of DSM-III R. Criteria efficiency for the diagnosis of borderline personality disorder. J Pers Disord 1991; 5:211–224.
69. Porter TL: The use of race in case presentation. [letter] Am J Psychiatry 1993; 150:1129.
70. Ishii-Kuntz M, Ihringer Tallman M: The subjective well-being of parents. J Fam Issues 1991; 12:58–68.
71. Slaby A, Andrew E: The emergency treatment of the depressed patient with physical illness. Int J Psychiatry Med 1987; 17:71–83.
72. Flomenbaum N, Altman M: Medical aspects of emergency psychiatry. New Dir Ment Health Serv 1985; 28:55–66.
73. Hammen CL, Gordon D, Burge D, et al: Maternal affective disorders, illness and stresses. Am J Psychiatry 1987; 144:736–741.
74. Nemiah J: The doctor and his patient. In: Foundations of Psychopathology. New York: Oxford University Press, 1961:289–304.
75. Mackinnon R, Michels R: The Psychiatric Interview in Clinical Practice. Philadelphia: WB Saunders, 1971:28–33.
76. Gaw A (ed): Culture, Ethnicity, and Mental Illness. Washington, DC: American Psychiatric Press, 1993.
77. Bernstein L, Berstein R: An overview of interviewing techniques. In Interviewing. A Guide for Health Professionals. New York: Appleton-Century-Crofts, 1985:21–33.

78. Malan DH: Unconscious communication. In Malan DH (ed): Individual Psychotherapy and the Science of Psychodynamics. London: Butterworth, 1979:16–23.
79. Freud A: The Ego and the Mechanisms of Defense. New York: International Universities Press, 1946.
80. Casement P: Forms of interactive communication. In On Learning for the Patient. New York: Guilford Press, 1985:72–101.
81. Knapp ML: Nonverbal Communication in Human Interaction. New York: Holt, Rinehart & Winston, 1978.
82. Ekman P, Friesen W, Ellsworth P: Emotion in the Human Face. New York: Pergamon Press, 1972.
83. Luborsky L: Expressive techniques: Listening and understanding. In Principles of Psychoanalytic Psychotherapy. New York: Basic Books, 1984:90–93.
84. Barrett-Lennard GT: The empathy cycle: Refinement of a nuclear concept. J Counsel Psychol 1981; 28:91–100.
85. Sullivan HS: The Psychiatric Interview. New York: WW Norton, 1970.
86. Strean H: Resolving Resistances in Psychotherapy. New York: John Wiley & Sons, 1985.
87. Wiens A: Structured clinical interviews for adults. In Goldstein G, Hersen M (eds): Handbook of Psychological Assessment, 2nd ed. New York: Pergamon Press, 1990:324–341.
88. Spitzer RL, Endicott JO, Robins E: Research diagnostic criteria. Rationale and reliability. Arch Gen Psychiatry 1978; 35:773–782.
89. Groth-Marnat G: The assessment interview. In Groth-Marnat G (ed): Handbook of Psychological Assessment, 2nd ed. New York: John Wiley & Sons, 1990:57–79.
90. Elliott R, Stiles W, Mahrer A, et al: Primary therapist response modes: Comparison of six rating systems. J Consult Clin Psychol 1987 55:218–223.
91. Rutter M, Cox A, Egert S, et al: Psychiatric interviewing techniques IV. Experimental study: Four contrasting styles. Br J Psychiatry 1981; 138:456–465.
92. Cox A, Holbrook D, Rutter M: Psychiatric interviewing techniques VI. Experimental study. Eliciting feelings. Br J Psychiatry 1981; 139: 144–152.
93. Cox A, Rutter M, Holbrook D: Psychiatric interviewing techniques. A second experimental study: Eliciting feelings. Br J Psychiatry 1988; 152:64–72.

CHAPTER

3 Physician-Patient Relationship

Stephen M. Sonnenberg
Loree Sutton
Robert J. Ursano

For centuries, healers had little understanding of disease processes and lacked the technology we now know is necessary to cure many diseases. Physicians had few medications, and surgery was only a last resort. In fact, the most important tool for healing was the relationship between the physician and the patient. Interpersonal relationships have a powerful influence on both morbidity and mortality.[1] Social connectedness can aid health in both direct and indirect ways: directly regulating many biological functions, decreasing anxiety, providing avenues for obtaining new information, and fostering alternative behaviors.[2] We know little about the basic mechanisms by which interpersonal relationships, and the physician-patient relationship in particular, operate.[3] However, clinical wisdom holds that both the reality-based elements of the physician-patient relationship—in modern times referred to as the working alliance or the therapeutic alliance[4, 5]—and the fantasy-based elements of the relationship affect the patient's pain, suffering, and recovery from illness.

Historically, physicians learned to interact with their patients in ways that relieved pain and promoted health.[6] Often the physician's main tools were reassurance, providing knowledge about the patient's disease, accepting the patient's feelings of distress as normal, and maximizing the patient's hope for the future. Although these interventions, based on wisdom and intuition, are no longer the only tools available to the physician, they continue to be an important part of the physician's and particularly the psychiatrist's therapeutic armamentarium.

Such nonspecific aspects of cure are often referred to as mystical or mysterious or, in biological studies, as the placebo effect. Oddly, these effects of interpersonal relationships are both one of the prized and one of the most denigrated aspects of all of medicine. Yet as clinicians we all strive to alleviate our patients' pain and suffering and return them to health as soon as possible. Many well-designed studies show that 20% to 30% of subjects respond to the placebo condition. The problem with placebos is not whether they work but that we do not understand how they work and, therefore, we do not have control over their effects. As a physician one strives to maximize one's interpersonal healing effects and, in this way as well as with other healing tools, increase the chances for our patients' relief of pain and recovery.

The physician-patient relationship is based on specific roles and motivations. These form the core ingredients of the healing process. In its most generic form the physician-patient relationship is defined by the coming together of an expert and a help seeker to identify, understand, and solve the problems of the help seeker. The help seeker (in modern terms, the patient) is motivated by the desire and hope for assistance and relief of pain.[7] A physician requires a genuine interest in people and a desire to help.[8] Simply stated, "the secret of the care of the patient is in caring for the patient."[9] Caring about and paying attention to a patient's suffering can yield remarkable therapeutic dividends. More than one attending physician has been reminded of this when a patient deferred making a treatment decision until he or she was able to consult with "my doctor," who turned out to be a medical student.

In today's technology-driven medicine, the importance and complexity of the physician-patient interaction are often overlooked. The amount of information the medical student or resident must learn frequently takes precedence over learning the fine points of helping the patient relax sufficiently to provide a thorough history or to allow the physician to palpate a painful abdomen. Talking with patients and understanding the intricacies of the physician-patient relationship are often given little formal attention in a medical curriculum. Even so, medical students, residents, and staff physicians recognize, often with awe, the skill of the senior physician who uncovers the lost piece of history, motivates the patient who had given up hope, or is able to talk to the distressed family without increasing their sense of hopelessness or fear.

The relationship between the physician and the patient is central to the healing of many patients and perhaps particularly so for many psychiatric patients. The physician who can skillfully recognize the patient's half-hidden comment that he or she has not been taking the prescribed medication, perhaps hidden because of feelings of shame, anger, or denial, is better able to ensure long-term compliance with medication as well as to motivate the patient to stay in treatment. Regardless of the type of treatment—

medication, biofeedback, hospitalization, psychotherapy, or the rearrangement of demands and responsibilities in the patient's life—the relationship with the physician is critical to therapeutic outcome.

Clinical Vignette 1

A 20-year-old female patient suffered a painful athletic injury. She was unsure exactly how her injury had occurred, but she did recall falling on her shoulder on the tennis court while running after a sharply hit ball. She went to the physician fearing that she had damaged her collarbone. When she was informed that there was no fracture, that her pain was due to a bruised muscle and would go away with ice, heat, and aspirin, she immediately felt better. Not only was she relieved, but also her perception and experience of the pain actually changed. "It doesn't seem to hurt as much now."

Clinical Vignette 2

Somewhat different was the situation of a 30-year-old male patient who developed chronic pain after an athletic injury. The patient had to convince himself to visit the physician. He felt he was being a "baby" to complain. One week after the injury he went to his family physician, who perfunctorily prescribed a strong painkiller and offered a follow-up appointment a month later. He left feeling that he had been a nuisance. The following week was a particularly bad one for the patient. The pain was severe. But the patient stopped taking the prescribed medication, did not keep the follow-up appointment, and never returned for help. This patient continued to experience pain, unnecessarily, for years. In large part this was because no hope was provided by the physician, and therefore follow-up care, including physical therapy and alternative medications, could not be provided.

The physician-patient relationship is also a source of information for the physician. The way in which the patient relates to the physician can help the physician understand the problems the patient is experiencing in her or his interpersonal relationships. The nature of the physician-patient relationship can also provide information about relationships in the patient's childhood family, in which interpersonal patterns are first learned. With this information the physician can better understand the patient's experience, promote cooperation between the patient and those who care for her or him, and teach the patient new behavioral strategies in an empathic manner, understanding the patient's subjective perspective, that is, the patient's feelings, thoughts, and behaviors.

Clinical Vignette 3

The patient, a 45-year-old single man, was hospitalized for treatment of a bleeding ulcer. The patient had no past history of ulcers. Despite reassurance, the patient continued to feel hopeless. A psychiatric consultant was called to evaluate the patient. She found him to be needy but could not understand why he was so pessimistic. The psychiatrist recognized the importance to this patient of showing interest in him, showing concern for his condition, and spending time with him. The patient's response was noteworthy; he clearly enjoyed the psychiatrist's company but seemed unusually sad when their times together ended. The psychiatrist asked the patient if this was a correct perception and, if so, why it was the case. The patient responded that the psychiatrist reminded him of his mother. Further inquiry revealed that the patient's mother had died several years ago of colon cancer. The psychiatrist inquired about the symptoms the mother had during her terminal illness. The symptoms were similar to the patient's symptoms: bleeding in the digestive tract and gastrointestinal pain.

The psychiatrist then understood the complex process through which the patient was feeling inordinately pessimistic. Transference was evident in the patient's experience of each departure as an unconscious reminder of the loss of his mother. The patient's identification with his mother (as part of managing her death) was also the source of his unspoken expectation that he, too, was dying of colon cancer. It was the pattern of the relationship between the psychiatrist and the patient, the sadness shown whenever the psychiatrist left, that provided the information necessary to help the patient. Increasing the patient's understanding of his medical condition, specifically how it was different from his mother's, relieved his emotional pain, and he began on the road to recovery.

These clinical vignettes illustrate that the physician-patient relationship is composed of both the reality-based component (the working alliance or therapeutic alliance) and the fantasy-based component (the transference) derived from the patient's patterns of interpersonal behavior learned in childhood. Either or both of these may maximize or limit the patient's sense of reassurance, available information, feelings of comfort, and sense of hope.[10] In this way, the nonspecific curative aspects of the physician-patient relationship may be enhanced or diminished.

Formation of the Physician-Patient Relationship

Assessment and Evaluation

The physician-patient relationship develops during the assessment and evaluation of the patient. The patient observes the thoroughness and sensitivity with which the physician collects information, performs the physical examination, and explains needed tests. At each step, the physician's clarification of the treatment goals and interventions either builds up the patient's expectation of help and feelings of safety or creates increasing dis-ease for the patient.[11] Alertness to the patient's fears and misunderstandings of the evaluation process can minimize unnecessary disruptions of the relationship and provide information on the patient's previous experiences with medical care and important authority figures. These past experiences form the patient's present expectations of either help or disappointment[12] (Table 3–1).

Rapport

Early in the relationship between a psychiatrist and a patient, the patient requests help with his or her pain, uncertainty, or

Table 3–1 Mechanisms Affecting the Formation and Structure of the Physician-Patient Relationship

Assessment and evaluation process
Development of physician-patient rapport
Therapeutic or working alliance
Transference
Countertransference
Defense mechanisms
Patient's mental status

discomfort. The psychiatrist initiates the "contract" of the relationship by acknowledging the patient's pain and offering help. In this action, the psychiatrist has recognized the patient's ill health and acknowledged the need for and possibility of removing the disease or illness. In this first stage of the development of rapport, the way of relating between the physician and the patient, the physician-patient relationship has begun to organize the interactions. Through the physician's and the patient's shared recognition of the patient's pain, the basis for rapport—a comfortable pattern of working together—is established.

The psychiatrist's ability to empathize, to understand in feeling terms the patient's subjective experience, is important to the development of rapport. Empathy is particularly important in complex interpersonal behavioral problems in which the environment (family, friends, caretakers) may wish to expel the patient and the patient has, therefore, lost hope. Suicidal patients, adolescents involved in intense family conflicts, and patients in conflict with their medical caregivers can often be convinced to cooperate with the evaluation only when the psychiatrist has shown accurate empathy early in the first meeting with the patient. When the physician acknowledges the patient's pain, the patient feels less alone and inevitably more hopeful.[13] This rapport establishes a set of principles and expectations of the physician-patient interaction. On this basic building block, more elaborate goals and responsibilities of the patient can be developed.

Clinical Vignette 4

A young man sought treatment for ill-defined reasons: he was dissatisfied with his work, his social life, and his relationship with his parents. He was unable to say how he thought the psychiatrist could help him, but he knew he was experiencing emotional pain: he felt sadness, anxiety, inhibition, and loss of a lust for living. He wanted help. The psychiatrist noted the patient's tentative style and heard the patient describe his ambivalence toward his controlling and directing father. With this in mind, the psychiatrist articulated the patient's wish for help and recognized with him his confusion about what was troubling him. She suggested that through discussion they might define together what he was looking for and how she might help him. This description of the evaluation process as a joint process of discovery established a rapport based on shared work that removed the patient's fears of control and allowed the patient to feel heard, supported, and involved in the process of regaining his health.

The Therapeutic or Working Alliance

For a patient to trust and work closely with a physician it is essential that there be a reality-based relationship outside the conflicted ones for which the patient is seeking help.[14, 15] With more disturbed patients considerable skill is required for the physician to reach this reality-based part of the patient and decrease the patient's fears and expectations of attack or humiliation. Even for healthy patients, the physician must bridge the gap between the patient and the physician that is always present because of their different backgrounds and perceptions of the world. This gap is an expectable result of differences between the physician's and the patient's culture, gender, ethnic background, socioeconomic class, religion, age, or role in the physician-patient relationship. The experienced physician makes communication across the gap seem effortless, using a different "language" for each patient. The student often sees this as an art rather than as a skill to be learned.

The therapeutic alliance is extremely important in times of crisis such as suicidality, hospitalization, and aggressive behavior. But it is also the basis of agreement about appointments, fees, and treatment requirements. In psychiatric patients, this core component of the physician-patient relationship can be disturbed and require careful tending. Frequently, the psychiatrist may feel that he or she is "threading a needle" to reach and maintain the therapeutic alliance while not activating the more disturbed elements of the patient's patterns of interpersonal relating.

The therapeutic or working alliance must endure in spite of what may, at times, be intense, irrational, delusional, characterologic, or transference-based feelings of love and hate. The working alliance must outweigh or counterbalance the distorted components of the relationship. It provides a stable base for the patient and the physician when the patient's feelings or behaviors may impair reflection and cooperation. The working alliance embodies the mutual responsibilities both physician and patient have accepted to restore the patient's health. Likewise, the working alliance must be strong enough to ensure that the treatment goes forward even when both members of the dyad may doubt that it can. The alliance requires a basic trust by the patient that the physician is working in his or her best interests, despite how the patient may feel at a given moment. Patients must be taught to be partners in the healing process and to recognize that the physician is a committed partner in that process as well. The development of common goals fosters the physician and patient seeing themselves as having reciprocal responsibilities: the physician to work in a physicianly fashion to promote healing, the patient to participate actively in formulating and supporting the treatment plan, "try on" more adaptive behaviors in the chosen mode of treatment, and take responsibility for his or her actions to the extent possible.[16]

Important to the reality-based relationship with the patient is the physician's ability to recognize and acknowledge the limitations of her or his knowledge and work collaboratively with other physicians. When this happens, patients are most often appreciative, not critical, and experience a strengthening of the alliance because of the physician's commitment to finding an answer. When a patient loses confidence in the physician, it is often because of unacknowledged shortcomings in the physician's skills.

The patient may lose motivation to maintain the alliance and seek help elsewhere. Alternatively, the patient may seek no help.

Transference and Countertransference

Transference is the tendency we all have to see someone in the present as like an important figure from our past.[17] This process occurs outside our conscious awareness and is probably a basic means used by the brain to make sense of current experience by seeing the past in the present and limiting the input of new information. Transference is more common in settings that provoke anxiety and provide few cues to how to behave—conditions typical of a hospital. Transference influences the patient's behavior and can distort the physician-patient relationship, for good or ill.[18]

Although transference is a distortion of the present reality, it is usually built around a kernel of reality that can make it difficult for the inexperienced clinician to recognize rather than react to the transference. The transference can be the elaboration of an accurate observation into the "total" explanation or the major evidence of some expected harm or loss. Often the physician may recognize transference by the pressure she or he feels to respond in a particular manner to the patient—for example, always to stay longer or not abruptly leave the patient.[19]

Transference is ubiquitous. It is a part of day-to-day experience, although its operation is outside conscious awareness. Recognizing transference in the physician-patient relationship can aid the physician in understanding the patient's deeply held expectations of help, shame, injury, or abandonment that derive from childhood experiences.

Transference reactions, of course, are not confined to the patient; the physician also superimposes the past on the present. This is called countertransference, the physician's transference to the patient (Table 3–2). Countertransference usually takes one of two forms: concordant countertransference, in which one empathizes with the patient's position, or complementary countertransference, in which one empathizes with an important figure from the patient's past.[20] For example, concordant countertransference would be evident if a patient were describing an argument with his or her boss and the psychiatrist, perhaps after a disagreement with the psychiatrist's own supervisor and without having collected detailed information from the patient, felt "Oh yeah, what a terrible boss." Similarly, complementary countertransference would be evident if the same psychiatrist felt "This person (the patient) does not work very hard, no wonder the boss is dissatisfied" and felt angry at the patient as well. Paying close attention to our personal reactions, while refraining from immediate action, can inform us in an experiential manner about subtle aspects of the patient's behavior that we may overlook or not appreciate. In the preceding example, perhaps the psychiatrist, in recognizing the countertransference, would identify the patient's subtle need to fight with authority (concordant countertransference) or the patient's passive behavior that expressed hidden anger that the nurses on the ward might have noticed and responded to with feelings of anger (complementary countertransference).

Table 3–2 Types of Countertransference

Concordant countertransference
- The physician experiences and empathizes with *the patient's* emotional experience and perception of reality.

Complementary countertransference
- The physician experiences and empathizes with the emotional experience and perception of reality of *an important person from the patient's life.*

Countertransference occurs in all "sizes and shapes," more or less mixed with the physician's past but often greatly influencing the physician-patient relationship. The wish to save or rescue a patient is commonly experienced and indicates a need to look for countertransference responses. When a patient is seriously ill, such as with cancer, we may increasingly want to treat the patient more aggressively, with procedures that may hold little hope, create substantial pain, and perhaps even be against the patient's wishes. The physician's feelings of loss of a valued person (in the present and as a reminder of the past) or feelings of failure (loss of the physician's own power and ability) can often fuel such reactions. More subtle factors, such as the effects of being overworked, can result in unrecognized feelings of deprivation leading to unspoken wishes for a patient to quit treatment. When these feelings appear in subtle countertransference reactions, such as being late to appointments, becoming tired in an hour, or being unable to recall previous material, they can have powerful effects on the patient's wish to continue treatment.

Major developmental events in physicians' lives can also influence their perceptions of their patients. When a psychiatrist is expecting the birth of a child, she or he may be overly sensitive to or ignore the concerns of a patient worried about a significant illness in the patient's child. Similarly, a physician with a dying parent or spouse may be unable to empathize with a patient's concerns about loss of a job, feeling that it is trivial.

Clinical Vignette 5

A psychiatrist was called to evaluate an agitated older adult resident of a nursing home. After she had interviewed the energetic, sad, and anxious patient, the psychiatrist found herself unexpectedly sad, confused, and unsure about what to do. This was not a new case for the psychiatrist, who had treated many similar cases. In considering her response, her thoughts turned to her grandmother with whom she had lived when she was 8 years old and who had been displaced from her residence and moved to a nursing home in another city by well-meaning children who wanted her near them. After the move, her grandmother had become depressed and disoriented and died 3 months later. The psychiatrist recalled feeling confused at the time of her grandmother's death, wondering why she had died when she had just moved to an attractive new home. Recalling her confusion, the psychiatrist could think more clearly about her present patient and wondered if the patient might be depressed. She talked further with the nurses and found symptoms of depression in addition to the nighttime agitation. This new information altered her decision on the type of medication to begin with and the need for psychotherapy in addition to medication.

Table 3–3 Common Defense Mechanisms

Healthier Defenses	More Primitive Defenses
Sublimation	Splitting
Humor	Projection
Repression	Projective identification
Displacement	Omnipotence
Intellectualization	Devaluing
Reaction formation	Primitive idealization
Reversal	Denial
Identification with the aggressor	
Asceticism	
Altruism	
Isolation of affect	

Defense Mechanisms

All people, including patients, employ mechanisms of defense to protect themselves from the painful awareness of feelings and memories that can provoke overwhelming anxiety. Defense mechanisms are specific cognitive processes, ways of thinking, that the mind employs to avoid painful feelings.[21] They are often characteristic of a person and form a style of cognition.[22] Common defense mechanisms include projection, repression, displacement, intellectualization, humor, suppression, and altruism (Table 3–3).

Defense mechanisms may be more or less mature depending on the degree of distortion of reality and interpersonal disruption they lead to. This patterning of feelings, thoughts, and behaviors by defense mechanisms is involuntary and arises in response to perceptions of psychic danger.[23] The patient's characteristic defense mechanisms, the cognitive processes used to lower anxiety and unpleasant feelings, can greatly affect the physician-patient relationship. Defense mechanisms operate all the time; however, in times of high anxiety, such as in a hospital or during a life crisis, patients may become much less flexible in the defenses they use and may revert to using less mature defenses.

Clinical Vignette 6

A 36-year-old army first sergeant was hospitalized for the evaluation of acute paralysis of his right hand. When the results of a neurological work-up revealed no evidence of organic pathology, psychiatric consultation was obtained. The patient denied any past psychiatric history or significant alcohol or other substance abuse. He described a healthy family support system but then hesitated, saying, "You know, Doc, there's one thing I just haven't been able to talk about with anyone." He proceeded to speak of the extreme pressure he was feeling on the job, where he had found out that his boss (the company commander) was behaving unethically. The patient stated, "I feel like I'm between a rock and a hard place—if I report it, I'm being disloyal to my boss, but if I don't, I'm betraying my soldiers and the army." After further elaborating his feelings of anger and disgust toward his boss, the patient asked to terminate the interview but agreed to talk with the psychiatrist again in the morning.

Returning the next morning, the psychiatrist was greeted by the patient, who was brushing his teeth, using his right hand. "Hey, Doc, I'm good to go!" The patient then described what happened the evening before. "I was telling my wife about how I've got to get out of here and get back to work, because, after all, I'm the commander's 'right-hand' man. And you know what, Doc? My hand started to work! Get me out of here, I'm not crazy after all!" The patient then reviewed the process, aided by the psychiatrist, and was able to further his understanding of the link between his conflicted rage toward his boss and how it was expressed symbolically as an involuntary physical paralysis of his right hand. He resolved "I'm gonna do the right thing. I got to live with myself" and planned to report the commander's misconduct on return to work. He was discharged from the hospital later that day, having regained full use of his hand.

Clinical Vignette 7

A 20-year-old man came for consultation because of uncertainty about his career. He soon revealed that he felt profoundly sad, hopeless, helpless, even suicidal. He had a family history of depression. The physician and patient agreed to employ antidepressant medication aggressively. Yet over a period of several weeks the patient did not improve. When the physician asked why that might be happening, the patient revealed that he had frequently forgotten to take the prescribed medication and had forgotten to tell the physician that this was the case during two meetings. The physician explored the reasons for this, and together the physician and the patient learned that the patient felt ashamed of having been diagnosed as depressed and of having been considered to require medication. He felt he was not his own master and had experienced this as a severe blow to his self-esteem. Taking the medication was a reminder of this "flaw." Hearing himself say this and feeling the physician's empathic support, the patient recognized the irrationality of his behavior and felt relieved. In addition, the physician now understood better the intensity of the patient's feelings and changed the prescription to once-a-day dosage at bedtime to decrease the patient's sense of shame and increase compliance with the treatment.

Clinical vignettes 6 and 7 are examples of defense mechanisms (conversion and avoidance or repression) affecting the treatment relationship. In vignette 6 the conversion reaction that resulted in the paralysis expressed both the patient's anger and his conflict over what to do. In vignette 7 the physician knew that the forgetting was neither intentional nor conscious but was directed at denying the need for treatment. In these cases, recognizing the defenses was important to knowing how to relate to the patient (clinical vignette 6) and avoid a countertransference reaction of anger at the patient for lack of compliance (clinical vignette 7).

Research on the Physician-Patient Relationship

Research examining the physician-patient relationship has focused primarily on studies of psychotherapy. In general, the research confirms what clinicians have long recognized: the physician-patient relationship is central to behavioral change in nearly all treatment modalities.[24] The therapeutic alliance has been and continues to be the most studied aspect of the psychotherapy process.[25(p308)] Pioneered by Roger's[26] view of the therapeutic relationship as providing "necessary and sufficient conditions" of change, psychotherapy process-outcome studies have focused both on identifying the effects of particular components of the therapeutic alliance and on identifying the effects of the alliance on outcome.[25(p308)] Current research focuses on the patient's affective relationship to the therapist, the patient's capacity to work purposefully in therapy, the therapist's empathic ability, and the patient's and therapist's mutual agreement on the goals and tasks of therapy.[27] Horvath and Greenberg[11] developed the Working Alliance Inventory, noted for its measurement of the interaction between therapist and patient in terms of the bond and agreement on tasks and goals.[28]

Psychotherapy outcome research has used meta-analysis to attain efficient and maximally objective integrative summaries of existing studies.[29] Early studies focused on determining the extent of the benefit associated with psychotherapy in the existing literature as a whole, compared the outcomes of different treatments, and examined the impact of methodological features of studies on the reported effectiveness of treatments. Smith and colleagues[30] found an average effect size of 0.85 standard deviation unit for 475 studies comparing treated and untreated groups. This means that, after treatment, the average treated person was better off than 80% of the untreated sample.

Subsequent meta-analytic reviews of specific disorders likewise have yielded promising results. For depression, five meta-analytic reviews totaling 133 studies showed effect sizes ranging from 0.65 to 2.15 standard deviation units. For agoraphobia, three meta-analytic reviews totaling 95 studies showed effect sizes ranging from 1.2 to 2.10 units. For obsessive-compulsive disorder, two meta-analytic reviews totaling 43 studies showed effect sizes ranging from 1.34 to 1.37 units.[31(pp144–145)]

Orlinsky and colleagues[25] used meta-analysis for more than 2300 findings on process outcome from approximately 300 psychotherapy studies conducted between 1950 and 1992. They concluded that the strongest evidence supports the importance of the therapeutic alliance to outcome, with more than 1000 significant findings. The relationship of outcome to therapeutic alliance is particularly strong when the alliance is measured from the patient's perspective; for example, it is perhaps more important that the patient feels understood and valued than that the therapist thinks this is so. What therapists do, when they do it, and whether they are genuine in doing it all matter to patients, as does the level of the patient's emotional involvement in the process.[25(pp360–361)] From the perspective of the therapeutic alliance, the therapist contributes to helping the patient achieve a favorable outcome mainly through empathic, affirmative, collaborative, and self-congruent engagement with the patient.[32]

Although there are many therapies, each with its own theoretical basis and specific techniques, there is only modest evidence to suggest the superiority of one school or technique over another. Common factors, which include the therapeutic alliance, loom large as the major mediators of treatment outcome. Research on specific techniques and research on common factors, however, are not necessarily in opposition.[31(p167)] A growing number of researchers and clinicians assert that research cannot hope to separate the unique contributions of techniques and common factors to outcome. In this view, techniques are interpersonal and gain their meaning from the particular interaction of the individuals involved.[33–35] Studies are needed to investigate the change processes associated with each of the various psychotherapeutic approaches, to determine which are common to all and which are unique.[36]

Based on the existing evidence, the therapeutic alliance accounts for much, if not most, of the gains that result from therapy. This confirms the importance of the alliance for change. Further study is needed of the therapeutic alliance in treatment settings other than psychotherapy. In the interim, the data support the notion that physicians may enhance clinical outcomes by intentionally incorporating the components of the therapeutic alliance into their relationships with patients.[31(p163)]

Special Issues in the Physician-Patient Relationship

Phase of Treatment

The treatment phase, early, middle, or late (Table 3–4), affects the structure of the physician-patient relationship in terms of both the issues to be addressed and the task to be accomplished by the physician and the patient. The early stage of treatment involves developing a rapport, forming shared initial goals, and initiating the working alliance. Education of the patient is important in the success of the physician-patient relationship in this stage. In this way the patient learns what he or she can expect. In the middle stage of treatment, the physician and patient continuously refine their shared goals and various interventions are tried. While this takes place, transference and countertransference are likely to emerge. How these are recognized and managed is critical to whether the relationship continues and is therapeutic.

In the later phase of treatment, the assessment of the outcome and plans for the future are the primary focus. The physician and the patient discuss the end of their relationship in a process known as termination. Successes and disappointments associated with the treatment are reviewed. The physician must be willing to acknowledge the patient's disappointments, as well as recognize her or his own disappointments in the treatment. The therapeutic alliance is strengthened in this stage when the physician accepts expressions of the patient's disappointments, encourages such expressions when they are not forthcoming, and prepares the patient for the future. Such preparations include

Table 3–4 Key Features of Treatment Phases
Early: developing rapport, forming shared initial goals, initiating the working alliance
Middle: refining shared goal, using a variety of trial interventions
Late: assessing outcome, resolving presenting problems, planning for future

Table 3–5 Factors Affecting the Physician-Patient Relationship

Phases of treatment: early, middle, late
Treatment setting
Transition between inpatient and outpatient treatment
Managed care
Health and illness of the physician

orienting the patient as to when he or she might seek further treatment.[37] Solidifying the physician-patient relationship at the end of treatment can be critical to the patient's self-esteem and willingness to return if symptoms reappear (Table 3–5).

As a part of the termination process the physician and the patient must review what has been learned, discuss what changes have taken place in the patient and the patient's life, and acknowledge together the sadness and joy of their leave-taking. The termination involves a mourning process, even when treatment has been brief or unpleasant. Of course, when the physician-patient relationship has been rewarding and both physician and patient are satisfied with what they have accomplished, mourning is more intense and often characterized by a bittersweet sadness.

Treatment Settings

The physician-patient relationship takes place in a variety of treatment settings. These include the private office, community clinic, emergency room, inpatient psychiatric ward, and general hospital ward. Psychiatrists treating patients in a private office may find that the relative privacy of this setting enhances the early establishment of trust related to confidentiality. In addition, the psychiatrist's personality is more evident in the private office, where personal factors influencing choice of decor, room arrangement, and location play a role. However, in contrast to the hospital or community setting, the private office generally lacks other evidence of the physician's competence and humanness. In hospital and community settings, when a colleague greets the physician and the patient in the hall or the physician receives a call for a consultation by a colleague or a meeting, these events may indicate to the patient that the physician is qualified, skilled, and humane.

On the other hand, therapeutic work conducted in the community clinic, emergency room, and general hospital ward often requires the psychiatrist and patient to adapt rapidly to meeting one another, assessing the problem, establishing treatment goals, and ensuring the appropriate interventions and follow-up. The importance of protecting the patient's needs for time, predictability, and structure can run counter to the demands of a busy service and unexpected clinical and administrative requirements. The psychiatrist must stay alert to the patient's perspective. Not all interruptions can be avoided. But the patient can be informed and accommodated as much as possible, and any feelings of hurt, disappointment, or anger can be listened for by the physician and responded to empathically. At times, patients, particularly those with borderline personality disorder, may require transfer to another psychiatrist whose schedule can accommodate the patient's exquisite needs for stability.

The boundaries of confidentiality are necessarily extended in hospital and community settings to include consultation with other physicians, nursing staff, and family members.[38] Particular attention must always be given to the patient's need for and right to respect.

Regardless of the setting, patients receiving medications must be fully informed about the potential risks and benefits of and alternatives to the recommended pharmacological treatment.[39] This is an important component of maintaining the physician-patient relationship. Patients who are informed about and involved in decisions about medication respect the physician's role and interest in their welfare. Psychiatrists must also pay particular attention to the meaning a patient attaches to any prescribed medication, particularly when the time comes to alter or discontinue its use.[40]

Transition Between Inpatient and Outpatient Treatment

Many psychiatric treatments include the sheltered environment of a hospital for at least some time. The purpose of this environment is to provide the patient with a safe refuge, a moratorium during which stressors are reduced, supportive assistance is provided, and an inner equilibrium is reestablished in the mind and life of the patient. In this situation the patient is temporarily relieved of some elements of personal responsibility, at least compared with what is expected of that person in the community. This difference is reflected in the relationship between physician and patient. The change from inpatient to outpatient therapy involves the resumption of a greater degree of autonomy by the patient in the physician-patient dyad. The physician must actively encourage this separation and its hope for the future. This transition is delicate for any therapeutic pair.

So, too, is the extremely delicate situation that occurs when the patient must switch physicians for any reason. This often occurs when a patient leaves the hospital and begins outpatient work with a new therapist. Discussing with the patient the skills and abilities of the receiving physician can alleviate much anxiety and foster the new physician-patient relationship. The knowledge that the receiving physician is known and respected by the present physician is a powerful endorsement. In difficult cases in which the strength of the therapeutic alliance is critical to the stability of the patient, as is seen in some psychotic disorders and with some patients with borderline personality disorder, it may be helpful to hold a joint meeting before the transfer. At this meeting, both the new and the old physicians should be present; the patient can be scheduled for an appointment with the new physician in the same week.

Managed Care

Managed care, broadly defined as any care of patients that is not determined solely by the provider, currently focuses on the economic aspects of delivering medical care, with little attention thus far to its potential effects on the physician-patient relationship.[41] Discontinuity of care and the creation of unrealistic expectations on the part of patients have been raised as likely deleterious effects on that relationship.[42] Other issues that can affect the physician-patient relationship include the erosion of confidentiality, shrinkage of the types of reimbursable services, and diminished autonomy of the patient and the physician in medical decision-making. With neither party in complete control of decisions, the physician-patient relationship can become increasingly adversarial and subservient to external issues such as cost, quality of life, political expediency, and social efficiency.[43]

Psychiatrists can best serve their patients by continuing to conduct thorough diagnostic assessments covering the biological, psychological, and social aspects of the patients' condition to determine the most effective plan for treatment.[44] This plan should be openly shared with the patient regardless of whether economic considerations render it infeasible. The psychiatrist and patient may then work together to make the best of what is possible, both aware of the societal and individual factors influencing their actions. For a more detailed discussion of this topic, see Chapter 4.

Health and Illness of the Physician

Psychiatrists, like all people, become ill, and the illness can affect their ability to work effectively. Reactions of denial, projection, and hopelessness, to name but a few of the possibilities, can distort the psychiatrist's vision of the patient. The psychiatrist may be blinded to the patients' suffering or see it as if it were his or her own or, worse yet, as a hopeless situation. In some instances, a physician who is ill must leave a practice, temporarily or permanently, and in that situation therapy enters a late phase in which termination must take place. In some cases, when the onset of illness is devastating, this can be impossible; in other cases termination may have to be rapid. Sometimes, such as when the physician dies suddenly, colleagues must step in to conduct the termination of therapy or the patient's transfer and transition to another physician.[45, 46]

Depression and grief can also impair the physician's ability to make use of accurate empathy and medical decision-making. It is important for physicians to stay alert to these influences and seek clinical supervision or consultation to ensure accurate decision-making and a consistent physician-patient relationship. A thoughtful colleague who recognizes the role of depression and grief in the life course can both assist in any treatment that is needed and help to provide a necessary period of clinical supervision or consultation.

The Physician-Patient Relationship in Specific Populations of Patients

Cross-Cultural and Ethnic Issues

Addressing cross-cultural issues such as race, ethnicity, religion, and gender is vital to the establishment and maintenance of an effective physician-patient relationship. Psychiatry as practiced in the United States generally represents the value orientation of the American middle-class family, emphasizing individualism, scientific rationale, free expression of speech, and tolerance of dissent.[47] Accordingly, therapists may unconsciously make value judgments stemming from their personal cultural perspective, without adequate appreciation for the diversity of normal behavior.[3] For example, assertiveness may be seen as manipulativeness, stoicism as passivity, religious ritual as compulsion, competence as dominance, unselfishness as masochism, charm as seductiveness, lack of concern with appearance as depression, family orientation as dependency, and homosexuality as perversion. Even similarities in background may create misunderstanding, in that both physician and patient may make unjustified assumptions or fail to explore certain behaviors or symptoms because the reasons for them seem self-evident. Failure to clarify cultural assumptions, whether stemming from differences or similarities in background, may impede the establishment of a trusting therapeutic alliance, making effective treatment unlikely.[48]

Every individual is inevitably like everyone else, like someone else, and like no one else.[49] Thus, every physician-patient relationship involves the universal, the group-specific, and the unique aspects of each participant.[50] Maintaining a thoughtful awareness of and appreciation for the influence of cross-cultural issues can enrich and empower the physician-patient relationship.

When psychiatrists work with a patient who belongs to or identifies with a particular ethnic or minority group, they are well advised to learn about the culture of the patient and use caution in making assumptions based on stereotypical or popular beliefs. This is true even when the psychiatrist has the same ethnic or minority group background. Other significant cross-cultural factors include gender, sexual orientation, physical appearance, religious background, and personal experience.[51]

Ethnicity, culture, and race can stir deep unconscious feelings in many individuals that may surface as projections within the physician-patient relationship. The physician must strive to understand what it is like to live in the patient's world, however divergent its patterns or values may be from those of the physician's world. Maintaining therapeutic neutrality may be difficult and, in some cases, require the physician to seek further consultation.[52]

Children, Adolescents, and Families

Establishing an effective physician-patient relationship with children, adolescents, and families is one of the most challenging and rewarding tasks in the practice of psychiatry. Rather than being treated as "little adults," children and adolescents must be approached with an appreciation for their age-appropriate developmental tasks and needs. When physicians treat this population, they must establish a trusting relationship with both the patient and the parents. Preadolescent children face the psychosocial developmental tasks of establishing trust, autonomy, initiative, and achievement. By understanding the facets of normal childhood development, physicians may help parents understand the nature of their child's disturbance and work within the family system to manage effective mechanisms for coping and recovery.[53, 54]

Adolescent patients, facing the task of establishing an individual identity, pose particular challenges to the physician-patient relationship. Adolescents are particularly sensitive to any signals from the physician that their powers of decision, their intelligence, or their perceptions are being ignored. The critical time for engagement with the adolescent is often in the first session, sometimes even in the first few minutes.[55] Defiance, detachment, and aggression may be anticipated and defused with a steady therapeutic presence grounded in consistent boundaries and open acknowledgment of the adolescent patient's distress.[56]

In working with families, physicians in general and psychiatrists in particular must clearly address questions and concerns regarding all aspects of treatment and convey respectful compassion for all members. The therapeutic alliance, or "joining" with the family and patient, requires developing enough of a family consensus that treatment is worth the struggle involved. Taking sides and engaging with individual and family power struggles can be particularly destructive to the physician-patient relationship in families. Rather, it is the physician's ability to relate to the family as a multifaceted organism, massively interconnected, transcending the sum of its parts, that often allows treatment to progress and, in the best scenarios, for growth and understanding to occur.[57, 58]

Terminally Ill Patients

Terminally ill patients share concerns related to the end of the life cycle. Elderly patients at all levels of health face the developmental task of integrating the various threads of their life into a figurative tapestry that reflects their lifelong feelings, thoughts, values, goals, beliefs, experiences, and relationships and places them into a meaningful perspective. Patients newly diagnosed with a terminal illness such as metastatic cancer or acquired immunodeficiency syndrome may be particularly overwhelmed and initially unable to deal with the demands of their illness, especially if the patient is a younger adult or child. Psychiatrists may enhance the terminally ill patient's ability to cope by addressing issues related to medical treatment, pharmacotherapy, psychotherapy, involvement of significant others, legal matters, and institutional care.[59(pp275–276)] Patients struggling with spiritual or religious concerns may benefit from a religious consultation, a resource that is frequently unused.

Countertransference feelings ranging from fear to helplessness to rage to despair can assist the therapist greatly in maintaining the physician-patient relationship and ensuring appropriate care. Physicians working with patients with acquired immunodeficiency syndrome must frequently confront their own feelings and attitudes toward homosexuality.[60] Issues commonly encountered with disabled patients include inaccurate assumptions about their ability to function fully in all areas of human activity, including sex and vocation. Terminally ill patients may evoke reactions of unwarranted pessimism, thwarting the physician's ability to help the patient maximize hope for the quality of whatever time may remain. Patients and their family members often look to their physician for guidance.

Physicians, Important Persons, and Relatives

Treating other physicians, important persons, and personal relatives poses significant risks that must be actively addressed within the physician-patient relationship. Patients who are physicians are frequently expected to assume greater responsibility for their care and, if there is evidence of poor compliance, to "know better." Relinquishing control and acknowledging dependency run counter to the professional development of most physicians, who are accustomed to caring for others and may fear becoming a burden. Furthermore, they may refrain from asking pertinent questions to avoid further embarrassment and humiliation.[59(p4)]

Patients who are important persons or personal relatives pose similar challenges. With these patients and with other physicians, the treating physician may feel insecure and under increased pressure to perform flawlessly. Psychiatrists risk losing their usual assessment benchmarks when making exceptions to standard practice habits in recognition of a patient's special status. Difficult transferential issues for the physician include managing self-esteem, overidentification with the patient, ethical boundaries, and the potential dilemmas arising from ruptured treatment. Professional identification, awe of celebrity, and personal attachment exert tremendous pressures that can tax even the most seasoned psychiatrist in maintaining a healthy relationship with the patient. The psychiatrist may consult with uninvolved peers and, especially in the case of patients who are relatives, arrange for timely referrals to ensure appropriate treatment.[61]

Conclusion

The physician-patient relationship is essential to the healing process and is the foundation on which an effective treatment plan may be negotiated, integrating the best of what medical technology and human caring can provide. The centrality of this relationship is particularly true for psychiatric physicians and their patients. In the psychiatrist-patient relationship, empathy, compassion, and hope frequently serve as major means of alleviating pain and enhancing active participation in all treatment interventions: biological, psychological, and social.

The development of the physician-patient relationship depends on skilled assessment, the development of rapport through empathy, a strong therapeutic alliance, and the effective understanding of transference, countertransference, and defense mechanisms. Current research findings support the purposeful use of common therapy factors, of which the therapeutic alliance is the most powerful, to enhance clinical outcome.

The development of the physician-patient relationship is influenced by numerous factors, including the phase of treatment, the treatment setting, transitions between inpatient and outpatient care, managed care, and changes in the physician's health. The astute physician is attuned to the needs and characteristics of specific populations of patients, adopting the therapeutic approach that most effectively bridges the gap between physician and patient and leads to a healing relationship.

References

1. House JS, Landis KR, Umberson D: Social relationships and health. Science 1988; 241:540–545.
2. Hofer MA: Relationships as regulators: A psychobiologic perspective on bereavement. Psychosom Med 1984; 46:183–197.
3. Ursano RJ, Fullerton CS: Psychotherapy: Medical intervention and the concept of normality. In Offer D, Sabshin M (eds): The Diversity of Normal Behavior: Further Contributions to Normatology. New York: Basic Books, 1991:39–59.
4. Zetzel ER: Current concepts of transference. Int J Psychoanal 1956; 37:369–376.
5. Greenson R: The working alliance and the transference neurosis. Psychoanal Q 1965; 34:155–181.
6. Frank JD: Therapeutic factors in psychotherapy. Am J Psychother 1971; 25:350–361.
7. Sullivan HS: The Psychiatric Interview. New York: WW Norton, 1954.
8. Lidz T: The Person, revised edition. New York: Basic Books, 1983:xviii.

9. Peabody FW: The care of the patient. JAMA 1927; 88:877–882.
10. Meissner W: The concept of the therapeutic alliance. J Am Psychoanal Assoc 1992; 40:1059–1087.
11. Horvath AO, Greenberg LS: Development and validation of the Working Alliance Inventory. J Counsel Psychol 1989; 58:614–621.
12. Smith TC, Thompson TL: The inherent, powerful therapeutic value of a good physician-patient relationship. Psychosomatics 1993; 34: 166–170.
13. Marziali E, Alexander L: The power of the therapeutic relationship. Am J Orthopsychiatry 1991; 61:383–391.
14. Rawn M: The working alliance: Current concepts and controversies. Psychoanal Rev 1991; 78:379–389.
15. Friedman L: The therapeutic alliance. Int J Psychoanal 1969; 50:139–153.
16. Ursano RJ, Silberman EK: Individual psychotherapies. In Talbott JA, Hales RE, Yudofsky SC (eds): The American Psychiatric Press Textbook of Psychiatry. Washington, DC: American Psychiatric Press, 1988:876–884.
17. Freud S: The dynamics of transference. In Strachey J (trans-ed): The Standard Edition of the Complete Psychological Works of Sigmund Freud, Volume 12. London: Hogarth Press, 1958:97–108. Originally published in 1912.
18. Adler G: Transference, real relationship and alliance. Int J Psychoanal 1980; 61:547–558.
19. Sandler J, Dare C, Holder A: The Patient and the Analyst: The Basis of the Psychoanalytic Process. New York: International Universities Press, 1973.
20. Racker H: Transference and Countertransference. New York: International Universities Press, 1968.
21. Freud A: The Ego and the Mechanisms of Defense, revised edition. New York: International Universities Press, 1966.
22. Shapiro D: Neurotic Styles. New York: Basic Books, 1965.
23. Vaillant G: Ego Mechanisms of Defense. Washington, DC: American Psychiatric Press, 1992:237–248.
24. Lambert MJ, Bergin AE: Achievements and limitations of psychotherapy research. In Freedheim DK (ed): History of Psychotherapy: A Century of Change. Washington, DC: American Psychological Association, 1992:360–390.
25. Orlinsky DE, Grawe K, Parks BK: Process and outcome in psychotherapy—noch einmal. In Bergin AE, Garfield SL (eds): Handbook of Psychotherapy and Behavior Change, 4th ed. New York: John Wiley & Sons, 1994.
26. Rogers CR: The necessary and sufficient conditions of therapeutic personality change. J Consult Clin Psychol 1957; 21:95–103.
27. Gaston L: The concept of the alliance and its role in psychotherapy: Theoretical and empirical considerations. Psychotherapy 1990; 27: 143–153.
28. Horvath A, Luborsky L: The role of the therapeutic alliance in psychotherapy. J Consult Clin Psychol 1993; 61:561–573.
29. Strube MJ, Hartman DP: Meta-analysis: Techniques, applications, and function. J Consult Clin Psychol 1983;51:14–27.
30. Smith ML, Glass GV, Miller TI: The Benefits of Psychotherapy. Baltimore: The Johns Hopkins University Press, 1980.
31. Lambert MJ, Bergin AE: The effectiveness of psychotherapy. In Bergin AE, Garfield SL (eds): Handbook of Psychotherapy and Behavior Change, 4th ed. New York: John Wiley & Sons, 1994.
32. Docherty JP: The therapeutic alliance and treatment outcome. In Frances AJ, Hales RE (eds): American Psychiatric Association Annual Review, Volume 4. Washington, DC: American Psychiatric Press, 1985:529.
33. Karasu TB: Specificity versus nonspecificity. Am J Psychiatry 1986; 143:687–695.
34. Norcross JC, Goldfried MR (eds): Handbook of Psychotherapy Integration. New York: Basic Books, 1992.
35. Butler SF, Strupp HH: Specific and nonspecific factors in psychotherapy: A problematic paradigm for psychotherapy research. Psychotherapy 1986; 23:30–40.
36. Goldfried MR: Research issues in psychotherapy integration. J Psychother Integration 1991; 1:5–25.
37. Ursano RJ, Silberman EK: Psychoanalysis, psychoanalytic psychotherapy and supportive psychotherapy. In Hales RE, Yudofsky SC, Talbot JA (eds): American Psychiatric Press Textbook of Psychiatry. Washington, DC: American Psychiatric Press, 1994:1035–1060.
38. Wise MG, Rundell JR: Concise Guide to Consultation Psychiatry. Washington, DC: American Psychiatric Press, 1988:1.
39. Kessler DA: Communicating with patients about their medications. N Engl J Med 1991; 325:1650–1652.
40. Ursano RJ, Sonnenberg SM, Lazar SG: Concise Guide to Psychodynamic Psychotherapy. Washington, DC: American Psychiatric Press, 1991:5.
41. Goodman M, Brown J, Dietz P: Managing Managed Care: A Mental Health Practitioner's Survival Guide. Washington, DC: American Psychiatric Press, 1992:5.
42. Emanuel EJ, Brett AS: Managed competition and the patient-physician relationship. N Engl J Med 1993; 329:879–882.
43. Siegler M: Falling off the pedestal: What is happening to the traditional doctor-patient relationship? Mayo Clin Proc 1993; 68:461–467.
44. Engel GL: The clinical application of the biopsychosocial model. Am J Psychiatry 1980; 137:535–544.
45. Lasky R: Catastrophic illness in the analyst and the analyst's emotional reactions to it. Int J Psychoanal 1990; 71:455–473.
46. Simon JC: A patient-therapist's reaction to her therapist's serious illness. Am J Psychother 1990; 44:590–597.
47. Kinzie JD: Lessons from cross-cultural psychotherapy. Am J Psychother 1978; 32:511–520.
48. Cheng LY, Lo HT: On the advantages of cross-cultural psychotherapy: The minority therapist/mainstream patient dyad. Psychiatry 1991; 54:386–396.
49. Kluckhohn C, Murray HA: Personality formation: The determinants. In Kluckhohn C, Murray HA, Schneider DM (eds): Personality in Nature, Society and Culture. New York: Knopf, 1953:201–224.
50. Gabbard GO: Psychodynamic Psychiatry in Clinical Practice. Washington, DC: American Psychiatric Press, 1990:80–85.
51. Comas-Diaz L, Jacobsen FM: Ethnocultural transference and countertransference in the therapeutic dyad. Am J Orthopsychiatry 1991; 61:392–402.
52. Kleinman A: Rethinking psychiatry: From cultural category to personal experience. New York: Free Press, 1991:178–179.
53. Lewis M: General psychiatric assessment of children and adolescents. In Michels R (ed): Psychiatry, Volume 2, Chapter 20. Philadelphia: JB Lippincott; 1991:1–4.
54. Erikson EH: Childhood and Society. New York: WW Norton, 1950.
55. Katz P: The first few minutes: The engagement of the difficult adolescent. Adolesc Psychiatry 1990; 17:69–81.
56. Colson DB, Cornsweet C, Murphy T, et al: Perceived treatment difficulty and therapeutic alliance on an adolescent psychiatric hospital unit. Am J Orthopsychiatry 1991; 61:221–229.
57. Fleck S: The family and psychiatry. In Kaplan HI, Sadock BJ (eds): Comprehensive Textbook of Psychiatry, Volume IV. Baltimore: Williams & Wilkins, 1985:273–294.
58. Whitaker CA, Bumberry WM: Dancing with the Family: A Symbolic-Experiential Approach. New York: Brunner/Mazel, 1988:57–68.
59. Kaplan HI, Sadock BJ: Synopsis of Psychiatry, 6th ed. Baltimore: Williams & Wilkins, 1991.
60. McKusick L: The impact of AIDS on practitioner and client. Notes for the therapeutic relationship. Am Psychol 1988; 43:935–940.
61. Bridges N: Clinical dilemmas: Therapists treating therapists. Am J Orthopsychiatry 1993; 63:34–44.

CHAPTER

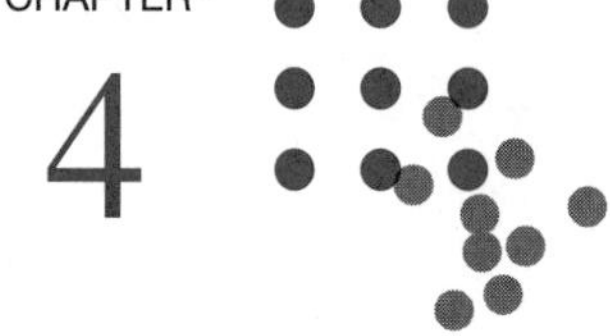

4 Professional Ethics and Boundaries of the Clinical Relationship

Richard S. Epstein

In the past several decades, advances in psychiatry have made it possible to treat mental disorders that were previously not amenable to successful intervention. There has been a dark side to this progress, however, because futuristic anticipation of subduing disease and forcing nature to surrender its secrets has led many practitioners to outrun their headlights. Like technical sorcerers of science fiction confusing promise with reality, we are in danger of being lulled into an intellectual arrogance that can cause us to forget what it means to be professionals. One manifestation of this process has been the defensive reliance by clinicians on reductionistic explanations for complex and multidetermined disorders, combined with a neglect of the important role of trust and empathy as curative factors in treating mental disorders.

A bewildering potpourri of treatment options and methods for financing health care presents psychiatrists with other sources of confusion. Patients' health and safety often depend on our ability to decide whether they require outpatient or inpatient treatment, brief psychotherapy, or long-term care. The psychiatrist's dilemma is similarly compounded by conflicts between the cost-determined restrictions of managed care and the sacred promise to advocate primarily for patients' welfare.

Building a cooperative and trusting relationship with patients has always been an essential factor enabling clinicians to foster the healing process, especially during ancient times, when few specific remedies were available. In most instances, modern technology augments but cannot substitute for a trusting physician-patient relationship. Patients seeking medical care must suspend ordinary social distance and critical judgment if they are to allow physicians to enter their physical and psychological space. Although neither the law nor medical ethics relieve patients from taking an active responsibility for treatment outcome,[1] society places a greater burden on the healer—a mandate to act with the special care and vigilance expected of a fiduciary[2, 3] or of a common carrier,[4(pp59–61)] as a precondition for granting licenses to practice.

As I review in this chapter, the ability to sustain a professional attitude and to practice within a set of coherent boundaries forms the foundation of proper psychiatric treatment, regardless of theoretical orientation or treatment modality. An understanding of psychiatric ethics plays a vital role in the psychiatrist's ability to keep proper boundaries, because these values provide a stable beacon in the cognitively perplexing fog that so often pervades the treatment situation.

Ethical Behavior and Its Relationship to the Professional Attitude

The term *professional* derives from medieval times, when scholastics were expected to "profess" their belief in a doctrine.[5(p17)] In modern times, a professional is assumed to be a learned person who has acquired special knowledge of a subject that is of vital importance for the welfare of the community. Having expertise is not enough, however. A professional is also obliged to adhere to certain societal responsibilities that are founded on a code of ethical behavior and an attitude of service to those in need. A professional commitment to ethical behavior and service must take precedence over monetary compensation.[5(p16)] All physicians, including psychiatrists, are bound by such a covenant—a sacred vow to place the patient's well-being before other considerations.[6] In Western medical tradition, this obligation derives from the teachings of Hippocrates in the fifth century BC. The oath of Hippocrates is the pledge predominantly recited at the graduation exercises at American medical schools,[7] and it contains three of the six core principles of modern medical ethics: *beneficence, nonmalfeasance,* and *confidentiality:*

> I will follow that system of regimen which according to my ability and judgement, I consider for the benefit of my patients, and abstain from whatever is deleterious and mischievous . . . . With purity and holiness I will pass my life and practice my Art . . . . Into whatever houses I enter,

Table 4–1 Six Basic Principles of Medical Ethics

Principle	Description
Beneficence	Applying one's abilities solely for the patient's well-being
Nonmalfeasance	Avoiding harm to a patient
Autonomy	Respect for a patient's independence
Justice	Avoiding prejudicial bias based on idiosyncrasies of the patient's background, behavior, or station in life
Confidentiality	Respect for the patient's privacy
Veracity	Truthfulness with oneself and one's patients

Adapted from Epstein RS: Keeping Boundaries. Maintaining Safety and Integrity in the Psychotherapeutic Process. Washington, DC: American Psychiatric Press, 1994:20.

> I will go into them for the benefit of the sick, and will abstain from every voluntary act of mischief and corruption; and, further, from the seduction of females or males, of freemen and slaves. Whatever, in connection with my professional practice or not, in connection with it, I see or hear, in the life of men, which ought not to be spoken of abroad, I will not divulge, as reckoning that all such should be kept secret.[8]

The other three general principles of medical ethics are *autonomy, justice,* and *veracity* (see Table 4–1 for a description and summary of all six ethical principles).[4(p20)] In 1973 the American Psychiatric Association adopted the American Medical Association's principles of medical ethics, publishing them along with special annotations applicable for psychiatric practice.[9] The American Psychiatric Association has produced six revisions of these annotations.[10] The seven sections of the American Medical Association principles are summarized in Table 4–2. Table 4–3 summarizes some of the more salient ethical annotations for psychiatrists.[10]

The Coherent Treatment Frame and the Role of Therapeutic Boundaries in Effective Psychiatric Treatment

The *frame* of a social interaction was defined by Goffman[11] as consisting of the spoken and unspoken expectations defining meaning and involvement in a given situation. For example, patients seek out a psychiatrist on the basis of a tacit assumption that the psychiatrist is a reliable and experienced clinician who has the ability to assist them in finding relief for distress. However, many patients tend to frame their treatment in pathological ways. For example, some attempt to pressure the psychiatrist into the role of a magical wizard who confers unconditional love and pleasure. Whatever method the patient employs to frame the relationship, any abrupt disappointment or rupture of these unspoken expectations often results in intense and disruptive feelings of mortification and betrayal. A sudden breach of a social frame can lead to the dissolution of one's sense of meaning and connection and is often accompanied by intense feelings of shame. By examining verbal and behavioral responses after violations of the treatment frame, Langs[12] was able to document that patients usually perceive the offending therapist as an unreliable and mentally unstable person—someone seeking perverse pleasure at another person's expense.

The psychiatrist's task is to provide a coherent therapeutic frame within which to contain the patient's illness. The psychiatrist's frame makes it secure to proceed with the specific therapeutic modality, just as the surgical suite provides a safe environment for operative techniques.

Table 4–2 Summary of the Principles of Ethics of the American Medical Association

Section	Statement of Principle
Preamble	The medical profession's ethical standards are designed primarily for the well-being of patients. As professionals, physicians are required to acknowledge a responsibility to patients, to society, to self, and to their colleagues.
Section I	Dedication to competent, compassionate care. Respect for human dignity.
Section II	Obligation to deal honestly with patients and colleagues and to expose physicians who are incompetent or fraudulent.
Section III	Respect for the law. Obligation to seek changes in laws harmful to patients' care.
Section IV	Respect for the rights of patients and colleagues. Within legal constraints, preservation of confidentiality.
Section V	Commitment to continued education, sharing of relevant knowledge, and obtaining necessary consultation.
Section VI	Except in emergency, freedom to decide whom to treat, with whom to associate, and the setting in which one serves.
Section VII	Acknowledge the responsibility to contribute to improving the community.

From American Psychiatric Association: The Principles of Medical Ethics. With Annotations Especially Applicable to Psychiatry. Washington, DC: American Psychiatric Association, 1993.

Table 4–3 Summary of Selected Ethical Principles for Psychiatrists

Principle	Annotations
Competent care	The psychiatrist must scrutinize the effect of his or her conduct on the boundaries of the treatment relationship.
Honest dealing	Sex with a current or former patient is unethical. Information given by patients should not be exploited. Contractual arrangements should be explicit. Fee splitting is unethical.
Confidentiality, respecting colleagues	Restraint in release of information to third parties. Adequate disguise of case presentations. Disclosure of lack of confidentiality in nontreatment situations. Sex with students or supervisees may be unethical.

From American Psychiatric Association: The Principles of Medical Ethics. With Annotations Especially Applicable to Psychiatry. Washington, DC: American Psychiatric Association, 1993.

Table 4–4 Factors Common to All Successful Psychotherapy

Principle	Method Applied
Inspiring trust	The therapist establishes an emotionally arousing, trusting, and confidential relationship.
Coherent structure	A structured setting is formed that is associated with the healing process.
Rationale explained	A reasoned treatment method is offered that plausibly explains the patient's problems.
Cooperative engagement	Therapist and patient actively work together in the program. Both believe that it will work.

From Frank JD, Frank JB: Persuasion and Healing. A Comparative Study of Psychotherapy, 3rd ed. Baltimore: The Johns Hopkins University Press, 1991. Reprinted by permission of Johns Hopkins University Press.

The treatment frame enables the patient to maintain a feeling of trust and connectedness while learning to deal with the unrealistic nature of his or her expectations. The frame comprises various boundary factors, including acting in a reliable way, showing respect for the patient's autonomy by explaining the potential risks and benefits of the treatment method, maintaining confidentiality, avoiding exploitation of the patient's sexual feelings, and resisting the patient's manipulative efforts by explaining the maladaptive nature of such behavior.[4, 13]

Frank and Frank[2] conducted an extensive review of the literature concerning psychotherapy outcome. They determined that four basic factors were common to all successful psychotherapies (Table 4–4) and that treatment efficacy relied on the ability of the therapist to form a structured, mutually trusting, confidential, and emotionally arousing relationship. Their findings sustain the argument that maintaining a coherent treatment frame is an essential part of all psychiatric treatment, regardless of the therapeutic paradigm being employed. These issues are important whether the patient is being treated solely with psychotropic medication management, behavior therapy, or psychoanalysis.

Boundary Violations

Psychiatric treatment cannot be conducted without psychiatrist and patient entering into each other's space, just as it is impossible to perform a bloodless laparotomy. Gutheil and Gabbard[14] termed such incursions that occur during the therapeutic process *boundary crossings.* They defined boundary *violations* as boundary crossings that cause injury to the patient. However, it is not always easy to be sure of the consequences of such a crossing, because harmful effects may be delayed or concealed. Many patients are unable to articulate their sense of injury, because the psychiatrist's aberrant behavior may appear so similar to exploitation they have experienced in previous pathological relationships. For example, patients who were sexually abused in childhood are more likely to acquiesce to an amorous advance by a psychiatrist and to avoid complaining about feeling used, because they fear the threat of the psychiatrist's rejection and retaliation. Certain nonsexual boundary crossings, such as conflicts of interest, might seem harmless on the surface but can interfere with patients' ability to feel safe in their psychiatrist's care and diminish their chances for optimal recovery. In this context, a boundary violation can be defined as any infringement that interferes with the primary goal of providing care or causes harm to the patient, the therapist, or the therapy itself.[4(p2)]

Before the 1970s, open discussion of the topic of sexual involvement between psychiatrists and patients was virtually taboo and considered "too hot to handle" as a subject for publication in scientific journals.[15] Professional societies demonstrated an inconsistent and confused attitude of "amused tolerance"[16(p161)] toward mental health practitioners who engaged in sexual behavior with their patients.

In the past 20 years, the public has become increasingly interested in the subject of psychiatric boundary violations, particularly those involving sexual exploitation. State licensing boards, professional ethics committees, and civil juries are much more likely than ever before to mete out strong sanctions against violators. These attitudinal changes have taken place in spite of the fact that Hollywood movies continue to romanticize the idea of psychiatrist-patient sexuality and almost always seem oblivious to the horrendous feelings of shame, betrayal, and devastation that patients experience when these things happen to them in real life.

The public's intolerance of sexual involvement between psychiatrists and patients has resulted in part from the increasing empowerment of the victims of incest, rape, and spousal abuse and a better understanding of the psychological sequelae of mental trauma, such as posttraumatic stress disorder. In addition, psychiatric patients have become more willing to expose unethical or exploitative behavior on the part of clinicians, particularly when it involves sexual activity. This trend has been augmented by the fact that courts and professional licensing bodies are now more inclined to render sanctions for injuries that are solely psychological in nature.

Quantitative estimates of the frequency of sexual boundary violations among mental health professionals derive from survey studies conducted during the past 20 years.[16–22] A review of these studies shows that from 5.5% to 13.7% of male mental health clinicians admitted to engaging in sexual activity with patients. Epstein[4(pp207–208)] calculated a crude weighted average from Schoener's[22] comprehensive review of survey studies reporting frequency of sexual violations by clinicians' gender. From 10 studies involving a total of 5816 respondents (excluding a large survey of nurses), an average of 7.4% of male and 2.3% of female clinicians admitted to engaging in sexual behavior with patients. These data suggest that male clinicians are about three times more likely to admit they have become sexually involved with patients. Although subsequent studies suggested that sexual exploitation by mental health practitioners might be occurring less frequently, increasing reports in the media of severe sanctions taken against offending therapists have probably diminished the value of self-report questionnaires.

Studies of nonsexual violations suggested that many mental health clinicians still have serious problems maintaining professional boundaries with patients.[21, 23] Epstein and colleagues[23] queried 532 psychiatrists about their behavior with patients within a prior 2-year period. They found that 19% of respondents reported engaging in a personal relationship with patients after treatment was terminated, 17% told patients personal details of their life to impress the patients, and 17% joined in activities with patients to deceive a third party such as an insurance company (Table 4–5). Simon[24] emphasized that when clinicians engage in nonsexual infringements of the treatment relationship, it is often a prelude to subsequent sexual behavior. Sexual involvement with patients often starts with excessive personal disclosure, accepting and giving gifts, requesting favors, and meeting patients outside the office setting. Like a seduction, the behavior escalates over time until it culminates in sexual contact.[24]

Regardless of the specific type of infringement involved, there are common elements to all boundary violations. Peterson[25] argued that such activity emanated from a disturbed and disconnected relationship. She suggested four basic behavioral themes in this regard: efforts on the part of the clinician to reverse roles with the patient, to intimidate the patient to maintain secrecy, to place the patient in a double bind, and to indulge professional privilege.[25] Indulgence of privilege is often accompanied by a sense of entitlement on the clinician's part, such that she or he regards the patient as a wholly owned subsidiary.

Epstein[4(pp89–110)] outlined the progression of boundary violations as they originate from dysregulation in the clinician's personal ego boundaries. Circumstances impairing the clinician's ability to cope with patients and their problems may include deficient knowledge, general stress, mental disorder, or a treatment-induced regression. These factors may lead the clinician to employ maladaptive intrapsychic or behavioral coping mechanisms that are manifest in the form of therapeutic boundary violations. Other general factors common to all boundary violations include a slippage of the original purpose of the treatment,[4(pp97–98)] pseudoeclecticism,[26] a narcissistic sense of specialness,[4(pp107–110), 27] and efforts to deprofessionalize the relationship by fostering an atmosphere of "pseudoequality" between clinician and patient.[25]

The double-binding messages that exploitative clinicians employ often represent a way for them to project their own disavowed feelings of shame and inadequacy onto vulnerable patients. For example, a therapist may deceive a patient suffering from low self-esteem and sexual dysfunction by encouraging a sexual relationship between them. The therapist may rationalize:

> You have told me that you feel unattractive and inadequate. Because therapy is supposed to help you with your problems, I will help show you how attractive and effective you are by having sex with you.

Psychotherapy and erotic behavior can both be construed as subcategories of the superordinate class of "activities that help people feel better."[4(p102)] In the preceding example, the exploitative therapist blurs the logical boundaries between the two subcategories and fails to inform the patient that this sexual behavior is likely to be harmful to the patient. Blurring of logical categories is an essential aspect of double-binding messages. Patients who are subjected to such reasoning are often in a dependent and cognitively regressed state and are unable to understand the logical absurdity of the double bind. They fear that if they refuse to comply with the therapist's suggestions, they will be rejected for failing to cooperate with the goals of therapy.

It is important to place the burgeoning literature on boundary violations in its social context. An aroused public has been exposed to recurring reports of psychiatrists and other mental health professionals who have been disciplined or sued for behavior such as sexual involvement with patients and spouses of patients, using information learned in patients' psychotherapy sessions to gain inside data on financial investments, and accepting large bequests from elderly patients. Each new scandal serves to erode society's trust in the integrity of psychiatry as a profession and makes it more difficult for the mentally ill to obtain needed treatment. Compounding this problem is the fact that many of these well-publicized reports of boundary violations involved highly trained psychiatrists who were leaders in their field and who served as important role models for students in professional training.

As has occurred many times before in history, societal changes tend to overshoot the mark, leading some observers to caution against a hysterical witch-hunt against suspected offenders. Slovenko[28] cautioned that the climate has become ripe for an increasing number of false accusations to be made against innocent clinicians. Gutheil[29] has documented such cases and provided guidelines for proper forensic psychiatric evaluation after allegations of sexual misconduct.

Table 4–5 Summary of Survey Results of Nonsexual Boundary Violations Among 532 Psychiatrists

Behavior	Percentage
Using touch (exclusive of handshake)	45
Treating relatives or friends	32
Personal relationships after termination	19
Personal disclosure	17
Colluding with patient against third party	17
Influencing patient for political causes	10
Using patient's communication for financial gain	7

From Epstein RS, Simon RI, Kay GG: Assessing boundary violations in psychotherapy: Survey results with the Exploitation Index. Bull Menninger Clin 1992; 56:150–166.

Components of the Coherent Psychiatric Frame

The purpose of the therapeutic frame is to protect the patient's safety and to promote recovery. It is the therapist's responsibility to structure the frame through word and deed. Langs[12] stressed that a healthy and secure therapeutic environment is predicated on reducing variability and uncertainty in the treatment setting as much as possible. Table 4–6 summarizes the major boundary factors of the coherent treatment frame. Careful attention to these boundary issues can help treating psychiatrists to communicate defining messages that strengthen the differentiation of role and identity between patient and practitioner.

There is an enormous diversity of opinion regarding the diagnosis and treatment of psychiatric disorders. This makes it difficult to devise a set of specific guidelines that are

Table 4–6 Major Boundary Issues Contributing to the Formation of a Coherent Treatment Frame

Boundary Issue	Function and Purpose	Implicit Message to Patient
Stability	Consistency as to time, place, location, parties involved, and treatment method	"The doctor is reliable. This treatment can contain my irrationality."
Avoiding dual relationships	Utmost fidelity to the primary purpose of helping the patient	"The doctor focuses her or his attention on my problem and is not sidetracked."
Neutrality and promoting autonomy of the patient	Avoiding abuse of power and promoting the patient's independence	"The doctor values my ideas and encourages me to exercise choices."
Noncollusive compensation	Scrupulous and forthright terms of remuneration for the clinician	"Aside from the payment, I don't have to gratify the doctor."
Confidentiality	To protect the patient's privilege of keeping his or her communications secret	"My thoughts and feelings belong to me, not to the doctor."
Anonymity	Avoids seductiveness and role reversal	"This is a place to bring *my* issues, not a forum for the doctor's personal problems."
Abstinence	Encourages verbalization rather than action in dealing with feelings and conflicts	"There is a big difference between wishes and reality."
Preserving the clinician's safety and self-respect	Discourages the patient's destructive behavior, sets a good role model for establishing healthy self-esteem	"It is possible to have a close relationship without someone getting hurt."

appropriate for psychiatrists adhering to a wide spectrum of theoretical orientations. Dyer[5(pp45–57)] emphasized how problematic it is to define a comprehensive ethical system, whether it is based on a set of specific rules (deontological ethics), on a list of values and goals (teleological ethics), or on consideration of the emotional and practical consequences of a given course of action (consequentialist ethics). A parallel dilemma exists when it comes to defining psychiatric boundaries. For this reason, guidelines for psychiatrists should enhance patients' safety, foster adherence to established clinical principles, and help to avoid specific consequences that are detrimental to either patient or practitioner. From a safety standpoint, each boundary issue can be examined from the point of view of clearly *indicated* procedures, *relatively risky* procedures, and *contraindicated* procedures.[4(pp113–117)] In the ensuing discussion of components of the psychiatric frame, lists of these various types of procedures are adapted from my earlier work on boundaries.[4(pp119–236)]

Riskier procedures that fall into the gray zone are not necessarily unethical or unsound. However, psychiatrists who engage in such activity should be aware of the circumstances under which they increase or reduce the chance for injury to either the patient or themselves. For example, under most conditions, it is probably unwise to attempt psychiatric treatment of one's next-door neighbor. Nevertheless, practitioners living in remote areas or working in confined ethnic communities might, as a matter of practicality, be forced to treat a patient for whom no reasonable alternative exists. The hazard of no treatment may outweigh other factors in this situation. However, the fact that psychiatrists sometimes must treat patients under risky circumstances does not mean they should forget about the highest treatment standards, just as the exigencies of battlefield surgery do not obviate the need to remember aseptic technique.

Psychiatrists should safeguard against any semblance of inappropriate behavior, even if the activity can be justified as harmless. For example, seeking social activities with patients outside the treatment setting can be interpreted by patients or their family members as seductive. Gutheil and Gabbard[14] have emphasized that the very appearance of undue familiarity with a patient may in and of itself hamper successful defense against false allegations of professional wrongdoing.

Stability

A stable and consistent treatment setting is analogous to the "holding environment" provided by parents in early childhood.[30] Patients with psychiatric illnesses find it difficult to entrust their lives to a psychiatrist whom they perceive to be unreliable. Indicated measures regarding stability include formulating an agreement with the patient for a treatment regimen to take place according to a specific method and schedule, encouraging truthful disclosure and cooperation, establishing a commitment to beginning and ending sessions on time, discouraging interruptions during treatment sessions, offering advance notice about when the psychiatrist will be absent, providing for coverage by another practitioner when the psychiatrist is off duty, maintaining coherent therapeutic demeanor, and maintaining relative consistency as to who participates in the treatment situation.

It is generally unwise for a psychiatrist to disparage a patient's complaints about issues like the psychiatrist's tardiness in starting sessions or to become defensive when explaining the meaning of the patient's distress about such complaints. Many psychiatrists experience patients' demands for consistency as a form of control and imprisonment. Out of anger, they may react to these patients as if their wishes for reliability and concern were infantile and irrational:

> Your complaints about my lateness are a reflection of your need to control me.

The psychiatrist's tardiness might in fact be creating tremendous anxiety because it reminds the patients of parents who never took their feelings into account.

Avoiding Dual Relationships

Psychiatrists should avoid treatment situations that place them in a conflict between therapeutic responsibility to patients and third parties. Examples of dual relationships in psychiatric practice include clinicians treating their own relatives and friends, the same therapist employing concurrent family and individual therapy paradigms with a patient, and clinicians testifying as forensic witnesses for current psychotherapy patients. Although it is common practice,[23] accepting psychotherapy patients referred by one's current or former patients embraces certain risks that must be considered.[32(pp60–62)] For example, a current patient might refer an attractive friend for therapy as a way of either seducing the therapist or sabotaging the treatment.[31(pp60–62)]

Role conflicts are quite widespread[32] and interfere with the practitioner's single-mindedness of purpose as a healer. Chodoff[33(pp457–459)] placed special emphasis on this issue by arguing that advocating for the needs of the mentally ill was one of psychiatry's primary societal responsibilities. By eroding public trust, dual relationships interfere with the ability of psychiatrists to carry out their vital functions in the community.

The burgeoning expansion of prepaid care in the United States in the past two decades has provoked concern about a new source of role conflict for psychiatrists. Managed care has been espoused as an important modality for reducing unnecessary treatment by encouraging preventive care and promoting cost-consciousness among physicians.[34] Stephen Appelbaum[35] argued that psychotherapists practicing under the old fee-for-service model were more inclined to provide unnecessarily prolonged treatment than those working under an organizational system that prevented direct monetary involvement between patient and practitioner.

On the other hand, increasing coverage of the population of the United States under a system of managed care has generated serious concerns regarding potential conflicts of interest.[36(pp113–126)] This disquietude is particularly noticeable in the field of psychiatry. Many managed care organizations have severely restricted the number of psychiatrists within a given community allowed to serve on their treatment panels. Patients' access to their regular treating practitioner have been further limited, even when the practitioner is allowed to enroll on the panel. For example, under the rules of some managed care organizations, a psychiatrist might be prevented from maintaining continuity of care for outpatients needing hospitalization. During their hospital stay, such patients must be attended by a preselected group of psychiatrists who conduct all hospital treatment for the plan.

Despite the contention that restricted managed care panels are necessary for lowering costs, it is important that both patients and clinicians be informed about the hazard such a system of care entails. Because participation on a panel is often contingent on cost-efficiency profiles, psychiatrists who derive a significant portion of their income from a given managed care organization are discouraged from advocating for patients needing more expensive care. With news reports of physicians claiming they were terminated from managed care contracts because they protested treatment denials, fear of retaliation for advocacy for patients has mounted.[37] Retired judge Marvin Atlas[38] has suggested that psychiatrists who fail to warn patients about the risks of their role conflicts would be exposing themselves to civil damages in the event of an adverse outcome. Although the extent of the legal duty to disclose risk factors under managed care is unresolved, Paul Appelbaum[39] proposed that mental health clinicians inform beginning patients that payment for treatment under managed care might be stopped before the patient feels ready to terminate.

Limitations on who may serve on a managed care panel and what functions the clinician may perform are other factors that have strong potential for creating disruption in the continuity of care. For example, Westermeyer[40] described seven case histories in which psychiatric patients treated under managed care committed suicide or suffered serious clinical deterioration. Clinically uninformed managed care practices appeared to serve as critical aggravating factors for each of these patients. In the cases of two individuals who committed suicide, the employer had switched contracts to different managed care companies and the patients were forced to transfer to new clinicians. These disruptions appeared to play an important role in the patients' suicides.

Although more research is required to evaluate the full ramifications of managed care for psychiatric populations, studies suggest that some groups face adverse outcomes under this system. For example, Rogers and colleagues[41] found that, on average, patients with depression who were treated by psychiatrists under prepaid treatment plans acquired new limitations in their physical or day-to-day functioning during a 2-year period, whereas those treated in the traditional fee-for-service setting did not.

Autonomy and Neutrality

Early in this century, Sigmund Freud recommended that psychoanalysts adhere to a position of *neutrality* with their patients by refraining from the temptation to take sides in the patients' internal conflicts or life problems.[42, 43] This advice has relevance for all psychiatric treatment, insofar as it espouses the idea that practitioners should maintain profound respect for their patients' autonomy and individuality. This is a fundamental therapeutic stance that fosters independence, growth, and self-esteem. It reinforces the idea that the clinician believes the patient to be the owner of his or her body, life, and problems. The patient receives the following message:

> The doctor tries to help by assisting me to learn about myself, not by trying to take control of me.

Indicated ways to encourage autonomy include encouraging informed consent by outlining the potential benefits, risks, and alternatives for a proposed treatment approach; explaining the rationale for the treatment; and fostering the patient's participation in the treatment process. Paradoxically, acutely suicidal patients often require the psychiatrist to assume temporary responsibility for their safety. In most instances this serves to augment the patient's sense of autonomy through a coherent modeling process,[44] because true independence is impossible without self-governance.

Clinical actions that may interfere with the patient's autonomy include giving advice regarding nonurgent major life decisions, attempting to exert undue influence on issues unrelated to the patient's health, being reluctant to allow patients to terminate treatment, seeking gratification by exerting power over patients, and using power over patients as a form of retaliation.

Coherent and Noncollusive Compensation

Although there are tremendous rewards to be obtained from working in an interesting and creative profession, it is better to derive them from one's collective professional endeavors than from one case. With a specific patient, monetary compensation is the only gratification psychiatrists should realistically expect.[27] When compensation is direct, there should be a set fee, and the patient should be responsible for the time. When compensation is indirect or salaried, the psychiatrist must avoid colluding either with the patient against the party paying for the treatment or with the third party against the patient (see the previous section on avoiding dual relationships). Whatever method is being used to pay for mental health treatment, a coherent and noncollusive arrangement imparts the message to the patient:

> The doctor has needs of her or his own, but they are limited to a salary or fee. Aside from financial obligations, I don't have to please, gratify, or nurture my doctor.

The practice of charging for missed appointments under the traditional fee-for-service paradigm is often misunderstood by patients, because their experience with physicians in other branches of medicine has usually been that they were charged on a fee-for-procedure, rather than fee-for-time, basis. Charging for missed appointments is justifiable from an ethical standpoint as long as the rationale is clearly explained to the patient at the beginning of treatment and the patient agrees to it. In addition, no attempt should be made to hide the fact of billing for missed appointments from third-party payers. Some states have an absolute prohibition against billing for missed appointments under Medicaid.[4(p169)] Within certain guidelines, and as of the date of this writing, it is permissible to bill the patient (but not Medicare) for missed appointments under the Medicare program.[4(pp169–170)] Readers are cautioned that regulations regarding Medicaid and Medicare are subject to periodic legislative revisions and may vary according to jurisdiction.

Generally risky compensation arrangements include working for a treatment organization that one perceives to be financially exploitative, accepting small gifts from patients, bartering goods or services in return for treatment, referring patients for treatments or procedures in which one has a proprietary financial interest, and neglecting the patient's failure to adhere to the original agreement regarding payment of fees. Certain practices are absolutely contraindicated and likely to be destructive, including fraudulent billing, accepting expensive gifts, fee splitting, colluding with the patient or third party, and using financial insider information.

Confidentiality

It is essential that psychiatrists treat their patients' communications as privileged. This means that patients alone retain the right to reveal information about themselves. Psychiatrists should caution their patients about the potential limitations to confidentiality and be prepared to explore the consequences of these exceptions. For example, if a patient is raising his or her mental health as an issue in litigation, some or all communications to a psychiatrist could be legally discoverable. Coherent boundaries with regard to confidentiality send the message to the patient:

> My thoughts and feelings belong to me. The doctor does not treat them as if they belong to him or her.

Indicated means of preserving confidentiality include obtaining proper authorization from patients before releasing information, explaining the need for confidentiality with parents of children and adolescents, and involving all participants in family and group psychotherapy in agreements about confidentiality. Problematical activities that may endanger confidentiality include stray communications with concerned relatives of patients in individual psychotherapy, discussion of privileged information with the psychiatrist's own family members, releasing information about deceased patients, and failing to disguise case presentations properly.

Anonymity

Many psychiatrists associate the principle of relative anonymity with Freud's advice to psychoanalysts[42]:

> The doctor should be opaque to his patients and, like a mirror, should show them nothing but what is shown to him.

Freud argued that it was dangerous for psychoanalysts to expose their own mental problems or intimate life details in a spurious attempt to place themselves on an "equal footing" with patients.[42(pp117–118)] The merit of this recommendation extends beyond its origin in psychoanalytic technique to a fundamental boundary issue applicable to all forms of psychiatric treatment. It serves as a reminder to both patient and clinician of the professional purpose of the relationship. Avoiding unnecessary personal disclosure to patients protects both patient and practitioner from a reversal of roles—one of the critical themes recurring in boundary violations in general.[25] Many patients experience excessive self-disclosure by the psychiatrist as seductive, and it has frequently been observed to be a precursor to subsequent sexual involvement.[45(p403)] By maintaining a policy of relative anonymity, the patient receives the following message about the treatment:

> This a place where I can bring my issues. The doctor doesn't burden me with his or her problems.

Certain forms of self-disclosure are indicated in the course of work with psychiatric patients, including apprising patients of the clinician's qualifications and treatment methods as part of informed consent, discussing reality factors related to the psychiatrist's health status or intentions regarding retirement that would affect the patient's treatment decisions, and using "reality checks" to help patients contain disturbed and frightening fantasies.

Abstinence

Abstinence means that psychiatrists should discourage direct forms of pleasure such as touching or sexuality in the course of their interactions with patients. For patients, actual gratification is best confined to realistic goals for recovery and emotional growth. Psychiatrists should limit themselves to the pleasure of getting paid for a job well done and the opportunity to participate in an interesting and creative profession. Although steadfast application of this boundary can be quite frustrating for both psychiatrist and patient, it pays excellent dividends in the long run by encouraging autonomy and a more mature way of dealing with impulses. The rule of abstinence as a therapeutic boundary has a function analogous to that of the incest taboo as a social organizer. In all known human cultures, the incest taboo has survival value because during childhood development it serves to strengthen the sense of individuality and personal boundaries so necessary for growth, independence, and social responsibility.[46]

From a practical standpoint, psychiatrists can strengthen their patients' boundaries in this regard by resisting such behaviors as physical touching, accepting gifts, socialization outside treatment, and sexual involvement. The patient receives the following messages from a clinician who is able to adhere to this principle:

> The doctor is more interested in my health than her or his own gratification and doesn't try to take possession of me. I am learning that I can have wishes that needn't result in action.

There are occasions when psychiatrists are obligated to employ physical procedures such as taking blood pressures, checking for extrapyramidal symptoms, restraining dangerous patients, or administering electroconvulsive therapy. Indeed, clinical touching of patients is considered an integral part of the physician-patient relationship because of its important role in physical examination and therapeutic procedures. Even though psychiatrists are physicians, they are obligated to use much more restraint in this regard than is expected of colleagues in other branches of medicine. It is probably too invasive for the same physician on a protracted basis to intrude simultaneously into the patient's psychological and physical spaces.

Other risky forms of gratification include embracing or kissing patients, eating and drinking with patients, socializing with patients outside the therapy setting, and failing to determine the meaning of recurrent or obsessive sexual fantasies about a patient. Engaging in sexual behavior with current or former patients is contraindicated because it is almost invariably destructive, even though the damage may not be manifest immediately. Although the issue of sexual relationships with former patients continues to stir debate among clinicians,[47, 48] the fact remains that a large portion of our society, including legislators, judges, juries, and licensing boards, view such behavior as highly unprofessional and destructive. Gabbard and Pope[49] emphasized that clinician defendants have frequently raised the posttermination argument in malpractice cases but have never prevailed with this approach.

Self-respect and Self-protection

It is essential that psychiatrists protect themselves from being exploited by patients. This principle is necessary to protect clinicians and patients alike. Many patients seeking treatment have endured abusive relationships in which being victimized became the price for maintaining human connectedness. For such patients, efforts to exploit the psychiatrist may represent an action-question that inquires:

> Must one of us be injured in order for us to have a close relationship?

By setting a proper role model for self-respect and self-caretaking, the psychiatrist imparts the following message to the patient:

> Relationships need not be structured on the basis that one or both parties must be exploited. If I as the doctor allow you to hurt me, I am setting a poor role model.

Psychiatrists should attempt to discuss the meaning of any exploitative behavior on the patient's part as soon as possible. With unstable or impulsive patients who are prone to acting out, confrontation should be timed to maximize safety. For example, it would be more prudent to interpret the manipulative aspects of a patient's suicidal behavior after the patient is admitted to a hospital. If a patient makes a sudden physical overture such as attempting a sexually provocative embrace, it must be dealt with the same urgency as a physical assault. The psychiatrist should inform the patient that such behavior is inconsistent with coherent treatment.[4(pp228–231)] It is generally risky to allow repeated exceptions such as last-minute prolongation of sessions, repeated lateness in paying fees, repeated intrusions into the psychiatrist's personal space in the form of late night phone calls, or taking items from the office.

Certain psychiatrists find themselves avoiding confrontation with an exploitative patient out of fear of the latter's narcissistic rage. This is an indication of an escalating situation that may lead to further boundary violations by either the patient or the psychiatrist. A useful explanation of this behavior is provided in Gabbard's[51] description of a subgroup of clinicians who become sexually involved with patients as part of a self-defeating pattern of behavior he termed "masochistic surrender." These practitioners are unable to defend against being tormented by certain highly demanding patients. They succumb to the patient's importunings, sometimes while in a dissociated state, even though they may know that their behavior is wrong. Gabbard thought that the aberrant behavior of these clinicians is rooted in an impaired ability to cope with their own aggressive feelings, resulting in their feeling that it would be sadistic to set limits on the patient.

Summary

The ethical and boundary issues discussed in this chapter were designed to stimulate a better understanding of an extremely thorny topic rather than to provide an exhaustive compendium. Table 4–7 summarizes selected indicators of potential boundary violations, along with remedial responses clinicians might employ to deal with these situations.

The difficulties psychiatrists may encounter in keeping boundaries derive from many sources. In the past, professional training programs have not addressed this issue systematically. It behooves psychiatrists to determine whether they have suffered deficiencies in training or adverse role modeling during the course of their professional development and whether their own emotional problems significantly interfere with maintaining coherent professional boundaries. A burgeoning literature regarding the

Table 4–7 Indicators of Potential Boundary Violations with Suggested Remedial Responses

Indicator	Suggested Remedial Response for Clinician
Clinician is frequently tardy starting sessions.	Avoid criticizing the patient for complaining about lateness. Reexamine reasons for tardiness in light of the patient's need for a stable treatment frame.
Clinician changes the treatment paradigm in midstream, for example, switching from individual therapy with Mr. A to couples therapy with Mr. A and Mrs. A.	Avoid dual relationships that may interfere with primary loyalty to the first patient. If dual relationships cannot be avoided, explain risks to patients according to principle of informed consent.
Clinician frequently advises patients on matters not related to the treatment process.	Consider whether this is a general pattern of need for control in one's nonclinical relationships. If so, consider ways to help the patient to make her or his own decisions.
Clinician often relates to the patient as if he or she were a personal friend.	Listen for signs that the patient feels burdened. Acknowledge the pattern of role reversal and the importance of the clinician's fiduciary obligations to the patient.
Clinician accepts gifts from the patient.	Try to explore the patient's motive for the gift. Consider refusing the gift by explaining that it might interfere with the effectiveness of treatment. Be prepared to work with the patient's and one's own feelings of shame in this regard.
Clinician feels overly resentful about having to keep boundaries because they feel too constraining and spoil the "fun" and creativity of being a therapist.	Remember that therapy is hard work that is often burdensome and frustrating and that boundaries are necessary for the patient's safety.
Clinician seeks contact with the patient outside therapy setting.	Avoid contact, and explain the reason to the patient. In settings where social contact is likely, discuss problems and options with the patient in advance.
Clinician is unable to confront patients who are late paying fees, remove items from the office, repeatedly try to prolong sessions, or torment therapist with insatiable demands.	Listen to the content of the patient's communications and dreams regarding people injuring one another. Explore fear of one's own anger, the patient's anger, or of setting limits.
Clinician often tries to impress patients with personal information about himself or herself.	Refrain from further disclosure and examine one's possible motives. Consider how such activity might relate to sexual feelings for patient or need to control the patient.
Clinician becomes sexually preoccupied with patient—for example, feels a pleasurable sense of excitement or longing when thinking of the patient or anticipating the patient's visit.	Consider that one's sexual feelings may portend the reenactment of an actual or symbolic incestuous scenario from the patient's past. Remember that incestuous behavior or its symbolic equivalent infantilizes the victim. Obtain supervision and/or personal psychotherapy if sexual preoccupations continue unabated.

psychological characteristics of clinicians who have problems in maintaining proper boundaries[4, 14, 27, 45, 51–54] might provide useful guidance in this regard.

Medical and psychiatric ethics are based on an ancient tradition of adherence to the values of trust and commitment to a healing relationship. These values transcend the uncertainty of our current scientific knowledge, because they are based on principles that augment a mature form of relatedness. The ethical psychiatrist follows these principles for the patient's well-being. In turn, this encourages the trust that is necessary for biological, psychodynamic, and behavioral treatments to be successful. By cultivating these values and the principles embodied within them, maintaining professional skills through training and continuing education, obtaining personal psychotherapy, and utilizing supervision and consultation when indicated, the ethical psychiatrist increases the chance that an effective partnership for healing will be forged.

References

1. Council on Ethical and Judicial Affairs: Patient Responsibilities, Volume IV. Chicago: American Medical Association, 1993:190–191. Code of Medical Ethics Reports, Report number 52.
2. Frank JD, Frank JB: Persuasion and Healing. A Comparative Study of Psychotherapy, 3rd ed. Baltimore: The Johns Hopkins University Press, 1991.
3. Simon RI: The psychiatrist as a fiduciary. Avoiding the double agent role. Psychiatr Ann 1987; 17:622–626.
4. Epstein RS: Keeping Boundaries. Maintaining Safety and Integrity in the Psychotherapeutic Process. Washington, DC: American Psychiatric Press, 1994.
5. Dyer AR: Ethics and Psychiatry. Toward Professional Definition. Washington, DC: American Psychiatric Press, 1988.
6. Webb WL: The doctor-patient covenant and the threat of exploitation. Am J Psychiatry 1986; 143:1149–1150.
7. Dickstein E, Erlen J, Erlen JA: Ethical principles contained in currently professed medical oaths. Acad Med 1991; 66:622–624.
8. Adams F (trans): Hippocrates: The Genuine Works of Hippocrates. New York: William Wood, 1929.
9. American Psychiatric Association. The principles of medical ethics with annotations especially applicable to psychiatry. Am J Psychiatry 1973; 130:1057–1064.
10. Principles of Medical Ethics with Annotations Especially Applicable to Psychiatry. Washington, DC: American Psychiatric Association, 1993.
11. Goffman E: Frame Analysis. An Essay on the Organization of Experience. Cambridge, MA: Harvard University Press, 1974.
12. Langs R: Making interpretations and securing the frame: Sources of danger for psychotherapists. Int J Psychoanal Psychother 1984–85; 10:3–23.
13. Simon RI: Treatment boundary violations: Clinical, ethical and legal considerations. Bull Am Acad Psychiatry Law 1992; 20:269–286.
14. Gutheil TG, Gabbard GO: The concept of boundaries in clinical practice: Theoretical and risk-management dimensions. Am J Psychiatry 1993; 150:188–196.
15. Dahlberg CC: Sexual contact between patient and therapist. Contemp Psychoanal 1970; 6:107–124.

16. Pope KS, Bouhoutsos JC: Sexual Intimacy Between Therapists and Patients. New York: Praeger Publishers, 1986.
17. Kardener SH, Fuller M, Mensh IN: A survey of physicians' attitudes and practices regarding erotic and nonerotic contact with patients. Am J Psychiatry 1973; 130:1077–1081.
18. Perry JA: Physicians' erotic and nonerotic physical involvement with patients. Am J Psychiatry 1976; 133:838–840.
19. Holroyd JC, Brodsky AM: Psychologists' attitudes and practices regarding erotic and nonerotic physical contact with patients. Am Psychol 1977; 32:843–849.
20. Gartrell N, Herman J, Olarte S, et al: Psychiatrist-patient sexual contact: Results of a national survey. I: Prevalence. Am J Psychiatry 1986; 143:1126–1131.
21. Borys DS, Pope KS: Dual relationships between therapist and client: A national study of psychologists, psychiatrists, and social workers. Prof Psychol Res Pract 1989; 20:283–293.
22. Schoener GR: A look at the literature. In Schoener GR, Milgrom JH, Gonsiorek JC, et al (eds): Psychotherapists' Sexual Involvement with Clients: Intervention and Prevention. Minneapolis, MN: Walk-In Counseling Center, 1990:11–50.
23. Epstein RS, Simon RI, Kay GG: Assessing boundary violations in psychotherapy: Survey results with the Exploitation Index. Bull Menninger Clin 1992; 56:150–166.
24. Simon RI: Sexual exploitation of patients. How it begins before it happens. Psychiatr Ann 1989; 19:104–112.
25. Peterson MR: At Personal Risk. Boundary Violations in Professional-Client Relationships. New York: WW Norton, 1992.
26. Epstein RS, Janowsky DS: Research on the psychiatric ward. The effects on conflicting priorities. Arch Gen Psychiatry 1969; 21:455–463.
27. Epstein RS, Simon RI: The Exploitation Index: An early warning indicator of boundary violations in psychotherapy. Bull Menninger Clin 1990; 54:450–465.
28. Slovenko R: Undue familiarity or undue damages? Psychiatr Ann 1991; 21:598–610.
29. Gutheil TG: Approaches to forensic assessment of false claims of sexual misconduct by therapists. Bull Am Acad Psychiatry Law 1992; 20:289–296.
30. Winnicott DW: Ego distortion in terms of true and false self. In The Maturational Processes and the Facilitating Environment. Studies in the Theory of Emotional Development. New York: International Universities Press, 1965. Article originally published in 1960.
31. Langs R: The Technique of Psychoanalytic Psychotherapy, Volume 1. New York: Aronson, 1973.
32. Pope KS, Vetter VA: Ethical dilemmas encountered by members of the American Psychological Association. A national survey. Am Psychol 1992; 47:397–411.
33. Chodoff P: Responsibility of the psychiatrist to his society. In Bloch S, Chodoff P (eds): Psychiatric Ethics, 2nd ed. New York: Oxford University Press, 1993:449–460.
34. Fries JF, Koop CE, Beadle CE, et al: Reducing health care costs by reducing the need and demand for medical services. N Engl J Med 1993; 329:321–325.
35. Appelbaum SA: Evils in the private practice of psychotherapy. Bull Menninger Clin 1992; 56:141–149.
36. McKenzie NF: The new ethical demand in the crisis of primary care medicine. In McKenzie NF (ed): The Crisis in Health Care. Ethical Issues. New York: Meridian, 1990.
37. McCormick B: What price patient advocacy? Am Med News March 28, 1994:1, 6.
38. Atlas M: Forum on health care reform. Presented at the American Psychiatric Association assembly meeting; November 5, 1993; Washington, DC.
39. Appelbaum PS: Legal liability and managed care. Am Psychol 1993; 48:251–257.
40. Westermeyer J: Problems with managed psychiatric care without a psychiatrist-manager. Hosp Community Psychiatry 1991; 42:1221–1224.
41. Rogers WH, Wells KB, Meredith LS, et al: Outcomes for adult outpatients with depression under prepaid or fee-for-service financing. Arch Gen Psychiatry 1993; 50:517–525.
42. Freud S: Recommendations to physicians practicing psychoanalysis. In Strachey J (trans-ed): The Standard Edition of the Complete Psychological Works of Sigmund Freud, Volume 12. London: Hogarth Press, 1958:118–119. Originally published in 1912.
43. Freud S: On beginning the treatment. Further recommendations on the technique of psychoanalysis. In Strachey J (trans-ed): The Standard Edition of the Complete Psychological Works of Sigmund Freud, Volume 12. London: Hogarth Press, 1958:140. Originally published in 1913.
44. Bratter TE: Responsible therapeutic eros: The psychotherapist who cares enough to define and enforce behavior limits with potentially suicidal adolescents. Counseling Psychol 1975; 5:97–104.
45. Schoener GR, Gonsiorek JC: Assessment and development of rehabilitation plans for the therapist. In Schoener GR, Milgrom JH, Gonsiorek JC, et al (eds): Psychotherapists' Sexual Involvement with Clients: Intervention and Prevention. Minneapolis, MN: Walk-in Counseling Center, 1990:401–420.
46. Parker S: The precultural basis of the incest taboo: Toward a biosocial theory. Am Anthropol 1976; 78:285–305.
47. Appelbaum PS, Jorgenson L: Psychotherapist-patient sexual contact after termination of treatment: An analysis and a proposal. Am J Psychiatry 1991; 148:1466–1473.
48. Brown LS, Borys DS, Brodsky AM, et al: Psychotherapist-patient sexual contact after termination of treatment. Am J Psychiatry 1992; 149:979–980.
49. Gabbard GO, Pope KS: Sexual intimacies after termination: Clinical, ethical, and legal aspects. In Gabbard GO (ed): Sexual Exploitation in Professional Relationships. Washington, DC: American Psychiatric Press, 1989:115–127.
50. Shor J, Sanville J: Erotic provocations and alliances in psychotherapeutic practice: Some clinical cues for preventing and repairing therapist-patient collusions. Clin Social Work J 1974; 2:83–95.
51. Gabbard GO: Psychotherapists who transgress sexual boundaries with patients. Bull Menninger Clin 1994; 58:124–134.
52. Twemlow SW, Gabbard GO: The lovesick therapist. In Gabbard GO (ed): Sexual Exploitation in Professional Relationships. Washington, DC: American Psychiatric Press, 1989:71–87.
53. Gabbard GO: Psychodynamics of sexual boundary violations. Psychiatr Ann 1991; 21:651–655.
54. Geis G, Pontell HN, Keenan C, et al: Peculating psychologists: Fraud and abuse against Medicaid. Prof Psychol Res Pract 1985; 16:823–832.

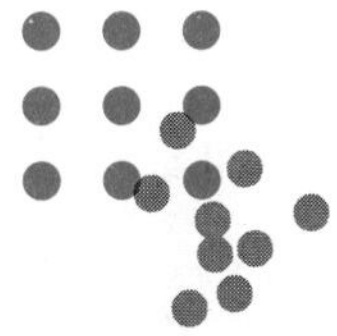

SECTION II

David A. Mrazek, Section Editor

A Developmental Perspective on Normal Domains of Mental and Behavioral Function

CHAPTER

5 A Psychiatric Perspective on Human Development

David A. Mrazek

The miracle of human development has always fascinated physicians. Psychiatrists and pediatricians have formally studied developmental processes and have used the knowledge gained from these investigations to create more effective strategies for care of patients. With the evolution of the specialty of geriatrics, interest in the developmental changes that occur after having achieved full maturation has further expanded the scope of investigations. With better understanding of the changes that predictably occur in the last half of life, it has become possible to link more effectively early precursors of illnesses to the later expression of developmental delays and deviations.

There are two classical approaches to the study of human development: the stage model and the longitudinal lines of development model. Each has distinct advantages and disadvantages. The more traditional approach is to examine each stage of development. Consequently, the unfolding of the many new capabilities of the infant is reviewed chronologically so that the child as a whole can be better understood. Thinking about development as a series of stages is a particularly useful approach for clinicians and therefore is the primary strategy used to organize this section on human development. There are five chapters that chronologically address the development of 1) infants, 2) preschool children, 3) school-age children, 4) adolescents, and 5) adults. The reader can turn to each of these chapters and come away with a clear understanding of the developmental changes that occur during each of these stages. Furthermore, the special risks associated with each period of development that are relevant to the onset of psychiatric illness are reviewed.

An alternative strategy used to teach development is to choose a particular aspect of human development and track it from birth until death. This is a helpful strategy for understanding the process of development and is useful for researchers who are searching for the antecedents of characteristics that occur during later developmental periods. However, the accurate charting of these lines of development has proved to be difficult. Clearly, it is not feasible for a single investigator to study the extensive changes that occur over the life span. In the rare longitudinal studies that span 10 or more years, the rule is that a series of principal investigators must work sequentially to achieve continuity. Consequently, most investigators become specialists in narrow age ranges of the developmental process and must work collaboratively with colleagues to link together the transitions from infancy to childhood or adolescence to the adult years.

In this chapter, an overview of five prominent lines of human development is presented so that the reader can quickly obtain a sense of the timetable of normal development. These five lines of development are 1) biological development, 2) cognitive development, 3) emotional development, 4) social development, and 5) moral development. In addition, a longitudinal review of periods of development that are associated with an increased risk for specific psychiatric disturbances is provided.

In the past century, there has been a scientific preoccupation with defining the relative contributions of genetic endowment and environmental experience to human development. Whereas early behavioralists adhered to the extreme view that children can be shaped almost exclusively by their environments, today evidence supports the theory that genes and experience interact in a transactional manner that leads to the unique development of an individual. The study of environmental contributions has steadily improved through the application of more careful methods of assessment and an appreciation of the value of examining the many components of children's early experiences.

However, the most explosive advances in the understanding of human development have been made as specific gene sequences have been identified and linked to physical and behavioral outcomes. In the past decade, the pace of new gene discovery has increased exponentially as the technology necessary for processing gene mapping has become more automated. It is expected that within a decade the human genome map will be virtually complete, and this achievement will set the stage for a far greater understanding of how genes function. The next phase will involve the investigation of how genes interact with each other and how they are regulated by the environment. Among the most exciting prospects are new opportunities for discovering how the passage of time and the gradual maturation of the individual affect the expression of genes that have remained silent but ominous from the beginning of fetal development. Future studies of cohorts of infants at known genetic risk for a trait or illness may well identify environmental factors associated with both the expression and the suppression of gene action.

The concept of studying development longitudinally has its origin in the studies of lives and was well established by Plutarch and popularized by Shakespeare. In many ways biographers strive to examine the origins of adult traits through consideration of the early experiences of their particular subject. This tradition was adopted by psychoanalysts, who searched for the origins of psychopathology through the exposition of a "genetic formulation." The choice of the word genetic to modify a formulation based on the experience of the individual is somewhat ironic. The term has largely been abandoned, because these formulations have little to do with the function of individual genes. Nonetheless, this focus on the influence of early experience on development may well have been a forewarning of the probable importance of intense early experience in gene expression that is only now becoming well appreciated. In all likelihood, the genetic formulations of the future will focus on how experience regulates gene expression at the molecular level.

The concept of parallel yet interacting lines of development was popularized by Anna Freud,[1] who created a classical monograph that articulated nine lines of development that were well described through adolescence. Although some of these conceptual lines have been abandoned, the overarching principle of a line of development has proved to be heuristically valuable and represents an important legacy of psychoanalytic theory to the field of human development. Other analysts have built on this model to create parallel lines extending into adulthood, such as some of the work underpinning self psychology. Erikson[2] further elaborated the evolution of domains of function in the creation of his epigenetic stage model. His paradigm continues to have a strong influence on psychiatric theory, as is well illustrated by Vaillant's work,[3] which is discussed extensively in Chapter 10.

Although lines of development are attractive conceptually, they are a deceptively simplistic representation of the complex evolution of personality. The concept of decalage was put forward by Piaget[4] to refer to a disengagement in the normal evolution of the parallel development of specific cognitive abilities. However, this concept is equally salient in the conceptualization of major distortions in emotional or social development. In this chapter, five broad lines of development are reviewed as they evolve over the course of the life span, and developmental time lines for each line are included. In each of the following chapters, there is a more detailed discussion of the five time lines as well as a discussion of the interactions that are typical within that stage of development and the stage-specific risk factors.

Biological Development

Genetic Considerations

The genes that an individual possesses contain all of the information required to define the individual. Some genes have strong penetrance and express themselves in virtually all environments. This is the traditional view of the influence of genes, and it has led to the erroneous conclusion that any genetic influence is immutable. It has become clear that many genes have only partial penetrance and that there are both physical and emotional environmental factors associated with their expression.

However, in considering the biological development of an individual, single genes that control such critical functions as physical growth appear to have a high degree of penetrance in a wide range of environments. It is true, for example, that although growth can be retarded by malnutrition, maltreatment, and iatrogenic interventions such as the use of systemic corticosteroids, the genes have a powerful impact on adult height. In fact, in normal environments monozygotic twins are nearly identical in adult height. Interestingly, the same is not true of weight, because a wider range of environmental factors can lead to adult variation in weight. In monozygotic twin pairs, adult weight can vary by more than 20%, although the majority of twins are actually much closer in size. However, it is difficult to disentangle the effects of gene action from those of twins' similar early environments.

A time line of biological development over the course of the life span is presented in Figure 5–1.

Neurological Considerations

Brain growth is a basic indicator of neurological development. The brain is already at approximately one third of its adult size at birth, and it grows rapidly, reaching 60% by approximately 1 year and 90% by 5 years of age. The final 10% of growth occurs during the next 10 years with attainment of full weight by 16 years of age. The processes of myelinization, synapse proliferation, and synaptic pruning occur in the course of the life span, but they are particularly active in the first years of life, when the functional structure of the brain is becoming defined. The visual cortex reaches peak synaptic density by 6 months of age; the frontal cortex does not peak until 1 year. The density of dendritic spines decreases to adult levels by the end of the second year of life, at which time glucose metabolism is also fully developed. The establishment of biological rhythms occurs in early infancy, and sleep becomes more organized and of shorter nocturnal duration. A stable pattern of temperament cannot be documented in the first months of life, but it gradually becomes established during the second year. During the preschool period, individual neurons and neural networks are preferentially preserved if they receive stimulation. Motor skills develop and activity levels increase, rapidly reflecting underlying neural development.

By the age of 7 years, considerable sensory integration has occurred. Handedness has been clearly established, and brain plasticity has decreased. By 10 years of age, limitations in the ability to learn to speak an unaccented second language reflect further changes in the development of the motor linguistic pathways. In the years of adolescence, full brain weight is achieved, but myelinization continues well into the fourth decade. By the end of the fifth decade, there is often evidence of the beginning of decline in specific neuronal functions, with vision and memory being particularly vulnerable. However, integrative capacities may reach a peak during the later decades.

Biological Development

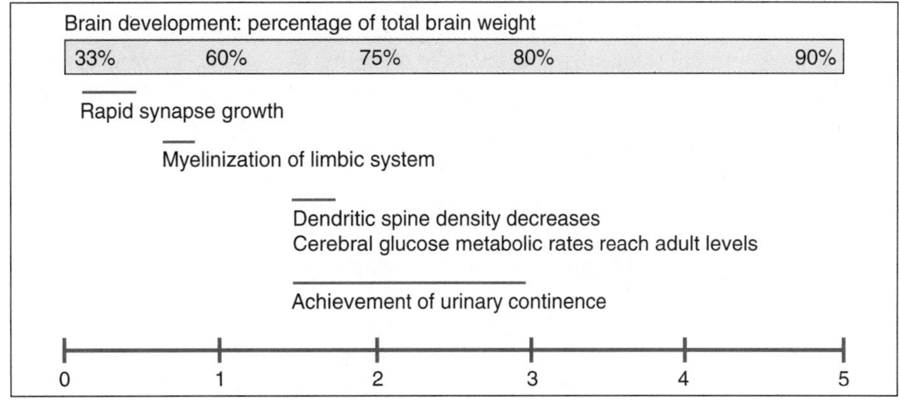

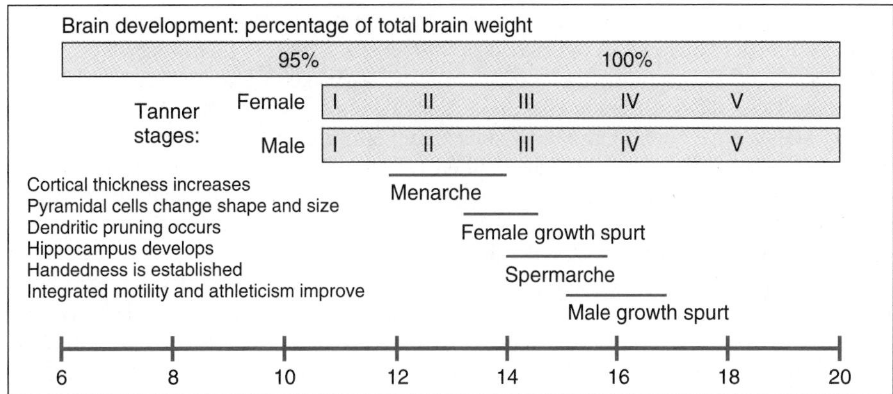

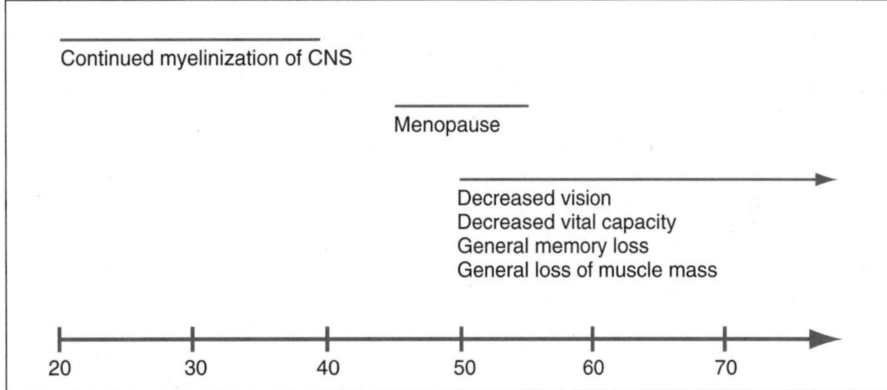

Figure 5–1 *Time line (in years) of biological development across the life span.*

Endocrinological Considerations

Although interesting changes in hormonal development occur in the first years of life, dramatic changes in both physical and emotional functions are triggered by the striking hormonal shifts associated with puberty that usher in the adolescent years. In girls, estradiol and progesterone production results in the onset of breast development, followed by the onset of pubic hair development and vaginal elongation. Axillary hair subsequently develops during stage 3 of pubic hair development. Menarche is usually attained 2 years after the onset of breast development and has been reported to occur at an average of 12.8 years of age in population studies, with wide variability in different cultural environments.[5] In boys, puberty begins when rising levels of pituitary hormones result in enlargement of the testes and subsequent increases in circulating testosterone. Spermatogenesis occurs after testicular enlargement at approximately 14 years of age. Pubic hair development is triggered by adrenal androgens and occurs in five stages during the course of about 2.5 years. Facial hair tends to develop between 14 and 15 years of age.

Growth hormone and gonadal hormones are both necessary to initiate the adolescent growth spurt. This occurs earlier in girls, usually during Tanner's breast stages 2 and 3, whereas in boys it does not occur until stage 4 of genital development. Both an acceleration of bone growth and a maturation of the skeletal structure as reflected by increased bone density and closing of epiphyses occur during this process.

Sexual function peaks early in the adult years in men,

but there is only a gradual decline in sexual function as measured by frequency of orgasm from 20 to 70 years. Women have consistent sexual functioning throughout the childbearing years and frequently become more orgasmic in their 30s. However, decreases in estrogen levels associated with menopause usually occur between 45 and 54 years of age. Men have no comparable menopausal change in hormonal levels.

Cognitive Development

The study of cognitive development provides a perspective on the evolution of the capacity to think. Increased cognitive abilities are an integral component required for the onset of language, and changes in thinking shape the course and ultimate level of emotional, social, and moral development. However, the acquisition of mental abilities has been charted as an independent sequence of mental accomplishments. Piaget established the field of cognitive development, and his stage theory of the evolution of cognitive processes has dominated this field.[6] Although specific aspects of his four primary stages have been modified by subsequent empirical experiments as well as by the development of a greater appreciation of the role of emotions and context in the utilization of cognitive abilities, his careful observations and brilliant deductions have provided the framework on which much of our knowledge of cognitive development has been built.

Piaget both introduced the concept of schemas, which represent units of cognition, and defined processes that result in schema modification, such as the classical interaction of assimilation and accommodation of new stimuli. A particularly important piagetian concept has been that of a decalage within cognitive development. In cognitive terms, this refers to an unevenness in development. For example, a child demonstrating cognitive abilities at the concrete operational stage of development with regard to conservation of volume while retaining preoperational forms of thinking as manifested by a persistent egocentrism demonstrates an unevenness in performance. Such distortion can also be seen across lines of development, and the concept of interlineal decalages is described more fully in the last section of this chapter.

Even newborns have the ability to learn through making associations between different states or experiences. There is evidence that cognitive "prewiring" exists that allows for the perceptual capacities of infants that are necessary to seek stimulation and interaction with adult caregivers. A key capacity required for these early cognitions is recognition of the invariant features of perceptual stimuli coupled with the ability to translate these invariant features across sensory modalities. Interestingly, infants can differentiate the human voice from other sounds innately but do not have to "learn" the complex characteristics of the structure and pitch of speech.

By 2 to 3 weeks of age, cross-modal fluency is demonstrated by the ability of infants to imitate facial expression. This requires the recognition of a visual schema of a facial expression to be linked with a proprioceptive tactile schema of producing a facial expression. By 3 months of age, infants can be classically conditioned, and their interest in stimuli led Piaget to suggest that this was a period dominated by attempts to make "interesting spectacles last."[6]

By 6 months of age, associations between "means" and "ends" have been demonstrated. This is followed by object permanence, which evolves during the second half of the first year. During the second year, the abilities evolve both to infer cause after observing an effect and, conversely, to anticipate effects after producing a causal action. A corollary of this new ability is becoming able to correctly sequence past events.

By the third year of life, children enter the preoperational stage. This stage has some similarity to adult thinking but is dominated by magical qualities and the tendency to focus on one perceptual attribute at a time. Idiosyncratic cosmological theories are the rule and are usually dominated by transductive reasoning, which attributes causality based exclusively on temporal or spatial juxtaposition. Throughout the preschool period, attention span and memory are limited and pretend play and fanciful thinking are common. Therefore, it is not surprising that this cognitive period is characterized by imaginary friends and talking pets. The preoperational stage is also the time during which explosive language development occurs. This development appears to be made possible by a genetically determined capacity for language, but it is clearly enhanced by experiential support and parental communication that is sensitive to the child's ability to process new words and language structure.

By age 6 or 7 years, children begin to use operational thinking. The concrete operational child has the ability to conserve both volume and quantity and can appreciate the reversibility of events and ideas. A shift from an egocentric perspective results in a new capacity to appreciate the perspective of others. These new cognitive skills are the result of new cognitive structures that are required to engage in logical dialogue and to develop an appreciation for more complex causal sequences. These are precisely the abilities that are required to benefit from the grade school curriculum.

Adolescence results in the development of a new processing capacity that involves the manipulation of ideas and concepts. Furthermore, the informational fund of knowledge is dramatically expanded and serves as a referent for verification of new data that are assimilated. A final major transition is to the new ability to reflect on cognition as a process. This is referred to as the development of a metacognitive capacity. This capacity allows adolescents to understand and empathize with the divergent perspectives of others to a greater degree. Furthermore, it is possible to engage in recursive thinking whereby the awareness that others can think about the domain of the adolescent's own thought is achieved. These cognitive skills represent the transition into the final stage of cognitive ability, referred to as the use of formal operations. This form of thinking is complex and is not achieved by many adults who remain at the stage of concrete operations. A specific product of this process is the ability to understand complex combinatorial systems that require a well-developed sense of reversibilities including inversion, reciprocity, and symmetry. New levels of problem solving are achieved that include the ability to recognize a core problem isomorph that has previously been solved within a new problem. Through the use of previously successful solutions, efficient parallel solutions can be developed and applied.

A time line of cognitive development during the course of the life span is presented in Figure 5–2.

Emotional Development

The emotional state of the newborn is largely assessed by facial expression and accompanying vocalizations. However, the communicative capacity of young infants has become increasingly well appreciated. In the first weeks of life, contentment and distress have been reliably monitored,[7] and they further differentiate during the first months of life. By 7 to 9 months, a transition occurs that is based on the earliest attainment of intersubjectivity. At this point infants begin to understand that their own inner experiences and feelings can be appreciated by other individuals.[8, 9] This leads to the possibility of developing affect attunement as parents match their own behavior with the behavior of their infant, which is accompanied by some sharing of internal feeling states. Furthermore, the instrumental use of emotions is evidenced by an infant pouting to elicit a parental response. Social referencing occurs by 12 months of age, as illustrated by infants' turning to examine their mothers' facial expressions when they are confronted with potentially fearful situations or objects.[10]

In the second year of life, a period of mixed emotions evolves and the rapprochement crisis occurs as infants become aware of their separateness from their primary attachment object and the limitations of their control on the primary object's behavior. After the infant has attained self-cognition, new more complex emotions of embarrassment and envy emerge that further evolve to create shame, pride, and then guilt by the end of the second year. Furthermore, object constancy, or the ability to reduce anxiety in response to the separation from the primary

Cognitive Development

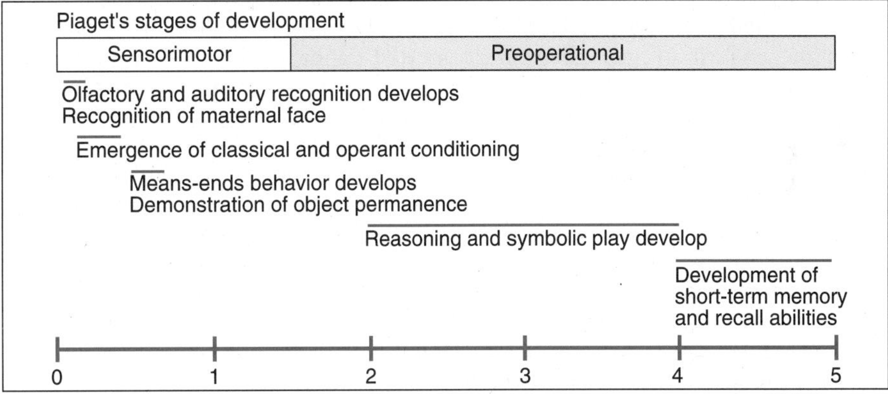

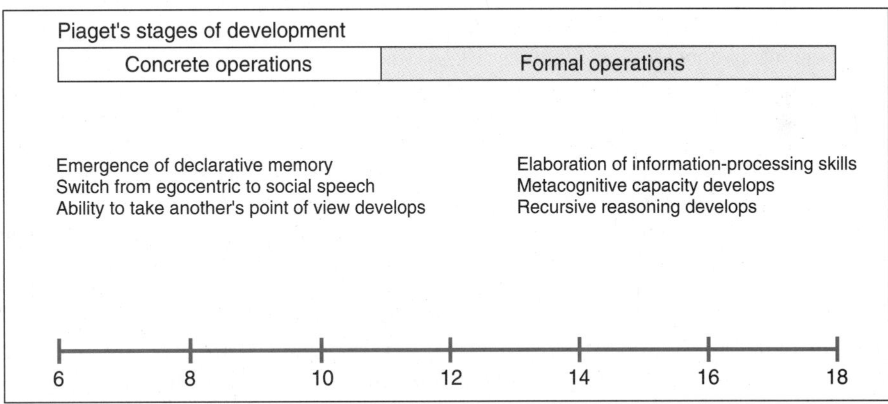

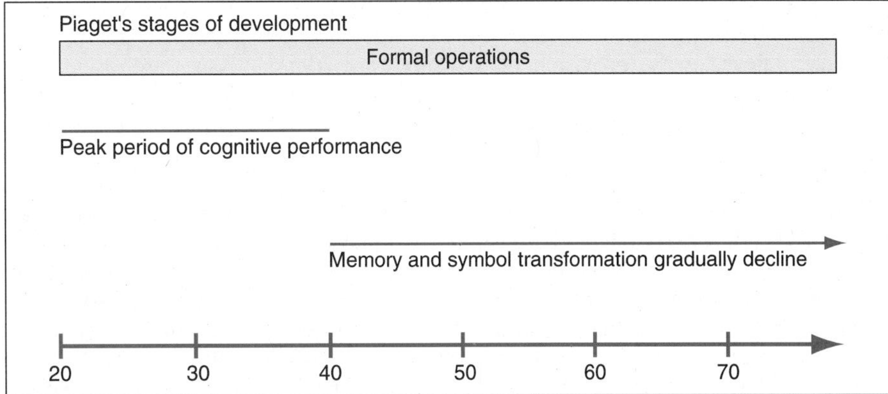

Figure 5–2 *Time line (in years) of cognitive development across the life span.*

caretaker, reflects the association of an emotional state with the memory of the affect modulation provided by the attachment figure.

During the preschool years, children begin to learn more effectively the nature of the relationship between emotions and behaviors. They begin to understand the culturally defined rules associated with affect expression and consequently begin to mask their emotions. This is also the period when the Oedipus complex is most evident, and the child must deal with conscious desire for the parent of the opposite sex and the potential retaliation from the same-sex parent. Clearly, this links positive affects with fearful and angry emotions.

As children move into the school years, they experience the full range of adult emotions, although there is at least a qualitative sense that during the prepubertal period there is less intense expression of affect. Although sadness is easily recognized from the second year of life, prolonged periods of depressed affect are rare during this period. However, temperamental styles tend to emerge and, specifically, behavioral inhibition can become more clearly appreciated within the context of increasing social and educational demands.[11]

In adolescence, emotions are more intensely displayed, and there is an emergence of a greater incidence of affective disorder and anxiety. Similarly, there is a dramatic increase in suicidal behavior that is in part associated with cognitive ability. At this point, there is a greater reflection on the existential crisis, which is now experienced from a more complex vantage point.

A perspective on the evolution of defense mechanisms as regulators of affect suggests that a hierarchy of more sophisticated and effective defensive strategies emerges throughout adolescence and adulthood.[12] A detailed review of the evolution of defense mechanisms during this period of development is included in Chapter 10. A time line of emotional development during the course of the life span is presented in Figure 5–3.

Social Development

It has become widely appreciated that infants are socially interactive from the first days of life. The strong tie that parents feel for their infants has been referred to as the parent-infant bond, and the process of bonding with infants has been extensively studied, particularly within the context of developing postnatal hospital procedures. Between 7 and 9 months of age, infants develop separation protest and a negative reaction to the approach of a stranger. During the second half of the first year, the attachment of the infant to his or her parents evolves. The primary role of the attachment figure is the provision of a secure base from which the infant can begin to explore a wider social environment.[13] It is within the context of the attachment relationship that the first eriksonian state of "basic trust" is achieved.

By 18 months, play begins to be more other directed, but this does not become the predominant form of play until the third year. Along with the striving toward autonomy that characterizes Erikson's second stage, there emerge more negative affective interactions within the context of the attachment relationship. This phenomenon is widely recognized within the popular culture as the arrival of the "terrible twos." However, the quality of the attachment relationship earlier in life has been shown to predict better preschool social adaptation and a stronger sense of self-worth. This has included the observation that patterns of social dominance become established during the third year of life and that insecure, attached preschoolers exhibit more conflict and aggression in the establishment of their social status. These early social strivings are compatible with Erikson's third stage, which has as its central developmental objective the achievement of initiative within the context of potential failure and guilt.

Gender differences emerge by 2 years of age. Boys are more aggressive and tend to play with toys that can be manipulated. Girls prefer doll play and artwork. By the end of the third year gender preference in play has emerged, and the preference is to play with children of the same sex. This preference remains throughout childhood. Associative play, which refers to play that involves other children and the sharing of toys but does not include the adopting of roles or working toward a common goal, becomes more prominent during the preschool years. Cooperative play also emerges, with a strong tendency to include elements of pretend play into the cooperative sequences. The cultural context begins to shape the nature of social interaction even at these earliest stages of development.

During the school years, the role of peers in shaping social behavior becomes predominant. Small groups form, and the concept of clubs becomes important. Shared activities, including the collection of baseball cards or doll clothes, are a common and important characteristic of this period. Sharing secrets and making shared rules also serve as organizing social parameters. Social humor develops, and appearance and clothing become an important social signaling system. It is a time of practicing and developing athletic, artistic, and social skills that are associated with Erikson's fourth stage of achievement of industry within the context of a sense of potential interpersonal inferiority.

In adolescence and throughout the adult years, social and sexual relationships play a complex and powerful role in shaping experience. With the onset of strong sexual impulses and increasing academic and social demands in adolescence, the role of peer influences in shaping both prosocial and deviant behavior becomes powerful and, in some cases, predominant. Adolescence is the period during which Erikson described the central objective to be the establishment of an individual identity, and there has been wide acceptance of this sense of self occurring within the context of the social and cultural experience. The roles of adulthood are complex and focused on the most basic issues of marriage, parenting, working, and dealing with death. These issues are discussed in detail in Chapters 9 and 10. A time line of social development during the course of the life span is presented in Figure 5–4.

Moral Development

The newborn infant lives in an interactive world but one that is free of moral directives or structure. However, by the second year of life the emergence of "moral emotions," such as embarrassment, shame, and guilt, demonstrates that the beginning of a code of moral behavior in the most primitive sense is being established. By 36 months, children demonstrate the internalization of parental stan-

Emotional Development

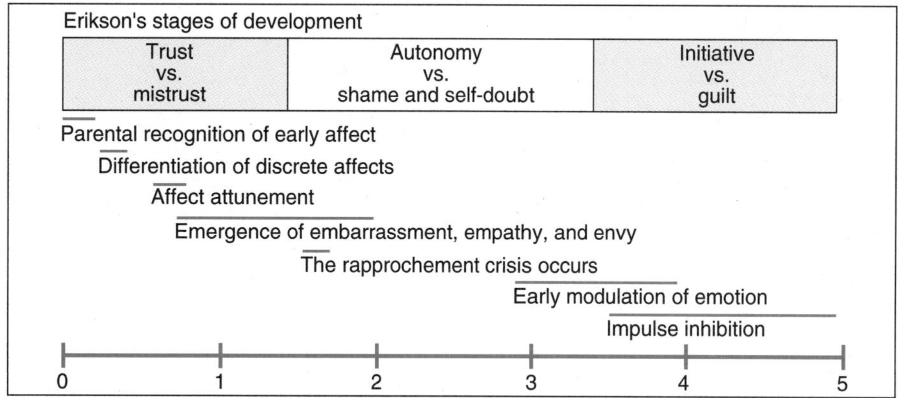

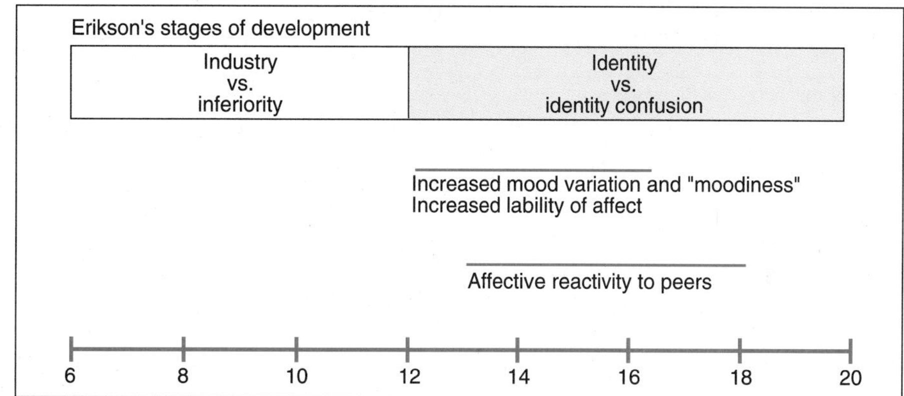

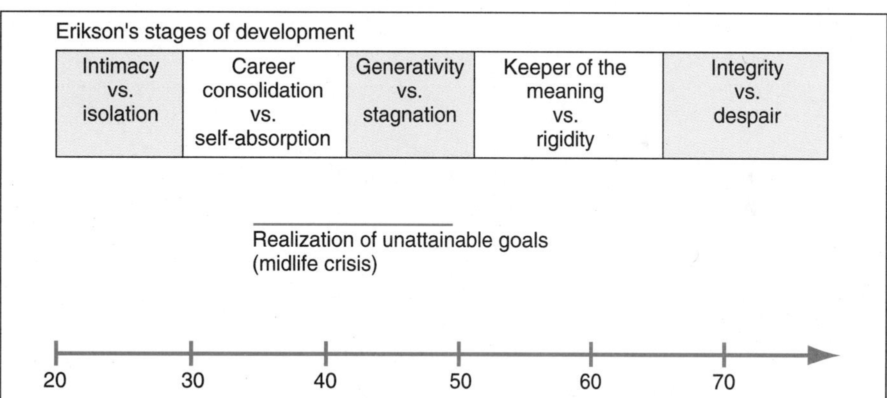

Figure 5–3 *Time line (in years) of emotional development across the life span.*

dards even when their parents are not available to provide cues or reinforcement. The importance of emotions in the early evolution of moral behavior is discussed extensively in Chapter 7 and represents a distinct departure from the more traditional perspective that moral development does not occur until the establishment of concrete operation.

During the school years, the importance of rules and adhering to them becomes well defined. The moral code tends to be one of absolutes with strong consequences for transgressors. Boys have been shown to be even less forgiving than girls, and extreme examples of children turning their parents in to authorities because of political resistance provide a sobering perspective on the strength of some children's convictions.

The later evolution of moral principles is a complex process. With the development of abstract reasoning, adolescents progress through Kohlberg's[14] stages of conventional morality, which entail meeting the expectations of others (stage 3) and subsequently accepting the maintenance of societal norms and rules as an appropriate standard (stage 4). These stages do not progress in a strictly sequential manner, nor have stages 5 and 6, which ultimately lead to the conviction that moral principles of justice should supersede those of human-made laws, been easily codified given the influence of the complex emotions on behavior and the well-documented moral inconsistencies that occur over the course of adult development.[15]

A time line of moral development during the course of the life span is presented in Figure 5–5.

Social Development

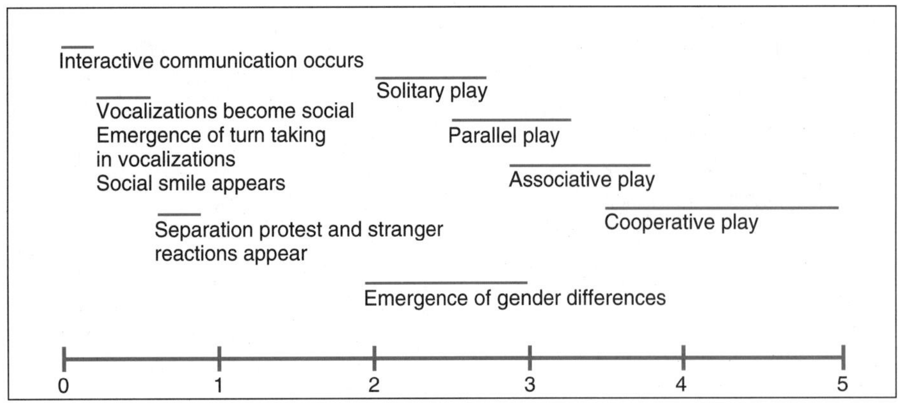

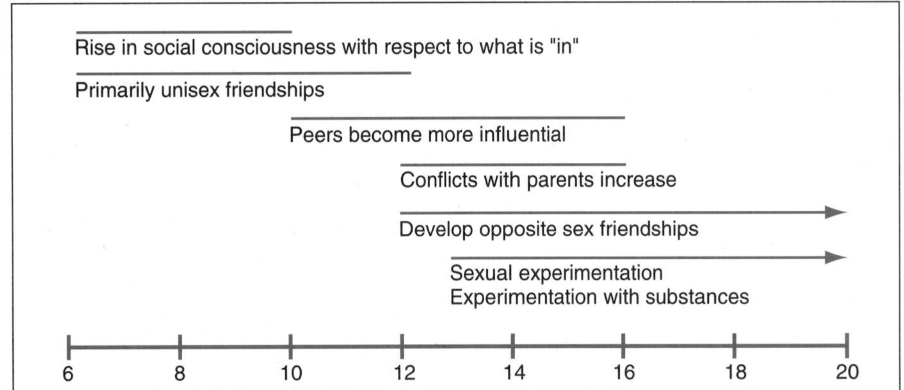

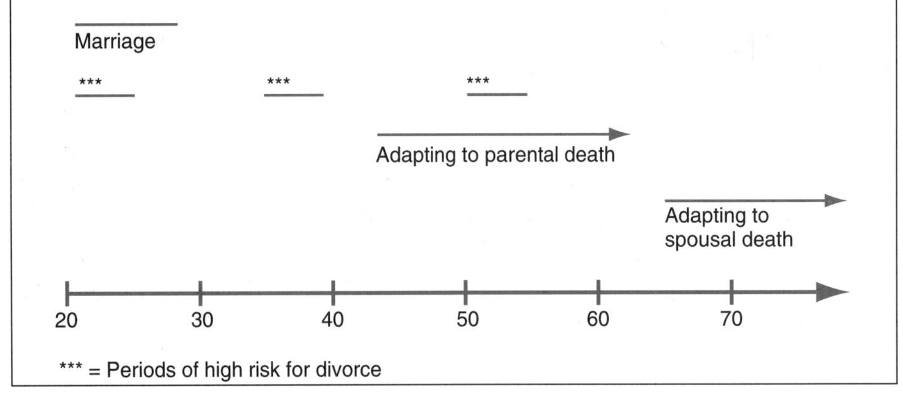

Figure 5–4 *Time line (in years) of social development across the life span.*

Developmental Psychopathology

Risk and Protective Factors

The risk and protective factor model is a paradigm that facilitates the understanding of developmental deviations. It can be applied at any stage of development and, in the chapters that follow, the stage-specific considerations that are relevant to infants, toddlers, children, adolescents, and adults are addressed. Risk factors have been divided into three large categories: those at the level of the individual, the family, and the community.

The first category of risk factors is defined at the level of the individual. Both physical and emotional considerations are relevant. Examples include vulnerable genes, deficits in perception, and intense anxiety. Variable possibilities for adaptation exist, but for something to be considered a risk factor there must be a demonstrated increase in the probability of subsequent emotional or behavioral disorder associated with the factor.

The second category of risk factors is conceptualized at the level of the family. One of the classic examples of a familial risk factor is being raised by a parent with a serious mental illness. It is difficult to define the mechanism by which this risk is transmitted, because a parent provides half of the child's genome and is also in a position to shape the child's early environment. Furthermore, the full range of family risk factors is quite broad and extends beyond the influence of single individuals within the family to include the impact of family dynamics on the development of the child. For example, a scapegoated child in a family environment that tolerates overt child maltreatment is at particularly high risk for the development of psychopathology.

The third category of risk factors is defined at the level of the community. Discrimination based on any ethnic or racial condition falls into this group of risk factors, as does social disadvantage. Although there is little controversy regarding the negative consequences of discrimination and poverty, the quantification of this risk has been particularly problematic. Community risk factors rarely occur in the absence of individual and familial risk factors, and their interactions have been difficult to disentangle.

The strategy that is usually used to determine the overall risk for developmental psychopathology is to add up the specific factors that a child must deal with to create an adversity index. This has been accomplished for young children[16] as well as applied to risk factors occurring later in development.[17, 18] Most individuals can cope with a small number of risk factors, particularly if protective factors are also present, but under the weight of multiple risk factors, the individual begins to show signs of disturbance. Curiously, the quantitative effects of protective factors have been less extensively studied, although investigations into the life course of resilient individuals provide some understanding of these factors.[19]

Resilient children represent one of the most fascinating opportunities to understand the mechanism by which risk and protective factors interact. The study of the children of schizophrenic mothers has been an area of investigation that is of particular interest for psychiatrists. Perhaps this is

Moral Development

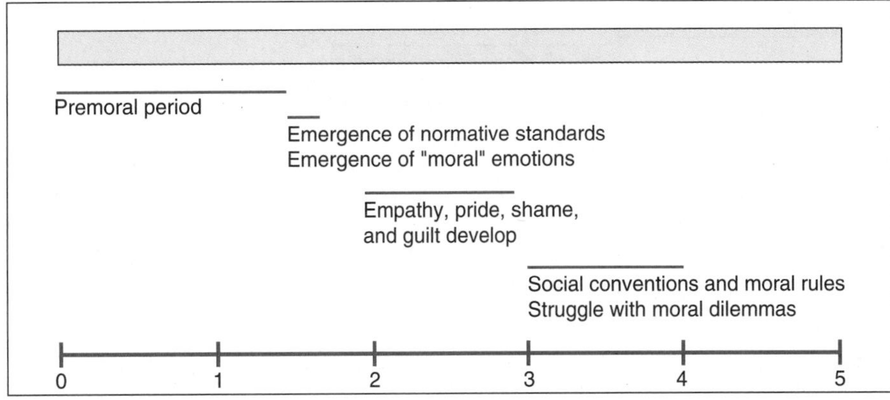

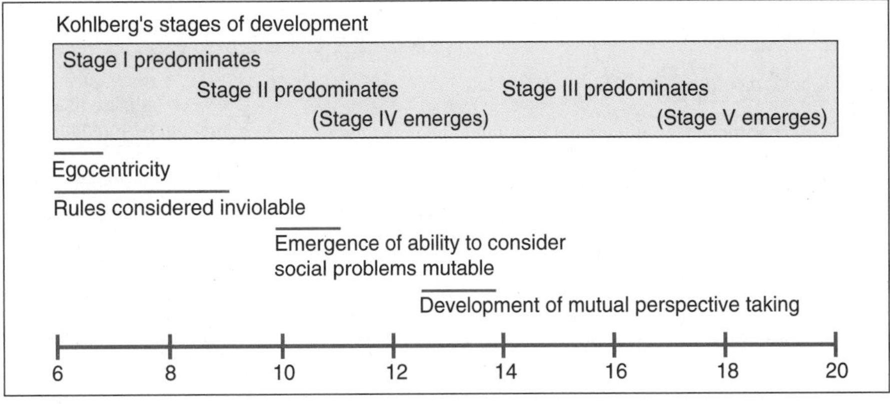

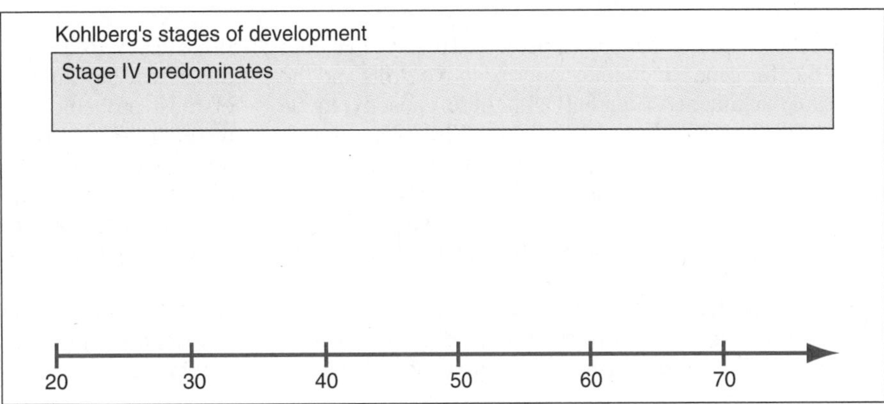

Figure 5–5 *Time line (in years) of moral development across the life span.*

Development of Psychopathology
Intervals represent periods of greatest risk for onset of illness

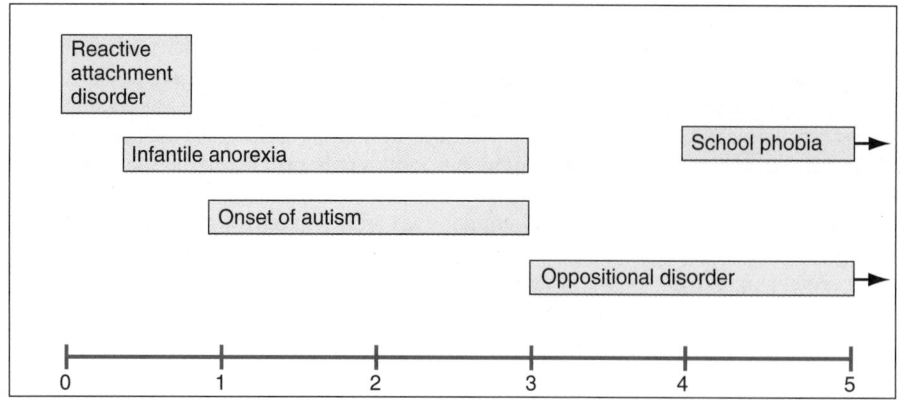

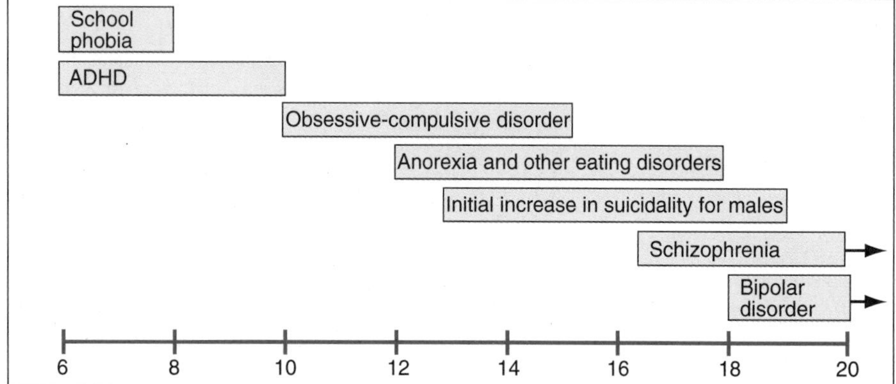

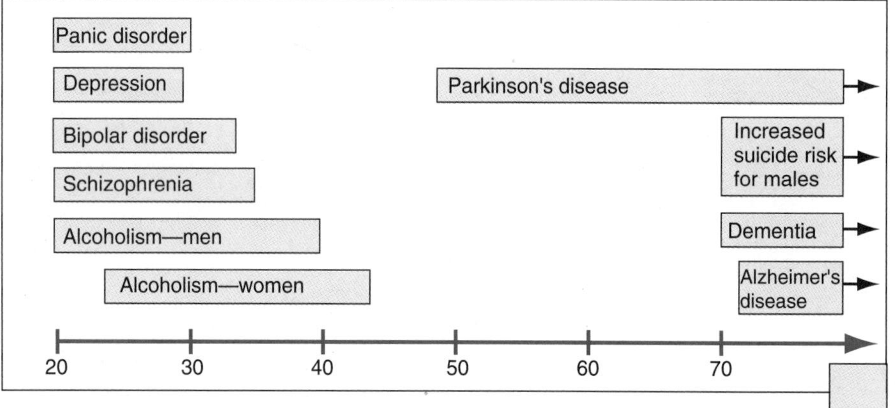

Figure 5–6 *Time line (in years) showing the development of psychopathology across the life span.*

because these children have been perceived to have had both a high risk for genes that confer poor adaptive skills and the misfortune of having a parent with little capacity to be sensitive to their developmental needs. What is striking is that some of these children turn out to be productive and happy adults despite what appear to be overwhelming odds.

A time line of the development of psychopathology during the course of the life span is presented in Figure 5–6.

High-Risk Periods for Psychopathology

Psychiatrists who treat children and adolescents are particularly aware of the precursors and onset of psychiatric illnesses. Two examples of age-specific vulnerabilities are discussed, but Figure 5–6 gives an overview of the periods of most probable onset for many of the major psychiatric disorders. The first example is autism, which is unusual in both its invariant early onset and its striking presentation. The second is suicide, which is particularly interesting because of episodic periods of particularly high risk during the developmental course.

Autism is a disease of early onset and has increasingly been shown to have a strong genetic basis. Nevertheless, the role of the environment in affecting the onset of autism is still striking, as demonstrated by the quite dramatic variability in the symptom presentations and ultimate adaptations of monozygotic twins. Autistic children appear normal at birth and during their first months of life but subsequently develop severe deficits in their capacity to form relationships and communicate with others. Once fully expressed, autism has a devastating impact on the subsequent development of afflicted children and has, unfortunately, proved highly resistant to intense treatment. What is perhaps most striking is the inevitability of early expression, with virtually no examples of onset later in childhood or adolescence.

Suicide provides a sharp contrast to autism. Suicide is highly associated with mental disorder in general and affective disorder in particular. Whereas the onset of suicidal thoughts does occur in rare cases in the preschool period, the capacity to commit suicide increases with age. After puberty the rate of suicide increases nearly 10-fold. The underlying explanation for this dramatic increase is complex and involves consideration of risk factors at the level of the individual, family, and community. However, the ultimate life course pattern is of particular interest in that there is a second dramatic increase in suicidality in the later years of life. The explanation for this second increase usually focuses on the increase in medical problems of the elderly, but the multiple emotional losses of these years also provide a vulnerable context for depression and despair.

Interlineal Decalage

Piaget defined uneven developmental progress of specific cognitive abilities as a decalage.[6] Psychiatrists must often help patients deal with a decalage across lines of development. Although the chapters in this section are largely devoted to the explanation of normal development, there has been a systematic effort to illustrate how deviations in development occur, particularly as they are associated with the onset of developmental psychopathology. Normality can be defined as multilineal progression of development without a decalage, or unevenness of progress, across any of the primary domains of function. Normal children learn to think, to make friends, to deal with intense affects, and to honor the customs of their society. Problems occur when development is uneven. The patterns of these interlineal decalages are varied and their complexity is in large part one of the persistent areas of fascination for psychiatrists. To illustrate this process, two straightforward decalages are discussed, as well as one more complex example of a severe arrest in development.

Cognitive delays can result in a decalage in which a teenager has the mental capacity of a second-grader while having the sexual urges and emotional swings of a normal child in high school. Although such a child's cognitive ability may not be perceived as abnormal in the context of a protected classroom, within the general population the child is clearly deviant and at high risk for impulsive behavior that will place him or her in jeopardy for negative social and academic experiences. Beyond the obvious limitations in achievement that must be dealt with, there are also emotional risks to be considered if intellectual limitations cannot be placed within a context that protects the child from ridicule and humiliation.

Emotional delays provide a similar potential for a variety of decalages. A child who is cognitively normal or even precocious may remain emotionally immature. The decalage can be widened if intensive academic effort and subsequent successes become the child's predominant strategy for dealing with social awkwardness or peer rejection. Temper tantrums that were expected in the early years become less easily tolerated in the child "genius" who must have family and social events orchestrated on her or his terms. In more severe cases, frustration and despair may interfere with adaptation in the same way as they do in the child who is cognitively delayed.

If a domain of function becomes arrested, the decalage becomes more severe. In these cases, overt psychopathology often results. A clear example is the development of conduct disorder and, subsequently, antisocial personality disorder. In these individuals, physical, cognitive, and social developments appear to be progressing well, but a specific deficit in the development of moral judgment occurs. In some cases the deficit is best described as the persistence of a primitive sense of right and wrong, but in others there is a deviant evolution of a degree of immorality that is abnormal at any stage of development. Given the resistance of adults with antisocial personality disorder to current treatments, there is a strong case for focusing on the origins of this development decalage with the expectation that earlier intervention may be more effective.

The Psychiatrist as a Developmentalist

All psychiatrists inevitably become students of development. The life histories of their patients demand developmental formulations to achieve a sense of understanding of the origins of the presenting symptoms and disturbing behaviors that bring the patients to psychiatric treatment. Perhaps one of the most poignant examples is Huntington's chorea. The gene associated with this disease has at long last been identified, and it is possible to know quite accurately whether an infant is destined to struggle with the symptoms of this crippling disability many decades in the future. Yet it is the life experiences of this individual that shape many of the coping strategies that determine the ultimate outcomes of these future struggles. Anticipating the challenges of later life and understanding the origins of the strengths and weaknesses of each patient are at the core of the therapeutic process, whether it involves influencing the balance of the patient's central neurotransmitters or identifying and supporting available community resources.

References

1. Freud A: The Ego and the Mechanisms of Defence. New York: International Universities Press, 1946.
2. Erikson E: Childhood and Society, 2nd ed, revised and expanded. New York: WW Norton, 1963.
3. Vaillant GE: Adaptation to Life. Boston: Little, Brown, 1977.
4. Piaget J: The Origins of Intelligence in Children. New York: International Universities Press, 1952.
5. Zacharias L, Rand WM, Wurtman RJ: A prospective study of sexual development and growth in American girls: The statistics of menarche. Obstet Gynecol Surv 1976; 31:325–337.
6. Piaget J, Inhelder B: The Psychology of the Child. New York: Basic Books, 1969.
7. Lewis M: The emergence of human emotions. In Lewis M, Haviland J (eds): Handbook of Emotions. New York: Guilford Press, 1994:223–226.
8. Trevarthen C: Communication and cooperation in early infancy: A description of primary intersubjectivity. In Bullowa MM (ed): Before

Speech: The Beginning of Interpersonal Communication. New York: Cambridge University Press, 1979:321–347.
9. Emde RN: The affective self: Continuities and transformations from infancy. In Call J, Galenson E, Tyson RL (eds): Frontiers of Infant Psychiatry II. New York: Basic Books, 1984:38–54.
10. Klinnert MD: The regulation of infant behavior by maternal facial expression. Infant Behav Dev 1984; 7:447–465.
11. Kagan J, Reznick JS, Gibbons J: Inhibited and uninhibited types of children. Child Dev 1989; 60:838–845.
12. Vaillant GE: The Wisdom of the Ego. Cambridge, MA: Harvard University Press, 1993.
13. Ainsworth MDS, Blehar MD, Waters E, et al: Patterns of Attachment: A Psychological Study of the Strange Situation. Hillsdale, NJ: Lawrence Erlbaum, 1978.
14. Kohlberg L: Development of moral character and moral ideology. In Hoffman ML, Hoffman LW (eds): Review of Child Development Research. New York: Russell Sage Foundation, 1964:383–432.
15. Gibbs JC: Kohlberg's moral stage theory: A piagetian revision. Hum Dev 1979; 22:89–112.
16. Sameroff AJ: Environmental context of child development. J Pediatr 1986; 109:192–200.
17. Rutter M: Resilience in the face of adversity: Protective factors and resistance to psychiatric disorder. Br J Psychiatry 1985; 147:598–611.
18. Rutter M: Family and school influences on behavioral development. J Child Psychol Psychiatry 1985; 26:349–368.
19. Mrazek PJ, Mrazek DA: Resilience in child maltreatment victims: A conceptual exploration. Child Abuse Negl 1987; 11:357–366.

CHAPTER

6 Infant Development: The First 3 Years of Life

Charles H. Zeanah
Neil W. Boris
Michael S. Scheeringa

For most clinicians treating individuals suffering from psychiatric disorders, early development is of great interest. How did the disorder begin? Were there early biological or psychosocial risk factors that could have led to early identification of the disorder or even its prevention? Is there anything unique or more important about events occurring in the first 3 years of life compared with other periods of development with regard to the ontogenesis of psychiatric disorders? More broadly, how do patterns of behavioral adaptation follow particular developmental trajectories and what factors are most influential with regard to establishing those trajectories?

Many factors may contribute to clinicians' interest in early development, and new knowledge from research on infant development in the past 25 years has afforded greater insight into clinical issues. Theories of development, which guided the teaching of clinicians for many years, have been supplemented, revised, and in some instances supplanted by data from scientifically rigorous investigations in developmental and cognitive psychology, ethology, neurobiology, chronobiology, behavioral genetics, and linguistics. Greater collaboration among researchers, clinicians, and theoreticians from these diverse disciplines has led to exploration of increasingly rich, interesting, and pressing clinical questions. Researchers who study infants are now attempting to characterize and measure formerly unapproachable constructs such as relationships and the dimensions of subjective experiences. These developments have made possible new insights in the realm of infant development, while also enriching our understanding of clinically relevant issues.

In this chapter, we present a broad overview of research on infant development relevant to clinical work on infancy and later phases of life. First, we briefly describe influential theories and models of development. Then we trace various lines of development through the first 3 years of life. Next, we consider various risk and protective factors as they affect infant development. Finally, we consider selective examples of psychiatric disorders that occur in infancy to illustrate the clinical application of developmental findings. Two overarching points are emphasized throughout. First, infants are active participants in their development, and individual differences in their characteristics and capacities have important implications for how infants are experienced by their caregivers. Second, the caregiving environment is the crucible within which individual differences in development in the first 3 years of life are shaped, preparing infants for transition to the broader influences of the preschool years and beyond.

Theories and Models of Development and the First 3 Years of Life

Theories of Development

Theories are important to the study of development for a number of reasons. They organize and prioritize large amounts of data regarding infant development, indicating which are the most salient and why. Often they also explain the importance of the early years for subsequent development, indicating how early developmental issues are related to broader issues of the life span. Generally, they move beyond mere descriptions of behavior and attempt to explain *why* individuals are motivated to behave in certain ways at certain times. Finally, they may generate meaningful and testable hypotheses for empirical research.

On the other hand, theories also have inherent liabilities. They are framed from particular points of view, often with specific agendas. A selective focus on one theory may obscure others of equal or greater value. Theories also inevitably lead to oversimplification of complex processes and events. They may create biases that affect how we interpret observations and how we make inferences from those observations. The history of psychology is filled with examples of adherence to a particular point of view, making it impossible to see disconfirming information. All of these factors urge us to be cautious about the uncritical use of theories to understand development.

Table 6–1 presents a brief summary of some of the major theories of development as they pertain to the first 3 years of life. Although others could have been selected, those presented have been the most influential with regard to

Table 6–1 Developmental Theories and the First 3 Years of Life

Theorist	Type and Focus of Theory	Stages or Phases
Sigmund Freud (1940)	Psychoanalytic drive theory (psychosexual stages)	Oral (birth to 18 mo) Anal (18–36 mo)
Jean Piaget (1952)	Cognitive	Sensory-motor intelligence (first 2 y) Modification of reflexes (birth–1 mo) Primary circular reactions (1–4 mo) Secondary circular reactions (4–10 mo) Coordination of secondary schemas (10–12 mo) Tertiary circular reactions (12–18 mo) Representational thinking (18–24 mo) Preoperational intelligence (2–6 y)
Erik Erikson (1951)	Psychoanalytic theory (psychosocial stages)	Trust versus mistrust (birth–18 mo) Autonomy versus shame or doubt (18–36 mo)
Margaret Mahler (1975)	Psychoanalytic theory (separation and individuation)	Autistic phase (birth–2 mo) Symbiosis (2–4 or 5 mo) Differentiation (4 or 5–8 or 9 mo) Practicing Early practicing: 8 or 9–12 mo Practicing proper: 12–18 mo) Rapprochement (18–24 mo) On the way to object constancy (24–36 mo)
John Bowlby (1969, 1973, 1980)	Attachment theory	Phase of limited discrimination (birth–2 mo) Phase of limited preference (2–7 mo) Phase of focused attachment and secure base (7–24 mo) Phase of goal-corrected partnership (24–36 mo)
Daniel Stern (1985)	Psychoanalytic theory (sense of self-development)	Sense of emergent self (forms birth–2 mo) Sense of core self (forms 2–3 mo) Sense of subjective self (forms 7–9 mo) Sense of verbal self (forms 18–20 mo)

clinical practice and research on early development. As noted in Table 6–1, the theories vary with regard to their particular focus on development, although most use stages to describe periods of discontinuity.

Models of Development

Whereas theories of development describe the evolution of particular issues such as cognition, aggression, attachment, or the sense of self, models of development are more concerned with the process by which development proceeds. How do individuals change or remain the same over time? What drives both continuities and discontinuities in development?

Although it is common to suggest that we are now beyond nature-nurture conflicts, this ancient debate actually continues in every aspect of science concerned with human development. Although the most extreme positions in the debate have been eliminated, the weight that different clinicians, investigators, and theorists give to environmental or to genetic influences varies enormously.

The field of behavioral genetics has made some important and even surprising contributions to this debate. Studies of twins and adopted siblings are able to determine the proportion of variance in various outcomes explained by genes, by shared environment, and by nonshared environment. Shared environment includes all aspects of environ-

Focus and Features	Strengths	Weaknesses
Attempted to describe the unfolding of innate drives, whose objects progressed from oral to anal during first 3 y of life.	Most sophisticated and comprehensive theory of human behavior ever developed. Accounts for the irrational component of behavior through construct of unconscious, which has been widely accepted. Clinically useful and generative; linked to important treatment concepts and techniques.	No systematic evidence for fixation-regression model. Constructs not well operationalized and as a result many of its major premises are untestable. Exclusive focus on aggression and libido as motivators of behavior to the exclusion of other seminal constructs. Derived in large part from reconstructive method and from populations of patients. Mechanistic view of person motivated by tension reduction.
Concerns how infants construct, organize, and transform information.	Most comprehensive theory of cognition ever proposed. Based on observable behaviors and replicated cross-culturally. Described qualitative differences in how children think.	Considerable evidence of uneven performance based on task and contextual factors. Evidence of sophisticated cognitive endowment in newborns that the theory cannot account for, especially in regard to cross-modal fluency and memory. Minimized social and familial contributions to cognition.
Accepted Freud's drive model but placed developmental issues in a social context.	Places Freud's intrapsychic metapsychology in a social context and introduces issues that are more obviously salient than psychosexual stages (trust instead of orality).	Stages imply qualitative changes that are not always supported by data. Theory ties clinical issues to particular stages of development. There are few efforts at validation of first two stages, and clinical implications are not well articulated.
Also accepted drive model but focused on emergence of psychological self, which she believed was not differentiated until the later part of the second year of life.	Deals with fundamental human dilemma of how to be with others and how to be alone. Developed in part from observing normal infants. Moved psychoanalysis to a focus on self-development.	Presupposes what it purports to demonstrate: that psychological birth gradually unfolds during first 2 y of life. Accepts fixation-regression. Logical inconsistencies. Derived in part from study of deviant behavior.
Describes the development of attachment, a biologically endowed motivational system responsible for maintaining felt security.	Careful attention to observable behavior. Has inspired more research than any other developmental theory. Describes how individual continuity occurs within model of developmental change. Major premises confirmed in cultures around the world. Places emotional intimacy as centerpiece of interpersonal relatedness.	Limited to one domain of infant-parent relationships. Overstates importance of early separations. Minimal attention to individual differences in infants as contributors to attachment.
Concerned with how the infant subjectively experiences the world; senses of self continue to function throughout the life span once they are formed.	Clear focus on subjective experience of infants in relationships. Abandoned stages in favor of model in which new capacities are added rather than effacing away older capacities. Freed clinical issues from being tied to particular stages in development. Derived primarily from empirical studies of development.	Clinical implications not well developed. Does not account for fantasies and distortions by infants.

mental contributions that two individuals in the same family have in common, such as social class, family warmth, and neighborhood. Nonshared environment refers to the aspects of environmental contributions that are unique and nonredundant for an individual, such as unique aspects of relationships with parents, peer relationships, and unexpected life events. There is considerable evidence to suggest that for the broad areas of intellectual capacities, personality traits, and many types of psychopathology, nonshared environmental contributors are more important than contributions from genes or from shared environment.[1] What matters most for a particular infant's development is neither the general characteristics of family size nor income nor warmth but instead the particular ways in which the family relates to that child.

Despite these contributions, behavioral genetic formulations are limited to explaining proportions of variance in relation to a particular outcome. They say nothing of the actual environment-gene transactions that underlie the changes. It now appears that gene-environment transactions are extraordinarily complex, with genes switching on and off at various points in development, often in response to various environmental perturbations.[2] Research associated with the human genome project may begin to fill in some of these important gaps in our understanding of developmental processes.

Transactional Model

Linear biological models suggest that insults at an early age might be expected to lead to adverse outcomes. This suggests that we should look for biological markers in infancy of subsequent emotional, behavioral, and cognitive disabilities. Nevertheless, longitudinal studies of child development suggest that biological risk factors considered alone are not strongly predictive of outcomes. Sameroff[2] cited one study in which the importance of 169 biomedical and behavioral variables assessed in infancy was examined in relation to the cognitive outcome of over 25,000 children 4 years later.[3] Although only 11 of the 169 variables involved family factors, parental social class and mother's educational level were more predictive of outcome than were all biological risk factors combined.

These and related results have led to the creation of linear environmental models of development. Here the idea is that the child's outcome is shaped by the quality of the caregiving environment. There is, in fact, abundant evidence that the environment contributes powerfully to the infant's outcome. Nevertheless, ample data also indicate that early adverse environments are not linked in straightforward ways with poor outcomes.[4] For example, the Kuaui Longitudinal Study followed children at high clinical risk from age 2 years through adulthood and found considerable variety and complexity of interactions among environmental factors.[5] Similar results from other studies suggest that linear environmental models are as inadequate as linear biological models.

Sameroff and Chandler[6] have proposed a *transactional model* of development in which genetic and environmental regulators of an individual's behavior transact continually over time, mutually influencing one another. In fact, Sameroff[2] has posited that much as the genotype acts as the biological regulator of infants' behavior, the *environtype* acts as the social regulator of the infants' behavior. For infants, the environtype comprises the cultural, familial, and parental characteristics that regulate infants' experiences and opportunities. This model describes individuals transacting continually with genotypic and environtypic regulators over time. Behavior at any point in time is a result of the dynamic interplay of genotype, environtype, and individual.

The transactional model is currently the most widely accepted description of the developmental process. It appears to account reasonably well for most developmental outcomes that have been studied except for those that follow the extremes of biological insults, such as certain chromosomal disorders, or extreme environmental adversities, such as intense deprivation. Still, the transactional model does not give predictive weight to any particular set of risk or protective factors, and the search for more precise predictive models continues.

Cultural Context of Development

One of the most important contexts for development is that of culture, which influences not only the developmental process but also the variables we choose to study and how we choose to study them. There is increasing recognition within the behavioral sciences that in a country as culturally diverse as the United States, we must face the challenges of better understanding and appreciating cultural diversity as it affects developmental processes.

Culture refers to a shared system of beliefs, attitudes, and values that characterize a particular social group who share a common history and heritage. Culture includes a world view of the group and describes normative assumptions that provide individuals within the group with a frame of reference for developing their own values and beliefs. Culture is crucial to understanding development, because one of the major means of transmitting cultural meanings, assumptions, and values is from caregivers to children during child-rearing.

Sameroff and Fiese[7] have emphasized the role of the cultural code in regulating development through processes of socialization and education. They believe that culture sets a broad developmental agenda for child-rearing, with individual differences apparent within the broad framework. A number of investigations of cultural influences on development provide support for these assertions.

Garcia-Coll and Meyer[8] have drawn several conclusions from their overview of some of the major research findings from investigations of cultural differences and similarities in child-rearing and their implications for infant development. First, despite enormous differences in child-rearing techniques around the world, parents are motivated by wanting to do what is best for their children. Second, despite differences in child-rearing, there is a remarkable consistency of some aspects of development across cultures, such as attaining communicative, intellectual, and social competence, although the meanings of what is competent may differ considerably. Third, the timing, content, and expression of certain developmental processes vary widely across different cultures. Finally, there appears to be a universality of gender differences in cultures around the world, with boys being more aggressive and girls being more nurturing.

This raises the question of what other universals exist with regard to development across different cultures. LeVine[9] suggested that there exists a universal hierarchy of parental goals that guide child-rearing behavior. At the most basic level, parents are concerned about the physical survival and health of their children. At the next level, parents are concerned about developing children's capacities for economic self-maintenance as adults. Finally, parents are concerned with developing their children's cultural values. There is a developmental sequence implied in this model, in which the first goal takes precedence over the other two and is the major concern of parents in the child's first 3 years of life.

The application of cultural universals may well be limited, at least beyond the broad outline provided by LeVine. What may be more important from the clinical perspective is identifying within-culture deviance from broadly accepted norms, with less regard for the content of the norms themselves.

Conceptual Framework

To describe the details of psychological development in the first 3 years of life, we follow selected lines of development with regard to their continuities, discontinuities, and content. These lines are *biological-neurological*, referring primarily

Biological Development:
0–24 months

0–2 months
Increasing organization of sleep patterns
Quantitative changes in brain development

2–6 months
Rapid growth of synapses
Rapid increase in cerebral glucose metabolism
Social smiling emerges
Diurnal sleep-wake cycles emerge

7–9 months
Growth in head circumference with rapid cerebral growth
Myelination of limbic system
Enhanced associative pathways
Improved inhibitory control of higher centers

18–20 months
Density of dendritic spines decreases
Cerebral glucose metabolic rates reach adult levels
Increasing lateral and anterior-posterior cerebral specialization of language centers

0 2 4 6 8 10 12 14 16 18 20 22 24

Figure 6–1 *Biological development during the first 2 years of life.*

to brain and central nervous system development and temperament (Fig. 6–1); *cognitive*, referring to changes in intellectual capacity and modes of thinking (Fig. 6–2); *emotional*, including the differentiation of discrete affects and emotional expression (Fig. 6–3); *communicative*, referring to understanding of and use of preverbal and verbal modes of communication; and *social*, referring to all aspects of relatedness and affiliative behavior with others (Fig. 6–4). (Moral development during the first 2 years of life is shown in a time line in Fig. 6–5.) Discussing these lines separately has some heuristic value, although all of the lines of development are interwoven and interdependent such that changes in one resonate through the others.

Rather than discuss each line of development in succession from birth to 3 years, we review findings relevant to each of the developmental lines within four different periods. These epochs are defined by three major periods of qualitative reorganization or discontinuity in infancy: 2 to 3 months, 7 to 9 months, and 18 to 20 months. (Table 6–2 summarizes emerging patterns of behavior at different points during the first 52 weeks of life.) These epochs describe periods of qualitative change in biological, cognitive, emotional, communicative, and social development in which new capacities for experiencing and relating emerge and are different in kind rather than in amount from earlier capacities. Thus, development between these points consists primarily of quantitative changes, whereas development across these points results in qualitative changes.

It is important to acknowledge that the described transition points can also be overemphasized. By focusing on these major transition points, their importance may be exaggerated at the expense of more minor transitions that are salient for some particular domain of development at a particular point in time. Nevertheless, there is considerable evidence that these specific developmental transitions include observable changes in cognitive, emotional, communicative, and social development.[10–14]

Cognitive Development:
0–24 months

0–2 months
Rapid development of olfactory and auditory recognition
Emergence of cross-modal fluency
Recognition of maternal face

2–3 months
Emergence of classical and operant conditioning
Development of habituation

7–9 months
Means-ends behavior develops
Demonstration of object permanence
Stranger reaction and separation protest appear
Exploration of novel properties of objects
Emergence of mastery motivation and symbolic play
Emergence of the discovery of intersubjectivity

18–20 months
Development of symbolic representation
Emergence of personal pronouns
Pretend play is progressively other directed

Figure 6–2 *Cognitive development during the first 2 years of life.*

Emotional Development:
0–24 months

0–2 months
Maternal recognition of contentment
Maternal recognition of interest
Maternal recognition of distress

2–3 months
Differentiation of joy from contentment
Differentiation of surprise from interest
Differentiation of sadness, disgust, and anger

7–9 months
Affect attunement
Emergence of instrumental use of emotion
Emergence of social referencing

9–24 months
Discriminates emotions by facial expressions and vocalizations

18–20 months
The rapprochement crisis occurs
Emergence of embarrassment, empathy, and envy

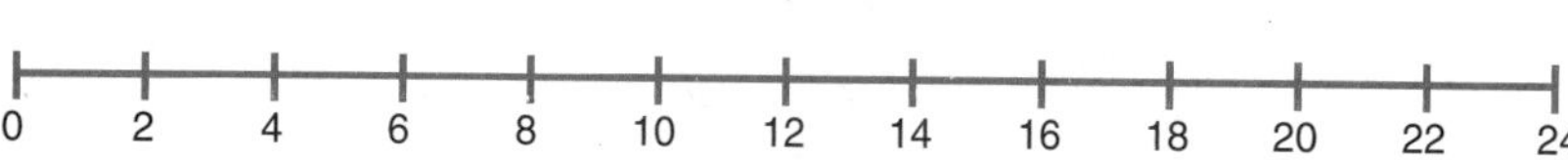

Figure 6–3 *Emotional development during the first 2 years of life.*

Social Development:
0–24 months

0–2 months
Interactive communication occurs
Stimulate social responses

7–9 months
Increasing evidence of intersubjectivity
Responds to caregiver empathy
Emergence of separation protest and stranger reactions

2–3 months
Vocalizations become social
Emergence of turn taking in vocalizations
Emergence of mutual imitation
Emergence of sound localization
Recognition of verbal affect

18–20 months
Words used for social functions
Language development enhances relatedness
Increased evidence of social relationships

2–7 months
Eye to eye contact begins
Emergence of the social smile
Emergence of social interaction
Diminished crying

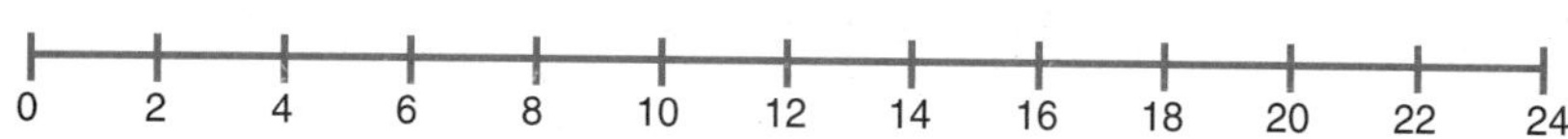

Figure 6–4 *Social development during the first 2 years of life.*

Moral Development:
0–24 months

0–18 months
Premoral period

18–20 months
Generate and monitor goals
Emergence of normative standards
Emergence of distress to standard violation
Emergence of the "moral emotions"

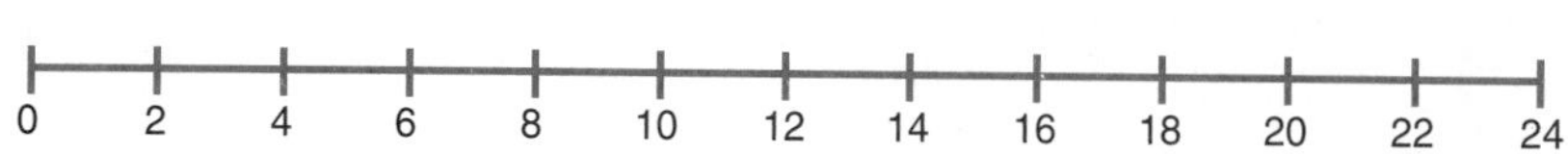

Figure 6–5 *Moral development during the first 2 years of life.*

Table 6–2 Emerging Patterns of Behavior During the First Year of Life

Neonatal Period (First 4 Weeks)	
Prone:	Lies in flexed attitude; turns head from side to side; head sags on ventral suspension
Supine:	Generally flexed and a little stiff
Visual:	May fixate face or light in line of vision; "doll's-eye" movement of eyes on turning of the body
Reflex:	Moro's response active; stepping and placing reflexes; grasp reflex active
Social:	Visual preference for human face
At 4 Weeks	
Prone:	Legs more extended; holds chin up; turns head; head lifted momentarily to plane of body on ventral suspension
Supine:	Tonic neck posture predominates; supple and relaxed; head lags on pull to sitting position
Visual:	Watches person; follows moving object
Social:	Body movements in cadence with voice of other in social contact; beginning to smile
At 8 Weeks	
Prone:	Raises head slightly farther; head sustained in plane of body on ventral suspension
Supine:	Tonic neck posture predominates; head lags in pull to sitting position
Visual:	Follows moving object 180 degrees
Social:	Smiles on social contact; listens to voice and coos
At 12 Weeks	
Prone:	Lifts head and chest, arms extended; head above plane of body on ventral suspension
Supine:	Tonic neck posture predominates; reaches toward and misses objects; waves at toy
Sitting:	Head lag partially compensated on pull to sitting position; early head control with bobbing motion; back rounded
Reflex:	Typical Moro's response has not persisted; makes defensive movements or selective withdrawal reactions
Social:	Sustained social contact; listens to music; says "aah, ngah"
At 16 Weeks	
Prone:	Lifts head and chest, head in approximately vertical axis; legs extended
Supine:	Symmetrical posture predominates, hands in midline; reaches and grasps objects and brings them to mouth
Sitting:	No head lag on pull to sitting position; head steady, tipped forward; enjoys sitting with full truncal support
Standing:	When held erect, pushes with feet
Adaptive:	Sees pellet, but makes no move to it
Social:	Laughs out loud; may show displeasure if social contact is broken; excited at sight of food
At 28 Weeks	
Prone:	Rolls over; pivots; crawls or creep-crawls (Knobloch)
Supine:	Lifts head; rolls over, squirming movements
Sitting:	Sits briefly, with support of pelvis; leans forward on hands; back rounded
Standing:	May support most of weight; bounces actively
Adaptive:	Reaches out for and grasps large object; *transfers* objects from hand to hand; grasp uses radial palm; rakes at pellet
Language:	Polysyllabic vowel sounds formed
Social:	Prefers mother; babbles; enjoys mirror; responds to changes in emotional content of social contact
At 40 Weeks	
Sitting:	Sits up alone and indefinitely without support, back straight
Standing:	Pulls to standing position; "cruises" or walks holding on to furniture
Motor:	Creeps or crawls
Adaptive:	Grasps objects with *thumb and forefinger;* pokes at things with forefinger; picks up pellet with assisted pincer movement; uncovers hidden toy; attempts to retrieve dropped object; releases object grasped by other person
Language:	Repetitive consonant sounds (mama, dada)
Social:	Responds to sound of name; plays peek-a-boo or pat-a-cake; waves goodbye
At 52 Weeks (1 Year)	
Motor:	Walks with one hand held (48 wk); rises independently, takes several steps (Knobloch)
Adaptive:	Picks up pellet with unassisted pincer movement of forefinger and thumb; releases object to other person on request or gesture
Language:	A few words besides mama, dada
Social:	Plays simple ball game; makes postural adjustment to dressing

From Behrman RE (ed): Nelson Textbook of Pediatrics, 14th ed. Philadelphia: WB Saunders, 1992:41.

Lines of Development and Their Discontinuities

First 2 Months of Life

The first 2 months of life were once considered a period of psychological inactivity or at least incomprehensibility. William James,[15] for example, considered the newborn to be a "blooming, buzzing confusion." In the conceptualizations of learning theorists, the newborn was a passive recipient of external influences, a tabula rasa, or blank slate, on which the environment drew particular characteristics. Following Freud's[16] ideas about a stimulus barrier, which was postulated to protect the young infant from potentially overwhelming environmental input, Mahler and colleagues[17] described the first 2 months of life as the relatively "autistic" phase of development.

All of these views of the first 2 months of life have been challenged by careful experimental work that began in the late 1960s and 1970s. From this work has emerged a new view of the human infant as organized, regulating, and interactive.[18] Nevertheless, the first 2 months may be thought of as a period of stabilization for infants as they adapt to postnatal life. During this period of stabilization, infants do not undergo major transitions or reorganizations but appear to consolidate earlier prenatal changes in neurological and psychological development.

Biological-Neurological Development

Although birth is a dramatic transition, change at the level of neuroanatomy and neurophysiology is much less striking. Brain growth and specialization, which began in fetal life, continue after birth; in some areas more sophisticated associative pathways continue to develop for many years.[19, 20] Three of the major arenas in which brain development proceeds and in which there appear to be important functional changes after birth are myelination of selected central nervous system tracts, synaptic proliferation and growth in selected areas of the brain, and synaptic pruning, in which the number of synapses are selectively reduced throughout the brain. During the first 2 months of life, changes in these domains are generally quantitative rather than qualitative.

On the other hand, growing physiological stability becomes apparent within a few days after birth. In this case, interaction with the environment facilitates the rhythmic organization of behavior.[18] Feeding is the first regularly recurring postnatal temporal event, and a cycle of behavioral and physiological regularity becomes organized around the interval between feedings. Notably, human infants seem able to adjust their rhythms to cycle lengths varying from 1 to 6 hours to accommodate cultural differences in feeding practices.

Other components of young infants' rhythmically organized behaviors are circadian rhythms (diurnal cycles) and ultradian rhythms (faster periodic functions such as heart and respiratory rates). Although circadian rhythms are generated endogenously, they are regulated by exogenous cycles, especially light-dark, temperature, and social cues. Environmental cues impose period and phase control on rhythmicity through a process called entrainment.[18] The pacemaker or oscillators regulating ultradian rhythms are less well understood, but study of recurrent physiological patterns temporally in phase with one another has led to interest in infants' states of consciousness or arousal.

The newborn's day and night are spent shifting between six states of arousal, listed in Table 6–3. At first, there is little stability in the duration of these states, although from birth there is some order in the direction of transitions between them. Compared with the two sleep states, which occupy two thirds of the newborn's day, the awake states are particularly unstable in the first few weeks, although they become progressively better organized and more sustained during the second month of life.[21]

Dyadic interaction, although once considered minimal or superfluous during this period of development, is probably of significant importance in regulating development of neural mechanisms that modulate and control central nervous system arousal. Caregivers regulate the newborn's behavioral, neurochemical, autonomic, and hormonal functions through different aspects of the relationship, such as the provision of nutrition, warmth, sensory stimulation, and especially rhythmical responsiveness.[18]

Rhythmicity is a behavioral referent to hypothesized differences in the central nervous system that are often referred to as temperament. All major theories of temperament suggest that temperamental dispositions are rooted in biological differences.[22] Nevertheless, although individual differences in newborns have been widely demonstrated, there is only modest convergence of measures of temperament.[23] In other words, meaningful differences in temperament appear to be difficult to ascertain within the first 2 months of life. This is not surprising given that behavioral genetics research comparing monozygotic and dizygotic twins has demonstrated virtually no genetic contributions to temperament in newborns.[24]

Cognitive Development

The human infant has a remarkable ability to learn. Newborns (and even third-trimester fetuses) can be conditioned to auditory stimuli successfully and reliably.[25] Infants at birth seem to prefer female voices, but they also "work" by nonnutritive sucking to recordings of their mothers' voices in preference to the voice of another woman. DeCasper and Spence[26] have reported that when mothers read Dr. Seuss' *The Cat in the Hat* to their fetuses once a day during the last 6 weeks of pregnancy, newborns found that

Table 6–3 Newborn States of Arousal

States of Arousal	Characteristics
Quiet sleep	Regular respirations, limited movements
Active sleep	Rapid eye movements, irregular respirations, large muscle paralysis Most common state in newborn period
Drowsy	Transitional state between sleep states and waking states
Quiet alert	Sustained gaze, limited movements, maximal alertness Limited in first few weeks
Active alert	Active movements, mild distress occasionally
Crying	Unable to attend to other stimuli

story much more familiar (as detected by patterns of nonnutritive sucking) than another story also read by their mothers soon after birth. This suggests that fetuses' early preference for their own mothers' voices may have developed as a result of hearing them in utero.

Early learning in the olfactory domain also indicates newborn recognition of mother. Macfarlane[27] demonstrated that 6-day-old infants reliably discriminate the smell of their mothers' milk. When the breast pad of a 6-day-old nursing infant's mother and the pad of another lactating woman were placed on either side of an infant's head, the infant turned preferentially toward the mother's pad. These behaviors may contribute importantly to parents' beliefs that their infants recognize them.

In addition to the capacity for rapid learning, research has documented that human newborns are born with a sophisticated biological endowment that Stern[13] has called their "prewired knowledge" of the world. This knowledge consists of various perceptual capacities enabling them to seek stimulation actively, to regulate their environment, and to interact with adult caregivers. At the core of these capacities is a remarkable ability to detect the invariant features of perceptual stimuli and to translate the invariant features across different sensory modalities.

Gaze fixation and visual following of the face, as documented by Fantz,[28] demonstrate that infants possess an unlearned preference for visual stimuli that conform to the characteristics of the human face. By 1 month of age, infants demonstrate by differential looking times that they can distinguish the features of their mother's face from that of an unfamiliar woman.

A similar case holds for auditory stimuli. Infants are born not only with a preference for the human voice but also with a preference for voices in the usual pitch ranges of females rather than males. Infants are able to recognize innately that speech is a special class of acoustic signals and that language is composed of discrete units.[29] This is quite important, because it would take several lifetimes to learn through trial and error how to distinguish between speech and nonspeech sounds.

Even more sophisticated forms of prewired knowledge are referred to as intermodal matching or *cross-modal fluency*. Meltzoff and Moore[30] first described the ability of 2- to 3-week-old infants to imitate human facial expressions. This capacity requires that infants match a visual schema of the facial expression with the proprioceptive-tactile schema of the act of producing the facial expression. This visual-proprioceptive cross-modal translation has been replicated in infants 36 hours old.[31] In another study, 1-month-old infants were given either a smooth or a rough pacifier. When shown both pacifiers, infants looked preferentially at the pacifier they had mouthed but never seen before.[32] This tactile-visual matching seems to be innate rather than learned. Finally, infants are able to match the intensity of events across modalities. For example, infants can indicate that a light of a certain brightness is comparable to a sound of a certain loudness.[33] Stern[13] has emphasized the importance of cross-modal fluency for interactional synchrony and for early self-other differentiation in human infants.

Although there has been great interest in the innate knowledge and learning capacities of newborns, it is important to remember that demonstrations of these capacities require setting up careful experimental conditions and conducting frequent trials that generate only a small amount of usable data. In fact, newborns have important limitations in their cognitive capacities, which become substantially more sophisticated beyond the first 2 months of life.

Emotional Development

Most observers agree that newborns exhibit two major forms of emotional expression: distress and contentment. Nevertheless, Lewis[34] has pointed out that the expression of interest also seems to be present at birth. He has proposed a model of differentiation of emotional expressions in which three major emotional states, contentment, interest, and distress, are present in the first 2 months of life and later differentiate into more specific emotional states. All of the studies of early emotions rely on inferring infants' emotional experience based on facial expressions of emotion and crying; still, most investigators agree that facial expressions are reasonable indices of emotional experience.[34]

Communicative Development

Biological, cognitive, and emotional developments in infants during the first 2 months have implications for the infants' communicative behaviors. A wide variety of spontaneous behaviors in the neonate, including diffuse motility, crying, smiling, startles, and mouthing movements, guarantees that the infant has an impact on the environment. The recurrence of these behaviors during the different states of sleep and wakefulness provides periodic opportunities to relate to significant others. As infants become better organized and more rhythmically regulated during the first 2 months, they also probably exert a more systematic impact on caregivers, who are highly attuned to interpreting who their infants are and what their infants' behaviors mean.[35, 36] In fact, interaction with adult caregivers is frequently initiated by infants through enactment of simple, recurring behaviors that stimulate affiliative responses by adult caregivers.

Infants prefer human faces and voices to inanimate objects or to nonspeech sounds.[37] Long before language symbols are available to infants, they are communicating interactively through crying, quieting, cuddling, looking, and occasional vocalizations. Caregivers, whose attributional processes are highly attuned to infant behaviors, respond to these communications and imbue them with elaborate meanings.[35]

Social Development

Infants are wonderful projective stimuli. They elicit interest and responses from caregivers, who unconsciously change their behaviors to optimize interaction with the infants.[37] Facial expressions are exaggerated in time and space. Speech is modified by amplified syntax, short length of utterance, nonsense sounds, and transformations of consonants (i.e., motherese). Vocal pitch is exaggerated and sound intensity is varied more dramatically when caregivers communicate with infants than when they speak with adults. The speed of speech is generally slowed down, with brief eruptions of speeded-up utterances. Gaze is maintained by adult caregivers with infants for much longer periods than with adults. These changes in adult behavior are testimony to the socially evocative power of human infants.

Klaus and Kennell[38] first popularized the term *bonding*

to describe parents' emotional ties to their newborn infants. They proposed that the first few hours after birth constituted a "sensitive period" for facilitating parental attachment to their children and suggested that providing or preventing an opportunity for parents to have intimate physical contact with their newborns has long-term effects on the parent-infant relationship. Although their assertions contributed to a useful demedicalization of the childbirth experience, they probably overstated the importance of the immediate period after birth and oversimplified attachment by dichotomizing it as present or absent. Early contact between parents and their newborns should be regarded as potentially helpful rather than essential. Goldberg[39] pointed out that the human parent-infant relationship is too complex a system to have its ultimate success or failure hinge on a few brief moments of time.

Several studies have investigated the onset of parents' reported feelings of affection for their infants, although methodological problems make generalization difficult. There appear to be wide variations in onset of affection from the first trimester of pregnancy to several weeks after birth. The clinical significance of these findings is not established, although it is clear that most U.S. mothers report feeling as if they love and have a relationship with their infants within the first several weeks after birth.[36]

Summary of Development in the First 2 Months

In contrast to earlier theories of development that held that the human newborn was disorganized, passive, reactive, or withdrawn, research on newborn behavior suggests a different view. Biological, cognitive, communicative, emotional, and social capacities, which are functionally integrated, enable infants to seek stimulation actively and to regulate their own behavior through interactions with the environment. The psychobiological endowment of infants at birth includes prewired knowledge of the world, such as cross-modal fluency, as well as a remarkable ability to detect and to remember invariant aspects of experiences. These capacities make the infant in the first 2 months of life a far more sophisticated social partner than most widely quoted developmental theories have recognized.

2- to 3-Month Transition

The first significant developmental transition occurs at about 2 to 3 months of age. A significant convergence of researchers[12, 40, 41] and theoreticians[13, 17] have noted dramatic qualitative changes in infants that occur at this time. Stern[13] has pointed out that parents also frequently remark about the qualitative change that occurs at this time because their infants become more focused, better organized, more communicative, and more enjoyable social partners.

Biological-Neurological Development

Development of the central nervous system at the time of the 2- to 3-month transition is beginning to be studied. Brain growth, which continues at a rapid pace after birth, results from growth of neurons and their connections. Growth of synapses in the cortex enters its most rapid phase from about 2 to 6 months of age. Midbrain-cortical visual pathways become myelinated at this time.[42]

Functional changes in the brain are also apparent after this transition at 2 months. Local rates of glucose metabolism, as determined by positron emission tomography, are believed to represent an important window into brain functioning. Maturation of patterns of glucose metabolism is apparent for the first time in large parietal, occipital, and temporal areas after the 2- to 3-month transition.[43] In addition, electrophysiological research corroborates functional changes. Emde and colleagues[40] documented changes in prominent electroencephalographic frequencies at 2 to 3 months. Although we have not yet moved beyond global correlations between developments at the level of brain functioning and newly appearing behavioral capacities, this is an area in which rapid progress may be anticipated within the next few years.[19] At present, a host of changes in infant behavior and capacities at 2 to 3 months of age have biological correlates that are only partially elucidated.

One of the hallmarks of the 2- to 3-month transition is the social smile. Interestingly, evidence suggests significant genetic contributions to the onset of social smiling. Onset of social smiling is better predicted by the date of the last menstrual period than by time elapsed since birth.[44] Furthermore, monozygotic twins are more concordant for onset of social smiling than are dizygotic twins.[45]

Another important maturational development for most infants is that the diurnal organization of sleep-wake cycles begins to appear at this time.[21, 46] Infants begin spending more of their time sleeping at night and having longer periods of sustained wakefulness during daylight hours, probably as a result of maturation of internal pacemakers.[18]

Most investigators believe that after the 2- to 3-month transition, behaviors reflecting temperamental dispositions are apparent. All of the major theories of temperament endorse the idea that temperament is rooted in biological differences.[22] The most influential view of temperament has been that of Thomas and colleagues[47, 48] in the New York Longitudinal Study. They viewed temperament as a child's behavioral style, the "how" of behavior as opposed to its content or motivation. Chess and Thomas[49] argued that nine dimensions of temperament best capture the salient features of individual differences in behavioral style. These categories are listed in Table 6–4.

Assessment instruments derived from any of the major theoretical perspectives on temperament have proved problematical. This may explain why few reliable individual differences in temperament have been identified in the first 6 months of life. One source of controversy is that assessments of temperament have typically been obtained from parental reports, but convincing evidence of subjectivity and bias in these reports has led to interest in laboratory-based or home-based measures. Nevertheless, there are no well-validated and widely accepted assessments for tapping a broad range of temperamental dispositions for infants in this age range.

Clinically, there has long been an interest in the construct of difficult temperament, which, despite different definitions, centers on various aspects of emotional expression. There are few clear links between difficult temperament in infancy and subsequent behavior problems unless contextual factors are taken into account. For example, in one study, there was no relationship between difficult temperament at 4 months of age and behavior problems at 3 years of age unless mothers were depressed.[50]

Table 6–4 New York Longitudinal Study Dimensions of Temperament

Temperament Dimensions	Description
Activity level	Overall level of motor activity
Rhythmicity*	Regularity of the infant's biological functioning
Approach-withdrawal*	Tendency for the infant to approach or withdraw around unfamiliar people
Adaptability*	Flexibility to adjust to changes in routine and to new environments
Intensity*	Intensity of the infant's emotional reactions, whatever their content
Mood*	Infant's tendency to display predominantly positive or negative moods
Distractibility	Tendency to react to sensory stimulation
Sensory threshold	Ease with which the infant can be distracted into more socially desirable responses
Persistence	Tendency to sustain attention

*Negative poles describe dimensions of difficult temperament.

Modified from Chess S, Thomas A: Temperament in Clinical Practice. New York: Guilford Press, 1986.

Results such as these suggest that assessing the fit between the infant's characteristics and the environment's responses to those characteristics ought to be clinically useful. Unfortunately, despite its appeal, goodness of fit has not yet been adequately operationalized in investigations.[47, 48, 51] We do not really know what goodness of fit means from an empirical standpoint—indeed, this seems unlikely until we develop improved measures of temperament.

Cognitive Development

At 2 to 3 months after birth, infants develop greatly enhanced cognitive capacities across a number of different types of learning. Infants demonstrate enhanced classical conditioning, operant conditioning, and habituation at about this time. In general, infants become more interested in exploring a wider range of the world around them. Piaget[52] designated this period of external focus as that of secondary circular reactions as the infant behaves to make interesting spectacles last.

Emotional Development

Further elaboration and development of the basic emotions of contentment, distress, and interest, which may be reliably observed in the first 2 months of life, begin after the transition at 2 to 3 months. By the time infants have reached 6 months of age, they exhibit a differentiation of contentment into joy and contentment, of interest into surprise and interest, and of distress into sadness, disgust, and anger.[34]

Lewis[34] has provided a timetable for the emergence of discrete emotional expression. Joy appears soon after the 2- to 3-month transition and is often elicited by familiar faces or events. Sadness appears at about the same time and has been reliably elicited in middle-class, U.S. infants when their mothers stop interacting with them. Disgust appears for the first time also, often in the context of an unpleasant new taste.

Anger is clearly evident somewhat later, perhaps between 4 and 6 months of age,[53] although it has been demonstrated as early as 2 months in specially designed experimental situations.[54] Because it includes a response designed to overcome some obstacle to a goal, the emergence of anger must be closely tied to the cognitive capacity needed to appreciate the relationship of a means to an end.[34] This suggests that at least a limited form of means-end differentiation must be available to human infants even before 7 months of age.

Communicative Development

Communicative behavior of infants changes after the 2- to 3-month transition. Infant vocalizations become more clearly social as infants begin to react to vocalizations from others and to coo responsively. Patterns of turn taking in vocalizations begin to appear at this time, suggesting far greater appreciation by infants of the behavior of their interactive partners.

Expressive communication at 2 to 3 months includes production of several different vowel sounds (e.g., ah, eh, uh) as well as some simple mutual imitation. Coos, squeals, and screams appear at about 2 months, followed by consonants at 4 to 6 months, as infants begin to babble using repetitive syllable sequences, such as da-da-da.[55]

Advances in receptive language are apparent after the 2- to 3-month transition as well. In addition to the enhanced ability to take into account the behavior of others, infants begin to localize the source of voice sounds and noisemakers. They attend and respond differently to different affects in caregivers, such as anger and playfulness.[55]

These enhanced receptive and expressive communicative capacities are central components of a blossoming of social behavior that appears concurrently. Essentially, these changes in communicative behavior make possible a qualitative advance in infants' abilities as social partners.

Social Development

Enhanced eye-to-eye contact, diminished crying, more sustained wakefulness and periods of quiet alertness, and blossoming of the social smile all contribute to a sense of the infant as a more playful and engaging social partner after the 2- to 3-month transition. Therefore, it is not surprising that a great deal of attention has been paid to infants' social behavior in the period from 2 to 7 months. Individual differences in infant-parent interactive behaviors, as measured by features such as matching emotional states, synchrony, reciprocity, and turn taking, have been related to infants' cognitive competence,[56] emotion regulation,[57] language development,[55] and sense of self.[13, 17]

Infants who are interacting with their caregivers between 2 and 7 months engage in alternating periods of engagement and disengagement, or time-outs. The interactive pattern of a dyad may be thought of as a mutual feedback system in which each partner's behavior affects the other's in ongoing transactions over time.[58, 59] Infants are more likely to respond to changes in their mothers' behavior if mothers are more responsive to changes in their behavior.[59]

What sustains play periods or social interaction for infants at this age is maintaining the level of stimulation within some optimal range.[37] If caregivers provide too little feedback, infants lose interest and turn their attention elsewhere. If caregivers are too stimulating, infants avert their gaze or otherwise interrupt or even terminate the interaction until the stimulation is reduced to a level that they can tolerate.

Although much of the literature on infant-parent interaction has emphasized matching affective states, infants and their caregivers actually spend little time in matching states, even when observed in situations designed to maximize opportunities for interaction.[60] This has led Tronick and colleagues[60, 61] to speculate that infants' coping strategies are challenged by their efforts to effect repair of mismatching affective states and interactive errors. These efforts would then stimulate efforts to attain reparation and effectance. Some preliminary work has demonstrated links between individual differences in infants' emotion regulation efforts at this age and subsequent development. For example, infants who used more positive efforts to elicit responsiveness from their mothers (when the mothers had been instructed to refrain from responding) were more likely to be securely attached at 1 year of age.[62]

Repeated patterns of social interaction are remembered and even anticipated by infants between 2 and 7 months. If mothers are instructed not to respond in their usual ways to infant displays, infants exhibit negative affect and behavioral dysregulation.[59] The nature of these early social expectations is believed to have great importance for how infants anticipate and experience intimacy in later relationships.[13, 63]

Summary of the 2- to 3-Month Transition

Dramatic changes in developmental capacities across a number of domains appear at 2 to 3 months after birth, changing both infants' behavior and the behavior of caregiving adults. All of these changes enhance infants' appeal to others as a more responsive and enjoyable social partner. The nature of caregivers' responsiveness to infants is associated with relationship characteristics that probably have far-reaching implications for infant development. Infants' efforts at adaptation within the goal-correcting system of interaction with their primary caregivers provide an early feel for what it is like to be with another in an intimate relationship.

7- to 9-Month Transition

At 7 to 9 months, another major developmental transition occurs. This has been one of the best studied transitions from biological, cognitive, communicative, and socioemotional perspectives. Emde[10] has termed this shift the "onset of focused attachment," and Stern[13] has termed it "the discovery of intersubjectivity." Both of these conceptualizations call attention to the enhanced importance of subjective experience for infants that develops at this time.

Biological-Neurological Development

Evidence for changes in brain development at this time is extensive. As Fischer and Rose[19] have pointed out, these have included changes in electroencephalographic frequency, power, and coherence; changes in patterns of glucose metabolism documented through positron emission tomographic scanning techniques; and a spurt of growth in head circumference and brain growth.[64–68] Research has also demonstrated that selected portions of the limbic system are myelinated at this time.[42] These documented changes are all compatible with a hypothesized qualitative change in central nervous system functioning that may be associated with other qualitative changes in motor, cognitive, emotional, and social domains of development.

Fischer and Rose[19] have suggested that biological changes associated with other developmental advances at these times must include connections between the frontal cortex and other regions because more sophisticated cognitive and communicative skills require coordination of components, which is a frontal region function. In keeping with this reasoning, a new rise in glucose metabolism in the frontal lobes occurs at the time of the 7- to 9-month transition.[43] Also, Bell and Fox[64] demonstrated that both electroencephalographic frequency and coherence change at the time of this transition, implying that they reflect improved inhibitory control of higher centers and enhanced associative pathway links. Having more sophisticated coordination of pathways probably makes possible the qualitatively different behavioral advances that are apparent at this time.

With regard to temperament, individual differences in the second half of the first year and first half of the second year may be a bit more stable than in the first 6 months of life, although the absence of an agreed upon "gold standard" assessment procedure has limited interpretability of findings. The general trend is for parental convergence about temperamental differences to increase during this time, although lack of convergence between parental report and observer ratings of temperament remains a formidable challenge.[69]

Cognitive Development

In the cognitive realm, dramatic advances are apparent. Infants are now able to use one scheme as a means of obtaining another scheme that is a desired goal. For example, infants know that they can pull a string to reach an attractive toy to which the string is attached. This means-end behavior is the prototype of all later problem-solving behavior. In addition, infants demonstrate object permanence; that is, infants purposefully remove a cloth covering a hidden object that seems to have disappeared under it. This suggests that infants possess an enhanced ability to retain a mental image of the absent object.

This enhanced capacity has been used to explain the development of stranger reaction and separation protest, which appear for the first time after the 7- to 9-month transition. Infants begin to protest separations from their primary caregivers and react with increased wariness or outright distress when approached by unfamiliar adults. Kagan and colleagues[41] pointed out that separation protest and stranger reactions require a second maturational ability to emerge, an enhanced capacity to anticipate possible events in the future.

Also in the cognitive realm, infants begin for the first time to explore novel properties of objects and to pursue novelty for its own sake. The notions of causality advance, and infants at this age develop a clearer understanding of the independence of objects and that these objects carry with them their own properties. Infants also begin to experiment with different ways of accomplishing goals when their initial efforts are thwarted.[52]

A tendency for infants to explore the unfamiliar and to attempt to master challenges through repeated practice appears in the latter part of the first year and has been termed *mastery motivation*. Mastery behaviors are believed to reflect an innate motivational system in human infants. As assessed in the laboratory, mastery has been shown to be stable over months and to be predictive of subsequent cognitive performance.[70, 71] Mastery behaviors are related to pleasurable exploration and curiosity and appear to represent early indicators of competence. To date, most efforts to capture these behaviors in the laboratory have been concerned with cognitive rather than social competence.

Progress toward symbolic or pretend play begins to emerge after the 7- to 9-month transition, although true pretend play does not appear until after the 18- to 20-month transition. Whereas before 9 months, infants' play with toys consists largely of banging, mouthing, or visually inspecting them, by about 12 months functional play appears. At this age, infants may hold a telephone receiver properly, then let it go, or hug a baby doll. Over the course of the next 6 months, other-directed play generally increases until true pretend play emerges.

Perhaps the most important cognitive development in terms of its social and communicative implications for the infant is the discovery of *intersubjectivity*.[72] This refers to a variety of changes in infant behavior that seem to indicate that infants now understand that their own inner experience, that is, their thoughts, feelings, and desires, can be appreciated by and shared with others. Furthermore, they also behave as if they understand the thoughts and desires of others. This ability to share thoughts and feelings with others represents a monumental discovery for infants, with far-reaching implications for the development of empathy and the subjective experience of intimacy. Interestingly, it has become a focus in research on autism, with some studies suggesting that intersubjectivity is one of the earlier social milestones never achieved by individuals with autism.[73]

Emotional Development

One of the more important clinical and developmental phenomena that intersubjectivity makes possible is *affect attunement*.[13] Affect attunement between mother and infant involves an emotional interchange in which the mother matches her behavior to the infant's behavior. This matching is not imitative; rather, it involves some aspect of an internal feeling state that is shared. Affect attunement appears to be an essential ingredient of empathy, intimacy, mirroring, and other clinical phenomena.

Emotions begin to be used instrumentally for the first time after the 7- to 9-month transition.[10] Smiling and pouting expressions mark infants' efforts to get their own way. For the first time, anger is often directed purposefully at another person. Parental report studies have suggested that parents as well as observers note that infants begin to use affects as a means to an end toward the latter half of the first year.[74]

Infants also begin to detect and share affective states with their social partners. *Social referencing* describes infants' use of cues from others to resolve affective uncertainty. If a mother and her 1-year-old are in a playroom and a noisy and flashing toy robot advances toward the infant, the infant looks at the mother's face. If the mother smiles encouragingly, the child is likely to smile and perhaps to approach the robot. If the mother looks frightened, on the other hand, the infant is likely to cry or to approach the caregiver for comfort. Hirshberg and Svejda[75] demonstrated that infants are just as likely to reference their fathers as their mothers.

Mahler and colleagues[17] suggested that exuberance and joy are the dominant emotions at around 1 year of age, noting that infants at this age also demonstrate a relative imperviousness to frustration. These observations have not yet been subjected to any attempt at empirical confirmation.

Communicative Development

The importance of intersubjectivity for communicative development cannot be overstated. After the 7- to 9-month transition, infants begin to behave not only as if they understand others but also as if they anticipate that others will understand them. Infants younger than 7 months may reach for desired objects, but they do not check back to the caregiver's face in an appeal for help. After 9 months, infants behave as if they attribute to the other person comprehension of their own intention and the capacity to satisfy that intention.

The emergence of *intentional communication* is one of the hallmarks of the 7- to 9-month transition, with major implications for the infant's new appreciation of both self and other. In contrast to Mahler,[17] who viewed infants at this age as only beginning to emerge from symbiotic unity with their mothers, Stern[13] has argued convincingly that it is only after infants develop intersubjectivity that they can even conceive of the kind of unity that Mahler presupposes to be present at birth.

Advances in symbolic functioning after the 7- to 9-month transition also have communicative implications. Infants understand by 8 to 10 months that a word is agreed upon to designate a specific object. By 1 year of age infants may have an expressive vocabulary of a few words, although gestural communication dominates in interactions until the latter part of the second year.[76]

Social Development

Of course, biological, cognitive, emotional, and communicative developments at the 7- to 9-month transition have major implications for infant social development. Stern[13] has emphasized that what infants discover at the 7- to 9-month transition is that their own inner subjective experiences may be shared with someone else. Intentional communications via gestures that convey "I want a cookie," affective sharing that conveys "This is exciting!" or joint referencing that conveys "Look at that toy" are all evidence of intersubjectivity. When this occurs, interpersonal relatedness has moved in part from overt actions and responses to the internal subjective states lying behind the actual behaviors. Stern[13] has emphasized that infants not only feel different to others but also experience others differently. At this point the infant not only experiences caregiver empathy through overt behavioral responses but also directly experiences the subjective empathic process of which these responses are only a part. Still, there is another monumentally important social development at this time—the infant "falls in love."

Although the attachment relationship between caregiver and infant begins to develop at birth, it becomes increasingly focused during the latter half of the first year as separation protest develops and stranger reactions appear. By the time the infant is 1 year old, the quality of the attachment relationship to a particular caregiver can be measured categorically. A laboratory procedure known as the Strange Situation Procedure involves observing how 11- to 20-month-old infants organize their behavior around attachment figures when they are mildly stressed by being in a strange room, encountering an unfamiliar adult, and being left briefly by their attachment figure.[77] The most important parts of the procedure from the standpoint of classifying the infant's attachment relationship are the two reunion episodes between infant and caregiver after separation. Infants' relationships with their caregivers are classified as secure or as one of several types of insecure, depending on their behavior in these reunion episodes.

The Strange Situation Procedure has been widely investigated and is the subject of considerable controversy. Dozens of studies exploring the reliability and validity of the procedure have been completed (for reviews, see Sroufe[78] and Zeanah and Emde[79]), and a few conclusions about infant attachment classifications are widely shared.

First, securely or insecurely attached infants in the strange situation experience different patterns of parent-infant interaction during the first year of life. Sensitive and responsive caregiving has been associated with secure attachment. The specific patterns of parenting associated with the different types of insecure attachments are less clear, but they lack the features of caregiving that are associated with secure attachments.

Second, infants assessed several months apart with the Strange Situation Procedure tend to maintain the same attachment classifications, barring major changes in family stresses and supports. This suggests that what is measured is something fairly robust rather than something transitory. When the security of attachment changes, it changes congruently with changes in stresses and social supports.

Neither infant behavior nor temperament in the first year has been shown to predict secure versus insecure attachment, but this is an active area of investigation at present. It is believed that temperament is related to the type of security or insecurity the infant exhibits. Attachment classifications are not within-child traits (as temperament is believed to be); instead, these classifications summarize salient features of the relationship pattern between an infant and a particular caregiver. The clearest evidence for this is that infants' attachment classifications with different caregivers may be different.[80] Moreover, Steele and associates[81] identified differential characteristics in mothers and in fathers that were predictive of mother-infant and father-infant attachment measured more than a year later.

Infants classified as securely or insecurely attached to their primary caregivers at 12 and 18 months differ emotionally and behaviorally in preschool and school-age years.[82–84] At present, one of the best predictors in infancy of later adaptation is the security of the infant's attachment to the primary caregiver as measured by the Strange Situation Procedure.

Summary of the 7- to 9-Month Transition

Infants emerge from this period of developmental transformation quite differently from the way they entered it—in cognitive, communicative, emotional, and social terms. After the 7- to 9-month transition, infants act as if they understand that their thoughts, feelings, and actions can be understood by another person, and they have strong preferences for caregivers with whom they have established relationships. The dual capacities for intersubjectivity and focused attachment underlie the specific changes in capacities that develop at this time. These changes continue to develop and to be refined throughout the next year, but their appearance for the first time after the 7- to 9-month transition makes infants at this age qualitatively different social experiencers and agents.[13] Under usual circumstances, after 7 to 9 months, infants have developed a strong preference for turning to a relatively small number of caregiving adults for nurturance and comfort. By having their caregiver function as a secure base, they can use their more sophisticated motor capacities for independent locomotion to explore the world exuberantly.

18- to 20-Month Transition

The final transition period of major reorganization in infancy occurs at age 18 to 20 months. Although this transition is marked dramatically by the appearance of language, it is actually the qualitative change in *symbolic representation* that underlies the child's remarkable advances in language, cognition, affect, and social functioning at this age. These advances predate the evolution of infants' moral development, which burgeons after the 18- to 20-month transition. After this transition, much of what follows in the third year involves further elaboration, refinement, and consolidation of the functions that emerge during the transition.

Biological-Neurological Development

Much remains to be learned about specific dimensions of brain development at 18 months and about the relationships between this development and changes in behavior at this time. Evidence suggests that there are important associations between changes in central nervous system structure and function and the spurt of capacities noted to appear in other domains of development across this period of reorganization.

One of the important spurts of brain growth in the first 2 years of life occurs at about 18 to 20 months.[19] Density of dendritic spines, which represent sites of synaptic contact, decreases postnatally and almost reaches adult levels by 21 months of age.[85] Myelination of structures associated with language appears at this time.[42] Associated behavioral changes need to be studied in relation to these anatomical developments.

Functional changes are apparent as well. Although local cerebral metabolic rates for glucose in infants qualitatively resemble those of adults by 1 year of age, they typically reach levels comparable to those of adults in the second year.[43]

Discontuities in event-related potentials between 13 and 20 months have been documented in association with processing of language. Specifically, by studying differential responses of brain electrical activity to comprehended and unknown words, investigators have demonstrated that different parts of the brain are involved in language comprehension.[86] Whereas diffuse patterns of activity were widely distributed over the anterior and posterior parts of both hemispheres in toddlers before 18 months, by 20 months they had become more localized to temporal and parietal regions of the left hemisphere.

These data suggest increasing lateral and anterior-posterior specialization of brain systems responsible for language comprehension at the 18- to 20-month transition. In fact, individual differences in language competence have been associated with the degree of specialization of brain function.[86]

In the realm of temperament, behavioral inhibition is a trait that has been reliably identified after the 18- to 20-month transition. Kagan and colleagues[87] have suggested that behavioral inhibition to the unfamiliar characterizes about 10% of middle-class white 2-year-olds and is counterbalanced by a roughly equal number of children deemed uninhibited. Descriptively, inhibited infants strongly avoid novel stimuli. Kagan and colleagues[87] have suggested that despite the poles of inhibited and uninhibited, behavioral responsivity in the face of novelty does not represent a continuum. Instead, they believe that behaviorally inhibited children represent a qualitatively different group. In support of this assertion, they have demonstrated stability of the trait for 4 years and associated it with physiological activation of the hypothalamic-pituitary-adrenal axis, the reticular activating system, and the sympathetic arm of the central nervous system.[87, 88] Furthermore, infants of adults with panic disorder exhibit high incidences of behavioral inhibition.[89] These results have led Kagan and colleagues to suggest that behavioral inhibition is a heritable trait that is mediated through central and peripheral nervous systems and predisposes infants to anxious and inhibited behavior in a variety of novel contexts.

Cognitive Development

A qualitative advance in symbolic representation at 18 to 20 months is believed to be the central cognitive development occurring at this time. More sophisticated symbolic representation makes possible significant advances in infants' understanding of causality, including the ability to infer causes based on observed effects and to anticipate effects based on their actions. They are also able to remember specific past events and sequences even when no sign of the event or sequence remains. This capacity allows the infant access to two versions of the same reality: a representation of the original act as performed by the other and a representation of their own anticipated performance of the act. This seems to require some representation of the self as an objective entity.

In fact, Lewis and Brooks-Gunn[90] and Kagan[91] have provided evidence of the emergence of an objective self at 18 months. Experimental studies have demonstrated toddlers' clear facial recognition of themselves in mirrors, in still photographs, and in videotapes. In addition, self-awareness has been demonstrated by self-descriptive utterances, by a variety of gestural directives, and by emotional reactions to success or failure. Personal pronouns begin to be used at this time. Gender identity appears to consolidate at this point, although it is not until about age 5 years that children attain gender constancy wherein they recognize that gender is an immutable characteristic of the individual.[92]

A further dramatic implication of symbolic representation occurs in the realm of pretend play. Whereas younger toddlers' play is generally self directed, by the time a child is 18 months the play has become progressively more other directed and is more sustained. True pretend play emerges at this time and becomes progressively richer and more complex.

The importance of all of these advances is that infants can, for the first time, entertain and maintain a formed wish of how they would like reality to be, even if this is different from fact.[13] Internal experience of social interactions now include wishes that involve past memories, present realities, and expectations of the future.

The gains of symbolic representation continue to be extended and refined after 18 months. By about 2 years of age children begin to compare themselves to various evaluative standards, such as "I am small" or "I am pretty." Children move into Piaget's preoperational stage in the third year of life. By this time, they have advanced sufficiently that we may consider the ways in which their thinking differs from that of adults. Piaget's work reminds us, for instance, that children's judgments are limited by their perceptions of objects and events and that they have difficulty attending to more than one perceptual attribute at a time.[52] Furthermore, egocentrism describes children's difficulty viewing events from any perspective other then their own. Similarly, toddlers at this age may have some difficulty differentiating between subjective experiences and objective reality. Piaget also noted that toddlers use transductive reasoning in which events are believed to be causally related merely by temporal or spatial juxtaposition.

Emotional Development

Emotional development at 18 months has been less carefully studied than cognitive or language development. The observational studies of Mahler suggest that the exuberance and ebullience of the previous 6 months change as infants become more irritable, more somber, and more clingy. Mahler and colleagues[17] view this as evidence of the rapprochement crisis in which toddlers are for the first time aware of their separateness from mother and of their own relative powerlessness and ineffectiveness. Stern[13] has argued that the somberness and irritability of this period derive from the toddlers' sense of verbal estrangement from their own experience.[13] That is, their well-developed sense of their own subjective experiences as lived cannot yet be adequately represented by language, leading to observable frustration and emotional turmoil. Nevertheless, it should be pointed out that there have not been systematic investigations validating the observations on which Mahler's and Stern's explanations are based, although this remains an important area for future research.

Some of the most important work on emotional development at this transition is that of Lewis and colleagues[93] on the emergence of self-conscious emotions including the emotions of embarrassment, empathy, and envy. They appear not to emerge until the toddler demonstrates self-recognition at about 18 months. Lewis[34] also asserts that the cognitive development of comparing one's behavior to an evaluative standard, which probably appears at around 24 months of age, is required for the development of self-conscious evaluative emotions such as guilt, pride, and shame.

Moral Development

Emde and colleagues[94, 95] have considered the implications of cognitive and emotional advances at the 18- to 20-month transition for the development of morality. Toddlers at this age are able to generate and to monitor the attainment of their goals much more competently than before. They are also able to construct value labels and normative standards based on the evaluations of others[91] and to react with distress to violations of these standards, including broken toys and disapproved of behaviors.[57] The emergence of the "moral emotions" of embarrassment, empathy, envy, pride, shame, and guilt at this age are core accompaniments of these various cognitive manifestations of moral development. These emotions have important implications for the infant's subjective experience of morality.

By about 24 months of age, infants begin to demonstrate an internalization of parental standards in the presence of parents, although consistent demonstrations of this in their parents' absence probably do not occur until at least 36 months of age.[95] Of course, different parental styles are associated with important individual differences in moral development. Considerable evidence in U.S. families suggests that power-assertive strategies by parents are associated with an increase in children's defiant behavior, whereas reasoning and negotiation on the part of the parent facilitate internalization of the parent's standards.[57]

Communicative Development

Language makes possible a dramatic advance in the infant's capacity for relatedness to others. Considerable variability in language production is so common that it is difficult to describe modal patterns. At 18 months, U.S. toddlers have a median expressive vocabulary of 50 words with a range of less than 10 for those at the 10th percentile to more than 200 words for those at the 90th percentile. Short-term stability in expressive language is high, but the long-term implications of differences at this age are largely unknown.[76]

Toddlers use words for a variety of different social functions between 18 and 24 months. Although language comprehension generally precedes production, Bretherton and Bates[96] found that the magnitude of the gap varied considerably from child to child. New evidence suggests that some infants may produce word utterances before they understand the meaning of the utterances, so that comprehension of a particular word does not always precede production of that word.

By age 24 months, the U.S. toddler has a median expressive vocabulary of about 200 words with a range of less than 50 for those at the 10th percentile to more than 500 words for those at the 90th percentile.[76] They begin to combine two or more words and to recognize that the combination means more than either word can convey in isolation. Nevertheless, toddlers' comprehension remains heavily dependent on social cues, as most parents who attempt to have their 2-year-olds "talk to grandma" on the telephone can attest. As toddlers' language learning progresses, they begin to realize that different forms of messages have different effects on different listeners. Two- and 3-year-olds are beginning to infer what listeners know and do not know, because they ask significantly more questions when interacting with adults instead of peers, simplify their speech when talking to younger children, and whine almost exclusively in the presence of their parents.

Stern[13] has pointed out that a toddler is on the way to being able to narrate his or her own life stories. This carries with it numerous possibilities for changing one's view of oneself. What toddlers tell in stories about themselves to others and to themselves and how they tell these stories probably have crucial developmental implications.

Social Development

Symbolic representation permits the child to appreciate more about social relationships. Most theories of development have emphasized conflicts between toddlers and their caregivers because of an increasing move by infants toward autonomy. Interestingly, however, as famous as the "terrible twos" are, there have been no investigations that have addressed the question of difficult behavior in 2-year-olds and whether or not it differs systematically from difficult behavior in 1- or 3-year-olds. A number of contextual factors are probably important, and it is plausible that different infants and toddlers are perceived as more or less challenging at different ages by different parents. As one example, Crockenberg[97] found that adolescent mothers who had both experienced rejection in childhood and received little support from partners after the birth of their infants were more likely to be angry and punitive with their toddlers. The toddlers, in turn, were angry and noncompliant and distanced themselves from their mothers.

In the third year of life, toddlers become far more aware of their relation to others in groups and more sensitive to being included or excluded. Along with increasing independence, toddlers develop a sense of personal space and possession.[10] At this age, toddlers are also able to perceive their own self-efficacy.[98] Social relationships, especially attachment relationships, become increasingly important referents for children's self-appraisal. Sroufe and Matas[99] showed that 2-year-old children with secure attachments to their primary caregivers showed more competent autonomous functioning in stressful problem-solving situations. In preschool years, securely attached infants were more socially competent and more ego resilient than anxiously attached infants.[82, 84]

With peers, children begin to move from having little to do with others to engaging in complex and mutually gratifying cooperative play. In naturalistic observations of interactive play, parallel play, in which children played in proximity but without interaction, emerged at around 18 months but did not become common until the end of the second year. Episodes of fleeting contact, which contained a clear invitation to interaction but were not sustained beyond one- or two-step exchanges, also emerged as early as 18 months but were more common in the third year.[100]

Dominance hierarchies appear in the third year, presumably as a means of controlling aggression. Aggressive interchanges in children's groups occur almost exclusively among members who are quite close to one another in the hierarchy. This implies, of course, that children are able to detect and to respond to subtle social cues about relationships. Troy and Sroufe[83] demonstrated the behavioral manifestations of such detection by studying patterns of victim-victimizer play in pairs of preschool children. They found, as predicted, that children with a history of secure attachment in infancy were neither victims nor victimizers, whereas children with a history of avoidant attachment were always engaged in victim-victimizer interactions when paired with another insecurely attached child.

Summary of the 18- to 20-Month Transition

Infants change profoundly during the 18- to 20-month transition. New biological developments appear to make possible significant advances in symbolic representation, which are in turn associated with dramatic cognitive, emotional, communicative, and social advances. Infants are substantially more verbal, both in understanding others' directives to them and in making their own intentions apparent to others, and this affects both their emotional experience and their social relatedness. Stern[13] has emphasized that the changes at 18 to 20 months also introduce a new sense of self, the verbal self, in which individuals experience both the power and the limitations of language for expressing their most important ideas and feelings.

After all of these dramatic changes, infants consolidate and enhance their new capacities during the third year of life as they prepare to move into wider social spheres of peer and teacher influences in the preschool years. By the time children reach their third birthdays they have available a sophisticated repertoire of skills for communicating and experiencing relationships. Qualitative features of their caregiving context during the first 3 years of life shape their expectations of relationship as they move into the broader social world.

Risk and Protective Factors

Throughout this review of development, we have set aside the biological and environmental factors that may adversely affect infant development and eventually lead to dysfunction. Given the greater understanding of development that is now available, it is important to address how maladaptive patterns appear and how they may influence lines of development. A central focus of the research in developmental psychopathology is on describing the processes of adaptive and maladaptive development and the mechanisms by which risk and protective factors influence developmental processes. The impressive cognitive and social competence of infants and the important biobehavioral shifts during this period of rapid developmental change support the notion that infancy is a critical time to study these mechanisms. Furthermore, the emphasis on longitudinal study of these mechanisms has major implications for prevention of mental disorders, and infancy has long been recognized as an important time for initiating preventive efforts.[101]

Research in developmental psychopathology has been influenced by increasingly sophisticated models of development designed to capture the complex interrelationships between biological, interpersonal, and wider social factors. Given this complexity, it is not surprising that research on how risk and protective factors affect development has rarely supported the notion that the transmission of risk is specific and linear in nature.[102] For example, maternal depression is related not just to an increased incidence of childhood depression but also to a host of other less specific outcomes.[103] Furthermore, multiple risk conditions from different domains (e.g., biological, psychological, or social) may occur simultaneously and may, in turn, be exacerbated or ameliorated by the infant's caregiving.[102, 104] This has led to the important observation that the total number of risk conditions affecting an infant may be more predictive of competence in later life than exposure to any specific single risk factor.[105]

Rutter[106] has suggested that the field must move toward understanding protective processes as well as documenting mechanisms by which risk conditions operate. Indeed, a risk condition that sets off a negative chain reaction in one infant may immunize another against future developmental deviance merely by allowing the infant to overcome that condition.[106] In this case, the presence of other risk conditions or of critical protective factors in the infant or environment is likely to account for the difference in outcome.

Illustrative Risk Conditions

Defining what constitutes a risk factor or condition is somewhat arbitrary, and many risk factors have been postulated. Nevertheless, the four illustrative areas that are reviewed in this section and summarized in Table 6–5 have been studied extensively. Most studies document effects on broad outcomes in groups of infants and families exposed to

Table 6–5 Developmental Risk Factors

Risk Factor	Biological Effect	Psychological Effect	Social Effect
Poverty	Malnutrition	Attachment problems	Family dysfunction, environmental threat
Child maltreatment	Trauma effects, failure to thrive	Disturbed affective responsiveness, poor social interaction, attachment problems	Antisocial behavior and conduct disorder
Maternal substance abuse	Impaired prenatal central nervous system development	Inconsistent and unpredictable parenting, attachment problems	Family dysfunction
Premature birth and serious illness in infancy	Delayed or disrupted central nervous system development, increased developmental disorders	Increased parental stress	Environmental destabilization

a given risk condition, and the results of these investigations provide only limited information about a particular infant and its family. We move from a discussion of broader social risk conditions toward more biological risk conditions, with the important caveat that risk conditions only rarely occur in isolation.

Poverty

Poverty has long been recognized as a powerful risk condition with myriad developmental implications. Its effects are considered to be largely nonspecific and may be mediated through many associated factors (e.g., teenage parenting, poor education) that are more common in families who are economically disadvantaged. In fact, poverty is probably best understood as a risk condition that is an aggregate of many separate risk factors. An approach to considering this topic has centered on breaking down poverty into its component parts, allowing the researcher to attempt to tease apart the critical specific factors that are most related to outcomes of interest.

Poverty is defined in the United States by household income—currently, the cutoff is $13,000 per year for a family of four. Approximately two thirds of poor infants are supported by welfare and the same number live in mother-only families.[107] Of the 700,000 poor children younger than 2 years old in the United States, 40% live in inner cities and 30% live in rural areas. More than one half of the parents of these children's have not completed high school, and approximately one half of all mothers in poverty began parenting in their teenage years.

There are biological risks associated with poverty, some of which exert influences before birth and contribute to the high neonatal and postneonatal mortality indices in this country. From a lack of prenatal care to poor peripartum nutritional status and higher rates of prenatal drug and alcohol exposure, infants born into poverty often face early hurdles. These problems may be compounded by the higher rates of lead intoxication and iron deficiency in poor infants compared with infants raised in more economically advantaged homes. Each of these variables has been shown via well-designed studies to have significant effects on cognitive function in infants; together they may have synergistic effects that are severe. Finally, rates of hospitalization are higher and lengths of stay longer for poor infants, suggesting a diminished access to preventive medical care.

These biological factors may be ameliorated or exacerbated by a host of psychological and social factors. As with biological risk, there are group differences in the prevalence and severity of the different component factors given later. Although they may be more common in poor families, none are exclusive to poor families, and the clinician is left having to screen for these problems in each individual case.

The most devastating effects of poverty may be on the family, including factors such as parenting style, responsiveness, and resulting family cohesiveness.[108] There has been some research focused on parenting style and its relationship to poverty. On the whole, data collected regarding caregiving environments in families faced with poverty suggest that infants may compete for parental attention against many instrumental factors to which parents must attend. Furthermore, there appears to be an overall pattern of reduced or inconsistent attentiveness to infants in these settings, often because of the parents' own history of inadequate nurturance (for a review, see Halpern[109]). The consequences of this intergenerational transmission of parenting vulnerability not uncommonly include hostile, intrusive interactions by toddlerhood.[110] These interactions appear to be associated with the increased incidence of anxious and disorganized attachment in samples with low socioeconomic status[110, 111] and may interact with other factors to predict insecure attachment across time in low-income families.[112]

The consequences of insecure and/or disorganized attachment have been addressed in longitudinal research. These patterns are predictive of subsequent behavioral problems, impulse control problems, low self-esteem, disordered peer relations, and poor cognitive performance.[83, 113–116] These associations are suggestive of the seeds of disruptive behavior disorders, and longitudinal studies suggest that socioeconomic status is a powerful predictor of, among other things, conduct disorder in children.[117, 118] The rates of disorder appear to be linked to high-deliquency neighborhoods where children are exposed to high rates of adult criminal behavior, substance abuse, and child maltreatment.[119] Here, the association of poverty with other risk factors for antisocial behavior may represent the final link in a chain reaction begun by poor perinatal nutrition, insufficient maternal responsiveness, and insecure or disorganized attachment.

In fact, it is the accumulation of biological, psychological, and/or social risk factors that accounts for the association of poverty with numerous adverse outcomes in childhood. Each of these factors appears to exert nonspecific effects, so that the exact mechanisms by which they are related to outcome are difficult to untangle and often inconsistent in different individuals. The clinician is faced with putting the individual puzzle together for each infant to reduce the toll of these complex effects on eventual outcome.

Child Maltreatment

Child maltreatment is another broad risk condition related in its etiology to complex interactions between separate risk factors and in its outcome to a variety of possible effects on young children. Physical abuse is the leading cause of death for children younger than 1 year old in the United States. In 1990, 160,392 children younger than 3 years old were abused and/or neglected. These cases account for more than 25% of all child abuse victims in the United States.[120] The first year of life has the highest incidence of child maltreatment in all years from birth to age 18 years, and more than two thirds of child victims of physical abuse are younger than 6 years old.[121] The so-called shaken infant syndrome is particularly devastating and is associated with high morbidity and mortality. Intracranial hemorrhages (typically in the subdural space) and retinal detachment that result, along with intra-abdominal injuries, account for most cases of death and disability related to physical abuse in this age group.[122]

Another common presentation of child maltreatment in infancy is the syndrome of failure to thrive. As many as 35% of all cases of failure to thrive are considered to be due to parental neglect, and it is estimated that 5% to 10% of all children who fail to thrive have also been physically abused.[121] Because severe malnutrition in the first 6 months of life may have permanent neurological sequelae, failure to thrive may be associated with significant morbidity in a minority of cases.

Although there appear to be associations between child maltreatment and poverty, unemployment, child disability, parental psychopathology, parental substance abuse, parental history of childhood maltreatment, and parental antisocial behavior, none of these conditions alone or in combination are either necessary or sufficient to predict abuse. Attempts to reconcile these facts have led to models designed to understand child maltreatment in the family and in the wider social contexts in which it occurs. In these contexts and influenced by any or all of the associated factors previously given, some parents may withdraw from their children, resulting in neglect; others may strike out at their children, leading to emotional or physical abuse; still others may use their children for sexual gratification. Frequently, different forms of maltreatment exist together in a given family, and there is some evidence that simply witnessing abuse of a sibling or violence between parents may be harmful to children.[123]

Researchers studying the outcomes related to child maltreatment are similarly challenged to integrate numerous coexisting factors. For infants, whose capacities to remember and integrate abusive experiences are different from those of older children, these issues are doubly complex. The limited data gathered prospectively regarding the effects of child maltreatment on the psychological functioning of infants and toddlers suggest problems in multiple domains of functioning. First, infants who have been abused have disturbed patterns of affective responsiveness.[124] Second, they tend to exhibit high levels of anger, especially in interaction with peers during toddlerhood, leading to disturbed patterns of social interactive behavior.[125, 126] These problems probably reflect the high levels of insecure and disorganized patterns of attachment in abused and neglected infants.[127–129] Third, they may also be the seeds of subsequent psychiatric disorders linked to abuse in infancy and childhood.

Child maltreatment in infancy is a serious problem in the United States and results in significant morbidity and mortality. Some of the morbidity may be apparent in early childhood as an abnormal pattern of social relatedness, and there may be significant long-term sequelae including the possibility of an increased incidence of major psychiatric disorders in adulthood.

Maternal Substance Abuse

Substance abuse has long been recognized as a major public health problem in the United States. Statistics indicating that each year between 100,000 and 375,000 women give birth to infants prenatally exposed to illicit drugs (not including alcohol and nicotine) have generated increasing public interest in this problem.[130] In particular, the rising incidence of crack cocaine use among pregnant women has led to increased research in this area, in part because of concern regarding direct toxic effects on infants and possible long-term developmental effects.

The tendency for pregnant substance abusers to use more than one drug and the large number of pre- and postnatal risk factors associated with substance abuse have complicated research in this area. There is no evidence that simple models linking prenatal drug exposure directly to any specific developmental outcome are valid. Instead, as with other broad risk conditions, the interplay among individual biological and psychosocial risk factors must be accounted for in determining the ultimate effect of prenatal drug exposure on infant outcome.

Several important issues in the prenatal period are related to abuse of drugs by pregnant women. First, the drug-using lifestyle is often associated with inadequate nutrition, which may itself affect fetal growth. Second, this problem may be exacerbated by the tendency for substance-abusing women not to receive adequate prenatal care. Third, the issue of the timing, dose, and duration of drug exposure is almost never controlled for in studies in this area, although these factors may be critical in determining possible structural effects on the developing central nervous system. Because these issues are difficult to account for even in the most well-designed studies, the relative effects of drug exposure itself remain obscured. Even the effects of alcohol, long known to have direct toxic effects on developing neurons as evidenced by the fetal alcohol syndrome, appear to be modified by factors unrelated to dosage of exposure.[131, 132]

There are also numerous postnatal factors associated with what has been called the culture of drug abuse that may independently affect infant outcome. First, drug abuse appears to be more common among women living in poverty, especially in the inner cities. Second, there appear to be high rates of parental psychopathology associated with substance abuse during pregnancy. Third, caregiving environments for infants whose mothers abuse drugs may be marked by disorganization, with infants often being exposed to multiple caregivers. Thus, there may be direct and indirect contributors to the high rates of insecure and disorganized attachment in infants prenatally exposed to drugs.[133]

Reports in the media of early research on the effects of prenatal exposure to drugs raised public concern that a generation of "crack infants" would be irreparably damaged, despite the fact that studies were often retrospective and did not control for many prenatal and postnatal associated risk factors. Prospective studies are now under way that attempt to account for drug-associated, environmental risk factors while also delineating possible specific neurobehavioral effects. Neurobehavioral effects are understood to be physiological effects on the developing nervous system that may have behavioral manifestations, such as difficulty with state regulation in the neonatal period. The infant's ability to manage these effects is seen to be partly determined by her or his interactions with the environment, which may serve to heighten or lessen these behavior patterns and their physiological triggers. As yet, there is no consistent picture of what these neurobehavioral effects might be even in the neonatal period, nor are there data on how these effects might be transformed over time (for a review, see Lester and Tronick[134]).

Infants prenatally exposed to drugs and to a collection of these associated risk factors are at high risk for adverse developmental outcome. As with many of the broad risk conditions, this outcome is best predicted by analysis of the number and severity of individual risk factors affecting the infant's proximal environment and the infant's neurobehavioral profile.

Premature Birth and Serious Illness in Infancy

Premature birth and serious medical illness in infancy represent obvious biological risk factors that may significantly influence infant outcome. Given the wide variability in the causes and limitations of severe medical conditions and premature birth, it is probably the interplay of aggregates of risk factors that may eventually lead to negative outcomes. Interestingly, even with great variability in biological risk factors in preterm infants, psychosocial and especially family factors are most predictive of outcome.[2]

Approximately 3% of births in the United States show evidence of major malformations and about 1% of children born weigh less than 1500 g.[135–137] This means that approximately 135,000 infants per year are at heightened risk for major developmental problems. However, these numbers do not account for many of the children who eventually suffer from developmental disorders; in fact, developmental disorders occur in 3 of every 1000 children, a majority of which are not diagnosed until after age 2 years. Most of these developmental disorders have a primarily biological basis (e.g., chromosomal abnormalities, inadequate fetal blood supply, infections), although 10% are idiopathic.[138]

Understanding the developmental pathways for children born biologically compromised is complicated by the fact that there is a wide range of degree of compromise even within types of disorders. This makes outcome research difficult because the groups studied may not be comparable. Furthermore, rates of biological compromise are not equally spread across socioeconomic strata or family composition. For instance, the rate of low birth weight (less than 2500 g) for healthy white women aged 20 to 30 years is 3%, whereas it is as high as 9% for minority teenagers of low socioeconomic status, a higher proportion of whom are single.[139] Although these rates are different primarily because of prenatal psychosocial determinants, these factors define the infant's postnatal environment as well. As for every infant, the particulars of the proximal environment of the medically compromised infant are powerful determinants of long-term functioning. There must also be some consideration regarding experiences common in this group of infants that are of relevance for later development. For instance, the number, length, and timing of hospitalizations in infancy and toddlerhood may affect development significantly.[140]

Research suggests that the etiology of medical compromise in infancy is likely to be less important than the severity of the compromise and the context in which it occurs. A seriously ill infant burdens parents in many ways, both direct and indirect. The stress of caring for the infant may affect marital and family relationships. It may also awaken feelings of shame and guilt in caretakers, thereby further compromising the formation of a stable early relationship. There are often significant financial and social burdens that compound these effects and may further destabilize the infant's proximal environment. Finally, the specific manifestations of the infant's medical status (for example, increased irritability resulting from neurological injury) may influence caregivers' responses.

These problems, common in families dealing with an ill infant, may themselves be potentiated or diminished by associated nonspecific factors, such as socioeconomic status or social support. Here, the context in which the stressors occur helps determine how these stressors affect a given infant and its family. Fortunately, intervention with parents of premature and seriously ill infants often helps to avert a negative chain reaction of parental stressors affecting the infant's caretaking environment and may improve eventual outcome.[141]

Like other broad risk conditions, prematurity and serious medical illness in infancy have direct biological effects that may be modified by associated psychological and social factors impinging on the infant's environment.

Conclusions

The field of developmental psychopathology and the study of risk and protective factors have provided a framework for understanding critical determinants of infant and family functioning and outcome. Poverty, child maltreatment, maternal drug abuse, and serious illness in infancy represent important high-risk conditions. Their eventual effects are determined largely by the associated risk conditions with which they cluster. The mechanisms by which these risk factors exert their effects are not well understood and may be different for different infants. Still, risk assessment has important clinical implications and future research will better identify these mechanisms. Better delineation of risk and protective factors may lead to better understanding of clinical disorders of infancy and beyond.

Disorders of Infancy and Developmental Psychopathology

Disorders of infancy are only beginning to be recognized formally, and the research base for them is necessarily preliminary. The first diagnostic classification system tailored specifically to infants and young children has been published and builds on the *Diagnostic and Statistical Manual of Mental Disorders*, Fourth Edition (DSM-IV).[142, 143]

Four different disorders are reviewed in this section: autism, regulatory disorders, posttraumatic stress disorder, and attachment disorders. Each was chosen to represent a different manifestation of psychopathology along a putative spectrum of more biological etiology in autism and regulatory disorders and less biological etiology in posttraumatic stress and attachment disorders. Table 6–6 provides symptoms and signs of these disorders as they appear developmentally during the first 3 years of life.

Autistic Disorder

Autism is an example of a disorder of infancy whose expression represents a final common pathway of a number of different biological abnormalities of the central nervous system, although qualitative differences in caregiving environments may be significant for affected individuals.

By definition, autism must be manifest in infancy, although how early it may be definitively diagnosed is

Table 6–6 Disorders of Infancy and Development in the First 3 Years

Disorder	First 2 Months	2–7 Months	7–18 Months	After 18 Months
Autism	No clear indicators despite some prenatal risk factors.	Failure to reach out in anticipation of pickup by familiar caregiver or to show interest in or affection toward family members.	Intersubjectivity does not develop. Also, intentional communication, affect sharing, means-end differentiation, and imitation are all restricted or absent.	Symbolic play is selectively deficient.
Regulatory disorder	Generally not apparent, although colic and sleep disturbances may be present. State regulation difficulties apparent.	Difficulty in organizing and maintaining a calm, alert, and positive emotional state. Also demonstrates over- or underreactivity to various sensory stimuli or motor difficulties.	Same as previous age range.	Same as previous age range.
Posttraumatic stress disorder	Not reported.	Simple phobic reactions reported.	Fewer symptoms of reexperiencing the traumatic event than in older children, but symptoms of numbing of responsiveness and hyperarousal similar to older children.	Similar to clinical picture in older children except less able to describe subjective experiences and new symptoms of fear and aggression are common.
Attachment disorder	Not apparent.	Not present. Precursors include interactive anomalies or unusual social behaviors.	Failure to exhibit a preferred caregiver at times when in need of comfort, or distortions in use of caregiver as a secure base, or signs and symptoms of grief after loss of primary caregiver.	Same as previous period. Secure base distortions may become more common than in previous period.

unclear. Nonspecific cognitive and social abnormalities, particularly those affecting parent-infant interaction, have been noted by parents and by investigators in the first few months of life, although it is not until after the transition at 7 to 9 months that a number of more specific indicators are apparent.[144–146] Soon after this transition, marked abnormalities in imitation, means-end differentiation, and affect sharing become apparent, as well as expressive delays in communication. Intersubjectivity, one of the hallmark developments at this time, is never attained beyond the most rudimentary form by individuals with autism.[72, 147] Furthermore, focused attachment may be attained, but attachment behavior is markedly deviant in individuals with autism.[148, 149] Symbolic play is selectively impaired and generally not present at all in the first 3 years of life. All of these features may make it possible to exclude a diagnosis of autism by the end of the first year, although it may be another 6 months before it can be diagnosed reliably.

In most cases, abnormalities are noted by parents in the first year of life, although parents most often seek help when the child is 18 to 24 months of age and not speaking.[150] Nonetheless, 3 years typically elapse between the time parents first expressed concern to the child's physician and the time when a definitive diagnosis is made, usually when the child is about 5 years of age.[151] This delay in diagnosis implies lack of recognition by professionals rather than lack of symptoms and signs in affected individuals. Studies indicate that reliable diagnoses may be made in the second year of life.[152, 153] Profound signs of the disorder that become apparent in infancy remain evident throughout the life span.

Regulatory Disorders

Regulatory disorders include behaviors that are presumed to reflect subtle central nervous system abnormalities that lead to sensory processing abnormalities, motor problems, and/or difficulties with regulation of emotion.[154] Regulatory disorders do not exert nearly as profound effects on development as do pervasive developmental disorders, although in case reports they may be associated with significant morbidity. Descriptions of these disorders are included in the Zero to Three diagnostic system but not in standard classification systems such as the DSM-IV.[143]

Regulatory disorders must include a distinct behavioral pattern coupled with a sensory, sensory-motor, or organizational processing difficulty that impairs the child's daily functioning.[142] Four types of regulatory disorders have been described: hypersensitive (with two patterns, fearful-cautious and negative-defiant), underreactive (with two patterns, withdrawn–difficult to engage and self-absorbed), motorically disorganized–impulsive, and other (a mixed picture). Clinically, infants who are affected may manifest impulsivity, affective lability, withdrawal, hyperarousal, sleep disorders, feeding problems, or other symptoms and signs. Although criteria for diagnosing the disorders are now available, the boundaries of these disorders remain unclear. The method for determining that the symptomatic behavior reflects central nervous system abnormalities is also unclear, although in one study infants with difficult temperament, as manifested by fussiness, were demonstrated to have higher baseline vagal tone and failure to suppress vagal tone during cognitive tests. These findings may reflect difficulties in regulating the autonomic nervous system.[155]

Regulatory disorders may be detected as early as the 2- to 3-month transition in some instances, especially if emotion regulation is a primary manifestation of the disorder. More commonly, regulatory disorders are likely to appear after the 7- to 9-month transition, when more obvious sensory, motor, and emotion regulation abnormalities may be detected. The course of the disorders is unknown, although Greenspan and Weider[154] suggested that regulatory disorders may represent the earliest presentation of some types of disruptive behavior disorders, as well as anxiety disorders. Future research on regulatory disorders needs to determine whether they represent a distinct type of disorder or whether problems in regulation represent a dimension of risk underlying a number of different types of disorders.

Posttraumatic Stress Disorder

Signs and symptoms of posttraumatic stress disorder in infants and young children resemble those of older children and adults suffering from the same disorder, including the classical triad of symptoms: reexperiencing, numbing of responsiveness, and hyperarousal. On the other hand, an investigation indicated that when the disorder develops in the first 3 years of life, it differs in important ways from the disorder in older children and adults.[156]

Several major developmental differences need to be addressed to understand the occurrence of posttraumatic stress disorder in this age group. First, what constitutes a traumatic experience for infants and toddlers may be quite different from that for older children and adults. Appreciating that an event is traumatic requires sophisticated attentional and perceptual processes and a degree of anticipation that become increasingly available after the 7- to 9-month transition. Experiences that are traumatic to an adult may not be appraised, understood, or experienced in the same way by an infant who experienced it with the adult. On the other hand, events that are not traumatic to adults may be traumatic to infants. Second, relational issues may be much more influential in the development of symptoms in infants who are traumatized. Clinicians must consider not only direct reactions to the traumatic event but also indirect effects mediated by the effect of the trauma on the caregiver. Third, infants and toddlers have limited verbal capacities to express their subjective experiences, requiring changes in criteria needed to identify the disorder. Fourth, symptoms are often different in infants than in older children and adults. Reexperiencing the trauma is likely to be more evident in play than in verbalization. Scheeringa and colleagues[156] noted that children often had recurrent recollections without obvious signs of distress; this is despite the fact that feeling distress is required by DSM-IV.[143]

After traumatic experiences, toddlers often lost previously acquired developmental skills such as toilet training and language capacities. They developed new fears of such things as toileting alone, the dark, and strangers. Separation anxiety and onset of aggression were also frequently noted.[156]

Drell and associates[157] have asserted that infants as young as a few months of age are capable of experiencing posttraumatic symptoms, although they suggested that the symptom picture may differ depending on developmental differences across the first 3 years of life. There have been only four reported cases of infants younger than 1 year of age with posttraumatic symptoms, but only two of these actually met criteria for a diagnosis of posttraumatic stress disorder.[156] Important directions for future research concern better delineating these developmental differences, including the requisite memory, representational, and perceptual capacities.

The course of posttraumatic stress disorder with onset in the first 3 years of life is unknown. Case reports have indicated that some children may be helped by treat-

Table 6–7 Patterns of Attachment

Characteristics	Secure Pattern	Avoidant Pattern	Resistant Pattern	Disorganized Pattern
Distress	Open display of distress and need for comfort	Inhibited display of distress	Exaggerated display of distress	Odd or contradictory display of distress
Soothing	Effective soothing; positive greeting	No soothing; avoidance instead of greeting	Ineffective soothing; no positive greeting because of distress	Ineffective soothing; usually no positive greeting; often odd or ambivalent greeting
Anger	Little angry behavior	Displaced anger	Angry, resistant behaviors	No predictable pattern
Stress	Low cortisol secretion	High cortisol secretion	No cortisol data	No cortisol data
Strategy for obtaining comfort	Coherent strategy of seeking comfort directly when needed	Coherent strategy of minimizing distress by displaced attention	Coherent strategy of exaggerating distress to mobilize caregiver	Incoherent strategy or significant lapse in organization of strategy
Parental characteristics	Sensitive, emotionally available caregiving, balanced perspective on childhood relationship experiences	Emotionally restricted caregiving; dismissing of painful relationship experiences and their effects	Inconsistent caregiving; unintegrated emotional response to relationship experiences	No data on caregiving; unresolved losses or traumatic childhood experiences

ment,[158, 159] but other reports suggest that individuals may remain symptomatic for years.[160, 161] Prognostic indicators are unknown.

Attachment Disorders

Attachment disorders are characterized by symptoms that reflect an absence of or a profound disturbance in an infant's attachment to one of a small number of preferred caregivers. Lieberman and Zeanah[162] proposed three major types of attachment disorders: disorders of nonattachment with indiscriminate or withdrawn patterns; disordered attachment (secure base distortions) with inhibited, role-reversed, and self-endangering patterns; and disrupted attachment disorders that reflect symptoms of grief after loss of an attachment figure.[162]

Attachment disorders are relational disorders in that they exist within individual infants but may be differentially expressed toward caregivers. Infant behaviors indicating a possible attachment disorder include lack of warm and affectionate interchanges, lack of or abnormal comfort seeking, excessive dependence or failure to use the caregiver's supportive presence, noncompliance, inhibited or reckless exploration, controlling behavior, and failure to reestablish emotional contact after separations.[163]

Although infants discriminate their mothers at birth and may even express limited preferences for their primary caregivers in the first few months of life, it is not until after the 7- to 9-month transition that a clear and strongly expressed preference for an attachment figure can be seen. For this reason, Zeanah[164] has suggested that attachment disorders not be diagnosed unless infants have a mental age of at least 10 months. Nevertheless, interactive precursors of attachment disorders and signs of affective disturbances may be evident in the first few months of life.

Although the course of insecure patterns of attachment has been delineated, the course of actual disorders of attachment is less clear, in part because of problems with the criteria for defining the disorder. By extrapolating with caution from follow-up studies of children raised in institutions and from the sequelae of insecure attachment, it appears that attachment problems in infancy may be related to disruptive behavior disorders and to some internalizing disorders in middle childhood.[165, 166]

Patterns of attachment are presented in Table 6–7.

Conclusions

Promising new conceptualizations of disorders based on developmental considerations are emerging. Nevertheless, developmental considerations remain insufficiently integrated into diagnostic schemes. Although it is clear that disorders of infancy share some similarities with disorders in older children and adults, important differences are also apparent. These differences derive primarily from the rapid pace of development in the first 3 years, the importance of the caregiving context for infant adaptation, and the difficulties in distinguishing between disorder and risk for disorder in infancy.

References

1. Plomin R, Daniels D: Why are children in the same family so different from one another? Behav Brain Sci 1987; 10:1–60.
2. Sameroff AJ: Understanding the social context of early psychopathology. In Noshpitz J (ed): Handbook of Child and Adolescent Psychiatry. New York: Basic Books, in press.
3. Broman SH, Nichols PL, Kennedy WA: Preschool IQ: Prenatal and Early Developmental Correlates. Hillsdale, NJ: Lawrence Erlbaum, 1975.
4. Rutter M: Pathways from childhood to adulthood. J Child Psychol Psychiatry 1989; 30:23–51.
5. Werner E: Risk, resilience and recovery: Perspectives from the Kauai longitudinal study. Dev Psychopathol 1993; 4:503–515.
6. Sameroff AJ, Chandler MJ: Reproductive risk and the continuum of caretaking casualty. In Horowitz FD, Hetherington EM, Scarr-Salpatek S, et al (eds): Review of Child Development Research, Volume 4. Chicago: University of Chicago Press, 1975:187–244.
7. Sameroff AJ, Fiese B: Transactional regulation and early intervention. In Meisels SJ, Shonkoff JP (eds): Handbook of Early Intervention. Cambridge, UK, Cambridge University Press, 1990:119–149.
8. Garcia-Coll C, Meyer E: Socio-cultural context of infant development. In Zeanah CH Jr (ed): Handbook of Infant Mental Health. New York: Guilford Press, 1993:56–69.
9. LeVine R: Childrearing as a cultural adaptation. In Liederman PH, Tulkin SR, Rosenfeld A (eds): Culture and Infancy: Variations in the Human Experience. New York: Academic Press, 1977:15–27.
10. Emde RN: The affective self: Continuities and transformations from infancy. In Call J, Galenson E, Tyson RL (eds): Frontiers of Infant Psychiatry II. New York: Basic Books, 1984:38–54.
11. Kagan J: Continuity and change in the opening years of life. In Emde RN, Harmaon RJ (eds): Continuities and Discontinuities in Development. New York, Plenum Publishing, 1984:15–39.
12. McCall RB, Eichorn DH, Hogarty PS: Transitions in early mental development. Monogr Soc Res Child Dev 1977; 42(3).
13. Stern D: The Interpersonal World of the Infant. New York: Basic Books, 1985.
14. Zeanah CH, Anders TF, Seifer R, et al: Implications of research on infant development for psychodynamic theory and practice. J Am Acad Child Adolesc Psychiatry 1989; 28:657–668.
15. James W: The Principles of Psychology. New York: Dover, 1890.
16. Freud S: Formulations on the two principles of mental functioning. In Strachey J (trans-ed): The Standard Edition of the Complete Psychological Works of Sigmund Freud, Volume 12. London: Hogarth Press, 1958:218–226. Originally published in 1912.
17. Mahler M, Pine F, Bergman A: The Psychological Birth of the Human Infant. New York: Basic Books, 1975.
18. Anders TF, Zeanah CH: Early infant development from a biological point of view. In Call J, Galenson E (eds): Frontiers of Infant Psychiatry II. New York: Basic Books, 1985:55–69.
19. Fischer KW, Rose SP: Dynamic development of coordination of components in brain and behavior: A framework for theory and research. In Dawson G, Fischer KW (eds): Human Behavior and the Developing Brain. New York: Guilford Press, 1994:3–66.
20. Dawson G: Development of emotional expression and emotion regulation in infancy: Contributions of the frontal lobe. In Dawson G, Fischer KW (eds): Human Behavior and the Developing Brain. New York: Guilford Press, 1994:346–379.
21. Anders TF, Keener M, Bowe T, et al: A longitudinal study of sleep-wake patterns in infants from birth to one year. In Call J, Galenson E (eds): Frontiers of Infant Psychiatry. New York: Basic Books, 1983:150–165.
22. Goldsmith HH, Buss AH, Plomin R, et al: Roundtable: What is temperament? Four approaches. Child Dev 1987; 58:505–529.
23. Woroby J: Convergence among assessments of temperament in the first month. Child Dev 1986; 57:47–55.
24. Riese M: Neonatal temperament in monozygotic and dizygotic twin pairs. Child Dev 1990; 61:1230–1237.
25. Papousek H: Experimental studies of appetitional behavior in human newborns and infants. In Stevenson HW, Hess EH, Rheingold HL (eds): Early Behavior: Comparative and Developmental Approaches. New York: John Wiley & Sons, 1967:249–277.
26. DeCasper A, Spence MJ: Prenatal maternal speech influences newborns' perceptions of speech sounds. Infant Behav Dev 1986; 9:133–150.
27. Macfarlane A: Olfaction in the development of social preferences in the human neonate. Ciba Found Symp 1975; 33:103–117.
28. Fantz R: Visual experience in infants: Decreased attention to familiar patterns relative to novel ones. Science 1964; 146:668-670.

29. Eimas P, Miller JL: Organization in the perception of speech by young infants. Psychol Sci 1992; 3:340–345.
30. Meltzoff AN, Moore MK: Imitation of facial and manual gestures by human neonates. Science 1977; 198:75–78.
31. Field T, Woodson R, Greenberg R, Cohen D: Discrimination and imitation of facial expressions by neonates. Science 1982; 218:179–181.
32. Meltzoff AN, Borton W: Intermodal matching by human neonates. Nature 1979; 282:403–404.
33. Lewkowicz D, Turkewitz G: Cross-modal equivalence in early infancy: Auditory-visual intensity matching. Dev Psychol 1980; 16:597–607.
34. Lewis M: The emergence of human emotions. In Lewis M, Haviland J (eds): Handbook of Emotions. New York: Guilford Press, 1994: 223–226.
35. Zeanah CH, Adners TF: Subjectivity in parent-infant relationships: A discussion of internal working models. Infant Ment Health J 1987; 8:237–250.
36. Zeanah CH, Zeanah PD, Stewart L: Parents' constructions of their infants' personalities before and after birth: A descriptive study. Child Psychiatry Hum Dev 1990; 20:191–206.
37. Stern D: The First Relationship: Mother and Baby. Cambridge, MA: Harvard University Press, 1977.
38. Klaus M, Kennell J: Mother-Infant Bonding. St Louis: CV Mosby, 1976.
39. Goldberg S: Parent-infant bonding: Another look. Child Dev 1983; 54:1355–1382.
40. Emde RN, Gaensbauer T, Harmon R: Emotional Expression in Infancy: A Biobehavioral Study. New York: International Universities Press, 1976:35–60.
41. Kagan J, Kearsley RB, Zelarzo PR: Infancy: Its Roots in Human Behavior. Cambridge, MA: Harvard University Press, 1978.
42. Ceaser P: Old and new facts about perinatal brain development. J Child Psychol Psychiatry 1993; 34:101–110.
43. Chugani HT: Development of regional brain glucose metabolism in relation to behavior and plasticity. In Dawson G, Fischer KW (eds): Human Behavior and the Developing Brain. New York: Guilford Press, 1994:153–175.
44. Hofer MA: The Roots of Human Behavior. San Francisco: WH Freeman, 1981.
45. Freedman D: Human Infancy: An Evolutionary Perspective. New York: John Wiley & Sons, 1974.
46. Anders TF, Keener MA, Kramer H: Sleep-wake state organization, neonatal assessment and development in premature infants during the first year of life. Sleep 1985; 8:193–206.
47. Thomas A, Chess S, Birch HG, et al: Behavioral Individuality in Early Childhood. New York: New York University Press, 1963.
48. Thomas A, Chess S, Birch HG: Temperament and Behavior Disorders in Children. New York: New York University Press, 1968.
49. Chess S, Thomas A: Temperament in Clinical Practice. New York: Guilford Press, 1986.
50. Wolkind SN, De Salis W: Infant temperament, maternal mental state and child behaviour problems. Ciba Found Symp 1982; 89:221–239.
51. Seifer R, Sameroff AJ: The concept, measurement and interpretation of temperament in young children: A survey of research issues. Adv Dev Behav Pediatr 1986; 7:1–43.
52. Piaget J; Cook M (trans): The Origins of Intelligence in Children. New York: International Universities Press, 1952. Originally published in 1936.
53. Stenberg CR, Campos JJ, Emde RN: The facial expression of anger in seven-month-old infants. Child Dev 1983; 54:178–184.
54. Lewis M, Alessandri S, Sullivan MW: Violation of expectancy, loss of control and anger in young infants. Dev Psychol 1990; 26:745–751.
55. McCormick L: Review of normal language acquisition. In McCormick L, Schiefelbusch R (eds): Early Language Intervention. Columbus, OH: Charles E Merrill Publishing, 1984:35–88.
56. Barnard KE, Hammond M, Booth CL, et al: Measurement and meaning of parent-child interaction. In Morrison FJ, Lord CE, Keating DP (eds): Applied Developmental Psychology, Volume 3. New York: Academic Press, 1989:39–80.
57. Lyons-Ruth K, Zeanah CH: The family context of infant mental health I: Affective development in the primary caregiving relationship. In Zeanah CH Jr (ed): Handbook of Infant Mental Health. New York: Guilford Press, 1993:14–37.
58. Beebe B, Jaffe J, Feldstein S, et al: Interpersonal timing: The application of an adult dialogue model to mother-infant vocal and kinesic interactions. In Field T, Fox N (eds): Social Perception in Infants. Norwood, NJ: Ablex Publishing, 1985:147–217.
59. Cohn JF, Tronick E: Mother-infant face-to-face interaction: Influence is bidirectional and unrelated to periodic cycles in either partner's behavior. Dev Psychol 1988; 24:386–392.
60. Tronick EZ, Cohn JF: Infant-mother face to face interaction: Age and gender differences in coordination and the occurrences of miscoordination. Child Dev 1989; 60:85–92.
61. Gianino A, Tronick EZ: The mutual regulation model: The infant's self and interactive regulation coping and defense. In Field T, McCabe P, Schneiderman N (eds): Stress and Coping. Hillsdale, NJ: Lawrence Erlbaum, 1988:47–68.
62. Cohn JF, Campbell S, Ross S: Infant response in the still-face paradigm at 6 months predicts avoidant and secure attachment at 12 months. Dev Psychopathol 1991; 3:367–376.
63. Beebe B, Lachmann FM: The contribution of mother-infant mutual influence of the origins of self and object representations. Psychoanal Psychol 1988; 5:305–337.
64. Bell MA, Fox N: The relations between frontal brain electrical activity and cognitive development during infancy. Child Dev 1992; 63:1141–1163.
65. Chugani HT, Phelps ME: Maturational changes in cerebral function in infants determined by ^{18}FDG positron emission tomography. Science 1986; 231:840–843.
66. Epstein HT: Phrenoblysis: Special brain and mind growth periods. Dev Psychobiol 1974; 7:217–224.
67. Fischer KW: Relations between brain and cognitive development. Child Dev 1987; 57:623–632.
68. Hagne I, Persson J, Magnusson, et al: Spectral analysis via fast Fourier transform of waking EEGs in normal infants. In Kellway P, Peterson I (eds): Automation of Clinical Electroencephalography. New York: Raven Press, 1973:103–143.
69. Seifer R, Sameroff A, Barrett LC, et al: Infant temperament measured by multiple observations and mother report. Child Dev 1994; 65:1478–1490.
70. Jennings KD, Yarrow LJ, Martin PP: Mastery motivation and cognitive development: A longitudinal study from infancy to 3.5 years of age. Int J Behav Dev 1984; 7:441–461.
71. Messer DJ, McCarthy ME, McQuiston S, et al: Relation between mastery behavior in infancy and competence in early childhood. Dev Psychol 1986; 22:366–372.
72. Trevarthen C: Communication and cooperation in early infancy: A description of primary intersubjectivity. In Bullowa MM (ed): Before Speech: The Beginning of Interpersonal Communication. New York: Cambridge University Press, 1979:321–347.
73. Baron-Cohen S: The autistic child's theory of mind: A case of a specific developmental delay. J Child Psychol Psychiatry 1989; 30:285–298.
74. Klinnert MD, Campos JJ, Sorce JF, et al: Emotions as behavior regulators: Social referencing in infancy. In Plutchik R, Kellerman H (eds): Emotion: Theory, Research, and Experience, Volume 2. New York: Academic Press, 1983:57–86.
75. Hirshberg L, Svejda M: When infants look to their parents: Infants' social referencing of mothers compared to fathers. Child Dev 1990; 61:1175–1186.
76. Fenson L, Dale PS, Reznick JS, et al: Variability in early communicative development. Monogr Soc Res Child Dev 1994; 59(5):1–173.
77. Ainsworth MDS, Blehar M, Waters E, et al: Patterns of Attachment. Hillsdale, NJ: Lawrence Erlbaum, 1978.
78. Sroufe LA: The role of infant-caregiver attachment in development. In Belsky J, Nezworski T (eds): Clinical Implications of Attachment. Hillsdale, NJ: Lawrence Erlbaum, 1988:18–40.
79. Zeanah CH, Emde RN: Attachment disorders in infancy. In Rutter M, Taylor E, Hersov L (eds): Child and Adolescent Psychiatry: Modern Approaches. Boston: Blackwell Scientific Publications, 1994:490–504.
80. Fox NA, Kimmerly NL, Schaefer WD: Attachment to mother/attachment to father: A meta-analysis. Child Dev 1991; 62:210–225.
81. Steele M, Steele H, Fonagy P: Associations among attachment classifications of mothers, fathers and their infants: Evidence for a relationship specific perspective. Presented at the Biennial Meeting of the Society for Research in Child Development; March 26,1993; New Orleans.

82. Arend R, Gove F, Sroufe LA: Continuity of individual adaptation from infancy to kindergarten: A predictive study of ego-resiliency and curiosity in preschoolers. Child Dev 1979; 50:950–959.
83. Troy M, Sroufe LA: Victimization among preschools: Role of attachment relationship history. J Am Acad Child Adolesc Psychiatry 1987; 26:166–172.
84. Waters E, Wippman J, Sroufe LA: Attachment, positive affect, and competence in peer group: Two studies in construct validation. Child Dev 1979; 50:821–829.
85. Huttenlocher PR: Synaptogenisis in the human cerebral cortex. In Fischer KW, Dawson G (eds): Human Behavior and the Developing Brain. New York: Guilford Press, 1994:137–152.
86. Mills DJ, Coffey-Corina SA, Neville HJ: Variability in cerebral organization during primary language acquisition. In Fischer KW, Dawson G (eds): Human Behavior and the Developing Brain. New York: Guilford Press, 1994:427–455.
87. Kagan J, Reznick, JS, Snidman N: The physiology and psychology of behavioral inhibition in children. Child Dev 1987; 58:1459–1473.
88. Kagan J, Reznick S, Snidman N: Biological bases of childhood shyness. Science 1988; 240:167–171.
89. Biederman J, Rosenbaum JF, Hirshfield DR, et al: Psychiatric correlates of behavioral inhibition in young children of parents with and without psychiatric disorders. Arch Gen Psychiatry 1990; 47:1459–1473.
90. Lewis M, Brooks-Gunn J: Social Cognition and the Acquisitional Self. New York: Plenum Publishing, 1979.
91. Kagan J: The Second Year: The Emergence of Self-awareness. Cambridge, MA: Harvard University Press, 1981.
92. Gouze K, Nadelman L: Constancy of gender identity for self and others in children between the ages of three and seven. Child Dev 1980; 51:275–278.
93. Lewis M, Sullivan MW, Stanger C, et al: Self-development and self-conscious emotions. Child Dev 1989; 60:146–156.
94. Emde RN, Buchsbaum HK: "Didn't you hear my mommy?": Autonomy with connectedness in moral self emergence. In Cicchetti D, Beeghly M (eds): Development of the Self in Transition. Chicago: University of Chicago Press, 1990:35–60.
95. Emde RN, Johnson WF, Easterbrooks A: The do's and don't's of early moral development: Psychoanalytic tradition and current research. In Kagan J, Lamb S (eds): The Emergence of Morality. Chicago: University of Chicago Press, 1988:245–277.
96. Bretherton I, Bates E: The emergence of intentional communication. In Uzgiris I (ed): New Directions for Child Development. San Francisco: Jossey-Bass, 1979: 81–100.
97. Crockenberg S: Predictors and correlates of anger toward and punitive control of toddlers by adolescent mothers. Child Dev 1987; 58:964–975.
98. Bandura A: Self-referent thought: A developmental analysis of self-efficacy. In Flavell JH, Ross L (eds): Social Cognitive Development: Frontiers and Possible Futures. Cambridge, UK: Cambridge University Press, 1981:200–239.
99. Matas L, Arend RA, Sroufe LA: Continuity of adaptation in the second year: The relationship between quality of attachment and later competence. Child Dev 1978; 49:547–556.
100. Whiteside MF, Busch F, Horner T: From egocentric to cooperative play in young children: A normative study. J Am Acad Child Psychiatry 1976; 15:294–313.
101. Mrazek PJ, Haggerty RJ (eds): Reducing Risks for Metal Disorders. Washington, DC: National Academy Press, 1994.
102. Seifer R, Sameroff AJ, Anagnostopolov R, et al: Child and family factors that ameliorate risk between 4 and 13 year of age. J Am Acad Child Adolesc Psychiatry 1992; 31:893–903.
103. Beardslee WR, Bernporad J, Keller MB, et al: Children of parents with major affective disorders: A review. Am J Psychiatry 1983; 140:825–832.
104. Sroufe LA, Rutter M: The domain of developmental psychopathology. Child Dev 1984; 55:17–29.
105. Sameroff AJ, Seifer RS, Barocas R, et al: IQ scores of 4-year-old children: Social-environmental risk factors. Pediatrics 1987; 79:343–350.
106. Rutter M: Psychosocial resilience and protective mechanisms. Am J Orthopsychiatry 1987; 57:316–331.
107. National Center for Children in Poverty: Five Million Children: A Statistical Profile of Our Poorest Young Citizens. New York: National Center for Children in Poverty, Columbia University, 1990.
108. Rutter M: Family and school differences on behavioral development. J Child Psychol Psychiatry 1985; 26:349–368.
109. Halpern R: Poverty and infant development. In Zeanah CH Jr (ed): Handbook of Infant Mental Health. New York: Guilford Press, 1993:73–87.
110. Lyons-Ruth K, Zoli D, Connell D, et al: Family deviance and family disruption in childhood: Associations with maternal behavior and infant maltreatment during the first two years of life. Dev Psychopathol 1989; 1:219–236.
111. Zeanah CH, Hirshberg L, Danis B, et al: Specificity of the adult attachment interview in a high risk sample. Presented at the Biennial Meeting of the Society for Research in Child Development; March 30, 1995; Indianapolis, IN.
112. Egeland B, Farber E: Infant-mother attachment: Factors related to its change over time. Child Dev 1984; 53:753–771.
113. Lewis M, Feiring C, McGuffog C, et al: Predicting psychopathology in six-year-olds from early social relations. Child Dev 1984; 55:123–136.
114. Easterbrooks A, Goldberg W: Security of toddler-parent attachment: Relation to the children's sociopersonality functioning during kindergarten. In Greenberg MT, Cicchetti D, Cummings EM (eds): Attachment in the Preschool Years: Theory, Research, and Intervention. Chicago: University of Chicago Press, 1990:221–244.
115. Cassidy J: Child-mother attachment and the self at age six. Child Dev 1988; 57:331–337.
116. Jacobsen T, Edelstein W, Volker H: A longitudinal study of the relation between representations of attachment in childhood and cognitive functioning in childhood and adolescence. Dev Psychol 1994; 30:112–124.
117. Kolvin FJ, Miller JW, Fleeting M, Kolvin PA: Social and parenting factors affecting criminal-offence rates: Findings from the Newcastle Thousand Family Study (1947–1980). Br J Psychiatry 1988; 152:80–90.
118. Offord DR, Alder RJ, Boyle MH: Prevalence and sociodemographic correlates of conduct disorder. Am J Soc Psychiatry 1986; 6:272–278.
119. Rutter M, Giller H: Juvenile Delinquency: Trends and Perspectives. New York: Penguin Books, 1983.
120. National Child Abuse and Neglect Data System, Working Paper 1, 1990 Summary Data Component. Washington, DC: U.S. Department of Health and Human Services, 1992. DHHS publication (ACF) 92-30361.
121. Schmitt BD, Krugman RD: Abuse and neglect of children. In Behrman RE (ed): Nelson Textbook of Pediatrics, 14th ed. Philadelphia: WB Saunders, 1992:78–83.
122. Waller AE, Baker SP, Szocka A: Childhood injury deaths: National analysis and geographic variations. Am J Public Health 1989; 79:310–315.
123. Rosenberg MS: New directions for research on the psychological maltreatment of children. Am Psychol 1987; 42:166–171.
124. Gaensbauer TJ, Mrazek DA: Differences in the patterning of affective expression in infants. J Am Acad Child Adolesc Psychiatry 1981; 20:673–691.
125. George C, Main M: Social interactions of young abused children: Approach, avoidance, and aggression. Child Dev 1979; 50:306–318.
126. Main M, George C: Responses of abused and disadvantaged toddlers to distress in agemates: A study in the daycare setting. Dev Psychol 1985; 21:407–412.
127. Schneider-Rosen K, Cicchetti D: The relationship between affect and cognition in maltreated infants: Quality of attachment and the development of visual self-recognition. Child Dev 1984; 55:648–658.
128. Pianta RC, Sroufe LA, Egeland B: Continuity and discontinuity in maternal sensitivity at 6, 24, and 42 months in a high-risk sample. Child Dev 1989; 60:481–487.
129. Carlson V, Cicchetti D, Barnett D, et al: Disorganized/disoriented attachment relationships in maltreated infants. Dev Psychol 1989; 24:525–531.
130. U.S. General Accounting Office: Drug-Exposed Infants: A Generation at Risk (Report to the Chairman, Committee on Finance, U.S. Senate). Washington, DC: Government Printing Office, 1990.
131. Abel EL, Sokol RJ: Incidence of fetal alcohol syndrome and economic impact of FAS-related anomalies. Alcohol Drug Depend 1987; 19:51–70.
132. Sampson PD, Streissguth AP, Barr HM, et al: Neurobehavioral effects of prenatal alcohol exposure: Part II. Partial least squares analysis. Neurobehav Toxicol Teratol 1989; 11:477–491.

133. Rodning C, Beckwith L, Howard J: Characteristics of attachment organization and play organization in prenatally drug-exposed toddlers. Dev Psychopathol 1990; 1:277–289.
134. Lester BM, Tronick EZ: The effects of prenatal cocaine exposure and child outcome. Infant Ment Health J 1994; 15:107–120.
135. Kalter H, Warkany J: Congenital malformations: Etiological factors and their role in prevention (first of two parts). N Engl J Med 1983; 308:424–431.
136. Kalter H, Warkany J: Congenital malformations (second of two parts). N Engl J Med 1983; 308:491-497.
137. Pharoah POD, Alberman ED: Annual statistical review. Arch Dis Child 1990; 65:147–151.
138. Kopp CB, Kaler SR: Risk in infancy: Origins and implications. Am Psychol 1989; 44:224–230.
139. National Center for Health Statistics: Advance Report of Final Natality Statistics, 1985. Monthly Vital Statistics Report, Volume 36. Washington, DC: National Center for Health Statistics, 1987.
140. Quinton D, Rutter M: Early hospital admissions and later disturbances of behavior: An attempted replication of Douglas findings. Dev Med Child Neurol 1976; 18:447–459.
141. Minde KK: Prematurity and serious medical illness in infancy: Implications for development and intervention. In Zeanah CH Jr (ed): Handbook of Infant Mental Health. New York: Guilford Press, 1993.
142. Zero to Three/National Center for Clinical Infant Programs: Diagnostic Classification: 0–3. Arlington, VA: Zero to Three, 1994:87–105.
143. American Psychiatric Association: Diagnostic and Statistical Manual of Mental Disorders, 4th ed. Washington, DC: American Psychiatric Association, 1994.
144. Short AB, Schopler E: Factors relating to age of onset in autism. J Autism Dev Disord 1988; 18:207–216.
145. Volkmar FR, Cohen DJ: Diagnosis of pervasive developmental disorders. In Lahey B, Kazdin A (eds): Advances in Clinical Child Psychology, Volume 11. New York: Plenum Publishing, 1988:249–284.
146. Volkmar FR, Stier DM, Cohen DJ: Age of recognition of pervasive developmental disorder. Am J Psychiatry 1985; 142:1450–1452.
147. Baron-Cohen S: From attention-goal psychology to belief-desire psychology: The development of a theory of mind and its dysfunction. In Baron-Cohen S, Tager-Flusberg H, Cohen DJ (eds): Understanding Other Minds: Perspectives from Autism. New York: Oxford University Press, 1993:59–82.
148. Sigman M, Mundy P: Social attachments in autistic children. J Am Acad Child Adolesc Psychiatry 1989; 28:74–81.
149. Sigman M, Ungerer J: Attachment behaviors in autistic children. J Autism Dev Disord 1984; 14:231–244.
150. Volkmar FR: Autism and the pervasive development disorders. In Zeanah CH Jr (ed): Handbook of Infant Mental Health. New York: Guilford Press, 1993:236–249.
151. Siegel B, Pliner C, Eschler J, et al: How autistic children are diagnosed: Difficulties in identification of children with multiple developmental delays. J Dev Behav Pediatr 1988; 9:199–204.
152. Hertzig M, Snow M, New E, Shapiro T: DSM-III and DSM-II-R diagnosis of autism and pervasive developmental disorder in nursery school children. J Am Acad Child Adolesc Psychiatry 1990; 29:123–126.
153. Kao BT, Frantantaro L, Palombo ML, et al: Early presentation of children with pervasive developmental disorders. Poster presented at the Ninth National Training Institute, Zero to Three/National Center for Clinical Infant Programs; December 1–4, 1994; Dallas, TX.
154. Greenspan S, Weider S: Regulatory disorders. In Zeanah CH Jr (ed): Handbook of Infant Mental Health. New York: Guilford Press, 1993:280–290.
155. DiGangi GA, DiPietro JA, Greenspan SA, et al: Psychophysiological characteristics of the regulatory disorder infant. Infant Behav Dev 1991; 14:37–50.
156. Scheeringa MS, Zeanah CH, Drell MJ, et al: Two approaches to the diagnosis of posttraumatic stress disorder in infancy and early childhood. J Am Acad Child Adolesc Psychiatry 1995; 34:191–200.
157. Drell M, Siegel CH, Gaensbauer TJ: Post traumatic stress disorder. In Zeanah CH Jr (ed): Handbook of Infant Mental Health. New York: Guilford Press, 1993:291–304.
158. MacLean G: Psychic trauma and traumatic neurosis: Play therapy with a four-year old boy. Can Psychiatr Assoc J 1977; 22:71–75.
159. Zeanah CH, Burk GS: A young girl who witnessed her mother's murder: Therapeutic and legal considerations. Am J Psychother 1984; 38:132–145.
160. Gaensbauer TJ, Chatoor I, Drell M, et al: Traumatic loss in a one-year-old girl. J Am Acad Child Adolesc Psychiatry 1995; 34:94–102.
161. Pruett KD: A chronology of defensive adaptations to severe psychological trauma. Psychoanal Study Child 1984; 39:591–612.
162. Lieberman A, Zeanah CH: Disorders of attachment. In Minde K (ed): Infant Psychiatry, Child and Adolescent Clinics of North America. Philadelphia: WB Saunders, 1995:571–588.
163. Zeanah CH, Mammen O, Lieberman A: Disorders of attachment. In Zeanah CH Jr (ed): Handbook of Infant Mental Health. New York: Guilford Press, 1993:332–349.
164. Zeanah CH: Beyond insecurity: A reconceptualization of attachment disorders of infancy. J Consult Clin Psychol, in press.
165. Lyons-Ruth K, Alpern L, Repacholi B: Disorganized attachment classification and maternal psychosocial problems as predictors of hostile aggressive behavior in the preschool classroom. Child Dev 1993; 64:572–585.
166. Tizard B, Hodges J: The effect of early institutional rearing on the development of eight-year-old children. J Child Psychol Psychiatry 1978; 19:99–118.

CHAPTER

7 Preschool Development

Robert B. Clyman

> Maturation is a useful concept, but in reality there is only development.[1]

The preschool period is a time of remarkable development. Toddlers who are "into everything" and require constant parental supervision become kindergartners who can play alone or with peers for extended lengths of time. The 2-year-old who struggles to put two words together to communicate a simple desire, like "me candy," turns into a 5-year-old who can tell complex, richly embellished stories. Toddlers who have just mastered the ability to recall information become preschoolers who surprise their parents when they remember events that happened 6 to 12 months earlier, events the parents themselves may have forgotten. In this chapter, I examine development from the beginning of the third year of life until the child enters the first grade. This broad definition of the preschool period encompasses rapid growth in all developmental domains, including biological, cognitive, linguistic, emotional, and moral development. I address each of these areas and sociocultural influences as well. I begin with a brief introduction to the field, followed by a discussion of a modern conceptual framework for considering a range of developmental issues in the preschool period. I conclude with a description of risk and protective factors and a developmental perspective on the ontogeny of psychopathology in this age group.

Overview of the Literature

The designation of the preschool period as a unique developmental epoch is relatively modern. Many observers of young children consider the preschool period to be a critical time during which children develop the skills that are necessary to move from the safe haven of the home into the broader social world of school. Historically, psychoanalytic thinkers helped to focus our attention on the importance of early childhood for the future life of the child. Currently, thinking about the preschool years has been influenced by the increase in infant and toddler daycare as an increasing number of women have moved into the out-of-home work force. Our understanding of development, as of all areas in social science, is embedded in a historical context.

Sigmund Freud[1a] emphasized the role of young children's thoughts and feelings in influencing their subsequent development, focusing on the child's oedipal fantasies. He left the field with a rich legacy of interest in children's individuality and the importance of understanding the meaning of events to children. His daughter, Anna Freud,[1b] developed the important concept of developmental lines through her observations of children. She examined the unfolding of different domains of development, much as Piaget[2] did in his fascinating explication of preschoolers' cognitive growth. Erik Erikson[2a] further directed our study to the prominent developmental themes of each age period, emphasizing the development of autonomy for toddlers and initiative for preschoolers. He also broadened psychoanalytic interest from the intrapsychic to the world of actual social relationships, anticipating an important focus of current empirical research.

Whereas psychodynamic clinicians have derived their hypotheses about child development predominantly from clinical experience with children and adults, modern developmental psychology requires that observations be subjected to the rigor of empirical research. Developmental studies, as in much of psychiatry, continue to struggle with integrating clinical and empirical insights. Researchers such as Sroufe[3] have extended studies of parent-infant attachment to the preschool period, demonstrating both continuities and discontinuities in attachment status through time, as well as delineating some of the negative correlates of insecure attachment. Cicchetti[4] has examined how normative and at-risk populations of children negotiate stage-salient developmental tasks either adaptively or maladaptively, shedding light on both normal development and the origins of some forms of psychopathology. Researchers have also focused on broader social influences on children's linguistic[5] and social[6] development. Currently, there is quite a bit of interest in development within the context of one's culture. These investigations are leading to a richer and more complex understanding of development in the preschool period.

Conceptual Framework

As children progress from infancy through the preschool years, they attempt to master specific developmental issues and to acquire certain skills. For example, with the advent of walking at the end of the first year of life, children begin to grapple with autonomy issues. However, these issues are not resolved completely within any single developmental period; they continue to be important throughout the life span.[7] More or less successful resolution of stage-specific issues leads to healthier or less successful adaptation for the child. Children who do not master stage-specific issues are not condemned to develop psychopathology, but they are at increased risk for subsequent developmental failures and the development of certain psychiatric disorders. This is particularly noticeable when the individual subsequently encounters the same issue in a different developmental form, such as when young physicians once again confront autonomy issues when they complete their long years of training and move into practice. It is often overlooked that this process is frequently positive, offering new opportunities for growth. Each new developmental stage enables the individual to rework past traumas, resolve problematical issues, and master new skills. This positive perspective emphasizes children's potential resilience to trauma and loss, an important area for future research.

Developments within different functional domains do not necessarily progress in concert. A child may be more advanced cognitively than socially, for example. Lines of development are not parallel lines. They interact, supporting or inhibiting growth in other domains, such as when a 3-year-old who has not yet developed much language has more difficulty in communicating needs and regulating frustration. Examples of developmental milestones in the preschool period for different developmental domains appear in Table 7–1.

Much of early development occurs within the context of the parent-child relationship. Parents tune in to what skills their young child has and what skills the child needs to acquire to move forward to the next phase of growth. Parents who structure their child's learning so that they provide most of what the child needs help the child acquire the next level of skill. Vygotsky[8, 9] referred to this as working in the "zone of proximal development." An example would be a parent helping a youngster with a puzzle by orienting the piece so that the child can see where it fits in the puzzle. Another example would be a parent watching a child struggle with the temptation to reach for a forbidden cookie and reminding the child not to take it. By reminding the child of the restriction, the parent helps the child to resist the temptation. Scaffolding the child's development, as this is called, requires that parents provide assistance when needed but do not provide unneeded help.

Modern models of development emphasize that not only do parents influence their children but children influence their parents. Children within the same family are born with different temperaments, and parents often remark on how different their children are. Over time, children and parents influence each other, mutually affecting the child's developmental trajectory. This is referred to as a transactional model of development. As children grow older, the influences of teachers, peers, and other adults become more important. Our knowledge base is most limited in understanding genetic contributions to these processes. Research suggests that genes may become activated at different times in development. We can expect further understanding of these processes to result in a major reorganization of our thinking about development in this age group.

These transactional processes result in both continuities and discontinuities in development. For example, there is substantial continuity in aggressive behavior from the preschool to the school-age period. But a happy infant can become a detached autistic 3-year-old, reflecting a major discontinuity in development. With these general models of development in the preschool period, we turn now to an examination of development in different domains.

Lines of Development

Biological Development

The field of behavioral genetics is changing the way we think about child development. Behavioral genetics research not only has demonstrated that there are genetic influences on children's development but also has provided the best evidence that environmental influences affect children. By conducting studies of monozygotic and dizygotic twins or of adopted children, researchers can begin to tease apart the genetic and environmental influences on children's cognitive, emotional, and social development.

This research has led to a number of surprising findings that are relevant for our understanding of the preschool period. First, parents have different effects on different children. This is referred to as the effects of the "nonshared environment."[10] In understanding children's development, we must focus on how each parent influences each child separately. It becomes more important to examine not the nurturing parent but how this nurturing parent shapes the development of each child individually.

Second, genetic influences vary with age. For example, although environmental influences explain significant variability in IQ in childhood, this is no longer true in adolescence.[11]

Third, nongenetic factors appear to be at least as important as genetic factors in the development of most psychiatric disorders.[12] An exception is autism. Concordance for developing autism is 65% for monozygotic but only 10% for dizygotic twins, indicating the influence of the genes.[13] This result is striking, because autism was initially thought to result entirely from environmental factors. Now it is an example of a disorder that is principally genetic in origin.

Despite these exciting findings, comparatively little is known about how nature and nurture interact. Understanding the factors that lead to the expression of genes that carry risk for psychopathology, particularly if the expression of the genes occurs before the first manifestation of the disorder, would contribute substantially to our ability to intervene with infants and young children to prevent psychiatric disorders.

We turn now to neurobiological development in the preschool period. A central principle of neural development is that while brain maturation influences children's behavior, environmental experience also influences neurobiological development. This is evident when we consider brain development. By 18 weeks of gestational age, nearly all cortical neurons have formed and migrated to their neural destination.[14] However, at birth, the average infant brain is only one third the weight of the adult brain. There is an important brain growth spurt at approximately age 4 years, and by the age of 5 years children's brains weigh

Table 7–1 Emerging Patterns of Behavior from 1 to 5 Years of Age*

15 Months	
Motor:	Walks alone; crawls up stairs
Adaptive:	Makes tower of three cubes; makes a line with crayon; inserts pellet in bottle
Language:	Jargon; follows simple commands; may name a familiar object (ball)
Social:	Indicates some desires or needs by pointing; hugs parents
18 Months	
Motor:	Runs stiffly; sits on small chair; walks up stairs with one hand held; explores drawers and waste baskets
Adaptive:	Makes a tower of four cubes; imitates scribbling; imitates vertical stroke; dumps pellet from bottle
Language:	10 words (average); names pictures; identifies one or more parts of body
Social:	Feeds self; seeks help when in trouble; may complain when wet or soiled; kisses parent with pucker
24 Months	
Motor:	Runs well; walks up and down stairs, one step at a time; opens doors; climbs on furniture; jumps
Adaptive:	Tower of seven cubes (six at 21 mo); circular scribbling; imitates horizontal stroke; folds paper once imitatively
Language:	Puts three words together (subject, verb, object)
Social:	Handles spoon well; often tells immediate experiences; helps to undress; listens to stories with pictures
30 Months	
Motor:	Goes up stairs alternating feet
Adaptive:	Tower of nine cubes; makes vertical and horizontal strokes but generally does not join them to make a cross; imitates circular stroke, forming closed figure
Language:	Refers to self by pronoun "I"; knows full name
Social:	Helps put things away; pretends in play
36 Months	
Motor:	Rides tricycle; stands momentarily on one foot
Adaptive:	Tower of 10 cubes; imitates construction of "bridge" of three cubes; copies a circle; imitates a cross
Language:	Knows age and sex; counts three objects correctly; repeats three numbers or a sentence of six syllables
Social:	Plays simple games (in "parallel" with other children); helps in dressing (unbuttons clothing and puts on shoes); washes hands
48 Months	
Motor:	Hops on one foot; throws ball overhand; uses scissors to cut out pictures; climbs well
Adaptive:	Copies bridge from model; imitates construction of "gate" of five cubes; copies cross and square; draws a man with two to four parts besides head; names longer of two lines
Language:	Counts four pennies accurately; tells a story
Social:	Plays with several children with beginning of social interaction and role-playing; goes to toilet alone
60 Months	
Motor:	Skips
Adaptive:	Draws triangle from copy; names heavier of two weights
Language:	Names four colors; repeats sentence of 10 syllables; counts 10 pennies correctly
Social:	Dresses and undresses; asking questions about meaning of words; domestic role-playing

*Data are derived from those of Gesell (as revised by Knobloch), Shirley, Provence, Wolf, Bailey, and others. After 5 y the Stanford-Binet, Wechsler-Bellevue, and other scales offer the most precise estimates of developmental level. In order to have their greatest value, they should be administered only by an experienced and qualified person.

From Behrman RE (ed): Nelson Textbook of Pediatrics, 14th ed. Philadelphia: WB Saunders, 1992:42.

90% as much as adults' brains.[15] Much of this increase in size is due to the growth of neurons and their connections. However, increases in brain mass do not tell the most important story.

Another important principle of neurobiological development is that synaptic connections strengthen in response to experience. Activation of both individual neurons and neural networks in response to stimulation increases their likelihood to survive. This is an important mechanism for the influence of environmental experience on brain development.[16]

Different brain systems develop at different rates, much as different functional systems develop at different rates. Synaptic density in the frontal cortex peaks at 1 year and pruning of synapses begins by 7 years of life.[17] This process occurs earlier in the human visual cortex, where synaptic density peaks at 6 months. Loss of synapses is under way by 1 year of life.

Functional evidence reveals that the brain's capacity for plasticity varies with age. Young children can recover language functions after the dominant hemisphere is damaged.[18] After age 8 years, however, progress is limited, suggesting that language is represented bilaterally in young children but that it may be represented unilaterally by the early school years.[19] With the development of new brain imaging tools, we can expect to see an increase in our knowledge of the relationship between brain structure and function, with a corresponding increase in our ability to treat neurodevelopmental disorders.

Motor development progresses rapidly during the preschool years.[20] This is particularly noticeable in the development of gross motor skills involving large body movements such as jumping and running. Whereas toddlers are often awkward in their gross motor movements, most American kindergartners can throw and catch a ball and ride a tricycle. Fine motor skills are more difficult for preschoolers to master. Their limited muscular control, patience, and judgment and short, stubby fingers make it difficult for them to draw, cut food with a knife and fork, pour milk from a pitcher without spilling, or tie a shoelace. Parents who can provide a sensitive scaffold for their children, accurately judging their children's abilities and helping them to master the next level of skill, are rewarded with children who take pride in their increasing mastery of new abilities.

As with all developmental milestones, the age at which children acquire bowel and bladder control varies among individuals within the normal range. Bowel control is established between 20 and 30 months. Daytime bladder control is acquired in the third year of life, and nighttime control develops between 3.5 and 4 years of age.

Activity level peaks in the third year of life and then decreases.[21] Individual differences in activity level reflect the influences of both nature and nurture. Genetic influences are reflected in the observation that monozygotic twins are more equal in their activity levels than are dizygotic twins.[22] However, children's activity levels are quite influenced by context (e.g., children are often more fidgety when they are expected to sit quietly, as in school), and cultural expectations of what is acceptable influence their level of activity as well. As is true for most developmental domains, genetic, familial, and cultural influences shape children's activity levels.

A time line of biological development from age 20 months to 5 years is presented in Figure 7–1.

Cognitive Development

Piaget[2] believed that the idiosyncratic and, at times, humorous ideas of preschoolers are not random thoughts. Rather, they reflect the activity of inquiring young minds operating according to a unique set of rules. He referred to these rules as the preoperational stage of reasoning. The transition from the sensory-motor to the preoperational stage at 18 to 24 months is marked by the development of the capacity for symbolic representation. The 2-year-old can store representations of objects in memory, even when not perceiving the objects. This enables the child to recall information. The child in the preoperational stage is capable of symbolic reasoning and symbolic play. A 3-year-old rides a broom as if it were a horse or pretends that a block is a car and races it around the room. This ushers in the young child's fascination with pretend play, which continues until it yields to the school-age child's interest in games, sports, and hobbies.

Parents often take delight in the creative oddities of young children's magical thinking. Piaget's classification of these idiosyncratic modes of reasoning is valuable as a way of characterizing the children's thought processes. Animism refers to endowing inanimate objects with the qualities of living things. For example, young children may say that the sun shines "because it wants to." Artificialism is the belief that all things are made for our use. The child who states that day turns into night because people need to sleep is demonstrating artificialism. Centration is the child's tendency to focus on only one aspect of a problem at a time. Young children can identify two rows of five identical objects as being of equal length (Fig. 7–2). Yet, if one of the rows is spread out, 3- and 4-year-old children say that the longer row has more objects, centrating on the length of the row (see Fig. 7–2). This experiment also indicates that preschoolers are unable to *conserve* number; the number of items is not conserved across a transformation. Development of this ability heralds the onset of the operational stage of thinking at about 7 years of age.

Bowel control established

Daytime bladder control established
Activity level peaks

Nighttime bladder control established

Cerebral growth spurt

Brain weight 90% of adult brain

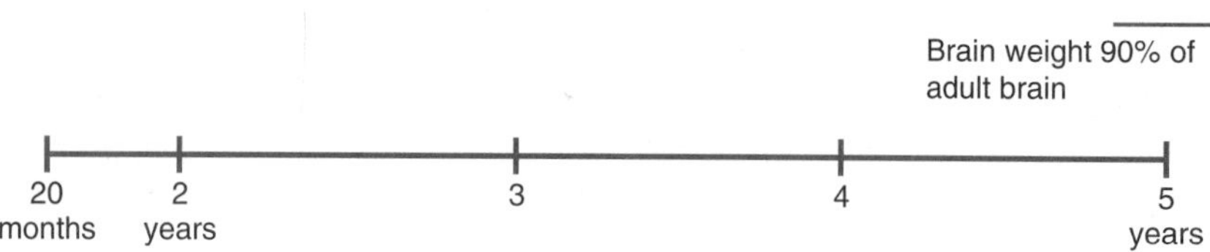

Figure 7–1 *Biological development during the preschool years (20 months to 5 years).*

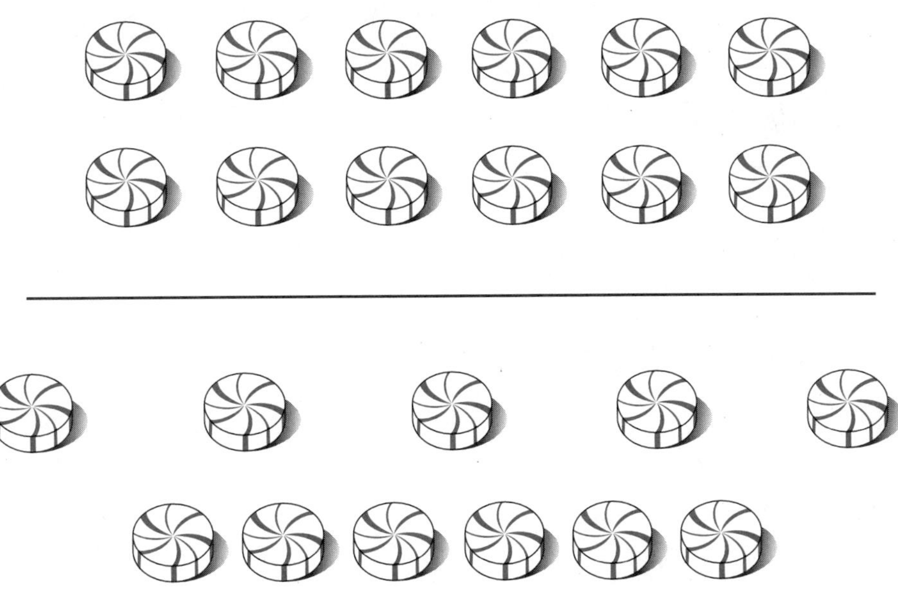

Figure 7–2 *Piaget's experiment on the conservation of numbers. When shown the arrangement of candies in the top two rows and asked whether one line has more or both lines are the same, the 4- or 5-year-old generally answers that both lines contain the same number of candies. Using the same candies, those in the lower row were pushed closer together and one candy was removed from the upper row, but the line was spread out so that it was longer. The child has watched this operation and has been told that he or she may eat the candies in the line that contains more. Even preoperational children, who can count, insist that the longer line has more, although they have gone through the exercise of counting off the candies in each line. (From Craig, Grace J. Human Development, 6/e, © 1992, p. 266. Reprinted by permission of Prentice Hall, Upper Saddle River, New Jersey.)*

Although Piaget noticed that young children had difficulty distinguishing surface appearances from underlying realities, careful research has now documented preschoolers' growing abilities to distinguish reality from appearance. Whereas 3-year-olds have difficulty [knowing that a stone that is painted to look like an egg is not an egg], older preschoolers readily discriminate the two.[23] This is known as the appearance-reality distinction.

Another well-known claim of Piaget's is that preschoolers are egocentric; they have difficulty taking others' perspectives. This claim derived from the following experiment: when shown a three-dimensional model of three distinct mountains, preschoolers were unable to report which mountain would be in front of which mountain if they were asked to imagine seeing the model from a different angle. This led to the incorrect view that young children are egocentric in all ways. It was thought for many years that young children lacked empathy, because empathy requires the adoption of another's perspective. This view delayed our understanding of the development of empathy and prosocial behavior in young children.

Problems with the piagetian view of egocentrism reflect a more general problem with piagetian stage theory. At the heart of the theory is the claim that all thinking in one age period is characterized by certain principles, which can be elucidated by observing children's performance on specific tasks. However, young children's performance is exceedingly sensitive to small contextual influences. When tasks are simplified for children or more familiar materials are used, children perform better.

Subsequent attempts to characterize both adults' and children's cognitive abilities have focused on how information is processed. This approach emphasizes children's limited information-processing capacities. For example, preschoolers have limited attention spans. They approach tasks in an unsystematic fashion, not focusing on the most relevant features of the task.[24] Their short-term memory capacity is limited.[25] However, when information is presented more slowly and the child already has some background in the area, performance improves, again demonstrating young children's sensitivity to the contextual demands of the task.

Although children in the preoperational period can recall information, their abilities remain quite limited at this age. However, research has indicated that their memory is more organized and more similar to adults' memory than was previously thought. They have a good capacity to form generalized event memories, or scripts, of commonly occurring events. These knowledge structures are general templates that represent the expected events in a familiar routine. Children as young as 3 years old can report what typically happens during familiar events or routines. These structures are quite important, as they organize young children's memories. For example, children use them to make inferences about what happened when recalling an event. If asked to retell a story they have just been told, young children tell it as if certain commonly occurring events occurred, even if they never happened in the story.[26] Preschoolers may be more able to recall generalized memories than specific memories of events, known as episodic memories.[27] Like adults' memory, children's memory enables them to anticipate future events. This ability also supports the preschoolers' growing ability to establish goals, to outline a plan of behavior to reach those goals, and to sustain the effort to accomplish those goals.

The development of scripts also supports the development of transference expectations. Transference expectations reflect the child's experience or fantasy of how adults act toward them. Children whose parents neglect and ignore their emotional needs, for example, may come to believe that adults, in general, would behave in this way toward them. Transference expectations form in response to children's normative needs to understand their world and to anticipate future events, whether those events are nap time in school or are emotionally charged issues such as whether parents act helpfully or punitively toward them.[28, 29]

These cognitive abilities also support preschoolers' developing talents for telling stories and engaging in

Cognitive Development:
20 months–5 years

COGNITIVE DEVELOPMENT

Begins to report recalled information

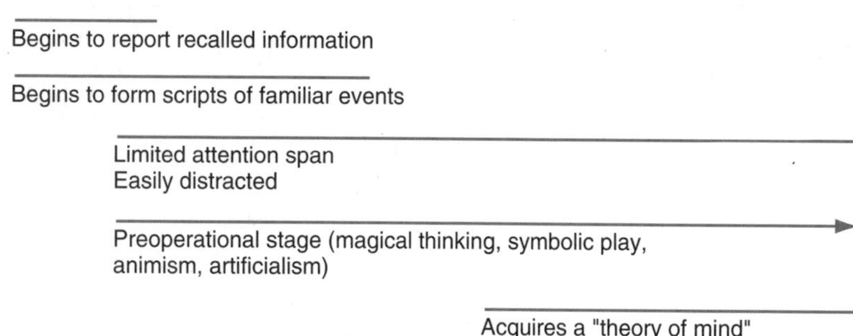

LANGUAGE DEVELOPMENT

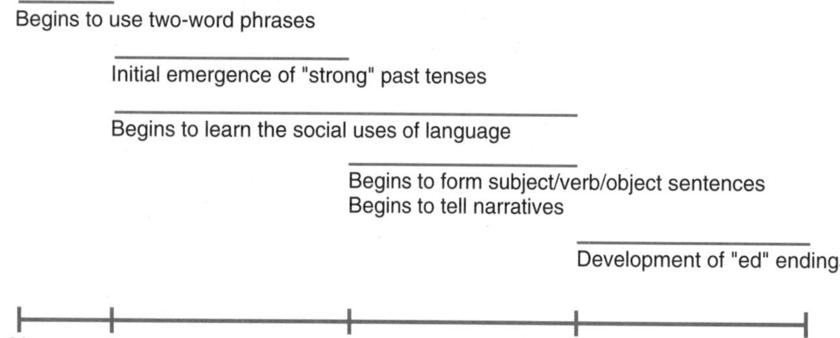

20 months | 2 years | 3 | 4 | 5 years

Figure 7–3 *Cognitive development during the preschool years (20 months to 5 years).*

imaginative play. They permit children to explore what Bruner[30] has termed "possible worlds." Children develop imaginary friends, play dress up, and create stories with doll figures. This forms the basis for play therapy. With the support and insight of the play therapist, children can try out more successful solutions to problematical situations or re-enact traumatic events, tolerating the disturbing emotions the events evoke within the safety of the therapeutic relationship. The ability to make narratives of experience helps the child make sense of emotions and relationships. The ability to tell coherent narratives about important issues and events in their lives is an important developmental achievement.

Understanding cognitive development is helpful for both psychiatrists and parents. Consider a few examples. Although young children are no longer in the sensory-motor stage, in which all reasoning occurs within the context of direct sensory experience, it is often quite helpful to teach them with concrete examples. When explaining a surgical procedure to a young child, a picture is worth more than a thousand words. Draw a picture. Or have the child draw a picture of what he or she thinks is wrong. It provides a clearer view of the child's understanding of the illness. Another example concerns the challenges of psychiatric diagnosis in young children. Because preschoolers normatively have a short attention span, substantial distractibility, and an unsystematic approach to tasks, it is often quite difficult to diagnose attention-deficit/hyperactivity disorder in young children.

A time line of cognitive development from age 20 months to 5 years is presented in Figure 7–3.

Language Development

Language acquisition is an enormous accomplishment. How do children, who are exposed predominantly to complex utterances, induce the multiplicity of grammatical rules that permit them to understand and converse in their language? Answers to this question have mostly been framed within the debate over the influences of nature versus nurture. Chomsky[31] has argued that language development is genetically driven by the formation of specific mental capacities, which he termed the language acquisition device (LAD). His view suggests a strong separation between language and cognition, and it downplays the role of social processes in language development. Others, such as Bruner,[5] have argued that adults scaffold language input for children. For Bruner, the process of learning language is shared; it is not solely an individual achievement. In a humorous vein, Bruner has suggested that language development requires not only a LAD but a LASS as well—a language acquisition support structure—the social environment that supports the child's growing linguistic abilities.

Linguistic development can be separated into four domains: sounds (phonology), words, methods of combining words (grammar), and sociocultural roles that language serves. Preschoolers are actively acquiring the capacity to pronounce different sounds, which becomes apparent when one compares how 3- and 4-year-olds talk. However, the capacity to form different sounds develops at different rates in this age group.

It is remarkable that children learn the meaning of individual words by listening to how they are used and trying to use them themselves. They tend to learn simpler forms first. A 2-year-old can say "no," but at 3 she or he can say "nobody" and "nothing." Language learning is an active process, and children make mistakes. Toddlers engage regularly in overextension when they use a word as if it refers to more than it actually does. They might say "daddy" to refer to all men. They engage in underextension when they restrict the meaning of a word. An example would be using "animal" to refer only to certain familiar mammals, such as cats and dogs, but not daddies or fish. Children by 2 to 3 years of age learn strong past-tense endings (such as "brought" or "sang"), because these endings are common and useful. They learn these verb forms before they learn to apply "ed" as a suffix to form the past tense for standard verbs, as in "teased." The development of "ed" endings, which occurs about age 4 years, leads them to switch to overgeneralized versions of verbs that take a strong past-tense ending (they say "bringed" and "singed"). By the end of the preschool period, most young children have sorted out the rules and use these verb forms correctly.

Why do we learn to say "I will let you play" but not "I will allow you play"? Children must learn to use grammar to organize words into sentences so that they can communicate their ideas and wishes. Toddlers begin the third year of life in the two-word phase. They are able to form propositions, typically by bringing a subject together with a verb or object: "Me cookie" or "Rover come." By the age of 3 years, children can form subject-verb-object sentences. Later, they develop the capacity for narrative. As Bruner and others have indicated, the linguistic environment supports language learning in children. Parents speak to their infants slowly in simple statements, using small vocabularies.[32] This use of "motherese" occurs across languages and social classes.[33] However, children learn grammar primarily through exposure to examples of correct syntax. It is uncommon for parents to correct their children's grammar. Strikingly, when they do, children usually ignore them. There are gender differences in language input as well. Mothers talk more to daughters. Concomitantly, girls are more advanced than boys in their language development.

Preschoolers acquire substantial knowledge of the social uses of language. Two-year-olds begin to understand that "Is the door shut" is often an indirect command and not a question.[34] Four-year-olds can take into account who their listener is when speaking. They alter their speech and use motherese when they speak with children who are younger than themselves.[33] Language development is a complex and fascinating field. Scrutiny of what young children learn in such a short time leaves us in awe of their accomplishments.

Emotional Development

Regulation of emotion is a principal developmental task of the preschool years.[35] The emotionally competent 6-year-old can increasingly regulate multiple emotions in diverse contexts. An increased capacity for regulation of emotion enables the child to make the transition from the normative dependency and supervision in the home to the broader social world of the school, where greater emotion regulation and self-regulation are expected.[36]

In contrast to earlier views, which conceptualized emotions as principally disorganizing behavior, research indicates that emotions also act as adaptive organizers of behavior. When confronted with a frightening stimulus, a child's fear organizes a fight-or-flight response. On seeing a novel, loud toy that can elicit either fear or pleasure, infants use adults' expressions of emotion to guide their behavior. They are more likely to approach the toy if the adult smiles or flee from it if the adult shows fear. [37] This is known as social referencing, and it indicates that emotions can serve functional roles, organizing children's behavior.

Since Arnold,[38] theories have characterized emotion regulation into two component processes. First, children appraise the meaning of the stimulus within the context of their values and goals. Most emotions are elicited through appraisal processes. It is precisely because a tiger that is leaping at us is threatening that we feel fear. Second, children modulate the behavioral expression of the emotion. Many of the skills that are used to interpret events, elicit emotions, modulate expression, and organize behavior develop in the preschool period.

Central to the social cognitive skills that underlie appraisal processes is a growing ability to think about emotions and relationships. At the end of infancy, toddlers can discriminate emotions by facial expression[39] and by differences in vocalizations.[40] Their knowledge of the situational elicitors of emotion increases.[41] They understand that individuals' desires and beliefs affect the emotions they feel in different situations.[42] Children understand that people are happy if they expect to obtain a goal, even if they are incorrect in their belief that they will obtain that goal.[43] They can evaluate others' intent,[44] and they increasingly understand the relationship between emotion and behavior.[45] These skills support the child's ability to interpret accurately the meaning of events as emotions are elicited during their day-to-day life.

There are substantial advances in their capacity to modulate the expression of emotion as well. They become better able to modulate their emotional arousal, and preschoolers develop increasingly sophisticated coping strategies to regulate the expression of emotions. They are able to use parents and teachers to organize their emotional responses to disconcerting events. Young children learn to abide by culturally defined rules of emotional expression, which includes learning to mask emotional expression in certain situations. For example, if 3- to 4-year-olds are promised a gift but are given one they do not want, they inhibit their display of disappointment if the adult who gave them the toy is present but they express their disappointment if they are alone.[46]

The interrelationship between cognitive and emotional development is apparent in preschoolers' growing ability to modulate their expression of emotions. Preschoolers develop a capacity to inhibit and delay behavioral plans,[47, 48] begin to use problem solving in a reflective and planful manner, act in accordance with internalized standards when not in the caregiver's presence,[49] and develop a sense of personal responsibility for their own actions.[36] The role of neural development in these processes, particularly in the frontal lobes, remains an important area of investigation.

One of the most important advances in emotion modulation skills is the ability to use symbolization, language,[4, 50] and narrative[51] to express emotions. By the age of 3 years, children can communicate about past, current, and future emotions.[52] However, there are large individual differences in this domain. In a naturalistic, home-based study, 3-year-olds varied from almost never talking about their feelings to talking about them every 2 minutes with their mothers.[53] Peers and siblings also play an important role in the development of emotion language. One study found that although children who were 2 years 9 months old talked more with their mothers about their feelings, by 3 years 11 months they talked more with their older siblings. Interestingly, the children were more likely to comment on their siblings' feelings than their mothers' feelings, suggesting that siblings provide an opportunity for learning about others' emotions that may be less available to only children.[54]

As indicated, preschoolers are able to tell coherent narratives or stories about their experiences. This not only enables them to organize their understanding of the meaning of events but also supports their expressing it in language rather than in action. Play therapy is helpful to children in part because it promotes the development of these skills. This is particularly noticeable when young children learn to put angry feelings into words instead of acting aggressively.

One of the central principles of emotional development is that it occurs within the context of relationships. Although, as we discuss later in the section on sociocultural influences, peers, siblings, and teachers play an increasingly important role in children's development, children's primary caregivers are always critical in their emotional development. Interest in how young children develop emotionally within the context of the parent-child relationship has developed primarily from psychoanalytic observations. These investigations have focused on preschoolers' progressive physical and intrapsychic separation from their parents. Children are increasingly able to tolerate being at both a physical and a psychological distance from their parents for longer lengths of time. Winnicott[55] described this as the ability to be alone. Mahler and colleagues[56] characterized this process as the fourth subphase of separation-individuation, which they described with the unusual phrase "on the way to libidinal object constancy." The word libidinal in psychoanalytic usage refers to Freud's conceptualization of the sexual drive. Object refers to the people to whom the individual is relating, in contrast to the index child or subject. Object constancy refers to the ability to calm oneself, self-soothe, and reduce and tolerate anxiety in response to separation from the primary caregiver. Object constancy has been thought to depend on the 2-year-old's capacity to recall an image of the caregiver as soothing, even when the caregiver is absent. However, object constancy is not an act of memory but is an emotional skill that builds on the child's growing capacity for recall.[29] Many psychoanalytic theorists have linked difficulties in acquiring object constancy with the disorganizing anxiety seen in patients with borderline personality disorder.[57]

Object constancy arises from the sense of "basic trust"[58] that the infant develops from emotionally sensitive and competent caregiving. Bowlby[59] characterized this process as the development of a secure attachment to the caregiver, as reviewed in Chapter 6. In the preschool period, attachment researchers have focused on the development of internal working models of the attachment relationship, an idea that derives from the work of psychoanalytic object relations theorists.[60, 61] The hypothesis is that children construct a mental model involving emotions, memories, and sets of expectations of how their caregivers act toward them. Are they warm and nurturing, responding helpfully when you are hurt, or are they harsh and punitive? Internal working models may develop from young children's ability to form scripts of repeatedly occurring events.[28, 29, 62] These expectations become a frame, or internal context, within which children appraise the meaning of events. These appraisals then elicit the children's emotional reactions, organizing their behavior. For example, a child who expects her or his father's frustration to turn into abusive anger may feel anger or fear and then hide. Research is under way to test a number of hypotheses about children's internal working models of relationships.[63]

The notion of the Oedipus complex is quite related to these ideas. In its simplest form, the oedipal hypothesis postulates that young children emotionally and sexually desire the parent of the opposite sex, are angry at the parent of the same sex, with whom they perceive themselves in competition for the opposite-sex parent, but also fear retribution from this parent. Fundamentally, the Oedipus complex involves developing a set of feelings and ideas about one's parents and how they feel and are likely to act toward one. The ideas about internal working models of relationships and the Oedipus complex both acknowledge the preschooler's ability to form expectations about others' actions, which then organize their emotions and behavior. They differ in a number of important ways, however. Whereas internal working models are thought to be constructed from actual experiences, Freud hypothesized that oedipal thoughts develop from the child's internal fantasies. Furthermore, the theory of the Oedipus complex involves hypotheses about the specific content of those fantasies (e.g., envy, hatred, and fear of the parent of the opposite sex). Both theories claim that these mental structures are critical in the lives of preschoolers and are intimately involved in personality formation. Both theories would benefit from further specification of the mechanisms by which internal working models and oedipal fantasies affect behavior. Further research should help us to understand these developmental processes.

A time line of emotional development from age 20 months to 5 years is presented in Figure 7–4.

Sociocultural Influences

Much of children's socialization occurs within the context of the parent-child relationship. Vygotsky[8, 9] has been influential in his observations of how parents scaffold their children's development in the zone of proximal development. Parents influence their children's development predominantly through their moment to moment, day-to-day interactions with their children. They experience delight in their toddlers' growing motoric abilities, supporting the development of pride and self-esteem. They offer them choices when appropriate, supporting their toddlers' sense of themselves as agents who can have a positive impact on their environment. They teach them social mores as well as moral

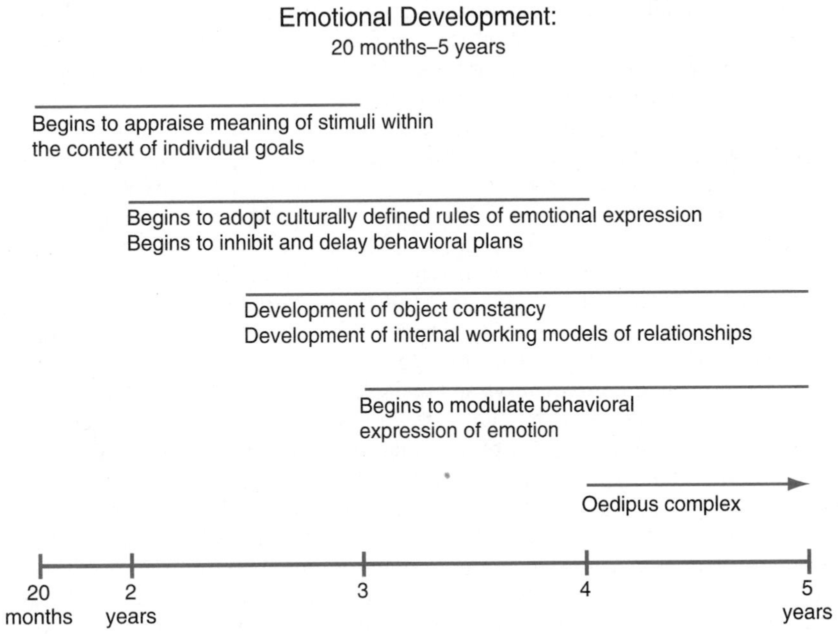

Emotional Development:
20 months–5 years

Begins to appraise meaning of stimuli within the context of individual goals

Begins to adopt culturally defined rules of emotional expression
Begins to inhibit and delay behavioral plans

Development of object constancy
Development of internal working models of relationships

Begins to modulate behavioral expression of emotion

Oedipus complex

20 months | 2 years | 3 | 4 | 5 years

Figure 7–4 *Emotional development during the preschool years (20 months to 5 years).*

rules, promoting prosocial and attenuating aggressive behavior. They talk with the toddlers, recalling events of the day and reading stories, encouraging the development of language. They support their enjoyment of imaginative, pretend play, which enhances symbolic thinking and social understanding. They take pleasure in their developing ability to play with peers, supporting a healthy separation from the parents, and their developing autonomy. Above all, children learn about healthy, reciprocal relationships by loving and being loved by their parents.

Baumrind[64] has delineated four general styles of parenting (Table 7–2). The authoritarian style is demanding, is controlling, and makes frequent use of threats and punishment. This parenting style correlates with having children who are moody, irritable, aggressive, and at higher risk for developing disruptive behavior disorders. Indifferent parents set few limits, engage in less monitoring of their children's behavior, and often appear detached. Their children tend to be demanding, tend to be less compliant, and have poorer interpersonal skills with peers. The permissive style is loving, is emotionally available, tends to set few limits, and is accepting and encouraging. The children are often impulsive and have behavioral problems. The authoritative parenting style is characterized as caring, emotionally available, setting appropriate limits, and maintaining structure and reasonable expectations for the children. The children in turn are more independent, have better social skills, and are more self-confident.

Siblings and peers become increasingly important to young children during the preschool years. Preschoolers tend to spend more time with peers and less time with adults than toddlers do. In turn, siblings and their peers affect the development of social and cognitive skills in their younger brothers and sisters.[65] Children who compete with siblings for toys or for their parents' attention may be more motivated to decipher what others think and feel, which may support the development of social cognitive skills.[20] These skills can then be used either to please or to annoy their siblings.[6] An interesting finding in this area is that, although young children are more likely to be rivalrous with their siblings than with unrelated peers, they are also more likely to be more cooperative and nurturing with their siblings than with other children.[20]

There are sex differences in the development of children's peer relationships that are evident by age 2 years. Boys are more aggressive, are more likely to engage in

Table 7–2 Parenting Styles

Style	Characteristics	Clinical Correlation in Children
Authoritarian	Demanding, controlling, threatening, punishing	Moodiness, irritability, aggressivity, risk for development of behavior disorders
Indifferent	Sets few limits, decreased monitoring of behavior, detachment	Demanding, less compliant, poor peer relationships
Permissive	Loving, emotionally available, sets few limits, accepting, encouraging	Impulsivity, behavior problems
Authoritative	Caring, emotionally available, appropriate limit setting, maintains structure, reasonable expectations	Independent, stronger social skills, confident

rough-and-tumble play, and are more apt to play with objects that can be manipulated, such as blocks or trucks. Girls often prefer doll play, dress up, and artwork. However, as with virtually all group differences, children of both sexes engage in both types of play. Children in all cultures prefer to play with same-sex partners, which is known as gender segregation. These preferences are evident by 33 months and increase during the school years. There is a long history of debate over whether sex differences reflect the influence of nature or nurture. Observations of parents clearly document differences in their behavior toward children of different sexes. It remains unclear, however, which behaviors reflect larger genetic or environmental influences.

Much of children's cognitive and social learning occurs through play. Early research[66] suggested that preschoolers progress through four stages of play: solitary play, in which children play alone; parallel play, in which children play side by side but limit their interactions; associative play, in which children share toys but do not adopt roles or cooperate to reach a goal; and cooperative play, in which the latter features become prominent. Solitary play and parallel play decrease and associative play and cooperative play increase during the preschool years. However, children continue to engage in all forms of play. In the preschool years, children increasingly enjoy pretend play, which allows them to try out new roles and experiences and master difficult feelings. By the beginning of elementary school, children become more interested in rule-governed games, which support the growth of collaborative problem solving.

Daycare has become an important caregiving environment for young children. This has raised questions about its influence on children's development. Some studies suggest that children may be less likely to develop secure attachments to their parents if they have more experience in daycare. However, children may also develop secure attachments to their daycare providers. Intellectual and linguistic development may actually improve for middle-class children cared for in good daycare centers.[67] These children tend to be more self-sufficient and less dependent on their parents. Findings are mixed on other variables: children may be more knowledgeable about and more comfortable in social situations, yet they may be less compliant and more aggressive than children not exposed to daycare.[68] These studies suggest that the quality of the daycare is the critical variable. Larger daycare centers are less likely to let children initiate activities, and they tend to emphasize rules to maintain order. Teachers may be less likely to be sensitive to the individual needs of children.[68] A major federally funded, multisite study is under way to investigate these questions.

There has been increasing recognition of the importance of cultural influences on children's development. Children develop within a culture, acquiring many of its expectations and patterns outside their awareness. The meaning of their behavior can then be understood only within the context of those cultural patterns and norms. For example, when children are evaluated for depression, we must understand whether the child's culture values concealing or expressing emotion. Children who learn not to express emotion may be seen as having a flat facial affect, which can be misinterpreted as reflecting depression. It is essential to understand the functional meaning of a behavior as it is understood within the child's culture.

These issues have become more prominent as we have increasingly appreciated the cultural and class bias in previous developmental studies. Most studies of child development, including those reviewed in this chapter, have focused predominantly on middle-class, white families. This has made it difficult to know what is universal and what is culture specific in children's development. This is critical because research indicates that cultural variability is prevalent in children's development. Another example is the cross-cultural differences in siblings' roles. Many non-Western, nonindustrialized cultures encourage children to be important caregivers for their younger siblings.[69] Parents' use of praise[70] and children's attention-seeking behavior [71, 72] show marked cross-cultural variation. Many cultures do not value independence and assertiveness in children to the extent that they are valued in the majority American culture, instead emphasizing caretaking and mutual responsibility.[73] These differences have an important impact on children's social development.

A time line of social development from age 20 months to 5 years is presented in Figure 7–5.

Moral Development

Why do children learn to behave in accordance with societal standards? It is not simply a matter of learning social mores and moral rules. Some children know what is expected of them but are not motivated to comply. Other children want to follow their parents' directives, but they find themselves becoming angry and aggressive and then regretting their destructive actions. These observations illustrate the com-

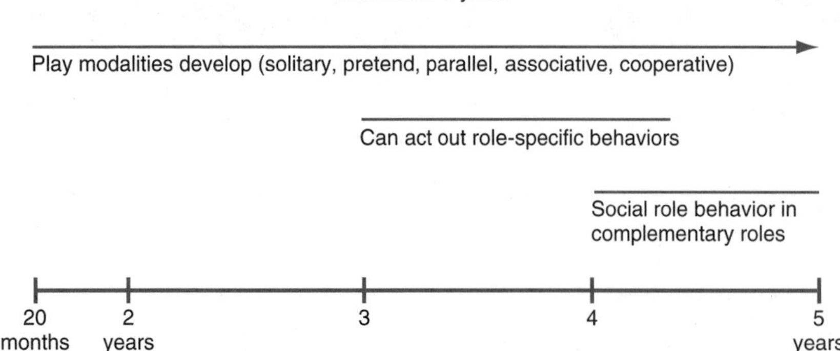

Figure 7–5 *Social development during the preschool years (20 months to 5 years).*

plexity of the cognitive, emotional, and motivational processes involved in moral behavior. Central to these processes is the principle that moral development, like emotional development in general, occurs within the context of relationships. Parents influence their children's moral development through their moment to moment interactions with them. They communicate their expectations both explicitly and implicitly. They model acceptable behavior, both self-consciously and without forethought. They help their children to regulate their anger and aggression and to act prosocially, learning to share their toys and to act fairly with their friends. Children internalize their parents' expectations within the context of a loving relationship with them.

The value of a broad perspective in understanding moral development has been articulated. This view emphasizes the central role that emotions play in organizing moral behavior, the early development of moral motives and behavior in the infant and toddler years, the importance of shared experience with others in internalizing moral emotions and values, and the role of nonconscious information processing in moral behavior.[49, 74] This view stands in contrast to the historically important views of Piaget [2] and Kohlberg,[75] who argued that moral development begins with the acquisition of perspective taking, with the onset of concrete operations about the age of 7 years.

The development of moral emotions is a critical process for children's moral development.[49] In the first years of life, infants express the basic or darwinian emotions, which include anger, happiness, sadness, fear, surprise, and disgust. These emotions appear to be neurobiologically hard-wired, are tied to characteristic facial expressions of emotion, and appear across cultures.[76] Beginning in the second year of life and continuing through the preschool years, the moral emotions of empathy, pride, shame, and guilt develop. Unlike the basic emotions, they do not all have characteristic facial expressions, are more internal yet appear to develop from shared experience, and arise either in situations of conflict or in response to internalized standards. Like all emotions, they play functional roles in motivating and organizing children's behavior. Only when they are particularly intense are they likely to disorganize or dysregulate children's behavior.

Moral emotions begin to develop in the second year of life. Toddlers show anxiety when internalized standards are violated, such as when they are presented with a flawed toy or doll.[77] This emotion signals a violation of a norm. Empathy also develops quite early. Infants in the first year of life cry in response to another's distress. By the end of the second year of life, toddlers comfort others who are hurt or crying, patting them gently or bringing them a favorite blanket.[78] This finding was critical historically in focusing research attention on early moral development.[79] Empathy, like pride, is important in the acquisition of the "do's" of moral development.[80] Although parents (and researchers) tend to focus on the "don'ts," that is, children's misbehavior, children often act in accordance with parental and societal standards without a sense of struggle or conflict. Early games involving turn taking and reciprocity, such as an infant and an adult handing a shiny toy back and forth, may set the stage for sharing and early prosocial behavior. Empathy can motivate children's prosocial behavior in the absence of conflict. A twin study has demonstrated that both empathic concern and prosocial behavior are under some genetic control, although to different degrees at different ages.[81] This should not surprise us, because altruistic behavior may increase the likelihood that a social group reproduces, therefore increasing the probability that altruism is selected for in evolution. [82] This view stresses the role empathy plays as a critical mediator of early moral development.

Pride also develops early in childhood. Like embarrassment, shame, and guilt, it evokes a relationship with a significant other who has set a standard that the child has internalized. Pride involves pleasure over meeting that standard and may be expressed with one's head held high, a puffed-up posture, and a puffed-up feeling. Young children are excited and proud when they experience themselves as agents who can have an important effect on people and events in their world.[58] In contrast, shame and embarrassment evoke an image of the significant other casting a disapproving look, and the child wishes he or she could escape from being seen. Shame and embarrassment are remarkably visual emotions. Guilt is an auditory emotion in that we readily evoke the significant other's disapproving voice. Guilt appears later than the other moral emotions, although it may develop from earlier reparative behaviors.[83] Whereas guilt appears to be invoked when a child feels that an act was bad, shame appears to arise when it is the self that is evaluated negatively.[84]

Moral emotions evoke a sense of shared experience with important others that is central to the process of moral internalization. By the end of the first year of life, children engage in social referencing, looking to an adult when they are uncertain and modifying their behavior depending on the adult's emotional response. This interpersonal emotional signaling is transformed into internal emotional signaling with the development of moral emotions. Moral emotions alert us to possible or actual rule violations, invoking an auditory or visual representation of the significant other's emotional response.

The acquisition of moral and social rules also develops from shared experience. Young toddlers who are repeatedly told not to approach a stove become older toddlers who utter "no" or "hot" to themselves when they walk near it. However, rule internalization is quite tentative at this age, and toddlers typically regulate their behavior "under the watchful eyes of the caregiver."[80] It is not until later that they learn to withstand temptation by themselves without direct adult support. But we believe there is developmental continuity in these processes from quite an early age.

The acquisition of regulatory rules often occurs outside conscious awareness.[29, 49] Just as children learn to use grammatical rules before they learn in school how to articulate those rules, young children learn to behave in accordance with parental and cultural standards before they can articulate, or are even conscious of, those standards. Indeed, a child can acquire moral and social rules even if adults never verbalize them to the child. Much of psychological research is directed at articulating the rules that govern human behavior, even though individuals are not conscious of those rules. This is particularly true for moral and social standards.

As the child moves directly into the preschool period, social cognitive processes become increasingly important in mediating development in the moral sphere. Young children

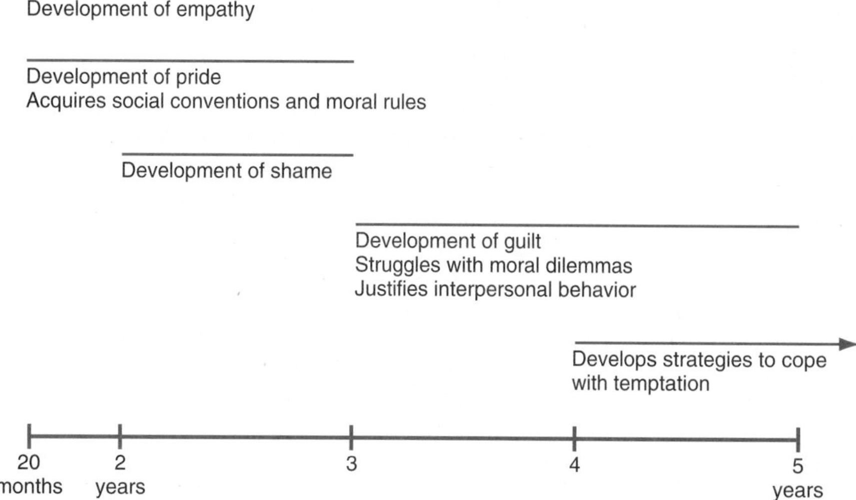

Figure 7–6 *Moral development during the preschool years (20 months to 5 years).*

are increasingly able to appraise the meaning of others' behavior and to interpret social cues. They develop an understanding that others have feelings and intentions. This is referred to as acquiring a theory of mind, realizing that others have thoughts, feelings, and desires as we do. Children begin to deceive others in the preschool years, perhaps because they understand that others can hold beliefs that are not true. Ironically, this is a developmental achievement.[85]

Preschoolers begin to justify their prosocial actions. In response to teacher's directives, they explain that one should obey authority figures or indicate that they fear punishment. However, when justifying prosocial behavior toward friends or peers, they refer to their relationships with them or comment on their needs.[86] By the end of the third year of life, children can distinguish between social conventions (e.g., not to place your elbows on the table) and moral rules (e.g., not to hurt others), and they know that moral violations are considered more serious.[87]

Children also develop more sophisticated strategies for coping with temptation. Mischel[47, 88] offered children a choice of an immediate reward or a more desirable prize after some delay. Few young preschoolers spontaneously develop delay strategies, but they are developed by 5 to 6 years of age. However, when the researchers provided the children with strategies, such as trying to distract themselves, they were able to use them to resist the temptation. Similarly, parents teach their children to regulate temptation within the zone of proximal development.

The development of preschoolers' capacity for narrative permits them to talk about moral events and to consider alternative outcomes. Moral themes are frequent in young children's doll play. Children as young as 3 years old can struggle with simple moral dilemmas, if presented to them in an age-appropriate form.[51] They struggle, for example, with whether they should help an injured peer even if it means disobeying a parental directive. There may be substantial variations in how children resolve moral dilemmas depending on their caregiving environment.[63]

Psychoanalysts have focused on the oedipal narrative as central to moral development. In this view, the resolution of this conflict leads the child to internalize the same-sex parent's standards and ideals, resulting in the formation of the superego. The Oedipus complex builds on preschool children's ability to narrate experience, think about other's feelings, experience guilt, and entertain alternative possible worlds. Whether the Oedipus complex is central to moral development and personality formation continues to be debated both within and outside psychoanalytic circles.[89] We know, however, that the traditional psychoanalytic view did not adequately address females' experiences or moral development before the age of 4 years and that it overemphasized the role of fear of retribution and guilt without adequately appreciating the part played by empathy and reciprocity in young children's moral development.

Nowhere in developmental psychology is it more evident that one must be thoughtful about one's implicit and explicit assumptions than in discussions of moral development. Freud and Kohlberg principally focused on moral development in boys, giving short shrift to moral development in girls. Similarly, it is critical that we address cultural variations in values and behavior. Only then can we have a valid and useful understanding of moral development.

A time line of moral development from age 20 months to 5 years is presented in Figure 7–6.

Risk and Protective Factors

Modern theories of developmental psychopathology suggest that psychiatric disorders develop from the interaction of risk and protective factors in development. Studies indicate that children with more risk factors and fewer protective factors are more likely to develop a number of different psychiatric disorders. Risk and protective factors operate at multiple levels of influence. There can be child factors such as prematurity or attentional problems, genetic factors, nongenetic biological factors such as closed head injuries, parental influences such as maltreatment, family influences such as the protective value of growing up with caring grandparents or other concerned adults, community influences such as the availability of treatment services, and societal influences such as the current prevalence and toleration of violence in America.

These risk and protective factors can influence all domains of children's development. For example, children who are maltreated are more likely to have language delays and to be angry and aggressive. These risks interact with the availability of community services, such as early intervention programs. Preschoolers may be particularly sensitive to the influence of risk and protective factors because development is so rapid in this period. Their influence is best understood within the broader context of developmental psychopathology, the subject to which we now turn.

Developmental Psychopathology

Developmental psychopathology posits that the ontogeny of psychiatric disorders can best be examined within the context of normal development.[4, 90] The meaning of temper tantrums can be understood only if we know the child's age: temper tantrums in a 2-year-old have a different meaning than a tantrum in a 10-year-old. Atypical development provides an "experiment in nature"[91] that illuminates our understanding of normal development. Just as the normal functioning of the islets of Langerhans was determined by studying diabetic patients, we can learn about normal development by studying psychopathological variations.

Multivariate, transactional models are used to understand the reciprocal influence that the child and the caregiving environment have on each other over time. The balance of risk and protective factors is critical in influencing the child's outcome. Risk is considered probabilistically. Inability to master developmental tasks at one age places the child at increased risk for subsequent developmental difficulties. But later developmental challenges offer new opportunities for emotional growth. Outcomes are often evaluated as healthier or less optimal adaptations to exigent conditions, both environmental and genetic. Psychopathology is often evaluated dimensionally, examining, for example, more or less aggression, emphasizing the continuities between normal and atypical development. This view stands in contrast to the biomedical, categorical perspective found in the *Diagnostic and Statistical Manual of Mental Disorders*, Fourth Edition. The perspective of developmental psychopathology can best be illustrated with an example.

The disruptive behavior disorders, including attention-deficit/hyperactivity disorder, oppositional defiant disorder, and conduct disorder, are the most common reason for presentation to child psychiatric clinics.[92] Disruptive behavior is particularly common in the preschool period. However, judging whether oppositional and aggressive behavior reflects a psychiatric disorder is often difficult in preschoolers, because some defiant and aggressive behavior is normative in this age group as children struggle to define themselves, separate from parents, and modulate their strong emotions.

There is growing evidence of continuity in disruptive behavior patterns from preschool to later childhood. Examining 3-year-olds with disruptive behavior problems, Richman and colleagues[93] found that the problems persisted, both at home and in school, in 62% of the children at age 8 years. However, stability of behavior problems was associated with a range of risk factors operating at multiple levels of influence, including family factors (marital conflict, maternal depression, punitive child-rearing styles) and social factors (including poor housing and financial difficulties). Child factors are important as well. Children with early language difficulties are subsequently at risk for both emotional and behavioral disorders.[94] Early disruptive behavior is associated with other outcomes, such as internalizing disorders, reading difficulties, and low school achievement.[94, 95] Severe behavior problems in preschoolers can also predict multiple difficulties into adolescence.[96] Protective factors operate as well. For example, stable family functioning can prevent early temperamental difficulties from developing into later behavioral disorders.

Developmental psychopathology models continually confront us with the complexity of preschoolers' development. In our work with young children, both those who are at risk and those who are developing well, we often feel both joy and amazement as we see what young children can do, what they can learn, what they can feel, and what they can understand. Indeed, our joy and amazement are not unlike the glee preschoolers experience in their encounter with the world.

References

1. Spitz R, Emde R, Metcalf D: Further prototypes of ego formation. Psychoanal Study Child 1970; 25:417–444.

1a. Freud S: Three essays on the theory of sexuality. In Strachey J (trans-ed): The Standard Edition of the Complete Works of Sigmund Freud, Volume 7. London: Hogarth Press, 1953:125–243. Originally published in 1905.

1b. Freud A: The writings of Anna Freud, Volume 7, Normality and Pathology in Childhood: Assessments of Development. New York: International Universities Press, 1965.

2. Piaget J: The Origin of Intelligence in Children. New York: International Universities Press, 1952.

2a. Erikson E: Identity and the Life Cycle. Psychological Issues, Monograph 1. New York: International Universities Press, 1959.

3. Sroufe LA: Infant-caregiver attachment and patterns of adaptation in preschool: The roots of maladaptation and competence. Minn Symp Child Psychol 1983; 16:41–81.

4. Cicchetti D: The emergence of developmental psychopathology. Child Dev 1989; 55:1–7.

5. Bruner J: Child's Talk. New York: WW Norton, 1983.

6. Dunn J: The Beginnings of Social Understanding. Cambridge, MA: Harvard University Press, 1988.

7. Stern D: The Interpersonal World of the Infant. New York: Basic Books, 1985.

8. Vygotsky LS: Mind in Society: The Development of Higher Psychological Processes. Cambridge, MA: Harvard University Press, 1978.

9. Vygotsky LS: Thought and Language. Cambridge, MA: The MIT Press, 1986.

10. Plomin R, Daniels D: Why are children in the same family so different from each other? Behav Brain Sci 1987; 10:1–16.

11. Loehlin JC, Horn JM, Willerman L: Modeling IQ change: Evidence from the Texas Adoption Project. Child Dev 1989; 60:993–1004.

12. Plomin R: The Emanuel Miller Memorial Lecture 1993: Genetic research and identification of environmental influences. J Child Psychol Psychiatry 1994; 35:817–834.

13. Rutter M, Bailey A, Bolton P, Le Couteur A: Autism: Syndrome definition and possible genetic mechanisms. In Plomin R, McClearn GE (eds): Nature, Nurture, and Psychology. Washington, DC: American Psychological Association, 1993:269–284..

14. Sidman RL, Rakic P: Neuronal migration, with special reference to developing human brain: A review. Brain Res 1973; 62:1–35.

15. Lowery GH: Growth and Development of Children, 8th ed. Chicago: Year Book Medical Publishers, 1986.

16. Changeux JP, Danchin A: Selective stabilisation of developing synapses as a mechanism for the specification of neuronal networks. Nature 1976; 264:705–712.

17. Huttenlocher PR: Synaptic density in human frontal cortex—developmental changes and effects of aging. Brain Res 1979; 163:195–205.
18. Dennis M, Whitaker HA: Language acquisition following hemidecortication: Linguistic superiority of the left over the right hemisphere. Brain Lang 1976; 3:404–433.
19. Woods BT, Teuber HL: Changing patterns of childhood aphasia. Ann Neurol 1978; 3:273–280.
20. Berger KS: The Developing Person Through the Lifespan, 3rd ed. New York: Worth Publishers, 1994.
21. Eaton WO, Yu AP: Are sex differences in child motor activity level a function of sex differences in maturational status? Child Dev 1989; 60:1005–1011.
22. Saudino K, Eaton W: Heredity and infant activity level: An objective twin study. Paper presented to the International Society for the Study of Behavioral Development; 1989; Jybaskyla, Finland. Cited by: Berger KS: The Developing Person Through the Lifespan, 3rd ed. New York: Worth Publishers, 1994:215.
23. Flavell JH, Flavell ER, Green FL: Development of the appearance-reality distinction. Cognitive Psychol 1983; 15:95–120.
24. Zinchenko VP, Chzhi-Tsin V, Tarakanov VV: The formation and development of perceptual activity. Sov Psychol 1963; 2:3–12.
25. Case R, Khanna F: The missing links: Stages in children's progression from sensorimotor to logical thought. New Dir Child Dev 1981; 12:21–32.
26. Nelson K, Gruendel J: Generalized event representations: Basic building blocks of cognitive development. In Lamb ME, Brown AL (eds): Advances in Developmental Psychology, Volume 1. Hillsdale, NJ: Lawrence Erlbaum, 1981:131–158.
27. Nelson K: Event Knowledge: Structure and Function in Development. Hillsdale, NJ: Lawrence Erlbaum, 1986.
28. Bretherton I: Attachment theory: Retrospect and prospect. Monogr Soc Res Child Dev 1985; 50:3–35.
29. Clyman RB: The procedural organization of emotions: A contribution from cognitive science to the psychoanalytic theory of therapeutic action. J Am Psychoanal Assoc 1991; 39(suppl):349–382.
30. Bruner J: Actual Minds, Possible Worlds. Cambridge, MA: Harvard University Press, 1986.
31. Chomsky N: Aspects of the Theory of Syntax. Cambridge, MA: The MIT Press, 1975.
32. Snow CE: Mother's speech to children learning language. Child Dev 1972; 43:549–565.
33. Shatz M, Gelman R: The development of communication skills: Modification in the speech of young children as a function of listener. Monogr Soc Res Child Dev 1973; Vol 5:1–38.
34. Shatz M: Children's comprehension of question-directives. J Child Lang 1978; 5:39–46.
35. Maccoby EE: Social Development. New York: Harcourt Brace Jovanovich, 1980.
36. Kopp CB: Regulation of distress and negative emotions: A developmental view. Dev Psychol 1989; 25:343–354.
37. Klinnert MD, Emde RN, Butterfield P, Campos JJ: Social referencing: The infant's use of emotional signals from a friendly adult with mother present. Dev Psychol 1986; 22:427–432.
38. Arnold MB: Emotion and Personality. New York: WH Freeman, 1960.
39. Haviland JM, Lelwica M: The induced affect response: 10-week-old infants' responses to three emotional expressions. Dev Psychol 1987; 23:97–104.
40. Fernald A: Human maternal vocalizations to infants as biologically relevant signals: An evolutionary perspective. In Barkow JH, Cosmides L, Tooby J (eds): The Adapted Mind: Evolutionary Psychology and the Generation of Culture. Oxford, UK: Oxford University Press, 1992: 391–428.
41. Denham SA: Social cognition, prosocial behavior, and emotion in preschoolers: Contextual validation. Child Dev 1986; 57:194–201.
42. Wellman HH, Woolley JD: From simple desires to ordinary beliefs: The early development of everyday psychology. Cognition 1990; 35:245–275.
43. Harris PL, Johnson CN, Hutton D, et al: Young children's theory of mind and emotion. Cogn Emotion 1989; 3:379–400.
44. Dodge KA, Pettit GS, McClaskey CL, Brown MM: Social competence in children. Monogr Soc Res Child Dev 1986; 51 G7-20 (2):1–85.
45. Denham SA, Bouril B, Belouad F: Preschoolers' affect and cognition about challenging peer situations. Child Study J 1994; 24:1–21.
46. Cole PM: Children's spontaneous control of facial expression. Child Dev 1986; 57:1309–1321.
47. Mischel W: Metacognition and the rules of delay. In Flavell JH, Ross L (eds): Social Cognitive Development: Frontiers and Possible Futures. New York: Cambridge University Press, 1983:240–271.
48. Gottman J: The world of coordinated play: Same- and cross-sex friendship in young children. In Gottman JM, Parker JG (eds): Conversations of Friends: Speculations on Affective Development. Cambridge, UK: Cambridge University Press, 1986:139–191.
49. Emde RN, Clyman RB: "We hold these truths to be self-evident": The origins of moral motives in individual activity and shared experience. In Noshpitz J (ed): Handbook of Child and Adolescent Psychiatry. New York: John Wiley & Sons, in press.
50. Greenberg MT, Kusche CA, Speltz M: Emotion regulation, self-control, and psychopathology: The role of relationships in early childhood. In Cicchetti D, Toth SL (eds): Internalizing and Externalizing Expressions of Dysfunctions: Rochester Symposium on Developmental Psychopathology, Volume 2. Hillsdale, NJ: Lawrence Erlbaum, 1991:21–55.
51. Buchsbaum HK, Emde RN: Play narratives in 36-month-old children. Psychoanal Study Child 1990; 45:129–155.
52. Bretherton I, Fritz J, Zahn-Waxler C, Ridgeway D: Learning to talk about emotions: A functionalist perspective. Child Dev 1986; 57:529–548.
53. Dunn J, Brown J, Beardsall L: Family talk about feeling states and children's later understanding of others' emotions. Dev Psychol 1991; 27:448–455.
54. Brown J, Dunn J: Talk with your mother or your sibling? Developmental changes in early family conversations about feelings. Child Dev 1992; 63:336–349.
55. Winnicott DW: The capacity to be alone. Int J Psychoanal 1958; 39:416–420.
56. Mahler MS, Pine F, Bergman A: The Psychological Birth of the Human Infant. New York: Basic Books, 1975.
57. Kernberg O: Borderline Conditions and Pathological Narcissism. New York: Jason Aronson, 1975.
58. Erikson EH: Childhood and Society, 2nd ed. New York: WW Norton, 1950.
59. Bowlby J: Attachment and Loss, Volume 1, Attachment. New York: Basic Books, 1969.
60. Klein M: Contributions to Psycho-Analysis 1921–1945. London: Hogarth Press, 1948.
61. Fairburn WRD: Object-Relations Theory of the Personality. New York: Basic Books, 1954.
62. Main M, Kaplan K, Cassidy J: Security in infancy, childhood, and adulthood: A move to the level of representation. Monogr Soc Res Child Dev 1985; 50:66–104.
63. Buchsbaum HK, Toth S, Clyman RB, et al: The use of a narrative story stem technique with maltreated children: Implications for theory and practice. Dev Psychopathol 1993; 4:603–625.
64. Baumrind D: Current patterns of parental authority. Dev Psychol Monogr 1971; 4:1–103.
65. Lamb ME: Social and emotional development in infancy. In Bornstein MH, Lamb ME (eds): Developmental Psychology: An Advanced Textbook, 2nd ed. Hillsdale, NJ: Lawrence Erlbaum, 1988:359–410.
66. Parten M: Social participation among preschool children. J Abnorm Soc Pscyhol 1932; 27:243–269.
67. Clarke-Stewart A: Day-care: A new context for research and development. Minn Symp Child Psychol 1984; 17:61–100.
68. Cole M, Cole SR: The Development of Children. New York: Scientific American Books, 1989.
69. Weisner T: Sibling interdependence and child caretaking: A cross-cultural view. In Lamb ME, Sutton-Smith B (eds): Sibling Relationships: Their Nature and Significance Across the Lifespan. Hillsdale, NJ: Lawrence Erlbaum, 1982:305–327.
70. Whiting BB, Whiting JWM: Children of Six Cultures: A Psychocultural Analysis. Cambridge, MA: Harvard University Press, 1975.
71. LeVine RA: Child rearing as cultural adaptation. In Leiderman PH, Tulkin SR, Rosenfeld A (eds): Culture and Infancy. New York: Academic Press, 1977:15–27.
72. LeVine RA: Anthropology and child development. New Dir Child Dev 1980; 8:71–86.
73. Whiting JWM, Child I: Child Training and Personality: A Cross-Cultural Study. New Haven, CT: Yale University Press, 1953.

74. Emde RN, Biringen Z, Clyman RB, Oppenheim D: The moral self of infancy: Affective core and procedural knowledge. Dev Rev 1991; 11:251–270.
75. Kohlberg L: The Philosophy of Moral Development. San Francisco: Harper & Row Publishers, 1982.
76. Ekman P: Universals and cultural differences in facial expressions of emotion. Nebr Symp Motiv 1971; 19:207–283.
77. Kagan J: The Second Year: The Emergence of Self-awareness. Cambridge, MA: Harvard University Press, 1981.
78. Zahn-Waxler C, Radke-Yarrow M, King R: Child rearing and children's prosocial initiations toward victims of distress. Child Dev 1979; 50:319–330.
79. Radke-Yarrow M, Zahn-Waxler C, Chapman M: Children's prosocial dispositions and behavior. In Hetherington EM (ed), Mussen PH (Series ed): Handbook of Child Psychology, Volume 4, Socialization, Personality, and Social Development. New York: John Wiley & Sons, 1983:469–545.
80. Emde R, Johnson WF, Easterbrooks MA: The do's and don'ts of early moral development: Psychoanalytic tradition and current research. In Kagan J, Lamb S (eds): The Emergence of Morality. Chicago: University of Chicago Press, 1988:
81. Zahn-Waxler C, Robinson J, Emde R: The development of empathy in twins. Dev Psychol 1992; 28:1038–1047.
82. Wilson EO: Sociobiology: The New Synthesis. Cambridge, MA: Harvard University Press, 1975.
83. Zahn-Waxler C, Kochanska G: The origins of guilt. In Thompson RA (ed): The 36th Annual Nebraska Symposium on Motivation: Socioemotional development. Lincoln, NE: University of Nebraska Press, 1990:183–258.
84. Lewis M: Self-conscious emotions and development of self. In Shapiro T, Emde RN (eds): Affect: Psychoanalytic Perspectives. Madison, CT: International Universities Press, 1992:45–73.
85. Hay DF: Prosocial development. J Child Psychol Psychiatry 1994; 35:29–71.
86. Eisenberg N, Lundy T, Shell R, Roth K: Children's justifications for their adult and peer-directed compliant (prosocial and nonprosocial) behaviors. Dev Psychol 1985; 21:325–331.
87. Smetana JG, Braeges JL: The development of toddlers' moral and conventional judgments. Merrill-Palmer Q 1990; 36:329–346.
88. Flavell JH: Cognitive Development, 2nd ed. Englewood Cliffs, NJ: Prentice Hall, 1985.
89. Kohut H: The Restoration of the Self. New York: International Universities Press, 1977.
90. Sroufe LA, Rutter M: The domain of developmental psychopathology. Child Dev 1984; 55:1184–1199.
91. Bronfenbrenner U: The Ecology of Human Development: Experiments by Nature and Design. Cambridge, MA: Harvard University Press, 1979.
92. Robins LN: Conduct disorder. J Child Psychol Psychiatry 1991; 32:193–212.
93. Richman N, Stevenson J, Graham PJ: Preschool to School: A Behavioral Study. London: Academic Press, 1982.
94. Stevenson J, Richman N, Graham G: Behavior problems and language abilities at three years and behavioral deviance at eight years. J Child Psychol Psychiatry 1985; 26:215–230.
95. Campbell SB: Behavior Problems in Preschool Children: Clinical and Developmental Issues. New York: Guilford Press, 1990.
96. Lerner JA, Inui TS, Trupin EW, Douglas E: Preschool behavior can predict future psychiatric disorders. J Am Acad Child Psychiatry 1985; 24:42–48.

CHAPTER

8 School-Age Development

Theodore Shapiro

The age span primarily discussed in this chapter on school-age development is 6 years to pubescence. Demarcating this period as school age is an artifact of Western civilization, industrialization, and the public school system. In the preindustrial era, most instruction took place at home, where the practical issues of life as well as preparation for adulthood were addressed. Alternatively, in aristocratic homes, tutors often taught reading and writing as well as liturgical and scholarly enterprises. Even within the constraints of these cultural and temporal variables, many facts support the concept that this period of childhood is a discrete discontinuous stage in which new skills and neurodevelopmental capacities evolve.

Freud and Piaget both recommended that this period be demarcated because of its uniqueness. Freud[1] characterized it as a period that follows the resolution of the Oedipus complex and subsequent reorganizations in behavior and moral acuity. Piaget [2] emphasized that in this period the child achieves a new stage of operational thinking and develops a new capacity for learning. This period has been variously named by different observers, each using a label that reflects a particular vantage point; the many different labels offer some insight into the theoretical positions of the respective authors. For example, Freud called the period "latency" to designate that early infantile sexuality is repressed and remains latent until puberty. Erikson[3] called it the "age of industry," signifying the tendency of children during this stage to be persistent and task oriented. Sullivan[4] simply referred to it as the "juvenile era," offering an explanation of the consolidation of early attachments and the potential move into adolescence. Piaget[2] provided a detailed description of the concrete operations that bridge the preoperational stage and the later advent of abstract operations.

Each of these models is based on the concept that there is a discontinuity from early toddlerhood. Thomas and Chess[5] argued that this period simply be called "middle childhood," with the warning that more specific names represent theoretical vantage points with strong biases. These perspectives reflect the evidence linking continuities from early childhood into adulthood. Werner[6] provided an alternative perspective of discontinuity and hierarchical reorganization indicating that new functions emerge that are not easily derived from prior stages. Shapiro and Perry[7] argued that the behaviors that become apparent during the period of middle childhood cannot be clearly foretold from the epigenetic sequences of the prior lives of children. Indeed, this is a period marked by a greater capacity and opportunity to learn. These achievements have sufficient consistency across cultures to be considered a maturational discontinuity. These new capacities have been recognized repeatedly by new social roles as well as new cognitive capacities, both within and outside the scientific framework. Freud also implied that hierarchical reorganizations of all developmental capacities occurred during middle childhood. From a theoretical vantage point, Spitz[8] and his followers[9] developed the concept of biodevelopmental shifts based on a maturational succession of organizers that evolve in average expectable environments.

The end of this period is also defined by the emergence of puberty and is associated with the onset of adolescent behaviors that are shaped by cultural expectations. However, puberty is not equivalent to adolescence, despite the reality that adolescence is often initiated by social rituals that presuppose biological maturity.

Middle childhood has been divided into early and late stages. In schools, the curriculum of pre–fourth-graders focuses on reading and writing before the introduction of integrative studies such as social sciences and literature. Psychoanalysts argue that the superego is now relatively new but that morality becomes a crucial issue. Gesell and Ilg[10] provided the best behavioral descriptions of normal school-age children. Gesell's original studies began in the 1930s, but these descriptions hold true even within our current culture.

Gesell and Ilg[10(p131)] wrote, "There is a kind of quieting down at seven. Six-year-olds tended to produce brash reactions and bursts of activities. The 7-year-old goes into lengthy periods of calmness and self-absorption." They further remarked, "At home, as at school, the child's personal social behavior shows an increasing awareness of both self and of others. He is more companionable . . . . He is not a good loser. He tattletales. If a playground situation grows too complex and things go badly, the 7-year-old runs home with a more or less righteous declaration, 'I am quitting.' Let us be duly grateful for his germinating righteousness. It is evident that the 7-year-old is developing an ethical sense." About 8-year-olds, Gesell and Ilg continued, "Eight is more a person by adult standards and in terms of adult-child relationships. One converses with an 8-year-old with lessening condescension . . . . There are three traits which characterize the dynamics of his behavior: speediness, expansiveness, evaluativeness. The 9-year-old is no longer a mere child, nor is he yet a youth. Nine is an intermediate age in the middle zone which lies between the kindergarten and the junior high school teens."

Within a short time span, there are rapid changes in these descriptions and significant behavioral reorganization. There is a growing preoccupation with self but also an increased interest in peer relationships. An expanded moral and social orientation helps the child first to bridge the preschool period with the new period and, later, to move into the period of adolescence. Thus, middle childhood can be understood as a bridge as well as a stage in its own right.

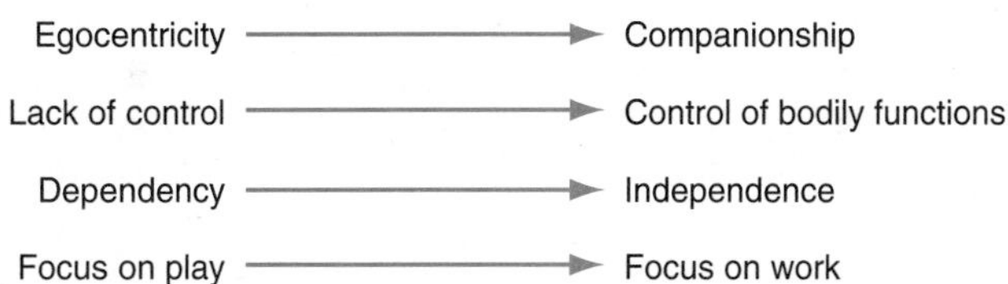

Figure 8–1 *Anna Freud's view of developmental lines. (Adapted from Freud A: A psychoanalytical view of developmental psychopathology. In The Writings of Anna Freud, Volume VIII. New York: International Universities Press, 1981:57–95. Originally published in 1974.)*

Conceptual Framework

The concept of lines of development outlined throughout this section on development provides a means of considering development in a linear manner. Anna Freud's[11] concepts of developmental lines (Fig. 8–1) moving from egocentricity to companionship, from body tyranny to mastery over one's body, and from dependency to independence all represent examples of the tasks that are partly accomplished during middle childhood. All lines must progress on schedule for there to be horizontal continuity. There are times, however, when some functions and skills lag behind others, and yet we may describe a child as being in middle childhood.

From the earliest of times, children of 6 and 7 years were believed to have achieved the capacity for some degree of independent action. Darwin proposed the general maxim for mammals of "small broods, long caretaking." In our culture, children remain dependent well into adolescence, but it is recognized that 6- and 7-year-olds are able to attend school and learn the basic skills that are necessary for later education and adaptation. Preschool and kindergarten currently provide early socialization experiences that previously occurred naturally within the family and community. Preschool gatherings are preparatory for "real" school work. Kohlberg and Gilligan[12] commented that all cultures recognize "two great stages of transformation and development," one at 5 to 7 years and the other in adolescence.

Although Aries[13] has suggested that early Western cultures did not recognize early childhood, the Roman Catholic Church considered the age of 7 years to be the age of reason. In recognition of the 7-year-old's increased cognitive capacity, the Catholic Church deemed this age the appropriate time for first communion. Similarly, the early English kings determined that the age of 7 years was significant for common law. Children younger than age 7 years were believed to be incapable not only of criminal intent but also of taking an oath to testify in a courtroom. At 7, boys apprenticed as tradesworkers and artisans to learn specific skills.[14]

During the industrial revolution, children were employed as laborers in factories, and because of their size they were often given specific positions such as chimney sweeps and mine crawlers. These activities placed them at increased risk for a variety of industrial diseases and physical abuse. In the United States, the child labor laws were among the first laws to protect children in our society; they were later expanded to curtail abusive labor practices involving adults.

Freud looked at the period of latency as a major step in the developmental course. The Oedipus complex is considered a nuclear conflict.[15] Freud was presaged by Diderot and St. Augustine regarding the moral development of children. Diderot[15a] wrote, "If the little savage were left to himself, preserving all his foolishness and adding to all the small sense of a child in the cradle the violent passions of a man of thirty, he would strangle his father and lie with his mother." Augustine concurred with this, saying, "If babies are innocent, it is not for lack of will to do harm, but for lack of strength."[16]

The Oedipus complex provides a basic human formula containing the permutations of the experiences of the developing child directed toward the first two important objects of dependence, mother and father. Freud's[17] hierarchy of anxieties or danger signals includes the threat of castration as a mental deterrent to the wishes of this period and leads to repression of the constellations that are again revived in postadolescent children. Bornstein,[18] an early freudian, suggested that there is "a persistent denial of the struggle against the breakthrough of instinctual impulses" during the early period. The former lively desires are repressed, and the latency child directs energy to the accomplishment of age-appropriate tasks.

There is sufficient variation in the course of middle childhood to lead some observers to question the capacity of the theory-driven model to explain the phenomena encountered. Longitudinal studies that traverse latency suggest a more linear developmental course.[19–21] With the emergence of industriousness, an increase in number and kinds of relationships, and the importance of belonging to peer groups, five emergent patterns of development have been described. The first is the most frequent and is characterized by a steady developmental progression such as that described by Offer and Offer[20] and Neubauer and Flapan[22] for some children during adolescence. A second group has behavioral difficulties early in life that are resolved during middle childhood. A third group presents with early behavior problems and develops new problems in middle childhood that are associated with new stressors. A fourth group has early behavioral problems that persist into middle childhood. A fifth demonstrates entirely new problems in middle childhood.

A more specific group of children known as *difficult children* was also distinguished by Chess and Thomas.[23] Difficult children express early behaviors that are correlated with later school problems, social difficulties, and psychiatric disorders. They show slower adaptability to new situations and intense negative reactions to stimuli.

The children who experienced persistent difficulties from preschool through latency were described by Richman and colleagues[24] in a London epidemiological study. Polysymptomatic 3-year-olds were found to show persistent trouble when they were followed up at 7 and 9 years of age. Early epidemiological studies by LaPouse and Monk[25] and McFarland and colleagues[26] demonstrated that with advancing age there is a decrease in the prevalence of behavior disorders in middle-class school-age children.

Biological Development

As early as 1935, Schilder[27] described the gradual cephalocaudad maturation and intersensory integration of the developing child with specific documentation of the discontinuities that seem to occur at ages 6 and 7 years. Many investigators[2, 14, 26–31] documented the increasing regularity of mature performance on a variety of visual-motor and neuroperceptual tests by the age of 7. Seven-year-olds appreciate two simultaneous stimuli. They can make visual-motor and intersensory integrations other than those that existed before differentiation, and they follow Sherrington's[32] earlier rule of a developmental progression from proximal to distal receptors during ontogenesis. Seven-year-olds can cross the midline. They have established handedness, eyedness, and footedness. Furthermore, haptic-auditory and auditory-visual integrations are more reliable.[33]

Motility is better integrated, motor sequencing behaviors are performed more accurately and smoothly, and athletic prowess begins to become apparent. Some of these achievements, although not well localized in the central nervous system, have been called soft neurological or nonfocal neurological signs if there is a delay in their occurrence. Whatever the merit of soft signs in regard to frank brain maturation or evidence of lesion, they seem to mature in a regular sequence, and if three or more are present in children older than 7 years, associations with psychopathology have been demonstrated.[34, 35]

As early as 1946, Ames[36] showed that children 7 years old understand the difference between days and months. They have achieved the sequencing of days, months, and seasons. These developmental achievements are in line with related cognitive achievements described by Piaget.[2]

Brain developmental landmarks also converge during this period to recommend a maturational discontinuity. The brain attains about 90% of its total weight by age 7, at which time microscopical structural studies show a broad degree of differentiation. Hippocampal development and the functions related to hippocampal memory are completed by middle childhood.[37] These achievements are thought to be responsible for the passage from procedural memory to the emergence of declarative memory. In procedural memory we recall how to do something or how to get somewhere with easy access to motor patterns that facilitate the task. In declarative memory we have the map of the territory to be traversed in verbal narrative form that can be used or transmitted to others. Rabinowicz[31] suggested that age 7 years encompasses a period of cortical remodeling, in which cortical thickness increases and pyramidal cell shape and size undergo accelerated change. In addition, the many dendritic connections that were stimulated by external stimuli during early childhood reach a high point at about age 7 and begin to level off in latency, with dendritic pruning following.[38]

In earlier studies in the Soviet Union, Pavlov stimulated Luria[39] and his group to demonstrate how speech and language become a second signal system that supersedes motor impulses, achieving highest performance levels at age 6 years. In addition to these studies, Lenneberg[40] and others showed that when children acquire lesions of the central nervous system after age 7, alternative possibilities for language development become less possible and there is a strong tendency to show fixity of aphasia problems after the seventh birthday. Thus, earlier brain plasticity diminishes by middle childhood. On a more general level, children brought up unilingually find it difficult to speak an unaccented second language after age 10 years, suggesting that neurodevelopmental motor linguistic pathways become more rigidly defined during this period. Studies of neurotransmitters should provide firm evidence of a biodevelopmental shift at age 7.

The time line in Figure 8–2 presents biological development from age 6 to 12 years.

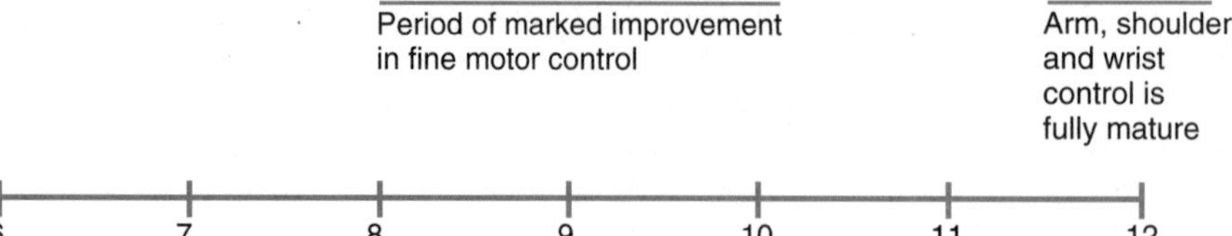

Figure 8–2 *Biological development in the school-age child (6 to 12 years).*

Cognitive Development

Piaget was not content with a description of how children of various ages perform on normative tests. Instead, he asked how they arrive at a particular answer and what cognitive mechanism underlies their reasoning. Although Piaget's original data set was derived from his own three children, his followers were able to generalize his findings and concepts and to achieve a new understanding of the invariant sequences in cognitive development. Despite subsequent refinements, Piaget's basic developmental theory has remained intact across time and cultures.

The initial cognitive organization of the child registered in loose sensory-motor organizations gives way to the preoperational stage after the child attains object permanence. However, it is not until about age 7 that concrete operations are achieved. In fact, it is the attainment of concrete operations that permits children to learn in school and utilize school instruction effectively.

A number of significant transformations become possible with operational intelligence. There is a switch from egocentric to social speech. There is also a shift from egocentrism with a new capacity to take another person's vantage point. From one part of the room an examiner can ask what the room would look like from another's perspective. There is a shift to conservation of material volume and quantity and a shift from irreversible to reversible operations. At this point children can begin to understand that their speech and language are useful for social aims rather than simply for conveying desires and wishes.

Although there are observations that suggest prior understanding of empathy, the more formal capacity for taking another's vantage point on a perceptual task suggests a newfound possibility for perspective taking, with an appreciation of another's vantage both emotionally and perceptually. Up to age 7 years, simple repetition or monologues are possible, but preschool children do not have true topic maintenance. Explanations are often noncausal and are cast in a merely sequential juxtaposition of desires, wishes, or events. Preoperational children use the word "because" without specificity to its meaning. By contrast, the concrete operational child can engage in logical dialogue and produce causal sequences. These achievements are essential features of formal education that can now be engaged in properly. The child can now make predictions about relationships or about sequences. In fact, the latency-age child can reproduce a chain of related circumstances based on past experiences. In anticipation of going on a trip, the child can say, "When we get to Aunty's home, we'll go to the room that she has for us, and we'll put our toys away, and then we can go downstairs and have dinner, and then you can tuck me into the new bed. What fun!" This sequence suggests that memories are operative but also that forward reasoning and forward-looking adaptive reassuring discussion based on past experiences are possible.

The child of this age can also understand that transformations of form can take place even though there is a constant material basis in reality. In fact, the toy industry created "transformers" that are based on the idea that a basic material module can be changed from one form into another by manipulation of its parts. Noticing that the actors in a theater are actually children or adults who take on parts and then return to their former roles as ordinary persons is a feature of the conservation of this period. This conservation of person is also demonstrated materially. For example, colored liquid in a shallow pitcher is conserved as the same quantity when it is poured into a tall tubular pitcher, as are a row of coins whether spread out or piled together, by virtue of numeration. These achievements indicate that there are shifts in the child's mental strategies available to assimilate new tasks in formal elementary education and logic. These new strategies permit comprehension and production of sequential relationships in story lines and also the integration of stories into larger generalized categories above and beyond the immediate task orientation.

Neopiagetians have challenged the strict sequential notions that mark the original model of Piaget, but they do not take issue with the idea of the constant set of transformations and the increasing capacity for new mental strategies and varying forms of logical integration that are characteristic of this period. Kendler and Kendler[41] showed that children of age 7 can solve particular cognitive experimental sequences that demonstrate that they now use integrative reasoning, insight, and inferential behavior. The eminent developmental psychologist White[42] offered a comprehensive summary of the discontinuity and developmental achievements of middle childhood, again recommending that the hierarchical arrangement that was suggested by Werner[6] on theoretical grounds was valid. These new cognitive strategies are also geared toward change in language representation. White described the new capacity to maintain a constant orientation toward an invariant dimension even though the surroundings are varied. The increased dependence on distance receptors of audition and visualization also becomes most prominent at this point. Kagan and colleagues[43] essentially agreed with White's and Freud's earlier notions about the seminal changes that occur during this stage of life; thus, they suggested that this new mode of thinking that evolves supersedes prior modes and builds toward major consequences for later adolescent thinking. These are not simply epigenetic in their organization based on cumulative achievements; they are indeed new skills based on new integrative cognitive structures.

The time line in Figure 8–3 presents cognitive development from age 6 to 12 years.

Emotional Development

If we look at emotions as native dispositions represented by the seven emotions of Darwin, we observe, as have Klinnert and colleagues,[44] that the emotional life of infants and toddlers is reciprocally modulated in relation to the caretaking environment by feedback behaviors defined as social referencing. Mahler and associates[45] described the checking and "refueling" that take place during development in 2- to 3-year-olds. Two lines of investigation address the precursors to emotional development in latency that are significant. One pertains to the follow-up studies on security of attachment at 18 months using the strange situation paradigm of Ainsworth and colleagues.[46] The other line of research concerns temperamental variation in early childhood and its predictive value for emotional modulation and expression during middle childhood. Sroufe and Fleeson[47] showed that by the time securely attached children are 8, 9, and 10 years old, they are more socially adaptive and have better peer interactions.

Cognitive Development:
6–12 years

Piaget's stages of development

Concrete operations

Role learning, categorization, or elaboration to enhance performance

Switch from egocentric to social speech
Understanding of temporal sequences and the differences between day, time, and month emerges
Understanding of the conservation of material volume emerges
Make-believe play (role-playing)

Emergence of declarative memory
Ability to take another's point of view emerges
Shift from irreversible to reversible operations occurs
Ability to understand logical principles develops (e.g., reciprocity, classification, class inclusion, seriation, and number)

Increasing awareness of one's own abilities and comprehension (or lack thereof)

Development of competence motivation

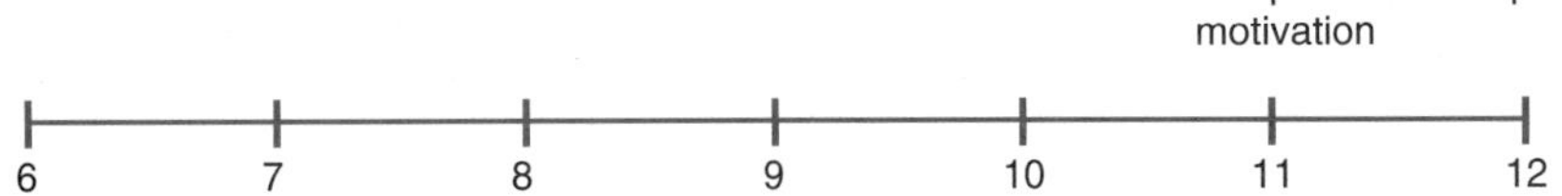

Figure 8–3 *Cognitive development in the school-age child (6 to 12 years).*

The work of Chess and Thomas[23] has already been cited with regard to the continuities and discontinuities that they found in the difficult child. Richman and colleagues'[24] follow-up of 3-year-old behavioral descriptions indicates continuity when extremes of emotion and behavior are coded at 3 but not when there is only moderate behavioral description.

Although epidemiological studies show that depression is not highly prevalent in middle childhood, it is now clear that major depressive disorders do occur rarely[48, 49]; there is a rising rate of emotional disorders in early adolescence, followed by a steep continuing rise of incidence into late adolescence. Kagan and associates[50] showed that early behavioral and emotional inhibition often evolves in middle childhood as anxiety disorders that match parental anxiety and may reflect a genetic origin. This method of tracking the extremes from early childhood suggests a useful research strategy for the study of the genetic determinants of behavior.

The modulation of emotions by new cognitive structures was thought to occur as a result of a signal of anxiety triggered by perceived dangers concerning bodily harm and castration. This was thought at times to take the form of behavioral separation anxiety.[17] In the latter forms, school avoidance and school reluctance may be the major features of manifest anxiety seen in the clinic.[51] The idea that the modal latency-age child is more emotionally contained than the exuberant preschooler has not been found across cultures, just as the postulated diminution of sexuality was shown to be culturally bound.[52, 53] These findings notwithstanding, Ramsey[54] found that rates of masturbation in boys rose from 10% at age 7 to more than 80% at age 13.

There are also suggestions that development provides a trigger for gene expression at various times in childhood. Thus, it may not be only the condition of changing dependency that is central to the emergence of mood disorders. Support for the discontinuity model is provided by the observation that children with the earliest expression of major depression seem to have a different course from those with a later onset.[49] It is during this period of middle childhood that peer socialization takes on new significance, becoming an additional boost to feelings of approval and self-esteem.

Sociocultural Development

Erikson[3] provided ego dimensions to the freudian developmental model. However, the epigenetic model maintains that prior stages have strong influences on the later stages of development. His model differs from the hypothesized discontinuity model insofar as traversing a stage-phase boundary does not permit the developing child to leave behind the faults that characterized a prior stage. By contrast, the discontinuity model offers the possibility for reorganizations without the necessary continuing major impact of earlier dynamisms. Sociocultural behavior of middle childhood has been described most extensively for middle-class U.S. culture, although some poor and inner-city populations have been studied. Many behaviors of middle childhood can be construed as new aspects of the socialization process that is fostered by schooling, community involvement, and the move away from the family.

Children of this age form clubs that mimic parental social groups. Clubs during middle childhood have specific characteristics, such as every member demanding to be an officer. The "natural club" of the school-age child borrows from larger societal forms, but unlike the Cub Scouts or Brownies, it does not have the rules offered by prior structures. The rules are provided by a new oligarchy of strong-minded children experimenting with leadership.

Secrets and collecting are important. The tendency to collect everything from bottle caps to baseball cards has led to widespread advertising that stimulates peer pressure. More sports-minded children can become devoted to collecting enormous quantities of statistics regarding their favorite sport. Children who may not perform as well in athletics often turn to other collecting rages. If you cannot hit home runs, you can at least have at your fingertips the names and years and records of the Babe Ruths and Mickey Mantles of history to impress your peers. The traditional image of the child emptying pockets stocked with pieces of string, small stones, and other personal treasures is typical of this period. Stamp collecting and coin collecting have their origins and fascinations during this period and lead to increased knowledge that parallels and enhances the learning of geology, geography, and history. Devotion to particular forms of attire also becomes clearly delineated at this point as social consciousness rises with respect to what is "in" and what is "gross." Children may also become rather cruel toward each other with regard to teasing and name-calling. Particular styles of dress become associated with idealized figures and are treasured with regard to early crushes and devotions that become paramount in adolescence.

The concept of a joke can be appreciated in a new way during middle childhood as "knock-knock" jokes are replaced by more pointed stories with clear punch lines. The school-age child can be reduced to hysterical laughter by bathroom humor. Explicit virtuoso performances of burps or flatus are exceedingly popular. The titter that is created by these demonstrations sometimes evolves into belly laughs that adults find silly or inappropriate.

Mastery of the body is also a prominent theme during latency. A latency-age child may shoot baskets or practice the piano for hours. Boys may endlessly grease and pound a new baseball glove to make the perfect pocket. Girls of this age are likely to dance or exercise for hours on end.

The unisex friendships of this period lead to a number of avoidant practices that emerge in groups. The frequent culturally determined "cooties," a mythical contagious disease that comes from touching a person of the opposite sex, serves the function of maintaining a safe sexual distance. The notion of contamination by those who are sexually active and the reaction formation of expressing disgust at the thought of kissing and turning away from romantic scenes in films represent prominent behaviors during this period. The tendency to establish same-sex groupings becomes more pronounced at ages 7 and 8 years.[55]

Shame is another social regulator. Any suggestion of romantic attachment or interest in someone of the opposite sex may lead to titters among latency children, with shame and embarrassment as a deterrent. During this time, boys and girls are trained to "one-up" each other, with the threat of potential humiliation. Skill at sports, dance, or other physical prowess often leads to increased socialization and enhanced self-esteem and competence during middle childhood. Peers have little tolerance of boys who deviate from clear gender role play.[56] Anthropological investigations show that most cultures provide rituals that accompany the transition to adult male status and that preparation for these rituals begins during middle childhood.[57]

Anthropologists have indicated that in cultures other than middle-class U.S. culture and also within ghetto cultures, sexuality is not as dormant. Freud[1] believed that each culture had its own avenue for expression of sexuality. In more modern terms, we can see that variations in latency are determined by aspects of permission and prohibition within each culture. Erikson[3] described the variations in Native American and urban U.S. cultures. Maccoby[58] conducted studies modifying our notion of the latent period in middle-class U.S. samples. Nonetheless, although some cultures do not appear to show a latency, most take some notice of prepubertal status, because it is during the next phase that most of the rites and privileges of young adulthood are bestowed by ceremonial or ritual behaviors, permitting children to enter into adult practices. It is a time when respect for parents and larger cultural institutions begins to be solidified.

Moral development may be looked at as an independent line only insofar as it describes the capacity of the child to act in accord with conscience and moral imperatives rather than primitive egocentric and non–socially concerned values. Freud's belief that the superego was formed as a residue of identifications and drive resolution at the end of the oedipal stage has been modified by new evidence of internal control in accord with the development of moral injunction during the preschool years.[59] Nonetheless, the internalized "oughts" and "shoulds" of the latency period represent a new cognitive advance and a new capacity to contain emotions that sometimes leads to exceedingly rigid exercise of moral restraint. It is a period when an 8-year-old can turn on his or her father for the slightest moral infraction for the sake of obeying the code. It is a time when children receiving religious education chide their parents for not following the rules and not attending church. The notion of "Do as I say, not as I do" is easily contested, and latency-age children frequently recognize parental hypocrisy preceding the more widely recognized phenomenon of adolescent protest. There is a tendency for good and bad to take on absolute valence, allowing little room for shades of gray.

Gilligan[60] has found in naturalistic observations that the quality of mercy that was involved in human interactions and concern for interaction are more characteristic of girls and are less prominent in boys, who preferentially seek blind justice. This may be what Freud alluded to in his turn-of-the-century dichotomy between the sexes.

Piaget[28] studied how children followed varying systems of rules. He observed boys playing a game of marbles and, feigning ignorance, asked how the game worked. He concluded that there were stages in the acquisition of morality. From 4 to 7 years, children appear egocentric. That is, they are not able to take another's perspective; they follow a fluctuating set of rules that is governed by some inner dictates. From 7 to 11 years, rules are followed more carefully, and only at 11 or 12 years are absolute rules scrupulously demanded in rule-governed games. He also found that 5- to 9-year-old children believe that rules are inviolable, originating in some absolute authority. However,

10- or 11-year-old children question this and show the ability to consider social contracts mutable. Piaget similarly studied ethical questions, showing that younger children believe that if something bad is done, punishment must follow, whereas older children take motivation into account, asking what the individual meant to do. Children's sense of fairness also begins to evolve during this time, and the idea of "it isn't fair" emerges. Kohlberg and colleagues[61–63] used piagetian techniques to study the response to moral dilemmas at various ages.

The six stages of moral development patterns gathered by Kohlberg[61] were believed to have an invariable sequence, mimicking Piaget's idea (Table 8–1). The first two stages were called preconventional morality. The vast majority of 10-year-olds were found to be at this level. The first stage is egocentric, with the rights of others being irrelevant. Action at this stage is deferred to avoid punishment. The second-stage child acknowledges that other people have interests too, but the child's own interest prevails at this level. Conventional morality, stage 3, involves being good by living up to what people generally expect of one. By stage 4, the child is oriented toward maintaining the society norm. At postconventional morality, a child may consider questions from both a moral and a legal point of view, even acknowledging that there might be conflict. At stage 6, there is consideration of a universal moral principle of justice that may override human law. Walker[64] found some support for Kohlberg's sequencing of stages but not for the existence of significant differences between the sexes. Smetana and colleagues[65] studied third-, sixth-, and ninth-graders and found little support for Gilligan's differential between boys and girls, commenting that there were few sex differences between interpersonal considerations and issues of justice in the children studied. As noted earlier, the precursors of moral judgment are already present in 3-year-olds, according to Buchsbaum and Emde,[59] but there is a consolidation of moral rules during latency marked by excessive rigidity, only to become more broadly conceived in light of reason and human condition as adolescence proceeds.

Figures 8–4, 8–5, and 8–6 present time lines for emotional, moral, and social development in 6- to 12-year-olds.

Risk and Protective Factors

During latency the prevalence of categorical psychiatric disorders rises, and children begin to present with prepubertal depression in midlatency at 9 years. Children with an early onset of illness have a worse prognosis.[49] Attention-deficit/hyperactivity disorder also begins to appear as the

Table 8–1 Kohlberg's Stages of Moral Development

Level	Stage	Description
Preconventional: Emphasis on avoiding punishments and getting rewards	Stage 1 Might makes right (punishment and obedience orientation).	Children at this stage are egocentric and experience difficulty with perspective taking when considering moral dilemmas. Motives and intentions are ignored when judging the goodness or badness of a behavior.
	Stage 2 Look out for number one (instrumental and relativist orientation).	Recognition that others have different points of view occurs at this stage, but this understanding is still somewhat limited. Action is viewed as right if it satisfies one's needs. The reason to be nice to people is so they will be nice to you.
Conventional: Emphasis on social rules and conformity to social norms	Stage 3 "Good girl" and "nice boy."	Approval is more important than any specific reward. The individual has newly acquired abilities for mutual perspective taking. In this stage, a person can anticipate what another person is feeling and knows that other people also have this ability.
	Stage 4 Law and order.	The individual can now take into consideration societal laws when deciding a course of action. A behavior is considered right if it involves obeying rules established by authority.
Postconventional: Emphasis on moral principles and values	Stage 5 Social contract, legalistic.	Rules are regarded as more flexible, with the aim of furthering human values. They are not absolute. This stage emphasizes fair procedures for interpreting and chang- ing the law when the law is destructive or unethical. Ethics are considered when evaluating laws.
	Stage 6 Universal ethical principles.	At this stage, there is the recognition that some principles and values (i.e., "life is sacred") transcend laws, and that some moral obligations are valid for humanity.

From Kohlberg L: Development of moral character and moral ideology. In Hoffman ML, Hoffman LW (eds): Review of Child Development Research. New York: Russell Sage Foundation, 1964:383–432.

Emotional Development:
6–12 years

Emergence of emotional control
Vacillates from one emotional extreme to another

Increasing sensitivity to attitudes of others

Decrease in "sensitivity"
Increasing feelings of anticipation and impatience

Becomes more independent, dependable, and obedient
Development of a sense of empathy

Increased mood variation
and "moodiness"

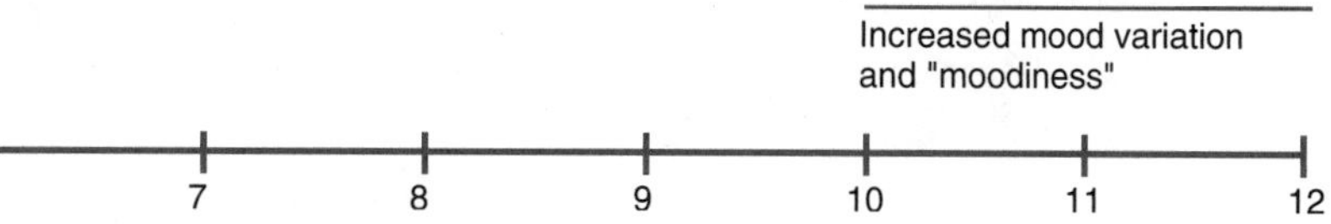

Figure 8–4 *Emotional development in the school-age child (6 to 12 years).*

school years intrude on free play, and separation disorders emerge as well, as schooling away from home becomes mandatory.[51] Children who are prone to conduct disorders show their symptoms more prominently when new demands of school are introduced. There are more opportunities to lie and steal and act in a disruptive manner in the confines of a school, where an unfamiliar demand structure is imposed.

Factors associated with the onset of psychopathology include "turning on" genes but can be understood also within the context of risk and protective factors. Sameroff and Chandler[66] have examined the notion put forward by Passamanick and Lilienfeld[67] of a continuum of reproductive casualty and found that as children enter the middle years, social influences become most significant among the factors that account for the variance in the expression of disorder. In fact, if problems related to early biological hazards are considered, the latency-age child's problems are better accounted for on the basis of sociofamilial factors than biological factors. If three or more risk factors are present, such as extreme poverty, a single-parent family, and child abuse, the rate of disorder is high regardless of the occurrence of early anoxia, prematurity, or complications of delivery.

On the other hand, early influences may also be included in the equation if we consider the impact of programs such as Head Start, whose effects are not seen early but seem to be present later.[68] Nonetheless, as Richman and

Moral Development:
6–12 years

Kohlberg's stages of moral development

Egocentric	Preconventional	Conventional

Shame is social regulator

Egocentricity
Limited ability to take another's point of view

Rules considered inviolable

Rules are followed more carefully
Internalization of "oughts" and "shoulds"
Recognition of hypocrisy
Conscious of attitudes and actions of others

Learns to be fair and to understand justice

Begins to consider social
contracts mutable

Plays rule-governed
games scrupulously

Figure 8–5 *Moral development in the school-age child (6 to 12 years).*

Social Development:
6–12 years

Understands that people can have multiple roles
Likes some social routines

Interested in secrets, collecting, and organized games and hobbies
Off-color humor emerges
Primarily unisex friendships
Explains actions by referring to events of immediate situation

Redefines status relationships with friends
Same-sex groupings prominent
Punchlines emerge in humor
Focus on peoples' physical appearances as opposed to their personality dispositions

Adoption of group's values, speech patterns, and manners
Strong peer group affiliation

Rise in social consciousness with respect to what is "in"
Increased self-regulation
Best friends rise in importance

Understands that emotions have internal causes
Recognizes that people can have conflicting feelings and can sometimes mask true feelings

Relates actions to personality traits and feelings
Sees friends as people who understand each other and share thoughts and feelings

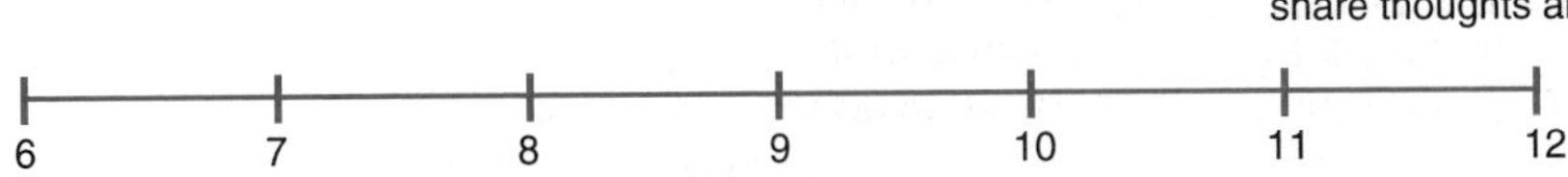

Figure 8–6 *Social development in the school-age child (6 to 12 years).*

colleagues[24] have shown, multiple symptoms at 3 years offer a poor prognostic sign for later expression of disorder. However, we do not yet know whether strain trauma or ongoing insult is the key factor in sustaining such early propensities.

Developmental Psychopathology

The middle years are marked by an enormous new availability of skills and coping mechanisms permitting children to expand their achievements when appropriate support systems are available. The emergence of disorder can be understood from the perspective of factors that enhance or inhibit the new roles and skills of the period. In the arena of friendships and initial attempts at removal from the home, we can see that a deficient support system at home distorts the attempts to make friends and to participate in team sports. We also know that sexual dimorphism is at its height in this period and that too early an introduction to behaviors that are more appropriate after puberty may interfere with the establishment of sexual role and the integration of arousal and tenderness that seem essential for later intimacy and conjugal living. As Erikson[3] noted, this is a period of industry in which the habits of work and the tools for the intellectual work to come are forged. If these are interfered with because the sheer requirements of survival are uppermost, then the time necessary for learning and adaptation is lost.

Clinical Vignette 1

Josh, a 7-year-old, was in second grade for about 1 month when he had a mild febrile illness that kept him at home for 2 days. Because the next day was Friday and his mother was at home from her 3-day-a-week job, she permitted Josh to recover over the long weekend. He and his 5-year-old brother Kevin played well. His mother seemed quite pleased that the three of them had these days to spend together.

On Monday morning, Josh did not want to go to school. He protested that his stomach hurt, he had a headache, and he felt worried that his mother would be hurt at her job. His mother worried that Josh was ill again and called in sick. Within 40 minutes, Josh seemed content and happy, and he played comfortably at her side. Still, he seemed reluctant to let her out of his sight. He promised that he would go to school in the morning, but the next day he was again reluctant and wept bitterly as his mother became increasingly anxious and angry. By the week's end a struggle ensued each morning, and his mother sought consultation.

Josh's immediate history included the fact that his father and mother separated when he was 5 years old. Although his father had been conscientious in his visitation, there had been an altercation about child support between Josh's father and mother, and unpleasant accusations were exchanged. Josh overheard the argument and became progressively worried about his mother and his own safety.

Josh's mother suffered from panic anxiety for many years and found it difficult to engage socially. She was somewhat phobic, was generally fearful, and would hover about her children when she became anxious about their safety.

Josh was a normal full-term infant but had developed an elevated bilirubin level that required ultraviolet light treatment. He also had two febrile seizures before he was 18 months old and was temporarily given phenobarbital. He had frequent otitis media and was a "slow to warm" child with a cautious restrictive temperament.

His motor and language landmarks were all well within normal limits. When he began kindergarten, he took longer to accomplish the planned separation than his peers. Otherwise, he was a bright, imaginative youngster who did well in one-on-one interactions.

This case demonstrates the interplay between biological predispositions and current stressors that permits the expression of emergent pathological conditions in the middle school years. Although Josh was vulnerable as an infant, having suffered seizures and having a withdrawing temperament, his mother's panic and his parents' separation augmented his rising anxiety. This anxiety was reinforced by his mother's own anxiety and worry, and he became angry that he could not contain either of their feelings. These feelings added to his anticipation of abandonment and regressive clinging. The vulnerabilities of this stage of development can thus interact with the accidents of life that are all too common for children in this age group.

The tasks and challenges in this period represent an amalgam of evolutionarily specific cognitive and emotional maturation and opportunities that can be integrated in an enriched or impoverished environment as the case may be. There is probably no developmental period that has a more determining effect on the next stage and no other period in which the environment has so much to offer in the favor of the developing child.

References

1. Freud S: Three essays on the theory of sexuality. In Strachey J (trans-ed): The Standard Edition of the Complete Psychological Works of Sigmund Freud, Volume 7. London: Hogarth Press, 1953:125–243. Originally published in 1905.
2. Piaget J: The Child's Conception of the World. New York: Harcourt, Brace, 1929.
3. Erikson E: Childhood and Society, 2nd ed, revised and expanded. New York: WW Norton, 1963.
4. Sullivan HS: Conceptions of modern psychiatry. Psychiatry 1940; 3:1–117.
5. Thomas A, Chess S: Temperament and Development. New York: Brunner/Mazel, 1977.
6. Werner H: Comparative Psychology of Mental Development. New York: International Universities Press, 1957.
7. Shapiro T, Perry R: Latency revisited: The significance of age 7 plus or minus 1. Psychoanal Study Child 1976; 31:79–105.
8. Spitz RA: The First Year of Life: A Psychoanalytic Study of Normal and Deviant Development of Object Relations. New York: International Universities Press, 1965.
9. Emde RN, Gaensbauer T, Harmon R: Emotional Expression in Infancy: A Bio-Behavioral Study. New York: International Universities Press, 1976.
10. Gesell AL, Ilg FL: Child Development: An Introduction to the Study of Human Growth. New York: Harper & Row Publishers, 1949.
11. Freud A: The Assessment of Normality in Childhood. New York: International Universities Press, 1965.
12. Kohlberg L, Gilligan C: The adolescent as a philosopher. Boston: Daedalus 1971; 100:1051–1086.
13. Aries P; Baldick R (trans): Centuries of Childhood: A Social History of Family Life. New York: Alfred A Knopf, 1962.
14. Pinchbeck I, Hewett M: Children in English Society, Volume 1. London: Routledge & Kegan Paul, 1969.
15. Shapiro T: Varieties of oedipal distortions in severe character pathologies: Developmental and theoretical considerations. Psychoanal Q 1977; 46:559–579.

15a. Diderot D: Rameau's Nephew. London: Penguin Books, 1966:113.

16. Rudnytsky P, Spitz EH (eds): Freud and Forbidden Knowledge. New York: New York University Press, 1994:150.
17. Freud S: Inhibitions, symptoms and anxiety. In Strachey J (trans-ed): The Standard Edition of the Complete Psychological Works of Sigmund Freud, Volume 20. London: Hogarth Press, 1959:75–175. Originally published in 1926.
18. Bornstein B: On latency. Psychoanal Study Child 1951; 6:279–285.
19. Thomas A, Chess S: Development in middle childhood. Semin Psychiatry 1972; 4:331–341.
20. Offer D, Offer JB: From Teenage to Young Manhood: A Psychological Study. New York: Basic Books, 1975.
21. Hauser ST, Powers S, Noam GG: Adolescents and Their Families. New York: Free Press, 1991.
22. Neubauer P, Flapan D: Developmental groupings in children. J Am Acad Child Adolesc Psychiatry 1976; 15:646–664.
23. Chess S, Thomas A: Origins and Evolution of Behavior Disorders: From Infancy to Early Adult Life. New York: Brunner/Mazel, 1984.
24. Richman N, Stevenson J, Graham P: Preschool to School. London: Academic Press, 1982.
25. LaPouse R, Monk MA: Fear and worries in a representative sample of children. Am J Orthopsychiatry 1959; 29:803.
26. McFarland J, Allen L, Honzik M: A Developmental Study of the Behavior Problems of Normal Children Between 21 Months and 14 Years. Berkeley, CA: University of California Press, 1954.
27. Schilder P: The Image and Appearance of the Human Body, 2nd ed. New York: International Universities Press, 1950.
28. Piaget J: The Moral Judgment of the Child. New York: Free Press, 1948.
29. Pollock M, Goldfarb W: The face-hand test in schizophrenic children. Arch Gen Psychiatry 1957; 77:635–642.
30. Pollock M, Gordon E: The face-hand test in retarded and nonretarded emotionally disturbed children. Am J Ment Defic 1960; 64:758–776.
31. Rabinowicz T: The differentiated maturation of the cerebral cortex. In Falkner F, Tanner JM (eds): Human Growth: A Comprehensive Treatise, Volume 2. New York: Plenum Publishing, 1986:385–410.
32. Sherrington C: Man on His Nature. New York: Doubleday, 1953.
33. Birch HG, Lefford A: Visual differentition, intersensory integration, and voluntary motor control. Monogr Soc Res Child Dev 1967; 32(2):1–82.
34. Hertzig M: Stability and change in nonfocal neurologic signs. J Am Acad Child Adolesc Psychiatry 1982; 21:231–236.
35. Schaffer D: Soft neurological signs and later psychiatric disorder. J Child Psychol Psychiatry 1978; 19:63–65.
36. Ames LB: The development of the sense of time in the young child. J Genet Psychol 1946; 68:97–125.
37. Koppitz EM: Psychological Evaluation of Children's Human Figure Drawings. New York: Grune & Stratton, 1968.
38. Huttenlocher PR: Synaptic density in human frontal cortex: Developmental changes and effects of aging. Brain Res 1979; 163:195–205.
39. Luria AR: The Role of Speech in the Regulation of Normal and Abnormal Behavior. New York: Liveright, 1961.
40. Lenneberg EH: In search of a dynamic theory of aphasia. In Lenneberg EH, Lenneberg EL (eds): Foundations of Language Development: A Multidisciplinary Approach, Volume 2. New York: Academic Press, 1975:3–20.

41. Kendler TS, Kendler HH: Inferential behavior in children as a function of age and subgoal constancy. J Exp Psychol 1962; 64:460–466.
42. White SH: Evidence for a hierarchical arrangement of learning processes. Adv Child Dev Behav 1965; 2:187–220.
43. Kagan J, Klein RE, Finley GE, et al: A cross-cultural study of cognitive development. Monogr Soc Res Child Dev 1979; 44(5):1–77.
44. Klinnert MD, Emde RN, Butterfield P, et al: Social referencing: The infant's use of emotional signals from a friendly adult with mother present. Dev Psychol 1986; 22:427–432.
45. Mahler MS, Pine F, Bergman A: The Psychological Birth of the Human Infant: Symbiosis and Individuation. New York: Basic Books, 1975.
46. Ainsworth MDS, Blehar MD, Waters E, et al: Patterns of Attachment: A Psychological Study of the Strange Situation. Hillsdale, NJ: Lawrence Erlbaum, 1978.
47. Sroufe LA, Fleeson J: Attachment and the construction of relationships. In Hartup W, Rubin Z (eds): Relationships and Development. New York: Cambridge University Press, 1984:51–71.
48. Puig Antich J, Rabinovich H: Relationship between affective and anxiety disorders in children. In Gittelman R (ed): Anxiety Disorders of Childhood. New York: Guilford Press, 1986:136–156.
49. Kovacs M: Depressive disorders in childhood: Longitudinal study of co-morbidity. Arch Gen Psychiatry 1989; 46:776–782.
50. Kagan J, Reznick JS, Gibbons J: Inhibited and uninhibited types of children. Child Dev 1989; 60:838–845.
51. Shapiro T, Jegede O: School phobia: A babel of tongues. J Autism Child Schizophr 1973; 3:168–186.
52. Malinowski B: The Sexual Life of Savages in North-Western Melanesia. New York: Harcourt, Brace, 1929.
53. Ford CS, Beach FA: Patterns of Sexual Behavior. New York: Harper & Row Publishers, 1951.
54. Ramsey CV: The Sexual Development of Boys. Am J Psychol 1943; 56:217–233.
55. Campbell EH: The social-sex development of children. Genet Psychol Monogr 1939; 21:461–552.
56. Fagot BI: Consequences of moderate cross-gender behavior in preschool children. Child Dev 1977; 48:902–907.
57. Gilmore DD: Manhood in the Making: Cultural Concepts of Masculinity. New Haven, CT: Yale University Press, 1990.
58. Maccoby EE: Gender and relationships: A developmental account. Am Psychol 1990; 45:513–520.
59. Buchsbaum HK, Emde RN: Play narrations in 36-month-old children: Early moral development and family relationships. Psychoanal Study Child 1990; 40:129–155.
60. Gilligan C: In a Different Voice: Psychological Theory and Women's Development. Cambridge, MA: Harvard University Press, 1982.
61. Kohlberg L: Development of moral character and moral ideology. In Hoffman ML, Hoffman LW (eds): Review of Child Development Research. New York: Russell Sage Foundation, 1964:383–432.
62. Colby A, Kohlberg L, Gibbs J, et al: A longitudinal study of moral judgment. Monogr Soc Res Child Dev 1983.
63. Colby A, Kohlberg L: The Measurement of Moral Judgment, Volume I, Theoretical Foundations and Research Validation. Cambridge, UK: Cambridge University Press, 1987.
64. Walker LJ: A longitudinal study of moral reasoning. Child Dev 1989; 60:157–166.
65. Smetana JG, Killen M, Turiel E: Children's reasoning about interpersonal and moral conflicts. Child Dev 1991; 52:629–644.
66. Sameroff AJ, Chandler MJ: Reproductive risk and the continuum of caretaking casualty. In Horowitz FD (ed): Review of Child Development Research, Volume 4. Chicago: University of Chicago Press, 1975:187–244.
67. Passamanick B, Lilienfeld H: Retrospective studies on the epidemiology of reproductive casualty: Old and new. Merrill-Palmer Q 1966; 12:7–26.
68. Consortium for Longitudinal Studies: As the Twig Is Bent . . . Lasting Effects of Preschool Programs. Hillsdale, NJ: Lawrence Erlbaum, 1983.

CHAPTER

9 Adolescent Development

John E. Schowalter
Kenneth E. Towbin

Adolescence is the developmental phase that spans the transition from relatively complete child-like reliance on parents to nearly complete self-reliance for the management of one's own life.[1] Although the term adolescence did not have its current meaning before the middle of the 19th century, young people have always had to make the transition from being considered dependent children to being regarded as independent adults. This transition occurs in almost all societies. Although the Bible, St. Augustine, and Shakespeare have commented on the joys, dangers, and sorrows of this transition period, it has been studied only in this century.[2] In premodern times, the passage to adulthood was demarcated by a puberty rite. Before enacting the rite one was a child; after completing it one was an adult. This ritual was far more explicit than it is today. The contemporary steps include a variety of experiences such as first communion, bar mitzvah and bat mitzvah, paying the full cost for social events, and being granted certain privileges such as driving legally, consuming alcohol, voting, and performing military service.

It appears that different societies have different time frames for this transition, and even the same society is likely to modify the steps and ages over time. The clearer and narrower a society is in its definition of and expectations for adulthood, the more smoothly the child passes through adolescence. Greater freedom fosters greater latitude for the young person and generates greater confusion about what constitutes an adult to the individual, his or her parents, and society.

Adolescence is a period of many changes. Near the time of puberty, there is a sudden increase in the size of hands and feet, height, body hair, and genitalia. Boys experience a voice change and an increase in muscle mass; girls develop breasts and begin menstruation. Thinking also changes. Particularly for boys, sexual thoughts become more common, explicit, and intrusive, and there is an upsurge of aggressive feelings and urges. However, the timing of these changes is highly variable.

Although girls generally begin pubertal changes about 2 years before boys do, the range of normalcy for both sexes is wide. Some girls begin their growth spurt as early as age 9 or 10 years and are physically adults 4 or 5 years before late-developing boys even begin their pubertal changes. Consequently, one contribution to the emotional chaos of this age group stems from the widely divergent physical and emotional development of its members. A seventh- or eighth-grade classroom is filled with ever-changing strangers, and teachers must cope with the diversity of physical and emotional maturity within the constraints of the same curriculum, textbooks, sports matches, and social events. Not only is there a disparity in appearance among students, but how individual students feel about themselves is often in flux as well. It is not unusual for a young adolescent to feel and behave maturely and independently in one context and then childishly and dependently in another.

It is useful to divide adolescence into three overlapping biopsychosocial phases (Table 9–1) that are epigenetic in that each leads to the next. However, there are wide variations among individuals with regard to the age at onset and duration of each phase. On average, girls precede boys into each phase. Early adolescence typically begins near the end of grade school or the beginning of middle school. This phase is characterized by the growth spurt, beginning development of secondary sex characteristics, greater social separation from parents and family, and greater affinity with peers. These shifts are often manifested by changes in attitude, clothing, and hairstyle. It is common for adolescents and their parents to harbor doubts about whether the changes in body and thought are normal, and reassurance is often sought from the family physician or pediatrician about these fears. Masturbation begins or becomes more frequent, and although there may be strong romantic crushes on older and unobtainable persons, the peer group remains predominantly unisexual. Concerns about possible homosexuality are common, especially for boys.

Midadolescence typically occurs during the middle teenage years, and sexual experimentation between teenagers usually begins at this time. As the individual gains a more consolidated and surer sense of self, there is more serenity and less uncertainty about sexual orientation. Late adolescence, which typically takes place during the late teens, is a time of assuming adult responsibilities and perspectives rather than focusing on earlier conflicts related to dependency. This requires decisions about school, work, leaving home, and romantic relationships and commitments.

Table 9–2 shows a set of tasks that are accomplished by psychologically healthy adults.[3] These tasks are seldom fully

Table 9–1 Phases of Adolescence

Phase	Age (Years)	Characteristic
Early	11–13	Growth spurt, development of secondary sex characteristics, beginning of social separation from parents and family, greater affinity with peers
Middle	14–16	Consolidation of sense of self, increased sexual experimentation, decreased sense of threat from adults
Late	17–19	Concerns about entering adult life—work, independence, intimacy

completed by the end of the teenage years or even the early 20s but represent key development objectives for this period.

Historical Perspectives

Kett[1] claimed that "every generation of intellectuals since 1820 has been convinced that an acceleration of the velocity of social change has disrupted traditional harmony and has had a calamitous effect on youth," but it seems clear that the industrial revolution of the late 19th century was crucial for the structuring of adolescence as we now know it. Earlier, teenagers had been expected to perform tasks that required strong backs, good endurance, a willingness to work for little pay, and little experience. Machines became the ideal substitute for this work force, and in the late 19th century there was a diminishing need for teenagers in the workplace. This displacement continues and has had important economic ramifications for society and personal implications for adolescents and their parents. Before this century, children in this country were usually considered an asset for the family. In the mainly agricultural society, they helped around the house and out in the fields. Usually, formal education was available only for boys in the upper classes. Apprenticeships granted to teenagers who were not required for family work provided the opportunity for these boys to learn trades other than those of their fathers.

Kett believed that the adolescent as a type of individual was "invented" by the American psychologist G. Stanley Hall, who influenced public opinion of teenagers. Hall was struck by the religiosity of many young people and, in a paper published in 1882,[2] stated that religious conversions are most dramatic for persons in their second decade of life.

Table 9–2 Ideal Task Accomplishment to Attain Adolescence

- Disengagement from parents along with ability to make decisions about one's life
- Value system respecting self and others
- Solid employment, possibly beginning a vocation
- Fixed sexual identity
- Long-term sexual relationship

Hall theorized that religious awakening and sexual awakening had many similarities and that through maturation they both began at about the same time. Hall conceived of adolescence as a "new start" or recapitulation of an earlier age. Some psychoanalysts proposed similar theories about the possibility of experiential traits being passed genetically.[1] Hall[4] focused on the importance of biological heritage and minimized social factors. When the Boy Scouts began in the United States in 1910, its leaders were influenced by Hall's anthropomorphic notions. For example, it was believed that adolescents should be in the outdoors because this was how young people traditionally learned to look after themselves and to become independent.

Hall's theory, which stressed recapitulation and biological inevitability, was reassuring to parents and educators because it explained teenage behavior without attributing blame. Adolescence was just a difficult time. Kett noted that although Hall originally conceived the age of adolescence as extending into the early 20s, his educator followers shifted the time frame of adolescence to be coincidental with secondary school. Eventually adolescence became synonymous with the years between the end of primary school and the leaving of school in the middle to late teens.

Sigmund Freud[5] in Three Essays on the Theory of Sexuality declared that puberty was not when sexuality emerged. Rather, humans experience an active and varied array of sexual wishes and feelings from the time of infancy. Freud believed puberty was the time when the genital zone attained primacy. He proposed that this occurred when the earlier oral, anal, and phallic sexual instincts come under the sway of the reproductive function. Psychoanalysts have debated the preeminent importance of the first 3 years of life, the oedipal period of about ages 4 to 6 years, and the period of adolescence for adult development.

Anna Freud[6] in the mid-1930s published in German *The Ego and the Mechanisms of Defence.* Focusing on the adolescent years, she described the mind's defense mechanisms and highlighted their use for adaptation during adolescence. She theorized that at this time a relatively strong id, enhanced by the biological changes of puberty, confronts a relatively weak ego, which can become disorganized by quickly shifting parental and social expectations. She gave examples of ego defenses used by adolescents to help counter increased drives, such as "ascetism" and "intellectualization." Ascetism acts to dampen all urges toward pleasure, and intellectualization is a method by which feelings and urges are contemplated and studied rather than felt and acted on. Whereas the ascetic adolescent flees from instincts, those who use intellectualization turn toward their instincts but only through thought. She described the common ego defenses used by adolescents against the regressive pull toward remaining a dependent child.[7] Examples include "displacement" of incestuous libido from parents onto other adults, such as popular musicians, movie stars, and cult figures, and the "reversal of affect," an example of which is the changing of respect for and dependence on parents into their opposites of belittlement and rebellion. Table 9–3 lists the characteristic adolescent ego defenses.

Blos[8] stressed that the two primary and interacting developmental themes for adolescents are the revival of the Oedipus complex and the need to disengage from the close

Table 9–3 Characteristic Adolescent Ego Defenses
Asceticism
Intellectualization
Displacement
Reversal of affect

childhood-based ties to parents. Blos proposed that a major problem arises when the adolescent withdraws emotionally from the parents and from the parents' values. This leaves the adolescent bereft of accustomed moral underpinnings just at the time when sexual and aggressive fantasies and urges are greatest.

Psychoanalysts emphasized that adolescence was a time of Sturm und Drang—storm and stress. By the 1960s and 1970s, research began to indicate that emotional upheaval was not necessary for a successful transition from childhood to adulthood. Offer and colleagues[9, 10] studied high school students in Chicago and reported that a large majority displayed relatively little turmoil. Although these youngsters became more attached to and influenced by peers, they were still most powerfully influenced by their parents. In 1976 Rutter and colleagues[11] reported on studies demonstrating that major turmoil during adolescence was not a developmental necessity. Rutter believed that adolescents often feel more misery than is noticed by parents and other adults but that the degree of turmoil and its psychiatric importance had been exaggerated in earlier clinical reports. This view opened the way to a more modern, empirically driven view of cognitive and emotional development during adolescence.

Conceptual Framework

The conceptual framework draws on concepts of continuity and linkage. The sections of this chapter consider biological, cognitive, social, and moral development as separate pathways, but each has its inception in childhood and merges imperceptibly into adulthood. Thus, development can be viewed as a continuous process that begins with the absolute helplessness and dependency of an infant and proceeds toward the capacity to fulfill one's own requirements and effect propagation of the species. At any one point there is continuity, connections with the previous and succeeding points on this continuum. For example, adolescents' first experiences with members of the opposite sex are influenced by prior experiences with same-sex relationships in childhood and in turn may affect later decisions about their adult choice of a sexual partner.

Moreover, this continuum is composed of a number of simultaneous developmental events that occur at different levels in different domains (Fig. 9–1). These events and domains are said to be linked. That is, they are related to one another and influence one another but are not epigenetically dependent on one another. At any one moment an individual may be more mature in one domain than in another. Yet the interplay of these domains affects overall development in a fundamental way. For illustration, one domain, such as heightened motor skills, may interact with a separate domain, such as enhanced cognitive abilities, resulting in improved athletic performance. Increased strength and reflex speed do not activate the ability to perceive weaknesses and form a strategy for defeating an opponent. However, when they are combined, the player may be more victorious on the field. Subsequent varsity success may affect self-image and peer social status.

At each arbitrarily defined phase there are tasks, responsibilities, and pressures that are particularly characteristic of that time. Across individuals, no matter how different the sources of these demands and pressures may be, the conflicts of a particular developmental phase are remarkably similar. Thus, it has been argued that adolescence recapitulates the struggles of toddlerhood but at a different level.[8] One similarity between these two developmental phases is the conflict between wishes for self-sufficiency and the recognition that one's capacities are not yet at a level that permits these strivings to be fulfilled. However, major differences exist. The limitations of adolescence are derived from much broader realms than those of the toddler. The immediate source of limitations on strivings for adulthood may be physical, familial, cultural, or social. Moreover, the pressures on adolescents stem from both internal and external sources. Examples of internal sources are sexual urges and capacities, longings for self-sufficiency, awareness of new capabilities, and feelings of dependency and uncertainty. Some examples of external sources are the tacit requirements for being a responsible member of society,

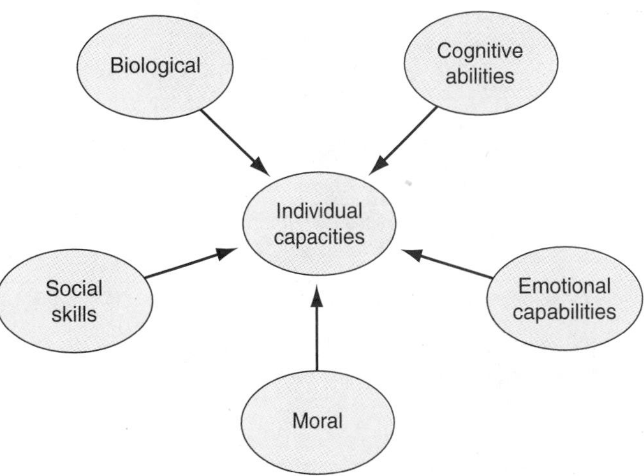

Figure 9–1 *Interplay of developmental domains.*

expanded parental expectations, and more intense and complex peer pressures that exert demands to "fit in."

The negotiation of these conflicting pressures is determined by the interplay of biological, social, familial, cultural, and psychological factors. Although there is continuity in some of these domains, there are also discontinuous events. Falling ill with a chronic viral disease, suffering a traumatic physical injury, experiencing war, living in a period of economic decline, or experiencing sudden parental death may not be related to what has come before but certainly influences what follows. Models of development cannot take these more random events into account, but the factors that influence successful accommodation to them are probably rooted in the same elements that promote optimal adaptation to the predictable conflicts of development. There is a bias in the assumption that these unpredictable events typically exert an adverse effect on development. Positive developmental consequences of unpredictable events are also possible.

Biological Development

Adolescence is related but not identical to puberty. Puberty is a biological event, whereas adolescence is a period designated by society. The biological changes of puberty may predate or may not have occurred by the age that society has designated as the definition of adulthood. Puberty originates from the Latin *puber*, which refers to "being of marriageable age." This linguistic link implies an emerging capacity for reproduction. There is a prominent implication of the primacy of biological capacities in the understanding of this stage of development. These biological changes are both the most rapid and the most striking of the physical changes that the body experiences after infancy. By the end of this stage of development, the body has reached adult stature and sexual appearance. Biological changes include maturation of sexual organs and capacities, cardiovascular function, body composition, height, and weight. A time line of biological development from age 13 to 18 years is presented in Figure 9–2.

The development of secondary sex characteristics in both sexes has been well documented.[12, 13] In girls, puberty usually commences with breast development, although 15% may show growth of pubic hair first. Before these observable changes, ovarian secretion of estradiol and progesterone produces an increase in vaginal length and cytological transformation of the cells in the vaginal lining.[14]

Biological Development:
13–18 years

FEMALE DEVELOPMENT

Breast development*

Stage I	Stage II	Stage III	Stage IV	Stage V

Pubic hair development in females*

Stage I	Stage II	Stage III	Stage IV	Stage V

Menarche (average onset = 12.8)

Growth spurt

Muscle mass decreases, bone density increases, LH and FSH secretion increases, satisfaction with weight decreases

MALE DEVELOPMENT

Testicular and penile development*

Stage I	Stage II	Stage III	Stage IV	Stage V

Pubic hair development in males*

Stage I	Stage II	Stage III	Stage IV	Stage V

Spermarche (average onset = 14.3)

Growth spurt

Facial hair emerges
Deepening of male voice

Muscle mass develops, bone width and density increase, LH and FSH secretion increases

*Although the sequence of these events is constant, the length of time spent in each stage is highly variable

Figure 9–2 *Biological development during the adolescent period (ages 13 to 18 years).*

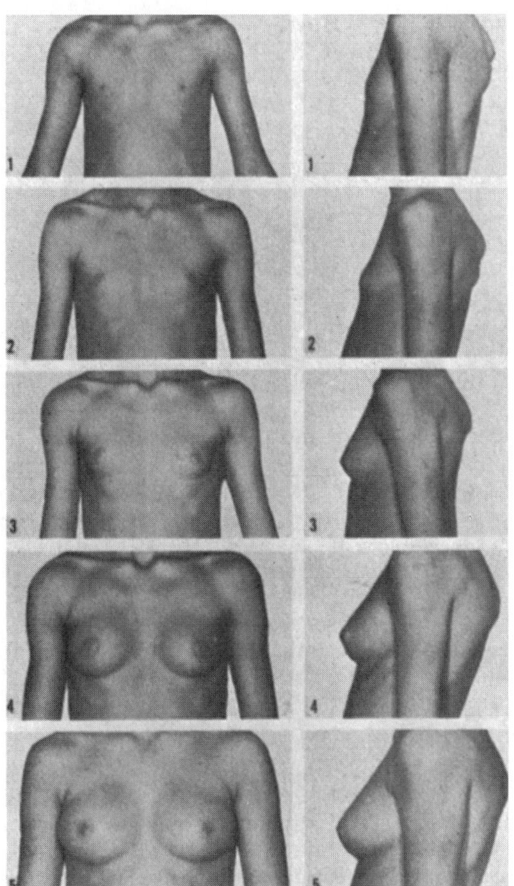

Figure 9–3 *Sex maturity ratings of breast changes in adolescent girls. (Courtesy of J. M. Tanner, MD, Institute of Child Health, Department of Growth and Development, University of London, London, UK.)*

Breast development (Fig. 9–3) follows a predictable sequence under the influence of ovarian estradiol and progesterone production. Asymmetrical growth is common.[12] The average age for the onset of breast development (thelarche) is 11.2 years (Fig. 9–4). Stage I consists of only a raised papilla. In stage II a breast bud is visible with enlargement of the areola. In stage III there is an enlarged breast without separation of the contours between the areola and the breast itself. Stage IV is defined by further enlargement and projection of the areola and papilla to form a secondary mound above the level of the breast. In stage V there is an adult breast contour with elevation of the papilla only (Table 9–4; see Fig. 9–3).

Pubic hair development also has five stages.[12] The average age for the onset of pubic hair growth is 11.9 years (see Fig. 9–4). Pubic hair growth is largely under the control of adrenal androgens, although some contribution from estrogens may be important.[15] Pubic hair growth may lag behind breast stages as shown in Figure 9–4. In stage I there is no pubic hair. Stage II is characterized by straight or only slightly curly hair that has little pigmentation and primarily appears on the labia (Fig. 9–5). Stage III shows the characteristically dark curly hair that spreads from the labia over the mons. By this time the mons itself has gained in size as a result of increased fat deposition. Stage IV shows the entire mons overspread by thick dark pubic hair that does not yet extend as far as the medial aspect of the thigh. Stage V shows the typical adult distribution, which includes the areas of the medial thigh (see Table 9–4 and Fig. 9–5). In girls, axillary hair develops during the later portions of stage III or during stage IV and appears at an average age of 13.2 years.[14] Activation of the apocrine glands in the vulva and axilla and on the face coincides with the appearance of pubic and axillary hair.

Typically, within 2 years of the onset of breast development menarche is attained (see Fig. 9–4). Although the average age for menarche is reported to be 12.8 years,[16] the range is between 10 and 16 years. After menarche, from 2 to as long as 5 years, menstrual cycles are typically anovulatory.[14] The sequence of maturational events in girls is shown in Figure 9–6.

In nearly all boys, the onset of puberty begins with testicular enlargement. Enlargement is a consequence of cellular proliferation of the seminiferous tubules caused by rising levels of luteinizing hormone (LH) and follicle-stimulating hormone (FSH).[15] Prepubertal testes respond to a variety of tropic substances with production of testosterone. The appearance of sustained increases in levels of circulating testosterone lags behind measures of testicular volume, implying separate mechanisms in the induction of testosterone secretion by Leydig's cells and the proliferation of seminiferous tubules. Spermatogenesis occurs after the increase in testicular volume. An approximate estimate for spermarche is based on the average age of conscious ejaculation, which is 14.3 years.[14]

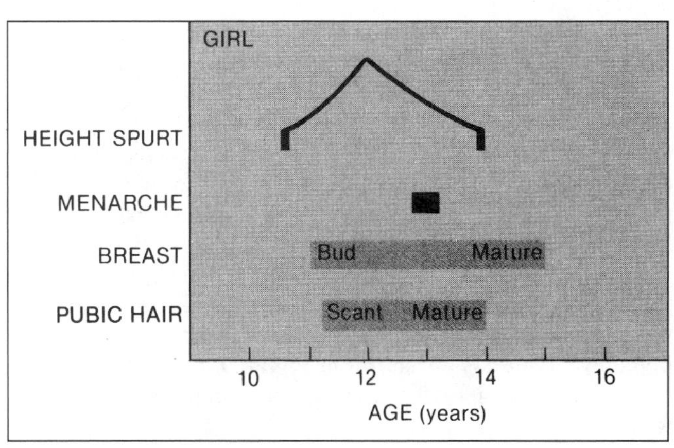

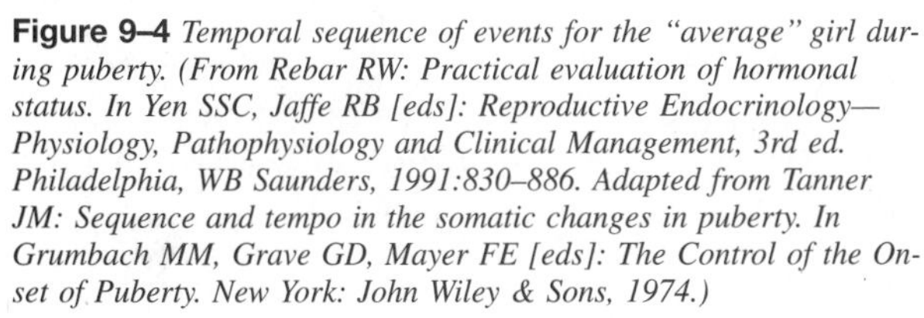

Figure 9–4 *Temporal sequence of events for the "average" girl during puberty. (From Rebar RW: Practical evaluation of hormonal status. In Yen SSC, Jaffe RB [eds]: Reproductive Endocrinology—Physiology, Pathophysiology and Clinical Management, 3rd ed. Philadelphia, WB Saunders, 1991:830–886. Adapted from Tanner JM: Sequence and tempo in the somatic changes in puberty. In Grumbach MM, Grave GD, Mayer FE [eds]: The Control of the Onset of Puberty. New York: John Wiley & Sons, 1974.)*

Table 9–4 Classification of Sex Maturity Stages in Girls

Sex Maturity Rating Stage	Pubic Hair	Breasts
I	Preadolescent	Preadolescent
II	Sparse, lightly pigmented, straight, medial border of labia	Breast and papilla elevated as small mound; areolar diameter increased
III	Darker, beginning to curl, increased amount	Breast and areola enlarged, no contour separation
IV	Coarse, curly, abundant but amount less than in adult	Areola and papilla form secondary mound
V	Adult feminine triangle, spread to medial surface of thighs	Mature; nipple projects, areola part of general breast contour

Data from Tanner JM: Growth at Adolescence, 2nd ed. Oxford, UK: Blackwell Scientific Publications, 1962.

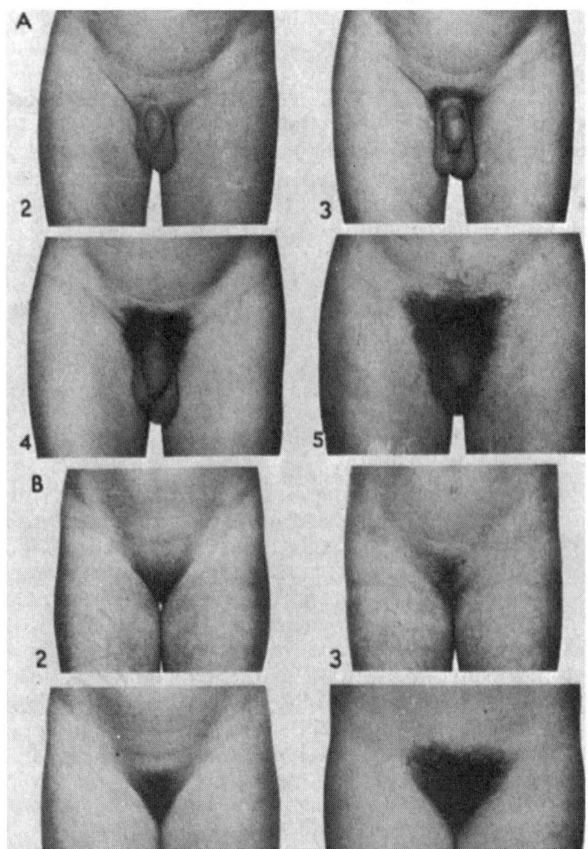

Figure 9–5 *Sex maturity ratings of pubic hair changes in adolescent boys and girls. (Courtesy of J. M. Tanner, MD, Institute of Child Health, Department of Growth and Development, University of London, London, UK.)*

The stages of male genital development are based on testicular and penile length and are associated with increases in serum testosterone levels[13] (Fig. 9–7). Stage I is characterized by testicular length less than 2.0 cm. Stage II is defined by testicular length between 2.5 and 3.2 cm and is usually associated with scrotal thinning. Stage III reflects growth of the penis and lengthening of the testis to between 3.3 and 4.0 cm. Stage IV is characterized by lengthening of the penis and testicular enlargement to 4.1 to 4.9 cm in length, with darkening of the scrotum. Stage V corresponds to adult testicular size (greater than 5 cm). Usually the left testicle hangs lower in the scrotum and the right testicle is larger.[15]

Male pubic hair development is also under control of adrenal androgens and their precursors (see Fig. 9–7) and may not be synchronous with genital development.[12] In stage I there is no genital hair. Stage II is characterized by sparse growth of slightly pigmented straight hair primarily at the base of the penis. Stage III corresponds to hair that is dark, curly, and distributed over the mons. Stage IV hair is spread over the mons but does not reach the medial aspect of the thigh. In stage V hair growth has reached the adult distribution (Table 9–5). For boys, the average time from the emergence of the first pubic hair to reaching the adult pattern is 2.7 years.[14]

Male axillary and facial hair growth is affected by testosterone and is not tightly linked to the appearance of other sexual features. The typical adult pattern of facial hair occurs within 2 years of Tanner's stage II pubic hair development.[14] Male facial hair emerges at an average age of 14.9 years at the lateral aspects of the lip and moves medially.[17] Chin hair usually appears last. The deepening of the male voice is a consequence of enlargement of the larynx and thickening of the vocal chords. These changes are under the control of testosterone and its metabolites and correspond to the male growth spurt. The sequence of maturational events in boys is shown in Figure 9–8.

Puberty changes the distribution of muscle, fat, and water in the body. In girls, muscle mass continues to develop until menarche and then declines. In boys, muscle mass, which is under androgenic stimulation, develops throughout adolescence and is accompanied by increases in bone density. In girls, fat distribution continues throughout puberty and by the end of puberty lean body stores of fat are double those of boys. In boys, intracellular water increases during puberty to 39%, whereas in girls it decreases to 29%.[14]

A variety of factors affect the onset of puberty, including, but not limited to, genetic endowment, adequate

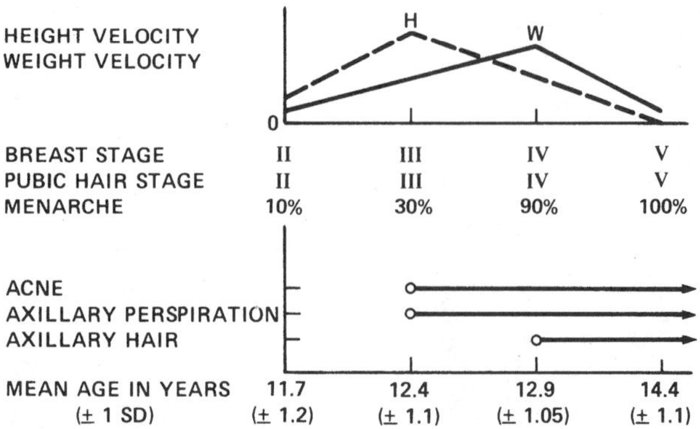

Figure 9–6 *Sequence of maturational events in girls. (Adapted from Marshall WA, Tanner JM: Variations in pattern of pubertal changes in girls. Arch Dis Child 1969; 44:291.)*

Major Actions of Testosterone and Dihydrotestosterone in Male Sexual Development

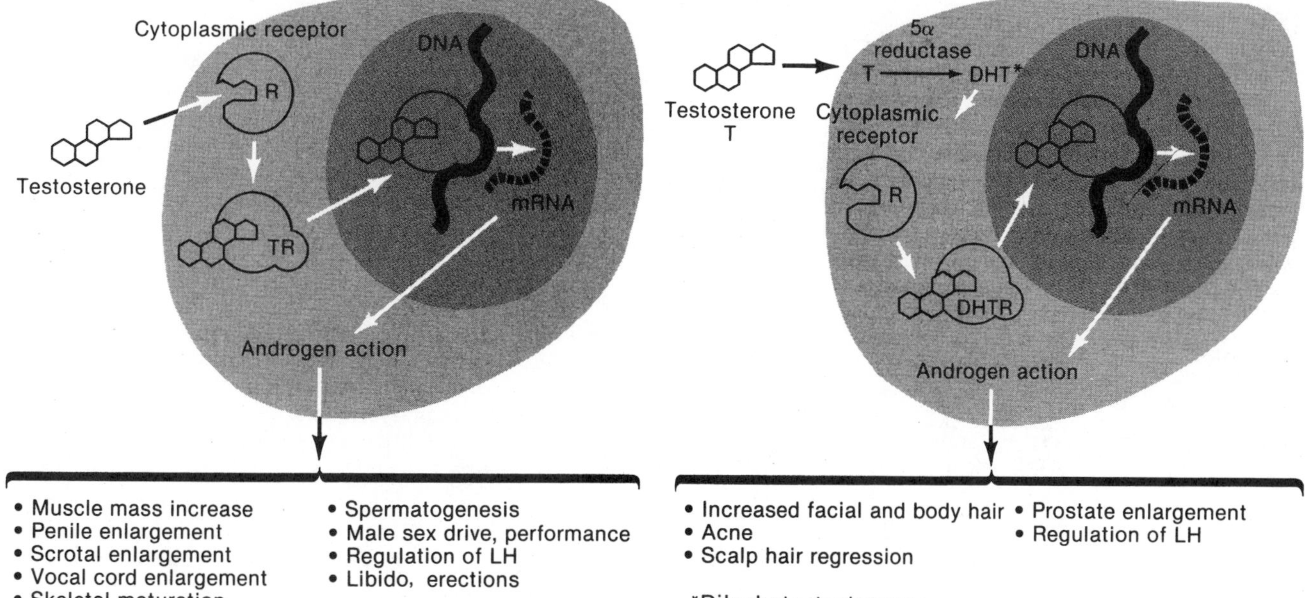

Figure 9–7 *Illustration of the major actions of testosterone and dihydrotestosterone at puberty. (From Schowalter JE: Adolescent development. In Wyngaarden JB, Smith LW, Bennett JC: Cecil Textbook of Medicine, 19th ed. Philadelphia: WB Saunders, 1992:1331.)*

nutrition, and general health status, as well as environmental factors such as altitude and physiological factors such as prolonged heavy exercise. There may also be an association between deprivation of exposure to light and earlier onset of puberty. Girls who are blind from birth or who reside in extreme latitudes where there is little light for protracted periods may have earlier onset of puberty on average.[18] The importance of nutrition for the onset of menarche is highlighted by data that suggest that menarche in America now occurs more than a year earlier than it did in the mid-19th century.[14, 19]

Long before body changes appear there are gradual increases in levels of circulating FSH and LH, which are produced in response to secretion of gonadotropin-releasing hormone into the portal pituitary circulation. Gonadotropin-releasing hormone is secreted in a nocturnal circadian rhythm in pulses; consequently, gonadotropin-releasing hormone, LH, and FSH follow a similar nocturnal pulsatile pattern throughout childhood. As adolescence approaches, the rate and amount of secretion of gonadotropin-releasing hormone increase and the pattern changes to day and night pulses. As much as 2 years before increases in circulating gonadotropins, circulating adrenal androgenic hormones—dehydroepiandrosterone and 17-ketosteroid—increase in both sexes. As puberty nears, LH and FSH levels increase sharply. LH in boys increases the secretion of testosterone, which reaches adult levels within a year.

Both growth hormone (GH) and gonadal hormones are needed to initiate and sustain the adolescent growth spurt. GH is one of the most important influences on height and may be excreted at significantly higher levels in taller children than in their smaller peers during childhood.[19] The secretion of GH is under the control of GH-releasing hormone and somatostatin. In addition, estrogen, thyroxine, and glucocorticoids affect GH secretion. The timing of GH spikes is dependent on diminishing levels of somatostatin,

Table 9–5 Classification of Sex Maturity Stages in Boys

Sex Maturity Rating Stage	Pubic Hair	Penis	Testes
I	None	Preadolescent	Preadolescent
II	Scanty, long, slightly pigmented	Slight enlargement	Enlarged scrotum, pink texture altered
III	Darker, starts to curl, small amount	Longer	Larger
IV	Resembles adult type, but less in quantity; coarse, curly	Larger; glans and breadth increased in size	Larger, scrotum dark
V	Adult distribution, spread to medial surface of thighs	Adult size	Adult size

Data from Tanner JM: Growth at Adolescence, 2nd ed. Oxford, UK: Blackwell Scientific Publications, 1962.

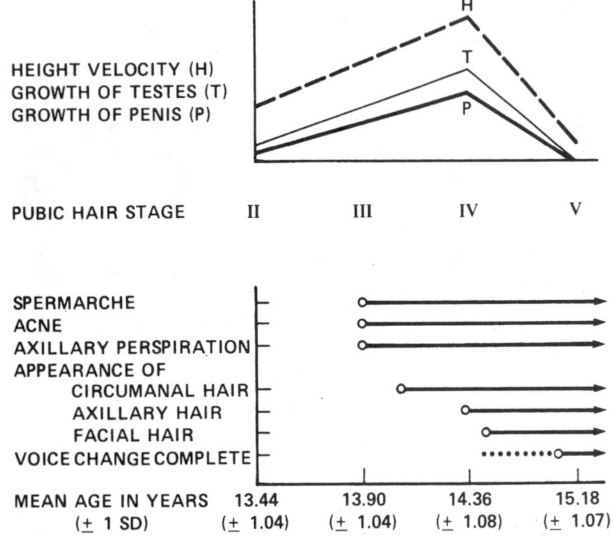

Figure 9–8 *Sequence of maturational events in boys. (Adapted from Marshall WA, Tanner JM: Variations in pattern of pubertal changes in girls. Arch Dis Child 1969; 44:291.)*

and the amplitude of the GH spikes is directly related to GH-releasing hormone levels. GH-releasing hormone also appears to have a role in facilitating GH gene transcription.

The adolescent growth spurt depends on GH levels. Throughout childhood, GH levels are similar in both sexes. Under the influence of rising levels of gonadal steroids and GH, the growth spurt appears earlier in female development. The female growth spurt typically occurs during breast stages II and III, whereas the male growth spurt occurs during genital stage IV.[14, 15, 19] The circadian timing of GH secretion is the same in both sexes but the magnitude of the GH spike is greater in boys.

There are changes in body proportions as well as composition during adolescence. The relationship between the shoulders and hips changes depending on sex. In boys the shoulders increase in comparison with the hips, whereas the hips widen relative to the shoulders in girls. Similarly, the relationship between leg and trunk lengths changes. In boys the lengthening of the femur is greater in proportion to overall bone growth than it is in girls. This leads to longer legs in boys. Growth of the bones of the face also affects appearance between childhood and adulthood. Mandibular length increases and the frontal sinuses evolve. This results in the protrusion of the jaw, a more upright alignment of the incisors, and creation of a brow ridge. The nose extends downward and forward to a greater extent as well.[14]

The physical changes of puberty and adolescence produce a wide variety of psychological effects. These changes affect the way others look at adolescents and how adolescents view themselves. The rate and timing of these physical changes have a powerful effect on later psychological, social, and emotional development. The individual may be thrust into roles or responsibilities prematurely or, conversely, may be denied access to privileges. The influence of hormones on the behavior of adolescents has also come to be questioned. "Raging" hormones continue to be advanced as an explanation for teenage behaviors. However, many studies show inconsistent or modest correlations between hormone levels and types of adolescent behavior.[20]

Cognitive Development

The child's cognitive apparatus undergoes dramatic transformations throughout adolescence. This maturation of the child's capacity for thinking and memory is as significant as the physical changes that unfold throughout this time. The transformation itself is mediated by the emergence of novel cognitive skills that allow the manipulation of ideas and permit the adolescent to assimilate more highly complex information. The adolescent's informational catalog expands, allowing the verification of new facts. Among the most important developments is the emergence of the ability to reflect on cognition itself; this is referred to as the development of metacognitive capacity facilitating both understanding and empathy.[21]

Piaget's theories[22] provide a fundamental starting point for understanding childhood cognitive development[23] despite problems in the staging of skills at certain developmental times. Most of Piaget's descriptions and sequences of skills have proved to be valid, but consensus is lacking on whether the skills aggregate or can be demarcated in a manner that supports piagetian developmental stages.[23]

A major contribution of Piaget was the description of the ways in which the child's conscious mind is transformed and recasts itself from an efficient but heavily subjective, relatively concrete, memory and organizational tool into an exquisite "conceptual processor" during preadolescence and adolescence. But contemporary theory has suggested that there are limitations that must be acknowledged when trying to generalize from the capacities of preoperational and operational stages. It may be that there are some skills that come "on line" at one phase of development but do not readily generalize to other functions as Piaget suggested. Logical skills in particular may display the least generalization. "Conditional reasoning begins to appear in elementary school years or earlier, but remains incomplete and imperfectly used even in adulthood. . . . Truly abstract thought is a rarity and, if it appears in the adult at all, it seems to be dependent on specialized training."[24]

In comparison with its developmental forerunners, the processing skill of the adolescent is capable of much higher levels of abstracting and conceptualizing. This higher level processing capacity is linked closely to abilities to grasp novel attributes and perceive critical elements. As a result, concepts can now be manipulated as things in freestanding objects that may be uncoupled from actual experience. With this ability, critical elements can be applied across situations or subtracted out of a logical string of assumptions. Similarly, novel attributes can be generalized to other problems. Consequently, the adolescent begins to understand and apply concepts in imaginative ways, outside the circumstances in which they were first learned or even without having observed them firsthand. When actions are under consideration, the more powerful processing skill permits the adolescent to imagine the outcome of a theoretical or conceptualized intervention without actually having experienced the situation or needing to perform the action directly. The adolescent acquires far greater capacities for comparing outcomes and imagining emotional consequences and, as a result, acquires far greater abilities to understand, integrate, and relate experiences and ideas.

For Piaget and Inhelder,[25] logical reasoning is "a transformation of thought that permits the handling of hypotheses and reasoning with regard to propositions removed from concrete and present observation." It is this ability that undergoes rapid growth just before and during adolescence. These mechanisms equip the child with additional cognitive abilities such as a combinatorial system, an ability to understand combinations of objects, an acquisition of new propositional combinations, and an appreciation of reversibilities like inversion, reciprocity, and symmetry.[26]

Consequently, adolescents are able to understand, organize, and relate information in new ways. As Flavell and coworkers[23] have described, adolescents are able to entertain ideas about possible alternatives that are not immediately in front of them. Adolescents readily grasp possibilities that are beyond the realm of reality or that may contradict all previous assumptions they have held. In addition, novel problem-solving methods become available. Deductions can be made from hypotheses that are no longer fashioned exclusively from facts that are known or apparent. Adolescents can conceive of outcomes from mental experiments that are based on concepts alone. Abstract ideas can be entertained. The consequences of living under the simultaneous coexistence of two competing value systems, neither one of which the adolescent has ever known, can be imagined and explored. Such skills extend beyond an ability to imagine or the creativity of manipulating these ideas; they are based on an ability to think beyond one's self and one's subjective experience.

Adolescents can understand the relationships between objects outside subjective experience. Adolescents learn to work from "intrapropositional versus interpropositional knowledge."[26] "Formal operational thinkers understand that logical arguments have a disembodied and passionless life of their own, at least in principle. Concrete-operational thinkers have enough trouble seeing what logically follows from credible premises, let alone from premises that actually contradict one's knowledge, beliefs, or values."[23]

These ideas formed the foundations of cognitive sciences for adolescence throughout the 1960s and 1970s. But during the past decade there has been an elaboration and expansion of Piaget's concepts and they have been interwoven with discoveries from other lines of inquiry. Information-processing theory and the concept of metacognition have been major contributions to these modifications of traditional piagetian views.

Information-processing theory posits alternative explanations for several of the most basic tenets that underlie Piaget's constructs of cognitive development at this stage. A key acquisition of the adolescent in Piaget's schema of this period is the ability to understand abstract theoretical concepts. He proposed that greater logical skills were at the core of this competence.[25] However, an inviting alternative hypothesis from information theory suggests that the success of the adolescent, compared with the child in this arena, has less to do with logic than with experience and knowledge. Information theory suggests that the amount of knowledge possessed by the individual influences both learning efficiency and techniques. The developmental difference between children and adolescents stems from the latter's "ability to access and flexibly use competencies they are known to possess. Development consists in part of going from the context-dependent state where resources are welded to the original learning situation to a *relatively* context independent state where the learner extends the ways in which initially highly constrained knowledge and procedures are used."[27] The hypothesis draws from observations of problem-solving techniques used by children and adolescents. In a series of studies,[28] younger children appeared to reason through new problems one at a time. On the other hand, the more experienced adolescents or adults were able to 1) more readily distill the critical features of the new problem and 2) recognize how the new problem resembled other, more familiar problems.[28]

Three mechanisms by which this efficiency occurs have been suggested: 1) more thorough processing of information, 2) greater capacity to transfer different learning strategies from one kind of problem solving to new problems, and 3) greater familiarity with the problems and solutions.[29] The greater success of the more experienced individual when presented with a novel problem does not appear to be attributable to more refined logic skills. One line of development through childhood to adulthood involves improvement in the completeness with which data are scanned and processed with increasing age.[29] Children tend to overlook or prematurely cease scanning information compared with adolescents.

A second factor influencing efficiency may be that more experienced solvers possess a better ability to withstand the confusion of new vocabulary, unfamiliar subjects, or new ideas [30] and to place the problem in the context of what they know. This ability to place the problem in the context of other knowledge is called transfer processing.[29] "Transfer components are processes involved in carrying over retained information from one situational context to another."[29] One factor promoting facility with transfer skills is experience. "Novices tend to use key words in the problem format when they are asked to sort problems into types; in contrast, experts generally sort on the basis of underlying conceptual identities."[27] Information theory suggests that when the common elements of a problem can be discerned, the access to knowledge about this type of problem is greater and an approach to its solution is more likely to be found.

Familiarity with the type of problem is another important advantage of experience.[31] With greater experience and knowledge, an individual is more likely to recognize a familiar pattern—a so-called problem *isomorph*—within the new problem.[32] Experience increases the individual's ability to recognize the pattern and to transfer knowledge of the solution from a similar problem to the new one. The techniques of problem solving also change as a result of this knowledge. Instead of working through to find the solution each time, the more experienced individual relies on familiar strategies, rote learning, and analogy. If the isomorph is discerned, the method is applied, and the solution can be recalled; the answer to the new problem follows by analogy.

Metacognition, as used by Brown[27] and Flavell[23] and their coworkers, refers to "any knowledge or cognitive activity that takes as its objects, or regulates, any aspect of any cognitive enterprise."[23] In other theories, metacognition is encompassed in the wider category of executive control or processes.[27, 29] The ability to think about thinking means that the adolescent can consider her or his own thinking styles, aptitudes, and limitations. Moreover, this reflective capacity can be applied to understanding others. A deeper appreciation of the way others think and how their thinking influences their behavior reaches the grasp of the adolescent.

A typical school-age child who is asked to reason out the behaviors involved in an interpersonal exchange between two others is inclined to draw on only the interactions that were perceivable at the time—in the here and now. Such a child has only a rudimentary capacity to understand what prior experiences may have contributed to the thoughts or feelings that influenced the exchange.

Unlike the younger child, the adolescent with metacognitive skills understands something about the act of thinking and the antecedents of feelings. The adolescent thinks about the perceivable elements of the exchange—the overt proximal emotional and environmental factors—but also understands that thought and perception may be influenced by a host of internal events that lie beyond what is visible. The modal adolescent is aware of a wider array of internal states, subjective motives, and unique historical forces; adolescents know that each person possesses an inner life and a past that impinge on current behavior and thought. Thus, the adolescent is aware that people have unique histories that affect their assumptions and perceptions and influence their thinking and actions. Adolescents also know that thinking itself can be influenced by fatigue or emotion. This permits typical adolescents to compare their observations with knowledge of behaviors or influences that are foreign to their subjective experience.

Some elements of metacognition begin to appear in childhood and are relatively well established in the later part of childhood. One component of metacognition that commences in childhood but is extended considerably throughout adolescence is cognitive monitoring.[21] In one study, two groups of children, one of school-age children and another of preschoolers, were asked to memorize a small series of simple items and decide for themselves when they were ready to recall them from memory.[33] The younger children were significantly less prepared despite their claims of readiness; the older children were considerably more competent. Tasks such as this hinge on an ability to understand one's own thinking or gauge one's own learning ability.

In adolescence, the ability to reflect on thinking moves to a higher level. This next level, which relies on so-called recursive reasoning, permits one to reflect on another's thinking about oneself. The capacity to "think about your thoughts about my thoughts and so on"[34] is an important cognitive and developmental milestone. On reaching it, the adolescent acquires a greater understanding of thought and behavior.

The applications of recursive thinking have educational and interpersonal relevance. In literature, they permit the more developed adolescent to imagine how the protagonist would think about how the antagonist would regard the protagonist's thoughts. This sort of "mind game" is the basis for a variety of theatrical intrigues. For example, character A attempts to outthink or "psych out" character B by anticipating what B would predict of A's line of reasoning. A may even attempt to lead B in a certain direction, anticipating that this would encourage B's presumption. A then exploits B's predictability. A acts in a different way than B has assumed in order to gain the advantage of surprise.

It is no coincidence that this ability to conceive of ways in which peers, parents, and authority figures think about how one is thinking is associated with a time of immense social self-consciousness and preoccupation for the adolescent. In interpersonal endeavors, recursive thinking permits adolescents to imagine misunderstandings and distortions that may arise between themselves and their friends and respond in ways that repair mistakes. They can imagine what reactions would follow from what others think about them. Conversely, these abilities can be used to tease or manipulate others at a more sophisticated level of destructiveness. These skills may also be applied to test taking and essay assignments, in which the student thinks about the instructor's thoughts about her or his likely responses to the question.

In summary, a number of salient features distinguish the cognitive development of adolescents. The capacity to grasp conceptual underpinnings and to manipulate them as objects themselves appears consistently across nearly all theories of cognitive development and might be regarded as the most significant. Information theory departs from the traditional piagetian reliance on development in logic skills during this phase. Information theory asserts that larger foundations of information and better skills in discerning the isomorphic features shared by new and familiar problems are critical. In addition, more thorough scanning skills, flexible use of learning strategies, and control or monitoring of information processing appear to be important.[29] Development of metacognitive skills has emerged as a vital developmental activity during adolescence based on studies of knowledge transfer and executive function processes.[23]

A time line of cognitive development from age 13 to 18 years is presented in Figure 9–9.

Emotional Development

During adolescence, emotional development is advanced and shaped by experience and cognitive maturation. The emotional life of children in middle childhood can be characterized as relatively concrete, instantaneous, and circumstantial. They have access to a wide array of emotions, can distinguish subtle gradients of difference, and can identify these emotions in others as readily as they recognize them in themselves. They worry about how others think of them and display empathy for their friends. However, a deeper appreciation of others' sentiments is limited by the school-age child's ability to understand the mental lives and motives of others who have a different sense of time, experience, and memory. In contrast, adolescents are capable of perceiving a range of events from an individual's distant history that may be influential at the present time. They can reason that events well outside their shared experience with an individual might be strongly influential, and they can reason backward from the sequence of events and emotions to speculate on motives or feelings that might be at work. Capacities for abstraction permit adolescents to consider factors outside their own immediate emotional experience. Consequently, adolescents are more emotionally interactive than at any previous period of development.

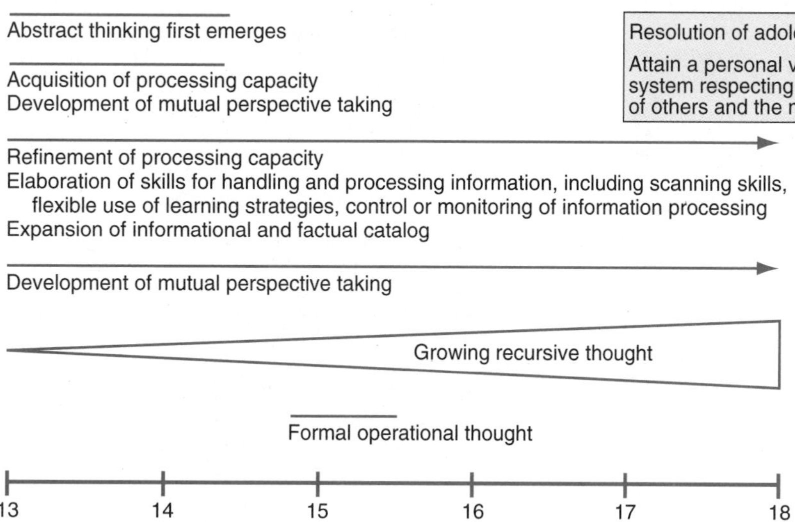

Figure 9–9 *Cognitive development during the adolescent period (ages 13 to 18 years).*

Emotions can be more thoroughly understood and explored within the context of the various cognitive changes that occur during adolescence. Emotions in adolescence exert an increasingly important role in guiding behavior. They become a sustaining motivation for behaviors and mediate the adolescent's relationship with peers and family.

There are differences of opinion about whether adolescents are actually more emotional than school-age children. Psychoanalytic theory proposes that emotionality arises as a consequence of efforts by the ego to integrate conflicts between wishes or drives and social demands. The theory suggests that these developmental conflicts achieve a comfortable equilibrium during the latency years before puberty and are remnants of what was incompletely resolved in toddlerhood. The intrusion of the biological drives of adolescence is believed to upset this equilibrium and force the conflict to resurface in a new way and at a different level. Just as in toddlerhood, the child is confronted with internal pressures that must be brought into alignment with social and familial demands. The social demands on adolescents have different objects and aims, but the task of accommodation remains much the same. Similarly, the outlets available for managing the conflict in adolescence are more diverse and are influenced by more mature cognitive and physical capacities.

Psychoanalytic theory proposes that this conflict is not only typical of adolescence but is inevitable in the developmental process. Consequently, a lack of overt conflict should be viewed as atypical. "Convenient as this may be, it signifies a delay of normal development and as such, is a sign to be taken seriously. These are children who have built up excessive defenses against their drive activities and are now crippled by the results, which act as barriers against the normal maturational processes of phase development."[7]

Empirical investigations do not support this hypothesized increase in emotionality.[35] Direct sampling of adolescents revealed no greater quantity of emotional feeling than is found among children in the preteenage period. In addition, research on nonclinical populations does not support the concept of a disruption of the equilibrium from middle childhood. Investigation suggests that emotional tone remains quite stable from middle childhood through adolescence.[36] Moreover, the stability of these measures was observed across several different cultures.[36] Overall, the empirical investigations offer little support for the idea that adolescence is a period of emotional turmoil, just as there is minimal support for the concept of a normative period of intense conflict between parents and adolescents.

One way to reconcile the difference between the clinical observations and the research findings is to observe the quantitative increase in emotional disorders arising during this time. A variety of studies support the premise that anxiety and depression rise steeply, particularly among girls, during adolescence.[37] Clinicians are in the position of treating adolescents with these disorders and are thus at risk of erroneously generalizing their experience to the entire population. "Office epidemiology" may be quite an accurate reflection of incidence trends of psychopathology but is inappropriate when generalized or applied as prevalence in the nonclinical population.

Another way to reconcile these different perspectives draws on studies of the means by which adolescents resolve conflict compared with the methods used by younger children. The cognitive set of adolescents promotes seeking advice and looking to peers for sympathy. There are cultural and sexual differences in the quantities of and conventions surrounding these exchanges.[38] However, whatever culture is being considered, there are differences in the amounts of discussion and intimate exchange that occur in adolescence

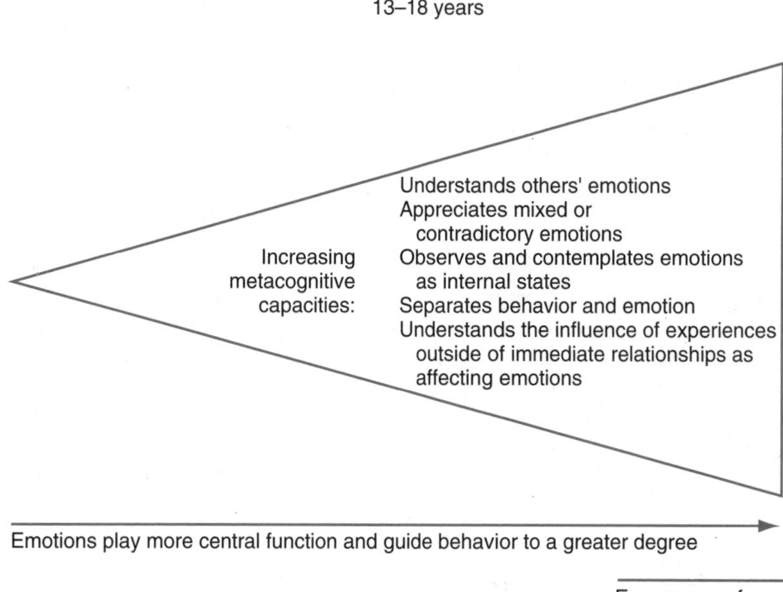

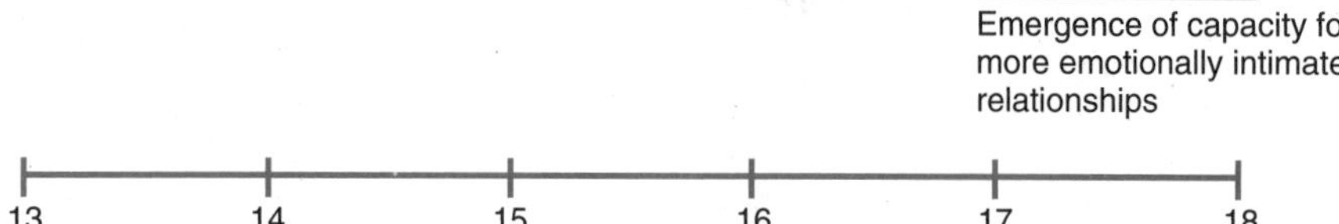

Figure 9–10 *Emotional development during the adolescent period (ages 13 to 18 years).*

compared with earlier periods of development.[37] Thus, emotional expression and discussion about conflict may increase in adolescence and lead to the distorted perception that the actual amount of turmoil has increased. This is analogous to the incorrect presumption of increasing crime rates that follows the expanded availability of police. The ease of reporting decreases barriers to detection and rates appear to rise. Thus, although the emotional life of adolescents is more complex and more interpersonal than that of younger children, it does not appear that the developmental changes of adolescence are in themselves sources of increased emotionality.

A time line of emotional development from age 13 to 18 years is presented in Figure 9–10.

Social Development

Unlike the relatively clear biological criteria defining puberty, the demarcation of adolescence is variable because it is basically designated by society; that is, society determines the criteria for adolescence. At times there are social pressures that dictate whether a larger or a smaller proportion of the teenage population are considered to be adults. For example, when the economy is depressed, teenagers competing with adults for jobs are an economic threat. Conversely, when there is a war, the demand for military personnel defines that it is appropriate for strong and vigorous teenagers to become soldiers. Enright and colleagues,[39] taking a developmentalists' perspective, studied this bias by tracing articles published in the *Journal of Genetic Psychology* from the 1890 through 1945. This span encompassed two periods of depression and both world wars. The research focused specifically on the attributes assigned to teenagers during these four periods. Through the two depressions, youth tended to be described as relatively child-like and immature, obviously still needing time before becoming adults. During the two wars, youth were more often described as mature and developmentally ready to fight for their country.

Two examples illustrate how the perception of the maturity of teenagers has changed in this century. The first was in response to the Great Depression, when, in 1938, Congress passed the first federal labor laws to protect adults, many of whom had families to support. The second was during the Vietnam War. The age of legal maturity at that time was defined as 21 years, but soldiers were drafted at age 18. The media made much of the fact that the government had 18-year-olds fight and die for 3 years before they were allowed to buy alcohol legally or vote. In response, Congress lowered the age of majority to 18 years. Since then, there has been mounting concern about teenagers' deaths caused by drunken driving. Therefore, although the voting age and age of entry into military service have remained at 18 years, most states have raised the legal age for drinking alcohol to 21.

Just as state and national policies affect who is considered to have reached adulthood, so do more local and personal pressures such as family and ethnic expectations. These may favor a teenager being regarded as an adult earlier or later than would be true for another youth.

Poverty is an important factor that influences crucial aspects of life such as nutrition, health care, housing, recreation, and education. Other factors, such as race or ethnicity, can also affect many facets of life. For example, minority adolescents are much more likely to be raised by a single parent. This in turn is associated with a higher likelihood of poverty, less education, increased drug use, and, for a woman, raising a child as a single parent. Similarly,

African-American and Hispanic youth have been shown to be at a greater risk for certain injuries and illnesses. The greatest risk for African-American adolescents, particularly male adolescents, is that of being murdered. The homicide rate for 15- to 20-year-old black males is almost six times that for white males.[40] In the 15- to 24-year-old age range, homicides accounted for 57% of the deaths of black males in 1991, and two thirds of these deaths were caused by guns. According to the National Commission on Children, "teenage boys of all races are more likely to die from gunshot wounds than from all natural causes combined."[41]

Suicide rates are higher for white than for African-American teenagers.[42] This ratio, however, has remained relatively stable compared with the widening racial gap for homicides. As with homicides, firearms have become increasingly popular for committing suicide.

Age at onset and type of sexual experiences are associated with social and ethnic background. The family is the first and foremost conveyor of culture. A child's expectations for sexual activity stem mostly from parent or parents, relatives, and neighbors. African-American adolescents of both sexes are more likely than their Hispanic or other white peers to have had sexual intercourse at each age through the teens.[43] Although education and economic variables are influential in the timing of first sexual experiences, timing is also powerfully molded by what is considered normative.[44] Early sexual activity in turn is linked to early pregnancy and to a greater likelihood of contracting sexually transmitted diseases. Condom and other contraceptive use is more common as adolescents become older. Self-esteem and sexual activity are linked to the adolescents' personal beliefs.[45] If the teenager believes that sexual experience is a positive activity, abstinence lowers self-esteem and participation raises it. The teenager develops a mental value about sexual activity through his or her experiences during the first 12 years of life.

Early sexual experience is not only a social issue, it is also a serious health risk. All sexually transmitted diseases are more common among poor and minority teenagers than in any other groups. There has been an increase in sexually transmitted diseases in adolescents. Syphilis cases doubled among teenagers between 1975 and 1987, and the frequency of human immunodeficiency virus infection is rising. In 1993 racial and ethnic minorities accounted for 51% of all reported cases of acquired immunodeficiency syndrome in boys older than age 13 years and for 75% in girls in the same age group.[46] In children younger than age 13 years, minorities accounted for 84% of cases. Of minority cases, 66% were African-American and 32% were Hispanic. In patients older than age 13 years, the rate of acquired immunodeficiency syndrome for African-American girls was almost 15 times that for white girls, and for boys the corresponding ratio was almost 5:1. Although the syndrome is seldom diagnosed during the teenage years, it is often at this time that human immunodeficiency virus infection is contracted. Acquired immunodeficiency syndrome does not occur until 7, 10, or more years after infection. In a study of African-American young people, aged 9 to 15 years, rates of foreplay even among the 35% who were sexually active were quite low, but among those who were sexually active, 24% of boys and 35% of girls had had anal intercourse, a strong risk factor for human immunodeficiency virus infection.[47] Only about 60% of these youngsters reported that they used a condom during their last intercourse. In 1989, 92% of births to African-American adolescent mothers occurred outside marriage. Pregnant adolescents are more likely than other mothers to deliver low-birth-weight infants, who in turn are more likely than average-sized infants to have developmental delays.

Early sexual activity, alcohol and other drug use, early pregnancy, and sexually transmitted diseases are all intercorrelated.[48] They all embody risk taking and increase the likelihood of injury, disease, and further poverty. An estimated 25% of 10- to 17-year-olds engage in behaviors that create a serious danger to themselves or others.[49] Drug and alcohol use correlates with decreased use of condoms. Drug use may reduce sexual inhibitions, and sexual favors may be sought in exchange for drugs or money for drugs. Transmission of human immunodeficiency virus arises from unprotected sexual intercourse or the injection of drugs.

Parents often feel unappreciated by teenagers or envious of the increasing beauty, strength, or intelligence of their offspring. Giving up control over their children may also represent to parents that they are aging and less needed. The ability to exchange points of view can moderate this conflict. Extremes can be destructive; too few parental rules can be just as much a problem as too many. When parents are absent psychologically, teenagers may increase their misbehavior to learn what limits exist. If there are no parental limits, social limits become salient.

Selman and coworkers[50] have described an invariant sequence of five stages of moral perspectives. Selman's third stage usually comes just before or during preadolescence and permits the child to put her or his viewpoint aside and take the perspective of another person. The fourth stage occurs in the early teens and includes mutual perspective taking, the ability to take the perspective of a neutral third-party observer. Obviously, the ability to accomplish these stages is related to intelligence and the quality of social morality displayed by parents and mentors to the adolescent throughout childhood. This sequence of moral stages cannot be accelerated, but it can be slowed or stopped.

Conflicts between teenagers and their parents typically intensify about the time of puberty and begin to subside after secondary sexual characteristics become evident.[20] Most parent-child quarrels begin over minor issues and do not escalate. Baumrind[51] has classified parental discipline into authoritarian, authoritative, and permissive types. Permissiveness is characterized by too few rules, whereas authoritarian parenting is quite strict and does not balance punishment with praise for positive behaviors. The authoritative approach includes consistency, firmness, and a warmth for the adolescent as well as reinforcement of his or her mature responses.[51] Authoritative parenting appears to be associated with the acquisition of positive social attributes.[52] It is also remarkable that the overall incidence of family abuse and neglect is, if anything, higher for adolescents than it is for younger children.[53]

Peers become more influential as a child enters adolescence, and peer pressure can be socially positive or negative. Adolescents seem most susceptible to peer pressure in early adolescence, and this begins to lessen after age 13 or 14 years.[20] Most early teenagers believe that their parents are not objective enough to help them resolve doubts about parental values and viewpoints. To a large extent, during early adolescence, the peer group comes to represent the stamp of normality and an assurance of acceptance. Typically, adolescents who have many friends possess high self-esteem. Friends may change their individual behaviors to conform to the group, or groups may be formed because of shared peer interests. Both processes probably occur.[54] Teenagers often quit groups that are not sufficiently homogeneous or have unacceptable expectations.

It is common for parental abuse or neglect to push adolescents into associations with adverse peer influences. Boys seem more influenced by group pressures toward antisocial behavior, but otherwise the relationships between gender and group conformity do not show consistent findings. Under peer pressure, cigarette and alcohol use may rise,[55] but so may school grades.[56] Not all groups or group members are equal. Some group members are more influential than others, and some groups are more demanding of members. Peer groups in early adolescence tend to be rather narrow, same-gender cliques, but they become mixed-gender, larger, and more loosely structured by later adolescence. Adolescents who cannot make friends usually manifest emotional, social, and academic problems. Their self-esteem tends to be low. Peer acceptance and support are less available to these individuals.[57]

Schools are where adolescents typically spend most of the time that they are not at home. Doing poorly in school and dropping out of school are highly correlated with having behavioral, social, and legal problems.[58] According to the Educational Testing Service, fewer than half of American 17-year-olds have the skills and basic knowledge required for college or for many entry-level jobs.[59] About one in eight adolescents drops out of school. Four of five prison inmates are high school dropouts, [60] and dropouts are nearly twice as likely as high school graduates to be unemployed.[61] School offers one possible way for adolescents from families and neighborhoods that have powerful antisocial tendencies to learn other values and other paths to being successful. Friendships, skills, and mentoring are all positive attributes that can be obtained through school.

The decision to drop out of high school carries with it potential risks that are seldom foreseen by the teenagers themselves. Part-time work during high school may be positive or negative, depending on the experiences provided and whether or not educational and social opportunities are critically curtailed. Part-time work for more than 15 to 20 hours per week usually undermines basic education.[62]

Young people who enter the marketplace while still in their teens or early 20s have lower incomes. For example, between 1973 and 1986 the real median income for working persons 24 years old or younger fell 26% in general, 19.4% for white non-Hispanics, 18.5% for Hispanics, and 46.7% for African-Americans.[63] Youth do best who gain on-the-job training or apprenticeships that lead to promotions and greater responsibility.

A paradox of independence is produced for youth who attend college, live away from home, and have their parents help pay for it all. The young person living away from home is legally an adult but remains financially unemancipated. Graduate or professional school further prolongs the interval between adolescence and adulthood. Some young people cannot tolerate this protracted period of dependency and

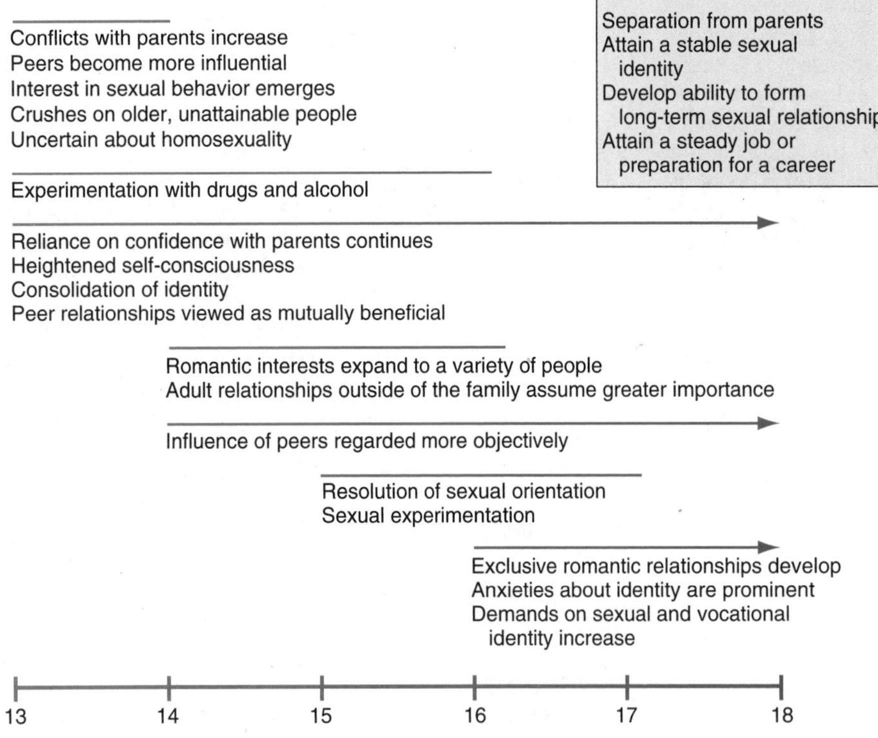

Figure 9–11 *Social development during the adolescent period (ages 13 to 18 years).*

either quit school or stop taking money to achieve financial liberation from their parents. Others reject financial responsibility and are content with absolute fiscal dependency.

A time line of social development from age 13 to 18 years is presented in Figure 9–11.

Risk and Protective Factors

A review of the epidemiology of serious psychiatric disorders points to adolescence as a time of increased risk. It has been established that incidence rates for depression,[64, 65] bipolar affective disorder,[66] panic disorder,[67] obsessive-compulsive disorder,[68] anorexia nervosa,[69] bulimia nervosa,[70] substance abuse,[71] antisocial behavior,[72] and schizophrenia[73] either peak or display a major increase during adolescence. Why adolescence should be the developmental period of greatest risk for so many chronic psychiatric disorders is unclear. A variety of childhood and adolescence risk factor models have been proposed. These share a view that the interplay of biological, familial, social, and cultural forces is critical to the emergence of serious disorders. Parallel to models of infant development, it appears that illness in adolescence evolves from the combination of biological vulnerability and adversity in familial and community environments.

An example of this transactional view is Patterson's[74] model of antisocial behavior. Patterson proposed that childhood noncompliance plus lack of parental monitoring, harsh discipline, lack of parental involvement, and negative coercion creates a reinforcing feedback loop that encourages childhood noncompliance. When the child goes to school, the pattern of noncompliance travels from the household to the schoolroom. In school, the consequence of these behaviors leads to academic failure, impoverished self-esteem, and incompetence in peer relationships.

Another example is the interactional model, which links low birth weight, low family cohesiveness, and inability to obtain support in school to later delinquency. Low birth weight, especially with brain damage, and an unsupportive family increase the child's risk for poor school achievement, impulsivity, behavior disorders, school dropout, and, finally, in adolescence, delinquency.

It appears that most risk factors are not specific for particular disorders. Highly dissimilar symptoms may be produced under the burden of multiple stressors. A great deal of effort has been devoted to discovering which risks might be specific for particular psychiatric disorders. However, "a series of studies in a variety of domains have found that, except at the extremes of biological deviation, it is the number rather than the nature of risk factors that is the best determinant of outcome."[75] Examples of individual biological variables include male sex, low birth weight, mental retardation, and prenatal exposure to large amounts of alcohol.

The potency of any particular stressor appears to vary with age and sex. Boys appear more vulnerable to both physical and psychosocial stressors from the prenatal period to about age 10 years; girls grow more vulnerable to stressors during their teens.[76] Similarly, maternal inattention during childhood plus residence in high-crime neighborhoods in adolescence appears to associate with substance abuse in adolescence.[77] In addition, temperamental features seem relevant. The combination of difficult temperament and parental psychopathology appears to produce a particularly malignant prognosis.[78] A variety of parental and familial attributes have been proposed to influence the onset of child and adolescent psychiatric illness. Examples that have been advanced include high levels of parental personality disorder and depression, expressed emotion, unavailability of mother, marital discord, and low degree of family cohesion. Hill[20] suggested that "early puberty, authoritarian or permissive parenting, family disruption, large impersonal schools, and the availability of a negative peer culture" are important. In addition, "a low level of parental monitoring of the adolescent's behavior [is] a risk factor for involvement with antisocial peers."[20, 79]

Goodness of fit is another concept from temperament research that is relevant for adolescent development and risk. Chess and Thomas[80] defined goodness of fit as that which "results when the environmental expectations, demands, and opportunities are consonant with the individual's temperament and other characteristics so that he can master them effectively." Conversely, "poorness of fit" occurs "when the environmental demands are excessive for the individual's capacities, so that excessive stress and an unhealthy developmental course may be the result."[80] In this paradigm, stress accompanies developmental progress even when the fit between parent and child is good. The difference between good fit and poor fit is the degree to which parents provide support, modulation, and buffering so that stress and demands are no greater than the child's capacities to assimilate them.[80] When adolescents possess biological vulnerabilities and there is a poor fit between them and their parents, the risks of a poor adaptation and maximal expression of the vulnerability are increased.

A risk paradigm that is more specific for adolescents focuses on how personality traits can be reinforced or reduced by the responses that they evoke from the wider community environment. Scarr and McCartney[81] proposed a reinforcing loop that reverberates between the individual, home, and extrafamilial environment. They suggested that genes affect the children's and adolescents' behaviors, which, in turn, select or shape the experiences that individuals have outside the family milieu. The loop is completed when these extrafamilial experiences further encourage the same genetic traits.[81] This model implies that when worried parents report that their adolescent is associating with "bad company" their concern should not be dismissed. It appears that such affiliations are an influential, separate variable that is associated with delinquency and social adjustment problems later.[54] Conversely, involvement with prosocial activities such as the school science club, athletics, a violin quartet, or community volunteer organizations reinforces an adolescent's socially adaptive behavior. This paradigm also underscores that adolescents' behaviors affect their parents' behaviors. For example, parental self-esteem can be enhanced through pride or lowered through shame, and these changes in turn influence the parent's actions toward the teenager.

Biological factors appear to be relatively important during the early years, but in adolescence interpersonal factors and behaviors take center stage. Rutter[82] has suggested that certain family factors raise the likelihood of adolescents' having greater difficulty coping with their impulses and with the rules of society. Rutter cited severe marital discord, large family size with physical or psychological overcrowding, maternal mental disorder, and paternal antisocial behavior as examples of these family risk factors. Furthermore, attending impoverished schools, living in dangerous neighborhoods, and becoming involved in social welfare or correctional institutions such as foster or residential care and juvenile detention facilities add to overall emotional stress. These further jeopardize the adolescent because, typically, they emerge in the context of preexisting biological and psychological risk factors.

There is less research on protective factors than on risk factors. One might consider protective factors to be the obverse of risk factors, but this would be an oversimplification. Clearly, physical health, normal or high IQ, and economic advantage play a role. Having above average intelligence influences school success and facilitates problem solving. Yet, protective factors, like risk factors, usually are not specific to outcome. Anthony[71] coined the term "invulnerable" to describe children who emerged from adverse backgrounds without the trauma and scars that would be predicted. He proposed that these individuals possessed internal resources that made it possible for them to absorb extraordinary amounts of stress without becoming traumatized or overwhelmed.

Garmezy[83] advanced a more interpersonal view on observing similar phenomena. He stressed three categories of protective factors: "(1) personality dispositions in the child, (2) a supportive family milieu, and (3) an external support system that encourages and reinforces a child's coping efforts and strengthens these by reinforcing the child's positive values." Garmezy suggested that such adolescents (and children) were more successful in eliciting helping responses from adults and making use of their support. In a similar way, they may also be more successful in making relationships with peers and responding to the support peers offer.[84] Such skills increase the chances of parents, peers, and teachers being available to support and guide decisions and challenges that would be difficult to face alone. Better quality advice and chances to consider the entire set of possible alternatives also increase the likelihood of a favorable outcome. O'Grady and Metz[85] submitted that adolescents who feel in charge of their lives and know how to obtain help are highly resilient, even when otherwise at risk. The Kauai Longitudinal Study has also reported that the ability to find and use an external support system is a significant protective factor for adolescents who were otherwise considered in jeopardy.[86]

There are suggestions that sex differences may be relevant to resilience too. Girls appear to possess a wider range of coping skills than boys, particularly in forming relationships.[38] The community is also a source of protection for adolescents. Scouting or youth clubs, school extracurricular activities, and church involvement provide safe activities for teenagers to acquire friends, find supportive adults, and develop new competencies.

Conclusion

Increasing attention to adolescent development in the past decade has resulted in substantial changes in our understanding of social, familial, cognitive, and biological characteristics of this period. A great deal is still outside our understanding, and tenacious myths about adolescents persist.[87] However, new findings place adolescent development into greater harmony with the principles of the preceding developmental epochs. The revised view of these changes during adolescence suggests that they are paradoxically dramatic and yet remarkably similar to those of antecedent periods and much less tumultuous than was once presumed. It is intellectually reassuring to be able to place normal adolescence within the context of the constitutional and experiential past. Increasingly, adolescence emerges as a time in which innate capacities are extended under the influence or guidance of secure familial, cultural, and social supports. Noxious forces oppose these changes from within the same domains, but their impact is no greater during this time than at others. The view of adolescence as a time much influenced by preceding risk and protective factors, rather than only as a major metamorphosis triggered by unpredictable interactions between the influences of hormones, peer pressures, and the increased separation from parents, seems most accurate.

References

1. Kett JP: Rites of Passage: Adolescence in America, 1790 to the Present. New York: Basic Books, 1977.
2. Hall GS: The moral and religious training of children. Princeton Rev 1882; 10:26–48.
3. Schowalter JE: Normal adolescent development. In Kaplan HI, Sadock BJ (eds): Comprehensive Textbook of Psychiatry, 6th ed. Baltimore: Williams & Wilkins, 1995:2161–2167.
4. Hall GS: Adolescence: Its Psychology and Its Relations to Anthropology, Sociology, Sex, Crime, Religion and Education. New York: Appleton, 1904.
5. Freud S: Three essays on the theory of sexuality. In Strachey J (trans-ed): The Standard Edition of the Complete Psychological Works of Sigmund Freud, Volume 7. London: Hogarth Press, 1953:125–243. Originally published in 1905.
6. Freud A: The Ego and the Mechanisms of Defence. New York: International Universities Press, 1946.
7. Freud A: Adolescence. In Eissler RS, Freud A, Hartmann H, et al (eds): The Psychoanalytic Study of the Child, Volume 13. New York: International Universities Press, 1958.
8. Blos P: On Adolescence: A Psychoanalytic Interpretation. New York: Free Press, 1962.
9. Offer D: The Psychological World of the Teenager. New York: Basic Books, 1969.
10. Offer D, Ostrov E, Howard KI: Adolescence: What is normal? Am J Dis Child 1989; 143:731–736.
11. Rutter M, Graham P, Chadwick OFD, et al: Adolescent turmoil: Fact or fiction. J Child Psychol Psychiatry 1976; 17:35–56.
12. Marshall WA, Tanner JM: Variation in the pattern of pubertal changes in girls. Arch Dis Child 1969; 44:291–303.
13. Marshall WA, Tanner JM: Variation in the pattern of pubertal changes in boys. Arch Dis Child 1970; 45:13–25.
14. Wheeler MD: Physical changes of puberty. Endocrinol Metab Clin North Am 1991; 20:1–14.
15. Odell WD: Endocrinology of sexual maturation. In DeGroot LJ (ed): Endocrinology, 3rd ed. Philadelphia: WB Saunders, 1995:1938–1952.
16. Zacharias L, Rand WM, Wurtman RJ: A prospective study of sexual development and growth in American girls: The statistics of menarche. Obstet Gynecol Surv 1976; 31:325–337.
17. Lee PA: Normal ages of pubertal events among American males and females. J Adolesc Health Care 1980; 1:26–29.
18. Cardinali DP, Vacas MI: Pineal gland, photoperiodic responses, and puberty. J Endocrinol Invest 1984; 7:157–165.
19. Brook CGD, Hindmarsh PC: The somatotropic axis in puberty. Endocrinol Metab Clin North Am 1992; 21:767–782.
20. Hill P: Recent advances in selected aspects of adolescent development. J Child Psychol Psychiatry 1993; 34:69–99.
21. Flavell JH: Cognitive monitoring. In Dickson WP (ed): Children's Oral Communication Skills. New York: Academic Press, 1981.

22. Gelman R, Baillargeon R: A review of piagetian concepts. In Flavell JH, Markman EM (eds): Handbook of Child Psychology, Volume 3, Cognitive Development. New York: John Wiley & Sons, 1983:167–230.
23. Flavell JH, Miller PH, Miller SA: Cognitive Development, 3rd ed. Englewood Cliffs, NJ: Prentice Hall, 1993.
24. Mandler JR: Representation. In Flavell JH, Markman EM (eds): Handbook of Child Psychology, Volume 3, Cognitive Development. New York: John Wiley & Sons, 1983:420–494.
25. Piaget J, Inhelder B: The Psychology of the Child. New York: Basic Books, 1969.
26. Inhelder B, Piaget J: The Early Growth of Logical Thinking from Childhood to Adolescence. New York: Basic Books, 1958.
27. Brown AL, Bransford JD, Ferrara RA, et al: Learning, remembering, and understanding. In Flavell JH, Markman EM (eds): Handbook of Child Psychology, Volume 3, Cognitive Development. New York: John Wiley & Sons, 1983:77–167.
28. Lovett SB, Flavell JH: Understanding and remembering. Children's knowledge about the differential effects of strategy and task variables on comprehension and memorization. Child Dev 1990; 61:1842–1858.
29. Sternberg RJ, Powell JS: The development of intelligence. In Flavell JH, Markman EM (eds): Handbook of Child Psychology, Volume 3, Cognitive Development. New York: John Wiley & Sons, 1983:341–419.
30. Chi MTH, Feltovich P, Glaser R: Categorization and representation of physics problems by experts and novices. Cognitive Sci 1981; 5:121–152.
31. Glaser R, Chi MTH: Overview. In Chi MTH, Glaser R, Farr J (eds): The Nature of Expertise. Hillsdale, NJ: Lawrence Erlbaum, 1988.
32. Brown AL: Learning and development. The problem of compatibility, access, and induction. Hum Dev 1982; 25:89–115.
33. Flavell JH, Friedrichs AG, Hoyt JD: Developmental changes in memorization processes. Cognitive Psychol 1970; 1:324–340.
34. Flavell JH: The development of children's knowledge about the mind: From cognitive connections to mental representations. In Astington JW, Harris PL, Olson ER (eds): Developing Theories of Mind. Cambridge, UK: Cambridge University Press, 1988:244–267.
35. Larson R, Lampman-Petraitis C: Daily emotional states as reported by children and adolescents. Child Dev 1989; 60:1250–1260.
36. Offer D, Ostrov E, Howard KI: The Adolescent: A Psychological Self-portrait. New York: Basic Books, 1981.
37. Buhrmester D: Intimacy of friendship, interpersonal competence, and adjustment during pre-adolescence and adolescence. Child Dev 1990; 61:1101–1111.
38. Seiffge-Krenke I: Developmental processes in self-concept and coping behavior. In Bosma H, Jackson S (eds): Coping and Self-concept in Adolescence. Berlin: Springer-Verlag, 1990.
39. Enright RD, Levey VM Jr, Harris D, Lapsley DK: Do economic conditions influence how theorists view adolescence? J Youth Adolesc 1987; 16:541–559.
40. National Center for Health Statistics: Advance Report of Final Mortality Statistics, 1991. Hyattsville, MD: National Center for Health Statistics, 1993:2. Monthly Vital Statistics Report 42(suppl).
41. National Commission on Children: Just the Facts: A Summary of Recent Information on America's Children and Their Families. Washington, DC: National Commission on Children, 1993:12.
42. National Center for Health Statistics: Vital Statistics, Mortality Data and Multiple Cause-of-Death-Detail. Hyattsville, MD: U.S. Department of Health and Human Services, Public Health Service, 1988.
43. Mott FL, Haurin RJ: Linkages between sexual activity and alcohol and drug use among American adolescents. Fam Plann Perspect 1988; 20:128–136.
44. Furstenberg FF Jr, Morgan SP, Moore KA, et al: Race differences in the timing of adolescent intercourse. Am Soc Rev 1987; 52:511–518.
45. Miller B, Christensen R, Olson TD: Self-esteem in relation to adolescent sexual attitude and behavior. Youth Society 1987; 19:93–111.
46. Centers for Disease Control: AIDS among racial/ethnic minorities—United States, 1993. MMWR Morb Mortal Wkly Rep 1994; 43:644–655.
47. Stanton B, Li X, Black M, et al: Sexual practices and intentions among preadolescent and early adolescent low-income urban African-Americans. Pediatrics 1994; 93:966–973.
48. Elster AB, Kuznets NJ: AMA Guidelines for Adolescent Preventive Services (GAPS). Chicago: American Medical Association, 1994.
49. Dryfoos G: Adolescents at Risk. New York: Oxford University Press, 1990.
50. Brion-Meisels S, Selman R: Early adolescent development of new interpersonal strategies: Understanding and intervention. School Psychol Rev 1984; 13:278–291.
51. Baumrind D: Current patterns of parental authority. Dev Psychol Monogr 1971; 1:1–103.
52. Hill P: Research on adolescents and their families: Past and prospect. In Irwin CE (ed): Adolescent Social Behavior and Health. San Francisco: Jossey-Bass, 1987:13–31.
53. Council on Scientific Affairs, American Medical Association: Adolescents as victims of family violence. JAMA 1993; 207:1850–1856.
54. Kandel DB: Homophily, selection and socialization in adolescent friendships. Am J Sociol 1978; 84:427–436.
55. Fisher LA, Bauman KE: Influence and selection in the friend-adolescent relationship: Findings from studies of adolescent smoking and drinking. J Appl Soc Psychol 1988; 18:289–314.
56. Epstein JL: The influence of friends on achievement and affective outcomes. In Epstein JL, Karweir NL (eds): Friends in School. New York: Academic Press, 1983.
57. East PL, Hess LE, Lerner RM: Peer social support and adjustment of early adolescent peer groups. J Early Adolesc 1987; 7:153–163.
58. Rutter M: School effects on pupil progress: Research findings and policy implications. Child Dev 1983; 54:1–29.
59. Applebee AN, Langer JA, Mullis IVS: Crossroads in American Education. Princeton, NJ: Educational Testing Service, 1989.
60. Committee for Economic Development: The Unfinished Agenda: A New Vision for Child Development and Education. New York: Committee for Economic Development, 1991:11.
61. US Congress, Office of Technology Assessment: Worker Training: Competing in the New International Economy. Washington, DC: Government Printing Office, 1990:163.
62. William T. Grant Commission on Work, Family and Citizenship: The Forgotten Half: Pathways to Success for America's Youth and Young Families. Washington, DC: William T. Grant Foundation, 1988:46.
63. Johnson C, Sum A: Declining Earnings of Young Men: Their Relation to Poverty, Teen Pregnancy and Family Formation. Washington, DC: Children's Defense Fund, 1987.
64. Angold A: Childhood and adolescent depression. I. Epidemiological and aetiological aspects. Br J Psychiatry 1988; 152:601–617.
65. Joyce PR, Oakley-Browne AM, Wells JE, et al: Birth cohort trends in major depression: Increasing rates and earlier onset in New Zealand. J Affect Disord 1990; 18:83–90.
66. Akiskal HS, Downs J, Jordan P, et al: Affective disorders in referred children and younger siblings of manic depressives. Arch Gen Psychiatry 1985; 42:996–1003.
67. von Korff MR, Eaton WW, Keyl PM: The epidemiology of panic attacks and panic disorder: Results of three community surveys. Am J Epidemiol 1985; 122:970–981.
68. Rasmussen SA, Eisen JL: Epidemiology and clinical features of obsessive-compulsive disorder. Psychiatr Clin North Am 1992; 15: 743–758.
69. Lucas AR, Beard CM, O'Fallon WM, Kurland LT: 50-year trends in the incidence of anorexia nervosa in Rochester, Minn.: A population-based study. Am J Psychiatry 1991; 148:917–922.
70. Kendler K, MacLean C, Neale M, et al: The genetic epidemiology of bulimia nervosa. Am J Psychiatry 1991; 148:1627–1637.
71. Anthony EJ: The syndrome of the psychologically invulnerable child. In Anthony EJ, Koupernik C (eds): The Child in His Family: Children at Psychiatric Risk, Volume 3. New York: John Wiley & Sons, 1974:529–544.
72. Rutter M, Giller H: Juvenile Delinquency: Trends and Perspectives. New York: Guilford Press, 1983.
73. Angermeyer MC, Kuhn L: Gender differences in age at onset of schizophrenia. Eur Arch Psychiatry Neurol Sci 1988; 237:351–364.
74. Patterson GR: Performance models for antisocial boys. Am Psychol 1986; 41:432–444.
75. Sameroff AJ: Conceptual issues in prevention. In Prevention of Mental Disorders, Alcohol, and Other Drug Use in Children and Adolescents. U.S. Department of Health and Human Services OSAP Prevention Monograph-2. Rockville, MD: Office of Substance Abuse Prevention, 1989:23–53.
76. Mrazek PJ, Haggerty RJ (eds): Reducing Risks for Mental Disorders: Frontiers for Preventive Intervention Research. Washington, DC: National Academy Press, 1994.

77. Cohen P, Brook JS, Cohen J, et al: Common and uncommon pathways to adolescent psychopathology and problem behavior. In Rubins LN, Rutter M (eds): Straight and Devious Pathways from Childhood to Adulthood. Cambridge, UK: Cambridge University Press, 1990:242–258.
78. Rutter M, Quinton D: Parental psychiatric disorder: Effects on children. Psychol Med 1984; 14:853–880.
79. Patterson GR, Stouthamer-Loeber M: The correlation of family management practices and delinquency. Child Dev 1984; 33:1299–1307.
80. Chess S, Thomas A: Origins and Evolution of Behavior Disorders: From Infancy to Early Adult Life. New York: Brunner/Mazel, 1984.
81. Scarr S, McCartney K: How people make their own environments: A theory of genotype environment effects. Child Dev 1983; 54:424–435.
82. Rutter M: Protective factors in children's responses to stress and disadvantage. In Kent MW, Rolf JE (eds): Primary Prevention in Psychopathology, Volume 3, Social Competence in Children. Hanover, NH: University Press of New England, 1979.
83. Garmezy N: Developmental aspects of children's responses to the stress of separation and loss. In Rutter M, Izard CE, Read P (eds): Depression in Young People. New York: Guilford Press, 1986:297–323.
84. Rutter M: Psychiatric Disorder in parents as a risk factor for children. In Prevention of Mental Disorders, Alcohol, and Other Drug Use in Children and Adolescents. U.S. Department of Health and Human Services OSAP Prevention Monograph-2. Rockville, MD: Office of Substance Prevention, 1989:157–189.
85. O'Grady D, Metz JR: Resilience in children at high risk for psychological disorder. J Pediatr Psychol 1987; 12:3–23.
86. Werner EE, Smith RS: Overcoming the Odds: High Risk Children from Birth to Adulthood. New York: Cornell University Press, 1992.
87. Offer D, Schonert-Reichl K: Debunking the myths of adolescence: Findings from recent research. J Am Acad Child Adolesc Psychiatry 1992; 31:1003–1014.

CHAPTER

10 Adult Development

William R. Beardslee
George Vaillant

The study of adult development is evolving within the context of new empirical investigations. Rich theoretical conceptualizations,[1] psychologically informed biographies,[2] and empirical cohort-based research[3] have all contributed to the knowledge base. Although these data have limitations in terms of a lack of cross-cultural comparisons and an overemphasis on male development, enough evidence has accumulated to suggest well-founded conceptualizations of adult development.

The central thesis of this chapter is that development occurs in multiple dimensions throughout the course of adulthood. First, current biological perspectives on adult development are reviewed. Next, the importance of a developmental perspective for understanding serious psychopathology and resiliency is discussed. Last, theoretical perspectives of developmental stages in adulthood are discussed within the context of three longitudinal empirical studies.

This chapter builds naturally on the preceding review of developmental stages from infancy through adolescence and relies on the integrative framework of Erik Erikson. Broadly, adult development represents a continued assimilation of and accommodation to both the external world and inner life. Adult development occurs in response to a series of predictable and unpredictable challenges. Such development follows a probable but not invariant sequence as each stage builds on what has gone before. Adult development, although sequential, is not invariably tied to specific ages. For example, puberty in girls may normally occur at age 10 years or at age 16 years. If puberty does not occur, the vicissitudes of menopause will not occur either. Most adults reach puberty, but other stages of adult development may not be attained.

Four factors render our understanding of adult development difficult. First, there must be a cultural belief that adult development does, in fact, occur. Second, the duration of empirical longitudinal studies that span the entire range of adult development will, by definition, exceed the productive life of a single researcher. Third, longitudinal studies must be understood within the context of cohort effects, cultural characteristics, and historical biases. Finally, the observer must maintain a constancy in perspective while documenting development in others.

The most challenging of these issues is that development in adulthood occurs during a much longer time interval than earlier developmental phases. The specific stages of childhood described in previous chapters may span only 1 or 2 years, which renders their detailed documentation much more feasible.

Although the current emphasis on diagnosis within psychiatry has allowed for progress in the study of cross-sectional psychopathology, diagnostic systems have only minimally incorporated developmental principles and, consequently, have obscured the developmental variation that characterizes some disorders. For example, the diagnostic criteria used to establish depression are identical for children and adults despite the fact that a depressed 8-year-old presents with different symptoms than a depressed 80-year-old because of differences in psychological, linguistic, and neurological maturation. Also, some anxiety disorders that begin in childhood have been shown to evolve into a major depressive disorder later in life. The genotype remains constant, but the phenotype changes with development.

An additional cause for difficulty in the study of adult development is the fact that individuals are greatly affected by the time in which they live. The profound changes in family structure in the United States in the 20th century provide contemporary illustration. In 1960, 5% of all births occurred to unmarried mothers; by 1988, this figure had risen to 26%. Furthermore, in 1910 only 1% of children experienced parental divorce. In 1993, almost *50%* of all children experienced parental divorce during childhood and lived in a single-parent family for at least 5 years.[4]

There has been a significant increase in children raised in poverty, and young parents with young children have disproportionately fewer resources. Between 1971 and 1991, although the number of children younger than 6 years old increased by less than 10%, the number of children who were poor increased by 60%.[4] These factors have a profound implication for the mental health and development of adults and children.

A transactional model facilitates the understanding of developmental evolution. The interactions between constitutional and genetic predispositions in an individual, the effects of early childhood experience and caregiving, and the individual's interaction with broader society reciprocally affect outcome for a long time period. Although initial transactional models primarily emphasized the influence of factors on the developing child and young adult, more recent models have stressed that the patterns of influence are mutual. Endogenous characteristics that develop within a child, adolescent, or adult (e.g., puberty or schizophrenia) can have a profound impact on the environment of the family.

Finally, the need for utilizing caution when considering the certainty of prediction in adult development is demonstrated by empirical studies. Discontinuities are not uncommon in studies of adult development,[5, 6] and simple linear developmental lines are often difficult to discern.

In most studies there are clear correlations between certain childhood and adult characteristics such as intelligence or endomorphy, but these consistencies are less evident as the complexity of the characteristic increases. For example, schizoid children rarely grow up to be schizophrenic adults. In contrast, children with profound mental retardation or autism experience lifelong disabilities. In populations of healthy individuals, the discontinuities are particularly evident and emphasize the degree of change that adults undergo over time. One reason for these changes is the gradual penetrance in adult life of genetic predispositions (e.g., Huntington's disease, alcoholism, and bipolar disorder). Identical twins are often more similar in personality at age 60 years than they were at age 10.[7]

Knowledge of adult development has evolved from four sources: 1) theoretical conceptualizations of development; 2) detailed studies of individual lives; 3) empirical examinations of discrete phenomena over time; and 4) most rarely, studies that have attempted to integrate conceptual theoretical frameworks with empirical data. The synthesis of these results coupled with an awareness of the inner life based on ego psychology provides a heuristic overall framework.

Biological Perspectives

A developmental perspective is useful in understanding the biological changes of adulthood (Fig. 10–1). Most individuals pass through puberty, which leads to the achievement of sexual intimacy and procreation. By the age of 65 years, an individual has undergone many biological developmental transformations that are quite independent from the decrements of function that result strictly from the aging process. The adaptive responses to the penetrance of genetically controlled diseases such as bipolar depression or alcoholism vary with age and the course of the illness. The biological bases for these differences are less well understood than the equally important environmental forces that affect the individual. Careful longitudinal and cross-sectional studies are required to differentiate genetically determined developmental changes from those that are environmentally determined. For example, although epiphyseal closure is genetically determined, it occurs at puberty, and the onset of puberty is powerfully affected by environmental factors. The languages one speaks, or even dreams in, are entirely environmentally determined and can be acquired at any age. However, the accent that characterizes speech becomes fixed within a biologically determined period, usually at about the age of 14 years.

Myelinization of the central nervous system continues to occur until the fifth decade.[8] This may offer a partial explanation for why simple cognitive operations, such as memory and symbol transformation, decline after about age 20 years, but more complex associational skills continue to improve until about age 30 years. Continued brain development may explain why sensitivity to simple sensations

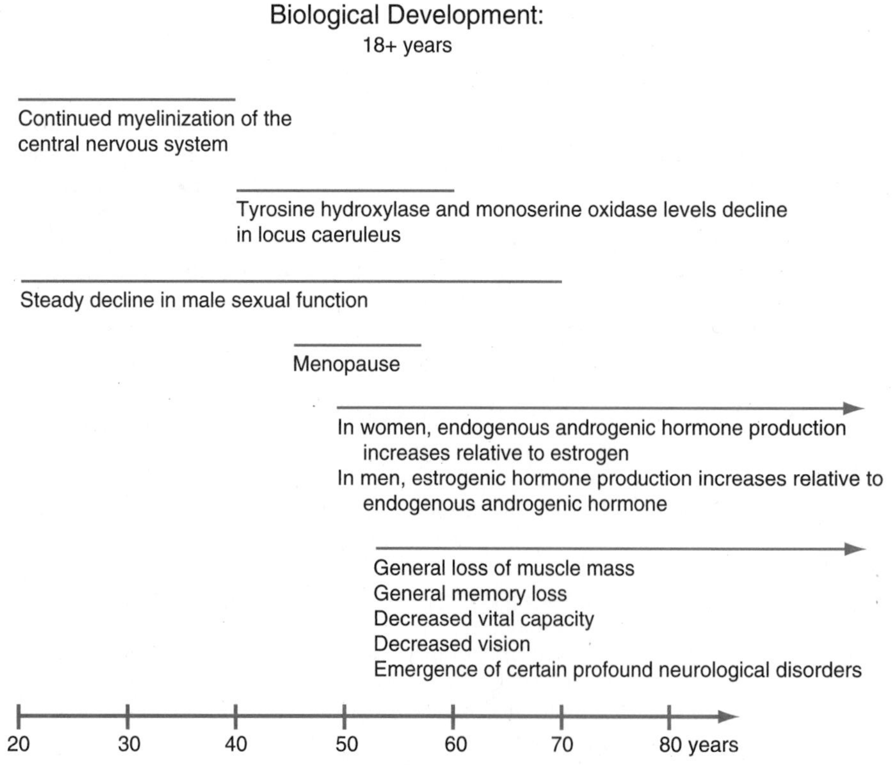

Biological Development:
18+ years

Continued myelinization of the central nervous system

Tyrosine hydroxylase and monoserine oxidase levels decline in locus caeruleus

Steady decline in male sexual function

Menopause

In women, endogenous androgenic hormone production increases relative to estrogen
In men, estrogenic hormone production increases relative to endogenous androgenic hormone

General loss of muscle mass
General memory loss
Decreased vital capacity
Decreased vision
Emergence of certain profound neurological disorders

20 30 40 50 60 70 80 years

Figure 10–1 *Biological development from age 18 years through adulthood.*

such as night vision usually peaks at about age 10 years, but reaction time peaks at age 20. Similarly, appreciation of spatial transformations is best at age 30 years, whereas the ability to delay gratification probably peaks after age 40. Whereas records for sprinting are held by 20-year-olds, those for long distance races are held by 30-year-olds. Mathematicians and physicists often do their best work before 35 years of age, but philosophers and playwrights often create their finest pieces after this age. In general, peak cognitive performance usually occurs between the ages of 10 and 40 years and then begins to decline. However, skills of one type often develop to compensate for losses in other areas. For example, 50-year-olds have dramatically better driving records than do 20-year-olds. In contrast, suicide becomes an increasingly high risk with increasing age.

There are predictable developmental changes in stage 4 and rapid eye movement sleep,[9] electroencephalograms,[10] extrapyramidal symptoms, and brain neurochemistry, but the significance of these changes is not known. For example, extrapyramidal symptoms after administration of neuroleptic agents at age 20 years are quite different from those at age 60 and appear unrelated to brain impairment. The initial manifestations of the gene responsible for Huntington's disease vary with age.

In the locus caeruleus between ages 40 and 60 years, tyrosine hydroxylase, which is the rate-limiting enzyme in the synthesis of norepinephrine, declines while the activity of monoamine oxidase, the rate-limiting factor for the breakdown of norepinephrine, increases. These changes suggest that the activity of the locus caeruleus may be significantly attenuated in the middle years.[12]

In terms of adult development, it is important not to confuse the results of injury and disease. After age 55 years, there is a considerable decline in a variety of biological functions, including a general loss of muscle mass, loss of memory, decreased vital capacity, and diminished vision, as well as the emergence of certain profound neurological disorders such as Alzheimer's disease. Thus, these deficits may reflect disease rather than developmental decline in some elderly persons. Some octogenarians can carry out almost every cognitive and physical function as well as an average 40-year-old despite some loss of abilities in memory and flexibility. In addition, the cross-sectional evidence suggesting that general intelligence declines between ages 20 and 70 years is probably an artifact of cohort effects on educational opportunities as opposed to biological processes. Prospective studies do not support declines in general intelligence.[13]

During puberty, predictable shifts occur in sex hormones that are known to affect cerebral functioning. Particularly in women, changes in the reproductive system are marked during the years of adulthood. In early adulthood, most women menstruate and are able to bear children. Between the ages of 45 and 54 years, a series of endocrine changes accompany menopause, including changes in the balance and production of female hormones. After age 50 years in women, endogenous androgenic hormone production increases relative to estrogens. Although wide individual differences exist, these hormonal changes may facilitate a shift toward increased female dominance that occurs within some couples after the age of 50 years.[14] For men, no single biological change occurs, but there is considerable evidence of changes in sexual functioning and, in biological terms, the degeneration of the prostate gland over time.

The relative importance of sexual life compared with other facets of intimacy can increase at any point between 15 and 65 years of age. Although there is a steady decline in male sexual function from ages 20 to 70 years in terms of the mean number of orgasms per week, the reverse is true for women. Studies have shown that women become increasingly orgasmic with age, at least into their 30s.

The importance of a developmental perspective in dealing with fundamental psychopathology has been illustrated by using schizophrenia.[11] The psychopathology of schizophrenia can best be explained by a developmental hypothesis that acknowledges the underlying brain abnormalities that are present long before the disorder of schizophrenia appears in young adulthood. During childhood and adolescence, the individual with these biological abnormalities appears developmentally normal. It is in early adulthood that predictable stressors may place high demands on these vulnerabilities, which leads to the expression of symptoms.

Similarly, studies of Parkinson's disease suggest that both the general symptoms and the monoamine oxidase concentration in the globus pallidus change depending on the age at onset of the disease.[15] Various metabolic diseases and brain disorders (e.g., traumas, tumors, and injuries resulting from war) are similarly affected by age at onset. The same underlying structural abnormality may lead to different symptoms depending on the developmental stage of the individual. In short, the manifestations of disorders of the nervous system are heavily influenced by the developmental level of the adult.

Developmental and Cohort Effects

The importance of a developmental perspective is emphasized by studies of substance abuse and addiction across the life span. Secular trends have a strong impact on drug use; different drugs have been "in fashion" during different decades. Consequently, it is important to separate social trends and cohort effects from more universal patterns of adult development. Despite these difficulties, there is substantial evidence that adults at different life stages use drugs for different reasons. In adolescence and young adulthood, drugs are used for novelty and excitement. In middle life, drug abuse is more likely to be linked to social and family rituals. Finally, drug abuse is often the result of an effort to produce calm and to reduce the raw anxiety-producing effects of novelty and change in late life.[15a]

Typically, most stimulant drug use occurs before age 20 years. Specifically, inhalants, such as glue (in glue sniffing) and tobacco (in cigarette smoking), are among the first drugs to be abused. These rapid-acting agents are more likely to produce dependence in young adults. Furthermore, by adjusting their behavioral repertoire, young adults often use alcohol and barbiturates in ways that create excitation. In contrast, the peak use of sedative drugs occurs after age 45 years when these drugs are used not to party but to calm (Fig. 10–2). Cessation of illegal drug use by adults in midlife appears linked to emotional maturation, which allows for greater tolerance of depression and the replacement of drugs with intimate relationships.[15a]

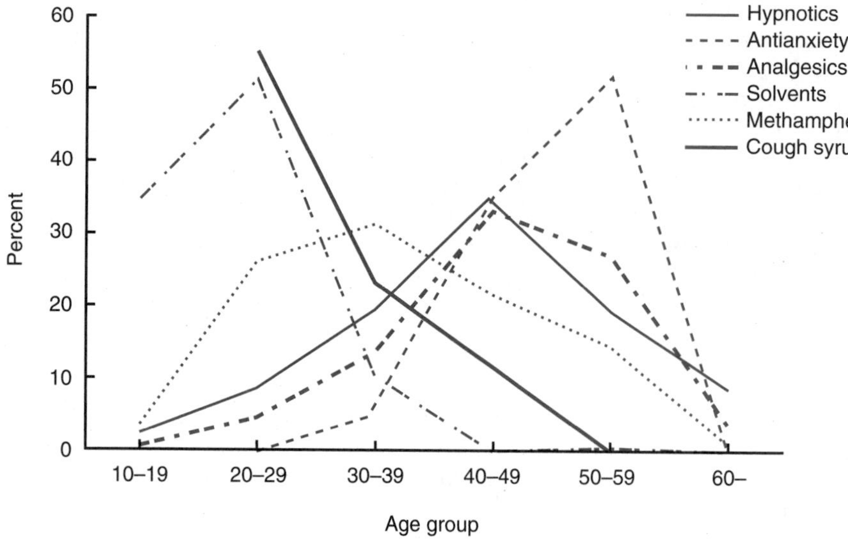

Figure 10–2 *Age distribution of psychiatric patients with substance use disorder. (From Fukui S, Watanabe N, Iyo M, et al: An Epidemiological Survey of Drug Dependence. 1987 Report of Studies of Etiological Factors and Pathological Conditions of Drug Dependence. Tokyo: Ministry of Health and Welfare, 1988:169–182.)*

More generally, there is a developmental pattern to the onset of disorder. Antisocial behavior is more common in adolescents, schizophrenic symptoms in young adulthood, and affective disorder in middle life.[11]

Elder[16] illustrated a cohort effect on adult development by examining individuals who grew up during the Great Depression. In a prospective study of children at the Institute of Human Development at Berkeley, he demonstrated the differential effects of World War II and the Great Depression by following a 1920s cohort and a 1930s cohort from birth into adulthood. In the 1920s cohort, boys grew up to be more successful and competent, whereas girls fared relatively poorly. Conversely, in the 1930s birth cohort the boys fared relatively badly and the girls did well.

Elder provided a cohort-based explanation that considered a variety of social, economic, and psychological factors. For example, because of paternal unemployment, the boys in the 1920s cohort were forced to enter adulthood earlier. Therefore, they left home at a younger age and avoided some of the family problems created by the unemployment of their fathers. Ninety percent of these men served in the armed services in World War II, which offered them a moratorium and allowed them to extend their adolescence and to take advantage of the GI bill. In contrast, the girls remained dependent on their families during adolescence, and their self-esteem was negatively affected by their relative poverty during high school. These girls married at a young age and tended to drop out of work.

In contrast, the boys in the 1930s cohort were unable to avoid the emotional impact of the Great Depression and the anger of their unemployed fathers. Effectively, many did not have a father during boyhood. In adolescence, they "lost" their mothers to war-related jobs and grew up with lower aspirations. Although 70% of these men served in the Korean War, this experience did not offer them the moratorium or the financial benefits available to World War II veterans. The girls in this cohort fared better partially because, apparently, it was easier for a girl to be poorly dressed in grade school than in high school. These girls also tended to provide comfort to their stressed mothers.

A study of depression also emphasizes the importance of the cohort effect. There is increasing evidence that cohorts born in subsequent decades in this country and in Europe during the 20th century have increasingly greater rates of depression and an earlier onset of symptoms.[17] However, a developmental perspective is also necessary for understanding the onset of depression. Although depression was once thought to begin during early or middle adulthood, it is now accepted that its onset is much earlier[17] and that it is associated with more severe psychopathology.[18] In addition, some of the developmental challenges that occur during adulthood, such as child-rearing, are also risk factors for the onset of affective disorder. Studies show that mothers who have several children younger than the age of 6 years and who lack adequate social and financial support are at particularly high risk for the onset of major depressive disorder.[19]

Risk Factors, Protective Factors, and Resilience

Resilient individuals do well despite being at high risk for negative outcomes. There is convergent evidence identifying a set of factors that contribute to resilience. Garmezy and colleagues[20] have proposed broad categories of such protective factors, including self-esteem, positive social orientation, family cohesion, and availability of an external support system.

In adulthood, resilience depends on the ability to find, use, and internalize social supports. Maturity of ego defense is an important characteristic of resilience throughout the life span. The specificity of stressors appears to be less important than the relative number of risk and protective factors. This suggests that the number of protective factors minus the number of risk factors provides a crude but useful index for predicting outcome. Luck, the timing of the stressor, and the individual's fundamental sense of self-esteem and self-efficacy also affect outcome.[21]

Data from a number of ongoing longitudinal studies illustrate different facets of resilience over time. Werner and Smith[22] conducted a 30-year study on the island of Kauai and followed up infants from different cultural backgrounds into adulthood. Many were at high psychosocial risk because of family dysfunction and poverty, but approximately one fifth of these high-risk youngsters demonstrated good adult adjustment. The protective factors were categorized as those within the child, within the family, and within the environment.

In terms of factors related to the individual child, the absence of distress in early life and good sleeping and eating habits were important protective factors. Similarly, being affectionate (for girls), being active (for boys), the absence of behavior problems at age 10 years, and the presence of high intelligence were associated with good adult outcomes. Other studies have confirmed the importance of positive temperament, above-average intelligence, and sociability.[23, 24] The presence of a close and caring relationship with at least one parent or other caregiver during early childhood has been shown to enhance resiliency.[23, 25]

Within the family, high educational level of the opposite-sex parent and warm relationships with both parents proved important. The presence of rules and structures in the household strongly supported adolescent development, as did having mothers who worked. Families with four or fewer children and with at least a 2-year interval between children were also protective.[22]

In terms of protective factors within the community, relationships outside the family and external support systems such as churches, youth groups, schools, and recreational activities were important.[25–27] Good secondary schools also had a positive effect.[28]

In adulthood, second-chance opportunities occurring at major life transitions were protective. These included marriage or entry into a long-term relationship, the birth of a child, finding a supportive employer, entering the military service, or joining a church group.[25] More generally, two kinds of protective factors in adulthood have been identified: those that arise from social supports and personality attributes that affect the ability of an individual to master stress.[29]

The best model for understanding development is one that integrates clearly defined behavioral tasks and functions in the external world, such as having friends, with innate and developing capacities within the individual, such as coping skills. Vaillant and Vaillant[30] studied a sample of adolescent boys until age 50 years; these boys had been at risk because of poverty and recent immigrant status. They found the most important predictor of success to be "competence." Clausen[31] similarly described "planful competence" as a core integrative construct that predicted successful adult outcome. Competence reflected the presence of regular part-time work, performance of household chores, participation in extracurricular activities, good school grades relative to IQ, and ability to plan.

In the study by Vaillant and Vaillant,[30] competence measured what the individuals *did*, not what they *reported* about their feelings. Examination of adult outcomes in objective behavioral terms led to three important findings. First, the capacity to work in early adolescence was strongly correlated with good mental health in midlife. Second, the boys who were most successful in adolescence in terms of competence were much more likely to be successful in adulthood, in terms of both their paid jobs and their capacity to have relationships with others. Third, the presence of positive attributes in the family environment was more predictive of outcome than was the presence of negative attributes. Similarly, the positive presence of planful competence outweighed the presence of negative factors.

The complex interactions between risk factors and protective factors and the emergence of resilience over time are illustrated in a different way by two investigations conducted in London. The study by Quinton and Rutter[32] of difficulties in parenting provides an illustration of complex development transitions. This study followed up a group of girls who had been placed in residential or group homes as youngsters. Those girls who, after leaving the residential home, entered positive family environments were more likely to make positive decisions later in life, such as in the selection of a supportive spouse. They also developed better parenting skills. Similarly, those who had good school experiences were more likely to demonstrate planning in terms of career choice and marriage partners. On the other hand, the youngsters who did not have positive family experiences tended to marry quickly and to make poor choices in life. These women more frequently divorced and displayed difficulties in parenting their own children. Thus, the capacity to plan emerged as crucially important in making choices about marriage partners. This, in turn, was strongly related to success in child-rearing.

Brown and Harris[33] demonstrated that a complex interactional model of risk and protective factors was associated with the onset of depression in a group of women living in London. They found that the absence of close confiding relationships in adulthood coupled with the presence of unusual stresses preceded depression in women. Focusing on earlier events, Rutter[34] demonstrated that it was the loss of care for the child and the degree of the disruption in the child's life after the death of a parent that predicted a negative outcome rather than parental loss per se.

Developmental Formulations of Adulthood

Most theorists believe that development involves an increase in cognitive and affective differentiation that leads to a greater capacity to relate to the environment. The observations by Piaget[35] of the dual processes of assimilation and accommodation and the invariate sequence of stages in the development of intelligence have supported this fundamental belief. He also described the stages in the development of intelligence and the cognitive structures or schemas that underlie the learning paradigm. Individuals progress from one cognitive stage to the next through periods of disequilibrium. The process of equilibration involves coming into balance in the new phase.

Piaget's approach has been applied in adults to moral development,[36] the development of self-understanding,[37] and the development of interpersonal understanding.[38] Kohlberg[36] delineated six stages of moral development: stage 1, a premoral level with a punishment and obedience orientation; stage 2, a naive and straightforward hedonism; stage 3, a level involving conforming to avoid disapproval; stage 4, a level entailing conforming to avoid criticism by legitimate authorities in the development of guilt; stage 5, morality of contract in which there is an agreement to maintain and respect impartial laws; and stage 6, morality of individual principles in which the individual conforms to avoid self-condemnation. Processes similar to those described by Piaget were hypothesized to occur in the development of each stage. Although these stages of moral development provide some support for a stage sequential perspective, this work has been criticized for not addressing gender-specific differences.

A second model, based on the principles of ego psychology, is compatible both with the developmental frameworks presented in this chapter and with the work of Loevinger.[39] This model attempts to describe and characterize inner states, processes, and functions that manifest themselves in a wide array of behavioral situations that correspond to behavioral functioning. Ego defenses and ego maturation are viewed as critical organizing constructs across the life span. This formulation of the ego proposes a mediating function in the inner life that facilitates the completion of complex behavior tasks. In psychoanalytic terms, the ego resolves conflicting impulses and, in contemporary terms, it performs executive and organizing functions such as focusing attention.

Differences in ego functioning explain the mechanism by which individuals cope with conflict or stress. Longitudinal studies of development have found conceptualizations of increasing capacities of the ego and maturing defensive structure to be useful.[21, 40] Vaillant's work illustrates a heuristic framework of ego development parallel to shifts in diagnostic domains. Ratings of defenses were based on both objective behaviors (as is Axis II in the *Diagnostic and Statistical Manual of Mental Disorders,* Fourth Edition) *and* awareness of inner states.[6, 21] The "immature" defenses, which are common to character disorders, include denial through fantasy, dissociation, projection, passive aggression, hypochondriasis, and acting out. There is also a set of neurotic defenses that are traditionally described for neurosis. Examples are intellectualization (isolation, undoing, and rationalization), repression, displacement (including phobias and conversions), reaction formation, and disassociation (neurotic denial and counterphobia)[21] (Table 10–1).

Finally, there are "mature" defenses such as altruism, sublimation, suppression, anticipation, and humor. These defenses are particularly relevant to the adulthood stage because many of them are thought to appear only in late adolescence or adulthood. Altruism entails doing for others as one would have done for oneself; the person engaging in altruistic behavior is at least partially gratified, and such behavior contributes to self-efficacy. Sublimation allows the expression of intense (if attenuated) emotion without either adverse consequences or loss of pleasure. Suppression involves the semiconscious decision to postpone paying attention to a particular inner impulse. Anticipation involves realistic and effective planning for the future rather than denying it; it incorporates thinking and planning about affective issues as well as cognitive ones. All of the mature defenses integrate sources of conflict and thus do not involve characteristic modes of self-deception. Unlike other defenses, mature defenses allow subjects to experience themselves, their relationships, their ideas, and their feelings fully and without ignoring important parts of either external reality or their internal lives.

The relative maturity of defenses was ascertained by comparing the proportion of an individual's mature defenses with the proportion of her or his immature defenses. Two major findings emerged. Immature defenses were negatively correlated with good adjustment and positively correlated with psychopathology. The reverse was true for mature defenses. They were associated with health whether health was defined as the presence of successful objective life adjustment, the absence of psychopathology, or the achievement of subjective satisfaction. Men characterized by passivity, pessimism, self-doubt, fear of sex, and dependence were more likely to use immature defenses. In general, adolescents also utilized immature defenses, whereas adults in middle life typically used mature defenses. Between the ages of 15 and 30 years, there was a gradual evolution in both of the longitudinal samples from the use of immature defenses to the use of mature defenses.[21, 40] Figure 10–3 provides a graphical representation of changes in the use of defenses over time. As with Kohlberg's data, such evidence strongly suggests a maturational process that occurs during the course of adulthood, and it lays the groundwork for a stage sequential approach.

Eriksonian Model of Adult Development

The question of whether there are stages that characterize adult life in the same way that there are clear stages in childhood and adolescence is still debated. However, the adult developmental sequence illustrated by Erikson's model has been widely found to be useful.[42, 43] These tasks have the advantage of being less ethnocentric than either an

Table 10–1 Contrasting Ways of Altering the Conscious Representation of a Conflict

Defense	DSM-III Phenomenological Diagnosis*	
No defense	309.9	Adjustment reaction with atypical features
Psychotic defense		
Denial	298.8	Brief reactive psychosis
Immature defenses		
Projection	301.0	Paranoid personality disorder
Passive aggression	300.4	Dysthymic disorder
Acting out	301.7	Antisocial personality disorder
Fantasy	301.2	Schizoid personality disorder
Neurotic (intermediate) defenses		
Dissociation	300.15	Atypical dissociative disorder
Displacement	300.29	Simple phobia
Isolation (or intellectualization)	300.3	Obsessive-compulsive disorder
Repression	300.02	Generalized anxiety disorder
Reaction formation	—	
Mature defenses		
Suppression	—	
Sublimation	—	
Altruism	—	

*Diagnosis assumes that conscious representation of the conflict was carried to pathological extremes and that the other criteria for the diagnosis were met. DSM-III, *Diagnostic and Statistical Manual of Mental Disorders,* Third Edition.

Data from Vaillant GE: The Wisdom of the Ego. Cambridge, MA: Harvard University Press, 1993.

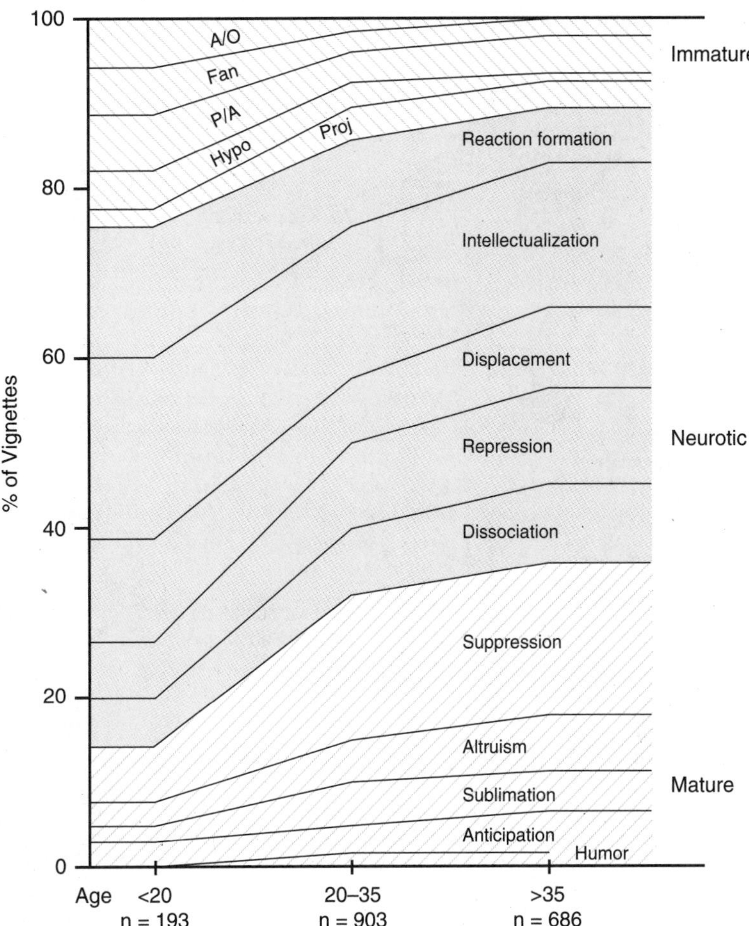

Figure 10–3 *Shifts in distribution of defensive vignettes shown by 95 subjects at adolescence, young adulthood, and middle age. A/O indicates acting out; Fan, fantasy; P/A, passive aggression; Hypo, hypochondriasis; Proj, projection. (From Vaillant GE: Natural history of male psychological health, Arch Gen Psychiatry 1976; 33:535–545. Copyright 1976, American Medical Association.*

individual-centered stage sequential model or a defense-centered model. Erikson's model suggests that a term such as Havinghurst's *developmental task* is a more appropriate construct than *stage of development*.[43] A modification of Erikson's model of the adult life cycle is presented in Figure 10–4 as a spiral staircase. This model depicts the growing adult's ego capacity to master and feel at ease in an increasingly complex social radius. The spiral depicted in Figure 10–4 contains two stages, career consolidation (stage 6a) and keeper of the meaning (stage 7a), that have been added to Erikson's original eight stages.

The key to understanding the sequential nature of adult ego development lies in the appreciation of both the relative complexity and the inner threat of the tasks and commitments that must be mastered. The twin anxieties of young adulthood involve the abilities to commit to one person and to commit to one job without sacrificing autonomy. Older adults, having mastered these tasks, may serve as mentors in the process.

There is correspondence between the accomplishment of tasks in the external world, such as maintaining a long-term intimate relationship, and ego development. This framework is valuable not only for organizing the unfolding of development in normal individuals but also for providing a useful framework for understanding how psychopathology may affect development at different stages.

In the empirical studies, those individuals who achieved generativity almost always had also evolved to stages of identity formation, achievement of intimacy, and career consolidation. This proved true both for men and for women.[21]

Erikson's task of identity versus identity diffusion, stage 5, reflects mastering the last task of childhood: the sustained separation from social, residential, economic, and ideological dependence on one's family of origin. Such separation derives as much from the identification and internalization of important childhood figures as it does from the ability to master modern life. Identity is not just a product of egocentricity, of running away from home, or of marrying to escape the family. There is a world of difference between the instrumental act of running away from home and the developmental task of knowing where one's family's values end and one's own values begin.

Men and women who fail to reach stage 5, identity, never achieve independence from their family of origin, or they remain dependent on institutions indefinitely. In middle life, such individuals remain dependent on others and never commit themselves either to occupational specialization or to sustained intimate friendships. Many schizophrenic individuals with stable community adjustment fall in this category.

Mastery of the task of intimacy versus isolation (stage 6) serves as the gateway to adult development. Intimacy is defined as living with another person in an *interdependent, committed,* and *intimate* fashion for years. Although marriage, heterosexuality, and orgasm are not necessarily criteria

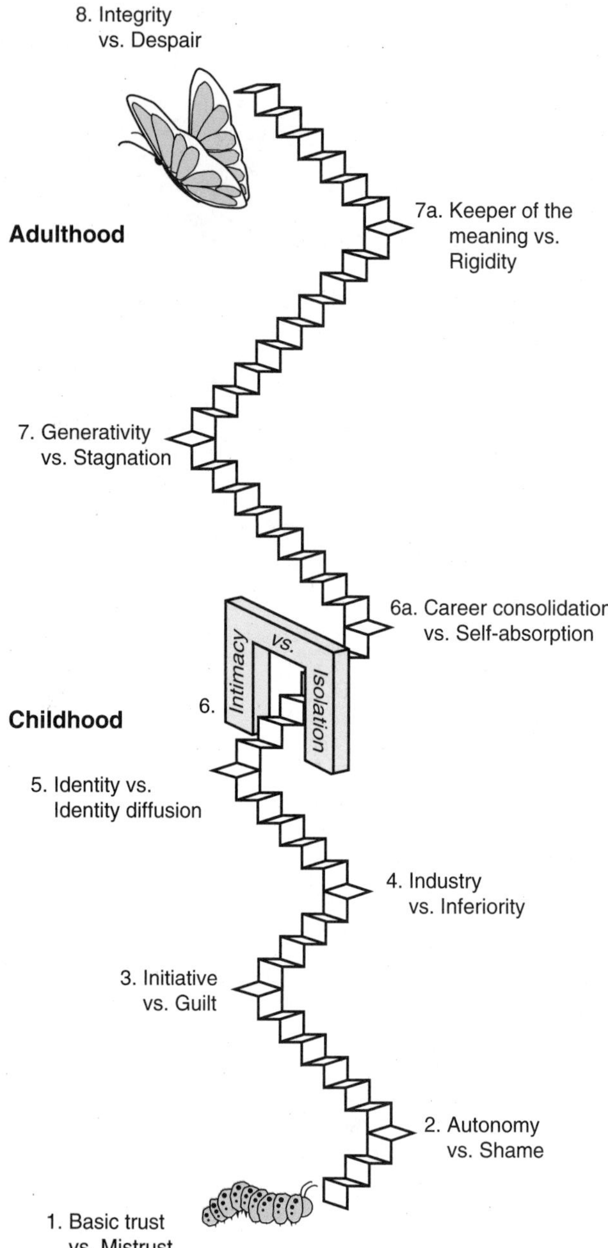

Figure 10–4 *A model of adult development. This is essentially Erik Erikson's model of the adult life cycle with the addition of stages 6a and 7a. (Modified and reprinted by permission of the publisher from The Wisdom of the Ego by George E. Vaillant, Cambridge, Mass: Harvard University Press, Copyright © 1993 by the President and Fellows of Harvard College.)*

for intimacy, intimacy is initially achieved most often with a spouse. Adolescents and adults with pervasive developmental disorders are usually incapable of close mutual interdependence. For many young adults, especially those who seek psychotherapy, mastery of interpersonal intimacy is a major focus of treatment.

The creation of a stage between intimacy and generativity reflects the importance of achieving a stable career identity. The construction of this stage distinguishes the development of identity within one's family of origin from the development of identity within the world of work. The internalized (usually familial) mentors important to achieving identity are rarely the same as the (rarely familial) mentors important to achieving an identity in the world of work. This task has been described as career consolidation, which involves the achievement of vocational identity that, like intimacy, reflects reciprocity. Put differently, the task of career consolidation is rarely accomplished before the achievement of intimacy but is characterized by *commitment, compensation*, *contentment*, and *competence*. In behavioral terms, this task involves making a clear, specialized career identification as measured by personal satisfaction and appreciation by others. These four concepts distinguish a career from a job. Career consolidation involves the transformation of preoccupation with self into a specialized role valued by both self and society.

One of the tasks of mature adult development is to compensate for societal imperatives rather than to accommodate to them. The study by Broverman and colleagues[44] showed that both men and women attributed a specific cluster of traits including independence, rationality, and self-direction to the ideal man, independent of their level of education. Both sexes attributed a different cluster of traits such as warmth, emotional expressiveness, and relatedness to the ideal woman. Prospective studies suggest that by midlife a major developmental task for women is to achieve the traits of *independence*, *rationality,* and *self-direction*.[6, 14] Similarly, it becomes equally enriching for men in midlife to achieve *warmth*, *emotional expressiveness,* and *relatedness*.[6, 14]

Selfless generativity (stage 7) reflects a clear capacity to care for and guide the next generation. Generativity means assuming sustained responsibility for building the community and for the growth, well-being, and leadership of others. It can entail serving as a consultant, guide, mentor, or coach to young adults in the society. In Figure 10–4, we have split off certain facets of Erikson's concept of generativity and relabeled them as stage 7a, keepers of the meaning. Generativity and its virtue, *care*, require taking care of one person rather than another.[2] Keeper of the meaning and its virtue, *wisdom*, involve a nonpartisan and less personal approach to others. Thus, the tasks of a generative coach or partisan parent of adolescent children are vastly different from the tasks of a supreme court judge or chair of a historical society.

The generative individual cares for an individual in a direct, future-oriented relationship—as, for example, a mentor or a teacher to a student. In contrast, the keeper of the meaning speaks for past cultural achievements and guides groups, organizations, and bodies of people toward the preservation of traditions. Care and justice, as Gilligan[45] underscored, have always been different dimensions of development. However, the term wisdom is preferable to justice, for it is less value-laden.

Further empirical justification for Erikson's model has been provided by data from three different major longitudinal studies of adults: 1) the Grant Foundation study of Harvard men[6]; 2) the core city study of the men in Boston enrolled in the early 1930s[30] and 3) the Terman study of women in northern California.[3, 46, 47] Individuals in these studies reached different stages at different ages in a manner that was relatively independent of social class and education. Those individuals who did not reach earlier stages (such as intimacy) were much less likely to reach higher stages (such as generativity).[21]

There are several heuristic advantages to depicting Erikson's model in Figure 10–4 as a spiral rather than simple structure. First, this representation underscores that during adult life individuals evolve rather than merely grow. Second, the spiral conveys the concept that with maturational change past progress is not lost. Third, the model suggests that as in climbing a spiral staircase, failure to attain one landing makes it unlikely that one will attain the next. Fourth, the left and right sides of the model reflect the rhythmic changes in malleability of character that occur during the life span. The oedipal years (stage 3), adolescence (stage 5), midlife (stage 7), and old age (stage 8) are often times of personal change and instability. These periods of life often involve reworking ascribed identity and questioning conventional morality. They are times of heightened introceptiveness, affective lability, and fresh instinctual conflict.

On the right side of the spiral, the life periods of autonomy, industry, career consolidation, and keeper of the meaning are represented. During these periods, individuals are preoccupied with the preservation of sameness and autonomy and are involved in following and maintaining rules. Such individuals are more likely to be concerned with absorbing, observing, and promulgating the past traditions than with reworking their culture. During the life span there appears to be an oscillation with a still longer amplitude than the journey depicted in the spiral staircase model. At some point in life, there are suddenly more yesterdays than tomorrows. At this point one seemingly retraces the stairs one has climbed. If the steps from infancy through childhood to adolescence lead sequentially to mastering one's body, one's external environment, and, finally, one's emotions, then from age 40 years to senescence the steps lead in the reverse direction. Like the adolescent, the 40-year-old in crisis struggles with feelings; like the 10-year-old, the 60-year-old struggles to resist the changing times; and the 80-year-old, like the toddler, is preoccupied with an unruly, unsteady body. Neugarten[48] has written that if 40-year-olds "see the environment as one that rewards boldness and risk-taking, sixty year olds seem to see the environment as complex and dangerous, no longer to be reformed in line with one's own wishes and to see the self as conforming and accommodating to outer world demands."

Grief

Although it is believed that as one ages one becomes more accepting of death, increases in age also increase the likelihood of experiencing the loss of a loved one or a family member. Bereavement, or grief, usually occurs after such a loss. Uncomplicated grief is believed to proceed through a series of anticipated stages.[49] The initial stage, which occurs during the first few weeks after the loss, is characterized by feelings of shock and disbelief. The second or intermediate phase takes place during the first year after the loss; it is distinguished both by feelings of loneliness and by thoughts about the death, why it happened, and how it could have been prevented. Usually by the beginning of the second year after the loss, the individual begins the recovery phase; during this time the individual begins to seek out social situations and move on with life.[50, 51] Lehman and colleagues[52] pointed out that little is known about the actual duration of grief, and in their studies of parents and spouses who were experiencing unexpected loss, grief often continued to be experienced 4 to 7 years after the loss.

Unexpected or sudden deaths often result in more severe and long-lasting periods of grief than those that were anticipated.[52–54] Death of one's spouse, regardless of the nature of the death, can have a significant impact on the health of the individual, with it "not being uncommon for the remaining spouse to become seriously ill or to die within two years."[50, 54] A gender difference in the period of greatest risk has been observed, with widowers being at increased risk for the first year after loss and widows during the first 3 months.[55] Widowers who remarry appear to have lower mortality rates than those who do not.[56]

The effects of loss do not appear to lessen with increased age. Lesher and Bergey[57] found that the loss of a child resulted in a number of negative effects in elderly bereaved mothers. These mothers experienced high levels of "psychological distress" as well as changes in "health, functional activities, family cohesion and psychological well being." The authors pointed out that not only does the loss of a child have an impact on the older individual's sense of life order, but it may also have a strong impact on the quality of their life. This can be due to the assistance that the child could have provided or to the decreased contact with their deceased child's spouse and/or children that can result.

As individuals pass from childhood through adolescence and into early adulthood, most have developed a belief that death is irreversible, final, and inevitable.[50] Kubler-Ross[58] has identified five stages that occur when individuals are confronted with death: 1) denial and isolation, 2) anger, 3) bargaining, 4) depression, and 5) acceptance. These stages are useful in understanding the experience of dying, but it should be noted that they do not necessarily occur in a particular order and that all stages may not be experienced by every individual. For example, an individual's response to death may be influenced by their age: those of a younger age may be more likely than older persons to experience stages of denial and anger.[59]

Several investigators prefer to chart adult development in terms of *transitions* and developmental crises. In some sense, transitions are a by-product of normal development. Certainly, the process of development is more than the achievement of chronological landmarks such as one's graduation, first job, marriage, and first child. Development creates transitions, and transitions then influence development.

The crises associated with transitions often have more to do with three nondevelopmental factors than they do with the process of development. The first factor is psychopathology. For example, individuals who have a particularly troubled adolescence are also likely to have a particularly troubled middle life. Similarly, a tendency to serious depression makes almost any change a crisis. However, community studies of people during adolescence and middle age suggest that such assumptions of inevitable developmental crisis are unwarranted.[60, 61]

The second factor associated with crisis during developmental transitions involves poorly culturally mediated changes in role. For example, an uncelebrated retirement or a perfunctory civil marriage ceremony may lead to greater instability of adjustment and to later crises. Nonindustrialized cultures frequently ritualize adolescence, menopause, and old age more effectively than do modern industrialized cultures. Smooth transitions appear to be facilitated by cultural, ritual, and sacramental celebrations.

The third factor associated with the crises of life transitions occurs when the transitions take place outside of the appropriate temporal sequence. Widowhood is a greater developmental crisis at 40 years than at 80. Menopause may be a crisis at 30 years of age but a welcome fact of life at 50. In contrast, the death of a child is always a crisis because it runs counter to the expectations of adult development.

Conclusion

In reflection on the course of development, several points deserve emphasis. The first is that within the various eriksonian stages an emphasis on identity formation and identity is the key to each stage. A firm sense of personal identity is a critical achievement of adult development. This identity can change as the individual grows and develops, but identity nonetheless provides both an internal anchor and a stable way of relating to others in the world. Erikson emphasized that the adolescent process of identity formation ends only when an individual develops a new kind of identification and, indeed, long-term commitments both to others and to work. Furthermore, before an identity is formed, there is often a psychosocial moratorium during which an individual postpones making life choices. Erikson emphasized the dynamic interaction between the inner sense of self and the manner in which individuals have responded to and dealt with those around them. In simple terms, youngsters evolve from being dependent on their parents and going to school to maintaining jobs of their own, functioning independently, and developing close intimate relationships. In broader terms, mastering the task entails mastering internal conflicts so as to be able to engage in working and loving. Erikson emphasized that identity formation is not simply an internal process of selecting identification during childhood but a process through which others often "through subsocieties identify the young individual."[42]

From a clinical perspective, it is well worth determining the fundamental identity of the person under consideration and where along the various stages of adult development the individual falls. A second consideration is how the individual deals with her or his own children. The stages of adult development are closely tied to functions related to child-rearing. In the stage of career consolidation, one component is the need for the provision of adequate resources to raise a family. In the later stages, characterized by generativity, individuals proceed from being concerned mainly with their own children to becoming concerned about broader issues such as the next generation in general. This occurs as their own children become parents and as people of the next generation assume leadership positions and become mentors and teachers. The final stage, keeper of the meaning, includes being a wise grandparent or, in figurative terms, embodying family wisdom and cultural wisdom.

Although development does take place during adulthood, simple cross-sectional approaches will not lead to the uncovering of developmental processes. This is because the time frames in which adult development occur are so large that it is not possible to see them in short periods.

Another major emphasis of this chapter is that the study of adult development is an evolving field. At present there are various competing ways of thinking about development. Combining knowledge of the inner life with observable behaviors can be effectively organized around the framework of ego psychology. Broad domains for inquiry have been identified that are likely to remain robust in the future. These include the importance of measurement of observable behaviors, the necessity of a stage sequential approach, and awareness of qualities within individuals, such as ego identity, that acquire stability over time but can also evolve. These are the building blocks that must be incorporated into any reasonable formulation of adulthood.

References

1. Kegan R: The Evolving Self. Cambridge, MA: Harvard University Press, 1982.
2. Erikson E: Childhood and Society. New York: WW Norton, 1963.
3. Terman MD, Oden MH: The Gifted Group at Midlife. Genetic Studies of Genius. Stanford, CA: Stanford University Press, 1959.
4. Carnegie Task Force: Starting Points: Meeting the Needs of Our Youngest Children. New York: Carnegie Corporation of New York, 1994.
5. Rutter M: Developing Minds. New York: Basic Books, 1993.
6. Vaillant GE: Adaptation to Life. Boston: Little, Brown, 1977.
7. Bouchard TJ, Lykken DT, McGue M, et al: Source of human psychological differences: The Minnesota study of twins reared apart. Science 1990; 250:223–228.
8. Yakovlev PI, Lecours AR: The myeogenetic cycles of regional maturation of the brain. In Minkowski A (ed): Regional Development of the Brain in Early Life. Oxford, UK: Blackwell Scientific Publications, 1967.
9. Roffwarg HP, Munzio JN, Dement WC: Ontogenetic development of the human sleep-dream cycle. Science 1966; 152:604–619.
10. Woodruff DS: Brain electrical activity and behavior relationships over the life span. In Baltes PB (ed): Life-Span Development and Behavior. New York: Academic Press, 1978.
11. Weinberger DR: Implication of normal brain development for the pathogenesis of schizophrenia. Arch Gen Psychiatry 1987; 44:660–669.
12. Roose SP, Perdes H: Biological considerations in the middle years. In Oldham JM, Liebert, RS (eds): The Middle Years. New Haven, CT: Yale University Press, 1989:179–190.
13. Schaie KW, Parham IA: Cohort-sequential analyses of adult intellectual development. Dev Psychol 1977; 13:649–653.
14. Guttman D: The cross-cultural perspective: Notes toward a comparative psychology of aging. In Birren JE, Schaie KW (eds): Handbook of the Psychology of Aging. New York: Van Nostrand Reinhold, 1977:302–326.
15. Robinson DS, Sourkes TL, Nies A: Monoamine metabolism in human brain. Arch Gen Psychiatry 1977; 34:89–92.
15a. Vaillant GE: Addictions over the life course: Therapeutic implication. In Edwards G, Dare C (eds): Psychotherapy, Psychological Implications and Addictions. Cambridge, UK: Cambridge University Press, 1996.
16. Elder GH: Studying lives in a changing society: Sociological and personological explorations. In Rabin AI, Zucker RA, Frank S (eds): Studying Persons and Lives. New York: Springer-Verlag, 1990.
17. Institute of Medicine: Reducing Risks for Mental Disorders: Frontiers for Preventive Intervention Research. Washington, DC: National Academy Press, 1994.
18. Weissman MM, Gammon GD, John K, et al: Children of depressed parents: Increased psychopathology and early onset of major depression. Arch Gen Psychiatry 1987; 44:847–853.
19. Weissman MM, Leif PJ, Bruce ML: Single parent women. A community study. Soc Psychiatry 1987; 22:29–36.
20. Garmezy N, Masten A, Tellegen A: The study of stress and competence in children. Child Dev 1984; 55:97–111.
21. Vaillant GE: The Wisdom of the Ego. Cambridge, MA: Harvard University Press, 1993.
22. Werner EE, Smith RS: Overcoming the Odds: High Risk Children from Birth to Adulthood. Ithaca, NY: Cornell University Press, 1992.

23. Rutter M: Resilience in the face of adversities. Br J Psychiatry 1985; 147:598–611.
24. Rutter M, Tizard J, Whitmore R: Education, Health and Behavior. London: Longman, 1970.
25. Werner EE, Smith RS: Vulnerable but Invincible: A Study of Resilient Children. New York: McGraw-Hill, 1982.
26. Jones MB, Offord DR: Reduction of antisocial behavior in poor children by nonschool skill-development. J Child Psychol Psychiatry 1989; 30:737–750.
27. Werner EE: High-risk children in young adulthood: A longitudinal study from birth to 32 years. Am J Orthopsychiatry 1989; 59:72–81.
28. Rutter M: Protective factors in children's response to stress and disadvantage. In Kent R (ed): Primary Prevention of Psychopathology. Hanover, NH: University Press of New England, 1979.
29. O'Grady D, Metz JR: Resilience in children at high risk for psychological disorder. J Pediatr Psychol 1987; 12:3–23.
30. Vaillant GE, Vaillant CO: Natural history of male psychological health: Work as a predictor of positive mental health. Am J Psychiatry 1981; 138:1433–1439.
31. Clausen JA: American Lives: Looking Back at the Children of the Great Depression. Toronto: Free Press, 1993.
32. Quinton D, Rutter M: Parental Breakdown: The Making and Breaking of Intergenerational Links. Aldershot, UK: Gower Publishing, 1988.
33. Brown GW, Harris TO: Depression. In Brown GW, Harris TO (eds): Life Events and Illness. New York: Guilford Press, 1989:49–94.
34. Rutter M: Maternal Deprivation Reassessed. Harmondsworth, UK: Penguin, 1981.
35. Piaget J: The Moral Judgement of the Child. London: Kegan Paul, 1932.
36. Kohlberg L: Continuities in childhood and adult moral development revisited. In Baltes PB, Schaie KW (eds): Life Span Developmental Psychology: Personality and Socialization. New York: Academic Press, 1973.
37. Damon W, Hart D: The development of self-understanding from infancy through adolescence. Child Dev 1982; 52:841–864.
38. Selman RL: The Growth of Interpersonal Understanding. New York: Academic Press, 1980.
39. Loevinger J: Ego Development. San Francisco: Jossey-Bass, 1976.
40. Haan N: Coping and Defending. New York: Academic Press, 1977.
41. Fukui S, Watanabe N, Iyo M, et al: An Epidemiological Survey of Drug Dependence. 1987 Report of Studies of Etiological Factors and Pathological Conditions of Drug Dependence. Tokyo: Ministry of Health and Welfare, 1988:169–182.
42. Erikson E: The problem of ego identity. J Am Psychoanal Assoc 1956; 4:56–121.
43. Havinghurst R: Developmental Tasks and Education. New York: David McKay, 1972.
44. Broverman I, Voger S, Broverman D, et al: Sex-role stereotypes: A current appraisal. J Soc Issues 1972; 28:59–78.
45. Gilligan C: In a different voice: Women's conception of the self and morality. Harvard Educ Rev 1977; 47:481–517.
46. Oden MH: The fulfillment of promise: 40-year follow-up of the Terman gifted group. Genet Psychol Monogr 1968; 77:3–93.
47. Sears RR: The Terman gifted children study. In Mednick SA, Harway M, Finello KM (eds): Handbook of Longitudinal Research. New York: Praeger Publishers, 1984:398–414.
48. Neugarten BL: Personality in Middle and Late Life. New York: Atherton, 1964.
49. Schulz R: The Psychology of Death, Dying and Bereavement. Reading, MA: Addison-Wesley, 1978.
50. Dworetzky JP: Human Development. St Paul, MN: West Publishing, 1995.
51. National Institute of Mental Health: Health Professionals and the Bereaved. Washington, DC: National Academy Press, 1988.
52. Lehman DR, Wortman CB, Williams AF: Long-term effects of losing a spouse or child in a motor vehicle crash. J Pers Soc Psychol 1987; 52:218–231.
53. Parkes CM, Weiss RS: Recovery from Bereavement. New York: Basic Books, 1983.
54. Stroebe W, Stroebe MS: Bereavement and Health: The Psychological and Physical Consequences of Partner Loss. New York: Cambridge University Press, 1987.
55. Mellstrom D, Nilsson A, Oden A, et al: Mortality among the widowed in Sweden. Scand J Soc Med 1982; 19:33–41.
56. Helsing KJ, Comstock GW, Szklo M: Causes of death in a widowed population. Am J Epidemiol 1982; 116:524–532.
57. Lesher EL, Bergey KJ: Bereaved elderly mothers: Changes in health, functional activities, family cohesion, and psychological well-being. Int J Aging Hum Dev 1988; 26:81–91.
58. Kubler-Ross E: On Death and Dying. New York: Macmillan Publishing, 1969.
59. Pattison EM: The Experience of Dying. Englewood Cliffs, NJ: Prentice Hall/Spectrum, 1977.
60. Farrell MP, Rosenberg SD: Men at Midlife. Boston: Auburn House, 1981.
61. Offer D, Offer J: From Teenage to Young Manhood. New York: Basic Books, 1975.

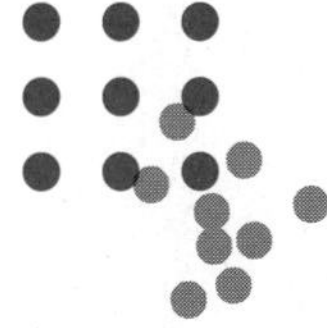

SECTION 

Charles B. Nemeroff,
Section Editor

Scientific Foundations of Psychiatry

CHAPTER

11 Introduction

Charles B. Nemeroff

Since its origin in the 17th century, the discipline of psychiatry has undergone a continuous evolution. The driving force in this process has been the introduction of new knowledge and the emergence of new bodies of information that bear on the understanding of psychiatric disorders. Historically , the epistemological basis of psychiatry derived from several disciplines including religion, anthropology, and clinical medicine. Subsequently, the fields of both psychology and sociology substantially influenced the development of psychiatry. More recently, several emergent scientific disciplines including genetics, molecular biology, neurobiology, pharmacology, epidemiology, and cognitive neuroscience have gained prominence and exerted a remarkable influence on biomedical research in general and psychiatry in particular. Thus, the evolution of the discipline of psychiatry has followed the course determined by progress in the biological and social sciences from which it is derived.

This section spans both the external social manifestations of pathology (from a given scientific perspective) and the intrapsychic and neurobiological domains. In this way, Epidemiology, Chapter 12, describes the frequency of pathological conditions (as they are defined by nosological systems, e.g., the *Diagnostic and Statistical Manual of Mental Disorders* and the *International Classification of Diseases*) in the population; Social Psychology, Chapter 18, describes the interpersonal and social processes that cause or subserve psychopathology; Psychoanalytic Theories, Chapter 19, provides a historical depiction of the evolution of this important body of knowledge in the understanding and treatment of psychopathology, and describes the different schools of thought that emanated from Freud's seminal theory; Cognitive Psychology and Neurophysiology, Chapter 17, and Cognitive Neuroscience, Chapter 16, describe the cognitive and neuropsychological manifestations of psychopathology and their putative neurobiological substrates; Genetics, Chapter 13, describes the mechanisms of heredity and their role in the pathogenesis of psychiatric disease; Pathophysiologic Basis of Psychiatric Disorders, Chapter 15, describes the biological manifestations of psychopathology, whereas Molecular and Neurobiological Mechanisms in the Treatment of Psychiatric Disorders, Chapter 14, describes the cellular and subcellular basis of psychopathology. By design, this section has focused on the primary contemporary sources from which psychiatry has drawn. It has necessarily excluded discussion of related but less relevant (to contemporary psychiatry) disciplines such as anthropology, sociobiology, philosophy, and religion. (For these the reader is referred to Appendix I, A Brief History of Psychiatry.)

The aforementioned course of development could be said to be true of all of the medical disciplines. However, psychiatry is unique among these disciplines in its admixtures of scientific thought and the various emphases placed on specific perspectives that have historically informed its theoretical orientation and clinical practices (e.g., psychodynamic, psychopathological, and pharmacological). For a period in this century, American psychiatry appeared to be moving away from mainstream medicine and had eschewed the medical model. This process, in large part, reflected the dominant influence of one school of thought (psychoanalytic theory). Thus, the conceptual basis and practices of psychiatry have been formed through a dialectical process related to emergent knowledge and theories, and the fundamental principles of clinical medicine forged into the clinical practices of the field.

Psychiatry currently finds itself at some intermediate point in the excursion of the epistemological pendulum that oscillates between the psychodynamic (metaphysical) and the biological (physical) systems of understanding. This artificial dichotomy between the psychodynamic and neurobiological is surely being dismantled by the growing evidence that the brain affects behavior and behavior affects the brain. Indeed, psychoanalysis and molecular neurobiology are not only not mutually exclusive but also inexorably linked, as we have previously proposed.[1] As Baxter and colleagues[2] have shown, the psychotherapy of obsessive-compulsive disorder has profound neurobiological consequences as measured with positron emission tomography. As psychiatry continues to redefine its identity and form of clinical expression (made more complicated by the tumultuous changes in health care economics), it serves an important function for clinical medicine as a whole by providing a vehicle for the introduction of humanistic, interpersonal, and intrapsychic dimensions to the practice of medicine. As we approach the new millennium in this period of postmodern technological globalized culture, these are the perspectives that medicine needs and for which psychiatry deserves rightful recognition.

References

1. Levy ST, Nemeroff CB: From psychoanalysis to neurobiology. Natl Forum 1993; 73:18–21.
2. Baxter LR, Schwartz JM, Bergman KS, et al: Caudate glucose metabolic rate changes with both drug and behavior therapy for obsessive-compulsive disorder. Arch Gen Psychiatry 1992; 49:681–689.

CHAPTER

12 Epidemiology

Mauricio Tohen
Evelyn Bromet

Epidemiological research assesses the distribution of mental disorders in the population and the risk factors associated with their onset, duration, and recurrence. This information is fundamental to the development of effective intervention and prevention programs. Since the 1978 report of the President's Commission on Mental Health[1] that emphasized the need for basic data on the incidence, prevalence, and predictors of mental disorders, significant methodological developments have changed the face of epidemiological research and led to new descriptive and analytical findings on psychiatric disorders.[2] Advances also occurred in other areas of epidemiology for which information was lacking,[3, 4] such as the relationship between physical and mental disorders, cross-national comparisons of illness distribution, genetics, and the natural history and course of psychiatric disorders. This progress was accompanied by a proliferation of doctoral and postdoctoral psychiatric epidemiology training programs in centers throughout the United States funded by the National Institute of Mental Health (NIMH).[5]

Two fundamental requirements that distinguish epidemiological research from other clinical investigations are the inclusion of representative samples and the application of systematic methods for determining diagnosis or outcome. The specific type of sample and choice of mental health measure depend on the goal of the study. Three types of samples are used in epidemiology. For studies of rare disorders, identified patients are usually ascertained from registries or a representative set of psychiatric treatment facilities. However, because only a minority of individuals with diagnosable disorders are ever treated for psychiatric problems within the mental health care system, these sources may omit true case patients who do not present for treatment. Another source for epidemiological samples is an institution, such as a psychiatric hospital, general medical facility, school, or workplace. There has been an expansion of mental health research in primary medical care settings because individuals with psychological disorders are relatively heavy users of such services.[6] Such studies have focused on the recognition and treatment of mental disorders and the specific patterns of health service use by patients with diagnosable psychiatric conditions. For studies aimed at establishing prevalence and incidence rates, the population-based survey is the optimal method. Complex sampling procedures have been developed to ensure random selection for both one-stage and two-stage studies.

With respect to definitions of "caseness," the unavailability of methods for obtaining reliable diagnostic-level information efficiently and at a reasonable cost was the central methodological impediment to conducting research that could provide even basic data on the distribution and recurrence of mental disorders. In the past, case definitions ranged from scoring above a threshold on a symptom inventory to receiving mental health services. The development of structured diagnostic interview schedules tailored to clear, operationalized diagnostic criteria was the crucial element underlying the progress we have seen in psychiatric epidemiology. The need for uniform methods of eliciting and quantifying clinical information became evident with the findings of the United States–United Kingdom project,[7] in which previously observed cross-national differences in the distributions of schizophrenia and affective disorders in hospitalized patients disappeared when consistent diagnostic procedures were administered. The feasibility and benefits of structured, or semistructured, interview schedules that could systematically elicit criteria for objectively defined disorders further became evident after the appearance and widespread use of instruments such as the Schedule for Affective Disorders and Schizophrenia (SADS),[8] the companion interview for the Research Diagnostic Criteria.[9] The SADS and the Research Diagnostic Criteria were originally developed for use by psychiatrists in the multisite Collaborative Study of the Psychobiology of Depression sponsored by the NIMH.[10] Two community-based studies demonstrated that master's-level mental health professionals could successfully administer the lifetime version of the SADS (SADS-L) for epidemiological purposes.[11, 12] Puig-Antich and colleagues developed a similar instrument for use with children (Puig-Antich J, Orvaschel H, unpublished), the Kiddie-SADS, that was subsequently modified for epidemiological studies.[13] Other standardized psychiatric interviews that are widely used are the Present State Examination[14] and its successor, the Schedule for Clinical Assessment in Neuropsychiatry[15]; the Structured Clinical Interview for DSM-III-R[16]; and the Diagnostic Interview for Genetic Studies developed by the NIMH-sponsored centers for genetic linkage research.[17]

Robins[3] was among the first to advocate the development of fully structured diagnostic interview schedules that could be administered in the community by non–mental health professionals or lay interviewers. Because semistructured instruments require clinical knowledge and judgment, she argued, other more cost-effective instruments were needed that were fully structured and did not require clinical expertise. Although some such instruments were developed before the introduction of the *Diagnostic and Statistical Manual of Mental Disorders,* Third Edition (DSM-III), the best known and most widely used of this family of instruments is the Diagnostic Interview Schedule.[18] The Diagnostic Interview Schedule was originally designed for the five-site Epidemiological Catchment Area (ECA) study of DSM-III disorders.[19] The ECA methodology and findings are described in more detail later. Subsequent versions of the Diagnostic Interview Schedule incorporated revised DSM-III (DSM-III-R) as well as *Diagnostic and Statistical Manual of Mental Disorders,* Fourth Edition (DSM-IV) criteria. Another structured instrument is the Composite International Diagnostic Interview developed by Robins in collaboration with the World Health Organization[20] and NIMH.[21] The Composite International Diagnostic Interview was used in the National Comorbidity Study (NCS), which provided the first prevalence estimates of mental disorders in the United States as a whole.[22] The design and findings of the NCS are also described in detail later. In the field of children's mental health, fully structured diagnostic interview schedules have also been designed, such as the Diagnostic Interview Schedule for Children.[23, 24]

As a result of the development of structured diagnostic interview schedules, the need to establish the prevalence of specific disorders was finally realized, at least within the limits of our current ability to operationalize mental disorders and within the constraints inherent in interview data.[25] Estimates suggest that approximately 12% of children[26] and 15% of adults[27] currently meet criteria for one or more mental disorders. However, more precise estimates cannot be made until more sensitive diagnostic tools become available.

This chapter reviews the extensive descriptive and analytical findings of epidemiological research on mental disorders, emphasizing the design and findings from the major studies of the past two decades as well as continued challenges to conducting epidemiological research with respect to reliability and validity. We begin with a brief overview of the scope and methods that characterize epidemiological research, focusing on the strengths and limitations of the different approaches. We then turn to a discussion of the growth of psychiatric epidemiology and important findings from the two largest descriptive studies of the past decade.

Scope of the Epidemiological Inquiry

The word epidemiology is derived from the Greek words *epidemos* ("among the people") and *logos* ("speech"). MacMahon and Pugh[28] defined epidemiology as the study of "the patterns of disease occurrence in human populations and of the factors that influence these patterns." Some of the earliest research in epidemiology was conducted in England. In 1662, John Graunt[29] published *Natural and Political Observations . . . Made upon the Bills of Mortality.* Using birth and mortality records collected by parish clerks, Graunt studied the variations in birth and death patterns by sex, urban-rural residence, and seasonality, hypothesizing that such data could provide clues toward understanding human disease. He is also credited with constructing the first known life table. The Englishman John Snow is regarded as the founder of epidemiology. Snow[30] studied an outbreak of cholera in London during 1848 that became known as the Broad Street Pump Incident; he hypothesized that the outbreak was associated with the discharge of fecal waste into the water supply. He noted that in the same neighborhoods served by two water companies, the mortality rate among residents served by the company whose source was from a heavily polluted part of the Thames River was eight to nine times higher than that of residents served by the other company whose water was drawn from a less contaminated part of the river. By turning off the offending company's pump, known as the Broad Street pump, he successfully reduced the level of mortality, thus demonstrating that prevention efforts could be initiated even if the specific cause (in this case, a microorganism) was not known.

Modern epidemiology goes beyond establishing the incidence, causes, and prevention of infectious diseases. Following MacMahon and Pugh's definition, epidemiology encompasses the study of all acute and chronic diseases, including mental disorders. Although the scope of epidemiology can be stated simply, the requirements of such research are formidable.[31] These entail the ability to define a disorder accurately and reliably, to establish its time of onset, to identify an unbiased sample of cases, and to delineate the risk factors and moderators. Because the ultimate goal of epidemiological research is to understand the cause of disease and prevent its occurrence, epidemiology is the backbone of public health. Psychiatric epidemiology thus takes a comprehensive and systematic approach to the study of mental illness, one that progresses from descriptive work on establishing rates, to analytical research aimed at identifying risk factors and biological or psychosocial variables that might modify the effects of these risk factors, to experimental research on the impact of treatment or preventive and rehabilitative interventions in reducing psychiatric morbidity.

Clinical Epidemiology

Whereas classical epidemiology is concerned with identifying the causes of disease and is the basic science for public health, clinical epidemiology has been described as the study of the outcome of illness[32] or the basic science for clinical medicine.[33] Clinical epidemiology follows the principles of population-based epidemiology in a clinical setting. It is interested in the outcome of illness and determination of its variation. Modern examples include two countywide longitudinal studies of first-admission psychosis,[34, 35] which included patients from all facilities in the respective geographical regions, or a follow-up study of first-episode psychotic patients admitted to The McLean Hospital in Belmont, Massachusetts.[36] In addition to studying the course of the condition, clinical epidemiology evaluates prognostic factors differentially affecting outcome. It also evaluates "costs" associated with treatment and outcome. Costs are measured not only in terms of the provisions of services and ancillaries but also by the cost to society secondary to the disability in patients. Another domain of clinical epidemiology is evaluation of the use of diagnostic and screening tests vis-à-vis a patient's outcome.

Epidemiological Methods

Measures of Disease Frequency

Epidemiological studies examine the incidence and prevalence rates of disorders in populations at risk and the factors associated with onset and recurrence. A rate is determined by the number of cases (the numerator) divided by the population at risk (the denominator).

Incidence

Incidence rates refer to new cases that arise in a healthy population during a fixed time. The most commonly applied incidence rate in psychiatric epidemiology is the cumulative incidence rate, also known as the incidence proportion,[37] that is, the proportion of a population at risk that has a disease during a specified time. The range is from 0 to 1. The numerator includes new cases of the illness, and the denominator is composed of individuals at risk of becoming diseased for the first time. In cumulative incidence, the duration of the observation needs to be defined (e.g., new cases in 1 month, 1 year, or 5 years). For example, we wished to determine the cumulative incidence rate of depressive and anxiety disorders in a sample of mothers of young children during the year after the accident at the Three Mile Island nuclear power plant. A total of 312 women with small children living within 10 miles of the plant were interviewed with the SADS-L.[12] Of them, 84 met research diagnostic criteria for major depression or generalized anxiety disorder *before* the accident. Forty-five cases occurred during the year after the accident, of which 26 were first-onset or incident cases. The 1-year cumulative incidence rate is thus 26 divided by 228 (the total sample less those with a prior history, or 312 − 84), or 11.4%.

Cumulative incidence is appropriate when a study has a fixed cohort design, that is, when all of the members of the cohort are observed for the same time. However, when attrition occurs, the cumulative incidence rate is a less desirable measure. Individuals lost to follow-up who would have become case patients are excluded from the numerator, whereas the denominator, which is the total population, remains unchanged. Moreover, as we will see in the discussion on the ECA, those who become lost to follow-up are often a biased subgroup of the original study population.[38] Therefore, cumulative incidence should be considered most reliable when there is a small loss to follow-up during the specified time. When loss to follow-up occurs or when the occurrence of a health outcome is measured in a dynamic cohort, that is, when members of the cohort come in and out, different statistical adjustments must be employed.[37]

$$\text{Cumulative incidence} = \frac{\text{number of new cases}}{\text{total population at risk}}$$

In epidemiology, incidence rate refers to the number of new cases occurring in a specified time period divided by the sum of time periods of the observation for all individuals in the population at risk, or person-time.[39] In effect, this statistic measures the instantaneous force of morbidity or disease occurrence.[39] Miettinen[40] also referred to it as incidence density. The denominator person-time is the observational experience during which a particular outcome may occur. The range of an incidence rate is 0 to infinity. The incidence rate is measured in units of the reciprocal of time (time^{-1}). For example, suppose an investigator wishes to calculate the incidence rate of suicide in 100 patients with mania during the 5-year period after initial diagnosis. The numerator is the number of patients who committed suicide, and the denominator is 100 patients × 5 years, or 500 person-years. If five suicides occur, the incidence rate of suicide will be 5 divided by 500 person-years. The units of incidence rates are time^{-1}. Because the units and the numerical value of an incidence rate are difficult to interpret, incidence rates are usually compared with each other to obtain incidence rate ratios.

$$\text{Incidence rate} = \frac{\text{number of new cases}}{\text{person-years}}$$

Prevalence

Prevalence rates measure the proportion of individuals who have the disease at a specified point or period in time. Incidence refers only to new-onset cases, whereas prevalence includes all new, recurrent, or chronic cases in the numerator and the entire population, including those with a history of the disorder, in the denominator. The point prevalence rate is the proportion of a population affected by a disease at a given point in time. For example, the point prevalence of schizophrenia is the number of individuals with schizophrenia in a community divided by the population of that community. Period prevalence refers to the proportion of a population affected by a disease during a specified time period, such as 6 months, 1 year, or lifetime. In the Three Mile Island example, the 1-year period prevalence rate of anxiety and depression among the mothers of young children was 45 divided by 312, or 14.4%.[12] Prevalence rates are influenced by the duration of a disease. For nonchronic disorders, such as major depression, the point prevalence is usually lower than the period prevalence. For chronic conditions, such as schizophrenia, the point prevalence and period prevalence are expected to be similar.

$$\text{Prevalence rate} = \frac{\text{number of cases}}{\text{total population at risk}}$$

In general, prevalence data are less useful than incidence data for etiological research. Prevalence is determined not just by factors that cause a disease but by factors secondary to the disease itself. On the other hand, prevalence measures are useful in public health or service utilization situations. For instance, the geographical location and planning of specific services of a community mental health center are usually based on findings from prevalence studies.

Measures of Association

Incidence rates can be used to calculate two types of effects. One is the attributable risk, or the absolute effect. The attributable risk is the difference between two incidence

Odds ratio

A = 30	B = 60
C = 10	D = 80

Odds ratio = A/B ÷ C/D = AD/BC = 30.80/60.10 = 4

Figure 12–1 *Calculation of relative risks using a ratio of the odds of exposure of case patients to that of control subjects.*

rates. This is most commonly used in comparing rates of exposed with nonexposed populations. For example, the Three Mile Island study included a sample of mothers of young children living near another nuclear power plant in Pennsylvania. The risk of depression and anxiety attributable to the Three Mile Island accident was the incidence rate in the exposed population (11.4%) minus that in the comparison population (3.2%), or 8.2%. The second type of effect is the relative risk, which is the ratio of the incidence rates of the exposed and unexposed groups. In the same example, the relative risk was 3.56. In case-control studies, it is not possible to estimate incidence rates. Relative risks, however, can be calculated with an odds ratio, which is the ratio of the odds of exposure of the case patients to that of the control subjects (Fig. 12–1).

Quality of Case Assessments and Risk Factor Identification

The calculations defined in the preceding assume a fundamental requirement of epidemiological research, the ability to define a case. In epidemiology, particularly psychiatric epidemiology in which classification is based on self-report or interviewer-based rating scales and questionnaires, several features of an instrument are tested. An instrument's sensitivity (proportion of those with true-positive results identified as such by the study instrument) and specificity (proportion of those with true-negative results identified as such by the study instrument) are one set of measures (Table 12–1). For an instrument to be useful in epidemiology, it should have high sensitivity and at least moderately high specificity.

To identify cases accurately, an instrument used for case identification must be reliable and valid. Reliability refers to the reproducibility of a measure, that is, the consistency of measurement regardless of the rater, the situation, or the time of administration. Interrater agreement is usually calculated with statistical methods, such as κ, that control for chance agreement. Test-retest reliability, or temporal stability, is calculated with product-moment or intraclass correlation coefficients. Validity refers to whether a construct is measured accurately. This concept is more difficult to establish in psychiatry because there is no "gold standard" or biological marker for the disorders under study. The one exception is Alzheimer's disease, for which considerable progress has occurred in developing test batteries that accurately predict autopsy findings of plaques and tangles that exemplify this disorder. That is, these measures are believed to have high positive predictive values. Table 12–1 illustrates a numerical example of these measures.

Table 12–1 Measures of Reliability and Validity

	Test criterion		
Reference criterion	*a* (9)	*b* (1)	*a + b* (10)
	c (70)	*d* (34)	*c + d* (104)
	a + c (79)	*b + d* (35)	N (114)

Sensitivity	$a/(a + b) = 9/10 = .90$
Specificity	$d/(c + d) = 34/104 = .33$
PV+	$a/(a + c) = 9/79 = .11$
PV−	$a/(b + d) = 34/35 = .97$
Sensitivity	Proportion of those with the condition who have a positive test result
Specificity	Proportion of those without the condition who have a negative test result
Predictive value of a positive test result (PV+)	Proportion of those with a positive test result who have the condition
Predictive value of a negative test result (PV−)	Proportion of those with a negative test result who do not have the condition

Risk factors are characteristics whose presence increases the odds for development of a disease. A true risk factor must exist before a disease develops. For example, being male and having a family history of alcoholism are risk factors for the development of alcoholism.[41] When a variable cannot be definitively proved to predate the onset of a disorder, it is best conceptualized as a correlate. For example, socioenvironmental factors, such as adverse life events and chronic strain, that are statistically associated with the development of depressive disorders should usually be regarded as correlates because it is usually not possible to disentangle the causal sequence of these relationships.

Types of Epidemiological Studies

In general, epidemiological studies are designed to find associations between exposures and health outcomes. A main concern in epidemiological studies is the selection of study groups on the basis of either disease status or exposure status. Epidemiological studies (Table 12–2) can be classified as 1) experimental, 2) quasi-experimental, and 3) nonexperimental or observational.

Table 12–2 Types of Study Designs

- Experimental
- Quasi-experimental
- Nonexperimental (observational)
  - Longitudinal
    - Case-control studies
    - Cohort studies
      - Prospective
      - Retrospective
  - Cross-sectional

Experimental Studies

The main distinction of experimental studies is that the investigator assigns the status of exposure or nonexposure to each subject. The assignment to the exposure group becomes part of the study protocol. Once subjects are assigned to exposed or nonexposed groups, they are observed for a time, and observations about changes in morbidity are recorded. The most common experimental design is the clinical trial, in which clinical populations are exposed to a specific treatment protocol to measure an outcome, usually resolution of symptoms. To ensure the integrity of a clinical trial, three main elements are necessary[40]: 1) randomization, to ensure comparability of the populations; 2) placebo, to ensure comparability of the effects; and 3) "blinding," to ensure comparability of information.

In randomization, subjects are randomly assigned to different exposure groups to attempt to ensure that subjects in each group have similar clinical and demographical characteristics. It is possible that with a small sample size, the groups may have different characteristics in spite of randomized allocation. If these characteristics are factors that could affect the outcome, they then need to be controlled in subsequent analyses. Of course, in many cases, not all factors predicting a good or a poor outcome are known. Randomization should theoretically achieve a balance of unknown factors in the different groups.

To control comparability of extraneous effects of a specified treatment, experimental studies use placebo-controlled groups. A placebo controls for factors that may affect the outcome of the study independently of the exposure status. That is, if subjects in an open trial are aware of what medication they receive, this knowledge could bias their response to the treatment. Similarly, subjects who are aware of being in an untreated control group could respond over time in a biased fashion. Thus, one goal in assigning patients at random to treatment or placebo control groups is to minimize observation bias. In a single-blind study, only the patient is unaware of the actual treatment. In a double-blind study, the investigator and the subject of investigation are unaware of treatment assignment. In a triple-blind study, the data analyst is also not informed of the meaning of the group assignment code.

Quasi-experimental Studies

Natural experiments that permit comparisons of two populations, one that receives an exposure and the other that does not, are referred to as quasi-experimental studies. To be considered quasi-experimental, baseline data must have been collected before the exposure event. Without that requirement, the study is simply a retrospective observational study. For example, during the course of the Three Mile Island investigation, the comparison site underwent widespread unemployment owing to massive layoffs resulting from a recession in the steel industry. Penkower and colleagues[42] were able to chart the long-term effects of husbands' layoff and to identify prior-event predictors from interview data obtained before the layoffs occurred. Even though the investigator does not have full control over the exposures and environments, these designs still permit an understanding of the influence of different environmental constraints.

Nonexperimental Studies

Nonexperimental studies are divided into cross-sectional and longitudinal designs.

Cross-sectional Designs

Cross-sectional designs are typically employed in surveys aimed at providing data on the distribution of disorders in the population. Differences in rates by basic demographical data are also usually derived. In epidemiology, cross-sectional designs are employed when causal hypotheses are not being tested. For example, when a community wants to investigate the distribution of an illness to decide on the need for psychiatric services, a cross-sectional survey is appropriate. Even though cross-sectional data are limited in terms of the level of inference that can be drawn, such surveys must still assess a well-defined population at risk with reliable assessment tools to be epidemiologically useful. Surveys that are based on volunteers or instruments with no established psychometric utility are not regarded as using epidemiological methodology.

Cross-sectional studies include not only current symptoms but also retrospective data on age at onset of the disorder. With sophisticated statistical modeling techniques, it is possible to develop informed hypotheses about links between potential risk factors and disease. However, the true test of such hypotheses must be drawn from data obtained prospectively.

Longitudinal Designs

Longitudinal designs are divided into case-control and cohort studies and are characterized by a time interval between cause and effect. In cross-sectional studies, there is no interval between exposure and illness, which are measured at the same point in time.

Case-Control Studies. In case-control studies, subjects are defined in terms of having (case patients) or not having (control patients) the disease of interest. The groups are compared in terms of history of exposure. In general, two types of control groups are used: hospital control groups and population control groups. The selection of the control group is a key point in terms of validity. Control subjects should be selected independently of exposure status. Case and control patients may be matched on different characteristics, the key issue being that control patients should represent those individuals who, if they had the disease, would be selected as case patients.[40] One of the most widely cited case-control studies focused on the role of stressful life events in the onset of depression.[43] In this study, women treated for depression were assessed about their previous life events, and a control group of non-depressed women were similarly assessed. Calculations were then made of the excess risk of depression associated with the occurrence of life events.

Among the strengths of case-control studies are their feasibility and relatively low cost. Case-control studies allow the evaluation of multiple hypotheses and are the ideal design for investigating rare diseases, such as anorexia nervosa. The primary limitation of case-control studies is potential recall bias, particularly in the control patients for whom there may be no corroborating record information. In addition, it is often difficult to obtain suitable data on rare exposures.

Case-control studies can assess whether a risk factor is more prevalent in case than in control patients but cannot establish the rate of disease after exposure to that risk factor. For the purpose of estimating the true rate of disease associated with an exposure, the prospective cohort study design is the appropriate methodology.

Cohort Studies. In cohort studies, subjects are identified in terms of exposure or nonexposure status and are observed for a specified time to determine the presence or absence of a health outcome. Cohort studies are divided into prospective and retrospective. In prospective cohort studies, the exposure or nonexposure status is defined when the study is initiated. The subjects of investigation are followed up into the future to determine disease or nondisease status. In retrospective studies, the status of exposed or nonexposed is defined in the present. In prospective cohort studies, exposures of the present are evaluated; in retrospective cohort studies, exposures of the past are being evaluated. Cohort groups share the common exposure status and are observed to ascertain the presence or absence of a disease or outcome.

Retrospective Cohort Studies. A second retrospective design is the retrospective cohort study, in which subjects are identified from archival data collected many years previously and located in the present. In other words, exposure status is defined in the past, and illness status is defined in the present. A classic example of this type of design is a study entitled *Deviant Children Grown Up,*[44] in which 524 individuals who had been evaluated 30 years earlier in a child guidance clinic, along with demographically matched school-based control subjects, were assessed with respect to subsequent psychopathological processes and sociopathic behaviors. The data in the agency records served as predictor variables in the analysis. This design has the advantage of obtaining information in a timely and cost-effective manner. The primary disadvantage, however, is that the interval experiences are reconstructed for long periods and, in the absence of objective records, may be subject to considerable recall bias. Another disadvantage is that the samples themselves may not be representative of individuals with the exposure. Furthermore, some studies have reported considerable loss to follow-up through either mortality or mobility. For example, in a long-term "follow-back" study of patients from a clinic in Switzerland, Ciompi[45] assessed only 289 of the original 1642 patients, or 18%.

Prospective Cohort Studies. In prospective cohort studies, subjects are identified in terms of exposure or nonexposure status and observed forward for a specified interval to determine the presence or absence of a health outcome. Cohort studies are similar to an experimental study with the exception that exposure or nonexposure status is not assigned by the investigator. To illustrate, Solomon[46] identified a sample of Israeli soldiers who fought in the war between Israel and Lebanon and soldiers who were not on active duty at the time. After the war, they were followed up for several years to determine the onset of long-term war-related mental disorders. The prevalence of subsequent psychiatric illness was significantly higher in the soldiers exposed to war than in soldiers not exposed.

The sources of cohort groups are variable. The most powerful type of cohort is the birth cohort drawn from the general population. Two British birth cohorts have been used to study a range of diseases, including schizophrenia.[47] Another powerful source of a cohort is a community. In 1947, Essen-Moller began a longitudinal study of the 2550 inhabitants of Lundby, Sweden; the cohort was subsequently followed up for more than 25 years.[48] Often, healthy cohorts are identified from specific settings, particularly universities and medical facilities. For example, a well-known study in American psychiatry is Vaillant's[49] 40-year study of initially healthy Harvard University undergraduates. Another common population targeted for cohort research is an occupational group. To minimize bias in determining whether an occupational condition is associated with an adverse health outcome, members of occupational cohorts must be identified at the point of hire. Because most disorders occur infrequently, another cohort source frequently used in psychiatry is the offspring of mentally ill adults, such as children of individuals with alcoholism, children of individuals with schizophrenia, and children of depressed parents.

For comparison groups, a cohort study can use an internal subset of the population under study, by comparing exposed with unexposed members of the cohort, or an external comparison. A comparison cohort can be selected from a similarly defined population (e.g., mothers living near Three Mile Island were compared with mothers similarly sampled from around another nuclear power plant), or the cohort can be compared with the general population (e.g., symptoms among women living near Three Mile Island can be compared with norms established for the same measure for women of the same age).

The major strength of the cohort design is the possibility of estimating a temporal relationship between exposure and disease. With a cohort study, it is possible to study rare exposures and to evaluate multiple outcomes from a single exposure. The limitation of cohort studies is primarily one of feasibility because most such studies are expensive and involve study populations who are difficult to recruit and maintain for follow-up.

Threats to Validity in Epidemiological Studies

An essential feature of epidemiological studies is a comparison of two groups in terms of presence or absence of exposure or presence or absence of disease. For the measurements to be comparable, the investigator should ensure absence of bias. Biases can be divided into three general types: selection bias, information or observation bias, and confounding bias.

Selection Bias

Selection bias can arise when the sampling procedure is influenced a priori by the disease or the exposure. For example, studies of employed populations are limited by the "healthy worker effect" because disabled individuals or those who were adversely affected by aspects of the work environment will not be in the cohort.[50] The Three Mile Island investigation compared unionized nuclear power plant workers at Three Mile Island with workers at a comparable power plant in western Pennsylvania.[12] Because of union regulations, the workers at Three Mile Island could not transfer to a less stressful type of power plant without losing their seniority and benefits, but the comparison site employees could and did transfer. Thus, because of the bias introduced by the different union regulations, the two samples were not comparable.

Another example, referred to as self-selection bias, occurs when subjects who have been exposed to an event are more likely to participate in a study if they have the disease or prodromal stages of the disease under study. A similar type of selection bias can occur when subjects are solicited from newspaper or other similar advertisements. To illustrate, in a study of individuals who responded to an advertisement seeking healthy volunteers as control subjects in a mental health study, Halbreich and coworkers[51] reported that one third had a history of diagnosable mental disorders. Selection bias can also occur when the mortality rate is elevated as a result of the exposure. Thus, concentration camp survivors or survivors of major earthquakes are not necessarily representative of individuals who underwent those stresses.

When an investigator suspects selection bias at the start of a study, it is usually difficult to isolate the source because it is often impossible to obtain sufficient information about the nonrespondents. As we will see later in the chapter, Kessler and associates[22] conducted a special study of nonrespondents to the NCS and discovered that they had a higher rate of psychiatric illness than did the sample interviewed without special procedures. On the other hand, considerable detail has accumulated about individuals who drop out of longitudinal studies. Such individuals tend to be at both ends of the spectrum, that is, they have either the highest or the lowest degree of psychiatric illness. Each longitudinal study needs to include an analysis of the bias imposed by attrition.

Information (Observation) Bias

In case-control studies, information bias occurs when the details about prior exposure are obtained in a noncomparable manner or are subject to poor recall. To minimize such bias in case-control studies, exposure data should be collected without knowledge of disease status. This procedure is known as blindness. However, because of selective recall, when the sole source of information is the affected individual, this type of bias sometimes presents insurmountable problems. For instance, in studies of life events and onset of depression, it is likely that subjects who present with the disease under study will have a more accurate recollection of life events than will individuals without depression. Subjects themselves may break the blind feature built into a study. In research on occupational lead exposure, an attempt was made to keep the interviewers blind as to exposure status by putting all questions about employment at the end of the interview.[52] However, the subjects frequently volunteered information about their jobs early in the interview. Another example comes from clinical trials in which raters can sometimes accurately guess which subjects are receiving placebo and which are not and hence bias the results about the drug's effects.

Confounding Bias

Confounding bias results when a third factor that is a cause of the disease under study is also associated with the exposure. A confounding factor is a cause of the disease under study independent of its association with the exposure. For instance, if unemployment is considered a cause of suicidal behavior, and at the same time alcoholism is related to both unemployment and suicidal behavior, then alcoholism would be a confounding variable for a study designed to measure the association between unemployment and suicidal behavior. In such a study, the measure of association between unemployment and suicidal behavior should be adjusted by the presence or absence of alcoholism.

Major Population-Based Studies

Historical Overview

Dohrenwend and Dohrenwend[53] divided the growth of psychiatric epidemiological research into three periods, or generations. This section describes the key studies and prevalence rates from each of these periods.

First-Generation Research

The first-generation studies took place for the most part before World War II. These studies are characterized by their reliance on known cases, usually individuals in mental hospitals, to define mental illness. There were three extraordinary studies conducted during this time. The first was a prevalence study performed in 1885 in Massachusetts in which case patients were identified through key informants, such as general practitioners and clergy, and hospital records.[54] This study, the first known American prevalence study, identified 2632 "lunatics" and 1087 "idiots" in need of care.

The second landmark study in the history of psychiatric epidemiology was an etiological study of pellagra, a common disorder found in patients in mental hospitals. In the early 1920s, Goldberger and colleagues[55] demonstrated with the case-control method that pellagra was associated with nutritional deficiency. Although no specific nutrient was identified, dietary changes were instituted that dramatically reduced the level of morbidity from this disease in institutional settings.

The third landmark study conducted before World War II was an ecological analysis of hospital patients, *Mental Disorders in Urban Areas*.[56] This pioneering study examined the geographical distribution of all first-admission patients hospitalized between 1922 and 1934 in mental hospitals in Chicago. They found that the central area of the city, which had the greatest degree of social disorganization, had the highest rates of admissions for patients with schizophrenia (46% of all admissions). The rates decreased progressively with distance away from the center, reaching a low of 13% in the outermost area. This study became influential in mental health research because the investigators interpreted the results as indicating that adversity in the social environment played an etiological role in the occurrence of severe mental illness. Critics argued that downward social drift could have accounted for the high number of cases from the central urban area. Because the study used an ecological design, the data could not be used to test causal hypotheses about the relative role of personal versus environmental risk factors. Nevertheless, the debate about the causal contributions of these risk factors led to an extensive body of research on the contribution of social factors to the onset of mental illness.

In general, the median prevalence rate among the various first-generation studies relying on key informants and agency records was 3.6%.[53] Compared with findings from later studies, this design is generally believed to result in an underestimate of the true prevalence of mental disorders.

Second-Generation Studies

World War II represented a turning point in psychiatric epidemiology.[4, 53] A number of events converged during this time. First, mental illness accounted for the largest proportion of men rejected for military service. The fact that such large numbers of (untreated) recruits failed the psychological screen emphasized that treated patients, who served as the foundation of previous prevalence estimates, represented the tip, and as we now know, a biased tip, of the iceberg. Second, healthy men who fought in the war frequently suffered from combat stress reactions when faced with the overwhelming horrors of battle, indicating that stress can play an etiological role in the onset of mental disorders under some circumstances. Some of these individuals were subsequently discharged because of psychiatric illness.[57] Also, psychologists in the armed forces developed the Neuropsychiatric Screening Adjunct, which became a forerunner of symptom questionnaires administered after the war.

In 1946, Congress passed the National Mental Health Act (Public Law 79-487), enabling the creation in 1949 of the NIMH as a separate agency within the National Institutes of Health. This facilitated governmental support of training, prevention, and epidemiological research in mental health. The second-generation studies profited from this financial support. Growing conceptually out of the experiences of World War II that suggested a major role for stress in relation to mental disorders, these studies focused on early childhood and contemporaneous sources of stress believed to influence psychological well-being adversely.

In the early 1950s, three major studies were initiated to examine the prevalence of and risk factors associated with psychosomatic and affective symptoms in the general population, the Midtown Manhattan Study,[58] the Nova Scotia Stirling County research,[59] and the University of Michigan's national survey of mental health.[60] These early representatives of the second-generation studies used lengthy symptom questionnaires, modified in large part from the Neuropsychiatric Screening Adjunct, which were directly administered to carefully selected samples of the population. The underlying assumption of these studies was that mental illness existed along a unidimensional continuum of severity, and that impairment ratings by psychiatrists who reviewed the symptom questionnaires were appropriate and suitable reflections of true mental illness. This conceptualization of mental illness as existing along a continuum was congruent with the paradigm of social disruption as an etiological factor of psychiatric illness.

The common denominator of the early second-generation studies was the direct interview of all subjects with supplementation of data from other sources, such as medical or community records. The care and elegance of the data collection in the earlier studies are important to emphasize. For example, in the Stirling County study, 1010 adults were assessed initially by a lay interviewer using a structured questionnaire.[59] Further information was collected from general practitioners and psychiatrists practicing in the area. All of the information was evaluated by research psychiatrists using the DSM-I nosology. The prevalence of mental illness was estimated to be 20%. The Midtown Manhattan Study[58] used a similar methodology; social workers were hired to collect the interview data. On the basis of psychiatrists' ratings of impairment, this study reported that 23.4% of the sample was severely impaired.

In the late 1950s, Hollingshead and Redlich[61] conducted a landmark study of the impact of social class on the treatment experiences of psychiatric patients, drawing on treated patients from the city of New Haven, Connecticut. Similar to the Chicago study of Faris and Dunham,[56] major differences were found across socioeconomic strata. The most influential finding was that regardless of diagnosis, the type of therapy patients received varied according to their class of origin. Patients from the working and lower classes were more likely to be treated with electroconvulsive therapy or medications. In contrast, patients from the upper classes were mostly treated with psychotherapy. Researchers also found a higher treated prevalence for the lower social classes.

Later second-generation studies used abbreviated assessment methods empirically derived from the lengthy symptom inventories and eliminated the role of psychiatrists in case identification. These studies continued to focus on the role of social adversity in the occurrence of psychiatric symptoms. However, these studies have been criticized for not adequately assessing the full range of psychiatric symptoms, particularly those associated with psychosis, aggression, and substance use, and hence drawing biased conclusions about both rates and risk factors (such as female gender). Furthermore, although many such studies were longitudinal (e.g., the New Haven study of stressful life events and symptoms[62]), they were unable to disentangle cause and effect because they were not prospective, that is, they did not start with a healthy cohort and detect whether or under what conditions the risk factors under observation led to new cases of individuals with high symptom counts. The primary limitation, however, was the assessment of symptoms rather than diagnosable-level disorder.

Nevertheless, it became clear that mental illness was a public health problem and that most individuals with significant symptoms never received psychiatric treatment. In part on the basis of these community studies, including the highly influential *Social Class and Mental Illness,* President Kennedy delivered a message to Congress on mental illness and mental retardation in 1963 that set the stage for the Community Mental Health Centers Act.

Third-Generation Studies

As noted earlier, the 1978 President's Commission on Mental Health highlighted the need for descriptive data not only on the prevalence of psychiatric illness in the general population but also on the services required for its treatment. The methodology for the third-generation epidemiological studies reflected the view in American psychiatry in the early 1970s that mental illness could be delineated into discrete, operational categories. These changes in nosology were exemplified in the 1970s with the development of the

Feighner criteria at Washington University in St. Louis[63, 64] and culminated in the creation of DSM-III a decade later. By operationalizing diagnoses with specific criteria, it was possible to create structured diagnostic assessments to elicit the symptoms needed for these categories. Preliminary evidence about the utility of using diagnostic procedures in community samples was obtained in a third-wave follow-up of the New Haven study noted before. In this study, Weissman and colleagues[11] successfully administered the SADS-L in a community population. Encouraged by these results, Bromet and colleagues[12] used a modified (reorganized) version of the SADS-L to study the effects of the Three Mile Island accident. These studies demonstrated that structured diagnostic instruments designed for clinical investigations could produce meaningful findings when administered in population-based studies.

The third-generation studies, thus, are characterized primarily by the use of structured diagnostic assessment procedures. In the next sections, we describe the two largest third-generation studies, the NIMH-sponsored ECA project[19, 65, 66] and the NCS.[22] Many other important investigations focusing on diagnosable mental disorders have been conducted in the past decade. These include (but are not limited to) the National Vietnam Veterans Readjustment Study,[67] the prevalence study of major depressive disorder and alcohol abuse or dependence in white-collar employees of Westinghouse Electric Corporation,[68] the prevalence and risk factor study of psychiatric disorders in an Israeli birth cohort,[69, 70] and the social risk factor study of adults residing in metropolitan Toronto.[71]

It is also important to note the progress in studying the epidemiology of children's disorders. Since Rutter's[72] pioneering research of children living on the Isle of Wight and in an inner-city area of London, several community studies have been conducted using structured diagnostic assessment procedures. These studies have been conducted in several countries, including Canada (Ontario),[73] United States (New York State,[74] Pittsburgh[23]), Puerto Rico,[75] New Zealand,[76] and France.[77] In a review of prevalence studies, Costello[78] concluded that the rate of diagnosable mental disorders in children and adolescents may be as high as 18% to 20%.

The Epidemiological Catchment Area Study

In response to the President's Commission on Mental Health report, the NIMH sponsored the ECA project to determine the prevalence of mental disorders in specific sites and the proportion receiving mental health services.[19] The ECA project would not have been feasible without the experience generated by previous population-based studies and the improved methodology in the assessment of psychiatric disorders with structured diagnostic instruments. Parallel to the planning of the ECA study, the American Psychiatric Association published the DSM-III,[79] which had clearly defined operational criteria that facilitated case definition. Thus, the concept of a case as a discrete entity that had been achieved in the late 1970s permitted the categorical determination of psychiatric caseness as opposed to the dimensional assessment of symptom impairment. As a prelude to the ECA, the NIMH cosponsored the development of the Diagnostic Interview Schedule. The mandate for this instrument was that it would elicit information needed to make DSM-III diagnoses and be fully structured so that nonclinicians, or lay interviewers, could administer it. Since its creation,[18] a number of studies have assessed its reliability. Reliability has been found to vary depending on the diagnosis under consideration and to be better when the Diagnostic Interview Schedule is compared with itself in the hands of a physician[80] than when it is compared with other semistructured diagnostic instruments.[81]

Design of the Study

The ECA study estimated the prevalence of mental disorders in designated catchment areas with at least 200,000 persons. The enumeration within catchment areas included individuals living in the community as well as institutionalized individuals. In the selection of ECA sites, the availability of special populations was considered (e.g., minority and ethnic groups, urban and rural populations, the elderly). Catchment areas were selected within New Haven, Connecticut; Baltimore, Maryland; Raleigh-Durham, North Carolina; St. Louis, Missouri; and Los Angeles, California. In each location, approximately 3000 individuals were assessed initially.[82] The sampling was not intended to provide national estimates; rather, the focus on specific geographical sites facilitated the project's goal of linking mental health assessments to service use information.

The ECA study had three missions: estimating the lifetime and current prevalence of psychiatric disorders in the selected catchment areas; estimating the 1-year cumulative incidence of psychiatric disorders; and examining the service use of the catchment area populations. The basic design involved face to face baseline interviews with random samples of adults selected from the catchment areas, 6-month telephone follow-up interviews to obtain interim information on medical and psychiatric service use, and 1-year face to face interviews with the original sample. The initial response rate ranged from 68% (Los Angeles) to 79% (St. Louis and Durham).[83] Overall, 12% of the original respondents did not participate in the follow-up interview either because they could not be tracked or because they refused to participate. In an analysis of factors associated with attrition, Eaton and collaborators[38] reported that failure to be tracked was associated with being male, young, unmarried, and Hispanic; refusal to participate was associated with being older, married, and uneducated. These biases must be kept in mind when the incidence and follow-up findings are considered.

In addition to data on psychiatric disorders (including substance abuse or dependence and cognitive impairment), each ECA site obtained extensive information on demographical characteristics. However, each site selected which additional risk factors they would examine. Because the ECA study was conducted under a collaborative agreement, the core data are available for analysis through a public-use data tape.

Prevalence

Overall, 32.2% of the adults included in the five sites met criteria for one or more of the assessed mental disorders during their lifetime (Table 12–3 and Fig. 12–2), and 15.4% experienced a Diagnostic Interview Schedule–DSM-III mental disorder in the last month (Table 12–4). Phobias and alcohol abuse and dependence were the most common

Table 12–3 Lifetime Prevalence Rate of Specific Diagnostic Interview Schedule (DIS)–DSM-III Disorders*

Disorder	Estimated Prevalence Rate (% Population)
Any DIS disorder covered	32.2
Any DIS disorder except cognitive impairment, personality disorder, and substance abuse	19.6
Substance use disorders	16.4
Alcohol abuse and dependence	13.3
Drug abuse and dependence	5.9
Schizophrenia and schizophreniform disorders	1.5
Affective disorders	8.3
Manic episode	0.8
Major depressive episode	5.8
Dysthymia	3.3
Anxiety disorders	14.6
Generalized anxiety disorder	8.5
Phobia	12.5
Panic	1.6
Obsessive-compulsive disorder	2.5
Somatization disorder	0.1
Personality disorder	
Antisocial personality	2.5
Cognitive impairment (severe)	1.3

*Based on five ECA sites, standardized to the 1980 U.S. census.

From Regier DA, Boyd JH, Burke JD Jr, et al: One-month prevalence of mental disorders in the United States. Based on five Epidemiologic Catchment Area sites. Arch Gen Psychiatry 1988; 45:977–986. Copyright·1988, American Medical Association.

mental disorders.[65] The lifetime prevalence for phobia was 12.5%, and the 1-month prevalence was 6.2%. The rates for drug abuse and dependence were 5.9% for lifetime and 1.3% for 1-month prevalence.

The ECA study investigators did extensive analyses of the variation in prevalence rates by demographical characteristics. For lifetime diagnosis, 36% of men at some point suffered from an addictive or mental disorder, compared with 30% of women (Table 12–5 and Fig. 12–3). As seen in Table 12–5, some differences also emerged by age groups, with age groups younger than 30 and 30 to 44 years having the highest lifetime prevalence rates. Interestingly, individuals older than 65 years reported lower prevalence rates, suggesting a possible underreporting of symptoms in this age group.[66] Furthermore, Regier and Kaelber[82] suggested that it is possible that individuals with psychiatric disorders tend disproportionately to die prematurely. Table 12–5 also indicates that the rates overall are higher in African-Americans than in whites and Hispanics, but this is confounded by social strata because rates are similar across ethnic groups when social class is controlled.[82] Similarly, individuals who did not complete high school had a higher prevalence of mental disorders than did those who graduated from high school (see Table 12–5). Lifetime prevalence rates were also associated with unemployment (especially in men) and with being separated or divorced (see Table 12–5).

The pooled 1-month prevalence rates for the five sites (see Table 12–4) was 15.4% for all ages for any DSM-III disorder. The age group 25 to 44 years had the highest overall rate of 17.3%. Although this age pattern was also true for women, men aged 18 to 24 years had the highest overall rate. This occurred because of the peak in rates of drug abuse and dependence in men in this age group. Anxiety disorders were most prevalent at 11.7% in women 25 to 44 years old, compared with only 4.7% for men in the same group. The overall prevalence for all affective disorders was 5.1%; the highest age group was women 25 to 44 years old.

Incidence

As noted, the 12-month follow-up assessment was included primarily for purposes of calculating cumulative 1-year incidence rates. Of the 20,291 individuals assessed initially, 88% completed the 1-year follow-up assessment.[84] Incidence rates proved to be difficult to calculate. Incidence rates require that the denominator include only healthy individuals at risk for development of a first onset of disease during a defined period. Because of problems with recall, ECA respondents sometimes reported symptoms inconsistently across the two waves of interviews. Thus, Eaton and colleagues[85] presented estimates for seven disorders, adjusting for these unreliability problems. These included major depressive disorder, panic disorder, phobia, obsessive-compulsive disorder, drug abuse and dependence, alcohol abuse and dependence, and cognitive impairment. Overall, phobias had the highest incidence rate (4.0%); panic disorder and obsessive-compulsive disorder had the lowest (0.6% and 0.7%, respectively). The female/male ratio for phobias was approximately 3:1. Women also had a higher rate of obsessive-compulsive disorder. The opposite was found for drug abuse and dependence, with men having a much higher 1-year incidence rate. Also as expected, older age groups had virtually no new cases of drug abuse and dependence. Interestingly, the incidence of alcohol abuse and dependence was somewhat associated with age; a slight increase was found after the age of 60 years and even more after 75 years. For 1.6% with new onsets of major depressive disorder, women, especially those in their mid-40s, were at highest risk (female/male ratio was more than 2:1).

During the 1-year follow-up period, 6% of the total population had one or more new disorders.[84] Also, 5.7% of those with a history of a mental disorder suffered a relapse or a new condition in the 1-year period for a total of 12.3% of new cases in 1 year.

Institutionalized Sample

The ECA investigators interviewed individuals institutionalized in psychiatric hospitals, halfway houses, nursing homes, and prisons. Not surprisingly, rates were much higher in these institutionalized populations. Estimates of lifetime prevalence of 65% and 1-year prevalence of 51% were reported.[82] Also, not surprisingly, the prevalence of different diagnoses varied depending on the type of institution.[66]

Mental Health Services

A major mission of the ECA study was to provide information on the use of mental health services and the use of medical and other professional services by individuals with diagnosable mental disorders.[84–86] Although 28.1% of the sample had diagnosable mental or addictive disorders,

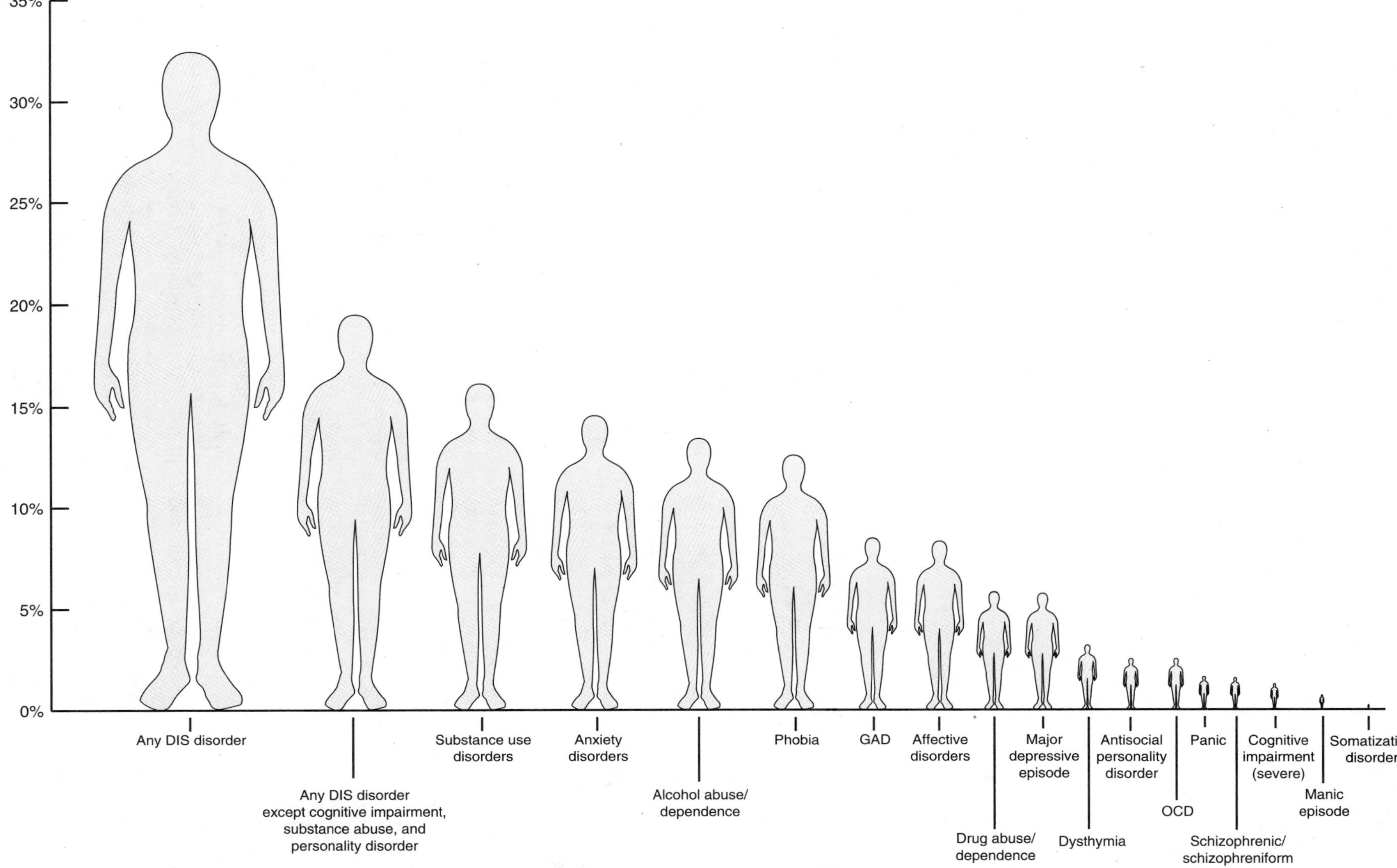

Figure 12–2 *Estimated lifetime prevalence rates of a specific Diagnostic Interview Schedule (DIS)–DSM-III disorder at five ECA sites. GAD, Generalized anxiety disorder; OCD, obsessive-compulsive disorder. (Data from Regier DA, Boyd JH, Burke JD Jr, et al: One-month prevalence of mental disorders in the United States. Based on five Epidemiologic Catchment Area sites. Arch Gen Psychiatry 1988; 45:977–986.)*

Table 12–4 One-Month Prevalence Rate (%) of Specific Diagnostic Interview Schedule (DIS)–DSM-III Disorders*

	Any DIS Disorder	Any DIS Disorder Except Cognitive Impairment, Substance Use, and Antisocial Personality	Drug Abuse and Dependence	Schizophrenia	Schizophreniform Disorders	Anxiety Disorders
Both Sexes						
All ages	15.4	11.2	1.3	0.6	0.1	7.3
18–24	16.9	11.0	3.5	0.7	0.1	7.7
25–44	17.3	13.0	1.5	0.9	0.1	8.3
45–64	13.3	10.7	0.1	0.4	0.0	6.6
65+	12.3	7.4	0.0	0.1	0.0	5.5
Men						
All ages	14.0	7.6	1.8	0.6	0.1	4.7
18–24	16.5	8.4	4.8	0.7	0.2	4.9
25–44	15.4	8.2	2.3	0.8	0.1	4.7
45–64	11.9	7.5	0.1	0.6	0.1	5.1
65+	10.5	4.5	0.0	0.1	0.0	3.6
Women						
All ages	16.6	14.5	0.7	0.6	0.1	9.7
18–24	17.3	13.5	2.4	0.7	0.0	10.4
25–44	19.2	17.7	0.8	1.1	0.2	11.7
45–64	14.6	13.7	0.0	0.3	0.0	8.0
65+	13.6	9.4	0.0	0.1	0.0	6.8

* Based on five ECA sites.

From Regier DA, Boyd JH, Burke JD Jr, et al: One-month prevalence of mental disorders in the United States. Based on five Epidemiologic Catchment Area sites. Arch Gen Psychiatry 1988; 45:977–986. Copyright 1988, American Medical Association.

only 14.7% (23 million) received care. Conversely, although 22% of respondents who had recently used a medical care facility met criteria for a DSM-III disorder, 17% of nonusers had a diagnosable illness.[87] The disorders making the greatest contribution were alcohol abuse and dependence in men and major depression in women.

Again, pooling across sites, the ECA study found that 0.9% received inpatient treatment in a specialty mental and addictive disorders facility during a 1-year period. For all inpatient and outpatient services combined, 14.7% received some type of mental or addictive disorder service each year, indicating that a disproportionate number of individuals suffering from mental and addictive disorders did not receive treatment.

Table 12–6 shows mental health visits of individuals with a specific mental disorder who used the health and mental health services within the last year. Among individuals with any Diagnostic Interview Schedule–DSM-III disorder, 28.5% sought some type of mental health treatment from either a mental health clinician or medical physician. Although the diagnosis of schizophrenia is believed to be among the least reliable, it was surprising that only 64.3% of respondents with this diagnosis sought help. Interestingly, a similar proportion of individuals with panic disorders and somatization disorders, 58.8% and 69.7%, respectively, used such services in the last 12 months.

Comorbidity of Mental and Substance Use Disorders

The ECA study provided valuable data about the prevalence of comorbidity of alcohol and substance use disorders with mental disorders.[65, 88] Before the ECA study, most of the information about comorbidity came from populations in treatment settings. Since the early 1950s, it has repeatedly been found that patients in clinical settings typically present themselves for treatment because they have more than one disorder, a phenomenon first described by Berkson.[89] Thus, clinical populations provide a biased (and inflated) view of comorbidity.

The ECA study defined comorbid as the occurrence of more than one disorder and did not require that the disorders overlap temporally. Up to 29% of individuals with a mental disorder suffer from a comorbid substance use disorder. Similarly, individuals with alcohol use disorder have twice the risk of having a comorbid mental disorder and more than five times the risk of having a comorbid drug use disorder. Of all mental disorders, antisocial personality disorder carried the highest risk of having a comorbid substance use disorder, 83.6%, which translates to nearly 30 times the odds of having a substance use disorder compared with the general population. Bipolar disorder had the next highest prevalence of substance use disorder (60.7%), and the odds of having a substance use disorder were 7.9 times higher than that of the general population. Interestingly, the rate of substance use disorder in respondents with bipolar disorder was higher than in those with major depressive disorder or schizophrenia. Furthermore, 26.7% of respondents with bipolar I disorder had a comorbid drug dependence disorder. The cause for such high prevalence of substance use disorder comorbidity in patients with bipolar disorder remains unclear.[90, 91]

Table 12–4 One-Month Prevalence Rate (%) of Specific Diagnostic Interview Schedule (DIS)–DSM-III Disorders* *Continued*

Phobia	Panic	Obsessive-Compulsive Disorder	Affective Disorders	Manic Episode	Manic-Depressive Episode	Dysthymia
6.2	0.5	1.3	5.1	0.4	2.2	3.3
6.4	0.4	1.8	4.4	0.6	2.2	2.2
6.9	0.7	1.6	6.4	0.6	3.0	4.0
6.0	0.6	0.9	5.2	0.2	2.0	3.8
4.8	0.1	0.8	2.5	0.0	0.7	1.8
3.8	0.3	1.1	3.5	0.3	1.6	2.2
3.6	0.4	1.7	3.4	0.4	1.5	2.2
3.5	0.3	1.2	4.5	0.5	2.2	2.8
4.8	0.5	0.6	3.1	0.2	1.2	2.0
2.9	0.0	0.7	1.4	0.0	0.4	1.0
8.4	0.7	1.5	6.6	0.4	2.9	4.2
9.1	0.4	1.8	5.3	0.8	2.9	2.2
10.2	1.1	1.9	8.2	0.6	3.9	5.1
7.0	0.7	1.2	7.2	0.2	2.6	5.4
6.1	0.2	0.9	3.3	0.0	0.9	2.3

Among individuals with alcohol use disorders, the most common comorbid mental disorder was anxiety disorder, with a prevalence of 19.4%. For individuals with drug use disorder, 22% suffered from a mental disorder. Again, anxiety disorder was the most prevalent with 28.3%.

Summary

When the second-generation community studies reported rates of more than 20% with significant impairment, the common reaction was disbelief and criticism of the methodology. Ironically, the rates in the five ECA sites confirmed the high prevalence of untreated mental disorder and the concomitant underuse of mental health specialty services by individuals fitting these DSM-III disorders. At the same time, such individuals were relatively more likely to use general medical services compared with those without disorder. Because the ECA study was conducted in five specific sites, each selected because it contained unique population characteristics, the findings could not be readily extrapolated to the United States as a whole. As a result, a further investigation was needed to fulfill the original objective of the President's commission, to determine the true prevalence of mental disorder in the United States.

The National Comorbidity Survey

The NCS was designed to estimate the prevalence and comorbidity of psychiatric and substance use disorders in the mainland United States. Only two (second-generation) national studies of the prevalence of psychiatric symptoms in the United States had been conducted previously, both by University of Michigan investigators. The NCS was designed by Kessler and colleagues[22] at the same university and is the only population-based study administered to a nationally representative sample in the United States using a structured diagnostic interview. The NCS built on the knowledge and experience of the ECA study. As a single study, it had the advantage of uniformly including a set of demographical and psychosocial risk factors.

The NCS used a stratified probability sampling procedure and focused on individuals aged 15 to 54 years. It included only noninstitutionalized individuals in 48 states. A total of 8098 individuals were interviewed, which represented 82.6% of the targeted population. To understand the full impact of nonresponse, a random sample of the initial refusers were reapproached and given further incentives to participate in a short form of the original interview. These individuals were subsequently found to have elevated rates of psychiatric illness. Therefore, a nonresponse adjustment weight was included in the analysis.

Subjects were administered a modified version of the Composite International Diagnostic Interview,[20] referred to as the University of Michigan Composite International Diagnostic Interview. The NCS obtained estimates of 14 DSM-III-R diagnoses, including alcohol abuse and dependence, antisocial personality disorder, drug abuse and dependence, dysthymia, generalized anxiety disorder, panic disorder, social phobia, agoraphobia, simple phobia, major depression, and nonaffective psychosis (schizophrenia, schizophreniform disorder, schizoaffective disorder, delusional disorder, and atypical psychosis). In addition, to

Table 12–5 Epidemiological Catchment Area Study Lifetime Prevalence Rate of Any Psychiatric Disorder

	N	Lifetime Prevalence (%)
Total	19,640	
Sex		
Men	8,419	36
Women	11,221	30
Age (y)		
<30	4,872	37
30–44	4,650	39
45–64	4,194	27
65+	5,912	21
Ethnicity		
White	13,091	32
Black	4,697	38
Hispanic	1,606	33
Education		
Not complete high school	8,818	36
High school or more	10,565	30
Occupational status of men (30–64 y)		
Total	3,452	35
Unemployed	774	48
Unskilled	599	40
Skilled or higher	2,061	30
Rural/urban		
Urban	4,694	34
Rural	2,107	32
Marital history		
Married and never divorced or separated	9,216	24
Single and never cohabited for 1 y	3,424	33
Ever divorced or separated	5,906	44
Unmarried and cohabited	986	52

address the ECA finding that psychotic disorders had poor reliability and validity when assessed by nonclinicians,[80, 81] NCS individuals endorsing psychotic symptoms in the survey were reinterviewed by telephone by a clinician with the Structured Clinical Interview for DSM-III-R.[16]

Table 12–7 presents the NCS 1-year and lifetime prevalence rates of the various psychiatric disorders. Lifetime prevalence rates are the proportion of individuals who ever experienced a disorder, and 1-year prevalence represents the proportion of individuals who experienced a disorder in the year before the interview. The lifetime prevalence for any DSM-III-R disorder was 48.7%, and the 12-month prevalence was 27.7%. When grouped into their larger category, the lifetime prevalence rates were 24.9% for anxiety disorder, 26.6% for substance abuse and dependence, and 19.3% for affective disorder. As expected, anxiety and affective disorders were more common in women, and substance abuse was more common in men.

An important focus of the NCS was the assessment of comorbidity. Interestingly, whereas 21% of the sample experienced only one disorder, 14% met criteria for three or more lifetime disorders. Furthermore, among individuals with a lifetime disorder, 53.9% had three or more lifetime disorders. Among individuals with a disorder occurring in the past 12 months, 58.9% experienced three or more disorders. The level of comorbidity was most dramatic for individuals with a severe disorder in the past 12 months, defined as active mania, nonaffective psychosis, or active disorder of other types that either resulted in hospitalization or created severe role impairment. In that subset of respondents, 89.5% had three or more disorders.

The findings on the demographical risk factors for each of these disorders suggested that in addition to gender, the expected pattern of associations was obtained. Specifically, affective disorders occurring in the past 12 months were more frequent in 15- to 24-year-olds, Hispanics, respondents with the lowest income, and respondents who had not graduated from college. Anxiety disorders occurred more frequently in 15- to 24-year-olds, respondents in the three lower income categories (less than $70,000 per annum), and those without a college degree. Substance abuse was found less frequently in African-Americans and more frequently in 15- to 44-year-olds, respondents earning $0 to $19,000 per annum, and non–college graduates. All of these risk factors were also associated with having three or more disorders. No significant results were found for region of the country where the respondent resided (e.g., the Midwest, Northeast, West, and South). However, although residing in a major metropolitan versus a rural area was not a risk factor for the individual disorders, respondents from major metropolitan areas were four times more likely than those from rural areas to have three or more disorders.

The NCS also examined the health services use patterns of the respondents. Only 40% of individuals with a mental disorder received professional care, and only 25% received their care in the mental health specialty sector. On the other hand, 60% of individuals with three or more comorbid disorders received professional help, 40% in the mental health specialty sector. Furthermore, one third of persons with three or more comorbid disorders received professional help in the past year compared with only 20% of those with one disorder. These findings indicate that the use of health services is concentrated in the segment of the population with a high degree of comorbidity.

Future Directions

The progress in enumerating the rates of mental disorders in adults in the general population, and documenting the extent of unmet need, has been extensive. Similar research on children is about to be undertaken. It should be borne in mind that the results of these studies are only as good as the instruments that are used for the assessment and the memories of the respondents who are asked to recall their internal states throughout their lifetimes. Until we have a means of verifying self-reports against a gold standard, these data will always be subject to criticism about measurement.[25]

Against this progress in descriptive epidemiology, there is a need to expand our knowledge from a clinical epidemiology perspective. Thus, whereas community stud-

Gender

Men

Women

0% 10% 20% 30% 40% 50% 60%

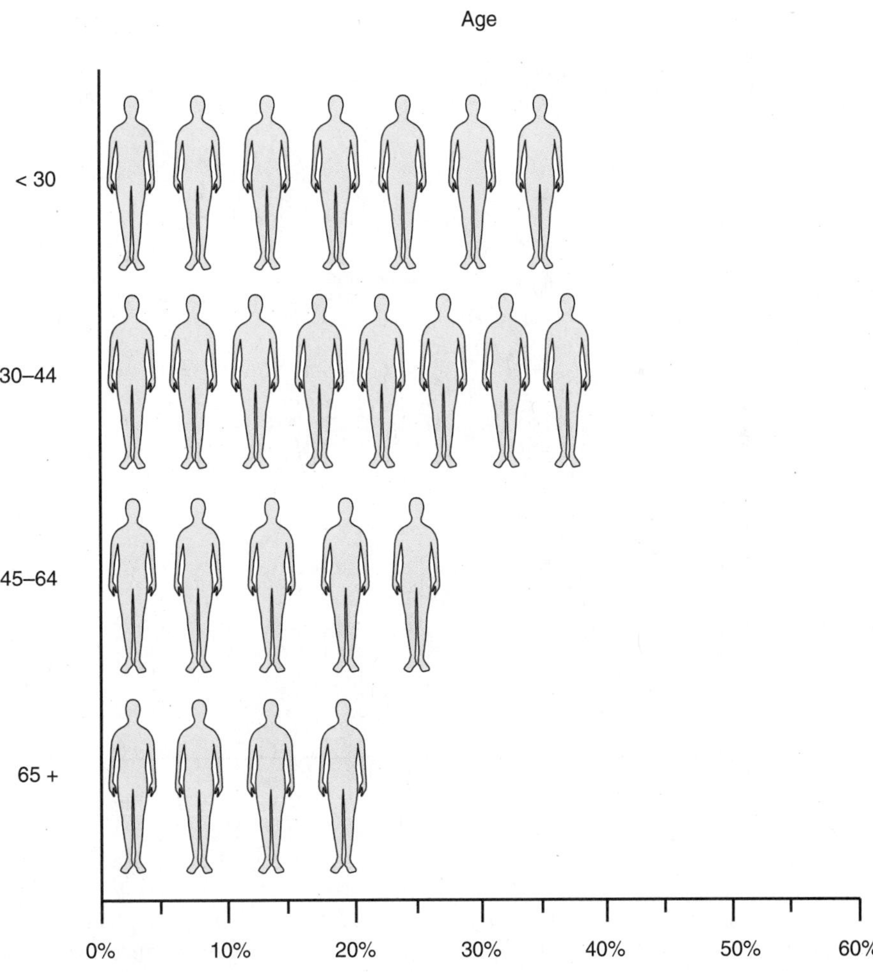

Figure 12–3 *Estimated lifetime prevalence rates of any psychiatric disorder at five ECA sites. (Data from Regier DA, Boyd JH, Burke JD Jr, et al: One-month prevalence of mental disorders in the United States. Based on five Epidemiologic Catchment Area sites. Arch Gen Psychiatry 1988; 45:977–986.)*

Illustration continued on following page

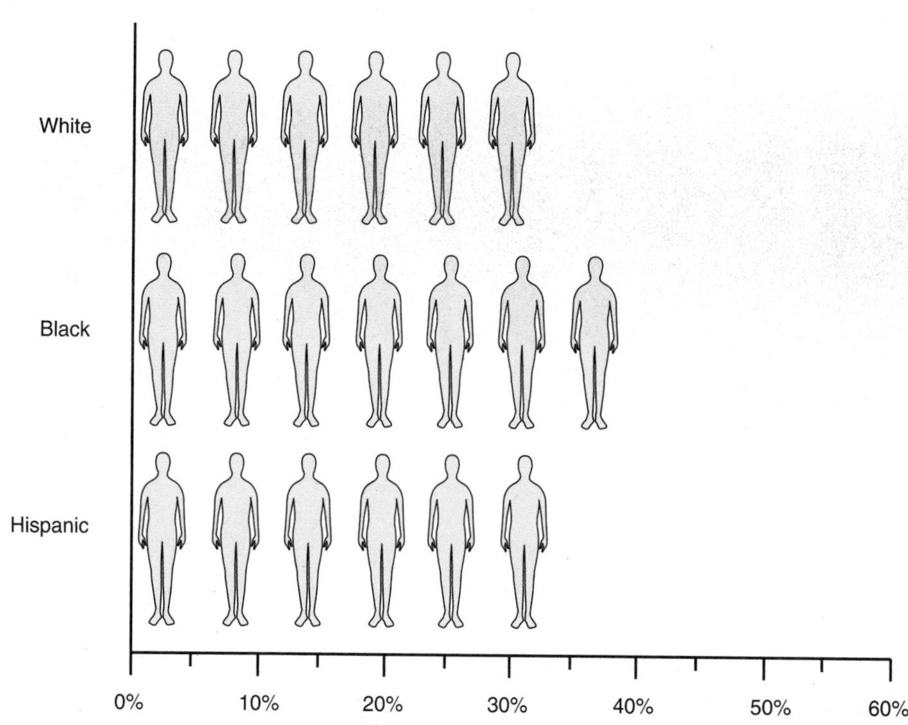

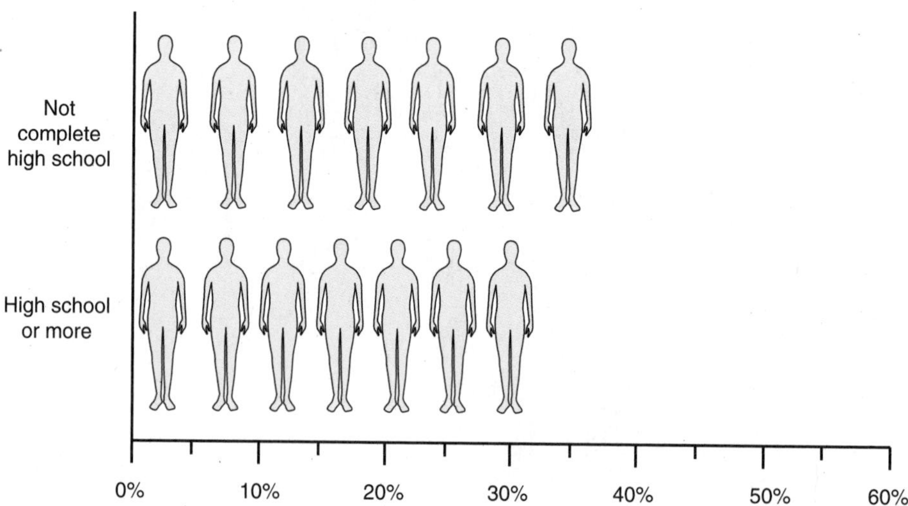

Figure 12-3 *Continued*

ies now use sophisticated sampling techniques and state-of-the-art assessment tools, many clinical studies of onset and course suffer from poor sampling schemes and psychometrically unproven measurement tools. Four specific issues need to be strengthened in clinical studies so that they can be regarded as epidemiologically informative. These include sampling strategies, incorporation of longitudinal diagnoses, obtaining good historical data on prior and current treatment experiences, and assessing the full range of biological and psychological risk factors.

Sampling

The majority of clinical studies rely on consecutive admissions rather than first-episode or even first-admission samples. This is a fundamental shortcoming because the samples are biased by chronically ill users of service.[92] Thus, conditions such as nonaffective acute remitting psychosis, found in patients in the first-contact study of the World Health Organization, have gone unnoticed in clinical research conducted in the United States.[93] To understand such basic issues as the course of alcohol abuse or the course of major depression, and the risk factors associated with better or worse prognosis, it is crucial to identify samples at the time of their first episode of disorder. Several studies of schizophrenia and other psychotic disorders have been undertaken that are a step in this direction. Some of these investigations enroll first-admission patients as study participants. Others are focused on the onset of disorder in children of mentally ill parents. Of course, both types of study design contain their own limitations, including variations in onset in the first-admission studies and sampling biases in the offspring studies. Nevertheless, to have a clearer understanding of the patterns of course and their risk factors, such research designs are crucial to implement.

Another epidemiologically important source of archival

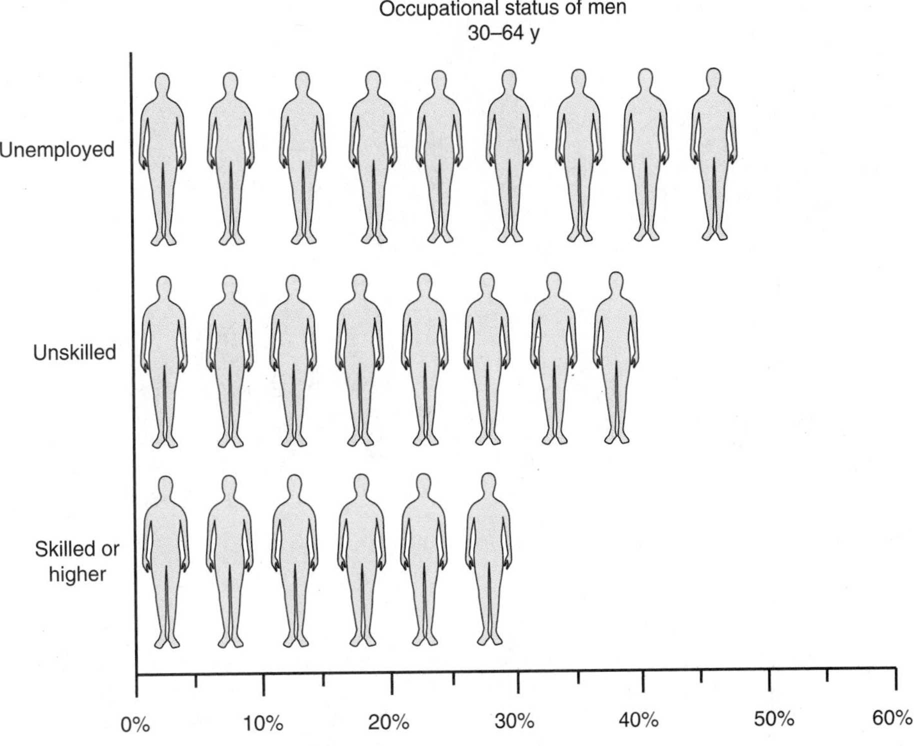

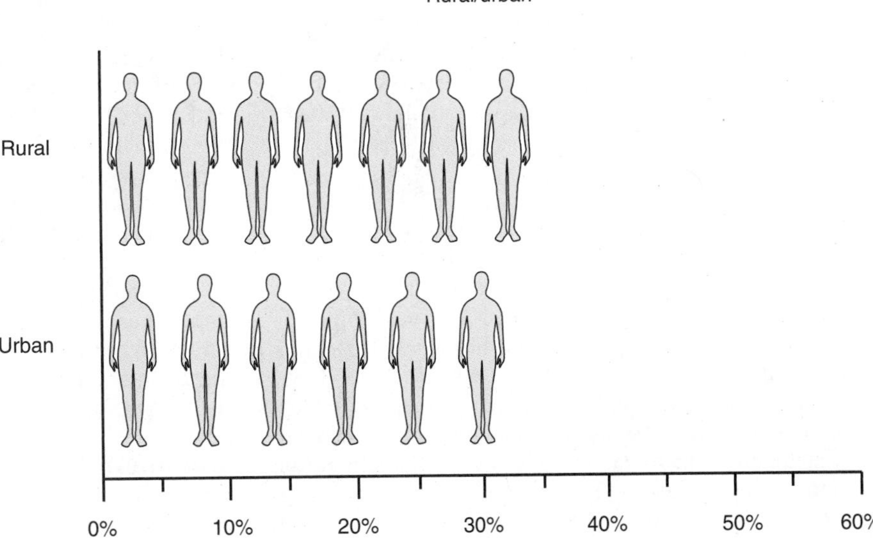

Figure 12-3 *Continued*

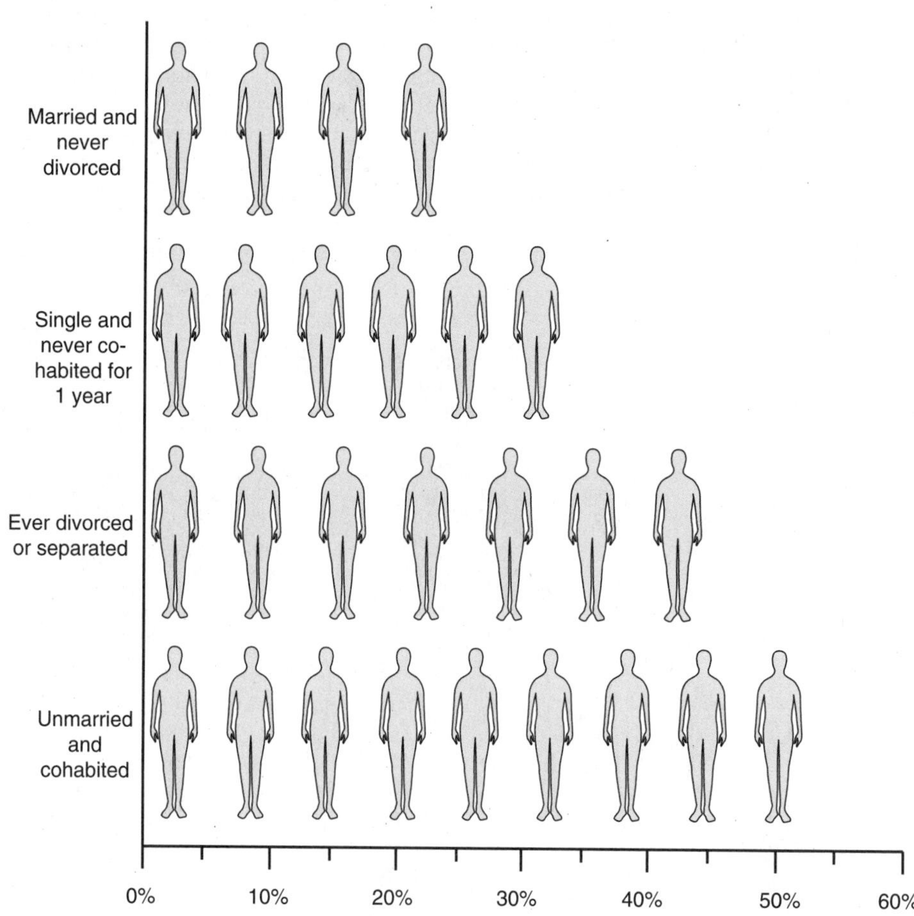

Figure 12-3 *Continued*

data derives from case registries. Although such registries rely on clinical diagnosis, and thus contain no information on reliability of measurement, Eaton and colleagues[94] have shown that they are extremely valuable sources of information for examining basic issues about risk of rehospitalization and mortality. In their study of four case registers (Victoria, Australia; Maryland, United States; Denmark; and Salford, England), they showed that more than 50% of the samples had one or more subsequent hospitalizations. Early age at onset was a significant predictor of rehospitalization, whereas sex and length of hospitalization did not have significant effects.

Diagnosis

In spite of evidence to the contrary,[95, 96] diagnostic decisions are thought to be more reliable in samples composed of chronically ill patients, in which structured assessments and informative records can be combined with information from relatives to form reasonably reliable diagnoses. However, when a sample is composed of first-admission or first-episode patients without extensive records, diagnoses may be far less reliable. One study found that the agreement between facility and research diagnosis of first-admission psychotic patients was low ($\kappa = .49$) and varied depending on the type of facility.[97] Better agreement was found between the researchers and the university facility than between researchers and the state facility, with the community hospitals falling between.

The initial research diagnosis in a first-admission sample may also be unstable. Fennig and coworkers[98] have shown that the initial diagnosis in a first-admission psychotic sample is difficult to determine (primarily because of substance abuse comorbidity) and can change over time. Thus, longitudinal approaches to diagnosis need to be implemented, as was done in the study by Tohen and colleagues[99, 100] of outcome in mania.

If a first-admission sample with a particular disorder is selected on the basis of a cross-sectional diagnosis, it will contain false-positives and exclude potential false-negatives. The false-positives are not a major problem because individuals later discovered to have a different disorder can be dropped from a study. The false-negatives are a greater impediment because they will have been excluded from the sample even though their symptom pattern might evolve into the disorder. Thus, longitudinal diagnoses are valuable from both perspectives.

Treatment Experiences

Considerable emphasis has been given to understanding the treatment needs of individuals in the general population who

Table 12–6 Epidemiological Catchment Area Study Mental Health Visits in Service Sector in 1 Year

Diagnosis	Proportion with Mental Health Visits (%)
Any Diagnostic Interview Schedule–DSM-III disorder	28.5
Any Diagnostic Interview Schedule–DSM-III disorder except substance abuse	31.9
Any mental disorder with comorbid substance use	37.4
Substance use disorder	23.6
Alcohol abuse and dependence	22.0
Drug abuse and dependence	29.8
Schizophrenia and schizophreniform disorders	64.3
Affective disorders	45.7
Manic episode	60.9
Major depressive episode	53.9
Dysthymia	42.1
Anxiety disorders	32.7
Phobia	31.1
Panic	58.8
Obsessive-compulsive disorder	45.1
Somatization disorder	69.7
Antisocial personality	31.1
Severe cognitive impairment	17.0

From Regier DA, Narrow WE, Rae DS, et al: The de facto US mental and addictive disorders service system: Epidemiologic Catchment Area prospective 1-year prevalence rates of disorders and services. Arch Gen Psychiatry 1993; 50:85–94.

are found to have diagnosable mental disorders and to characterizing the treatment experiences of the chronically mentally ill. Ironically, we have little information on the pathways into and through formal and nontraditional sources of care. Because clinical research has shown that adherence to a treatment protocol is the most important risk factor for recovery, an important way to improve our ability to predict illness course is to integrate treatment experiences into the prognostic equation.

Risk Factors

Most epidemiological studies have relied on psychosocial and demographical risk factors and failed to consider potential familial and biological variables. Progress has been made to integrate familial variables, although the sources of information on familial mental disorders have often been meager and inadequate. Biological research has often relied on small, clinically diagnosed samples. It seems timely to integrate the two types of research under a single umbrella.

Conclusion

The ultimate goal of epidemiology is to identify the causes of disease to provide information useful to disease prevention. Current studies of mental disorders in children, adults, and elderly persons have made considerable progress in methods for defining disorders reliably. Understanding the risk factors for these disorders, and the efficacy of different treatment protocols for alleviating their morbidity, is required for the development of effective public health education and treatment programs.[101]

Table 12–7 National Comorbidity Survey Lifetime and 12-Month Prevalence Rates (%)

Disorders	Male Lifetime Rate	Male 12-Month Rate	Female Lifetime Rate	Female 12-Month Rate	Total Lifetime Rate	Total 12-Month Rate
Affective disorders						
Major depressive episode	12.7	7.7	21.3	12.9	17.1	10.3
Manic episode	1.6	1.4	1.7	1.3	1.6	1.3
Dysthymia	4.8	2.1	8.0	3.0	6.4	2.5
Anxiety disorders						
Panic disorder	2.0	1.3	5.0	3.2	3.5	2.3
Agoraphobia without panic disorder	3.5	1.7	7.0	3.8	5.3	2.8
Social phobia	11.1	6.6	15.5	9.1	13.3	7.9
Simple phobia	6.7	4.4	15.7	13.2	11.3	8.8
Generalized anxiety disorder	3.6	2.0	6.6	4.3	5.1	3.1
Substance use disorders						
Alcohol abuse without dependence	12.5	3.4	6.4	1.6	9.4	2.5
Alcohol dependence	20.1	10.7	8.2	3.7	14.1	7.2
Drug abuse without dependence	5.4	1.3	3.5	0.3	4.4	0.8
Drug dependence	9.2	3.8	5.9	1.9	7.5	2.8
Any substance abuse and dependence	35.4	16.1	17.9	6.6	26.6	11.3
Nonaffective psychosis*	0.6	0.5	0.8	0.6	0.7	0.5
Any National Comorbidity Survey disorder	48.7	27.7	47.3	31.2	48.0	29.5

* Schizophrenia, schizophreniform disorder, schizoaffective disorder, delusional disorder, and atypical psychosis.

References

1. The President's Commission on Mental Health: Report to the President from the President's Commission on Mental Health. Washington, DC: U.S. Government Printing Office, 1978.
2. Tsuang MT, Tohen M, Zahner G (eds): Textbook in Psychiatric Epidemiology. New York: John Wiley & Sons, 1995.
3. Robins LN: Psychiatric epidemiology. Arch Gen Psychiatry 1978; 35:697–702.
4. Weissman MM, Klerman GL: Epidemiology of mental disorders: Emerging trends in the United States. Arch Gen Psychiatry 1978; 35:705–712.
5. Bromet EJ: Research training in psychiatric epidemiology and biostatistics. Int J Methods Psychiatr Res, in press.
6. Regier DA, Goldberg ID, Taube CA: The de facto US mental health service system: A public health perspective. Arch Gen Psychiatry 1978; 35:685–693.
7. Cooper JE, Kendell RE, Gurland BJ, et al: Psychiatric Diagnosis in New York and London: A Comparative Study of Mental Hospital Admissions. Institute of Psychiatry, Maudsley Monographs 20. London: Oxford University Press, 1972.
8. Endicott J, Spitzer RL: A diagnostic interview: The Schedule for Affective Disorders and Schizophrenia. Arch Gen Psychiatry 1978; 35:837–844.
9. Spitzer RL, Endicott J, Robins E: Research diagnostic criteria: Rationale and reliability. Arch Gen Psychiatry 1978; 35:773–782.
10. Katz MM, Secunda SK, Hirschfeld RMA, Koslow SH: NIMH clinical research branch collaborative program on the psychobiology of depression. Arch Gen Psychiatry 1979; 36:765–771.
11. Weissman MM, Myers JK, Harding PS: Psychiatric disorders in a U.S. urban community: 1975–1976. Am J Psychiatry 1978; 135:459–461.
12. Bromet EJ, Parkinson DK, Schulberg HC, et al: Mental health of residents near the Three Mile Island reactor: A comparative study of selected groups. J Prev Psychiatry 1982; 1:225–276.
13. Orvaschel H: Psychiatric interviews suitable for use in research with children and adolescents. Psychopharmacol Bull 1985; 21:737–745.
14. Wing JK, Cooper JE, Sartorius N: Measure and Classification of Psychiatric Symptoms: An Instructional Manual for the PSE and CATEGO Programs. Cambridge, UK: Cambridge University Press, 1974.
15. Wing JK, Babor T, Brugha T, et al: SCAN: Schedule for Clinical Assessment in Neuropsychiatry. Arch Gen Psychiatry 1990; 47:589–593.
16. Spitzer RL, Williams JBW, Gibbon M, First MB: The Structured Clinical Interview for DSM-III-R (SCID). I: History, rationale, and description. Arch Gen Psychiatry 1992; 49:624–629.
17. Nurnberger JI, Blehar MC, Kaufman CA, et al: Diagnostic Interview for Genetic Studies. Rationale, unique features and training. Arch Gen Psychiatry 1994; 51:849–859.
18. Robins LN, Helzer JE, Croughan JL, Ratcliff KS: National Institute of Mental Health Diagnostic Interview Schedule: Its history, characteristics, and validity. Arch Gen Psychiatry 1981; 38:381–389.
19. Regier DA, Myers JK, Kramer M, et al: The NIMH Epidemiologic Catchment Area (ECA) Program: Historical context, major objectives, and study population characteristics. Arch Gen Psychiatry 1984; 41:934–941.
20. World Health Organization: Composite International Diagnostic Interview (CIDI), Version 1.0. Geneva: World Health Organization, 1990.
21. Wittchen H-U, Robins LN, Cottler LB, et al: Cross-cultural feasibility, reliability and sources of variance in the Composite International Diagnostic Interview (CIDI). Br J Psychiatry 1991; 159:645–653.
22. Kessler RC, McGonagle KA, Zhao S, et al: Lifetime and 12-month prevalence of DSM-III-R psychiatric disorders in the United States: Results from the National Comorbidity Survey. Arch Gen Psychiatry 1994; 51:8–19.
23. Costello E, Costello A, Edelbrock C, et al: Psychiatric disorders in pediatric primary care. Arch Gen Psychiatry 1988; 45:1107–1116.
24. Jensen P, Roper M, Fisher P, et al: Test-retest reliability of the Diagnostic Interview Schedule for Children (DISC 2.1). Arch Gen Psychiatry 1995; 52:61–71.
25. Fennig S, Bromet E: Issues of memory in the Diagnostic Interview Schedule. J Nerv Ment Dis 1992; 180:223–224.
26. Institute of Medicine: Research on Children and Adolescents with Mental, Behavioral, and Developmental Disorders: Mobilizing a National Initiative. Washington, DC: National Academy Press, 1989.
27. Regier DA, Boyd JH, Burke JD Jr, et al: One-month prevalence of mental disorders in the United States. Based on five Epidemiologic Catchment Area sites. Arch Gen Psychiatry 1988; 45:977–986.
28. MacMahon B, Pugh TF: Epidemiology: Principles and Methods. Boston: Little, Brown, 1970.
29. Graunt S: Natural and Political Observations . . . Made upon the Bills of Mortality. Baltimore: The Johns Hopkins University Press, 1939. Originally published in 1662.
30. Snow J: On the mode of communication of cholera. In Snow on Cholera. New York: The Commonwealth Fund, 1936. Originally published in 1855.
31. Lilienfeld DE, Stolley PD: Foundations of Epidemiology, 3rd ed. New York: Oxford University Press, 1994.
32. Weiss NS: Clinical Epidemiology. New York: Oxford University Press, 1985.
33. Sackett DL, Haynes RB, Tugwell P: Clinical Epidemiology. Boston: Little, Brown, 1985.
34. Beiser M, Iacono WG, Erickson D: Temporal stability in the major mental disorders. In Robins LN, Barrett JE (eds): The Validity of Psychiatric Diagnosis. New York: Raven Press, 1989:77–98.
35. Bromet EJ, Schwartz JE, Fennig S, et al: The epidemiology of psychosis: The Suffolk County Mental Health Project. Schizophr Bull 1992; 18:243–255.
36. Tohen M, Stoll AL, Strakowski SM, et al: The McLean First-Episode Psychosis Project: Six-month recovery and recurrence outcome. Schizophr Bull 1992; 18:273–282.
37. Selvin S: Statistical Analysis of Epidemiologic Data. New York: Oxford University Press, 1991.
38. Eaton WW, Anthony JC, Tepper S, Dryman A: Psychopathology and attrition in the Epidemiologic Catchment Area Study. Am J Epidemiol 1992; 135:1051–1059.
39. Rothman KJ: Modern Epidemiology. Boston: Little, Brown, 1986.
40. Miettinen OS: Theoretical Epidemiology. New York: John Wiley & Sons, 1985.
41. Merikangas KR: The genetic epidemiology of alcoholism. Psychol Med 1990; 20:11–22.
42. Penkower L, Bromet EJ, Dew MA: Husbands' layoff and wives' mental health: A prospective analysis. Arch Gen Psychiatry 1988; 45:994–1000.
43. Paykel ES, Myers JK, Dienelt MN, et al: Life events and depression: A controlled study. Arch Gen Psychiatry 1969; 21:753–760.
44. Robins LN: Deviant Children Grown Up. Baltimore: Williams & Wilkins, 1966.
45. Ciompi L: The natural history of schizophrenia in the long term. Br J Psychiatry 1980; 136:413–420.
46. Solomon Z: Combat Stress Reaction: The Enduring Toll of War. New York: Plenum Publishing, 1993.
47. Crow TJ, Done DJ: Prenatal exposure to influenza does not cause schizophrenia. Br J Psychiatry 1992; 161:390–393.
48. Hagnell O, Lanke J, Rorsman B, Ojesjo L: Are we entering the age of melancholy? Depressive illnesses in a prospective epidemiological study over 25 years: The Lundby Study, Sweden. Psychol Med 1982; 12:279–289.
49. Vaillant GE: The Natural History of Alcoholism. Cambridge, MA: Harvard University Press, 1983.
50. Monson RR: Occupational Epidemiology. Boca Raton, FL: CRC Press, 1980.
51. Halbreich U, Bakhai Y, Bacon K, et al: The normalcy of self-proclaimed "normal volunteers." Am J Psychiatry 1989; 146:1052–1055.
52. Parkinson DK, Ryan C, Bromet EJ, Connell MM: A psychiatric epidemiologic study of occupational lead exposure. Am J Epidemiol 1986; 123:261–269.
53. Dohrenwend BP, Dohrenwend BS: Perspectives on the past and future of psychiatric epidemiology: The 1981 Rema Lapouse lecture. Am J Public Health 1982; 72:1271–1279.
54. Jarvis E: Insanity and Idiocy in Massachusetts: Report of the Commission on Lunacy, 1855. Cambridge, MA: Harvard University Press, 1971.
55. Terris M (ed): Goldberger on Pellagra. Baton Rouge, LA: Louisiana State University Press, 1964.
56. Faris REL, Dunham HW: Mental Disorders in Urban Areas: An Ecological Study of Schizophrenia and Other Psychoses. Chicago: University of Chicago Press, 1939.

57. Grinker K, Spiegel S: Men Under Stress. Philadelphia: Blakiston, 1945.
58. Srole L, Langner S, Michael ST, et al: Mental Health in the Metropolis: The Midtown Manhattan Study. New York: McGraw-Hill, 1962.
59. Leighton DC, Harding JS, Macklin DB, et al: Psychiatric findings of the Stirling County Study. Am J Psychiatry 1963; 119:1021–1026.
60. Gurin G, Veroff J, Feld J: Americans View Their Mental Health. New York: Basic Books, 1960.
61. Hollingshead A, Redlich FS: Social Class and Mental Illness. New York: John Wiley & Sons, 1958.
62. Myers JK, Lindenthal JJ, Pepper MP: Life events and psychiatric impairment. J Nerv Ment Dis 1971; 152:149–157.
63. Robins E, Guze SB: Establishment of diagnostic validity in psychiatric illness: Its applications to schizophrenia. Am J Psychiatry 1970; 126:983–988.
64. Feighner JP, Robins E, Guze SB, et al: Diagnostic criteria for use in psychiatric research. Arch Gen Psychiatry 1972; 26:57–63.
65. Regier DA, Boyd JH, Burke JD: One-month prevalence of mental disorders in the United States based on five Epidemiologic Catchment Area sites. Arch Gen Psychiatry 1985; 45:977–986.
66. Robins LN, Locke BZ, Regier DA: An overview of psychiatric disorders in America. In Robins LN, Regier DA (eds): Psychiatric Disorders in America: The Epidemiologic Catchment Area Study. New York: Free Press, 1991:328–366.
67. Kulka RA, Schlenger WE, Fairbank JA, et al: Trauma and the Vietnam War Generation: Report of Findings from the National Vietnam Veterans Readjustment Study. New York: Brunner/Mazel, 1990.
68. Bromet EJ, Parkinson DK, Curtis EC, et al: Epidemiology of depression and alcohol abuse/dependence in a managerial and professional work force. J Occup Med 1990; 32:989–995.
69. Dohrenwend BP, Levav I, Shrout PE, et al: Socioeconomic status and psychiatric disorders: The causation-selection issue. Science 1992; 255:946–952.
70. Levav I, Kohn R, Dohrenwend BP, et al: An epidemiological study of mental disorders in a 10-year cohort of young adults in Israel. Psychol Med 1993; 23:691–707.
71. Turner RJ, Marino F: Social support and social structure: A descriptive epidemiology. J Health Soc Behav 1994; 35:193–212.
72. Rutter M: Isle of Wight studies, 1964–1974. Psychol Med 1976; 6:313–332.
73. Offord DR, Boyle MH, Szatmari P, et al: Ontario Child Health Study. II. Six-month prevalence of disorder and rates of service utilization. Arch Gen Psychiatry 1987; 44:832–836.
74. Velez CN, Johnson J, Cohen P: A longitudinal analysis of selected risk factors for childhood psychopathology. J Am Acad Child Adolesc Psychiatry 1989; 28:861–864.
75. Bird HR, Canino G, Rubio-Stipec M, Gould MS: Estimates of the prevalence of childhood maladjustment in a community survey in Puerto Rico. Arch Gen Psychiatry 1988; 45:1120–1126.
76. Anderson J, Williams W, McGee R, Silva P: Cognitive and social correlates of DSM-III disorders in preadolescent children. J Am Acad Child Adolesc Psychiatry 1989; 28:842–846.
77. Fombonne E: The Chartres Study: I. Prevalence of psychiatric disorders among French school-aged children. Br J Psychiatry 1994; 164:69–79.
78. Costello EJ: Developments in child psychiatric epidemiology. J Am Acad Child Adolesc Psychiatry 1989; 28:836–841.
79. American Psychiatric Association: Diagnostic and Statistical Manual of Mental Disorders, 3rd ed. Washington, DC: American Psychiatric Press, 1980.
80. Helzer JE, Robins LN, McEvoy LT, et al: A comparison of clinical and diagnostic interview schedule diagnoses. Arch Gen Psychiatry 1985; 42:657–666.
81. Anthony JC, Folstein M, Romanoski MR, et al: Comparison of the lay Diagnostic Interview Schedule and a standardized psychiatric diagnosis. Arch Gen Psychiatry 1985; 42:667–675.
82. Regier DA, Kaelber R: ECA study. In Tsuang MT, Tohen M, Zahner G (eds): Textbook in Psychiatric Epidemiology. New York: John Wiley & Sons, 1995.
83. Leaf PJ, Myers JK, McEvoy LT: Procedures used in the Epidemiologic Catchment Area study. In Robins LN, Regier DA (eds): Psychiatric Disorders in America. New York: Free Press, 1991:11–32.
84. Regier DA, Narrow WE, Rae DS, et al: The de facto US mental and addictive disorders service system: Epidemiologic Catchment Area prospective 1-year prevalence rates of disorders and services. Arch Gen Psychiatry 1993; 50:85–94.
85. Eaton WW, Kramer M, Anthony JC, et al: The incidence of specific DIS/DSM-III mental disorders: Data from the NIMH Epidemiologic Catchment Area Program. Acta Psychiatr Scand 1992; 79:163–178.
86. Narrow WE, Regier DA, Rae DS, et al: Use of services: Findings from the National Institute of Mental Health Epidemiologic Catchment Area Program. Arch Gen Psychiatry 1993; 50:95–107.
87. Kessler LG, Burns BJ, Shapiro S, et al: Psychiatric diagnoses of medical service users: Evidence from the Epidemiologic Catchment Area Program. Am J Public Health 1987; 77:18–24.
88. Regier DA, Farmer ME, Rae DS, et al: Comorbidity of mental health disorders with alcohol and other drug abuse. JAMA 1990; 264:2511–2518.
89. Berkson J: Limitations of the application of fourfold table analysis to hospital data. Biometrics 1946; 2:47–53.
90. Tohen M, Goodwin FK: Epidemiology of bipolar disorder. In Tsuang MT, Tohen M, Zahner GW (eds): Textbook in Psychiatric Epidemiology. New York: John Wiley & Sons, 1995.
91. Tohen M: Bipolar Disorder and Comorbid Substance Use. The Decade of the Brain, Volume 5. New York: The National Alliance of the Mentally Ill, 1994:1–2.
92. Cohen P, Cohen J: The clinician's illusion. Arch Gen Psychiatry 1984; 41:1178–1183.
93. Susser E, Wanderling J: Epidemiology of nonaffective acute remitting psychosis vs schizophrenia. Arch Gen Psychiatry 1994; 51:294–301.
94. Eaton WW, Mortensen PB, Herrman H, et al: Long-term course of hospitalization for schizophrenia. Part I. Risk for rehospitalization. Schizophr Bull 1992; 18:217–228.
95. Lipton AA, Simon FS: Psychiatric diagnosis in a state hospital: Manhattan State revisited. Hosp Community Psychiatry 1985; 36:368–373.
96. Mukherjee S, Shukla S, Woodle J, et al: Misdiagnosis of schizophrenia in bipolar patients: A multiethnic comparison. Am J Psychiatry 1983; 140:1571–1574.
97. Fennig S, Craig TJ, Karant M, Bromet E: A comparison of facility and research diagnoses in first admission psychotic patients. Am J Psychiatry 1994; 151:1423–1429.
98. Fennig S, Kovasznay B, Rich C, et al: Six-month stability of psychiatric diagnoses in first-admission patients with psychosis. Am J Psychiatry 1994; 151:1200–1208.
99. Tohen M, Waternaux CM, Tsuang MT: Outcome in mania: A four-year prospective follow-up of 75 patients utilizing survival analysis. Arch Gen Psychiatry 1990; 47:1106–1111.
100. Tohen M, Tsuang MT, Goodwin DC: Prediction of outcome in mania by mood-congruent or mood-incongruent psychotic features. Am J Psychiatry 1992; 149:1580–1584.
101. Cooper B: Single spies and battalions: The clinical epidemiology of mental disorders. Psychol Med 1993; 23:891–907.

CHAPTER

13 Genetics

Janet L. Sobell
Steve S. Sommer

Each year, many thousands of original publications expand our knowledge of human genetics. An increasing number of these papers use the powerful new tools of molecular biology that are revolutionizing our understanding of biology. Clinical genetics, the medical application of human genetics, has traditionally focused on rare single-gene or congenital diseases. However, advances indicate that human genetics will provide many medically relevant insights for almost all disease, including psychiatric illness. These insights will increasingly result in 1) disease reclassification based on molecular etiology; 2) targeted prevention strategies; 3) novel diagnostic strategies; and 4) gene-based therapies. As a by-product, the focus of clinical medicine will necessarily shift from the current focus on disease diagnosis and treatment in individual patients to the prevention of disease in genetically predisposed families.

The goal of this chapter is to provide the reader with certain core information to help in critically reviewing the psychiatric genetics literature. The material is presented in five parts: 1) basic human genetics; 2) introduction to psychiatric genetics; 3) molecular (DNA) diagnosis; 4) selected laboratory methodology; and 5) summary and future directions. The interested reader may supplement the information herein by consulting a diversity of excellent texts and review articles that frequently appear in the medical literature (see bibliography).

Basic Human Genetics

Selected core concepts are presented in this section and in the glossary after the text of the chapter. All terms included in the glossary are italicized when they are initially used in the text or in the definition of other terms in the glossary; additional terms are also included so that the glossary can serve as a broader resource.

The human genome, contained in all nucleated cells, is composed of some 100,000 *genes,* of which only a small minority have been characterized. Nucleated cells contain two copies of the genome (diploid cells) except for oocytes and sperm, which contain one copy (haploid cells), and megakaryocytes and striated muscle cells, which contain multiple copies (polyploid or multinucleated cells). Genes are encoded for by duplex *deoxyribonucleic acid (DNA),* which forms a double helical structure (Fig. 13–1). The backbone of each strand of the helix consists of a deoxyribose sugar molecule and phosphates. One of four nitrogen-containing bases (*nucleotides* or *base pairs:* adenine, thymine, cytosine, and guanine) is attached to each sugar ring. The nucleotides "base pair" by hydrogen bonds to one another (adenine pairs with thymine, and guanine pairs with cytosine) to form the double helix. From this DNA template, genes are expressed by *transcription* of one strand of the DNA into *ribonucleic acid (RNA),* processing of the RNA to mature *messenger RNA (mRNA),* and *translation* of the mRNA into a protein product. The translation process involves "reading" the nucleotide code in which units of three bases *(codons)* encode for a specific *amino acid* or a termination signal (stop or *termination codon*). The translation of these nucleotide codons results in the creation of a specific protein product (i.e., polypeptide or amino acid chain) for each gene. Gene transcription and translation are often tissue-specific; for example, tyrosine hydroxylase is expressed primarily in brain and adrenal glands, whereas phenylalanine hydroxylase is expressed primarily in liver. The processes of transcription and translation are highly regulated, involving myriad chemical signals, such as transcription factors.

In mammalian genes, the actual DNA template includes regions that code for the protein product, regulatory regions that are involved in gene expression, and intervening sequences *(introns).* During RNA processing, the introns are spliced out; thus, the mature mRNA includes nucleotides that code for the protein product plus flanking regions that may contain regulatory sequences but are not translated into protein (*5′ and 3′* untranslated regions). The sequences that are retained in the mature mRNA are referred to as *exons.*

The 100,000 or so human genes are arrayed at specific points, or *loci,* on the 23 pairs of chromosomes. Humans have 22 pairs of *autosomes* plus the sex chromosomes, XX for females and XY for males. Alternative forms of a gene at the same *locus* are known as *alleles.* Alleles at a given locus may be identical *(homozygous)* or different *(heterozygous).* Other selected aspects of the human genome structure are presented in Table 13–1.

Inherited genetic diseases can be categorized mechanistically into three broad groups: chromosomal aberrations, single-gene defects, and *multifactorial* diseases. In chromosomal anomalies, many genes arrayed on a chromosome may be lost, gained, or translocated. Examples of chromosomally mediated diseases include Turner's syndrome (loss of one X chromosome in females) and Down's syndrome or trisomy 21 (extra copy of chromosome 21).

Mutations that disrupt the normal function of single genes may produce diseases with classical *mendelian* inheritance. Several thousand severe single-gene disorders with autosomal dominant, autosomal recessive, or sex-linked inheritance have been described and are estimated to affect 125 per 10,000 live births.[1] In addition, defects in nonnuclear mitochondrial genes are responsible for a few

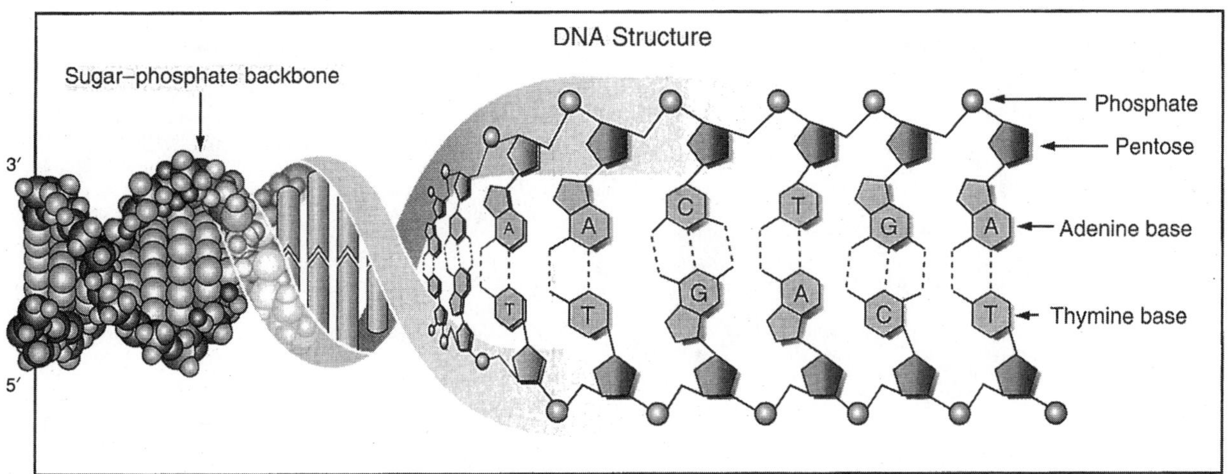

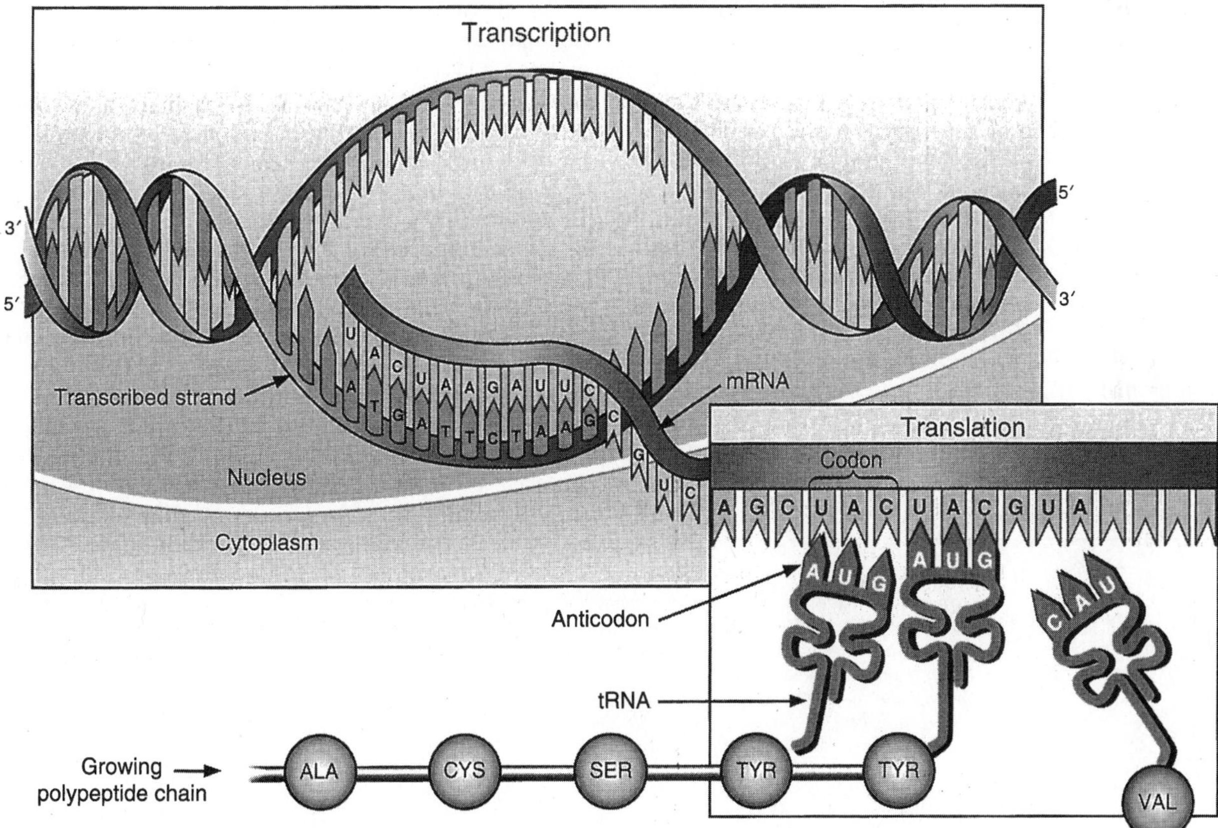

Figure 13–1 *DNA structure, transcription, and translation.* (A) *Depiction of the double-stranded DNA helix; the enlargement displays base pairing of the nitrogenous bases (guanine [G] with cytosine [C] and adenine [A] with thymine [T]). The bases face inward from the sugar (pentose)–phosphate backbone.* (B) *Depiction of transcription in the nucleus and translation in the cytoplasm. Transcription, proceeding from the 5′ end to the 3′ end, creates a complementary heterogeneous RNA (hnRNA) copy from one DNA strand, and introns are spliced from the hnRNA (not shown) to produce messenger RNA (mRNA). Note that RNA has uracil (U) paired to adenine in place of thymine. The mRNA serves as a template for translation by transfer RNA (tRNA) of the nucleotide codons into a polypeptide chain.* (A and B *from Rosenthal N: DNA and the genetic code. N Engl J Med 1994; 331:39–41. Reprinted by permission of The New England Journal of Medicine. Copyright 1994, Massachusetts Medical Society.)*

Table 13–1 Selected Aspects of Mammalian Genome Structure

The number of chromosomes in mammals can vary markedly by more than a factor of 10, but total genome size is similar (about 3×10^9 base pairs).
About 10% of all genes are on the X chromosome, whereas only a few genes are on the Y chromosome; almost all, if not all, genes on the X chromosome of one mammal are on the X chromosome of another mammal.
There are 30,000–100,000 genes in mammals.
About 3% of the genome contains protein coding sequences.
Genes in the same metabolic pathway are generally scattered throughout the genome.
Most genes are interrupted by introns, which typically account for about 95% of the gene sequence.
The average percentage of guanine and cytosine nucleotides (G + C content) is 40%, but *isochores* of higher G + C content exist.
Genes are preferentially found in high G + C isochores (up to 80% G + C).
About 70% of the genome is unique sequence, 20% is moderately repetitive, and 10% is highly repetitive.
In primates, the two most abundant repetitive sequences (*Alu* and *Line 1*) and many *pseudogenes,* which compose about 10% of the human genome, are the result of past retrotransposition events.
Centromeres and *telomeres* are composed of highly repeated simple sequences.
Microsatellites, composed of tandem repetitive sequences of 2 or 3 base pairs, are greatly enriched in the human genome and are often highly polymorphic.
The *mutation* rate of microsatellites generally increases with an increasing number of repeated units; once a certain threshold of size is reached, the microsatellite becomes unstable, i.e., the size often increases manyfold and the germline mutation rate approaches 1.0.
Polymerase slippage events may be the major cause of nonrandomness in genome sequence; among the important practical consequences of polymerase slippage are 1) diseases of trinucleotide repeats (e.g., Huntington's chorea); 2) the generation of high frequencies of *minisatellite* and microsatellite sequences; and 3) the rapid mutation of minisatellite and microsatellite sequences, which then provides highly informative polymorphic markers useful in gene mapping and in DNA-based disease diagnosis.
Most CpG dinucleotides are *methylated* and highly susceptible to mutation.
"CpG islands," which are found at the beginning of many genes, have a high G + C content and a high frequency of unmethylated CpG dinucleotides.

inherited diseases (e.g., Leber's hereditary optic atrophy). Mitochondria reside in the cellular cytoplasm, and their genomes are transmitted maternally through ova (i.e., sperm do not contribute mitochondria to the zygote). Pedigrees illustrating each of these forms of inheritance are presented in Figure 13–2; in addition, an example of genomic *imprinting,* in which disease occurrence or disease severity is dependent on whether the aberrant gene was inherited maternally or paternally, is included. Four common confounders of segregation are also illustrated: consanguinity, incomplete *penetrance,* new *mutation,* and *assortative mating.* It is useful to bear these segregation patterns in mind while ascertaining family histories in patients.

Although each gene typically codes for a single protein product, different mutations in the gene may result in different diseases. The exact genetic configuration of an individual *(genotype)* produces the observable traits *(phenotype).* For example, depending on the particular mutation in the β-globin gene, diseases as diverse as sickle cell anemia, congenital cyanosis, or hereditary polycythemia may result (Table 13–2). Likewise, detailed study generally reveals that one disease phenotype results from mutations in different single genes; for example, the hemophilia phenotype may be due to mutations in factor VIII, factor IX, or the factor VIII binding site of von Willebrand's factor (see Table 13–2).

The overwhelming majority of common human diseases are the result neither of single-gene mendelian inheritance, or transmission, nor of mitochondrial transmission. Rather, they are multifactorial and, most likely, genetically heterogeneous in nature (Table 13–3). Multifactorial connotes that the disease is the result of the action of several, or even many, predisposing genes plus "environmental" factors (the term environmental is necessarily

Figure 13–2 *Segregation patterns for single-gene disease. Squares indicate males, circles indicate females, and triangles indicate stillbirths or spontaneous abortions. Solid symbols indicate individuals with disease, and for didactic purposes, half-shaded symbols indicate* carriers. *In clinical situations, carrier status is usually unknown, so the pattern of inheritance must be inferred from the available family structure data. Pedigree I, autosomal dominant inheritance. The probability of transmitting the disease to an offspring is 50%; males and females are affected with equal likelihood. Pedigree II, autosomal recessive inheritance. On average, one in four is affected as a result of matings between two carriers who do not have the illness; family members outside of the sibship are rarely affected. Pedigree III, X-linked recessive inheritance. The disease appears in males who receive the defective gene from their generally asymptomatic carrier mothers;* male-to-male transmission rules out X-linked inheritance. *Pedigree IV, Y-linked inheritance. Male to male inheritance occurs; 100% of male offspring will inherit the defective gene. Pedigree V, mitochondrial inheritance. Mitochondria are maternally inherited, so all offspring of affected females are affected; in practice,* heteroplasmy *produces marked variation in disease severity among family members. Pedigree VI, imprinting. In this example, only the maternal copy of the gene is expressed; if the maternal copy is mutated, disease occurs. The following pedigrees illustrate confounders of the segregation pattern. Pedigree VII, consanguinity. In this pedigree, an X-linked disease such as hemophilia A occurs in a female owing to consanguineous mating. Pedigree VIII, incomplete penetrance. The disease gene is inherited, but disease expression is prevented because of modifying effects of environmental factors or other genes; incomplete penetrance is especially common in autosomal dominant disease. Pedigree IX, new mutation. New mutations are commonly found in individuals with severe sex-linked or autosomal dominant disease; these mutations are generally eliminated within a few generations, whereas autosomal recessive mutations are generally thousands of years old. Pedigree X, assortative mating. Nonrandom mating in which selection of a mate is based partially on the genotype of interest. The pedigree shows nonrandom or assortative mating for an autosomal dominant trait.*

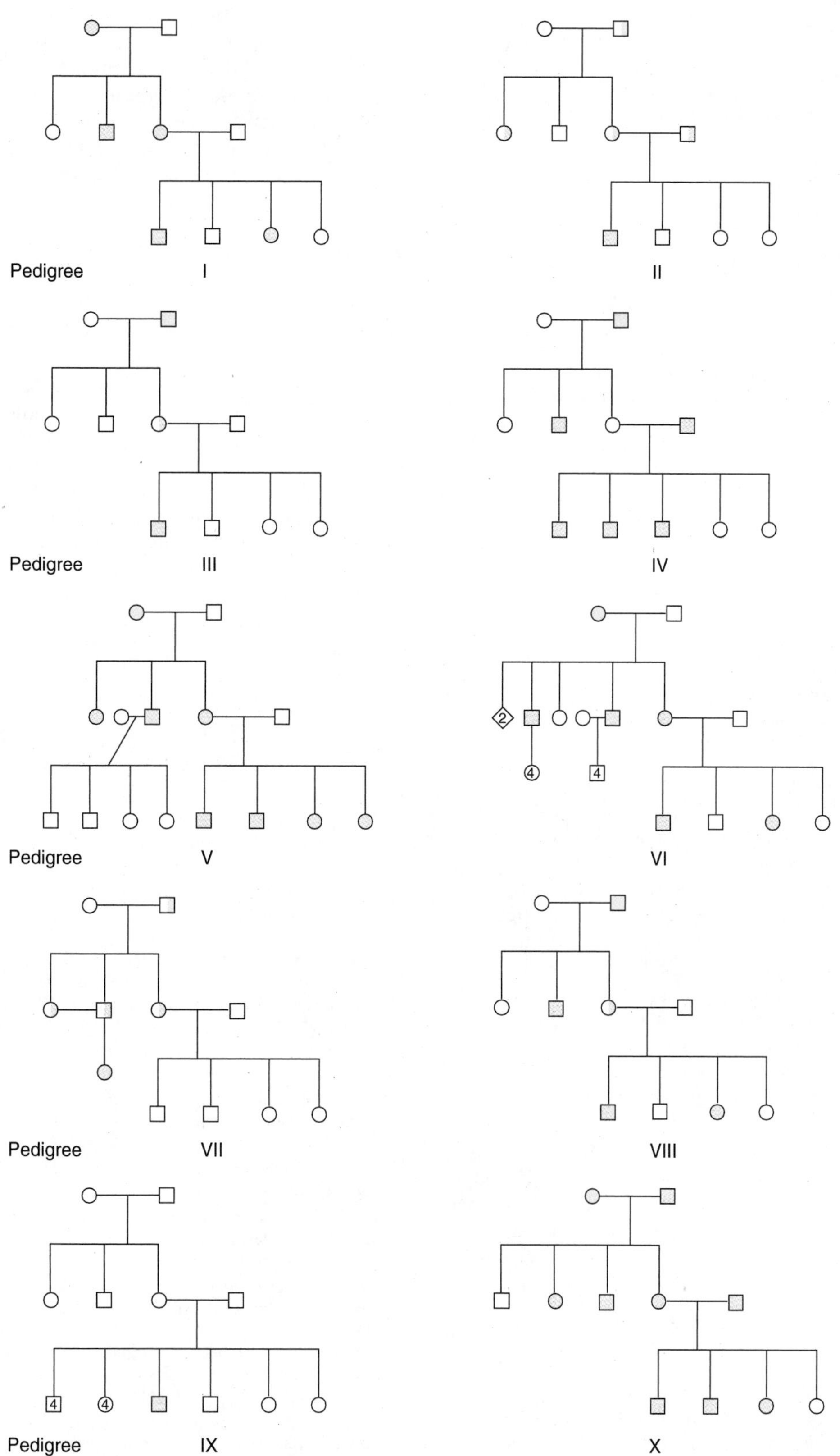

Figure 13–2 *See legend on opposite page*

Table 13–2 Genes, Diseases, and Phenotypes

One Gene → Multiple Diseases
β-Globin
Sickle cell anemia
Thalassemia
Congenital Heinz-body hemolytic anemia
Congenital cyanosis
Hereditary polycythemia
Cystic fibrosis transmembrane conductance regulator (CFTR)
Cystic fibrosis
Congenital bilateral absence of vas deferens
Androgen receptor (AR)
Testicular feminization (complete and incomplete)
Reifenstein's syndrome
Infertile male syndrome
Spinal and bulbar muscular atrophy (Kennedy's syndrome)
One Disease Phenotype → Multiple Genes
Thalassemia
α-Globin
β-Globin
Unlinked to globin
Hemophilia
Factor VIII
Factor IX
von Willebrand's factor
Phenylketonuria
Phenylalanine hydroxylase
Dihydropteridine reductase
Guanosine triphosphate cyclohydrolase I
6-Pyruvoyltetrahydropterin synthase

vague, because these factors may be myriad and may include prenatal as well as postnatal exposures). Genetic heterogeneity refers to the fact that the cause of disease in one family or population subgroup may be different from that in others. Most multifactorial diseases display genetic heterogeneity.

For common multifactorial diseases, including many psychiatric disorders, the identification of predisposing genes in different families or population subgroups, the delineation of specific mutations in these genes, and the understanding of gene-environment interactions remain major challenges. Strategies used in psychiatric genetics research are described in the following.

Introduction to Psychiatric Genetics

The causes of the major psychiatric diseases, including schizophrenia, bipolar disorder, and alcoholism, have long been postulated to include genetic predisposition. Data from twin, adoption, and family studies generally support a genetic component (Tables 13–4 and 13–5). Twin studies are especially useful in determining whether familial aggregation of disease is due to common genetic or common environmental factors. If twin *concordance rates* are elevated among monozygotic twins who have identical genomes and also a shared environment, but substantially less so among dizygotic twins who share environment but only 50% of their genes on average, genetic factors are implicated in disease predisposition. Similar rates of concordance in monozygotic and dizygotic twins suggest that environmental factors are of predominant importance (e.g., the monozygotic and dizygotic concordance rates for measles are essentially equal[2]). Unusual patterns of segregation in monozygotic and dizygotic twins may also suggest novel disease mechanisms. As an example, in most twin studies of Parkinson's disease, the concordance rates for monozygotic and dizygotic twins are similar to the population risk. These data suggest that neither genetics nor environment plays a role in disease causation. One possible mechanism compatible with such twin data is the existence of *prion* analogues for membrane or extracellular proteins, which occur in only 3% of individuals during their lifetime.[3]

As shown in Table 13–4, concordance rates in monozygotic twins are significantly greater than in dizygotic twins for a number of psychiatric illnesses, suggesting a genetic contribution. However, despite the evidence of a genetic component to many common psychiatric diseases, simple mendelian modes of transmission have not been convincingly demonstrated as major mechanisms of disease. However, there may be small subsets of families in which single genes, transmitted in a mendelian fashion, are responsible for disease. For example, a small percentage of Alzheimer's disease displays autosomal dominant inheritance (see later).

To dissect the genetic predisposition to the major psychiatric diseases, a number of molecular genetic epidemiology research strategies have been applied to psychiatric disorders. These approaches have included linkage analysis, *marker*-based *association studies,* and candidate gene–based association studies.

Table 13–3 Genetics and Disease: General Principles

- One disease phenotype can often be caused by defects in more than one gene *(genetic heterogeneity).*
- Detailed analysis generally reveals that some mutations in a gene give rise to one disease phenotype, whereas others may give rise to different disease phenotypes.
- The disease phenotypes associated with a defective gene are often difficult to predict from a knowledge of the gene (e.g., self-mutilation and hypoxanthine phosphoribosyltransferase *[HPRT]* deficiency; bilateral absence of the vas deferens in cystic fibrosis transmembrane conductance regulator *[CFTR]* deficiency; motor neuron death in androgen receptor deficiency).
- Defining the gene that causes a disease can aid in prevention and sometimes suggest novel therapies.
- Most of the common diseases are *multifactorial* in nature with a substantial genetic predisposition.
- *Somatic* mutations can cause multiple diseases, such as cancer, neurodegenerative disease, autoimmune disease, and paroxysmal nocturnal hemoglobinuria.
- The majority of mutations are neutral; of the mutations that affect function, deleterious mutations are much more frequent than advantageous mutations.
- Almost all "genetic deaths" are due to *dominant* expression of deleterious mutations. This is so because almost all *recessive* mutations for severe disease are mildly deleterious in the heterozygote (carrier) form; because heterozygotes are so much more common, most recessive mutant alleles are lost owing to the occasional deleterious effects in heterozygotes.
- There is a high level of redundancy in gene function in mammals implying that *gene disruption* (i.e., gene inactivation) experiments in *transgenic animals* will often yield subtle phenotypes; also, the level of expression of a gene in a tissue is frequently not a good measure of the relative functional importance of the gene product in that tissue.

Table 13–4 Population Risk and Twin Concordance for Selected Psychiatric and Nonpsychiatric Diseases

Disease	Population Lifetime Risk	Twin Concordance*	Reference
Measles	—	MZ 97.4% DZ 94.3%	2
Parkinson's disease	2.5%	MZ 3% DZ 9%	3
Schizophrenia	1%	MZ 48% DZ 15%	4
Bipolar disorder	1%	MZ 79% DZ 19%	5
Unipolar depression†	2%–5%	MZ 58% DZ 23%	5–8
Panic disorder	1%–5%	MZ 24% DZ 11% MZ 31% DZ 0%	9 10

*Probandwise concordance rates are presented. For concordant twins independently ascertained, both ill twins are counted, as is appropriate when systematic ascertainment procedures have been used. MZ, Monozygotic; DZ, dizygotic.

†Rates are the weighted average of three independent twin studies that uses the probandwise concordance method.

Linkage Analysis

In genetic diseases that exhibit classical mendelian patterns of segregation, the application of linkage analysis has met with dramatic success in the past few years. Genes responsible for mendelian diseases such as cystic fibrosis, Duchenne's muscular dystrophy, familial amyotrophic lateral sclerosis, and Huntington's chorea have been identified. These advances have provided hope that the genes for major mental illnesses may also be identified. However, the application of linkage analysis in the major psychiatric disorders, which are multifactorial rather than mendelian, is fraught with difficulties. These include the lack of clear evidence for the involvement of a major single gene and the difficulty in sharply defining the disease phenotype. Are alcohol abuse and major depressive disorder sometimes variable expressions of the same underlying genotype *(variable expressivity)?* Are bipolar I disorder and schizophrenia variable expressions of the same underlying genotype? Nonetheless, intensive searches for genetic linkage in psychiatric disorders have been undertaken.

Linkage analysis is an approach for identifying a gene involved in disease causation that takes advantage of the fact that genetic loci close to one another on the same chromosome are likely to be coinherited, that is, linked loci cosegregate. An unknown disease-conferring locus may be identified by following the cosegregation of a *polymorphic* "marker" of known chromosomal location with the disease in a family or in a group of families. These markers may include protein polymorphisms, *restriction fragment length polymorphisms (RFLPs),* or, most frequently, *variable number tandem repeats* (e.g., *microsatellites*) (Fig. 13–3). To be *informative* in a family, key individuals must have two different alleles (i.e., be heterozygous) at the marker locus so that the cosegregation of a particular marker with disease can be followed unambiguously through the family. Once marker genotypes and disease status are identified for each family member, a statistical analysis is performed to determine whether a particular marker locus is linked to a disease-conferring locus. A ratio is computed of the probability of observing the pattern of cosegregation of the marker allele and the disease under the assumption of linkage with the probability of observing the same pattern under the assumption of no linkage between the marker and a disease-causing locus. These probabilities depend on a number of factors or parameters, including a hypothesized mode of inheritance, specific frequencies of the wild-type and mutant alleles, and particular gene penetrances.

The probability that a particular genetic locus and a marker allele will be linked depends on how closely the two are situated relative to one another on a given chromosome. The shorter the distance, the more likely the two are inherited nonindependently. During the meiotic process that gives rise to haploid ova and sperm, segments of DNA may be physically exchanged between the two chromosomes of a pair (e.g., between the two chromosomes 8 or the two chromosomes 12). These crossing over or *recombination* events result in the separation and independent assortment of gene loci that initially cosegregated (Fig. 13–4). Thus, the

Table 13–5 Risk to Relatives of Affected Individuals

Diagnosis in Affected Individual	Lifetime Risk in General Population	Lifetime Risk* in First-Degree Relatives	Reference
Schizophrenia	1% 2% in spouses of patients	Parents 6% Children 13% Siblings 9% Siblings when one parent has schizophrenia 17% Offspring of two parents with schizophrenia 46%	11
Bipolar disorder	1%	Bipolar 7.8% (1.5%–17.9%) Unipolar 11.4% (0.5%–22.4%)	12, 13
Unipolar depression	2%–5%	Bipolar 0.6% (0.3%–2.1%) Unipolar 9.1% (5.9%–18.4%)	12, 13
Panic disorder	1%–5%	7.7%–20.5%	14, 15
Alcoholism	5%–10% (males) 1%–3% (females)	25%–35% (males) 5%–10% (females)	6

*Includes only age-corrected data that adjust for the fact that not all relatives have lived through the risk period.

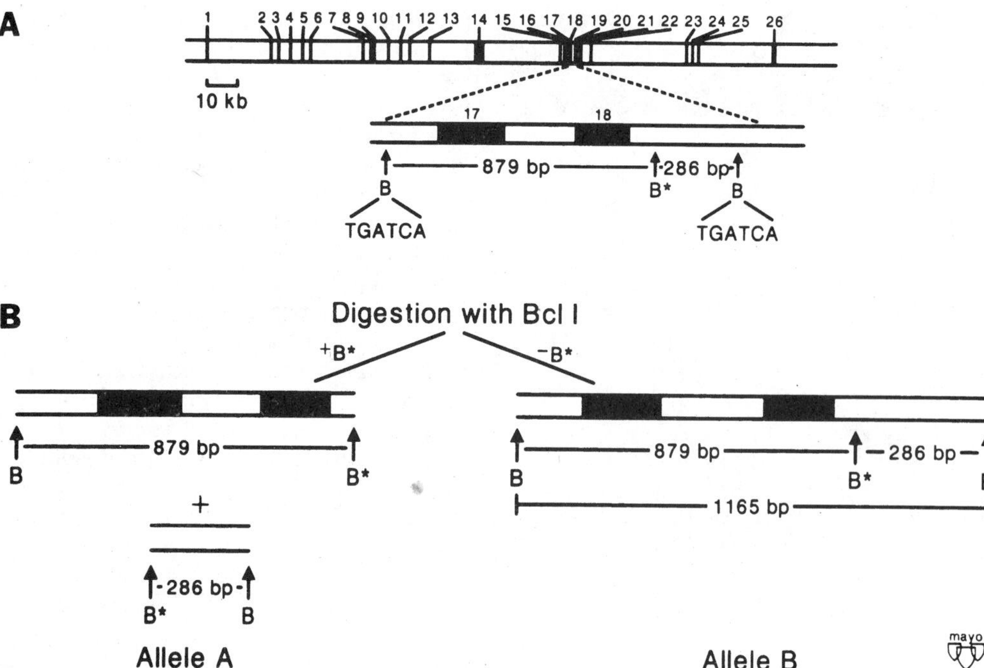

Figure 13–3 *Diagram of RFLP in the human factor VIII gene that is recognized by the* restriction endonuclease *(restriction enzyme)* Bcl *I.* (A) *The human factor VIII gene with its 26 exons is shown to scale. The 26 exons are shaded, whereas the 25 introns and the sequences flanking the first and last exons are unshaded.* (B) *Expanded portion of gene covering exons 17 and 18 is shown, and positions of* Bcl *I sites (B) are indicated. The presence or absence of the middle site, denoted by* B*, *is due to variation of sequence at a single base pair, which renders that site susceptible to cleavage with* Bcl *I in one case (+) and resistant to cleavage in another (−). If cleavage occurs, an 879–base pair and a 286–base pair fragment are produced (allele A). If cleavage does not occur, a 1165–base pair fusion fragment is produced (allele B).* (A *and* B *from Sommer SS, Sobell JL: Application of DNA-based diagnosis to patient care: The example of hemophilia A. Mayo Clinic Proc 1987; 62:387–404.)*

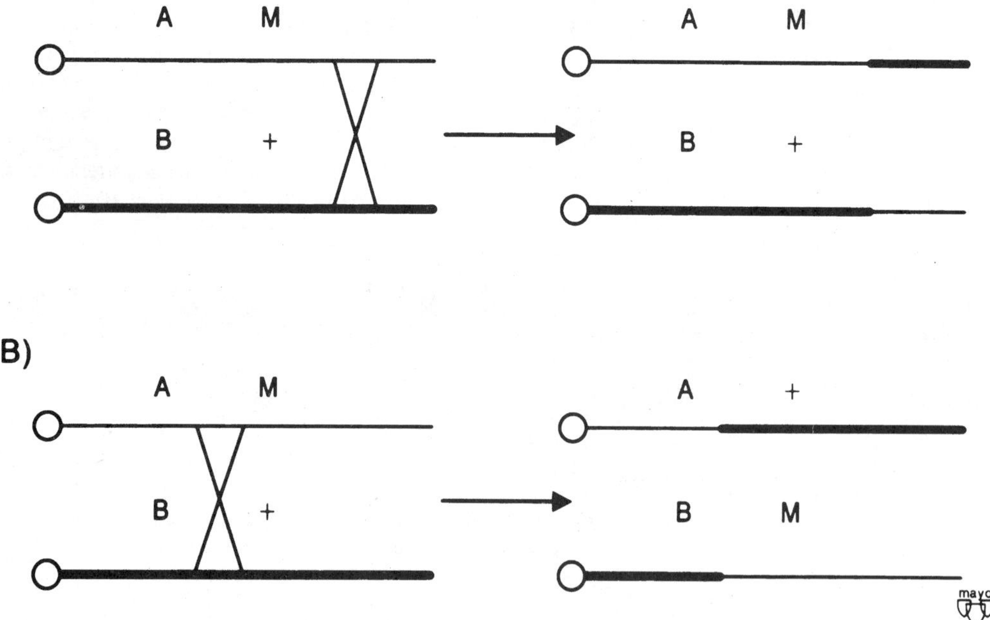

Figure 13–4 *Diagram showing potential for alteration in linkage relationships with recombination during* meiosis. *Before meiotic recombination, RFLP allele A is linked to the mutation (M), and RFLP allele B is linked to the functional gene (+).* (A) *Meiotic recombination distal to both the polymorphism and the mutation has no effect on the linkage relationship. Likewise, meiotic recombination proximal to both the polymorphism and the mutation also has no effect on linkage (not illustrated).* (B) *Recombination between the polymorphism and the mutation changes their linkage relationship.* (A *and* B *from Sommer SS, Sobell JL: Application of DNA-based diagnosis to patient care: The example of hemophilia A. Mayo Clinic Proc 1987; 62:387–404.)*

probability of cosegregation versus independent assortment (i.e., random inheritance) of loci on the same chromosome will depend on the frequency with which the loci are separated by recombination. On average, segments that are 1 million base pairs apart on a chromosome will be separated by recombination in 1% of meioses. The recombinational distance is expressed in units of *centimorgans (cM).*

In linkage analyses, the probability of linkage is computed for different *recombination fractions* (theta, θ, where θ can vary between 0 and ½. If there is complete linkage between two loci, θ is equal to 0; if there is independent segregation of the two loci, then θ is equal to ½. A ratio is computed of the probability of observing the pattern of cosegregation of the marker and the disease under the assumption of linkage at a specified level of recombination ($0 \leq \theta < ½$) with the probability of observing the same pattern under the assumption of no linkage (i.e., $\theta = ½$) between the marker and an unknown disease-causing locus. The $\log_{10}$ of this odds ratio is called the *lod score.* By expressing the odds ratio in lod scores, the scores may be summed across families. In diseases with clear mendelian inheritance, lod scores of 3 and above are accepted as significant evidence of linkage for a given θ, and scores of −2 and below are accepted as significant evidence against linkage for a given θ. More stringent criteria (e.g., lod scores of 5) have been recommended for linkage analyses conducted when the mode of transmission is unknown and many parameters have been estimated and tested at various levels, such as is often the case in analyses of multifactorial diseases.

In addition to analysis based on this maximal likelihood approach, other analytical strategies have been developed that do not require specification of the mode of transmission or penetrance. These "model-free" or *nonparametric* methods include the affected sib pair and the affected pedigree member methods. Briefly, these methods compare the observed number of shared alleles between specified affected members with the expected number of shared alleles based on mendelian expectations given specific parental mating types. As an example, consider a hypothetical family in which the parental *haplotypes* at the marker locus are *AB* and *CD,* and the affected child has haplotype *AC.* If there were no linkage between the marker locus and the unknown disease or trait locus, then siblings would be expected to share marker alleles with the index case in accordance with mendelian expectations. That is, 25% of sibs would be expected to share no marker alleles with the index case (haplotype *BD*); 50% would share one (half the sibs would have either the *A* or the *C* allele); and 25% would share both (haplotype *AC*). Significant deviations from these expectations would indicate linkage between the marker locus and an unknown causative locus. Various analytical formats for these types of data have been developed and are reviewed in the bibliography.

Historically, the application of linkage analysis used genomic markers based on protein *polymorphisms* in the few genes that had been mapped (e.g., histocompatibility antigens, ABO blood groups). The approach has become more powerful with the use of highly polymorphic DNA markers such as microsatellites, which have been mapped at close intervals through the human genome. This has permitted genome-wide linkage analyses in addition to studies of particular candidate genes or specific chromosomal regions. Regardless of the exact markers used, the principle of linkage analysis remains the same: individuals are genotyped at the marker loci, and statistical analyses attempt to demonstrate cosegregation of particular loci with the disease or trait of interest. The use of multipoint linkage analyses, in which linkage to two or more markers is evaluated simultaneously, facilitates the chromosomal localization and eventual identification of the disease locus. A search for linkage may be conducted by a series of analyses that investigate multiple genetic markers, multiple models of disease transmission (e.g., dominant or recessive, single locus versus two loci), multiple levels of penetrance, multiple allele frequencies, and multiple disease definitions.

Because the basis of linkage analysis is the cosegregation of markers with disease in families or sets of relatives, accurate disease phenotypes are essential. However, when the boundaries of the disease phenotype are not clearly definable, such as is the case with many psychiatric disorders, linkage analysis has been attempted by using hierarchical definitions of disease. In schizophrenia research, the most narrow disease definition may include only schizophrenia. The phenotype is broadened by the inclusion of "spectrum" disorders such as schizoaffective disorder and schizotypal personality disorder, with the broadest phenotype sometimes defined to include any mental illness. To circumvent the problems inherent in clinical disease definitions, attempts have been made to use a variety of other indicator traits or biological markers of disease (e.g., deficits in smooth pursuit eye tracking) to characterize family members.

Sometimes diseases or traits involve quantitative measures rather than qualitative measures (e.g., blood pressure, IQ). *Quantitative traits* may be evaluated by use of quantitative trait loci statistical approaches. The quantitative trait loci approach involves a search for genes that influence continuously distributed phenotypes *(continuous traits).* Data from quantitative trait loci analysis[16] suggested that reading disability, as measured by continuous scores on a battery of psychometric tests, was associated with a major quantitative trait locus on chromosome 6. These authors analyzed data on reading performance from 114 sib pairs genotyped for DNA markers localized to 6p21.3 and from 50 dizygotic twin pairs. On the basis of these data, the position of the quantitative trait loci was narrowed to a small region within the human leukocyte antigen complex.

The elucidation of novel modes of inheritance suggested that these may also play a role in psychiatric diseases. One novel mode is characterized by a phenomenon known as *anticipation.* Diseases that display anticipation show a pattern of increasing severity of phenotype or an earlier age at disease onset in successive generations. The genetic basis of the phenotypic variation is the expansion of a DNA trinucleotide repeat *(trinucleotide repeat expansion),* that is, the number of repeated units is variable between generations (Table 13–6). Once a threshold level of expansion is reached, the disease phenotype occurs. The unstable expanded allele is likely to expand further in a subsequent meiosis, producing more severe disease by more fully disrupting gene function. Novel human genes containing trinucleotide repeat expansion sequences have been identified, and it has been estimated that 50 to 100 genes containing trinucleotide

Table 13–6 Examples of Diseases Resulting from Trinucleotide Repeat Expansions

Disease	Expanded Trinucleotide*	Number of Repeat Units: Unaffected	Carriers, Mildly Affected	Affected	Gene	Location in Gene
Fragile X syndrome	CGG	6–52	48–200	230–>1000	*FMR1*	5′ untranslated region
Huntington's chorea	CAG	10–29	30–35	36–121	Huntington	Coding region
Dentatorubral-pallidoluysian atrophy	CAG	8–25	Not known	54–68	*DRPLA*	Coding region
Myotonic dystrophy	CTG	5–37	50–80	99–2000	Myotonin-protein kinase	3′ untranslated region
Spinal and bulbar muscular atrophy	CAG	11–31	Not known	40–62	Androgen receptor	Coding region

*C, Cytosine; G, guanine; A, adenine; T, thymine.

repeat expansions may be expressed in the human brain. Bipolar disorder and schizophrenia have been identified in families with evidence of anticipation, and candidate trinucleotide repeat expansion sequences are being explored in these pedigrees.

Other genetic phenomena that have been implicated or postulated to be involved in human diseases with unusual inheritance patterns include *mosaicism, uniparental disomy,* and *pseudoautosomal inheritance.* Pseudoautosomal inheritance has been postulated to be involved in a subset of schizophrenia.

Application of Linkage Analysis and Related Strategies in Psychiatric Disease

Linkage analyses in psychiatric diseases have for the most part been disappointing, with no major genes yet identified for schizophrenia, bipolar disorder, major depression, or panic disorder. These data have been reviewed elsewhere[4, 15, 17–19]; selected linkage studies are discussed briefly here.

As one exception to these generally disappointing findings, positive findings have been reported for a large Dutch pedigree segregating for borderline mental retardation and abnormal behavior in males.[20, 21] The abnormal behavior included impulsive aggression, arson, attempted rape, and exhibitionism. Initial linkage studies assigned a genetic locus for this disorder to Xp11–21, a region including the genes for monoamine oxidase A and B *(MAOA, MAOB).* A maximal multipoint lod score of 3.69 was obtained with a microsatellite polymorphism in the structural gene for monoamine oxidase A (Xp11.23–11.4). Results of 24-hour urine analysis in family members demonstrated dramatic elevations for monoamine oxidase substrates and reduced amounts of monoamine oxidase products in the affected males, intermediate levels in carriers, and normal levels in unaffected males. Further biochemical analyses suggested a deficiency or absence of monoamine oxidase A activity. On examination of *MAOA* cDNA from family members, a *nonsense mutation* was identified in exon 8, resulting in the substitution of a termination codon for the normal glutamine 296 codon. Thus, truncation of the protein underlies the isolated, complete monoamine oxidase A deficiency in the affected males and appears to be responsible for the observed behavioral phenotypes. Further analyses are necessary to establish the frequency of monoamine oxidase A deficiency in the population, to determine what level of deficiency correlates with behavioral phenotypes, and to identify specific neurochemical alterations that underlie these behaviors.

Schizophrenia

Schizophrenia and bipolar disorder illustrate the difficulties that can occur in applying linkage analysis to psychiatric diseases. In schizophrenia, the literature is replete with negative linkage reports; several positive linkages have failed to be replicated or have yet to be replicated. A now well-known example of an unreplicated linkage is that which was reported in 1988 between markers mapped to 5q11–q13 and schizophrenia in five Icelandic and two British pedigrees.[22] This region was of interest because of the cosegregation of schizophrenia with a partial trisomy of chromosome 5 in a single family with one affected male proband and an affected maternal uncle.[23] The linkage analysis performed by Sherrington and colleagues[22] involved analyses under three different definitions of "affected." Under a dominant gene model with high penetrance, a maximal lod score of 6.49 ($\theta = 0.14$) was found with use of the broadest definition of affected status, which included schizophrenia spectrum disorders as well as other illnesses such as alcoholism. When only schizophrenia and schizophrenia spectrum diagnoses were used, a lod score of 4.33 was found; for schizophrenia alone, a lod score of 3.22 was achieved.

In sharp contrast to these findings, Kennedy and colleagues[24] examined chromosome 5q and found strong exclusionary evidence for linkage in a large, geographically isolated Swedish pedigree. St. Clair and colleagues[25] examined 15 Scottish families using the same *probes* and reported no evidence of linkage using four separate models of affected status. Detera-Wadleigh and colleagues[26] reported similar negative results in a study of five North American caucasian families in which three different models of affected status were used.

The inconsistent findings were initially thought by some to be evidence of genetic heterogeneity; however, specific criticisms of these studies included the use of too high a penetrance parameter by Sherrington, the inclusion of "fringe" phenotypes by these same investigators, and the inclusion of families with cases of bipolar disorder by both St. Clair and Detera-Wadleigh.[27, 28] When data on families from Sweden, Scotland, the United States, London, and Wales were combined, linkage was solidly rejected with lod scores as low as –40.[29]

It now appears more likely that the positive results of Sherrington and colleagues were spurious. This is supported by an extension of their initial work. When highly polymorphic microsatellite markers were used to increase the number of informative meioses, the initial high lod score for the broadly defined phenotype was greatly deflated. With use of a more narrow definition of disease (schizophrenia and spectrum disorders), the lod score was approximately 3. However, when additional families were added to the original sample, the authors reported no evidence for linkage.[30] These studies of chromosome 5 emphasize the importance of replication of initial linkage findings in independent samples; this, however, may not always be possible, as described later (see section on pitfalls and problems in linkage analysis).

In addition to chromosome 5, attention has been focused on several other regions: the long arm of chromosome 11, the pseudoautosomal region of the sex chromosomes, chromosome 22, and most recently chromosomes 3 and 8. Interest in chromosome 11 was aroused by several facts, including the mapping of the genes for tyrosine hydroxylase and the D_2 and D_4 dopamine receptors to 11p15.5. In addition, a report of albinism cosegregating with schizophrenia (the gene coding for tyrosinase, responsible for the oculocutaneous form of albinism, maps at 11q14–21) and reports of two families in which psychotic illness cosegregated with translocations in this region[17] also contributed to the interest in chromosome 11. However, analyses of markers on both 11q and 11p have failed to support linkage.[17]

Involvement of the pseudoautosomal region of the sex chromosomes in schizophrenia has been postulated by Crow[31] as an explanation for the observation that affected siblings tend to be of the same sex more often than of opposite sex. During the male meiotic process to produce sperm, particular regions of the X and Y chromosomes undergo recombination. Thus, genes located in these regions are not inherited in a sex-linked manner, but rather they are inherited in the same manner as autosomal genes. If a predisposing dominantly acting gene were on the X chromosome, then in families in which schizophrenia was transmitted paternally, affected offspring most likely would be female. If the predisposing dominantly acting gene were on the Y chromosome, then affected offspring most likely would be male. This pattern would not be expected when the disease was maternally transmitted. Although Crow[32, 33] has presented evidence of this pattern of disease concordance in some families, other analyses have been negative or only weakly positive.[17]

In contrast to linkage studies involving probes for specific chromosomal regions, genome-wide searches for linkage have been undertaken by a number of laboratories. From one endeavor, preliminary evidence of linkage was suggested for chromosome 22q.[34] At least three independent studies have been published, including one by the original investigators. Polymeropoulos and colleagues,[35] using 10 highly informative polymorphic markers in 105 families segregating for schizophrenia or schizoaffective disorder, found no conclusive evidence for linkage by the lod score method under a variety of transmission models. Similarly, affected sibling pair and affected pedigree member analyses yielded nonsignificant, inconclusive, or only weakly suggestive evidence in favor of linkage. Coon and colleagues[36] tested for linkage using 10 highly polymorphic chromosome 22 markers in nine families and found suggestive evidence for linkage to the distal end of the chromosome. The highest lod score was 2.09 under autosomal recessive inheritance. Other analyses, including nonparametric methods and a candidate gene linkage analysis, were either inconclusive or only suggestive. Likewise, no strong or consistent linkages have been reported for chromosomes 3, 8, or others.

Bipolar Disorder

Although a number of linkage studies reported positive results in bipolar illness, none of the linkages have been conclusively replicated. A well-known example is that involving an Old Order Amish pedigree segregating for bipolar and other affective disorders.[17] In studies of candidate gene regions, a positive linkage to 11p15 was reported. This region was chosen for study because the genes for tyrosine hydroxylase and the dopamine D_4 receptor map to 11p15.1. However, this linkage was not replicated in numerous other studies.[17] Furthermore, when additional Amish pedigree members were considered in the analysis, the initial findings could not be replicated.[17]

Preliminary findings of a positive linkage in bipolar illness have been reported for chromosome 18.[37] By using a disease model that included bipolar I disorder, bipolar II disorder with major depression, schizoaffective disorder, and recurrent unipolar illness, a study of 22 pedigrees yielded positive lod scores under two different models of disease transmission (dominant, 50% penetrance; recessive, 85% penetrance). At a recombination fraction of 1%, five pedigrees had lod scores in the range of 1.08 to 2.38. Nonparametric analyses were also performed, with both yielding evidence of linkage (affected sibling pair analysis: $P < .002$ at D18S21; affected pedigree member analysis [multilocus results for five loci]: $P < .0001$ and $P = .0007$ depending on weighting functions used). Whereas several other investigators have found suggestive evidence for linkage to chromosome 18 markers, others have had negative findings.

Assuming that linkage exists in a subset of families, candidate genes in the 50-cM linked region are being explored. Two of the many possible candidate genes in this region are the α-subunit of a guanine nucleotide–binding protein and a corticotropin receptor gene. To date, no mutations in these genes have been identified.

McInnis and colleagues[38] have attempted to demonstrate that disease in a subset of families with bipolar disorder may exhibit anticipation and thereby may be due to the expansion of unstable trinucleotide repeat DNA sequences. The investigators compared the age at onset and disease severity between two generations of 34 unilineal families segregating for bipolar disorder. Evidence for an earlier age at onset and for more severe illness in the second generation was found in a subset of these families, even when the potential confounding effects of drug abuse, death of affected individuals before ascertainment, and cohort effects were taken into account. Follow-up studies will endeavor to identify trinucleotide repeat expansions that may be involved in disease.

Alzheimer's Disease

Of the diseases relevant to psychiatry, the most progress has been made on the genetics of Alzheimer's disease. Like the major psychiatric disorders, Alzheimer's disease exhibits familial clustering, with an estimated threefold increased frequency of disease in first-degree relatives of probands compared with the general population.[39] A small subset of families, usually with early onset of illness, exhibit autosomal dominant inheritance; however, the overwhelming majority of cases appear to be sporadic or multifactorial in inheritance. Interestingly, a strong correlation exists between Down's syndrome (trisomy 21) and early-onset Alzheimer's disease.

Unlike schizophrenia or bipolar disorder, Alzheimer's disease can be diagnosed reliably, albeit at autopsy, from brain tissue that shows pathognomonic neurofibrillary tangles and amyloid plaques. One caveat is that Alzheimer's disease must be distinguished from Gerstmann-Sträussler-Scheinker disease, which may also exhibit typical Alzheimer's plaques and tangles in brain tissue and a clinical course similar to that of an Alzheimer-type progressive dementia, although an unusually severe one. Gerstmann-Sträussler-Scheinker disease is associated with a mutation in the prion protein gene on chromosome 20p, and these cases must be separated from Alzheimer's disease in genetic studies.

The amyloid precursor protein gene *(APP)* was considered a strong candidate for involvement in Alzheimer's disease on the basis of the occurrence of amyloid plaques, the mapping of *APP* to chromosome 21, and the finding of genetic linkage in the same region as *APP* in a few large families with early-onset autosomal dominant Alzheimer's disease. When several instances of recombination between the marker locus and the *APP* locus were found in linked families, the gene was eliminated as a major disease candidate. However, mutations in *APP* have been shown to be causative in a few families with autosomal dominant disease. These mutations appear to account for less than 1% of all Alzheimer's cases. Interestingly, although the mutations cluster in exons 16 and 17 of the *APP* gene, the phenotypes associated with each mutation are distinct, with some conferring classical Alzheimer's disease and others predisposing to other entities, such as hereditary cerebral hemorrhage of the Dutch type. Variable clinical phenotypes even exist within families with the same mutation.[39]

Genetic linkages in Alzheimer's disease have also been reported on chromosomes 14 and 19. Linkage to chromosome 14q was found in approximately 70% of families with early-onset cases.[39] Although several candidate genes have been proposed, no specific mutations have thus far been delineated. Linkage to chromosome 19 was first observed in families with late-onset Alzheimer's disease. In investigations of cerebrospinal proteins that bound amyloid β-peptide with high affinity, apolipoprotein E (apo E) was identified. Analysis of the brains of familial Alzheimer's disease patients showed that senile plaques, neurofibrillary tangles, and cerebral vessel amyloid deposits react with antisera to apo E. In addition, the apo E gene was localized to the region of chromosome 19 in which linkages had been reported.

There are three known forms of apo E, termed apo E2, E3, and E4, that occur in the general population. The E4 allele has been shown to be associated with older-onset Alzheimer's disease, but this allele is neither necessary nor sufficient for causation of Alzheimer's disease. The effects of gene dosage (i.e., number of copies of the predisposing allele) appear to be complex, with individuals homozygous for the E4 allele having the highest risk of disease. As estimated by Corder and colleagues,[40] each occurrence of an E4 allele increases risk by a factor of more than 4. However, the effects of gene dosage and sex also appear to be complex, with females heterozygous for the E4 allele having a risk equal to that of males with two E4 alleles. The complicated effects of gene dosage, sex, history of familial versus sporadic disease, late versus early onset, and other variables for risk of Alzheimer's disease are areas of intense investigation. The pathophysiological mechanism for involvement of apo E4 in Alzheimer's disease is also unknown and under study.

The progress to date on the genetics of Alzheimer's disease illustrates the concept that neuropsychiatric diseases are likely to be etiologically and genetically complex. The subset of Alzheimer's disease families with autosomal dominant inheritance is an invaluable resource for the conduct of traditional (i.e., lod score–based) linkage approaches, but these families represent a small minority of Alzheimer's disease. Other approaches to understanding the genetic basis of complex and common disorders are essential. These have included nonparametric linkage analyses and association studies (see later).

Pitfalls and Problems in Linkage Analysis

The application of linkage analysis to multifactorial diseases has been a problem, as illustrated by studies in schizophrenia, bipolar disorder, and other psychiatric conditions. In schizophrenia, the approach is compromised by uncertainties in the mode of transmission, *genetic heterogeneity,* boundaries of clinical illness (e.g., should schizophrenia spectrum patients be included as affected family members?), variable age at onset of illness, incomplete penetrance of susceptible genotypes, biases due to decreased reproduction by ill individuals, *assortative mating,* and difficulty in ascertaining large families with multiple affected individuals. In lod score–based linkage analysis, a hypothesized mode of inheritance must be specified. Misspecification of the mode may result in the false exclusion of linkage (although some have argued that if consistent results are achieved under both dominant and recessive models, the probability of error decreases). Furthermore, as argued by Greenberg,[41] linkage approaches are not a powerful design for detecting susceptibility loci, that is, genes that increase risk but that are neither necessary nor sufficient for disease expression.

The interpretation of the lod score in the analysis of multifactorial disorders is also a problem. Although in mendelian diseases, with known modes of inheritance, a lod score of 3 is considered evidence in favor of linkage, the same criterion is not applicable to analyses of multifactorial disorders. This is because these analyses most often involve multiple statistical tests, and with each test conducted, there is an increased probability of obtaining false-positive results in favor of linkage. The multiple testing results from the need to investigate a variety of parameter estimates, including different models of disease transmission, levels of penetrance, and definitions of affected status, as discussed briefly before. Thus, adjustment of the lod score must be undertaken or the results of such analyses must be interpreted cautiously. Even if evidence of linkage is found, replication of the initial results presents other difficulties and may require large sample sizes.

Alternative model-free methods such as affected sib pair analysis and affected pedigree member analysis have been used. Although these methods bypass some of the assumptions made in likelihood-based linkage analysis (estimation of penetrance and specification of mode of transmission), there are other limitations. As with family-based studies, the ascertainment of sibs with identical diagnoses can be a problem. The accurate estimation of marker allele frequencies is essential, and the effects of *noninformative* pairs may greatly compromise the approaches. Statistical power for a given number of affected relative pairs is highly dependent on the recombination fraction, the informativeness of polymorphic markers, and the relationship of the relative pairs available (e.g., grandparent-grandchild, sibs). Large sample sizes are necessary when there is even moderate genetic heterogeneity, and statistical power is highly decreased even with modest rates of recombination.

Association Studies

As an alternative to linkage-based approaches, association studies have been undertaken in psychiatric genetics. Association studies are research strategies that use unrelated diseased individuals (cases) and nondiseased individuals (controls) in an attempt to demonstrate that a particular risk factor is more prevalent among those affected (or, conversely, that a putative protective factor is more prevalent among the unaffected individuals). In traditional epidemiological studies, risk factors might include cigarette smoking, cholesterol levels, radiation exposure, and similar environmental variables. Family history of disease was also often examined as a surrogate for genetic predisposition.

Specific genotypes have been examined as risk factors. In most studies, these genotypes have been defined on the basis of either polymorphic markers at or near the locus (or loci) of interest or "anonymous polymorphic markers" that define alleles in a chromosomal region for which the mapped genes are not yet known. The polymorphic systems used to define genotypes have included RFLPs, variable number tandem repeats, and other markers. Because these markers rarely, if ever, define alleles with functional differences, these studies require both linkage of disease to a particular marker allele and the presence of strong *linkage disequilibrium* between an unknown causative mutation and that particular allele. Therefore, these types of association studies are referred to as linkage disequilibrium studies. It is unlikely that both criteria for success will be met if multiple independent mutations cause disease, as is often the case for X-linked and autosomal dominant diseases and for some autosomal recessive diseases, such as phenylketonuria. If multiple mutations occur, a single marker allele may not be associated with disease because some mutations may occur by chance in chromosomes containing a particular marker allele, whereas other mutations may occur in the chromosomes with the other allele. Thus, the results of a marker-based study can be negative even if a correct locus (or region) has been chosen for study. In addition, false-positive results can occur because marker allele frequencies may differ dramatically between individuals of different ethnic backgrounds (referred to as *population stratification*).

Application of Association Strategies in Psychiatric Diseases

A notable set of linkage disequilibrium studies have involved the relationship of particular alleles of the D_2 dopamine receptor gene *(DRD2)* to alcoholism. These *DRD2* alleles (designated *A1* and *A2*) were defined on the basis of a RFLP. The alleles are not of functional consequence; that is, the RFLP itself does not result in an altered protein structure or in altered expression of the gene. Nearly a dozen studies have appeared in the literature, and *meta-analyses* have been performed.[42] The data have alternatively been interpreted as indicating that *DRD2* is an important single-locus determinant of susceptibility to severe substance abuse or, in contrast, that the reported associations are spurious because of population stratification. Thus far, specific mutations in *DRD2* that might be associated with alcoholism, generalized substance abuse, or any other psychiatric abnormality have not been found. As one example, the *DRD2* gene was examined in 113 individuals with alcoholism and other subjects, and although three sequence changes that altered the amino acid structure of the protein were identified, none was associated with alcoholism.[43] In addition, there is no indication that the *DRD2* RFLP marker is linked to another causative gene.

Association studies that do *not* depend on linkage disequilibrium have also been conducted. In this approach, genes of neurobiological interest are first examined at the DNA level in a subset of affected individuals to search for DNA sequence variations affecting protein structure or expression (VAPSEs).[44] VAPSEs are identified by DNA sequencing; if a sequence change alters the protein coding sequence or disrupts a consensus sequence affecting *splicing* or gene regulation, it is a VAPSE. Many VAPSEs are of functional significance. Once a VAPSE of likely functional significance is found in a relevant candidate gene, the prevalence of the sequence change in a large group of affected individuals and ethnically similar control subjects can be determined. If the VAPSE is significantly more prevalent among the diseased individuals than among the control subjects, an etiological association with disease is suggested. Further investigations are warranted: 1) performing additional case-control studies of these VAPSEs to confirm or refute the initial association; 2) conducting family-based linkage studies in those specific families with the variant allele; and 3) searching in affected individuals for additional VAPSEs in the *same* candidate gene and demonstrating that different mutations in the same gene, all likely to disrupt gene function, are associated with disease.

Assessment of Likely Functional Significance of Sequence Changes

When a sequence change is identified, the likelihood of its being of functional significance (i.e., altering normal function) can be assessed initially by determining the type of mutation. Some mutations (e.g., nonsense changes, frameshifts, and deletions of one or more exons) virtually always disrupt gene function. However, the majority of changes in coding regions are expected to be *missense* changes. The likelihood of a missense change altering the function of the allele may be estimated by the level of *evolutionary conservation* of the residue. For example, analyses of the relationship between missense mutations causing hemophilia B and the extent to which residues in factor IX are conserved during evolution have indicated that almost all missense mutations affecting function occur at residues conserved in the nine available mammalian factor IX sequences. This same relationship has been found for other genes in which many mutations have been described (e.g., p53, phenylalanine hydroxylase, cystic fibrosis transmembrane conductance regulator).

These data also suggest that a significant proportion of the residues conserved in multiple mammals is not essential. In their comparison of missense mutations causing hemophilia B and amino acid sequence alignments of factor IX and related coagulation proteases, Bottema and colleagues[45] proposed that most residues in factor IX were of two extreme types. At least 25% and possibly up to 40% were "critical" residues in which any missense changes would disrupt function. Most of the remaining residues functioned as "spacer" residues in which virtually all possible missense changes would be tolerated, but the main chain was necessary to keep the critical residues in proper register. This model, the critical-spacer model of protein structure, implies that important versus inconsequential amino acid substitutions in a human protein can be predicted by analysis of appropriately diverged sequences (for the factor IX and related genes, this represents 2.5+ billion years). Four levels of evolutionary conservation for the factor IX and related genes were defined: generic, partially generic, specific, and nonconserved residues. Specific residues are defined as those conserved in the available factor IX sequences but different in the three members of the gene family (factor VII, factor X, and protein C); partially generic residues are defined as those conserved in the factor IX gene and in one or two other members of the gene family; and generic residues are defined as those conserved in all members of the gene family. Relative to residues that are not conserved in mammalian factor IX sequences, deleterious missense mutations are 5-fold more likely to occur in factor IX specific residues, 13-fold more likely to occur in partially generic residues, and 33-fold more likely to occur in generic residues.

The potential importance of missense changes may also be assessed if in vitro cell culture assays of protein activity are available. The mutant proteins can be analyzed to determine the functional parameters of the mutant protein (e.g., receptor-binding properties) or in *expression analysis* to determine the effect of specific mutations on level of gene expression. However, these assays do not capture the complexity of the intact organism in its ecosystem, so data generated must be interpreted with caution, especially if the assays fail to document a disruption of function. In vivo studies, through the use of *transgenic* animals, may provide additional data.

Testing of Sequence Changes for Disease Associations

If sequence changes are determined to be of likely functional significance, disease associations may be tested in a number of approaches. Powerful, yet indirect, evidence of the gene's involvement in disease would be the delineation of other sequence changes of likely functional significance in the same gene in additional patients. The cosegregation of particular variant alleles with disease in pedigrees with multiple affected members or in sib pairs would be strong evidence of a disease association. Alternatively, the frequency of the sequence change may be compared between unrelated patients with the disease of interest and ethnically similar control subjects. The strength of association between the sequence change and disease is measured by the *odds ratio,* and the ability to detect an elevated risk is correlated to sample size, among other parameters. In addition to these epidemiologically based determinants of association, the demonstration of a biological relationship in experimental animal models between the sequence variant and disease symptoms (or surrogate animal measures of human symptoms) would be compelling evidence of the etiological importance of the sequence change.

If negative results are obtained from association or linkage studies, it is important to determine the level of association (i.e., level of elevated risk in the case of association studies and likelihood of linkage in linkage analysis) that could have been detected given the sample size and the presumed degree of genetic heterogeneity. Conversely, to guard against false-positive associations, replication of the positive results in an independent sample is essential. Sequential testing protocols for such replicative experiments within the structure of VAPSE-based association studies have been developed.

Another study design issue of importance in both linkage disequilibrium and VAPSE-based studies is that allele frequencies can vary as a function of ethnicity. If the distribution of ethnicities varies between cases and unrelated control subjects, spurious associations (either positive or negative) may result. To avoid potential confounding by ethnicity, an alternative control group can be used. Falk and Rubinstein[46] initially described a case-control study design that used a control group composed of the parental *alleles* not inherited by the case patients (hereafter referred to as nontransmitted alleles). An odds ratio statistic, termed the haplotype relative risk, was computed as the odds of the presence of a particular marker (or VAPSE) among either of the two alleles transmitted to the affected child divided by the odds of the presence of the marker (or VAPSE) among either of the two nontransmitted alleles. However, the haplotype relative risk failed to distinguish individuals who were homozygous for the marker (or VAPSE) from those who were heterozygous. Both groups were combined and compared with the baseline group, consisting of individuals without the marker (or VAPSE). Recognizing that the haplotype relative risk was really a weighted average of two odds ratios (homozygotes for marker compared with homozygotes for the wild type; heterozygotes for marker compared with homozygotes for the wild type), Schaid and Sommer[47] proposed genotype relative risk statistics. The genotype relative risk computes each of these odds ratios separately.[47] To test the significance of the genotype relative risks, an unconditional likelihood test, which assumes that Hardy-Weinberg equilibrium assumptions are met, and a conditional likelihood test (i.e., Hardy-Weinberg equilibrium assumptions are not met) were derived.

An additional advantage of the genotype relative risk approach over earlier statistics is the use of likelihood approaches that can also incorporate regression models to test for interactions between genetic and environmental risk factors. Thus, the effects of polygenes as well as the effects of environment, plus the interaction of these factors, may be examined.

Genotype-to-Phenotype Analysis

An additional aspect of VAPSE-based studies makes the approach attractive. When sequence changes of likely functional significance are identified but found not to be associated with the particular disease of interest, further studies may be conducted to determine whether the genotype is associated with another neuropsychiatric disorder, differential response to pharmacotherapy, or other phenotypes. These genotype-to-phenotype studies may be conducted by investigators with large genetic epidemiology resources that couple extensive medical records with DNA samples (e.g., DNA resources developed on members of a large health maintenance organization or from population-based epidemiological samples). With such a resource, all individuals with the genotype of interest may be identified, and their medical histories may be compared with age- and sex-matched subjects with the normal genotype. Useful hypotheses regarding the physiological consequences of a sequence change (i.e., the consequences of a defect in a particular pathway) may be developed and tested in this manner.

The rate-limiting step in the conduct of VAPSE-based association studies is the identification of sequence changes of likely functional significance. However, the advent of laboratory methodologies based on the amplification of nucleic acids by the *polymerase chain reaction* and the ongoing identification of the universe of candidate genes through the Human Genome Project have made the approach a feasible adjunct to existing approaches for the study of genetic predisposition to multifactorial disease.

Molecular (DNA) Diagnosis

Once specific predisposing genes are identified, disease diagnosis, prognosis, therapy, and ultimately prevention can be tailored for the specific disorder on the basis of its molecular profile. These advances are most likely to occur incrementally, with the identification of a limited number of disease susceptibility genes as the first step. If the predisposing gene is large and if many mutations are involved in disease in different families, the rapid identification of causative mutations in each family may be difficult. In this case, the most powerful approach to disease diagnosis, including prenatal diagnosis to identify carriers, would be indirect DNA-based diagnosis, as is currently performed for diseases such as hemophilia A. Indirect DNA diagnosis involves the application of linkage analysis to determine which members of a pedigree possess an unknown, but causative, mutation for the disease of interest. Indirect DNA diagnosis by linkage analysis is described here with use of an example to illustrate the difficulties that can be encountered.

The principles of indirect diagnosis are illustrated by a Southern blot (Fig. 13–5) of an informative *Bcl* I RFLP (see Fig. 13–3) in two hypothetical families with hemophilia A (Fig. 13–6). Hemophilia A is an X-linked coagulopathy diagnosed by a combination of clinical findings and protein assays. Unfortunately, the defective gene, factor VIII, is too large for efficient identification of the causative mutation in most families. However, polymorphisms of little or no functional significance are available within the introns (e.g., the *Bcl* I polymorphism mentioned before) and in regions flanking the gene. These polymorphisms have been used successfully to perform linkage analyses to determine which members of a family are carriers of a defective factor VIII allele.

Indirect diagnosis requires participation of family members, and nonpaternity, cryptic adoption, and mix-up in the nursery can result in diagnostic error. In addition, recombination between polymorphic markers and the mutation can lead to error (see Fig. 13–4). Genetic heterogeneity may also lead to diagnostic error. For example, if the affected patient has a rare defect in the autosomally located von Willebrand factor gene that disrupts only the factor VIII binding site in the von Willebrand protein, the preceding diagnostic logic would be incorrect. That is because the *Bcl* I RFLP would be unlinked to the true causative mutation in the von Willebrand factor gene. This and possibly other undiscovered mechanisms of genetic heterogeneity in hemophilia A may result in errors in a small percentage of families with the disease. Finally, new mutations, which occur in a significant fraction of families with severe X-linked or autosomal dominant diseases, can lead to uncertainty in diagnosis. Family members who do not inherit the polymorphism linked to the mutated allele can be diagnosed as noncarriers with an accuracy equivalent to that achieved in families with documented familial disease. However, those who do inherit the marker linked to the mutation may be normal rather than carriers, depending on when the mutation originated in the family.

As mentioned before, the ultimate goal of molecular diagnosis is direct analysis because many of the uncertainties of indirect analysis are circumvented. Once the causative mutation has been identified in the proband, any at-risk family member can be tested directly. Issues such as nonpaternity, adoption, recombination, and the point of origin of the mutation become moot. However, although direct diagnosis is almost always more accurate than indirect diagnosis, technical artifact (e.g., sample mix-up) and confusion between a neutral polymorphism and a causative mutation are the major pitfalls. Sometimes, the putative mutation is a large deletion, a frameshift, or a nonsense mutation. These mutations are highly likely to cause disease. However, missense changes are frequently observed. If no other sequence changes are found in the regions of likely

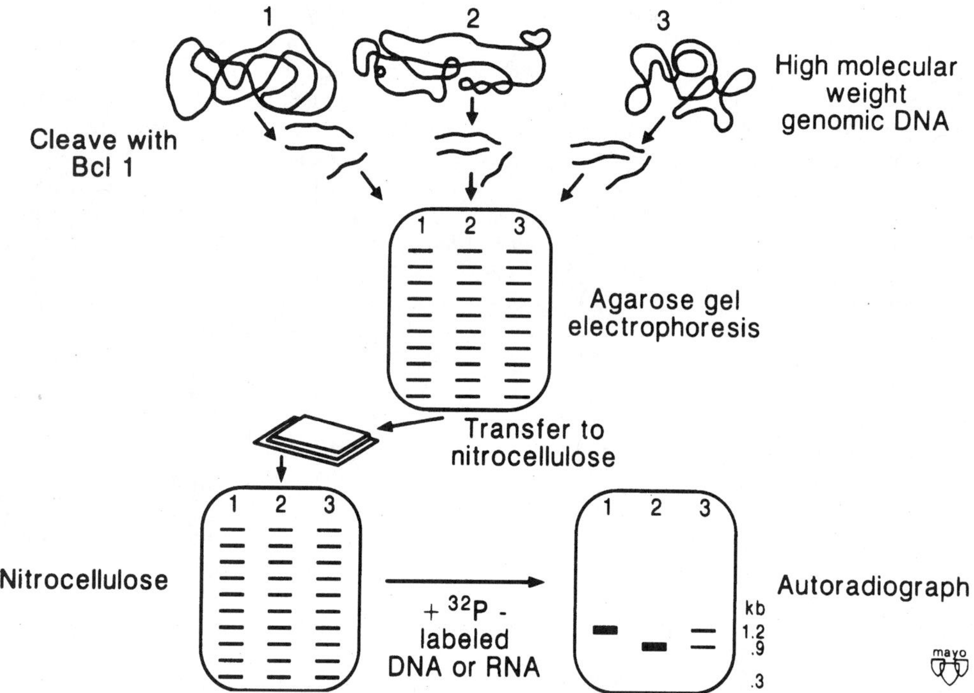

Figure 13–5 *Southern blot analysis of the* Bcl *I RFLP in the factor VIII gene in three females. DNA is cleaved with the restriction enzyme* Bcl *I (i.e., digested with* Bcl *I). Cleaved DNA is separated on the basis of size by agarose gel* electrophoresis. *The gel is then placed in contact with a piece of nitrocellulose, and by capillary action, buffer flows through gel onto nitrocellulose filter. This procedure causes the DNA fragments to flow out of the gel and bind to the filter. A replica of the DNA fragments in the gel is created on the filter.* Hybridization *is performed with a labeled probe complementary to exons 17 and 18.* Autoradiography *reveals specific DNA fragments with which the probe hybridizes. Female 1 has two copies of the 1165–base pair (1.2-kb) fusion fragment. Female 2 has two copies of the 879–base pair (0.9-kb) fragment and of the 286–base pair (0.3-kb) fragment produced by the presence of the* Bcl *I site, which is labeled* B* *in Figure 13–3. Because the probe used in this example was complementary only to exons 17 and 18, the 286–base pair fragments, although present, are not detectable by autoradiography. Female 3 is heterozygous for each allele; consequently, both a 1165–base pair and an 879–base pair fragment are seen at 50% of the intensity of homozygotes. (From Sommer SS, Sobell JL: Application of DNA-based diagnosis to patient care: The example of hemophilia A. Mayo Clinic Proc 1987; 62:387–404.)*

functional significance and the common missense polymorphisms have been previously characterized, the missense change is highly likely to be a causative mutation. If the mutation is in an amino acid conserved during 2+ billion years of evolutionary divergence, the missense change is almost certain to be the causative mutation. In addition, in vitro or in vivo studies with the mutated protein may be helpful.

Selected Laboratory Methodology

All molecular approaches for delineating the genetic predisposition to psychiatric diseases, including linkage analyses, marker-based association studies, and VAPSE-based association studies, and all approaches for direct DNA diagnosis converge on mutations in genes of interest. Mutations that may lead to disease can be classified at present as 1) chromosomal aberrations, 2) submicroscopic deletions or insertions, 3) microdeletions or insertions (<50 base pairs), and 4) single base pair substitutions. Chromosomal anomalies (e.g., duplications, deletions, translocations) may be detected by karyotyping and fluorescent in situ hybridization studies. Smaller deletions (or insertions) have traditionally been detected by Southern blotting (see Fig. 13–5). Microdeletions or insertions may be detected by DNA amplification followed by electrophoresis on thin acrylamide gels, allowing resolution of sequences differing by as little as one base pair.

However, the great majority of disease-causing mutations are single base pair changes that result in missense, nonsense, or splicing mutations or mutations that alter the level of expression of a normal protein product. Of these, missense changes, in which a single nucleotide change results in the substitution of one amino acid for another, have been the most common type of deleterious mutation in coding regions.

A variety of methods have been developed for rapidly screening and sequencing genetic material to identify and characterize sequence variants. Most if not all of these methods depend on the rapid amplification of DNA as the initial step. DNA can be efficiently amplified 10^6-fold or more through the polymerase chain reaction, resulting in the availability of a sufficient amount of material for analysis (Fig. 13–7). Direct gene sequencing must ultimately be conducted to identify novel sequence variants. A multitude of sequencing strategies, based primarily on the dideoxy sequencing approach (Fig. 13–8), have been developed for use with double-stranded DNA, single-stranded DNA, or RNA templates.

However, direct sequencing techniques are time-consuming and labor-intensive. Rapid and highly sensitive methods are preferable for screening gene regions of multiple individuals simultaneously in lieu of the direct sequencing of all samples. A brief review of several screening approaches is presented in Table 13–7 but is by no means inclusive. After a putative sequence change is identified by screening, the exact change is identified through sequencing (see Fig. 13–8).

Once the sequence change is elucidated, to rapidly and accurately identify individuals who are heterozygous or homozygous for a particular genetic marker or VAPSE, one of several laboratory methods is used (Table 13–8).

The development of more rapid and efficient methods for screening DNA and RNA samples, for identifying sequence changes of likely functional significance, and for testing these sequence changes for disease associations will be essential for identifying genes of etiological importance in psychiatric and other multifactorial disorders.

Summary and Future Directions

Several genetic epidemiology approaches are being employed in humans to delineate genetic predisposition in multifactorial psychiatric illnesses. These methods include parametric pedigree-based linkage analyses (including candidate gene–based linkage analysis and genome-wide searches), nonparametric methods such as affected sib pair analysis, quantitative trait loci analysis, and association studies (linkage disequilibrium and VAPSE-based candidate gene studies).

In addition to these genetic epidemiology approaches, powerful laboratory-based approaches for identifying new candidate genes and for defining the interactions between genes and between genes and environment are being developed. Of the mammalian systems, the mouse promises to be the most widely studied because of its well-defined classical genetics, short generation time, and ease of experimental manipulation. Genome-wide linkage analysis of second-generation offspring from two (usually inbred) strains with no overlapping distributions of a quantitative trait can map genes responsible for the trait. The success of this approach depends on the presence of one or a few genes that determine most of the genetic variation between the strains. Once specific genes are mapped, the relevant genes may be isolated by the methods of positional cloning that have been successful in elucidating human disease genes.

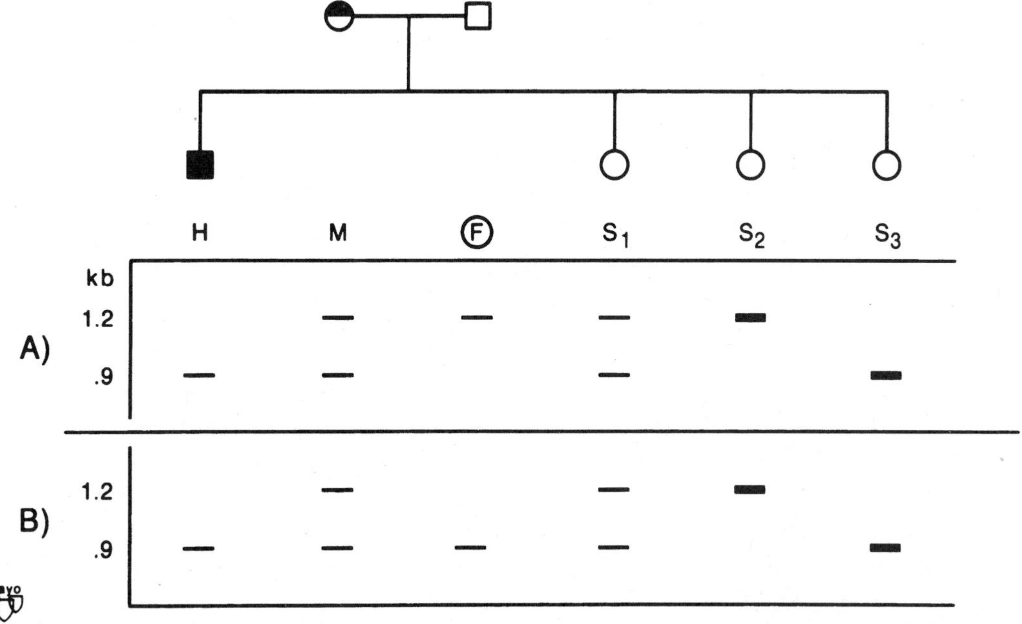

Figure 13–6 *Indirect DNA-based diagnosis for hemophilia A.* (A) Southern blot *for a hypothetical family in which the sisters of an affected individual desire carrier testing. An RFLP at a* Bcl *I restriction endonuclease site in intron 18 is informative in this family. The individual with hemophilia (H) has the 0.9-kb allele. The mother (M) is heterozygous for the polymorphism. Thus, her two X chromosomes can be distinguished by this RFLP, a necessary prerequisite for diagnosis in this family. The father (F) of H has to have the 1.2-kb allele on his one X chromosome. Sister one (S_1) is a carrier; she inherited the 1.2-kb allele from F because that is the only allele that he has. Thus, she received the 0.9-kb allele from M. Because H has the disease and, by inference, a mutation in the factor VIII gene, the mutated gene is linked to the 0.9-kb marker in M. Thus, S_1 is a carrier because she received that 0.9 kb allele from M. Sister two (S_2) is a noncarrier because she received the factor VIII gene linked to the 1.2-kb allele. This gene is known to be of normal function because the mother is an asymptomatic carrier. Sister three (S_3) has two copies of the 0.9-kb allele. Thus, F could not be her biological father because he transmits the 1.2-kb allele to all of his female offspring. Regardless of true paternity, S_2 is a carrier because she must have received the 0.9-kb allele from M,* unless there was an adoption that the family is not discussing or there was a mix-up in the nursery. (B) *Same Southern blot data as in A, except that F now has the 0.9-kb allele. F does not have hemophilia; he is among the 23% of caucasian males who have this polymorphic allele. In this family, S_1 is a noncarrier; she must inherit the 0.9-kb allele from F because that is the only allele that he has. Thus, the 1.2-kb allele was inherited from M, and this allele is linked to a functional factor VIII gene. S_2 remains a noncarrier because she did not inherit the 0.9-kb allele from M, and F is not her biological father. S_3 is a carrier. Thus, analysis of the biological father is critical for correctly diagnosing the carrier status of S_1.* (A and B *from Sommer SS, Sobell JL: Application of DNA-based diagnosis to patient care: The example of hemophilia A. Mayo Clinic Proc 1987; 62:387–404.)*

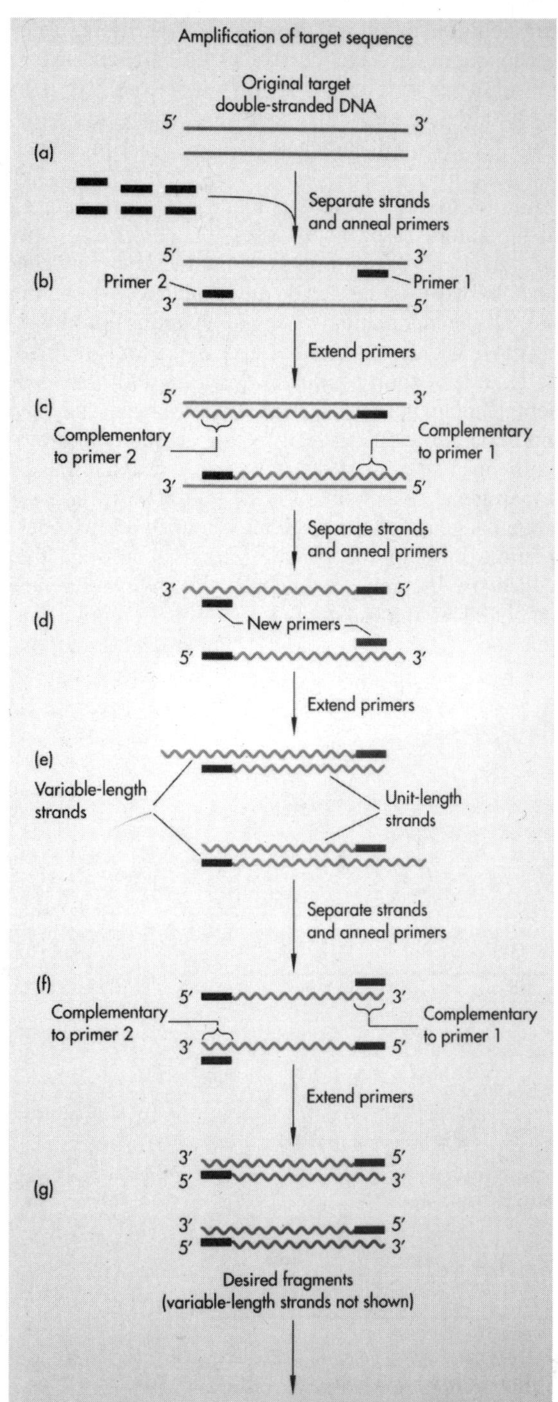

Figure 13–7 *Polymerase chain reaction.* (a) *The starting material is a double-stranded DNA molecule.* (b) *The strands are separated by heating the reaction mixture and then cooled so that the primers anneal to their complementary regions in the template DNA (one on each strand).* (c) *DNA* polymerase *(e.g.,* Taq *polymerase) synthesizes new strands of DNA, complementary to the template, that extend a variable distance beyond the position of the primer binding site on the other template.* (d) *The reaction mixture is heated again; the original and newly synthesized DNA strands separate. Four binding sites are now available to the primers, one on each of the two original strands and the two new DNA strands (for simplicity, subsequent events involving the original strands are omitted).* (e) *DNA polymerase synthesizes new complementary strands, but the extension of these chains is limited precisely to the target sequence. The two newly synthesized chains thus span exactly the region specified by the primers.* (f *and* g) *The process is repeated, typically for a total of 30 cycles, and results in the exponential increase in the region spanned by the two primers.* (a *to* g *from Recombinant DNA 2/E by Watson, Gilman, Witkowski, and Zoller. Copyright © 1992 by James D. Watson, Michael Gilman, Jan Witkowski, and Mark Zoller. Used with permission of W. H. Freeman and Company.)*

Analysis of quantitative trait loci in animals can elucidate unknown genes that contribute to a particular trait. Conversely, the analysis of transgenic animals can elucidate the phenotypes associated with alteration of specific genes of interest. Transgenic animals are genetically modified to express foreign genes or to alter function of an endogenous gene (Fig. 13–9). The technology is most well developed and most actively used in the mouse. Complete loss of gene function can be created by *insertional mutagenesis* in a random fashion or by *homologous recombination* in a targeted fashion (Fig. 13–10). These transgenic animals can be bred to generate mice homozygous for nonfunctional alleles. These transgenic "knockouts" provide a powerful experimental system for understanding the role of particular genes in development and in disease states. Different lines of transgenic animals may be bred to explore the interaction of two or more genes.

The use of antisense oligonucleotides provides another means for elucidating the role of particular genes. In these experiments, short synthetic DNA sequences are designed to hybridize to a specific mRNA- or gene-regulating region of interest. The binding blocks the translation of the mRNA into functional protein or the expression of the gene. The amount and timing of the gene expression can thus be regulated and studied without the effort of creating a knockout animal. The use of antisense sequence in therapeutic strategies is illustrated in Figure 13–11.

These described experimental systems attempt to examine and manipulate known genes; of the 100,000 estimated genes in the human genome, only a fraction have been defined. The elucidation of the sequence of the entire human genome is one of the goals of the Human Genome Project. However, as important, the Human Genome Project will also delineate the genomes of other organisms, including *Escherichia coli* (bacteria), *Saccharomyces cerevisiae* (yeast), *Caenorhabditis elegans* (nematode), *Drosophila melanogaster* (fruit fly), and the mouse. These sequences will provide perspective on the human sequence and greatly enhance the utility of these experimental systems for understanding gene organization, regulation, and gene-gene as well as gene-environment interaction.

Glossary

Allele One of two or more alternative forms of a DNA sequence; for example, most persons have two functional (normal) alleles of the gene coding for phenylalanine hydroxylase, whereas carriers of phenylketonuria have one functional allele and one mutant allele.

Table 13–7 Selected Screening Strategies for Unknown Mutations

Method	Basis of Method	References and Comments
Chemical or enzymatic cleavage of heteroduplexes	Chemicals such as osmium tetroxide, hydroxylamine, or carbodiimide or enzymes such as RNase A, RNase I, mut S, or T4 endonuclease VII are used to cleave heteroduplexes formed between complementary wild-type and mutant sequences. Wherever a single base pair sequence change has occurred, the heteroduplex will contain a base pairing mismatch. Chemicals or enzymes either will cleave at mismatches or will protect mismatched nucleotides from cleavage.	Reviewed in reference 48. For chemical cleavage, a single base pair mismatch can be detected with high sensitivity in segments ranging up to 400–500 base pairs, but the method is laborious.
Denaturing gradient gel electrophoresis	Differences in denaturing properties between wild-type and mutant double-stranded sequences are monitored on one- or two-dimensional denaturing gels as follows. Heteroduplexes are formed between the wild-type and test sequences based on base pair complementarity. The heteroduplexes are then electrophoresed at a precisely constant temperature through a thin gel that contains increasing concentrations of a chemical denaturant. The DNA migrates until a partially denatured intermediate forms that has a much slower mobility than duplex DNA. If a single base pair mismatch has occurred in the heteroduplex, the melting or denaturing properties of that strand will differ from homoduplexes formed by wild-type–wild-type strands. Differential migration patterns in the gel matrix will be observed (usually through radioactive labeling and autoradiography), indicating the presence of a base pairing mismatch due to sequence changes. An alternative approach is temperature gradient gel electrophoresis that uses heat, in lieu of chemicals, as the denaturant.	Reviewed in reference 48. Up to 500–600 base pairs may be screened at a time with high sensitivity, but the technique requires technical skill and can be time-consuming.
Single-strand conformational polymorphism (SSCP) analysis	Electrophoretic differences between single-stranded wild-type and mutant sequences are distinguished by amplifying the DNA (or RNA) followed by electrophoresis on a nondenaturing gel. Characteristic secondary structures will dictate the migration pattern of the wild-type and mutant sequences through the matrix. Single base pair changes will result in a variant secondary structure that will not migrate at the same rate as wild-type sequences. To detect a high fraction of mutations, SSCP analysis is often performed under two to four conditions. A variation of SSCP, restriction endonuclease fingerprinting (REF), can screen 1- to 2-kb segments with virtually 100% sensitivity. In REF, a highly redundant SSCP pattern is generated by amplifying a 1- to 2-kb segment, digesting separately with five to six sets of restriction endonucleases, combining the samples, end labeling, heat denaturing, and electrophoresing on a nondenaturing gel.	SSCP analysis reviewed in reference 48. Convenient and rapid, but the sensitivity of the technique varies dramatically with sequence composition, segment size, and other experimental conditions. If performed under only one condition, the sensitivity is typically in the range of 70%–95% for segments of 200 base pairs. For REF, see reference 49. REF is more laborious but has almost 100% sensitivity for hemizygous segments up to 2 kb.
Dideoxy fingerprinting (ddF)	ddF is a hybrid technique combining dideoxy sequencing with SSCP analysis. A single dideoxy termination reaction is performed, followed by electrophoresis of the sample on a nondenaturing gel. From the point of the mutation onward, the dideoxy termination segments contain mutant sequence. If any one of these segments migrates abnormally, the presence of a mutation can be detected.	See references 50 and 51. Owing primarily to the introduction of great redundancy in the SSCP phenomenon, ddF is nearly 100% sensitive for all types of single base pair mutations in segments between 200 and 300 base pairs.

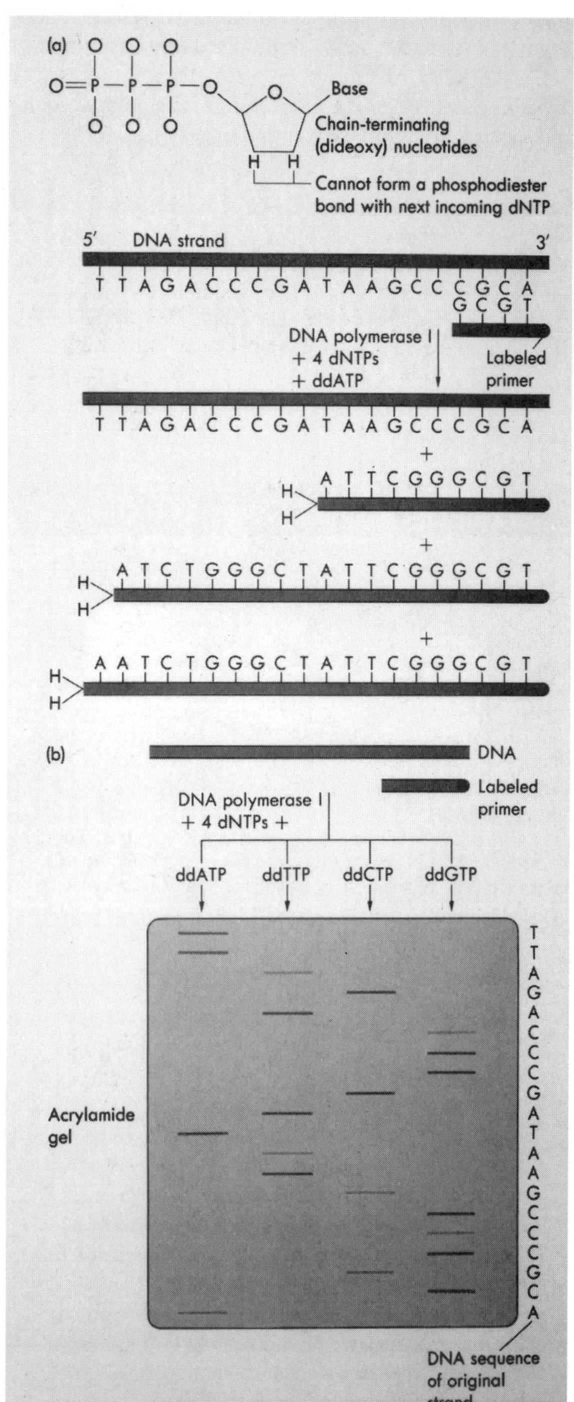

Figure 13–8 *The Sanger dideoxy chain termination method of DNA sequencing. The sequencing reaction consists of a DNA strand to be sequenced, a short labeled (e.g. , radioactively) piece of DNA (the primer) that is complementary to the end of that strand, and deoxyribonucleic acids (dNTPs; adenine, guanine, cystosine, and thymine) in optimal ratios with dideoxynucleotides (ddNTPs).* (a) *The ddNTPs are chemically altered dNTPs that cannot form phosphodiester bonds with dNTPs. When DNA polymerase is added to the reaction, normal polymerization will begin from the primer; however, when a ddNTP is incorporated, the growth of that chain will stop. If the correct ratio of ddNTPs to dNTPs is used, a series of labeled strands will result, the lengths of which are dependent on the location of a particular base relative to the end of the DNA.* (b) *A DNA strand to be sequenced, along with labeled primer, split into four DNA polymerase reactions, each containing one of the four ddNTPs. The resultant labeled fragments are separated by size on an acrylamide gel, and autoradiography is performed; the pattern of the fragments gives the DNA sequence. (*a *and* b *from Recombinant DNA 2/E by Watson, Gilman, Witkowski, and Zoller. Copyright © 1992 by James D. Watson, Michael Gilman, Jan Witkowski, and Mark Zoller. Used with permission of W. H. Freeman and Company.)*

Alternative splicing The removal of introns and joining (i.e., splicing together) of exons in transcribed nuclear RNA at alternative sites to create different mRNAs from the same underlying DNA template.

Alu family A set of dispersed, related sequences of approximately 300 base pairs in the human genome.

Amino acid Twenty α–amino acids are the basic units of proteins; the amino acids differ by the functional group (termed residue) attached to the α-carbon of the carboxylic acid moiety.

Anticipation Increasing severity or earlier onset of disease in successive generations in a pedigree; anticipation is found in diseases due to expansion of triplet repeats.

Association studies Research strategies that use unrelated diseased individuals (cases) and non-diseased unrelated individuals or non-inherited parental alleles as controls in an attempt to demonstrate that a particular risk

Table 13–8 Selected Screening Strategies for Known Mutations

Method	Basis of Method	References and Comments
Allele-specific oligonucleotides	Oligonucleotide DNA sequences that are perfectly complementary to the allele of interest are synthesized, labeled, and hybridized to amplified DNA and incubated at a temperature that dissociates duplexes with one or more base mismatches but does not dissociate the perfectly matched duplexes. Subjects with the allele of interest are identified.	Reviewed in reference 52.
Polymerase chain reaction (PCR) amplification of specific alleles (PASA) Allele-specific amplification Amplification refractory mutation system	An alternative approach to allele-specific oligonucleotides that does not use radioactively labeled probes but takes advantage of PCR methodology to rapidly and selectively amplify only the variant allele. A PCR primer is designed so that the 3′ end matches the mutant sequence. Amplification occurs efficiently when genomic DNA with the mutation is present, but amplification is inefficient for the mismatched wild-type genomic DNA. The amplified allele can be detected by simple agarose gel electrophoresis. Haplotypes can be determined in the absence of relatives by using double PASA.	See reference 53. In one study, successful PASA assays were achieved for each of 69 attempted assays. A mutation can generally be detected in the presence of a 40+-fold excess of wild-type DNA.
Primer extension method Single-nucleotide primer extension (SNuPE)	In a solid-phase version of the assay, a DNA region is amplified by use of a biotin-labeled oligonucleotide primer. The biotinylated DNA is immobilized on an avidin matrix and denatured to a single strand. A second primer set is used to amplify a region beginning near the site of variation. At this site of variation, a radioactively labeled nucleoside triphosphate base is incorporated into the newly synthesized complementary DNA strand and is detected by autoradiography.	Reviewed in reference 52. SNuPE can typically detect the mutant allele in the presence of a 1000-fold excess of wild-type DNA.
Restriction endonuclease digestion Primer-specified restriction map modification	If a sequence change creates or abolishes a recognition sequence for a restriction endonuclease, individuals with the variant or marker allele may be rapidly identified by PCR, restriction endonuclease digestion, and agarose gel electrophoresis of the created fragments. If a restricton site does not occur, one sometimes may be created artificially by PCR with specially designed primers.	See references 54 and 55.
Oligonucletoide ligation assay Ligase chain reaction PCR-mediated ligase detection reaction	The basis of these methods is the use of PCR primers that anneal at sequences adjacent to one another and that are complementary to the mutant sequence. A ligation reaction is performed that will ligate the primers together only when they exactly match the template. If the template has a wild-type sequence, the ligation will not occur. There are various adaptations of this basic scheme.	Reviewed in references 52 and 56.

factor (e.g., a particular allele) is more prevalent among those affected (or, conversely, that a putative protective factor is more prevalent among the unaffected individuals); association studies in psychiatric genetics are of two general classes: 1) linkage disequilibrium studies and 2) candidate gene (VAPSE)–based studies.

Assortative mating Nonrandom mating in which a member of a particular subpopulation is more likely (positive) or less likely (negative) to mate with other members of that subpopulation.

Autoradiography A technique that captures the image formed in a photographic emulsion as a result of the emission of either light or radioactivity from a labeled component that is placed next to the unexposed film.

Autosomes Chromosomes other than the sex chromosome; humans have 22 pairs of autosomes and 1 pair of sex chromosomes.

Base pair Verb: Partnership of purines with pyrimidines in forming the double helix of DNA; adenosine pairs with thymine, and guanine pairs with cytosine; noun: distance along DNA is measured in base pairs or in kilobases (1 kb = 1000 base pairs).

Carrier A phenotypically normal individual who is heterozygous for a recessive or X-linked mutant allele.

Centimorgan (cM) A unit of measure of recombination frequency; 1 cM is equal to a 1% chance that a marker at one genetic locus will be separated from a marker at a second locus owing to crossing over in a single generation; in the human genome, 1 cM is, on average, equal to 1 million base pairs.

Centromere Central constriction of a chromosome; during DNA replication, the chromosomal material duplicates into sister chromatids, which are connected at the centromere.

Codon A group of three nucleotides that code for an amino acid or a termination signal.

Complementary DNA (cDNA) A DNA sequence that is generated from an mRNA template; this sequence, which is single stranded and complementary to the mRNA, contains the coding region of the gene plus additional upstream and downstream sequences but does not contain intronic sequences.

Compound heterozygote An individual with an autosomal recessive disease caused by two different mutations, each in a different allele of the gene.

Concordance rates The rate of co-incidence of a disorder among monozygotic or dizygotic twins; there are two methods of calculating concordance, pairwise and probandwise; the pair method counts every pair only once, whereas the proband method can count a pair of twins twice if each twin were independently ascertained; probandwise rates are commonly used because these can be compared directly with population rates.

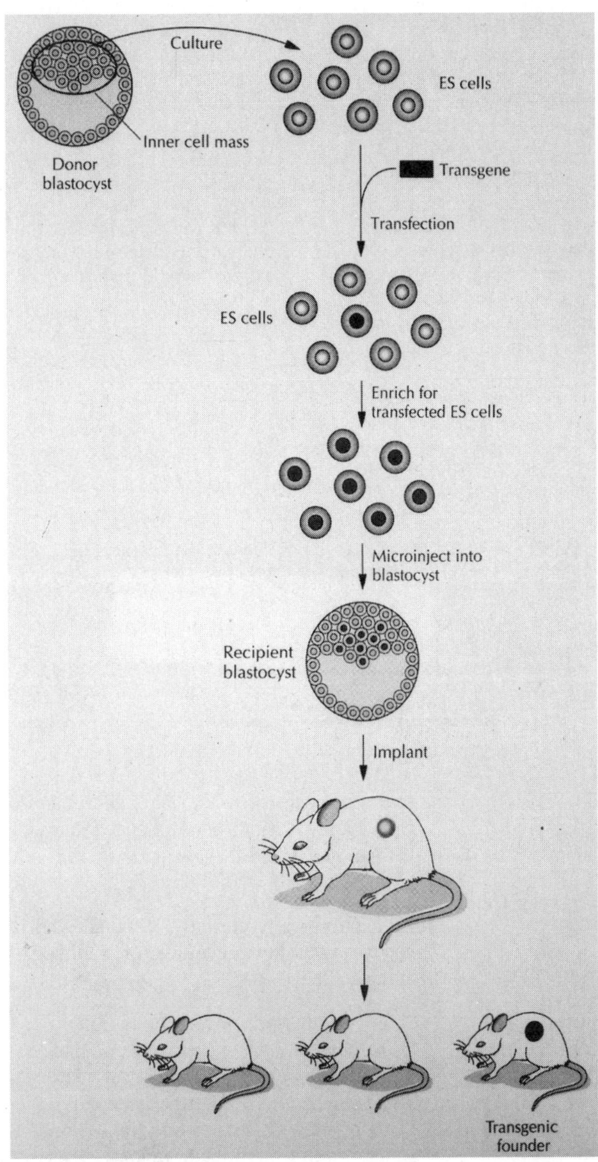

Figure 13–9 *Establishment of* transgenic *mice with genetically engineered embryonic stem (ES) cells. An embryonic stem cell culture is initiated from the inner cell mass of a mouse blastocyte. The embryonic stem cells are transfected with a* transgene. *After growth, the transfected cells are identified by either polymerase chain reaction analysis or a positive-negative selection procedure (see Fig. 13–10) in which the non-transfected cells are selectively eliminated. Populations of transfected cells can be cultured and inserted into blastocytes, which are then implanted into foster mothers. Transgenic lines can be established by breeding crosses from founder mice that carry the transgene in their germlines. (From Glick BR, Pasternak JJ: Molecular Biotechnology: Principles and Applications of Recombinant DNA. Washington, DC: ASM Press, 1994.)*

Conserved amino acid An amino acid that is identical through evolutionary time; sometimes substitutions of certain chemically similar amino acids are allowed.

Continuous trait A trait in which the possible phenotypes do not occur in discrete classes but rather occur in a continuous range from one extreme to the other (e.g., blood pressure, IQ).

Cosegregation The coinheritance of two genetic traits or alleles.

CpG The dinucleotide that is often methylated at the 5-carbon atom of the pyrimidine ring (5-methylcytosine). Methylated CpG dinucleotides are dramatic hotspots of mutations.

Denaturation The melting, by breakage of hydrogen bonds, of double-stranded DNA into single strands.

Deoxyribonucleic acid (DNA) The macromolecule, usually composed of two polynucleotide chains in a double helix, that is the carrier of the genetic information in cells and many viruses.

Dominant (trait) Those conditions that are expressed in heterozygotes who have one copy of the normal (wild-type) allele and one copy of a variant, or mutant, allele.

Electrophoresis The separation of molecules on the basis of differential mobility in an electric field (secondary to size and conformation differences) by passing an electric current through a gel matrix (e.g., agarose, acrylamide).

Endonuclease An enzyme that breaks internal phosphodiester bonds in DNA or RNA.

Epistasis Interaction between two genes such that one gene interferes with or prevents expression of the other.

Evolutionary conservation The extent to which amino acid residues have been retained in particular genes through billions of years of evolutionary time; the degree of evolutionary conservation can be estimated by comparing amino acid sequences in one organism (e.g., *Homo sapiens*) with other evolutionarily distant organisms (e.g., mice, reptiles, fish); residues that have been highly conserved over evolutionary time (i.e., are identical or only conservatively substituted in highly distant organisms) are most likely essential for the function of the gene.

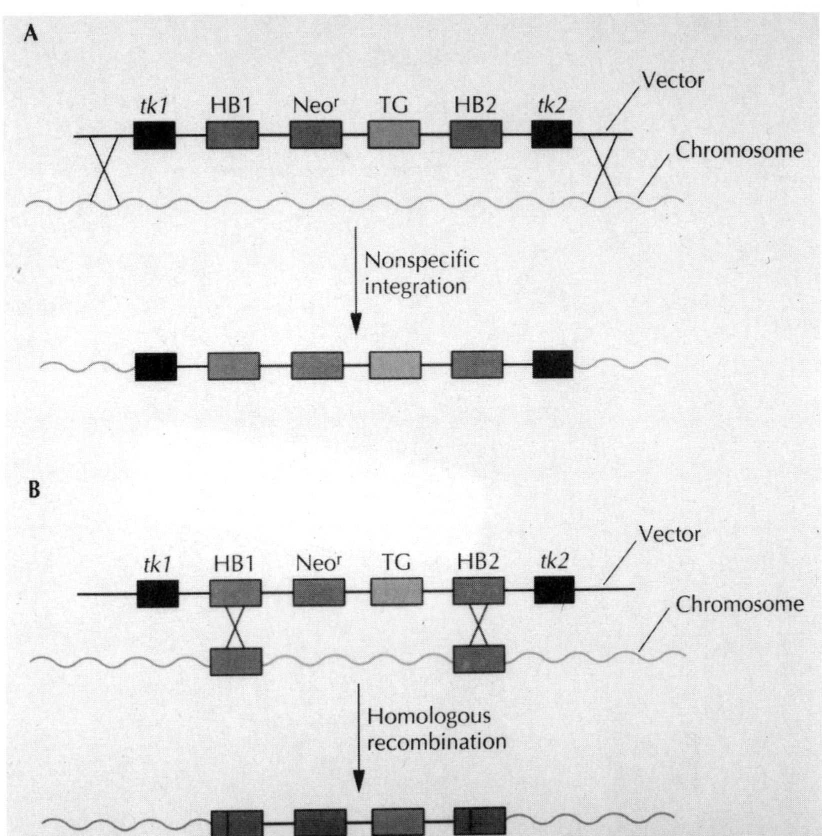

Figure 13–10 *Positive-negative selection of cells that have undergone homologous recombination.* (A) *Result of nonspecific integration: both genes for thymidine kinase* (tk1, tk2), *the two DNA sequences that are homologous to a specific chromosomal region in the recipient cells (HB1, HB2), a gene (Neo^r) that confers resistance to the cytotoxic compound G418, and the transgene (TG) are incorporated into the chromosome. After transfection, cells are selected for resistance to both G418 and gancyclovir, which becomes cytotoxic to cells that synthesize thymidine kinase. Other nonhomologous integrations may occur and produce inserts with one or the other of the thymidine kinase genes. After treatment with G418 and gancyclovir, all cells with nonspecific integration of the input DNA are killed.* (B) *Result of homologous recombination: the product of a double crossover between homologous blocks (HB1, HB2) of DNA on the vector DNA and on chromosomal DNA does not contain either of the two thymidine kinase genes* (tk1, tk2). *After treatment with G418 and gancyclovir, only cells that have undergone homologous recombination survive. (*A *and* B *from Glick BR, Pasternak JJ: Molecular Biotechnology: Principles and Applications of Recombinant DNA. Washington, DC: ASM Press, 1994.)*

Exon Any segment of an *interrupted gene* that is represented in the mature mRNA.

Expression analysis An in vitro assay for the transcription of DNA and its translation into a protein product.

5′ and 3′ ends These numbers refer to the ribose carbons of adjacent nucleotides that are connected by phosphodiester bonds during the polymerization of DNA or RNA; nucleic acid synthesis in vivo is always in the 5′ to 3′ direction; thus, the 5′ end is the beginning of the nucleic acid, and any extension of an oligonucleotide by DNA polymerase occurs by addition to the 3′ end of the oligonucleotide; in duplex DNA, the two strands are oriented in the opposite direction (antiparallel).

Frameshift mutation A mutation involving a deletion or insertion that is not an exact multiple of 3 base pairs, which changes the reading frame of the gene; after a frameshift mutation, the protein sequence is garbled and often prematurely terminated.

Gene The segment of DNA that is involved in producing a polypeptide chain (protein) or an RNA molecule of physiological function, such as transfer RNA; it includes a region preceding (5′ untranslated region) and following (3′ untranslated region) the protein coding (or RNA) region as well as intervening sequences (introns) between individual coding segments (exons).

Gene disruption The entire loss, not simply alteration in level, of gene activity.

Genetic heterogeneity Phenotypically identical traits or diseases caused in different families, or population subgroups, by different genes.

Genotype The genetic composition of an organism (i.e., alleles at a specific genetic locus) as distinguished from its appearance (phenotype).

Haplotype The alleles present at a particular combination of polymorphic loci in a defined region of DNA, or the pattern of polymorphism on a particular chromosome.

Heteroplasmy The simultaneous occurrence of both mutated and nonmutated mitochondrial genomes in the cytoplasm of the cell; depending on the proportion of genomes that are mutated, the phenotype of the individual will differ; thus, in mitochondrially inherited diseases, the phenotypes of family members may differ dramatically depending on "dosage."

Heterozygous Having two different alleles at a given locus; heterozygous individuals may be termed heterozygotes.

Homologous recombination The exchange of genetic material between complementary DNA sequences (i.e., homologues).

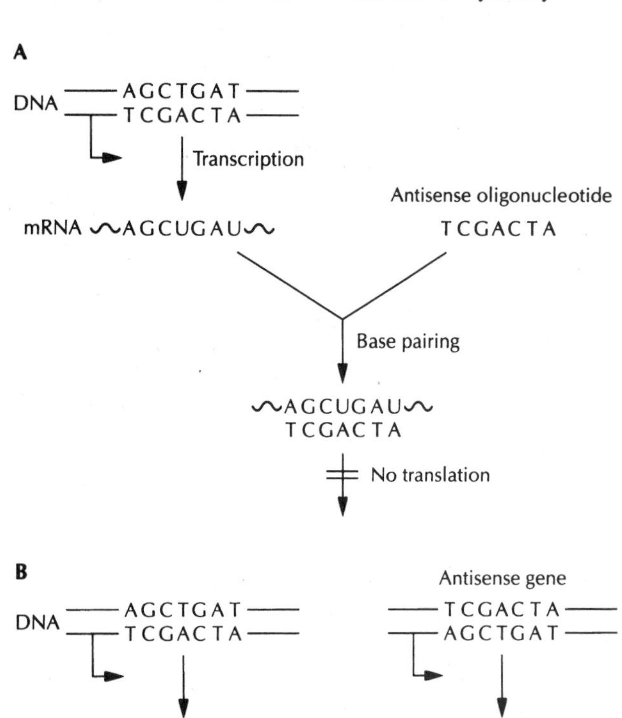

Figure 13–11 *Two strategies using antisense oligonucleotide therapy for inhibition of specific mRNAs. The right-angled, rightward pointing arrows show the direction of transcription from the lower DNA strand of the DNA duplexes of a chromosome.* (A) *Antisense oligonucleotide strategy. An oligonucleotide that has an antisense sequence to the region of a target mRNA is introduced into a cell; by base pairing to the target mRNA, it prevents the* translation *of this mRNA.* (B) *Antisense gene strategy. An expressible gene that is cloned in its reverse orientation is introduced into a cell. The RNA that is transcribed from this construct is the antisense sequence of the normal mRNA. When the antisense RNA base pairs with the mRNA, translation of the mRNA is prevented. The antisense RNA does not contain signals for the initiation of translation.* (A *and* B *from Glick BR, Pasternak JJ: Molecular Biotechnology: Principles and Applications of Recombinant DNA. Washington, DC: ASM Press, 1994.)*

Homologues The two members of a pair of corresponding chromosomes.

Homozygous Having the same two alleles at a given locus; homozygous individuals may be termed homozygotes.

Hybridization The pairing of complementary RNA and DNA strands to give an RNA-DNA hybrid.

Imprinting A change in gene expression that occurs during passage through the male or female germline with the result that the paternal and maternal alleles have different properties in the early embryo; may be caused by DNA *methylation.*

Insertional mutagenesis Loss of function of an allele by the integration of a transgene, carried in a plasmid or retrovirus, into the genome; insertional mutagenesis occurs in a random manner, because the plasmid or retrovirus containing the transgene does not have a preferred site for integration.

Interrupted gene A gene that contains both exonic and intronic sequences, that is, sequences that represent the protein product (exons) as well as additional sequences than interrupt the coding region (introns); the introns are spliced out in the production of mRNA.

Intron Any segment of an interrupted gene that is not represented in the mature RNA product; introns are part of the primary nuclear transcript but are spliced out to produce mRNA, which is then transported to the cytoplasm for translation into a polypeptide.

Isochore Long DNA segments, typically several hundred *kilobases,* that are homogeneous in guanine and cytosine nucleotides (G + C content); they can be subdivided into a small number of families characterized by different G + C levels; it has been estimated that G + C–rich isochore families represent about 31% of the mammalian genome; very rich G + C isochores represent 3% to 5%.

Kilobase (kb) 1000 base pairs.

Line 1 A set of dispersed, related sequences in the human genome; although the full length is approximately 5 kb, the sequences are often truncated.

Linkage disequilibrium The cosegregation of two or more genetic markers more frequently than would be expected; linkage disequilibrium implies that a group of markers has been inherited coordinately; typically a specific mutation occurs on a chromosome with an ancient haplotype and the mutation cosegregates with that haplotype because insufficient time has passed to reach equilibrium through random recombination.

Locus, loci The position on a chromosome at which the gene for a particular trait resides; a locus may be occupied by any one of the alleles of the gene.

Lod score Lod is an abbreviation for logarithm of the odds; the lod score is a measure of the confidence in establishing a putative genetic linkage, that is, the logarithm of the probability of obtaining the observed data if linkage is assumed divided by the probability of obtaining the observed data if nonlinkage is assumed; by convention, a lod score of 3 or more is interpreted as evidence of linkage (observed data are more likely to have been observed if the marker and disease locus were linked than if they were unlinked), and a lod score of −2 or less is interpreted as evidence against linkage; however, the lod 3 criterion was developed for application in mendelian traits or diseases and is based on an estimated prior probability of linkage, but in diseases with an unknown mode of transmission, there is no such meaningful prior probability and therefore more stringent criteria must be applied.

Markers A genetic polymorphism in a region of DNA that allows the differentiation of different forms of a gene or chromosomal region.

Meiosis Cell division resulting in the formation of germ cells with half of the full chromosomal content (i.e., haploid genomes).

Mendelian inheritance Classical inheritance in which a single nuclear gene defect causes disease that is transmitted in an autosomal dominant, autosomal recessive, or sex-linked fashion.

Messenger RNA (mRNA) The sequence of nucleotides generated from a DNA template that contains the region of the gene coding for the amino acid (protein) product (coding region) plus additional sequences on either end that do not directly represent protein but are involved presumably in regulation of protein synthesis.

Meta-analyses Statistical analyses in which data from several different studies are culled and reanalyzed; the approach is particularly useful when there is a specific question to answer and at least a few relatively strong studies that come to different conclusions.

Methylation The addition of a methyl group to a macromolecule; DNA methylation is believed to be one mechanism by which imprinting and X chromosome inactivation are regulated.

Microsatellite Repetitive DNA sequences of 5 base pairs or less (usually 2 to 3) that are polymorphic in the population with regard to the number of these repeated units.

Minisatellites Repetitive DNA sequences of 15 to 70 base pairs that are polymorphic in the population with regard to the number of these repeated units.

Missense mutation A DNA sequence change that results in the substitution of one amino acid for the normally occurring amino acid.

Mitochondrial DNA Nonnuclear unique DNA that is contained in cytoplasmic organelles called mitochondria; mitochondrial DNA is present in many copies per cell, is maternally inherited, and evolves 5 to 10 times as rapidly as genomic DNA; it encodes 22 transfer RNA molecules, 2 ribosomal RNA molecules, and about 13 proteins.

Mitosis Process of nuclear division through which one cell gives rise to two daughter cells with identical genetic material.

Morbid risk The probability that a person who survives through the period of greatest susceptibility or manifestation will develop a disease (i.e., the denominator for calculating risk is corrected for age, thus including only those at risk).

Mosaicism Condition in which an individual has two or more genetically distinct cell lines derived from a single zygote, but differing because of mutation during embryogenesis.

Multifactorial inheritance Refers to inheritance due to the effects of polygenes plus environmental components.

Mutation A change in DNA sequence; in sperm and ova, referred to as germline mutations and are transmissible to offspring; in nongerm cells, referred to as somatic or acquired mutations.

Mutational hotspot A site in a DNA molecule at which the mutation rate is higher than at other sites; recombinational hotspots also occur at which the rate of recombination is greater than in other regions.

Nondisjunction The failure of two homologous chromosomes to separate during *meiosis* I, or of two chromatids of a chromosome to separate in meiosis II or *mitosis,* so that both pass to the same daughter cell and one daughter cell receives none.

Noninformative When two alleles of a chromosome pair have identical marker patterns, the inheritance of one allele versus another will not be distinguishable in offspring; therefore, these alleles will not be useful in linkage studies in which the coinheritance of a particular marker allele with disease is sought.

Nonmendelian inheritance Pattern of disease inheritance not due to the effect of defects in a single nuclear gene, such as multifactorial inheritance, uniparental disomy, genomic imprinting, anticipation and trinucleotide repeat expansions, and mitochondrial inheritance.

Nonparametric models In a statistical genetics context, models that do not require specification of particular parameters including mode of inheritance and penetrance.

Nonsense mutation A mutation that results in premature protein termination because of the substitution of a translational termination signal in place of a normally occurring amino acid.

Nucleotide The basic units constituting DNA and RNA; a nucleotide is a molecule with three components: a heterocyclic ring of carbon and nitrogen atoms (the nitrogenous base), a five-carbon sugar in ring form (pentose), and a phosphate group; the nitrogenous base can be either a purine (adenine or guanine) or a pyrimidine (thymine, cytosine, or uracil).

Odds ratio Ratio of the odds of exposure among the diseased to the odds of exposure among the nondiseased in retrospective (case-control) studies; the odds ratio approximates the *relative risk* when the disease of interest is rare and when sampling is unbiased with regard to the risk factor of interest.

Oligonucleotide A short segment of single-stranded DNA that is typically less than 50 nucleotides; automation of the chemical synthesis of oligonucleotides has made any desired oligonucleotide sequence readily available for application in methods such as the polymerase chain reaction.

Penetrance A population parameter denoting the percentage of individuals with a particular gene or gene combination that exhibits the corresponding phenotype to any degree.

Phenotype The observable manifestations of a specific genotype.

Pleiotropy Multiple physiological effects of a single mutation in an individual.

Polygenic inheritance Multiple small effects of many genes acting together in an additive fashion.

Polymerase Enzymes that catalyze the formation of DNA or RNA in the presence of existing DNA or RNA templates.

Polymerase chain reaction (PCR) A method that can routinely amplify a segment of DNA by more than 1 million–fold; PCR consists of multiple repetitions of three steps.

Polymerase chain reaction amplification of specific alleles (PASA) A PCR-based method for amplifying one particular allele preferentially to another that varies by only one base pair; alternatively known as allele-specific amplification or amplification refractory mutation system.

Polymerase slippage Small insertions and deletions of nucleotides during DNA replication or repair that are due to the aberrant movement of the polymerase in either the 3′ or the 5′ direction.

Polymorphism Difference in DNA sequence among individuals; by convention, sequence differences occurring in at least 1% of a population are considered polymorphisms; less common sequence differences are termed rare variants.

Population stratification Statistical bias that occurs in allelic association studies when one population under study varies in ethnic background from the other groups under study; because populations often differ in underlying allele frequencies, when a particular allele is examined for association with disease, it is essential that study subjects be ethnically homogeneous to prevent spurious associations.

Positional cloning The use of various cloning strategies to identify, isolate, and characterize a gene when that unknown gene is mapped on the basis of linkage studies.

Prions Cellular proteins that are capable of pathological conformational rearrangements and that can catalyze similar rearrangements of other prion molecules; prion analogues can occur with multiple gene products, in unicellular as well as in multicellular organisms, in proteins with or without a secreted component, and in a context in which extracellular transmissibility is either observed (e.g., kuru in humans) or not observed (ureidosuccinate transport in the presence of ammonium ion and enhancement of ocher suppression in yeast).

Probe Single-stranded DNA or RNA molecules of specific base sequence, labeled either radioactively or immunologically, that are used to detect the complementary base sequence by hybridization.

Promoter The sequence elements, generally located 5′ to the gene, that fix the site of initiation of transcription and control mRNA quantity and tissue specificity.

Pseudoautosomal inheritance Small regions of the X and Y chromosomes that behave like autosomal chromosomes during meiosis and exchange genetic material that can be transmitted to offspring.

Pseudogene DNA sequences with the structures of expressed genes but that are incapable of producing active protein products because of the acquisition of mutations or the loss of regulatory signals.

Quantitative trait A trait (e.g., height, IQ) usually measured on a continuous scale that results from the combined action of multiple genes and their interplay with environmental factors.

Recessive (trait) Those conditions that are clinically manifested only in individuals homozygous for the mutant gene (i.e., both alleles of the gene are mutant).

Recombination During the generation of the sex chromosomes (meiosis), chiasmata are formed and certain chromosomal segments are exchanged between homologous chromosomes (crossing over) so that genes located on the same chromosome are not always inherited together.

Recombination fraction (θ, theta) The probability that a recombination event will occur between two gene sequences; measured by determining the probability that two genotypes (or their phenotypes) are coinherited (cosegregate).

Relative risk The ratio of the incidence of disease among those exposed to a risk factor to the incidence of disease among the unexposed (see *odds ratio*).

Restriction endonuclease A bacterial enzyme that recognizes a specific DNA sequence and cleaves phosphodiester bonds.

Restriction fragment length polymorphism (RFLP) An operational term that is derived from analysis of Southern blots; polymorphisms that may be detected by digesting DNA with *restriction endonucleases,* and when the digested DNA is subjected to gel electrophoresis, the resulting fragments can be identified by their differential, size-determined migration; RFLPs are inherited in a mendelian fashion so the cosegregation of a particular RFLP allele with disease (and, hence, a putative disease gene) can be followed in a pedigree to determine whether linkage (nonrandom cosegregation of the RFLP marker and a hypothesized disease locus) exists; the overwhelming majority of RFLPs are of no functional significance.

Ribonucleic acid (RNA) A nucleic acid usually generated from a DNA template but that contains uracil in place of the thymine base and a ribose sugar instead of the deoxyribose sugar.

Segregation analysis Statistical analysis to determine the underlying pattern of inheritance (transmission mode) of a disorder in families.

Somatic mutation An alteration of DNA sequence that is acquired in nongerm cells.

Southern blotting A nucleic acid hybridization method used to locate particular nucleic acid sequences from a larger segment; typically, DNA fragments are separated electrophoretically, denatured, transferred from a gel to a membrane filter, and then exposed to radioactive DNA or RNA under conditions of renaturation; after autoradiography, the hybridized fragment is detectable.

Splicing The removal of intervening sequences (introns) in the generation of mature mRNA.

Splicing junction, splice donor site The nucleotide sequences immediately surrounding the sites of breakage and reunion in the splicing out of introns and uniting of exons to form mRNA in an interrupted gene; the left splicing junction is called the donor and is at the left end of the intron; the right junction is called the acceptor and is at the right end.

Susceptibility gene A gene that is neither necessary nor sufficient for disease causation but that contributes with other genes or environmental factors in disease causation.

Telomere Tips of the chromosomes.

Termination codon Nucleotide codon that signals the end of translation.

Transcription The process of RNA synthesis from a DNA strand as a template that is catalyzed by RNA polymerase.

Transgene A gene from one source that has been incorporated into the genome of another organism.

Transgenic animal An experimental animal in which foreign DNA, usually a human gene, has been incorporated into the germline so that all successive generations will express the gene.

Transition, transversion Transitions are sequence changes that occur when one pyrimidine base (cytosine, thymine, or uracil) is changed to the other, or when one purine base (guanine or adenine) is changed to the other; in contrast, transversions change a purine to a pyrimidine or vice versa.

Translation The synthesis of a chain of linked amino acids (protein) on the mRNA template.

Transposition The movement and random reinsertion of a DNA sequence (transposon or insertion sequence) at a new location in the genome; transposons are DNA sequences; retroposons mobilize by an RNA form.

Trinucleotide repeat expansions Triplet nucleotides that are polymorphic in repeat number and can expand or contract in successive generations; expansion of unstable triplet repeats has been implicated in several neuropsychiatric diseases including Huntington's chorea.

Uniparental disomy Situation in which both chromosomes of a pair have been transmitted by the same parent, whereas none is transmitted by the other parent.

Variable expressivity Differences in the nature and severity of the phenotype arising from a particular genotype.

Variable number tandem repeats (VNTRs) Repetitive DNA sequences that may be variable in number of base pairs in the repeat; VNTRs include *microsatellites* (repeated units of 5 base pairs or less) and *minisatellites* (repeated units of 15 to 70 base pairs).

Variants affecting protein structure or expression (VAPSEs) An operational term that derives from analysis of DNA sequence; refers to sequence variants that change protein sequence or alter consensus sequences in regulatory regions or splice junctions; as opposed to RFLPs or variable number tandem repeats, VAPSEs have a substantial probability of being of functional significance.

Bibliography

General Genetics Texts

Gelehrter TD, Collins FS: Principles of Medical Genetics. Baltimore: Williams & Wilkins, 1990.
A short text with a goood glossary that reviews basic gene structure and expression, principles of mendelian and nonmendelian inheritance, cytogenetics, and some biochemical and molecular genetic features of selected human genetic diseases.

Griffiths AJF, Miller JH, Suzuki DT, et al (eds): An Introduction to Genetic Analysis, 5th ed. New York: WH Freeman, 1993.
Nicely illustrated text with an excellent treatment of the mutational process.

Hartl DL: Genetics, 3rd ed. Boston: Jones & Bartlett Publishers, 1994.
Nicely illustrated, introductory college-level text in genetics. Informative problem sets follow each chapter.

Vogel F, Motulsky V (eds): Human Genetics, Problems and Approaches, 2nd ed. Berlin: Springer-Verlag, 1986.

There is a good section on the mutational process. For readers with serious interest in human genetics, this magnificent book is worth buying because its more than 2400 references serve as a useful compendium of papers before the "PCR era."

Molecular Biology

Lewin B (ed): Genes V. New York: Oxford University Press, 1994.
Contains an excellent glossary in addition to detailed descriptions of basic genetic mechanisms of DNA replication, transcription, and translation as well as cell structure and regulation.

Sherman TG, Watson SJ: Molecular Biology Technology: A Primer. Kalamazoo, MI: Upjohn Company, 1992.
A short primer of the basics of molecular biology technology including gene structure, cloning, and expression, written as a guide for clinicians.

Watson JD, Gilman M, Witkowski J, Zoller M (eds): Recombinant DNA, 2nd ed. New York: WH Freeman, 1992.
An excellent short text that includes many useful diagrams on basic molecular biology principles and laboratory techniques.

Specialized Texts

Buyse ML (ed): Birth Defects Encyclopedia, Volumes 1 and 2. Center for Birth Defects Information Services. Oxford, UK: Blackwell Scientific Publications, 1990.
An illustrated compendium of congenital and other anomalies of clinical relevance.

Emery AEH, Rimoin DL (eds): Principles and Practice of Medical Genetics, Volumes 1 and 2, 2nd ed. New York: Churchill Livingstone, 1990.
Standard text for clinical geneticists.

Khoury MJ, Beaty TH, Cohen BH: Fundamentals of Genetic Epidemiology. New York: Oxford University Press, 1993.
Introduction to the design and analysis of genetic epidemiology studies, including segregation, linkage, and association designs.

King RA, Rotter JI, Motulsky AG (eds): The Genetic Basis of Common Diseases. New York: Oxford University Press, 1992.
Review chapters on the genetic basis of nonmendelian multifactorial diseases including autoimmune disorders, hypertension, infertility and gynecological disorders, cancer, neurological disorders, and psychiatric disorders.

McKusick VA (ed): Mendelian Inheritance in Man. Catalogs of Autosomal Dominant, Autosomal Recessive, and X-Linked Phenotypes, Volumes 1 and 2, 10th ed. Baltimore: The Johns Hopkins University Press, 1992.
Catalog of more than 6000 phenotypes of proven or possible mendelian inheritance; also available on-line (OMIM: Online Mendelian Inheritance in Man).

Scriver CR, Beaudet AL, Sly WS, Valle D (eds): The Metabolic Basis of Inherited Disease, 7th ed. New York: McGraw-Hill, 1995.
A three-volume review of mendelian diseases for which the defective gene products are known.

References

1. Sankaranarayanan K: Ionizing radiation and genetic risks. I. Epidemiological, population genetic, biochemical and molecular aspects of Mendelian diseases. Mutat Res 1991; 258:3–49.
2. Vogel F, Motulsky V: Human Genetics, Problems and Approaches, 2nd ed. Berlin: Springer-Verlag, 1986.
3. Sommer SS, Rocca WA: Prion analogues and twin studies in Parkinson's disease. Neurology 1996; 46:273–275.
4. Prescott CA, Gottesman II: Genetically mediated vulnerability to schizophrenia. Psychiatr Clin North Am 1993; 16:245–267.
5. Bertelsen A, Harvald B, Hauge M: A Danish twin study of manic depressive disorders. Br J Psychiatry 1977; 130:330–351.
6. Nurnberger JI, Goldin LR, Gershon ES: Genetics of psychiatric disorders. In Winokur G, Clayton P (eds): The Medical Basis of Psychiatry. Philadelphia: WB Saunders, 1986:486–521.
7. Torgersen S: Genetic factors in moderately severe and mild affective disorders. Arch Gen Psychiatry 1986; 43:222–226.
8. McGuffin P, Katz R: The genetics of depression and manic-depressive disorder. Br J Psychiatry 1989; 155:294–304.
9. Kendler K, Neale M, Kessler R, et al: A population-based twin study of panic disorder in women. Psychol Med 1993; 23:397–406.
10. Torgersen S: Genetic factors in anxiety disorders. Arch Gen Psychiatry 1983; 40:1085–1089.
11. Gottesman II: Schizophrenia Genesis. New York: WH Freeman, 1991.
12. McGuffin P, Katz R: Nature, nurture and affective disorder. In Deakin JWF (ed): The Biology of Depression. London: Gaskell, 1986:26–51.
13. Reich T, Cloninger CR, Suarez B, Rice J: Genetics of the affective disorders. In Wing JK, Wing L (eds): Handbook of Psychiatry, Psychoses of Unknown Aetiology. Cambridge, UK: Cambridge University Press, 1982:147–159.
14. Weissman M, Wickramaratne P, Adams P, et al: The relationship between panic disorder and major depression: A new family study. Arch Gen Psychiatry 1993; 50:767–780.
15. Woodman CL, Crowe RR: The genetics of panic disorder. In Asnis GM, Van Praag HM (eds): Panic Disorder: Clinical, Biological, and Treatment Aspects. New York: John Wiley & Sons, 1995:66–79.
16. Cardon LR, Smith SD, Fulker DW, et al: Quantitative trait locus for reading disability on chromosome 6. Science 1994; 266:276–279.
17. O'Donovan MC, Owen MJ: Advances and retreats in the molecular genetics of major mental illness. Ann Med 1992; 24:171–177.
18. Craddock N, McGuffin P: Approaches to the genetics of affective disorder. Ann Med 1993; 25:317–322.
19. Kaufmann CA, Malaspina D: Molecular genetics of schizophrenia. Psychiatr Ann 1993; 23:111–122.
20. Brunner HG, Nelen M, van Zandvoort P, et al: X-linked borderline mental retardation with prominent behavioral disturbance: Phenotype, genetic localization, and evidence for disturbed monoamine metabolism. Am J Hum Genet 1993; 52:1032–1039.
21. Brunner HG, Nelen M, Breakefield XO, et al: Abnormal behavior associated with a point mutation in the structural gene for monoamine oxidase A. Science 1993; 262:578–580.
22. Sherrington R, Brynjolfsson B, Petursson H, et al: Localization of a susceptibility locus for schizophrenia on chromosome 5. Nature 1988; 336:164–167.
23. Bassett AS, Jones BD, McGillivray BC, Pantzar JT: Partial trisomy chromosome 5 cosegregating with schizophrenia. Lancet 1988; 1:799–801.
24. Kennedy JL, Guiffra LA, Moises HW, et al: Evidence against linkage of schizophrenia to markers on chromosome 5 in a northern Swedish pedigree. Nature 1988; 336:167–170.
25. St. Clair D, Blackwood D, Muir W, et al: No linkage of chromosome 5q11–q13 markers to schizophrenia in Scottish families. Nature 1989; 339:305–309.
26. Detera-Wadleigh SD, Goldin LR, Sherrington R, et al: Exclusion of linkage to 5q11–13 in families with schizophrenia and other psychiatric disorders. Nature 1989; 340:391–393.
27. Lander ES: Splitting schizophrenia. Nature 1988; 336:105–106.
28. Byerley WF: Genetic linkage revisited. Nature 1989; 340:340–341.
29. McGuffin P, Sargeant M, Hetti G, et al: Exclusion of a schizophrenia susceptibility gene from the chromosome 5q11–q13 region: New data and a reanalysis of previous reports. Am J Hum Genet 1990; 47:524–535.
30. Mankoo B, Sherrington R, Brynjolfsson J, et al: New microsatellite polymorphisms provide a highly polymorphic map of chromosome 5 bands q11.2–q13.3 for linkage analysis of Icelandic and English families affected by schizophrenia. [abstract] Psychiatr Genet 1991; 2:17.
31. Crow TJ, DeLisi LE, Johnstone EC: Concordance by sex in sibling pairs is paternally inherited. Evidence for a pseudoautosomal locus. Br J Psychiatry 1989; 155:92–97.
32. Crow TJ: Sex chromosomes and psychosis: The case for pseudoautosomal locus. Br J Psychiatry 1988; 153:675–683.
33. Crow TJ, DeLisi LE, Johnstone EC: In reply . . . A locus close to the telomere. Br J Psychiatry 1990; 156:416–420.
34. Pulver AE, Karayiorgou M, Wolyniec P, et al: Sequential strategy to identify a susceptibility gene for schizophrenia: Report of potential linkage on chromosome 22q12–q13.1: Part 1. Am J Med Genet 1994; 54:36–43.
35. Polymeropoulos MH, Coon H, Byerley W, et al: Search for a schizophrenia susceptibility locus on human chromosome 22. Am J Hum Genet 1994; 54:93–99.
36. Coon H, Holik J, Hoff M, et al: Analysis of chromosome 22 markers in nine schizophrenia pedigrees. Am J Med Genet 1994; 54:72–79.
37. Berrettini WH, Ferraro TN, Goldin LR, et al: Chromosome 18 DNA markers and manic-depressive illness: Evidence for a susceptibility locus. Proc Natl Acad Sci USA 1994; 91:5918–5921.
38. McInnis MG, McMahon FJ, Chase GA, et al: Anticipation in bipolar affective disorder. Am J Hum Genet 1993; 53:385–390.

39. St. Clair D: Genetics of Alzheimer's disease. Br J Psychiatry 1994; 164:153–156.
40. Corder EH, Saunders AM, Risch NJ, et al: Protective effect of apolipoprotein E type 2 allele for late onset Alzheimer disease. Nature Genet 1994; 7:180–184.
41. Greenberg DA: Linkage analysis of "necessary" disease loci versus "susceptibility" loci. Am J Hum Genet 1993; 52:135–143.
42. Pato CN, Macciardi F, Pato MT, et al: Review of the putative association of dopamine D2 receptor and alcoholism. Am J Med Genet 1993; 48:78–82.
43. Gejman PV, Ram A, Gelernter J, et al: No structural mutation in the dopamine D2 receptor gene in alcoholism or schizophrenia. Analysis using denaturing gradient gel electrophoresis. JAMA 1994; 271:204–208.
44. Sobell JL, Heston LL, Sommer SS: Delineation of genetic predisposition to multifactorial disease: A general approach on the threshold of feasibility. Genomics 1992; 12:1–6.
45. Bottema CDK, Ketterling RP, Ii S, et al: Missense mutations and evolutionary conservation of amino acids: Evidence that many of the amino acids in factor IX function as "spacer" elements. Am J Hum Genet 1991; 49:820–838.
46. Falk CT, Rubinstein P: Haplotype relative risks: An easy reliable way to construct a proper control sample for risk calculations. Ann Hum Genet 1987; 51:227–233.
47. Schaid DJ, Sommer SS: Genotype relative risks: Methods for design and analysis of candidate gene association studies. Am J Hum Genet 1993; 53:1114–1126.
48. Grompe M: The rapid detection of unknown mutations in nucleic acids. Nature Genet 1993; 5:111–117.
49. Liu Q, Sommer SS: Restriction endonuclease fingerprinting (REF): A sensitive method for screening mutations in long contiguous segments of DNA. Biotechniques 1995; 18:470–477.
50. Sarkar G, Yoon H-S, Sommer SS: Dideoxy fingerprinting (ddF): A rapid and efficient screen for the presence of mutations. Genomics 1992; 13:441–443.
51. Sommer SS, Vielhaber EL: Phage promoter-based methods for sequencing and screening for mutations. In Mullis KB, Ferre F, Gibbs RA (eds): The Polymerase Chain Reaction. Boston: Birkhauser, 1994:214–221.
52. Syvanen A-C, Landegren U: Detection of point mutations by solid-phase methods. Hum Mutat 1994; 3:172–179.
53. Bottema CDK, Sarkar G, Cassady, et al: Polymerase chain reaction amplification of specific alleles: A general method of detection of mutations, polymorphisms, and haplotypes. Methods Enzymol 1993; 218:388–402.
54. Haliassos A, Chomel JC, Grandjouan S, et al: Detection of minority point mutations by modified PCR technique: A new approach for a sensitive diagnosis of tumor-progression markers. Nucleic Acids Res 1989; 17:8093–8099.
55. Sorscher EJ, Huang Z: Diagnosis of genetic disease by primer-specified restriction map modification, with application to cystic fibrosis and retinitis pigmentosa. Lancet 1991; 337:1115–1118.
56. Wiedmann M, Wilson W, Czajka J, et al: Ligase chain reaction (LCR)—overview and applications. PCR Methods Appl 1994; 3:S51–S64.

CHAPTER

14 Molecular and Neurobiological Mechanisms in the Treatment of Psychiatric Disorders

Michael J. Owens
Jeff J. Mulchahey
Steven C. Stout
Paul M. Plotsky

Poetic descriptions of the human central nervous system (CNS) have estimated the number of neuronal building blocks in the brain to exceed the number of stars in the cosmos. The fact that individual neurons can make multiple connections with many other neurons in the brain gives rise to a system of enormous complexity. Given this complexity, it is not surprising that neuroscience has not yet been able to provide cellular and molecular descriptions of some of the more abstract features of the human brain such as consciousness and memory. However, remarkable progress has been made in understanding many of the fundamental building blocks of the brain, and our collective insight into the workings of this, the most complicated structure known to humans, is increasing daily. This chapter explores some of these fundamental mechanisms as a prelude to understanding the aberrations associated with certain psychopathologies as well as the pharmacological interventions used to ameliorate those pathologies.

Despite the complexities of the brain, the neural components of the brain can be reduced to a relatively simple stylized model. The archetypal neuron consists of a cell that is specialized for the reception, processing, and transmission of various forms of information. The neuron functions as both an analog device, integrating the effects of numerous inputs, and a digital device, which is either off (quiescent) or on (producing action potentials, all of which are virtually identical). It is the sum of neuronal activities, across many neurons within many populations of neurons, that gives rise to the higher order activities of the brain such as cognition and consciousness. The key functional property of neurons is their ability to communicate among themselves through the process of neurotransmission. It is at the level of neurotransmission that the brain is most susceptible to neuropharmacological intervention.

The specialization of the neuron for information processing does not relieve the neuron of the burden of being a cell. Thus, in addition to its cellular specializations, the neuron maintains a full repertoire of cellular activities, including ongoing transcription of messenger ribonucleic acids (mRNAs) from a nucleus containing a normal genetic complement, translation of mRNAs into proteins, posttranslational modification of proteins, maintenance of a lipid bilayer membrane replete with transmembrane differences in ion distributions as a result of ion pumping, energetic substrate–dependent transportation of intracellular constituents along a network of microtubules, and production of those energetic substrates. Interference with any of these routine cellular functions of the neuron—such as inhibition of transcription or translation by certain antibiotics, inhibition of the membrane Na^+,K^+-ATPase (sodium-potassium adenosinetriphosphatase) by cardiac glycosides, or uncoupling of oxidative phosphorylation and ATP production by metabolic poisoning—disrupts the activities of the CNS. However, these agents lack specificity for the brain, much less for any particular subsystem of the brain, and therefore have little utility as therapeutic agents.

Neuronal Cell Biology

The prototypical neuron consists of a cell body, or soma, and specialized functional cellular structures. These structures are the dendrites, the axon, and the nerve terminals. In general, these are the sites of information integration and processing, intracellular information transmission, and intercellular communication, respectively. Because intercellular communication occurs across synaptic junctions, the dendritic and terminal components may also be referred to as postsynaptic and presynaptic elements, respectively.

Neurons are similar to most other eukaryotic cells in that the internal and external environments differ. The presence of Na^+,K^+-ATPase molecules in the neuronal cell membrane establishes an unequal distribution of ions across the cell membrane such that the interior is enriched in potassium ions while sodium ions are removed from the interior. This unequal distribution of ions across the neuronal cell membrane in turn establishes an electrical potential difference across the cell membrane. The potential difference resulting from the unequal distribution of ions across a membrane may be calculated using a simplified version of the Nernst equation, which takes the form

$$E = \frac{58}{z} \log_{10} \frac{[X]_1}{[X]_2} \qquad (1)$$

where E is the resulting potential difference, in millivolts
z is the charge on the ion
$[X]_1$ is the ion concentration on one side of the membrane
$[X]_2$ is the ion concentration on the other side of the membrane

The following table gives the approximate concentrations of the major ionic constituents of a model neuronal environment as well as their calculated Nernst potentials. The external concentration is used as the numerator in the Nernst equation.

Ion	External Concentration (mmol/L)	Internal Concentration (mmol/L)	Nernst Potential (mV)
K^+	2.25	124	−101
Na^+	109	10.4	+59
Cl^-	77.5	1.5	−99

The observation that the typical neuron displays a resting membrane potential of approximately −90 mV with respect to the exterior suggests that potassium and chloride ions are the major contributors to the resting potential.

The Nernst equation has been modified to take into account the relative permeability of the neuronal membrane to these ions and thus the relative contributions of the various ionic species to the resting membrane potential. The relative permeabilities are taken into consideration in the Goldman-Hodgkin-Katz equation:

$$E = \frac{RT}{F} \log_e \frac{P_K[K^+]_o + P_{Na}[Na^+]_o + P_{Cl}[Cl^-]_i}{P_K[K^+]_i + P_{Na}[Na^+]_i + P_{Cl}[Cl^-]_o} \qquad (2)$$

where P_K, P_{Na}, and P_{Cl} are permeability coefficients
R is the universal gas constant
T is the absolute temperature
F is Faraday's constant

Experimental evidence has demonstrated that the membrane potential faithfully follows changes in sodium and potassium concentrations and the distribution of chloride ions follows that predicted on the basis of membrane potential. Therefore, Equation 2 is often simplified by omitting the chloride terms and expressing the membrane permeability for sodium as a ratio to the potassium permeability:

$$E = \frac{RT}{F} \log_e \frac{[K^+]_o + \alpha[Na^+]_o}{[K^+]_i + \alpha[Na^+]_i} \qquad (3)$$

where $\alpha = P_{Na}/P_K$

The salient feature of Equation 3 is the demonstration that the membrane potential of a neuron appears to be dependent on the internal and external concentrations of sodium and potassium and the relative permeability of the membrane to these two ions.

Action Potential

A cellular property unique to neurons is their electrical excitability combined with the ability to transmit this electrical signal to other locations in the brain. This electrical excitability takes the form of an action potential and is illustrated in Figure 14–1, which shows membrane potential plotted as a function of time and demonstrates a neuron with a resting potential of −60 mV; the negative term means that the interior is negative with respect to the exterior of the neuron. Under appropriate conditions a relatively slow depolarization occurs that, once the appropriate threshold is reached, leads to a phase of rapid regenerative depolarization, known as the rising phase. This rapid depolarization

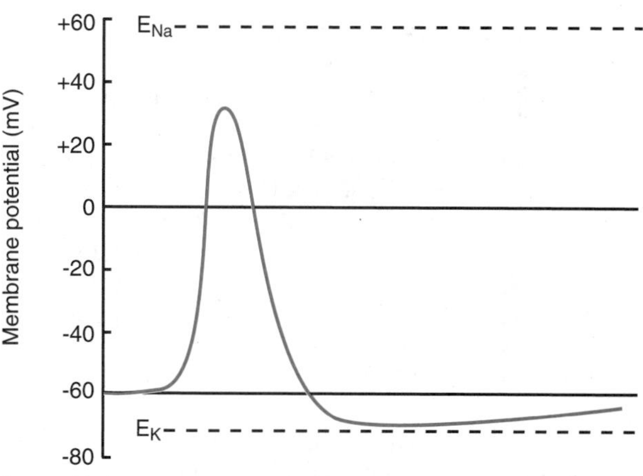

Figure 14–1 *Drawing of a stylized neuronal action potential in which membrane potential is plotted versus time. The initial membrane potential is −60 mV. Depolarization of the membrane leads to a regenerative decrease (i.e., the interior becomes less negative with respect to the exterior) in membrane potential. The membrane potential passes electroneutrality and tends toward the equilibrium potential for sodium (E_{Na}). Inactivation of sodium channels prevents the membrane potential from reaching E_{Na}. The rising positive membrane potential is slowed and reversed by activation of potassium channels, which drives the membrane potential toward E_K. The membrane potential overshoots the initial resting membrane potential and hyperpolarizes the membrane through potassium influx. The membrane potential slowly returns to the resting state as potassium channels are inactivated and the membrane Na^+,K^+-ATPase restores the ion distribution and membrane potential to their initial resting states.*

overshoots electrical neutrality and peaks at approximately +40 mV. The rise in membrane potential is blunted and ultimately reverses into a falling phase in which the membrane potential returns toward the resting value. The return overruns the resting potential for a brief period of hyperpolarization, after which the membrane potential returns to the original value.

Experiments using artificial amounts of extracellular sodium have demonstrated that the depolarization and overshoot are due to the movement of sodium into the neuron. Thus the rising phases of membrane potential are due to increases in membrane sodium conductance, which allow the membrane potential to rise toward the Nernst potential for sodium. Other experiments demonstrated an increased efflux of radiolabeled potassium from neurons during an action potential. This efflux would tend to reduce the positive potential resulting from the influx of sodium, as would the increase in potassium conductance, which would tend to bring the membrane potential toward the Nernst potential for potassium. These alterations in membrane ion conductances occur through specialized membrane proteins that function as ion-specific channels for sodium or potassium. Because each channel protein has a conductance that is constant across all such molecules, an increase in conductance occurs by means of an increase in the number of ion channels that are open at any given moment. Increased sodium conductance, increased sodium current, and sodium channel opening are synonyms for this phenomenon.[1]

Voltage clamp experiments have been used to examine the behavior of ion channels as a function of membrane voltage. When neurons are clamped at initial membrane voltages at or near the resting potential, depolarization results in large increases in sodium conductance. When the same neurons are clamped at initial voltages above the resting membrane voltage, depolarization results in smaller increases in sodium conductance; the decrease in depolarization-induced sodium current is proportional to the increase in initial voltage. That the decrease in sodium conductance is not a result of the initial membrane voltage approaching the equilibrium voltage for sodium is shown by the fact that the depolarization-induced sodium current fails to occur at initial voltages below the equilibrium voltage for sodium. These findings demonstrate that the sodium channels are voltage gated and illustrate the phenomenon of sodium channel inactivation in which the sodium conductance decreases as membrane voltage depolarizes. This inactivation limits both the magnitude and the duration of the action potential.[2]

A second key feature of the action potential is an increase in potassium conductance. The opening of potassium channels is also voltage gated, with the increase in membrane potential associated with the rising and overshoot phases of the action potential acting directly on the potassium channels to increase their conductance. The resulting efflux of potassium combines with sodium channel inactivation to limit the magnitude and duration of the action potential. Potassium channels are activated more slowly than are sodium channels, which prevents the electrical potential changes resulting from the increase in sodium conductance being offset by increases in potassium conductance. Potassium channels are also inactivated as the membrane potential returns to the initial resting potential. The hyperpolarization in the later phase of the action potential occurs because the slowly inactivated potassium channels allow greater potassium conductances at this time than in the quiescent membrane. This elevated potassium conductance allows the membrane potential to tend toward the equilibrium potential for potassium, at a time when sodium channels have been inactivated. The relative time courses of the membrane potential during an action potential and of the ionic conductances of sodium and potassium[2] are shown in Figure 14–2. In drawing the ionic conductances, it is important to realize that both sodium and potassium conductances show transient increases during the action potential, which are drawn as positive (upward) deflections of those lines. In the case of sodium, the increase in conductance results in an increase in membrane potential. However, in the case of potassium, the increase in conductance results in a decrease in membrane potential. Agents that disrupt the function of the excitable neuronal membrane impair the production of action potentials. Such agents may be specific blockers of ion channels such as tetrodotoxin or tetraethylammonium or nonspecific disrupters of the organization of the neuronal membrane such as alcohols or local anesthetics. The terms *nonspecific* and *specific* in this instance are relative, because these agents are certainly not selective for a particular population of neurons.

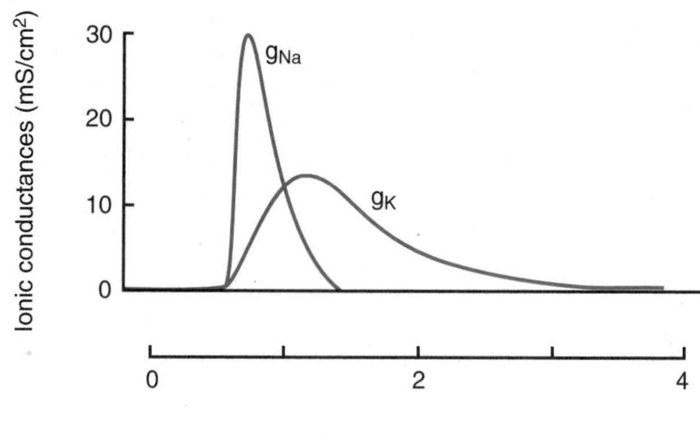

Figure 14–2 *Drawing of the changes in ion flux across the membrane that accompany the changes in membrane potential illustrated in Figure 14–1. Ion flux is shown as conductance* (g) *for sodium and potassium.*

Information Processing by Neurons

We have examined the electrical and ionic properties of the resting and transiently excited neuronal membrane as these events might occur in a patch of membrane in isolation. For action potentials to effect intra- and intercellular communication, they must occur within the context of being generated in one part of the neuron, propagated to another part of a neuron, and ultimately communicated to a neighboring neuron.

The soma, or cell body, of the neuron is the primary site of transsynaptic communication to a neuron. Specialized branched cell processes called dendrites are elaborated by the neuron and dramatically increase the surface area of the neuron available for synaptic input. Synapses may be either electrical or chemical in nature, depending on the medium used for communication. Electrical synapses consist of pre- and postsynaptic elements in tight apposition across a synaptic cleft. Specialized gap junctions, formed by a regular array of specialized transmembrane proteins, permit the flow of ions and other small molecules between the presynaptic cell and the postsynaptic cell. Electrical events in the presynaptic cell are communicated to the postsynaptic cell by means of the same ion movements that give rise to the electrical events of the neuronal membrane.

More common than the electrical synapse is the chemical synapse, which relies on a neurotransmitter released from the presynaptic cell to communicate information about electrical events in the presynaptic cell to specialized receptors on the postsynaptic cell. A chemical synapse is illustrated in Figure 14–3, which shows several ultrastructural features of both pre- and postsynaptic elements, such as the presence of vesicles and mitochondria in the presynaptic element and the apposition of densely stained membrane at the synapse.[3] Much of our understanding of chemical synaptic neurotransmission was developed from experiments on the motor end plates of the neuromuscular junction that were subsequently confirmed by results for neuron-neuron synapses.[4]

When a microelectrode is used to study the membrane potential around postsynaptic elements of the neuronal membrane, several important observations can be made. The first is that the membrane potential is not static. On appropriate stimulation of the presynaptic elements, synapse activation occurs and the postsynaptic membrane potential deviates from the resting potential. Deviations from the resting potential that decrease the negative resting potential tend to drive the membrane potential into the regenerative type of membrane depolarization seen in the action potential. These positive deviations in membrane potential are said to be excitatory postsynaptic potentials (EPSPs).[5] Alternatively, the postsynaptic membrane potential may be driven more negative and thus away from the regenerative depolarization of the action potential. These negative deviations in membrane potential are said to be inhibitory postsynaptic potentials (IPSPs).[6] The identity of the neurotransmitters and their specific postsynaptic receptors and the ionic basis of the EPSPs or IPSPs that result from the neurotransmitters are discussed in detail later in this chapter.

A second series of important observations concerns the quantal release of neurotransmitter. If the resting membrane potential about a synapse is examined in detail, it is found to contain small fluctuations of electrical noise. These fluctuations are distributed randomly in time and are smaller in magnitude than are the EPSPs and IPSPs. Statistical analyses have indicated that these fluctuations, or miniature potentials, are not noise but represent the smallest unit of neurotransmitter release. A comparison with electrophoretic application of known amounts of exogenous neurotransmitter indicates that these smallest units, or quanta, of neurotransmitter consist of approximately 10,000 molecules of neurotransmitter. When the ultrastructure of the synapse is taken into account, the quanta of neurotransmitter release are thought to correspond to the vesicles of the presynaptic nerve terminal.[7]

A third series of important observations concerns the magnitude and duration of the various postsynaptic potentials. An individual postsynaptic potential displays a rapid onset followed by a slower decay toward the initial resting membrane potential. This implies that the postsynaptic potential is a temporally constrained event. If the recording electrode is moved away from the postsynaptic area, the magnitude of the postsynaptic potential decays with distance from the postsynaptic region. This implies that the postsynaptic potential is a spatially constrained event. When these implications are combined with the observation that an individual EPSP is insufficient to generate an action potential, we conclude that action potentials occur only if an adequate number of EPSPs are summed over time or over membrane area to exceed the threshold for regenerative depolarization. This summation of postsynaptic potentials over time is known as temporal summation and the

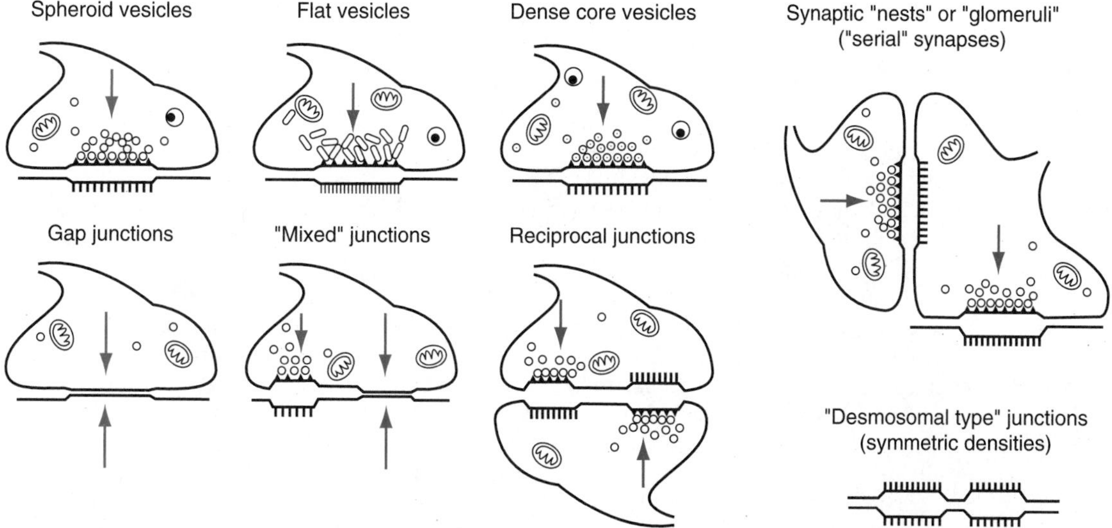

Figure 14–3 *Drawing of synapse ultrastructure illustrating the major types of synaptic junctions. Synaptic transmission is chemical at synapses where there are neurotransmitter-containing vesicles; conduction at gap junctions is electrical. The desmosomal-type junctions occur primarily in sympathetic ganglia. (From Bodian D: Neuron junctions: A revolutionary decade. Anat Rec 1973; 174:73–88. Copyright © 1973 John Wiley & Sons. Reprinted by permission of Wiley-Liss, Inc., a subsidiary of John Wiley & Sons, Inc.)*

summation over the space of the membrane area is known as spatial summation.[8] The postsynaptic potentials, both inhibitory hyperpolarizing IPSPs and excitatory depolarizing EPSPs, summed over space and time, determine the firing rate of the postsynaptic neuron. The ability of the neuron to integrate synaptic inputs is an example of analog information processing within the nervous system.

Given an adequate summation of EPSPs, the postsynaptic neuron is stimulated to produce an action potential. The generation of action potentials occurs in the initial segment of the axon. This unmyelinated region of the neuron is the region that has the lowest threshold and thus is the most sensitive to depolarization. The mechanism underlying this increased sensitivity is thought to involve an increased density of ion channels in this region. Because of the differences in volume between the initial segment of the axon and the neuronal cell body and dendrites, the passive electronic spread of the action potential back into the soma and dendrites is damped and the action potential is usually not propagated back to the synapses. This means that the soma and dendrites do not reach the threshold to generate an action potential unless the cell body is partially depolarized before the initial segment generates an action potential.[9]

Axonal Conduction

The action potential is propagated along the axon from the initial segment. Our understanding of this propagation is based on a model for the axon that relates the axon to a cable surrounded by a leaky insulator. This cable model relates the transverse resistance and transverse capacitance across the axon membrane to the longitudinal resistance of the external medium and the longitudinal resistance of the axoplasm. These cable properties of the axon can be modeled mathematically. The equation from this model that is relevant to this discussion is

$$V_x = V_0 e^{-x/\lambda} \quad (4)$$

where V_x is the membrane potential at position x
V_0 is the membrane potential at an initial position
e is the base of the natural logarithm
λ is a space constant depending on the membrane geometry

The salient feature of Equation 4 is that it describes the passive electrotonic spread of a local membrane potential disturbance along the axon and shows that this membrane potential decays as a function of distance. This implies that on either side of an action potential there exists a region of depolarized membrane. The local circuit theory suggests that localized ion fluxes occur across the axon membrane and account for these local changes in membrane potential.

The fact that an action potential passively depolarizes the axon membrane on either side of the action potential means that the areas of membrane adjacent to the action potential reach their thresholds for regenerative depolarization and generate their own action potentials. Action potentials propagate along nonmyelinated fibers by depolarizing the axon membrane to threshold ahead of the action potential. A consequence of this is that a stimulus that generates an action potential in midaxon results in action potentials that travel in both "forward" (orthodromic) and "backward" (antidromic) directions along the axon. This situation does not occur in vivo because 1) axons are rarely stimulated to depolarize at regions other than the initial segment and 2) the voltage-dependent inactivation of the various ion channels involved in generating an action potential means that the membrane behind the action potential is (transiently) refractory to another depolarization and thus action potentials do not reverse themselves. A second consequence of this axon model is that the space constant contains the terms for internal and external longitudinal resistance. Decreases in either resistance increase the rate of electrotonic spread and thus increase the rate of action potential movement along the axon. The constancy of the internal environment means that the external resistance is unlikely to change, as this is dependent on the ionic composition of the extracellular space. Physiologically relevant changes in internal resistance do occur: the larger the diameter of the axon, the lower the internal longitudinal resistance and the greater the rate of action potential travel along the axon.[2, 10]

Action potentials are conducted along myelinated axons by a mechanism involving the same fundamental principles as conduction along a nonmyelinated fiber. The myelin coating formed from many closely packed layers of Schwann cell membrane contains no extracellular channels. As a result, the combined axon membrane–myelin sheath has a much higher transverse resistance and a much lower transmembrane capacitance than does a nonmyelinated axon. Typically, there are 160- and 400-fold differences, respectively, in these parameters in myelinated axons compared with nonmyelinated axons. The myelin sheath is not continuous over the length of the axon and the discontinuities, which occur approximately every millimeter, are termed nodes of Ranvier. The axonal membrane at the nodes shows decreased transverse resistance and increased transmembrane capacitance compared with both axons within the myelin and nonmyelinated axons. Compared with the nonmyelinated axons, membranes at the nodes have approximately one fifth the resistance and three times the capacitance. This causes current flow across the membrane induced by local currents to be much greater at the nodes than in the internode regions.

As a result of these differences in membrane architecture, the electrotonic spread of depolarization occurs over a greater distance in myelinated axons than it does in nonmyelinated axons. Because the membrane between the nodes is relatively nonexcitable, action potentials occur primarily at the nodes. Therefore, the transmission of the action potential along the axon is discontinuous and occurs from node to node. This conduction is said to be saltatory in nature. Saltatory conduction is a more rapid means of action potential conduction because large portions of the axon are bypassed as the action potential "jumps" from node to node.[10] Saltatory conduction in myelinated axons is not at present a target for pharmacological invention. However, certain neuromuscular disorders (e.g., amyotrophic lateral sclerosis) are marked by degeneration of the myelin sheaths with an accompanying degradation in axonal conduction. Treatment of these degenerative diseases focuses on improving the effectiveness of synaptic transmission from the remaining functional axons rather than on altering axonal conduction.

Synaptic Transmission

On reaching the end of the axon, the action potential invades the presynaptic nerve terminals and depolarizes them. Depolarization of the presynaptic terminals results in an influx of calcium ions, which initiate an energy-dependent movement of synaptic vesicles to the presynaptic membrane. The vesicles fuse with the presynaptic membrane and release their contents into the synaptic cleft.[11] The movement and fusion of the vesicles are parts of a complex process that appears to occur along actin microfilaments in a manner somewhat analogous to other intracellular transport processes that occur along microtubules.[12]

The synaptic vesicles contain the chemical neurotransmitters that communicate with the postsynaptic terminal through interaction with specific receptor proteins on the postsynaptic membrane. The neurotransmitters can generally be classified into two broad categories: low-molecular-weight amines and peptides. At this point we are concerned with the differences in synthesis and packaging of these different classes of neurotransmitter. The origin of synaptic vesicles is the Golgi apparatus located in the cell body. As a final step in the progression from endoplasmic reticulum and Golgi apparatus, nascent vesicles bud off the distal Golgi and are transported along the axon at the slow axoplasmic transport rate of 1 mm/d. The two broad categories of transmitter differ in their mode of synthesis. The peptide transmitters are synthesized by the protein synthetic machinery in the cell body and are packaged into and transported with the vesicles. In the case of the various amine transmitters, the enzymatic proteins required for their synthesis are packaged and transported with the vesicles; the final synthesis of these transmitters occurs in the vesicle at the presynaptic terminal.

The arrival of the action potential at the presynaptic terminal has two consequences: 1) release of neurotransmitter into the synaptic cleft and 2) fusion of the vesicle membrane with the neuronal cell membrane and an increase in membrane area. As a result of this, plasma membrane is recycled from the cell membrane and vesicles are re-formed in an endocytotic process. The amine-based transmitters are synthesized locally and the vesicle complement is restored locally. The extra membrane of peptide-based terminals is recycled to the Golgi apparatus, and vesicles are formed there as synthesis of the peptide occurs.[13] The recycled nature of vesicular components means that at times of intense stimulation and transsynaptic activity, the vesicle content of the presynaptic terminal may be depleted transiently. The synapse fatigues in this case and the fidelity of transmission across the synapse falls. This might occur, for example, after tetanic stimulation of a motor neuron, which typically occurs only during experimental stimulation at supraphysiological levels. However, pharmacological agents (e.g., reserpine) that interfere with the synthesis or storage of peptide or other neurotransmitters also deplete the presynaptic terminal of available transmitters and diminish synaptic fidelity.

Neurotransmitter released from presynaptic terminals diffuses across the synaptic cleft and impinges on specific receptors on the postsynaptic membrane. These receptors are typically (i.e., approximately 90% of all CNS receptors) ligand-gated ion channels whose ionic conductivity is increased by the presence of the ligand. Although transmitter passage across the synaptic cleft is by passive diffusion, the distance involved is small, on the order of 200 Å. Although the exact concentration of transmitter in the cleft is unknown, the concentration gradients are likely to be quite high. These two factors combine to reduce the delay in transsynaptic communication to the order of milliseconds.[14]

A second important type of neurotransmitter receptor is one in which the presence of the neurotransmitter in the extracellular space of the synapse is communicated indirectly to internal cellular constituents. The neurotransmitter, the "first messenger" in this scheme, cannot permeate the cell membrane. The neurotransmitter interacts with a specific cell surface receptor that communicates the presence of the transmitter to the interior of the postsynaptic cell by generating second messengers. The second messengers are low-molecular-weight species such as cyclic nucleotides, calcium ions, or phosphoinositols that diffuse rapidly throughout the cell. The second messengers interact with intracellular acceptors, typically protein kinases, and activate them. These kinases phosphorylate specific acceptor proteins, which are the third messengers of this cascade. The phosphorylation of these proteins alters their biological activity; this is illustrated in general form in Figure 14–4. Two important features exist in this second-messenger scheme. First, each step of this cascade utilizes activation of catalytic enzymes, each of which generates multiple copies of the next effector. Thus there is an amplification of the neurotransmitter effect through the cascade. Second, the time scale of responses can range from immediate changes in ion flux through channels to intermediate-term changes in cellular metabolism to long-term changes in gene expression.

These cell surface receptors belong to a superfamily of proteins patterned after bacteriorhodopsin and share a highly homologous structure with seven membrane-spanning hydrophobic helices.[15, 16] These receptors have been termed G protein–coupled receptors because a protein that binds the guanine nucleotides guanosine triphosphate (GTP) and guanosine diphosphate (GDP) serves to couple the cell surface receptor to specific intracellular effector systems (see Fig. 14–4). To date, all of the adrenergic, dopaminergic, muscarinic, and peptidergic, all but one of the serotoninergic, and some of the glutamatergic receptors are members of this family. Figure 14–5 (see Color Plate I) illustrates the general structure, topology, and ligand binding domain of a typical G protein–coupled receptor.

Each G protein is a heterotrimer composed of a single α, β, and γ subunit. Different α subunits confer specific functional activity on the different types of G proteins, whereas the β- and γ-subunits appear to be similar in all G proteins. In the absence of drug or transmitter bound to their receptors, G proteins exist as heterotrimers that are bound to GDP and are unassociated with the receptor or with the intracellular effector proteins. When a receptor is activated by drug or transmitter binding, a conformational change in the receptor causes its association with the α-subunit of the G protein. This leads to a conformational change of the α-subunit and to the exchange of GDP for GTP on the α-subunit and dissociation of the β- and γ-subunits (which stay together) from the α-subunit. After association with GTP, the α-subunit releases the

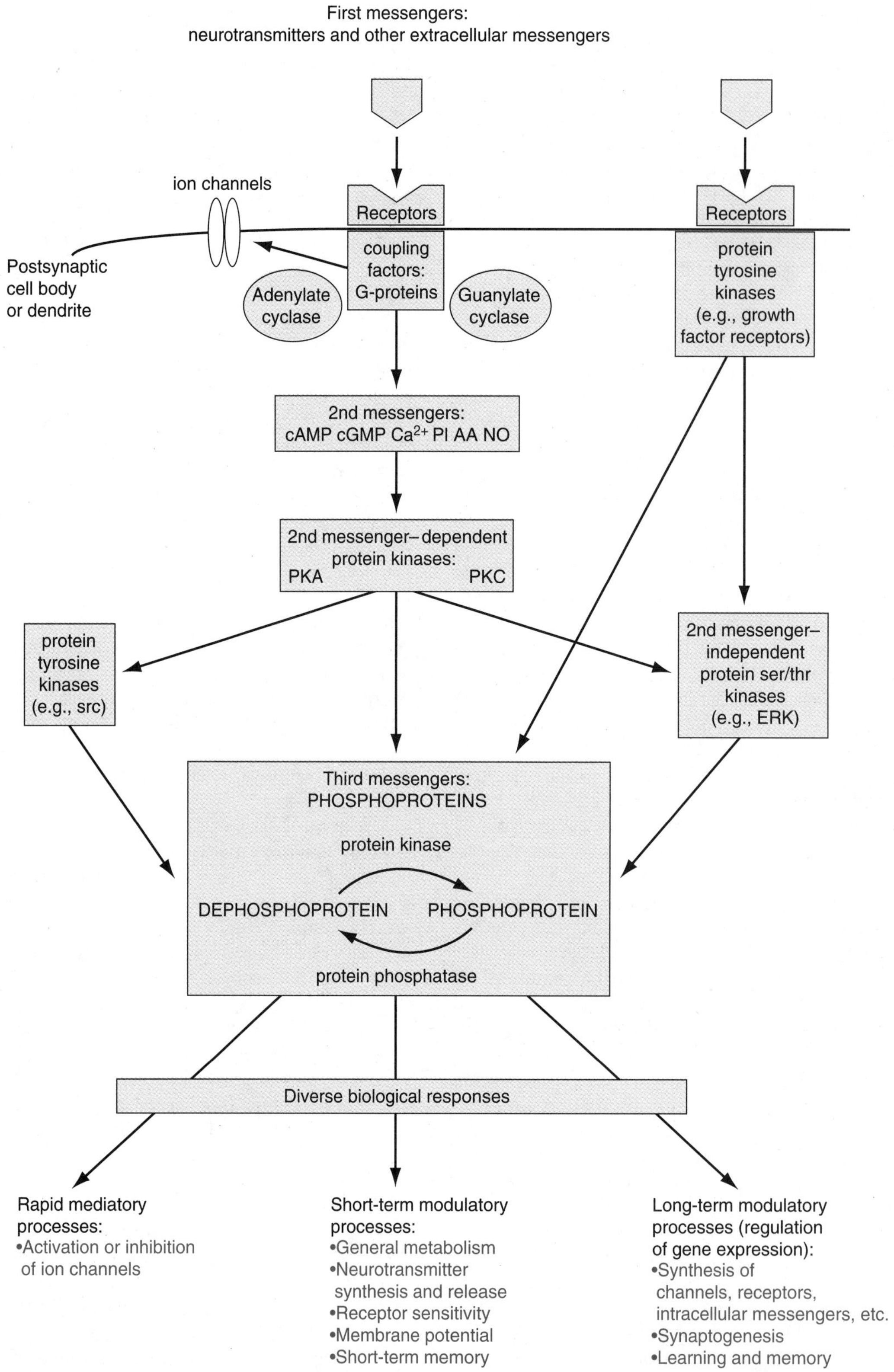

First messengers:
neurotransmitters and other extracellular messengers

ion channels

Receptors

Receptors

Postsynaptic
cell body
or dendrite

coupling
factors:
G-proteins

Adenylate
cyclase

Guanylate
cyclase

protein
tyrosine
kinases
(e.g., growth
factor receptors)

2nd messengers:
cAMP cGMP Ca^{2+} PI AA NO

2nd messenger–dependent
protein kinases:
PKA PKC

protein
tyrosine
kinases
(e.g., src)

2nd messenger–
independent
protein ser/thr
kinases
(e.g., ERK)

Third messengers:
PHOSPHOPROTEINS

protein kinase

DEPHOSPHOPROTEIN PHOSPHOPROTEIN

protein phosphatase

Diverse biological responses

Rapid mediatory
processes:
•Activation or inhibition
of ion channels

Short-term modulatory
processes:
•General metabolism
•Neurotransmitter
synthesis and release
•Receptor sensitivity
•Membrane potential
•Short-term memory

Long-term modulatory
processes (regulation
of gene expression):
•Synthesis of
channels, receptors,
intracellular messengers, etc.
•Synaptogenesis
•Learning and memory

Figure 14–4 *Representation of the role played by intracellular signal transduction pathways in regulation of synaptic transmission in the brain. These pathways mediate the multiple actions of neurotransmitters. The figure illustrates the cascade of events, which can all be modified by other intracellular events or actions of different neurotransmitters or can lead to amplification of the signal produced by a single neurotransmitter. As shown at the bottom, these intracellular events lead to a vast array of physiological effects. (Adapted from Duman RS, Nestler EJ: Signal transduction pathways for catecholamine receptors. In Bloom FE, Kupfer DJ [eds]: Psychopharmacology: The Fourth Generation of Progress. New York: Raven Press, 1995:303–320.)*

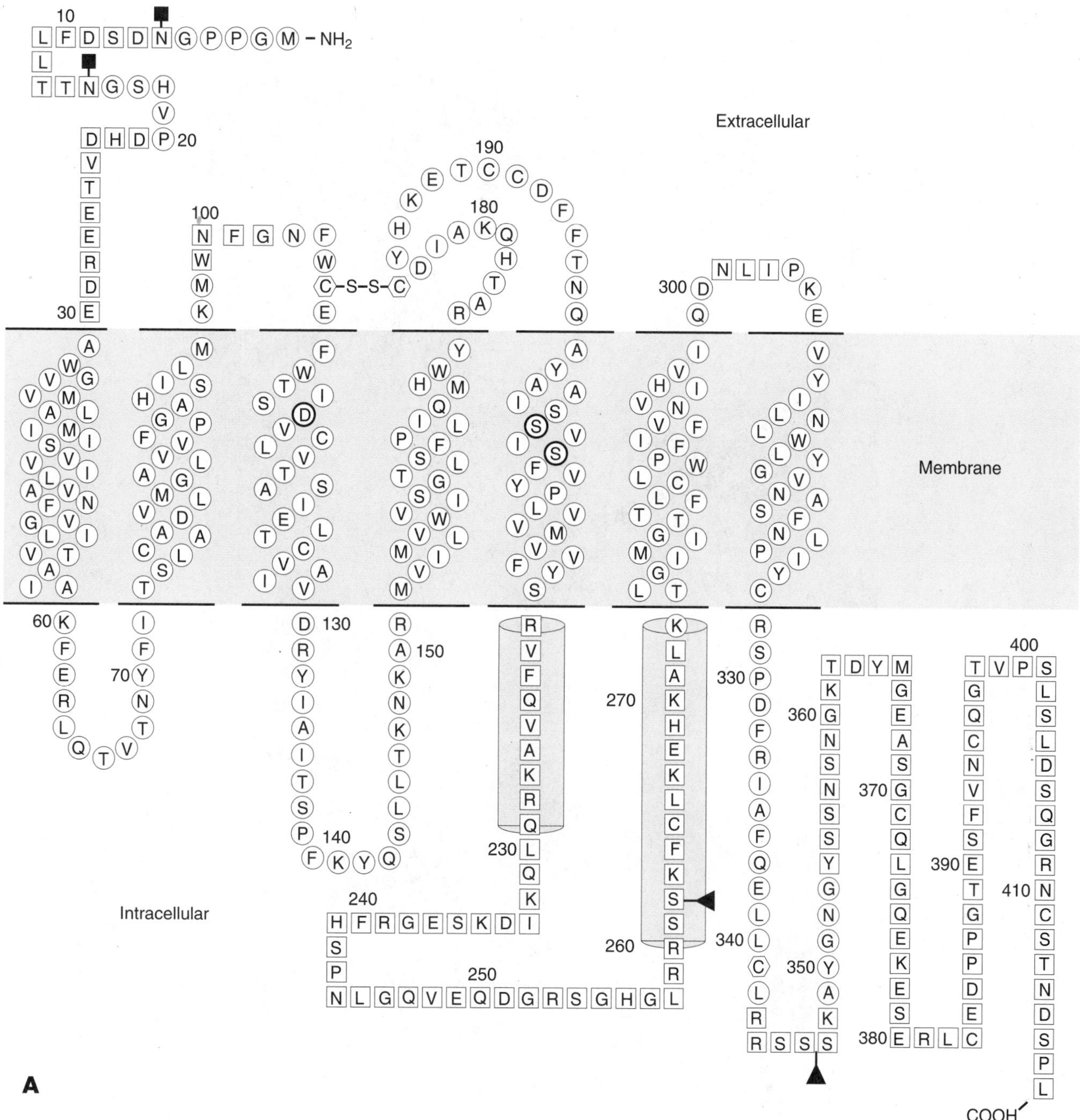

Figure 14–5 (A) *Representative G protein–coupled receptor. The hamster β_2-adrenergic receptor is presented as a model for the receptor superfamily having seven membrane-spanning domains. The extracellular space is at the top and the cytoplasmic region is at the bottom. The seven putative membrane-spanning helices are shown in the middle. This motif is present in all members of this receptor superfamily, and members of a particular receptor subfamily typically show sequence homologies of upward of 75% in this region. Amino acid residues are identified by their standard one-letter abbreviations and are numbered from the amino-terminal end of the protein. Residues that can be removed without affecting ligand binding are shown in square boxes. Residues shown in bold circles (Asp^{113}, Ser^{204}, and Ser^{207}) are involved in ligand binding (see Fig. 14–5C and Color Plate I). The solid squares attached to the two Asn residues near the amino-terminal end indicate glycosylation sites. The proposed disulfide bond between Cys^{106} and Cys^{184} is shown. Solid triangles represent potential sites of phosphorylation by protein kinase A based on the presence of the Arg/Lys-Arg-X-(X)-Ser/Thr consensus sequence. The large cylinders delineate the amphiphilic helices in the third cytoplasmic loop, which cannot be deleted without affecting G protein coupling. This third cytoplasmic loop and the carboxyl-terminal end of the receptor show the greatest sequence divergence within subtypes and across receptor types. The former may vary in length from approximately 65 to 175 residues; the latter varies from 20 to 165 residues in length and contains a variable number of potential protein kinase A phosphorylation sites. (From Strader CD, Sigal IS, Dixon RAF: Mapping the functional domains of the β-adrenergic receptor. Am J Respir Cell Mol Biol 1989; 1:81–86.)*

Illustration continued on following page

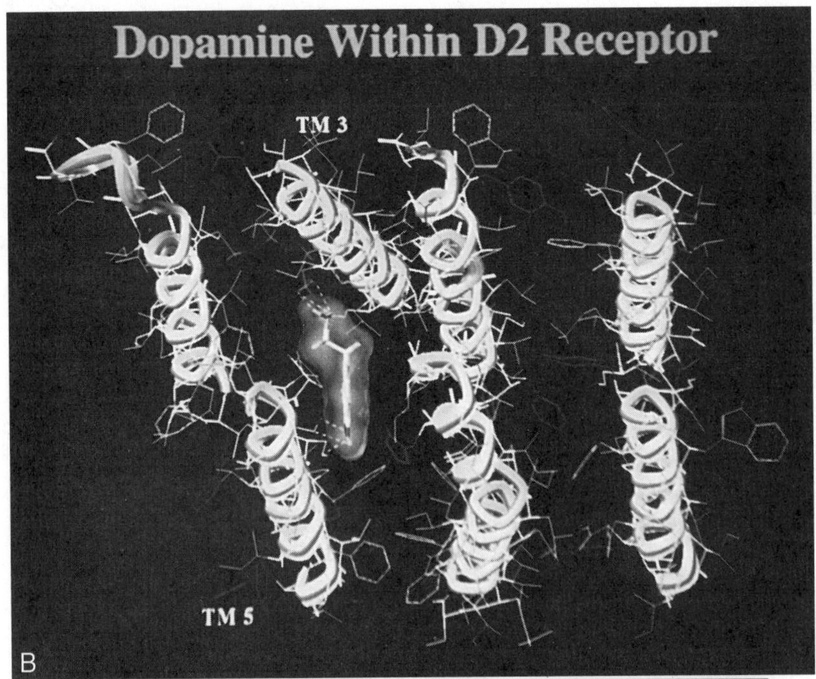

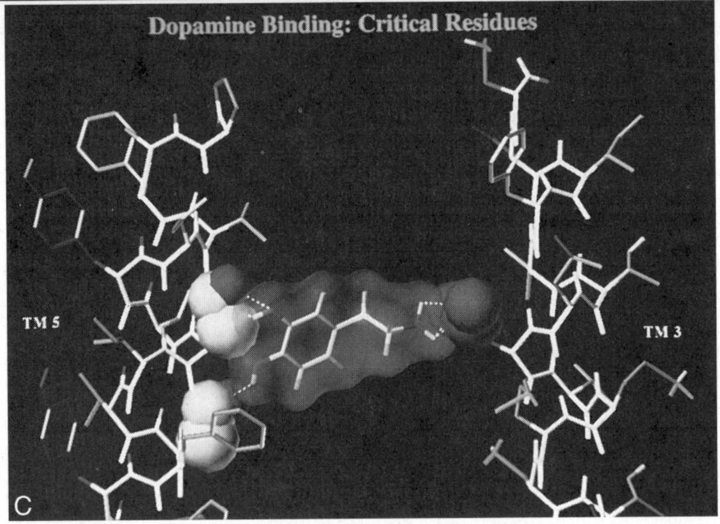

Figure 14–5 *Continued* (B) *Computer model of dopamine bound to the* D_2 *receptor. Shown is an oblique view of dopamine resting within the ligand binding domain formed by the transmembrane segments of the human* D_2 *receptor. Only the transmembrane portion of the receptor is shown; the intracellular region is below the plane of the illustration. The color scheme for the elemental structure of dopamine is as follows: C, white; N, dark blue; O, red; H, light blue. Dopamine is shown surrounded by a transparent green surface that approximates its molecular volume. The yellow dotted lines between the dopamine molecule and the receptor represent putative interactions between the ligand and the receptor. The receptor side chains are color coded for the following properties and amino acids: hydrophobic, green; acidic, red; basic, blue; neutral or polar, orange; Ser, green-blue; Pro, red-orange; Cys, magenta. The putative receptor helices are highlighted light blue–magenta ribbon. Transmembrane domains 3 and 5 (TM3 and TM5) are labeled for orientation. The figure was produced using the molecular modeling software SYBYL on a Silicon Graphics Indigo Elan. The illustration is not intended to reflect a quantitative reality. Distances between the transmembrane segments are intentionally large to facilitate visual examination. (See Color Plate I.)* (C) *Critical residues involved in dopamine binding to the ligand recognition site. This illustration highlights the interaction between dopamine (shown within its blue volume contour) and the aspartic acid (red) in TM3 and the two serine residues (green-blue) in TM5. The portions of the aspartic acid and serine residues that interact with dopamine are rendered in space-filling mode; the hydrogen atoms are shown as dark red. The figure was produced using the molecular modeling software SYBYL on a Silicon Graphics Indigo Elan. (See Color Plate I.)* (B *and* C *courtesy of L. Taylor, PhD, and H. Akil, PhD, Mental Health Research Institute, University of Michigan, Ann Arbor, MI.)*

receptor, generating a free α-subunit that can directly regulate the functional activity of various intracellular effector proteins. The system returns to the inactive state when the drug or transmitter is released from the receptor and the inherent GTPase activity of the α-subunit itself hydrolyzes GTP to GDP. The latter action leads to reassociation of the free α subunit with the β-γ-dimer to restore the original heterotrimer.

Agents that mimic at least some of the effects of endogenous compounds by interacting with the appropriate receptor are termed agonists. Compounds that lack intrinsic pharmacological activity but cause inhibition of the actions of a specific agonist are said to be antagonists. Partial agonists bind to a specific receptor but do not possess full biological activity at that receptor, even at maximally effective doses.[17] Therefore, in the presence of an agonist, a partial agonist can act as a functional antagonist. Agonists and antagonists are available for most, if not all, chemical synapses.

Neurotransmitter action is terminated in part by the cessation of transmitter release from the presynaptic terminal. Transmitters are also inactivated rapidly by the action of degradative enzymes specific for the transmitters as well as by specific reuptake mechanisms that sequester released neurotransmitter in the presynaptic terminal. In addition to pharmacological agents that mimic or block the action of neurotransmitters by acting as agonists or antagonists at the postsynaptic receptor, agents are available that block the hydrolysis or reuptake of released neurotransmitter and thus prolong or increase the rate of synaptic activation. These agents are specific for a particular neurotransmitter. In addition, calcium ionophores or channel blockers may influence neurotransmitter release, albeit in a nonspecific manner.

Presynaptic Inhibition

The amount of neurotransmitter released from the presynaptic terminal is directly related to the size of the action potential invading that terminal. Minor decrements in resting membrane potential in the terminal reduce the magnitude of the action potential. This is because the action potential occurs from a less negative membrane potential and the less negative membrane potential causes increased potassium conductance and inactivation of sodium channel conductance in the presynaptic terminal. The net result of a decrease in presynaptic terminal depolarization is a reduction in the magnitude of the postsynaptic response. This mechanism for reducing the magnitude of the postsynaptic response by altering the presynaptic membrane potential is known as presynaptic inhibition. This inhibition takes place without the occurrence of IPSPs in the postsynaptic terminal and has a longer duration than do IPSPs. The observation at the electron microscopic level that presynaptic terminals can also receive synaptic input provides a morphological basis for presynaptic inhibition. This also requires a modification of the stylized archetypal neuron presented earlier. We see that afferent connections may alter not only the summation occurring on the soma and dendrites leading up to the generation of an action potential but also the communication of that action potential to a postsynaptic cell through presynaptic inhibition.[18, 19]

Neurotransmitters

In this section, we briefly review the synthesis and metabolism of the major neurotransmitter systems and then show in tabular form the current receptors and effector systems associated with each. Many of these neurotransmitters and their receptors are highlighted in greater detail in the section on neuropharmacological mechanisms. Those seeking more detailed general information regarding neurotransmitter neurobiology are encouraged to read the books by Cooper[20] and Siegel[21] and their colleagues and by Bloom and Kupfer.[22]

Catecholamines

Paton[23] suggested in 1958 that a substance must meet several criteria for acceptance as a neurotransmitter:

1. The presynaptic neuron should contain the substance and should be capable of synthesizing it.
2. The substance should be released on stimulation of the presynaptic axons.
3. Application of the substance to the postsynaptic cell should mimic the effects of normal synaptic transmission.
4. The actions of the substance should be affected by competitive agonists or antagonists in the same manner as is synaptic transmission.

Originally a fifth criterion was included, namely that enzymes should exist in the vicinity of the synapse that would be capable of destroying the substance. Given our present understanding of the mechanisms by which neurotransmission is terminated, this may be stated more generally as:

5. A cellular mechanism should exist to terminate rapidly the action of the substance.

The principal catecholamines found in the nervous system are dopamine, epinephrine, and norepinephrine. These compounds are synthesized from dietary tyrosine or dietary phenylalanine after the latter is hydroxylated by hepatic phenylalanine hydroxylase. The overall scheme is shown in Figure 14–6. Tyrosine is transported into neurons by an active process in which tyrosine is accumulated against a concentration gradient. Within the cytoplasm, tyrosine is converted to dopa and then to dopamine by the actions of tyrosine hydroxylase and dopa decarboxylase, respectively. The latter enzyme is also known as L-amino-acid decarboxylase. Dopamine is then taken up into the vesicles. In neurons that utilize norepinephrine, the vesicles are also the site of dopamine conversion to norepinephrine by dopamine β-hydroxylase. The rate-limiting step in this process involves the action of tyrosine hydroxylase. This enzyme is subject to feedback inhibition by dopamine and norepinephrine. In cells that produce epinephrine, such as the cells of the adrenal medulla, the granules also contain the enzyme phenylethanolamine *N*-methyltransferase, which catalyzes the conversion of norepinephrine to epinephrine.

The actions of epinephrine and norepinephrine are terminated by transport out of the synapse back into the presynaptic terminal and then by repackaging into vesicles

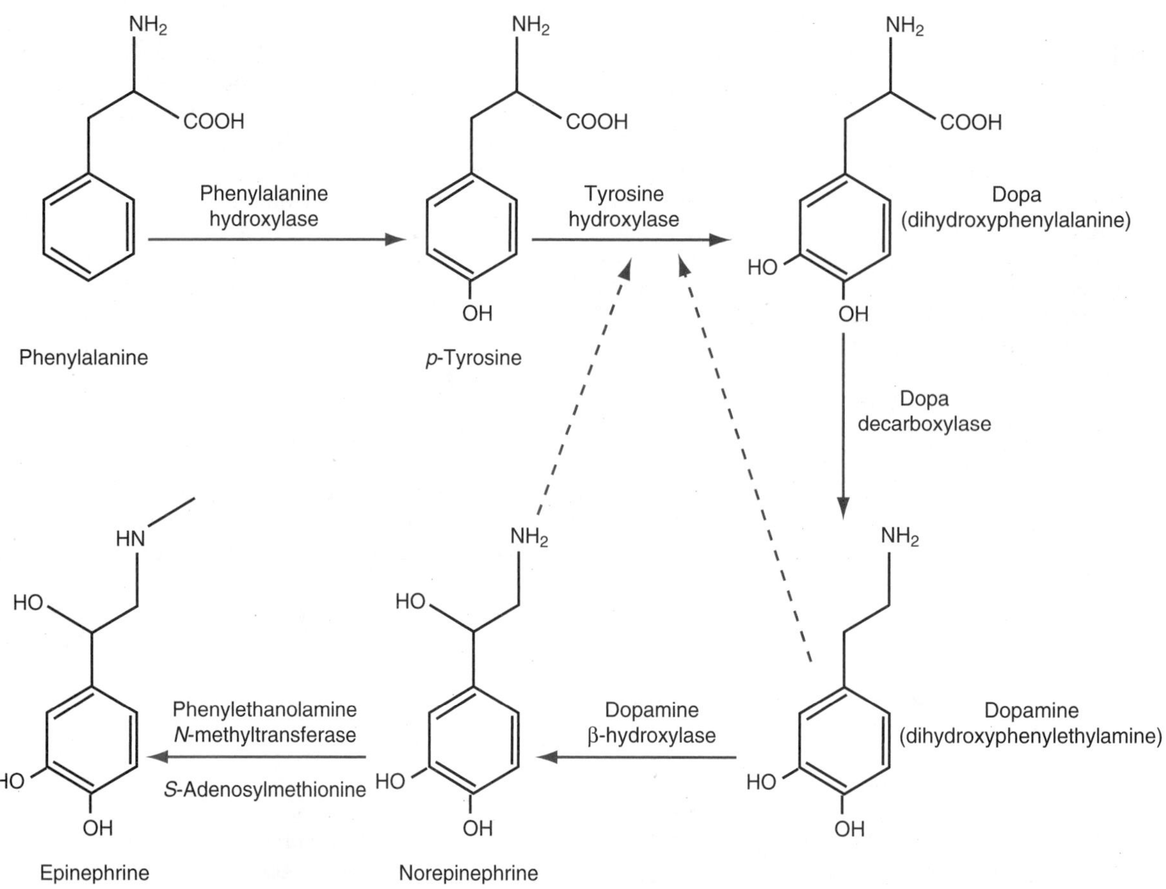

Figure 14–6 *Biochemical pathway for the endogenous synthesis of catecholamines. Tyrosine hydroxylase is the rate-limiting enzyme in this pathway. The dashed lines indicate product feedback inhibition by dopamine and norepinephrine on tyrosine hydroxylase.*

or by oxidation and methylation. Oxidation is performed by monoamine oxidase (MAO), which is present on mitochondrial membranes within the terminal, and methylation by catechol *O*-methyltransferase. The metabolism of epinephrine and norepinephrine is shown in Figure 14–7. Both enzymes are found in the liver and kidneys in high amounts. However, only MAO is found at the synapse. Circulating epinephrine and norepinephrine are primarily O-methylated. These products are excreted in the urine and provide useful measures of secretory rates from peripheral sympathetic sources. Products that are not excreted are oxidized to 3-methoxy-4-hydroxymandelic acid, which is then also excreted in the urine.

Norepinephrine that is not repackaged into vesicles after uptake from the synapse is oxidized by MAO to the physiologically inactive compounds 3,4-dihydroxymandelic acid and 3,4-dihydroxyphenylglycol. These metabolites may be then methylated to 3-methoxy-4-hydroxyphenylglycol and 3-methoxy-4-hydroxymandelic acid. The major means by which the action of norepinephrine is terminated at the synapse is uptake and recycling by the presynaptic nerve terminal, with oxidation by MAO making a smaller contribution to inactivation.

The postsynaptic receptors and effectors for epinephrine and norepinephrine were originally subdivided on the basis of their differential sensitivity to certain pharmacological agents. Initially, α-adrenergic receptors were identified by the ability of phentolamine to act as an antagonist at these receptors and β-adrenergic receptors were identified by the antagonist properties of propranolol. Later work resulted in further subdivision of these receptor types as increasingly selective agonists and antagonists became available. Thus, α_1-adrenergic receptors are sensitive to phenylephrine but not clonidine, whereas the converse holds for α_2-adrenergic receptors. Similarly, β_1-adrenergic receptors are sensitive to dobutamine but not to salbutamol, whereas the converse

Figure 14–7 *Routes of catabolism of epinephrine and norepinephrine. The upper portion illustrates the pathways for circulating epinephrine and norepinephrine. The liver is the primary site of catabolism, and the conjugates are primarily sulfates and glucuronides. The lower portion illustrates the pathways involved in nerve terminals. DOMA and DOPEG enter the circulation before the formation of VMA and MOPEG. Note the convergence of the two pathways into common final products, albeit with different intermediates. MAO, Monoamine oxidase; COMT, catechol O-methyltransferase.*

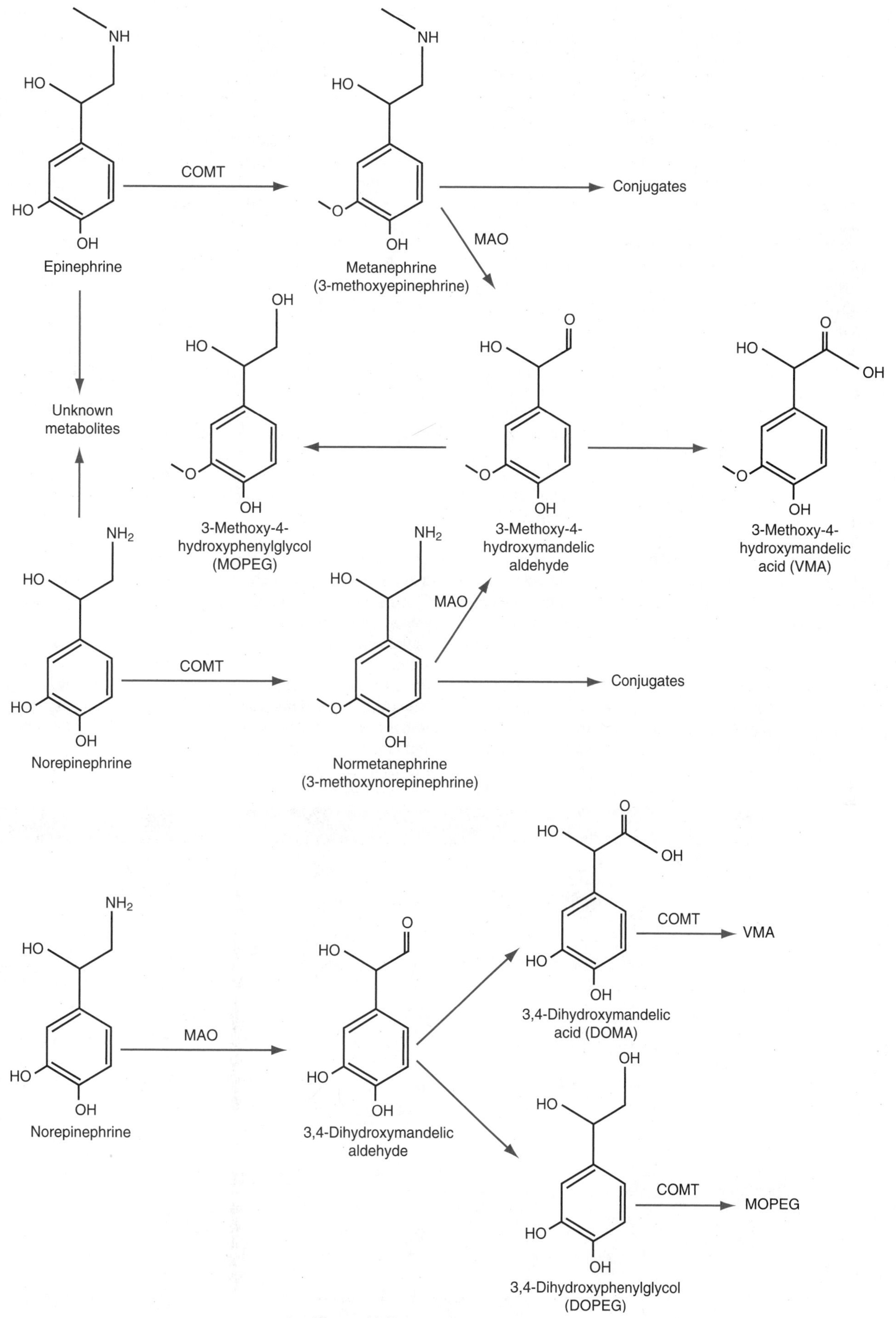

Epinephrine
COMT
Metanephrine (3-methoxyepinephrine)
Conjugates
MAO
Unknown metabolites
3-Methoxy-4-hydroxyphenylglycol (MOPEG)
3-Methoxy-4-hydroxymandelic aldehyde
3-Methoxy-4-hydroxymandelic acid (VMA)
Norepinephrine
COMT
Normetanephrine (3-methoxynorepinephrine)
MAO
Conjugates
Norepinephrine
MAO
3,4-Dihydroxymandelic aldehyde
3,4-Dihydroxymandelic acid (DOMA)
COMT
VMA
3,4-Dihydroxyphenylglycol (DOPEG)
COMT
MOPEG

Figure 14–7 *See legend on opposite page*

holds for β_2-adrenergic receptors. In addition, epinephrine is a much more potent agonist at β_2-adrenergic receptors than at β_1-adrenergic receptors. The powerful tools of molecular cloning have identified additional members of this family of receptors. The basis for this identification is close sequence homology of the predicted protein sequences of the DNA clones with the sequences originally cloned for the adrenergic receptors, as well as sensitivity to adrenergic compounds in various receptor expression assay systems.[15]

The α_1-adrenergic receptors appear to be linked to the phosphatidylinositol second-messenger system. When cells expressing these receptors are challenged with the agonist epinephrine, a rise in cytoplasmic concentrations of inositol 1,4,5-trisphosphate and calcium ions occurs. Activation of this pathway also leads to activation of protein kinase C. The α_2-adrenergic receptors act via the cyclic adenosine monophosphate (cAMP) pathway. Adrenergic stimulation of these cells decreases cAMP levels through a decrease in adenylate cyclase mediated by activation of an inhibitory member of the G protein family, G_i. This leads ultimately to a reduction in the activity of protein kinase A. The β-adrenergic receptors couple positively to the cAMP pathway. After stimulation of β-adrenergic receptors, activation of adenylate cyclase is mediated by a stimulatory member of the G protein family, G_s, and results ultimately in an increase in the activity of protein kinase A. Many members of the family of adrenergic receptors have been cloned by molecular biological techniques. The characteristics of the adrenergic receptors are summarized in Table 14–1, which presents information on present and past nomenclature of the receptors, their effector mechanisms, and the genes to which the receptors correspond. All of the adrenergic receptors identified thus far contain seven hydrophobic regions that are believed to be membrane-spanning domains.

Dopamine acts as a neurotransmitter at more than one type of receptor.[24] The D_1 and D_5 receptors are coupled to adenylate cyclase and cAMP formation in a manner similar to the β-adrenergic pathway, and therefore dopamine agonists increase cAMP in cells expressing D_1 or D_5 receptors. Released dopamine is removed from the synapse by an active uptake mechanism. The catecholamine is also inactivated by MAO and catechol *O*-methyltransferase in pathways that are homologous to those shown for epinephrine and norepinephrine.[16, 25] The characteristics of the dopaminergic receptors are summarized in Table 14–2 and are discussed in greater detail in the section on antipsychotic drugs. All of the dopamine receptors identified thus far also contain seven hydrophobic regions that are believed to be membrane-spanning domains.

Acetylcholine

The first neurotransmitter to be identified functionally in the vertebrate nervous system was the *Vagusstoff,* characterized for its actions on frog heart by Loewi.[26] Chemical identification of acetylcholine (ACh) as the Vagusstoff followed shortly thereafter.[27] The fact that ACh is the transmitter of the neuromuscular junction facilitated early work in the field of transsynaptic communication, and indeed most of the mechanistic models for synaptic transmission were developed initially at the neuromuscular junction. The neuromuscular junction was used to define nicotinic ACh transmission on the basis that nicotine would activate these receptors whereas curare would block them. Phenomenological characterization of the nicotinic receptor indicated that it is a membrane protein containing an integral ion channel that opens when the receptor binds its ligand and hence depolarizes the postsynaptic cell. Protein chemistry combined with molecular biology identified the nicotinic receptor as a heteropentamer with four unique subunits constituting the functional receptor. The receptor contains two of one of the subunits (α). Each subunit has four putative transmembrane domains.[28] An additional type of ACh

Table 14–1 Characteristics of Adrenergic Receptors

	α_1-Adrenoceptors		
Nomenclature	α_{1A}	α_{1B}	α_{1D}
Previous or alternative names	α_{1a}, α_{1C}	α_{1b}	$\alpha_{1A/D}$
Effector	$G_{q/11}$	$G_{q/11}$	$G_{q/11}$
Result	Increased intracellular Ca^{2+}	Increased intracellular Ca^{2+}	Increased intracellular Ca^{2+}
Gene	*α1C*	*α1B*	*α1A*
	α_2-Adrenoceptors		
Nomenclature	α_{2A}	α_{2B}	α_{2D}
Previous or alternative names	—	—	—
Effector	$G_{i/o}$	$G_{i/o}$	$G_{i/o}$
Result	Inhibition of adenylate cyclase	Inhibition of adenylate cyclase	Inhibition of adenylate cyclase
Gene	*α2A*	*α2B*	*α2C*
	β-Adrenoceptors		
Nomenclature	β_1	β_2	β_3
Previous or alternative names	—	—	Atypical β
Effector	G_s	G_s	G_s
Result	Activation of adenylate cyclase	Activation of adenylate cyclase	Activation of adenylate cyclase
Gene	*β1*	*β2*	*β3*

Table 14–2 Characteristics of Dopaminergic Receptors

Nomenclature	D_1	D_2	D_3	D_4	D_5
Previous or alternative names	D_{1A}	D_{2A}	D_{2B}	D_{2C}	D_{1B}
Effector	G_s	$G_{i/o}$	$G_{i/o}$	$G_{i/o}$	G_s
Result	Activation of adenylate cyclase	Inhibition of adenylate cyclase*	Inhibition of adenylate cyclase*	Inhibition of adenylate cyclase*	Activation of adenylate cyclase
Gene	*d1*	*d2*	*d3*	*d4*	*d5*

*Controversial at present.

receptor, the muscarinic receptor, was first identified on the basis of activation by muscarine and inhibition by atropine and later through pharmacological and molecular studies.

The postsynaptic events produced by activation of muscarinic receptors occur more slowly than do those produced by activation of nicotinic receptors. This suggested that muscarinic activation does not involve direct activation of an ion channel. The muscarinic receptor was isolated and cloned by the group of investigators who elucidated the structure of the nicotinic receptor. The muscarinic receptor was found to be of insufficient size to form an ion channel. Sequence homology with the β-adrenergic receptors, complete with the seven-transmembrane-domain topology, and reconstitution experiments involving G proteins indicated that the G protein system is the intracellular effector of the muscarinic receptor.[29] Subsequent molecular cloning work has identified five related members of the muscarinic receptor family. The characteristics of these and of four types of nicotinic receptor are summarized in Table 14–3.

Serotonin

Serotonin is produced by enzymatic modification of dietary tryptophan. Tryptophan is hydroxylated by the enzyme tryptophan hydroxylase and then decarboxylated by an L-amino-acid decarboxylase (5-hydroxytryptophan decarboxylase) to form serotonin. This pathway is illustrated in Figure 14–8. Serotonin is also referred to as 5-hydroxytryptamine or 5-HT. Serotonin is similar to the catecholamines in that the major mechanism by which synaptic activation is terminated is transport into the presynaptic terminal. MAO is also capable of deamidating serotonin to produce 5-hydroxyindoleacetic acid, which is excreted in the urine. The characteristics of the 15 known types of serotoninergic receptors[16, 30] are summarized in Table 14–4.

γ-Aminobutyric Acid and Glycine

γ-Aminobutyric acid (GABA) and glycine act as fast inhibitory neurotransmitters in the CNS. Glutamate and aspartate act as fast excitatory neurotransmitters in the CNS. This type of neurotransmission accounts for the vast majority of intercellular communication in the CNS. GABAergic inhibition at $GABA_A$ receptors results in rapid IPSPs that derive from an increase in chloride conductance.[31] These IPSPs tend to stabilize the electronegative resting membrane potential and reduce the excitability of the postsynaptic cell. Voltage clamp experiments combined with noise analysis indicated that the chloride channels are in one of four conductance states, which are influenced by the

Table 14–3 Characteristics of Muscarinic and Nicotinic Acetylcholine Receptors

Muscarinic Acetylcholine Receptors

Nomenclature	M_1	M_2	M_3	M_4	M_5
Previous or alternative names	—	—	—	—	—
Effector	$G_{q/11}$	$G_{i/o}$	$G_{q/11}$	$G_{i/o}$	$G_{q/11}$
Result	Increased phosphoinositide metabolism	Inhibition of adenylate cyclase	Increased phosphoinositide metabolism	Inhibition of adenylate cyclase	Increased phosphoinositide metabolism
Gene	*m1*	*m2*	*m3*	*m4*	*m5*

Nicotinic Acetylcholine Receptors

Nomenclature	Muscle	Ganglionic	Neuronal CNS	α7 neuronal
Previous or alternative names	—	Epibatidine	—	α-Bungarotoxin binding site
Effector	Sodium/potassium/calcium channel	Sodium/potassium/calcium channel	Sodium/potassium/calcium channel	Sodium/potassium/calcium channel
Result	Cellular depolarization	Cellular depolarization	Cellular depolarization	Cellular depolarization
Gene	—	—	—	—

NH_2 COOH

Tryptophan

Tryptophan hydroxylase

NH_2 COOH

HO

5-Hydroxytryptophan

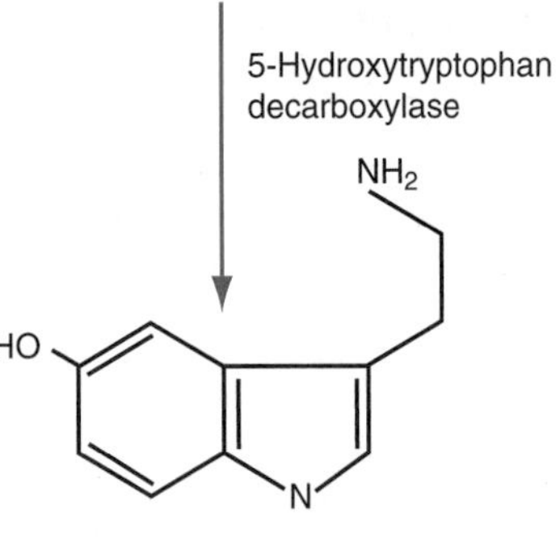

Serotonin

Figure 14–8 *Biosynthesis of endogenous serotonin. The source of tryptophan is dietary proteins. 5-Hydroxytryptophan decarboxylase is similar to dopa decarboxylase (L-amino-acid decarboxylase).*

presence or absence of the ligand. This suggested that the $GABA_A$ receptor is a chloride channel. The $GABA_A$ receptor also appears to be a target for the benzodiazepines and barbiturates insofar as benzodiazepines increase the frequency of chloride channel openings and barbiturates increase the average open time of the channel.[32] A detailed description of the molecular events occurring at the $GABA_A$ receptor is presented later in this chapter. The $GABA_B$ receptor has not been characterized as completely as the $GABA_A$ receptor[16] (Table 14–5). The inhibitory effects of GABA at these receptors display slower onsets than at $GABA_A$ receptors and appear to involve alterations in adenylate cyclase activity.

The glycine receptor has many similarities to the $GABA_A$ receptor. Application of glycine to neurons expressing glycine receptors results in a hyperpolarization that varies with alterations in chloride concentration. The glycine-gated chloride channel is slightly smaller than the $GABA_A$ chloride channel (5.2 versus 7.4 Å) and displays four conductance states, which are similar to those of the $GABA_A$ chloride channel.[32] The glycine receptor also consists of two glycoproteins, each of which has four transmembrane domains and is homologous to the $GABA_A$ receptor subunits.[16]

Glutamate

Glutamate is the major mediator of fast excitatory synaptic transmission in the CNS. The postsynaptic receptors forglutamate appear to be ligand-gated ion channels selective for cations. Of the multiple types of glutamate receptors, the best characterized are those that are activated by *N*-methyl-D-aspartate (NMDA) and are referred to as NMDA receptors. Excessive excitation of NMDA receptors results in neurotoxicity. Other glutamate receptors are insensitive to NMDA but are activated by quisqualic acid or by kainic acid. These are known as Q- and K-type receptors and are also referred to as non-NMDA receptors. The selective ligand α-amino-3-hydroxy-5-methyl-4-isoxazolepropionic acid (AMPA) has supplanted quisqualate as the definitive ligand for those receptors. Glutamate, like other amino acid neurotransmitters, is rapidly removed from the synaptic cleft by an uptake mechanism and repackaged for subsequent rerelease.[33]

Voltage clamp and patch clamp investigations of glutamate receptors have demonstrated that activation of these receptors results in an increase in intracellular calcium and that this increase can be blocked by magnesium. The elevation in intracellular calcium accounts for the cytotoxicity that occurs after overstimulation of NMDA receptors. Conversely, NMDA receptors have been found to be essential for the production of many types of long-term potentiation. This in vitro model of learning may depend on alterations in intracellular metabolism secondary to the NMDA-induced influx of calcium for the long-term changes observed in cellular responses within this model. A protein kinase C–like protein appears to be the intracellular target for calcium.[34]

Non-NMDA receptors do not show the sensitivity to magnesium displayed by NMDA receptors. Some Q-type receptors are coupled to inward ion currents that are delayed in onset and are altered by manipulations of G proteins. Because the ion currents can be mimicked with inositol triphosphate and blocked with calcium chelation, these responses are thought to arise from calcium activation of chloride channels.[35] Molecular cloning of the various glutamate receptors has resolved the confusion over which glutamatergic effects are mediated by direct activation of ion channels and which are mediated by intracellular messengers or effectors. The molecular structures of glutamate receptors reveal a heterogeneity of structures, which may be divided into two subfamilies. The first is a group composed of the NMDA, AMPA, and kainate receptors. These display a four-transmembrane-region topology reminiscent of the GABA and glycine receptors; however, studies of the topology of these receptors suggest that the standard model is not entirely accurate. These receptors form integral ligand-gated ion channels and, because they directly alter ion flux across the cell membrane, are referred to as ionotropic glutamate receptors. The members of the second subfamily of glutamate receptors display a seven-transmembrane-region topology and are similar in structure to other receptors that couple to G proteins. These glutamate receptors have

Table 14–4 Characteristics of Serotonin Receptors

Nomenclature	5-HT_{1A}	5-$HT_{1D\alpha}$	5-$HT_{1D\beta}$	5-HT_{1E}	5-HT_{1F}
Previous or alternative names	—	5-HT_{1D}	5-HT_{1B}	—	5-$HT_{1E\beta}$
Effector	$G_{i/o}$	$G_{i/o}$	$G_{i/o}$	$G_{i/o}$	$G_{i/o}$
Result	Inhibition of adenylate cyclase	Inhibition of adenylate cyclase	Inhibition of adenylate cyclase	Inhibition of adenylate cyclase	Inhibition of adenylate cyclase
Gene	*5-ht1A*	*5-ht1D*	*5-ht1B*	*5-ht1E*	*5-ht1F*
Nomenclature	5-HT_{2A}	5-HT_{2B}	5-HT_{2C}	5-HT_3	5-HT_4
Previous or alternative names	5-HT_2, D	5-HT_{2F}	5-HT_{1C}	M	—
Effector	$G_{q/11}$	$G_{q/11}$	$G_{q/11}$	Cation channel	G_s
Result	Increased phosphoinositide metabolism	Increased phosphoinositide metabolism	Increased phosphoinositide metabolism	Neuronal depolarization	Activation of adenylate cyclase
Gene	*5-ht2A*	*5-ht2B*	*5-ht2C*	*5-ht3*	*5-ht4*
Nomenclature	5-HT_{5A}	5-HT_{5B}	5-HT_6	5-HT_7	5-HT_{1P}
Previous or alternative names	5-$HT_{5\alpha}$	5-$HT_{5\beta}$	—	5-HT_X	5-$HT_{1\text{-like}}$
Effector	Unknown	Unknown	G_s	G_s	Unknown
Result	Unknown	Unknown	Activation of adenylate cyclase	Activation of adenylate cyclase	Unknown
Gene	*5-ht5A*	*5-ht5B*	*5-ht6*	*5-ht7*	Not cloned

been shown to interact with various G proteins. Because their effects on cellular processes are indirect and are manifest through various alterations in cellular metabolism, these receptors are referred to as metabotropic glutamate receptors.[16] The characteristics of the various glutamate receptors are summarized in Table 14–6.

Neuropeptide Transmitters

Table 14–7 contains an incomplete list of peptides that have been localized within the CNS. These peptides have been implicated as neurotransmitters because of their localization within discrete neurons of the CNS. The inclusion of the hypothalamic peptides in this list may seem inappropriate because of their role in the neuroendocrine regulation of pituitary function. However, these peptides have also been localized to neurons outside the neurohemal zone of the hypothalamus and thus appear to function as neurotransmitters in addition to their neuroendocrine functions. Similarly, many of these peptides were first identified elsewhere in the body. Their roles were elucidated and their names applied for effects in peripheral tissue before their identification in brain.

Table 14–5 Characteristics of γ-Aminobutyric Acid Receptors

Nomenclature	$GABA_A$	$GABA_B$
Previous or alternative names	—	—
Effector	Chloride channel	$G_{i/o}$
Gene	*gabra1–gabra6, gabrg1–gabrg3, gabrd*	—
Structure	Four transmembrane regions	

The peptides readily fulfill the first four of the Paton criteria described earlier. The demonstration of specific means of terminating the action of these neuropeptides has been more difficult. Specific reuptake mechanisms do not appear to be present for the peptides. However, most of the peptides have short half-lives in biological matrices because of the action of nonspecific endo- and exopeptidases. The list in Table 14–7 is incomplete because of the rapid pace at which additional peptides are being added to this list.

The receptors for many of these peptides have been identified and their structures determined. Most appear to belong to the bacteriorhodopsin superfamily of macromolecules that have seven transmembrane regions and couple to various members of the G protein family of intracellular effectors. Members of this receptor family are capable of coupling to multiple members of the G protein family. The cellular responses mounted by neuropeptide receptor–expressing cells therefore depend on the complement of G proteins also expressed by those cells. It is thus impossible to define specific target cell responses for a given neuropeptide, as these vary across target cell types. Some of the neuropeptides have multiple subtypes of receptors, which, as was the case for the classical neurotransmitters, were discovered through the development of receptor subtype–selective ligands or molecular cloning. Implicit in this statement is the fact that several peptide as well as nonpeptide ligands have been developed for some of the neuropeptide receptors and these ligands may act as agonists or antagonists.

Neuropeptides are similar to other peptides in that they are synthesized in the ribosomal and Golgi compartments of the perinuclear cell. Like other peptides, the neuropeptides are commonly synthesized as larger precursor molecules from which the final biologically active peptide is excised.

Table 14–6 Characteristics of Glutamate Receptors

Metabotropic Glutamate Receptors							
Nomenclature	$mGlu_1$	$mGlu_2$	$mGlu_3$	$mGlu_4$	$mGlu_5$	$mGlu_6$	$mGlu_7$
Previous or alternative names	$mGluR_1$	$mGluR_2$	$mGluR_3$	$mGluR_4$	$mGluR_5$	$mGluR_6$	$mGluR_7$
Effector	$G_{q/11}$	$G_{i/o}$	$G_{i/o}$	$G_{i/o}$	$G_{q/11}$	$G_{i/o}$	$G_{i/o}$
Result	Stimulation of phospho-lipase C	Inhibition of adenylate cyclase	Inhibition of adenylate cyclase	Inhibition of adenylate cyclase	Stimulation of phospho-lipase C	Inhibition of adenylate cyclase	
Gene	*mglu1*	*mglu2*	*mglu3*	*mglu4*	*mglu5*	*mglu6*	*mglu7*

Ionotropic Glutamate Receptors			
Nomenclature	NMDA	AMPA	Kainate
Previous or alternative names	α_{1a}, α_{1C}	Quisqualate	—
Effector	Sodium/potassium/ calcium channel	Sodium/potassium/ calcium channel	Sodium/potassium/ calcium channel
Result	Cellular depolarization	Cellular depolarization	Cellular depolarization
Gene	*nmda1, nmda2A–nmda2D*	*glu1–glu4*	*glu5–glu7, ka1, ka2*

The precursor may be common to several cell types, with the cellular complement of processing enzymes determining the final product. The synthesis of endorphin and corticotropin (ACTH) from a common precursor, proopiomelanocortin, is an example of this.[36] In the case of calcitonin gene–related peptide, knowledge of one gene product, calcitonin, led to the identification of a second product of the same gene, calcitonin gene–related peptide, before a biological function was ascribed to the latter product.[37]

An intriguing development in the biology of neuropeptide-based neurotransmission is the finding that the neuropeptides are frequently colocalized to cells that also produce "classical" nonpeptide neurotransmitters. As would be predicted from these observations, the peptide and nonpeptide neurotransmitters that are colocalized within a neuron are coreleased on stimulation of that neuron. However, the molar ratios of the two types of released neurotransmitter are not constant. This suggests that neurons are capable of altering the relative proportions of the transmitters they release.[38, 39] The mechanisms underlying the shifts in proportions of neurotransmitter that are synthesized or released are poorly understood. However, changes in the humoral milieu of the neuron and frequency modulation of input to the neuron are the two leading, and not mutually exclusive, mechanisms thought to be responsible for shifts in neurotransmitter proportions within a neuron.

Steroids

The classical model of steroid action postulates that extracellular steroids impinge on the cell membrane from external sources. The abundance of intracellular steroid receptors creates a concentration gradient down which the steroid diffuses into the cell. Once the steroid is inside the cell and bound to a cytoplasmic receptor, a conformational transformation occurs such that a DNA binding domain is exposed on the receptor. The receptor translocates to the

Table 14–7 Peptide Neurotransmitters

Angiotensin
Atrial natriuretic peptide
Bombesin
Calcitonin
Calcitonin gene–related peptide
Cholecystokinin
Corticotropin
Corticotropin-releasing factor
Dynorphin
β-Endorphin
Leu-enkephalin
Met-enkephalin
Galanin
Gastrin
Gonadotropin-releasing hormone
Growth hormone
Growth hormone–releasing hormone
Insulin
Motilin
Neuropeptide Y
Neurotensin
Oxytocin
Pancreatic polypeptide
Prolactin
Secretin
Somatostatin
Substance K
Substance P
Thyrotropin-releasing hormone
Vasoactive intestinal polypeptide
Vasopressin (arginine vasopressin, antidiuretic hormone)

nucleus and binds to specific response elements in the regulatory regions of various steroid-responsive genes to alter transcription of those genes.

This model holds for both peripheral targets of steroids and neurons in the CNS. Neurons that are responsive to circulating steroid hormones function in large part as sensors for the feedback component of a neuroendocrine negative feedback. As an example, the hypothalamic production of gonadotropin-releasing hormone stimulates the anterior pituitary to produce the gonadotropins luteinizing hormone and follicle-stimulating hormone. The gonadotropins stimulate the gonads to produce sex steroids. The sex steroids have among their targets cells in the hypothalamus that bind those steroids specifically and maintain homeostatic levels of the steroids by restraining the production of gonadotropin-releasing hormone. The steroids may be viewed in this context as another afferent to the CNS. This afferent also impinges on behavioral systems, as cyclic changes in sex steroids have profound behavioral effects in some mammalian species.

It has been known since 1942 that steroids also have rapid anesthetic and sedative effects that could not be accounted for on the basis of the classical model of steroid action.[40] We now know of the existence of another class of steroids that have neurotransmitter-like actions in the CNS. Steroids of this class are referred to as neurosteroids and are subdivided further into neuroactive and neuroinactive steroids. Neuroactive steroids are those that are active on neural tissue, regardless of their site of origin. Neuroinactive steroids are those that are synthesized in the brain but are inactive on neural tissue. The relationships among these steroids are illustrated in Figure 14–9. Neurosteroid synthesis within the brain occurs through enzymes distributed heterogeneously throughout the brain and localized almost exclusively to glia. This synthesis may occur by metabolism of parent steroids or by local synthesis from cholesterol.[41]

The mechanisms of action of the steroids alphaxalone, allopregnanolone, pregnenolone, and allotetrahydrodeoxycorticosterone (alloTHDOC) are known. These steroids interact with the $GABA_A$ receptor. This interaction is an allosteric effect at the receptor, with an increase in the frequency and duration of opening of the $GABA_A$ receptor chloride channel induced by agonists. Benzodiazepine binding to the $GABA_A$ receptor is also potentiated by the agonists. All of these steroids appear to interact at a single site on the $GABA_A$ receptor, but it is unclear whether they act on all subunits of all $GABA_A$ receptors. It is through this interaction with the $GABA_A$ receptor that these steroids exert their reported sedative, anticonvulsant, and anxiolytic (i.e., benzodiazepine-like) effects in vivo.[42] It is interesting to note that in preclinical studies alloTHDOC levels have been observed to rise in the brain at times of stress. This rise is secondary to an increase in adrenal steroid production as a result of activation of the hypothalamic-pituitary-adrenal (HPA) axis by stress. The brain alloTHDOC levels achieved are similar to those reported to be effective in relieving behavioral and neurochemical indices of stress in some experimental paradigms.[43]

In addition, pregnenolone sulfate acts as an allosteric modulator at the NMDA receptor to enhance its response to glutamate. As was seen at the $GABA_A$ receptor, the effects of pregnenolone sulfate at the NMDA receptor occur as a result of increasing the frequency and the duration of opening of the channel.[44] This explains the ability of pregnenolone sulfate to potentiate the convulsant actions of NMDA in vivo.

Nitric Oxide

Nitric oxide (NO) was identified initially as a potent endothelium-derived vasodilator. This gaseous compound is synthesized through the actions of NO synthase, and an isoform of this enzyme has been detected in neural tissue.

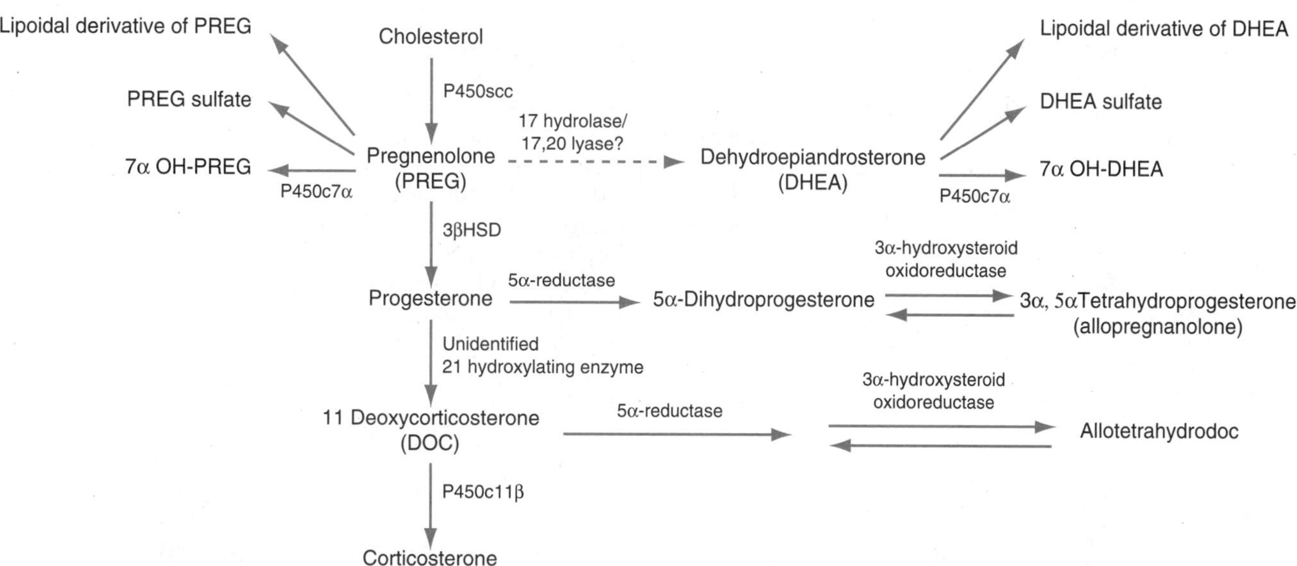

Figure 14–9 *Pathways of neurosteroid biosynthesis in the brain. Solid arrows refer to enzyme activities demonstrated in the brain; the dashed arrow refers to enzyme activity not demonstrated in the brain. Allotetrahydrodoc, indicates allotetrahydrodeoxycorticosterone. (From Mellon SH: Neurosteroids: Biochemistry, modes of action, and clinical relevance. J Clin Endocrinol Metab 1994; 78[5]:1003–1008; © The Endocrine Society.)*

The vasodilator actions of NO led initially to the hypothesis that within the CNS, NO produced by neurons coordinates neural activity with local blood flow.[45] This occurs because NO synthase is activated, although not induced, by increased cytoplasmic calcium levels associated with neuronal activation. Therefore, increased neural traffic would activate NO synthase, producing additional NO, with local vasodilatation being the result. However, the diffusible nature of NO has led to the suggestion that it may also serve to integrate local neuronal activity. NO permeates the cell membrane and binds to guanylate cyclase. This activates the enzyme and increases the intracellular concentration of the second messenger cyclic GMP (cGMP). Because of the widespread distribution of NO production within the brain, NO is the major stimulus for cGMP production in the brain. Glutamate activation of NMDA receptors leads to calcium influx, which activates NO synthase, probably by means of a calmodulin-mediated conformational change in NO synthase. The increased NO produced as a result of this activation diffuses rapidly over a localized region of the brain, where its actions are classified as mediation of slow synaptic transmission despite a brief life of 5 to 10 seconds.[46]

NO has also been implicated as a retrograde messenger in hippocampal models of long-term potentiation (LTP). NO produced by activation of postsynaptic cells diffuses to the presynaptic element and induces an undefined structural alteration that reinforces traffic through that synapse. Within the cerebellum, NO synthesized by basket and granule cells inhibits the Purkinje cells by altering the activity of guanylate cyclase and thus altering the level of cGMP. Other mechanisms that have been implicated in the action of NO are activation of the cyclooxygenase or ADP-ribosylation pathways as well as generation of cytotoxic free radicals.[47] Thus, although the full repertoire of NO actions may remain to be elucidated, it is clear that the gaseous nature of this compound allows its effects to extend beyond the limits of the synapse and allows it to act as a local modulator that may serve to link populations of neurons that are functionally disparate but locally adjacent.[48]

Carbon monoxide (CO) appears to function in intercellular communication in a role homologous to that of NO. This gaseous compound is synthesized endogenously by cells on the CNS by means of the enzyme heme oxygenase. A requirement for CO in hippocampal LTP, an in vitro model for learning and memory formation, is well established. Inhibitors of heme oxygenase or CO production block the induction of LTP. In the intact organism, CO appears to function in the hypothalamus to suppress appetite. The mechanism of CO action is similar to that of NO. Both compounds activate soluble guanylate cyclase, increase cGMP levels, and activate cGMP-dependent protein kinase. This suggests that CO and NO systems may interact with additive effects.[49]

Neuropharmacological Mechanisms

> On the other hand, and this seems to be a distinct advantage of this "pharmacopsychology," we might be able to learn from the specific effect of a given drug on a specific psychic symptom something about the true nature of this symptom. (Emil Kraepelin, 1892[49a])

More than 100 years later, this insightful statement remains a logical avenue for research into the neurobiological basis of neuropsychiatric disorders, particularly in light of the armamentarium of techniques that have become available in the past 30 years. Based to some extent on this tenet, elucidation of the monoamine transporter antagonism properties of tricyclic antidepressants and the dopamine receptor antagonism properties of antipsychotic drugs suggested decreased monoamine function and increased dopaminergic function in depression and schizophrenia, respectively. Unfortunately, in both cases, one is faced with the conundrum that therapeutic efficacy is delayed several weeks, although antagonism of transporters and dopamine receptors occurs immediately. Moreover, in the case of antidepressants, not all monoamine transporter antagonists are effective antidepressants (e.g., cocaine). Nevertheless, characterization of the pharmacology of psychotherapeutic drugs continues to provide details of how the brain functions normally and how beneficial treatments for psychiatric illnesses alter brain function.

For each class of psychotherapeutic drugs, our discussion of their cellular and molecular mechanisms of action is generally separated into three distinct actions. First, each drug (ligand) interacts directly with some cellular protein (e.g., receptor, enzyme). Ions such as lithium and magnesium, alcohols, and volatile anesthetics are exceptions. The binding of drugs to these receptors can be described in terms of both potency and selectivity compared with other receptors. Second, an immediate neurobiological response is produced by binding of these drugs to their respective receptors. This can be described at a system, cellular, or subcellular level. Finally, and most important, as well as least known, are the long-term alterations in function that appear to mediate the therapeutic response. The reader should keep in mind that pharmacotherapy is a function of mechanism of action and several other variables not considered here (such as pharmacokinetics and side effect profiles).

Antidepressants

Immediate Actions of Antidepressant Drugs

Beginning with work in the middle to late 1950s, it was shown that most antidepressant drugs are primarily either antagonists of one or more monoamine transporters or inhibitors of MAO type A (MAOIs). The tricyclic antidepressants and several miscellaneous antidepressants also interact with a number of other neurotransmitter receptors. Although some of these interactions are known to be responsible for the side effect profile of these compounds (i.e., α_1-adrenergic, muscarinic, and histaminergic), it is possible, although not known, that binding to others (e.g., 5-HT_{2A}) may be involved in the efficacy of these compounds. Table 14–8 lists the affinities of a number of antidepressants in their ability to antagonize the serotonin and norepinephrine transporters (SERT and NET, respectively). The affinity is expressed as a constant, usually denoted by K_d or K_i. Under ideal circumstances, the constant represents the concentration of drug necessary to occupy 50% of the available receptors. Therefore, the smaller the number, the more potent the compound. Table 14–9 lists the

Table 14–8 Affinity (K_i) of Various Antidepressants for the Serotonin and Norepinephrine Transporters

	SERT			NET		
Method*	[³H]Ligand	[³H]5-HT (Cells)	[³H]5-HT (Brain)	[³H]Ligand	[³H]NE (Cells)	[³H]NE (Brain)
Paroxetine	0.06	0.05	0.7	59	310	33
Sertraline	0.32	1.1	3.4	1,595	1,717	220
Citalopram	0.5	4.8		4,874	30,300	3,900
Clomipramine	0.52	0.5				96
Fluoxetine	2.1	3.1	13	473	2,188	271
Fluvoxamine	1.6	14	7.1	913	4,748	1,116
Imipramine	12	8.2	42		65	23
Amitriptyline	17	11	75	8.5	100	18
Venlafaxine	21	102	39	1,065	210	
Nortriptyline		85	201		17	3
Desipramine	141	46	249	0.3	4	0.6
Doxepin	115		247			18
Nefazodone	239	549	137	554	713	570
Trazodone	258	690	304	>10,000	6,892	
Maprotiline		6,700	3,333	1.8		7
Bupropion			14,900			2,200

*[³H]Ligand refers to the ability of the particular antidepressant to displace the selective ligands [³H]citalopram and [³H]nisoxetine from the rat SERT and NET, respectively. [³H]5-HT or [³H]NE refers to the ability of the drugs to inhibit the uptake of the radiolabeled monoamines into cells expressing the cloned human SERT or human NET (cells) or into freshly prepared rat brain synaptosomes (brain). The ability of a drug to displace the [³H]ligand is highly correlated with its ability to inihibit monoamine uptake.

Data compiled from Owens MJ, Morgan WN, Plott SE, et al: In vitro inhibition of the rat and human serotonin and norepinephrine transporters by the antidepressant nefazodone and its metabolites. Soc Neurosci Abstr 1995; 21:766.

relative selectivities of a number of antidepressants for the SERT and NET, expressed as the unitless ratio of the affinity of NET antagonism to that of SERT antagonism. A value of 1 represents equipotency; values greater than 1 indicate SERT selectivity; values less than 1 indicate NET selectivity. Keep in mind that although this ratio is constant, as the concentration or dose of drug increases, the in vivo selectivity may disappear as transporters or receptors become occupied by the drug in question. Moreover, many of these compounds have active metabolites that may not have the same selectivity as the parent compound. A final consideration for in vivo selectivity is the amount of plasma protein binding for a given drug. It is much more difficult to increase the free drug concentrations of highly protein-bound drugs with relatively modest changes in dosage. Thus, highly protein-bound drugs that exhibit selectivity in vitro are more likely also to show it in vivo regardless of dose.

As a class, the tricyclic antidepressants are relatively potent (K_i values between 1 and 100 nM) antagonists of muscarinic, histamine$_1$, and α_1-adrenergic receptors. Their affinity for these receptors is not thought to contribute to their therapeutic efficacy but is responsible for their side effect profile. Trazodone, nefazodone, and the tricyclic agents are also potent 5-HT$_{2A}$ antagonists (K_i values less than 10 nM for trazodone and nefazodone and less than 100 nM for the tricyclic agents). Although modulation of serotoninergic transmission is one of the consequences of effective antidepressant therapy, it is not known whether 5-HT$_{2A}$ antagonism is important or beneficial per se.

Within minutes after exposure to monoamine transporter antagonists, the ability of neurons to transport 5-HT

Table 14–9 Relative Selectivity* of Various Antidepressants for the Serotonin and Norepinephrine Transporters in Vitro

Assay Type	[³H]Ligand	[³H]-Monoamine (Cells)	[³H]-Monoamine (Brain)
Citalopram	9748	6313	
Sertraline	4984	1561	65
Paroxetine	983	6200	47
Fluvoxamine	567	339	157
Fluoxetine	225	706	21
Venlafaxine	51	2.1	5.4
Trazodone	>40	10	23
Nefazodone	2.3	1.3	4.2
Amitriptyline	0.5	9	0.2
Imipramine		8	0.5
Nortriptyline		0.2	0.01
Bupropion			0.15
Doxepin			0.07
Desipramine	0.002	0.09	0.002
Maprotiline			0.002

*Relative selectivity is expressed as the unitless ratio of the affinity of NET antagonism to SERT antagonism. A value of 1 indicates equipotency; values greater than 1 indicate SERT selectivity; values less than 1 indicate NET selectivity. Refer to Table 14–8 for explanation of assay type.

Data are compiled from Table 14–8.

and norepinephrine out of the synapse and back into the cell is inhibited in vivo in a dose-dependent manner. This leads to an increase in synaptic concentrations of the particular monoamine and was initially thought to be the mechanism by which antidepressants produce their effect. However, it was quickly realized that there were several flaws in this theory. First, this effect occurs immediately, whereas therapeutic efficacy is delayed at least several weeks. Second, other drugs that inhibit monoamine uptake such as cocaine and amphetamine are not true antidepressants. Moreover, some antidepressants such as bupropion and iprindole are weak uptake inhibitors. In vivo microdialysis studies in laboratory animals have shown that antidepressants such as the SERT antagonists acutely increase extracellular 5-HT concentrations in 5-HT terminal fields, with larger increases observed in somatodendritic regions of the raphe nuclei than in forebrain projection areas. This increase in 5-HT in the somatodendritic region produces a strong negative feedback inhibition of serotoninergic activity and effectively attenuates further 5-HT release. Similar findings related to noradrenergic activity have been reported with imipramine or desipramine.

As described earlier, MAO is present in the outer mitochondrial membrane, where it keeps intracellular (i.e., cytoplasmic) monoamine concentrations low. The MAOIs used clinically, mostly phenelzine and tranylcypromine, are nonselective inhibitors of both the A and B isoforms of MAO. In vivo, 5-HT and norepinephrine are metabolized by MAO-A, whereas dopamine is metabolized by both forms. The therapeutic efficacy of nonselective MAOIs is due to their actions on MAO-A, because clorgyline, moclobemide, and brofaromine, which selectively inhibit this isoform, are clearly effective in the treatment of endogenous depression, whereas selective MAO-B inhibitors such as deprenyl are ineffective. After administration, MAOIs irreversibly (phenelzine, tranylcypromine) or reversibly (moclobemide, brofaromine) inhibit MAO. This leads to increased cytoplasmic concentrations of 5-HT and norepinephrine available for repackaging in synaptic vesicles via the vesicular monoamine transporter. For a constant rate of monoamine synthesis, MAO inhibition would theoretically lead to a greater amount of 5-HT or norepinephrine available per synaptic vesicle, increasing the quanta of 5-HT or norepinephrine released per neuronal impulse. This acute effect was initially thought to be the major mechanism of action. However, as with the monoamine transporter antagonists, therapeutic benefits are delayed by several weeks.

Long-Term Changes Produced by Antidepressant Treatment

It is now clear that elucidation of the chronic or delayed effects of antidepressant treatment would yield a better description of the pharmacological actions of antidepressants with respect to their mechanism of action. Because both transporter antagonists and MAOIs interact with monoamine-containing neurons, we first describe the long-term actions of antidepressants on these neurons with emphasis on serotoninergic and noradrenergic neurons (Fig. 14–10). This is followed by current knowledge of the effects of antidepressant treatment on postsynaptic neuronal functioning.

It has consistently been shown that after chronic antidepressant treatment in rats, serotoninergic neuronal firing rates are not different from those in control animals.

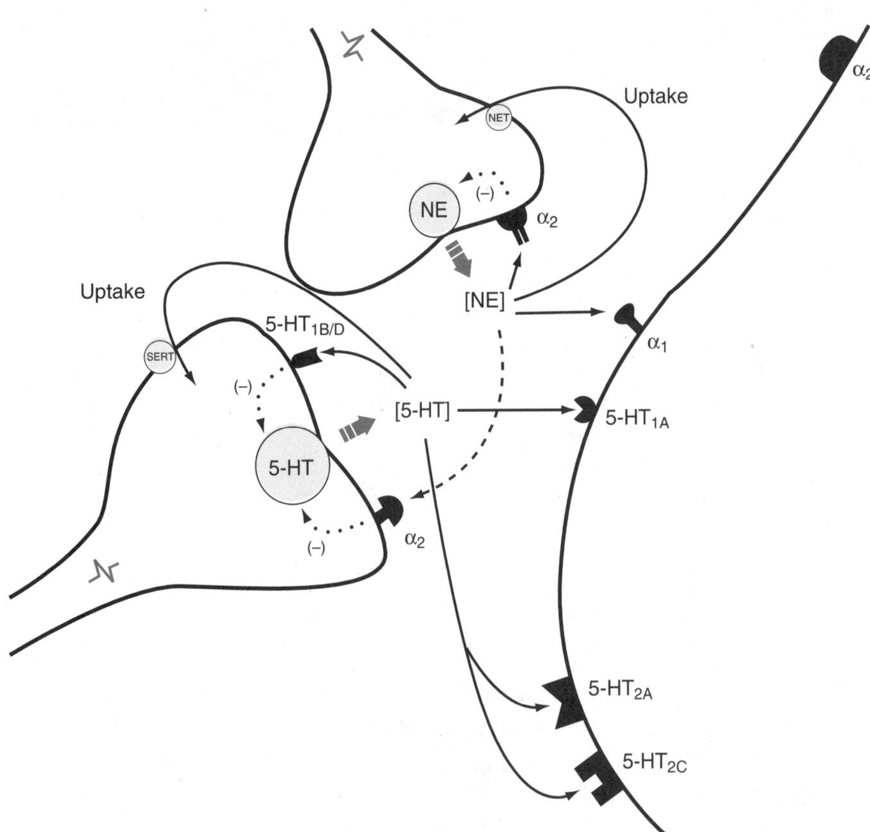

Figure 14–10 *Representation of the modulation of 5-HT and norepinephrine neurotransmission in terminal fields (e.g., hippocampus). Note that α_2-receptors are depicted using different symbols depending on their location, as evidence suggests that they may be pharmacologically distinct. (From Blier P, Mongeau R, Weiss M, de Montigny C: Modulation of serotonin neurotransmission by presynaptic alpha-2-adrenergic receptors: A target for antidepressant pharmacotherapy?* In *Mendlewicz J, Brunello N, Langer SZ, Racagni G [eds]: New Pharmacological Approaches to the Therapy of Depressive Disorders. International Academy for Biomedical and Drug Research Series, Volume 5. Basel: S Karger AG, 1993:74–82.)*

Table 14–10 Effects of Various Antidepressant Treatments on 5-Hydroxytryptamine Neurotransmission

Treatment	Somatodentritic 5-HT Autoreceptor ($5\text{-}HT_{1A}$) Responsiveness	Terminal 5-HT Autoreceptor ($5\text{-}HT_{1B/1D}$) Responsiveness	Terminal 5-HT α_2-Receptor Responsiveness	Postsynaptic 5-HT Receptor Responsiveness	Net Effect on 5-HT Neurotransmission
Tricyclic antidepressants	0	0	?	↑	↑
5-HT uptake inhibitors	↓	↓	0	0	↑
Electroconvulsive therapy	0	0	0	↑	↑
MAO inhibitors	↓	0	↓	0 or ↓	↑
$5\text{-}HT_{1A}$ agonists	↓	0	?	0	↑
Norepinephrine uptake inhibitors	?	?	↓	0	↑ or ?
Lithium	?	?	?	?	↑

However, in vivo microdialysis studies revealed that extracellular 5-HT concentrations are significantly increased in forebrain regions with smaller increases observed in the raphe nuclei after chronic fluvoxamine administration.[50] Less consistent are reports of increased tryptophan hydroxylase activity and basal 5-HT synthesis. These findings suggest that the efficiency of 5-HT release is increased so that more 5-HT is released into the synapse after the same amount of neuronal firing. At this time, no consistent effects on SERT mRNA expression or SERT binding have been reported (various investigators have reported increases, decreases, or no effect on either of these parameters). Whereas neither transporter antagonists nor MAOIs appear to alter somatodendritic $5\text{-}HT_{1A}$ receptor binding or mRNA expression, chronic administration of both selective SERT antagonists and MAOIs decreases the functional activity of this receptor, leading to decreased negative feedback on serotoninergic neurons. Similarly, SERT antagonists decrease the functional activity of terminal $5\text{-}HT_{1B}$ receptors without altering receptor density (the $5\text{-}HT_{1B}$ receptor is the rat homologue of the human $5\text{-}HT_{1D}$ receptor). This action would also serve to produce less negative feedback for identical quanta of 5-HT release. Serotoninergic terminals also possess an inhibitory α_2-autoreceptor that exhibits decreased functional activity after administration of drugs that would theoretically augment noradrenergic function (e.g., MAOIs, NET antagonists) but not after administration of the SERT antagonist paroxetine. As shown in Table 14–10, these actions on serotoninergic neurons by a number of antidepressant treatments would augment serotoninergic neurotransmission during chronic treatment.

The effects of chronic antidepressant treatment on noradrenergic neurotransmission are less clear than are the effects on 5-HT. Nestler and colleagues[51] have observed that all classes of antidepressants decrease tyrosine hydroxylase and tyrosine hydroxylase mRNA concentrations after long-term administration. Previous studies have shown that tyrosine hydroxylase activity directly reflects the physiological activity of tyrosine hydroxylase–containing cells. In addition, both acute administration and long-term administration of MAOIs decrease spontaneous firing rates of locus caeruleus noradrenergic neurons. These findings, taken together, imply a decrease in noradrenergic neurotransmission after antidepressant treatment. However, chronic administration of antidepressants that are transporter antagonists produces minimal or no change in basal firing rates. Moreover, there is some evidence from in vivo microdialysis studies that chronic MAOIs or NET antagonism produced by desipramine but not fluoxetine increases extracellular norepinephrine in terminal fields. Finally, there is some evidence, although it has not been consistently observed, that tricyclic antidepressants and possibly MAOIs decrease the number or function of somatodendritic α_2-adrenergic receptors in the locus caeruleus. This would imply augmented noradrenergic transmission after chronic antidepressant treatment. Antidepressant effects on the NET are also inconsistent. Decreases in radioligand binding to the NET were reported after desipramine and electroconvulsive shock, but administration of desipramine and amitriptyline increased NET mRNA expression.

Chronic antidepressant treatment also results in a number of changes in postsynaptic neurons. One of the most consistent of these findings is the observation that tricyclic antidepressants and electroconvulsive shock, but apparently not SERT-selective antagonists, desensitize norepinephrine receptor–coupled adenylate cyclase in the brain. This is usually accompanied by down-regulation of β_1-adrenergic receptors[52, 53] and decreased β_1-adrenergic receptor mRNA expression. The decrease in β-adrenergic receptor density is confined to receptors in the high-affinity state (i.e., receptors directly coupled with nucleotide regulatory G proteins) and may be neuroanatomically selective (e.g., amygdala). This response is observed with many antidepressants, but the global functional consequences are unclear.

Long-term administration of most tricyclic antidepressants, MAOIs, and the atypical antidepressant mianserin down-regulates the number of cortical $5\text{-}HT_{2A}$ receptors. These receptors are coupled to phosphatidylinositol turnover. Whereas SERT antagonists do not appear to alter $5\text{-}HT_{2A}$ receptor density, long-term sertraline administration can desensitize agonist-stimulated phosphatidylinositol hydrolysis (i.e., decreased second-messenger production). Because both agonists and antagonists of the $5\text{-}HT_{2A}$ receptor can decrease $5\text{-}HT_{2A}$ receptor density, the relevance of this finding is also unknown. Moreover, electroconvulsive shock actually increases 5-HT_{2A} receptor density and mRNA expression. Antidepressant treatments apparently do not consistently alter postsynaptic 5-HT_{1A} receptor number; however, electrophysiological studies have consistently shown that tricyclic antidepressants and electroconvulsive shock increase postsynaptic 5-HT–mediated responses in the hippocampus (see Table 14–10). The receptors responsible are thought to be postsynaptic 5-HT_{1A} receptors.

It has been reported that chronic treatment with antidepressants of every major class decreases the functional activity of the NMDA subtype of glutamate receptor in the frontal cortex, but not limbic regions, by reducing the ability of the coagonist glycine to bind to its recognition site on the receptor complex and by reducing the proportion of high-affinity glutamate recognition sites.[54] Finally, changes in benzodiazepine and GABA_B receptors have been reported after long-term tricyclic antidepressant administration; however, the data are rather inconsistent.

Much interest has focused on intracellular adaptations after long-term drug treatment. At least two major types of intracellular adaptations can result in long-term alterations in neuronal activity. The first includes altered phosphorylation states on a number of intracellular proteins including cell surface receptors, cytosolic proteins (e.g., synapsins), second-messenger–dependent protein kinases, and various third-messenger phosphoproteins. A second major intracellular adaptation, and one we have discussed briefly before, is alteration in genomic expression of various neuronal proteins involved in neuronal activity. These intracellular pathways represent the primary mechanisms by which chronic drug treatment or environmental stimuli regulate neuronal function (see Fig. 14–4).

Because most of these intracellular sites subserve both norepinephrine and serotonin receptors, these intracellular adaptations could represent a common pathway for antidepressants that differentially affect norepinephrine and 5-HT systems in the short term. Indeed, antidepressant treatments have been shown to alter the expression and activity of various G protein subunits, adenylate cyclase, and cAMP-dependent protein kinases in brain. In addition to the changes already described, posttranscriptional changes might alter long-term neuronal functioning after antidepressant treatment. These changes include alterations in RNA processing, protein turnover (rates and sites), protein and RNA trafficking within the cell, and qualitative changes in the amounts and types of transcription factors expressed in certain populations of neurons. Detailed descriptions of intracellular adaptations to drug treatment can be found in Hyman and Nestler,[55] Duman and Nestler,[56] and Nestler and Duman.[57] Although continued study of these intracellular adaptations may eventually lead to a complete understanding of how antidepressant treatments work, these findings, which are undeniably real but still in their infancy, have not and cannot yet be assimilated into a generic mechanism of action of antidepressants.

Antipsychotic Drugs

The widely held dopamine hypothesis of the pathophysiology of schizophrenia is based on two main lines of evidence: 1) almost all clinically useful antipsychotic drugs are dopamine receptor antagonists and 2) dopamine agonists, drugs that increase the synaptic availability of dopamine such as dextroamphetamine, can produce positive symptoms of psychosis (i.e., hallucinations, delusions, and thought disorders) indistinguishable from those in paranoid schizophrenia. Indeed, the ability of antipsychotic drugs to produce an antipsychotic action, as well as extrapyramidal symptoms, has been attributed primarily to their ability to block the D_2 receptor subtype in the mesolimbocortical and nigrostriatal dopamine systems, respectively. Although the inhibitory effects of these antipsychotics on classical D_2 receptors appear to correlate superbly with their clinical antipsychotic potency (Fig. 14–11), the only exception being clozapine, this neurochemical effect alone cannot explain all the clinically relevant differences among these drugs. Indeed, this D_2 antagonism should be viewed as the initial molecular event that leads to chronic alterations and adaptations in neuronal functioning. Similarly to the tricyclic antidepressants, antipsychotic drugs, depending on their chemical class, bind to α-adrenergic, serotoninergic, muscarinic, and/or histaminergic receptors. Indeed, the first antipsychotic, chlorpromazine, was developed from the antihistamine promazine as an adjunct to anesthesia. Except for their serotoninergic actions, binding to these other sites is implicated primarily in their side effect profile.

Since the advent of antipsychotic drug use in the treatment of schizophrenia, there has been a search for superior antipsychotic drugs, as use of the "typical," "classical," or "traditional" D_2-blocking antipsychotics often does not result in full remission of symptoms or, in many cases, even a significant improvement. This search has focused on compounds with an improved therapeutic profile (i.e., improved efficacy for both positive and negative symptoms and decreased side effects). These compounds, of which clozapine is considered the prototypical agent, have been termed atypical antipsychotics. Clozapine differs from typical antipsychotics (e.g., haloperidol, chlorpromazine) in producing minimal or no extrapyramidal symptoms in humans or catalepsy in rodents at therapeutic doses. Perhaps more important, clozapine, unlike typical antipsychotics, improves both positive and negative symptoms of schizophrenia. The fact that clozapine differs clinically from typical antipsychotics and the data showing that clozapine is a relatively weak D_2 antagonist have been the dominant impetus for the suggestion that the original dopamine hypothesis of schizophrenia may need revising.

Neurobiological Actions of Antipsychotics: Focus on Clozapine

Based on studies of clozapine's activity, the mechanism of action of atypical antipsychotics is thought to involve its differential actions in various subpopulations of dopamine neurons, differential binding to different dopamine receptor subtypes, or additional binding to other neurotransmitter receptors. First, we compare and contrast the neurophysiological effects of clozapine and those of typical antipsychotic agents. Some of these differences may confer an atypical profile on clozapine. Second, we describe the receptor-binding profile of a number of putative atypical antipsychotic agents. These differences in receptor binding are likely to be responsible for the neurophysiological differences between clozapine and other typical antipsychotics.

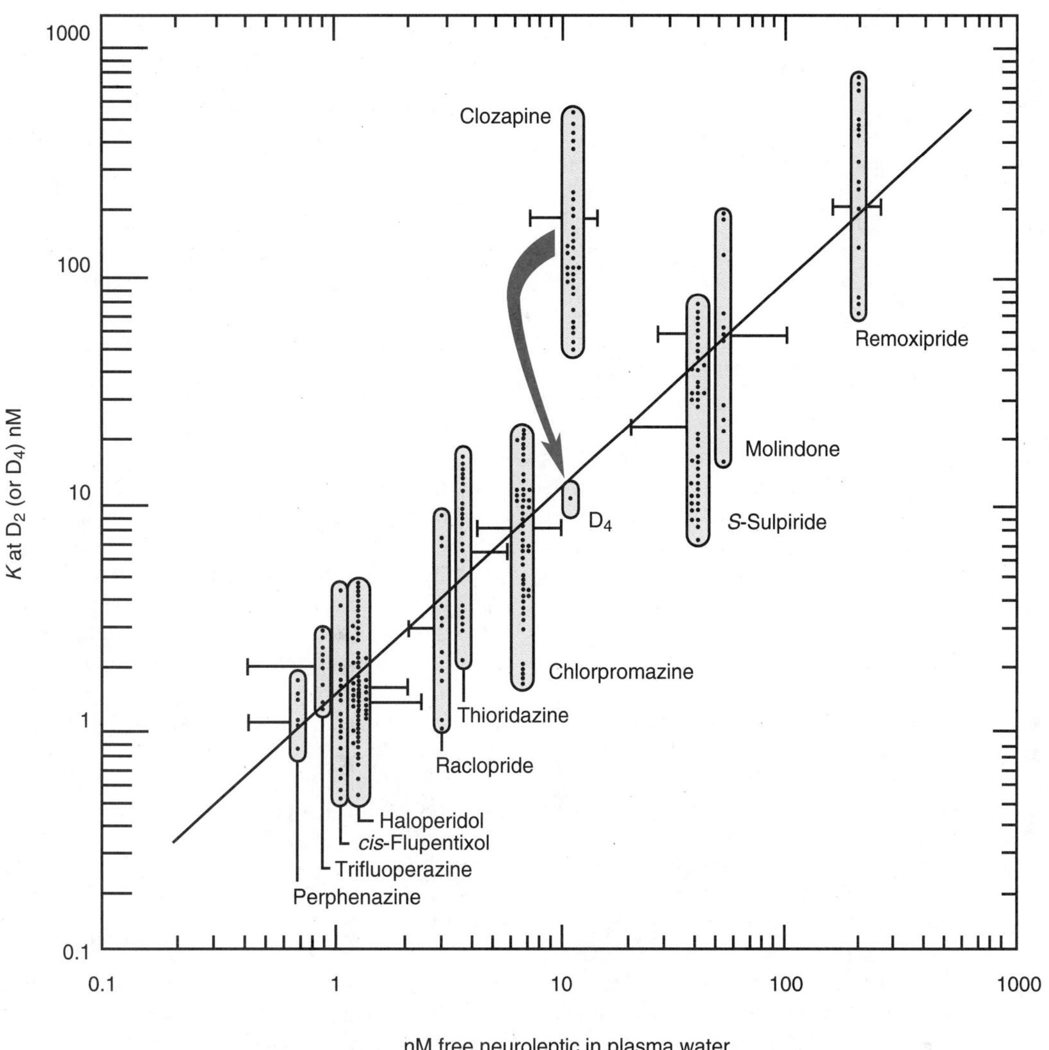

Figure 14–11 *The neuroleptic dissociation constants* (K) *at the dopamine D_2 receptor closely match the free neuroleptic concentrations in the patients' plasma water. Each point indicates a* K *value. Clozapine is the only drug that does not fit the D_2 correlate, but its affinity at D_4* (arrow) *does. The plasma molarities for* cis-*flupentixol and for S-sulpiride are half those published for the racemates, which are used clinically. (Reprinted by permission of Elsevier Science Inc. from Dopamine receptor sequences: Therapeutic levels of neuroleptics occupy D_2 receptors, clozapine occupies D_4, by Seeman P, Neuropsychopharmacology 7:261–284. Copyright 1992 by the American College of Neuropsychopharmacology.)*

It has been suggested that clozapine, unlike typical antipsychotics, possesses relative mesolimbic dopaminergic specificity compared with its actions on nigrostriatal dopamine neurons and that this may underlie its relative lack of extrapyramidal symptoms and tardive dyskinesia liability. Much of this evidence has come from electrophysiological studies of midbrain dopamine neurons. In general, dopamine neurons originating in the ventral tegmental area (VTA; A_{10} cell group) project to the nucleus accumbens, amygdala, and neocortex and constitute the mesolimbocortical dopamine system. In contrast, the dopamine cells of the substantia nigra (A_9 cell group) project primarily to the caudate putamen and make up the nigrostriatal dopamine system. The pioneering work of Bunney and colleagues[58] showed that acute administration of haloperidol increases the firing rate of VTA and substantia nigra dopamine neurons. This response is probably the result of decreased negative feedback on dopamine cells after D_2 receptor blockade. In contrast, acute clozapine administration increases the firing rate of VTA neurons only. Of perhaps more physiological significance are the changes observed after long-term administration of these compounds. On a time scale similar to that in which antipsychotics exert their clinical effects, typical antipsychotics such as haloperidol significantly decrease the number of spontaneously active dopamine neurons encountered in the VTA and substantia nigra. Subsequent examination revealed that these cells enter into a state of depolarization-induced block (inactivation) and decreased dopaminergic function. It is hypothesized that prolonged activation of the dopamine neurons leads to inactivation of sodium channels so that they do not open in response to further membrane depolarization. These partially depolarized neurons are functionally inactive because they cannot develop further action potentials in response to excitatory stimuli. Clozapine differs from typical antipsychotics in that chronic administration does not induce depolarization block of dopamine neurons in the substantia nigra but does induce inactivation of dopamine neurons of the VTA.[59, 60] The delayed onset of depolarization block in the VTA is thought to be related to the slow onset of action of all antipsychotic drugs, including clozapine, whereas the lack of extrapyramidal symptoms with clozapine is hypothesized to be the result of preservation of the activity of the substantia nigra neurons. Although depolarization block has been widely accepted as a primary consequence of chronic antipsychotic treatment, other findings have questioned somewhat the functional importance of depolarization block in the mechanism of action of antipsychotics, clozapine included, as the release of dopamine from nerve terminals may be much more independent of cell firing than was previously thought.

The electrophysiological actions are thought to result in neurochemical differences as well. Studies have shown that short-term administration of typical antipsychotic drugs results in more prominent effects on dopamine metabolism in the striatum than in mesolimbocortical areas; in contrast, clozapine appears to augment dopamine turnover to a relatively greater degree in mesolimbic areas.[61] Based on the electrophysiological findings suggesting that increased firing of dopamine neurons after acute antipsychotic drug administration is secondary to a lack of negative feedback related to D_2 autoreceptor blockade, the data suggest that clozapine preferentially alters mesolimbocortical dopamine neurons. There is some evidence that clozapine may preferentially increase dopamine metabolism in the prefrontal cortex.[62] This effect, together with the relatively weaker D_2 receptor blockade produced by clozapine than by typical antipsychotic agents, may lead to a net increase in mesocortical dopamine activity. Indeed, the hypofrontality theory states that the negative symptoms of schizophrenia may be the result of a cortical dopamine deficit. Thus, one could speculate that the beneficial effect of clozapine on both negative and positive symptoms may be due to its ability to increase cortical and decrease nucleus accumbens dopamine activity, respectively. However, other studies have suggested that dopamine release from nerve terminals may not be significantly affected by the presence of depolarization block.[63]

Dopamine Receptors

It appears that there is indeed some regional specificity for clozapine versus typical antipsychotics, and logic and physical chemistry dictates that this must have some basis in selective binding of clozapine to certain dopamine receptor populations or other additional receptors. These findings are explored here. Although we mentioned that findings have suggested that the dopamine hypothesis of schizophrenia needs revision, newer findings from studies using positron emission tomography have provided further proof that the D_2 receptor is involved in the pathophysiology of schizophrenia and the mechanism of action of antipsychotic agents. It has been reported that drug-naive schizophrenic patients have increased numbers of D_2 receptors in the putamen. Moreover, chemically distinct antipsychotic agents occupy from 65% to upward of 90% (in the case of haloperidol) of D_2 receptors in the caudate putamen at clinically relevant doses.[64–66] Notably, clozapine differs from typical antipsychotic agents in that it occupies only 40% to 60% of D_2 receptors in the striatum, whereas 80% to 90% occupancy is observed in limbic areas.[67]

The cloning of the D_2 receptor has enabled the simultaneous visualization of the distribution of D_2 receptors and mRNA in rat, primate, and human brain (Fig. 14–12 [see Color Plate I]). Along with the anterior pituitary, where dopamine regulates prolactin secretion, highest concentrations are observed in the nigrostriatal and mesolimbic dopamine systems. D_2 receptors are located both postsynaptically and presynaptically. Presynaptically, they probably act as autoreceptors either on the somatodendritic portion of the dopamine neuron or on presynaptic terminals. Increases in D_2 receptor binding and receptor supersensitivity are observed after long-term antipsychotic treatment through mechanisms that are thought to include both transcriptional (i.e., increased mRNA synthesis) and posttranscriptional (i.e., not related to changes in receptor synthesis) processes.

Shortly after the initial cloning of the D_2 receptor, it was found that different isoforms of the same receptor are synthesized through alternative RNA splicing. The two different isoforms vary by 29 amino acids in the third cytoplasmic loop near the G protein recognition site. Although this difference does not appear to result in binding differences between D_2 ligands, its location near the G protein regulatory site may result in differences in intracellular transduction mechanisms.

The D_3 receptor has been cloned and studied.[68, 69] This receptor displays considerable homology with the D_2 receptor but has 10 to 100 times higher affinity for dopamine than do D_2 receptors. Moreover, the D_3 receptor appears to be expressed predominantly in the mesolimbic dopaminergic system (see Fig. 14–12 [Color Plate I]). Like the D_2 receptor, the D_3 receptor has high affinity for antipsychotic drugs in vitro. Typical antipsychotic agents such as haloperidol are 10 to 20 times more potent at D_2 receptors than at D_3 receptors. However, atypical antipsychotic drugs such as clozapine and several substituted benzamides are only two to three times more potent at the D_2 receptor. Thus, the ratio of binding in vitro to the D_3 receptor versus the D_2 receptor is higher for several atypical antipsychotic drugs. This, combined with the localization of D_3 receptors primarily in the mesolimbic system, might underlie the ability of atypical antipsychotic agents such as clozapine to treat schizophrenia while sparing the nigrostriatal dopamine system. However, drug affinities derived from in vitro binding studies can be misleading. Only free drug in the extracellular compartment is available in vivo for binding to a given receptor. This fraction of total drug is dependent on a number of bioavailability and pharmacokinetic considerations, including fractional protein binding, lipophilicity, and elimination kinetics. Therefore, selectivity based on in vitro binding affinities may not be apparent in vivo. For example, at commonly used clinical doses the D_2 receptors are blocked by about 80%, whereas D_3 receptors are blocked by only 2% to 40%.[70, 71] At present there are no neuroleptics that block D_3 receptors more readily than D_2 receptors. Moreover, there are no agonists that discriminate between these receptors, as the affinities of agonists at the D_3 receptor are similar to that at the high-affinity state of the D_2 receptor. Finally, although a selective D_3 antagonist would be of considerable interest as an antipsychotic, preliminary genetic linkage studies have not found evidence for a link between D_3 receptor abnormalities and schizophrenia.

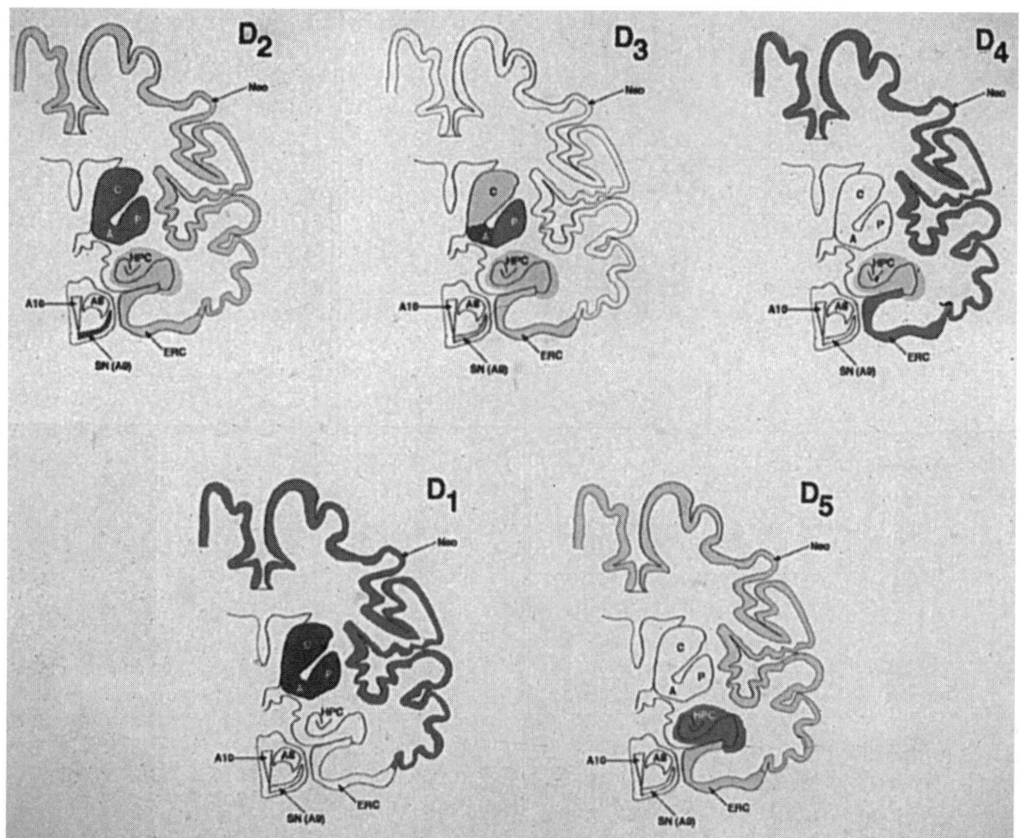

Figure 14–12 *Brain region location of mRNA for human dopamine receptors (see Color Plate I). Cx, Cerebral cortex; L, lateral ventricle; 3, third ventricle; C, caudate nucleus; P, putamen; G, globus pallidus; AC, nucleus accumbens; ICJ, islands of Calleja; H, hypothalamus; O, olfactory tubercle; AM, amygdala; Hipp, hippocampus; VTA, ventral tegmental area; SN, substantia nigra. (Courtesy of James Meador-Woodruff, MD, University of Michigan, Ann Arbor, MI. Modified by permission of Elsevier Science Inc. from Dopamine receptor sequences: Therapeutic levels of neuroleptics occupy D_2 receptors, clozapine occupies D_4, by Seeman P, Neuropsychopharmacology 7:261–284. Copyright 1992 by the American College of Neuropsychopharmacology.)*

The D_4 receptor is the latest in the D_2 receptor family to be cloned.[72] The D_4 receptor displays homology with both D_2 and D_3 receptors. In general, the D_4 receptor displays affinities for dopamine agonists and antagonists lower than or equal to those of the D_2 receptor. The finding that clozapine exhibits greater than 10-fold higher affinity for the D_4 receptor than for the D_2 receptor is of considerable interest. Moreover, the affinity constant of clozapine for the D_4 receptor is similar to the free concentration of clozapine observed during antipsychotic treatment[70–72] (see Fig. 14–11). Several variants of the D_4 receptor found in the human population have different antipsychotic binding properties. Using a data subtraction technique, Seeman and colleagues[73] found a sixfold increase in D_4 receptors in striatal tissue in schizophrenia compared with Parkinson's disease. D_4 receptors were determined by subtracting [^{3}H]raclopride binding (in the presence of guanine nucleotide) from [^{3}H]emonapride binding, which label D_2 and D_3 receptors and D_2, D_3, and D_4 receptors, respectively. This increase in D_4 receptors may actually represent the increases in D_2 receptors reported in the past.

Areas of high D_4 receptor mRNA expression include the frontal cortex and other limbic regions, with relatively less in the striatum (see Fig. 14–12 [Color Plate I]). This distribution differs from that of the D_2 and D_3 receptors and may partly explain the lack of extrapyramidal symptoms with clozapine. In addition, the D_4 receptor may represent frontal cortical labeling observed with [^{11}C]clozapine in a study using positron emission tomography.[74]

Although the existence of the D_1 receptor has been known since the late 1970s, it was not until 1990 that the receptor was cloned from rat and human tissue by four groups simultaneously. The D_1 receptor, unlike the D_2 receptor, stimulates the production of cAMP and is distributed similarly to D_2 receptors (see Fig. 14–12 [Color Plate I). It has since been shown that these two receptors (D_1 and D_2) can interact either synergistically or antagonistically through G proteins or second messengers. Indeed, Seeman and associates[75] have found this interaction uncoupled in schizophrenic brains, possibly resulting in excessive D_2 activity and inability of antipsychotic agents to bind efficiently to their receptors. However, this uncoupling is not the result of an altered amino acid sequence of the D_1 receptor.

In general, most antipsychotics currently in use bind to both D_2 and D_1 receptors, although generally with lower affinity to D_1 than to D_2 receptors. No correlation has been found between the atypical nature of an antipsychotic and its D_1 affinity, although as a group atypical antipsychotic drugs are less potent at the D_1 receptor.[76] However, Farde and colleagues[67] reported that clozapine displaces the D_1 ligand ^{11}C-Sch-23390 used in positron emission tomography more efficiently than do typical antipsychotic drugs.

The D_5 receptor has been isolated and cloned from human[77] and rat tissue. This receptor has considerable homology with the D_1 receptor and is considered a second member of the D_1 receptor subfamily. Like the D_1 receptor, the D_5 receptor is positively coupled to adenylate cyclase and cAMP production, and it exhibits affinities for various agonists and antagonists much like those of the D_1 receptor with the notable exception of dopamine itself, which is about 10 times more potent at the D_5 receptor. This suggests that the D_5 receptor may be important in maintaining dopaminergic tone. The D_5 receptor is expressed at lower concentrations than is the D_1 receptor, with highest concentrations found in the hippocampus and hypothalamus and lower concentrations in cortex (see Fig. 14–12 [Color Plate I]). Until a selective antagonist can be found, the function of the D_5 receptor in antipsychotic drug action remains unknown.

Other Receptors

It has been hypothesized that clozapine's atypical actions may be due, at least in part, to actions at other neurotransmitter receptors such as certain serotonin (5-HT) receptor subtypes. The involvement of 5-HT neural circuits in the mechanism of action of atypical antipsychotic drugs was postulated partly because 5-HT is known to exert a regulatory action on dopamine neurons. Neurochemical studies suggest that 5-HT projections tonically inhibit mesolimbic and nigrostriatal dopaminergic activity. Moreover, 5-HT may directly inhibit dopamine release from striatal nerve terminals. These findings led to the hypothesis that 5-HT_{2A} antagonists might decrease the inhibition of dopamine activity produced by chronic antipsychotic drug treatment (i.e., depolarization block, postsynaptic D_2 antagonism) and functionally increase dopaminergic activity in certain areas. This also suggests that there may be relative differences in the optimal magnitude of dopaminergic blockade needed in different brain areas. Furthermore, complete dopaminergic blockade may not be beneficial for negative symptoms and may result in extrapyramidal symptoms.

Many of the data suggesting the involvement of 5-HT_{2A} receptors have come from Meltzer and colleagues,[76] who examined the receptor-binding profile of a large series of antipsychotic drugs. They noted that typical and atypical antipsychotics can be distinguished on the basis of lower D_2 and higher 5-HT_{2A} pK_i values (a logarithmic measure of drug affinity for its receptor) of atypical compounds. Absolute potency at the 5-HT_{2A} receptor alone is not the determining factor, but atypical antipsychotic drugs appear to have 5-HT_{2A} pK_i/D_2 pK_i ratios of at least 1.1 (>13-fold higher affinity). Likewise, Seeman[70] reported that antipsychotic agents with less propensity to cause rigidity have higher 5-HT_{2A}/D_2 ratios. 5-HT_{2A} blockade, however, cannot account for the atypical actions of all purported atypical antipsychotic agents, because the 5-HT_{2A}/D_2 blocking profiles of several are similar to that of classical antipsychotic drugs.

There is some evidence that serotonin receptor subtypes other than the 5-HT_{2A} receptor may play a role in the action of atypical antipsychotic drugs. The 5-HT_{2C} receptor has been implicated in the mechanism of action of these drugs, because clozapine has a higher affinity for 5-HT_{2C} receptors than for D_2 receptors. However, chlorpromazine also has a higher affinity for 5-HT_{2C} receptors than for D_2 receptors. Indeed, most typical and atypical antipsychotics bind weakly to 5-HT_{2C} receptors labeled with [^{3}H]mesulergine.

Two cloned 5-HT receptors that are positively coupled to adenylate cyclase have been tentatively identified as the 5-HT_6 and 5-HT_7 receptors.[78–80] These receptors are of particular interest, as clozapine and several other antipsychotics display high affinity for these sites in vitro.

The σ-receptors have been implicated in schizophrenia because a stereoisomer of certain related benzomorphans (opiates) possesses profound psychotomimetic properties and σ-antagonists might therefore possess antipsychotic properties. Indeed, a number of drugs possessing preclinical antipsychotic activity, including haloperidol, bind to the σ-receptor. However, a critical review of the literature showed that the psychotomimetic and dysphoric effects of these opiates have been attributed to the wrong stereoisomer (the psychotomimetic effects are produced by the (−) enantiomer, whereas the (+) enantiomer is what is defined as the σ-site).[81] In addition, classical σ-ligands such as pentazocine, dextromethorphan (+)-3-(3-hydroxyphenyl)-*N*-n-propylpiperidine [(+)-3-PPP], and 1,3-di-*o*-tolylguanidine do not block or cause psychotomimetic behaviors. Finally, clozapine is essentially devoid of activity at the σ-receptor.

Phencyclidine acts as an antagonist at the NMDA subtype of the glutamate receptor and can cause profound schizophrenia-like symptoms. This implies that mechanisms that decrease NMDA receptor (glutamatergic) function may produce psychosis and that the glutamatergic system might be hypofunctional in schizophrenia. Based on known glutamatergic neurobiology, this is not inconsistent with the dopamine hypothesis of schizophrenia, although there is little pharmacological evidence for effective antipsychotic actions of glutamate agonists or antipsychotic actions on glutamatergic neurons.

There has been an explosion of information regarding the neurotransmitter role of neuropeptides in the past decade. Indeed, opioid peptides, cholecystokinin, and neurotensin can regulate dopaminergic activity in laboratory animals. For example, haloperidol increases neurotensin and neurotensin mRNA concentrations in the mesolimbic and nigrostriatal dopamine systems, whereas the atypical antipsychotic clozapine increases neurotensin activity only in the mesolimbic system. The endogenous opioid peptide precursor proenkephalin is also increased in the nigrostriatal system after antipsychotic administration. Unfortunately, at present few peptidergic ligands are available for detailed preclinical studies predictive of antipsychotic activity, although, as is the case with many psychiatric disorders, peptide-based drugs may hold great promise in the future. Finally, as is the case with antidepressant drugs, intracellular adaptations in second- and third-messenger systems, transcriptional factors, and so forth probably play an important role in the molecular mechanism of antipsychotic drug efficacy, although detailed investigation in this area has just begun.

Anxiolytics and Sedative-Hypnotics

Soon after the introduction of chlordiazepoxide in 1960, benzodiazepines became the most commonly prescribed psychotropic drugs, popular for their superior safety and dependence liability compared with barbiturates. By 1977 it was established that benzodiazepines potentiate GABA-induced chloride flux by interacting with high-affinity benzodiazepine receptors in the brain. It has since been conclusively demonstrated that the benzodiazepine receptor (BZR) is a component of the inhibitory $GABA_A$ receptor and that the anxiolytic and sedating pharmacological effects of benzodiazepines are due to their actions at the BZR. Further progress, including molecular cloning of the $GABA_A$ receptor, has yielded detailed knowledge of the actions of benzodiazepines and suggested strategies for improving the safety and efficacy of current drugs. In this section, we discuss benzodiazepines and nonbenzodiazepines that act at the BZR, other drugs such as barbiturates that also act at the $GABA_A$ receptor complex but at a different site, and miscellaneous anxiolytics such as buspirone that do not act primarily at the $GABA_A$ receptor.

Benzodiazepines and the $GABA_A$ Receptor

The substance GABA functions as a ubiquitous inhibitory neurotransmitter in the CNS by binding to $GABA_A$ receptors and opening channels permeable to chloride and bicarbonate anions ($GABA_B$ receptors are G protein–coupled receptors and are not considered here). Because both the resting membrane potential and the chloride equilibrium potential vary with cell type and ion concentrations, the opening of chloride channels may cause a slight depolarization or hyperpolarization. More important, the increased chloride conductance holds the neuron at a negative membrane potential and opposes depolarization toward the threshold potential in response to excitatory stimuli. Thus, GABA and drugs, such as the benzodiazepines, that potentiate GABA's actions are inhibitory compounds. How or where in the brain this neuronal inhibition is relevant to treatment of anxiety disorders is unclear.

Early evidence that benzodiazepines act at the $GABA_A$ receptor included findings that diazepam potentiates GABA-induced chloride flux in the spinal cord and that the effect of diazepam can be blocked by GABA synthesis inhibitors or the $GABA_A$ receptor antagonist bicuculline. In the late 1970s, high-affinity benzodiazepine binding sites were purified from rat brain membranes and the affinity of various benzodiazepines for these sites correlated well with their therapeutic potency.[82] A direct linkage between these binding sites (BZRs) and $GABA_A$ receptors was demonstrated by potentiation of benzodiazepine binding to brain homogenates in response to GABA and the copurification of $GABA_A$ and BZRs by benzodiazepine affinity chromatography.[83]

Biochemical purification and cloning revealed that the $GABA_A$ receptor consists of several subunits of varying electrophoretic mobility and that a large gene family of $GABA_A$ receptor subunits exists.[84] Currently, at least 15 genes for rat $GABA_A$ receptor subunits have been discovered. These cloned subunits can be subdivided by sequence homology into families of six α-subunits, four β-subunits, three γ-subunits, one δ-subunit, and one ρ-subunit.[85] Further sequence analysis placed the $GABA_A$ receptor in a superfamily of closely related ligand-gated ion channels. By analogy to the nicotinic ACh receptor, $GABA_A$ receptors are believed to be heteromeric assemblies of five subunits surrounding a pore, each of the subunits possessing four transmembrane domains (Fig. 14–13).

Transfected cell lines expressing various combinations of recombinant subunits have revealed that GABA-responsive anion channels can be formed from α- and β-subunits alone but that the presence of a γ_2- or γ_3-subunit is required to confer potentiation by benzodiazepines.[86, 87] These findings, along with other biochemical experiments, have led to the current notion that the BZR resides on the α-subunit or α-γ-interface and that the γ-subunit relays information from the BZR to the GABA binding site on the β-subunit. The roles of other subunits are less clear. The δ-subunit may serve as a structural substitute for γ in receptors nonresponsive to benzodiazepines. The newly discovered ρ-subunit is expressed primarily in the retina and is of unknown function.

The "information" relayed to the β-subunit in response to benzodiazepine binding is an increase in the affinity of the receptor for GABA. This cooperativity is reciprocal; the presence of GABA also increases benzodiazepine affinity. As this mechanism suggests, benzodiazepines do not have any physiological effect in the absence of GABA. These points distinguish benzodiazepines from barbiturates, which prolong the duration of channel open time and at high concentrations can gate chloride current in the absence of GABA.

The many benzodiazepines in clinical use share the same mechanism of action but vary in potencies (Table 14–11) and pharmacokinetic properties. Rate of entry into the CNS, entry into and out of lipid compartments, and rate of elimination all determine a drug's suitability for a particular clinical use; the shorter lived benzodiazepines such as midazolam and triazolam are commonly used as anesthetics or sedative-hypnotics and the longer acting drugs as anxiolytic agents. An additional principle governing the time course of benzodiazepine action is hepatic biotransformation to active metabolites. For example, desmethyldiazepam is a major active metabolite of diazepam and other compounds. Finally, a particular benzodiazepine's set of potencies at individual $GABA_A$ receptor subunit assemblies may influence its behavioral profile. For example, triazolam and alprazolam, benzodiazepines with some unusual clinical properties including antipanic efficacy, reportedly have higher affinities than does diazepam for certain recombinant $GABA_A$ receptor assemblies.[88]

Doses of benzodiazepines required to produce anxiolytic effects are generally lower than those producing sedation, hypnosis, or physical dependence. In light of this fact, structural variants have been sought whose maximal effect at any dose would be similar to the desired effects of a low-dose classical benzodiazepine. Such a profile is characteristic of partial agonists (partial allosteric modulators), which at full receptor occupancy produce a partial response. Preclinical studies indicated that the partial agonists bretazenil and imidazenil may be anticonvulsant and anxiolytic, with low risk of sedation, ataxia, tolerance, or physical dependence.[89] The efficacy of these agents is unproved in the clinical setting.

Unlike antidepressants, benzodiazepines produce their effects acutely and do not require long-term administration. Although tolerance does not develop to the anxiolytic effects, long-term use may result in tolerance and the risk of

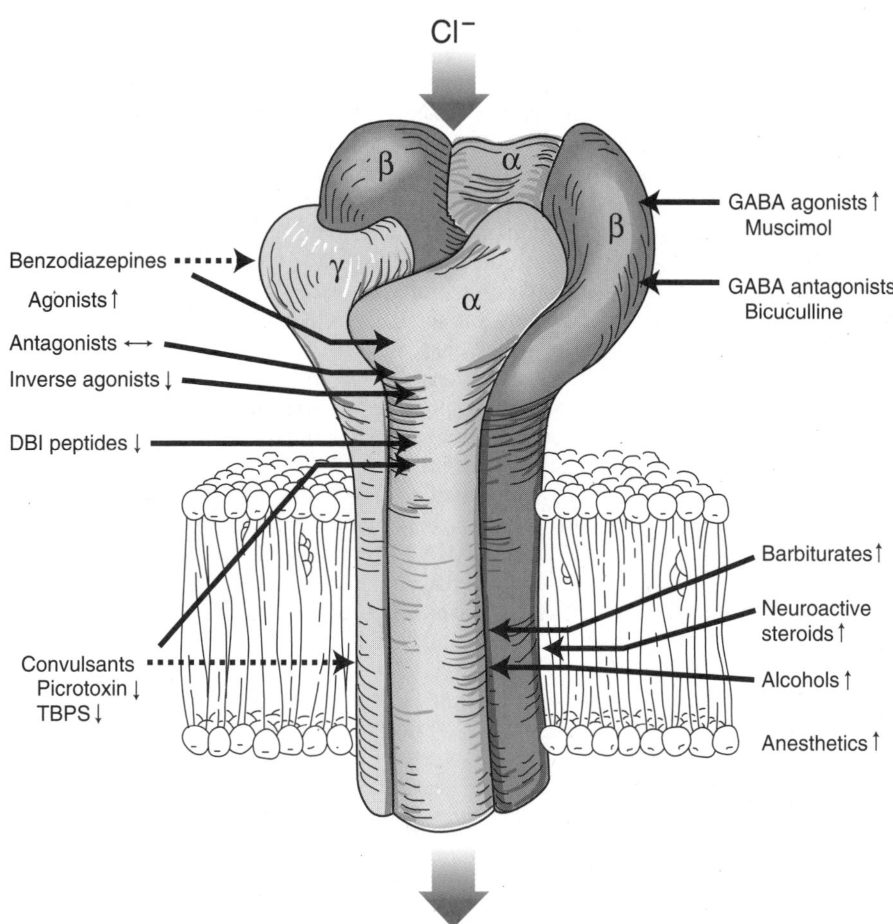

Figure 14–13 *Hypothetical structure of a $GABA_A$ receptor containing five pore-forming subunits surrounding a chloride channel. Shown are the variety of compounds that interact at one or more sites associated with the $GABA_A$ receptor to modulate chloride ion conductance positively (↑) or negatively (↓). The BZR ligands include both positive and negative modulators and interact with a site on the α-subunit; positive modulators such as the barbiturates and volatile anesthetics interact more directly with the chloride channel itself. The latter compounds have also been shown to interact with other receptors and channels. (Adapted from Paul SH: GABA and glycine. In Bloom FE, Kupfer DJ [eds]: Psychopharmacology: The Fourth Generation of Progress. New York: Raven Press, 1995:87–94.)*

dependence. Various pharmacodynamic explanations for the development of tolerance and dependence have been proposed, including receptor desensitization, down-regulation, and changes in subunit expression. The contradictory data implicating a purely functional desensitization or a down-regulation of receptor number after chronic benzodiazepine treatment[90–92] may reflect variations in experimental design. Alternatively, a shift in $GABA_A$ receptor subunit composition may underlie either the apparent down-regulation or desensitization. In support of this hypothesis, reduced α_1- and γ_2-subunit mRNA expression in various brain regions of chronic benzodiazepine-treated rats has been reported by several groups.[92–94] Finally, it remains an intriguing but insufficiently tested hypothesis that endogenous ligands such as neurosteroids or diazepam binding inhibitor peptides (see next section) may mediate some of the chronic benzodiazepine effects. In summary, unlike the acute actions of benzodiazepines, the chronic pharmacodynamic mechanisms are poorly understood.

Benzodiazepine Receptor Ligands and Bidirectional Allosteric Modulation of the $GABA_A$ Receptor

Many compounds lack the benzodiazepine structure but bind to the BZR, including cyclopyrrolines, β-carbolines, pyrazoquinolines, imidazopyridines, and triazolopyridazines. Such ligands are to be distinguished from barbiturates, which bind to the $GABA_A$ receptor but not at the BZR site. With the exception of alpidem, these nonbenzodiazepines have not been used clinically, but many show promise in preclinical testing, such as the partial agonist Ro 19-8022, which does not cause tolerance.[95]

The most surprising discovery to result from study of these compounds was that certain β-carbolines such as ethyl-β-carboline-3-carboxylate (β-CCE) and methyl-6,7-dimethoxy-4-ethyl-β-carboline-3-carboxylate (DMCM) inhibit GABA-induced chloride currents and have proconvulsant, anxiogenic effects. Other β-carbolines instead resemble benzodiazepines in their physiologic and behavioral effects. BZR antagonists such as flumazenil block the effects of either the anticonvulsant or proconvulsant agents. Thus, unlike most receptors, for which ligands can be divided into agonists, partial agonists, and antagonists, the BZR also responds to full and partial inverse agonists. Many authors now prefer the terms positive or negative allosteric modulator, rather than agonist or inverse agonist. The newer terms distinguish BZR ligands from true agonists at the $GABA_A$ receptor (e.g., GABA, muscimol) and also describe a mechanism whereby BZR ligands bind, alter the conformation of several receptor subunits, and modulate the affinity of the GABA binding site.[96]

Figure 14–14 summarizes the spectrum of effects of compounds acting at the BZR. Full agonists such as midazolam maximally potentiate GABA binding and are assigned an intrinsic activity of +1.0, whereas Ro 19-4603 maximally inhibits GABA binding and has an intrinsic activity of −1.0. In other words, midazolam and Ro 19-4603 are full positive and negative allosteric modulators, respectively. Flumazenil, a benzodiazepine derivative useful in treating benzodiazepine overdose and perhaps some hepatic encephalopathies or in precipitating benzodiazepine withdrawal in animal studies, possesses zero intrinsic activity. Partial allosteric modulators have fractional positive or negative intrinsic activity.

The discovery of BZRs and the phenomenon of bidirectional modulation prompted the search for natural anxiolytic or anxiogenic ligands in the brain.[97] Numerous candidate ligands have been identified to date, including the diazepam binding inhibitor peptides, β-carbolines, and benzodiazepines themselves, but none have been proved conclusively to regulate GABAergic tone. Considering the unique bidirectional modulatory site on the $GABA_A$ receptor, it is plausible that the brain can synthesize endogenous anxiolytics as well as anxiogenics, and preliminary evidence has appeared to this effect.[98]

Table 14–11 Affinity of Various Benzodiazepine Receptor Ligands for the Benzodiazepine Receptor

Benzodiazepine Receptor Ligands*	K_i (nM)†
Ethyl-β-carboline-3-carboxylate (β-CCE)‡	0.64
Brotizolam	0.85
Clonazepam	1.3
Etizolam	2.2
Lorazepam	2.5
Flunitrazepam	2.7
Triazolam	2.8
Midazolam	3.4
Loprazolam	4.4
Diazepam	5.7
Estazolam	6.0
DMCM‡	6.6
Nordiazepam	6.6
Nitrazepam	7.1
Flurazepam	10
Temazepam	11
Bromazepam	13
Oxazepam	13
Alprazolam	14
Zopiclone‡	22
Tetrazepam	24
Clorazepate	42
Halazepam	65
Prazepam	78
Cl 218.872‡	85
Adinazolam	95
Premazepam	120
Demoxepam	220
Chlordiazepoxide	250

*BZR ligands are arranged in order of decreasing potency.

†K_i values for the inhibition of [^{3}H]diazepam binding to rat cerebrocortical synaptosomes are adapted from IC_{50} values as determined by Haefely W, Kyburz E, Gerecke M, Mohler H: Recent advances in the molecular pharmacology of benzodiazepine receptors and in the structure-activity relationships of their agonists and antagonists. Adv Drug Res 1985; 14:165–322.

‡Nonbenzodiazepine compounds that bind to BZRs, as discussed in the text.

In addition to the important discovery of bidirectional $GABA_A$ receptor modification at the BZR site, nonbenzodiazepine BZR ligands have provided the basis for distinguishing pharmacologic subtypes of BZRs[99] such as the BZ_1 and BZ_2 subtypes. The BZ_1 subtype has high affinity for the triazolopyridazine CL 218,872 and predominates overall, especially in the cerebellum. In contrast, the lower affinity BZ_2 subtype is enriched in a few sites such as hippocampus and spinal cord. β-Carbolines also display a higher affinity for BZ_1 receptors and bind preferentially in cerebellum. In the late 1980s, immunohistochemical and in situ hybridization studies as well as pharmacologic analysis of recombinant expressed subunits established that the BZ_1 and BZ_2 subtypes represent receptor populations enriched in α_1- versus α_2- or α_3-subunits, respectively.

The BZ_1-BZ_2 classification scheme, although informative with respect to α-subunit heterogeneity, is of unclear clinical significance. Preclinical experiments with CL 218,872 at first suggested that BZ_1-selective agents might serve as nonsedating anxiolytics, but further behavioral experiments have not supported this claim. Most classical benzodiazepines such as diazepam and clonazepam do not differentiate between BZ_1 and BZ_2, whereas the BZ_1-selective compounds abecarnil, quazepam, and zolpidem give conflicting results in behavioral tests. As a further complication, some of the putative subunit-selective agents are partial allosteric modulators as well.

Further study of receptor diversity and drug selectivity beyond BZ_1 and BZ_2 is an important area of investigation. Other α-subunit differences, such as the greater GABA potentiation of benzodiazepine binding to α_3- than α_2-recombinant subunits or the unique pharmacology of the α_6-subtype, which is expressed in cerebellar granule cells, remain to be fully explored. Other pharmacologic classifications based on affinities of other BZR ligands besides CL 218,872 have been proposed but have not been refined and tested sufficiently to determine their usefulness. It is clear that consideration of individual, molecular $GABA_A$ receptor subtypes rather than broad classifications such as BZ_1-BZ_2 would ultimately be most informative in characterizing a BZR ligand's pharmacodynamic properties. Understanding the behavioral pharmacology of these ligands at the subunit level is, however, a monumental undertaking in light of the thousands of potential receptor subunit combinations and overlapping expression patterns at the gross and cellular level.

In summary, benzodiazepines and other ligands have led to the discovery of a unique, bidirectional allosteric modulatory site at which one or more endogenous ligands modify GABAergic neurotransmission. Many structural classes of compounds show affinity for the BZR, providing a rich basis for basic science discovery and therapeutic drug design. Partial allosteric modulators may possess a more favorable side effect profile than may classical benzodiazepines. Receptor heterogeneity may play an important role in determining neuroanatomical differences in the response to a particular BZR ligand. The latter topic is perhaps the most challenging to study, but it may yield important advances in our understanding of the neuroanatomy and

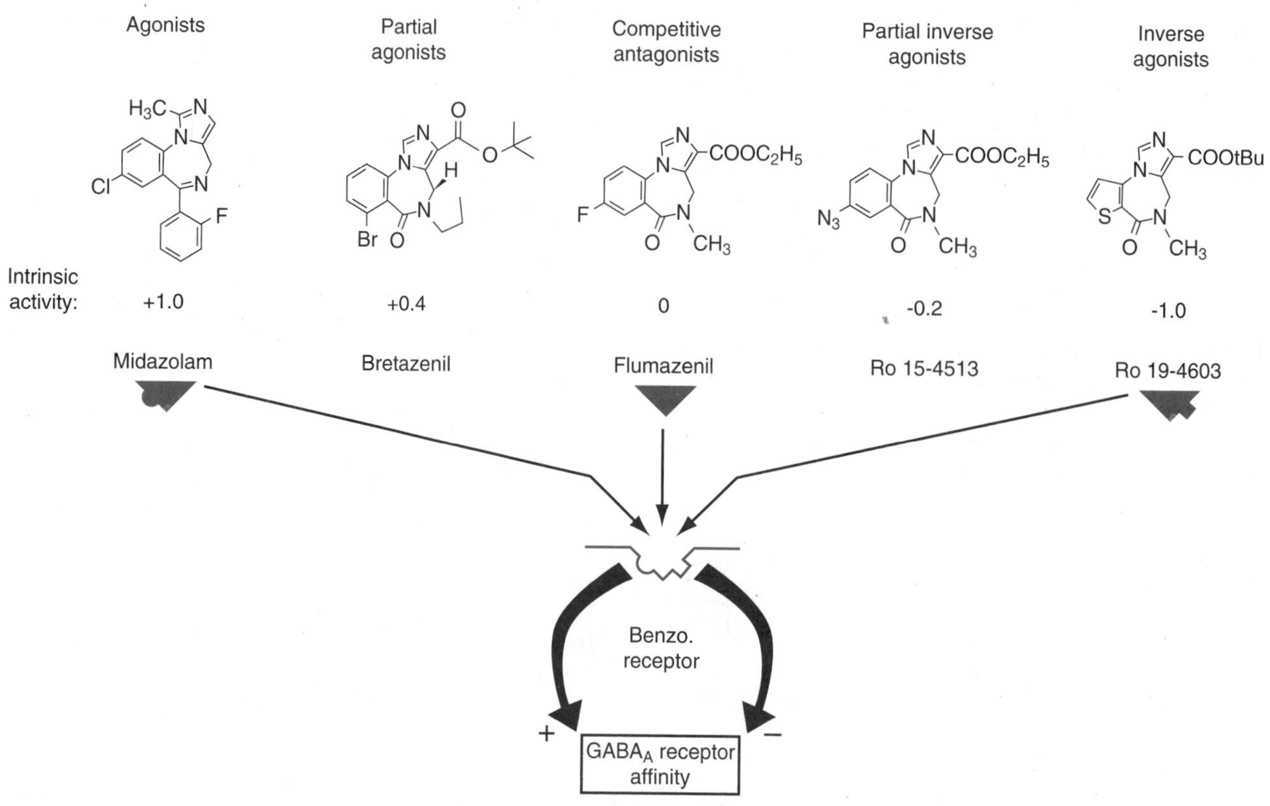

Figure 14–14 *The spectrum of BZR ligands, from full agonists to full inverse agonists (full positive and negative allosteric modulators, respectively). These compounds are thought to stabilize the BZR in a form that either increases or decreases GABA$_A$ receptor affinity, with the exception of antagonists (intrinsic activity of zero), which bind to the receptor but preferentially stabilize neither conformation. Partial agents (fractional intrinsic activity) submaximally stabilize the benzodiazepine receptor in one or the other conformation. (From Haefely W: The GABA-benzodiazepine interaction fifteen years later. Neurochem Res 1990; 15:169–174.)*

molecular biology of anxiety, as well as the development of drugs that improve the efficacy and side effect profile of benzodiazepines.

Barbiturates and Other Drugs That Bind to the GABA$_A$ Receptor

Many different classes of compounds interact with the GABA$_A$ receptor complex, apart from the benzodiazepine binding site, but at sites more directly associated with the chloride ion channel. These compounds include barbiturates, ethanol, anesthetics such as halothane or propofol, endogenous neurosteroids, the antagonist bicuculline, and the chloride channel blocker picrotoxin. Of primary interest in this chapter are barbiturates and ethanol, although the remaining structures and their sites of action may point the way to future drug development. Since the discovery and development of benzodiazepines and the explosion of information about the GABA$_A$ receptor, barbiturate and related drug mechanisms have been relatively little investigated.

As indicated in the previous sections, barbiturates differ from benzodiazepines by prolonging chloride channel open time rather than increasing the probability of GABA-mediated openings. Furthermore, at high concentrations barbiturates open chloride channels in the absence of GABA. Rather than displacing benzodiazepines from the BZR, barbiturates enhance benzodiazepine affinity. This observation proves that the binding sites are distinct and also provides the theoretical basis for an important drug-drug interaction. The barbiturates' more direct effects on GABA$_A$ receptors may be responsible for their poorer therapeutic index, side effects, and dependence liability compared with benzodiazepines. In addition, barbiturates exert non-GABAergic CNS effects such as inhibition of presynaptic calcium entry and inhibition of nonsynaptic voltage-gated sodium and potassium channels.[100] These actions are thought to result from nonselective lipophilic interactions with cell membranes. The stronger, less selective actions of barbiturates compared with benzodiazepines may be important for their utility as anticonvulsants and anesthetics.

Ethanol interacts with the GABA$_A$ receptor and many other membrane proteins, in an indirect and poorly understood manner involving changes in lipid mobility. Interestingly, only the long-splice variant of the γ_2-subunit, which contains a protein kinase C phosphorylation site, is sensitive to ethanol in vitro.[101] Many behavioral effects of ethanol, particularly sedation, are probably due to an elevation of chloride flux through the GABA$_A$ receptor complex. Therefore, a number of complex interactions exist between ethanol and other drugs, including the well-known profound sedation after simultaneous ethanol and benzodiazepine or barbiturate administration and the cross-tolerance between these agents. Because ethanol does not increase chloride conductance by acting at the BZR, "pure" benzodiazepine antagonists such as flumazenil are ineffective in reversing the behavioral effects of ethanol. However, partial negative allosteric modulators (partial inverse agonists) such as Ro 15-4513 have received attention as potential drugs to oppose the actions of ethanol. Such agents will be brought to clinical trials with caution, if at all, because of the proconvulsant nature of negative allosteric modulators and ethical considerations. Finally, chronic ethanol exposure has been reported to down-regulate or desensitize the $GABA_A$ receptor, which may underlie the physical dependence caused by chronic alcoholism as well as the efficacy of benzodiazepines in treating ethanol withdrawal.

The primary alternative to benzodiazepines for the treatment of anxiety has been buspirone. Buspirone does not directly interact with $GABA_A$ receptors but most likely owes its efficacy to serotoninergic mechanisms.[102] Autoradiographic, electrophysiological, biochemical, and behavioral studies all indicate that buspirone acts as a partial agonist at $5\text{-}HT_{1A}$ receptors. Binding of buspirone to $5\text{-}HT_{1A}$ receptors on neurons of the dorsal raphe nucleus inhibits neuronal firing and reduces serotoninergic output. Buspirone also has weak to moderate affinity for D_2 receptors and reportedly functions as a weak D_2 agonist. However, the doses at which buspirone is effective suggest that its anxiolytic mechanism of action is serotoninergic and not dopaminergic. Because buspirone has a mechanism of action unrelated to that of benzodiazepines, it is not surprising that it has distinct anxiolytic properties not reported for the benzodiazepines.

The β-blocking drugs (e.g., propranolol) are used as anxiolytics primarily for acute or situational anxiety. Although a central mechanism of action has not been ruled out, β-blockers most likely mediate their effect by blockade of peripheral β-adrenergic receptors. Inhibition of stress-induced sympathetic activity reduces tremor; hence, β-blockers are commonly taken by musicians and others experiencing situational anxiety. Furthermore, it has been hypothesized that emotions are influenced by visceral sensory feedback and that β-adrenergic blockade may reduce anxiety by reducing the sensation of physiological stress arousal.[103]

Clonidine is another antihypertensive agent that has anxiolytic properties as well. In a manner analogous to buspirone's action at $5\text{-}HT_{1A}$ receptors, clonidine is an agonist at central α_2-adrenergic receptors and inhibits firing of noradrenergic neurons in the locus caeruleus and other nuclei. The anxiolytic effects of clonidine may be due to a combination of central noradrenergic attenuation and consequent sympathetic nervous system inhibition.

Mood-Stabilizing Drugs

For more than 40 years, lithium has been used effectively in the treatment of mania and bipolar disorder. The anticonvulsants carbamazepine and valproic acid have also been used in these disorders. Although lithium is also an effective adjunct to antidepressants in the treatment of major depression, we summarize its known actions, together with those of carbamazepine and valproic acid, in this section on mood stabilizers based on the ability of these drugs to attenuate or abolish the labile mood shifts observed between the manic and depressive phases of bipolar disorder.

Lithium

Because of its situation in the periodic table, lithium shares many of the physiochemical properties of sodium and potassium and has ready access to the intracellular milieu via sodium channel transport. However, its ionic radius is closer to that of the divalent cations magnesium and calcium. Because of its ionic nature, lithium is distributed evenly in body water, and plasma concentrations therefore reflect cerebrospinal fluid or extracellular fluid concentrations (0.6 to 1.0 mmol/L at therapeutic concentrations). Lithium has been reported to act at a number of cellular sites, but many of these reports have not provided meaningful data regarding an agreed-upon mechanism of action. For interested readers, the numerous biochemical actions of lithium have been reviewed in detail by Lenox and Manji.[104]

One pharmacological action of lithium that has been well replicated is its inhibition ($K_m \approx 0.8$ mmol/L) of the conversion of inositol monophosphate to *myo*-inositol by inhibiting the action of the enzyme inositol monophosphatase. This leads to a reduction in the amount of free inositol, which is required for production of phosphatidylinositol 4,5-bisphosphate and normal recycling of the phosphoinositide pathway. This can lead to a decrease in intracellular signaling in brain systems that utilize phosphatidylinositol hydrolysis as a second-messenger pathway (e.g., α_1, m_1, m_3, m_5, $5\text{-}HT_{2A}$, and D_1 receptors). Although this reduction in free inositol concentrations is real and consistent, it has not been conclusively demonstrated that phosphatidylinositol hydrolysis signaling systems are, in fact, diminished.

In addition to its effects on the phosphatidylinositol 4,5-bisphosphate transduction system, several studies reported that lithium appears to alter (either decrease or increase) adenylate cyclase–mediated production of cAMP. Lithium administration is also associated with changes in the amount of cAMP-dependent protein phosphorylation in specific brain regions. A series of studies have shown that the pharmacologically relevant actions of lithium (i.e., chronic and somewhat stable after lithium removal) are probably exerted proximally to adenylate cyclase at the level of the G proteins. Because G proteins are also involved in the phosphatidylinositol 4,5-bisphosphate signaling system, they represent a logical point at which lithium could alter the two major second-messenger–generating systems in the CNS. A series of studies have shown that chronic lithium may reduce the activation of G_i (G_i normally inhibits adenylate cyclase) by stabilizing the inactive undissociated α-β-γ heterotrimeric form of G_i.[105, 106] In addition, Avissar and Schreiber[107] have reported that lithium, carbamazepine, and electroconvulsive shock attenuate G_s as well as G_i and G_o protein function. Contrasting data have been obtained on whether the absolute concentrations of G proteins are altered by lithium treatment. For example, either no changes[106, 108, 109] or small decreases[110] have been reported for $G\alpha_s$ and $G\alpha_i$. In addition, Colin[110] and Li[108] and their colleagues observed reductions in mRNA levels for $G\alpha_s$, $G\alpha_{i1}$, and $G\alpha_{i2}$.

Based on the lithium-induced changes in phosphatidylinositol hydrolysis mentioned earlier, it was hypothesized that there might also be changes in the activity or amount of protein kinase C isozymes that are responsive to this hydrolysis and are capable of phosphorylating a number of important intracellular proteins, including G proteins, thereby altering their activity. Indeed, after long-term administration, both lithium and valproic acid appear to decrease protein kinase C activity, which has been postulated to lead to a number of cellular events that ultimately lead to changes in the production of nuclear transcription factors such as *fos,* subsequent changes in gene expression, and ultimately neurotransmission.[111] These include augmentation of 5-HT neurotransmission[112, 113] (see Table 14–2), potentiation of several cholinergic transmitter functions, and reduction of certain aspects of dopaminergic transmission.

Carbamazepine and Valproate

The anticonvulsants carbamazepine and valproate (valproic acid) have been successfully used in the acute and prophylactic treatment of bipolar disorder. Like lithium, both of these agents, especially carbamazepine, exert effects on a multiplicity of neurotransmitter and second-messenger systems. Because anticonvulsants are often effective in treating lithium nonresponders and, furthermore, some patients respond selectively to one or another anticonvulsant, mechanisms of action unique to each drug may be important for their antimanic or antidepressant effects. The individual effects of each of these drugs may produce common downstream effects (e.g., intracellular adaptations) by convergent pathways, as we have suggested for antidepressants and antipsychotics.

Carbamazepine is a tricyclic compound structurally related to imipramine. As an antiepileptic, it is notable for its efficacy in virtually all types of seizures except absence seizures. Its most overt acute effect is an inhibition of voltage-gated sodium channels by selectively binding to the inactivated state of the channel. It has been reported that carbamazepine may increase potassium conductance in addition to decreasing sodium conductance.[114] In short, carbamazepine's anticonvulsant properties most likely derive from the use-dependent suppression of cell excitability and reduction of sustained bursting of action potentials.[115] Acute anticonvulsant actions may also be dependent on peripheral-type (P-type) BZRs. The P-type BZR, unlike the flumazenil-sensitive central receptor responsible for modulating CNS GABAergic activity via the GABA-BZR-chloride channel complex, is localized on the mitochondrial membrane and may regulate cholesterol transport and indirectly the synthesis of neurosteroids that act at $GABA_A$ receptors. The suppression of amygdala-kindled seizures by carbamazepine is sensitive to P-type receptor ligands but not to flumazenil.[116]

The antimanic or antidepressant mechanisms of carbamazepine's actions are much less clear. Many different systems are involved, with none unequivocally linked to its therapeutic profile.[116] Furthermore, the primary molecular targets of the drug have not been deduced. However, it should be noted that, like lithium and electroconvulsive shock, carbamazepine has been shown to attenuate receptor-coupled G_s, G_i, and G_o protein function.[107] Inhibition of norepinephrine-stimulated adenylate cyclase activity, decreased GABA turnover, and increased substance P sensitivity and substance P concentrations are also effects shared with lithium. Chronic carbamazepine, like lithium and valproate, increases hippocampal $GABA_B$ receptor density. Complex interactions between P-type receptors and $GABA_A$ and $GABA_B$ receptors may play an important role in the mood-stabilizing action of carbamazepine. The prominent role of GABAergic mechanisms in the mechanisms of action of lithium, valproate, and benzodiazepines supports this hypothesis.

Valproic acid or its salt, sodium valproate, is a simple branched-chain carboxylic acid first used as an organic solvent and serendipitously discovered to have anticonvulsant properties. Unlike carbamazepine, valproate is effective in preventing absence seizures. The anticonvulsant properties of valproate are generally attributed to elevation of GABA, an effect that occurs within minutes of valproate exposure in some brain regions.[117, 118] Several metabolic explanations for the increase in GABA have been proposed. Originally, this effect was attributed to inhibition of the enzyme GABA-α-oxoglutarate aminotransferase, but the effect on the enzyme is weak at therapeutic concentrations. Valproate's efficacy may instead be due to inhibition of another enzyme involved in GABA catabolism, succinate-semialdehyde dehydrogenase, or enhancement of GABA synthesis by glutamic acid decarboxylase. Valproate may also increase GABA release. Inhibition of GABA uptake is not likely to be a major effect of valproate. Some evidence that valproate may enhance postsynaptic responses to GABA has been reported; however, most of the experiments used extremely high valproate concentrations. Unlike the actions of carbamazepine, the anticonvulsant properties of valproate are not influenced by P-type BZR receptor ligands. Non-GABAergic mechanisms of action that have been suggested for valproate's anticonvulsant effects include a direct effect on membrane channels similar to that of carbamazepine and a potent decrease in brain content of the excitatory amino acid aspartate.

The chronic effects of valproate relevant to its mood-stabilizing properties are unknown. In addition to the interaction with GABA and aspartate, potentially relevant effects that have been reported include increased CNS serotonin and dopamine concentrations and changes in cGMP levels. A more exhaustive list of putative mechanisms, many of them confounded by conflicting evidence, is presented elsewhere.[117, 118] At present, little is known regarding an actual molecular mechanism responsible for the efficacy of valproate or carbamazepine.

Psychostimulants

Psychostimulants in clinical use include amphetamine and the related compounds methamphetamine, methylphenidate, and pemoline. Although the usefulness of these agents in clinical medicine is limited because of their high abuse potential, pemoline being an exception, they are widely prescribed for narcolepsy and attention-deficit/hyperactivity disorder in both children and adults.[119] The efficacy of stimulants in the treatment of attention-deficit/hyperactivity disorder is not well understood but is postulated to result from a relative enhancement of attentional or "slow rate" behaviors and not a direct action on locomotor activity.

Psychostimulants acutely elevate synaptic concentrations of monoamine neurotransmitters through two major mechanisms: stimulating neurotransmitter release and inhibiting neuronal uptake. Inhibition of MAO occurs chiefly at high amphetamine doses but cannot be ruled out as a potential third mechanism of action. Amphetamine and related compounds are distinguished from cocaine, which has similar behavioral effects but functions exclusively as an uptake blocker. To complicate matters further, several differences exist between the different psychostimulants in their acute mechanisms of action. These differences are noted here, although their relevance to long-term therapeutic efficacy is not understood.

We focus on dopaminergic effects as central to behavioral responses to amphetamine, although noradrenergic stimulation in the lateral hypothalamus may be responsible for the short-term anorexic effect and less potent effects at serotoninergic synapses may contribute to toxic paranoid psychoses. Amphetamine-stimulated dopamine release is blocked by dopamine uptake antagonists but not by depletion of calcium ions, suggesting that amphetamine stimulates dopamine release in a manner other than vesicular exocytosis. According to the exchange-diffusion model, amphetamine competes with extracellular dopamine as a substrate for the presynaptic dopamine transporter and is transported into the nerve terminal down its concentration gradient in exchange for cytoplasmic dopamine. In this manner, amphetamine both blocks uptake and stimulates release of a cytoplasmic pool of dopamine. In a stably transfected cell line expressing the dopamine transporter, these effects occur at similar drug concentrations.[120] In further support of the model, amphetamine-induced dopamine release is not sensitive to neuronal inhibition by dopamine autoreceptors, and reserpine pretreatment, which depletes vesicular stores of dopamine, does not prevent the effect of amphetamine on dopamine release.

Methylphenidate and other related nonamphetamine stimulants differ in their acute pharmacodynamic effects. Most important, methylphenidate promotes release of vesicular rather than cytoplasmic dopamine, and this release is sensitive to reserpine pretreatment. In cells transfected with the human monoamine transporters but lacking secretory vesicles, methylphenidate causes little or no monoamine release at concentrations that block uptake.[120] Although methylphenidate is similar to amphetamine in its potency at inhibiting dopamine uptake, methylphenidate may not be as effective in the long-term treatment of attention-deficit/hyperactivity disorder. The difference in ability to affect cytoplasmic neurotransmitter release may in part underlie this clinical observation, although a mechanistic explanation in terms of chronic drug action is not available. Fenfluramine is structurally related to the stimulants but instead functions as an anorexic drug with mild behavioral depressant properties. Like amphetamine, fenfluramine, 3,4-methylenedioxyamphetamine, and 3,4-methylenedioxymethamphetamine (MDMA; "ecstasy") appear to act by an exchange-diffusion model wherein their transport via the SERT is accompanied by an equimolar release of serotonin.

Chronic stimulant effects appear to be at least as complex as the multiple acute mechanisms. Tolerance develops rapidly to the anorexic but not necessarily the stimulant effects; in fact, sensitization of locomotor responses to amphetamine may occur. Preclinical studies, largely focused on models of drug addiction rather than therapeutic stimulant use, have determined that the development of tolerance versus sensitization is complex and is correlated with both the dose and the temporal pattern of drug exposure. Broadly, constant long-term exposure to steady-state drug levels has been shown to result in tolerance, whereas intermittent amphetamine exposure over several days may induce sensitization. Adaptations in the mesocorticolimbic dopamine pathway are hypothesized to account for the development of either tolerance or sensitization.[121, 122] The balance of D_2 autoreceptor inhibition of dopamine synthesis and/or release or the desensitization of these autoreceptors appears to be of central importance, although many other factors, including glutamatergic modulation of dopamine release, plasticity of postsynaptic receptors or signal transduction, and shifts in intracellular dopamine compartments, may be involved. A complete discussion of these processes is beyond the scope of this chapter; furthermore, it is unclear whether these dopaminergic adaptations in this reward pathway resemble chronic mechanisms relevant to therapeutic actions of psychostimulants.

Large doses of methamphetamine, fenfluramine, 3,4-methylenediopyamphetamine, or MDMA cause depletion of monoamines and axonal degeneration. The axonal degeneration in response to MDMA is specific to serotoninergic terminals. The neurochemical basis of neurotoxicity in response to certain stimulants is not entirely clear but is likely to involve toxic metabolites of the drugs and/or of dopamine itself and probably involves excitotoxic glutamate release as well. Interestingly, methylphenidate and pemoline, which release vesicular rather than cytoplasmic dopamine stores, do not appear to cause monoamine depletion or neurotoxicity.

Cognitive Enhancers

Drugs directed largely toward the amelioration of cognitive decline in Alzheimer's disease (AD) involve a variety of partially understood pharmacodynamic mechanisms. The most common strategy has been to improve cholinergic function. Evidence for a deficit in cholinergic neurotransmission in AD includes the findings of reduced choline acetyltransferase activity in the cortex and hippocampus and degeneration of cholinergic neurons in the nucleus basalis of Meynert. Neuronal damage and multiple neurotransmitter defects may account for the limited success of cholinergic strategies. In this section, cholinergic and noncholinergic treatment strategies are discussed, including drugs already approved as well as those under development.

Cholinergic Agents

Current drugs targeted toward improvement of cholinergic function include cholinesterase inhibitors, ACh precursors, and muscarinic receptor agonists. Muscarinic receptors are designated with an uppercase M for those discriminated by pharmacological mechanisms and a lowercase m for those characterized by cloning strategies. Two other classes, presynaptic M_2 receptor antagonists and nicotinic agonists, have been investigated but are not currently prescribed. The nootropics, discussed in the next section, also influence cholinergic function.

Physostigmine and tetrahydroaminoacridine (THA, tacrine) are the most commonly used acetylcholinesterase inhibitors for AD.[123, 124] Physostigmine inhibits acetylcholinesterase by interacting with the catalytic site, whereas

THA produces allosteric inhibition. A 30% inhibition of acetylcholinesterase has been observed in patients with AD who are treated with THA (80 to 160 mg/d). Of the two inhibitors, THA has become the drug of choice because of its demonstrated therapeutic efficacy, although minimal, in major clinical trials and its five to six times longer duration of action than that of physostigmine. The greater efficacy of THA may also be due, in part, to additional modes of action. In addition to acetylcholinesterase inhibition, THA may enhance ACh release as well as release of other neurotransmitters such as glutamate, inhibit MAO-A and -B, inhibit monoamine transport, and interact directly with cholinergic receptors. The monoamine effects are observed only at high concentrations of the drug and therefore are unlikely to contribute to its therapeutic properties. In contrast, a 30% inhibition of muscarinic receptor binding is observed at therapeutic concentrations of THA.

Conflicting data have made it difficult to establish whether THA increases or decreases ACh release and by what mechanism. THA may stimulate ACh release by blockade of presynaptic potassium channels or by direct or indirect action at M_1 receptors. In support of the latter hypothesis, THA produces an increase in ACh release in the cortex in AD, which is prevented by the M_1 antagonist pirenzepine. Partial recovery of somatostatin production in patients with AD treated with THA may be an important mechanism, because somatostatin has been shown to stimulate ACh release.[125, 126] In contrast, THA has been found to diminish ACh release in control human and rat brain slices. This inhibitory effect may result from the elevated synaptic ACh concentrations causing a feedback inhibition of ACh release via presynaptic, inhibitory M_2 receptors. Indeed, the nature of THA's noncholinesterase effects may depend on the absolute and relative numbers of remaining nerve terminals and receptor types.

A second cholinergic strategy, precursor loading, has not proved effective in controlled studies, although it is still sometimes attempted in combination with other strategies. Lecithin (phosphatidylcholine) increases high-affinity choline uptake, but it has not been demonstrated that ACh synthesis or release is increased.

The finding that muscarinic antagonists (e.g., scopolamine) produce learning deficits in laboratory animals and humans suggests that muscarinic agonists may serve as cognitive enhancers. However, the agonists arecoline, bethanecol, and RS-86 have so far proved ineffective in treatment of AD. These agents are all weak agonists and are not receptor subtype selective. Therefore, much research has been aimed at the development of subtype-selective compounds. Although it is unclear at present, selective affinity for M_1 receptors appears to be the most desirable pharmacological property of a muscarinic agonist, because presynaptic M_2 autoreceptors in the hippocampus and cortex are coupled negatively to adenylate cyclase and inhibit ACh release. Based on the latter observation, M_2 antagonists are being developed as an alternative approach for enhancing cholinergic activity; these agents have shown promising results in animal studies but have not yet reached clinical trials.[127] Finally, it should be cautioned that muscarinic receptor distribution is considerably more complex than the distribution of presynaptic M_2 receptors and postsynaptic M_1 receptors. M_2 receptors are also located on postsynaptic densities, and there are also a third pharmacologic receptor subtype designated M_3 and five cloned receptor subtypes (m_1 through m_5). The most favorable selectivity profile of an agonist for the individual molecular receptor types remains to be determined.

Nicotinic ACh receptors have also been targeted as possible sites for agonist treatment. A nicotinic agonist strategy for cognitive enhancement is supported by the finding that, like muscarinic antagonists such as scopolamine, the nicotinic antagonist mecamylamine produces memory impairment in animals.[128] Nicotine itself improves learning and memory in patients with AD, but its side effect profile prohibits chronic treatment.

Each of the cholinergic treatment strategies has limitations that may explain the failure to produce a more effective drug. The neuronal degeneration in AD confounds attempts at cholinergic replacement. Muscarinic agonists may also be limited in efficacy because of loss of receptor-effector coupling and defects in phosphoinositide hydrolysis. Furthermore, tonic receptor stimulation does not resemble physiological, phasic stimulation. Finally, it is thought that the pathology of AD involves other transmitters including monoamines, amino acids, and peptides such as somatostatin and corticotropin-releasing factor (CRF), although some of these neurotransmitter deficits may be ameliorated by certain of the cholinergic agents; for example, THA elevates somatostatin levels and muscarinic agonists probably enhance NMDA or other glutamate receptor function. The combination of one or more cholinergic agents with noncholinergic agents described in the remainder of this section may provide the most benefit in improving cognitive function.

Nootropics and Miscellaneous Other Drugs

The term nootropic refers to the pyrrolidone GABA derivative piracetam and structurally related compounds (e.g., aniracetam, oxiracetam, pramiracetam).[129] These drugs have been shown to prevent cognitive deficits induced by scopolamine in laboratory animals, but clinical trials have yielded mixed results. Despite their structure, nootropics are not GABA-like; the mechanism by which they may improve cognitive function is unknown. One hypothesis is that these drugs stimulate adenylate kinase and improve the metabolic status of neurons. Nootropics have also been proposed to protect against hypoxia through one or more vascular mechanisms. Third, nootropics have been shown to increase cholinergic transmission by increasing ACh synthesis or release. Pramiracetam, but not piracetam or aniracetam, increases high-affinity choline uptake in rat hippocampus. Reduction of brain ACh concentrations in response to electroshock stimulus can be prevented by oxiracetam, further supporting the hypothesis that nootropics act by increasing ACh synthesis. Interestingly, the cognitive effect of nootropics appears to be steroid dependent, because adrenalectomy, inhibition of steroid synthesis, and aldosterone receptor antagonism all block the memory-enhancing effects of nootropics but not physostigmine or arecoline in mice.[130] The variety of implicated mechanisms, lack of an identified molecular target, and contrasting results with different nootropic agents all defy a coherent understanding of how these drugs work.

Vinpocetine is a vinca alkaloid that has shown some efficacy in improving memory in normal volunteers and patients with dementia. Vinpocetine produces increases in cerebral blood flow, as well as increases in neuronal ATP synthesis, and also functions as an anticonvulsant.[129] A proposed mechanism, at least for the latter effect, is inhibition of adenosine uptake. Extracellular adenosine inhibits neuronal calcium influx and protects against excitotoxicity. Vinpocetine also inhibits a calcium/calmodulin-dependent isoform of cyclic-nucleotide phosphodiesterase, thus elevating cAMP and/or cGMP. It is not known whether the cognitive enhancement induced by vinpocetine is due primarily to effects on extracellular adenosine levels or intracellular cyclic nucleotides or whether the vascular, metabolic, or neuroprotective effects are most important.

Co-dergocrine is a mixture of four ergot alkaloids commonly used as a treatment for dementia and other symptoms of aging. Like vinpocetine, co-dergocrine improves both circulation to underperfused regions of the brain and neuronal ATP production. The activity of co-dergocrine as an α-adrenoreceptor antagonist may underlie one or both of these effects, but the mechanisms are unclear. Co-dergocrine also interacts with dopamine and serotonin receptors. Its activity as a D_2 agonist is responsible for an increase in hippocampal ACh release and a decrease in striatal ACh release in response to co-dergocrine.[131] Thus, in addition to neuroprotective effects, these drugs produce neurochemical changes that are particularly well suited to treatment of dementia in patients with Parkinson's disease. Finally, co-dergocrine has been reported to have mild antidepressant activity, which may be due to its interaction with monoamine receptors or its inhibition of cyclic-nucleotide phosphodiesterase.

A variety of other drugs have been used or are currently under investigation, most of which involve neuroprotective or neurotransmitter replacement mechanisms similar to those already discussed.[132] Acetylcarnitine is similar to the nootropic drugs in that it may have cholinergic properties, either as a direct agonist or as an ACh precursor, and it may also have a neuroprotective effect by stimulating glutathione synthesis. Phosphatidylserine has been suggested to stabilize neuronal membranes or enhance ACh release. Alkylxanthines such as caffeine have been attempted for treatment of dementia because of their psychostimulant and purported cognitive enhancing properties. Like vinpocetine, alkylxanthines inhibit one or more cyclic-nucleotide phosphodiesterase isozymes. However, most of these agents are also adenosine antagonists and thus produce an undesirable cerebral vasoconstriction. Denbufylline may be safer and more effective in the treatment of dementia because it functions more strongly as a phosphodiesterase inhibitor than as an adenosine antagonist. Calcium channel blockers have been investigated for treatment of dementia based on the observations that cytosolic calcium concentrations increase with aging and that a high intracellular calcium concentration is associated with various forms of neuronal death.[133] Nimodipine, an L-type calcium channel blocker, slowed the progression of memory loss in AD in one clinical trial. L-Deprenyl (selegiline), an MAO-B inhibitor approved for treatment of Parkinson's disease, has also shown positive cognitive effects in patients with AD. Increased MAO-B activity has been observed in the brain in AD. Increases in dopamine levels, for example, in mesocortical pathways, are thought to underlie the beneficial effects of L-deprenyl. Prevention of neurotoxin formation could theoretically be involved as well.

Despite only disappointing to modest success with existing drugs for the treatment of AD, advances have yielded several novel and promising pharmacological strategies that are hoped to lead to truly efficacious therapy in the near future.

Neuronal Plasticity

The term *neuronal plasticity* has several meanings. In the context of neuronal damage, the brain of adult mammals responds to injury with varying degrees of success by both regeneration and collateral sprouting. Some neuronal systems, primarily the thin unmyelinated axons of monoaminergic projections, respond to injury with remarkable plasticity. These fibers are capable of reinnervating denervated targets after axotomy, and in some cases this reinnervation restores lost function.[134] In the context of the developing mammalian brain, it is clear that far more neurons and synapses arise during morphogenesis of the CNS than persist into adulthood. Only the neural circuits that are reinforced through early activation and use are retained. As an example of this phenomenon, monocular deprivation of neonates results in a failure to maintain appropriate binocular synaptic input to the visual cortex. Similarly, allowing neonates to view only simple vertically striped environments results in adults that are unable to recognize the same pattern in other orientations.

It is also known that there are critical developmental periods, during gestation and in the neonatal period, when the immature brain is irreversibly altered by the presence of gonadal steroids.[135] The results of perinatal exposure to gonadal steroids, referred to as *organizational effects,* are the permanent imprinting on the brain circuitry of masculine or feminine patterns of behaviors and gonadotropin secretion that are expressed in adulthood. Manipulations of gonadal steroids during the critical developmental interval of experimental mammals can alter or reverse the normal sexual dimorphisms observed in hypothalamic architecture, gonadotropin secretion, and behavior. However, in the context of this chapter neural plasticity refers to the ability of the adult brain to undergo biochemical and ultrastructural changes in response to different external stimuli. These changes, which occur in the absence of injury, indicate that neural connections are adapting to their internal and external environment. In the case of the gonadal steroids, their *activational effects* occur after the perinatal critical period and result from the exposure of the brain to hormones during endocrine events such as puberty, the reproductive cycle, and pregnancy.[136] The activational effects of gonadal steroids, unlike their organizing effects, were thought initially to be mediated by alterations in gene expression with attendant alterations in protein synthesis or by alterations in electrical properties rather than by alterations in neuronal structure.[137] It is now known that the adult brain undergoes rapid reversible changes in neuronal structure in response to changes in the endocrine environment. These changes include increases in the number of synapses, the number of axodendritic synapses, and the synaptic density in various periventricular brain regions.[136] These observations suggest that the plasticity seen in hypothalamic neurons may be an important physiological mechanism of feedback in the hypothalamic-pituitary-gonadal axis. Similar studies and findings are appearing for the HPA axis, although studies of this axis are comparatively immature.

Another relevant form of neural plasticity occurs in drug addiction. Some aspects of drug addiction can occur relatively rapidly in response to acute administration of a drug of abuse. However, most changes in brain function associated with addiction occur gradually over time in response to prolonged drug exposure. These progressive changes, once acquired, can persist for some time after the cessation of chronic drug administration. These changes are described by the terms tolerance, sensitization, dependence, and withdrawal. Addiction is defined as the sum of these effects, which presumably arise as the result of adaptive changes occurring in specific brain areas.[138] There are, of course, behavioral ramifications of this suite of characteristics defining addiction, and these behaviors are of great clinical relevance.

Dependence and Tolerance

The locus caeruleus and the mesolimbocortical dopamine systems have been implicated as central components of drug addiction. Despite the fact that these two systems can influence one another, they appear to regulate distinct aspects of drug addiction. The locus caeruleus mediates physical opiate dependence but has little involvement in the opiate reinforcement. The mesolimbic dopamine system mediates the reinforcing properties of many drugs of abuse but plays little role in physical dependence.[139, 140]

Within the locus caeruleus, the acute effect of opiates is an inhibition of neuronal firing rates. This occurs by means of an activation of potassium channels and an inhibition of sodium channel conductance. Potassium channels are activated by a direct coupling of the channel to the opioid receptor via a G protein. The inhibition of sodium channel conductance appears to be mediated by reduced levels of cAMP and thus reduced levels of activated cAMP-dependent protein kinase.[141] After prolonged opiate treatment, locus caeruleus neurons develop tolerance to the acute inhibitory actions of opiates and firing rates return toward normal levels. Maintenance of this restored level of firing depends on the continued presence of opiates. Cessation of opiate inputs leads to a marked elevation, to levels above normal rates, in locus caeruleus neuronal electrical activity. This elevation in firing rate is effected by an increase in intracellular cAMP.[142]

Chronic administration of opiates increases expression of the G proteins G_i and G_o,[143] adenylate cyclase,[144] cAMP-dependent protein kinase, and several protein substrates for protein kinase such as tyrosine hydroxylase.[145] This up-regulation of the cAMP pathway occurs in the absence of changes in other protein kinase pathways. The excitation of locus caeruleus neurons during opiate withdrawal appears to be necessary and sufficient for producing behavioral signs of physical opiate withdrawal, and the time course in which the up-regulated cAMP pathway returns to normal levels after opiate withdrawal parallels both the return to normal firing rates in the locus caeruleus and the amelioration of behavioral signs of withdrawal. The mechanisms of tolerance overlap to some extent those underlying dependence. Up-regulation of the cAMP pathway makes it more difficult for opiates to inhibit the activity of locus caeruleus neurons via inhibition of the cAMP system. The up-regulated cAMP system also increases desensitization of the opiate receptor by increased phosphorylation of the receptor. The tolerant state is therefore characterized by desensitized opiate receptors and an up-regulated cAMP system.[138] These combine to reduce the ability of opiates to reduce cAMP levels and inhibit neuronal firing in the locus caeruleus.

Psychological Dependence

Drugs of abuse are positive behavioral reinforcers insofar as drug use leads to additional use of the drug. This repeated drug use leads to adaptive changes in the brain that are relevant to reinforcement, and these adaptive changes may represent the basis for the psychological dependence accompanying drug abuse. The identification of the mesolimbic dopamine system as the likely site of mediation of the reinforcing properties of drugs of abuse has led to the discovery of a set of common actions of morphine, cocaine, and ethanol in this brain system.[138]

The effects observed in the locus caeruleus after chronic opiate administration have also been observed in the nucleus accumbens. These effects include an up-regulation of adenylate cyclase and cAMP-dependent protein kinase, a decrease in G_i levels with an attendant increase in functional activity in the cAMP pathway, and an increase in tyrosine hydroxylase phosphorylation. Similar intracellular adaptations are also observed in the nucleus accumbens after chronic treatment with cocaine or ethanol.[146]

The VTA appears to be refractory to up-regulation of the cAMP pathway by chronic opiate or cocaine treatment. This occurs despite decreases in G_i and G_o expression as a result of these chronic treatments. Also altered by chronic opiate or cocaine treatment are levels of tyrosine hydroxylase and three major neurofilament proteins. These levels are increased and decreased, respectively, in these states. Chronic ethanol treatment produces similar changes in the levels of these proteins.[147, 148]

Chronic cocaine treatment induces D_1 dopamine receptor supersensitivity in the nucleus accumbens. This supersensitivity occurs in the absence of alterations in the amount of D_1 receptor that is expressed. Because D_1 receptors are positively coupled to the cAMP pathway, the increase in adenylate cyclase and cAMP-dependent protein kinase combined with a decrease in G_i without offsetting changes in G_s may explain the D_1 receptor supersensitivity. This D_1 receptor supersensitivity is manifest electrophysiologically and is the only alteration in neuronal firing activity that has been documented in the mesolimbic dopamine system as a result of chronic treatment with drugs of abuse.[138, 149] An overall view of the biochemical changes associated with drug abuse–induced neural plasticity are summarized in cartoon form in Figure 14–15.

Unfortunately, the behavioral complexity of drug abuse is such that it is impossible to correlate a specific biochemical change, and the accompanying physiological change(s), in the mesolimbic dopamine system with a particular behavior. However, it is encouraging to observe common biochemical alterations as a consequence of chronic drug treatment in both the areas of the brain seemingly responsible for physical dependence (i.e., the locus caeruleus) and

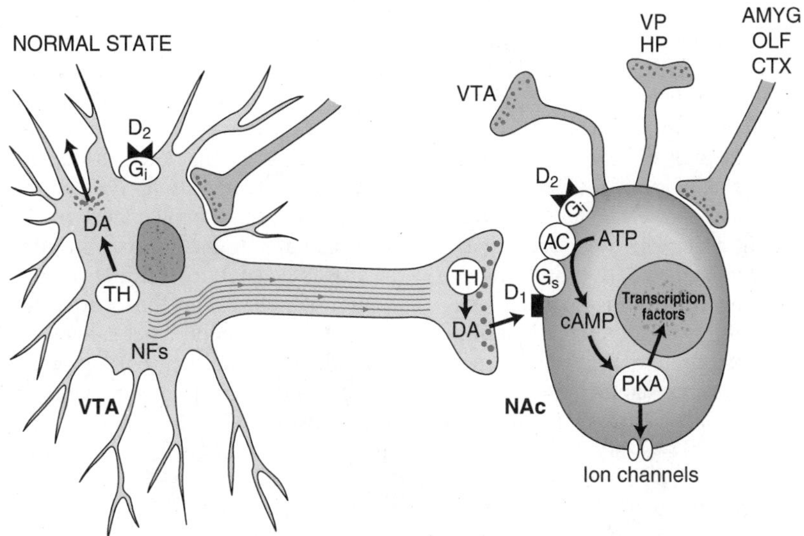

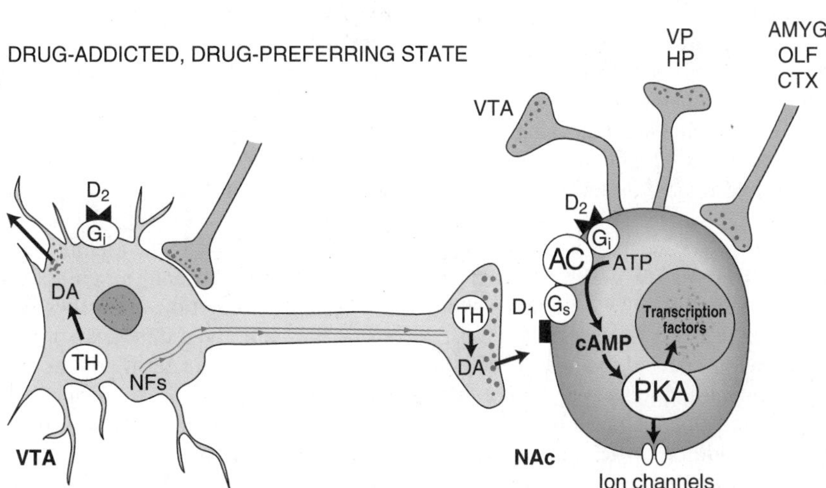

Figure 14–15 *Cartoon scheme illustrating biochemical parameters associated with some aspects of the drug-addicted and drug-preferring state. The top portion depicts a normal VTA neuron projecting to the nucleus accumbens (NAc). The ventral tegmental neuron expresses tyrosine hydroxylase (TH), presynaptic D_2 dopamine receptors (D_2) coupled to inhibitory G proteins (G_i), and neurofilaments (NFs) and synthesizes dopamine (DA). The nucleus accumbens neuron expresses TH, components of the intracellular cAMP system (AC, adenylate cyclase; PKA, protein kinase A, cAMP-dependent protein kinase), and postsynaptic D_1 and D_2 dopamine receptors coupled to stimulatory (G_s) and inhibitory (G_i) G proteins, respectively. These neurons also synthesize DA. Afferent and efferent connections are shown with ventral pallidum (VP), hippocampus (HP), amygdala (AMYG), olfactory cortex (OLF), and other cortical areas (CTX). The lower portion depicts the drug-addicted, drug-preferring state such as occurs after chronic administration of cocaine, ethanol, or morphine. The relative size of the lettering and circles indicates the relative expression of the various components of this system. The drug-addicted, drug-preferring state corresponds to increased expression of tyrosine hydroxylase and decreased expression of neurofilaments in the VTA. The decreased expression of neurofilaments causes a reduction in axonal transport and a reduction in the availability of dopamine at VTA projections to the nucleus accumbens. The drug-addicted, drug-preferring state also correlates with increased expression of adenylate cyclase activity and a corresponding increase in the activity of protein kinase A in the nucleus accumbens. This, combined with a decrease in G_i protein expression, leads to an increase in the phosphorylation state of various protein kinase A substrates such as ion channels and nuclear transcription factors. The overall result of these changes is a D_1 receptor supersensitivity in the drug-addicted, drug-preferring state. (From Nestler EJ, Hope BT, Widnell KL: Drug addiction: A model for the molecular basis of neural plasticity. Neuron 1993; 11:995–1006. © by Cell Press.)*

those seemingly responsible for psychological dependence (i.e., the mesolimbic dopamine system).

Long-Term Potentiation

Hippocampal neurons in the CA1 region have become a standard model for the study of LTP and memory. LTP involves a lasting increase in the electrical responses, and therefore increased synaptic efficacy, after a brief high-frequency stimulation of monosynaptic afferents to CA1.[150] LTP is thus another form of synaptic plasticity. In addition to the relevance of LTP to learning and memory, this phenomenon illustrates an important principle of cellular and molecular neurobiology. Initial investigations into LTP sought a singular underlying mechanism to explain the increase in synaptic efficacy. Early results implicated NMDA receptor–mediated increases in postsynaptic cystolic calcium as the cause of the increased responsiveness of the postsynaptic cell. Additional research in a variety of fields has identified intracellular sequelae of increased intracellular calcium. In the case of hippocampal LTP, these include activation of calcium/calmodulin-dependent protein kinase II and protein kinase C. The persistence of activity-induced changes is a logical prerequisite for a molecular explanation of LTP, and the activation of calcium/calmodulin-dependent protein kinase II and protein kinase C is persistent.[151] Later work identified a presynaptic component in LTP, leading to a search for retrograde communication in this model system. Elucidation of the NO and CO systems provided candidates for the retrograde communicator. The observations that inhibitors of the CO or NO systems blocked LTP and that LTP-invoked activation of guanylate cyclase and cGMP-dependent protein kinase was obligatory for LTP suggest strongly that the CO and NO systems are involved in LTP.[152] Additional study has shown that metabotropic and AMPA glutamate receptor activation is obligatory for LTP[153] and that adrenal steroids regulate LTP in a biphasic manner.[154] We can conclude that, rather than a single crucial molecular event evoking LTP, this neuroplasticity arises from a series of interrelated molecular events of a particular cascade form.[155]

Gene-Environment Interactions

Persuasive preclinical[156–165] and clinical[166–171] studies support the thesis that life experiences, especially those occurring during the pre- and neonatal periods of CNS development, exert a significant influence on phenotypic development at the cellular and organismal levels. Developing a comprehensive understanding of the nature and the mechanism underlying this plasticity remains a major goal of biological psychiatry.

In vertebrates, the identity of individual neurons is not necessarily determined by lineage but can be influenced by signals received from neighboring cells and other epigenetic factors.[172–175] This feature also carries over to development of actual patterns of neuronal connectivity; hence the pattern of synaptic wiring is not fully developed at birth but instead emerges as a result of activity-dependent mechanisms modulated by sensory experience. The importance of epigenetic factors, of intrinsic (diffusible factors, surface molecules) or extrinsic (sensory input, social experiences, learning) origins, in neural development may be inferred from the likelihood that insufficient genetic information is present in the estimated 10^5 genes in the mammalian genome to specify individually each of the approximately 10^{15} synaptic connections in the mature nervous system. Overall, it appears that the magnitude of these environmental influences diminishes but does not completely disappear with age. Thus, adverse environmental conditions during the early postnatal period (perhaps the first 3 years of life in humans) exert a more profound influence on CNS development than do similar events in later life. Initially, this variable degree of plasticity may serve to fine-tune each individual's genetically prescribed pattern of neuronal circuitry for survival in its specific habitat. Cajal[176] was among the first to postulate that development and learning shared a common process of neuronal remodeling. This view has also been embraced by Kandel and colleagues,[177] who suggested that learning with its associated alterations in neuronal gene expression and the resultant synaptic reorganization can be considered as a late, and continuous, stage in neuronal differentiation. It is currently assumed that the molecular mechanisms underlying developmental plasticity also mediate, at least in part, the synaptic plasticity evident in processes such as learning, memory, and the response to injury, which occur throughout life. This scheme, then, provides a general mechanism that may account for individual variability within a population in behavior, neuroendocrine responses to actual or perceived challenges, as well as serve as a foundation for vulnerabilities leading to subsequent pathophysiology and pathopsychology.

Our current understanding of CNS developmental processes postulates the existence of a fundamental genetic program. This genetic program presumably directs the interrelationships among larger categories of neurons via mechanisms including cell differentiation and chemoaffinity for the establishment of appropriate synaptic connections. As has been amply demonstrated in numerous species, the developing nervous system contains an excessive number of synaptic connections, many of which are lost during development.[178, 179] This process of synaptic sculpting, which occurs in response to the level of impulse activity along each connection,[179, 180] leads to a more precise pattern of synaptic activity in the mature nervous system. Activation of developing neuronal assemblies substantially increases the specific formation and efficiency of a neuronal group while reducing the redundancy of connections. This process has been viewed in terms of the selective stabilization of neuronal wiring.[172, 175] In this formulation, three successive stages must emerge in order that synaptic plasticity be achieved: an unstable state, a stable state, and a regressive state. Nerve fiber outgrowth leads to the formation of the unstable state. In the unstable state, nerve fibers either become stabilized or are broken down (i.e., regressive state) in response to impulse traffic. The characteristics of "mature" neuronal assemblies, represented by the transition from the unstable to the stable state, is highly dependent on a number of factors, including 1) the point in development at which it occurs, 2) the activity of the excitatory presynaptic fibers, and 3) the ability of the postsynaptic cell to be stimulated. Neural activity within a developing network selectively stabilizes only the emerging contacts (presynaptic) whose postsynaptic (receiving) cell is receptive to the process at a given and decisive moment. To reiterate, the activation of a specific gene is not necessary for construction of a specific individual synaptic contact; rather, the fine structuring of synaptic contacts follows a pattern determined by epigenetic factors that build on a foundation specified by a basic genetic constellation of less finely structured neuronal networks. This high degree of flexibility leads to individual variability even among organisms sharing the same genes (i.e., identical twins).

Communication between the environment and the genome is bidirectional. In addition to the "genome-outward" flow of information occurring during differentiation, the synaptic activity leading to alterations in synaptic efficiency results in part from environmental alterations in gene expression. Multiple lines of evidence indicate that the tropic interactions that influence brain development are critical throughout life, mediating processes as diverse as learning, memory, and regrowth after injury.[172, 174, 178–180] Impulse activity, through activation of second-messenger systems and initiation of calcium fluxes, regulates tropic interactions in the brain by modulating gene expression for a variety of proteins, thus permitting the conversion of millisecond-to-millisecond signaling into long-term changes in neural circuit function. Cellular responses to the external environment are capable of altering gene expression within those responsive cells at the microscopic level of fine structure and biochemistry. However, the early environmental experiences of an individual are also capable of permanently altering the behavior of the CNS on a macroscopic level. The mechanistic aspects of this long-term imprinting by early experience remain to be fully elucidated but are likely to involve alterations in gene expression via processes of DNA methylation or demethylation, activation of transcription factors, and changes in protein phosphorylation state, which are discussed later.

Aspects of the organism's environment are perceived via sensory neurons and, thus, this information is first analyzed in primary cortical sensory areas. It then flows to unimodal and then to polymodal sensory association cortices. Additional information arrives from the limbic system. This ensures an appropriate and integrated response by the organism; however, it must be noted that these input filters are subject to individual modulation during development, so the perception of the stimulus may be quite different between individuals and, as a consequence, the final behavioral or endocrine output may also vary. Among factors influencing an organism's perception and processing of environmental input are its arousal state and its previous experience, which may initiate cascades leading to long-term adaptations in synaptic activity mediated via changes in protein phosphorylation and gene expression that would serve to produce prolonged, and some relatively stable, alterations in brain function. From this perspective, early experiences would be expected to exert important and perhaps permanent influences on brain function in response to the occurrence or failure of occurrence of particular experiences at times when relevant systems are undergoing development. Therefore, it is important to realize that this complex gene-environment interaction leads to a situation in which the environment affects the expression of genes and the gene products partially create selective filters through alterations in CNS neuronal assemblies so that the actual environment perceived by the developing individual and the organism's response repertoire is highly individualized.

Maturational development of the mammalian visual system provides a particularly good example of the importance of gene-environment interactions. In his 1932 review, von Senden[181] reported that in children born with binocular cataracts a delay of treatment until an age greater than 10 years resulted in permanent impairment of the ability to perceive form. Later studies of the effects of visual deprivation in developing cats and monkeys also illustrated profound deficits in visual abilities. For instance, unilateral visual deprivation imposed by suturing of the eyelid resulted in animals with cells in the retinal ganglion and lateral geniculate nucleus normally responsive to a visual stimulus; however, few cortical cells in area 17 (striate cortex) were activated by presentation of visual stimuli to the previously deprived eye.[182] As shown by Hubel and colleagues,[183] this type of sensory deprivation during postnatal development actually altered the structure of the visual cortex so that cortical columns receiving input from the normal eye were greatly widened at the expense of those receiving input from the deprived eye.

It has been appreciated for some time that neurotransmitters act as tropic factors during periods of brain development by regulating the expression of genes that control cellular differentiation.[184] However, this tropic function continues beyond the stage of differentiation via similar mechanisms. Development of the visual cortex in response to visual input is at least partially dependent on noradrenergic input to and subsequent activation of the β-adrenergic receptor signaling cascade in the cortical neurons. Infusion of exogenous norepinephrine into the catecholamine terminal–depleted visual cortex or the cortex of an animal with monocular lid suture restored cortical plasticity to visual input; furthermore, activation of visual cortex β-adrenergic receptor systems with specific agonists or postreceptor processes using dibutyryl cAMP restored visual perception.[185, 186] Activation of β-adrenergic receptors initiates a cascade beginning with increased cAMP and leading to augmented expression of nuclear transcription factors, including *FOS* and cAMP response element binding protein that transduce receptor-binding events into modulation of gene expression. These results suggest that presynaptic input is vital in programming β-adrenergic responsiveness during a critical period of development and that interruption of transsynaptic events occurring at this time can lead to lasting alterations in neuronal responsiveness.

Maternal Deprivation and Neonatal Handling Experiments

Studies of maternal deprivation provide a striking example of how genetic factors, development, and experience interact in early life and how environmental deprivation can dramatically alter developmental processes. Exposure of young children to severe social and sensory deprivation is associated with withdrawal, lack of curiosity, general delay in motor and speech development, and susceptibility to infection.[187] Classical studies carried out in the 1960s first demonstrated that rearing under conditions of social isolation resulted in severe behavioral abnormalities that persisted into adulthood.[159, 188] Subsequent studies of primates[156, 189, 190] reexamined the organizing influence of early experience on behavior, cardiovascular and sympathetic nervous system responsiveness, and immune function. In a longitudinal study of rhesus macaques by Higley and associates,[191] the effects of developmental change, experimental history, sex, and individual variation on the response of the catecholaminergic, serotoninergic, and adrenocortical systems to separation-induced stress were assessed from infancy through adolescence. Subjects reared for the first 6 months of life either with their mothers or in peer groups were compared in terms of developmental changes in response to repeated separation stress assessed by subjecting them to four sequential 4-day social separations when they were 6 and 18 months old. Social separation consistently increased cerebrospinal fluid 3-methoxy-4-

hydroxyphenylglycol, a major norepinephrine metabolite, decreased levels of the dopamine metabolite homovanillic acid, and resulted in increased levels of the serotonin metabolite 5-hydroxyindoleacetic acid after the first but not the fourth separation. Plasma cortisol increased rapidly immediately after separation and remained higher than the baseline value on day 4 of both the first and fourth separations. Interindividual differences were highly stable, with significant correlations both within and between years for each of the three metabolites and cortisol. Thus, this study indicates that rearing conditions lead to long-term alterations in sympathetic nervous system and sympathoadrenal responsiveness. Higley and colleagues[192] also showed that in peer- and mother-reared groups, early rearing experiences that predisposed monkeys to increased fear-related behaviors produced excessive alcohol consumption under normal living conditions and this behavior was accentuated by the stressor of social separation. Beginning when infant bonnet macaques were 11 weeks old, Andrews and Rosenblum[156, 193] housed and observed dyads under different maternal foraging demand conditions, consisting of a low-foraging-demand (LFD) condition, a high-foraging-demand (HFD) condition, and a variable-foraging-demand (VFD) condition. Differences between the LFD and VFD groups were minimal during this period; however, increased maternal grooming and shorter separation bouts were observed in the VFD group than in the LFD group. On challenge by brief introductions to a novel environment, the frequency of breaking dyadic contact and levels of play were significantly lower for the VFD infants than for the LFD infants, perhaps as a consequence of less secure attachment. Similarly, animals raised under the VFD regimen exhibited a longer latency during adolescence to separate from their mother to explore a novel physical environment, suggesting that these effects of early rearing persist.

Complementary studies have been performed with rodents illustrating that different neonatal rearing conditions lead to lifelong changes in behavior, HPA axis and sympathoadrenal responsiveness, altered vulnerabilities to disease, and changes in the CNS.[158, 162, 165, 194] These findings clearly demonstrate that rudimentary, adaptive responses to stress could be modified by environmental events leading to stable differences in HPA responsivity that are mediated by effects on the differentiation of neurons that are ultimately involved in the negative feedback regulation of the HPA axis. These studies, which we discuss at some length, underscore the plasticity within brain regions that regulate the HPA axis, elucidate potential mechanisms underlying these long-term functional alterations, and provide a model for understanding how individual differences in responses to stress emerge.

As adults, handled (MS15) rats exhibited attenuated fearfulness in novel environments and decreased HPA responses to a wide variety of stressors, whereas animals exposed to maternal separation (MS180) showed hyperresponsivity. These rearing manipulations, imposed from neonatal day 2 to 12 or longer, after which the animals were reared normally and tested as adults, involved removing rat pups from their maternal cage, placing the animals together in small containers in an incubator, and either 15 (HMS15) or 180 (HMS180) minutes later returning the animals to their cage and their mothers. In response to a wide variety of stressors HMS15 rats showed smaller increases in ACTH and both total and free corticosterone (the principal glucocorticoid in the rat) and a faster return to basal levels after termination of stress than did nonhandled (HMS0) animals.[164] The integrated plasma hormone response to stress (prestress to 120 minutes after stress) was usually 40% to 50% lower in the HMS15 rats, with these differences apparent at puberty and as late as 24 to 26 months of age. There were no differences between HMS15 and HMS0 animals in adrenal sensitivity to ACTH, pituitary sensitivity to CRF, plasma corticosteroid-binding globulin levels, or the metabolic clearance rate for ACTH or corticosterone. Rather, HMS0 and HMS180 animals showed increased secretion of both hormones during and immediately after stress. Interestingly, the handling effects on HPA function were specific to conditions of stress, as these animals did not differ in basal ACTH or corticosterone levels at any time point over the diurnal cycle and differences in HPA activity observed during stress could not be accounted for by altered prestress, basal glucocorticoid levels. Therefore, differences in plasma ACTH levels among these differentially reared animals suggest that the mechanism underlying the differences in adrenocortical activity is located at or above the level of the pituitary and may be related to differential sensitivity of glucocorticoid negative feedback processes (i.e., the processes by which glucocorticoids act at pituitary and neural sites to damp HPA activity).

Indeed, Meaney and colleagues[195] found that exogenously administered corticosterone or dexamethasone given 3 hours before a 20-minute period of restraint stress suppressed ACTH responses to a greater extent in HMS15 than in HMS0 animals, suggesting that HMS15 animals are more sensitive to the negative feedback effects of circulating glucocorticoids on HPA activity. Studies have demonstrated significant and tissue-specific differences in glucocorticoid receptor–binding capacity as a function of rearing conditions, with HMS15 rats exhibiting increased glucocorticoid receptor but not mineralocorticoid receptor binding capacity, number, and mRNA in the hippocampus and frontal cortex but not in septum, amygdala, hypothalamus, or pituitary.[164, 196–198] The difference in hippocampal glucocorticoid receptor levels appeared to be related to the decreased HPA responsivity to stress in HMS15 animals by enhancing the efficiency of negative feedback inhibition by circulating glucocorticoids of the HPA axis. These findings are consistent with data revealing that the hippocampus is a critical site for glucocorticoid-mediated inhibition of HPA activity.[199, 200]

The negative feedback differences between HMS15 and HMS0 animals could have occurred in response to basal corticosterone levels and were reflected in differences in hypothalamic synthesis of the ACTH secretagogues CRF and arginine vasopressin.[201] Similarly, hypothalamic CRF mRNA levels were about 2.5-fold higher in HMS0 and HMS180 rats than in HMS15 animals.[202] Thus, under basal conditions, hypothalamic CRF and arginine vasopressin synthesis appeared to be elevated in HMS0 and HMS180 rats, a difference that occurred in the presence of basal glucocorticoid levels. Because HMS15, HMS0, and HMS180 animals did not differ in basal levels of ACTH or corticosterone, it seems likely that the differences in CRF and arginine vasopressin represent changes in the readily releasable storage pools of these peptides in axon terminals of neurons of the paraventricular nucleus located in the median eminence. On excitation by a stressor, release of CRF and arginine vasopressin from median eminence nerve terminals was enhanced in HMS0 and HMS180 rats compared with the HMS15 animals.[164]

Plotsky and Meaney[201] studied animals that were separated from their mothers once a day for 0, 15, 60, 180, or 360 minutes from days 2 to 14 of life and then studied as adults. The long-term effects of HPA responses to stress were qualitatively different depending on the duration of maternal separation. As adults, animals that had been exposed to repeated maternal separation of 180 to 360 minutes per day for the first 2 weeks of life showed significantly increased plasma ACTH and corticosterone responses to either restraint or novelty stress compared with control animals separated for 0 minutes. The animals exposed to the 15-minute period of separation showed reduced plasma ACTH or corticosterone responses to stress. These findings underscore the different sequelae associated with handling versus maternal separation.

At this juncture, the question arises of the mechanism by which early experiences are translated into long-term alterations in glucocorticoid receptor density and other elements of the HPA axis. Experiments to address these issues are in progress, and a putative sequence of events has emerged. Early experience affects neurochemical differentiation in the hippocampus by specifically altering the sensitivity of hippocampal cells to corticosterone through an effect on glucocorticoid receptor gene expression and, thus, receptor density. This effect is independent of processes such as neuron survival, because adult rats from these different rearing groups did not differ in hippocampal neuron density,[203] although they might have exhibited alterations in the dendritic branching patterns and complexity of hippocampal neurons.[204] The effects of early environment on the development of hippocampal glucocorticoid receptor density exhibit the common characteristics of a developmental effect: 1) there is a specific critical period during which the organism is maximally responsive to the effects of rearing conditions; 2) the effects of altered rearing during the first 21 days of life on glucocorticoid receptor density endure throughout the life of the animal; and 3) a substantial degree of specificity to the rearing conditions is present, in that early handling (HMS15) increased whereas maternal separation (HMS180) decreased hippocampal glucocorticoid but not mineralocorticoid receptor gene expression (note that both types of adrenal steroid receptors are coexpressed in virtually all hippocampal neurons). Such variations in neuronal differentiation are likely to underlie important individual differences in tissue sensitivity to hormonal signals and thus represent a biochemical basis for environmental programming of neural systems.

The temporal pattern for the rearing effect on hippocampal glucocorticoid receptor density and mRNA corresponds to the normal developmental changes occurring over the early postnatal life,[205] with glucocorticoid receptor density low on postnatal day 3 and then steadily increasing toward adult values, which are achieved by about the third week of life. During this period of ontogenetic development, environmental events can influence the development of this receptor population. It is important to note that the developmental pattern for glucocorticoid receptor binding in regions not affected by neonatal handling, such as the hypothalamus, amygdala, and septum, is identical to that of the hippocampus, and thus it is unlikely that the handling effect on glucocorticoid receptor density in the hippocampus can be explained simply by the status of the glucocorticoid receptor system during the first weeks of life.

The hypothalamic-pituitary-thyroid axis is also activated by neonatal handling, leading to systemic elevations of thyroxine and increased intracellular levels of the biologically more potent thyroxine metabolite triiodothyronine. Furthermore, the pituitary-thyroid axis is a major regulator of HPA development.[203, 205] Neonatal treatment with either thyroxine or triiodothyronine resulted in significantly increased glucocorticoid receptor binding capacity in the hippocampus of adult animals but, as with early handling, neither thyroxine nor triiodothyronine treatment affected hypothalamic or pituitary glucocorticoid receptor density. In addition, administration of propylthiouracil, a thyroid hormone synthesis inhibitor, to MS15 pups for the first 2 weeks of life completely blocked the effects of handling on hippocampal glucocorticoid receptor binding capacity. These results are consistent with the idea that the thyroid hormones might, at least in part, mediate the effects of neonatal handling on the development of the forebrain glucocorticoid receptor system. However, studies of hippocampal culture systems showed that the effect of triiodothyronine was not directly mediated on hippocampal cells but rather occurred at some distal site.

Thyroid hormones exert pervasive effects throughout the developing CNS, including the regulation of central serotoninergic (5-HT) neurons.[206] Studies have shown that thyroid hormones as well as neonatal handling increase 5-HT turnover in the hippocampus of the neonatal rat.[207, 208] 5,7-Dihydroxytryptamine lesions of raphe 5-HT neurons dramatically reduced the ascending serotoninergic input to the hippocampus, and neonatal day 2 rat pups treated with 5,7-dihydroxytryptamine showed a reduction of hippocampal glucocorticoid receptor density as adults.[207] Thus, it appears that thyroid hormone actions on hippocampal glucocorticoid receptor development may be mediated via a serotoninergic mechanism. This is further supported by the observation that incubation of hippocampal cell cultures with increasing concentrations of 5-HT was associated with increased glucocorticoid receptor binding, an effect that required a minimum of 4 days of treatment to appear, suggesting that the effect of 5-HT involves increased synthesis of receptors.[209, 210] Moreover, this effect of 5-HT on glucocorticoid receptor binding appears to be restricted to the neurons, as no effects of 5-HT on glucocorticoid receptor binding were observed in hippocampal glia–enriched cell cultures.

The effect of 5-HT on glucocorticoid receptor density in cultured hippocampal cells was blocked by the 5-HT_2 receptor antagonists ketanserin and mianserin. The 5-HT_2 agonists 1-(2,5-dimethoxy-4-iodophenyl)-2-aminopropane (DOI), trifluoromethylphenylpiperazine (TFMPP), and quipazine and the stable cAMP analogue 8-bromo-cAMP were also effective in increasing glucocorticoid receptor binding in hippocampal culture, whereas selective agonists or antagonists of the 5-HT_{1A} or 5-HT_3 receptors were without effect on glucocorticoid receptor binding.[209, 210] Interestingly, exposure of cultured hippocampal cells to 5-HT produced a fourfold increase in cAMP levels, which was blocked by ketanserin and at least partially mimicked by quipazine, TFMPP, and DOI.[210] Overall, these observations suggest that changes in cAMP concentrations may mediate the effect of 5-HT on glucocorticoid receptor synthesis in hippocampal cells.

The cyclic nucleotide–dependent protein kinase inhibitor H8 completely blocked the effects of 5-HT (10 nmol/L) on glucocorticoid receptor binding in hippocampal cell cultures, but the protein kinase C inhibitor H7 was without effect.[210] These findings suggest that activation of protein kinase A might, at some point, be involved in the serotoninergic regulation of hippocampal glucocorticoid receptor development. However, the 5-HT_{2A} receptor has not been linked to cyclic nucleotide but rather to phospholipase C–related second-messenger systems.[211] Several 5-HT receptors (5-HT_4, 5-HT_6, 5-HT_7) that directly stimulate adenylate cyclase activity have been cloned and their mRNAs are expressed in the rat hippocampus.[212] Of particular interest is the observation that the 5-HT_7 receptor binds ketanserin with high affinity.

The studies of 5-HT turnover by Smythe and associates[208] have provided useful insights into why the hippocampus is selectively affected by neonatal rearing conditions. In rat pups handled during the first 7 days of life and killed immediately after handling on day 7, serotonin turnover was significantly increased in the hippocampus but not in the hypothalamus or amygdala (regions in which handling has no effect on glucocorticoid receptor density). This suggests that handling selectively activates specific ascending 5-HT pathways,[213] and this response to handling, coupled with the existence of a developing glucocorticoid receptor system, underlies the sensitivity of this receptor system in specific brain regions to regulation by environmental events during the first week of life. Neonatal handling also stimulated a fourfold increase in hippocampal tissue cAMP levels in neonates that was almost completely abolished by concurrent treatment with either ketanserin or the thyroid hormone synthesis inhibitor propylthiouracil.

The regulation of gene transcription by cAMP[214–218] has been shown to be mediated by various transcription factors, including cyclic nucleotide response element binding proteins (CREBs); cyclic nucleotide response element binding modulators (CREMs), most of which seem to be antagonists for CREBs; and the activating transcription factor family (ATF-1, ATF-2, ATF-3). In addition to the CREB-CREM-ATF family, nerve growth factor–inducible factors (NGFI-A and NGFI-B) and activator protein-2 (AP-2) have been shown to be inducible by cAMP.[219, 220] The promoter region of the human and mouse glucocorticoid receptor gene contains numerous binding sites for most of these transcription factors, providing a mechanism whereby cAMP might increase glucocorticoid receptor expression.[221, 222]

Using in situ hybridization and immunocytochemical methods, neonatal handling was found to induce a modest increase in hippocampal AP-2 mRNA expression, an 8- to 10-fold increase in NGFI-A mRNA, an increase in NGFI-A immunoreactivity, no changes in either CREB or phosphorylated CREB staining, and elimination of CREM staining in the hippocampus. Most CREM isoforms are believed to function as CREB antagonists at the cyclic nucleotide response element binding sites; thus, a reduction in CREM might function to enhance CREB-regulated gene transcription. J. Diorio and M.J. Meaney (personal communication, 1995) have shown that the handling-induced increase in hippocampal NGFI-A mRNA expression is blocked by ketanserin, thus completing the circle putatively linking these factors, thyroid hormones, and serotonin effects on hippocampal glucocorticoid receptor mRNA expression and receptor density. Of further interest is the observation that in hippocampal cell culture systems, the effects of 5-HT on glucocorticoid receptor levels persisted after 5-HT withdrawal from the medium for at least 50 days. Thus, the effect of 5-HT on glucocorticoid receptor density observed in hippocampal culture cells mimics the long-term effects of early environmental events.

Because this effect continued in the absence of 5-HT in vitro and there was no in vivo evidence of sustained 5-HT turnover or 5-HT innervation of the hippocampus,[208] it is unlikely that a sustained increase in hippocampal exposure to 5-HT can be invoked as an explanation. Alternatively, handling may induce a "structural" change in the glucocorticoid receptor gene (and/or the promoter region), which sustains a difference in basal transcription rates throughout the life of the animal. This would represent a most intriguing example of receptor imprinting occurring in response to an environmental signal. Obviously, considerable research remains to be performed in this area. However, it may be speculated that the process of DNA methylation, which is quite active during early development, may contribute to inactivation of selected genes, thus rendering gene expression tissue specific.[223] The glucocorticoid receptor promoter region is rich in methylation sites. If some of these sequences serve as binding sites for enhancers, such as the cAMP-inducible transcription factors discussed earlier, and the binding of these factors is enhanced during early development, then methylation at these sites could be attenuated by the presence of the protein-DNA binding. This would then leave these sites unmethylated and available in later life, thus affording a greater number of potential sites in the promoter for enhanced gene expression. Although this scenario is highly speculative, handling does increase NGFI-A expression and might also increase CREB binding through a decrease in CREM expression. These postulated mechanisms, although only partially supported by available data, offer logical pathways leading to early environmental influences on the differentiation of neuronal populations.

Glucocorticoids exert numerous effects throughout the CNS and particularly in the hippocampus, including regulation of $GABA_A$ subunit expression,[224] modulation of mRNA for the growth-associated protein GAP-43 (whose expression is correlated with axonal growth and neuronal plasticity) and neurotropic factors,[225] and hippocampal neuronal survival and dendritic morphology.[226–229] These effects of glucocorticoids may significantly alter signal processing in the animal. Environmental effects on the development of HPA responses to stress last throughout the life of the animal, and these differences partially contribute to individual differences in vulnerability to stress-induced illness.[170, 230] Together, these data provide an interesting and compelling example of how a cascade of neural processes induced by aspects of an animal's early environment may lead to lifelong individual variability and may either enhance or reduce vulnerability to pathology in later life.

References

1. Hill AV: Trails and Trials in Physiology. London: Edward Arnold, 1965.
2. Huxley AF: Reflections on Muscle. Liverpool, UK: Liverpool University Press, 1980.
3. Bodian D: Neuron junctions: A revolutionary decade. Anat Rec 1973; 174:73–88.
4. Katz B: The Release of Neural Transmitter Substances. Liverpool, UK: Liverpool University Press, 1969.
5. Coombs JS, Eccles JC, Fatt P: Excitatory synaptic action in motoneurones. J Physiol (Lond) 1955; 130:374–395.
6. Coombs JS, Eccles JC, Fatt P: The specific ionic conductances and the ionic movements across the motoneuronal membrane that produce the inhibitory postsynaptic potential. J Physiol (Lond) 1955; 130:326–373.
7. Kuffler SW, Yoshikami D: The number of transmitter molecules in a quantum: An estimate from iontophoretic application of acetylcholine at the neuromuscular synapse. J Physiol (Lond) 1975; 251:465–482.
8. Coombs JS, Curtis DR, Eccles JC: The generation of impulses in motoneurones. J Physiol (Lond) 1957; 139:232–235.
9. Eccles JC: From electrical to chemical transmission in the central nervous system. Notes Rec R Soc London 1976;30:219–230.
10. Hodgkin AL: The Conduction of the Nervous Impulse. Liverpool, UK: Liverpool University Press, 1964.
11. Torri-Tarrelli F, Grohavaz F, Fesce R, Ceccarelli B: Temporal coincidence between synaptic vesicle fusion and quantal secretion of acetylcholine. J Cell Biol 1985; 101:1386–1399.
12. Gray EG: Synaptic vesicles and microtubules in frog motor endplates. Proc R Soc Lond B Biol Sci 1978; 203:219–227.
13. Miller TM, Heuser JE: Endocytosis of synaptic vesicle membrane at the frog neuromuscular junction. J Cell Biol 1984;98:685–698.
14. Katz B, Miledi R: Input/output relation of a single synapse. Nature 1966; 212:1242–1245.
15. Bylund DB, Eikenberg DC, Hieble JP, et al: International Union of Pharmacology nomenclature of adrenoceptors. Pharmacol Rev 1994; 46:121–136.
16. Watson SP, Girdlestone D: 1995 Receptor and ion channel nomenclature supplement. Trends Pharmacol Sci 1995.
17. Ross EM: Pharmacodynamics: Mechanisms of drug action and the relationship between drug concentration and effect. In Gilman AG, Rall TW, Nies AS, Taylor P (eds): The Pharmacological Basis of Therapeutics. New York: Permagon Press, 1990:33–48.
18. Eccles JC, Eccles RM, Magni F: Central inhibitory action attributable to presynaptic depolarization produced by muscle afferent volleys. J Physiol (Lond) 1961; 159:147–166.
19. Frank K, Fuortes MGF: Presynaptic and postsynaptic inhibition of monosynaptic reflexes. Fed Proc 1957; 16:39–40.
20. Cooper JR, Bloom FE, Roth RH: The Biochemical Basis of Neuropharmacology. New York: Oxford University Press, 1991.
21. Siegel GJ, Agranoff BW, Albers RW, Molinoff PB: Basic Neurochemistry. New York: Raven Press, 1994.
22. Bloom FE, Kupfer DJ: Psychopharmacology: The Fourth Generation of Progress. New York: Raven Press, 1995.
23. Paton WDM: Central and synaptic transmission in the nervous system. Annu Rev Physiol 1958; 20:431–470.
24. Kebabian JW, Calne DB: Multiple receptors for dopamine. Nature 1979; 277:93–96.
25. Civelli O: Molecular biology of the dopamine receptor subtypes. In Bloom FE, Kupfer DJ (eds): Psychopharmacology: The Fourth Generation of Progress. New York: Raven Press, 1995:155–162.
26. Loewi O: Über humorale Übertragbarkeit der Herznervenwirkung. Pflugers Arch Gesamte Physiol Menschen Tiere 1921; 189:239–242.
27. Dale HH, Dudley HW: The presence of histamine and acetylcholine in the spleen of the ox and the horse. J Physiol (Lond) 1929; 68:97–123.
28. Numa S, Noda M, Takahashi H, et al: Molecular structure of the nicotinic acetylcholine receptor. Cold Spring Harb Symp Quant Biol 1983; 48:57–69.
29. Haga K, Haga T, Ichiyama A, et al: Functional reconstitution of purified muscarinic receptors and inhibitory guanine nucleotide regulatory protein. Nature 1985; 316:731–733.
30. Hoyer D, Clarke DE, Fozard JR, et al: International Union of Pharmacology classification of receptors for 5-hydroxytryptamine (serotonin). Pharmacol Rev 1994; 46:157–203.
31. Hill DR, Bowery NG: ^{3}H-Baclofen and ^{3}H-GABA bind to bicuculline-insensitive $GABA_B$ sites in rat brain. Nature 1981; 290:149–152.
32. Bormann J, Hamill OP, Sakmann B: Mechanism of anion permeation through channels gated by glycine and γ-aminobutyric acid in mouse cultured spinal neurons. J Physiol (Lond) 1987; 385:243–286.
33. Monaghan DT, Bridges RJ, Cotman CW: The excitatory amino acid receptors: Their classes, pharmacology and distinct properties in the function of the central nervous system. Annu Rev Pharmacol Toxicol 1989; 29:365–402.
34. Schoepfer R, Monyer H, Sommer B, et al: Molecular biology of glutamate receptors. Prog Neurobiol 1994; 42:353–357.
35. Sugiyama H, Ito I, Hirono C: A new type of glutamate receptor linked to inositol phospholipid metabolism. Nature 1987; 325:531–533.
36. Douglass J, Civelli O, Herbert E: Polyprotein gene expression: Generation of diversity of neuroendocrine peptides. Annu Rev Biochem 1984; 53:665–715.
37. Amara SG, Jones V, Rosenfeld MG, et al: Alternative RNA processing in calcitonin gene expression generates mRNAs encoding different polypeptide products. Nature 1982; 298:240–244.
38. Hökfelt T, Elfvin LG, Elde R, et al: Occurrence of somatostatin-like immunoreactivity in some peripheral sympathetic noradrenergic neurons. Proc Natl Acad Sci USA 1977; 74:3587–3591.
39. Hökfelt T, Everitt B, Holets VR, et al: Coexistence of peptides and other active molecules in neurons: Diversity of chemical signalling potential. In Iversen LL, Goodman E (eds): Fast and Slow Chemical Signalling in the Nervous System. New York: Oxford University Press, 1986:205–231.
40. Selye H: Correlations between the chemical structure and the pharmacological actions of the steroids. Endocrinology 1942; 30:437–453.
41. Mellon SH: Neurosteroids: Biochemistry, modes of action, and clinical relevance. J Clin Endocrinol Metab 1994; 78:1003–1008.
42. Majewsha MD, Harrison NL, Schwartz RD, et al: Steroid hormone metabolites are barbiturate-like modulators of the GABA receptor. Science 1986; 232:1004–1007.
43. Gee KW, Bolger MB, Brinton RE, et al: Steroid modulation of the chloride ionophore in rat brain: Structure-activity requirements, regional dependence, and mechanism of action. J Pharmacol Exp Ther 1988; 246:803–812.
44. Morrow AL, Pace JR, Purdy RH: Characterization of steroid interactions with gamma-aminobutyric acid receptor–gated chloride ion channels: Evidence for multiple steroid recognition sites. Mol Pharmacol 1990; 37:263–270.
45. Furchgott RF, Zawadzki JV: The obligatory role of endothelial cells in the relaxation of arterial smooth muscle by acetylcholine. Nature 1980; 286:373–376.
46. Garthwaite J: Nitric oxide signalling in the nervous system. Semin Neurosci 1993; 5:171–180.
47. Grossman A: Editorial: NO news is good news. Endocrinology 1994; 134:1003–1005.
48. Edelman GM, Gally JA: Nitric oxide: Linking space and time in the brain. Proc Natl Acad Sci USA 1992; 89:11651–11652.
49. Dawson TM, Snyder SH: Gases as biological messengers: Nitric oxide and carbon monoxide in brain. J Neurosci 1994; 14:5147–5159.

49a. Kraepelin E: Über die Beeinflussung einfacher psychischer Vorgänge durch einige Arzneimittel. Jena: Fischer, 1892.

50. Bel N, Artigas F: Chronic treatment with fluvoxamine increases extracellular serotonin in frontal cortex but not in raphe nucleus. Synapse 1993; 15:243–245.
51. Nestler EJ, McMahon A, Sabban EL, et al: Chronic antidepressant administration decreases the expression of tyrosine hydroxylase in the rat locus coeruleus. Proc Natl Acad Sci USA 1990; 87:7522–7526.
52. Vetulani J, Sulser F: Action of various antidepressant treatments reduces reactivity of noradrenergic cyclicAMP generating system in limbic forebrain. Nature 1975; 257:495–496.
53. Pryor JC, Sulser F: Evolution of the monoamine hypotheses of depression. In Horton RW, Katona C (eds): Biological Aspects of Affective Disorders. London: Academic Press, 1990:77–94.
54. Paul IA, Nowak G, Layer RT, et al: Adaptation of the *N*-methyl-D-aspartate receptor complex following chronic antidepressant treatments. J Pharmacol Exp Ther 1994; 269:95–102.
55. Hyman SE, Nestler EJ: The Molecular Foundations of Psychiatry. Washington, DC: American Psychiatric Press, 1993.
56. Duman RS, Nestler EJ: Signal transduction pathways for catecholamine receptors. In Blomm FE, Kupfer DJ (eds): Psychopharmacol-

ogy: The Fourth Generation of Progress. New York: Raven Press, 1995:303–320.
57. Nestler EJ, Duman RS: Intracellular messenger pathways as mediators of neural plasticity. In Bloom FE, Kupfer DJ (eds): Psychopharmacology: The Fourth Generation of Progress. New York: Raven Press, 1995:695–704.
58. Bunney BS, Chiodo LA, Grace AA: Midbrain dopamine system electrophysiological functioning: A review and new hypothesis. Synapse 1991; 9:79–94.
59. Chiodo LA, Bunney BS: Typical and atypical neuroleptics: Differential effects of chronic administration on the activity of A9 and A10 midbrain dopaminergic neurons. J Neurosci 1983; 3:1607–1619.
60. Chiodo LA, Bunney BS: Possible mechanisms by which repeated clozapine administration differentially affects the activity of two subpopulations of midbrain dopamine neurons. J Neurosci 1985; 5:2539–2544.
61. Deutch AY, Moghaddam B, Innis RB, et al: Mechanisms of action of atypical antipsychotic drugs: Implications for novel therapeutic strategies for schizophrenia. Schizophr Res 1991; 4:121–136.
62. Moghaddam B, Bunney BS: Acute effects of typical and atypical antipsychotic drugs on the release of dopamine from prefrontal cortex, nucleus accumbens, and striatum of the rat: An in vivo microdialysis study. J Neurochem 1990; 54:1755–1760.
63. Ichikawa J, Meltzer HY: Differential effects of repeated treatment with haloperidol and clozapine on dopamine release and metabolism in the striatum and the nucleus accumbens. J Pharmacol Exp Ther 1991; 256:248–357.
64. Farde L, Hall H, Ehrin E, et al: Quantitative analysis of D_2 dopamine receptor binding in the living human brain by PET. Science 1986; 231:258–260.
65. Farde L, Wiesel FA, Halldin C, et al: Central D_2-dopamine receptor occupancy in schizophrenic patients treated with antipsychotic drugs. Arch Gen Psychiatry 1988; 45:71–76.
66. Farde L, Nordstrom AL, Weisel FA, et al: Positron emission tomographic analysis of central D_1 and D_2 dopamine receptor occupancy in patients treated with classical neuroleptics and clozapine. Relation to extrapyramidal side effects. Arch Gen Psychiatry 1993; 49:538–544.
67. Farde L, Weisel FA, Nordstrom AL, Sedvall G: D_1- and D_2-dopamine receptor occupancy during treatment with conventional and atypical neuroleptics. Psychopharmacology (Berl) 1989; 99(suppl):S28–S31.
68. Sokoloff P, Giros B, Martres MP, et al: Molecular cloning and characterization of a novel dopamine receptor (D_3) as a target for neuroleptics. Nature 1990; 247:146–151.
69. Sokoloff P, Martres MP, Giros B, et al: The third dopamine receptor (D_3) as a novel target for antipsychotics. Biochem Pharmacol 1992; 43:656–666.
70. Seeman P: Receptor selectivities of atypical neuroleptics. In Meltzer HY (ed): Novel Antipsychotic Drugs. New York: Raven Press, 1992:145–154.
71. Seeman P: Dopamine receptor sequences: Therapeutic levels of neuroleptics occupy D_2 receptors, clozapine occupies D_4. Neuropsychopharmacology 1992; 7:261–284.
72. Van Tol HHM, Bunzow JR, Guan H, et al: Cloning of the gene for a human dopamine D_4 receptor with high affinity for the antipsychotic clozapine. Nature 1991; 350:610–614.
73. Seeman P, Hong-Chang G, Van Tol HHM: Dopamine D_4 receptors elevated in schizophrenia. Nature 1993; 365:441–445.
74. Lundberg T, Lindström LH, Hartvig P, et al: Striatal and frontal cortex binding of 11-C-labelled clozapine visualized by positron emission tomography (PET) in drug-free schizophrenics and healthy volunteers. Psychopharmacology (Berl) 1989; 99:8–12.
75. Seeman P, Niznik HB, Guan HC, et al: Link between D_1 and D_2 dopamine receptors is reduced in schizophrenia and Huntington diseased brain. Proc Natl Acad Sci USA 1989; 86:10156–10160.
76. Meltzer HY, Matsubara S, Lee JC: Classification of typical and atypical drugs on the basis of dopamine D_1, D_2 and serotonin$_2$ pK_i values. J Pharmacol Exp Ther 1989; 251:238–246.
77. Sunahara RK, Guan HC, O'Dowd BF, et al: Cloning of the gene for a human dopamine D_5 receptor with higher affinity for dopamine than D_1. Nature 1991; 350:614–619.
78. Monsma FJ, Shen Y, Ward RP, et al: Cloning and expression of a novel serotonin receptor with high affinity for tricyclic psychotropic drugs. Mol Pharmacol 1993; 43:320–327.
79. Shen Y, Monsma FJ, Metcalf MA, et al: Molecular cloning and expression of a 5-hydroxytryptamine$_7$ serotonin receptor subtype. J Biol Chem 1993; 268:18200–18204.
80. Roth BL, Craigo SC, Choudhary MS, et al: Binding of typical and atypical antipsychotic agents to 5-hydroxytryptamine-6 and 5-hydroxytryptamine-7 receptors. J Pharmacol Exp Ther 1994; 268:1403–1410.
81. Musacchio JM: The psychotomimetic effects of opiates and the σ receptor. Neuropsychopharmacology 1990; 3:191–199.
82. Mohler H, Okada T: Benzodiazepine receptors: Demonstration in the central nervous system. Science 1977; 198:849–851.
83. Martin JL: The benzodiazepines and their receptors: 25 years of progress. Neuropharmacology 1987; 26:957–970.
84. Burt DR, Kamatchi GL: $GABA_A$ receptor subtypes: From pharmacology to molecular biology. FASEB J 1991; 5:2916–2923.
85. Wisden W, Seeburg PH: $GABA_A$ receptor channels: From subunits to functional entities. Curr Opin Neurobiol 1992; 2:263–269.
86. Pritchett DB, Lüddens H, Seeburg PH: Importance of a novel $GABA_A$ receptor subunit for benzodiazepine pharmacology. Nature 1989; 338:582–585.
87. Knoflach F, Drescher U, Scheurer L, et al: The γ3-subunit of the $GABA_A$-receptor confers sensitivity to benzodiazepine receptor ligands. FEBS Lett 1991; 293:191–194.
88. Ducic I, Puia G, Vicini S, Costa E: Triazolam is more efficacious than diazepam in a broad spectrum of recombinant $GABA_A$ receptors. Eur J Pharmacol 1993; 244:29–35.
89. Giusti P, Ducic I, Puia G, et al: Imidazenil: A new partial positive allosteric modulator of γ-aminobutyric acid (GABA) action at $GABA_A$ receptors. J Pharmacol Exp Ther 1993; 266:1018–1028.
90. Hu X, Ticku MK: Chronic benzodiazepine agonist treatment produces functional uncoupling of the GABA–benzodiazepine receptor ionophore complex in cortical neurons. Mol Pharmacol 1994; 45:618–625.
91. Miller LG, Greenblatt DJ, Barnhill JG, Shader RI: Chronic benzodiazepine administration. I. Tolerance is associated with benzodiazepine receptor downregulation and decreased γ-aminobutyric acid$_A$ receptor function. J Pharmacol Exp Ther 1988; 246:170–176.
92. Kang I, Miller LG: Decreased $GABA_A$ receptor subunit mRNA concentrations following chronic lorazepam administration. Br J Pharmacol 1991; 103:1285–1287.
93. O'Donovan MC, Buckland PR, McGuffin P: Levels of $GABA_A$ receptor subunit mRNA in rat brain following flurazepam treatment. J Psychopharmacol 1992; 6:364–369.
94. Zhao T-J, Chiu TH, Rosenberg HC: Reduced expression of gamma-aminobutyric acid type A/benzodiazepine receptor gamma2 and alpha5 subunit mRNAs in brain regions of flurazepam-treated rats. Mol Pharmacol 1994; 45:657–663.
95. Jenck F, Moreau J-L, Bonetti EP, et al: Ro 19-8022, a nonbenzodiazepine partial agonist at benzodiazepine receptors: Neuropharmacological profile of a potential anxiolytic. J Pharmacol Exp Ther 1992; 262:1121–1127.
96. Haefely W: The GABA-benzodiazepine interaction fifteen years later. Neurochem Res 1990; 15:169–174.
97. Leonard BE: Commentary on the mode of action of benzodiazepines. J Psychiatr Res 1993; 27:193–207.
98. Rothstein JD, Garland W, Puia G, et al: Purification and characterization of naturally occurring benzodiazepine receptor ligands in rat and human brain. J Neurochem 1992; 58:2102–2115.
99. Doble A, Martin IL: Multiple benzodiazepine receptors: No reason for anxiety. Trends Pharmacol Sci 1992; 13:76–81.
100. MacDonald RL, McLean MJ: Anticonvulsant drugs: Mechanisms of action. Adv Neurol 1986; 44:713–735.
101. Wafford KA, Burnett DM, Leidenheimer NJ, et al: Ethanol sensitivity of the $GABA_A$ receptor expressed in *Xenopus* oocytes requires 8 amino acids contained in the γ2L subunit. Neuron 1991; 7:27–33.
102. Taylor DP: Serotonin agents in anxiety. Ann N Y Acad Sci 1990; 600:545–557.
103. Tyrer P: Anxiolytics not acting at the benzodiazepine receptor: Beta blockers. Prog Neuropsychopharmacol Biol Psychiatry 1992; 16:17–26.
104. Lenox RH, Manji HK: Lithium. In Schatzberg AF, Nemeroff CB (eds): Textbook of Psychopharmacology. Washington, DC: American Psychiatric Press, 1995:303–349.
105. Manji HK, Hsiao JK, Risby ED, Potter WZ: The mechanisms of action of lithium. Arch Gen Psychiatry 1991; 48:505–512.

106. Masana MI, Bitran JA, Hsiao JK: In vivo evidence that lithium inactivates G_i modulation of adenylate cyclase in brain. J Neurochem 1992; 59:200–205.
107. Avissar S, Schreiber G: Ziskind-Somerfeld research award. The involvement of guanine nucleotide binding proteins in the pathogenesis and treatment of affective disorders. Biol Psychiatry 1992; 31:435–459.
108. Li PP, Tam YK, Young LT, Warsh JJ: Lithium decreases G_s, $G_{i\text{-}1}$ and $G_{i\text{-}2}$ alpha-subunit mRNA levels in rat cortex. Eur J Pharmacol 1991; 206:165–166.
109. Manji HK, Bitran JA, Masana MI, Potter WZ: Signal transduction modulation by lithium: Cell culture, cerebral microdialysis and human studies. Psychopharmacol Bull 1991; 27:199–208.
110. Colin SF, Chang HC, Mollner S, et al: Chronic lithium regulates the expression of adenylate cyclase and G_i-protein alpha subunit in rat cerebral cortex. Proc Natl Acad Sci USA 1991; 88:10634–10637.
111. Manji HK, Lenox RH: Long term action of lithium: A role for transcriptional and posttranscriptional factors regulated by protein kinase C. Synapse 1994; 16:11–28.
112. Blier P, de Montigny C: Short-term lithium administration enhances serotonergic neurotransmission: Electrophysiological evidence in the rat CNS. Psychopharmacology (Berl) 1985; 113:69–77.
113. Blier P, de Montigny C, Tardif D: Short term lithium treatment enhances responsiveness of postsynaptic 5-HT_{1A} receptors without altering 5-HT autoreceptor sensitivity: An electrophysiological study in the rat brain. Synapse 1987; 1:225–232.
114. Zona C, Tancredi V, Palma E, et al: Potassium currents in rat cortical neurons in culture are enhanced by the antiepileptic drug carbamazepine. Can J Physiol Pharmacol 1990; 68:545–547.
115. Macdonald RL: Carbamazepine: Mechanisms of action. In Levy RH, Drefuss FH, Mattson RH (eds): Antiepileptic Drugs, 3rd ed. New York: Raven Press, 1989:447–455.
116. Post RM, Weiss SRB, Chuang D-M: Mechanisms of action of anticonvulsants in affective disorders: Comparisons with lithium. J Clin Psychopharmacol 1992; 12:23S–35S.
117. Cotariu D, Zaidman JL, Evans S: Neurophysiological and biochemical changes evoked by valproic acid in the central nervous system. Prog Neurobiol 1990; 34:343–354.
118. Löscher W: Effects of the antiepileptic drug valproate on metabolism and function of inhibitory and excitatory amino acids in the brain. Neurochem Res 1993; 18:485–502.
119. Chiarello RJ, Cole JD: The use of psychostimulants in general psychiatry: A reconsideration. Arch Gen Psychiatry 1987; 44:286–292.
120. Wall SC, Gu H, Rudnick G: Biogenic amine flux mediated by cloned transporters stably expressed in cultured cell lines: Amphetamine specificity for inhibition and efflux. Mol Pharmacol 1995; 47:544–550.
121. Kalivas PW, Stewart J: Dopamine transmission in the initiation and expression of drug- and stress-induced sensitization of motor activity. Brain Res Rev 1991; 16:223–241.
122. Grace AA: The tonic/phasic model of dopamine system regulation: Its relevance for understanding how stimulant abuse can alter basal ganglia function. Drug Alcohol Depend 1995; 37:111–129.
123. Håkansson L: Mechanism of action of cholinesterase inhibitors in Alzheimer's disease. Acta Neurol Scand Suppl 1993; 149:7–9.
124. Adem A: The next generation of cholinesterase inhibitors. Acta Neurol Scand Suppl 1993; 149:10–12.
125. Araujo DM, Lapchak PA, Collier B, Quirion R: Evidence that somatostatin enhances endogenous acetylcholine release in the rat hippocampus. J Neurochem 1990; 55:1546–1555.
126. Alhainen K, Sirviö J, Helkala E-L, et al: Somatostatin and cognitive function in Alzheimer's disease—the relationship of cerebrospinal fluid somatostatin increase with clinical response to tetrahydroaminoacridine. Neurosci Lett 1991; 130:46–48.
127. Doods HN, Quirion R, Mihm G, et al: Therapeutic potential of CNS-active M_2 antagonists: Novel structures and pharmacology. Life Sci 1993; 52:497–503.
128. Elrod K, Buccafusco JJ: Correlation of the amnestic effects of nicotinic antagonists with inhibition of regional brain acetylcholine synthesis in rats. J Pharmacol Exp Ther 1991; 258:403–409.
129. Nicholson CD: Pharmacology of nootropics and metabolically active compounds in relation to their use in dementia. Psychopharmacology (Berl) 1990; 101:147–159.
130. Mondadori C, Bhatnager A, Borkowski J, Hüsler A: Involvement of a steroidal component in the mechanism of action of piracetam-like nootropics. Brain Res 1990; 506:101–108.
131. Imperato A, Obinu MC, Dazzi L, et al: Co-dergocrine (Hydergine) regulates striatal and hippocampal acetylcholine release through D_2 receptors. Neuroreport 1994; 5:674–676.
132. Schneider LS, Tariot PN: Emerging drugs for Alzheimer's disease: Mechanisms of action and prospects for cognitive enhancing medications. Med Clin North Am 1994; 78:911–934.
133. Branconnier RJ, Branconnier ME, Walshe TM, et al: Blocking the Ca^{2+}-activated cytotoxic mechanisms of cholinergic neuronal death: A novel treatment strategy for Alzheimer's disease. Psychopharmacol Bull 1992; 28:175–181.
134. Azmitia EC, Buchan AM, Williams JH: Structural and functional restoration by collateral sprouting of hippocampal 5-HT neurons. Nature 1978; 274:374–376.
135. Gorski RA: Gonadal hormones and the development of neuroendocrine function. In Martini L, Ganong WF (eds): Frontiers in Neuroendocrinology. London: Oxford University Press, 1971:237–290.
136. Frankfurt M: Gonadal steroids and neuronal plasticity: Studies in the adult rat hypothalamus. Ann N Y Acad Sci 1994; 743:45–59.
137. McEwen BS: Gonadal steroids: Humoral modulators of nerve cell function. Mol Cell Endocrinol 1980; 18:151–164.
138. Nestler EJ, Hope BT, Widnell KL: Drug addiction: A model for the molecular basis of neural plasticity. Neuron 1993; 11:995–1006.
139. Aghajanian GK: Tolerance of locus coeruleus neurons to morphine and suppression of withdrawal response by clonidine. Nature 1978; 267:186–188.
140. Bozarth MA: New perspectives on cocaine addiction: Recent findings from animal research. Can J Physiol Pharmacol 1989; 67:1158–1167.
141. Alreja M, Aghajanian GK: Opiates suppress a resting sodium-dependent inward current in addition to activating an outward potassium current in locus coeruleus neurons. J Neurosci 1993; 13:3525–3532.
142. Kogan JH, Nestler EJ, Aghajanian GK: Elevated basal firing rates and enhanced responses to 8-Br-cAMP in locus coeruleus neurons in brain slices from opiate-dependent rats. Eur J Pharmacol 1992; 211:47–53.
143. Nestler EJ, Erdos JJ, Terwilliger RZ, et al: Regulation of G-proteins by chronic morphine treatment in the rat locus coeruleus. Brain Res 1989; 476:230–239.
144. Duman RS, Tallman JF, Nestler EJ: Acute and chronic opiate-regulation of adenylate cyclase in brain: Specific effects in the locus coeruleus. J Pharmacol Exp Ther 1988; 246:1033–1039.
145. Guitart X, Hayward M, Nisenbaum LK, et al: Identification of MARPP-58, a morphine- and cyclic AMP–regulated phosphoprotein of 58 kDa, as tyrosine hydroxylase: Evidence for regulation of its expression by chronic morphine in the rat locus coeruleus. J Neurosci 1990; 10:2649–2659.
146. Terwilliger RZ, Beitner-Johnson D, Sevarino KA, et al: A general role for adaptations in G-proteins and the cyclic AMP system in mediating the chronic actions of morphine and cocaine on neuronal function. Brain Res 1991; 548:100–110.
147. Nestler EJ, Terwilliger RZ, Walker JR, et al: Chronic cocaine treatment decreases levels of the G-proteins $G_{i\alpha}$ and $G_{o\alpha}$ in discrete regions of rat brain. J Neurochem 1990; 55:1079–1082.
148. Beitner-Johnson D, Guitart X, Nestler EJ: Neurofilament proteins and the mesolimbic dopamine system: Common regulation by chronic morphine and chronic cocaine in the rat ventral tegmental area. J Neurosci 1992; 12:2165–2176.
149. Henry DJ, White FJ: Repeated cocaine administration causes persistent enhancement of D_1 dopamine receptor sensitivity within the rat nucleus accumbens. J Pharmacol Exp Ther 1991; 258:882–890.
150. Voronin LL: Quantal analysis of hippocampal long-term potentiation. Rev Neurosci 1994; 5:141–170.
151. Lisman J: The CaM kinase II hypothesis for the storage of synaptic memory. Trends Neurosci 1994; 17:406–412.
152. Hawkins RD, Zhuo M, Arancio O: Nitric oxide and carbon monoxide as possible retrograde messengers in hippocampal long-term potentiation. J Neurobiol 1994; 25:652–665.
153. Izquirdo I: Pharmacological evidence for a role of long-term potentiation in memory. FASEB J 1994; 8:1139–1145.
154. McEwen BS: Corticosteroids and hippocampal plasticity. Ann N Y Acad Sci 1994; 746:134–142.

155. Shaw CA, Lanius RA, van den Doel K: The origin of synaptic neuroplasticity: Crucial molecules or a dynamical cascade? Brain Res Brain Res Rev 1994; 19:241–263.
156. Andrews MW, Rosenblum LA: The development of affiliative and agonistic social patterns in differentially reared monkeys. Child Dev 1994; 65:1398–1404.
157. Anisman JD, Zacharko RM: Depression: The predisposing influence of stress. Behav Brain Sci 1982; 5:89–137.
158. Denenberg VH: Critical periods, stimulus input, and emotional reactivity: A theory of infantile stimulation. Psychol Rev 1964; 71:335–351.
159. Harlow HF, Harlow MK: Social deprivation in monkeys. Sci Am 1962; 207:136–146.
160. Hofer MA: Early relationships as regulators of infant physiology and behavior. Acta Paediatr 1994; 397:9–18.
161. Insel TR: Long-term neural consequences of stress during development: Is early experience a form of chemical imprinting? In Carroll BJ, Barrett JE (eds): Psychopathology and the Brain. New York: Raven Press, 1991:133–152.
162. Levine S, Haltmeyer GC, Karas GG, Denenberg VH: Physiological and behavioral effects of infantile stimulation. Physiol Behav 1967; 2:55–63.
163. McEwen BS: Stressful experience, brain, and emotions: Developmental, genetic, and hormonal influences. In Gazzaniga MS, Bizzi E, Black IB, et al (eds): The Cognitive Neurosciences. Cambridge, MA: The MIT Press, 1994:1117–1135.
164. Meaney MJ, Tannenbaum B, Francis D, et al: Early environmental programming of hypothalamic-pituitary-adrenal responses to stress. Semin Neurosci 1994; 6:247–259.
165. Piazza PV, Deminiere J-M, Maccari S, et al: Individual vulnerability to drug self-administration: Action of corticosterone on dopaminergic systems as a possible pathophysiological mechanism. In Willner P, Scheel-Kruger J (eds): The Mesolimbic Dopamine System: From Motivation to Action. New York: John Wiley & Sons, 1991:473–494.
166. Ambelas A: Life events and mania: A special relationship? Br J Psychiatry 1987; 150:235–240.
167. Benes FM: Developmental changes in stress adaptation in relation to psychopathology. Dev Psychopathol 1994; 6:723–739.
168. Breslau N, Davis GC, Andreski P, Peterson E: Traumatic events and posttraumatic stress disorder in an urban population of young adults. Arch Gen Psychiatry 1991; 48:216–222.
169. Brown GW, Bifulco A, Harris TO: Life events, vulnerability and onset of depression. Br J Psychiatry 1987; 150:30–42.
170. Chrousos GP, Gold PW: The concepts of stress and stress system disorders. JAMA 1992; 267:1244–1252.
171. Kendler KS, Kessler RC, Walters EE, et al: Stressful life events, genetic liability, and onset of an episode of major depression in women. Am J Psychiatry 1995; 152:833–842.
172. Purves D, Lichtman JW: Principles of Neural Development. Sunderland, MA: Sinauer Associates, 1985.
173. Hatten ME: The role of migration in central nervous system neuronal development. Curr Opin Neurobiol 1993; 3:38–44.
174. Rahmann H, Rahmann M: Neuronal plasticity. In Freeman SJ (trans): The Neurobiological Basis of Memory and Behavior. New York: Springer-Verlag, 1992:187–277.
175. Whitaker-Azmitia PM: The role of serotonin and serotonin receptors in development of the mammalian nervous system. In Zagon IS, McLaughlin PJ (eds): Receptors in the Developing Nervous System: Neurotransmitters, Volume 2. London: Chapman & Hall, 1993:43–53.
176. Cajal SR: New Ideas on the Structure of the Nervous System in Man and Vertebrates (translation of Swanson N, Swanson LW: Les nouvelles idées sur la structure des centres nerveux chez l'homme et chez les vertébrés). Cambridge, MA: The MIT Press, 1990.
177. Kandel ER, Jessell TM, Schacher S: Early experience and the fine tuning of synaptic connections. In Kandel ER, Schwartz JH, Jessell TM (eds): Principles of Neural Science, 3rd ed. New York: Elsevier, 1991:945–958.
178. Black I: Trophic interactions and brain plasticity. In Gazzaniga MS, Bizzi E, Black IB, et al (eds): The Cognitive Neurosciences. Cambridge, MA: The MIT Press, 1995:9–17.
179. Jessell TM: Neuronal survival and synapse formation. In Kandel ER, Schwartz JH, Jessell TM (eds): Principles of Neural Science, 3rd ed. New York: Elsevier, 1991:929–944.
180. Rakic P, Cameron RS, Komuro H: Recognition, adhesion, transmembrane signaling and cell motility in guided neuronal migration. Curr Opin Neurobiol 1994; 4:63–69.
181. von Senden M, Heath P (trans): Space and Sight. Glencoe, IL: Free Press, 1960. Originally published in 1932.
182. Wiesel TN, Hubel DH: Single-cell responses in striate cortex of kittens deprived of vision in one eye. J Neurophysiol 1963; 26:1003–1017.
183. Hubel DH, Wiesel TN, LeVay S: Plasticity of ocular dominance columns in monkey striate cortex. Philos Trans R Soc Lond Ser B 1977; 278:377–409.
184. Wagner JP, Seidler FJ, Lappi SE, et al: Role of presynaptic input in the ontogeny of adrenergic cell signaling in rat brain: Beta receptors, adenylate cyclase and c-*fos* protooncogene expression. J Pharmacol Exp Ther 1995; 273:415–426.
185. Bear MF, Daniels JD: The plastic response to monocular deprivation persists in kitten visual cortex after chronic depletion of norepinephrine. J Neurosci 1983; 3:407–416.
186. Kasamatsu T: Enhancement of neuronal plasticity by activating the norepinephrine system in the brain: A remedy for amblyopia. Hum Neurobiol 1982; 1:49–54.
187. Spitz RA: Hospitalism: An inquiry into the genesis of psychiatric conditions in early childhood. Psychoanal Study Child 1945; 1:53–74.
188. Harlow HE, Dodsworth RO, Harlow MK: Total social isolation in monkeys. Proc Natl Acad Sci USA 1965; 54:90–97.
189. Laudenslager ML, Rasmussen KL, Berman CM, et al: Specific antibody levels in free-ranging rhesus monkeys: Relationships to plasma hormones, cardiac parameters, and early behavior. Dev Psychobiol 1993; 26:407–420.
190. Suomi SJ: Models of depression in primates. Psychol Med 1983; 13:465–468.
191. Higley JD, Suomi SJ, Linnoila M: A longitudinal assessment of CSF monoamine metabolite and plasma cortisol concentrations in young rhesus monkeys. Biol Psychiatry 1992; 32:127–145.
192. Higley JD, Hasert MF, Suomi SJ, Linnoila M: Nonhuman primate model of alcohol abuse: Effects of early experience, personality, and stress on alcohol consumption. Proc Natl Acad Sci USA 1991; 88:7261–7265.
193. Andrews MW, Rosenblum LA: Attachment in monkey infants raised in variable- and low-demand environments. Child Dev 1991; 62:686–693.
194. Ader R, Grota LJ: Effects of early experience on adrenocortical reactivity. Physiol Behav 1969; 4:303–305.
195. Meaney MJ, Aitken DH, Sharma S, et al: Postnatal handling increases hippocampal type II, glucocorticoid receptors and enhances adrenocortical negative-feedback efficacy in the rat. Neuroendocrinology 1989; 51:597–604.
196. Bhatnagar S, Shanks N, Meaney MJ: Hypothalamic-pituitary-adrenal function in handled and nonhandled rats in response to chronic stress. J Neuroendocrinol 1995; 7:107–119.
197. O'Donnell D, Larocque S, Seckl JR, Meaney MJ: Postnatal handling alters glucocorticoid, but not mineralocorticoid messenger RNA expression in the hippocampus of adult rats. Brain Res Mol Brain Res 1994; 26:242–248.
198. Sarrieau A, Sharma S, Meaney MJ: Postnatal development and environmental regulation of hippocampal glucocorticoid and mineralocorticoid receptors in the rat. Dev Brain Res 1988; 43:158–162.
199. De Kloet ER: Brain corticosteroid receptor balance and homeostatic control. Front Neuroendocrinol 1991; 12:95–164.
200. Jacobson L, Sapolsky RM: The role of the hippocampus in feedback regulation of the hypothalamic-pituitary-adrenal axis. Endocr Rev 1991; 12:118–134.
201. Viau V, Shanna S, Plotsky PM, Meaney MJ: The hypothalamic-pituitary-adrenal response to stress in handled and nonhandled rats: Differences in stress-induced plasma ACTH secretion are not dependent upon increased corticosterone levels. J Neurosci 1993; 13:1097–1105.
202. Plotsky PM, Meaney MJ: Early, postnatal experience alters hypothalamic corticotropin-releasing factor (CRF) mRNA, median eminence CRF content and stress-induced release in adult rats. Mol Brain Res 1993; 18:195–200.
203. Meaney MJ, Aitken DH, Sapolsky RM: Thyroid hormones influence the development of hippocampal glucocorticoid receptors in the rat: A mechanism for the effects of postnatal handling on the development of the adrenocortical stress response. Neuroendocrinology 1987; 45:278–283.
204. McEwen BS: Steroid hormone effects on brain: Novel insights

connecting cellular and molecular features of brain cells to behavior. In de Kloet ER, Sutanto W (eds): Methods in Neurosciences: Neurobiology of Steroids, Volume 22. San Diego, CA: Academic Press, 1994:525–542.

205. Meaney MJ, O'Donnell D, Viau V, et al: Corticosteroid receptors in rat brain and pituitary during development and hypothalamic-pituitary-adrenal (HPA) function. In McLaughlin P, Zagon I (eds): Receptors and the Developing Nervous System. London: Chapman & Hall, 1994:163–202.
206. Savard P, Merand Y, Di Paolo T, Dupont A: Thyroid hormone regulation of serotonin metabolism in developing rat brain. Brain Res 1984; 292:99–108.
207. Mitchell JB, Iny LJ, Meaney MJ: The role of serotonin in the development and environmental regulation of hippocampal type II corticosteroid receptors. Dev Brain Res 1990; 55:231–235.
208. Smythe JW, Rowe W, Meaney MJ: Neonatal handling alters serotonin turnover and serotonin type 2 receptor density in selected brain regions. Dev Brain Res 1994; 80:183–189.
209. Mitchell JB, Rowe W, Boksa P, Meaney MJ: Serotonin regulates type II, corticosteroid receptor binding in cultured hippocampal cells. J Neurosci 1990; 10:1745–1752.
210. Mitchell JB, Betito K, Rowe W, et al: Serotonergic regulation of type II corticosteroid receptor binding in hippocampal cell cultures: Evidence for the importance of serotonin-induced increases in cAMP levels. Neuroscience 1992; 48:631–639.
211. Sanders-Bush E, Tsutsumi M, Burris KD: Serotonin receptors and phosphatidylinositol turnover. Ann N Y Acad Sci 1990; 600:224–235.
212. Lucas JJ, Hen R: New players in the 5-HT receptor field: Genes and knockouts. Trends Pharmacol Sci 1995; 16:246–262.
213. Tork I: Anatomy of the serotonergic system. Ann N Y Acad Sci 1990; 600:9–35.
214. de Groot RP, Sassone-Corsi P: Hormonal control of gene expression: Multiplicity and versatility of cyclic adenosine 3′,5′-monophosphate-responsive nuclear regulators. Mol Endocrinol 1993; 5:145–153.
215. Habener J: Cyclic AMP response element binding proteins: A cornucopia of transcription factors. Mol Endocrinol 1990; 4:1087–1094.
216. Montminy MR, Gonzalez GA, Yamamoto KK: Regulation of cAMP-inducible genes by CREB. Trends Neurosci 1990; 13:184–188.
217. Vallejo M: Transcriptional control of gene expression by cAMP-response element binding proteins. J Neuroendocrinol 1994; 6:587–596.
218. Yamamoto KK, Gonzales GA, Biggs WH III, Montminy MR: Phosphorylation-induced binding and transcriptional efficacy of nuclear factor CREB. Nature 1988; 334:494–498.
219. Imagawa M, Chiu R, Karin M: Transcription factor AP-2 mediates induction by two different signal-transduction pathways. Protein kinase C and cAMP. Cell 1987; 51:251–260.
220. Vaccarino FM, Hayward MD, Le HN, et al: Induction of immediate early genes by cyclic AMP in primary cultures of neurons from rat cerebral cortex. Mol Brain Res 1993; 19:76–82.
221. Leclerc S, Xie B, Roy R, Govindan MV: Purification of a human glucocorticoid receptor gene promoter–binding protein. J Biol Chem 1991; 266:8711–8719.
222. Strahle U, Schmidt A, Kelsey G, et al: At least three promoters direct expression of the mouse glucocorticoid receptor gene. Proc Natl Acad Sci USA 1992; 89:6731–6735.
223. Eden S, Cedar H: Role of DNA methylation in the regulation of transcription. Curr Opin Genet Dev 1994; 4:255–259.
224. Orchinik M, Weiland NG, McEwen BS: Adrenalectomy selectively regulates $GABA_A$ receptor subunit expression in the hippocampus. Mol Cell Neurosci 1994; 5:451–458.
225. Chao HM, McEwen BS: Glucocorticoids and the expression of mRNAs for neurotrophins, their receptors and GAP-43 in the rat hippocampus. Brain Res Mol Brain Res 1994; 26:271–276.
226. Gould E, Woolley CS, McEwen BS: Short-term glucocorticoid manipulations affect neuronal morphology and survival in the adult dentate gyrus. Neuroscience 1990; 37:367–375.
227. McEwen BS, Cameron H, Chao HM, et al: Adrenal steroids and plasticity of hippocampal neurons: Toward an understanding of underlying cellular and molecular mechanisms. Cell Mol Neurobiol 1993; 13:457–482.
228. Sapolsky RM, Uno H, Rebert CS, Finch CE: Hippocampal damage associated with prolonged glucocorticoid exposure in primates. J Neurosci 1990; 10:2897–2902.
229. Woolley CS, Gould E, McEwen BS: Exposure to excess glucocorticoids alters dendritic morphology of adult hippocampal pyramidal neurons. Brain Res 1990; 531:225–231.
230. McEwen BS, Steller E: Stress and the individual: Mechanisms leading to disease. Arch Intern Med 1993; 153:2093–2101.

CHAPTER

15

Pathophysiological Basis of Psychiatric Disorders: Focus on Mood Disorders and Schizophrenia

Charles B. Nemeroff
Dominique L. Musselman
Kalpana I. Nathan
Alan F. Schatzberg
Michael B. Knable
Joel E. Kleinman
Daniel R. Weinberger
Clinton D. Kilts
Jay M. Weiss

From the time of Hippocrates and Galen, physicians have speculated on the hormonal and biological basis of mental disorders. The 19th century "German School" of psychiatrists searched for the neuropathological basis of behavior disturbances yet to be defined as psychiatric disorders. Indeed, Freud believed that the "whole range of human behavior, normal and pathological" could ultimately be explained in neurochemical and neurohistological terms.

Yet, the elucidation of the pathophysiological basis of mental illness has to await the clearer delineation of psychiatric disorders and the methodological and technological advances that would enable noninvasive studies of brain structure and function in vivo and analysis of brain anatomy and biochemistry at the cellular and molecular levels in postmortem tissue and animal models. With the advent of these capabilities have come remarkable advances in the elucidation of the biological basis of the major psychiatric disorders. Indeed, entire volumes have been devoted to this topic. However, space constraints preclude a comprehensive review of this subject. Instead, we have chosen three major areas that are representative of the research strategies and focus on the most extensively studied and best understood groups of disorders: mood disorders and psychotic disorders. Specifically, we review 1) the biology of mood disorders, 2) the biology of schizophrenia, and 3) animal models of depression and schizophrenia.

MOOD DISORDERS

Neurochemical Hypotheses

The initial models of mood disorders posited a biochemical deficiency in selected neurotransmitter systems that were believed to regulate affect. These specifically hypothesized that biogenic amine metabolism played a key role in the pathophysiological process of depression. Pioneering studies were conducted in the United States by Bunney and Davis,[1] Prange,[2] and Schildkraut,[3] who largely focused on alterations of catecholamine systems. Schildkraut[3] is credited for formally proposing the catecholamine hypothesis of affective disorders, which inspired much of the biological research conducted in the last 30 years. However, substantial

This chapter was adapted from Weiss JM, Kilts CD: Animal models of depression and schizophrenia; Nathan KI, Musselman DL, Schatzberg AF, Nemeroff CB: Biology of mood disorders; and Knable MB, Kleinman JE, Weinberger DR: Neurobiology of schizophrenia. In Schatzberg AF, Nemeroff CB (eds): The American Psychiatric Press Textbook of Psychopharmacology. Washington, DC: American Psychiatric Press, 1995:81–123, 439–499.

data have implicated alterations in several other neuromodulatory systems in mood disorders.

European investigators initiated their studies of the serotoninergic system in the 1960s, positing a serotoninergic deficiency as a prime cause of depressive symptoms.[4, 5] This line of research was further stimulated by the seminal observations of Asberg and colleagues,[6] who reported that a subgroup of drug-free depressed patients had low cerebrospinal fluid (CSF) concentrations of 5-hydroxyindoleacetic acid (5-HIAA) and, moreover, that these patients were at greater risk for attempting or committing suicide, particularly by violent means. The association between indices of low serotonin (5-hydroxytryptamine [5-HT]) turnover and impulsive violent behavior has been consistently replicated in several studies,[7–9] but it may not be specific to depression.[10, 11] Although the last decade has seen a marked increase in the number and kinds of evidence supporting a role of 5-HT in the pathophysiological mechanism of depression, a major impetus for the role of 5-HT systems in depression has come from the efficacy of the selective serotonin reuptake inhibitors (SSRIs), such as paroxetine, fluoxetine, and sertraline.

Janowsky and coworkers[12] hypothesized that adrenergic-cholinergic imbalances were responsible for pathological variations in mood. A relative increase in acetylcholine (ACh) synaptic availability in comparison to norepinephrine (NE) availability was posited to be associated with depression; contrariwise, a relative increase in NE activity in comparison to ACh activity was posited to be associated with mania.

Several of these theories were derived in part from pharmacological observations. Reserpine, a rauwolfia alkaloid antihypertensive drug, was observed to produce depressive symptoms in a substantial number of patients—symptoms believed to result from depletion of 5-HT, NE, and perhaps dopamine (DA) or epinephrine. Reserpine was also noted to produce symptoms consistent with increased cholinergic activity. The putative antidepressant effect of monoamine oxidase inhibitors (MAOIs) was posited by physicians working in tuberculosis sanitoriums who noted the mood-elevating effects of iproniazid, an antitubercular drug. Monoamine oxidase (MAO) was known to degrade intraneuronal NE and 5-HT, and MAOIs alleviated depressive symptoms. Imipramine, a tricyclic compound chemically similar to chlorpromazine, was developed for the treatment of schizophrenia but was noted to be a better mood elevator than an antipsychotic. Tricyclic antidepressants (TCAs) blocked the reuptake of both 5-HT and NE into presynaptic neurons and were also anticholinergic. The importance of 5-HT was also highlighted by the studies of Shopsin and colleagues,[13, 14] who reported that administration of *p*-chlorophenylalanine, an inhibitor of 5-HT synthesis, reversed the antidepressant action of both imipramine and the MAOI tranylcypromine.

Neuroendocrine and Neuropeptide Hypothesis

Several psychiatric disorders, particularly major depression, are associated with specific neuroendocrine alterations. Furthermore, certain endocrine disorders, most notably thyroid and adrenal diseases, are associated with higher than expected rates of psychiatric morbidity, specifically depression and anxiety disorders. Neuroendocrine abnormalities have long been posited to provide a unique "window to the brain," revealing information about the pathophysiological involvement of central nervous system (CNS) neurotransmitter systems in particular psychiatric disorders. This so-called neuroendocrine window strategy is based on extensive basic science and clinical literature indicating that the secretion of the peripheral endocrine organs is controlled by their respective pituitary trophic hormones. These, in turn, are controlled largely by the secretion of the hypothalamic hypophysiotropic hormones. Interestingly, there is now considerable evidence that the secretion of these hypothalamic releasing hormones is controlled by many of the classic neurotransmitters, such as 5-HT, ACh, and NE, all increasingly implicated in the pathophysiological process of mood and anxiety disorders. Also, there is mounting evidence that components of the neuroendocrine axes themselves, such as corticotropin-releasing factor (CRF), may directly contribute to depression.

Hypothalamic-Pituitary-Adrenal Axis

The hypothalamic-pituitary-adrenal (HPA) axis (Fig. 15–1) has been intensely studied in patients with major depression. CRF, composed of 41 amino acids, is the major physiological mediator of corticotropin (ACTH) and β-endorphin secretion from the anterior pituitary.[15] CRF-containing neurons project from the hypothalamic paraventricular nucleus to the median eminence.[16] Activation of this circuit occurs in response to stress, resulting in an increase in

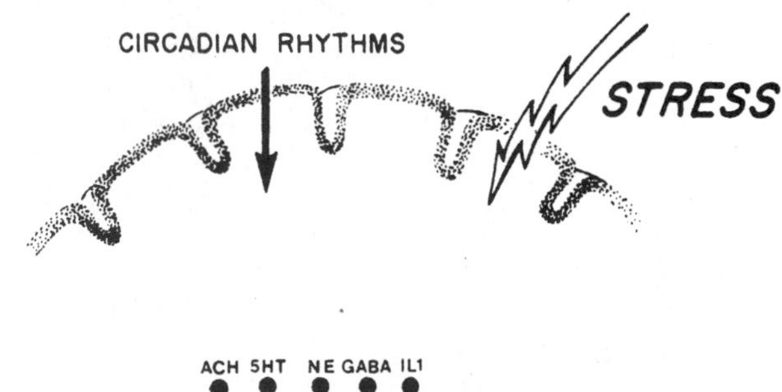

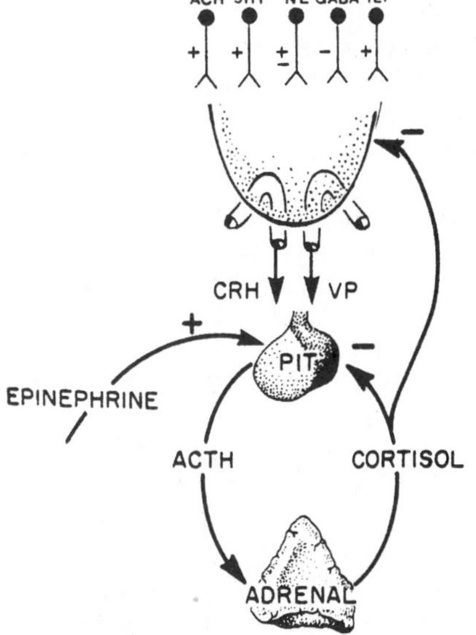

Figure 15–1 *The hypothalamic-pituitary-adrenal axis. ACH, Acetylcholine; 5HT, 5-hydroxytryptamine; NE, norepinephrine; GABA, γ-aminobutyric acid; IL1, interleukin 1; CRH, corticotropin-releasing hormone; VP, arginine vasopressin; PIT, anterior pituitary; ACTH, corticotropin. (From Martin JB, Reichlin S: Clinical Neuroendocrinology, 2nd ed. Philadelphia: FA Davis, 1987:160.)*

Table 15–1 Alterations in the Activity of the Hypothalamic-Pituitary-Adrenal Axis in Major Depression*

↑ CRF concentrations in CSF
Blunted ACTH and β-endorphin responses after intravenous CRF administration
↓ Density of CRF receptors in frontal cortex of suicide victims
Pituitary gland enlargement
Adrenal gland enlargement in major depression and in suicide victims
↑ Cortisol production, hypercortisolemia, and ↑ CSF cortisol concentrations
Plasma glucocorticoid, ACTH, and β-endorphin nonsuppression after dexamethasone administration
↑ Urinary free cortisol concentrations
↑ 5-HTP–induced cortisol secretion
↑ ACTH-induced cortisol secretion
↑ ACTH and cortisol responses to CRF after dexamethasone pretreatment

*CRF, Corticotropin-releasing factor; ACTH, corticotropin; 5-HTP, 5-hydroxytryptophan.

From Nathan KI, Musselman DL, Schatzberg AF, Nemeroff CB: Biology of mood disorders. In Schatzberg AF, Nemeroff CB (eds): The American Psychiatric Press Textbook of Psychopharmacology. Washington, DC: American Psychiatric Press, 1995:445.

synthesis and release of ACTH, β-endorphin, and other proopiomelanocortin products (see Fig. 15–1). There are a multitude of reports documenting HPA axis hyperactivity in drug-free patients with major depression, including CNS (i.e., CRF), pituitary (i.e., ACTH), and adrenal (i.e., glucocorticoid) involvement (Table 15–1). There is considerable evidence that CRF neurons throughout the CNS coordinate the endocrine, behavioral, autonomic, and immune responses to stress.

Involvement of CRF in the pathophysiological process of depression is suggested by elevated CRF concentrations in CSF, which have been documented in multiple studies of drug-free patients with major depression[17–22] as well as suicide victims,[23] although not all studies agree.[24] There is virtually universal agreement that CSF CRF concentrations are elevated in depressed dexamethasone suppression test (DST) nonsuppressors.[24, 25] These elevations of CRF concentrations in CSF are believed to be due to central CRF hypersecretion.[26] Reduction of CRF concentrations in CSF has been reported in healthy volunteer subjects after administration of desipramine (DMI).[27]

One method to assess the activity of the HPA axis is by the use of the CRF stimulation test. CRF is administered intravenously (usually in a dose of 1 μg/kg), and the subsequent ACTH (or β-endorphin) and cortisol response is measured during a 2- to 3-hour period.[28, 29] In drug-free depressed patients, the ACTH and β-endorphin response to exogenously administered ovine CRF is attenuated compared with that of normal comparison subjects.[30–35] The blunted ACTH response to CRF occurs in depressed DST nonsuppressors but not in DST suppressors.[36] The diminished ACTH response to CRF is probably due, at least in part, to chronic hypersecretion of CRF from the median eminence, which results in down-regulation of adenohypophysial CRF receptor number with resultant decreased pituitary responsivity to CRF, as has previously been demonstrated in laboratory animals.[37–41] Further evidence for hyperactivity of hypothalamic CRF neurons in depression has been provided by Raadsheer and coworkers,[42, 43] who reported that depressed patients, in postmortem tissue, exhibit a fourfold increase in the numbers of CRF-containing paraventricular hypothalamic neurons and an increase in CRF mRNA expression as well. Moreover, decreased CRF receptor number in the frontal cortex has been reported in postmortem tissue of suicide victims.[44]

Structural changes in components of the HPA axis have been reported in depression; thus, depressed patients exhibit pituitary gland enlargement at magnetic resonance imaging (MRI),[45] which significantly correlates with cortisol concentrations, a measure of HPA axis activity, after dexamethasone administration.[46] Furthermore, enlargement of the adrenal cortex has been reported post mortem in suicide victims[47, 48]; and in depressed patients by use of computed tomography (CT) and MRI,[30, 49, 50] a finding probably due to chronic ACTH hypersecretion.

This adrenocortical hypertrophy most likely explains the normal plasma cortisol response to CRF in depressed patients, a sharp contrast to the blunted ACTH and β-endorphin response to the peptide.[30–32, 34, 35, 51] For each pulse of ACTH, depressed patients with an enlarged adrenal cortex would be expected to secrete greater quantities of glucocorticoids than control subjects do. Adrenocortical hypertrophy probably underlies the markedly enhanced cortisol response to high doses of ACTH in depression.[52–56]

Another measure of HPA axis hyperactivity well documented in depression is cortisol hypersecretion, reflected in elevated plasma glucocorticoid concentrations,[57, 58] increased levels of cortisol metabolites,[59] elevated 24-hour urinary free cortisol concentrations, and nonsuppression of plasma hydroxycorticosteroid levels after the administration of dexamethasone. Because the initial study of Carroll[60] and subsequent claims for diagnostic utility,[61] the DST has generated remarkable controversy.[62] The rate of cortisol nonsuppression after dexamethasone administration has been generally found to be correlated with the severity of depression (e.g., almost all patients with major depression with psychotic features exhibit DST nonsuppression).[63–66] Moreover, as noted before, DST nonsuppressors have been found to have CSF CRF concentrations higher than those of DST suppressors.[24, 25]

The increased rate of DST nonsuppression in depressed patients may in part be due to the more rapid metabolism of dexamethasone than occurs in depressed patients.[67] In summary, the well-documented HPA axis hyperactivity in depressed patients can be explained by hypersecretion of CRF and secondary pituitary and adrenal gland hypertrophy, although impaired negative feedback at various CNS sites and the pituitary are also likely to contribute. HPA axis activity, including the DST response, usually normalizes after recovery from depression,[60, 68] and its absence may predict early relapse or poor prognosis,[63] as do persistently elevated CSF CRF concentrations. DST nonsuppression, like hypercortisolemia,[59] hypersecretion of CRF,[69, 70] blunting of the ACTH response to CRF,[71] and adrenal gland hypertrophy,[72] all appear, in fact, to be state dependent.

Hyperactivity of the HPA axis also occurs in patients with bipolar disorder.[73, 74] This increased HPA activity has been observed in mixed states,[75–77] mania,[78] and depression in rapid-cycling patients.[79]

Hypothalamic-Pituitary-Thyroid Axis

In the last 30 years, the hypothalamic-pituitary-thyroid (HPT) axis has been the subject of intense scrutiny in patients with mood disorders. Hypothyroidism has long been known to be associated with a markedly depressed mood. In addition, patients with rapid-cycling bipolar disorder exhibit evidence of hypothyroidism, with some responding to thyroid hormone treatment.[80–82] Thyroid hormone supplementation (usually triiodothyronine [T_3]) has been reported to increase the rapidity of action of TCAs[83, 84] and is as effective as lithium in converting depressed TCA nonresponders to responders.[85]

Thyrotropin-releasing hormone (TRH) was the first hypothalamic releasing factor to be chemically characterized; it is a tripeptide (pGlu-His-Pro-NH_2). Released from the median eminence, TRH is transported in the hypothalamo-hypophysial portal system to the anterior pituitary (Fig. 15–2). There, TRH binds to the TRH receptors on the pituitary thyrotrophs, increasing the synthesis and release of thyroid-stimulating hormone (TSH) by activation of the phosphatidylinositol hydrolysis second-messenger system. Released into the general circulation, TSH binds to TSH receptors in the thyroid, causing the release of thyroid hormones, T_3 and thyroxine (T_4). In turn, thyroid hormones act at the anterior pituitary to inhibit TSH release and at the hypothalamus to inhibit TRH synthesis and secretion. TRH is widely distributed in extrahypothalamic brain areas, where it functions as a CNS neurotransmitter. Receptors for T_3 are also widely distributed throughout the mammalian brain.

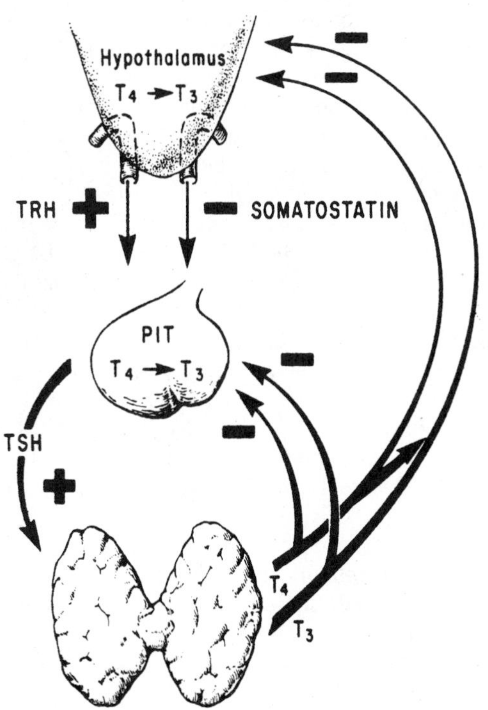

Figure 15–2 *The hypothalamic-pituitary-thyroid axis. T_4, Thyroxine; T_3, triiodothyronine; TRH, thyrotropin-releasing hormone; PIT, pituitary; TSH, thyroid-stimulating hormone. (From Wilson JD, Foster DW: Williams Textbook of Endocrinology, 8th ed. Philadelphia: WB Saunders, 1992:169.)*

Table 15–2 Alterations in the Activity of the Hypothalamic-Pituitary-Thyroid Axis in Depression*

↑ CSF TRH concentrations
↓ Nocturnal plasma TSH levels
Blunted or exaggerated TSH response to TRH stimulation
↓ ΔΔTSH (difference between 11 PM ΔTSH and 8 AM ΔTSH after TRH administration)
Presence of antimicrosomal thyroid or antithyroglobulin antibodies

*TRH, Thyrotropin-releasing hormone; TSH, thyroid-stimulating hormone.

From Nathan KI, Musselman DL, Schatzberg AF, Nemeroff CB: Biology of mood disorders. In Schatzberg AF, Nemeroff CB (eds): The American Psychiatric Press Textbook of Psychopharmacology. Washington, DC: American Psychiatric Press, 1995:448.

The initial report of elevated CSF concentrations of TRH in depressed patients was published more than 15 years ago[86] and subsequently confirmed by Banki and colleagues.[87] In a subsequent study of moderately depressed patients, we did not observe elevated CSF TRH concentrations.[88] Elevated CSF concentrations of TRH are believed to be a reflection of increased extracellular fluid concentrations of the tripeptide, probably the result of central TRH hypersecretion.[26] The increase in pituitary gland size reported in depressed patients[45] may be due in part to TRH hypersecretion. Hatterer and colleagues[89] have reported low CSF levels of transthyretin, the thyroid hormone transport globulin, in treatment-refractory depressed patients, which suggests that this may be a factor in low central thyroid hormone and high central TRH levels.

Arguably, the most sensitive measure of HPT activity is the TSH response to TRH (200 to 500 μg intravenously). This response is greater than normal in hypothyroidism and blunted in hyperthyroid patients. More than 20 years ago, two groups reported that about 25% of depressed patients with major depression exhibit a blunted TSH response to TRH.[90, 91] This is not secondary to hypersecretion of somatostatin (SRIF); in fact, depressed patients have been shown to exhibit considerably reduced CSF concentrations of SRIF compared with nondepressed control subjects.[92, 93] The blunted TSH response to exogenously administered TRH is probably at least partly due to chronic hypersecretion of TRH from median eminence (i.e., elevated TRH release from the hypothalamus, causing down-regulation of anterior pituitary TRH receptors), with resultant diminished anterior pituitary responsiveness to TRH. After long-term administration of TRH, blunting of the TSH response to TRH stimulation has been observed in rats.[94] Adinoff and colleagues[95] found an inverse relationship between the blunted TSH response to TRH and CSF TRH concentrations in 13 drug-free alcoholic men. Moreover, Maeda and coworkers[96] demonstrated that repeated TRH administration in humans produces the blunted TSH response to TRH observed in depressed patients. Further basic and clinical studies documenting TRH hypersecretion and TRH receptor down-regulation are needed.

Two HPT axis measures have demonstrated excellent diagnostic sensitivity in depression compared with the standard TRH stimulation test (Table 15–2). Duval and col-

Table 15–3 Grades of Hypothyroidism*

Grade	T_3 and T_4	Basal TSH	TSH Response to TRH	Antithyroid Antibodies
I	↓	↑	↑	Often present
II	Normal	↑	↑	Often present
III	Normal	Normal	↑	Often present
IV	Normal	Normal	Normal	Present

*T_3, Triiodothyronine; T_4, thyroxine.

From Nathan KI, Musselman DL, Schatzberg AF, Nemeroff CB: Biology of mood disorders. In Schatzberg AF, Nemeroff CB (eds): The American Psychiatric Press Textbook of Psychopharmacology. Washington, DC: American Psychiatric Press, 1995:448.

leagues[97] performed a standard TRH (200 μg) stimulation test on subjects at 8 AM and 11 PM. The difference between the 11 PM ΔTSH and the 8 AM ΔTSH, designated the ΔΔ TSH, is markedly lower in depressed patients than in control subjects, with a diagnostic specificity of 95% and a diagnostic sensitivity of 89%. Another purportedly more sensitive indicator of depression than the TRH stimulation test is diminished nocturnal plasma TSH concentrations.[98–100]

In contradistinction to the blunted TSH response to TRH, approximately 15% of depressed patients exhibit an exaggerated TSH response to TRH.[101] Patients with normal levels of T_3, T_4, and TSH who exhibit an exaggerated TSH response to TRH are defined as having grade III hypothyroidism (Table 15–3). In grade I hypothyroidism, plasma concentrations of T_3 and T_4 are decreased, plasma TSH concentrations are elevated because of the loss of the negative feedback on the pituitary, and TSH response to TRH is markedly exaggerated. In grade II hypothyroidism, plasma concentrations of thyroid hormones are normal, but basal plasma TSH concentrations are elevated, and the TSH response to TRH is exaggerated.

Depressed patients have also been reported to have a higher than expected prevalence rate of symptomless autoimmune thyroiditis, as defined by the abnormal presence of circulating antimicrosomal thyroid or antithyroglobulin antibodies.[102–104] There is a higher frequency of symptomless autoimmune thyroiditis (i.e., 50%) in depressed patients who are DST nonsuppressors.[104, 105] These patients may be designated as having grade IV hypothyroidism (see Table 15–3), that is, antithyroid antibodies are present, but they have normal T_3, T_4, and TSH levels and TRH-induced TSH response.[106]

Abnormalities of the HPT axis have also been reported in patients with bipolar disorder, as demonstrated by an exaggerated TSH response to TRH and elevated basal plasma concentrations of TSH[105, 107] (Table 15–4). In fact, a higher prevalence rate of hypothyroidism (grades I, II, and III) has been reported in bipolar patients who experience rapid cycling of their mood than in bipolar patients who do not.[80, 82] Other abnormalities of the HPT axis have been documented in bipolar patients, including a blunted TSH response to TRH, a blunted or absent nocturnal surge in concentrations of plasma TSH,[108, 109] and the presence of antithyroid microsomal or antithyroglobulin antibodies.[110, 111] The presence of antithyroid antibodies is apparently not a result of lithium treatment, although lithium can exacerbate the process.[112]

Table 15–4 Alterations in the Activity of the Hypothalamic-Pituitary-Thyroid Axis in Bipolar Disorder

Blunting of the TSH response to TRH
Exaggeration of the plasma TSH response to TRH stimulation
Blunted or absent nocturnal surge in plasma TSH concentration
Presence of antimicrosomal thyroid or antithyroglobulin antibodies

From Nathan KI, Musselman DL, Schatzberg AF, Nemeroff CB: Biology of mood disorders. In Schatzberg AF, Nemeroff CB (eds): The American Psychiatric Press Textbook of Psychopharmacology. Washington, DC: American Psychiatric Press, 1995:449.

Hypothalamic–Growth Hormone Axis

Mood disorders are also associated with alterations in the activity of the growth hormone (GH) axis. GH is synthesized and secreted from the anterior pituitary somatotrophs (Fig. 15–3). GH secretion is modulated by two hypothalamic hormones, growth hormone–releasing hormone (GH-RH) and SRIF, as well as by the classic neurotransmitters (e.g., DA, NE, and serotonin) that innervate these peptidergic neurons. GH-RH, located primarily in the arcuate nucleus of the hypothalamus, stimulates the synthesis and release of GH. In contrast, SRIF inhibits GH release; it is found predominantly in the periventricular nucleus of the hypothalamus. SRIF, but not GH-RH, is widely distributed in the CNS, including the cerebral cortex, hippocampus, and amygdala. Both GH-RH and SRIF, released from nerve terminals in the median eminence, are transported by the hypothalamo-hypophysial portal system, where they act on the anterior pituitary somatotrophs.

GH release is stimulated by levodopa,[113] a DA precursor, and by apomorphine, a DA receptor agonist.[114] GH release also occurs after the administration of the 5-HT precursors L-tryptophan and 5-hydroxytryptophan (5-HTP).[115, 116] The 5-HT receptor antagonists methysergide and cyproheptadine attenuate the GH response to hypoglycemia.[117] NE and clonidine, a central α-adrenergic agonist, inhibit GH secretion.[117] Under normal basal conditions, GH is secreted in pulses that are highest during the initial hours of the night.[118] In depressed patients, multiple studies have revealed dysregulation of GH secretion (Table 15–5); nocturnal GH secretion is diminished in these individuals,[119] whereas daytime GH secretion is exaggerated in unipolar and bipolar depressed patients.[120]

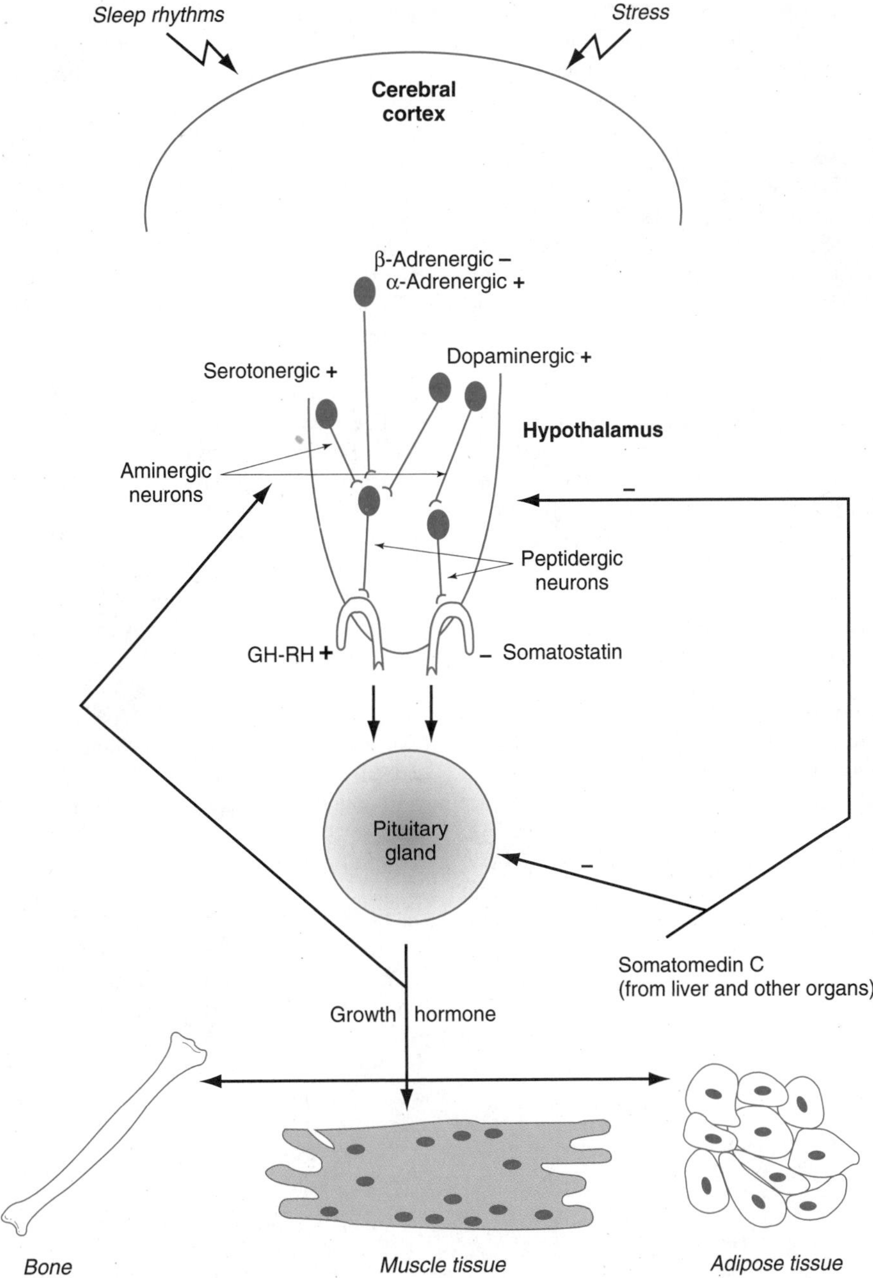

Figure 15–3 *The hypothalamic–growth hormone axis. GH-RH, Growth hormone–releasing hormone.*

Furthermore, a multitude of studies have documented a marked attenuation of the GH response to clonidine (and, to a lesser extent, apomorphine) in depressed patients.[121–124]

The GH-RH stimulation test has been studied in depressed patients, and the results are discordant. Two groups reported a diminished GH response to GH-RH in depressed patients.[125–127] However, Krishnan and colleagues[128] found no differences between depressed patients and nondepressed control subjects in the plasma concentrations of GH after GH-RH stimulation. These discrepant findings may be due to various factors that can influence the GH response to GH-RH, including sex, age, menstrual cycle, plasma somatomedin concentrations, and body weight.[128]

Table 15–5 **Alterations of the Hypothalamic–Growth Hormone Axis in Depression***

↓ Nocturnal GH secretion in depression
↑ GH secretion during the day (unipolar and bipolar)
↓ Response of GH to clonidine and apomorphine in depression
↓ CSF SRIF concentrations
?↓ GH response to GH-RH

*GH, Growth hormone; GH-RH, growth hormone–releasing hormone.

From Nathan KI, Musselman DL, Schatzberg AF, Nemeroff CB: Biology of mood disorders. In Schatzberg AF, Nemeroff CB (eds): The American Psychiatric Press Textbook of Psychopharmacology. Washington, DC: American Psychiatric Press, 1995:450.

Further studies using GH-RH will assist in the development of a standardized GH-RH stimulation test and should clarify the response of GH to GH-RH in depressed patients.

In several studies, CSF concentrations of SRIF have been reported to be reduced in depressed patients.[92, 93, 129–131] These decreased CSF concentrations of SRIF correlate inversely with plasma cortisol concentrations after dexamethasone administration[132]; in fact, exogenous glucocorticoids reduce SRIF concentrations in CSF.[133] In patients with bipolar disorder, blunting of noradrenergic-stimulated GH has been observed during mania.[134] Table 15–5 presents a summary of the alterations of the hypothalamic-GH axis in depression.

Hypothalamic-Pituitary-Gonadal Axis

Despite the high frequency of depression in women and the purportedly increased occurrence of depression during and after menopause, data on the hypothalamic-pituitary-gonadal axis in patients with mood disorders are remarkably limited. The hypothalamic-pituitary-gonadal axis is organized in a "hierarchical" fashion. Driven by a "pulse generator" in the arcuate nucleus of the hypothalamus, gonadotropin-releasing hormone (Gn-RH) secretion occurs in a pulsatile fashion.[135] Gn-RH, a decapeptide, causes secretion of luteinizing hormone (LH) and follicle-stimulating hormone (FSH) from anterior pituitary gonadotrophs[136] (Fig. 15–4). Changes in plasma LH concentrations are often used as an index of pulsatile Gn-RH secretion.[137] In the follicular phase of the menstrual cycle, LH pulses of nearly constant amplitude occur with regular frequency (i.e., every 1 to 2 hours).[138] In the luteal phase, LH pulse amplitude (reflecting Gn-RH secretion) is more variable, with pulse frequency declining to one pulse every 2 to 6 hours.[139] Gonadal steroids inhibit the hypothalamic secretion of Gn-RH as well as the secretion of LH and FSH from the adenohypophysis. Interestingly, Gn-RH secretion is also inhibited by CRF[139] and β-endorphin.[140]

More than 20 years ago, Sachar and colleagues[141] found no significant differences in plasma concentrations of LH and FSH in depressed postmenopausal women compared with nondepressed matched control subjects. In contrast, decreased plasma LH levels were reported in depressed postmenopausal women compared with matched control subjects.[142] The gonadotropin response to exogenous Gn-RH administration has also been studied. Normal LH and FSH responses to a high dose of Gn-RH have been reported in depressed patients,[143] whereas a decreased LH response to a lower dose of Gn-RH has been reported in premenopausal and postmenopausal depressed patients.[142] Unden and colleagues[144] observed no change in baseline or TRH- and LH–releasing hormone (LH-RH)–stimulated LH or FSH concentrations (200 μg TRH and 100 μg LH-RH combined, intravenously) in depressed patients. Interestingly, plasma LH concentrations are increased in those individuals who have recovered from a manic state—possibly a trait phenomenon.[145] Closer scrutiny of the hypothalamic-pituitary-gonadal axis in depression is clearly warranted.

Other Brain Peptides

Investigation of other CNS peptides in mood disorders is limited. The neurohypophysial hormone arginine vasopressin, a nonpeptide that also stimulates ACTH secretion[146] and potentiates CRF-induced ACTH release,[147] is of interest. Unlike the ACTH response to CRF, the ACTH response to arginine vasopressin is unchanged in depression.[148]

Role of Monoamine and Amino Acid Neurotransmitters and Receptors

Earlier we provided some historical perspective on the work concerning the role of monoamine neuronal dysfunction in

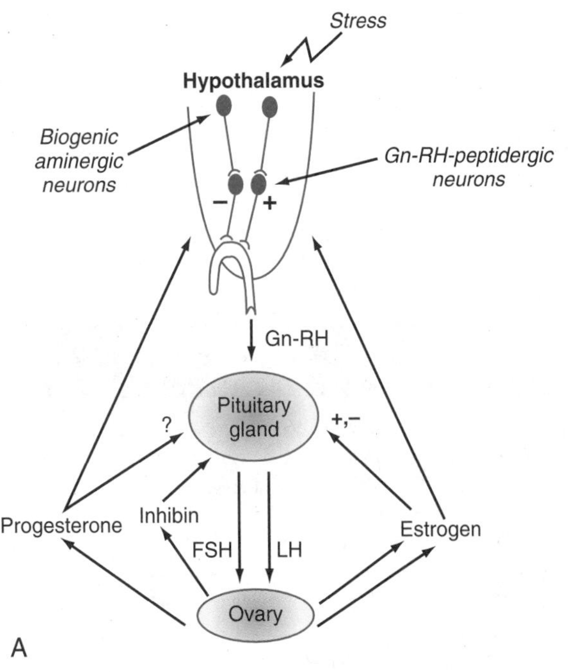

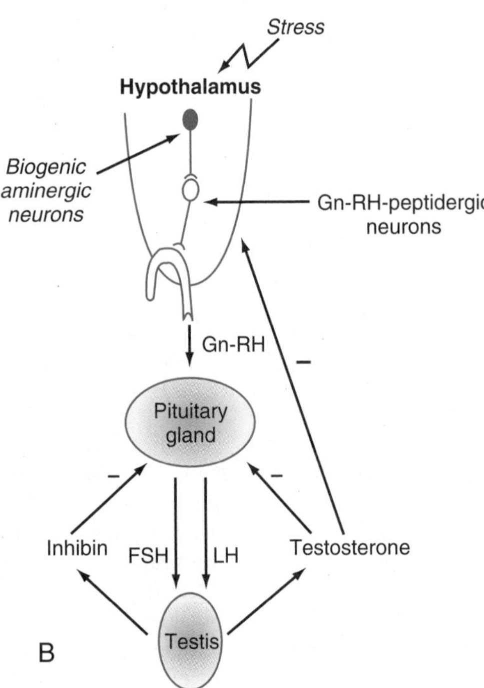

Figure 15–4 *The hypothalamic-pituitary-gonadal axis in the female* (A) *and in the male* (B). *Gn-RH, Gonadotropin-releasing hormone; FSH, follicle-stimulating hormone; LH, luteinizing hormone.*

the pathophysiological mechanism of mood disorders. In this section, the field is reviewed in more detail.

Norepinephrine

The catecholamine hypothesis of affective disorders proposed that some forms of depression are associated with a relative deficiency of catecholamines, particularly NE, at functionally important synaptic sites in the CNS, whereas in contrast, mania is associated with a relative catecholamine excess.[3] In early studies, urinary levels of 3-methoxy-4-hydroxyphenylglycol (MHPG), the major metabolite of CNS NE, were reported to be significantly reduced in depressed patients compared with control subjects.[149] MHPG concentrations were reported to be elevated in bipolar patients when they were manic, compared with the levels when these patients were depressed.[150] Table 15–6 summarizes the findings relevant to the NE system in depression.

Much research in this area has emphasized the use of catecholamine measures to discriminate among subtypes of depressed patients. Early reports indicated that bipolar depressed patients demonstrated significantly lower urinary MHPG levels than did unipolar patients or healthy control subjects.[151] It now appears that low urinary MHPG levels are characteristic of bipolar I depressed patients but not of bipolar II depressed patients, who have MHPG levels similar to those of unipolar patients.[152, 153] Although unipolar depressed patients have higher urinary MHPG levels than do bipolar I patients, some unipolar patients do demonstrate low MHPG levels. These patients may be more likely to develop hypomania or mania than are unipolar patients with high MHPG levels.[153]

Overall, with regard to catecholamine excretion, unipolar depressed patients are more heterogeneous than are bipolar I patients; unipolar patients demonstrate MHPG levels over a wide range of values. MHPG levels may help to biochemically classify unipolar depressed patients.[154, 155] The subtype with low MHPG levels may have low NE output or release. These patients appear to respond well to predominantly noradrenergically active antidepressants,[149] although this finding has not always been replicated.[156] More recent data suggest that patients with low MHPG levels also respond to treatment with fluoxetine.[157] De Bellis and colleagues[70] reported that CSF MHPG levels in nine depressed patients, which were no different from those of control subjects, decreased significantly after treatment with the SSRI fluoxetine, suggesting that this drug may alter NE turnover.

Patients with high MHPG levels have high NE output, which may reflect receptor dysfunction or may be secondary to cholinergic hyperactivity.[158] Such patients also frequently exhibit hypercortisolemia and respond poorly to both noradrenergic TCAs and fluoxetine.

Schildkraut and colleagues[159] reported that discriminant function analysis of urinary catecholamines and metabolites yielded a depression-type (D-type) score that more clearly separated unipolar, nonendogenous depression from bipolar depressions than did urinary MHPG levels alone. In a subsequent report,[153] D-type scores provided greater sensitivity and specificity in differentiating among depressed patients with bipolar or schizoaffective disorder and those individuals with unipolar depression and all other depressions than were seen with use of individual catecholamine and metabolite measures or the sum of the catecholamines and their metabolites. Bipolar I depressed patients had significantly lower D-type scores than did subjects with all other depressive subtypes, including those with bipolar type II depression. Patients with bipolar II disorder demonstrated D-type scores similar to those with unipolar depression.

Table 15–6 Alterations in the Norepinephrine System in Depression
↑ or ↓ 3-methoxy-4-hydroxyphenylglycol
↑ α_2-Adrenergic binding in platelets
Blunted growth hormone response to clonidine
↑ β-Adrenergic receptors in postmortem brain of patients who committed suicide

From Nathan KI, Musselman DL, Schatzberg AF, Nemeroff CB: Biology of mood disorders. In Schatzberg AF, Nemeroff CB (eds): The American Psychiatric Press Textbook of Psychopharmacology. Washington, DC: American Psychiatric Press, 1995:451.

NE appears to play an important role in the control of the HPA axis. Several studies have reported the relationship between measurements of the HPA axis and catecholamine systems. Although early hypotheses suggested that NE may have an inhibitory effect on HPA activity, investigators have reported significant positive correlations between cortisol and MHPG levels in depressed patients.[160, 161] Similar findings have been reported for plasma cortisol and epinephrine levels.[161] These data suggest that simultaneous elevation of HPA axis and NE activity is a feature of some depressed patients. This simultaneous increase in activity could plausibly be explained by increased ACh or CRF secretion.

Catecholamine levels have been measured in patients in the manic phase of bipolar disorder. Bipolar patients during manic episodes demonstrated significantly higher plasma NE and epinephrine levels than when they were depressed or euthymic.[162] Swann and colleagues[163] reported that CSF MHPG and NE levels were higher in manic patients than in either depressed patients or control subjects. Others have reported that plasma MHPG concentrations are higher during the manic rather than the depressive phase in bipolar patients.[150] In a later report, Swann and colleagues[164] noted that environmental sensitivity had a significant effect on urinary NE excretion. Manic patients whose episodes were "environmentally sensitive" demonstrated elevated NE excretion, compared with patients with manic episodes that were unrelated to external stressors.

Adrenergic Receptors

The α_1-receptor is not coupled to the adenylate cyclase system but is linked to processes that regulate cellular calcium ion fluxes. In contrast, α_2-receptors, present both presynaptically and postsynaptically, are inhibitory to the adenylate cyclase system. Activation of the presynaptic α_2-receptor inhibits NE release in the CNS. Increased numbers of α_2-receptor binding sites in platelets of depressed patients have been reported.[165] There is also increased α_2-receptor density in the brains of suicide victims.[166] These studies support the theory of supersensitivity of α_2-receptors in depression, although these findings are not universal. Moreover, treatment with antidepressants has been associated with decreases in the density and sensitivity of these receptors.

Activation of the α_2-receptor inhibits adenylate cyclase and produces a corresponding decrease in cyclic adenosine monophosphate, which mediates several physiological responses, one of which is platelet aggregation. Garcia -Sevilla and coworkers[167] assessed the functional status of α_2-receptors in depressed patients by measuring both inhibition of adenylate cyclase activity and induction of platelet aggregation. They concluded that platelet aggregation is a better marker to assess receptor changes in depression. Mooney and colleagues[168] reported that some depressed patients demonstrate decreased responsivity of α_2-receptors to inhibition by epinephrine.

An indirect method for studying α_2-receptors is to challenge subjects with the α_2-receptor agonist clonidine. Administration of clonidine induces GH secretion, primarily through an action on postsynaptic receptors. Several abnormalities in GH release in depression have been reported (see earlier). The GH response to clonidine is attenuated in unipolar depressed patients,[123, 169] indicative of decreased responsiveness of postsynaptic α_2-adrenergic receptors. Siever and colleagues[170] reported that the GH response to clonidine was blunted in both acute and remitted patients compared with control subjects, suggesting that this may represent a trait marker in depression.[171]

The β-adrenergic receptor subtypes are postsynaptic and stimulate the adenylate cyclase system. Mann and coworkers[171] reported increased β-adrenergic receptor density in the postmortem brains of people who committed suicide and have confirmed these findings in several subsequent studies. In contrast, Crow and associates[172] reported a decreased density of hippocampal β-adrenergic receptors in the postmortem brains of depressed patients. It is possible, however, that previous antidepressant treatment may have resulted in β-adrenoreceptor down-regulation in these patients.

Serotonin

For more than two decades, serotonin has been hypothesized to play a role in the pathogenesis of affective illness.[173] The metabolic pathway for serotonin is described in Figure 15–5. This has been a particularly burgeoning area of research, partly because of the introduction of SSRI antidepressants. The permissive hypothesis of serotonin function postulated a deficit in serotoninergic neurotransmission that permits the expression of bipolar affective disorder but is not sufficient in itself to cause it.[174] According to this hypothesis, both mania and depression are characterized by low CNS 5-HT activity but differ in high versus low NE availability.

A remarkable number of studies have demonstrated that there is reduction in the CSF concentration of 5-HIAA, the principal metabolite of 5-HT, in drug-free depressed patients, particularly those who have had suicide attempts[7, 175, 176] (Table 15–7). Asberg and coworkers[6] hypothesized low concentrations of 5-HIAA as a marker for suicide risk in depressed patients. Subsequent studies have largely confirmed these observations.[8, 177, 178] Low CSF 5-HIAA concentrations appear to be associated with more impulsive methods of suicide,[179] suggesting an

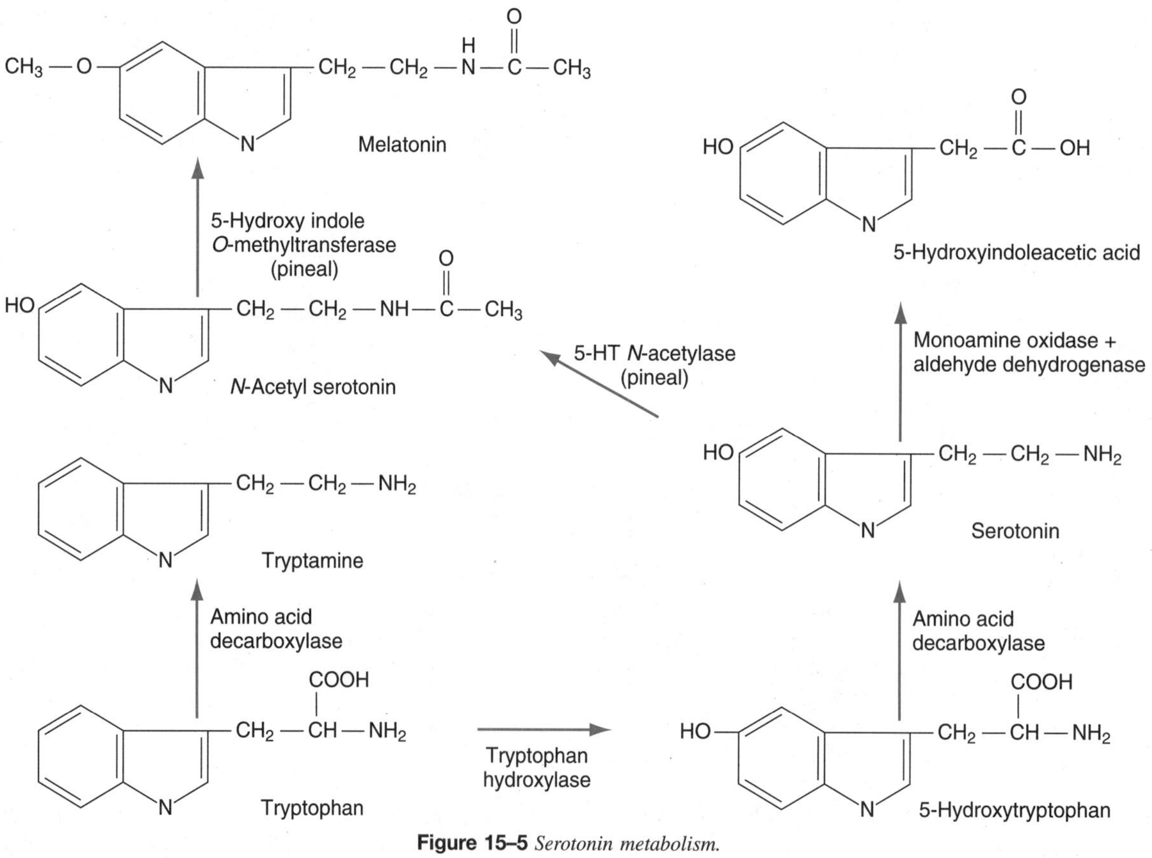

Figure 15–5 *Serotonin metabolism.*

Table 15–7 Alterations in the Serotonin (5-HT) System in Depression

Plasma tryptophan concentrations
↓ CSF 5-HIAA
↑ Postsynaptic 5-HT_2 receptors in brain and platelets
↓ Serotonin transporter ([^{3}H]imipramine or [^{3}H]paroxetine) binding in brain and platelets
Platelet 5-HT uptake in platelets
Blunted prolactin response to fenfluramine

From Nathan KI, Musselman DL, Schatzberg AF, Nemeroff CB: Biology of mood disorders. In Schatzberg AF, Nemeroff CB (eds): The American Psychiatric Press Textbook of Psychopharmacology. Washington, DC: American Psychiatric Press, 1995:455.

association between decreased levels of 5-HIAA and suicide, aggression, or poor impulse control. Indeed, low CSF 5-HIAA levels have also been associated with aggression or poor impulse control in impulsive violent criminal offenders[180] and arsonists.[181]

Drugs that target the 5-HT transporter site, thereby selectively inhibiting reuptake of 5-HT (e.g., fluoxetine, sertraline, paroxetine, and fluvoxamine), have all been shown to be effective antidepressants. In addition to SSRIs, there is growing interest in agents that specifically act at one or another of the many recently identified 5-HT receptor subtypes.

There are three main classes of 5-HT receptors: 5-HT_1, 5-HT_2, and 5-HT_3 receptors. The 5-HT receptors are composed of the following subtypes: 5-HT_{1A}, 5-HT_{1B}, 5-HT_{1D}, 5-HT_{1E}, and 5-HT_{1F} subtypes. The 5-HT_{1A} receptor has been implicated in the pathophysiological mechanism of depression and anxiety. This receptor has a high affinity for 5-HT, and long-term treatment with antidepressants in rats results in reduction of 5-HT_{1A} receptor sensitivity.

Long-term antidepressant treatment decreases the density of 5-HT_2 receptors; in contrast, electroconvulsive therapy increases them.[182] Mann and colleagues[171] reported an increased number of postsynaptic 5-HT_2 receptors in the brains of depressed patients. This suggests a relative deficiency of presynaptic serotonin release in depression that may lead to an increased number of postsynaptic 5-HT_2 receptors.[22]

Binding to platelet membranes and 5-HT–induced shape change and aggregation have been commonly used to study 5-HT_2 receptors. Beigon and colleagues[183] suggested that the increase in 5-HT_2 receptor binding in platelets is a state-dependent marker in major depression. In their study of 15 depressed patients, receptor binding was measured at baseline and again after 1 and 3 weeks of treatment with maprotiline. A significant decrease in 5-HT_2 receptor binding was observed in responders but not in nonresponders.

The human platelet concentrates 5-HT from plasma through the 5-HT transporter in a manner identical to that of 5-HT neurons in the CNS; thus, platelets have been suggested as a model for central 5-HT neurons. Drugs such as [^{3}H]imipramine and [^{3}H]paroxetine bind to the 5-HT transporter on the presynaptic nerve terminal and in the platelet. A reduction in the number of platelet [^{3}H]imipramine binding sites in depressed patients has been reported by several groups.[184–186] Also, Stanley[187] and Perry and colleagues[188] reported decreased density of [^{3}H]imipramine binding sites in the frontal cortex and hypothalamus and in the hippocampus and occipital cortex, respectively, in depressed patients.

In contrast, the report of the World Health Organization Collaborative Study[189] argued that [^{3}H]imipramine binding is not a valid biological marker of endogenous depression. This multicenter study investigated data from 154 depressed patients and 130 control subjects. No significant differences in [^{3}H]imipramine binding between depressed patients and control subjects were observed. There were marked discrepancies in findings among different centers, perhaps reflecting different biochemical techniques used for platelet isolation and membrane preparation. A meta-analysis of all the platelet [^{3}H]imipramine binding data has revealed a significant reduction in the density of the 5-HT transporter in depressed patients compared with that of control subjects.[190]

In more recent years, [^{3}H]imipramine has been found to have less specificity than [^{3}H]paroxetine.[191] Nemeroff and coworkers[192] reported that [^{3}H]paroxetine binding sites are reduced in the platelets of drug-free depressed patients and, moreover, that never-treated depressed patients exhibited reductions in both platelet [^{3}H]imipramine and [^{3}H]paroxetine binding. The latter observation suggests that prior antidepressant treatment is not responsible for the observed reduction in 5-HT transporter binding in depressed patients.

Serotoninergic systems are involved in the regulation of secretion of a variety of hormones, including cortisol, prolactin, and GH. Administration of fenfluramine, which increases 5-HT release from presynaptic nerve terminals, increases plasma concentrations of ACTH, cortisol, and prolactin and increases body temperature as well. Stahl and colleagues[193] reported that fenfluramine-induced hyperthermia was blunted in drug-free depressed patients.

In normal volunteers, administration of L-tryptophan, a 5-HT precursor, produces a robust increase in plasma prolactin concentrations. Prolactin responses to L-tryptophan and to the 5-HT–releasing agent fenfluramine are blunted in depression.[169, 194] Because patients with other diagnoses also demonstrate a blunted prolactin response to fenfluramine, its specificity and sensitivity in depression need to be scrutinized further before it can be of clinical use.

Cortisol secretion induced by 5-HTP has been reported to be increased in unmedicated depressed patients compared with nondepressed control subjects and to be decreased after treatment with antidepressants.[195] Noting a significant negative correlation between baseline plasma cortisol levels and the cortisol response to 5-HTP in nondepressed control subjects, Koyama and Meltzer[195] postulated that 5-HT plays an important role in the stimulation of basal plasma cortisol secretion.

As a potent stimulator of the HPA axis, increased 5-HT availability could play a role in the characteristic increased HPA axis activity of psychotic depression. Indeed, Schatzberg and Rothschild[196] noted that increased 5-HT uptake into platelets and increased CSF levels of 5-HIAA have been observed in patients with psychotic major depression. These findings highlight the need for further studies on increased serotoninergic activity in psychotic depression. Table15–7 summarizes the alterations in the 5-HT system in depression.

Dopamine, Dopamine β-Hydroxylase, and Monoamine Oxidase

Enhanced dopaminergic activity may play a significant pathophysiological role in psychotic depression. Compared with nonpsychotic depressed patients, psychotically depressed patients have been reported to have lower serum DA β-hydroxylase (DBH) activity and higher plasma DA and homovanillic acid (HVA) concentrations.[197–199] The metabolic pathway for DA is described in Figure 15–6.

Several studies have provided data supporting the view that this increased DA activity in psychotic depression occurs as a result of increased glucocorticoid secretion. Glucocorticoids may induce tyrosine hydroxylase activity, the rate-limiting step in the biosynthesis of DA and NE. The administration of dexamethasone increases plasma DA and HVA concentrations in healthy control subjects,[200, 201] and the administration of corticosterone or dexamethasone to rats increases central DA turnover.[202, 203] Schatzberg and coworkers[198] hypothesized that enhancement of DA activity by glucocorticoids may contribute to the development of psychosis or delusional thinking in depressed patients.

Platelet MAO activity has been studied as a putative biological marker in mood disorders. Bipolar patients and their relatives were reported to have lower platelet MAO activity than that of unipolar patients or control subjects.[204–206] Low MAO levels are found primarily in bipolar I (but not bipolar II) subjects.[206] Although MAO activity appears to be under strong genetic control and is linked to affective disorders, these results have not been widely replicated.[207] Schatzberg and colleagues[208] reported that MAO activity was significantly higher in patients with psychotic depression than in those with nonpsychotic depression or in healthy control subjects.

High platelet MAO activity has been reported to correlate with elevated urinary free cortisol levels and DST nonsuppression.[209, 210] The association between high platelet MAO activity and DST nonsuppression has been replicated by several groups.[211, 212] Thus, mean 4 PM plasma cortisol concentrations after dexamethasone administration are significantly higher in patients with high MAO activity. Several hypotheses have been put forth for this finding. MAO could be a genetic marker of a risk for DST nonsuppression in the face of developing depression. If elevated MAO activity is correlated with a corresponding increase in hypothalamic MAO, a decrease in central noradrenergic tonic inhibition of HPA axis activity could result in DST nonsuppression. Also, increased central MAO activity could be associated with serotoninergic supersensitivity and elevated HPA axis activity. Conversely, it is possible that increased glucocorticoid activity is associated with elevated levels of catecholamines, which then results in an increase in platelet MAO activity. Further studies are clearly needed.

DBH catalyzes the hydroxylation of DA to NE. In several studies, DBH activity has been measured in major psychiatric disorders, including schizophrenia and affective disorders. However, results have generally been consistent only in patients with unipolar psychotic depression who have been reported to demonstrate low DBH levels. For example, Sapru and associates[213] measured DBH activity in 280 adult male psychiatric patients with no previous exposure to psychoactive drugs and reported lower serum DBH activity in patients with psychotic major depression compared with control subjects. No differences between control subjects and patients with schizophrenia, bipolar depression, or nonpsychotic major depression were found. Low DBH

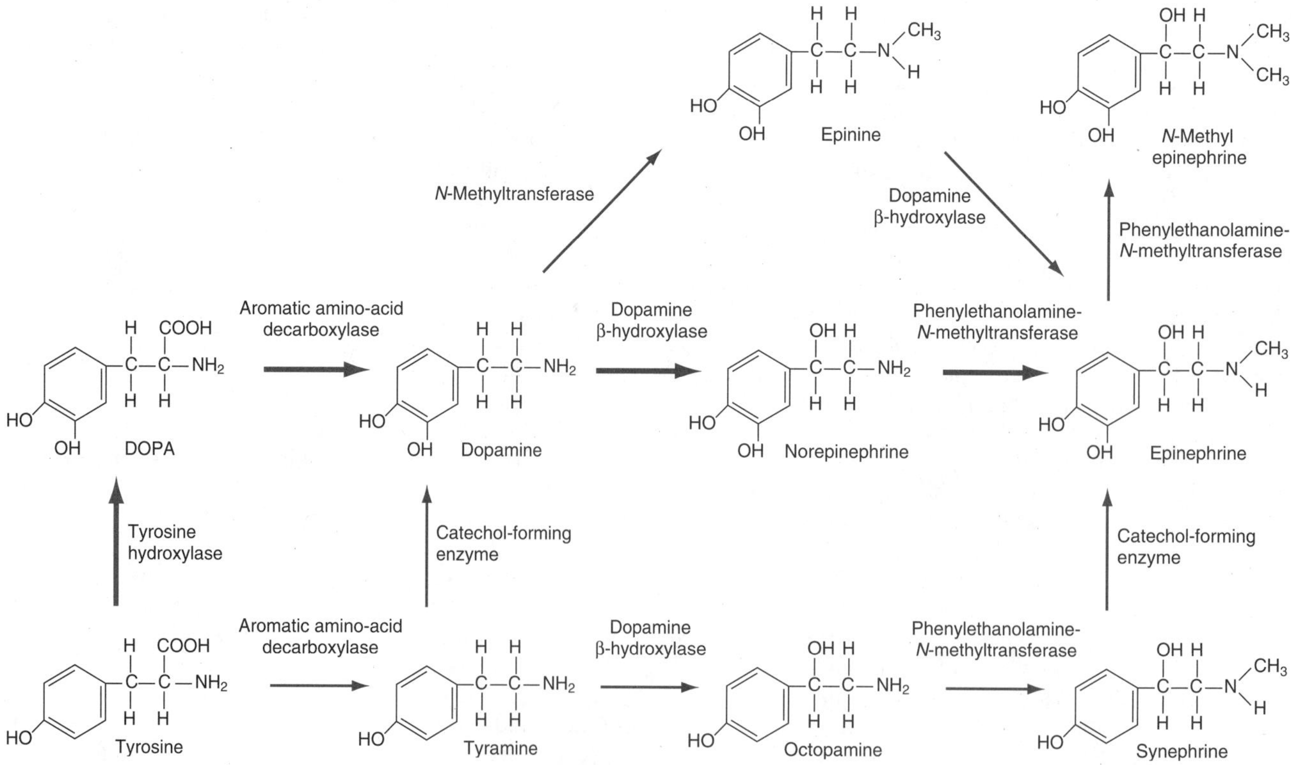

Figure 15–6 *Metabolic pathways of dopamine.*

activity has therefore been hypothesized to be a risk factor for psychotic depression.

γ-Aminobutyric Acid

γ-Aminobutyric acid (GABA) exerts inhibitory electrophysiological effects in almost all areas of the CNS. GABA is a major regulator of many CNS functions, such as seizure threshold; it also exerts inhibitory input to other neurotransmitter systems, such as NE and DA. The metabolic pathway for GABA is described in Figure 15–7. Some data suggest that GABA metabolism may be altered in affective disorders.

Two major types of GABA receptors, $GABA_A$ and $GABA_B$, have been identified. $GABA_A$ receptors are coupled to chloride ion channels and are associated with benzodiazepine binding sites, whereas $GABA_B$ receptors are associated with calcium ion transport. $GABA_B$ agonists such as baclofen enhance cyclic adenosine monophosphate production during exposure to other neurotransmitters such as NE, although they themselves have little effect on the second-messenger response. A decrease in GABAergic activity may play a role in depression by regulating receptor responses to catecholamines. For example, baclofen potentiates down-regulation of β-adrenergic receptor number in response to imipramine.[214]

The role of GABA in epilepsy has been extensively studied, and antiepileptic drugs appear to have direct or indirect actions on GABA neurons. The antiepileptic agents valproic acid and carbamazepine were serendipitously noted to have mood-stabilizing effects, decreasing the intensity and frequency of the manic phases of bipolar disorder. In addition to valproic acid, other antimanic agents (e.g., lithium and carbamazepine) may stabilize mood in part by increasing GABAergic transmission, leading to the hypothesis that GABA deficiency plays a role in mania.[215]

Gold and coworkers[216] reported that the CSF GABA concentration is significantly lower in depressed patients; several studies have reported reduced plasma concentrations of GABA in depression.[217, 218] Honig and colleagues[219] directly measured GABA in brain tissue from patients undergoing cingulotomy for intractable depression and reported that GABA concentrations were inversely correlated with severity of depression. However, low levels of GABA are not specific to cases of depression or mania because they are also seen in patients with alcoholism.[220]

Acetylcholine

The metabolic pathway for ACh is described in Figure 15–8. Janowsky and associates[12] hypothesized an increased ratio of cholinergic to adrenergic activity in depression and the reverse in mania. Pharmacologically induced changes in ACh activity result in dramatic alterations in mood. Increases in cholinergic activity (induced by cholinergic agonists such as arecoline and cholinesterase inhibitors such as physostigmine) may reduce manic symptoms in bipolar patients or worsen depressive symptoms in depressed patients.

In contrast, Schatzberg and Mooney[221] suggested that increased ACh activity may result in increased catecholamine output as well as elevation in cortisol secretion in a subgroup of depressed patients. Thus, ACh activity may not be reciprocal to catecholamine activity.

Sitaram and coworkers[222] proposed that bipolar disorder may be characterized by a state-independent cholinergic hypersensitivity in conjunction with a state-dependent noradrenergic supersensitivity (during late depression and early mania), which return to normal during remission. The researchers administered arecoline during the second non–rapid eye movement sleep period, which resulted in significantly more rapid onset of rapid eye movement (REM) sleep in currently depressed as well as in remitted depressed patients compared with control subjects. This finding of a supersensitive cholinergic response in patients with major depressive disorder has been replicated.[223, 224]

Brain Imaging Studies

Remarkable advances in the last decade in structural and functional brain imaging have now been applied to the study of mood disorders. Although there are many reports of ventricular enlargement in patients with schizophrenia, the literature also contains many CT and MRI studies reporting increased ventricle size in patients with unipolar and bipolar disorders. However, many of these studies are confounded by numerous methodological problems. For example, most of these studies estimate lateral ventricle size by using a ventricular brain ratio. More consistent, however, are the CT and MRI studies of increased ventricular size in depression in geriatric patients (those individuals older than 65 years). The structural alterations in the CNS of patients with mood disorders are summarized in Tables 15–8 and 15–9. In addition, hyperintensities of gray and white matter (Table 15–10) have repeatedly been reported in MRI studies of geriatric patients with affective disorder, particularly those with "late-onset depression" (i.e., elderly depressed patients experiencing their first depression after age 60 years). Subcortical hyperintensities in the elderly are age dependent and may reflect pathological changes stemming from genetic, perinatal, posttraumatic, demyelinating, and infectious factors,[225] or from infarctions due to arteriosclerotic involvement of the small lacunar arterioles that supply the basal ganglia and subcortical white matter.[226] Study of nondepressed control subjects has revealed that increasing age is also associated with reduction of the size of the putamen[227] and caudate nuclei[228] as well as of the size of the midbrain[229] and pituitary gland.[45, 230]

To assess whether abnormal brain structure is associated with abnormal brain function, investigators have used CT and MRI studies of the CNS in association with neuroendocrine stimulation tests and neuropsychological testing, monitoring patients' clinical course, response to treatment, and so on. For example, plasma cortisol concentrations after dexamethasone administration are significantly correlated with ventricle-to-brain ratio[231] and pituitary volume.[46] Furthermore, in depressed elderly patients, caudate hyperintensities are associated with an increased risk for the development of delirium induced by TCAs and electroconvulsive therapy[232–234] as well as neuroleptic-induced parkinsonism.[235]

The controlled positron emission tomography studies are summarized in Table 15–11. Of particular interest is the decreased neuronal activity of the caudate and putamen reported in patients with both unipolar and bipolar depression. This is consistent with the MRI-documented morphological abnormalities of the basal ganglia (i.e., reduced size and increased prevalence of hyperintensities within these structures). Vulnerability to affective dysfunction might

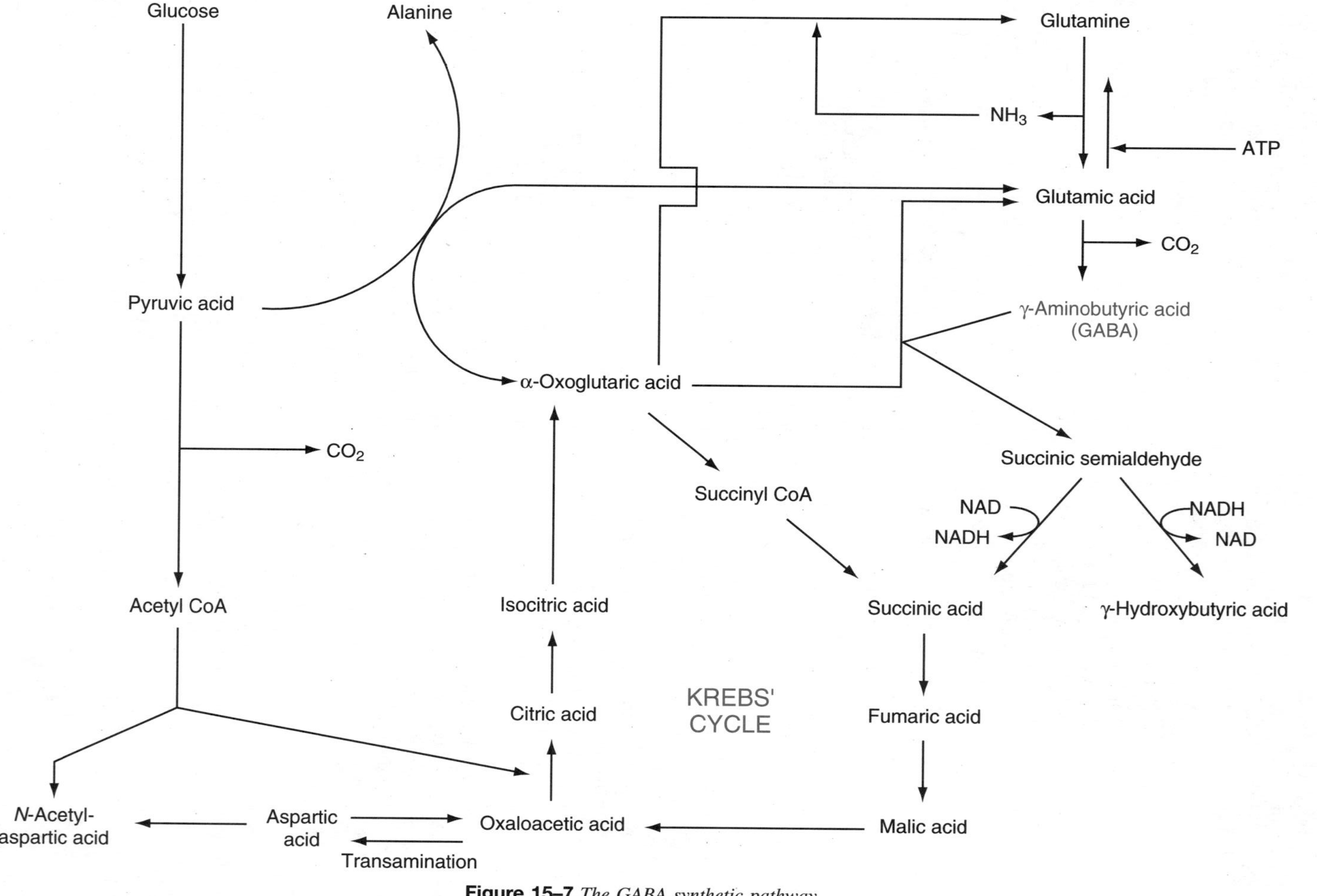

Figure 15–7 *The GABA synthetic pathway.*

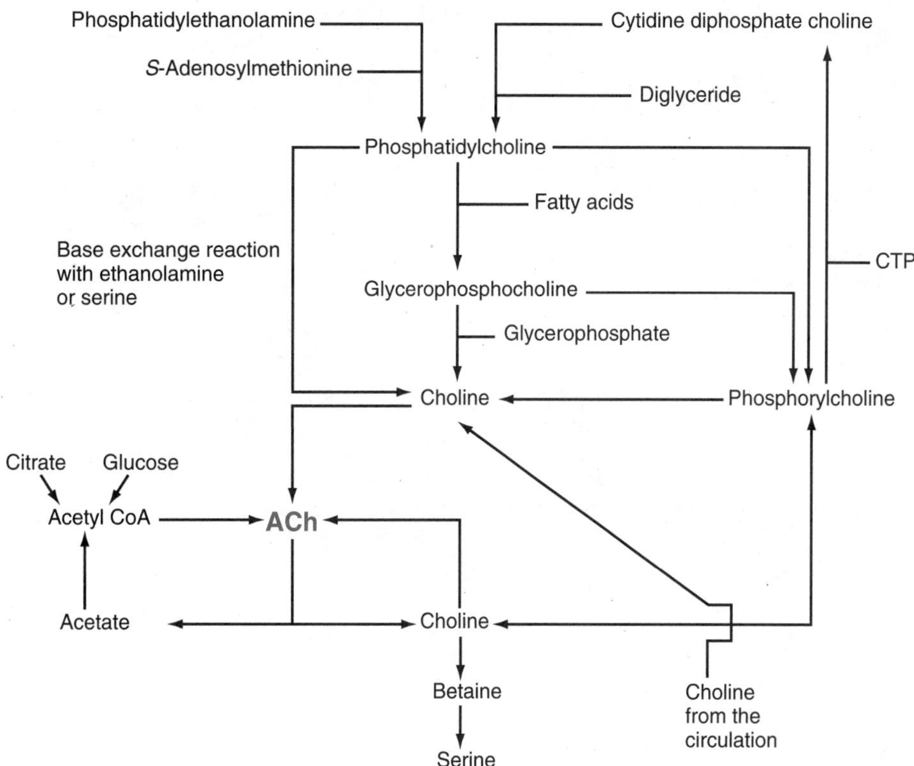

Figure 15–8 *Acetylcholine (ACh) metabolism.*

derive from disruption of connections between the basal ganglia or from interruption of pathways connecting the basal ganglia to other parts of the brain, specifically the limbic system and prefrontal cortex.[236, 237] This speculation would be consistent with the findings of subcortical hyperintensities (deep white matter and periventricular) found at MRI and the abnormal cortical neuronal activity reported in patients with depression and mania.

Undoubtedly, structures within the basal ganglia circuit requiring further scrutiny include the globus pallidus and amygdala as well as brain structures with neuronal pathways leading to or from the basal ganglia: the thalamus, subthalamic nucleus, hippocampus, and relevant cortical areas.

Table 15–8 Brain Computed Tomography Alterations

Major Depression
↑ Lateral ventricular size (geriatric depression*)[641–643]
↑ Third ventricular width[644,645]
↔ Cortical atrophy
Bipolar Disorder
↔ Cortical atrophy
No cerebral asymmetry
Cerebellar atrophy (also in schizophrenic patients)[646]

*Geriatric depression is depression in patients older than 65 years.

From Nathan KI, Musselman DL, Schatzberg AF, Nemeroff CB: Biology of mood disorders. In Schatzberg AF, Nemeroff CB (eds): The American Psychiatric Press Textbook of Psychopharmacology. Washington, DC: American Psychiatric Press, 1995:460.

Table 15–9 Brain Magnetic Resonance Imaging Alterations

Major Depression
↑ Ventricular size (geriatric depression*)[641–643,647]
↑ Prevalence of subcortical (gray and white matter) hyperintensities (geriatric depression*)[648] (late-onset depression†)[649]
↑ Prevalence of periventricular hyperintensities (geriatric depression*)[648]
↑ Prevalence of hyperintensities of the basal ganglia (late-onset depression†)[649,650]
↓ Cerebellar volume and smaller cerebellar vermis[229]
Smaller brain stem and medulla[229]
Smaller temporal lobe[651]
No significant structural changes in corpus callosum[652]
↓ Caudate volume[653]
↑ Prevalence of hyperintensities of the caudate (geriatric depression*)[647,648]
↓ Putamen volume[227]
↑ Pituitary gland volume[45]
Bipolar Disorder
↓ Temporal lobe volume bilaterally[654]
No significant structural changes in corpus callosum[655]
↑ Frequency of subcortical hyperintensities[649,656,657]

*Geriatric depression is depression in patients older than 65 years.

†Late-onset depression is depression that first appears in a patient after age 60 years.

From Nathan KI, Musselman DL, Schatzberg AF, Nemeroff CB: Biology of mood disorders. In Schatzberg AF, Nemeroff CB (eds): The American Psychiatric Press Textbook of Psychopharmacology. Washington, DC: American Psychiatric Press, 1995:460.

Table 15–10 Increased Frequency of Hyperintensities on Magnetic Resonance Imaging Scans of Patients with Mood Disorders

Study	Major Depression	Bipolar Disorder
Coffey et al,[648] 1990	+	
Dupont et al,[656] 1990		+
Swayze et al,[657] 1990		+
Figiel et al,[649] 1991	+	+
Rabins et al,[647] 1991	+	
Figiel and Nemeroff,[650] 1993	+	

Further research is required to determine the diagnostic specificity of morphological and functional abnormalities associated with the major mood disorders. Furthermore, the stability or state dependency of these alterations is not known (e.g., the ventriculomegaly associated with major depression). One prospective study by Vita and colleagues[238] reports ventricle-to-brain ratios increased in size during a 3-year period in depressed patients. Yet one retrospective study found no significant increase in ventricle-to-brain ratio in bipolar patients.[239] Prospective longitudinal studies might help determine whether patients afflicted with a major mood disorder exhibit structural and functional brain alterations before, during, or as a result of affective episodes and, furthermore, whether these findings "normalize" with clinical improvement.

Postmortem Brain Studies

A renaissance in neuropathology fueled by in vivo findings (i.e., neuroimaging) and improved techniques has allowed testing a number of the peripheral findings in postmortem specimens of patients dying by suicide, many with a prior diagnosis of depression. Initial studies of NE, 5-HT, and their metabolites in many of these patients have not yielded any consistent finding, perhaps because these compounds are so unstable post mortem.[9, 172] Receptors and reuptake sites that are considerably more stable post mortem have proved more reliable and have confirmed some of the peripheral platelet studies of the 5-HT transporter and the 5-HT_2 receptor. Perry and associates[188] found decreased imipramine binding in brain tissue from suicide victims. Mann and coworkers[171] found increased 5-HT_2 β-adrenergic receptors in the frontal cortex of suicide victims; the increase was not found in the Crow study.[172] Meana and colleagues[166] reported an increase in α_2-receptor (which inhibits NE release) in the brains of patients committing suicide.

Table 15–11 Brain Positron Emission Tomography Alterations

Major Depression
↓ Glucose metabolic rates in the cortex[658] and basal ganglia[659]
Bipolar Disorders
↓ Global cerebral activity during depression[660]
↑ Global cerebral activity during depression[661]

From Nathan KI, Musselman DL, Schatzberg AF, Nemeroff CB: Biology of mood disorders. In Schatzberg AF, Nemeroff CB (eds): The American Psychiatric Press Textbook of Psychopharmacology. Washington, DC: American Psychiatric Press, 1995:461.

One of the more intriguing new findings involves studies of CRF and its receptors in suicide victims and depressed patients. There appears to be an increase both in mRNA, which makes CRF, and in the number of CRF neurons in the periventricular nucleus of the hypothalamus of depressed patients.[42, 43] Moreover, suicide victims (most likely depressed patients) have an increase in CRF binding in the frontal cortex.[44] These studies clearly warrant further work.

SCHIZOPHRENIA

Schizophrenia, the most common of the so-called functional psychoses, is characterized by episodes of formal thought disorder, delusions, and hallucinations—the classic "positive symptoms." "Negative symptoms," such as avolition, flat affect, cognitive problems, and lack of concern for personal hygiene and social conventions, tend to be chronic and resistant to treatment.

Early descriptions of schizophrenia noted familial aggregation of the illness. We begin our discussion with a brief review of the genetics of schizophrenia and the extent to which environmental factors may contribute to the illness. Speculation that schizophrenia symptoms result from dysfunction of several brain areas has existed since the early descriptions of the illness. After a century of attempts to identify neuropathological correlates of schizophrenia we have only recently begun to develop some consensus. We review data largely from modern studies using neuropathological and neurochemical techniques as well as structural and functional neuroimaging in schizophrenia.

Genetics and Obstetrical Complications

It is well established that schizophrenia occurs more commonly in the family members of affected individuals. However, most cases of schizophrenia occur without a positive family history, raising the possibility that cases can arise sporadically. Although results from family, twin, and adoption studies provide compelling evidence for a genetic contribution to schizophrenia, the nature of the inherited defect and its degree of penetrance remain obscure. Schizophrenia occurs at similar prevalence rates throughout most regions of the world, despite diversity of cultural, racial, and socioeconomic groups. This observation also lends support to the concept of an inherited vulnerability with a relatively stable gene frequency.

Family and twin studies estimate the risk of schizophrenia in first-degree relatives and dizygotic twins of schizophrenic patients to be 10 to 15 times that of the general population. However, several of these studies were conducted in Europe when diagnostic criteria for schizophrenia were less stringent than today. Therefore, cases that now would be diagnosed as schizophrenia spectrum disorders or other atypical psychoses were likely included. Studies that have attempted to exclude atypical cases postulate a risk for first-degree relatives that is somewhat less than that stated in older studies.[240, 241] Monozygotic twins of schizophrenic patients have a concordance rate for schizophrenia of approximately 30% to 80%, depending on ascertainment methods.[242–244] Because monozygotic twins do not have concordance rates of 100%, nongenetic factors must also contribute to pathogenesis.

Further support for a genetic vulnerability in schizophrenia comes from the following observations in adoption studies: 1) children of schizophrenic mothers who are adopted by normal adults have an increased risk for schizophrenia,[245, 246] and 2) children of normal adults who are adopted away and raised by schizophrenic parents do not have an increased risk for schizophrenia.[247]

Linkage analysis assumes that if a putative disease locus is in proximity to a known genetic marker, the two segments of genetic material will remain in proximity after meiosis, even if recombination takes place. Several studies have attempted to "link" a schizophrenic gene to specific chromosomal markers without reliable success.

Linkage analyses of genes for two neurotransmitter receptor proteins have been completed. The gene encoding the serotonin 5-HT_2 receptor subtype has been mapped to chromosome 13. Hallmayer and coworkers[248] have excluded linkage of the 5-HT_2 locus with schizophrenia in a Swedish kindred. Moises and colleagues[249] have excluded linkage of markers coding for parts of the DA D_2 receptor and for porphobilinogen deaminase (the deficient enzyme in acute intermittent porphyria) on chromosome 11 to Californian and Swedish pedigrees with schizophrenia.

In genetic association studies, a population with a pathological phenotype is compared with control subjects with regard to the frequency of alleles of known genetic markers. The classic markers are the ABO and Rh blood groups and the human leukocyte antigen (HLA) system. A previously replicated finding of a weak association of paranoid schizophrenia with the HLA-A9 locus[250] has not been confirmed by a new study of 33 families.[251] Crocq and colleagues[252] have reported that schizophrenic patients have an increased frequency of homozygosity of a polymorphism of the DA D_3 receptor gene.

It is not entirely surprising that cytogenetic and "candidate gene" linkage studies have not generated positive results. Molecular biological techniques have been more successfully applied to disorders with known modes of inheritance and clinically homogeneous phenotypes. In schizophrenia research, large kindred samples need to be collected to make accurate assessments of inheritance and penetrance, to identify populations at risk for developing the illness, and to examine the role of specific genes. Genetic modeling strategies based on available pedigree data[241] seem to support a complex multifactorial pattern of inheritance rather than a single-gene model.

A history of obstetrical complications in schizophrenic patients may indicate that an environmental effect is more important than genetic vulnerability in producing psychosis. However, it may be argued that abnormal development of the CNS based on genetic underpinnings may predispose to obstetrical complications. To resolve this controversy, several authors have tried to determine whether obstetrical complications were more common in schizophrenic individuals who did not have a family history of the disorder. However, lack of a family history of illness does not rule out a genetic cause of disease. Several studies support[253, 254] and some refute[255–257] the proposed relationship between obstetrical complications and theoretically sporadic cases of schizophrenia. There is also a division of opinion as to whether a history of obstetrical complications is related to ventriculomegaly as measured by CT scan in schizophrenic adults.[253, 258–262] The proposition that monozygotic twins discordant for schizophrenia might be discriminated by obstetrical complications or lower than normal birth weight has not been supported in a Scandinavian study.[263]

Another approach for evaluating prenatal risk factors in schizophrenia has been the epidemiological analysis of adverse intrauterine events. Several studies have examined the frequency of schizophrenia in offspring born to mothers who were pregnant during documented influenza epidemics. O'Callaghan and associates[264] in the United Kingdom and Mednick and colleagues[265] in Finland reported significantly increased rates of schizophrenia in offspring of mothers who were in their second trimesters of pregnancy during the 1957 influenza A2 pandemic. Kendell and Kemp[266] reported that offspring in their second trimesters of development during the 1957 influenza epidemic in Edinburgh were at increased risk. These authors were not able to demonstrate increased risk when Scottish national data from the 1918 and 1957 epidemics were examined. The findings of Bowler and Torrey[267] in the United States and those of Done and coworkers[268] in the United Kingdom do not support a relationship between prenatal exposure to influenza and risk for schizophrenia. Susser and Lin[269] have described an increased risk for schizophrenia in female offspring exposed to severe food deprivation in their first trimesters of development during the Dutch Hunger Winter of 1944 to 1945.

Brain Abnormalities in Schizophrenia

There is an extensive literature on abnormal clinical neurological signs in schizophrenia. "Soft" neurological signs are not typically ascribable to a focal lesion in the CNS and are thought to reflect disordered motor or sensory function at a complex, integrative level. Soft signs include dysdiadochokinesia, astereognosis, agraphesthesia, mirror phenomena, mild choreiform and tic-like movements, primitive reflexes, and sensory extinction phenomena. "Hard" neurological signs localize lesions to specific tracts, nuclei, or nerves or discrete cortical areas. Hard signs that occur in isolation from other traditional hard signs, however, may not support the presence of discrete lesions.

Various studies of neurological signs have important methodological differences, but most authors agree on an increased frequency of such signs in schizophrenic patients. Merriam and coworkers[270] found that neurological signs of prefrontal impairment correlated with deficit symptoms but not with age, presence of movement disorder, chronicity of illness, or psychological testing. King and associates,[271] in a study of 16 schizophrenic patients, found that soft signs correlated with presence of tardive dyskinesia, exposure to neuroleptic drugs, presence of positive and negative symptoms, and cognitive impairment but not with ventricular size on CT scan. Schroder and colleagues[272] found that the presence of soft signs was correlated with Brief Psychiatric Rating Scale measures of thought disorder and with third ventricular width as measured by CT scan. Two studies have supported the observation that neurological signs are more common in the normal relatives and in the psychiatrically ill relatives of schizophrenic patients.[273, 274]

Neuropsychological deficits have received increased emphasis in research on schizophrenia. Deficits in attention, memory, and "executive functions" have been observed repeatedly. These deficits implicate primarily prefrontal cortex and medial temporal lobe structures—brain areas in which altered structure and function have been found (see later). Neuropsychological abnormalities in schizophrenia are not thought to be epiphenomena of ongoing psychosis or of medication status and tend to predict long-term disability.[275]

Ventricular Enlargement and Cortical Sulcal Dilatation

The most widely replicated finding in studies of the brains of schizophrenic patients was also one of the earliest published observations. The increased ventricular size and decreased brain volume that were observed by early neuropathologists[276–278] have been replicated in postmortem specimens to which modern diagnostic criteria and quantitative measurement techniques have been applied.[279, 280]

Enlargement of the lateral and third ventricles and cortical sulci has also been demonstrated in a large number of CT studies. Despite a number of methodological problems that arise in attempting to measure cerebral structures by CT for between-group comparisons,[281] a majority of studies confirm the presence of ventricular and cortical sulcal enlargement. Shelton and Weinberger,[282] in a comprehensive review, concluded that lateral ventricular enlargement was found in 75%, third ventricular enlargement in 83%, and cortical changes in 67% of the papers they surveyed. The proportion of schizophrenic patients with ventricles greater than 2 standard deviations larger than the control means has ranged from 3% to 35%.[283] No consistent relationship has been demonstrated between ventricular size in schizophrenic individuals and age, duration of neuroleptic exposure, electroconvulsive therapy, or duration of illness.[282] Further evidence against ventricular enlargement as an epiphenomenon is found in the observation of ventricular enlargement in "first-break" schizophrenic patients[284–286] and in affected twins of monozygotic pairs discordant for schizophrenia.[287, 288] Ventricular enlargement also appears to be stable when patients are observed prospectively.[289, 290] MRI studies have confirmed the presence of ventricular enlargement.[288, 291–295]

Clinical correlations of ventriculomegaly in schizophrenic patients include poor premorbid adjustment, cognitive impairment, more negative symptoms, diminished response to neuroleptics, and greater frequency of extrapyramidal movement disorders. However, these findings have been contested by some investigators.[281, 282, 296]

Basal Ganglia

The basal ganglia are a group of functionally and anatomically related subcortical gray matter structures lying in the forebrain and midbrain. The caudate nucleus, claustrum, globus pallidus, putamen, subthalamic nucleus, and substantia nigra are considered parts of the basal ganglia. The nucleus accumbens lies in the anteroventral striatum and is included as part of the basal ganglia in this discussion. Dysfunction of the basal ganglia may contribute to the stereotypies, dyskinesias, catatonia, and possibly cognitive deficits seen in schizophrenic patients. Also, abnormalities attributed to limbic, frontal, and temporal cortices can be produced by dysfunction of the rich interconnections between these structures and the basal ganglia.

Traditional neuropathological techniques have been applied to the study of the basal ganglia of schizophrenic patients; the conflicting results are summarized in Table 15–12.

It is difficult to draw any firm conclusions from this small group of studies, but several interesting findings deserve comment. The putamen and caudate, which compose the neostriatum, and the nucleus accumbens have been reported to have normal volume and area but decreased neuronal diameter. In addition, studies from two different brain collections have revealed decreased volume of the internal segment of the globus pallidus, a finding that was reported in earlier studies.[277, 297] Decreased neuronal diameter in the nucleus accumbens may allow "hypersensitivity" to normal amounts of DA. Decreased volume of the

Table 15–12 Postmortem Neuropathological Studies in Basal Ganglia of Schizophrenic Subjects

Study	Number of Subjects/Control Subjects	Findings
Dom et al,[662] 1981	5 drug-free cases from Vogt collection, 5 control subjects	Decreased cell diameter of Golgi II neurons in neostriatum and nucleus accumbens
Bogerts et al,[330] 1983	6 drug-free cases from Vogt collection, 6 control subjects	Decreased total volume of lateral substantia nigra, decreased neuron volume in medial substantia nigra
Bogerts et al,[308] 1985	13 drug-free cases from Vogt collection, 9 control subjects	Reduced volume of internal globus pallidus; normal volume of putamen, caudate, and nucleus accumbens
Brown et al,[279] 1986	41/29 (affective disorder control subjects)	No difference in areas of lenticular nuclei or caudate
Pakkenberg,[329] 1990	12/12	Reduced total number of neurons in nucleus accumbens with normal neuron numbers in ventral pallidum
Bogerts et al,[309] 1990	18/21	Decreased volume of internal globus pallidus with normal volumes of external globus pallidus, putamen, caudate, and nucleus accumbens
Heckers et al,[300] 1991	23/23	Increased striatal volume on left, increased volume of globus pallidus on right

From Knable MB, Kleinman JE, Weinberger DR: Neurobiology of schizophrenia. In Schatzberg AF, Nemeroff CB (eds): The American Psychiatric Press Textbook of Psychopharmacology. Washington, DC: American Psychiatric Press, 1995:483.

Table 15–13 Magnetic Resonance Imaging Studies of the Basal Ganglia in Schizophrenia

Study	Number of Subjects/Control Subjects	Findings
Kelsoe et al,[291] 1988	24/14	Normal area of caudate, globus pallidus, putamen
Young et al,[293] 1991	31/33	Normal size of caudate; inverse relationship between negative symptom scale and caudate size
Jernigan et al,[298] 1991	42/24	Increased volume of lenticular nucleus; lenticular size correlates with age at onset
DeLisi et al,[301] 1991	30/15/20*	No difference in caudate or lenticular volume
Swayze et al,[299] 1992	54/48/47†	Enlarged putamen in male subjects bilaterally

*First-break patients/long-term patients/neurological control subjects.

†Forty-eight bipolar patients and 47 control subjects.

From Knable MB, Kleinman JE, Weinberger DR: Neurobiology of schizophrenia. In Schatzberg AF, Nemeroff CB (eds): The American Psychiatric Press Textbook of Psychopharmacology. Washington, DC: American Psychiatric Press, 1995:483.

substantia nigra may indicate that there is a deficiency of afferent striatonigral or corticonigral projections. Such a deficiency could allow dysregulated nigrostriatal and mesolimbic dopaminergic transmission.

In Table 15–13, the results of MRI volumetric studies of the basal ganglia are presented for comparison to the pathological studies listed before. In general, the results tend to confirm the neuropathological findings of normal striatal volume. However, two MRI studies[298, 299] and one neuropathological study[300] have found increased size of the neostriatum or its component parts. These findings are interpreted by the authors as possible evidence of defective pruning of synaptic connections during neuronal development. However, the enlargement of basal ganglia structures has not been seen in studies of first-break patients[301, 302] and has been shown to be the result of treatment effects with classic antipsychotic drugs.[302–304]

Limbic System

The limbic system has been defined in different ways. In general, a group of interconnected structures in the medial temporal lobe, diencephalon, subcortical gray matter of the forebrain, and septal aspects of the frontal lobe are considered parts of the limbic system. In a broad sense, limbic structures are thought to subserve the integration of sensory input and motoric responses with affective or emotional data. These structures are among the oldest phylogenetic components of the CNS. Areas that are often included in discussion of the limbic system are the hippocampus; the cytoarchitecturally related parahippocampal, entorhinal, and insular cortices; and the amygdala, septal nuclei, hypothalamus, nucleus accumbens, anterior thalamus, cingulate cortex, and olfactory bulbs.

The most intensive neuropathological investigation of postmortem tissue from schizophrenic patients has been focused on the hippocampus and surrounding structures. Table 15–14 summarizes neuropathological studies of this area, and Table 15–15 presents data from MRI studies.

These studies strongly implicate medial temporal lobe abnormalities in schizophrenia. The findings of reduced volume of the amygdala, hippocampus, parahippocampal gyrus, and entorhinal cortex have been replicated in the majority of neuropathological and neuroimaging studies. Abnormal cellular orientation and lamination, heterotopic cell groups, and reductions in neuron size and number that occur in the absence of gliosis suggest damage to medial temporal lobe areas in the prenatal period. Cellular migration from the ventricular surface to the cerebral cortex is essentially complete by the fifth fetal month. Therefore, pathological orchestration of neuronal migration in schizophrenia may occur before this time. Few studies have used modern diagnostic and neuropathological methods to examine other limbic structures. Two studies of the nucleus basalis of Meynert[305, 306] do not demonstrate differences between schizophrenic patients and control subjects. Benes and colleagues[307] have reported reduced neuron density in layer V of cingulate cortex, layer VI of prefrontal cortex, and layer III of motor cortex. These findings were associated with reduced glial numbers and normal neuron/glia ratio and neuron size. This concatenation of observations does not support the idea of a degenerative neuronal process underlying the schizophrenic syndrome.

Several studies noted in Tables 15–12 to 15–15 have reported findings in the basal ganglia and in mesial temporal structures. Bogerts and coworkers[308] described specimens from the Vogt collection that had decreased volume of the internal globus pallidus. These same subjects also had decreased volumes of the amygdala, hippocampus, and parahippocampal gyrus. In a later study, Bogerts and coworkers[309] replicated the findings of decreased volume of the internal globus pallidus and hippocampus in a new collection. The report by Jernigan and colleagues[298] regarding decreased medial temporal and orbitofrontal cortical volumes also included the finding of enlarged lenticular nucleus. However, findings by Young and associates[293] of decreased left parahippocampal volume and lack of normal asymmetry in amygdala volume were reported from subjects who had normal volumes of basal ganglia structures.

Neocortex

Remarkably few studies regarding disease of neocortical areas in schizophrenia are available. Sporadic reports of reduced cortical thickness and neuron number have been noted in the older neuropathological literature.[310] There have been a few reports of reduced neuron number and density in the prefrontal regions of the frontal lobes.[307, 311, 312] MRI reports of decreased temporal lobe volume[288, 313, 314] often do not distinguish whether decreased volume could be explained solely by hippocampal or medial temporal cortical thinning. Disease of lateral temporal neocortex has long been a speculative origin of positive schizophrenic symptoms and language abnormali-

Table 15–14 Neuropathological Studies of the Hippocampal Region in Schizophrenia

Study	Method	Number of Subjects/Control Subjects	Findings
Kovelman and Scheibel et al,[663] 1984	Pyramidal cell orientation and density	10/8	Pyramidal cell disarray in cornu ammonis (CA) interface CA_1/CA_2 and presubiculum/CA_1 interface in anterior hippocampus
Bogerts et al,[308] 1985	Volumetric study of 20-μm sections from the Vogt collection (left hemisphere only)	13/9	Reduced volume of amygdala, hippocampal formation, parahippocampal gyrus
Brown et al,[279] 1986	Computer-assisted determination of area at level of interventricular foramina	41/29*	Enlarged temporal horn of lateral ventricle and reduced thickness of parahippocampal cortex
Roberts et al,[664] 1986	Computer-assisted densitometry of glial fibrillary acidic protein	5/7	No gliosis in left hippocampal area
Jakob and Beckmann et al,[665] 1986	Qualitative histopathology and cell counts	64/10	Abnormal lamination and heterotopic cells in rostral entorhinal and ventral insular cortices; reduced cell counts in insular cortex layers II and III
Colter et al,[666] 1987	Computer-assisted determination of cortical area at level of interventricular foramina	17/11*	Reduced volume of gyral component of parahippocampal gyrus
Altshuler et al,[667] 1987	Pyramidal cell orientation and density in the Yakovlev collection	7/6	No difference between schizophrenic subjects and control subjects; hippocampal disarray correlated with severity of behavioral impairment in schizophrenic subjects
Falkai et al,[668] 1988	Volume and cell counts in entorhinal region in the Vogt collection	13/11	Neuron loss and decreased volume of left entorhinal cortex
Christison et al,[669] 1989	Computerized analysis of pyramidal cell size, shape, and orientation	17/32†	Normal hippocampal pyramidal cell size, shape, and orientation in left and right CA_1
Jeste and Lohr,[670] 1989	Computer-assisted volume and pyramidal cell density of CA_1–CA_4 in the Yakovlev collection	13/25†	Decreased volume of bilateral anterior and posterior CA_4; decreased pyramidal cell density in bilateral anterior and posterior CA_3/CA_4
Altshuler et al,[671] 1990	Computerized shape analysis and area determinations of single coronal sections at the level of the mamillary bodies	12/17/10‡	No difference in hippocampal area; reduced parahippocampal area on right; abnormal right hippocampal and parahippocampal shape
Bogerts et al,[309] 1990	Volume of hippocampal formation	18/21	Decreased volume of right and left hippocampal formation
Arnold et al,[672] 1991	Qualitative histopathology	6/16	Aberrant surface invaginations, lamination patterns, heterotopias, and qualitative neuron loss in entorhinal cortex
Benes et al,[673] 1991	Pyramidal cell disarray, number and size, and camera lucida determination of volume in posterior hippocampus	14/9	No difference in posterior hippocampal volume; reduced number of neurons in CA_1; smaller pyramidal cell neurons CA_1–CA_4
Conrad et al,[628] 1991	Pyramidal cell disarray in right hippocampus	11/7	Increased disarray at CA_1/CA_2 and CA_2/CA_3 interfaces

*Control subjects with affective disorders.

†Leukotomized and nonschizophrenic control subjects.

‡Nonschizophrenic and nonschizophrenic suicide control subjects.

From Knable MB, Kleinman JE, Weinberger DR: Neurobiology of schizophrenia. In Schatzberg AF, Nemeroff CB (eds): The American Psychiatric Press Textbook of Psychopharmacology. Washington, DC: American Psychiatric Press, 1995:485.

Table 15–15 Magnetic Resonance Imaging Studies* of the Hippocampal Region in Schizophrenia

Study	Number of Subjects/Control Subjects	Findings
DeLisi et al,[674] 1988	24/18	Decreased volume of the anterior amygdalo-hippocampal region bilaterally; decreased volume of right posterior amygdalo-hippocampal region
Suddath et al,[313] 1989	17/17	Decreased volume of bilateral temporal lobe gray matter, especially in region of amygdala and anterior hippocampus
Barta et al,[315] 1990	15/15	Decreased volume of left amygdala, right temporal lobe, and right superior temporal gyrus
Bogerts et al,[675] 1990	35/25	Decreased volume of left amygdalo-hippocampal region in male first-break schizophrenic subjects
Suddath et al,[288] 1990	15/15†	Decreased volume of left temporal lobe and of bilateral anterior hippocampus
Rossi et al,[314] 1991	16/10‡	Reduced bilateral temporal lobe volume
Jernigan et al,[298] 1991	42/24	Reduced volume of cortical areas containing medial temporal lobe and orbitofrontal cortex
Young et al,[293] 1991	31/33	Amygdala smaller on left in control subjects but not in schizophrenic subjects; parahippocampal gyrus smaller on left in schizophrenic subjects but not in control subjects
Shenton et al,[316] 1992	15/15	Decreased volume of gray matter in left anterior amygdalo-hippocampal area, left parahippocampal gyrus, and left superior temporal gyrus

*All were computer-assisted volumetric studies.

†Control subjects are discordant monozygotic twins.

‡Bipolar control subjects.

From Knable MB, Kleinman JE, Weinberger DR: Neurobiology of schizophrenia. In Schatzberg AF, Nemeroff CB (eds): The American Psychiatric Press Textbook of Psychopharmacology. Washington, DC: American Psychiatric Press, 1995:486.

ties. The MRI studies of Barta[315] and Shenton[316] and colleagues have found decreased volumes of the superior temporal gyrus. A number of CT and MRI studies that describe generalized reductions in thickness of cerebral cortex suggest that the proposed developmental defect in cortical maturation may not be restricted to medial temporal or frontal neocortex.[295, 317, 318]

Technological advances in the imaging of brain function have produced the most provocative evidence for dysfunction of neocortex in schizophrenia. Single-photon emission CT and positron emission tomography have been used to measure regional cerebral blood flow and local cerebral metabolic rate of glucose. These techniques and their merits have been reviewed comprehensively by Berman and Weinberger.[319] Such studies have not revealed consistent abnormalities in global cerebral metabolism or in lateralization of brain function in schizophrenic patients. Original reports by Ingvar and Franzen[320, 321] of decreased frontal lobe metabolic activity ("hypofrontality") in schizophrenic patients have been confirmed by some investigators but disputed by others.

The concept that hypofrontality may exist as a state-dependent phenomenon has emerged. When measurements of regional cerebral blood flow during cognitive tasks are performed, schizophrenic patients are consistently hypofrontal. Weinberger and coworkers[322] demonstrated a lack of activation of dorsolateral prefrontal cortex in schizophrenic patients given an automated version of the Wisconsin Card Sorting Test during xenon Xe133 regional cerebral blood flow measurement. Physiological dysfunction of dorsolateral prefrontal cortex in schizophrenia during the Wisconsin Card Sorting Test has also been replicated using hexamethylpropyleneamineoxime single-photon emission CT.[323] Prefrontal cortical dysfunction may be a discrete abnormality in schizophrenia because regional differences in cerebral metabolism are not observed during a visual continuous performance vigilance test[324] or during Raven's Progressive Matrices.[325] In studies of monozygotic twins discordant for schizophrenia, diminished activation of the dorsolateral prefrontal cortex during the Wisconsin Card Sorting Test is invariably associated with the illness, is not present in unaffected co-twins, is not affected by long-term neuroleptic exposure,[326] and is correlated with diminished hippocampal volume in the affected twins.[327]

Thalamus and Brain Stem

Lesch and Bogerts[328] have described decreased volume of the central nucleus of the thalamus. One report of decreased neuron numbers in the dorsomedial nucleus of the thalamus has appeared.[329] These thalamic nuclei deserve further study because of their interconnections with limbic structures and prefrontal cortex. Bogerts and coworkers[330] have also described a decreased size of mesencephalic ventral tegmental cells when schizophrenic subjects are compared with control subjects. An MRI study also found thalamic abnormalities in schizophrenia patients compared with healthy subjects.[331]

Cerebellum

Reduced size of the cerebellar vermis has been described in some schizophrenic patients with CT scanning[332, 333] and in a postmortem study.[334] In an effort to control for vermian atrophy from other causes, Lohr and Jeste[335] have not been able to replicate this finding in a postmortem sample. Moreover, Weinberger and colleagues[286] did not observe reduced size of the cerebellar vermis in first-break patients. These results suggest that to the extent that cerebellar disease has been associated with schizophrenia, it is likely to be an epiphenomenon.

Neurochemical Alterations

Dopamine

The DA hypothesis of schizophrenia has served as a major impetus for research for more than 30 years. In early studies, Carlsson and Lindquist[336] reported that DA turnover is increased in laboratory animals treated with antipsychotic drugs. Subsequently, it was shown that the clinical efficacy of neuroleptics was correlated with their ability to displace radioligands from DA D_2 receptors.[337, 338] Pharmacological induction of DA hyperactivity in laboratory animals produced behavioral alterations that are thought to be similar to the attentional problems seen in schizophrenic patients.[339, 340] In parallel with laboratory investigations, psychiatrists also noted that psychotic symptoms could be observed in patients exposed to drugs such as amphetamine or levodopa.[341, 342]

Investigations of DA function in schizophrenic patients in the past have been constrained by the methodological problems inherent in studies of CSF metabolites and postmortem neurochemical measures. In general, CSF DA and HVA concentrations in schizophrenic patients have not been shown to differ from those of control subjects.[343]

Studies of plasma HVA concentrations have been reviewed by Davis and colleagues.[344] Whereas some studies have found that plasma HVA levels correlate with severity of symptoms and response to neuroleptic treatment, plasma HVA concentrations are affected substantially by changes in renal clearance, an issue that has not been adequately addressed in these studies. Likewise, the possibility that increased plasma concentrations of HVA in drug-free schizophrenic patients may simply reflect alterations in peripheral autonomic function that accompany psychosis has also been generally disregarded.[345]

Studies of DA and HVA in postmortem brain tissue have yielded inconsistent results.[344] Three studies have reported increased postmortem DA concentrations. Bird and coworkers[346] found increased concentrations of DA in the nucleus accumbens and anterior perforated substance in schizophrenic patients. Crow and associates[347] found an increased concentration of DA that was restricted to the caudate nucleus. Reynolds[348] described increased DA concentration in the amygdala of schizophrenic patients that was more prominent on the left.

Postmortem studies of DA receptor binding in schizophrenic brains have demonstrated an increased number of DA D_2 receptors in the caudate, putamen, and nucleus accumbens. These changes have been reported in more than 20 studies[344, 349] and would seem to imply that a primary abnormality of the DA receptor may underlie dopaminergic dysfunction in schizophrenia. Although chronic neuroleptic treatment is also known to increase the number of DA D_2 receptors, a number of studies have reported increased D_2 receptor binding in patients who have been drug free for prolonged periods.

Attempts to measure D_2 receptor density in vivo with positron emission tomography have produced discordant results. Wong and colleagues,[350] using [^{11}C]spiperone in 10 drug-naive schizophrenic subjects, found increased binding in the caudate nucleus. This group has replicated these findings.[351] Two studies using [^{11}C]raclopride have not replicated this finding.[352, 353] No group differences between 12 schizophrenic patients and control subjects could be detected in one study with [^{76}Br]bromospiperone.[354] Interpretation of these results requires consideration of several problems. First, raclopride has a lower affinity for DA receptors than spiperone does and may be more easily displaced by endogenous ligand. Second, the studies have used different mathematical models for data analysis that are not easily compared. Third, the studies may have used patients with different severity or lengths of illness. DA receptor number may be state dependent and vary under such conditions. Finally, spiperone and bromospiperone bind to serotoninergic and adrenergic receptors and may complicate data analysis for this reason.

Fewer studies exist concerning the DA D_1 receptor. Interest in this receptor was initially not great because the clinical efficacy of neuroleptics was not correlated with displacement of ligands from the D_1 receptor. Cross[355] and Seeman[356] and coworkers have reported that D_1 binding in schizophrenic brains was not different from that in control brains. In contrast, Hess and colleagues[357] reported decreased D_1 binding in caudate and putamen in schizophrenic brains.

An abnormal functional interaction between D_1 and D_2 receptors in schizophrenia has been suggested by Seeman and coworkers.[358] Pretreatment of striatal homogenates with the D_1 antagonist Sch-23390 prevents the ability of DA to inhibit binding of the D_2 antagonist raclopride. This D_1-D_2 linkage is present in brain tissue from Parkinson's disease patients but not in schizophrenia. A link between the two receptor subtypes is proposed to be mediated by a G protein. This intriguing study has not yet been replicated.

There have been reports of elevations in the density of D_3 receptors[359] and D_4 receptors[360–362] in postmortem tissue of schizophrenic patients. It seems increasingly unlikely that simple hyperdopaminergia can account for the many clinical manifestations of schizophrenia. The mesocortical, mesolimbic, and nigrostriatal DA circuits differ from each other substantially in their anatomical and functional organizations.[363] Alterations in these projections may occur in different combinations to produce the variability of the schizophrenic syndrome.

Weinberger[364] has proposed that many of the negative symptoms of schizophrenia are primarily related to dysfunction of prefrontal cortex and that positive symptoms may reflect disinhibited subcortical DA activity as a result of a neocortical abnormality. Damage to the prefrontal cortex in rats potentiates the behavioral effects of amphetamine[365] and apomorphine.[366] Ibotenic acid lesions of medial prefrontal cortex in rats increase behavioral and biochemical evidence of DA hyperactivity in the basal ganglia, especially when the animals are stressed.[367]

Cortical modulation of subcortical DA release, in turn, may depend on intact cortical dopaminergic innervation. If mesocortical projections to frontal cortex are damaged with

6-hydroxydopamine in rodents, there is an increase of DA turnover and DA binding sites in the striatum.[368–370] Thus, cortical hypodopaminergia may play a role in some aspects of the schizophrenic syndrome.

The hypothesis that hypofrontality of schizophrenia may be related to deficient mesocortical DA activity is supported by several cerebral blood flow studies. Geraud and coworkers[371] found that piribedil restored nearly normal frontal blood flow in drug-free schizophrenic patients selected for hypofrontality as measured with ^{133}Xe single-photon emission CT. Weinberger and colleagues[372] found a positive correlation between CSF HVA concentration and prefrontal regional cerebral blood flow during the Wisconsin Card Sorting Test. Daniel and associates[373] demonstrated improved blood flow to dorsolateral prefrontal cortex during performance of the Wisconsin Card Sorting Test when six drug-free schizophrenic patients were administered intravenous apomorphine.

Defective subcortical DA transmission may also be altered by aberrant input to dopaminergic neurons from the medial temporal structures that have been implicated in the neuropathological literature on schizophrenia. Ibotenic acid lesions of ventral hippocampus in rats cause increased amphetamine-induced locomotion, increased DA concentrations in the nucleus accumbens, and decreased concentrations of dihydroxyphenylacetic acid and HVA in the medial prefrontal cortex.[374] Thus, a medial temporal cortical defect (which has been proposed in schizophrenia) may differentially affect DA transmission in subcortical and cortical systems in a manner consistent with current models of the illness.

Future advances in the study of dopaminergic abnormalities in schizophrenia will likely follow the developments of molecular biology. D_3, D_4, and D_5 receptors have now been cloned. The D_3 and D_5 receptors are located primarily in limbic areas of the brain.[375, 376] mRNA encoding the D_4 receptor is located in frontal cortex, midbrain, and amygdala and is bound with high affinity by clozapine.[377]

Glutamate

The ability of cortical neurons to modulate subcortical DA activity is probably dependent on glutamate projections because glutamate is the dominant neurotransmitter of cerebral cortex. Three principal glutamate receptors have been named for their affinity for the synthetic glutamate analogues *N*-methyl-D-aspartate (NMDA), quisqualate, and kainate.

Abnormal glutamate transmission has been suspected in schizophrenia for several reasons. Data concerning cortical hypofunction logically imply decreased cortical output. Destruction of cortical glutamatergic fibers increases the susceptibility of animals to the behavioral effects of dopaminergic drugs.[366] Glutamate normally stimulates the inhibitory neurotransmitter GABA in the striatum, whereas DA inhibits GABA release. Thus, similar behavioral effects could be produced by deficient corticostriatal glutamate activity or excessive mesostriatal DA activity.[378] It has also been shown that the normal phasic depolarization of ventral tegmental neurons is dependent on the presence of NMDA receptor–mediated effects.[379]

Glutamatergic system dysfunction in schizophrenia is also predicted by the phencyclidine model of psychosis. Phencyclidine binds to a receptor located within the ion channel formed by the NMDA receptor complex and prevents the normal neuronal events produced by binding of glutamate to the NMDA receptor.[378]

The decreased concentration of glutamate in the CSF of schizophrenic patients reported by Kim and associates[380] has not been replicated by other authors.[381–383] Perry[383] was unable to demonstrate differences in levels of glutamate measured in six regions of postmortem brain tissue in schizophrenic and control subjects. Toru and coworkers[384] measured glutamate concentrations in multiple brain areas and found decreases in the angular gyrus of schizophrenic patients. Using synaptosomal preparations from postmortem schizophrenic brain tissue, Sherman and coworkers have reported deficient glutamate release with veratridine-induced depolarization[385] or on exposure to NMDA or kainic acid.[386] The results of glutamate receptor binding studies, summarized in Table 15–16, have been somewhat more consistent in showing evidence of decreased glutamate reflected by increased excitatory amino acid binding.[384, 387]

Although it would be difficult to say that these results can be condensed to form a glutamatergic hypothesis of schizophrenia, they do seem to emphasize the possible complexities of reciprocal interactions between dopaminergic and glutamatergic systems. Decreased binding of glutamate receptor ligands in the hippocampus may imply abnormal cellular development or cell loss in this area. This is supported by the findings of Harrison and colleagues,[388] who have reported a decrease in mRNA expression of the NMDA receptor in the CA_3 region of the hippocampus in postmortem brain tissue from schizophrenic individuals. Increased numbers of prefrontal cortical glutamate receptors and glutamate reuptake sites may indicate an abnormally rich glutamatergic innervation of prefrontal cortex by other cortical projection neurons. Abnormal elimination of transient synaptic connections during development could explain such a finding. In the basal ganglia, decreased glutamate reuptake sites may indicate a reduction in the number of glutamatergic projections to subcortical areas, with increased MK-801 binding representing a "denervation supersensitivity" phenomenon. Indeed, in all the brain areas mentioned, one may argue that abnormalities in glutamate receptor binding do not reflect anything at all about anatomical connections but are purely functional in nature. It will be left for future research to determine whether glutamate receptor abnormalities in schizophrenia arise as a primary feature of the illness, in response to abnormalities in other neurotransmitter systems, or as an artifact of drug treatment.

Serotonin

Early theories implicating 5-HT in the pathogenesis of schizophrenia were based on the observation that D-lysergic acid diethylamide (LSD), an agonist for 5-HT receptors, could produce a psychosis with some features similar to that of schizophrenia. Animal studies have provided evidence for modulation of DA activity by 5-HT,[389, 390] and interest in the 5-HT system in schizophrenia has been rekindled because many atypical neuroleptics (e.g., clozapine, ziprasidone, sertindole, risperidone, olanzepine, and seroquel) have 5-HT_2 receptor antagonist properties.[391]

Table 15–16 Glutamate Receptor Binding Studies in Postmortem Schizophrenic Brain Tissue*

Study	Method	Number of Subjects/Control Subjects	Results
Kerwin et al,[676] 1988	[^{3}H]kainate and glutamate in hippocampal homogenates	11/9 (kainate)† 10/7 (glutamate)†	Decreased kainate and glutamate binding in left hippocampus
Toru et al,[384] 1988	[^{3}H]kainate in homogenates from multiple brain areas	14/10‡	Increased binding in prefrontal cortex and angular gyrus Negative correlation between [^{3}H]kainate binding and glutamate levels in frontal cortex and thalamus
Kornhuber et al,[387] 1989	[^{3}H]MK-801 (PCP binding site ligand) in homogenates from multiple brain areas	10/7†	Increased binding in putamen
Deakin et al,[677] 1989	[^{3}H]D-aspartate (glutamate reuptake sites) and [^{3}H]kainate in homogenates from seven cortical areas	14/14†	Increased binding of both ligands in bilateral orbital frontal cortex Negative correlation of aspartate binding in left polar temporal cortex and dopamine concentration in left amygdala
Kerwin et al,[678] 1990	[^{3}H]glutamate (for glutamate and NMDA sites), kainate, CNQX (for quisqualate sites) in medial temporal lobe with autoradiography	8/7†	Decreased kainate binding in bilateral CA_4/CA_3 region, DG, PHG, and left CA_2/CA_1 Decreased CNQX binding in bilateral CA_4 and left CA_3 regions
Weissman et al,[679] 1991	[^{3}H]TCP (for PCP sites) in homogenates of multiple brain regions	44/18§	Mild decrease in binding in occipital cortex in schizophrenic subjects and suicide victims. No change in putamen
Simpson et al,[680] 1992	[^{3}H]D-aspartate in homogenates of basal ganglia	19/22	Reduced binding in putamen and lateral pallidum
Simpson et al,[681] 1992	[^{3}H]TCP binding in frontal and temporal cortex, hippocampus, and amygdala	13/14	Bilateral increase in binding in orbital frontal cortex

*CA, Cornu ammonis; CNQX, 6-cyano-7-nitroguinoxaline-2,3-dione; DG, dentate gyrus; NMDA, *N*-methyl-D-aspartate; PCP, phencyclidine; PHG, parahippocampal gyrus; TCP, *N*-(1-[2-thienyl] cyclonexyl) piperidine.

†Receiving neuroleptics at death.

‡No neuroleptics for 40 days before death.

§Includes nonpsychotic suicide control subjects.

There have been few consistently replicated abnormalities of serotoninergic neurotransmission in schizophrenia despite a considerable number of studies. Measurements of brain and CSF 5-HT and 5-HIAA concentrations have produced conflicting results. However, several studies have replicated a correlation between low CSF 5-HIAA levels and the presence of ventriculomegaly and cortical thinning in schizophrenic patients.[391] Postmortem studies of 5-HT receptors have focused mainly on the 5-HT_2 receptor subtype. In the nucleus accumbens[392] and striatum,[393] there is reportedly no difference between schizophrenic subjects and control subjects in 5-HT_2 receptor binding. Binding sites in frontal cortex have been reported to be decreased[394–397] or unchanged.[398, 399] Laruelle[397] has also reported increased binding of paroxetine to 5-HT transporter sites in prefrontal cortex.

Norepinephrine

The noradrenergic system in schizophrenia has been investigated less intensely than other neurotransmitter systems. The noradrenergic system is implicated in schizophrenia for several reasons. Neuroleptics may produce some therapeutic effects through adrenergic receptors.[400] Elevations of plasma and CSF NE levels have been reported in a number of studies.[401] CSF concentrations of NE and MHPG have been correlated with severity of negative symptoms.[402, 403] A few studies have found elevated levels of NE in limbic areas of postmortem schizophrenic brain tissue,[404, 405] but conflicting studies also exist.[347, 406] No consistently replicated abnormality of adrenergic receptors has emerged.

Peptides and Other Neurochemicals

Cholecystokinin (CCK) is a 33–amino acid peptide that was originally isolated in the gastrointestinal tract. CCK is also present in high concentrations in the brain, coexists with DA in mesolimbic neurons, and is thought to act as a neurotransmitter or neuromodulator. Several radioimmunoassay studies have revealed decreased concentrations of CCK in temporal lobe structures of schizophrenic brain.[407–409] Two other studies did not confirm this finding.[410, 411]

Farmery and coworkers[412] reported a 20% decrease in CCK receptor binding in frontal cortex homogenates and a 40% decrease in binding in hippocampal homogenates from postmortem schizophrenic tissue. Using quantitative autoradiography, Kerwin and colleagues[413] have noted decreased CCK binding sites in the cornu ammonis region of hippocampus, subiculum, and parahippocampal gyrus in schizophrenic patients.

Considerable information supports a role for neurotensin in the mechanism of action of antipsychotic drugs and in the pathophysiological process of schizophrenia.[414]

Although abnormalities have been reported in AC, GABA, endogenous opiates, TRH, somatostatin, substance P, vasoactive intestinal polypeptide, synapsins, and microtubular associated proteins, none of these findings has been consistently replicated.

Conclusion

Researchers at the beginning of the 20th century implicated dysfunction of frontal and temporal cortices in psychosis. More recent schizophrenia research has produced findings that support their suspicions, although the nature and etiology of frontal and temporal lobe dysfunction remain unknown. Whereas a genetic predisposition to schizophrenia is well established, research findings in schizophrenia lead one to conclude that multifactorial and, in part, environmentally derived insults to the brain probably contribute to the pathological process of schizophrenia. Monozygotic twins do not have uniformly high concordance rates for schizophrenia, and the unaffected members of monozygotic twin pairs that are discordant for schizophrenia do not share with their ill twins the markers of structural brain disease described before. In addition, there is some evidence that people with schizophrenia may have an increased frequency of obstetrical complications or may have been exposed to viral infections or malnutrition during fetal life that could alter brain development.

As a result of the genetic and environmental factors that may have contributed to the development of schizophrenia, one can observe several reproducible structural and physiological abnormalities of the brain in schizophrenic patients. These include enlargement of the cerebral ventricles, dilatation of cortical sulci, reduction in the size of several anteromedial temporal lobe structures, and hypometabolism of dorsolateral prefrontal cortex during cognitive tasks. Clinical and neuropathological evidence supports the idea that these abnormalities result from a fixed "lesion" that is acquired early in life and that results in a relatively nonprogressive psychotic syndrome. A lack of gliosis in neuropathological studies supports the notion that the neuronal lesions of schizophrenia are acquired before birth. The onset of psychotic symptoms in adolescence or early adulthood may occur because of a disturbance or failure in maturation of a frontotemporolimbic neural network during a critical period of development.

In light of the structural brain abnormalities observed in schizophrenia, alterations in neurotransmitter function may be regarded as secondary to neuron loss or altered neuron development. This hypothesis is supported by 1) findings in laboratory animals that cortical lesions can differentially affect DA neurotransmission in subcortical areas and in distant cortical areas, 2) the correlation between prefrontal regional cerebral blood flow in schizophrenic patients during cognitive tasks and CSF metabolites of DA, and 3) the correlation between hippocampal size and activation of prefrontal cortical blood flow in schizophrenic patients.

However, the possibility exists that primary dysfunction of dopaminergic or other neurotransmitter systems may underlie the schizophrenic syndrome. Future research with more rigorously defined postmortem samples will be necessary before one can reliably conclude that increased concentrations of DA, altered DA receptor function, or alterations in other neurotransmitters occur in schizophrenic patients independently of drug treatment artifacts and structural brain abnormalities.

ANIMAL MODELS OF DEPRESSION AND SCHIZOPHRENIA

Researchers have historically lacked validated animal models with which to study psychiatric disorders, although animal models of both depression and schizophrenia have more recently played a significant role in the development of treatments for these disorders. Nevertheless, animal models of these disorders have yet to achieve their potential because existing models remain imperfect approximations of their target disorders. However, the ability to study physiological and environmental processes under experimental control that is not possible when human patients are the subject population renders animal models of such apparent value for development of effective treatments that efforts to improve animal models are continuously ongoing. This section briefly summarizes the development of these models to date.

Types of Animal Models

Animal models can be divided into two categories. The first category includes models termed *animal assay* models. Models in this category use behavioral and physiological responses of animals to assess processes, usually physiological, that already existing evidence indicates are important in a disorder. For example, considerable evidence (see earlier) indicates that alteration in the activity of DA neurons is important in the pathogenesis of schizophrenia and Parkinson's disease. Rats show turning (rotational) behavior when receptors for DA in the brain are stimulated. The sensitivity of receptors and activity of the nigroneostriatal dopaminergic system in the brain can be assessed in animals by measuring turning (rotational) behavior; thus, this response in the animal serves as an assay for a physiological function of importance in behavior disorders. The second category consists of models that can be called *homologous* models. These models endeavor to re-create the human disorder in animals. In these models, treatments are administered to animals in the hope of causing the animals to resemble individuals who are afflicted with the disorder.

Both the animal assay and homologous models are useful. The first type finds its major use in drug screening and development of new drugs. By permitting one to determine how various compounds affect physiological processes that are important in disease, these models make it possible to rapidly assess the potential utility of novel drugs and, in some cases, to discover new drugs that unexpectedly affect an important physiological process. Of course, a limitation of this type of model is that it must assume a priori that a particular physiological process is important in a disorder, and the usefulness of the model rests on this assumption. The second type of animal model is also valuable, perhaps even more so than the first. Once perfected, a homologous model reproduces a disorder (as closely as can be done) in an animal. Unlike the animal assay type, a model of this type does not assume that a particular physiological abnormality underlies a disorder. Consequently, because the perfected homologous model reproduces a disorder, it is then possible to study the model as a means to discover the underlying cause (i.e., physiological defect) in the disorder. In addition, such a model can be used to test for totally novel treatments for the disorder; that is, because a perfected homologous model reproduces the disorder without making any assumptions regarding its physiological basis, one can test any type of potential treatment on the animal model to see whether it can reverse the disorder. Because the physiological basis of any disorder in medicine can theoretically be discovered if one produces a disorder in animals, and completely new treatments can be tested, major advances in understanding and treatment of a disorder frequently follow the development of an adequate homologous model.

Criteria for Evaluating Animal Models

Soon after animal models of behavior disorders, particularly depression, came into use, criteria were proposed by which such models could be evaluated. Although these criteria have been constructed primarily for evaluation of homologous models, animal assays can also be evaluated by applying to them those aspects of the criteria applicable to such models. Interestingly, a considerable degree of consensus has developed in regard to one particular set of criteria, which has been widely accepted throughout the field despite occasional recommendations for some modifications.

Criteria Proposed by McKinney and Bunney

The criteria that have been widely accepted are those proposed by McKinney and Bunney[415] in 1969. They proposed that the usefulness and validity of an animal model of any behavior disorder could be determined on the basis of the similarity of the animal model to the human disorder with respect to four criteria:

1. Etiology
2. Symptoms
3. Biochemistry
4. Response to treatment

In other words, the "goodness" or validity of an animal model of any behavioral-psychological-psychiatric disorder can be determined by the extent to which the animal model 1) is produced by etiological factors similar to those that produce the human disorder, 2) resembles the human disorder in manifestations or symptoms, 3) has an underlying pathophysiological basis similar to that of the human disorder, and 4) responds as does the human disorder to appropriate therapeutic treatments. Before these particular criteria are commented on further, other suggestions and amplifications are described.

Criteria Proposed by Abramson and Seligman

Abramson and Seligman,[416] in a volume that reviewed a wide variety of animal models, proposed a different set of criteria:

1. Is the analysis of the laboratory phenomenon (model) thorough in describing the essential features of its cause, prevention, and cure?
2. Is the similarity of symptoms convincingly demonstrated?
3. To what extent are physiology, cause, cure, and prevention similar to the human disorder?
4. Does the model describe in all instances a naturally occurring psychopathological process or only a subgroup?

In actuality, these criteria do not suggest anything markedly different from those proposed by McKinney and Bunney but appear to address issues such as the quality of the research that is carried out to establish the model (i.e., Is the analysis thorough enough? Are symptoms convincingly demonstrated?). The third criterion seems to repeat the criteria proposed by McKinney and Bunney[415] with the exception that etiology is omitted from this particular list. Finally, the last criterion simply asks for judgment regarding whether the model reproduces a particular subgroup of a disorder; however, once this issue is settled, the same criteria would be used to evaluate the model whether it represented some global disorder or a subgroup.

Criteria Proposed by Willner

The most significant attempt to improve the simple schema presented by McKinney and Bunney[415] was offered by Willner.[417] He suggested that animal models should be evaluated for different types of validity—predictive validity, face validity, and construct validity. Each of these categories was said to possess five characteristics. Predictive validity is determined by whether a model correctly predicts an aspect of the disorder, for example, identifies 1) pharmacological antidepressant treatments of 2) different types 3) without showing false-positives or 4) false-negatives and 5) by whether drug dosages effective in the model correlate in potency with those found to be effective in the clinic. Face validity is said to be determined by whether a model approximates the clinical characteristics of a disorder. For example, in the case of depression, face validity is determined by whether 1) antidepressant effects are present only with chronic administration and whether the symptoms of the model 2) resemble a number of the symptoms of depression that are 3) specific to depression and 4) found in particular subtypes of depression; and 5) the model should not show characteristics not seen clinically. Finally, construct validity requires that 1) the behavioral features of the model and 2) the features of the disorder that the model seeks to reproduce can be unambiguously interpreted, 3) are homologous, and stand in an established 4) empirical and 5) theoretical relationship to the specific disorder.

Whereas these criteria constitute a long and detailed list, it is unclear how they substantially contribute to those proposed by McKinney and Bunney earlier. For example, predictive validity, which Willner applied only to antidepressant medications, would seem to be subsumed under the McKinney and Bunney criterion of response to treatment. Moreover, the first characteristic listed by Willner under face validity—that antidepressant medication has therapeutic effects only on chronic administration—would seem to be an aspect of this criterion rather than of some other. Thus, what Willner described as predictive validity as well as the chronicity requirement for the effects of drugs could well be seen simply as a more elaborate description of McKinney and Bunney's last general criterion. (It can also be noted that Willner's schema omits any mention of nonpharmacological treatments, which not only are effective in ameliorating depression but conceivably can be modeled in an animal.) A similar judgment can be made regarding face validity, which would seem subsumed under McKinney and Bunney's requirement of symptom similarity; moreover, the specific requirements proposed by Willner for this category may be excessively restrictive. In particular, it is unclear why a model that includes all salient clinical features of depression (which presumably are also reversible by antidepressant treatment) would be of lesser value if the model showed additional changes as well; depression in humans is rarely uncontaminated by other changes or disturbances.

Potentially the most significant contribution embodied in Willner's suggestions is the addition of construct validity. By pointing out the need to define characteristics clearly and unambiguously, Willner drew attention to the fact that attributes of the human disorder are often poorly described, which makes modeling exceedingly difficult. However, the need for construct validity could be said to apply to every aspect of both the animal response being generated (and measured) and the human behavior that one attempts to match in an animal model, all of these characteristics falling within the criteria of McKinney and Bunney. In other words, these aspects of construct validity, like many of the Abramson and Seligman criteria, appear to set requirements for how any criterion, including those proposed by McKinney and Bunney, should be established and evaluated, but such requirements do not themselves expand the actual list of criteria proposed by McKinney and Bunney.

There is, however, one exception to this in Willner's criteria; it is that aspect of construct validity stipulating that responses seen in the animal model should "stand in theoretical relationship to [for example] depression." This stipulation could be regarded as trivial, one that might be fulfilled by, as an example, conceptually linking reduced motor activity in rats to psychomotor retardation in humans. However, defining a theoretical basis for a model normally would be understood to require more than this. What would be expected by this requirement is to *establish a link across different levels of analysis,* such as linking a syndrome of different behaviors to an underlying generalized cognitive deficit or physiological defect. Thus, this criterion potentially expands the scope of homologous models by promoting modeling not only of responses or syndromes of responses but also of *processes* involved in abnormal behavior. For example, one might model deficits in the appreciation of pleasure (for depression) or the inability to properly exclude irrelevant stimuli (for schizophrenia). Moreover, it can be argued that ultimately the most satisfactory and appropriate models for behavior disorders will reflect critical processes.

Despite potential positive attributes of this suggestion, it is also important to consider the appreciable dangers in using the criterion described. To model a critical process, one must make two major assumptions: 1) that the particular process one addresses is affected (disturbed) in the disorder; and 2) that the behavioral change measured in the animal validly represents that process, rather than this change being caused by some other, unrelated influence. In short, adopting this approach means that one is no longer strictly bound by symptom similarity of the behavior seen in the model to what is seen in the disorder; the link to the disorder is accomplished through a series of theoretical formulations. In considering this course, it should be recalled that the field of abnormal psychology is emerging from a long period during which disorders were defined by hypothetical underlying processes; these were usually psychodynamic in nature. Today, proponents of theoretically based models are likely to replace psychodynamic processes with physiological ones as the appropriate basis for abnormal psychology. For example, in the case of depression, "anger turned inward" is likely to be replaced by "deficits in brain dopaminergic transmission mediating pleasure." However, although aspects of the latter formulation may be easier (and more fashionable) to measure than the former, the underlying concerns with respect to modeling are similar. This is because even a physiologically based formulation of an underlying deficit is presently a conjecture. Little is *actually known* at present about the pathophysiological mechanism underlying abnormal psychological conditions; no reliable physiological abnormalities denote any diagnostic group, and the wealth of information we process in the physiological realm relates largely to drug action that describes processes involved in counteracting or ameliorating abnormal responses, which ultimately may relate only indirectly to what is physiologically disturbed in the affected patient. As a result, although theoretically based models are likely to provide interesting and valuable information about the relationship of certain behaviors to physiological changes, they face no fewer fundamental problems in establishing their validity as models of diagnostic categories than did the psychodynamic formulations they have replaced.

The thrust of the *Diagnostic and Statistical Manual of Mental Disorders,* Third Edition (DSM-III), which is continued in the third edition, revised (DSM-III-R) and the fourth edition (DSM-IV), has been to move away from diagnosis related to theoretical constructs and toward diagnosis based on directly observable markers. This trend is accentuated in the recent call for basing the diagnosis of depression on behavioral "signs" rather than even on reported symptoms.[418, 419] Consequently, reproducing the symptoms or signs of abnormal psychological conditions in animal models, and finding these symptoms to be ameliorated by effective treatments, must continue to be the goals of models at present, or one risks slipping back to pre–DSM-III diagnosis. The appropriate goal for models is to achieve empirical validity, regardless of theoretical validity. For depression, this pursuit is aided by its considerable repertoire of motor and vegetative symptoms. For schizophrenia, on the other hand, symptoms and signs in the human disorder are predominantly evidence of cognitive disturbance, so that reproducing these specific symptoms in an animal model is much more difficult. As will be seen in the discussion of models for schizophrenia, attempting to duplicate disturbed processes appears to be the most productive avenue at present, despite the conceptual risks.

In conclusion, the concise, straightforward schema proposed by McKinney and Bunney[415] therefore appears to be the most adequate set of criteria for evaluating animal models suggested up to the present. As Sir Martin Roth[420] commented in addressing the diagnosis of affective disorders, "Good classifications are simple and parsimonious."

Models of Depression

In this section, a description of each model is given. These descriptions begin with the procedural aspects by which the model is produced, and then the attributes of the model are summarized, particularly those that permit evaluation according to the criteria of McKinney and Bunney.[415] The allocation of models to either the animal assay category or the homologous model category can occasionally be somewhat arbitrary, but heavy emphasis is placed here on face validity with respect to symptoms. For example, in accord with the view that a fundamental aspect of depression is a slowing, or retardation, of function,[418, 421, 422] models are here classified as homologous when reduced motor activity is the primary symptom shown by the animal despite the fact that the model may be deficient in other ways. Conversely, models of depression are not classified as homologous when hyperactivity is a significant feature, except in those cases when the model shows evidence that functioning is otherwise generally retarded or that the hyperactivity seen in the model is due to agitation.

Animal Assay Models

As stated previously, animal assay models are essentially used to screen for antidepressant drugs. Consequently, these models are described in terms of their ability to detect pharmacological agents useful in the treatment of depression. Such models are therefore described not only regarding whether they respond to antidepressant medications but also whether they respond to drugs or treatments that are not antidepressant in nature or fail to respond to known antidepressant treatments or both. Whether a model responds to acute or long-term drug administration is also noted.

Muricide

Some rats will spontaneously kill mice when the mice are presented to the rat. Horovitz and coworkers[423] noted that administration of imipramine, iproniazid (MAOI), and *d*-amphetamine blocked the tendency of such rats to kill mice and that this effect could not be attributed to drug-induced debilitation or sedation. Subsequent studies confirmed that TCAs, (e.g., DMI, imipramine), MAOIs, and amphetamines have this effect, but antihistamines were also found to do so.[424, 425] Antidepressants accomplished this effect with acute administration.

Yohimbine Lethality

The drug yohimbine can be administered to mice in dosages that are lethal; administration of sublethal doses was found to be lethal when accompanied by the administration of TCAs and MAOIs.[426] Malick[427] reported that atypical antidepressants (bupropion, nomifensine, mianserin, iprindole) also produced this effect, whereas antipsychotics and most tranquilizers did not. An important exception is that electroconvulsive shock does not potentiate lethality; also, anticholinergics and antihistaminics do. Drugs have these effects when they are administered acutely.

Amphetamine Potentiation

Amphetamine produces a number of effects in rats, including hypothermia,[428] increased locomotor activity,[429] and improved shuttle box avoidance performance.[430] Antidepressants, both TCAs and MAOIs, have been found to potentiate these responses. As with the models described previously, these effects are observed after acute administration of drug. It can be noted that the various effects measured in conjunction with this test derive from the catecholamimetic action of amphetamine; consequently, amphetamine potentiation primarily detects ability of a drug or treatment to potentiate catecholaminergic neurotransmission.

Kindling

Electrical stimulation of certain brain regions (e.g., amygdala, cortex) apparently sensitizes the brain region to initiate seizure activity so that after such stimulation considerably less electrical stimulation is required to initiate seizure activity than is the case in animals that have not previously been given electrical stimulation. Babington and Wedeking[431] reported that TCAs reduced the likelihood of development of seizures in "kindled" animals. Other drugs, such as tranquilizers and sedatives, also blocked kindled seizures. However, only the antidepressants that were tested (amitriptyline, nortriptyline, imipramine) blocked seizures initiated in the amygdala at considerably lower doses than were needed to block seizures kindled in the neocortex; all other drugs tested were equipotent against seizures initiated at both sites. Subsequently, electroconvulsive shock was found to produce the same effect,[432] but MAOIs did not. Drugs are effective when given acutely.

Circadian Rhythm Readjustment

Rats are normally active during the dark period of the day and are quiet (less active) during the light period. If the light-dark periods are exchanged, the animals must readjust their activity to this shift in the light-dark cycle. The rapidity with which animals will shift their activity to the new dark period and decrease their activity to the new light period is facilitated by administration of the TCA imipramine or the MAOI pargyline.[433] A stimulant (amphetamine) and a benzodiazepine (chlordiazepoxide) were not effective. In treatments reported to be effective, drugs were administered repeatedly (i.e., for 10 days before the light-dark shift and for approximately 2 weeks thereafter).

Lesions of the Olfactory Bulbs

Bilateral lesions of the olfactory bulbs produce a number of behavioral effects. This procedure generally results in hyperactivity in novel situations such as the open field[434] and exaggerated responses to excitatory stimuli.[435] Perhaps related to the hyperactivity, animals with olfactory bulb lesions also show deficits in passive avoidance performance[436, 437] as well as superior performance in the two-way shuttle avoidance task[436] that is highly dependent on high levels of motor activity for good acquisition.[438] However, olfactory bulb lesions also produce poor performance in one-way avoidance,[439] suggesting that decreased fearfulness may contribute to both poor passive avoidance and enhanced shuttle avoidance (shuttle avoidance is performed better in animals whose fear level is low). Activity in the Porsolt swim test has been reported to be unaffected by bulbectomy,[440] but bulbectomy was found to increase activity in a swim task that emphasized escape attempts.[441] Lesions of the olfactory bulbs were initially reported to produce a sustained elevation of circulating corticosterone in the rat, therefore mimicking the hypercortisolemia seen in severe depression, but this response may have been generated as an acute reaction to the measurement procedures.[442]

Regarding pharmacological tests, deficits in avoidance behavior, particularly passive avoidance, produced by bulbectomy were found to be reversed by TCAs (amitriptyline, imipramine, chlorimipramine), atypical antidepressants (mianserin, viloxazine), and a 5-HT uptake inhibitor; this deficit was exaggerated by tranquilizers and neuroleptics.[435, 437, 443, 444] Drugs were effective in such tests when given chronically. Increased open-field activity of bulbectomized animals was found to be diminished by 5-HT uptake inhibitors, which were effective when given acutely as well as chronically.[445]

Differential Operant Responding for Low Reinforcement

Seiden, O'Donnell, and colleagues[446–450] have screened a wide variety of drugs for their effects on responding by rats when the animals are reinforced for a low rate of responding. In this task, an animal is taught to press a lever to receive a food reward. After the response is acquired, the animal is placed on a "differential reinforcement of low rate 72-second" schedule, which requires the animal to wait 72 seconds after making a response before making another response to obtain the food reward; making a second response in less than 72 seconds after the first causes no reinforcement to be obtained and simply resets the timing sequence so that the animal must wait an additional 72 seconds before responding to receive a reward. In several studies,[446–450] these investigators found that electroconvulsive shock and a variety of antidepressant drugs including TCAs (DMI, imipramine, nortriptyline, chlorimipramine), MAOIs (tranylcypromine, iproniazid, phenelzine), atypical antidepressants (iprindole, mianserin, trazodone), and SSRIs (zimeldine, fluoxetine) all improved the ability of animals to inhibit reward in responding and obtaining reward. Danysz and coworkers[451] found similar detection of antidepressants. This effect was usually seen with acute administration of drug, but further improvements in performance were seen when the drug was administered repeatedly. Antipsychotic, psychomotor stimulant, narcotic analgesic, anxiolytic, antihistaminic, and anticholinergic agents did not improve performance. Seiden and colleagues[451a] described findings indicating that the improved ability to perform on a differential reinforcement of low rate schedule could not be explained simply by the possibility that antidepressant treatment decreased response rate because anxiolytics and phenothiazines also decreased response rate but did so to such an extent that number of reinforcements decreased dramatically. However, Pollard and Howard[452] found in two studies that nonantidepressant drugs (chlorpromazine, haloperidol, and buspirone) could reduce response rate moderately to produce an increase in reinforcements similar to antidepressants and argued that this test is not specific for antidepressant drugs.

Isolation-Induced Hyperactivity

When rats were housed individually as soon as they were weaned, they were found to be hyperactive as adults when tested in a novel environment. Garzon and Del Rio[453, 454] found this hyperactivity (i.e., increased activity of isolated rats relative to nonisolated rats) to be attenuated or abolished by TCAs (amitriptyline, clomipramine, DMI), MAOIs (phenelzine, clorgyline), and atypical antidepressants (iprindole, mianserin, trazodone). The hyperactivity of isolated rats was not affected by antipsychotic medication (chlorpromazine, haloperidol), anxiolytics (chlordiazepoxide, diazepam), and amphetamine. These investigators have tested several drugs in an attempt to elucidate the neurotransmitter mechanism underlying the hyperactivity. The activity difference between isolated and nonisolated rats is abolished by the postsynaptic DA receptor agonist apomorphine and also by higher doses of nomifensine, which blocks DA as well as NE reuptake; interestingly, the lowest dose of nomifensine used (5 mg/kg intraperitoneally) markedly increased the difference between isolated and nonisolated animals. Hyperactivity of isolated animals was also blocked by cyproheptadine, a 5-HT receptor antagonist, as well as by salbutamol, a β-adrenergic receptor agonist. On the basis of this array of pharmacological results, the nature of isolation-induced hyperactivity does not appear easily explained in relation to any one particular monoamine. All of the drug effects described were seen with acute administration. One potential concern in the use of this testing procedure, which was emphasized by the investigators and considered throughout their studies, is that many of the drugs used will affect motor activity of normal (nonisolated) animals, so that drugs can eliminate differences between isolated and nonisolated animals by either markedly increasing or decreasing activity in general; care must be taken to use doses of drug that do not change normal motor patterns considerably.

Summary Observations Regarding Animal Assay Models

Animal assays are, almost by definition, useful (or not useful) depending on their ability to screen for drugs or other potential treatments for depression. As noted in the preceding descriptions, many of these models detect antidepressant medication when the drug is administered acutely. The first observation that can be made is that although this might at first appear to be a deficiency because antidepressant medication is effective in patients only after repeated administration, it may not be so in an animal assay model. A drug screen can be viewed as most useful if it specifically detects effective antidepressant medication when the drug is given only once and therefore is highly efficient. In evaluating animal assays, it needs to be kept in mind that such assays use responses of animals, whether behavioral or physiological, in a manner that is not different from an in vitro assay; that is, the response of the animal, even if it is a behavioral one, is no more than a "readout" of drug action. As one increasingly requires that the drug mimic the effects observed in human patients (i.e., effectiveness when administered only chronically), one is effectively moving to criteria that are applicable to homologous models, and one is requiring the behavioral response of the animal to resemble the behavioral response of the depressed patient. Consequently, an animal assay that responds to acute administration of a treatment is as useful as, and perhaps more useful than, one that requires chronic administration of the treatment.

Lesioning of the olfactory bulbs produces one of the more interesting models described under the category of animal assays. This model has one of the best profiles for detection of known antidepressants, responding to TCAs and atypical antidepressants as well as SSRIs, whereas stimulants (amphetamine) and the anticholinergic atropine were ineffective; however, the single MAOI that was tested (tranylcypromine) was ineffective. The ability of olfactory bulbectomy to act as a screen for antidepressant medication may appear anomalous at first, given the nature of the manipulation, but studies have determined that neurotransmitter changes resulting from lesions of the olfactory bulbs may account for the ability of this seemingly unusual procedure to generate a model of relevance to depression. For instance, all effective TCAs potentiate the effects of released NE by blocking reuptake,[455] which was a key observation that led to the catecholamine hypothesis of depression.[1, 456] As noted earlier in this chapter, this hypothesis originally proposed that a deficit in brain NE, which NE reuptake blockers and MAOIs corrected, was responsible for depression. Lesions of the olfactory bulbs produce a marked depletion of NE in the forebrain, possibly by interruption of noradrenergic axons as they course by the olfactory bulbs in projection to the neocortex.[443, 457] Moreover, Shipley and colleagues[458] reported that 40% of neurons of the locus caeruleus (LC) project to the rat olfactory bulb, which is 10 times as many LC cells as project to any other part of the cerebral cortex; consequently, altered activity of a significant number of the noradrenergic cells that innervate the forebrain is likely to follow a lesion of the olfactory bulbs.

As could be expected, the consequences of bulbectomy are not simple; lesions of the olfactory bulbs affect not only NE but 5-HT, cholinergic, and GABAergic systems as well.[459] Moreover, the behavioral effects of bulbectomy cannot be reproduced simply by reducing forebrain NE.

Homologous Models

As stated previously, the models discussed in this section represent those in which the animal shows responses similar to those seen in clinical depression. Inclusion of the model in this section does not require the symptom profile to be extensive—the animal may manifest only one particular response that appears similar to what is seen in clinical depression—although animal models included in this section may also reproduce a number of changes, behavioral or physiological, that can be related to depressive responses.

Reserpine-Induced Reduction of Motor Activity

Reserpine and reserpine-like compounds, such as tetrabenazine, inactivate the ability of synaptic vesicles to retain monoamines; as a consequence of this action, release of monoamines follows administration of these drugs, and there is then a long-term reduction in monoamine stores resulting in depletion of DA, NE, epinephrine, and 5-HT in the brain and the periphery. The depletion of amines produces a variety of physiological and behavioral effects, and antidepressants have been shown to counteract a number of these. Domenjoz and Theobald[460] first reported that imipramine could block the ability of reserpine to potentiate hypnotic effects. Costa and associates[461] then reported that reserpine-induced decreases in rectal temperature and heart rate and increases in diarrhea and ptosis were blocked by imipramine. These effects would normally cause this model to be classified as an animal assay, but reserpine will also decrease motor activity, and antidepressants will counteract this effect as well. Vernier and coworkers[462] reported that imipramine would antagonize reserpine-induced sedation, which was quantified largely by decreased motor activity. In addition to imipramine, other TCAs also antagonize reserpine-induced (or tetrabenazine-induced) depression of motor activity. MAOIs have a similar effect.[463] The "reserpinized rodent" constitutes one of the earliest, if not the earliest, animal model of depression, and the observation that reserpine suppresses motor activity was apparently a key factor in development of the catecholamine hypothesis of depression.

Given the ability of TCAs and MAOIs to potentiate the action of monoamines, in retrospect it is not surprising that these substances antagonize effects of reserpine on a variety of responses, including the ability of reserpine to depress motor activity. On the other hand, a variety of compounds that do not appear to be effective antidepressant medications, such as amphetamine and cocaine, also yield positive results in antagonizing reserpine-induced reduction of motor activity. Thus, this test apparently detects the ability of a treatment or drug to potentiate central aminergic transmission, rather than the test's being specific for antidepressant action. Effects described before are also seen with acute administration of drug, rather than requiring chronic administration. Finally, the test is not known to detect non-TCAs such as iprindole.

Depression of Active Responding Induced by 5-Hydroxytryptophan

On the basis of early studies suggesting that LSD produced psychoactive effects by interacting with serotoninergic receptors, Aprison hypothesized that 5-HT might be importantly involved in behavioral states. Consequently, Aprison and coworkers[464] injected the 5-HT precursor 5-HTP into pigeons, and subsequently rats, and observed that the treatment produced marked suppression of active responding for food reinforcement. This reduction in active behavior seen after increased 5-HT release due to administration of 5-HTP was blocked by TCAs (amitriptyline, imipramine) as well as by non-TCAs (mianserin, iprindole).[465] Features of the model that do not reproduce what is seen in depression include 1) acute administration of the antidepressants was effective in blocking the behavioral depression and 2) drugs that block 5-HT reuptake (e.g., fluoxetine) increased 5-HTP–induced behavioral depression markedly.[466] Thus, this model would predict, paradoxically, that antidepressants exacerbate rather than prevent depression.

Swim Test Immobility

Proposed by Porsolt and colleagues,[467] this test involves placing a rodent (rat or mouse) into a beaker of water and determining the amount of time that the animal remains immobile. The typical procedure that has been used is to place the animal in the tank for 15 minutes on day 1; as a result of this exposure, active coping attempts are extinguished so that the animal ceases movement by the end of the session. The following day, the animal is returned to the water tank for 5 minutes, when immobility is quantified (timed). Between the first and second exposure to the swim tank, the drug (or other treatment) is given, often a single drug administration shortly before the immobility test or two or three drug administrations during the 24 hours intervening between the first and second exposure to the swim tank. Effective antidepressants cause animals to show less immobility on the second (test) exposure than is shown by vehicle-treated or untreated animals.

This test detects a wide range of antidepressant treatments including all TCAs tested (e.g., imipramine, DMI, amitriptyline, nortriptyline), MAOIs (nialamide, iproniazid), atypical antidepressants (iprindole, mianserin, nomifensine), and electroconvulsive shock.[467, 468] Deprivation of REM sleep, which is therapeutic in depression, is also detected by this test.[469] The test does not respond to anxiolytics or phenothiazines. The test will, however, show "false-positive" responses to a variety of different substances,[470] particularly stimulants (amphetamine and caffeine). Also, a significant weakness of this test, considering present preference for antidepressant medication, is its poor detection of SSRIs, which was noted early by Porsolt and colleagues.[471, 472]

Perhaps because of its ease of use and ability to detect drugs of antidepressant potential, the Porsolt swim test is the most widely used pharmacological test for antidepressants at present. A number of interesting and significant characteristics have been discovered regarding this model. First, drugs work when given acutely, which does not reproduce the clinical efficacy of antidepressant drugs that require repeated administration; however, larger effects are often seen when drugs have been given repeatedly before the test. (In this regard, effects of SSRIs need to be assessed after chronic administration of drug.) Second, although the test was initially described as "behavioral despair," there is little evidence that exposure of animals to this test situation produces a significant degree of anything that might be called despair; rather, immobility in the standard test situation appears to be explained, at least in part, by the animals' learning to adopt an immobile posture with the rear feet or tail balanced on the bottom of the swim tank, thereby supporting the head above the top of the water.[470, 473] Thus, effective drugs appear to cause the animal on the test day to attempt active behavior instead of continuing to practice a previously learned immobile posture. Modifications of the original test situation using water of greater depth to prevent the animal from standing on the bottom of the tank have been employed in several situations[470, 474, 475]; under these conditions, the immobility that is measured represents more unambiguously a loss of motivation to engage in active coping attempts than is the case when the animal can partially resolve its dilemma by standing on the floor of the tank. Third, although despair has not been shown to characterize the model, stress may well be involved in its ability to detect antidepressant effects. Borsini and colleagues[476] showed that the initial exposure to the swim tank, although typically done to extinguish active behavior, produces consequences similar to known stressors (cold, restraint, and foot shock) and that exposure to the swim tank on the day before the test considerably enhances the capacity of the test to detect antidepressants. Thus, the swim test, as usually conducted, appears to determine how treatments counteract "stress-induced" immobility. Fourth, antidepressant medication particularly increases "escape-like" motor activity occurring early in the swim test, which can be discriminated from general increases in motor activity that can be detected late in swim tests of long duration.[477, 478] This discriminates between antidepressant action and nonspecific stimulation of motor activity in the swim test.

Clonidine Withdrawal

Whereas acute administration of the drug clonidine causes rats to be inactive in the swim test, it is also possible to produce long-lasting inactivity in this test in drug-free animals. A procedure to accomplish this was reported by Hoffman and Weiss.[479] When clonidine was administered to rats for 2 weeks and was then abruptly withdrawn, the animals, which were now drug free, showed a depression of activity in the swim test that lasted for several weeks. The long-lasting nature of this reduction in motor activity permits examination of the effects of long-term treatment regimens. Only DMI has been tested to date. When given daily for 2 weeks, DMI reversed the depression of swim test activity seen in this model; when the chronic administration of DMI was halted, activity in the swim test again became depressed. It was also observed that DMI did not increase swim test activity after being given for only 1 day. Further studies of this model have not been conducted.

Tail Suspension Test

When a mouse is suspended in the air by its tail, it will struggle to free itself. Steru and coworkers[480] reported that antidepressant drugs increase the amount of time spent in such struggling. Struggling is increased by TCAs, MAOIs, and atypical antidepressants; it is not increased by neuroleptics, anxiolytics, or anticholinergics. Struggling time is, however, also increased by psychostimulants (e.g., *d*-amphetamine). Drugs work in this test when given acutely, and consequently this model has been proposed to be, and has been used exclusively as, a screening technique for pharmacological treatments. However, because effective treatments counteract a form of immobility (i.e., cessation of struggling), the test is thought to be related to the Porsolt swim test and is here listed as a homologous model.

Neonatal Clomipramine

In this model, rat pups are injected with clomipramine (15 mg/kg) twice daily on postnatal days 8 through 21. When tested at 90+ days of age, these animals show decreased sexual activity, intracranial self-stimulation, aggressive behavior, and motor hyperactivity in a novel situation.[481–483] Relative to control animals that had been injected neonatally with saline, clomipramine-injected rats also showed changes in sleep behavior that have been associated with depression, including 1) reduced latency to enter REM sleep after sleep onset and 2) frequent onset of REM periods.[484, 485] On the basis of these behavioral effects, the investigators who developed the procedure proposed it as a means to model endogenous, as opposed to reactive, depression.[486] One drawback to this model appears to be the hyperactivity evidenced by the animals because patients manifesting endogenous depression are likely to be the most seriously affected who will show psychomotor retardation rather than hyperactivity. Testing of treatment efficacy on this model has been limited; preliminary data were given[486] showing that imipramine treatment for 4 days reduced locomotor hyperactivity of the neonatal clomipramine-treated animals. Although this treatment uses an inducing stimulus that seems to have little relation to whatever normal physiological conditions may give rise to the susceptibility of depression, the investigators offered the underlying hypothesis that a physiological defect is present in endogenous depression and that giving neonatal clomipramine somehow reproduces this defect.

Lesions of the Dorsomedial Amygdala in Dogs

When lesions are made electrolytically in the dorsomedial amygdala of dogs, one of the most dramatic syndromes resembling severe depression is produced. Fonberg[487–489] has reported that these animals display lethargy, negativism, reluctance to eat, and (to the extent that this can be judged in a dog) saddened facial expression. In terms of symptom profile, the appearance of these animals ranks with the "monkey separation" model (see next section) as producing the most similarity to what is observed in severe retarded depression. The effect of antidepressant medication on this syndrome has not yet been reported. Despite its dramatic appearance, the model has been little studied and perhaps is likely to remain so in view of the problems of using dogs as subjects. Also, some questions can be raised as to its relevance. Fonberg has reported that lesions of the lateral hypothalamus, which are now well known to disturb dopaminergic axons ascending to the striatum and forebrain, produce in the dog a similar phenomenon, thus raising the question of whether the dorsolateral amygdala lesions simply produce a variant of the "lateral hypothalamic syndrome" that is produced by lesions of DA inputs of the basal ganglia. If this is the case, it would mean that either 1) the model is unrelated to clinical depression or 2) the resemblance of these dogs to what is seen in severe retarded depression indicates that clinical depression involves disturbance of these dopaminergic systems, which is simply seen in extreme form when these brain lesions are made in the dogs.

Isolation- or Separation-Induced Depression in Monkeys

Behavioral responses that appear similar to what is seen in severe depression have been elicited by separating young monkeys from their mothers and normal social setting or from their juvenile peers. After separation, animals are initially highly active, accompanied by much vocalization; this is labeled the stage of "agitation" or "protest," which usually lasts 24 to 36 hours. After this, the behavior pattern changes markedly; the animal then shows decreased activity, huddling and self-clasping, dejected and saddened facial expression, and generally decreased activity and exploration.[490, 491] This constellation of depressive-type behaviors can persist for 5 or 6 days before gradually remitting; however, in some cases, it lasts even longer. Depression-related behaviors are diminished by long-term administration of imipramine, and symptoms reappear if the drug is withheld.[492] Also, the drug appears not to work soon after it is administered but requires long-term administration, thus paralleling what is seen with antidepressants in humans.

Studies exploring underlying biochemical changes in this model are of interest. Kramer[493] has shown that 1) animals that are isolated for long periods have NE levels in the CSF that are approximately half the levels seen in normal animals, and 2) animals having low CSF levels of NE are more susceptible to showing depression-like symptoms when separated than are animals with higher NE levels. Also, Porsolt and colleagues[494] reported that acute administration of imipramine, which blocks NE reuptake, increased both motor activity and vocalization during the protest stage, making responses during this initial stage more extreme. These data suggest that NE and adrenergic receptors in the brain are importantly involved in this type of depression. Suggested hypotheses include 1) a decreased CSF NE level in susceptible animals is indicative of low NE release and, consequently, supersensitive adrenergic receptors in these animals; or 2) animals susceptible to depression, having low CSF NE levels, are vulnerable to NE depletion in the brain when they are subjected to stress, which would result in depression.

Separation of Siberian Hamsters

Siberian dwarf hamsters (*Phodopus sungorus* Pallas) form stable male-female mating pairs that normally remain together even after pups are born, with the male participating in rearing activities. Crawley[495] developed a model in which Siberian hamster pairs, maintained in the laboratory, were separated 3 to 4 weeks after they had formed mating pairs; thereafter, animals were housed in individual cages. During the period after separation (3 to 4 weeks was generally monitored), the male hamsters showed 1) decreased daily running-wheel activity, 2) decreased activity when tested in the open field, 3) increased body weight, and 4) decreased social interaction when an unfamiliar animal of the opposite sex was introduced into the cage. Separated females showed a smaller decrease in running-wheel activity and no change in the other measures. All of the changes described could be reversed by reuniting the separated pair. The changes in behavior could not be attributed to the isolation (i.e., single housing) of animals after separation because similar changes were not seen in animals that had been maintained in single-sex groups and then were individually housed. Effects of one antidepressant, imipramine, were tested in this model. Daily administration of imipramine for 2 weeks (10 mg/kg) after separation eliminated a number of activity-related changes shown by male hamsters in the open field (but not total distance traversed in the open field) and also did not eliminate the increase in body weight or the decrease in social encounters with an unfamiliar animal of the other sex. Regarding neurochemical differences, males were found to show evidence of decreased 5-HT turnover (decreased release?), as indicated by lower 5-HIAA/5-HT ratios in cortex, diencephalon, and mesencephalon.[496] Further studies of this model have not been reported.

Exhaustion Stress

Hatotani and colleagues[497] exposed female rats to forced running in an activity wheel until the animals were exhausted as indicated by rectal temperature reaching 33°C or less. After exposure to three sessions of forced running, each separated by a 24-hour rest period, spontaneous motor activity was marked by complete suppression of diurnal peaks in spontaneous motor activity seen in normal animals. Motor activity was returned to normal by daily injections of imipramine; a therapeutic response was seen only after the drug was administered for longer than 10 days. The other characteristic described for this model is that there is a marked increase in intensity of histochemical fluorescence of NE cell bodies in the brain accompanying the exhaustion-induced decrease in motor activity, thereby indicating that activation of NE neurons in the brain appears to be increased by the exhaustion-stress procedure. Conversely, fluorescence of DA neurons of the tuberoinfundibular system in the hypothalamus was much weaker in stressed animals, which was thought to indicate decreased activity in these DA neurons.

Chronic Mild Stress

First introduced by Katz, Roth, and Carroll, this model is generated by exposing rats to a succession of different stressful conditions across a period of either 2 weeks[498] or 3 weeks[499]; the stressful conditions consist of mild uncontrollable foot shock, cold swim, changing of housing conditions, reversal of light-dark periods, and food and water deprivation. The sequence of stressors is concluded with exposure to 95-dB noise and bright light for 1 hour, followed by testing of spontaneous motor activity in an open field; the effect measured in these studies is a decrease in open-field activity seen in chronically stressed animals relative to animals that have not been exposed to the chronic stress regimen. Whereas changes were sometimes of small magnitude (20% to 30% relative to nonstressed animals), a reduction in open-field activity nevertheless reliably characterized chronically stressed animals in a number of studies. Katz and colleagues[500–505] principally analyzed effects of treatment and showed that the decrease in activity in the open field could be reduced by TCAs (imipramine, amitriptyline), an MAOI (tranylcypromine), atypical antidepressants (mianserin, bupropion, iprindole), and electroconvulsive shock and was not consistently reversed by an anticholinergic, antihistaminic, anxiolytic, or neuroleptic drug; this profile indicated that the decreased activity in the open field produced by "chronic stress" is selectively responsive to antidepressant medications. Katz and colleagues also reported that stress-induced elevations in corticosteroids were antagonized by antidepressant medication.

An interesting effect reported in one paper of the series has been followed up by a considerable amount of research because of its hypothesized relevance to depression. Katz[506] reported that the chronic stress regimen decreased the hedonic value of a stimulus and that this change could be reversed by treatment with imipramine. It was found in this study that normal rats would ingest increasingly larger amounts of fluid that contained progressively larger concentrations of sucrose or saccharin, but greater consumption of more palatable solutions was not seen when consumption was measured within 24 to 48 hours after conclusion of the 3-week chronic stress regimen. When chronically stressed rats were treated with imipramine during the 3-week stress procedure, the amount of sucrose solution they ingested was equivalent to that ingested by unstressed animals, although the interpretation of this therapeutic effect is complicated by the fact that the imipramine treatment decreased saccharin consumption in the control animals that were exposed to no stress at all. Nevertheless, these results indicate that the tendency of rats to take in larger than normal amounts of a palatable solution was reduced by the chronic stress regimen.

Subsequent studies have followed up on this result on the assumption that it may model what Klein[507] has termed the principal characteristic of depression, the inability to experience pleasurable events. Reward and hedonic effects have been related to the dopaminergic system of the brain.[508] Tekes and coworkers[509] showed that the chronic stress regimen decreased indices of DA turnover in the brain and that these changes in DA turnover were antagonized by chronic treatment with a TCA (amitriptyline) and an MAOI (deprenyl). Moreau and colleagues[510] found that a similar stress regimen increased the threshold for electrical self-stimulation through electrodes in the DA-rich cells of the ventral tegmental area and that this reduction in self-stimulation was countered by DMI. Willner and colleagues[511–515] have published a number of studies showing that chronic mild stress decreases intake of palatable solutions, that these effects can be counteracted by treatment with antidepressants, and that chronic stress alters DA turnover and DA receptors in the brain. Whereas these studies make clear that the chronic stress regimen does alter various aspects of DA systems in the brain, the interpretation of changes in intake that were observed is more ambiguous. For example, studies do not appear to demonstrate that animals exposed to the chronic stress regimen ever lose their preference for palatable substances (sucrose, saccharin) in comparison to tap water, but only that the degree to which they will overconsume these palatable substances in comparison to tap water decreases in animals that are exposed to chronic stress. Thus, it is not evident that the chronic stress regimen has not simply decreased total consumption rather than affecting preference. It is well known that stressful conditions will decrease consumption of both food and liquid.[516, 517] From the clinical perspective, the emphasis of these studies on the DA system raises the question of why antidepressants that preferentially potentiate DA transmission, such as bupropion, appear to be no faster acting or better, and perhaps less so, than classic TCAs that block NE uptake or SSRIs.

Uncontrollable Shock (or "Learned Helplessness")

In the late 1960s, several studies showed that exposing animals, both rats and dogs, to electric shocks that they could not control resulted in different responses than were seen in animals that received the same shocks while having control over them. Seligman, Maier, and Solomon found that exposing dogs to uncontrollable shock caused animals to be unable to acquire an active (shuttle) avoidance-escape response.[518–520] At the same time, Weiss[517] observed that exposure of rats to uncontrollable shock decreased subsequent food and water intake in the home cage and caused body weight loss, these changes being virtually absent in animals that received the same shocks while exerting control over them. In these studies, the rats also became more fearful after receiving uncontrollable shock than they did after receiving controllable shock. In the mid-1970s, both Seligman and Maier found that the avoidance-escape deficit resulting from uncontrollable shock could be produced in rats as well as in dogs.[521, 522] At about this time, Seligman[523] hypothesized that exposure to uncontrollable events produces a depression-like response and that exposure of animals to uncontrollable shock therefore constituted a model for the study of depression. Subsequently, Weiss and colleagues[474] showed that uncontrollable shock, but not controllable shock, decreased active behavior, and increased immobility, in a swim test.

Perhaps because it has been studied more widely than any other, the uncontrollable shock model has been found to reproduce the largest list of symptoms found in human depression. In 1982, Weiss and coworkers[524] listed the various effects of uncontrollable shock and showed that these symptoms correspond closely to those listed in DSM-III, which was used at that time as the basis for diagnosis of depression in humans. These symptoms now include 1) decreases in food and water consumption, 2) loss of body weight, 3) loss of ability to initiate normal active behavior, 4) loss of normal grooming activity, 5) loss of normal competitiveness and play-like activities, 6) alteration of sleep patterns, particularly marked by early morning awakening, 7) loss of responding for rewarding brain stimulation, and 8) increased errors in discrimination tasks.

Responsivity to antidepressant treatment of animals exposed to uncontrollable shock has been examined by different investigators. All studies concerned with this issue have measured the ability of antidepressant treatment to reverse the deficit avoidance-escape performance produced by uncontrollable shock. Poor performance of active avoidance-escape responses after uncontrollable shock was first reported to be reversed by DMI[525] and then by nortriptyline.[526] Sherman and colleagues[527] then conducted a large study in which the avoidance-escape deficit was reversed by a wide variety of antidepressant medications (including TCAs, atypical antidepressants, and MAOIs) and electroconvulsive shock, whereas it was not corrected by stimulants or antipsychotic medications. Martin and colleagues[528, 529] have also found deficits to be reversed by SSRIs as well as by TCAs and MAOIs. In these studies, drugs have generally been given for only a few days (1 to 3 days) between the uncontrollable shock and testing, although Leshner and coworkers[525] tested effects after 7 days of drug administration. Although this might suggest beneficial effects of acute drug administration, Telner and Singhal[526] reported no effects early in drug application but positive effects later. A difficulty with establishing efficacy after long-term (i.e., 2-week) drug administration is that the symptoms in this model tend to dissipate (see later).

Regarding the pathophysiological mechanism that underlies the behavioral symptoms produced by uncontrollable shock, investigations have again focused on reduced motor activity produced by uncontrollable shock. Studies of the physiological mechanism underlying this deficit have been extensive, with disturbance of central NE, 5-HT, cholinergic, and GABAergic systems and opioids hypothesized by different investigators to be responsible for the deficit. Of these various formulations, the most well developed hypotheses are those emphasizing disturbance of NE and 5-HT; not only are these hypotheses based on data showing that pharmacological manipulation of these systems can produce or reverse the behavioral deficit, but most important, studies are also included showing that uncontrollable shock alters the implicated neurotransmitter system to produce changes potentially able to mediate the behavioral deficit observed after shock.

The noradrenergic hypothesis is the most detailed and specific; it states that strong uncontrollable shock decreases NE to increase burst firing of LC cells by reducing transmitter available to stimulate inhibitory somatodendritic α_2-receptors on LC cell bodies.[530] These findings in turn suggest that depressive symptoms in the uncontrollable shock model result from an excess of NE released in the terminal regions to which the LC neurons project (e.g., hippocampus, cortex, forebrain), which would be the presumed consequence of hyperactivity of LC neurons. This formulation appears to complement the findings of Henn, Martin, and colleagues, who have reported that β-adrenergic receptors are up-regulated in animals that are susceptible to behavior-depressing effects of uncontrollable shock[528, 531] in that both higher-than-normal release of NE from LC terminals and up-regulated β-receptors would potentiate postsynaptic noradrenergic activity.

A final point relevant to this model concerns the controversial issue of interpretation. The model produced by exposure of animals to uncontrollable shock is often called the learned helplessness model, a term derived from the original interpretation offered by Seligman, Maier, and colleagues. These investigators hypothesized that the poor avoidance response after exposure to uncontrollable shock occurred because the animals learned that they were helpless during exposure to the shock, that "nothing I do matters." This cognition was said to cause the various consequences that followed uncontrollable shock; in fact, Seligman's[523] original hypothesis linking the consequences of uncontrollable shock to depression argued that as evidence of this, depressed individuals made many comments indicative of their feeling helpless. In contrast, Weiss[532, 533] and others[534, 535] argued that the inference of the "I am helpless" cognition to animals was extremely difficult, if not impossible, to test and that a simpler explanation was available—exposure to uncontrollable shock (as opposed to shock that can be controlled) is extremely stressful, and the depression-like symptoms observed are produced by this high degree of stress. According to this view, the depression-like symptoms resulting from uncontrollable shock are stress induced. Shortly after this controversy crystallized, the last symptom listed in the second paragraph of this section—that uncontrollable shock causes increased errors in discrimination tasks—was reported. When first described, this finding was thought to demonstrate that exposure to uncontrollable shock diminished an animal's ability to make associations as would be predicted if uncontrollable shock indeed led to a learned helplessness cognition.[536] However, Minor and coworkers[537, 538] carefully analyzed the phenomenon in further studies and found that the deficits in learning ability seen in these experiments could be accounted for by increased emotionality or fearfulness produced by uncontrollable shock. These studies linked the effects to changes in the concentration of NE in the forebrain, thus suggesting that deficits in discrimination learning were produced by a stress-induced change. At present, despite the durability of the learned helplessness label for the model being discussed here, there is no substantial evidence that the consequences of uncontrollable shock in animals involve a learned helplessness cognition.

Models Using Selective Breeding (Genetic Selection)

Despite the ability of homologous models to approximate symptoms seen in depression and respond to treatments effective in combating human clinical depression, each of the various models described before nevertheless lacks elements found in the human disorder. Attempts to correct this and other shortcomings of existing animal models have given rise to a salient new development in this area—the use of selective breeding procedures to attempt to produce populations of animals that either 1) have a higher likelihood of showing the appropriate characteristics than is the case in a normal population of animals or 2) display characteristics of the disorder to a more pronounced extent than is seen in normal populations. Thus, investigators are now attempting to incorporate into their models the clinical observation that not all individuals appear to be equally likely to become depressed in that there is often a genetic component to the expression of behavior disorders.

The models described in this section often use standard procedures that have been described previously for various models (e.g., uncontrollable shock, swim test), and therefore the models included here could have been described under previously defined models. However, in that genetic selection procedures constitute recent, and perhaps the most promising, developments presently ongoing in construction of animal models of depression, these models are addressed here in a separate section.

The first model considered is one in which animals were selectively bred for susceptibility and resistance to a behavioral deficit produced by uncontrollable shock.[531] Henn and colleagues exposed animals to uncontrollable grid shock and then tested animals for their ability to depress a lever to escape from grid shock. In a normal population of Sprague-Dawley rats used by these investigators, only 5% to 20% of the animals showed impaired escape behavior (i.e., long latencies of more than 20 seconds to escape) after receiving uncontrollable shock. Long latencies, which the investigators termed "failure to escape," can be attributed to decreased motor activity, and hence it is a depression-like symptom generated in the uncontrollable shock model. These investigators repeatedly tested for, and then bred, animals that showed failure to escape after uncontrollable shock and also bred animals that performed the escape response well (i.e., showed short escape latencies). After four generations of selective breeding, the proportion of animals showing failure to escape had increased to 45% among offspring bred for this characteristic, whereas 0% of animals bred for rapid escape showed poor escape performance. The authors also reported that among animals bred for susceptibility to poor escape performance, uncontrollable shock also reduced appetite and caused weight loss.

Effects of antidepressant treatment have been assessed on animals selectively bred for poor escape performance. Henn and colleagues[531] reported that when such animals were given placebo (or vehicle), they showed normal escape performance after 3 to 5 weeks of repeated escape testing. In contrast, antidepressant treatment was reported to produce normal escape responding after 5 days. Effective antidepressants were said to include TCAs, MAOIs, and atypical antidepressants, although details were not given.

Another model derives from rats initially selected to be highly responsive to cholinergic agonists.[539] In this model, animals were originally differentiated by the extent to which various responses (decreased body temperature, body weight, and drinking behavior) were affected by potentiation of ACh (by use of the anticholinesterase drug diisopropyl fluorophosphate), and selective breeding was then undertaken to establish animals that were sensitive or resistant to pharmacological manipulation of cholinergic activity. Two lines have been developed, the Flinders sensitive line and the Flinders resistant line. On the basis of the hypothesis that depressed individuals are hypersensitive to cholinergic agonists, it was suspected that the "sensitive" animals (Flinders sensitive line) might show an increased propensity to exhibit depressive symptoms. Consistent with this hypothesis, these Flinders sensitive line rats showed reduced motor activity (measured in the open field and the swim test) relative to the Flinders resistant line, and this difference was exaggerated by exposure to uncontrollable foot shock.[540] Flinders sensitive line rats also show increased REM sleep,[541] which may relate to differences in REM sleep shown by depressed patients. This model has also been reported to respond to several different antidepressant drugs including SSRIs.[539] Of considerable interest regarding underlying pathophysiological mechanisms, studies indicate that despite the initial selection of these animals because of sensitivity to cholinergic agonists, affecting cholinergic receptors pharmacologically does not alter the reduced motor activity shown in the model, whereas intervening with drugs that affect NE systems (imipramine, DMI) does counteract this symptom.[542] Thus, the hypoactivity in the model appears related to classic catecholaminergic systems that have been previously linked to depression.

These investigators have also begun to explore the possibility that the fawn-hooded rat might constitute an animal model of depression[543] and have compared fawn-hooded animals with the Flinders lines. The fawn-hooded rat shows reduced sensitivity to serotoninergic drugs and consequently has been characterized as showing deficient serotoninergic neurotransmission.[544, 545] In view of the antidepressant effects of SSRIs, it has been suggested that the fawn-hooded animal might constitute a depression-susceptible rat. Overstreet and coworkers[543] found that the fawn-hooded rat showed decreased motor activity after exposure to uncontrollable shock, although the extent of this deficiency was not as great as they had found in the Flinders sensitive line. They observed that the fawn-hooded rat, as opposed to its normal progenitor (the Wistar rat), showed a marked preference for alcohol, and consequently the investigators argued that the fawn-hooded rat may also be a model for alcoholism. Antidepressant drugs have not yet been tested in this model.

Finally, in a series of brief reports, Golda and Petr[546] proposed that the spontaneously hypertensive rat derived from the Wistar line can be used as an animal model of depression. They have demonstrated that exposure of the spontaneously hypertensive rats to grid shock results in a decrease in motor activity that can be seen up to 9 weeks after exposure to the shock. The stress-induced suppression of motor activity has been dissociated from changes in spontaneous exploratory activity[547] and threshold for reaction to shock.[548] Effects of a variety of drugs in reversing this shock-induced decrease in motor activity have been reported by these same investigators[547, 549]; however, only one drug related to classic antidepressants (an MAOI) was tested and showed positive results. A significant question that remains regarding these studies is whether the depression in motor activity produced in these studies represents a response other than that produced by conditioned fear (freezing behavior by the rats). The brief reports that present the findings do not make clear whether motor activity was tested in a location different from the one in which the animals initially received inescapable grid shock; if the location is the same, the phenomenon being investigated (i.e., long-term suppression of motor activity) could simply reflect the durability of conditioned fear and consequently not be related to reduced motor activity that is analogous to a depression-like symptom.

Models of Schizophrenia

The disruption of normal cognitive operations is the hallmark of schizophrenia. As such, it can be argued that schizophrenia is a uniquely human disorder that is not amenable to being modeled in animals. At the least, it can be asserted that the inability of animal models to incorporate elements of language that are invaluable to the expression and examination of schizophrenia creates an enormous barrier to model development. Nevertheless, the potential benefits for understanding neurobiological processes and improving treatment that would accrue from the study of valid models of a disorder as prevalent and debilitating as schizophrenia have resulted in the proposal of a variety of animal models related to schizophrenia.[550, 551] Animal assay models exist for screening of antipsychotic drugs. In addition, a variety of animal models of schizophrenia that can be classified as homologous have been generated on the basis of hypotheses that describe underlying deficits in schizophrenia in both physiological and psychological terms.

Animal Assay Models

Animal behavioral models stressing their predictive pharmacology represent by far the greatest effort in the development and use of animal models of schizophrenia. The demonstrated efficacy of neuroleptics, both phenothiazine and nonphenothiazine drugs, in the treatment of psychosis[552, 553] established the basis for testing the effects of these drugs on responses of animals and then screening for potentially new antipsychotic medications by assessing the ability to produce similar effects. As with animal assays for depression, such models reflect pharmacological similarity of the responses that are measured to the pharmacology of schizophrenia; these responses observed in the animal may bear little or no relevance to the symptoms of schizophrenia.

Conditioned Avoidance Responding

Perhaps the most studied pharmacological model has been the inhibitory effects of neuroleptic antipsychotics on the conditioned avoidance responding (CAR) to aversive stimuli.[554, 555] In this test, subjects (usually rodents) are conditioned to make an active response (e.g., locomotion in a shuttle box, pole climbing) to avoid or escape foot shock. Neuroleptic administration results in a deficit in avoidance responding, with escape behavior impaired only by higher drug doses. The differential effect of neuroleptics on avoidance and escape behavior distinguishes neuroleptics from other avoidance-disrupting drugs such as barbiturates, MAOIs, and benzodiazepines that exhibit overlapping dose-effect relationships for avoidance and escape behavior.[556] In addition to drug specificity, CAR paradigms exhibit significant positive correlations between the potency of antipsychotics to inhibit avoidance responding (median effective dose [ED_{50}] values) and their clinical potency reflected in their average administered daily dose.[557] However, the model has several features that limit its relationship to the pharmacology of schizophrenia. First, inhibition of avoidance responding by neuroleptic antipsychotics exhibits tolerance with repeated drug administration.[558–560] Second, the atypical antipsychotic drug clozapine is not effective in the CAR test.[560] Whereas CAR paradigms have use as a screening technique for neuroleptic antipsychotics, they appear to be of limited value in identifying mechanistically novel antipsychotics.

Catalepsy Test

The induction of catalepsy (inability to correct an externally imposed body posture)[561] represents an additional animal behavioral screen for neuroleptic antipsychotics.[555] Drug-induced catalepsy, however, is neither specific nor sensitive for antipsychotic drugs, exhibits tolerance with repeated administration, and demonstrates a poor correlation with the therapeutic potency of antipsychotics.[550] Although they have virtually no strength as an animal behavioral model of antipsychotics, catalepsy tests do have value in the study of the neuropharmacology of extrapyramidal function[561] and as a rapid behavioral screen for predicting the motor side effects of potential antipsychotic drugs.

Paw Test

The paw test[562] is a relatively recent addition to pharmacological behavioral models related to schizophrenia. The paw test reflects the effect of drug administration to rats on the spontaneous retraction of their extended forelimbs and hindlimbs.[563] Neuroleptic antipsychotics increase the time to retraction of the hindlimb and forelimb with equipotent effects for both limbs, whereas atypical antipsychotics increase hindlimb retraction time at lower doses than those required to increase forelimb retraction time. From these observations, it was proposed that drug effects on hindlimb retraction time and forelimb retraction time are separate measures of the antipsychotic potential and liability for extrapyramidal side effects, respectively, of tested drugs. The paw test appears superior to previously developed screening techniques in that it distinguishes neuroleptic from atypical antipsychotics, with members of the latter class exhibiting positive effects rather than being false-negative results in the test. As a pharmacological model of schizophrenia, the paw test shows antipsychotic drug specificity and lack of effect of anticholinergics on the hindlimb retraction time; another positive aspect of the model is that drug-induced increases in the hindlimb retraction time do not develop tolerance with the repeated administration of antipsychotic drugs.[563] Whereas additional tests of antipsychotic drug sensitivity and specificity are needed to establish the predictive strength of this model, the paw test appears to represent a unique behavioral screen for the distinct clinical pharmacology of neuroleptic and atypical antipsychotics.[564]

Self-stimulation Paradigms

Neuroleptic administration produces an inhibition of operantly conditioned lever pressing for intracranial electrical stimulation[555] or intravenous administration of cocaine.[565] Both paradigms appear to be models of the dopaminergic pharmacology of brain reward mechanisms, and drug effects are typically interpreted as an induction of an anhedonic state.[566] Intracranial electrical self-stimulation (ICSS) paradigms may also, or alternatively, model the effects of neuroleptics on motor function, because the inhibitory effects of flupenthixol on ICSS obtained when ICSS is delivered after lever pressing are not observed in rats that obtain ICSS by nose poking, a motorically simple task.[566] An inhibition of ICSS and an increase in cocaine self-administration are exhibited by many neuroleptic and atypical antipsychotics.[555, 565] A notable exception is clozapine, which actually decreases cocaine self-administration.[565] These authors also reported an excellent correlation, for a limited number of antipsychotics other than clozapine, between drug potency for increasing cocaine intake by self-administration and their average daily clinical dose for antipsychotic effects. Antipsychotic drug specificity and tolerance development represent unresolved issues for both paradigms. Collectively, these self-stimulation administration paradigms would seem better able to predict the negative effect of a drug on DA-mediated reward mechanisms than its antipsychotic potential.

Homologous Models

These models aspire to a direct relevance between the behavior shown in the animal model and behavioral responses seen in schizophrenia or underlying processes that are thought to define schizophrenia. Homologous animal models of schizophrenia can be subdivided into three types. The first type reflects the previously made point that the signs and symptoms of schizophrenia express disturbances in cognitive operations, and these can be represented only in nonhuman animals by theoretically based constructs. Modeling of psychophysiological processes thought to be disturbed in schizophrenia has largely focused on deficits in information processing and stimulus filtering.[340, 567, 568] As might be expected, such animal models do not necessarily reproduce observable consequences (symptoms) seen in the disorder; moreover, it has been shown that deficits in these processes and the diagnostic symptoms of schizophrenia in patients may not covary over time.[569]

A second type of model reproduces a salient symptom seen in schizophrenia, the disturbance of social behavior. The third type of model reproduces physiological disturbances linked theoretically to the etiology of schizophrenia. With respect to these models, it can be noted that progression from knowledge of etiology to development of models represents the most rational approach to establishing models, but pharmacological models of schizophrenia are an excellent example of the reverse progression.[570] A defect (overactivity) of brain DA function, which neuroleptic medication presumably counteracts, has been taken as an etiological fact of schizophrenia, and models then reproduce the "hyperdopaminergic" state in animals to study the consequences of this state.

Latent Inhibition Paradigms

The latent inhibition (LI) of conditioned responses by preexposure to a to-be-conditioned stimulus is a well studied model of selective attention.[571] Operationally, it is proposed that the neutral presentation of a stimulus retards the subsequent learning of conditioned associations to the stimulus.[572] Conceptually, LI paradigms are models of the ability to accurately categorize a stimulus on the basis of its changing salience. The phenomenon of LI attempts to reproduce attentional defects in schizophrenia that are expressed as the use of inefficient and inflexible processing strategies to filter stimuli. LI also contains parallels with nonattentional constructs of schizophrenia such as deficits in the control of behavior by context[573] and the influence of prior experience on the perception of current events.[574]

The empirical strength of LI paradigms as models of brain functions affected by schizophrenia is derived from animal behavioral pharmacology and human behavioral studies. Initial interest in LI paradigms stemmed from the effects of amphetamine,[575, 576] a drug thought to induce psychosis (see later section on chronic amphetamine intoxication). More recent studies of LI have emphasized the response of these paradigms to antipsychotic drugs.[577–580] For example, haloperidol administration to rats facilitates the LI of conditioned response suppression by stimulus preexposure.[577, 578] The facilitation of LI by haloperidol exhibits a potency similar to its clinical potency, is self-limiting at higher doses, and is nontolerating with repeated drug administration.[580] Also, LI is enhanced by structurally diverse neuroleptic antipsychotics as well as affected by atypical antipsychotics, although clozapine, fluperlapine, amperozide, and olanzapine *decrease* LI.

Significantly, the effects of typical and atypical antipsychotics on LI, although distinct, are confined to the effect of stimulus preexposure on conditioned suppression; conditioned responses in the absence of stimulus preexposures were found to be unaffected by drug administration.[580] This pattern of effect is not mimicked by anxiolytics, sedative hypnotics, antidepressants, a nonantipsychotic phenothiazine, or morphine.[580] A challenge for this model will be defining conditions (e.g., a deficit in LI) that produce a convergence for all efficacious antipsychotic drugs on a common behavioral effect or an appreciation of the mechanisms (e.g., 5-HT–DA actions) underlying the distinct effects on LI of neuroleptic versus atypical antipsychotics as a key to understanding their distinct clinical pharmacology.[564]

Human behavioral studies lend further support to LI phenomena as animal models of symptoms or psychopathological constructs of schizophrenia. With a variation of LI paradigms used in animals, Baruch and coworkers[581] demonstrated that LI of a learned stimulus association by stimulus preexposure was absent in patients with acute schizophrenia; normal control subjects and a chronic schizophrenic group exhibited clear LI. These results led to the proposal that LI paradigms represent a model of the positive symptoms and causal mechanisms (i.e., hyperdopaminergia) of acute but not chronic schizophrenia.[581] However, a more plausible, testable hypothesis based on the animal pharmacology of LI is that differences in antipsychotic medication underlie the group differences in LI performance. Importantly, all three groups readily learned the stimulus association in the absence of stimulus preexposure. DA receptors negatively modulate LI in both animal and human paradigms. The administration of apomorphine, amphetamine, and D_1 or D_2-D_3 DA receptor agonists inhibits LI in rats (Kilts CD, et al, unpublished data, 1996), whereas amphetamine administration inhibits LI in normal human subjects.[582] LI paradigms appear to be promising models of brain functions sensitive to schizophrenia, antipsychotic drugs, and DA receptor activation.

Blocking Paradigms

Blocking paradigms, like LI tasks, represent models of selective attention and the influence of context and prior experience on current perception and learning.[583] Blocking tasks[584] also involve a stimulus preexposure, conditioning, and behavioral testing component. Stimulus preexposure, unlike LI paradigms, involves the conditioned association of the stimulus (CS-A) with an unconditioned stimulus. In conditioning, a compound stimulus (CS-A plus CS-B) is presented, followed by the same unconditioned stimulus. In testing, the conditioned response to CS-B is measured; preexposure (prior association of CS-A and the unconditioned stimulus) weakens ("blocks") the response to CS-B. As models of the differential processing of a stimulus of different relevance, LI and blocking tasks differ in the simultaneous presentation of different stimuli (blocking) versus sequential processing of the same stimulus (LI). Blocking tasks were used initially as models of amphetamine-induced or amphetamine-exacerbated psychosis.[585] The negative effect of amphetamine on the blocking effect was antagonized by haloperidol administration.[585] However, the ability of blocking tasks to detect a range of antipsychotic drugs has not yet been tested. It can be noted that testing of humans indicates the presence of a deficit in the stimulus-blocking effect in schizophrenia.[586] Acutely ill schizophrenic patients fail to exhibit blocking of conditioned associations to CS-B by CS-A; normal control subjects and patients with anxiety disorder or chronic schizophrenia exhibit a clear blocking effect. The validity of blocking behavior as an animal model, distinct from LI, of brain functions relevant to schizophrenia must await the results of the study of the sensitivity, specificity, and potency of the effects of antipsychotic drugs and the assessment of tolerance development with repeated drug administration.

Prepulse Inhibition of the Startle Reflex

An additional animal model of the information-processing–stimulus-filtering deficits of schizophrenia is represented by the inhibition of the startle reaction to an acoustic or tactile stimulus when the startling stimulus is preceded by a weak prestimulus (hence, prepulse inhibition, or PPI).[587] The PPI effect is often proposed to represent an animal behavioral model of sensorimotor gating functions. The model is proposed to reproduce gating deficits found in schizophrenia and, on the basis of this hypothesis, has been used to probe the neural and pharmacological substrates of schizophrenia.[340, 588-590] Parallels between rats and humans in the graded response and threshold for PPI defined by a range of prepulse intensities and in the startle stimuli[590] support the contention that similar operations underlie PPI in both species. Like LI and blocking paradigms, PPI (of the eye blink reflex) is absent or dramatically reduced in patients with schizophrenia compared with normal control subjects.[340, 587–591] Like LI,[592] PPI is also diminished in psychosis-susceptible individuals.[593] However, deficits in PPI are not unique to schizophrenia but are also observed in patients with Huntington's disease or obsessive-compulsive disorder.[590, 594]

As behavioral models of stimulus-filtering functions that are disrupted by schizophrenia, PPI paradigms differ from LI with respect to modulation by DA receptors and effects of antipsychotic drugs. PPI is inhibited by the administration of D_2, but not D_1, DA receptor agonists, although D_1 receptor agonists potentiate the disruptive effects of D_2 receptor activation on PPI.[595] In contrast, the LI of a conditioned response suppression by stimulus preexposure is inhibited by the activation of either D_1 or D_2-D_3 DA receptors in the absence of apparent interactive effects between receptor subtypes (Kilts CD, et al, unpublished data, 1996). The specific DA projections involved in modulating PPI and LI also appear to differ because the selective activation of DA receptors in the nucleus accumbens inhibits PPI of the startle reflex[589, 596] but does not affect the LI of conditioned suppression.[597] These differences suggest that LI and PPI of the startle reflex represent distinct aspects of stimulus filtering with different neural mechanisms. These paradigms would therefore have distinct strengths and applications as models of the psychobiological "symptom" of information-processing deficits in schizophrenia. Differences between LI and PPI are also seen in response to antipsychotic drugs. LI in normally functioning animals is significantly affected by antipsychotic drug administration; neuroleptic antipsychotics enhance the negative impact of stimulus preexposure on associative learning. In contrast, sensorimotor gating measured by PPI is not affected by the administration of antipsychotic drugs to normally functioning animals.[590] Antipsychotic drugs do antagonize decreases in PPI of the startle reflex produced by apomorphine[590, 596, 598] or isolation rearing.[599] That a deficit in PPI is needed to reveal an effect of antipsychotic drugs may represent a source of strength for the PPI model because the substrates of drug action in schizophrenia are those brain functions that are degraded by the genetic and psychosocial factors unique to this disorder. In other words, a "defect state" may be a requirement of valid animal models of antipsychotic drug effects in schizophrenia.

The hypothesis that antipsychotic drug effects on induced deficits in PPI in animals represent a model of the pharmacology of sensorimotor gating abnormalities in schizophrenia[590, 596] is not supported, however, by the apparently negligible effect of antipsychotic medication on PPI deficits in schizophrenic patients.[340] This inconsistency highlights a means for validating animal models—the testing of predictions from the model in human behavioral studies. Are the modeled behaviors (e.g., PPI, LI) differently affected in distinct symptom subtypes of schizophrenia, by different classes of antipsychotic drugs in a within-subject crossover design, or by sex of the patients? The attempt to correlate results of clinical behavioral research with animal behavioral models represents both the best effort in model testing and the ultimate goal of animal modeling—to learn about the clinical condition. The study of PPI phenomena in humans may reveal highly useful information concerning the neurobiology of stimulus-processing deficits in schizophrenia but not about the mode of action of antipsychotic drugs. Perhaps Carlton's[600] assessment of the restricted relevance of animal behavioral models is partly correct in that *complete* relationship between an animal model and schizophrenia is not a necessary requirement and places too much strain on the model.

Rodent Interaction

The degradation of social skills in schizophrenia is a hallmark of this disorder[601] and the distinguishing feature of subgroups of schizophrenia.[602, 603] Depreciation of social skills is associated with the chronic phase of schizophrenia and the deficit form[602] or negative syndrome[603] of schizophrenia. A modification of the rat social interaction (SI) paradigm, developed and tested as an animal behavioral model of anxiolytic drug activity,[604] has been proposed as an animal model of the effects of antipsychotic drugs on social behaviors affected by schizophrenia.[605] Active, nonaggressive behavioral interactions between pairs of familiar or unfamiliar rats were timed after the acute administration of antipsychotic or nonantipsychotic drugs. Antipsychotic drug administration significantly altered SI behaviors between unfamiliar, but not familiar, pairs compared with vehicle-injected control pairs; neuroleptic antipsychotics decreased SI, whereas atypical antipsychotics increased SI. As a comparison, diazepam administration enhanced SI in both familiar and unfamiliar pairs. SI paradigms thus have possible use as behavioral screens for drugs of potential value in the treatment of the deficits in social skills observed in schizophrenia. Several considerations support a cautious use of these models. The effectiveness of clozapine in this test may be explained in part by the anxiolytic properties of this drug.[606] Also, the negative influence of neuroleptic antipsychotics on SI is difficult to reconcile with their beneficial (i.e., ameliorative) effects on negative symptoms.[607] A critical test of the model strength of SI will be the determination of antipsychotic drug effects after their chronic administration.

Social Behavior in Monkeys

An obvious limitation of the use of SI models is the conceptual distance between interactive behavior in rodent pairs and deficits in social skills and social withdrawal exhibited by schizophrenic patients in complex human social contexts. These deficiencies have been addressed by an ethological analysis of monkeys in the context of their complex, well-organized social structure.[608] Observed social interactions are compiled into a behavioral ethogram. Monkeys exhibit a wide and rich repertoire of social behaviors and thus better approximate the social setting of humans. For instance, drug effects on the interactive behavior of the alpha and beta males and the females of a social group can be described and changes analyzed in terms of group social structure or individual social bonds.[609] Monkey social behavior in models of schizophrenia has largely been studied in conjunction with amphetamine-induced social isolation,[609–611] which is thought to be analogous to social withdrawal symptoms seen in the negative (or deficit) forms of schizophrenia.

Amphetamine administration to monkeys markedly reduces the duration and number of both active and passive social behaviors with a resulting increase in spatial distance between socially living monkeys.[608, 609, 611] Amphetamine-induced social isolation is observed after either chronic or acute drug administration, and different social behaviors are differentially affected. For instance, acute amphetamine administration 1) decreased behavioral items of the ethogram such as grooming and huddling, 2) had no significant effect on looking at other animals, and 3) increased submissive behaviors.[609, 610] The social withdrawal observed in monkeys after amphetamine administration and the complex pattern (compared with rodents) of drug-induced stereotyped behaviors have been proposed as models of both negative and positive symptoms, respectively, of schizophrenia in a single paradigm.[608] The amphetamine-induced social isolation in monkeys has characteristics of a deficient ability to interpret communicative signals or a hyperdopaminergic state. The validity of this model has not been demonstrated beyond a shared lack of effect of noradrenergic and opiate receptor antagonists, benzodiazepines, and neuroleptic antipsychotics on deficits in social function in schizophrenia and this animal behavioral model.[608] However, the assertion that neuroleptics lack effect is dubious for both the clinical symptoms and animal behaviors, and the needed test of efficacy for the atypical antipsychotics on amphetamine-induced social isolation in monkeys has apparently not been conducted. That this model is produced by a dopaminomimetic drug limits its application as a screen for novel antipsychotics and as a tool for studying the mechanism of schizophrenia. However, this animal model is unique in reproducing degraded complex social behavior of the negative, or deficit, form of schizophrenia. A more systematic analysis of the monkey behaviors associated with social withdrawal induced by other nonpharmacological means and more thorough analysis of the behavioral pharmacology of antipsychotic drugs would seem worthwhile in the development and testing of such a model.

Chronic Amphetamine Intoxication

Animal behavioral models based on an induced hyperdopaminergic state derive from the long-held belief in the involvement of the neurotransmitter DA in the neurochemical pathology of schizophrenia.[344, 600] Indirect evidence for a hyperactivity of DA neurons innervating the subcortical limbic system in schizophrenia is inferred from the behavioral symptoms of patients, symptom exacerbation by dopaminomimetics,[612, 613] and their therapeutic response to antidopaminergic treatment.[614] As noted earlier in this chapter, more recent reformulations of the DA hypothesis of schizophrenia include postulating a hypoactivity of DA neurons innervating the prefrontal cortex as the neural basis of the negative (deficit) symptom complex in schizophrenia.[344] The behavioral effects of the drug-induced activation of brain DA receptors has long been proposed as an animal model of psychotic symptoms.[615–617] Models based on the effects of chronic amphetamine intoxication in cats and monkeys emphasize elicited behaviors that are interpreted as parallels of motor and cognitive symptoms of schizophrenia.[616, 618] Motor disturbances observed in the end stage of chronic amphetamine administration in animals include restless shifting and awkward postures; behavioral effects include fragmented, perseverative, or abortive behaviors with situationally irrelevant responses and reduced or inappropriate social behaviors. Nielsen and coworkers[618] also described apparent amphetamine-induced hallucinatory behavior in monkeys consisting of behavioral sequences oriented toward nonexistent stimuli. Not surprisingly, treatment with neuroleptic antipsychotics resulted in a rapid cessation of these effects of chronic amphetamine administration. Chronic amphetamine intoxication models thus produce animal behavioral analogues of even the most human of the positive and negative symptoms of schizophrenia and historically have added considerable momentum to the purported role of DA in the neurochemical pathology of schizophrenia. However, a caution in interpreting these models is necessitated by the possibility that effects of amphetamine and other dopaminomimetics may reflect actions on neural mechanisms related to treatment but not to etiology. The use of in vivo functional brain imaging techniques (e.g., positron emission tomography) may demonstrate parallels between the functional neuroanatomy of schizophrenia[619, 620] and that of chronic amphetamine intoxication and thus strengthen the model beyond its behavioral parallels.

Hippocampal Damage

Models in which the hippocampus of animals is damaged have gained added significance with the demonstration that changes in the volume of the hippocampus (and amygdala) represent one of the most consistently observed components of the neuropathology of schizophrenia.[316, 621] Bilateral lesions of the hippocampus in animals affect specific behaviors (e.g., attention, arousal, habituation), cognitive operations (e.g., learning, memory), and physiological reactions (e.g., skin conductance) that parallel a constellation of deficits associated with schizophrenia.[622] Behavioral deficits after hippocampal lesions can be reversed by the administration of clinically efficacious antipsychotics.[622]

More recent formulations of the hippocampal lesion model have shown the model to reproduce diverse phenomenological aspects of schizophrenia. Bilateral lesions of the ventral hippocampus of young adult (42-day-old) rats produced by intracerebral microinjection of the excitatory amino acid neurotoxin ibotenic acid resulted in changes in postoperative behavior as well as pharmacological and biochemical estimates of brain DA systems.[623] Specifically, hippocampal damage increased spontaneous exploratory behavior and amphetamine-induced locomotion while inducing an increase in the estimated activity of DA neurons innervating the limbic (ventral) striatum and a decrease in the activity of DA neurons of the medial prefrontal cortex. Hippocampal damage in these studies was not associated with an altered behavioral responsivity to environmental stimuli (stressors). This paradigm has also been strengthened by the addition of developmental features. Schizophrenia represents a disorder with a defined developmental latency; the index episode typically occurs at postpubertal ages in late adolescence or early adulthood.[624] Moreover, the neuroanatomical alterations associated with schizophrenia (e.g., decreased volume of the amygdaloid-hippocampal complexes of the temporal lobes) are thought to represent early developmental disease that remains functionally quiescent until adolescence or adulthood.[625, 626] In the animal model described here, ibotenic acid–induced hippocampal damage of the rats at postnatal day 7 results in a delayed emergence of an enhanced (relative to sham-operated control animals) locomotor response to a novel environment, intraperitoneal injection of saline or amphetamine, or a swim stressor.[627] Behavioral effects of lesions were noted at postpubertal postnatal day 56, but not prepubertal day 35, after lesion on postnatal day 7. Behavioral effects were interpreted as being suggestive of an enhanced response of mesolimbic DA neurons to stressful environmental and pharmacological stimuli. The neonatal hippocampal damage model thus possesses analogues of the postpubertal onset and stress vulnerability of schizophrenia and of the neurochemical construct of limbic DA dysregulation.[627]

Despite the similarities described, the observed changes in hippocampal volume[316, 621] or cytoarchitecture[628] in adult schizophrenic patients represent subtle, asymmetric changes, in contrast to the robust loss of neuropil, gliosis, and cavitation observed in the hippocampus of lesioned animals. Also, changes in neuroanatomy associated with schizophrenia are not confined to the hippocampal formation.

High Ambient Pressure

The psychotogenic effect of exposure to high ambient pressure[629] has led to the conclusion that high pressure–induced changes in neurotransmission and behavior represent a method by which schizophreniform psychosis can be produced.[630] In addition to neurological and other psychiatric symptoms, divers experiencing high pressure exhibit neuroleptic-reversible delusions, hallucinations, paranoid thoughts, and agitation.[629] The exposure of rats to environments of high ambient pressure results in neuroleptic-reversible increases in spontaneous locomotor activity and correlated increases in the DA content of the nucleus accumbens and caudate putamen.[630] The high pressure–induced behavioral-neurochemical model has its strength in parallels with a key component of the DA hypothesis of schizophrenia—the hypothetical overactivity of mesolimbic DA neurons. An additional strength of the model is that the inducing condition (high pressure) does not involve a presumption of underlying causes of schizophrenia but rather makes possible studies of the mechanistic bases and pharmacology of its consequences in an attempt to understand these aspects of psychotic disorders. An obvious weakness of the model is its lack of relevance to inducing conditions to schizophrenia.

Models Using Selective Breeding (Genetic Selection)

Even those animal models of schizophrenia that are arguably best able to reproduce symptoms or psychophysiological constructs of schizophrenia (e.g., LI, blocking, PPI) have multiple shortcomings. An example is the apomorphine-induced deficit in PPI of the startle reflex in which an induced behavioral deficit is a prerequisite for demonstrating antipsychotic drug effects[590]; this manipulation produces a short-lived behavioral deficit that differs from the enduring deficiency that characterizes schizophrenia. As with animal models of depression, behavioral genetic techniques offer a promising approach by which models may be improved. The technique, however, has yet to be used extensively.

The one area in which genetic selection techniques have been applied has been drug response. It will be recalled that drug-produced interference with CAR has been used as a screening technique for antipsychotic medication. Genetically distinct strains of mice differ greatly in the effect of neuroleptic antipsychotics on CAR[631] and induction of catalepsy,[632] and these observations constituted the impetus for developing pharmacogenetic models of response to neuroleptic antipsychotics. A significant proportion (7% to 30%) of newly admitted patients with schizophrenia exhibit little or no therapeutic benefit from neuroleptic therapy.[564, 633] A smaller subgroup of patients demonstrates a rapid and robust response to antipsychotics.[634] Selective breeding programs have been used to develop genetic animal models of neuroleptic response and nonresponse in gerbils[635] and in mice.[636] By use of the cataleptic response to haloperidol administration, a significant bidirectional response to selection has been demonstrated in mice; by the seventh generation, the haloperidol nonresponsive line exhibited no catalepsy after haloperidol (2 mg/kg), whereas the haloperidol responsive line exhibited a robust cataleptic response of long duration to 1 mg/kg.[636] Behavioral differences in drug response to haloperidol were not attributable to differences between lines in the pharmacokinetics of haloperidol. The response to selection generalized to D_2 DA receptor antagonists other than haloperidol, suggesting that alterations in brain D_2 receptor density or function may underlie the difference in response.

Selective breeding techniques for good and poor CAR learning have long been known to result in the generation of distinct lines of rats.[637–639] The three major strains of rats resulting from successful bidirectional selection for CAR acquisition include the Roman, Syracuse, and Australian High and Low Avoidance strains.[639] Although these breeding programs have demonstrated convincingly the hereditary influences on CAR, the effect of genetic selection on the response of CAR to antipsychotic drug administration has not been systematically examined. Finally, genetic selection programs with respect to the LI model are presently under development.

Summary Observations Regarding Models of Schizophrenia

The signs and symptoms of schizophrenia reflect cognitive disturbances that have no prima facie duplication in animal behavior. As such, animal behavioral models of schizophrenia have sought validation in pharmacological parallels as well as in parallels with psychophysiological and neurochemical constructs of schizophrenia. The utility of such models in elucidating the neurobiology of schizophrenia or as targets for the rational development of mechanistically novel antipsychotics with improved efficacy and decreased side effects will be dependent on an increased number of modelable aspects of schizophrenia. Noninvasive, in vivo imaging techniques will, as noted before, play a major role in the discovery of the neurobiological facts of schizophrenia. The application of improved techniques of MRI has identified a neuropathology of schizophrenia[316, 640] that suggests a disorder in neocortical-limbic communication. Similarly, the application of functional brain imaging techniques to schizophrenia has demonstrated that schizophrenia has a functional neuroanatomy represented by alterations in functional neural circuits.[619, 620] In solving the mysteries of schizophrenia, these findings provide important clues as to the *what* and *where* of the effects of schizophrenia on the brain and leads in defining *why* such effects occur and *how* they affect cognitive processes. These findings also furnish needed facts concerning the neurobiology of schizophrenia for use as targets for animal modeling and model validation.

Finally, future animal behavioral models related to schizophrenia should manifest "appropriate" psychophysiological deficits before models are used to probe the neurochemistry, neuroanatomy, and pharmacology of schizophrenia. The reverse order has been typically pursued. In particular, it needs to be recognized that the psychopharmacology of schizophrenia is often unique because drugs interact with the neurochemical and neuroanatomical abnormalities that underlie the disorder. The dependency of pharmacology on a defect state for accurate assessment suggests that the search for novel treatments for schizophrenia using animal models needs to proceed from the development of valid symptom models.

References

1. Bunney WE Jr, Davis JM: Norepinephrine in depressive reactions: A review. Arch Gen Psychiatry 1965; 13:483–494.
2. Prange A: The pharmacology and biochemistry of depression. Dis Nerv Syst 1964; 25:217–221.
3. Schildkraut JJ: The catecholamine hypothesis of affective disorders: A review of supporting evidence. Am J Psychiatry 1965; 122:509–522.
4. Coppen A: Depressive states and indolealkylamines. Adv Pharmacol 1968; 6:273–291.
5. Lapin I, Oxenkrug G: Intensification of the central serotonergic process as a possible determinant of thymoleptic effect. Lancet 1969; 1:132–136.
6. Asberg M, Traskman L, Thoren P: 5-HIAA in the cerebrospinal fluid: A biochemical suicide predictor? Arch Gen Psychiatry 1976; 33: 1193–1197.
7. Roy A, De Jong J, Linnoila M: Cerebrospinal fluid monoamine metabolites and suicidal behavior in depressed patients. Arch Gen Psychiatry 1989; 46:609–612.
8. Traskman L, Asberg M, Bertilsson L, et al: Monoamine metabolites in CSF and suicidal behavior. Arch Gen Psychiatry 1981; 10:253–261.
9. Van Praag HM: Depression, suicide, and the metabolites of serotonin in the brain. J Affect Disord 1982; 4:21–29.
10. Linnoila VM, Virkkunen M: Aggression, suicidality and serotonin. J Clin Psychiatry 1992; 53(suppl):46–51.
11. Virkkunen M, Rawlings R, Tokola R, et al: CSF biochemistries, glucose metabolism, and diurnal activity rhythms in alcoholic, violent offenders, fire setters, and healthy volunteers. Arch Gen Psychiatry 1994; 51:20–27.
12. Janowsky DS, El-Yousef MK, Davis JM, et al: A cholinergic-adrenergic hypothesis of mania and depression. Lancet 1972; 2:573–577.
13. Shopsin B, Gershon S, Goldstein M, et al: Use of synthesis inhibitors in defining a role for biogenic amines during imipramine treatment in depressed patients. Psychopharmacol Commun 1975; 1:239–249.
14. Shopsin B, Friedman E, Gershon S: Parachlorophenylalanine reversal of tranylcypromine effects in depressed outpatients. Arch Gen Psychiatry 1976; 33:811–819.
15. Vale W, Spiess J, Rivier C, Rivier J: Characterization of a 41-residue ovine hypothalamic peptide that stimulates secretion of corticotropin and β-endorphin. Science 1981; 213:1394–1397.
16. Swanson LW, Sawchenko PE, Rivier J, et al: Organization of ovine corticotropin-releasing factor immunoreactive cells and fibers in the

rat brain: An immunohistochemical study. Neuroendocrinology 1983; 36:165–186.

17. Arato M, Banki CM, Nemeroff CB, et al: Hypothalamic-pituitary-adrenal axis and suicide. Ann N Y Acad Sci 1986; 487:263–270.
18. Banki CM, Bissette G, Arato M, et al: Cerebrospinal fluid corticotropin-releasing factor–like immunoreactivity in depression and schizophrenia. Am J Psychiatry 1987; 144:873–877.
19. Banki CB, Karmacsi L, Bissette G, et al: CSF corticotropin-releasing hormone and somatostatin in major depression: Response to antidepressant treatment and relapse. Eur Neuropsychopharmacol 1992; 2:107–113.
20. France RD, Urban B, Krishnan KRR, et al: CSF corticotropin-releasing factor–like immunoreactivity in chronic pain patients with and without major depression. Biol Psychiatry 1988; 23:86–88.
21. Nemeroff CB, Widerlov E, Bissette G, et al: Elevated concentrations of CSF corticotropin-releasing factor–like immunoreactivity in depressed patients. Science 1984; 226:1342–1344.
22. Risch SC, Lewine RJ, Kalin NH, et al: Limbic-hypothalamic-pituitary-adrenal axis activity and ventricular-to-brain ratio in affective illness and schizophrenia. Neuropsychopharmacology 1992; 6:95–100.
23. Arato M, Banki CM, Bissette G, et al: Elevated CSF CRF in suicide victims. Biol Psychiatry 1989; 25:355–359.
24. Roy A, Pickar D, Paul S, et al: CSF corticotropin-releasing hormone in depressed patients and normal control subjects. Am J Psychiatry 1987; 144:641–645.
25. Pitts AF, Kathol RG, Gehris TL, et al: Elevated cerebrospinal fluid corticotropin-releasing hormone and arginine vasopressin in depressed patients with dexamethasone nonsuppression. Soc Neurosci Abstr 1990; 16:454.
26. Post RM, Gold P, Rubinow DR, et al: Peptides in cerebrospinal fluid of neuropsychiatric patients: An approach to central nervous system peptide function. Life Sci 1982; 31:1–15.
27. Veith RC, Lewis N, Langohr JI, et al: Effect of desipramine on cerebrospinal fluid concentrations of corticotropin-releasing factor in human subjects. Psychiatry Res 1992; 46:1–8.
28. Hermus AR, Pieters GF, Smals AG, et al: Plasma adrenocorticotropin cortisol and aldosterone responses to corticotropin-releasing factor: Modulatory effect of basal cortisol levels. J Clin Endocrinol Metab 1984; 58:187–191.
29. Watson SJ, Lopez JF, Young EA, et al: Effects of low dose ovine corticotropin-releasing hormone in humans: Endocrine relationship and beta-endorphin/beta-lipotropin responses. J Clin Endocrinol Metab 1986; 66:10–15.
30. Amsterdam JD, Marinelli DL, Arger P, et al: Assessment of adrenal gland volume by computed tomography in depressed patients and healthy volunteers: A pilot study. Psychiatry Res 1987; 21:189–197.
31. Gold PW, Chrousos GP, Kellner C, et al: Psychiatric implications of basic and clinical studies with corticotropin-releasing factor. Am J Psychiatry 1984; 141:619–627.
32. Gold PW, Loriaux DL, Roy A, et al: Responses to corticotropin releasing hormone in the hypercortisolism of depression and Cushing's disease: Pathophysiologic and diagnosis implications. N Engl J Med 1986; 314:1329–1335.
33. Holsboer F, Haack D, Gerken A, et al: Plasma dexamethasone concentrations and different suppression response of cortisol and corticosterone in depressives and controls. Biol Psychiatry 1984; 19:281–291.
34. Kathol RG, Jaeckle RS, Lopez JR, Meller WH: Consistent reduction of ACTH responses to stimulation with CRH, vasopressin and hypoglycaemia in patients with major depression. Br J Psychiatry 1989; 155:468–478.
35. Young EA, Watson SJ, Kotun J, et al: Beta-lipotropin–beta-endorphin response to low-dose ovine corticotropin releasing factor in endogenous depression. Arch Gen Psychiatry 1990; 47:449–457.
36. Krishnan KRR, Rayasam K, Reed D, et al: The CRF corticotropin-releasing factor stimulation test in patients with major depression: Relationship to dexamethasone suppression test results. Depression 1993; 1:133–136.
37. Aguilera G, Wynn PC, Harwood JP, et al: Receptor-mediated actions of corticotropin-releasing factor in pituitary gland and nervous system. Neuroendocrinology 1986; 43:79–88.
38. Holmes MC, Catt KJ, Aguilera G: Involvement of vasopressin in the down-regulation of pituitary corticotropin-releasing factor receptors after adrenalectomy. Endocrinology 1987; 121:2093–2098.
39. Wynn PC, Aguilera G, Morell J, et al: Properties and regulation of high-affinity pituitary receptors for corticotropin-releasing factor. Biochem Biophys Res Commun 1983; 110:602–608.
40. Wynn PC, Hauger RL, Holmes MC, et al: Brain and pituitary receptors for corticotropin-releasing factor: Localization and differential regulation after adrenalectomy. Peptides 1984; 5:1077–1084.
41. Wynn PC, Harwood JP, Catt KJ, et al: Corticotropin-releasing factor (CRF) induces desensitization of the rat pituitary CRF receptor–adenylase cyclase complex. Endocrinology 1988; 122:351–358.
42. Raadsheer FC, Hoogendijk WJG, Stan FC, et al: Increased numbers of corticotropin releasing hormone expressing neurons in the hypothalamic paraventricular nucleus of depressed patients. Neuroendocrinology 1994; 60:436–444.
43. Raadsheer FC, Van Heerikhuize JJ, Lucasen PJ, et al: Increased corticotropin releasing hormone (CRH) mRNA in the paraventricular nucleus of patients with Alzheimer's disease and depression. Am J Psychiatry, 1995; 152:1372–1376.
44. Nemeroff CB, Owens MJ, Bissette G, et al: Reduced corticotropin-releasing factor (CRF) binding sites in the frontal cortex of suicides. Arch Gen Psychiatry 1988; 45:577–579.
45. Krishnan KRR, Doraiswamy PM, Lurie SN, et al: Pituitary size in depression. J Clin Endocrinol Metab 1991; 72:256–259.
46. Axelson DA, Doraiswamy PM, Boyko OB, et al: In vivo assessment of pituitary volume using MRI and systemic stereology: Relationship to dexamethasone suppression test results in patients with affective disorder. Psychiatry Res 1992; 46:63–70.
47. Zis KD, Zis A: Increased adrenal weight in victims of violent suicide. Am J Psychiatry 1987; 144:1214–1215.
48. Szigethy E, Conwell Y, Forbes NT, et al: Adrenal weight and morphology in victims of completed suicide. Biol Psychiatry 1994; 36:374–380.
49. Rubin RT, Heist K, McGeoy SS, et al: Neuroendocrine aspects of primary endogenous depression, XI: Serum melatonin measures in patients and matched controls. Arch Gen Psychiatry 1992; 49:558–567.
50. Nemeroff CB, Krishnan KRR, Reed D, et al: Adrenal gland enlargement in major depression: A computed tomographic study. Arch Gen Psychiatry 1992; 49:384–387.
51. Holsboer F, Von Bardeleben U, Gerken A, et al: Blunted corticotropin and normal cortisol response to human corticotropin-releasing factor in depression. [letter] N Engl J Med 1984; 311:1127.
52. Amsterdam JD, Winokur A, Abelman E, et al: Cosyntropin (ACTH) stimulation test in depressed patients and healthy subjects. Am J Psychiatry 1983; 140:907–909.
53. Jaeckle RS, Kathol RG, Lopez JF, et al: Enhanced adrenal sensitivity to exogenous ACTH stimulation in major depression. Arch Gen Psychiatry 1987; 44:233–240.
54. Kalin NH, Risch SC, Janowsky DS, et al: Plasma ACTH and cortisol concentrations before and after dexamethasone. Psychiatry Res 1982; 7:87–92.
55. Krishnan KRR, Ritchie JC, Saunders WB, et al: Adrenocortical sensitivity to low dose ACTH administration in depressed patients. Biol Psychiatry 1990; 27:930–933.
56. Linkowski P, Mendlewicz J, LeClerq R, et al: The 24 hour profile of ACTH and cortisol in major depressive illness. J Clin Endocrinol Metab 1985; 61:429–438.
57. Carpenter W, Bunney W: Adrenal cortical activity in depressive illness. Am J Psychiatry 1971; 128:31–40.
58. Gibbons JL, McHugh PR: Plasma cortisol in depressive illness. J Psychiatr Res 1962; 1:162–171.
59. Sachar E, Hellman L, Fukushima D, et al: Cortisol production in depressive illness. Arch Gen Psychiatry 1970; 23:289–298.
60. Carroll BJ: Pituitary-adrenal function in depression. Lancet 1968; 1:1373–1374.
61. Carroll BJ: Use of the dexamethasone test in depression. J Clin Psychiatry 1982; 43:44–50.
62. Arana GW, Mossman D: The DST and depression: Approaches to the use of a laboratory test in psychiatry. Neurol Clin 1988; 6:21–39.
63. Arana GW, Baldessarini RJ, Ornsteen M: The dexamethasone suppression test for diagnosis and prognosis in psychiatry. Arch Gen Psychiatry 1985; 42:1193–1204.
64. Evans DL, Nemeroff CB: Use of dexamethasone suppression test using DSM III criteria on an inpatient psychiatric unit. Biol Psychiatry 1983; 18:505–511.
65. Krishnan KRR, France RD, Pelton S, et al: What does the

dexamethasone suppression test identify? Biol Psychiatry 1985; 20:957–964.
66. Schatzberg AF, Rothschild AJ, Bond TC, et al: The DST in psychotic depression: Diagnostic and pathophysiologic implications. Psychopharmacol Bull 1984; 20:362–364.
67. Ritchie J, Belkin BM, Krishnan KRR, et al: Plasma dexamethasone concentration and the dexamethasone suppression test. Biol Psychiatry 1990; 27:159–173.
68. Nemeroff CB, Evans DL: Correlation between the dexamethasone suppression test in depressed patients and clinical response. Am J Psychiatry 1984; 141:247–249.
69. Nemeroff CB, Bissette G, Akil H, et al: Neuropeptide concentrations in the cerebrospinal fluid of depressed patients treated with electroconvulsive therapy: Corticotropin-releasing factor, beta-endorphin and somatostatin. Br J Psychiatry 1991; 158:59–63.
70. De Bellis MD, Geracioti TD Jr, Altemus M, et al: Cerebrospinal fluid monoamine metabolites in fluoxetine-treated patients with major depression and in healthy volunteers. Biol Psychiatry 1993; 33: 636–641.
71. Amsterdam JD, Maislin G, Winokur A, et al: The oCRF test before and after clinical recovery from depression. J Affect Disord 1988; 14:213–222.
72. Rubin RT, Phillips JJ, Sadow TF, et al: Adrenal gland volume in major depression: Increase during the depressive episode and decrease with successful treatment. In Proceedings of the Annual Meeting of the American College of Neuropsychopharmacology; December 1992; San Juan, Puerto Rico.
73. Kiriike N, Izumiya Y, Nishiwaki S, et al: TRH test and DST in schizoaffective mania, mania, and schizophrenia. Biol Psychiatry 1988; 24:415–422.
74. Stokes PE, Sikes CR: Hypothalamic-pituitary-adrenal axis in affective disorders. In Meltzer HY (ed): Psychopharmacology: The Third Generation of Progress. New York: Raven Press, 1987:589–607.
75. Evans DL, Nemeroff CB: The dexamethasone suppression test in mixed bipolar disorder. Am J Psychiatry 1983; 140:615–617.
76. Krishnan KRR, Maltbie AA, Davidson JRT: Abnormal cortisol suppression in bipolar patients with simultaneous manic and depressive symptoms. Am J Psychiatry 1983; 140:203–205.
77. Swann AC, Stokes PE, Casper R, et al: Hypothalamic-pituitary-adrenocortical function in mixed and pure mania. Acta Psychiatr Scand 1992; 85:270–274.
78. Godwin CD, Greenberg LB, Shukla S: Predictive value of the dexamethasone suppression test in mania. Am J Psychiatry 1984; 141:1610–1612.
79. Kennedy SH, Tighe S, McVey G, et al: Melatonin and cortisol "switches" during mania, depression, and euthymia in a drug-free bipolar patient. J Nerv Ment Dis 1989; 177:300–303.
80. Bauer MS, Whybrow PC: Rapid cycling bipolar affective disorder, I: Associations with grade I hypothyroidism. Arch Gen Psychiatry 1990; 47:427–432.
81. Bauer MS, Whybrow PC: Rapid cycling bipolar affective disorder, II: Treatment of refractory rapid cycling with high-dose levothyroxine: A preliminary study. Arch Gen Psychiatry 1990; 47:435–447.
82. Cowdry RW, Wehr TA, Zis AP, et al: Thyroid abnormalities associated with rapid-cycling bipolar illness. Arch Gen Psychiatry 1983; 40:414–420.
83. Prange AJ, Wilson IC, Rabon AM, et al: Enhancement of imipramine antidepressant activity by thyroid hormone. Am J Psychiatry 1969; 126:457–469.
84. Prange AJ, Loosen PT, Wilson IC, et al: The therapeutic use of hormones of the thyroid axis in depression. In Post CR, Ballenger J (eds): Neurobiology of Mood Disorders. Baltimore: Williams & Wilkins, 1980:311–322.
85. Joffe RT, Singer W, Levitt AJ, et al: A placebo-controlled comparison of lithium and triiodothyronine augmentation of tricyclic antidepressants in unipolar refractory depression. Arch Gen Psychiatry 1993; 50:387–394.
86. Kirkegaard CJ, Faber J, Hummer L, et al: Increased levels of TRH in cerebrospinal fluid from patients with endogenous depression. Psychoneuroendocrinology 1979; 4:227–237.
87. Banki CM, Bissette G, Arato M, et al: Elevation of immunoreactive CSF TRH in depressed patients. Am J Psychiatry 1988; 145:1526–1531.
88. Roy A, Wolkowitz DM, Bissette G, Nemeroff CB: Differences in CSF concentrations of thyrotropin-releasing hormone in depressed patients and normal subjects: Negative findings. Am J Psychiatry 1994; 151: 600–602.
89. Hatterer JA, Herbert J, Hidaka C, et al: CSF transthyretin in patients with depression. Am J Psychiatry 1993; 150:813–815.
90. Kastin AJ, Ehrensing RH, Schalch DS, et al: Improvement in mental depression with decreased thyrotropin response after administration of thyrotropin-releasing hormone. Lancet 1972; 2:740–742.
91. Prange AJ Jr, Wilson IC, Lara PP, et al: Effects of thyrotropin-releasing hormone in depression. Lancet 1972; 2:999–1002.
92. Bissette G, Widerlov E, Walleus H, et al: Alterations in cerebrospinal fluid concentrations of somatostatin-like immunoreactivity in neuropsychiatric disorders. Arch Gen Psychiatry 1986; 43:1148–1151.
93. Rubinow DR, Gold PW, Post RM, et al: CSF somatostatin in affective illness. Arch Gen Psychiatry 1983; 40:409–412.
94. Nemeroff CB, Bissette G, Martin JB, et al: Effect of chronic treatment with thyrotropin-releasing hormone (TRH) or an analog of TRH (linear–beta-alanine TRH) on the hypothalamic-pituitary-thyroid axis. Neuroendocrinology 1980; 30:193–199.
95. Adinoff B, Nemeroff CB, Bissette G, et al: Inverse relationship between CSF TRH concentrations and the TSH response to TRH in abstinent alcohol-dependent patients. Am J Psychiatry 1991; 148: 1586–1588.
96. Maeda K, Yoshimoto Y, Yamadori A: Blunted TSH and unaltered PRL responses to TRH following repeated administration of TRH in neurologic patients: A replication of neuroendocrine features of major depression. Biol Psychiatry 1993; 33:277–283.
97. Duval F, Macher JP, Mokrani MC: Difference between evening and morning thyrotropin responses to protirelin in major depressive episode. Arch Gen Psychiatry 1990; 47:443–448.
98. Bartalena L, Placidi GF, Martino E, et al: Nocturnal serum thyrotropin (TSH) surge and the TSH response to TSH-releasing hormone: Dissociated behavior in untreated depressives. J Clin Endocrinol Metab 1990; 71:650–655.
99. Goldstein J, Van Cauter E, Linkowski P, et al: Thyrotropin nyctohemeral pattern in primary depression: Difference between unipolar and bipolar women. Life Sci 1980; 27:1695–1703.
100. Weeke A, Weeke J: The 24-hour pattern of serum TSH in patients with endogenous depression. Acta Psychiatr Scand 1980; 62:69–74.
101. Extein I, Pottash ALC, Gold MS: The thyrotropin-releasing hormone test in the diagnosis of unipolar depression. Psychiatry Res 1981; 5:311–316.
102. Gold MS, Pottash AC, Extein I: Symptomless autoimmune thyroiditis in depression. Psychiatry Res 1982; 6:261–269.
103. Nemeroff CB, Simon JS, Haggerty JJ, et al: Antithyroid antibodies in depressed patients. Am J Psychiatry 1985; 142:840–843.
104. Reus VI, Berlant J, Galante M, et al: Proceedings of the 41st Annual Meeting of the Society of Biological Psychiatry. Washington, DC: Society of Biological Psychiatry, 1986.
105. Haggerty JJ, Simon JS, Evans DL, et al: Relationship of serum TSH concentration and antithyroid antibodies to diagnosis and DST response in psychiatric inpatients. Am J Psychiatry 1987; 144:1491–1493.
106. Haggerty JJ, Evans DL, Golden RN, et al: The presence of anti-thyroid antibodies in patients with affective and non-affective psychiatric disorders. Biol Psychiatry 1990; 27:51–60.
107. Loosen PT, Prange AJ Jr: Serum thyrotropin response to thyrotropin-releasing hormone in psychiatric patients: A review. Am J Psychiatry 1982; 139:405–416.
108. Sack DA, James SP, Rosenthal NE, et al: Deficient nocturnal surge of TSH secretion during sleep and sleep deprivation in rapid-cycling bipolar illness. Psychiatry Res 1988; 23:179–191.
109. Souetre E, Salvati E, Wehr TA, et al: Twenty-four hour profiles of body temperature and plasma TSH in bipolar patients during depression and during remission and in normal control subjects. Am J Psychiatry 1988; 145:1133–1137.
110. Lazarus JH, McGregor AM, Ludgate M, et al: Effect of lithium carbonate therapy on thyroid immune status in manic depressive patients: A prospective study. J Affect Disord 1986; 11:155–160.
111. Myers DH, Carter RA, Burns BH, et al: A prospective study of the effects of lithium on thyroid function and on the prevalence of antithyroid antibodies. Psychol Med 1985; 15:55–61.
112. Calabrese JR, Gulledge AD, Hahn K, et al: Autoimmune thyroiditis in manic-depressive patients treated with lithium. Am J Psychiatry 1985; 142:1318–1321.

113. Boyd AE, Levovitz HE, Pfeiffer JB: Stimulation of growth hormone secretion by L-dopa. N Engl J Med 1970; 283:1425–1429.
114. Lal S, Martin JB, de la Vega C, et al: Comparison of the effect of apomorphine and L-dopa on serum growth hormone levels in man. Clin Endocrinol (Oxf) 1975; 4:277–285.
115. Imura H, Nakai Y, Hoshimi T: Effect of 5-hydroxy-tryptophan (5-HTP) on growth hormone and ACTH release in man. J Clin Endocrinol Metab 1973; 36:204–206.
116. Muller EE, Brambilla F, Cavagnini F, et al: Slight effect of L-tryptophan on growth hormone release in normal human subjects. J Clin Endocrinol Metab 1974; 39:1–5.
117. Toivola PTK, Gale CC, Goodner CJ, et al: Central alpha-adrenergic regulation of growth hormone and insulin. Hormones 1972; 3: 193–213.
118. Finkelstein JW, Boyar RM, Roffwarg HP, et al: Age-related change in the twenty-four-hour spontaneous secretion of growth hormone. J Clin Endocrinol Metab 1972; 35:665–670.
119. Schilkrut R, Chandra O, Osswald M, et al: Growth hormone during sleep and with thermal stimulation in depressed patients. Neuropsychobiology 1975; 1:70–79.
120. Mendlewicz J, Linkowski P, Kerkhofs M, et al: Diurnal hypersecretion of growth hormone in depression. J Clin Endocrinol Metab 1985; 60:505–512.
121. Charney DS, Henninger GR, Steinberg DE, et al: Adrenergic receptor sensitivity in depression: Effects of clonidine in depressed patients and healthy controls. Arch Gen Psychiatry 1982; 39:290–294.
122. Checkley SA, Slade AP, Shur P: Growth hormone and other responses to clonidine in patients with endogenous depression. Br J Psychiatry 1981; 138:51–55.
123. Matussek N, Ackenheil M, Hippius H, et al: Effects of clonidine on growth hormone release in psychiatric patients and controls. Psychiatry Res 1980; 2:25–36.
124. Siever LJ, Uhde TW, Silberman EK, et al: Growth hormone response to clonidine as a probe of noradrenergic receptor responsiveness in affective disorder patients and controls. Psychiatry Res 1982; 6:171–183.
125. Lesch KP, Laux G, Erb A, et al: Attenuated growth hormone response to growth hormone RH in major depressive disorder. Biol Psychiatry 1987; 22:1495–1499.
126. Lesch KP, Laux G, Pfuller H, et al: Growth hormone response to GH-releasing hormone in depression. J Clin Endocrinol Metab 1987; 65:1278–1281.
127. Risch SC: Growth hormone–releasing factor and growth hormone. In Nemeroff CB (ed): Neuropeptides and Psychiatric Disorders. Washington, DC: American Psychiatric Press, 1991:93–108.
128. Krishnan KRR, Manepalli AN, Ritchie JC, et al: Growth hormone–releasing factor stimulation test in depression. Am J Psychiatry 1988; 145:190–192.
129. Agren H, Lundqvist G: Low levels of somatostatin in human CSF mark depressive episodes. Psychoneuroendocrinology 1984; 9: 233–248.
130. Gerner RH, Yamada T: Altered neuropeptide concentrations in cerebrospinal fluid of psychiatric patients. Brain Res 1982; 238: 298–302.
131. Rubinow DR, Gold PW, Post RM, et al: Somatostatin in patients with affective illness and in normal volunteers. In Post RM, Ballenger JC (eds): Neurobiology of Mood Disorders. Baltimore: Williams & Wilkins, 1984:369–387.
132. Rubinow DR: Cerebrospinal fluid somatostatin and psychiatric illness. Biol Psychiatry 1986; 21:341–365.
133. Wolkowitz OM, Rubinow DR, Breier A, et al: Prednisone decreases CSF somatostatin in healthy humans: Implications for neuropsychiatric illness. Life Sci 1987; 41:1929–1933.
134. Dinan TG, Yatham LN, O'Keane VO, Barry S: Blunting of noradrenergic-stimulated growth hormone release in mania. Am J Psychiatry 1991; 148:936–938.
135. Knobil E: The GnRH pulse generator. Am J Obstet Gynecol 1990; 163:1721–1727.
136. Midgely AR, Jaffe RB: Regulation of human gonadotropins: Episodic fluctuation of LH during the menstrual cycle. J Clin Endocrinol Metab 1971; 33:963–969.
137. Clarke IJ, Cummins JT: The temporal relationship between gonadotropin releasing hormone (GnRH) and luteinizing hormone (LH) secretion in ovariectomized ewes. Endocrinology 1982; 111:1737–1739.
138. Reame N, Sauder SE, Kelch RP, et al: Pulsatile gonadotropin secretion during the human menstrual cycle: Evidence for altered pulse frequency of gonadotropin releasing hormone secretion. J Clin Endocrinol Metab 1984; 59:328–337.
139. Jaffe RB, Plosker S, Marshall L, et al: Neuromodulatory regulation of gonadotropin-releasing hormone pulsatile discharge in women. Am J Obstet Gynecol 1990; 163:1727–1731.
140. Ferin M, Van de Wiele R: Endogenous opioid peptides and the control of the menstrual cycle. Eur J Obstet Gynecol Reprod Biol 1984; 18:365–373.
141. Sachar EJ, Schalch DC, Reichlin S, et al: Plasma gonadotrophins in depressive illness: A preliminary report. In Williams TA, Katz MM, Shield JA Jr (eds): Recent Advances in the Psychobiology of the Depressive Illnesses. Washington, DC: U.S. Department of Health and Welfare, 1972:229–233.
142. Brambilla F, Maggioni M, Ferrari E, et al: Tonic and dynamic gonadotropin secretion in depressive and normothymic phases of affective disorders. Psychiatry Res 1990; 32:229–239.
143. Winokur A, Amsterdam J, Caroff S, et al: Variability of hormonal responses to a series of neuroendocrine challenges in depressed patients. Am J Psychiatry 1982; 139:39–44.
144. Unden F, Ljunggren JG, Beck-Friis J, et al: Hypothalamic-pituitary-gonadal axis pulse detection. Am J Physiol 1988; 250:E486–E493.
145. Whalley LJ, Kutcher S, Blackwood DHR, et al: Increased plasma LH in manic-depressive illness: Evidence of a state-independent abnormality. Br J Psychiatry 1987; 150:682–684.
146. Landon J, James VHT, Stoker DJ: Plasma cortisol response to lysine-vasopressin in comparison with other tests of human pituitary-adrenocortical function. Lancet 1965; 2:1156–1159.
147. Von Bardeleben U, Holsboer F, Stalla GK, et al: Combined administration of human corticotropin-releasing factor and lysine vasopressin induces escape from dexamethasone suppression in healthy subjects. Life Sci 1985; 37:1613–1618.
148. Carroll BT, Meller WH, Kathol RG, et al: Pituitary-adrenal axis response to arginine vasopressin in patients with major depression. Psychiatry Res 1993; 46:119–126.
149. Maas JW, Fawcett JA, Dekirmenjian H: Catecholamine metabolism, depressive illness and drug response. Arch Gen Psychiatry 1972; 26:252–262.
150. Halaris AE: Plasma 3-methoxy-4-hydroxyphenyl-glycol in manic psychosis. Am J Psychiatry 1978; 135:493–494.
151. Schildkraut JJ, Orsulak PJ, LaBrie RA, et al: Toward a biochemical classification of depressive disorders, I: Differences in urinary excretion of MHPG and other catecholamine metabolites in clinically defined subtypes of depression. Arch Gen Psychiatry 1978; 35:1427–1433.
152. Muscettola G, Potter WZ, Pickar D, et al: Urinary 3-methoxy-4-hydroxyphenylglycol and major affective disorders: A replication and new findings. Arch Gen Psychiatry 1984; 41:337–342.
153. Schatzberg AF, Samson JA, Bloomingdale KL, et al: Toward a biochemical classification of depressive disorders, X: Urinary catecholamines, their metabolites, and D-type scores in subgroups of depressive disorders. Arch Gen Psychiatry 1989; 56:260–268.
154. Schatzberg AF, Orsulak PJ, Rosenbaum AH, et al: Towards a biochemical classification of depressive disorders, V: Biochemical heterogeneity of unipolar depression. Am J Psychiatry 1982; 139: 471–475.
155. Schildkraut JJ, Orsulak PJ, Schatzberg AF, et al: Possible pathophysiological mechanisms in subtypes of unipolar depressive disorders based on differences in urinary MHPG levels. Psychopharmacol Bull 1981; 17:90–91.
156. Janicak PG, Davis JM, Chan C, et al: Failure of urinary MHPG levels to predict treatment response in patients with unipolar depression. Am J Psychiatry 1986; 143:1398–1402.
157. Rosenbaum AH, Schatzberg AF, Bowden CL, et al: MHPG as a predictor of clinical response to fluoxetine: Proceedings of the 18th Collegium Internationale Neuro-Psychopharmacologicum Congress, Nice, France. Clin Neuropharmacol 1992; 15(pt B):209B.
158. Schildkraut JJ, Orsulak PJ, Schatzberg AF, et al: Urinary MHPG in affective disorders. In Post RM, Ballenger JC (eds): Neurobiology of Mood Disorders. Baltimore: Williams & Wilkins, 1984:519–528.
159. Schildkraut JJ, Orsulak PJ, LaBrie RA, et al: Toward a biochemical classification of depressive disorders, II: Application of multivariate discriminant function analysis to data on urinary catecholamines and metabolites. Arch Gen Psychiatry 1978; 35:1436–1439.

160. Rosenbaum AH, Maruta T, Schatzberg AF, et al: Toward a biochemical classification of depressive disorders, VII: Urinary free cortisol and urinary MHPG in depressions. Am J Psychiatry 1983; 140:314–318.
161. Stokes PE, Frazer A, Casper R: Unexpected neuroendocrine-transmitter relationships. Psychopharmacol Bull 1981; 17:72–75.
162. Maj J, Ariano MG, Arena F, et al: Plasma cortisol, catecholamine and cyclic AMP levels, response to dexamethasone suppression test and platelet MAO activity in manic-depressive patients: A longitudinal study. Neuropsychobiology 1984; 11:168–173.
163. Swann AC, Koslow SH, Katz MM, et al: Lithium carbonate treatment of mania. Arch Gen Psychiatry 1987; 44:345–354.
164. Swann AC, Secunda SK, Stokes PE, et al: Stress, depression and mania: Relationship between perceived role of stressful events and clinical and biochemical characteristics. Acta Psychiatr Scand 1990; 81:389–397.
165. Halaris A, Piletz J: Platelet adrenoceptor binding as a marker in neuropsychiatric disorders. 17th Annual Collegium Internationale Neuro-Psychopharmacologicum Congress, 1990. Abstract 28.
166. Meana JJ, Barturen F, Garcia-Sevilla JA: Alpha$_2$-adrenoceptors in the brain of suicide victims: Increased receptor density associated with major depression. Biol Psychiatry 1992; 31:471–490.
167. Garcia-Sevilla JA, Padro D, Giralt T, et al: Alpha$_2$-adrenoceptor–mediated inhibition of platelet adenyl cyclase and induction of aggregation in major depression. Arch Gen Psychiatry 1990; 47: 125–132.
168. Mooney JJ, Schatzberg AF, Cole JO, et al: Rapid antidepressant response to alprazolam in depressed patients with high catecholamine output and heterologous desensitization of platelet adenyl cyclase. Biol Psychiatry 1988; 23:543–559.
169. Siever LJ, Murphy DL, Slater S, et al: Plasma prolactin change following fenfluramine in depressed patients compared to controls: An evaluation of central serotonergic responsivity in depression. Life Sci 1984; 34:1029–1039.
170. Siever LJ, Trestman RL, Coccaro EF, et al: The growth hormone response to clonidine in acute and remitted depressed male patients. Neuropsychopharmacology 1992; 6:165–177.
171. Mann JJ, Stanley M, McBride PA, McEwen BS: Increased serotonin$_2$ and β-adrenergic receptor binding in the frontal cortices of suicide victims. Arch Gen Psychiatry 1986; 43:954–959.
172. Crow TJ, Cross AJ, Cooper SJ, et al: Neurotransmitter receptors and monoamine metabolites in the brains of patients with Alzheimer-type dementia and depression, and suicides. Neuropharmacology 1984; 23:1561–1569.
173. Copper A, Prange AJ Jr, Whybrow PC, et al: Abnormalities of indoleamines in affective disorders. Arch Gen Psychiatry 1972; 26:474–478.
174. Prange AJ Jr, Wilson IC, Lynn CW, et al: L-Tryptophan in mania: Contribution to a permissive hypothesis of affective disorders. Arch Gen Psychiatry 1974; 30:56–62.
175. Asberg M, Thoren P, Traskman L, et al: "Serotonin depression"—a biochemical subgroup within the affective disorders? Science 1976; 191:478–483.
176. Gibbons RD, Davis JM: Consistent evidence for a biological subtype of depression characterized by low CSF monoamine levels. Acta Psychiatr Scand 1986; 74:8–12.
177. Banki CM, Arato M, Papp Z, et al: Biochemical markers in suicidal patients: Investigations with cerebrospinal fluid amine metabolites and neuroendocrine tests. J Affect Disord 1984; 6:341–350.
178. Brown GL, Ebert MH, Boyer PF, et al: Aggression, suicide and serotonin: Relationships to CSF amine metabolites. Am J Psychiatry 1982; 139:741–746.
179. Traskman-Bendz L, Alling C, Oreland L, et al: Prediction of suicidal behavior from biologic tests. J Clin Psychopharmacol 1992; 12(suppl):21s–26s.
180. Linnoila VM, Virkkunen M, Scheinin M, et al: Low cerebrospinal fluid 5-hydroxyindoleacetic acid concentration differentiates impulsive from non-impulsive violent behavior. Life Sci 1983; 33:2609–2614.
181. Virkkunen M, Nuutila A, Goodwin FK, et al: Cerebrospinal fluid monoamine metabolite levels in male arsonists. Arch Gen Psychiatry 1987; 44:241–247.
182. Gonzalez-Heydrich J, Peroutka SJ: Serotonin receptors and reuptake sites: Pharmacologic significance. J Clin Psychiatry 1990; 51(suppl): 5–12.
183. Beigon A, Essar N, Israeli M, et al: Serotonin 5-HT$_2$ receptor binding on blood platelets as a state dependent marker in major affective disorder. Psychopharmacology (Berl) 1990; 102:73–75.
184. Briley M, Langer SZ, Raisman R, et al: Tritiated imipramine binding sites are decreased in platelets of untreated depressed patients. Science 1980; 209:303–305.
185. Langer SZ, Raisman R: Binding of [^{3}H]imipramine and [^{3}H]desipramine as biochemical tools for studies in depression. Neuropharmacology 1983; 22:407–413.
186. Lewis DA, McChesney C: Tritiated imipramine binding distinguishes among subtypes of depression. Arch Gen Psychiatry 1985; 42: 485–488.
187. Stanley M, Virgilio J, Gershon S: Tritiated imipramine binding sites are decreased in the frontal cortex of suicides. Science 1982; 216: 1337–1339.
188. Perry EK, Marshall EF, Blessed G, et al: Decreased imipramine binding in the brains of patients with depressive illness. Br J Psychiatry 1983; 142:188–192.
189. World Health Organization Collaborative Study: Validity of imipramine platelet binding sites as a biological marker for depression. Pharmacopsychiatry 1990; 23:113–117.
190. Ellis PM, Salmond C: Is platelet imipramine binding reduced in depression? A meta-analysis. Biol Psychiatry 1994; 36:292–299.
191. Nemeroff CB, Knight DL, Krishnan KRR: Reduced platelet [^{3}H]-paroxetine and [^{3}H]-imipramine binding in major depression. Soc Neurosci Abstr 1991; 17:1472.
192. Nemeroff CB, Knight DL, Franks J, et al: Further studies on platelet serotonin transporter binding in depression. Am J Psychiatry 1994; 151:1623–1625.
193. Stahl SM, Hauger RL, Rausch JL, et al: Down regulation of serotonin receptor subtypes by nortriptyline and adinazolam in major depressive disorder: Neuroendocrine and platelet markers. Presented at the 18th Annual Collegium Internationale Neuro-Psychopharmacologicum Congress; June 1992; Nice, France.
194. Cowen PJ, Charig EM: Neuroendocrine responses to tryptophan in major depression. Arch Gen Psychiatry 1987; 44:958–966.
195. Koyama T, Meltzer HY: A biochemical and neuroendocrine study of the serotonergic system in depression. In Hippius H, Klerman GL, Matussek N (eds): New Results in Depression Research. New York: Springer-Verlag, 1986:169–188.
196. Schatzberg AF, Rothschild AJ: Serotonin activity in psychotic (delusional) major depression. J Clin Psychiatry 1992; 53(suppl): 52–55.
197. Devanand DP, Bowers MB, Hoffman FJ, et al: Elevated plasma homovanillic acid in depressed females with melancholia and psychosis. Psychiatry Res 1985; 15:1–4.
198. Schatzberg AF, Rothschild AJ, Langlais PJ, et al: A corticosteroid/dopamine hypothesis for psychotic depression and related states. J Psychiatr Res 1985; 19:57–64.
199. Sweeney D, Nelson C, Bowers M, et al: Delusional versus nondelusional depression: Neurochemical differences. Lancet 1978; 2:100–101.
200. Rothschild AJ, Langlais PJ, Schatzberg AF, et al: Dexamethasone increases plasma free dopamine in man. J Psychiatr Res 1984; 18:217–223.
201. Wolkowitz OM, Sutton ME, Doran AR, et al: Dexamethasone increases plasma HVA but not MHPG in normal humans. Psychiatry Res 1985; 16:101–109.
202. Rothschild AJ, Langlais PJ, Schatzberg AF, et al: The effects of a single dose of dexamethasone on monoamine and metabolite levels in rat brain. Life Sci 1985; 36:2491–2501.
203. Wolkowitz OM, Sutton ME, Koulu M, et al: Chronic corticosterone administration in rats: Behavioral and biochemical evidence of increased central dopaminergic activity. Eur J Psychopharmacol 1986; 122:329–338.
204. Gershon ES, Goldin LR, Lake CR, et al: Genetics of plasma dopamine-β-hydroxylase erythrocyte catechol-*O*-methyltransferase and platelet monoamine oxidase in pedigrees of patients with affective disorders. In Usdin E, Sourkes L, Youngs MBH (eds): Enzymes and Neurotransmitters in Mental Disease. New York: John Wiley & Sons, 1980:281–299.
205. Leckman JF, Gershon ES, Nichols AS, et al: Reduced MAO activity in first-degree relatives of individuals with bipolar affective disorders: A preliminary report. Arch Gen Psychiatry 1977; 34:601–606.
206. Samson JA, Gudeman JE, Schatzberg AF, et al: Toward a biochemical classification of depressive disorders, VIII: Platelet monoamine

oxidase activity in subtypes of depressions. J Psychiatr Res 1985; 19:547–555.
207. Maubach M, Diebold K, Fried W, et al: Platelet MAO activity in patients with affective psychosis and their first-degree relatives. Pharmacopsychiatry 1981; 14:87–93.
208. Schatzberg AF, Rothschild AJ, Langlais PJ, et al: Psychotic and nonpsychotic depressions, II: Platelet MAO activity, plasma catecholamines, cortisol, and specific symptoms. Psychiatry Res 1987; 20:155–164.
209. Agren H, Oreland L: Early morning awakening in unipolar depressives with higher levels of platelet MAO activity. Psychiatry Res 1982; 7:245–254.
210. Schatzberg AF, Rothschild AJ, Gerson B, et al: Toward a biochemical classification of depressive disorders, IX: DST results and platelet MAO activity. Br J Psychiatry 1985; 146:633–637.
211. Meltzer HY, Lowy MT, Locascio JJ: Platelet MAO activity and the cortisol response to dexamethasone in major depression. Biol Psychiatry 1988; 24:129–142.
212. Pandey GN, Sharma RP, Janicak PG, et al: Monoamine oxidase and cortisol response in depression and schizophrenia. Psychiatry Res 1992; 44:1–8.
213. Sapru MK, Rao BSSR, Channabasavana SM: Serum dopamine-beta-hydroxylase activity in classical subtypes of depression. Acta Psychiatr Scand 1989; 80:474–478.
214. Enna SJ, Karbon EW, Duman RS: GABA-B agonist and imipramine-induced modifications in rat brain beta-adrenergic receptor binding and function. In Bartholine G, Lloyd KG, Morselli PL (eds): GABA and Mood Disorders: Experimental and Clinical Research. New York: Raven Press, 1986:23–49.
215. Bernasconi R: The GABA hypothesis of affective illness; influence of clinically effective antimanic drugs on GABA turnover. In Emrich HM, Aldenhoff JB, Lux HD (eds): Basic Mechanisms in the Action of Lithium. New York: Elsevier, 1982:183–192.
216. Gold BI, Bowers MB, Roth RH, et al: GABA levels in CSF of patients with psychiatric disorders. Am J Psychiatry 1980; 137:362–364.
217. Petty F, Schlesser MA: Plasma GABA in affective illness. J Affect Disord 1981; 3:339–343.
218. Petty F, Sherman AD: Learned helplessness induction decreases in vivo cortical serotonin release. Pharmacol Biochem Behav 1983; 18:649–650.
219. Honig A, Bartlett JR, Bouras N, et al: Amino acid levels in depression: A preliminary investigation. J Psychiatr Res 1989; 22:159–164.
220. Petty F: Plasma concentrations of GABA and mood disorders: A blood test for manic depressive disease? Clin Chem 1994; 40:296–302.
221. Schatzberg AF, Mooney JJ: Noradrenergic and cholinergic mechanisms in depressive disorders: Implications for future treatment strategies. In Meltzer HY, Nerozzi D (eds): Current Practices and Future Developments in the Pharmacotherapy of Mental Disorders. New York: Elsevier, 1991:91–97.
222. Sitaram N, Gillin JC, Bunnery WE Jr: Cholinergic and catecholaminergic receptor sensitivity in affective illness: Strategy and theory. In Post RM, Ballenger JC (eds): Neurobiology of Mood Disorders. Baltimore: Williams & Wilkins, 1984:519–528.
223. Dube S, Kuman N, Ettedgui E, et al: Cholinergic REM induction response: Separation of anxiety and depression. Biol Psychiatry 1985; 20:408–418.
224. Jones D, Kelwala S, Bell J, et al: Cholinergic REM sleep induction response correlation with endogenous major depressive type. Psychiatry Res 1985; 14:99–110.
225. Valk J, van der Knaap MS: Magnetic Resonance of Myelin, Myelination, and Myelin Disorders. Berlin: Springer-Verlag, 1989.
226. Roman GC: Senile dementia of the Binswanger type: A vascular form of dementia in the elderly. JAMA 1987; 258:1782–1788.
227. Husain MM, McDonald WM, Doraiswamy PM, et al: A magnetic resonance imaging study of putamen nuclei in major depression. Psychiatry Res 1991; 40:95–99.
228. Krishnan KRR, Husain MM, McDonald WM, et al: In vivo assessment of caudate volume in man: Effect of normal aging. Life Sci 1990; 47:1325–1329.
229. Shah SA, Doraiswamy PM, Husain MM, et al: Posterior fossa abnormalities in major depression: A controlled MRI study. Acta Psychiatr Scand 1992; 85:474–479.
230. Lurie SN, Doraiswamy PM, Figiel GS, et al: In vivo assessment of pituitary gland volume with MRI: Effect of age. J Clin Endocrinol Metab 1990; 71:505–508.
231. Rao VP, Krishnan KRR, Goli V, et al: Neuroanatomical changes and hypothalamo-pituitary-adrenal axis abnormalities. Biol Psychiatry 1989; 26:729–732.
232. Figiel GS, Krishnan KRR, Brenner JC, et al: Radiologic correlates of antidepressant-induced delirium: The possible significance of basal ganglia lesions. J Neuropsychiatry Clin Neurosci 1989; 1:188–190.
233. Figiel GS, Coffey CE, Djang WT, et al: Brain magnetic resonance imaging findings in ECT-induced delirium. J Neuropsychiatry Clin Neurosci 1990; 2:53–58.
234. Figiel GS, Krishnan KRR, Doraiswamy PM: Subcortical structural changes in ECT-induced delirium. J Geriatr Psychiatry Neurol 1991; 3:172–176.
235. Figiel GS, Krishnan KRR, Doraiswamy PM, et al: Caudate hyperintensities in elderly depressed patients with neuroleptic-induced parkinsonism. J Geriatr Psychiatry Neurol 1991; 4:86–89.
236. Alexander GE, Delong MR, Strick PL: Parallel organization of functionally segregated circuits linking basal ganglia and cortex. Annu Rev Neurosci 1986; 9:357–381.
237. Krishnan KRR: Organic bases of depression in the elderly. Annu Rev Med 1991; 42:261–266.
238. Vita A, Saccleti E, Cazzullo C: A CT scan follow-up study of cerebral ventricular size in schizophrenia and major affective disorder. Schizophr Res 1988; 1:165–166.
239. Woods BT, Yurgelun-Todd D, Benes FM, et al: Progressive ventricular enlargement in schizophrenia: Comparison to bipolar affective disorder and correlation with clinical course. Biol Psychiatry 1990; 27:341–352.
240. Schulz SC: Genetics of schizophrenia: A status report. In Tasman A, Goldfinger SM (eds): American Psychiatric Press Review of Psychiatry, Volume 10. Washington, DC: American Psychiatric Press, 1991:79–97.
241. Tsuang MT, Gilbertson MW, Faraone SV: The genetics of schizophrenia: Current knowledge and future directions. Schizophr Res 1991; 4:157–171.
242. Kendler KS: Overview: A current perspective on twin studies of schizophrenia. Am J Psychiatry 1983; 140:1413–1425.
243. McGue M: When assessing twin concordance use the probandwise not the pairwise rate. Schizophr Bull 1992; 18:171–176.
244. Torrey EF: Are we overestimating the genetic contribution to schizophrenia? Schizophr Bull 1992; 18:159–169.
245. Heston LL: Psychiatric disorders in foster home reared children of schizophrenic mothers. Br J Psychiatry 1966; 112:819–825.
246. Rosenthal D, Wender PH, Kety SS, et al: Parent-child relationships and psychopathological disorder in the child. Arch Gen Psychiatry 1975; 32:466–476.
247. Wender PH, Rosenthal D, Rainer JD, et al: Schizophrenics' adopting parents: Psychiatric status. Arch Gen Psychiatry 1977; 34:777–784.
248. Hallmayer J, Kennedy JL, Wetterberg L, et al: Exclusion of linkage between the serotonin 2 receptor and schizophrenia in a large Swedish kindred. Arch Gen Psychiatry 1992; 49:216–219.
249. Moises HW, Gelernter J, Giuffra LA, et al: No linkage between D_2 dopamine receptor gene region and schizophrenia. Arch Gen Psychiatry 1991; 48:643–647.
250. Owen MJ, McGuffin P: DNA and classical genetic markers in schizophrenia. Eur Arch Psychiatry Clin Neurosci 1991; 240: 197–203.
251. Campion D, Leboyer M, Hilliaire D, et al: Relationship of HLA to schizophrenia not supported in multiplex families. Psychiatry Res 1992; 41:99–105.
252. Crocq MA, Lannfelt L, Mayerova A, et al: Dopamine D_3 receptor polymorphism in psychiatric patients. Presented at the 31st Annual Meeting of the American College of Neuropsychopharmacology; December 1992; San Juan, Puerto Rico.
253. Lewis SW, Murray RM: Obstetrical complications, neurodevelopmental deviance and risk of schizophrenia. J Psychiatr Res 1987; 21:413–422.
254. O'Callaghan E, Larkin C, Kinsella A, et al: Obstetric complications, the putative familial-sporadic distinction, and tardive dyskinesia in schizophrenia. Br J Psychiatry 1990; 157:578–584.
255. McCreadie RG, Hall DJ, Berry IJ, et al: The Nithsdale schizophrenia surveys X: Obstetric complications, family history and abnormal movements. Br J Psychiatry 1992; 161:799–805.
256. Nimgaonkar VL, Wessely S, Murray RM: Prevalence of familiality, obstetric complications, and structural brain damage in schizophrenic patients. Br J Psychiatry 1988; 153:191–197.

257. Reddy R, Mukherjee S, Schnur DB, et al: History of obstetric complications, family history, and CT scan findings in schizophrenic patients. Schizophr Res 1990; 3:311–314.
258. Owen MJ, Lewis SW, Murray RM: Obstetric complications and cerebral abnormalities in schizophrenia. Psychol Med 1988; 15: 27–41.
259. Cannon TD, Mednick SA, Parnas J: Genetic and perinatal determinants of structural brain deficits in schizophrenia. Arch Gen Psychiatry 1989; 46:883–889.
260. Williams AO, Reveley MA, Kolakowska T, et al: Schizophrenia with good and poor outcome, II. Cerebral ventricular size and its clinical significance. Br J Psychiatry 1985; 146:239–246.
261. Farmer A, Jackson R, McGuffin P, Storey P: Cerebral ventricular enlargement in chronic schizophrenia: Consistencies and contradictions. Br J Psychiatry 1987; 150:324–330.
262. Nasrallah HA, Charles GT, McCalley-Whitters M, et al: Cerebral ventricular enlargement in subtypes of chronic schizophrenia. Arch Gen Psychiatry 1982; 39:774–777.
263. Onstad S, Skre I, Torgersen S, Kringlen E: Birthweight and obstetric complications in schizophrenic twins. Acta Psychiatr Scand 1992; 85:70–73.
264. O'Callaghan E, Sham P, Takei N, et al: Schizophrenia after prenatal exposure to 1957 A2 influenza epidemic. Lancet 1991; 337:1248–1250.
265. Mednick SA, Machon RA, Huttunen MO, et al: Adult schizophrenia following prenatal exposure to an influenza epidemic. Arch Gen Psychiatry 1988; 45:189–192.
266. Kendell RE, Kemp IW: Maternal influenza in the etiology of schizophrenia. Arch Gen Psychiatry 1989; 46:878–882.
267. Bowler AE, Torrey EF: Influenza and schizophrenia. [letter] Arch Gen Psychiatry 1990; 47:875–877.
268. Done DJ, Johnstone EC, Frith CD, et al: Complications of pregnancy and delivery in relation to psychosis in adult life: Data from the British perinatal mortality survey sample. Br Med J 1991; 302:1576–1580.
269. Susser ES, Lin SP: Schizophrenia after prenatal exposure to the Dutch Hunger Winter of 1944–1945. Arch Gen Psychiatry 1992; 49:983–988.
270. Merriam AE, Kay SR, Opler LA, et al: Neurologic signs and the positive-negative dimension in schizophrenia. Biol Psychiatry 1990; 28:181–192.
271. King DJ, Wilson A, Cooper SJ, Waddington JL: The clinical correlates of neurologic soft signs in chronic schizophrenia. Br J Psychiatry 1991; 158:770–775.
272. Schroder J, Niethammer R, Geider FJ, et al: Neurologic soft signs in schizophrenia. Schizophr Res 1992; 6:25–30.
273. Kinney DK, Yurgelun-Todd DA, Woods BT: Hard neurologic signs and psychopathology in relatives of schizophrenic patients. Psychiatry Res 1991; 39:45–53.
274. Rossi A, De Cataldo S, Di Michele V, et al: Neurologic soft signs in schizophrenia. Br J Psychiatry 1991; 157:735–739.
275. Goldberg TE, Gold JM, Braff DL: Neuropsychological functioning and time-linked information processing in schizophrenia. In Tasman A, Goldfinger SM (eds): American Psychiatric Press Review of Psychiatry, Volume 10. Washington, DC: American Psychiatric Press, 1991:60–78.
276. Hecker E: Die Hebephrenie. Arch Pathol Anat Physiol Klin Med 1871; 52:394.
277. Vogt C, Vogt O: Alterations anatomiques de la schizophrenie et d'autres psychoses dites functionelles. In Proceedings of the First International Congress of Neuropathology. Turin, Italy: Rosenberg & Sellier, 1952; 1:515–532.
278. Yakovlev PI, Hamlin H, Sweet WH: Frontal lobotomy neuroanatomical observations. J Neuropathol Exp Neurol 1950; 9:250–285.
279. Brown R, Colter N, Corsellis JAN, et al: Postmortem evidence of structural brain changes in schizophrenia. Arch Gen Psychiatry 1986; 43:36–42.
280. Pakkenberg B: Post-mortem study of chronic schizophrenic brains. Br J Psychiatry 1987; 151:744–752.
281. Cleghorn JM, Zipursky RB, List SJ: Structural and functional brain imaging in schizophrenia. J Psychiatry Neurosci 1991; 16:53–74.
282. Shelton RC, Weinberger DR: X-ray computerized tomography studies in schizophrenia: A review and synthesis. In Nasrallah HA, Weinberger DR (eds): Handbook of Schizophrenia, Volume I, The Neurology of Schizophrenia. Amsterdam: Elsevier, 1986:207–250.
283. Jernigan TL: Anatomical and CT scan studies of psychiatric disorder. In Berger PA, Brodie KH (eds): American Handbook of Psychiatry, Volume 8, Biological Psychiatry, 2nd ed. New York: Basic Books, 1986:213–235.
284. Nyback H, Wiesel FA, Berggren BM: Computed tomography of the brain in patients with acute psychosis and in healthy volunteers. Acta Psychiatr Scand 1982; 65:403–414.
285. Schulz SC, Koller MM, Kishore PR, et al: Ventricular enlargement in teenage patients with schizophrenia spectrum disorders. Am J Psychiatry 1983; 140:1592–1595.
286. Weinberger DR, DeLisi L, Perman GP, et al: Computed tomography in schizophreniform disorder and other acute psychiatric disorders. Arch Gen Psychiatry 1982; 39:778–793.
287. Reveley AM, Reveley MA, Clifford CA, et al: Cerebral ventricular size in twins discordant for schizophrenia. Lancet 1982; 2:540–541.
288. Suddath RL, Christison GW, Torrey EF, et al: Anatomical abnormalities in the brains of monozygotic twins discordant for schizophrenia. N Engl J Med 1990; 322:789–794.
289. Illowsky BP, Juliano DM, Bigelow LB, Weinberger DR: Stability of CT scan findings in schizophrenia: Results of an 8 year follow-up study. J Neurol Neurosurg Psychiatry 1988; 51:209–213.
290. Sponheim SR, Iacono WG, Beiser M: Stability of ventricular size after the onset of psychosis in schizophrenia. Psychiatry Res 1991; 40:21–29.
291. Kelsoe JR, Cadet JL, Pickar D, et al: Quantitative neuroanatomy in schizophrenia. Arch Gen Psychiatry 1988; 45:533–541.
292. Gur RE, Mozley D, Resnick SM, et al: Magnetic resonance imaging in schizophrenia. I. Volumetric analysis of brain and cerebrospinal fluid. Arch Gen Psychiatry 1991; 48:407–412.
293. Young AH, Blackwood DHR, Roxborough H, et al: A magnetic resonance imaging study of schizophrenia: Brain structure and clinical symptoms. Br J Psychiatry 1991; 158:158–164.
294. Degreef G, Ashtari M, Bogerts B, et al: Volumes of ventricular system subdivisions measured from magnetic resonance images in first episode schizophrenic patients. Arch Gen Psychiatry 1992; 49: 531–537.
295. Zipursky RB, Lim KO, Sullivan EV, et al: Widespread cerebral gray matter volume deficits in schizophrenia. Arch Gen Psychiatry 1992; 49:195–205.
296. Pfefferbaum A, Zipursky RB: Neuroimaging studies of schizophrenia. Schizophr Res 1991; 4:193–208.
297. Hopf A: Über histopathologische Veranderungen im Pallidum und Striatum bei Schizophrenie. In Proceedings of the First International Congress on Neuropathology. Turin, Italy: Rosenberg & Sellier, 1952; 3:629–635.
298. Jernigan TL, Zisook S, Heaton RK, et al: Magnetic resonance imaging abnormalities in lenticular nuclei and cerebral cortex in schizophrenia. Arch Gen Psychiatry 1991; 48:881–890.
299. Swayze VW 2d, Andreasen NC, Alliger RJ, et al: Subcortical and temporal structures in affective disorder and schizophrenia: A magnetic resonance imaging study. Biol Psychiatry 1992; 31: 221–240.
300. Heckers S, Heinsen H, Heinsen Y, Beckmann H: Cortex, white matter, and basal ganglia in schizophrenia: A volumetric postmortem study. Biol Psychiatry 1991; 29:556–566.
301. DeLisi L, Hoff AL, Schwartz JE, et al: Brain morphology in first-episode schizophrenic-like psychotic patients: A quantitative magnetic resonance imaging study. Biol Psychiatry 1991; 29: 159–175.
302. Chakos MH, Lieberman JA, Bilder RM, et al: Increase in caudate nuclei volumes of first episode schizophrenic patients taking antipsychotic drugs. Am J Psychiatry 1994; 151:1430–1436.
303. Chakos MH, Lieberman JA, Alvin J, et al: Caudate nuclei volumes in schizophrenic patients treated with typical antipsychotics or clozapine. [letter] Lancet 1995; 345:456–457.
304. Keshaven MS, Reynold CF III, Miewald J, Montrose D: Slow-wave sleep deficits and outcome in schizophrenia and schizoaffective disorder. Acta Psychiatrica Scandinavica 1995; 91:289–292.
305. Arendt T, Bigl Y, Arendt A, et al: Loss of neurons in the nucleus basalis of Meynert in Alzheimer's disease, paralysis agitans, and Korsakoff's disease. Acta Neuropathol 1983; 61:101–108.
306. El-Mallakh R, Kirch DG, Shelton R, et al: The nucleus basalis of Meynert, senile plaques, and intellectual impairment in schizophrenia. J Neuropsychiatry Clin Neurosci 1991; 3:383–386.
307. Benes FM, Davidson J, Bird E: Quantitative cytoarchitectural studies

of the cerebral cortex of schizophrenics. Arch Gen Psychiatry 1986; 43:31–35.
308. Bogerts B, Meertz E, Schonfeldt-Bausch R: Basal ganglia and limbic system pathology in schizophrenia. Arch Gen Psychiatry 1985; 42:784–791.
309. Bogerts B, Falkai P, Haupts M, et al: Post-mortem volume measurements of limbic system and basal ganglia structures in chronic schizophrenics. Schizophr Res 1990; 3:295–301.
310. Kirch DG, Weinberger DR: Anatomical neuropathology in schizophrenia: Post-mortem findings. In Nasrallah HA, Weinberger DR (eds): Handbook of Schizophrenia. Amsterdam: Elsevier, 1986: 325–348.
311. Benes FM, Bird ED: An analysis of the arrangement of neurons in the cingulate cortex of schizophrenic patients. Arch Gen Psychiatry 1987; 44:608–616.
312. Colon EJ: Quantitative cytoarchitectonics of the human cerebral cortex in schizophrenic dementia. Acta Neuropathol (Berl) 1979; 20:1–10.
313. Suddath R, Casanova MF, Goldberg TE, et al: Temporal lobe pathology in schizophrenia: A quantitative magnetic resonance imaging study. Am J Psychiatry 1989; 146:464–472.
314. Rossi A, Stratta P, Di Michele V, et al: Temporal lobe structure by magnetic resonance in bipolar affective disorders and schizophrenia. J Affect Disord 1991; 21:19–22.
315. Barta PE, Pearlson GD, Powers RE, et al: Auditory hallucinations and smaller superior temporal gyral volume in schizophrenia. Am J Psychiatry 1990; 147:1457–1462.
316. Shenton ME, Kikinis R, Jolesz FA, et al: Abnormalities of the left temporal lobe and thought disorder in schizophrenia: A quantitative magnetic resonance imaging study. N Engl J Med 1992; 327:604–612.
317. Weinberger DR, Torrey EF, Neophytides AN, et al: Structural abnormalities in the cerebral cortex of chronic schizophrenic patients. Arch Gen Psychiatry 1979; 36:935–939.
318. Pfefferbaum A, Zipursky RB, Lim KO, et al: Computed tomographic evidence for generalized sulcal and ventricular enlargement in schizophrenia. Arch Gen Psychiatry 1988; 45:633–640.
319. Berman KF, Weinberger DR: Functional localization in the brain in schizophrenia. In Tasman A, Goldfinger S (eds): American Psychiatric Press Review of Psychiatry, Volume 10. Washington, DC: American Psychiatric Press, 1991: 24–59.
320. Ingvar DH, Franzen G: Abnormalities of cerebral blood flow distribution in patients with chronic schizophrenia. Acta Psychiatr Scand 1974; 50:425–462.
321. Ingvar DH, Franzen G: Distribution of cerebral activity in chronic schizophrenia. Lancet 1974; 2:1484–1486.
322. Weinberger DR, Berman KF, Zec RF: Physiologic dysfunction of dorsolateral prefrontal cortex in schizophrenia. I. Regional cerebral blood flow evidence. Arch Gen Psychiatry 1986; 43:114–124.
323. Rubin P, Holm S, Friberg L, et al: Altered modulation of prefrontal and subcortical brain activity in newly diagnosed schizophrenia and schizophreniform disorder. Arch Gen Psychiatry 1991; 48:987–995.
324. Berman KF, Zec RF, Weinberger DR: Physiologic dysfunction of dorsolateral prefrontal cortex in schizophrenia. II. Role of neuroleptic treatment, attention, and mental effort. Arch Gen Psychiatry 1986; 43:126–135.
325. Berman KF, Illowsky BP, Weinberger DR: Physiologic dysfunction of dorsolateral prefrontal cortex in schizophrenia. IV. Further evidence for regional and behavioral specificity. Arch Gen Psychiatry 1988; 45:616–622.
326. Berman KF, Torrey EF, Daniel DG, Weinberger DR: Regional cerebral blood flow in monozygotic twins discordant and concordant for schizophrenia. Arch Gen Psychiatry 1992; 49:927–934.
327. Weinberger DR, Berman KF, Suddath R, et al: Evidence of dysfunction of a prefrontal-limbic network in schizophrenia: A magnetic resonance imaging and regional cerebral blood flow study of discordant monozygotic twins. Am J Psychiatry 1992; 149:890–897.
328. Lesch A, Bogerts B: The diencephalon in schizophrenia: Evidence of reduced thickness of the periventricular gray matter. Eur Arch Psychiatry Neurol Sci 1984; 234:212–219.
329. Pakkenberg B: Pronounced reduction of total neuron number in mediodorsal thalamic nucleus and nucleus accumbens in schizophrenics. Arch Gen Psychiatry 1990; 47:1023–1028.
330. Bogerts B, Hantsch J, Herzer M: A morphometric study of the dopamine-containing cell groups in the mesencephalon of normals, Parkinson patients and schizophrenics. Biol Psychiatry 1983; 18: 951–969.
331. Andreasen NC, Arndt S, Swayze V, et al: Thalamic abnormalities in schizophrenia visualized through magnetic resonance image averaging. Science 1994; 266:294–298.
332. Weinberger DR, Kleinman JE, Luchins DJ, et al: Cerebellar atrophy in chronic schizophrenia. Lancet 1979; 1:718–719.
333. Heath RG, Franklin DE, Schraberg D, et al: Gross pathology of the cerebellum in patients diagnosed and treated as functional psychiatric disorders. J Nerv Ment Dis 1979; 167:585–592.
334. Weinberger DR, Kleinman JE, Luchins DJ, et al: Cerebellar atrophy in schizophrenia: A controlled postmortem study. Am J Psychiatry 1980; 137:359–361.
335. Lohr JB, Jeste DV: Cerebellar pathology in schizophrenia, a neuronometric study. Biol Psychiatry 1986; 21:865–875.
336. Carlsson A, Lindquist M: Effect of chlorpromazine or haloperidol on formation of 3-methoxytyramine and normetanephrine in mouse brain. Acta Pharmacol Toxicol 1963; 20:140–144.
337. Creese I, Burt DR, Snyder SH: Dopamine receptor binding predicts clinical and pharmacological potencies of antipsychophrenic drugs. Science 1976; 192:481–483.
338. Seeman P, Lee T, Chau-Wong M, et al: Antipsychotic drug doses and neuroleptic/dopamine receptors. Nature 1976; 261:717–719.
339. Mathysse S: Role of dopamine in selective attention. Adv Biochem Psychopharmacol 1977; 16:667–669.
340. Braff DL, Geyer MA: Sensorimotor gating and schizophrenia: Human and animal model studies. Arch Gen Psychiatry 1990; 47:181–188.
341. Ellinwood EH: Amphetamine psychosis I: Description of the individuals and the process. J Nerv Ment Dis 1967; 144:274–283.
342. Angrist BM, Sathanathan G, Gershon S: Behavioral effects of L-dopa in schizophrenic patients. Psychopharmacology (Berl) 1973; 31:1–12.
343. Widerlov E: A critical appraisal of CSF monoamine metabolite studies in schizophrenia. Ann N Y Acad Sci 1988; 537:309–323.
344. Davis KL, Kahn RS, Ko G, et al: Dopamine in schizophrenia: A review and reconceptualization. Am J Psychiatry 1991; 148:1474–1486.
345. Potter WZ, Hsiao JK, Goldman SM: Effects of renal clearance on plasma concentrations of homovanillic acid. Methodologic cautions. Arch Gen Psychiatry 1989; 46:558–562.
346. Bird ED, Spokes EGS, Iversen LL: Increased dopamine concentrations in limbic areas of brain from patients dying with schizophrenia. Brain 1979; 102:347–360.
347. Crow TJ, Baker HF, Cross AJ, et al: Monoamine mechanisms in chronic schizophrenia. Postmortem neurochemical findings. Br J Psychiatry 1979; 134:249–256.
348. Reynolds GP: Increased concentration and lateral asymmetry of amygdala dopamine in schizophrenia. Nature 1983; 305:527–529.
349. Hyde TM, Casanova MF, Kleinman JE, et al: Neuroanatomical and neurochemical pathology in schizophrenia. In Tasman A, Goldfinger SM (eds): American Psychiatric Press Review of Psychiatry, Volume 10. Washington, DC: American Psychiatric Press, 1991:7–23.
350. Wong DF, Wagner HN, Tune LE, et al: Positron emission tomography reveals elevated D_2 dopamine receptors in drug naive schizophrenics. Science 1986; 244:1558–1563.
351. Tune LE, Wong DF, Pearlson GD, et al: Dopamine D_2 receptor density estimation in schizophrenia: A positron emission tomography study with 11C-*N*-methylspiperone. Psychiatric Res 1993; 49:219–237.
352. Farde L, Wiesel F, Hall H, et al: No D_2 receptor increase in PET study of schizophrenia. Arch Gen Psychiatry 1987; 44:671–672.
353. Farde L, Wiesel FA, Stone-Elander S, et al: D_2 dopamine receptors in neuroleptic-naive schizophrenic patients. Arch Gen Psychiatry 1990; 47:213–219.
354. Martinot JL, Peron-Magna P, Huret JD, et al: Striatal D_2 dopaminergic receptors assessed with positron emission tomography and [^{76}Br] bromospiperone in untreated schizophrenic patients. Am J Psychiatry 1990; 147:44–50.
355. Cross AJ, Crow TJ, Owen F: ^{3}H-fluphenthixol binding in postmortem brains of schizophrenics: Evidence for a selective increase in dopamine D_2 receptors. Psychopharmacology (Berl) 1981; 74:122–124.
356. Seeman P, Bzowej NH, Guan HC, et al: Human brain D_1 and D_2 dopamine receptors in schizophrenia, Alzheimer's, Parkinson's and Huntington's diseases. Neuropsychopharmacology 1987; 1:5–15.
357. Hess EJ, Brancha HS, Kleinman JE, et al: Dopamine receptor subtype imbalance in schizophrenia. Life Sci 1989; 40:1487–1497.

358. Seeman P, Niznik H, Guan H, et al: Link between D_1 and D_2 dopamine receptors is reduced in schizophrenia and Huntington diseased brain. Proc Natl Acad Sci U S A 1989; 86:10156–10160.
359. Knable MB, Hyde TM, Herman MM, et al: Quantitative autoradiography of dopamine-D1 receptors, D2 receptors, and dopamine uptake sites in postmortem striatal specimens from schizophrenic patients. Biol Psychiatry 1994; 36:827–835.
360. Seeman P, Guan HC, Van Tol HHM: Dopamine D_4 receptors are elevated in schizophrenia. Nature 1993; 365:441–445.
361. Murray AM, Hyde TM, Knable MB, et al: Pharmacological characterizations of the binding of [^{3}H]-YMO9151-2 to D_4 dopamine receptor subtypes in basal ganglia and cortex of schizophrenics and controls. Soc Neurosci Abstr 1994; 20:1261.
362. Reynolds GP, Mason SL: Are striatal dopamine D_4 receptors increased in schizophrenia? J Neurochem 1994; 63:1576–1577.
363. Bachneff SA: Positron emission tomography and magnetic resonance imaging: A review and a local circuit neurons hypo(dys)function hypothesis of schizophrenia. Biol Psychiatry 1991; 30:857–886.
364. Weinberger DR: Implications of normal brain development for the pathogenesis of schizophrenia. Arch Gen Psychiatry 1987; 44: 660–669.
365. Iversen SD: The effect of surgical lesions to frontal cortex and substantia nigra on amphetamine responses in rats. Brain Res 1971; 31:295–311.
366. Scatton B, Worms P, Lloyd KG, et al: Cortical modulation of striatal function. Brain Res 1982; 232:331–343.
367. Jaskiw GE, Karoum F, Weinberger DR: Persistent elevations in dopamine and its metabolites in the nucleus accumbens after mild subchronic stress in rats with ibotenic acid lesions of the medial prefrontal cortex. Brain Res 1990; 534:321–323.
368. Carter CJ, Pycock CJ: Behavioral and biochemical effects of dopamine and noradrenaline depletion within medial prefrontal cortex of rat. Brain Res 1980; 192:163–176.
369. Pycock CJ, Kerwin RW, Carter CJ: Effect of lesions of cortical dopamine terminals on subcortical dopamine in rats. Nature 1980; 286:74–77.
370. Pycock CJ, Kerwin RW, Carter CJ: Effect of 6-hydroxydopamine lesions of medial prefrontal cortex in rat. J Neurochem 1980; 34:91–99.
371. Geraud G, Arne-Bes MC, Guell A, et al: Reversibility of hemodynamic hypofrontality in schizophrenia. J Cereb Blood Flow Metab 1987; 7:9–12.
372. Weinberger DR, Berman KF, Illowsky BP: Physiologic dysfunction of dorsolateral prefrontal cortex in schizophrenia. III. A new cohort and evidence for a monoaminergic mechanism. Arch Gen Psychiatry 1988; 45:609–615.
373. Daniel DG, Berman KF, Weinberger DR: The effect of apomorphine on regional cerebral blood flow in schizophrenia. J Neuropsychiatry 1989; 1:377–384.
374. Lipska BK, Jaskiw GE, Chrapusta S, et al: Ibotenic acid lesion of the ventral hippocampus differentially affects dopamine and its metabolites in the nucleus accumbens and prefrontal cortex in the rat. Brain Res 1992; 585:1–6.
375. Sokoloff P, Giros B, Martres M, et al: Molecular cloning and characterization of a novel dopamine receptor (D_3) as a target for neuroleptics. Nature 1990; 347:146–151.
376. Sunahara RK, Guan HC, O'Dowd BF, et al: Cloning of the gene for a human D_5 receptor with higher affinity for dopamine than D_1. Nature 1991; 350:614–619.
377. Van Tol H, Bungow JR, Guan HC, et al: Cloning of the gene for a human dopamine D_4 receptor with high affinity for the antipsychotic clozapine. Nature 1991; 350:610–614.
378. Zukin SR, Javitt DC: The brain NMDA receptor, psychotomimetic drug effects, and schizophrenia. In Tasman A, Goldfinger SM (eds): American Psychiatric Press Review of Psychiatry, Volume 10. Washington, DC: American Psychiatric Press, 1991: 480–498.
379. Johnson SW, Seutin V, North RA: Burst firing in dopamine neurons induced by *N*-methyl-D-aspartate: Role of electrogenic sodium pump. Science 1992; 258:665–667.
380. Kim JS, Kornhuber HH, Schmid-Burgk W, et al: Low cerebrospinal fluid glutamate in schizophrenic patients and a new hypothesis on schizophrenia. Neurosci Lett 1980; 20:379–382.
381. Gattaz WF, Gatz D, Beckmann H: Glutamate in schizophrenics and healthy controls. Arch Psychiatr Nervenkr 1982; 231:221–225.
382. Gattaz WF, Gasser T, Beckmann H: Multidimensional analysis of the concentration of 17 substances in the CSF of schizophrenics and controls. Biol Psychiatry 1985; 20:360–366.
383. Perry TL: Normal cerebrospinal fluid and brain glutamate levels in schizophrenia do not support the hypothesis of glutamatergic neuronal dysfunction. Neurosci Lett 1982; 28:81–85.
384. Toru M, Watanabe S, Shibuya H, et al: Neurotransmitters, receptors and neuropeptides in post-mortem brains of chronic schizophrenic patients. Acta Psychiatr Scand 1988; 78:121–137.
385. Sherman AD, Davidson AT, Baruah S, et al: Evidence of glutamatergic deficiency in schizophrenia. Neurosci Lett 1991; 121:77–80.
386. Sherman AD, Hegwood TS, Baruah S, et al: Deficient NMDA-mediated glutamate release from synaptosomes of schizophrenics. Biol Psychiatry 1991; 30:1191–1198.
387. Kornhuber J, Mack-Burkhardt F, Riedere P, et al: ^{3}H-MK801 binding sites in postmortem brain regions of schizophrenic patients. J Neural Transm 1989; 77:231–236.
388. Harrison PJ, McLaughlin D, Kerwin RW: Decreased hippocampal expression of a glutamate receptor gene in schizophrenia. Lancet 1991; 337:450–452.
389. Dickinson SL, Curzon G: Roles of dopamine and 5-hydroxytryptamine in stereotyped and non-stereotyped behavior. Neuropharmacology 1983; 22:805–812.
390. Korsgaard S, Gerlach J, Christensson E: Behavioral aspects of serotonin-dopamine interaction in the monkey. Eur J Pharmacol 1985; 118:245–252.
391. Bleich A, Brown SL, Kahn R, et al: The role of serotonin in schizophrenia. Schizophr Bull 1988; 14:297–315.
392. Mackay AVP, Doble A, Bird ED, et al: ^{3}H-Spiperone binding in normal and schizophrenic post-mortem human brain. Life Sci 1978; 23:527–532.
393. Owen F, Cross AJ, Crow TJ, et al: Neurotransmitter receptors in brain in schizophrenia. Acta Psychiatr Scand 1981; 63:20–28.
394. Bennett JP, Enna SJ, Bylund DB, et al: Neurotransmitter receptors in frontal cortex of schizophrenics. Arch Gen Psychiatry 1979; 36:927–934.
395. Mita T, Hanada S, Nishimo N, et al: Decreased serotonin S_2 and increased dopamine D_2 receptors in chronic schizophrenics. Biol Psychiatry 1986; 21:1407–1414.
396. Arora RC, Meltzer HY: Serotonin 2 (5-HT_2) receptor binding in the frontal cortex of schizophrenic patients. J Neural Transm 1991; 85:19–29.
397. Laruelle M, Toti R, Abi-Dargham A, et al: Selective abnormalities of prefrontal serotonergic markers in schizophrenia: A post-mortem study. Arch Gen Psychiatry, in press.
398. Whitaker PM, Crow TJ, Ferrier IN: Tritiated LSD binding in frontal cortex in schizophrenia. Arch Gen Psychiatry 1981; 38:278–280.
399. Reynolds GP, Rossor MN, Iversen LL: Preliminary studies of human cortical 5-HT_2 receptors and their involvement in schizophrenia and neuroleptic drug action. J Neural Transm Suppl 1983; 18:273–277.
400. Van Kammen D: The biochemical basis of relapse and drug response in schizophrenia: Review and hypothesis. Psychol Med 1991; 21:881–895.
401. Van Kammen D, Kelley M: Dopamine and norepinephrine activity in schizophrenia. Schizophr Res 1991; 4:173–191.
402. Van Kammen D, Peters J, Yao J, et al: Norepinephrine in acute exacerbations of chronic schizophrenia. Arch Gen Psychiatry, 1990; 47:161–168.
403. Pickar D, Breier A, Hsiao J, et al: Cerebrospinal fluid and plasma monoamine metabolites and their relation to psychosis. Arch Gen Psychiatry 1990; 47:641–648.
404. Farley IJ, Price KS, McCullogh E, et al: Norepinephrine in chronic paranoid schizophrenia: Above normal levels in limbic forebrain. Science 1978; 200:456–458.
405. Kleinman JE, Karoum F, Rosenblatt JE, et al: Postmortem neurochemical studies in chronic schizophrenia. In Usdin, E, Hanin I (eds): Biological Markers in Psychiatry and Neurology. New York: Pergamon Press, 1982.
406. Bird ED, Spokes EG, Iversen LL: Brain norepinephrine and dopamine in schizophrenia. Science 1979; 204:93–94.
407. Crow TJ, Ferrier IN, Johnstone EC, et al: Neuroendocrine aspects of schizophrenia. In Fink G, Whalley LJ (eds): Neuropeptides: Basic and Clinical Aspects. Edinburgh: Churchill-Livingstone, 1982:222–239.
408. Roberts GW, Ferrier IN, Lee Y, et al: Peptides, the limbic lobe and schizophrenia. Brain Res 1983; 288:199–211.
409. Ferrier IN, Crow TJ, Farmery SM, et al: Reduced CCK in the limbic

lobe in schizophrenia: A marker for the defect state in schizophrenia. Ann N Y Acad Sci 1985; 448:495–500.
410. Perry RH, Dockray GJ, Dimaline R, et al: Neuropeptides in Alzheimer's disease, depression and schizophrenia. J Neurol Sci 1981; 51:465–472.
411. Kleinman JE, Hong J, Iadarola M, et al: Neuropeptides in human brain—postmortem studies. Prog Neuropsychopharmacol Biol Psychiatry 1985; 9:91–95.
412. Farmery SM, Owen F, Poulter M, et al: Reduced high affinity cholecystokinin binding in hippocampus and frontal cortex of schizophrenic patients. Life Sci 1985; 36:473–477.
413. Kerwin R, Robinson P, Stephenson J: Distribution of CCK binding sites in the human hippocampal formation and their alteration in schizophrenia: A post-mortem autoradiographic study. Psychol Med 1992; 22:37–43.
414. Nemeroff CB, Bissette G, Prange AJ Jr, et al: Neurotensin: Central nervous system effects of a hypothalamic peptide. Brain Res 1977; 128:485–496.
415. McKinney WT, Bunney WE: Animal model of depression. Arch Gen Psychiatry 1969; 21:240–248.
416. Abramson LY, Seligman MEP: Modeling psychopathology in the laboratory: History and rationale. In Maser JD, Seligman MEP (eds): Psychopathology: Experimental Models. San Francisco: WH Freeman, 1977:1–26.
417. Willner P: The validity of animal models of depression. Psychopharmacology (Berl) 1984; 83:1–16.
418. Parker G, Hadzi-Pavlovic D, Boyce P, et al: Classifying depression by mental state signs. Br J Psychiatry 1990; 157:55–65.
419. Mitchell PB, Potter WZ: Major depression: The validity of a diagnosis. [letter] Depression 1993;1:180.
420. Roth M: A classification of affective disorders based on a synthesis of new and old concepts. In Meyer E, Brady JV (eds): Research in the Psychobiology of Human Behavior. Baltimore: The Johns Hopkins University Press, 1976:75–114.
421. Nelson JC, Charney DS: The symptoms of major depressive illness. Am J Psychiatry 1981; 138:1–13.
422. Cohen RM, Weingartner H, Smallberg SA, et al: Effort and cognition in depression. Arch Gen Psychiatry 1982; 39:593–597.
423. Horovitz ZP, Ragozzino PW, Leaf RC: Selective block of rat mouse-killing by antidepressants. Life Sci 1965;4:1909–1912.
424. Sofia RD: Effects of centrally active drugs on four models of experimentally-induced aggression in rodents. Life Sci 1969; 8:705–716.
425. Sofia RD: Structural relationship and potency of agents which selectively block mouse killing (muricide) behavior in rats. Life Sci 1969;8:1201–1210.
426. Quinton RM: The increase in the toxicity of yohimbine induced by imipramine and other drugs in mice. Br J Pharmacol 1963; 21:51–66.
427. Malick JB: Yohimbine potentiation as a predictor of antidepressant action. In Enna SJ, Malick JB, Richardson E (eds): Antidepressants: Neurochemical, Behavioral, and Clinical Perspectives. New York: Raven Press, 1981:141–155.
428. Morpurgo C, Theobald W: Influence of imipramine-like compounds and chlorpromazine on the reserpine-hypothermia in mice and the amphetamine-hyperthermia in rats. Med Pharmacol Exp 1965; 12:226–232.
429. Halliwell G, Quinton RM, Williams FE: A comparison of imipramine, chlorpromazine and related drugs in various tests involving autonomic functions and antagonism of reserpine. Br J Pharmacol 1964; 23:330–350.
430. Carlton PL: Potentiation of the behavioral effects of amphetamine by imipramine. Psychopharmacologia 1961; 2:364–376.
431. Babington RG, Wedeking PW: The pharmacology of seizures induced by sensitization with low intensity brain stimulation. Pharmacol Biochem Behav 1973; 1:461–467.
432. Babington RG: Antidepressives and the kindling effect. In Fielding S, Lal H (eds): Antidepressants. Mount Kisco, NY: Futura Publishing, 1975:113–124.
433. Baltzer V, Weiskrantz L: Antidepressant agents and reversal of diurnal activity cycles in the rat. Biol Psychiatry 1975; 10:199–209.
434. Janscar S, Leonard BE: The effects of olfactory bulbectomy on the behaviour of rats in the open field. Ir J Med Sci 1980; 149:80–81.
435. Cairncross KD, Cox B, Forster C, et al: The olfactory bulbectomized rat: A simple model for detecting drugs with antidepressant potential. [proceedings] Br J Pharmacol 1977; 61:497P.
436. Archer T, Soderberg U, Ross SB, et al: Role of olfactory bulbectomy and DSP4 treatment in avoidance learning in the rat. Behav Neurosci 1984; 98:496–505.
437. Rigter H, van Riezen H, Wren A: Pharmacological validation of a new test for the detection of antidepressant activity of drugs. Br J Pharmacol 1977; 59:451–452.
438. Weiss JM, Krieckhaus EE, Conte R: Effects of fear conditioning on subsequent avoidance and movement. J Comp Physiol Psychol 1968; 65:413–421.
439. King MG, Cairncross KD: Effects of olfactory bulb section on brain noradrenaline, corticosterone and conditioning in the rat. Pharmacol Biochem Behav 1974; 2:347–353.
440. Gorka Z, Earley B, Leonard BE: Effect of bilateral olfactory bulbectomy in the rat, alone or in combination with antidepressants, on the learned immobility model of depression. Neuropsychobiology 1985; 13:26–30.
441. Stockert M, Serra J, De Robertis E: Effect of olfactory bulbectomy and chronic amitriptyline treatment in rats. ^{3}H-imipramine binding and behavioral analysis by swimming and open field tests. Pharmacol Biochem Behav 1988; 29:681–686.
442. van Riezen H, Leonard BE: Effects of psychotropic drugs on the behavior and neurochemistry of olfactory bulbectomized rats. In File SE (ed): Psychopharmacology of Anxiolytics and Antidepressants. New York: Pergamon Press, 1991:231–250.
443. Cairncross KD, Schofield SPM, Bassett JR: Endogenous brain norepinephrine levels following bilateral olfactory bulb ablation. Pharmacol Biochem Behav 1975; 3:425–427.
444. van Riezen H, Schnieden H, Wren AF: Olfactory bulb ablation in the rat: Behavioural changes and their reversal by antidepressant drugs. Br J Pharmacol 1977; 60:521–528.
445. Earley B, Leonard BE: Effect of two specific-serotonin re-uptake inhibitors on the behaviour of the olfactory bulbectomized rat in the 'open field' apparatus. In Burrows GD, Norman TR, Dennerstein L (eds): Clinical and Pharmacological Studies in Psychiatric Disorders. London: John Libbey, 1985:234–240.
446. McGuire PS, Seiden LS: Differential effects of imipramine in rats as a function of DRL schedule value. Pharmacol Biochem Behav 1980; 13:691–694.
447. McGuire PS, Seiden LS: The effects of tricyclic antidepressants on performance under a differential-reinforcement-of-low-rates schedule in rats. J Pharmacol Exp Ther 1980; 214:635–641.
448. O'Donnell JM, Seiden LS: Effects of monoamine oxidase inhibitors on performance during differential reinforcement of low response rate. Psychopharmacology (Berl) 1982; 78:214–218.
449. O'Donnell JM, Seiden LS: Differential-reinforcement-of-low-rate 72-second schedule: Selective effects of antidepressant drugs. J Pharmacol Exp Ther 1983; 224:80–88.
450. O'Donnell JM, Seiden LS: Effect of the experimental antidepressant AHR-9377 on performance during differential reinforcement of low response rate. Psychopharmacology (Berl) 1985; 87:283–285.
451. Danysz W, Plaznik A, Kostowski W, et al: Comparison of desipramine, amitriptyline, zimeldine and alaproclate in six animal models used to investigate antidepressant drugs. Pharmacol Toxicol 1988; 62:42–50.
451a. Seiden LS, O'Donnell JM: Effects of antidepressant drugs on DRL behavior. In Seiden LS, Balster RL (eds): Behavioral Pharmacology the Current Status. New York: Alan R. Liss, 1985:323–338.
452. Pollard GT, Howard JL: Similar effects of antidepressant and non-antidepressant drugs on behavior under an interresponse-time > 72-s schedule. Psychopharmacology (Berl) 1986; 89:253–258.
453. Garzon J, Fuentes JA, Del Rio J: Antidepressants selectively antagonize the hyperactivity induced in rats by long-term isolation. Eur J Pharmacol 1979; 59:293–296.
454. Garzon J, Del Rio J: Hyperactivity induced in rats by long-term isolation: Further studies on a new model for the detection of antidepressants. Eur J Pharmacol 1981; 74:287–294.
455. Richelson E, Pfenning M: Blockade by antidepressants and related compounds of biogenic amine uptake into rat brain synaptosomes: Most antidepressants selectively block norepinephrine uptake. Eur J Pharmacol 1984; 104:277–286.
456. Schildkraut JJ, Kety SS: Biogenic amines and emotion. Science 1967; 156:23–33.
457. Cairncross KD, Schofield S, King HG: The implication of noradrenaline in avoidance learning in the rat. Prog Brain Res 1973; 39:481–485.

458. Shipley MT, Halloran FJ, De La Torre J: Surprisingly rich projection from locus coeruleus to the olfactory bulb in the rat. Brain Res 1985; 329:294–299.
459. Leonard BE, Tuite M: Anatomical, physiological, and behavioral aspects of olfactory bulbectomy in the rat. Int Rev Neurobiol 1981; 22:251–286.
460. Domenjoz R, Theobald W: Zur Pharmakologie des Tofranil®(*N*-(3-dimethylaminopropyl)-iminodibenzylhydrochlorid). Arch Int Pharm 1959; 120:450–489.
461. Costa E, Garattini S, Valzelli L: Interactions between reserpine, chlorpromazine, and imipramine. Experientia 1960; 16:461–463.
462. Vernier VG, Hanson HM, Stone CA: The pharmacodynamics of amitriptyline. In Nodine JH, Moyer JH (eds): Psychosomatic Medicine, the First Hahnemann Symposium. Philadelphia: Lea & Febiger, 1962:683–690.
463. Howard JL, Soroko FE, Cooper BR: Empirical behavioral models of depression, with emphasis on tetrabenazine antagonism. In Enna SJ, Malick JB, Richardson E (eds): Antidepressants: Neurochemical, Behavioral, and Clinical Perspectives. New York: Raven Press, 1981:107–120.
464. Aprison MH, Takahashi R, Tachiki K: Hypersensitive serotonergic receptors involved in clinical depression—a theory. In Haber B, Aprison MH (eds): Neuropharmacology and Behavior. New York: Plenum Publishing, 1978:23–53.
465. Nagayama H, Hingtgen JN, Aprison MH: Postsynaptic action by four antidepressive drugs in an animal model of depression. Pharmacol Biochem Behav 1981; 15:125–130.
466. Nagayama H, Hingtgen JN, Aprison MH: Pre- and postsynaptic serotonergic manipulations in an animal model of depression. Pharmacol Biochem Behav 1980; 13:575–579.
467. Porsolt RD, Anton G, Blavet N, Jalfre M: Behavioural despair in rats: A new model sensitive to antidepressant treatments. Eur J Pharmacol 1978; 47:379–391.
468. Borsini F, Meli A: Is the forced swimming test a suitable model for revealing antidepressant activity? Psychopharmacology (Berl) 1988; 94:147–160.
469. Hawkins J, Phillips N, Moore JD, et al: Emotionality and REMD: A rat swimming model. Physiol Behav 1980; 25:167–171.
470. De Pablo JM, Parra A, Segovia S, Guillamon A: Learned immobility explains the behavior of rats in the forced swimming test. Physiol Behav 1989;46:229–237.
471. Porsolt RD, Bertin A, Blavet N, et al: Immobility induced by forced swimming in rats: Effects of agents which modify central catecholamine and serotonin activity. Eur J Pharmacol 1979; 57:201–210.
472. Satoh H, Mori J, Shimomura K, et al: Effect of zimeldine, a new antidepressant, on the forced swimming test in rats. Jpn J Pharmacol 1984; 35:471–473.
473. Hawkins J, Hicks RA, Phillips N, et al: Swimming rats and human depression. [letter] Nature 1978; 274:512–513.
474. Weiss JM, Goodman PA, Losito BG, et al: Behavioral depression produced by an uncontrollable stressor: Relationship to norepinephrine, dopamine, and serotonin levels in various regions of the rat brain. Brain Res Rev 1981; 3:167–205.
475. Abel EL: Alarm substance emitted by rats in the forced-swim test is a low volatile pheromone. Physiol Behav 1991; 50:723–727.
476. Borsini F, Lecci A, Sessarego A, et al: Discovery of antidepressant activity by forced swimming test may depend on pre-exposure of rats to a stressful situation. Psychopharmacology (Berl) 1989; 97:183–188.
477. Kitada Y, Miyauchi T, Satoh A, et al: Effects of antidepressants in the rat forced swimming test. Eur J Pharmacol 1981; 72:145–152.
478. Armario A, Gavalda A, Marti O: Forced swimming test in rats: Effect of desipramine administration and the period of exposure to the test on struggling behavior, swimming, immobility and defecation rate. Eur J Pharmacol 1988; 158:207–212.
479. Hoffman LJ, Weiss JM: Behavioral depression following clonidine withdrawal: A new animal model of long-lasting depression? Psychopharmacol Bull 1986; 22:943–949.
480. Steru L, Chermat R, Thierry B, Simon P: The tail suspension test: A new method for screening antidepressants in mice. Psychopharmacology (Berl) 1985; 85:367–370.
481. Vogel G, Neill D, Hagler M, et al: Decreased intracranial self-stimulation in a new animal model of endogenous depression. Neurosci Biobehav Rev 1990; 14:65–68.
482. Neill D, Vogel G, Hagler M, et al: Diminished sexual activity in a new animal model of endogenous depression. Neurosci Biobehav Rev 1990; 14:73–76.
483. Hartley P, Neill D, Hagler M, et al: Procedure- and age-dependent hyperactivity in a new animal model of endogenous depression. Neurosci Biobehav Rev 1990; 14:69–72.
484. Vogel G, Hartley P, Neill D, et al: Animal depression model by neonatal clomipramine: Reduction of shock induced aggression. Pharmacol Biochem Behav 1988; 31:103–106.
485. Vogel G, Neill D, Kors D, et al: REM sleep abnormalities in a new animal model of endogenous depression. Neurosci Biobehav Rev 1990; 14:77–83.
486. Vogel G, Neill D, Hagler M, et al: A new animal model of endogenous depression: A summary of present findings. Neurosci Biobehav Rev 1990; 14:85–91.
487. Fonberg E: Effects of small dorsomedial amygdala lesions on food intake and acquisition of instrumental alimentary reactions in dogs. Physiol Behav 1969; 4:739–743.
488. Fonberg E: The role of the hypothalamus and amygdala in food intake, alimentary motivation and emotional reaction. Acta Biol Exp 1969; 29:335–358.
489. Fonberg E: Control of emotional behaviour through the hypothalamus and amygdaloid complex. Ciba Found Symp 1972; 8:131–161.
490. McKinney WT, Suomi SJ, Harlow HF: Depression in primates. Am J Psychiatry 1971; 127:49–56.
491. Kaufman IC, Rosenblum LA: The reaction to separation in infant monkeys: Anaclitic depression and conservation-withdrawal. Psychosom Med 1967; 29:648–675.
492. Suomi SJ, Seaman SF, Lewis JK, et al: Effects of imipramine treatment of separation-induced social disorders in rhesus monkeys. Arch Gen Psychiatry 1978; 35:321–325.
493. Kraemer GW: Causes of changes in brain noradrenaline systems and later effects on responses to social stressors in rhesus monkeys: The cascade hypothesis. Ciba Found Symp 1986; 123:216–233.
494. Porsolt RD, Roux S, Jalfre M: Effects of imipramine on separation-induced vocalizations in young rhesus monkeys. Pharmacol Biochem Behav 1984; 20:979–981.
495. Crawley JN: Evaluation of a proposed hamster separation model of depression. Psychiatry Res 1984; 11:35–47.
496. Crawley JN: Preliminary report of a new rodent separation model of depression. Psychopharmacol Bull 1983; 19:537–541.
497. Hatotani N, Nomura J, Kitayama I: Changes in brain monoamines in the animal model for depression. Adv Biosci 1982; 40:65–72.
498. Roth KA, Katz RJ: Further studies on a novel animal model of depression: Therapeutic effects of a tricyclic antidepressant. Neurosci Biobehav Rev 1981; 5:253–258.
499. Katz RJ, Roth KA, Carroll BJ: Acute and chronic stress effects on open field activity in the rat: Implications for a model of depression. Neurosci Biobehav Rev 1981; 5:247–251.
500. Katz RJ: Animal model of depression: Effects of electroconvulsive shock therapy. Neurosci Biobehav Rev 1981; 5:273–277.
501. Katz RJ, Roth KA, Schmaltz K: Amphetamine and tranylcypromine in an animal model of depression: Pharmacological specificity of the reversal effect. Neurosci Biobehav Rev 1981; 5:259–264.
502. Katz RJ, Hersh S: Amitriptyline and scopolamine in an animal model of depression. Neurosci Biobehav Rev 1981; 5:265–271.
503. Katz RJ, Baldrighi G: A further parametric study of imipramine in an animal model of depression. Pharmacol Biochem Behav 1982; 16:969–972.
504. Katz RJ, Sibel M: Animal model of depression: Tests of three structurally and pharmacologically novel antidepressant compounds. Pharmacol Biochem Behav 1982; 16:973–977.
505. Katz RJ, Sibel M: Further analysis of the specificity of a novel animal model of depression—effects of an antihistaminic, antipsychotic and anxiolytic compound. Pharmacol Biochem Behav 1982; 16:979–982.
506. Katz RJ: Animal model of depression: Pharmacological sensitivity of a hedonic deficit. Pharmacol Biochem Behav 1982; 16:965–968.
507. Klein DF: Differential diagnosis and treatment of the dysphorias. In Simpson GM, Gallant DM (eds): Depression: Behavioral, Biochemical, Clinical and Treatment Concepts. New York: Spectrum Press, 1975:127–154.
508. Wise RA, Rompre PP: Brain dopamine and reward. Annu Rev Psychol 1989; 40:191–225.
509. Tekes K, Tothfalusi T, Magyar K: Irregular chronic stress related selective presynaptic adaptation of dopaminergic system in rat

striatum: Effects of (–)deprenyl and amitriptyline. Acta Physiol Pharmacol Bulg 1986; 12:21–28.
510. Moreau JL, Jenck F, Martin JR, et al: Antidepressant treatment prevents chronic unpredictable mild stress-induced anhedonia as assessed by ventral tegmentum self-stimulation behavior in rats. Eur J Pharmacol 1992; 2:43–49.
511. Muscat R, Towell A, Willner P: Changes in dopamine autoreceptor sensitivity in an animal model of depression. Psychopharmacology (Berl) 1988; 94:545–550.
512. Sampson D, Willner P, Muscat R: Reversal of antidepressant action by dopamine antagonists in an animal model of depression. Psychopharmacology (Berl) 1991; 104:491–495.
513. Muscat R, Papp M, Willner P: Antidepressant-like effects of dopamine agonists in an animal model of depression. Biol Psychiatry 1992; 31:937–946.
514. Willner P, Muscat R, Papp M: Chronic mild stress-induced anhedonia: A realistic animal model of depression. Neurosci Biobehav Rev 1992; 16:525–534.
515. Muscat R, Sampson D, Willner P: Dopaminergic mechanism of imipramine action in an animal model of depression. Biol Psychiatry 1990; 28:223–230.
516. Pare WP: Stress and consummatory behavior in the albino rat. Psychol Rep 1965; 16:399–405.
517. Weiss JM: Effects of coping responses on stress. J Comp Physiol Psychol 1968; 65:251–260.
518. Overmier JB, Seligman MEP: Effects of inescapable shock upon subsequent escape and avoidance learning. J Comp Physiol Psychol 1967; 63:28–33.
519. Seligman MEP, Maier SF: Failure to escape traumatic shock. J Exp Psychol 1967; 74:1–9.
520. Seligman MEP, Maier SF, Solomon RL: Unpredictable and uncontrollable aversive events. In Brush FR (ed): Aversive Conditioning and Learning. New York: Academic Press, 1971:347–400.
521. Maier SF, Albin RW, Testa TJ: Failure to learn to escape in rats previously exposed to inescapable shock depends on nature of escape response. J Comp Physiol Psychol 1973; 85:581–592.
522. Seligman MEP, Beagley G: Learned helplessness in the rat. J Comp Physiol Psychol 1975; 88:534–541.
523. Seligman MEP: Depression and learned helplessness. In Friedman RJ, Katz MM (eds): The Psychology of Depression: Contemporary Theory and Research. Washington, DC: VH Winston, 1974:83–125.
524. Weiss JM, Bailey WH, Goodman PA, et al: A model for neurochemical study of depression. In Spiegelstein MY, Levy A (eds): Behavioral Models and the Analysis of Drug Action. Amsterdam: Elsevier Science Publishing, 1982:195–223.
525. Leshner AI, Remler H, Biegon A, et al: Desmethylimipramine (DMI) counteracts learned helplessness in rats. Psychopharmacology (Berl) 1979; 66:207–208.
526. Telner JI, Singhal RL: Effects of nortriptyline treatment on learned helplessness in the rat. Pharmacol Biochem Behav 1981; 14:823–826.
527. Sherman AD, Sacquitne JL, Petty F: Specificity of the learned helplessness model of depression. Pharmacol Biochem Behav 1982; 16:449–454.
528. Martin P, Soubrie P, Puech AJ: Reversal of helpless behavior by serotonin uptake blockers in rats. Psychopharmacology (Berl) 1990; 101:403–407.
529. Martin P, Soubrie P, Simon P: The effect of monoamine oxidase inhibitors compared with classical tricyclic antidepressants on learned helplessness paradigm. Prog Neuropsychopharmacol Biol Psychiatry 1987; 11:1–7.
530. Weiss JM: Stress-induced depression: Critical neurochemical and electrophysiological changes. In Madden J IV (ed): Neurobiology of Learning, Emotion and Affect. New York: Raven Press, 1991: 123–154.
531. Henn FA, Johnson J, Edwards E, Anderson D: Melancholia in rodents: Neurobiology and pharmacology. Psychopharmacol Bull 1985; 21: 443–446.
532. Weiss JM, Stone EA, Harrell N: Coping behavior and brain norepinephrine level in rats. J Comp Physiol Psychol 1970; 72: 153–160.
533. Weiss JM: Coping behavior: Explaining behavioral depression following uncontrollable stressful events. Behav Res Ther 1980; 18:485–504.
534. Anisman H, Bignami G: A comparative neurochemical, pharmacological, and functional analysis of aversively motivated behaviors: Caveats and general consideration. In Anisman H, Bignami G (eds): Psychopharmacology of Aversively Motivated Behavior. New York: Plenum Publishing, 1978:487–512.
535. Anisman H, Shanks N, Zakman S, et al: Multisystem regulation of performance deficits induced by stressors: An animal model of depression. In Iverson MTM (ed): Animal Models in Psychiatry, Volume 2. Clifton, NJ: Humana Press, 1991:1–55.
536. Jackson RL, Maier SF, Rapaport PM: Exposure to inescapable shock produces both activity and associative deficits in the rat. Learn Motiv 1978; 9:69–98.
537. Minor TR, Jackson RL, Maier SF: Effects of task-irrelevant cues and reinforcement delay on choice-escape learning following inescapable shock: Evidence for a deficit in selective attention. J Exp Psychol Anim Behav 1984; 10:543–556.
538. Minor TR, Pelleymounter MA, Maier SF: Uncontrollable shock, forebrain norepinephrine, and stimulus selection during choice-escape learning. Psychobiology 1988; 16:135–145.
539. Overstreet DH: The Flinders sensitive line rats: A genetic animal model of depression. Neurosci Biobehav Rev 1993; 17:51–68.
540. Overstreet DH: Selective breeding for increased cholinergic function: Development of a new animal model of depression. Biol Psychiatry 1986; 21:49–58.
541. Shiromani PJ, Overstreet D, Levy D, et al: Increased REM sleep in rats selectively bred for cholinergic hyperactivity. Neuropsychopharmacology 1988; 1:127–133.
542. Schiller GD, Pucilowski O, Wienicke C, et al: Immobility-reducing effects of antidepressants in a genetic animal model of depression. Brain Res Bull 1992; 28:821–823.
543. Overstreet DH, Rezvani AH, Janowsky DS: Genetic animal models of depression and ethanol preference provide support for cholinergic and serotonergic involvement in depression and alcoholism. Biol Psychiatry 1992; 31:919–936.
544. Aulakh CS, Wozniak KM, Hill JL, et al: Differential neuroendocrine responses to the 5-HT agonist *m*-chlorophenylpiperazine in Fawn-Hooded rats relative to Wistar and Sprague-Dawley rats. Neuroendocrinology 1988; 48:401–406.
545. Wang P, Aulakh CS, Hill JL, Murphy DL: Fawn-Hooded rats are subsensitive to the food intake suppressant effects of 5-HT agonists. Psychopharmacology 1988; 94:558–562.
546. Golda V, Petr R: Behaviour of genetically hypertensive rats in an animal model of depression and in an animal model of anxiety. Activ Nerv Sup 1986; 28:274–275.
547. Golda V, Petr R: Animal model of depression: Drug induced changes independent of changes in exploratory activity. Activ Nerv Sup 1987; 29:114–115.
548. Golda V, Petr R: Animal model of depression: Retention of motor depression not predictable from the threshold of reaction to the inescapable shock. Activ Nerv Sup 1987; 29:113–114.
549. Golda V, Petr R: Animal model of depression: Effect of nicotergoline and metergoline. Activ Nerv Sup 1987; 29:115–117.
550. Dunn LA, Kilts CD, Nemeroff CB: Animal behavioral models for drug development in psychopharmacology. In Moos WH, Clark JS (eds): Modern Drug Discovery Technology. New York: VCH and Ellis Horwood 1990:259–280.
551. Lyon M: Animal models of mania and schizophrenia. In Wilner P (ed): Behavioral Models in Psychopharmacology: Theoretical, Industrial and Clinical Perspectives. Cambridge, UK: Cambridge University Press, 1990:253–310.
552. Kane JM: Neuroleptic treatment of schizophrenia. In Henn FA, DeLisi LE (eds): Handbook of Schizophrenia, Volume 2, Neurochemistry and Neuropharmacology of Schizophrenia. New York: Elsevier Science Publishing, 1987:179–226.
553. Cott JM, Kurtz NM: New pharmacological treatments for schizophrenia. In Henn FA, DeLisi LE (eds): Handbook of Schizophrenia, Volume 2, Neurochemistry and Neuropharmacology of Schizophrenia. New York: Elsevier Science Publishing, 1987:203–207.
554. Cook L, Catania AC: Effects of drugs on avoidance and escape behavior. Fed Proc 1964; 23:818–835.
555. Worms P, Broekkamp CLE, Lloyd KG: Behavioral effects of neuroleptics. In Coyle JT, Enna SJ (eds): Neuroleptics: Neurochemical, Behavioral, and Clinical Perspectives. New York: Raven Press, 1983:93–117.
556. Arnt J: Pharmacology specificity of conditioned avoidance response inhibition in rats: Inhibition by neuroleptics and correlation to

dopamine receptor blockade. Acta Pharmacol Toxicol 1982; 51: 321–329.
557. Kuribara H, Tadokoro S: Correlation between antiavoidance activities of antipsychotic drugs in rats and daily clinical doses. Pharmacol Biochem Behav 1981; 14:181–192.
558. Nielsen M, Fjalland B, Pedersen V, Nymark M: Pharmacology of neuroleptics upon repeated administration. Psychopharmacology 1974; 34:95–104.
559. Bregnan GB, Chieli T: Classical neuroleptics and deconditioning activity after single or repeated treatments. Arzneimittelforschung 1980; 30:1865–1870.
560. Sanger DJ: The effects of clozapine on shuttle-box avoidance responding in rats: Comparison with haloperidol and chlordiazepoxide. Pharmacol Biochem Behav 1985; 23:231–236.
561. Sanberg PR, Bunsey MD, Giordano M, Norman AB: The catalepsy test: Its ups and downs. Behav Neurosci 1988; 102:748–759.
562. Ellenbroek BA, Peeters BW, Honig WM, et al: The paw test: A behavioural paradigm for differentiating between classical and atypical neuroleptic drugs. Psychopharmacology (Berl) 1987; 93: 343–348.
563. Ellenbroek B, Cools AR: The paw test: An animal model for neuroleptic drugs which fulfills the criteria for pharmacological isomorphism. Life Sci 1988; 42:1205–1213.
564. Kane J, Honigfeld G, Singer J, et al: Clozapine for the treatment resistant schizophrenic. Arch Gen Psychiatry 1988; 45:789–796.
565. Roberts DCS, Vickers G: Atypical neuroleptics increase self-administration of cocaine: An evaluation of a behavioural screen for antipsychotic activity. Psychopharmacology (Berl) 1984; 82:135–139.
566. Ettenberg A, Koob GF, Bloom FE: Response artifact in the measurement of neuroleptic-induced anhedonia. Science 1981; 213: 357–359.
567. Freedman R, Waldo MR, Bickford-Wimer P, Nagamoto H: Elementary neuronal dysfunctions in schizophrenia. Schizophr Res 1991; 4:233–243.
568. Neuchterlein KH, Dawson ME: Information processing and attentional functioning in the developmental course of schizophrenic disorders. Schizophr Bull 1984; 10:160–203.
569. Penn DL, van der Does AJW, Spaulding WD, et al: Information processing and social cognitive problem solving in schizophrenia. J Nerv Ment Dis 1993; 181:13–20.
570. Iversen SD: Is it possible to model psychotic state in animals? J Psychopharmacol 1987; 1:154–156.
571. Lubow RE, Weiner I, Feldon J: An animal model of attention. In Spiegelstein MY, Levy A (eds): Behavioral Models and the Analysis of Drug Action. Proceedings of the 27th Oholo Conference. Amsterdam: Elsevier North-Holland, 1982:89–107.
572. Lubow RE: Latent inhibition. Psychol Bull 1973; 79:398–407.
573. Lubow RE: Latent Inhibition and Conditioned Attention Theory. New York: Cambridge University Press, 1989.
574. Hemsley DR: An experimental psychological model for schizophrenia. In Hafner H, Gattaz WF, Janzarik W (eds): Search for the Causes of Schizophrenia. Berlin: Springer-Verlag, 1987:179–188.
575. Solomon CR, Crider A, Winkleman JW, et al: Disrupted latent inhibition in the rat with chronic amphetamine or haloperidol-induced supersensitivity: Relationship to schizophrenic attention disorder. Biol Psychiatry 1981; 16:519–537.
576. Weiner I, Lubow RE, Feldon J: Abolition of expression but not acquisition of latent inhibition by chronic amphetamine in rats. Psychopharmacology (Berl) 1984; 83:194–199.
577. Weiner I, Feldon J: Facilitation of latent inhibition by haloperidol in rats. Psychopharmacology (Berl) 1987; 91:248–253.
578. Christison GW, Atwater GE, Dunn LA, et al: Haloperidol enhancement of latent inhibition: Relation to therapeutic action? Biol Psychiatry 1988; 23:746–749.
579. Feldon J, Weiner I: The latent inhibition model of schizophrenic attention disorder. Haloperidol and sulpiride enhance rats' ability to ignore irrelevant stimuli. Biol Psychiatry 1991; 29:635–646.
580. Dunn LA, Atwater GE, Kilts CD: Effects of antipsychotic drugs on latent inhibition: Sensitivity and specificity of an animal behavioral model of clinical drug action. Psychopharmacology (Berl) 1993; 112:315–323.
581. Baruch I, Hemsley DR, Gray JA: Differential performance of acute and chronic schizophrenics in a latent inhibition task. J Nerv Ment Dis 1988; 176:598–606.
582. Gray NS, Pickering AD, Hemsley DR, et al: Abolition of latent inhibition by a single 5 mg dose of *d*-amphetamine in man. Psychopharmacology (Berl) 1992; 107:425–430.
583. Gray JA, Feldon J, Rawlins JNP, et al: The neuropsychology of schizophrenia. Behav Brain Sci 1991; 14:1–35.
584. Kamin LJ: Predictability, surprise, attention and conditioning. In Campbell BA, Church RM (eds): Punishment and Aversive Behaviour. New York: Appleton-Century-Crofts, 1969:279–296.
585. Crider A, Solomon PR, McMahon MA: Disruption of selective attention in the rat following chronic *d*-amphetamine administration: Relationship to schizophrenic attention disorder. Biol Psychiatry 1982; 17:351–360.
586. Jones SH, Gray JA, Hemsley DR: Loss of the Kamin blocking effect in acute but not chronic schizophrenics. Biol Psychiatry 1992; 32:739–755.
587. Braff D, Stone C, Callaway E, et al: Prestimulus effects on human startle reflex in normals and schizophrenics. Psychophysiology 1978; 15:339–343.
588. Swerdlow NR, Geyer M, Braff D, Koob GF: Central dopamine hyperactivity in rats mimics abnormal acoustic startle in schizophrenics. Biol Psychiatry 1986; 21:23–33.
589. Swerdlow NR, Braff DL, Masten VL, Geyer MA: Schizophrenic-like sensorimotor gating abnormalities in rats following dopamine infusion into the nucleus accumbens. Psychopharmacology (Berl) 1990; 101:414–420.
590. Swerdlow NR, Braff DL, Taaid N, et al: Assessing the validity of an animal model of deficient sensorimotor gating in schizophrenic patients. Arch Gen Psychiatry 1994; 51:139–154.
591. Braff DL, Grillon C, Geyer MA: Gating and habituation of the startle reflex in schizophrenic patients. Arch Gen Psychiatry 1992; 49:206–215.
592. Baruch I, Hemsley DR, Gray JA: Latent inhibition and "psychotic proneness" in normal subjects. Pers Individual Differences 1988; 9:777–783.
593. Simmons RF: Schizotypy and startle prepulse inhibition. Psychophysiology 1990; 27(suppl):S6.
594. Swerdlow NR, Benbow CH, Zisook S, et al: A preliminary assessment of sensorimotor gating in patients with obsessive compulsive disorder. Biol Psychiatry 1993; 33:298–301.
595. Peng RY, Mansbach RS, Braff DL, et al: A D_2 dopamine receptor agonist disrupts sensorimotor gating in rats: Implications for dopaminergic abnormalities in schizophrenia. Neuropsychopharmacology 1990; 3:211–217.
596. Swerdlow NR, Keith VA, Braff DL, Geyer MA: The effects of spiperone, raclopride, SCH 23390 and clozapine on apomorphine inhibition of sensorimotor gating of the startle response in the rat. J Pharmacol Exp Ther 1991; 256:530–536.
597. Killcross AS, Robbins TW: Differential effects of intra-accumbens and systemic amphetamine on latent inhibition using an on-baseline, within-subject conditioned suppression paradigm. Psychopharmacology (Berl) 1993; 110:479–489.
598. Swerdlow NR, Geyer MA: Clozapine and haloperidol in an animal model of sensorimotor gating deficits in schizophrenia. Pharmacol Biochem Behav 1993; 44:741–744.
599. Geyer MA, Wilkinson LS, Humby T, et al: Isolation rearing of rats produces a deficit in prepulse inhibition of acoustic startle similar to that in schizophrenia. Biol Psychiatry 1993; 34:361–372.
600. Carlton PL: Theories and models in psychopharmacology. In Lipton MA, DiMascio A, Killam KF (eds): Psychopharmacology: A Generation of Progress. New York: Raven Press, 1978:553–561.
601. Mueser KT, Bellack AS, Douglas MS, et al: Prevalence and stability of social skill deficits in schizophrenia. Schizophr Res 1991; 5:167–176.
602. Carpenter WT, Heinrichs DW, Wagman AMI: Deficit and nondeficit forms of schizophrenia: The concept. Am J Psychiatry 1988; 145:578–601.
603. Kibel DA, Lafont I, Liddle PF: The composition of the negative syndrome of chronic schizophrenia. Br J Psychiatry 1993; 162:744–750.
604. Gardner C, Guy A: A social interaction model of anxiety sensitive to acutely administered benzodiazepines. Drug Dev Res 1984; 4:207–216.
605. Corbett R, Hartman H, Kerman LL, et al: Effects of atypical antipsychotic agents on social behavior in rodents. Pharmacol Biochem Behav 1993; 45:9–17.
606. Spealman RD, Kelleher RT, Goldberg SR, et al: Behavioral effects of

clozapine: Comparison with thioridazine, chlorpromazine, haloperidol and chlordiazepoxide in squirrel monkeys. J Pharmacol Exp Ther 1982; 224:127–134.

607. Meltzer HY, Sommers AA, Luchins DJ: The effect of neuroleptics and other psychotropic drugs on negative symptoms in schizophrenia. J Clin Psychopharmacol 1986; 6:329.

608. Ellenbroek BA: The ethological analysis of monkeys in a social setting as an animal model for schizophrenia. In Birkhauser (ed): Animal Models in Psychopharmacology Advances in Pharmacological Sciences. Basel: Springer-Verlag, 1991:265–284.

609. Ellenbroek BA, Willemen APM, Cools AR: Are antagonists of dopamine D_1 receptors drugs that attenuate both positive and negative symptoms of schizophrenia? Neuropsychopharmacology 1989; 2:191–199.

610. Miczek K, Yoshimura H: Disruption of primate social behavior by *d*-amphetamine and cocaine: Differential antagonism by antipsychotics. Psychopharmacology (Berl) 1982; 76:163–171.

611. Arnett L, Ridley R, Gamble S, et al: Social withdrawal following amphetamine administration to marmosets. Psychopharmacology (Berl) 1989; 99:222–229.

612. Angrist B, Pedselow E, Rubinstein M, et al: Amphetamine response and relapse risk after depot neuroleptic discontinuation. Psychopharmacology (Berl) 1985; 85:277–301.

613. Davidson MK, Lindsey JR, Davis JK: Requirements and selection of an animal model. Isr J Med Sci 1987; 23:551–555.

614. Creese I, Burt DR, Snyder SH: Dopamine receptor binding predicts clinical and pharmacological potencies of antischizophrenic drugs. Science 1976; 192:481–483.

615. Ellinwood EH Jr, Sudilovsky A, Nelson LM: Behavioral analysis of chronic amphetamine intoxication. Biol Psychiatry 1972; 4:215–225.

616. Ellinwood EH Jr, Kilbey MM: Chronic stimulant intoxication models of psychosis. In Hannin I, Usdin E (eds): Animal Models in Psychiatry and Neurology I. Oxford, UK: Pergamon Press, 1977:61–74.

617. Ellison G, Eison MS, Huberman HS: Stages of constant amphetamine intoxication: Delayed appearance of paranoid-like behaviors in rat colonies. Psychopharmacology (Berl) 1978; 56:293–299.

618. Nielsen EB, Lyon M, Ellison G: Apparent hallucinations in monkeys during around-the-clock amphetamine for seven to fourteen days. Possible relevance to amphetamine psychosis. J Nerv Ment Dis 1983; 171:222–233.

619. Liddle PF, Firston KJ, Frith CD, et al: Patterns of cerebral blood flow in schizophrenia. Br J Psychiatry 1992; 160:179–186.

620. Tamminga CA, Thaker GK, Buchanan R, et al: Limbic system abnormalities identified in schizophrenia using positron emission tomography with fluorodeoxyglucose and neocortical alteration with deficit syndrome. Arch Gen Psychiatry 1991; 49:522–530.

621. Bogerts B, Lieberman JA, Ashtari M, et al: Hippocampus-amygdala volumes and psychopathology in chronic schizophrenia. Biol Psychiatry 1993; 33:236–246.

622. Schmajuk NA: Animal models of schizophrenia: The hippocampally lesioned animal. Schizophr Bull 1987; 13:317–327.

623. Lipska BK, Jaskiw GE, Chrapusta S, et al: Ibotenic acid lesions of ventral hippocampus differentially affect dopamine and its metabolites in the nucleus accumbens and prefrontal cortex in rat. Brain Res 1992; 585:1–6.

624. Kendler KS, Tsuang MT, Hays P: Age at onset in schizophrenia. A familial perspective. Arch Gen Psychiatry 1987; 44:881–890.

625. Weinberger DR: Implications of normal brain development for the pathogenesis of schizophrenia. Arch Gen Psychiatry 1987; 44: 660–669.

626. Crow TJ: Temporal lobe asymmetries as the key to the etiology of schizophrenia. Schizophr Bull 1990; 16:433–443.

627. Lipska BK, Jaskiw GE, Weinberger DR: Postpubertal emergence of hyperresponsiveness to stress and amphetamine after neonatal excitotoxic hippocampal damage: A potential animal model of schizophrenia. Neuropsychopharmacology 1993; 9:67–75.

628. Conrad AJ, Abebe T, Austin R, et al: Hippocampal pyramidal cell disarray in schizophrenia as a bilateral phenomenon. Arch Gen Psychiatry 1991; 48:413–417.

629. Stoudemire A, Miller J, Schmitt F, et al: Development of an organic affective syndrome during a hyperbaric diving experiment. Am J Psychiatry 1984; 141:1251–1254.

630. Abraini JH, Ansseau M, Fechati T: Pressure-induced disorders in neurotransmission and spontaneous behavior in rats: An animal model of psychosis. Biol Psychiatry 1993; 34:622–629.

631. Fuller JL: Strain differences in the effects of chlorpromazine and chlordiazepoxide upon active and passive avoidance in mice. Psychopharmacologia 1970; 16:261–271.

632. Fink JS, Swerdloff A, Reis DJ: Genetic control of dopamine receptors in mouse caudate nucleus: Relationship of cataleptic response to neuroleptic drugs. Neurosci Lett 1982; 32:301–306.

633. Kolakowska T, Williams AO, Arden M, et al: Schizophrenia with good and poor outcome. I: Early clinical features, response to neuroleptics and signs of organic dysfunction. Br J Psychiatry 1985; 146:229–239.

634. Garver DL, Zemlan F, Hirschowitz J, et al: Dopamine and non-dopamine psychoses. Psychopharmacology (Berl) 1984; 84:138–145.

635. Upchurch M, Schallert T: A behavioral analysis of the offspring of "haloperidol-sensitive" and "haloperidol-resistant" gerbils. Behav Neural Biol 1983; 39:221–228.

636. Hitzemann R, Daines K, Bieir-Langing CM, Zahniser NR: On the selection of mice for haloperidol response and non-response. Psychopharmacology (Berl) 1991; 103:244–250.

637. Bignami G: Selection for high rates and low rates of avoidance conditioning in rat. Anim Behav 1965; 13:221–227.

638. Brush FR, Froehlich JC, Sakellaris PC: Genetic selection for avoidance behavior in the rat. Behav Genet 1979; 9:309–316.

639. Brush FR: Genetic determinants of individual differences in avoidance learning: Behavioral and endocrine characteristics. [reviews] Experientia 1991; 47:1039–1050.

640. Breier A, Buchanan RW, Elkashef A, et al: Brain morphology and schizophrenia. Arch Gen Psychiatry 1992; 49:921–926.

641. Abas MA, Sahakian BJ, Levy R, et al: Neuropsychological deficits and CT scan changes in elderly depressives. Psychol Med 1990; 20: 507–520.

642. Jacoby RJ, Levy R: Computed tomography in the elderly: Affective disorder. Br J Psychiatry 1980; 136:270–275.

643. Pearlson GD, Rabins PV, Kim WS, et al: Structural brain CT changes and cognitive deficits in elderly depressives with and without reversible dementia. Psychol Med 1989; 19:573–583.

644. Iacono WG, Smith GN, Moreau M, et al: Ventricular and sulcal size at the onset of psychosis. Am J Psychiatry 1988; 145:820–824.

645. Schlegel S, Maier W, Philipp M, et al: Computed tomography in depression: Association between ventricular size and psychopathology. Psychiatry Res 1989; 29:221–230.

646. Lippman S, Manshadi M, Baldwin H, et al: Cerebellar vermis dimensions on computerized tomographic scans of schizophrenia and bipolar patients. Am J Psychiatry 1982; 139:667–668.

647. Rabins PV, Pearlson GF, Aylward E, et al: Cortical magnetic resonance imaging changes in elderly inpatients with major depression. Am J Psychiatry 1991; 148:617–620.

648. Coffey CE, Figiel GS, Djang WT, et al: Subcortical hyperintensity on magnetic resonance imaging: A comparison of normal and depressed elderly subjects. Am J Psychiatry 1990; 147:187–189.

649. Figiel GS, Krishnan KRR, Doraiswamy PM, et al: Subcortical hyperintensities on brain magnetic resonance imaging: A comparison between late age onset and early onset elderly depressed subjects. Neurobiol Aging 1991; 12:245–247.

650. Figiel GS, Nemeroff CB: The mesolimbic motor circuit and its role in neuropsychiatric disorders. Adv Physiol 1993; 4:351–357.

651. Hauser PH, Altshuler LL, Berettini W, et al: Temporal lobe measurement in primary affective disorder by magnetic resonance imaging. J Neuropsychiatry Clin Neurosci 1989; 1:128–134.

652. Husain MM, Figiel GS, Lurie SN, et al: MRI of corpus callosum and septum pellucidum in depression. Biol Psychiatry 1991; 29:300–301.

653. Krishnan KRR, McDonald WM, Escalona PR, et al: Magnetic resonance imaging of the caudate nuclei in depression. Arch Gen Psychiatry 1992; 49:553–557.

654. Altshuler LL, Conrad A, Haruser P, et al: Reduction of temporal lobe volume in bipolar disorder: A preliminary report of magnetic resonance imaging. Arch Gen Psychiatry 1991; 48:482–483.

655. Hauser PH, Dauphinais D, Berrettinin W, et al: Corpus callosum dimensions measured by magnetic resonance imaging in bipolar affective disorder and schizophrenia. Biol Psychiatry 1989; 26: 659–668.

656. Dupont RM, Jernigan TL, Butters N, et al: Subcortical abnormalities detected in bipolar affective disorder using magnetic resonance imaging: Clinical and neuropsychological difference. Arch Gen Psychiatry 1990; 1:55–60.

657. Swayze VW, Andreasen NC, Alliger RJ: Structural brain abnormali-

ties in bipolar affective disorder. Arch Gen Psychiatry 1990; 47:1054–1059.
658. Baxter LR, Phelps MC, Mazziotta JC, et al: Cerebral metabolic rates for glucose in mood disorders studied with positron emission tomography (PET) and (F-18)-fluoro-2-deoxyglucose (FDG). Arch Gen Psychiatry 1985; 42:441–447.
659. Buchsbaum MS, Wu J, DeLisi LE, et al: Frontal cortex and basal ganglia metabolic rates assessed by positron emission tomography with F2-deoxyglucose in affective illness. J Affect Disord 1986; 10:137–152.
660. Baxter LR, Schwartz JM, Phelps ME, et al: Reduction of prefrontal cortex glucose metabolism common to three types of depression. Arch Gen Psychiatry 1989; 46:243–250.
661. Kishimoto H, Takazu O, Ohno S, et al: ^{11}C-glucose metabolism in manic and depressed patients. Psychiatry Res 1987; 22:81–88.
662. Dom R, DeSaedeleer J, Bogerts B, et al: Quantitative cytometric analysis of basal ganglia in catatonic schizophrenics. In Perris C, Struwe G, Jansson B (eds): Biological Psychiatry. Amsterdam: Elsevier, 1981:723–726.
663. Kovelman JA, Scheibel AB: A neurohistological correlate of schizophrenia. Biol Psychiatry 1984; 19:1601–1621.
664. Roberts GW, Colter N, Lofthouse R, et al: Gliosis in schizophrenia. Biol Psychiatry 1986; 21:1043–1050.
665. Jakob H, Beckmann H: Prenatal developmental disturbances in the limbic allocortex in schizophrenics. J Neural Transm 1986; 65: 303–326.
666. Colter N, Battal S, Crow TJ, et al: White matter reduction in the parahippocampal gyrus of patients with schizophrenia. Arch Gen Psychiatry 1987; 44:1023.
667. Altshuler L, Conrad A, Kovelman JA, et al: Hippocampal cell disorientation in schizophrenia: A controlled neurohistologic study of the Yakovlev collection. Arch Gen Psychiatry 1987; 44:1094–1098.
668. Falkai P, Bogerts B, Rozumek M: Limbic pathology in schizophrenia: The entorhinal region. Biol Psychiatry 1988; 24:515–521.
669. Christison GW, Casanova MF, Weinberger DR, et al: A quantitative investigation of hippocampal pyramidal cell size, shape, and variability of orientation in schizophrenia. Arch Gen Psychiatry 1989; 46:1027–1032.
670. Jeste DV, Lohr JB: Hippocampal pathologic findings in schizophrenia. Arch Gen Psychiatry 1989; 46:1019–1024.
671. Altshuler L, Casanova M, Goldberg T, et al: The hippocampus and parahippocampus in schizophrenic, suicide, and control brains. Arch Gen Psychiatry 1990; 47:1029–1034.
672. Arnold SE, Hyman BT, Van Hoese GW, et al: Some cytoarchitectural abnormalities of the entorhinal cortex in schizophrenia. Arch Gen Psychiatry 1991; 48:625–632.
673. Benes FM, Sorenson I, Bird E: Reduced neuronal size in posterior hippocampus of schizophrenic patients. Schizophr Bull 1991; 17: 597–608.
674. DeLisi L, Dauphinais ID, Gershon ES: Perinatal complications and reduced size of brain limbic structures in familial schizophrenia. Schizophr Bull 1988; 14:185–191.
675. Bogerts B, Ashtari M, Degreef G, et al: Reduced temporal limbic structure volume on magnetic resonance images in first episode schizophrenia. Psychiatry Res 1990; 35:1–13.
676. Kerwin RW, Patel S, Meldrum BS, et al: Asymmetrical loss of glutamate receptor subtype in left hippocampus in schizophrenia. Lancet 1988; 1:583–584.
677. Deakin J, Slater P, Simpson M, et al: Frontal cortical and left temporal glutamatergic dysfunction in schizophrenia. J Neurochem 1989; 52:1781–1786.
678. Kerwin R, Patel S, Meldrum B: Quantitative autoradiographic analysis of glutamate binding sites in the hippocampal formation in normal and schizophrenic brain post mortem. Neuroscience 1990; 39:25–32.
679. Weissman AD, Casanova MF, Kleinman JE, et al: Selective loss of cerebral cortical sigma but not PCP binding sites in schizophrenia. Biol Psychiatry 1991; 29:41–54.
680. Simpson M, Slater P, Royston M, et al: Regionally selective deficits in uptake sites for glutamate and gamma-aminobutyric acid in the basal ganglia in schizophrenia. Psychiatry Res 1992; 42:273–282.
681. Simpson M, Slater P, Royston M, et al: Alterations in phencyclidine and sigma binding sites in schizophrenic brains. Schizophr Res 1992; 6:41–48.

CHAPTER

16 Cognitive Neuroscience

Robert S. Goldman
Irma C. Smet
Malini Singh

What Is Cognitive Neuroscience?

The study of the manner in which the brain performs cognitive functions provides a unique challenge to the neurosciences. Cognitive neuroscience is concerned with the structural and functional properties of brain regions as they relate to the multifaceted aspects of cognitive behavior—how we sense, perceive, speak, remember, and synthesize the external environment into consciousness. The task of cognitive neuroscience is to map macrocognitive phenomena such as language to the underlying neuroanatomical substrate, its neural circuitry, its molecular underpinnings, and ultimately the level of the gene. In the past two decades, much has been learned about cognitive phenomena from the constituent disciplines of cognitive neuroscience: neuropsychology, neurology, psychiatry, neuroimaging, neurobiology, computer science, and cognitive psychology. The emergence of cognitive behavior from the underlying neuroanatomical substrate represents a fascinating, if elusive, process of scientific discovery. Although cognitive neuroscience is represented by a collection of disciplines, its goal is to provide a framework or process for integration in the study of cognitive phenomena. That is, the experimental information gained from these disciplines allows coordinated knowledge of brain systems to proceed both reductionistically (from macrocognitive to cellular levels) and laterally (from cognitive theories to neuropsychological theories).

The proper domain of cognitive neuroscience is vast. Motor functioning, attention, language, memory, executive control, vision, emotion, sensory functions, and consciousness are only subsets of this domain. Each of these areas is associated with a large body of literature. In this chapter, we selectively focus on a few critical areas of cognitive neuroscience—namely, memory, language, and executive functions—and discuss these areas in depth. We highlight the structural and functional organization of these systems and discuss the relevant research from the cognitive neurosciences that address these areas. The reader is referred to a number of more comprehensive sources, where appropriate, for greater detail and discussion.

Themes in the Neural Organization of Cognitive Functions

Modern cognitive neuroscience traces its roots along the time lines of the various subdisciplines that define its core. For simplicity, we suggest that the central theme of cognitive neuroscience has been, and to a large degree continues to be, the issue of localization versus holism in conceptualizing how cognitive functions are organized in the brain. We will discuss some of the critical theoretical perspectives that have shaped cognitive neuroscience. Many of these principles are endemic to our discussion of memory, language, and executive function.

Localizationism Versus Holism

Historically, the 19th century physician and neuroanatomist Francis Gall is largely credited for specifically linking cognitive functions to the brain. Gall was a phrenologist who posited a strictly localizationist perspective: he suggested that a myriad of brain regions underlie everything from the esoteric functions of "acquisitiveness" and "sublimity" to more basic cognitive functions such as calculation and language. Although the notion that behaviors have a biological basis in the brain was sound, Gall's one-to-one correspondence between arbitrary brain regions and descriptive behavioral contents was, of course, largely fictional when considered from a modern perspective. It was not until the middle of the 19th century that a localizationist doctrine was put on a firm scientific footing. The French neurologist Paul Broca thoroughly described the case of an individual who could not speak grammatically, utter full sentences, or write, yet who had no damage to the oral facial musculature or laryngeal complex. On postmortem examination, Broca discovered a lesion in the inferior posterior left frontal lobe. Broca suggested that this region was therefore specialized for speech. Twelve years later, Carl Wernicke discovered (again using the case study approach) a type of aphasia characterized by impairment in language comprehension, but in this case the lesion was located in the left temporoparietal cortex. To reconcile the different lesion sites and their relationship to language, Wernicke proposed that separate areas of the brain were specialized for motor and sensory components of speech. The notion of separate but interconnected regions defining a cognitive system was the forerunner for much of the current work in language and cognitive neuroscience in general.

The findings of this functional localizationist approach led to the characterization of brain regions based on their particular anatomical characteristics. Beginning in 1901, Korbinian Brodmann undertook a series of landmark studies on the cytoarchitectonics of the mammalian cortex. It had been known before Brodmann that there were six layers of the human isocortex based on cell type and size. Brodmann extended this work on cytoarchitectonics to the subdivision of areas of cortex with similar cellular and laminar structure; he subdivided the human cerebral cortex into 47 areas. The result is a cytoarchitectonic map of the human cerebral cortex. Its development is critical to the interpretation and replication of findings in cortical localization. This system is the predominant one utilized today, especially with the use of single-cell recordings in animals and functional neuroimaging studies in humans. In a number of places we refer to Brodmann's areas with respect to localization of particular cognitive functions. Brodmann's map is depicted in Figure 16–1.

Existing concurrently with the localizationist trends in neuroscience is the notion of holism. The neurologist H. Hughlings Jackson, a contemporary of Broca, objected to the notion that disturbances in higher cortical functions should be seen as resulting from local brain damage. He noted that a lesion that disturbs speech does not necessarily indicate that speech is strictly localized to that structure. Rather, he suggested that impairment in complex functions can occur in the presence of widely distributed lesions. In fact, Jackson[1] warned that only lesions, not functions, can be strictly localized. The antilocalizationist tradition described much of early to middle 20th century thinking as revealed in the

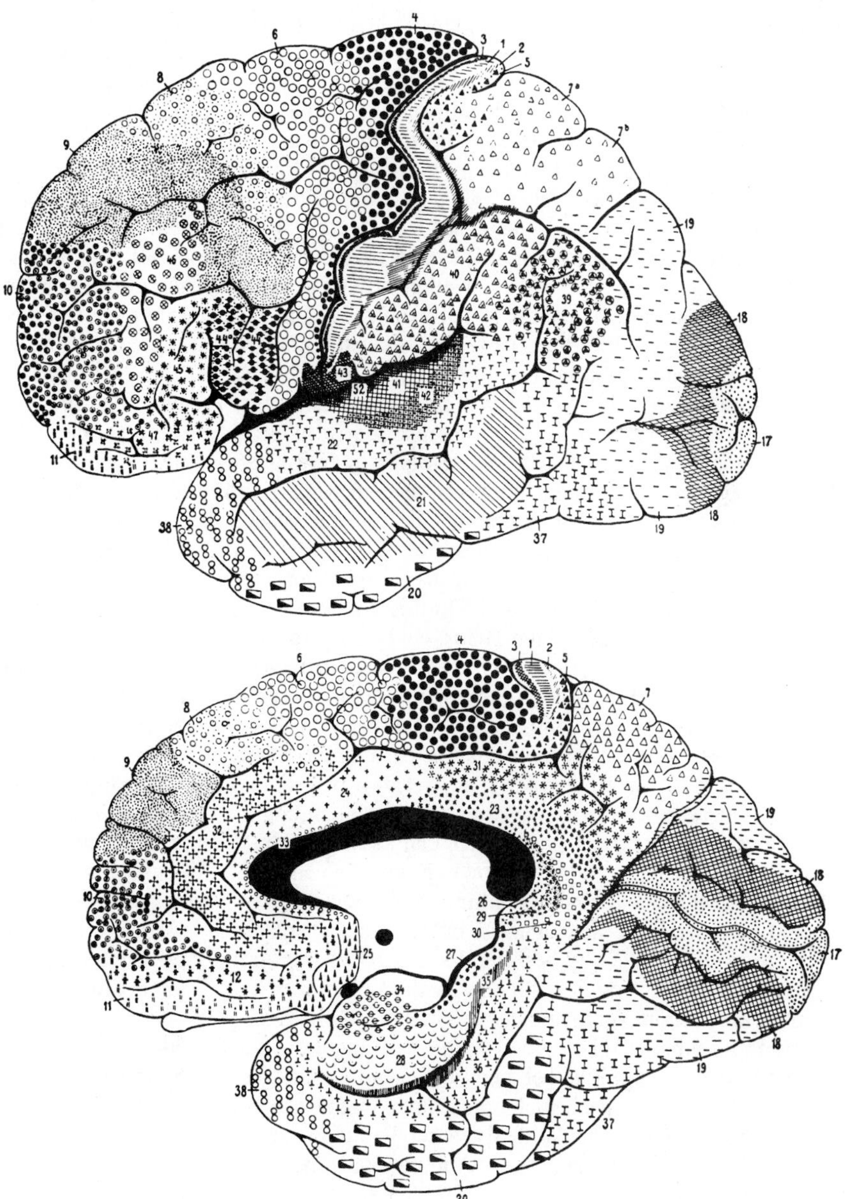

Figure 16–1 *Brodmann's cytoarchitectural map of the human cerebral cortex, lateral view; each symbol represents a distinct area of the cerebral cortex, numbered as shown. (From Brodmann K: Vegleichende Lokalisation lehre der Grosshirnrinde ihren Prinzipien dargestelt auf Grund des Zellenbaues. Leipzig: JA Barth, 1909.)*

views of Karl Lashley, whose series of ablation studies in the rat called into question the notion that behavior could result from specific neural locations. Lashley espoused a theory of mass action that suggested that brain lesions produce impairment in functions proportional to the amount of tissue that is destroyed. Borrowing from gestalt psychology, Lashley also advocated the notion of equipotentiality, which refers to the capacity of any part of a functional area to produce a given behavior. Equipotentiality was an influential concept because it embodied the idea that brain regions, through their redundant organization, could be plastic with respect to function. The remarkable degree of experientially based neural plasticity has since been demonstrated in the mammalian brain.

Current Theoretical Conceptualization of Brain Organization: A Rapprochement

The weight of evidence suggests that localizationism and holism in their extreme are not satisfactory perspectives from which to consider complex cognitive processes. Current thinking in the cognitive neurosciences strikes a balance between local and holistic organization of functions. The current emphasis on "connectivity," as both a theoretical heuristic and a set of models of neural behavior, has its roots in the earlier traditions. The localizationist perspective of Wernicke introduced the rudimentary idea that interconnected brain regions could work in a serial fashion to perform a set of operations such as language. The Russian neuropsychologist Alexander Luria, who influenced much contemporary thinking in cognitive neuroscience, was himself influenced by the idea of connectivity. Luria's approach was a rapprochement between localizationism and holism. He enlarged the concept of interconnected cortical zones subserving cognition. On the basis of the clinical examination of carefully considered human brain lesions, he reasoned that higher cortical functions resulted from complex functional systems: "every psychological function can be regarded as a complicated functional system which is a result of a constellation of simultaneous and successive participation of several cortical zones."[2]

It is also clear that Luria's approach was resonant with the cognitive models of language and other functions that were first being introduced in the 1950s. By borrowing from the then emerging fields of machine intelligence, the model of the brain as a digital computer operating in a serial processing framework was introduced. In this model, brain functions were seen as the constellation of interconnected neural networks, each operating in serial, to produce macrocognitive processes from series of local microcognitive operations. Although the early artificial intelligence and information-processing traditions of cognitive psychology offered elegant models, they were limited by their underlying assumptions. First, the cognitive models that postulated the premise of connectivity between local networks did not explicitly link the cognitive realm with the underlying anatomical substrate, lending these theories a lack of neural reality. For example, this yielded models of attention that "worked" from a cognitive perspective but did not suggest an underlying neural mechanism. The other main problem with the idea of a computational model based on serial processing is that of time. The computational speed of individual neurons is on the order of a few milliseconds, but functions can be performed in a few hundred milliseconds. This requires only 100 serial steps, yet the artificial intelligence models postulated many more steps.[3] Furthermore, it is likely that neurons compute functions that are more complex than individual instructions in computer programs.

Current connectionist theories of brain within the cognitive sciences have begun to offer models with greater neural and computational realism. In the computer realm, the development of massively parallel computing has suggested that extremely complex functions can be performed simultaneously, not in a serial fashion. The obvious extrapolation to neural science is to think of brain functions as having a parallel architecture, which would perform several operations simultaneously. In contrast to serial processing, parallel processing allows the relatively slow individual neurons to accomplish tasks in rapid real time. The other current concept applied to neural processing is that of distributed processing. Distributed processing refers to the coordination of functions that are distributed within and across brain regions. A particular function is therefore emergent from neural processing that is both parallel and distributed. This concept of neural function represents a compromise between local and holistic perspectives. The model of brain in terms of parallel distributed processing (PDP) is both a heuristic framework from which to view neural organization and a formal set of models within cognitive science. The formal elements of PDP involve the relationship of neural science and computer science and have been applied to the development of models of language, memory, vision, motor learning, and memory. In the course of this chapter, we make reference to PDP models, but the reader is referred to other sources for more detailed descriptions.[4, 5]

As a heuristic framework, the notion that higher cortical functions are best described as parallel and distributed is quite influential to most current thinking in the cognitive neurosciences. From a structural perspective, the neuroanatomical studies of Goldman-Rakic[6, 7] have demonstrated extensive parallelism and distribution with respect to neuronal connectivity, especially in the frontal lobes. Her studies of the frontal lobes have demonstrated that parallelism between distributed brain regions in performing complex cognitive operations such as memory is a neural reality. A number of lesion analytical and functional neuroimaging investigations have also demonstrated that language functions, for example, involve parallel and distributed processes.

Attention is now turned to the discussion of important work in the cognitive neuroscience of memory, language, and executive functions. These areas have been chosen because of their historical importance in the cognitive and neural sciences and because they richly illustrate the workings of complex systems. However, it is recognized that selectivity and focus preclude the discussion of many other interesting systems such as the vision and motor systems.

Memory

Memory functioning—broadly defined as the storage and recall of past experience—is of major interest and importance in cognitive neuroscience. The intensity of research in the area of memory has been especially great in the past decade, when the fields of cognitive psychology and neuropsychology converged to offer unified models of memory functioning on the basis of experimentation in normal and brain-damaged humans, as well as lesion studies in animals. Functional neuroimaging (mostly positron emission studies at this writing) has also begun to yield valuable insights into the patterns of neuroanatomical connectivity involved in aspects of memory. This section sheds light on some of the basic concepts and findings in the cognitive neuroscience of memory. Because this field is relatively massive, the reader is referred to comprehensive sources for further details.[8, 9]

Historically, the debate between the localizationist and holistic views of neural processing has been nowhere sharper than in the search for regionally specific entities involved in memory. The search for the "engram" or memory trace led Lashley[10] to conclude that memories are distributed throughout the brain, not localized within a discrete or unitary structure. The debate has been given a more sophisticated focus with the finding that there is indeed some regional specificity in aspects of memory but the realization that memory as a complex process requires multiple brain regions, probably operating in a parallel fashion.

Major Subdivisions of Memory Systems

Methods of Study

Two basic methods have contributed to the present knowledge of memory. These are the lesion analytical method and cognitive studies of normal individuals. Still in its infancy, functional neuroimaging as a technique (positron emission tomography [PET] and functional magnetic resonance imaging) also offers the potential to validate existing models of memory and to suggest newer theories based on patterns of anatomical connectivity observed during the performance of memory tasks. By far, the lesion analytical method has contributed the most to an understanding of both the cognitive and neuroanatomical aspects of memory functioning. The lesion analytical technique refers not to a unitary procedure but to the generic study of brain injury and its effect on memory. In the case of humans, this is exemplified by the study of amnesias as a result of surgical ablations, Korsakoff's disease, and head trauma, for example. In animals, the lesion technique considers brain structure a dependent variable, the goal of research being to study the effects on memory of carefully placed chemical or structural anatomical lesions. Often, the method of study influences the theories that ensue. In the case of memory, the lesion method has led to a view that memory is subdivided into separate systems (e.g., implicit versus explicit memory) with different neuroanatomical loci.[11] The cognitive psychological studies of normal individuals stemming from the information-processing tradition have led to an emphasis on memory processes such as encoding, storage, and retrieval that have been tied to anatomical regions.[12]

Memory Systems

Current research on the cognitive neuroscience of memory has considered memory from the perspective of multiple systems rather than a unitary system. Figure 16–2 illustrates the subdivisions between memory systems. A number of systems have been proposed, and the distinction between these systems is not impermeable. The most basic distinction

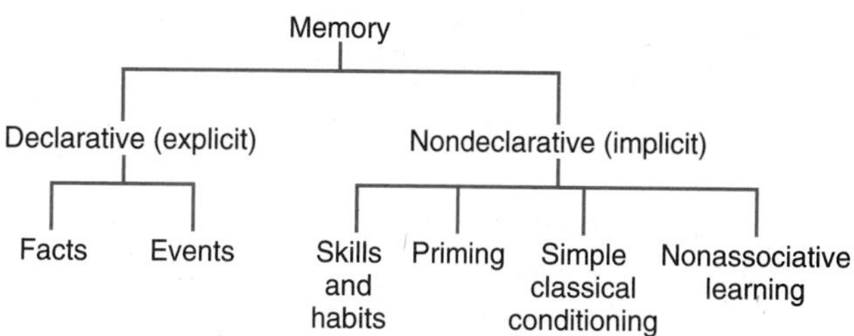

Figure 16–2 *Subdivision of major memory systems. Declarative (explicit) memory requires conscious awareness of past experience; nondeclarative (implicit) memory refers to the effects of previous experience on current behavior without conscious recollection. (Reprinted with permission from Squire LR, Zola-Morgan S: The medial temporal lobe memory system. Science 1991; 253:1380–1386. Copyright 1991 American Association for the Advancement of Science.)*

between memory systems is that of explicit versus implicit memory. Explicit memory is also referred to as declarative memory and implicit memory is also known as nondeclarative memory. What is considered explicit about this type of memory is that it requires conscious awareness of past experience. Tests of explicit memory typically involve the ability to recall or simply to recognize previously experienced events. One major aspect of explicit memory is episodic or autobiographical memory, which is the ability to remember personal events over time. This refers to the individual's ability to remember not only that something occurred but also the context in which it occurred. Another type of explicit memory system that involves the short-term registering of information is termed working memory. Memory systems research in the past 10 years has also focused on implicit memory. Implicit memory does not involve conscious awareness. It refers to the effects of previous experience on current behavior without conscious recollection. Explicit memory and implicit memory along with their hypothesized cognitive and neuroanatomical correlates are described more fully in the following.

Explicit Memory and the Medial Temporal Lobe System

The case of H.M.[13] described in the context of other amnesias by Markowitsch and Pritzel[14] is used to illustrate some of the major dissociations between memory systems. As suggested, studies of brain lesions in humans have provided a wealth of information regarding the cognitive and anatomical organization of memory system. H.M. received a bilateral resection of medial temporal regions secondary to intractable epileptic seizures. The surgery included the hippocampus bilaterally, as well as the uncus and amygdala. After the surgery, H.M. demonstrated a profound anterograde amnesia, which involved inability to transfer new information into long-term storage, resulting in rapid forgetting. He also manifested a temporally graded retrograde amnesia, which is defined as the inability to recall information that occurred shortly before the traumatic brain event. In the case of H.M., the retrograde amnesia was for events occurring some years before the surgery. He had good ability to remember events that occurred in earlier decades. The paradigm used to test for the retrograde memory utilized a measure of famous faces, which involves identifying historical figures from different decades. On this measure,

H.M. demonstrated preserved retrograde memory for the decades preceding the injury. Psychological testing also revealed normal levels of intellectual functioning, normal abstract reasoning, and normal semantic knowledge of vocabulary.

Memory researchers often draw a distinction between storage and retrieval processes. Storage refers to the transfer of perceptually encoded information into a form that can be accessed at a later time. Short-term memory was a concept introduced by the information-processing theorists to describe the storage of brief elements of information. H.M. was clearly able to learn tasks that relied on short-term memory but was essentially unable to process this information further in a form that would allow more permanent access. H.M. also did not have a retrieval failure, because he was clearly able to recall events in his past in sufficient detail. H.M. was also able to exhibit nearly intact performance on motor learning tasks[15] and fragment-cued recall procedures,[16] tasks of implicit rather than explicit retrieval.

On the basis of H.M. and other cases of medial temporal lobe damage in humans, it has been concluded that the medial temporal lobe, including the hippocampus, and adjacent anatomical structures enable the formation of explicit memories. In humans, it has been shown that a lesion confined solely to the hippocampus (field CA_1 of the hippocampus) can produce a mild amnestic syndrome, one that is not as pervasive as that of H.M.[17] It would then appear that the parahippocampal and perirhinal cortical regions are also necessarily involved in explicit memory.

Studies in animals can provide a good model for human amnesia. In animals, of course, the amnesia must be inferred on the basis of analogous nonlinguistic tasks that still somewhat manage to preserve the phenomenon of context. The classical tasks used in this literature are paradigms that contain a delay involving the animal's ability to match subsequent objects to previously encountered stimuli. In studies with monkeys, it has been nicely shown that a progression of lesions involving the medial temporal lobe system are involved in producing an amnestic syndrome. It was found that lesions in the hippocampal region produced a memory impairment but that as the lesions progressively included adjacent brain regions (anterior entorhinal cortex and perirhinal cortex), the memory impairment increased in severity.[18] Lesions confined to the amygdaloid complex do not have a clear effect on explicit memory functions.[19]

According to Zola-Morgan and Squire,[18] the medial temporal lobe system essentially coordinates the organization of information that originated in other brain regions. The medial temporal lobe system may thereby act as a temporary site to store information that is cortically distributed until the information is permanently coded. That the medial temporal lobe is not the repository of permanently stored information is clearly shown in the case of H.M., who was able to access information that occurred long before the surgery. Furthermore, the fact that humans and animals are able to "retrieve" information after damage to this brain region also suggests that the hippocampus and related structures are not critically involved in memory retrieval processes. From a theoretical perspective, Moscovitsch[20] has postulated that the role of the hippocampal formation is directly responsible for the experience of "consciousness" of memory. That is, the hippocampal formation "binds" a memory trace that was consciously experienced. As discussed later, the neocortical regions may be involved in transmitting conscious information to the hippocampus for consolidation.

Cellular Basis of Memory

On the basis of lesion analytical studies, the hippocampus and related structures have been implicated as a site for the consolidation of memory. The question naturally arises of the properties of the neurons in this area that might permit the association of information. Neuroanatomically (Fig. 16–3), the hippocampal formation consists of the fields of Ammon's horn (regions CA_1, CA_2, CA_3), the dentate gyrus, and the subiculum. Afferent pathways from the entorhinal cortex project to the hippocampus via the perforant pathway and synapse on the granular cells in the dentate gyrus. The entorhinal cortex itself receives cortical inputs from polysensory associational regions in the frontal, temporal, and

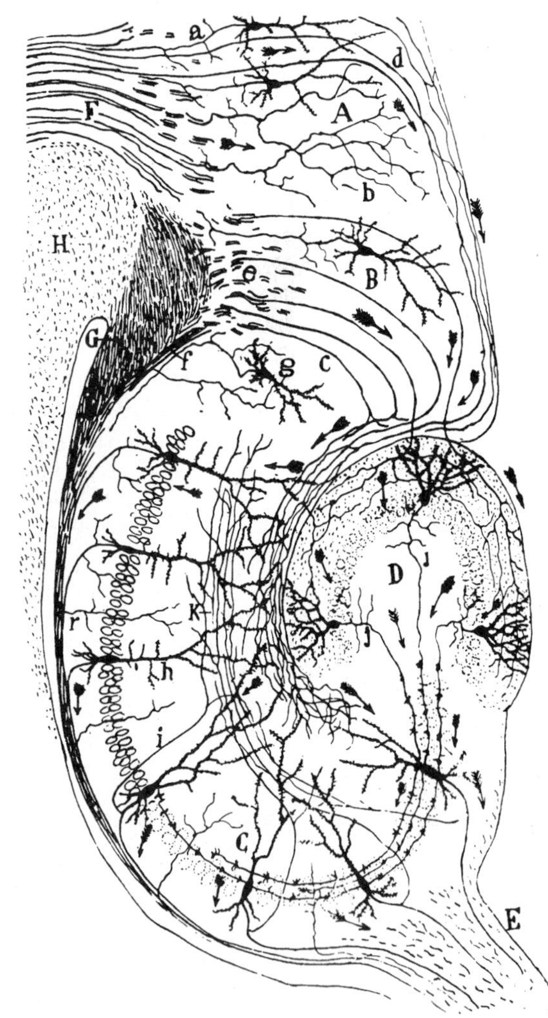

Figure 16–3 *Some of the structure and connections of the hippocampus (Ammon's horn) as drawn by Ramon y Cajal. A, Entorhinal cortex; B, subiculum; C, hippocampus; D, dentate gyrus; E, fimbria of fornix; F, fibers of the cingulum entering the entorhinal cortex (A); K, Schaffer collaterals; a, axons entering the cingulum; b, fibers of the cingulum terminating in the entorhinal cortex; g, pyramidal cell of the subiculum; h, pyramidal cells of the hippocampus; i, ascending collaterals from the hippocampal pyramidal cells; j, granule cell axons; r, collaterals from axons in the alveus. (From Ramon y Cajal S: Histologie du Système Nerveux de l'Homme et des Vertébrés. Paris: Maloine, 1911.)*

parietal lobes. Within the hippocampal formation, the granule cells in region CA_3 also project to the CA_1 region through the fimbria fornix, which also projects to the subiculum. The subiculum is the major efferent pathway, projecting to a number of cortical regions but also projecting back to the entorhinal cortex, completing the loop.

For learning and memory to occur, there must be plastic changes such that the structure and functional characteristics of nerve cells and their interconnections are altered. Much of the research into the processes of synaptic plasticity underlying learning and memory has been conducted in invertebrates[21, 22] through examination of reflexive learning processes (habituation, sensitization, and classical conditioning).

Regarding the mammalian brain, Bliss and Lomo[23] were the first to demonstrate that repeated stimulation of the afferent pathways to the dentate granule cells of the hippocampus of the rabbit produced an excitatory potential in the postsynaptic hippocampal neurons lasting for hours. Recording in intact animals has shown potentials that lasted for days and weeks. They termed this increased facilitation as a result of repeated stimulation long-term potentiation (LTP). The conceptual relationship between the phenomenon of LTP and cognitive neuroscience was prefigured by Hebb.[24] Hebb first postulated that an increase in synaptic strength occurs when the presynaptic and postsynaptic aspects of a synapse are coactive. He postulated that the accumulation of these synaptic units underlies the cellular basis of associative memory. The hebbian postulate is as follows: "When an axon of a cell A is near enough to excite cell B or repeatedly or persistently takes part in firing it, some growth or metabolic change takes place in both cells such that A's efficiency, as one of the cells firing B, is increased."[24(p62)]

The hebbian postulate has formed the criteria from which to determine whether LTP occurs in a specific neural region (not limited to the hippocampus). With respect to area CA_1 of the hippocampus, studies have shown that LTP occurs only when a number of input pathways have been stimulated. This is known as the criterion of cooperativity. When distinct weak and strong excitatory inputs impinge on a pyramidal nerve cell, the weak input becomes potentiated through association with a strong input. This is known as the criterion of associativity. Finally, the criterion of specificity refers to the fact that strong repeated stimulation in one synaptic pathway is specific only to that stimulated pathway. Unstimulated synapses on the same cell do not demonstrate LTP.

The events surrounding LTP are schematically described here (Fig. 16–4); the reader is referred to a detailed explanation of the cellular and molecular aspects of LTP.[22, 25] Studies of the CA1 region of the hippocampus reveal that LTP is mediated by the neurotransmitter glutamate. Glutamate acts on the *N*-methyl-D-aspartate (NMDA) receptor. Pharmacological blockade of NMDA receptors has been shown to block LTP. The events leading to the induction of LTP involve the action of NMDA and non-NMDA membrane channels. Through the action of these channels, calcium enters the spines of the postsynaptic dendrites. Calcium then acts as a second messenger to activate protein kinases, which then remain persistently active and thereby strengthen synaptic connections. The longer term maintenance of the synaptic transmission also involves increases in presynaptic transmitter release. The behavioral relevance of LTP can be seen in a series of experiments by Morris and colleagues.[26] They demonstrated that LTP could be blocked in rats by in vivo administration of 2-amino-5-phosphonovaleric acid and the degree of blocking was dose dependent. They then utilized a water maze learning test, which necessitates spatial memory and presumably requires an intact hippocampus. On administration of 2-amino-5-

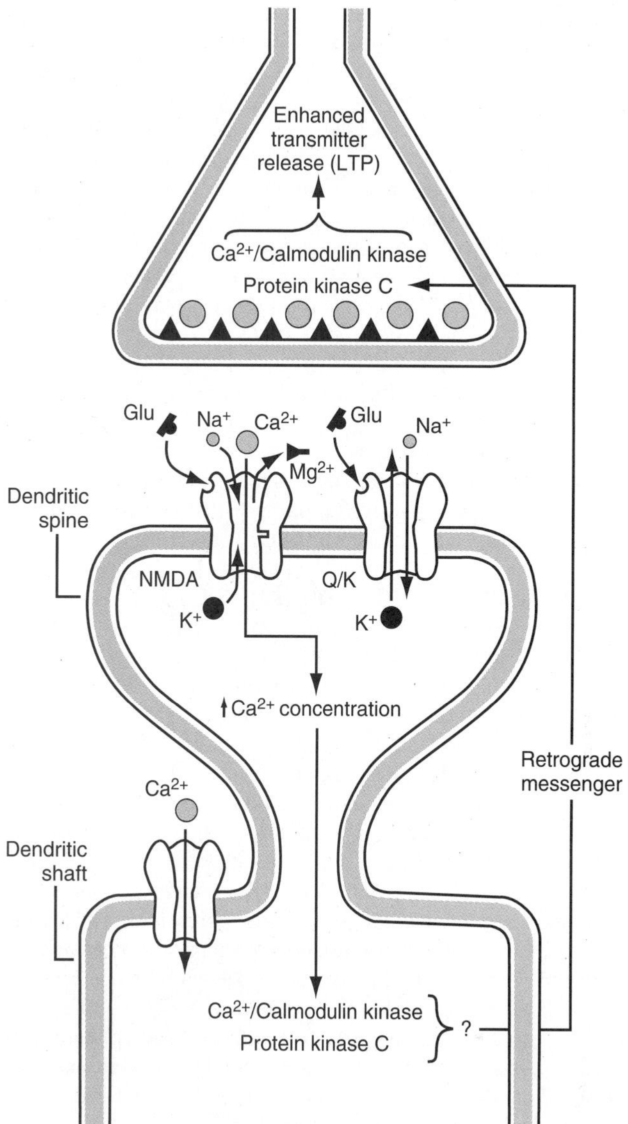

Figure 16–4 *The events surrounding the induction of LTP are portrayed. As a result of the tetanic stimulation of the postsynaptic membrane, depolarization relieves the magnesium (Mg^{2+}) blockade of the NMDA channel, allowing sodium (Na^{+}), potassium (K^{+}), and calcium (Ca^{2+}) to flow through the NMDA channel. The increase of calcium in the dendritic spine then triggers calcium-dependent kinases, which induce LTP. The maintenance of transmitter release is thought to occur by release of a retrograde messenger that acts on the presynaptic terminal. The voltage-dependent calcium channels in the dendritic shaft remain closed. (Adapted from Kandel ER: Cellular mechanisms of learning and the biological basis of individuality. In Kandel E, Schwartz JH, Jessell TM [eds]: Principles of Neural Science, 3rd ed. Norwalk, CT: Appleton & Lange, 1991:1021.)*

phosphonovaleric acid, the learning of the water maze task was retarded. Most important, the learning curve at the level of behavior and the blocking curve at the cellular level were correlated.

LTP has been stressed as a cellular mechanism of informational connectivity in the hippocampus. Brief mention should also be made of long-term depression (LTD). LTD is the opposite of LTP and refers to "use-dependent long-lasting decreases in synaptic strength."[27] LTD may have a number of advantages and work in parallel with LTP with respect to memory functioning. LTD may help to reset synapses that have been potentiated by LTP, to prevent saturation. It may serve as a cellular mechanism of forgetting[28] and, finally, may also form an active inhibitory system to attenuate signals from adjacent potentiated synapses. The specific role of LTD in the coordination of memory is still unclear. For a detailed description of the potential cellular and molecular mechanisms involved in LTD, the reader is referred to other sources.[27, 29]

Long-Term Potentiation and Computational Neuroscience

Studies of LTP and LTD are typically conducted with tetanic stimulation applied directly to neurons, yet these cellular phenomena, if they underlie learning and memory, must somehow occur naturally, on the basis of endogenous stimulation. Some "memorable" event in the environment must occur, which the animal responds to and thereby sets into motion the necessary synaptic events. Computational neuroscience has begun to offer models linking the behavioral events with the potential neural circuitry. The notion of the hebbian postulate has been at the core of computational neuroscience attempts to model the behavior of networks of neurons. Computational models use the hebbian postulate as the basis from which to infer connectivity between neurons in the performance of neural computations. The phenomena of LTP and LTD provide an example in which neural cytoarchitecture and the underlying cellular and molecular levels may actually conform to the principles of association and connectivity. Computational models have been developed to further our understanding of the manner in which learning and memory emerge from the properties of synaptic plasticity embodied in the circuitry of the hippocampus.[5, 30] The attraction of computational models is that they may clarify the link between aspects of LTP and LTD within local networks of associated neurons at the cellular level and the events at the behavioral level. This may prove quite useful to working out the as yet poorly understood spatial-temporal aspects of LTP and LTD that provide efficient information processing.

Diencephalon and Memory

Neuropsychological studies of patients with Wernicke-Korsakoff disease have yielded insight into the contribution of the diencephalon (dorsal and anterior thalamic nuclei and the mamillary bodies of the hypothalamus) to memory. Wernicke-Korsakoff disease is usually associated with a thiamine deficiency and is typically seen in individuals with alcoholism. However, it can also be seen in those with other nutritional deficiencies, infections, and brain tumors.[14] The memory deficit is characterized by impairment of explicit memory as seen by dense anterograde amnesia and variable retrograde amnesia. These patients are also frequently apathetic and indifferent and have diminished initiative.

The effects of damage caused by alcoholic and nonalcoholic lesions to the anterior and medial thalamic nuclei as well as to the mamillary bodies are diverse. The diencephalic region is connected with the hippocampal region; the mamillary bodies are connected to the hippocampus via the fornix and to the anterior thalamus via the mamillothalamic tract. The mediodorsal thalamic component of the system is also interconnected with the frontal lobes. Patients with Korsakoff's disease typically manifest frontal lobe damage, which is seen in the phenomenon of confabulation. Confabulation occurs clinically in testing a subject's episodic memory when the individual begins to fill in gaps with irrelevant information. Aside from this frontal component, which is often seen in alcoholism and may represent an independent lesion, the diencephalic amnesia is largely similar to the kinds of memory deficits observed with damage to the medial temporal lobe system. This suggests that, at least at a functional level, anatomical damage in this subcortical system produces an impairment in the consolidation of information. Whether the medial temporal lobe and diencephalic regions work in parallel or have distinct functions with respect to memory is thus far unclear.[31, 32]

Basal Forebrain and Memory

Another neuroanatomical region that plays a direct role in explicit memory is the basal forebrain. The basal forebrain region is located where the diencephalon meets the cerebral hemispheres and includes a number of brain structures such as the septal area, diagonal band of Broca, nucleus accumbens septi, olfactory tubercle, and substantia innominata. Figure 16–5 illustrates the rostral cholinergic projections in the rat brain. The contribution of this brain region to memory has been a relatively recent discovery. Human neuropsychological studies have generally found two classes of patients with damage in the basal forebrain and concomitant memory impairment—those with Alzheimer's disease and those with vascular disease. The basal forebrain region sends cholinergic projections from the medial septal area to the hippocampus. The relevance of the cholinergic projections to memory was first demonstrated in normal individuals given scopolamine, a centrally acting cholinergic antagonist. Drachman and Leavitt[33] demonstrated that scopolamine significantly impeded the ability of normal individuals to demonstrate free recall. Anticholinergics impair initial encoding as well as retrieval. The effect was reversed by physostigmine, a cholinergic agonist. It has been suggested that normal cholinergic activity acts on cognition by narrowing the focus of attention to behaviorally relevant stimuli.[34] Reduced cholinergic activity, according to this hypothesis, would then diffuse attention and reduce the efficiency of selective processing of information to be encoded and retrieved.

The facts that cholinergic activity has been found to be reduced in normal aging and that Alzheimer's disease produces pathological changes in the basal forebrain cholinergic system have led to the cholinergic hypothesis of normal and pathological aging.[35] This also spurred the development of cholinomimetic agents to reverse the effects of dementia. The cholinergic hypothesis, however, is limited in scope for the following reasons. Alzheimer's disease

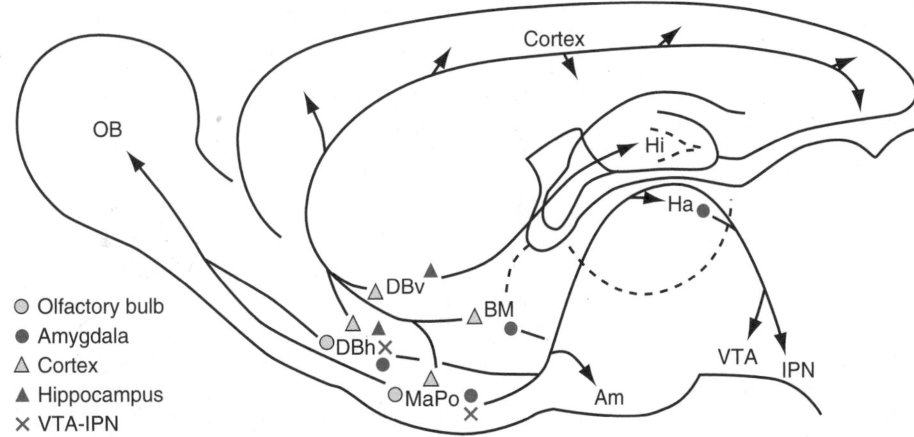

Figure 16–5 *Sagittal view of some projections of the rostral cholinergic column in the rat. The symbols (○, ●, △, ▲, ×) refer to the origin within the rostral cholinergic column of afferents to the olfactory bulb, amygdala, and so on. Am, Amygdala; BM, nucleus basalis; DBh, horizontal limb of diagonal band; DBv, vertical limb of diagonal band; Ha, habenula; Hi, hippocampus; IPN, interpeduncular nucleus; MaPo, magnocellular preoptic area; OB, olfactory bulb; VTA, ventral tegmental area. (From Fibiger HC, Vincent SR: Anatomy of central cholinergic neurons. In Meltzer HY [ed]: Psychopharmacology: The Third Generation of Progress. New York: Raven Press, 1987:213.)*

affects multiple neurotransmitter systems and the effects on memory are quite profound, causing something akin to a global amnesia by the later stages of the disease. Alzheimer's disease produces impairment in retrograde memory, episodic memory, knowledge of semantic information, and working memory. The effects of scopolamine, on the other hand, are specific to the disruption of new learning, leaving intact other aspects of memory. The point here is that the cholinergic system plays a role in memory (although its full role is not clear at this time) and is implicated in normal and pathological aging but is only one locus in the network of brain regions involved in memory.

Affective Valence and Neuromodulatory Systems

Memory functioning requires a system for establishing valence between memorable events. That is, some events are more memorable than others. Affect and its associated chemical neuromodulators probably serve a valence capacity by facilitating the storage of emotionally charged experiences. The underlying assumption here is that emotionally tinged experiences activate neurobiological pathways that facilitate their storage. In evolutionary terms, it is highly adaptive to remember experiences that are learned under arousing conditions.

A number of neuromodulators play a role in affective responding and also influence memory storage. Chief among them is the noradrenergic system. The central noradrenergic system involves the locus caeruleus in the midbrain reticular formation, the amygdala, and the stria terminalis (a major afferent and efferent pathway to the amygdala). The noradrenergic system is known to be involved in mediating emotionally related responses in mammals. A number of experiments, largely in animals, have confirmed that the noradrenergic system also influences postlearning retention of affective and nonaffective information.[36] The earliest studies found that posttraining electrical stimulation of the reticular formation improved appetitively motivated learning tasks. With respect to hormonal influences, it was found that when rats were given systemic injections of epinephrine after training, their task memory was enhanced for up to 1 month.[37] This has since been shown on a variety of learning tasks, including inhibitory avoidance tasks, discrimination learning tasks, and appetitively motivated tasks. A number of findings have converged to suggest that central norepinephrine (NE) receptors in the amygdala are involved in the postlearning consolidation of information. For example, intraamygdala injection of NE enhanced the retention of inhibitory avoidance learning.[38] Furthermore, intraamygdala injections of propranalol, a ß-adrenergic antagonist, blocked the memory-enhancing effect of NE.[39]

Lesion analytical studies of brain-injured adults also suggest that the amygdala is critical to the acquisition of conditioned emotional responses. A case study[40] found a dissociation between the role of the amygdala in human conditioning and the role of the hippocampus in the declarative memory of conditioned stimuli. When the lesion was confined to the amygdala (sparing the hippocampus), there was an inability to acquire conditioned autonomic responses despite intact declarative knowledge of the stimuli that were paired with the unconditioned stimulus. Conversely, when the lesion was confined to the hippocampus (with a spared amygdala), normal autonomic conditioning occurred in the absence of declarative memory for the stimuli.

Other neuromodulatory systems are involved in memory. Studies of the GABAergic and opioid peptidergic systems suggest a converging mechanism for memory consolidation with respect to the release of NE.[36] GABAergic and opioid peptidergic systems themselves play an inhibitory role on the noradrenergic system; they inhibit the release of NE. Administration of intraamygdala opiate antagonists such as naloxone facilitates NE (by blocking the opiate inhibition of noradrenergic release) and, most important, also results in greater posttraining retention. GABAergic antagonists such as picrotoxin also enhance retention by potentiating NE release in the amygdala. Overall, the role of the noradrenergic and related systems in memory may lie in the release of adrenal epinephrine after stressful or emotional stimuli. Activation of NE in the locus caeruleus–amygdala system, which ultimately has extensive connectivity with a number of brain regions, then serves to consolidate the storage of these memories. On a cellular level this may occur by the production of LTP, because noradrenergic compounds have been found to enhance LTP.[41]

Frontal Lobe Contribution to Explicit Memory

The process of storing and retrieving episodes is complex. Let us say, for example, that one is attempting to recall a pleasant Sunday picnic. The experience is encoded as an episode in the context of some temporally graded sequence of events. One might recall the event in the sequence in which it occurred, such as planning for the picnic, arriving at the event, leaving for home. One also recalls the interplay of other factors as they intersect with the relevant events: the food one ate, the conversations that might have taken place that day, the weather, the mood one was in, and so forth. The complexity required for organizing, storing, and retrieving information in a spatial-temporal context probably requires more than the medial temporal lobe system.

It is probable that interactive processing between the medial temporal lobe system and the frontal lobes is necessary for explicit memory. The frontal lobe provides an executive input to the medial temporal lobe system, imbuing memory with "intelligence."[42] The frontal lobes, through their extensive reciprocal connectivity with the hippocampal formation, probably provide input to ordering and placing experience in a spatial-temporal context. The frontal lobes in a sense add goal orientation to memory.

A number of cognitive tasks illustrate the contribution of frontal lobe functioning to memory. Measures of free recall typically reveal the organizational component of frontal mechanisms in memory. Free recall tasks involve the learning of lists of words. Words are presented in trials, with learning indexed by the ability to recall additional words on subsequent trials. Patients with frontal lobe lesions perform poorly on these measures despite accurate recognition memory. However, frontal lobe damage per se does not appear to produce anything like the anterograde memory impairment seen with medial temporal lobe involvement. Instead, patients with prefrontal lesions are unable to generate appropriate strategies to organize the presented information in a form that would facilitate recall, despite the intact ability to recognize having been presented with the information.

For humans and animals, there are also tasks that illustrate the dissociation between the hippocampal and frontal contributions to memory. On measures of conditional discrimination learning, which involves learning the association between sets of stimuli, hippocampal lesions do not produce deficits in the absence of delay. That is, hippocampal lesions result in normal conditional learning, but once delay is involved, the information cannot be stored for longer intervals. Frontal lesions, in contrast, produce impairment of the ability to learn the discrimination[43, 44] in the first place. In measures of delayed matching in humans and animals, the task is to study a stimulus and subsequently learn to make different responses on the basis of the stimulus. Damage to the hippocampal formation typically does not affect performance when the interval between stimuli is brief. Damage to the prefrontal cortex, on the other hand, results in severe impairment even with brief delays because of the inability to display conditional learning.[44, 45]

A number of other tasks are also typically impaired in humans with frontal lesions. These include memory for temporal order,[46, 47] source memory,[48, 49] and metamemory.[50, 51] Again, the deficits that these seemingly disparate tasks have in common appear to involve the fact that the frontal lobes provide a "top-down" organization to memory. In the case of the concept of metamemory, the frontal lobes appear to allow a self-awareness of memory processes. This enables animals, and especially humans, to guide and systematically search memory to achieve a variety of goals. The role of the frontal cortex in allocating and controlling attentional processes may also affect the myriad memory tasks that have demonstrated frontal lobe involvement.[51] For example, patients with frontal lobe lesions are often unable to inhibit irrelevant information while performing a cognitive task, which may affect such measures as free recall, with intrusive information being recalled instead of the salient stimuli.

Working Memory

We have discussed in general terms the frontal contribution to memory. Given that the frontal lobes contribute executive control to memory, it is important to consider whether the frontal cortex may itself form a specialized memory system. From a memory-processing perspective, it is likely that the medial temporal lobe system is involved in transferring information to longer term storage, which may then be distributed to areas other than the hippocampal formation and accessed from a number of modalities. The frontal lobes are involved in organizing information at the level of encoding and retrieval. Memory researchers in the cognitive neurosciences have considered the unique role of the frontal lobes as that of working memory. Working memory is a form of explicit memory that is concerned with the temporary storage of information in the context of performing a goal-directed task. The concept of working memory evolved from the notion of short-term memory. Baddeley and Hitch[52] were the first to provide a human cognitive model for the concept of working memory, and the neuroanatomical localization of this to the frontal lobes has been largely advanced by the extensive work of Goldman-Rakic and colleagues.[6, 7, 53]

Figure 16–6 illustrates the major components of the cognitive model of working memory. The model provided by Baddeley and Hitch[52] provides for a dynamic system of temporary and limited storage. It is composed of a central executive and two "slave" systems, a visual-spatial sketchpad, and a phonological loop. The phonological loop is seen as a memory store that holds phonological information for a brief period and is also combined with an articulatory control process. The articulatory control process (articulatory loop) can hold information for longer periods through such processes as subvocal rehearsal. Evidence for a phonologically based short-term store comes from studies demonstrating that acoustic processes are involved in short-term learning. During a test of immediate learning, when phonemically dissimilar words (e.g., black, car, stone) are

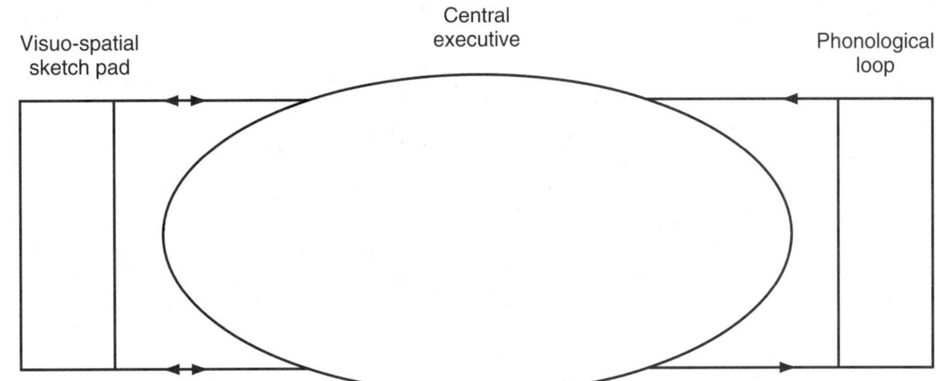

Figure 16–6 *A simplified representation of the Baddeley and Hitch (1974) working memory model. (From Baddeley A: Working memory. In Gazzaniga MS, Bizzi E, Black IB, et al [eds]: The Cognitive Neurosciences. Cambridge, MA: The MIT Press, 1995:760. © The MIT Press.)*

presented, immediate recall is superior to the condition when phonemically similar words are presented (e.g., car, park; can, pan). Neuropsychological evidence for a short-term store also comes from studies of individuals with amnesia, in whom immediate recall is usually intact. Evidence for the articulatory process is also seen in the word length effect; longer words decay faster because rehearsal takes longer. Also, suppressing subvocal rehearsal increases forgetting.

The visual-spatial sketchpad is a subsystem that is specialized to process and store visual material, spatial forms, and linguistic information that has been transformed into imagery. Research to date suggests that this system functions independently of the phonological system.[54] For example, studies that have utilized imagery to mediate verbal recall have demonstrated that the visual-spatial sketchpad is disrupted by interference from the visual system, whereas the phonological sketchpad is disrupted only by verbal information.[55] The ability to disrupt these systems by modality-specific information suggests that the phonological loop and visual-spatial sketchpad involve separate information buffers. Evidence from animal[56] and human[57] lesion studies has also indicated that the visual and spatial inputs of the visual-spatial sketchpad are mediated by separate brain systems. Bilateral occipital components appear to be involved in the visual aspects, whereas parietal regions are more involved in the spatial component of the system.

The central executive aspect of the working memory system appears to exert control over the flow of activity between the slave systems and provides the input to long-term memory. However, this is also the least well understood component of working memory. Baddeley[58] utilized the supervisory attentional system (SAS) model developed by Shallice[59] to describe the functioning of this system. The SAS, more thoroughly described later, essentially performs two operations; the first is contention scheduling, which involves activation of hierarchically organized schemas that modulate behavior. The supervisory aspect of the attentional system is a higher level, limited-capacity system that activates or inhibits schemas to coordinate the performance of the slave subsystems. Presumably, the SAS resides within the prefrontal cortex. The interaction of slave systems with the central executive probably reflects the interplay between the frontal lobe mechanisms of executive control of input received from parietal, temporal, and occipital systems of perception and association.

Anatomical Evidence of Working Memory

The notion of a limited-capacity working memory system would suggest that the prefrontal cortex is specialized for the temporary, goal-directed storage of information in parallel with other brain regions. Although the detailed role of the central executive remains unclear, evidence from the animal and human experimental literature suggests that the prefrontal cortex is specialized with respect to working memory. The work of Goldman-Rakic and colleagues[6, 7, 53] has helped to elucidate the neuroanatomy of working memory systems in primates. From the perspective of the working memory model provided by Baddeley, the research of Goldman-Rakic and colleagues has identified elements of the visual-spatial sketchpad in primates. They have utilized the concept of representational memory as underlying working memory. The classical example of this is versions of the delayed response task (Fig. 16–7). In the original form of this task, the animal is shown the location of a food morsel, which is then hidden behind a screen. After a delay period lasting several seconds, the animal is shown two locations. To receive a reward, the animal must recall in which of the two locations the food had been placed before the delay interval. Extensive work with animals has demonstrated that the delayed response task requires intact bilateral dorsolateral prefrontal cortical activity; lesions in Brodmann's area 46 have reliably produced a deficit on this task.

According to Goldman-Rakic, the essence of the delayed response paradigm and analogous tasks in humans is that of short-term representational memory or the animal's ability to develop an internal representation of the environment in the absence of external stimuli at the time when the response must be made. If representational memory was not available, the human or animal would have to rely on the external cues and would engage in a pattern of stereotyped, stimulus-bound behavior. Lesions of the prefrontal cortex produce such a pattern of perseverative behavior in animals and humans.

Research by Wilson and colleagues[53] has found that different regions of the prefrontal cortex are segregated with respect to the working memory of object and spatial features. Physiological recording of neuronal activity during the delayed response test revealed that when the animal is representing object-oriented information (features of the visual stimulus), firing of neurons in the inferior prefrontal convexity is time locked to the delay interval. In contrast, when

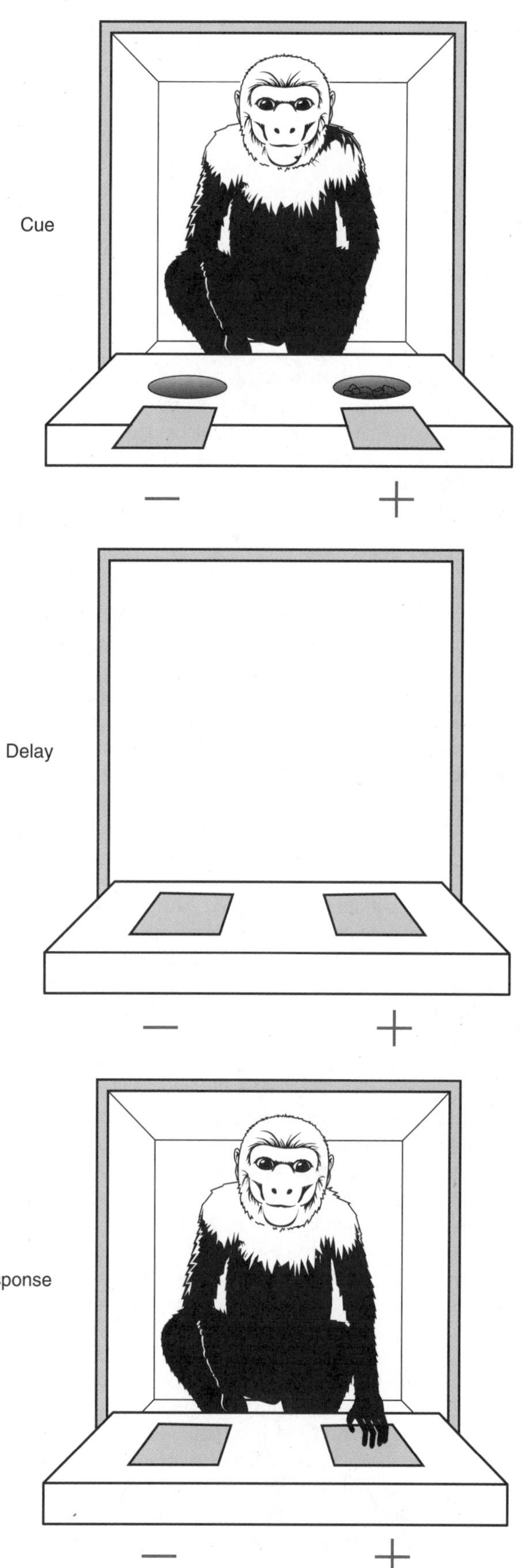

the animal is demonstrating working memory for spatial location, neurons in the dorsolateral prefrontal cortex are responsive during the delay interval.

The model of neuronal connectivity implicated in this model suggests that parallel systems are involved in working memory. From the perspective of a system of working memory, what differentiates areas of the prefrontal cortex may be specialization with respect to types of information processed. That is, the prefrontal cortex may be a kind of multipurpose working memory center, with each area concerned with a different domain. The prefrontal cortex functions as the coordinating element in a parallel distributed cortical-cortical network. Figure 16–8 shows that the frontal lobe may be specialized with respect to working memory for "what" an object is versus "where" in space the object may be located. In the case of spatial working memory (the where), the dorsolateral prefrontal cortex, frontal cortex, and parietal areas are interconnected; the dorsolateral prefrontal cortex projects to the parietal region, and both areas project to the same targets in more than a dozen cytoarchitectonic areas (e.g., supplementary motor cortex, anterior cingulate, posterior cingulate, parahippocampal gyrus).[7] In the case of working memory for object information, the frontal lobe may receive its input from inferior temporal lobe regions, which may provide information about the categorical attributes (the what) of foveal visual stimuli.

A number of in vivo functional neuroimaging studies of humans have been performed in an attempt to anatomically map brain regions involved in working memory.[60–62] Most of these have been PET studies rather than functional magnetic resonance imaging studies because the PET technology was implemented earlier. Both techniques utilize a hemodynamic model to image local changes in cortical activity while various cognitive tasks are performed. The advantage of these techniques is that they can pinpoint the cortical areas involved in the performance of a relatively specific cognitive function. Of course, the cognitive task and its associated function must be specified in relatively discrete terms and must occur in real time. The elucidation of the brain function is then only as good as the task specification. Although functional neuroimaging can suggest brain regions functionally involved in performing a cognitive operation, blood flow studies cannot suggest what is unique about that brain region. Also, when distributed brain regions are simultaneously activated, the technique itself does not immediately reveal the functional connectivity between those regions. Unlike the electrophysiological studies of working memory, imaging cannot suggest whether a brain region is in a sense storing information or transmitting information or is in some other way involved in the performance of an operation. With these caveats in mind, some

Figure 16–7 *Delayed response test. The animal is shown the location of a food morsel, which is then hidden behind a screen. After a delay period lasting several seconds, the animal is shown two locations. To receive a reward, the animal must recall in which of the two locations the food had been placed before the delay interval. (Adapted from Goldman-Rakic PS: Circuitry of the prefrontal cortex and the regulation of behavior by representational knowledge. In Plum F [ed]: Handbook of Physiology, Section 1, The Nervous System, Volume V, Higher Functions of the Brain. Bethesda, MD: American Physiological Society, 1987:373–417.)*

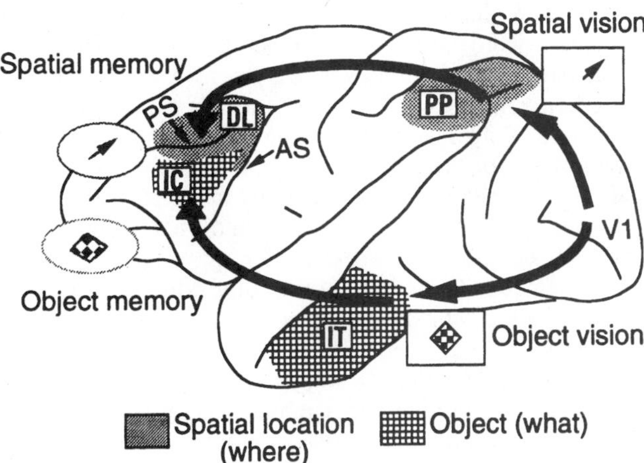

Figure 16–8 *Diagram depicting the what versus where segregation of the frontal lobe for working memory. PS, Principal sulcus; AS, arcuate sulcus. The posterior parietal (PP) cortex is involved with spatial features; the inferior temporal (IT) cortex is concerned with object recognition. Each of these areas projects to the dorsolateral (DL) and inferior convexity (IC) of the prefrontal cortices, which is involved in the working memory for spatial location and object identity, repectively. (Reprinted with permission from Wilson FAW, Scalaidhe SPO, Goldman-Rakic PS: Dissociation of object and spatial processing domains in primate prefrontal cortex. Science 1993; 260:1955–1957. Copyright 1993 American Association for the Advancement of Science.)*

interesting data have emerged and should continue to emerge in the neuroimaging of memory. We touch on a few of the findings.

Paulesu and coworkers[61] set out to map the neuroanatomical regions that are involved in the phonological storage and subvocal rehearsal mechanisms of the articulatory loop of the working memory system. Subjects were required to perform two tasks. The first task consisted of the presentation of phonologically dissimilar consonants. Subjects rehearsed the stimuli silently and were asked to remember them. Two seconds after each sequence, a probe consonant was shown and the subjects were asked to decide if it was the same as a previously presented stimulus. This task rests on the assumption that the visually presented letters are transformed into a phonological code and access the articulatory loop through the subvocal rehearsal system. The control task for this consisted of the presentation of Korean letters, which could be visually encoded but could not be phonologically coded because the subjects were English speakers. To determine whether distinct neuroanatomical substrates are involved in phonological storage versus subvocal rehearsal, a second task was used. This consisted of judging phonological similarity by asking subjects to determine whether presented consonants rhyme. The control for this task involved asking subjects to determine whether a Korean letter was similar to a Korean target letter. The intent of the rhyming task was that this presumably engages the subvocal rehearsal system to make decisions about rhyming but does not require phonological storage.

For the phonological short-term memory task, the region of maximal activation was seen in the area around the left supramarginal gyrus (Brodmann's area 40), suggesting that this area may represent the phonological store. This activation was not seen with the rhyming task. For the rhyming task, activation was seen in the inferior frontal lobe (Broca's area); this brain region appears to mediate the subvocal rehearsal system. A number of other brain regions were activated for both tasks, as part of a general network of language planning and motor execution (supplementary motor area, cerebellum). Overall, this study demonstrated that phonological storage and subvocal rehearsal processes of verbal working memory are mediated by anatomically distinct and distributed regions. Furthermore, this study suggests that the brain region mediating processing of phonological codes also mediates storage of information.

With respect to spatial working memory, Jonides and colleagues[63] utilized two tasks, a spatial memory task and an object memory task. In the spatial memory task, subjects had to remember the locations of three dots for a brief period. The object memory task consisted of unfamiliar geometrical figures that the subject needed to recall for a brief period. As with most functional imaging studies of cognition, control conditions for each of the tasks are also customarily included; control conditions approximate the experimental condition in all but the critical cognitive operation. In this case, the critical cognitive operation was the respective temporary storage of either spatial or object information. The results of the study (Fig. 16–9) revealed areas of cortical activation subserving the spatial memory task that included Brodmann's area 47 (ventral to area 46) in the right prefrontal cortex, which is consistent with the electrophysiological studies of the monkey.[6] Significant activations in parietal and occipital cortex were also found. Activation in the parietal and occipital regions is probably consistent with the visual-spatial nature of the task; frontal-parietal connectivity was also demonstrated in the monkey.[6] In addition, premotor cortex was involved in the performance of this spatial memory task. The object memory task showed a different pattern of activation. In this task, prefrontal cortical activation was seen in Brodmann's area 6 in the left hemisphere; the left parietal cortex was activated, as was the left inferior temporal cortex and anterior cingulate. Because the object memory task was more of a symbolic recognition task, the areas of activation paralleled areas of involvement reported in studies of verbal working memory[62] and neuropsychological studies of linguistic or symbolic representation.[64] To date, most of the PET studies involving some form of working memory for words, letters, digits, abstract shapes, and faces have largely revealed activation in the anterior prefrontal cortex with the activation generally implicating area 46 and adjacent regions.

The advantages of functional magnetic resonance imaging over PET are that it is completely noninvasive, provides higher spatial resolution, and allows a greater number of study conditions because of the lack of radiation exposure. Cohen and colleagues[65] used functional magnetic resonance imaging to investigate nonspatial working memory. The task for the working memory condition consisted of repeated letters; the subject had to note when a letter repeated with an intervening nonidentical letter (e.g., A-F-A). This is a working memory task because the subject has to remember the identify and sequence of letters. The control condition for this task consisted of any occurrence of the letter X, which requires only perceptual identification and does not involve a memory component. The results of this study showed that the greatest areas of activation for the working memory task were in Brodmann's areas 46 and 45, corresponding to the middle and inferior frontal gyri. The results of this study were generally consistent with those of PET studies demonstrating prefrontal cortical activation during working memory. The high spatial resolution of functional magnetic resonance imaging may allow future studies to determine whether the prefrontal cortex is topographically organized with respect to encoding spatial versus verbal information

Functional Neuroimaging and Memory Processes

As stated earlier, the basic research in memory considers memory functioning from both processing and systems perspectives. We have discussed some of the relevant research on the medial temporal system and its role in explicit memory, as well as the frontal contributions to memory systems. Functional neuroimaging studies have also been applied to the mapping of auditory-verbal long-term memory in normal individuals. As noted earlier, studies using the lesion analytical framework have found that patients with frontal lobe damage typically perform poorly on free recall tasks, but this does not directly implicate this brain region as involved in "normal" processing.

In a PET activation study, Grasby and coworkers[66] utilized measures of subspan and supraspan free recall to determine the common and distinct neuroanatomical regions involved in verbal long-term memory. In subspan memory tasks, subjects needed to remember a series of lists containing five words. In the supraspan task, subjects were required to recall word lists 15 words in length. The terms subspan and supraspan refer to the different amounts of information that need to be processed and stored. The subspan 5-word list can be remembered using a phonological short-term memory store, whereas the 15-word list requires long-term memory in addition to short-term memory processes. With respect to unique regions involved in the performance of the two tasks, activation in the dorsolateral prefrontal cortex was seen bilaterally in the performance of the supraspan task. The interpretation of this finding is that the frontal cortex is necessary for the organization and implementation of strategies for dealing with large amounts of information, which can then be more efficiently encoded. There were also differences in other brain regions (increased activity in the precuneus), suggesting that visual processes may have been used as a mnemonic strategy to recall larger amounts of information. Areas of common activation for both the subspan and supraspan tasks included the thalamus, anterior cingulate, medial temporal lobe (right parahippocampal gyrus), superior temporal cortex, and cerebellum. The multiple brain regions involved in auditory-verbal memory probably represent a distributed system for memory function. The medial temporal lobe and other structures are involved in short-term recall, and the prefrontal cortex is active when word lists exceed the immediate memory span. A PET activation study[67] using briefer subspan word lists found regions of activation in the medial temporal lobe. The finding of temporohippocampal activation with short lists suggests that this system receives auditory-verbal input in parallel with the phonological input store of the working memory system.

Tulving and colleagues[68–70] have performed PET activation studies to map the regions involved in the

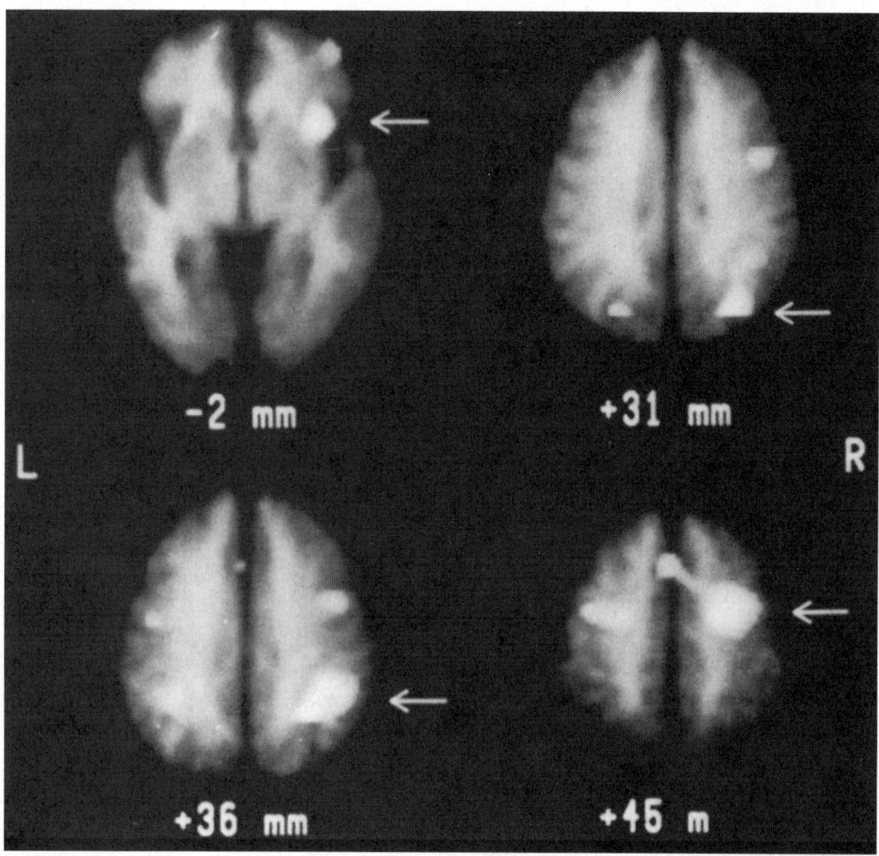

Figure 16–9 *PET images from a study of spatial working memory displaying areas of statistically significant activation. Examining the images from top to bottom and from left to right, foci of activation were found in prefrontal cortex (Brodmann's area 47), parietal cortex (Brodmann's area 40), occipital cortex (Brodmann's area 19), and premotor cortex (Brodmann's area 6). (From Smith EE, Jonides J: Working memory in humans: Neuropsychological evidence. In Gazzaniga MS, Bizzi E, Black IB, et al [eds]: The Cognitive Neurosciences. Cambridge, MA: The MIT Press, 1995:1009–1020. © The MIT Press.)*

encoding versus retrieval of information in episodic memory. With respect to encoding information, it has been a well-established finding that the level of encoding or processing of a stimulus determines its subsequent retrieval. This is referred to as the "level of processing effect."[71] Incoming stimuli can be processed at different levels, with superficial levels signifying the processing of pitch, color, form, and other perceptual attributes of stimuli. Deeper levels of semantic analysis involve meaning and lead to better retrieval of episodic information. In the context of using PET to examine the level of processing effect, subjects were required to process information in either a shallow or a deep fashion. In the shallow processing condition, the subject examined each word and decided whether it contained the letter "a." In the deeper processing condition, the subject studied each word and decided whether its referent was living or nonliving. Subjects who performed deeper processing demonstrated superior retrieval. The image analysis revealed that when subjects performed deeper as opposed to shallow processing, the deeper encoding was associated with increased activity in the left inferior prefrontal cortex (Brodmann's areas 45, 46, 47, and 10).

In a PET activation study of episodic retrieval,[68] subjects were given a series of novel, meaningful sentences that elicited deep semantic processing. The next day subjects were presented auditorily with either old sentences (from the day before) or new sentences while they underwent PET scanning. The pattern of findings revealed increased activation in the right dorsolateral prefrontal cortex and adjacent regions, as well as in the left cingulate sulcus. Other major regions of activation were seen in the parietal lobe, bilaterally. The parietal activation was seen in the right homotopical area (Brodmann's area 40) to Wernicke's area on the left. With respect to the processing of old sentences, there were also areas of decreased activation in the temporal lobes of both hemispheres. This decreased activity may reflect the diminished processing requirements for identifying and comprehending information that was previously familiar. The finding of lateralized prefrontal activation with respect to encoding (increased left dorsolateral activity) and retrieval (increased right dorsolateral activity) has led Tulving and coworkers[69] to propose that these processes reflect a hemispherical asymmetry in the frontal contribution to episodic memory. In this model, the left prefrontal cortex is involved in encoding novel information and the right prefrontal cortex is involved in retrieving the information that has been encoded. Although the frontal cortex is involved in information encoding, it is unlikely that the frontal cortex is the storage site for episodic memory. From the perspective of a neural network, it is probable that the frontal lobe is involved in transforming information and that, in conjunction with regions such as the parietal lobe, the information is placed into a spatial-temporal context.

Implicit Memory

As defined earlier, implicit memory refers to the influence of past experience on current behavior that is not conscious or intentional. In other words, retention of linguistic, visual, or motor information can occur in the absence of explicit retrieval of that information. An example of the manner in which explicit memory and implicit memory can be dissociated is given by the results of a fragment stem completion task,[72] which illustrates the priming effect. Priming refers to the increased facilitation of identifying a stimulus that occurs as a result of having had prior exposure to that stimulus,[73] even though the individual may have no conscious recollection of the exposure. On a repetition priming test, subjects examine long lists of infrequently occurring words and are then asked to perform explicit and implicit retrieval operations. In one task, subjects are asked to utilize explicit memory to recognize whether a word had appeared on the list by indicating yes or no to a series of presented words. With a fragment completion condition, incomplete words (fragments) were presented and subjects were required to complete them; the fragments were either of previously presented words or of novel words. It was found that the completion rate for previously presented words was significantly higher than that for novel words. More important, the probability of producing a correct fragment was independent of the probability of recognizing a word (explicit retrieval), indicating that explicit memory and implicit memory were separate. Manipulations of depth of encoding also revealed that explicit and implicit memory processes are functionally dissociable. As described earlier, it is well established that increasing the depth of encoding facilitates later explicit retrieval.[71] However, a number of studies have clearly demonstrated that deep encoding has no bearing on the magnitude of the priming effect, again suggesting that explicit memory and implicit memory refer to separate systems.[74] A number of other experimental paradigms with normal individuals reliably show that the priming effect necessitates implicit memory and is functionally separate from conscious, explicit retrieval strategies.[73]

As with studies of explicit memory, the examination of individuals with amnesia has provided valuable information concerning the cognitive and neuroanatomical aspects of implicit memory. With respect to priming, individuals with amnesia often demonstrate normal performance when utilizing implicit retrieval strategies. The patient H.M. discussed earlier was reported to demonstrate intact nonword priming.[75] Although there is some variability in the priming effect in individuals with amnesia,[73] most findings suggest that priming does not activate stored representations of information, because access to this information is disrupted in patients with amnesia. In fact, when patients with amnesia are required to utilize explicit retrieval strategies on stem completion tasks, performance is impaired but their priming effect remains normal.[76]

Therefore, priming does not appear to depend on the medial temporal lobe memory system that is involved in the retrieval of stored representations. According to Tulving and Schacter,[77, 78] priming effects are based on experience-induced changes in a presemantic perceptual representation system. The perceptual representation system is itself composed of a number of domain-specific subsystems, each subserving different aspects of words and objects. The perceptual representation system can function independently of semantic aspects of memory. This observation is based on studies of brain-damaged patients who demonstrate intact ability to access perceptual knowledge of words or objects but cannot access the semantic aspects for the same items.[78] PET activation studies of lexical processing also reveal that different brain regions are involved in the processing of perceptual and semantic characteristics. On the basis of numerous studies with brain-damaged and normal individuals, it is probable that the perceptual representation subsystems for priming are a visual word form system representing the orthographical features of words, a system that represents structural relations among parts of objects, and an auditory word form system that mediates phonological or acoustic information. The likely brain regions associated with each of these subsystems are the extrastriate cortex, inferior temporal region, and perisylvian cortex.

Although the priming effect is the most extensively studied aspect of explicit memory, it is important to note that the learning of motor skills and habits and the phenomenon of classical conditioning fall under the rubric of implicit memory. These processes may be considered as part of implicit memory because behavior changes and learning occur without conscious awareness. For example, patients with amnesia such as H.M. are able to demonstrate relatively intact motor skill learning even though unable to recall the episodes during which the training occurred. Skill learning processes are also dissociable from priming and are probably mediated by different brain regions. Patients with Alzheimer's disease demonstrate impaired word stem completion priming but can usually acquire motor skills.[79] On the other hand, patients with Huntington's disease, a disorder involving basal ganglia, do not acquire motor skill learning but are able to show normal word stem completion priming.[79] This behavioral dissociation between priming and skill learning suggests that the latter may be mediated by the corticostriatal loop that mediates motor programming, namely the basal ganglia, thalamus, and motor, premotor, and sensorimotor cortex.[80]

Language

Language as a species-specific ability in humans is intrinsic to the development of knowledge and understanding. It endows us with a capacity unique to the human species to structure and organize experiences through the manipulation of categorical and abstract concepts. With increasing internalization of language comes the capacity for disengagement from the environment so that concepts exist independently of their immediate context, as internal representations. Through this capacity to organize and form internal representations of experiences, a stable construction of reality is made possible.[81, 82]

Language is thus an integral part of mentation. Language is also central to modes of communication. Both of these aspects of language have been subjects of study for many disciplines, including philosophy, psycholinguistics, psychology, and cognitive sciences. Furthermore, the disconnection of language from other cognitive processes and the disruptions in its communicative functions have been subjects of investigation in the fields of neurology, neurosurgery, neurophysiology, and neuropsychology. Multidisciplinary efforts have led to a burgeoning body of research on language in normal and brain-damaged individuals, and the converging findings have greatly advanced our understanding of language as a complex human ability.

Regardless of the discipline within which the study of language is attempted, its essential features are common. Language is governed by a set of rules that link its various components. The basic units of a sound-based language (as opposed to a sign-based language, for example) are classified in terms of phonemes, morphemes, lexicon, syntax, semantics, prosody, and discourse. Phonemes are the smallest units of sound; morphemes are the smallest meaningful word units that when combined form words; syntax refers to the relational features by which words are combined, that is, grammar; lexicon refers to the words or vocabulary of a language; semantics refers to the meaning of words and sentences; prosody means the inflection and rhythm of utterances; and discourse involves the combination of sentences within any given context and constitutes narratives.[83]

Inasmuch as a comprehensive description of language from all vantage points is beyond the scope of this section, the focus is on providing an overview of knowledge about language and its dysfunctions within the framework of cognitive neuroscience. A brief presentation of the methodologies applied within these disciplines is therefore pertinent to an understanding of language.

Methodology

The study of brain-language relations in normal and brain-damaged individuals has involved a combination of methods. Clinical assessments of language disturbance include Mental Status Examination and neuropsychological evaluations using diagnostic language batteries. In the neurobiological traditions, the use of animal models to gain insights into neural mechanisms has been inadequate because language is uniquely human. Some investigations of linguistic abilities in chimpanzees, like Sarah[84] and Washoe,[85] have suggested only the most rudimentary capabilities devoid of the aspects that most distinguish human language, especially the generative capacity of syntax. The neurobiological approach has had the most extensive yield from lesion analytical studies of acquired language disorders, primarily involving aphasia. In this method, lesion-deficit correlational analyses are performed using data from a variety of electrophysiological and neuroimaging techniques, including computed tomography, magnetic resonance imaging, single-photon emission computed tomography, and PET. Cognitive neuroscience has combined traditional experimental designs with methods based on computational models and neuroimaging techniques such as PET. The methods of cognitive neuroscience have enabled investigations of language functions and neural mechanisms at various levels of processing, including phonological, lexical, and syntactic.

Important Issues in Language Research

From a historical standpoint, one of the earliest questions about language has pertained to the concept of cerebral dominance and differential lateralization. A second area of investigation that has gained considerable interest because of cross-disciplinary research efforts is concerned with structural and functional localization of language. Researchers are concerned with whether specific regions of the brain are specialized for specific linguistic functions, including speaking, comprehending, reading, and writing. Furthermore, with the growing influence of cognitive neuroscience, researchers are investigating whether specific language operations are localized in different levels of processing (e.g., phonological, orthographical, lexical, syntactic) and studying specific neural substrates associated with these processing networks. They are also interested in studying the patterns of connectivity between these neural networks. A third area that continues to generate great interest relates to neurodevelopmental aspects of language. Some of the questions in this area deal with the acquisition and development of language, as well as with the organization of the brain for language abilities in children.

The centrality of these issues to an understanding of language is reflected in the emergence of different models for language, which are described in greater detail in later sections. Briefly, these models can be broadly classified into traditional and current models when placed in a historical context. The traditional models were essentially localizationist (Wernicke, Broca, early contributions of Geschwind); the current models are more "hybrid"[86] in that they reflect a conceptualization of language processing as being both localized and distributed.

Because a great deal of what is understood about language and continues to intrigue investigators has emerged from studies of deficits and their neuroanatomical correlates in the various language disorders, especially aphasia, a description of these is important and is provided next. For more detailed reviews of language disorders, the reader is referred to other sources.[87, 88]

Acquired Language Disorders: Aphasia and Alexia

As previously noted, the clinical approach to diagnosis and understanding of language disturbance involves various assessment techniques, including a detailed Mental Status Examination and use of diagnostic batteries. The language functions that are typically examined through these techniques include conversational speech, repetition, comprehension of spoken language, word finding, reading, and writing.[89] For a formal analysis of language deficits, the neuropsychological batteries that are used either in their entirety or selectively include the Boston Diagnostic Aphasia Examination,[90] Multilingual Aphasia Examination,[91] and Neurosensory Center Comprehensive Examination for Aphasia.[92] For details of these tests the reader is referred to Lezak.[93]

Aphasia

Aphasia is the loss or impairment of linguistic abilities as a result of brain damage associated with any one of multiple causes, including vascular disease, tumors, traumatic injury, and degenerative dementias. It results in a breakdown of generally multiple but selective aspects of language functioning. Thus, the impairments might be in the functions enumerated earlier (e.g., repetition, comprehension, word finding), which would in turn differentially involve the components of language including lexicon, syntax, and semantics. Aphasia has been distinguished from disorders of perception in that even when there is damage to the auditory apparatus, as in deaf individuals, information can be received and comprehended through other sensory modalities, such as vision or touch.[94] Although individuals with language impairments might also exhibit signs of dysarthria, dysphonia, and oral apraxia, aphasia has been distinguished from these disorders. For example, dysarthria is an articulatory disturbance involving distorted speech sounds (because of incoordination in the speech apparatus) but language processing remains basically intact.

The long-standing finding of different patterns of language impairment linked with specific neuroanatomical sites has led to several classification schemes for organizing clinical and research data on aphasia. Classifications based on syndromes or clusters of symptoms have been most favored. The major aphasia subtypes that are now widely accepted are presented in Table 16–1. The subtypes of aphasia have been further subdivided in terms of their neuroanatomical loci into perisylvian (Broca's, Wernicke's, conduction, and global) and extrasylvian (transcortical-motor, transcortical-sensory, mixed, anomic, and subcortical) aphasias.[89] The impairment and preservation of the ability to repeat appear to coincide with this dichotomy. Figure 16–10 depicts some of the regions of the left cerebral cortex that are involved in language functioning.

Broca's aphasia involves nonfluent, effortful speech with short phrases and lengthy pauses. Defects in grammatical language involving omissions of certain obligatory syntactic categories, such as prepositions, articles, conjunctions, auxiliary verbs, and suffixes, are typical of the clinical picture. This defect is termed agrammatism and gives a telegraphic quality to the patient's speech. Patients also have difficulty with repeating sentences. Although naming is also impaired, these patients show some capacity to benefit from phonetic or contextual cuing.[89] Impairments in reading aloud and writing are also present. Comprehension is relatively preserved, but sentences may be misunderstood because of problems in comprehending critical grammatical words and certain forms of syntactic constructions such as reversible passive sentences.[95] Because of defective articulatory programming, patients with Broca's aphasia tend to misproduce speech sounds such as "p" and "b"; they also have problems in discrimination of such phonemes.[96] This pattern of language impairment is often seen together with right hemiplegia.

When damage occurs only to Broca's area (inferior left frontal gyrus, which includes Brodmann's areas 44 and 45), the result is a milder and transitory form of aphasia.[94] On the other hand, it is now well known that the lesion sites associated with the typical clinical picture of severe Broca's aphasia extend beyond Broca's area. Such lesions also involve most of the frontal operculum, the premotor and motor regions posterior and superior to the frontal operculum, the basal ganglia, and the insula.[94, 97, 98]

In Wernicke's aphasia, speech is fluent; the most marked defects are in comprehension and repetition. Although comprehension of both auditory and visual input is affected, some patients show more impairment in the comprehension of spoken words (word deafness), whereas in others defects in written comprehension may be more severe (word blindness). Another feature of this type of aphasia is the misuse of words and misproduction of speech sounds. Because of their problems in selecting the right word to convey the intended meaning, these patients substitute a word (or words) for the correct one, resulting in semantic paraphasic errors and circumlocution. They also make phonemic paraphasic errors by adding or omitting phonemes or missequencing the order of phonemes in a word. Because of an abundance of words, often incorrect ones involving

Table 16–1 Clinical Features Associated with Subtypes of Aphasia

Type of Aphasia	Speech or Verbal Output	Repertoire	Comprehension	Naming	Other Features*	Regions Involved
Broca's	Nonfluent	Impaired	Largely preserved	Often impaired	Right hemiparesis; may be depressed	Left posterior inferior frontal
Wernicke's	Fluent; paraphasic	Impaired	Impaired	Impaired	May be agitated; ambiguous; paranoid	Left posterior superior temporal
Conduction	Fluent; paraphasic	Impaired	Impaired	Often impaired	±Right hemisensory defect ±Right arm and facial weakness	Left supramarginal gyrus or left auditory cortex
Global	Nonfluent	Impaired	Impaired	Impaired	Right hemiparesis; right hemisensory defect	Left frontal parietal temporal
Transcortical motor	Nonfluent	Intact or largely preserved	Impaired	Impaired	+Right hemiparesis	Left frontal, anterior or superior to Broca's area
Transcortical sensory	Fluent; paraphasic	Intact or largely preserved	Impaired	Impaired	±Right hemiparesis	Left temporoparietal areas surrounding Wernicke's area
Anomic	Fluent	Intact or largely preserved	Largely preserved	Impaired	No definite motor signs	Left temporoparietal or frontal
Subcortical†	Fluent or articulatory disturbances may be present	Intact or may be impaired	Impaired	Intact or impaired	±Right hemiparesis	Caudate; thalamus

*+, Often present; ±, sometimes present.

†Variable symptoms depending on subcortical area affected.

paraphasias and neologisms, their speech is characterized as empty.

The underlying neuropathology in Wernicke's aphasia is associated with damage in the posterior region of the left auditory association cortex (posterior region of the superior temporal gyrus, area 22). Lesions can also extend into the posterior inferior temporal lobe, the second and third temporal gyri (areas 20, 21, 37), and the angular gyrus (area 39),[94, 98] depending on the nature of the language deficits. For example, when word deafness is more severe, the damage extends deeper into the first temporal gyrus involving Heschl's gyrus. When word blindness is more severe, the lesion involves the angular gyrus in the adjoining parietal cortex.[89]

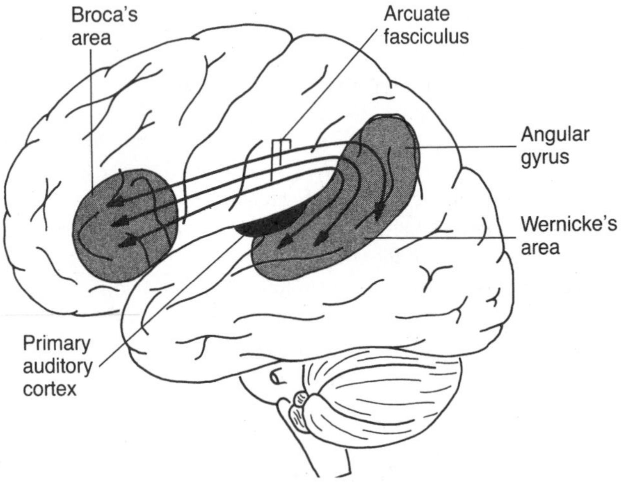

Figure 16–10 *Left cerebral hemisphere showing areas of particular relevance to language processing. (From Burt AM: Textbook of Neuroanatomy. Philadelphia: WB Saunders, 1993:469.)*

Just as in Wernicke's aphasia, conduction aphasia is characterized by fluent speech but severe problems with repetition and paraphasic output with primarily phonemic substitutions. Unlike patients with Wernicke's aphasia, patients with conduction aphasia show well-preserved comprehension of spoken language. Naming is disturbed because of paraphasic errors. Reading aloud is defective, but silent reading for comprehension is preserved. Writing may be disturbed, with spelling errors involving omissions, missequencing, and substitution of letters. The neuropathology in conduction aphasia most commonly involves the fibers of the arcuate fasciculus. This results in a disconnection between the linguistic areas in the temporal and frontal lobes.[99] It is thought that repetition is impaired precisely because of this disruption in the transfer of information from the auditory regions to the articulatory regions.[98] In contrast, speech and comprehension may remain intact because Broca's and Wernicke's areas are themselves relatively spared. The pathology has also been found to include the supramarginal gyrus (area 40) and, occasionally, aspects of the left auditory cortex.[99]

In global aphasia, most language functions are impaired, including fluency of speech, comprehension, repetition, naming, reading, and writing. This type of aphasia is accompanied by right hemiplegia. Lesions usually involve most of the perisylvian area, which includes frontal and parietotemporal language areas.

Transcortical motor aphasia involves difficulties in the production of speech and naming, but repetition is intact and comprehension of spoken language is relatively well preserved. This type of aphasia is associated with lesions in the frontal lobe anterior to Broca's area, including damage to the pathways that connect Broca's area with the supplementary motor areas in the frontal lobe.[100]

Transcortical sensory aphasia is characterized by fluent speech and intact repetition, but like patients with Wernicke's aphasia these patients make paraphasic errors, have defective comprehension for spoken and written language, and have impaired naming, reading, and writing. Lesions are located posterior to the perisylvian region in the parietal-temporal and parietal-occipital junctions.[101]

In anomic aphasia, the central feature is a fairly focal deficit in word finding in both spoken and written language. The defect is clearly seen in confrontation naming and other word-finding tasks. Attempts to substitute for missing words often result in circumlocution. Typically, other language abilities including repetition and comprehension are well preserved, although in some cases comprehension may be somewhat compromised. Anomic aphasia is a common syndrome associated with various causes. Its underlying pathological process is also variable and has been found to involve frontal, temporal, and parietal areas of the dominant hemisphere as well as nondominant and subcortical areas.[87]

Computed tomographic studies have linked aphasia with left-sided lesions in areas lying outside the cerebral cortex. This finding suggests that language is also subserved by subcortical areas. Subcortical aphasia is characterized by mutism in the early stage of the disorder, followed by articulatory disturbances and paraphasic output. Paraphasia appears to resolve when the patient has to repeat sentences. Comprehension is commonly impaired, and other language disturbances may also be involved. One distinguishing feature of this type of aphasia is the transient nature of the severe language defects seen in the early stages.[89] The neuropathology in subcortical aphasia has been found to vary in terms of localization. Most commonly, subcortical aphasia is associated with lesions in the thalamus, caudate, and putamen.[102]

Some inconsistent findings have raised questions about the role of subcortical damage in aphasia. For example, it has been noted that aphasia can resolve even in the presence of persisting subcortical abnormalities. Conversely, in some cases, aphasia does not follow damage to subcortical areas. In some instances, evidence from functional neuroimaging studies has been used to understand such discrepancies. PET studies reveal that structural damage in an area might result in hypometabolism in distant, intact areas. Metter and coworkers[103] found that aphasia was associated with the presence of cortical hypometabolism after structural lesions in subcortical areas. Thus, there is some suggestion that changes in cortical hypometabolism accompanying subcortical lesions might be a factor associated with the presence or absence of aphasia rather than the lesion in the subcortical region.

Alexia

Alexia refers to impairments in the ability to read and comprehend written language. Although it can occur in the presence of aphasia, it can also be a relatively circumscribed defect associated with specific lesions. It is distinguished from dyslexia in that alexia is an acquired inability to read, caused by brain damage. In contrast, dyslexia is a developmental disorder of reading in childhood that typically occurs in the presence of normal intellectual abilities. Historically, Dejerine classified alexia into two main subtypes: alexia with agraphia and alexia without agraphia. This classification is still being used, but other varieties of alexia have been introduced. Detailed descriptions of various alexic syndromes by Benson[104] and colleagues are documented in the literature on alexia. Advances in cognitive neuroscience have led to further delineation of the reading disorders based not only on functional manifestations and neuroanatomy but also on operations at the levels of orthographical, phonological, lexical, and semantic processing. Models of reading as elaborated by Friedman and colleagues[105] clearly reflect the more current trends. Following a classification strategy based on syndromes, the major subtypes of alexia as classified by Benson and Geschwind[87] are summarized in this section.

Alexia without agraphia (also termed posterior alexia or pure alexia) is the inability to read written material while writing remains intact. Although the ability to read visually presented material is lost, the ability to decode words through auditory mechanisms may be preserved. Hence, if words are spelled out aloud or the individual has some persevered ability for letter-by-letter reading, some degree of compensation is possible.[105] The location of the damage involves the left occipital lobe, specifically, the pathways that connect the visual and language systems.[106] The primary visual input area and secondary visual association cortex are disconnected from the angular gyrus (inferior parietal lobule, area 39), which is part of the frontotemporoparietal language system that is responsible for integrating visual, auditory, and tactile information. Alexia has also been found to accompany blindness in the right visual field (right hemianopia) caused by lesions involving the splenium of the corpus callosum. In such cases, there is inability to read in the right visual field. The damage also results in a disconnection of visual input in the right visual cortex from the language processing areas of the left side.[106] Thus, when material is presented in the left visual field, the right hemisphere may be intact to receive input from the left field, but the damage to the splenium precludes transfer of this information to the left temporoparietal region, including the angular gyrus, for the processing of language to be carried out.

Alexia with agraphia (central alexia) is the inability to produce and comprehend written language. In some cases, alexia with agraphia might be associated with aspects of other language impairment, such as anomia, or even an entire aphasic syndrome, such as Wernicke's or transcortical sensory aphasia. In fact, it was mentioned earlier in reference to Wernicke's aphasia that some individuals with Wernicke's aphasia exhibit more severe deficits in the comprehension of written material compared with spoken material. In alexia with agraphia, damage is located in the angular gyrus itself and the surrounding inferior parietal region of the dominant hemisphere.

Among the other variants of alexia, Benson and Geschwind[87] have included third alexia and deep alexia. Third alexia (anterior alexia) is characterized by inability to comprehend syntactic structure, particularly of sentences. This type of alexia is often seen together with Broca's aphasia, which involves defects in the comprehension of syntactic structure. Lesions causing this type of alexia are located in the posterior inferior frontal cortex, often including subcortical regions. Deep dyslexia is characterized by substitution errors in reading involving whole words, a condition that is also termed semantic paralexia. The underlying pathology involves extensive damage to the language region.

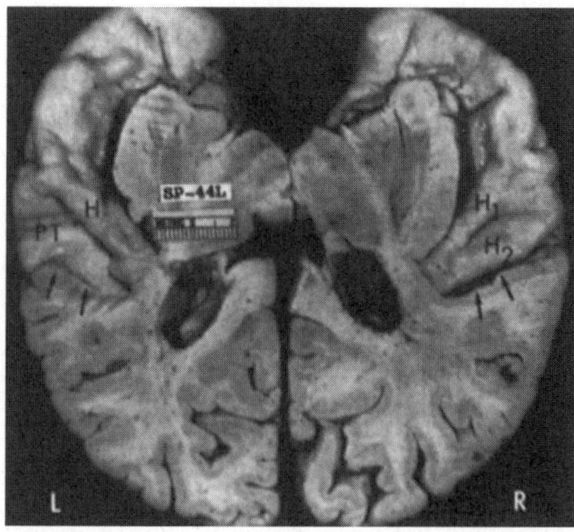

Figure 16–11 *The upper surfaces of the temporal lobes (supratemporal planes), illustrating the most typical type of asymmetry in the planum temporale (PT)—namely, larger on the left side. The arrows denote the posterior (inferior in figure) borders of the PT. Note that the right PT, which lies posterior to H_2, is extremely narrow. A doubling or bifurcation of Heschl's gyrus (H) into two rostrocaudal segments (H_1 and H_2) is more common on the right side. (From Galaburda AM: Anatomical asymmetries. In Geschwind N, Galaburda AM [eds]: Cerebral Dominance: The Biological Foundations. Cambridge, MA: Harvard University Press, 1984:11–25.)*

Concepts of Neuroanatomical Dominance and Localization in Language

Dominance

As previously noted, Broca's discovery of the connection between aphasia and damage to the left hemisphere was the precursor of all contemporary investigations of the structural and functional organization of the brain. Broca pointed out the significance of the left inferior frontal area, and Wernicke predicted the importance of the left temporoparietal region. The early localizationist theories of Broca and Wernicke were subsequently challenged by holist theories that proposed that the different linguistic functions were not linked to specific regions; rather, there was one central language system. In the mid-1960s, the localizationist view was revived when Geschwind pointed out the evidence for cortical-cortical disconnections and their relationship to brain functions.

Geschwind and colleagues[107–109] have provided compelling evidence for anatomical asymmetries, including asymmetry for language. In their study of 100 human brains, Geschwind and Levitsky[108] confirmed an earlier documented observation of asymmetry in the left planum temporale, which is related to linguistic functioning. They found that the planum on the left side was larger in 67% of adult brains and was about 1 cm longer and one third larger in area. Galaburda and colleagues[109] have further pointed out that rather than just the simple fact of gross anatomical asymmetry, it is the extent of the cytoarchitectonic regions involved that is important in determining the neuroanatomical substrate for dominance for language. Galaburda and colleagues also mapped the extent of these areas in the planum and its environs and found that the volume of the temporoparietal cortex on the left side was seven times larger than that on the right side (Fig. 16–11).

In the past two decades, functional mapping studies of language disorders have clearly established dominance of the left hemisphere for language functions through the use of radiological techniques. Compelling evidence for dominance of the left side has come from the studies of Bellugi and colleagues[110–112] on language disorders in deaf individuals. Bellugi and coworkers[110] found that left side lesions in deaf individuals who used American Sign Language resulted in aphasia and a loss of ability to sign. Corina and associates[111] found that although there was left side lateralization for both spoken and sign language, there was no asymmetry for other types of gestures, such as symbolic gestures (goodbyes) or arbitrary gestures. This suggests that signing in deaf language is separate from nonlinguistic movement. In another study, Haglund and colleagues[112] found that the left hemisphere was the cortical site for various aspects of linguistic ability in deaf individuals, including comprehension of American Sign Language and hand shape formation in sign language.

Studies of the relationship between handedness and dominance for language have suggested that in about 98% to 99% of right-handed individuals the left side is dominant for language. About 1% to 2% of right-handed individuals show right side dominance.[113] This reversed pattern of dominance (i.e., right side dominance) is therefore considered to be exceptional and has been reported in a few studies.[114] Benson and Geschwind[87] noted that some authors have suggested that left-handed individuals tend to have either right or left side dominance with more than half (about two thirds) showing evidence for left side dominance. On the other hand, other authors have suggested that individuals who indicate a preference for their left hand have bilateral hemispherical involvement.

Investigations of the role of the right hemisphere in right-handed individuals have shown its mediation in aspects of paralinguistic functions, including prosody, vocal inflection, melodic aspects of speech, stress, and affective processing of language.[115, 116] Lesions on the right side have been found to result in aprosodia, with an anterior lesion being related to the quality of production and a posterior lesion being associated with disturbance in the comprehension of the affective components of spoken language.[116] One PET study of the comprehension of metaphorical sentences found the expected activation of sites in the left side but, in addition, found activation in various sites of the right hemisphere. This suggests involvement of the right side in figurative aspects of linguistic tasks.[117]

Localization

Although the issue of neuroanatomical dominance for language abilities in right-handed adults has been more or less settled for many years, the debate over localization has evolved into new directions. One classical approach to localization has been syndromic, with attempts made to find structural substrates for each of the subtypes of aphasia. This method involves lesion-syndrome correlations.[118]

However, although classification of aphasia in terms of syndromes has great clinical utility, some authors have pointed out that there are theoretical problems with this approach.[119] Perusal of even the brief descriptions of the aphasia subtypes in the preceding section suggests two problems with respect to the use of the lesion-syndrome correlational method for localization: 1) a given impairment associated with a particular syndrome may or may not occur in different individual cases, and 2) the same impairment might fall into more than one subtype. Thus, first, there are individual differences in the dissociation between functions even within a syndrome. Second, despite different neuropathologies, two subtypes of aphasia might have overlapping sets of impairments. This variability in the patterns of impairment might account for some of the variability in lesion sites associated with the syndromes, that is, the failure to find clear-cut correlations between a syndrome and a lesion site.

In one large-scale study, Willmes and Poeck[120] found that the association between the type of aphasia and localization of lesion was not clear-cut. They concluded that this lack of one-to-one correspondence between syndrome and lesion reflects deviations that cannot simply be explained in terms of exceptions from the rule. They also found that over time patients' symptom patterns changed, leading to diagnostic changes. Thus, they proposed that rather than a static association between sets of symptoms and specific lesions, the dynamic course of the nature of both lesions and impairments should be considered.

An approach to localization that has yielded an extensive literature on neuroanatomical correlates of language focuses on specific linguistic functions and processes. As stated earlier, this approach uses data from lesion-deficit correlational studies, and functional neuroimaging techniques have further made it possible to identify brain regions that are activated during the performance of language tasks even in normal individuals. In the past few years, investigations into the neural correlates of specific functions, such as naming, comprehension, and reading, have led to the well-established conclusion that these functions are not unitary. Rather, they are complex language processes that involve various components of language, including phonology, lexicon, syntax, and semantics. Thus, the new direction in localization research involves attempts to find the loci for specific language operations within the various component processes and, in turn, to map these components onto brain regions.

Current Developments

Evidence from various sources has clearly established that linguistic functions are multifaceted in terms of both neural mechanisms and components of processing. As a result, impairment of a function does not involve global loss; instead, there are selective patterns of dissociation even between aspects of a specific linguistic function. This finding has given rise to the view that the various aspects of a function have corresponding neural mechanisms that are localized in different regions of the brain. The different regions are interconnected in ways that are thought of as forming neural networks. A breakdown in their connections results in selective patterns of dissociation. Because these networks can involve distant regions of the brain, the earlier ideas of localization of a function in terms of dichotomous subdivisions such as anterior versus posterior and sensory versus motor regions are now considered untenable. In addition, the patterns of dissociation suggest differential breakdown of the interconnections between levels of processing. Some of the patterns of dissociation observed in functions such as word finding and comprehension are presented to elucidate the involvement of different regions.

Although word-finding deficits can be part of an aphasic syndrome or might constitute a fairly circumscribed impairment, many different patterns of naming deficits have been documented in the literature. This finding has suggested that defects in naming are subserved by different regions of the brain. Most commonly, naming difficulties are associated with damage in posterior regions, including the left posterior temporal and inferior parietal cortex.[83, 86] Mesulam[86] pointed out that word-finding deficits associated with damage in Wernicke's area are more severe than naming impairments caused by lesions in other areas. With respect to the nature of the lexical defect associated with this region, it is thought that the words themselves may not be lost but the ability to access the lexicon to find the correct word that best matches the intended meaning is compromised.[83, 86] Thus, Mesulam posited that Wernicke's area lies on the "lexical-semantic pole" of language processing. Damasio and Damasio[83] also pointed out that damage in the posterior perisylvian regions impairs the ability to arrange phonemes into words, as well as to select words, resulting in phonemic and paraphasic errors.

The posterior perisylvian cortex is considered to be important for word finding and lexical processing, but there is also evidence for the involvement of anterior regions. Impaired ability to initiate words can also be due to defects in articulatory programming as seen in patients with anterior lesions (such as Broca's aphasia or transcortical motor aphasia).[87] Further evidence for both anterior and posterior involvement comes from investigations of category-related word deficits. Many researchers have been studying word deficit profiles, which has led to an increased specificity in linking impairments in particular classes of words with specific regions. These studies have examined the patterns of localization for various categories of word forms and concepts, including common and proper nouns, verbs, adjectives, color, animate versus inanimate objects, and concepts for activities, events, and experiences.[83, 121–123]

Lexical deficits involving nouns (both common and proper) have been associated with damage in the posterior perisylvian region.[83, 122, 123] Conversely, it has been suggested that damage to anterior regions (left frontal) compromises the production of verbs.[83, 122–124] These studies thus present evidence for a double dissociation between verbs and nouns and anterior and posterior lesions. The evidence that naming difficulties can be localized in both anterior and posterior regions clearly challenges the earlier anterior-posterior dichotomy with respect to expressive deficits.[86]

Damasio and Damasio[83] reported the case of a patient (named Boswell) with lesions in the anterior and middle temporal lobes. He had word-finding deficits involving proper and common nouns (including names of people, places, animals) but was intact with respect to adjectives (concepts such as beautiful, ugly), states and activities (love, jumping, swimming), abstract relational concepts (above, under, before), and even nouns such as wrench, an object with action-oriented representation; he was also intact with respect to syntax. In another patient (KJ-1360) who had a lesion in the left frontal region (left premotor cortex, specifically), Damasio and Tranel[123] noted that the retrieval of nouns was intact but the retrieval of verbs was impaired.

Efforts to map naming defects (both within and across several categories) onto brain regions have suggested that the names for a wide variety of objects and living things have different neural substrates.[122] For example, dissociations between proper nouns and common nouns have been noted. Damasio[94] noted that a defective retrieval of proper nouns was associated with lesions in the left temporal pole (area 38) and medial temporal surface; when the retrieval of both common and proper nouns was impaired, the lesions included the lateral and inferior temporal lobe (areas 20 and 21). Damage to the left occipital region was associated with an impaired ability for a wide range of nouns and for naming colors.[83] The fact that patterns of deficit are not internally consistent within conceptual categories has led to several attempts to interpret factors that might account for these differential patterns of deficits.

For example, Warrington and Shallice[121] reported some cases of patients who had more difficulty with naming living things and food than with naming inanimate objects. Rapp and Caramazza[125] noted some of the interpretations for this differential breakdown within animate and inanimate categories. Thus, it has been suggested that the dissociation between names for animate and inanimate objects might occur in terms of neural representations for factors such as complexity and familiarity[126] or sensory-specific features.[121] In one case, Warrington and Shallice[121] observed that the names of objects that were better preserved had distinct sensory features (color, shape), whereas representations of inanimate objects rely on "functional attributes." Other authors also suggest that representations of certain objects (such as concrete nouns) might rely on visual aspects, whereas representations of action words (concrete verbs) might rely on motor images (e.g., Goldberg[64]). Rapp and Caramazza[125] argued that the sensory-specific hypothesis is not entirely satisfactory because the wide range of impairments observed within categories cannot be fully explained in terms of this hypothesis. They suggested that the selective patterns of dissociation within categories might occur in terms of some objects having similarities in meaning (semantic features) because of shared features; for example, both fruits and vegetables might be associated with plants. Such interpretations are at best only hypotheses that need to be further investigated.

As in the case of naming, studies have found that comprehension of language also involves multiple neuroanatomical regions. For the comprehension of auditory input, information is processed through areas of the temporal lobe, including the auditory association cortices, angular gyrus, and Wernicke's area. However, the involvement of anterior regions (particularly Broca's) in the comprehension of syntactic structure of sentences has also been noted by several authors.[83, 86, 127] Thus, Mesulam[86] pointed out that Broca's area lies on the "syntactic-articulatory" pole of the language processing network. In one study,[127] PET activity was assessed while normal college students engaged in three tasks in which they had to judge whether sentences were acceptable or unacceptable. Tasks 1 and 2 involved both the construction and assignation of meaning to the syntactic structure of sentences (task 1 also involved increased memory processing). In task 3 they were required to read the words but not construct the syntactic structure or assign its meaning. Subtraction of PET activity in task 2 from that in task 1 showed increased activation in pars opercularis of Broca's area. It is of note that this evidence supporting an involvement of Broca's area in syntactic comprehension contests the traditional anterior-posterior dichotomy with respect to receptive language.

Current Model of Language

In the past decade, neurolinguistic research has been greatly influenced by the application of cognitive theories and computational models to the study of language processes. Combined with functional neuroimaging techniques, these methodologies have enabled the analyses of much smaller units of language processing. The evidence has led to the development of the current information-processing or PDP model for language that has supplemented the traditional Wernicke-Geschwind model as well as earlier cognitive models of language.

The traditional Wernicke-Geschwind model was more anatomically based and reflected a view of language functioning in terms of interconnections and disconnections between hierarchically arranged regions of the brain. According to this view, language was processed through a serial flow of information in the interconnecting pathways and cortical regions. For example, in a simple repetition task, the information flows through the following pathways: auditory input received by the auditory apparatus passes through the medial geniculate nucleus, primary auditory cortex (Brodmann's 41), and higher order auditory cortex (area 42) to the angular gyrus (area 39) and Wernicke's area (area 22). Thereupon, the arcuate fasciculus transfers the information to Broca's area, where syntactic processing and articulatory programming for production take place.

The application of cognitive theories to neuropsychological processes led to the development of information-processing models for language (as for other mental activities). However, the earlier models also tended to posit that information traversed across regions and across levels of processing (phonological, syntactic, semantic) in a serial fashion.

Within the framework of the current PDP model, linguistic operations are considered to be performed in more complex ways. One feature that characterizes this model is that any given task is thought to involve many operations that are localized within the various components of language (e.g., orthographical, semantic, phonetic, syntactic). These components, in turn, are subserved by different regions in the brain; that is, they are distributed.[128] Investigations in this area therefore entail two stages: first, an attempt is made to locate the operations within the components or levels of processing; second, attempts are made to map these components onto specific brain areas. A second feature of this model is that it posits a view that the various linguistic operations that constitute performance are carried out interactively through various routes in a parallel, concurrent, and simultaneous fashion. At least, in normal or near-normal performance this is the case. In defective language processing, the flow of information through the expected routes is disturbed. As suggested earlier, the concept of parallel processing emerged from a realization that the notion of a serial transfer of information did not account for the rapidity with which mental processes are carried out.

Given the complexity of linguistic phenomena and the technical and methodological limitations involved in applying a heuristic computational model to the empirical analyses of language processes, this field of inquiry is still in its infancy. However, to provide a flavor of some of the developments in the area of neurolinguistic research, a few aspects of some current investigations are described here.

Work in the area of reading elucidates some of the efforts being made to understand the manner in which the processing operations involved might be accounted for within a PDP framework. Friedman and colleagues[105] have proposed two networks involved in a reading model. One network links the orthographical and phonological systems (orthographical-phonological), and in the second network, orthographical and phonological systems are mediated by the semantic system (orthographical-semantic-phonological). Friedman and associates[105] noted that with the presentation of a word to the visual modality, a process of visual analysis ensues by which visual features are analyzed. Whereas a child beginning to read identifies letters in a serial order and from left to right, a skilled reader processes the letter identities in an automatic and parallel fashion. This letter identification then activates orthographical units, which, in turn, are connected to semantic and phonological units.

The PDP model presupposes that there are multiple routes within the networks involved in reading.[105, 128] Thus, one route is presumed to link the orthographical and semantic levels directly, bypassing phonology. In fact, Posner and coworkers[128] pointed out that skilled reading involves this route. Another route involves phonological mediation so that visually presented words have to be sounded out, which in turn activates the meaning code (orthographical-phonological-semantic). Alternatively, mediation may also be achieved between orthography and phonology via semantics. Yet another route links orthography and phonology so that words can be at least read out loud even if they are not understood.

Thus, within the framework of a PDP model, varieties of reading deficits can be accounted for in terms of defects at one level of the network or a dissociation between the interconnecting routes. In fact, the influence of the PDP model is clearly seen in the classification of alexia by Friedman and associates.[105] Thus, pure alexia is thought of as involving a defect in the automatic, parallel processing of letters by the visual analysis system.[105] Because the PDP model posits many other routes within the network, a defect in the automatic visual analysis may be compensated by the involvement of the phonological system so that letters can be sounded out to further process the word, a strategy termed letter-by-letter reading. In another type of reading problem, words can be pronounced without being comprehended, which is considered to be the result of a possible dissociation between the orthographical and semantic systems.

Whereas investigators such as Friedman and coworkers[105] presented a PDP view of reading in terms of the component processes in the major networks, the studies of Petersen and colleagues[128–130] on single-word reading, using PET technology, have focused on the localization of operations at a neural level. In these studies, patterns of PET activation are assessed while subjects perform a variety of reading operations. Some findings from the studies of Petersen and colleagues that relate to one level of processing, visual analysis of words, are described here. The involvement of areas of the extrastriate visual cortex in visual processing has been reported in some PET studies. Petersen and coworkers[129] found that in a task that required passive attention to visually presented nouns, areas of the extrastriate visual cortex showed bilateral activation. In another study, Petersen and Fiez[130] further attempted to determine the specific reading operations that might have caused the activations in this area. Specifically, they tried to determine whether the extrastriate visual cortex was activated by simply observing visual features or by processing at some other higher level, which might involve analysis of letters, letter-like stimuli, recognizable words, and word-like visual stimuli. Subjects were shown real common nouns, strings of letter-like forms (false font), strings of random consonants (letter-string stimuli), and pseudowords that followed spelling rules of typical English words but were not real words. Presentations of all types of visual stimuli gave rise to lateral activations in the extrastriate regions of the hemispheres, but a differential activation pattern was also found. Thus, the findings revealed that the left medial extrastriate cortex showed activation for both real words and pseudowords but not for the two types of letter-string stimuli. According to the authors, this finding suggests that the left medial region in the extrastriate cortex is involved in processing combinations of letters at the level of orthographical analysis.

Neurodevelopmental Aspects of Language

Any description of the relationship between the brain and language would be incomplete without entering into some neurodevelopmental aspects of language. As a comprehensive discussion of this subject is beyond the scope of this section, the focus is on presenting central theoretical issues. Some of these issues help shed light on the ways in which the brain is organized for language in children. For discussions of language disorders in children, the reader is referred to Yule and Rutter.[131]

Language Acquisition

One central issue addresses the notion of the innateness of language. Interest in this concept was stimulated by the pioneering work of Chomsky,[132] who espoused the view of an innate human capacity to know the universal rules of grammar. Chomsky drew attention to the fact that despite differences in the languages of the world, all human languages have the same universal features. Consequently, learning a language is something that "happens" to a child.[132]

The fact that there are universal regularities in the acquisition of language supports the notion of an innate capacity. Thus, according to Lenneberg,[133, 134] an infant's language capabilities are linked with physical maturation and there is therefore a correlation between language development and motor development. Thus, by about 15 months of age, when the motor milestone of self-propulsive gait is attained, an infant has a vocabulary of 3 to 50 words; by 18 to 24 months, when a child begins to run (with falls), many two-word utterances are observed.[134, 135] By about 3 to 4 years of age, a child acquires the capability for many fully grammatical utterances.[136]

Research on the linguistic capabilities of neonates is an area of interest in studying language acquisition. There is evidence to suggest that quite young infants can discriminate between linguistic and nonlinguistic stimuli.[137] Mehler and colleagues[138] also reported evidence that neonates as young as 4 days old have a preference for listening to their mothers' language as determined by increased sucking when listening to the maternal language. Furthermore, 4-day-old infants can also discriminate between two unfamiliar languages. In contrast, although 2-month-old infants showed a preference for their mothers' language, they did not show the same ability to discriminate between unfamiliar languages. These authors interpreted this to mean that younger infants have a sensitivity to certain aspects (e.g., prosody) of all utterances to which they are exposed, wherease older ones tend to concentrate on languages whose structure is similar to the maternal language and neglect dissimilar utterances.

In the literature dealing with the issue of language acquisition, much consideration has been given to the relative influences of genetic and environmental factors. Individual differences in performance raise questions about the relative contributions of these factors in language acquisition. On the one hand, it has been thought that if language is indeed an innate capacity with associated neural mechanisms, then language functions and malfunctions must also have a genetic basis.

Evidence for a genetic basis has come from many sources, especially from research in the area of developmental language disorders. Based on a review of relevant studies, Stromswold[136] reported the finding of a higher incidence of language impairment in families of children with developmental disorders than in families of children without such impairment. Familial aggregation with respect to language disorders has frequently been noted in dyslexia, a developmental reading disorder. Pennington[139] noted that in some studies the estimates of familial risk for dyslexia ranged from 35% to 40%. Although familial aggregation can be due to both genetic and environmental factors, the evidence from twin studies tends to support the view of a strong heritability factor in dyslexia.[139] For example, in one study, which used a multiple regression model to determine the influence of both genetic and environmental factors, Defries and coworkers[140] found that in 64 pairs of monozygotic twins and 55 pairs of dizygotic twins, the contribution of hereditable factors was about 30%; this estimate was noted to have risen to 50% with the accrual of additional data.[139] Other twin studies have reported higher concordance rates for monozygotic twins (ranging between 82% to 86%) compared with dizygotic twins (ranging from 48% to 56%) with respect to language disorders.[141, 142]

With respect to the view of language as an innate capacity, it is generally believed that language can be acquired without explicit instruction. For example, Stromswold[136] reported that even children who are unable to speak and therefore cannot be corrected are capable of acquiring normal receptive language. In addition to the evidence that supports genetic contributions to language functions and dysfunctions, there is indirect support for the role of environmental exposure from studies of individuals raised in severely deprived environments. Studies of "wild" children raised in conditions of extreme linguistic, social, and emotional deprivation essentially suggested an innate hypothesis for language acquisition but also suggested that the environment can have some modifying influences.

Curtiss[143] studied the case of Genie, who was found at the age of 13 years 7 months after a period of 12 years of deprivation. During this time, she was subjected to conditions of not only profound deprivation but also extreme abuse by her father. She was physically restrained in a "potty-chair" for most of the day and at night was tied to a sleeping bag. She was punished for even the slightest vocalization. Even after being discovered and rehabilitated, Genie had severe language impairments. Although she made progress with comprehension, she had almost no expressive language skills. However, it has been noted that Curtiss did not comment on the structural organization of the left hemisphere. Curtiss[144] also studied the case of Chelsea, a deaf woman who was linguistically but not socially deprived until the age of 32 and even after speech and language training continued to have significant linguistic impairment. Skuse[145, 146] reviewed nine cases of children subjected to profound deprivation that affected many developmental aspects by the time they were discovered. After some years of rehabilitation, however, most of the children made significant progress in terms of language acquisition with the exception of Genie. The fact that Genie's linguistic deprivation had been for the longest period and extended into puberty supports the notion of a critical period for language development.[133, 143]

Brain Organization and Language Development

It is thought that if language is indeed an innate capacity, there must be a neural basis for this capacity that is present from birth. In this regard, there has been some debate about the concepts of equipotentiality and differential lateralization at birth.

Equipotentiality of the brain for language means that both sides are capable of performing linguistic functions. Equipotentiality also suggests plasticity of the brain and a capacity for reorganization even after injury so that language functions can be transferred from one hemisphere to the other. Indeed, lesion data for childhood aphasia and earlier reports of hemispherectomy studies have suggested functional recovery with respect to language until puberty, as evidenced by ipsilateral and contralateral transfer of linguistic functions. Thus, it has been reported that if there is damage to the left side in infancy but the right side remains intact, the child can still develop normal language.[134, 147]

In early childhood, after the onset of language but before age 4 years, damage to the language areas results in transient aphasia. After puberty, by about age 14 years, the prognosis begins to worsen, and similar lesions in adulthood can cause irreversible deficits.[133, 134] There is some disagreement about the extent of recovery after left hemispherectomy even in children.[148] Nevertheless, the findings do appear to suggest that the recovery is better when the damage is earlier rather than later.[136]

Some authors, such as Lenneberg,[133] have taken these findings about the capacity for transfer of function in young children to mean that the brain is symmetrically organized to begin with and only gradually becomes asymmetrically specialized, resulting in a diminished capacity for recovery with age. However, there is now increasing evidence that the brain is asymmetrical with respect to linguistic ability from birth. In fact, the planum temporale, which Geschwind and Levitsky[108] found to be larger on the left side in adult brains, has also been found to be larger on the left side as early as the 29th week of gestation.[149] Dichotic listening studies have shown a right ear (left hemisphere) advantage for speech sounds (syllables) and a left ear (right hemisphere) advantage for musical sounds in 4-month-old infants[150] as well as 4-day-old neonates.[151]

If the brain is lateralized for linguistic functions from birth, a question arises about the evidence for greater recoverability of language when damage occurs early enough in life. One interpretation of this recoverability is that there is greater neuroplasticity in the young brain, as evident from the capacity of surviving neurons to make new synaptic connections even after injury.

Lenneberg's view of the critical period for language development (from birth to the early teens) was that both hemispheres are involved in language functions at first, but by puberty the left becomes more specialized. A later view relates the concept of critical period to the notion of neural plasticity. In any case, it is thought that the critical period is correlated with innate mechanisms, and that language development is most susceptible to the limiting effects of both biological and environmental factors if these extend beyond this critical period.

Executive Functioning and the Frontal Lobes

Historical Overview

Early discussions concerning frontal lobe function revolved around stormy debates about whether the frontal association cortex subserved the highest intellectual and moral function. Most researchers now agree that the study of frontal lobes represents an important aspect of humans' higher mental functions, which are often referred to as executive processes.

Historically, some of the earliest documented interest in frontal lobe functioning was precipitated by observed behavioral and personality changes in individuals after frontal lobe damage. One can scarcely engage in dialogue concerning the impact of frontal lobe injury without being reminded of the well-publicized case of Phineas Gage.[152] Gage had survived an explosion that blasted a 3 foot 7 inch iron tamping bar through the front of his head. His injury affected primarily the left frontal lobe from the medial orbital region upward to the precentral region. Before this accident, Gage was described as being of average intelligence and was "energetic and persistent in executing all his plans of operation."[153(p439)] The following is a description of his personality after trauma:

> The equilibrium or balance, so to speak, between his intellectual faculties and animal propensities seems to have been destroyed. He is fitful, irreverent, indulging at times in the grossest profanity, manifesting but little deference for his fellows, impatient of restraint or advice when it conflicts with his desires, at times pertinaciously obstinate, yet capricious and vacillating, devising many plans of operation, which are no sooner arranged then they are abandoned in turn for others appearing more feasible. A child in his intellectual capacity and manifestations, he has the animal passions of a strong man.[154(p153)]

Patients with frontal lobe damage have been studied extensively in the past century, leading to descriptions of numerous abnormalities and theories concerning frontal lobe functioning. The quest to understand the nature of the frontal lobes has been aided by increasingly sophisticated neuroradiological, electroencephalographic, and neurophysiological techniques. In addition, a proliferation of animal research, particularly employing primates, has allowed direct observation of frontal anatomy via ablations, dissections, and various neurobehavioral and neurophysiological manipulations.

Anatomical Connectivity

The frontal lobes of the human brain comprise all the tissue anterior to the central sulcus. Four major subdivisions of the frontal lobes have been suggested: 1) the motor area, 2) the premotor area, 3) the prefrontal area, and 4) the basomedial portion of the lobes.[155] The motor area or motor strip occupies the precentral gyrus and is responsible for execution of motor movement. Damage to this area may result in paralysis, a plight often seen in patients suffering from cerebrovascular accidents. The premotor area lies anterior to the motor area and serves to integrate motor components for the accomplishment of complex acts. The latter two subdivisions are often considered as one prefrontal region, often simply referred to as the prefrontal cortex.

Two prefrontal areas, namely, the orbitomedial prefrontal cortex and the dorsolateral prefrontal cortex, have been targeted in much of the research concerning executive processes. Most generally, dorsolateral damage has been associated with impairment in the regulation and integration of cognitive activities. Disruption to emotional and social functioning is frequently seen with damage to the orbitomedial areas of the prefrontal cortex. Walsh[155] further delineated the roles of the orbital and medial aspects of the frontal cortex and pointed out that the former is most associated with ongoing behavior and the latter with the initiation and maintenance of activity.

The importance of the frontal lobes for human activity is reflected in their neuroanatomy. The frontal lobes in humans are far larger than those in any other animals, including the higher primates,[156] constituting roughly one third of the human cerebral cortex.[6, 157] The functional role of the frontal system in providing executive control to behavior is probably related to the extensive reciprocal anatomical connectivity between the frontal lobes and other brain regions involved in information processing. Numerous afferent and efferent connections of the frontal lobe have been demonstrated. The extracortical and transcortical connections of the frontal lobes are exceedingly complex, especially where the prefrontal cortex is involved.[158] Although there are many unanswered questions regarding neural connectivity, a number of elaborate models based primarily on primate research have been proposed. In general, brain connectivity encompasses three major types: cortical-cortical, thalamic-cortical, and subcortical-cortical (Fig. 16–12). The following is a synopsis of the major connections between the frontal lobe and the rest of the brain. For a detailed review of brain connectivity, the reader is referred to the works of Pandya and Yeterian[159] and Goldman-Rakic.[7]

Cortical-cortical connections of the frontal lobes take on a number of distinct forms.[158] First, as previously mentioned, connections within the frontal lobes themselves involve projections from tertiary cortex in the prefrontal areas to the premotor cortex and to the motor cortex. Second, there are reciprocal connections between the prefrontal cortex (Brodmann's areas 8, 9, and 46) and the temporal, auditory, and visual association regions, as well as the medial temporal lobes. Third, there is another set of reciprocal connections connecting the prefrontal areas and the anterior and medial temporal regions. Fourth, there are connections between prefrontal areas and the limbic system, including a reciprocal connection between the amygdala and the frontal lobe.

Thalamic-cortical connections include projections to the prefrontal lobe from the pulvinar, anterior nuclei, and dorsomedial nucleus of the thalamus. In addition, via the dorsomedial nucleus, information from limbic areas and the hypothalamus is relayed to the frontal lobes for processing of emotions and internal states.

Subcortical-cortical connections include projections from the frontal cortex to various subcortical structures including the caudate nucleus, superior colliculus, and hypothalamus. Particular attention has been paid to the interconnectivity of the frontal lobe and basal ganglia via the corticostriate projection system. Lesions in either area are associated with similar cognitive impairments, such as decreased cognitive flexibility or set switching.[160]

Examination of the connectivity of the frontal lobes has revealed that the pattern of connectivity is best viewed from within the context of a parallel and distributed anatomical network. In a series of experiments using a double-labeling paradigm, Goldman-Rakic[7] and colleagues (Fig. 16–13) have found that association cortices are connected with other brain regions in parallel. For example, the dorsolateral prefrontal cortex projects to multiple brain regions in parallel with posterior parietal association cortex. As discussed earlier, this type of connectivity has significant functional implications for processes such as spatial working memory.

Development

The human frontal lobes are the latest area to develop, reflecting a unique phylogenetic status on the evolutionary ladder. In terms of brain maturation, a number of studies have suggested a hierarchical progression of development that begins with primary sensory and motor areas and ends with the maturation of association and prefrontal regions around the time of puberty or beyond.[161] Support for a hierarchical pattern of development is suggested by research on a number of aspects of the brain including morphology, myelination, metabolism, and electrophysiological activity.[162–164] As one might expect given the complexity of the brain, there is evidence of a hierarchical pattern of development within specific areas of the brain, such as the frontal lobes, as well. For example, Yakovlev[162] found evidence that the orbital prefrontal areas of the brain mature before the dorsolateral regions.

Evidence for columnar organization and synaptogenesis[165, 166] suggests that hierarchical development does not solely explain the entire brain maturation process. For example, when Rakic and colleagues[166] investigated the initial development of synaptogenesis, they found that simultaneous development of this process occurred in all cell layers and areas of the cortex studied. Therefore, it may be naive to assume that specific regions related to certain

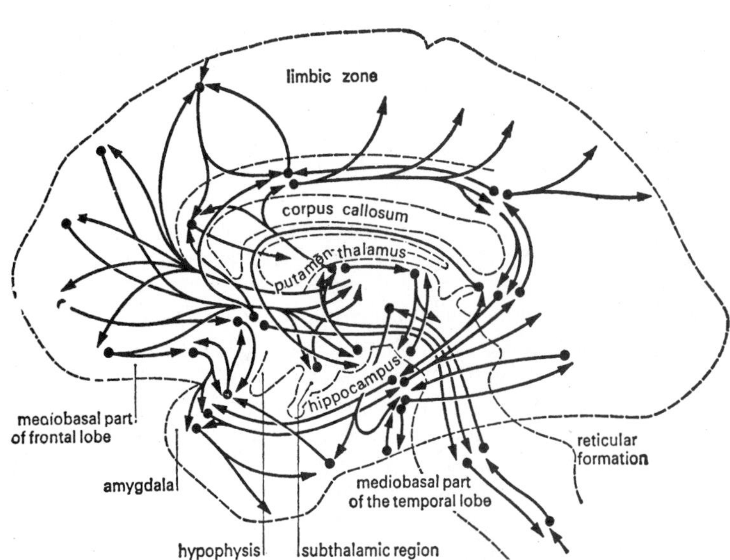

Figure 16–12 *Illustration of some of the patterns of frontal lobe connectivity. (From Luria AR: The Working Brain: An Introduction to Neuropsychology. London: Penguin Books, 1973:85.)*

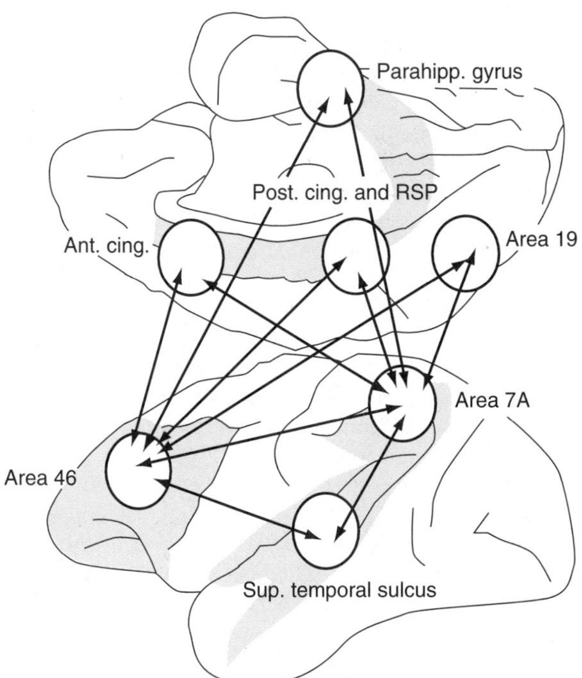

Figure 16–13 *Illustration of the parallel connectivity of the frontal and parietal regions. Area 46 and area 7A project to more than a dozen common targets; five of these areas are illustrated. (From Goldman-Rakic PS: Changing concepts of cortical connectivity: Parallel distributed cortical networks. In Rakic P, Singer W [eds]: Neurobiology of Neocortex. New York: John Wiley & Sons, 1988:187. Copyright 1988 John Wiley & Sons. Reprinted by permission of John Wiley & Sons, Ltd.)*

abilities follow a hierarchy of biological development alone. It may well be that a selective survival ensues based on behavioral demands.[161] Undoubtedly, the process of maturation involves a number of developmental principles, probably including an intimate interaction between behavior and biology.

What is known about the biological maturation of the brain has led to a plethora of research on progressive changes in the abilities of children. These studies have allowed further insight into the role of the frontal lobes through the association of structural changes with functional changes. The classical test for dorsolateral prefrontal cortex function in nonhuman primates and children is the delayed response task,[167] described earlier. Infant monkeys between 1 and 2 months of age performed poorly on delayed response tasks and their performance was similar to that of adult monkeys with prefrontal ablations.[168] By 4 months of age, the healthy monkeys were performing perfectly on tasks of this type. Likewise, there was a steady increase in performance with age in human infants, with perfect performance being mastered at approximately 12 to 18 months.[169] In a number of studies, changes in performance on delayed response tasks have been found to correlate with changes in electrical and metabolic activity of the frontal regions of the brain. Increases in frontal electroencephalographic activity in individual infants were observed at the time that each infant was improving on delayed response tasks.[170] Chugani and associates[171] have used PET to measure glucose uptake in localized regions of the brains of healthy, awake infants. They found that beginning around 8 months, glucose utilization increases specifically in the frontal cortex. Furthermore, this increase directly corresponds to increases in the performance of delayed response tasks.

The classical test for dorsolateral prefrontal cortex function in human adults is the Wisconsin Card Sorting Test (WCST).[172] In this task, the patient is presented with four target cards that have printed stimuli that differ with respect to number, color, and form. Subjects are then given a deck of cards and asked to match the cards to one of the target cards. The examiner provides feedback concerning whether or not the match was correct. It is the task of the subject to use that feedback to determine the correct sorting principle. To complicate matters, the correct sorting principle changes, without advance warning, after a number of correct matches are made. Here, as in delayed response tasks, the subject must flexibly switch to a new response or "sort," based on examiner feedback, after having been rewarded for a different response. The subject must remember which sorting criteria were most recently tried and found incorrect and which sorting criterion is now correct. The WCST is most often used to assess executive functioning in adults, although some studies have employed this test to assess progressive developmental change in children. It has generally been found that performance on the WCST peaks at approximately age 18 years, with a gradual improvement with age up until that point.[173] Improvement included a progressive lessening of perseverative responses and an increase in flexible thinking as children approached adulthood.

Numerous other neuropsychological instruments have been used to assess progressive changes in the frontal lobe functioning of children. In a study of 72 children between the ages of 3 and 8 years inclusive, Diamond[167] found a significant improvement on seven different measures of abilities associated with the frontal cortex, with a leveling off from 6 to 8 years of age. On all tests, the same pattern was found: progressive increases with age in the ability to inhibit preferred responses, execute a sequence of actions, and remember sequential information. These increased abilities may result from the child's increasing ability to use language to guide behaviors and put information in the proper sequence. There was also a strong positive relationship between electroencephalographic activity and ability to perform these tasks.[170] The striking similarity between cycles of electroencephalographical coherence and cycles of cognitive growth has been noted in other studies.[174] In general, there is strong evidence that a sequence of changes in the attentional, executive, and self-reflective processes of children occurs as they grow older that parallel changes in electroencephalographical coherence. Furthermore, findings overwhelmingly suggest that these changes are frontally mediated.

Theories of Frontal Lobe Functioning

Some of the influential theories of the role of the prefrontal cortex and behavior are discussed here (Table 16–2). All theories impute to the frontal lobes a functional role as an executive control system for other cognitive and motor processes. The theories differ with respect to the specific mechanisms involved and the extent to which cognitive and neuroanatomical parameters are delineated.

Some of the earliest theories of frontal lobe functioning were put forth before the advent of neuroimaging techniques and were largely based on behavioral sequelae of individuals with known frontal lobe damage. Miller and colleagues[175] proposed a test-operate-test-exit system of monitoring behavior based on feedback loops. In this theory, a fourfold division of brain function based on external and internal representations is proposed. The external representations include sensory modalities and their association areas, and internal representations consist of frontal association and limbic areas. Basic information is gathered by external representation areas, formed into sequences and plans by the limbic and subcortical areas, and stored in frontal regions where intentional behavior is commanded. In contrast to the test-operate-test-exit theory, which suggests that behavior begins in the posterior brain and is transferred to the frontal lobes, Teuber[176] postulated that the reverse may be true. He emphasized the role of the motor system in sensory function by suggesting that an anticipatory discharge travels from the motor to sensory areas in preparation for voluntary behaviors.

A number of workable models of mental functions have arisen from the neuropsychology literature. Many of these theories expanded on the work of Luria.[177] Luria proposed three functional brain units that have different neuroanatomical representations: 1) regulation and wakefulness of mental tone; 2) reception, analysis, and storage of information; and 3) programming, regulation, and verification of mental activity. The first brain unit, regulation and wakefulness of mental tone, is largely seated in the reticular activating system. Luria described this unit as being nonspecific in nature, setting the tone for all brain activity, unlike the more specific sensory or motor systems. Through activation from stimuli in the outside world, metabolic processes, and feedback from other brain areas, the reticular activating system exerts excitatory and inhibitory action on all sensory and motor functioning by regulating periods of wakefulness and sleep. The first functional unit works closely with higher levels of cortical functioning. The second functional unit, reception, analysis, and storage of information, is thought to be seated in the posterior cortex. In general terms, this functional unit captures the processes we commonly refer to as perception and memory. The processing of information is thought to proceed in a sequential and hierarchical manner via the primary, secondary, and tertiary zones. According to Luria, the third functional unit, programming, regulation, and verification of mental activity, occurs in the frontal lobes. This unit operates not only to create programs but also to evaluate them through feedback from the other two units. Through the vast connections among all brain areas, "the tertiary portions of the frontal lobes are in fact a super-structure above all parts of the cerebral cortex, so that they perform a far more universal function of regulation of behavior."[177(p89)]

Luria also proposed a hierarchical pattern of organization for both the anterior and posterior brain. He suggested that the posterior brain can be divided into primary (sensory), secondary (association), and tertiary (interpretive) cortices. The processing of incoming information becomes increasingly complete and elaborate as it proceeds successively through these areas. The primary areas are responsible for receiving information in its primary form, the secondary areas for synthesizing those elements into a functional organization, and the tertiary areas for integrating informa-

Table 16–2 Theories of Frontal Lobe Functioning

Basis	Author	Description
Psychological assessment	Miller, Gallanter, and Pribram[175]	Postulated test-operate-test-exit feedback loops by which the frontal lobe organizes and coordinates behaviors transferred from the posterior brain.
Psychological assessment	Teuber[176]	Postulated that anticipatory discharges travel from the frontal lobe to the posterior brain, influencing motor system and sensory functions.
Psychological or anatomical	Luria[177]	Postulated three brain units, each unit having different neuroanatomical representation. Unit 3 is located in frontal lobes and exerts regulatory functions over the behavior of the other two units in the posterior brain through interactive and sequential processing.
Psychological or information processing	Norman and Shallice[178]	Postulated that the frontal lobes primarily function as an SAS over cognitive units and schemas during nonroutine behavior.
Anatomical or animal studies	Fuster[157]	Postulated that frontal lobes generally function in the temporal integration of behavior through three subordinate functions: anticipation, provisional memory, and control of interference.
Neuroanatomical or animal studies	Goldman-Rakic[6]	Postulated that prefrontal cortex maintains a representational memory of symbolic, mnemonic, and sensory information from nonprefrontal areas. These memory units exert inhibitory and excitatory influences on behavior through PDP.
Neuroanatomical or computational neuroscience	Mesulam[86]	Postulated that the frontal lobes, through interconnectivity with other brain areas, exert executive control over neural networks subserving different information processing capacities via PDP.

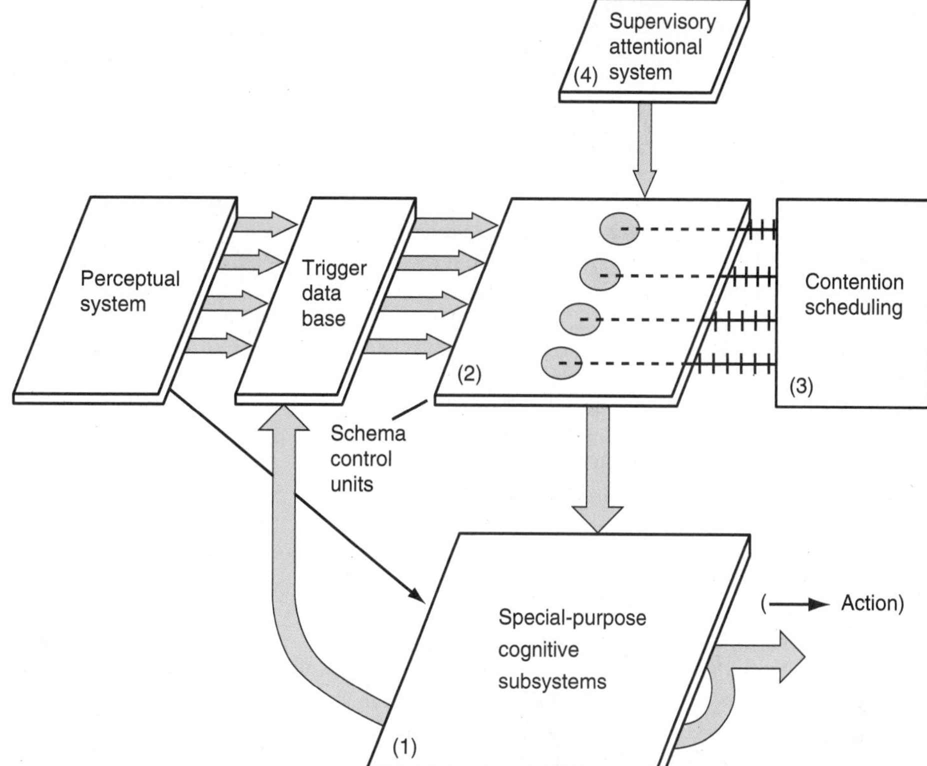

Figure 16–14 *Components of the Norman and Shallice[178] model for the supervisory attentional system. Thick dashed lines refer to control information, thin continuous lines refer to the specific information processed by special-purpose cognitive subsystems, and hatched lines refer to inhibitory interaction between the activation levels of schemas in contention scheduling. (From Shallice T, Burgess PW, Baxter DM, Schon F: The origins of utilisation behavior. Brain 1989; 112:1587–1598. By permission of Oxford University Press.)*

tion across modalities (e.g., visual, auditory) into complex schemes needed for higher level processing. For example, if one were to perceive an ordinary cube, the processing sequence would go something like this: perception of single lines in various orientations by primary visual cortex, synthesis of these lines into the configuration of a block by the secondary association areas, and integration of that configuration and input from other areas, such as language areas, which would result in correctly identifying the perception as a cube. In much the same manner as the posterior brain, Luria contended that the frontal lobes process information in a sequential and hierarchical manner with information proceeding from the prefrontal cortex (tertiary zone) and premotor cortex (secondary zone) to the motor cortex (primary zone). One interesting difference is that the progression of information in the anterior cortex occurs in descending order, beginning with the highest levels of activity and moving toward the more basic levels. This allows motor plans and programs to be formed by the prefrontal and premotor areas before execution by the motor cortex.

An information-processing model of brain function that closely parallels the neuropsychological model of Luria has been suggested by Norman and Shallice.[178] Expanding on the general executive component found in most theories of cognitive psychology, Norman and Shallice proposed a model of brain functioning based on four components—1) cognitive schemas, 2) schemas, 3) contention scheduling, and 4) SAS—that form a hierarchical system of functioning (Fig. 16–14). The basic assumption in this model is that the processes involved in control of action and thought can be divided into two levels of processing. The cognitive units are the most basic part of the model and refer to specific brain functions, such as language. Schemas generally refer to the integration of multiple cognitive units into well-learned, goal-directed programs. Acting as a lateral inhibitory mechanism, the contention scheduling unit selects between competing schemas largely as a function of activation. In the accomplishment of routine tasks associated with well-learned behavioral sequences, such as eating when you are hungry, there is little need to select among alternative behaviors. However, consider the conflictual situation in which you are late for a meeting and are hungry. This is a basic example of a situation in which contention scheduling must choose between schemas that compete for the same resources. The resultant selection is largely dependent on input from the SAS, which, through modulation of schema activation levels, biases the selection made by the contention scheduling unit. It is the role of the SAS to handle nonroutine goal achievement in a flexible manner. Norman and Shallice postulated that the SAS is a frontal function and operates only when contention scheduling fails or there is no known solution. Earlier, we stated that the SAS is thought to form the central executive component of the working memory model offered by Baddeley.[58]

A number of theories of frontal lobe functioning have arisen from animal research. Fuster[157] proposed a theory of executive processing that is based on the need to form a temporal gestalt. He theorized that prefrontal functioning consists of at least three distinctive subordinate functions (provisional or short-term memory, preparatory set, interference control) that cooperate under the superordinate function of temporal organization of behavior. In addition, Fuster maintained that these functions can be identified as correlating with a specific region of the prefrontal cortex. Provisional memory allows one to refer any event in the behavioral sequence to preceding events and to the original scheme of action. For this to occur, relevant events must be temporally represented and retained. Anticipatory set or preparation implies both foresight and preparatory action. Using past experiences, the organism is able to prepare for a variety of possible contingencies. Preparation involves adjusting sensory and motor apparatus before each event to increase the chances that stimuli are received and responded to. Certain phenomena of neuroelectrical activation that precede expected events in structured behavioral tasks suggest involvement of the dorsolateral prefrontal cortex as a whole. Interference control is accomplished by the inhibition of both internal and external stimuli. Fuster contended that there is substantial evidence that the control of interference is carried out by inhibitory counterinfluences originating in the orbital and perhaps medial prefrontal cortex. The temporal structures of behavior have a unifying purpose or goal, that is, the structuring of goal-directed behavior.

Extensive research on monkeys provided the basis for the Goldman-Rakic[6] model of prefrontal function. This theory postulates that the prefrontal cortex maintains active representation or "representational memory" of mnemonic, sensory, and symbolic information that originated in nonprefrontal areas despite the absence of external contingencies or discriminative stimuli. The prefrontal cortex keeps the memory of this information activated long enough to modulate behavior. Goldman-Rakic contended that different representational memory units reside in different areas of the prefrontal cortex and that these units are highly related on a functional as well as anatomical basis. In addition, these representational memory units are thought to exert both inhibitory and excitatory influences on the motor area, thereby effecting behavioral control. Earlier, we discussed the application of this theory to consider the unique role that the prefrontal cortex plays in working memory.

Mesulam[86] proposed an interesting perspective on the role of the frontal lobes and the executive control of behavior, one that borrows from computational neuroscience concerning neural networks and behavior. Neural networks refer to constellations of neurons that subserve a particular function. Networks vary in magnitude depending on the task at hand. They can refer to smaller local networks that may subserve a simple function such as the analysis of a shape or involve large-scale networks necessary to process complex problem-solving tasks. It is important to keep in mind that cognitive problems are solved not merely by segmented or hierarchical processing but by simultaneous and interactive networks. This is in contrast to Luria's model, which stressed sequential processing. Considering the extensive parallel and distributed anatomical connectivity of the frontal lobes, Mesulam reasoned that the connectivity of the frontal lobes underlies their functional role in executive function. Through their interconnections with multiple brain regions, the frontal lobes provide executive control over a number of neural networks that subserve different information-processing capacities.

According to this model, the frontal lobes can activate other networks, inhibit networks, or have an effect on the combination of networks that are active. Basic sensory or motor information is handled by other networks but coordinated by the frontal system. In this sense, the frontal lobes allow for the higher level internal representation of the state of particular networks. Extrapolating from neuropsychological studies of brain lesions, some support for a network model is seen in the fact that frontal lobe syndromes are produced by damage directly to the frontal lobes but are more frequently seen when connectivity between the frontal system and other networks is disrupted.

Assessment of Frontal Lobe Functioning

Neuropsychological Assessment

There is an extensive literature concerning the evaluation of frontal lobe functioning with various neuropsychological assessment techniques. The majority of these studies are based on assessment of individuals with known frontal lobe damage or animals with experimentally induced lesions. Dubois and colleagues[179] suggested that the skills needed for the elaboration, control, and execution of goal-directed behaviors form the basis of studies involving the prefrontal cortex. These abilities would necessarily include planning, mental flexibility, impulse control, working memory, and evaluation of one's behavior, that is, executive processes.

Evaluation of executive processes is fraught with numerous obstacles. First, there are few assessment procedures that allow enough flexibility in response or ability to consider alternative ways of thinking, which are central elements of executive processing. Consider the paradox of having to structure an examination technique that assesses the ability of subjects to make structure for themselves.[93] Second, executive functioning is the final stage of a processing sequence, relying heavily on information provided by other brain areas. It follows that successful execution of the frontal lobe functions depends, in great part, on the integrity of the remainder of the brain. Effective executive processing is an unlikely occurrence if the information needed from non–frontal lobe regions is missing or inaccurate. Third, frontal lobe functioning encompasses a number of abilities, making a complete assessment of such processes an arduous, if not impossible, task at best. Fourth, many of the neuropsychological instruments used in the assessment of executive processes are weakly constructed and insensitive to obscure changes in the presence of compensatory strategies that occur after frontal lobe damage. Despite these obstacles, the quest to better understand the cognitive processes that belie the functioning of the frontal lobes, as well as the desire to prognosticate level of adaptive functioning in patients with known impairment, has maintained the strong interest in employing neuropsychological assessment techniques. Many of these neuropsychological tasks have also been used in the context of functional neuroimaging to better delineate cognitive and neuroanatomical correlates. Table 16–3 details several of the assessment procedures used to evaluate the integrity of the frontal lobes in performing cognitive operations.

The WCST is one of the most widely used instruments in assessing executive processes. Presumably, this task requires a number of elements that constitute executive processing including visual-spatial working memory, deductive reasoning, problem solving, and cognitive flexibility or ability to shift set. Milner[172] found that patients with static frontal lobe lesions, especially lesions located in the dorsolateral prefrontal cortex, had greater difficulty switching set during the WCST than patients with either temporal or orbital frontal lobe lesions. In a follow-up study, Milner[180] demonstrated a lateralized effect, with left frontal lobe lesions being associated with more impairment on the WCST than right frontal lobe damage. A number of sorting tasks, particularly those that assess the ability to change mental set, appear sensitive to frontal lobe damage. In part, poor performance on these types of tasks could be related to disinterest or random responding.[156] Vilkki[181] found that patients with anterior lesions performed significantly poorer on the category identification and sorting tasks of the Colour Form Size Test. Sorting tasks, however, are not differentially sensitive to frontal lobe dysfunction, as diffuse or generalized damage can produce similar results. Anderson and colleagues[182] evaluated 91 patients with focal brain lesions by using the WCST and found no significant differences in performance between patients with frontal and non–frontal lobe lesions. This would lead one to conclude that sorting tasks are not diagnostic unless normal functioning is observed on a number of non–frontal lobe tests. In addition, because of the heterogeneity of executive processes, the absence of impairment on sorting tasks does not exclude frontal lobe damage, at least in certain areas.[156]

Fluency tasks, both verbal and design, have frequently been included in neuropsychological evaluations as a measure of the ability to generate, maintain, and switch set. In general, verbal fluency tasks require a patient to generate verbally as many words as possible in a specified amount of time that belong to certain categories or begin with the same letter. A number of studies have found decreased verbal fluency in patients with frontal lobe damage, with left frontal lobe lesions resulting in greater suppression of word production than right frontal lobe lesions.[183] Impairments in a number of brain regions have been associated with diminished verbal fluency, presumably because of the heavy reliance on memory and language abilities in these tasks. However, some research has noted differences in the type of errors made on fluency tasks by patients with frontal lobe damage compared with patients with damage to non–frontal lobe areas. In a comparison of patients with anterior and posterior left hemisphere lesions, Vilkki[184] found that patients with posterior lesions committed more errors involving the repetition of a previous correct response, whereas patients with anterior lesions gave more new, although incorrect, words that were a perseveration of a previous category. The author concluded that these different types of perseverations, which were termed "recurrent" and "stuck-in-set," are characteristic of posterior and anterior left hemisphere damage, respectively.

Some evidence of laterality in frontal lobe functioning has been observed through the use of design fluency tasks. Like verbal fluency tests, design fluency tests require a patient to generate as many different designs as possible within a specified time that adhere to a given criterion. For example, a patient may be asked to make designs limited to five lines. A number of trials are given, each differing in criterion demands. In a study assessing 100 patients with unilateral cortical excisions, Gotman and Milner[185] found patients with right frontal lobe lesions to be most impaired on a design fluency task, with milder deficits noted in patients with left frontal lobe and temporal lesions. This study emphasizes the importance of both side and lesion site in the performance of fluency tasks. In a study conducted by Smith and Milner,[186] patients with unilateral frontal or temporal excisions and normal control subjects were compared in recalling the frequency of abstract designs. Their findings suggested that patients with frontal lobe excisions (right more than left) were most impaired in recalling the occurrence of designs and patients with right temporal lobe excisions most defective in recognition tasks. The authors concluded that the frequency estimation impairments found in patients with frontal lobe excisions may represent a disorderly search process in memory.

A number of tests have been designed to assess planning and foresight, including maze tests and the Tower of London test. Maze tests generally assess visual-motor planning and consist of a number of labyrinths, each with increasing difficulty.[156] The task of the patient is to proceed through the maze without hitting a dead end. Karnath and colleagues[187] found that patients with acute frontal lobe lesions required more learning trials to pass through a covered maze compared with a normal control group. The Tower of London[188] is a task designed to assess planning abilities by requiring patients to solve a series of novel

Table 16–3 Tests Commonly Used to Assess Executive Functions

Function	Test
Abstract thinking	Comprehension subtest of Wechsler Adult Intelligence Scale–Revised, Gorham's Proverbs Test
Concept formation, social judgment	Similarities subtest of Wechsler Adult Intelligence Scale–Revised
Concept formation and cognitive flexibility including establishing, maintaining, and shifting cognitive set	Wisconsin Card Sorting Test Halstead Categories Test
Cognitive flexibility and psychomotor speed	Trail Making Test, part B
Cognitive set maintenance and impulse control	Stroop Color-Word Test
Planning and impulse control	Porteus Maze Test
Visuospatial working memory and problem solving	Tower of London
Cognitive productivity	Controlled Oral Word Association Test (verbal fluency) Ruff Figure Fluency Test (design fluency)

problems that successively increase in difficulty. The patients are presented with three pegs and three colored beads. They are then shown a picture depicting a certain arrangement of the beads on the sticks and asked to duplicate the configuration in a specified number of moves. As the patients are allowed only a limited number of moves, a trial-and-error approach generally results in an unsuccessful attempt to achieve the desired goal. Rather, success follows the patient's ability to solve the problem mentally before behaviorally carrying out the solution. A number of studies have found that patients with anterior lesions require more moves to arrive at the correct solution than normal control subjects or patients with lesions in other areas of the brain.[188, 189] A study examining regional cerebral blood flow (RCBF) during the execution of this task in normal individuals found that greater planning activity was correlated with increased activation in the left prefrontal cortex.[190]

Few studies are as colorful or unusual as those carried out by Lhermitte.[191] He observed that patients with frontal lobe damage frequently exhibited stimulus-bound behavior in the form of imitation and/or utilization. Imitation behavior refers to the tendency of patients to imitate the actions of others, even when they are told not to. Utilization behavior is observed when patients pick up any object they are presented with and begin to use it, regardless of appropriateness to context. For example, when Lhermitte presented a patient with frontal lobe damage with a hypodermic syringe, the patient attempted to give the examiner a shot without being told to do so. In a subsequent study, Lhermitte and coworkers[192] noted the presence of imitation and/or utilization behavior in all but 1 of the 29 patients with frontal lobe lesions who were studied. Results of computed tomography suggested the presence of damage to the inferior half of the anterior part of one or both frontal lobes in all patients. Imitation and utilization behaviors were virtually absent in a normal control group.

Despite massive research suggesting that frontal lobe damage is linked to impaired performance on various neuropsychological measures, a number of studies put forth evidence to the contrary. Test insensitivity, heterogeneity of frontal lobe functioning, and test reliance on the integrity of the remainder of the brain probably played a part in these contradictory findings. A frequent observation has been the sparing of intellectual functioning, at least on psychological tests, in patients with frontal lobe injury. Such was the case with Phineas Gage, whose plight was described earlier in the chapter. Joseph[193] pointed out that psychometrical evidence of normal intelligence does not necessarily imply that one has the ability to use such functioning in an adaptive manner. The well-publicized case of E.V.R.[194] is one example in which neuropsychological assessment failed to detect the presence of obvious maladaptive functioning. At age 35 years, E.V.R., a bright, college-educated accountant, was diagnosed with a large orbitofrontal meningioma. After a bilateral frontal ablation to remove the tumor, E.V.R. demonstrated severe, chronic behavior changes including impulsivity, poor judgment, social inappropriateness, and disorganization. However, an extensive neuropsychological evaluation 2 years postoperatively revealed E.V.R.'s IQ to be in the bright range of abilities. His performance on all measures of memory, attention, executive functioning, and language was also above the average range.

Behavioral-Neuroanatomical Correlates

Disrupted neurobehavioral functioning in a number of psychiatric and neurological disorders has revealed several interesting aspects of the role of the frontal lobes in behavior. Studies involving dementias of the frontal lobe type, particularly Pick's disease, have provided some information concerning the role of the frontal lobes. Pick's disease is quite distinguishable from the better known Alzheimer's type in that in the former basic memory functions are relatively spared early in the disease course. The initial presentation of Pick's disease largely involves the presence of striking changes in personality and social appropriateness. Memory dysfunction, if apparent, is secondary to motivational or attentional factors rather than faulty learning. Patients with Pick's disease consistently perform poorly on a wide variety of tests sensitive to frontal lobe dysfunction. A number of studies using radioactive tracers and neuroimaging techniques have confirmed the predominance of frontal lobe abnormalities in these patients.[195, 196]

Many of the studies involving the association of affective disorders and frontal lobe functioning have emerged from the literature on stroke. Starkstein and associates[197] have found that the left frontal opercular region is the area most frequently damaged in patients suffering from poststroke depression. Similarly, using computed tomography, Robinson and Szetela[198] have demonstrated that the closer the lesion is to the frontal pole, the more severe the ensuing depression. After reviewing the relationship between frontal lobe impairment and affective dysfunction, Baxter and colleagues[199] concluded that left prefrontal hypometabolism was the most consistent and severe finding in major depression, bipolar depression, and obsessive-compulsive disorders.

As noted earlier, the orbital prefrontal cortex has been associated with emotional dyscontrol. This association arose from observations of mania after surgical procedures involving the prefrontal region. As alluded to, the ability of the prefrontal cortex to perform its duties efficiently depends heavily on the integrity of the remainder of the brain. Therefore, a secondary mania can occur with lesions to other areas of the brain, particularly the limbic and subcortical areas. The extensive connections (direct or indirect) between these areas and the orbital prefrontal cortex probably hold the key to this phenomenon. An example of secondary mania was noted during a study of three patients who developed mania after damage to subcortical areas including the caudate nucleus or internal capsule.[200] When evaluated by PET, all three patients showed significant hypometabolism in the right basotemporal cortex.

Kinsbourne[201] has suggested that different types of emotional dysfunction are associated with particular areas of the cortex, including the frontal lobes. His theory is based on a number of neuropsychological, neuroanatomical, and neuroimaging findings associated with various affective disorders. This theory purports separate, although interactive, roles for each quadrant (right, left, anterior, posterior) of the cerebral cortex. The role of the left anterior (frontal) cortex is to program an action, the right anterior cortex searches for context, the left posterior cortex analyzes meaning, and the right posterior cortex interprets the emotion. In general, the role of the left hemisphere is thought to be the continuation of ongoing activity, whereas the right hemisphere is generally involved in the arresting of ongoing behavior. Kinsbourne believed that changes in the environmental stimuli may disrupt the self-regulating process of emotional organization and control. Consequences of behavior are continually monitored by the left posterior cortex in relation to the current behavioral program, which is maintained by the left frontal region. Ongoing behavior is maintained as long as it matches the anticipated state of affairs. A mismatch is accompanied by an arrest in ongoing behavior that is the result of switching control to the right frontal region. This arrest is accompanied subjectively by a surge of negative emotion (right posterior cortex). It is thought that the right hemisphere provides the left frontal lobe with an interpretive context in which to reprogram behavior to fit with new conditions. If no solution is found to the unexpected event, a surge of negative emotion (right posterior) ensues and cessation of ongoing behavior (left anterior) continues, possibly to the point of a reactive depression.

Therefore, the suspension of ongoing activity by the left frontal lobe after a catastrophic event is accompanied by a shift in control to the right frontal lobe in an effort to control the emotional reaction by searching for an appropriate interpretive context on which the frontal lobe may reprogram behavior. It is thought that the increase in right frontal lobe activity corresponds to a simultaneous decrease in right posterior activity, which results in impaired detection of emotional cues and decreased sensitivity to pleasurable stimuli (anhedonia). Together, impaired function of the left frontal and right posterior regions results in rumination without goal-oriented activity and anhedonia with flat affect, both of which are core symptoms of endogenous depression. Aside from the neuropsychological evidence,[202] a number of RCBF studies have found support for Kinsbourne's theory, including the work of Kuhl and colleagues[203] and Guenther and associates.[204]

A surge in the study of schizophrenia has provided a wealth of knowledge concerning the functioning of the prefrontal cortex. It is generally agreed that cognitive abnormalities associated with schizophrenia often involve difficulties in executive processing. Some of the earliest and best known studies involving neuroimaging techniques in the assessment of cognitive abilities in this population were carried out by Weinberger and colleagues. In their initial study (Fig. 16–15), Weinberger and associates[205] compared the metabolic brain activity of 24 normal control subjects and 20 medication-free patients with chronic schizophrenia while resting, performing a number matching task, and performing the WCST. They found that brain activation, as determined by RCBF, did not differ between the groups during the resting condition or number matching task. However, they found significant differences in RCBF during the WCST, with activation of the dorsolateral prefrontal cortex being lower in the patients with schizophrenia. Many other studies employing RCBF[206–208] and functional brain imaging[209] have found evidence to support the "hypofrontality" hypothesis in schizophrenia. However, not all studies have found frontal hypometabolism in patients with schizophrenia.[210, 211] The heterogeneous nature of schizophrenia probably accounts for these contradictory findings. A number of researchers including Volkow and colleagues[212] and Andreasen and associates[213] have found that hypofrontality was most related to patients with a predominance of negative symptoms.

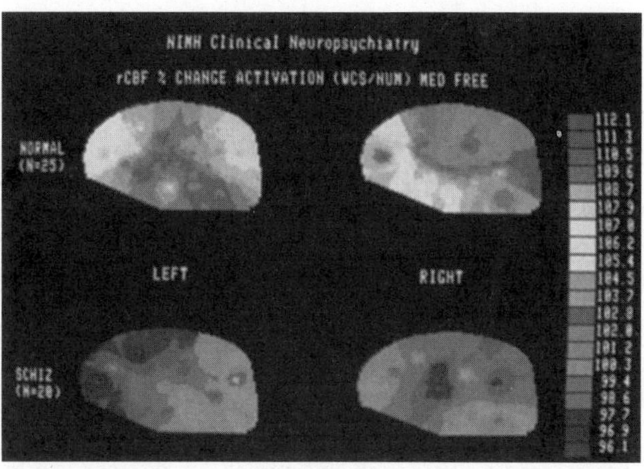

Figure 16–15 *RCBF map showing lack of activation in the dorsolateral prefrontal cortex of schizophrenic patients performing the WCST. The map shows the percentage change in RCBF from the control task (number matching task) relative to the experimental task (WCST). (From Weinberger DR, Berman KF, Zec RF: Physiologic dysfunction of dorsolateral prefrontal cortex in schizophrenia. I. Regional cerebral blood flow evidence. Arch Gen Psychiatry 1986; 43:114–124.)*

Attention

In view of what is known about the role of the prefrontal cortex, it is readily apparent that the primary role of this brain region involves the integration and modulation of cognitive functioning. It is unlikely that such functioning arises out of specialized modules alone.[214] Rather, these abilities, like other executive processes, are the result of extensive neuronal networks composed of reciprocal connections between many brain areas and the prefrontal cortex. Given the onerous task of managing vast amounts of incoming and outgoing information, it stands to reason that attentional abilities are of great importance to frontal lobe functioning.

The area of attention as it relates to the frontal lobes has provided a rich field of study. Like many of the other general areas of cognition (e.g., memory, language), attention represents a vast and complex phenomenon. This is, in part, due to the many facets of attention itself. Underlying all cognitive activity, there must be some tonic form of activation that provides the background in which all other cortical activity occurs. Luria[177] referred to this capacity as his first functional brain area and noted that the reticular activating system in the brain stem provided the core structure subserving brain activation. In general, this is referred to as alertness or wakefulness. However, one's ability to pay attention to specific stimuli is thought to be subserved by higher cortical areas, including the prefrontal cortex. The psychological process of attention can broadly be defined in terms of divided, focused, and sustained abilities. Divided attention occurs when multiple stimuli are attended to simultaneously. We can often find ourselves participating in divided attention tasks at parties when we tune into two different conversations at one time. Focused attention refers to the ability to inhibit irrelevant stimuli in the service of attending to a particular stimulus. Often this type of attention requires one to inhibit automatic responses that conflict with the task at hand. Sustained attention requires the ability to maintain attention over time.

Differences in the role of the right versus left prefrontal regions have long been suspected. The greater frequency of left neglect than right neglect with the occurrence of contralateral lesions has provided much of the initial basis on which hemispherical differences were suggested. Mesulam[215] found that right-sided prefrontal infarcts more often resulted in contralateral hemineglect than comparable areas of left-sided damage. A study of directed attention by Deutsch and colleagues[216] suggested a general role for the right hemisphere in attention and vigilance. When examining the data from 121 RCBF studies that employed different stimuli (i.e., verbal, visual, spatial) requiring differing levels of effort, they found consistently greater right frontal activity compared with its left counterpart. Moreover, this observed hemispherical difference was greatest for tasks that were the most demanding.

A number of studies have employed cognitive event-related potentials to study attentional processes independent of sensory concerns. Humans with focal lesions of the dorsolateral prefrontal cortex frequently demonstrate impairment in inhibiting irrelevant sensory input from the primary sensory areas as well as an impairment in the ability to focus attention and detect novel stimuli.[214] The neurophysiological evidence suggests that impaired attention occurs within a 20- to 500-ms window after presentation of the stimulus. Much of the research exploring focused sustained attention has employed dichotic paradigms. In these types of tasks, different stimuli are presented simultaneously to each of the bilateral sensory fields (i.e., an ear, a hand, a visual field) and subjects are required to attend to the stimuli in one field while suppressing the stimuli in the contralateral field. Knight and colleagues[217] compared normal control subjects with patients with unilateral prefrontal lesions during dichotic listening tasks. They found that normal subjects attended equally well to stimuli to the left and right ear. The subjects with left prefrontal lesions had slightly diminished processing of stimuli in either ear, although their performance did not significantly differ from that of normal control subjects. Consistent with earlier evidence of a predominant role for the right prefrontal cortex in attention, patients with right prefrontal damage exhibited a significant decrease in selective attention detection capacity in the left ear. This finding was evident only if the interstimulus interval was greater than 200 ms. The observation that impaired attentional capacity occurs only after long interstimulus intervals provides support for Fuster's[218] "synthetic temporal function" hypothesis, which purports that frontal lesions impair the ability to bridge temporal discontinuities in the environment. For an extensive review of the use of event-related potentials in investigating attentional processes, the reader is referred to Knight.[219]

As suggested earlier, Mesulam[86] has proposed a neurocognitive network of attention involving a number of neural circuits participating in PDP. According to this model, interactive, multifocal neural pathways that are both localized and distributed give rise to multiple possibilities and flexibility with respect to attentional behavior. Much of this model is based on neglect behavior, which can be separated into perceptual, motor, and limbic components. In general, the perceptual component refers to the diminished awareness that a sensory event has occurred within the neglected field, the motor component refers to the diminution or absence of exploratory behaviors, and the limbic component refers to a devaluation or amotivation of the neglected hemispace. According to Mesulam, neglect behavior in both humans and monkeys consistently follows lesions to one of three areas: the dorsolateral parietal cortex, the dorsolateral premotor-prefrontal cortex, and the cingulate gyrus. These three areas provide local networks that provide the basis for a large-scale neural model of attention. Each local network or component participates in mapping the environment in slightly different ways. For example, in the case of visual hemineglect, Mesulam suggested that the posterior parietal cortex provides sensory (visual) awareness, the prefrontal area provides a map of exploratory movements (i.e., eye movements), and the cingulate gyrus provides a map for assigning value to the spatial coordinates. Within these areas, specific cytoarchitectonic structures interact through extensive reciprocal and monosynaptic connections. In the area of the dorsolateral prefrontal cortex, the frontal eye fields (Brodmann's area 8) play a critical role in directed attention. Although lesions in other brain regions, such as subcortical structures, are known to cause neglect, these areas have been found to connect to at least two of the three central components.

Morecraft and associates[220] have examined whether or not the monosynaptic and reciprocal connections between the three components of Mesulam's model (posterior parietal, dorsolateral prefrontal eye fields, cingulate gyrus) arise from axonal collaterals. They injected one of two different retrogradely fluorescent dyes into each of the frontal eye fields and posterior parietal cortex of three monkey brains to determine the degree of source overlap and axonal collateralization in the neural inputs of the posterior parietal cortex and frontal eye fields. Although large numbers of cingulate cortex neurons were retrogradely labeled with each of the two dyes, less than 1% of them were labeled with both tracers. Other cortical areas including premotor, temporal, orbital frontal, premotor, parahippocampal, opercular, and insular regions contained neurons labeled with one of the two dyes, although virtually no neurons were double labeled. Moreover, overlap between the two populations of retrogradely labeled neurons was much more extensive at the cortical than at the thalamic level. The lack of double labeling in the presence of marked single labeling suggested that these areas project to the inferior parietal and frontal eye fields not through axon collaterals but rather through two distinct and only partially overlapping populations of neurons.

Conclusion

The focus of this chapter has been the cognitive neuroscience of memory, language, and executive functions. As stated earlier, the term cognitive neuroscience does not refer to a single discipline; it connotes the integration of work from several fields examining brain-behavior relationships as they subserve specific mental processes. In the context of discussing complex cognitive systems, we have attempted to detail the contributions of lesion analytical work in humans and animals, as well as studies of normal processing. The exciting research that has emanated from in vivo functional imaging, especially with respect to memory, holds promise for further understanding of the manner in which the brain is specialized to process and store information.

Within the realm of theory, we have also stressed the growing consensus that neural processing and the emergence of cognition occur in a parallel and distributed fashion. Although this idea may be heuristically tenable, the specific mechanisms allowing simultaneity in information processing are difficult to model, from both cognitive and neuroanatomical perspectives. Work in computational neuroscience, aided by functional imaging and electrophysiological techniques, should permit the development of increasingly realistic and integrated models of cognition and brain. The advantage of in vivo studies is that normal processes can be examined in non–brain-damaged subjects. Although this marks a departure from the long tradition of lesion analytical studies in the neurosciences, newer imaging technologies offer to broaden, not to replace, lesion work. Rather than localizing whole functions to discrete areas of damage (as was the earlier tradition), the current emphasis continues to be on the contribution of a discrete area to a particular functional network. This approach characterizes present research on language, in which the role of regional specificity is understood within the context of a distributed functional and neuroanatomical system. The frontal lobes and executive control of behavior have proved to be an area that is rich in theory, but delineating the specific role of the frontal lobes in behavior and underlying neuronatomical mechanisms has proved somewhat elusive. Advances in characterizing frontal circuitry and the specialized role of the prefrontal cortex in such functions as representational memory have elucidated the complex contribution of this region to the regulation of behavior.

References

1. Jackson HJ: On affections of speech from disease of the brain. Brain 1878; 1:304–330.
2. Luria AR: Neuropsychology in the local diagnosis of brain damage. Cortex 1964; 1:3–18.
3. Feldman JA, Ballard DH: Connectionist models and their properties. Cogn Sci 1982; 6:205–254.
4. Rumelhart DE, McClelland JL, PDP Research Group: Parallel Distributed Processing, Volume 1. Cambridge, MA: The MIT Press, 1986.
5. Churchland PS, Sejnowski TJ: The Computational Brain. Cambridge, MA: The MIT Press, 1992.
6. Goldman-Rakic PS: Circuitry of the prefrontal cortex and the regulation of behavior by representational knowledge. In Plum F (ed): Handbook of Physiology, Section 1, The Nervous System, Volume V, Higher Functions of the Brain. Bethesda, MD: American Physiological Society, 1987:373–417.
7. Goldman-Rakic PS: Changing concepts of cortical connectivity: Parallel distributed cortical networks. In Rakic P, Singer W (eds): Neurobiology of Neocortex. New York: John Wiley & Sons, 1988:177–202.
8. Christianson SA (ed): The Handbook of Emotion and Memory: Research and Theory. Hillsdale, NJ: Lawrence Erlbaum, 1992.
9. Squire LR, Butters N (eds): Neuropsychology of Memory. New York: Guilford Press, 1992.
10. Lashley KS: In search of the engram. Symp Soc Exp Biol 1950; 4:454–482.
11. Gabrieli JDE: A systematic view of human memory processes. J Int Neuropsychol Soc 1995; 1:115–118.
12. Blaxton TA: A process-based view of memory. J Int Neuropsychol Soc 1995; 1:112–114.
13. Scoville WB, Milner B: Loss of recent memory after bilateral hippocampal lesions. J Neurol Neurosurg Psychiatry 1957; 20:11–21.
14. Markowitsch HJ, Pritzel M: The neuropathology of amnesia. Prog Neurobiol 1985; 25:189–287.
15. Milner B, Corkin S, Teuber HL: Further analysis of the hippocampal amnesic syndrome: Fourteen year follow-up study of H.M. Neuropsychologia 1968; 6:215–234.
16. Warrington EK, Weiskrantz L: The effect of prior learning on subsequent retention in amnesic patients. Neuropsychologia 1974; 12:419–428.
17. Zola-Morgan S, Squire LR, Amaral DG: Human amnesia and the medial temporal region: Enduring memory impairment following a bilateral lesion limited to field CA1 of the hippocampus. J Neurosci 1986; 6:2950–2967.
18. Zola-Morgan S, Squire LR: Neuroanatomy of memory. Annu Rev Neurosci 1993; 16:547–563.
19. Zola-Morgan S, Squire LR, Amaral DG: Lesions of the amygdala that spare adjacent cortical regions do not impair memory or exacerbate the impairment following lesions of the hippocampal formation. J Neurosci 1989; 9:1922–1936.
20. Moscovitsch M: Recovered consciousness: A hypothesis concerning modularity and episodic memory. J Clin Exp Neuropsychol 1995; 17:276–290.
21. Kandel ER, Abrams T, Bernier L, et al: Classical conditioning and sensitization share aspects of the same molecular cascade in *Aplysia.* Quant Biol 1983; 48:821–830.
22. Kandel ER: Cellular mechanisms of learning and the biological basis of individuality. In Kandel E, Schwartz JH, Jessell TM (eds): Principles of Neural Science, 3rd ed. Norwalk, CT: Appleton & Lange, 1991:1009–1031.
23. Bliss TVP, Lomo T: Long-lasting potentiation of synaptic transmission in the dentate area of the anaesthetized rabbit following stimulation of the perforant path. J Physiol (Lond) 1973; 232:331–356.
24. Hebb DO: The Organization of Behavior: A Neuropsychological Theory. New York: John Wiley & Sons, 1949.
25. Shepherd GM: Neurobiology, 3rd ed. New York: Oxford University Press, 1994.
26. Morris RGM, Anderson E, Lynch GS, Baudry M: Selective impairment of learning and blockade of long-term potentiation by an *N*-methyl-D-aspartate receptor antagonist, AP5. Nature 1986; 319: 774–776.
27. Linden DJ, Connor JA: Long-term synaptic depression. Annu Rev Neurosci 1995; 18:319–357.
28. Tsumoto T: Long-term depression in cerebral cortex: A possible substrate of "forgetting" that should not be forgotten. Neurosci Res 1993; 16:263–270.
29. Linden DJ: Long-term synaptic depression in the mammalian brain. Neuron 1994; 12:457–472.
30. Traub RD, Miles R: Neuronal Networks of the Hippocampus. Cambridge, UK: Cambridge University Press, 1991.
31. McKee RD, Squire LR: Equivalent forgetting rates in long-term memory for diencephalic and medial temporal lobe amnesia. J Neurosci 1992; 12:3765–3772.
32. Markowitsch HJ, von Cramon DY, Schuri U: Mnestic performance profile of a bilateral diencephalic infarct patient with preserved intelligence and severe amnesic disturbances. J Clin Exp Neuropsychol 1993; 15:627–652.
33. Drachman DA, Leavitt J: Human memory and the cholinergic system. A relationship to aging? Arch Neurol 1974; 30:113–121.
34. Meador KJ, Moore EE, Nichols ME, et al: The role of cholinergic systems in visuospatial processing and memory. J Clin Exp Neuropsychol 1993; 15:832–842.
35. Bartus RT, Dean RL, Flicker C: Cholinergic psychopharmacology: An integration of human and animal research on memory. In Meltzer HY (ed): Psychopharmacology: The Third Generation of Progress. New York: Raven Press, 1987:219–232.
36. McGaugh J: Affect, neuromodulatory systems, and memory storage. In Christianson SA (ed): The Handbook of Emotion and Memory: Research and Theory. Hillsdale, NJ: Lawrence Erlbaum, 1992: 245–268.
37. Gold PW, van Buskirk R: Facilitation of time-dependent memory processes with posttrial amygdala stimulation: Effect on memory varies with footshock level. Brain Res 1975; 86:509–513.
38. Liang KC, McGaugh JL, Yao HY: Involvement of amygdala pathways in the influence of posttraining amygdala norepinephrine and peripheral epinephrine on memory storage. Brain Res 1990; 508:225–233.

39. Liang KC, Juler R, McGaugh JL: Modulating effects of posttraining epinephrine on memory: Involvement of the amygdala noradrenergic system. Brain Res 1986; 368:125–133.
40. Bechara A, Tranel D, Damasio H, et al: Double dissociation of conditioning and declarative knowledge relative to the amygdala and hippocampus in humans. Science 1995; 269:1115–1118.
41. Gold PE, Delanoy RL, Merrin J: Modulation of long-term potentiation by peripherally administered amphetamine and epinephrine. Brain Res 1984; 305:103–107.
42. Moscovitch M: A neuropsychological model of memory and consciousness. In Squire LR, Butters N (eds): Neuropsychology of Memory, 2nd ed. New York: Guilford Press, 1992:5–22.
43. Petrides M: Deficits on conditional associative-learning tasks after frontal and temporal-lobe lesions in man. Neuropsychologia 1985; 23:601–614.
44. Winocur G: The hippocampus and prefrontal cortex in learning and memory: An animal model approach. In Squire LR, Butters N (eds): Neuropsychology of Memory, 2nd ed. New York: Guilford Press, 1992:429–439.
45. Milner B: Some effecs of frontal lobectomy in man. In Warren JM, Akert K (eds): The Frontal Granular Cortex and Behavior. New York: McGraw-Hill, 1964:313–334.
46. Moscovitch M: Confabulation and the frontal system: Strategic vs. associative retrieval in neuropsychological theories of memory. In Roediger HL, Craik FIM (eds): Varieties of Memory and Consciousness: Essays in Honor of Endel Tulving. Hillsdale, NJ: Lawrence Erlbaum, 1989:133–156.
47. Shimamura AP, Janowsky JS, Squire LR: Memory for temporal order in patients with frontal lobe lesions and patients with amnesia. Neuropsychologia 1990; 28:803–813.
48. Schacter DL: Memory, amnesia, and frontal lobe dysfunction. Psychobiology 1987; 15:21–36.
49. Janowsky JS, Shimamura AP, Squire LR: Source memory impairment in patients with frontal lobe lesions. Neuropsychologia 1989; 27:1043–1056.
50. Metcalfe J, Shimamura AP (eds): Metacognition: Knowing about Knowing. Cambridge, MA: The MIT Press, 1994.
51. Shimamura AP: Memory and frontal lobe function. In Gazzaniga M (ed): The Cognitive Neurosciences. Cambridge, MA: The MIT Press, 1995:803–813.
52. Baddeley AD, Hitch G: Working memory. In Bower GA (ed): The Psychology of Learning and Motivation, Volume 8. New York: Academic Press, 1974:47–89.
53. Wilson FAW, Scalaidhe SPO, Goldman-Rakic PS: Dissociation of object and spatial processing domains in primate prefrontal cortex. Science 1993; 260:1955–1957.
54. Gathercole SE: Neuropsychology and working memory: A review. Neuropsychology 1994; 8:494–505.
55. Baddeley AD, Lieberman K: Spatial working memory. In Nickerson R (ed): Attention and Performance VIII. Hillsdale, NJ: Lawrence Erlbaum, 1980.
56. Ungerleider LG, Mishkin M: Two cortical visual systems. In Ingle DJ, Goodale MA, Mansfield RJW (eds): Analysis of Visual Behavior. Cambridge, MA: The MIT Press, 1982:549–586.
57. Farah MJ, Hammond KM, Levine DL, Calvanio R: Visual and spatial mental imagery: Dissociable systems of representation. Cogn Psychol 1988; 20:439–462.
58. Baddeley AD: Working Memory. Oxford, UK: Oxford University Press, 1986.
59. Shallice T: Specific impairments of planning. Philos Trans R Soc Lond Ser B 1982; 298:199–209.
60. Becker JT, Mintun MA, Diehl D, et al: Functional neuroanatomy of verbal memory as revealed by word list recall during PET scanning. Soc Neurosci Abstr 1993; 19:1079.
61. Paulesu E, Frith CD, Frackowiak RSJ: The neural correlates of the verbal component of working memory. Nature 1993; 362:342–345.
62. Petrides M, Alivisatos B, Evans AC, Meyer E: Dissociation of human mid-dorsolateral from posterior dorsolateral frontal cortex in memory processing. Proc Natl Acad Sci USA 1993; 90:873–877.
63. Jonides J, Smith EE, Koeppe RA, et al: Spatial working memory in humans as revealed by PET. Nature 1993; 363:623–625.
64. Goldberg E: Gradiential approach to neocortical functional organization. J Clin Exp Neuropsychol 1989; 11:489–517.
65. Cohen JD, Forman SD, Braver TS, et al: Activation of the prefrontal cortex in a nonspatial working memory task with functional MRI. Hum Brain Mapping 1994; 1:293–304.
66. Grasby PM, Frith CD, Friston KJ, et al: Functional mapping of brain areas implicated in auditory-verbal memory function. Brain 1993; 116:1–20.
67. Becker JT, Mintun MA, Diehl DJ, et al: Functional neuroanatomy of verbal free recall: A replication study. Hum Brain Mapping 1994; 1:284–292.
68. Kapur S, Craik FIM, Tulving E, et al: Neuroanatomical correlates of encoding in episodic memory: Levels of processing effect. Proc Natl Acad Sci USA 1994; 91:2008–2011.
69. Tulving E, Kapur S, Craik FIM, et al: Hemispheric encoding/retrieval asymmetry in episodic memory: Positron emission tomography findings. Proc Natl Acad Sci USA 1994; 91:2016–2020.
70. Tulving E, Kapur S, Markowitsch HJ, et al: Neuroanatomical correlates of retrieval in episodic memory: Auditory sentence recognition. Proc Natl Acad Sci USA 1994; 91:2012–2015.
71. Craik FIM, Tulving E: Depth of processing and the retention of words in episodic memory. J Exp Psychol Gen 1975; 104:268–294.
72. Tulving E, Schacter DL, Stark H: Priming effects in word-fragment completion are independent of recognition memory. J Exp Psychol Learn Mem Cogn 1982; 8:336–342.
73. Schacter DL, Chiu P, Ochsner KN: Implicit memory: A selective review. Annu Rev Neurosci 1993; 16:159–182.
74. Bowers JS, Schacter DL: Implicit memory and test awareness. J Exp Psychol Learn Mem Cogn 1990; 16:404–416.
75. Gabrieli JDE, Keane MM: Priming in the patient H.M.: New findings and a theory of intact and impaired priming in patients with memory disorders. Soc Neurosci Abstr 1988; 14:1290.
76. Graf P, Squire LR, Mandler G: The information that amnesic patients do not forget. J Exp Psychol Learn Mem Cogn 1984; 10:164–178.
77. Tulving E, Schacter DL: Priming and human memory systems. Science 1990; 247:301–306.
78. Schacter DL: Understanding implicit memory: A cognitive neuroscience approach. Am Psychol 1992; 47:559–569.
79. Butters N, Heindel WC, Salmon DP: Dissociation of implicit memory in dementia: Neurological implications. Bull Psychon Soc 1990; 28:359–366.
80. Heindel WC, Salmon DP, Butters N: The biasing of weight judgements in Alzheimer's and Huntington's disease: A priming or programming phenomenon? J Clin Exp Neuropsychol 1991; 13:189–203.
81. Bunowski J, Bellugi U: Language, name and concept. Science 1970; 168:669–673.
82. Guidano VF, Liotti G: Cognitive Processes and Emotional Disorders. New York: Guilford Press, 1983.
83. Damasio AR, Damasio H: Brain and language. Sci Am 1992; 267(3):89–95.
84. Gardner RA, Gardner BT: Teaching sign language to a chimpanzee. Science 1969; 165:664–672.
85. Premack D: Intelligence in Ape and Man. Hillsdale, NJ: Lawrence Erlbaum, 1976.
86. Mesulam MM: Large scale neurocognitive networks and distributed processing for attention, language and memory. Ann Neurol 1990; 28:587–613.
87. Benson DF, Geschwind N: Aphasia and related disorders: A clinical approach. In Mesulam MM (ed): Principles of Behavioral Neurology, 3rd ed. Philadelphia: FA Davis, 1985:193–238.
88. Heilman KM, Valenstein E: Clinical Neuropsychology, 3rd ed. New York: Oxford University Press, 1993.
89. Benson DF: Aphasia. In Heilman KM, Valenstein E (eds): Clinical Neuropsychology, 3rd ed. New York: Oxford University Press, 1993:17–36.
90. Goodglass H, Kaplan E: The Assessment of Aphasia and Related Disorders. Philadelphia: Lea & Febiger, 1972.
91. Benton AL, Hamsher K: Multilingual Aphasia Examination. Iowa City, IA: University of Iowa, 1978.
92. Spreen O, Benton A: Neurosensory Center Comprehensive Examination for Aphasia. Victoria, British Columbia, Canada: Neuropsychology Laboratory, University of Victoria, 1969.
93. Lezak MD: Neuropsychological Assessment, 3rd ed. New York: Oxford University Press, 1995.
94. Damasio AR: Aphasia. N Engl J Med 1992; 326:531–539.

95. Caramazza A, Berndt RS: Semantic and syntactic processes in aphasia: A review of the literature. Psychol Bull 1978; 85:898–918.
96. Blumstein SE, Cooper WE, Zurif ED, Caramazza A: The perception and production of voice-onset time in aphasia. Neuropsychologia 1977; 15:371–383.
97. Naeser MA, Hayward RW: Lesion localization in aphasia with cranial computed tomography and the Boston Diagnostic Aphasia Exam. Neurology 1978; 28:545–551.
98. Damasio AR, Geschwind N: The neural basis of language. Annu Rev Neurosci 1984; 7:127–147.
99. Damasio AR, Damasio H: The anatomical basis of conduction aphasia. Brain 1980; 103:337–350.
100. Freedman M, Alexander MP, Naeser MA: Anatomical basis of transcortical motor aphasia. Neurology 1984; 34:409–417.
101. Kertesz A, Sheppard A, Mackenzie R: Localization in transcortical sensory aphasia. Arch Neurol 1982; 39:475–478.
102. Naeser MA, Alexander MP, Helm-Estabrooks N, et al: Aphasia with predominantly subcortical lesion sites: Description of three capsular/putaminal aphasia syndromes. Arch Neurol 1982; 39:2–14.
103. Metter EJ, Kempler D, Jackson C, et al: Cerebellar glucose metabolism in chronic aphasia. Neurology 1987; 37:1599–1606.
104. Benson DF: Alexia and the neuroanatomical basis of reading. In Pirozzolo FJ, Wittrock MC (eds): Neuropsychological and Cognitive Processes in Reading. New York: Academic Press, 1981:69–92.
105. Friedman RF, Ween JE, Albert ML: Alexia. In Heilman KM, Valenstein E (eds): Clinical Neurology, 3rd ed. New York: Oxford University Press, 1993:37–62.
106. Damasio AR, Damasio H: The anatomical basis of pure alexia. Neurology 1983; 33:1573–1583.
107. Geschwind N: Disconnection syndrome in animals and man. Brain 1965; 88:237–294.
108. Geschwind N, Levitsky W: Human brain. Left-right asymmetries in temporal speech region. Science 1968; 161:186–187.
109. Galaburda AM, LeMay M, Kemper TL, Geschwind N: Right-left asymmetries in the brain. Science 1978; 199:852–856.
110. Bellugi U, Poizner H, Klima ES: Brain organization for language: Clues from sign aphasia. Hum Neurobiol 1983; 2:155–170.
111. Corina DP, Vaid J, Bellugi U: The linguistic basis of left hemispheric specialization. Science 1992; 255:1258–1260.
112. Haglund MM, Ojemann GA, Lettich E, et al: Dissociation of cortical and single unit activity in spoken and signed languages. Brain Lang 1993; 44:19–27.
113. Gling I, Gloning K, Haub G, Quatember R: Comparison of verbal behavior in right-handed and non right-handed patients with anatomically verified lesion of one hemisphere. Cortex 1969; 5:43–52.
114. Fischer RS, Alexander MP, Gabriel C, et al: Reversed lateralization of cognitive functions in right handers: Exceptions to classical aphasiology. Brain 1991; 744:245–261.
115. Ross ED, Mesulam MM: Dominant language functions of the right hemisphere? Prosody and emotional gesturing. Arch Neurol 1979; 36:144–148.
116. Ross ED: The aprosodias. Arch Neurol 1981; 38:561–569.
117. Bottini G, Corcoran R, Sterzi R, et al: The role of the right hemisphere in the interpretation of figurative aspects of langauge. A positron emission tomography activation study. Brain 1994; 117:1241–1253.
118. Cappa SF, Vignolo LA: CT scan studies of aphasia. Hum Neurobiol 1983; 2:129–134.
119. Whitaker HA: Two views on aphasia classification. Brain Lang 1984; 21:1–2.
120. Willmes K, Poeck K: To what extent can aphasic syndromes be localized? Brain 1993; 116:1527–1540.
121. Warrington EK, Shallice T: Category-specific semantic impairments. Brain 1984; 107:829–853.
122. Damasio AR: Category-related recognition defects as a clue to the neural substrates of knowledge. Trends Neurosci 1990; 13:95–98.
123. Damasio AR, Tranel D: Nouns and verbs are retrieved with differently distributed neural systems. Proc Natl Acad Sci USA 1993; 90:4957–4960.
124. Micelli G, Silver MC, Villa G, Caramazza A: On the basis for the agrammatic's difficulty in producing main verbs. Cortex 1984; 20:207–220.
125. Rapp BC, Caramazza A: Disorders of lexical processing and the lexicon. In Gazzaniga M (ed): Cognitive Neuroscience. Cambridge, MA: The MIT Press, 1995:901–913.
126. Funnel E, Sheridan J: Categories of knowledge? Unfamiliar aspects of living and non-living things. Cogn Neuropsychol 1992; 9:135–153.
127. Caplan D: The cognitive neuroscience of syntactic processing. In Gazzaniga M (ed): Cognitive Neuroscience. Cambridge, MA: The MIT Press, 1995:871–879.
128. Posner MI, Petersen SE, Fox PT, Raichle ME: Localization of cognitive operations in the human brain. Science 1988; 240:1627–1631.
129. Petersen SE, Fox PT, Posner MI, et al: Positron emission tomographic studies of the processing of single-words. J Cogn Neurosci 1989; 1:153–170.
130. Petersen SE, Fiez JA: The processing of single words studied with positron emission tomography. Annu Rev Neurosci 1993; 16:509–530.
131. Yule W, Rutter M: Language Development and Disorders. Oxford, UK: MacKeith Press, 1987.
132. Chomsky N: Language and Problems of Knowledge. Cambridge, MA: The MIT Press, 1988.
133. Lenneberg EH: Biological Foundations of Language. New York: John Wiley & Sons, 1967.
134. Lenneberg EH: On explaining language. Science 1969; 164:635–643.
135. Brown R: A First Language: The Early Stages. Cambridge, MA: Harvard University Press, 1973.
136. Stromswold K: The cognitive and neural bases of language acquisition. In Gazzaniga M (ed): Cognitive Neuroscience. Cambridge, MA: The MIT Press, 1995:855–870.
137. Mehler J, Christophe A: Maturation and learning of language in the first year of life. In Gazzaniga M (ed): Cognitive Neuroscience. Cambridge, MA: The MIT Press, 1995:943–954.
138. Mehler J, Jusczyk PW, Lambertz G, et al: A precursor of language acquisition in young infants. Cognition 1988; 29:143–178.
139. Pennington BF: Diagnosing Learning Disorders. A Neuropsychological Framework. New York: Guilford Press, 1991.
140. Defries JC, Fulker DW, LaBuda MC: Reading disability in twins: Evidence for a genetic etiology. Nature 1987; 329:537–539.
141. Locke JL, Mather PL: Genetic factors in the ontogeny of spoken language: Evidence from monozygotic and dizygotic twins. J Child Lang 1989; 16:553–559.
142. Lewis BA, Thompson LA: A study of developmental speech and language disorders in twins. J Speech Hear Res 1992; 35:1086–1094.
143. Curtiss S: Genie: A Psycholinguistic Study of a Modern Day "Wild Child." New York: Academic Press, 1977.
144. Curtiss S: The independence and task-specificity of language. In Bornstein A, Bruner J (eds): Interaction in Human Development. Hillsdale, NJ: Lawrence Erlbaum, 1989:105–137.
145. Skuse DH: Extreme deprivation in early childhood I: Diverse outcomes for 3 siblings from an extraordinary family. J Child Psychol Psychiatry 1984; 25:523–541.
146. Skuse DH: Extreme deprivation in early childhood II: Theoretical issues and a comparative review. J Child Psychol Psychiatry 1984; 25:543–572.
147. Dennis M, Whitaker HA: Language acquisition following hemidecortication: Linguistic superiority of the left over the right hemisphere. Brain Lang 1976; 3:404–433.
148. St James-Roberts I: A reinterpretation of hemispherectomy data without functional plasticity of the brain. I: Intellectual functions. Brain Lang 1981; 13:31–53.
149. Wada JAR, Clarke R, Hamm A: Cerebral hemispheric asymmetry in humans. Arch Neurol 1975; 32:239–246.
150. Entus AK: Hemispheric asymmetry in processing of dichotically presented speech and nonspeech stimuli by infants. In Segalowitz SJ, Gruber FA (eds): Language Development and Neurological Theory. New York: Academic Press, 1977:63–73.
151. Bertoncini JJ, Morais R, Bijeljac-Babic S, et al: Dichotic perception and laterality in neonates. Brain Cogn 1989; 37:591–605.
152. Harlow JM: Recovery after severe injury to the head. Publ Mass Med Soc 1868; 2:327–346.
153. Kolb B, Wishaw IQ: Fundamentals of Human Neuropsychology, 2nd ed. New York: WH Freeman, 1985.
154. Blumer D, Benson DF: Personality changes in frontal and temporal lobe lesions. In Benson DF, Blumer D (eds): Psychiatric Aspects of Neurologic Disease, Volume I. New York: Grune & Stratton, 1975: 151–169.

155. Walsh KW: Neuropsychology, A Clinical Approach. New York: Churchill Livingstone, 1994.
156. Stuss DT, Benson DF: The Frontal Lobes. New York: Raven Press, 1986.
157. Fuster JM: The Prefrontal Cortex: Anatomy, Physiology, and Neuropsychology of the Frontal Lobe. New York: Raven Press, 1989.
158. Kolb B, Wishaw IQ: Fundamentals of Human Neuropsychology, 3rd ed. New York: WH Freeman, 1990.
159. Pandya DN, Yeterian EH: Architecture and connections of cortical association areas. In Peters A, Jones EG (eds): Cerebral Cortex, Volume 4. New York: Plenum Publishing, 1984:3–61.
160. Eslinger PJ, Grattan LM: Frontal lobe and frontal-striatal substrates for different forms of human cognitive flexibility. Neuropsychologia 1993; 31:17–28.
161. Stuss DT: Biological and psychological development of executive functions. Brain Cogn 1992; 20:8–23.
162. Yakovlev PI: Morphological criteria of growth and maturation of the nervous system in man. Res Publ Assoc Res Nerv Ment Dis 1962; 39:3–46.
163. Orzhekhovskaya NS: Frontal-striatal relationships in primate ontogeny. Neurosci Behav Physiol 1981; 11:379–385.
164. Bell M, Fox N: The relations between frontal brain activity and cognitive development during infancy. Child Dev 1992; 63:1142–1163.
165. Goldman-Rakic PS: Modular organization of prefrontal cortex. Trends Neurosci 1984; 7:419–424.
166. Rakic P, Bourgeois JP, Eckenhoff ME, et al: Concurrent overproduction of synapses in diverse regions of the primate cerebral cortex. Science 1986; 232:232–235.
167. Diamond A: Frontal lobe involvement in cognitive changes during the first year of life. In Carey S, Gelman R (eds): The Epigenesis of Mind: Essays on Biology and Knowledge. Hillsdale, NJ: Lawrence Erlbaum, 1991:67–110.
168. Diamond A, Goldman-Rakic P: Comparative development in human infants and infant rhesus monkeys of cognitive functions that depend on prefrontal cortex. Neurosci Abstr 1986; 12:742.
169. Diamond A, Doar B: The performance of human infants on a measure of frontal cortex function, the delayed response task. Dev Psychobiol 1989; 22:272–294.
170. Fox N, Bell M: Electrophysiological indices of frontal lobe development: Relations to cognitive and affective behavior in human infants over the first year of life. Ann N Y Acad Sci 1990; 608:677–698.
171. Chugani H, Phelps M, Maziotta J: Positron emission tomography study of human functional development. Ann Neurol 1987; 22:487–497.
172. Milner B: Effects of different brain lesions on card sorting: The role of the frontal lobes. Arch Neurol 1963; 9:90–100.
173. Milner B, Petrides M, Smith M: Frontal lobes and temporal organization of memory. Hum Neurobiol 1985; 4:137–142.
174. Case R: The role of the frontal lobes in the regulation of cognitive development. Brain Cogn 1992; 20:51–73.
175. Miller GA, Gallanter EH, Pribram KH: Plans and the Structure of Behavior. New York: Holt, Reinhart, & Winston, 1960.
176. Teuber HL: The riddle of frontal lobe function in man. In Warren JM, Akert K (eds): The Frontal Granular Cortex and Behavior. New York: McGraw-Hill, 1964:410–444.
177. Luria AR: The Working Brain. New York: Basic Books, 1973.
178. Norman DA, Shallice T: Attention to action: Willed and automatic control of behavior. In Davidson RJ, Schwartz GE, Shapiro D (eds): Consciousness and Self-regulation. Advances in Research and Theory. New York: Plenum Publishing, 1986:1–18.
179. Dubois B, Verin M, Teixeira-Ferreira C, et al: How to study frontal lobe functions in humans. In Thierry AM, Glowinski J, Goldman-Rakic PS, Christen Y (eds): Motor and Cognitive Functions of the Prefrontal Cortex. New York: Springer-Verlag, 1994:1–16.
180. Milner B: Report on section of the "frontal lobes" at the 17th International Symposium of Neuropsychology Neuropsychologia 1975; 13:129–133.
181. Vilkki J: Problem solving deficits after focal cerebral lesions. Cortex 1988; 24:119–127.
182. Anderson SW, Damasio H, Jones RD, Tranel D: Wisconsin Card Sorting Test performance as a measure of frontal lobe damage. J Clin Exp Neuropsychol 1991; 13:909–922.
183. Benton AL: Differential behavioral effects of frontal lobe disease. Neuropsychologia 1968; 6:53–60.
184. Vilkki J: Differential perseverations in verbal retrieval related to anterior and posterior left hemisphere lesions. Brain Lang 1989; 36:543–554.
185. Gotman M, Milner B: Design fluency: The invention of nonsense drawings after focal cortical lesions. Neuropsychologia 1977; 15:653–674.
186. Smith ML, Milner B: Estimation of frequency of occurrences of abstract designs after frontal or temporal lobectomy. Neuropsychologia 1988; 26:297–306.
187. Karnath H, Wallesch C, Zimmermann P: Mental planning and anticipatory processes with acute and chronic frontal lobe lesions: A comparison of maize performance in routine and nonroutine situations. Neuropsychologia 1991; 29:271–290.
188. Shallice T: Specific impairments in planning. In Broadbent DE, Weiskrantz L (eds): The Neuropsychology of Cognitive Function. London: The Royal Society, 1982:199–209.
189. Owen AM, Roberts AC, Polkey CE, et al: Extra-dimensional versus intra-dimensional set shifting performance following frontal lobe excision, temporal lobe excision or amygdalo-hippocampectomy in man. Neuropsychologia 1991; 29:993–1006.
190. Morris RG, Ahmed S, Syed GM, Toone BK: Neural correlates of planning ability: Frontal lobe activation during the Tower of London test. Neuropsychologia 1993; 31:1367–1378.
191. Lhermitte F: Utilization behavior and its relation to the lesions of the frontal lobes. Brain 1983; 106:237–255.
192. Lhermitte F, Pillon B, Serdaru M: Human autonomy and the frontal lobes. Part I: Imitation and utilization behavior: A neuropsychological study of 75 patients. Ann Neurol 1986; 19:326–334.
193. Joseph R: Neuropsychology, Neuropsychiatry, and Behavioral Neurology. New York: Plenum Publishing, 1990.
194. Eslinger PJ, Damasio AR: Severe disturbance of higher cognition after bilateral frontal lobe ablation: Patient EVR. Neurology 1985; 35:1731–1741.
195. Neary D, Snowden JS, Shields RA, et al: Single photon emission tomography using ^{99m}Tc-HM-PAO in the investigation of dementia. J Neurol Neurosurg Psychiatry 1987; 50:1101–1109.
196. Risberg J: Frontal lobe degeneration of non-Alzheimer type. III. Regional cerebral blood flow. Arch Gerontol Geriatr 1987; 6:225–233.
197. Starkstein SE, Robinson RG, Price TR: Comparison of cortical and subcortical lesions in the production of post-stroke mood disorders. Brain 1987; 110:1045–1059.
198. Robinson RG, Szetela B: Mood change following left hemispheric injury. Ann Neurol 1981; 9:447–453.
199. Baxter LR, Schwartz JM, Phelps ME, et al: Reduction of prefrontal cortex glucose metabolism common to three types of depression. Arch Gen Psychiatry 1989; 46:243–250.
200. Starkstein SE. Robinson RG: Affective disorders and cerebral vascular disease. Br J Psychiatry 1989; 155:79–85.
201. Kinsbourne M: Hemispheric interactions in depression. In Kinsbourne M (ed): Cerebral Hemisphere Function in Depression. Washington, DC: American Psychiatric Press, 1988:135–162.
202. Flor-Henry P, Fromm D, Schlopflocher D: Neuropsychological test performance in patients before and after drug therapy. Biol Psychiatry 1984; 19:55–72.
203. Kuhl DE, Metter JE, Riege WH: Patterns of cerebral glucose utilization in depression, multiple infarct dementia and Alzheimer's disease. In Sokoloff L (ed): Brain Imaging and Brain Function. New York: Raven Press, 1985:211–226.
204. Guenther W, Moser E, Mueller-Spahn F: Pathological cerebral blood flow during motor function in schizophrenia and endogenously depressed patients. Biol Psychiatry 1986; 21:889–899.
205. Weinberger DR, Berman KF, Zec RF: Physiologic dysfunction of dorsolateral prefrontal cortex in schizophrenia. I: Regional cerebral blood flow evidence (rCBF). Arch Gen Psychiatry 1986; 43:114–125.
206. Buchsbaum MS, Cappelletti J, Ball R, et al: Positron emission tomographic image measurement in schizophrenia and affective disorders. Ann Neurol 1984; 15(suppl):157–165.
207. Weinberger DR, Berman KF, Illowsky BP: Physiological dysfunction of the dorsolateral prefrontal cortex in schizophrenia. Arch Gen Psychiatry 1988; 454:609–615.
208. Sagawa K, Kawakatsu S, Shibuya I, et al: Correlation of regional cerebral blood flow with performance on neuropsychological tests in schizophrenic patients. Schizophr Res 1990; 3:241–246.
209. Buchsbaum MS, Nuechterlein KH, Haier RJ, et al: Glucose metabolic rate in normals and schizophrenics during the Continuous Perfor-

mance Test assessed by positron emission tomography. Br J Psychiatry 1990; 156:216–227.

210. Gur RE, Gur RC, Skolnick BE, et al: Brain function in psychiatric disorders. III. Regional cerebral blood flow in unmedicated schizophrenics. Arch Gen Psychiatry 1985; 42:329–334.
211. Berman KF, Illowsky BP, Weinberger DR: Physiological dysfunction of dorsolateral prefrontal cortex in schizophrenia. IV. Further evidence for regional and behavioral specificity. Arch Gen Psychiatry 1988; 45:616–622.
212. Volkow ND, Wolf AP, VanGelder P, et al: Phenomenological correlates of metabolic activity in 18 patients with chronic schizophrenia. Am J Psychiatry 1987; 144:151–158.
213. Andreasen NC, Rezai K, Alliger R, et al: Hypofrontality in neuroleptic naive patients and in patients with chronic schizophrenia. Arch Gen Psychiatry 1992; 49:943–958.
214. Knight RT: Attention regulation and the human prefrontal cortex. In Thierry AM, Glowinski J, Goldman-Rakic PS, Christen Y (eds): Motor and Cognitive Functions of the Prefrontal Cortex. New York: Springer-Verlag, 1994:160–173.
215. Mesulam MM: A cortical network for directed attention and unilateral neglect. Ann Neurol 1981; 10:309–325.
216. Deutsch G, Papanicolaou AC, Bourbon WT, Eisenberg HM: Cerebral blood flow evidence of right frontal activation in attention demanding tasks. Int J Neurosci 1987; 36:23–28.
217. Knight RT, Hillyard SA, Woods DL, Neville SJ: The effects of frontal cortex lesions on event-related potentials during auditory selective attention. Electroencephalogr Clin Neurophysiol 1981; 52:571–582.
218. Fuster JM: The Prefrontal Cortex. New York: Raven Press, 1980.
219. Knight RT: Evoked potential studies of attention capacity in human frontal lobe lesions. In Levin HS, Eisenberg HM, Benton AL (eds): Frontal Lobe Function and Dysfunction. New York: Oxford University Press, 1991:139–153.
220. Morecraft RJ, Geula C, Mesulam MM: Architecture of connectivity within a cingulo-fronto-parietal neurocognitive network for directed attention. Arch Neurol 1993; 50:279–284.

CHAPTER

17 Cognitive Psychology: Basic Theory and Clinical Implications

W. Edward Craighead
Stephen S. Ilardi
Michael D. Greenberg
Linda W. Craighead

This chapter discusses the cognitive aspects of human functioning and development within the context of a biopsychosocial interactive model. It provides an overview of major theoretical conceptualizations and the relevant empirical data regarding several psychological aspects of the development of normal and abnormal behavioral patterns and of effective biopsychosocial treatments. Among clinical psychiatrists and psychologists, there has been a tendency to divide the biopsychosocial factors of human functioning into the "bio" (e.g., physiological reactions to stressors), the "psych," which includes both cognition (e.g., intellectual functioning, cognitive appraisals) and emotion (e.g., feelings), and the "social" (e.g., environmental causative and ameliorative factors). Indeed, the organization of this section of this textbook reflects the partitioning of human functioning into various components. This subdivided biopsychosocial model has provided a heuristic framework for empirical advances, but successful clinical work requires the recognition that these components function in a continuously dynamic and interactive system. Over the life span, an individual's biological, psychological, and social systems—both normal and pathological—are interwoven in the developmental fabric of life.

In a historical sense, particularly in the field of psychiatry, Piaget's[1–3] theoretical model of human development has been most frequently associated with the word cognitive. His writings and observational data on the stages of human development have had a substantial impact on the study of children and adolescents as well as psychiatric theory and clinical practice with children, adolescents, and families. Piaget's work, in conjunction with that of later developmental psychologists, has highlighted the importance of taking the cognitive development, as well as the biological and social development, of the patient into account in the assessment and treatment of children and adolescents.[4] Furthermore, Piaget's work earlier in this century helped delineate the subsequent areas of inquiry about human psychological functioning and adaptation, and to some extent it has influenced the mainstream of cognitive psychology; however, his greatest legacy is clearly his seminal contributions to the study of human development and developmental psychology, of which cognitive development is only a portion. The focus of Piaget's theory was also considered cognitive when set in apposition to Freud's focus on emotion in his theory of psychosexual development.

Cognitive psychology developed as a distinct subarea of the broader field of experimental psychology and separate from developmental psychology during the 1950s and 1960s.[5] It is generally accepted in psychology that a "cognitive revolution"[6] had occurred by 1970[7]; by that date cognitive psychology had evolved as an independent subarea of psychological theory and scientific inquiry. Ashcraft[8(p37)] has defined cognitive psychology as "the scientific study of human memory and mental processes .... *Memory* refers to the mental processes of retaining information for later use and retrieving such information, and the mental storage system that allows this retention and retrieval. *Cognition* refers to the collection of mental processes and activities used in perceiving, remembering, and thinking, and the act of using those processes." Although cognitive psychology subsumes the areas of intellectual development (with the associated clinical fields of intelligence testing, academic achievement assessment, and neuropsychological assessment), the psychological aspects of neuroscience in general, and social cognition,[9] these topics are discussed in detail in the next two chapters. This chapter focuses instead on other major areas of cognitive psychology: attention, memory, and several of the most important "higher order" cognitive processes. Each of these topics is reviewed in detail, including both their relevant empirical findings and their clinical applications, in subsequent sections of this chapter. They are best understood, however, within the context of the history of cognitive psychology.

Historical Development of Cognitive Psychology

Early Psychology

The importance of psychological factors in human functioning has been understood and noted from ancient times. The beginning of psychology as an independent discipline, however, is usually not dated until 1879, which marks the establishment of Wundt's psychological laboratory in Leipzig, Germany. Wundt identified immediate experience and conscious mental processes as the substantive areas with which psychology should concern itself. To study these topics, he developed a scientific method of detailed, rigorous, and inward self-observation, which has become known as introspection. He trained numerous psychologists who continued his focus on this science of the mind. One of the foremost among them was Titchener, who joined the faculty of Cornell University in 1892. Titchener continued to focus his research efforts on understanding the structures (components) of the conscious mind via introspection; his topics of study and his methods of limited introspection he called *structuralism*.

Before the beginning of this century the other major approach to the study of human consciousness was initiated by William James,[10] a Harvard physician turned philosopher and psychologist, who focused on the processes by which the mind functions in human adaptation. This use of introspection to study how the mind functions came to be called *functionalism*, and it was subsequently championed by influential theoreticians and practical-minded investigators, the most notable of whom were Angell and Dewey.

These early psychologists were clearly studying cognitive processes; for example, James espoused a theory of memory that anticipated the prevailing contemporary view of short-term and long-term memory as described later in this chapter. However, during the first quarter of this century the study of cognitive processes was largely precluded by the development of another major school of psychology, *behaviorism*, with a markedly different empirical methodology and focus.

Rise of Behaviorism

The origins of behaviorism may be traced to multiple influences from throughout the world; behaviorism resulted from the confluence of numerous experiments and theoretical conceptualizations of human behavior in the first quarter of this century. Watson,[11] the most important person in the development of behaviorism, defined psychology as the science of behavior, which limited the scope of psychological inquiry to directly observable, objectively verifiable events and behaviors. This approach stood in direct contrast to the more subjective introspection of structuralism and functionalism.

Watson's work at The Johns Hopkins University, as well as the conditioning research in Russia and the animal behavior research in Europe (especially England), sharply focused early 20th century psychology on the study of behavior. There were, of course, exceptions to this primarily behavioral focus. For example, the 1927 assembly of the world's greatest psychologists at the dedication of the new psychology and chemistry building at Wittenburg College predicted that the "battlefield" for study in psychology in the 1930s would be "emotions."[12] Nevertheless, with the emphasis on external influences, stimuli and responses, and learning, behaviorists ruled the day in basic psychological research. Consequently, during the next 50 years, "several theories of learning were proposed to explain the acquisition of responses . . . . Generally, these premises adhered to the basic methodological tenets of behaviorism: focus upon stimuli and responses, reliance upon objective evidence, and rejection of consciousness . . . . several important theorists, notably Thorndike, Hull, Tolman, Guthrie, Mowrer, and Skinner, carved out individual positions within the realm of behaviorism."[13(pp71–72)]

Behaviorism is the conceptual framework within which behavioral therapy was developed.[14] By drawing on behavioristic principles of learning,[13, 15] the primary core of experimental psychology, behavioral therapists developed several clinical interventions including applied behavioral analysis (use of operant conditioning), systematic desensitization,[16] and several exposure procedures for anxiety disorders. The point is that clinical psychiatrists, psychologists, and social workers utilized findings from basic psychological research (primarily behavioral learning principles) to develop clinical interventions, and these were then evaluated by basic scientific methodologies; these are the two hallmarks of behavioral therapy. As shall be seen momentarily, as the basic science of psychology became more cognitive in focus and clinicians continued to draw on basic psychology during the 1960s, the resulting clinical interventions became more cognitive. Before we discuss specific implications and applications of cognitive psychology for clinical practice, however, the questions of how and why basic psychological research moved back from behaviorism to a cognitive focus must be answered.

Emergence of Cognitive Psychology

During the 1940s, a number of developments led psychologists to recognize the limitations of classical behaviorism, including its use of conditioning and a genetic tabula rasa, to explain complex human behaviors. These events included 1) development of complex learning theories that focused on internal cognitive processes, 2) explanations of language development, 3) development of the computer and the associated concepts of information processing, and 4) the more practical applications of psychological research necessitated by World War II.[8] These events, coupled with ensuing developments during the next two decades, produced the cognitive revolution in psychology and the emergence of cognitive psychology, first as a major subarea of experimental psychology and later as one of the primary and relatively independent areas of basic psychological inquiry (alongside the experimental, social and personality, developmental, and clinical areas).

One of the major developments in experimental psychology of the 1940s was the formulation of sophisticated learning theories to explain the complex processes of human functioning and behavior acquisition.[17] These theories posited the existence of a number of "intervening variables" and "hypothetical constructs"[18] between the environmental stimulus and the person's response as a means of explaining the variance in individuals' behavior. This represented an implicit indication of the significance of internal mediators in human adaptation, although at that point in history every attempt was made to tie these mediators to external and observable variables. The assertion that the acquisition of all behaviors could be accounted for on the basis of the stimulus-response learning model came under increasing scrutiny during the 1950s and 1960s, as experimental findings and theoretical explanations from a number of psychology's subdisciplines appeared to belie the explanatory efficacy of the stimulus-response model.[19]

The study of language behavior, highlighted in the now famous debate between Skinner[20] and Chomsky[21] over language acquisition, suggested strongly that language cannnot be viewed as simply a set of associations acquired according to operant conditioning principles.[7] Likewise, findings in the area of human memory indicated that people are not mere passive receptacles of new information; rather, they engage in active strategies (e.g., "chunking") in the encoding and retrieval of information—strategies that necessarily occur inside the "black box" of the human. The field of perception also provided numerous examples of the influence of intrasubject events (i.e., cognition) on perceptual processes. Finally, Bandura's[22] elegant demonstrations of observational learning, or modeling, pointed to yet another set of phenomena that were not easily reconciled within the stimulus-response model.

As Kuhn[6] has observed, however, paradigm shifts in scientific disciplines do not occur simply by virtue of the appearance of data that do not fit the predictions of the existing scientific paradigm; rather, there must also emerge a rival theoretical model that appears to do a better job of acccounting for the existing empirical data. In the case of psychology's cognitive revolution, the appearance of the computer (another black box that processes information) provided psychology with a compelling metaphor of human cognition and suggested a model within which human thought might take on an objective (or at least scientifically testable) rather than purely subjective existence.[15] Betweeen 1955 and 1965, the computer metaphor inspired numerous attempted theoretical formulations of human cognition according to principles of linear information processing.

Another major event that underscored the significance of cognitive or mental processes in human functioning was World War II. Although the application of learning theory to clinical problems during World War II marked the beginning of contemporary behavioral therapy,[14] several other areas in which psychology laboratory findings were needed demonstrated the inadequacy of the stimulus-response learning theory or black box approach to understanding human mental processes. Major limitations of the behavioral approach were evident in the need for practical and applied information regarding vigilance and attention for radar operators, decision-making and problem-solving processes, and human factors, for example, person-machine interactions.[8, 23]

The preceding developments coalesced into the area of psychology referred to as cognitive, and by 1967 Neisser[24] provided a seminal summary of cognitive psychology reviewing in detail information-processing approaches and findings from related models and empirical data regarding internal mental processes of human functioning. Later, Neisser[25] leveled major criticisms at cognitive research models, emphasizing the sterility of laboratory research, given its focus on visual and auditory problems in settings with only limited external validity to real-world functioning. Despite its limitations, cognitive psychology has made major advances in our understanding of internal cognitive processes. In particular, fairly extensive findings regarding attention and memory have resulted in numerous clinical applications; furthermore, there are several clinically applicable findings derived from research on higher order cognitive functions including problem solving, development and modification of schemata, and automatic versus conscious processing.

Applying Cognitive Theories to Clinical Problems: The Beginning

These developments in basic psychology were at first largely independent of clinical applications. Addressing data from both basic experimental psychology and the clinical area, Bandura[22] proposed a new paradigm, *social learning theory*, representing an original integration of operant and respondent learning with symbolic cognitive processes. Building on the phenomenon of observational learning (modeling), the theory proposed that behavior acquisition may occur solely as a result of cognitive processes (e.g., attention, retention). Although not denying that new behaviors could be learned via conditioning, he proposed that cognitive processes could mediate the acquisition of new behavior. Bandura[26, 27] further proposed that behavior is not simply determined by an individual's environment (the orthodox behaviorist position) but rather that person and environment reciprocally influence one another; he labeled this *reciprocal determinism.*

Significantly, Bandura made extensive use of information-processing models of cognition in formulating his social learning theory model and applying it to clinical problems. He thereby set the stage for the development of a new clinical approach—*cognitive-behavioral therapy.* This approach differs from behavioral therapy because it incorporates cognition as both a mechanism and a target of clinical change and it replaces environmental determinism with an acknowledgment of reciprocal determinism betweeen the individual and the environment.

Perhaps more than those of other theoretical orientations, behaviorally oriented psychiatrists have continued to draw heavily on basic cognitive psychology in the development of cognitive-behavioral therapy.[15, 22, 28–30] Indeed, as Craighead[31] reported, about 70% of the members of the Association for the Advancement of Behavior Therapy now describe themselves as cognitive-behavioral. The developments within cognitive psychology have applications, however, that go beyond cognitive-behavioral therapy. In addition to the material discussed in this chapter, the relevance of cognitive psychology to clinical practice is also apparent in Chapter 16. The historical developments identified in this chapter are outlined in Table 17–1. In the following sections of this chapter, we review the general findings regarding attention, memory, and higher order cognitive processes and give exemplars of their application to various areas of psychopathology and treatment interven-

Table 17–1 Historical Developments in Cognitive Psychology

Theoretical Paradigm	Inception Date	Seminal Contributors	Description
Structuralism	1880s	Wundt, Titchener	The study of immediate experience and conscious mental processes through a scientific method of detailed and rigorous self-observation (introspection)
Functionalism	1890s	James, Dewey	The study of human consciousness focused on the processes by which the mind functions in human adaptation
Behaviorism	1910s–1950s	Watson, Skinner	The science of behavior, limiting the scope of inquiry to objectively verifiable behavioral events; cognition largely ignored
Social learning theory	1960s	Bandura	Focus on behavioral acquisition mediated by cognitive processes (e.g., modeling)
Cognitive psychology	1960s, 1970s	Neisser	Seminal integration of findings from areas such as linguistics, information processing theory, social learning theory, and perception to formulate comprehensive theoretical model

tions. Figure 17–1 provides an overall schematic of the interactions of the cognitive processes that are discussed in this chapter. The reader may wish to refer to this schematic when beginning to read each section of the chapter.

Attention

As discussed earlier in this chapter, the information-processing activities of the human brain may be broadly subdivided into such categories as perception, short-term memory, long-term memory, and numerous higher order functions (e.g., problem solving, judgment). It is important to note, however, that there are inherent limits on the degree to which these various processes may be carried out simultaneously (this fact should be readily apparent to anyone who has ever tried to drive a car through traffic, carry on a conversation, listen to the radio, and recall the directions to one's destination all at the same time); in other words, the sum total of mental resources available for processing information at any given time is finite.[32, 33] The purposeful allocation of one's finite mental resources is a process known as attention.[8]

Because the volume of information encountered in the environment typically far exceeds the brain's available processing capacity, it follows that only a limited subset of available data is ever selected for processing by the attentional system. Thus, the direction of attention has profound implications regarding the adaptive functioning of the individual, inasmuch as it falls to the attentional system to identify and select the most salient pieces of data in need of processing at each moment. The attentional system serves, in this respect, as a type of executive controller, which continually sets and adjusts priorities among the myriad potential processing options. Inefficient or erratic allocation of attention could, by extension, engender maladaptive behavioral responses (in the driving example, devotion of excessive attention to ruminative thoughts about a previous argument could lead to impairment of the driver's ability to recognize and avoid a traffic hazard). Chronic misallocation of attentional resources could, as shown later, be indicative of serious psychopathology.

Although it has long been known that attentional focus is a necessary precondition for many complex modes of cognition, such as abstract reasoning,[10, 34] there has emerged, in the past two decades, an increasing recognition among cognitive psychologists that some mental processes occur in the complete or partial absence of attentional focus.[35–37] Such cognitive processes are often referred to as *automatic*, because they seem to operate without conscious awareness or involvement. In essence, each cognitive process could be located on a continuum ranging from fully automatic to fully conscious (or, to use a term often preferred by cognitive psychologists, *controlled*),[37] based on the degree of attentional focus required for any particular process to occur. Furthermore, it is believed that many

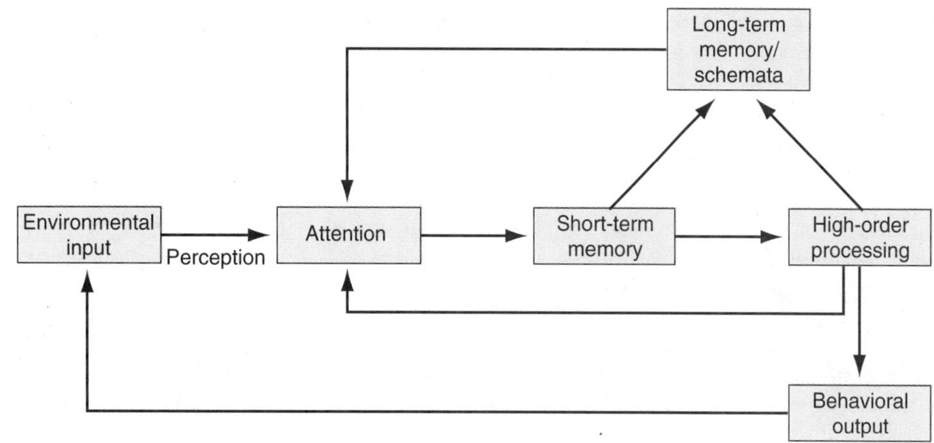

Figure 17–1 *Human cognition.*

complex cognitive processes that initially require conscious attention become automatic, with repeated practice, as a result of their being "overlearned."[35] For example, the typical 4-year-old devotes considerable attention to the task of tying a shoelace, as such an undertaking represents a novel challenge, but an adult accomplishes this feat relatively automatically, presumably by virtue of many years of practice.

One of the most important characteristics of automatic cognitive processes is that they consume a relatively small portion of available mental resources; by contrast, it is believed that a person's total attentional resources are occupied by the processing of just one demanding conscious task.[8] Automatic cognition, therefore, appears to make possible the phenomenon of parallel processing, in which one or more automatic processes occur in the background while attention is accorded to a more demanding task in the foreground of conscious awareness. Such background processing is often profoundly advantageous with respect to the individual's adaptive functioning. It has been suggested, however, that some automatic cognitive processes may be etiologically involved in certain forms of psychopathology, to the extent that the end products of automatic processing (so-called automatic thoughts), which come to fruition without the benefit of attentional inspection, turn out to be aberrant or distorted.[28]

The following sections examine various ways in which the functioning, or malfunctioning, of attentional processes may be involved in four relatively common psychiatric disorders: generalized anxiety disorder (GAD), major depression, attention-deficit/hyperactivity disorder (ADHD), and borderline personality disorder (BPD).

Anxiety Disorders

In general, information selection by the attentional system tends to follow a principle of salience; that is, people tend to attend to pieces of information that are perceived to be of greatest importance at any given moment. Accordingly, it has been consistently observed that various emotional states (e.g., anxiety, sadness, anger) produce a selectivity bias for environmental cues congruent with those states.[38–41] Thus, an individual in an anxious state gives heightened attention to threat-related cues,[39, 40] as such cues are usually particularly salient to the feelings of anxiety; this selectivity process may in turn filter out and discard information not congruent with the anxious mood state. Such a mood-congruent attentional bias helps orient the individual to the source of danger, which may in turn help ensure that the individual formulates an appropriate response to the threatening situation. To the extent that there is a reasonable goodness of fit between the level of anxious arousal and the level of genuine threat posed to the individual by the environment, the mood congruence attentional bias serves an adaptive function. When the level of anxiety is consistently incommensurate with the environmental context, however, a state of pathological anxiety ensues.

Barlow's *anxious apprehension model*[42] suggests that pathological anxiety, such as that observed in GAD, may arise from a chronic misapprehension, or overestimation, of the level of threat posed by a wide array of situations, many of them benign. It is further proposed that, once the anxious arousal of a patient with GAD is triggered by the misapprehension of threat, there is a narrowing of external attention to the perceived danger, concurrent with a ruminative internal self-focus on negative expectancies regarding the situation's outcome. Two deleterious consequences of such an attentional bias predictably ensue: 1) the patient disregards or discounts information that could serve to correct the original misapprehension of threat, and 2) the patient's attentional resources are so thoroughly consumed by the focus on negative expectancies that few resources are available for constructive problem solving and adaptive responding.

Consider the situation in which one encounters a stranger at a party. The patient with GAD may immediately begin to feel somewhat anxious as a result of an overestimation of threat ("I'll probably embarrass myself horribly by saying something stupid"), which occurs automatically. The increase in anxious arousal leads to a narrowing of attention, which causes the patient to ignore the stranger's friendly smile and focus instead on ruminative negative thoughts. This attentional narrowing consumes mental processing resources to the extent that the patient is unable to engage in a conversation, and the encounter ends with the patient having validated his or her negative self-fulfilling prophecy ("I knew I would embarrass myself").

There are numerous clinical implications of Barlow's anxious apprehension model regarding psychotherapeutic interventions for pathological anxiety, many of which address the proposed dysregulations of the patient's attentional system described earlier. First, the patient with anxiety may be taught to attend to the physiological cues of anxious arousal (e.g., rapid shallow breathing or increased heart rate) and to reinterpret such arousal as less threatening by virtue of its being partially under the patient's control, via such techniques as progressive relaxation.[42, 43] The patient may also learn to identify the tendency toward self-focus that accompanies anxious arousal and to shift attentional focus away from self and toward the discovery of a satisfactory response to the situation at hand. Such an adaptive response is, in turn, made more probable by the widening of attentional focus that is believed to occur after the patient's successful lessening of physiological arousal (e.g., through the application of relaxation techniques). Empirical studies of the efficacy of this clinical approach generally suggest that it is highly effective in the treatment of both GAD[44] and panic disorder.[45]

A somewhat related cognitive model of pathological anxiety has been proposed by Beck and Emery[46] in the *schema theory* of anxiety. Central to this theory is the mechanism of cognitive appraisal, with anxiety as the feeling state resulting from the appraisal of threatening stimuli. The appraisal process, in turn, is believed to be influenced by cognitive structures known as schemata, which consist of stored information abstracted from previous experience.[47] Schema-guided appraisal is held to take place automatically, that is, largely outside conscious awareness and reflection; for example, a hiker who has stepped next to a snake probably makes a quick appraisal of danger and experiences substantial anxiety without the need for time-consuming conscious processing of snake-related material stored in long-term memory (although, in a sense, the activated

Table 17–2 Prominent Clinical Exemplars of Cognitive Psychology

DSM Syndrome	Relevant Cognitive Psychological Finding	Clinical Application*
Major depressive disorder	Mood-congruent bias in recall and encoding of memory	CBT: Patient is trained to examine noncongruent memories (positive or neutral) to compensate for schematic distortion.
	Occurrence of negativistic automatic thoughts regarding self, world, and future	CBT: Patient is directed to challenge automatic thoughts and to generate rational alternatives and is subsequently taught to challenge underlying negative beliefs.
	Deficits in problem solving	IPT: Patient is instructed in the use of problem-solving techniques, primarily in the interpersonal domain.
Generalized anxiety disorder	Heightened attention to environmental threat cues	CBT: Patient is directed to use relaxation techniques as means of ameliorating the anxiety state, thereby attenuating attentional bias.
	Overestimation of environmental threat	CBT: Patient is trained to undertake rational evaluation of all relevant environmental stimuli.
	Schematic bias in retrieval of threat-related memories	CBT: Threat-related schemata are modified via integration of successful coping experiences.
Borderline personality disorder	Poor regulation of emotion secondary to lack of attentional control	DBT: Patient is trained in the use of numerous attentional control techniques (e.g., core mindfulness; see Linehan).
	Deficits in problem solving secondary to attentional dyscontrol	DBT: Patient is directed to shift attention from rumination over difficulties to discovery of more adaptive responses to problem. Also, patient receives direct training in social problem-solving skills.

*CBT, Cognitive-behavioral therapy; IPT, interpersonal psychotherapy; DBT, dialectical behavioral therapy.

"snake schema" contains a preprocessed distillation of such information).

Predictably, schema theory views pathological anxiety as the result of faulty schemata that lead to habitual, and largely automatic, overappraisal of danger; pathological appraisal often takes place automatically, without benefit of the scrutiny that accompanies attentional focus. Accordingly, Beck's therapeutic approach to ameliorating pathological anxiety involves helping the patient allocate more attentional resources to the appraisal process, as a corrective to faulty schematic processing. To return to the example of meeting a stranger at a party, the patient with GAD could be taught to attend to the initial automatic misappraisal of threat ("I'll probably embarrass myself") and give conscious attentional consideration to the genuine level of threat posed. In this case, the patient might challenge the automatic misappraisal by purposefully shifting attention to an examination of evidence from past experiences and recalling that many such previous encounters with strangers led to noncatastrophic outcomes. Clinical exemplars of applications from cognitive psychology to the treatment of anxiety disorders are presented in Table 17–2.

Major Depression

It has been consistently observed that individuals suffering from major depression are prone to a negativistic bias in cognitive processing.[48, 49] Within Beck's influential cognitive model of depression,[28, 50] these depressotypic negative thoughts are held to be centrally involved in the onset and maintenance of the depressive episode. In addition, Beck's model proposes that many depressive thoughts occur automatically, in the absence of attentional awareness. For example, a depressed student, on receiving an A on an examination, may think, "I can't believe I missed those easy questions; I'm so stupid"—a negatively biased assessment, the quick and effortless occurrence of which is suggestive of automatic, as opposed to conscious, processing.[8] Two investigations of cognitive processing in dysphoric college students provide modest empirical support for the hypothesis that such depressotypic thoughts may occur automatically,[51, 52] although it should be noted that the automaticity hypothesis has not heretofore been tested directly with a sample of clinically depressed subjects.[48, 53]

The *cognitive therapy* of depression of Beck and colleagues,[50] a treatment approach arising from the cognitive model, has received extensive empirical validation as a highly effective treatment modality for unipolar major depression, with an efficacy rate in controlled outcome trials consistently equal to that of antidepressant medications.[54, 55] The cognitive therapy protocol focuses on amelioration of depressive symptoms via a reduction in the occurrence of negativistic depressive thoughts. Because many of these thoughts are held to arise automatically, the first step in the cognitive restructuring process involves helping the patient to monitor, through a shift in attentional focus, the occurrence of automatic thoughts.[50] As noted previously, this type of attentional shift from automatic to more controlled processing appears to help facilitate a more accurate and less biased appraisal of relevant information. Thus, the depressed student receiving the A, on shifting attention to the biased conclusion—"I'm so stupid"—would be more capable of subjecting such a thought to considerable scrutiny ("I've made one of the highest grades on this test, so I must not be that stupid"). Not surprisingly, this type of cognitive restructuring appears to catalyze an improvement in depressive mood.[56–58]

Additional roles of attentional processes in depression have been noted by investigators. In a manner similar to that observed with anxiety disorders, it appears that the attention of depressed patients is selectively focused on environmental cues congruent with the depressed state,[48] such as cues related to themes of failure or rejection. Beck[28] has identified several negativistic "cognitive errors" that may arise from the depressive attentional bias; for example, *selective abstraction* is a process in which the depressed patient attends selectively to information consistent with negativistic themes (e.g., "I missed three items on this test") and filters out counterbalancing positive cues ("I received one of the highest grades in this class"). Cognitive errors are believed to be linked to the occurrence of negative automatic thoughts (e.g., "I really blew it on this test")[59] (see Table 17–2).

Another prominent dysregulation of the attentional system in major depression has been identified by Rehm in the *self-control model* of depression,[60] in which it is noted that depressed patients often devote excessive attentional focus to ruminative appraisal of self. By extension, *self-management therapy* for depression[61] assists patients in shifting attentional focus away from self, thereby freeing up mental processing resources for the formulation of more effective behavioral responses.

Attention-Deficit/Hyperactivity Disorder

ADHD is a syndrome characterized by a deficiency in sustained attentional focus, typically accompanied by poor inhibitory control of behavior.[62] Although it has been discovered that a substantial number of adults meet formal criteria for ADHD in the *Diagnostic and Statistical Manual of Mental Disorders,* Fourth Edition (DSM-IV),[63] the bulk of research activity on cognitive processing anomalies in ADHD has been confined to children and adolescents. This literature has provided robust documentation of the difficulty encountered by children with ADHD in sustaining and maintaining attention to various higher order cognitive tasks.[64] Such difficulties appear to be especially prominent in the presence of environmental distractors.[65, 66] In general, it appears that the attentional system of children with ADHD frequently functions inefficiently, so that relevant stimuli often go unidentified, irrelevant stimuli (distractors) are accorded disproportionate attention, and even on occasions when attention is given to appropriate environmental information, such attention is often broken off prematurely; that is, the children frequently respond to environmental stimuli before consideration of all relevant data.[67] In light of the profound and far-ranging importance of attentional processes discussed earlier, it is not surprising that children with ADHD frequently experience deficits in social and academic functioning.

Various stimulant medications, most notably methylphenidate, have been shown to be efficacious in the acute treatment of ADHD.[62, 68] However, as noted by Kendall and MacDonald,[64] there are numerous limitations to stimulant therapy that highlight the need for effective psychosocial interventions for ADHD: 1) some children with ADHD do not respond to stimulant medication; 2) medication appears to be limited in its effect on some higher order cognitive processes, such as problem solving; 3) medication may not ameliorate long-standing deficits in social skills; 4) some children experience difficulties complying with medication regimens; and 5) gains made during medicaton therapy are often not maintained after termination of treatment. Cognitive-behavioral treatment interventions for ADHD, therefore, would appear to constitute a potentially valuable supplement and/or alternative to medication. A major multisite clinical trial is evaluating the comparative effectiveness of combining medication and cognitive-behavioral treatment.

Cognitive-behavioral therapy for ADHD is predicated on the concept that treatment interventions should directly address the cognitive deficiencies, many of them attentional, prominent among children with ADHD.[69] A number of cognitive-behavioral approaches have been formulated and subjected to clinical evaluation.[70–72] These various approaches tend to concentrate on teaching children strategies to assist them in attending to salient stimuli and ignoring irrelevant information in the pursuit of goal-directed behavior, as well as training and practice in maintaining attention on the relevant environmental field before shifting attentional focus internally to the formation of a behavioral response. Cognitive-behavioral interventions have generally been found effective in increasing attentional efficiency among children with ADHD, including improvements on tests of sustained attention[73–75] and complex problem solving.[76] However, the efficacy of these interventions appears to be less pronounced in more severe cases of ADHD,[64] perhaps owing to the fact that a moderately well-developed capacity for attentional focus may be a prerequisite to the successful acquisition and application of many cognitive-behavioral techniques.

Borderline Personality Disorder

One of the primary diagnostic criteria for BPD in DSM-IV is "affective instability due to a marked reactivity of mood."[63] In fact, inability to regulate emotional states has been identified as one of the hallmarks of BPD.[77, 78] The significance of this finding for the present discussion lies in the fact that there exists a strong reciprocal relationship between emotion regulation and attentional focus: an increase in emotional arousal narrows attention to a focus on emotion-relevant stimuli[38–41, 79]; conversely, the ability to shift attention away from affect-inducing stimuli may be central to the process of emotion modulation.[80–82] Therefore, it has been hypothesized that the characteristic difficulties with emotion regulation of the patient with BPD may be directly linked to a relative lack of attentional control.[78]

Although BPD has gained an extraordinary reputation among mental health professionals as one of the most difficult to treat and intractable psychiatric syndromes, a cognitive-behavioral approach to BPD—Linehan's[78, 83] *dialectical behavioral therapy*—has been shown in a series of clinical trials to be highly effective in ameliorating many of the more serious symptoms of BPD, including parasuicidal behavior and impulsive angry outbursts.[84–86] Significantly, the dialectical behavioral therapy protocol includes numerous interventions that seek to address the dysregulations in attention characteristic of patients with BPD.

A central goal of the dialectical behavioral therapy approach is the cultivation of core mindfulness, a frame of mind described by Linehan as "[being] in control of attentional processes—that is, what one pays attention to and how long one pays attention to it."[87(p65)] The patient with BPD is taught to recognize the connection between attentional fixation on distressing stimuli and a commensurate escalation in affective arousal, especially problematical negative affective states such as rage and depression. Thus, there is explicit recognition in dialectical behavioral therapy that enhanced attentional control is a primary treatment goal.

The dialectical behavioral therapy protocol includes a number of specific strategies employed to facilitate more efficient and adaptive functioning of the borderline patient's attentional system (see Table 17–2). Attentional exercises include 1) teaching the patient purposefully to fix attention on neutral sensory stimuli (e.g., the feeling of one's hand on a cool surface), 2) monitoring internal thought processes and deliberately shifting attentional focus away from each thought that arises, and 3) focusing all available attentional resources on what would otherwise constitute an automatic process (such as washing dishes) as a means of interrupting ruminative cognitive processing. The patient is also taught a plethora of attentional distraction techniques; these are strategies that most people (but not those with BPD) appear to employ almost automatically in times of emotional distress (e.g., engaging in exercise, calling a friend, listening to soothing music) as a means of reducing the intensity of emotional arousal. In fact, it would be fair to state that the majority of treatment interventions incorporated in the dialectical behavioral therapy protocol address, in some manner, the patient's suboptimal attentional control. The demonstrated efficacy of this treatment approach would appear to validate the importance of psychiatrists attending carefully to the attentional processes of patients with BPD.

Conclusion

The purposeful allocation of one's finite mental resources is a process known as attention.[8] Attentional processes have profound implications regarding adaptive functioning, inasmuch as it falls to the attentional system to identify and select the most salient pieces of information in need of processing at each moment. Inefficient or erratic allocation of attention may engender maladaptive behavioral responses. Furthermore, it has been noted that a subset of cognitive processes appears to occur in the absence of attentional focus; such processes are often referred to as automatic.[36] Some automatic processes may also be etiologically involved in certain forms of psychopathology to the extent that automatic thoughts, which occur without the benefit of attentional inspection, turn out to be aberrant or distorted.[28] Dysregulations of the attentional system appear to play a central role in several clinical disorders such as GAD, major depression, ADHD, and BPD. Consequently, efficacious cognitive-behavioral interventions for these disorders have accorded considerable attention to the development of strategies designed to facilitate more efficient and adaptive functioning of the attentional system.

Memory

The second major area of study in cognitive psychology involves the investigation of memory. In the most generic sense, memory refers to the components of an information-processing system that support the encoding, storage, and retrieval of information over time. A familiar example is that of the electronic computer, in which information is encoded into a string of binary digits (or bits), stored as a series of electrostatic differentials on a silicon chip, and subsequently retrieved for use by a microprocessor. Computer memory gives the machine the capacity to retain information for subsequent use. By sequentially retrieving individual packets of data, the computer can execute a complicated set of instructions, at a time arbitrarily removed from the occasion on which those instructions were written. Given the appropriate organization and memory content, the computer can respond intelligently (within limited domains) to the demands that are placed on it. The adaptive implications of electronic memory are therefore profound.

Clearly, any analogy between computer memory and human memory is at best inexact. Setting aside the obvious difference in physical substrates, computers and humans appear to possess different mnemonic talents. Humans, for example, are typically poor at remembering large strings of digits with pinpoint accuracy. By contrast, computers are limited in the kinds of information they can store and in the flexibility with which they can employ stored information. Nevertheless, both computer memory and human memory possess the same fundamental, descriptive properties. Both involve the transformation of external, physical stimuli into internal, symbolic representations. Both involve the structured storage of internal representations and the capacity for subsequent retrieval and decoding. And for both computers and humans, memory is the primary, necessary component of experientially informed, adaptive behavior.

The systematic study of human memory long predates the development of electronic computers. Beginning with the works of Ebbinghaus and of William James in the late 1800s, psychologists have spent the better part of a century in trying to identify and to understand human memory functions. The sum of these investigations has been an increasingly fine-grained empirical approach to the study of memory,[8, 88, 89] as well an increasing recognition that human memory consists of several distinct subsystems with different properties. Thus, it is often suggested that memory is composed of short-term and long-term stores, with the former referring to the limited capacity for conscious rehearsal and focused recollection of new material and the latter referring to a much broader capacity to recollect stored information after it has been removed from immediate consciousness.

Several other important distinctions have been developed in the past 25 years of research on memory. *Procedural memory*, for example, refers to recollection for skills and physical operations, procedures that can be remembered automatically and without conscious awareness (e.g., complex motor activity such as riding a bicycle). By contrast, *declarative memory* refers to the process of conscious recollection, as of information or experience.[90] A further distinction has been drawn between *episodic* and *semantic* memories, or the capacities to recall autobiographical events versus abstract information or images.[91] These sorts of distinctions have proved important in research efforts to isolate different neural mechanisms corresponding to different memory systems. The distinctions have also proved significant in clinical settings, in which distortions and deficits in memory have been associated with certain kinds of psychopathology.

The limits of the current chapter do not permit a comprehensive review of the research literature in cognitive psychology on human memory. For current purposes, it is sufficient to point out that the study of memory has become a useful adjunct to the cognitive perspectives on psychopathology. The central theme of these perspectives is an emphasis on maladaptive thinking in the genesis and maintenance of psychiatric disorders. Once granted the premise that dysfunctional thoughts and/or cognitive biases may play a pivotal role in the dynamics of psychopathology,[28, 50, 92] it follows that memory may serve as a cognitive mediator in many forms of mental disorders; an extensive empirical literature has developed through efforts to test this premise.

The following sections of this chapter present a brief overview of memory-related research for two particular psychiatric disorders, depression and posttraumatic stress disorder (PTSD). Because the memory deficits associated with these disorders have been substantially documented by researchers, a review of the findings may prove useful for clinical and diagnostic purposes. The findings also carry a more general set of implications. To the extent that human memory processes are vulnerable to emotional dysfunction, all adaptive behavior is potentially compromised, because behavioral adaptation cannot take place in the absense of (accurate) recollection. Memory deficits may therefore pose an additional set of behavioral problems quite apart from their immediate role in psychiatric disorders. In consequence, the formulation of psychiatric treatment plans requires professional recognition of the potential behavioral impact of memory biases and deficits.

Clinical Depression, Memory, and Schematic Bias

One of the most important contemporary perspectives on clinical depression derives from the cognitive model of Beck and associates.[28, 50, 92] The model posits that clinical depression may often involve a set of cognitive biases, that these biases can exert an influence on individual perceptions and beliefs, and that the biases may ultimately serve to maintain depressive affect. Beyond the attentional biases noted earlier, Beck and colleagues postulated a cognitive triad of negative thoughts concerning the world, the self, and the future and suggested that the triad may lead to a pattern of systematically inaccurate and deleterious inferences regarding the contingencies in a person's life. Because these inferences fail to reflect the full range of plausible interpretations of reality, they may come to exert an increasingly powerful and circular influence on the person's mood state. The tendency to make negativistic inferences can over time become more and more generalized, corresponding to the description by Beck and colleagues[50] of an overactive and idiosyncratic depressive schema.

Beck's cognitive theory of depression is predicated on the notion that cognitive mechanisms (e.g., perception, memory, and appraisal) play an active role in the disorder processes. The cognitive substrates of major depression have received increasing attention in the empirical literature,[49, 93–95] with results that strongly implicate maladaptive or deficient cognitive processes as an important element in depressive syndromes. In particular, a good deal of effort has been devoted to the study of memory in depression and to the differences in memory function between depressed and nondepressed individuals. Most of these studies fall into two broad categories, examining 1) generic impairment of memory associated with depression and dysphoric affect and 2) mood congruence effects in memory, such that depressed individuals are negatively biased in their capacity to recall affectively toned materials. These categories are reviewed in turn.

Clinical depression, as defined by the parameters of DSM-IV,[63] includes at least two symptoms that bear directly on memory function: impairment of concentration and fatigue or exhaustion. Thus, depression by definition implies some tendency toward deficit in the human capacity to remember. Empirical studies have repeatedly documented significant memory deficits in clinically and subclinically depressed individuals, although idiosyncratic patterns of results have been associated with different strategies for testing memory performance. In general, memory decrements have been most commonly documented for explicit (i.e., consciously directed) memory, across a wide variety of recall and recollection tasks.[96–101] By contrast, research findings on implicit memory (i.e., automatic or unconscious recollection, as in tests of lexical priming) are sparse and inconsistent.[98, 99] Pending the outcome of further research on implicit memory tasks, depression-related memory impairment appears to be most prominent in tests of consciously directed memory retrieval.

An interesting and related finding in the study of depressive memory deficits involves the role of information structure in moderating recall. Structure, in this context, refers to the degree to which information can be hierarchically organized or chunked into easily encodable fragments (e.g., the digit clusters of a phone number) as opposed to an unstructured, inchoate mass (e.g., an unstructured list of digits). Because of the limited capacity of short-term memory storage for individual list items (i.e., about seven), structured information ordinarily facilitates superior encoding for later memory retrieval.[8, 89] For depressed individuals, however, there is evidence that information structure may be less effective in facilitating memory performance. Findings by several researchers[102–104] have indicated that memory deficits in depressed individuals may be moderated by the level of structure in memory test materials, such that the deficits are somewhat more pronounced in experimental tasks with less structured materials. This finding complements the work of several other researchers[105–107] suggesting that depressed individuals may be less effective or less motivated in the employment of mnemonic strategies (i.e., optimally organizing or encoding new material to facilitate later recall). Taken together, the studies imply that depressed individuals, compared with nondepressed individuals, may be less attentive to structural cues in informational materials or else less successful in employing structural cues to boost subsequent memory performance; further study is required to clarify the issue.

In sum, depression (clinical and subclinical) has been linked to impaired performance in a variety of memory experiments, and additional research has suggested that the effect may partly reflect deficits in the recognition or employment of informational structure in stimulus materials. It remains to be demonstrated conclusively whether similar impairments obtain for implicit memory processes (in which the subject is unaware of any conscious recollection). There is a different line of research, however, that bears more directly on depression and automatic (or unconscious) memory processes. According to the theory of depression of Beck and colleagues,[28, 50, 92] the depressed individual is prone to make negativistic inferences and generalizations and prone to consequent biases in recall and recognition memory (e.g., through selective abstraction, overgeneralization, magnification, minimization). These memory biases have been more broadly described as mood-congruent recall, referring to distortions in memory based on current mood state. Mood-congruent recall is an implicit, automatic memory process (to the extent that mood state may exert a systematic effect on the content of memory retrieval, without conscious awareness or intention on the part of the individual).

Extensive empirical research has demonstrated mood-congruent (negativistic) memory distortions in depressed individuals across multiple tasks and settings.[108–116] Mood congruence effects have been demonstrated in both clinical (inpatient) and subclinical populations, as well as in empirical manipulations designed to elicit dysphoric moods in college students. Furthermore, these effects have been noted in tasks of autobiographical recall, as well as in tests of recall and recognition for verbal or textual materials.[117] Once again, idiosyncratic patterns of memory bias have been obtained in individual studies, but in the aggregate these studies suggest that depressed individuals, in comparison with nondepressed control subjects, may be more prone to recollect negatively toned experiences (and stimulus items) and less prone to recollect postively toned experiences (and stimulus items).

On a related topic, these findings lend fuel to a long-running debate on the subject of depressive distortion versus realism. Depressive realism refers to the hypothesis that depressed individuals may actually be more accurate than nondepressed persons in their recollections and perceptions (i.e., nondepressed people may actually distort memory in a positive direction). Several empirical studies have found that both depressed and nondepressed individuals may be prone to memory biases, albeit in different patterns,[118, 119] and reviewers have concluded that depressed people may be either more accurate or less accurate in recall, depending on the specific tasks that are employed in memory research.[120, 121] In general, mood-congruent recall appears to be a fairly robust phenomenon among both depressed and nondepressed individuals (see Matt and coworkers[94] for a meta-analytical review). The data regarding events with negative valence are sometimes consistent with the depressive realism hypothesis, with nondepressed individuals filtering out negative experiences, but the data regarding positive events have nearly always been inconsistent with the depressive realism hypothesis, with depressed individuals recalling fewer positive events than in fact have occurred.[122]

Research on depression and memory is an ongoing endeavor. Patterns of empirical results have grown increasingly complex as investigators have employed different memory tasks, studied different memory subsystems, and recruited research subjects based on different diagnostic criteria. For clinical purposes, two generic findings are important to remember. First, depression is associated with general impairment for explicit memory tasks (recognition and recall). Second, depression is also associated with a mood-congruent memory bias. Taken individually, either of these symptoms may interfere with adaptive coping, because accurate memory is necessary for adaptive and intelligent behavioral responses. In combination, the two symptoms can have a substantial impact on an individual's perceptions of the self, the world, and the future (Beck's cognitive triad[28, 50]), serving both to impair behavior and to maintain depressive affect. In consequence, memory disturbance in depression can be an important focus for clinical intervention,[50] and it should ideally be considered in the formulation of a comprehensive treatment package.

Posttraumatic Stress Disorder, Repression, and Memory Impairment

The diagnosis of PTSD was first formally added to the psychiatric nomenclature in 1980, when the disorder was included in the *Diagnostic and Statistical Manual of Mental Disorders,* Third Edition (DSM-III)[123] after political lobbying by organized veterans' groups.[124] PTSD is an unusual disorder classification, because it is one of the few disorders in DSM-IV that is defined on the basis of an etiology as well as a symptom profile; to suffer from PTSD, one must first have been exposed to traumatic circumstances, these involving perceptions of death or physical injury, intense fear, helplessness, or horror.[63] Survivors of PTSD suffer from a persistent and aversive tendency to reexperience the traumatic event, as manifested by symptoms of intrusion, dissociation, and hyperarrousal. These symptoms can include recurrently intrusive images or dreams, hallucinatory flashbacks, intense psychological distress (caused by symbolic reexposure), blunted affect, social withdrawal, hopelessness, amnesia, avoidant behavior, irritability, insomnia, hypervigilance, and impaired concentration. When experienced in combination, these symptoms may often result in a highly debilitating syndrome that operates to the exclusion of adaptive coping behavior.

Memory mechanisms in PTSD have become the focus of a major controversy. The disorder by definition involves a pathological response to memories that are so traumatic as to be at once unforgettable (hence the intrusive symptoms) and intolerable to remember (hence the dissociation). The resulting heterostasis leads to emotional and physical dysregulation and presents a challenge to fundamental beliefs regarding security, efficacy, and prospect for future well-being.[125] Although the symptoms of PTSD have been widely documented in cases of demonstrated physical trauma,[125] conflict and criticism have arisen in regard to putative cases in which the traumatic events cannot be objectively documented apart from the recollections of the survivor. By itself this might not represent a bone of contention, except that many clinicians and researchers believe that trauma memories can be entirely repressed for long periods, sometimes returning (along with PTSD symptoms) only years after the traumatic event took place. These claims have led other researchers to question the validity of completely repressed, unverifiable traumatic memories, particularly given established empirical findings that human episodic memory is often reconstructed, suggestible, and inaccurate.[126]

As in the case of depression, two sorts of memory deficits have commonly been associated with PTSD. Several empirical studies have investigated general memory function among PTSD survivors by using standardized tests of short-term and long-term memory, as well as tasks of cued recall and free recall. Findings have been noteworthy for significant memory impairment among PTSD survivors compared with control subjects, across a number of different memory tests and stimulus materials.[127–130] It is currently unclear whether PTSD memory deficits derive from some (unidentified) neuropsychological sequelae of extreme stress exposure or are simply concomitant to prolonged symptoms of hypervigilance, emotional distress, or comorbid depression. It is clear from these data that PTSD is associated with significant proactive interference in memory, such that survivors are impaired in their ability to encode and to retrieve new information.

The second type of memory deficit in PTSD involves symptoms of amnesia for, and intrusion of, memories for the initial traumatic event. These symptoms represent a functional deficit in memory, such that the survivor is alternately confronted with emotionally disturbing recollections and unable to access the traumatic memory. Amnesia and intrusion have both been clearly documented among known survivors of trauma (e.g., veterans and accident victims[125]). Nevertheless, the vicissitudes of amnesia and intrusion imply by their nature some distortion in the memory process for traumatic events; in consequence, some researchers have questioned whether PTSD victims are entirely accurate in their recollections. At least one study has suggested that memories for trauma may shift over time, with significant alterations in reports of perceived threat and emotional distress.[131] Loftus[126] has further argued that it is often difficult to assess the reality basis for specific claims of repressed trauma memory and that the processes of traumatic repression have never been subjected to a rigorous program of scientific examination.

Questions about the accuracy (or inaccuracy) of repressed memory are difficult to address. The cognitive psychology literature includes several empirical demonstrations of human suggestibility in the retrieval of memories in the context of a laboratory[132, 133]; however, these studies may be inapplicable to PTSD, because the research subjects were never exposed to any psychological trauma. Several other studies have examined the accuracy of highly vivid autobiographical memories (called "flashbulb" memories), with mixed findings of inaccuracy and unreliability in subjects' recollections.[134, 135] Here again, findings based on nontrauma populations may fail to generalize to trauma survivors, because of the unique quality (e.g., inescapability, intense aversiveness) of trauma experiences. And yet, although the prevalence of amnesic and dissociative symptoms in PTSD has been validated by studies of trauma survivors,[136, 137] these studies do not address the validity of more controversial cases that reportedly involve complete (and asymptomatic) repression over long periods. Empirical efforts to document long-term traumatic repression continue to meet with significant methodological and conceptual criticisms.[138, 139]

It is unfortunately the case that the most extreme claims of traumatic repression cannot be subjected to direct empirical study, because the traumatic events cannot be confirmed after the fact or (ethically) controlled in the setting of a research laboratory. Although further investigation may serve to clarify issues regarding memory accuracy and repression in PTSD, research findings are unlikely to offer any conclusive standard for the validation of traumatic memories for specific individuals.[126] Thus, the practicing psychiatrist must recognize the possibility of suggestibility and bias in retrieval of traumatic memories[126, 140, 141] while maintaining a stance of openness and compassion in helping trauma survivors to clarify and to reintegrate their memories of traumatic events.[125] In sum, PTSD is a disorder of unbearable and inescapable recollection, and both research and therapy will continue to focus on the elucidation of memory for trauma.

Conclusion

Human memory is the central, essential ingredient in an information-processing system more sophisticated than any electronic computer ever designed. Human cognition supports operations more diverse by far than those of a computer, ranging from complex mathematical and spatial reasoning, to artistic and literary endeavors, to athletic prowess and interpersonal awareness. Memory is the substrate of these many skills and the foundation for human consciousness. And to the extent that we are each more than the sum of our biological components, it is in large part the texture of our own unique memories that makes us so.

Over the course of the past century, the empirical effort of cognitive psychologists has led to an increasingly refined understanding of the interlocking mechanisms that constitute human memory. This understanding has begun to be applied to the domain of clinical assessment and psychopathology. Researchers have documented the role of memory deficits and biases in several mental disorders, including (but not limited to) depression and PTSD. The results of these investigations have suggested that memory, just as it plays an essential role in adaptive human functioning, may also play a central role in maladaptive, pathological functioning. The cognitive perspectives on psychopathology place an emphasis on the role of schematic memory bias in its contribution to various forms of psychiatric disorder, and corresponding psychotherapeutic techniques have been developed to address bias in memory.[28, 50] The study of memory in psychopathology seems likely to become only more important with the passage of time, and ongoing research should lead to further improvement in the therapeutic technologies for cognitive intervention.

Higher Order Cognitive Processing

The current chapter has made frequent reference to the obvious correspondences between the information-processing capabilities of humans and computers. For example, perception and attention are generally analogous to computerized data input. Likewise, human short-term memory functions similarly to a computer's working memory buffer, and long-term memory serves a storage function similar to that of computer random-access memory (or hard-disk space). To this point, however, we have not addressed the human equivalent of computerized algorithmic information processing or the manner in which information is organized and manipulated in meaningful ways. In a computer, algorithmic processing is a function that is typically carried out by computer software; in humans, such processes have come to be described by several different terms including problem solving, schematic processing, and automatic processing. We refer to these processes as higher order because they involve the algorithmic manipulation of existing information rather than the more elementary processes of acquisition and storage of information. Following is a brief discussion of higher order cognitive processes, particularly as they apply to clinical research and practice.

Problem Solving

Anderson[142(pp199–200)] stated that "human cognition is always purposeful, directed to achieving goals and to removing obstacles to those goals." In that sense, all cognitive activity might be considered problem solving. Within the field of cognitive psychology, however, problem solving has referred to fairly narrow realms of empirical research. Ashcraft[8(p576)] defined problem solving as the "rather slow and deliberate cognitive processing . . . in which a problem has been presented to the individual, the solution to the problem is not immediately obvious, and the individual is often uncertain what to do next." As such, it would seem that similarities to the clinical situation would be immediately obvious; however, early empirical work on problem solving developed outside the clinical arena and was not seen as particularly relevant either to understanding psychopathology or to facilitating clinical treatment.

Basic research on problem solving has made some differentiation between the concepts of problem solving and the concepts of learning, which were the major early influences on the development of behavioral therapies. Bruner[143] described the psychology of learning as focused on the aquisition and extinction of specific responses, whereas the psychology of problem solving was focused on the utility of learning, that is, whether having learned one response, a person could solve other problems without the occurrence of any further explicit learning. The clinical applications of problem solving reflect this distinction, as the goal is to teach the patient a general strategy for coping independently with problems as they arise rather than just addressing a specific (i.e., presenting) problem. As indicated throughout this chapter, tensions between the more mental (introspective) and the more overt (behavioral) conceptualizations of human functioning have been evident over the course of the history of psychology. In current clinical practice, however, problem solving is an excellent example of how both perspectives can be integrated. Problem solving is first modeled by the therapist; then the patient is coached through a number of current problem situations as well as possible future problem situations. Throughout, the mental steps of problem solving as an explicit strategy for coping with new situations are labeled and reinforced. Behavioral strategies are also utilized as needed to carry out the chosen solution. Mental processes are again emphasized as the patient evaluates the results of attempting the initial solution and decides whether the solution is adequate or whether further problem solving is needed. The effectiveness of problem solving is usually determined by the patient's ability to apply the strategy to new situations (i.e., generalization).

The early empirical work on problem solving began during the 1920s when Gestalt psychologists[5] studying perception concluded that humans tended to perceive and deal with integrated, cohesive wholes. Findings from their work suggested that humans tend to fill in missing parts of familiar patterns and often misperceive, or have difficulty perceiving, something because of their prior exposure. Thus, human perception does not work like an objective or camera image. In extending this work with animals, Kohler observed that Gestalt principles also applied to the animals' perceptions about relationships among real-life objects and how a particular object could be used. As Kohler studied animals' attempts to solve real-life problems (such as how to reach a banana), he noted that they often came up with novel uses of objects to solve their problems. He called these sudden perceptions of useful or proper relations insight.

These observations about insight, the generation of novel response options (also called creativity), represented significant contributions of Gestalt psychology, but at the time they had little impact on clinical work. Behaviorism and insight via psychoanalysis were then the primary clinical models, and problem-solving research had provided little in terms of specifying how such adaptive insights might be encouraged. One positive contribution, however, was the documentation of the utility of using analogies in efforts to solve problems. The use of analogy refers to seeing an already solved problem as similar to a current one and adapting the old solution to the new situation. Research (summarized in Ashcraft[8]) following up on these earlier findings has enumerated several ways of increasing subjects' use of analogies such as giving explicit hints and explicitly describing the cause-and-effect connections in the original problem.

Other Gestalt psychologists made significant contributions by documenting two fundamental processes that tended to interfere with, or limit, adaptive problem solving. Duncker[144] described the phenomenon of functional fixedness, which refers to the tendency to use objects and concepts in the problem environment only in their customary and usual way. Luchins[145] described a related difficulty, negative set, which refers to a bias or tendency to solve problems in one particular way, using a single specific approach even when a different approach might be more productive. Unfortunately, consistent with Neisser's later criticism[25] of cognitive research, these phenomena were demonstrated in laboratory subjects attempting to solve cognitive problems; little effort was made to demonstrate that such processes probably also affect many common everyday problems that people face. Thus, although this early work undoubtedly influenced later psychiatrists who developed problem-solving therapy, there has been little explicit connection. Nonetheless, these demonstrations provide interesting empirical support for the conclusion that human thinking (and consequent behavior) can be overly rigid and that this rigidity may compromise effective problem solving. As can be seen in the current discussion of schemata and their particular application to personality disorders (i.e., rigid or inflexible behavior patterns), the cognitive processes noted in this early research help explain the recurrent clinical observation that patients often have difficulty in looking at their problems and potential resources in a new ways; instead they use already established strategies or patterns of relating, despite some awareness that new strategies might be more effective.

The beginnings of the cognitive revolution in the 1950s brought renewed attention to cognitive problem solving as the mental activities ignored by the behaviorist tradition became more legitimate topics of inquiry. Many critics had contended that prior research was limited by the Gestalt assumption that the process must be studied as a whole and could not be broken down into component processes. Newell and Simon[146] exemplified the modern approach to the study of problem solving. Their methodology involved the extensive analysis of verbal protocols, that is, subjects' verbalizations as they attempted to solve (often lengthy) mental problems. Many researchers still considered the use of verbal protocols too introspective and inadequately rigorous, but these in-depth analyses of human mental processes ultimately led Newell and Simon to their most important conceptual contribution—the idea that human thought could be conceived of as internal symbol manipulation, or the processing of information. Their analogy to algorithmic information processing in computers proved useful; data input was similar to perception, data representation was similar to memory, and data manipulation was similar to problem solving.

This conceptualization served as the foundation for the information-processing approach, which has since dominated the field of cognitive psychology. Newell and Simon created a computer simulation (called the General Problem Solver) to emulate human problem-solving processes (based on their earlier study of verbal protocols). Although later researchers found some instances of particular problems in which the model failed to do an adequate job of simulating human problem solving, the work on the General Problem Solver made a significant contribution in establishing the fundamental role of means-ends analysis in human thinking—defined as "solving problems by repeatedly determining the difference between the current state and the goal or subgoal, then finding and applying an operator that reduces this difference."[8(pp602–603)] Means-ends thinking (generating specific step-by-step means by which a problem could be resolved) was one of several types of social problem-solving thinking emphasized in the clinical application of problem solving developed by Spivak and Shure.[147] The others were alternative thinking (generating numerous solutions to problems), which derived from cognitive work on brainstorming; consequential thinking (the ability to anticipate the consequences that may occur as a result of emitting a particular behavior); causal thinking (ability to relate one event to another over time and understand why one event led to a particular action from another person); and perspective taking (ability to view the problem from the perspective of other persons involved in it).

Beginning with the work of D'Zurilla and Goldfried[148] and Spivack and Shure,[147] the clinical relevance of the cognitive processes involved in problem solving has been increasingly recognized. In their overview of problem solving, Goldfried and Davison[149(p186)] concluded that "much of what we view clinically as 'abnormal behavior' . . . may be more usefully construed as ineffective behavior with its negative consequences, such as anxiety, depression, and the creation of secondary problems." Deficits in problem solving have been documented as nonspecific deficits associated with many psychiatric disorders (e.g., schizophrenia). Problem-solving techniques are considered standard cognitive-behavioral interventions with applications to such diverse problems as depression, suicidal behavior, anxiety, marital problems, and adolescent social problems.[150–153] Applications with children have focused on reducing aggressive behavior,[154] reducing impulsive behavior,[155] and teaching social competence in prevention programs.[156]

To understand the clinical relevance of basic cognitive research in problem solving, it is useful to point out that the more purely cognitive aspects are only part of what psychiatrists think of as problem-solving therapies. Goldfried and Davison[149(p187)] specified that "the major objective in problem solving is to *identify* the most effective alternative, which may then be followed by other self-control operations to stimulate and maintain performance of the selected course of action. Thus, problem solving becomes a crucial initial phase in a more general self-control process, often described by such terms as 'independence,' 'competence,' and 'self-reliance.' " Similarly, other descriptions of problem-solving therapy make the distinction between the cognitive skills needed to generate and evaluate alternative solutions and the social skills needed to implement the intended solution. Thus, training in various behavioral skills may be incorporated into problem-solving therapies.

In the current practice of problem-solving therapies, there is general agreement on the five steps central to most problem-solving applications. These steps may be traced to observations deriving from empirical work on problem solving in cognitive psychology, although actual explicit empirical links have never been established. These five steps, first enumerated by D'Zurilla and Goldfried,[148] are 1) developing a general orientation or set to recognize problems, 2) defining the specifics of the the problem and what needs to be accomplished, 3) generating alternative courses of action, 4) deciding among the alternatives by evaluating their consequences, and 5) verifying the results of the decision process and determining whether the alternative selected is achieving the desired outcome. If the outcome is not satisfactory, the process is repeated. These basic steps of clinical problem solving, at times combined with components of Spivak and Shure's[147] program (e.g., taking the perspective of other persons), have formed the core of the empirically validated problem-solving therapies that are usually identified as a type of cognitive-behavioral therapy.

Although developed within a psychodynamic framework rather than being based on basic cognitive psychology, interpersonal psychotherapy employs problem solving in ameliorating the four interpersonal problem areas it addresses: grief, interpersonal role disputes, role transitions, and interpersonal deficits.[157] In each of these areas, the therapist and patient identify specific problems to be solved and work out solutions to those problems; of course, there is a good deal of focus on the patient's feelings about the process of therapy and the life experiences associated with the implementation of the solutions in the problem areas. Perhaps it is this general interpersonal problem-solving focus of interpersonal psychotherapy that underlies its apparent effectiveness with diverse clinical problems such as anxiety, eating, and marital discord.[158]

Schema Theory

When Beck initially proposed his cognitive model for depression,[28, 50] he suggested that depressive affect may derive, in part, from patterns of maladaptive thinking. Beck hypothesized that depressed individuals may suffer from a cognitive triad of negative beliefs about the world, the self, and the future and furthermore that this triad might be maintained (or exacerbated) by cognitive errors, or flaws in information processing. The depressed individual was hypothesized to engage in patterns of dichotomous thinking, arbitrary inference, overgeneralization, and selective abstraction, these resulting in a systematic bias toward negativistic and depressogenic beliefs. Finally, Beck and colleagues[50] suggested that new information about particular experiences or situations is processed through the medium of an established, organized, cognitive structure based on the abstraction of relevant prior experience. This organized, cognitive structure is called a *schema*, and it has become one of the primary elements in the cognitive perspective on depression (as well as the cognitive perspective on other forms of mental disorder).

The concept of schema was originally developed by researchers in cognitive psychology, in the context of the early studies of human memory. Investigators found that memory, although sometimes incredibly accurate for the details of complicated events, is often quite abstract and sketchy and sometimes even distorted in the process of recollection. Findings of inaccuracy and bias did not seem consistent with a memory mechanism that encodes events in the manner of a tape recording. The schema construct was formulated in an attempt to explain how memory might be organized to produce the inaccuracies and incompleteness that are often observed in human recall.[159] The fundamental premise of schema theory is that new information is somehow screened by and amalgamated into existing cognitive structures. Experiences that are relevant to any particular domain become abstracted and incorporated into a corresponding schema, which then influences the interpretation of new experience and the encoding and recollection of new memories.

In their review of the empirical literature in cognitive psychology on schemata, Alba and Hasher[159] pointed out that schema has never been formally defined and that the term actually derives from a loose set of theories about the organization and construction of memory. In vernacular use, schema has become synonymous with more general mentalistic constructs such as categories and prototypes.[89, 160] These distinctions become important in the interpretation of particular research studies, because idiosyncratic definitions of schema can potentially influence the methods and findings of corresponding research. Nevertheless, schema theories generally postulate the existence of a set of memory structures that can selectively direct attention and can subsequently influence memory encoding through abstraction, interpretation, and integration. Schemata have been hypothesized to function in many different cognitive domains, ranging from person perception (e.g., stereotypes[88]) to interpersonal knowledge (e.g., scripts[161]) to general semantic representations and understandings (e.g., categories and prototypes[160]). Schema theory has been popular in empirical research in cognitive psychology, and over time the schema construct has gradually been exported to investigations in other disciplines among the behavioral sciences.

The application of schema theory to the study of psychiatric disorders represents one of the most important elements in the cognitive perspective on psychopathology. Although Beck is most widely known for his theories about depression, he has also written about the cognitive bases for other emotional disorders (including anxiety and anger[28]), as well as the cognitive basis for the personality disorders.[162] In all of these theories, the central credo involves the influence of schematic bias in the interpretation of new information and the encoding of new memory. Thus (for example) in depression, the overgeneralized operation of negativistic schemata is hypothesized to lead to faulty and depressogenic inferences about events and experiences in an individual's life.[50] An example of a depressogenic schema is the attributional cognitive style of the reformulated learned helplessness theory.[163] These authors, employing the attribution theory domain of personality and social psychology research,[164] postulated that depressed individuals explain negative life events to themselves and others by attributing the causes of these events to internal, stable, and global factors. In subsequent writings, this group extended the theory by further hypothesizing that depressed individuals attribute positive life events to external (e.g., luck), unstable, and specific causes.

Although the data pertinent to this theory have been mixed (especially for negative events) and indicate that this cognitive style is characteristic of only a subset of depressed individuals, it is a good example of the integration of a cognitive schema with a prior behavioral model (learned helplessness)[165] of depression. Another example of the role of schemata in psychopathology is observed in the personality disorders, wherein an individual is hypothesized to suffer from a self-perpetuating and treatment-resistant "early maladaptive schema," which essentially involves a dysfunctional set of assumptions and interpretations regarding oneself in relation to other people and/or the environment.[166] Cognitive theory can be extended, by analogy, to many of the other forms of psychiatric disorders.

Cognitive schemata are believed to exert their influence at many different levels of information processing. Schemata are hypothesized to direct the selectivity of attention, as well as the interpretation of ambiguous information, and the integration of new experiences into an existing cognitive matrix. For this reason, schema theory can be used as an overarching, explanatory framework for much of the clinical psychopathology research on attentional mechanisms, memory biases, and reasoning processes. Findings in support of schema theory are often focused on demonstrations of cognitive bias, consistent with prior clinical predictions.[167–169] More generally, much of the research that is described elsewhere in this chapter (particularly in the sections on attention and memory) bears directly on the validity and usefulness of schemata in understanding mental disorders. The sum of this research bears testimony that schema theory may be the single most important contribution of cognitive psychology to the ongoing investigation of psychiatric dysfunction.

Automatic Versus Conscious Processing

As noted previously, mental processes exist that appear to occur in the absence of attentional focus and thus outside conscious awareness; these processes are frequently described as being automatic.[35–37] It was further noted that complex mental processes, such as driving to work, initially require considerable attentional focus but may eventually become automatic as a result of overlearning.[35] Automatic cognitive processes often facilitate adaptive functioning, inasmuch as they permit the individual to engage in numerous cognitive operations concurrently (i.e., parallel processing). However, it has also been suggested that some automatic thoughts, such as appraisals, may turn out to be aberrant or distorted.[46] And because such thoughts are not subjected to the scrutiny that accompanies conscious attentional focus, aberrant automatic thoughts are unlikely, under most circumstances, to be corrected.

This model of automatic cognitive processes, drawn from constructs generated in basic cognitive psychology, has been implicated in the etiology and maintenance of numerous forms of psychopathology, most prominently GAD[42, 46] and unipolar depression.[28, 50] For example, the patient with GAD is hypothesized to engage in automatic overestimation of potential threat in a variety of environmental contexts, many of them benign.[46] This automatic misappraisal is believed to be influenced, in large measure, by the operation of faulty schemata, cognitive structures that represent the preprocessed distillation of various threat-related experiences stored in long-term memory. Likewise, depressed patients have been observed to engage frequently in a variety of negativistic automatic thoughts, presumably influenced by the operation of schemata concerning themes of rejection and failure.

Successful cognitive-behavioral treatment approaches to both GAD and depression, accordingly, have incorporated interventions designed to assist patients in shifting attentional focus to a deliberate evaluation of automatic thoughts as they occur, as a means of detecting and correcting distortions that might otherwise engender distressing affect and maladaptive behavioral responses. In a sense, this cognitive-behavioral approach may be viewed as one in which "unconscious" (i.e., automatic) cognitive processes are made more conscious. It is fitting that, at the end of a chapter on the history and clinical applications of cognitive or mental processes, the focus turns to the concept of the unconscious, which has occupied a central role in much of clinical theory and practice throughout this century.

While remaining perhaps the most fascinating subject for the psychiatrist, the unconscious is simultaneously the greatest conundrum facing clinical theory, research, and practice. At the beginning of this century, Freud made the unconscious the primary focus of psychotherapy by suggesting that pathological symptoms may often derive from unconscious mental conflict and repression of emotion.[170, 171] These ideas rapidly gained popularity and resulted in a proliferation of psychotherapies based on variations of psychoanalytic theory.

The rise of behaviorism and its applications in behavioral therapies in the 1950s and 1960s, however, led many psychiatrists to reject psychoanalysis, based on the premise that freudian constructs (e.g., unconscious conflict, defense mechanisms) could not be directly observed and were therefore incompatible with scientific methodology. Whereas strict behaviorism focuses exclusively on the external contingencies that elicit observable behaviors and thereby rejects the usefulness of internal cognitive processes, its offspring, cognitive behaviorism, focuses on the manner in which human appraisals, beliefs, and recollections can influence behaviors (as well as emotional experience). The cognitive-behavioral theories of psychopathology stress the importance of mediating cognitive processes in the ongoing relationship between emotional responses and external stimuli. In fact, various cognitive-behavioral psychotherapists have attempted to provide explanations of the unconscious and integrate those concepts into clinical interventions.[172–174] Thus, psychotherapists are no longer left to choose between the dichotomy of the psychodynamic concepts of the unconscious and the behavioral rejection altogether of the unconscious. Rather, almost all current models of clinical intervention accept the notion of unconscious or automatic processing, regardless of the name attached to the construct within each model. Unresolved are the issues of how and why unconscious processing affects consciously directed or controlled cognitive processing as well as overt behavior. Is the unconscious emotionally motivated, or does it simply reflect adaptive mental coping processes that allow humans to function in an increasingly complex world? Continued advances in cognitive psychology and neuroscience should soon answer some of these complex questions.

One prominent example among the myriad attempts to address these questions is the debate and research on the nature of the relationship between cognition and emotion. Some researchers have argued that emotional experience cannot take place in the absence of some level of cognitive functioning.[175–178] Others have taken the position that primitive emotional responses can occur independently of any cognitive mediation.[179–181] The issue has been clouded by semantic confusion regarding the exact meaning of cognition. The distinction among behaviors, cognition, and emotion is demonstrated by the DSM-IV diagnostic category of bereavement.[63, 182] Bereavement describes a period of intense dysphoria that is experienced in response to the loss of a loved one and can include many of the symptoms of a major depressive episode. Presumably, bereavement cannot take place until an individual becomes aware of the loss (a cognitive event) and overwhelmed by the recognition that life can never again be the same.

For the practicing psychiatrist, the exhaustive search for primary causes may be less valuable than the recognition of the potential for bidirectional influences in pathological states. The purpose of the current chapter has been to examine some of the interactions among cognition, behavior, and (dysfunctional) affective states and thereby to acquaint the psychiatrist with the role of cognition in psychopathological syndromes. In conclusion, as noted at the beginning, these cognitive processes must be considered within a broad biopsychosocial model of whole human beings and the context in which they live and function.

Conclusion

Psychology's beginning as an independent discipline is usually dated as 1879, which marked the establishment of Wundt's psychological research laboratory. Wundt identified immediate experience and conscious mental processes, which were cognitive in nature, as the substantive areas for study by psychology. That focus of inquiry was maintained in the United States by the structuralism of Titchener and the functionalism of James and others. Early in this century, however, the rise of behaviorism, with its emphasis on external influences on behavior acquisition and observation as a methodology, marked a hiatus in research regarding cognitive psychological processes. A number of factors, including the development of complex learning theories, discussions regarding language development, use of computers as a metaphor for human information processing, and practical applications needed during World War II, all contributed to the cognitive revolution in psychological research during the 1950s and 1960s. Cognitive psychology is now one of the major areas of psychological inquiry alongside experimental, developmental, social and personality, and clinical.

The major synthesis of cognitive psychology with clinical practice has been forged by cognitive-behavioral therapists. There are, however, other major applications and implications of cognitive psychology, including the work reviewed in this chapter regarding attention, memory, and higher order cognitive processes such as problem solving, schema construction and modification, and automatic processing (see also Chapter 16).

The purposeful allocation of one's finite mental resources is a process known as attention.[8] Attentional processes have profound implications regarding adaptive functioning, inasmuch as it falls to the attentional system to identify and select the most salient pieces of information in need of processing at each moment. Inefficient or erratic allocation of attention may engender maladaptive behavioral responses. Furthermore, it has been noted that a subset of cognitive processes appear to occur in the absence of attentional focus; such processes are often referred to as automatic.[36] Dysregulations of the attentional system appear to play a central role in several clinical disorders, such as GAD, major depression, ADHD, and BPD. Consequently, efficacious cognitive-behavioral interventions for these disorders have accorded considerable attention to the development of strategies designed to facilitate more efficient and adaptive functioning of the attentional system.

Human memory is the central, essential ingredient in an information-processing system more sophisticated than any electronic computer. Human cognition supports operations more diverse by far than those of a computer, ranging from complex mathematical and spatial reasoning, to artistic and literary endeavors, to athletic prowess and interpersonal awareness. During the past century, the empirical effort of cognitive psychologists has led to an increasingly refined understanding of the interlocking mechanisms of human memory. This understanding has now been applied to the domain of clinical assessment and psychopathology. Researchers have documented the role of memory deficits and biases in several mental disorders, including (but not limited to) depression and PTSD. The results of these investigations have suggested that memory, just as it plays an essential role in adaptive human functioning, may also play a central role in maladaptive, pathological functioning. The cognitive perspectives on psychopathology place an emphasis on the role of schematic memory bias in its contribution to various forms of psychiatric disorder, and corresponding psychotherapy techniques have been developed to address bias in memory.[28, 50]

Problem solving is the complex mental process of using previously learned information to identify solutions to new problems. Although the specific empirical links between basic research and clinical practice have been sparse, the conceptual connections have provided several clinical procedures that are identifiable within self-control, cognitive-behavioral, and interpersonal psychotherapies.

The concept of schema was developed by cognitive psychologists studying memory. The schema construct was formulated to explain how memory is organized and why it produces the inaccuracies and incompleteness often observed in human recall. The incorporation and abstraction of new experiences into relevant schemata serve to influence the interpretation of future experience and thereby the encoding and recollection of new memories. Schemata, therefore, affect all levels of human cognitive processing and may well be the most significant contribution to date in cognitive psychology. The development and modification of schemata are central to Beck's and others' models of cognitive-behavioral conceptualizations of psychopathology and therapeutic change.

Finally, material is frequently processed automatically while conscious processing occurs on a parallel cognitive track. This raises intriguing questions regarding the similarities and differences in various conceptualizations of the unconscious. Answers to questions raised about automatic processes may well be the most significant future contributions cognitive psychology and neuroscience integration can offer clinical practice.

References

1. Piaget J: The Origins of Intelligence in Children. New York: WW Norton, 1963. Originally published in 1936.
2. Piaget J: Intelligence and Affectivity. Palo Alto, CA: Annual Reviews, 1981. Originally published in 1954.
3. Piaget J, Inhelder B: The Psychology of the Child. New York: Basic Books, 1969.
4. Meyers AW, Craighead WE: Cognitive Behavior Therapy with Children. New York: Plenum Publishing, 1984.
5. Leahey TH: A History of Psychology: Main Currents in Psychological Thought, 3rd ed. Englewood Cliffs, NJ: Prentice Hall, 1992.
6. Kuhn TS: The Structure of Scientific Revolutions. Chicago: University of Chicago Press, 1962.
7. Dember WN: Motivation and the cognitive revolution. Am Psychol 1974; 29:161–168.
8. Ashcraft MH: Human Memory and Cognition, 2nd ed. New York: HarperCollins College Publishers, 1994.
9. Shantz CU: The development of social cognition. In Hetherington EM (ed): Review of Child Development Research, Volume 5. Chicago: University of Chicago Press, 1975.
10. James W: The Principles of Psychology. New York: Dover, 1890.
11. Watson JB: Psychology as the behaviorist views it. Psychol Rev 1913; 20:158–177.
12. Reyert M: Feelings and Emotions: The Wittenberg Symposium. Worcester, MA: Clark University Press, 1928.
13. Kazdin AE: History of Behavior Modification: Experimental Foundations of Contemporary Research. Baltimore: University Park Press, 1978.
14. Craighead WE, Craighead LW, Ilardi SS: Behavior therapies in historical perspective. In Bongar B, Beutler LE (eds): Comprehensive Textbook of Psychotherapy: Theory and Practice. New York: Oxford University Press, 1995:64–83.
15. Craighead LW, Craighead WE, Kazdin AE, Mahoney MJ: Cognitive and Behavioral Interventions: An Empirical Approach to Mental Health Problems. Needham, MA: Allyn & Bacon, 1994.

16. Wolpe J: Psychotherapy by Reciprocal Inhibition. Stanford, CA: Stanford University Press, 1958.
17. Osgood CE: Method and Theory in Experimental Psychology. New York: Oxford Univerity Press, 1953.
18. MacCorquodale K, Meehl PE: On a distinction between hypothetical constructs and intervening variables. Psychol Rev 1948; 55:95–107.
19. Breger L, McGaugh JL: Critique and reformulation of "learning theory" approaches to psychotherapy and neurosis. Psychol Bull 1965; 63:338–358.
20. Skinner BF: Verbal Behavior. New York: Appleton-Century-Crofts, 1957.
21. Chomsky N: A review of Verbal Behavior by B.F. Skinner. Language 1959; 35:26–58.
22. Bandura A: Principles of Behavior Modification. New York: Holt, Rinehart & Winston, 1969.
23. Hunter W: Psychology in the war. Am Psychol 1946; 1:479–481.
24. Neisser U: Cognitive Psychology. New York: Appleton-Century-Crofts, 1967.
25. Neisser U: Cognition and Reality: Principles and Implications of Cognitive Psychology. San Francisco: WH Freeman, 1976.
26. Bandura A: Behavior therapy and the models of man. Am Psychol 1974; 29:859–869.
27. Bandura A: Social Learning Theory. Englewood Cliffs, NJ: Prentice Hall, 1977.
28. Beck AT: Cognitive Therapy and the Emotional Disorders. New York: International Universities Press, 1976.
29. Mahoney MJ: Cognition and Behavior Modification. Cambridge, MA: Ballinger Publishing, 1974.
30. Meichenbaum D: Cognitive-Behavior Modification: An Integrative Approach. New York: Plenum Publishing, 1977.
31. Craighead WE: There's a place for us: All of us. Behav Ther 1990; 21:2–23.
32. Eysenck MW: Attention and Arousal: Cognition and Performance. New York: Springer-Verlag, 1982.
33. Williams JMG, Watts FN, MacLeod C, Matthews A: Cognitive Psychology and Emotional Disorders. Chichester, UK: John Wiley & Sons, 1988.
34. Hunter WS: General Psychology. Chicago: University of Chicago Press, 1923.
35. Logan GD, Klapp ST: Automatizing alphabet arithmetic: I. Is extended practice necessary to produce automaticity? J Exp Psychol Learn Mem Cogn 1991; 17:179–195.
36. Posner MI, Snyder CRR: Facilitation and inhibition in the processing of signals. In Rabbitt PMA, Dornic S (eds): Attention and Performance V. New York: Academic Press, 1975.
37. Shiffrin RM, Schneider W: Controlled and automatic human information processing: II. Perceptual learning, automatic attending, and a general theory. Psychol Rev 1977; 84:127–190.
38. Gotlib IH, McCann CD: Construct accessibility and depression: An examination of cognitive and affective factors. J Pers Soc Psychol 1984; 47:427–439.
39. MacLeod C, Matthews AM, Tata P: Attentional bias in emotional disorders. J Abnorm Psychol 1986; 95:15–20.
40. Matthews AM, MacLeod C: Selective processing of threat cues in anxiety states. Behav Res Ther 1985; 23:563–569.
41. Segal ZV, Cloitre M: Methodologies for studying cognitive features of emotional disorder. In Dobson KS, Kendall PC (eds): Psychopathology and Cognition. San Diego, CA: Academic Press, 1993:19–50.
42. Barlow DH: Anxiety and Its Disorders: The Nature and Treatment of Anxiety and Panic. New York: Guilford Press, 1988.
43. Barlow DH, Cerny JA: Psychological Treatment of Panic. New York: Guilford Press, 1988.
44. Barlow DH, Rapee RM, Brown TA: Behavioral treatment of generalized anxiety disorder. Behav Ther 1992; 23:551–570.
45. Barlow DH: Long-term outcome for patients with panic disorder treated with cognitive-behavioral therapy. J Clin Psychiatry 1990; 51(suppl A):17–23.
46. Beck AT, Emery G: Anxiety Disorders and Phobias: A Cognitive Perspective. New York: Basic Books, 1985.
47. Dombeck MJ, Ingram RE: Cognitive conceptions of anxiety. In Dobson KS, Kendall PC (eds): Psychopathology and Cognition. San Diego, CA: Academic Press, 1993:54–81.
48. Engel RA, DeRubeis RJ: The role of cognition in depression. In Dobson KS, Kendall PC (eds): Psychopathology and Cognition. San Diego, CA: Academic Press, 1993:83–119.
49. Haaga DA, Dyck MJ, Ernst D: Empirical status of the cognitive theory of depression. Psychol Bull 1991; 110:215–236.
50. Beck AT, Rush AJ, Shaw BF, Emery G: Cognitive Therapy of Depression: A Treatment Manual. New York: Guilford Press, 1979.
51. Bargh JA, Tota ME: Context-dependent automatic processing in depression: Accessibility of negative constructs with regard to self but not others. J Pers Soc Psychol 1988; 54:925–939.
52. Wenzlaff RM, Wegner DM, Roper DW: Depression and mental control: The resurgence of unwanted negative thoughts. J Pers Soc Psychol 1988; 55:882–892.
53. Moretti MM, Shaw BF: Automatic and dysfunctional cognitive processes in depression. In Uleman JS, Bargh JA (eds): Unintended Thought. New York: Guilford Press, 1989.
54. Craighead WE, Evans DD, Robins CJ: Unipolar depression. In Turner SM, Calhoun KS, Adams HE (eds): Handbook of Clinical Behavior Therapy, 2nd ed. New York: John Wiley & Sons, 1992:99–116.
55. Dobson KS: A meta-analysis of the efficacy of cognitive therapy for depression. J Consult Clin Psychol 1989; 57:414–419.
56. DeRubeis RJ, Evans MD, Hollon SD, et al: How does cognitive therapy work? Cognitive change and symptom change in cognitive therapy and pharmacotherapy for depression. J Consult Clin Psychol 1990; 58:862–869.
57. Persons JB, Burns DD: Mechanism of action of cognitive therapy: Relative contribution of technical and interpersonal intervention. Cogn Ther Res 1985; 9:539–551.
58. Teasdale JD, Fennell MJV: Immediate effects on depression of cognitive therapy interventions. Cogn Ther Res 1982; 6:343–352.
59. Robins CJ, Hayes AM: An appraisal of cognitive therapy. J Consult Clin Psychol 1993; 61:205–214.
60. Rehm LP: A self-control model of depression. Behav Ther 1977; 8:787–804.
61. Rehm LP: Self-management therapy for depression. Adv Behav Res Ther 1984; 6:83–98.
62. Barkley RA: Attention Deficit Hyperactivity Disorder: A Handbook for Diagnosis and Treatment. New York: Guilford Press, 1990.
63. American Psychiatric Association: Diagnostic and Statistical Manual of Mental Disorders, 4th ed. Washington, DC: American Psychiatric Association, 1994.
64. Kendall PC, MacDonald JP: Cognition in the psychopathology of youth and implications for treatment. In Dobson KS, Kendall PC (eds): Psychopathology and Cognition. San Diego, CA: Academic Press, 1993:387–427.
65. Ceci SF, Tishman J: Hyperactivity and incidental memory: Evidence for attentional diffusion. Child Dev 1984; 55:2192–2203.
66. Radosh A, Gittelman R: The effect of appealing distractors on the performance of hyperactive children. J Abnorm Child Psychol 1981; 9:179–189.
67. Douglas VI: Treatment and training approaches to hyperactivity: Establishing internal or external control. In Whalen C, Henker B (eds): Hyperactive Children: The Social Ecology of Identification and Treatment. New York: Academic Press, 1980.
68. Rapport MD, Kelly KL: Psychostimulant effects on learning and cognitive functioning in children with attention deficit hyperactivity disorder: Findings and implications. In Matson JL (eds): Hyperactivity in Children: A Handbook. New York: Pergamon Press, 1990.
69. Whalen CK, Henker B, Hinshaw SP: Cognitive-behavioral therapies for hyperactive children: Premises, problems and prospects. J Abnorm Child Psychol 1985; 13:391–410.
70. Pelham WE, Hinshaw SP: Behavioral intervention for attention deficit–hyperactivity disorder. In Turner SM, Calhoun KS, Adams HE (eds): Handbook of Clinical Behavior Therapy. New York: John Wiley & Sons, 1992:259–283.
71. Hinshaw SP, Henker B, Whalen CK: Self-regulation for hyperactive boys: A training manual. Manuscript, University of California at Los Angeles, 1981; available from S.P. Hinshaw, Department of Psychology, University of California, Berkeley, CA.
72. Kendall PC, Braswell L: Cognitive-Behavioral Therapy for Impulsive Children, 2nd ed. New York: Guilford Press, 1993.
73. Brown RT: Impulsivity and psychoeducational intervention in hyperactive children. J Learn Disabil 1980; 13:249–254.
74. Brown RT, Wynne ME, Medinis R: Methylphenidate and cognitive therapy: A comparison of treatment approaches with hyperactive boys. J Abnorm Child Psychol 1985; 13:69–87.
75. Kirby EA: Durable and generalized effects of cognitive behavior modification with attention deficit disorder children. Presented at the

Annual Meeting of the American Psychological Association; August 1984; Toronto.
76. Abikoff H: Efficacy of cognitive training interventions in hyperactive children: A critical review. Clin Psychol Rev 1985; 5:479–512.
77. Grotstein JS: The borderline as a disorder of self-regulation. In Grotstein JS, Solomon MF, Lang JA (eds): The Borderline Patient: Emerging Concepts in Diagnosis, Psychodynamics, and Treatment. Hillsdale, NJ: The Analytic Press, 1987:347–384.
78. Linehan MM: Cognitive-Behavioral Treatment of Borderline Personality Disorder. New York: Guilford Press, 1993.
79. Cornsweet DJ: Use of cues in the visual periphery under conditions of arousal. J Exp Psychol 1969; 80:14–18.
80. Derryberry D, Rothbart MK: Emotion, attention, and temperament. In Izard CE, Kagan J, Zajonc RB (eds): Emotions, Cognition, and Behavior. Cambridge, UK: Cambridge University Press, 1984:132–166.
81. Derryberry D, Rothbart MK: Arousal, affect, and attention as components of temperament. J Pers Soc Psychol 1988; 55:958–966.
82. Gottman JM, Katz LF: Effects of marital discord on young children's peer interaction and health. Dev Psychol 1990; 25:373–381.
83. Linehan MM: Cognitive and behavior therapy for borderline personality disorder. In Tasman A, Hales RE, Frances AJ (eds): American Psychiatric Press Review of Psychiatry, Volume 8. Washington, DC: American Psychiatric Press, 1989:84–102.
84. Linehan MM, Armstrong HE, Suarez A, Douglas A: Cognitive-behavioral treatment of chronically parasuicidal borderline patients. Arch Gen Psychiatry 1991; 48:1060–1064.
85. Linehan MM, Heard HL, Armstrong HE: Naturalistic follow-up of a behavioral treatment for chronically parasuicidal borderline patients. Arch Gen Psychiatry 1993; 50:971–974.
86. Shearin EN, Linehan MM: Dialectical behavior therapy for borderline personality disorder: Theoretical and empirical foundations. Acta Psychiatr Scand Suppl 1994; 89:61–68.
87. Linehan MM: Skills Training Manual for Treating Borderline Personality Disorder. New York: Guilford Press, 1993.
88. Fiske ST, Taylor SE: Social Cognition, 2nd ed. New York: McGraw-Hill, 1991.
89. Glass AL, Holyoak KJ: Cognition, 2nd ed. New York: Random House, 1986.
90. Cohen N, Squire L: Preserved learning and retention of pattern analyzing skills in amnesia: Dissociation of knowing how and knowing that. Science 1980; 210:207–209.
91. Tulving E: Episodic and semantic memory. In Tulving E (ed): Organization of Memory. New York: Academic Press, 1972.
92. Beck AT: Cognitive therapy of depression: New perspectives. In Clayton PJ, Barrett JE (eds): Treatment of Depression: Old Controversies, New Approaches. New York: Raven Press, 1983:265–290.
93. Dagleish T, Watts FN: Biases of attention and memory in disorders of anxiety and depression. Clin Psychol Rev 1990; 10:589–604.
94. Matt GE, Vazquez C, Campbell WK: Mood-congruent recall of affectively toned stimuli: A meta-analytic review. Clin Psychol Rev 1992; 12:227–255.
95. Mineka S, Sutton SK: Cognitive biases and the emotional disorders. Psychol Sci 1992; 3:65–69.
96. Brand AN, Jolles J, Gispen de Wied C: Recall and recognition memory deficits in depression. J Affect Disord 1992; 25:77–86.
97. Colby CA, Gotlib IH: Memory deficits in depression. Cogn Ther Res 1988; 12:611–627.
98. Danion J, Willard-Schroeder D, Zimmerman M, et al: Explicit memory and repetition priming in depression: Preliminary findings. Arch Gen Psychiatry 1991; 48:707–711.
99. Elliott CL, Greene RL: Clinical depression and implicit memory. J Abnorm Psychol 1992; 101:572–574.
100. Sweeny JA, Wetzler S, Stokes P, Kocsis J: Cognitive functioning in depression. J Clin Psychol 1989; 45:836–842.
101. Watts FN, Sharrock R: Cued recall in depression. Br J Clin Psychol 1987; 26:149–150.
102. Channon S, Baker JE, Robertson MM: Working memory in clinical depression: An experimental study. Psychol Med 1993; 23:87–91.
103. Channon S, Baker JE, Robertson MM: Effects of structure and clustering on recall and recognition memory in clinical depression. J Abnorm Psychol 1993; 102:323–326.
104. Watts FN, Dalgleish T, Bourke P, Healy D: Memory deficit in clinical depression: Processing resources and the structure of materials. Psychol Med 1990; 20:345–349.
105. Hertel PT, Hardin TS: Remembering with and without awareness in a depressed mood: Evidence of deficits in initiative. J Exp Psychol 1990; 119:45–59.
106. Hertel PT, Rude SS: Recalling in a state of natural or experimental depression. Cogn Ther Res 1991; 15:103–127.
107. Watts FN, Cooper Z: The effects of depression on structural aspects of the recall of prose. J Abnorm Psychol 1989; 98:150–153.
108. Bradley BP, Mogg K, Williams R: Implicit and explicit memory for emotional information in non-clinical subjects. Behav Res Ther 1994; 32:65–78.
109. Denny EB, Hunt RR: Affective valence in memory in depression: Dissociation of recall and fragment completion. J Abnorm Psychol 1992; 101:575–580.
110. Holtgraves T, Athanassopoulou M: Depression and processing information about others. J Res Pers 1991; 25:445–453.
111. Puffet A, Jehin-Marchot D, Timsit-Berthier M, Timsit M: Autobiographical memory and major depressive states. Eur Psychiatry 1991; 6:141–145.
112. Richards A, Whittaker TM: Effects of anxiety and mood manipulation in autobiographical memory. Br J Clin Psychol 1990; 29:145–153.
113. Ruiz-Caballero JA, Moreno JB: The role of affective focus: Replication and extension of mood congruence and memory. Pers Individual Differences 1993; 14:191–197.
114. Watkins PC, Mathews A, Williamson DA, Fuller RD: Mood-congruent memory in depression: Emotional priming or elaboration? J Abnorm Psychol 1992; 101:581–586.
115. Williams JM, Scott J: Autobiographical memory in depression. Psychol Med 1988; 18:689–695.
116. Yang JA, Rehm LP: A study of autobiographical memories in depressed and nondepressed elderly individuals. Int J Aging Hum Dev 1993; 36:39–55.
117. Rubin DC: Remembering Our Past: Studies in Autobiographical Memory. Cambridge, UK: Cambridge University Press, 1995.
118. Dykman BM, Abramson LY, Albright JS: Effects of ascending and descending patterns of success upon dysphoric and nondysphoric subjects' encoding, recall, and predictions of future success. Cogn Ther Res 1991; 15:179–199.
119. Dykman BM, Abramson LY, Alloy LB, Hartlage S: Processing of ambiguous and unambiguous feedback by depressed and nondepressed college students: Schematic biases and their implications for depressive realism. J Pers Soc Psychol 1989; 56:431–445.
120. Alloy LB, Abramson LY: Depressive realism: Four theoretical perspectives. In Alloy LB (ed): Cognitive Processes in Depression. New York: Guilford Press, 1988:3–30.
121. Alloy LB, Albright JS, Abramson LY, Dykman, BM: Depressive realism and nondepressive optimistic illusions: The role of self. In Ingram RE (ed): Contemporary Psychological Approaches to Depression. New York: Plenum Publishing, 1990.
122. Kennedy RE, Craighead WE: Differential effects of depression and anxiety on recall of feedback in a learning task. Behav Ther 1988; 19:437–454.
123. American Psychiatric Association: Diagnostic and Statistical Manual of Mental Disorders, 3rd ed. Washington, DC: American Psychiatric Association, 1980.
124. Kirk SA, Kutchins H: The Selling of DSM: The Rhetoric of Science in Psychiatry. Hawthorne, NY: Walter de Gruyter, 1992.
125. Herman JL: Trauma and Recovery. New York: Basic Books, 1992.
126. Loftus EF: The reality of repressed memories. Am Psychol 1993; 48:518–537.
127. Bremner JD, Scott TM, Delaney RC, et al: Deficits in short-term memory in posttraumatic stress disorder. Am J Psychiatry 1993; 150:1015–1019.
128. Gil T, Calev A, Greenberg D, et al: Cognitive functioning in posttraumatic stress disorder. J Traumatic Stress 1990; 3:29–45.
129. Sutker PB, Allain AN, Johnson JL: Clinical assessment of long-term cognitive and emotional sequelae to World War II prisoner-of-war confinement: Comparison of pilot twins. Psychol Assessment 1993; 5:3–10.
130. Uddo M, Vasterling JJ, Brailey K, Sutker PB: Memory and attention in combat related post traumatic stress disorder. J Psychopathol Behav Assessment 1993; 15:43–52.
131. Schwarz ED, Kowalski JM, McNally RJ: Malignant memories: Post-traumatic changes in memory in adults after a school shooting. J Traumatic Stress 1993; 6:545–553.
132. Barnier AJ, McConkey KM: Reports of real and false memories: The

relevance of hypnosis, hypnotizability, and context of memory test. J Abnorm Psychol 1992; 101:521–527.
133. Jacoby LL, Whitehouse K: An illusion of memory: False recognition influenced by unconscious perception. J Exp Psychol 1989; 118:126–135.
134. Weaver CA: Do you need a "flash" to form a flashbulb memory? J Exp Psychol 1993; 122:39–46.
135. Wright DB: Recall of the Hillsborough disaster over time: Systematic biases of "flashbulb" memories. Appl Cogn Psychol 1993; 7:129–138.
136. Herbst PR: From helpless victim to empowered survivor: Oral history as a treatment for shattered survivors of torture. Women Ther 1992; 13:141–154.
137. Zimering R, Cadell JM, Fairbank JA, Keane TM: Post-traumatic stress disorder in Vietnam veterans: An experimental validation of the DSM-III diagnostic criteria. J Traumatic Stress 1993; 6:327–342.
138. Williams LM: Recall of childhood trauma: A prospective study of women's memories of childhood abuse. J Consult Clin Psychol 1994; 62:1167–1176.
139. Loftus EF, Garry M, Feldman J: Forgetting sexual trauma: What does it mean when 38% forget? J Consult Clin Psychol 1994; 62:1177–1181.
140. Berliner L, Loftus E: Sexual abuse accusations: Desperately seeking reconciliation. J Interpers Violence 1992; 7:570–578.
141. Gutheil TG: True or false memories of sexual abuse? A forensic psychiatry view. Psychiatr Ann 1993; 23:527–531.
142. Anderson JR: Cognitive Psychology and Its Implications, 2nd ed. New York: WH Freeman, 1985.
143. Bruner JS: Beyond the information given. In Anglin J (ed): Studies in the Psychology of Knowing. New York: WW Norton, 1973.
144. Duncker K: On problem solving. Psychol Monogr 1995; 58(whole issue 270).
145. Luchins AS: Mechanization in problem solving. Psychol Monogr 1942; 54(whole issue 248).
146. Newell A, Simon HA: Human Problem Solving. Englewood Cliffs, NJ: Prentice Hall, 1972.
147. Spivak G, Shure MB: Social Adjustment of Young Children: A Cognitive Approach to Solving Real-life Problems. San Francisco: Jossey-Bass, 1974.
148. D'Zurilla TJ, Goldfried MR: Problem solving and behavior modification. J Abnorm Psychol 1971; 78:107–126.
149. Goldfried MR, Davison GC: Clinical Behavior Therapy. New York: John Wiley & Sons, 1994.
150. D'Zurilla T: Problem-Solving Therapy: A Social Competence Approach to Clinical Intervention. New York: Springer-Verlag, 1986.
151. Nezu AM, Nezu CM, Perri MG: Problem Solving Therapy for Depression. New York: John Wiley & Sons, 1989.
152. Nezu A, D'Zurilla T: Social problem-solving and negative affective conditions. In Kendall PC, Watson D (eds): Anxiety and Depression: Distinctive and Overlapping Features. New York: Academic Press, 1980:285–315.
153. Robin AL: A controlled evaluation of problem-solving communication training with parent adolescent conflict. Behav Ther 1981; 12:593–609.
154. Camp BW, Bash MAS: Think Aloud: Increasing Social and Cognitive Skills—A Problem Solving Program for Children. Champaign, IL: Research Press, 1985.
155. Kendall PC, Braswell L: Cognitive-Behavioral Therapy for Impulsive Children. New York: Guilford Press, 1985.
156. Kirschenbaum DS, Ordman AM: Prevention interventions for children: Cognitive behavioral perspectives. In Meyers AW, Craighead WE (eds): Cognitive Behavior Therapy with Children. New York: Plenum Publishing, 1984:377–409.
157. Klerman GL, Weissman MM, Rounsaville BJ, Chevron ES: Interpersonal Psychotherapy of Depression. New York: Basic Books, 1984.
158. Weissman MM, Markowitz JC: Interpersonal psychotherapy: Current status. Arch Gen Psychiatry 1994; 51:599–606.
159. Alba JW, Hasher L: Is memory schematic? Psychol Bull 1983; 93:203–231.
160. Barsalou LW: Deriving categories to achieve goals. In Bower GH (ed): The Psychology of Learning and Motivation: Advances in Research and Theory, Volume 27. San Diego, CA: Academic Press, 1991.
161. Schank RC, Abelson R: Scripts, Plans, Goals, and Understanding. Hillsdale, NJ: Lawrence Erlbaum, 1977.
162. Beck AT, Freeman AM: Cognitive Therapy of Personality Disorders. New York: Guilford Press, 1990.
163. Abramson LY, Seligman MEP, Teasdale J: Learned helplessness in humans: Critique and reformulation. J Abnorm Psychol 1978; 87:49–75.
164. Weiner B, Frieze I, Kukla A, et al: Perceiving the Causes of Success and Failure. Morristown, NJ: General Learning Press, 1971.
165. Seligman MEP: Helplessness: On Depression, Development, and Death. New York: WH Freeman, 1975.
166. Young JE: Cognitive Therapy for Personality Disorders: A Schema-Focused Approach. Sarasota, FL: Professional Resource Exchange, 1990.
167. Dohr KB, Rush AJ, Bernstein IH: Cognitive biases and depression. J Abnorm Psychol 1989; 98:263–267.
168. Drennen WT: Negative schemas and depression in normal college student volunteers. Psychol Rep 1991; 68:521–522.
169. Golin S: Schema congruence and depression: Loss of objectivity in self- and other-inferences. J Abnorm Psychol 1989; 98:495–498.
170. Freud S; Strachey J (trans-ed): Introductory Lectures on Psychoanalysis. New York: WW Norton, 1977. Originally published in 1917.
171. Freud S; Strachey J (trans-ed): New Introductory Lectures on Psychoanalysis. New York: WW Norton, 1989. Originally published in 1933.
172. Meichenbaum D, Gilmore JB: The nature of unconscious processes: A cognitive-behavioral perspective. In Bowers KS, Meichenbaum D (eds): The Unconscious Reconsidered. New York: John Wiley & Sons, 1984.
173. Mahoney MJ: Human Change Processes: The Scientific Foundations of Psychotherapy. New York: Basic Books, 1991.
174. Safran JD, Segal ZV: Interpersonal Process in Cognitive Therapy. New York: Basic Books, 1990.
175. Lazarus RS: A cognitivist's reply to Zajonc on emotion and cognition. Am Psychol 1981; 36:222–223.
176. Lazarus RS: On the primacy of cognition. Am Psychol 1984; 39:124–129.
177. Lazarus RS: Thoughts on the relations between emotion and cognition. Am Psychol 1982; 37:1019–1024.
178. Parrot W, Sabini J: On the "emotional" qualities of certain types of cognition: A reply to arguments for the independence of cognition and affect. Cogn Ther Res 1989; 13:49–65.
179. Murphy ST, Zajonc RB: Affect, cognition, and awareness: Affective priming with optimal and suboptimal stimulus exposures. J Pers Soc Psychol 1993; 64:723–739.
180. Zajonc RB: Feeling and thinking: Preferences need no inferences. Am Psychol 1980; 35:151–175.
181. Zajonc RB: On the primacy of affect. Am Psychol 1984; 39:117–123.
182. American Psychiatric Association. Diagnostic and Statistical Manual of Mental Disorders, 3rd ed, revised. Washington, DC: American Psychiatric Association, 1987.

CHAPTER

18 Social Psychology: Theory, Research, and Mental Health Implications

Eugene W. Farber
Nadine J. Kaslow

Trends in the behavioral sciences have led to a convergence of biological, psychological, and social theories and research into a biopsychosocial understanding of clinical phenomena.[1] Increasingly, theories of psychological development and functioning are emphasizing the importance of understanding the interpersonal nature of psychological functioning, interpersonal interactions, and the person-environment relationship. Social psychology, which may be defined broadly as the study of social influences on psychological functioning, focuses on social processes and the social context in which behavior is embedded.

This chapter provides a comprehensive overview of the vast field of social psychology, emphasizing theory and research and addressing mental health implications.[2–4] The chapter begins by addressing the ways in which social factors influence the psychological processes of the individual, with particular attention to the self, person perception, and social cognition. The social cognition section addresses attributions and attitudes. This is followed by a review of the literature on interpersonal interaction and relationships, including altruism and helping behavior, affiliative behavior, and aggressive behavior. Next, attention is turned to the functioning of social groups, including the family. Finally, the influence of sociocultural variables is considered.

Social Psychological Views on Self

Theory and Research Findings

The Interpersonal Nature of Self

Interest in the role of social factors in understanding the self is consistent with the trends in personality, social, and clinical psychology toward systematic examination and articulation of the person-environment relationship in personality functioning as a whole.[5–7] From a social psychological perspective, the self is presumed to be influenced by social relationships and the interpersonal context.[8, 9] After a brief historical overview of theories focusing on the interpersonal nature of self is presented, representative social psychological models of self-functioning are provided and relevant research findings are described.

Historical Precedents. Current efforts to understand the self in the context of the social world of the individual are not without significant historical precedence. For example, William James[10] posited that one component of the self was a social self determined in part by relationships with significant others. James maintained that because one's social roles and impact on others are varied, each individual has multiple social selves (e.g., self at work, self with family) with varying degrees of integration and internal consistency. Charles Cooley[11] asserted that the self emerges from one's interpretations of the reactions of important others in the social environment (i.e., looking glass self). Similarly, George Herbert Mead's[12] symbolic interactionism approach posited that self-knowledge derives from a process of taking the role of the other in social interaction. According to this view, the individual internalizes norms and expectations of the social group (the generalized other) in the course of social interaction. This internalization of the generalized other provides the basis for self-reflection, including the capacity to evaluate one's gestures and deeds and anticipate others' responses to one's behavior. Consistent with these ideas, H. S. Sullivan's[13] clinical theory included a characterization of the self-system consisting of the good-me, bad-me, and not-me personifications. The self-system is defined interpersonally on the basis of perceived responses of significant others beginning early in life. Current object relations theorists and adherents to self psychology[14–17] underscore the importance of the interpersonal contributions to self-development and self-functioning.

Social Psychological and Clinical Models. As articulated by Deaux[5] in her cogent review of social psychological perspectives on the self, a cognitive information-processing framework forms a cornerstone on which social psychological theories of self have been developed.[18] This social psychological emphasis on cognitive aspects of self contrasts with clinical theories that highlight the emotional aspects of self.[5] Social psychological and clinical perspectives on self also differ with respect to the structural stability of self. Specifically, social psychologists tend to view self as changeable, depending on the interpersonal context and role expectations; psychiatrists tend to conceptualize self as relatively stable, enduring, and slow to modify.[5] Theorizing regarding the self includes elements from both social and clinical theories of self.[8, 19–25]

Social Psychological Models of Self

To illustrate current social psychological thinking with regard to self-functioning, a few examples of social psychological theories of self are described briefly here and summarized in Table 18–1. The models include self-verification theory, self-evaluation maintenance model, self-discrepancy theory, and Deaux's model for understanding the association between self-definition and mental health.

Self-verification Theory. Self-verification theory[23, 26] posits that individuals seek to validate core elements of their self-conceptions to facilitate a sense of continuity and predictability in the experience of self and the social world. According to this model, a stable self-concept provides a sense of internal continuity and familiarity in a highly changeable social environment (serving the epistemic goal of self-verification) and increases the likelihood that interpersonal identities and associated role expectations remain relatively predictable (thereby serving the pragmatic goal of self-verification). In the service of these epistemic and pragmatic goals, individuals structure their social environment to maximize the likelihood that self-verification will occur. This is accomplished in the following ways: pursuing social relationships and selecting social situations that confirm core self-conceptions; displaying cues that communicate how one perceives oneself and wants to be perceived by others (identity cues); interacting in ways that maximize the likelihood of eliciting feedback from others that confirms predominant self-conceptions; and selectively attending to and processing interpersonal feedback consistent with one's conceptions of self. According to self-verification theory, the degree of certainty or conviction with which a given self-conception is held determines the intensity of the epistemic and pragmatic desire to find verification for that view of self, even if it is a negative self-concept.

Table 18–1 Theories of Self: Representative Examples

Model	Basic Tenets
Self-verification theory	Individuals use their social relationships to validate core aspects of their self-concepts.
Self-evaluation maintenance model	Regulation of self-regard is influenced by the performance of others in one's social environment.
Self-discrepancy theory	Persons seek a state of affairs in which their self-concept (qualities that oneself and others presume that one possesses) is perceived to be congruent with how they and others believe they should or ought to be.
Deaux's social psychological model	Self consists of social and personal identities, expressions of self that one aspires toward, and life tasks and personal projects.

Self-evaluation Maintenance Model. The self-evaluation maintenance model[24] provides a social psychological conceptualization of regulation of self-regard. This model assumes that individuals wish to maintain positive self-regard and that the process of self-evaluation is influenced by the social environment. Specifically, one's self-evaluation may be influenced by the successful performance of others experienced as psychologically close to oneself (i.e., closeness of relationship or shared characteristics). The nature of this influence (i.e., positive or negative) is determined by the extent to which the success of the other occurs in a domain that is important to one's core self-definition (referred to as relevance). The self-evaluation maintenance model predicts that to the degree that an individual is psychologically close to another person and that other person performs well in a domain low in self-relevance, the individual's self-evaluation may be increased by the association with the psychologically close and accomplished other person (reflection process). However, the success of this close other may lower one's self-evaluation if the performance domain is high in self-relevance and the close other's performance exceeds one's own performance (comparison process). Hence, the relevance of the performance domain to core self-conceptions determines the degree to which the reflection or comparison process will be salient in the formulation of the self-evaluation. Further, according to the self-evaluation maintenance model, to the extent that degree of psychological closeness is minimal and the other's performance is judged unremarkable, the influence of the reflection and comparison processes on self-evaluation will be diminished.

Self-discrepancy Theory. Self-discrepancy theory[20] is a social psychologically based conceptualization of specific domains of the self and standpoints on the self (internal or external), with the relationships between these domains and standpoints posited to influence affective experience of self. The domains of self consist of three self-representations, including the actual self (qualities that oneself and others presume that one possesses), ideal self (qualities that oneself and others would like one to aspire toward), and ought self (qualities that oneself and others believe one should possess owing to duty, obligation, or responsibility). The two standpoints from which self is evaluated include one's own viewpoint and internal representations of the perspective of significant others. The combination of actual self-representations and the two standpoints on the self (i.e., actual-own, actual-other) constitute the self-concept, whereas the remaining combinations (i.e., ideal-own, ideal-other, ought-own, ought-other) are self-guides. These self-guides, standards by which one evaluates oneself, represent socially acquired values and objectives for self that one strives to attain. According to self-discrepancy theory, individuals seek a state of affairs in which the self-concept is perceived to be congruent with relevant self-guides. As such, self-regulation processes involving the relationship between the self-concept and self-guides influence one's feelings about self and perceptions and judgments of others.

Deaux's Social Psychological Model. In Deaux's[5] social psychological model for understanding the association between self-definition and mental health, self-definition consists of social and personal identities, possible selves (selves that one aspires toward or fears one will become),[27] and life tasks or personal projects. This definition underscores the notion of self as consisting of specifically defined domains of functioning rather than a global entity, incorporates goals and aspirations as motivational elements, and stresses that self is personally defined on the basis of experience. Distal influences on self-definition include demographical and sociocultural variables, social structure, and socialization processes. Challenges or threats to one's self-definition may come from such internal sources as discrepancies between one's current self-evaluation and the self one would like to be.[5] These standards may be self-generated (internally defined goals for oneself), be provided by others (expectations of others), or represent comparisons with others (social comparison). External challenges to self-definition that may force a redefinition of self include positive or negative major life events and acute or chronic stressors (e.g., illness, change of employment status, changes in significant relationships, discrimination).

This model posits that individuals selectively attend to and interpret environmental information in a manner that is consistent with self-definition. However, when presented with salient self-relevant positive or negative information (including internal and external sources of threat) that challenges the self-definition, individuals typically engage in a self-evaluation process. This self-evaluation process may consist of self-regulation and self-reconstruction activities (e.g., self-esteem maintenance, self-affirmation, self-esteem protection) or social regulation and reconstruction (e.g., self-verification, self-monitoring, behavioral disconfirmation).

Impression Management. The aforementioned social psychological models address how interpersonal interactions influence self-definition and functioning. It is also the case that one's self-presentation influences one's social relationships. More specifically, individuals strive to control the impressions that others form about them (impression management). People are invested in presenting themselves in a certain way (performing) in social situations and make efforts to control the impression that others have of the situation.[28] Successful impression management includes an awareness of social expectations regarding behavior in a specific situation, a desire to act within social expectations, and the capacity to present oneself in such a way that the desired impression is conveyed. One's behavior in social interactions is guided by the impressions one forms of others. As such, it is adaptive to be cognizant of others' views of oneself and to portray oneself in an acceptable manner. This enhances the capacity to comprehend, regulate, and anticipate social interaction patterns. Several motivational determinants influence one's chosen self-presentation in a social interchange. People stress the commonalities between themselves and what is expected of them and present a personally and socially desirable public image to ensure social compatibility, solidarity with others, and social approval.

Research on the Interpersonal Nature of Self

Research supporting the position that self is constructed and maintained in the context of relationships with others is found in diverse areas of study, including animal psychology, child development, and cognitive psychology. For example, an animal study of self-recognition in chimpanzees whose faces were unknowingly painted with red marks demonstrated that chimpanzees raised with opportunities for social interaction were able to recognize themselves in a mirror more readily than were those raised in social isolation.[29] On the basis of these results, the investigator hypothesized that social interaction may have facilitated enhanced self-recognition in these chimpanzee subjects. Self-recognition may be an important component in the formation of a sense of self. Investigations in child development provide ample evidence that beginning in infancy, there is an active interactional process of engagement between the infant and primary caretaker, with particular interactional patterns contributing to the formation of the subjective and interpersonal world of the individual, including representations of self.[30, 31]

Information-processing models from cognitive psychology have been used in conceptualizations of self as witnessed by the increased use of the term self-schema, hierarchically organized (i.e., possessing supraordinate and subordinate subcategories) and enduring sets of beliefs about oneself that include semantic (i.e., abstract and procedural knowledge) and episodic (i.e., memory of life events) components.[25] Investigators examining processes involved in social cognition have focused on the role of self-schemas in the perception, processing, and organization of information about self and others in everyday social discourse.[32] Further, the schema concept has been integrated into psychodynamic conceptualizations of intrapsychic self-organization that incorporate representations of self in relationship with others, including the role-relationship model configuration approach,[21, 22] core conflictual relationship theme model,[33] and structural analysis of social behavior method.[34]

Self in Health and Illness

Issues of physical health and illness influence both one's self-definition and the quality and nature of one's interpersonal world. In turn, one's self-definition influences how one responds to health-related concerns. To heighten the extent to which individuals can exercise control over their own health behaviors and associated environmental stresses, individuals may be taught self-management and self-control techniques. Learning the array of cognitive and behavioral coping strategies that increase people's ability to manage their illness and associated affective responses also enhances capacity for effective self-regulation. In other words, self-efficacy is an important variable in responding to health-related concerns.

Mental Health Implications: Social Psychological Views on Self

Mental health professionals have increasingly appreciated the need to understand self-functioning in an interpersonal context. This shift in focus has been influenced by attachment theory,[35] interpersonal psychiatry,[13] psychoanalytic object relations theory,[36] feminism,[37, 38] and family systems theory.[39, 40] Each of these approaches emphasizes that because self is socially derived, the nature and quality of the relationship between the therapist and patient is centrally relevant to helping the patient make changes in self-functioning.

Models of Self and Clinical Interventions

The social psychological model articulated by Deaux[5] offers a general road map of processes influencing self-functioning and provides a reference for identifying multiple points of departure for various clinical intervention strategies. For example, the problem can be conceptualized in terms of its impact on the components of the self-definition (i.e., social and personal identities, possible selves, life tasks or personal projects), and appropriate clinical interventions can be formulated according to the evaluation of where the problem is affecting self-experience the most. Further, interventions may be tailored according to the internal or external challenges to the self-definition identified in the clinical assessment of the patient's presenting concerns. These interventions may be informed by the self-verification model,[26] self-evaluation maintenance model,[24] and self-discrepancy model.[20]

Self-verification Theory. One implication of self-verification theory for psychotherapy is that the focus should be on facilitating change in the self-conceptions of the patient while maintaining sensitivity to the epistemic and pragmatic implications of relinquishing these core negative self-conceptions.[26] This can be accomplished by accompanying challenges to current self-conceptions with suggestions and guidance regarding newly defined and emerging behavioral patterns and positive self-conceptions. In this model, the notion of transference is reconceptualized in terms of the tendency of the patient to engage in interactional patterns aimed at organizing the therapist to respond in ways that confirm the patient's negative views of self.[26] Accordingly, the therapist must be alert to such patterns and resist responding in a way that verifies the patient's negative self-conceptions while maintaining a focus on slowly and delicately challenging negative self-views, starting with more innocuous material and gradually moving toward more core elements of the self-concept.

Self-evaluation Maintenance Model. According to the self-evaluation maintenance model, clinical interventions designed to facilitate changes in the environment or the patient's perceptions of the environment may promote enhanced self-regard.[24] For example, helping patients identify circumstances in which their performance on self-relevant tasks exceeds those of others would presumably result in enhanced self-regard. Similarly, helping patients redefine the domains relevant to self-definition or lower the relevance of a given domain may enhance self-regard in instances when the comparison process is resulting in lowered self-esteem and changing environmental variables is not feasible.

Self-discrepancy Theory. A number of therapeutic strategies that target emotional distress are suggested by self-discrepancy theory.[20] First, this theory provides a conceptual means for the therapist and patient to map and predict specific emotional responses to perceived disparities between perceived self-conceptions and desired self-goals (i.e., self-concept–self-guide discrepancies). For example, experiencing a discrepancy between actual self-conception and expectations regarding qualities one believes one ought to possess is likely to generate agitation-related emotions (e.g., guilt, self-concept). Alternatively, experiencing a discrepancy between one's perception of current actual self-functioning and beliefs about the ideal state of self that a significant other desires for one may generate dejection-related emotions (e.g., shame, embarrassment). Second, the therapist can focus on altering the patient's currently held conceptions of self in a manner that makes the self-concept less discrepant with core self-guides. Third, the patient can be helped to modify self-guides to be less discrepant with current self-conceptions. Finally, by minimizing the patient's exposure to circumstances associated with difficulties or by encouraging cognitive rehearsal of positive self-statements, the patient's access to discrepancies can be altered.

General Comments. In general, a social psychological perspective on self can serve a useful heuristic function for therapists. This viewpoint underscores the importance of assessing an individual's self-definition in the context of his or her social environment. In other words, information should be gleaned about the person's perceptions of positive and negative aspects of self-in-relation in terms of interpersonal and occupational functioning. People's aspirations, goals, and social role expectations should be examined. This assessment entails examining psychological symptoms in terms of current interactional patterns and stressors and taking a socialization history at the level of the family, community, and sociocultural environments. For individuals in whom self-definition appears to be negative or diffuse, intervention involves creating a social context in which a more positive and clearer articulation of self can occur.

Person Perception

Theory and Research Findings

Definition and Conceptual Overview

Perception is the process through which environmental stimuli are received and interpreted. Person perception, also referred to as social perception, pertains to the ways in which we formulate impressions of others. Social psychological research has demonstrated a tendency for people to formulate viewpoints on human nature and behavior that influence their understanding of the behavior of others. These perspectives permit rapid evaluation of persons and interpersonal circumstances and inferences about the enduring personality qualities of other people with use of limited observable information. Individualized versions of these perspectives have been referred to as implicit personality theories, unstated assumptions about human characteristics and attributes that are assumed to covary.[41]

Affect in Person Perception. In forming initial impressions of social and intellectual qualities of others, people typically make evaluative assessments based on either positive or negative affective reactions. These judgments are often distorted by perceptual biases, most notably the halo effect (information that is consistent with the affective evaluation is attended to selectively, and discrepant information is ignored) and the person-positivity bias (the propensity to formulate positive evaluations more readily than negative ones).[42]

Cognition in Person Perception. Person perception also involves cognitive components because individuals actively seek to develop coherent and meaningful impressions of others. In forming person perceptions, the perceiver is typically influenced by stereotypes, rigid and oversimplified views of groups of people in which all group members are viewed as possessing certain traits. The perceiver is also influenced by the salient features (central traits) of the other, particularly in regard to physical appearance, verbal behavior, and nonverbal communication. This information, whether averaged (mean value of traits) or added (sum of the trait values), is integrated with other perceptual input regarding the situational context.

Other Influences in Person Perception. Researchers studying person perception have found that the accuracy of such affective and cognitive evaluations in part varies as a function of the attribute being judged. For example, whereas people tend to be relatively accurate in their assessments of physical attributes, less accuracy is noted in judgments about others' internal states (e.g., feelings, personality characteristics, attitudes). In addition, perceptions of others are influenced strongly by self-perceptions, a phenomenon referred to as the self-referencing effect.

Person Perception in Health and Illness

The physician-patient relationship is influenced in part by the affective and cognitive evaluations that each makes about the other. These person perception variables affect interactional styles between physicians and their patients, which in turn may influence the nature and quality of medical care. Patients' perceptions of their physicians as paternalistic, interested in mutuality in decision-making regarding care, or expecting the patient to have primary responsibility for decision-making contribute to differential physician-patient interactional dynamics.[43] Similarly, the degree to which the physician's impression of the patient is that of a passive novice, an informed partner, or the consumer in charge of care affects physician-patient interactions.

Mental Health Implications: Person Perception

Cognitive and Affective Influences

The issue of person perception has clinical relevance for the cognitive interpretation of interpersonal situations. Many of the cognitive distortions (e.g., overgeneralization, magnification, and minimization) observed in depressed persons,[44] anxious individuals,[45] and people with personality disorders[46] influence person perception in a maladaptive fashion. Thus, although person perception research has demonstrated a normative tendency to base rapid evaluations of others and interpersonal situations on limited information, this process is likely to become a problem when cognitive distortions are operative. For example, the depressed person with low self-esteem and a pessimistic attributional style who interprets others as judgmental in virtually every interpersonal interaction on the basis of a few interchanges in which he or she is criticized is overgeneralizing on the basis of limited data (e.g., "Others are always critical of me."). This is likely to interfere with the development of trusting relationships.

With regard to affective influences on person perception, research demonstrating that individuals' moods affect their perceptions of others has accumulated. For example, some investigators have found that depressed persons have negative perceptions of others.[47] This selective attention to the negative attributes of others represents a negative halo effect. Further, the prevalence of negative perception of self, world, future, and others seen in depressed people suggests a disruption of the person-positivity bias. In addition, there is evidence that in both depressed and nondepressed subjects, positive or negative views of self are correlated with positive or negative views of significant others.[48] This association may be decreased when the other person is relatively unimportant to the life of the perceiver.[48] These findings suggest that it behooves therapists working with depressed patients to use a cognitive-interpersonal framework[49, 50] to modify distorted cognitions and interpersonal processes involving person perception that perpetuate the depressive cycle and reestablish the person-positivity biases.

Implicit Personality Theories

The notion of implicit personality theories that influence person perception is applicable clinically to the understanding of individual conceptualizations of the social world. This may have particular relevance for the clinical understanding of personality disorders. For example, patients with paranoid personality disorder (*Diagnostic and Statistical Manual of Mental Disorders,* Fourth Edition [DSM-IV] cluster A) may hold an implicit personality theory of others as potentially attacking, blaming, and controlling.[34] Patients with borderline personality disorder (DSM-IV cluster B) may perceive others as simultaneously rejecting and abandoning and needing dependent others.[34] Patients with obsessive-compulsive personality disorder (DSM-IV cluster C) may believe that others expect them to be perfect regardless of their own wants and needs.[34] To address these maladaptive implicit personality theories and associated interactional patterns, effective psychotherapy helps patients identify dysfunctional person perceptions, develop an affective and cognitive awareness of the cause of these beliefs and the functions they serve, and learn more adaptive implicit personality theories.[34] In addition, therapists' awareness of implicit personality theories early in treatment can assist in assessment and identification of interpersonal patterns that are likely to be enacted in the therapeutic relationship.

Influences on Clinical Judgment

A final example of the clinical implications of person perception research relates to the finding that judgments about overt qualities are generally more accurate than judgments about internal states. It follows that therapists are likely to be more accurate in making judgments based on overt behavior of their patients than they are in making judgments about the internal experiences of their patients. Thus, efforts should be devoted to developing an empathic awareness of the patient's internal experiences. Further, to the extent that affective states influence person perception, it is important for therapists to maintain a sensitivity to their own feelings as they formulate perceptions of patients' problems and dynamics.

Social Cognition

Social cognition, the ways in which social events are comprehended and interpreted, yields insights about the interaction of person and situational variables in constructing personal knowledge, personality, and interpersonal relationships. Responses to social situations depend on one's understanding of the circumstance and can be influenced by social consensus. Social psychological study of social cognition phenomena provides insight into the ways in which construals of social situations affect social discourse. Relevant areas of social psychological inquiry include research on attributions and attitudes.

Theory and Research Findings: Attribution Theory

Definition

Attribution theory focuses on causal explanations generated by an individual to account for why a particular event or set of outcomes has occurred.[51] Such inferences, which provide a means through which to make sense of events, influence interpersonal behavior, individual personality functioning, and affective experiences. Representative examples of attribution theory are presented in Table 18–2.

Table 18–2 Attribution Theories: Representative Examples

Model	Basic Tenets
Heider's model	Individuals attribute the causes of events to dispositional or situational factors.
Kelly's model	Individuals attribute the causes of behavior to the actor, the entity, or the circumstances. Consensus, consistency, and distinctiveness information is used to formulate an attribution to one of these three sources. Causal schemas also influence attributions when one or more of these types of information is not available.
Achievement model	Affective responses in achievement situations are influenced by the extent to which success or failure is attributed to internal or external causes, stable or variable causes, and controllable or uncontrollable causes.
Depression model	Attribution of events to internal, stable, and global causes increases the risk of helplessness, hopelessness, and depression in the actor.

Table 18–3 Major Attributional Biases

Bias	Description
Fundamental attribution error	A bias toward attributing behavior to dispositional factors and underestimating situational influences on the behavior in question
Actor-observer bias	A bias toward attributing one's own acts to situational factors while attributing others' behavior to dispositional factors
Self-serving (hedonic) bias	A propensity to attribute one's own successes to dispositional factors while attributing failures to situational factors

Historical Overview

Heider,[52] the originator of attribution theory, analyzed the manner in which people explain everyday occurrences. According to Heider, causes of events can be dispositional (i.e., personal) or situational (i.e., environmental). Individuals may attribute the causes of events to internal factors (e.g., personality traits or dispositions) or external variables (e.g., environmental circumstances). Heider's work has served as a foundation for later research and theorizing in this area.

Kelley,[53] another pioneer in the study of causal attributions, maintained that covariation of cause and effect is the cornerstone of the attribution process. Kelley asserted that individuals seek to discern systematic patterns of relations and make inferences about cause and effect on the basis of these sequences of events. In accord with Heider's distinction between dispositional and situational causal attributions, Kelley postulated that behavior may be attributed to the person engaging in the behavior (actor), the person toward whom the behavior is directed (entity), or the setting in which the behavior is manifested (circumstances). Individuals use consensus (knowledge of the behavior of others in similar situations), consistency (knowledge of the behavior of the actor in other situations), and distinctiveness (similarities or differences in behavior in the presence of different others) information to formulate an attribution to one of three sources (actor, entity, or circumstances). The most likely type of attribution can be predicted if consensus, consistency, and distinctiveness data are available. Typically, individuals do not have access simultaneously to all three types of information. As such, information that is lacking is filled in by reliance on causal schemas, consisting of general beliefs regarding the causes of behavior.

Attributional Biases

Most people exhibit three major types of attributional biases in everyday social interactions: the fundamental attribution error, the actor-observer bias, and the self-serving (hedonic) attributional bias. These biases are described here and summarized in Table 18–3.

The fundamental attribution error, a bias toward attributing behavior to dispositional factors in the actor while underestimating the influence of situational variables,[54] typically occurs in the context of understanding the behavior of others. The actor-observer bias[55] is noted when individuals attribute their own acts to situational factors and minimize the role of dispositional qualities, attributing the others' behavior to dispositional factors. Actor-observer differences may be a function of greater self-knowledge than knowledge of others or related to different perspectives between actors and observers that lead to different perceptual interpretations. The actor-observer difference has received inconsistent support in the research literature.[56]

Whereas the fundamental attribution error and the actor-observer bias are presumably attribution processes based on cognitive and rational assumptions, it has been suggested that the self-serving (hedonic) attribution bias is based primarily on motivational factors. The hedonic bias reflects a wish to present oneself in the best possible light. As such, individuals evidence a propensity to attribute their successes to dispositional factors and their failures to situational causes.[57] People tend to extend this attributional bias to important others in their interpersonal sphere (e.g., spouse, political candidate supported).

Attributions and Achievement

Attributional principles applied to affective responses in achievement situations[58] provide a means for understanding ways that successes and failures trigger searches for causal attributions. For example, when failure is attributed to internal, stable, and uncontrollable causes (e.g., lack of ability), a negative affective response is likely to ensue, subsequent expectations of success are likely to be lowered, and self-esteem is likely to suffer. In contrast, an individual is likely to experience positive feelings and self-esteem may be bolstered if successes in achievement contexts are attributed to one's own ability.

Attributions and Depression

Attributional theory has been employed to understand the phenomena of learned helplessness and depression.[59] It has been demonstrated that attribution of negative events to internal, stable, and global causes (pessimistic attributional style) increases the risk that an individual will experience helplessness, hopelessness, and depression.[60, 61] Empirical tests of the relation between these attributional processes and depression reveal that depressed psychotherapy patients may begin to view life events and problems as less global and uncontrollable as their depressive symptoms lessen.[62] For some patients, there appear to be concurrent changes in symptoms and attributional processes, suggesting a possible functional association between symptom remittance and attributional change.[62]

Attributions in Health and Illness

Pessimistic Attributional Style. Theorists have posited that an active, optimistic, and hopeful outlook may be associated with physical health and effective coping with illness.[63] Conversely, feelings of helplessness and hopelessness, passivity, and pessimism may increase susceptibility to physical illness and be associated with less effective coping with illness. It has been suggested that there is a link between an attributional style associated with the development of depression (pessimistic explanatory style) and increased vulnerability to physical illness.[63] More specifically, individuals who feel helpless and manifest a pessimistic explanatory style when confronted with loss or failure may be vulnerable to becoming depressed, a condition associated with neurophysiological changes that are correlated with immune suppression and concomitant increased disease vulnerability.[63] Data have accumulated supporting the association between explanatory style and illness. For example, healthy college students with a pessimistic explanatory style compared with those not exhibiting pessimism for negative events endorse more illness, poorer health, and less active coping and lifestyle patterns for preventing and managing medical symptoms.[64, 65] In addition, this pessimistic attributional style places young adults at increased risk for physical problems in middle and late adulthood.[66]

Positive Illusions. A collection of attributional processes referred to as positive illusions has been identified as being associated with health and illness.[67] These positive illusions, which include an unrealistically positive view of self, an excessive sense of control over life circumstances, and an overly optimistic view of the future, may influence health habits.[67] Specifically, individuals who have a sense of control over negative events may be more likely to practice good health habits and more accurately ascertain aspects of the health situation that are controllable than those who experience a lack of instrumentality.

General Comments. On the basis of the aforementioned findings, it has been suggested that treatment interventions with medically ill persons focus on enhancing the individual's sense of control over his or her health and treatment regimen.[68] This approach can increase adherence to medical regimens and improve adjustment to medical procedures and conditions. In general, the association between specific attributions and illness should not be interpreted to mean that certain attributional patterns cause illness; rather, attributional processes may be one of a complex set of factors contributing to illness susceptibility and course.

Mental Health Implications: Attribution Theory

Attributional Approaches and Maladaptive Cognitions

Research findings from studies of causal attributions have been applied clinically in a cognitive approach that involves identifying, challenging, and altering maladaptive attributional processes.[69, 70] This intervention method assumes that when attributions leading to maladaptive responses are replaced with more desirable attributions, more adaptive responses are likely to occur.[71] For example, a patient presenting with complaints of low self-esteem may be helped to identify and alter tendencies to attribute personal difficulties to her or his own perceived interpersonal deficits rather than a combination of situational and personal factors.

Attribution retraining programs are most appropriate when individuals make unrealistic attributions that lead to a range of psychological difficulties including depression, social anxiety and shyness, and marital or family problems.[72] These programs teach individuals to identify unrealistic attributions associated with dysfunctional reactions and formulate more realistic attributions in these situations.[71]

Investigation of change processes in psychotherapy suggests that a patient's attributions of positive behavior change to internal causes is associated with maintenance of therapeutic gains.[72] Attributional retraining most likely is not the treatment of choice for individuals who make realistic attributions but nevertheless respond in maladaptive ways or for persons whose unrealistic attributions do not result in problematical response styles.[71]

Attributional Approaches and Interpersonal Problems

In addition to their application with individuals, principles of attribution theory have been applied clinically to problems in interpersonal relationships. For example, research investigating the influence of attributional processes in marital relationships has suggested that marital dissatisfaction and distress are related to viewing negative marital events caused by one's partner as having stable and global qualities.[73] One implication of these findings is that marital dissatisfaction may be ameliorated to some degree in marital therapy by helping the couple identify and alter unrealistic causal attributions regarding the respective partner's behavior. Thus, for example, one spouse who attributes marital problems to his perception that his spouse has never been committed to the relationship can consider possible alternative attributions of cause of marital distress.

Theory and Research Findings: Attitude Theory

Definition

Attitudes, stable and enduring views held toward ideas, objects, or persons, include cognitive, affective, and behavioral elements. Attitudes guide responses to life events, permitting rapid interpretation and understanding of one's world, often without the need for deliberate conscious processing.[74] As such, attitudes provide a mechanism by which to interpret and formulate responses to the complexities and ambiguities of daily living in an economical fashion. After reviewing learning and reinforcement, social judgment, consistency, and functional theories of attitudes (Table 18–4), this section examines the association between behavior and attitudes and between persuasion and attitude change.

Attitude Theories

Learning and Reinforcement Theories. Learning and reinforcement theories, founded on principles of behaviorism, are derived from basic experimental psychology. Two major examples of learning and reinforcement theory regarding attitude formation and change are conditioning[75] and associationist (stimulus-response)[76] perspectives. These approaches emphasize the influence of environmental contingencies in the formation, maintenance, and alteration of attitudes. For example, a classical conditioning view of attitude formation might predict that a child whose mother berates his depressed father as a "good for nothing, lazy bum" will associate laziness with depression and thereafter adopt the attitude that depression is bad behavior.

Social Judgment Theory. Social judgment theory emphasizes the interplay of cognitive and affective attitudinal components and assumes that perceptions and judgments mediate attitude change.[77] According to this approach, individuals are most likely to have their attitudes influenced by information that is similar to their own attitudinal set (i.e., latitude of acceptance), may be influenced by information about which their attitudinal set is not clearly defined and affectively neutral (i.e., latitude of noncommitment), and are least likely to change their attitude when confronted with data inconsistent with their attitudinal set (i.e., latitude of rejection). An individual who as a child learned that depression was bad and a sign of laziness is unlikely to change this view in light of education received in school suggesting that depression is a natural response to stress or a biological condition associated with a neurochemical imbalance. For this individual, such information falls within the latitude of rejection.

Consistency Theories. Consistency theories posit that attitude formation and change are organized by a need to impose structure and order on one's understanding of the environment. Major consistency models include Heider's balance theory,[52] Osgood and Tannenbaum's congruity theory,[78] Festinger's dissonance theory,[79] and Bem's self-perception theory.[80] To illustrate consistency theories, the cognitive dissonance and self-perception perspectives are reviewed briefly.

Cognitive Dissonance Theory. Cognitive dissonance theory holds that a discrepancy between simultaneously held attitudinal cognitions (dissonance) produces psychological tension, requiring attitudinal changes to reestablish consistency (consonance). The degree to which this dissonance causes psychological tension is a function of the personal importance of the cognitions and the number of dissonant

Table 18–4 Attitude Theories: Representative Examples

Model	Basic Tenets
Learning and reinforcement theories	Environmental contingencies, including conditioning and associational processes, determine the formation, maintenance, and alteration of attitudes.
Social judgment theory	Attitudes are most likely to be influenced by information that is similar to one's own attitudinal set, may be influenced by information about which one's attitudes are not clearly defined, and are least likely to be influenced by information that is inconsistent with one's attitudinal set.
Consistency theory	Attitude formation and change are organized by a need to impose structure and order on one's understanding of the environment. An example of a consistency theory is cognitive dissonance theory.
Functional theories	Individuals form and maintain attitudes that are consistent with their needs and motives.

cognitions relative to consonant cognitions. Dissonance theory predicts that once a decision has been made, the alternative chosen is increasingly viewed as correct and the unchosen option is seen as less desirable than when it was considered before the decision was made. Dissonance may be ameliorated by decreasing the number or importance of discrepant beliefs, increasing the number or significance of consonant beliefs, or altering dissonant beliefs in accord with other simultaneously held attitudes.

Self-perception Theory. An alternative approach that accounts for research findings regarding dissonance is self-perception theory.[80] According to this perspective, individuals infer their attitudes through observing their own behavioral responses and the conditions under which they occur. From this view, attitudes are formed on the basis of self-attributions. Efforts have been undertaken to understand specific conditions under which the cognitive dissonance and self-perception framework is most applicable in attitude formation and change.[81]

Functional Theories. Functional theories hold that individuals form and maintain attitudes consistent with their needs and motives. Three functional theories have been proposed,[82–84] the most developed of which is that of Katz, which posits that particular attitudes may be adopted for adjustive, instrumental, or utilitarian purposes because they maximize rewards and minimize punishments. The ego-defensive or externalizing functions of attitudes allow maintenance of desired views of self and the world while protecting the individual from acknowledgment of unpleasant realities. Attitudes serving a knowledge function assist people in formulating meaning about events in their world. Finally, attitudes may serve a value expression function. This model suggests a complex interplay among different attitudinal beliefs, necessitating different change strategies based on the function of the attitude being targeted for change.

Attitudes and Behavior

Early interest in attitude formation and change was propelled by the assumption that attitudinal sets could predict behavioral responses. However, the relation between attitudes and behavior is complex[85]; research suggests that strength and temporal stability of the attitudinal conviction,[86, 87] relevance and salience of the attitude relative to a particular behavioral response,[88, 89] and situational factors[90] all contribute to the specificity with which a specific set of behaviors might follow from a given set of attitudes. Interest in predicting behavioral responses from attitudinal beliefs prompted efforts to develop models of the attitude-behavior relationship. Representative models are discussed here and summarized in Table 18–5.

Among the most prominent of these is the reasoned action model.[91] According to this model, the strength of intentions to act (i.e., behavioral intention) is determined by one's attitudes toward the behavior and perceptions of the social desirability of the behavior (i.e., subjective social normative beliefs). Attitudes about the behavior and beliefs about the appropriateness of the behavior mutually influence whether one will behave in accord with a given attitude. The strength of the behavioral intention is considered the best predictor of a given response.

Table 18–5 Models of Attitude-Behavior Relationships: Representative Examples

Model	Basic Tenets
Reasoned action model	The strength of intentions to act is determined by one's attitudes toward the behavior and perceptions of the social desirability of the behavior.
Cognitive dissonance model	Individuals alter attitudes in a manner consistent with their behavior to reduce dissonance.
Self-perception model	Individuals infer their attitudes through observation of their own behaviors and the conditions under which they occur.

In addition to studying the influence of attitudes on behavioral responses, social psychologists have investigated the ways behavior influences attitudes. Laboratory research demonstrates that in specific experimental situations, attitudes are formed in accord with certain behaviors. Cognitive dissonance theory[79] and self-perception theory[80] predict that attitudes are influenced by one's behavioral responses. In a review of attitude research, Cooper and Croyle[92] concluded that behavior is most influential in changing attitudes when a given behavior is performed without coercion, its benefits are small, and it results in potentially undesirable consequences for which the individual feels responsible.

Persuasion and Attitude Change

The persuasion process involves efforts to alter attitudinal beliefs. This process of attitude change is influenced by the source (person appealing for attitude change), message (what is presented and how it is delivered), channel (paths by which the message is received), and receiver (characteristics of the recipient of persuasive communications).[93] A vast literature investigates the ways these variables, separately and in combination, influence the success or failure of persuasive communication.[93, 94] Further, it has been suggested that the study of persuasion is important for altering behaviors relevant to mental health issues.[74] Representative persuasion models are discussed here and summarized in Table 18–6.

Elaboration Likelihood Model. The elaboration likelihood model attempts to account for diverse findings regarding the persuasion process.[95] This model focuses on the degree to which the persuasive message is cognitively elaborated on by the message recipient, with this elaboration ranging on a continuum from minimal to thorough message consideration. The elaboration likelihood model posits two major pathways to persuasion, the central and peripheral routes. Whereas the central route involves change in attitudinal beliefs as a result of considering the merits of the content of the communication, the peripheral route involves attitudinal shifts as a function of attending to contextual cues. Motivation level (e.g., personal relevance of the issue, individual differences, contextual influences) and capacity to process message contents (e.g., understandability of the message, cognitive and intellectual factors, environmental

Table 18–6 Persuasion Models: Representative Examples

Model	Basic Tenets
Elaboration likelihood model	Persuasion can result from considering the merits of the content of a communication (central route to persuasion) or from attention to contextual cues (peripheral route to persuasion). Motivation level and capacity to process message contents influence which of these two paths to persuasion will be adopted in a given attitude situation.
Heuristic-systematic model	Attitude change is influenced by systematic processing of the persuasive argument or through the use of simple decision rules with regard to a given message.

distractions) influence whether the central or peripheral route to persuasion will be adopted with respect to a given attitude situation. Specifically, when motivation and capacity to process the message are high, the individual carefully scrutinizes the merits of a persuasive communication (central route) and attitude change is influenced by the strength of the message. Conversely, when motivation and capacity to process the message are low, attitudes are likely to be affected by cues peripheral to the persuasive message.

Heuristic-Systematic Model. The heuristic-systematic model,[96] another leading model of the persuasion process, posits that attitude change is influenced by systematic processing of the persuasive argument (akin to the central route in the elaboration likelihood model). Attitude change may in addition be influenced through heuristic processing, in which inferences or heuristic devices (i.e., simple decision rules) are used to make attitudinal formulations with regard to a given message. For example, an individual who believes that the statements of an expert can be routinely trusted may agree with a persuasive message delivered by an expert without carefully studying the content of the message. The heuristic-systematic model differs from the elaboration likelihood model in conceptualizing heuristic and systematic processing as parallel modes of assessing persuasive messages.[94]

Attitudes in Health and Illness

People's attitudes affect whether they practice adaptive or maladaptive health behaviors. According to the health belief model proposed to explain health-related behavior, individuals' decisions regarding their responses to threats of illness are influenced by sociocultural and demographical factors, perceptions of the threat of the condition, expectations regarding the ability to minimize such a threat, and personal and environmental cues regarding appropriate courses of action.[97] People are likely to take steps to minimize the risk of contracting a medical problem if the following conditions occur: 1) they view themselves as vulnerable to a particular health condition; 2) they deem the condition to be personally consequential; 3) they believe that a specific course of action would minimize vulnerability to the condition and that limitations associated with such actions are outweighed by the potential benefits to be accrued; and 4) they perceive themselves as capable of performing these actions (i.e., self-efficacy).[97] Researchers have begun to examine the efficacy of using the health belief model to inform prevention and intervention approaches for medically ill individuals and those at risk for specific illnesses.

The theory of reasoned action has also been applied to the study of health behaviors and to recommendations for promoting adaptive health behaviors and discouraging maladaptive health behaviors. Accordingly, it has been suggested that information aimed at promoting behaviors that reduce health risk should focus on behavioral or normative beliefs influencing the behavior in question. The goal of such interventions is to bolster intentions to engage in or abstain from the target behavior.

Mental Health Implications: Attitude Theory

Attitudes and Mental Outlook

Only recently have mental health professionals attended to the interplay between attitudes and mental outlook.[74] It has been postulated that whereas individuals who evidence positive mental health possess flexible attitudes that are adaptive to the context, persons with psychological difficulties evidence maladaptive attitudes that impair their capacity to cope effectively with life's challenges. This suggests that helping patients identify and modify maladaptive attitudes about self and others can enhance their psychological functioning.[74]

Clinical Applications

Dissonance Approaches. Cooper and Aronson[74] have suggested several clinical applications of attitude theory and research. One method employs dissonance techniques that coax the patient to adopt attitudinal beliefs contrary to currently held maladaptive attitudes. This induced compliance approach may involve requiring the patient to engage in a behavior that is inconsistent with the attitude targeted for change while carefully balancing the variables of reward and freedom of choice in behaving in counterattitudinal ways. Such an intervention is most effective if rewards are sufficiently low and perceived freedom of choice is sufficiently high that dissonance can be generated by the inconsistency between the maladaptive attitude targeted for change and the counterattitudinal behavior. In the event that rewards are too high or freedom of choice is low, dissonance may be minimized by attribution of counterattitudinal behavior to one of these factors. For example, a chronically ill medical patient who expresses profound mistrust of health care providers because of their lack of genuine concern for their patients is encouraged by the therapist to consider volunteering in a medical clinic. If the patient freely chooses to follow this recommendation, and feels rewarded by meaningfully filling her or his time and enhancing the well-being of others with similar medical problems, her or his attitude of mistrust is likely to become dissonant with the behavior. To reconcile this discrepancy, the patient may begin to view health care professionals in a more positive light.

A second approach outlined by Cooper and Aronson[74] draws on the prediction from dissonance theory that individuals more highly value that which they have worked hard for or suffered to attain. From this perspective, one might hypothesize that a patient who enters therapy with problems that are rated equally important is likely to feel the greatest improvement in self-esteem when an amelioration is noted of the problem that the patient invested the most time and effort in addressing.

Persuasion Models. Social psychological models of persuasion, such as the elaboration likelihood model, have also been applied to the study of attitude change in psychotherapy.[98] The elaboration likelihood model predicts that change in psychotherapy is likely to be longer lasting to the extent that persuasion occurs through the central route, because this route involves substantive cognitive elaboration of persuasive messages by the therapist. Specifically, the central route to attitude change in therapy increases the likelihood that the therapist's persuasive messages will be personalized (i.e., assimilated into the patient's attitudinal and meaning schemas) and internalized (i.e., claimed as part of the patient's own attitude system).[98] Cooper and Aronson[74] noted, however, that for individuals whose motivation for therapy and capacity to process therapeutic message contents are limited, careful consideration of peripheral persuasion variables may maximize the change process.

Attitude Theory and Cognitive Therapy. A number of specific clinical intervention strategies have been developed that incorporate social psychological models of attitude formation and change. These strategies have been delineated by adherents to a cognitive therapy approach. These include reattribution techniques, problem-solving strategies, and modification of dysfunctional cognitions.[46, 69, 99–102] For example, a cognitive approach to negative attitudes about self might focus on identifying internal self-statements that maintain these attitudes and suggesting alternative self-statements that are more consistent with enhanced self-regard.

Interpersonal Relationships

Whereas the preceding sections covered issues related to self-functioning, person perception, and social cognition within an interpersonal context, this section is concerned specifically with interpersonal relationships. The study of interpersonal relationships spans a multitude of behavioral domains relevant to social psychology. In keeping with the purpose of this chapter, the following discussion focuses on selected topics pertinent to a social psychological perspective and its mental health implications: prosocial behavior and altruism, affiliation, and aggression.

Theory and Research Findings: Prosocial Behavior and Altruism

There is considerable evidence that interpersonal relatedness offers certain evolutionary advantages that enhance species survival.[103] For example, ethological research reveals that under certain conditions, animals may exhibit helpful or altruistic behavior. Helping behaviors are more common among related animals of the same species (kin selection) than between animals that are unrelated. In social animals, there are many examples of helpful behavior among relatives, including protecting and defending offspring or alerting members of one's social group when a predator is observed. These behaviors are classified as helpful because the helper and the recipient of help obtain reproductive gains. Such helpful tendencies are referred to as mutualism or cooperation.[104]

Models of Altruism

Definition. Altruism refers to instances in which there is no reproductive gain attributable to the helping behavior.[104] Altruistic acts benefit others (who are not offspring), with no apparent short- or long-term benefits obtained by the helper. In the context of debate among theorists and researchers regarding the extent to which truly altruistic behavior occurs, a number of theories have been proposed to explain altruistic behavior in animals and humans.[104–106]

The Models. Trivers[107] asserted that altruistic acts serve to increase the chance of survival of the individual's genes at the expense of the altruist.[105] Trivers[107] further posited that deferred reproductive gain may be obtained by participation in reciprocal altruism, in which individuals take turns helping each other. According to this view, there is short-term loss for the helper but ultimately greater long-term reproductive gain.

In contrast to the aforementioned view, Simon[106] proposed a model of successful altruism according to which the adoption of socially appropriate behaviors that are culturally transmitted may enhance the fitness of the species. Further, on the basis of Gould's[108] argument that selection operates at several different levels (e.g., genes, organisms, species), Guisinger and Blatt[103(p106)] postulated that "populations of altruists might have had a selective advantage over selfish populations in the evolutionary past." As such, these authors[103(p106)] concluded that recent models of evolution "account for the development of an altruistic, cooperative, interpersonally related self."

Many psychological inquiries with regard to prosocial behavior and altruism in humans have assumed that prosocial acts are ultimately motivated by self-serving factors rather than a specific desire to benefit others. In reviewing this matter, Batson[109] identified two categories of self-serving motives that typically are manifested in contemporary examinations of the problem of altruism. The first approach incorporates a reinforcement model, according to which the impetus for altruistic acts is the desire to avoid punishment or seek reward (e.g., self-rewarding acts of helping in response to internalized values and norms). The second view conceptualizes altruism as motivated by a need to reduce aversive internal arousal states.

An alternative model proposed by Batson[109] is intended to account for altruism without invoking self-serving motives by establishing empathy as the key factor that drives altruistic behavior. According to this model, adopting the perspective of the other in need can generate vicarious empathy in the helper that then leads to a desire for the other's need to be reduced. Because empathic emotion is distinguished from that of a distress response, it is argued that helpful acts resulting from empathic determinants are carried out with the intention of enhancing the welfare of the other rather than the self. Although presenting empirical tests of the model, Batson cautions that further study is needed to

Table 18–7 Factors Influencing Helping Behavior
Mood of the helper
Empathy for the needs of the helpee
View of helpee as similar to oneself
Perception of helpee as attractive and likable
Attributions regarding whether the helpee is deserving of assistance
Diffusion of responsibility
Ambiguity regarding whether the situation is one in which help is needed
Concerns that one might do more harm than good
Evaluation apprehension

determine whether this conceptualization provides clear evidence for truly altruistic motivations.

Helping Behavior

In investigations of helping behavior, social psychologists have been invested in determining the factors that influence whether an individual will engage in helping others, focusing on characteristics of the helper, the person who is in need of help, and the situation (Table 18–7). For example, individuals are most likely to engage in helping behavior if they are in a good mood and experience empathy for the needs of the person requiring help. Perception of the person in need as similar to oneself, attractive, likable, and deserving of help also enhances the likelihood of helping behavior. Evaluations of whether an individual warrants help depend largely on attributional processes, particularly regarding the issue of whether the cause of the problem is within or outside the realm of control of the individual needing assistance. Attribution of cause to external factors is likely to evoke increased empathy in the helper, whereas attribution to internal factors may result in disdain and lowered interest in helping.

Among the situational variables that influence helping behavior is the bystander effect,[110] the empirical finding that individuals are less likely to help when multiple others are present. Factors contributing to the bystander effect include the perception that others at the scene will respond or have responded to the problem (diffusion of responsibility), perceptual ambiguity with regard to whether the situation is one in which an individual requires assistance, concerns that one might do more harm than good, and fears that others might evaluate negatively one's efforts to help (evaluation apprehension).

Mental Health Implications: Prosocial Behavior and Altruism

In general, the theory and research findings regarding prosocial behavior and altruism suggest that helping behavior, whether or not it is truly altruistic, is an adaptive process. One implication for mental health treatment is that it is important to focus on fostering helping behavior in patients with maladaptive interpersonal behavior patterns.

Empathy

Another implication of the altruism literature is that empathy is central to the promotion of helpful interpersonal behavior. Thus, individuals in therapy who demonstrate an inability or unwillingness to help others may lack appropriate empathy. For example, the relative absence of prosocial behavior typical of an individual with an antisocial personality disorder diagnosis may be understood, in part, as resulting from a lack of empathic awareness of the feelings and needs of others. As such, one objective of the therapy might be to assist the patient in empathic skill development in the hope that this would contribute to the individual's increased attention to the interpersonal consequences of his or her behavior. Unlike persons with antisocial personality disorders who typically have a socially unaware stance, individuals who help others at the expense of their own needs and well-being (e.g., "masochism" or "self-defeating personality style") may need to be taught both to be less focused on others and to increase their empathy toward neglected aspects of self.

Facilitation of Helping Behavior

As noted before, social psychological research suggests a number of conditions under which the likelihood of helping behavior is increased that may be of clinical relevance. These include enhancing mood, highlighting similarities of self with those in need, and facilitating external attributions of cause for difficulties. For example, a mother whose 16-year-old son fails a math class is more likely to help her son if she attributes the cause of his failure to difficult subject material rather than to lack of effort. If the mother is furious at her son for his seeming lack of effort, the therapist might encourage her to consider alternative perspectives regarding the causes of her son's difficulties, including such uncontrollable factors as the complexity of the subject matter. This may enable her to be more understanding of his difficulties and more willing to facilitate his management of the situation.

Prosocial Behavior, Altruism, and the Therapist

The broad issues of prosocial behavior and altruism raise important questions about therapists' motives as helping professionals. Because for many health care professionals the desire to help others is a powerful motivator, it is essential that they thoughtfully consider the degree to which their helping behavior is self versus other motivated. Ultimately, this requires therapist's to examine their own views with regard to the question of whether true altruism is a possibility within the realm of human relationships.

Theory and Research Findings: Affiliative Behavior in Animals

As investigations of prosocial behavior illustrate, there is adaptive value in forming and maintaining interpersonal relationships. An area of theory and research on relationships that has received considerable attention in the social psychological literature is affiliative behavior. Interpersonal attraction, attachment, close relationships, love, and sexuality are key topics encompassed within the rubric of affiliative behaviors. Although most social psychological investigations of affiliative behavior have been conducted with humans, considerable work on affiliative behavior (e.g., courtship and sexual behavior, parent-child attachment) has been conducted with animals within an evolutionary perspective. Certain parallels may be observed between animal and human social behavior, and insight about human social interaction can be gleaned from studying animals, although it is important to emphasize that the nature and qualities of human social interaction are not attributable solely to evolutionary and biological influences and processes and are not directly parallel to animal behavior.[111] Further, although an evolutionary perspective can provide useful insights, adoption of such a viewpoint does not imply strict genetic determinism or unmodifiability of evolved behavioral patterns.[112] Despite these caveats, however, findings on affiliative behavior in the animal world can inform our understanding of affiliative processes in humans.

Courtship and Sexual Behavior

One aspect of ethological research on the affiliative component of interpersonal relationships involves courtship and sexual behavior. To ensure that sexual reproduction occurs, species-specific behavior patterns have evolved that determine the time, place, and manner in which mating occurs. These courtship rituals communicate sexual interest, convey that intentions are not aggressive, and help ensure that the animals involved are members of the same species (conspecifics) to increase the likelihood that mating will produce fertile offspring. Ethological study suggests that the ultimate decision to mate is typically made by the partner who carries the major cost of reproduction.[113, 114] The social organization of mating varies among species and may include the coming together of male and female only once for the purpose of mating, polygyny, polyandry, or monogamy. Presumably, the mating system maximizes reproductive success in that species.

Attachment

Adaptive Significance. Parent-child attachment has received considerable attention from ethologists and animal psychologists. Investment in parental care for offspring is theorized to involve a cost-benefit tradeoff; the increased likelihood that offspring will survive is weighed against potential costs of parental care. Attachment phenomena are virtually ubiquitous in birds and mammals, with extended dependency periods in which offspring are fed, cleaned, sheltered, and protected by the parent. From this perspective, attachment facilitates survival of the offspring.

Imprinting. In many species, this attachment process is enhanced by imprinting, a learned attachment that forms at the earliest phases of development. Imprinting is most likely to occur during specific, critical periods of development. If imprinting is not achieved during those times, it is difficult to attain.[115]

Primate Research on Attachment. Given that the social relationships within many nonhuman primate communities are remarkably similar to those observed in human societies, it is not surprising that some of the most influential animal work on attachment has been with primates. For example, Suomi's[116] summary of the research with rhesus monkeys reveals that nonhuman primates maintain long-term relationships with specific members of their social troop, which may be interrupted intermittently for short periods and severed by loss (e.g., death, emigration). Although the termination of these relationships is stressful for the majority of rhesus monkeys, there is variability in an individual's reactions to such losses, ranging from symptoms akin to human affective disorders to relatively brief and mild negative responses.

Harlow[117] raised newborn rhesus monkeys separated at birth from their mothers. These baby monkeys were reared in cages with surrogate mothers, including a wire mesh figure equipped with a nipple that provided milk and a soft terry cloth figure. The rhesus newborns were drawn more to the terry cloth figures than to the wire mesh figures, particularly when confronted with stress. These findings suggest that attachment is associated primarily with physical comfort (contact comfort) rather than the provision of nutritional sustenance.[117] The behavior of these monkeys is similar to that observed in young children, who seek out their primary caretaker for nurturance in response to stress and who are comforted by soft toys (e.g., stuffed animals) or blankets. Some psychoanalytic theorists have inferred that these soft and cuddly "transitional objects" serve as symbols of maternal nurturance.[17]

Implications of Primate Attachment Research. Findings from the longitudinal studies of Harlow's monkeys provide insights into the importance of early attachment behavior in overall social development in nonhuman primates and humans. Specifically, socially isolated young monkeys reared with no opportunities for attachment engage in rocking behavior, clasp themselves, and huddle in a corner in the cage. When brought into contact with normally reared age-mates, these socially isolated monkeys fail to demonstrate age-appropriate social behavior (e.g., play, sexual behavior, parenting). Similarly, human infants institutionalized at birth and reared in relative social isolation with minimal social stimulation, despite adequate nutrition and body care, manifest impaired social development, poor peer relations, and patterns of social behavior that include extreme apathy or excessive attention-seeking behavior.[35] These difficulties persist throughout life, and as these children reach adolescence, they often evidence elevated levels of aggression, delinquency, and social indifference. It has been argued that the work with socially isolated rhesus monkeys provides an analogue for socially deprived human infants.

Researchers have examined whether the deficits noted in nonhuman primates reared in isolation could be reversed by use of "therapist" monkeys, reared normally and 3 months younger than the "patient" monkeys.[118] Within a few weeks, previously socially isolated monkeys join in play with the therapist monkeys, their autistic-like behaviors decline, and these improvements become more marked over time. Although more vulnerable to deteriorating under stress, these monkeys exhibit relatively normal adult social behaviors. These findings suggest that sequelae of early social deprivation may be ameliorated with adequate social contact, at least in nonhuman primates. Whereas research on reversal of social deprivation in humans is limited, one study found that orphans raised by a mentally retarded woman or an attendant in an institutional setting fared better than their counterparts who remained in the orphanage where they received minimal one-to-one attention and care and limited emotional and intellectual stimulation.[119]

Taken together, these animal psychology studies suggest that early attachment experiences influence, but are not the sole determinants of, later social adjustment. There appears to be a degree of plasticity such that early social deprivation can be mediated by later reparative social intervention. These findings may have significant implications for intervention studies with socially deprived and socially impaired children.

Theory and Research Findings: Affiliative Behavior in Humans

Interpersonal Attraction

Definition. Social psychologists define interpersonal attraction as an attitude pertaining to the degree of liking for another person along a continuum from strong liking (positive valence) to intense disliking (negative valence).[120] Similar to other attitudinal phenomena, attraction consists of cognitive, affective, and behavioral components. Attraction is a component of the process of the development of interpersonal relationships.[121]

Theories. As reviewed by Berscheid[120] and Derlega and colleagues,[121] cognitive consistency, reinforcement, exchange, and developmental theories have been applied to the understanding of interpersonal attraction. Representative attraction theories are discussed here and summarized in Table 18–8.

Cognitive consistency theories[52, 79, 122] highlight the influence of the need for internally consistent beliefs on interpersonal attraction. Reinforcement theories[123, 124] are founded on the proposition that individuals like those who reward them and satisfy their needs (e.g., provide reinforcement) and dislike people who withdraw rewards (e.g., invoke punishment) or impose costs that outweigh the benefits of ongoing interaction. Exchange theories[125] assume that interpersonal attraction is influenced by the mutuality, rather than quantity, of rewards. Such an approach emphasizes the two-way nature of attraction processes. According to a developmental or stage theory,[126] attraction occurs according to a logical sequence, beginning with casual contact and progressing to varying degrees of mutual intimacy.

Variables Influencing Attraction. Researchers have identified a number of factors that influence attraction (Table 18–9). One such variable is similarity. Specifically, to the extent that individuals are similar on the dimensions of attitudinal beliefs, values, interests, background, and personality, the likelihood of attraction will be enhanced.[123] Thus, despite the common folklore that "opposites attract," partners tend to be similar to one another (i.e., matching principle). Differences, however, can be a basis for mutual attraction to the extent that each individual offers something of importance or value that the other lacks and desires (i.e., completion principle; complementarity hypothesis).

Table 18–8 Attraction Theories: Representative Examples

Model	Basic Tenets
Cognitive consistency theories	Attraction is influenced by the need for internally consistent beliefs.
Reinforcement theories	Attraction is influenced by patterns of reinforcement and punishment.
Exchange theories	Attraction is influenced by mutuality of rewards.
Developmental theories	Attraction occurs according to a logical sequence from casual contact to increased degrees of intimacy.

Table 18–9 Factors Influencing Attraction

The extent to which the other is similar to oneself
Complementarity of personal attributes
Physical attributes
Propinquity

Physical attractiveness is another variable that influences interpersonal attraction. Physically attractive people are more popular and responded to more positively than those who are not physically attractive. In addition, individuals with comparable levels of physical attractiveness are more likely to form relationships with each other than with those of different levels of physical attractiveness.

Proximity, also referred to as propinquity, is a final variable influencing interpersonal attraction. Research reveals that individuals are likely to be attracted to those in physical proximity. Investigators suggest that propinquity is associated with liking because people who are physically close tend to be familiar and have characteristics in common, and they are available for social contact. Further, there often is psychological and social incentive or pressure to like those with whom interaction is common or required.

Close Relationships

Social psychological research findings have led to the development of a number of theories regarding interpersonal relationships, two of which are described briefly here. One theory, developed by Berscheid,[127] posits that in close relationships, partners engage in interwoven behavioral patterns (action sequences) that occur with minimal self-reflection. Interruptions of these action sequences activate heightened emotion, either negative or positive, depending on whether the disruption interferes with the attainment of goal objectives. The extent of emotional influences on relationships depends on the degree to which core behavioral patterns are intertwined. A second model distinguishes communal relationships typified by mutuality and genuine concern for the well-being of the other (e.g., family and romantic relationships, friendships) and exchange relationships (e.g., business dealings, casual acquaintanceships) based on a benefits-debts structure in which one gives to another to pay debts for previously received benefits.[128] Individuals may differ in their perceptions of a given relationship as either communal or exchange in nature, and conflicts may arise if these views are discrepant and not resolved.

Love

Although romantic love has long been a focus of writers, poets, and songwriters, only relatively recently have psychologists turned their attention to the empirical study of love.[129] Although some have argued that love is an intense form of liking, research suggests that liking and love are qualitatively distinct.[130] Whereas liking combines affection and respect, romantic love involves distinct physiological manifestations, dependence on the other for need fulfillment, reciprocity such that each member promotes the welfare of the other and is responsive to the other's needs (i.e., mutuality), and feelings of trust and an associated willingness to self-disclose. The affective experience and psychological significance of romantic love differ across such dimensions as sex, culture, and epoch and may be expressed verbally or nonverbally and through material or nonmaterial symbols.

Passion, often a hallmark of the initial phases of romantic love, is complemented over the long term by a mutuality in the relationship referred to by social psychologists as companionate love.[131] Companionate love, defined as "the affection we feel for those with whom our lives are deeply intertwined,"[131(p177)] is characterized by warmth and affection, trust and caring, and an acceptance of one's partner's foibles. It has been asserted that companionate love serves as the basis for healthy and satisfying long-term romantic attachments.

Attachment

Attachment Behavioral System. Attachment theory has as its cornerstone a system of reciprocal interactions that facilitate psychological safety and security (i.e., attachment behavioral system).[35, 132, 133] According to Bowlby's theory of attachment, as a consequence of evolutionary processes, children possess emotional and behavioral systems that organize and direct them to seek proximity and to bond with their primary caretakers when they feel distressed or threatened. The nature and quality of parental responses in such instances influence the child's development. Children's internal working models (i.e., self and object representations; schemas) of the attachment figure and the self in relation to this figure influence their attachment style and the quality of their interpersonal relationships.

Attachment in Children. The bulk of attachment research has been conducted with young children and their primary caretakers. This research reveals four attachment bonds (Table 18–10) most noted when an infant and the primary caretaker are reunited after a brief, experimentally controlled separation.[134, 135]

Securely attached children are social, able to explore their environment freely, and resilient when faced with stressful situations. In contrast, avoidant children tend to be anxious with their primary caretakers and angry or attention-seeking with others. Anxious-ambivalent children are typically fearful of the environment, affectively unstable, and inordinately clinging to others. Finally, disorganized-disoriented children often exhibit signs of disorganization and contradictory behaviors, particularly on reunion with their primary caretaker. This attachment style is most often observed in children whose primary caretaker manifests unresolved feelings and incoherent thinking about attachment-related traumas and losses.[135, 136] Longitudinal research shows that attachment behavior patterns are stable over time, predictive of school behavior and peer interactions, and consistent with the quality of parenting received and parental attachment style.[137–139]

Table 18–10 Types of Childhood Attachment Bonds and Behavioral Correlates

Attachment Bond	Behavioral Hallmarks
Secure	Social, freely explore the environment, respond with resilience to stress
Avoidant	Anxious with primary caretaker, angry or attention seeking with others
Anxious-ambivalent	Fearful, affectively unstable, excessive clinging behavior
Disorganized-disoriented	Disorganized and contradictory behaviors, particularly on reunion with primary caretaker

Attachment in Adults. Therapists and researchers have begun to turn their attention to attachment patterns in adults.[140, 141] Similar to infant attachment patterns, adult attachment has biological origins and may be characterized by a strong interest in the other, a desire to remain physically close to and spend time with the other, reliance on ongoing access to the other, dependence on the other for support in the face of physical or emotional threats, and feelings of discomfort and distress on separation.[142, 143] However, unlike attachment patterns in children, the primary adult attachment objects are typically peers, adult patterns of relating are more reciprocal, and attachment figures are often also sexual partners.[144] Adult attachment is influenced significantly by working models of the attachment object and self that have their origins in childhood attachment experiences with primary caretakers.[145] Work in adult attachment theory addresses the establishment and maintenance of primary emotional partnerships of adult life, the effects of early and current attachment experiences on the development of psychopathological conditions, and the use of attachment theory to guide therapeutic interventions.

Sexuality

Sexual behavior is an important channel of expression in certain types of interpersonal relationships, and its patterns of expression may symbolize underlying relational dynamics.[146] In humans, sexual behavior serves more than the purely biological functions of procreation and physiological release; it is also an important means of expressing love, closeness, and a need for human contact. Sexual behavior is manifested in diverse ways determined by a complex interplay among one's relationships, life situations, and the broad sociocultural context. Although normative sexual behavior has received systematic empirical study, beginning with the survey research of Kinsey and colleagues[147, 148] and continuing to the present day,[149] much current psychological research focuses on sexual dysfunction and its treatment.[150, 151]

Clinically oriented researchers have attempted to describe well-functioning sexual relationships.[152, 153] Heiman and coworkers[152] delineated relationship variables specific to sexual functioning that characterize healthy sexual interactions. Relationship factors often associated with satisfying sexual involvements include erotic attraction, love, relational flexibility, emotional closeness and intimacy, trust and commitment, openness to receptive and expressive communication, autonomy, and responsibility. Sexual factors include pleasure and arousal from sexual involvements, compatibility with regard to frequency and variety, sexual self-awareness and acceptance, and acknowledgment and acceptance of one's partner's sexuality. The presence and importance of these considerations may vary across individuals and relationships.[152] Further, evaluation of the health of a sexual relationship depends partially on the frame of reference of the individuals making such an assessment.

Mental Health Implications: Affiliative Behavior

Interpersonal Attraction, Close Relationships, and Love

Derlega and coworkers[121] delineated specific mental health applications of social psychological research on interpersonal attraction and love attitudes and styles. They suggested that appreciating the individual factors defined by social psychological research as contributing to interpersonal attraction in relationships enhances understanding of the goodness of fit and working alliance between therapist and patient. For example, a patient's attraction to the therapist may be influenced by the extent to which the therapist is perceived as similar on domains that the patient considers highly significant (e.g., sex, ethnicity, beliefs and values, personality style). The therapist's experience of rapport with the patient may be influenced similarly. The attraction between therapist and patient is probably strengthened by the extent to which time is shared, because increased experience allows a greater sense of mutual understanding, which in turn enhances the experience of interpersonal attraction and compatibility.

Clark and Bennett[154] briefly presented implications for mental health practice of Berscheid's[127] theory of emotion in relationships and Clark and Mills'[128] work on communal and exchange relationships. They recommended that couples and families be encouraged to define interactional patterns based more on communal than exchange norms. This work may include specific behavioral and social learning interventions (e.g., communication training, behavior exchange) commonly used in couples and family therapy.

Derlega and colleagues[121] also conceptualized an association between the six love styles defined by Lee[155] and interpersonal behaviors and their manifestations in psychotherapeutic relationships. For example, one love style, entitled Eros by Lee,[155] is akin to the social psychological notion of passionate love. In the therapeutic relationship, this style may be expressed as a rapidly forming intense therapist-patient bond characterized by high emotion and self-disclosure.[121] Conversely, the love style termed Storge by Lee[155] has parallels to the social psychological concept of companionate love. When this style is evident in a therapeutic alliance, the relationship is marked by a steady evolution of a bond of mutual respect, care, and concern.[121] Different types of therapeutic alliances may influence the course and nature of the treatment.

Attachment

The construct of attachment is pivotal to the understanding of relatedness across the life span.[156] As such, attachment theory and the associated empirical findings have useful clinical implications for assessing and treating dysfunctional parent-child, peer, dyadic romantic, family, and therapist-patient relationships.[137, 140, 141, 157] Attachment theory also provides a meaningful framework for conceptualizing various psychiatric disorders in individuals and families.[140, 157] In an attachment theory–based approach to psychotherapy, the therapist provides new and more adaptive models of relating such that individuals may move from insecure or anxious attachments to the development and maintenance of secure attachments.[141] This process is facilitated by the therapist's provision of a secure base, examination of relationships and expectations of significant people, exploration of the therapist-patient relationship, reflection on links between parental expectations and the patient's working models of relationships, and development of an understanding of the appropriateness of these working models for guiding current and future relationships.[137]

Sexuality and Sex Therapy

As discussed herein, sexuality is highly significant in the development and maintenance of certain relationships, especially romantic involvements. Sex therapy, a specialized clinical approach to sexual dysfunction, aims to help couples develop healthier and more satisfying sexual interactions. In the past two decades, sex therapists have developed techniques to address myriad forms of sexual dysfunction including disorders of sexual desire, problems with sexual arousal, orgasmic difficulties, and sexual pain. Many sex therapists highlight the connection between sexual problems and relational conflicts and espouse that treatment of sexual dysfunction occur in the context of couples therapy.[146] They emphasize understanding both the ways in which sexual problems influence romantic relationships and the manner in which relational conflicts are reflected in particular sexual complaints. Thus, specific sexual problems are most effectively treated with a combination of sex therapy principles and a focus on maladaptive relational patterns.

Theory and Research Findings: Aggressive Behavior

Definition

Multiple definitions of aggression have been proposed by social scientists. This reflects both the diverging views regarding the nature and determinants of aggressive behavior and the social norms that provide a context for evaluating whether an aggressive behavior is socially sanctioned (e.g., murder in self-defense versus murder to commit a crime). For this discussion, aggressive action is defined as any verbal or physical behavior or set of behaviors emitted with the intention to harm or damage someone or something. Biological, affective, cognitive, developmental and socialization, and sociocultural influences on aggressive behavior are reviewed here and summarized in Table 18–11.

Biological Influences

Aggressive communication patterns in animal populations offer some insight into the biological and evolutionary roots

Table 18–11 Factors That Influence Aggression

Factor	Behavioral Correlates
Biological	Aggressive behavior results from a buildup and discharge of biologically rooted aggressive energy (hydraulic models).
Affective	Aggression is a response to frustration associated with the thwarting of important goals (frustration-aggression model).
Cognitive	Aggression is influenced by cognitive interpretation of events, including causal attributional processes, beliefs about the consequences of aggressive behavior, deindividuation processes, and degree of self-consciousness in the actor.
Developmental-social	Aggression is influenced by developmental history and socialization processes.
Sociocultural	Aggression is influenced by social norms, laws, and customs that demarcate expressions of aggression that are prosocial, socially sanctioned, and antisocial.

of human aggression. Aggressive behavior between species typically involves predation and defense, wherein a predator attacks potential prey and is met with a counterattack. Most animal behavior researchers regard conflict occurring between same-species members as prototypical of aggressive behavior,[158] and many restrict use of the term aggression to instances of conflict between conspecifics. Conflict between members of the same species appears to be almost universal in the animal world. Prominent adaptive functions of this aggression include securing limited resources (e.g., food, mating partners), eliminating competitors, and demarcating territorial boundaries. Animals have evolved mechanisms for limiting the extent, severity, and costs of aggressive interactions, including territoriality, dominance hierarchies, ritualized fighting, and threat and appeasement displays.

There are parallels between animals and humans in the overt communication of aggression. For instance, threat and appeasement behaviors are common elements of human social interaction. Examples of territoriality and human dominance hierarchies are found at the level of the family, the community, and the culture. Borrowing from animal models of aggression founded on darwinian principles of evolution, some theorists have argued that aggression among humans regulates hierarchical relationships and is a competitive strategy used to acquire scarce resources and to defend against attack. Thus, aggression is not inherently negative, because it may enhance survival of the individual and the species. A significant danger in humans, however, is posed by the emergence of culturally derived methods for promulgating violent acts against others that are not subject to the controls routinely observed in animals that evolved to provide natural inhibitions on aggressive interactions.[159]

With regard to human aggression, some theorists have conceptualized aggression as rooted in biological instinct. For example, from a psychoanalytic perspective, Freud[160] posited the existence of an innate aggressive drive called Thanatos, or the death instinct, which he assumed made aggression an inevitable element of human psychological functioning. Adopting an ethological frame of reference, Lorenz[158] asserted that individuals express aggression when their internal aggressive energy level is sufficiently intense that environmental stimuli (releasers) induce an aggressive response. These conceptualizations employ a hydraulic metaphor of the mechanism of human aggression and view aggression as a biologically rooted phenomenon that is difficult, if not impossible, to control. Critics of such instinct theories maintain that human aggression is determined by an interplay of biological and cultural variables, learning history, affective and cognitive factors, and reactions to present threats and frustrations.

Affective Factors

Certain discussions have pointed out that anger serves important adaptive functions in self-defense and mastery as well as in regulating interpersonal relationships.[161] The adaptive value of anger is linked to its modulation and expression in the context of social discourse, with parental and peer socialization and broad cultural influences playing central roles in shaping the development and manifestation of anger responses in individuals. Lemerise and Dodge[161] underscored that problems in the regulation and expression of angry emotions appear to be linked to interpersonal difficulties.

Theoretical discussions of aggression often elaborate on the role of frustration and anger in the manifestation of aggressive behavior. According to the frustration-aggression hypothesis,[162] frustration occurs when goals are thwarted, and aggression is a response to this frustration. Later modifications of this model recognized that aggression was only one of several responses to frustrating situations. Indeed, research reveals that not all aggressive acts follow from angry emotional states, and anger does not always result in aggressive behavior. Other theorists have posited that aggressive action results in reduction of subsequent angry feelings and aggression (i.e., catharsis). In this regard, a mixture of results has been found; some studies reveal decreases in aggression after an aggressive act and others indicate that aggressive behavior may increase the likelihood of subsequent aggression.[159]

Cognitive Factors

A third set of factors contributing to the emergence of an aggressive response involves the cognitive interpretation of events. In this regard, the causal attributional process is a key cognitive variable that influences aggressive behavior. Attribution theory predicts that angry emotional responses are likely to emerge when frustrating or aggressive behavior in the other is perceived as intentional and under the other's internal control, whereas anger and aggressive responses are less likely if the frustrating act is attributed to circumstances outside the other's sphere of control.[58]

Additional cognitive variables that affect the expression of aggression include beliefs regarding consequences of aggressive behavior, deindividuation, and the role of self-consciousness in aggression.[159] With regard to beliefs about consequences, in many instances, aggressive behavior may be inhibited by a belief that such acts will result in retaliation. Deindividuation refers to a lack of awareness of self resulting from such situational variables as anonymity, heightened arousal, and sensory overload. Research reveals that aggressive behavior is more likely when individuals are in a deindividuated state than when they are not manifesting deindividuation. In a related vein, research has yielded a negative correlation between degree of self-focus and aggressive behavior; individuals who are more self-conscious are less likely to engage in aggressive acts than are those who are externally focused.

Developmental and Socialization Factors

Two psychosocial factors influencing the development and expression of aggression are reinforcement history and the effects of modeling.[159] Socialization, which occurs during the course of development, represents a coalescing of reinforcement and modeling experiences related to when, how, and against whom it is appropriate to express aggression. Individuals whose aggressive behavior was reinforced or rewarded are likely to engage further in aggressive behaviors, whereas individuals whose aggressive behavior was not reinforced are less likely to demonstrate aggressive acts in the future. Further, modeling of aggressive behavior provides a means of learning to be aggressive without the requirement that aggressive acts be reinforced.[163]

Sociocultural Factors

Social norms, a key sociocultural variable studied by social psychologists in research on aggression, typically influence the socialization process. These norms represent a means by which culture influences manifestations of aggression. Social norms differentiate between types of aggressive behavior that is prosocial, socially sanctioned, and antisocial. To function effectively in society, it is important to internalize these social norms and to adapt to changes in such norms. Other sociocultural factors that influence aggressive behavior include societal and moral values, laws, and customs.[159]

Mental Health Implications: Aggressive Behavior

Social psychological research underscores the multidimensional nature of aggression, suggesting that clinical assessment and intervention address the biological, affective, cognitive, interpersonal, situational, and sociocultural influences on aggressive behavior. Individuals who, on the basis of a thorough assessment, have a history of being temperamentally irritable and easily aroused in infancy, prone to aggressive acts at the slightest provocation, and raised in a family in which aggressive behavior is a primary means of solving problems require an intervention different from that for people who are temperamentally calm, reinforced for nonaggressive behavior, and uncertain regarding how to manage angry feelings and aggressive impulses when confronted with anger-inducing situations.

Clinical Techniques: Intervention

An array of clinical techniques have been developed for helping individuals effectively modulate and manage aggression. These include exploring interpersonal patterns in which aggression arises; teaching cognitive restructuring techniques regarding attributional processes and beliefs about the consequences of anger; using functional family therapy approaches and parent management training; and employing myriad cognitive-behavioral techniques including problem-solving skills training, social skills training, and the use of reinforcement and punishment contingencies. These techniques may be used individually or in combination, depending on the clinical indications as gleaned from the multidimensional assessment.

Clinical Techniques: Prevention

The social psychological literature also suggests strategies for preventing aggressive behavior. For instance, it is useful to help individuals reduce their levels of frustration, teach people ways to control their aggressive behavior, provide instruction regarding the conditions under which it is appropriate to express aggressive behavior and acceptable ways in which to do so, and offer alternative models of self-expression. In addition, it is important to decrease the individual's sense of deindividuation, enhance empathy for the potential victim, and construct situations in which the benefits of cooperation outweigh the potential benefits for antagonistic or aggressive behavior. Further, education regarding the disinhibiting effects of alcohol and drugs and the potential association between media violence and increased levels of aggressive behavior may provide a preventive approach to aggression.

Behavior in Groups

Theory and Research Findings

Characteristics and Social Functions of Groups

An individual's social world is composed of group affiliations. Involvement in familial, work, social, and activity groups provides several potential benefits, including the satisfaction of survival, psychological, informational, and identity needs. In some instances, however, the group dynamics and organization may compromise or hinder the gratification of these needs.[164]

A group is a social unit in which members interact and are interdependent, such that there is mutual influence among the members. Groups vary across such dimensions as size, duration, purpose, tasks, goals, and patterns and rules of communication. Groups are in addition characterized by particular rules and expectations (i.e., group norms), and members typically adopt specific roles in the group vis-à-vis other group members and the group as a whole. Further, the extent to which group members experience a sense of connectedness to the group as a whole is reflective of the level of group cohesiveness. Each of these factors contributes to the group patterns that constitute the group culture (i.e., beliefs, norms, and behaviors that shape the group).

Group Influence

Factors influencing group behavior are discussed here and summarized in Table 18–12.

Social Facilitation, Social Inhibition, and Social Loafing. The study of group influence on behavior has been an

Table 18–12 Group Influence Factors

Factor	Description
Social facilitation	The presence of others enhances performance on simple or familiar tasks.
Social inhibition	The presence of others inhibits performance on complex or novel tasks.
Social loafing	The presence of others leads to lowered work effort when individual efforts are perceived to be anonymous and not subject to social evaluation.
Identity functions	Personal identity may in part be influenced by group affiliations.
Conformity	Groups may exert a pressure toward uniformity that appears related to wishes for group members to be informationally correct and positively regarded by others in the group.
Minority influence	A minority faction can influence group activities and viewpoints when specific conditions are obtained.

important area of social psychological inquiry.[165] For instance, research on task performance in the presence of others reveals that in some situations, individual task performance is enhanced by the mere presence of others (i.e., social facilitation), whereas in other circumstances task performance is compromised by the presence of others (i.e., social inhibition). Social facilitation appears to be observed when the task is simple or familiar; social inhibition appears to occur when the task is complex or novel.[166] In contrast to the findings from social facilitation research, other studies have shown that the presence of others may result in a tendency to work less hard on a task when others are present than when one is alone. This phenomenon, known as social loafing, tends to emerge when people perceive that their individual efforts will be anonymous and thus not subject to social evaluation.[167]

Group Influences on Identity and Deindividuation. Another related area studied by social psychologists involves the impact of the group on identity functions. One's sense of identity is defined partially according to one's group affiliations (e.g., familial, occupational, social). As such, identification with specific groups helps one delineate a sense of self. One model of such processes is social identity theory,[168] according to which individuals seek a positive valuation of their own group in contrast to other groups as a means of attaining a favorable social identity. In contrast, group involvement may influence identity functioning, such that one's self-awareness and sense of personal identity are lessened while identification with the group identity is enhanced. This process is referred to as deindividuation. Research on deindividuation suggests that anonymity, high group cohesiveness, involvement in collective action, and external attentional focus contribute to a reduction in self-awareness in an individual group member.[169]

Conformity. Conformity is an additional process manifested in groups that exerts influence on the individual. In a classic set of studies, experimental subjects asked to make simple judgments regarding the length of lines often gave the wrong answer with the full realization of the correct response, simply because they did not want to disagree with the responses of other participants, who actually were experimental confederates.[170] In general, it has been hypothesized that group dynamics include a pressure toward uniformity, with a tendency for participants to have antipathy for or spurn individuals in the group who differ from other members. Conformity of group members is likely to be observed to the extent that there is high group cohesiveness, there are high levels of commitment to the group, and group viewpoints are unanimous. Size of the group, at least up to a certain point, may also influence this process. The wishes to be informationally correct and regarded positively by others appear to be two motivational factors contributing to group conformity.[171]

Minority Group Influence. Whereas researchers on conformity focus on majority group influence, others underscore the impact of minority influence on group behavior.[172] These researchers have demonstrated that a powerful faction within a group holding a minority position with regard to a given issue can sway the majority opinion. The likelihood of successful minority group influence is enhanced when the individual adhering to a minority view persists in expressing his or her position and does so in a flexible although firm, logically consistent and coherent fashion. This presentation style is likely to be perceived as indicative of confidence in the correctness of the position being advocated. Additional factors influencing the persuasive effectiveness of the minority view include the degree to which the position is consistent with the predominant social culture and the extent to which the individual presenting the minority viewpoint agrees with the majority view regarding most other group issues. At present, controversy exists with regard to the similarities and differences of the social processes associated with majority (i.e., conformity) and minority (i.e., innovation) influences.

Group Decision-Making

One function that groups serve is that of decision-making. Evidence suggests that groups are often more effective than individuals in making decisions or solving problems, particularly when the collective and cooperative efforts of the individuals in the group are needed to accomplish the various components of the task at hand (additive tasks). Successful group performance is aided by a cooperative, rather than competitive, group atmosphere in which members work together to attain goals that benefit the group as a whole. Groups are susceptible to specific social processes (Table 18–13) that may exert a potentially deleterious

Table 18–13 Group Decision-Making Processes

Group polarization	The tendency for groups to arrive at more extreme positions (i.e., more risky or conservative decisions) than would individual group members alone
Group-think	A phenomenon in which cohesive groups make decisions without allowing intragroup dissent or receiving input from knowledgeable outsiders

influence on the process of making thoughtful and productive decisions.

Group Polarization. Social psychological research reveals that groups either arrive at more risky decisions than do individual group members alone (the risky shift) or shift toward a more conservative decision than do individual group members alone. Whether a group position moves toward the more conservative or risky extreme depends partially on the extent to which individual group members hold conservative or risky positions before group discussion. This phenomenon of arriving at more extreme positions by group discussion is referred to as group polarization.[173]

Group-Think. Group-think[174] is a process of group decision-making in which cohesive group members with a powerful, dynamic leader make decisions without allowing intragroup dissent or receiving input from knowledgeable outsiders. Notable characteristics of this group-think process include feelings of invulnerability, high levels of conviction regarding the moral correctness of group positions, group rationalizations, stereotypical portrayals of out-groups, and active suppression of dissenting perspectives to create the illusion of uniformity of opinion within the group. Not surprisingly, this process often results in faulty decisions and sometimes catastrophic consequences.

The Familial Group

The family is one of the most powerful and important group structures in our society,[175] and there are many similarities between the functioning of familial and nonfamilial groups.[176] Further, one's roles and functions in social groups are influenced by one's roles and functions in one's family of origin (i.e., parents, grandparents, extended family, siblings) and family of creation (i.e., partner, children, grandchildren).

General Systems Theory. General systems theory,[177] which provides the theoretical underpinnings of family systems theory, is also applicable to nonfamilial groups. According to systems theory, a system is a group of interacting elements. Family systems attempt to find a balance between change and homeostasis to facilitate adaptation of the family and its individual members across the life cycle. Family systems exchange information through feedback loops, circular response patterns in which there is a return flow of information within the system. Interactions reflect circular causality, in which single events are viewed as both cause and effect and are considered to be reciprocally related. Families may be characterized in terms of their structure (i.e., organization) and function. The key structural property is wholeness (i.e., the whole is greater than the sum of its parts). Family units consist of interdependent subsystems that carry out distinctive functions to maintain themselves and sustain the system as a whole. Boundaries separate these subsystems and protect their integrity while allowing interaction between subsystems. To maintain their structure, family systems have rules that enable them to function productively. Within each unit, individuals play a number of roles, exhibiting a predictable set of behaviors that may be influenced by family of origin, sex, and generation within the nuclear family. All behavior (e.g., roles, communication patterns, symptoms) manifested serves a systemic function.

Groups and Families in Health and Illness

Collaboration among medical providers is central to effective care of patients. Because medical providers routinely make important decisions in the context of work groups, it is important to be cognizant of the dynamics of group behavior described. When decisions are being made about such matters as delicate health procedures or life and death decisions, efforts should be made to foster a group environment that minimizes the likelihood of faulty group decision-making stemming from group polarization or group-think phenomena. This process increases the chances that an integrated biopsychosocial strategy will be adopted and maintained.

This biopsychosocial approach is also important in family medicine.[178] In these instances, important decisions about a patient's care are often best managed by involving patients, their families, and health care providers in a collaborative process. Given the systemic phenomena that typify family functioning as described before, the family context within which the illness progression unfolds is a key component in developing and implementing effective treatment strategies as well as maximizing treatment adherence.

Mental Health Implications: Group Behavior

The vast clinical literature regarding both group therapy and family therapy is beyond the scope of this discussion. Thus, the following section covers only general points related to the mental health implications of social psychological principles for small groups, including families. Given the profound influence of group involvement on one's sense of self and interpersonal relationships, it is reasonable to assume that membership in family groups, groups at work or school, or community-based groups is associated with the quality of one's mental health functioning.[164] Involvement in group activities is often sought as a means of gaining help in managing personal and social problems.

Group Therapy

Group therapy was popularized during the 1930s and early 1940s, concurrent with the shift in American psychology from an intrapsychic to a more social or interpersonal view of human psychological functioning. This shift paved the way for more widespread acceptance of multiperson treatment situations. The group therapy movement was advanced further by the work of Lewin,[179] which emphasized group dynamics and leadership roles, as well as by the efforts of Rogers,[180] which focused on human growth, authenticity, interpersonal style, and communication. These divergent lines of thought led to the development of a variety of groups, including psychotherapy groups, human potential groups, and self-help groups.[164, 181, 182] The discussion that follows is limited to psychotherapy groups.

Psychotherapy Groups. Psychotherapy groups are organized for the specific purpose of dealing with intrapsychic, behavioral, and interpersonal difficulties encountered in daily living. For illustrative purposes, a brief review of the interpersonal or transactional approach to group psychotherapy is presented, because social psychological principles can be applied easily to understanding the nature and efficacy of this commonly used approach.

Yalom,[183] who has contributed substantively to the understanding and implementation of psychotherapy groups, posited that groups provide an interpersonal context within which the members manifest their maladaptive interpersonal patterns, receive feedback about these patterns, and gain opportunities to learn new and more authentic modes of relating to others. In this regard, groups function as social microcosms reflecting each participant's social universe. According to Yalom, a number of therapeutic factors facilitate change in group therapy. These include the instillation of hope, universality, imparting of information, altruism, corrective recapitulation of the primary family group, development of socializing techniques, imitative behavior, interpersonal learning, group cohesiveness, catharsis, and existential factors. Forsyth[181] has evaluated these change factors from a social psychological perspective, suggesting that social comparison, social learning, self-insight, social influence, and social provisions processes are all relevant to the understanding of change processes in therapeutic groups.

Clinical Applications of Group Behavior Principles

Many of the social psychological processes described, as pertains to small group behavior in general, may have particular applicability to group psychotherapy. For example, it is essential for the therapist to facilitate establishment of group norms that maximize the likelihood that the therapeutic factors associated with change will exert full influence. Such norms may pertain to group procedure (e.g., attendance; participation and communication rules; length, frequency, and duration of sessions), communication of support and empathy, values (e.g., self-disclosure, honesty, acceptance), and goals (e.g., improved psychological adjustment, enhanced relationship satisfaction). In addition, group cohesiveness is a key component to a successful therapeutic group in that group cohesion is associated with acceptance and support among group members and the formation of authentic intragroup relationships. Further, high levels of group cohesion are associated with more stable group functioning.[183]

The therapist's awareness of some potential pitfalls of group decision-making processes is also essential (i.e., group polarization, group-think). For instance, the group polarization phenomenon (e.g., risky shift) may be addressed effectively by the presence of a cotherapy team rather than a single therapist; the two therapists may assist group members in arriving at a more moderate position.[183] Careful attention to minimizing the conditions under which groupthink may occur is also important to sidestep potentially catastrophic group decisions. In this regard, it is crucial that group leaders monitor their own inclinations to dominate group processes and suppress intragroup dissent.

Culture and Psychological Functioning

Theory and Research Findings

Definitions of Culture

Increasingly, attention within academic and applied psychology and clinical psychiatry has been focused on how culture influences psychological functioning.[184–188] Myriad definitions of culture have been proposed by social scientists across a range of disciplines. For our purposes, culture is defined as a collective organization of behaviors, ideas, attitudes, values, beliefs, and customs shared by a group of people and socially transmitted across generations through language or other modes of communication. As this sociopsychological definition suggests, cultural processes are of core importance to individual psychological functioning because they influence the behavioral and attitudinal aspects of a range of personal and social activities. Factors that influence the manner in which cultural patterns are manifested in interpersonal relationships include gender, ethnicity, race, socioeconomic status, educational background, neighborhood and geographical region of residence, country of origin, transmigration patterns, religious and political affiliations, and stage in the life cycle.

Table 18–14 Study of Culture and Psychological Functioning

Approach	Description
Etic	Seeks to identify universal psychological principles applicable across different cultures
Emic	Seeks to examine psychological phenomena identified as being different across cultures

Research and theoretical work in this area are conducted with specific reference to distinctions between investigations that seek to identify universal psychological principles that apply across cultures (i.e., etic approaches) and those that examine psychological phenomena identified as being different across cultures (i.e., emic approaches) (Table 18–14). Researchers and theoreticians have also investigated such phenomena as ethnocentrism, stereotypes, and prejudice as they influence everyday interpersonal functioning. As Triandis and Brislin[189] have noted, psychological research findings include both universal and culture-specific components, making it important to conduct inquiries with the awareness of such so that the risk of false generalizations can be avoided. For purposes of illustration, the following discussion briefly reviews some of the contributions of cultural psychology to the understanding of the basic social psychological phenomena covered in this chapter. Table 18–15 summarizes social psychological factors influenced by culture.

The Self

Work has elucidated cultural factors that influence self-definition and self-functioning.[190, 191] For example, Markus and Kitayama[190] delineated two distinct cultural represen-

Table 18–15 Social Psychological Factors Influenced by Culture

Internal Processes	Interpersonal Processes
Self	Affiliation
Person perception	Aggression
Social cognition	Group behavior

tations of the individual. The independent construal of self, seen in many Western cultures, is characterized by a view of self as an autonomous entity. This construal emphasizes understanding oneself in terms of individual thoughts, feelings, personality characteristics, and behavior patterns. A primary normative task is to develop and maintain this unique individuality and independence, with an emphasis on self-expression, self-realization, and self-assertion. Esteem is based on validation and realization of internal attributes and self-defined goals and expectations, with others serving social comparison and reflected appraisal roles.

Interdependent construals of self, observed in many non-Western cultures, emphasize the definition of self in terms of one's social context. Self is defined in terms of the ways in which one is connected to important others, and thus, the interdependent self is relatively unbounded. Further, its structure is flexible; internal attributes may change or be expressed differentially according to the characteristics and dynamics of the social context. According to this view, a primary normative task is to maintain connectedness to one's social world, with an emphasis on identifying and maintaining one's social position. Individuals behave according to role expectations and in a manner consistent with the realization of the goals of the social group. Esteem is based on the capacity to contribute to the group and maintain harmonious relations, with others serving the function of providing a context for self-definition.

Person Perception

Given that culture influences nonverbal and verbal communication patterns, and interpretations of these patterns in others, there are likely to be cultural differences in person perception.[192] This variability is based on one's learning history and cultural context. For example, attractiveness variables will differ according to cultural norms, thereby influencing formation of impressions. Even when individuals from diverse cultural groups arrive at similar perceptions of others, they may differ with regard to the implications or behavioral consequences of these judgments.

Social Cognition

According to Triandis and Brislin,[189] three major approaches have been incorporated to study the relation of culture and cognition. The universalist perspective examines similarities in cognitive functioning. The evolutionist model is concerned with alterations in cognition attributable to one's cultural activities. Finally, the relativist view identifies differences in cognition among cultural groups. As these models suggest, it is important to understand the influence of cultural factors in social cognitive processes, including attributions[193] and attitudes.[194]

For illustrative purposes, only attributional processes are addressed from a cultural perspective. Attributional theories may be limited in their cross-cultural applicability because cultures differentially define success and failure and vary in their conceptualization of specific factors that influence attributional processes (e.g., effort, luck).[193] Differences in attributional processes can influence the negotiation of intercultural communication and the development of relationships between persons of different cultural backgrounds. Research reveals that a number of attributional patterns typically described in individuals from the United States are not characteristic of individuals from other cultures. For example, findings from studies on the self-serving attributional bias conducted with several cultural groups were inconsistent with the results of research in the United States. Further, the degree to which the fundamental attribution error emphasizes internal versus situational factors is associated with the cultural values along the independence-interdependence continuum. Specifically, situational factors appear to be salient for persons in cultures valuing interdependence over independence, whereas internal predispositions are more influential for persons in cultures valuing independence over interdependence.

Interpersonal Relationships

Triandis and Brislin[189] outlined general ways in which culture influences interpersonal interactions. They noted that cultural groups vary with regard to social perception and the manner in which these perceptions inform evaluations of others. In addition, persons across cultural groups differ in terms of their interactional patterns and styles. Cultural factors influencing these interactional patterns include such variables as in-group versus out-group status, verbal communication norms, and nonverbal behaviors (e.g., extent of touching and eye contact, volume and rate of speech, physical proximity or distance).

Cross-cultural researchers have only more recently begun to examine such interpersonal variables as attraction and love, and thus there is a relative dearth of research on this topic.[192] One study reported that romantic love is valued more by Americans and Germans than by Japanese. This may be attributable to the fact that romantic love is experienced as more important in cultures with fewer strong extended family ties than in societies in which marital relationships are influenced and reinforced by one's extended family network.[195] This and other findings suggest considerable cross-cultural variability in attitudes toward and emphasis on various types of love.[192]

Group Behavior

Whereas the tendency of individuals to organize themselves into groups appears to be a universal phenomenon, the attributes used to define group membership, group structure and norms, and the degree of predictability of individual behavior from group processes vary across cultures.[189] Research examining behavior toward in-group versus out-group members has revealed significant cross-cultural differences.[189]

One group behavior variable that has received empirical attention from a cross-cultural perspective is group productivity.[192] Researchers have found that the phenomenon of social loafing is not universally observed across cultures. Indeed, in certain Asian cultures, individual performance may be enhanced rather than impeded by involvement in a group, even when one's performance is anonymous and not subject to social evaluation. This process, referred to as social striving, appears to occur more commonly in cultures that emphasize interdependence over independence.

Culture in Health and Illness

Culture affects definitions and causal explanations of health and illness as well as the nature and quality of help-seeking behavior. Given that one's ethnomedical system influences one's involvement in the health care system as either patient or health professional, it is essential to inquire about the patient's "explanatory models" of health and illness and to be cognizant of the match between the physician's and the patient's world view vis-à-vis illness and its treatment.[186] Further, it behooves health providers and patients to acknowledge that medicine as practiced in hospitals forms a subculture consisting of specific values, beliefs, and practices (i.e., the culture of medicine). In this regard, interactions between patients and health care providers can be viewed as cross-cultural communications, with all participants working to comprehend one another's world views.

Mental Health Implications: Culture

Work emphasizing the understanding of psychological functioning from a cultural perspective has led mental health practitioners to recognize culture as central to the conceptualization, assessment, and treatment of emotional and behavioral disorders as well as dysfunctional interactional patterns. A cultural perspective has significant implications for the definition and conceptualization of normal and abnormal behavior and for the development and implementation of culturally sensitive interventions. In fact, some have argued that the practice of dichotomizing behavior as either normal or abnormal reflects historically Western scientific cultural constructions.[196] There is considerable evidence to suggest that culture influences many of the psychological and social variables typically associated with psychological development, including child-rearing practices and customs, constellation and structure of family life, communication and affect expression, social support networks, frequency and quality of life stress, the ways in which difficulties are defined and managed, and values regarding help-seeking behavior for emotional distress.[196] Therefore, as cultural differences across these domains vary, the manifestations of psychological and personality functioning and dysfunction will also differ.[196] This is particularly applicable to disorders that are thought to derive more from social and environmental influences than from biological factors.

Culture-Bound Assumptions

Implicit in Western models of psychiatric nosology are a number of culture-bound assumptions regarding mental health and psychiatric disorder. Examples of U.S. culture-bound biases articulated by Lewis-Fernandez and Kleinman[197] include 1) the emphasis on individuality and autonomy (egocentric view of self) as opposed to a more interdependent emphasis (sociocentric view of self); 2) the view that psychopathological conditions have either an organic or a psychological cause but not both simultaneously (mind-body dualism versus a more integrated somatopsychological view); and 3) a regard for cultural factors in psychological functioning as epiphenomena underneath which is a universally knowable biological reality. The tendency to organize one's understanding of behavior according to these biases must be monitored carefully in work with patients, and it is essential for therapists and researchers to contextualize behavior and experience and use relevant cultural norms to understand behavioral difficulties and their adaptational value.[197]

Psychiatric Epidemiology and Diagnostic Classification

Cross-cultural social scientists have investigated psychiatric epidemiology across cultures, with particular attention to schizophrenia spectrum disorders and mood disorders. This work has primarily been conducted by use of an etic approach. Although there is considerable evidence that supports the universality of schizophrenia, cross-cultural differences in symptom expression and course have been reported.[198] An additional area of work that approaches diagnostic classification from an emic perspective is that of culture-bound syndromes or folk diagnostic categories, "certain recurrent, locality-specific patterns of aberrant behavior and experience that appear to fall outside conventional Western psychiatric diagnostic categories."[199(p75)] These disorders reflect symptom patterns that are linked to the cultural context within which they are embedded. Examples of culture-bound syndromes in Western societies include anorexia nervosa and the type A behavior pattern.[199]

Clinical Intervention

In addition to their influence in assessment and diagnosis, cultural variables have implications for psychotherapeutic endeavors. In this regard, cultural considerations are important in understanding the conditions under which mental health treatment may be sought, the type of approaches that would be most effective, the clinical stance of the therapist within the treatment setting, and the nature of the therapeutic relationship. Effective psychotherapy requires sensitivity to differences that may affect the therapist's and the patient's perspective on the problem, treatment method, and therapeutic process and objective. Thus, it is important for therapists to be cognizant of the patient's culturally defined values and belief systems, definitions of normality and psychopathology, problem-solving styles, communication patterns, interpersonal customs, and family role behaviors. This cultural perspective is essential in working with adults,[184] children,[200, 201] and families.[202]

Conclusion

In a discussion of the place of social psychology in the Decade of the Brain, Cacioppo and Berntson[203] proposed a multilevel analysis for understanding psychological phenomena, integrating various biopsychosocial variables and the interaction among them. In this regard, they maintained that "the level of organization of psychological phenomena can vary from the molecular, to the cellular, to the tissue, to the organ, to the system, to the organism, to the physical environment, to the sociocultural context."[203(p1020)] The focus of this chapter has been to highlight the social, interpersonal, and sociocultural tiers of this multilevel approach to understanding psychological functioning.

Throughout this chapter, efforts were made to articulate mental health implications of social psychological theory and research findings to illustrate the interface between social psychology and clinical psychiatry. Several basic assumptions, articulated cogently by Leary and Maddux,[204] guide the work of mental health professionals whose clinical activities incorporate a social psychological perspective. First, emotional and behavioral dysfunction is understood within the interpersonal and sociocultural context within which it is embedded. Second, the social milieu and its associated norms and values contribute to definitions of normality and abnormality. Third, clinical conceptualization, diagnosis, and assessment involve the therapist's attributional and attitudinal processes and those person perception operations that contribute to impression formation and maintenance. Fourth, psychotherapeutic interventions with individuals, couples, families, or groups are conceptualized as quintessentially social relationships that have as major objectives the enhancement of both individual identity and healthy interpersonal relatedness, inextricably interwoven processes.[103] As such, a social psychological perspective has important implications for clinical work in general, and psychiatry in particular, because it underscores the value of attending to the patient's social environment in addition to his or her neurobiological, internal psychological, and behavioral functioning.

References

1. Engel GL: The clinical application of the biopsychosocial model. Am J Psychiatry 1980; 137:535–544.
2. Lindzey G, Aronson E (eds): The Handbook of Social Psychology, Volume I, Theory and Method, 3rd ed. New York: Random House, 1985.
3. Lindzey G, Aronson E (eds): The Handbook of Social Psychology, Volume II, Special Fields and Applications, 3rd ed. New York: Random House, 1985.
4. Synder CR, Forsyth DR: Handbook of Social and Clinical Psychology: The Health Perspective. New York: Pergamon Press, 1991.
5. Deaux K: Focusing on the self: Challenges to self-definition and their consequences for mental health. In Ruble DN, Costanzo PR, Oliveri ME (eds): The Social Psychology of Mental Health: Basic Mechanisms and Applications. New York: Guilford Press, 1992:301–327.
6. Higgins ET: Personality, social psychology, and person-situation relations: Standards and knowledge activation as a common language. In Pervin LA (ed): Handbook of Personality: Theory and Research. New York: Guilford Press, 1990:301–338.
7. Magnusson D: Personality development from an interactional perspective. In Pervin LA (ed): Handbook of Personality: Theory and Research. New York: Guilford Press, 1990:193–222.
8. Baumeister RF: Neglected aspects of self theory: Motivation, interpersonal aspects, culture, escape, and existential value. Psychol Inq 1992; 3:21–25.
9. Markus H, Cross S: The interpersonal self. In Pervin LA (ed): Handbook of Personality: Theory and Research. New York: Guilford Press, 1990:576–608.
10. James W: The Principles of Psychology. Cambridge, MA: Harvard University Press, 1981. Originally published in 1890.
11. Cooley CF: Human Nature and the Social Order. New York: Charles Scribner, 1902.
12. Mead GH: Mind, Self, and Society. Chicago: University of Chicago Press, 1934.
13. Sullivan HS: The Interpersonal Theory of Psychiatry. New York: WW Norton, 1953.
14. Fairbairn WRD: Psychoanalytic Studies of Personality. London: Tavistock, 1954.
15. Guntrip H: Schizoid Phenomena, Object Relations and the Self. New York: International Universities Press, 1969.
16. Kohut H: The Restoration of the Self. New York: International Universities Press, 1977.
17. Winnicott DW: The Maturational Processes and the Facilitating Environment: Studies in the Theory of Emotional Development. New York: International Universities Press, 1965.
18. Markus H: Self-schemata and processing information about the self. J Pers Soc Psychol 1977; 35:63–78.
19. Bandura A: Social Foundations of Thought and Action. New York: Prentice Hall, 1986.
20. Higgins ET: Self-discrepancy: A theory relating self and affect. Psychol Rev 1987; 94:319–340.
21. Horowitz MJ: Introduction to Psychodynamics: A New Synthesis. New York: Basic Books, 1988.
22. Horowitz MJ (ed): Person Schemas and Maladaptive Interpersonal Patterns. Chicago: University of Chicago Press, 1991.
23. Swann WB Jr: Self-verification: Bringing social reality into harmony with self. In Suls J, Greenwald AG (eds): Psychological Perspectives on the Self, Volume II. Hillsdale, NJ: Lawrence Erlbaum, 1983:33–66.
24. Tesser A: Social versus clinical approaches to self psychology: The self-evaluation maintenance model and Kohutian object relations theory. In Curtis RC (ed): The Relational Self: Theoretical Convergences in Psychoanalysis and Social Psychology. New York: Guilford Press, 1991:257–281.
25. Westen D: The cognitive self and the psychoanalytic self: Can we put our selves together? Psychol Inq 1992; 3:1–13.
26. McNulty SE, Swann WB Jr: Psychotherapy, self-concept change, and self verification. In Curtis RC (ed): The Relational Self: Theoretical Convergences in Psychoanalysis and Social Psychology. New York: Guilford Press, 1991:213–237.
27. Markus H, Nurius P: Possible selves. Am Psychol 1986; 41:954–969.
28. Goffman E: The Presentation of Self and Everyday Life. Garden City, NY: Doubleday Anchor, 1959.
29. Gallup GG: Self-recognition in primates: A comparative approach to the bidirectional properties of consciousness. Am Psychol 1977; 32:329–338.
30. Beebe B, Lachman FM: The contribution of mother-infant mutual influence in the origins of self- and object-representations. Psychoanal Psychol 1988; 5:305–337.
31. Stern DN: The Interpersonal World of the Infant: A View from Psychoanalysis and Developmental Psychology. New York: Basic Books, 1985.
32. Strauman TJ, Higgins ET: The self construct in social cognition: Past, present, and future. In Segal ZV, Blatt SJ (eds): The Self in Emotional Distress: Cognitive and Psychodynamic Perspectives. New York: Guilford Press, 1993:3–40.
33. Luborsky L, Crits-Christoph P: Understanding Transference: The CCRT Method. New York: Basic Books, 1990.
34. Benjamin LS: Interpersonal Diagnosis and Treatment of Personality Disorders. New York: Guilford Press, 1993.
35. Bowlby J: Attachment and Loss, Volume I, Attachment, 2nd ed. New York: Basic Books, 1982.
36. Greenberg JR, Michell SA: Object Relations in Psychoanalytic Theory. Cambridge, MA: Harvard University Press, 1993.
37. Gilligan C: In a Different Voice. Cambridge, MA: Harvard University Press, 1982.
38. Jordan JV, Kaplan AG, Miller JB, et al (eds): Women's Growth in Connection. New York: Guilford Press, 1991.
39. Gurman AS, Kniskern DP (eds): Handbook of Family Therapy, Volume I. New York: Brunner/Mazel, 1981.
40. Gurman AS, Kniskern DP (eds): Handbook of Family Therapy, Volume II. New York: Brunner/Mazel, 1991.
41. Schneider DJ, Hastorf AH, Ellsworth PC: Person Perception, 2nd ed. Reading, MA: Addison-Wesley Publishing, 1979.
42. Sears DO: The person-positivity bias. J Pers Soc Psychol 1983; 44:233–250.
43. Shelton S: The doctor-patient relationship. In Stoudemire A (ed): Human Behavior: An Introduction for Medical Students, 2nd ed. Philadelphia: JB Lippincott, 1994:3–21.
44. Beck AT, Rush J, Shaw B, Emery G: Cognitive Therapy of Depression. New York: Guilford Press, 1979.
45. Beck AT, Emery G, Greenburg RL: Anxiety Disorders and Phobias: A Cognitive Perspective. New York: Basic Books, 1985.
46. Beck AT, Freeman A (eds): Cognitive Therapy of Personality Disorders. New York: Guilford Press, 1990.
47. Tabachnik N, Crocker J, Alloy LB: Depression, social comparison, and the false-consensus effect. J Pers Soc Psychol 1983; 45:688–699.
48. Gara MA, Woolfolk RL, Cohen BD, et al: Perception of self and other in major depression. J Abnorm Psychol 1993; 102:93–100.
49. Gotlib IH, Herman CL: Psychological Aspects of Depression: Toward a Cognitive-Interpersonal Integration. Chichester, UK: John Wiley & Sons, 1992.
50. Safran JD, Segal ZV: Interpersonal Process in Cognitive Therapy. New York: Basic Books, 1990.
51. Weiner B: Attribution in personality psychology. In Pervin LA (ed): Handbook of Personality: Theory and Research. New York: Guilford Press, 1990:465–485.
52. Heider F: The Psychology of Interpersonal Relations. New York: John Wiley & Sons, 1958/1980.

53. Kelley HH: Attribution theory in social psychology. In Levine D (ed): Nebraska Symposium on Motivation, Volume XV. Lincoln, NE: University of Nebraska Press, 1967:192–238.
54. Ross L: The intuitive psychologist and his shortcomings: Distortions in the attribution process. Adv Exp Soc Psychol 1977; 10:173–220.
55. Jones EE, Nisbett RE: The actor and the observer: Divergent perceptions of the cases of behavior. In Jones EE, Kanouse DE, Kelley HH, et al (eds): Attribution: Perceiving the Cause of Behavior. Morristown, NJ: General Learning Press, 1971:79–94.
56. Monson TC, Snyder M: Actors, observers, and the attribution process: Toward a reconceptualization. J Exp Soc Psychol 1977; 13:89–111.
57. Bradley GW: Self-serving biases in the attribution process: A reexamination of the fact or fiction question. J Pers Soc Psychol 1978; 13:420–432.
58. Weiner B: An Attributional Theory of Motivation and Emotion. New York: Springer-Verlag, 1986.
59. Abramson LY, Seligman MEP, Teasdale JT: Learned helplessness in humans: Critique and reformulation. J Abnorm Psychol 1978; 87:49–74.
60. Abramson LY, Metalsky GI, Alloy LB: Hopelessness depression: A theory-based subtype of depression. Psychol Rev 1989; 96:358–372.
61. Burns MO, Seligman MEP: Explanatory style, helplessness, and depression. In Synder CR, Forsyth DR (eds): Handbook of Social and Clinical Psychology: The Health Perspective. New York: Pergamon Press, 1991:267–284.
62. Firth-Cozens J, Brewin CR: Attributional change during psychotherapy. Br J Clin Psychol 1988; 27:47–54.
63. Seligman MEP: Learned Optimism. New York: Alfred Knopf, 1990.
64. Lin EH, Peterson C: Pessimistic explanatory style and response to illness. Behav Res Ther 1990; 28:243–248.
65. Peterson C: Explanatory style as a risk factor for illness. Cognitive Ther Res 1988; 12:119–132.
66. Peterson C, Seligman MEP, Vaillant GE: Pessimistic explanatory style as a risk factor for physical illness. A thirty-five year longitudinal study. J Pers Soc Psychol 1988; 55:23–27.
67. Taylor SE: Positive Illusions: Creative Self-Deception and the Healthy Mind. New York: Basic Books, 1989.
68. Rodin J, Salovey P: Health psychology. Annu Rev Psychol 1989; 10:533–579.
69. Forsterling F: Attributional retraining: A review. Psychol Bull 1985; 98:495–512.
70. Weiner B: An Attributional Theory of Motivation and Emotion. New York: Springer-Verlag, 1986.
71. Forsterling F: Attributional conceptions in clinical psychology. Am Psychol 1986; 41:275–285.
72. Murdock NL, Altmaier EM: Attribution-based treatments. In Synder CR, Forsyth DR (eds): Handbook of Social and Clinical Psychology: The Health Perspective. New York: Pergamon Press, 1991:563–578.
73. Bradbury RN, Fincham FD: Attributions in marriage: Review and critique. Psychol Bull 1990; 107:3–33.
74. Cooper J, Aronson JM: Attitudes and consistency theories: Implications for mental health. In Ruble DN, Costanzo PR, Oliveri ME (eds): The Social Psychology of Mental Health: Basic Mechanisms and Applications. New York: Guilford Press, 1992:279–300.
75. Staats AW: An outline of an integrated learning theory of attitude formation and function. In Fishbein M (ed): Readings in Attitude Theory and Measurement. New York: John Wiley & Sons, 1967:373–376.
76. Hovland C, Janis I, Kelley HH: Communication and Persuasion. New Haven, CT: Yale University Press, 1953.
77. Sherif CW, Sherif M, Nebergall RE: Attitude and Attitude Change: The Social Judgement Approach. Philadelphia: WB Saunders, 1965.
78. Osgood CE, Tannenbaum PH: The principle of congruity in the prediction of attitude change. Psychol Rev 1955; 62:42–55.
79. Festinger LA: A Theory of Cognitive Dissonance. Stanford, CA: Stanford University Press, 1957.
80. Bem DJ: Self-perception theory. Adv Exp Soc Psychol 1972; 6:1–62.
81. Fazio RH, Zanna MP, Cooper J: Dissonance and self-perception: Integrative view of each theory's proper domain of application. J Exp Soc Psychol 1977; 13:464–479.
82. Katz D: The functional approach to the study of attitudes. Public Opin Q 1960; 24:163–204.
83. Kelman HC: Processes of opinion change. Public Opin Q 1961; 25:57–78.
84. Smith MB, Bruner JS, White RW: Opinions and Personality. New York: John Wiley, 1956.
85. Ajzen I, Fishbein M: Attitude-behavior relations: A theoretical analysis and review of empirical research. Psychol Bull 1977; 184:888–918.
86. Kelley S Jr, Mirer TW: The simple act of voting. Am Political Sci Rev 1974; 68:572–591.
87. Schwartz SH: Temporal instability as a moderator of the attitude-behavior relationship. J Pers Soc Psychol 1978; 36:714–715.
88. Bordiga E, Campbell B: Belief relevance and attitude-behavior consistency: The moderating role of personal experience. J Pers Soc Psychol 1982; 42:239–247.
89. Snyder M, Kendzierski D: Acting on one's attitudes. Procedures for linking attitude and behavior. J Exp Soc Psychol 1982; 18:165–183.
90. Andrews KH, Kandel DB: Attitude and behavior. Am Sociol Rev 1979; 44:298–310.
91. Ajzen I, Fishbein M: Understanding Attitudes and Predicting Social Behavior. Englewood Cliffs, NJ: Prentice Hall, 1980.
92. Cooper J, Croyle RT: Attitudes and attitude change. Annu Rev Psychol 1984; 35:395–426.
93. McGuire WJ: Attitudes and attitude change. In Lindzey G, Aronson E (eds): The Handbook of Social Psychology, Volume II, 3rd ed. New York: Random House, 1985:233–346.
94. Chaiken S, Stangor C: Attitudes and attitude change. Annu Rev Psychol 1987; 38:575–630.
95. Petty RE, Cacioppo JT: The elaboration likelihood model of persuasion. Adv Exp Soc Psychol 1986; 19:123–205.
96. Chaiken S, Liberman A, Eagly AH: Heuristic and systematic information processing within and beyond the persuasion context. In Uleman JS, Bargh JA (eds): Unintended Thought. New York: Guilford Press, 1989:212–252.
97. Rosenstock IM; Strecher VJ, Becker MH: Social learning theory and the health belief model. Health Educ Q 1988; 15:175–183.
98. Cacioppo JT, Claiborn CD, Petty RE, Heesacker M: General framework for the study of attitude change in psychotherapy. In Synder CR, Forsyth DR (eds): Handbook of Social and Clinical Psychology: The Health Perspective. New York: Pergamon Press, 1991:523–539.
99. Beck AT: Cognitive Therapy and the Emotional Disorders. New York: International Universities Press, 1976.
100. Heppner PP, Hillerbrand ET: Problem solving training: Implications for remedial and preventive training. In Synder CR, Forsyth DR (eds): Handbook of Social and Clinical Psychology: The Health Perspective. New York: Pergamon Press, 1991:681–698.
101. Meichenbaum D: Cognitive Behavior Modification. New York: Plenum Publishing, 1977.
102. Spivack G, Platt JJ, Shure MB: The Problem Solving Approach to Adjustment. San Francisco: Jossey-Bass, 1976.
103. Guisinger S, Blatt SJ: Individuality and relatedness: Evolution of a fundamental dialectic. Am Psychol 1994; 49:104–111.
104. Alcock J: Animal Behavior: An Evolutionary Approach, 5th ed. Sunderland, MA: Sinauer Associates, 1993.
105. Ridley M, Dawkins R: The natural selection of altruism. In Rushton JP, Sorrentino RM (eds): Altruism and Helping Behavior: Social, Personality, and Developmental Perspectives. Hillsdale, NJ: Lawrence Erlbaum, 1981:19–39.
106. Simon HA: A mechanism for social selection and successful altruism. Science 1990; 250:1665–1668.
107. Trivers RL: The evolution of reciprocal altruism. Q Rev Biol 1971; 46:35–57.
108. Gould SJ: Ontogeny and phylogeny revisited and reunited. Bioessays 1992; 14:275–279.
109. Batson CD: Prosocial motivation: Is it ever truly altruistic? Adv Exp Soc Psychol 1987; 20:65–122.
110. Latane B, Darley JM: The Unresponsive Bystander: Why Doesn't He Help? New York: Appleton-Century-Crofts, 1970.
111. Hinde RA: Individuals, Relationships, and Culture: Links Between Ethology and the Social Sciences. New York: Cambridge University Press, 1987.
112. Buss DM: Evolutionary social psychology: Prospects and pitfalls. Motivation Emotion 1990; 14:265–286.
113. Sakaluk SK: Is courtship feeding by male insects parental investment? Ethology 1986; 73:161–166.
114. Thornhill R: Sexual selection and nuptial feeding behavior in *Bittacus apicalis* (Insecta: Mecorptera). Am Naturalist 1976; 110:529–548.

115. Lorenz KZ: Studies on Animal and Human Behavior. Cambridge, MA: Harvard University Press, 1970.
116. Suomi SJ: Primate separation models of affective disorders. In Madden J (ed): Neurobiology of Learning, Emotion, and Affect. New York: Raven Press, 1991:195–214.
117. Harlow H: The nature of love. Am Psychol 1958; 13:673–685.
118. Suomi SJ, Harlow HF: Social rehabilitation of isolate-reared monkeys. Dev Psychol 1972; 16:487–496.
119. Skeels H: Adult status of children with contrasting early life experiences. Monogr Soc Res Child Dev 1966; 31.
120. Berscheid E: Interpersonal attraction. In Lindzey G, Aronson E (eds): The Handbook of Social Psychology, Volume II, 3rd ed. New York: Random House, 1985:413–484.
121. Derlega VJ, Hendrick SS, Windstead BA, Berg JH: Psychotherapy as a Personal Relationship. New York: Guilford Press, 1991.
122. Newcomb TM: The Acquaintance Process. New York: Holt, Rinehart & Winston, 1961.
123. Byrne D: The Attraction Paradigm. New York: Academic Press, 1971.
124. Lott AJ, Lott BE: The role of reward in the formation of positive interpersonal attitudes. In Huston TL (ed): Foundations of Interpersonal Attraction. New York: Academic Press, 1974:171–192.
125. Thibaut JW, Kelley HH: The Social Psychology of Groups. New York: John Wiley, 1959.
126. Levinger G, Snoek DJ: Attraction in Relationship: A New Look at Interpersonal Attraction. Morristown, NJ: General Learning Press, 1972.
127. Berscheid E: Emotion. In Kelley HH, Berscheid E, Christensen A, et al (eds): Close Relationships. New York: WH Freeman, 1983:110–168.
128. Clark MS, Mills J: Interpersonal attraction in exchange and communal relationships. J Pers Soc Psychol 1979; 37:12–24.
129. Sternberg R, Barnes ML: The Psychology of Love. New Haven: Yale University Press, 1989.
130. Rubin A: Liking and Loving: An Invitation to Social Psychology. New York: Holt, Rinehart & Winston, 1973.
131. Berscheid E, Walster EH: Interpersonal Attraction, 2nd ed. Reading, MA: Addison-Wesley Publishing, 1978.
132. Bowlby J: Attachment and Loss, Volume II, Separation: Anxiety and Anger. New York: Basic Books, 1973.
133. Bowlby J: Attachment and Loss, Volume III, Loss: Sadness and Depression. New York: Basic Books, 1980.
134. Ainsworth MDS, Blehar MC, Waters E, Wall S: Patterns of Attachment: A Psychological Study of the Strange Situation. Hillsdale, NJ: Lawrence Erlbaum, 1978.
135. Main M, Solomon J: Procedures for identifying infants as disorganized/disoriented during the Ainsworth Strange Situation. In Greenberg M, Cicchetti D, Cummings EM (eds): Attachment in the Preschool Years. Chicago: University of Chicago Press, 1990:121–160.
136. Crittenden PM: Relationships at risk. In Belsky J, Nezworski T (eds): Clinical Implications of Attachment. Hillsdale, NJ: Lawrence Erlbaum, 1988.
137. Bowlby J: A Secure Base. New York: Basic Books, 1988.
138. Main M, Kaplan N, Cassidy J: Security in infancy, childhood, and adulthood: A move to the level of representation. Monogr Soc Res Child Dev 1985; 50:66–104.
139. Sroufe LA, Egeland B, Kreutzer T: The fate of early experience following developmental change: Longitudinal approaches to individual adaptation in childhood. Child Dev 1990; 61:1363–1373.
140. Sperling MB, Berman WH (eds): Attachment in Adults: Clinical and Developmental Perspectives. New York: Guilford Press, 1994.
141. West ML, Sheldon-Keller AE: Patterns of Relating: An Adult Attachment Perspective. New York: Guilford Press, 1994.
142. Hazan C, Shaver PR: Romantic love conceptualized as an attachment process. J Pers Soc Psychol 1987; 52:511–524.
143. Shaver PR, Hazan C: Adult romantic attachment: Theory and evidence. Adv Pers Rel 1993; 4:29–70.
144. Weiss RS: Attachment in adult life. In Parkes CM, Stevenson-Hinde J (eds): The Place of Attachment in Human Behavior. New York: Basic Books, 1982:171–184.
145. Bartholomew K, Horowitz L: Attachment styles among young adults: A test of a four category model. J Pers Soc Psychol 1991; 61:226–244.
146. Mason MJ: Family therapy as the emerging context for sex therapy. In Gurman AS, Kniskern DP (eds): Handbook of Family Therapy, Volume II. New York: Brunner/Mazel, 1991:479–507.
147. Kinsey AC, Pomeroy WB, Martin CE: Sexual Behavior in the Human Male. Philadelphia: WB Saunders, 1948.
148. Kinsey AC, Pomeroy WB, Martin CE, Gebhard PH: Sexual Behavior in the Human Female. Philadelphia: WB Saunders, 1953.
149. Janus SS, Janus CL: The Janus report on Sexual Behavior. New York: John Wiley & Sons, 1994.
150. Kaplan HS: The New Sex Therapy: Active Treatment of Sexual Dysfunction. New York: Brunner/Mazel, 1974.
151. Masters WH, Johnson VE: Human Sexual Inadequacy. Boston: Little, Brown, 1970.
152. Heiman JR, LoPiccolo L, LoPiccolo J: The treatment of sexual dysfunction. In Gurman AS, Kniskern DP (eds): Handbook of Family Therapy. New York: Brunner/Mazel, 1981:592–630.
153. Masters W, Johnson V, Kolodny R: On Sex and Human Loving. Boston: Little, Brown, 1983.
154. Clark MS, Bennett ME: Research of relationships: Implications for mental health. In Ruble DN, Costanzo PR, Oliveri ME (eds): The Social Psychology of Mental Health: Basic Mechanisms and Applications. New York: Guilford Press, 1992:166–198.
155. Lee JA: The Colors of Love. New York: Bantam, 1973.
156. Hazan C, Shaver PR: Attachment as an organizational framework for research on close relationships. Psychol Inq 1994; 5:1–22.
157. Doane JA, Diamond D: Affect and Attachment in the Family: A Family-Based Treatment of Major Psychiatric Disorder. New York: Basic Books, 1994.
158. Lorenz K: On Aggression. New York: Harcourt Brace & World, 1966.
159. Krebs DL, Miller DT: Altruism and aggression. In Lindzey G, Aronson E (eds): Handbook of Social Psychology, Volume II, 3rd ed. New York: Random House, 1985:1–71.
160. Freud S: Civilization and its discontents. In Strachey J (trans-ed): The Standard Edition of the Complete Psychological Works of Sigmund Freud, Volume 21. London: Hogarth Press, 1961:59–145. Originally published in 1930.
161. Lemerise EA, Dodge KE: The development of anger and hostile interactions. In Lewis M, Haviland JM (eds): Handbook of Emotions. New York: Guilford Press, 1993:537–546.
162. Dollard J, Doob LW, Miller ME, et al: Frustration and Aggression. New Haven, CT: Yale University Press, 1939.
163. Bandura A: Aggression: A Social Learning Analysis. Englewood Cliffs, NJ: Prentice Hall, 1973.
164. Levine JM, Moreland RL: Small groups and mental health. In Ruble DH, Costanzo PR, Oliveri ME (eds): The Social Psychology of Mental Health: Basic Mechanisms and Applications. New York: Guilford Press, 1992:126–165.
165. Paulus PB (ed): Psychology of Group Influence, 2nd ed. Hillsdale, NJ: Lawrence Erlbaum, 1989.
166. Green RG: Alternative conceptions of social facilitation. In Paulus PB (ed): Psychology of Group Influence, 2nd ed. Hillsdale, NJ: Lawrence Erlbaum, 1989:15–51.
167. Harkins SG, Szymanski K: Social loafing and group evaluation. J Pers Soc Psychol 1989; 56:934–941.
168. Tajfel H, Turner JC: The social identity theory of intergroup behavior. In Worchel S, Austin WG (eds): Psychology of Intergroup Relations, 2nd ed. Chicago: Nelson-Hall, 1986:7–24.
169. Prentice-Dunn S, Rogers RW: Deindividuation and the self-regulation of behavior. In Paulus PB (ed): Psychology of Group Influence, 2nd ed. Hillsdale, NJ: Lawrence Erlbaum, 1989:87–109.
170. Asch S: Opinions and social pressure. Sci Am 1955; 193:31–35.
171. Campbell JD, Fairey PJ: Informational and normative roots to conformity: The effect of faction size as a function of norm extremity and attention to the stimulus. J Pers Soc Psychol 1989; 57:457–468.
172. Moscovici S: Social influence and conformity. In Lindzey G, Aronson E (eds): The Handbook of Social Psychology, Volume II, 3rd ed. New York: Random House, 1985:347–412.
173. Isenberg DJ: Group polarization: A critical review and meta-analysis. J Pers Soc Psychol 1986; 50:1141–1151.
174. Janis IL: Groupthink: Psychological Studies of Policy Decisions and Fiascos, 2nd ed. Boston: Houghton Mifflin, 1982.
175. Kaslow NJ, Celano MP: Family therapy. In Gurman AS, Messer SB (eds): Modern Psychotherapies: Theory and Practice. New York: Guilford Press, in press.
176. McGrath JE: Groups: Interaction and Performance. Englewood Cliffs, NJ: Prentice Hall, 1984.
177. von Bertalanffy L: General Systems Theory: Foundations, Development, and Applications. New York: George Braziller, 1968.
178. McDaniel SH, Hepworth J, Doherty WJ: Medical Family Therapy: A

Biopsychosocial Approach to Families with Health Problems. New York: Basic Books, 1992.

179. Lewin K: Field Theory in Social Science. New York: Harper & Brothers, 1951.
180. Rogers C: Carl Rogers on Encounter Groups. New York: Harper & Row, 1970.
181. Forsyth DR: Change in therapeutic groups. In Snyder CR, Forsyth DR (eds): Handbook of Social and Clinical Psychology: The Health Perspective. New York: Pergamon Press, 1991:664–680.
182. Klein RH, Bernard HS, Singer DL (eds): Handbook of Contemporary Group Psychotherapy: Contributions from Object Relations, Self Psychology, and Social Systems Theories. Madison, CT: International Universities Press, 1992.
183. Yalom ID: The Theory and Practice of Group Psychotherapy, 3rd ed. New York: Basic Books, 1985.
184. Gaw AC (ed): Culture, Ethnicity, and Mental Illness. Washington, DC: American Psychiatric Press, 1992.
185. Kim U, Berry JW (eds): Indigenous Psychologies: Research and Experience in Cultural Context. Newbury Park, CA: Sage, 1993.
186. Kleinman A: Rethinking Psychiatry: From Cultural Category to Personal Experience. New York: Free Press, 1988.
187. Marsella AJ, Tharp RG, Ciborowski TJ (eds): Perspectives on Cross-Cultural Psychology. New York: Academic Press, 1979.
188. Price-Williams DR: Cultural psychology. In Lindzey G, Aronson E (eds): The Handbook of Social Psychology, Volume II, 3rd ed. New York: Random House, 1985:993–1042.
189. Triandis HC, Brislin RW: Cross-cultural psychology. Am Psychol 1984; 39:1006–1016.
190. Markus H, Kitayama S: Culture and the self: Implications for cognition, emotion, and motivation. Psychol Rev 1991; 98:224–253.
191. Triandis H: The self and social behavior in differing cultural contexts. Psychol Rev 1989; 96:506–520.
192. Matsumoto D: People: Psychology from a Cultural Perspective. Pacific Grove, CA: Brooks/Cole, 1994.
193. Duda JL, Allison MT: The attributional theory of achievement motivation: Cross-cultural considerations. Int J Intercultural Rel 1989; 13:37–55.
194. Davidson AR: Culture and attitude structure and change. In Marsella AJ, Tharp RG, Ciborowski TJ (eds): Perspectives on Cross-Cultural Psychology. New York: Academic Press, 1979:137–157.
195. Simmons CH, vonKolke A, Shimizu H: Attitudes toward romantic love among American, German and Japanese students. J Soc Psychol 1986; 126:327–336.
196. Foulks EF: Transcultural psychiatry and normal behavior. In Offer D, Sabshin M (eds): The Diversity of Normal Behavior: Further Contributions to Normatology. New York: Basic Books, 1991:207–238.
197. Lewis-Fernandez R, Kleinman A: Culture, personality, and psychopathology. J Abnorm Psychol 1994; 103:67–71.
198. World Health Organization: Schizophrenia: An International Follow-up Study. New York: John Wiley & Sons, 1979.
199. Simons RC, Hugnes CC: Culture-bound syndromes. In Gaw AC (ed): Culture, Ethnicity, and Mental Illness. Washington, DC: American Psychiatric Press, 1993:75–99.
200. Canino IA, Spurlock J: Culturally Diverse Children and Adolescents: Assessment, Diagnosis, and Treatment. New York: Guilford Press, 1994.
201. Vargas LA, Koss-Chioino JD (eds): Working with Culture: Psychotherapeutic Interventions with Ethnic Minority Children and Adolescents. San Francisco: Jossey-Bass, 1992.
202. McGoldrick M, Pearce JK, Giordano J (eds): Ethnicity and Family Therapy. New York: Guilford Press, 1982.
203. Cacioppo JT, Berntson GG: Social psychological contributions to the Decade of the Brain: Doctrine of multilevel analysis. Am Psychol 1992; 47:1019–1028.
204. Leary MR, Maddux JE: Progress toward a viable interface between social and clinical-counseling psychology. Am Psychol 1987; 42:904–911.

CHAPTER

19 Psychoanalytic Theories

Lawrence B. Inderbitzin
Steven T. Levy

Historical Developments and Basic Concepts

Robert A. Paul

Origins

Psychoanalysis is a clinical therapy originally developed by Sigmund Freud (1856 to 1939) for the treatment of the neuroses. By extension, the term refers as well to a theory of psychopathology underlying the therapeutic practice; a general theory of the mind, based on the understanding arising from the clinical procedure; and a mode of research into mental life that is inherent in and inextricably intertwined with the clinical therapeutic process.

Although the contemporary practice of psychoanalysis derives historically from Freud's original work, it has evolved greatly (like any other discipline). The writings of Freud can no longer be regarded as constituting a definitive contemporary account of psychoanalysis. Furthermore, Freud's career as the first psychoanalyst covered a 50-year span, during which time his own thought changed, often dramatically.

Despite these caveats, the most effective way of presenting psychoanalytic ideas is to begin at the beginning and to retrace the steps by which Freud, initially working alone, originated the practices and theories that can be recognized as distinctively psychoanalytic.

Freud and 19th Century Science

Freud was trained as a neurologist at the University of Vienna at a time when many of the fundamentals of contemporary neurology were first being developed and established. From 1876 to 1882, he worked in the physiological laboratory directed by Ernst Brücke, where he made a number of technical and research contributions to the evolving science of neurology. Brücke, together with scientists such as Emil Du Bois–Reymond, Rudolph Virchow, and the towering figure of Hermann Helmholtz, represented a new school of thought, radically innovative in its day, that sought to apply strictly scientific, positivistic principles of investigation and explanation to the life sciences and to the study of human life in particular.[1] From his immersion in this milieu, Freud learned to understand biological and psychological phenomena in terms of known physicochemical laws, without any admixture of extraneous "vitalistic" ideas ascribing human mental or cultural life to nonmaterial forces. Freud was also a student during the first great impact of the darwinian revolution on European biology and always considered himself a darwinian thinker.[2, 3]

In 1882, Freud joined the department of internal medicine, presided over by Hermann Nothnagel, and shortly thereafter transferred to the department of the great brain anatomist and psychiatrist Theodor Meynert; both influenced Freud by their adherence to a deterministic, scientific psychology. The scientists of the so-called Helmholtz school were not pure mechanists, however, in their approach to the human psyche. Rather, they subscribed to a philosophical position that can be described as dual-aspect monism.[4] Although rejecting the cartesian dualism, according to which there are two different kinds of substances (one material and occupying space, the other mental and not occupying space), dual-aspect monists held that whereas there is only one substance, it can be apprehended by us in two different aspects. Studied from a strictly objective, scientific point of view, matter, including the matter that forms the neurological system, possesses only *quantitative* characteristics, such as mass, velocity, and energy, but viewed phenomenologically, as it appears to subjective conscious awareness, matter possesses *qualities* as well, such as color, smell, and taste. Freud always retained as an ideal for psychology that it should be able to account for mental life in both quantitative and qualitative terms.

In the mid-1880s, as Freud began to shift from laboratory science to the private practice of neurology, he realized that there were few effective treatments for the cases of "neuroses" turning up in his consulting room. He therefore leapt at the chance to visit Paris for a year, supported by a prestigious fellowship, to study the methods for the treatment of hysteria then being pioneered by Jean Martin Charcot of the Pathological Laboratory at the Saltpêtrière. Freud was impressed by the clinical use of hypnosis by the French; he returned to France in 1889 to improve his hypnotic technique under Bernheim, the foremost rival of Charcot. During the later 1880s, Freud attempted to remove neurotic symptoms from patients by means of hypnotic suggestion in his clinical work.[5]

By the early 1890s, Freud had begun making his own modifications in hypnotic treatment—in part, he claimed, because he was not a particularly good hypnotist. Dispensing with the induction of a state of hypnosis, he retained the arrangement whereby the patient lies supine on a couch while the psychiatrist sits out of the patient's field of vision so that their only communication is by voice.

Under the influence of his senior colleague in Vienna, the neurologist Josef Breuer, Freud came to believe that one could remove hysterical symptoms not by direct suggestion, but by getting patients to recall certain unpleasant memories that were apparently forgotten but retrievable under hypnosis.[6] As his technique developed and he dispensed with hypnotic induction, Freud instructed patients that the desired memory would come to them when he pressed his hand to the patient's forehead. Later, in response to a remark of one of his patients, he eliminated the pressure technique too, asking the patient to begin with the symptom and then simply to say whatever came to mind prompted by association to the symptom. Ultimately, he would dispense even with the starting point of the symptom, letting the patient begin at whatever conscious "surface" the patient chose at each session; this technique is known as *free association.* Given his deterministic views of the mind, Freud was confident that a chain of associations would lead from any initial conscious idea to the pathogenic idea that had been excluded from consciousness but whose existence could be established either by direct observation under hypnosis or by deduction from the phenomenology of the symptoms.

Also in the early 1890s, Freud became convinced that neurotic disorders were invariably the result of disturbances in sexual life or of a struggle against memories or ideas of an erotic nature. Exactly what gave him this firm conviction is not clear, although he claimed that he was establishing as explicit theory only what had long been unofficial, off-the-record clinical wisdom among the best practitioners.[7] During this period in his career, Freud postulated that a class of neurological disorders called actual neuroses, to be distinguished from psychoneuroses, were caused by a toxic accumulation of some as yet unknown material correlate of sexual energy, to which he gave the name libido. The actual neuroses, according to this view, included the anxiety neuroses (more common in women) and neurasthenia (more common in men), whose symptoms included hypochondria and general lassitude.[8] These were actual neuroses in the sense that they were real organic affectations of the nervous symptoms rather than the effect of more "psychological," "qualitative" factors, such as troublesome memories (although of course, being a dual-aspect monist, he assumed that memories too had a material, quantitative existence in the neurological system).

In a number of works written in the years 1894 and 1895, Freud conceptualized the first unified formulation of a clinical technique, a theory of psychopathology, and a more general theory of the mind, each of which depends on and implies the others.[8, 9] We may begin our exposition with the clinical technique.

Hysteria as a Model: Clinical Treatment

Freud knew that in Breuer's treatment of the famous patient Anna O. from 1880 to 1882, the somatic symptoms of hysteria disappeared when, in a state of hypnosis and working backward from the most recent appearance of a symptom, the patient could remember each previous occasion on which it had occurred until she finally recalled the original moment of its inception; when, still in hypnosis, she relived the scene in which the symptom first appeared, verbalizing it to the psychiatrist and experiencing the emotions appropriate to the original scene, the symptom disappeared permanently. Anna O. referred to the procedure as "chimney sweeping" or "the talking cure"; Breuer called it the cathartic method, positing a process of "abreaction" whereby the long stifled affects of the original scene, trapped in a split-off state of consciousness because the patient was in a "hypnoid state" at the time they were acquired, were finally discharged in the act of expressing the memory aloud. Hysterical patients were thus said to be "suffering from reminiscences."[6(p7)]

In adapting Breuer's technique, Freud went beyond dispensing with hypnosis. He proposed that the reason the memory of the original scene at which a symptom had been acquired could not be recalled voluntarily, and was thus preserved with its initial quota of affect undischarged, was not simply that the patient was in a hypnoid state. It was that this split-off state had been induced *intentionally* by the patient with the express purpose of warding off the pain or "unpleasure" associated with the memory. The patient's ego—the great mass of interconnected ideas forming the patient's conscious personality—had deliberately excluded the pathogenic memory from consciousness to defend itself from an affect that would otherwise have proved too painful to feel, either because of disgust, shame, or moral repugnance at the idea on the part of the patient's ego or because the intensity of the emotions accompanying the experience was too great to be borne.

In treatment, the patient had to be induced to overcome the defensive motivation for keeping the "incompatible idea" out of awareness and in an "unconscious" state with the assistance of the psychiatrist. By interpreting the patient's symptoms and utterances in such a way as to reconstruct the original pathogenic idea, the analyst could weaken the patient's "resistance" to remembering the repressed memory. In hysterics, because of a constitutional capacity for turning warded off affects, by a process called *conversion,* into a somatic symptom, neurotic symptoms bore a real or symbolic connection with or resemblance to the warded off idea.

Knowing this, the psychiatrist could decipher the symptom and arrive at the unconscious idea and tell it to the patient. For example, in the case of "a girl, who blamed herself because, while she was nursing her sick father, she had thought about a young man who had made a slight impression on her,"[6(pp135–181), 8(p48)] the somatic hysterical symptoms were a condition of awkward gait, abasia, and pains in the leg. This symptom complex was "overdetermined": it had many different sources converging at a single somatic location, the thigh, chosen because there had already been some real organic disturbance there, in this case neuralgic pain. The patient had been in the habit of resting her father's foot on her *thigh* while she changed his bandages; she had taken a *walk* with the young man when her father took a turn for the worse; and, at a more symbolic level, she felt that she was *"stuck"* in her life and "could not take a *step* forward" in a metaphorical sense that took on literal reality as her symptom.

Freud's original theory of the origin and nature of psychoneurotic symptoms is thus a "trauma" theory: a moment arrives in the patient's life when a strongly felt idea rises that is so disturbing it is incompatible with the other ideas and ideals of the patient's ego. Instead of experiencing the conflict between the unwanted idea or feeling and the offended sensibility of the ego, and dealing with it in a conscious and productive way, the patient defensively avoids the conflict by undertaking a psychological maneuver that keeps the idea out of consciousness, thus rendering it unconscious. In hysteria, the defensive mechanism is repression, whereby the idea is prevented by a counterforce working against its efforts to achieve conscious recognition and eventual discharge. The affect from the repressed idea is then converted into a somatic symptom that is itself a veiled expression of the banished idea.

Freud believed that other neurotic syndromes, in particular obsessions, compulsions, and phobias, had the same traumatic pathogenesis; they differed from hysteria and from each other, however, in that in the absence of the capacity for somatic conversion, another avenue of defense and attempted substitute discharge had to be sought. In the case of obsessions, the affect from the memory of the original traumatic idea was detached from the idea and "displaced," that is, attached to another, seemingly trivial idea, which now took on the force of the original idea.[9] Phobias worked by displacing the original affect into some external object, which could then be rendered innocuous by the simple tactic of being avoided.[9] A chance encounter with the phobic object, however, would reanimate the original traumatic idea, and the patient would experience intense anxiety.

Anxiety, in Freud's view at that time, was the feeling associated with strangulated libido that had not been properly discharged through a completed act of sexual intercourse. Freud thought that the original trauma in cases of the psychoneuroses would be the arising of an erotic idea, fantasy, or wish to which the patient's ego would respond with disgust, shame, or moral indignation. Because of the defense against the discordant idea, the pleasure normally associated with a sexual experience was converted into the unpleasure of anxiety. It then became the aim of the neurotic symptom to avoid this anxiety by conversion into physical pain, by compulsive rituals and verbal formulas, or by phobic avoidances.

Freud's Early Model of the Mind

The model of the mind underlying Freud's clinical thinking and his views on pathogenesis and nosology in the early and middle 1890s can be briefly summarized as follows. The mind is to be seen as a system of interconnected neurons, each capable of receiving a certain charge or "cathexis" of electrochemical energy and of discharging it across the synapse or "contact barrier" to a neighboring neuron, thus setting up patterns of flow of energic force through the system.[10] The goal of each individual neuron and of the system as a whole is to rid itself of cathexis by means of discharge; because this would be inconsistent with continued life, the compromise goal is to bring the entire network into relative equilibrium. A rise in cathexis in a neuron or complex of neurons is something to be avoided and is described as unpleasure; pleasure is achieved by discharging the buildup of cathexis, preferably into the motor system for use in actions taken to reduce the tension.

The mind is located at the boundary between the somatic system of the organism and the external environment. Inputs of stimuli, experienced as a demand for action to reduce the unpleasure, come from the external world in the

Table 19–1	Secondary Process Thinking
	Preserves logic
	Rules of causality exist
	Consistent with outside reality
	"Waking language"

form of perception and also from sources internal to the body in response to the various somatic needs; the latter are the "drives." Thus, for example, an internal stimulus signaling hunger creates tension in the neuronal system, which must then energize the organism to seek food and thus restore equilibrium.

Two different modes of finding discharge are possible. In the more primitive one, which is present from birth, the mind, in response to a demand for action to discharge cathexis, produces a perception by recathexis of the memory of something that previously accompanied an experience of the satisfaction of the drive or need. In dreams, neurosis, psychosis, and hallucination, this perception serves the pseudofunction of allowing an avenue in discharge. (If the stimulus comes from the environment, a similar illusory discharge might be provided by a defensive operation, for example, by simply denying the presence of a threatening situation by closing the eyes.) In this mode, the mind obeys the impulse to discharge stimulation as efficiently and quickly as possible, without raising the issue of whether the measures taken are effective in responding to the stimulus. This mode of operation is called the primary process, which is governed by the pleasure principle.

The distinctive feature of the so-called secondary process (Table 19–1)—normal ordinary waking thought—is that developmentally we learn that the discharge provided by the primary process does not produce satisfaction in the form of the elimination of the stimulus. Thus, a process of "reality testing" governed by the reality principle is instituted to decide whether a perception is really something in the world capable of satisfying the need, for example, the actual breast instead of a hallucination of the breast. It does this by inhibiting the free or "unbound" flow of cathexis along avenues of previous satisfaction, instead making a trial run of tiny amounts of energy through the system, which, as "thought," allows critical examination of the results of the trial run before immediate action is taken along the line of least resistance. To make such thought possible, the neuronal system has to keep high degrees of cathexis "bound" within the system so that only minute differentials can be invested in the process of thinking without concomitant action.

Trauma Theory of Neurosis

Neurosis occurs when a trauma introduces a stimulus into the mind to which it cannot adequately respond in accordance with reality. This may be because the stimulus is an internal impulse that is too intense or is rejected by the rest of the ego; or it may be the result of an external stimulus that for some reason cannot be processed, bound, and discharged in the usual way. To prevent the unpleasure that the stimulus would otherwise cause, the mind initiates a "countercathexis" and by a constant expenditure of psychic energy prevents the emergence into conscious awareness of the unwanted idea. This may take the form of simple repression or may occur through some other defensive maneuver, for example, thinking hard about a contrasting idea instead.

Before Freud's theory of infantile sexuality, sexuality nevertheless played a special and potentially pathogenic role related to what Freud at that time thought of as its belated onset during adolescence. Memories with a sexual content from the presexual era of childhood, be they of internally generated sexual sensations, of perceptions of sexual stimuli in the environment, or of actual stimulation or "seduction" by an older person, would become traumatic only retrospectively during adolescence, when the newly enhanced flow of energy in the form of libidinous cathexis encounters a network of neurons previously unprepared for the high intensities flowing through it. A child who has spontaneously masturbated, who has witnessed a sexual scene between adults, or who has been seduced or molested by an adult remembers the scene, but the memory does not become traumatic and thus pathogenic until a later scene, occurring after pubescence, causes recathexis of the earlier one and now poses an unmanageable threat to the psychic system. The mind can then respond only by a defensive, unrealistic, primary process move, such as repression ("I just won't think about that.").

By 1896, Freud had become convinced, and publicly stated, that all psychoneuroses—hysteria, obsessional neurosis, and phobias—as well as paranoid delusions were caused by premature sexual experiences undergone in childhood and reexperienced traumatically after the increase of sexual feelings in adolescence. This is the so-called seduction hypothesis, because the most usual source for such premature sexual stimulation of children is abuse by elders, whether parents, other relatives, teachers and caretakers, or others.[11, 12]

By the next year, Freud had modified his views on seduction as the *invariable* cause of hysteria and other neuroses, realizing that what he had taken to be literal memories from childhood had usually themselves undergone tendentious distortion, indicating the influence of a conflict between impulse and defense.[13] He was led to postulate that adolescence is not in fact the first appearance of sexual feeling, but that there is an early efflorescence of libido in children before a reactive "latency" sets in after about 6 or 7 years of age. When, therefore, one encountered memories of scenes of sexual trauma from early childhood in the course of psychoanalytic treatment by free association, one could not be certain a priori whether the memory represented a recollection of an actual historical event, a wishful or defensive fantasy elaborated by the child, or—most likely—memories of real events modified by unconscious fantasy distortions. Because repression (or another defense) would have kept the memory-fantasy from interaction with the rest of the mind, it would never have been subjected to secondary process critical examination and reality testing and so would continue to have the force of a "real" memory whether it had actually occurred or not: that is, it would operate with the force of a real trauma because it possessed "psychic reality."

During this era, the aim of psychoanalytic treatment was to let the unconscious idea become conscious so that it could lose its force as a traumatic stimulus and the cathexis associated with it could be discharged realistically instead of through the pseudodischarge of symptom formation. The traumas were always assumed to be memories of sexual experiences in childhood, whether endogenous or initiated by others, whether real or fantasies. The patient could not alone bring these memories to consciousness, precisely because they were traumatic and thus were sealed off from consciousness by defenses. During the process of free association in analysis, these defenses become manifest as resistances, that is, obstacles to continued association, such as forgetting what one is talking about or falling silent. At this point, the psychiatrist could intervene by interpreting to the patient his or her own reconstruction of what underlying traumatic memory the symptoms and free associations indicate.

During this period, too, Freud began to notice what would only later become the core idea of psychoanalytic practice, that is, the *transference*. This is a process whereby the patient in analysis "transfers" onto the psychiatrist wishes, fantasies, fears, and defenses deriving from the complex of repressed, traumatic ideas and feelings. At this time, Freud believed that the positive transference, often dominated by an erotic flavor, assisted the treatment by making the patient receptive to the psychiatrist's interventions. The negative transference, in which the psychiatrist is seen as the source or object of hostile feelings, Freud saw merely as an obstacle to treatment that must be overcome by the psychiatrist's urging. Only later would he realize that the most effective treatment comes precisely from the reliving by the patient of both positive and negative dimensions of the unconscious complexes in the clinical arena, with the psychiatrist serving *both* as intensely loved or hated object *and* as relatively neutral observer who could interpret to the patient the unconscious forces in conflict.

References

1. Bernfeld S: Freud's earliest theories and the school of Helmholtz. Psychoanal Q 1944; 13:341–362.
2. Ritvo LB: Darwin's Influence of Freud: A Tale of Two Sciences. New Haven: Yale University Press, 1990.
3. Sulloway F: Freud: Biologist of the Mind. New York: Basic Books, 1979.
4. Makari GD: In the eye of the beholder: Helmholtzian perception and the origins of Freud's 1900 theory of transference. J Am Psychoanal Assoc 1994; 42:549–580.
5. Freud S: A case of successful treatment by hypnosis. In Strachey J (trans-ed): The Standard Edition of the Complete Psychological Works of Sigmund Freud, Volume 1. London: Hogarth Press, 1966:115–128. Originally published in 1892–1893.
6. Breuer J, Freud S: Studies on hysteria. In Strachey J (trans-ed): The Standard Edition of the Complete Psychological Works of Sigmund Freud, Volume 2. London: Hogarth Press, 1955. Originally published in 1893–1895.
7. Freud S: On the history of the psycho-analytic movement. In Strachey J (trans-ed): The Standard Edition of the Complete Psychological Works of Sigmund Freud, Volume 14. London: Hogarth Press, 1957:1–66. Originally published in 1914.
8. Freud S: The neuro-psychoses of defense. In Strachey J (trans-ed): The Standard Edition of the Complete Psychological Works of Sigmund Freud, Volume 3. London: Hogarth Press, 1962:41–61. Originally published in 1894.
9. Freud S: Obsessions and phobias: Their psychical mechanisms and their aetiology. In Strachey J (trans-ed): The Standard Edition of the Complete Psychological Works of Sigmund Freud, Volume 3. London: Hogarth Press, 1962:69–82. Originally published in 1894.
10. Freud S: Project for a scientific psychology. In Strachey J (trans-ed): The Standard Edition of the Complete Psychological Works of Sigmund Freud, Volume 1. London: Hogarth Press, 1966:281–387. Originally published in 1895.
11. Freud S: The aetiology of hysteria. In Strachey J (trans-ed): The Standard Edition of the Complete Psychological Works of Sigmund Freud, Volume 3. London: Hogarth Press, 1962:187–222. Originally published in 1896.
12. Freud S: Further remarks on the neuro-psychoses of defense. In Strachey J (trans-ed): The Standard Edition of the Complete Psychological Works of Sigmund Freud, Volume 3. London: Hogarth Press, 1962:162–185. Originally published in 1896.
13. Freud S: Letter of September 21, 1987 to Wilhelm Fliess. In Strachey J (trans-ed): The Standard Edition of the Complete Psychological Works of Sigmund Freud, Volume 1. London: Hogarth Press, 1966:259–260. Originally published in 1897.

Mark E. James

Development and Major Concepts

Dreams

Freud's study of dreams, during his self-analysis and in his work with patients, resulted in his more elaborate understanding of the workings of the mind.[1, 2] The analysis of dreams continues to hold a prominent position in psychoanalytic theory. Dreams provide a wealth of information about the influence of unconscious wishes and fantasies and the role of defensive processes in the shaping of mental content. Without the benefit of contemporary electrophysiological data (which show dreaming to be generated by specific patterns of brain activity during the sleep cycle), Freud believed that dreams functioned to preserve sleep, to prevent awakening, in the presence of nocturnal stimuli, both exogenous (e.g., noise, tactile stimulation) and endogenous (e.g., hunger, the need to urinate). In particular, unconscious wishes related to the sexual and aggressive drives, and the anxieties that accompany their conscious recognition, are a significant source of endogenous stimulation that must be managed to preserve sleep. Dreams then give expression to unconscious wishes in disguised form and generally represent their fulfillment or gratification. Analysis of dreams can therefore provide conscious access to unconscious drives, wishes, fantasies, and associated repressed infantile memories, providing a "royal road to the unconscious."

The dream that is remembered on awakening is referred to as the *manifest dream.* It is the product of mental activity that has woven together a number of conscious and unconscious elements into a hallucinated experience that is recalled like a story or a play. Its component elements include sensory stimuli occurring during sleep, the day residue, and the latent dream content. The *day residue* consists of experiences of events of the preceding day or days, often associated in the mind with unconscious wishes. The *latent dream content* is the set of unconscious infantile urges, wishes, and fantasies that seek gratification during the dreaming state of blocked motor discharge and regression.

Freud hypothesized a *dream censor* whose function is to keep the unconscious latent content from conscious

Table 19–2 Primary Process Thinking
Does not follow rules of logic
Spatial and temporal relationships are not preserved
Thoughts and actions are equivalent
"Dream language"

awareness, thereby preventing the emergence of anxiety and awakening from sleep. The surreal and fantastic quality of the remembered manifest dream is a reflection of the influence of *primary process* unconscious mentation (Table 19–2; depiction of immediate gratifications, absence of the rules of logic of conscious thought, merging of past and present, absence of negatives, loss of distinction between opposites, and representation of a whole by a part) and of the activity of the *dream work,* a set of mental mechanisms designed to disguise and distort the latent content in keeping with the function of the dream censor.

The specific mechanisms of the dream work include condensation, displacement, symbolization, and projection. *Condensation* is a process by which several unconscious elements are represented by a single image or event in the dream. In *displacement,* the psychic intensity or emotional charge belonging to a latent element is attached to a more neutral or innocuous dream image, creating a shift of emotional emphasis and directing attention away from an unconsciously charged element. *Symbolization* is a mechanism by which an unconscious idea is represented in the dream by something else, usually associatively connected (e.g., a gun symbolizing a penis). Freud emphasized that there are few symbols common to everyone; symbols that are chosen by an individual are most often unique to that individual. The mechanism of *projection* results in the depiction of unconscious wishes or motives as originating in other figures in the dream, placing them outside oneself. Finally, the various images and themes of the dream are organized by the process of *secondary elaboration* into the relatively coherent story line of the manifest dream (Fig. 19–1).

In psychoanalytic treatment, the analysis of dreams attempts to take this process backward, starting with the patient's narration of the dream and then observing the patient's associations to the manifest elements, with the goal of obtaining insight into her or his unconscious wishes, infantile memories and fantasies, and processes of defense and resistance. Even with our revised neurophysiological understanding of the origin of dream activity, the process of dream analysis continues to provide a rich source of data about the associative connections between mental representations, memories, unconscious wishes and fantasies, and the construction of thought.[3, 4]

Childhood Sexuality

In his analyses of adult patients and observations of children, Freud[5] became convinced of the influence of early sexual fantasies on the formation of neurotic symptoms and of the universality of sexual wishes throughout life, including early childhood. The term *sexuality* is used in this context to refer not exclusively to adult genital sexuality but to a variety of body stimulations that are pleasurable and sensually gratifying. He postulated a developmental sequence of body zones that become primary foci of erotic sensations and mental organization (Table 19–3): oral, anal (including perianal and urethral), and genital (phallic). During development, there is a more or less orderly progression from one zone to the next, with pleasure being derived from sucking, biting, tasting, touching, looking, smelling, filling, emptying, penetrating, and being penetrated. The urge to do each of these, in relation to each specific erotogenic zone, is referred to as a *component instinct.* In adult sexuality, the component instincts come together in forepleasure and sexual intercourse. If one of the component instincts predominates exclusively in adult sexual behavior, a *perversion* results. In the neuroses, the component instincts have been repressed and become the unconscious source of symptom formation.

Each phase of psychosexual development brings with it specific types of mental organization involving where pleasurable sensations are localized, means of accomplishing gratification, persons or objects of most significance to the fulfillment of erotic strivings, and characteristic fantasies and conflicts. *Fixation* (Table 19–4) at a particular phase of development may occur if there is insufficient mastery of issues pertinent to that phase. This will result in a continued, unresolved emphasis in a person's behavior that influences later personality functioning (e.g., the anal organization of the obsessional character). *Regression* (Table 19–4), a return to a less mature level of mental organization, may occur in the context of stressors or conflict that overtaxes the adaptive

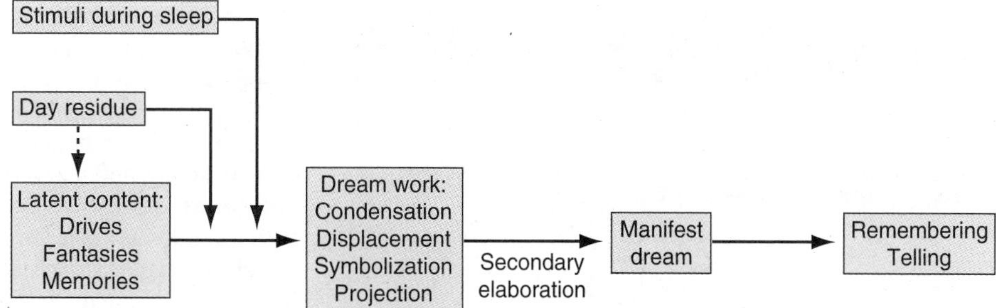

Figure 19–1 *Dream formation.*

Table 19–3 Freud's Stages of Psychosexual Development

Stage
Oral: birth to 18 mo
Anal: 18 mo to 3 y
Genital: 3 to 6 y
Latency: 6 y to puberty
Adolescence: puberty

capacities of an individual. Regression, which often serves defensive or self-protective purposes, may be determined in its degree by the level of fixation in psychosexual development.

The first of the phases described by Freud is the *oral phase* (Table 19–5), which encompasses approximately the first 18 months of life. During this phase, the mouth, lips, and tongue are the primary source of sensual gratification. The activities of sucking, swallowing, mouthing, and biting as well as the experience of being held during feeding form a cognitive template for the organization of fantasy and relatedness to others. The infant at this stage is dependent on mother for nurturance, protection, and sustenance. A favorable outcome of this stage is the establishment of a capacity to feel trust and safety in a dependent relationship, a sureness that needs will be recognized and gratified, and a minimum of conflict about aggressive wishes occurring during moments of frustration. Excessive neglect or deprivation during this period may result in adult feelings of interpersonal insecurity, mistrust, envy, depression, excessive dependency, anticipation of rejection by others, and proneness to moments of diffuse rage.[6, 7]

The *anal phase* (see Table 19–5) emerges with the development of increasing neuromuscular control of the anal and urethral sphincters and takes place from about 18 months to 3 years. Sensual pleasure becomes most highly localized in the anal and rectal mucosa. Fantasy organizes around anal pleasure and anal functions, such as withholding, expelling, and controlling. Because of the child's increased motor skills, language development, and emerging autonomy, she or he is expected to take more of an active part in self-care activities, including using the toilet. Related to toileting, power struggles may ensue around the child's soiling or withholding. Anger is felt toward those in control of this educative process, but the child also wishes to please them. The child in the anal phase experiences considerable ambivalence around expelling versus retaining (giving versus keeping), obedience and submission versus defiance and protest, and cleanliness and orderliness versus messiness. The working through of these areas of intense ambivalence can be complicated if the parents are overly controlling, critical, punitive, or rigidly intolerant of the child's expressions of aggression and willfulness. Fixation at this stage results in a personality organized around anal erotism and its associated conflicts and characterized by wishes to dominate and control people or life situations, rigidity, defiance and anger toward authority, neatness, orderliness, parsimony, frugality, and obstinacy.[8–11]

The *phallic* or *phallic-oedipal* or *genital phase* (see Table 19–5) occurs from the ages of 3 to about 5 or 6 years. At the onset of this period, sensual pleasure has become most highly focused around the genitals, and masturbatory sensations more closely resemble the usual sense of the word *sexual.* The child at this time has become even more autonomous and has more sophisticated motor and language development, conceptual capabilities, and elaborate fantasies. The child is better able to recognize feelings of love, hate, jealousy, and fear; has a more distinct recognition of the anatomical difference between the sexes; and appreciates that the parents have an intimate sexual relationship from which the child is excluded. Thinking about relatedness to others shifts from the largely dyadic quality of the prephallic phases to an appreciation of relational triangles.

Table 19–4 Responses to Developmental Stress

Response	Description
Regression	Use of behavioral and emotional solutions from a developmental phase earlier than the present conflict
Fixation	Overreliance on behavioral and emotional solutions from the phase in which the conflict occurs

Table 19–5 Characteristics of Developmental Phases

Phase	Characteristics
Oral	Urgency of needs
	Extreme dependency
	No consideration of others
	Low frustration tolerance
	Separation anxiety
Anal	Need for control and autonomy
	Orderliness, obstinacy, punctuality
	Beginning dyadic relationships
	Conflict over autonomy and compliance
	Guilt
Genital	Oedipus complex
	Emergence of genital sexuality
	Concerns about self-image
	Shift from dyadic to triadic relationships
Latency	Waning of Oedipus complex
	Decreased emphasis on sexual gratification
	Focus on same-sex relationships
	Emphasis on development of autonomous ego functions
Adolescence	Recapitulates early phases
	Separation from family
	Important bonds with peers
	Revival of sexual interest
	Identity formation

Freud recognized in his patients' associations that there were regularly occurring incestuous fantasies and wishes toward the parent of the opposite sex that were involved in the formation of neurotic difficulties. He termed this phenomenon the *Oedipus complex,* in reference to the story of Oedipus, who unknowingly killed his father and married his mother. In the midst of the Oedipus complex, the child wishes to possess exclusively the parent of the opposite sex and to eliminate the parent of the same sex. The jealousy and murderous rage felt toward the same-sex parent are accompanied by fears of retaliation and physical harm. Because these fantasies are associatively linked to pleasurable genital sensations, the child has specific unconscious fears of being castrated, which Freud referred to as the *castration complex.*

The oedipal phase proceeds differently in boys and girls. The little boy has maintained his primary attachment to his mother, but he now wants to sleep with her, see her naked, touch her, and marry her. He feels jealousy and hostility toward his father, seen as his rival. His fears of retaliatory castration, as well as wanting to maintain his loving relationship with father, lead him to renounce his wishes and to strengthen his identification with father. He seeks to become more like father and to find someone else like mother.

Freud's ideas about the girl's Oedipus complex have stirred much criticism and controversy. Freud[12, 13] believed that the little girl comes to recognize her lack of a penis with feelings of loss, narcissistic injury, anger with mother, and envy of men. She turns toward father to provide her with a penis substitute in the form of a baby. She fantasizes a rivalry with mother and fears punishment, loss of love, and genital damage. Eventually she returns to her identification with mother. Whereas the castration complex leads to the resolution of the Oedipus complex in boys, the castration complex precedes and creates the Oedipus complex in girls. A number of contemporary theorists have disputed Freud's views of feminine development, citing observational evidence of girls' primary feminine identification, positive experience of their female genitals, and wishes to have a baby before the oedipal situation.[14–18] Envy of men may be seen, in a sociohistorical context, as a by-product of cultural devaluation of women (in an egalitarian society, a predominating sense of penis envy may indicate neurotic or narcissistic difficulties). Boys too are susceptible to fantasies of genital inferiority on comparing their small penises to the large adult genitals.[19]

Successful passage through the phallic phase includes resolution of the Oedipus complex and repression of oedipal fantasies. The child internalizes the parental prohibitions and moral values and demonstrates a greater capacity to channel instinctual energies into constructive activities. Excessive conflict or traumatization during this phase may lead to a personality organized around oedipal fantasies and conflicts or a proneness to defensively regress to anal or oral organization.

During the *latency phase* (see Table 19–5), from age 6 years to puberty, play and learning take a prominent position in the child's behavior as cognitive processes mature further. Although Freud believed that the sexual urges become relatively quiescent during this phase, observation indicates that they are expressed in derivative form in the child's play.[20] At puberty, and through adolescence, genital urges once again predominate, but there is now a consolidation of sexual identity and a movement toward adult sexuality (Fig. 19–2).

Libido Theory

Freud's continued consideration of the sources and nature of the sexual drives led to his dynamic model of the mind referred to as *libido theory* (Table 19–6). This theory attempted to explain the observation that behavior and mental activity are not only triggered by external stimuli (as in the reflex arc) but also generated by primary internal processes. As a biologist, Freud hoped to understand the somatic origins of mental activity and used the concept of *instinct* (*Treib,* "drive") to do so. The psychoanalytic use of the term instinct differs from that of biology, which refers to innate, inherited, unlearned, stereotypical, species-specific behaviors. Freud defined instinct as "a concept on the frontier between the mental and the somatic, as the psychical representative of the stimuli originating within the organism and reaching the mind, as a measure of the demand made upon the mind for work in consequence of its connection with the body."[21] Regardless of the specifics of their physiological origins, derivatives of the instincts are experienced mentally as compelling urges and a source of motivation.

Although Freud had given up the idea that sexual traumatization was always the cause of psychoneurotic symptoms, he maintained the view that the sexual instinct played an etiological role in the neuroses and that sexual stimulation exerted a predominant force on mental activity throughout life. Freud termed this force *libido.* The discharge of libido is experienced as pleasure; the welling up of libido without discharge is felt as tension or unpleasure. According to the *pleasure principle,* the individual seeks pleasure (through the discharge of libidinal tension) and avoids unpleasure. The primary process quality of unconscious mentation follows the pleasure principle as it maintains its focus on the gratifications of wishes. As the mind develops, conscious mentation becomes more governed by the *reality principle,*[22] involving a shift from fantasy to perception of and action on reality. The secondary process form of conscious thought follows the reality principle. Under the influence of the reality principle, gratification of wishes may be delayed with the aim of eventually achieving greater pleasure.

The sexual instinct has four defining components: source, pressure (or impetus), aim, and object.[5, 21] *Source* refers to the biological substrate of the instinct. *Pressure* is the amount of force or "demand for work" of the instinct. The *aim* is the action designed to accomplish release of tension and satisfaction. An *object* is the target of desire, the person or thing through which gratification is accomplished. Freud[21, 23] went on to theorize that libido can be invested in or attached to representations of others in the mind or to the mental structures themselves, a phenomenon referred to as *cathexis.* Libido invested in mental representations of others is termed *object libido;* cathexis of the libido to the ego or self-representation is referred to as *ego libido.* Although the libido theory has been criticized because it was based on 19th century German scientism, it has served as a useful metaphor to understand pleasure, attachments, and the dynamic processes of mental activity.

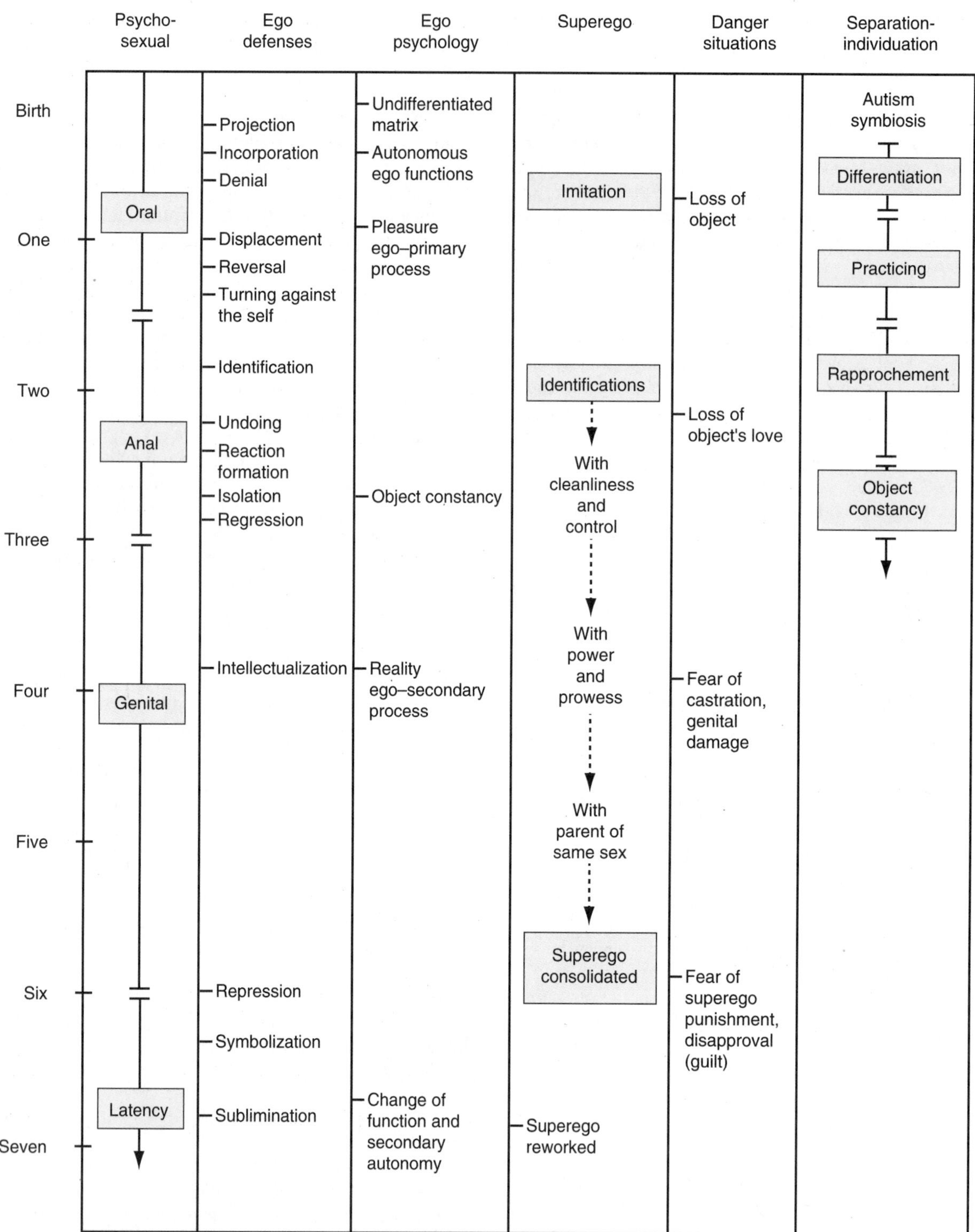

Figure 19–2 *Parallel lines of development. (From Inderbitzin LB, James ME: Psychoanalytic psychology. In Stoudemire A [ed]: Human Behavior: An Introduction for Medical Students, 2nd ed. Philadelphia: JB Lippincott, 1994:131.)*

Table 19–6	Libido (Drive) Theory
Assumes that biological "needs" (drives) fuel behavior	
The aim of behavior is to gratify the drive	
Drives are either sexual or aggressive in nature	

From the Topographical to the Structural Model

As psychoanalytic theory developed during the 20 years after Freud's writing of The Interpretation of Dreams (1900),[1] it was built on the foundation of the *topographical theory* (Table 19–7). This theory was able to explain the

Table 19–7 Topographical Theory

Unconscious
Contents
Drives
Repressed ideas and affects
Uses primary process thinking
Conscious
Contents
Sensory input from environment
Nonrepressed feelings and ideas
Uses secondary process thinking
Preconscious
Has access to both the conscious and the unconscious
Mental effort brings some preconscious material to the conscious
Uses secondary process thinking

observations that patients under hypnosis, or using free association, were able to become consciously aware of memories or motives for which they had no prior conscious awareness, the causal role of these elements in symptom formation and other psychological events, and the apparent opposition the mind exerted against the awareness or recall of these unconscious elements.

According to the topographical theory (Fig. 19–3) three regions or systems of the mind exist as defined by their relationship to conscious thought: the conscious, preconscious, and unconscious. The *conscious* mind registers sensations from the outside world and from internal processes and is the agency of ordinary wakeful thought. Conscious mentation follows the reality principle and uses secondary process logic. The *preconscious* includes mental contents that can be accessed into consciousness by the focusing of attention. The *unconscious* is defined from three basic angles: descriptively, it consists of all mental processes and contents operating outside conscious awareness; dynamically, these processes and contents are kept actively repressed or censored by the expenditure of mental energy to prevent the anxiety or repugnance that would accompany their conscious recognition; and as a mental system, it is a part of the mind that operates in accordance with the pleasure principle using primary process logic.

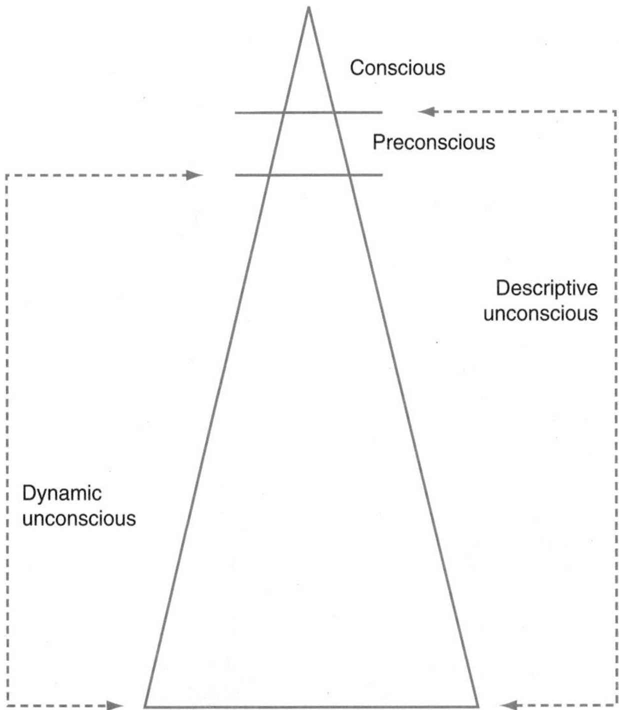

Figure 19–3 *Topographical theory. (From Bernstein AE, Warner GM [eds]: An Introduction to Contemporary Psychoanalysis. Northvale, NJ: Jason Aronson, 1981:11.)*

Over time, Freud encountered clinical phenomena that were not adequately accounted for by the topographical model. Resistance to free association did not appear to be governed by conscious processes, but rather was operating unconsciously. In addition, the topographical model did not help explain self-defeating behavior and the unconscious need for punishment. In time, Freud revised his theory of mental systems to include the structural model, but the useful conception of the dynamic unconscious and the particular qualities of conscious, preconscious, and unconscious mentation have been retained.

Theory of Narcissism

Freud[23] was led to his theory of narcissism (Fig. 19–4) by his consideration of a number of psychological phenomena including psychosis, hypochondria, different types of loving or erotic attachments, and relationship of self-love or self-regard to the judgmental processes of the conscience. The term narcissism was derived from the myth of Narcissus, who fell in love with his own reflection, and hence refers broadly to self-love. Freud noted that although a narcissistic attitude had been described as a component of certain psychiatric disorders, narcissism was seen more extensively and could be considered a part of normal development. Using the terminology of libido theory, Freud observed that psychotic individuals, with their turning inward and away from the external world and with their megalomaniacal preoccupations, appeared to have withdrawn libido from objects and attached it to the ego (self); however, phenomena similar to megalomania, such as magical thinking and overestimation of wishes and thoughts, could be seen early in normal development. Therefore, during earliest infancy, libido is originally attached to the ego, a state of *primary narcissism.* Libido then becomes progressively attached to love objects in the form of object libido. This can be withdrawn back to the ego, referred to as *secondary narcissism.*

In all mental functioning, it is then possible to observe the balance between libido deployed toward objects and libido withdrawn into the ego. For example, when a person is in love, much libido is attached to the loved object, even to the extent that the person feels himself or herself diminished (from decreased ego libido). During physical

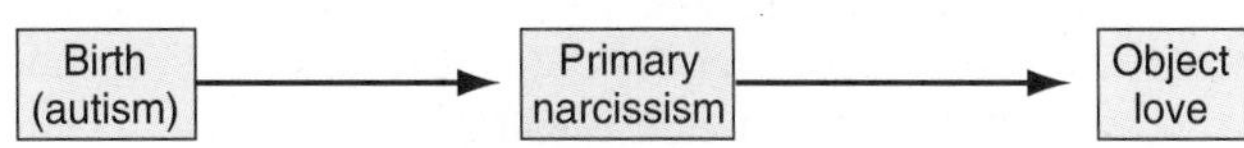

Figure 19–4 *Freud's theory of narcissism (1914).*

illness or hypochondriacal states, libido is pulled toward the ego so the person appears preoccupied with the body and uninterested in the world. According to the pleasure principle, the mind seeks to discharge libido, and if it is dammed up, symptoms will result. In neurotic persons, excess object libido has accumulated and, undischarged, produces anxiety. In psychotic persons, ego libido has been prevented from being discharged outward, so it is discharged inward, resulting in hypochondriacal anxiety and megalomania.

Narcissistic phenomena are involved in certain love and erotic relationships. In infancy, the primary attachment to mother has a self-preservative quality involving ego libido and is referred to as an *anaclitic* attachment. Some adults continue to seek out anaclitic love attachments, wishing to be fed and protected. Other individuals may form narcissistic attachments, looking for someone who resembles oneself, the way one was, or the way one would like to be. Often the love of parents for their children may involve a revival of their own narcissism, reflected in the overvaluation or overindulgence of a child.

Internal judgmental processes and self-regard are also addressed by the theory of narcissism. In normal adults, most evidence of the operation of ego libido has been repressed. A new target of self-love has been constructed, the *ego ideal,* consisting of ideas and wishes for how one would like to be. Similarly, love objects may become the subject of this idealization. Freud theorized a separate psychic agency that attends to ensuring narcissistic satisfaction and measuring the self in comparison to the ideal. This agency (later to become part of the superego) is involved in processes of self-reflection, censoring, and repression. Living up to the ideal, loving oneself, and being loved reflect attempts to restore a state comparable to the primary narcissism of infancy.

Melancholia

In Mourning and Melancholia (1917), Freud[24] developed a theory to explain processes of guilt, internal self-punishment, and depression. To do this, he contrasted states of grief or mourning with the condition of melancholia. Both have in common the experience of pain and sadness, and both are brought on by the experience of loss, but the person in mourning maintains her or his position of self-regard, whereas the person with melancholia feels dejected, loses interest in the world, shows a diminished capacity to love, inhibits all activities, and exhibits low self-regard in the form of self-reproaches and self-revilings. In mourning, libido is gradually withdrawn from the object attachment; in melancholia, the ego feels depleted or comes under attack as though "one part of the ego sets itself over against the other, judges it critically, and as it were, takes it as its object." This critical agency (again a theoretical forerunner of the superego) comes to operate independently of the ego.

The self-accusations of the person with melancholia seem to fit best with criticisms that might be leveled against the lost object. In the case of suicidal impulses, the melancholic person seems to be directing at himself or herself the sadism and murderous wishes felt toward the disappointing or lost other. Freud theorized that in the context of the loss of an ambivalently held object, the ego incorporates, or forms a narcissistic identification with, the object. Hostility originally felt toward the object is now directed at the self, giving rise to feelings of torment, suffering, and self-debasement. The predisposition to melancholia, then, results from a tendency to form narcissistic object attachments and to form narcissistic identifications with objects. The development of mania in some patients is accounted for by the liberation of the previously bound libido, which is then available for massive motor discharge.

Dual-Instinct Theory

Over time, Freud's theory of aggression evolved. He had originally considered two types of instincts, the sexual and the ego (self-preservative) instincts, and considered sadism to represent a fusion of the two, with hostility occurring in the context of frustrated libidinal strivings. This theory, however, did not adequately address psychological situations in which destructive tendencies seemed to be operating independently of libidinal or self-preservative drives. In addition, certain types of pathological conditions seemed to defy the pleasure principle in that experiences of unpleasure appeared to repeat over and over, a phenomenon referred to as the *repetition compulsion.*[25–27] Patients with traumatic neuroses were observed to think and dream repeatedly of the painful experiences that brought on their disorder. Other patients with masochistic qualities tend to unconsciously set up life situations in which they suffer. Some individuals in psychoanalytic treatment manifest *negative therapeutic reactions,* in which insights that ought to lead to symptomatic improvement produce worsening instead.

Freud concluded that there must be a separate instinct of aggression, whose aim is destruction. The aggressive drive is at work in impulses to harm, in the desire for control and power, in sadistic or masochistic behaviors, in guilt and depression, and in the persecutory fears of paranoid individuals. Freud theorized two general forces at work in the human psyche: the *life instinct* (Eros or libido), operative in positive, synthetic, constructive activities; and the *death instinct* (Thanatos), which propels the human organism toward destruction, disarray, and eventually entropy. Although the concept of a death instinct has largely been rejected by most psychoanalysts, the concept of an aggressive drive and its related conflicts has been of considerable clinical utility.

Structural Model

On the basis of the preceding considerations, Freud[28, 29] revised his theory of the mind into what is now known as the structural or tripartite model (Fig. 19–5 and Table 19–8). He conceived of three mental agencies operating in the psyche: the id, the ego, and the superego. The *id* is the biological source of instinctual drives, operating unconsciously and following the pleasure principle. The activity of the id creates a motivational push toward gratification of sexual and aggressive wishes.

The *ego* grows out of the id early in human development; it was defined by Freud as the "organized portion of the id." Its functions include perception, interpretation of perceptions, voluntary movement, modulation of affects and impulses, cognition, memory, judgment, and adaptation to reality. Subject to conflicting forces from the id, the superego, and reality, the ego synthesizes mental compromises that provide maximal gratification of instinctual

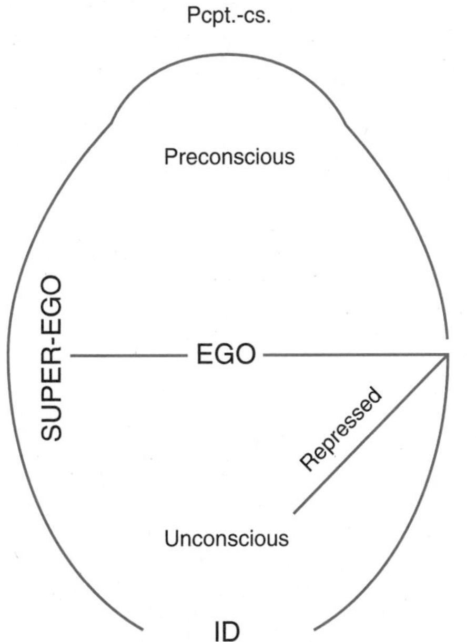

Figure 19–5 *Representation of Freud's structural theory. Pcpt.-cs., Precipitant conscious. (From Bernstein AE, Warner GM [eds]: An Introduction to Contemporary Psychoanalysis. Northvale, NJ: Jason Aronson, 1981:16.)*

wishes but at the same time accord with reality and the moral demands of the superego.

The *superego,* which develops as an outgrowth of both the ego and id, consists of the moral standards, values, and prohibitions that have been internalized throughout childhood and adolescence. It is the source of internal punishment, which is felt as guilt, and of internal reward. Early in development, the superego has a harsh or archaic quality and

Table 19–8 Structural Theory

Id
First developmentally
Completely unconscious
Contains all drives
Ruled by pleasure principle
No awareness of reality
Ego
Second structure to develop
Operates on reality principle
Mediates conflict among id, ego, and superego
Provides reality testing
Monitors quality of interpersonal relations
Provides synthesis and coordination
Carries out primary autonomous functions
Defends against anxiety
Superego
Third structure to develop
Self-criticism based on moral values
Self-punishment
Self-praise based on ego ideal
Most functions are unconscious

Freud's first formulation:
dammed-up libido ------------------------► anxiety

Freud's second formulation:
dammed-up libido ----------► defense (repression) + anxiety

Freud's final formulation:
infantile wish ----------------► danger situation (conflict)
anxiety (as a signal) -----------------------► defense

Figure 19–6 *Schematic representation of the evolution of Freud's theory of anxiety. (From Bernstein AE, Warner GM [eds]: An Introduction to Contemporary Psychoanalysis. Northvale, NJ: Jason Aronson, 1981:32.)*

is experienced with a sadistic severity. During maturation under optimal conditions, it becomes less harsh and comes to include loving components as well. In the structural model, the ego ideal (discussed earlier) is considered a component of the superego, accounting for feelings of shame and pride.

Anxiety and Symptom Formation

With the elaboration of the structural theory, Freud progressively viewed the nature of anxiety (Fig. 19–6) and the origin of symptoms (Fig. 19–7) differently from those of his first model. According to his original theory, anxiety resulted from the accumulation of undischarged sexual tensions, caused by inadequate sexual activity in the actual neuroses or by the action of repression in the psychoneuroses. Later, it became clear that anxiety was more closely related to fear, occurring in response to perceived dangers, either external or internal. This led to a focus on the function of the ego, one of whose functions is to anticipate and negotiate danger situations.[28] A dangerous or traumatic situation is one in which excessive stimulation threatens to overcome the ego.

The original traumatic situation is birth, at which time the immature psychic apparatus of the newborn cannot manage the stimuli surrounding birth and the upsurge of instinctual tensions accompanying extrauterine life. During subsequent development, other characteristic danger situations arise (Table 19–9). Because of the helplessness and vulnerability of the infant, the major danger during the oral phase is *loss of the primary object,* typically mother. Later, as the child has greater autonomy and a sense of the individuality of the parents, *loss of the object's love* comes to be the foremost danger. During the phallic phase, the principal danger is the threat of *castration or body injury.*

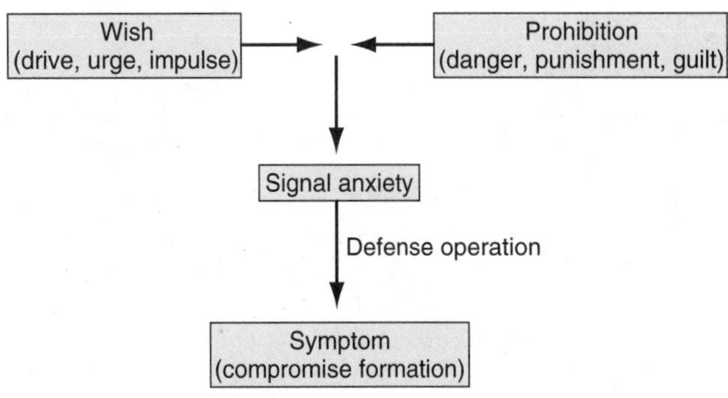

Figure 19–7 *Freud's theory of symptom formation.*

Table 19-9 Typical Situations of Danger
Fear of instincts (traumatic overstimulation)
Fear of object loss
Fear of loss of love
Fear of castration (body injury)
Fear of guilt (moral anxiety)

Further on, as the superego has become more developed, the primary danger is *guilt,* the internalized punishment or loss of love of the superego.

In this model, then, the ego is able to anticipate the potentially traumatic danger situations associated with unconscious wishes or impulses that are pushing toward conscious awareness. It mobilizes a small amount of alerting anxiety, referred to as *signal anxiety,* which in turn activates repression or any of a number of defensive operations to prevent the wish or impulse from emerging into conscious awareness. (Anna Freud's development of the theory of ego defense mechanisms is discussed in the section on ego psychology.)

The ego has as one of its tasks the continual formation of *compromises* between the forces of id wishes, the prohibitions and moral standards of the superego, and the dictates of reality. If these compromises are successful, anxiety will operate predominantly on a signal level and behavior will be both gratifying and acceptable in reality. A *symptom neurosis* occurs if these compromises are felt as uncomfortable, painful, or maladaptive. For example, in the development of a phobia, a conflictual unconscious wish and its associated fantasies have been successfully displaced outward, or externalized, and attached to something in the environment that can be avoided. Although the compromise works, in that it prevents conscious recognition of the wish and its associated unconscious fears, the resulting phobic avoidances may lead to a restriction of adaptive functioning. In the neuroses, there is a recognition of the difficulties created by one's symptoms and a desire to change. In the *character neuroses,* on the other hand, problem behaviors and modes of experiencing, which result from rigid and repetitive use of particular defense constellations, are felt as relatively comfortable and *ego-syntonic.* Because character-disordered individuals often resist the notion that their life difficulties are a result of internal processes, a first order of business in their psychoanalytic treatment is to transform their defenses and compromises into *ego-dystonic* experiences with a resulting motivation to change.

References

1. Freud S: The interpretation of dreams. In Strachey J (trans-ed): The Standard Edition of the Complete Psychological Works of Sigmund Freud, Volumes 4 and 5. London: Hogarth Press, 1958. Originally published in 1900.
2. Freud S: On dreams. In Strachey J (trans-ed): The Standard Edition of the Complete Psychological Works of Sigmund Freud, Volume 5. London: Hogarth Press, 1958:629–714. Originally published in 1901.
3. Reiser MF: Memory in Mind and Brain: What Dream Imagery Reveals. New York: Basic Books, 1990.
4. Winson J: Brain and Psyche: The Biology of the Unconscious. New York: Vintage Books, 1985.
5. Freud S: Three essays on the theory of sexuality. In Strachey J (trans-ed): The Standard Edition of the Complete Psychological Works of Sigmund Freud, Volume 7. London: Hogarth Press, 1953:123–246. Originally published in 1905.
6. Abraham K: The first pregenital stage of the libido. In Selected Papers. London: Hogarth Press, 1916:248–279.
7. Meissner WW: Theories of personality and psychopathology: Classical psychoanalysis. In Kaplan HI, Sadock BJ (eds): Comprehensive Textbook of Psychiatry/IV, 4th ed. Baltimore: Williams & Wilkins, 1985:337–418.
8. Abraham K: Contributions to the theory of the anal character. In Selected Papers. London: Hogarth Press, 1921:370–392.
9. Freud S: Character and anal erotism. In Strachey J (trans-ed): The Standard Edition of the Complete Psychological Works of Sigmund Freud, Volume 9. London: Hogarth Press, 1959:167–176. Originally published in 1908.
10. Shengold L: Halo in the Sky: Observations on Anality and Defense. New Haven: Yale University Press, 1988.
11. Salzman L: Treatment of the Obsessive Personality. Northvale, NJ: Jason Aronson, 1980.
12. Freud S: The dissolution of the Oedipus complex. In Strachey J (trans-ed): The Standard Edition of the Complete Psychological Works of Sigmund Freud, Volume 19. London: Hogarth Press, 1958:173–182. Originally published in 1924.
13. Freud S: Some physical consequences of the anatomical distinction between the sexes. In Strachey J (trans-ed): The Standard Edition of the Complete Psychological Works of Sigmund Freud, Volume 19. London: Hogarth Press, 1961:241–260. Originally published in 1925.
14. Stoller R: Primary femininity. J Am Psychoanal Assoc 1976; 24(suppl): 59–78.
15. Kleeman JA: Freud's views on early female sexuality in the light of direct child observation. J Am Psychoanal Assoc 1976; 24(suppl):3–27.
16. Blum G: Masochism, the ego ideal, and the psychology of women. J Am Psychoanal Assoc 1976; 24(suppl):157–191.
17. Chehrazi S: Female psychology: A review. J Am Psychoanal Assoc 1986; 34:141–162.
18. Gilligan C: In a Different Voice: Psychological Theory and Women's Development. Cambridge, MA: Harvard University Press, 1982.
19. Horney K: The dread of woman: Observations on a specific difference in the dread felt by men and women respectively for the opposite sex. Int J Psychoanal 1932; 13:348–360.
20. Sarnoff C: Latency. Northvale, NJ: Jason Aronson, 1976.
21. Freud S: Instincts and their vicissitudes. In Strachey J (trans-ed): The Standard Edition of the Complete Psychological Works of Sigmund Freud, Volume 14. London: Hogarth Press, 1957:109–140. Originally published in 1915.
22. Freud S: Formulations on the two principles of mental functioning. In Strachey J (trans-ed): The Standard Edition of the Complete Psychological Works of Sigmund Freud, Volume 12. London: Hogarth Press, 1958:213–226. Originally published in 1911.
23. Freud S: On narcissism: An introduction. In Strachey J (trans-ed): The Standard Edition of the Complete Psychological Works of Sigmund Freud, Volume 14. London: Hogarth Press, 1957:67–104. Originally published in 1914.
24. Freud S: Mourning and melancholia. In Strachey J (trans-ed): The Standard Edition of the Complete Psychological Works of Sigmund Freud, Volume 14. London: Hogarth Press, 1957:237–258. Originally published in 1917.
25. Freud S: Beyond the pleasure principle. In Strachey J (trans-ed): The Standard Edition of the Complete Psychological Works of Sigmund Freud, Volume 18. London: Hogarth Press, 1955:1–64. Originally published in 1920.
26. Freud S: The ego and the id. In Strachey J (trans-ed): The Standard Edition of the Complete Psychological Works of Sigmund Freud, Volume 19. London: Hogarth Press, 1961:1–66. Originally published in 1923.
27. Freud S: The economic problem of masochism. In Strachey J (trans-ed): The Standard Edition of the Complete Psychological Works of Sigmund Freud, Volume 19. London: Hogarth Press, 1961:155–172. Originally published in 1924.
28. Freud S: Inhibitions, symptoms, and anxiety. In Strachey J (trans-ed): The Standard Edition of the Complete Psychological Works of Sigmund Freud, Volume 20. London: Hogarth Press, 1959:75–176. Originally published in 1926.
29. Freud S: New introductory lectures on psycho-analysis. In Strachey J (trans-ed): The Standard Edition of the Complete Psychological Works of Sigmund Freud, Volume 22. London: Hogarth Press, 1964:1–182. Originally published in 1933.

Lucy LaFarge
Richard B. Zimmer

Other Early Theories

Early dissenting analysts diverged from Freud on the issue of the sexual etiology of the neuroses. Many of these analysts abandoned instinct theory altogether and emphasized the role of the environment in the genesis of personality and neurotic symptoms. Others retained a role for sexuality as one of a host of needs pressing for satisfaction and leading to potential conflict and symptom formation. As a group, these analysts rejected the idea that infantile sexuality and the Oedipus complex were universal.

Alfred Adler

Alfred Adler (1870 to 1937) was the first among the early followers of Freud to break with him. Initially, Adler[1] asserted the psychic centrality of the individual's efforts to compensate for actual organ inferiority. Later, the idea of compensation was incorporated into his concept of the *masculine protest,* in which both men and women sought to overcome feelings of inferiority through attempts to feel "like a real man," powerful and complete. Adler came to believe that the masculine protest was more central to human motivation than the sexual drive. The disagreement between Freud and Adler over the importance of sexuality in human motivation proved to be irreconcilable, and Adler resigned from the Vienna Psychoanalytic Society in 1911, establishing the school he called *individual psychology.* Ultimately, he repudiated other central tenets of freudian theory, including the universality of the Oedipus complex and the doctrine of psychic determinism.

According to Adler, the universal compensatory strivings for superiority implicit in the masculine protest were given direction by a *personal goal* or *self-ideal,* a personal fiction that each individual created. This goal, largely outside of conscious awareness, was the primary determinant of motivation, and the drives became subordinate to it; thus, motivation was driven by a vision of the future rather than by the past. All psychological processes, including behavior and perceptions of the self and of the environment, were organized around the goal.

Adler believed that the psychology of the individual could not be considered separately from the person's relation to her or his social milieu. He thought that people were born with an innate capacity for *social interest,* which found its first expression in the relationship with the mother. In its most mature form, the capacity for social interest could manifest in wishes to improve society and the lot of humanity.[2] Socialization occurred primarily through the maturation of social interest rather than through the repression of drives because of guilt or anxiety.

Adler minimized the importance of specific diagnostic categories of psychopathology and believed in the dynamic unity of mental disorders. All psychological disorders, he believed, were due to heightened feelings of inferiority, which led to an exaggerated compensatory need for superiority. In conjunction with underdeveloped social interest, this resulted in socially maladaptive behaviors based on distortions in perception and logic.

Adler placed less emphasis than did Freud on insight in treatment and did not see the revival of instinctual wishes toward early objects in the transference as an important part of the therapeutic process. In adlerian therapy, the therapist would help bring the patient's guiding goal more into conscious awareness; "mistaken" perceptions and goals of superiority based on self-aggrandizement and depreciation of others, rather than on useful accomplishments, would be demonstrated to be unrealistic, and the therapist would actively encourage the development of social interest in the patient as well as efforts to seek new, more socially adaptive forms of behavior.

Carl Jung

Carl Jung (1875 to 1961), initially a strong supporter of Freud and a central figure in the analytical movement, broke with Freud in 1913 to form his own school, *analytical psychology.* Jung, who had begun his psychotherapeutic and research efforts working with the severely disturbed patients in the Burgholzli asylum in Zurich, doubted from the first the universal role of sexuality in the etiology of neurosis.[3] Ultimately, he came to see Freud's libido theory and Adler's striving for power as complementary models, each explaining a different aspect of a relatively superficial level of neurotic conflict. Each model might fruitfully be applied to a specific group of patients. Even for those patients for whom sexual conflicts were paramount, Jung believed, the infantile sexuality and incestuous strivings that Freud observed in his adult patients were secondary formations, the result of a psychopathological process rather than its cause. Adults who failed in the adaptive task of forming mature ties with new objects turned their libido, now freighted with adult sexual desires, back on their early objects.

According to Jung, the neuroses described by Freud and Adler were caused by unconscious conflicts that originated in the patient's early development within the matrix of his or her family. The analysis of these conflicts gave rise to the kinds of personal transferences that Freud delineated, in which the analyst was perceived as a new edition of an early object. Their treatment progressed along the lines of classical analysis. However, Jung observed, as these conflicts and the transferences associated with them were resolved, a second, deeper layer of transference imagoes often emerged. These transferences, mythical or primitive in character, seemed far removed from the realistic qualities of the patient's parents. They were often extreme, idealizing or intensely bad; they came in pairs of opposites; and Jung found that they frequently represented a projected part of the self. Jung believed that these transferences were impersonal in character, arising from the deep layer that he named the *collective unconscious,* the repository of inherited, primordial *archetypes* that gave form to human thought. These imagoes, which predated individual development, gave rise to disturbances in conscious experience just as instinctual conflicts did. Only by integrating them with conscious self-experience could the person find meaning in life. This notion of a spiritual factor that lives through the individual rather than arising within the individual lends a mystical cast to Jung's work. From the viewpoint of contemporary mainstream psychoanalysis, Jung's impersonal archetypes resemble the phenomena of narcissism, and Jung indicates that these transferences frequently emerged after a blow to the patient's secure sense of self. Jung's 1916 paper, On the Psychology of the Unconscious, would thus be one of the first descriptions of primitive narcissistic transferences.[4]

Although Jung's work has remained isolated from mainstream psychoanalysis, his contributions address many issues that have only later come to interest more orthodox analysts. His linkage of specific forms of psychopathology to the failure to accomplish specific developmental tasks throughout the life cycle foreshadows Erikson's work. He was among the first to introduce the concept of the *supraordinate self,* in which ego and unconscious are viewed as components of a larger structure. In addition, he was an early advocate of the analyst's productive use of the countertransference.[5]

Otto Rank

Otto Rank (1884 to 1939) was one of Freud's most beloved early disciples. He joined the Vienna Psychoanalytic Society in 1905 as a largely self-educated, impoverished young man with no professional credentials. Freud gave him a position as the paid secretary of the society and encouraged him to pursue gymnasium and university education. Rank's initial interest was in psychoanalytic theory as it applied to the arts, literature, and mythology. His first publication, "The artist," dealt with the role of sexuality and the unconscious in the creative process.[6] In *The Myth of the Birth of the Hero,* he traced common themes in hero myths of different cultures and discussed their psychological and philosophical implications.[7]

Rank was drawn to the work of Sandor Ferenczi, and in 1924 they collaboratively published The Development of Psychoanalysis,[8] in which they asserted the therapeutic value of specific modifications of psychoanalytic technique, for which Ferenczi had coined the term *active therapy.* In the same year, Rank[9] published *The Trauma of Birth,* probably his boldest and most important theoretical contribution. In this work, Rank asserted that at the deepest level, all anxiety derived from the experience of separation from the haven of the mother's womb at birth. In the oedipal situation, Rank thought, the horror of incest was derived not from fear of retaliatory castration at the hands of the father but rather from the dread of the image of the maternal genitalia and the ambivalently held wish to return to the mother's womb. Implicit in this work was a shift of attention away from oedipal and toward preoedipal conflicts. Rank deemphasized the centrality of the relation with the father in genesis of neurosis and placed a greater importance on the relation with the mother. These shifts anticipated by decades later trends in psychoanalytic thinking, particularly with regard to the understanding of narcissism. Technically, Rank suggested setting a time limit for treatment at the outset to bring separation anxieties to the fore. Although Freud initially hailed this work, his enthusiasm for it gradually waned because he thought that it challenged central tenets of psychoanalytic theory. Rank insisted his ideas constituted an extension of rather than a rebellion against Freud's thinking but was unable to elicit sufficient acceptance from Freud, and in 1926 he broke with Freud and the Vienna group.

After this break, there was a growing divergence between Rank's thinking and that of mainstream psychoanalysis. Rank[10] placed increasing emphasis on the *will* of the individual as a central element of the psyche and as the focus of treatment. Rank began to see the essence of neurosis as the denial of will. The goal of therapy, he believed, was *psychological rebirth.* The patient would be helped to create a personality for herself or himself that allowed the constructive expression of will. The patient could then consciously mobilize the will in the service of either inhibiting or carrying through to realization instinctual impulses. Rank emphasized the overcoming of guilt, which he believed was implicit in the exercise of will. In his *will therapy,* the focus was not on the understanding of the transference as a new edition of earlier relationships but rather on the use of the immediacy of the therapeutic relationship to enable the patient to assert and strengthen his or her own will.

Sandor Ferenczi

Sandor Ferenczi (1873 to 1933), although a courageous clinical innovator who frequently challenged Freud's beliefs, remained personally loyal to Freud and dependent on his approval throughout his life. Unlike others of Freud's original disciples, he never made a final break with Freud.

Ferenczi's work drew extensively on Freud's central theoretical assertions: the importance of sexuality in motivation, psychic determinism, the centrality of the Oedipus complex, and the concept of the transference. At the same time, he expanded psychoanalytic theory in new directions. He emphasized the importance of introjection as a psychic mechanism.[11] In his paper Stages in the Development of the Sense of Reality,[12] he traced the steps in the gradual relinquishing of infantile feelings of omnipotence and how traces of these stages manifested in varying forms of adult psychopathological conditions. He believed in the importance of aggression as well as libido in psychic life and emphasized the importance of the death instinct in the genesis of symptoms as well as the relative weakness of the life instincts (libidinal and self-preservative) at the onset of life.[13] In these respects, he anticipated (and undoubtedly influenced) the later pioneering work of his analysand, Melanie Klein. Although a believer in the importance of fantasy, Ferenczi also believed in the importance of external reality and thought that real trauma was a frequent cause of neurotic symptoms and character disorder. In his last published paper, Confusion of Tongues Between Adults and the Child,[14] he suggested that the explicitly sexual fantasies of children were induced by the parents' overly sexual behavior toward them and that these traumatic seductions were played out in the analytical situation through enactments, often accompanied by intense hostile feeling toward the analyst that was covered over by an attitude of compliance. This paper outraged Freud, who saw it as a return to his altered seduction theory, but Ferenczi died before the disagreement could turn into an open confrontation between the two.

Ferenczi strove to maximize the clinical usefulness of psychoanalytic theory, and much of his work focused on innovations in technique. In his *active therapy,* he recommended enjoining the patient to confront phobically avoided situations, prohibiting symptomatic acts, or prescribing the symptom. He distinguished this technique from that of pure suggestion by emphasizing the need to analyze fully the patient's reactions to the analyst having made these interventions. He advocated the broadening of the field of clinical data to be interpreted beyond the patient's verbal productions to include the physical appearance of the patient and the patient's behavior toward the analyst. His *elasticity of technique,* wherein the analyst would tolerate the patient's unpleasant or antipathetic behavior and would "yield to the patient's pull, without ceasing to pull in his own direction," sought explicitly to bring the patient's actions and unspoken attitudes more into interpretive focus.[15] In his *relaxation technique,* he emphasized the importance of encouraging the freest possible expression of transference feelings, both libidinal and aggressive, and advocated as well the analyst's open acknowledgment of errors and limitations of understanding.[16] Although at times criticized for being too flexible in his technqiue, Ferenczi believed strongly in the necessity of complete character analysis for the analyst to enable the analyst to withstand intense transferences, to maintain an interpretive stance, and to avoid the induction of enactments with patients.

Karen Horney

Karen Horney (1885 to 1952), a German-born psychoanalyst trained in Berlin, first assumed a critical stance toward freudian theory on the issue of the psychology of women. In an important series of papers written in the 1920s, Horney[17, 18] argued that Freud's model of feminine development was phallocentric, a masculine fantasy that protected men from their unconscious fear of women. Freud's hypothesis that the little girl experienced herself as masculine until the phallic phase was incorrect, Horney contended; the girl's experience was from the first uniquely feminine and included an early awareness of the vagina. Although the girl did experience penis envy during the phallic phase, this envy, which Horney termed *primary penis envy,* did not have the universal meaning and importance that Freud attributed to it. What analysts observed in the treatment of adult women was *secondary penis envy,* a fantasy of masculinity that served as a defense against the girl's oedipal wish for her father's love. Secondary penis envy was further reinforced by women's awareness of the real deprivations that the culture inflicted on them. Horney's arguments have been of central importance in feminist critiques of Freud and ultimately in the reworking of views of feminine psychology within mainstream psychoanalysis.

Horney radically challenged Freud's views on women, but she did so from a vantage point within freudian metapsychology. After her emigration to the United States in 1932, she gradually came to reject Freud's instinct theory and his model of a tripartite mental structure. Horney believed that humans were not the tragic figures that Freud depicted, driven by biological endowment to seek sexual and aggressive satisfaction and inevitably meeting conflict. Normal and neurotic development were qualitatively different, and sexual and aggressive wishes were less important to each than Freud had postulated. Normal development was not inherently conflictual. The neurotic child sacrificed the pursuit of pleasure and the fulfillment of his or her unique potential, which Horney termed the *real self,* to ensure safety in an environment that the child perceived as hostile and dangerous.[19] Horney argued that this perception of danger was an objective one, rather than a fantasy originating in the child's own wishes. Ultimately, neurosis was the result of environment; the neurotic child responded to the parents' failure to love her or him as she or he was; and neurotic symptoms were importantly determined by cultural norms. The oedipal wishes that Freud observed were largely disguised wishes for safety, important only in neurotic persons. Aggression was reactive. Although childhood influences shaped character, current defensive needs rather than infantile wishes were the chief determinants of current behavior and of the patient's transference. The analyst should focus on the here and now, interpreting current wishes and defensive structures so that the patient's unconflicted potential could emerge.[20] Horney's theoretical divergence, and the alterations in technique that emerged from it, led to the loss of her teaching position within the orthodox New York Psychoanalytic Institute and to the foundation of her own school, the Association for Advancement of Psychoanalysis.[21] Her emphasis on the current context of analysis has been absorbed into mainstream psychoanalysis; her concepts of the real self and human potential have contributed to the broader expanse of dynamic psychotherapies.

Harry Stack Sullivan

Harry Stack Sullivan (1892 to 1949), an American psychiatrist who was not formally trained as a psychoanalyst, melded elements of psychoanalysis, the psychobiology of Adolf Meyer, and sociological concepts to develop the *interpersonal theory of psychiatry.*[22] Like Horney, with whom he shared collegial discussions, Sullivan rejected Freud's instinct theory and emphasized the central influence of the environment on individual development. Sullivan envisioned a succession of developmental phases during which the individual used growing cognitive capacities to adapt to the interpersonal roles offered by significant objects and society. At first the passive recipient of the roles assigned by the mother, the child soon learned to elicit desired roles in objects and to avoid undesirable ones that caused anxiety. In contrast with other analysts, Sullivan held that anxiety was exclusively interpersonal in origin: the infant became anxious because he or she experienced anxiety in the mother. Later experiences triggered anxiety because they evoked the recollection of the contagious anxiety felt with early objects. Conflict and neurotic symptoms arose when the individual's wish for satisfaction threatened the *self-system* of roles that was constructed to avoid these remembered interactions. Although the earliest phases were crucial in establishing the foundations of the personality, adolescence and adulthood afforded significant opportunities for growth and change. Sullivan rejected the notion of infantile sexuality and argued that sexual wishes became an important source of conflict only at adolescence.

Sullivan's emphasis on the shaping influence that early objects exert on the child, and the parallel influence that the therapist, as participant-observer, exerts on the patient, have made an important contribution to the broader field of psychoanalysis. Sullivan spent a major part of his career working with individuals with schizophrenia, and his writings in this area offer a valuable perspective on the psychology of severe mental illness. In Sullivan's view, the weak self-system of the person with schizophrenia was unable to bar dissociated material from consciousness at times when conflictual wishes triggered anxiety. The autism, bizarreness, and loss of ego boundaries seen in schizophrenia reflected the eruption of infantile layers of experience that were normally screened by later modes of thought. The therapist working with the person with schizophrenia must attempt to build a relationship that would anchor the patient in a more mature, reality-based mode of functioning. Similarly, a therapeutic community in which these patients' capacity for relating was strengthened would also strengthen their capacity to tolerate anxiety and to function in reality.[23] These views have had a lasting influence on the psychotherapy and hospital treatment of schizophrenia.

References

1. Adler A: Study of Organ Inferiority and Its Psychical Compensation: A Contribution to Clinical Medicine. New York: Nervous and Mental Diseases Publishing Company, 1917. Originally published in 1907.
2. Adler A: Social Interest: A Challenge to Mankind. London: Faber & Faber, 1938. Originally published in 1933.
3. Freud S, Jung C; McGuire W (ed): The Freud/Jung Letters. London: Hogarth Press, 1974.
4. Jung C: Two Essays on Analytical Psychology. Princeton, NJ: Bollingen, 1953.
5. Jung C: Modern Man in Search of a Soul. New York: Harcourt, Brace & World, 1933.
6. Rank O: The artist. J Otto Rank Assoc 1980; 15:1. Originally published in 1907.
7. Rank O: The Myth of the Birth of the Hero. New York: Brunner, 1952. Originally published in 1909.
8. Ferenczi S, Rank O: The Development of Psychoanalysis. Nervous and Mental Disease Monograph Series 40, 1924. New York: Nervous and Mental Diseases Publishing Company, 1925.
9. Rank O: The Trauma of Birth. London: Routledge, 1929. Originally published in 1924.
10. Rank O: Will Therapy. New York: Knopf, 1936.
11. Ferenczi S: Introjection and transference. In First Contributions to Psychoanalysis. London: Hogarth Press, 1952:35–93. Originally published in 1909.
12. Ferenczi S: Stages in the development of the sense of reality. In First Contributions to Psychoanalysis. London: Hogarth Press, 1952:213–239. Originally published in 1913.
13. Ferenczi S: The unwelcome child and his death instinct. In Balint M (ed): Final Contributions to Psychoanalysis. London: Hogarth Press, 1955:102–107. Originally published in 1929.
14. Ferenczi S: Confusion of tongues between adults and the child. In Balint M (ed): Final Contributions to Psychoanalysis. London: Hogarth Press, 1955:156–167. Originally published in 1933.
15. Ferenczi S: The elasticity of psychoanalytic technique. In Balint M (ed): Final Contributions to Psychoanalysis. London: Hogarth Press, 1955:87–101. Originally published in 1928.
16. Ferenczi S: The principles of relaxation and neocatharsis. In Balint M (ed): Final Contributions to Psychoanalysis. London: Hogarth Press, 1955:108–125. Originally published in 1930.
17. Horney K: On the genesis of the castration complex in women. Int J Psychoanal 1924; 5:49–65.
18. Horney K: The flight from womanhood: The masculinity-complex in women as viewed by men and women. In Strouse J (ed): Women and Analysis. New York: Grossman, 1974:171–186. Originally published in 1926.
19. Horney K: Neurosis and Human Growth. New York: WW Norton, 1950.
20. Horney K: New Ways in Psychoanalysis. New York: WW Norton, 1939.
21. Quinn S: A mind of her own: The life of Karen Horney. New York: Summit, 1987.
22. Sullivan HS: The Interpersonal Theory of Psychiatry. New York: WW Norton, 1953.
23. Sullivan HS: Clinical Studies in Psychiatry. New York: WW Norton, 1956.

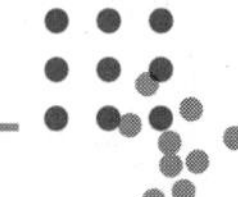

Ego Psychology and Modern Structural Theory

Steven T. Levy
Lawrence B. Inderbitzin

Consolidation of Ego Psychology

Ego psychology refers specifically to a systematic and coordinated conceptualization of various mental activities grouped together by virtue of their similar aims and behavioral manifestations, especially associated with delay or control of instinctual discharge on the one hand and with adaptation to reality opportunities and dangers on the other. More generally, ego psychology is often equated with Freud's last mental model, the structural hypothesis of id, ego, and superego, and refers to all those theoretical, clinical, and technical concepts and therapeutic practices based on or expressed in Freud's structural terms. As discussed in a later section, those modern psychoanalytic ideas most clearly recognizable as direct descendants of freudian thinking are usually referred to as modern ego psychology or contemporary structural theory.

Freud's ego psychology represented his last and most comprehensive and integrative understanding of how the mind works, both normally and pathologically. The Ego and The Id (1923) and Inhibitions, Symptoms, and Anxiety (1926) represent the formal presentation of Freud's theory of the ego, but ego concepts can be traced throughout Freud's work.[1–3] Defense, a central ego concept, appears early (1894 and 1896) in Freud's writings, referring there mainly to the avoidance of painful reality experiences encoded as memories, which leads to the damming up of affect and subsequent psychopathological processes. Even as Freud turned his attention to the study of instinctual life during the first two decades of the 20th century, concepts crucial to his later theory of the ego, for example, the secondary process (rational thinking), the reality principle, and a detailed examination of repression, were now focusing on how this defense is aimed at warding off instinctual manifestations rather than the "reality" contained in memories. With The Ego and The Id and Inhibitions, Symptoms, and Anxiety, Freud replaced an untenable model of the mind based on the property of consciousness of mental activity with a tripartite system of structures whose interactions, conscious and unconscious, fit best with clinical observations. The ego, now more than the instinctual id, became the subject of intense analytical inquiry. The nature of psychopathology was redefined with emphasis on deformation of ego activities rather than instinctual and external reality considerations as the enduring variables in what was considered mentally abnormal. It was to the ego that the analyst directed attention during treatment.

Equally important, the groundwork was laid for the expansion of psychoanalysis into a more comprehensive general psychology of all human behavior by Freud and ego psychologists like Hartmann, Anna Freud, Erikson, Rapaport, and many others. In their work, the structure and function of the ego, which had previously been conceptualized mainly in opposition to the id, were explored in relation to the ego's interaction with reality (especially object relations) as well as with the other psychic structures. The development of individual ego functions was described in detail. Hartmann[4] explored the ego as an organ of adaptation, mediating between instinctual demands, reality or environmental opportunities and constraints, and superego ideals and inhibitions. Individual defensive functions were described in detail, especially by Anna Freud.[5] The ego was seen to be a complex structure emerging, as Freud had noted, out of the perceptual apparatus, gradually assuming an executive role in forging compromises among the psychic structures and external reality. An expansion of our understanding of ego development and functioning included detailing the ways in which external controls, initially embedded in relations with parental objects, were gradually internalized, becoming the substrate for ego functions formally carried out by parental figures. This laid the foundation for the development of psychoanalytic object relations theory. The consolidation of ego psychology also led to direct child observation research, allowing study of how external relationships led to structuralization of the ego and examination of the details of mother-child interactions. Concepts such as reality testing, sublimation, altruism, modes of internalization, ideal formation, and self-esteem regulation were all explored in detail and coordinated with earlier psychoanalytic conceptualizations. Although there was considerable overlap in the work of the pioneer ego psychologists, their main areas of emphasis and lasting contributions are described separately. Their work extended Freud's structural view of the mind in many directions in building psychoanalysis into a broadly appealing theory and science of human psychology that profoundly influenced psychiatric thinking about psychopathology and therapeutics and deeply affected 20th century thought and behavior in general.

Anna Freud

Before the publication of Anna Freud's *The Ego and the Mechanisms of Defense*[5] in 1936, there were widely divergent views of ego psychology dominated by interest in primitive aspects of the ego revealed in infancy and in psychosis. Anna Freud's clear and systematic approach was grounded in an empirical study of the defensive functions of the ego that immediately forced themselves on the attention of analysts listening to "normal" and neurotic analysands.

Table 19–10 Ten Mechanisms of Defense (Anna Freud)

Mechanism	Description
Repression	This process consists of the expelling and withholding from conscious awareness of an idea or feeling. It may operate by excluding from awareness what was once experienced on a conscious level, or it may curb ideas and feelings before they have reached consciousness.
Regression	This means a return to a previous stage of development or functioning, to avoid the anxieties or hostilities involved in later stages; a return to earlier points of fixation embodying modes of behavior previously given up.
Reaction formation	This is a method for the management of unacceptable impulses by permitting expression of the impulse in antithetical acceptable form.
Isolation	This process is characterized by the intrapsychic splitting or separation of affect from content, resulting in repression of either idea or affect or the displacement of affect to a different or substitute content.
Undoing	A forbidden offensive act is ritualistically and magically nullified by atonement, often by religious or self-punitive expiation.
Introject (identification)	Introjection nullifies or negates the loss by taking on characteristics of the object, thus in a sense internally preserving the object.
Projection	Unacceptable impulses or ideas are attributed to someone or something else.
Turning against the self	Aggressive impulses originally directed toward someone else (the object) are directed back to the self.
Reversal	This is turning into the opposite and often applies to affects.
Sublimation (displacement)	The gratification of an impulse whose goal is retained, but whose aim or object is changed from a socially objectionable one to a socially valued one.

She categorized and developed the first theory of mechanisms of defense (Table 19–10), providing vivid clinical illustrations. In discussing the preliminary stages of defense that are first used by the ego to avoid pain from the external world, she succeeded in integrating two main themes in the development of the ego concept: defense and relations with external reality.

Taking Sigmund Freud's Inhibitions, Symptoms, and Anxiety as her starting point, she advocated a shift of the analyst's attention to the ego as "the proper field for observation" and as the only way to get a picture of its functioning in relationship to the two other psychic structures, id and superego. In contrast to impulses of the id that push toward consciousness, the unconscious aspects of the ego do not push toward the surface and therefore offer a greater challenge to the analyst. "All the defensive measures of the ego against the id are carried out silently and invisibly"[5(p8)] and must be inferred from their influence on the patient's associations. This requires a shift in the analyst's *method of observation.* This may represent her most important contribution, but it is also one that Kris[6] predicted could easily pass unnoticed. Her more detailed methodical attention to the mind's surface, which included manifestations of unconscious ego activities, provided a much clearer view of the actual workings of the mental apparatus.

In describing three types of transference (transference of the libidinal impulses, transference of defense, and acting out), Anna Freud emphasized the importance of interpreting transference of defense first to effect the dynamic struggle at the exact point where it is occurring. The conflict between emergent wishes and the defenses against them is a repetition in the here and now of earlier infantile struggles, and learning how and why the patient's defenses take the particular form also provides valuable information about the development of the ego. Her recommendation that the analyst listen from a point equidistant from id, ego, and superego emphasized the importance of neutrally observing the influence of all three psychic institutions. However, the analyst's activity (interventions) always begins with and is directed toward the ego, and in this sense the analyst is actually nearer to the ego than to the id or superego. The ego wards off not only derivatives of instinctual drives but also *affects* that are intimately connected with the drives. She advocated that priority be given to the interpretation of the defenses against affects as well as defenses against instinctual drives.

Anna Freud emphasized that repression occupies a unique place among the various mechanisms of defense, because of both its effectiveness and its potential dangerousness. Although she explored the possibility of classifying defenses according to the developmental phase in which they first appear and also systematically according to what they accomplish, her conclusions were cautious and tentative. In relation to the motives for defense, she stressed *objective anxiety* (fear of environmental consequences) in infantile neurosis, *superego anxiety* (fear of guilt and shame) in the neurosis of adults, and, more generally, *instinctual anxiety* or dread of the strength of the drives. She introduced two special types of defense not previously well described: identification with the aggressor and altruism. The former involves becoming like a feared person (identification) to appease and avoid being a passive victim, and the latter uses defensive surrender of one's own instinctual impulses that are experienced as dangerous for the advantage of someone else. She also described the asceticism and intellectuality of puberty as examples of defense motivated by fear of the strength of the instincts. Finally, Anna Freud emphasized and illustrated the adaptive nature and purpose of defense. Her broad perspective encompassed the whole range of mental life from normal to pathological. In her much later work, *Normality and Pathology in Childhood: Assessment of Development,*[7] she emphatically and enthusiastically pursued the subject of normality: what it is, how it develops, how it can be impeded or facilitated, and how it can be practically evaluated by use of her concept of developmental lines.

Heinz Hartmann

Heinz Hartmann's contributions to psychoanalytic theory, appearing mainly between 1930 and 1960, can profitably be considered, following his own design, an attempt at " 'synchronization' of Freud's unsystematized and unevenly developed contributions, and formulation of psychoanalytic propositions in a manner suitable for establishing psychoanalysis as 'a general psychology.' "[8(p425)] Especially in need of revision, amplification, and reorganization were the theory of aggression, ego development, economic and energic propositions, preoedipal development, narcissism, relations among and especially within the psychic structures, and propositions concerning the relation between the ego and the external world, viewed from the perspective of biological adaptation. Hartmann, along with his regular collaborators, Ernst Kris and Rudolph Loewenstein, in a brilliant series of papers beginning with Hartmann's classic and groundbreaking monograph Ego Psychology and the Problem of Adaptation[4] appearing in 1939 and first translated into English by David Rapaport in 1951, created an elegant and comprehensive general psychology firmly rooted in freudian thinking, retaining its biological and developmental perspectives and its profound discoveries about unconscious mental life and instinctual vicissitudes, and emphasizing the ego as the organ of adaptation.

Hartmann wished to maintain the biological perspective inherent in Freud's theorizing while emphasizing the *ego's* biological connections and pushing psychoanalysis in the direction of a general psychology. Freud's biological perspectives, there being several, nonetheless centered on the mind as a vehicle for the discharge of psychic energy. Most of his "biologizing" was linked primarily to the drives or instincts and those economic principles that could explain mental events in terms of the management of instinctual energy or force within the mind. Conceptual links were drawn between the physical sciences, the nervous system, and psychology. The ego played a management role in Freud's economics of psychic energy, later called libido. Hartmann sought to establish a separate biological substrate for the ego in the concept of adaptation. The ego was to maintain a dynamic equilibrium among instinctual pressures, internal ideals and prohibitions, and the external environment. Its aims were safety and optimal adaptation to inner and outer demands. It did not develop solely out of the id but had its own history, the id and ego differentiating from each other after a common or undifferentiated phase during infancy. The ego had its own substrate, consisting of what Hartmann called the primary autonomous functions, including perception, mobility, and memory, which subserved the ego's adaptational aims and arose outside the realm of conflict, in what he termed the conflict-free sphere. These ego apparatuses were preadapted to an average expectable environment the organism was born into. Their development could be traced, and temperamental or inherited variations in ego functions among individuals could be detected. These primary ego functions could be drawn into conflict and serve nonego aims, losing their *autonomy* (independence) from instinctual and environmental demands. Likewise, functions could arise within conflictual settings and over time become *secondarily autonomous* from their conflictual origins, coming to serve ego aims through a *change in function.* For example, the sexual "research" of childhood could become adult curiosity and interest in accumulating knowledge. Many such sublimations are examples of how genetic continuity is consistent with a change of function. Hartmann emphasized that it is a mistake to assume that a current function or meaning can be equated with or reduced to its historical precursors and referred to this common type of error as a *genetic fallacy.*

The ego is defined as a group of mental functions with similar adaptive aims, including a regulatory or coordinating function, an idea further developed by Nunberg,[9] who referred to the synthetic function of the ego. Waelder[10] described, in similar terms, the importance of viewing all ego functions from the perspective of an ego-coordinated interaction of trends within the mind representing all the psychic agencies in their instinctual and inhibiting modes. He referred to this as the principle of multiple function. Hartmann attempted to carry over and further develop Freud's energy proposals, emphasizing especially a more complex conceptualization of aggression alongside of libido in the working of the ego and, in fact, of all the psychic structures.[11] He attempted a parallel or symmetrical theory of libido and aggression, reaching for developmental, even anatomical zonal parallels as well as hypotheses about similar pleasure in discharge of aggressive and libidinal energies. He developed proposals about how aggressive and libidinal energies are taken over by the ego, lose their aggressive and sexual characteristics, become neutralized ego energy in a manner analogous to the way mental activities with instinctual aims could undergo a change in function, become relatively autonomous of their origin, and participate in the ego's adaptive efforts.

Hartmann can be seen here to be attempting a refinement and symmetry between functional and economic principles to preserve Freud's economic point of view about mental forces and energies in coordination with newer ideas about ego structure and function and their development. Hartmann encouraged the development of psychoanalytically informed infant and child observational research to confirm or disconfirm as well as fill in knowledge about hypotheses developed theoretically and from adult clinical work. His collaborative work "Comments on the formation of psychic structure" summarizes many of these developmental hypotheses and clinical observations.[11]

Hartmann recognized that a comprehensive and coherent psychoanalytic theory was of necessity going to be complex, as was the human behavior it was designed to explain. Hartmann attempted to develop psychoanalytic theory to its most systematically complete point. He began with Freud's natural science model of mental functioning, preserving and refining Freud's clinical and theoretical contributions while considerably advancing structural, developmental, and adaptational perspectives. Unfortunately, Hartmann's work, with its uncompromising theoretical vigor and complexity, became the center of theoretical and even clinical orthodoxy within psychoanalysis during the mid-20th century in America. His formidable edifice of elegant and singularly "freudian mainstream" theorizing (it is an interesting sidelight that Hartmann was probably the only analyst to have been a patient of both Breuer and Freud, the former as family physician, the latter as analyst) posed a difficult challenge for analysts wishing to view human behavior from other than a natural science model, for example, a historical, linguistic, or informational model. Whatever the short-term inhibiting consequences of how his work came to be viewed by some, Hartmann's contributions to the development of psychoanalytic theory and practice come right after Freud's own in their power and influence on modern psychoanalytic ways of understanding human behavior.

David Rapaport

David Rapaport's work has been elegantly summarized by Gill and Klein.[12] Like Hartmann, his varied and prolific contributions were devoted to the integration and systematization of psychoanalytic theory; however, his creative legacy went far beyond this. The central organizing theme in all of his work was an unrelenting adherence to the principle of codetermination of drive and environment (reality) in all theoretical formulations. He consistently argued that psychoanalytic observations do not support the view either that behavior is shaped by one's drives alone or, at the other extreme, that environmental experiences (reality relations) can alone explain development and behavior.

Rapaport worked diligently to integrate the contributions of Hartmann and Erikson, which he thought of as complementary and essential. He argued, "The crucial characteristic of this [Erickson's] psychosocial theory of ego development, and of Hartmann's adaptation theory (in contrast to the culturalist theories) is that they offer a conceptual explanation of the individual's social development by tracing the unfolding of the genetically social character of the human individual."[12(p20)]

A dominant theme in Rapaport's work was the exploration of the relatively stable delaying and inhibiting characteristics of the psychic apparatus, and thus the pervasiveness of structure in all mental functioning. His views were consistent with and built on the contributions of Hartmann and his collaborators, Kris and Loewenstein. Rapaport was concerned not only with the so-called macrostructures (id, ego, superego) but also with all levels and forms of structures ranging from ideas and precepts to controls and identifications. He wrote, "Yet in the course of the development of psychological and psychoanalytic knowledge, this discovery [that basic drives are at the heart of all human psychological processes] proved to be only a partial explanation of human behavior. We have learned that no dynamics of forces alone can explain what a human being does. We know from biology and social studies also, that functions, once established, structuralize, i.e., they form steady states which are resistive to change. In psychological life, too, we find such automatized functions, which do not have to be created anew, which behave as structures."[12(p12)]

His primary interest was the nature of thinking, which culminated in his monumental work, *Organization and Pathology of Thought.*[3] He was interested in not only the form and content of thought but also the structure of thinking. His studies ranged from primary models of thinking through creative thinking and the socialization of thought. This work was based on extensive experimentation, particularly on dreams and pathological thought processes. He believed that psychoanalytic theory could provide the most useful conception of the nature and function of consciousness. He believed that consciousness is an organization subserving cognition and that rather than being a unitary phenomenon, there are many varieties of consciousness corresponding to different cognitive organizations. His theoretical and experimental contributions to states of consciousness have yet to be fully explored.

Rapaport was concerned with the absence of a learning theory, which he considered a major gap in psychoanalysis. Here, too, structure was a linchpin underlying his theoretical and experimental explorations. "Whether or not all structure formation (in that broad sense which takes account of the epigenetic-maturational matrix) should be considered learning (i.e., abiding change wrought by experience) is both an empirical and a conceptual problem. But it seems that all learning may be looked upon as a process of structure formation. The processes of verbal learning and habit formation may well be considered subordinate to this broader category, though their study may or may not be revealing of the relationship between process and structure."

Using Hartmann's theory of the ego's autonomy in relation to the id as a starting point, Rapaport provided a complementary theory of the ego's relative autonomy from the environment. Following Hartmann, he insisted that the ego's autonomy is only *relative* and that this is a basic condition of mental health. It is through such relativity that drive structures and reality relatedness can serve as each other's guarantees. Autonomy can be lost to either the drives or the environment. Rapaport showed not only how this can occur but also how autonomy is protected.

Otto Fenichel

Fenichel, like Rapaport, was an extraordinary systematizer, but Fenichel's creative efforts were far more clinically directed. Much of his work can be characterized as a diligent and exhaustive effort at applying structural concepts to psychoanalytic technique and to psychopathology. His "Problems of psychoanalytic technique" remains a classic.[13] He believed that the theory of technique had not been sufficiently developed according to rational criteria, and he set out to rectify the situation. He outlined a theory of psychoanalytic treatment and described the process of interpretation according to dynamic, economic, and structural aspects. His discussion of transference, and special technical problems, reflected his balanced viewpoint and his avoidance of polarized positions. He warned against the dangers of one-sided analysis of either ego or id and against the excessive use of free-floating attention by the analyst, almost to the exclusion of logical activity and scrutiny as a means of guiding the analyst's interventions. He insisted "the subject matter, not the method, of psychoanalysis is irrational."[13(p13)]

In his encyclopedic work, *The Psychoanalytic Theory of Neurosis,* Fenichel[14] presented a comprehensive survey of the analytical literature and a detailed psychoanalytic theory of psychoneurosis informed by structural concepts. The work is a tour de force not written for the nonprofessional; it remains the most extensive and detailed statement on the theory of neurosis, mechanisms of symptom formation, and forms of symptom and character neurosis. This book also represents the best reference source to the psychoanalytic literature up to the time of its publication.

References

1. Freud S: The ego and the id. In Strachey J (trans-ed): The Standard Edition of the Complete Psychological Works of Sigmund Freud, Volume 19. London: Hogarth Press, 1961:1–66. Originally published in 1923.
2. Freud S: Inhibitions, symptoms, and anxiety. In Strachey J (trans-ed): The Standard Edition of the Complete Psychological Works of Sigmund Freud, Volume 20. London: Hogarth Press, 1959:75–176. Originally published in 1926.
3. Rapaport D: Organization and Pathology of Thought. New York: Columbia University Press, 1951.
4. Hartmann H: Ego Psychology and the Problem of Adaptation. New York: International Universities Press, 1939.
5. Freud A: The Ego and the Mechanisms of Defense. New York: International Universities Press, 1946. Originally published in 1936.
6. Kris E: The ego and the mechanisms of defense. A. Freud. [book review] Int J Psychoanal 1938; 19:139.
7. Freud A: Normality and Pathology in Childhood: Assessment of Development. New York: International Universities Press, 1965.
8. Schafer R: An overview of Heinz Hartmann's contributions to psychoanalysis. Int J Psychoanal 1970; 51:425–446.
9. Nunberg H: The synthetic function of the ego. Int J Psychoanal 1931; 12:123–140.
10. Waelder R: The principle of multiple function. Psychoanal Q 1930; 5:45–62.
11. Hartmann H, Kris E, Loewenstein RM: Comments on the formation of psychic structure. Psychol Issues 1946; 4:27–55.
12. Gill M, Klein G: The structuring of drive and reality. In Gill MM (ed): Collected Papers of David Rapaport. New York: Basic Books, 1967; 8–34.
13. Fenichel O: Problems of psychoanalytic technique. Psychoanal Q 1945.
14. Fenichel O: The Psychoanalytic Theory of Neurosis. New York: WW Norton, 1945.

Arnold D. Richards

Modern Structural Theory

This section of psychoanalytic theory was developed primarily by Americans who trained in the late 1940s and early 1950s and were analyzed and supervised, for the most part, by psychoanalytic émigrés from Central Europe. This group of analysts subsequently developed a distinctive theoretical point of view that has come to be referred to as modern structural theory, although modern conflict theory or modern structural-conflict theory might be more suitable designations. Jacob Arlow, David Beres, Charles Brenner, Martin Wangh, and Leo Rangell were the original group who developed this point of view. After they completed their psychoanalytic training, Arlow, Beres, Brenner, and Wangh met and subsequently with their teachers and supervisors (Hartmann, Kris, Lewin, Loewenstein, and others) critically examined the received psychoanalytic wisdom of the time. It was out of this examination, which focused on concepts of anxiety, repression, defense, and symptom formation, that the modern structural viewpoint emerged.

Modern structural theory is an outgrowth of ego psychology as described in the preceding section inasmuch as it devotes "considerable attention to the role, function, and characteristics of the ego."[1] Yet Boesky[2] pointed out that structural theory is not synonymous with ego psychology, because ego psychology admits consideration of the essential interrelatedness of all three mental structures. Beres[3] and Arlow[1] suggested that "id/ego/superego psychology" would be a more appropriate designation of modern structural theory.

Fundamentals of Freud's Structural Theory

Freud's structural theory of 1923, as already noted, proposed the division of mental organization into the psychic "agencies" or "structures" of id, ego, and superego.[4] Freud held that persistent patterns of functioning, repetitive in nature and more or less predictable, could be grouped together as a component structure of the mind. This viewpoint replaced an earlier concept of mental organization that Freud had developed, the topographical theory, in which the mind was "sectioned" into unconscious, preconscious, and conscious layers. What are the three structures, or psychic agencies, that Freud proposed? Persistent wishes from the past, operating as continuous stimuli to the mind and giving rise to innumerable, repetitive, relatively predictable patterns of mental representation collectively constitute the id. It is the vast reservoir of motivation, or motivation dynamic, consisting of sexual and aggressive wishes, self-centered and often antisocial.

Another source of motivation dynamic is the ideal aspirations, the moral and behavioral imperatives, the judgments of right and wrong. Freud called this group of relatively stable mental functions the superego not only because it developed later in the life of the mind than the ego but also because it functioned as an observer and critic, seeming to stand above and beyond the self, passing judgment on it.

The third structural component of the psyche includes those functions that serve to integrate and mediate the aims—at times complementary, at times contradictory—of the other agencies. At the same time, this component takes into account the nature of the objective, realistic situation in which individuals find themselves. Freud designated this agency the ego in recognition of its status as executant for the other agencies of the mind. The ego is the mediator between the internal and external world—between the world of thoughts and feelings on one hand, and the world of perception and objects on the other.

Freud's Structural Model in a Modern Key

Modern structural theory embraces the presuppositions underlying Freud's structural hypothesis: that psychoanalysis is primarily a psychology of conflict. That is to say that psychoanalysis approaches mental life from the standpoint of intrapsychic forces in conflict and the compromises that are the outcomes of such intrapsychic conflict. The concept of compromise formation is essential to this viewpoint because it exemplifies the interrelatedness of the id, ego, and superego and all psychic phenomena.[2] Modern structural theory has progressively refined and amended Freud's hypothesis in the interest of achieving a better theoretical understanding of the meaning of conflict, a fuller appreciation of the range of conflicts and compromise formations, and a more powerful clinical approach to the psychoanalytic treatment of such conflicts.

Initially, this approach led to an espousal of structural concepts as more useful, clinically, than concepts associated with Freud's older topographical model. Even within the realm of Freud's structural model, certain explanatory viewpoints (e.g., the dynamic and the genetic) were given precedence over others (e.g., the economic and the energic). Arlow and Brenner's coauthored book of 1964, *Psychoanalytic Concepts and the Structural Theory,*[5] was an important articulation of this viewpoint. It has been underscored by Boesky,[2] who observed that Freud's concepts of psychic energy are no longer accepted by those who espouse modern structural theory. "These theorists do not, for example, go along with Rapaport's ideas about energy and discharge thresholds linked to transformations of psychic energy and his defining structure in energic terms."[2(p120)]

Along with this selective use of structural concepts was a revisionist trend aimed at loosening the dependency of a psychoanalytic psychology of conflict from Freud's model of the three psychic agencies. Beres[3] gave voice to this trend in an influential paper, "Structure and function in psychoanalysis." He argued that Freud always understood the psychic structures as "functional groups" and that his emphasis was always on issues of organization and process. Believing that theoretical concepts are ways of organizing clinical phenomena, Beres urged analysts to follow the functional direction of Freud's theorizing, an approach that views id, ego, and superego as metaphorical rather than concrete structural entities. Beres pointed out that, in fact, Freud never actually propounded a structural theory. He intended the structural hypothesis to be but one of the several metapsychological viewpoints to be brought to bear on clinical phenomena. In fact, Freud never used the term structure in introducing or amplifying the tripartite model.[2] Beres'[3(p53)] cautionary advice that analysts retain the structural theory while "be[ing] aware of the dangers inherent in overemphasis on structure" has generated a range of theoretical responses.

One set of responses, associated with the work of Arlow and Brenner, has been to dissociate modern structural theory from the metapsychological propositions that Freud imported into *his* structural theory. Arlow[1] was explicit in noting that "while the clinical aspects of the structural theory have an enriching impact on psychoanalysis, the metapsychological propositions that were carried along with it had the opposite effect." He argued for jettisoning economic concepts, such as cathexis and decathexis, that are far removed from clinical observation. The modern structural emphasis on unconscious fantasy as an ego function, an emphasis growing out of an early paper by Beres[6] and an influential body of work by Arlow, is consonant with this trend. Without reverting to Freud's biological or economic concepts, Beres[3] invoked structural theory to define unconscious fantasy in a clinically illuminating way as "the product of the multiple functions of id, ego, and superego. It is modified by id, organized by ego functions, and distorted and repressed by superego demands." Abend[7] underscored that unconscious fantasies are a variety of compromise formation formed out of the loving and hating wishes accompanying affects and defenses against these wishes in the mind of the small child.

Structural Theory Beyond Freud

The progressive loosening of modern structural theory from Freud's formulations of id, ego, and superego has resulted in a more clinically based focus on the components of psychic conflict (drive derivatives, anxiety, depressive affect, defenses, reality, and moral considerations) accompanied by an enlargement of the experiential and dynamic realm of conflict. Thus, modern structural theory can be seen as a kind of systems theory because it stresses the interrelatedness of all psychic structures and the associated behaviors.

These several trends—the jettisoning of Freud's energy concepts, the expansion of the components of conflict, and the adoption of an experience-near clinical language to describe conflict—come together in the work of Brenner, whose contributions of the past four decades chronicle the successive steps in the emergence of modern structural theory as a wide-ranging psychology of conflict and compromise formation. Brenner's *Elementary Text Book of Psychoanalysis*[8] can be viewed as the first overview of this theoretical landscape by a member of this group. His collaborative effort with Arlow, *Psychoanalytic Concepts and the Structural Viewpoint,*[5] endorsed Freud's structural model at the expense of the topographical model while deemphasizing the role of economic concepts within structural theory proper. Then, in a series of papers in the 1970s and leading to the publication of *The Mind in Conflict,* Brenner proceeded to a substantive revision of Freud's structural theory.[9–12] He not only argued against the extraanalytical (i.e., biological) presuppositions that Freud imported to the structural model but also called into question the theoretical soundness of Freud's definitions of the three psychic structures.

These revisions, taken together, constitute a new language for structural theory. As early as 1971, Brenner argued against the broad, biological meaning Freud imputed to the drives. He defended Freud's theory of the aggressive drive, which derived from "the accumulation of psychoanalytic evidence," but not his theory of a biological death instinct. He went on to redefine the drives as "generalizations" about two classes of "wishes" corresponding to two types of motivation. The language of drives, thus, was replaced by a language of wishes—wishes as uniquely individual drive derivatives. Brenner did not see the id, Freud's repository of the drive, as being as constitutionally determined from the beginning of life and as relatively independent of experience as Freud did. Drawing on the available psychoanalytic evidence, he stressed that from birth, drive-related activities, whether libidinal or aggressive, are influenced by experiential factors that gain expression in ego development. Because clinical analysis could not support the idea that ego development is separate from drive expression and drive gratification, it followed for Brenner that a sharp distinction between ego and id, even a sharp "heuristic" distinction, could not be maintained. Furthermore, what psychoanalytic theory included under the notion of ego functions is distinguishable from drive, and drive derivatives, only in situations of conflict. Ego functions are the executants of drives and therefore come into opposition to drives only when drive derivatives evoke unpleasure and defense. Thus, conflict is the sine qua non of structural theory. In a paper of 1971, "Some problems in the psychoanalytic theory of instinctual drives," he supported this point by appealing to Anna Freud, who held that "in the absence of conflict, there is no division among the mental agencies, or in other words, no id, ego or superego."[10]

In stressing the role of the ego in drive gratification from the beginning of life, Brenner was implicitly parting company with Freud, who was content to locate repressed wishes first in the unconscious, or the topographical model, and ultimately in the "id of the structural model."

In the elementary textbook, Brenner[7] had accepted the traditional view of the superego as one agency of the psychic apparatus. In articles published during the next two decades (1959 to 1982), he significantly enlarged our appreciation of this mental agency by drawing attention to the role of both masochism and libidinal gratification in superego formation. In *The Mind in Conflict,* Brenner[12] radically redefined the superego, construing it to be a compromise formation functionally analogous to other compromise formations revealed by psychoanalytic investigation: neurotic symptoms, dreams, delusions, character traits, and so forth. He continued to stress that the superego was a structure that entered into psychic conflict along with id and ego. However, insofar as id and ego were presumably *not* compromise formations, Brenner's formulation of 1982 appeared to forgo the symmetry of the three intrapsychic agencies of Freud's structural theory.

Structural Affect Theory

Among modern structural-conflict theorists, Charles Brenner and Leo Rangell have taken the lead in showing how affect theory helps us to define the unique constellation of conflicts presented by each analysand. Their dialogue of several decades in the literature demonstrates both the basic assumptions of modern structural-conflict theory and the divergence of viewpoint of some of its leading proponents. As early as 1953, Brenner[13] began to set out a position at issue with Freud's theories of actual and traumatic neurosis. He argued that the anxiety associated with traumatic states derives from the conflicts evoked by the traumatic situation, rather than a "rupture of the stimulus barrier that is from the sexually quantitative variations in psychic energy or excitation."[13(p21)] Brenner likewise disputed the belief, long held by Freud and most analysts, that anxiety as a differentiated affect could be experienced from birth or early infancy. Brenner differentiated between the infant's reaction to danger and the child's (and adult's) experience of anxiety on the basis of the maturation of ego functions. In the relative absence of these functions, the traumatically distressed infant could be said to experience an "extreme unpleasure" that was the anlagen of later experiences of anxiety as well as of depression; the capacity to be anxious or depressed in a dangerous situation, on the other hand, was a developmental achievement in the sense that these specific affects presupposed not only pleasurable or unpleasurable sensations but specific ideational content associated with such sensations.

Affects, then, originated early in life, when ideas first became linked to sensations of pleasure and unpleasure. According to this formulation, the development of affects and their differentiation from one another went hand in hand with the subsequent development of ego and superego.

Rangell,[14] although endorsing the essential role of affects in the psychoanalytic process, has presented a unitary theory of anxiety that contrasts with Brenner's point of view. According to Rangell, Brenner limited anxiety to signal anxiety, believing as he did that anxiety occurs only when there is an ego able to anticipate danger. Rangell, on the other hand, argued that anxiety, as a reaction to existing traumatic states, includes both the early involuntary reactions and later signal reactions experimentally brought about by the ego. Rangell, in fact, stressed the interdependence of the two types of anxiety reaction; traumatic states, he reminded us, invariably precede signal anxiety. Further, what Brenner understood as infantile unpleasure, which lacks the ideational component of anxiety, Rangell saw as an anxious state of psychic helplessness that may already possess psychological meaning. In the "Psychoanalytic theory of affects" (1918), Rangell[15] disputed Brenner's theory of ideation within the very concept of affect. For Rangell, ideation and affect represented "separate derivatives of instinctual drives as modified and influenced by ego and superego activity."

Brenner's differentiation between anxiety and depression, the two principal categories of emotion, demonstrates the clinical utility of this modern structural approach to affect. For Brenner, time made the difference: anxiety concerns something bad that will happen in the future, depression something bad that has already happened. Following from his clinical sensitivity to the link of negative affect to both past and future events, Brenner[11] introduced the term *calamity* to replace Freud's concept of "danger" and "danger situations." Calamity, he argued, connotes bad experiences that either are impending or have already happened. It therefore can refer to either anxiety or depressive affects. Danger, in contrast, has primarily a future orientation and is less connected with the idea of past events or circumstances that are associated specifically with depressive affect. Thus, the major situations of classical theory, loss of object, loss of the object's love, and castration anxiety, were recast as the three calamities of childhood.

Here again, Rangell offered a thoughtful critique of Brenner's viewpoint. Referring to the claim that depressive affect is on a par with anxiety as a cause of defense, Rangell asserted that for him, anxiety "occupies a superordinate position since in contrast to any of the other affects anxiety is never absent in the intrapsychic sequence of events prior to the institution of defensive activity."[16(p18)] Issues of conceptual superordinacy notwithstanding, Brenner's theory of affect has been especially useful in bringing pathology within the orbit of modern conflict psychology. By situating the anlagen of depression in amorphous unpleasure of early life, he showed how adult depression, no less than adult anxiety, yields to analytical unraveling with respect to its essential structure and meaning. Like symptoms of anxiety, depressive symptoms are crystallizations of complex affect, that is, compromise formations issuing from the various wishes, fears, defenses, self-punitive trends, and environmental pressures brought to bear at a given point in time. Whether or not patients are consciously aware of being depressed, the affect of a depressive patient has the same complex structure as does any other fantasy, thought, action, or symptom.[12]

Brenner's theoretical formulations on affect culminated in the therapeutic precepts set forth in *The Mind in Conflict.*[12] There, he enjoined his colleagues to view unpleasurable affect as a symptom masking unsatisfactory compromise formation and to proceed with the work of analysis by looking for the cause of the particular genre of unpleasure that gains expression in symptom.

In agreement with Schafer,[17] Brenner[12] noted that it is misleading to consider defense only in terms of specific mechanisms. Brenner's position was that any mental content or ego function can be used for defense, defined here as a process that is in the service of a reduction of unpleasure. Apfelbaum and Gill[18] stressed that a given mental function can alternate as defense or wish and that defenses may operate synergistically rather than separately. Building on the work of Schafer, Brenner, and Apfelbaum and Gill, Inderbitzin and Levy[19] have elaborated the specific uses of external reality as defense.

Rangell has located his ideas about anxiety in a broad conceptualization of "the unconscious intrapsychic process," which includes the signal theory of anxiety, thoughts as trial action, choice conflicts in addition to the conventional oppositional type of intrapsychic conflicts, and an unconscious decision-making function located in the ego. This introduces an active dimension of "executive functions of the ego" to unconscious human functioning. Unconscious choice is executed and fashioned throughout the intrapsychic process by unconscious ego will. Rangell stressed that no matter how much is known of previous individual history and patterning, final psychic outcome cannot be predicted. Psychic determinism, introduced by psychoanalysis, is relative. This view is additive and reciprocal to Hartmann's and Rapaport's concepts of relative autonomy. Above determinism, there is a distinctly individual uncertainty and unpredictability. With the degree of freedom that accompanies relative autonomy comes responsibility and accountability. This incorporates a moral dimension into psychoanalytic theory.

Rangell's approach of adding new findings while retaining valid discoveries that preceded them, what he referred to as "total composite psychoanalytic theory," is characteristic of all the modern conflict structuralists' approach to theory building and advance.

Conclusion

As the foregoing summary tries to make clear, modern structural theory is continuously evolving. Within the spectrum of psychoanalytic theories, it puts forward an evolutionary as opposed to a revolutionary viewpoint, because it takes Freud's conflict psychology, his depiction of the human psyche as the locus of dynamic forces in conflict, as a conceptually and clinically adequate perspective. To be sure, it is a perspective subject to ongoing emendation, refinement, and expansion, as the work of Arlow, Brenner, Rangell,[16] and others demonstrates. It is noteworthy that Brenner,[20] in his most recent writings, had dispensed entirely with Freud's structural model of id, ego, and superego in expounding conflict and compromise formation. Arlow, for his part, has long argued against the clinical-explanatory importance of a structural model with reified psychic agencies: "Id, ego, and superego," he has remarked, "exist not in the patient but in psychoanalytic textbooks" (personal communication, 1991). Yet, other prominent structuralists continue to believe that Freud's structural model remains the most illuminating and clinically useful way to understand these same concepts. Clearly, there is no "last word" in modern structural theory, and future decades will witness continuing growth in our understanding of, and clinical approaches to, "the mind in conflict."[21]

References

1. Arlow J: Conflict, regression, and symptom formation. Int J Psychoanal 1963; 44:12–22.
2. Boesky D: The concept of psychic structure. J Am Psychoanal Assoc 1988; 365(suppl):113–135.
3. Beres D: Structure and function in psychoanalysis. Int J Psychoanal 1965; 46:53–63.
4. Freud S: The ego and the id. In Strachey J (trans-ed): The Standard Edition of the Complete Psychological Works of Sigmund Freud, Volume 19. London: Hogarth Press, 1961:3–66. Originally published in 1923.
5. Arlow J, Brenner C: Psychoanalytic Concepts and the Structural Theory. New York: International Universities Press, 1964.
6. Beres D: The unconscious fantasy. Psychoanal Q 1962; 31:309–328.
7. Abend S: Unconscious fantasies, structural theory, compromise formation. J Am Psychoanal Assoc 1990; 38:61–73.
8. Brenner C: An Elementary Text Book of Psychoanalysis. New York: International Universities Press, 1954.
9. Brenner C: The psychodynamic concept of aggression. Int J Psychoanal 1971; 52:137–144.
10. Brenner C: Some problems in psychoanalytic theory of the instinctual drives. In Marcus IM (ed): Currents in Psychoanalysis. New York: International Universities Press, 1971:216–223.
11. Brenner C: Depressive affect, anxiety and psychic conflict in the phallic-oedipal phase. Psychoanal Q 1979; 43:177–197.
12. Brenner C: The Mind in Conflict. New York: International Universities Press, 1982.
13. Brenner C: An addendum to Freud's theory of anxiety. Int J Psychoanal 1953; 34:18–24.
14. Rangell L: On the psychodynamic theory of anxiety. J Am Psychoanal Assoc 1955; 7:632–662.
15. Rangell, L: A further attempt to resolve the problem of anxiety. 1968; J Am Psychoanal Assoc 16:371–404.
16. Rangell L: The Human Core. Madison, CT: International Universities Press, 1990.
17. Schafer R: Aspects of Internalization. New York: International Universities Press, 1968.
18. Apfelbaum B, Gill MM: Ego analysis and the relativity of defense: Technical implications of the structural theory. J Am Psychoanal Assoc 1989; 37:1071–1096.
19. Inderbitzin L, Levy S: On grist for the mill: External reality as a defense. J Am Psychoanal Assoc 1994; 42:763–778.
20. Brenner C: The mind as conflict and compromise formation. J Clin Psychoanal 1994; 3:473–478.
21. Richards A: Psychoanalysis, the Science of Mental Conflict: Essays in Honor of Charles Brenner. Hillsdale, NJ: Analytic Press, 1986.

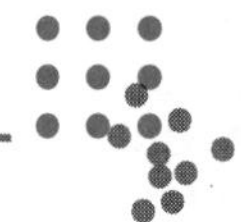

Beth Seelig
Sybil A. Ginsburg

Object Relations Theory

There is no unitary theory of object relations; rather, it is a variety of theories that differ from each other in important ways and are often contradictory. For some theorists, object relations refers primarily to interpersonal relations; others emphasize that the concept refers not to external interpersonal relationships but to specific intrapsychic structures. In this latter sense, object relations theory can be defined as "a system of psychological explanation based on the premise that the mind is comprised of elements taken in from outside, primarily aspects of the functioning of other persons. This occurs by means of the processes of internalization. This model of the mind explains mental functions in terms of relations between the various elements internalized."[1] The concept of an inner world inhabited by mental representations of the self and of objects is central to all object relations theories. This inner world is constructed by the individual through the more or less successful integration of the internalized representations of real significant external figures with whom the subject has interacted. In Schafer's terms, "Internalization refers to all those processes by which the subject transforms real or imagined regulatory interactions with his environment, and real or imagined characteristics of his environment, into inner regulations and characteristics."[2(p9)] It is the internalized mental representations of self and objects that influence external interpersonal relations.

Most object relations theorists have worked with patients who suffered from severe, frequently psychotic, psychopathological conditions. Finding previous theories insufficient to conceptualize or treat these disorders, they have searched for new ways in which their patients could be understood. Although all acknowledge their debt to Freud as the originator of the psychoanalytic theory of the mind, object relations theorists were dissatisfied with Freud's psychoanalytic libido theory, which stressed that the motivational force of human beings to relate to others results from internal drives for need gratification.

The term *object* occurred in Freud's writings as early as 1905, and he defined the object of an instinct in 1915 as "the thing in regard to which or through which the instinct is able to achieve its aim."[3] According to libido theory, the object is the creation of the drives. Where there is no inner tension, the *pleasure principle* reigns, and there is simply a state of quiescence (as with the satiated infant falling asleep at the breast). The prototype for the earliest object relationship is the suckling infant, in whom hunger causes buildup of tension, which is discharged during nursing. The breast is the original object, which gradually becomes associated with need satisfaction in the first few weeks of life. Freud's choice of the term object, which he used to describe the significant other in human relationships, demonstrates the influence of the mechanistic approach that was guiding his conceptualization. (Freud's libido theory is more fully discussed in an earlier section of this chapter.)

His libido theory was criticized for its disregard of the person as a social animal in conjunction with a growing recognition that the existence and quality of our relationships with others determine our adaptations from infancy onward. Freud's struggle to incorporate object relations can be traced in a series of papers culminating in Beyond the Pleasure Principle in 1920.[3–6]

The attempt to reconcile and integrate the role of the object in the internal world with drive theory was continued by ego psychologists, especially Hartmann (see previous section), as well as some object relations theorists (Klein, Mahler, Kernberg, and others). This represents one major trend in the development of object relations theory. In contrast, others such as Fairbairn, Sullivan, and more recently Mitchell view drive theory and object relations models as incompatible and favor discarding drive theory. These two different strategies for dealing with object relations provide an orienting framework for understanding the complexities of the various object relation theories we present. However, the reader must also be alerted to the important differences in theory that exist among various contributors within each of these strategies (e.g., Klein versus Hartmann, Greenberg versus Mitchell).

Melanie Klein

Melanie Klein was a student of Freud. She lived in England and was a contemporary of Anna Freud. Klein and Anna Freud diverged in their work, and each became the leader of a group of psychoanalysts in England. Klein's branch of psychoanalysis became called the kleinian school. Anna Freud was the leader of the ego psychologists. Melanie Klein has been called the first object relations theorist. A third school of psychoanalysis also developed in England that was theoretically between the ego psychologist followers of Anna Freud and the kleinians: the British Middle School. It included Winnicott, Fairbairn, Guntrip, and Balint, whose ideas are presented later.

Klein's theoretical formulations grew out of her observations of the psychotic children she treated. Although some of her controversial ideas have never gained acceptance in mainstream American psychoanalytic thought, her formulations about the importance of aggression and envy, particularly in the understanding of more primitively organized patients, as well as her understanding of primitive defensive operations, have been central in the thinking of later object relations theorists.

Klein believed that fantasy exists from the beginning of life and is by definition the mental expression of the instincts. She conceptualized the neonate as having an active inner world of fantasy based on its innate libidinal and aggressive drives and their aims. The death instinct is central to Klein's theories. It finds its expression in earliest infancy in aggression against the object and the self.

Klein modified Freud's theories of psychological development drastically. As mentioned, she focused predominantly on infancy, describing two psychological "positions" during the first year of life (which was for Freud the oral stage of development). These are the paranoid-schizoid position (Table 19–11) during the first 6 months of life and the depressive position during the second 6 months. The paranoid-schizoid position is characterized by the defenses of projection, introjection, projective identification, splitting, idealization, omnipotence, and denial.[7]

Table 19–11 Characteristic Defenses of Paranoid-Schizoid Position
Projection
Introjection
Projective identification
Splitting
Idealization
Omnipotence
Denial

These defenses are termed primitive defenses because they have their origin in early development, in contrast to the higher level defenses that evolve later. *Projection* is the defensive externalization of a threatening internal impulse, idea, or feeling. Because this is the predominant defense of earliest infancy, the young infant believes that the dangerous impulse, idea, or feeling, which actually originated from within as a manifestation of its own intense drives, is coming from an external source. Therefore, the feared threat is perceived as external rather than internal. This results in anxiety about being attacked from without, termed paranoid anxiety. *Introjection* takes place when an external object is taken inside (in fantasy, of course) and becomes part of the internal rather than the external world. The paranoid position is characterized by projection and introjection taking place in cycles. *Projective identification,* as conceptualized by Klein, is a complicated primitive defense that involves the projection of an internal object (usually a bad one) into an external object, followed by identification with the external object that is now experienced by the infant as having been contaminated by the bad object. *Splitting* is the intrapsychic separation of the object into different partial objects. Typically, an unrealistically all-good (idealized) object and an equally unrealistically all-bad object are constructed. For Klein, the innate aggressive drive of the infant is central and the paranoid-schizoid position is viewed as a "normal" early psychosis from which the infant gradually emerges. In the course of normal development, in the presence of adequate parenting that provides the consistent availability of predominantly benign external objects, the cycle of projection and introjection gradually results in the introjection of more benign aspects of the external object (parent or other caretaker), and the bad internal object is gradually detoxified.

In the depressive position, infants, who have now developed the capacity to accept the existence of an external good object (for example, the nurturing breast of mother), are for the first time "grateful" to caretakers. However, this too presents a problem, for the infants now fear that their attacks on the giving object (which in the paranoid position they had felt justified in making) will damage the good object. This leads to infants' making efforts to repair the damage as well as to the emergence of self-directed aggression (guilt). Just as paranoid anxiety was central during the paranoid-schizoid position, depressive anxiety takes center stage during the depressive position. Infants now fear that their aggression will destroy those they love and result in the loss of caretakers. The depressive anxiety is defended against by denial and by a fantasy of being omnipotently able to restore the (idealized) good object. This is the "manic defense," for Klein a normal part of the depressive position in the second 6 months of life.[8]

Klein's conceptualization of the primitive defensive operations and the important role of destructive envy and of aggression in the psychopathological processes of borderline and psychotic states has proved to be of great clinical and theoretical utility to later nonkleinian object relations–oriented psychoanalysts. However, few now accept her ideas about universal early infantile paranoid-schizoid and depressive positions. In addition, her efforts to telescope the Oedipus complex into the first year of life have not generally been found to be useful and are not discussed in this section.

The British Middle School

The theorists who are considered to be part of this group include Donald W. Winnicott, Michael Balint, W. R. D. Fairbairn, and Harry Guntrip. All were born in the 1890s and died in their early 70s. Guntrip was analyzed first by Winnicott and later by Fairbairn. Fairbairn's publications and lectures were sparse, but Guntrip wrote extensively about his second analyst's theories; he elaborated and amended them, mostly with Fairbairn's approval. J. D. Sutherland has compared and contrasted the work of the British Middle School.[9]

Donald W. Winnicott

Donald W. Winnicott was both a practicing pediatrician and a psychoanalyst for most of his professional life. He worked with many categories of patients—including regressed adults, disturbed and delinquent adolescents, and problem children—and treated mother–infant-toddler pairs. Working with such a diverse population of patients, he experienced the deficiencies of both the libido and the structural theories. The libido theory focuses on drives and anergic concepts; the structural theory concentrates on oedipal development and, in Freud's formulation, places the "narcissistic neuroses" (i.e., the psychoses) in a separate group without a framework for treatment. Although he found the existing theories to be a problem, Winnicott attempted to fit his ideas within them. He handled his disagreement with Freud's ideas by reinterpreting them to meet his need to deal with highly disturbed early relationships. For example, he reworked the Oedipus complex to emphasize Klein's conflict between love and hate, rather than Freud's conflict between instinctual desires and fear of castration. (Winnicott acknowledged a debt to Klein, in particular with reference to the depressive position.) Another way in which Winnicott reinterpreted freudian theory was to focus on the central function of an early maternal "holding environment." This primacy of early bonding contradicted Freud's concept of "primary narcissism," which stated that the infant is at first not oriented toward others and that relationships become important only later, secondarily to drive frustration. Winnicott simply changed Freud's meaning and said that what he *really* meant by primary narcissism was the state of early dependence on the mother. Winnicott frequently presented his papers only as lectures. He was a gifted teacher as well as physician. His editors, particularly Masud Kahn, organized his work into collected volumes of papers.[10]

Every individual, according to Winnicott, develops *true* and *false selves.* Insofar as the mother is empathically tuned in to her child, without intruding on the child, there is a core of feeling of wholeness and goodness from which the true self develops. With appropriate "mirroring," the child learns to play, to be creative, and to be alone with comfort. Those developmental achievements *create* the *fundamental organizer,* the true self (at times also called the *ego* by Winnicott). However, insofar as there is a mismatch in the relationship, the child's development is stunted, and the child develops a false self. In healthy people, the false self is relatively minimal. It is represented by politeness and social manners; however, in extreme states of illness, it may be the main self-representation. The genesis of such a severe pathological process is based on the seduction of the infant into complying with the imposed demands of the unempathic mother. The infant then develops false relationships; the child learns to live by imitating, becomes less spontaneous and creative, and is unable to play. A lifelong feeling of unreality and futility results. One positive function of the false self is that it protects the nascent true self from a damaging environment.[11(pp140–152)] Therapy of individuals with a dominant false self begins with accepting that self, and it proceeds through periods of negative transference and great dependence toward a more full development and expression of the (previously hidden) true self.

Winnicott regarded psychoneuroses as grouped around defenses (especially repression), in contrast with psychoses, which result from annihilation anxiety and the breakdown of defenses. He believed that the breakdown has its roots in the original breakdown of "good enough" mothering and a consequent inadequate development of the true self. Winnicott maintained that the psychoses are analyzable and that there is a gradation from normality through psychoneuroses and psychopathy to psychosis.[11(pp124–139)] However, psychotic patients *do* bring particular transference and countertransference problems to the analysis. Because psychotic patients evoke annihilation anxiety in the analyst, countertransference hate is inevitable and is difficult to cope with, despite such compensations as being paid and being able to end the hour. These patients answer love by evoking hate; this is really a test to see whether the analyst can hate them "objectively." The task of the analyst is to keep the hate latent, as the mother must when the infant frustrates her, until the patient has become healthier through the analytical process. The analyst must then tell the patient about the way the hatred had been evoked and how the analyst held it in abeyance until the patient was stronger.[12(pp194–203)]

Winnicott's *transitional object* is a concrete real external object (unlike the intrapsychic objects that we have being discussing). It is the infant's first "not me" possession and is imbued with attributes of both mother and infant. The transitional object evolves out of activities occurring in the "space" between infant and mother. These activities generally have close links to the mouth or the mother's body. For example, the child may at first put a fist or thumb in the mouth or stroke the corner of a blanket. The blanket gradually becomes special and essential to the child (the familiar security blanket). A stuffed toy such as a teddy bear or even a hard toy may become a transitional object. This process is based on the facilitating, appropriate response of the mother. The blanket may become smelly, yet it must not be washed; and the teddy bear may become tattered, yet it must accompany the toddler everywhere. The evolution of the transitional object is the precursor of the child's ability to play. As an intermediary object, the transitional object also serves as a precursor of the ability to be alone. There is wide variation as to when the transitional object develops, but it frequently evolves from about 4 to 12 months.[13]

Michael Balint

Michael Balint must be discussed in conjunction with Sandor Ferenczi, his analyst and mentor. Ferenczi's attempts to analyze severely traumatized individuals and his unorthodox practices profoundly affected Balint's theoretical views and their reception in the analytical community from the 1930s through the 1970s. Before Ferenczi's death in 1933, Freud had distanced himself from his former disciple for transgressing the boundaries of analytical neutrality and confidentiality with experiments such as "mutual analysis." Balint agreed that some of Ferenczi's practices toward the end of his career were unacceptable. However, Balint pointed out that Ferenczi had made important contributions toward an understanding of the nature of regression and in the recognition and treatment of adults who had been physically and sexually traumatized in childhood. An overreaction on the part of the strictly freudian classical psychoanalytic community took place, and Ferenczi's contributions were "repressed" for decades.[14, 15] Indeed, Balint's own ideas, many of which were based on Ferenczi's, were also suspect as being "fringe."

Balint adhered to the general principles of the economic (libido) theory and of the structural (ego) theory. He did not formulate any complete theoretical framework of his own. However, his emphasis on the dyadic nature of the analytical relationship, his idea of a *basic fault,* his discussion of *benign* and *malignant regression,* and his proposals concerning analytical technique foreshadow current object relational and deficit theories. For example, his conceptualization that a critical primary developmental phase must be surmounted for an individual to be able to have effective object relationships reverberates within the developmental theory of Mahler. His idea that patients with a basic fault have deficient development, lack structure, and tend to feel empty and dead is reminiscent of Kohut.[16]

For patients suffering from a basic fault, Balint believed a departure from classical technique to be necessary to provide an atmosphere in which they may grow and feel understood. Benign regression is viewed as a useful and even necessary stage of such analyses. Balint proposed that at certain critical moments in treatment, after the analyst had established himself or herself as a trustworthy, new object and when regressive tension is at its height, the analyst must accept and sometimes facilitate moments of acting out on the part of the patient. This acting out will provide a *new beginning* after which analytical progress, as measured by structural development and successful adult relationships, will occur. The crucial factor is the establishment and testing of a new primary object relationship in the therapeutic setting, rather than the acting out. Benign regression is "aimed at recognition" (of the patient by the analyst), as opposed to malignant regression, which is "aimed at gratification" (again of the patient by the analyst). In the malignant form, the demand for gratification is pressing, is never ending, and has an addictive quality. Rather than a yearning that occurs *within* the patient in the context of a dyadic analytical relationship, an individual who develops a malignant regression craves and actually demands the *participation* of the analyst. Balint stated that the acting out in benign regression is not part of the compulsion to repeat, because it is a new, never previously performed act.[14]

W. R. D. Fairbairn

In his preface to a collection of Fairbairn's papers, Ernest Jones (a disciple and biographer of Freud) stated, "Instead of starting where Freud did, from the stimulation of the nervous system . . . from erotogenic zones . . . Dr. Fairbairn starts from the center of the personality, the ego, and depicts . . . its endeavor to reach an object where it may find support."[17(pv)]

W. R. D. Fairbairn was uncomfortable with libido theory's emphasis on the drive to obtain pleasure as well as with the tenets of scientific materialism. Both were at odds with his early training in philosophy and theology. Because he lived in Edinburgh, he was geographically separated from contact with analytical colleagues. Fairbairn formulated his unique theoretical framework stressing the importance of parents' imparting to the infant a sense of being a valued human being.[9] He called the ego a *primary unity,* which he believed to be present in *pristine* form from the earliest weeks of life. With the proper nurturing, the infant, who relates to others innately, as do animals (i.e., is object seeking from the start), develops into a healthy human being capable of achieving intimacy with others. Although Fairbairn used the terminology of drive theory, and credited Melanie Klein, he defined the terms in his own way.[10(pp151–187)] For example, he stated that the libido is *object* seeking, not *pleasure* seeking.[17(pp28–58)] He did not view pleasure as an end in itself. Rather, for Fairbairn, the erogenous zones were of importance secondarily as pathways to relationships with others.

Focusing on the early oral phase of development, Fairbairn described the earliest object relationship as being with the mother's breast. If the infant is subjected to unsatisfactory nurturing, this will result in an excess of oral sadism, which in turn results in the infant's fearing that she or he will destroy the libidinal object (mother). This anxiety about the infant's own destructive potential sets the stage for a libidinal fixation in this stage. A *schizoid tendency* results, and the individual treats others as *partial objects* rather than as people with inherent value.[17(pp3–27)]

In the ideal situation, there would be no split in the ego. Realistically, there is always some. To the extent that the imparting of a sense of self-worth is lacking in the earliest mother-child relationship, the infant compensates by building up a separate inner world. The original ego is split into three parts: 1) The *central* (conscious) *ego* is also called the *self* and is attached to the ideal object (ego ideal). 2) A repressed *libidinal* (needy) *ego* is attached to the exciting (or libidinal) object. 3) A repressed *antilibidinal* (rejecting) *ego* is attached to the rejecting object. This third ego is hostile toward the second and reinforces its repression by the central ego.[18] The degree and nature of the split determine the pathological process. Because pleasure is not an end in itself, the oedipal conflict is not primary. Rather, the extent and type of the divided self determine the existence as well as the outcome of the oedipal conflict. The needy, libidinal self is expressed during that developmental phase by sexual attachment to the exciting object, usually to the parent of the opposite sex. In general, hedonism represents a breakdown of the mother-child bond, such that emotional longings are perceived as sexual.

According to Fairbairn, aggression is a reaction to frustration and not a primary drive. He did not believe that there is a death instinct; rather, destructive tendencies are expressions of a sadomasochistic relationship with internalized bad objects.[17(pp59–81)] According to Fairbairn, human civilization predisposes toward a breakdown in the prolonged, intimate maternal-infant bonding seen in other higher animals. When the mother is unavailable to satisfy the young infant, the infant's anxiety becomes intense; it is this separation anxiety that precipitates the splitting of the unitary ego. Hence, infantile dependence is a core issue, and development requires stage-appropriate separation from the primary object. Healthy adulthood requires *mature dependence,* which involves giving as well as taking. The goal of psychotherapy is to elucidate and repair the splits in the unitary (central) self (ego), so that it may succeed in the task of forming adaptive relationships to others. Resistance to therapy occurs because of an attachment of the divided self to disparate bad objects (i.e., one subself is attached to a forbidden object, and another to a rejecting object).

Harry Guntrip

Harry Guntrip was a minister and a pastoral counselor who had analyses first with Winnicott and later with Fairbairn. He was disturbed by aspects of Freud's instinct theory that seemed to him to be mechanistic and amoral. Guntrip believed the emphasis of any psychology should be on social and interpersonal relationships. Freud's pessimistic view of a human nature that innately seeks only gratification, is "hostile to good personal relationships," and is "socialized only under very heavy pressure"[19(p79)] was anathema to Guntrip's "moral standpoint."[20(p9)] Widely read and erudite, and with an interest in the historical development of psychodynamic theories, Guntrip also believed that the theories could be studied scientifically. He reviewed, compared, and contrasted the contributions of numerous other workers. In addition to Klein, Fairbairn, and Winnicott, he included Harry Stack Sullivan, Alfred Adler, Karen Horney, Erich Fromm, and others. He discussed the relationships of both Klein (whom he credited with providing the first major challenge to Freud) and Fairbairn to Freud and to one another, and to some extent to Winnicott.[19(pp161–348)]

For Guntrip, the crucial issue was to "stay born." He theorized that all psychopathological processes originate in the earliest years of life as a result of inadequate mothering. He modified Fairbairn's concept of the split, weakened ego to include regressive withdrawal from *internal* as well as *external* objects (see section on Fairbairn). The regressed individual has to cope with a sense of deadness. The struggle to feel alive and connected was termed the *schizoid problem* by Guntrip and was central to his theory. Fairbairn approved Guntrip's modification of his own theory to include this hypothesis that a pathological process results in a split in the *libidinal self* such that one part regresses to a *schizoid position* and seeks a state of safety, as would be found only in the womb. The dead feeling associated with this totally regressed state brings with it a terrifying anxiety about dissolution of the self. In a desperate attempt to keep the self in existence, the suffering individual defensively revitalizes the negative internal objects. However, the individual is now left with *antilibidinal self-persecution.*[20(pp168–213)] Psychotherapy must help patients cope with the anxiety. The therapist is viewed as a nurturing figure who coaxes the helpless patient back to an investment in life and to a renewed hope for positive external relationships and consequent achievement of some internal equilibrium.

Guntrip's difficult personal history may shed some light on the polarity of his theory, in which the patient is seen as a victim who is continually fighting a sense of isolation and hopelessness. His mother did not want children and was overtly rejecting. At age 3.5 years, Harry Guntrip discovered his infant brother dead in his mother's lap. Subsequently, he was sent to live with an aunt, away from this mother who "was unable to support life."[20(p217)]

John Bowlby

John Bowlby's work has been widely read not only in the psychoanalytic community but also among anthropologists, ethologists, public health advocates, and the general public. An analyst who was analyzed by Joan Reviere and supervised by Melanie Klein, Bowlby began his study of the attachment of children to their caregivers in the late 1940s. His work was contemporaneous with that of Spitz, who observed the profound depression produced in infants who were deprived of human contact.[21] He came to differ with Spitz in his interpretation of the meaning of the observations, but the actual observations are highly consistent with each other. Bowlby collaborated initially with James Robertson in his naturalistic observations of young children who are separated from their mothers (much more briefly than the anaclitically depressed infants observed by Spitz) because of the mother's hospitalization.[22] The observations clearly confirmed that separation produced extreme distress in children and that there were significant long-term adverse effects on the children as a result of even relatively brief separations. These initial observations, combined with the fact that there was at the time no adequate theoretical framework for understanding the profound effects of separation, led Bowlby to research and formulate theories about attachment, separation reactions, related anxiety, depression, and psychopathological processes originating in disturbances in attachment. His observations as well as those of others, including observations of both humans and animals, and Bowlby's theoretical formulations are set forth in a three-volume work, *Attachment and Loss.*[23]

Bowlby's major thesis was that the child's tie (attachment) to the object, for which he preferred the term attachment-figure, is primary and instinctive (in the sense of instincts shared by humans and animals rather than in Freud's sense of instinctual drives). This attachment is *not* secondary to the gratification of any drive. It is independent of the need for food and warmth and of any other striving. He strongly opposed the theoretical position that there is *ever* an early objectless state. Bowlby buttressed his argument with observations of nonhuman primates. He made the point that human infants are born in such a helpless state that the majority of the observable early attachment behavior must be on the part of the mother, whereas in some other primates, the baby is able to cling from the time it is born. In all primates, great distress is observed when mother and baby are separated, and the effects of separation are long lasting, producing visible anxiety and a marked increase in clinging at ages when the clinging is decreasing in unseparated animals. He referred to the work of Harlow and colleagues,[24] whose experimental work on maternal deprivation in monkeys is now considered classic. Harlow's observations supported Bowlby's thesis that there is a primary need for clinging and contact. His motherless monkeys strongly preferred to cling to a soft cloth dummy mother that provided no nourishment than to a hard wire dummy mother that was equipped with a bottle of milk. In addition, monkeys raised without their mothers were highly abnormal in interaction with other monkeys later in life, despite the fact that their needs of nourishment, shelter, and warmth had been met.

Bowlby went on to extend his observations of attachment behaviors and responses to separation across various cultures, citing anthropological observations. "No form of behavior is accompanied by stronger feeling than is attachment behavior. The figures towards whom it is directed are loved and their advent is greeted with joy. So long as a child is in the unchallenged presence of a principal attachment-figure, or within easy reach, he feels secure. A threat of loss creates anxiety, and actual loss sorrow: both, moreover, are likely to arouse anger."[23(p209)] For Bowlby, the unpleasurable affects of anxiety, grief, and anger were *secondary* to the thwarting of attachment. His theoretical position, therefore, was harmonious to a great extent with that of Winnicott, Fairbairn, and Guntrip.

Edith Jacobson

Edith Jacobson's contributions to the development of object relations theory grew out of her interest in the development of affects and the treatment of affective disorders. She proposed that affects are the expression of the drives and that they are intimately connected to both self and object representations from the beginning of development: "there is no doubt that long before the infant becomes aware of the mother as a person and of his own self, engrams are laid down of experiences which reflect his responses to maternal care in the realm of his entire mental and body self."[25(pp34–35)] Jacobson emphasized not only the infant's innate drives but also the role of the mother or other parenting figure in molding and shaping the character both of the developing affect dispositions that are the expression of the drives and the images of self and object as they differentiate in the course of development. "The earliest relationship between mother and child is of a truly symbiotic nature, for not only does the helpless infant need the mother and feed on her, but the mother also needs and—emotionally—even feeds on the child."[25(p56)] Out of this original symbiotic relationship with the mother, the child gradually differentiates from the originally undifferentiated self-object state in which the child's own affects were unable to be distinguished from those of the mother. Gradually, a progressively more complex and well-integrated image of the self develops, and this self becomes progressively more differentiated from the internal image of the object, which also becomes progressively more complex and integrated. This process is facilitated by the mother (and of course by other important people in the child's life), and therefore problems in parenting can lead to difficulties in this process. Early in the course of normal development, the child goes through a psychological stage in which the child tends to mentally separate the good aspects of the object, which are associated with positive affects, from the bad aspects of the object, which are associated with negatively charged aggressive affects. If development proceeds normally, these good and bad images become integrated into a more complete and realistic object image that combines both good and bad attributes. In some more pathological situations, an all-good self-object representation develops that is invested with libidinal drive derivatives. This all-good self-object representation coexists with but is dissociated from an all-bad self-object representation invested with aggressive drive derivatives. This is the characteristic structure of the intrapsychic world of borderline and psychotic patients, who remain chronically unable to integrate the various aspects of their internal representations of objects and of themselves.

As development proceeds, the intrapsychic structures described by Freud differentiate out of the original undifferentiated matrix. Subsequent identifications with important external objects continue to contribute to the gradual evolution of all the intrapsychic structures. The early nucleus of what will eventually become the child's superego is described by Jacobson as being the early bad internal object representation that is linked with punishing and prohibiting affect (the "No!" of the parent). Simultaneous with the beginning of the development of the punitive superego is the development of internal idealized images of the parents and of the ideal self that contribute to the gradual formation of the ego ideal. The ego ideal, according to Jacobson, is "composed of idealized parental and self images and of realistic ego goals as well as realistic self and object representations."[25(p111)]

Margaret Mahler

In the 1950s, Margaret Mahler led an extensive research project that studied a syndrome she termed symbiotic child psychosis.[26, 27] In an effort to understand the overwhelming disabilities of these children, she and her colleagues soon began a parallel study of normal youngsters. In a controlled nursery school setting, with and without the mothers' being present, they made extensive observations of numerous children from the fifth month through the third year of life. The case histories of five of these children are included in their 1975 book.[28] One of Mahler's collaborators, John McDevitt, has since done a 25-year follow-up of Donna, one of the five.[29]

Mahler primarily used the libido theory's drive model in describing the first few weeks of life, which are centered on achieving homeostasis and which she called the "normal autistic phase." According to Mahler, the newborn does not differentiate internal from external stimuli; there is only tension and satiation. By the second month, the infant begins the "normal symbiotic phase," in which there is a relationship characterized by an "omnipotent fusion," a "delusion of a common boundary" with "the need-satisfying object." From the infant's perspective, mother and child are a "dual unity." If the symbiotic period progresses normally, the infant begins to develop "memory islands" and a "core sense of self," which are preparatory for the "hatching" that will occur at about 5 months. In her description of this period, Mahler used the concepts of libido theory but also referred to both Rene Spitz's observations of the first months of life* and to Winnicott's concept of the holding environment.

What follows these earliest months, the period from about 5 months to beyond 3 years, is termed "the psychological birth of the human infant" by Mahler. During this time, the stages of the separation-individuation process

* Spitz[30] has made important contributions to object relations theory. He observed infants during their first year of life and made a timetable for important responses to others. His descriptions of the 1-month smiling response, the 3-month recognition of the human face, and the 7- to 8-month stranger anxiety are well known.

occur. Mahler formulated a series of subphases of this process. In summary, the subphases are

1. Differentiation: 4 to 8 or 9 months. During these months, there is the "first tentative" pushing away from "completely passive lap-babyhood." The 5- to 6-month-old infant gradually begins to creep. During this time, transitional objects develop (a term coined by Winnicott and discussed earlier in this section). The infant soon begins differentiating, with more or less anxiety, the faces of strangers from primary caretakers.
2. Practicing
   a. Early: 7 months to about 1 year. This subphase overlaps with differentiation. Infants begin to crawl and stand. They become upset if they end up too far away, frequently paddling back to mother for "emotional refueling."
   b. Practicing subphase proper: about 12 to 18 months. This subphase begins with walking and ushers in a "love affair with the world." The children are frequently elated, curious, and adventurous. They are delightful to observe but must be carefully watched because they are likely to dash blithely into precarious situations. They tend to be impervious to minor falls and other mishaps.
3. Rapprochement: gradually, from about 15 to 22 months or more, the carefree behavior gives way to anxiety about separation and fear of "object loss." The toddler is learning that "the world is *not* his oyster."[28(p78)] The child alternates between demanding, negativistic, challenging behavior and seeking love and approval by "wooing" behavior.
4. "The child on the way to object constancy": 24 months to 3 years and beyond.

Mahler was careful to blur the boundaries of each of the subphases. She stated that for all of our lives, we are "both fully 'in' and at the same time basically separate from the world 'out there'."[28(p3)] The optimal unfolding of phases depends on the emotional availability of the mothering person. If it is disrupted in the earliest months, the result can be the development of an infantile psychosis *either* because of lack of maternal availability or empathy or because, for constitutional reasons, the infant is unable to respond to the mothering. Regardless of whether the cause is environmental or constitutional, if the symbiotic mother-infant relationship fails to provide safe "anchoring" or discourages hatching, the separation-individualization process cannot proceed normally. Later phases may also be disrupted, for example, by overprotective mothering, which inhibits independence, or because of precocious motor development, which may lead the infant to separate physically from the mother before psychological readiness for that degree of separation. In addition, Mahler stated that the rapprochement subphase lays "the foundation for subsequent relatively stable mental health or borderline pathology."[31(p494)] However, she also emphasized that there are many individual paths taken to the achievement of object constancy. Using the case histories of the observed toddlers, Mahler demonstrated how children are capable of shaping themselves to their environment. Acknowledging a debt to Hartmann's work on adaptation, she described how several children adapted, with varying degrees of success, to the personalities of their mothers.

In later work, Mahler and McDevitt began to trace the "emergence of the sense of self" during the first 15 months of life.[32(pp 827–848)]

Otto Kernberg

Otto Kernberg, like Jacobson before him, believed that it is possible to integrate an ego psychological approach to the understanding of mental functioning with an objects relations perspective. His major contributions have stemmed from his work on the psychoanalysis and psychotherapeutic treatment of patients with severe character disorders, particularly those with borderline personality organization, as well as patients with narcissistic character. This section summarizes his contributions to object relations theory.

The primitive defenses of splitting and projective identification, first described by Klein, are central to the diagnosis of borderline personality disorder as conceived by Kernberg. His depiction of the landscape of the mind also owes some of its salient features to Jacobson, who first suggested that internal representations of self and object with an associated affect are the nuclei of the early development of the psyche. Kernberg's depiction of the inner world of borderline and psychotic patients is, however, uniquely his. Splitting breaks up the internal representations of objects and of the self into part object representations, each with an associated affect. Thus, objects are perceived as either all good or all bad in relationship to the self. Projective identification, first conceptualized by Klein as a primitive defense of the paranoid-schizoid position[33] (see section on Klein), was further elaborated by Kernberg. The central feature of projective identification, according to Kernberg, is that projective identification always involves the projection of an internal object relation with its associated affect. When projection is effective, the subject eliminates the unacceptable impulse or idea from any connection with the self. In contrast, in projective identification, the connection to the unacceptable contents is preserved along with the tie between the part self and the part object. The connection cannot be totally eliminated.

Kernberg envisioned the inner world of the borderline or psychotic patient as being populated by numerous unintegrated part self–part object dyads that are each linked by a predominant affect. These internal nuclei are kept separate by the defense of splitting. The borderline individual projects these pathological inner contents onto any significant other with whom he or she interacts. Which of these self-object–affect structures is active can shift from moment to moment; this results in the chaotic and shifting pattern of relationships that is the essence of what is observed clinically in patients with borderline psychopathological disorders (who can be described as being stably unstable). Depending on what happens in the course of an interaction, the relationship between the patient and the other can shift rapidly, for example, from that of the good nurturing mother interacting with the blissfully nursing infant with a sense of mutual pleasure, to that of the rageful depriving mother interacting with the rageful deprived infant. Such a shift can occur instantaneously in the course of an interview if the interviewer does something that is perceived by the patient as being depriving or attacking.

Differentiating between a borderline patient and one who is actually psychotic at such a moment can be difficult.

For Kernberg, this differentiation is dependent on the response of the patient to clarification and interpretation of the projective identification that take place in the course of the interview. In response to the careful sequence of clarification, confrontation, and interpretation in the clinical interview, the borderline patient will improve in the ability to test reality. The structurally psychotic patient will rigidify or get worse. Neurotic patients do not rely primarily on the more primitive defenses, using predominantly higher level defenses (e.g., repression, reaction formation, isolation, undoing, rationalization, and intellectualization; see Table 19–10). Kernberg relied on a classical ego psychological framework for his understanding of neurotic patients. However, because he saw psychopathological disorders to be a continuum, lower level neurotic patients tend to have some borderline features (i.e., in some situations, they will habitually use primitive defensive operations), and higher level borderline patients have access to many of the higher level defenses of the neurotic.

Conclusion

Greenberg and Mitchell[10] have summarized the work of many theorists; their work exemplifies the major trends and the current liveliness and creativity in the field of object relations theory. They categorized many of the object relations theories discussed in this chapter in one of three ways. Some were considered to be proponents of the *drive-structural model,* which is based on libido theory, with ego structure developing in response to intrapsychic conflict. The theories of others were categorized as adhering to the *relational-structural model,* which emphasizes the primacy of relationships, with the self evolving out of a dyadic interaction. A third category included those who have attempted an *accommodation* of the two models. The struggles of human beings are observed and treated differently, depending on the theoretical framework. The drive model philosophically considers the person a unique, pleasure-seeking individual; the relational model focuses on the person as a social animal.

Since their joint publication, Greenberg and Mitchell have written independently and have reached somewhat different conclusions about the models. Mitchell[34] has maintained that the drive theory must be discarded as outdated. He has attempted to present a unified relational model, in which different relational theories are either integrated or shown to be incompatible. He has stressed that sexuality is to be considered a medium for the expression of self in relationship with others and not *only* determined by biological urges. Also, he maintained that accommodators are incorrect in their use of a "developmental tilt"[34(p133)] to attempt to validate both models, that is, in applying the relational model to the preoedipal developmental stages and the drive model to oedipal development. Rather, for Mitchell, a psychopathological process reflects the pervasiveness of problems through all developmental stages, and past experience provides a blueprint for how the present is approached throughout the life cycle. Psychoanalysis aims to understand this blueprint, so that the analysand's "relational world"[34(p289)] may be altered.

Greenberg[35] maintained that both the drive and the relational models are valuable and should be used even though they are philosophically incompatible. The dual-instinct theory is clinically relevant: drive endowment is constitutionally and individually variable; conflict is inherent in human development; and somatic sources *do* account for the urgency of certain behaviors. However, the Oedipus complex must be expanded beyond its reduction by the drive theory to incestuous, parricidal wishes. Human behavior oscillates between the need to relate and the need to be separate. The goal of the analytical situation, which itself is a paradox because it is both social and private, is to bring to consciousness and facilitate *rerepresentation* of pathological ego representations. Hence, analysis is both interpretive and interactive, and its success permits increased flexibility in human relationships.

References

1. Moore BE, Fine BD: Psychoanalytic Terms and Concepts. New Haven, CT: Yale University Press, 1990.
2. Schafer R: Aspects of Internalization. New York: International Universities Press, 1968.
3. Freud S: Instincts and their vicissitudes. In Strachey J (trans-ed): The Standard Edition of the Complete Psychological Works of Sigmund Freud, Volume 14. London: Hogarth Press, 1957:109–140. Originally published in 1915.
4. Freud S: On narcissism: An introduction. In Strachey J (trans-ed): The Standard Edition of the Complete Psychological Works of Sigmund Freud, Volume 14. London: Hogarth Press, 1957:67–102. Originally published in 1914.
5. Freud S: Mourning and melancholia. In Strachey J (trans-ed): The Standard Edition of the Complete Psychological Works of Sigmund Freud, Volume 14. London: Hogarth Press, 1957:237–258. Originally published in 1917.
6. Freud S: Beyond the pleasure principle. In Strachey J (trans-ed): The Standard Edition of the Complete Psychological Works of Sigmund Freud, Volume 18. London: Hogarth Press, 1955:3–64. Originally published in 1920.
7. Klein M: Notes on some schizoid mechanisms. In Envy and Gratitude, 1946–1963. New York: Dell, 1975:43–47. Originally published in 1946.
8. Klein M: Mourning and its relation to manic-depressive states. In Love, Guilt and Reparation, 1921–1945. New York: Free Press, 1975:344–369. Originally published in 1940.
9. Sutherland JD: The British object relations theorists: Balint, Winnicott, Fairbairn, Guntrip. J Am Psychoanal Assoc 1980; 28:828–858.
10. Greenberg JR, Mitchell SA: Object Relations in Psychoanalytic Theory. Cambridge, MA: Harvard University Press, 1983.
11. Winnicott DW: The Maturational Process and the Facilitating Environment. New York: International Universities Press, 1965.
12. Winnicott DW: Collected papers: Through paediatrics to psychoanalysis. In Hate in the Countertransference. New York: Basic Books, 1958:194–203, 1965. Originally published in 1947.
13. Winnicott DW: Playing and Reality. New York: Basic Books, 1971:1–25.
14. Balint M: The benign and the malignant forms of regression. In New Perspectives in Psychoanalysis. Sandor Rado Lectures 1957–1963. New York: Grune & Stratton, 1963.
15. Dupont J: The Clinical Diary of Sandor Ferenczi. Cambridge, MA: Harvard University Press, 1988.
16. Balint M: The Basic Fault, Part 1. London: Tavistock Publications, 1968:3–29.
17. Fairbairn WRD: Psychoanalytic Studies of the Personality. London: Tavistock Publications, 1952.
18. Fairbairn WRD: Synopsis of an object-relations theory of the personality. Int J Psychoanal 1963; 44:224–225.
19. Guntrip H: Personality Structure and Human Interaction. New York: International Universities Press, 1961.
20. Guntrip H: Schizoid Phenomena, Object Relations and the Self. New York: International Universities Press, 1969.
21. Spitz RA: Anaclitic depression. Psychoanal Study Child 1946; 2:313–342.
22. Robertson J, Bowlby J: Responses of young children to separation from their mothers. Courr Cent Int Enf 1952; 2:131–142.
23. Bowlby J: Attachment and Loss. New York: Basic Books, 1969.

24. Harlow HF, Harlow MK: Social deprivation in monkeys. Sci Am 1962; 207:136–146.
25. Jacobson E: The Self and the Object World. New York: International Universities Press, 1964.
26. Mahler MS, Goslinger BJ. On symbiotic child psychosis: Genetic, dynamic and restitutive aspects. Psychoanal Study Child 1955; 10:195–212.
27. Mahler MS: On human symbiosis and the vicissitudes of individuation. In Mahler MS (ed): Infantile Psychosis, Volume I. New York: International Universities Press, 1968.
28. Mahler MS, Pine F, Bergman A: The Psychological Birth of the Human Infant. Symbiosis and Individuation. New York: Basic Books, 1975.
29. McDevitt J: Conflict and compromise formation: A 25-year follow-up study. Presented at the Annual Meeting of the American Psychoanalytic Association; April 28, 1992; Washington, DC.
30. Spitz RA: The First Year of Life: A Psychoanalytic Study of Normal and Deviant Development of Object Relations. New York: International Universities Press, 1965.
31. Mahler MS: Rapprochement subphase of the separation-individuation process. Psychoanal Q 1972; 41:487–506.
32. Mahler MS, McDevitt JB: Thoughts on the emergence of the sense of self, with particular emphasis on the body self. J Am Psychoanal Assoc 1982; 30:827–848.
33. Klein M: Love, guilt, and reparation. In Love, Guilt and Reparation, 1921–1945. New York: Free Press, 1975:306–343. Originally published in 1937.
34. Mitchell SA: Relational Concepts in Psychoanalysis, an Integration. Cambridge, MA: Harvard University Press, 1988.
35. Greenberg JR: Oedipus and Beyond: A Clinical Theory. Cambridge, MA: Harvard University Press, 1991.

Other Psychoanalytic Perspectives

Henry F. Smith

Erik H. Erikson

Erikson, a psychoanalyst and integrative theoretician, made several major contributions to psychoanalytic theory and to the practice of American psychiatry.

Development of Ego Psychology

To the theoretical development of ego psychology, Erikson added three components: first, an epigenetic model; second, a theory of the relationship between internal and external reality; and third, a psychosocial theory of development throughout the life cycle.

Epigenesis and the Life Cycle

The concept of epigenesis was borrowed by Erikson from embryology. It refers to the view that all developmental processes unfold in a succession of stages, with each stage having a lawful relationship to every other stage. Erikson considered each stage of psychological development to have its own critical developmental task. Furthermore, he believed that the achievements and failures of earlier stages influence later stages, whereas later stages modify and transform earlier ones.

Erikson divided the entire life cycle into eight stages, thus extending into adulthood Sigmund Freud's notion of infantile psychosexual stages while at the same time broadening Anna Freud's concept of the developmental lines of childhood. As shown in Table 19–12, Erikson linked each *psychosexual* stage to a particular body zone or zones.[1] In each stage, the individual negotiates a phase-specific *psychosocial* developmental task toward the achievement of specific *strengths.* In this model, each individual evolves a mode of interpersonal and intrapsychic functioning with emergent social capacities uniquely adapted to a particular social milieu. The "crises" of each stage are normative, not pathological ones, and the developmental tasks are never fully resolved in each stage but continue to be worked out throughout the life span.

To simplify, life begins with the oral-sensory stage of infancy, marked by the potential development of what Erikson called basic trust toward the achievement of a sense of hope. In early childhood, the second or anal-muscular stage, the toddler struggles with the task of developing a sense of autonomy toward the capacity for strength of will. Relative degrees of failure at this stage may predispose the child to shame and doubt. Next, Erikson's play age, coinciding with the nursery school–age or preschool-age child, is marked by the genital-locomotor stage or third stage of development. Here the child's task is to develop a sense of initiative as opposed to further shame and guilt. The lasting achievement of this stage is a sense of purpose. In the fourth stage, the school-age child in what is traditionally called the stage of latency tries to master the crisis of industry versus inferiority toward the development of a sense of competence. At puberty, the fifth stage, the task of adolescence is to navigate the familiar "identity crisis" (see later) as each individual struggles with a degree of "identity confusion." The lasting outcome of this stage can be a

Table 19–12 Erikson's Stages of Development

Psychosexual Stage	Psychosocial Crisis	Basic Strength
Oral-sensory (infancy)	Basic trust versus basic mistrust	Hope
Anal-muscular (early childhood)	Autonomy versus shame and doubt	Will
Genital-locomotor (play age)	Initiative versus shame and guilt	Purpose
Latency (school age)	Industry versus inferiority	Competence
Puberty (adolescence)	Identity versus identity confusion	Fidelity
Genitality (young adulthood)	Intimacy versus isolation	Love
Procreativity (adulthood)	Generativity versus stagnation	Care
Generalization of sensual modes (old age)	Integrity versus despair	Wisdom

Modified from Erikson EH: The Life Cycle Completed. New York: WW Norton, 1985:32–33. Originally published in 1982. © by WW Norton.

capacity for fidelity. Young adulthood, at the stage of genitality or sixth stage, is marked by the crisis of intimacy versus isolation, out of which may come the achievement of a capacity for love. In the procreative period of adulthood, the seventh stage, the individual may develop a capacity for generativity at the risk of stagnation.

Out of this struggle comes the ability to care. Finally, Erikson viewed the wisdom of old age, the eighth stage, as a summation of all the achievements of the previous seven stages. Similarly, he considered that all of the modes of functioning in the previous psychosexual stages come into play at this stage. Hence, the task of old age is to develop a sense of integrity at the risk of despair.

Far from being a simple linear model, Erikson used his hierarchical schema to explore increasingly complex interactions between earlier and later stages over time and between internal and external factors that influence development. Although his mixing of internal and external frames of reference always continued to cloud the conceptual status of his theory, it was Erikson's singular capacity to integrate so many separate components of the individual's development and to provide tools for their investigation in research models.

Practical Uses of the Model

Locating a patient on Erikson's epigenetic schema has proved to be of practical use not only to the child psychiatrist assessing and treating children but also to the psychiatrist evaluating adults in such settings as consultation-liaison work. With some appreciation of the patient's history and current state, one can more easily assess the hospitalized patient's capacity for trust, for example, or predict and understand the individual surgical patient's response to the trauma of surgery.

Adolescence and the Concept of Identity

One of Erikson's lasting impacts has been on the field of adolescence and the concept of identity. Each of the developmental stages has a psychosocial crisis that needs to be negotiated; for the adolescent, that crisis is the identity crisis. Whereas the term identity crisis has come into popular use to denote troubled teenagers with pathological antisocial behavior, Erikson's original intention, as with the crises of each of the other developmental stages, was to designate a normative phase-specific internal conflict, something "silent, inner, and unconscious."[2]

The inevitable presence of an internal identity crisis does not predict the degree of anguish individual adolescents may experience or the specifics of their outward behavior, both of which may vary considerably as research has demonstrated.[3] The alternative to the formation of a sense of identity is identity confusion, which is also, to one degree or another, a normative experience for every adolescent. On the other hand, the state of identity confusion can form the basis for a core disturbance and future psychopathological process.

If Erikson's terminology is confusing, the difficulty may stem both from the complexity of the concepts he is trying to integrate and from his attempt to speak throughout from internal and external frames of reference. If he intended the term identity to connote "a persistent sameness within oneself (self-sameness) and a persistent sharing of some kind of essential character with others,"[4] Erikson used the term deliberately to refer at different moments, first, to a "*conscious* sense of individual identity"; second, to an "*unconscious* striving for a continuity of personal character"; third, to a "criterion for the silent doings of *ego synthesis*"; and fourth, to a "maintenance of *inner solidarity with a group's ideals* and identity" (italics added). Thus, in the definition of the term identity, we can see the mix of internal and external frames of reference. Overall, Erikson viewed adolescence as a kind of psychosocial "moratorium," a time when society sanctioned the postponement of definitive commitments while sexual and cognitive maturation continued.

Erikson sometimes attributed his interest in the identity crisis to his own upbringing. Born in Germany the illegitimate son of Danish Lutheran parents, he was raised as a Jew. Not knowing his Nordic ancestry, he was rejected both by anti-Semitic classmates for his Judaism and by Jews, who taunted him for his Nordic features, leaving him with a persistent interest in the search for identity. Academically, his interest in adolescence stemmed from his work with Anna Freud, who was his personal psychoanalyst and teacher, and from his collaborative work with his friend Peter Blos. His views of adolescence and the tools he provided for its investigation have paved the way for much research in the field.[3, 5, 6]

Psyche, Soma, and Society: An Integrated Tripartite View

It is the concept of individual development within a social matrix and the interaction between the two to which Erikson gave his stamp. He had a complex view of this interaction, describing how at each stage of development the specific caretaker within the social matrix responds to the individual's stage and needs in accordance with the caretaker's own phase-specific capacities and needs. Thus, the developing individual and his or her caretaker mutually influence each other in a manner specific to each dyad. The paradigm of this mutual interplay can be used to describe the interaction between parents and children, children and their teachers, psychotherapists and patients, societies and their members, or any one individual and another throughout the life cycle.

As he bridged psyche and culture, his theory, like Freud's, was always firmly rooted in the individual's experience of her or his own body, thus forming a tripartite interaction of *soma* (body), *psyche,* and *ethos* (society). He demonstrated this most clearly in his studies of children of the Sioux and Yurok cultures in his seminal book, *Childhood and Society.*[7] Reflecting later on his work with Sioux children, he noted that training in groups is "the method by which a group's basic ways of organizing experience . . . is transmitted to the infant's early bodily experiences and, through them, to the beginnings of his ego."[1] Erikson concluded that every society responds to each developmental phase with institutions specific to that culture and so determines for each individual growing up in that culture the manner and extent of resolution of every developmental phase. Through this process, a given community preserves its own ecological balance.

Within these same theoretical points of reference, Erikson's study of historical individuals, especially Martin

Luther[8] and Mahatma Gandhi,[9] made major contributions to the field of psychobiography.

If Erikson's work bridged psychiatry, psychoanalysis, and sociology, he remained, throughout his life, a clinical psychoanalyst and a contributor to the clinical literature. In one of his last writings, he wrote that he considered psychoanalysis to be the best laboratory for the study of the individual in his or her historical context and "the prime method for the study of the *developmental* and *historical relativity* in human experience. And only such study can confirm what is, indeed, invariantly human."[1]

Interaction and Relativism

In recent decades, it has become evident how modern Erikson's views were. He anticipated future developments in research on infancy, especially the importance of the mutual interaction between caretaker and child. At the same time, his view of the complex determinants of individual development is compatible with the views of modern structural theory (see previous section). His idea that syntonic functions of the ego can be used for defensive purposes, for example, is consistent with Brenner's[10] view that any aspect of psychic functioning can be used in the service of defense. Finally, Erikson's abiding interest in the role of interaction in development and in the psychoanalytic situation, together with his appreciation of relativism in scientific observation, positions him far from the positivism of the 19th century and in the forefront of contemporary scientific discourse.

References

1. Erikson EH: The Life Cycle Completed. New York: WW Norton, 1985. Originally published in 1982.
2. Erikson EH: Identity: Youth and Crisis. New York: WW Norton, 1968.
3. Offer D, Offer JB: From Teenage to Young Manhood: A Psychological Study. New York: Basic Books, 1975.
4. Erikson EH: Identity and the Life Cycle. New York: International Universities Press, 1959.
5. Hauser S, Powers SI, Noam GG: Adolescents and their Families. New York: Free Press, 1991.
6. Hauser S, Smith HF: The development and experience of affect in adolescence. J Am Psychoanal Assoc 1991; 39(suppl):131–165.
7. Erikson EH: Childhood and Society. New York: WW Norton, 1950.
8. Erikson EH: Young Man Luther: A Study in Psychoanalysis and History. New York: WW Norton, 1958.
9. Erikson EH: Gandhi's Truth. New York: WW Norton, 1969.
10. Brenner C: The Mind in Conflict. Madison, CT: International Universities Press, 1982.

Robert M. Galatzer-Levy

Self Psychology

Self psychology is a major new development in psychoanalysis. It emerged in response to less than satisfactory clinical results of older analytical methods in work with certain patients whose problems can be conceptualized as centering on their experience of self. This group of patients includes people who suffer directly from experiences of a depleted or fragmented self and patients with a range of driven behaviors that can be understood as attempts to invigorate the self or maintain its coherence. Self psychology includes distinctive ways of investigating psychological life as well as unique theories of psychological function and development, pathogenesis, and treatment. Its concepts are applicable not only to psychoanalysis but also to psychotherapy, crisis intervention, liaison psychiatry, organizational psychiatry, study of life course development, and understanding of social institutions and history. This section describes self psychology and emphasizes its clinical implications.

Within psychoanalysis, Freud[1] posited that psychological investment in the self antedated and always remained more important than interest in others or the external world. Although he theorized about the self and the vicissitudes of narcissism, Freud was pessimistic about psychoanalytic investigation of the self. He believed psychoanalytic study of people with predominantly narcissistic interests was impossible because transference, the intense emotional response of the patient to the analyst that is the analyst's major investigational tool,[2] did not develop in persons whose main interest was in their selves. Despite these difficulties, Paul Federn[3] explored many phenomena of the enfeebled and fragmented self. British object relations theorists W. R. D. Fairbairn[4] and Donald Winnicott[5] were the first to show that the self develops and continues to exist in a context of internal and external relations with others. During the same period, Erik H. Erikson[6, 7] discussed the importance of personal identity in the psychology of adolescents and young adults. These psychoanalytic developments took place within a wider social context. In the United States and Europe, concern to find personal significance in life and a valued place for the self was reflected in philosophical, literary, and political movements.[8–10] In the Third World, the search for personal and group identity in the face of oppression emerged as a similarly important topic.[11] However, it remained for Heinz Kohut to develop a coherent psychoanalytic theory of the self in health and illness.

Kohut's work appeared in a series of seminal papers and three major books that reflect the evolution of his thought as he tried to understand patients with disorders of the self, frame a coherent theory of self-development, and apply his theories to creativity and history.[12–14] In his early writings, the extent of his departure from traditional analytical thought was obscured by his use of traditional terminology. In the course of his work, Kohut claimed an increasing clinical significance for his findings. Initially, he addressed issues involving only patients with narcissistic personality disorders. Later, he saw disorders of the self as the basis for a wide range of pathological processes, including much that more traditional analysts believe results from unresolved conflict. Today, many psychoanalytically oriented psychiatrists are profoundly influenced by Kohut's thinking. Self psychology also has many critics. Kohut's theories gave rise to extensions, for example, by integrating them with object relations theory,[15] extending them to a life course developmental psychology,[16] and elaborating them from an intersubjective viewpoint.[17] The ideas that led to self psychology started with a profound change in ideas about how psychoanalysts should understand people.

Conceptual Background

Freud and his followers tried to understand psychological life in terms of biology. Their ideal was scientific objectivity. They believed the analyst's human tendency to identify with the subjects of study impeded objectivity.[18] In contrast, Kohut[19] viewed empathic comprehension as the fundamental mode of psychoanalytic investigation. It is the knowledge of the other's experience, what it is like to be in that person's shoes. Empathy is the understanding of another's complex psychological experience as a whole. Kohut likened it to vicarious introspection. It is not sympathy, nor does it necessarily entail good intentions toward the other person. (Confidence artists are empathic with their prey.) Using this empathic method, Kohut attempted to create an "experience-near" psychology, explaining psychological events in terms of meanings and motives comprehensible from ordinary experience. He contrasted this with freudian metapsychology, with its postulated experience-distant forces, energies, and structures.

Kohut held that the meaning of self could be empathically comprehended. He used the term self to refer to a center of initiative, experience, or the core of personal being. Kohut largely ignored the long history of the idea of self in religion, philosophy, and psychology. He did not address the conceptual complexities that result from attempts to be more precise about the idea[20] or the evidence that the self experience varies dramatically across cultures. Like Freud,[21, 22] who claimed that the sexual quality of experience was immediately apparent, Kohut claimed the self-experience was directly knowable to us all. Many other authors have addressed the question of the meaning of the self. They have put forward such ideas as the continuing experience of one's affective responses[23] or the sense of that which absolutely belongs to one.[24, 25]

Part of the difficulty is that awareness of the self is minimal unless the self is threatened. Aspects of the self then come into sharp focus. There is a profound need to experience the self as coherent in time and space and to feel that the self is alive. Coherence in time means that one feels like a person who has a continuity of history, that one is the same person across the life course. Coherence in space refers to the sense that the various aspects of one's person are active, with common intention and within one's control. The concept of *bipolar self* (Fig. 19–8) refers to Kohut's metaphorical description of the self as having two poles, one of ideals and ambitions, the other a sense of the grandiose self. The former involves the sense of being vigorous and coherent because one is associated with what is good and powerful, for example, the sense of well-being that a young girl might have by virtue of taking care of an infant like her admired mother, or the similar sense that an adult might have when working in accord with professional ideals. The grandiose pole of the self consists in the sense of being personally valuable and appreciated, as a child may feel by virtue of the glowing enthusiasm of parents.

Kohut's singular contribution was the idea of the *self-object.* Clinical observation led him to believe that the self could survive and prosper only in the context of experiences with others. These clinical experiences find support by observations of infants and young children that consistently show that appropriate psychological interactions with others are essential for early psychological development.[26] These experiences Kohut called self-objects, that is, objects (in the psychoanalytic sense of intrapsychic representation of other people) that are necessary for the well-being of the self. Kohut was speaking of intrapsychic experiences, *not* interpersonal relations. Intrapsychic experience may be contingent on interpersonal events. For example, the sense that one is appreciatively responded to usually requires some sort of active response from another person, but how that person's actions are experienced depends on many factors besides the actions themselves.

Kohut[13] described two main types of self-object. *Idealized self-objects* embody what is admirable, strong, and vigorous. The self feels alive and coherent by virtue of

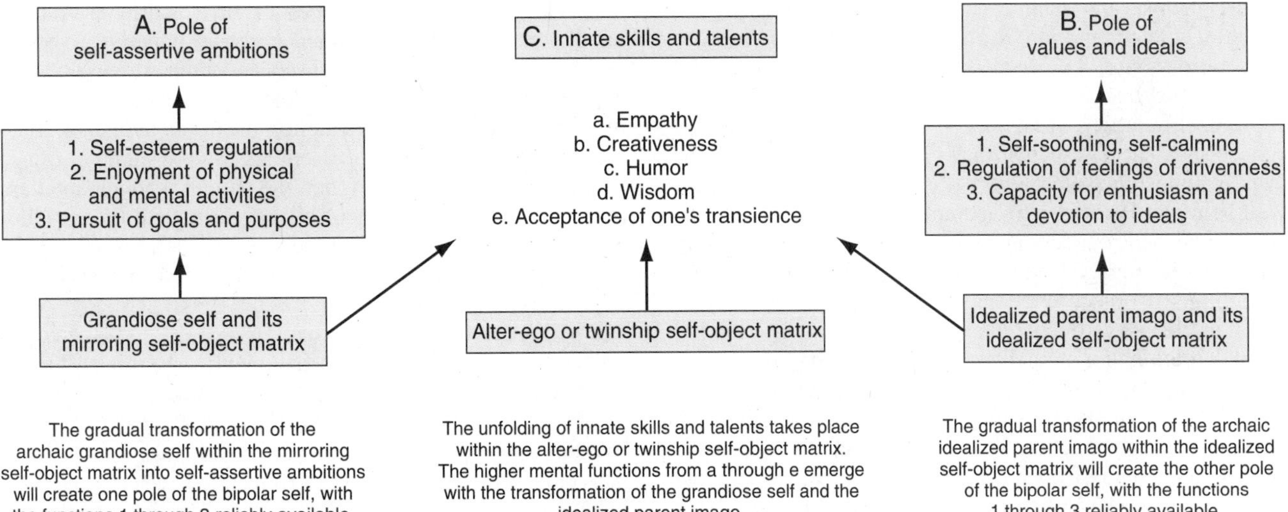

Figure 19–8 *Structure and functions of the supraordinate bipolar self (normal development). (From Ornstein P, Kay J: Developments of psychoanalytic self psychology: A historical-conceptual overview. Annu Rev Psychiatry 1990; 9:303–322.)*

proximity to the idealized self-object. The youngster who feels like "a chip off the old block," the student who is enlivened in the presence of a brilliant teacher, and the religious person who feels safe in God's presence have idealized self-object experiences. *Mirroring self-objects* contribute to the sense of self through their support of the grandiose pole of the self. Kohut described three major types of mirroring self-object:

- In *merger,* the self is maintained through the sense that the person and self-object form a unity that is powerful and alive in a way the person could not be by himself or herself. The sense of merger can be found in the feeling that "we" do something. Outside the analytical situation, it is commonly seen in athletic, professional, and military activities. (Note that these experiences do not involve psychotic confusion about the self and other, but a feeling state of commonality.)
- *Alter ego (or twinship) self-object* induces a sense of personal coherence by virtue of having a partner who is like oneself.
- The *mirroring self-object proper* supports the sense of personal value and coherence through its accurate, valuing appreciation of the person. The person who feels valuable and whole when a parent's or friend's eyes light up as she or he comes into a room or who feels similarly in response to authentic praise of accomplishment is experiencing such a mirroring self-object.

Further clinical studies have extended the types of self-objects. For example, Wolf[27] observed that an adversary is needed for certain types of self-development. Whenever the representation of a person, institution, or idea serves to support the experience or development of the self, we say that it serves self-object functions.

Self-objects remain essential throughout life. Contrary to psychoanalytic theories like Mahler's that characterize maturity in terms of autonomy,[28] self psychology views mature people as ordinarily dependent on others for appreciation, comradeship, meaning, and solace. The nature of the people and institutions that embody self-objects changes with maturation.[16] They become more numerous and more complex, often serving many psychological functions beyond their self-object function. Compare the self-object functions of an infant's caretakers and those of a spouse in a successful marriage. The infant's caretaker is usually almost the sole support of the infant's psychological well-being and provides for material care of the infant. The adult's spouse is one among many supports for the partner's self and is engaged in a highly complex relationship involving self-object functions, erotic gratification, collaboration in life tasks from parenting to finance, and the creation and celebration of a mutual history. The urgency with which the self-object is needed is different. Separation of the young child from the caretaker results in almost immediate distress and can quickly become a psychological catastrophe.[29] Adults can often, with varying degrees of distress, tolerate separation from the embodiment of a self-object function for extended periods. Commonly, the evocation of the self-object through memory is sufficient.[30] Because they believe that self-object functions are always embedded within more complex relations with people, Galatzer-Levy and Cohler[16] introduced the term *essential other.* It refers to the total experience of people and institutions that sustain and support the development of the self.

Disorders of the Self

The study of self psychology began with the realization that many symptoms of psychological distress could be understood as arising from disorders of the self. These symptoms take two major forms: symptoms involving direct experiences of an endangered, enfeebled, or fragmented self; and symptoms arising from unsatisfactory attempts to protect the endangered self. In practice, these symptoms may appear in the same patient, but for expository purposes, separating them is useful. Sometimes the symptoms of self pathology are acute (Fig. 19–9), but more often they are chronic states whose intensity varies as the self is felt to be more or less in danger.

Symptoms that directly express the enfeeblement or fragmentation of the self include certain depressive states, traumatic states, hypochondriasis, some forms of rage, and direct experiences of profound disorganization. "Empty" depressions arising from a sense of an enfeebled self are characterized by feeling that life is drab, meaningless, pointless, and tedious. These states are differentiated from "guilt" depression, in which the patient feels that he or she is in some way bad, defective, or immoral. They reflect an experience of loss of significance because the self is unable to value aspects of the internal world or see how they can be part of a personally meaningful situation. In empty depression, people may act in ways that otherwise would be rejected because the value placed on the self is so low that it is not adequately protected. Many authors have seen empty depression as the characteristic psychological state of our times, feelings of triviality and insignificance being widespread in many populations.[8] Traumatic states occur when current experience cannot be integrated into preexisting visions of the self. The sense of unreality, being destructively overwhelmed, depersonalization, and derealization commonly associated with trauma can be understood in terms of a self unable to maintain its coherence. After trauma, people commonly describe themselves or their world as "shattered," meaning that continued personal coherence seems impossible. Hypochondriacal states often represent the experience of a fragmented or dysfunctional self. Using the most powerful available metaphor, the body, hypochondriacal patients insist that something is profoundly, often life-threateningly wrong. When the patient is understood as referring to a threat to her or his psychological life and the demands for help are understood as pleas for assistance with this state, the psychiatrist can comprehend and help the hypochondriacal patient.[31]

A common response to feeling the self endangered is rage.[32] Narcissistic rage is a major public health problem. The most common cause of violence and homicide is the rage engendered when people feel "disrespected." Spousal murders most commonly result when an already demoralized person is confronted by an apparently trivial inconsiderate behavior and responds with murderous rage. Precipitants of such murder include smoking the last cigarette in the house or failure to pick up the newspaper.[33] Communal chronic narcissistic rage may be a major factor in world history when maintaining group dignity or compensating for past inequi-

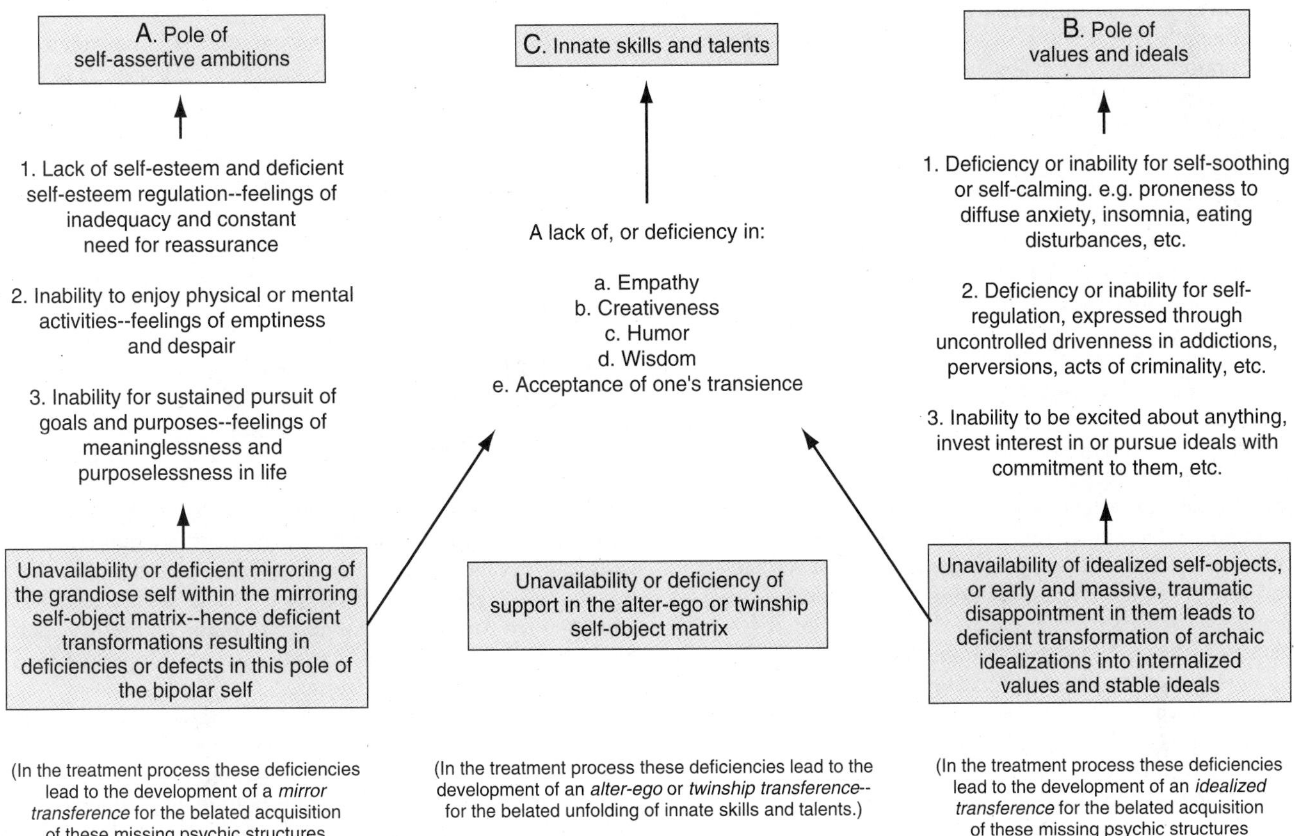

Figure 19–9 *Structure and functions of the supraordinate bipolar self (deficient or derailed development). (From Ornstein P, Kay J: Developments of psychoanalytic self psychology: A historical-conceptual overview. Annu Rev Psychiatry 1990; 9:303–322.)*

ties leads to hatred and destructiveness lasting for centuries. Narcissistic rage varies from the momentary fury, familiar to anyone who has stubbed a toe, to lifelong states, like those of Shakespeare's Richard III, who dedicated his life to revenge against a world that inadequately valued him. Like many activities in the service of the self, narcissistic rage is often rationalized. Perpetrators often describe violence as necessary to achieve a goal, but closer examination usually shows that the violence did little to effect its supposed aim. The physical child abuse that often is a manifestation of the narcissistic rage resulting from a sense of inadequacy in caring for the child is commonly rationalized as "educating" the youngster. Narcissistic rage often joins other psychological action designed to invigorate the self. Acting on a punitive ideal can express rage and unite the person with a higher good. Teachers who harshly attack students' productions often simultaneously act out of narcissistic rage and feel invigorated by living up to an ideal that joins them to an admired community.

States involving the direct experience of fragmentation in which patients cannot organize experience or recognize their coherent wishes are overwhelmingly distressing. Any solution to this state, including the psychotic reorganization of experience, feels better. Indeed, such states are most commonly seen briefly with the onset of overt psychosis. Patients commonly describe this state as "going crazy" and may attempt desperately to hang on to some organizing principle. These states are psychiatric emergencies, because many patients report that death is preferable to the continuation of the intense anxiety they experience. Many other symptoms are understandable as attempts to repair an impaired or endangered self. These include relations with others designed to achieve urgently needed self-object experiences and activities designed to soothe or stimulate the self.

Pathogenesis of Disorders of the Self

When development goes well, self-objects ensure that the painful experiences of living are not overwhelming. The child may experience painful and distressing events but not to such an extent that the capacity to maintain a cohesive and vigorous sense of self is threatened. Responsive self-objects maintain a milieu in which the child feels safe, appreciated, and able to comfortably idealize others in a developmentally appropriate way. The environment empathically comprehends and supports the child.[26] In such an environment, the child thrives. She or he can increasingly maintain self-object functions that were performed by others in their physical absence. There are several ways in which this happens. Biological maturation increases the child's capabilities. The child takes on certain capacities through becoming like the person who embodied the self-object function and being increasingly able to evoke the memory and function of that person when he or she is away. A first prerequisite for such development is that the child have "good enough" experiences with others to internalize. A youngster who has been insufficiently valued or who has been blocked from comfortably admiring a powerful caretaker cannot take in these capacities. Classical psychoanalytic theory[34, 35] and early self psychology studies[13] emphasize the role of frustration as a motive for developing psychological structure. The loss of the other's self-object function, if not too overwhelming, leads the youngster to take on that function for herself or himself. Although such processes certainly occur, the extent to which normal development is driven by loss of others is unclear, but the availability of adequate others to perform self-object function is essential to healthy development.

Several types of self-object failures seem to lead to later disorders of the self. Early deprivation of human responsiveness is psychologically and physically devastating to infants.[36] Less severe deprivations may result in serious lack of adequate experiences with caretaking self-objects. For example, children of depressed mothers do not receive ordinary enthusiastic responsiveness, engagement, and mirroring.[37, 38] Many difficulties in life may deprive a child of needed self-object experiences. These include loss of a parent, parents who are psychologically unavailable because of personal pathological processes or life circumstances, caretakers who are made anxious by and therefore avoid developmentally appropriate demands (e.g., for the opportunity to idealize), and caretakers deficient in empathy who do not comprehend the child's developmental needs.

When self-object functions become unavailable to such an extent that the person cannot provide that function from the abilities and memories already available, a psychological emergency ensues. In this circumstance, the person uses less broadly adaptive means to try to compensate for the missing but needed psychological functions. At this point, pathological functioning is manifested either in direct expression of a distressed self or as problem compensatory activities.

Community and Self Psychology

Many people experience psychological distress because they are in need of the self-object functions that can come from communities and social groups. Complaints of alienation from work and school may be translated as statements that these institutions do not provide needed support for the self and its development. Certain people can find needed self-object functions only in the contexts of groups and organizations, like Alcoholics Anonymous and similar recovery groups, that assist their members in regulating otherwise unmanageable destructive psychological states. Diagnosing self-object needs and aiding the patient in finding ways to meet them are of enormous help to many people. The psychiatrist in the role of consultant to social service agencies and courts may play a particularly significant role in helping to provide institutional solutions to people's self-object needs. For example, the recognition that youngsters need *at least one* reliable caretaker suggests that the preservation of one strong relationship take precedence over other concerns in recommending custody and visitation arrangements for children of divorce.[39] Psychiatric administrators and psychiatric consultants to management can ease the tasks of the institutions by recognizing the self-object needs of both providers and recipients of services. For example, in business settings, the psychological need of people for admirable leaders commonly goes unappreciated to the great detriment of the institution.[40, 41] The ideas of self psychology are useful guides to thinking through a wide range of issues involving communities and organizations.

Criticisms of Self Psychology

Self psychology's exclusive focus on the self and self-objects has resulted in extensive criticism on clinical and theoretical grounds. The self psychology approach abandons or minimizes the importance of many factors that traditional analysts view as centrally important.[42] Self psychologists dismiss the concept of primary sexual and aggressive drives, along with the idea that people's major struggles arise in managing those drives. Instead, they see observed instances of driven sexuality and aggression as breakdown products that emerge from a self threatened with fragmentation or depletion. Similarly, self psychologists view rivalries, including the Oedipus complex, which are so important in classical psychoanalytic theory, as pathological malformations of intergenerational support.[43] Self psychology has been faulted for a polyanna view of human nature in which the darker side of life is pasted over as "fragmentation products" rather than confronted.

Self psychologists posit that the embodiment of self-object functions in other people is a normal lifelong process. Thus, self psychology predicts that extensive interpersonal interdependence is normative throughout life. Students of Mahler,[44, 45] who see development as moving toward independence, and students of Lacan,[46] who view the need for mirroring as inevitably distorting of the true self, regard these self psychology ideas as promoting psychological infantilism.

Prospects for Self Psychology

The combination of therapeutic usefulness, consonance with contemporary developmental research, and focus on problems important to our society has led to a growing interest in self psychology. Its ideas are applied to an ever-widening spectrum of normal and pathological states. Self psychology finds an audience among psychoanalysts and analytically oriented therapists. It is finding increasing links to other fields. Developmental psychology studies, especially studies of infants, suggest details of how self-object experience is created in the interpersonal world of the young child[26] and in later life.[16] Links with philosophical and social science studies of the construction of experience have led to extensions of self psychology to the study of *intersubjectivity,* the ways in which the experience of reality is mutually constructed between analyst and patient.[17, 47] The finding that needed self-objects are also the objects of fear and terror and that patients seem often to spoil the needed self-object has led to explorations of ways in which self-objects may be thought of in terms of object relations theories.[15] The best ideas of self psychology, like those of psychoanalysis in general, rapidly become invisible as part of the implicit assumptions that first therapists and later the public make about psychological function. Today, many analysts and therapists who would not describe themselves as self psychologists use ideas from self psychology freely in their work. Clearly, the area of influence of self psychology will continue to grow, and some variant of its theories will remain important in conceptualizing and treating many forms of psychological distress.

References

1. Freud S: Psycho-analytic notes on an autobiographical account of a case of paranoia (dementia paranoides). In Strachey J (trans-ed): The Standard Edition of the Complete Psychological Works of Sigmund Freud, Volume 12. London: Hogarth Press, 1958:3–82. Originally published in 1911.
2. Freud S: Formulations regarding the two principles of mental functioning. In Strachey J (trans-ed): The Standard Edition of the Complete Psychological Works of Sigmund Freud, Volume 12. London: Hogarth Press, 1958:215–226. Originally published in 1911.
3. Federn P: Ego Psychology. New York: Basic Books, 1952.
4. Fairbairn W: An Object Relations Theory of Personality. New York: Basic Books, 1952.
5. Winnicott D: The Maturational Process and the Facilitating Environment. New York: International Universities Press, 1965.
6. Erikson E: Childhood and Society, 2nd ed. New York: WW Norton, 1963.
7. Erikson E: Identity Youth and Crisis. New York: WW Norton, 1968.
8. Lasch C: The Culture of Narcissism: American Life in an Age of Diminishing Expectations. New York: WW Norton, 1979.
9. Keniston K: The Uncommitted: Alienated Youth in American Society. New York: Dell Books, 1960.
10. Keniston K: Inburn: An American Ishmael. In White RW (ed): The Study of Lives: Essays in Honor of Henry A. Murray. New York: Atherton-Aldine, 1963:43–71.
11. Fannon F; Ferrington C (trans): The Wretched of the Earth. New York: Grove Paperback, 1968.
12. Ornstein P: The Search for the Self: Selected Writings of Heinz Kohut: 1950–1978. New York: International Universities Press, 1978.
13. Kohut H: The Analysis of the Self. New York: International Universities Press, 1971.

13a. Kohut H: The Restoration of Self. New York: International Universities Press, 1977.

14. Kohut H: How Psychoanalysis Cures. Chicago: University of Chicago Press, 1984.
15. Becal H, Newman K: Theories of Object Relations: Bridges to Self Psychology. New York: Columbia University Press, 1990.
16. Galatzer-Levy R, Cohler B: The Essential Other: A Developmental Psychology of the Self. New York: Basic Books, 1993.
17. Stolorow R, Atwood G: Contexts of Being: The Intersubjective Foundations of Psychological Life. Hillsdale, NJ: Analytic Press, 1992.
18. Hartmann H: Understanding and explaining. In Essays in Ego Psychology. New York: International Universities Press, 1927:369–404.
19. Kohut H: Introspection, empathy, and psychoanalysis: An examination of the relationship between mode of observation and theory. In Ornstein P (ed): The Search for the Self, Volume 1. New York: International Universities Press, 1959:205–232.
20. Meissner W: Can psychoanalysis find its self? J Am Psychoanal Assoc 1986; 34:379–400.
21. Freud S: Three essays on the theory of sexuality. In Strachey J (trans-ed): The Standard Edition of the Complete Psychological Works of Sigmund Freud, Volume 7. London: Hogarth Press, 1953:130–243. Originally published in 1905.
22. Freud S: Fragment of an analysis of a case of hysteria. In Strachey J (trans-ed): The Standard Edition of the Complete Psychological Works of Sigmund Freud, Volume 7. London: Hogarth Press, 1953:7–122. Originally published in 1905.
23. Emde R: The prerepresentational self and its affective core. Psychoanal Study Child 1983; 38:165–192.
24. Goldberg A: The scientific status of empathy. Annu Psychoanal 1983; 11:155–169.
25. Goldberg A: Self psychology and alternatives to internalization. In Lichtenberg J, Kaplan S (eds): Reflections on Self Psychology. Hillsdale, NJ: Analytic Press, 1983:297–312.
26. Stern D: The Interpersonal World of the Infant. New York: Basic Books, 1985.
27. Wolf E: Treating the Self: Elements of Clinical Self Psychology. New York: Guilford Press, 1988.
28. Mahler M, Pine F, Bergman A: The Psychological Birth of a Human Infant. New York: Basic Books, 1975.
29. Bowlby J: Separation, Anxiety and Anger: Attachment and Loss, Volume 2. New York: Basic Books, 1973.
30. Cohler B, Galatzer-Levy R: Self, coherence and meaning in the second half of life. In Nemiroff R, Colarusso C (eds): New Dimensions in Adult Development. New York: Basic Books, 1990:214–259.
31. Galatzer-Levy R: The opening phase of psychotherapy of hypochondriasis. Int J Psychoanal Psychother 1982; 9:389–413.
32. Kohut H: Thoughts on narcissism and narcissistic rage. Psychoanal Study Child 1972; 27:360–400.
33. Katz J: Seductions of Crime: Moral and Sensual Attractions in Doing Evil. New York: Basic Books, 1988.
34. Freud S: On narcissism: an introduction. In Strachey J (trans-ed): The Standard Edition of the Complete Psychological Works of Sigmund Freud, Volume 14. London: Hogarth Press, 1957:73–102. Originally published in 1914.
35. Freud S: Remembering, repeating and working through: Further recommendations on the technique of psychoanalysis II. In Strachey J (trans-ed): The Standard Edition of the Complete Psychological Works of Sigmund Freud, Volume 12. London: Hogarth Press, 1958:146–156. Originally published in 1914.
36. Spitz R: Hospitalism: An inquiry into the genesis of psychiatric conditions in early childhood. Psychoanal Study Child 1945; 1:53–72.
37. Radke-Yarrow M, Cummings E, Kuczynski L, et al: Patterns of attachment in two- and three-year olds in normal families and families with parental depression. Child Dev 1985; 56:884–893.
38. Cohler B: Parenthood, psychopathology, and child-care. In Cohler BS, Weisman S, Cohen R (eds): Parenthood: A Psychodynamic Perspective. New York: Guildford Press, 1984:119–148.
39. Wallerstein JS, Johnston JR: Children of divorce: recent findings regarding long-term effects and recent studies of joint and sole custody. Pediatr Rev 1990; 11:197–204.
40. Levinson D: The Seasons of a Man's Life. New York: Alfred A Knopf, 1978.
41. Badaracco J, Ellsworth R: Leadership and the Quest for Integrity. Boston: Harvard Business School Press, 1988.
42. Wallerstein RS: One psychoanalysis or many? Int J Psychoanal 1988; 69:5–21.
43. Kohut H: Introspection, empathy and the semi-circle of mental health. Int J Psychoanal 1982; 63:395–407.
44. Settlage C: Childhood to adulthood: Structural change in development toward independence and autonomy. In Nemiroff R, Colarusso C (eds): New Dimensions in Adult Development. New York: Basic Books, 1990:26–43.
45. Settlage CF, Curtis J, Lozoff M, et al: Conceptualizing adult development. J Am Psychoanal Assoc 1988; 36:347–369.
46. Turkle S: Psychoanalytic culture: Jacques Lacan in the social appropriation of psychoanalysis. In Smith J, Morris H (eds): Telling Facts: History and Narration in Psychoanalysis. Baltimore: The Johns Hopkins University Press, 1992:220–263.
47. Stolorow R, Brandchaft B, Atwood G: Psychoanalytic Treatment: An Intersubjective Approach. Hillsdale, NJ: Analytic Press, 1987.

Jonathan E. Dunn

Intersubjectivity

Intersubjectivity in psychoanalysis refers to the dynamic interplay between the analyst's and the patient's subjective experiences in the clinical situation. To some extent, all schools of psychoanalysis agree on the significance of intersubjectivity in psychoanalytic work. However, in the current psychoanalytic literature, the concept of intersubjectivity constitutes a major epistemological and clinical challenge to the "classical" paradigm, which is grounded in the positivist scientific orientation.* Intersubjectivity embodies the notion that the very formation of the therapeutic process is derived from an inextricably intertwined mixture of the clinical participants' subjective reactions to one another. Knowledge of the patient's psychology is considered contextual and idiosyncratic to the particular clinical interaction. This interactional nexus is considered the primary force of the psychoanalytic treatment process.

The intersubjective position is that mental phenomena cannot be sufficiently understood if approached as an entity that exists "within" the patient's mind, conceptually isolated from the social matrix from which it emerges. These theorists see the analyst and the patient together constructing the clinical data from the interaction of both members' particular psychic qualities and subjective realities. The analyst's perceptions of the patient's psychology are always shaped by the analyst's subjectivity. Conversely, the patient's psychology is not conceptualized as something discoverable by an external, unbiased observer.[4–8]

The intersubjective theorists believe that a positivistically oriented search for a latent psychic reality beyond the analytical interaction is clinically and epistemologically misguided. They also construe the fundamental operation of mind as based in its striving for relational connection and communication, rather than discharge and gratification of endogenous instinctual pressures. For these reasons, the intersubjectivists contend that their method constitutes a new and more powerful scientific paradigm for psychoanalysis.[1, 9–11]

Intersubjectivists believe that their method is truer to the nature of human psychology. They view it as less mechanistic and less likely to reify mental life (i.e., assigns less material-like metaphors to essentially nonmaterial phenomena). Intersubjectivist theorists consider their method intrinsically more sensitive to the patient's relational needs, because it facilitates greater acuity to how the analyst's own psychology affects the patient's psychic activity and the treatment process.[12–19]

The positivistic, classical model of psychoanalysis, in contrast to an intersubjective one, shares aspects of the physical scientist's relationship to the object of investigation. The analyst is considered capable of situating himself or herself objectively enough outside the patient's psychic life, able to identify the constituents of the patient's mental processes that are seen to be operating within the patient, relatively independent of the analyst's influence. These classical theorists hold that the intersubjective interaction between analyst and patient forms only the *manifest* layer of the psychic data and that an underlying core substance of mind, rather than the clinical interaction, is the true motive force of the therapeutic process.

Classical analysts try to subordinate the intersubjective aspects of the psychiatrist-patient interaction to an understanding of the patient's mental processes in a way different from that of intersubjectivists. Classical psychoanalysis is distinguished from the intersubjective approach by its emphasis on a primordial existence of mental life that is separate from the immediate clinical interaction. Notions of biologically based instinctual urges and drives of the human body ground such assumptions.[20–22] Classical analysts view the drives' sequential development throughout the child's formative years (oral, anal, phallic, and genital) as cutting across history and culture. They surmise that because human beings share the same biological heritage, they must also share essential features of unconscious fantasy and pathogenic conflict; the form of mind changes, but not its substance.*

Classical analysts do not deny the subjectivity of knowledge, nor do they ignore the fact that reality can never be absolutely known. However, they take the idea that ego functioning contains an element of autonomy from internal and external pressures to mean that, to some extent, a person can accurately perceive the nature of an object outside his or her personal frame of reference. The irreducibility of our subjectivity does not doom us to *total* ignorance and misconception—it is not, in other words, an all-or-nothing proposition.[24] Classical analysts believe that the concept of the analyst as an objective observer is valid (although they may say that in a technical sense it needs to be less rigidly applied, that is, better adapted to the unique nature of human psychology and thus to the psychoanalytic situation). In their view, psychoanalysis should continue to refine its positivism-based methods, expanding the analyst's ability to "bracket out" distorting prejudices and thereby developing a greater capacity for objective observation.[25–28]

In the classical analytical view, a positivistic *striving* toward an *ideal* of objective truth facilitates a sufficiently appropriate uncertainty and openness in the clinical situation. This should be compared with pursuing an *idealization* of objective truth, in which pathological aspects of the analyst's narcissism dominate her or his clinical functioning. A rigid demand for absolutes in this approach leads to a dogmatic, authoritarian, and grandiose analytical sensibility. The classical analyst argues that the intersubjective critique may apply to the latter situation but not to the former. Classical theorists believe that the analyst can be aware of the interpersonal forces in the treatment while appreciating how these forces represent the intrapsychically driven, unconscious fantasies they consider to exist autonomously from the clinical interaction. Consequently, these analysts do not believe that the patient's humanity is deemphasized by their therapeutic strategy, nor do they believe that their

* The term *positivism* is used in this section in a general way, similar to how the intersubjective writers typically employ it in their critiques of the classical model. This use refers primarily to the classical notion that an attempt to factor out the observer's subjectivity through specific clinical postures can to some extent be done in a beneficial manner (these postures are discussed in the body of the section). Ironically, many positivist scientists[1–3] have denounced Freud's attempts to forge a positivistic method for a human psychology as vehemently as have the intersubjectivists.

*Fenichel wrote, "The instinctual needs are the raw material formed by the social influence; and it is the task of a psychoanalytic sociology to study the details of this shaping. Different 'biological constitutions' contain manifold possibilities; yet they are not realities but potentialities. It is experience, that is, the cultural conditions, that transform potentialities into realities, that shape the real mental structure of man by forcing his instinctual demands into certain directions, by favoring some of them and blocking others, and even by turning parts of them against the rest."[23(p588)] method inherently conceals the dynamically fluid intersubjective components of the clinical encounter.[29, 30]

The echo of the intersubjective-positivistic debate can be heard in all the challenges to classical freudian theory. This dispute bears on some of the central intellectual tensions spurring the growth of psychoanalysis since its inception. The debate can be traced to some of the contradictions in Freud's writing, especially in his concepts of countertransference (which is discussed in the next section of this review) and of ego development (taken up in the discussion of intersubjectivity and theoretical models).

References

1. Hoffman IZ: Some practical implications of a social constructivist view of the psychoanalytic situation. Psychoanal Dialogues 1992; 2:287–304.
2. Hook S: Psychoanalysis, Scientific Method and Philosophy. New York: New York University Press, 1959.
3. Popper KR: Conjectures and Refutations: The Growth of Scientific Knowledge. New York: Basic Books, 1963.
4. Hoffman IZ: Discussion: Towards a social-constructivist view of the psychoanalytic situation. Psychoanal Dialogues 1991; 1:74–105.
5. Ogden TH: The dialectically constituted/decentered subject of psychoanalysis. I. The Freudian subject. Int J Psychoanal 1992; 73:517–526.
6. Ogden TH: The dialectically constituted/decentered subject of psychoanalysis. II. The contributions of Klein and Winnicott. Int J Psychoanal 1992; 73:613–626.
7. Ogden T: The analytic third: Working with intersubjective clinical facts. Int J Psychoanal 1994; 75:3–19.
8. Spezzano C: Affects in Psychoanalysis: A Clinical Synthesis. Hillsdale, NJ: Analytic Press, 1993.
9. Atwood G, Stolorow R: Structures of Subjectivity: Explorations in Psychoanalytic Phenomenology. Hillsdale, NJ: Analytic Press, 1984.
10. Stolorow R, Brandchaft B, Atwood G: Contexts of Being: The Intersubjectivity Foundation of Psychological Life. Hillsdale, NJ: Analytic Press, 1992.
11. Spezzano C: The three faces of two person psychology. Psychoanal Dialogues, in press.
12. Stolorow R, Brandchaft B, Atwood G: Psychoanalytic Treatment: An Intersubjectivity Approach. Hillsdale, NJ: Analytic Press, 1987.
13. Benjamin J: The Bonds of Love: Psychoanalysis, Feminism and the Problem of Domination. New York: Pantheon Books, 1987.
14. Natterson J: Beyond Countertransference: The Therapist's Subjectivity in the Therapeutic Process. Northvale, NJ: Jason Aronson, 1991.
15. Mitchell S: Relational Concepts in Psychoanalysis: An integration. Cambridge, MA: Harvard University Press, 1988.
16. Aron L: The patient's experience of the analyst's subjectivity. Psychoanal Dialogues 1991; 1:29–51.
17. Greenberg J: Oedipus and Beyond. Cambridge, MA: Harvard University Press, 1991.
18. Renik O: Analytic interaction: Conceptualizing technique in light of the analyst's irreducible subjectivity. Psychoanal Q 1993; 62:553–571.
19. Modell A: The Private Self. Cambridge, MA: Harvard University Press, 1993.
20. Draenos S: Freud's Odyssey. New Haven, CT: Yale University Press, 1982.
21. Shengold L: Halo in the Sky. New York: Guilford Press, 1988.
22. Ritvo LB: Darwin's Influence on Freud: A Tale of Two Sciences. New Haven, CT: Yale University Press, 1990.
23. Fenichel O: The Psychoanalytic Theory of Neurosis. New York: WW Norton, 1945.
24. Whitebook J: A scrap of independence: On the ego's autonomy in Freud. Psychoanal Contemp Thought 1993; 16:359–382.
25. Brenner C: Psychoanalysis and science. J Am Psychoanal Assoc 1986; 16:675–696.
26. Brenner C: Psychoanalysis: Philosophy or science. In Hanley C, Lazerowitz M (eds): Psychoanalysis and Philosophy. New York: International Universities Press, 1973:35–45.
27. Blight JG: Must psychoanalysis retreat to hermeneutics? Psychoanalytic theory in the light of Popper's evolutionary epistemology. Psychoanal Q 1986; 4:147–206.
28. Wallerstein R: Psychoanalysis as a science: A response to the new challenges. Psychoanal Q 1986; 55:414–451.
29. Arlow J, Brenner C: The psychoanalytic process. Psychoanal Q 1990; 59:678–692.
30. Abrams S: The psychoanalytic process: The developmental and the integrative. Psychoanal Q 1990; 59:650–677.

Ralph E. Roughton

Relational Perspective, Interpersonal Psychoanalysis, and Social Constructivism

Relational Perspective

There is a momentum in contemporary psychoanalytic writing toward the full appreciation that the analyst's personal involvement in the analytic process is both inevitable and useful.[1–6] This relational perspective does not constitute a new psychoanalytic theory but, in fact, links together loosely a wide range of theoretical models, including interpersonal psychoanalysis, British object relations theory, self psychology, intersubjectivity, and social constructivism. The relational perspective addresses a different understanding of the role of the analyst as well as different ways of thinking about the basic motivational forces in human development.

This cluster of otherwise diverse and often competing theories has in common a greater emphasis on the actual here-and-now interaction between analyst and analysand, whether this is viewed in interpersonal or intrapsychic terms. It encompasses the participant observation of the interpersonalists, the projective identification and transference-countertransference focus of the British object relationists, the empathic immersion and self-object phenomena of the self psychologists, the analyst's stance *within* the observational field of the intersubjectivists, and the social constructivists' emphasis on the effect of the analyst's personal emotional presence on the analysand's experience.

These theoretical perspectives also have in common a deemphasis of Freud's drive theory as the basic motivational force and a greater emphasis on some version of the idea that the human organism seeks attachment and relations with others, not just drive discharge, as a basic motivational system. In this relational perspective, the individual as a separate entity is not the basic unit of study. Rather, the focus is on the interactional field, whether as mother-infant or analyst-analysand.[1]

The dividing line between this relational perspective and the work of some contemporary classical analysts is less than sharp and clear, particularly in the clinical interchange. As in most psychoanalytic controversies, theoretical explanations tend to sharpen conceptual differences, even when clinical practice reveals much similarity and overlap in what is actually said and done. Some writers, Winnicott and Loewald, for example, continued to use the terms *drive* and *instinct* but expanded their meanings to include a relational perspective. Loewald[7] redefined instinct not as an innate given but as developing out of interactions between the infant and the infant's human environment. Although they may differ in degree and in balance, drive theorists and relational theorists agree—as Freud himself repeatedly stressed—that both innate and experiential factors are influential, and it seems more useful to view the two stances as dialectical rather than as dichotomous.

Nevertheless, there are significant differences of emphasis, and certain points are more easily clarified by highlighting the contrasting points of view. The more rigorously analysts adhere to classical theory, the more they will work from the perspective of a one-person psychology, in which the locus of the psychoanalytic process is within the analysand's mind and in which everything is understood through the prism of intrapsychic compromise formation, unconscious fantasy, and psychic reality. Resistance and transference are the unfolding of the analysand's inner world in this new analytical setting, in which repetition of old experiences and response patterns is fostered, and the interpretive focus is on intrapsychic defensive operations that interfere with free association. The actual person and the behavior of the analyst are considered less important in determining the nature of transference and resistance. The analyst's position outside the observational field is thought to allow a more objective perspective from which to make confident interpretations of the analysand's intrapsychic experience and to monitor the analyst's own countertransference reactions that might have a negative impact on the interpretive work.

However, there has been an evolution of thinking among many analysts on these issues, so that differences between classical and relational perspectives are less striking than when each is presented in its most defining form. Many analysts may still accept the basic tenets of classical theory yet incorporate a degree of relational perspective in their clinical writing and may, for example, work comfortably within a clinical perspective that focuses on the here and now in the transference,[8] that recognizes countertransference as an ongoing source of data,[9] and that considers enactments to be inevitable and to provide useful insight.[6, 10–12]

Nevertheless, the relational perspective is defined by its much greater emphasis on a two-person psychology, both in the developing individual and in the clinical experience. The infant and the analysand both seek contact and interaction. Development and therapeutic effect both are seen as mediated through relationships. The locus of the psychoanalytic process is the interactive field of the two persons, even though the primary purpose is the understanding of the inner world of the analysand. As such, there is a tilt toward viewing the analytical relationship more in interpersonal terms rather than solely through the prism of the analysand's intrapsychic experience. Analysts are more likely to use their acknowledged subjectivity as a tool than to distance themselves behind a presumed objectivity. Transference is more often interpreted in its immediate manifest response to the actual person and behavior of the analyst than as a distorted perception of a neutral, objective analyst. Although interpretation and insight are still considered essential aspects of the analytical process, the therapeutic effects of the relationship are accorded a more prominent place.

Object relations, self psychology, and intersubjectivity are discussed elsewhere; the remainder of this section concentrates on interpersonal psychoanalysis and social constructivism as important embodiments of the relational perspective.

Interpersonal Psychoanalysis

In the late 1930s, a divergent approach to psychoanalytic theory and practice began to coalesce in the work of Harry Stack Sullivan, Erich Fromm, Frieda Fromm-Reichmann, and Karen Horney around some commonly held assumptions. They shared the belief that classical drive theory was fundamentally flawed and that freudian theory underemphasized social and cultural influences in explaining normal and pathological developments of personality. In discarding drive theory and emphasizing cultural influences, these analysts have often been misunderstood as having a "sociological" view of the individual as molded passively by the environment; their clinical work has been criticized as being superficial and ignoring passions and deeper conflicts. As Greenberg and Mitchell[13] pointed out, however, this is a serious misreading of their work. Deep, intense passions and conflicts are not ignored, but these analysts rejected the idea that they arise as derivatives of instinctual drives. Rather, they see passion and conflict arising in the relationships with others, whether real or imagined.

At about the same time that this interpersonal tradition was developing in the United States, another major contribution to the shift from a drive model to a relational model came from W. R. D. Fairbairn in Edinburgh, working in relative isolation from his kleinian colleagues in England. Unlike Sullivan, Fairbairn did not emphasize cultural factors so much as challenge the basic understanding of libido theory and assumptions about psychosexual development. Still working within the freudian framework, he sought to redefine the basic motivational principle of libido not as pleasure seeking but as object seeking. Fairbairn, like others who are now identified under the umbrella of the relational perspective, saw the human experience as a search for contact and attachment, not as a set of instinctual tensions seeking release.[13]

Fairbairn had an important influence on British object relations theory and deserves recognition, along with Sullivan, as one of the seminal thinkers in what has lately been characterized as the relational perspective. It would not be correct, however, to identify him with interpersonal psychoanalysis, which is the movement that diverged sharply from classical psychoanalysis under the influence of Sullivan and those who followed him in the United States.

Sullivan introduced the term *interpersonal* in 1927, and it is his name that has been most closely identified with that perspective. He saw the human mind as inherently dyadic and from earliest infancy in constant responsive interaction with its caretakers. Research on infants supports such a view.[14] Although the terms interpersonal and intrapsychic have come to represent a dichotomy in much of psychoanalytic discourse, Sullivan did not reject the concepts associated with the intrapsychic perspective so much as object to the exclusion of the interpersonal from the classical perspective. What he did uncompromisingly oppose was drive theory because, as understood at that time, the drives as the primary motive force arose independently in the id and were sheltered from the interpersonal field. As Mitchell[15] has pointed out, the concept of drive has been increasingly "interpersonalized" in later theoretical developments, so that contemporary interpersonalists find the concept less objectionable.

Sullivan was not an integrative theorizer or a compelling writer in the ways that Freud was. In addition, he was not a rebel from orthodox psychoanalysis, as were other innovators. He came from the world of general psychiatry with a talent for working with patients suffering from schizophrenia in an operationalist methodology, and he tended not to use the language of psychoanalysis but to develop his own nomenclature. These factors, apart from the perceived merit of his ideas, have made him less known to more traditional psychoanalysts. Even some contemporary interpersonalists believe that Sullivan's theories lacked a sufficient conception of the inner world.[15] For example, he explained mental disorder as the result of inadequate interpersonal communication due to the interfering effect of anxiety.[16] Those who have studied his work stress that what sounds naive in his explanations is nevertheless grounded in a depth of understanding of the human condition and a respect for the uniqueness for the individual, and this allowed him to be uncommonly effective with patients. These therapeutic principles have endured and are now finding new credibility in the current interest in the relational perspective. More in-depth study of Sullivan's ideas and of interpersonal psychoanalysis than can be presented here is available for those interested.[1, 13, 15–20]

Social Constructivism

Hoffman[2, 5, 21–23] has introduced a new paradigm for understanding the psychoanalytic situation, which he calls social constructivism. The "social" part of the term refers to the analyst's personal presence and involvement in the analytical situation, and thus it is linked to the interpersonal and the relational perspectives. However, Hoffman emphasized that beyond the shift from drive to relational issues of those perspectives, his new paradigm proclaims a shift from a positivist to a constructivist model as well. That is, not only is the analyst personally involved in the analytical situation, but personal involvement is wedded to the construction of meaning for the patient, because the analyst's understanding is always a function of her or his perspective at any given moment. In Hoffman's view, the analyst is continually implicated in "constructing" the patient's experience, and not to attend to that aspect of the analytical relationship is to miss the vital issue.

Constructivism generally refers to the concept that meanings are generated, as texts are interpreted, rather than there being one true meaning awaiting discovery. Hoffman's social constructivism goes further. It is not simply an interpreting of reality but a shaping of it through the mutual and reciprocal influences in the interpersonal analytical relationship. He also contrasted his view with the constructivism of Schafer,[24] which he described as concerned primarily with the effect that the analyst's theoretical bias or occasional countertransference has on the way the analysand's story emerges. Hoffman objected to Schafer's view of countertransference as occasional and undesirable and to be overcome. He wanted to free analysts to be themselves and to speak their minds, constrained only by the purposes of the analysis.[2, 5, 23]

Lest this sound like casting off all knowledge and previous experience in favor of uncharted spontaneity, Hoffman[2] was quick to assure his readers that he was advocating a subtle diminishing of the authority of theory in favor of a subtle increase in respect for the analyst's awareness of and use of personal subjective experience in guiding what he or she does and says. Subjective experience, for both analyst and analysand, is a continuous stream, only a small fraction of which can be attended to at any given moment. What is selected from that stream of experience is influenced by the unconscious determinants that include the patient's transference and the analyst's countertransference. Hoffman's point is that it is impossible to avoid the analyst's influence in this subtle selection. Therefore, rather than attempting to control subjectivity and remain outside the action, analysts should feel free in their subjectivity and embrace the uncertainty of this freedom.[23]

Hoffman made the point that patients are extremely sensitive to certain facets of their analysts' ambiguous responses to them. What is often called distortion in the transference is instead a highly selective attention to something present in the analyst, something that one patient notices but another will ignore.[21] As Racker[25] has said, interpreting the transference fully means being receptive to the patient's interpretation of the countertransference.

Hoffman[2(p302)] was careful to place these innovations within a firm psychoanalytic frame, and he detailed its features, which include "a circumscribed time and place; the asymmetry of personal expression in the process; a primary interest in exploring the patient's experience, . . . a commitment by the analyst to critical reflection on his or her own participation; and a sense of the relationship as a whole as a means of promoting the patient's development. Every interaction in this context is experienced by the analyst as a psychoanalytic interaction. There are no exceptions. . . . the stamp of the analytic situation should never be lost on the participants."

Social constructivism is Hoffman's term, and it is his papers that most fully explore these concepts. Nevertheless, Gill's contribution to this concept must also be acknowledged, as Hoffman carefully does. Through a series of works in the past 15 years, Gill's thinking about transference and mutual influence and constructivism has evolved in this direction, although he may not have gone as far as Hoffman. Gill's[4(p156)] view of transference is "the analysand's plausible experience of the relationship. It is based on the contributions of both participants to the here-and-now interaction as well as on their respective past experiences." Countertransference is defined similarly as based on contributions of both participants in present interaction and from past experiences. Although Gill kept his roots in classical theory, he adopted a constructivist perspective, and he insisted that psychoanalysis is both a one-person and a two-person psychology, that the innate and experiential are always working together, and that the analytical situation is a continuing interaction between two participants that must be the subject of mutual exploration.[4]

Conclusion

This brief excursion through the changing landscape of psychoanalysis highlights one important aspect: how we regard the influence of other people on the individual, whether it is the mother of the developing infant or the analyst of the adult analysand. Sullivan and Fairbairn differed radically from Freud about a basic concept, yet Sullivan led a revolution while Fairbairn quietly influenced an evolution. The contemporary proponents of both tracks seem to be converging again, along with contemporary classical analysts who are also finding their way to a greater appreciation of the relational perspective. Despite some territorial arguments,[26, 27] they are all heading in the same general direction and proving that psychoanalysis remains vital, largely because of its capacity for evolving modification.

References

1. Mitchell SA: Relational Concepts in Psychoanalysis: An Integration. Cambridge, MA: Harvard University Press, 1988.
2. Hoffman IZ: Some practical implications of a social-constructivist view of the psychoanalytic situation. Psychoanal Dialogues 1992; 2:287–304.
3. Renik O: Analytic interaction: Conceptualizing technique in light of the analyst's irreducible subjectivity. Psychoanal Q 1993; 62:553–571.
4. Gill MM: Psychoanalysis in Transition: A Personal View. Hillsdale, NJ: Analytic Press, 1994.
5. Hoffman IZ: Dialectical thinking and therapeutic action in the psychoanalytic process. Psychoanal Q 1994; 63:187–218.
6. Roughton RE: Repetition and interaction in the analytic process: Enactment, acting out, and collusion. Annu Psychoanal 1994; 22:275–290.
7. Loewald HW: Instinct theory, object relations, and psychic-structure. J Am Psychoanal Assoc 1978; 26:493–506.
8. Gill MM: Analysis of Transference, Volume 1, Theory and Technique. Madison, CT: International Universities Press, 1982.
9. Jacobs TJ: On countertransference enactments. J Am Psychoanal Assoc 1986; 36:673–695.
10. Chused JF: The evocative power of enactments. J Am Psychoanal Assoc 1991; 39:615–629.
11. McLaughlin JT: Clinical and theoretical aspects of enactment. J Am Psychoanal Assoc 1991; 39:595–614.
12. Renik O: Countertransference enactment and the psychoanalytic process. In Horowitz MJ, Kernberg OF, Weinshel EM (eds): Psychic Structure and Psychic Change. Madison, CT: International Universities Press, 1993:135–158.
13. Greenberg JR, Mitchell SA: Interpersonal psychoanalysis. In Object Relations in Psychoanalytic Theory. Cambridge, MA: Harvard University Press, 1983:79–115.
14. Stern D: The Interpersonal World of the Infant. New York: Basic Books, 1985.
15. Mitchell SA: The intrapsychic and the interpersonal: Different theories, different domains, or historical artifacts? Psychoanal Inquiry 1988; 8:472–496.
16. Levenson E: The Ambiguity of Change: An Inquiry into the Nature of Psychoanalytic Reality. New York: Basic Books, 1983.
17. Guntrip H: H. S. Sullivan's interpersonal theory of psychiatry. In Personality Structure and Human Interaction. New York: International Universities Press, 1961:174–191.
18. Mullahy P: Psychoanalysis and Interpersonal Psychiatry: The Contributions of Harry Stack Sullivan. New York: Science House, 1970.
19. Sullivan HS: The Collected Works of Harry Stack Sullivan, Volumes 1 and 2. New York: WW Norton, 1953, 1956.
20. Antonovsky AM: Object relations theory and interpersonal theory: Some comparative comments. Psychoanal Contemp Thought 1987; 10:533–555.
21. Hoffman IZ: The patient as interpreter of the analyst's experience. Contemp Psychoanal 1983; 19:389–422.
22. Hoffman IZ: Toward a social-constructivist view of the psychoanalytic situation. Psychoanal Dialogues 1991; 1:74–105.
23. Hoffman IZ: Expressive participation and psychoanalytic discipline. Contemp Psychoanal 1992; 28:1–15.
24. Schafer R: The Analytic Attitude. New York: Basic Books, 1983.
25. Racker H: Transference and Countertransference. New York: International Universities Press, 1968.
26. Bachant JL, Richards AD: Review essay: Relational concepts in psychoanalysis: An integration by Stephen A. Mitchell. Psychoanal Dialogues 1993; 3:431–460.
27. Mitchell SA: Reply to Bachant and Richards. Psychoanal Dialogues 1993; 3:461–480.

Otto F. Kernberg

Lacan

Jacques Lacan was one of the major and probably the most controversial of the theoreticians influencing the development of psychoanalytic thinking during the second half of this century. Whereas his influence has been particularly marked in France, his thinking has had indirect influences on both French mainstream psychoanalysis and contemporary psychoanalysis in general. Paradoxically, the impact of French psychoanalysts who argued with him has fostered psychoanalytic exploration in new domains and raised the awareness of his work throughout the psychoanalytic community.

Lacan was a member of the Paris Psychoanalytic Society in 1953 when he was asked to resign because of his suggested modification of psychoanalytic technique. In 1964, he founded the École Française de Psychanalyse and, eventually, the École Freudienne de Paris. Although his disagreements with the French psychoanalytic establishment and with the International Psychoanalytic Association centered on his innovations in technique, the major impact of his ideas was in the realm of theory, particularly of metapsychology and early development.

Major Contributions

Lacan's central proposal was that the freudian unconscious is structured like a natural language.[1, 2] He conceived of the unconscious as a kind of discourse, without differentiating between thought and language.[3] Following de Saussure's[4] description of the arbitrary relationship between phonic and conceptual aspects of language, Lacan established a relationship between the "signifiers" (linguistic symbols) and the underlying "signified" (their unconscious contents). The discourse of the unconscious refers to the main unconscious conflicts and fantasies described by Freud, centering on the Oedipus complex.

Lacan viewed the unconscious as disrupting conscious discourse, particularly by means of negation and ambiguity, creating an openness of meaning that permits the interpretation of "another scene," a text behind the text. Slips, dreams, and so on reveal the "true speech" of the "subject" who free associates.

Lacan differentiated between communication to the other (with a lowercase o) as the object and communication to the Other (with a capital O) representing the unconscious as linguistic discourse. The conscious speech of the patient communicates unconscious messages that directly reach the unconscious of the analyst, who in addition to deciphering the hidden messages behind the patient's conscious discourse expresses direct messages to the patient's unconscious, in part beyond his or her own awareness, while addressing the patient's consciousness.

Metaphor and Metonymy

The two principal characteristics of unconscious discourse, in Lacan's view, are metaphor and metonymy, roughly corresponding to Freud's description of, respectively, condensation and displacement as characteristics of the primary process. Lacan used Freud's method of dream interpretation, proposing that the analyst interpret the distortions in the patient's chains of signifiers, because the signified erupts into conscious language by means of metonymy and metaphor at particular "nodal" points of communication where conscious and unconscious meanings become condensed. These nodes of condensed meanings in the patient's conscious discourse are a dominant focus of the lacanian analyst's attention.

The interpretation of displacements and condensation in conscious discourse thus opens the road to unconscious meanings. In the course of psychoanalytic communication, the analyst tries to decode the eruption of unconscious meanings in herself or himself and the patient; the analyst communicates these to the patient, who now receives his or her own message "in inverted form," that is, elaborated by the analyst. Lacan's technique encourages the analyst to be largely silent, an effort to maximally stimulate the patient's unconscious desire for communication at the same time that the awareness of the impossibility of full expression of unconscious desire evolves throughout the hours.[5]

Drives, Needs, Desire, and Wishes

Lacan[6] developed Freud's concepts of drive by differentiating physiological or biological "needs" from the psychological experience of needs, or "desire": desire reflects basic, general, diffuse psychic notions, in contrast to "wishes," which are more concrete, circumscribed forms of desire. The original physiological shortcomings and needs of the infant bring about a psychic experience of void that creates a primary desire for completion or fulfillment. For Lacan, this desire for completion is the original determinant of the ideational contents of the unconscious—of unconscious fantasies and wishes. The desire for completion takes the form of the phallus, that is, a symbolic, self-satisfying, autonomous, complete entity that at first cannot be differentiated practically from primary narcissism and from the wish fulfillment of symbiotic oneness.[1]

The rupture of the infant's symbiotic fusion with mother reopens the infant's basic sense of void and the desire for refusion with mother to again become the phallus. Primary fantasies include the wish first to *be* the phallus, then to become mother's phallus. These fantasies form the prototype of later oedipal wishes as well as of the desire to re-fuse with mother in a narcissistic regression. Still later, the fantasy of becoming father's phallus and of becoming father himself as the symbolic phallus concludes by transforming the earliest desire for completion into the structured Oedipus complex.

The experience of birth and postnatal separation from mother constitutes the earliest trauma activating the infant's primary sense of incompleteness and void, and it is the origin of castration anxiety together with the awareness of the unbridgeable incompleteness of both sexes who will need each other to achieve completion. This desire for completion, for becoming the phallus (at all the levels described), can never be satisfied.

The reality principle enters with the awareness of the impossibility of obtaining or restoring the desired symbiotic fusion; it is represented symbolically by the "law of the father." The law of the father (or the name of the father) symbolized as phallus intrudes into the symbiotic relationship between infant and mother; prevents the infant from being everything for mother; and condemns the infant to an eternal desire (for completion) that can never be fully satisfied, to castration anxiety (because of this radical separation and loss), and to the earliest fantasy about completion represented by the parental pair. Lacan[7] analyzed the *Fort-Da* game described by Freud[8] as the acceptance of renunciation and the simultaneous entry into the realm of the symbolic, that is, linguistic discourse and the rules governing social life.

The desire for completion also becomes the desire of mother to accept the child as a substitute phallus. The complex interaction of the desire of both participants has multiple meanings. The desire for the Other also stands for the desire for the phallus and at root for completion. A key concept for Lacan was that the *desire for the desire of the other* (originally the mother) constitutes the basic form of love and gives a narcissistic frame to all love relations.

Psychic Reality

Lacan[1, 2] divided the realm of psychic reality into three major areas: the symbolic, the imaginary, and the real. The imaginary refers to pictorial fantasy influenced by unconscious processes and originates in an early stage of development (from 6 to 18 months of age) that Lacan called the mirror stage.[9] The infant's self-discovery of his or her image in the mirror initiates the capacity for self-reflection. The ego is therefore for Lacan a fantastic, alienated, or "specular self" that does not correspond to the authentic self *(je),* the subject of unconscious discourse. The mirror stage therefore initiates a radical split between unconscious discourse, on the one hand, and conscious and preconscious discourse and fantasy, on the other. It is in the realm of the imaginary that the desire for completion, the various phases of desire for the other, and the desire to become or obtain the phallus are played out. The ego *(le moi)* is therefore an alienating and alienated agency, center of all the resistance to the exploration of the unconscious.

The symbolic, in contrast, represents, first of all, the order represented by natural language, the structure of the unconscious, but also the father's law (the name of the father) that disrupts the identification of the infant with mother, originating castration anxiety and leading eventually to the acceptance of the oedipal situation. The symbolic thus encodes the oedipal prohibitions, the acknowledgment of triangularity and the impossibility of becoming mother's phallus. It is thus the locus of social and conventional reality, as opposed to the imaginary realm, in which unconsciously determined preconscious wishes and fantasies are played out.

It is difficult to describe what is included in the concept of the real, which, by definition, includes everything not included in the imaginary or the symbolic. The real may refer to ordinary reality insofar as it is not included as part of psychic reality as well as to the ultimate limits of psychic reality given by death. It appears as the traumatic, which defies both symbolization and imagination. A later concept of Lacan must be mentioned here, namely, that of *jouissance*.[1, 7, 10] This is a sense of total enjoyment and gratification linked to an illusory attainment of fusion in extreme pleasure that erases all differences and differentiation, combines heightened sexual pleasure with extreme aggression, and ultimately signifies emotional death. The fulfillment of *jouissance,* eliminating all differences between sexes and generations in reaching total narcissistic completion, erases the barrier between the symbolic and the imaginary realms and is equivalent to the real as the death of the ego.

If *jouissance* reflects a projection of illusory totality and completion (and total destruction) into the future, the concept of foreclosure *(forclusion)* refers to Lacan's interpretation of one primitive form of the mechanism of denial in which there is a failure to establish the symbolic.[2] This implies an incapacity to insert oneself into the symbolic order, into the triangular structure of the Oedipus complex, and to acknowledge the law of the father—that is to say, into ordinary reality—and is represented by psychotic regression, particularly the emergence of hallucination. Psychotic developments, for Lacan, cover a "hole" or blank space in the symbolic universe where the foreclosed name of the father should be.[11]

Technique

With regard to treatment, lacanian literature contains little description of extended clinical material. Lacan's formulations imply that the patient initially speaks about herself or himself without being able to speak to the analyst. Only gradually does the analyst's help, in reflecting to the patient her or his own unconscious communications to the analyst, permit the patient to become aware of unconscious desire. This development signals the beginning of the completion of treatment. The patient shifts from "empty words" to a period of "full words" when the ability to incorporate unconscious discourse into conscious discourse increases. The patient gradually has to let the id speak and to overcome the self-deceptive function of the conscious system of language.

The psychoanalytic "cure" thus consists of a gradual approach to unconscious discourse, but the dialectic between the conscious and unconscious split is never fully resolved. In fact, a complete collapse of the tension between the symbolic and the imaginary realms can lead to a sense of nothingness equivalent to (psychic) death. In this connection, Lacan pointed to the dialectic of a *jouissance* as joyful liberty to let oneself be experienced by one's own unconscious and a *jouissance* as a total reality of fusion between consciousness and unconsciousness, which implies death.

For Lacan, the concept of transference referred not to the moment to moment shifts in unconscious object relations activated in the psychoanalytic situation but to the gradual replication of the oedipal situation in the analysis: the patient's unconscious addresses itself to the analyst's unconscious as the Other, reflecting both the order of the symbolic and the oedipal father. The analyst, in turn, in carrying out her or his interpretive function, enacts the symbolic order interfering with the imaginary relation between the patient and the analyst as a primitive, maternal object. The transference thus expresses both the patient's desire to reestablish a symbiotic completion with the analyst as primordial mother and the relation to the oedipal father as the "subject of supposed knowledge." The mostly silent analyst gradually contributes to resolving both transferential currents by an interpretive "question and answer game."

Comment

I have tried in this brief outline to convey the global and ambiguous way in which Lacan described the psychoanalytic situation as interplay of overlapping and crisscrossing, conscious and unconscious messages between patient and analyst. The most controversial aspect of lacanian technique is the variable duration of the hour. Lacan proposed that the dominance of empty words justifies interrupting an hour when no real communication from the unconscious is evolving. He also recommended stopping a session after a significant piece of work has been achieved. The underlying principle is that the unconscious speaks irrespective of the "objective" duration of the hour, and the analyst has to listen to his or her own unconscious as well as to the patient's to decide an optimal duration of their interchange. In general, the lacanian analyst is extremely attentive to the linguistic aspects of the patient's discourse. There is an almost exclusive focus on the verbal in contrast to the analysis of nonverbal behavior.

The ambiguity of lacanian language and even of central concepts has been widely criticized.[3, 12] We have seen this exemplified in the multiple meanings Lacan attributed to such central concepts as the other, the phallus, the symbolic, and the real. Lacan conveyed the impression that he demonstrated his theory—that the unconscious speaks directly to the unconscious of the other—by means of an ambiguous and evocative presentation of his theories, as if to speak directly to the unconscious of the reader. Green[13, 14] has addressed Lacan's neglect of the affective aspects of unconscious functioning, stressing that drives are expressed not only in cognitive discourse but in the affective implications of unconscious fantasy and internalized object relations.

The absence of detailed, well-documented clinical evidence for many of Lacan's assertions, and of clinical illustrations in the use of key concepts such as the symbolic, the imaginary, and the real, is another problem area. The sharpest criticism, however, is warranted by the lack of a detailed, explicit technique in Lacan's writings and that of his school in general; the almost total neglect of areas such as nonverbal communication, character analysis, the interplay of concrete transference, and countertransference developments; and the almost exclusive focus on linguistic structure and content in the hours.

On the positive side, Lacan has strongly influenced an entire generation of French psychoanalysts. André Green's studies on affect,[13] his analysis of the "narcissism of death,"[15] and his important work on the negative[16] have sources in Lacan's study of foreclosure. Green's study of the structure of subjectivity is in reaction to Lacan's neglect of the affective aspects of the unconscious. Chasseguet-Smirgel's[17, 18] description of the archaic Oedipus, of primitive narcissistic wishes for merger into a utopian world without boundaries linked to regressive fantasies about the content of mother's body, and her description of perversion as the rupture of boundaries between sexes and generations may be considered to have roots in Lacan's stress on the early Oedipus complex. The study by Marty and colleagues[19] of psychosomatic disorders and the contributions of Aulagnier[20] to psychosis have roots in Lacan's concept of foreclosure. Laplanche's[21] theories about the "enigmatic" function of mother's linguistic communication to the infant and its role regarding the origins of primal fantasy also have roots in Lacan's formulation about the imaginary and the symbolic order. Then, too, Lacan's emphasis on Freud's concept of *Nachträglichkeit* (that is, the retrospective modification of early experience in the light of later trauma) has raised questions regarding linear models of development in a way that has strongly influenced French psychoanalytic thinking.

In short, the concept of the oedipal situation as a permanent structure of the content of the mind as well as a basic developmental principle and the description of fantastic aspects of the primitive oedipal situation have been provocative contributions regarding early development that have stimulated important work in the psychoanalytic literature. Lacan's criticism of ego psychology, in terms of its fostering an alienating theoretical distancing from the unconscious realm of psychic reality, has contributed to a shift of that pendulum.

References

1. Lacan J: Écrits. Paris: Seuil, 1966.
2. Lacan J: Le Séminaire, Livre I, Les Écrits Techniques de Freud. Paris: Seuil, 1975.
3. Bär EB: Understanding Lacan. Psychoanal Contemp Sci 1974; 3:473–545.
4. Saussure F de; de Mauro T (ed): Cours de Linguistique Générale. Paris: Payot, 1978.
5. Lacan J: Le Séminaire, Livre II, Le Moi dans la Théorie de Freud et dans la Technique de la Psychanalyse. Paris: Seuil, 1978.
6. Lacan J; Miller JA (ed); Sheridan A (trans): The Four Fundamental Concepts of Psycho-Analysis. London: Hogarth Press and the Institute of Psycho-Analysis, 1977.
7. Lacan J: Le Séminaire, Livre XX, Encore. Paris: Seuil, 1975.
8. Freud S: Beyond the pleasure principle. In Strachey J (trans-ed): The Standard Edition of the Complete Psychological Works of Sigmund Freud, Volume 18. London: Hogarth Press, 1955:7–64. Originally published in 1920.
9. Lacan J: The mirror state as formative of the function of the I as revealed in psychoanalytic experience. In Sheridan A (trans): Écrits: A Selection. New York: WW Norton, 1977.
10. Miller JA (ed); Porter D (trans): The Seminar of Jacques Lacan. New York: WW Norton, 1986.
11. Lacan J: Le Séminarie, Livre III, Les Psychoses. Paris: Seuil, 1981.
12. Bowie M: Freud, Proust and Lacan: Theory as Fiction. London: Cambridge University Press, 1987.
13. Green A: Le Discours Vivent: La Conception Psychanalytique de l'Affect. Paris: Presses Universitaires de France, 1973.
14. Green A: On Private Madness. Madison, CT: International Universities Press, 1993.
15. Green A: Narcissism de Vie. Narcissisme de Mort. Paris: Les Éditions de Minuit, 1983.
16. Green A: Le Travail du Négatif. Paris: Les Éditions de Minuit, 1993.
17. Chasseguet-Smirgel J: Creativity and Perversion. New York: WW Norton, 1984.
18. The archaic matrix of the Oedipus complex in utopias. In Sexuality and Mind. New York: New York University Press, 1986.
19. Marty P, M'Uzan M de, David C: L'Investigation Psychosomatique. Sept Observations Cliniques. Paris: Presses Universitaires de France, 1963.
20. Aulagnier P: La Violence de l'Interprétation: Du Pictogramme à l'Énoncé. Paris: Presses Universitaires de France, 1975.
21. Laplanche J; Fletcher J, Stanton M (eds): Seduction, Translation, and the Drives. London: Psychoanalytic Forum, Institute of Contemporary Arts, 1992.

Glossary of Psychoanalytic Terms*

Abreaction The discharge of affect associated with a traumatic memory. Abreaction may be brought about by hypnosis or free association.

Adaptive point of view A metapsychological framework that considers how the developing mind is influenced by environmental realities. In this model, the ego is thought of as the "organ" of adaptation.

Aggressive drive One of the primary instinctual drives, aggression includes the urge to harm or destroy, the urge to dominate or prevail over others, and strivings toward mastery. The aggressive drive is a major source of intrapsychic conflict.

Anal Stage of psychosocial development from about 18 months to 3 years during which pleasures and conflicts center on defecation and urination and their symbolic derivatives. In addition, with increased cognitive and motor development, issues of mastery, autonomy, obedience, and defiance are observed.

Cathexis The attachment of mental energy to a thought or memory, resulting in an increased emotional or motivational intensity associated with the thought or memory.

Character (personality) disorder Habitually and generally inflexible patterns of behavior that are ego-syntonic, that is, cause little subjective discomfort and are experienced as appropriate, reasonable, and justified. Such behavior may actually cause problems in adaptive functioning and interpersonal relationships.

Compromise formation An activity of the ego that attempts to solve conflicts between opposing forces operating in the mind, in particular the gratification of instinctual wishes that are prohibited by the superego or by reality. Compromises may take many forms, including character traits, neurotic symptoms, dreams and fantasies, adaptive behavior, and transference.

Conscious The portion of mental activity and content that is directly available to immediate perception (as opposed to unconscious or preconscious). Conscious mentation obeys rational, secondary process logic.

---

* From Moore BE, Fine BD (eds): Psychoanalytic Terms and Concepts. New Haven, CT: American Psychoanalytic Association and Yale University Press, 1990. © Yale University.

Countertransference Attitudes and feelings of the psychiatrist toward the patient. As narrowly defined, countertransference comes about as a result of activation of wishes, fantasies, or conflicts from the psychiatrist's life. More broadly defined, countertransference also includes reactions to the patient's projections or role enactments. Countertransference responses have the potential to have a negative impact on the therapeutic approach to the patient and also to provide data about unconscious processes occurring in patient and psychiatrist.

Defense mechanism Specific unconscious operations used by the ego to protect against the fantasied dangers associated with conscious awareness of unconscious wishes. Examples include repression, displacement, reaction formation, projection, isolation, and undoing.

Depressive position In kleinian theory, a constellation of internal object relations, defenses, and anxieties in which others are viewed ambivalently (as containing both goodness and badness, as opposed to the split objects of the paranoid-schizoid position) and in which fear and guilt are felt around the fantasy that one's aggressive impulses may destroy the needed and loved object.

Developmental point of view Metapsychological perspective that emphasizes the progressive unfolding of stages of development and focuses on the contribution of childhood experience to the psychology of the adult.

Dynamic-motivational point of view Metapsychological perspective that considers the actions of mental forces (wishes or needs inherent in the nature of humans), which may be in opposition to one another, resulting in conflict and compromise.

Dynamic unconscious The contents and processes of the system unconscious, which are kept outside conscious awareness by repression.

Ego In the structural model, the mental agency that is positioned between the physiologically based instinctual urges and the outer world. Its functions include mediating between the pressures of the id, superego, and reality and the variety of processes of perception, cognition, memory, motor behavior, and learning.

Ego ideal The portion of superego functions that includes goals, ideals, and standards of thought and behavior. It is involved in the experience of self-esteem, pride, and shame.

Empathy A mode of knowing or perceiving the emotional or psychological state of another, in which the quality of experience of one person is momentarily shared by another.

Envy A primitive emotion of desire, of wanting what the other has, combined with a hostile wish to destroy or spoil the source of that which is desired.

Fixation The persistence of modes of gratifying impulses, reacting defensively to perceived dangers, and relating to objects that belong to earlier stages of psychosexual development. Points of fixation can be returned to in the process of regression.

Free association The basic activity in psychoanalytic treatment in which the patient reports everything that comes to mind without the usual selectiveness used in conventional discourse.

Id In the structural model, the collection of unconscious drives and drive derivatives that continually push for gratification.

Insight The conscious recognition and comprehension of previously unconscious mental content and conflicts, as occurs during psychoanalytic treatment. Insight is typically accompanied by adaptive behavioral changes.

Instinctual drives Innate motivational forces originating within the organism that seek discharge or gratification. In Freud's theory, drives are characterized by their source, aim, and object. The two basic instincts are the sexual and the aggressive.

Internalization A process by which aspects and functions of need-gratifying relationships are taken into the self and represented in its psychic structure. Types of internalization include incorporation, introjection, and identification.

Interpretation The principal type of therapeutic intervention in psychoanalytic treatment that brings to the patient's attention observations about his or her mental processes and their underlying motives, conflicts, compromises, wishes, needs, and patterns of object relations. The expected outcome of interpretation is insight, psychic structural change, and symptomatic improvement.

Latency Stage of psychosexual development between the approximate ages of 5 and 12 years in which the sexual drives and conflicts are less apparent and the major activities of the child are learning and other socially approved channels of gratification.

Libido Term originally used to refer to sexual desire but later used by Freud to describe the metapsychological concept of mental "energy" that could be deployed toward and attached to various mental representations or psychic structures.

Metapsychology An abstract conceptual framework used to organize, systematize, and orient clinical observations.

Narcissism In its original use, narcissism refers to self-love, but the term was elaborated theoretically by Freud to refer to the libidinal cathexis of the self (or ego). In modern theory, aspects of character organization, self-experience, affect regulation, and object relations are discussed along the dimension of normal versus pathological narcissism.

Neurosis A set of psychiatric syndromes characterized by abnormalities of emotions, attitudes, behavior, and thought and that have in common (in psychoanalytic theory) their origins in unconscious psychic conflict. Classic neuroses include hysteria, obsessions, phobias, and certain types of depression. The symptoms of neurosis are ego-dystonic, that is, are recognized by the patient as abnormal and alien to the self.

Object As defined by Freud, a person or thing through which instinctual needs can be gratified. The inner mental schemas or constructions that conceptualize other persons are referred to as object representations. The theory of object relations examines the relationship of the self to internal objects and the interpersonal enactments of these mental phenomena.

Object constancy A developmental achievement in which mental representations of love objects are experienced as constant and stable, despite their availability or unavailability.

Oral The stage of psychosexual development occurring in the first 18 months of life, during which the oral and perioral areas provide the major source of sensual pleasure. Because the infant is extremely dependent during this stage, optimal development requires considerable parental attunement to the needs of the infant; if this is provided satisfactorily, the infant should acquire a sense of trust and a sense that the world is safe and that the infant's needs will be met.

Paranoid-schizoid position In kleinian theory, the earliest and most primitive mental organization, in which there is a predominance of the defenses of projective identification, splitting, primitive denial, and idealization. During moments of frustration in this stage, there is the experience of diffuse rage and persecutory anxiety.

Phallic-oedipal Stage of psychosexual development from approximately 3 to 6 years of age, during which the genitals become the major source of sensual pleasure. During this stage, the child develops an intense desire to possess exclusively the parent of the opposite sex and to eliminate the other parent who is perceived as a rival. The jealous conflict of this triangular relationship, with accompanying fantasies of retaliation by castration, leads eventually to identification with the parents and the development of the superego.

Pleasure-unpleasure principle The tendency of the mental apparatus to seek pleasure and avoid unpleasure. According to Freud's libido theory, pleasure is attained through drive discharge, and unpleasure represents the buildup of undischarged mental energy.

Preconscious In the topographical theory, mental content and processes that are not conscious but can be readily accessed by the direction of attention.

Primary process Type of mentation associated with the unconscious, characterized by irrationality and a predominant emphasis on wish fulfillment and drive discharge. Primary process logic involves many of the mechanisms and qualities seen in dreams, including symbolization, displacement, condensation, absence of negatives, and timelessness.

Psychic determinism A central idea of psychoanalysis, which asserts that all psychological events are influenced and shaped by past experiences that nothing in mental life occurs solely by chance.

Psychosexual development The sequence of development of the instinctual drives as theorized by Freud, in which the expression of drives centers on and is organized around specific erotogenic zones (oral, anal, genital) that shift in emphasis as the infant grows and develops.

Regression A shift in the organization of mental functioning to a more developmentally immature level, often occurring defensively in the context of anxiety associated with higher level functioning but also seen in sleep and dreaming, love and sex, esthetic and religious experiences, and psychoanalytic treatment.

Repetition compulsion A controversial concept that descriptively refers to the tendency to repeat certain distressing or painful experiences during the course of life; also referred to as the neurosis of destiny.

Resistance The opposition to free association and other aspects of participation in psychoanalytic treatment, activated to prevent the emergence of unconscious wishes and their associated anxieties.

Secondary process Rational, logical, linear, controlled thought that characterizes conscious mentation and follows the rules of aristotelian logic.

Self The total person including the body and the psychic organization; the center of subjectivity; the nuclear core of the personality.

Self-object In self psychology as developed by Kohut, objects who provide an interpersonal function that optimally contributes to the maintenance of cohesive self-experience (e.g., mirroring or idealizability).

Separation-individuation Developmental process elaborated by Mahler in which the infant progressively emerges from the symbiotic unity with mother and forms a sense of individual selfhood and a sense of differentiation from love objects. The subphases of this process include "hatching" (differentiation), practicing, rapprochement, and "on the way to object constancy."

Structural model Also known as the tripartite model, Freud's later model of the mind that divides the mind into three structures: id, ego, and superego.

Superego Mental structure that includes the functions of moral standards, ideals, prohibitions, and conscience and generates the affects of guilt and shame.

Therapeutic alliance The rational, conscious relationship between patient and psychiatrist based on the mutual agreement to work together cooperatively for the patient's benefit.

Topographical model Freud's first systematic model of the mind classifying three regions of mental functioning: conscious, preconscious, and unconscious.

Transference The unconscious displacement of feelings, attitudes, and expectations from important persons of childhood onto the person of the analyst or the analytic relationship.

Unconscious Set of mental processes and content that operates outside conscious awareness. Unconscious mentation tends to be irrational; obeys primary process logic; and may be revealed through dreams, parapraxes, and free associations.

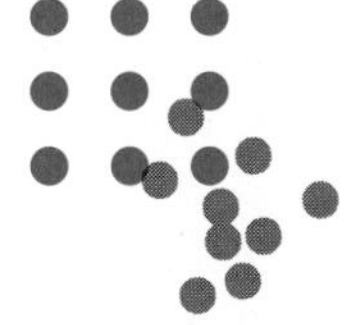

SECTION IV

Andrew E. Skodol, Section Editor

Manifestations of Psychiatric Illness

CHAPTER

20 Psychopathology Across the Life Cycle

Andrew E. Skodol
David Shaffer
Barry Gurland

Psychopathology is the study of the nature and causes of mental disorders. Because definitive etiologies for most mental disorders have not been identified, psychopathology for the most part is focused on the myriad manifestations of psychiatric illness. An elusive concept itself, mental disorder has been defined in the *Diagnostic and Statistical Manual of Mental Disorders*, Fourth Edition (DSM-IV)[1(pxxi)] as "a clinically significant behavioral or psychological syndrome or pattern that occurs in an individual and that is associated with present distress (e.g., a painful symptom) or disability (i.e., impairment in one or more important areas of functioning) or with a significantly increased risk of suffering death, pain, disability, or an important loss of freedom."

The manifestations of psychiatric illness can be grouped into five broad domains of human functioning: 1) consciousness, orientation, memory, and intellect; 2) speech, thinking, perception, and self-experience; 3) emotions; 4) physical functioning; and 5) behavior and adaptive functioning. These five areas encompass the processes by which humans know about themselves and the world around them; how they think, reason, learn, and express themselves; how they feel and express these feelings; how they perceive their bodies and experience their sensations and essential functions; and how they act and react to both internal and external stimuli.

Each of these major domains of psychopathology is the subject of one of the chapters in this section. Also, Chapter 21 discusses techniques and tests to elicit the manifestations of psychiatric illness during a psychiatric evaluation of a patient and Chapter 22 addresses the specialized area of neuropsychological testing. Chapter 28 describes the variation of the manifestations of psychiatric illness depending on the particular ways in which mental distress or disorder is conceived, experienced, and expressed according to a person's cultural context. Chapter 29 discusses the sorting of the individual manifestations of mental disorder into syndromes and their arrangement in a classificatory scheme that facilitates communication between mental health professionals and promotes efforts both to understand the pathogenesis of the conditions and to treat them. Finally, Chapter 30 describes a new and comprehensive system of assessing and diagnosing very young children.

In this chapter, we discuss the ways in which psychiatric illness presents across the life cycle and in which the manifestations of disorder may vary according to the patient's developmental life stage (e.g., infancy, childhood, adolescence, adulthood, and late life). We also discuss variation by gender, because psychiatric disturbance often takes different forms in men and in women. Fundamental to our discussion is the notion that different life stages (and genders) are associated with differential incidence and prevalence rates of particular mental disorders as a result of the developmental tasks of the epoch and corresponding stressors.[2] Thus, developmental considerations may help to explain both the origins of individual disorders and their course.[3] In addition, age appears to have a pathoplastic effect on the manifestations of psychiatric illness such that the same disorder may have different manifestations at different ages.

Continuity, Persistence, and Progression Across the Life Cycle

Epidemiological research suggests that considerable stability or continuity of mental disorders can be observed from childhood into adolescence, at least for broad diagnostic groupings. In particular, behavior disorders in childhood are associated with increased risk of behavior disorders in adolescence, especially for boys, and childhood emotional disorders are associated with increased risk of adolescent emotional disorders, especially for girls.[4] The more severe the disorder, the more likely it is to persist.[5] In addition, epidemiological surveys of adults indicate that the age at onset of disorders for many patients was during adolescence, further reinforcing the notion of persistence or progression of disorders from childhood across the life cycle.[6]

Stress-Diathesis Model of Psychopathology

Theories of the causes of mental disorders are many and are the subjects of other chapters. For simplicity, we take the position that etiology in psychopathology is multifactorial. Most mental disorders are likely to be caused by both a predisposition or vulnerability at the level of brain biochemistry and experience with acute life events or chronic stressful life circumstances. Such a model helps to explain why a person with a strong family history of depression, for

Table 20–1	Pathoplastic Effects of Age
	Age specificity of disorders
	Usual age at onset
	Age effects on symptom expression

example, may be asymptomatic for long periods but may experience depression after a loss. In a population-based survey of female twin pairs, severely stressful events such as the death of a close relative, assault, serious marital problems, and divorce or breakup significantly predicted the onset of major depression in the month of occurrence. For individuals at highest genetic risk for depression, the probability of onset of major depression was significantly higher after stressful events than for individuals at lowest genetic risk, suggesting "genetic control of sensitivity to the depression-inducing effects of stressful life events."[7(p833)] Some disorders, however, may be exclusively caused by disease processes that directly alter brain structure and function or by exogenous or environmental factors such as drugs or toxins. A few disorders may be the result solely of psychosocial stressors.

Pathoplastic Effects of Age

Age appears to influence psychopathology in three ways (Table 20–1). A few mental disorders appear almost to be age specific and not to occur outside a certain age range. Feeding disorder of infancy or early childhood (failure to thrive) is a disturbance restricted to the first several years of life, because of a child's total dependence on caregivers for food during this time. Dementia of the Alzheimer's type is much more common after the age of 65 years; few cases develop before age 50.

More commonly, disorders that may occur at virtually any age have a usual onset at certain stages in life. Mental retardation, learning disorders, disruptive behavior disorders, and elimination disorders, among others, usually have their onset and are first diagnosed during childhood. The median age at onset for the first psychotic episode of schizophrenia is in the middle to late 20s.

Most mental disorders can occur at various times in life's stages. Some of these are expressed differently depending on age. For example, although the core symptoms of major depression are the same regardless of a person's age, in children somatic symptoms, irritable mood, and social withdrawal may be especially common. In depressed elderly persons, cognitive symptoms such as memory loss, disorientation, and distractibility may predominate.

Problems of Childhood

Individual Differences

Children differ from each other in ways that affect their psychological functioning from birth. They differ in intelligence, in temperament, and in genetic endowment for both risk for and resilience against mental disorder.

Intelligence is the ability to reason, plan, think abstractly, solve problems, understand, and learn. Average intelligence is associated with a score of 100 (IQ) on a standardized intelligence test. About two thirds of children have IQs between 85 and 115 and about 95% between 70 and 130. Estimates of the heritability of IQ range from 0.4 to 0.8,[8] indicating that heredity plays a larger role than environment. Higher intelligence is correlated with successful adaptation in life, and substantially reduced intelligence is associated with developmental and behavioral problems and functional impairment (see the discussion of mental retardation).

Children also differ at birth in certain fundamental behavioral predispositions, such as emotionality, activity, and sociability, called temperament.[9] Thus, some children are born with a calm and placid nature; others are inclined to be active and energetic. Thomas and colleagues[10] found that some children showed particular clusters of temperamental characteristics. "Difficult" children had irregular sleeping and eating patterns, tended to withdraw from new situations, were not adaptable, and had intense and negative reactions to stimulation. "Easy" children were biologically regular, adaptive, and in good moods; they had positive reactions to new situations and reactions to stimuli that were mild in intensity. "Slow-to-warm-up" children had initial withdrawal responses, slow adaptation, and mild reactions. Some aspects of temperament have been shown to be remarkably stable throughout childhood and adolescence and into adult life.[11, 12] Shy, inhibited temperament may predispose to the development of childhood anxiety disorders and to inhibited, avoidant personalities in adult life.[13] Difficult temperament is thought to be a predisposition for behavior disorders.[14] The concept of goodness of fit between an individual's capacities and behavioral style and the expectations and demands of others in the environment may be important in determining outcome.

Inheritance has been shown to play a role in the development of certain developmental disabilities, enuresis, schizophrenia, and mood and anxiety disorders. As mentioned earlier, heredity does not indicate with certainty that an individual will develop a mental disorder. Instead, a susceptibility is inherited, and some life experiences or other environmental factors are often required for a disorder to become manifest. Factors that lead to greater resilience in the face of adversity[15] and consequently lessen the risk of mental disorder, such as intelligence, adaptability, and sociability, also have genetic components.

Types of Problems

Psychopathology in childhood falls into four major groups of problems (Table 20–2). Many of the disorders of childhood appear to be severe forms of problems that are more or less continuously distributed, common, and "normal" occurrences. Thus, clinical depression may appear to be a severe form of sadness and disappointment, conduct disorder a severe form of aggressiveness, and anorexia nervosa a severe form of adolescent dieting and dissatisfaction with body

Table 20–2	Psychopathology in Childhood
	Developmental problems
	Emotional problems
	Behavioral problems
	Problems in physical functioning

shape.[16] However, although dieting and concerns about body shape may be relatively common among young women, anorexia nervosa is actually quite rare, suggesting a discontinuity between normal problems and psychopathology. Therefore, identification of a clinically significant disorder involves consideration of both the quantitative severity of a disturbance and its persistence and qualitative distinctions, such as the impact of the problems on the child's functioning, continued development, and adaptation to life.[17] Differences between cases and noncases may depend on fundamental differences in biology, personality, or social environment.

Estimates are that 5% to 15% of 9- to 10-year-old children suffer from an emotional or behavior disorder of sufficient severity to cause impairment in everyday functioning.[18] Overall rates of mental disorders and rates of individual disorders are lower when impairment criteria are more stringent and higher when they are relaxed. Rates are lowest when the need for treatment is included in the criteria for disorder. Rates vary by the age range of the population studied, whether the children are evaluated in clinical settings or in the community, and the period of time over which the disorder can be present.[19] Rates are also influenced by who provides information and how many sources of information are used. In general, children are usually more aware of their emotional problems than are their parents, but parents report more behavioral problems (understandably) than do their children. The more people who provide information on symptoms, the more diagnoses are made. More boys than girls are affected until the age of 11 years; more girls than boys are affected from age 12 years and older. The co-occurrence of several disorders (i.e., comorbidity) is common in childhood.[20] As can be seen in Table 20–3, comorbidity both within and between disorder types can be observed. Thus, children with learning disorders are likely to have more than one and are likely to have communication and behavior disorders as well. Children with behavior disorders may also have more than one and are likely to have learning and communication disorders. Mood and anxiety disorders co-occur and are found in children with learning and behavior disorders, in addition.

Table 20–3 Common Patterns of Comorbidity in Childhood

Disorder Type or Specific Disorder	Comorbid Disorders
Intellectual (mental retardation)	Attention-deficit/hyperactivity disorder Pervasive developmental disorders Stereotyped movement disorder Mood disorders Disorders due to general medical condition
Learning disorders	Other learning disorders Conduct disorder Oppositional defiant disorder Attention-deficit/hyperactivity disorder Major depressive disorder Dysthymic disorder Communication disorders Medical conditions (e.g., lead poisoning, fetal alcohol syndrome)
Motor skills disorders (developmental coordination disorder)	Communication disorders
Communication disorders	Other communication disorders Learning disorders Motor skills disorders Enuresis Attention-deficit/hyperactivity disorder
Pervasive developmental disorders	Mental retardation Pica Communication disorders General medical conditions
Anxiety disorders	Other anxiety disorders Major depressive disorder Behavioral disorders
Depressive disorders	Anxiety disorders
Behavioral disorders	Other behavioral disorders Learning disorders Communication disorders Mood disorders Anxiety disorders Substance use disorders Somatoform disorders Tourette's disorder Mental retardation
Feeding disorders	Mental retardation
Elimination disorders	Other elimination disorders Parasomnias Oppositional defiant disorder Conduct disorder
Tourette's disorder	Obsessive-compulsive disorder Attention-deficit/hyperactivity disorder Learning disorders

Data from American Psychiatric Association: Diagnostic and Statistical Manual of Mental Disorders, 4th ed. Washington, DC: American Psychiatric Association, 1994.

Developmental Problems

Childhood is a time of growth, physical and social maturation, and the acquisition of skills necessary to deal independently and successfully with the environment. Children who are greatly delayed in their development or who never acquire the requisite skills or maturity associated with their developmental stage have developmental problems. Developmental disorders fall into five main types: intellectual, learning, motor skills, communication, and pervasive developmental disorders.

Significantly subaverage intelligence recognized before the age of 18 years and accompanied by impairment in adaptive functioning is called mental retardation. Approximately 1% of the population is estimated to be mentally retarded. Boys are slightly more likely to be diagnosed with mental retardation than are girls.[1]

Intelligence is defined by the IQ, which is measured by a standardized, individually administered test, such as the Wechsler Intelligence Scale for Children–Revised or the Stanford-Binet Intelligence Scale. Subaverage intelligence is indicated by a score of approximately 70 or below on one of these tests, corresponding to approximately two standard deviations below mean intelligence scores. Mental retardation is commonly specified by degree of severity as mild, moderate, severe, or profound (Table 20–4). Impairment in

Table 20–4 Severity of Mental Retardation

Level	IQ Range	% of Population with Mental Retardation*
Mild	50–55 to 70	80
Moderate	35–40 to 50–55	12
Severe	20–25 to 35–40	7
Profound	Below 20–25	1

*Data from Scott S: Mental retardation. In Rutter M, Taylor E, Hersov L (eds): Child and Adolescent Psychiatry: Modern Approaches, 3rd ed. Oxford: Blackwell Scientific Publications, 1994:616–646.

mental retardation is the inability to meet functional standards for the person's age and sociocultural group and is exhibited by deficits in communication skills, self-care, home living, interpersonal relations, self-direction, academic skills, work, leisure, health, or safety.

The causes of mental retardation can be grouped from most to least common as follows[1]:

1. Alterations in embryonic development, such as those caused by chromosomal abnormalities or fetal exposure to drugs or toxins.
2. Environmental deprivation and other mental disorders, such as autism.
3. Problems of pregnancy and the perinatal period, such as fetal malnutrition, hypoxia, infection, trauma, or prematurity.
4. Hereditary abnormalities, such as inborn errors of metabolism or chromosomal aberrations.
5. Medical conditions of infancy or childhood, such as central nervous system (CNS) infection or trauma, or lead poisoning.

Physical causes are evident in the majority of cases of moderate to profound retardation. A disadvantaged environment is more likely in mild retardation.[21]

Mental retardation may be recognized at birth if it is due to a condition like Down's syndrome with physical manifestations. Likewise, it can be noted readily after a severe medical illness affecting the CNS. Severe retardation is commonly associated with lifelong functional impairment and shortened life expectancy. Milder forms of mental retardation may be responsive to appropriate training and support so that impairment in adaptive functioning is no longer apparent.

Children with mental retardation often have other problems besides their intellectual deficits and may be diagnosed with behavioral, emotional, or other developmental disorders as well.

When a child's performance on standardized achievement tests falls substantially below what would be expected given her or his IQ, age, and schooling, the child is said to have a learning disorder. Learning disorders may involve primarily subaverage reading, mathematical, or writing ability. Significant underachievement in reading affects 3% to 10% of school-age children, with boys outnumbering girls by 3 or 4 to 1.[22] Learning deficits adversely affect the child's academic functioning or other activities of daily living that require proficiency with these skills. Vision or hearing impairment may also interfere with academic achievement. Learning disorders are diagnosed in children with limited sight or hearing only when the deficits are even greater than would be expected given the sensory problem. Children with learning disorders also often have other behavioral and emotional problems.[23, 24]

Specific learning disorders are usually diagnosed when formal training in reading, mathematics, or writing begins in school. If the child is significantly above average in intelligence, the learning deficits may not be recognized until after several years of school. Most untreated learning disorders persist into adult life, with consequent emotional and behavioral problems and varying degrees of functional impairment depending on environmental opportunities and demands.[22]

Motor skills disorder involves marked impairment in motor coordination. Incoordination is of such a degree of severity that it limits the child's ability to locomote or to perform tasks in school (such as handwriting) or otherwise interferes with activities of daily living, such as getting dressed. Developmental coordination disorder has been estimated to affect as many as 6% of children between the ages of 5 and 11 years,[1] with boys outnumbering girls by 2:1 to 4:1.[25] The problems of coordination indicative of a motor skills disorder would be distinguished from those associated with neurological disorders such as cerebral palsy. Motor skills problems also tend to persist, at least into the teens, with self-esteem and school problems typical of other learning disorders.[26]

Communication disorders subsume problems in self-expression using language, in understanding language, in articulating appropriate speech sounds, and in speech fluency and timing. Communication problems may be acquired as a result of CNS infection, toxin exposure, or trauma or may be developmental, that is, not associated with neurological insults of known origin. Children may not develop an age-appropriate amount of speech, range of vocabulary, complexity of speech, or appropriate grammatical construction. If these problems significantly interfere with academic achievement or social development, an expressive language disorder is diagnosed. If a child is also unable to understand words and sentences, a receptive-expressive language disorder is present. If a child has a significant problem in pronouncing or articulating sounds required for speech, the impairment is referred to as phonological disorder. If a child has a problem in the fluency or patterning of speech, such that there are sound, syllable, or word repetitions plus frequent pauses, broken words, and sound prolongations, the problem is called stuttering.

The developmental types of expressive or mixed language disorders affect approximately 3% to 5% of children; the acquired types are more rare.[1] Phonological disorder occurs in 2% to 3% of children and stuttering in about 1%. The sex ratio for language disorders and stuttering has been estimated as three boys to one girl.[27]

Communication disorders become evident as language becomes more complex. Severe problems with expressive or receptive language of a developmental type (i.e., not acquired through CNS disease) are evident in the first 2 or 3 years of life. More subtle disturbances may not become apparent until the demands of formal schooling. Articulation and stuttering problems are also usually apparent before the child begins school. In many instances, communication disorders are time limited or reversible. The prognosis for acquired types of language disturbance may be poorer than for the developmental type and depends on the nature and severity of CNS damage.

Sometimes children have many different problems in development, involving communication, social skills, and behavior. When these problems are extremely deviant for the child's developmental stage, they are diagnosed as pervasive developmental disorders.[28] The subtypes of the pervasive developmental disorders are discussed in Chapter 35. The prototype disturbance is called autistic disorder. Children with autistic disorder fail to develop the abilities to interact socially and to communicate effectively and frequently have restricted and stereotyped behavior patterns and interests. They are socially isolated, uninterested in peer activity or sharing, and apparently unable to have reciprocal interactions either nonverbally or emotionally with others.[29] They also either do not speak or speak in limited or idiosyncratic ways. A typical repetitive, stereotyped behavior is hand or finger flapping. Boys are five times more likely than girls to have autism. Moderate mental retardation is a common additional problem. Autistic disorder is rare, affecting only about 2 to 5 children in 10,000.[1]

The most severe developmental problems are evident in infancy. The infant with autism may manifest limited eye contact, facial responsiveness, and smiling and may be difficult to hug or appear to dislike physical contact. Restricted social relationships emerge, however, after the third or fourth year of life. For children with other pervasive developmental disorders, infancy may be normal, with the onset of the abnormal behavior occurring months or even years after birth. In milder forms, such as Asperger's syndrome,[30] in which communication skills are spared, a pervasive developmental disorder may not be recognized until preschool or the actual beginning of school. The course after diagnosis is variable, depending on the subtype. In some cases, there is limited improvement; in other cases, there is progressive deterioration. Pervasive developmental disorders cause lifelong impairment: persons with intellectual impairment need supervised living and working situations; those with normal intelligence and higher levels of language acquisition may achieve a degree of independence by their 30s.[29] Outcome studies indicate that approximately two thirds of children with autism are unable to lead an independent existence, one fourth make some social and educational gains, and one tenth have a normal social life with adequate functioning at work or at school.[31]

Emotional Problems

The emotional problems of children involve anxiety and depression. Although these problems have counterparts in adults, children frequently experience and express their disturbances of feelings or emotions differently than adults. Because of their more limited vocabulary and understanding of emotional life, children may not express their emotional distress verbally as well as some adults do. Thus, even in the emotional disorders of childhood, disturbances in behavior and in physical functioning are apt to be prominent in the clinical presentation. Children are not unlike so-called alexithymic adults, whose expression of emotions is indirect and nonverbal.

Pathological childhood anxiety and age-appropriate childhood anxiety tend to have the same age distribution.[32] Thus, animal phobias appear in early childhood, when normal children may also have milder fears of animals; pathological and normal performance anxieties occur in late childhood; and social anxiety, both mild and severe, has its usual onset in adolescence.[33] An exception is pathological separation anxiety, which has a peak age at onset in community and clinical samples in late childhood,[34, 35] although normal, developmentally appropriate separation anxiety occurs during the first year of life. Rates of anxiety disorders tend to decline with increasing age in childhood and adolescence.[19]

A child with separation anxiety fears separation from home or from attachment figures, such as parents. A common first expression occurs when the child is faced with going to school (or preschool) for the first time. The young child may refuse to go to school, may exhibit clinging behavior, or may complain of physical symptoms such as headache or stomachache. Other, early, non–school-related manifestations of separation anxiety include insistence on sleeping with parents, nightmares, and fears of the dark. Separation anxiety may be precipitated by a stressful event, such as a family death or illness or a move or change of schools. Older children express the fear that calamity will happen either to themselves or to the person(s) to whom they are attached. The course of separation anxiety may wax and wane, but whenever a developmentally appropriate separation is imminent, such as going away to college, a susceptible person is anxious in anticipation of it and may actually avoid the separation or come home prematurely. Separation anxiety may predispose to the development of panic disorder and agoraphobia in late adolescence or early adulthood.[36] Separation anxiety disorder is more common among girls. About 4% of children may have the disorder.[1] Children with separation anxiety disorder may also have mood disorders.

Selective mutism is an emotional condition in which a child has ceased speaking in certain situations (e.g., at school), although the child has normal or near-normal speech and does, in fact, speak in other situations (e.g., with friends or parents).[37] It is often associated with temperamental and behavioral features such as negativism, shyness, oppositional tendencies, and poor peer relations.[38] The syndrome is more common in girls than in boys. Reluctance to speak when first entering school occurs in about 1% of children[39] and usually remits spontaneously. When it persists beyond 6 months, it can become chronic to a degree, often in the context of a disturbed family.[40]

Fear of social or performance situations in which a child is exposed to the scrutiny of others and is afraid of being humiliated or embarrassed is called social phobia. Shy or fearful temperament is a predisposing factor. Social phobia may be manifest by the young child by crying, tantrums, clinging to familiar figures (parents), or mutism. The slightly older child may not wish to play with peers or may refuse to go to school. Social phobia may be more limited (i.e., restricted to a performance situation like speaking in class) or more generalized (i.e., involving a fear of most social situations). The prevalence of social phobia in children is about 1%.[41, 42] The course of social phobia is often characterized by exacerbations caused by life stressors and social demands followed by remissions when situations pass or stabilize.

Some children may be excessive worriers in general. They may worry about school performance, athletic prowess, appearance and popularity, parental expectations, potential catastrophic events, and so on. Children who worry excessively are said to have generalized anxiety disorder. About 3% to 4% of preadolescent children may be affected.[41, 42] They may also be excessively conforming and perfectionistic and insecure to the point of extreme self-consciousness and needs for reassurance. Generalized anxiety is also likely to have a fluctuating course, with more symptoms during times of stress.

Children may develop compulsive behavioral rituals involving counting, checking, washing, or ordering. Boys are more likely to be affected than girls, especially before age 7.[43] Preoccupation with rituals and obsessional thoughts may lead to impaired school performance. Parents are likely to bring compulsive behaviors to clinical attention as they do in the case of the behavior disorders. Children are less likely than are adults to recognize their behaviors as excessive and unreasonable.

Children may also develop posttraumatic stress disorder (PTSD) after a severely traumatic event.[44, 45] Girls may be more vulnerable than boys.[36] In children, distressing dreams are usually nightmares; reliving experiences are often reenactments of the traumatic event in play. Separation difficulties may occur. Memory problems, avoidance of situations reminiscent of the trauma, and hyperarousal symptoms are also reported.[46] Diminished interest and responsiveness may be evident only to others, as children tend not to report such complaints on their own. Children with PTSD sometimes feel they will never live to be adults or become preoccupied with "telling" the future. Somatic complaints such as headaches and stomachaches are common.

Moody periods are common in children, but children may also exhibit prolonged and persistent disturbances of mood, usually depression. The prevalence of major depression among young children appears to be between 0.5% and 2.5%.[47] Again, feelings of depression may not be experienced by children in the same way as by adults or may not be readily articulated.[48] Children who are depressed may be more likely to complain of boredom or of being unable to have fun. They may become socially withdrawn and tend to want to stay at home rather than attend school.[47] Depressed children cry and express self-criticism and thoughts about death. Energy level is significantly diminished, and depressed children tend to sleep significantly more than usual. Eating habits may change. Irritability and somatic complaints may be prominent symptoms. In prepubertal children, depressive episodes tend to occur in association with behavior or anxiety disorders.[49] Although prepubertal depression has been shown to be strongly familial,[50] depressive episodes are frequently triggered by some type of loss, such as the death of a parent, a divorce, a serious illness, or a move to a new town or neighborhood, often in the context of chronic adversity.[51] In childhood, the sex ratio for depressive disorders is about 1:1.[52, 53] By adolescence, more girls than boys are affected.[54, 55]

Although the vast majority of preadolescent children with depressive episodes recover within 2 years,[56] up to 70% are likely to have another episode within 5 years.[57] Children who also have chronic mild depression have a poorer short-term outcome.[58] Patients whose symptom picture most resembles that of severe adult-like presentations and who do not have comorbid conduct disorder are more likely to have continuity of depressive illness into adult life. Older depressed children may have a worse prognosis than younger ones.[59, 60]

The manifestations of mania in younger children may involve irritability, emotional lability, or admixtures of dysphoria and hypomania, as well as more typical symptoms of hyperactivity, grandiosity, pressure of speech, and distractibility.[61, 62] As many as one third of children with major depressive episodes may show bipolar disorder by adolescence.[63] Early-onset bipolar disorders may have a poorer prognosis than later onset disorders.

Behavior Problems

Behavior problems in children fall into the general groupings of oppositional behavior, hyperactivity, excessive aggressiveness, and conduct disturbance. An appropriate degree of control over behavior is a necessary development for a child to function in a family, in school, and with peers.

A certain amount of oppositional behavior toward parents is a normal phenomenon in the preschool years (e.g., the "terrible twos"). When oppositional behavior is excessive, given a child's developmental stage, and adversely affects social or academic functioning, it is pathological. Oppositional children are negative, hostile, and defiant. They frequently lose their temper; are argumentative with adults; defy rules and expectations set by adults; are easily annoyed and deliberately annoy others; and are angry, resentful, spiteful, and vindictive. In the preschool years, oppositional children are often those who have difficult temperaments (e.g., high reactivity, difficulty being soothed) and who are hyperactive. When the problem is not associated with hyperactivity, it is often the result of a family in which parents have not been able to set appropriate standards for behavioral compliance in their children or to set limits with appropriate punishments when expectations for behavior are deliberately opposed. Oppositional behavior is sometimes a forerunner of conduct disorder[64, 65] (Table 20–5). Oppositional behavior causing significant social or academic impairment is diagnosed as oppositional defiant disorder. The disorder is common among children in the community with a psychiatric condition and may affect nearly 6% of children overall.[66] Oppositional defiant disorder is twice as common in boys as in girls 12 years of age or younger. In adolescence, more girls may have the disorder.

Hyperactivity is also common in young children. Hyperactivity is not a problem unless it is severe enough to preclude a child's focusing attention on learning or play activities. The hyperactive child is constantly fidgeting and squirming, moves about constantly as if driven by a motor, and shows signs of impulsivity. Much of the motor activity is not goal directed and has a disorganized, chaotic quality. Thus, qualitative differences in activity as well as quantitative differences are significant.[67] Hyperactive children do not play well and demand constant attention and supervision. The inattentive child is easily distracted and forgetful, seems unable to organize activities, cannot follow instructions, and does not appear to listen.

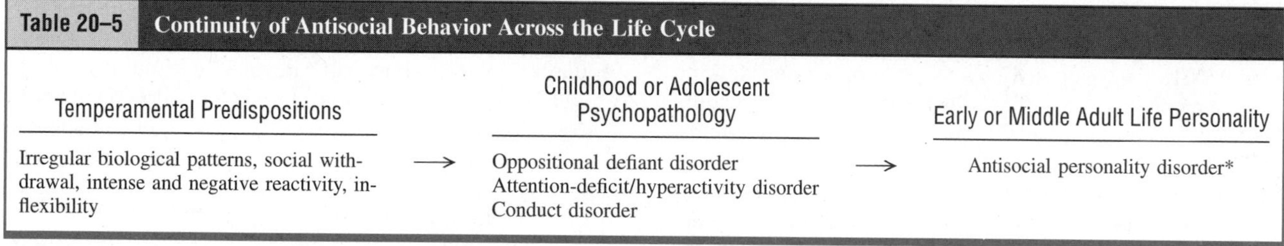

Table 20–5 Continuity of Antisocial Behavior Across the Life Cycle

Temperamental Predispositions		Childhood or Adolescent Psychopathology		Early or Middle Adult Life Personality
Irregular biological patterns, social withdrawal, intense and negative reactivity, inflexibility	→	Oppositional defiant disorder Attention-deficit/hyperactivity disorder Conduct disorder	→	Antisocial personality disorder*

*Comorbidity with substance-related disorders is likely.

Sometimes hyperactivity is evident from the age of 3 years, but more often it is diagnosed after the child begins school, when the behaviors may become disruptive and interfere with forming peer relations and with learning. Hyperactivity with attention deficits occurs 4 to 10 times more commonly in boys than girls and affects about 3% to 5% of children.[1] Without treatment, these problems tend to persist into adolescence. After that, more than half of affected children appear to develop into normal adults. About one third go on to have problems with delinquency and antisocial behavior.[68, 69] A small percentage (about 10%)[70] have continuing subtle problems into adult life, which lead them to be emotionally labile with problems controlling moods and temper and to be disorganized and distractible with problems in sustaining effort and completing tasks.[71] Adults with persisting, residual attention-deficit/hyperactivity disorder have elevated rates of other mental disorders during their lifetimes, histories of scholastic failure, and impaired cognitive and global functioning.[72]

Assertiveness, aggressiveness, and expression of anger are also on a continuum of severity and adaptiveness in children. Children can be excessively passive, or they can have a problem with too much aggression if they repeatedly and consistently hit, bite, or kick others; destroy property (including toys); or injure animals. When excessive aggression toward other people or animals, destruction of property, deceitfulness or theft, or other serious violations of parental or school rules are repetitive and persistent, a conduct disturbance exists. Conduct disturbance beginning in childhood tends to be much more common in boys than girls.[73] Boys and girls also differ in their antisocial behaviors. Boys tend to have fighting, stealing, and school discipline problems; girls exhibit lying, truancy, running away, substance abuse, and prostitution.

The causes of conduct disturbance are multiple and include genetic and environmental factors.[74] Excessive aggressiveness has been shown to be hereditary. Parental neglect and poor quality of parenting also exert strong influences on childhood antisocial behavior.[75] Growing up in a family in which violence and abuse are modeled by parents may also promote aggressive patterns of dealing with problems by children. Physical abuse of children themselves tends to provoke a panoply of negative, impulsive, angry, and aggressive behaviors. Television and the movies provide reinforcement for the aggression-prone child's behavior. Lack of consequences for inappropriate aggressiveness, excessive physical punishment, and inconsistency of parental response to hurtful or destructive acts of children all tend to exacerbate conduct problems. Conduct disorder is sometimes seen as early as 5 or 6 years of age. It is most frequently diagnosed in later childhood or early adolescence, however, and is rare in onset after age 16 years. Early onset, hyperactivity or inattention, poor peer relationships, and family discord and disorganization predict a worse prognosis, with a significant number of children developing antisocial personality as adults.[76, 77] Children with conduct disorder also often have problems with mood and anxiety disturbances and substance abuse.

Disturbances in Physical Functioning

A number of developmental tasks of childhood involve primarily physical functions. These include developing proper eating and sleeping habits,[78] bowel[79] and bladder[80] control, and sexual identity.[81] Disturbances may occur in these functions during childhood.

The eating disturbances of early childhood are rumination, failure to thrive (feeding disorder), and pica.[82] Rumination involves regurgitation and rechewing of food, without any structural anomaly or physiological disturbance to account for it. The problem is rare and is diagnosed most often in the first year of life. This early-onset syndrome occurs in developmentally normal children in association with a disturbed mother-child relationship.[83] Rumination may also be associated with mental retardation and may occur somewhat later in these children. It usually remits spontaneously.

Failure to thrive is a syndrome that also most commonly begins during the first year of life and consists of a child not eating enough to grow or in fact losing weight. Again, the feeding disturbance occurs in the absence of a medical condition, such as a disorder of intestinal absorption, which could cause weight loss. The behavior may remit after hospitalization, but long-term problems including mental retardation, developmental delays, and behavior problems are common.[84]

Pica is a syndrome of eating nonnutritional substances, such as paint, plastic, string, or hair.[85] Older children eat animal droppings, sand, insects, leaves, or pebbles. Pica usually begins in infancy or the first years of life. It may be associated with mental retardation, or it may develop as a result of child neglect. It usually remits spontaneously, although it may occasionally persist into adolescence and rarely into adulthood. Pica in early childhood has been shown to be associated with bulimic symptoms in adolescence.[86]

Developing a regular sleep pattern is also a task of early childhood. Abnormal behavioral or physiological events occurring in association with sleep are called parasomnias.[87] The common parasomnias are nightmares, sleep terrors, and sleepwalking.[88] Nightmares are extremely frightening dreams that rapidly awaken children and leave them frightened and unable to go back to sleep. Sleep terrors involve awakening in a panic without recall of a dream and being confused, disoriented, and somewhat unresponsive to others.[89] Sleepwalking involves rising from bed and walking about, unresponsive to others. Disturbed sleep may also be the result of an emotional disorder (such as the nightmares of PTSD) or a general medical condition, such as epilepsy. Nightmares are common in children before the age of 5 years; more girls than boys may have them. Sleep terrors are much rarer and occur most often in school-age boys. Sleepwalking is more common (1% to 5%)[1] in school-age and prepubescent children. Most often parasomnias resolve on their own during adolescence.

When toilet training becomes significantly delayed, a child may have an elimination problem. A 4-year-old child (or a child with a mental age of at least 4 years) who repeatedly passes feces into clothing or onto the floor has encopresis. Encopresis may occur in children who have never had bowel control or whose previously established bowel control is interrupted by psychosocial stress.[79] Constipation caused by physical disease or anxiety with resulting overflow incontinence is the most common mechanism. Encopresis is familial, is strongly related to the sphincter abnormality of enuresis, and may be preceded by an early history of sluggish bowel movements. Therefore, constitutional determinants of bowel motility are likely to be important in many cases. Usually the incontinence is involuntary; occasionally, it may be deliberate and suggest an oppositional pattern of behavior. The latter children are often generally aggressive and from socially disadvantaged families. Encopresis is more common in boys than in girls.[90] Encopresis can be a persistent problem with exacerbations and remissions, but it usually resolves by late childhood.

A child who repeatedly voids urine into clothing or bedding after the age (or mental age) of 5 years has enuresis. Enuresis can also be primary (i.e., the child has never been continent) or secondary. Enuresis is two to three times more common in boys than in girls.[91] At age 5 years, the prevalence is about 7% in boys and 3% in girls. After age 5, the spontaneous remission rate is about 5% to 10% per year, with all but about 1% of cases having remitted by adolescence. Enuresis has been shown to occur in families and to be associated with biological dysfunctions in circadian rhythms and bladder function, as well as other developmental delays.[80] Inadequate or inconsistent toilet training and psychosocial stressors, such as entering school or the birth of a sibling, may also predispose to elimination problems. Elimination disorders frequently co-occur with disruptive behavior disorders.

Interest in sexuality and sexual play are common in childhood. Sexual activities between children may be heterosexual or homosexual. The concept of a sexual identity as a boy or as a girl has usually developed by the age of 3 years.[92] Occasional cross-gender behavior in dressing or play also occurs in many normal children. When a child, usually a boy, actually develops a strong and persistent preference to be the other sex, the child has a gender identity problem. Such children may insist that they are the opposite sex, dress and play as if they are, and prefer friends of the other sex. They may also repudiate aspects of their own sex, such as having a penis. Most children with a gender identity disorder no longer report cross-gender identification or discomfort with or sense of inappropriateness in gender role by adolescence.[1] About three quarters of boys with a childhood history, however, develop a homosexual or bisexual orientation.[93] A small number of adolescents with a cross-gender identification seek sex reassignment surgery or hormone therapy or exhibit chronic gender confusion or dysphoria.

Disorders of movement may also afflict children. Tics are sudden, rapid, recurrent, nonrhythmic stereotyped motor movements or vocalizations that are not caused by medications or other drugs or by general medical conditions. Motor tics can be simple, abrupt movements such as eye blinking, head jerks, or shoulder shrugs or more complex behaviors such as facial expressions or arm gestures. Vocal tics can vary from simple throat-clearing sounds to more complex speech, including obscenities.[94] Tics ordinarily appear during childhood or early adolescence. They may be transient or chronic. Although twin and family studies indicate that genetic factors are involved in the etiology of tic disorders,[95] these disorders are also exacerbated by stress. In the rare (4 to 5 cases per 10,000)[1] prototype disorder, Tourette's disorder, there are both motor and vocal tics, but either may also occur alone. Tics are up to three times more common in boys than in girls. Tourette's disorder is often seen in association with obsessive-compulsive disorder.

Another motor abnormality of children that is unrelated to a general medical disorder is characterized by repetitive, seemingly driven, and nonfunctional motor behavior, such as hand shaking or waving or body rocking. The movements may also cause bodily injury, such as in head banging, self-biting, picking at the skin, or hitting one's own body. So-called stereotyped movement disorders may be associated with mental retardation. Stereotyped movements may also be precipitated by stressful events and may be persistent or may subside after adolescence. The motor movements are similar to those seen in pervasive developmental disorders, but in stereotyped movement disorders, severe social skills and communication deficits are absent. Boys tend to have head banging as a symptom, whereas in girls self-biting may be more prevalent.

Table 20–6 summarizes the estimated prevalence and sex distribution of DSM-IV mental disorders seen in children.

Problems of Adolescence

Adolescence is the period of life between puberty and age 19 years. For the great majority of children, the physiological events of puberty signify the end of childhood. Achievement of financial independence from the family of origin through work and formation of love relationships outside the family usually signify the end of adolescence and the beginning of adulthood. In the modern world, these goals may not be attained until the early or middle 20s. There are many important developmental phases in adolescence. Although moody, confused, and rebellious "adolescent turmoil" is no longer considered the norm for young people, some emotional troubles are fairly common. These may turn out to be symptomatic of nothing more than the stresses and strains of normal development, or they may be the early signs of significant psychological disturbance.

Table 20–6 Prevalence and Sex Distribution of Mental Disorders of Childhood

Type of Problem	Specific Disorder	Estimated Prevalence*	Predominant Sex
Developmental			
Intellectual	Mental retardation	Rare	Male
Learning	Reading disorder	Less common	Male
Motor skills	Developmental coordination disorder	Common	Male
Communication	Expressive language disorder	Less common	Male
	Mixed receptive-expressive language disorder	Less common	Male
	Phonological disorder	Less common	Male
	Stuttering	Rare	Male
Pervasive	Autistic disorder	Very rare	Male
	Rett's disorder	Very rare	Female (only)
	Childhood disintegrative disorder	Very rare	Male
	Asperger's disorder	Very rare	Male
Emotional			
Anxiety	Separation anxiety disorder	Less common	Female
	Specific phobia	Less common	Female
	Social phobia	Rare	Female
	Generalized anxiety disorder	Less common	Female
	Obsessive-compulsive disorder	Rare	Equal
	Posttraumatic stress disorder	NK	Female
	Selective mutism	Very rare	Female
Mood	Major depressive disorder	Rare	Equal
Behavioral	Oppositional defiant disorder	Common	Male
	Attention-deficit/hyperactivity disorder	Less common	Male
	Conduct disorder, childhood onset	Common	Male
Physical functioning			
Eating	Rumination disorder	NK	Male
	Feeding disorder	NK	Equal
	Pica	NK	NK
Sleep	Nightmare disorder	NK	Female
	Sleep terror disorder	NK	Male
	Sleepwalking disorder	Less common	Equal
Elimination	Encopresis	Rare	Male
	Enuresis	Common	Male
Sexual	Gender identity disorder	Less common	Male
Tic	Tourette's disorder	Very rare	Male

*Prevalence estimates are as follows: common, >5%; less common, 2%–5%; rare, 1%–2%; very rare, <1%; NK, not known.

Adolescent Development

Early in adolescence, children become more independent of parents and mature sexually. Passage through puberty can be stressful. In middle adolescence, children attempt to further their development of an independent identity, experiment with sexual behavior, develop intellectual capacities such as reason and abstraction, and acquire values and morals. In late adolescence, the task is separation, with the concurrent development of a plan for work and discovery of loving relationships outside the nuclear family.

Types of Problems

Common problems of adolescence are listed in Table 20–7. Rarely, schizophrenia may have a late adolescent onset. As might be expected, comorbidity is common among disorders of adolescence. Table 20–8 summarizes these patterns.

Table 20–7 Psychopathology in Adolescence

Identity problems
Emotional problems
Behavioral problems
Problems in self-image and physical functioning

Identity Problems

Identity issues are at the crux of adolescent development. Therefore, distress about issues concerning long-term goals, values, peer loyalties, sexual orientation and behavior, and lifestyle is common in this age group. Although most identity problems are worked through during adolescence without serious sequelae, unresolved problems may indicate the presence of mood or anxiety disorders or form the nucleus for the development of behavioral or characterological problems in adulthood.

Emotional Problems

In response to disappointments in life, adolescents may become transiently depressed. These periods of low mood are not usually sustained or impairing. From 2% to 10% of teenagers, with more girls affected than boys,[96] develop a full-blown major depressive episode.[47, 97] Suicide is the third leading cause of death among teenagers in the United States, and major depression, especially among girls, is a commonly associated disorder.[98] About one third of adolescents with clinical depression have a parent with a mood disorder.

Table 20–8 Common Patterns of Comorbidity in Adolescence

Disorder Type or Specific Disorder	Comorbid Disorders
Mood disorders	Anxiety disorders Substance use disorders Eating disorders
Anxiety disorders	Other anxiety disorders Mood disorders
Substance use disorders	Substance-induced disorders Other substance use disorders Conduct disorder
Conduct disorder	Substance use disorders Mood disorders
Pathological gambling	Mood disorders Substance use disorders Anxiety disorders
Trichotillomania	Substance use disorders Mood disorders Anxiety disorders
Eating disorders	
Anorexia nervosa	Major depressive disorder Obsessive-compulsive disorder Substance use disorders Avoidant personality disorder General medical conditions
Bulimia nervosa	Major depressive disorder Dysthymic disorder Anxiety disorders Substance use disorders Borderline personality disorder
Narcolepsy	Mood disorders Substance-related disorders Generalized anxiety disorder Sleepwalking disorder Enuresis
Body dysmorphic disorder	Mood disorders Anxiety disorders Personality disorders

Data from American Psychiatric Association: Diagnostic and Statistical Manual of Mental Disorders, 4th ed. Washington, DC: American Psychiatric Association, 1994.

Episodes of major depression, like less serious adjustment problems, may be precipitated by a breakup of a romantic relationship, an academic disappointment, a family argument, or the suicide of a friend or family member.

Episodes of mood disorder during adolescence may be a continuation of childhood-onset disorder. The risk of recurrence of major depression of childhood is up to 40%[57] within a 2-year period. Ninety percent of adolescents with a major depressive episode may recover within 2 years,[99] although each episode may last nearly 6 months. Children and adolescents with major depressive disorder have an elevated risk of recurrence of mood disorders into young adulthood as well.[60] In about 10% to 15% of adolescents with recurrent depressive episodes, mania, with excitement and extreme energy, can develop and alternate with episodes of depression, suggesting a bipolar mood disorder.[99]

Major depression in adolescents is frequently accompanied by anxiety, substance use, behavior (young men only), and eating (young women only) disorders.[100] Comorbidity is associated with more suicidal behavior and treatment seeking.

The most common age at onset for panic disorder is late adolescence.[101] About 1 in 200 adolescents may develop panic disorder.[102, 103] Panic disorder is characterized by sudden, unexpected panic attacks, which consist of a feeling of intense fear and a constellation of characteristic symptoms, such as palpitations, sweating, trembling, shortness of breath, choking, chest pain, nausea, dizziness, paresthesias, hot flashes, and feelings of going crazy or of dying. Panic disorder is more common among young women than young men. The course tends to be chronic, with waxing and waning of symptoms. Naturalistic follow-up studies suggest that at least 30% of affected people can be symptom free and another 50% have symptomatic improvement during follow-up periods ranging from 1 to 8 years.[101]

Social phobia also has a common onset in the teens.[104] Between 1% and 2% of teenagers may be affected.[55, 105] Fears of being humiliated or embarrassed in front of others may develop abruptly after a humiliating experience or may develop more gradually, in the context of a childhood history of social inhibition or shyness. In adolescents, social phobia may lead to poor school performance, avoidance of dating, and general social isolation. The duration is frequently lifelong (Table 20–9), although the severity of symptoms may fluctuate depending on life's demands. By early to middle adult life, a limited social phobia, such as in speaking in front of a group, may become a more generalized and pervasive pattern of social inhibition, feelings of inadequacy, and hypersensitivity to negative evaluation characteristic of avoidant personality disorder.[106] In the community, social phobia is more common among women, although more men may seek treatment for it.

Obsessive-compulsive disorder has a modal age at onset between 6 and 15 years for boys and may affect as many as 2% of adolescents.[102, 107] Obsessive-compulsive disorder is characterized by persistent and intrusive anxiety-provoking thoughts. The obsessions of children and adolescents most often involve contamination, danger to self or others, symmetry, or moral issues.[108] A person may perform repetitive behaviors, such as hand washing, ordering, or checking, or mental acts, such as praying, counting, or repeating words. Compulsive behaviors are performed rigidly, according to rules that are aimed at reducing anxiety or preventing something from happening. Among children and adolescents, rituals are more common than obsessions; washing rituals are the most common. Predominant symptoms often change over time. Symmetry and counting are common during grade school, excessive washing occurs frequently in early adolescence, and thoughts and behaviors with sexual themes arise in later adolescence. The course of obsessive-compulsive disorder is chronic, with waxing and waning of symptoms. In a 2-year follow-up of adolescents, symptoms and impairment persisted.[109] Thirty percent to 50% of adult patients with obsessive-compulsive disorder report a childhood or adolescent onset.[110, 111]

Behavior Problems

Experimentation with psychoactive substances is common in adolescence. More than 50% of 14-year-old boys and girls have had experience drinking alcohol.[112] Although use of most substances of abuse is widespread in the 18- to 24-year age group, alcohol, tobacco, and marijuana are the drugs of choice of adolescents.[113] Initially, pathological drug use in the teens is in the form of episodes of intoxication, that is, clinically significant, maladaptive behavioral and physiological changes secondary to recent substance ingestion. Eight percent of 8th-graders, 18% of 10th-graders, and 30% of 12th-graders reported that they had been intoxicated with alcohol in the past month.[112] The maladaptive changes of intoxication may include inappropriate sexual or aggressive behavior; mood lability; impaired judgment or increased risk taking; or impaired social, academic, or occupational functioning. Substance withdrawal is rare in adolescence, but it may occur if the drug has been taken in sufficiently high quantities for a sufficiently long time. Substance abuse or dependence (i.e., maladaptive patterns of substance use leading to social, occupational, legal, or physical problems) may also develop in adolescence, although an early onset of these types of problems usually suggests additional conduct problems. Most substance-related problems are more common in boys than in girls.

Recurrent substance intoxication often leads to substance abuse. Although the adverse social consequences of substance abuse often remain relatively stable over time,[114] abuse evolves into dependence most commonly with drugs that have a high potential for the development of tolerance, withdrawal, and patterns of compulsive use. These substances include alcohol, cocaine, opioids, and sedative, hypnotic, and anxiolytic drugs. The course of substance dependence is extremely variable, ranging from complete remission after successful treatment or the development of a life-threatening physical ailment secondary to drug use to chronicity. Early use of drugs or alcohol by adolescents predicts persisting problems.[115] Use of drugs by adolescents has been shown to be associated with elevated rates of delinquency, unemployment, divorce, and abortions in young adulthood.[116] Co-occurring mental disorders, such as mood disorders and personality disorders, increase the risk of poor outcomes.

Conduct problems of adolescence may be a continuation of childhood problems or may arise de novo during the teenage years. Estimates of the prevalence of conduct disorder range from 6% to 16% in boys and 2% to 9% in girls younger than age 18 years, depending on the population studied and methods of case ascertainment.[1] Conduct problems of adolescence are more serious than conduct problems of childhood. The greater freedom, independence, and physical strength of adolescents increase the risk that aggressive or destructive behavior will harm others. Conduct problems that commonly emerge during adolescence include burglary, mugging, armed robbery, rape, and use of knives and guns in arguments and fights.

Persistence of childhood conduct problems into adolescence and evolution of more severe aggressive and destructive behaviors portend a continuation of antisocial behavior and substance abuse in adult life. However, onset of conduct disorder in adolescence suggests a better prognosis.[117] Conduct disorder has also been shown to be associated with premature death, virtually always from violent causes.[118, 119]

Teenage boys are particularly vulnerable to developing pathological gambling. Gambling behavior can become an addiction with greater and greater amounts of time and money spent on gambling, with deleterious financial, social, and sometimes legal consequences. Gambling may be regular or episodic, but the course is chronic. Gambling behavior increases during times of stress. Pathological gambling frequently becomes associated with mood, anxiety, and substance use disorders[120] by middle age.

Trichotillomania is the behavior of recurrent pulling out of one's own hair.[121] Common areas of the body for hair pulling are the scalp, eyebrows, eyelashes, and beard. There is an increasing sense of tension that is relieved after hair pulling. The behavior shares features of both impulsive and compulsive behavior problems.[122] Trichotillomania appears to be more common among girls than boys. The peak ages at onset are between 5 and 8 years and again about age 13. The symptoms may be continual with significant hair loss resulting or may be episodic. Trichotillomania is commonly associated with mood, anxiety, and substance use disorders.[123, 124]

Problems in Self-image and Physical Functioning

Disturbances in body image and eating behavior have peak ages at onset during adolescence and early adulthood. A girl with anorexia nervosa (90% of those with eating disorders are female) refuses to maintain her body weight above minimally normal and has an intense fear of becoming fat. In addition, she has a disturbance in the way her weight and body shape are experienced, such that she denies the seriousness of her low weight and places excessive importance on her weight and shape for self-esteem. Girls with anorexia nervosa become amenorrheic. They may also engage in binge-eating and purging behavior.[125] The prevalence of anorexia nervosa among late adolescent and early adult females is between 0.5% and 1%.[1] Anorexia nervosa occurs most commonly in industrialized countries,[126] where

Table 20–9 Continuity of Social Anxiety Across the Life Cycle

Temperamental Predispositions		Childhood or Adolescent Psychopathology		Early or Middle Adult Life Personality
Shy, inhibited, fearful of strangers and novel situations, high reactivity	⟶	Social phobia*	⟶	Avoidant personality disorder†

*Other anxiety disorders, such as separation anxiety disorder or generalized anxiety disorder, may also occur.

†Comorbidity with other personality disorders, such as dependent personality disorder, and with mood and anxiety disorders is likely.

the ideal of physical attractiveness is to be thin, and may be increasing over time.[127] The onset is often after a stressful life event. Patients with anorexia nervosa may experience episodes of major depression[128] or have obsessions and compulsions about issues in addition to food, weight, and body shape. The course of anorexia nervosa is variable, ranging from a single adolescent episode to a chronic, lifelong, and deteriorating course. Factors associated with a good prognosis include an early age at onset, hysterical personality, good parent-child relationship, early treatment, and high socioeconomic status. Factors associated with a poor prognosis include bulimia, vomiting, and compulsivity.[129] Mortality in serious cases may be 10%.[1]

In bulimia nervosa, there are recurrent episodes of binge-eating in which large amounts of food are consumed in an out-of-control mode, accompanied by compensatory behavior to prevent weight gain, such as self-induced vomiting; misuse of laxatives, diuretics, or enemas; fasting; or excessive exercise. Bulimia nervosa is more common than anorexia nervosa; it is estimated to occur in 1% to 3% of adolescent and young adult women.[1] Patients with bulimia nervosa may also have mood disorders, anxiety disorders, problems with substance abuse or dependence, or other problems of impulse control. The mean age at onset is slightly later for bulimia nervosa than that for anorexia nervosa. The behavior usually persists for several years, at least, and may be chronic or intermittent. Persistence of disturbed eating behaviors into early adulthood is accompanied by the development of personality disorders in many cases. Bulimia nervosa has been shown to be associated with borderline personality disorder in contrast with anorexia nervosa, which was found to be associated with avoidant personality disorder.[130]

Although adolescents tend to sleep late, excessive daytime sleepiness may become a problem during adolescence. Excessive sleepiness may indicate the onset of narcolepsy, a rare disorder characterized by sleep attacks, accompanied by cataplexy (sudden, bilateral loss of muscle tone), and/or hypnopompic or hypnogogic hallucinations or sleep paralysis.[131] The excessive sleepiness of narcolepsy is persistent over time. Poor nocturnal sleep may develop later in middle age. Persons developing narcolepsy may have had a childhood history of a parasomnia, such as sleepwalking disorder, or an elimination disorder, such as enuresis. Comorbidity with major depressive disorder, dysthymic disorder, generalized anxiety disorder, and substance-related disorders on a concurrent or lifetime basis is also common.[1] There are equal numbers of males and females with narcolepsy.

A preoccupation with an imagined or exaggerated defect in appearance may develop in adolescence. Unlike the normal concerns of adolescents with their physical appearances, excessively time-consuming concerns that cause great distress or interfere with functioning suggest body dysmorphic disorder. Common complaints involve imagined or slight defects of the face or head or preoccupation with the shape or size of some body part.[132] The obsessive preoccupation with the perceived defect and frequently accompanying mirror checking and excessive grooming behaviors suggest a continuity with obsessive-compulsive disorder or with the weight and shape preoccupations and accompanying behaviors of anorexia nervosa. The course of body dysmorphic disorder is fairly continuous, although the severity of the symptoms may fluctuate. Persons with the disorder may seek repeated and unnecessary surgical corrections of their perceived disfigurements, which rarely result in improvements in their conditions.[133] Men and women are equally likely to be diagnosed with the disorder.

Table 20–10 summarizes the estimated prevalence and sex distribution of DSM-IV mental disorders commonly seen in adolescents.

Problems of Early Adulthood

The period between the ages of 20 and 30 years is commonly referred to as early adulthood.

Table 20–10 Prevalence and Sex Distribution of Mental Disorders of Adolescence

Type of Problem	Specific Disorder	Estimated Prevalence*	Predominant Sex
Emotional			
Mood	Major depressive disorder	Common	Female
	Bipolar disorder	NK	Equal
Anxiety	Panic disorder	Very rare	Female
	Social phobia	Rare	Female
	Obsessive-compulsive disorder	Rare	Male
Behavioral			
Substance related	Alcohol intoxication	Very common	Male
	Substance abuse	Common	Male
Disruptive	Conduct disorder	Very common	Male
Impulse control	Pathological gambling	Very rare	Male
	Trichotillomania	Rare	Female
Self-image and physical functioning			
Eating	Anorexia nervosa	Very rare	Female
	Bulimia nervosa	Less common	Female
Sleep	Narcolepsy	Very rare	Equal
Somatoform	Body dysmorphic disorder	NK	Equal

*Prevalence estimates are as follows: very common, >10%; common, 5%–10%; less common, 2%–5%; rare, 1%–2%; very rare, <1%; NK, not known.

Table 20–11 Psychopathology in Early Adulthood
Emotional problems
Problems of behavior and adaptive functioning
Problems in physical functioning
Problems in reality testing

Early Adult Development

Developmental tasks of early adulthood include achieving emotional and financial independence from parents and forming intimate relationships with people outside the family of origin. Stage-specific stressors include leaving home, education and career choice, in some cases service in the armed forces, finding and maintaining employment, courtship and marriage, and sexual relations, among others.

Types of Problems

Problems of young adulthood fall mostly into the categories listed in Table 20–11. By the end of early adulthood, people have passed through the ages of greatest risk for first onset of the majority of recognized mental disorders. Comorbidity between disorders becomes the rule rather than the exception. In a population survey in the United States, 14% of those evaluated had three or more lifetime disorders and accounted for more than 50% of the mental disorders found, both on a lifetime basis and in the year before the assessment.[134]

The relationships between comorbid "disorders" are complex. Whether they indeed represent independent entities with distinctive etiologies, pathogenetic mechanisms, or outcomes or merely reflect different ways in which fundamental psychopathological disturbances are manifest over time, between sexes, or across aspects of psychological functioning remains to be determined. In some cases, one disorder is clearly antecedent to another. Examples include disorders of childhood, such as separation anxiety disorder or conduct disorder, that evolve into adult versions, in these cases panic disorder with agoraphobia or antisocial personality disorder, respectively. Sometimes, as in the case of attention-deficit/hyperactivity disorder, residual symptoms persist and form the basis for developing problems such as substance abuse or personality dysfunction. At other times, a second disorder may develop as a consequence of a primary disorder, in reaction to it or as a complication. Examples include major depressive disorder developing after a person has been incapacitated by panic disorder with agoraphobia or sedative, anxiolytic, or alcohol abuse developing because the person attempted to self-medicate for the condition. Alternatively, disorders appear more or less contemporaneously and reflect an underlying diathesis or vulnerability. Thus, patients present with several disorders, all suggestive of a problem of generalized impulsivity, such as bulimia nervosa, a substance use disorder, and an impulse control disorder (e.g., kleptomania). Personality disorders often develop in the context of underlying traits affecting specific capacities, such as impulse control or interpersonal relatedness, as dysfunction becomes widespread.

Table 20–12 summarizes patterns of comorbid mental disorders in early adulthood.

Emotional Problems

Although disturbances in mood can occur at any age, the peak ages of onset of mood disorders are probably in the 20s. Mood disturbances may be acute and episodic or insidious and chronic. They may be relatively mild or severe and may be accompanied by psychotic features or suicidal behavior. The most common mood disorders are major depressive

Table 20–12 Common Patterns of Comorbidity in Early Adulthood

Disorder Type	Comorbid Disorders
Mood disorders	Other mood disorders Anxiety disorders Eating disorders Substance-related disorders Personality disorders
Anxiety disorders	Other anxiety disorders Mood disorders Substance-related disorders Eating disorders Somatization disorder Personality disorders
Dissociative disorders	Mood disorders Posttraumatic stress disorder Substance-related disorders Somatoform disorders Personality disorders
Substance use disorders	Other substance-related disorders Mood disorders Anxiety disorders Personality disorders Schizophrenia and other psychotic disorders Eating and sleep disorders Impulse control disorders
Impulse-control disorders	Mood disorders Anxiety disorders Substance-related disorders Eating disorders Personality disorders
Personality disorders	Other personality disorders Psychotic disorders Mood disorders Anxiety disorders Eating disorders Substance-related disorders Impulse control disorders Somatoform disorders
Sexual disorders	
Sexual dysfunctions	Other sexual dysfunctions Mood disorders Anxiety disorders Substance-related disorders
Paraphilias	Sexual dysfunctions Personality disorders
Somatoform disorders	Mood disorders Anxiety disorders Substance-related disorders Dissociative disorders Personality disorders
Factitious disorders	Substance-related disorders Personality disorders

Data from American Psychiatric Association: Diagnostic and Statistical Manual of Mental Disorders, 4th ed. Washington, DC: American Psychiatric Association, 1994.

disorder, dysthymic disorder, bipolar disorder, and cyclothymic disorder.

Major depressive disorder is characterized by episodes of severe depression that impair functioning. The lifetime risk for major depressive disorder is estimated to be between 10% and 25% and the point prevalence in adult women from 5% to 9%.[1] About twice as many women are affected as men. Initial episodes of major depressive disorder are often precipitated by a psychosocial stressor. More than 50% of people who have a major depressive episode have a second episode, and as the number of episodes increases, the likelihood of having subsequent episodes and the severity of the episodes also increase.[135] The time period between episodes generally decreases with recurrences. About two thirds of episodes of major depressive disorder resolve completely, about 40% within 3 months and 60% within 6 months.[136, 137] Chronicity or partial remission characterizes the others. Five percent to 10% of persons develop bipolar disorder. Dysthymic disorder sometimes precedes the development of major depressive disorder. Panic disorder, obsessive-compulsive disorder, both anorexia nervosa and bulimia nervosa, substance-related disorders, and several different personality disorders are often found in association with major depressive disorder.

Dysthymic disorder is characterized by milder depressive symptoms, more often cognitive (e.g., low self-esteem, pessimism, feelings of inadequacy) than vegetative (e.g., insomnia, loss of appetite), that are chronic.[138] It has an insidious onset, usually persists for years, and may be complicated by episodes of superimposed major depressive disorder (so-called double depression).[139] Dysthymic disorder is about half as common as major depressive disorder. The sex ratio for dysthymic disorder is 1:1. Persons with dysthymic disorder with or without concomitant major depressive episodes had a poorer outcome than persons with major depression alone during a 2-year follow-up period.[140] Dysthymic disorder is often found in persons with personality disorders and substance use disorders.

Manic episodes characterize bipolar I disorder. Manic episodes are periods of persistently elevated, expansive, or irritable mood. Bipolar I disorder is relatively rare compared with major depressive disorder, affecting 0.4% to 1.6% of persons on a lifetime basis.[1] Bipolar I disorder is equally common in men and women. The first episode of what eventually becomes bipolar I disorder is more likely to be a depressive episode in women than in men, whose initial episode is more likely to be manic. About 90% of persons with bipolar I disorder have recurrent episodes.[141, 142] Patients with bipolar I disorder have more lifetime episodes, in general, than patients with recurrent major depressive disorder.[143] Subsyndromal symptoms between episodes may occur in as many as 50% of patients and substantially increase the risk of relapse into full mood episodes.[144] From 15% to 25% of patients with bipolar I disorder have persistent mood disturbance and functional impairment.[143, 145] If a person has hypomanic episodes characterized by shorter duration of mood elevation and less impact on functioning than in a manic episode, the person is said to have bipolar II disorder.[146] Bipolar disorders are often accompanied by anxiety, eating, and substance-related disorders and attention-deficit/hyperactivity disorder. Substance dependence is associated with recurrence of mood episodes.[147] Bipolar II disorder may be comorbid with borderline personality disorder.

Cyclothymic disorder is characterized by a chronic mood disturbance with numerous periods of hypomanic and depressive symptoms that are not as severe as in bipolar I disorder or major depressive disorder. Persons with cyclothymic disorder are at increased risk for a bipolar disorder.

Although several anxiety disorders have their onset most often in childhood or adolescence, as previously described, others have increased risk for onset in early adult life. In particular, many cases of acrophobia (fear of heights) and situational phobias, such as of elevators, flying, or closed places, develop in early adulthood.[1] There is a rise in the rate of panic disorder in women in early and middle adult life.[148] Obsessive-compulsive disorder has a later age at onset in women than in men, during the 20s rather than the teens. Acute stress disorder and PTSD can occur at any age but are prevalent in young adults.

Disorders such as panic disorder, other specific phobias, social phobia, and generalized anxiety disorder, which are more likely to begin in childhood or adolescence, may persist or recur during early adult life. The lifetime prevalence of panic disorder in the adult population is estimated to be between 1.5% and 3.5%; the 1-year prevalence rate is between 1% and 2%.[1] Phobias are common in the community. The lifetime rate is estimated to be between 10% and 11% and the 1-year rate about 9%. Specific phobias are twice as common in women as in men.[149] The lifetime prevalence rate of social phobia ranges between 3% and 13%. Generalized anxiety disorder is thought to have a lifetime prevalence of about 5% and a 1-year prevalence of about 3% and is more common among women than among men.[150] Obsessive-compulsive disorder has estimated rates of 2.5% and 1.5% to 2.1% for lifetime and current prevalences, respectively. When rates vary widely, the degree of associated distress or resulting impairment also tends to vary. Episodes of panic disorder may be precipitated by disruptions in important interpersonal relationships; social phobia may occur after new demands in school or the workplace for speaking to a group. Childhood phobias that persist into adulthood remit infrequently.[1] Women with early adult onset panic disorder tend to have attacks that persist into older age.[148] Comorbidity with other anxiety disorders is common for all types of anxiety disorders. High percentages of people with anxiety disorders also suffer from mood disorders and may develop substance-related disorders as a result of efforts to treat their anxiety with alcohol or medications.

Although psychological reactions to extremely stressful events can occur, like the events themselves, at any age, much of what is known about these reactions has been learned from populations of young adults. These populations include soldiers in combat,[151] refugees,[152] and community subjects who have experienced crime victimization, natural or human-made disasters, or life-threatening illness or injury.[153–155]

Immediately after an event in which a person experiences or witnesses actual or threatened death or serious injury or threat to physical integrity, which arouse feelings of helplessness, fear, or horror, an acute stress reaction may occur. These reactions are characterized by 1) dissociative symptoms, such as feeling numb or detached, derealization, or depersonalization; 2) reexperiencing symptoms, such as recurrent images, thoughts, dreams, or flashbacks of the traumatic event; 3) avoidance of stimuli that arouse recollections of the trauma; and 4) symptoms of hyperarousal, such as hypervigilance, exaggerated startle response, and difficulty sleeping. Acute stress reactions resolve within a month of a stressor and may serve an adaptive function, limiting painful thoughts and feelings associated with the stressor.[156] When the symptoms persist, the disorder is known as PTSD. Dissociative symptoms are less prominent in PTSD than in acute stress disorder. PTSD may also have a delayed onset, months or even years after the traumatic event. The lifetime prevalence of PTSD may be as low as 1% or as high as 14% in community populations.[1]

The severity, duration, and proximity of a person's exposure to a traumatic event influence the risk of developing either an acute stress disorder or PTSD.[157] Social support, family history, childhood experiences, personality variables, and preexisting mental disorders also affect risk. Men and women appear equally vulnerable.

Reexperiencing, avoidance, and hyperarousal symptoms may fluctuate over the course of the PTSD. Intrusion symptoms may be more common early in the course and avoidant symptoms may become more common later.[158] About one half of cases resolve in a few months; others may persist for years. PTSD is frequently accompanied by mood, psychoactive substance use, personality, and other anxiety disorders.[159]

Dissociative disturbances may occur in the absence of reexperiencing or avoidance symptoms, often in response to severe stress.[160] Dissociative states all involve isolation of memory and emotions from normal states of consciousness, disturbance in sense of identity or sense of self, and experiences of intense absorption or focused concentration.[161] The exact prevalences of dissociative amnesia, fugue (inability to recall one's past, unexpected travel), depersonalization, and identity (multiple personality) disorders are not known, but all are probably relatively rare. The course of dissociative problems is usually chronic but fluctuating, with exacerbations occurring in association with episodes of stress or trauma. Dissociative disturbances may be more common among women.

Dissociative amnesia is seen in association with conversion disorder, mood disorders, or a personality disorder. Fugue states may be seen, in addition, in PTSD and in association with substance-related disorders. Depersonalization can be seen in substance-related disorders and hypochondriasis. Persons with dissociative identity disorder may also have mood disorders, eating disorders, sexual disorders, substance-related disorders, or borderline personality disorder.[1]

Milder, time-limited reactions to stressors of any severity may also occur. These are common occurrences that might follow the breakup of a romantic relationship or the loss of a job. The symptoms may be of depression, anxiety, or disturbance of conduct. They cause temporarily decreased performance at school or work or impairment in social relationships. Provided that the consequences of the stressor are resolved (i.e., the person resumes dating or obtains a new job), the course of the symptoms and impairment should be less than 6 months.

Behavior and Adaptive Functioning

Problems with various types of impulsive behaviors and problems with adaptive functioning in general seem particularly prone to become manifest in early adulthood. These problems may develop, in part, secondary to the increased stresses of movement away from the protective environments of school and family that characterize the period.

Although experimentation with substances ordinarily begins in adolescence and some personal, social, or legal problems secondary to maladaptive patterns of use (abuse) may have already occurred, the full syndrome of dependence on alcohol or other substances may not emerge until the 20s. Dependence on substances is characterized not only by symptoms of physiological dependence, such as tolerance or withdrawal, but also by a pattern of loss of control over substance use.[162] The prevalence of substance abuse or dependence varies widely depending on the substance. Alcohol dependence and nicotine dependence are common, with lifetime prevalence estimates ranging between 15% and 20%. Amphetamine and cannabis dependences affect 2% to 4% of the population and opioid dependence less than 1%.[1] The course of substance dependence is variable and depends somewhat on the class of substance and its route of administration. In general, frequent substance intoxication may lead to repeated episodes of substance abuse, which can develop into substance dependence. For example, during a 4-year follow-up period, 30% of alcohol-abusing men had progressed to alcohol dependence.[163] Episodes and recurrences are commonly precipitated by stressors or accompany episodes of other mental disorders, such as major depressive disorder. For drugs of abuse, men are more likely to have substance-related problems than are women.

A childhood history of conduct disorder or attention-deficit/hyperactivity disorder frequently precedes the development of substance abuse or dependence. A history of mood or anxiety disorders is common in persons with nicotine dependence. Concurrent antisocial personality disorder is common in people with substance use disorders that involve illegal and expensive drugs such as cocaine, heroin, or amphetamines. Substance use disorders can develop in the context of PTSD and often complicate the course of mood, anxiety, and psychotic disorders. Co-occurring mental disorders often lead to further complications secondary to substance use and a poorer overall prognosis.

Other problems of impulse control involving assaultive acts or destruction of property (intermittent explosive disorder), fire setting (pyromania), or stealing (kleptomania) may begin in early adult life.[164] Social gambling may progress to become pathological gambling.

Of major significance in the 20s is the stabilization of patterns of perceiving, relating to, and thinking about the environment and oneself that we call personality. Also, however, in the 20s, the potential for the development of inflexible and maladaptive traits that cause distress or interfere with effective social and occupational functioning may arise. Thus, personality disorders may become evident.

The standard guidelines for the diagnosis of personality disorders refer to a pattern of inner experience and behavior that has an onset in adolescence or early adulthood and is stable and of long duration. Although some traits or behaviors that are forerunners of adult personality disorders, such as mood lability and impulsivity for borderline personality disorder or conduct disorder for antisocial personality disorder, are often evident in childhood or adolescence,[165, 166] it is rare for a full-blown personality disorder to be present before age 20 years. Furthermore, because adolescent development is often a period of rapid growth and change, it is difficult to conceptualize a stable personality pattern during the teenage years.

Personality disorders presumably arise from interactions between a person's temperamental traits and predispositions and his or her experiences with parents, siblings, peers, and others.[167] Innately high versus low levels of arousal, activity, and sociability may either become reinforced by life's experiences to harden into exaggerated and inflexible personalities or be balanced by a fortuitous combination of chance and parental planning over the years leading to adulthood. How stable personality disorder manifestations are over time and how long they remain stable are currently unknown, despite the assumptions in the definition of personality disorder. The prevalence of individual personality disorders ranges from about 2% to 3% for the more common varieties, such as schizotypal, antisocial, borderline, and histrionic, to 0.5% to 1% for the least common, such as narcissistic and avoidant.[1] The manifestations of some personality disorders, such as borderline and antisocial, may become less evident over time. Others, such as obsessive-compulsive personality disorder, may become exaggerated with advancing age.

Personality disorders fall into three clusters (Table 20–13) that have some descriptive validity: the odd-eccentric cluster (paranoid, schizoid, and schizotypal), the dramatic-emotional cluster (antisocial, borderline, histrionic, and narcissistic), and the anxious-fearful cluster (avoidant, dependent, and obsessive-compulsive).[168] The disorders in each of the three clusters may share some underlying common vulnerability factors involving cognition, affect and impulse control, and behavioral maintenance or inhibition, respectively, and may have a spectrum relationship to certain syndromal mental disorders.[169] Thus, paranoid or schizotypal personality disorders may be observed to be premorbid antecedents of delusional disorders or schizophrenia; borderline personality disorder is seen in association with mood and anxiety disorders and with disorders of impulse control, such as bulimia nervosa, attention-deficit/hyperactivity disorder, or a substance use disorder; and avoidant personality disorder is seen with generalized social phobia. Comorbidity between personality disorders[170] and related other mental disorders is substantial.[171] Cluster A personality disorders and antisocial and narcissistic personality disorders are diagnosed more frequently in men than in women. Borderline, histrionic, and dependent personality disorders are diagnosed more frequently in women than in men.

Disturbances in Physical Functioning

Certain disturbances in physical functioning are likely to become manifest in early adult life. These include disturbances in sexual functioning, sleep disturbances, and some physical complaints that cannot be fully explained on the basis of a known general medical condition.

Sexual experimentation begins in adolescence and, although some adolescents may have ongoing sexual relations, sexual behavior becomes an expected part of life in the 20s. Thus, the 20s seem to be a common period for the onset of sexual dysfunctions. Premature ejaculation is a common problem in young men and is often present from their first experiences with intercourse. With further sexual experience and aging, most men learn to control and delay orgasm. Premature ejaculation may recur after a period of sexual abstinence or secondary to performance anxiety with a new partner. Vaginismus (involuntary spasm of the muscles of the vagina) is a problem that can affect young women having their first experiences with intercourse. Inhibited orgasm is also a problem of younger women; orgasmic capacity in women increases with age. Disorders of sexual arousal (e.g., deficient desire or excitement) usually develop during adulthood, after a period of normal sexual interest, in association with psychological distress, stressful life events, or interpersonal difficulties. The exact prevalence of the psychosexual dysfunctions is unknown, although problems with desire and orgasm are more common among women.[172, 173] Psychosexual dysfunctions are likely to have significant adverse affects on marital and other interpersonal relationships.

Paraphilias are disorders of sexual aim. Persons with paraphilias are sexually aroused by fantasies, urges, and behaviors that involve nonhuman objects, suffering or humiliation, children, or other nonconsenting persons. Paraphilias include exhibitionism (exposure of genitals), fetishism (use of inanimate objects), frotteurism (touching or rubbing), pedophilia (sexual activity with children), sexual masochism (self-suffering), sexual sadism (sexual excite-

Table 20–13 Descriptive Features of Personality Disorders in Three Clusters

Cluster	Specific Disorder	Descriptive Features
Odd-eccentric	Paranoid	Distrust and suspiciousness; others' motives interpreted as malevolent
	Schizoid	Detachment from social relationships; restricted range of emotional expression
	Schizotypal	Discomfort in close relationships; cognitive or perceptual distortions; eccentricities of behavior
Dramatic-emotional	Antisocial	Disregard for and violation of the rights of others
	Borderline	Instability in interpersonal relationships, self-image, and affects; marked impulsivity
	Histrionic	Excessive emotionality and attention seeking
	Narcissistic	Grandiosity, need for admiration, lack of empathy
Anxious-fearful	Avoidant	Social inhibition, feelings of inadequacy, hypersensitivity to negative evaluation
	Dependent	Submissive and clinging behavior; need to be taken care of
	Obsessive-compulsive	Preoccupation with orderliness, perfectionism, and control

Adapted from American Psychiatric Association: Diagnostic and Statistical Manual of Mental Disorders, 4th ed. Washington, DC: American Psychiatric Association, 1994: 629–673.

ment derived from the suffering of others), transvestic fetishism (cross-dressing), and voyeurism (watching). Paraphilias have a usual age at onset from late adolescence into early adult life. Except for sexual masochism (male-to-female ratio of 20:1), paraphilias are almost never found in women. The actual prevalence of paraphilias is also unknown, but pedophilia, voyeurism, and exhibitionism are most commonly found in clinics specializing in their treatment.[1] Multiple paraphilias may coexist; when one subsides, another may emerge or become more prominent.[174] Sexual dysfunctions and personality disorders may be comorbid.

Disturbances of sleep, including both insomnia[175] and hypersomnia,[176] commonly develop in young adults. Insomnia and hypersomnia may occur in association with another mental disorder, a general medical condition, or use of a substance or may be independent of other pathologic conditions (primary). Insomnia is much more common than hypersomnia in association with other mental disorders, such as major depressive disorder, bipolar disorder, or a psychotic disorder. Sleep disorders related to another mental disorder are more common in women because of the parallel increased prevalence of mood and anxiety disorders among women.[1]

Primary insomnia often begins acutely after a period of psychosocial or medical stress. The common complaint of young adults is difficulty falling asleep. Women are more often affected than men. Because of conditioning and hyperarousal, a sleeping problem can become persistent. Some cases remit after resolution of the stressor; others are chronic or episodic for many years. Insomnia secondary to another mental disorder (e.g., schizophrenia, mood and anxiety disorders)[177] or a medical condition (e.g., chronic obstructive pulmonary disease, asthma)[178] usually follows the course of the underlying disorder. The course of insomnia related to substances depends on the particular substance involved. Primary hypersomnia rarely resolves without treatment.

Certain disturbances characterized by physical complaints without known medical etiology have a high incidence rate in early adulthood. Specifically, conversion reactions, hypochondriasis, and somatization disorder can be first diagnosed in this age group.

Conversion disorder is a rare disturbance characterized by unexplained symptoms or deficits affecting voluntary motor or sensory functions. Conversion disorders are more common in women than in men.[1] Psychological stressors or conflicts invariably precede the initiation or exacerbation of the symptoms. The onset is usually abrupt and symptoms remit within 2 weeks. Recurrences are common, and a single recurrence predicts future problems. Paralysis and blindness have a better prognosis than tremor or seizures.[179]

Hypochondriasis is a preoccupation with fears of having or the belief that one has a serious disease. It is equally common in men and in women. The course is usually chronic, with waxing and waning of symptoms. Hypochondriasis is often seen in association with anxiety disorders[180] or depression. Comorbid personality disorder suggests a poorer prognosis.

People with somatization disorder have multiple physical complaints involving pain, gastrointestinal symptoms, sexual symptoms, and pseudoneurological symptoms that cause them to seek repeated medical evaluations and treatments. The disorder is more common among women, with a prevalence estimated as 0.2% to 2.0%.[1] Initial symptoms, often menstrual complaints, commonly present during adolescence, and the full syndrome is typically present by age 25 years (symptoms begin before age 30 by definition). The course is chronic but fluctuating.[181] Conversion disorder may progress to somatization disorder.[182] Major depressive disorder, panic disorder, substance-related disorders, and cluster B personality disorders are frequently comorbid.[1]

Rarely, a person may intentionally produce or feign physical symptoms to become a patient, but not for obvious reasons. So-called factitious disorders are more common in men than in women. The course may be episodic or chronic. The onset usually follows a hospitalization for a bona fide general medical condition or another mental disorder. Severe personality psychopathology is usually present.

Problems in Reality Testing

Problems in reality testing are reflected in abnormalities of speech, thinking, perception, and self-experience. They are suggestive of psychotic disorders, such as schizophrenia. Although schizophrenia and its counterpart disorder of briefer duration, schizophreniform disorder, may have an onset in late adolescence (or in later adulthood), the most common age at onset is in early adult life. There is a distinct sex difference in median age at onset for the first psychotic episode of schizophrenia: for men the onset is in the early to middle 20s; for women the onset is in the late 20s. The lifetime prevalence of schizophrenia is estimated to be between 0.5% and 1%.[1]

The onset of schizophrenia may be acute, but more often an insidious prodrome develops before the first psychotic episode.[183] The usual prodrome consists of the gradual onset of social withdrawal, loss of interest in school or work, poor personal hygiene, and unusual behavior. As mentioned earlier, cluster A personality disorders may be evident before the onset of schizophrenia.

The symptoms of the acute phase of schizophrenia consist of delusions; hallucinations; disorganized speech; grossly disorganized or catatonic behavior; and/or negative symptoms such as affective flattening, alogia, or avolition. Schizophrenia inevitably has a significant negative impact on functioning in work, social relations, and self-care. In the first 6 months of a schizophrenia-like illness, the disorder is called schizophreniform disorder. About one third of patients receiving this diagnosis recover fully; the other two thirds eventually progress to schizophrenia or schizoaffective illnesses.[184] Good prognostic signs in schizophreniform disorder are an acute onset (i.e., without prodromal deterioration), good premorbid social and occupational functioning, confusion and perplexity as part of the acute psychotic episode, and absence of blunted or flat affect.

The long-term course of schizophrenia is variable, but few persons recover fully. Some may experience good control of positive symptoms with medications and have reasonably stable clinical courses. Others show progressive deterioration with increasing functional disability. Factors associated with a better prognosis in schizophrenia include good premorbid adjustment, acute onset, later age at onset, being female, precipitating events, associated mood disturbance, brief duration of active phase symptoms, good

Table 20–14 Good Versus Poor Prognostic Factors in Schizophrenia

Characteristic	Prognosis	
	Good	**Poor**
Premorbid adjustment	Good	Poor
Mode of onset	Acute	Insidious
Age at onset	Late	Early
Sex	Female	Male
Precipitating events	Present	Absent
Mood disturbance	Present	Absent
Duration of psychotic symptoms	Brief	Prolonged
Interepisode functioning	Good	Poor
Residual symptoms	Few	Many
Structural brain abnormalities	Absent	Present
Neurological examination	Normal	Abnormal
Family history	Mood disorder	Schizophrenia

From American Psychiatric Association: Diagnostic and Statistical Manual of Mental Disorders, 4th ed. Washington, DC: American Psychiatric Association, 1994:283.

interepisode functioning, minimal residual symptoms, absence of structural brain abnormalities, normal neurological examination, a family history of mood disorder, and no family history of schizophrenia (Table 20–14). The paranoid subtype of schizophrenia appears to be the least severe; the disorganized subtype is the most severe.[185, 186] Comorbid substance-related disorders may complicate the course of schizophrenia.

Patients who have illness episodes that are characterized by major episodes of mood disturbance, either depressed or manic, accompanied by schizophrenia-like psychotic symptoms and whose delusions and hallucinations are also present when mood symptoms are not, are said to have schizoaffective disorder. The prognosis for schizoaffective disorder, in general, and especially the bipolar type, is better than that for schizophrenia, as might be expected given the factors described as good prognostic signs in schizophrenia.[187, 188] Compared with schizophrenia, schizoaffective disorder occurs more frequently in women.[1]

The vast majority of disorders with typical onset in early adult life persist or recur in middle adult life. Some of these disorders may also have their initial onset after age 30 years. Table 20–15 summarizes the estimated prevalence and sex distribution of mental disorders of early adulthood.

Problems of Middle Adult Life

Middle Adult Development

Middle adult life may be applied to ages 30 to 65 years, which are characterized developmentally by consolidation and generativity in career and family life. Although potentially the most productive years of life, they are also fraught with obstacles and frustrations in the achievement of personal goals. Common stressors include marriage and divorce, parenting, career setbacks, recognition of unattainable goals, and death of parents. Any of these may serve as the focus of a midlife crisis.

Types of Problems

Psychosocial stressors may precipitate episodes of already existing disorders of virtually any type or initiate disorders de novo. Relatively few disorders have a typical onset between 30 and 65 years (Table 20–16). They include particular anxiety, psychotic, sleep, and substance-related disorders and disorders associated with general medical conditions.

Anxiety Disorders

Although panic disorder most frequently presents in late adolescence, there is a second peak in age at onset distribution in the middle 30s.[101] Onset after age 45 years is unusual. The lifetime and 1-year prevalences of panic disorder thus peak between the ages of 30 and 44 years.[149] Panic attacks with intense fear and discomfort and accompanying symptoms are more likely to be spontaneous and unexpected early in the course of panic disorder. With long-standing, chronic panic disorder, the recurrence of attacks tends to become associated with various situations that predispose to or precipitate them. Thus, in an effort to avoid situations from which escape might be difficult or help unavailable, a patient with recurrent panic attacks may develop agoraphobia.

Psychotic Disorders

A psychotic disorder with onset from middle to late adult life is delusional disorder.[189] Delusional disorder differs symptomatically from the schizophrenia-related conditions discussed previously in having delusions involving situations that can occur in real life (nonbizarre), such as being followed, poisoned, infected, loved at a distance, or deceived by a spouse or lover, or having a disease. Behavior is not obviously odd or bizarre. Patients with delusional disorder are likely to have premorbid personalities that are extroverted, dominant, and hypersensitive, in contrast to patients with schizophrenia, whose premorbid personalities are typically introverted, submissive, and schizoid.[190] In addition, delusional disorder usually has a much less severe impact on overall psychosocial functioning. Delusional disorder, in general, is equally common among men and women, although the jealous subtype may be more common among men. It is a rare disorder, affecting only about 3 persons in 10,000.[1] The course of delusional disorder is quite variable. It may remit without relapse, have full periods of remission with subsequent relapses, or become chronic. Delusional disorders may develop in the context of obsessive-compulsive or body dysmorphic disorders, if the affected person becomes unable to recognize that her or his belief (obsession) or preoccupation is excessive or unreasonable, that is, loses the ability to test reality.

Sleep Disorders

Breathing-related sleep disorders most frequently lead to clinical evaluation in persons between 40 and 60 years of age. Excessive sleepiness or insomnia is caused by obstructive or central sleep apnea syndrome or central alveolar hypoventilation syndrome. Women may develop obstructive sleep apnea after menopause. The prevalence of obstructive sleep apnea may be as high as 10% and even higher in the elderly.[1] Technically, these disorders are neurological or

Table 20–15 Prevalence and Sex Distribution of Mental Disorders in Early Adulthood and Middle Adult Life

Type of Problem	Specific Disorder	Estimated Prevalence*	Predominant Sex†
Emotional			
Mood	Major depressive disorder	Very common	Female
	Dysthymic disorder	Very common	Female
	Bipolar I disorder	Rare	Equal
	Bipolar II disorder	Very rare	Female
	Cyclothymic disorder	Very rare	Equal
Anxiety	Specific phobia	Very common	Female
	Social phobia	Very common	Female
	Panic disorder‡	Less common	Female
	Obsessive-compulsive disorder	Less common	Equal
	Acute stress disorder	NK	NK
	Posttraumatic stress disorder	Less common or common	NK
	Generalized anxiety disorder	Less common	Female
Dissociative	Dissociative amnesia	NK	NK
	Dissociative fugue	Very rare	NK
	Depersonalization disorder	NK	NK
	Dissociative identity disorder	NK	Female
Adjustment	Adjustment disorder	Very common	Equal
Behavior, adaptive functioning			
Substance use	Alcohol dependence	Very common	Male
	Amphetamine dependence	Less common	Male
	Cannabis dependence	Less common	Male
	Cocaine abuse	Very rare	Equal
	Hallucinogen abuse	Very rare	Male
	Inhalant abuse	NK	Male
	Nicotine dependence	Very common	Male
	Opioid dependence	Very rare	Male
	Sedative dependence	Rare	Female
Substance-induced	Alcohol-induced persisting amnestic disorder§	NK	Male
Impulse control	Intermittent explosive disorder	Rare	Male
	Kleptomania	Rare	Female
	Pyromania	Rare	Male
	Pathological gambling	Less common	Male
Personality	Paranoid personality disorder	Rare	Male
	Schizoid personality disorder	NK	Male
	Schizotypal personality disorder	Less common	Male
	Antisocial personality disorder	Less common	Male
	Borderline personality disorder	Less common	Female
	Histrionic personality disorder	Less common	Female
	Narcissistic personality disorder	Very rare	Male
	Avoidant personality disorder	Very rare	Equal
	Dependent personality disorder	NK	Female
	Obsessive-compulsive personality disorder	Rare	Male
Physical functioning			
Sexual dysfunction	Premature ejaculation	NK	Male (only)
	Vaginismus	NK	Female (only)
Paraphilias	All	NK	Male
Sleep	Primary insomnia	NK	Female
	Primary hypersomnia	NK	NK
	Breathing-related sleep disorder§	Common	Male
Somatoform	Conversion disorder	Very rare	Female
	Hypochondriasis	NK	Equal
	Somatization disorder	Rare	Female
	Pain disorder§	Very common	Female
Factitious	Factitious disorder	NK	Male
Reality testing	Schizophrenia	Very rare	Equal
	Schizophreniform disorder	Very rare	Female
	Schizoaffective disorder	Very rare	Female
	Delusional disorder§	Very rare	Equal

*Prevalence estimates are as follows: very common, >10%; common, 5%–10%; less common, 2%–5%; rare, 1%–2%; very rare, <1%; NK, not known.

†NK, Not known.

‡Second peak in incidence in middle adult life.

§Peak in age at onset in middle adult life.

Table 20–16 Disorders with Onset in Middle Adult Life

Panic disorder
Delusional disorder
Breathing-related sleep disorder
Substance-induced disorders
Disorders due to general medical conditions
Pain disorder

respiratory in nature but are encountered by psychiatrists evaluating patients with problems related to sleeping.[191] Central sleep apnea is common among elderly persons with CNS or cardiac disease. The course of breathing-related sleep disorders is chronic.

Substance-Related Disorders

Because the peak onset of alcohol dependence is in the 20s to middle 30s, some alcohol-related disorders, which tend to develop in the context of dependency, may not become problems until middle adult life. These include episodes of alcohol withdrawal, amnestic syndrome, and dementia (Table 20–17). Alcohol-induced persisting amnestic disorder (Korsakoff's syndrome) is a severe impairment in memory secondary to thiamine deficiency and is associated with prolonged heavy alcohol ingestion. Korsakoff's syndrome usually develops after the age of 40 years and usually persists indefinitely, leading a person to require lifelong custodial care. Amnestic syndrome can also develop after prolonged and heavy use of sedatives, hypnotics, or anxiolytic drugs. Unlike the course of alcohol-induced disorder, the course of amnestic disorder associated with other sedative drugs is more variable and full recovery is possible. An amnestic syndrome can also develop after treatment with anticonvulsants or with exposure to environmental toxins, such as lead, mercury, insecticides, or industrial solvents. Full syndromes of dementia may also develop and persist after chronic alcohol ingestion or from other drugs or toxins.

General Medical Conditions

Because medical conditions have increased incidence during adult life, psychopathological conditions resulting from the direct physiological effects of general medical conditions are on the rise. General medical conditions (and their treatments) can cause delirium, dementia, amnestic disorder, psychotic disorder, mood disorder, anxiety disorder, catatonic disorder, sexual dysfunction, sleep disorder, and personality disorder. A general medical condition is likely to be the cause of a psychiatric syndrome under the following circumstances[1]:

1. A temporal relationship can be observed between the onset, exacerbation, or remission of the general medical condition and that of the mental disorder.
2. There are features of the psychiatric disturbance that are atypical of the primary mental disorder. Included would be an atypical age at onset, unusual symptoms, or symptoms that are disproportionately severe given the overall clinical picture.
3. There is an association established in the medical literature between the general medical condition and the psychiatric syndrome.
4. Previous episodes or a family history of the primary mental disorder is absent.

The actual age at highest risk, the sex distribution, and the clinical course of these disturbances are determined by the underlying medical condition. Neurological, endocrine, neoplastic, cardiovascular, infectious, and miscellaneous other medical illnesses have been implicated in the etiology of secondary mental disorders.[192] Medical conditions can also act as psychosocial stressors,[193] in which case the prognosis also depends on the management of the stress and the treatment of the mental disorder.

Pain is a common problem among adults. Estimates are that from 10% to 15% of adults in the United States have some work impairment in any given year caused by back pain alone.[1] Pain may be associated with a general medical condition only, in which case it is not considered a mental disorder. When psychological factors are judged to play an important role in the onset, severity, exacerbation, or maintenance of pain, then a mental disorder is present, whether or not a medical condition also plays a role. Most pain syndromes that present to mental health professionals are chronic. Women appear to have a greater risk for at least certain chronic pain conditions, such as headaches and musculoskeletal pain. Pain disorder is often associated with mood and anxiety disorders.

The estimated prevalence and sex distribution of the few mental disorders with a peak in age at onset in middle adult life are included in Table 20–15.

Problems of Late Life

Late Life Development

The developmental demands of late life are many. Coping with physical illness, disability, or a diminished capacity for physical activity; adapting to retirement or reduced productivity at work; and dealing with grief after the loss of friends or a spouse are all frequent and challenging tasks. Maintaining emotional equilibrium by finding a new balance

Table 20–17 Continuity of Substance-Related Problems Across the Life Cycle

Early Adolescent Psychopathology		Late Adolescent Psychopathology		Psychopathology of Early Adulthood		Psychopathology of Middle Adult Life
Substance intoxication	→	Substance abuse	→	Substance dependence	→	Substance withdrawal Substance-induced persisting amnestic disorder Substance-induced persisting dementia

Table 20–18 Psychopathology in Late LIfe

Memory impairment
Emotional problems
Substance abuse
Problems in physical functioning
Problems in reality testing

between desirable and undesirable events and circumstances[194] is a major undertaking.

Types of Problems

Risk for mood disturbances in late life remains high. Other emotional problems, substance abuse, and problems in physical functioning and in reality testing may occur. But peak age of risk is mainly for memory impairment associated with the dementias[195] (Table 20–18).

Memory Impairment

Dementia is characterized by multiple cognitive deficits, invariably including memory impairment but also such deficits as aphasia, apraxia, agnosia, and disturbance in executive functioning (e.g., planning, organization, abstraction). Dementia represents a decline in cognitive abilities that interferes with successful adaptive functioning. The decline in memory and intellectual functioning of dementia must be distinguished from analogous declines that occur with normal aging processes.[196, 197] The cause of dementia (Table 20–19) may be degenerative CNS conditions such as Alzheimer's or Parkinson's disease; nondegenerative CNS conditions such as cerebrovascular disease, Huntington's disease, subdural hematoma, normal-pressure hydrocephalus, viral and prion encephalitides, or brain tumor; or systemic illnesses such as anemia, renal or hepatic failure, hypothyroidism, vitamin B_{12} or folic acid deficiency, niacin deficiency, hypercalcemia, neurosyphilis, or human immunodeficiency virus infection.[198, 199] Chronic use of or exposure to substances, including alcohol and environmental toxins, may also cause dementia. States of delirium related to the side effects of medications, acute infections, and other conditions may be mistaken for dementias.

Not all of the potential causes of dementia are increased in prevalence in late life. The most common types, however, such as the Alzheimer's type and vascular type, usually present after age 65 years and progressively increase in frequency with increasing age. From 2% to 4% of the population older than 65 years are estimated to have Alzheimer's dementia. In most ethnic groups, the majority of dementias are due to Alzheimer's disease; vascular dementia is less common.[200, 201] After age 85 years, 20% of the population is estimated to have a dementia. Women may be slightly more likely to develop Alzheimer's disease than men. Men are more likely to develop vascular dementia.[201] Other causes of dementia in the elderly are much less common.[202]

The course of dementia may be progressive, static, or remitting, depending on the underlying cause and the availability of effective treatment. The course of Alzheimer's disease is slowly progressive, with an insidious onset, gradual loss of cognitive functions, and eventual neurological impairment.[203] The average duration from symptom onset to death is 8 to 10 years. Vascular or multiinfarct dementia has a more abrupt onset and a stepwise and fluctuating course corresponding to the events of cerebrovascular disease.[204, 205] Depression may be comorbid with dementia.[206, 207]

The elderly are also at highest risk for developing deliria. Delirium is a disturbance of consciousness, with reduced ability to focus, sustain, or shift attention. There are changes in cognitive functioning, such as memory impairment or disorientation; the development of perceptual disturbances, such as illusions and hallucinations; and agitation. The symptoms develop rapidly and tend to fluctuate during the course of the day.

There are many causes for delirium. General medical conditions include systemic infections, metabolic disorders, fluid and electrolyte imbalances, hepatic or renal disease, thiamine deficiency, postoperative states, hypertensive encephalopathy, postictal states, and head trauma. Many substances, including prescribed medications, may also produce delirium. The elderly are particularly susceptible to developing delirium because many of the medical conditions mentioned have an increased prevalence in this age group and the CNS vulnerability of the population is increased. In the age group older than 65 years, 10% of those hospitalized have a delirium on admission and another 10% to 15% develop a delirium while hospitalized.[1] The in-hospital fatality rate for elderly delirious patients is 25% to 33%.[208] Because more women survive to an advanced age, more cases of delirium are encountered among women.

Emotional Problems

Problems with depressed mood are common among the elderly. Although the prevalence of major depressive disorder is only about 1% to 2%,[209, 210] other depressive disorders including dysthymic disorder and atypical depres-

Table 20–19 Causes of Memory Impairment Disorders in Late Life

Disease or Illness Class	Specific Type
Central nervous system diseases	Alzheimer's disease Parkinson's disease Cerebrovascular disease Pick's disease Creutzfeldt-Jakob disease Subdural hematoma Brain tumor Epilepsy Infections
Systemic illnesses	Anemia Renal failure Hepatic failure Hypertension Heart disease Diabetes Fluid and electrolyte imbalances Vitamin deficiencies Infections
Toxins	Medications Substances Environmental toxins

sion raise the rates to between 2% and 4%, and when subthreshold but clinically significant depressive symptoms are included the rates rise to between 10% and 15% or higher.[200, 211, 212] Women continue to be at greater risk for depression during late life.[213] One form of so-called minor depression, that is, depression that is not stress related and whose symptoms are below the threshold for major depression, has been found to be unique among persons older than age 60 years[214]: depressive complaints coupled with cognitive impairment. In addition, wide swings in mood (emotional lability) and sudden expressions of strong emotions (emotional incontinence) can occur in elderly patients with brain lesions.

Depressive symptoms and depressive disorders are common in people with physical illnesses and physical disability[215–217] but tend to improve as physical status improves.[218] Depression may increase the severity, awareness, and reporting of the symptoms of physical illness.[219] A majority of people older than the age of 65 years have at least one chronic physical disorder,[220] so it is not surprising that comorbidity between depressive disorders and physical illnesses is substantial among the elderly.

Both depressive and manic mood disturbances resulting from the direct physiological effects of general medical conditions are seen in the elderly. The causes may be Alzheimer's disease, Parkinson's disease, stroke, vascular dementia, and other CNS, cardiovascular, traumatic, metabolic, neoplastic, and endocrine diseases. Because the elderly are more likely to be taking prescribed medications for medical conditions, substance-induced mood disturbances are also encountered.

The elderly are at risk for suicide,[221, 222] particularly after the first onset of a major depressive disorder late in life,[221, 223] after a psychosocial stressor such as divorce or bereavement,[224] or in the context of alcoholism[222] or a serious physical illness.[225] With advancing age, the frequency of attempted suicide decreases but the frequency of completed suicide increases.

Depression-induced cognitive impairment, also known as depressive dementia or pseudodementia, is a particular problem among the elderly.[226, 227] Patients with pseudodementia cannot recall material presented to them to remember but can recognize familiar material, whereas patients with irreversible dementias are impaired in both free recall and recognition memory. Mild cognitive impairment, detectable by neuropsychological testing, and complaints of difficulty with memory occur in many cases of "pure" depressive disorder in elders. In approximately 10% of depressive disorders in elders (15% of cases referred to clinics for memory disorders), a more prominent dementia-like syndrome presents. Depressive symptoms usually respond to treatment with concomitant improvement in cognitive impairment. However, most patients with more severe depressive pseudodementia eventually develop a true dementia in subsequent years.[228, 229]

Problems with anxiety are common among the elderly, affecting up to 20% of the population older than age 65 years at any given time.[230] Specific phobias are the most common disturbance, with an estimated 1-month prevalence rate of 4.8%.[149] Although most anxiety disorders in the elderly have an onset at an earlier stage in life, a few persons may experience the first onset in late life. Agoraphobia may develop in late life, precipitated by physical illness or a traumatic incident.[231] Anxiety disorders, as well as mood disorders, may be secondary to general medical conditions, such as cardiovascular, pulmonary, and neurological diseases. Use of prescription medications and withdrawal from alcohol or sedative, hypnotic, or anxiolytic drugs may also cause anxiety symptoms.

Substance Abuse

Contrary to common clinical opinion, substance abuse late in life may affect a significant minority of elderly persons. Increasing biological sensitivity to most psychoactive drugs, aggravation of common comorbid medical conditions by substances, and the occurrence of drug interactions between psychoactive substances and prescribed medications all make excessive substance use a likely clinical problem for the elderly.[232] Elderly patients with substance use disorders may present with uncontrolled medical illnesses; with secondary substance-related disorders such as amnestic syndrome, delirium, or dementia; or with general and nonspecific signs and symptoms of deterioration, such as poor personal hygiene, malnutrition, muscle weakness, gait disturbances, frequent falls or other injuries, or mood or behavior changes.

Alcohol problems are the most common substance use problems among the elderly, with a prevalence of 4% to 20% depending on the setting in which the patients are seen.[232] Although alcohol abuse tends to decline with advancing age, in part because of premature deaths among early-onset alcohol abusers, up to one half or more of elders with problem drinking have onset in middle or late life.[233, 234] These disorders may be precipitated by age-specific stressors such as retirement or loss of significant others through death. The course and outcome of late-onset alcoholism may be better than for early-onset alcoholism, with milder symptoms and more frequent spontaneous remission.[235, 236] Rates of alcoholism after age 85 years are negligible.

Another common substance-related problem among the elderly is dependence on sedative, hypnotic, or anxiolytic drugs. These drugs are most often prescribed to elderly patients for insomnia or anxiety and are taken sometimes for many years, with physical dependence resulting. Benzodiazepines are associated with excessive daytime sedation, ataxia, and cognitive impairment, and cessation of treatment may result in recurrence, rebound, or frank withdrawal symptoms.

Disturbances in Physical Functioning

Sleep disorders and problems with pain are among the most common disturbances in physical functioning in the elderly. Sleep disturbances have been found to affect 12% to 15% of the population older than age 65 years.[237] Sleep disturbances in the elderly may be a consequence of depression or a risk factor for developing depression. Psychosocial stressors, medical illness, and increasing physical limitations in general all contribute to the disturbances of sleep and mood in the elderly. The course of sleep disturbance in the elderly often depends on the identification of an underlying condition and its successful treatment.

Medical and psychiatric illnesses make pain a special problem among the elderly. Psychosocial stressors may interfere with a patient's ability to cope with the pain of a

Table 20–20 Prevalence and Sex Distribution of Mental Disorders in Late LIfe

Type of Problem	Specific Disorder	Estimated Prevalence*	Predominant Sex
Memory impairment	Dementia of Alzheimer's type	Less common	Female
	Vascular dementia	Rare	Male
Emotional			
Mood	Major depressive disorder	Rare	Female
	Other depressive disorders	Less common	Female
	Minor depression	Very common	Female
Anxiety	Specific phobia	Common	Female
	Panic disorder	Very rare	Female
	Generalized anxiety disorder	Rare	Female
	Obsessive-compulsive disorder	Very rare	Equal
Substance use	Alcohol abuse or dependence	Rare	Male
Physical functioning			
Sleep	All sleep disorders	Very common	NK
Somatoform	Pain disorder	Very common	NK
Reality testing	All nonaffective psychotic disorders	Very rare	Equal

*Prevalence estimates are as follows: very common, >10%; common, 5%–10%; less common, 2%–5%; rare, 1%–2%; very rare, <1%; NK, not known.

medical condition. Common painful medical conditions in the elderly include degenerative disorders (e.g., rheumatoid arthritis and osteoarthritis), diabetic neuropathy, vascular disease (intermittent claudication, vasculitis), radiculopathies, trigeminal neuralgia, neoplasms, and fractures.[238] Mental disorders in the elderly that can present with pain as a major complaint include major depressive disorder, dysthymic disorder, panic disorder, and any of the somatoform disorders.

Reality Testing

Late-onset schizophrenia or paraphrenia is a psychotic illness with a first onset after age 65 years. Seven percent of hospitalized patients with schizophrenia appear to have had an onset after age 60 years and 3% after age 70.[239] In paraphrenia, distinctive psychopathological features include more frequent persecutory delusions and auditory hallucinations and less frequent formal thought disorder and negative symptoms. A common way in which the circumstances of the elderly may shape the expression of a delusion is the so-called partition delusion that some strangers, substance, or force enters the patient's home through the walls. This phenomenon is thought to be related to the social isolation and homebound existence common in the elderly.[240] The premorbid personalities of persons developing schizophrenia late in life are schizoid or paranoid. Occupational adjustment, however, has usually been adequate until middle adult life.[241] Once the condition develops, the course is chronic with a poor prognosis. Paraphrenia is significantly more common in women than in men.

Other conditions that may cause psychotic syndromes in the elderly are early-onset schizophrenia, delusional disorder, mood disorders with psychotic features, Alzheimer's and vascular dementias, and other medical conditions, substances, and prescribed medications.

Table 20–20 summarizes the estimated prevalence and sex ratio of selected mental disorders of late life.

Conclusion

Psychopathology occurs throughout the life cycle, from infancy to death. Certain forms of psychopathology are limited to specific stages in life, but most can occur at any stage. Particular disorders have a peak age at onset during specific intervals of the life cycle. Some seem related to the developmental themes of the stage in which they tend to develop. The manifestations of psychopathology may change in expression in relationship to age. Men and women differ in their susceptibilities to certain disorders, the age at which they are at greatest risk, certain symptom patterns, and in some cases in their prognoses.

Given the wide range of psychopathology encountered in the life cycle, clinicians must cast a wide net in collecting diagnostically relevant information. They must exert good clinical judgment in interpreting the information collected, including a judicious weighing of the evidence supporting diagnostic criteria. They must view patients through the filter of their cultural context. And they must apply accepted diagnostic algorithms to reach the most accurate diagnosis for each patient's problem. The remaining chapters in this section are meant to assist in these endeavors.

References

1. American Psychiatric Association: Diagnostic and Statistical Manual of Mental Disorders, 4th ed. Washington, DC: American Psychiatric Association, 1994.
2. Rutter M: Pathways from childhood to adult life. J Child Psychol Psychiatry 1989; 30:23–51.
3. Rutter M, Taylor E, Hersov L (eds): Child and Adolescent Psychiatry: Modern Approaches, 3rd ed. Oxford, UK: Blackwell Scientific Publications, 1994.
4. Costello EJ, Angold A: Developmental epidemiology. In Cicchetti D, Cohen DJ (eds): Developmental Psychopathology, Volume 1, Theory and Methods. New York: John Wiley & Sons, 1995:23–56.
5. Cohen P, Cohen J, Brook J: An epidemiological study of disorders in late childhood and adolescence: 2. Persistence of disorder. J Child Psychol Psychiatry 1993; 34:869–877.
6. Burke KC, Burke JD Jr, Regier DA, et al: Age at onset of selected mental disorders in five community populations. Arch Gen Psychiatry 1990; 47:511–518.
7. Kendler KS, Kessler RC, Walters EE, et al: Stressful life events, genetic liability, and onset of an episode of major depression in women. Am J Psychiatry 1995; 152:833–842.
8. Plomin R: The role of inheritance in behavior. Science 1990; 248:183–188.
9. Buss AH, Plomin R: A Temperament Theory of Personality Development. New York: John Wiley & Sons, 1975.

10. Thomas A, Chess S, Birch HG: Temperament and Behavior Disorders in Children. London: University of London Press, 1968.
11. Kagan J, Resnick JS, Snidman N: Biological bases of childhood shyness. Science 1988; 240:167–171.
12. Chess S, Thomas A: Temperamental individuality from childhood to adolescence. J Am Acad Child Adolesc Psychiatry 1977; 16:218–226.
13. Biederman J, Rosenbaum JF, Hirschfeld DR, et al: Psychiatric correlates of behavioral inhibition in young children of parents with and without psychiatric disorders. Arch Gen Psychiatry 1990; 47:21–26.
14. Thomas A, Chess S: Genesis and evolution of behavioral disorders: From infancy to early adult life. Am J Psychiatry 1984; 141:1–9.
15. Rutter M: Resilience in the face of adversity: Protective factors and resistance to psychiatric disorder. Br J Psychiatry 1985; 147:598–611.
16. Rutter M, Sandberg S: Epidemiology of child psychiatric disorder: Methodological issues and some substantive findings. Child Psychiatry Hum Dev 1985; 15:209–233.
17. Rutter M: Isle of Wight revisited: Twenty-five years of child psychiatric epidemiology. J Am Acad Child Adolesc Psychiatry 1989; 28:633–653.
18. Cox AD: Diagnostic appraisal. In Rutter M, Taylor E, Hersov L (eds): Child and Adolescent Psychiatry: Modern Approaches, 3rd ed. Oxford, UK: Blackwell Scientific Publications, 1994:22–33.
19. Cohen P, Provet AG, Jones M: Prevalence of emotional and behavioral disorders in childhood and adolescence. In Levin B, Petrila J (eds): Mental Health Services: A Public Health Perspective. Oxford, UK: Oxford University Press, 1996:193–209.
20. Caron C, Rutter M: Comorbidity in child psychopathology: Concepts, issues, and research strategies. J Child Psychol Psychiatry 1991; 32:1064–1080.
21. Scott S: Mental retardation. In Rutter M, Taylor E, Hersov L (eds): Child and Adolescent Psychiatry: Modern Approaches, 3rd ed. Oxford, UK: Blackwell Scientific Publications, 1994:616–646.
22. Maughan B, Yule W: Reading and other learning disabilities. In Rutter M, Taylor E, Hersov L (eds): Child and Adolescent Psychiatry: Modern Approaches, 3rd ed. Oxford, UK: Blackwell Scientific Publications, 1994:616–646.
23. Jorm AF, Share DL, Matthews R, et al: Behavior problems in specific reading retarded and general reading backward children: A longitudinal study. J Child Psychol Psychiatry 1986; 27:33–43.
24. Rourke BP, Fuerst DR: Learning Disabilities and Psychosocial Functioning: A Neuropsychological Perspective. New York: Guilford Press, 1991.
25. Baker L, Cantwell DP: Developmental coordination disorder. In Kaplan HI, Sadock BJ (eds): Comprehensive Textbook of Psychiatry, Volume 2, 6th ed. Baltimore: Williams & Wilkins, 1995:2257–2260.
26. Loose A, Henderson SE, Elliman D, et al: Clumsiness in children—do they grow out of it? A 10-year follow-up study. Dev Med Child Neurol 1991; 33:55–68.
27. Baker L, Cantwell DP: Expressive language disorder. In Kaplan HI, Sadock BJ (eds): Comprehensive Textbook of Psychiatry, Volume 2, 6th ed. Baltimore: Williams & Wilkins, 1995:2260–2264.
28. Rutter M, Schopler E: Classification of pervasive developmental disorders: Some concepts and practical considerations. J Autism Dev Disord 1992; 22:459–482.
29. Lord C, Rutter M: Autism and pervasive developmental disorders. In Rutter M, Taylor E, Hersov L. (eds): Child and Adolescent Psychiatry: Modern Approaches, 3rd ed. Oxford, UK: Blackwell Scientific Publications, 1994:569–593.
30. Tantum D: Asperger's syndrome. J Child Psychol Psychiatry 1988; 29:245–253.
31. Campbell M, Shay J: Pervasive developmental disorders. In Kaplan HI, Sadock BJ (eds): Comprehensive Textbook of Psychiatry, Volume 2, 6th ed. Baltimore: Williams & Wilkins, 1995:2277–2293.
32. Klein RG: Anxiety disorders. In Rutter M, Taylor E, Hersov L (eds): Child and Adolescent Psychiatry: Modern Approaches, 3rd ed. Oxford, UK: Blackwell Scientific Publications, 1994:351–373.
33. Öst L-G: Age of onset in different phobias. J Abnorm Psychol 1987; 96:223–229.
34. Bird HR, Canino G, Rubio-Stipec M, et al: Estimates of the prevalence of childhood maladjustment in a community survey in Puerto Rico. Arch Gen Psychiatry 1988; 45:1120–1126.
35. Last CG, Perrin S, Hersen M, et al: DSM-III-R anxiety disorders in children: Sociodemographic and clinical characteristics. J Am Acad Child Adolesc Psychiatry 1992; 31:1070–1076.
36. Mattison RE: Separation anxiety disorder and anxiety in children. In Kaplan HI, Sadock BJ (eds): Comprehensive Textbook of Psychiatry, Volume 2, 6th ed. Baltimore: Williams & Wilkins, 1995:2345–2351.
37. Tancer NK: Elective mutism: A review of the literature. In Lahey BB, Kazdin AE (eds): Advances in Clinical Child Psychology, Volume 14. New York: Plenum Publishing, 1992:265–288.
38. Bishop DVM: Developmental disorders of speech and language. In Rutter M, Taylor E, Hersov L (eds): Child and Adolescent Psychiatry: Modern Approaches, 3rd ed. Oxford, UK: Blackwell Scientific Publications, 1994:546–568.
39. Brown J, Lloyd H: A controlled study of children not speaking at school. J Assoc Workers Maladjusted Child 1975; 3:49–63.
40. Sluckin A, Foreman N, Herbert M: Behavioral treatment programmes and selectivity of speaking at follow-up in a sample of 25 selective mutes. Aust Psychol 1991; 26:132–137.
41. Anderson JC, Williams S, McGee R, et al: DSM-III disorders in preadolescent children. Arch Gen Psychiatry 1987; 44:69–76.
42. Costello EJ, Costello AJ, Edelbrock C, et al: Psychiatric disorders in pediatric primary care: Prevalence and risk factors. Arch Gen Psychiatry 1988; 45:1107–1116.
43. Swedo S, Rapoport JL, Leonard HL, et al: Obsessive compulsive disorder in children and adolescents: Clinical phenomenology of 70 consecutive cases. Arch Gen Psychiatry 1989; 46:335–341.
44. Yule W, Williams R: Posttraumatic stress reactions in children. J Trauma Stress 1990; 3:279–295.
45. Yule W: Posttraumatic stress disorder in child survivors of shipping disasters: The sinking of the "Jupiter." Psychother Psychosom 1992; 57:200–205.
46. Yule W: Posttraumatic stress disorders. In Rutter M, Taylor E, Hersov L (eds): Child and Adolescent Psychiatry: Modern Approaches, 3rd ed. Oxford, UK: Blackwell Scientific Publications, 1994:392–406.
47. Harrington R: Affective disorders. In Rutter M, Taylor E, Hersov L (eds): Child and Adolescent Psychiatry: Modern Approaches, 3rd ed. Oxford, UK: Blackwell Scientific Publications, 1994:330–350.
48. Rutter M: Depressive feelings, cognitions, and disorders: A research postscript. In Rutter M, Izard CE, Read PB (eds): Depression in Young People: Developmental and Clinical Perspectives. New York: Guilford Press, 1986:491–519.
49. Angold A, Costello EJ: Depressive comorbidity in children and adolescents: Empirical, theoretical, and methodological issues. Am J Psychiatry 1993: 150:1779–1791.
50. Harrington RC, Fudge H, Rutter M, et al: Child and adult depression: A test of continuities with data from a family study. Br J Psychiatry 1993; 162:627–633.
51. Goodyer IM, Wright C, Altham PME: Maternal adversity and recent stressful life events in anxious and depressed children. J Child Psychol Psychiatry 1988; 29:651–667.
52. Fleming JE, Offord DR, Boyle MH: Prevalence of childhood and adolescent depression in the community: Ontario Child Health Study. Br J Psychiatry 1989; 155:647–654.
53. Velez CN, Johnson J, Cohen P: A longitudinal analysis of selected risk factors for childhood psychopathology. J Am Acad Child Adolesc Psychiatry 1989; 28:861–864.
54. Kashani JH, Beck NC, Hoeper EW, et al: Psychiatric disorders in a community sample of adolescents. Am J Psychiatry 1987; 144:584–589.
55. McGee R, Feehan M, Williams S, et al: DSM-III disorders in a large sample of adolescents. J Am Acad Child Adolesc Psychiatry 1990; 29:611–619.
56. Kovacs M, Feinberg TL, Crouse-Novak MA, et al: Depressive disorders in childhood: I. A longitudinal prospective study of characteristics and recovery. Arch Gen Psychiatry 1984; 41:229–237.
57. Kovacs M, Feinberg TL, Crouse-Novak MA, et al: Depressive disorders in childhood: II. A longitudinal study of the risk for a subsequent major depression. Arch Gen Psychiatry 1984; 41:643–649.
58. Asarnow JR, Goldstein MJ, Carlson GA, et al: Childhood-onset depressive disorders. A follow-up study of rates of rehospitalization and out-of-home placement among child psychiatric inpatients. J Affect Disord 1988; 15:245–253.
59. Kovacs M, Gatsonis C, Paulauskas S, et al: Depressive disorders in childhood: IV. A longitudinal prospective study of comorbidity and risk for anxiety disorders. Arch Gen Psychiatry 1989; 46:776–782.
60. Harrington RC, Fudge H, Rutter M, et al: Adult outcomes of childhood and adolescent depression: I. Psychiatric status. Arch Gen Psychiatry 1990; 47:465–473.

61. Carlson GA: Child and adolescent mania—diagnostic considerations. J Child Psychol Psychiatry 1990; 31:331–341.
62. Strober M, Hanna G, McCracken J: Bipolar disorder. In Last CG, Hersen M (eds): Handbook of Child Psychiatric Diagnosis. New York: John Wiley & Sons, 1989:299–316.
63. Geller B, Fox L, Clark K: Rate and predictors of prepubertal bipolarity during follow-up of 6- to 12-year-old depressed children. J Am Acad Child Adolesc Psychiatry 1994; 33:461–468.
64. Schachar R, Wachsmuth R: Oppositional disorder in children: A validation study comparing conduct disorder, oppositional disorder and normal control children. J Child Psychol Psychiatry 1990; 31:1089–1102.
65. Loeber R, Lahey BB, Thomas C: Diagnostic conundrum of oppositional defiant disorder and conduct disorder. J Abnorm Psychol 1991: 100:379–390.
66. Rey JM: Oppositional defiant disorder. Am J Psychiatry 1993; 150:1769–1778.
67. Taylor E: Syndromes of attention deficit and overactivity. In Rutter M, Taylor E, Hersov L (eds): Child and Adolescent Psychiatry: Modern Approaches, 3rd ed. Oxford, UK: Blackwell Scientific Publications, 1994:285–307.
68. Barkley RA, Fischer M, Edelbrock CS, et al: The adolescent outcome of hyperactive children diagnosed by research criteria: I. An 8-year prospective follow-up study. J Am Acad Child Adolesc Psychiatry 1990; 29:546–557.
69. Farrington DP, Loeber R, van Kammen WB: Long-term criminal outcomes of hyperactivity-impulsivity-attention deficit and conduct problems in childhood. In Robins LN, Rutter M (eds): Straight and Devious Pathways from Childhood to Adulthood. Cambridge, UK: Cambridge University Press, 1990:62–81.
70. Mannuzza S, Klein RG, Bessler A, et al: Adult outcome of hyperactive boys: Educational achievement, occupational rank, and psychiatric status. Arch Gen Psychiatry 1993; 50:565–576.
71. Wender PH, Reimherr FW, Wood D, et al: A controlled study of methylphenidate in the treatment of attention deficit disorder, residual type, in adults. Am J Psychiatry 1985; 142:547–552.
72. Biederman J, Faraone SV, Spencer T, et al: Patterns of psychiatric comorbidity, cognition, and psychosocial functioning in adults with attention deficit hyperactivity disorder. Am J Psychiatry 1993; 150:1792–1798.
73. Offord DR, Boyle MH, Szatmari P, et al: Ontario Child Health Study: I. Six month prevalence of disorder and service utilization. Arch Gen Psychiatry 1987; 44:832–836.
74. Earls F: Oppositional-defiant and conduct disorders. In Rutter M, Taylor E, Hersov L (eds): Child and Adolescent Psychiatry: Modern Approaches, 3rd ed. Oxford, UK: Blackwell Scientific Publications, 1994:308–329.
75. Kolvin I, Miller FJW, Fleeting M, et al: Social and parenting factors affecting criminal-offence rates: Findings from the Newcastle Thousand Family Study (1947–1980). Br J Psychiatry 1988; 152:80–90.
76. Robins LN: Conduct disorder. J Child Psychol Psychiatry 1991; 32:193–212.
77. Zoccolillo M, Pickles A, Quinton D, et al: The outcome of conduct disorder: Implications for defining adult personality disorder and conduct disorder. Psychol Med 1992; 22:971–986.
78. Wolke D: Sleeping and feeding across the lifespan. In Rutter M, Hay DF (eds): Development Through Life: A Handbook for Clinicians. Oxford, UK: Blackwell Scientific Publications, 1994:517–557.
79. Hersov L: Faecal soiling. In Rutter M, Taylor E, Hersov L (eds): Child and Adolescent Psychiatry: Modern Approaches, 3rd ed. Oxford, UK: Blackwell Scientific Publications, 1994:520–528.
80. Shaffer D: Enuresis. In Rutter M, Taylor E, Hersov L (eds): Child and Adolescent Psychiatry: Modern Approaches, 3rd ed. Oxford, UK: Blackwell Scientific Publications, 1994:505–519.
81. Paikoff RL, Brooks-Gunn J: Psychosexual development across the lifespan. In Rutter M, Hay DF (eds): Development Through Life: A Handbook for Clinicians. Oxford, UK: Blackwell Scientific Publications, 1994:558–582.
82. Minde K, Minde R: Infant Psychiatry: An Introductory Textbook. London: Sage Publications, 1986.
83. Mayes SD, Humphrey FJ 2nd, Handford HA, et al: Rumination disorder: Differential diagnosis. J Am Acad Child Adolesc Psychiatry 1988; 27:300–302.
84. Oates RK, Peacock A, Forrest D: Long-term effects of nonorganic failure to thrive. Pediatrics 1985; 75:36–40.
85. Bicknell DJ: Pica: A Childhood Symptom. London: Butterworth, 1975.
86. Marchi M, Cohen P: Early childhood eating behaviors and adolescent eating disorders. J Am Acad Child Adolesc Psychiatry 1990; 29:112–117.
87. Mahowald MW, Ettinger MG: Things that go bump in the night: The parasomnias revisited. Neurophysiol Clin 1990; 7:119–143.
88. Anders TF: Neurophysiological studies of sleep in infants and children. J Child Psychol Psychiatry 1982; 23:75–83.
89. Thorpy MJ: Disorders of arousal. In Thorpy MJ (ed): Handbook of Sleep Disorders. New York: Marcel Dekker, 1990:531–550.
90. Bellman M: Studies on encopresis. Acta Paediatr Scand [Suppl] 1966; 170:1.
91. Oppel WC, Harper PA, Rider RV: Social, psychological and neurological factors associated with enuresis. Pediatrics 1968; 42:627–641.
92. Ehrhardt AA, Meyer-Bahlburg HFL: Effects of prenatal sex hormones on gender-related behavior. Science 1981; 211:1312–1318.
93. Green R: The "Sissy Boy Syndrome" and the Development of Homosexuality. New Haven, CT: Yale University Press, 1987.
94. Leckman JF, Cohen DJ: Tic disorders. In Rutter M, Taylor E, Hersov L (eds): Child and Adolescent Psychiatry: Modern Approaches, 3rd ed. Oxford, UK: Blackwell Scientific Publications, 1994:455–466.
95. Pauls DL, Leckman JF: The inheritance of Gilles de la Tourette syndrome and associated behaviors: Evidence of autosomal dominance transmission. N Engl J Med 1986; 315:993–997.
96. Angold A, Rutter M: Effects of age and pubertal status on depression in a large clinical sample. Dev Psychopathol 1992; 4:5–28.
97. Cicchetti D, Toth SL: Developmental psychopathology and disorders of affect. In Cicchetti D, Cohen DJ (eds): Developmental Psychopathology, Volume 2, Risk, Disorder, and Adaptation. New York: John Wiley & Sons, 1995:369–420.
98. Shaffer D, Piacentini J: Suicide and attempted suicide. In Rutter M, Taylor E, Hersov L (eds): Child and Adolescent Psychiatry: Modern Approaches, 3rd ed. Oxford, UK: Blackwell Scientific Publications, 1994:407–424.
99. Strober M, Lampert C, Schmidt S, et al: The course of major depressive disorder in adolescents: I. Recovery and risk of manic switching in a follow-up of psychotic and nonpsychotic subtypes. J Am Acad Child Adolesc Psychiatry 1993; 32:34–42.
100. Rohde P, Lewinsohn PM, Seeley JR: Comorbidity of unipolar depression: II. Comorbidity with other mental disorders in adolescents and adults. J Abnorm Psychol 1991; 214–222.
101. Fyer AJ, Mannuzza S, Coplan JD: Anxiety disorders. In Kaplan HI, Sadock BJ (eds): Comprehensive Textbook of Psychiatry, Volume 1, 6th ed. Baltimore: Williams & Wilkins, 1995:1191–1204.
102. Whitaker A, Johnson J, Shaffer D, et al: Uncommon troubles in young people: Prevalence estimates of selected psychiatric disorders in a nonreferred adolescent population. Arch Gen Psychiatry 1990; 47:487–496.
103. Lewinsohn PM, Hops H, Roberts RE, et al: Adolescent psychopathology: I. Prevalence and incidence of depression and other DSM-III disorders in high school students. J Abnorm Psychol 1993; 103:133–144.
104. Schneier FR, Liebowitz MR, Beidel DC, et al: Social phobia. In Widiger TA, Frances AJ, Pincus HA, et al (eds): DSM-IV Sourcebook, Volume 2. Washington, DC: American Psychiatric Association, 1995: 507–548.
105. Cohen P, Cohen J, Kasen S, et al: An epidemiological study of disorders in late childhood and adolescence: I. Age- and gender-specific prevalence. J Child Psychol Psychiatry 1993; 34:851–867.
106. Skodol AE, Oldham JM, Hyler SE, et al: Patterns of anxiety and personality disorder comorbidity. J Psychiatr Res 1995; 29:361–374.
107. Flament MF, Whitaker A, Rapoport JL, et al: Obsessive compulsive disorder in adolescence: An epidemiologic study. J Am Acad Child Adolesc Psychiatry 1988; 27:764–771.
108. Rapoport JL, Swedo S, Leonard H: Obsessive-compulsive disorder. In Rutter M, Taylor E, Hersov L (eds): Child and Adolescent Psychiatry: Modern Approaches, 3rd ed. Oxford, UK: Blackwell Scientific Publications, 1994:441–454.
109. Berg CZ, Rapoport JL, Whitaker A, et al: Childhood obsessive compulsive disorder: A two-year prospective follow-up of a community sample. J Am Acad Child Adolesc Psychiatry 1989; 28:528–533.

110. Karno M, Golding J: Obsessive compulsive disorder. In Robins L, Regier DA (eds): Psychiatric Disorders in America: The Epidemiologic Catchment Area Study. New York: Free Press, 1991:204–209.
111. Carter AS, Pauls DL, Leckman JF: The development of obsessionality: Continuities and discontinuities. In Cicchetti D, Cohen DJ (eds): Developmental Psychopathology, Volume 2: Risk, Disorder, and Adaptation. New York: John Wiley & Sons, 1995:609–632.
112. Johnston LD, O'Malley PM, Bachman JG: National Survey Results on Drug Use from the Monitoring the Future Study, 1975–1992, Volume 1: Secondary School Students. Rockville, MD: National Institute on Drug Abuse, 1993.
113. Farrell M, Taylor E: Drug and alcohol use and misuse. In Rutter M, Taylor E, Hersov L (eds): Child and Adolescent Psychiatry: Modern Approaches, 3rd ed. Oxford, UK: Blackwell Scientific Publications, 1994:529–545.
114. Helzer JE: Psychoactive substance abuse and its relation to dependence. In Widiger TA, Frances AJ, Pincus HA, et al (eds): DSM-IV Sourcebook, Volume 1. Washington, DC: American Psychiatric Association, 1994:21–32.
115. Robins LN, Przybeck TR: Age of onset of drug use as a factor in drug and other disorders. In LaRue Jones C, Battjes RJ (eds): Etiology of Drug Abuse: Implications for Prevention. Rockville, MD: National Institute on Drug Abuse, 1985. National Institute on Drug Abuse Research Monograph 56.
116. Kandel D, Davies M, Karus D, et al: The consequences in young adulthood of adolescent drug involvement. Arch Gen Psychiatry 1986; 43:746–754.
117. Robins LN: Deviant Children Grown Up. Baltimore: Williams & Wilkins, 1966.
118. Rydelius PA: The development of antisocial behavior and sudden violent death. Acta Psychiatr Scand 1988; 77:398–403.
119. Yeager CA, Lewis DO: Mortality in a group of formerly incarcerated juvenile delinquents. Am J Psychiatry 1990; 147:612–614.
120. Roy A, Adinoff B, Roehrich L, et al: Pathological gambling: A psychobiological study. Arch Gen Psychiatry 1988; 45:369–373.
121. Swedo SE: Trichotillomania. In Hollander E (ed): Obsessive-Compulsive–Related Disorders. Washington, DC: American Psychiatric Press, 1993:93–111.
122. Skodol AE, Oldham JM: Phenomenology, differential diagnosis, and comormidity of the impulsive/compulsive spectrum of disorders. In Oldham JM, Hollander E, Skodol AE (eds): Impulsivity and Compulsivity. Washington, DC: American Psychiatric Press, 1996:1–36.
123. Swedo SE, Leonard HL, Rapoport JL, et al: A double-blind comparison of clomipramine and desipramine in the treatment of trichotillomania (hair-pulling). N Engl J Med 1989; 321:497–501.
124. Christenson GA, MacKenzie TB, Mitchell JE: Characteristics of 60 adult chronic hair pullers. Am J Psychiatry 1991; 148:365–370.
125. Halmi KA: Review: Classification of the eating disorders. J Psychiatr Res 1985; 19:113–120.
126. Pate JE, Pumariega AJ, Hester C, et al: Cross-cultural patterns in eating disorders: A review. J Am Acad Child Adolesc Psychiatry 1992; 31:802–809.
127. Lucas AR, Beard CM, O'Fallon WM, et al: Fifty-year trends in the incidence of anorexia nervosa in Rochester, Minnesota: A population-based study. Am J Psychiatry 1991; 148:917–922.
128. Herzog DB, Keller MB, Sacks NR, et al: Psychiatric comorbidity in treatment-seeking anorexics and bulimics. J Am Acad Child Adolesc Psychiatry 1992; 31:810–818.
129. Steinhausen H-C, Rauss-Mason C, Seidel R: Follow-up studies of anorexia nervosa: A review of four decades of outcome research. Psychol Med 1991; 21:447–451.
130. Skodol AE, Oldham JM, Hyler SE, et al: Comorbidity of DSM-III-R eating disorders and personality disorders. Int J Eating Disord 1993; 14:403–416.
131. Regestein QR: Narcolepsy. In Widiger TA, Frances AJ, Pincus HA, et al (eds): DSM-IV Sourcebook, Volume 1. Washington, DC: American Psychiatric Association, 1994:627–638.
132. Phillips KA: Body dysmorphic disorder: The distress of imagined ugliness. Am J Psychiatry 1991; 148:1138–1149.
133. Hollander E, Phillips KA: Body image and experience disorders. In Hollander E (ed): Obsessive-Compulsive–Related Disorders. Washington, DC: American Psychiatric Press, 1993:17–48.
134. Kessler RC, McGonagle KA, Zhao S, et al: Lifetime and 12-month prevalence of DSM-III-R psychiatric disorders in the United States: Results from the National Comorbidity Survey. Arch Gen Psychiatry 1994; 51:8–19.
135. Maj M, Veltro F, Pirozzi R, et al: Pattern of recurrence of illness after recovery from an episode of major depression: A prospective study. Am J Psychiatry 1992; 149:795–800.
136. Keller M, Lavori P, Mueller T, et al: Time to recovery, chronicity, and levels of psychopathology in major depression: A 5-year prospective follow-up of 431 subjects. Arch Gen Psychiatry 1992; 49:809–816.
137. Coryell W, Akiskal H, Leon A, et al: The time course of nonchronic major depressive disorder. Arch Gen Psychiatry 1994; 51:405–410.
138. Keller MB, Klein DN, Hirschfeld RMA, et al: Results of the DSM-IV mood disorders field trial. Am J Psychiatry 1995; 152:843–849.
139. Keller MB, Shapiro RW: "Double-depression": Superimposition of acute depressive episodes on chronic depressive disorders. Am J Psychiatry 1982; 139:438–442.
140. Wells K, Burnam A, Rogers E: The course of depression in adult outpatients: Results from the medical outcomes study. Arch Gen Psychiatry 1992; 49:788–794.
141. Keller MB: Chronic and recurrent affective disorders: Incidence, course, and influencing factors. In Kemali D, Racagni G (eds): Chronic Treatments in Neuropsychiatry. New York: Raven Press, 1985:111–120.
142. Keller MB, Lavori PW, Coryell W, et al: Bipolar I: A five-year prospective follow-up. J Nerv Ment Dis 1993; 181:238–245.
143. Winokur G, Coryell W, Keller M, et al: A prospective follow-up of patients with bipolar and primary unipolar affective disorder. Arch Gen Psychiatry 1993; 50:457–465.
144. Keller MB, Lavori PW, Kane JM, et al: Subsyndromal symptoms in bipolar disorder: A comparison of standard and low serum levels of lithium. Arch Gen Psychiatry 1992; 49:371–376.
145. Carlson GA, Kotin J, Davenport YB, et al: Follow-up of 53 bipolar manic-depressive patients. Br J Psychiatry 1974; 124:134–139.
146. Dunner DL: Subtypes of bipolar affective disorder with particular regard to bipolar II. Psychiatr Dev 1983; 1:75–86.
147. Tohen M, Waternaux CM, Tsuang MT: Outcome in mania: A 4-year prospective follow-up of 75 patients using survival analysis. Arch Gen Psychiatry 1990; 47:1106–1111.
148. Regier DA, Boyd JH, Burke JD Jr, et al: One-month prevalence of mental disorders in the United States, based on five Epidemiologic Catchment Area sites. Arch Gen Psychiatry 1988; 45:977–986.
149. Eaton WW, Dryman A, Weissman MM: Panic and phobia. In Robins LN, Regier DA (eds): Psychiatric Disorders in America: The Epidemiologic Catchment Area Study. New York: Free Press, 1991:155–179.
150. Blazer DG, Hughes D, George LK. Generalized anxiety disorder. In Robins LN, Regier DA (eds): Psychiatric Disorders in America: The Epidemiologic Catchment Area Study. New York: Free Press, 1991:180–203.
151. Kulka RA, Schlenger WE, Fairbank JA, et al: Trauma and the Vietnam War Generation. New York: Brunner/Mazel, 1990.
152. Kinzie JD, Boehnlein JK, Leung PK: The prevalence of posttraumatic stress disorder and its clinical significance among Southeast Asian refugees. Am J Psychiatry 1990; 147:913–917.
153. Helzer JE, Robins LN, McEvoy L: Post-traumatic stress disorder in the general population: Findings of the Epidemiologic Catchment Area Survey. N Engl J Med 1987; 317:1630–1634.
154. Breslau N, Davis GC, Andreski P, et al: Traumatic events and posttraumatic stress disorder in an urban population of young adults. Arch Gen Psychiatry 1991; 48:216–222.
155. Davidson J, Hughes D, Blazer DG, et al: Post-traumatic stress disorder in the community: An epidemiological study. Psychol Med 1991: 21:713–721.
156. Koopman C, Classen C, Cardena E, et al: When disaster strikes, acute stress disorder may follow. J Trauma Stress 1995; 8:29–46.
157. March JS: What constitutes a stressor? The "criterion A" issue. In Davidson JRT, Foa EB (eds): Posttraumatic Stress Disorder: DSM-IV and Beyond. Washington, DC: American Psychiatric Press, 1993:37–54.
158. Blank AS: The longitudinal course of posttraumatic stress disorder. In Davidson JRT, Foa EB (eds): Posttraumatic Stress Disorder: DSM-IV and Beyond. Washington, DC: American Psychiatric Press, 1993:3–22.
159. Davidson JRT, Foa EB: Diagnostic issues in posttraumatic stress disorder: considerations for DSM-IV. J Abnorm Psychol 1991; 100:346–355.
160. Spiegel D, Cardena E: Disintegrated experience: The dissociative disorders revisited. J Abnorm Psychol 1991; 100:366–378.
161. Putnam FW: Development of dissociative disorders. In Cicchetti D,

Cohen DJ (eds): Developmental Psychopathology, Volume 2: Risk, Disorder, and Adaptation. New York: John Wiley & Sons, 1995: 581–608.
162. Rounsaville BJ, Kranzler HR: The DSM-III-R diagnosis of alcoholism. In Tasman A, Hales RE, Frances AJ (eds): American Psychiatric Press Review of Psychiatry, Volume 8. Washington, DC: American Psychiatric Press, 1989:323–340.
163. Hasin DS, Grant B, Endicott J: The natural history of alcohol abuse: Implications for definitions of alcohol use disorders. Am J Psychiatry 1990; 147:1537–1541.
164. McElroy SL, Hudson JI, Pope HG, et al: The DSM-III-R impulse control disorders not elsewhere classified: Clinical characteristics and relationship to other psychiatric disorders. Am J Psychiatry 1995: 149:318–327.
165. Rey JM, Morris-Yates A, Singh M, et al: Continuities between psychiatric disorders in adolescents and personality disorders in young adults. Am J Psychiatry 1995; 152:895–900.
166. Bernstein DP, Cohen P, Skodol AE, et al: Childhood antecedents of adolescent personality disorders. Am J Psychiatry 1996; 153:907–913.
167. Millon T, Davis RD: The development of personality disorders. In Cicchetti D, Cohen DJ (eds): Developmental Psychopathology, Volume 2: Risk, Disorder, and Adaptation. New York: John Wiley & Sons, 1995:633–676.
168. Kass F, Skodol AE, Charles E, et al: Scaled ratings of DSM-III personality disorders. Am J Psychiatry 1985; 142:627–630.
169. Siever LJ, Davis KL: A psychobiological perspective on the personality disorders. Am J Psychiatry 1991; 148:1647–1658.
170. Oldham JM, Skodol AE, Kellman HD, et al: Diagnosis of DSM-III-R personality disorders by two structured interviews: Patterns of comorbidity. Am J Psychiatry 1992; 149: 213–220.
171. Oldham JM, Skodol AE, Kellman HD, et al: Comorbidity of Axis I and Axis II disorders. Am J Psychiatry 1995; 152:571–578.
172. Nathan SG: The epidemiology of the DSM-III psychosexual dysfunctions. J Sex Marital Ther 1986; 12:267–281.
173. Spector IP, Carey MP: Incidence and prevalence of the sexual dysfunctions: A critical review of the empirical literature. Arch Sex Behav 1990; 19:389–408.
174. Abel GG, Becker JV, Cunningham-Rathner J, et al: Multiple paraphilic diagnoses among sex offenders. Bull Am Acad Psychiatry Law 1988; 16:153–168.
175. Reynolds CF III, Kupfer DJ, Buysse DJ, et al: Subtyping DSM-III-R primary insomnia. In Widiger TA, Frances AJ, Pincus HA, et al (eds): DSM-IV Sourcebook, Volume 1. Washington, DC: American Psychiatric Association, 1994:607–618.
176. Regestein QR: Primary hypersomnia. In Widiger TA, Frances AJ, Pincus HA, et al (eds): DSM-IV Sourcebook, Volume 1. Washington, DC: American Psychiatric Association, 1994:619–626.
177. Nofzinger EA: Sleep disorders related to another mental disorder. In Widiger TA, Frances AJ, Pincus HA, et al (eds): DSM-IV Sourcebook, Volume 1. Washington, DC: American Psychiatric Association, 1994:681–696.
178. Sateia MJ: Sleep disorders associated with a general medical condition. In Widiger TA, Frances AJ, Pincus HA, et al (eds): DSM-IV Sourcebook, Volume 1. Washington, DC: American Psychiatric Association, 1994:711–725.
179. Toone BK: Disorders of hysterical conversion. In Bass C (ed): Physical Symptoms and Psychological Illness. London: Blackwell Scientific Publications, 1990:207–234.
180. Barsky AJ, Barnett MC, Cleary PD: Hypochondriasis and panic disorder: Boundary and overlap. Arch Gen Psychiatry 1994; 51:918–925.
181. Guze SB, Cloninger CR, Martin RL, et al: A follow-up and family study of Briquet's syndrome. Br J Psychiatry 1986; 149:17–23.
182. Kent D, Tommasson K, Coryell W: Course and outcome of conversion and somatization disorders: A four-year follow-up. Psychosomatics 1995; 36:138–144.
183. Keith SJ, Matthews SM: The diagnosis of schizophrenia: A review of onset and duration issues. In Widiger TA, Frances AJ, Pincus HA, et al (eds): DSM-IV Sourcebook, Volume 1. Washington, DC: American Psychiatric Association, 1994:393–417.
184. Beiser M, Fleming JAE, Iacono WG, et al: Refining the diagnosis of schizophreniform disorder. Am J Psychiatry 1988; 144:695–700.
185. Kendler KS, Gruenberg AM, Tsuang MT: Outcome of schizophrenia subtypes defined by four diagnostic systems. Arch Gen Psychiatry 1984; 41:149–154.
186. Fenton WS, McGlashan TH: Natural history of schizophrenia subtypes. I: Longitudinal study of paranoid, hebephrenic, and undifferentiated schizophrenia. Arch Gen Psychiatry 1991; 48:969–977.
187. Kendler KS: Schizophrenia and other psychotic disorders. In Skodol AE, Spitzer RL (eds): An Annotated Bibliography of DSM-III. Washington, DC: American Psychiatric Press, 1987:85–93.
188. Kendler KS: The nosologic validity of mood-incongruent psychotic affective illness. In Widiger TA, Frances AJ, Pincus HA, et al (eds): DSM-IV Sourcebook, Volume 1. Washington, DC: American Psychiatric Association, 1994:461–475.
189. Kendler KS: Demography of paranoid psychosis (delusional disorder): A review and comparison with schizophrenia and affective illness. Arch Gen Psychiatry 1982; 39:890–902.
190. Kendler KS: The nosological validity of paranoia (simple delusional disorder)—a review. Arch Gen Psychiatry 1980; 37:699–706.
191. Thorpy MJ: Breathing-related sleep disorder. In Widiger TA, Frances AJ, Pincus HA, et al (eds): DSM-IV Sourcebook, Volume 1. Washington, DC: American Psychiatric Association, 1994:639–642.
192. Popkin MK, Tucker GJ: Mental disorders due to a general medical condition and substance-induced disorders: Mood, anxiety, psychotic, catatonic, and personality disorders. In Widiger TA, Frances AJ, Pincus HA, et al (eds): DSM-IV Sourcebook, Volume 1. Washington, DC: American Psychiatric Association, 1994:243–276.
193. Popkin MK, Callies AL, Colon EA: A framework for the study of medical depression. Psychosomatics 1987; 28:27–33.
194. Baltes PB: Theoretical propositions of life-span developmental psychology: On the dynamics between growth and decline. Dev Psychol 1987; 23:611–626.
195. Gurland B: Epidemiology of psychiatric disorders. In Sadavoy J, Lazarus LW, Jarvik LF, Grossberg GT (eds): Comprehensive Review of Geriatric Psychiatry, 2nd ed. Washington, DC: American Psychiatric Press, 1996:3–41.
196. Crook TH, Bartus RT, Ferris SH, et al: Age-associated memory impairment: Proposed diagnostic criteria and measures of clinical change—report of a National Institute of Mental Health work group. Dev Neuropsychol 1986; 2:261–276.
197. Blackford RC, LaRue A: Criteria for diagnosing age associated memory impairment: Proposed improvements from the field. Dev Neuropsychol 1989; 5:295–306.
198. Miller BL, Chang L, Oropilla G, et al: Alzheimer's disease and frontal lobe dementias. In Coffey CE, Cummings JL (eds): The American Psychiatric Press Textbook of Geriatric Neuropsychiatry. Washington, DC: American Psychiatric Press, 1994:389–404.
199. Reichman WE: Nondegenerative dementing disorders. In Coffey CE, Cummings JL (eds): The American Psychiatric Press Textbook of Geriatric Neuropsychiatry. Washington, DC: American Psychiatric Press, 1994:370–388.
200. Livingston G, Hawkins A, Graham N, et al: The Gospel Oak Study: Prevalence rates of dementia, depression and activity limitation among elderly residents in inner London. Psychol Med 1990; 20:137–146.
201. Folstein MF, Bassett SS, Anthony JC, et al: Dementia: Case ascertainment in a community survey. J Gerontol 1991: 46:M132–M138.
202. Fratiglioni L, Grut M, Forsell Y, et al: Prevalence of Alzheimer's dsease and other dementias in an edlerly urban population: Relationship with age, sex, and education. Neurology 1991; 1:1886–1892.
203. Cummings JL, Benson DF: Dementia: A Clinical Approach, 2nd ed. Boston: Butterworth-Heinemann, 1992.
204. Loeb C, Gandolfo C: Diagnostic evaluation of degenerative and vascular dementia. Stroke 1983; 14:339–401.
205. Small GW: Revised ischemic score for diagnosing multi-infarct dementia. J Clin Psychiatry 1985; 46:514–517.
206. Larson EB, Reifler BV, Sumi SM, et al: Diagnostic evaluation of 200 elderly outpatients with suspected dementia. J Gerontol 1985; 40:536–543.
207. O'Connor DW, Roth M: Coexisting depression and dementia in a community survey of the elderly. Int Psychogeriatr 1990; 2:45–53.
208. Tune L, Ross C: Delirium. In Coffey CE, Cummings JL (eds): The American Psychiatric Press Textbook of Geriatric Neuropsychiatry. Washington, DC: American Psychiatric Press, 1994:351–365.
209. Blazer D, Hughes D, George LK : The epidemiology of depression in an elderly community population. Gerontologist 1987; 27:281–287.
210. Weissman MM, Bruce ML, Leaf PJ, et al: Affective disorders. In Robins LN, Regier DA (eds): Psychiatric Disorders in America: The Epidemiologic Catchment Area Study. New York: Free Press, 1991:53–80.

211. Blazer D, Williams CD: The epidemiology of dysphoria and depression in an elderly population. Am J Psychiatry 1980; 137:439–444.
212. Gurland B, Copeland J, Kuriansky J, et al: The Mind and Mood of Aging. New York: Haworth Press, 1983.
213. Dewey ME, de la Camara C, Copeland JRM, et al: Cross-cultural comparison of depression and depressive symptoms in older people. Acta Psychiatr Scand 1993; 87:369–373.
214. Blazer D, Woodbury M, Hughes DC, et al: A statistical analysis of the classification of depression in a mixed community and clinical sample. J Affect Disord 1989; 16:11–20.
215. Gurland BJ, Wilder DE, Berkman C: Depression and disability in the elderly: Reciprocal relations and changes with age. Int J Geriatr Psychiatry 1988; 3:163–179.
216. Turner RJ, Noh S: Physical disability and depression. J Health Soc Behav 1988; 29:23–37.
217. Wells KB, Rogers W, Burnam MA, et al: Course of depression in patients with hypertension, myocardial infarction, or insulin-dependent diabetes. Am J Psychiatry 1993; 150:632–638.
218. von Korff M, Dworkin S, LeResche L: Graded chronic pain status: An epidemiological evaluation. Pain 1990; 40:279–291.
219. Barsky AJ, Goodson JD, Lane RS, et al: The amplification of somatic symptoms. Psychosom Med 1988; 50:510–519.
220. Verbrugge LM: Longer life but worsening health? In Lee PR, Estes CL (eds): The Nation's Health, 3rd ed. Boston: Jones & Bartlett Publishers, 1990:14–34.
221. Pierce D: Deliberate self-harm in the elderly. Int J Geriatr Psychiatry 1987; 2:105–110.
222. Hawton K, Fagg J: Deliberate self-poisoning and self-injury in older people. Int J Geriatr Psychiatry 1990; 5:367–373.
223. Conwell Y, Olsen K, Caine ED, et al: Suicide in later life: Psychologicial autopsy findings. Int Psychogeriatr 1991; 3:59–66.
224. Livingston BM, Kim K, Leaf PJ, et al: Depressive disorders and dysphoria resulting from conjugal bereavement in a prospective community sample. Am J Psychiatry 1990; 147:608–611.
225. Conwell Y, Rotenberg M, Caine ED: Completed suicide at age 50 and over. J Am Geriatr Soc 1990; 38:640–644.
226. Stoudemire A, Hill C, Gulley LR, et al: Neuropsychological and biomedical assessment of depression-dementia syndromes. J Neuropsychiatry Clin Neurosci 1989; 1:347–361.
227. Rabins PV, Pearlson GD: Depression induced cognitive impairment. In Burns AK, Levy R (eds): Dementia. London: Chapman & Hall, 1994:667–679.
228. Kral V: The relationship between senile dementia, Alzheimer's type, and depression. Can J Psychiatry 1983; 28:304–306.
229. Kral VA, Emery OB: Long-term follow-up of depressive pseudodementia of the aged. Can J Psychiatry 1989; 34:445–446.
230. Blazer D, George LK, Hughes D: The epidemiology of anxiety disorders: An age comparison. In Salzman C, Lebowitz BD (eds): Anxiety in the Elderly. New York: Springer-Verlag, 1991:17–30.
231. Lindesay J: Phobic disorders in the elderly. Br J Psychiatry 1991; 159:531–541.
232. Atkinson RM, Ganzini L: Substance abuse. In Coffey CE, Cummings JL (eds): The American Psychiatric Press Textbook of Geriatric Neuropsychiatry. Washington, DC: American Psychiatric Press, 1994:297–321.
233. Atkinson RM: Aging and alcohol use disorders: Diagnostic issues in the elderly. Int Psychogeriatr 1990; 2:55–72.
234. Liberto JG, Oslin DW, Ruskin PE: Alcoholism in older persons: A review of the literature. Hosp Community Psychiatry 1992; 43:975–984.
235. Atkinson RM: Late onset problem drinking in older adults. Int J Geriatr Psychiatry 1994; 9:321–326.
236. Moos RH, Brennan PL, Moos BS: Short-term processes of remission and nonremission among late-life problem drinkers. Alcohol Clin Exp Res 1991; 15:948–955.
237. Ford DE, Kamerow DB: Epidemiologic study of sleep disturbances and psychiatric disorders: An opportunity for prevention? JAMA 1989; 262:1479–1488.
238. Schuster JM, Goetz KL: Pain. In Coffey CE, Cummings JL (eds): The American Psychiatric Press Textbook of Geriatric Neuropsychiatry. Washington, DC: American Psychiatric Press, 1994:333–350.
239. Harris MJ, Jeste DV: Late-onset schizophrenia: An overview. Schizophr Bull 1988; 14:39–55.
240. Pearlson GD, Petty RG: Late-life–onset psychoses. In Coffey CE, Cummings JL (eds): The American Psychiatric Press Textbook of Geriatric Neuropsychiatry. Washington, DC: American Psychiatric Press, 1994:261–277.
241. McGlashan TH: Late-onset schizophrenia. In Widiger TA, Frances AJ, Pincus HA, et al (eds): DSM-IV Sourcebook, Volume 1. Washington, DC: American Psychiatric Association, 1994:441–445.

CHAPTER

21 Clinical Evaluation and Treatment Planning: A Multimodal Approach

Francine Cournos
Deborah L. Cabaniss

Every psychiatric evaluation must be specific to the context in which it occurs. The evaluation of a patient in the psychiatric emergency room is different from the evaluation of a graduate student applying for psychoanalysis, a member of a couple who seeks consultation for marital distress, or an indicted prisoner who is being evaluated for competence to stand trial. In each case, the evaluation and treatment plan are tailored to the situation.

In this chapter, we present an outline of the most thorough approach to psychiatric evaluation—that is, the one most typically followed when someone is admitted to a psychiatric inpatient unit. The complete psychiatric evaluation consists of the psychiatric interview; physical examination, including neurological assessment; laboratory testing; and, as appropriate, neuropsychological testing, structured interviews, and brain imaging. The results of the evaluation are then used to assess risk; reach tentative and, if possible, definitive diagnoses; and complete initial and comprehensive treatment plans. Clearly, the length, detail, and order of the evaluation need to be modified when it is conducted in different settings. The clinician needs to assess the goals of the interview, the patient's tolerance for questioning, and the time available. Table 21–1 shows the variation of the psychiatric evaluation with the type of setting.

Psychiatric Interview

Despite the advent of brain imaging tests, standardized diagnostic criteria, and structured rating scales, the psychiatric interview (Table 21–2) remains the cornerstone of clinical evaluation in psychiatry. Whether it is conducted in a busy psychiatric emergency room, an inpatient ward, or an outpatient office, the psychiatric interview is essential for establishing rapport with the patient, initiating the therapeutic alliance, eliciting the psychiatric history, and conducting the mental status examination. When conducted skillfully, the interview may appear to be a relaxed and casual conversation, but it is actually an extremely precise diagnostic tool composed of specific elements: the identifying information, the chief complaint, the history of present illness, the past psychiatric history, the personal history, the family history, the medical history, the substance use history, and the Mental Status Examination (MSE). The essential features of the psychiatric interview are highlighted here. For a more complete discussion of the psychiatric interview, see Chapter 2.

Before beginning, the psychiatrist should introduce himself or herself, explain the purpose of the interview, and try to make the patient as comfortable as possible. The interview gives the most accurate information when the psychiatrist and patient speak in a language in which they are both fluent. When this is not possible, a translator should be used, preferably one with mental health training or experience. Even then, some of the subtleties of the patient's communications are lost.

Identifying Information

Most interviewers find it helpful to begin with a few questions designed to identify the patient in a general way. Asking the patient's name, age, address, marital status, and occupation provides a quick general picture and begins the interview with emotionally neutral material. If the interviewer chooses to begin in this way, it is important to complete this section rapidly and then give the patient a chance to respond to open-ended questions. This allows the interviewer to get a more accurate sense of the patient's spontaneous speech patterns, thought processes, and thought content. If the patient becomes too disorganized in response to this change, the psychiatrist can revert to more focused questions to structure and organize the interview. If it is possible, within the context of the interview, other pieces of identifying information, such as the patient's ethnic group and religious affiliation, should be obtained.

Chief Complaint

At the start, the interviewer wants to ascertain exactly why the patient is seeking psychiatric help at this time. The

Table 21–1 Psychiatric Evaluation and Treatment Planning

Setting	Psychiatric Interview and Mental Status Examination	Physical or Neurological Examination, Laboratory Assessments, Brain Imaging	Treatment Planning
Emergency room	Most often lengthy and extensive, except as limited by patient's ability or willingness to communicate.	Physical examination is often performed; other tests and examinations are ordered as indicated.	Primary focus is on disposition.
Psychiatric inpatient unit	Extensive, but complete information may be obtained in a series of interviews over time.	Physical and neurological examinations and laboratory tests are always performed. Other tests and examinations are ordered as indicated.	Comprehensive and formal plans are developed.
Consultation liaison service	Depth of interview is highly variable depending on reasons for referral and patient's medical condition. An attempt is made to obtain a complete MSE.	Most medical information is obtained from the chart. Psychiatric consultant may request further assessment.	Recommendations focus on reasons for referral and are made to the primary treatment team.
Outpatient office or clinic	Urgency of situation is assessed. In nonurgent situations, the initial interview usually focuses on the chief complaint and MSE.	Medical information is obtained as needed, usually by referral to a general practitioner or specialist.	Planning may be formal or informal, depending on applicable regulatory and reimbursement requirements.
Third-party interviews (e.g., for court, disability determinations)	Interview addresses the reason for referral and may be narrowly focused but contains a complete MSE.	Assessments are ordered according to the purpose of the interview.	Not usually relevant except for recommendations pertaining to the purpose of the interview.

interviewer may begin with a fairly general question, such as "What brings you to the hospital at this time?" The patient may have a long history of psychiatric illness, but the chief complaint refers only to the acute problem that necessitates the current intervention. The interviewer should try to help the patient distinguish the chief complaint from any chronic problems, as in the following example:

> ***Interviewer:*** *Can you tell me what brings you to see a psychiatrist at this time?*
> ***Patient:*** *Well, I have had schizophrenia for 25 years.*
> ***Interviewer:*** *I see. But my guess is that something happened recently that has prompted you to come in today, rather than several months ago.*
> ***Patient:*** *Oh yes. Yesterday my wife kicked me out of the house. I'm homeless.*

Table 21–2 Psychiatric Interview

Greeting
Identifying information
Chief complaint
History of present illness
Past psychiatric history
Personal history
Family history
Medical history
Substance use history
Mental status examination

Here the patient's chief complaint is homelessness; the schizophrenia is part of his psychiatric history. Although a psychotic patient may offer a chief complaint that seems incoherent or unrealistic, it is important to collect the chief complaint in the patient's words and later look to other sources of information for additional history. Similarly, in response to the question, "What brings you to seek psychotherapy at this time?" a patient may begin to answer by detailing his or her childhood, but the interviewer should help the patient to focus on current issues that precipitated the consultation. Some patients may not be able to cite a chief complaint: "My wife sent me" or "There's no problem. I don't know why the police picked me up." But even these answers give the interviewer information about the patient's current situation, which can be elaborated on by asking the patient for more details.

History of Present Illness

Having obtained the chief complaint, the interviewer should clarify the nature of the present illness. By definition, the present illness begins with the onset of signs and symptoms that characterize the current episode of illness. For example, the present illness of a manic patient with chronic bipolar disorder who was asymptomatic for the past 3 years would begin with the onset of the current episode of mania. The interviewer should determine the duration of the present illness, as well as precipitating factors such as psychosocial stressors, substance use, discontinuing medication, and medical illnesses. The patient should be allowed to tell the story, and the clinician should follow up with specific diagnostic questions. For example, a patient who tells a story of 6 months of sadness after the death of a relative should then be asked about vegetative symptoms of depression, suicidal ideation, and guilty rumination.

Past Psychiatric History

The interviewer should ask for information regarding any previous episodes of psychiatric illness or treatment, including hospitalization, medications, outpatient therapy, substance use treatment, self-help groups, and consultation with culture-specific healers such as shamans. The duration and effectiveness of treatment should be ascertained, as well as the patient's general experience of her or his psychiatric treatment to date.

Personal History

No interview is complete without some understanding of the patient's background and life circumstances (Table 21–3).

Table 21–3 Personal History

Personal History
Prenatal History
Wanted versus unwanted pregnancy
History of maternal malnutrition or maternal drug use (including prescription drugs)
Circumstances of birth (vaginal delivery versus cesarean section)
History of birth trauma
Birth order
Early Childhood (0–3 y)
Temperament
Major milestones, including speech and motor development
History of toilet training
Early feeding history, including breast-feeding
Early behavioral problems, (e.g., nightmares and night terrors, enuresis and encopresis, aggressive behavior)
Early relationships with parents and siblings
History of significant early illnesses or hospitalizations
History of early separations from caregivers
Middle Childhood—Latency (3–11 y)
Early school history, including any evidence of cognitive impairment
Relationships with siblings and peers
Early personality development
History of behavioral problems (e.g., separation anxiety, school phobia, aggressive behavior)
Adolescence (12–18 y)
Psychosexual development, including experience of puberty and menarche, masturbatory history, and early sexual behavior
Later school history
Later personality development
History of behavioral or emotional problems (e.g., substance abuse, eating disorders)
Adulthood
Marital history or history of relationships with significant others
History of child-rearing
Sexual history
Occupational and educational history
Religious history
Current living situation

Within the constraints of the interviewer's time and the patient's tolerance for further questioning, the clinician should inquire about the patient's upbringing, educational and vocational history, interpersonal relations, and current social situation. It is important to inquire about the patient's sexual history and to ask about risk factors for human immunodeficiency virus (HIV) infection, such as a history of multiple partners or unprotected vaginal and anal intercourse. This information is relevant not only for the assessment and diagnosis of the present illness but also for treatment planning.

Family History

The interviewer should ask the patient specifically about any relatives with a history of psychiatric illness or treatment, suicide, or substance use. This information may be of diagnostic importance. For example, a patient who presents with a first episode of acute psychosis may have any one of a number of disorders, but a family history of affective disorders may lead the interviewer to suspect a diagnosis of bipolar disorder or major depression with psychotic features rather than schizophrenia. This information is also important for treatment planning, particularly if the patient's primary caregivers are also psychiatrically ill or also abuse substances.

Medical History

A careful review of a patient's medical history is an important part of the psychiatric interview because medical conditions can dramatically affect psychiatric status. Many medical disorders, such as endocrinological conditions (thyroid disease, pheochromocytomas, pituitary adenomas), neurological disorders (Parkinson's disease, neoplasms, Wilson's disease, stroke syndromes, head trauma), and infectious diseases (HIV infection, meningitis, sepsis) can have manifestations that include psychiatric symptoms (see Chapter 26). When such a disorder is suspected, rigorous inquiry is essential. A review of all of the patient's medications, including over-the-counter preparations, is important, because many of these substances can produce or exacerbate psychiatric symptoms. For example, propranolol taken for hypertension may produce symptoms of depression, and scopolamine taken for motion sickness may induce delirium. Finally, the toll of chronic, debilitating medical conditions or the acute onset of a catastrophic physical illness may be accompanied by secondary psychiatric symptoms that can be fully understood only in the context of the patient's medical condition.

Substance Use History

The interviewer should inquire about which substances are used, under what circumstances, and the quantity, variety, and duration of use (Table 21–4). A question such as "Do you drink alcohol?" is likely to be answered with a quick "No." A better question, such as "How much alcohol do you drink?" communicates to the patient that the clinician is not making a value judgment and is more likely to elicit an accurate answer. The interviewer must be sure to ask about past and current drug injection, including the sharing of injection equipment, to assess for HIV risk factors (Table 21–5).

Table 21–4 Substance Use History

Survey of drugs that have been used. Include
- Alcohol
- Opioids (heroin, methadone, codeine)
- Stimulants (cocaine, crack, amphetamines)
- Depressants (benzodiazepines, barbiturates)
- Hallucinogens (cannabis, lysergic acid diethylamide [LSD], mescaline)
- Phencyclidine
- Nicotine
- Caffeine
- Over-the-counter preparations

Pattern of usage
- Age of first use
- Period of heaviest use
- Pattern or frequency of current use
- Route of administration (injected, intranasal, inhaled, oral)
- Periods of sobriety

Symptoms of tolerance or dependence.

Medical history, including HIV status and other substance use–related disorders—note ongoing substance use despite knowledge that it could worsen medical conditions.

History of treatment for substance use.

Legal history—note relationship to drug use.

Table 21–5 Human Immunodeficiency Virus Risk Factors

Parenteral

Use of shared needles or drug works in the course of drug injection or amateur tattooing

Receipt of blood, blood products, or organ transplant in the United States between 1978 and 1985

Maternal-fetal transmission (pediatric cases)

Occupational exposure among health care workers and laboratory technicians through needle-stick injuries and other significant exposures (uncommon)

Unsafe Sexual Activity

Most common for men: unprotected anal intercourse with other men; unprotected vaginal or anal intercourse with women who are known to be HIV-positive, engage in prostitution, or are injection drug users or sexual partners of injection drug users; multiple heterosexual partners

Most common for women: unprotected anal or vaginal intercourse with men who are known to be HIV-positive, are injection drug users, are the sexual partners of injection drug users, are bisexual, or have hemophilia or coagulation disorder; multiple heterosexual partners

Cofactors

Compromise of the skin or mucous membranes, especially through the presence of sexually transmitted diseases, which increases the likelihood of transmission on exposure to HIV-infected body fluids

Use of noninjection drugs, especially alcohol and crack cocaine, through association with high-risk sexual activity

Environmental Context

Risk behavior while living or traveling in geographic areas with high rates of HIV infection, through increased likelihood of exposure to HIV-infected body fluids

Mental Status Examination

The MSE is a structured way to assess a patient's mental state at a given time. Unlike the parts of the interview that focus on the history, the MSE provides a descriptive snapshot of the patient at the interview. Much of the information needed for the evaluation of appearance, behavior, and speech is gathered without specific questioning during the course of the interview. However, the interviewer generally wants to ask specific questions to assess the patient's mood, thought process and content, and cognitive functioning. Bearing in mind the outline of the MSE (Table 21–6) ensures that the interview is comprehensive. The components of the MSE are described in the following paragraphs.

Appearance. The interviewer should note the patient's general appearance, including grooming, level of hygiene, and attire.

Behavior. This includes patient's level of cooperativeness with the interview, motor excitement or retardation, abnormal movements (e.g., tardive dyskinesia, tremors), and maintenance of eye contact with the interviewer.

Speech. The psychiatrist should carefully assess the patient's speech for rate, fluency, clarity, and softness or loudness. The interviewer may want to question the patient directly about his or her speech. For example, the psychiatrist can gain valuable diagnostic information by asking a patient with pressured speech if she or he is able to modulate the rate of the speech or by asking whether a dysarthric patient is aware of not speaking clearly. A bipolar patient

Table 21–6 Mental Status Examination

I. Appearance
II. Behavior (includes attitude toward the interviewer)
III. Speech
IV. Mood and affect
V. Thought
  A. Thought process
  B. Thought content
VI. Perception
  A. Hallucinations
    1. Auditory
    2. Visual
    3. Other (somatic, gustatory, tactile)
  B. Illusions
VII. Cognition
  A. Level of awareness
  B. Level of alertness
  C. Orientation
    1. Person
    2. Place
    3. Time
  D. Memory
    1. Immediate
    2. Short term
    3. Long term
  E. Attention (digit span)
  F. Calculations
  G. Fund of knowledge
  H. Abstractions
    1. Similarities
    2. Proverbs
  I. Insight
  J. Judgment

who is in the midst of a manic episode is not able to slow down her or his speech; a fast-talking anxious person is able to do so. Similarly, a patient whose dysarthria is secondary to ill-fitting dentures is aware of this problem whereas an intoxicated person is not. It is helpful to clarify whether patients with a speech abnormality feel that this is their normal speech pattern or a new problem.

Mood and Affect. The interviewer should be aware of the patient's mood and affect. This may be evident from the way in which the patient answers other questions and tells the history, but specific questions are often indicated. The patient's mood is a pervasive affective state, and it is often helpful simply to ask, "What has your mood been like lately?" or "How would you describe your mood?" In contrast, affect is the way in which one modulates and conveys one's feeling state from moment to moment. The clinician judges the congruity between the material the patient is presenting and the accompanying affect, that is, sadness when discussing the death of a loved one or happiness when describing a child's accomplishments. This reveals whether the affect is labile (shifts too rapidly) and whether it is appropriate to the content of the material (see Chapter 25).

Thought. The clinician should assess the patient's thought process and content. Thought process is the form of the patient's thoughts—are they organized and goal directed or are they tangential, circumstantial, or loosely associated? (See Chapter 24 for definitions and examples.) If the patient's thought processes are difficult to understand, the clinician can indicate his or her difficulty in following what is being said and then assess the patient's response to this intervention. Some patients, such as patients with stroke who have nonfluent aphasias, may appear to have disorganized speech but be aware that they are not making sense, whereas those with fluent aphasias, psychosis, and delirium are not necessarily aware of their impairment. The psychiatrist should ask specifically about the patient's thought content, including delusions (grandiose, persecutory, somatic), hallucinations (auditory, visual, tactile, and olfactory), obsessions, phobias, and suicidal and homicidal ideation. Although these questions should be asked with tact and empathy, they should always be asked. Patients are generally relieved that the interviewer has broached the subject of suicide, and simply asking the question does not give patients ideas they have not had before.

Cognition. Every psychiatric interview should include some assessment of the patient's cognitive functioning (see also Chapter 23). This includes the patient's level of awareness, alertness, and orientation (to person, place, and time). If there is a question about the patient's memory, formal memory testing may be done to assess short-term, intermediate, and long-term memory. A patient who can answer questions for 30 minutes is clearly attentive, but any doubts about the patient's attentiveness should prompt a formal assessment—for example, asking the patient to recite a series of digits forward and backward. Before assessing the patient's calculations and fund of knowledge, it is important to ascertain the patient's level of education. Formal assessment of the patient's ability to abstract may be unnecessary for a patient who has used abstract constructions throughout the interview, but the interviewer may want to ask formally for interpretations of similes and proverbs. It is often helpful to begin with simple constructions, for example, asking the patient the meaning of such phrases as "He has a warm heart" or "Save your money for a rainy day." Patients whose native language is not English may have difficulty in this area that does not reflect a lack of ability to abstract.

The interviewer should gain a full understanding of the patient's insight into the illness by asking why, in the patient's opinion, he or she is currently in need of psychiatric care and what has caused the problems. Finally, the interviewer should learn about the patient's judgment. This is best assessed in terms of the circumstances of the patient's life—for example, asking a mother how she would deal with a situation in which she had to leave her children to go to the store or asking a chronically ill person what he does when he sees that he is running out of medicine.

The interviewer may want to use the Mini-Mental State Examination (Mini-MSE) to quantify the degree of cognitive impairment of a patient with obvious cognitive abnormalities. This can be useful as an initial diagnostic tool as well as a means of assessing changes in cognitive function over time. The Mini-MSE is outlined in Figure 21–1.

Physical Examination

The physical examination is an important part of the comprehensive psychiatric evaluation for several reasons. First, many patients who present with psychiatric symptoms may have underlying medical problems that are causing or exacerbating the presenting symptoms. For example, an agitated, delirious patient may be septic or an asthmatic patient with a new onset of paranoia may have a steroid-induced psychosis. Second, the patient's physical capacity to tolerate certain psychiatric medications, such as tricyclic antidepressants or lithium, must be assessed. Finally, many patients who present to a psychiatrist have had inadequate medical care and should be routinely examined to assess their general level of physical health. This is especially true for patients with chronic mental illness or substance abuse. In some settings, such as emergency rooms and inpatient wards, the psychiatrist may want to perform the physical examination; in others it may be more appropriate to refer the patient to a general practitioner for this purpose. Genital, rectal, and breast examinations can usually be included even for anxious and paranoid patients, but when they must be postponed, care should be taken to complete them at a later time. A same-sex chaperone is necessary for the security of both the patient and the examiner.

Certain aspects of the information obtained in the psychiatric interview should alert the psychiatrist to the need for a physical examination. Any indication (Table 21–7) from the history that the psychiatric symptoms followed physical trauma, infection, medical illness, or drug ingestion should prompt a full physical examination. Similarly, the acute onset of psychiatric symptoms in a previously psychiatrically healthy individual, as well as symptoms arising at an unusual age, should raise questions about potential medical causes (Table 21–8).

For example, new-onset psychosis or mania in a previously healthy 65-year-old would make one pursue a medical condition as the cause, because these disorders do not commonly present at this age. Any gross physical abnormalities,

Maximum Score	Score	
		ORIENTATION
5	( )	What is the (year) (season) (date) (day) (month)?
5	( )	Where are we: (state) (county) (town) (hospital) (floor)?
		REGISTRATION
3	( )	Name 3 objects: 1 second to say each. Then ask the patient all 3 after you have said them. Give 1 point for each correct answer. Then repeat them until he learns all 3. Count trials and record. Trials
		ATTENTION AND CALCULATION
5	( )	Serial 7's. 1 point for each correct. Stop after 5 answers. Alternatively spell "world" backwards.
		RECALL
3	( )	Ask for the 3 objects repeated above. Give 1 point for each correct.
		LANGUAGE
9	( )	Name a pencil, and watch (2 points) Repeat the following "No ifs, ands or buts." (1 point) Follow a 3-stage command: "Take a paper in your right hand, fold it in half, and put it on the floor" (3 points) Read and obey the following: CLOSE YOUR EYES (1 point) Write a sentence (1 point) Copy design (1 point)
________		Total score
		ASSESS level of consciousness along a continuum ________ Alert Drowsy Stupor Coma

Figure 21–1 *Mini-Mental State Examination. (Reprinted with permission from Folstein MF, Folstein SE, McHugh PR: Mini-mental state: a practical method for grading the cognitive state of patients for the clinician. J Psychiatr Res 1975; 12:189–198. Elsevier Science Ltd., Pergamon Imprint, Oxford, England.)*

such as gait disturbances, skin lesions, eye movement abnormalities, lacerations, flushed skin, or drooling, should raise the interviewer's suspicion that there might be an underlying medical condition. Urinary or fecal incontinence is also highly suggestive of a medical etiology. Stigmata of drug or alcohol use or abuse, such as dilated or pinpoint pupils, track marks, evidence of skin popping, or frank evidence of intoxication (e.g., alcohol on the breath), should also signal the need for a more thorough physical examination. Abnormalities of speech, such as impaired fluency or dysarthria, may indicate the presence of an underlying medical disturbance. Many mood problems may be caused by physical disorders, and even apparently healthy patients with dysthymia may have hypothyroidism that can be treated medically. Finally, any cognitive disturbances, such as disorientation, fluctuating level of alertness, inattentiveness, or memory problems, are, until proved otherwise, evidence of a physical problem that is causing psychiatric symptoms. In such situations, careful attention should be paid to the patient's vital signs, neurological examination (see the next section), and any indications of infection. In a hospital setting, a physical examination, including a careful assessment of the patient's vital signs (including orthostatic measurements), cardiovascular status, and pulmonary status, precedes the prescription of most psychiatric medications. Psychiatrists should pay particular attention to a patient's cardiovascular status (e.g., electrocardiographic abnormalities, orthostatic hypotension, decreased cardiac ejection fraction) before beginning tricyclic antidepressants, which may induce cardiac conduction disturbances and thus must be used with caution for patients with such cardiac abnormalities as arrhythmias or other conduction abnormalities. Patients taking medications such as low-potency neuroleptics, monoamine oxidase inhibitors, and tricyclic antidepressants should be assessed for orthostatic hypotension, especially if they are elderly. If β-blockers such as propranolol are being considered, patients should be evaluated for the presence of asthma, which may be exacerbated by these drugs.

Table 21–7 Indications for Physical Examination
History of medical illness
Current symptoms of medical illness, particularly fever, neurological symptoms, or cardiovascular abnormalities
Evidence while taking history of altered mental status or cognitive impairment
History or physical evidence of trauma, particularly head trauma
Rapid onset of symptoms
New onset of psychosis, depression, mania, panic attacks
New onset of visual, tactile, or olfactory hallucinations
New-onset psychiatric symptoms after age 40 y
Family history of physical illness that could cause psychiatric illness

Physical examination may also be warranted during treatment with medication if physical symptoms arise. For example, fever and a change of mental status during a course of neuroleptics require a full physical and neurological examination to rule out neuroleptic malignant syndrome. Urinary retention induced by medications with anticholinergic side effects requires an abdominal examination to assess bladder fullness. Anticholinergic-induced constipation may warrant abdominal or rectal examination to assess for impaction. When patients are seen in office-based practices, the psychiatrist most often obtains a careful medical history and may complete simple procedures such as blood pressure checks but may refer the patient to another physician for a complete physical examination.

Neurological Examination

In the hospital setting, every patient should have a thorough neurological examination. Patients who have a history of neurological disturbances, such as strokes, seizure disorders, central nervous system neoplasms, dementias, and movement disorders, should be carefully evaluated, perhaps by a neurologist. The neurological examination should be particularly designed to rule out any lateralizing neurological signs, which would point toward the presence of a focal lesion. Unilateral weakness or abnormalities in pupil size or eye movements might suggest a focal neoplasm, infection (such as toxoplasmosis), intracranial bleeding, or a stroke, which may explain such psychiatric symptoms as confusion, sudden onset of speech difficulties, psychosis, or even depression. Stiffness and cogwheel rigidity are classical signs of Parkinson's disease, which may be associated with such psychiatric symptoms as depression, psychosis, and dementia.

Patients with acquired immunodeficiency syndrome should also be carefully evaluated neurologically, because many neurological manifestations of advanced HIV-related illness (including HIV encephalopathy, toxoplasmosis, and cryptococcal meningitis) and the medicines administered to treat these illnesses may produce psychiatric symptoms, including depression, delirium, dementia, mania, and psychosis. Gait should be carefully examined in psychiatric patients, because certain neurological conditions in which gait disturbances are prominent, such as normal-pressure hydrocephalus, tertiary syphilis (tabes dorsalis), and combined system disease (caused by vitamin B_{12} deficiency), may produce a variety of psychiatric symptoms.

Psychological and Neuropsychological Testing

Psychological and neuropsychological tests are standard instruments used to measure specific aspects of mental functioning. They are usually administered by psychologists or other professionals who have been trained in their use and interpretation. In most cases, several tests, often referred to as a battery, are performed together. These test results must then be interpreted in the context of the broad clinical picture of the patient. The neuropsychological evaluation is discussed in detail in Chapter 22.

Because of the time and expense involved, testing is usually reserved for situations in which there is some uncertainty about a patient's diagnosis, cognitive capacity, or psychological functioning. There are, however, times when

Table 21–8 Physical Illnesses That May Present with Psychiatric Symptoms

Neurological	Metabolic
Amyotrophic lateral sclerosis	Acute intermittent porphyria
Epilepsy—particularly partial complex seizures (e.g., temporal lobe epilepsy)	Electrolyte imbalance
Huntington's disease	Hepatic encephalopathy
Multiinfarct dementia	Hepatolenticular degeneration (Wilson's disease)
Normal-pressure hydrocephalus	Hypoxemia
Parkinson's disease	Uremic encephalopathy
Pick's disease	**Nutritional**
Stroke syndromes (cerebrovascular disease)	Vitamin B_{12} deficiency
Rheumatological (Autoimmune)	Central pontine myelinolysis
Systemic lupus erythematosus	Folate deficiency (megaloblastic anemia)
Temporal arteritis	General malnutrition
Infectious	Nicotinic acid deficiency (pellagra)
Acquired immunodeficiency syndrome	Thiamine deficiency (Wernicke-Korsakoff syndrome)
Brain abscess	**Traumatic, Particularly Head Trauma**
Encephalitis	**Toxic**
Meningitis	Environmental toxins
Syphilis, particularly neurosyphilis	Intoxication with alcohol or other drugs
Tuberculosis	**Neoplastic**
Viral hepatitis	Carcinoma (general)
Endocrine	Central nervous system tumors (primary or metastatic)
Adrenal hypoplasia (Cushing's syndrome)	Endocrine tumors
Diabetes mellitus	Pancreatic carcinoma
Hypo- or hyperparathyroidism	
Hypo- or hyperthyroidism	
Hypothalamic dysfunction	
Panhypopituitarism	
Pheochromocytoma	

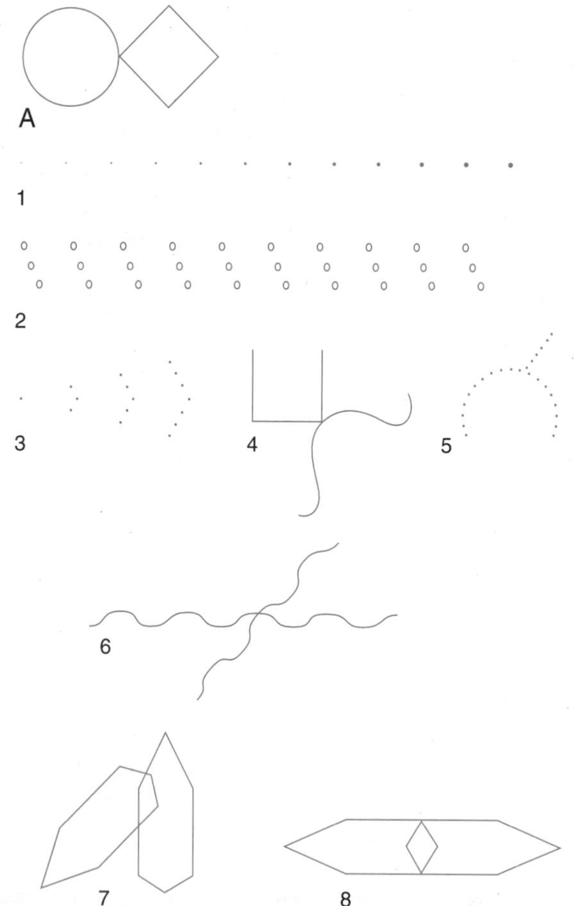

Figure 21–2 *Bender Visual-Motor Gestalt Test.*

psychological testing is essential—for example, IQ testing to establish the severity of mental retardation. In addition, giving simple tests of cognitive functioning, such as asking the patient to copy Bender Gestalt diagrams (Fig. 21–2), can be helpful as one aspect of assessing central nervous system impairment caused by a medical condition. Psychological and neuropsychological testing can be particularly useful in the assessment of children with academic or behavioral difficulties in school. Table 21–9 lists some of the most commonly used tests.

Structured Clinical Instruments and Rating Scales

Structured instruments and rating scales have been developed primarily for research purposes. They allow investigators to compare findings in different studies by ensuring that similar data and criteria have been used to establish diagnoses and to measure the presence and severity of psychiatric symptoms and their response to treatment. Many types of mental health professionals, and in some cases nonclinicians, can be trained to administer these rating scales.

Although most practicing clinicians do not commonly use structured instruments to assess or follow up patients, a small number of rating scales have come to be used routinely in clinical practice. For example, the Abnormal Involuntary Movement Scale (Fig. 21–3) is often used to monitor patients receiving antipsychotic medication for the presence of tardive dyskinesia, and the Global Assessment of Functioning Scale (Fig. 21–4), which is a slight modification of the Global Assessment Scale, is now used in Axis V in the *Diagnostic and Statistical Manual of Mental Disorders,* fourth edition (DSM-IV).

Table 21–10 shows some of the most commonly cited structured instruments and rating scales. Hundreds of other specialized scales are also in use to assess such diverse areas as personality disorder, aggressive behavior, sexual practices, stressful life events, and quality of life.

Table 21–11 gives an example of how these different rating scales approach the assessment of two symptoms: guilt, a purely subjective state of mind, and suicide risk, an inclination that is assessed using both subjective and behavioral components.

Laboratory Assessments

A variety of laboratory tests can aid in the clinical evaluation of the psychiatric patient (Table 21–12).

Serological Evaluations. Blood tests are particularly helpful in ruling out medical causes of psychiatric symptoms.

Toxicology. When the clinician suspects that the ingestion of a substance has caused the presenting symptoms, a urine toxicology screen and blood alcohol level determination (Table 21–13) are indicated. (It is important to remember that an alcohol level of zero may indicate that the symptoms are due to a withdrawal syndrome and thus does not rule out alcohol as an inciting factor.) If the patient is known to be

Table 21–9 Common Psychological and Neuropsychological Tests

Name of Test	General Purpose
Bender Gestalt Test	Subject's reproduction of geometric designs used to screen for neuropsychiatric impairment
Halstead-Reitan Battery	Complex battery of tests that give a detailed picture of neuropsychiatric functioning
Minnesota Multiphasic Personality Inventory*	Multiple true-false questions designed to assess psychopathology and personality
Rorschach Test	Ten inkblot designs; subject's associations used to assess thinking disturbances and psychological conflicts and defenses
Thematic Apperception Test	Emotionally suggestive pictures portraying one or more people; used to elicit stories that reveal psychological development and motivation
Wechsler Adult Intelligence Scale–Revised	Eleven subscales; used to assess verbal and performance IQ in adults
Wechsler Intelligence Scale for Children–Revised	Twelve subscales; used to assess verbal and performance IQ in children 6 to 16 y old

*Can be self-administered.

INSTRUCTIONS: Complete Examination Procedure before making ratings.
MOVEMENT RATINGS: Rate highest severity observed.
Rate movements that occur upon activation one *less* than those observed spontaneously.

Code: 0 = None
1 = Minimal, may be extreme normal
2 = Mild
3 = Moderate
4 = Severe

		(Circle One)				
FACIAL AND ORAL MOVEMENTS:	1. Muscles of Facial Expression e.g., movements of forehead, eyebrows, periorbital area, cheeks; include frowning, blinking, smiling, grimacing	0	1	2	3	4
	2. Lips and Perioral Area e.g., puckering, pouting, smacking	0	1	2	3	4
	3. Jaw e.g., biting, clenching, chewing, mouth opening, lateral movement	0	1	2	3	4
	4. Tongue Rate only increase in movement both in and out of mouth, NOT inability to sustain movement	0	1	2	3	4
EXTREMITY MOVEMENTS:	5. Upper *(arms, wrists, hands, fingers)* Include choreic movements, (i.e., rapid, objectively purposeless, irregular, spontaneous), athetoid movements (i.e., slow, irregular, complex, serpentine). Do NOT include tremor (i.e., repetitive, regular, rhythmic)	0	1	2	3	4
	6. Lower *(legs, knees, ankles, toes)* e.g., lateral knee movement, foot tapping, heel dropping, foot squirming, inversion and eversion of foot	0	1	2	3	4
TRUNK MOVEMENTS:	7. Neck, shoulders, hips e.g., rocking, twisting, squirming, pelvic gyrations	0	1	2	3	4

GLOBAL JUDGMENTS:	8. Severity of abnormal movements	None, normal Minimal Mild Moderate Severe	0 1 2 3 4
	9. Incapacitation due to abnormal movements	None, normal Minimal Mild Moderate Severe	0 1 2 3 4
	10. Patient's awareness of abnormal movements Rate only patient's report	No awareness Aware, no distress Aware, mild distress Aware, moderate distress Aware, severe distress	0 1 2 3 4

Figure 21–3 *Abnormal Involuntary Movement Scale. (From Guy W: ECDEU Assessment Manual for Psychopharmacology Revised. Rockville, MD: National Institute of Mental Health, 1976:534.)*

taking certain psychiatric medications, such as lithium, tricyclic antidepressants, and anticonvulsants, levels of these medications should be tested, as toxic levels may cause a variety of psychiatric symptoms.

Complete Blood Count. The complete blood count is part of the general laboratory evaluation of a new patient. It is used to screen for multiple problems, most commonly infections and anemia. In cases in which alcoholism is suspected or the mean corpuscular volume indicates a macrocytic anemia, vitamin B_{12} and folate levels should be tested. Vitamin B_{12} deficiency may lead to combined system disease, which can present with psychiatric symptoms such as irritability and forgetfulness in the early stages and dementia or frank psychosis in the later stages. The complete blood count is routinely used to monitor white blood cell counts in patients taking clozapine. Additional emergency complete blood counts may be necessary if such a patient develops fever, malaise, or other symptoms of infection.

Blood Glucose. The blood glucose test is an inexpensive, essential test in the evaluation of patients with a new onset of central nervous system dysfunction, psychosis, affective disorders, and anxiety disorders. Hypoglycemia may produce lethargy and vegetative symptoms that may mimic those of depression, and hyperglycemia may produce anxiety and delirium. This test is clearly indicated for known diabetics who present with the first onset of psychiatric symptoms.

Kidney Function Tests. The blood urea nitrogen and creatinine levels are important measures of kidney function. Kidney function tests are used to screen for kidney failure and hypovolemic states (in which blood urea nitrogen and creatinine levels increase). It is essential to perform these tests before beginning therapy with lithium, which is cleared by the kidneys.

Liver Function Tests. These tests, which check for levels of various enzymes in the liver, are indicated when there is some suspicion that liver disease is present. They help the clinician to screen for hepatitis, alcoholism, and biliary tract disease. They include creatine kinase, which is often elevated in neuroleptic malignant syndrome as well as in other conditions in which muscle rigidity is prominent.

Thyroid Function Tests. Both hypothyroidism and hyperthyroidism can mimic the symptoms of psychiatric disorders. Hyperthyroidism may mimic anxiety disorders, psy-

Consider psychological, social, and occupational functioning on a hypothetical continuum of mental health–illness. Do not include impairment in functioning due to physical (or environmental) limitations.

Code	(**Note:** Use intermediate codes when appropriate, e.g., 45, 68, 72.)
100 | 91	**Superior functioning in a wide range of activities, life's problems never seem to get out of hand, is sought out by others because of his or her many positive qualities. No symptoms.**
90 | 81	**Absent or minimal symptoms** (eg., mild anxiety before an exam), **good functioning in all areas, interested and involved in a wide range of activities, socially effective, generally satisfied with life, no more than everyday problems or concerns** (e.g, an occasional argument with family members).
80 | 71	**If symptoms are present, they are transient and expectable reactions to psychosocial stressors** (e.g, difficulty concentrating after family argument); **no more than slight impairment in social, occupational, or school functioning** (e.g., temporarily falling behind in schoolwork).
70 | 61	**Some mild symptoms** (e.g., depressed mood and mild insomnia) **OR some difficulty in social, occupational, or school functioning** (e.g., occasional truancy, or theft within the household), **but generally functioning pretty well, has some meaningful interpersonal relationships.**
60 | 51	**Moderate symptoms** (e.g., flat affect and circumstantial speech, occasional panic attacks) **OR moderate difficulty in social, occupational, or school functioning** (e.g., few friends, conflicts with peers or co-workers).
50 | 41	**Serious symptoms** (e.g., suicidal ideation, severe obsessional rituals, frequent shoplifting) **OR any serious impairment in social, occupational, or school functioning** (e.g., no friends, unable to keep a job).
40 | 31	**Some impairment in reality testing or communication** (e.g., speech is at times illogical, obscure, or irrelevant) **OR major impairment in several areas, such as work or school, family relations, judgment, thinking, or mood** (e.g., depressed man avoids friends, neglects family, and is unable to work; child frequently beats up younger children, is defiant at home, and is failing at school).
30 | 21	**Behavior is considerably influenced by delusions or hallucinations OR serious impairment in communication or judgment** (e.g., sometimes incoherent, acts grossly inappropriately, suicidal preoccupation) **OR inability to function in almost all areas** (e.g., stays in bed all day; no job, home, or friends).
20 | 11	**Some danger of hurting self or others** (e.g., suicide attempts without clear expectation of death; frequently violent; manic excitement) **OR occasionally fails to maintain minimal personal hygiene** (e.g., smears feces) **OR gross impairment in communication** (e.g., largely incoherent or mute).
10 | 1	**Persistent danger of severely hurting self or others** (e.g., recurrent violence) **OR persistent inability to maintain minimal personal hygiene OR serious suicidal act with clear expectation of death.**
0	Inadequate information.

Figure 21–4 *Global Assessment of Functioning Scale. (From American Psychiatric Association: Diagnostic and Statistical Manual of Mental Disorders, 4th ed. Washington DC: American Psychiatric Association, 1994:32.)*

Table 21–10 Common Structured Instruments and Psychiatric Rating Scales

Name of Scale	General Purpose
Abormal Involuntary Movement Scale	Brief structured assessment of abnormal movements; used to rate presence and severity of tardive dyskinesia
Beck Depression Inventory*	Twenty-item rating scale for depression; focuses on mood and cognition
Brief Psychiatric Rating Scale	Eighteen-item scale that rates current severity of psychopathology
Diagnostic Interview Schedule	Diagnostic instrument developed for use by nonclinicians to conduct community surveys
Global Assessment of Functioning Scale	Overall psychosocial functioning rated on a scale from 0 to 100; used as Axis V of DSM-IV
Hamilton Depression Rating Scale	A 17- to 21-item scale that rates the severity of depressive symptoms; strong focus on somatic problems
Nurses' Observation Scale for Inpatient Evaluation	Eighty items used to rate the behavior of hospitalized patients by staff
Overt Aggression Scale	Rates aggression in four categories: verbal, physical against self, physical against objects, physical against other people
Personality Disorder Examination	Items that rate six areas of personality functioning, which are analyzed by computer with a series of algorithms to generate personality disorder diagnoses
Present State Examination	Continually updated semistructured diagnostic interview used in international research and tied to the manual on the International Classification of Diseases (most recently ICD-10)
Schedule for Affective Disorders and Schizophrenia	Semistructured questions, similar to the Structured Clinic Interview for DSM-IV but more detailed, for establishing diagnoses of affective disorders and schizophrenia
Structured Clinical Interview for DSM-IV	Semistructured questions used to establish DSM-IV Axis I and Axis II diagnoses
Symptom Checklist* (SCL-90)	Nine-item self-report instrument used to assess psychopathology

*These instruments are self-administered.

chosis, or mania, and hypothyroidism may mimic dysthymia and depression. Thyroid function tests are therefore indicated in cases of new onset of a major mental illness. In addition, thyroid function should always be tested when initiating lithium therapy, because lithium may cause hypothyroidism.

Syphilis Screening. These tests should be done for any patient with new-onset psychosis. They have become particularly important with the increasing incidence of syphilitic infection associated with the HIV epidemic. Positive serologic results in the presence of unexplained psychiatric symptoms necessitate a lumbar puncture to test for neurosyphilis.

Blood Cultures. Blood cultures are indicated in the evaluation of medically ill patients who develop fever and psychiatric symptoms such as confusion, disorientation, and agitation, because this delirium may be secondary to sepsis.

HIV Testing. Psychiatric patients who present with known risk factors for HIV infection, including injection drug use and unsafe sexual practices (see Table 21–5), should be approached for consent to HIV testing, especially in geographic areas with high numbers of reported cases of acquired immunodeficiency syndrome. This also applies to patients who present with multiple sexually transmitted diseases or tuberculosis. HIV should always be suspected in cases of unexplained central nervous system dysfunction and when psychiatric illness is accompanied by suggestive medical findings such as thrush or swollen lymph nodes. HIV testing requires consent of the patient and should be preceded and followed by counseling.

Pregnancy Testing. The serologic test for the presence of human chorionic gonadotropin β-subunit may assist in ruling out pregnancy before the initiation of therapy with lithium, benzodiazepines, or other medications associated with fetal malformations. It is advisable to perform pregnancy testing for all women of childbearing age before initiating therapy with any psychotropic medication.

Urine Testing. Urine testing is indicated in two situations. Urine tests for pregnancy are often indicated in the emergency room setting in which an immediate result is required before the initiation of drug therapy, but they are less accurate than serologic evaluation. Urinalysis may be indicated for geriatric patients with new onset of central nervous system dysfunction or psychosis, because urinary tract infections may manifest themselves in this manner in the elderly.

Cerebrospinal Fluid Evaluation. Lumbar puncture may be indicated to test for infections, including meningitis, neurosyphilis, toxoplasmosis, and cerebrospinal fluid tuberculosis. It is indicated in the evaluation of patients with symptoms such as confusion, disorientation, decreased alertness, or dementia when accompanied by fever (Table 21–14). It is also an important part of the evaluation of patients who have new-onset seizures or who are suspected of having neuroleptic malignant syndrome, because these symptoms may be caused by central nervous system infections. In cases in which increased cerebrospinal fluid pressure is suspected, lumbar puncture should be preceded by computed tomographic (CT) scanning to evaluate for mass lesions.

Electrocardiogram. Because it is important to screen for conduction disturbances and cardiac arrhythmias before beginning therapy with tricyclic antidepressants, an electrocardiogram should precede the initiation of therapy. An electrocardiogram is also indicated before beginning certain other psychotropic medications that may produce electrocardiographic changes (Tables 21–15 and 21–16). An electrocardiographic tracing of a patient who took an overdose of tricyclic antidepressants is shown in Figure 21–5.

Brain Imaging

Several methods of brain imaging are available when routine laboratory examination proves insufficient for diagnostic purposes. Table 21–17 lists the indications for brain imaging.

Electroencephalography

An electroencephalogram (EEG) gives the clinician a visual picture of the electrical activity of the brain. Electrodes placed on the scalp measure electrical activity in the most superficial layer of the cortex. By noting the frequency, amplitude, and distribution of the waveforms produced on an EEG, a skilled reader can determine the presence and location of epileptiform activity (often indicated by spike waves), generalized slowing of electrical activity (e.g., in delirium or as a result of a drug effect), or the patient's stage of sleep. An EEG may be indicated in the evaluation of patients with known seizure disorders who present with psychiatric symptoms. Obtaining an EEG of a sleep-deprived patient may increase the likelihood of finding electrical abnormalities. A history of brain injury or head trauma is an indication for an EEG in the work-up of mental status changes or psychiatric symptoms. The patient with new-onset psychosis should also have an EEG, because partial complex seizures may produce psychosis. Symptoms suggesting temporal lobe epilepsy (Fig. 21–6), such as hyperreligiosity, hyposexuality, and hypergraphia, also in-

Table 21–11 Comparison of Rating Scales for Assessing Guilt and Suicide Risk

Rating Scale	Guilt	Suicide Risk
Beck Depression Inventory. Patient picks best answer.	3 = I feel as though I am very bad or worthless. 2 = I feel quite guilty. 1 = I feel bad or unworthy a good part of the time. 0 = I don't feel particularly guilty.	3 = I would kill myself if I had the chance. 2 = I have definite plans about committing suicide. 1 = I feel I would be better off dead. 0 = I don't have any thoughts of harming myself.
Symptom Checklist. Patient rates on five-point scale from not at all to extremely.	How much were you bothered by Blaming yourself for things? The idea that you should be punished for your sins? Feelings of guilt?	How much were you bothered by Thoughts of ending your life? Thoughts of death or dying?
Structured Clinical Interview for DSM-IV. Semistructured interview. Rater selects: 1 = Absent or false 2 = Subthreshold 3 = Threshold or true	*Interviewer asks:* "How did you feel about yourself? (worthless?)" If no, "What about feeling guilty about things you had done or not done? (nearly every day?)" *Interviewer rates:* Feelings of worthlessness or excessive or inappropriate guilt (which may be delusional) nearly every day (not merely self-reproach or guilt about being sick).	*Interviewer asks:* Were things so bad that you were thinking a lot about death or that you would be better off dead? What about thinking of hurting yourself? *Interviewer rates:* Recurrent thoughts of death (not just fear of dying), recurrent suicidal ideation without a specific plan, or a suicide attempt or specific plan for committing suicide.
Schedule for Affective Disorders and Schizophrenia. Semistructured interview. Rater selects answers on six-point scale from not at all to extreme.	*Interviewer asks:* Do you blame yourself for anything you have done or not done? What about feeling guilty? Do you feel you have done anything wrong? (Do you deserve punishment?) Do you feel you have brought this on yourself? *Interviewer rates:* Feelings of self-reproach or excessive or inappropriate guilt for things done or not done, including delusions of guilt. *Further questions:* Assess delusions of guilt or sin.	*Interviewer asks:* When people get upset or depressed or feel hopeless, they may think about dying or even killing themselves. Have you? (Have you thought how you would do it? Have you told anybody about suicidal thoughts? Have you actually done anything?) *Interviewer rates:* Suicidal tendencies, including preoccupation with thoughts of death or suicide. *Further questions:* Assess gestures, attempts, risk-rescue factors, medical lethality.
Hamilton Depression Rating Scale. Rater selects best answer.	0 = Feeling of guilt or absent. 1 = Self-reproach, feelings of having let people down. 2 = Ideas of guilt or rumination over past errors or sinful deeds. 3 = Present illness is a punishment; delusions of guilt. 4 = Hears accusatory or denunciatory voices and/or experiences, threatening visual hallucinations.	0 = Thoughts of suicide absent. 1 = Feels life is not worth living. 2 = Wishes he or she were dead or any thoughts of possible death to self. 3 = Suicide ideas or gesture. 4 = Attempts at suicide (any serious attempt rates 4).
Brief Psychiatric Rating Scale. Rater selects answer on seven-point scale where 1 = Not present 7 = Extremely severe	Overconcern or remorse for past behavior. Rate on the basis of patient's subjective experiences of guilt as evidenced by verbal report with appropriate affect; do not infer guilt feelings from depression, anxiety, or neurotic defenses.	

Table 21–12 Common Laboratory Tests for Evaluation of Psychiatric Patients

Serologic
Toxicology screen (blood)
Complete blood count
Blood glucose
Kidney function tests
Liver function tests
Thyroid function tests
Syphilis serology
HIV antibody test
Pregnancy test
Blood cultures
Vitamin B_{12} and folate levels
Urine
Toxicology screen (urine)
Dipstick for protein and glucose
Pregnancy test
Lumbar Puncture
Electrocardiogram
Chest Radiograph

Table 21–13 Toxicology Screens

Drug	Amount per mL	Approximate Duration of Detectability (d)*
Alcohol	300 μg	1
Amphetamines	500 ng	2
Barbiturates	1000 ng	1–3
Benzodiazepines	300 ng	3
Cocaine	150 ng	2–3
Opiates	300 ng	2
Phencyclidine	25 ng	8
Tetrahydrocannabinol carboxylic acid	<15 ng	3–20

*May vary widely depending on amount ingested, compound, physical state of subject, and other factors.

Modified from Council on Scientific Affairs, The American Medical Association: Scientific issues in drug testing. JAMA 1987; 257:3110–3114. Copyright 1987, American Medical Association. See also Gold MS, Dackis CA: Role of the laboratory in the evaluation of suspected drug abuse. J Clin Psychiatry 1986; 47(suppl): 17–23.

dicate that an EEG should be obtained, including nasopharyngeal leads, to best evaluate electrical activity in the temporal lobes. EEGs may be useful in the assessment of insomnia and other sleep disturbances.

Abrupt onset of psychiatric symptoms such as psychosis, mania, or personality change suggests a medical etiology and may be an indication for electroencephalography. Delirium can be diagnosed from an EEG, but this is often unwieldy and unnecessary, because the diagnosis of delirium can be made clinically and followed up with laboratory testing. Visual, olfactory, and tactile hallucinations are suggestive of central nervous system dysfunction, which may warrant evaluation by electroencephalography.

Evoked Potentials

Evoked potentials are electrical responses that are recorded from the central nervous system. Visual, auditory, or somatosensory stimuli may be used to elicit these responses. By using this technique, the integrity of the central nervous system components of the sensory systems can be assessed. Visual evoked responses are recorded while a subject is exposed to flashing lights or a moving visual stimulus. They are particularly useful in demonstrating optic nerve lesions and can aid in the diagnosis of multiple sclerosis. Brain stem auditory evoked responses can be used to assess central nervous system damage to the auditory system and are elicited by exposure of the subject to click stimuli in either ear. Again, they are most useful in diagnosing multiple sclerosis, although they may also be useful in the diagnosis of brain

Table 21–14 Indications for Lumbar Puncture (Cerebrospinal Fluid Evaluation) in Psychiatric Patients

- Rapid onset of new psychiatric symptoms, including dementia, delirium, psychosis
- New-onset psychiatric symptoms with fever
- New-onset neurological symptoms (e.g., seizures, paralysis)
- Suspected neuroleptic malignant syndrome (e.g., while taking antipsychotics, patient develops fever, tremor, anemia, obtundation)
- New-onset psychiatric symptoms with a known history of HIV infection or neoplasm (if space-occupying lesion is suspected, brain imaging should precede lumbar puncture)

Table 21–15 Indications for Electrocardiography

- Assessment of cardiac functioning before beginning
  - Tricyclic antidepressants
  - Lithium
  - Thioridazine
  - β-Blockers
  - Electroconvulsive therapy
- Drug overdoses (need varies with substance or substances ingested)

Table 21–16 Common Electrocardiographic Abnormalities Seen with Psychotropic Medication

Medication	Abnormality
Tricyclic antidepressants	Increased PR, QRS, or QT intervals
Lithium	T wave flattening or inversion Sinoatrial block Sick sinus syndrome
Antipsychotics	
Thioridazine	Increased QT interval
Clozapine	Sinus tachycardia

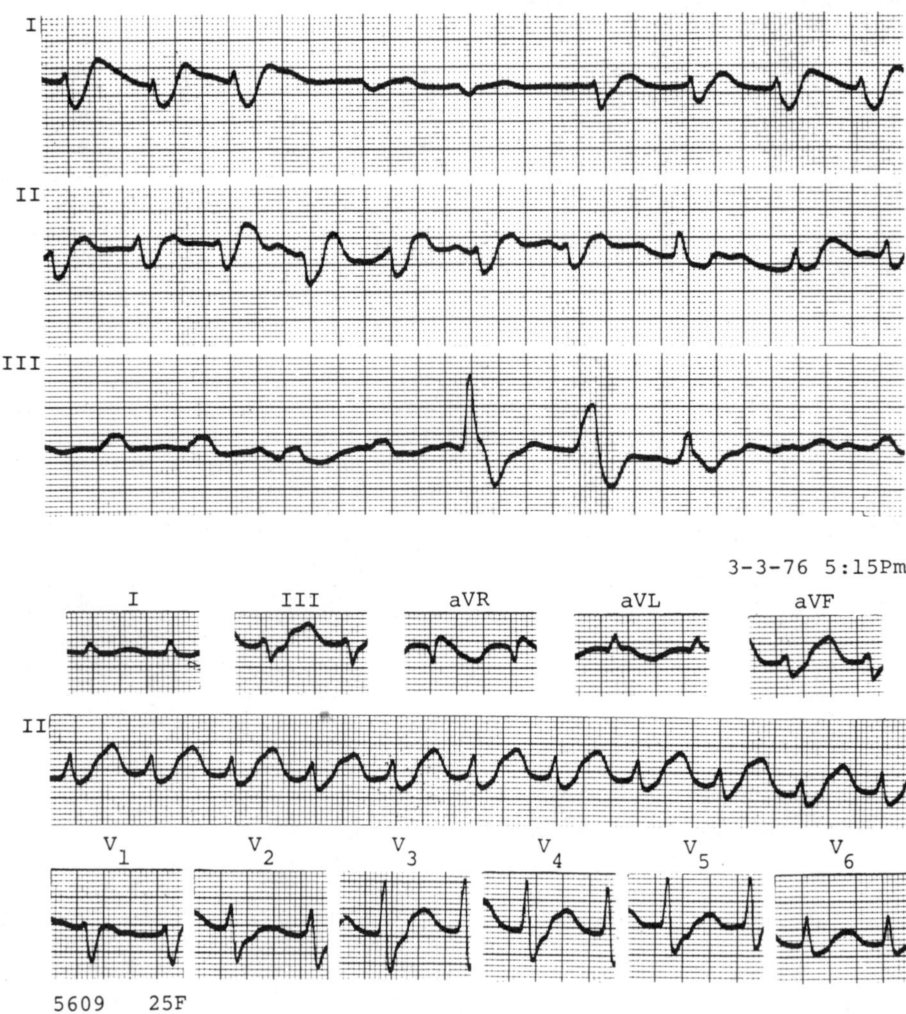

Figure 21–5 *Tricyclic antidepressant overdose. The patient was a 25-year-old woman who took 500 mg of imipramine (Tofranil) 4 hours before the 5 PM tracing was recorded. The three standard limb leads show wide QRS complexes of varying morphology. The exact rhythm cannot be determined. She had severe hypotension at this time. Fifteen minutes later, the tracing shows probable supraventricular rhythm with intraventricular conduction defect. (From Chou T-C: Electrocardiography in Clinical Practice, 3rd ed. Philadelphia: WB Saunders, 1991:481.)*

stem infarcts. Somatosensory evoked responses can be measured after the subject is exposed to stimulation of peripheral nerves. They are most useful in assessing spinal cord function intraoperatively. Although evoked potentials have been studied in psychiatric illness, there are currently no clinical indications for use of this procedure in the diagnosis and treatment of psychiatric patients. Ongoing investigations may reveal uses for this technique.

Table 21–17 Indications for Brain Imaging
History of head trauma
Focal neurological findings on physical examination
New-onset psychiatric systems after age 40 y (including psychosis, affective disorder, personality change)
Rapid onset of psychiatric symptoms
History of neurological symptoms (including seizures)
Evidence of cognitive impairment
Abnormal electroencephalogram
Abnormal lumbar puncture

Computed Tomographic Scans

The CT scan can be a powerful tool in psychiatric evaluation. In a CT scanning, the brain is visualized by measuring differences in the density of the various tissue components (cerebrospinal fluid, blood, bone, gray and white matter). Data obtained when x-ray photons pass through the brain tissue onto a detector are processed by a computer, which generates a three-dimensional view of the brain. The brain can be viewed in coronal, sagittal, or transverse sections. A CT scan should be part of the initial psychiatric evaluation when the clinician suspects such abnormalities as mass lesions (central nervous system neoplasms, toxoplasmosis [Fig. 21–7], abscesses, and hemorrhage), calcifications, atrophy, or areas of infarction. Bone abnormalities, calcifications, and areas of hemorrhage are particularly well visualized on CT scans;

details of brain tissue are not. Lesions in the posterior fossa and the brain stem are often not well visualized on CT scans because of surrounding bone structures. Mass lesions should be suspected in situations in which focal or lateralizing abnormalities, such as focal weakness, unilateral disturbances in reflexes, and increased pupillary size, are found during the neurological examination. The work-up of a patient with dementia should include a CT scan to look for brain atrophy or lacunar infarctions. A CT scan is also a part of the evaluation of new-onset psychosis, acute onset of aphasia or memory loss, and neglect syndromes. The evaluation of normal-pressure hydrocephalus, a syndrome characterized by a wide-based gait, dementia, and urinary incontinence, should also include a CT scan. Although CT scans have been shown to demonstrate certain abnormalities in some psychiatric illnesses (e.g., large ventricular size in some patients with schizophrenia), they cannot yet confirm a diagnosis of psychiatric illness. Instead, they serve to rule out medical disorders.

Magnetic Resonance Imaging

In magnetic resonance imaging, electromagnetic radiation rather than ionizing radiation is used to measure electrical changes in the brain's structure when it is exposed to a strong magnetic field. As with CT scanning, the data are processed by a computer to produce visual images of the brain. This technique produces an image that is superior to the CT scan in differentiating gray from white matter and in clearly visualizing individual brain structures. Although the absence of x-radiation makes the technique safer than CT scanning, the expense of magnetic resonance imaging and the ready availability of CT scanning in most medical facilities usually make CT scanning the brain imaging technique of choice in the initial work-up of the psychiatric patient. Exceptions would include cases in which the clinician suspects a small lesion in an area that is difficult to visualize and cases in which a demyelinating condition (e.g., multiple sclerosis) is suspected (Fig. 21–8).

Positron Emission Tomography, Single Photon Emission Computed Tomography, and Regional Cerebral Blood Flow

Whereas CT and magnetic resonance imaging provide visualization of brain structure, positron emission tomography (PET), single photon emission computed tomography (SPECT), and regional cerebral blood flow allow investigators to study brain functioning. With PET and SPECT, this is done by injecting radiolabeled organic compounds, such as glucose, into the blood stream and tracking these compounds as they are metabolized in brain tissue. This information is relayed to a computer, which produces visual images of the working brain. When multiple images are obtained over time, it is possible to learn which areas of the brain are stimulated during various types of mental activity. PET and SPECT differ principally in that different types of radioactive isotopes are used for labeling: in PET, positron-emitting isotopes are used, and SPECT uses single photon–emitting isotopes. The isotopes used in SPECT have longer half-lives than those used in PET, which allows SPECT to visualize the brain over longer periods. Nevertheless,

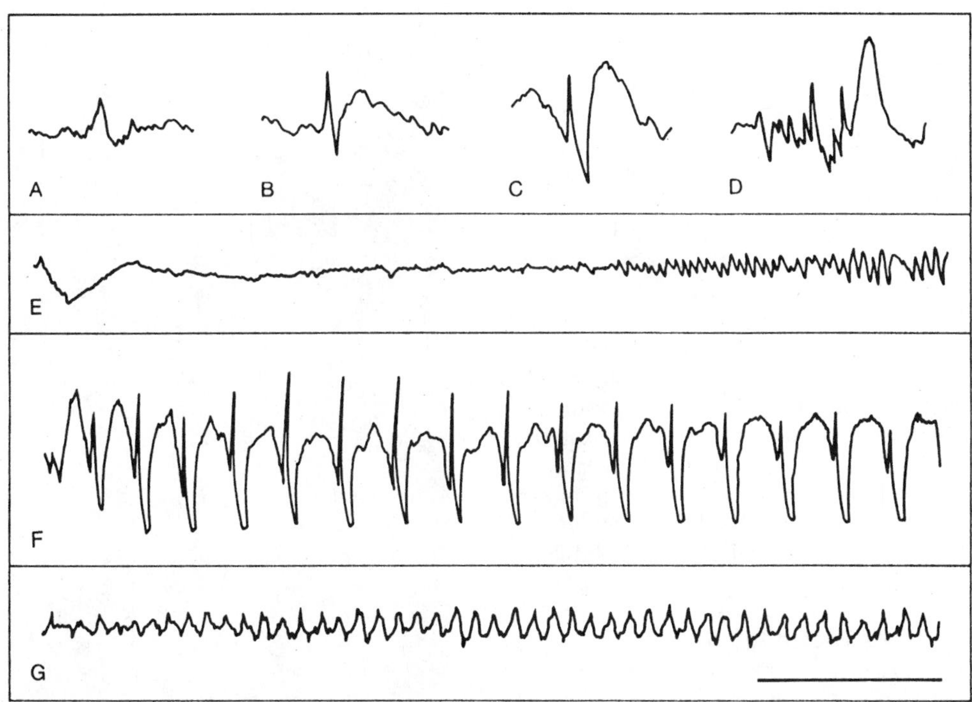

Figure 21–6 *Examples illustrate waveforms of typical interictal EEG transients and ictal EEG discharges.* (A) *Interictal sharp wave.* (B) *and* (C) *Interictal spike-and-wave complexes.* (D) *Interictal polyspike-and-wave complex.* (E) *Recruiting rhythm typical of generalized convulsion onsets.* (F) *Repetitive spike-and-wave discharges typical of absence seizures.* (G) *Rhythmic pattern seen with temporal lobe seizures. Line at the bottom right of the figure represents 1 second. (From Wyngaarden JB, Smith LH Jr, Bennett JC: Cecil Textbook of Medicine, 19th ed. Philadelphia: WB Saunders, 1992:2208.)*

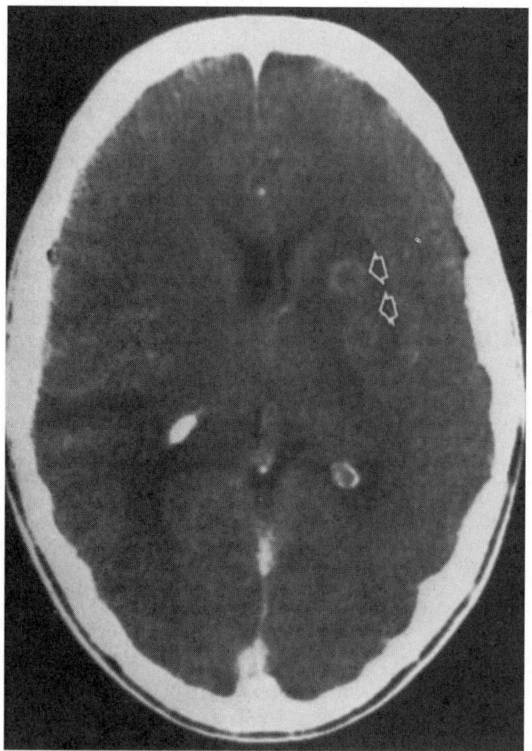

Figure 21–7 *A contrast-enhanced CT scan of two toxoplasmosis lesions* (arrows) *in a patient with acquired immunodeficiency syndrome. Both lesions are circular, white, and surrounded by dark areas that indicate cerebral edema. The adjacent anterior horn of the lateral ventricle is compressed, and the normally calcified choroid plexus, which is large, white, and circular, is pushed posteriorly—signs of swelling of the cerebral hemisphere. (From Kaufman DM: Clinical Neurology for Psychiatrists, 3rd ed. Philadelphia: WB Saunders, 1990:438.)*

PET technology still offers better visualization of brain structures. Most drugs can also be radiolabeled and tracked with this method. PET and SPECT are now used only for research purposes in psychiatry, although they are gaining utility in localizing seizure foci in neurology.

Regional cerebral blood flow enables investigators to assess cerebral activity by measuring blood flow to different areas of the brain. This technique is based on the principle that the amount of blood flowing to a given region of the brain correlates positively with the amount of mental activity occurring there. Subjects inhale a gas (usually xenon), which is distributed in the blood and emits γ-radiation, measurable through detectors on the scalp. Investigators can visualize the regional cerebral blood flow and use the data to hypothesize about relative metabolic activity in different regions of the brain. As with PET and SPECT, there are no current clinical indications for regional cerebral blood flow measurements in psychiatry.

Special Assessment Techniques

In certain situations, special assessment techniques may be indicated in the psychiatric evaluation of patients who are unable or unwilling to cooperate. These situations include the assessment of patients who are mute, have amnesia, or intentionally provide false information. In general, special techniques are employed only after all conventional ways to obtain the necessary information have been exhausted.

Hypnosis can aid in the recovery of repressed memories. For example, a patient who presents with a conversion symptom may be able to recall the forgotten traumatic events that precipitated it. The usefulness of hypnosis is limited by the patient's susceptibility to the procedure and by concern that the interviewer's suggestions can produce false memories. (See also Chapter 77.)

Another approach available for similar purposes is to use a sedative during the interview to produce disinhibition and allow the patient to speak more freely or access otherwise unavailable memories. Intravenous amobarbital sodium (Amytal Sodium) is the best known of the medications used for this purpose. Caution must be exercised to avoid oversedation, to monitor for side effects of the medication, and to ensure that the interviewer does not inappropriately influence the patient's answers.

The assessment of a patient who is suspected of intentionally providing false information or malingering can become uncomfortable and problematic, because it may require techniques that seem at odds with the establishment of the therapeutic alliance. A careful assessment of the patient's motives, confronting the patient with inconsistencies, physical assessment of implausible somatic complaints, and the use of other informants, prior medical records, and other documents can all help to establish the validity of what the patient is saying. When the case involves the commission of a crime, an assessment of the patient's capacity to understand his or her actions may be important for the disposition plan.

However, because psychiatric evaluation depends on

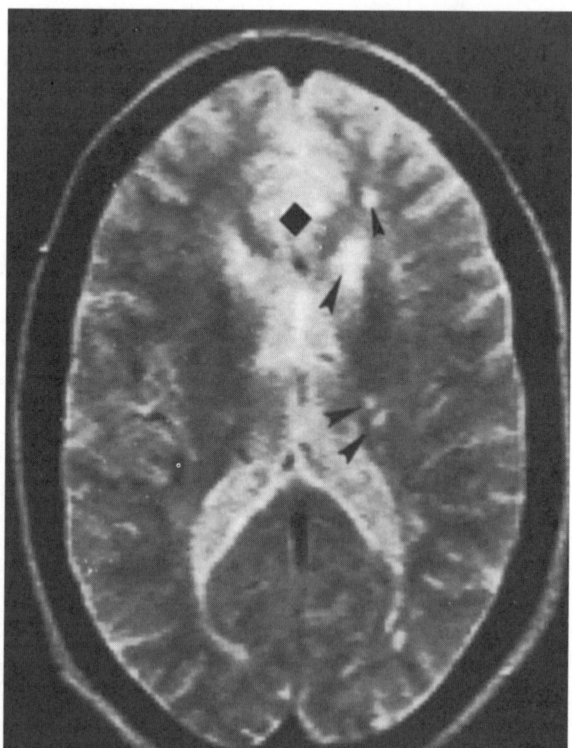

Figure 21–8 *This magnetic resonance image shows multiple cerebral plaques in a patient with multiple sclerosis. As is typical, the lesions are white and are clustered in the white matter deep in the cerebral hemispheres, particularly in the periventricular regions* (arrowheads) *and the frontal lobe* (diamond). *(From Kaufman DM: Clinical Neurology for Psychiatrists, 3rd ed. Philadelphia: WB Saunders, 1990:447.)*

what the patient tells the interviewer and there are few objective means of clarification, it is best for the interviewer not to be overly concerned about the possibility of being intentionally misled. Establishing the truthfulness of the patient's story usually takes place over an extended period.

Treatment Planning

The psychiatric evaluation is the basis for developing the case formulation, initial treatment plan, initial disposition, and comprehensive treatment plan.

Case Formulation

The case formulation is the summary statement of the immediate problem, the context in which the problem has arisen, the tentative diagnosis, and the assessment of risk. The latter two areas are described next in more detail.

Assessment of Risk

The assessment of risk is the most crucial component of the formulation because the safety of the patient, the clinician, and others is the foremost concern in any psychiatric evaluation. Four areas are important: suicide risk, assault risk, life-threatening medical conditions, and external threat.

Suicide Risk. The risk of suicide is the most common life-threatening situation mental health professionals encounter. Its assessment is based on both an understanding of its epidemiology, which alerts the clinician to potential danger, and the individualized assessment of the patient. Suicide is the eighth leading cause of death in the United States. In the past century, the rate of suicide has averaged 12.5 per 100,000 people. Studies of adults and adolescents who commit suicide reveal that more than 90% of them suffered from at least one psychiatric disorder and as many as 80% of them consulted a physician in the months preceding the event. An astute risk assessment therefore provides an opportunity for prevention.

For those who complete suicide the most common diagnoses are affective disorder (45% to 70%) and alcoholism (25%). In certain psychiatric disorders, there is a significant lifetime risk for suicide, as listed in Table 21–18. Panic disorder is associated with an elevated rate of suicidal ideation and suicide attempts, but estimates of rates of completed suicide are not well established.

Suicide rates increase with age, although rates among young adults have been steadily rising. Women attempt suicide more often than men, but men are three to four times more likely than women to complete suicide. Whites have higher rates of suicide than other groups.

A patient may fit the diagnostic and demographic profile for suicide risk, but even more essential is the individualized assessment developed by integrating information from all parts of the psychiatric evaluation. This includes material from the present illness (e.g., symptoms of depression, paranoid ideation about being harmed), past psychiatric history (e.g., prior attempts at suicide or other violent behavior), personal history (e.g., recent loss), family history (e.g., suicide or violence in close relatives), medical history (e.g., presence of a terminal illness), and the MSE (e.g., helplessness, suicidal ideation).

The most consistent predictor of future suicidal behavior is a prior history of such behavior, which is especially worrisome when previous suicide attempts have involved serious intent or lethal means. Among the factors cited as having an association with risk of suicide are current use of drugs and alcohol; recent loss, such as of a spouse or job; social isolation; conduct disorders and antisocial behavior, especially in young men; the presence of depression, especially when it is accompanied by hopelessness, helplessness, delusions, or agitation; certain psychotic symptoms, such as command hallucinations and frightening paranoid delusions; fantasies of reunion by death; and severe medical illness, especially when it is associated with loss of functioning, intractable pain, or central nervous system dysfunction. Table 21–19 lists risk factors for suicide. It

Table 21–18 Estimated Lifetime Rates of Completed Suicide by Diagnosis

Major affective disorders: 10%–15%
Alcoholism: 10%–15% (comorbid depression usually present)
Schizophrenia: 10% (often during a postpsychotic depressive state)
Borderline and antisocial personality disorders: 5%–10%

Table 21–19 Risk Factors for Suicide

Category	Risk Factors for Suicide
Demographic	White Male Older age Divorced, never married, or widowed Unemployed
Historical	Previous suicide attempts, especially with serious intent, lethal means, or disappointment about survival Family history of suicide Victim of physical or sexual abuse
Psychiatric	Diagnosis: affective disorder, alcoholism, panic disorder, psychotic disorders, conduct disorder, severe personality disorder (especially antisocial and borderline) Symptoms: suicidal or homicidal ideation; depression, especially with hopelessness, helplessness, anhedonia, delusions, agitation; mixed mania and depression; psychotic symptoms, including command hallucinations and persecutory delusions Current use of alcohol or illicit drugs Recent psychiatric hospitalization
Environmental	Recent loss such as that of a spouse or job Social isolation Access to guns or other lethal weapons Social acceptance of suicide
Medical	Severe medical illness, especially with loss of functioning or intractable pain Delirium or confusion caused by central nervous system dysfunction
Behavioral	Antisocial acts Poor impulse control, risk taking, and aggressiveness Preparing for death (e.g., making a will, giving away possessions, stockpiling lethal medication) Well-developed, detailed suicide plan Statements of intent to inflict harm on self or others

should be noted that assisted suicide is now more openly discussed among people with terminal illnesses and has gained some measure of acceptability, particularly among those suffering from acquired immunodeficiency syndrome. Nonetheless, the vast majority of people who are bereaved or suffer from a serious medical illness do not end their lives by suicide. Although suicidal intent may be lacking, patients who are delirious and confused as a result of a medical illness are also at risk of self-injury.

It is essential to be clear about whether the patient has passive thoughts about suicide or actual intent. Is there a plan? If so, how detailed is it, how lethal, and what are the chances of rescue? The possession of firearms is particularly worrisome, because nearly two thirds of documented suicides among men and more than a third among women have involved this method.

Factors that may protect against suicide include convictions in opposition to suicide; strong attachments to others, including spouse and children; and evidence of good impulse control.

In addition to the assessment of risk factors, it is important to decide whether the possibility of suicide is of immediate concern or represents a long-term ongoing risk.

Risk of Assault. Unlike those who commit suicide, most people who commit violent acts have not been diagnosed with a mental illness, and data clarifying the relationship between mental illness and violence are limited. The most common psychiatric diagnoses associated with violence are substance-related disorders. Conduct disorder and antisocial personality disorder, by definition, involve aggressive, violent, and/or unlawful behavior.

In the absence of comorbid substance–related disorders, most people with such major mental illnesses as affective disorders and schizophrenia are not violent. But data from the National Institute of Mental Health Epidemiological Catchment Area Study suggest that these diagnoses are associated with a higher rate of violence than that found among individuals who have no diagnosable mental illness.

Table 21–20 lists risk factors for violence. As with suicide, the best predictor of future assault is a history of past assault. Information from the psychiatric evaluation that helps in this assessment includes the present illness (e.g., preoccupation with vengeance, especially when accompanied by a plan of action), psychiatric history (e.g., childhood conduct disorder), family history (e.g., exposure as a child to violent parental behavior), personal history (e.g., arrest record), and the MSE (e.g., homicidal ideation, severe agitation). Other predictors of violence include possession of weapons and current illegal activities. There is considerable overlap between risk factors for suicide and those for violence.

Life-Threatening Medical Conditions. It is essential to consider life-threatening medical illness as a potential cause of psychiatric disturbance. Clues to this etiology can be found in the present illness (e.g., physical complaints), family history (e.g., causes of death in close family members), medical history (e.g., previous medical conditions and treatments), physical examination (e.g., abnormalities identified), and MSE (e.g., confusion, fluctuation in levels of consciousness). Laboratory assessment, brain imaging, and structured tests for neuropsychiatric impairment may also be essential.

Table 21–20 Risk Factors for Violence

Category	Risk Factors
Demographic	Young Male Limited education Unemployed
Historical	Previous history of violence to self or others, especially with high degree of lethality History of animal torture Past antisocial or criminal behavior Violence within family of origin Victim of physical or sexual abuse
Psychiatric	Diagnosis: substance-related disorders, antisocial personality disorder; conduct disorder; intermittent explosive disorder; pathological alcohol intoxication; psychoses (e.g., paranoid, toxic) Symptoms: physical agitation; intent to kill or take revenge; identification of specific victim(s); psychotic symptoms, especially command hallucinations to commit violence and persecutory delusions Current use of alcohol or other drugs
Environmental	Access to guns or other lethal weapons Living under circumstances of violence Membership in violent group
Medical	Delirium or confusion caused by central nervous system dysfunction Disinhibition caused by traumatic brain injuries and other central nervous system dysfunctions Toxic states related to metabolic disorders (e.g., hyperthyroidism)
Behavioral	Antisocial acts Agitation, anger Poor impulse control; risk taking or reckless behavior Statements of intent to inflict harm

Probably the most common life-threatening medical situations that the psychiatrist evaluates are acute central nervous system changes caused by medical conditions and accompanied by mental status alterations. These include increased intracranial pressure or other cerebral abnormalities, severe metabolic alterations, toxic states, and alcohol withdrawal. Patients may be at risk of death if these states are not quickly identified.

External Threat. Some patients who present for psychiatric evaluation are at risk as a result of life-threatening external situations. Such patients can include battered women, abused children, and victims of catastrophes who lack proper food or shelter. Information about these conditions is usually obtained from the present illness, the personal history, the medical history, and physical examination.

Differential Diagnosis

The differential diagnosis is best approached by organizing the information obtained in the psychiatric evaluation into five domains of mental functioning according to the disturbances revealed by the evaluation (see Table 21–21 and the subsequent chapters in this section for more detail). After organizing the information into these five domains,

Table 21–21 Categorizing Features of Mental Disturbance

Area of Mental Functioning	Examples of Relevant Evidence of Disturbance
Consciousness, orientation, and memory	Abnormalities on interview or MSE, especially impairments in awareness; alertness; orientation to person, place, time; immediate, short-term or long-term memory; attention; calculations; fund of knowledge; abstractions Past history of foregoing Positive substance use history Risk factors for HIV; positive HIV antibody result Focal neurological findings on physical examination Laboratory and brain imaging abnormalities Impairments on neuropsychological testing
Speech, thinking, perception, and self-experience	Abnormalities on interview or MSE, especially disturbances of speech, thinking, reality testing, and presence of hallucinations, delusions Past history of foregoing
Emotions	Abnormalities on interview or MSE, especially labile, depressed, expansive, elevated, irritable mood, and inappropriate affect, anger, or anxiety Past history of foregoing Positive scores for mood disturbance on structured interviews
Physical signs and symptoms; physiological disturbances	Physical or neurological findings indicative of medical or mental disorder Laboratory abnormalities Past medical illnesses Positive substance use history
Behavior and adaptive functioning	Personality dysfunction Impaired social or occupational functioning Impaired activities of daily living Impulsive, compulsive, or avoidance behaviors History of behavioral or functional disturbances Personal history (highest levels of achievement)

the psychiatrist looks for the psychopathological syndromes and potential diagnoses that best account for the disturbances described. A complete diagnostic evaluation includes assessments on each of the five axes of DSM-IV (Table 21–22).

Disturbances of consciousness, orientation, and memory are most typically associated with delirium related to a general medical condition or a substance use disorder. Memory impairment and other cognitive disturbances are the hallmarks of dementia. Results of the history, physical examination, laboratory testing, and brain imaging often help in defining the specific etiology. It is important to elicit risk factors for HIV infection and, when they are present, to encourage voluntary HIV antibody testing. Neuropsychological testing is particularly useful in the diagnosis of subcortical dementia, such as that caused by Huntington's disease and HIV infection. Dissociative disorders and severe psychotic states may also present with disturbances in this domain without evidence of any medical etiology. Cognitive impairment caused by mental retardation is established by intelligence testing.

Disturbances of speech, thinking, perception, and self-experience are common in psychotic states that can be seen in patients with such diagnoses as schizophrenia and mania, as well as in central nervous system dysfunction caused by substance use or a medical condition. Disturbances in self-experience are also common in dissociative disorders and certain anxiety, somatoform, and eating disorders. Cluster A personality disorders may be associated with milder forms of disturbances in this domain.

Disturbances of emotion are most typical of affective and anxiety disorders. These disturbances may also be caused by substance use disorders and general medical conditions. Mood and affect disturbances accompany many personality disorders and may be especially pronounced in borderline personality disorder.

Physical signs and symptoms and any associated abnormalities revealed by diagnostic medical tests and past medical history are used to establish the presence of general medical conditions, which are coded on Axis III. When a medical disorder is causally related to a psychiatric disorder, a statement of this relationship should appear on Axis I. Physical signs and symptoms may also suggest diagnoses of mood or anxiety disorders or states of substance intoxication or withdrawal. Physical symptoms for which no medical etiology can be demonstrated after thorough assessment suggest somatoform or factitious disorders or malingering.

Information about behavior and adaptive functioning is useful for diagnosing personality disorders, documenting psychosocial and environmental problems on Axis IV, and assessing global functioning on Axis V. This information is also useful for diagnosing most psychiatric disorders, which typically include criteria related to abnormal behaviors and functional impairment.

When all information has been gathered and organized, it may be possible to reach definitive diagnoses, but sometimes this must await further evaluation and the development of the comprehensive treatment plan.

Table 21–22 DSM-IV Multiaxial System

Axis I:	Clinical disorders Other conditons that may be a focus of clinical attention
Axis II:	Personality disorders Mental retardation
Axis III:	General medical conditions
Axis IV:	Psychosocial and environmental problems
Axis V:	Global assessment of functioning

From American Psychiatric Association: Diagnostic and Statistical Manual of Mental Disorders, 4th ed. Washington DC: American Psychiatric Association, 1994.

Initial Treatment Plan

The initial treatment plan follows the case formulation, which has already established the nature of the current problem and a tentative diagnosis. The plan distinguishes between what must be accomplished now and what is postponed for the future. Treatment planning works best when it follows the biopsychosocial model.

Biological Intervention. This includes an immediate response to any life-threatening medical conditions and a plan for the treatment of other less acute physical disorders, including those that may contribute to an altered mental status. Prescription of psychotropic medications in accordance with the tentative diagnosis is the most common biological intervention.

Psychosocial Intervention. This includes immediate plans to prevent violent or suicidal behavior and address adverse external circumstances. An overall strategy must be developed that is both realistic and responsive to the patient's situation. Developing this strategy requires an awareness of the social support systems available to the patient; the financial resources of the patient; the availability of services in the area; the need to contact other agencies, such as child welfare or the police; and the need to ensure child care for dependent children.

Initial Disposition

The primary task of the initial disposition is to select the most appropriate level of care after completion of the psychiatric evaluation. Disposition is primarily focused on immediate goals. After referral, the patient and the treatment team develop longer term goals.

Hospitalization. The first decision in any disposition plan is whether hospitalization is required to ensure safety. There are times when a patient presents with such severe risk of harm to self or others that hospitalization seems essential. In other cases the patient could be managed outside the hospital, depending on the availability of other supports. This might include a family who can stay with the patient or a crisis team in the community able to treat the patient at home. The more comprehensive the system of services, the easier it is to avoid hospitalization. Because hospitalization is associated with extreme disruption of usual life activities and in and of itself can have many adverse consequences, plans to avoid hospitalization are usually appropriate as long as they do not compromise safety.

Day Programs, Crisis Residences, and Supervised Housing. These interventions provide ongoing supervision but at a lower level than that available within the hospital. They are most often used to treat patients with alcohol and substance use disorders or severe mental illness. Crisis housing can be useful when a patient cannot safely return home, when caregivers need respite, and when the patient is homeless. Other forms of supervised housing usually have a waiting period and may not be immediately available.

There are many different types of and names for day-long programming, including partial hospitalization, day treatment, psychiatric rehabilitation, and psychosocial clubs. Depending on the nature of the program, it may provide stabilization, daily medication, training in social and vocational skills, and treatment of alcohol and substance use problems. Long-term day programs should generally be avoided if a patient is functioning successfully in a daytime role, such as in a job or as a homemaker. In these instances, referral to a day program may promote a lower level of functioning than the patient is capable of.

Outpatient Medication and Psychotherapy. The most common referral after psychiatric evaluation is to psychotherapy and/or medication management. In office-based settings, the psychiatrist decides whether she or he has the time and expertise to treat the patient and makes referrals to other practitioners as appropriate. Hospital staff usually have a broad overview of community resources and refer accordingly. There are high rates of dropout when patients are sent from one setting to another. These can be reduced by providing introductions to the treatment setting and/or conducting follow-up to ensure that the referral has been successful.

Comprehensive Treatment Planning

The psychiatric evaluation usually continues beyond the initial disposition. The providers assuming responsibility for the patient, who may be inpatient staff, outpatient staff, or private practitioners, complete the evaluation and take responsibility for developing the comprehensive treatment plan. This plan covers the entire array of concerns that affect the course of the patient's psychiatric problems. In hospital settings, the initial treatment plan is usually completed within 24 to 72 hours after admission and the comprehensive treatment plan approximately 10 days after admission.

The comprehensive treatment plan usually includes more definitive diagnoses and a well-formulated management plan with central goals and objectives. For severely ill or hospitalized patients, every area is usually covered (Table

Table 21–23 Areas Covered by Comprehensive Treatment Plan

Mental health
- Diagnoses on five axes
- Psychiatric management, including medications

Physical health
- Medical diagnoses
- Medical management, including medications

Personal strengths and assets

Rehabilitation needs
- Educational
- Occupational
- Social
- Activities of daily living skills
- Use of leisure time

Living arrangements

Social supports and family involvement

Finances
- Personal finances
- Insurance coverage
- Eligibility for social service benefits

Legal or forensic issues

Central goals and objectives

Listing of treatment team members

Evidence of participation by patient and, as appropriate, family members and others

Criteria for discharge from treatment

21–23). It is best for the patient and, as appropriate, the family, to have input into the plan. The comprehensive treatment plan guides and coordinates the direction of all treatment for an extended time, usually months, and is periodically reviewed and updated. For more focal psychiatric problems (e.g., phobias, sexual dysfunctions) and more limited interventions (e.g., brief interpersonal, cognitive, and behavioral therapies in office-based practices), the comprehensive treatment plan may focus on only several of the possible areas.

Conclusion

The psychiatric evaluation is a method of collecting present and past psychological, biological, social, and environmental data for the purpose of establishing a comprehensive picture of the patient's strengths and problems, including the psychiatric diagnoses, and developing treatment plans. It is the essential beginning of every course of psychiatric treatment and, when carried out successfully, integrates a multimodal approach to understanding mental illness and providing clinical care.

Bibliography

American Psychiatric Association: Diagnostic and Statistical Manual of Mental Disorders, 4th ed. Washington, DC: American Psychiatric Association, 1994.

Beck AT, Kovacs M, Weisman A: Hopelessness and suicidal behavior. JAMA 1975; 234:1146–1149.

Blumenthal SJ, Kupfer DJ (eds): Suicide over the Life Cycle. Washington, DC: American Psychiatric Press, 1990.

Folstein MF, Folstein SE, McHugh PR: "Mini-mental state." A practical method for grading the cognitive state of patients for the clinician. J Psychiat Res 1975; 12:189–198.

Frances RJ, Franklin JE: A Concise Guide to Treatment of Alcohol and Addictions, Washington, DC: American Psychiatric Press, 1989:62.

Guy W: ECDEU Assessment Manual for Psychopharmacology Revised. Rockville, MD: National Institute of Mental Health, 1976.

Hasin DS, Skodal AE: Standardized diagnostic interviews for psychiatric research. In Thompson C (ed): The Instruments of Psychiatric Research. New York: John Wiley & Sons, 1989:19–57.

Johnson J, Weissman MM, Klerman GL: Panic disorders, comorbidity, and suicide attempts. Arch Gen Psychiatry 1990; 47:805–808.

Jones WK, Curran JC: Epidemiology of AIDS and HIV infection in industrialized countries. In Broder S, Merigan TC, Bolognesi D (eds): Textbook of AIDS Medicine. Baltimore: Williams & Wilkins, 1994:91–108.

Kandel ER, Schwartz JH, Jessell TM: Principles of Neural Science. New York: Elsevier, 1991.

Kaplan H, Sadock B: Comprehensive Textbook of Psychiatry, Volumes 1 and 2. Baltimore: Williams & Wilkins, 1989.

Leon R: Psychiatric Interviewing—A Primer. New York: Elsevier, 1982.

Lowinson JH, Ruiz P, Millman RB, Langrad JG (eds): Substance Abuse—A Comprehensive Textbook. Baltimore: Williams & Wilkins, 1992.

MacKinnon RA, Michels R: The Psychiatric Interview in Clinical Practice. Philadelphia: WB Saunders, 1971.

MacKinnon RA, Yudofsky SC: The Psychiatric Evaluation in Clinical Practice. Philadelphia: JB Lippincott, 1991.

Michels R, Cooper AM, Guze SB, et al (eds): Psychiatry. Philadelphia: JB Lippincott, 1977.

Miles CP: Conditions predisposing to suicide: A review. J Nerv Ment Dis 1977; 164:231–246.

Monahan J, Steadman HS: Violence and Mental Disorder. Chicago: University of Chicago Press, 1994.

Ohimer E, Ohimer S: The Clinical Interview Using DSM-III-R. Washington, DC: American Psychiatric Press, 1989.

Oldham J: Personality Disorders: New Perspectives on Diagnostic Validity. Washington, DC: American Psychiatric Press, 1991.

Spitzer RL, Endicott J: Schedule for Affective Disorders and Schizophrenia (SADS). New York: New York State Psychiatric Institute, 1978.

Tardiff K: Concise Guide to Assessment and Management of Violent Patients. Washington, DC: American Psychiatric Press, 1989.

Trzepacz P, Baker R: The Psychiatric Mental Status Examination. New York: Oxford University Press, 1993.

Weisman AD, Worden WJ: Risk rescue rating in suicide assessment. Arch Gen Psychiatry 1972; 26:553–560.

Weissman MM, Klerman GL, Markowitz JS, Ouellette R: Suicidal ideation and suicide attempts in panic disorder and attacks. N Engl J Med 1989; 321:1209–1214.

Wyngaarden JB, Smith LH, Bennett JC: Cecil Textbook of Medicine, 19th ed. Philadelphia: WB Saunders, 1992.

Yudofsky SC, Silver JM, Jackson W, et al: The Overt Aggression Scale for the objective rating of verbal and physical aggression. Am J Psychiatry 1986; 43:35–39.

CHAPTER

22 Neuropsychological Testing

Larry J. Seidman

Neuropsychology is the study of brain-behavior relationships. Its subject matter overlaps considerably that of a number of related fields, especially behavioral neurology, neuropsychiatry, and cognitive neuroscience. Neuropsychology is implemented most tangibly by the utilization of clinical tests and experimental procedures designed to elucidate brain-behavior relations in normal individuals or in persons with dysfunctional or damaged brain tissue. The procedures and techniques used by neuropsychologists in the clinic have also had rapid application to research settings. For example, neuropsychological tasks such as the Wisconsin Card Sorting Test[1] have been used to demonstrate that most patients with schizophrenia have cognitive deficits similar to those seen in patients with frontal network (brain) dysfunction.[2] Paradigms derived from animal and human neuropsychology are particularly useful in identifying intact or disordered components of information processing, such as attention and memory, that are fundamental to all human behavior.[3] As the field of psychiatry has increasingly incorporated new biological (especially neural) knowledge, the role of neuropsychology has grown accordingly. In this chapter, the major focus is on the neuropsychologist's contribution to the clinical practice of psychiatry.

Assessment of Brain Dysfunction: Overview of Neuropsychological Testing

In psychiatric settings until the 1970s, psychological evaluation of patients with suspected brain dysfunction usually consisted of a psychodiagnostic test battery[4] primarily oriented to personality dynamics. A clinical psychologist would attempt to determine the presence or absence of "organicity" (brain damage) on the basis of pathognomonic "organic" signs derived primarily from an individually administered Wechsler intelligence test and the Bender Gestalt, Draw-A-Person, Minnesota Multiphasic Personality Inventory, and Rorschach tests, supplemented typically by specialized memory tests. Although this clinical process had some success in identifying brain dysfunction, it was limited on both empirical and conceptual grounds.[5–7] Many organic test impairments were associated with confounding factors (e.g., poor motivation, psychosis, low IQ) and thus produced false-positive diagnoses, and many manifestations of brain damage (e.g., language deficits, memory problems) were not reflected in the single visual-motor test (i.e., Bender Gestalt) typically used to assess organicity, leading to false-negative diagnoses.

The basic assumption underlying the concept of organicity—that is, that brain damage is unitary—was also faulty. Rather, the manifestations of brain dysfunction vary dramatically depending on the size, location, and period of brain development during which a lesion occurs and the lesion type, to name a few influential factors.[6] Other personal variables such as age, sex, education, and handedness mediate the expression of brain dysfunction on neuropsychological tests.[8] The organicity construct has gradually been replaced by the neuropsychological approach. In this model, the neuropsychologist specialist attempts to determine whether the clinical picture and test data represent some neurobehavioral syndrome.[9]

The traditional psychological battery remains useful in identifying neurological information when none is suspected. That is, when a psychologist is asked to do a psychological evaluation of intellectual capacity and personality dynamics (Table 22–1), he or she may identify unexpected brain impairment on the basis of the organic signs or test patterns. These may then be validated by the more specialized neuropsychological, neurological, and brain imaging assessments. When brain dysfunction is clearly part of the original differential diagnosis or if there is known brain damage and the referring clinician wants an assessment of functional strengths and weaknesses, a neuropsychological assessment should be requested. The two approaches may be appropriately used conjointly when both personality and neuropsychological factors are to be assessed, such as in articulating various aspects of complex neuropsychiatric disorders such as temporal lobe epilepsy (Table 22–2) or attention-deficit/hyperactivity disorder[10, 11] (Table 22–3). For such cases, a careful evaluation of personality and neuropsychological function may enhance goal setting and choice of type of psychotherapy or other treatment interventions.[12, 13]

Since the 1950s, the practice of clinical neuropsychological assessment has progressed dramatically. Whereas neuropsychological testing was initially a series of specialized procedures known only to a few[9] and utilized primarily in neurological and neurosurgical settings,[35] it has been used increasingly in rehabilitation and psychiatric settings during the past decade[36] and there are now a few thousand practitioners in the field.

Table 22–1 Selected Referral Issues for Psychodiagnostic Testing

Is thought disorder present?
Provide differential diagnosis between borderline personality organization and schizophrenia.
How suicidal is the patient?
Clarify the nature of the patient's intrapsychic conflicts in male-female relationships.
Help identify the roots of transference (currently contributing to an impasse in psychotherapy).
Describe the patient's apparent attitudes toward achievement.
What psychological conflicts are interfering with intellectual efficiency?

Neuropsychological Examination Compared with Other Examinations

Neuropsychological testing provides information regarding diagnosis; cognitive, perceptual, and motor capacities or deficits; and treatment recommendations (Table 22–4). Experienced clinicians use test data to determine the presence or absence of brain dysfunction, to localize the damage, and to establish the etiology of the lesion.[37] Moreover, a comprehensive functional assessment can lead to neurologically meaningful subgroups of disorders (as in different types of developmental disorders, verbal and nonverbal) that may have relevance to treatment, such as in the application of differential strategies of cognitive rehabilitation or school placement.[13, 38]

Most neuropsychologists, regardless of theoretical orientation, agree on a number of basic characteristics that define clinical neuropsychological evaluations. The goal in a neuropsychological examination is to reflect reliably, validly, and as completely as possible the behavioral correlates of brain functions.[5, 6, 9] The greatest relevance of testing lies in treatment planning and implications for daily life. Especially in neuropsychological work with children, the clinician is oriented to the impact of neuropsychological strengths and weaknesses in school, family, and other settings.[39]

All neuropsychological approaches assess some aspects of intelligence, reasoning and abstraction, attention (sustained and selective), "executive" and self-control functions (set shifting, planning, and organizational capacity), learning and memory, language, perceptual (i.e., auditory and visual) and constructional tasks, and sensory and motor functions. Comprehensive test batteries can be quite lengthy, because the human brain-behavior relationship is quite complex.[9] Test data are interpreted in the context of many factors including the age, sex, education, and handedness of the patient.[8]

Table 22–2 Selected Tests Useful in the Neuropsychological Assessment of Adults with Temporal Lobe Epilepsy

Neuropsychological Tests
Wechsler Adult Intelligence Scale–Revised[14]
Wechsler Memory Scale–Revised (particularly Logical Memory Stories, Visual Reproductions, and Paired Associate Learning Tests)[15]
Peterson and Peterson tasks (auditory and visual consonant trigrams)[16]
California Verbal Learning Test[17]
Rey-Osterrieth Complex Figure[18]
Boston Naming Test[19]
Controlled Word Association Tests of Verbal Fluency[20]
Wisconsin Card Sorting Test[1]
Personality Tests
Minnesota Multiphasic Personality Inventory–2[21]
Thematic Apperception Test[22]
Bear-Fedio Temporal Lobe Inventory[23]
Rorschach Inkblot Test[24]

Data from Greenberg M, Seidman LJ: The neuropsychology of temporal lobe epilepsy. In White RF (ed): Clinical Syndromes in Adult Neuropsychology: The Practitioner's Handbook. Amsterdam: Elsevier Science Publishing, 1992.

Table 22–3 Selected Tests Useful in the Neuropsychological Assessment of Children and Adolescents with Attention-Deficit/Hyperactivity Disorder

Neuropsychological Tests
Wechsler Intelligence Scale for Children, third edition[25]
Wide Range Achievement Test, third edition[26]
Stroop test[27]
Auditory Continuous Performance test[28]
Visual Continuous Performance test[29]
Wisconsin Card Sorting Test[1]
Wide Range Assessment of Memory and Learning[30]
Rey-Osterrieth Complex Figure: Waber-Holmes developmental scoring system[31]
Cancellation tests[28]
Motor response inhibition tests[32]
Finger-Tapping test[33]
Personality Tests
Thematic Apperception Test[22]
Sentence Completion Tests[34]

Data from Seidman LJ, Biederman J, Faraone SV, et al: Effects of family history and comorbidity on the neuropsychological performance of children with ADHD: Preliminary findings. J Am Acad Child Adolesc Psychiatry 1995; 34:1015–1024.

Table 22–4 Typical Goals of Neuropsychological Testing

Reliably, validly, and as completely as possible, measure the behavioral correlates of brain functions.
Differential diagnosis—identify the characteristic profile associated with a neurobehavioral syndrome.
Establish possible localization, lateralization, and etiology of a brain lesion.
Determine whether neuropsychological deficits are present (i.e., cognitive, perceptual, or motor) regardless of diagnosis.
Describe neuropsychological strengths, weaknesses, and strategy of problem solving.
Assess the patient's feelings about his or her syndrome.
Provide treatment recommendations (i.e., to patient, family, school).

Although the data-gathering approach of the neuropsychologist can be well integrated with a psychodynamic orientation,[12, 36] a few distinctions between the approaches are noteworthy. In the psychodynamic approach, the examiner reduces test structure to assess "projective" components and to discern underlying motives, wishes, and thought processes,[4] whereas the neuropsychologist is usually structuring and encouraging, attempting to find out what the patient can best achieve and by what process.[40] Moreover, neuropsychologists conducting a clinical assessment typically make use of the history, symptom data, and medical records, as well as test data per se, rather than relying on test data alone.

The neuropsychological evaluation covers the same functions as the Mental Status Examination used by psychiatrists and neurologists[41] but in a more elaborated, deep, and quantified manner.[28] When contrasted with the typical Mental Status Examination, neuropsychological testing is the following: broader, in that more differentiated functions are assessed; deeper, in that far more items compose a task or function, usually arranged from simple to difficult; and more quantified, in that there is more sophisticated scoring of data as well as the provision of normative data on different samples. In addition, the administration of neuropsychological testing is more standardized. The neurologist's assessment of cranial nerves, sensory-motor function, and coordination (more "elementary" functions) and the neuropsychologist's assessment of "higher" cognitive functions complement each other well.[28]

Types of Referral Questions in Psychiatry

The neuropsychological examination has three general aims: 1) identification of neuropsychological dysfunction leading to inferences regarding the presence, type, and etiology of brain dysfunction; 2) comprehensive assessment of cognitive, perceptual, and motor strengths and weaknesses as a guide for treatment; 3) assessment of the level of performance over a broad range, for both initial evaluation and measurement of change over time.

Differential Diagnosis

Although experienced neuropsychologists may achieve a greater than 90% accuracy in diagnosing brain dysfunction,[37, 42] the referring clinician needs to discuss with the neuropsychologist the merits of using neuropsychological examination (comprehensive or brief) compared with other methods such as the neurological evaluation or specialized neurodiagnostic techniques. For example, neuropsychological evaluation is labor-intensive (a full battery typically takes 3 to 8 hours to administer, not to mention scoring, interpretation, and report writing) and is thus expensive. On the other hand, it has low invasiveness compared with such procedures as computed tomography or lumbar puncture. Moreover, the neuropsychological examination is unique in providing a comprehensive, empirically grounded picture of mental function. Neuropsychological evaluation may be especially helpful when the clinician wants both differential diagnostic information and a profile of adaptive strengths and weaknesses or when neuropsychological testing is perceived as a less threatening diagnostic procedure by a patient who is resistant to other testing.

For many disorders, such as Alzheimer's disease, there are no reliable and valid in vivo laboratory tests, and these can be best diagnosed with the aid of neuropsychological profiles.[43] Other disorders, such as schizophrenia or schizophreniform psychoses associated with temporal lobe epilepsy, may present broadly overlapping and confusing pictures on clinical psychiatric and electroencephalographic evaluation that may be clarified by neuropsychological testing. For example, a distinctly focal and lateralized neuropsychological deficit (e.g., verbal memory deficit and mild word-finding difficulty in the absence of other neuropsychological deficits) is more characteristic of temporal lobe epilepsy than of schizophrenia.[10, 44]

The neuropsychologist frequently encounters many typical neuropsychiatric differential diagnostic questions, but the conceptual framework of the diagnostic process differs substantially from the organic versus functional dichotomy of earlier approaches. She or he may frame the question, "Is there neuropsychological deficit consistent with focal or diffuse brain dysfunction?" (i.e., restricted executive deficits associated with frontal lobe dysfunction versus widespread impairment consistent with a dementing process). The neuropsychologist may ask, "Can this clinical symptom picture be correlated with test scores to identify a cluster of deficits characterizing a specific subtype of neurobehavioral syndrome?" (e.g., such as the high rate of forgetting found in Alzheimer's disease). Alternatively, the neuropsychologist may conclude that cognitive dysfunction is indeed present but may be static or not essential to the syndrome being evaluated (i.e., developmentally based language problem in a case of adult-onset traumatic brain injury).

Clinical Vignette 1

In this vignette, a neuropsychological examination led to the unexpected identification of a focal brain lesion that accounted for the patient's current clinical picture. A 69-year-old woman had been seen regularly for at least 5 years by her treating psychiatrist. She had a long history of bipolar disorder and was treated with lithium carbonate. At the time she was evaluated by the neuropsychology service, she had been admitted to an inpatient psychiatric service because of increasingly agitated behavior. During the course of her stay she repeatedly complained about a "lithium tremor in my right hand." This was initially interpreted as irrational because 1) the patient often spoke in a thought-disordered way familiar to her doctor and her current complaint was not considered unusual for her and 2) it was considered unlikely that lithium would cause a unilateral tremor self-reported by the patient but not diagnosed by the physician. Neuropsychological testing was requested and revealed a number of putative abnormalities pointing to left frontal cerebral dysfunction. Despite the fact that the patient was right-handed dominant, she was consistently and significantly slower on the Finger-Tapping test[33] with her right hand. On the Boston Naming Test[19] she made a significant number of paraphasic naming errors and had long latencies of response. On Trail Making B[45] she made many perseverative errors and missed a target stimulus on the right side of the test page. Subsequently, a computed tomographic scan revealed a large cyst affecting primarily her left frontal lobe. The patient was transferred to the neurosurgery service, where the cyst was successfully drained before her discharge. Because we could not follow up this patient, we never learned whether her mood symptoms were alleviated by the surgical treatment.

Adapted from Seidman.[12]

Characterization of Adaptive Strengths and Weaknesses and Treatment Planning

Probably the greatest contribution of the neuropsychological examination compared with that of neurological or other neurodiagnostic evaluation is in providing a broad description of the patient's capacities and deficits and the impact of these resources and limitations on the patient's adaptation to the world. This profile is essential for treatment planning, which may include rehabilitation efforts generally and psychotherapy specifically.[7, 11, 13]

For example, although it may be clear that a patient has schizophrenia, the disorder is heterogeneous with respect to manifestations of brain dysfunction[2, 44, 47] and it may be quite helpful to determine the types of vocational training or education the patient can utilize.[48] Subtle learning disabilities may be identified in a student who is anxious and depressed about failures in school but is unable to pinpoint the cause. Referrals of this type are wide ranging; they include high school students who have a specific spelling disability, college students who are quite bright but are unable to learn required foreign languages, and graduate students in mathematics, science, or medicine who are failing subjects requiring visual-spatial analysis. All of these people may benefit from counseling about career choice, recommendations for compensatory learning strategies, and psychotherapy to deal with the impact on self-esteem, mastery, and identity.[12]

Identification of a neurologically based cognitive deficit may also help a patient come to terms more realistically with narcissistic injuries associated with failure experiences. Some patients are greatly relieved when they learn that the basic origin of their problem is in their brain and not in their mind or "self." Others, of course, become depressed because they perceive damage to the brain as irremediable. Neuropsychological data can aid the family of a handicapped or vulnerable child (e.g., with schizophrenia or learning disability) by helping them develop realistic expectations for their child so that secondary emotional problems can be minimized and a maximally supportive environment can be constructed.[11]

Clinical Vignette 2

In this vignette, neuropsychological examination identified a nonverbal learning disability, attentional problems, and depression and was used to help frame the patient's psychotherapy. A 21-year-old man was referred with the goal of assessing the reasons for his lifelong school difficulties. It was clear to the referring psychiatrist that the patient had significant conflicts regarding achievement, variable motivation, and problems with assertiveness; however, the psychiatrist suspected that primary cognitive difficulties might be contributing to the picture. On the Wechsler Adult Intelligence Scale–Revised,[14] the patient had a Verbal IQ of 121, a Performance IQ of 100, and a Full-Scale IQ of 113, certainly indicative of college-level intellectual ability. However, he showed significant discrepancies between rather high verbal reasoning abilities and rather poor arithmetical calculation and visual-spatial skills. Moreover, he worked rather slowly on all visual-motor tasks, and his piecemeal strategy[40] for constructing the Rey-Osterrieth Complex Figure[18, 31] was developmentally immature. He approached the figure by drawing small details, without recognizing the gestalt, and this inefficient strategy appeared to be responsible for his poor reconstruction of the figure on recall conditions. He also demonstrated attentional difficulties on a continuous performance test indicating difficulties in sustaining attention. These difficulties were entirely consistent with the results of a pediatric neuropsychological examination done when he was 7 years old, on the basis of which a "developmental perceptual organization disorder" was reported.

Personality testing with the Minnesota Multiphasic Personality Inventory and the Thematic Apperception Test indicated mild depression, poor self-esteem, anxiety about achievement, and a defensive style emphasizing minimization and denial. These traits were reformulated as, in part, secondary reactions to a primary, lifelong learning disability. The patient was effectively treated once or twice weekly with supportive, psychoeducational psychotherapy by a psychotherapist who was sophisticated in combining neuropsychology and psychotherapy. Moreover, he was adjunctively treated with fluoxetine (Prozac) at 20 mg/d, which contributed to considerable improvement. He felt more energetic and decisive and more able to focus and sustain his attention. Over time, this progress led to an improved social life; a more balanced focus on school, work, and play; and better school performance.

Adapted from Seidman.[12]

Assessment of Change of State

Many patients have fluctuating mental states, such as in schizophrenia and affective disorder, medical illness (e.g., renal disease, diabetes), or abuse of drugs or alcohol or as a result of somatic therapies (medication or electroconvulsive therapy). Repeated testing is often desirable to clarify the patient's cognitive capacities.[7] The effects of a treatment such as electroconvulsive therapy on cognitive function (e.g., verbal memory functions) can persist for months.[3] Monitoring cognitive status by repeated testing allows an objective measure of subjective complaints and of recovery of function. Baseline testing early in the course of an illness such as schizophrenia or brain tumor can be compared with later evaluations to clarify the course of the disorder or to assess the impact of various interventions.

Clinical Vignette 3

In this vignette, the issue of stability of neuropsychological functioning early in the course of schizophrenia and the problem of distinguishing capacity from performance are addressed. As is apparent in Table 22–5, there were dramatic fluctuations over a year when testing was done three times at approximately 6-month intervals. Moreover, changes were not equivalent across tasks;

Table 22–5 Repeated Neuropsychological Assessment—Clinical Vignette 3

Function	Test Variable	Time 1	Time 2	Time 3
Intelligence	Wechsler Adult Intelligence Scale			
	Verbal IQ	101	105	97
	Performance IQ	88	113	102
	Full-Scale IQ	95	108	99
	Verbal-Performance difference	+13	−8	−5
Abstraction	Visual-Verbal test	24	12	10
Attention (sustained visual)	Continuous Performance test, omission %	3.7	0	
	Late errors (raw)	7	2	
	Omissions (raw)	8	2	
	Reaction time (s)	0.47	0.44	
Executive	Wisconsin card categories		2	2
	Perseverative response		36	26
Language	Boston naming (selected items)	9/15	11/15	10/15
	Spelling	7/14	11/14	10/14
	Verbal fluency (FAS), percentile	7	84	80
Motor	Finger-tapping speed			
	Right	43.6	50.4	44.8
	Left	40.6	48.2	41.4
	Asymmetry, % difference	6.9	4.1	7.6

Adapted from Seidman LJ: The neuropsychology of schizophrenia: A neurodevelopmental and case study approach. J Neuropsychiatry Clin Neurosci 1990; 2:301–312.

Clinical Vignette 3 *continued*

performance on certain tasks was fairly stable and performance on others changed markedly along with the exacerbations and remissions of the patient's psychosis.

The patient was an 18-year-old single man, right-handed, a high school student when his behavior began to deteriorate about the beginning of his senior year. Six months later he had a florid psychotic episode including acute catatonic symptoms resulting in a 7-month inpatient psychiatric hospitalization. The patient had a good premorbid history, was a better than average student without evidence of learning disabilities, and had no documented neurological problems. However, he was drinking alcohol and using some drugs at least once or twice weekly during the period before hospitalization. He had a normal electroencephalogram and a mildly abnormal computed tomographic scan including slightly enlarged lateral ventricles, unilateral visibility of the right temporal horn, and prominence of the anterior interhemispheric tissue.

The patient was initially given the neuropsychological battery 4 months (time 1) into his first hospitalization. This was after his acute catatonic symptoms had abated, and he was cooperative with the evaluation. Although he was not fully stable at that time, he was quite testable and had been receiving a stable dose of medication for about 6 weeks (haloperidol, 20 mg/d). His second evaluation (time 2) took place 7 months later, when as an outpatient he was in significant remission and had not been taking any medication for more than a month. The third evaluation (time 3) took place 6 months later, when he had been readmitted after decompensation and was once again taking haloperidol (20 mg/d). He remained quite engageable and cooperative throughout all three examinations, during which he was tested by the same examiner.

In reviewing Table 22–5 it is clear that the overall neuropsychological performance parallels the patient's change in clinical status, from initial acute psychosis (time 1) to outpatient remission (time 2) to reexacerbation of the psychosis (time 3). Whereas he was quite impaired in some areas at time 1 (e.g., verbal fluency at the seventh percentile), his overall picture suggested average intellectual abilities and only mild to moderate attention and conceptual dysfunction.

At time 2, during the patient's best clinical state, he was dramatically improved in all areas previously assessed but showed significant impairment on the Wisconsin Card Sorting Test, which had not been previously administered. At time 3, when most of the tests were readministered, he declined most significantly on the Wechsler Adult Intelligence Scale, less so on other tasks, and remained impaired on the Wisconsin Card Sorting Test.

This vignette illustrates that in patients early in the course of an illness in which significant clinical fluctuation may occur, a cross-sectional assessment may accurately measure performance but not accurately measure capacity. A related issue demonstrated here is that repeated evaluations may help identify a person's underlying capacities or deficits. We assume that trait contributions (i.e., reliable enduring capacities or deficits) can best be determined by tasks that remain relatively constant, whereas state effects can best be seen on tests that vary most in association with exacerbation or remission of the illness. By both criteria, time 2 is the time most likely to yield trait and capacity data. At this point, overall performance is relatively high and psychosis relatively minimal. At time 2 most of the patient's test scores are at their highest and thus the signal/noise ratio is probably clearest. It is of interest that at this point in time the patient performed rather badly on the Wisconsin Card Sorting Test (as he did 6 months later), had a lower

Verbal IQ than Performance IQ, had some difficulties on visual confrontation naming and spelling, and had rather negligible dominance of motor speed. These deficits were apparent in the context of good overall performance, good motor tapping speed, excellent sustained attention, and only mild or marginally impaired conceptual dysfunction (Visual-Verbal test). The data suggest that the difficulties in time 2 (Wisconsin Card Sorting Test, verbal skills) are due to trait deficits probably reflecting the subtle cerebral dysfunction of schizophrenia. It is not unusual for executive deficits, in particular, to be associated with brain abnormalities in schizophrenia.[46]

Adapted from Seidman.[47]

The Flexible, Hypothesis-Testing Approach to Assessment

The assessment of the multiple functions that has been described can be performed with various degrees of depth and flexibility. For example, we have noted that a comprehensive examination may last from 3 to 8 hours, whereas a shortened screening examination may take only an hour or two, covering the same functions more superficially. Moreover, even briefer "bedside" evaluation may be most appropriate for patients who cannot be tested by conventional methods.[28] The increasing prevalence of patients presenting with cognitive disorders (especially elderly patients), combined with resource limitations, may redefine the way in which neuropsychologists practice.[49] Milberg[49] noted that evaluations must be "efficient, designed to reflect current knowledge of brain function and the developmental characteristics of older patients." He suggested that specialized microbatteries should be developed to serve as brief, cognitively specific assessment instruments.

Neuropsychological evaluations differ not only in length but also in conceptual focus and in selection of the particular instruments that compose a battery of tests. In general, three batteries are used commonly throughout the United States: the Halstead-Reitan Battery,[5, 42] the Luria-Nebraska Battery,[50] and a flexible, hypothesis-testing approach typified by the Boston process neuropsychological approach.[37, 39, 40, 51] The decision to use one or the other of these approaches depends to some extent on the training of the practitioner, the nature of the referral questions, and a number of other factors discussed in more detail elsewhere.[7]

Neuropsychological examination requires attention to the outcome of problem solving and, perhaps more important, to the process of performing tasks[40] (Table 22–6). Reitan[42] has articulated four types of analyses that clinicians use to evaluate neuropsychological data: 1) *level of performance* refers to the absolute deviation and dispersion of individual test scores compared with normative expectancies and within-patient (across different tests for the same subject) scatter of scores; 2) *left-right comparisons* are made on sensory, perceptual, and motor performances, presented to or executed by the two sides of the body; 3) *pathognomonic signs* are special features of extremely poor performance or specific clusters of test scores pointing clearly to the existence of discrete disorders; and 4) *differential patterns* are large arrays of test profiles that are predictive of disease or damage.

The Boston process neuropsychological approach[37, 40, 51] is not a battery of identical items or tests routinely administered, such as the Halstead-Reitan and Luria-Nebraska batteries, but rather reflects a flexible, hypothesis-testing, qualitative approach to neurobehavioral syndrome analysis.[6, 52] The Boston process approach involves a combination of qualitative and psychometric features that reflects the integration of the behavioral neurological orientation exemplified by Geschwind[53] and Luria[9] with the rigorous quantification of the American research tradition in psychology. Many neuropsychologists around the world use variations of the clinical, qualitative process approach in that they have a flexible approach to battery construction in the context of relatively shared neurobehavioral knowledge.[6]

The process approach starts with a small set of core measures and then focuses in more specifically and intensively as hypotheses are developed. On the assumption that neurological dysfunction is reflected in psychological tests, the examiner looks for nonspecific indicators of impairment at the same time that she or he scans for highly selective deficits, or a configuration of deficits, that allow the inference that a lateralized or localized brain dysfunction is present.[51]

Some of the nonspecific (nonlocalizing) deficits found commonly are the following: impairment in conceptual thinking, slowing and "stickiness" of ideational processes, perseveration, reduced scope of attention, stimulus boundedness, and impairment of memory.[51] The set of lateralizing and localizing signs and deficits is too extensive to list completely here but broadly speaking includes disorders of functions previously addressed, such as many aspects of language, attention, visual-spatial performance, and motor ability.[51–53]

The Boston approach, when oriented toward a relatively comprehensive examination, usually includes but is not limited to tests such as these: the Wechsler Adult Intelligence Scale–Revised[14]; the Wechsler Memory Scale–Revised[15]; the Rey-Osterrieth Complex Figure,[18] a test of visuoconstructional and organizational ability; the Wisconsin Card Sorting test,[1] which assesses the capacity to shift set; the Boston Naming Test,[19] a measure of visual confrontation naming ability; and the Visual-Verbal Test,[54] a measure of abstraction ability. Certain tasks or brief batteries may be utilized for specific populations of patients, such as the Dementia Rating Scale[55] or the Boston Diagnostic Apha-

Table 22–6 Analyses Used by Clinicians to Evaluate Neuropsychological Data

Level of performance relative to normative expectation
Level of performance compared with patient's own premorbid ability (e.g., variation across test scores)
Process of problem solving (e.g., constructing a figure in a piecemeal, disorganized strategy)
Pathognomonic signs or clusters of deficits (e.g., high rate of forgetting in Alzheimer's disease)
Comparison of the two sides of the body on sensory, motor, and perceptual performance
Identification of differential patterns of test scores associated with specific disease

sia Examination.[56] Descriptions of many of these tests can be found in more comprehensive texts.[6]

The process approach[40] utilizes the four basic principles of interpretive analysis described earlier but emphasizes the way in which the patient attains a score and the preserved functions that the scores reflect rather than the achievement per se. For example, a dynamic serial picture of the process of problem solving is recorded while a patient is putting the Wechsler Adult Intelligence Scale–Revised Block Designs together (Fig. 22–1). In this way, such behaviors as featural priority (emphasis on details), contextual priority (emphasis on the gestalt), and hemispatial priority (the tendency to work on one side of visual space) can be assessed. Right hemisphere–damaged patients tend to work on the right side of space and use a detail-oriented strategy, whereas left hemisphere–damaged patients tend to work in the reverse field and with the reverse strategy.[37, 40]

Kaplan[40] suggested that qualitative data may, in fact, better reflect an underlying brain lesion, because impairment may be demonstrated even if the final score is correct. This perspective is partially supported by a study by Heaton and collaborators.[57, 58] They demonstrated that clinicians who rated Halstead-Reitan Battery results had better success in classifying brain damage than did a psychometric formula approach relying heavily on level of performance. The authors believed that the superiority of the clinicians was related to their ability to supplement test scores with consideration of the qualitative and configural features of their data. The process approach is consistent with this interpretation in that it is performed by highly trained clinicians rather than technicians.

The process or flexible approach seems well suited to psychiatry because problem-solving approaches are less likely to be affected by motivational deficits than are level of performance and pathognomonic signs. Process variables are probably less susceptible to conscious faking, as a patient would be unlikely to know the neurological rules governing the process, and may also be less susceptible to practice and repetition effects, which can confound the interpretation of scores.

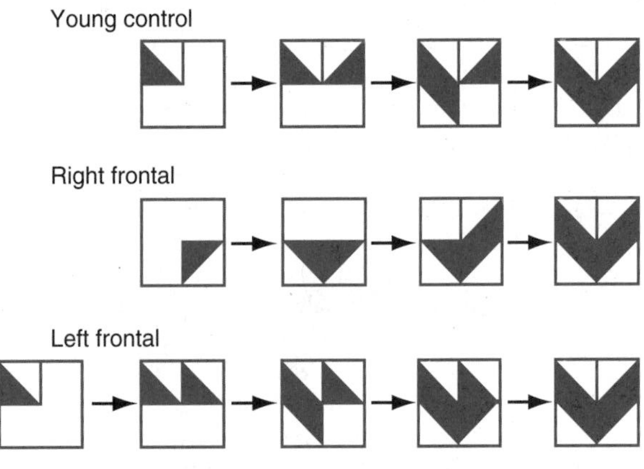

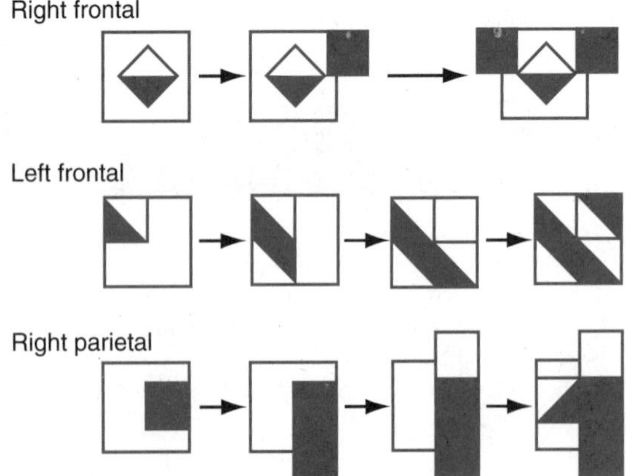

Figure 22–1 *Block Design: feature versus context. (From Kaplan E: The process approach to neuropsychological assessment of psychiatric patients. J Neuropsychiatry Clin Neurosci 1990; 2:72–87.)*

Limitations of Reliability and Validity

Despite the obvious role of quantification in neuropsychological testing, interpretation of test data ultimately depends on the knowledge base, training, and skill of the clinician. Neuropsychological test scores are an indirect measure of the status of the brain, as contrasted with direct measures of structure by computed tomography or function by positron emission tomography. In a psychiatric setting, where problems of motivation, effort, cooperation, and stage of the illness are ubiquitous, analysis of neuropsychological data must go beyond the level of performance deficits, because many studies have shown performance to be especially affected by functional (emotional) factors. Process analyses oriented to focal syndromes and focused on the relative efficiency of the two sides of the body and hemispace may enhance predictive validity.[40]

The patient's clinical state may change, and repeated testing when the patient's clinical status is optimal often clarifies the nature of the diagnosis. Selective deficits found in the context of otherwise good performance when patients are tested in their best state can be considered most valid. Neuropsychologists must also take into account the effect of medication on neuropsychological function and distinguish medication effects from the patient's adaptive ability. Different medications are likely to produce different effects. For example, Trimble and Thompson[59] have demonstrated that, for epileptic patients and normal subjects, anticonvulsants have negative effects on most measures of neuropsychological testing. On the other hand, Cassens and colleagues[60] have demonstrated that (traditional) antipsychotic medications have negligible or mildly positive effects on most measures of neuropsychological testing in chronic schizophrenia, with the possible exception of a negative effect on motor performance. Spohn and Strauss[61] have indicated that typical neuroleptic (antipsychotic) medications tend to improve attentional performance, such as on versions of the Continuous Performance Test.[62]

Clinical Vignette 4

In this vignette, the patient is a 30-year-old man with a 13-year history of schizophrenia. This case illustrates the beneficial clinical effects of one of the newer "atypical" antipsychotic medications, clozapine (Clozaril), on neuropsychological function, suggesting that certain com-

Figure 22–2 *Clock drawing by a schizophrenic man. Note the excessive detail and elaboration of the clock, which is unusual for normal volunteers or brain-injured patients. The patient did set the clock correctly, to read "10 after 11" (clinical vignette 4).*

ponents of schizophrenic "dementia" are reversible in some patients.[63]

This patient's first episode of psychosis occurred in high school shortly before the end of the junior year. At age 17 years, he was admitted to the hospital in an acutely agitated state, hallucinating and suicidal. After some remission was achieved with 40 mg/d of haloperidol, the patient was given a psychodiagnostic test battery that included a Wechsler Adult Intelligence Scale. At that time, he had a Verbal IQ of 121, a Performance IQ of 111, and a Full-Scale IQ of 121.

During the next 5 years, the patient was hospitalized 10 times for a total of 27 months of hospitalization. On one of those occasions (4 years after initial testing), he was readministered the Wechsler Adult Intelligence Scale–Revised,[14] receiving a Verbal IQ of 109 (a 17-point drop), a Performance IQ of 112, and a Full-Scale IQ of 111. Although the patient was not subsequently hospitalized, he remained in a chronically disorganized phase of illness until his medication was changed from typical neuroleptics to clozapine in the 12th year of the illness. Within months of the start of this treatment, the patient's illness diminished significantly, leaving residual paranoid delusions and only episodic, mild disorganization. The patient demonstrated a remarkable increase in insight and sociability.

Shortly before clozapine treatment began, the patient had a neuropsychological evaluation. At that point, his IQ estimate was only 83, and he was grossly impaired on an Auditory Continuous Performance Test (15 of 30), on the Wisconsin Card Sorting Test (0 categories sorted, 125 perseverative responses), and on the Wechsler Memory Scale–Revised, Logical Memories Immediate Recall (5 of 50). He had mild olfactory deficits on the University of Pennsylvania[64] Smell Identification Test (31 of 40). Two and a half years later, after 12 months of clozapine treatment, the patient showed dramatic improvement in neuropsychological functions. His IQ estimate was now 113, relatively close to his premorbid range. At this point, he performed within normal limits on the Auditory Continuous Performance Test (29 of 30), Logical Memories (31 of 50), and the University of Pennsylvania Smell Identification Test (37 of 40). Although his performance on the Wisconsin Card Sorting Test was significantly improved from the previous evaluation, he remained se-

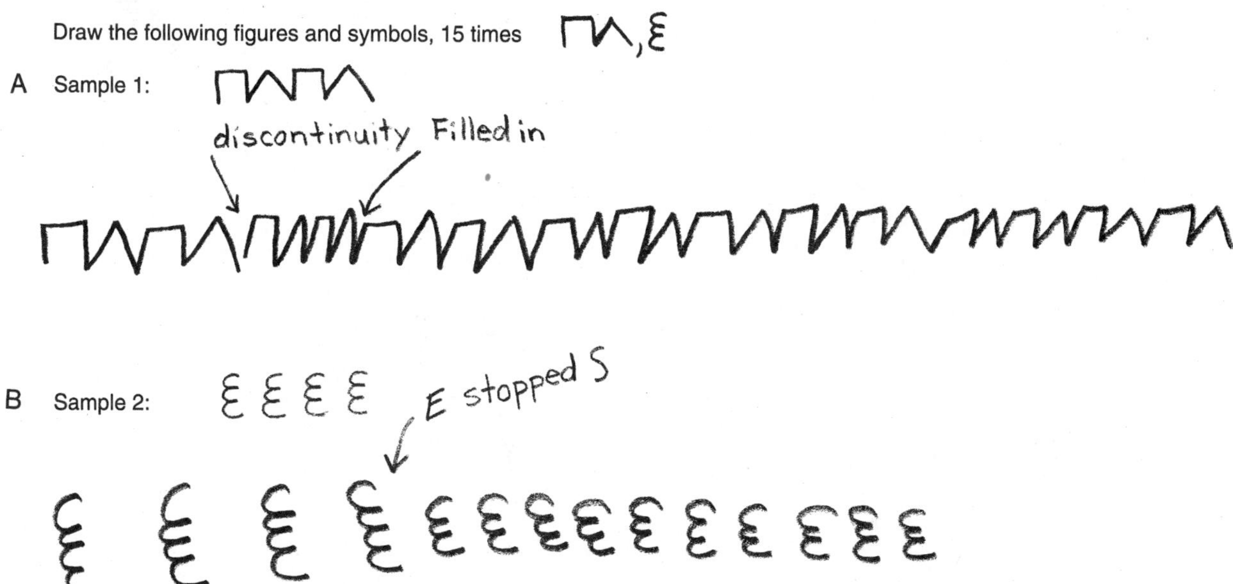

Figure 22–3 *Graphic sequences.* (A) *The subject has trouble with smooth continuity in drawing an open square and triangle because of concretely assuming that only two pairs of figures should be drawn attached. The subject later fills in the missing figures.* (B) *The subject draws an extra loop on the first four renditions of multiple loops. This perseverative tendency probably reflects attention dysfunction in this schizophrenic man (clinical vignette 4).*

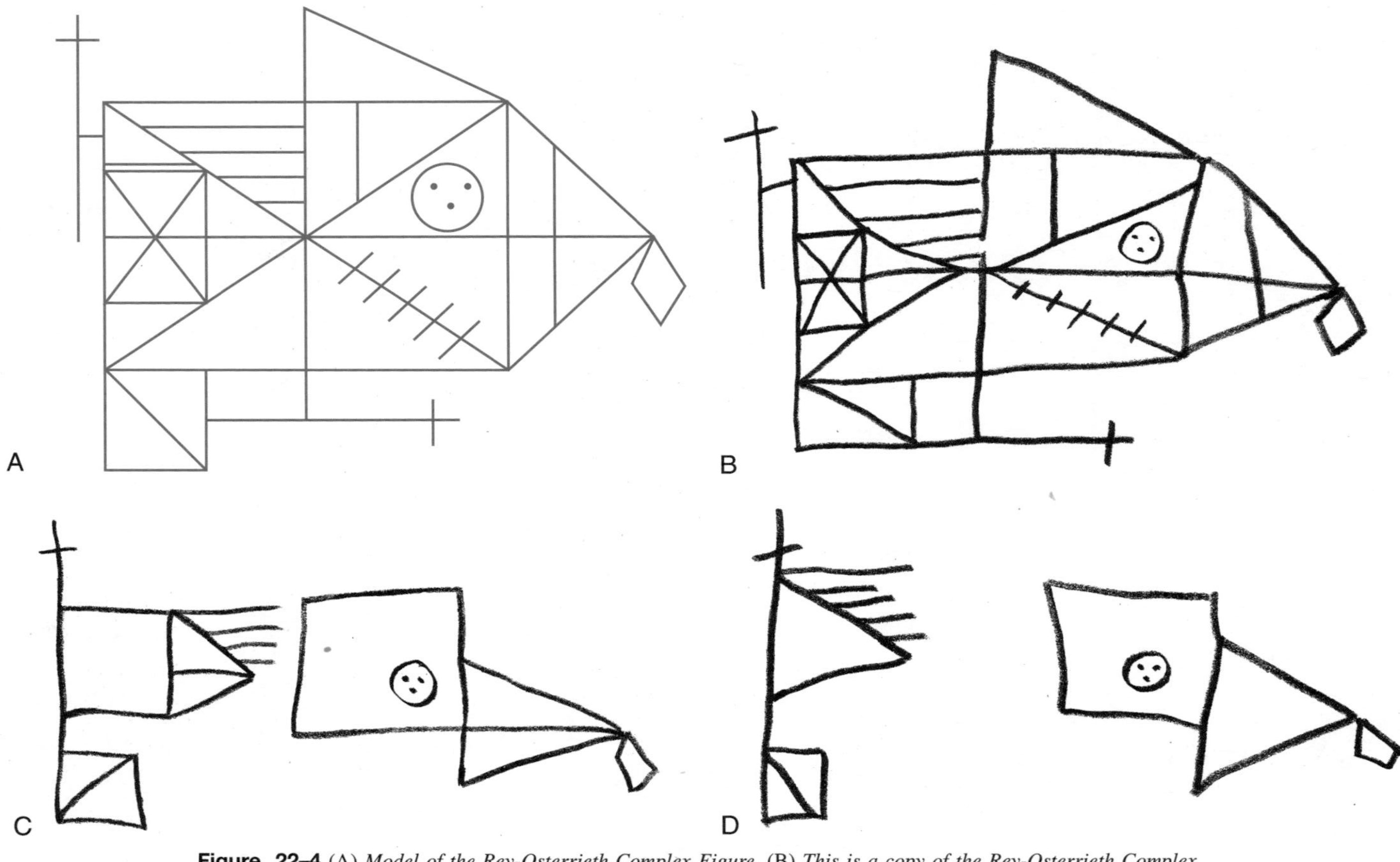

Figure 22–4 (A) *Model of the Rey-Osterrieth Complex Figure.* (B) *This is a copy of the Rey-Osterrieth Complex Figure. Although it looks superficially correct, the patient constructed it in a segmented style, focusing on small features and gradually building up the whole figure.* (C) *This is the immediate "incidental" recall—the subject was not told to memorize the figure for later retrieval. This is a remarkably fragmented reconstruction in which the patient remembers many of the details in rough proximity to their appropriate place but is unable to create a whole (gestalt).* (D) *On 20-minute delayed recall, the patient lost more information, retaining only individual fragments of the original design. These data were produced by a man with schizophrenia (clinical vignette 4), despite substantial clinical and neuropsychological improvement after treatment with clozapine.*

Clinical Vignette 3 *continued*

verely compromised on this task (3 categories sorted, 68 perseverative responses). Thus, in this case neuropsychological and symptomatic improvements were strongly associated with the introduction of a new medication. Illustrations relevant to this vignette are presented in Figures 22–2 through 22–4.

Conclusion

This chapter contains a relatively broad overview of the role of neuropsychological testing in psychiatric practice. The increased recognition that many psychiatric syndromes (e.g., schizophrenia) can be understood as neuropsychological disorders[65] requires greater attention to the functional capacities and deficits of the affected individuals. Moreover, the increasing prevalence of disorders of cognitive functioning, especially in the elderly, is leading to an increased need for neuropsychological assessment. Neuropsychological testing can be helpful in diagnosis, treatment planning, and assessing change over time, such as in response to interventions (e.g., medications). Neuropsychological assessment can include both cognitive and personality measures, so that the patient's cognitive problems can be understood psychodynamically in terms of meaning, experience, conflict, and adaptive capacity. The flexible use of assessment, at the bedside or in extended evaluation, may be of great benefit to both patient and clinician.

One final note regarding the use of neuropsychological tests in research. Neuropsychological tests have many applications in neuropsychiatric research, although caution must be exercised in drawing inferences about brain localization from individual cognitive deficits.[66] Our ability to infer the neuroanatomy of any neuropsychiatric disorder from cross-sectional neurocognitive studies is limited by many factors, such as variations in clinical stage or state, the effects of medications, and the interpretive difficulties posed by developmental alterations in brain organization found in many psychiatric illnesses.[2]

References

1. Grant DA, Berg EA: A behavioral analysis of degree of reinforcement and ease of shifting to new responses in a Weigl-type card sorting program. J Exp Psychol 1948; 38:404–411.
2. Goldberg E, Seidman LJ: Higher cortical functions in normals and in schizophrenia: A selective review. In Steinhauer SR, Gruzelier JH, Zubin J (eds): Handbook of Schizophrenia, Volume 5, Neuropsychology, Psychophysiology and Information Processing. Amsterdam: Elsevier, 1991:595–597.
3. Squire LR: The neuropsychology of memory dysfunction and its assessment. In Grant I, Adams KM (eds): Neuropsychological Assessment of Neuropsychiatric Disorders. New York: Oxford University Press, 1986:268–299.
4. Holt RR (ed): Diagnostic Psychological Testing, revised ed. New York: International Universities Press, 1968.
5. Reitan RM, Davison LA: Clinical Neuropsychology: Current Status and Applications. Washington, DC: VH Winston & Sons, 1974.
6. Lezak MD: Neuropsychological Assessment, 3rd ed. New York: Oxford University Press, 1995.
7. Weiss JL, Seidman LJ: The clinical use of psychological and neuropsychological tests. In Nicholi A (ed): The New Harvard Guide to Psychiatry. Cambridge, MA: Harvard University Press, 1988:46–69.
8. Heaton RK, Grant I, Matthews CG: Differences in neuropsychological test performance associated with age, education and sex. In Grant I, Adams KM (eds): Neuropsychological Assessment of Neuropsychiatric Disorders. New York: Oxford University Press, 1986:100–120.
9. Luria AR: Higher Cortical Functions in Man, 2nd ed. New York: Basic Books, 1980.
10. Greenberg M, Seidman LJ: The neuropsychology of temporal lobe epilepsy. In White RF (ed): Clinical Syndromes in Adult Neuropsychology: The Practitioner's Handbook. Amsterdam: Elsevier Science Publishing, 1992:345–379.
11. Weinstein CS, Seidman LJ, Feldman J, et al: Neurocognitive disorders in psychiatry: A case example of diagnostic and treatment dilemmas. Psychiatry 1991; 54:65–75.
12. Seidman LJ: Listening, meaning, and empathy in neuropsychological disorders: Case examples of assessment and treatment. In Ellison J, Weinstein CS, Hodel-Malinofsky T (eds): The Psychotherapist's Guide to Neuropsychiatry: Diagnostic and Treatment Issues. Washington, DC: American Psychiatric Press, 1994:1–22.
13. Weinstein CS, Seidman LJ: The role of neuropsychological assessment in adult psychiatry. In Ellison J, Weinstein CS, Hodel-Malinofsky T (eds): The Psychotherapist's Guide to Neuropsychiatry: Diagnostic and Treatment Issues. Washington, DC: American Psychiatric Press, 1994:53–106.
14. Wechsler D: Wechsler Adult Intelligence Scale–Revised. New York: Psychological Corporation, 1981.
15. Wechsler D: The Wechsler Memory Scale–Revised. New York: Psychological Corporation, 1987.
16. Peterson LR, Peterson MJ: Short term retention of individual verbal items. J Exp Psychol 1959; 58:193–198.
17. Delis DC, Kramer JH, Kaplan E, Ober BA: California Verbal Learning Test–Adult Version. San Antonio, TX: The Psychological Corporation, 1987.
18. Osterrieth P, Rey A: Le test de copie d'une figure complexe. Arch Psychol 1944; 30:206–356.
19. Kaplan E, Goodglass H, Weintraub S: The Boston Naming Test. Philadelphia: Lea & Febiger, 1983.
20. Borkowski JG, Benton AL, Spreen O: Word fluency and brain damage. Neuropsychologia 1967; 5:135–140.
21. Hathaway SR, McKinley JC: The Minnesota Multiphasic Personality Inventory–2. Minneapolis, MN: Regents of The University of Minnesota, 1989.
22. Morgan CD, Murray HA: A method for investigating fantasies: The thematic apperception test. Arch Neurol Psychiatry 1935; 34:289–306.
23. Bear D, Fedio P: Quantitative analysis of interictal behavior in temporal lobe epilepsy. Arch Neurol 1977; 34:454–467.
24. Rorschach H: Psychodiagnostics: A Diagnostic Test Based on Perception. Bern, Switzerland: Hans Huber, 1942.
25. Wechsler D: Manual for the Wechsler Intelligence Scale for Children–Revised. New York: Psychological Corporation, 1971.
26. Wilkinson GS: The Wide Range Achievement Test 3. Wilmington, DE: Jastak Associates, 1993.
27. Golden CJ: Stroop Color and Word Test: A Manual for Clinical and Experimental Use. Chicago: Stoelting, 1978.
28. Weintraub S, Mesulam M-M: Mental state assessment of young and elderly adults in behavioral neurology. In Mesulam M-M (ed): Principles of Behavioral Neurology. Philadelphia: FA Davis, 1985:71–123.
29. Conners CK: Conners' Continuous Performance Test: Computer Program 3.0, Users Manual. Toronto, Canada: Multi-Health Service, 1994.
30. Adams W, Sheslow D: The Wide Range Assessment of Memory and Learning. Wilmington, DE: Jastak Associates, 1990.
31. Waber D, Holmes JM: Assessing children's copy productions of the Rey-Osterrieth Complex Figure. J Clin Exp Neuropsychol 1985; 7:264–280.
32. Benson DF, Stuss DT: Motor abilities after frontal leukotomy. Neurology 1982; 32:1353–1357.
33. Reitan RR, Wolfson D: The Halstead-Reitan Neuropsychological Test Battery: Theory and Clinical Interpretation. Tucson, AZ: Neuropsychology Press, 1985.
34. Rotter J: Incomplete Sentence Blank. New York: Psychological Corporation, 1977.
35. Costa L: Clinical neuropsychology: A discipline in evolution. J Clin Neuropsychol 1983; 5:1–11.
36. Allen J, Lewis L (eds): Neuropsychology in a psychodynamic setting. Bull Menninger Clin 1986; 50:1–132.

37. Milberg WP, Hebben N, Kaplan E: The Boston process neuropsychological approach to neuropsychological assessment. In Grant I, Adams KM (eds): Neuropsychological Assessment of Neuropsychiatric Disorders. New York: Oxford University Press, 1986:65–86.
38. Yozawitz A: Applied neuropsychology in a psychiatric center. In Grant I, Adams KM (eds): Neuropsychological Assessment of Neuropsychiatric Disorders. New York: Oxford University Press, 1986:121–146.
39. Holmes-Bernstein J, Waber DP: Developmental neuropsychological assessment: The systemic approach. In Boulton AA, Baker GB, Hiscock M (eds): Neuromethods: Neuropsychology. Clifton, NJ: Humana Press, 1990:311–371.
40. Kaplan E: The process approach to neuropsychological assessment of psychiatric patients. J Neuropsychiatry Clin Neurosci 1990; 2:72–87.
41. Strub RL, Black FW: The Mental Status Examination in Neurology, 2nd ed. Philadelphia: FA Davis, 1985.
42. Reitan RM: Theoretical and methodological bases of the Halstead-Reitan neuropsychological test battery. In Grant I, Adams KM (eds): Neuropsychological Assessment of Neuropsychiatric Disorders. New York: Oxford University Press, 1986:3–30.
43. Moss MS, Albert MS: Neuropsychology of Alzheimer's disease. In White RF (ed): Clinical Syndromes in Adult Neuropsychology: The Practitioner's Handbook. Amsterdam: Elsevier Science Publishing, 1992:305–343.
44. Seidman LJ, Cassens G, Kremen WS, et al: The neuropsychology of schizophrenia. In White RF (ed): Clinical Syndromes in Adult Neuropsychology: The Practitioner's Handbook. Amsterdam: Elsevier Science Publishing, 1992:381–449.
45. Army Individual Test Battery: Manual of Directions and Scoring. Washington, DC: War Department, Adjutant General's Office, 1944.
46. Seidman LJ, Yurgelun-Todd D, Kremen WS, et al: Relationship of prefrontal and temporal lobe MRI measures to neuropsychological performance in chronic schizophrenia. Biol Psychiatry 1994; 35:235–246.
47. Seidman LJ: The neuropsychology of schizophrenia: A neurodevelopmental and case study approach. J Neuropsychiatry Clin Neurosci 1990; 2:301–312.
48. Liberman RP, Massell HK, Mosk MD, et al: Social skills training for chronic mental patients. Hosp Community Psychiatry 1985; 36:396–402.
49. Milberg W: Issues in the assessment of cognitive function in dementia. Brain Cogn, in press.
50. Golden CJ, Hammeke T, Purisch A: Manual for The Luria-Nebraska Neuropsychological Battery. Los Angeles: Western Psychological Services, 1980.
51. Goodglass H, Kaplan E: Assessment of cognitive deficit in the brain-injured patient. In Gazzaniga M (ed): Handbook of Behavioral Neurobiology, Volume 2, Neuropsychology. New York: Plenum Publishing, 1979.
52. Goldberg E, Costa LD: Qualitative indices in neuropsychological assessment: Extension of Luria's approach to executive deficit following prefrontal lesions. In Grant I, Adams KM (eds): Neuropsychological Assessment of Neuropsychiatric Disorders. New York: Oxford University Press, 1986:48–64.
53. Geschwind N: Specializations of the human brain. Sci Am 1979; 241(3):108–117.
54. Feldman MJ, Drasgow J: The Visual-Verbal Test. Los Angeles: Western Psychological Services, 1959.
55. Mattis S: Dementia Rating Scale (DRS) Manual. Odessa, FL: Psychological Assessment Resources, 1988.
56. Goodglass H, Kaplan E: The Assessment of Aphasia and Related Disorders, 2nd ed. Philadelphia: Lea & Febiger, 1983.
57. Heaton RK, Grant WZ, Anthony WZ, Lehman RA: A comparison of clinical and automated interpretation of the Halstead-Reitan battery. J Clin Neuropsychol 1981; 3:121–141.
58. Adams KM, Brown GG: The role of the computer in neuropsychological assessment. In Grant I, Adams KM (eds): Neuropsychological Assessment of Neuropsychiatric Disorders. New York: Oxford University Press, 1986:87–99.
59. Trimble MR, Thompson PJ: Neuropsychological Aspects of Neuropsychiatric Disorders. New York: Oxford University Press, 1986:321–346.
60. Cassens G, Inglis AK, Appelbaum PS, et al: Neuroleptics: Effects on neuropsychological function in chronic schizophrenic patients. Schizophr Bull 1990; 16:477–499.
61. Spohn HE, Strauss ME: The relation of neuroleptic and anticholinergic medication to cognitive functions in schizophrenia. J Abnorm Psychol 1989; 98:367–380.
62. Rosvold HE, Mirsky AF, Sarason I, et al: A continuous performance test of brain damage. J Consult Psychol 1956; 20:343–350.
63. Buchanan RW, Holstein C, Breier A: The comparative efficacy and long-term effect of clozapine treatment on neuropsychological test performance. Biol Psychiatry 1994; 36:717–725.
64. Doty RL: The Smell Identification Test Administration Manual. Haddonfield, NJ: Sensonics, 1984.
65. Seidman LJ: Schizophrenia and brain dysfunction: An integration of recent neurodiagnostic findings. Psychol Bull 1983; 94:195–238.
66. Keefe RSE: The contributions of neuropsychology to psychiatry. Am J Psychiatry 1995; 152:6–15.

CHAPTER

23 Consciousness, Orientation, and Memory

Keith H. Claypoole
Gary J. Tucker

There is a danger in presenting consciousness, orientation, and memory as distinct topics. By discussing these phenomena individually, a separation may be implied that is not actually present, either functionally or biologically. Consciousness, orientation, and memory are three closely linked and interdependent biological processes: a person cannot be oriented without intact memory; memory is related critically to one's level of consciousness. Consequently, it is not surprising that these seemingly disparate functions are mediated or affected by the same neurotransmitters and neuroanatomical structures.[1]

Perhaps most confusing are the many synonyms used to describe these functions; for example, consciousness has been referred to variously as awareness, attention, arousal, and vigilance.[2] Despite the disparity and confusion in terms, their unitary nature is evident in their overall function, that is, each is a key aspect of cognition or how an individual "knows" the world or the environment.

The usual definition of cognition is an intellectual process by which knowledge is gained by perceptions or ideas. It comes from the Latin *cognitio*. In essence, cognition is how an individual knows or relates to the world. Alterations of an individual's relationship to and knowledge of the world due to cerebral dysfunction have been well described historically. Soranus, in AD 100, portrayed a condition he called phrenitis, a disease associated with acute fever in which the patient made foolish gesticulations and had disturbed perceptions. At times, the patient would be completely unresponsive as well. Soranus attributed this condition to a disturbance of the brain.[3]

Changes in States and Levels of Consciousness

Most disturbances of the central nervous system are due to either psychological or physical insult and may be evident by changes in an individual's level of consciousness. A change in consciousness manifests itself functionally in the way the person responds to the surrounding environment. Plum and Posner,[4] in their classic monograph on stupor and coma, classified the spectrum of changes in consciousness as alterations of "stimulus-response" (Table 23–1). This model provides a useful empirical method for the physician to classify levels of consciousness. Accordingly, alert wakefulness (or the normal state) is a condition in which a subject is able to respond immediately and appropriately in all sensory modalities to stimuli. As consciousness becomes increasingly impaired, responses become delayed or incomplete and require increasing levels of external stimulation until no response, or only primitive responses, can be elicited. A classification of levels of consciousness that is limited to deficits, however, cannot encompass the range of disturbances seen in psychiatric illness. It is useful mainly for the conditions that usually confront the neurologist. A broader (psychiatric) perspective on alterations in consciousness begins with a level of consciousness in which responses to stimuli are increased, a state called hypervigilance.[5] Many psychiatric conditions associated with increased anxiety or arousal are also associated with hypervigilance.[6, 7] A hypervigilant individual may respond in an almost random manner to any stimuli in the environment and can become distracted or unable to focus attention. If anxiety persists, the person can become immobilized and completely unable to function (Table 23–2). The hypervigilant state follows the well-known inverted U association of anxiety and performance: a small amount of anxiety increases performance, but increasing amounts of anxiety cause a decrement in function. Hypervigilance can be induced by drugs (e.g., amphetamines), is common in paranoid conditions, may be apparent in agitated depressive states, and has been described as a key component of post-traumatic stress disorder.[8]

At the other end of the psychiatric spectrum of disturbances in consciousness are conditions closer to coma, such as akinetic mutism and catatonia. The akinetic state, frequently called the locked-in syndrome, is often related more to distinct pathological changes in the central nervous system. It is not unusual for a psychiatric consultant to be asked to see a patient who does not have clear neurological lesions but remains in a persistent vegetative or coma-like state that is neither clearly catatonia nor truly coma. The patient usually recovers with no neurological residual. In many of these coma-like states, there is no apparent cause. Similarly, the cause of catatonia can be unclear. Catatonia

Table 23–1 Alterations of Consciousness

State*	Definition
Hypervigilance	Increased scanning of environment, arousal Difficulty in focusing or shifting attention
Alert wakefulness	Subject responds immediately in all sensory modalities
Lethargy	State of drowsiness, inaction, indifference Responses delayed or incomplete May need increased stimulation to respond
Obtundation	More indifferent May maintain wakefulness but little more
Stupor	Subject can be aroused by vigorous and continuous external stimulation
Coma	Psychological and motor responses to stimulation either completely lost or reduced to rudimentary responsiveness, e.g., withdrawal, sucking, chewing, swallowing
Catatonia	Dramatic reduction of psychomotor activity presenting as rigidity, waxy flexibility, mutism, and negativism
Partial Alterations of Consciousness	
Dissociation	Unintegrated perceptions
Depersonalization	Feels detached from world
Derealization	Environment seems unreal
Déjà vu	Feeling of familiarity
Jamais vu	Feeling of unfamiliarity
Unilateral neglect	Unawareness of a body part

*The causes are the same for all states: anxiety, stress, paranoia, drugs, and central nervous system damage.

is characterized by marked nonresponse to the environment and thereby represents a profound, but reversible, alteration of consciousness.[4, 9, 10]

Partial Alterations in Consciousness

The changes in consciousness that occur in daily life can represent normal or psychopathological functions.[5] These changes are primarily mediated by responses to sensory stimuli and the ability to sustain a focus of attention that causes a partial change in the level of consciousness. For example, at the simplest level, a person going to the dentist is anxious about the experience and is likely to focus considerable attention on the drill. Under these circumstances, it is likely that pain, and the intensity of the slightest sensory input of any kind, will be heightened. However, if the person tries to focus attention on music from a cassette player with headphones (that the dentist thoughtfully provides), or simply on an image of more interest and less threat, such as a placid scene, then pain and discomfort are diminished. Purposeful shifting of the focus of attention underlies many relaxation techniques as well as hypnosis. Consequently, cortical activity can modify sensory input and thereby modify attention, arousal, and anxiety (anxiety can also modify consciousness as well).

Table 23–2 Types of Experience from People in Hypervigilant States

When I try to read something, each bit I read starts me thinking in 10 different directions at once.

When I try to concentrate on the major issues, I find myself paying attention to all sorts of tiny things instead of the important things.

Often I find myself paying attention to the silliest little things going on around me, and I waste a lot of energy that way.

I am attending to everything at once and as a result, I do not really attend to anything.

If I am distracted by too much noise, I can't move. If I am walking across the room, for example, and someone turns on the radio, I may freeze in my tracks for a moment or two.

When people are talking, I have to think what the words mean. I can pay attention to one person, but if there are three or four people speaking at once, I get confused.

Noises all seem to be louder—as if someone had turned up the volume.

If I am talking to someone and they cross their legs or scratch their heads, for example, I get distracted and forget what I am saying.

Cortical input (thought) can also modify motor activity. A person engaged in technical rock climbing often gets into a position in which he or she feels anxious or frightened and becomes "frozen" or immobilized, with a sensation of weakness in all muscles ("sewing machine leg"). As attention is focused on the situation and it becomes apparent that movement without some type of action is impossible, the person begins to control the fear. With this control, muscle strength and motor activity return.

In psychopathological states, the functions of cognitive input, or sensory and motor function, are more clearly related to partial alterations of consciousness (see Table 23–1). Dissociation has been defined by Spiegel[11] as "a separation of mental events that would ordinarily be processed together—a discontinuity of memory, identity, perception, motor function, or consciousness." Conditions such as dissociative identity disorder, dissociative fugue, hypnotic trance, or conversion disorder would all be classified as partial alterations of consciousness in that one's consciousness of the body (e.g., people who cannot move their legs) is separated from awareness, but, in general, the rest of the ability to relate to the world is intact. A similar type of splitting of consciousness can be seen with central nervous system damage. In many patients with stroke, and particularly in lesions of the right temporoparietal and thalamus region, a "neglect syndrome" results, which has also been described as "a denial of illness." For example, a patient with a paralyzed arm denies that the arm is paralyzed; even when shown the paralyzed arm, the person states, "That is not my arm."[12, 13]

It is becoming increasingly clear how arousal or anxiety levels are related to these partial disturbances of consciousness. Studies of the biological causes of posttraumatic stress disorder and its accompanying dissociated state, the partial alteration of consciousness called psychic numbing, implicate similar neurotransmitter systems (e.g., the noradrenergic system, which is highly related to anxiety and arousal).[8] Depersonalization has also been related in previous studies to heightened levels of anxiety and arousal, as has posttraumatic stress disorder.[14] In these studies, patients have reported experiences in which they felt there was a veil between themselves and their world, with a sense of being distant and detached. This is comparable to the state of derealization in which a person feels detached or separated from the immediate environment, rather than from her or his body. However, many people also experience depersonalization or derealization with febrile states, which shows that these are physiological responses of the body that can occur in response to a number of different etiological factors.

Other varieties of partial alterations of consciousness, such as déjà vu (in which the patient experiences a feeling of familiarity in an unfamiliar place) or its converse, jamais vu (in which the patient experiences feelings of unfamiliarity in a familiar place), have also been associated with increased anxiety levels.[14] Levels of consciousness as reflected in levels of attention, arousal, and anxiety (even mood) are clearly related to memory functions, as the studies of posttraumatic stress disorder and mood have shown.[8] Mood, anxiety, and level of consciousness are crucial determinants of which memory traces are or are not retained.[15, 16]

Physiology of Alterations in Consciousness

All of the alterations of consciousness are related to the same brain regions and the same neurotransmitter systems.[1] Usually cited are the brain stem and the reticular structures, but also involved are the cingulate cortex, the thalamus, and sensory and motor input from the parietal and frontal cortex (Fig. 23–1). Whereas most physicians associate changes of arousal exclusively with midbrain activity, arousal is also affected by sensory and motor input.

The complexity of the neurotransmitter systems that are potentially involved in alterations of consciousness is most clearly exemplified by the neurotransmitter systems that affect sleep (which is certainly an alteration of consciousness). For example, the histamine and cholinergic systems are related to wakefulness, whereas drowsiness is caused by antihistamines and anticholinergic drugs. These systems are found primarily in the brain stem (mesencephalon, medulla, and pontine areas). The brain stem dorsal raphe nuclei also affect sleep, which implicates the serotoninergic system. Increased serotonin levels produce sleep (the serotonin precursor tryptophan has been used as a sleep medication), and certain serotonin antagonist agents (parachlorophenylalanine) cause marked wakefulness. In the same way, the noradrenergic system, similarly located in the brain stem and, primarily, in the locus caeruleus, when stimulated, increases alertness and arousal. Agents that antagonize noradrenergic functions (e.g., propranolol) increase sleep. Dopamine, too, is related to sleep. Thus, neuroleptics cause sedation. Although many of these neurotransmitters are found in other locations, they are primarily located in subcortical regions.[17]

Sleep is an important example of an alteration of consciousness because sleep is really a suspension of consciousness. Sleep has a clear pattern of cycles and stages when it is studied with electroencephalography. However, sleep differs from coma in that the comatose patient cannot be aroused, and the electroencephalogram in coma fails to show the usual cycles and stages of sleep; the impact of cortical, sensory, and motor input is not apparent.

Memory Functions

Memory is, perhaps, one of the most pervasive aspects of consciousness. Memory helps to define identity and bestow self-awareness by providing a sense of continuity from our recall of past experience, promotes our capacity to adapt to the present, and allows us to benefit from learning and experience to prepare for the future. Although it is integral to almost every aspect of cognition and behavior, it is far from perfect, because our memories may be subject to alteration and decay. Understanding how memory works and what its limitations and potentials are is often made confusing by its numerous categorizations and overlapping terms. For clinical purposes, memory is often subdivided into three basic types—immediate, recent, and remote—on the basis of the time interval between presentation of the stimuli and retrieval. Immediate memory corresponds to the registration of information as a memory trace for several seconds and roughly corresponds to sensory memory described in the following. Recent memory generally refers to the ability to learn new information and recall day-to-day events. Remote memory is typically considered to represent recall of life events, which occurred before trauma or other neuropathological insult that induces memory disturbance. The functional components of memory are usually separated into three distinct areas: 1) *registration,* the ability to obtain the information and make it available to be stored; 2) the storage or *retention* of this information or activity; and 3) the ability

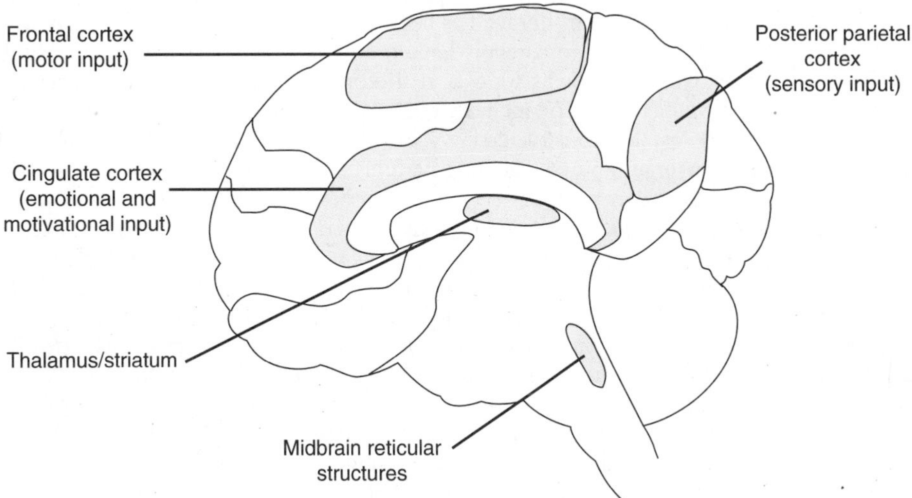

Figure 23–1 *Interacting brain regions that relate to consciousness.*

to *recall* the information. Each of these areas (registration, retention, and recall) can be separately evaluated.

The traditionally hypothesized model of memory is that of a temporally based storage system that postulates three stages: sensory memory, short-term memory, and long-term memory[18] (Fig. 23–2). In the sensory memory stage, information is considered to enter primarily through the visual or auditory sensory systems and remain briefly available to the individual immediately after presentation. Sensory memory rapidly decays unless it is considered salient and is attended to and encoded or registered, which allows transfer to the next stage, short-term memory. Sensory memory for visual stimuli is termed iconic memory and is considered to last no more than half a second, possibly corresponding to the persistence of the visual trace on the retina. Sensory memory for auditory information is termed echoic memory and may endure for several seconds. Echoic memory allows a persisting representation of auditory stimuli to enable one to nearly replay the tape, so to speak, of what has most recently been heard.

Considered an intermediate level of memory storage, short-term memory usually refers to maintenance of information available for a brief period; it may be maintained by rehearsal to facilitate retention and storage in long-term memory or risk being lost through decay or displacement. The capacity of short-term memory is usually considered limited (7 ± 2 bits or chunks of information) and is easily disrupted by being displaced from the introduction of subsequent information. Regardless of whether the information is new, or old information retrieved from long-term memory, the requirement to mentally manipulate and analyze information in short-term memory invokes the concept of a working or active memory. It is assumed that the longer the information is maintained in the short-term memory storage by elaboration processes such as rehearsal, the more likely it will be registered and consolidated into long-term memory.

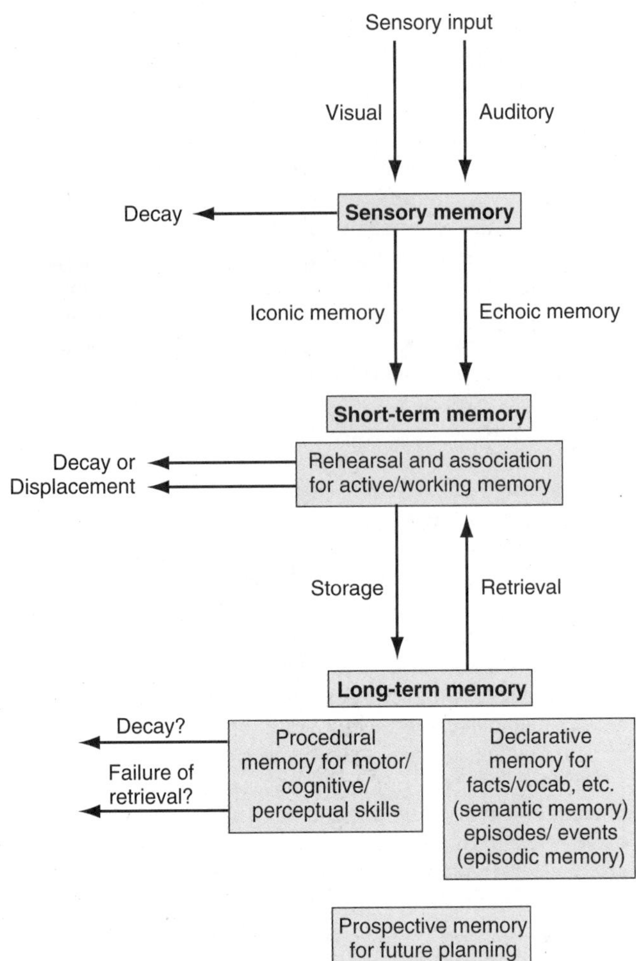

Figure 23–2 *Model of human memory.*

Long-term memory, sometimes called permanent memory, implies storage and subsequent retrieval back into working memory through recall or recognition of information after a delayed interval. These retrieved memories may be maintained by association with new short-term memory information and integrated or synthesized for the active or working memory process. Long-term memory is variably measured after intervals of minutes to hours or days, with the actual retention of long-term memory often regarded as permanent. The capacity of long-term storage has been considered to be unlimited; prominent researchers have proposed that memories may be stored for as long as a lifetime,[19] whereas others believe that long-term memory retrieval may be faulty, with details lost or reconstructed.[20]

From work with brain-injured patients, natural divisions between various forms of long-term memory have been observed. Foremost is the distinction between declarative memory for facts and episodes, which can be brought to mind as a proposition or an image, and procedural memory for motor skills and other cognitive operations. Incorporating the distinction between conscious and nonconscious memory is the view that amnesia impairs declarative memory, which is directly accessible to conscious recollection, and spares procedural memory, which is not.[21, 22] Amnestic patients have demonstrated the capability of retaining various forms of learning for motor, perceptual, and cognitive skills, which are outside of conscious awareness, as illustrations of intact procedural memory. Procedural memory abilities to learn cognitive operations or behavioral and motor skills are not accessible as specific facts, are not stored with respect to specific time or place, and do not appear to require the integrity of the medial temporal regions that declarative memory does. Thus, procedural memory is implicit because it is available only by engaging in specific operations and is essentially a memory without record. Declarative memory is available to conscious awareness and implies the explicit ability to report facts, data, and events of daily life experiences. Declarative memory permits storage of information in association with particular times and places and affords a sense of familiarity about previous events, allowing knowledge bases to be accessed for applications other than those to which learning initially occurred.[23] Declarative memory is typically impaired in amnesia because this kind of information can no longer be brought to mind as a knowledge base or image. The distinction between implicit procedural memory and explicit declarative memory can be characterized as the difference between "knowing how" and "knowing that."

A primary subdivision of declarative memory that has also emerged from research with amnestic patients is that of episodic and semantic memory.[24] Episodic memory refers to the memory for events that can be placed within a temporal framework or that have happened at a particular time in a person's life. As such, episodic memory stores the cumulative events in an individual's life and, in essence, functions as an autobiographical memory. Head-injured patients frequently experience medial temporal lobe dysfunction, with lost recollections of time- and place-specific experiences as demonstrated by varying lengths of pretraumatic and post-traumatic amnesia, and may be considered specifically susceptible to these episodic memory deficits.[24] In contrast to episodic memory, semantic memory refers to knowledge of organized information, such as facts, concepts, and vocabulary, for which a time relationship is not an essential aspect. Semantic memory does not refer to particular events in a person's past and is information that is explicitly known and available for recall. The ability to recall intact or "old" semantic knowledge in amnestic patients is in contrast with their impaired capacity for acquiring new episodic information, although recall of episodic information acquired well before the onset of amnesia may be retained.

An additional memory category that has developed from cognitive rehabilitation efforts with head-injured patients is known as prospective memory. Prospective memory refers to an individual's capacity to remember the impending need to complete a project or perform a particular activity at a specified future time or place. For instance, not remembering to turn off the oven after cooking dinner and not obtaining the required change before taking the bus are examples of prospective memory difficulties that are common complaints of head-injured patients. Prospective memory difficulty is often attributed to frontal lobe dysfunction in such patients; the executive abilities of planning, organizing, and integrating information available from memory may be compromised in the context of otherwise relatively preserved declarative memory.

Amnesia does not appear to necessarily reflect damage to cortical regions in which memory is processed or stored, but it is hypothesized to involve damage to the neural system that normally participates in memory storage without itself being a site of storage.[23] Before the turn of the century, neuropathological studies of patients with Korsakoff's syndrome first identified the significance of the midline diencephalic regions in amnesia. The other primary brain region that was initially linked to normal memory functioning, the medial temporal lobes, was established in the noted surgical case of H. M., who developed severe and lasting amnesia after bilateral temporal resection, including removal of the amygdala, uncus, hippocampal gyrus, and anterior two thirds of the hippocampus.[23] Amnesia due to medial temporal damage has since been observed to be associated with a variety of conditions, including traumatic head injury, posterior artery occlusion, stroke, viral encephalitis, and various degenerative neurological disorders.

Whereas the hippocampal region has traditionally been regarded as the most crucial site for memory, a more functional view of the neural memory system must also integrate the amygdala, because both the hippocampus and amygdala receive input from sensory-specific cortical areas and from multimodal association areas.[23] Extensive afferent and efferent pathways to and from the neocortex converge on the parahippocampal gyrus,[25] providing both hippocampus and amygdala with interconnections to ongoing cortical activity at memory storage sites. Compatible with systematic studies of the variable effects of brain lesions is Mishkin's[26] proposal that the structures critical for the medial temporal and diencephalic structures to function as a neural memory system must also incorporate additional structures with strong interconnections, such as the mamillary nuclei, which project to the anterior nucleus and receive input from the hippocampal formation through the fornix, and the ventromedial frontal cortex, which receives projections from the anterior nucleus and the thalamic nucleus. The neurotransmitter systems in these areas (e.g., glutamate, opiate, and midbrain systems mentioned before) also mediate and influence these memory functions.

Different pathophysiological mechanisms are involved with various organic conditions and result in different forms of memory disturbances. For example, globally impaired memory is a hallmark of the diffuse cerebral atrophy associated with the generalized cognitive decline of dementia. Severe memory deficits may also occur in relative isolation, as in Korsakoff's syndrome, in which the patient may deny memory deficits while providing confabulatory answers. Transient memory difficulty may arise from inattention in lethargic conditions or agitated, hypervigilant, or confusional states. Whereas memory disturbances are often the primary initial complaint of early organic brain disease, not all memory difficulties are organic in origin. Patients presenting with psychiatric disturbances, especially psychotic or clinically depressed and anxious patients, often display memory dysfunction on a mental status examination. Because memory testing requires optimal attention, motivation, and effort on the patient's part, memory disturbance is readily misdiagnosed. The differential diagnosis of dementia versus depression, for example, may be an extremely difficult clinical task in the early stages and require integration of neurological, radiological, psychiatric, and neuropsychological evaluations to ensure accurate diagnosis and provide appropriate treatment and psychosocial-vocational adjustments.

Clinical Vignette

Ms. A, a married, right-handed, 37-year-old social worker, was evaluated approximately 6 months after an episode of adenovirus encephalitis. The neurological examination was nonfocal and unremarkable. She was able to follow two-step commands but not three-step commands. She could complete six digits forward and repeat a four-word list immediately, but she had no recall after 1 minute. She showed pronounced affective lability, with exaggerated emotional responses, and obsessive thought patterns.

Like other amnestic patients, she performed poorly on formal tests of new learning ability (anterograde amnesia), with a significant loss for memories before her encephalitis (retrograde amnesia). She was oriented to person and place, but not time. Although visual-spatial functions and praxis were intact, she displayed subtle paraphasia, reduced verbal comprehension, and severe word-finding difficulties. She was able to sustain her attention for long periods when engaged in familiar activities, but her attention broke down rapidly for complex and unfamiliar demands, particularly when a new learning component was required, such as following a recipe. She was observed to be able to carry out a number of prior learned activities competently, such as household chores of laundry and cleaning, paint-by-number oil paintings, and driving in familiar places, demonstrating the relative intactness of her procedural memory abilities. She exhibited moderate impairment in attempting to learn new verbal information (semantic memory) and could not recall her previous day's activities, reflecting a deficit in episodic memory. Because of her organically based inability to generalize learning to unfamiliar situations, rehabilitation efforts were conducted within her home environment to capitalize on her relatively spared procedural memory. Owing to her declarative memory deficits, she was unable to meaningfully participate in psychotherapy. Close family members became engaged in counseling to gain a better understanding of the nature of her memory disturbance, express their feelings of loss, and receive assistance in maintaining a more predictable schedule and structured environment to minimize Ms. A's emotional instability.

Intelligence

One important aspect of how a person negotiates or knows the world is called intelligence. Both the normal levels of consciousness and intact memory functions are developmentally necessary to intelligence, although there have been documented cases of adult patients who remain capable of demonstrating relatively preserved levels of measured intelligence after the onset of amnesia. Intelligence has been defined as "an aggregate or global capacity of an individual to act purposefully, to think rationally, and to deal effectively with his/her environment."[27] Thorndike and colleagues[28] clearly delineated the multimodal nature of intelligence when they defined three key areas: 1) abstract or verbal intelligence, the ability to use symbols; 2) practical intelligence, the facility to manipulate objects; and 3) social intelligence, the facility to deal with human beings.

The origins of modern-day intelligence tests date to Termin's individually administered Stanford Revision of the Binet-Simon test in 1916. These early standardized intelligence tests were used in public schools for identifying and tracking the intellectual development of cognitively delayed children, with the goal of providing improved curricula and remedial teaching. Numerous individually administered intelligence tests have been developed since then; however, the Wechsler Adult Intelligence Scale–Revised (WAIS-R) has become the standard and most widely used instrument for the clinical assessment of intelligence for patients between the ages of 16 and 74 years.[29] The WAIS-R provides information that reflects overall or global intellectual functioning (Full-Scale IQ) and is divided into two subdomains of intelligence, verbal and nonverbal or visual-spatial performance functions. The verbal scale is composed of six subtests: information, digit span, vocabulary, arithmetic, comprehension, and similarities. The performance scale consists of five subtests: picture completion, picture arrangement, block design, object assembly, and digit symbol. Each of these 11 subtests measures somewhat different, but interrelated, abilities within the verbal and performance domains (Table 23–3); each yields a separate subtest scale score, having a mean of 10 and a standard deviation of 3.

Among verbal subtests, digit span and arithmetic rely heavily on intact attention and concentration abilities and are typically considered sensitive to brain injury in either hemisphere as well as to attentional disturbance from acute psychiatric disturbance. For patients who experience frontal lobe disease, the subtests that measure abstract verbal reasoning and knowledge of social understanding—similarities and comprehension—are often more adversely affected. Subtests measuring general fund of knowledge and word definition—information and vocabulary—are traditionally considered more robust and resistant to decline, but they too may decrease in cases of severe organic or psychiatric disturbance. The performance subtests that primarily measure nonverbal or visual-spatial abilities are typically considered less associated with level of education than are verbal subtests; in general, they are more susceptible to increased variability or decline in cases of head injury, particularly trauma to the temporoparietal regions of the nondominant hemisphere.

Verbal subtest scale scores are combined to yield a Verbal IQ, which is generally considered a measure of dominant hemisphere function. Visual-spatial subtests are combined to generate a Performance IQ, which is more typically a measure of nonhemispheric function. Together, they comprise the Full-Scale IQ. The three IQ scores are standardized on a stratified sampling plan for age, sex, race, occupation, and urban or rural residence to have a mean of 100 and a standard deviation of 15 points.[29] Accordingly, approximately one third of the U.S. population is expected to have a Full-Scale IQ between 85 and 100; another third falls between 100 and 115.

Because of the standard error of measurement of the WAIS-R, an obtained Full-Scale IQ of 100 at the 50th percentile indicates that at the .05 level of prediction, a

Table 23–3 Wechsler Adult Intelligence Scale–Revised

Subtests	Cognitive Abilities Evaluated
Verbal	
Information	Long-term general and academic knowledge
Digit span	Short-term auditory memory for numbers
Vocabulary	Basic word knowledge and long-term memory
Arithmetic	Verbally oriented numerical reasoning skills
Comprehension	Knowledge of socially appropriate behaviors
Similarities	Abstract and associative verbal reasoning
Performance	
Picture completion	Discernment of essential visual details
Picture arrangement	Visual perceptual synthesis and sequencing
Block design	Visual-motor reproduction of abstract designs
Object assembly	Visual-motor gestalt of part-whole relationships
Digit symbol	Psychomotor speed and visual-motor coordination

patient's "true" Full-Scale IQ falls between 95 and 105. When the clinical goal is to determine whether a patient's intellectual functioning has declined, the standard error of measurement is an important conceptualization to be taken into account.[30] Thus, an IQ score should not be thought of as a precise quantitative measure; rather, it should be considered an index of the approximate level of intelligence at which the patient is currently functioning, because many medical and psychiatric illnesses may adversely affect measured levels of intelligence. Analysis of individual subtest results, as well as of Verbal IQ and Performance IQ scores, are typically used for clinical inference and diagnosis to compare a patient's current IQ performance with estimates of premorbid levels of functioning, to evaluate a patient's individual performance against normative and clinical samples, and to contrast and compare a patient's different areas of subtest functioning to illustrate underlying brain-behavior relationships or deficits of the individual.

Clinical Evaluation

It is important to develop some ability to distinguish primary neurological disorders from primary psychiatric disorders. Perhaps most discriminating in this evaluation is the patient's longitudinal, medical, and psychiatric history. The central nervous system has only a limited number of responses to any type of disturbance (Table 23–4), so identical symptoms may be due to a variety of causes. For example, for a patient who experiences dementia symptoms, it is equally possible that the cognitive changes are due to depression, a toxin in the blood, head trauma, a tumor, a seizure disorder, encephalitis, or even a stressful situation. The longitudinal history of the symptom's manifestation is often the best way to differentiate the cause of the symptom. With the current emphasis on diagnosis and specific diagnostic criteria, it is easy to think the task is done by observing that the patient's current symptoms fit the diagnostic criteria; however, this reflects the patient's symptoms only at a moment in time. One must look at the patient's longitudinal history as well. The cross-sectional picture can provide a clue that the disturbance is due to a medical condition, not a primary psychiatric illness, especially if the patient does not exactly fit certain diagnostic criteria (see Table 23–4). In patients with a psychiatric illness history, it is important to rule out the recurrence of psychiatric illness (also, the presence of a family history of mental illness should be considered). Second, most dementias do not manifest themselves as abrupt changes in personality and behavior. Most dementias have a history that develops for months to years. Often, the patient with cognitive symptoms of a more psychological origin complains more of cognitive loss, highlights failures, and shows performances that are inconsistent in different modalities; social skills often decrease as well. The opposite is often the case in early stages of dementia; the personality and social skills are retained, and patients may offer minimal complaint about cognitive loss.

The classic symptoms associated with central nervous system dysfunction have been described for a number of years. Bleuler[31] first described the concept of an organic "psychosyndrome" in 1924 (Table 23–5). These classic symptoms are still the ones we evaluate in the clinical examination.[32]

Table 23–4 Major Cognitive and Behavioral Systems Areas

Cognitive
Orientation
Affect modulation
Memory
Intelligence
Judgment
Behavioral
Arousal
Mood
Anxiety
Perception
Personality
Motor

Evaluation of Orientation

The changes in orientation most often seen in central nervous system dysfunction relate to knowing time, place, and person. The sequence of the loss of these functions often correlates with the severity of insult to the brain (Table 23–6). For example, orientation to time is generally the first function lost and usually indicates early or mild damage. In light of the diagnostic significance of orientation to time, the Mini-Mental Status Examination explores time orientation by requesting the patient to provide day of the week, month, date, year, and season. Orientation to place is often lost next; last, in cases with the most severe damage, a person does not know who he or she is. It is common for early symptoms of brain damage to be manifested as trouble in geographical orientation (i.e., the complaint of becoming lost in a familiar environment, even though there is no problem in recognizing the place). It is not uncommon on hospital units that have a large number of patients with brain damage to have a patient's name on the door so that the patient can find his or her room. However, orientation can be the least reliable of the clinical symptoms of brain damage because some patients can become so well trained that the first thing they do when they wake up in the morning is to ask the date to tell the physician when she or he visits.

Evaluation of Intelligence

When evaluating intelligence, an experienced psychiatrist often estimates the actual IQ with relative accuracy. However, specific testing is needed to obtain the most reliable and replicable estimate as well as to delineate specific cognitive

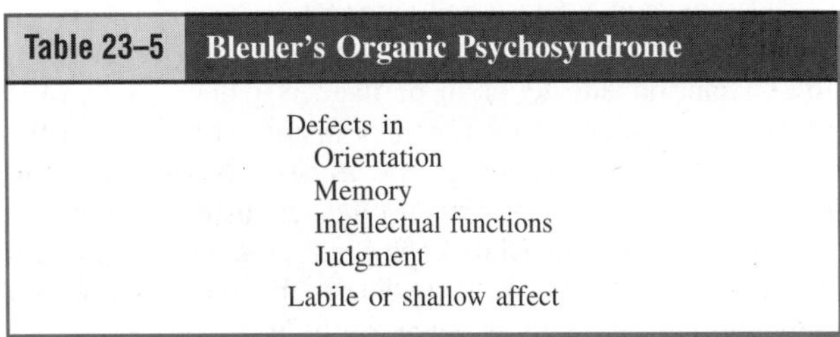

Table 23–5 Bleuler's Organic Psychosyndrome

Defects in
- Orientation
- Memory
- Intellectual functions
- Judgment

Labile or shallow affect

Table 23–6 Major Causes of Disorientation

Sensory deprivation
Fluctuating levels of consciousness
Damage to central nervous system, particularly causing memory impairment
Drugs and toxins
Fever
Hyperarousal or hypervigilance

defects. In most cases of generalized or diffuse brain damage, verbal functions are often better preserved than visual-spatial functions. Thus, with brain damage, one will often see marked disparity between the verbal and performance scores on the WAIS-R; in normal people, they tend to be more equal. Consequently, although one may have a good verbal interaction with a patient, there may be severe deficits in the visual-spatial performance areas that may not be readily apparent and should be closely evaluated. Useful measures of visual-spatial performance are the figure drawings and sentence writings in the Mini-Mental Status Examination, the Bender Gestalt Test, the block design and other WAIS-R performance subtests, and the various tests for apraxia and agnosia.[33]

Evaluation of Memory

Gross memory functions are relatively easy to evaluate clinically, and both recent and remote memory, as well as retention and recall, should be tested during evaluation. A good deal of information can be learned about a patient's memory and recall from the linear and sequential or disorganized way in which the patient relates his or her history and recent life events and from confirmation of this history by others. The ability to recall numbers forward and backward is also a good test of recent memory (registration). Most adults should be able to repeat six numbers forward and five backward. This ability may decrease slightly with age, and most patients should be given at least two trials. It is also useful to start out slowly by asking patients to remember and repeat only two or three numbers before progressing to larger strings of numbers. Intactness of remote memory is suggested by the logical sequence and order in which the patient conveys past information but is often best confirmed by others. There are some patients who tend to confabulate, which means that they attempt to fill in blanks in their memory with material that they create to hide these deficits. A simple test to check for confabulation is to ask the patient, Have you seen me before? Frequently, patients who confabulate will assure you that they have met you and will talk about where and when this took place.

Dissociated states and amnestic conditions often present a difficult problem in differential diagnosis. Most often, amnesia due to brain damage is patchy, with little pattern, or it can be total for brief historical periods in the patient's life, as in transient global amnesia. Fugue states and amnesia related to emotional changes usually relate to traumatic or psychosocial precipitants and usually have a clear onset; often, there is some gain to the individual for not remembering (e.g., to manage guilt, it is to her or his advantage not to remember). Frequently, the patient can be tested by asking questions in a number of different areas; for example, when a patient claims to have complete amnesia from birth on, she or he can often still perform various mathematical functions, be aware of what day it is, and name the months of the year. Quantification and specification of cognitive difficulties evident on mental status examinations are best left to specialized neuropsychological testing.

Evaluation of Judgment and Insight

Mental status examination involves an estimate of judgment. Most questions about judgment center on topics that demonstrate that the patient is aware of what normal, social interaction or responses are. For example, a frequently asked question is, What should you do if you are in a theater and notice a fire? Alternatives might be, Why are laws necessary? Why should you keep away from bad company? These types of questions check a patient's ability to judge and respond to social situations but are still somewhat superficial. Judgment must be examined in the context of recent behavior. A patient may have the sense to exit a burning building but still be a severe suicidal or homicidal risk.

Insight is simply measured in terms of the patient's understanding of his or her condition as either a psychological or medical condition. How the psychiatrist approaches the patient and prescribes treatment depends very much on the patient's conceptualization of the illness. For example, if someone has somatoform disorder and is absolutely convinced that something is wrong with his or her brain and body, then it becomes difficult, initially, to approach the individual primarily as a psychiatric patient. In other words, if the patient believes the problem to be physical rather than psychological, the patient will show little insight into his or her own condition.

Conclusion

The biologically and psychologically interdependent functions of consciousness, orientation, and memory are the primary aspects of how we negotiate life. They are so basic that we often take them for granted because, in most cases, they function automatically. However, their evaluation is critical in each patient because they are indicators of how the central nervous system is functioning and of the current and future capacities of the patient to function independently.

References

1. Mesulam MM: Large scale neurocognitive networks and distributed processing for attention, language and memory. Ann Neurol 1990; 28:597–613.
2. Benson DF: The Neurology of Thinking. New York: Oxford University Press, 1994.
3. Ackernecht E: A Short History of Psychiatry. New York: Hafner, 1959.
4. Plum F, Posner J: Diagnosis of Stupor and Coma, 2nd ed. Philadelphia: FA Davis, 1972.
5. Silverman J: A paradigm for the study of altered states of consciousness. Br J Psychiatry 1968; 114:1201–1218.
6. Tucker GJ, Harrow M, Detre T, et al: Perceptual experiences in schizophrenic and non-schizophrenic patients. Arch Gen Psychiatry 1969; 20:159–165.
7. Harrow M, Tucker GJ, Shield P: Stimulus overinclusion in schizophrenic disorders. Arch Gen Psychiatry 1972; 27:40–45.
8. Murburg M (ed): Catecholamine Function in Posttraumatic Stress Disorder. Washington, DC: American Psychiatric Press, 1994.
9. Taylor MA: Catatonia. Neuropsychiatry Neuropsychol Behav Neurol 1990; 3:48–72.

10. Popkin M, Tucker GJ: Secondary and drug induced mood, anxiety, psychotic, catatonic and personality disorders: A review of the literature. J Neuropsychiatry 1992; 4:369–385.
11. Spiegel D (ed): Dissociation. Washington, DC: American Psychiatric Press, 1994.
12. Weinsten EA, Kahn RL: Denial of Illness. Springfield, IL: Charles C Thomas, 1955.
13. Mesulam MM: Attention, confusional states, and neglect. In Mesulam MM (ed): Principles of Behavioral Neurology. Philadelphia: FA Davis, 1985:125–168.
14. Brauer R, Harrow M, Tucker GJ: Depersonalization phenomena in psychiatric patients. Br J Psychiatry 1970; 117:509–515.
15. McGaugh J: Affect, neuromodulatory systems, and memory storage. In Christianson S (ed): Handbook of Emotion and Memory. Hillsdale, NJ: Lawrence Erlbaum, 1992:245–268.
16. Cahill L, Prius B, Weber M, McGaugh J: β-Adrenergic activation and memory for emotional events. Nature 1994; 371:702–704.
17. Culebras A: Neuroanatomic and neurologic correlates of sleep disturbances. Neurology 1992; 42(suppl 6):19–27.
18. Squire LR: Short-term memory as a biological entity. In Deutch LD, Deutch JA (eds): Short-Term Memory. New York: Academic Press, 1975:2–40.
19. Tulving E: Cue dependent forgetting. Am Scientist 1974; 62:78–82.
20. Loftus EF, Loftus GR: On the permanence of stored information in the human brain. Am Psychol 1980; 35:409–420.
21. Cohen NJ, Squire LR: Preserved learning and retention of pattern analyzing skill in amnesia: Association of knowing how and knowing that. Science 1980; 210:207–209.
22. Squire LR: Comparisons between forms of amnesia: Some deficits are unique to Korsakoff's syndrome. J Exp Psychol Learn Mem Cogn 1982; 8:560–571.
23. Squire LR: Memory and Brain. New York: Oxford University Press, 1987.
24. Squire LR: The neuropsychology of human memory. Annu Rev Neurosci 1982; 5:241–273.
25. Van Hoesen GW: The parahippocampal gyrus. Trends Neurosci 1982; 5:345–350.
26. Mishkin M: A memory system in the monkey. Philos Trans R Soc Lond Ser B 1982; 298:85–95.
27. Wechsler D: The Measurement of Adult Intelligence. Baltimore: Williams & Wilkins, 1944.
28. Thorndike EL, Bergman EO, Cobb MV: The Measurement of Intelligence. New York: Arno Press, 1973.
29. Wechsler D: Wechsler Adult Intelligence Scale–Revised. New York: Psychological Corporation, 1981.
30. Matarazzo JD: Psychological assessment vs. psychological testing. Am Psychol 1990; 45:999–1017.
31. Bleuler E: Textbook of Psychiatry. New York: Macmillan, 1924.
32. Trzepacz P, Baker R: The Psychiatric Mental Status Examination. New York: Oxford University Press, 1993.
33. Folstein MF, Folstein SE, McHugh PR: "Mini-mental state" . . . A practical method for grading the cognitive state of patients for the clinician. J Psychiatr Res 1975; 12:189–198.

CHAPTER

24

Alterations of Speech, Thought, Perception, and Self-experience

Ralph E. Hoffman
Thomas H. McGlashan

No laboratory test has yet been developed that defines or determines the severity of any psychiatric disorder. Neither is there a laboratory probe that characterizes the content of an individual's thoughts. Instead these determinations are based to a large extent on the verbal productions of patients. The routine psychiatric "laboratory" exists as interactions between psychiatrist and patient, primarily although not exclusively conversational in nature, designed to elicit characteristic signs and symptoms. Some principles of psychiatric phenomenology may be worth making explicit to put this unique interview process in perspective.

First, psychiatric disorders do not intrude on all realms of brain or cognitive function equally. To quote Hughlings Jackson[1(p411)]: "In every insanity there is morbid affection of more or less of the highest cerebral centres or, synonymously, of the highest level of evolution of the cerebral sub-system. . . ." In other words, it is precisely our advanced and most developed faculties, those faculties that define us as human and as individuals, that are altered by psychiatric conditions. These include a person's willfulness, the rich tapestry of emotions directing that willfulness, the ability to know and judge one's own behavior and that of others, and the ability to express in words complex ideas, including ideas about how one experiences oneself and one's own mental processes. These domains, by virtue of their complexity, are often difficult to objectify.

Second, these higher level processes are integrative; consciousness examined, therefore, via a psychiatric interview does not cleave readily along the traditional subdivisions of mental capacity, that is, perception, belief, emotion, thought, and language. Each of these domains informs, guides, and constrains the others. Given that psychiatric disorders involve higher level mental processes, it is the rule rather than the exception that a psychiatric disorder in a particular person will also cut across different higher level capacities, producing alterations that interweave language, belief, thought, perception, and emotion. Recognizing how these different capacities are realigned with respect to each other—rather than identifying an impairment within a single domain—offers the most informative phenomenological approach to the patient.

Third, contextual factors that shape personal beliefs, expectations, and behaviors must always be attended to. These factors include personal and family history, cultural background, and current circumstances. All too often we are left having to make difficult distinctions between the boundary of normalcy and pathological conditions when such information becomes critical. When does healthy vigilance in a dangerous environment cross over to paranoia? When does mourning the loss of a loved one become a morbid preoccupation? Under what settings might a loose association in fact really be a poetic turn of phrase? When is experiencing an angelic presence a predictable outcome of religious worship rather than a delusion? Along these lines, it should be kept in mind that psychiatric manifestations fall along a continuum, ranging from normal variants to the most extreme cases.[2] The presence of intermediate phenomena that, in isolation, are not readily classified as either pathological or normal has been clearly documented.[2]

With these caveats in mind, we shall attempt to characterize major aspects of psychiatric phenomenology.

Disorders of Speech

Patients produce a range of speech behaviors that have clinical significance. Central to this discussion is the concept of *formal thought disorder*. This term unfortunately ignores the linguistic nature of deviant discourse but has heuristic value insofar as it implies that such deviance reflects how ideas flow from one to another during the course of speaking rather than the specific content of ideas themselves.

The sine qua non of formal thought disorder is looseness of association or derailment. These terms refer to speech that the psychiatrist cannot "follow," that is, where the overall intention or point of the utterance becomes lost as the speaker shifts idiosyncratically from one frame of reference to another.[3] Consider the following example taken from Hoffman and coworkers[4]:

> ***Interviewer:*** *Tell me about where you live.*
> ***Patient:*** *I live in one place and then another place. They're black and white you know. That's why I love Christmas and stuff because, you know, it's different colors. I used to live in Brooklyn.*

Here the patient seems to be responding to the interviewer's prompt but switches to a Christmas motif that fails to elaborate on the "where I live" theme and does not, in itself, make a point. Of note is that each of the sentences, when considered separately is quite ordinary and grammatical. Deviance reflects the juxtaposition of phrases and sentences.

A more complex form of derailment is illustrated by the following [5]:

> ***Interviewer:*** *Did you ever try to hurt yourself?*
> ***Patient:*** *I cut myself once when I was in the kitchen trying to please David. I was scared for life because if David didn't want me then no man would.*

Here the patient seems to be talking about two frames of reference, the first pertaining to cutting herself, presumably while preparing food, and the second pertaining to reasons for being suicidal. The shift is without warning, that is, the patient did not help the listener by saying, "I never intentionally hurt myself but I was so upset about David that . . . ."

Another related type of discourse production deviance is flight of ideas. Some authors have not distinguished flight of ideas from derailment,[3] but there is some empirical evidence that the two terms can be refer to similar but distinct phenomena.[6] Flight of ideas also refers to speech with shifts in frame of reference, but when the shifts in frame of reference are less idiosyncratic. At times, such shifts can be instigated by similarity of sound of particular words rather than topical relationships (clang association). Most important, the speaker seems to retain the ability to flesh out particular themes or topics when he or she is able to remain within a particular frame of reference. In contrast, looseness of association suggests a sustained inability to fully and coherently elaborate on *any* theme or topic. Flight of ideas is associated with mania and various medical conditions or substance-induced psychotic states (e.g., thyrotoxicosis, amphetamine-induced psychosis). This form of thought disorder is typically accompanied by pressured speech, that is, speech produced at an abnormally rapid rate that is difficult to interrupt.[3]

A less severe type of formal thought disorder is referred to as tangentiality. Here the shifts in frame of reference are less abrupt and, at any particular time, the speaker seems to offer a coherent message. Over time, however, the speaker clearly strays from the original frame of reference. For example:

> ***Interviewer:*** *Can you tell me where you live?*
> ***Patient:*** *I live in Connecticut. We live in a 50-year-old Tudor house that is very much a home. The house shows my personality. It is comfortable and modest. My husband's personality is very different. He is a very closed-off person who makes people feel ill at ease.*

An even milder form of formal thought disorder is circumstantiality. Here the shifts in frame of reference occur but the speaker is able to return to the original conversational point:

> ***Interviewer:*** *What are your thoughts about politics?*
> ***Patient:*** *Well, I'm most interested in national politics, you know, what the President is doing. I think that a lot of our problems are up to him to solve. But I don't know then again if any human being can pull off what he's gotta do. People always promise more than they deliver. That's been my experience all along, teachers, bosses, parents. My life is just one disappointment followed by the next. It gettin' so that I just expect the worst. And that's probably gonna be the case with our new President.*

Formal thought disorder, if prominent, is generally associated with the more severe psychiatric illnesses (e.g., schizophrenia, bipolar disorder, psychotic or mood disorders that are due to general medical conditions or that are substance induced) but does not occur inevitably in these conditions. Milder examples of formal thought disorder are frequently seen in patients with a range of diagnoses, including major depressive disorder, schizotypal personality disorder, and cyclothymic disorder.

Of note is that each of the segments just discussed does not demonstrate any intrinsic alterations in inferential reasoning. Instead, difficulties reflect the flow of sentences and the degree that each coheres to a common theme or topic. Actual breakdowns in reasoning are referred to as illogical thinking. A now classic example was cited by Arieti[7]:

> *I am a virgin. The Virgin Mary is a virgin. Therefore I am the Virgin Mary.*

Perseveration reflects the repeated use of particular words or phrases. It is commonly seen in patients with memory impairments resulting from dementia or lesions involving the hippocampal system and less often in patients with schizophrenia.

Another speech impairment is defined by reduced conversational output and is referred to as poverty of speech. Spontaneous speech is markedly diminished or absent, and responses to questions are met with replies consisting of only a few words. Poverty of speech, or alogia, can be seen in schizophrenia and depression. Patients with anterior aphasia also demonstrate poverty of speech because of impairment in the motor areas of the brain dedicated to speech production. Patients with so-called fluent aphasia (associated with posterior lesions) can also demonstrate poverty of speech during their recovery process; it is likely that these patients curtail their speech production as they become increasingly aware of its intrinsic disorganization. Extreme poverty of speech is known as mutism and can be seen in schizophrenia, dissociative disturbances, catatonic syndromes, and a wide range of brain lesions. Catatonic syndromes are also associated with echolalia, in which the speaker automatically reproduces words or phrases uttered by the interviewer. Thought blocking is extreme poverty of speech that occurs episodically. Patients with this symptom report either that their minds "just go blank" or that they are flooded with racing thoughts and cannot sort out a particular message to articulate. Thought blocking is often accompanied by considerable anxiety, which often worsens this symptom. When the patient perseverates on the same word, phrase, or theme, especially if the patient is vague or elliptical, poverty of content of speech can occur even if a normal amount of speech is produced. Poverty of content of speech is most closely associated with schizophrenia and various aphasic syndromes.

Concrete speech involves the use of literal meaning. Verbalizing in conceptually abstract, contextual frames is absent, as is the ability to use metaphor:

> ***Question:*** *What happened recently that brought you into the hospital?*
> ***Answer:*** *A taxi came.*

At times, patients produce "lower level" impairments in word construction and selection and in sentence syntax, which provide important clinical information. Consider, for instance, the following utterances:

> *he is a* grašsical *person*[8]
> *he still had* fooch *with* teykrimez, *I'll be willing to betcha*[9]

These nonwords are characteristic of patients with aphasia caused by impairment of dominant cerebral hemisphere speech centers but can also be produced sporadically by patients with severe schizophrenia.

Another type of lexical deviance occurring in schizophrenic and aphasic speech reflects words inappropriately combined with grammatical endings or other words:

> *attain* vigoration *and strength*[8]
> *stated not necessarily* factuated[10]
> *that's a lie-truth*[11]

Slips of the tongue are nonwords that reflect the exchange of phonemes within a phrase:

> soul hecond *path (intended: whole second path)*[9]

or the fusion of words within a phrase:

> *a prettiotic idea (intended: a pretty idiotic idea)*[12]

In general, spontaneously produced nonwords that are not slips of the tongue are referred to as neologisms in the psychiatric literature and paraphasias in the neurology literature.

Patients can also demonstrate word-finding problems that result in inappropriate insertion of lexical elements into sentences. A "mild" example is

> *He owns a store on Fifth Avenue, and that's never mentioned because that is his* side-kick *(intended: side-line).*[13]

An example of a more severe error in word selection corresponds to a noun inappropriately inserted into a verb slot of sentence structure:

> *fish* school *in their own communities*[13]

Psychotic and aphasic patients, moreover, may also produce paragrammatisms, that is, utterances in which word order or word combinations deviate from acceptable syntactic forms. An example (which also includes a paraphasia) that still expresses the remnants of grammatical structure follows:

> *That's why, you know, the fact there was no stigmatism (sic) attached to that clearly explained in the record why you were put back.*[8]

More deviant utterances of this type are referred to as word salad or incoherence:

> *The honest bring-back-to-life doctors agents must take John Black out through making up design meaning straight neutral underworld shadow tunnel.*[9]

Severely psychotic patients may produce sporadic neologistic or paragrammatical constructions. Prolonged social isolation or sustained alienation from other human beings, coupled with bizarre ideation, may, over time, lead the schizophrenic patient to disregard the constraints of ordinary language. If persistently expressed during most utterances, such deviance is much more likely to be produced by patients with aphasia caused by a detectable lesion of the dominant hemisphere.[14] Patients with temporal lobe epilepsy may at times produce mild, episodic word generation difficulties and paragrammatisms, but these generally occur in the absence of formal thought disorder as defined earlier.

With stuttering, there is a clear interruption of the flow, rhythm, and completeness of syllables, words, and phrases, but meaning and context are unaffected. Speech is spasmatic and uncoordinated, and, like other dysarthrias, appears related to problems in the muscular coordination of speech.

Finally, it should noted most of us are far from perfect speakers. Slips of the tongue, errors in word selection, garbled words, tangentiality, and even frank looseness of associations can be produced sporadically by normal individuals, especially under conditions of heightened arousal or fatigue. Therefore, an important aspect of speech behavior is self-monitoring and subsequent correction of momentary speech irregularities. A failure to recognize and correct one's own speech irregularities may be an important clue that a significant pathological condition is being expressed. Table 24–1 summarizes disorders of speech.

Disorders of Thought

First, a simple observation. Many psychiatric disorders present with repetitive mental content, and almost all psychiatric disorders impose some curtailment on content variance. Consider, for instance, the psychotic person who harbors the belief that the Central Intelligence Agency is spying on him. He might find evidence for this belief in unaccounted-for clicks on the telephone (thus, the telephone is being bugged); cars whose license plates contain the letters C, I, or A; or myriad other pieces of data that he is condemned to discover in his daily life. Almost independently of the range of input information received, the patient ends up drawing the same conclusion and is unwilling to consider alternative explanations for experiences. Depressed patients often have certain negative ideas that they constantly return to. Their minds can become remarkably adept at discovering evidence in daily experience that they are worthless or that they do not deserve to live. Heroin addicts cannot help but think about the next fix, their "works" (the tools used to inject the drug), and the person who supplies the drug. Patients with posttraumatic stress disorder are condemned to relive certain memories of the trauma.

How does psychiatric nomenclature distinguish among these experiences? First consider delusions. These are false beliefs that are not widely endorsed by other members of the societal group. However, this cannot be all that there is to the definition, because we are all liable to have false beliefs

Table 24–1 Disorders of Speech

Disorder	Definition
Looseness of association	Idiosyncratic shifts in frame of reference, failure in elaborating topic
Flight of ideas	Shifts in frame of reference but greater coherence and meaning within the frame
Clang association	Shift in frame of reference driven by phonetic similarity of words rather than topical relationships
Pressured speech	Speech produced at an abnormally high rate
Tangentiality	Less abrupt shifts in frame of reference; at any given time, message is coherent, with deviation from initial topic
Circumstantiality	Similar to tangentiality but with return to the original topic
Illogical thinking	Breakdowns in reasoning
Perseveration	Inappropriate repetition of words or phrases
Poverty of speech	Reduced conversational output
Neologism	Nonword phonetic combinations used as words
Paragrammatism	Ungrammatical word sequences
Word salad or incoherence	Combination of words or phrases that renders utterance devoid of decodeable meaning
Mutism	Persistent total absence of speech
Thought blocking	Episodic interruption of speech

whether they are societally endorsed or not. Delusions are false beliefs that are invulnerable to invalidation even if the patient is presented with overwhelming evidence to the contrary. For instance, a delusional patient will believe that her room is bugged even after the room has been completely torn apart looking for the bug.

In contrast, obsessions are preoccupations that the patient is able to acknowledge are irrationally based. Compulsions are repetitive actions due to obsessions. There are a number of fairly typical obsessions, including a preoccupation with dirt, contamination, or disease, which may be accompanied by ritualized behavior such as repeated hand washing. Repetitive checking is another typical obsessive syndrome, in which the individual is preoccupied with permitting certain potentially dangerous situations to go uncorrected (e.g., leaving home without unplugging appliances, leaving doors unlocked). Repeated verification of the fact that no such risk exists only temporarily alleviates the anxiety associated with the preoccupation. It is as if the patient cannot retain the memory that the front door was checked minutes earlier. Checking is often conducted in a ritualized fashion, for instance, by repeating the check a predetermined number of times while repeating the Lord's Prayer. A third common syndrome is obsessional orderliness. Here, certain objects need to be arranged in precise order, at times to an absurd degree. Obsessions are generally associated with anxiety and the expectation that terrible consequences will occur (e.g., the house will burn down, the family will be killed) if ritualized behaviors are not completed. Even though the patient will acknowledge that these preoccupations are not rationally based, they can come to dominate his or her entire life. These preoccupations are future oriented. Patients are condemned to ask themselves repeatedly, "What can I can do to avert future disaster?"

Ruminations generally have a basis in a true past experience of the patient. A typical example is a preoccupation with the loss or betrayal of a loved one. Ruminations, in general, are concerned with the irreversibility of certain past events and are associated with affects such as remorse and sadness.

When severe, obsessions and ruminations can assume psychotic proportions. In other words, the patient's awareness of the irrationality of the preoccupation is lost. Persistent compulsions can evolve into belief, as illustrated in the following vignette.

Clinical Vignette 1

A 19-year-old man had a long-standing compulsion to pick up trash on the street and endlessly sort through this collection at home. The elusive nature of "insight" was particularly striking in this patient. Although he found these habits disturbing and attempted to resist them, over time he began to express the conviction that these activities were his "special mission" in life and, later, that the objects were commanding him to perform the rituals.

Adapted from Fenton and McGlashan.[15]
Copyright 1986, the American Psychiatric Association. Reprinted by permission.

Delusions commonly invoke "unseen" forces or processes (aliens, secret agents, the devil) because they de facto are difficult or impossible to verify by direct experience. This contributes to the irrefutability of the delusion. A more subtle example of this same phenomenon (in this case accompanied by a clinical depression) is as follows:

Clinical Vignette 2

A 38-year-old woman read in the newspaper that an automobile accident resulting in the death of a boy occurred on a country road near her home. She determined that she had driven down that road the same night, although she could not recall seeing the boy. Nonetheless, she became convinced that she killed him. Police reports and the absence of any telltale damage to her car did not diminish her belief. What haunted her was that she could not go back in time to view the accident. This "opportunity" to absolutely ascertain the truth was forever lost. She consequently attempted to give money to the family of the deceased and attempted to arrange for her own arrest.

The "invisibility" of delusional material also applies to many somatic delusions, such as the belief that the insides of one's body are rotting (typically associated with psychotic depression or schizophrenia). A common delusion among patients with schizophrenia in rural Africa is that a snake has occupied one's intestines. In these cases, the fact that one cannot directly look inside one's own body sustains the delusional conviction.

Certain common themes cut across a spectrum ranging from normal to psychotic. Many otherwise normal individuals can be said to have overvalued ideas. These are pet peeves (e.g., the government collects too many taxes) or fixed beliefs (e.g., all men cannot be trusted) that are viewed as meritorious and, therefore, are often shared with or imposed on other people. In contrast, an obsession is a preoccupation that is associated with anxiety, is often viewed as being unhelpful or irrational because day-to-day activities are disrupted, and may thereby be kept entirely private by the patient. In cases of characterological narcissism, all the ideas arising from an individual are more or less overvalued: "What I do, think, or say should be paid attention to by others." Grandiosity takes this theme one step further: "What I do, think, or say is better than what others do, think, or say." Grandiose delusions reflect the extreme case, namely, fixed beliefs that go beyond attributions of individual value or worth by distorting reality, for example, "I am really a rock star, the Pope, Jesus Christ, the next President, the illegitimate son of Queen Elizabeth." The mirror opposite of this spectrum is also evident. A failure to positively endorse one's own ideas or self-worth can evolve into hopelessness, suicidality, and a sense of worthlessness.

Another theme that is expressed across the spectrum of normality to psychosis involves attributing negative intentions to other persons or groups of people. The normal variant is suspiciousness, that is, a cautious attitude derived from the possibility that certain individuals may be harboring malevolent wishes. In contrast, a phobia reflects fearfulness, not related to the intentions of others but instead to the nonhuman environment (fear of heights, elevators, dogs, and so forth). Paranoia reflects a level of suspiciousness that alters routine activities in nonadaptive ways and is accompanied by a tendency to misinterpret ambiguous events or actions in a fashion that reinforces the attribution of malevolent intentions of others. Intrinsic to the nature of paranoia is the belief in some more or less organized "plot." For instance, if a person has become paranoid at work it is often accompanied by the belief that one or more individuals share a common goal (e.g., coworkers are trying to get the patient fired), rather than a general, free-floating fearfulness. This leads inexorably to certain types of inferences that are consistent with the paranoid orientation, for instance, that a filing error committed while the patient was working was actually "planted" by a coworker. This belief orientation can reach the level of a paranoid delusion, in which reality testing is consistently and obviously distorted to maintain the belief orientation that others are intending harm.

Frequently associated with a paranoid orientation is self-referential thinking. Individuals with this symptom believe that people are paying special attention to them on the street or that strangers seem to be talking about them behind their backs. It is not uncommon for patients with grandiosity to become self-referential, because grandiosity leads to an expanded sense of self-importance; these inflated self-opinions lead to the expectation that others are paying special attention to the patient. Self-referential thinking, in turn, can lead to frank paranoid ideation. A typical reasoning process is as follows: if other people are paying so much attention to me, they might wish to thwart my exceptional abilities or in some way stand in my way (e.g., to become the next Christ). This trend in symptom development is fostered by the fact that the actions and behavior of the grandiose individual are generally not endorsed by others and may, for obvious reasons, be thwarted by others. Thus, it is not uncommon that the initial grandiosity due to a manic disorder evolves into a primarily paranoid orientation.

Other kinds of thought content disturbances reflect how patients perceive their own mental or perceptual processes. A common example of this sort of disturbance is racing thoughts. Here, thoughts and mental images occur so rapidly that patients themselves cannot keep track of what they are thinking. Often, but not inevitably, racing thoughts are accompanied by speech irregularities such as looseness of association or tangentiality. Some patients can compensate for such thought content disturbances by reducing the rate or amount of speech produced.

Some patients, particularly those who have paranoid tendencies, report that others can read their minds (referred to as thought broadcasting) or that they themselves are capable of mind reading. Other patients report receiving messages from the television or radio. This is a special form of self-referential thinking; these patients have the uncanny sense that the radio or television announcer, song, or commercial somehow has broadcast a message directly to them. Thought control refers to the belief that other individuals or powers can actually direct the content of one's own thoughts. A related, usually milder, self-referential focus is seen with magical thinking. In magical thinking, one's own thoughts, feelings, or behaviors are believed unrealistically to influence external events and history, for example, wishing harm on another can actually make it happen. Magical thinking is frequently seen in earlier developmental stages, as in the child's chant, "step on a crack, break your mother's back."

Often, many disordered elements of thought present simultaneously. The following clinical vignette is an illustration.

Clinical Vignette 3

When Mr. S entered the hospital he was 26 years old, was single, and had been continuously ill for 9 years, during which time he had been hospitalized 12 times. Despite adequate medication, he could slip into a confused state replete with paralyzing ambivalence and a fragmented delusional paranoid experience in which he felt assaulted by painful tactile hallucinations. During some agitated periods, Mr. S seemed to be experiencing an elemental dread about possessing some powerful, aggressive, evil force capable of destroying his most cherished objects and himself. Once, while pacing, he said to his therapist, "Get out of here! I'm insane! You're breathing my air!" Later, he told his therapist that mental illness could be passed through the air like germs. While agitated, he often hid his face and later told his therapist it was so he could not see the flesh peeling off his evil skull, the sight of which could destroy the therapist by driving him insane.

Adapted from McGlashan.[16]

Mr. S's world was filled with delusions (he was assaulted by the therapist), magical thinking (psychosis is contagious by proximity), grandiosity (he had the power to destroy others), and projected paranoid ruminations (the therapist should fear him and avoid his destructiveness).

A variety of repetitive thoughts, obsessions, ruminations, or delusions may be depressive and self-destructive in content, especially among the mood disorders, schizophrenic disorders (Mr. S's experiences bordered on the depressive spectrum), and borderline personality disorders. Hopelessness, feelings of personal worthlessness, and guilt are frequent cognitive schema that accompany downturns in mood. In their most severe forms, such ideas become delusional reality as convictions that one is dead, dying, doomed, or dangerous. Unrealistic worries about one's health, or hypochondriasis, can become nihilistic somatic delusions that one's brain is dust or one's insides have turned to excrement.

Suicidal thoughts are also common and often of major concern. Passive suicidal ideation consists of wishes to be dead, but with no clear intent or plan. Active thoughts about killing or hurting oneself, especially if elaborated into a plan, represent incremental leaps in dangerousness and often require hospitalization and careful monitoring. Unfortunately, such ideation can be unpredictable and not always congruent with a depressed mood, as in psychotic states:

Clinical Vignette 4

A 22-year-old man with two prior episodes of disorganized schizophrenia stopped his neuroleptic medication. Two months later he lost a bet when his favorite soccer team was beaten in World Cup competition. After the game, while watching a late night television talk show, he became disgusted with what he considered to be a poor performance of the talk show host and decided to kill himself. He took a massive and potentially lethal overdose of a relative's benzodiazepines and was later taken to the emergency department when he could not be aroused by his family.

Tables 24–2 and 24–3 summarize disorders of thought content.

Table 24–2 Disorders of Thought Content

Disorder	Definition
Delusion	False belief not endorsed by social group, relatively impervious to invalidation
Obsession	Preoccupation acknowledged by patient to be irrational and associated with anxiety
Compulsion	Repetitive actions based on obsession
Rumination	Preoccupation generally associated with the irreversibility of past events
Overvalued idea	Frequently endorsed idea, often imposed on others
Grandiosity	Belief that one's ideas, capacities, or actions are generally superior to those of others
Suspiciousness	A cautious attitude based on possible malevolent intentions of others
Phobia	Persistent and irrational fear of delineated aspects of nonhuman environment (e.g., "germs," heights)
Paranoia	Level of suspiciousness altering thinking and behavior in nonadaptive ways

Perceptual Disturbances

Sensory impressions of the external world obviously form the basis of much conscious experience. However, much of our conscious experience is generated internally. How do I know that I am thinking of a particular person? I "see" an image of that person in my mind, or inwardly "say" the name. Indeed, we can experience internally generated images involving one or more of all five sensory realms. We can "hear" a piece of music as well as imagine the smell of coffee, a feeling of cotton on the forearm, or hitting a good tennis backhand. All are different kinds of internally generated images that reaccess representational capabilities emerging from the senses. We ordinarily do not label such internally generated images as indicative of psychopathology.

As indicated in our introductory remarks, there is a continuum between ordinary self-generated imagery and pathological hallucination.[2, 5] Consider first illusions, namely, external sensory impressions that have been temporarily imbued with a novel interpretation. An example is seeing a cloud pattern that resembles the profile or face of, for instance, a famous figure or one's father. This experience in itself would not be considered pathological. This same experience becomes a delusional perception if the person maintains the conviction that the face was not an accidental pattern but was in some sense an actual visual re-creation of Abraham Lincoln's face (or the father) that was somehow intended by some force or agency. Here, pathology is intrinsic to inferences that are generated about the percept rather than the percept itself.

At the other end of the axis are hallucinations, which in their purest form are percepts that occur spontaneously (i.e., in the absence of particular sensory triggers).

Illusions and hallucinations are underappreciated aspects of normal experience. Preoccupation with another

Table 24–3 Alterations in the Experience of One's Own Thought and Perception

Disorder	Definition
Racing thoughts	Thoughts or images experienced as occurring at excessive rate
Thought broadcasting	One's own thoughts experienced as being transmitted to another person or agency
Thought control	Other people or forces controlling or directing one's thoughts
Magical thinking	An irrational belief that thoughts can change external events without intervening actions
Referential thinking	Perceptions of other people's actions or speech accompanied by belief that they are directed to or are in reference to the self

person (e.g., a lost loved one, a feared authority figure) can result in a fleeting visual illusion among normal individuals—momentarily seeing the longed-for person in a crowd or at a distance. A person in mourning may see the silhouette of the lost person in a shadow or hear that person's voice speaking. A common, normal experience is to misperceive indistinct sounds as a spoken word corresponding to one's own name. Complex visual scenes and sounds can be experienced during daydreams or at the onset of sleep or waking.[17, 18] When especially vivid, such imagery is referred to as hypnagogic hallucination when occurring at sleep onset and hypnopompic hallucination when occurring during drowsiness on waking from sleep. Dreams themselves are clearly hallucinations. Imagery can be quite vivid, and ordinarily the dreamer has the sustained conviction of the reality of the dream. A reasonable position is to assert that illusion and hallucination are not intrinsically pathological; pathology reflects the relative intractability of beliefs that emerge in response to the experience. For instance, the normal individual quickly realizes that the identity of a misapprehended person was mistaken; the momentary hallucination of a daydream is not retained as an accurate reflection of reality. The psychotic person, on the other hand, may not able to mentally correct the original misapprehension.

Psychotic states can result in hallucinations related to any one of the five senses. Visions of objects or persons, smells, and tactile sensations can be reported by patients with schizophrenia, mood disorders, similar states caused by medical conditions or induced by drugs, and various forms of epilepsy.

Among schizophrenic patients, however, the most common sensory modality of hallucinations is auditory. Auditory hallucinations can consist of various meaningless sounds (e.g., buzzes, hums, or rumbles), but most commonly spoken words, phrases, or sentences are heard.[5] Hallucinated speech consists of one or many voices that ordinarily have distinct acoustic characteristics (such as male versus female, high versus low pitched). For schizophrenic patients, hallucinated voices tend to use words and phrases that are constrained in terms of meaning. For instance, one voice will tend to be highly critical (repetitively using the same words, such as "you are ugly"), whereas another voice will repeat reassuring words, such as, "I love you." Hallucinations often express words or phrases that are not grammatical language, for instance, strings of numbers or jumbled phrases. These hallucinations are also tend to be repeated, and in time special meanings are attributed to them by the patient. For instance, one schizophrenic patient repeatedly heard the spoken numbers "three-nine" and came to believe that this was a message from her brother, who was 39 years old. Later, she concluded her brother was actually speaking to her.

Sometimes the acoustic qualities of the hallucinated voice are the same as the patient's own speaking voice. This suggests that these hallucinations are related to normal inner speech, that is, the words that we ordinarily say inwardly to ourselves. Nonetheless, such imagistic experiences are identified by the patient as hallucinations because they are experienced as alien, out of their control, and generated by an outside or nonself agency (such as another person or the Central Intelligence Agency). In other words, attribution of alien willfulness appears to be a primary determinant of the level of distress and pathology associated with the hallucination.[5] Vividness of voices (loudness and clarity of the speech percepts) and the degree that the spoken message deviates from thoughts of patients also contribute to the level of distress experienced by patients in response to these symptoms.

Voices are also commonly reported by patients with certain types of dissociative disorders. These voices can occur with distinct acoustic characteristics associated with particular internalized "personalities." However, these hallucinations generally yield running commentaries or conversational speech that lack the recurrent or idiosyncratic semantic content of voices experienced by patients with schizophrenia.

The British psychiatric tradition uses the term pseudohallucinations to refer to hallucinatory experiences that have the actuality or objectivity of externally derived percepts but nonetheless are known by the subject to have no external correlate.[19] This definition is often difficult to put into practice because the insight of a patient regarding the origin of these experiences often fluctuates from hour to hour. An alternative definition deriving from the German school associates pseudohallucinations with vivid images that are heard or seen from within.[20] Many such hallucinations (such as afterimages or visual imagery during drowsiness) are nonpathological. Pseudohallucinations are often reported by patients with psychotic disorders. In general, the hallucinated voices reported by patients with dissociative identity disorder are "heard from within."

So-called functional hallucinations are also intermediate phenomena; they are percept-like and are attributed to an external reality but are triggered by an external stimulus. These experiences are not classified as illusions because perceptual representations clearly depart from information derived from an external stimulus. Functional hallucinations of voices are often reported by psychiatric patients, prompted by, for instance, the background blur of indistinct voices in a crowd, running water, or even the hum of a refrigerator. For a given patient, the content and vocal characteristics of voices triggered by external sound are generally similar or identical to their spontaneous hallucinated voices.

Table 24–4 summarizes disorders of perception.

Table 24–4 Disorders of Perception

Disorder	Definition
Illusions	Sensory impressions temporarily imbued with a novel interpretation
Delusional perception	Delusional misinterpretation of a perception or illusion
Hallucination	Percept occurring in the absence of any particular sensory triggers
Pseudohallucination	Hallucinatory percept known by the subject to be self-derived or experienced as occurring from within the mind
Functional hallucination	Percept-like, triggered by an external stimulus but clearly departing from information intrinsic to stimulus

Disorders of Identity and Will

Some of the most fascinating expressions of psychopathology emerge as disorders of self-experience, variably manifested as problems of will, identity, self-integration, or self-awareness.

Disorders of will (also known as conative functions) are seen most commonly in psychotic states. Loss of willfulness is seem at its most extreme in catatonic waxy flexibility, echolalia, and echopraxia, but in milder forms it can frequently be detected in schizophrenia, depression, obsessive-compulsive disorder, and posttraumatic states. Mania, in contrast, might be characterized as an overabundance of willful intentions.

Patients who experience thought control believe that certain of their thoughts are willed by some agency or person outside their mind or body. Often, different instances of thoughts that are experienced as being controlled have similar content. For instance, a patient might involuntarily and repetitively experience the thought of wanting to kill a spouse. If experienced as his or her own thought, this experience would be classified as an obsession. If the patient believes that the thoughts are placed in her or his head by the devil, these experiences would be identified as thought control of delusional proportion.

Another example of a disorder of will is so-called the delusion of passivity. In this delusion, patients believe that their actions are controlled by some other being or agency.

Among the most striking forms of identity disturbance are distortions of body image, which contain sensory and cognitive elements to varying degrees. With the phantom limb phenomenon after an amputation, for example, the lost arm or leg retains its perceptual reality. In some forms of transsexualism, body distortion is more ideational, that is, the person harbors the conviction that he is really a female trapped in a male body. In this case, reality testing of the actual anatomy is retained, unlike some cases of severe anorexia nervosa in which the patient insists that she is obese despite clear and objective evidence to the contrary. A variety of body image distortions are displayed in body dysmorphic disorder. These are usually cosmetic in nature; imagined defects in appearance become overwhelming obsessions and compel afflicted patients to seek out plastic surgery or other body-altering treatments on repeated occasions. If these ruminations reach delusional intensity and conviction, the *Diagnostic and Statistical Manual of Mental Disorders,* Fourth Edition (DSM-IV),[21] identifies the syndrome as delusional disorder, somatic type. In this disorder, distortions may become more bizarre (such as a belief of having two heads) and may be accompanied by hallucinations of foul body odor or of insects crawling under the skin (formication).

Dissociation and its related disorders form sets of phenomena that are rich in complexity, often perplexing diagnostically, and occasionally sensational and dramatic in presentation. Dissociation refers to the splitting off of thoughts, feelings, or behaviors from everyday integrated awareness. The dissociative process may involve specific ideas, moods, or deeds, or it may involve complex patterns of behavior, that is, personality states.

It is important to note that dissociation is a normal adaptive mental function. Our everyday tasks of focusing attention and compartmentalizing experience involve dissociation. Normal dissociation is also displayed more explicitly in the phenomenon of hypnosis. The ability to enter different levels of hypnotic trance may be normally distributed in the population. Some people cannot experience hypnosis; other people enter deep trances easily (somnambulists); most people range somewhere in between. The trance state is a mixture of intense absorption with one idea or activity, dissociation from other experiences and sensations, and heightened suggestibility to instruction and demand characteristics of the social situation.[22, 23] In dissociated hypnotic trance states, anesthesia can occur by suggestion,[24] and other alterations in consciousness can be induced that mimic many of the DSM-IV dissociative disorders, for example, positive and negative (pseudo)hallucinations, voluntary muscle (conversion) paralysis, posthypnotic amnesias, and posthypnotic suggestion.

The phenomenology of posttraumatic disorders may represent another form of normal dissociation insofar as dissociation represents a normal response to major stress ("I am not here" or "This is not happening to me") that fosters adaptation under extreme conditions. The subsequent interaction between reexperiencing memories (often with hallucinatory vividness) and symptoms of distancing or numbing may also represent dissociation at work in modulating the psychological processing and integration of trauma. When the dissociative process is prolonged and perseverative, however, it becomes pathological, and disorder supersedes adaptation.

A relatively common dissociative disorder of self-experience is depersonalization. Patients with this syndrome report that they feel detached or estranged from themselves. Other associated symptoms include feeling like an automaton, a sense that one is actually outside one's own body, or feeling that parts of one's body are detached from each other.[20] A related symptom is derealization, which consists of the experience that one's self is somehow removed from the world, or that the immediate sensations of the environment are unreal or somehow inaccessible. This constellation of experience can be seen normally at times of exhaustion or bereavement and is associated with many psychiatric disorders, including schizophrenia, panic disorder, substance-induced states, and dissociative disorders, or it may occur as a separate disorder. The most intense and concrete form of derealization may be hysterical conversion, in which sensory anesthesia or motor paralysis ensues based on a dissociated idea.

Other dissociative disorders less frequently encountered involve amnesias, that is, whole time periods lost to memory, usually associated with some negative experience. Rarely, patients may develop a fugue state, that is, amnesia of their entire past in which they adopt a new identity in life. Most publicized but perhaps rarest of all is dissociative identity disorder, or the appearance of more than one distinct identity or personality states in the same person. Several personality states are the rule, usually manifested one at a time and usually dissociated from each other with varying levels of awareness. These identities or personality states have their own characterological profiles. When a person with dissociative identity disorder is in a particular personality, he or she may talk and dress differently and even assume a different name.

Some psychotic syndromes appear related to dissociation and depersonalization, at least on a phenomenological level. One such entity is Capgras' syndrome, in which patients report that other people are no longer real or are doubles. These beliefs can extend to family members and friends, that is, individuals who are known intimately by the patient. The experience is captured in the well-known movie *Invasion of the Body Snatchers*.

Another rare disorder of identity is called pseudologia phantasica. In this disorder, patients are compelled to enact certain belief orientations or assume certain roles even though they know that it is "all an act." An example of this disorder is given in the following vignette.

Clinical Vignette 5

A 28-year-old woman, during a period of 2 years, was compelled to portray herself as the daughter of a famous actress. This included changing her name, writing factitious letters from the actress to herself, and arranging for herself to receive faked telephone calls and telegrams. All the while she was very afraid that she would be discovered as a fraud.

Probably related to pseudologia phantasica is Munchausen's syndrome. The syndrome is named after Baron von Munchausen, a German soldier and traveler of the 18th century who was legendary for his exaggerated tales of accomplishment. The medical use of the term is restricted to patients who feign medical disorders. These individuals, for instance, may swallow blood and induce vomiting to mimic a bleeding ulcer or present in an emergency department with all the signs and symptoms of a perforated appendix. These individuals are often successful in obtaining extensive medical treatment, including multiple major surgical interventions. Patients who feign the symptoms of mental disorders to become patients (but not for external incentives, such as obtaining financial benefits) are diagnosed as having factitious disorders.

Finally, dissociation is common among psychotic disorders as an obvious curtailment or incongruity of feeling with respect to expressed ideas. The former is referred to as blunted affect, the latter as inappropriate affect. Both are common in schizophrenia.

Clinical Vignette 6

Mr. B's onset of schizophrenia came at age 14. By age 21 he had experienced 3 hospitalizations covering a total of 2½ years. He seldom experienced differentiated feelings and reported bafflement with people who did. In one therapy session he said, "I have an assumption that I'm alive," and he noted that he couldn't "hold onto" feelings about people from the past like his mother and father. He said "You see, I would die if I was feeling . . . I don't have natural reality like others because I'm not living. I'm always in a place of ever death . . . you have a language that I don't understand though I know you want me to learn it. You want me to want."

Adapted from McGlashan.[16]

Agnosias are massive deficits in self-experience usually related to brain damage. They consist of failures to recognize major changes in one's self and functioning. For example, in autotopagnosia, there is denial of hemiparesis and/or blindness (usually left sided) secondary to right parietal lesions, most frequently resulting from stroke. Sometimes the raw sensory data are intact but the patient is unable to interpret their significance and meaning. In visual agnosia, objects and people are seen but not recognized. In astereognosis, objects cannot be recognized by touch. In prosopagnosia, faces cannot be identified.

The most common and striking agnostic deficit is anosognosia, in which the patient steadfastly refuses to acknowledge that she or he has any illness despite overwhelming evidence to the contrary. Sometimes disability is acknowledged cognitively but not affectively or conatively. The patient persistently ignores the problem and behaves as though it is not there even when the presence of the disorder is acknowledged on direct questioning. This anosodiaphoria or indifference to disability is seen in a milder, functional form as *la belle indifférence*, or calmness in the face of disability associated with conversion hysteria.

Unawareness of illness can take many other forms and is commonly part of psychiatric disorders, especially the psychoses.[25] Some form and degree of illness denial or lack of awareness can be seen in most cases of schizophrenia, although the effect of this deficit on judgment and treatment compliance is hard to predict.

Table 24–5 Disorders of Integrated (Self) Experience

Disorder	Definition
Distortions of will	Misattribution of personal responsibility for mental and/or behavioral events, the self experienced as passively controlled or actively manipulating others' thoughts, feelings, or behaviors
Distortions of body image	Misapprehension of body sensation, anatomy, or function
Dissociation	Splitting off of thoughts, feelings, or behaviors from everyday integrated conscious awareness
Depersonalization	Estrangement or detachment from a sense of personal, existential presence
Derealization	Perception of the world without a simultaneous feeling or conviction of its reality
Blunted affect	Diminution or absence of associated feeling
Inappropriate affect	Incongruous association of idea and feeling
Agnosia	Deficits in recognition and understanding
Anosognosia	Deficit in recognizing and/or understanding obvious neurologically determined disability
Unawareness of illness	Truncated insight into psychiatrically determined disability ranging from inattention to complete denial

Insight is a complex construct with many levels, and loss of insight can become manifest at every one. Complete insight into schizophrenic illness, for example, involves understanding the nature of schizophrenia as a psychotic mental disorder and the lifelong treatment implications of having that diagnosis. At a less than complete level, patients acknowledge that something is wrong and that they need help. Insight is further truncated in patients who deny illness but recognize that others think differently and want the patients to accept treatment for everyone's peace of mind. Many patients deny vehemently that illness is present when asked, but nonetheless behave in total compliance with the treatment expectations presented to them. Finally, there are those, unfortunately all too common, who are unaware of their illness and noncompliant with treatment. Here, lack of insight has a profound and often destructive effect on judgment.

Table 24–5 summarizes disorders of self-experience.

Conclusion

Our psychiatric nomenclature reflects the fact that disorders of speech, thought, perception, and self-experience reflect a continuum ranging between normal and extremely disturbed. We have tended to discuss each manifestation singly. However, it should be again stressed that symptoms in one realm commonly cross over and influence or induce symptoms in other realms. For instance, a patient with a delusion or severe obsession might be pulled conversationally off track during a clinical interview, producing tangentiality or circumstantiality. A pattern of illusory misperceptions, for instance, momentarily seeing the face of a deceased relative on multiple occasions, could induce the delusion that the relative has come back to life. Moreover, this process could work in reverse; delusional preoccupations often induce misperceptions that support the delusion.

No particular sign or symptom is pathognomonic of these disorders. Clinical assessment is instead designed to generate a gestalt consisting of multiple signs and symptoms that tend to cluster together, which identifies particular psychiatric disorders. These disorders are discussed individually in later chapters.

References

1. Hughlings Jackson J: Factors of insanities. In Taylor J, Holmes G, Walshe FMR (eds): Selected Writings of John Hughlings Jackson, Volume II. London: Hodder & Stoughton, 1932:411–421.
2. Strauss JS: Hallucinations and delusions as points on continua function. Arch Gen Psychiatry 1969; 21:581–586.
3. Andreasen NC: Thought, language and communication disorders: I. Clinical assessment, definition of terms, and evaluation of their reliability. Arch Gen Psychiatry 1979; 36:1315–1321.
4. Hoffman RE, Kirstein L, Stopek S, Cichetti D: Apprehending schizophrenic discourse: A structural analysis of the listener's task. Brain Lang 1982; 15:207–233.
5. Hoffman RE: Verbal hallucinations and language production processes in schizophrenia. Behav Brain Sci 1986; 9:503–548.
6. Hoffman RE, Stopek S, Andreasen NC: A comparative study of manic versus schizophrenic speech disorganization. Arch Gen Psychiatry 1986; 43:831–838.
7. Arieti S: Schizophrenia. In Arieti S (ed): American Handbook of Psychiatry, Volume III, New York: Basic Books, 1974:575.
8. Hoffman RE, Sledge W: A microgenetic model of paragrammatisms produced by a schizophrenic speaker. Brain Lang 1984; 21:147–173.
9. Chaika EA: A linguist looks at "schizophrenic" language. Brain Lang 1974; 1:257–276.
10. Vetter H (ed): Language Behavior in Schizophrenia. Springfield, IL: Charles C Thomas, 1968.
11. Bleuler E: Dementia Praecox or the Group of Schizophrenias. New York: International Universities Press, 1950.
12. Fromkin VA: A linguist looks at "A linguist looks at 'schizophrenic language'." Brain Lang 1975; 2:498–503.
13. Hoffman RE, Sledge W: An analysis of grammatical deviance occurring in spontaneous schizophrenic speech. J Neurolinguistics 1988; 3:89–101.
14. Lecours AR, Vanier-Clement MV: Schizophrenia and jargonaphasia: A comparative description with comments on Chaika's and Fromkin's respective looks at "schizophrenic" language. Brain Lang 1976; 3:516–565.
15. Fenton WS, McGlashan TH: The prognostic significance of obsessive-compulsive symptoms in schizophrenia. Am J Psychiatry 1986; 143:437–441.
16. McGlashan TH: Aphanisis: The syndrome of pseudo-depression in chronic schizophrenia. Schizophr Bull 1986; 8:118–134.
17. Foulkes D, Fleisher S: Mental activity in relaxed wakefulness. J Abnorm Psychol 1975; 84:66–75.
18. Foulkes D, Vogel G: Mental activity at sleep onset. J Abnorm Psychol 1965; 70:231–243.
19. Taylor FK: On pseudo-hallucinations. Psychol Med 1981; 11:265–271.
20. Jaspers K: Zur Analyse der Trugwahrnehmungen (Liebhaftigkeit und Realittsurteil). Z Gesamte Neurol Psychiatr 1911; 6:460–535.
21. American Psychiatric Association: Diagnostic and Statistical Manual of Mental Disorders, 4th ed. Washington, DC: American Psychiatric Association, 1994.
22. Spiegel H, Spiegel D: Trance and Treatment: Clinical Uses of Hypnosis. Washington, DC: American Psychiatric Press, 1987.
23. Orne MT: The nature of hypnosis: Artifact and essence. J Abnorm Soc Psychol 1959; 58:277–299.
24. McGlashan TH, Evans FJ, Orne MT: The nature of hyponotic analgesia and placebo response to experimental pain. Psychosom Med 1969; 30:227–246.
25. Prigatano GP, Schacter DL (eds): Awareness of Deficit After Brain Injury. New York: Oxford University Press, 1991.

CHAPTER

25 Emotions

Robert Kohn
Martin B. Keller

Behavioral, Neurological, and Cognitive Components of Emotion

Emotion is a subjectively experienced feeling that is related to affect and mood. The experience of emotion occurs through a set of expressive behaviors, the function of the nervous system, and cognitive perception or appraisal. Emotion has behavioral, somatic, and psychic components.

Charles Darwin's work on facial expression pioneered the role of expressive behaviors in emotion.[1] Darwin stated that the complex behavioral actions associated with emotions occur to relieve or gratify sensations or desires and that the same movements are repeatedly performed through force of habit. Furthermore, when the opposite state of mind is induced, there is an involuntary tendency to perform movements of the opposite nature. He believed that the behavioral expression of emotion is driven by the nervous system independent of will and, to a large part, independent of habit.

The basic patterns of emotional expression are present at birth and vary little with age and across cultures. By 3 months of age, infant and adult facial expressions of certain emotions are similar.[2, 3] The facial expressions and emotions of infants differ little cross-culturally.[4] It is this nonverbal expression of emotion that the infant uses to communicate with the parent and that the parent uses to determine the needs of the infant. Although emotional expression is considered innate, it can be modified through learning and maturation.[5]

Ten basic, fundamentally different expressions of emotion have been proposed by Izard[6] (Table 25–1). These different emotions can be combined with one another to produce distinct behavioral reactions within and between individuals.[5] The basic emotions are differentiated not only by behavioral expression but also at the psychophysiological and neurobiological levels. The expressive behavioral tradition for the study of emotion assumes that it is the expressive behavior that results in the experience of affect through autonomic or central nervous system activation and that facial expression is the primary component of emotion.[5]

A related theory, known as the James-Lange theory,[7] proposes that body changes that differ between the basic emotions are a response to a predisposing event, but the sensation of these body changes and not the event leads to the expression of the emotion. The view that emotional expression is hard-wired is incomplete, because the behavioral, experiential, and somatic or physiological components of emotion are often not correlated.[5]

The role of the nervous system in the study of emotion was initiated by Walter Cannon[8] in experiments in which he surgically removed areas of animal brains. These studies of emotion as primarily a function of the brain suggested that the areas of the brain associated with emotion are phylogenetically more ancient and primitive. Pathological emotions involve the deep brain structures more than the cerebral cortex. Emotional activation may occur without the activation of higher cognitive processes and perhaps through connections with the retina.[9, 10] The deep brain structures that may mediate emotions include the limbic system (including the hypothalamus, septum, hippocampus, amygdala, and cingulum) as well as other bodies (such as the thalamus, locus caeruleus, median raphe nuclei, and dentate nuclei of the cerebellum) and the connections between them. This general neuroanatomical pathway for emotion was originally posited by Papez.[11] Research attempting to locate brain structures associated with specific emotions has been conducted in humans through insertion of electrodes that stimulated or coagulated different parts of the cortex and the deep brain.[12, 13] The subjective emotions elicited in these studies were accompanied by motor and autonomic changes only in the deep brain structures. Site-specific emotional expression has not been demonstrated; the emotion expressed varies under somewhat different conditions, and different structures may produce similar emotional responses.[6, 14, 15]

The neocortex and the cortex have also been demonstrated to play a role in emotion. Orbitomedial frontal leukotomy, for example, reduces anxiety.[16, 17] Laterality of cortical involvement has been demonstrated by some investigators, although the evidence is conflicting.[18] The right side of the cortex is more involved in unpleasant emotions, the left in pleasurable emotions.[19, 20] Perception and expression of emotion may be a right hemisphere function. Right hemisphere damage impairs the ability to express emotions through inflection of the tone of voice.[21]

Neurotransmitters and their presynaptic and postsynaptic receptors seem to mediate emotion within the central

Table 25–1	Izard's Ten Basic Emotions
	Anger
	Contempt
	Disgust
	Fear
	Guilt
	Interest
	Joy
	Sadness or distress
	Shame
	Surprise

nervous system. The possible role of norepinephrine in depression has been suggested by the catecholamine deficiency hypothesis. Many antidepressant drugs increase synaptic concentrations of norepinephrine, whereas reserpine, a catecholamine-depleting drug, causes depressive symptoms.[22, 23] The indolamine hypothesis postulates that depression results from deficits in serotonin. The γ-aminobutyric acid, noradrenergic, and serotoninergic systems have all been shown to mediate forms of anxiety.

A third approach to the study of emotion has been based on the cognitive characterization of emotion. Two competing cognitive explanations have been posited, the appraisal theory and Lang's bioinformational approach. The appraisal theory[24] suggests that emotion is a result of the individual's appraising the context of a situation, attributing a causal relationship after the perception of a generalized, undifferentiated arousal state. There is little evidence to support this theory in its entirety, because emotion can occur in the absence of arousal.[5] Emotion has also been viewed by alternative appraisal theories as an adaptive behavior, which follows changes in the environment that are evaluated in terms of their potential impact on the individual.[25, 26] The appraisal model suggests that an evaluation or appraisal of the environment is connected to the initial stimulus preceding and modifying the emotion. Appraisal theory has difficulty explaining irrational emotions,[5] unless information is appraised and processed by use of an unconscious process.[27]

An alternative cognitive explanation of emotion is the bioinformational approach.[28] Emotion involves processing and accessing information stored in memory. Information on both the stimulus and the response is stored in memory. This information is then interpreted on the basis of the significance of the event, allowing expression of the appropriate emotion in intensity consistent with the stimulus.

Research into emotional states based on factor-analytical approaches has resulted in various models to characterize the range of emotional expression. Factor analysis of dimensions of affect and personality has given rise to dimensional models, which are considered theoretical models to describe not only emotion but also personality. Dimensional models usually attempt to describe emotions in only two or three bidirectional dimensions, such as Eysenck's[29] two-factor model. One axis is called introversion-extroversion, and the other neuroticism-stability. In Eysenck's biological theory, emotions are associated with an individual's level of arousal that is set either too high or too low by the reticular activating system. Extroverts seek out greater stimulation because of low levels of arousal, whereas introverts, who have high levels of arousal, need less stimulation. Neuroticism is theorized to involve the autonomic nervous system; neurotic individuals have increased reactivity in the autonomic nervous system. Emotion results from the interaction of these two axes and the limbic system.

An alternative approach is the circumplex model, in which emotions are placed in a circular order reflecting their relationship to other emotions. The opposite emotion is on the other side of the circle. Tellegen[30] created a circumplex model that is divided into eight sections: strong engagement, high negative affect, unpleasantness, low positive affect, disengagement, low negative affect, pleasantness, and high positive affect. This model can be used to capture the distinction between an anxious, depressed, or manic mood or affect as well as to demonstrate that these moods are a continuum. An anxious mood is considered to be a high negative affect, with descriptors such as distressed, fearful, hostile, jittery, nervous, and scornful. A depressed mood in the circumplex model would be a low positive affect, including descriptors such as being drowsy, dull, sleepy, and sluggish. A manic affect would be captured by terms in the high positive affect dimension: active, elated, enthusiastic, excited, peppy, and strong.

Assessment of Mood and Affect in the Clinical Interview

Two terms are often used to refer to an individual's emotion: affect and mood (Table 25–2). In the absence of a psychopathological process, affect fluctuates with time and context and ranges from sadness to anger to elation, depending on the emotional state. Affect can be expressed through autonomic responses, body movements, and alterations in speech to concrete or abstract stimuli. Observing a violent act exemplifies a concrete stimulus that could lead to the expression of fear; hearing the abstract term love could result in the expression of an elated affect. Speech changes that reflect affect include tone of voice, vocalization, and word selection. Visible autonomic changes that may reflect changes in affect include sweating, trembling, blushing, and becoming flush. Changes in posture, alterations in facial expression, reactive responses, and grooming movements are body changes seen in expression of affect. Reactive movements include movements of the body and face made in response to a novel stimulus, such as in a startle response, when an individual jumps or turns and looks at the stimulus. Changes in facial movements of the mouth, nose, and eyes are found with different affective states. Manipulation of one's appearance is common in states of discomfort; individuals may fix their hair, clean their nails, scratch, or straighten their clothes.

Table 25–2	Affect and Mood
Affect	The observable behavior seen in the expression of emotion. Affect responds to changes in emotional states.
Mood	A sustained and pervasive emotion. Mood is frequently the reported emotional state.

Table 25–3 Disturbances in Affect

Blunted	Severe reduction in the intensity of emotional expression
Fixed	Display of only one particular emotion, and absence of range and mobility of affect
Flat	Near-absence of affective expression
Inappropriate	Emotional expression and thought content do not coincide
Labile	Repeated, rapid, and abrupt variability in affective expression occurs
Restricted or constricted	Mild to moderate reduction in emotional expression

Affect has three functions: self-perception, communication, and motivation.[31] Self-perception is the emotional value judgment or the affective response associated with affect. This function of affect tells one whether an experience is good or bad. A smile or an accelerated heart rate is an example of self-perception. The expression of affect communicates to others our emotional response to events, interactions, behavior, and situations. Affect precedes a behavioral response or motivates it. For example, anger is a precursor to aggression.

Social and cultural norms determine whether an affect is appropriate or disturbed for a given situation. Disturbances in affect (Table 25–3) may be quantitative or qualitative and include blunted, fixed, flat, inappropriate, labile, and restricted or constricted affect.[32(p763)] An appropriate affect, the normal condition, is exemplified by people who are able to express the full range of emotions in a manner consistent with their thoughts and speech.

Evaluation of affect consists of monitoring gestures, body movements, and facial expressions. Because adults are frequently capable of controlling facial expression in attempts to intentionally or unintentionally suppress their affect, other behavioral gestures may give clues to the underlying affect. The quality, duration or mobility, appropriateness, intensity, range, and reactivity or control over the affect should be considered.

The range of the affect is characterized by the variety of emotional expressions noted in a session. Normal individuals express different feelings at different times. Patients who appropriately express many different emotions have a full or broad range of affect. A restricted range of affect is seen in individuals who have a limited emotional expression, whereas a fixed or immobile affect is found in those who display only one type of emotion. The intensity of affect—the strength of the emotional expression—normally varies according to the situation. Those with limited emotional expression may have a blunted or a flattened affect. The mobility of affect is the ease and speed with which one moves from one type of emotion to another. Changes in the type and intensity of emotional expression normally occur gradually. Reduced mobility in affect is also referred to as constricted affect. When the affect is extremely constricted to one emotion, it is called a fixed or immobile affect. When no affect is displayed, it is reported to be flat. Pathologically increased mobility of affect is referred to as labile. The reactivity is the extent to which the affect changes in response to an environmental stimulus. When the patient does not respond to the examiner's provocation, such as joking, the affect is nonreactive[33, 34] (Table 25–4).

Table 25–4 Description of Affect

Parameter of Affect	Normal	Abnormal
Appropriateness	Appropriate Congruent	Inappropriate Incongruent
Intensity	Normal	Blunted Exaggerated Flat Heightened Overly dramatic
Mobility	Mobile	Constricted Fixed Immobile Labile
Range	Full range	Restricted range
Reactivity	Reactive Responsive	Nonreactive Nonresponsive

Adapated from The Psychiatric Mental Status Examination by Paula T. Trzepacz and Robert W. Baker.

Mood and affect are related but differ in their pattern of stability over time. Affect fluctuates, whereas mood is a more pervasive and sustained emotional state.[32(p768)] Unlike affect, which is observed, mood is not always readily discernible or observed but may need to be reported. An alexithymic person is unable to verbalize or has difficulty describing or being aware of emotions or moods. Mood colors an individual's perception of the environment. Mood can be characterized as dysphoric, elevated, expansive, irritable, or euthymic (Table 25–5). Mood is described by its quality, stability, reactivity, intensity, duration, and congruence with thought content (Table 25–6). A particular mood is not necessarily abnormal or pathological but must be evaluated in the context of the patient's entire history and psychiatric mental status examination.

Emotional Expression of Anxiety

Spectrum of Anxiety

Anxiety is an emotion characterized by apprehension and anticipation of future danger or misfortune associated with feelings of dysphoria or somatic symptoms of tension.[32(p764)] The perceived danger may be either an internal or an external fear. The physiological manifestations of anxiety (Table 25–7) may present as symptoms of activation of the autonomic nervous system. Anxiety is a normal reaction to

Table 25–5 Mood States

Dysphoric	Includes sustained emotional states, such as sadness, anxiety, or irritability
Elevated	Exaggerated feeling of well-being, euphoria, or elation
Expansive	Lack of restraint in expressing feelings
Irritable	Easily annoyed or angered
Euthymic	Mood in the normal range

Table 25–6 Clinical Assessment of Mood

Evaluate its quality	How do you feel? What is your mood like?
Evaluate its stability	Do you always feel like this?
Evaluate its reactivity	Does your mood ever change? When does your mood change?
Evaluate its intensity	What is it like to feel this way? On a scale of 1 to 10, how would you rate your mood?
Evaluate its duration	How long have you felt this way?
Evaluate whether the mood is congruent with the thought content	

a situation where immediate danger exists and may result in physical harm. Anxiety is also a normal response to situations that pose a threat to self-esteem or psychological well-being. Pathological anxiety occurs in situations where there is no real physical or psychological danger or when the emotional reaction is disproportionate in intensity to the actual danger.[35]

Etiology of Anxiety

Traditionally, the emotion of anxiety has been dichotomized into fear and neurotic anxiety. Fear, or objective anxiety, as conceptualized by Freud,[36, 37] consisted of three components: a real external danger; an accurate perception of the danger as potentially harmful; and an emotional response of anxiety, which varied in intensity proportional to the magnitude of the objective danger. Neurotic anxiety, as Freud described it, was also a psychobiological process; however, the danger was from within, in the form of forbidden instinctual drives that were punished in childhood, repressed, and subsequently about to escape from the individual's control.[38] Fear and anxiety may be present in varying proportions in a given situation. Elucidating the cause of the affect is more important clinically than determining whether the emotion is fear or anxiety.[39]

More recent theories of the emotion of anxiety can be divided into stimulus-oriented theories and response-oriented theories. The former construct suggests that stimulus events serve to initiate the emotional response. It is the nature of the event—the thoughts, feelings, and situation associated with the event—that precipitates the response. An example of a stimulus-oriented theory is Goldstein's[40] catastrophic reaction. A situation that represents a threat to the individual's existence, physical or psychological, is necessary for impairment of objective behavior resulting in the subjective experience of anxiety.

Table 25–7 Physiological Manifestations of Anxiety

- Elevated blood pressure
- Cardiac discomfort
  - Palpitations
  - Tachycardia
- Diaphoresis
- Dizziness
- Dry mouth
- Irregularities in breathing
  - Hyperventilation
- Musculoskeletal disturbances
  - Restlessness
  - Tremors
  - Weakness

The response-oriented approach focuses on the resultant affect. The response-oriented theorists hold that the anxiety response is the same regardless of the stimulus. Anxiety is an innate emotion resulting from a neurophysiological response that can be modified through learning. Pathological anxiety differs from normal anxiety by the increased intensity, frequency, and duration of the neurophysiological response.

The trait-state dichotomy[41] of anxiety is an outgrowth of the response-oriented theorists. Trait is viewed as a personality feature, whereby the individual consistently behaves anxiously despite the situation. State refers to momentary feelings of anxiety. Despite some detractors to this theoretical distinction,[42] the validity of this dichotomy has been shown in research demonstrating trait anxiety to remain stable over time and to be impervious to stress, despite circumstances.[35] The stimuli that elicit anxiety according to trait-state anxiety theory (Fig. 25–1) may be either intrapsychic or from environmental sources. Anxiety from situations that threaten personal adequacy is found more often in individuals with high trait anxiety.

Other cognitive theories of anxiety are outgrowths of the response-oriented view. Beck and colleagues[43] believed that anxiety results from a misperception of danger or an unrealistic heightened expectation of harm. The degree of the anxiety is directly proportional to the anticipated severity of the adversity and the degree to which the individual cognitively distorts these fears (Table 25–8).

Clinical Presentation of Anxiety

Anxiety is an emotion that may be present in many psychiatric disorders as well as other medical conditions (Table 25–9). Anxiety may be a prominent feature in numerous neurological disorders, hypoxic states, and endocrine disorders. Uremia, posthepatitis syndrome, infectious mononucleosis, porphyria, febrile illnesses and chronic infections, systemic malignancies, carcinoid syndrome, and hypoglycemia have been implicated in producing states of anxiety. Inflammatory diseases and some vitamin deficiencies have also been implicated. A number of toxic agents have been shown to result in anxiety.[44]

Anxiety is a common symptom in psychosis, mood disorders, organic disorders, delirium and dementia, and somatoform disorders. Anxiety is the prevailing mood state in the *Diagnostic and Statistical Manual of Mental Disorders,* Fourth Edition (DSM-IV) anxiety disorders: panic disorder without agoraphobia, panic disorder with agoraphobia, agoraphobia without history of panic disorder, specific phobia, social phobia, obsessive-compulsive disorder, posttraumatic stress disorder, acute stress disorder, generalized anxiety disorder, anxiety disorder due to a general medical condition, substance-induced anxiety disorder, and anxiety disorder not otherwise specified (NOS). Anxiety is also the prominent feature in adjustment disorders with anxiety.

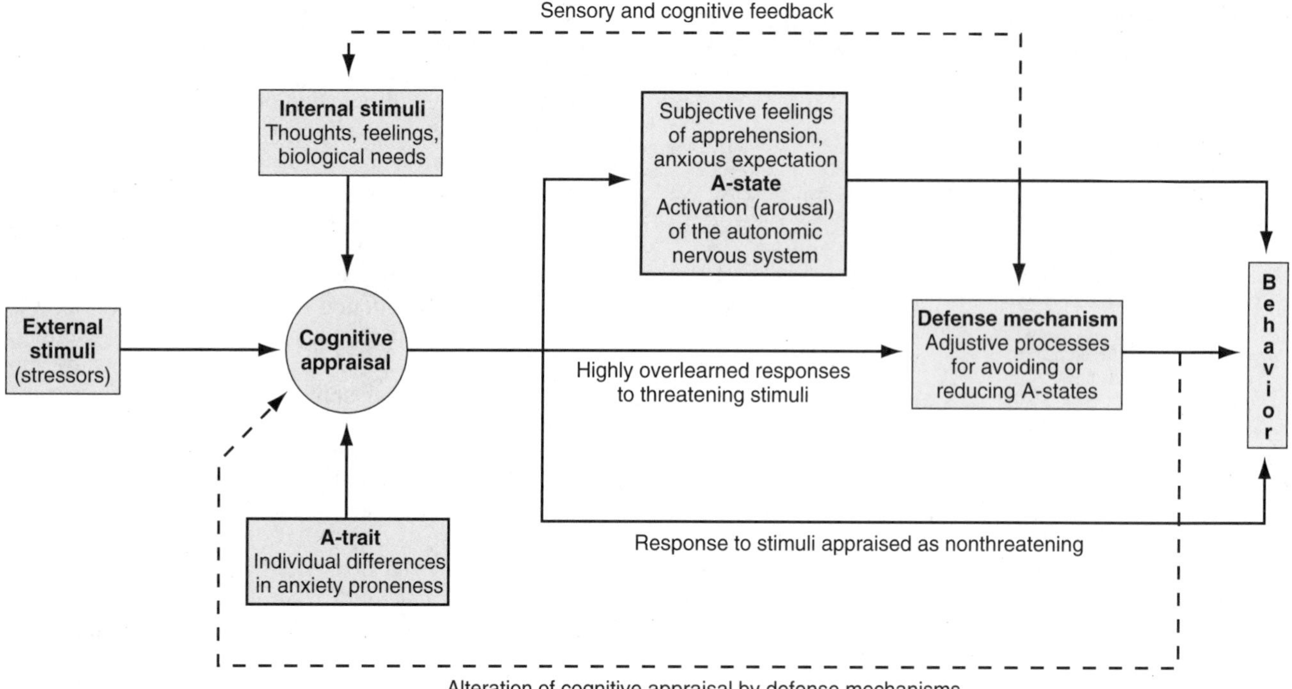

Figure 25–1 *A trait-state conception of anxiety. (From Spielberger CD: Theory and Research on Anxiety. In Spielberger CD [ed]: Anxiety and Behavior. New York: Academic Press, 1966:17.)*

The clinical presentation of the anxiety symptoms varies with the specific disorder. Panic attacks may be present in nearly all the specific anxiety disorders. A panic attack is described as a sudden, discrete period of intense apprehension, fearfulness, or terror associated with physical symptoms including shortness of breath, palpitations, and chest discomfort. During a panic attack, the individual frequently has feelings of impending doom, a fear of losing control, a sense of imminent danger, and an urge to escape. Panic attacks are divided into three characteristic types by the onset of the attack in relation to the presence or absence of a situational stimulus (Table 25–10). Unexpected panic attacks occur spontaneously, unassociated with a situational trigger. Situationally bound panic attacks occur immediately on exposure to or in anticipation of a situational cue. Situationally predisposed panic attacks are more likely to occur on exposure to a specific stimulus but do not necessarily occur immediately. Unexpected panic attacks are necessary for a diagnosis of one of the panic disorders. Situationally bound panic attacks are characteristic of social and specific phobias. The situationally predisposed panic attack occurs in panic disorder, specific phobias, or social phobias.

Table 25–8	Theories of Anxiety
	Objective-neurotic
	Stimulus-oriented
	Response-oriented
	Trait-state
	Cognitive

Clinical Vignette 1

A 45-year-old man was seen in the emergency department. He was dressed in a hospital gown and was observed to be hyperventilating, clutching his chest. He kept yelling out, "I'm dying, I'm having a heart attack, I can't breathe." His electrocardiographic, laboratory, and physical examination findings were all normal except for an elevated blood pressure. The patient was diaphoretic and restless and also complained of thirst. This was his third presentation this week to the emergency department. The patient was admitted to the coronary care unit on the other two occasions, with no evidence of a myocardial infarction. He appeared to be irritable and anxious. His speech was loud. When interviewed, he acknowledged feeling "wound up, nervous, and anxious." His affect during the interview was labile, full range, reactive, and mainly appropriate but exaggerated. He stated that he did not know what caused these attacks and that they came "out of the blue." Between episodes, he felt somewhat "nervous" but mainly "all right."

The characteristic presentation of anxiety in phobic disorders is a persistent, irrational fear of a specific object, activity, or situation that results in a desire to avoid it. When exposed to the stimulus, the phobic individual experiences intense, autonomic symptoms associated with fear. The response is frequently difficult to distinguish from the anxiety of panic disorder, which is characteristically spontaneous and not situationally provoked. Anxiety symptoms associated with increased arousal, reexperience of a traumatic event, and avoidance of stimuli reminiscent of the trauma are characteristic of both acute stress disorder and

Table 25–9 Anxiety Presenting in Medical Conditions

Neurological disorders	Cerebral neoplasms, cerebral syphilis, cerebral trauma, cerebrovascular disease, encephalitis, epilepsy, Huntington's disease, migraine, multiple sclerosis, postconcussional syndrome, subarachnoid hemorrhage, Wilson's disease
Hypoxia	Anemia, cardiac arrhythmias, cardiovascular disease, pulmonary insufficiency
Endocrine disorders	Adrenal dysfunction, disorders of female virilization, parathyroid dysfunction, pheochromocytoma, pituitary dysfunction, thyroid dysfunction
Inflammatory diseases	Polyarteritis nodosa, rheumatoid arthritis, systemic lupus erythematosus, temporal arteritis
Vitamin deficiencies	Pellagra, vitamin B_{12} deficiency
Other systemic disorders	Carcinoid syndrome, chronic infections, febrile illnesses, hypoglycemia, infectious mononucleosis, porphyria, posthepatitis syndrome, uremia, systemic malignancies
Toxic agents	Alcohol, amphetamines, arsenic, benzene, cannabis, caffeine, carbon disulfide, mercury, organophosphates, penicillin, phosphorus, sulfonamides, sympathomimetic agents, vasopressors

Adapted from Cummings JL: Clinical Neuropsychiatry. New York: Grune & Stratton, 1985:214. Copyright © 1985 by Allyn and Bacon. Adapted by permission.

posttraumatic stress disorder. Obsessions, persistent ideas, thoughts, impulses, or images that are intrusive and inappropriate result in the distress and anxiety characteristic of obsessive-compulsive disorder. The associated compulsion is a repetitive behavior or mental act, the goal of which is to prevent or reduce anxiety resulting from the obsession. Generalized anxiety disorder is characterized by excessive worrying, often about routine life circumstances. The object of worry may shift from one concern to another. Associated with generalized anxiety disorder are physiological symptoms, including muscle tension presenting as trembling, twitching, feeling shaky, or muscle aches or soreness. Autonomic aspects to the anxiety may be present, including cold, clammy hands; dry mouth; sweating; nausea or diarrhea; urinary frequency; and trouble swallowing. Individuals with generalized anxiety disorder frequently have an exaggerated startle response.

Emotional Expression of Depression

Spectrum of Depression

Depression refers not only to an emotional state that is characterized by brief or mild periods of sadness or being "down" but also to a clinical condition characterized by depressed mood. A sense of helplessness or loss of self-esteem is often present in a depressed mood. Sadness, dejection, self-reproach, helplessness, despair, feelings of rejection, pessimism, and boredom may be terms used to describe the dysphoric, painful, or unpleasant feelings associated with depression.[45] Depressed mood states are present in simple unhappiness, grief or bereavement, demoralization, and mood disorders.

Demoralization is a condition of low self-esteem, helplessness, hopelessness, sadness, and anxiety.[46] Demoralization is experienced in a variety of situations including severe physical illness, chronic illness, and conditions of marginalization as well as psychiatric disorders. The degree to which an individual is demoralized can be considered her or his psychological temperature and may provide a conceptual continuity of depressive symptoms from normalcy to clinical disorder.

Sadness appropriate to a real loss is part of mourning or grief. The depressed affect accompanying grief differs from other depressed states by a sense of relief felt with the expression of grief.[47] A depressed mood accompanied by poor appetite, weight loss, and insomnia commonly occurs during bereavement. If bereavement is also associated with morbid preoccupation with worthlessness, guilt about things other than actions taken or not taken by the survivor at the time of death, thoughts of death other than the survivor's feeling that he or she would be better off dead or should have died with the deceased person, prolonged and marked functional impairment, marked psychomotor retardation, or hallucinatory experiences other than thinking that he or she hears the voice of or transiently sees the image of the deceased person, this suggests that the bereavement is beyond the expected norm and that a major depressive episode is present. The duration and expression of normal bereavement vary considerably among different cultural groups.

Etiology of Depression

Theories of the origins of pathological depressed mood states can be found in the hippocratic writings of the fifth and fourth centuries. These early writings defined melancholia to

Table 25–10 Types of Panic Attacks and DSM-IV Anxiety Disorder

Type	Onset	Situational Trigger	DSM-IV Diagnoses
Unexpected	Spontaneous	Unassociated	Panic disorder
Situationally bound	Immediate	On exposure	Social phobia Specific phobia
Situationally predisposed	Not always immediate	On exposure	Panic disorder Social phobia Specific phobia

be a prolonged state of depression, with associated aversion to food, despondency, sleeplessness, irritability, and restlessness. Of the four humors, blood, yellow bile, black bile, and phlegm, an excess of black bile was thought by the ancient Greeks to play a distinct role in the development of melancholia. The introduction of the term depression as a substitute for melancholia in the mid-1800s began to signify a psychological and not merely physiological understanding of depressive mood states. Modern conceptualizations of the etiological origins of the emotion of depression encompass a broad theoretical spectrum, including early environmental, personality, psychodynamic, cognitive, life events and social stress, and neurobiological theories.

Early environmental theories considered parental loss, parental separation, and parental style to be risk factors for depression. There is little evidence in experimental controlled studies to support a relationship between parental loss by death in childhood and depression in adulthood.[48, 49] The role of parental separation appears to be more complex; separations involving family discord, such as divorce, may have a long-term impact. However, methodological issues in this area of research continue to create speculation as to the validity of such findings,[50] in particular the lack of adequate accounting of the effects of genetic and environmental factors preceding the loss. Parental styles from rejecting and indifferent to overprotective and controlling have been posited to predispose to adult depression; however, evidence of a causal relationship has yet to be demonstrated.

There are four major models for the role of personality in depression: vulnerability model, complication model, spectrum model, and pathoplasty model. The vulnerability or predispositional model considers that certain antecedent personality characteristics render an individual vulnerable to the development of depression. An example of this model is Cloninger's[51] theory that neurobiological processes interact with heritable personality traits. He stated that there are three underlying dimensions of personality defined by their stimulus-response characteristics that are genetically and neuroanatomically based: novelty seeking, harm avoidance, and reward dependence (Fig. 25–2). Susceptibility to reactive dysphoria is primarily determined by high reward dependence and reduced by high harm avoidance and high novelty seeking.[52] The complication model is the reverse of the predispositional model. According to this model, clinical depression leads an individual to change the way she or he interacts with others or perceives herself or himself. The spectrum model proposes a continuum between temperament and the mood disorders. Pessimism, moodiness, passivity, negativity, and low energy may be personality characteristics that represent the same genetic endowment in normal or milder depressive states as in pathological syndromes. Akiskal and Akiskal[53] have suggested that cyclothymic, depressive, and hyperthymic temperaments represent the subclinical foundations from which affective episodes arise (Table 25–11). The mechanism postulated by the fourth model, the pathoplasty model, that symptomatic expression and course of depression are influenced by personality characteristics, has not been demonstrated in studies measuring personality attributes before the development of a depressive episode.[54–57]

The psychodynamic understanding of depression has evolved with the development of psychoanalytic theory. It holds that depression is the result of disturbance of self-esteem in the context of failed interpersonal relationships. These childhood relationships are internalized and reactivated with the onset of depression. These object relationships are also externalized into current relationships. There is a close relationship between the individual's intimate interpersonal interactions and the maintenance of self-esteem in depression.[58]

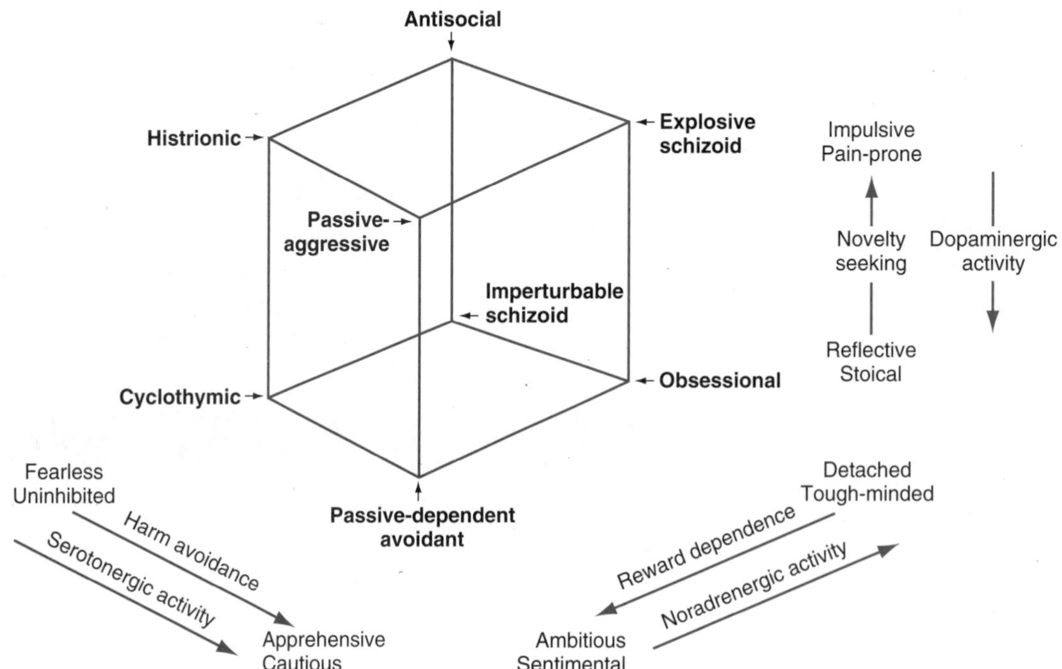

Figure 25–2 *Three-way interaction of personality and monoaminergic transmission. (From Cloninger CR: A unified biosocial theory of personality and its role in the development of anxiety states. Psychiatr Dev 1986; 4:167–226. By permission of Oxford University Press.)*

Table 25–11 Spectrum of Temperament and Mood

Temperament	Clinical Features
Cyclothymic temperament	Hypersomnia versus decreased sleep Introverted versus uninhibited Taciturn versus talkative Unexplained tearfulness versus jocularity Psychomotor inertia versus restlessness Lethargy versus eutonia Dulling of senses versus keen perceptions Slow-witted versus sharp thinking Shaky self-esteem Pessimistic brooding versus optimism
Depressive temperament	Gloomy, humorless, or incapable of fun Given to worry, brooding or pessimistic Introverted, passive, or lethargic Long sleeper or insomnia Preoccupied with inadequacy and failure Skeptical, overcritical, or complaining Self-critical, self-reproachful, and guilty Reliable, dependable, and devoted
Hyperthymic temperament	Cheerful, overoptimistic, or exuberant Warm, people seeking, and extroverted Overtalkative and jocular Overconfident, self-assured, or grandiose Short sleeper High energy level, full of plans Overinvolved and meddlesome Uninhibited, stimulus seeking

The best known cognitive theory of depression is Beck's.[59] Beck claimed that the principal etiological agent in the development of depression is inaccurate cognitions. It is these distorted thoughts that result in the self-defeating and pathological emotional responses experienced by individuals with depression. The study of dogs exposed to inescapable shock has led to the learned helplessness model of depression. Seligman[60] found that animals developed a passive acceptance of the condition in subsequent situations when escape was possible. In the learned helplessness condition, the animal was unable to initiate adaptive responses. This model was thought to apply to depression, when individuals perceive themselves as helpless and behave passively.

Theories of social stress have examined stressful life events[61] and social support[62, 63] as etiological factors in the development of depression. Such studies have demonstrated a cause-and-effect role for these social risk factors; however, these models can explain only a small proportion of the variance for the occurrence of depression.

Physiological explanatory models have become the primary focus in understanding the origins of depression. Subcortical and limbic brain structures and their ascending projections are believed to mediate depression. Biochemical theories have implicated disturbances in norepinephrine, serotonin, and dopamine in the pathogenesis of depression. None of these etiological mechanisms, biological or psychological, is sufficient to explain the development of the pathological expression of the emotion of depression.

Clinical Presentation of Depression

A dominating depressed mood state may be seen in numerous general medical disorders (Table 25–12) as well as in psychiatric disorders. A number of neurological conditions may result in a depressed mood. In cerebrovascular disease, depression is more common with frontal lobe lesions than with posterior hemisphere lesions, and it is more common with left- rather than right-sided infarcts.[64] Cardiopulmonary disease, renal disease and uremia, systemic neoplasms, porphyria, Klinefelter's syndrome, postoperative states, and acquired immunodeficiency syndrome may all present with disorders of emotion, often depression. Less common but documented are deficiencies of vitamin B_{12}, folate, and vitamin C resulting in depression. Endocrine disorders, inflammatory diseases, bacterial and viral infections, and a broad spectrum of pharmaceutical agents may result in development of depressed mood states. Of the hypertensive drugs, reserpine, methyldopa, and propranolol have been the most widely implicated in the literature.[44]

Table 25–12 Depression Presenting in Medical Conditions

Neurological disorders	Central nervous system infections, cerebral neoplasms, cerebral trauma, cerebrovascular disease, epilepsy, Huntington's disease, hydrocephalus, multiple sclerosis, narcolepsy, Parkinson's disease, progressive supranuclear palsy
Endocrine disorders	Addison's disease, Cushing's syndrome, hyperaldosteronemia, hyperparathyroidism, hyperthyroidism, hypoparathyroidism, hypothyroidism
Inflammatory diseases	Polyarteritis nodosa, rheumatoid arthritis, Sjögren's syndrome, systemic lupus erythematosus, temporal arteritis
Vitamin deficiencies	Folate, vitamin B_{12}, vitamin C
Other systemic disorders	Acquired immunodeficiency syndrome, cardiopulmonary disease, Klinefelter's syndrome, porphyria, postoperative states, renal disease, uremia, systemic neoplasms
Toxic agents	Analgesics, antibacterial and antifungal agents, antiinflammatory agents, antineoplastic drugs, cardiac and hypertensive drugs, neurological agents, psychotropic drugs, sedatives and hypnotics, steroids and other hormonal agents, stimulants and appetite suppressants

Adapated from Cummings JL: Clinical Neuropsychiatry. New York: Grune & Stratton, 1985:184. Copyright © 1985 by Allyn and Bacon. Adapted by permission.

Depression is a mood state that is at some point present in almost all of the DSM-IV mood disorders: major depressive disorder, dysthymic disorder, depressive disorder NOS, bipolar I disorder, bipolar II disorder, cyclothymic disorder, bipolar disorder NOS, mood disorder due to a general medical condition, substance-induced mood disorder, and mood disorder NOS. A depressed mood also predominates in adjustment disorders with depressed mood. Depressed mood may also color other psychiatric disorders including the anxiety disorders, dementia, schizophrenia, and schizoaffective disorder, depressive type.

The mood disturbance characterized by a major depressive episode involves both cognitive and vegetative symptoms. These vegetative symptoms, referred to as such because they are unconscious and involuntary, include changes in appetite or weight, sleep, energy, and psychomotor activity. The cognitive changes include feelings of worthlessness or guilt; difficulty in thinking, concentrating, or making decisions; and recurrent thoughts of death or suicidal ideation, plans, or attempts. Loss of interest or anhedonia, the inability to experience pleasure, is another cardinal feature. Although not necessary for a diagnosis of a major depressive episode, a depressed mood is usually present. The mood in a major depressive episode is often described as depressed, sad, hopeless, empty, discouraged, or down. The depressed mood is not always acknowledged or recognized by the patient and may need to be inferred from the patient's demeanor or facial expression. The affect is revealed by the slowed and hypophonic speech produced.[65] "Facial masking" with little or no facial muscle response to emotional stimuli is often seen.[66] The posture is frequently bowed, steps are shortened, and there is a general lack of spontaneous activity.[67] In children and adolescents, an irritable mood rather than a sad mood may be present. Individuals with major depressive episodes may also demonstrate other emotional states including irritability, anxiety, phobias, obsessive ruminations, and excessive worry, in particular about physical complaints.

The depressed mood seen in individuals with dysthymic disorder differs little from that found in major depressive disorder, except in the number and duration of the associated cognitive and vegetative features. The DSM-IV mood disorders field trials[68] suggested that cognitive symptoms are more characteristic of dysthymia than vegetative symptoms are. The depressed mood found in dysthymic disorder is typically described as sad or "down in the dumps" and is chronic (at least 2 years in duration).

The depressed mood in an adjustment disorder with depressed mood is a response to an identifiable psychosocial stressor but is not severe enough to meet criteria for another Axis I disorder. The dominant features include a depressed mood, tearfulness, and feelings of hopelessness.

Clinical Vignette 2

A 35-year-old woman presented to the outpatient clinic. She appeared disheveled with stains on her clothes, sullen, and tearful. She sat in the chair with a slumped posture, at times looking down at the floor. Her speech was of a normal rate and tone. She appeared to be sad. Her affect during the interview was flat and constricted but reactive and appropriate. She displayed a full range of affect. These clinical observations of her affect and the following interview provided a subjective report of her emotional state.

Interviewer: What brought you to the clinic?

Patient: I feel weak, my stomach hurts.

Interviewer: What is your mood like?

Patient: I'm nervous.

Interviewer: Do you mean you are anxious or sad?

Patient: Sad, very sad.

Interviewer: How long have you been this way?

Patient: A long time.

Interviewer: Days, weeks, months?

Patient: Two months.

Interviewer: So, you didn't always feel this way.

Patient: Oh, no! Thank goodness no [with a chuckle].

Interviewer: How about now, in the last 2 months?

Patient: Most of the time I'm down, but there are times I feel better, particularly when I have company.

Interviewer: How sad do you feel? Is this the worst that you have ever felt?

Patient: I'm not sure what you mean.

Interviewer: Well, let's say 1 is your worst and 10 is when you are feeling the best.

Patient: I guess I'm a 2. I'm not yet to the point of killing myself.

Emotional Expression of Euphoria

Euphoria is defined as intense elation often associated with feelings of grandeur. Euphoria, elation, exultation, and ecstasy are synonyms that describe exceedingly pleasurable mood. These emotions can be a part of normal experience. Euphoric states are achieved during sexual pleasure, when one is in love, after achieving a long-sought goal, or just when life is going well. Religious experiences can also result in feelings of euphoria. When euphoria goes beyond the range of normal experience and becomes a psychiatric problem, mania or hypomania is present.

Euphoric mood states may be induced by numerous drugs, neurological conditions, systemic medical disorders (Table 25–13), and psychiatric illnesses. The psychiatric

Table 25–13 Euphoria Presenting in Medical Conditions

Neurological disorders	Huntington's disease, postencephalitic Parkinson's disease, Wilson's disease, general paresis of syphilis, viral encephalitis, cerebral neoplasms, cerebral trauma, thalamotomy, cerebrovascular accidents, multiple sclerosis, temporal lobe epilepsy, Pick's disease, Kleine-Levin syndrome, Klinefelter's syndrome
Other systemic disorders	Uremia, dialysis dementia, hyperthyroidism, pellagra, carcinoid syndrome, vitamin B_{12} deficiency
Toxic agents	Amphetamines, baclofen, bromide, bromocriptine, cimetidine, cocaine, hydralazine, isoniazid, levodopa, metrizamide, procarbazine, procyclidine, phencyclidine, sympathomimetics, yohimbine

Adapated from Cummings JL: Clinical Neuropsychiatry. New York: Grune & Stratton, 1985:191. Copyright © 1985 by Allyn and Bacon. Adapted by permission.

conditions in which euphoric mood predominates are among the DSM-IV mood disorders: bipolar I disorder, bipolar II disorder, cyclothymic disorder, bipolar disorder NOS, mood disorder due to a general medical condition, substance-induced mood disorder, and mood disorder NOS. Euphoria is also characteristic of schizoaffective disorder, bipolar type. Euphoric mood states are characterized as being either a manic episode or a hypomanic episode.

The elevated mood of a manic episode is described as euphoric, unusually good, cheerful, or high. It is viewed as excessive and may seem to have an infectious quality. The quality of the mood is expansive with indiscriminate enthusiasm for interpersonal, sexual, and occupational interactions. Speech during a manic episode is pressured, loud, rapid, and difficult to interrupt. Lability and irritability of mood are often seen in manic episodes. The expression of the euphoric mood seen in a hypomanic episode is similar to that of a manic episode; however, it is not as severe and consequently does not result in psychotic features, hospitalization, or marked impairment in social or occupational functioning as seen in manic episodes.

Emotional Expression of Apathy

Apathy is characterized by a dulled emotional tone associated with detachment or indifference. The apathetic individual is often described as a "bump on a log." Abulia refers to conditions of severe apathy, the loss of will to act, and inability to make decisions or to set goals. This differs from avolition, one of the negative symptoms of schizophrenia, in that the wish to do something is present, but the desire is without energy.[69] The abulic patient may be immobile, be virtually unresponsive, or appear even comatose. Harry Stack Sullivan introduced a psychodynamic explanation for the existence of apathy as an emotion expressed in personality development.[70] He considered apathy an early security operation, a means of reducing awareness and susceptibility to interpersonal tension and of dealing with anxiety.

Bleuler[71] pointed out that apathy to the extent that there is no affect probably does not even occur in psychoses or in the most severe organic brain injury. Lack of interest in almost everything that occurs is seen among some individuals with schizophrenia and dementia. DSM-IV includes negative symptoms as a characteristic of schizophrenia. Affective flattening, alogia, and avolition may all characterize the emotional expression of apathy (Table 25–14). Individuals with severe major depressive episode may also present as apathetic, because they may not be able to discern their own feelings. Frontal lobe syndromes involving the orbital regions typically result in unresponsiveness to environmental stimuli. Individuals with frontal lobe syndromes often lack initiative and are unmotivated and disinterested in their daily activities. Apathy is also characteristically seen in Alzheimer's disease and other dementias, delirium, Huntington's disease, Korsakoff's syndrome, and Parkinson's disease. Individuals with right hemisphere strokes compared with left-sided lesions have a greater risk of presenting with apathy.[72]

Table 25–14 Characteristics of Apathy

Affective flattening	The face appears immobile, unresponsive with poor eye contact and reduced body language. Range of emotional expression is diminished most of the time.
Alogia	Poverty of speech is manifested by brief, laconic, and empty replies. Fluency and productivity of speech are decreased.
Avolition	There is inability to initiate and persist in goal-directed activities.

Emotional Expression of Hostility, Anger, and Rage

Hostility, anger, and rage are aggressive emotions. These emotions are characterized by heightened vigilance in response to a sense of threat. Often there is a tendency to act and engage the threatening stimulus. There is heightened physiological tone in preparation for a behavioral response. This behavioral response varies with societal and cultural norms and ranges from the adaptive-constructive response of assertiveness to the destructive response of violence.[73]

Individual differences in expressing and experiencing aggressive emotions may be cultural, developmental, and temperamental. An infant's temperament at birth may predispose to increased expression of aggressive emotions in adulthood.[74] Organic brain injuries may result in violent acts. Psychological and social contributions may increase the likelihood that an individual will express anger, hostility, or rage. For example, children from violent families or who are abused often become violent and abusive themselves.[75] Stimulant use, alcohol use, and other drugs of abuse can increase the experience of aggressive emotions; in addition, disinhibition increases the risk of violent behavior.

Aggressive emotions are present in aspects of everyday life and are present as part of the range of emotional expression in many psychiatric disorders. There are a number of psychiatric disorders in which the behavioral outcome of aggressive emotions is violence either toward others (as in antisocial personality disorder, intermittent explosive disorder, and sexual sadism) or directed toward oneself (as in borderline personality disorder).

Disturbances of Affect Incongruent with Mood

In certain neuropsychiatric disorders, the emotion expressed by the patient, the mood, is dissociated from the affect, what is observed. There are primarily three conditions in which this is seen: pseudobulbar palsy, ictal affective alterations, and dysprosody.

Patients with pseudobulbar palsy have exaggerated emotional expression with unintended laughing or unmotivated crying, and sometimes a mixture of both. The emotion expressed may be unrelated to the mood or in disproportionate intensity to the emotion experienced. The emotions expressed are difficult for the patient to discontinue. Dysarthria and dysphagia are associated features in many individuals with pseudobulbar palsy. Most cases are a result of bilateral vascular accidents involving the cerebral cortex or the internal capsule. Bilateral interruption of descending cortical fibers disinhibits responses integrated at the lower central nervous system. Exaggerated emotional expression results from release of intrinsic motor programs of the limbic system and related subcortical structures.[76]

Mood changes may be induced by focal seizure activity. Laughter is more common than crying as an ictal manifestation, but both may occur in the same patient. The laughter is stereotyped, inappropriate, and not stimulus induced. The patient views the expressed affect not as pleasurable, but rather as disagreeable.[77]

Prosody is the affective and inflectional coloring of speech. Prosody involves speech melody, pauses, intonation, stresses, and accents during articulation. Neurological insults to the basal ganglia, cerebellum, and brain stem may result in dysprosody as well as dysarthria. Dysprosody reduces the patient's ability to communicate emotion.

Conclusion

Emotions are a feeling state that is described in the psychiatric mental status examination by affect and mood. Affect and mood are not separate entities, although they are often considered as such. Any observable event or body feeling from which the psychiatrist makes an inference about affect could also be incorporated into determining the mood.[78] The important point in the description of emotions in the mental status examination is to obtain both a subjective report and an objective evaluation. It is the patient's described and observed emotion that allows the psychiatrist to properly distinguish and subsequently make a diagnosis of disorders that are related to anxiety, depression, euphoria, apathy, hostility, and anger.

References

1. Darwin C: The Expression of the Emotions in Man and Animals. London: John Murray, 1872.
2. Emde RN, Kligman DH, Reich JH, Wade TD: Emotional expression in infancy: Initial studies of social signaling and an emergent model. In Lewis M, Rosenblum L (eds): The Development of Affect. New York: Plenum Publishing, 1978:125–148.
3. Emde RN: Levels of meaning for infant emotions: A biosocial view. In Collins WA (ed): Minnesota Symposia on Child Psychology, Volume 13, Development of Cognition, Affect and Social Relations. Hillsdale, NJ: Lawrence Erlbaum, 1980:1–37.
4. Bowlby J: Attachment and Loss, Volume 2, Separation: Anxiety and Anger. New York: Basic Books, 1973.
5. Barlow DH: Anxiety and Its Disorders: The Nature and Treatment of Anxiety and Panic. New York: Guilford Press, 1988.
6. Izard CE (ed): Human Emotions. New York: Plenum Publishing, 1977.
7. James W: The Principles of Psychology. New York: Holt, 1890.
8. Cannon WB: Bodily Changes in Pain, Hunger, Fear and Rage, 2nd ed. New York: Appleton-Century-Crofts, 1929.
9. Moore RY: Retinohypothalamic projection in mammals: A comparative study. Brain Res 1973; 49:403–409.
10. Zajonc RB: On the primacy of affect. Am Psychol 1984; 39:151–175.
11. Papez JW: A proposed mechanism of emotion. Arch Neurol Psychiatry 1937; 38:725–743.
12. Delgado JMR: Physical control of the mind. In Karbias EM, Andrews LM (eds): Man Controlled: Readings in the Psychology of Behaviour Control. London: Collier-Macmillan, 1972:40–68.
13. Smirnov VM: Neurophysiological study of human emotion. In Symposium 3: Integrative Forms of Conditioned Reflexes. Presented at the XVIII International Congress of Psychology; August 1966:116–118; Moscow.
14. Panksepp J: Toward a general psychobiological theory of emotions. Behav Brain Sci 1982; 5:407–422.
15. Plutchik R: Emotion: A Psychoevolutionary Synthesis. New York: Harper & Row, 1980.
16. Marks IM, Birley JLT, Gelder MG: Modified leucotomy in severe agoraphobia: A controlled serial enquiry. Br J Psychiatry 1966; 112:757–769.
17. Tan E, Marks IM, Marset P: Bimedial leucotomy in obsessive-compulsive neurosis: A controlled serial enquiry. Br J Psychiatry 1977; 118:155–164.
18. Leventhal H, Tomarken AJ: Emotion: Today's problems. Annu Rev Psychol 1986; 37:565–610.
19. Fox NA, Davidson RJ: EEG asymmetry in response to the approach of a stranger and maternal separation in 10 month old infants. Dev Psychol 1986; 23:233–240.
20. Mayes A: The physiology of fear and anxiety. In Sluckin W (ed): Fear in Animals and Man. Berkshire, UK: Van Nostrand, 1979.
21. Ross ED, Mesulam MM: Dominant language functions of the right hemisphere? Prosody and emotional gesturing. Arch Neurol 1979; 36:144–148.
22. Bunney WE, Davis JM: Norepinephrine in depressive reactions. Arch Gen Psychiatry 1965; 13:483–494.
23. Schildkraut JJ: The catecholamine hypothesis of affective disorders: A review of the supporting evidence. Am J Psychiatry 1965; 122: 509–522.
24. Schacter S, Singer J: Cognitive, social and physiological determinants of emotional state. Psychol Rev 1962; 69:379–397.
25. Lazarus RS: Emotions and adaptation: Conceptual and empirical relations. In Arnold WJ (ed): Nebraska Symposium on Motivation, Volume 16. Lincoln, NE: University of Nebraska Press, 1968:175–266.
26. Lazarus RS, Averill JR, Opton EM: Towards a cognitive theory of emotion. In Arnold M (ed): Feelings and Emotion. New York: Academic Press, 1970:207–232.
27. MacLeod C, Mathews A, Tata P: Attentional bias in emotional disorders. J Abnorm Psychol 1986; 95:15–20.
28. Lang PJ: The cognitive psychophysiology of emotion: Fear and anxiety. In Tuma AH, Maser JD (eds): Anxiety and the Anxiety Disorders. Hillsdale, NJ: Lawrence Erlbaum, 1985:131–170.
29. Eysenck HJ: The Biological Basis of Personality. Springfield, IL: Charles C Thomas, 1967.
30. Tellegen A: Structures of mood and personality and their relevance to assessing anxiety, with an emphasis on self report. In Tuma AH, Maser JD (eds): Anxiety and the Anxiety Disorders. Hillsdale, NJ: Lawrence Erlbaum, 1985:681–706.
31. Othmer E, Othmer SC: The Clinical Interview Using DSM-IV, Volume 1, Fundamentals. Washington, DC: American Psychiatric Press, 1994.
32. American Psychiatric Association: Diagnostic and Statistical Manual of Mental Disorders, 4th ed. Washington, DC: American Psychiatric Association, 1994.
33. Manschreck TC, Keller MB: The mental status examination I. General appearance and behavior, emotional state, perception, speech and language, and thinking. In Lazare A (ed): Outpatient Psychiatry: Diagnosis and Treatment, 2nd ed. Baltimore: Williams & Wilkins, 1989:160–187.
34. Trzepacz PT, Baker RW: The Psychiatric Mental Status Examination. New York: Oxford University Press, 1993.
35. Spielberger CD, Rickman RL: Assessment of state and trait anxiety. In Sartorius N, Andreoli V, Cassano G, et al (eds): Anxiety: Psychobiological and Clinical Perspectives. New York: Hemisphere Publishing, 1990:69–83.
36. Freud S: Inhibitions, symptoms and anxiety. In Strachey J (trans-ed): The Standard Edition of the Complete Psychological Works of Sigmund Freud, Volume 20. London: Hogarth Press, 1959:77–174. Originally published in 1926.
37. Freud S: The Problem of Anxiety. New York: WW Norton, 1936.
38. Spielberger CD: Theory and research on anxiety. In Spielberger CD (ed): Anxiety and Behavior. New York: Academic Press, 1966.
39. Uhde TW, Nemiah JC: Panic and generalized anxiety disorders. In Kaplan HI, Sadock BJ (eds): Comprehensive Textbook of Psychiatry, 5th ed. Baltimore: Williams & Wilkins, 1989:952–972.
40. Goldstein K: Human Nature in the Light of Psychopathology. Cambridge, MA: Harvard University Press, 1940.
41. Cattell RB, Scheier IH: The Meaning and Measurement of Neuroticism and Anxiety. New York: Ronald Press, 1961.
42. Allen BP, Potkay CR: On the arbitrary distinction between states and traits. J Pers Soc Psychol 1981; 41:916–928.
43. Beck AT, Laude R, Bohnert M: Ideational components of anxiety neurosis. Arch Gen Psychiatry 1974; 31:319–325.
44. Cummings JL: Clinical Neuropsychiatry. New York: Grune & Stratton, 1985.
45. Hamilton M: Symptoms and assessments of depression. In Paykel ES

(ed): Handbook of Affective Disorders. New York: Guilford Press, 1982:3–11.
46. Dohrenwend BP, Shrout PE, Egri G, et al: Measures of nonspecific psychological distress and other dimensions of psychopathology in the general population. Arch Gen Psychiatry 1980; 37:1229–1236.
47. Jacobson E: Depression. New York: International Universities Press, 1974.
48. Crook T, Eliot J: Parental death during childhood and adult depression: A critical review of the literature. Psychol Bull 1980; 87:252–259.
49. Tennant C, Bebbington P, Hurry J: Parental death in childhood and risk of adult depressive disorders. Psychol Med 1980; 10:289–299.
50. Tennant C: Parental loss in childhood: Its effect in adult life. Arch Gen Psychiatry 1988; 45:1045–1050.
51. Cloninger CR: A systematic method for clinical description and classification of personality variants: A proposal. Arch Gen Psychiatry 1987; 44:573–588.
52. Cloninger CR: A unified biosocial theory of personality and its role in the development of anxiety states. Psychiatr Dev 1986; 4:167–226.
53. Akiskal HS, Akiskal K: Cyclothymic, hyperthymic, and depressive temperaments as subaffective variants of mood disorders. In Tasman A, Riba MB (eds): American Psychiatric Press Review of Psychiatry, Volume II. Washington, DC: American Psychiatric Press, 1992:43–62.
54. Angst J, Clayton P: Premorbid personality of depressive, bipolar, and schizophrenic patients with special reference to suicidal issues. Compr Psychiatry 1986; 27:511–532.
55. Hirschfeld RMA, Klerman GL, Lavori P, et al: Premorbid personality assessments of first onset of major depression. Arch Gen Psychiatry 1989; 46:345–350.
56. Lewinsohn PM, Hoberman HM, Rosenbaum M: A prospective study of risk factors for unipolar depression. J Abnorm Psychol 1988; 97:251–264.
57. Nystrom S, Lindegard B: Predisposition for mental syndromes: A study comparing predisposition for depression, neurasthenia and anxiety states. Acta Psychiatr Scand 1975; 51:69–76.
58. Gabbard GO: Psychodynamic Psychiatry in Clinical Practice: The DSM-IV Edition. Washington, DC: American Psychiatric Press, 1994.
59. Beck AT: Depression: Causes and Treatment. Philadelphia: University of Pennsylvania Press, 1967.
60. Seligman MEP: Depression and learned helplessness. In Friedman RJ, Katy MM (eds): The Psychology of Depression: Contemporary Theories and Research. New York: John Wiley & Sons, 1974.
61. Brown GW, Harris T: Social Origins of Depression. London: Tavistock, 1978.
62. Aneshensel CS, Stone JD: Stress and depression: A test of the buffering model of social support. Arch Gen Psychiatry 1982; 39:1392–1396.
63. Williams AW, Ware JE, Donald CA: A model of mental health, life events, and social supports applicable to general populations. J Health Soc Behav 1981; 22:324–336.
64. Robinson RG, Kubos KL, Starr LB, et al: Mood disorders in stroke patients. Brain 1984; 107:81–93.
65. Greden JF, Albala AA, Smokler IA, et al: Speech pause time: A marker of psychomotor retardation among endogenous depressives. Biol Psychiatry 1981; 16:851–859.
66. Schwartz GE, Fair PL, Salt P, et al: Facial muscle patterning to affective imagery in depressed and nondepressed subjects. Science 1976; 192:489–491.
67. Kupfer DJ, Weiss BL, Foster FG, et al: Psychomotor activity in affective states. Arch Gen Psychiatry 1974; 30:765–768.
68. Keller MB, Klein DN, Hirschfeld RMA, et al: Results of the DSM-IV mood disorders field trial. Am J Psychiatry 1995; 152:843–849.
69. Edgerton JE, Campbell RJ (eds): American Psychiatric Glossary, 7th ed. Washington, DC: American Psychiatric Press, 1994.
70. Mullahy P (ed): The Contributions of Harry Stack Sullivan. New York: Hermitage House, 1952.
71. Bleuler E: Textbook of Psychiatry. New York: Macmillan, 1924.
72. Marin RS, Fogel BS, Hawkins J, et al: Apathy: A treatable syndrome. J Neuropsychiatry Clin Neurosci 1995; 7:23–30.
73. Yager J: Clinical manifestations of psychiatric disorders. In Kaplan HI, Sadock BJ (eds): Comprehensive Textbook of Psychiatry, 5th ed. Baltimore: Williams & Wilkins, 1989:553–582.
74. Chess S, Thomas A: Temperament in Clinical Practice. New York: Guilford Press, 1986.
75. Kempe CH, Helfer RE (eds): The Battered Child, 3rd ed, revised and expanded. Chicago: University of Chicago Press, 1980.
76. Cummings JL, Benson DF, Houlihan JP, Gosenfeld LF: Mutism: Loss of neocortical and limbic vocalization. J Nerv Ment Dis 1983; 171:255–259.
77. Sethi PK, Rao S: Gelastic, quiritarian, and cursive epilepsy. A clinicopathological appraisal. J Neurol Neurosurg Psychiatry 1976; 39:823–828.
78. Owens H, Maxmen JS: Mood and affect: A semantic confession. Am J Psychiatry 1979; 136:97–99.

CHAPTER

26 Physical Signs and Symptoms

Philip R. Muskin

Mental disorders are syndromes consisting of sets of symptoms. The terminology that psychiatrists use to refer to these syndromes is one of convention. The research that helps define our terminology has limitations and, therefore, describes only a portion of any sample of patients.[1] The *Diagnostic and Statistical Manual of Mental Disorders,* Fourth Edition (DSM-IV) and the *International Classification of Diseases,* ninth revision (ICD-9) present categories for a large number of mental disorders. However, how individuals experience their symptoms and what is described to the physician may not fit easily into phenomenological nosological systems such as DSM-IV and ICD-9. The brain, in response to mental activity in the person's mind, may express the disorder only psychologically, that is, with thoughts and emotions. The brain also has control over the body via both humoral and neuronal systems and may express the disorder physiologically. Therefore, the consequences of mental distress can be expressed psychologically, along with somatic manifestations, or mental distress can be expressed somatically, with minimal psychological experience.

How a patient experiences and expresses distress has an important impact on the physician's ability to arrive at an accurate diagnosis. Of the numerous factors that influence the experience and expression of symptoms, culture is one of the most powerful.[2] Whether or not symptoms are believed to be medical or psychological may have implications for what happens to the person being evaluated. The outcome of the evaluation—that is, the symptoms are medical or are mental—has personal meaning for the individual, may have legal importance, or may have an impact on the role the person plays in society.[1] People with mental problems potentially suffer from the stigma and prejudice attached to psychiatric disorders.

Developed industrial nations, particularly those with Western cultures, are more likely to focus on psychological symptoms as the core manifestations of psychiatric illness; in contrast, somatization is much more the norm in non-Western cultures and underdeveloped countries. Thus, the prevalence of disorders such as depression and anxiety may vary widely across cultures, depending on the criteria used for the diagnosis. An individual's acceptance of receiving a psychiatric diagnosis, rather than receiving a medical diagnosis for the same set of symptoms, is influenced by the stigma attached to psychiatric disorders in that person's culture. Personal characteristics and cultural beliefs also influence the expression of symptoms in nonsomatic forms and thus determine what information the physician is able to obtain from the patient. The information the physician obtains clearly plays a crucial role in arriving at an accurate psychiatric diagnosis.

The powerful role that culture plays is not only a major point of interest of cross-cultural psychiatry but also one with considerable practical significance. The United States is a heterogeneous culture with many different points of view regarding mental illness. People from other countries bring with them their cultural views. In addition, there is a large population of immigrants who have lived in the United States for years but retain the cultural beliefs of their country of origin. The psychological framework that defines psychiatric disorders for physicians may not be one that any portion of a particular population of patients subscribes to. There is no absence of stigma associated with mental illness in the United States. Physicians inevitably encounter patients from cultures whose metaphors of distress vary widely. Many patients are likely to present with a variety of physical complaints, particularly to their primary care physicians; a significant portion of these patients have psychiatric problems.[3] Despite the importance of mental disorders in detracting from the overall well-being of patients, the accurate diagnosis of these disorders in primary care settings is quite low.[3, 4]

Evaluation of Physical Signs and Symptoms

All patients presenting with "psychiatric" symptoms require a careful and complete physical examination. Routine blood tests should include a complete blood count; determination of serum glucose and electrolyte levels; testing for hepatic, renal, and thyroid function; and testing for syphilis. Urinalysis, an electrocardiogram, and a chest radiograph should also be obtained. A thorough medical history and a family history of medical illness are crucial components of an adequate psychiatric evaluation. In many cases, the psychiatrist is the only physician who considers the possibility that a patient should have counseling and then testing to determine his or her human immunodeficiency virus status.

Psychiatric disorders can alter the way in which patients manage their health and health care. Patients with depression are at risk for metabolic disturbances secondary to anorexia.

Of particular importance is dehydration, which may alter serum electrolytes and magnify certain of the side effects of antidepressant treatment, such as orthostatic hypotension. Patients who are admitted with dehydration or who have been found at home in a dehydrated and malnourished state should be screened for depression. Agitated states, such as mania and schizophrenia, place patients at risk for a variety of medical problems. Increased motor activity for days or even weeks can affect joints and can lead to malnutrition and exhaustion. Inattention to intercurrent medical problems because of impaired judgment and agitation may lead to severe infections that would otherwise be easily treated.

Patients with mood disorders, both depressed and bipolar, as well as patients with a broad range of psychoses may become noncompliant with medication regimens to which they were previously adherent. Failure to take necessary medications or to follow a restricted diet exacerbates the underlying medical disorder. In every case in which the judgment of the patient is in question as part of the precipitant of the medical disorder and in which the patient has malnutrition or dehydration with or without an obvious mood disturbance, a psychiatric disorder is a worthwhile diagnostic consideration.

Physical Manifestations of Anxiety

Anxiety is an internal feeling state of fear in which the person does not know the cause of the fear. It is not a pleasant experience. Research has shown that anxiety at low levels of intensity can be motivating and increase performance.[5] As the intensity of anxiety increases, the person experiences greater degrees of discomfort and dysfunction. Whether it is of low or high intensity, anxiety is commonly associated with physical symptoms. Panic attacks, one form of anxiety disorder, always have a somatic component. There is no organ system that can *not* be affected by anxiety, and the differential diagnosis for such patients must always include a medical condition (Table 26–1).

As a rule, symptoms that have persisted for long periods, change over time but do not worsen, or match no known medical condition should be considered as potential symptoms of anxiety. Hall[6] has shown, however, that this rule is often violated in patients with medical conditions that are difficult to diagnose. Patients with panic disorder typically present to primary care physicians for medical evaluation, convinced that they have a medical disorder.[7] A typical presentation is that of a young woman with complaints of chest pain and shortness of breath, convinced she is having a heart attack. The intensity of the symptoms and the conviction that something must be wrong medically to generate such discomfort are often convincing to the patient's physician as well.[8]

Patients with anxiety often complain of feeling weak, having fatigue even with normal duration of sleep, and becoming exhausted with minimal exertion. Patients may offer no complaint of feeling anxious and may not appear anxious, or they may complain of feeling anxious regarding their physical symptoms. We separate *signs* (the observable phenomena or laboratory results) from *symptoms* (subjective experiences that patients offer as their chief complaint). The signs of anxiety are irritability, pacing, or restlessness during the history or physical examination. There can be a cold, clammy feeling to the skin and a fine tremor. In cases of severe hyperventilation, a patient may demonstrate Chvostek's sign, which is tetany (tonic muscular contractions, tremors, and parasthesias) caused by a low serum calcium level resulting from the hyperventilation-induced respiratory alkalosis. At electrocardiography, a sinus tachycardia may be observed, and patients may have elevated systolic blood pressure. A systolic ejection murmur of mitral valve prolapse may be heard in some patients with panic disorder,[9] but mitral valve prolapse does not appear to cause panic disorder.[10]

Symptoms of anxiety are the subjective experiences that patients offer as their chief complaint. These symptoms commonly affect the cardiovascular, pulmonary, gastrointestinal, nervous, or genitourinary systems. It is not known why one organ system is affected in one patient but not in another;

Table 26–1 Physical Manifestations of Anxiety by Organ System

Cardiovascular System
Palpitations
Tachycardia
Substernal pressure, precordial pain not related to exertion
Facial flushing
Feelings of having a heart attack
Pulmonary System
Shortness of breath
Sense of inability to get enough air (sense of suffocation)
Repeated yawning or sighing
Feeling of a tight band around the chest or throat
Excessive dryness of the mouth
Gastrointestinal System
Epigastric discomfort, pain, distress, fullness
Belching, heartburn
Feeling of being unable to swallow
Nausea
Diarrhea or constipation
Anorexia or overeating to calm anxieties
Nervous System
Difficulty concentrating, poor memory
Dizziness, lightheadedness, syncope (typically no loss of consciousness)
Insomnia, including difficulty falling and staying asleep
Nightmares
Headaches
Blurred vision
Numbness or tingling of the extremities and/or periorally
Tremors, muscle pain or stiffness
Weakess of extremities
Inability to sit still or to relax, feeling of being tense
Genitourinary System
Increased frequency of urination
Alterations in menses
Decreased libido
Impotence, anorgasmia, dyspareunia

however, patients have varying tolerance for symptoms. People may ignore symptoms in one organ system but focus their attention as well as their physician's attention on symptoms in another system that they find more distressing.[8]

Patients may have one, some, or all of the symptoms listed in Table 26–1. This is not an exhaustive list, and patients may complain of many other physical problems. It must always be kept in mind that patients may have both a psychiatric disorder and a medical disorder. A thorough medical evaluation of the patient's complaint must precede the final decision that the symptoms originate exclusively from an anxiety disorder. It is never appropriate to tell the patient that her or his symptoms are "all in your head." Every patient deserves to understand that a psychiatric diagnosis refers to a real illness.

Clinical Vignette 1

Mr. T was a 20-year-old college senior who had seen several physicians before a psychiatric consultation. He complained of nausea with one or two episodes of vomiting. Repeated medical work-ups were not revealing, and his family physician told his parents that he had a severe psychiatric disorder. Although handsome, he dated rarely. He was a straight A student and an athlete. The psychiatrist was able to elicit all the symptoms of panic disorder and a history of repeated panic attacks. The only symptoms that Mr. T cared about were the nausea and vomiting, because he feared he would vomit on a date or in a public situation and would be embarrassed. Treatment with desipramine at a dose of 300 mg abolished all of Mr. T's symptoms. He graduated from college, became an executive who traveled around the world for his company, and married some years later.

Physical Manifestations of Mood Disorders

Mood disturbance, like anxiety, commonly presents with physical symptoms. An unhappy emotion can be a normal reaction to a variety of life events, and most people would refer to this as depression. A sense of bereavement is also a normal response to life events, including the loss of a relationship, the death of an important individual, the loss of a body function, or the loss of a body part. The sadness in these situations may be accompanied by some somatic symptoms, typically a decrease in appetite or some disturbance in sleep. It is not surprising that people experience some depression under such circumstances. Sadness, depression, and feeling blue may be experienced in reaction to some physical malady or may be a component of the disorder that causes the physical complaints. Some patients have such severe agitation that they do not experience themselves as depressed and do not appear depressed to their physicians.

Many women experience some degree of mood alteration after the birth of a child. A woman may fail to distinguish the progression from postpartum blues into mood disorder because she is sleep deprived, fatigued, and normally occupied by the activities of caring for a newborn. Postpartum depression can be a serious illness, endangering the life of both mother and child. It is not a rare disorder, occurring in approximately 15% of women.[11] As is the case with anxiety, patients with depression often go to their primary care physicians with somatic, not psychological, complaints. Almost five times as many patients with depression spend days in bed with physical symptoms as people in the general population.[12] Studies using structured psychiatric interviews have shown that the point prevalence of major depressive disorder ranges from 4.8% to 8.6% in primary care outpatient settings. Of adult medical inpatients, 14.6% met criteria for major depressive disorder.[13]

People with depression typically present with complaints of fatigue, insomnia, lack of energy, and poor appetite. Many people continue to go to work and maintain their routine in spite of how miserable they feel. Typically, patients have a medical rationale to explain their physical complaints, such as anemia or the possibility that they have cancer. Patients with insomnia commonly believe that their insomnia is the cause of the other physical symptoms. Many patients have a variety of vague physical discomforts when they are depressed, such as headaches, backaches, and muscle aches. They may also have gastrointestinal symptoms such as indigestion, change in food preferences, or decreased appetite.

Without being questioned specifically, patients may not talk about decreased interests in usual activities, decreased sexual interest, feelings of low self-esteem, or suicidal thoughts. The alterations in concentration and memory that occur in depression may be concealed because patients fear that they are senile. As with anxiety disorders, patients may experience sadness about their lack of energy and other physical symptoms and not mention any other changes in their emotions. Mood-congruent delusions, as part of a delusional depression, may have a surface validity and not seem obviously delusional, such as a patient's conviction that he or she has cancer.

Severely depressed patients may present with a picture resembling that of a dementia. Slowed thinking, long response time to questions, inability to pay attention, and failure on cognitive testing (typically "I don't know" rather than an incorrect answer) may convince family and physician that the person has an "organic" problem.

In patients with serious medical illness, the diagnosis of depression can be missed, because many disease states and medical treatments can cause the vegetative symptoms associated with depression. Although it is understandable that someone might be sad as a reaction to a medical illness, the reasonable nature of the reaction does not rule out the possibility of a mood disorder. Why only some people develop a mood disorder during or after unfortunate life events, such as a serious physical illness or the loss of a significant person, is not yet known.

Clinical Vignette 2

Mr. C was referred for an inpatient neurological evaluation because of the conviction of his outpatient doctor that he had a depression. He complained of fatigue, sadness, and inability to perform the necessary exercises after his recent hip replacement. He had been started with a selective serotonin reuptake inhibitor before admission without effect. Although unhappy about his inability to regain full use of his leg and afraid he would not be able to dance at his daughter's wedding, he had no other symptoms of depression and the inhibitor was discontinued on admission. His "heavy" eyes and blurred vision led the ophthalmologist to perform an edrophonium (Tensilon) test, which was positive. He was diagnosed with myasthenia gravis and eventually had surgery for a thymoma. The subsequent hospital course was extremely difficult. After several weeks, Mr. C became tearful, anxious, and severely indecisive about his care. He was unable to sleep and was fearful that he would die in spite of continued improvement medically. After two weeks of treatment with a selective serotonin reuptake inhibitor for his depression, and a benzodiazepine to treat his insomnia, Mr. C felt less depressed. He was no longer tearful and was able to engage actively in decisions regarding discharge planning. Mr. C. left the hospital walking, smiling, and ready to enjoy his daughter's wedding.

Physical Disorders Causing Secondary Mental Symptoms

Numerous medical disorders have behavioral components, such as the mood disruption that occurs with many different endocrine disorders or the psychiatric symptoms that may occur with a disorder such as systemic lupus erythematosus. Many different aspects of the experience of being physically ill can exert either a psychological or a physiological effect on patients with the medical disorder. A patient's mental status or a patient's ability to experience and to express emotion may change as a result of the direct effects of a medical condition on the patient's brain. Cerebrovascular accidents have a direct effect on brain tissue. Conditions that alter blood flow to the brain, such as arrhythmias, hypotension, or vascular disease, also alter the person's ability to think. Systemic disorders including sepsis, disturbances in electrolyte and glucose metabolism, and a variety of intoxications all have effects on the brain and thus influence thinking and emotion.

Medical illness also has global effects on the body, such as fatigue. There may be changes in the person's appetite, sleep, or libido. From a psychodynamic perspective, medical illness has a regressive effect on the psychological functioning of the patient such that she or he may be less able to cope with the demands of the current situation.[14] Regression means that the person employs methods of coping with the world that were appropriate at an earlier stage of psychological development. A patient may also have psychological reactions, such as anxiety or depression, in response to the alterations in cognitive function.

Psychiatric patients (i.e., patients who have a psychiatric diagnosis known to their physicians) may have medical disorders that are not diagnosed because the presenting symptom appears to be mental (so-called functional) rather than physical (so-called organic). This is the reverse of the situation described in the sections on the physical manifestations of anxiety and of mood disorders, in which patients present with symptoms that are taken to be the result of a general medical condition rather than the somatic manifestations of a psychiatric disorder. Hall[6] noted nine mythological characteristics of patients who are believed to have functional medical complaints (Table 26–2). If the physician holds these myths to be axiomatic truths, her or his belief will impede the appropriate evaluation of the patient's underlying or concomitant medical disorder. The nine characteristics in Table 26–2 are a reminder that every clinical situation must be fully evaluated, no matter how obvious it seems that the complaints are functional.

In a review of 658 consecutive psychiatric outpatients, careful medical evaluation revealed that 9.1% of the psychiatric cases had a medical illness that produced the psychiatric symptoms.[15] Depression, confusion, and anxiety were the most common presentations. Cardiovascular and endocrine disorders were most commonly the cause of the psychiatric symptoms. Infections, pulmonary disease, gastrointestinal problems, hematological disorders, a variety of central nervous system disorders, and cancers were also found as the actual etiology of the "psychiatric" symptoms.

Clinical Vignette 3

Ms. P, a 38-year-old successful businesswoman, mother of two teenagers, was seen in psychiatric consultation 2 days after the removal of a pheochromocytoma because she was feeling sad. She gave a history of several years of intermittent episodes of palpitations, headaches, tremulousness, and flushing. Her physician had told her she was overwhelmed by being a "supermom" and anxious because of chronic marital problems. Ms. P was told to see a psychotherapist, a recommendation she did not follow. She would not have consulted an endocrinologist and would not have had succesful surgery for her pheochromocytoma, had a friend not heard a radio program about medical disorders that cause anxiety-like symptoms.

No convenient system exists to connect any one medical disorder with a particular set of psychiatric symptoms. Disorders such as systemic lupus erythematosus, acquired immunodeficiency syndrome, and pancreatic carcinoma regularly have a psychiatric presentation, particularly symptoms of mood disorders. This is of special importance in patients with acquired immunodeficiency syndrome.[16–20] Patients with hallucinations, especially visual hallucinations, should receive a full work-up to exclude a medical etiology for their symptoms.

Table 26–2	Mythological Characteristics of Patients with Functional Medical Complaints
1)	A history of anxiety or unusual behavior since childhood or adolescence
2)	The patient evidences a multiplicity of symptoms that involve several organ systems
3)	The patient evidences unusual symptoms that are difficult for the physicians to deal with
4)	A history of atypical response or failure to respond to treatment
5)	A history of doctor shopping
6)	A failure to carry out the physician's recommendations
7)	The absence of concern in the face of serious complaints
8)	Symptom onset concomitant with, or exacerbated by, particular people or stressful life events
9)	Apparent secondary gain resulting from physical symptoms

From Hall RCW (ed): Psychiatric Presentation of Medical Illness: Somatopsychic Disorders. New York: SP Medical & Scientific Books, 1980:4.

Clinical Vignette 4

A 44-year-old executive was admitted for inpatient treatment of ophthalmic herpes. When seen for a pain consultation, she was found to be agitated and "psychotic." The psychiatric consultant noted that she had a fluent aphasia, was extremely distressed at her sudden inability to communicate, and was not psychotic. A computed tomographic scan showed several lesions scattered on the left side of her brain. A glioblastoma with satellite lesions was a strong consideration, so a brain biopsy was performed. This procedure led to a diagnosis of toxoplasmosis. The patient gave no risk factors for human immunodeficiency virus infection except for unprotected sex several years before the admission. She tested positive for human immunodeficiency virus. Her "psychosis" cleared with treatment of the opportunistic infection and the resolution of the aphasia.

Intoxication and Withdrawal

It is always important to consider that a patient is intoxicated by any one of a variety of substances, particularly when the presentation is one of anxiety, agitation, confusion, paranoid ideation, or psychosis. It must also be considered that the same presentation can occur in patients withdrawing from a substance. Patients who are intoxicated have positive serum or urine toxicologic test results, whereas patients who are withdrawing typically have none of the substance in their blood or urine. However, in cases of chronic substance abuse, particularly with alcohol, patients may have serum levels of alcohol that, for them, are too low to prevent withdrawal. When this fact is not recognized, the patient's behavior can be a source of confusion in the diagnostic evaluation. The physician may not realize that the anxious patient is actually delirious. Patterns of substance abuse vary considerably, and many patients use more than one substance simultaneously. In complex cases, it is worth considering the possibility that the patient is withdrawing from a substance that was not included in the history.

Clinical Vignette 5

An 87-year-old woman was admitted to the neurology department with confusion and agitation. She was not able to give a coherent history, but her family reported that she had been a department store executive and that she was devoutly religious. Her medical evaluation was completely negative except for the change in her mental status. During the next day her agitation worsened. Her daughter reported that her mother had several large shopping bags of medications in her bedroom, accumulated over many years of receiving prescriptions. In her delirious state the patient denied taking any of these medications except for "my Centrum at bedtime." The psychiatric consultant suggested that Centrum (a multivitamin) might actually be Centrax (prazepam, a benzodiazepine with a long half-life). The psychiatrist suggested that the patient was in a withdrawal delirium from the benzodiazepine. An intramuscular administration of lorazepam brought the delirium under control, with rapid improvement in the patient's agitation. The patient was detoxified using oral lorazepam during the next week. She remained fully oriented and without confusion. Her family removed her collection of medications before her discharge home.

Many medical disorders may have psychiatric presentations with either depression or anxiety symptoms. There are also patients who present with symptoms that are mixtures of agitation and depression or mixtures of lethargy and anxiety. In some clinical situations, agitation may be difficult to differentiate from anxiety. Anxiety is typically a feeling that remains throughout the day, with increases or decreases in the intensity of the feeling and a clear sensorium. Agitation is often accompanied by confusion, disorientation, and a fluctuating level of consciousness. Some patients have a pattern of agitation alternating with sedation. Of particular diagnostic importance are symptoms in an elderly patient that are thought to represent anxiety, but the patient is actually suffering from a delirium. Delirium may be the presenting picture in elderly patients and may be the consequence of a variety of metabolic, hemodynamic, infectious, and pharmacological factors. The possibility of an anticholinergic delirium should always be entertained for a geriatric patient who seems anxious. Numerous medications that are commonly prescribed for geriatric patients have anticholinergic side effects. Although the potency of the anticholinergic effect for any one drug may be small, the additive effects of several drugs can produce an anticholinergic delirium.[21]

A complete evaluation always includes an investigation of the patient's medications. This includes medications that are currently prescribed and ones the patient still possesses from prior prescriptions. Psychiatric symptoms can be caused by such a large number of medications that it is always worthwhile to consult a reference when a patient is taking a medication new to the physician.[22] See Tables 26–3 and 26–4 for guides regarding medical disorders that may present with symptoms suggestive of a depression or of an anxiety disorder.

Physical Symptoms Without Known Etiology

It should be obvious by now that physical presentations of psychiatric disorders are a common occurrence. It is not

Table 26–3 Medical Disorders with Depression-Like Symptoms

Acquired immunodeficiency syndrome
Cancer: intracranial tumors, pancreatic carcinoma, and others
Central nervous system: Parkinson's disease, multiple sclerosis
Diabetes
Heavy metal toxicity: lead, mercury (agitation, apathy, psychosis)
Hyperthyroidism or hypothyroidism (lethargy and anxiety)
Hyperadrenalism (Cushing's disease)
Adrenocortical insufficiency (Addison's disease)
Hyper- or hypoparathyroidism
Pernicious anemia
Systemic lupus erythematosus
Viral infections: hepatitis, pneumonia

Table 26–4 Medical Disorders with Anxiety-Like Symptoms

Acquired immunodeficiency syndrome
Cardiac disease: arrhythmias, anginal variants
Central nervous system disorders: multiple sclerosis, head injury, encephalitis, Wilson's disease, Huntington's disease, vitamin B_{12} deficiency
Hyper- or hypothyroidism
Hyper- or hypoparathyroidism
Hypoglycemia (islet cell adenoma or medication induced)
Intracranial tumors
Pheochromocytoma
Porphyria
Virilizing syndromes in women: adrenal, ovarian, pituitary (tumors and disorders)
Withdrawal: particularly early phases of alcohol, barbiturate, and benzodiazepine withdrawal

surprising that some psychiatric disorders involve complaints of physical problems, without an underlying anxiety disorder or affective illness. These patients are people for whom psychological matters are expressed via their bodies. It is estimated that as many as 10% of all medical patients have no medical illness but still receive a diagnostic evaluation and medical treatment.[23]

Patients who have either somatoform or factitious disorders assume the rights that accompany the role of the physically sick without the organic pathology on which the role is based. The individual is presumed to be weakened by the underlying disease. In being sick a person is excused from the everyday responsibilities of a society, without being blamed and without penalty. A sick person is not expected to recover by force of will alone and can expect to be cared for by others. However, certain obligations accompany the sick role. The person who claims to be ill is expected to seek medical attention in order to discover the cause of the symptoms. He or she is expected to accept appropriate treatment for the malady. The person is expected to desire to return to being well.

What is unique to a patient with a somatoform or factitious disorder, and is often extremely frustrating to the person's physician, is that such a patient takes on the sick role for psychological, not physiological, reasons. The psychology that results in the person's complaint of a somatic problem may be unconscious, or it may be part of a conscious plan to create or fake a medical problem.

Patients with somatizing disorders do have an illness; they experience themselves as not being well. This experience impairs their lives. They may or may not have a disease; that is, there may or may not be objective evidence of organic impairment. Although people may use somatic symptoms for either conscious or unconscious gain, it is possible that both a psychiatric illness and a medical disease are present. Some patients have clear evidence of disease but claim not to have an illness—that is, they do not have an experience of being ill—and they are noncompliant with treatment. Some of this group of patients have psychosis, delirium, or dementia as the source of their denial of illness. There may be a small group who have maladaptive denial of physical illness.[24]

Somatic expression of psychological problems occurs commonly and typically is not severe enough to lead to medical attention. The queasy stomach before an examination and the headache in anticipation of or during an undesirable activity are well known. For some people, psychic experiences are readily translated into bodily experiences and such individuals seek treatment for their physical ailments, unaware of this unconscious mechanism.

Physicians may play a role in the continuation of the psychiatric disorder by too readily accepting the patient's complaints without a thorough evaluation of the patient's history and without obtaining a detailed history of prior treatment. Of equal importance is the failure of physicians to realize that the patient's somatic complaints are metaphors for psychic suffering and the patient's need to be taken care of by someone. If the patient's needs are not understood and no attempt is made to understand the kind of help the person requires, she or he has little choice but to persist in the physical complaints. A physician may find it impossible to believe that the patient is unaware of what appear to be obvious dynamic issues. The physician's anger or neglect may motivate the patient to seek "better" care, which often translates into consulting a different medical doctor, not pursuing psychiatric treatment.

It is impossible to review every symptom with which patients may present, and any physical complaint could be a symptom of a somatoform disorder. However, certain major points regarding these disorders are worth reviewing. A patient with a somatoform disorder frequently consults several physicians simultaneously or in rapid sequence. In contrast to the average medically ill patient who tries to give an adequate history but leaves out many details, a patient with somatoform disorders describes symptoms in exquisite detail, including dates of onset of the complaints, the character of the symptoms, and the precipitants of the symptoms, as well as results of previous laboratory and physical examinations. Although the evaluation of the complaints typically does not yield positive findings, some patients have organic disease exacerbated by a somatoform disorder and positive physical findings emerge during the work-up. In some cases a clue to the physician is that the patient's complaints exceed what would be expected from the physical or laboratory findings. In other cases, physical or laboratory abnormalities initially lend support to the patient's complaints but are eventually found not to be etiologically related to the presumed illness.

In conversion disorders, the patient presents with dysfunction of systems typically under voluntary control, such as the motor system, or the symptoms involve the special senses. Patients may have seizure-like symptoms without any evidence of a seizure disorder or may have confirmed electroencephalographic findings that do not correlate with the symptoms. DSM-IV does not require that there be an unconscious conflict that is expressed via the physical dysfunction, but there must be evidence of a precipitant for the symptoms. The symptoms are often notable for lacking anatomical validity; for example, glove anesthesia of the hand is not in keeping with the innervation of the hand. The symptoms do have causality that is logical from a psychological and symbolic perspective. The patient who is "blind" may have a need not to "see." Coming to an understanding of the precipitant for the disorder through careful questioning, sometimes aided by hypnosis or an interview using amobarbital (Amytal), is of great value in the resolution of the symptoms. Some physicians may find it impossible to believe that patients who have a conversion disorder are not aware that their psychology is the "cause" of the symptoms.

Patients with conversion disorders are not necessarily hysterical in demeanor. Whereas some patients may seem unnaturally calm about their malady, a phenomenon known as la belle indifférence, patients may also present with extreme distress caused by the sudden alteration in their physical functioning. The spectrum of intentionality in patients with medically unexplained motor or sensory symptoms or deficits runs from conversion to malingering. Conversion is unconscious and yields psychological gains that are outside the person's awareness. Malingering is entirely conscious and for the purpose of more readily apparent external incentives.

Clinical Vignette 6

A psychiatric consultation was requested for Ms. H, a 33-year-old woman who was admitted with paresis of the right hand. Her symptoms had developed slowly during the previous day, and she had a history of a stroke 5 years before this admission. The patient was obese and had taken oral contraceptives, which had been discontinued a month before the admission. Ms. H was tearful about the sudden change in her physical condition and expressed concern about how her mother would manage the care of her 6-year-old son. Further questioning revealed Ms. H's guilty feeling that an angry encounter with her ex-husband might have precipitated this stroke. Her belief was that she should never lose her temper. She also revealed that she went to church daily, prayed often, and occasionally "spoke in tongues." She was hypnotized during the consultation and was highly hypnotizable using the Hypnotic Induction Profile.[25] During the trance she talked about wishing to punch her ex-husband. The psychiatrist suggested before ending the trance that Ms. H would have greater use of her hand with progressively increasing strength in the hand over the next day. Ms. H had a complete recovery the next day and was able to use her hand without difficulty. She was referred for outpatient psychotherapy to resolve the difficulties with her ex-husband, with whom she had continued contact because of their child.

In somatization disorder, formerly known as Briquet's syndrome, patients have multiple complaints that have persisted for many years and have resulted in medical treatment. Patients may have a history of numerous surgical procedures and of taking many different medications. To fulfill the diagnostic criteria, patients must have complaints involving multiple organ systems and a history that begins relatively early in life, before age 30 years. People with somatization disorder suffer greatly from their constant attempts to obtain treatment. They are at risk of becoming physically dependent on prescribed medications. They may also suffer serious adverse effects from unnecessary medications that are prescribed or from taking combinations of medications. They have morbidity resulting from surgical and medical procedures and may engage in numerous treatments simultaneously that put them at risk.

Pain is a frequent complaint of many patients. Pain is a subjective experience and all pain, no matter what the origin, can be modulated by the person's emotional state. Because there is no test for pain, the physician must always consider the possibilities that the discomfort is caused by some general medical condition not yet diagnosed and that the pain is a psychological symptom. The patient's subjective experience does not guide the diagnosis in differentiating pain derived from an undiscovered physical source from pain that is a symptom of a somatoform disorder.

Patients who present with chronic pain syndromes should also be evaluated for depression. Even when there is evidence that such a patient is clinically depressed, the chronic pain may still stem from a medical illness. However, treatment for the pain is not successful unless the mood disorder is treated. As tolerance for pain varies considerably, it can be difficult to assess a patient's complaint. Patients' pain is real, as is their suffering, even if the treatment does not involve analgesics. Tricyclic antidepressants have been shown to be effective in the treatment of certain pain syndromes, without accompanying depression.[26] In the absence of depression, selective serotonin reuptake inhibitors have not been shown to be particularly effective as analgesics.[26]

Whether the patient's pain is best treated with analgesics, antidepressants, psychotherapy, or a combination of therapies must be determined clinically. Physicians who are not well trained in the use of oral and parenteral narcotic analgesics often encounter a problem that results in patient-physician discord. Undertreatment of pain with narcotic analgesics is well documented,[27–29] as is an unsubstantiated fear of causing addiction in spite of the low incidence of iatrogenic addiction.[30] Undertreatment of pain can result in patients' using manipulative techniques to obtain narcotic analgesics.[31] The failure to recognize that a patient is not being adequately treated for pain can result in anger at the physician to the point that the patient may want to leave the hospital.[32]

The fear of being ill can reach such proportions that it causes great suffering to the individual. In hypochondriasis, patients persist in the belief that they are or will become ill and complain of symptoms for which no medical cause can be found. Their fears of illness endure despite medical evidence to the contrary. The fear is not delusional; that is, the person can consider the possibility that he or she is not ill. The fear of having an illness should not occur only during a panic attack, and the fear must last for a period of 6 months or more. Transient fears of having an illness may occur in stressful settings, but this is not hypochondriasis; medical students often fear having the illness that they are studying. Patients with hypochondriasis have a high degree of psychiatric comorbidity, particularly mood and anxiety disorders.[33] Hypochondriac patients without other Axis I disorders appear to have a lifestyle of worrying about their body, misinterpreting bodily experiences as signifying illness, and increasing their discomfort by their focusing on the physical experience. These people are different from the patients who develop hypochondriasis in response to a life stress or secondary to another physical disorder.

Clinical Vignette 7

Ms. A consulted a psychiatrist because of feelings of depression, anxiety, and a history of difficulties in relationships with men. She had an overwhelming fear that she had acquired immunodeficiency syndrome but had no physical symptoms with the exception of fatigue. Although she could consider the possibility that she was not infected, she believed her sexual history had exposed her to the virus. At the age of 28 years, she had had sexual experiences with nine men. The idea of being tested to rule out acquired immunodeficiency syndrome was too frightening because she was convinced that she would test seropositive, and she refused human immunodeficiency virus testing. Treatment of her depression with fluoxetine and psychotherapy focused on her overstimulating relationship with her father as a little girl resulted in complete disappearance of her fears after several months. She started a relationship with a man and, when appropriate, recommended that they both be tested for human immunodeficiency virus before becoming involved sexually. They eventually married and had several children. The hypochondriasis did not return when she developed a postpartum depression (requiring antidepressant treatment) after the birth of her first child.

Body dysmorphic disorder is a preoccupation with a defect of physical appearance in an individual who has a consensually normal appearance. This bodily defect may be imagined or it may be an exaggeration of an actual but insignificant physical attribute.[34] Patients who have anorexia nervosa, who regard their body as excessively fat in spite of a thin appearance and restricted caloric intake, are not included in the body dysmorphic diagnostic category. The disorder was previously termed dysmorphophobia, and patients with such beliefs were described by Morselli more than 100 years ago.[34] Patients' preoccupation with their "deformity" can result in withdrawal from social engagement, repeated consultations with physicians, and attempts to correct the imagined defect with plastic surgery or cosmetic maneuvers. Individuals with delusional beliefs about a physical defect are diagnosed as having delusional disorder, somatic type. However, it may be difficult to make this distinction.[35] Treatment of patients diagnosed with body dysmorphic disorder using antipsychotics has not been particularly successful. It has also been argued that the distinction between body dysmorphic disorder and obsessive-compulsive disorder may be blurred in some patients.[36]

Clinical Vignette 8

In spite of her family's assurances and the attention of several men, Ms. B believed that her hair was thinning and that this made her unattractive. She had consulted several dermatologists for remedies that would increase hair growth, and she wore a baseball cap at all times. If she went out for a social engagement she wore some other type of head cover. Her experience of hair loss was extremely distressing. She complained of feeling depressed and having low self-esteem, but she had no other symptoms of a mood disorder. Her psychiatrist recommended she start sertraline, at a dose that was raised to 200 mg daily during a period of 2 weeks. After 8 weeks of treatment, Ms. B felt considerably better about her appearance. Although no noticeable change could be observed in the quantity of her hair, she felt comfortable going out without any type of head cover.

Factitious Symptoms

Perhaps no group of patients produces more negative reactions in physicians than those who create medical conditions or overtly lie about being ill. Such patients are likely to engender anger, not sympathy, when the situation is discovered. Physicians commonly fail to distinguish people who have psychological needs that are met by assuming the role of being sick (factitious disorder) from people who feign illness for reasons for personal gain (malingering). Any physical presentation may be factitiously produced, and patients may develop serious medical conditions secondary to their induction of symptoms. Such patients may precipitously leave the hospital when confronted with the discovery of their behavior, but they may also become acutely suicidal. It is difficult for many nonpsychiatric physicians to comprehend why people would make themselves ill to assume the sick role. This failure to understand results from a failure to appreciate that the sick role confers special rights, which the patient may seek above any other consideration. Patients may feign physical illness, psychological illness, or a combination of both.[37]

Clinical Vignette 9

A 28-year-old nurse presented with a long history of aseptic blisters over her entire body. These were painful and resulted in scarring of her skin. She gave a history of numerous work-ups, none of which yielded a cause for her condition. She also gave a history of the violent death of her husband and young child in a motor vehicle accident. The pastor of her church confirmed that she had come to him during her grief. During her hospital stay, she was a model patient who was well liked by all of the staff. When the work-up for the continued blistering was negative, the staff suspected that she might be inducing her symptoms. A search of her room revealed a syringe and a container of insecticide. Confrontation of the patient with this information resulted in an overt suicide attempt. A discussion with the patient revealed that she held the fixed conviction that no one would care for her if she were not medically ill. She was aware of her need to obtain concern and caring by being ill and could conceive of no other alternative for herself. It was necessary to hospitalize her in the psychiatric service, because she remained dangerously suicidal once her behavior was known and her creation of the "illness" was prevented.

There are also patients who assume the sick role for different kinds of personal gain. These include obtaining relief from financial responsibilities by pretending to be ill, obtaining money from disability insurance, eluding legal proceedings, or avoiding other unpleasant life events. Malingering is not considered a psychiatric disorder but rather is a conscious behavior in which the sick role is created because of external incentives.

Conclusion

For a physician, nothing is more rewarding than solving the diagnostic puzzle of a patient with a complex presentation of physical and psychological signs and symptoms, helping to return the patient to health. This challenge exists for psychiatrists and nonpsychiatrists, both of whom see many such patients. Patients report their symptoms and their subjective experience, but it is the physician who puts that information into a differential diagnostic formulation. The physician's understanding of the role of culture and cultural biases toward mental illness and of the physical components of mood and anxiety disorders results in a consideration of a psychiatric diagnosis, even if the patient offers no complaint of psychological symptoms. Instances in which patients' physical complaints are part of mood and anxiety disorders may cause diagnostic confusion for physicians who consider only medical diagnoses.

There are patients who insist that they have a medical problem and whose claim is not confirmed by physical examination or laboratory testing. The psychological need to have a physical complaint is the psychiatric disorder for this group of patients. At the other end of this physical-psychiatric continuum are patients, without obvious physical discomfort to suggest a medical condition, who may be misdiagnosed as having a psychiatric disorder because their presentation is atypical or their complaints are primarily in the domain of how they feel or how they think. Our unique role as physicians enables us to pay attention to all symptoms without the bias of a mind-body dualism. When it comes to the diagnostic consideration of a psychiatric versus a medical condition we know that it is not either/or but often is both. This is the modern practice of medicine, in which we seek to understand and care for the entire patient.

REFERENCES

1. Becker J, Kleinman A: Psychosocial Aspects of Depression. Hillsdale, NJ: Lawrence Erlbaum, 1991.
2. Kleinman A: Rethinking Psychiatry. New York: Free Press, 1988.
3. Ormel J, Van Den Brink W, Koeter MWJ, et al: Recognition, management and outcome of psychological disorders in primary care: A naturalistic follow-up study. Psychol Med 1990; 20:909–923.
4. Sherbourne CD, Wells KB, Hays RD, et al: Subthreshold depression and depressive disorder: Clinical characteristics of general medical and mental health specialty outpatients. Am J Psychiatry 1994; 151:1777–1784.
5. Yerkes RM, Dodson JD: The relationship of strength of stimulus to rapidity of habit formation. J Comp Neurol 1908; 18:459–482.
6. Hall RCW (ed): Psychiatric Presentation of Medical Illness: Somatopsychic Disorders. New York: SP Medical & Scientific Books, 1980.
7. Sheehan DV, Sheehan KH: The classification of anxiety and hysterical states. Part II. Toward a more heuristic classification. J Clin Psychopharmacol 1982; 2:386–393.
8. Muskin PR: Panics, prolapse and PVCs. Gen Hosp Psychiatry 1985; 7:219–223.
9. Gorman JM, Fyer AJ, Gliklich J, et al: Mitral valve prolapse and panic disorders: Effect of imipramine. In Klein DF, Rabkin JG (eds): Anxiety—New Research and Changing Concepts. New York: Raven Press, 1981:317–326.
10. Crowe RR, Gaffney G, Kerber R: Panic attacks in families of patients with mitral valve prolapse. J Affect Disord 1982; 4:121–125.
11. O'Hara MW, Zekoski EM, Philipps LH, Wright EJ: Controlled prospective study of postpartum mood disorders: Comparison of childbearing and nonchildbearing women. J Abnorm Psychol 1990; 99:3–15.
12. Wells KB, Golding JM, Burnam MA: Psychiatric disorder and limitations in physical functioning in a sample of the Los Angeles general population. Am J Psychiatry 1988; 145:712–717.
13. Feldman E, Mayou R, Hawton K, et al: Psychiatric disorder in medical inpatients. Q J Med 1986; 74:485–489.
14. Strain JJ, Grossman S: Psychological Care of the Medically Ill. New York: Appleton-Century-Crofts, 1975.
15. Hall RCW, Popkin MK, Devaul R, et al: Physical illness presenting as psychiatric disease. Arch Gen Psychiatry 1978; 35:1315–1320.
16. Perry SW, Tross S: Psychiatric problems of AIDS inpatients at the New York Hospital: Preliminary report. Public Health Rep 1984; 99:200–205.
17. Dilley JW, Ochitill HN, Perl M, et al: Findings in psychiatric consultations with patients with acquired immune deficiency syndrome. Am J Psychiatry 1985; 142:82–86.
18. Navia BA, Jordan BD, Price RW: The AIDS dementia complex: I. Clinical features. Ann Neurol 1986; 19:517–524.
19. Navia BA, Cho ES, Petito CK, Price W: The AIDS dementia complex: II. Neuropathology. Ann Neurol 1986; 19:525–535.
20. Johannet C, Muskin PR: Mood and behavioral disorders in hospitalized AIDS patients. Psychosomatics 1990; 31:55–59.
21. Tune L, Carr S, Hoag E, Cooper T: Anticholinergic effects of drugs commonly prescribed for the elderly: Potential means for assessing risk of delirium. Am J Psychiatry 1992; 11149:1393–1394.
22. Drugs that cause psychiatric symptoms. Med Lett Drugs Ther 1993; 35:65–70.
23. Ford CV: The somatizing disorders. Psychosomatics 1986; 27:327–337.
24. Strauss DH, Spitzer RI, Muskin PR: Maladaptive denial of physical illness: A proposal for DSM-IV. Am J Psychiatry 1990; 147:1168–1171.
25. Spiegel H: Manual for Hypnotic Induction Profile: Eye-Roll Levitation Method. New York: Soni Medica, 1973.
26. Max MB, Lynch SA, Muir J, et al: Effects of desipramine, amitriptyline, and fluoxetine on pain in diabetic neuropathy. N Engl J Med 1992; 326:1250–1256.
27. Marks RM, Sachar EJ: Undertreatment of medical inpatients with narcotic analgesics. Ann Intern Med 1973; 78:173–181.
28. Sriwatanakul K, Weis OF, Alloza JL, et al: Analysis of narcotic analgesic usage in the treatment of postoperative pain. JAMA 1983; 250:926–929.
29. Perry SW: Undertreatment of pain on a burn unit. Gen Hosp Psychiatry 1984; 6:308–316.
30. Kanner RM, Foley KM: Patterns of narcotic use in a cancer pain clinic. Ann N Y Acad Sci 1981; 362:161–172.
31. Weissman DE, Haddox JD: Opioid pseudoaddiction—an iatrogenic syndrome. Pain 1989; 36:363–366.
32. Albert HD, Kornfeld DS: The threat to sign out against medical advice. Ann Intern Med 1973; 79:888–891.
33. Barsky AJ, Wyshak G, Klerman GL: Psychiatric comorbidity in DSM-III-R hypochondriasis. Arch Gen Psychiatry 1992; 49:101–108.
34. Phillips KA: Body dysmorphic disorder: The distress of imagined ugliness. Am J Psychiatry 1991; 148:1138–1149.
35. Thomas CS: Dysmorphophobia and monosymptomatic hypochondriasis. [letter] Am J Psychiatry 1985; 142:1121.
36. Tynes LL, White K, Steketee GS: Toward a new nosology of obsessive compulsive disorder. Compr Psychiatry 1990; 31:465–480.
37. Phillips MR, Ward NG, Ries RK: Factitious mourning: Painless patienthood. Am J Psychiatry 1983; 140:420–425.

CHAPTER

27 Behavior and Adaptive Functioning

Susan C. Vaughan
John M. Oldham

To function adaptively means to behave in such a way that one's attitudes and actions are well matched to the demands and constraints of the external environment and that one's sense of internal discomfort or distress is minimized. Therefore, by definition, the ability to adapt depends both on the individual's behavioral repertoire and on the external environment. This chapter focuses on the ingredients that shape personality and the ways in which personality in turn affects behavior. Several systems for thinking about personality are described. In addition, the domains in which individuals are typically expected to function are reviewed, with particular attention to the ways in which various personality styles affect functioning in each domain. Patterns of behavior that are frequently pathological in nature, such as impulsive, compulsive, and avoidant behaviors, are examined. Finally, approaches to the assessment of behavior and adaptive functioning in the psychiatric interview are reviewed.

Personality Style

Clinical Vignette 1

Mr. A, a successful 48-year-old attorney, is married and has three children. He has enjoyed the position of partner in his large corporate law firm for many years, although he continues to work long hours. He often wishes he had enough time and energy to really enjoy his children, but he does manage to spend weekends with his family at their country home. He feels satisfied with his work and particularly enjoys his days in court, where he is known as a polished orator and a tough opponent who is likely to make clever legal arguments. His wife sometimes complains that he is too dedicated to work and too worried about money to enjoy the rewards of his labor. She wishes he would let loose and have fun more often, but she is generally satisfied with their marriage.

As a baby, Mr. A was considered easy, seldom ruffled by the inevitable delays of gratification in being fed and changed. He was a bright and cheerful child until age 10 years, when his father was killed in a car accident while driving home from work. After his father's death, his mother noticed that he became serious and sad, responding to the loss by becoming the "little man" of the family and by always watching out for his little brother, 3 years younger. His mother was particularly worried about this because her sister had a history of severe depression. In high school, he was class president and an excellent track-and-field athlete. No one was surprised when he studied government in college and entered law school.

Clinical Vignette 2

Mr. B is a 35-year-old divorced advertising executive. He enjoys his powerful role within his company and is well known for his impressively slick presentations. However, one problem for Mr. B in his career has been his difficulty keeping personal and work lives separate; during his fling with a junior colleague, his coworkers noted that he was more concerned with flirting than with finishing an important project. He seems to delight in the macho image he projects, basking in the attention of women at work and annoying other men with his tales of previous romantic conquests. These behaviors have kept Mr. B from being promoted to an even more prominent position. Mr. B's family suspects that he will never have a successful marriage until he stops being a "ladies' man."

As a baby, Mr. B was fussy and difficult owing to repeated bouts of colic in the first year of life. Once he recovered, however, he rapidly became the family entertainer. The youngest of five children, he was known for his antics and pranks. When he entered adolescence, Mr. B became engrossed in bodybuilding and football, quickly learning that his athletic prowess made him the heartthrob of his high-school class. Mr. B's father had also been a star athlete and responded to his athletic interests by coaching and encouraging him.

Although Mr. B was intelligent and graduated near the top of his high school class, he was far more interested in organizing parties. College was initially rough for Mr. B, who by then had become accustomed to being on top at high school. In college, he changed his major several times, trying to figure out what image he was trying to build for himself. His fantasies of becoming a National Football League defensive back were dashed by a knee injury during his junior year, which was largely the result of his overtraining and insistence on pushing himself to his limits. After this, Mr. B devoted himself to learning all about the business world instead. Network-

Clinical Vignette 2 *continued*

ing and social chatter came naturally to Mr. B, allowing him to rise rapidly within the advertising world. In fact, he proposed to his wife soon after they met at a business cocktail party; she was his boss' date for the evening. The marriage ended less than 2 years later when she discovered the affair with his coworker.

An individual's personality style has a great influence on his or her behavior and adaptive functioning. Personality is shaped from a blend of inborn temperament, genetic strengths and vulnerabilities, and the impact of positive and negative life experiences. Psychiatry is moving toward an improved understanding of human behavior that focuses on the ways that these factors interact with one another.

There is evidence of striking variation among neonates in their capacity to tolerate frustration, which reflects their inborn temperaments.[1] Such individual differences in temperament form the biological substrate that interacts with early development. Temperament affects the degree to which different infants are susceptible to distress as well as their variations in attachment style.[2] Mr. A's high tolerance for frustration was an advantage as an infant; his mother considered him an easy baby who was not too demanding. In contrast, only when Mr. B's repeated bouts of colic in his first year of life ended could he assume the role of family prankster.

Genetic factors of various types also play a role in development, particularly when they interact with environmental factors. Mr. A's mother was correct to be concerned that both his father's death when Mr. A was young and her sister's history of depression placed him at higher risk. Brown and Harris[3] have demonstrated a clear link between early loss of a parent and vulnerability to depression in the face of later stressful life events. Yet inherited characteristics can also be protective; because Mr. A is intelligent, he was able to become a talented lawyer. In contrast, Mr. B has no family history of mental illness. His hypermasculine style is reminiscent of his father's and is influenced both by genetics and by his relationship with his father. In general, genetic factors account for between 30% and 60% of the variance in adult personality traits.[4]

Life experiences also have an impact on an individual and affect her or his behavior for better or worse. After his father's death, Mr. A developed responsibility and conscientiousness atypical of a 10-year-old in addition to incurring a greater risk of depression. In contrast to the death of Mr. A's father, which was beyond his control, Mr. B's knee injury was probably the result of his own actions. His injury ended his dream of playing professional football but helped point him in the direction of a successful business career. Considering whether particular experiences are the result of fate in contrast to whether they are partially brought about by the person's own actions can be important in thinking about their impact and meaning.

In practice, the reciprocal interactions of the intrapsychic experiences of a person and environmental influences make the evaluation of how these factors interact difficult. Wachtel[5] referred to this reciprocity as a cyclical process. Mr. A's affective state after the loss of his father probably colored his behavior in the world as well as his experience of relationships and events in daily life. Separating aspects of functioning related to his affective state from external reality would be a problem and probably impossible.

Personality styles have been described in a variety of ways with use of different models of normal personality variation. These models are either categorical or dimensional in nature. In a categorical model, a person is described as meeting or not meeting the criteria for various diagnostic categories. In a dimensional model of personality, a person is evaluated in terms of the blend of various traits or factors he or she possesses, measured on a continuum. In general, as a person moves toward the extreme end of a given continuum in the dimensional model, she or he becomes more likely to meet the criteria for a categorical diagnosis. Some dimensional models set a threshold beyond which a given characteristic is likely to be a problem or pathological.

The categorical model is a more common approach to diagnosis within clinical psychiatry and within medicine in general. However, if Mr. A does not have obsessive-compulsive personality disorder, the unique characteristics of his personality style will not be captured within a categorical model. In addition, the categorical model suggests that the categories in which diagnoses are given are not overlapping.[6] In contrast, a dimensional model allows the retention of important information about a person's blend of traits but says less about how pathological these patterns are and is more difficult to use clinically than a straightforward categorical diagnosis.[7]

The personality disorders outlined in the *Diagnostic and Statistical Manual of Mental Disorders,* Fourth Edition (DSM-IV) provide an example of a categorical system. In DSM-IV terms, Mr. A does not meet the full criteria for any of the 10 personality disorders even though he shows some features of obsessive-compulsive personality disorder. He is excessively devoted to work to the exclusion of leisure and has a tendency to be overly cautious with money. In contrast, Mr. B would receive a diagnosis of histrionic personality disorder because he is often sexually seductive, is uncomfortable when he is not the center of attention, and consistently uses his physical appearance to draw attention to himself. He is emotionally shallow and tends to portray himself as a "hip" advertising executive. Although others may not see their relationships with him as intimate, Mr. B tends to assume that his relationships are more intimate than they actually are. However, a diagnosis of histrionic personality disorder would still mean overlooking those aspects of Mr. B's personality that are narcissistic in nature but do not meet full criteria for narcissistic personality disorder.[8]

Oldham and Morris[9] translated each of the personality disorders of the DSM-IV system into a less pathological collection of categories that describe normal personality styles. In their system, a cross between a categorical and a dimensional model, conscientiousness is the positive personality trait that in excess becomes obsessive-compulsive personality disorder. In Mr. A's case, both the positive aspects of his conscientiousness in helping him to achieve his goals at work and the negative impact of this trait on his wife and children when he works too hard are evident. In this model, being dramatic is a character style that when overdone becomes histrionic; self-confidence in excess becomes narcissism. A literature review by Widiger and Costa[10] supports the hypothesis that DSM-IV personality

Table 27–1 Oldham and Morris' Personality Style–Personality Disorder Continuum

Style	DSM-IV Disorder
Vigilant	Paranoid
Solitary	Schizoid
Idiosyncratic	Schizotypal
Adventurous	Antisocial
Mercurial	Borderline
Dramatic	Histrionic
Self-confident	Narcissistic
Sensitive	Avoidant
Devoted	Dependent
Conscientious	Obsessive-compulsive

disorders represent extreme variants of normal personality traits. Table 27–1 summarizes the personality style–personality disorder continuum described by Oldham and Morris.

A continuum model such as this one acknowledges that whereas too much of a good thing may constitute a disorder, everyone's personality consists of traits that can be adaptive or maladaptive. The quantity rather than the quality of a given trait is often what makes it a problem or adaptive. Similarly, flexibility and variability are important determinants of a person's adaptive capacity.

Examples of dimensional models of personality include the five-factor model,[11] Cloninger's seven-factor model,[12, 13] and the biogenic spectrum model of Siever and Davis.[14] The five-factor model of personality was first suggested by McDougall[15] in 1932 and was elaborated and updated by Digman[16] and McCrae and Costa[17] among others. In the five-factor model, personality traits are described in terms of a taxonomy of five dimensions. These include neuroticism, extraversion, openness to experience, agreeableness, and conscientiousness. Someone with an obsessive-compulsive personality style, such as Mr. A, is likely to score high on the factor of conscientiousness in the five-factor model. Conscientiousness encompasses the degree to which competence, order, dutifulness, achievement, self-discipline, and deliberation are likely to be important to an individual. In addition, those with obsessive-compulsive disorder are likely to score high in terms of neuroticism, meaning that they have excess amounts of traits such as anxiety, hostility, depression, and self-consciousness. Those with obsessive styles or personality disorders typically score low on factors such as extraversion, openness, and agreeableness. In contrast, Mr. B scores high on traits such as gregariousness and excitement seeking (extraversion) as well as fantasy and artistic sensibility (openness). However, he has particular difficulty being appropriately conscientious. Table 27–2 summarizes the factors of the five-factor model and their relationship to DSM-IV categories.

A second dimensional model of personality is Cloninger's seven-factor model of temperament and character (Table 27–3). In this model, a patient's behavior is evaluated on seven separate dimensions. Four of the seven dimensions are related to temperament and have been shown to be independently heritable, manifested early in life, and

Table 27–2 The Five-Factor Model

Factor	Traits	DSM-IV Example
Neuroticism	Anxiety Hostility Depression Self-consciousness Impulsiveness Vulnerability	High in borderline Low in schizoid
Extraversion	Warmth Gregariousness Assertiveness Activity Excitement seeking Positive emotions	High in histrionic Low in avoidant
Openness	Fantasy Esthetics Feelings Actions Ideas Values	High in schizotypal Low in paranoid
Agreeableness	Trust Straightforwardness Altruism Compliance Modesty Tendermindedness	High in dependent Low in narcissistic
Conscientiousness	Competence Order Dutifulness Achievement striving Self-discipline Deliberation	High in obsessive-compulsive Low in antisocial

involved in early perceptual memory and habit formation.[13] These four dimensions include novelty seeking, harm avoidance, reward dependence, and persistence. Mr. A is particularly attuned to avoiding harm, and his behavior is typically characterized by a high degree of persistence; he is cautious and thoughtful in approaching new situations and doggedly pursues his goals. Mr. B ranks high on Cloninger's dimensions of novelty seeking and reward dependence; he is quickly bored by things that are not new and exciting and actively seeks the approval and attention of others. Figure 27–1 is a schematic representation of Cloninger's model.

Table 27–3 Cloninger's Seven-Factor Model of Temperament and Character

Temperament Factor	Behavioral Effect
Harm avoidance	Behavioral inhibition
Reward dependence	Motivation for behavior
Novelty seeking	Initiation of exploration
Persistence	Maintenance of behavior
Character Factor	**Self-Concept Effect**
Self-directedness	Sense of self as autonomous
Cooperativeness	Sense of self as part of community
Self-transcendence	Sense of self in the universe

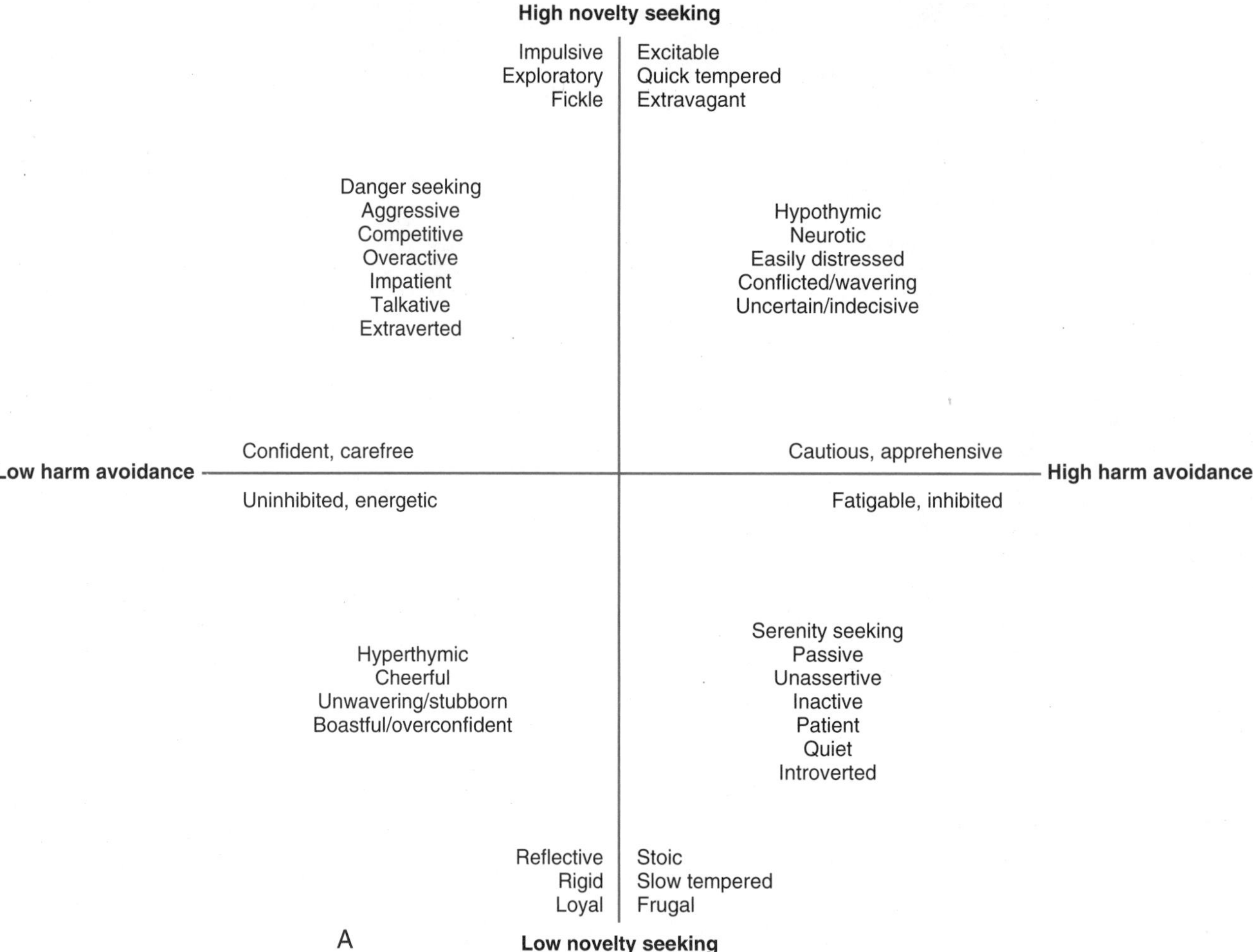

Figure 27–1 *Cloninger's model: harm avoidance, reward dependence, and novelty seeking. (*A *to* C *from Cloninger CR: A systematic method for clinical description and classification of personality variants: A proposal. Arch Gen Psychiatry 1987; 44:573–588. Copyright 1987, American Medical Association.)*

Cloninger also describes three dimensions of character, namely, self-directedness, cooperativeness, and self-transcendence. The blend of these three characteristics that an individual possesses helps to determine self-concept, such as whether the individual identifies himself or herself as an autonomous individual, as an integral part of humanity, and as a part of the universe as a whole. Those with low degrees of self-directedness and low degrees of cooperativeness are more likely to have personality disorders.[18] Someone as relatively well adapted as Mr. A is likely to rate high on the traits of self-directedness, cooperativeness, and self-transcendence. In contrast, Mr. B may be less self-directed and less cooperative than Mr. A.

A third dimensional model of personality is the biogenic spectrum model of Siever and Davis.[14] This model proposes that certain personality styles and disorders are associated with and are characterological variants of various Axis I disorders. Thus, personality disorders are not extreme variants of normal but are characterological variants of Axis I disorders. For example, Mr. A's obsessive-compulsive style may be a variant of anxiety disorder; Mr. B's histrionic personality disorder may be a variant of an impulse-control disorder. Table 27–4 presents details of the biogenic model.

Table 27–4 The Biogenic Model and DSM-IV

Axis I Disorder	Example of Axis II Variant
Mood	Borderline
Anxiety	Avoidant
Impulse-control	Antisocial
Psychotic	Schizoid

Domains of Functioning

Each person's unique personality style is reflected in the various domains in which the person functions. DSM-IV's Axis V, the Global Assessment of Functioning, provides a 100-point scale with which to rate a person's overall level of adaptation. It provides a useful global rating of adaptive function that assesses the degree of symptoms and the capacity to function in social and occupational spheres.[8] These domains are somewhat overlapping. Oldham and Morris' model of normal personality derived from the DSM

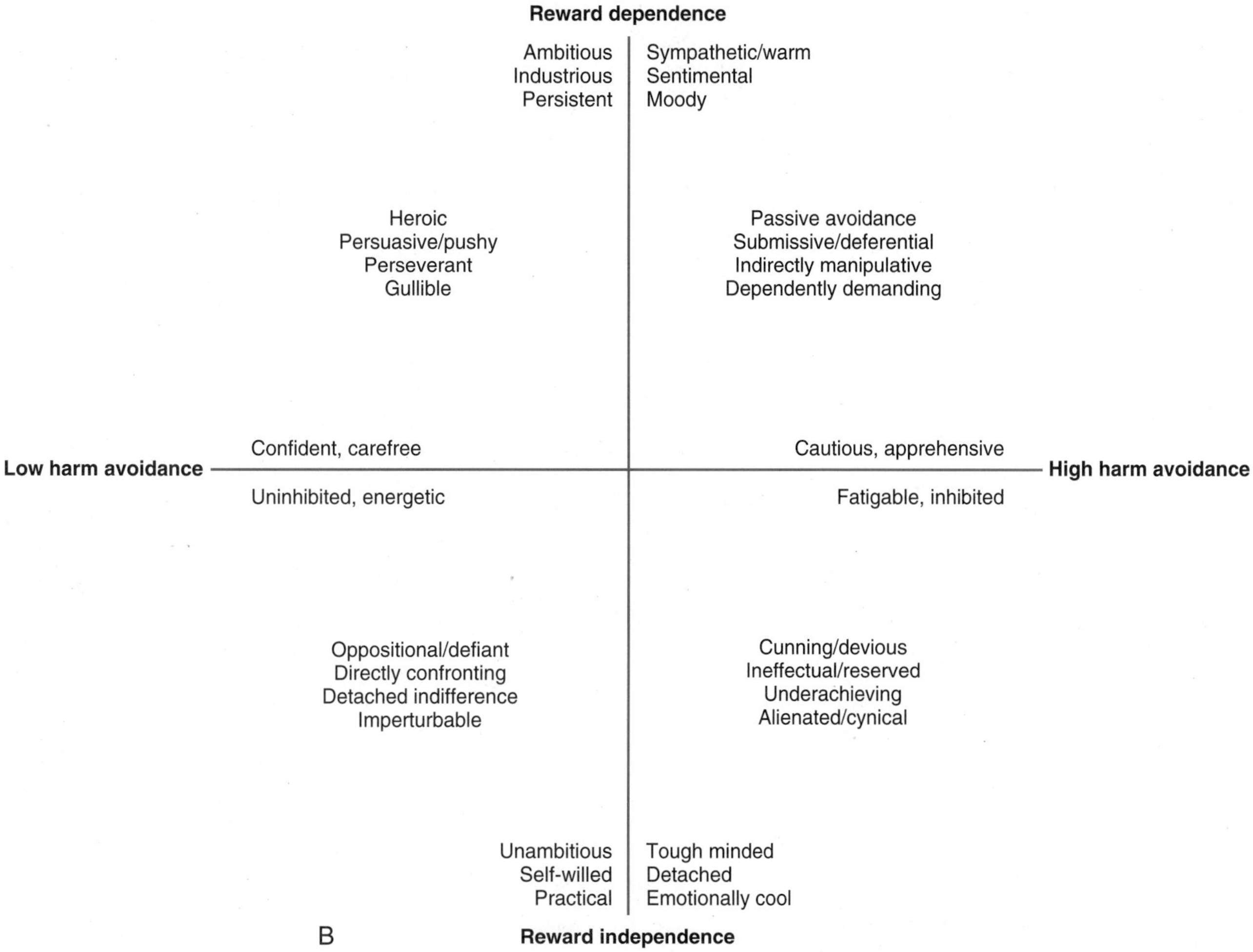

Figure 27–1 *Continued*

Illustration continued on following page

categories provides a framework for thinking about how different personality styles predispose people to emphasize or minimize the importance they assign each domain and to function more or less effectively in each area.

Social and Interpersonal Functioning

Interpersonal styles greatly affect social functioning, which in turn has a large impact on both work and leisure time functioning. Distinctive individual personality styles affect a person's perception of the importance of relationships with others as well as the quality and depth of the bonds they can form. Those with solitary traits are unlikely to crave and seek close relationships, whereas those with a devoted style become uneasy and feel incomplete if they are not with others. Vigilant people are cautious of the attentions of others, whereas dramatic types thrive on the admiration of their peers. Those who are mercurial often run "hot" and "cold" in their relationships with others, sometimes expressing their feelings in ways that offend others; sensitive types are easily affected by the perspectives and behavior of others but tend to keep their feelings to themselves.

The Social Adjustment Scale[19] provides a quantitative way to investigate several types of interpersonal functioning (Table 27–5), including a person's relationships with family of origin, spouse or partner, children, work colleagues, and friends and acquaintances. Some questions assess the degree of overt fighting and friction that is present in these relationships and whether it causes the person to minimize or avoid contact with others. The degree to which a person feels reticent about being reasonably open within each relationship and the degree to which others are depended on to provide various forms of help, such as advice and financial support, are also important indicators of the quality of interpersonal connections. In addition, the scale provides a way to assess whether someone initiates contact with others; whether the individual feels an urge to be defiant or rebellious; and whether the individual feels overly concerned, guilty, or resentful within each relationship. Inherent in these assessments of functioning is an assumption that to be successful, relationships should be interpersonally relatively free of friction and arguments, reciprocal, and supportive. In addition, each person's experience of the relationship should be comfortable and relatively conflict free.

Benjamin's Structural Analysis of Social Behavior (Fig. 27–2) provides another means of assessing recurrent patterns in a person's interactions with others.[20] It has three dimensions: the focus of the interaction, the tone of the interaction (loving versus hating), and whether the interaction is characterized by interdependence versus indepen-

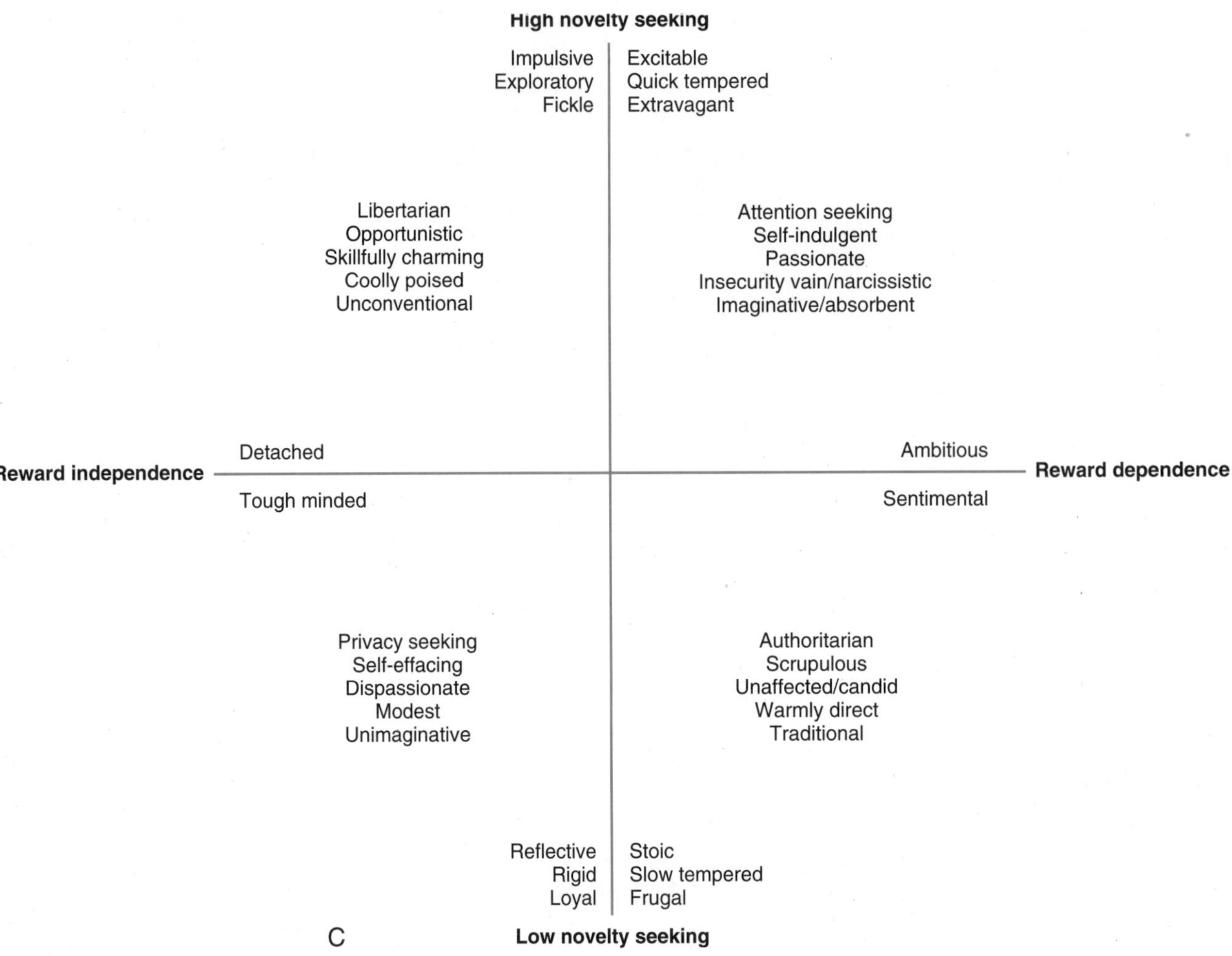

Figure 27–1 *Continued*

dence. The focus in the Structural Analysis of Social Behavior can be on another person; on oneself in relation to another person; or on inward, internal aspects of the self. As an example, a woman cleans house and runs errands with her family in mind; the focus is on others, and the tone of the action is friendly. The act of running the household suggests that the woman influences others in the family, so the score on the third dimension is in the controlling-interdependent direction. The Structural Analysis of Social Behavior is widely used in research settings to describe and quantify a person's mode of interpersonal functioning in various relationships.

Occupational Functioning

Assessing adaptive occupational functioning requires examining the ways in which an individual completes tasks, takes and gives orders, delegates responsibilities, and cooperates with others. Job situations also require an ability to balance demands, obey regulations, and make decisions. Clearly, success in these tasks in part depends on one's capacity for interpersonal functioning. A patient who is mercurial in personal relationships is also likely to have difficulty with coworkers. Work is often the central domain of concern for those with conscientious styles and for those with aggressive styles. For people with these styles of functioning, work is synonymous with fun. In contrast, for those with other personality styles, occupational functioning can be a problem because it is given too little importance. Leisurely people get by with the bare minimum of work, whereas those who are adventurous like challenges but tend to have difficulty with authority at work. Those with a devoted style tend to remain loyal even to jobs they dislike; thus, the problem with work for them is an intrapersonal problem rather than an interpersonal one.

Weissman's Social Adjustment Scale also provides a means of evaluating a person's occupational functioning. The scale focuses on both externally observable behaviors, such as number of days lost in a month and the degree of impairment of performance at work, as well as internal states, such as feeling inadequate, angry, and distressed at work. In addition, whether a person is distressed, disinterested, and bored by work is also assessed. These questions begin to suggest what adaptive occupational functioning comprises, namely, that it consists of being engaged and feeling satisfied about and competent at work. In addition, the Social Adjustment Scale assesses whether these positive internal states are reflected in work performance and relationships with superiors and subordinates.

Leisure

The capacity to enjoy leisure depends in part on other external demands and responsibilities as well as financial and other resources. A single mother with four young children must work harder than many mothers and is less likely to have time, money, and energy available for leisurely pursuits. Yet leisure is more than time left over from work and family. The gusto with which leisure activities are pursued and the types of activities that are chosen are affected by a person's characteristic style. In contrast to the work domain, those with a leisurely style are likely to enjoy their free time and to have myriad hobbies and interests; those with conscientious styles may approach leisure as another job, by working hard at trying to have fun. Those with aggressive styles may choose competitive leisure pursuits, such as sports, in which they can pit their prowess against others; solitary types may prefer solo leisure pursuits that do not involve others.

The Social Adjustment Scale may be used to evaluate how well developed and specific a patient's interests are as well as the frequency with which such activities are pursued. It can be helpful in assessing whether a person's leisure time contacts with others are diminished. The Social Adjustment Scale quantifies aspects of leisure, such as how many social events one has attended in the last month. The experience of loneliness or boredom during free time as well as the person's ability to compensate for these painful states yields a measure of leisure-time adaptation.

Table 27–5 The Social Adjustment Scale

Domain*	Assessment Questions
Work Outside home At home At school	Time lost? Impaired performance? Feelings of inadequacy? Friction with coworkers? Distress about work? Disinterest in work?
Social	Impaired leisure activities? Diminished contacts with others? Diminished social interactions? Reticence to have social contacts? Friction within social contacts? Hypersensitivity? Social discomfort? Loneliness? Boredom? Diminished dating? Disinterest in dating?
Interpersonal Extended family Spouse or partner Parental functioning Family unit	Friction? Reticence? Withdrawn? Dependency? Rebellion? Worry? Guilt? Resentment? Submissiveness? Domineering behavior? Lack of affection? Sexual interest, frequency, problems with partner? Lack of involvement? Impaired communication?

*Each domain is scored on a 5-point scale ranging from 1 (not a problem) to 5 (an extreme problem). In addition, a global score in each domain is assigned by use of this same scale.

Assessing Behavior and Adaptive Functioning in the Clinical Interview

Finding out about a patient's personality style, level of adaptive functioning, and usual patterns of behavior is one of the major tasks of the psychiatric interview. A psychiatrist gains important information from what a patient and those people close to the patient say about her or his behavior. However, a psychiatrist also gains invaluable information by closely observing the person during the interview itself. Whether the psychiatrist is quickly sizing up an agitated patient during a psychiatric emergency or carefully noticing how a patient shifts in the chair during a psychotherapy session, the ability to observe a patient's behavior is one of a psychiatrist's most important tools. A patient's appearance, attitude, and motor behaviors during an interaction with the psychiatrist provide important clues to personality, capacity for interpersonal interactions, and potentially problematical behavior patterns.

Appearance

Observing a patient's appearance includes making a judgment about the overall physical impression of the person reflected by grooming, clothing, poise, and posture. The ability to appear well-kept is impaired in many psychiatric disorders, ranging from the psychotic patient who appears disheveled after being up for several nights to the depressed patient dressed in dark, somber tones and slumped in the chair. Clothing often reveals aspects of personality; patients with extroverted, histrionic, or dramatic personalities often wear brightly colored, unusual clothes and are often garishly made up. Problems with appearance can suggest the possibility of other functional impairments as well.

The motivation and degree of volitional control over appearance must usually be inferred; the character of Klinger in the television series *M*A*S*H* appeared dressed in female clothing in an attempt to earn a discharge from the Army. On the other hand, a patient may try to disguise a psychiatric disorder by focusing on making her or his appearance as normal as possible.

Clinical Vignette 3

Mr. C, a young schizophrenic man, attempted to avoid hospitalization by beginning to shave more regularly and cutting his fingernails. However, he remained unwilling and unable to have his hair cut, attempting to disguise its length by wearing it up under a baseball cap when going outside.

At times, appearance may provide an important clue of an inconsistency in a patient's verbal presentation and suggest a serious behavior problem.

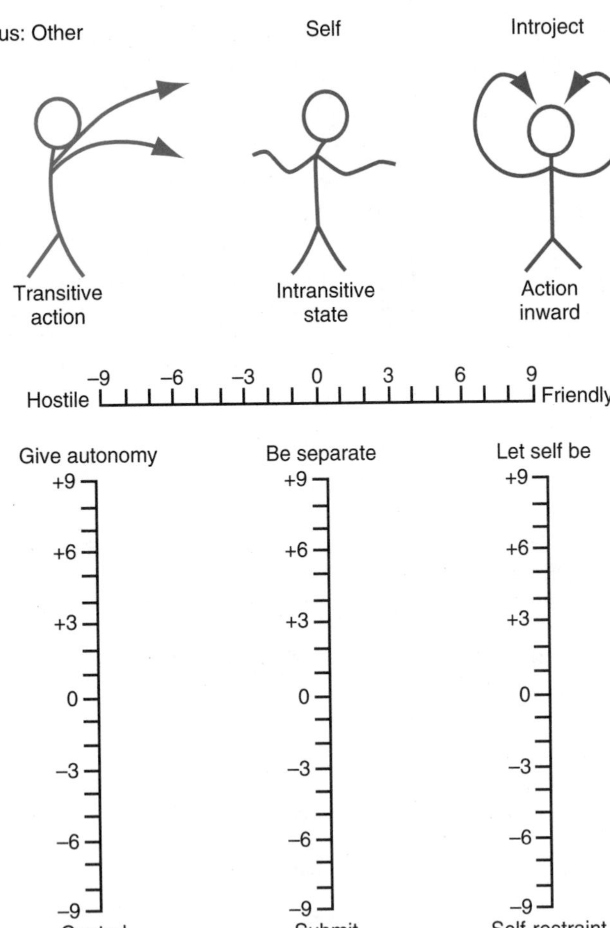

Figure 27–2 *The three dimensions of the Structural Analysis of Social Behavior model. Therapy content and process expressed in interactional terms can be coded in terms of the three dimensions: focus, love versus hate, and interdependence. Viewing all relationships in terms of these dimensions makes parallels among early and current relationships more apparent. (From Benjamin LS: Adding social and intrapsychic descriptors to Axis I of DSM-III. In Million T, Klerman GL [eds]: Contemporary Directions in Psychopathology: Toward the DSM-IV. New York: Guilford Press, 1986:608.)*

Clinical Vignette 4

Ms. D, a middle-aged woman, came to the emergency department claiming that she had run out of Valium and that her prescribing physician was out of town. Her story was convincing and the resident physician was about to give her a prescription when he noted on close examination that she had a dirty hem on both her pants and her jacket sleeves, which seemed inconsistent with her presentation of herself as an executive secretary. After pressing her for more details of her story and consulting with another emergency department, he determined that the patient was actually a homeless woman who got prescriptions from hospitals and then sold them on the street.

Attitude and Cooperation

The interviewer can also detect a patient's attitude and willingness to cooperate during an examination. Attitude and cooperation are related but not identical concepts; a paranoid patient may have a suspicious attitude but may cooperate by answering the interviewer's questions nonetheless. Often, however, a person's attitude and ability to cooperate are both affected by psychiatric illness. Patients may be friendly or hostile, seductive, defensive, or apathetic. During the psychiatric interview, they may seem attentive or disinterested and be frank or evasive and guarded. Again, each of these attitudes and the degree of cooperation a patient exhibits can depend on the underlying psychiatric state or can reflect a conscious manipulation on the part of the patient for the sake of achieving a desired goal. Attitude and degree of cooperativeness with an interviewer yield data about a patient's capacity to establish rapport and relate to others, thereby suggesting the person's general level of interpersonal functioning.

Motor Behavior

The astute examiner can also observe motor behaviors that provide clues to a patient's internal state. First, the overall level of activity should be noted. Behavioral activity is often quantitatively increased in patients with mania or anxiety disorders, whereas it may be decreased in those with depression or intoxication. In addition, impulsivity can sometimes be revealed by motor behaviors, as when a person pounds on a wall or hurls an object. Motor behavior can also provide clues to personality; the dramatic patient often gesticulates freely during conversation, whereas the obsessive patient often conveys a sense of constricted facial movements and gestures. The types of behaviors associated with overactivity may include restlessness, pacing, handwringing, or other forms of agitation. In contrast, psychomotor retardation is a slowing of the usual body movements. A depressed patient with psychomotor slowing may be observed sitting perfectly still, staring into space. Similarly, patients with underlying neurological disorders such as Parkinson's disease or those who are taking medicines that produce parkinsonism may exhibit motor slowing in the form of lack of facial expressiveness and loss of the body movements and gestures that often accompany speech.

Other types of motor behaviors may be unusual or qualitatively different from those observed in normal people. Tics are sudden, rapid, involuntary stereotyped movements or vocalizations. Examples of simple tics include facial grimaces, blinking, and neck jerking or shrugging as well as throat clearing, coughing, barking, or snorting vocal sounds. More complex motor tics include jumping, touching, or grooming behaviors as well as vocalizations consisting of complex phrases, socially unacceptable obscene words (coprolalia), or repeating of one's own words or the words of others (palilalia and echolalia, respectively). These tics are exacerbated by stress and anxiety and can be voluntarily suppressed for a time, although they are ultimately experienced as irresistible. They are generally believed to disappear during sleep.

Another clinically relevant way of approaching the task of assessing a patient's behavior was suggested by Seymour Halleck.[21] He suggested that in addition to focusing on appearance, attitude, and cooperation in the clinical evaluation, the interviewer can assess 1) the patient's physical and emotional attractiveness; 2) his or her means of seeking control and whether control is a central issue; and 3) the degree to which the patient is dependent, passive, aggressive, attention seeking, private, or exploitative in his or her behaviors. Although patients with different styles have different motives for and various ways of expressing these types of behaviors, examining their behavior in each of these categories is likely to provide a productive additional approach to evaluating behavior and adaptive functioning.

Problem Patterns of Behavior

Problem patterns of behavior, such as impulsivity, compulsivity, and avoidance, cut across diagnostic groups; looking for these patterns can be a fruitful way of characterizing aspects of maladaptive functioning. Each of these three patterns can arise from a wide array of psychiatric problems. For example, intoxicated people are often disinhibited and impulsive, acting in ways that they would not act if they were sober. However, a manic patient may also be impulsive, often spending money freely or engaging in sexual activity without considering the consequences of these actions. Labeling each of these patterns of behavior impulsive is an important first step in reaching a diagnosis. In addition, finding one type of impulsive behavior should prompt the psychiatrist to look for others and to predict that the patient may act impulsively in the future.

Impulsive Behaviors

Clinical Vignette 5

Mr. E, 34 years old, has a flair for choosing the right gifts for others. While shopping, he sees an expensive necklace that is perfect for his girlfriend and buys it. The time elapsed between seeing the necklace and finding himself at the register, credit card in hand, is less than 3 minutes. Although a little nervous about making such a big purchase, he decides he will pay off the necklace in several installments and give it to his girlfriend for Christmas.

Clinical Vignette 6

Ms. F, 23 years old, is undergoing evaluation in the emergency department after a suicide attempt by acetaminophen overdose. She reports that the attempt followed a fight with her boyfriend, after which she locked herself in the bathroom and swallowed several handfuls of pills before he broke the lock on the door and called for help. In the emergency department, Ms. F is tearful and angry that her boyfriend wants to break up with her. He has been restricted from visiting her in the emergency department because she attempted to strike his head and chest with her fists when he was initially allowed to see her. Her psychiatric history is notable for two past suicide attempts by pill ingestion, frequent episodes of binging on food and then purging, repeated episodes of burning herself with a cigarette and scratching her wrists with a steak knife, and problem weekend bouts of drinking accompanied by blackouts.

Impulsive behaviors are actions that arise without much delay between the formation of an idea or desire and its gratification in action. Not all impulsive behavior is pathological; in a muted and well-modulated form, impulsivity is closer to spontaneity, as Mr. E's necklace purchase suggests. Certain personality styles, such as dramatic characters, are more likely to be spontaneous or impulsive than others. Mr. E's capacity to decide rapidly results in the perfect gift for his girlfriend. In contrast, a person with a conscientious style might decide to think about the purchase for a few days, then return to buy the necklace only to find it gone.

However, in its more extreme forms, impulsivity is often pathological, as the case of Ms. F shows. A number of behaviors that seem dissimilar may have impulsivity as the common and uniting thread. In DSM-IV terms, Ms. F's history suggests a panoply of disorders including major depressive disorder, bulimia nervosa, impulse-control disorder not otherwise specified (cigarette burns), alcohol dependence, and a personality disorder such as borderline (stormy interpersonal relationships; self-injurious behaviors, such as substance abuse, suicide attempts, and self-mutilation). However, all of her problem behaviors may be more parsimoniously described as impulse-ridden than by reference to each DSM-IV diagnosis.

Another advantage of thinking about impulsivity as a distinct pattern of problem behavior is that impulsivity in one sphere is often accompanied by impulsive behaviors in other arenas. Thus, on learning that Ms. F has overdosed on pills, the emergency department psychiatrist should already be wondering about self-mutilation, eating disorders, and substance abuse. In a study of the relationship between impulsivity and eating disorders, Fahy and Eisler[22] reported that 51% of 67 bulimic subjects interviewed had at least one other form of impulsive behavior. These

Table 27–6 Impulsive, Compulsive, and Avoidant Patterns of Behavior

Pattern	Examples
Impulsive	Self-mutilation Suicide Substance abuse Pathological gambling Binging and purging Hair pulling Kleptomania Pyromania Paraphilias
Compulsive	Hand washing, checking Sexual compulsions Food restriction
Avoidant	Agoraphobia Simple phobias (e.g., acrophobia) Social phobia

subjects also reported more severe eating disturbances and were less quick to respond to treatment with medication than were bulimic subjects without other comorbid forms of impulsivity. In another study, 40 prisoners with antisocial personality disorders and self-injury while incarcerated showed significantly higher rates of impulsive behaviors such as fighting, rage outbursts, and drug use than did 40 prisoners with antisocial personality disorder who were not self-injurious in prison.[23] Sher and Trull[24] conceptualized the link between antisocial personality disorder and alcoholism in terms of each as a psychopathological form of disinhibition.

Behaviors that are frequently impulsive in nature include self-mutilation and suicide, substance abuse, pathological gambling, binging and purging eating behaviors, and hair pulling. In addition, urges to steal (kleptomania), to set fires (pyromania), or to engage in sexually perverse or unusual behaviors (paraphilias) also result in impulsive behaviors (Table 27–6).

Different types of impulsive behaviors are often experienced in similar ways by patients. One hallmark of impulsive acts is that they are often preceded by a growing internal sense of tension and discomfort that is reduced by the impulsive act itself. Whether the act is hair pulling (trichotillomania) that results in baldness or pathological gambling that has severe financial consequences, the person is likely to feel that she or he can no longer tolerate the internal tension and that giving in to the impulse will provide relief of an uncomfortable internal state.

Clinical Vignette 7

Ms. G, a 21-year-old woman with borderline personality disorder, carved the word "monster" on her arm. Of this act she said, "I was feeling so tense and angry, like there was a tornado inside of me. As I focused on the small red lines I made with the razor, I began to feel better. The physical pain let me center my attention on my body, and my angry feelings seemed to fade away."

A second characteristic of impulsive acts is that they are often frankly pleasurable at the moment of action even if the person is extremely remorseful afterward.

Clinical Vignette 8

Mr. H, a 23-year-old college senior, sought help for his paraphilia, namely, voyeurism. He would resist the urge to exhibit his genitals to a woman for weeks but would eventually feel that the desire was irresistible. As he noted the look of shock or surprise on the woman's face when he exhibited his penis, he would often ejaculate. However, after this, he would feel ashamed, remorseful, afraid that the woman would recognize him on the street, and convinced that she would notify the police and he would be arrested.

A third hallmark of impulsive behaviors is that patients are often relatively impervious to the consequences of their actions at the time and tend to underestimate their chances of being caught.

Clinical Vignette 9

Ms. I, a 50-year-old financially comfortable housewife, came for treatment after being arrested for shoplifting (kleptomania). She was puzzled by her urges, stating, "I feel compelled to steal things even though I don't need them and could easily buy them. Half the time I throw them away afterward." Although she felt that she could resist these urges if a security guard was in plain view, she recognized that the threat of being arrested did not deter her at the moment of the theft.

Patients with impulsive patterns of behavior also tend to underestimate the chances of being caught by a spouse or friend.

Clinical Vignette 10

Mr. J, a 43-year-old married executive, engaged in cross-dressing (transvestic fetishism). He frequently masturbated to orgasm while wearing his wife's lingerie, paying little attention to whether his wife would suspect him when she discovered the soiled undergarments.

In addition, the impulsive nature of the action itself may increase the odds of apprehension and punishment.

Clinical Vignette 11

Mr. K, a 35-year-old construction worker, experienced irresistible urges to set fires (pyromania). He often did so in a hasty and unpremeditated fashion at construction sites where he worked. Because his actions were poorly planned and executed, he was at risk of being seen setting the fires. Firefighters rapidly concluded that the fires were the result of arson. In addition, Mr. K tended to feel compelled to stay and watch the consequences of his actions, enjoying the sight of the fire itself as well as the various equipment used to extinguish it. This meant he was remaining at the scene of his crime for an extended time.

Another feature common to impulsive behaviors is that they often involve a binge, an episode of engaging in a behavior that seems out of control and cannot be terminated by the patient. Often, the binge ends only when an external constraint forces the patient to abandon the action. An eating binge and the relapse of an alcoholic person are often similarly described: "Once I started eating (drinking) I couldn't stop. I just kept on stuffing myself (ordering drinks) until I was too exhausted and sick (drunk and broke) to continue."

It is noteworthy that impulsively binging on a substance such as alcohol sets the stage for further impulsive behaviors secondary to intoxication.

Apart from the clinical utility of thinking of various impulsive behaviors in similar terms, there is also evidence of an underlying biological defect that commonly gives rise to a variety of impulsive behaviors. Linnoila and colleagues[25] reviewed a number of studies in support of the idea that low cerebrospinal fluid concentration of 5-hydroxyindoleacetic acid, the main by-product of serotonin metabolism, was related to impaired impulse control as well as increased aggressiveness. They cited several types of studies that supported this relationship, including studies demonstrating 1) that patients with unipolar depression who made violent suicide attempts often had low cerebrospinal fluid levels of 5-hydroxyindoleacetic acid, 2) that there is a strong negative correlation between lifetime aggressive behaviors and cerebrospinal fluid levels of 5-hydroxyindoleacetic acid, and 3) that young abstinent alcoholic men had lower cerebrospinal fluid levels of 5-hydroxyindoleacetic acid than control subjects did.

Compulsive Behaviors

Clinical Vignette 12

Ms. L is a 45-year-old accountant who audits the records of banks for the Federal Reserve. A married mother of two, she is frequently upset when she is unable to leave work on time to be with her family. However, her job demands attention to detail both in reviewing the records and in presenting her reports to her boss. She is frequently able to pick up banking record errors that others have not noticed. Of course, such careful attention to detail is time-consuming and often causes her to work overtime.

Clinical Vignette 13

Mr. M is a 48-year-old executive who suffers from obsessive-compulsive disorder. Despite treatment with a variety of medications including fluoxetine and clomipramine, he has been unable to rid himself of the idea that he has accidentally hit someone while driving to work. Any bump in the road that he notices sets off this obsessive worry, and he feels compelled to circle back to the scene to double-check that he is not guilty of a hit-and-run accident. Sometimes he is not reassured by this initial check and continues to circle the area until "something clicks" and he feels certain that he has not hit anyone. This behavior makes Mr. M as much as 2 hours late for work.

In its muted form, compulsivity can be seen as carefulness or attention to detail. It is easy to see how such attention to detail is helpful in a variety of settings in daily life. Many jobs, such as Ms. L's, depend on thoroughness and a willingness to keep working until the books are balanced to the last penny. However, compulsive behaviors become a problem when they begin to consume much more time than necessary and when they are a response to nonsensical thoughts (obsessions), as in Mr. M's case.

At first glance, compulsive patterns seem to be the opposite of impulsive patterns of behavior. In compulsive behaviors, a person repetitively behaves in a stereotyped way. Yet repeated impulsive behaviors can become difficult to distinguish from compulsive ones. Is a young female patient who repeatedly gives in to the urge to pull her hair out impulsive or compulsive or both?

In fact, there is evidence that impulsive and compulsive behaviors tend to co-occur in the same individual. In one study, impulsive aggression was found to be common in patients with obsessive-compulsive disorder.[26] The authors theorized that obsessive-compulsive disorder and impulsivity may both arise from a similar problem in the self-regulation of behavior due to a neuroanatomical lesion in the serotoninergic system. They found that treating the obsessive-compulsive disorder with serotonin reuptake inhibitors also decreased these patients' impulsive aggression.

Lopez-Ibor[27] also reviewed the literature on obsessive-compulsive disorder and impulse-control disorders and concluded that those with obsessive-compulsive disorder frequently have patterns of low control of impulses and that those with impulse-control disorders typically rate high on measures of control when their impulsivity is in the background. Lopez-Ibor's review supported the theory that common traits in impulsive and obsessive individuals are related to serotoninergic metabolic disturbances.

Polivy and coworkers[28] found that food restriction was correlated with binge-eating in veterans who had been prisoners of war. They compared 67 combat veterans with 198 prisoners of war and noted that binge-eating was significantly more prevalent in prisoners of war who had been food restricted while captive than among combat veterans in general. Although food restriction among prisoners of war was not internally motivated as it is in anorexia, this study suggested that food restriction temporally preceded binge-eating.

The compulsions of obsessive-compulsive disorder, food-restricting behaviors such as those found in anorexia nervosa, and compulsive sexual behavior are common types of compulsivity (see Table 27–6). Like impulsive behaviors, compulsions share common features and are experienced in similar ways by patients. However, the driving force behind compulsive behaviors is not the gratification of impulses, but rather the prevention or reduction of anxiety and distress.

Clinical Vignette 14

Ms. N is a 34-year-old woman with obsessive-compulsive disorder who has recurrent, intrusive thoughts about having been contaminated with germs by objects she has touched. These thoughts are pervasive and extremely anxiety producing. She attempts to neutralize them by compulsively cleaning her house and washing her hands. When treated by use of a technique called flooding in which she was not permitted to wash her hands despite her obsessional thought, she became overwhelmingly anxious and panicky.

The concept that compulsive behavior is an attempt to reduce anxiety is easy to understand when the behavior is a response to an obsessive thought. However, even when the compulsive behavior is sexual in nature, it is driven by the need for anxiety reduction rather than by sexual desire.[29]

Clinical Vignette 15

Mr. O is a 38-year-old man who is distressed by the compulsion to masturbate that he feels nearly every morning on awakening with an erection. He describes the activity in detached terms, stating, "I think it's a waste of time. I don't enjoy it. I'm often making a mental list of things I have to do at work or even watching morning television programs while I'm masturbating. But I feel nervous for the rest of the day if I don't do it."

Avoidant Behaviors

Clinical Vignette 16

Mr. P is a 55-year-old man who was robbed at gunpoint 1 year ago after visiting an automated teller machine to withdraw money. Since the robbery, he has felt somewhat afraid when using the automated teller machine in the daytime, although this fear has diminished over time. He has avoided needing to use the automated teller machine at night by carefully planning his finances since the robbery.

Clinical Vignette 17

Ms. Q is a 40-year-old woman who works in a university library. She has gradually become more accustomed to dealing with patrons at the reference desk but continues to prefer the solitary task of looking for books that are misshelved. Despite her boss's encouragement, she has decided not to apply for a higher level job that would involve teaching groups of new employees about the library computer system. She realizes that she is passing up a good career opportunity, but she also recognizes that the public speaking and writing on the board that this new position would entail are terrifying to her. She worries that she will stammer and blush and make a fool of herself in front of the group. Even now, she feels uncomfortable on her lunch break because she is reluctant to join other employees in the cafeteria.

As with impulsivity and compulsivity, avoidance in its modulated form can be positive; learning from past negative experiences and avoiding prior mistakes are important capacities. Mr. P's avoidance of automated teller machines at night seems a sensible and self-protective decision. In contrast, Ms. Q's fears about social interactions with others at work are a problem; avoiding social situations also means avoiding a chance for promotion.

One prevalent condition that gives rise to avoidant behavior is agoraphobia (see Table 27–6). The agora was a crowded open-air market in ancient Athens. The word agoraphobia literally means "fear of the agora."[30] Modern situations equivalent to the agora include those in which a person is outside of the home alone, in a crowd, standing in line, on a bridge or in a tunnel, or in a bus, train, or car. In each of these situations, help may not be readily available in the case of an emergency. Thus, agoraphobia is a condition in which a person has anxiety about being in places or situations from which escape is likely to be embarrassing or difficult. For many people with agoraphobia, the situation they dread is having a panic attack in public. Often what began as a spontaneous attack becomes linked to the situation in which the attack occurred so that the person becomes afraid of that particular place or activity.

Clinical Vignette 18

Mr. R is a 26-year-old man who had his first panic attack while attending church. Because he was sitting in the middle of a pew, he was forced to climb over several people to flee during the attack. He felt this was both scary and embarrassing. Since this initial attack, he has avoided sitting anywhere other than in the back row at the end of the pew while attending services. He feels relatively comfortable sitting in this location because he can escape quickly if another attack occurs. He is not bothered by sitting in the middle of a row at the movies or in a theater.

Avoidant behaviors usually arise from a patient's history of being fearful or concern that he or she will become fearful in a given situation. Because of the past history or the perceived threat, the anxiety-provoking situation is avoided. Avoiding the situation means avoiding the fear and anxiety the situation threatens to produce. One study showed that fear and avoidance ratings were highly correlated both at baseline level and after behavior therapy for agoraphobia.[31] In another study, panic disorder patients with agoraphobia were differentiated from panic disorder patients without agoraphobia by increased rates of anxiety-relevant cognitions in the agoraphobic group.[32]

The relationship between fear and avoidance also holds in other forms of avoidant behavior. Marshall and coworkers[33] studied 50 adults in a variety of settings that had the potential to induce phobic avoidance of heights. They found that catastrophic thinking (i.e., imagining various ways of falling) was especially common among those who were afraid of heights and that it was closely correlated with avoidance of height situations. Children with school phobias often avoid school by feigning illness. They are likely to become terrified when school attendance is enforced by their parents, clinging to the parent and crying to avoid being left at school alone.

Another feature common to avoidant behaviors is that they become self-reinforcing and tend to worsen in severity over time if left untreated.

Clinical Vignette 19

Mr. S is a 38-year-old man who began having panic attacks in his early 20s. After one unexpected attack while he was on the subway, he began to ride the bus instead. Before long, he had another panic attack on the bus, then began walking to work. Walking took about 1 hour, but he persisted until he had a panic attack in the street. After this attack, Mr. S avoided leaving his house unless accompanied by another person, often his brother who lives nearby. His agoraphobia forced him to quit work and apply for disability compensation.

A further common feature of avoidant behaviors is their tendency to heighten anticipatory anxiety and precipitate the very reactions that a person is afraid of.

Clinical Vignette 20

Ms. T, a 24-year-old student, recognized that she was mildly afraid of heights. However, she wished to climb the Mayan temple at Chichén Itzá during her vacation in Mexico. As she started the steep climb to the top, she began to feel anxious and to anticipate arriving at the top and being unable to descend from the monument. Pausing to try to calm down, she turned to look at the ground and began to feel overwhelmingly anxious and afraid of falling. She decided to descend at once but found that her legs felt shaky and weak, making the climb especially frightening. On making it down from the stairs, she vowed never to climb such a monument again.

Conclusion

In evaluating the adaptiveness of a person's behavior, an understanding of the strengths and weaknesses of various character styles and the constraints and demands of the external environment is essential. Behavior is the final common pathway for the expression of genetics, temperament, personality traits, and psychiatric symptoms. Behavior is an observable entity in a field where many important aspects of a patient's internal life must be inferred by the psychiatrist. Although some behaviors are clearly more adaptive than others, emphasizing the strengths of a person's capacities is important. Even pathological behaviors often represent a person's best attempt at adaptation; a paranoid patient who installs extra locks on the door may be doing the best she or he can in the face of illness to survive, to cope, and to adapt to the environment the patient perceives around her or him.

References

1. Thomas A, Chess S, Birch H, et al: Behavioral Individuality in Early Childhood. New York: New York University Press, 1963.
2. Rothbart MK, Ahadi SA: Temperament and the development of personality. J Abnorm Psychol 1994; 103:55–66.
3. Brown GW, Harris TO: Depression. In Brown GW, Harris TO (eds): Life Events and Illness. New York: Guilford Press, 1989:49–94.
4. Carey G, DiLalla DL: Personality and psychopathology: Genetic perspectives. J Abnorm Psychol 1994; 103:32–43.
5. Wachtel PL: Cyclical processes in personality and psychopathology. J Abnorm Psychol 1994; 103:51–54.
6. Livesley WJ, Schroeder ML, Jackson DN, et al: Categorical distinctions in the study of personality disorder: Implications for classification. J Abnorm Psychol 1994; 103:6–17.
7. Widiger TA, Frances AJ: Toward a dimensional model for the personality disorders. In Costa PT, Widiger TA (eds): Personality Disorders and the Five-Factor Model of Personality. Washington, DC: American Psychological Association, 1994:19–40.
8. American Psychiatric Association: Diagnostic and Statistical Manual of Mental Disorders, 4th ed. Washington, DC: American Psychiatric Association, 1994.
9. Oldham JM, Morris LB: The New Personality Self-Portrait: Why You Think, Work, Love and Act the Way You Do. New York: Bantam Books, 1995.
10. Widiger TA, Costa PT Jr: Personality and personality disorders. J Abnorm Psychol 1994; 103:78–91.
11. Widiger TA, Trull TJ, Clarkin JF, et al: A description of the DSM-III-R and DSM-IV personality disorders with the five-factor model of personality. In Costa PT, Widiger TA (eds): Personality Disorders and the Five-Factor Model of Personality. Washington, DC: American Psychological Association, 1994:19–40.
12. Cloninger CR: A systematic method for clinical description and classification of personality variants: A proposal. Arch Gen Psychiatry 1987; 44:573–588.
13. Cloninger CR, Svrakic DM, Przybeck TR: A psychobiological model of temperament and character. Arch Gen Psychiatry 1993; 50:975–990.
14. Siever LJ, Davis KL: A psychobiological perspective on the personality disorders. Am J Psychiatry 1991; 148:1647–1658.
15. McDougall W: Of the words character and personality. Character Personality 1932; 1:3–16.
16. Digman JM: Personality structure: Emergence of the five-factor model. Annu Rev Psychol 1990; 50:116–123.
17. McCrae RR, Costa PT Jr: Validation of the five-factor model across instruments and observers. J Pers Soc Psychol 1987; 52:81–90.
18. Svrakic DM, Whitehead C, Przybeck TR, et al: Differential diagnosis of personality disorders by the seven-factor model of temperament and character. Arch Gen Psychiatry 1993; 50:991–999.
19. Weissman MM, Klerman GL, Paykel ES, et al: Treatment effects on the social adjustment of depressed patients. Arch Gen Psychiatry 1974; 30:771–778.
20. Benjamin LS: Operational definition and measurement of dynamics shown in the stream of free associations. Psychiatry 1986; 49:104–129.
21. Halleck SL: Evaluation of the Psychiatric Patient: A Primer. New York: Plenum Publishing, 1994.
22. Fahy TA, Eisler I: Impulsivity and eating disorders. Br J Psychiatry 1993; 162:193–197.
23. Virkkunen M: Self-mutilation and antisocial personality disorder. Acta Psychiatr Scand 1976; 54:347–352.
24. Sher KJ, Trull TJ: Personality and disinhibitory psychopathology: Alcoholism and antisocial personality disorder. J Abnorm Psychol 1994; 130:92–102.
25. Linnoila M, Verkkunen M, George T, et al: Impulse control disorders. Int Clin Psychopharmacol 1993; 8:53–56.
26. Stein DJ, Hollander E: Impulsive aggression and obsessive-compulsive disorder. Psychiatr Ann 1993; 23:389–395.

27. Lopez-Ibor JJ: Impulse control in obsessive-compulsive disorder: A biopsychopathological approach. Prog Neuropsychopharmacol Biol Psychiatry 1990; 14:709–718.
28. Polivy J, Zetilin SB, Herman CP, et al: Food restriction and binge eating: A study of former prisoners of war. J Abnorm Psychol 1994; 103:409–411.
29. Coleman E: Is your patient suffering from compulsive sexual behavior? Psychiatr Ann 1992; 22:320–325.
30. Stedman's Medical Dictionary, 24th ed. Baltimore: Williams & Wilkins, 1982.
31. Cox BJ, Swinson RP, Fergus KD: Changes in fear versus avoidance ratings with behavioral treatments for agoraphobia. Behav Ther 1993; 24:619–624.
32. Ganellen RJ, Matuzas W, Uhlenhuth EH, et al: Panic disorder, agoraphobia and anxiety-related cognitive style. J Affect Disord 1986; 11:219–225.
33. Marshall WL, Bristol D, Barbaree HE: Cognitions and courage in the avoidance behavior of acrophobics. Behav Res Ther 1992; 30:463–470.

CHAPTER

28 Cultural Considerations in Psychopathology

Juan E. Mezzich
Roberto Lewis-Fernández

A modern approach to psychiatry, mindful of its international and historical roots, biopsychosocially conceptualized and centered on the person of the patient, must be culturally informed. In recognition of this, one of the innovative developments in the *Diagnostic and Statistical Manual of Mental Disorders,* Fourth Edition (DSM-IV), has been the incorporation of principles and components aimed at enhancing its cultural suitability and sensitivity.[1]

Proposals prepared by the National Institute of Mental Health Group on Culture and Diagnosis[2] have included a statement on cultural principles for the introduction to the manual, paragraphs on cultural considerations aimed at facilitating the application of diagnostic categories and their definitional criteria in multicultural settings, a glossary of culture-bound syndromes and idioms of distress, and guidelines for a cultural formulation.

This chapter focuses on cultural considerations pertinent to the use of criteria sets in culturally and ethnically diverse populations. In addition, brief comments on related culture-bound syndromes are offered.

Specific Cultural Considerations

Cognitive Disorders

Less attention has been paid to cultural variants of the cognitive disorders than to other psychopathological forms, probably because of the widespread assumption that this group of disorders is influenced exclusively by biological factors. Nevertheless, these disorders show several kinds of social, cultural, and ethnic influences. Given the etiologically based subtyping of the cognitive disorders, these influences are exerted, first, by effects on the nature and rates of the diseases that are the causative agents of these disorders.[3]

Socioeconomic factors influence the prevalence rates of diseases affecting the brain. Low industrialization of a country or the poverty of a particular social group tends to increase the rates of infectious diseases, nutritional disorders, toxic exposures (e.g., lead), head injuries, endocrinological abnormalities, and seizure disorders, among others.[4] This, in turn, may result in differences in the rates of the subtypes of dementia, of delirium, and of other specific cognitive syndromes.[5, 6]

Cultural factors, such as prohibitions against substance use and variations in sexual mores, also affect the rates of alcohol- and drug-related syndromes as well as of acquired immunodeficiency syndrome–related organic mental disorders.[7, 8] Ethnic determinants are also important. Hypertension and strokes have been suggested to be more prevalent among African-Americans and some Asian groups; this may result in different rates of multiinfarct dementia.[9] In addition, research on Alzheimer's dementia is currently evaluating reports of lower rates among the Chinese and Chinese-Americans as well as African-Americans.[9, 10]

The detection and assessment of the cognitive disorders are also influenced by social and cultural factors. Social groups that tolerate and even expect substantial decreases in decision-making and self-care among older persons may not regard as pathological milder degrees of disorientation among the elderly.[11] Educational level and cultural differences appear to exert separate but intermingled effects on the inappropriately high identification of cognitive impairment with the Mini-Mental State Examination among several ethnic groups, including Hispanic, Taiwanese, Chinese, and Southeast Asian populations.[12]

Substance Use Disorders

Sociocultural factors exert considerable influence over some aspects of substance use disorders and not others. The prevalence rates of alcohol and drug abuse and dependence vary significantly across cultures. Lifetime rates for alcoholism, for example, range from 23% among Native Americans to 0.45% among the population of Shanghai.[13] Specific local factors that affect degree of risk for substance-related disorders include patterns of use, attitudes toward substance consumption, accessibility of the drug, physiological reactions to the same drug, and family norms and patterns.[14] The local culture influences the definition of pathological substance use through differences in the perception of the impairment caused by high consumption and frequent intoxication.[15] Particular cultural views toward drinking in children, the value of moderation, the tolerance for intoxication, and the association of drinking with family activities and special social occasions appear to influence the degree of risk for alcoholism.[16] The availability of a substance also increases its rates of abuse and dependence.[13] Sociocultural factors such as religious proscriptions may exert their influence in this fashion.

Several aspects of substance use disorders appear to be less affected by cultural factors. Such aspects include the comorbidity patterns, the nature of dependence syndromes, the age at onset, and the results of laboratory tests and physical examinations.[14] For example, alcoholism is associated in many societies with abuse of other substances, mania, and antisocial personality as well as with depression and anxiety.[17] Alcoholism and drug abuse are reliably more common among men, although the sex ratio can vary from 2:1 to 40:1.[13, 18] Drug abuse is also more prevalent among urban populations, the less educated, and the young.[17] The physical symptoms as well as the temporal relationship between onset of use and dependence are substance specific and also fairly similar across cultures.[19]

Schizophrenia and Related Psychotic Disorders

The cross-cultural presentation and course of schizophrenia are among the best-studied aspects of cultural psychiatry. This research revealed significant cross-cultural differences as well as similarities. A "core" schizophrenic syndrome—consisting of a combination of certain positive and negative psychotic symptoms—has been found nearly everywhere, although the specific content of the hallucinations and delusions as well as the prevalence of visual and other nonauditory hallucinations varies.[20, 21] Significant cross-cultural variation has been found, however, in several features of the syndrome. Its distribution is not uniform, ranging from 1 in a 1000 in non-Western societies to more than 1% in the West; its highest prevalence is displayed in economically and technologically advanced, urbanized, and bureaucratized societies.[22, 23] Its phenomenology varies with cultural setting, with much higher rates of catatonia in India and of hebephrenia in Japan than in the West. Most important, the course of schizophrenia is markedly better in nonindustrialized countries, even when cultural differences in outcome assessment and in acuteness of presentation are taken into account.[24, 25] Variations in outcome are thought to be related in part to different attitudes toward persons with the disorder, a set of culturally patterned interactions studied under the rubric of expressed emotion.[26] Other cross-cultural variations with regard to schizophrenia include higher misdiagnosis among patients from devalued and ethnic minority groups[27]; differences in cultural and gender-related conceptions regarding the expression of emotion that complicate the assessment of flat affect[28]; and culturally syntonic experiences that may be mistaken for schizophrenic symptoms, such as the expected appearance of hallucinations among bereaved Native Americans[29] or reports of perceptual alterations among distressed Puerto Ricans.[30, 31]

Clinical Vignette 1

A 28-year-old mainland Chinese man living in the United States for several years was hospitalized in a psychiatric ward with delusions and hallucinations of 2 to 3 weeks' duration. These began after he took up the practice of *qi-gong*, a form of meditation, as treatment for his severe intermittent backaches and chronic exhaustion. According to the patient, feelings of *qi* ("vital energy") were circulating in the "wrong directions" in his body, and he heard the voices of supernatural beings commenting on how he should practice *qi-gong*. He denied depressed mood, appetite or weight changes, substance abuse, or a history of psychosis. The results of extensive medical evaluation, including electroencephalography and magnetic resonance imaging, were normal. Haloperidol substantially reduced his delusions and hallucinations, but follow-up information is unavailable because he did not keep his appointments after discharge.

Transient psychotic symptoms in connection with *qi-gong* practices are not uncommon, but duration for more than a few days is unusual. The patient's picture meets criteria in the Chinese classification system for *qi-gong*–induced psychosis (a DSM-IV culture-bound syndrome), and probably neurasthenia, because of his prodromal somatic symptoms. Brief duration of psychosis in the absence of confusion and emotional turmoil qualified the patient for a DSM-IV diagnosis of psychotic disorder not otherwise specified (NOS), but if psychosis were to persist, a diagnosis of schizophreniform disorder could also be considered.

Adapted from Mezzich and colleagues.[32]

Mood Disorders

Contemporary cross-cultural research on mood disorders has focused on unipolar depression syndromes, revealing extensive cultural patternings as well as significant similarities. For example, the World Health Organization Collaborative Study on Depression found a core depressive syndrome in the five countries studied, but it also revealed substantial cross-cultural differences in symptom presentation, affect conceptualization, level of severity, and influence of acculturation, despite a methodology that tended to accentuate similarities at the expense of local differences.[33]

Culture and other social factors, such as class and gender, influence the interpretation of and exposure to stressors that predispose to depression.[34] The specific characteristics of the dysphoria of depressive illness also vary cross-culturally. For example, among the Hopi, feelings of guilt, shame, and sinfulness are separate experiences displaying distinct relationships to subtypes of depression,[35] and reports of irritability, rage, and "nervousness" are prominent descriptors of depressive affect among Puerto Ricans and other Latinos.[36] The frequent combination of depression and anxiety noted around the world, particularly in primary care settings, has fueled the DSM-IV proposal for a mixed anxiety-depressive disorder.[37]

In addition, most cross-cultural studies have found a significantly higher rate of somatic complaints associated with depression (and anxiety) among non-Western groups than in Western settings, including the presence of unique symptoms (e.g., "heat or water in the head" and "crawling sensation of worms and ants" in Nigerian cultures).[33, 38] Emotional complaints are often present as well but may not be considered the source of distress or impairment. The mix of emotional and somatic symptoms has also been found to vary by sex in some studies.[39, 40] For example, a study comparing Puerto Ricans, Mexican-Americans, and Cuban-Americans on the Center for Epidemiologic Studies Depression Scale of depressive symptoms found that the women in all three groups tended to endorse depressive and somatic scale items together as a single factor significantly more often than the men did.[40]

Finally, the threshold at which dysphoria becomes disorder is affected by cultural factors. The 2-week duration criterion for major depression, an important proxy for pathological intensity, may vary among some non-Western groups. Manson and colleagues[35] found that the Hopi identify five distinct indigenous syndromes related to depression, only one of which shares significant parameters with Western depressive disorder. This folk syndrome, however, differed from major depression in its average duration of 1 week, not 2, although still causing comparable morbidity. On the basis of this research, these investigators called for a shortening of the duration criterion for major depressive disorder when it is used with Hopi patients.[35]

These findings raise serious issues about the operational criteria of the depressive disorders and tend to support the phenomenological expansion of the depression categories.[41]

Clinical Vignette 2

A 69-year-old traditional Hopi man was brought by his granddaughter to a general medical clinic. She reported finding her grandfather in his current deteriorated state on arriving to visit her family during a college break 2 days before. The patient described a 6-day history of weight loss; disrupted sleep; fatigue; agitation; difficulty being effective; loss of libido; trouble thinking clearly; and a sense of sinfulness, shame, and not being likable. The examining physician also noted psychomotor retardation and no evidence of psychosis or guilty ruminations.

The patient explained that he was suffering from *uu nung mo kiw ta,* an indigenous Hopi syndrome. This syndrome had afflicted him several times in the past, and he assured the physician that it would pass shortly, never lasting more than about 6 to 9 days. He attributed his presentation at the clinic to his granddaughter's insistence. He did not deny his marked deterioration from normal functioning but attributed it instead to his "heart being broken" over a shocking family revelation. He was planning to seek the help of a traditional healer when his granddaughter arrived. He received a diagnosis of depressive disorder NOS.

Case elaborated from illness description in Manson and colleagues.[35]

Anxiety Disorders

The effect of culture on anxiety is similar to that on depression. Cultural factors affect the precipitants, symptom presentations, pathological thresholds, and specific syndrome criteria of the anxiety disorders.[42] For example, the cross-cultural validity of criterion A for the *Diagnostic and Statistical Manual of Mental Disorders,* Third Edition, Revised (DSM-III-R) generalized anxiety disorder has been challenged because it restricts the diagnosis of chronic pathological anxiety to a disturbance stemming from undue worry in the absence of actual stressors or excessive worry after minor stress. This leaves out the much larger group of patients in developing societies and devalued minorities in the West who experience chronic pathological anxiety as a result of recurrent stress.[36]

Cultural and ethnic elements have been invoked to explain local differences in anxiety disorder prevalence that persist after controlling for other social factors. For example, the higher rate of simple phobia, social phobia, and agoraphobia among African-Americans compared with that in whites[43] has been attributed to the stress resulting from racial discrimination.[44] In fact, the cross-cultural epidemiological literature reveals a complex pattern of similarities and differences with regard to the anxiety disorders, and opinions differ as to the role of culture in this process.[45] For example, it is presently unclear why Mexicans born in Mexico compared with those born in the United States show a markedly lower rate of anxiety and other disorders. Suggested explanations include selective migration, different thresholds for perceiving and reporting a disorder stemming from distinct cultural interpretations of what constitutes a "hard life" and acceptable suffering, and a combination of both explanations.[46]

Multiple cross-cultural studies point to the coappearance of anxiety, depression, somatoform complaints, and dissociative symptoms among non-Western groups. A markedly somatic idiom predominates, often in the form of culturally specific symptoms.[38] These often coalesce distinctively as culture-bound syndromes characterized also by specific etiological factors, demographics, patterns of impairment, and help-seeking choices.[47] It is far from clear that this represents the comorbidity of Western disorders rather than a different organization of pathological experience.[48] Examples include *ataque de nervios* among Latinos, *koro* in Asian communities, and *taijin kyofusho* among the Japanese.[45] Each of these disorders exhibits significant differences that prevent simple one-to-one correlations with established Western categories.[49]

Clinical Vignette 3

A 42-year-old Puerto Rican man is referred to a regional mental health center by his town physician for treatment of chronic *nervios* (nerves). The patient describes a 4-year history of recurrent but intermittent symptoms of anxiety and depression since he hurt his back and was unable to return to agricultural work. He "awakens" with his symptoms several days a month but denies continuous symptoms for more than a few days. He feels partially handicapped by his symptoms, despite their intermittency, because he has been unable to sustain gainful work even after his back condition improved.

He describes exquisite reactivity to even minor stresses (e.g., watching crime news on television), resulting in acute nervousness, trembling, and crying. In addition, during his "bad days," he reports anxiety, sadness, difficulty falling asleep, irritability, a wish to isolate himself, chest pressure, easy fatigue, dizziness *(mareos),* "thinking too much," generalized worry that feels "out of control," low self-esteem, occasional tearfulness, and hearing his name called out when alone and sensing the presence of someone behind him. On one of these symptomatic days, he "saw" a man dressed in black who approached him and then disappeared, causing him intense fear. His irritability can lead to aggressive outbursts in which he breaks objects and insults his family, which he calls *ataques de*

Clinical Vignette 3 *continued*

nervios (nervous attacks). Later he regrets his actions during these episodes. He denies changes in appetite, history of substance abuse, symptoms of formal thought disorder, panic attacks, and past exposure to trauma.

Because of the intermittent nature of the symptoms, which persisted despite improvement of the acute precipitating stressor, the patient received DSM-IV diagnoses of anxiety disorder NOS and depressive disorder NOS.

Case composed by Roberto Lewis-Fernández from unpublished clinical material.

Somatoform Disorders

In a survey of international use of DSM-III and DSM-III-R, somatoform disorders were among the more problematic diagnoses,[50] probably because of their cross-cultural limitations.[51] First, many nosologies around the world do not distinguish between mood, anxiety, somatoform disorders, and dissociative disorders, because sufferers report single syndromes that cut across boundaries of the diagnostic categories.[52] Demarcating somatoform conditions in these settings may create artificial distinctions that confound accurate diagnosis. Examples include neurasthenia in China and other Asian settings, and *nervios* in Latin America.[53, 54]

Second, the idioms of distress of many societies rely on somatic complaints for the expression of nonpathological personal and social predicaments. Interpretation of these communication mechanisms as a somatoform disorder may result in overpathologization.[55] In addition, the use of somatic idioms varies according to intracultural factors, such as gender and class, which in turn may determine who receives a somatoform diagnosis. For example, conversion symptoms appear to be more common in rural and less educated sectors of non-Western societies, and particularly in family or social structures that allow few opportunities for protest.[51, 56]

Third, the symptom lists of DSM-III-R and DSM-IV do not canvas the rich variety of somatic symptoms reported in other parts of the world, such as the complaints of worms and ants in the head described earlier.[38] Examples of other common somatic symptoms include chronic fatigue; heat in the feet, chest, or head; painful "gas" that moves from the abdomen around the flank to the back; "brainache"; and feeling presences when alone or among others.

Fourth, in most of the world, the degree to which symptoms are medically unexplained is difficult to ascertain owing to the marked limitation of diagnostic tests and medical personnel. Moreover, the high prevalence of endemic disease in underdeveloped countries, often with protean and inchoate manifestations, may also confound the assessment of the somatoform disorders. This may result in overdiagnosis if organic causes are not identified or underdiagnosis if organic explanations are uncritically accepted for systemic illness.[51]

Clinical Vignette 4

A 45-year-old Igbo woman in Nigeria presents to a local general medical clinic complaining of multiple somatic symptoms occurring every day, most of the day, for 7 months. Among other symptoms, she is particularly distressed by sensations of heat in her head and "inside" her body, heaviness in her head and hammer-like headaches, dizziness, palpitations, the sense that her head is "breathing" and the feeling that there is water or worms in it, "painful" vision and decreased visual acuity, generalized weakness, pain in the "marrow of the bones" in her hands and legs, sweating, easy fatigue, itching all over her body, and minor cramping.

She complains that her body is "out of order" but that nobody seems to believe her. She denies depressed mood, significant sleep or appetite disturbances, and prior history of somatization, and her somatic descriptions are not of delusional proportion. She rejects the physicians' attributions of her symptoms to her concurrent menopause, explaining that in her experience with other women, her symptoms go beyond the average for this condition. However, she did note that she has been upset by the loss of her childbearing capacity. She explains that if the physicians do not find a physical cause, she will seek the help of a traditional healer.

The patient received a DSM-IV diagnosis of undifferentiated somatoform disorder.

Case elaborated from illness description in Ebigbo.[38]

Dissociative Disorders

Syndromes characterized by pathological dissociation are common worldwide, but the current concepts of dissociative disorders do not appear to account for their phenomenological variety.[52, 57] For example, a study performed in an outpatient psychiatric clinic in India found that more than 90% of dissociative disorder cases did not fulfill criteria for the specified categories, ironically receiving instead a DSM-III diagnosis of atypical dissociative disorder. Distressing trance states and possession trance episodes constituted most of these cases.[58] Many indigenous illness syndromes around the world display salient features of pathological dissociation. Some of these syndromes are characterized by involuntary possession trance—dissociative alterations in identity attributed to the invasion of external spirits or agents—distinguished from dissociative identity disorder by their episodic and remitting course, the nature and number of their alternative identities, and their gradual response to treatment. These syndromes have been identified in India, western Africa, China, Malaysia, Brazil, and the Caribbean, among many other settings.[31, 59, 60]

Other dissociative syndromes are characterized by alterations of consciousness and memory, during which the person runs around in an agitated state (Arctic *pibloktoq*); attacks others indiscriminately (Malayo-Indonesian *amok*); undergoes convulsive movements, screaming fits, and aggressive acts toward self or others (Caribbean *ataques de nervios*); or lies as if dead, suffering from specific perceptual alterations: the person can hear and understand what is happening but cannot see or move ("falling out" among African-Americans in the southern United States, Bahamian "blacking out," and Haitian *indisposition*).[57, 61, 62] The proposed dissociative trance disorder category in DSM-IV would provide a Western nosological niche for these disorders, although not without the risk of overpathologizing some culturally accepted instances of these behaviors.[52]

In fact, extensive cross-cultural research reveals that most dissociative experiences around the world are completely normal, usually forming part of religious and ritual events.[31] The Western emphasis on pathological experiences of dissociation that result from overwhelming trauma probably stems from the relative absence of normal dissociation among dominant Western groups and from the acknowledgment by mental health professionals of the sequelae of physical and sexual abuse.[63, 64] Depersonalization, considered one of the most common psychiatric symptoms in the West,[65] is a greatly desired goal for Hindu yogis, revealing the substantial cultural patterning of dissociative experience.[66]

Clinical Vignette 5

A 17-year-old recently married Hindu woman starts to undergo episodes of pathological possession trance 2 weeks after moving to her mother-in-law's house in a different village in India. Her first episode is preceded by a generalized convulsion, rolling on the ground, loud screaming, and a period of unconsciousness. On regaining semiconsciousness with a start, the woman speaks and behaves as the ghost of a dead cousin. Shouting loudly, she berates her in-laws and her new husband, who try to force the spirit out by pinching and other noxious stimuli. Minutes later, the woman again enters near-unconsciousness, moaning softly, signaling the temporary departure of the spirit. During a period of hours, she lapses between near-unconsciousness and full possession several times.

These attacks recur for 3 weeks, with mounting aggressiveness, despite the ministrations of traditional healers, who diagnose a "possession syndrome." The patient improves slightly only after her father travels to see her and takes her back on an extended visit to her family of origin following up a referral to a regional healing temple.

Adapted from Lewis-Fernández.[31]

Sexual Disorders

Research on cross-cultural influences on sexual disorders is limited, owing to the lack of uniform descriptive methodology and to the fact that the major ethnic minorities in the United States do not seek medical treatment for this class of complaints.[67] Some cross-cultural studies have concluded that the paraphilias as currently characterized in the DSM-IV are determined by specific features of Western society, such as demographical size and complexity (whereby individuals may escape social sanctions through anonymity), the nonavailability of partners, and the primacy of masturbatory activities as sexual outlets.[68, 69] Despite a few small clinical studies that found similar rates of sexual dysfunction among white and African-American populations,[70, 71] most cross-cultural research suggests that sexual response is influenced by cultural and ethnic considerations. Racist stereotypes, machismo, anxiety about infertility, and the tendency toward somatization of mood disorders as impotence have been cited as etiological factors of sexual dysfunction in African-American and Latino populations.[72, 73] In addition, the ethnographical literature shows that standards for sexual competence differ across the cultural spectrum and that many societies display a more flexible approach to issues of sexual orientation than is assumed by the diagnostic categories.[74, 75]

This cross-cultural diversity complicates the assessment of the sexual disorders. At present, it is unclear whether certain culture-bound syndromes involving sexual organs, such as *koro* among Asians (characterized by the fear of genital retraction) or *dhat* in India (involving obsession or anxiety about semen loss), should be categorized among the sexual or the somatoform disorders.[67]

Eating Disorders

Research has disclosed a significant cultural effect on the patterning and distribution of the eating disorders. An important determinant appears to be the Western premium on thinness as an esthetic and moral value.[76–78] Cases of eating disorder have been found in many non-Western societies and several ethnic minorities in the United States, but their presenting features often differ somewhat from the DSM-IV criteria for anorexia nervosa and bulimia nervosa.[79]

Groups at high risk include those experiencing rapid acculturation to Western society, such as immigrants or those living in areas undergoing accelerated industrialization.[80] For example, one study found a 12% prevalence of DSM-III eating disorders among Egyptian female college students in London and no evidence of these conditions among a similar sample in Cairo.[81] Bulimia nervosa appears more common than anorexia nervosa among U.S. minorities and is often associated with higher than average weight, female sex, and sometimes older age, for example, among some Native American groups.[82] Anorexia nervosa has been found among lower socioeconomic class samples in several cultures, but often characterized by "atypical" features, such as the absence of a distorted body image or of the fear of gaining weight.[83, 84] Cross-cultural studies have proposed more flexible diagnostic criteria for anorexia nervosa so that abdominal fullness, epigastric pain, or distaste for food may be accepted instead of intense fear of weight gain to account for the severe restriction of food intake or other weight-losing behavior.[85]

Adjustment Disorders

The effect of culture on the adjustment disorders is pervasive. Culturally based interpretations are essential to the appraisal of the psychosocial stressor, and culture also provides the repertoire of behavioral and emotional responses that pattern both normal and disordered reactions to stress.[86] Whereas some experiences are uniformly stressful (e.g., natural disaster), others may make sense only within particular cultural contexts (e.g., facing deadlines, witchcraft accusations).[87] In addition, the judgment of what constitutes a maladaptive response to a stressor must be made in relation to what exceeds cultural norms.[22] Diagnosis of an adjustment disorder may be a particular problem among refugee populations; these groups have undergone distressing experiences, but their intensively challenged coping styles may be unknown to caregivers in the host country.[88]

Personality Disorders

The current configuration of the personality disorders has received substantial cross-cultural challenge. Even the basic concept of personality as a set of individual internal traits is considered inseparable from Western cultural assumptions on individuality by many authors.[89] Difficulties in the reliable assessment of these disorders within Western cultures may be due to the degree to which these conditions are determined by social and contextual factors. These factors include adaptational strategies toward adverse communal environments (including the relative value of aggression or avoidance), family-based customs and traditions, occupational and educational options, and cultural methods of child-rearing.[90] It is striking, for example, that antisocial personality disorder is nearly absent among the Hutterites, an ethnoreligious enclave living for more than a century in the United States and Canada.[91] Intracultural diversity may be more important in this respect than cross-cultural difference. For example, in his studies of affective and personality disturbances among the Eskimo and the Yoruba, Leighton[92] was unable to disentangle cultural influences from "the much more powerful effects" of gender, age, and class.

Epidemiological assessment of DSM-III antisocial personality disorder has been performed as part of the Epidemiological Catchment Area study using a clearly operationalized survey instrument, the Diagnostic Interview Schedule.[18] This yielded similar prevalence rates in the United States and Puerto Rico.[93] However, low reliability rates for the diagnosis of personality disorders across standardized instruments raise serious doubts about the validity of this aspect of the Epidemiological Catchment Area study data.[94] One World Health Organization study was able to identify cases of most of the *International Classification of Diseases* personality disorders in 15 urban clinic samples in Africa, Asia, North America, and Europe,[95] but the cross-cultural validity of the definitions of these categories had been criticized earlier by Shepherd and Sartorius.[96]

The Case of Culture-Bound Syndromes and Idioms of Distress

Investigation of so-called culture-bound syndromes was geared for decades toward incorporation of these "exotic" categories into Western nosologies.[97] The term culture-bound was used to describe a certain number of psychiatric disorders whose phenomenologies made them distinct from Western categories and that theoretically could be singled out as unique to a particular cultural setting.[47] The clear implication was that Western categories were not culture-bound but rather universal, and that proper characterization would disclose a translation key for specific non-Western syndromes. However, these conditions have been studied more critically to understand instead the culture-bound nature of Western classification schemes themselves and to enable the appropriate treatment of patients whose understandings and presentations of illness conform to these indigenous categories.[98, 99]

Contemporary cultural psychiatry recognizes that all classification schemes are inherently cultural and subjects Western nosologies to the same kind of social analysis that it continues to apply to the indigenous nosologies.[100] In this modern sense, culture-bound syndrome is an inherited and controversial term that is used in practice to describe psychiatric categories, whether they are part of Western or non-Western nosologies, on whose emergence, manifestation, or course culture is thought to exert a particularly strong influence.[101, 102] The term continues to refer to relatively consistent illness categories with characteristic courses ("syndromes") and specific labels, some of which are discussed in this chapter (e.g., *amok, taijin kyofusho,* anorexia nervosa). The organizing principle that unifies a syndrome conceptually can be 1) a collection of symptoms, which can follow diverse classificatory schemes (descriptive); 2) a cause, including an immediate precipitating context (etiological); or 3) a response to treatment.[99]

Idiom of distress is a newer term, which was coined to refer to a more general level of analysis.[56] Rather than denoting specific syndromes, the term refers to the more general illness "languages" of social groups, the culturally preferred ways of expressing distress, such as by somatic complaints, psychologizing explanations, possession or witchcraft terminology, oppositional or violent behavior, illnesses due to "nerves," or attributions of inexplicable misfortune. In this sense, a given idiom of distress, such as somatization, can be expressed as multiple culture-bound syndromes, such as *ataques de nervios,* neurasthenia, "brain fag," and so on.

Contemporary use of this terminology allows us to understand certain difficulties in the integration of Western and non-Western categories of psychiatric illness.[52, 103] First, Western nosologies are based at present nearly exclusively on descriptive parameters. Wary of "theoretical" causes, our current diagnostic system privileges a formal definition of psychopathological processes. Most indigenous nosologies, on the other hand, distinguish illness from normality at least as much on the basis of contextual characteristics as by descriptive ones. These include assessments regarding the appropriateness of the symptom in the particular setting and at the specific time in question, the relative sufficiency of the precipitating stressors, and the nature and quality of the human relationships of the sufferer. This discrepancy between the organizing principles of Western and non-Western nosologies prevents an easy consolidation of pathological criteria across cultures.[99]

Second, nosologies also differ in the configuration of their phenomenologies.[22, 49, 99] The symptoms of many culture-bound syndromes, such as *amok* in Malaysia or *ataque de nervios* in Puerto Rico, are composed of a variety of behavioral and experiential elements that are considered by Western nosologists to belong in separate diagnostic categories. The characteristic presentations of these conditions exhibit diverse combinations of dissociative, psychotic, anxiety, depressive, characterological, and somatic symptoms.[52] Significant phenomenological variation occurs even among individual cases, which are nevertheless unified under a single nosological label.

These differences in definitions of illness and in phenomenological organization between Western and non-Western categories ensure that the two nosologies are not overlapping as global systems. From the psychiatric perspective, a cohort of individuals identified by a single indigenous label will prove to be diagnostically heterogeneous, or even nonpathological. The obverse is also true; homogeneous psychiatric cohorts will appear locally diverse. A nomographical, one-to-one relationship between Western and non-Western nosologies appears thus unattainable.[49] What is achievable is the systematic characterization of individual cases of persons suffering from culture-bound syndromes in terms of Western categories of psychiatric

Table 28–1 Components of the DSM-IV Outline for a Cultural Formulation

Cultural identity of the individual
Cultural explanations of the individual's illness
Cultural factors related to psychosocial environment and levels of functioning
Cultural elements of the relationship between the individual and the clinician
Overall cultural assessment for diagnosis and care

illness, retaining at the same time an account of their distinct definitions of illness, idioms of distress, unique symptoms, and other associated factors in the form of a cultural formulation[104] (Table 28–1). This iterative process of translation will result eventually in a comprehensive cultural psychiatry that integrates diverse local and professional classifications of psychiatric illness with the goal of more effective communication and care of patients.

Conclusion

New possibilities are emerging for the application of cultural information to diagnostic systems and the diagnostic process. This chapter has focused on some of the most conspicuous contributions aimed at enhancing the cultural suitability of DSM-IV and thus the use of diagnostic categories and criteria in multicultural settings. Other contributions, such as the glossary of culture-bound syndromes and idioms of distress and the guidelines for a cultural formulation, have been referred to succinctly. Cultural developments are also being worked into the family of classifications of the *International Classification of Diseases and Related Health Problems,* 10th revision.[105] All these efforts promise to increase the applicability and usefulness of the new diagnostic systems for our multicultural world. Further, they may encourage psychiatrists and the field as a whole to stay focused on the person of the patient and his or her context to augment the validity of diagnosis and the effectiveness of clinical care.

References

1. American Psychiatric Association: Diagnostic and Statistical Manual of Mental Disorders, 4th ed. Washington, DC: American Psychiatric Association, 1994.
2. Mezzich JE, Kleinman A, Fábrega H, Parron DL (eds): Culture and Psychiatric Diagnosis. Washington, DC: American Psychiatric Press, in press.
3. Lin K-M, Fábrega H: Cultural considerations on cognitive impairment in DSM-IV. In Widiger T, Frances AJ, Pincus HA, et al (eds): Sourcebook for DSM-IV. Washington, DC: American Psychiatric Press, in press.
4. Cruickshank JK, Beevers DG: Ethnic Factors in Health and Disease. London: Wright, 1989.
5. Spector RE: Cultural Diversity in Health and Illness. New York: Appleton-Century-Crofts, 1979.
6. Westermeyer J: Mental Health for Refugees and Other Migrants: Social and Preventive Approach. Springfield, IL: Charles C Thomas, 1989.
7. Agarwal DP, Goedde HW: Alcohol Metabolism, Alcohol Intolerance, and Alcoholism. Berlin: Springer-Verlag, 1990.
8. Kaslow RA, Francis DP: The Epidemiology of AIDS. New York: Oxford University Press, 1989.
9. de la Monte SM, Hutchins GM, Moore GW: Racial differences in the etiology of dementia and frequency of Alzheimer's lesions in the brain. J Natl Med Assoc 1989; 81:644–652.
10. Zhang M, Katzman R, Salmon D, et al: The prevalence of dementia and Alzheimer's disease in Shanghai, China: Impact of age, gender, and education. Ann Neurol 1990; 27:428–437.
11. Ikels C: Aging and disability in China: Cultural issues in measurement and interpretation. Soc Sci Med 1991; 32:649–665.
12. Williams CL: Issues surrounding psychological testing of minority patients. Hosp Community Psychiatry 1987; 38:184–189.
13. Helzer JE, Canino GJ (eds): Alcoholism—North America, Europe, and Asia: A Coordinated Analysis of Population Data from Ten Regions. London: Oxford University Press, 1992.
14. Westermeyer J, Canino GJ: Culture and substance related disorders. In Widiger T, Frances AJ, Pincus HA, et al (eds): Sourcebook for DSM-IV. Washington, DC: American Psychiatric Press, in press.
15. Osterberg E: Alcohol-related problems in cross-national perspectives: Results of the ISACE study. Ann N Y Acad Sci 1986; 472:10–20.
16. Vaillant G: Cultural factors in the etiology of alcoholism: A prospective study. Ann N Y Acad Sci 1986; 472:142–148.
17. Anthony JC, Helzer JE: Syndromes of drug abuse and dependence in America. In Robins L, Regier D (eds): Psychiatric Disorders in America. New York: Free Press, 1991:116–154.
18. Robins LN, Helzer JE, Weissman MM, et al: Lifetime prevalence of specific psychiatric disorders in three sites. Arch Gen Psychiatry 1984; 41:949–958.
19. Berger LJ, Westermeyer J: World traveler addicts in Asia: II. Comparison with "stay at home" addicts. Am J Drug Abuse 1977; 4:495–503.
20. Krassoievitch M, Pérez-Rincón H, Suárez P: Correlation entre les hallucinations visuelles et auditives dans une population de schizophrenes Mexicains. Confront Psychiatriques 1982; 15:149–162.
21. Ndetei DM, Vadher A: A comparative cross-cultural study of the frequencies of hallucination in schizophrenia. Acta Psychiatr Scand 1984; 70:545–549.
22. Kleinman A: Rethinking Psychiatry. New York: Free Press, 1988.
23. Warner R: Recovery from Schizophrenia: Psychiatry and Political Economy. New York: Routledge & Kegan Paul, 1985.
24. Sartorius N, Jablensky A, Korten A, et al: Early manifestations and first-contact incidence of schizophrenia in different cultures. Psychol Med 1986; 16:909–928.
25. Lin K-M, Kleinman A: Psychopathology and clinical course of schizophrenia: A cross-cultural perspective. Schizophr Bull 1988; 14:555–567.
26. Jenkins JH, Karno M: The meaning of expressed emotion: Theoretical issues raised by cross-cultural research. Am J Psychiatry 1992; 149:9–21.
27. Good BJ: Culture, diagnosis, and comorbidity. Cult Med Psychiatry 1992/93; 16:427–447.
28. Karno M, Jenkins JH: Cultural considerations in the diagnosis of schizophrenia and related disorders and psychotic disorders not otherwise classified. In Widiger T, Frances AJ, Pincus HA, et al (eds): Sourcebook for DSM-IV. Washington, DC: American Psychiatric Press, in press.
29. Hultkrantz A: The Religions of the American Indians. Berkeley, CA: University of California Press, 1979.
30. Guarnaccia PJ, Guevara-Ramos LM, Gonzáles G, et al: Cross-cultural aspects of psychotic symptoms in Puerto Rico. Res Community Ment Health 1992; 7:99–110.
31. Lewis-Fernández R: Culture and dissociation: A comparison of *ataque de nervios* among Puerto Ricans and "possession syndrome" in India. In Spiegel D (ed): Dissociation: Culture, Mind and Body. Washington, DC: American Psychiatric Press, 1994:123–167.
32. Mezzich JE, Good BJ, Lewis-Fernández R, et al: Cultural formulation guidelines. In Mezzich JE, Kleinman A, Fábrega H, et al (eds): Revised Cultural Proposals for DSM-IV. Technical report. Pittsburgh, PA: NIMH Group on Culture and Diagnosis. 1993:163–168.
33. Marsella AJ, Sartorius N, Jablensky A, Fenton FR: Cross-cultural studies of depressive disorders: An overview. In Kleinman A, Good BJ (eds): Culture and Depression: Studies in the Anthropology and Cross-Cultural Psychiatry of Affect and Disorder. Berkeley, CA: University of California Press, 1985:299–324.
34. Brown GW, Harris T: Social Origins of Depression: A Study of Psychiatric Disorder in Women. New York: Free Press, 1978.

35. Manson SM, Shore JH, Bloom JD: The depressive experience in American Indian communities: A challenge for psychiatric theory and diagnosis. In Kleinman A, Good BJ (eds): Culture and Depression: Studies in the Anthropology and Cross-Cultural Psychiatry of Affect and Disorder. Berkeley, CA: University of California Press, 1985: 331–368.
36. Lewis-Fernández R: Puerto Rico, los nervios, y la nueva psiquiatría transcultural. Rev Psiquiatría Puerto Rico, in press.
37. Katon W, Roy-Byrne PP: Mixed anxiety and depression. J Abnorm Psychol 1991; 100:337–345.
38. Ebigbo PO: Development of a culture specific (Nigeria) screening scale of somatic complaints. Cult Med Psychiatry 1982; 6:29–44.
39. Clark VA, Aneshensel CS, Frerichs RR, Morgan TM: Analysis of effects of sex and age in response to items on the CES-D scale. Psychiatry Res 1981; 5:171–181.
40. Guarnaccia PJ, Angel R, Worobey JL: The factor structure of the CES-D in the Hispanic Health and Nutrition Examination Survey: The influences of ethnicity, gender, and language. Soc Sci Med 1989; 29:85–94.
41. Manson SM, Good BJ: Cultural considerations in the diagnosis of DSM-IV mood disorders. In Widiger T, Frances AJ, Pincus HA, et al (eds): Sourcebook for DSM-IV. Washington, DC: American Psychiatric Press, in press.
42. Good BJ, Kleinman A: Culture and anxiety: Cross-cultural evidence for the patterning of anxiety disorders. In Tuma A, Maser J (eds): Anxiety and the Anxiety Disorders. Hillsdale, NJ: Lawrence Erlbaum, 1985.
43. Neal AM, Turner SM: Anxiety disorders research with African-Americans: Current status. Psychol Bull 1991; 109:400–410.
44. Brown DR, Eaton WW, Sussman L: Racial differences in prevalence of phobic disorders. J Nerv Ment Dis 1990; 178:434–441.
45. Guarnaccia PJ, Kirmayer LJ: Literature review on culture and the anxiety disorders (DSM-IV). In Widiger T, Frances AJ, Pincus HA, et al (eds): Sourcebook for DSM-IV. Washington, DC: American Psychiatric Press, in press.
46. Shrout PE, Canino GJ, Bird H, et al: Mental health status among Puerto Ricans, Mexican Americans, and non-Hispanic Whites. Am J Community Psychol 1992; 20:729–752.
47. Hughes CC, Simons RC, Wintrob RM: The 'culture-bound syndromes' and DSM-IV. In Widiger T, Frances AJ, Pincus HA, et al (eds): Sourcebook for DSM-IV. Washington, DC: American Psychiatric Press, in press.
48. Maser JD, Dinges N: Co-morbidity: Meaning and uses in cross-cultural clinical research. Cult Med Psychiatry 1992; 16:409–425.
49. Weiss M: Cultural comments on somatoform and dissociative disorders. In Mezzich JE, Kleinman A, Fábrega H, Parron DL (eds): Culture and Psychiatric Diagnosis. Washington, DC: American Psychiatric Press, in press.
50. Maser JD, Kaelber C, Weise RE: International use and attitudes toward DSM-III and DSM-III-R: Growing consensus in psychiatric classification. J Abnorm Psychol 1991; 100:271–279.
51. Kirmayer LJ, Weiss M: On cultural considerations for somatoform disorders in DSM-IV. In Widiger T, Frances AJ, Pincus HA, et al (eds): Sourcebook for DSM-IV. Washington, DC: American Psychiatric Press, in press.
52. Lewis-Fernández R: The proposed DSM-IV trance and possession disorder category: Potential benefits and risks. Transcult Psychiatr Res Rev 1992; 29:301–317.
53. Lin T-Y: Neurasthenia revisited: Its place in modern psychiatry. Cult Med Psychiatry 1989; 13:105–130.
54. Angel R, Guarnaccia PJ: Mind, body, and culture: Somatization among Hispanics. Soc Sci Med 1989; 28:1229–1238.
55. Kirmayer LJ, Robbins JM: Introduction: Concepts of somatization. In Kirmayer LJ, Robbins JM (eds): Current Concepts in Somatization: Research and Clinical Perspectives. Washington, DC: American Psychiatric Press, 1991:1–19.
56. Nichter M: Idioms of distress: Alternatives in the expression of psychosocial distress: A case study from South India. Cult Med Psychiatry 1981; 5:379–408.
57. González C, Lewis-Fernández R, Griffith EEH, et al: The impact of culture on dissociation: On enhancing the cultural suitability of DSM-IV. In Widiger T, Frances AJ, Pincus HA, et al (eds): Sourcebook for DSM-IV. Washington, DC: American Psychiatric Press, in press.
58. Saxena S, Prasad KVSR: DSM-III subclassification of dissociative disorders applied to psychiatric outpatients in India. Am J Psychiatry 1989; 145:261–262.
59. Ward CA (ed): Altered States of Consciousness and Mental Health: A Cross-Cultural Perspective. Newbury Park, CA: Sage, 1989.
60. Spiegel D, Cardeña E: Disintegrated experience: The dissociative disorders revisited. J Abnorm Psychol 1991; 100:366–378.
61. Cardeña E, Lewis-Fernández R, Bear D, et al: Dissociative disorders. In Widiger T, Frances AJ, Pincus HA, et al (eds): Sourcebook for DSM-IV. Washington, DC: American Psychiatric Press, in press.
62. Weidman HH: Falling-out: A diagnostic and treatment problem viewed from a transcultural perspective. Soc Sci Med 1979; 13B:95–112.
63. Ross CA: The dissociated executive self and the cultural dissociation barrier. Dissociation 1991; 4:55–61.
64. Martínez-Taboas A: Multiple personality disorder as seen from a social constructionist viewpoint. Dissociation 1991; 4:129–133.
65. Steinberg M: The spectrum of depersonalization: Assessment and treatment. In Tasman A, Goldfinger SM: American Psychiatric Press Review of Psychiatry, Volume 10. Washington, DC: American Psychiatric Press, 1991:223–247.
66. Castillo RJ: Culture, Trance and Mental Illness: Divided Consciousness in South Asia. Cambridge, MA: Harvard University; 1991. Doctoral dissertation.
67. Davis DL, Herdt G: Cultural issues and the sexual disorders of the DSM-IV. In Widiger T, Frances AJ, Pincus HA, et al (eds): Sourcebook for DSM-IV. Washington, DC: American Psychiatric Press, in press.
68. Rooth G: Exhibitionism. Arch Sex Behav 1973; 2:351–363.
69. Gebhard PH: Human sexual behavior. In Marshall DS, Suggs RC (eds): Human Sexual Behavior. New York: Basic Books, 1971: 206–217.
70. Fisher S: Personality correlates of sexual behavior in black women. Arch Sex Behav 1980; 9:27–35.
71. Finkle A, Finkle C: Sexual impotency. Urology 1978; 23:25–30.
72. Wyatt GE: Identifying stereotypes of Afro-American sexuality and their impact on sexual behavior. In Bass BA, Wyatt GE, Powell G: The Afro-American Family. New York: Grune & Stratton, 1982:333–346.
73. Espín OM: Cultural and historical influences on sexuality in Hispanic/Latin women. In Boston VC (ed): Pleasure and Anger: Exploring Female Sexuality. New York: Routledge & Kegan Paul, 1984:149–164.
74. Davis DL, Whitten RG: The cross-cultural study of human sexuality. Annu Rev Anthropol 1987; 16:69–98.
75. Herdt G: Developmental continuity as a dimension of sexual orientation across cultures. In McWhirter D, Reinisch J, Sanders P (eds): Homosexuality and Heterosexuality. New York: Oxford University Press, 1990:208–238.
76. Nichter M, Nichter M: Hype and weight. Med Anthropol 1991; 13:249–284.
77. Ritenbaugh C: Obesity as a culture-bound syndrome. Cult Med Psychiatry 1982; 6:347–361.
78. Banks CG: 'Culture' in culture-bound syndromes: The case of anorexia nervosa. Soc Sci Med 1992; 34:867–884.
79. Shisslak CM, Crago M, Yates A: Typical patterns in atypical anorexia nervosa. Psychosomatics 1989; 30:307–311.
80. Ritenbaugh C, Shisslak CL, Teufel N, et al: Eating disorders: A cross-cultural review in regard to DSM-IV. In Widiger T, Frances AJ, Pincus HA, et al (eds): Sourcebook for DSM-IV. Washington, DC: American Psychiatric Press, in press.
81. Nasser M: Comparative study of the prevalence of abnormal eating attitudes among Arab female students of both London and Cairo Universities. Psychol Med 1986; 16:621–625.
82. Rosen LW, Shafer CL, Dummer GM, et al: Prevalence of pathogenic weight-control behavior among Native American women and girls. Int J Eating Dis 1988; 7:807–811.
83. Suematsu H, Ishikawa H, Kuboki T, Ito T: Statistical studies on anorexia nervosa in Japan: Detailed clinical data on 1,011 patients. Psychother Psychosom 1985; 43:96–103.
84. Lee S, Chiu HFK, Chen C: Anorexia nervosa in Hong Kong: Why not more in Chinese? Br J Psychiatry 1989; 154:683–688.
85. Lee S: Anorexia nervosa in Hong Kong: A Chinese perspective. Psychol Med 1991; 21:703–711.
86. Jenkins JH, Kinzie JD: Culture and the diagnosis of adjustment disorders. In Widiger T, Frances AJ, Pincus HA, et al (eds):

Sourcebook for DSM-IV. Washington, DC: American Psychiatric Press, in press.
87. Fábrega H, Mezzich JE: Adjustment disorder and psychiatric practice: Cultural and historical aspects. Psychiatry 1987; 50:31–49.
88. Beiser M: Adjustment disorder in DSM-IV: Cultural considerations. In Mezzich JE, Kleinman A, Fábrega H, Parron DL (eds): Culture and Psychiatric Diagnosis. Washington, DC: American Psychiatric Press, in press.
89. Lewis-Fernández R, Kleinman A: Culture, personality, and psychopathology. J Abnorm Psychol 1993; 103:67–71.
90. Alarcón RD, Foulks EF: Cultural factors and personality disorders: A review of the literature. In Widiger T, Frances AJ, Pincus HA, et al (eds): Sourcebook for DSM-IV. Washington, DC: American Psychiatric Press, in press.
91. Favazza AR: Anthropology and psychiatry. In Kaplan HI, Sadock JD (eds): Comprehensive Textbook of Psychiatry, 4th ed. Baltimore: Williams & Wilkins, 1985:247–265.
92. Leighton AH: Culture and psychiatry. Can J Psychiatry 1981; 26:522–529.
93. Canino GJ, Rubio-Stipec M, Shrout P, et al: Sex differences in depression in Puerto Rico. Psychol Women Q 1987; 11:443–459.
94. Perry JC: Problems and considerations in the valid assessment of personality disorders. Am J Psychiatry 1992; 149:1645–1653.
95. Paris J: Personality disorders, parasuicide, and culture. Transcult Psychiatr Res Rev 1991; 28:25–39.
96. Shepherd M, Sartorius N: Personality disorder and the international classification of diseases. Psychol Med 1974; 4:141–146.
97. Simons RC, Hughes CC (eds): The Culture-Bound Syndromes: Folk Illnesses of Psychiatric and Anthropological Interest. Dordrecht, Netherlands: Reidel, 1985.
98. Good BJ: Medicine, Rationality, and Experience: An Anthropological Perspective. Cambridge, UK: Cambridge University Press, 1994.
99. Good BJ, Delvecchio Good MJ: Toward a meaning-centered analysis of popular illness categories: "Fright-illness" and "heart distress" in Iran. In Marsella AJ, White GM (eds): Cultural Conceptions of Mental Health and Therapy. Dordrecht, Netherlands: Reidel, 1982:141–166.
100. Lewis-Fernández R, Kleinman A: Cultural psychiatry: Theoretical, clinical and research issues. Psychiatr Clin North Am, in press.
101. Hahn RA: Culture-bound syndromes unbound. Soc Sci Med 1985; 21:165–171.
102. Guarnaccia PJ: *Ataques de nervios* in Puerto Rico: Culture-bound syndrome or popular illness? Med Anthropol 1993; 15:157–170.
103. Wig NN: DSM-III: A perspective from the Third World. In Spitzer RL, Williams JB, Skodol AE (eds): International Perspectives on DSM-III. Washington, DC: American Psychiatric Press, 1983.
104. Mezzich JE, Good BJ: On culturally enhancing the DSM-IV multiaxial formulation. In Widiger T, Frances AJ, Pincus HA, et al (eds): Sourcebook for DSM-IV. Washington, DC: American Psychiatric Press, in press.
105. Mezzich JE: International perspectives on psychiatric diagnosis. In Kaplan HI, Sadock BJ (eds): Comprehensive Textbook of Psychiatry, 6th ed. Baltimore: Williams & Wilkins, 1995:692–703.

CHAPTER

29 Psychiatric Classification

Michael B. First
Allen Frances
Harold Alan Pincus

There is a natural human predilection to categorize and classify for simplifying and organizing the wide range of observable phenomena and experiences that one is confronted with, thus facilitating both their understanding and their predictability. Many (if not most) of the mental disorders that afflict contemporary individuals have occurred in antiquity. For example, the first recorded depiction of mental illness dates to 3000 BC Egypt with a description of the syndrome senile dementia attributed to Prince Ptahhotep.[1] The current system for the diagnosis of mental disorders, the *Diagnostic and Statistical Manual of Mental Disorders,* Fourth Edition (DSM-IV),[2] is just the latest example from the long and colorful history of psychiatric classification.

Goals of a Classification System

Perhaps the most important goal of a psychiatric classification is to allow psychiatrists and researchers to communicate more effectively with each other by establishing a convenient shorthand for describing the mental disorders that they see.[3] For example, saying to a colleague that a patient has major depressive disorder can convey a great deal of information in only a few words. It indicates that depressed mood or loss of interest is an important part of the presenting symptoms; that the depression is not the kind of mood disturbance that lasts only a couple of days but rather that it persists for most of the day, nearly every day, for at least 2 weeks; that certain additional symptoms, like suicidal ideation and changes in appetite, sleep, and psychomotor activity, are likely to co-occur; that substance use and general medical conditions have been ruled out as etiological factors; and that there is no history of schizophrenia or manic or hypomanic episodes.

DSM-IV also facilitates the identification and management of mental disorders in both clinical and research settings. Most of the DSM-IV diagnostic labels provide considerable and important predictive power. For example, making a diagnosis of bipolar disorder suggests the choice of treatment options (e.g., mood stabilizers), that a certain course may be likely (e.g., recurrent and episodic), and that there is an increased prevalence of this disorder in family members. By defining more or less homogeneous groups of individuals for study, DSM-IV can also further efforts to understand the etiology of mental disorders. The classifications of the manual have been a reflection of, and a major contribution to, the development of an empirical science of psychiatry. DSM-IV also plays an important role in education. In its organization of disorders into major classes, the system offers a structure for teaching phenomenology and differential diagnosis. DSM-IV is also useful in psychoeducation by showing patients that their pattern of symptoms is not mysterious and unique but rather has been identified and studied in others.

Approaches to Classification

Historically, there have been two fundamental approaches to formulating systems of psychiatric classification: etiological and descriptive.[4] Etiology-based classification systems organize categories around pathogenetic processes so that disorders corresponding to a particular category share the same underlying cause. Although such systems tend to have relatively few categories and therefore are easy to use, their ultimate value is constrained by the limited extent to which underlying etiological factors have been elucidated. For example, the 16th century Swiss physician Paracelsus developed a classification system in which he divided psychotic presentations into three types of disorders on the basis of the presumed etiology. The first category, vesania, for disorders caused by poisons, is analogous to current-day substance-induced disorders. Insanity, for diseases caused by heredity, is analogous to modern disorders such as schizophrenia and bipolar disorder, which appear to have a strong familial component. His category of lunacy, which described a periodical condition influenced by the phases of the moon, has no analogous condition today because we know that the phases of the moon are not a direct cause of psychopathological conditions.

Because the etiological basis for most psychiatric conditions remains elusive, etiological classification systems tend to be based instead on a particular conceptualization of the process of mental disorders. Although such classifications may be heuristically useful to proponents of the particular conceptualization that forms the basis of the system, they are often considerably less useful for proponents of different etiological principles, which greatly limits their utility. For this reason, a descriptive approach to classification has proved to be of greater utility given our current understanding. The descriptive approach aims to eschew particular etiological theories and instead relies on clinical descriptions of presenting symptoms. This approach, advanced by the work of the 19th century psychiatrist Emil Kraepelin,[5] formed the basis for the system of classification of the *Diagnostic and Statistical Manual of Mental Disorders,* Third Edition (DSM-III) introduced in 1980. As a result, DSM-III and its successors, the *Diagnostic and Statistical Manual of Mental Disorders,* Third Edition, Revised (DSM-III-R) and DSM-IV, have proved to be useful in a variety of different settings and by psychiatrists of widely different backgrounds and conceptual orientations.

Organizing Principle of the DSM

Given that the manual lacks a specific etiological conceptualization, what is its organizing principle? The fundamental element is the syndrome, that is, a group or pattern of symptoms that appear together temporally in many individuals.[6] It is assumed that these symptoms cluster together because they are associated in some clinically meaningful way, which perhaps may reflect a common etiological process, course, or treatment response. Alternatively, individual symptoms could have been emphasized as the fundamental conceptual entities so that a person's disorder would be classified by enumerating all of his or her relevant symptoms. In fact, historically, there have been classifications that have been symptom based. For example, Boisser de Sauvages proposed a medical classification that arranged presenting symptoms into numerous classes, orders, and genera, comparable to the classification of plants and animals. This approach generated 2400 disorders, each of which was essentially a symptom.

Perhaps the most important advantage of the syndromal approach is in facilitating the management of mental disorders. The identification of psychiatric syndromes aims to define relatively homogeneous subpopulations of patients that share features like treatment response, course, family history, and biological markers. It is precisely this association between the syndromes and associated features that has made a syndromal classification system useful in clinical, research, and educational settings. The main disadvantage of syndromal classifications is the tendency for users to reify the syndromes and to treat them as if they were equivalent to the underlying disease entities. One should always keep in mind that the syndromal groupings that compose the manual reflect no more than the state of the art as it was during the time of drafting for that version of the classification. The principal reason for regular revisions in the manual's classification is to allow the syndromal definitions to be redrawn to reflect our evolving understanding of the pathophysiological mechanisms of mental disorders.

History of the Manuals

The predecessors of DSM-IV arose from the need to develop a classification system of mental disorders for statistical, epidemiological, and reporting purposes. The first official international classification of mental disorders, the sixth revision of the *International Classification of Diseases* (ICD-6), was considered unacceptable by most countries because of its heavy reliance on unproven etiological concepts. The *Diagnostic and Statistical Manual of Mental Disorders,* First Edition[7] (DSM-I) was published in 1952 as an alternative to ICD-6 and included glossary definitions of the various disorders. The *Diagnostic and Statistical Manual of Mental Disorders,* Second Edition[8] (DSM-II) was published in 1968. Like DSM-I, DSM-II retained many etiological concepts (e.g., neuroses). After reviewing early drafts of ICD-9 in the early 1970s, the American Psychiatric Association[9] opted to develop DSM-III because of concerns that the international nature of the ICD-9 resulted in inconsistent terminology and definitions and that the subtyping was inadequate for clinical and research use. DSM-III represented a major paradigm shift from the etiologically based frameworks of DSM-I and DSM-II. It adopted a descriptive approach that was meant to facilitate communication between mental health professionals operating under various theoretical orientations that continue to flourish in psychiatry and psychology.

Two innovations were introduced into DSM-III. Each DSM-III disorder was defined by use of explicit diagnostic criteria, which greatly improved the reliability of the system and provided researchers with well-defined categories for scientific study. DSM-III also included a multiaxial system for evaluation that facilitated the use of a biopsychosocial model of evaluation by separating (and thereby calling attention to) developmental and personality disorders (Axis II), physical conditions (Axis III), stressors (Axis IV), and level of adaptive functioning (Axis V) from the presenting diagnoses (Axis I). In 1987, DSM-III-R was published.[10] Although originally intended only as a fine-tuning to correct inconsistencies and problems identified after the publication of DSM-III,[11, 12] more substantive changes were made, many reflecting new evidence not available to the developers of DSM-III. Although the publication of DSM-III-R demonstrated that the system is self-correcting, DSM-III-R has been criticized as being too much of a change occurring too soon after the adoption of DSM-III.

DSM-IV was envisioned as a modification and refinement of previous editions of the manual rather than a radical reconceptualization.[13] The most significant change in DSM-IV is in the process by which DSM-III-R was revised to produce DSM-IV.[14] Prior revision efforts were guided almost exclusively by expert consensus. Although these experts were certainly familiar with the then-current state of knowledge about the psychiatric disorders, their decisions were subject to potential biases. In contrast, whenever possible, DSM-IV decisions were based on a systematic review of the then-current empirical database.

The method used to establish an empirical basis for changes in DSM-IV was divided into three stages. As a first step, the approximately 150 questions most deserving consideration for DSM-IV were identified.[15] Each of these then received an extensive and systematic review of the literature to determine what evidence was available and what additional evidence would need to be collected to support possible changes. One obvious shortcoming of relying on the literature reviews was that many important questions arose that were not addressed by the published literature. The second stage of the process was to conduct a series of approximately 40 data reanalyses of previously compiled

Table 29–1 DSM-IV Focused Field Trials

Schizophrenia
Mood disorders
Panic disorder
Mixed anxiety-depressive disorder
Obsessive-compulsive disorder
Posttraumatic stress disorder
Somatization disorder
Sleep disorders
Pervasive developmental disorders
Disruptive behavior disorders
Substance dependence
Antisocial personality disorder

data sets to supplement the evidence available from published studies. Although useful in generating new criteria sets for DSM-IV, the data reanalyses were limited by the fact that the data were collected before the DSM-IV process. Therefore, a series of 12 focused field trials were conducted (Table 29–1). Each field trial drew subjects from at least five different sites (with a minimum of 50 patients per site).[16] The field trials served to test the performance characteristics of the proposed criteria sets and to compare them with the DSM-III, DSM-III-R, and ICD-10 criteria sets. A summary of the results of the empirical review process as well as the rationale for the changes in DSM-IV is published in *The DSM-IV Sourcebook.*[17, 18]

The following example serves to illustrate this three-stage process. One of the main goals of the DSM-IV revision process was to improve the clinical utility of the criteria sets. In this regard, several of the DSM-III-R criteria sets had been identified as being particularly difficult to apply in clinical settings. One of the most cumbersome criteria sets was that for somatization disorder, which provided a list of 35 different unexplained physical symptoms, of which at least 13 were required for a diagnosis. A literature review was first conducted to investigate the performance characteristics of the DSM-III-R criteria set. It demonstrated, as expected, that the DSM-III-R definition was among the most reliable and valid in the manual. Any attempt to modify the criteria set would therefore have to result in a criteria set that defined the same group of patients as did DSM-III-R and be comparably reliable. A more user-friendly criteria set was generated through the data reanalysis process. Data sets of patients with somatization disorder were pooled, and different diagnostic algorithms were investigated. The resulting proposed criteria set required symptoms for a period of several years that occur in the following pattern: at least four pain symptoms, two gastrointestinal symptoms, one sexual symptom, and one conversion symptom. To ensure the generalizability of this proposed criteria set, a focused field trial was conducted that compared this simplified definition with the original DSM-III-R definition, along with DSM-III, ICD-10, and the historical definition of Briquet's syndrome. The field trial found that all of the definitions identified essentially the same group of patients with comparable reliability, providing empirical support for the DSM-IV decision to replace the DSM-III-R criteria set for somatization disorder.

SPECIFIC DISORDERS INCLUDED IN DSM-IV

The remainder of this chapter provides an overview of the various disorders included in the DSM-IV classification with special emphasis on changes from DSM-III-R.[19–21] More details concerning the specific disorders are contained in Section V.

DSM-IV Multiaxial System

The multiaxial system was first introduced by DSM-III[22] and, despite some concerns raised by its critics, is being retained (albeit in a modified form) in DSM-IV.[23] Use of the multiaxial system requires that information be noted on each of five different axes, each axis devoted to a different aspect of the evaluation process. Axes I, II, and III are the diagnostic axes and divide up the diagnostic pie into three domains. Because Axes II and III were created to highlight certain types of clinical disorders that were thought not to be given adequate attention by mental health professionals, we consider these first. Axis II was designed to draw attention to certain disorders that were thought to be overshadowed in the face of the more florid Axis I presentations. In DSM-III, Axis II was reserved for personality disorders in adults and specific developmental disorders in children. In DSM-III-R, the developmental disorders (i.e., mental retardation, pervasive developmental disorders, specific developmental disorders) were coded on Axis II along with the personality disorders. In DSM-IV, personality disorders remain on Axis II, but all of the developmental disorders (except mental retardation) have moved back to Axis I.

Axis III continues to provide an opportunity to note clinically relevant general medical conditions. The concept of clinically relevant is intended to be broad. For example, it would be appropriate to list hypertension on Axis III even if its only relationship to an Axis I disorder is its impact on the options for the choice of antidepressant medication.

The biggest change in the multiaxial system of DSM-IV is in Axis IV.[24] Whereas noting psychosocial stressors on DSM-III-R Axis IV (in which the severity of etiological stressors was also rated) was believed to be important in the understanding of the clinical situation, it was rarely used (except in research settings), probably because it was perceived as too complex a rating to make, with questionable clinical significance. In its place, DSM-IV provides the psychiatrist with the opportunity to list clinically relevant psychosocial and environmental problems (e.g., homelessness, poverty, divorce). To facilitate a comprehensive evaluation of such problems, DSM-IV includes a psychosocial and environmental checklist that allows the psychiatrist to indicate which types of problems are present and relevant (Fig. 29–1). Axis V in DSM-IV continues to be the Global Assessment of Functioning Scale (Fig. 29–2), although it has been modified in DSM-IV to include the uppermost 10 points of the scale (for "superior mental functioning"). An example of a DSM-IV multiaxial evaluation for a hypothetical patient is shown in Table 29–2.

DSM-IV Axis IV: Psychosocial and environmental problems

Check:

___ Problems with primary support group (childhood, adult, parent-child). Specify: ________

___ Problems related to the social environment. Specify: ________

___ Educational problems. Specify: ________

___ Occupational problems. Specify: ________

___ Housing problems. Specify: ________

___ Economic problems. Specify: ________

___ Problems with access to health care services. Specify: ________

___ Problems related to interaction with the legal system/crime. Specify: ________

___ Other psychosocial problems. Specify: ________

Figure 29–1 *DSM-IV Axis IV. (Modified from American Psychiatric Association: Diagnostic and Statistical Manual of Mental Disorders, 4th ed. Washington, DC: American Psychiatric Association, 1994:30.)*

Disorders Usually First Diagnosed in Infancy, Childhood, or Adolescence

Mental Retardation

A diagnosis of mental retardation requires a low score (70 or below) on an individually administered intelligence test as well as impairment in adaptive functioning. The areas of adaptive functioning specified in the criteria set were selected so that the criteria set is identical in wording with the definitions adopted by the American Association of Mental Retardation. Despite the apparent discrepancy in IQ cutoff scores (70 in DSM-IV, 75 for the American Association of Mental Retardation), the definitions are equivalent once one takes into account the 5-point measurement error built in to the DSM-IV IQ ranges.

Learning Disorders

In DSM-III-R, a diagnosis of learning disorder could not be given to a child with a sensory deficit (e.g., blindness or deafness) or a neurological condition because of concerns about the difficulty in determining how much of the low score on the requisite individually administered achievement test was due to a learning disorder versus how much was attributable to the sensory deficit or neurological condition. Because such children are certainly not immune to also having a learning disorder, DSM-IV allows a diagnosis of a learning disorder to be given if, in the psychiatrist's judgment, the measured learning disorder is greater than would be expected given the sensory deficit or neurological condition alone. In DSM-IV, the learning disorders are reading disorder, mathematics disorder, and disorder of written expression. In contrast to DSM-III-R, in DSM-IV learning disorders are coded on Axis I.

Pervasive Developmental Disorders

Pervasive developmental disorders are characterized by gross qualitative impairment in social relatedness, in language, and in repertoire of interests and activities. DSM-III-R included only two pervasive developmental disorders: autistic disorder and pervasive developmental disorder not otherwise specified (NOS). One problem encountered was that in many settings, the nonspecific diagnosis of pervasive developmental disorder NOS was considerably more frequent than the specific diagnosis of autistic disorder.[25] To provide more specificity in this area, DSM-IV has extracted from pervasive developmental disorder NOS three specific categories: Rett's disorder, childhood disintegrative disorder, and Asperger's disorder.

Rett's disorder, which has been diagnosed only in girls, is characterized by deceleration in head growth, loss of coordinated hand movements and social skills, and development of stereotyped movements. Childhood disintegrative disorder is characterized by normal development up to at least 2 years of age, which is followed by a marked decline involving a loss of previously acquired skills. Ultimately, a severe autistic-like clinical picture develops. In contrast, children with autistic disorder, by and large, do not have a period of normal development but have subtle evidence of the disturbance from birth. By far the most common of the three new disorders is Asperger's disorder, which resembles autistic disorder in its characteristic severe social impairment and restricted range of interests and activities but differs in that language development is preserved. Because of the sparing of language, individuals with Asperger's disorder tend to function at a higher level than do patients with autistic disorder.

Attention-Deficit/Hyperactivity Disorder

DSM-III-R included two categories for individuals who present with symptoms of inattention: attention-deficit/hyperactivity disorder for inattention accompanied by hyperactive-impulsive symptoms, and undifferentiated attention-deficit disorder for inattention that occurs in the absence of hyperactivity. Reflecting findings that support a unitary construct of attention-deficit/hyperactivity disorder, DSM-IV provides a single category with three subtypes reflecting the symptom patterns (predominantly inattentive, predominantly hyperactive-impulsive, combined). To reduce false-positives by ensuring that the symptoms are not situation specific, DSM-IV requires that the symptoms be present in two or more situations (e.g., at school, at work, and at home).

Conduct Disorder

The gender breakdown for the DSM-III-R diagnosis of conduct disorder is overwhelmingly male. Evidence suggests that this finding is partly the result of gender bias in the wording of the criteria items. One reason that the diagnosis is given to boys more often than to girls is because the behaviors listed in the criteria set are inherently more common in boys than in girls. Perhaps this is not surprising given that the early research that formed the basis for the diagnosis was carried out exclusively in boys. The addition of two more gender-neutral items ("staying out at night" and "intimidating others") should help mollify this problem. It

Consider psychological, social, and occupational functioning on a hypothetical continuum of mental health-illness. Do not include impairment in functioning due to physical (or environmental) limitations.

Code	(Note: Use intermediate codes when appropriate, e.g., 45, 68, 72.)
100–91	Superior functioning in a wide range of activities, life's problems never seem to get out of hand, is sought out by others because of many positive qualities. No symptoms.
90–81	Absent or minimal symptoms (e.g., mild anxiety before an examination), good functioning in all areas, interested and involved in a wide range of activities, socially effective, generally satisfied with life, no more than everyday problems or concerns (e.g., an occasional argument with family members).
80–71	If symptoms are present, they are transient and expectable reactions to psychosocial stressors (e.g., difficulty concentrating after family argument); no more than slight impairment in social, occupational, or school functioning (e.g., temporarily falling behind in school work).
70–61	Some mild symptoms (e.g., depressed mood and mild insomnia) OR some difficulty in social, occupational, or school functioning (e.g., occasional truancy, or theft within the household), but generally functioning pretty well, has some meaningful interpersonal relationships.
60–51	Moderate symptoms (e.g., flat affect and circumstantial speech, occasional panic attacks) OR moderate difficulty in social, occupational, or school functioning (e.g., few friends, conflicts with peers or coworkers).
50–41	Serious symptoms (e.g., suicidal ideation, severe obsessional rituals, frequent shoplifting) OR any serious impairment in social, occupational, or school functioning (e.g., no friends, unable to keep a job).
40–31	Some impairment in reality testing or communication (e.g., speech is at times illogical, obscure, or irrelevant) OR major impairment in several areas, such as work or school, family relations, judgment, thinking, or mood (e.g., depressed man avoids friends, neglects family, and is unable to work; child frequently beats up younger children, is defiant at home, and is failing at school).
30–21	Behavior is considerably influenced by delusions or hallucinations OR serious impairment in communication or judgment (e.g., sometimes incoherent, acts grossly inappropriately, suicidal preoccupation) OR inability to function in almost all areas (e.g., stays in bed all day; no job, home, or friends).
20–11	Some danger of hurting self or others (e.g., suicide attempts without clear expectation of death, frequently violent, manic excitement) OR occasionally fails to maintain minimal personal hygiene (e.g., smears feces) OR gross impairment in communication (e.g., largely incoherent or mute).
10–1	Persistent danger of severely hurting self or others (e.g., recurrent violence) OR persistent inability to maintain minimal personal hygiene OR serious suicidal act with clear expectation of death.
0	Inadequate information

Figure 29–2 *Global Assessment of Functioning Scale. (From American Psychiatric Association: Diagnostic and Statistical Manual of Mental Disorders, 4th ed. Washington, DC: American Psychiatric Association, 1994:32.)*

is of particular interest in conduct disorder to predict those individuals most likely to grow into adults with antisocial personality disorder. To this end, conduct disorder is subtyped on the basis of age at onset; onset before age 10 years predicts a high likelihood for a future diagnosis of adult antisocial personality disorder, more aggressive behavior, and poorer peer relationships.

Oppositional Defiant Disorder

This disorder describes a pattern of negativistic, hostile, and defiant behavior that causes clinically significant impairment or distress. One issue that arose during the DSM-IV deliberations was whether oppositional defiant disorder is better conceptualized as a milder form of conduct disorder without aggressive behavior rather than as a separate category (as it is in DSM-III-R).[26] Ultimately, it was decided to retain it as a separate category.

Pica

This category covers eating behavior characterized by the consumption of nonnutritive material (e.g., dirt). In contrast to DSM-III-R, DSM-IV allows this diagnosis in the presence of schizophrenia or a pervasive developmental disorder if the eating behavior is an independent focus of intervention or treatment.

Rumination Disorder

This feeding disorder is for infants who repeatedly regurgitate and rechew their food, often resulting in weight loss or failure to make expected weight gains.

Feeding Disorder of Infancy or Early Childhood

This category (often referred to as failure to thrive) was introduced into DSM-IV to cover situations in which infants and children fail to gain (or maintain) weight in the absence of an etiological general medical condition. Frequently, the failure to gain weight is related to an interactional problem between the infant and caretaker so that such children gain weight after being hospitalized and fed by someone else.

Tic Disorders

DSM-IV defines a tic as a "sudden, rapid, recurrent, nonrhythmic, stereotyped motor movement or vocalization." Three tic disorders are included in DSM-IV, different with respect to duration and types of tics: Tourette's disorder (a chronic tic disorder with both vocal and motor tics); chronic motor or vocal tic disorder; and transient tic disorder (for durations of less than 12 months). DSM-IV reduced the upper limit of age at onset from 21 to 18 years of age.

Communication Disorders

DSM-IV does not consider these disorders to be mental disorders; they are included to facilitate differential diagnosis and to increase recognition of these conditions among mental health professionals. These disorders include expressive language and mixed receptive-expressive language disorders (for problems in understanding or producing language); phonological disorder (for mechanical problems in articulation, such as a lisp); and stuttering.

Encopresis (Not due to a General Medical Condition)

Encopresis refers to the repeated passage of feces into inappropriate locations. DSM-IV distinguishes those situations in which the encopresis reflects overflow incontinence related to constipation by providing a different code for the "with constipation and overflow incontinence" type. In DSM-IV, the duration requirement has been reduced from 6 to 3 months to conform with clinical use.

Enuresis (Not due to a General Medical Condition)

Enuresis refers to repeated voiding of urine into bed or clothes. Because of the different treatment implications, three subtypes are provided to indicate when the behavior occurs (nocturnal only, diurnal only, nocturnal and diurnal). Although the specified frequency and duration threshold has been raised in DSM-IV (from twice per month to twice a week for 3 consecutive months), the psychiatrist is still encouraged to make the diagnosis regardless of duration if there is clinically significant impairment or distress.

Table 29–2 Example of DSM-IV Multiaxial Evaluation*

Axis I	296.23 Major depressive disorder, single episode, severe but without psychotic features, with postpartum onset 307.51 Bulimia nervosa
Axis II	301.6 Dependent personality disorder Frequent use of denial
Axis III	Rheumatoid arthritis
Axis IV	Partner relational problem
Axis V	GAF = 35 (current)

*GAF, Global Assessment of Functioning Scale score.

Separation Anxiety Disorder

Anxiety concerning separation from attachment figures is a developmentally appropriate behavior for most children during ages 1 to 3 years. When such behavior persists (or arises later) and is clinically significant (e.g., resulting in refusal to attend school), the diagnosis of separation anxiety disorder may apply.

Selective Mutism

The disorder refers to a pattern of behavior in which the child refuses to speak in certain situations (e.g., at school) despite speaking in other situations (e.g., when with parents). DSM-IV introduced several changes. The name was changed from the DSM-III-R elective mutism to reflect the observation that, in most cases, the behavior is more likely related to shyness rather than a willful attempt to be oppositional. In addition, several changes serve to reduce false-positives: the minimal duration of selective mutism is now 1 month; the diagnosis cannot be given if the behavior is confined to the first month of school; there must be clinically significant impairment; and the lack of speech cannot better be accounted for by a communication disorder or by lack of familiarity with the language required in the situation in which the child is quiet.

Reactive Attachment Disorder of Infancy or Early Childhood

This disorder describes two abnormal patterns of attachment resulting from grossly pathogenic care: inhibited attachments, in which the child is unable to respond appropriately in social situations (e.g., inhibited, hypervigilance, or ambivalent behavior); or disinhibited attachments, in which the child is indiscriminately sociable.

Stereotypic Movement Disorder

This disorder describes "repetitive, seemingly driven, and nonfunctional motor behavior," such as head banging and rocking. DSM-IV now allows this disorder to be diagnosed in the presence of mental retardation if the behavior is severe enough to become a focus of treatment, usually because of its self-injurious nature.

Delirium, Dementia, Amnestic Disorder, and Other Cognitive Disorders

In DSM-III-R, delirium, dementia, amnestic disorder, and other cognitive disorders were included in a section called organic mental disorders, which contained disorders that were due to either a general medical condition or substance use. In DSM-IV, the term *organic* has been eliminated because of the implication that disorders not included in that section (e.g., schizophrenia, bipolar disorder) do not have an organic component.[27] In fact, virtually all mental disorders have both psychological and biological components, and to designate some disorders as organic and the remaining disorders as nonorganic reflected a reductionistic mind-body dualism that is at odds with our understanding of the multifactorial nature of the etiological underpinnings of disorders.

DSM-IV substitutes the unitary organic disorders (e.g., organic mood disorder) with its two component parts (e.g., mood disorder due to a general medical condition and substance-induced mood disorder). Furthermore, DSM-IV places these disorders alongside their nonorganic counterparts in the classification. For example, mood disorder due to a general medical condition and substance-induced mood disorder are included in the mood disorders section of DSM-IV. Because of their central roles in the differential diagnosis of cognitive impairment, delirium, dementia, and amnestic disorder are contained in a single section in DSM-IV.

Delirium

Whereas both delirium and dementia are characterized by multiple cognitive impairments, delirium is distinguished by the presence of clouding of consciousness, which is manifested by an inability to appropriately maintain or shift attention. DSM-IV includes three types of delirium: delirium due to a general medical condition, substance-induced delirium, and delirium due to multiple etiologies.

Dementias

Dementia is characterized by clinically significant cognitive impairment in memory that is accompanied by impairment in one or more other areas of cognitive functioning (e.g., language, executive functioning). DSM-IV includes several types of dementia based on etiology, including dementia of the Alzheimer's type, vascular dementia, a variety of dementias due to general medical and neurological conditions (e.g., human immunodeficiency virus infection, Parkinson's disease), substance-induced persisting dementia, and dementia due to multiple etiologies.

Amnestic Disorders

In contrast to dementia, amnestic disorder is characterized by clinically significant memory impairment occurring in the absence of other significant impairments in cognitive functioning. DSM-IV includes amnestic disorder due to a general medical condition and substance-induced persisting amnestic disease.

Mental Disorders due to a General Medical Condition Not Elsewhere Classified

Catatonic Disorder due to a General Medical Condition

This is a new disorder in DSM-IV that was introduced as part of an effort to include the full range of disorders in the differential diagnosis of catatonic symptoms. Other disorders in the differential diagnosis include mood disorder (for which a new specifier, "with catatonic features," has been added), medication side effects (for which a section for medication-induced movement disorders has been added to DSM-IV), and schizophrenia.

Personality Change due to a General Medical Condition

In DSM-III-R, this category was called organic personality disorder. Its new name emphasizes that there is a change in the individual's baseline personality that is caused by the direct physiological effects of a general medical condition. DSM-IV indicates the most common specific changes in personality by the specification of subtypes (labile, disinhibited, aggressive, apathetic, and paranoid).

Substance-Related Disorders

The term *substance* in DSM-IV has a broader meaning than merely a drug of abuse. It also includes medication side effects and the consequences of toxin exposure. Two types of substance-related disorders are included in DSM-IV: substance use disorders (dependence and abuse), which describe the maladaptive nature of the pattern of substance use; and substance-induced disorders, which cover psychopathological processes caused by the direct effects of substances on the central nervous system.

Substance Dependence

In DSM-III, the concept of substance dependence was essentially synonymous with physiological dependence, because evidence of tolerance or withdrawal was required for the diagnosis to be made. DSM-III-R greatly broadened the category of dependence by allowing the diagnosis to be made with only evidence of compulsive use, a decision resulting in a heterogeneous category.

To provide more specificity for dependence in DSM-IV, subtyping for physiological dependence has been provided. A more complex set of course modifiers allows the psychiatrist to better describe the course of remission. Two types of remission, identifying two prognostically different groups, are provided: early remission for individuals who have been nondependent for less than a year, and sustained remission for those who have not been dependent for a year or longer. Alternative course specifiers are included to cover two special circumstances: "with agonist therapy" is for individuals whose remission occurs in the context of prescribed agonist treatment (e.g., methadone); "in a controlled environment" indicates that the individual's access to substances has been limited by being in a controlled environment (e.g., jail, therapeutic community).

Substance Abuse

The category of abuse is conceptualized as a maladaptive pattern of substance use leading to adverse consequences. Because virtually all individuals with substance dependence would automatically qualify for substance abuse, a diagnosis of abuse is not allowed for a particular class of substance if the individual currently has (or has had in the past) a pattern of use that qualifies for dependence. Four types of substance-related problems define substance abuse: impaired role functioning related to substance use, recurrent legal problems related to substance use, continued use despite social or interpersonal problems related to substance use, and use of substance in situations when it is physically hazardous.

Substance-Induced Disorders

It is crucial to consider substance-induced disorders in the differential diagnosis of every clinical presentation. There have been several changes in DSM-IV that serve to facilitate making this differential diagnosis. First, the criteria sets for the substance-induced disorders have been placed throughout the manual in those sections with which they share phenomenology. For example, the placement of substance-induced psychotic disorder alongside schizophrenia serves to remind the psychiatrist that substance use must be considered a possible cause for all schizophrenia-like clinical presentations. Furthermore, a number of new substance-induced disorders have been added to DSM-IV (e.g., cocaine-induced sexual dysfunction, alcohol-induced mood disorder). Guidelines for making the differential diagnosis between a substance-induced disorder and a primary disorder have been added to the criteria sets for these conditions. For example, it is suggested that the psychiatrist consider a non–substance-induced diagnosis only after the symptoms have persisted for a minimal period (i.e., about a month) after the cessation of the substance use. Finally, to emphasize the importance of the context in which the symptoms present, specifiers have been provided to indicate whether the symptoms had their onset during intoxication or withdrawal.

Schizophrenia and Other Psychotic Disorders

Schizophrenia

The definition of schizophrenia in DSM-IV has been simplified to emphasize that the active phase of schizophrenia is typically characterized by the presence of two or more psychotic symptoms.[28] The first four items composing the definition of the active phase are "positive" symptoms (i.e., delusions, hallucinations, disorganized speech, and disorganized or catatonic behavior); the fifth item covers "negative" symptoms, such as affective flattening, alogia (poverty of speech), and avolition (lack of goal-directed behavior). Furthermore, the required duration of the active phase symptoms has been increased from 1 week to 1 month to reduce false-positives and to increase compatibility with the ICD-10 definition of schizophrenia. The overall duration requirement for schizophrenia remains 6 months, which includes any combination of active, prodromal, and residual phase symptoms.

Schizoaffective Disorder

This disorder straddles the boundary between schizophrenia and mood disorder with psychotic features. Schizoaffective disorder is differentiated from mood disorder with psychotic features by the requirement that delusions and hallucinations occur outside of mood episodes (for at least 2 weeks preceding the onset of mood episodes or persisting for at least 2 weeks after mood episodes significantly remit). The boundary between schizoaffective disorder and schizophrenia is based on the relative duration of the mood symptoms compared with the total duration of the disturbance. In schizoaffective disorder, the mood symptoms are a significant part of the clinical picture, whereas in schizophrenia, the mood symptoms are no more than "brief" relative to the total duration of the disturbance.

Brief Psychotic Disorder

This category is for all psychotic episodes (not due to a general medical condition, substance, or mood episode) that remit within 1 month. In contrast, the DSM-III-R construct of brief reactive psychosis required that the psychotic symptoms occur in response to a severe stressor.

Psychotic Disorder due to a General Medical Condition and Substance-Induced Psychotic Disorder

DSM-III-R classified psychotic presentations that were due to a substance or general medical condition as organic delusional disorder or organic hallucinosis and included them in the organic mental disorders section. In their place, DSM-IV includes psychotic disorder due to a general medical condition and substance-induced psychotic disorder and places them in the schizophrenia and other psychotic disorders section.

Mood Disorders

This section begins with the criteria for mood episodes (major depressive episode, manic episode, hypomanic episode, mixed episode), which are the building blocks for the episodic mood disorders. The codable mood disorders (major depressive disorder, dysthymic disorder, bipolar I disorder, bipolar II disorder, cyclothymic disorder, mood disorder due to a general medical condition, and substance-induced mood disorder) are presented next. Finally, the many specifiers that provide important treatment-relevant information close this section.

Major Depressive Episode and Major Depressive Disorder

DSM-IV requires that in addition to meeting the symptomatic criteria for the episode, the disturbance must cause clinically significant distress or impairment before it can qualify for a major depressive episode. The often difficult to draw boundary between simple bereavement and a major depressive episode that is triggered by the loss of a loved one has been clarified by the provision that depressive episodes that persist for at least 2 months after a death be considered major depressive episodes. The occurrence of one or more major depressive episodes with no history of any manic, mixed, or hypomanic episodes warrants a diagnosis of major depressive disorder.

Manic Episode, Mixed Episode, and Bipolar I Disorder

A minimal duration of 1 week (or shorter if the patient is hospitalized) has been included in the definition of a manic episode. A mixed episode is defined as an episode characterized by an intermixing of manic and major depressive symptoms and, like manic episode, indicates the presence of bipolar I disorder.

Hypomanic Episode and Bipolar II Disorder

The symptom profile for a hypomanic episode is identical to that of a manic episode except for the requirement in hypomanic episode that the symptoms not be severe enough to cause marked impairment or result in hospitalization. The combination of hypomanic episodes and major depressive episodes warrants a diagnosis of bipolar II disorder.

Dysthymic Disorder

This disorder is characterized by a prolonged period of depressed mood (lasting at least 2 years) that is not severe enough to meet criteria for a major depressive episode.

Cyclothymic Disorder

This disorder is characterized by a prolonged period of hypomanic symptoms and depressive symptoms (lasting at least 2 years) that is not severe enough to meet criteria for a manic or major depressive episode.

Mood Disorder due to a General Medical Condition and Substance-Induced Mood Disorder

DSM-IV has replaced the DSM-III-R category organic mood disorder (included in the now-defunct organic mental disorders section) with these two disorders, which are included in the mood disorders section to facilitate differential diagnosis.

Mood Disorder Specifiers

Several new specifiers have been added to DSM-IV. The specifier "with atypical features" identifies a presentation of major depressive episode (e.g., mood reactivity, reverse vegetative symptoms, rejection sensitivity) that may have implications for treatment selection (e.g., initiating treatment with monoamine oxidase inhibitor antidepressants instead of tricyclic antidepressants). "With catatonic features" has been added to emphasize the association between catatonic presentations and mood disorders. "With rapid cycling" refers to a pattern of bipolar disorder episodes in which there have been at least four episodes in the past year. "With postpartum onset" identifies mood or psychotic episodes that occur within 4 weeks of delivery. "With full interepisode recovery" and "without full interepisode recovery" indicate the presence (or absence) of a period of full remission between the two most recent mood episodes.

Anxiety Disorders

Panic Disorder with or Without Agoraphobia

The frequency threshold for panic disorder was revised on the basis of results from literature review, data reanalysis, and field trial.[29] The DSM-IV definition requires recurrent unexpected panic attacks that are clinically significant as indicated by a month or more of worry about having more attacks or about the implications of the attacks (e.g., that the person is having cardiac problems) or a change in behavior (e.g., avoidance of situations).

Specific Phobia

Subtypes have been added to the DSM-IV definition reflecting the nature of the phobic stimulus. Animal type and natural environment type (e.g., darkness, heights, thunderstorms) are typical childhood fears that may persist into adulthood. Phobias of the situational type often have their onsets after a traumatic experience (e.g., development of claustrophobia after being stuck in an elevator for 4 hours). Blood-injection-injury type is distinguished by the individual's having a vasovagal (fainting) response on exposure to the phobic stimulus, as opposed to the flight response (i.e., removing oneself from the situation) that is more typical with the other types of phobias.

Social Phobia

This category is for individuals who are anxious in social situations for fear of being humiliated. Childhood presentations are covered by this criteria set and are no longer diagnosed as avoidant disorder of childhood, a DSM-III-R category that has been deleted from DSM-IV.

Obsessive-Compulsive Disorder

Obsessions and compulsions, both of which are repetitive and experienced as beyond the individual's control, are differentiated on the basis of their relation to anxiety. Obsessions cause marked anxiety or distress, whereas compulsions prevent or reduce anxiety or distress. For example, with contamination–hand washing, the ruminative and extremely distressing thought that the person has been contaminated by germs is counteracted by hand-washing behavior that reduces the anxiety brought on by the contamination obsession. Most obsessions and compulsions occur in such pairs.

Posttraumatic Stress Disorder

The DSM-III-R definition of the type of stressor associated with this presentation (i.e., events that are "outside the range of normal human experience") had to be changed because evidence indicates that it is inaccurate (i.e., community surveys indicate a relatively high lifetime prevalence of having been exposed to life-threatening experiences). The DSM-IV stressor involves experiences threatening to life or limb that are either directly experienced or witnessed.

Acute Stress Disorder

This new category can be conceptualized as an acute version of posttraumatic stress disorder that lasts for less than 1 month. In addition to the posttraumatic stress disorder symptoms of reexperiencing the trauma, avoiding stimuli associated with the trauma, and increased arousal, severe dissociative symptoms occur.

Generalized Anxiety Disorder

This disorder describes presentations characterized by chronic anxiety and worry that lasts at least 6 months.

Somatoform and Factitious Disorders

Somatization Disorder

This condition is characterized by multiple unexplained physical complaints occurring for a period of several years. To make the unwieldy DSM-III-R criteria set (i.e., 13 of 35 items) more user-friendly, the definition now consists of four symptom groupings (pain, gastrointestinal, sexual, and pseudoneurological).

Other Somatoform Disorders

- Undifferentiated somatoform disorder describes the more common somatoform presentation with fewer unexplained physical complaints than somatization disorder.

- Conversion disorder is for unexplained symptoms or deficits affecting voluntary motor or sensory functioning.
- Pain disorder is for pain presentations in which a psychological factor is judged to play an important role in the onset, exacerbation, or maintenance of the pain.
- Hypochondriasis and body dysmorphic disorder describe preoccupations with the belief that one has a serious illness or a physical defect, respectively.

Factitious Disorder
This condition describes presentations in which the individual intentionally produces or feigns physical or psychological symptoms. In contrast to malingering, in which the motivation is obvious external gain (e.g., disability benefits), the motivation in factitious disorder is a psychological need to assume the sick role.

Dissociative Disorders
- Dissociative amnesia describes presentations in which there is memory loss of information, usually of a personal nature, that is not due to substance use or a general medical condition.
- Dissociative fugue describes presentations in which the individual suddenly travels away from home, assumes a new identity, and cannot recall important elements of his or her past life.
- Dissociative identity disorder (formerly multiple personality disorder) describes the experience of having more than one personality or personality state.
- Depersonalization disorder is for episodes of depersonalization (feeling detached from one's mental processes or body) that are not due to another mental disorder or a result of substance use or a general medical condition.

Sexual and Gender Identity Disorders

Sexual Dysfunctions
These conditions are organized on the basis of which phase of the sexual response cycle is affected. Sexual dysfunctions are diagnosed only if the problem causes marked distress or interpersonal difficulty.

- Hypoactive sexual desire disorder is for problems with low sexual desire.
- Female sexual arousal disorder and male erectile disorder describe problems in sexual arousal.
- Female orgasmic disorder and male orgasmic disorder are for delays in (or complete lack of) orgasm.
- Premature ejaculation is for ejaculation that occurs too quickly.

Sexual Dysfunction due to a General Medical Condition and Substance-Induced Sexual Dysfunction
These disorders are now included in DSM-IV because they are important causes of sexual dysfunction that must be considered first and ruled out as part of the evaluation of every sexual dysfunction.

Paraphilias
Paraphilia is the DSM-IV term for "sexual deviation" or "sexual perversion." The hallmark of a paraphilia is recurrent, intense sexually arousing fantasies and sexual urges or behaviors generally involving 1) nonhuman objects, 2) the suffering or humiliation of oneself or one's partner, or 3) children or other nonconsenting persons. DSM-IV includes eight specific paraphilias:

- Exhibitionism (exposure of genitals to a stranger)
- Fetishism (use of nonliving objects)
- Transvestic fetishism (cross-dressing)
- Frotteurism (touching and rubbing against a nonconsenting person)
- Pedophilia (attraction to children)
- Sexual masochism (suffering humiliation or pain)
- Sexual sadism (inflicting suffering or humiliation on someone else)
- Voyeurism (observing unsuspecting strangers)

Gender Identity Disorder
This condition describes a persistent and impairing cross-gender identification accompanied by persistent discomfort with one's own gender. Individuals with severe gender identity disorder may seek a sex reassignment surgery to "correct" the problem.

Eating Disorders

Anorexia Nervosa
This disorder is characterized by the rigid maintenance of a body weight that is significantly below what it should be, motivated by a morbid fear of getting fat. DSM-IV identifies two types: binge-eating/purging type for individuals who regularly engage in binge-eating or purging behavior, and restricting type for those who do not.

Bulimia Nervosa
This disorder is characterized by regular binge-eating (i.e., eating an amount of food in a discrete period of time that is much more than most others would eat) accompanied by the use of an inappropriate mechanism to counteract the effect of the calories that are consumed during a binge. Some individuals (purging type) engage in purging behavior, like self-induced vomiting or abuse of laxatives, diuretics, or enemas; other individuals (nonpurging type) compensate by the use of other means, like excessive exercise or fasting.

Sleep Disorders
Sleep disorders are grouped into four sections on the basis of presumed etiology (primary, related to another mental disorder, due to a general medical condition, and substance induced). Two types of primary sleep disorders are included: dyssomnias (problems in regulation of amount and quality of sleep) and parasomnias (events that occur during sleep).

The dyssomnias include

- Primary insomnia
- Primary hypersomnia
- Circadian rhythm sleep disorder

- Narcolepsy
- Breathing-related sleep disorder

The parasomnias include

- Nightmare disorder
- Sleep terror disorder
- Sleepwalking disorder

Impulse-Control Disorders

Intermittent Explosive Disorder

This disorder, characterized by recurrent episodes of violent assaultive behavior, can be diagnosed only after all other possible causes for the aggressive behavior have been considered and ruled out. These include other mental disorders (e.g., schizophrenia, antisocial personality disorder), substance intoxication and withdrawal, general medical conditions, and no mental disorder (e.g., criminal behavior).

Other Impulse-Control Disorders

Other impulse-control disorders include

- Pathological gambling (failure to control impulses to gamble)
- Pyromania (fire setting)
- Kleptomania (stealing of objects not needed for personal use or their monetary value)
- Trichotillomania (hair pulling)

Adjustment Disorder

All DSM-IV categories (except NOS categories) take priority over adjustment disorder. This category is intended to apply for maladaptive reactions to psychosocial stressors that do not meet the criteria for any specific DSM-IV disorder. Adjustment disorder can be chronic in the case of chronic stressors.

Personality Disorders

These conditions are for personality patterns that significantly deviate from the expectations of the person's culture, are pervasive, and lead to significant impairment or distress. Ten specific personality disorders are included in DSM-IV:

- Paranoid personality disorder (pervasive distrust and suspiciousness of others)
- Schizoid personality disorder (detachment from social relationships and a restricted expression of emotions)
- Schizotypal personality disorder (acute discomfort with close relationships, perceptual distortions, and eccentricities of behavior)
- Antisocial personality disorder (disregard for the rights of others)
- Borderline personality disorder (instability of personal relationships, instability of self-image, and marked impulsivity)
- Histrionic personality disorder (extensive emotionality and attention seeking)
- Narcissistic personality disorder (grandiosity, need for admiration, and lack of empathy)
- Avoidant personality disorder (social inhibition, feelings of inadequacy, and hypersensitivity to negative evaluation)
- Dependent personality disorder (excessive need to be taken care of)
- Obsessive-compulsive personality disorder (preoccupation with orderliness, perfectionism, and mental and personal control at the expense of flexibility, openness, and efficiency)

Other Conditions That May Be a Focus of Clinical Attention

This section of DSM-IV is for problems that are not mental disorders but that may be a focus of attention or treatment by a mental health professional. *Psychological factors affecting medical condition* is intended to allow the psychiatrist to note the presence of psychological factors (e.g., Axis I or II disorder) that are adversely affecting the course of a general medical condition, including factors that interfere with treatment and factors that constitute health risks to the individual. Six specific *medication-induced movement disorders* have been included because of their importance in treatment and differential diagnosis; five are related to neuroleptic administration, and one (medication-induced postural tremor) is most often associated with the use of lithium carbonate. Although these are best considered medical conditions, by DSM-IV convention they are coded on Axis I.

Relational problems include parent-child, partner, and sibling relational problems. Relational problem related to a mental disorder or general medical condition applies to situations in which one member of the relational unit has a mental disorder or a general medical condition. In such situations, the relational dynamics can negatively affect the

Table 29–3 Criteria Sets and Axes Provided for Further Study

Postconcussional disorder
Mild cognitive disorder
Caffeine withdrawal
Postpsychotic depression of schizophrenia
Simple deteriorative disorder
Minor depressive disorder
Recurrent brief depressive disorder
Premenstrual dysphoric disorder
Mixed anxiety-depressive disorder
Factitous disorder by proxy
Dissociative trance disorder
Binge-eating disorder
Depressive personality disorder
Passive-aggressive personality disorder (negativistic personality disorder)
Defensive Functioning Scale
Global Assessment of Relational Functioning Scale
Social and Occupational Functioning Assessment Scale

Data from American Psychiatric Association: Diagnostic and Statistical Manual of Mental Disorders, 4th ed. Washington, DC: American Psychiatric Association, 1994.

individual's condition or vice versa (or both). *Problems related to abuse or neglect* (physical abuse, sexual abuse, and child neglect) have been introduced into DSM-IV because of the clinical and public health significance of these conditions.

Appendix Categories

DSM-IV aims to be on the trailing edge rather than the cutting edge of research.[30] New categories were considered for inclusion only if there was a substantial research literature behind them. Although there were proposals for more than 100 new categories to be introduced into DSM-IV, only a handful of new categories were added. Text and criteria for another 17 proposed categories have been included in a DSM-IV appendix, Criteria Sets and Axes Provided for Further Study (Table 29–3). These criteria sets have been included to provide a common language for researchers and psychiatrists who are interested in further investigating their potential utility and validity.

References

1. Mack AH, Forman L, Brown R, Frances A: A brief history of psychiatric classification. From the ancients to DSM-IV. Psychiatr Clin North Am 1994; 17:515–523.
2. American Psychiatric Association: Diagnostic and Statistical Manual of Mental Disorders, 4th ed. Washington, DC: American Psychiatric Association, 1994.
3. First MB: Trends in psychiatric classification: DSM-III-R to DSM-IV. Psychiatr Hung 1992; 7:539–546.
4. First MB: Principles of disease classification and diagnostic criteria. In Olesen J (ed): Headache Classification and Epidemiology. New York: Raven Press, 1994:17–26.
5. Kraepelin E: Compendium der Psychiatrie: Zum Gebrauche für Studirende und Aerzte. Leipzig: Verlag von Ambr. Abel, 1883.
6. First MB, Frances A, Widiger TA: DSM-IV and behavioral assessment. Behav Assess 1992;14:297–306.
7. American Psychiatric Association: Diagnostic and Statistical Manual of Mental Disorders. Washington, DC: American Psychiatric Association, 1952.
8. American Psychiatric Association: Diagnostic and Statistical Manual of Mental Disorders, 2nd ed. Washington, DC: American Psychiatric Association, 1968.
9. American Psychiatric Association: Diagnostic and Statistical Manual of Mental Disorders, 3rd ed. Washington, DC: American Psychiatric Association, 1980.
10. American Psychiatric Association: Diagnostic and Statistical Manual of Mental Disorders, 3rd ed, revised. Washington, DC: American Psychiatric Association, 1987.
11. Boyd JH, Burke JD, Gruenberg E, et al: The exclusion criteria of DSM-III, a study of the co-occurrence of hierarchy-free syndromes. In Tischler GL (ed): Diagnosis and Classification in Psychiatry. A Critical Appraisal of DSM-III. New York: Cambridge University Press, 1987; 403–424.
12. Spitzer R, Williams JBW: Revising DSM-III, the process and major issues. In Tischler GL (ed): Diagnosis and Classification in Psychiatry. A Critical Appraisal of DSM-III. New York: Cambridge University Press, 1987.
13. Frances A, Pincus HA, Widiger TA, et al: DSM-IV: Work in progress. Am J Psychiatry 1990; 147:1439–1448.
14. Widiger T, Frances A, Pincus H, et al: Toward a more empirical diagnostic system. Can Psychol 1991; 32:174–176.
15. Widiger T, Frances A, Pincus H, Davis W: DSM-IV literature reviews: Rationale, process, limitations. J Psychopathol Behav Assess 1990; 12:189–202.
16. Frances A, Davis W, Kline M, et al: The DSM-IV field trials: Moving towards an empirically-derived classification. Eur Psychiatry 1991; 6:307–314.
17. Widiger TA, Frances A, Pincus H, et al (eds): DSM-IV Sourcebook, Volume 1. Washington, DC: American Psychiatric Association, 1994.
18. Widiger TA, Frances A, Pincus H, et al (eds): DSM-IV Sourcebook, Volume 2. Washington, DC: American Psychiatric Association, 1996.
19. Williams JBW: Multiaxial diagnosis. In Skodol AE, Spitzer RL (eds): An Annotated Bibliography of DSM-III. Washington, DC: American Psychiatric Press, 1987:31–36.
20. First MB, Vettorello N, Frances AJ, Pincus HA: DSM-IV in progress: Changes in mood, anxiety, and personality disorders. Hosp Community Psychiatry 1993; 44:1034–1037.
21. First MB, Frances AJ, Pincus HA, et al: DSM-IV in progress: Changes in substance-related, schizophrenia, and other primarily adult disorders. Hosp Community Psychiatry 1994; 45:18–20.
22. Frances AJ, First MB, Pincus HA, et al: DSM-IV in progress: Changes in child and adolescent disorders, eating disorder, and the multiaxial system. Hosp Community Psychiatry 1994; 45:212–214.
23. Williams JBW, Goldman HH, Gruenberg A, et al: The multiaxial system. Hosp Community Psychiatry 1990; 41:1181–1182.
24. Skodol AE: Axis IV: A reliable and valid measure of psychosocial stressors? Compr Psychiatry, 1991; 32:503–515.
25. Volkmar FR: Autism and the pervasive developmental disorders. Hosp Community Psychiatry 1991; 42:33–35.
26. Loeber R, Lahey BB, Thomas C: Diagnostic conundrum of oppositional defiant disorder and conduct disorder. J Abnorm Psychol 1991; 100:379–390.
27. Spitzer RL, First MB, Williams JBW, et al: Now is the time to retire the term "organic mental disorders." Am J Psychiatry 1992; 149:240–244.
28. Andreasen NC: Schizophrenia and related disorders in DSM-IV: Editor's introduction. Schizophr Bull 1991; 17:25–26.
29. Frances A, Miele GM, Widiger TA, et al: The classification of panic disorders: From Freud to DSM-IV. J Psychiatr Res 1993; 27(suppl 1):3–10.
30. Pincus HA, Frances A, Wakefield-Davis W, et al: DSM-IV and the new diagnostic categories: Holding the line on proliferation. Am J Psychiatry 1992; 149:112–117.

CHAPTER

30

Diagnostic Classification in Infancy and Early Childhood

Stanley I. Greenspan
Serena Wieder

Knowledge about the mental health and development of infants has grown exponentially in the past two decades. Through systematic observation, research, and clinical intervention, a more sophisticated understanding has emerged of the factors that contribute to adaptive and maladaptive patterns of development and of the meaning of individual differences in infancy. This knowledge has led to an increasing awareness of the importance of prevention and early treatment in creating or restoring favorable conditions for the young child's development and mental health. Timely assessment and accurate diagnosis can provide the foundation for effective intervention before early deviations become consolidated into maladaptive patterns of functioning.

As a result of this growing knowledge base, a new diagnostic framework was formulated through an 8-year effort of ZERO TO THREE: National Center for Infants, Toddlers and Families. This framework is presented in detail in *Diagnostic Classification of Mental Health and Developmental Disorders of Infancy and Early Childhood* (DC:0–3).[1] It seeks to address the need for a systematic, developmentally based approach to the classification of mental health and developmental difficulties in the first 4 years of life. It is designed to complement existing medical and developmental frameworks for understanding mental health and developmental problems in the earliest years.

DC:0–3 categorizes emotional and behavioral patterns that represent significant deviations from normative development in the earliest years of life. Some of the categories presented represent new formulations of mental health and developmental difficulties. Other categories describe the earliest manifestations of mental health problems that have been identified among older children and adults but have not been fully described in infants and young children. In infancy and early childhood, these problems may have different characteristics, and prognosis may be more optimistic if effective early intervention can occur. This chapter summarizes the principles of assessment and diagnosis as well as the new diagnostic classifications for the first 3 years of life.

Discussions of diagnostic categories can be most helpful if they identify challenges to be overcome in the context of an understanding of adaptive coping and development. Understanding both adaptive capacities and challenges is part of the essential foundation for planning and implementing effective interventions. A detailed discussion of the principles of assessment, diagnosis, and intervention, along with case studies, is presented in *Infancy and Early Childhood.*[2]

Reflecting our current state of knowledge, the diagnostic categories presented in this chapter are descriptive, that is, they record presenting patterns of symptoms and behaviors. Some of the categories (e.g., those involving trauma) imply potential etiological factors; some (e.g., regulatory disorders) imply pathophysiological processes. However, at the moment, all that can be stated is that associations have been observed between some of these symptoms and processes (e.g., between a traumatic event and a group of symptoms, or between a sensory or motor pattern and a group of symptoms). Only further research will establish possible pathophysiological or etiological links among these observed phenomena.

This chapter describes a new diagnostic classification for the first 4 years of life. It is meant to complement the *Diagnostic and Statistical Manual of Mental Disorders,* Fourth Edition (DSM-IV). *Diagnostic Classification of Mental Health and Developmental Disorders of Infancy and Early Childhood,* published in 1994 by ZERO TO THREE/National Center for Clinical Infant Programs (now ZERO TO THREE: National Center for Infants, Toddlers and Families, Washington, DC) describes types of behaviors and problems not addressed in other schemas as well as the earliest manifestations of problems and behaviors that have heretofore been ascribed to older children. Because of the new system's comprehensive clinical and developmental approach, the authors have decided to include this overview, adapted from DC:0–3 with permission from ZERO TO THREE: National Center for Infants, Toddlers and Families, here. More information about DC:0–3 is available from ZERO TO THREE: National Center for Infants, Toddlers and Families, 734 15th Street, NW, 10th Floor, Washington, DC 20005, tel: 1-800-899-4301.

As an evolving framework, this conceptualization is not intended to include all possible conditions or disorders. It is an initial guide for mental health professionals and researchers to facilitate clinical diagnosis and planning as well as communication and further research. It is not intended to have legal or nonclinical applications.

Principles of Assessment

Many different assumptions and theories contribute to our approach to diagnosis and treatment. These assumptions come from both clinical practice and research. Developmental, psychodynamic, family systems, relationship, and attachment theory inform our work, as do observations of the way infants organize their experience, infant-caregiver interaction patterns, temperament, regulatory patterns, and individual differences in many domains of development.

Assessment and diagnosis must be guided by the awareness that all infants are participants in relationships. These relationships exist, usually, within families, and families themselves are part of the larger community and culture. At the same time, all infants have their own developmental progression and show individual differences in their motor, sensory, language, cognitive, affective, and interactive patterns.

Any intervention or treatment program should be based on as complex an understanding of the child's and family's circumstances as is possible to achieve. However, it is not uncommon for psychiatrists to give lip service to the importance of a comprehensive approach to diagnosis but then to address "favorite" variables in great detail, while giving only cursory regard to other influences on development (e.g., an evaluation consisting of a six-page description of the family system and a single sentence categorizing the infant's pattern of interaction with his or her caregiver). Psychiatrists may also be tempted to avoid assessing those areas of functioning in which the constructs or research tools are less well developed or that represent gaps in their own training.

Although these temptations are understandable, it is the responsibility of any psychiatrist who is charged with doing a full diagnostic work-up and planning an appropriate intervention program to take into account *all* the relevant areas of a child's functioning, using state-of-the-art knowledge in each area. These areas include the following:

Relevant Areas of a Child's Functioning

- Presenting symptoms and behaviors
- Developmental history: past and current affective, language, cognitive, motor, sensory, family, and interactive functioning
- Family functioning and cultural and community patterns
- Parents as individuals
- Caregiver-infant (child) relationship and interactive patterns
- The infant's constitutional-maturational characteristics
- Affective, language, cognitive, motor, and sensory patterns
- The family's psychosocial and medical history, the history of the pregnancy and delivery, and current environmental conditions and stressors

The process of gaining an understanding of how each area of functioning is developing for an infant or toddler usually requires a number of sessions. A few questions to the parents or caregiver about each area may be appropriate for screening but not for a full evaluation. A full evaluation usually requires a minimum of three to five sessions of 45 minutes or more each. A complete evaluation will usually involve taking the history; direct observation of functioning (i.e., of family and parental dynamics; caregiver-infant relationship and interaction patterns; the infant's constitutional-maturational characteristics; and language, cognitive, and affective patterns); and hands-on interaction assessment of the infant, including assessment of sensory reactivity and processing, motor tone and planning, language, cognition, and affective expression. Standardized developmental assessments, if needed, should always build on the clinical process described. They may be indicated when they are the most effective way to answer specific questions and when the child is sufficiently interactive and can respond to the requirements of the test.

The result of such a comprehensive evaluation should lead to preliminary notions about the following:

1. The nature of the infant's or child's difficulties as well as her or his strengths; the level of the child's overall adaptive capacity; and functioning in the major areas of development, including social-emotional relationships and cognitive, language, sensory, and motor abilities in comparison to age-expected developmental patterns.
2. The relative contribution of the different areas assessed (e.g., family relationships, interactive patterns, constitutional-maturational patterns, stress) to the child's difficulties and competencies.
3. A comprehensive treatment or preventive intervention plan to deal with 1 and 2.

Overview of the Classification System

Diagnostic Classification: 0–3 proposes a provisional multiaxial classification system. We refer to the classification system as provisional because it is assumed that categories may change as more knowledge accumulates. The diagnostic framework consists of the following:

Axis I	Primary diagnosis
Axis II	Relationship disorder classification
Axis III	Physical, neurological, developmental, and mental health disorders or conditions (described in other classification systems)
Axis IV	Psychosocial stressors
Axis V	Functional-emotional developmental level

The axes in this system are not intended to be entirely symmetrical with such other systems as DSM-IV and the *International Statistical Classification of Diseases and Related Health Problems,* 10th revision (ICD-10) because this system, in dealing with infants and young children, focuses on developmental issues. Dynamic processes, such as relationship and developmentally based conceptualizations of adaptive patterns (i.e., functional emotional developmental level), are therefore of central importance.

Use of the system will provide the psychiatrist with a *diagnostic profile* of an infant or toddler. Such a diagnostic profile focuses the psychiatrist's attention on the various factors that are contributing to the infant's difficulties as well as on areas in which intervention may be needed.

Axis I: Primary Diagnoses

The following are the Axis I primary diagnoses that have thus far been suggested.

100. Traumatic Stress Disorder

A continuum of symptoms related to a single event, a series of connected traumatic events, or chronic enduring stress.

1. Reexperiencing of the trauma, as evidenced by
   a. posttraumatic play
   b. recurrent recollections of the traumatic event outside play
   c. repeated nightmares
   d. distress at reminders of the trauma
   e. flashbacks or dissociation
2. Numbing of responsiveness or interference with developmental momentum
   a. increased social withdrawal
   b. restricted range of affect
   c. temporary loss of previously acquired developmental skills
   d. a decrease in play
3. Symptoms of increased arousal
   a. night terrors
   b. difficulty going to sleep
   c. repeated night waking
   d. significant attentional difficulties
   e. hypervigilance
   f. exaggerated startle response
4. Symptoms not present before
   a. aggression toward peers, adults, or animals
   b. separation anxiety
   c. fear of toileting alone
   d. fear of the dark
   e. other new fears
   f. self-defeating behavior or masochistic provocativeness
   g. sexual and aggressive behaviors
   h. other nonverbal reactions (e.g., somatic symptoms, motor reenactment, skin stigmas, pain, or posturing)

200. Disorders of Affect

Focuses on the infant's experience and on symptoms that are a general feature of the child's functioning rather than specific to a situation or relationship.

201. Anxiety Disorders of Infancy and Early Childhood

Levels of anxiety or fear, beyond expectable reactions to normal developmental challenges.

1. Multiple or specific fears
2. Excessive separation or stranger anxiety
3. Excessive anxiety or panic without clear precipitant
4. Excessive inhibition or constriction of behavior
5. Lack of development of basic ego functions
6. Agitation, uncontrollable crying or screaming, sleeping and eating disturbances, recklessness, and other behaviors

Criterion: Should persist for at least 2 weeks and interfere with appropriate functioning.

202. Mood Disorder: Prolonged Bereavement-Grief Reaction

1. Possible crying, calling, and searching for the absent parent, refusing comfort
2. Emotional withdrawal, with lethargy, sad facial expression, and lack of interest in age-appropriate activities
3. Eating and sleeping possibly disrupted
4. Regression in developmental milestones
5. Constricted affective range
6. Detachment
7. Sensitivity to any reminder of the caregiver

203. Mood Disorder: Depression of Infancy and Early Childhood

Pattern of depressed or irritable mood with diminished interest or pleasure in developmentally appropriate activities, diminished capacity to protest, excessive whining, and diminished social interactions and initiative. Disturbances in sleep or eating.

Criterion: At least 2 weeks.

204. Mixed Disorder of Emotional Expressiveness

Ongoing difficulty expressing developmentally appropriate emotions.

1. The absence or near-absence of one or more specific types of affects
2. Constricted range of emotional expression
3. Disturbed intensity
4. Reversal of affect or inappropriate affect

205. Childhood Gender Identity Disorder

Becomes manifest during the sensitive period of gender identity development (between approximately 2 and 4 years).

1. A strong and persistent cross-sex identification
   a. repeatedly states desire to be, or insistence that he or she is, the opposite sex

b. in boys, preference for cross-dressing or simulating female attire; in girls, insistence on wearing stereotypical masculine clothing
c. strong and persistent preferences for cross-sex roles in fantasy play or persistent fantasies of being the opposite sex
d. intense desire to participate in the games and pastimes of the opposite sex
e. strong preference for playmates of the opposite sex

4. Persistent discomfort with one's assigned sex or sense of inappropriateness in that role
5. Absence of nonpsychiatric medical condition

206. Reactive Attachment Deprivation-Maltreatment Disorder of Infancy

1. Persistent parental neglect or abuse, of a physical or psychological nature, undermines the child's basic sense of security and attachment.
2. Frequent changes in, or the inconsistent availability of, the primary caregiver.
3. Other environmental compromises that prevent stable attachments.

300. Adjustment Disorder

Mild, transient situational disturbances related to a clear environmental event and lasting no longer than 4 months.

400. Regulatory Disorders

Difficulties in regulating physiological, sensory, attentional, motor, or affective processes and in organizing a calm, alert, or affectively positive state. Observe at least one sensory, sensory-motor, or processing difficulty from the following list, in addition to behavioral symptoms.

1. Overreactivity or underreactivity to loud or high- or low-pitched noises
2. Overreactivity or underreactivity to bright lights or new and striking visual images
3. Tactile defensiveness or oral hypersensitivity
4. Oral-motor difficulties or incoordination influenced by poor muscle tone and oral-tactile hypersensitivity
5. Underreactivity to touch or pain
6. Gravitational insecurity
7. Underreactivity or overreactivity to odors
8. Underreactivity or overreactivity to temperature
9. Poor muscle tone and muscle stability
10. Qualitative deficits in motor planning skills
11. Qualitative deficits in ability to modulate motor activity
12. Qualitative deficits in fine motor skills
13. Qualitative deficits in auditory-verbal processing
14. Qualitative deficits in articulation capacities
15. Qualitative deficits in visual-spatial processing capacities
16. Qualitative deficits in capacity to attend and focus

401. Type I: Hypersensitive

- Fearful and cautious
  - Behavioral patterns: excessive cautiousness, inhibition, or fearfulness
  - Motor and sensory patterns: overreactivity to touch, loud noises, or bright lights
- Negative and defiant
  - Behavioral patterns: negativistic, stubborn, controlling, and defiant; difficulty in making transitions; prefers repetition to change
  - Motor and sensory patterns: overreactivity to touch and sound; intact visual-spatial capacities; compromised auditory processing capacity; good muscle tone and motor planning ability; shows some delay in fine motor coordination

402. Type II: Underreactive

- Withdrawn and difficult to engage
  - Behavioral patterns: seeming disinterest in relationships; limited exploratory activity or flexibility in play; appears apathetic, easily exhausted, and withdrawn
  - Motor and sensory patterns: underreactivity to sounds and movement in space; either overreactive or underreactive to touch; intact visual-spatial processing capacities, but auditory-verbal processing difficulties; poor motor quality and motor planning
- Self-absorbed
  - Behavioral patterns: creative and imaginative, with a tendency to tune into her or his own sensations, thoughts, and emotions
  - Motor and sensory patterns: decreased auditory-verbal processing capacities

403. Type III: Motorically Disorganized, Impulsive

Mixed sensory reactivity and motor processing difficulties. Some appear more aggressive, fearless, and destructive; others appear more impulsive and fearful.

- Behavioral patterns: high activity, seeking contact and stimulation through deep pressure; appears to lack caution
- Motor and sensory patterns: sensory underreactivity and motor discharge

404. Type IV: Other

500. Sleep Behavior Disorder

Only presenting problem; younger than 3 years of age; no accompanying sensory reactivity or sensory processing difficulties. Difficulty in initiating or maintaining sleep; may also have problems in calming themselves and dealing with transitions from one stage of arousal to another.

600. Eating Behavior Disorder

Shows difficulties in establishing regular feeding patterns with adequate or appropriate food intake. Absence of general regulatory difficulties or interpersonal precipitants (e.g., separation, negativism, trauma).

700. Disorders of Relating and Communicating

1. DSM-IV conceptualization pervasive developmental disorder or
2. Multisystem developmental disorder

Multisystem Developmental Disorder

1. Significant impairment in, but not complete lack of, the ability to form and maintain an emotional and social relationship with primary caregiver
2. Significant impairment in forming, maintaining, or developing communication
3. Significant dysfunction in auditory processing
4. Significant dysfunction in the processing of other sensations and in motor planning

701. Pattern A

These children are aimless and unrelated most of the time, with severe difficulty in motor planning, so that even simple intentional gestures are difficult.

702. Pattern B

These children are intermittently related and capable some of the time of simple intentional gestures.

703. Pattern C

These children evidence a more consistent sense of relatedness, even when they are avoidant or rigid.

Axis II: Relationship Disorder Classification

The diagnostic system also includes an Axis II for relationships classification. Three aspects of a relationship are considered: 1) behavioral quality of the interaction, 2) affective tone, and 3) psychological involvement. The types of relationship problems are as follows.

901. Overinvolved Relationship

Physical or psychological overinvolvement.

1. Parent interferes with infant's goals and desires
2. Overcontrols
3. Makes developmentally inappropriate demands
4. Infant appears diffuse, unfocused, and undifferentiated
5. Displays submissive, overly compliant behaviors
6. May lack motor skills or language expressiveness

902. Underinvolved Relationship

Sporadic or infrequent genuine involvement.

1. Parent insensitive or unresponsive
2. Lack of consistency between expressed attitudes about infant and quality of actual interactions
3. Ignores, rejects, or fails to comfort
4. Does not reflect infant's internal feeling states
5. Does not adequately protect
6. Interactions underregulated
7. Parent and infant appear to be disengaged
8. Infant appears physically or psychologically uncared for
9. Delayed or precocious in motor and language skills

903. Anxious-Tense Relationship

Tense, constricted with little sense of relaxed enjoyment or mutuality.

1. Parent is overprotective and oversensitive
2. Awkward or tense handling
3. Some verbally and emotionally negative interactions
4. Poor temperamental fit between parent and child
5. Infant compliant or anxious

904. Angry-Hostile Relationship

Harsh and abrupt, often lacking in emotional reciprocity.

1. Parent insensitive to infant's cues
2. Handling is abrupt
3. Infant frightened, anxious, inhibited, impulsive, or diffusely aggressive
4. Defiant or resistant behavior
5. Demanding or aggressive behaviors
6. Fearful, vigilant, and avoidant behaviors
7. Tendency toward concrete behavior

905. Mixed Relationship

Combination of the features described above.

906. Abusive Relationships

1. Verbally abusive relationship
   a. Intended to severely belittle, blame, attack, overcontrol, and reject the infant or toddler
   b. Reactions vary from constriction and vigilance to severe acting-out behaviors
2. Physically abusive relationship
   a. Physically harms by slapping, spanking, hitting, pinching, biting, kicking, physical restraint, isolation
   b. Denies food, medical care, or opportunity to rest
   c. May include verbal and emotional abuse or sexual abuse
3. Sexually abusive relationship
   a. Parent engages in sexually seductive and overstimulating behavior—coercing or forcing child to touch parent sexually, accept sexual touching, or observe others' sexual behaviors

b. Young child may evidence sexually driven behaviors such as exhibiting himself or herself or trying to look at or touch other children
c. May include verbal and emotional abuse or physical abuse

Axis III: Medical and Developmental Diagnoses

On Axis III, one indicates any coexisting physical (including medical and neurological), mental health, or developmental disorders. DSM-IV, ICD-9 or ICD-10, or *Diagnostic and Statistical Manual of Mental Disorders* for the primary care setting classifications are used. Occupational therapy, physical therapy, special education, and other designations are specified.

Axis IV: Psychosocial Stressors

On Axis IV, one identifies 1) the source of stress (e.g., abduction, adoption, loss of parent, natural disaster, parent's illness), 2) severity (mild to catastrophic), 3) duration (acute to enduring), and 4) overall impact (none, mild, moderate, severe).

Overall Impact of Stress

Mild effects	Causes recognizable strain, tension, or anxiety but does not interfere with infant's overall adaptation
Moderate effects	Derails child in areas of adaptation but not in core areas of relatedness and communication
Severe effects	Significant derailment in areas of adaptation

Axis V: Functional-Emotional Developmental Level

Axis V profiles the child's functional and emotional developmental level. It involves the following.

A. Essential processes or capacities
   1. Mutual attention: ability of dyad to attend to one another
   2. Mutual engagement: joint emotional involvement
   3. Interactive intentionality and reciprocity: ability for cause-and-effect interaction; infant signals and responds purposefully
   4. Representational-affective communication: language and play communicate emotional themes
   5. Representational elaboration: pretend play and symbolic communication that go beyond basic needs and deal with more complex intentions, wishes, or feelings
   6. Representational differentiation I: pretend play and symbolic communication in which ideas are logically related; knows what is real and unreal
   7. Representational differentiation II: complex pretend play; three or more ideas are logically connected and informed by concepts of causality, time, and space

B. Functional-Emotional Developmental Level Summary, which documents the child's achievement
   1. Has fully reached expected levels
   2. At expected level but with constrictions—not full range of affect; not at this level under stress; only with certain caregivers or with exceptional support
   3. Not at expected level but has achieved all prior levels
   4. Not at current expected level but some prior levels
   5. Has not mastered any prior levels

Conclusion

We have briefly reviewed the principles of assessment and diagnosis and outlined the new diagnostic classification system for infants, young children, and their families. The field of clinical work with infants and young children is a relatively new one. It has strong empirical support in the numerous studies of both normal and disturbed development and the rapidly expanding experience with a variety of clinical cases. As more experience is accumulated, the classification of challenges and difficulties will be refined and additional clinical strategies developed.

References

1. ZERO TO THREE Diagnostic Classification Task Force, Greenspan SI (chair), Weider S (co-chair and clinical director): Diagnostic Classification of Mental Health and Developmental Disorders of Infancy and Early Childhood. Arlington, VA: ZERO TO THREE/National Center for Clinical Infant Programs, 1994.
2. Greenspan SI: Infancy and Early Childhood: The Practice of Clinical Assessment and Intervention with Emotional and Developmental Challenges. Madison, CT: International Universities Press, 1992.

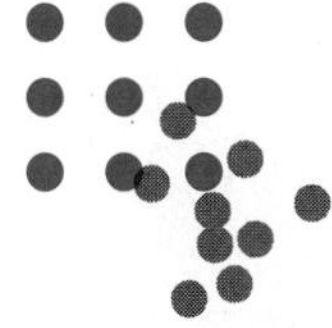

SECTION **V**

Harold Alan Pincus, Section Editor
Harold S. Koplewicz, Associate Section Editor for Childhood Disorders
Thomas R. Kosten, Associate Section Editor for Substance Use Disorders

Disorders

CHAPTER

31 Introduction

Harold Alan Pincus

During the past several decades, the science base in psychiatry has grown dramatically, with an enormous impact on our capacity to properly assess, diagnose, and provide effective and specific treatments. Earlier chapters clearly demonstrate this rich foundation of basic and clinical science.

One major result of and stimulus for the scientific revolution has been the development of the *Diagnostic and Statistical Manual of Mental Disorders,* Third Edition and, more recently, the Fourth Edition (DSM-IV). The development of an objective and reliable systematic taxonomy for mental disorders has been an essential element for the study of the pathophysiology, epidemiology, and psychobiology of these conditions, and for the development and assessment of treatments. Clearly, there are limitations in the use of such a descriptive, phenomenological system; for example, there are issues concerning the heterogeneity of the conditions and questions regarding the validity of some of the categories. Nonetheless, the DSM-IV is enormously useful as a way of organizing thinking about the clinical aspects of patients with mental disorders and for educating clinicians and students.

This section is intended to provide a comprehensive overview of each of the major disorder categories of DSM-IV, incorporating a systematic assessment and integration of current research. The DSM-IV process was an enormous and unique effort involving the gathering and arraying of available scientific information on psychiatric diagnoses. This allowed carefully documented decisions to be made on disorders to be included in the manual. This process, described in Chapter 29, has been adapted for the development of formal parameters for treatment in the American Psychiatric Association's practice guidelines project. The material contained in this section was informed by both the DSM-IV and the practice guidelines projects.

In general, the chapters are organized according to the following outline:

- *Definition* of the condition, as described in DSM-IV.
- *Epidemiology,* incorporating information about prevalence and incidence and comorbidity patterns.
- *Etiology and pathophysiology,* including information on family patterns and genetic findings as well as other empirical and theoretical information on biological and psychosocial mechanisms.
- *Diagnosis and differential diagnosis,* with information about the phenomenology and variations of presentation as well as consideration of special issues in the assessment of individuals with these conditions (i.e., psychiatric evaluation and history, physical examination, laboratory findings, and differences in developmental, gender, and cultural presentations).
- *Course and natural history,* consisting of patterns of onset, episodicity, and chronicity.
- *General and standard approaches to treatments,* including attention to the overall goals of care in the various phases and sites of treatment. The efficacy of specific treatments, their major side effects, and special issues in their implementation are discussed. Treatments include well-delineated psychotherapies, pharmacotherapies, and other somatic and psychosocial treatments; discussion of the role of the physician-patient relationship in psychiatric management is also included.
- *Special features influencing treatment* are presented in terms of the impact on clinical decision-making of such factors as psychiatric comorbidity (including substance use) and other aspects of clinical presentation (e.g., severity and specific subtypes of a disorder), general medical comorbidity, and demographic and other features related to the patient (e.g., age of the patient, pregnancy, and ethnic or cultural issues). Common problems in management when individuals fail to respond to initial sets of treatments are discussed.

Chapters also incorporate detailed references, clinical vignettes, and tables that outline DSM-IV criteria, diagnostic decision trees, and treatment decision trees.

The organization of this section follows DSM-IV, starting with disorders usually manifested in infancy or childhood and proceeding to cognitive disorders (and other disorders due to a general medical condition), substance-related disorders, and other major DSM-IV categories (e.g., schizophrenia and mood disorders). After the presentation of these disorders are two chapters on conditions that are not considered formal mental disorders but are clinically quite important: medication-induced movement disorders and relational conditions. Although there are separate chapters for childhood disorders, in keeping with the DSM-IV organizational pattern, aspects of these disorders (including diagnostic and treatment issues) are also discussed in other chapters.

Overall, this section is intended to provide a comprehensive picture of the full range of mental disorders, from etiology through treatment, based on the most up-to-date scientific information.

CHAPTER

32 Childhood and Adolescent Manifestations of Adult Disorders

Harold S. Koplewicz
Richard F. Morrissey
Stanley Kutcher

Although not specifically designated as disorders usually first diagnosed in infancy, childhood, or adolescence in the *Diagnostic and Statistical Manual of Mental Disorders,* Fourth Edition (DSM-IV), a number of psychiatric disorders are typically identified in young people whose presentation, course, and treatment may not precisely correspond to those of their adult counterparts. The purpose of this chapter is to delineate and describe these disorders as they may present in child and adolescent populations, and to describe several other disorders specific to this age group that have not been dealt with in previous chapters.

Mood Disorders

Major Depressive Disorder

Although the existence of true depressive disorders in children was in question for many years, the scientific consensus on this point is no longer in dispute. Although major depressive disorder (MDD) is relatively less common in children, its point prevalence approaches adult rates of 6% to 9% by late adolescence. Diagnostic criteria for MDD in children and adolescents are identical to those in adults apart from two caveats. First, in children and adolescents, depressed mood may manifest primarily as irritability. Second, calculations regarding weight loss may be made from failure to establish normal developmental weight gain, rather than actual loss. Especially for adolescents, care must be taken to distinguish fluctuating developmental problems accompanied by strong and variable feeling states from actual psychopathological processes.[1]

In prepubertal children, prevalence rates for boys and girls are roughly equal. By adolescence, the sex ratio approximates that of adults, with rates for girls about twice those for boys,[2] although this differential may not be true for early adolescence.[3] Point prevalence rates of major depression are estimated to be 1% to 2% for prepubertal children.[4] This rate, however, increases dramatically in adolescence; adolescent prevalence rates have been variously estimated at 4%,[5] 4.7%,[6] 8.9%,[3] and 9.4%,[7] depending on age and other demographical characteristics of the sample studied. The most common age at onset is estimated to be midadolescence[8–10]; early onset of MDD is associated with female sex, suicidal ideation, and longer episodes of MDD.[8]

Onset of MDD in childhood or adolescence is often the first episode of a chronic mood disorder characterized by relapse and functional impairments.[11, 12] Furthermore, investigations suggest a cohort effect; younger cohorts show both an earlier age at onset and an increased prevalence of the disorder.[13, 14]

Predictive risk factors for MDD in this population have not been well characterized, and those factors that have been correlated with depressive symptoms may not be associated with the syndrome. In addition, specific as opposed to nonspecific factors have not been clearly separated. At this point, the relatively specific risk factors for onset of MDD can be understood to be parental history of MDD, female sex, persistent subsyndromal depressive symptoms, and dysthymia.

Depressive disorders in children and adolescents are associated with a number of functional disturbances across a number of parameters. Cognitive difficulties, poor academic achievement, social-personal-family difficulties, and increased use of psychoactive substances have been described. Some of these may persist after the acute symptoms have improved or remitted and are hypothesized to increase the risk for further depressive episodes.[11] Suicide in adolescents is strongly associated with unrecognized and untreated depressive disorders.[15–17]

Evidence for familial aggregation is strong. Bottom-up studies have shown high rates of affective disorders in first-degree relatives of youngsters with MDD.[18, 19] Top-down studies showed similar results; at least one report suggested that by the age of 20 years, more than 50% of the offspring of depressed patients report having at least one major depressive episode themselves.[20] Hammen and coworkers[21] studied offspring of unipolar depressed, bipolar depressed, medically ill, and normal women and found that offspring of women with unipolar depression had the highest rates of disorder at repeated follow-up points. It is interesting to note that there is some evidence for the temporal association of major depressive episodes of mothers and children.[22]

Neurobiological studies show some differences yet some similarities between childhood and adolescent MDD and adult MDD in both basal and stimulation states. Neuroendocrine investigations have essentially identified that abnormalities of the hypothalamic-pituitary-adrenal axis are found relatively infrequently in children and adolescents. Hypothalamic-pituitary-thyroid abnormalities are similarly less frequent as well, although both hypothalamic-pituitary-adrenal and hypothalamic-pituitary-thyroid dysregulations, when they occur, do so in a fashion similar to the dysregulation found in older populations.[23] Dysregulated hypothalamic-pituitary growth hormone functioning has been demonstrated; abnormal basal and stimulation secretion occurs in depressed children and adolescents.[24] Studies of sleep physiology have been contradictory but as a whole suggest that a shortened rapid eye movement latency may occur concurrently with MDD, particularly in adolescence.[25] The abnormalities in neurobiological studies of childhood and adolescent depression have been interpreted as being suggestive of a primary dysregulation within serotonin system functioning.[23–27]

As with adults, the presence of disorders comorbid with major depression is striking. Garrison and colleagues[3] found major depression to be the diagnosis that overlapped most frequently with other psychiatric disorders in their study of young adolescents. The most common comorbid diagnoses were dysthymia and separation anxiety disorder (SAD). Lewinsohn and associates[2] found virtually all other categories of disorder to be related to unipolar depression; the highest associations were shown with eating disorders, substance use disorders, and anxiety disorders. An interesting study by Biederman and coworkers[28] compared children of parents with panic disorder and agoraphobia, with and without comorbid MDD. The presence of MDD alone in parents placed their children at risk for depression, but not for anxiety disorders; in contrast, children of parents with comorbid panic and MDD were at risk for both anxiety and MDD. Not surprisingly, comorbidity has been linked to more severe functional impairment. Ferro and coworkers[29] compared groups of inpatient children with major depression only, dysthymia only, and MDD with dysthymia ("double depression") and found that children with major depression only were the least impaired.

Depressive disorders in children and adolescents are persistent in spite of treatment, and their long-term course is, as noted before, characterized by relapse. Although a variety of psychosocial and biological interventions may be applied, the optimal method of treatment has not been identified. Studies of psychosocial methods are few, and no single psychological intervention has been clearly demonstrated to be effective in clinical samples, although preliminary evidence suggests that cognitive-behavioral strategies may be of value. Family therapy, which is often routinely prescribed, has no demonstrated benefit in ameliorating the symptoms of the disorder, but it is thought to be of benefit in families that experience difficulties related to the illness. Psychoanalytic therapy is unlikely to be of value.

Pharmacological treatments have not demonstrated efficacy of tricyclic antidepressants in childhood and adolescent depression. Selective serotonin reuptake inhibitors seem to be more promising and are usually better tolerated. Of particular importance in this group, the toxicity of selective serotonin reuptake inhibitors is significantly less than that of tricyclic antidepressants, particularly in overdose. Desipramine use has been associated with sudden death in children, although the causal relationship of its use in this rare event has not been clearly established. Electroconvulsive therapy[30, 31] or combined neuroleptic and selective serotonin reuptake inhibitor pharmacotherapy may be of value in psychiatrically depressed children and adolescents. Insufficient studies of other potential biological interventions have been reported.[32–34]

Unfortunately, no long-term studies of either psychosocial or biological treatments are available.

Dysthymic Disorder

The defining characteristic of dysthymic disorder is chronically depressed mood, which in children may be manifested as irritability "most of the day, more days than not" for a period of at least a year, with symptom-free periods lasting no longer than 2 months.[35] The initial 1-year period must be free of a major depressive episode. If such episodes occur later, it is justified to give both dysthymic disorder and MDD diagnoses, the so-called double depression.

Dysthymic disorder is underresearched in children and adults, especially compared with MDD, but several studies have begun to elucidate epidemiological and descriptive characteristics related to the disorder. Prevalence rates ranging from 4% to 8% are roughly comparable to those associated with MDD in childhood and adolescence. As in MDD, dysthymia in children and adolescents is associated with significant morbidity and often signals the onset of a chronic mood disorder. For example, Kovacs and colleagues[36] reported the partial results of a prospective longitudinal study that aimed to characterize the presentation, course, and outcome of childhood-onset dysthymic disorder. A group of 55 dysthymic school-age youngsters were compared with a group of 60 MDD children over time. Dysthymic disorder was associated with an earlier age at onset, more frequent symptoms of affective dysregulation, and greater overall risk of subsequent affective disorder. The authors concluded that childhood-onset dysthymia represents an early marker for recurrent affective illness.

Studies of comorbidity for dysthymic disorder are rare. Garrison and coworkers[3] found that 58% of young adolescents with dysthymic disorder also had major depression; the prevalence of double depression was placed at 2.7% in boys and 3.0% in girls in this sample. Those with double depression had the lowest scores on the Children's Global Assessment Scale, compared with those with major depression only or dysthymia only, indicating more impaired adaptive functioning. This study also found that not living with both natural parents was strongly associated with the presence of dysthymia, much more so than for major depression. Higher socioeconomic status also appeared to function as a protective factor for dysthymia in the sample.

There are no placebo-controlled studies of psychopharmacological interventions for dysthymic disorder in children and adolescents. Howland[37] concluded in his review of the adult literature on trials of pharmacotherapy of dysthymia that all classes of antidepressants have some effectiveness, with clinical response to monoamine oxidase inhibitors more favorable than that to tricyclic antidepressants. However, many investigators are reluctant to advise the use of these compounds in children and adolescents given the propensity for serious side effects. deJonghe and coworkers,[38] in a study of adults with dysthymia, concluded that both fluvoxamine and maprotiline were modestly effective in relieving depressive symptoms. Before conclusions can be drawn concerning efficacy in younger populations, however, more study is needed, especially in view of the equivocal results of controlled studies of psychopharmacological treatment of MDD in adolescents.

No psychosocial interventions are known to affect either the syndrome or the outcome of dysthymia in children and adolescents.

Bipolar Disorder

In contrast to diagnostic criteria for other major mood disorders, DSM-IV makes no special provisions for the diagnosis of bipolar disorder (I or II) in young people. To meet criteria for bipolar I disorder, children and adolescents must have experienced a clinical course characterized by the occurrence of one or more manic episodes or mixed affective episodes (both manic and depressed). Bipolar II disorder criteria require that young people have experienced one or more depressive episodes accompanied by at least one hypomanic episode. Bipolar disorder in young people is often confused with schizophrenia,[39] which has somewhat different precursors and outcome,[40] or with personality disorders, especially borderline personality disorder. Mixed episodes with both depression and mania are also more likely to occur in adolescents, and psychiatric symptoms are common.

Especially in younger adolescents, differential diagnosis may also be complicated by nonaffective psychoses, unipolar depression, organic syndromes, attention-deficit disorder, and disruptive behavior disorders.[41] Bowring and Kovacs[42] discussed four basic factors involved in attempting to arrive at a differential diagnosis of mania in children and adolescents: the low base rate of the disorder, its variable clinical presentation within and across episodes, its symptomatic overlap with more common disorders of childhood, and the constraints placed on symptom expression by the developmental level of the child.

There is evidence both in U.S. adult populations[43] and in Scandinavian child populations[44] that the frequency of bipolar disorder is between 1% and 2%. The Thomsen study[44] revealed no sex differences in incidence rates and a relatively poor prognosis, as evidenced by multiple hospital readmissions, although the focus was on "manic-depressive psychosis." Werry and McClellan[39] attempted to isolate predictors of follow-up status for childhood-onset schizophrenia and bipolar disorder. Premorbid adjustment and IQ proved to be the most important independent predictors of outcome for the group with bipolar disorder; in contrast, in the group with schizophrenia, premorbid personality abnormality and degree of recovery after initial hospitalization were the most important predictors.

The existence of major depressive episodes in prepubertal children may be an early marker of bipolar disorder; more than 30% of such youngsters were found to have bipolarity on 2- to 5-year follow-up,[45] especially those children with family histories of bipolar disorder. Similarly, Strober and Carlson[46] found that 20% of adolescents hospitalized for depression had a subsequent manic episode at 3- to 5-year follow-up. There is also evidence that children with dysthymic disorder are at increased risk for the later emergence of bipolar disorder.[36] Rapid onset of depression, psychiatric symptoms while depressed, and a history of bipolarity in first-degree relatives are features that might predict a bipolar course.

Familial aggregation in bipolar disorder has been described.[18, 19, 47, 48] Gershon[47] and Klein[48] and colleagues studied psychiatric disorders in children of patients with bipolar disorder; Gershon's group found no particular aggregation of disorder in the children, and Klein's study showed an increased risk for cyclothymia in offspring. Strober and associates,[19] using a sample of children with bipolar I disorder as a base, found increased rates of major depression and bipolar disorder in first-degree relatives, and Strober[49] found early age at onset to predict higher familial loading for bipolar disorder. Kutcher and Marton[18] compared relatives of adolescents with bipolar disorder with relatives of adolescents with unipolar disorder and normal control subjects and found that first-degree relatives of bipolar probands were significantly more likely to have a bipolar illness than were those of unipolar probands and control subjects; rates of unipolar illness were not significantly different between relatives of bipolar and unipolar probands. Todd and coworkers[50] studied a single extended bipolar pedigree and concluded that rates of affective and disruptive disorders in offspring were correlated with the degree of genetic relationship to an affected adult.

Rates of disruptive disorder in childhood may be no greater for offspring of patients with bipolar disorder than they are with other psychiatric disorders, but there may be a unique relationship between childhood problems and the development of mood disorders among groups at risk for bipolar disorder.[51] Interestingly, there is some evidence that children of mothers with bipolar disorder may be less at risk for psychosocial impairment than are children of mothers with unipolar disorder, whose chronic and recurring depressions may have more harmful consequences for their children[52] and at an earlier age.[53]

Elevations of thyroxine or free thyroxine have been found to be associated with mood disorders in adults. Sokolov and coworkers[23] studied thyroid functioning in 14 depressed and 13 manic adolescents and found elevated thyroxine levels in both groups compared with control subjects. In addition, triiodothyronine levels were found to be decreased, and reverse triiodothyronine levels increased for the manic adolescents, documenting the presence of thyroid function abnormalities in adolescent patients with bipolar disorder. Brain physiology in bipolar disorder has also received some attention. A report detailed a case study of an adolescent girl diagnosed with bipolar disorder who exhibited subcortical focal signal hyperintensities at magnetic resonance imaging of the brain, paralleling findings of some adult studies.[54]

As with adults, lithium treatment is the therapy of choice for children and adolescents with bipolar disorder,[46, 55] even though its efficacy has not been subject to rigorous double-blind investigation. Ordinarily, dosage is similar to that in adults (i.e., 600 to 1200 mg/d, in divided doses).[56] The therapeutic level is between 0.8 and 1.2 mEq; common adverse side effects in children are weight gain, stomachache, vomiting, nausea, tremor, enuresis, acne, and weight loss.[57] Weight gain and acne are often of particular concern to adolescents, especially because gains of up to 30 lb have been reported. These gains may reverse within a year of maintenance medication, however. The presence of comorbid personality disorder may also have treatment implications. Kutcher and colleagues[58] found that adolescents with bipolar illness and personality disorder differed significantly from a purely bipolar group in terms of increased lithium unresponsiveness.

Premature discontinuation of lithium maintenance therapy can have adverse effects for adolescent patients with bipolar disorder. Strober and associates[59] found that the relapse rate of bipolar illness in 13 adolescents with bipolar I disorder who discontinued prophylactic lithium therapy shortly after hospital discharge was nearly three times higher than the rate in patients who continued lithium without interruption. Two well-designed but uncontrolled studies[59a, 59b] have reported good outcome to valproate in acute adolescent mania. No comparative short- or long-term studies of either lithium or valproate are available.

Bilateral brief-pulse electroconvulsive therapy has been found to be a useful treatment of pharmacologically unresponsive acute adolescent manias, which suggests, much like in adults, that this treatment modality should be considered in a subgroup of seriously ill patients. Much further study of this and other biological interventions is necessary.

Anxiety Disorders

Anxiety disorders in children and adolescents include panic disorder, generalized anxiety disorder (GAD), obsessive-compulsive disorder (OCD), specific phobia, social phobia, and SAD. These are relatively common, affecting some 10% to 15% of the population. They often occur comorbidly with other anxiety disorders or other psychiatric illness, particularly MDD, dysthymia, attention-deficit/hyperactivity disorder, and Tourette's disorder. High rates of familial prevalence have been reported, and all the anxiety disorders are associated with significant disturbances in social, academic, and interpersonal functioning. Behaviorally inhibited children may be more likely to have an anxiety disorder, and anxiety disorders may predate the appearance of a mood disorder in some cases. The common problem of school refusal in children is often a symptom of an underlying anxiety disorder.[60]

Biederman and coworkers[28] have described the familial association of anxiety disorders in offspring of adults with panic disorder. "Behavioral inhibition" has also received a good deal of attention as a possible precursor of anxiety disorders in children. As originally conceptualized by Kagan and colleagues,[61, 62] behavioral inhibition refers to characteristics of a subgroup of normal children who are irritable as infants, fearful as toddlers, and cautious and introverted as school-age children. Rosenbaum and coworkers[63] suggested that behavioral inhibition to the unfamiliar may be one factor predisposing to the development of panic and agoraphobia later in life. Support for this hypothesis has been provided by Biederman and coworkers,[64, 65] who conducted a follow-up study of children with behavioral inhibition compared with control subjects. Among inhibited children, rates of anxiety disorders and psychiatric disorders in general were markedly higher than those for control children.

Specific Phobia

DSM-IV defines specific phobia as a "marked and persistent fear of clearly discernible, circumscribed objects or situations."[35] Responses to these stimuli "almost invariably" provoke an anxiety response, a situationally specific panic attack, and avoidance behavior, leading to marked distress or some functional impairment. To meet criteria, individuals older than 18 years also need to recognize that the fear is excessive or unreasonable. Subtypes are now specified: animal, natural environment (e.g., heights, water), blood-injection-injury, situational (e.g., airplanes, elevators), and other (e.g., loud sounds, vomiting). For individuals younger than 18 years, the duration of such symptoms must be at least 6 months.

Childhood fears and anxieties are among the most common of the psychological characteristics of youth and may be expressed in ways typical of children: crying, tantrums, freezing, or clinging. Objects of fear may also be developmentally idiosyncratic (e.g., anxiety about masks, balloons, or costumed figures). More commonly, fears of the dark, strangers, dogs, thunderstorms, and the like may reflect typical developmental phenomena and warrant nothing more than parental reassurance, talk, patience, and, perhaps, setting of limits. When are such symptoms significant enough to meet diagnostic criteria or warrant specialized treatment approaches? DSM-IV warns that fears do not warrant a diagnosis of specific phobia unless "there is significant interference with social, educational, or occupational functioning."[35] Does the fear of a dog en route prevent the child from attending school? Does concern about insects stand in the way of the child's going outside to play? Does fear of the physician prevent the child from having routine physical examinations or being examined when ill? When such functional impairments are clearly present, the psychiatrist should entertain the possibility of diagnosis and specialized intervention.

Specific fears appear to be linked with different developmental stages. Younger children exhibit fears of the dark, strangers, or animals; adolescents show health, social, and school-related fears.[66] Actual phobias concerning animals often begin even before elementary school and are not usually linked with a specific trauma.[67] Blood phobias have been estimated to occur in 2% to 4.5% of children and adults[68]; fears of blood are extremely common, especially in younger children. School phobia, a term that enjoyed popularity if not diagnostic status for many years, has now largely been abandoned in favor of school refusal, a term that highlights the behavioral character of a response that can have a number of etiological pathways, including depression; separation anxiety; or specific fears of school, peers, academic embarrassment, a teacher, gym, or objects or places encountered on the way to school. School refusal may also have more volitional underpinnings and be seen in conjunction with symptoms of oppositional behavior and conduct disorder.

Factors that may contribute to the development of a true phobia rather than developmentally normative fears are as yet little understood. A study of childhood anxiety disorders[69] compared anxiety-disordered children with groups of test-anxious children and control children. The study found that anxiety-disordered children showed significantly less self-competence and temperamental flexibility than did the other groups. Fathers of both anxiety-disordered children and test-anxious children were shown to have more obsessive-compulsive symptoms than did fathers of control children, supporting the notion of familial transmission of anxiety disorders.

Behavioral interventions are the treatment of choice for specific phobias. Techniques of systematic desensitization and progressive relaxation offer benefit, especially when done in the presence of the threatening stimulus.[70] Techniques involving modeling and flooding have also been employed with success, as have operant procedures employing contingency management programs.[71] Pharmacotherapy is not indicated, although short-term use of low-dose benzodiazepines may be of value in assisting the care with exposure therapy.

Social Phobia

Social phobia is defined in DSM-IV as a "marked and persistent fear" of social or performance situations in which one is exposed to unfamiliar people or when one's actions are witnessed by others.[35] For children, this presumes the capacity for age-appropriate relationships with familiar people and the existence of the fear in peer-related situations, not simply with adults. As with specific phobia, social phobia in children may take the form of crying, tantrums, freezing, or shrinking from social contact. Socially phobic children may refuse to participate in group play, prefer the periphery of peer activities, or attempt to remain close to adults with whom they are familiar and feel safe. School functioning is often affected. Socially phobic children exhibit an avoidance of speaking in front of others in class, writing on a blackboard where others may see, or even eating in a cafeteria with other children. Aversion to the use of a shared bathroom may also be seen, not because of fear of contamination, as might be present in OCD, but because of fears of being seen, heard, or smelled by other children when using the facility.

A major listing change of childhood and adolescent disorders in DSM-IV is the omission of avoidant disorder as a category on Axis I. It became apparent that there was insufficient evidence to distinguish avoidant disorder from social phobia. Francis and colleagues[72] examined characteristics of children with avoidant disorder, social phobia, and comorbid patterns, comparing them with normal control children, and found few distinguishing attributes between the anxiety disorder groups; this led the authors to question the validity of a distinct avoidant disorder. Similarly, Beidel[73] compared socially phobic and overanxious children with control subjects and found support for the validity of social phobia but less support for overanxious disorder. This was confirmed by the change in DSM-IV, which omitted avoidant disorder and overanxious disorder from the list of childhood disorders. There has also been some discussion in the literature concerning the distinction between social phobia and elective (now selective) mutism, that is, whether the latter may be a variant of the former.[74]

The prevalence and etiology of social phobia in children are little studied, and Judd[75] commented that of all the anxiety disorders, social phobia is the least understood. The picture is beginning to change, however, especially with data from the National Comorbidity Study, which has revealed a reasonably substantial 13.3% lifetime prevalence in the adult population (15 to 54 years). An epidemiological investigation in New Zealand of the prevalence of psychiatric disorders in 930 18-year-olds[76] revealed social phobia to be the second most prevalent disorder in this group (11.1%) , after major depressive episode (16.7%). There has also been more discussion about etiology[77]; current models include factors of biological preparedness to fear scrutiny by others, genetically transmitted predisposition to fear acquisition, and nongenetic familial and environmental factors. The authors also cited work examining behavioral inhibition in infants as an early marker of proneness to the development of anxiety disorders, including social phobia.

Much of what we currently know about onset of social phobia has emerged from retrospective studies of adults. Solyom and associates[78] compared groups of adults with social phobia, simple phobia, and agoraphobia and found that those with social phobias reported the age at onset of their symptoms in middle to late adolescence, a somewhat later onset than those with simple phobia reported for their symptoms. It may be that the acute sensitivity that adolescents are known to exhibit to peer acceptance and approval reaches a more pathological form in a subgroup of vulnerable individuals.

It is apparent that social phobia is frequently seen in conjunction with other psychiatric disorders. The National Comorbidity Study, focusing on adults, found high lifetime comorbidity with simple phobia (59%) and agoraphobia (45%) and moderate comorbidity with alcohol abuse (19%), major depression (17%), drug abuse (13%), and dysthymia (12%). Hovens and coworkers[79] reported similar comorbidity data specific to adolescent substance abusers in their finding that many had comorbid social phobia. Current clinical wisdom states that the course of this disorder appears to be chronic and unremitting, with a continuing fear of social scrutiny and evaluation, but there is a lack of prospective longitudinal research to bolster this claim.

Psychopharmacological treatments of children with social phobia that have received attention include fluoxetine[80] and buspirone.[81] Birmaher and colleagues[80] studied 21 children and adolescents with overanxious disorders, social phobia, and SAD (excluding OCD, panic, and depression) in an open trial and concluded that fluoxetine treatment may be an effective and safe treatment for childhood anxiety disorders. No significant side effects were reported. Buspirone was reported to be useful in a case study of a socially phobic and personality-disordered adolescent.[81] Controlled studies in adults with social phobia suggested some efficacy for phenelzine[82] and monoamine oxidase inhibitors in general[83]; summaries are available.[84] These are *not* recommended for use in children and adolescents. Psychotherapeutic approaches have traditionally included insight-oriented psychodynamic therapy, but there are no known studies demonstrating its effectiveness. Cognitive-behavioral approaches, including social skills training, show promise in enhancing social competence[85] but await proper evaluation.

Panic Disorder

The diagnosis of panic disorder, in children and adolescents as well as in adults, requires the presence of recurrent, unexpected panic attacks followed by at least 1 month of persistent concern or worry about the possible recurrence of an attack, the consequences of the attack, or behavioral change related to the attacks. Agoraphobia may or may not be present, and the attacks must not be a function of a medical condition, substance use, or other mental disorder.

It is only within the past 15 years that the existence of true panic disorder in children and adolescents has been clearly recognized. The frequency of panic disorder among the young is not known, although it is relatively rare in adults (0.6% to 1%).[86] The first clinical report to describe panic attacks in a child was published in 1984 by Van Winter and Stickler,[87] who highlighted both the existence of true panic and its familial aggregation in seven young patients of ages 9 to 17 years. Similar case study material was presented in subsequent years[88, 89]; somewhat more systematic descriptions have been given by Alessi and Magen[90] of panic disorder in a sample of hospitalized children and by Moreau[91] of panic in offspring of depressed parents. Age at onset varied fairly widely (age 3 to 18 years) across these studies, depending on the sample, but it is clear that prepubertal onset occurs in many cases, with an interval of about 3 years between onset and diagnosis.[92] The frequency of panic disorders increases with ascending pubertal stage[93] and peaks in adolescence and young adulthood. Assessment of panic disorder in children, like that of other disorders, is now routinely made by structured interviews, although self-reports have also been used.[94] Reviews on panic disorder in young people are available.[60, 95, 96]

As in the case of other anxiety disorders, comorbidity of panic disorder with other psychiatric disorders is common in children and adolescents. SAD and depression have been widely reported to co-occur with panic.[90, 91, 97] Attention has been paid to the comorbidity of behavioral disorders (i.e., attention-deficit/hyperactivity disorder, oppositional defiant disorder) and eating symptoms with panic disorder.[98] In keeping with research on adult panic disorder, mitral valve prolapse has also been found to occur in some children with panic disorder.[92]

Psychopharmacological studies of the treatment of panic disorders in adults have suggested the efficacy of tricyclic antidepressants, monoamine oxidase inhibitors, and benzodiazepines, but few studies have addressed their efficacy in children and adolescents in placebo-controlled, double-blind trials. Open trials and case studies have pointed to the potential usefulness of clonazepam for panic symptoms in prepubertal children[99] and panic disorder in adolescents.[100] Evidence of the usefulness of combined pharmacological and cognitive-behavioral interventions has been reported for adults with panic disorder,[101] but no scientifically valid studies of psychological treatments have been reported for children and adolescents.

Obsessive-Compulsive Disorder

OCD often has onset during childhood and adolescence. The prevalence of the disorder is approximately 1%; epidemiological studies describe the minority of children with this condition as receiving professional care. As in adults, OCD in children and adolescents is characterized by ego-dystonic intrusive, recurrent, and persistent thoughts, images, or impulses and repetitive, purposeful, intentional behaviors performed in response. These are accompanied by various degrees of distress and functional impairments.

The most common obsessions are fears of contamination, fears of harm to self, and fears of harm to a familiar person (often a parent). Common compulsions are washing, cleaning, checking, and counting. In the majority of cases, OCD is found comorbidly with another Axis I disorder; other anxiety disorders, tic disorders, major depression, and specific developmental disabilities are most frequent.

The natural history of OCD is that of a chronic psychiatric disorder characterized by periodic waxing and waning of symptom severity. Changes in symptom hierarchy may occur as well. With treatment, symptoms and functioning may in most cases be improved, although the majority of patients will continue to be somewhat symptomatic.

Familial-genetic studies suggest heritability for OCD, particularly in association with Tourette's disorder. OCD, tics, or Tourette's disorder is commonly found in first-degree relatives of children with OCD, and first-degree relatives of Tourette's disorder probands have increased rates of OCD. The exact pattern of inheritance is unknown, although autosomal dominance with variable penetrance and sex-influenced phenotypic expression has been postulated.

A number of neurobiological studies suggest that central nervous system serotonin dysfunction is a pathoetiological feature of OCD. However, dopaminergic dysfunction and subtle neuroendocrine abnormalities have also been described. Sydenham's chorea (autoimmune inflammation of the basal ganglia) may be associated with OCD in children, which suggests that antibody-mediated disturbance could underlie some cases of this disorder.

Treatment of childhood and adolescent OCD consists of psychological and pharmacological interventions. Cognitive-behavioral therapy is the psychological treatment of choice when exposure, response prevention, and anxiety management constitute the essential therapeutic components. Pharmacotherapy with medications that inhibit serotonin reuptake is well established as an effective treatment for childhood and adolescent OCD. Clomipramine, fluoxetine, fluvoxamine, and sertraline have been investigated with relatively similar results. Unlike in adults, for whom large doses of selective serotonin reuptake inhibitors may be required for symptom control, smaller doses may be beneficial in children. Combination therapy with clonazepam may be useful in optimizing response. The use of concomitant cognitive-behavioral therapy and medication treatments has been demonstrated to increase the magnitude of the initial treatment response and improve long-term outcome. Psychodynamic psychotherapy and family therapy are not indicated for the treatment of OCD but may be useful in ameliorating concurrent functional difficulties. Psychosurgery has been used with some success in improving OCD symptoms that have been previously resistant to maximized combined psychological-pharmacological interventions.

Separation Anxiety Disorder

SAD is a childhood-onset psychiatric disturbance characterized by "developmentally inappropriate and excessive anxiety concerning separation from home or from those to whom the individual is attached—usually parents."[35] It is accompanied by functional impairment and must be distinguished from developmentally appropriate fears, such as "stranger anxiety." This core cognitive feature is associated with various behaviors designed to avoid separation (tantrums, bed avoidance, school refusal) and symptoms of autonomic arousal when separation has occurred or is anticipated.

The reported prevalence of SAD is 3% to 5%; the peak age at onset occurs at 7 to 9 years. About 40% to 60% of children with SAD will demonstrate a comorbid psychiatric diagnosis, with other anxiety disorders and MDD being the most common. The clinical course of SAD is variable. The presence of comorbidity, later age at onset, and serious family psychiatric illness may be associated with a greater risk of chronicity. Childhood-onset SAD may furthermore be associated with an increased risk for development of panic disorder, depression, social phobia, or agoraphobia in adolescence and adulthood.

SAD has shown a familial pattern; increased rates of SAD have been reported in siblings of children with SAD. First-degree relatives of SAD probands demonstrate high rates of anxiety and depressive disorders. In addition, the offspring of panic-disordered probands show a threefold risk for SAD. This rate rises to 10-fold if parents demonstrate panic disorder plus major depression.

Treatment of SAD is primarily that of behavioral therapy, although controlled clinical trials are lacking. A variety of pharmacological interventions have been reported, usually as an adjunct to behavioral interventions. In the main, these are also uncontrolled. Currently, buspirone, fluoxetine, or low-dose clonazepam may be considered as part of a comprehensive medication plan. Family counseling may be of benefit in those cases in which family dysfunction complicates the clinical picture. Identification and effective treatment of an anxious parent will also often help in decreasing functional impairment in a child with SAD. The long-term effects (therapeutic or adverse) of various interventions for SAD are not known.

Generalized Anxiety Disorder

GAD often has onset in childhood. The core feature of GAD is excessive and functionally impairing worries across a variety of domains, including such things as personal safety, social interactions, and past and future events. Somatic disturbances are extremely common, with headaches and stomachaches predominating. In some cases, these children may be needlessly subjected to repeated and unnecessary medical investigations in an attempt to determine whether a specific medical diagnosis underlies their somatic complaints.

Prevalence rates of stringently diagnosed GAD are found to range between 2% and 4% with a female predominance. The natural history of this disorder is essentially unknown, although it may continue through adolescence into adulthood in a number of cases. Treatment of childhood GAD has been in the main defined by the theoretical orientation of the practitioner rather than by any valid scientific study. A variety of behavioral techniques have been described in case reports and small series of patients. These include modeling, cognitive self-control, relaxation training, and contingency management. Those few controlled studies that are available support the short-term efficacy of combined self-control and relaxation training. No evidence for efficacy of family therapy has been demonstrated, and analytically based psychotherapies might be considered to be contraindicated because they encourage rather than control ruminative thinking.

Pharmacological treatments of GAD have included buspirone, low-dose benzodiazepines such as lorazepam, and selective serotonin reuptake inhibitors. The results are difficult to interpret given the uncontrolled nature of these investigations. Current clinical practice suggests that if medications are considered in this disorder, buspirone may be a reasonable "first line." No long-term studies of any treatment modality are available.

Schizophrenia

Age at onset of schizophrenia is commonly noted to be in adolescence, but cases in younger children have been described, as summarized by Campbell and coworkers.[102] Presentation of the disorder in these children is similar to that in adults, including negative and positive signs[103]; the most commonly reported symptoms are auditory hallucinations, affective disturbance, thought disorder, and delusions.[104] Werry[105] noted that early-onset schizophrenia is more common in boys and is more frequently preceded by a premorbid schizotypal personality and by a high frequency of neurodevelopmental abnormalities. In children, hallucinations and delusions may be less elaborated than those in adults, and some care must be taken to differentiate some hallucinatory phenomena that occur in some normal children from true schizophrenic hallucinations. Similarly, disordered speech can be found in other childhood disorders (e.g., communication disorders, pervasive developmental disorder) and is not pathognomonic of schizophrenia. When schizophrenia does occur in childhood and adolescence, diagnostic, prognostic, and treatment ramifications are similar to those noted with adult-onset schizophrenia.[106]

McKenna and colleagues[107] conducted structured interviews of 71 children and their parents who had been referred to the National Institute of Mental Health for childhood-onset psychosis. With use of the Schedule for Affective Disorders and Schizophrenia for School-Age Children, Epidemiological Version, and portions of the Diagnostic Interview for Children and Adolescents, Parent Version, schizophrenia was diagnosed in 19 subjects, affective disorder in 14 subjects, and Asperger's disorder and pervasive developmental disorder in 6 subjects. Interestingly, a large group of reliably diagnosed, "multidimensionally impaired" children were also identified who did not have schizophrenia but who exhibited language or learning disorders, mood lability, and transient psychotic symptoms

(N = 21), highlighting the confusing nature of psychotic symptoms in childhood and the difficulty of establishing an appropriate diagnosis of schizophrenia in prepubertal children. Caplan,[108] in a review of the concept of thought disorder, has argued that a better defined construct of thought disorder can illuminate the distinction between childhood-onset schizophrenia and infantile autism, allowing exploration of the information-processing, linguistic, and biological correlates of thought disorder.

There has also been an intensified interest in exploring the neurobiological underpinnings of childhood-onset schizophrenia.[109] Findings to date suggest that childhood-onset schizophrenia exhibits a fairly high rate of family illness along with chromosomal or brain developmental abnormalities. Some research has also focused on cognitive processing in children with schizophrenia. Strandburg and associates[110] compared a group of children with schizophrenia with a group of normal children on the continuous performance task and recorded event-related potential data. Their findings suggested that the children with schizophrenia were deficient at several stages of information processing regarding cognitive control and strategic allocation of various control processing resources.

Using another paradigm, Caplan and Guthrie[111] studied blink rates as a putative measure of dopamine function in children with schizophrenia, children with schizotypal personality disorder, and normal children. Unlike the blink rates of adults not receiving neuroleptics, the blink rates of children with schizophrenia not receiving neuroleptics were significantly lower than those of normal children. Interestingly, there were no differences in blink rate between children with schizophrenia and children with schizotypal personality disorder, giving some credence to the concept of childhood-onset schizophrenia spectrum disorder. Similarities in thinking between children with schizophrenia and children with schizotypal personality disorder had been reported earlier by the same group.[112] Caplan and coworkers[113, 114] have also focused on the existence of thought disorder and schizophrenia in children with seizure disorders, suggesting possible anatomical substrates of thought disorder. At least one study investigating neuropathological findings in childhood schizophrenia has been reported,[115] which suggested the presence of a chronic derangement in the function of the neurons of the rostral brain stem tegmental area and medial thalamus.

Few outcome studies have focused solely on childhood-onset schizophrenia, but a study comparing youth hospitalized with schizophrenia, psychotic mood disorders, and personality disorders[116] suggested that those with schizophrenia had a poorer short-term (almost 4 years after discharge) outcome than the other groups did. Children with schizophrenia have been shown to improve with neuroleptic medication, and successful double-blind, placebo-controlled studies of haloperidol have been conducted with use of sound psychometric measures.[103] Clozapine has also been found to be effective in single-case studies[117, 118] and open trials[119]; clozapine concentrations were demonstrated to bear a consistent linear relationship to clinical benefit in children with schizophrenia.[120] McClellan and Werry[106] noted that strategies for medication management of the young patient with schizophrenia are best coordinated by a child and adolescent psychiatrist familiar with presentation of the disorder in this age group.

Regarding psychosocial interventions, a Scandinavian report[121] indicated some positive results with use of a psychoeducational program compared with more standard treatment. Fewer relapses during the next 2 years were evident in the psychoeducational group, but parents' cooperation was deemed to be a critical component to good outcome.

References

1. Golombek H, Kutcher S: Feeling states during adolescence. Psychiatr Clin North Am 1990; 13:443–454.
2. Lewinsohn PM, Hops H, Roberts RE, et al: Adolescent psychopathology. I. Prevalence and incidence of depression and other DSM-III-R disorders in high school students. J Abnorm Psychol 1993; 102:133–144.
3. Garrison CZ, Addy CL, Jackson KL, et al: Major depressive disorder and dysthymia in young adolescents. Am J Epidemiol 1992; 135:792–802.
4. Kashani JH, McGee RO, Clarkson SE, et al: Depression in a sample of 9-year-old children. Arch Gen Psychiatry 1983; 40:1217–1223.
5. Whitaker A, Johnson J, Shaffer D, et al: Uncommon troubles in young people: Prevalence estimates of selected psychiatric disorders in a nonreferred adolescent population. Arch Gen Psychiatry 1990; 47:487–496.
6. Kashani JH, Carlson GA, Beck NC, et al: Depression, depressive symptoms, and depressed mood among a community sample of adolescents. Am J Psychiatry 1987; 144:931–934.
7. Reinherz HZ, Giaconia RM, Lefkowitz ES, et al: Prevalence of psychiatric disorders in a community population of older adolescents. J Am Acad Child Adolesc Psychiatry 1993; 32:369–377.
8. Lewinsohn PM, Clarke GN, Seeley JR, et al: Major depression in community adolescents: Age at onset, episode duration, and time to recurrence. J Am Acad Child Adolesc Psychiatry 1994; 33:809–818.
9. Giaconia RM, Reinherz HZ, Silverman AB, et al: Ages of onset of psychiatric disorders in a community population of older adolescents. J Am Acad Child Adolesc Psychiatry 1994; 33:706–717.
10. Burke KC, Burke JD Jr, Regier DA, et al: Age at onset of selected mental disorders in five community populations. Arch Gen Psychiatry 1990; 47:511–518.
11. Harrington R, Fudge H, Rutter M, et al: Adult outcomes of childhood and adolescent depression. I. Psychiatric status. Arch Gen Psychiatry 1990; 47:465–473.
12. Garber J, Kriss MR, Koch M, et al: Recurrent depression in adolescents: A follow-up study. J Am Acad Child Adolesc Psychiatry 1988; 27:49–54.
13. Klerman G, Weissman MM: Increasing rates of depression. JAMA 1989; 261:2229–2235.
14. Ryan ND, Williamson DE, Iyengar S, et al: A secular increase in child and adolescent onset affective disorder. J Am Acad Child Adolesc Psychiatry 1992; 31:600–605.
15. Brent DA, Perper JA, Moritz G, et al: Suicide in affectively ill adolescents: A case-control study. J Affect Disord 1994; 31:193–202.
16. Brent D, Perper JA, Moritz G, et al: Suicide in adolescents with no apparent psychopathology. J Am Acad Child Adolesc Psychiatry 1993; 32:494–500.
17. Garrison CZ, Addy CL, Jackson KL, et al: A longitudinal study of suicidal ideation in young adolescents. J Am Acad Child Adolesc Psychiatry 1991; 30:597–603.
18. Kutcher S, Marton P: Affective disorders in first-degree relatives of adolescent onset bipolars, unipolars, and normal controls. J Am Acad Child Adolesc Psychiatry 1991; 30:75–78.
19. Strober M, Morrell W, Burroughs J, et al: A family study of bipolar I disorder in adolescence: Early onset of symptoms linked to increased familial loading and lithium resistance. J Affect Disord 1988; 15:255–268.
20. Weissman MM, Fendrich M, Warner V, et al: Incidence of psychiatric disorder in offspring at high and low risk for depression. J Am Acad Child Adolesc Psychiatry 1992; 31:640–648.

21. Hammen C, Burge D, Burney E, et al: Longitudinal study of diagnoses in children of women with unipolar and bipolar affective disorder. Arch Gen Psychiatry 1990; 47:1112–1117.
22. Hammen C, Burge D, Adrian C: Timing of mother and child depression in a longitudinal study of children at risk. J Consult Clin Psychol 1991; 59:341–345.
23. Sokolov ST, Kutcher SP, Joffe RT: Basal thyroid indices in adolescent depression and bipolar disorder. J Am Acad Child Adolesc Psychiatry 1994; 33:469–475.
24. Ryan ND, Dahl RE, Birmaher B, et al: Stimulatory tests of growth hormone secretion in prepubertal major depression: Depressed versus normal children. J Am Acad Child Adolesc Psychiatry 1994; 33:824–833.
25. Kutcher S, Williamson P, Marton P, et al: REM latency in endogenously depressed adolescents. Br J Psychiatry 1992; 161:399–402.
26. Dahl RE, Ryan ND, Puig-Antich J, et al: 24-Hour cortisol measures in adolescents with major depression: A controlled study. Biol Psychiatry 1991; 30:25–36.
27. Ryan ND, Birmaher B, Perel JM, et al: Neuroendocrine response to L-5-hydroxytryptophan challenge in prepubertal major depression: Depressed vs normal children. Arch Gen Psychiatry 1992; 49:843–851.
28. Biederman J, Rosenbaum JF, Bolduc EA, et al: A high risk study of young children of parents with panic disorder and agoraphobia with and without comorbid major depression. Psychiatry Res 1991; 37:333–348.
29. Ferro T, Carlson GA, Grayson P, et al: Depressive disorders: Distinctions in children. J Am Acad Child Adolesc Psychiatry 1994; 33:664–670.
30. Bertagnoli MW, Borchardt CM: A review of ECT for children and adolescents. J Am Acad Child Adolesc Psychiatry 1990; 29:302–307.
31. Crumley FE: More on ECT. J Am Acad Child Adolesc Psychiatry 1990; 29:840–841.
32. Ryan ND: Pharmacological treatment of child and adolescent major depression. Encephale 1993; 19:67–70.
33. Kutcher S, Boulos C, Ward B, et al: Response to desipramine treatment in adolescent depression: A fixed-dose, placebo-controlled trial. J Am Acad Child Adolesc Psychiatry 1994; 33:686–694.
34. Jain U, Birmaher B, Garcia M, et al: Fluoxetine in children and adolescents with mood disorders: A chart review of efficacy and adverse effects. J Child Adolesc Psychopharm 1992; 2:259–265.
35. American Psychiatric Association: Diagnostic and Statistical Manual of Mental Disorders, 4th ed. Washington, DC: American Psychiatric Association, 1994.
36. Kovacs M, Akiskal HS, Gatsonis C, et al: Childhood-onset dysthymic disorder: Clinical features and prospective naturalistic outcome. Arch Gen Psychiatry 1994; 51:365–374.
37. Howland RH: Pharmacotherapy of dysthymia. J Clin Psychopharmacol 1991; 11:83–92.
38. deJonghe F, Swinkels J, Tuynman-Qua H: Randomized double-blind study of fluvoxamine and maprotiline in treatment of depression. Pharmacopsychiatry 1991; 24:21–27.
39. Werry JS, McClellan JM: Predicting outcome in child and adolescent (early onset) schizophrenia and bipolar disorder. J Am Acad Child Adolesc Psychiatry 1992; 31:147–150.
40. Werry JS, McClellan JM, Chard L: Childhood and adolescent schizophrenic, bipolar, and schizoaffective disorders: A clinical and outcome study. J Am Acad Child Adolesc Psychiatry 1991; 30:457–465.
41. Krasa NR, Tolbert HA: Adolescent bipolar disorder: A nine-year experience. J Affect Disord 1994; 30:175–184.
42. Bowring MA, Kovacs M: Difficulties in diagnosing manic disorders among children and adolescents. J Am Acad Child Adolesc Psychiatry 1992; 31:611–614.
43. Weissman MM, Leaf PJ, Tischler GL, et al: Affective disorders in five United States communities. Psychol Med 1988; 18:141–153.
44. Thomsen PH, Moller LL, Dehlholm B: Manic-depressive psychosis in children younger than 15 years: A register-based investigation of 39 cases in Denmark. Acta Psychiatr Scand 1992; 85:401–406.
45. Geller B, Fox LW, Clark KA: Rate and predictors of prepubertal bipolarity during follow-up of 6- to 12-year-old depressed children. J Am Acad Child Adolesc Psychiatry 1994; 33:461–468.
46. Strober M, Carlson G: Bipolar illness in adolescents with major depression. Arch Gen Psychiatry 1982; 39:549–555.
47. Gershon ES, McKnew D, Cytryn L, et al: Diagnosis in school-age children of bipolar affective disorder patients and normal controls. J Affect Disord 1985; 8:283–291.
48. Klein DN, Depue RA, Slater JF: Cyclothymia in the adolescent offspring of parents with bipolar affective disorder. J Abnorm Psychol 1985; 94:115–127.
49. Strober M: Relevance of early age-of-onset in genetic studies of bipolar affective disorder. J Am Acad Child Adolesc Psychiatry 1992; 31:606–610.
50. Todd RD, Reich W, Reich T: Prevalence of affective disorder in the child and adolescent offspring of a single kindred: A pilot study. J Am Acad Child Adolesc Psychiatry 1994; 33:198–207.
51. Carlson GA, Weintraub S: Childhood behavior problems and bipolar disorder—relationship or coincidence? J Affect Disord 1993; 28:143–153.
52. Anderson CA, Hammen CL: Psychosocial outcomes of children of unipolar depressed, bipolar, medically ill, and normal women; a longitudinal study. J Consult Clin Psychol 1993; 61:448–454.
53. Radke YM, Nottelmann E, Martinez P, et al: Young children of affectively ill parents: A longitudinal study of psychosocial development. J Am Acad Child Adolesc Psychiatry 1992; 31:68–77.
54. Botteron KN, Figiel GS, Wetzel MW, et al: MRI abnormalities in adolescent bipolar affective disorder. J Am Acad Child Adolesc Psychiatry 1992; 31:258–261.
55. Hsu LKG, Starzynski JM: Mania in adolescence. J Clin Psychiatry 1986; 47:596–599.
56. Koplewicz HS, Klass E, Kafantaris V: The psychopharmacology of childhood and adolescent depression. In Koplewicz HS, Klass E (eds): Depression in Children and Adolescents. Chur, Switzerland: Harwood Academic Publishers, 1993:235–252.
57. Campbell M, Silva RR, Kafantaris V, et al: Predictors of side effects associated with lithium administration in children. Psychopharmacol Bull 1991; 27:373–380.
58. Kutcher SP, Marton P, Kornblum M: Adolescent bipolar illness and personality disorder. J Am Acad Child Adolesc Psychiatry 1990; 29:355–358.
59. Strober M, Morrell W, Lampert C, et al: Relapse following discontinuation of lithium maintenance therapy in adolescents with bipolar I illness: A naturalistic study. Am J Psychiatry 1990; 147:457–461.
59a. Papatheodorou G, Kutcher S, Katic M, Szalai J: The efficacy and safety of divalproex sodium in the treatment of acute mania in adolescents and young adults: An open clinical trial. J Clin Psychopharmacol 1995; 15:110–116.
59b. West SA, Keck PE Jr, McElroy SL, et al: Open trial of valproate in the treatment of adolescent mania. J Child Adolesc Psychopharmacol 1994; 4:263–267.
60. Black B: Separation anxiety disorder and panic disorder. In March J (ed): Anxiety Disorders in Children and Adolescents. New York: Guilford Press, 1995:212–234.
61. Kagan J, Reznick JS, Clarke C, et al: Behavioral inhibition to the unfamiliar. Child Dev 1984; 55:2212–2225.
62. Kagan J, Reznick JS, Snidman N: The physiology and psychology of behavioral inhibition in young children. Child Dev 1987; 58:1459–1473.
63. Rosenbaum JF, Biederman J, Gersten M, et al: Behavioral inhibition in children of parents with panic disorder and agoraphobia. Arch Gen Psychiatry 1988; 45:463–470.
64. Biederman J, Rosenbaum JF, Hirschfeld DR, et al: Psychiatric correlates of behavioral inhibition in young children of parents with and without psychiatric disorders. Arch Gen Psychiatry 1990; 47:21–26.
65. Biederman J, Rosenbaum JF, Bolduc-Murphy EA, et al: A 3-year follow-up of children with and without behavioral inhibition. J Am Acad Child Adolesc Psychiatry 1993; 32:814–821.
66. Marks IM: Fears, Phobias, and Rituals. New York: Oxford University Press, 1987.
67. Marks IM, Gelder MG: Different ages of onset in varieties of phobia. Am J Psychiatry 1966; 123:218–221.
68. Marks IM: Blood injury phobia: A review. Am J Psychiatry 1988; 145:1207–1213.
69. Messer SC, Beidel DC: Psychosocial correlates of childhood anxiety disorders. J Am Acad Child Adolesc Psychiatry 1994; 33:975–983.
70. Ultee CA, Griffioen D, Schellekens J: Reduction of anxiety in children: A comparison of the effects of systematic desensitization in

vitro and systematic desensitization in vivo. Behav Res Ther 1982; 20:61–67.
71. Babbitt RL, Parrish JM: Phone phobia, phact or phantasy? An operant approach to child's disruptive behavior induced by telephone usage. J Behav Ther Exp Psychiatry 1991; 22:123–129.
72. Francis G, Last CG, Strauss CC: Avoidant disorder and social phobia in children and adolescents. J Am Acad Child Adolesc Psychiatry 1992; 31:1086–1089.
73. Beidel DC: Social phobia and overanxious disorder in school-age children. J Am Acad Child Adolesc Psychiatry 1991; 30:545–552.
74. Black B, Uhde TW: Elective mutism as a variant of social phobia. J Am Acad Child Adolesc Psychiatry 1992; 31:1090–1094.
75. Judd LL: Social phobia: A clinical overview. J Clin Psychiatry 1994; 55:5–9.
76. Feehan M, McGee R, Raja SN, et al: DSM-III-R disorders in New Zealand 18-year-olds. Aust N Z J Psychiatry 1994; 28:87–99.
77. Rosenbaum JF, Biederman J, Pollock RA, et al: The etiology of social phobia. J Clin Psychiatry 1994; 55:10–16.
78. Solyom L, Ledwidge B, Solyom C: Delineating social phobia. Br J Psychiatry 1986; 149:464–470.
79. Hovens JG, Cantwell DP, Kiriakos R: Psychiatric comorbidity in hospitalized adolescent substance abusers. J Am Acad Child Adolesc Psychiatry 1994; 33: 476–483.
80. Birmaher B, Waterman GS, Ryan N, et al: Fluoxetine for childhood anxiety disorders. J Am Acad Child Adolesc Psychiatry 1994; 33:993–999.
81. Zwier KJ, Rao U: Buspirone use in an adolescent with social phobia and mixed personality disorder (cluster A type). J Am Acad Child Adolesc Psychiatry 1994; 33:1007–1011.
82. Liebowitz MR, Gorman JM, Fyer AJ, et al: Pharmacotherapy of social phobia: An interim report of a placebo control comparison of phenelzine and atenolol. J Clin Psychiatry 1988; 49:252–257.
83. Liebowitz MR: Social phobia. Mod Probl Pharmacopsychiatry 1987; 22:141–173.
84. Liebowitz MR, Schneier FR, Hollander E, et al: Treatment of social phobia with drugs other than benzodiazepines. J Clin Psychiatry 1991; 52(suppl):10–15.
85. LeCroy CW: Social skills training. In LeCroy CW (ed): Handbook of Childhood and Adolescent Treatment Manuals. New York: Lexington, 1994:126–169.
86. Von Korff MR, Eaton WW, Keyl PM: Epidemiology of panic attacks and panic disorder. Am J Epidemiol 1985; 122:970–981.
87. Van Winter JT, Stickler GB: Panic attack syndrome. J Pediatr 1984; 105:661–665.
88. Herskowitz J: Neurologic presentations of panic disorder in childhood and adolescence. Dev Med Child Neurol 1986; 28:617–623.
89. Vitiello B, Behar D, Wolfson S, et al: Panic disorder in prepubertal children. Am J Psychiatry 1987; 144:525–526.
90. Alessi NE, Magen J: Panic disorder in psychiatrically hospitalized children. Am J Psychiatry 1988; 145:1450–1452.
91. Moreau D, Weissman M, Warner V: Panic disorder in children at high risk for depression. Am J Psychiatry 1989; 146:1059–1060.
92. Vitiello B, Behar D, Wolfson S, et al: Diagnosis of panic disorder in prepubertal children. J Am Acad Child Adolesc Psychiatry 1990; 29:782–784.
93. Hayward C, Killen JD, Hammer LD, et al: Pubertal stage and panic attack history in sixth- and seventh-grade girls. Am J Psychiatry 1992; 149:1239–1243.
94. King NJ, Gullone E, Tonge BJ, et al: Self-reports of panic attacks and manifest anxiety in adolescents. Behav Res Ther 1993; 31:111–116.
95. Bradley SJ: Panic disorder in children and adolescents: A review with examples. Adolesc Psychiatry 1990; 17:433–450.
96. Leonard HL, Rapoport JL: Simple phobia, social phobia, and panic disorders. In Weiner JM (ed): Textbook of Child and Adolescent Psychiatry. Washington, DC: American Psychiatric Press, 1991:330–338.
97. Gittelman R, Klein DF: Relationship between separation anxiety and panic and agoraphobic disorders. Psychopathology 1984; 17(suppl 1):56–65.
98. Bradley SJ, Hood J: Psychiatrically referred adolescents with panic attacks: Presenting symptoms, stressors and comorbidity. J Am Acad Child Adolesc Psychiatry 1993; 32:826–829.
99. Biederman J: Clonazepam in the treatment of prepubertal children with panic-like symptoms. J Clin Psychiatry 1987; 48:38–41.
100. Kutcher SP, MacKenzie S: Successful clonazepam treatment of adolescents with panic disorder. J Clin Psychopharmacol 1988; 8:299–300.
101. Pollack MH, Otto MW, Rosenbaum JF, et al: Longitudinal course of panic disorder: Findings from the Massachusetts General Hospital Naturalistic Study. J Clin Psychiatry 1990; 51(suppl A):12–16.
102. Campbell M, Spencer EK, Kowalik SC, et al: Schizophrenic and psychotic disorders. In Weiner JM (ed): Textbook of Child and Adolescent Psychiatry. Washington, DC: American Psychiatric Press, 1991:223–239.
103. Spencer EK, Alpert M, Pouget ER: Scales for the assessment of neuroleptic response in schizophrenic children: Specific measures derived from the CPRS. Psychopharmacol Bull 1994; 30:199–202.
104. Russell AT, Bott L, Sammons C: The phenomenology of schizophrenia occurring in childhood. J Am Acad Child Adolesc Psychiatry 1989; 28:399–407.
105. Werry JS: Child and adolescent (early onset) schizophrenia: A review in the light of DSM-III-R. J Autism Dev Disord 1992; 22:601–624.
106. McClellan JM, Werry JS: Schizophrenia. Psychiatr Clin North Am 1992; 15:131–148.
107. McKenna K, Gordon CT, Lenane M, et al: Looking for childhood-onset schizophrenia: The first 71 cases screened. J Am Acad Child Adolesc Psychiatry 1994; 33:636–644.
108. Caplan R: Thought disorder in childhood. J Am Acad Child Adolesc Psychiatry 1994; 33:605–615.
109. McKenna K, Gordon CT, Rapoport JL: Childhood-onset schizophrenia: Timely neurobiological research. J Am Acad Child Adolesc Psychiatry 1994; 33:771–781.
110. Strandburg RJ, Marsh JT, Brown WS, et al: Event-related potential correlates of impaired attention in schizophrenia children. Biol Psychiatry 1990; 27:1103–1115.
111. Caplan R, Guthrie D: Blink rate in childhood schizophrenia spectrum disorder. Biol Psychiatry 1994; 35:228–234.
112. Caplan R, Perdue S, Tanguay PE, et al: Formal thought disorder in childhood onset schizophrenia and schizotypal personality disorder. J Child Psychol Psychiatry 1990; 31:1103–1114.
113. Caplan R, Shields WD, Mori L, et al: Middle childhood onset of interictal psychosis. J Am Acad Child Adolesc Psychiatry 1991; 30:893–896.
114. Caplan R, Guthrie D, Shields WD, et al: Formal thought disorder in pediatric complex partial seizure disorder. J Child Psychol Psychiatry 1992; 33:1399–1412.
115. Casanova MF, Carosella N, Kleinman JE: Neuropathological findings in a suspected case of childhood schizophrenia. J Neuropsychiatry Clin Neurosci 1990; 2:313–319.
116. McClellan JM, Werry JS, Ham M: A follow-up study of early onset psychosis: Comparison between outcome diagnoses of schizophrenia, mood disorders, and personality disorders. J Autism Dev Disord 1993; 23:243–262.
117. Jacobsen LK, Walker MC, Edwards JE, et al: Clozapine in the treatment of a young adolescent with schizophrenia. J Am Acad Child Adolesc Psychiatry 1994; 33:645–650.
118. Towbin KE, Dykens EM, Pugliese RG: Clozapine for early developmental delays with childhood-onset schizophrenia: Protocol and 15-month outcome. J Am Acad Child Adolesc Psychiatry 1994; 33:651–657.
119. Frazier JA, Gordon CT, McKenna K, et al: An open trial of clozapine in 11 adolescents with childhood-onset schizophrenia. J Am Acad Child Adolesc Psychiatry 1994; 33:658–663.
120. Piscitelli SC, Frazier JA, McKenna K, et al: Plasma clozapine and haloperidol concentrations in adolescents with childhood-onset schizophrenia: Association with response. J Clin Psychiatry 1994; 55:94–97.
121. Rund BR, Moe L, Sollien T: The Psychosis Project: Outcome and cost-effectiveness of a psychoeducational treatment programme for schizophrenic adolescents. Acta Psychiatr Scand 1994; 89:211–218.

CHAPTER

33 Mental Retardation

Ludwik S. Szymanski
Maija Wilska

Mental Retardation

Loneliness slowly sinks into you when
You (know you) are not perfect.
Syringes and needles can't cure
Loneliness and emptiness
Only understanding and caring will.
There is no prescribed medicine
That will cure it
But finding love and contentment will.
Don't lose heart and faith in yourself
Find the real you.[1]

This chapter is unique in that it does not deal with a specific disease but with a heterogenous group of persons with subaverage intellectual and adaptive functioning. They are at high risk for comorbid mental disorders of all types, the diagnosis and treatment of which often require special approaches and skills. For the purpose of clarity and ease of information retrieval, this chapter is divided into two major parts. The first one focuses on mental retardation itself, and the second one concentrates on the diagnosis, treatment, and prevention of mental disorders in persons with mental retardation.

MENTAL RETARDATION

Concept of Mental Retardation

Following are the basic concepts this chapter uses concerning mental retardation and the psychiatric approaches to it:

1. Mental retardation is not a specific disease. The term refers to a behavioral syndrome, describing the level of a person's functioning in defined domains. It does not have a single cause, mechanism, course, or prognosis and does not necessarily last a lifetime.
2. Mental retardation is not a unitary concept. Persons diagnosed as having mental retardation are not a homogeneous group but represent a wide spectrum of abilities, clinical presentations, and behavioral patterns.
3. Persons with mental retardation do not have unique personalities or behavioral patterns.
4. Maladaptive behaviors should not automatically be seen as part of the retardation or an expression of "organic personality disorder." As in all individuals, these behaviors may be related to life experiences; they can also be a symptom of comorbid mental illness existing with the retardation.
5. Mental disorders seen in persons with mental retardation are the same as those in the general population.
6. The most important contribution of psychiatrists in the field of mental retardation is the diagnosis, treatment, prevention, and research of mental disorders in persons with mental retardation.

Some common misconceptions about mental retardation are that it is a specific and lifelong disorder, with a characteristic behavioral phenotype that is associated with specific personality patterns and that comorbid mental disorders existing with mental retardation are different from those encountered in other individuals. Although mental retardation is listed as a mental disorder in the *Diagnostic and Statistical Manual of Mental Disorders,* Fourth Edition (DSM-IV),[1a] it is not a unique nosological entity with specific pathognomonic features. Instead, mental retardation describes the level of a person's intellectual and adaptive functioning below a cutoff point that is not even natural but is arbitrarily chosen in relation to the average level of functioning of the population at large. It is not necessarily lifelong. Strictly speaking, it is not a medical term. Its chief function is administrative, defining a group of persons who are in need of support and educational services. Thus, mental retardation does not have a single cause, mechanism, course, or prognosis. It has to be differentiated from the diagnosis (if known) of the underlying medical condition.

Definition of Mental Retardation and Its Evolution

One of the common misconceptions about mental retardation has been that it is defined by intelligence level alone (usually expressed as an intelligence quotient, or IQ). From earliest recorded history, however, the description of mental retardation included impairments in one or more areas of actual functioning.

The Talmud explicitly recognized that certain persons had significant impairments in cognitive capacity and included *shoteh* (a term describing persons with mental retardation or with mental illness) as well as deaf persons and minors among those who had limited legal capacity. With the advent of the Age of Enlightenment, attempts were made to define mental retardation. For example, Fitz-Herbert wrote in 1534: "And he who shall be said to be a sot and idiot from his birth, is such a person who cannot account or number 20 pence, nor can tell who was his father or mother, nor how old he is, etc. so as it may appear that he hath no understanding or reason what shall be for his profit, nor what for his loss."[2] Willis, in the 17th century, recognized that mental retardation could be of varying degrees: "Some are unable to learn their letters but can handle mechanical arts; others who fail at this can easily comprehend agriculture; others are unfit except to eat and sleep."[2] Edouard Sequin, in the last century, introduced the subclassification of mental retardation with four grades of severity on the basis of the person's abilities. In 1905, Alfred Binet and Theodore Simon, in France, published the first version of what became later an intelligence test. Actually, its goal was to assess which children require education in special classes. The first version classified children with mental retardation into idiots, imbeciles, and morons according to the number of test tasks they completed; the later versions gave the child's mental age.[3] These tests were soon translated into English and introduced to the United States by Henry Goddard. Many revisions and new tests followed. Lewis Terman's revision of 1916, known as the Stanford-Binet Intelligence Scale, introduced the concept of IQ and the classification of mental retardation according to its scores.

American Association on Mental Deficiency Definitions

The American Association on Mental Deficiency (currently the American Association on Mental Retardation) has published manuals on the classification of mental retardation. The 1910 definition required the presence of a mental defect and an inability to manage ordinary affairs (corresponding to today's impairment in cognitive capacity and adaptive behavior) and included the classifications of idiots (mental age of 2 years or younger), imbeciles (mental age of 2 to 7 years), and morons (mental age of 7 to 12 years). The definition published by that association in 1959 had three diagnostic criteria for mental retardation: subaverage intellectual functioning, impairment in adaptive behavior, and onset in the developmental period.[4] The subaverage intellectual functioning was meant to be one standard deviation or more below the population mean (IQ of approximately 85), and the developmental period referred to age 16 years or less. Five degrees of severity of mental retardation based on the IQ were introduced: borderline, mild, moderate, severe, and profound. In 1973, the definition was changed in that the IQ cutoff point was two standard deviations (approximate IQ of 70), thus eliminating the category of borderline mental retardation and retaining the other four degrees of severity. The developmental period was increased to 18 years or younger.

Current American Association on Mental Retardation Definition

In 1992 a new manual of classification was published, with the definition: "Mental Retardation refers to substantial limitations in present functioning. It is characterized by significantly subaverage functioning, existing concurrently with related limitations in two or more of the following applicable adaptive skill areas: communication, self-care, home living, social skills, community use, self-direction, health and safety, functional academics, leisure, and work. Mental retardation manifests before age 18."[5] The IQ cutoff point was defined as 70 to 75 to reflect the ±5-point error inherent in most tests. The subclassification of severity has been eliminated and replaced by classification according to the support needed in defined areas of functioning. This manual emphasizes the requirement for detailed assessment of individuals and their needs in all relevant domains, including psychological and emotional, and is by far the most modern and comprehensive available.

DSM-IV Definition

DSM-IV[1a] defines mental retardation in a manner generally compatible with the American Association on Mental Retardation definition.

DSM-IV Criteria

Mental Retardation

A. Significantly subaverage intellectual functioning: an IQ of approximately 70 or below on an individually administered IQ test (for infants, a clinical judgment of significantly subaverage intellectual functioning).

B. Concurrent deficits or impairments in present adaptive functioning (i.e., the person's effectiveness in meeting the standards expected for his or her age by his or her cultural group) in at least two of the following areas: communication, self-care, home living, social/interpersonal skills, use of community resources, self-direction, functional academic skills, work, leisure, health, and safety.

C. The onset is before age 18 years.

Severity	*Approximate IQ Range*	*Code*
Mild	50–55 to approx. 70	317
Moderate	35–40 to approx. 50–55	318
Severe	20–25 to approx. 35–40	318.1
Profound	Below 20–25	318.2
Undiagnosed		319

However, subclassification into degrees of severity is retained.

Mental retardation is coded on Axis II.

Epidemiology of Mental Retardation

Prevalence

The results of epidemiological studies of mental retardation depend on two major factors: the definition of mental retardation that is used and how the results are ascertained. There have been various models for estimating the prevalence of mental retardation. A model based on IQ score alone used the expected statistical distribution of intelligence levels. The past definition based only on an IQ that was one standard deviation or greater below the mean implied that almost 15% of the population could be classified as having mental retardation. With the introduction of the diagnostic criterion of impairment in adaptive behavior and an IQ cutoff at two standard deviations below the mean (approximately 70), the prevalence of mental retardation was commonly thought to be 3% of the population. More recent population-based studies, using multiple methods of ascertainment and a current definition of mental retardation, suggest that the prevalence might be closer to 1%. In the study of McLaren and Bryson,[6] the prevalence of mild mental retardation was 0.37% to 0.59%, whereas the prevalence of moderate, severe, and profound retardation was 0.3% to 0.4%. When age is considered, the highest prevalence is in the school-age group, when the child cannot meet the expectations of academic learning. Conversely, some persons who are diagnosed with mild mental retardation when of school age lose that diagnosis in adulthood, when their good adaptive skills are more relevant than their academic achievement.

Comorbidity Patterns

Other disorders frequently occur comorbidly with mental retardation. Mental retardation may be part of the clinical manifestation of a certain disorder or syndrome. Alternatively, an insult to the central nervous system (CNS) might cause both mental retardation and another disorder (for instance, seizures).

Central Nervous System Problems

The study of McLaren and Bryson[6] indicated that neurological disorders are frequently associated with mental retardation, especially when the retardation is severe: seizure disorders were associated with mental retardation in 15% to 30% of patients, cerebral palsy (CP) and other motor handicaps were found in association with mental retardation in 20% to 30% of patients, and sensory impairments were associated with mental retardation in 10% to 20% of patients.

Disturbance or injury during development often affects several functions of the CNS. In addition to the intelligence level, neuromotor, sensory, perceptional, and language functions are affected. The cumulative effect influences the developmental level and functioning; thus, these children should be carefully assessed and treated. These associated disabilities may be present alone or in different combinations, depending on the type, extent, and area of the injury. They are so interactive that when one symptom is present, the possible occurrence of all others has to be evaluated. Table 33–1 summarizes the various disorders associated with mild and severe mental retardation. It is to be noted that the additional disabilities are more often associated with severe than with mild mental retardation because of the more severe pathological brain condition.

Cerebral Palsy

CP is defined as "disorder of movement and posture secondary to a static encephalopathy, with the insult to the brain occurring prenatally, perinatally, or in early childhood."[7] The risk factors for the development of CP include disorders in pregnancy and the neonatal period. However, the majority of children with neonatal risk factors have no neurological symptoms later, and more than 75% of children with CP do not have risk factors in the neonatal period.[8] CP can be divided into spastic, athetoid, and mixed types. Mental retardation is found in about 50% of persons with CP, mostly those with spastic quadriplegia. Intelligence is intact in many athetoid forms.

Seizure Disorders

Seizure disorders are seen in 0.5% of the general population but in about 20% of persons with mental retardation. If the retardation is severe, seizures are twice as common. In prenatally affected, multiply disabled children, infantile

Table 33–1 Disorders Often Associated with Mental Retardation

Study	Subjects (Degree of Retardation; n; Age)	% with Seizures	CP	Visual Impairment	Hearing Disorder	Speech Disorder	Mental Disorder
Gustavson et al*	Severe; 161; school age	36	19%	10%	6%		
Gustavson et al†	Severe; 121; school age	30	18%	12%	4%		
McQueen et al‡	IQ <55; 221; school age	23	15.4%	13%	11%	65.6%	9%
Hagberg et al§	Mild; 91; school age	12	9%		7%		31%

*Data from Gustavson KH, Holmgren G, Jonsell G, Blomquist HK: Severe mental retardation in children in a northern Swedish county. J Ment Defic Res 1977; 21:161–180.

†Data from Gustavson KH, Hagberg B, Hagberg G, Sars K: Severe mental retardation in a Swedish county. II. Etiologic and pathogenetic aspects of children born 1959–1970. Neuropädiatrie 1977; 8:293–304.

‡Data from McQueen PC, Spence MW, Garner JB, et al: Prevalence of major mental retardation and associated disabilities in the Canadian maritime provinces. Am J Ment Defic 1987; 91:460–466.

§Data from Hagberg B, Hagberg G, Lewerth A, Lindberg U: Mild mental retardation in Swedish school children, II. Etiological and pathogenetic aspects. Acta Paediatr Scand 1981; 70:445–452.

spasms and their sequelae, myoclonic seizures, are often seen. Myoclonic seizures are common in many metabolic diseases. Careful evaluation and treatment are necessary to bring the seizures under control without reducing the learning capacity or causing behavior problems as a side effect of anticonvulsant treatment. Seizure disorders (especially partial complex ones) may be associated with behavioral and sensory manifestations. The latter may include illusions and hallucinations, but the person needs at least some communication skills to report them. Quick mood cycling may occur. Interictal mental disturbances may include mood disorders, anxiety, and certain personality traits such as exaggerated moral and religious preoccupations. Changes in attention and the ability to concentrate may be secondary to undiagnosed and untreated minor seizures, which are often difficult to recognize. Aggressive behavior in persons with mental retardation is often suspected to be the result of seizures, but such a relationship is not frequent. In some cases, a long-term electroencephalographic recording by telemetry with simultaneous videotaping of behavior is performed to clarify the possible relationship between the seizures and the behavior in question.

Sensory Impairments

Sensory problems are common in persons with mental retardation, but the prevalence data vary greatly, depending on the population studied (see Table 33–1), especially the type and the severity of the mental retardation–associated conditions. For example, among persons with Down syndrome, visual impairment and conductive hearing loss are seen in more than 50% of cases. Both greatly impair the child's learning and functioning, and thus early diagnosis and intervention are important. The diagnostic assessment may be more difficult than that in persons without mental retardation because the testing methods often rely on the patient's cooperation and verbal reporting, especially if the integrity of the sensory processing, rather than that of the sensory organ, is in question. Testing by auditory evoked potentials might be helpful in such instances.

Etiology and Pathophysiology of Mental Retardation

General Considerations

Intellectual abilities depend to a great degree on the integrity of the CNS. A variety of biomedical causes can disrupt this integrity and start the process leading to mental retardation. It should be kept in mind, however, that the term mental retardation describes the overall level of functioning, encompassing current intellectual and adaptive skills. These, in turn, are shaped by factors other than CNS integrity, such as the patient's general state of health and associated disabilities, environmental factors (such as nurturing, learning opportunities, supports), and psychological factors (such as the person's self-image, psychopathological characteristics, motivation). Thus, a biomedical cause, whether genetic or acquired, may be a primary cause that will start the process of developmental delay but will not necessarily be the only factor responsible for the functional outcome, which will depend on the synergistic, or cumulative, effects of all factors involved. It is important to know as much as possible about the "primary" cause for a number of reasons:

- *Treatment possibilities,* which can include early institution of diet in phenylketonuria (PKU) and thyroid hormone supplementation in congenital hypothyroidism
- *Prevention,* such as primary prevention of the recurrence of the same condition, using, for example, parental education to prevent fetal alcohol syndrome and enabling genetic counseling for the family
- *Early recognition and treatment of complications,* known to be associated with the particular mental retardation syndrome, such as hypothyroidism in Down syndrome
- *Research* on causation and prevention
- *Assessment of epidemiology,* which is important in public policy (planning for services) as well as in prevention
- *Understanding of prognosis* in association with a particular disorder
- *Support for the family* and other caregivers by dispelling misconceptions and anxieties related to uncertainty about the cause

For these reasons, it is important for physicians, including psychiatrists, to ascertain whether the persons with mental retardation to whom they provide care have had adequate and up-to-date etiological assessments that reflect current medical knowledge.

Approaches to Classification of the Causation of Mental Retardation

Many of the classification systems for mental retardation have been based on the timing of the insult to the CNS. In 1946, this approach was used by Yannet,[9] who divided the causes into prenatal, perinatal, and postnatal, plus genetic. In Heber's classification,[10] more emphasis was put on the presumed nature of the cause of retardation. The eight main categories were 1) infection; 2) intoxication; 3) trauma or physical agent; 4) disorder of metabolism, growth, or nutrition; 5) new growths; 6) unknown prenatal influences; 7) unknown or uncertain cause, with the structural reactions manifested; and 8) an uncertain or presumed psychological cause, with the functional reaction alone manifested. The successive classification systems developed by the American Association on Mental Retardation also followed the timing approach.

The goal of the etiological assessment is to elucidate the earliest developmental cause as well as other coexisting causative factors because their effects are usually interactive and cumulative.[6]

The prevalence of diagnosable (using current techniques) biomedical causes of mental retardation varies with the degree of the disability. When the retardation is severe, a prenatal cause can be identified in 59% to 73% of patients, but in mild mental retardation, such a cause can be identified in only 23% to 43% of patients (Table 33–2).

The classification used here reflects both the timing and the type of the causative process, which will affect the development and function of the CNS (Table 33–3).

Prenatal Causes: Genetic Disorders

Prenatal genetic disorders are characterized by changes in the genetic material, which may or may not have been inherited from the parents.

Table 33–2 Causes of Mental Retardation by Time of Insult to the Central Nervous System: Literature Summary

Study	Cohort (n; age)	% of Study Population* Prenatal	Perinatal	Postnatal	Unknown
		Studies of persons with severe mental retardation			
Gustavson et al†	161; 5–16 y	68	8	2	22
Gustavson et al‡	121; 5–16 y	73	10	5	12
McQueen et al§	221; 7–10 y	59	10	4	27
		Studies of persons with mild mental retardation			
Hagberg et al‖	91; school age	23	18	2	55
Blomquist et al¶	171; school age	43	7	7	43

*The percentages are of subjects in each study in whom the retardation was thought to be due to causation at the pre-, peri-, or postnatal period, respectively, or the cause could not be found.

†Data from Gustavson KH, Holmgren G, Jonsell G, Blomquist HK: Severe mental retardation in children in a northern Swedish county. J Ment Defic Res 1977; 21:161–180.

‡Data from Gustavson KH, Hagberg B, Hagberg G, Sars K: Severe mental retardation in a Swedish county. II. Etiologic and pathogenetic aspects of children born 1959–1970. Neuropädiatrie 1977; 8:293–304.

§Data from McQueen PC, Spence MW, Winsor EJT, et al: Causal origins of major mental handicap in the Canadian maritime provinces. Dev Med Child Neurol 1986; 28:697–707.

‖Data from Hagberg B, Hagberg G, Lewerth A, Lindberg U. Mild mental retardation in Swedish school children, II. Etiologic and pathogenetic aspects. Acta Paediatr Scand 1981; 70:445–452.

¶Data from Blomquist HK, Gustavson K-H, Holmgren G: Mild mental retardation in a northern Swedish county. J Ment Defic Res 1981; 25:169–185.

Table 33–3 Etiological Classification of Mental Retardation Based on the Timing and Type of the Central Nervous System Insult*†

Division and Group	Percent	Examples
Prenatal: Genetic Disorders	32	
Chromosomal aberrations		Trisomy 21, trisomy 13, cri du chat syndromes
Malformations due to microdeletions		Angelman's and Prader-Willi syndromes, Williams' syndrome, Rubinstein-Taybi syndrome
Monogenic mutations		Tuberous sclerosis, metabolic disorders, fragile X syndrome
Multifactorial mental retardation		"Familial" mental retardation
Malformations, Cause Unknown	8	
Malformations of the CNS		Holoprosencephaly, lissencephaly, neural tube defects
Multiple malformation syndromes		de Lange's syndrome, Sotos' syndrome
Prenatal: Disorders due to External Causes	12	
Maternal infections		Rubella and HIV, cytomegalovirus, and *Toxoplasma* infections
Toxins		Fetal alcohol syndrome, fetal hydantoin syndrome
Toxemia, placental insufficiency		IUGR, prematurity
Other		Radiation, trauma
Perinatal Causes	11	
Infections		Meningitis, herpes
Delivery problems		Asphyxia, trauma
Other		Hypoglycemia, hyperbilirubinemia
Postnatal Causes	8	
Infections		Meningitis, encephalitis
Toxins		Lead poisoning
Other CNS disorders		Cerebrovascular accidents, tumors, traumas
Psychosocial problems		
Unknown Causes	25	

*These data are based on the Finnish National Board of Social Welfare registry of persons with mental retardation who were receiving special services in the 1980s. There were about 19,000 persons in that registry. In about 4%, no etiological information was recorded (unpublished data).

†CNS, central nervous system; HIV, human immunodeficiency virus; IUGR, intrauterine growth retardation.

Chromosomal Aberrations

Down Syndrome. This syndrome is the best known example of prenatal genetic disorders. In 95% of cases, it is caused by trisomy 21, in which the extra chromosome 21 in the egg or sperm cell results from the nondisjunction in the meiotic stage. When such a gamete becomes fertilized, the fetus will have an extra chromosome 21 in all cells, for a total of 47 chromosomes. In cases of Down syndrome caused by translocation, there are 46 chromosomes, but chromosomal material from 47 chromosomes is present because an extra chromosome 21 is attached (translocated) to another chromosome, usually chromosome 14 (designated as t(14;21)). In about half of translocation cases, a parent (usually the mother) has a balanced translocation: 45 chromosomes with t(14;21). If a child has translocation Down syndrome, the parents should be examined for the presence of a balanced translocation. This is important in genetic counseling because when the mother or father has a t(14;21) translocation, there is a 1 in 10 or a 1 in 20 chance, respectively, of having a child with Down syndrome. In another variant, mosaicism, some cells have 47 chromosomes and others have 46 because of an error in one of the first cell divisions of the fertilized egg. The characteristic phenotype of Down syndrome is basically the same in trisomy 21 and in translocation. The main features are upward-slanted palpebral fissures, a low nasal bridge with epicanthal folds, a small mouth and ears, a single palmar crease (simian crease), a flat nasal bridge, short and wide palms, and a characteristic dermatoglyphic pattern (Fig. 33–1). Considerable hypotonia and a tendency toward respiratory problems are common. The level of retardation varies from severe to mild, with a mean IQ of approximately 50. The severity of symptoms in the mosaic form varies, and children with normal intelligence have been described. The global incidence of Down syndrome is 1 in 700 live births, but it rises with maternal age to about 1 in 40 live births in mothers older than 40 years of age. Children with Down syndrome are often described as "Prince Charming"—adorable and affectionate. However, various behavioral problems and psychopathological conditions can occur, even autistic disorder. Early diagnosis and intervention, including physical therapy and developmental stimulation, are essential to enable these children to reach their developmental potential.

Individuals with Down syndrome are at risk for associated health problems: congenital heart disease (in 40% of persons), gastrointestinal anomalies (in 12% of persons),

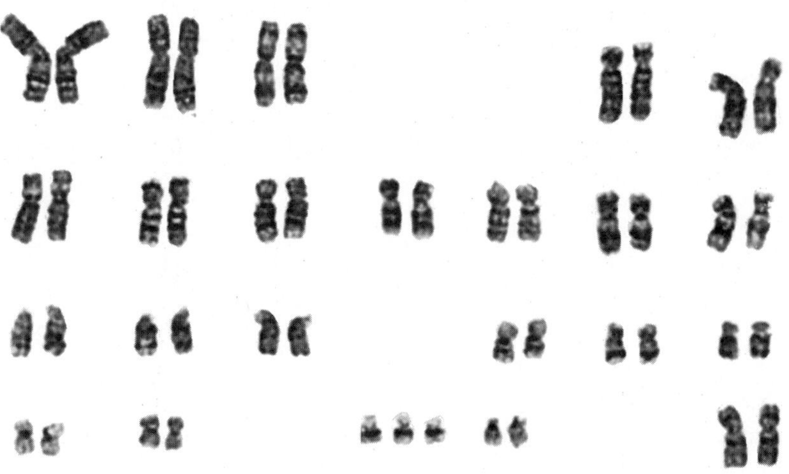

Figure 33–1 *"Drummer": a young man with Down syndrome and a trisomy 21 karyotype.*

nystagmus (in 30% of persons), and congenital cataracts (in 3% of persons).[11] Myopia and conductive hearing loss resulting from frequent ear infections are common. Hypothyroidism may be congenital or may develop later, the incidence increasing with age. It may often cause "reversible dementia," which is treatable with thyroid hormone replacement. It has been well documented that persons with Down syndrome usually have neuropathological changes of Alzheimer's dementia in their 30s, probably because of the increased dose of the gene for β-amyloid (involved in Alzheimer's disorder), which is on chromosome 21. It is important that the neuropathological changes usually are not accompanied by clinical symptoms of dementia until the fourth or fifth decade of life.

Deletions. A loss of part of a chromosome is called a deletion. The best known example is cri du chat syndrome, which is characterized by a high-pitched voice and is caused by a deletion in chromosome 5p3. It should be noted that most fetuses with chromosomal aberrations are not viable. About 40% to 50% of spontaneously aborted fetuses have a chromosomal anomaly. Only 2 of 10 fetuses with Down syndrome are born alive.

Malformation Syndromes due to Microdeletions

A new method of using DNA probes and fluorescence in situ hybridization has brought new light to many of the malformation syndromes previously classified as being of unknown origin. The same submicroscopic deletions (microdeletions) of DNA have been reported in chromosome 15q11–12 in the Prader-Willi and Angelman syndromes, despite the fact that these syndromes have different phenotypes. It has been discovered that because of the mechanism of imprinting, the Prader-Willi syndrome results when the microdeletion is in the chromosome of paternal origin, and the Angelman syndrome results when it is of maternal origin.[19, 20] Persons with the Prader-Willi syndrome have an excessive appetite and indiscriminate eating habits, leading to obesity. Because this syndrome has no clear pathognomonic features, it may remain undiagnosed, and such individuals might even be referred for psychiatric treatment because of an eating disorder. Obviously, psychological factors are not the primary cause here, but supportive psychotherapy might be helpful. The treatment is based on behavioral modification and imposing strict environmental limits on food intake as well as necessary educational and habilitative programming. It has also been found that one of four persons with the Rubinstein-Taybi syndrome has a microdeletion in chromosome 16p13.3.[21] The aortic stenosis in Williams' syndrome has been linked to the elastin gene on chromosome 7. Microdeletion in this location has been documented in up to 90% of the cases.[22] The phenotype of the Williams syndrome includes short stature, aortic stenosis or other congenital heart defects, and hypercalcemia in childhood. The facial appearance is characteristic and may include periorbital fullness, a long philtrum, full lips with open mouth, a stellate iris pattern, and early graying of hair. The behavioral phenotype may also be characteristic and includes an outgoing personality and overwhelming talkativeness that might even tax the caregivers' patience. The symptoms vary, however, and even autistic disorder and aggressiveness have been found in these individuals.

These syndromes had previously been classified as malformation syndromes of unknown origin (see further on), but because of the described findings of microdeletions, they are now placed in a separate category (Table 33–4).

Monogenic Mutations

A mutation in a gene results in production of a faulty protein (usually an enzyme) coded for by this gene. This, in turn, adversely influences the organism's development, producing a disorder specific to the mutation. The inheritance might be dominant or recessive, but the actual effect of the faulty gene also depends on the penetrance and expressivity.

Disorders with Autosomal Dominant Inheritance. Tuberous sclerosis is an example of the disorders in this group, which might be associated with mental retardation. It is caused by a mutation in a gene affecting the formation of the ectodermal layer of the embryo. Because the skin and the CNS develop from this layer, abnormalities are seen in both. The skin lesions include angiofibromas in the form of macules on the cheeks (adenoma sebaceum), with a butterfly-like distribution, especially after puberty. Café au lait spots or nonpigmented ash leaf–shaped areas are also found. Mental retardation, epilepsy, and calcifications in the brain are seen, as are tumors. Epileptic seizures often begin as infantile spasms, which should alert the physician to look for other symptoms of this disorder. If tuberous sclerosis is diagnosed, both parents should be examined carefully because the mutation is inherited in about 28% of cases. Because of the dominant inheritance, the risk of recurrence is 50% for each pregnancy. The expression of this gene mutation varies from small skin discolorations (which may indicate a carrier state) to multiple disabling conditions. It is a relatively rare disorder (with a prevalence of 1 in 30,000 to 1 in 50,000 live births), but it may be found in about 0.5% of persons with severe mental retardation.

Disorders with Autosomal Recessive Inheritance. Most metabolic disorders belong to this category. They are caused by single mutated genes that disturb the metabolism by deficient enzyme activity. The risk of healthy carrier parents having an affected child is 25% for each pregnancy. The diagnosis is made by detection of abnormal metabolic products in the urine, blood, or tissues and/or by low or absent enzyme activity. When there is high clinical suspicion and the possibility of gene detection, direct DNA techniques might be used. The metabolism of amino acids, carbohydrates, lipids, and mucopolysaccharides is affected in different disorders. A few examples of inborn errors of metabolism are given in Table 33–5. PKU is the best known and most common of the metabolic disorders, with a prevalence of about 1 in 10,000 live births. The enzymatic defect is diminished activity of phenylalanine hydroxylase, which leads to a high serum phenylalanine level, affecting, among other things, myelination of the CNS. It was described in 1934 by Folling in 10 children with mental retardation, hypertonia, and hyperreflexia, with a musty odor in urine and sweat. Seizures and tremors are common, as are eczema and psychotic manifestations. The clinical symptoms can be prevented by use of a low-phenylalanine diet soon after birth. In most developed countries, all newborns are screened for PKU. Increasingly, a lifelong low-phenylalanine diet is recommended to prevent later deterio-

Table 33–4 Examples of Various Malformation Syndromes Connected with Mental Retardation*

Syndrome	Features
Chromosomal aberrations	
Trisomy 21: Down syndrome	See text
Trisomy 13 syndrome	IQ < 50; growth retardation; polydactyly; holoprosencephaly; ear, eye, and scalp defects; CHD
Deletion 5p: cri du chat syndrome	IQ 20–50, growth retardation, microcephaly, cat-like cry, hypertelorism, epicanthus
Malformation syndromes due to microdeletions	
Prader-Willi syndrome	IQ 20–80, almond-shaped eyes, small hands and feet, cryptorchidism, hypotonia, obesity
Angelman's (happy puppet) syndrome	IQ < 50, ataxia, seizures, microbrachycephaly, large mouth, prognathism, jerky gait
Williams' syndrome	IQ 40–80, long philtrum, prominent lips, supravalvular aortic stenosis, loquatious, "cocktail party manners," hypercalcemia in infancy
Rubinstein-Taybi syndrome	IQ 20–85; growth retardation; beaked, long nose; broad thumbs; narrow palate
Malformation syndromes of unknown cause	
de Lange's syndrome	IQ < 50, growth retardation, microcephaly, hirsutism, synophrys, anteverted nostrils
Sotos' syndrome	Sometimes mental retardation, large size, macrocephaly, prognathism, downward-slanting palpebral fissures
Prenatal infections	
Congenital rubella	± Mental retardation, microcephaly, hearing loss, cataracts, CHD, microphthalmia, retinal pigmentation
Toxoplasmosis	± Mental retardation, hydrocephalus microcephaly, chorioretinitis, cataracts, intracranial calcifications, hepatosplenomegaly
Toxic agents	
Fetal hydantoin syndrome	± Mental retardation, growth retardation, short nose, hypertelorism, cleft lip, CHD

*CHD, Congenital heart disease.

Data from Jones KL: Smith's Recognizable Patterns of Human Malformation, 4th ed. Philadelphia: WB Saunders, 1988.

Table 33–5 Examples of Inborn Errors of Metabolism Causing Mental Retardation*

Disorder	Enzyme Defect	Onset/Life Expectancy	Clinical Features	Laboratory Diagnosis/Treatment
Aminoacidurias				
PKU	Phenylalanine hydroxylase	I/A	If not on diet: vomiting, musty odor, eczema, seizures, tremors, psychosis	U: ferric chloride test; gene locus 12q22–24; diet: low in phenylalanine
Homocystinuria	Cystathionine β-synthetase	I/A	Seizures, venous thromboses→cerebrovascular accidents, Marfan's habitus, malar flush, lens subluxation, often MR	U: cyanide-nitroprusside test
Lysosomal disorders				
Glycoproteinoses				
Mannosidosis	Mannosidase	6–36 mo/A	Coarse facial features, short stature, skeletal changes, hepatosplenomegaly, loose joints, hearing loss, ataxia	U: oligosaccharides
I-cell disease	Multiple lysosomal hydrolases	I/2–8 y	Early facial feature coarsening, short stature, stiffness of joints, gum hyperplasia	U: sialyl oligosaccharides
Mucopolysaccharidoses				
MPS I (Hurler's)	L-Iduronidase	I/10y	Early facial feature coarsening, hepatosplenomegaly, growth failure, corneal clouding, skeletal changes	U: heparan sulfate, dermatan sulfate
MPS II (Hunter's)	Iduronidate sulfatase	I/15 y	Symptoms milder and progression slower than in MPS I	U: heparan sulfate, dermatan sulfate
Sphingolipidoses				
Tay-Sachs (GM_2)	GM_2 ganglioside–*N*-acetylhexosaminidase	3–6 mo/2–3 y	Hypotonia→rigidity, macular cherry red spot→blindness, seizures, hyperacusis	Serum hexosaminidase assay
Metachromatic leukodystrophy	Arylsulfatase A deficiency	1–4 y/10–15 y	Gait disturbance, ataxia, motor incoordination	U: metachromatic cells, sulfatase A assay; sural nerve biopsy

*All disorders cause mental retardation except that in homocystinuria it does not occur in every case. Dietary treatment benefits patients with PKU and galactosemia. Prenatal diagnosis is available for all disorders. Inheritance is autosomal recessive, except for MPS II and Lesch-Nyhan, which are X linked. I, Infancy; A, adulthood; U, urinary; MR, mental retardation.

Adapted from Nellhaus G, Stumpf DA, Moe PG: Neurologic and muscular disorders, and Robinson A, Goodman SI, O'Brien D: Genetic and chromosomal disorders. In Kempe CH, Silver HK, O'Brien D (eds): Current Pediatric Diagnosis and Treatment, 8th ed. Los Altos, CA: Lange Medical Publications, 1984:628–711 and 992–1030.

ration in cognitive functions. Women with PKU who were successfully treated do not have clinical manifestations themselves but still have phenylalanine blood levels high enough to cause brain damage to a fetus if they become pregnant. To avoid this, they should start to follow the diet again before they become pregnant.

The phenylalanine hydroxylase gene has been mapped to 12q22–24.1. Prenatal diagnosis and carrier detection are possible.

The incidence of PKU varies among populations. In the United States, it is 1 in 8000 live births among whites and about 1 in 50,000 among African-Americans.

X-Linked Mental Retardation. Fragile X syndrome is the most common inherited form of mental retardation and, after Down syndrome, its most common genetic form. It is X linked, with dominant inheritance, and the penetrance is lower in females. Because of a constriction at the location Xq27.3, it appears as if the chromosome is fragile and a part of it is breaking off. Demonstrating this phenomenon requires a folate-poor cell culture medium. Fragile X syndrome was first reported by Lubs in 1969[11a] and was connected to the clinical syndrome by Harvey in 1977.[11b] It has been studied more consistently since the early 1980s, when the connection with folate-poor medium was identified. The gene, *FMR1* (fragile X-linked mental retardation), has been traced to an unstable region where there is a mutation consisting of repeats of the triplet nucleotide CCG (cytosines and guanine). The normal X chromosome has only 6 to 50 copies of this triplet; asymptomatic carrier females or males have up to about 200 copies (premutation), and affected males have up to 1000 copies (full mutation). Half the children born to carrier women receive the X chromosome with the mutated *FMR1* gene. It may remain as a premutation (in 20%) or increase to a full mutation (triplet repeat expansion), which causes mental retardation in males. Only a full mutation is associated with clinical symptoms, but only about half of females with a full mutation have cognitive deficits. The range of the triplet repeats can be demonstrated by the Southern blot technique, which is now used for the diagnosis of fragile X syndrome and the carrier state (Fig. 33–2). An excellent review of the fragile X syndrome has been provided by Sutherland, one of the pioneers in the research of this condition.[11c]

Figure 33–3 *A skillful weaver with fragile X syndrome.*

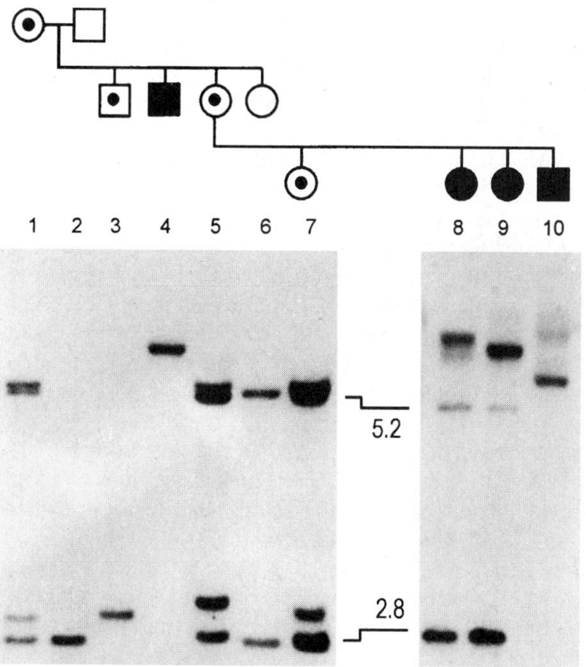

Figure 33–2 *Fragile X syndrome: molecular analysis by Southern blot and pedigree. Inheritance of the fragile X mutation and unstable element in a three-generation family. Genomic DNA was digested with* EcoRI *and methylation-sensitive* EagI *and probed with* StB*12.3 (provided by J. L. Mandel, MD). Double digestion allows the detection of methylation in addition to* CGG_n *amplification. Normal fragment sizes are 2.8 kb (kilobase) and 5.2 kb for active and inactive X chromosomes, respectively, as seen in the normal male and female (lanes 2 and 6). The normal fragment is lacking and is replaced in carrier males by a fragment larger than 2.8 kb (lane 3) and in affected males by a fragment larger than 5.2 kb (lanes 4 and 10), indicating methylation (inactivation) of the FMR1 gene. In carrier and affected females, in addition to enlarged premutation alleles (lanes 1, 5, and 7) or methylated full mutation (lanes 8 and 9) alleles or fragments, normal-sized fragments of 2.8 and 5.2 kb derived from a normal X chromosome are present.* □, *normal male;* ⊡, *carrier male;* ■, *affected male;* ○, *normal female;* ⊙, *carrier female;* ●, *affected female. (Courtesy of M. L. Väisänen, MSc, Department of Clinical Genetics, Oulu University Central Hospital, Oulu, Finland.)*

About 20% of the sons of carrier females, who have a premutation, have normal intelligence and phenotype but are carriers; they transmit the premutation to all their daughters who, through the expansion mechanism, might produce affected children. Fragile X syndrome is thought to occur in 1 in 1200 newborn boys and in 1 in 2400 newborn girls.

Prepubertal boys with this syndrome look quite normal. They are often restless and hyperactive and have a short attention span. Their developmental milestones, especially speech development, are delayed. After puberty, the characteristic phenotypical features may appear. They include an oblong face, prominent ears and jaw, and macroorchidism (Fig. 33–3). Most have moderate mental retardation, but retardation is more severe in others. Male carriers do not have mental retardation. Females with fragile X syndrome who have the full mutation and are symptomatic usually have learning disabilities or mild mental retardation. Behavioral symptoms have been described in these individuals—

hyperactivity and social withdrawal in about 50% and depression in about 25%.[12]

Males with fragile X syndrome were initially thought to be at high risk for autistic disorder because of a frequent behavioral pattern that included avoidance of eye contact, echolalia, abnormal staccato speech, stereotypic motor behavior, and unusual responses to sensory stimuli. They are usually able to relate to others, however, and most of them do not fulfill the diagnostic criteria for autistic disorder.

The Rett syndrome might be mentioned at this point. It is found in females only and has been thought to be X linked, but its genetics has not been clarified as yet. It has been postulated that there is a mutation that is lethal for males. Females, who have a normal second X chromosome, survive. The DSM-IV includes Rett's syndrome in the pervasive developmental disorders (PDD) category. Girls with this syndrome have normal development through the first 5 months of life. Between that age and about 4 years, head growth decelerates. Between 5 and 30 months of age, there is a loss of purposeful hand movements, and the characteristic "hand-washing" mannerism appears. Other symptoms include ataxia, tremor, poorly coordinated gait, teeth-grinding hyperventilation, and often seizure disorder. The deterioration is rapid at the beginning but slows later. Some skills may even be regained occasionally.[13]

The basic cause of Rett's syndrome has evaded research, but advances in the fields of neuropathology and neurochemistry have shed some light on it.[14–16] Armstrong[14] quantitated the dendritic tree in six cortical areas. He found reduction in length and branching and probably also in synapses. He postulated that the secondary increase in the synaptic density after 2 months of age, with a peak at 19 months, was disordered, which caused the deceleration of growth of the brain and head. Another finding has been a reduction in gangliosides GD1a (an integral component of synaptogenesis) and GT1b in certain brain regions. If this is confirmed, it would provide a chemical marker for diagnosis. In the later stages, the major involvement seems to be in the basal ganglia. This is suggested by rigidity, reduced dopamine and acetylcholine concentrations, and degeneration of the melanin-containing cells in the substantia nigra. In positron emission tomographic studies, the D_2 dopamine receptors are also reduced.

Multifactorial Mental Retardation

More than half the individuals with mild mental retardation have no other disability. Their speech development in childhood is delayed, and at school age they might be described as immature. Some of their first-degree relatives have a history of educational problems. A history of mental illness is also common in these families. The environmental factors and the family's socioeconomic situation are often suboptimal. However, with improvement in medical technologies, detailed assessment of such children has disclosed that biological factors could have contributed to the genesis of mental retardation. In a study of British children with mild mental retardation, genetic factors were estimated to be present in 20% and other biological factors were seen in an additional 37%. In almost 40% of the cases with a background of biological factors, the families also had a history of school problems. Thus, in these children, environmental and socioeconomic as well as genetic and biological factors are probably involved.[17, 18] This form of mental retardation has variously been called nonorganic, familial, cultural-familial, or retardation due to psychosocial disadvantage. Understanding the basic pathological features of this entity is vague. It is certain that many individuals with mental retardation have been labeled with these terms because of lack of a better alternative.

Prenatal Causes: Malformations and Malformation Syndromes of Unknown Cause

Various congenital (present at the time of birth but not necessarily genetic) structural malformations, or anomalies, are placed in this category. They usually occur during organogenesis of the embryo and are seen in about 3% of newborns. Up to 40% of persons with mental retardation of unknown cause have three or more major or minor anomalies.

Major malformations result from an intrinsic error in organogenesis, an example of which is cleft lip. Minor malformations, or dysmorphic features, such as epicanthal folds and simian palmar creases, do not cause functional problems, but they are a sign of disturbance in organogenesis. Deformation is defined as an abnormality of a body part caused by mechanical compression, such as club foot. Disruption is destruction of a previously normal structure. These should not be considered malformations because their origin is extrinsic and they usually occur later than malformations.[23]

Malformations may occur as single entities or in more or less defined combinations, or syndromes, that carry a specific name. With medical diagnostic advances, when the causation and pathogenesis of many of these syndromes are identified, they are better classified in another category. A good example is Down syndrome, which includes a number of malformations. With the elucidation of its genetic mechanism, it is now placed in the category of genetic disorders (chromosomal aberrations).

Malformations of the Central Nervous System

The development of the CNS begins at the third and fourth weeks of gestation when the neural plate twists itself into a neural tube; development and maturation continue several years after birth.

The CNS malformations may be connected with genetic abnormalities or may be caused by external insults and are then classified accordingly. Those with unknown causes are classified in this group.

Holoprosencephaly is connected with midfacial anomalies and may occur as part of other syndromes, for example, trisomy 13. Anencephaly originates from day 26 of gestation. Microcephaly may be connected with chromosomal anomalies; may have autosomal dominant, recessive, or X-linked inheritance; and may result from arrested brain growth caused by factors such as prenatal and neonatal viral infections as well as intracranial hemorrhage. Disturbances during the cell migration that occurs from 7 to 24 weeks of gestation may result in cortical gyrus anomalies—lissencephaly (nongyral cortex) and pachygyria (broad gyri). These may also be connected with chromosomal deletions. An example is the Miller-Dieker syndrome, with multiple major and minor anomalies. Agenesis of the corpus callosum also originates from a disturbance of cell migration and is connected with many syndromes. Occasionally it is also seen on neuroimaging studies of nonsymptomatic individuals. Hydrocephalus (enlargement of ventricles with increased cerebrospinal fluid volume) may be the result of an unknown malformation, but it can also have X-linked inheritance, develop in connection with meningomyelocele, or result from pre-, neo-, or postnatal infection, tumors, and other causes.

Neural tube defects are examples of severe CNS malformations known to be multifactorial—partly genetic and partly extrinsic in origin. Their incidence is between 1 and 2 in 1000 births.[23] They have assumed a new importance because it has been shown that they might be preventable to a large extent by vitamin (folic acid) supplementation before conception and in early pregnancy.[24] They range from anencephaly (which results in a nonviable child) to an asymptomatic, usually undiagnosed, occult spina bifida. Meningomyelocele is a neural tube defect characterized by various neurological deficits, depending on the level of involvement of the spinal cord. It is often associated with other CNS malformations, especially hydrocephalus, that may result in mental retardation. However, there are severely disabled individuals with meningomyelocele who have intact intelligence.

Malformation Syndromes of Unknown Origin

An estimated 50% or more of the malformation syndromes have no known cause. Many of these syndromes are known by the name of their discoverer (see Table 33–5). In clinical practice, however, one often encounters malformation syndromes that have not been formally described and named; these are sometimes called private syndromes. With improved genetic techniques, the cause of many of these malformations will certainly be delineated.

External Prenatal Causes

External prenatal causes include the deleterious effects of identifiable external factors on the developing fetus. These external prenatal causes are estimated to be responsible for 6% to 15% of mental retardation cases.[25, 26]

Maternal Infections

Viral infections in the mother can interfere with organogenesis, and the earlier in pregnancy they occur, the more severe their effect will be, as exemplified by congenital rubella. Rubella infection during the first month of pregnancy affects the organogenesis of 50% of embryos. Infection in the third month of pregnancy still disturbs the development of 15% of fetuses. Various systems are affected, and as a result, symptoms and impairments may vary and include mental retardation, microcephaly, hearing and vision impairment, congenital heart disease, and behavior problems. Fortunately, the incidence of congenital rubella has greatly decreased because of the availability of immunization for prospective mothers.

Congenital cytomegalovirus infection may result in microcephaly, sensorineural hearing loss, and psychomotor retardation. Antibodies against cytomegalovirus are found in about 80% of adults. Depending on the population, primary infections occur during 2% to 5% of pregnancies. Cytomegalovirus inclusion bodies are seen in urine specimens of newborns who were infected prenatally.

Congenital toxoplasmosis may result in significant problems in about 20% of infected infants (hydrocephalus, microcephaly, psychomotor retardation, vision and hearing impairment) and in milder developmental problems later in life.

Congenital human immunodeficiency virus infection has been increasing in importance. In a German study of 41 children born to human immunodeficiency virus–positive mothers, neurological symptoms were described at 1 to 7 years of age.[27] Human immunodeficiency virus encephalopathy was characterized by microcephaly, progressive neurological deterioration, mental retardation, cerebellar symptoms, and behavioral changes. Prophylactic intravenous immunoglobulin therapy with and without zidovudine was often able to prevent regression. Improvement was seen with zidovudine treatment.

Toxic Substances

The most important of the teratogenic substances is ethanol, which is the cause of fetal alcohol syndrome (FAS). The prevalence of this syndrome varies around the world, but its occurrence in industrialized countries is estimated to be about 1 in 1000 newborns. When used heavily during pregnancy, alcohol causes abnormalities in three main categories: 1) dysmorphic features, which originate in the period of organogenesis (Fig. 33–4); 2) pre- and postnatal growth retardation, including microcephaly; and 3) CNS dysfunction, including mild to moderate mental retardation, delay in motor development, hyperactivity, and attention deficit. The severity of the symptoms is related to the amount of alcohol ingested.[28] In a milder condition, called fetal alcohol effects (FAE), only two of the three main features are seen. Poor academic achievement and behavior problems are typical for these children. Social environmental factors during the early years have an important role in the outcome.

Some prescription drugs may have various teratogenic effects. Fetal hydantoin syndrome has long been known, and

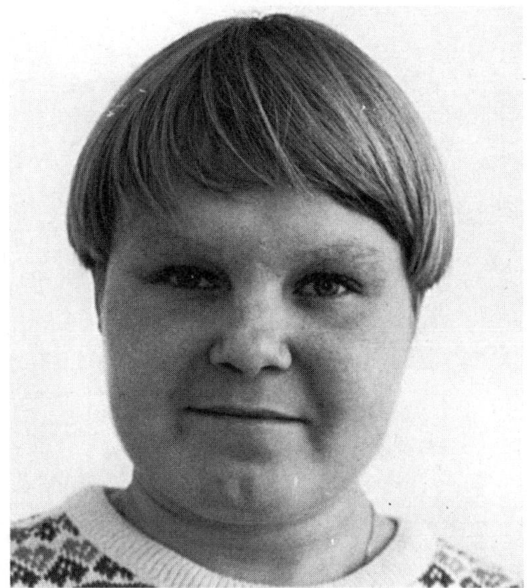

Figure 33–4 *A woman with facial features associated with fetal alcohol syndrome: 1) smooth philtrum, 2) thinned upper vermilion, 3) hypoplastic midface, 4) low and flat nasal bridge, 5) epicanthal fold, 6) short palpebral fissure, 7) low-set ears, and 8) microcephaly.*

alternative drugs are recommended for seizure control in pregnant women.

Toxemia of Pregnancy and Placental Insufficiency

Intrauterine growth retardation has many causes, the most important being maternal toxemia with its consequences, ending in insult to the CNS (Fig. 33–5). Prematurity may be of maternal or fetal origin. When it is connected with fetal developmental deviations, the prognosis depends on the infant's general condition. Prematurity and especially intrauterine growth retardation predispose to many perinatal complications, which may result in insult to the CNS and developmental problems.

Perinatal Causes

This period refers to 1 week before birth to 4 weeks after birth.

Infections

During the neonatal period, the most important infection, from the point of view of its developmental sequelae, is herpes simplex type 2. The neonate is infected during the delivery and may develop encephalitis within 2 weeks. Early treatment with acyclovir may alleviate the otherwise poor outcome—microcephaly, profound mental retardation, and neurological deficits. Neonatal bacterial infections might result in sepsis and meningitis, which, in turn, may cause hydrocephalus.

Delivery Problems

During delivery, asphyxia is the most important factor causing an insult to the CNS. It leads to cell death, which might be demonstrated with neuroimaging techniques as leukomalacia. Premature infants and those with intrauterine growth retardation are at special risk for damage to the cortex or thalamus, which, in addition to affecting intelligence, causes various symptoms of CP and seizure disorder, depending on the location of the pathological condition. It is important to know that asphyxia does not cause mental retardation alone.

Neurological symptoms during the neonatal period have a strong association with prenatal developmental deviations and later neurological integrity as well as intellectual level. For these reasons, infants with perinatal problems need a thorough examination for dysmorphic features and close follow-up because multiple disabilities might become evident later in life.

Other Perinatal Problems

Retinopathy of prematurity (formerly referred to as retrolental fibroplasia) was seen frequently when the use of 100% oxygen in neonates was common, resulting in blindness. It is often associated with other CNS damage, mental retardation, and other developmental problems. Extremely low birth weight infants are at risk for intracranial hemorrhage as well as hypoglycemia resulting from a lack of hepatic glycogen storage. These neonatal problems may have results similar to those of asphyxia. Hyperbilirubinemia may result from increased destruction of red cells (e.g., hemolysis due to maternal-child blood group incompatibility) or decreased excretion of bilirubin (e.g., due to an immaturity of liver function). The brain damage that may ensue results in manifestations of various degree, including CP, sensorineural hearing loss, and mental retardation.

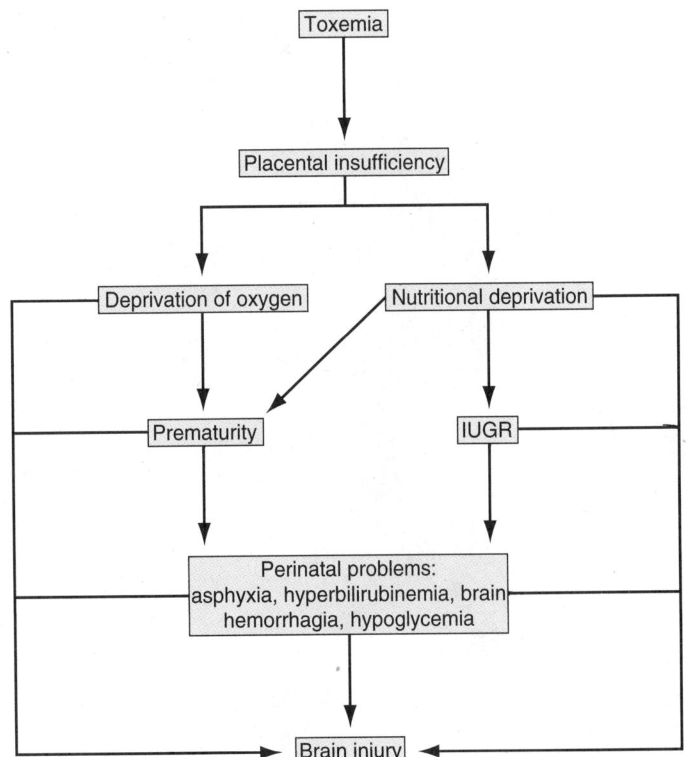

Figure 33–5 *Toxemia of pregnancy and its consequences.*

Postnatal Causes

Infections

Bacterial and viral infections of the brain during childhood may cause meningitis and encephalitis and result in permanent damage. The number of these complications has decreased because of improved treatment and the availability of immunizations such as that for measles.

Toxic Substances

Lead poisoning is still an important cause of mental retardation in the United States. The most frequent source of lead is pica—ingestion of flaking old lead-based paint. Other sources of lead are certain fruit tree sprays, leaded gasoline, some glazed pottery, and fumes from burning automobile batteries. Gastrointestinal symptoms dominate in acute poisoning. Headache may be associated with increased intracranial pressure, which may even lead to coma. Late manifestations include developmental retardation, ataxia, seizures, and personality changes.

Other Postnatal Causes

Among childhood malignancies, brain tumors are second in frequency after leukemias. Of these, 70% to 80% are gliomas, symptoms of which depend mostly on the location. Some are benign and treatable, but most have deleterious effects, resulting in various neuropsychiatric symptoms depending on their location and extent. In addition, treatment such as surgery and radiation might affect the integrity and function of the brain. Traffic accidents, drowning, and other traumas are the most common causes of death during childhood. Even greater is the number of children who become disabled. Near-drowning is often devastating, but even in these cases, improvement of functional capacity may be achieved by rehabilitation because of the ability of the developing brain to recover.

Psychosocial Problems

The developmental level of a growing individual depends on the integrity of the CNS and on environmental and psychological factors. The importance of environmental stimulation for child development has been appreciated since research on children in institutions showed that development was severely affected in a depriving environment, even if there was adequate physical care. Poverty predisposes the child to many developmental risks, such as teenage pregnancies, malnutrition, abuse, poor medical care, and deprivation. Severe maternal mental illness is another risk factor. Mothers with severe and chronic illness might have difficulty providing adequate care and stimulation. Children of mothers who have schizophrenia are at risk for the development of cognitive deficits (although these may not be secondary to maternal illness but may represent a genetically determined predisposition to schizophrenia). Psychotic illness in a child has been shown to be associated with a decline in cognitive abilities.

Unknown Causes

Despite detailed assessment, no cause can be identified in about 30% of cases of severe mental retardation and in 50% of cases of mild mental retardation.[6] This, of course, reflects the inadequacy of diagnostic techniques, rather than a lack of causation.

Diagnosis and Differential Diagnosis of Mental Retardation

Phenomenology and Variations in Presentation

The clinical presentation of persons with mental retardation is influenced by multiple factors, which can be grossly divided into biological (such as syndromes underlying the retardation), psychological (the level of the person's intellectual and adaptive functioning), and environmental (such as cultural expectations and services received). Their mutual relationship is illustrated in Figure 33–6.

The more severe the mental retardation, the earlier the child will come to medical attention because the developmental delay will be obvious earlier, and associated physical impairments will be more prevalent. Conversely, children with mild mental retardation may not be diagnosed until they reach school age, when they fail in academic learning. If the sociocultural environment does not value and stress early academic learning and early education is not available, mild mental retardation might go undetected, especially if the person has relatively good adaptive skills. A false-positive diagnosis of mental retardation can also occur, especially if psychological tests are not sensitive to cultural background, and there is a language barrier between the child and the tester.

The importance of the earliest diagnosis possible cannot be overstated because the prognosis will be much better if the intervention, which results from the diagnostic knowledge, is begun as early as possible.

Assessment of Mental Retardation

American Association on Mental Retardation's New Classification of Mental Retardation

The American Association on Mental Retardation has published a new manual for the classification of mental retardation, which includes an assessment outline[5]:

A. Step one: diagnosis of mental retardation
   Dimension I: intellectual and adaptive skills

This is essentially the step of ascertaining that the criteria for the diagnosis of mental retardation are met. The intellectual functioning is assessed in individual testing with one of the standardized intelligence tests appropriate for the person's cultural, linguistic, and social background and communication skills. (Psychological tests are discussed elsewhere in this book.) An appropriate amount of time and a suitable environment should be provided because many persons with mental retardation may be less than cooperative, having been tested many times before and viewing the tests as proof of their inadequacy. Even "nontestable" persons can be adequately assessed through prolonged observations, partial test completion, detailed history taking, and patience. Similar principles apply to the assessment of adaptive functioning. Standardized tests and scales, such as the Vineland Adaptive Behavior Scales and the American

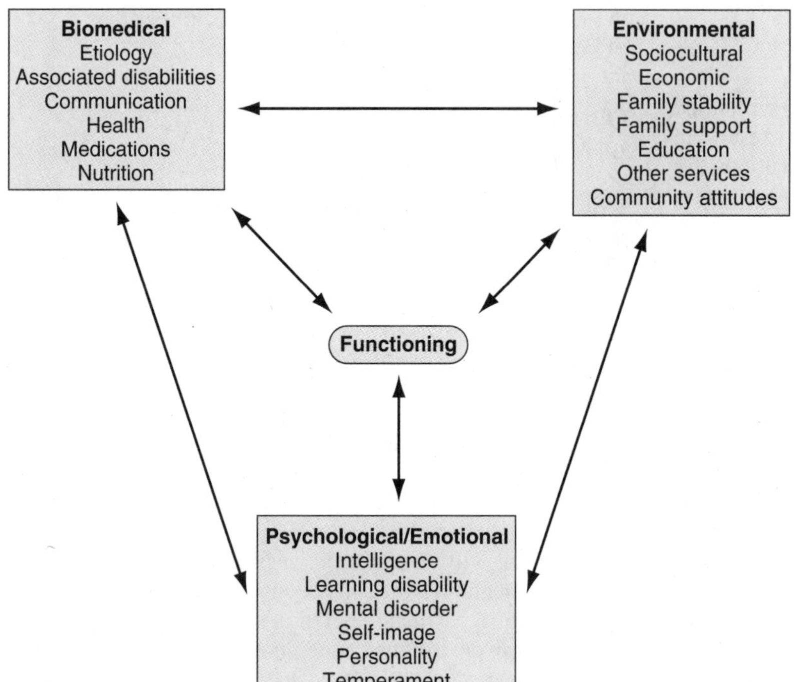

Figure 33–6 *Schematic representation of transactional relationship of various factors influencing the development of adaptive and maladaptive behaviors in persons with mental retardation.*

Association on Mental Retardation Adaptive Behavior Scales, as well as history and direct observations, are used.

B. Step two: classification and description
Dimension II: psychological and emotional considerations

This refers to the assessment of a person's strengths and weaknesses in the psychological-emotional domain or, in other words, psychiatric assessment. This procedure is described elsewhere in this chapter.

Dimension III: physical-health-etiology considerations

This is described in the following section.

Dimension IV: environmental considerations

This is a comprehensive description of the person's current environment: its nature, strengths, and weaknesses and its relationship to the person's development (e.g., poverty, family and its attitudes, availability of education and other services).

Biomedical Etiological Assessment of Mental Retardation

Biomedical causes of mental retardation have their origin in genetic or external factors or injury causing structural or functional disturbances of the CNS. The structural changes may or may not be recognizable by available clinical techniques, such as neuroimaging, computed tomography, magnetic resonance imaging, positron emission tomography, and single-photon emission computed tomography. Special staining methods have revealed changes in dendrites and synapses (hypoconnection) in some retardation syndromes.[29] As medical technology becomes more sophisticated, it is hoped that it will be possible to recognize the biological causes in an increasing number of individuals with mental retardation.

Mental retardation associated with syndromes and disorders with obvious phenotypical features is usually recognized earliest, such as in the case of Down syndrome. The diagnosis is then confirmed by chromosomal or other appropriate laboratory studies. If there was a suspicion of a family's risk for a genetic disorder before the birth (such as through prior genetic counseling), appropriate studies are performed in the neonatal period. Some cases of congenital mental retardation (e.g., PKU) are discovered in the course of routine neonatal screening. Newborns with perinatal risk factors like prematurity and asphyxia should be followed up closely for later manifestations of developmental delay. Other children might come to medical attention because of a delay in achieving developmental milestones or regression in a previously normal developmental pattern. Finally, many children with mental retardation will be referred for diagnostic assessment when they reach school age, because of failure in academic learning.

Elements of Biomedical Assessment

History. This is most important. The family history especially must be emphasized. Drawing the family tree is helpful in clarifying a possible occurrence of retardation or anomalies in any form. The risk of recessively inherited diseases increases if there has been intermarriage between the parents' families in earlier generations.

Physical Examination. This is essential and should also focus on searching for physical phenotypical manifestations of various mental retardation–associated syndromes, as well as a neurological examination, and growth measurements.

Diagnostic Studies. There is frequently discussion as to which diagnostic studies should be performed routinely. Most clinicians believe that the more complicated, invasive, and expensive studies should be performed only if there is clinical justification for them. Others believe that molecular genetic testing for fragile X syndrome as well as recent genetic techniques (e.g., chromosomal studies with G banding) should be used in every case of mental retardation, because etiologically notable abnormalities might occur even without dysmorphic features.

The diagnostic tree seen in Figure 33–7 is helpful in deciding which procedures are needed. Metabolic studies may be indicated even for patients with congenital anomalies because a metabolic disorder might coexist with a deviation in organogenesis. Conversely, dysmorphic features associated with metabolic disorders (such as facial features in mucopolysaccharidoses) might be erroneously considered nonspecific. Metabolic screening is important in every patient with progressive symptoms.

Neuroimaging techniques, such as computed tomography and magnetic resonance imaging, may help in understanding the basic pathological condition. For example, these modalities can detect intracranial calcifications in tuberous

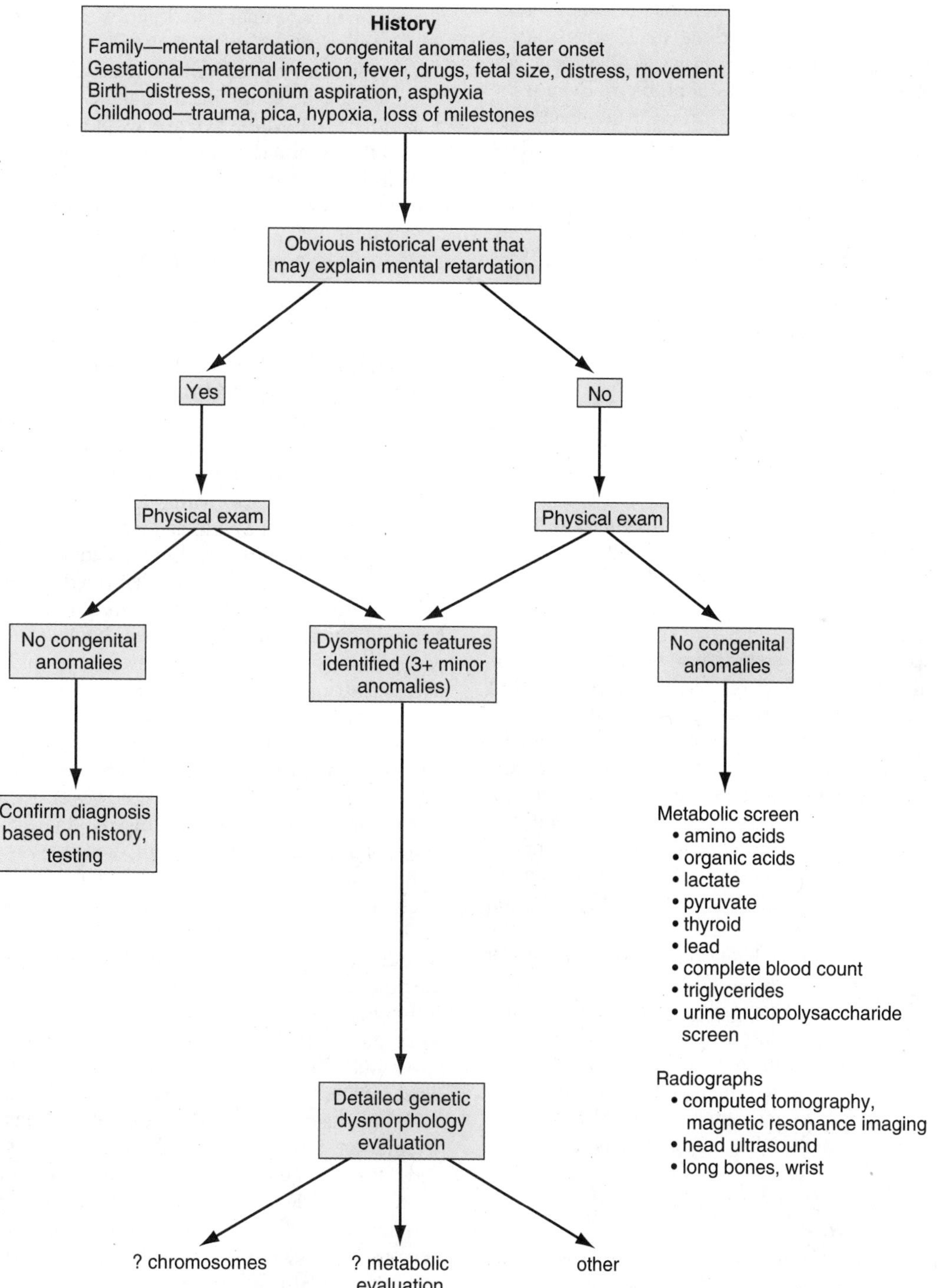

Figure 33–7 *Diagnostic approach to mental retardation of all ages. (From Szymanski LS, Kaplan LC: Mental retardation. In Wiener JM [ed]: Textbook of Child and Adolescent Psychiatry. Washington, DC: American Psychiatric Press, 1991:157.)*

sclerosis as well as hydrocephalus and tumors. Magnetic resonance imaging is especially helpful in evaluating diseases of the white matter. However, these techniques are not routine methods. It is often difficult to interpret the meaning of small deviations. Equally common is the lack of findings when one would expect them. Functional assessments with positron emission tomography have so far been used mostly for research purposes, with results that help explain the basic metabolism in certain disorders.[19]

Prenatal Diagnosis. Prenatal diagnostic methods are increasingly available. Amniocentesis with chromosomal studies is usually recommended for women 35 years or older. Prenatal diagnostic studies should be made available to everyone requesting them and should be used if there is a known risk for a genetic or congenital problem. Even if the parents do not plan a therapeutic abortion if the results are positive for a certain disorder, they will be able to prepare for the birth of a child with special needs and to marshal supports.

The currently available techniques include amniocentesis (chromosomal and metabolic disorders), chorionic villus sampling (chromosomal and molecular genetic studies), and maternal serum alpha-fetoprotein screening (for neural tube defects). Ultrasound scanning is often performed about the 20th week of gestation to screen for major malformations.

Carrier screening, which is increasingly available for certain recessive disorders, should be offered to all persons in high-risk populations, such as Ashkenazi Jews (for Tay-Sachs disease). Careful counseling is necessary to help the prospective parents decide on all available options if they are found to be positive for the particular trait.

Differential Diagnosis of Mental Retardation

The diagnosis of mental retardation itself should be relatively straightforward, as it reflects the current level of intellectual and adaptive functioning. Some persons with learning disorders or communication disorders might appear to have low functioning, but appropriate psychological and communication testing will demonstrate that the impairment is in the development of specific skills and is not generalized. Dementia can be diagnosed at any age, whereas mental retardation is diagnosed only if the onset is before age 18 years. However, both disorders might be diagnosed in persons younger than that age (see discussion of mental disorders due to a general medical condition further on). It is often asked how one differentiates between mental retardation and autistic disorder. Actually, such a question is incorrect because these disorders are not mutually exclusive; in fact, most persons with autism also have mental retardation. An uncomplicated mental retardation is not associated with qualitative impairment in social interaction and communication, which is diagnostic of autistic disorder.

Course and Natural History of Mental Retardation

The development of an individual with mental retardation depends on the type and extent of the underlying disorder, the associated disabilities and disorders, environmental factors (such as general health, education, treatment, and other services), and psychological factors (cognitive abilities, comorbid psychopathological conditions). Some general principles concerning the developmental trajectories of various mental retardation–associated disorders and syndromes are seen in Figure 33–8.

Life expectancy depends on a number of factors already discussed. Persons with profound mental retardation with multiple disabilities and an inability to ambulate or self-feed have a much shorter life expectancy, according to an extensive study conducted in California.[30]

When the patient is a person with mental retardation, even ordinary ailments require special diagnostic skills, as the person may be unable to describe the complaints because of communication difficulties. Physical pain and other discomforts are often communicated by these individuals through their behavior, such as aggression or self-injurious behavior (SIB). Many syndromes predispose the person to certain health problems that have to be anticipated. Illnesses typical of Down syndrome have been discussed. Nonambulatory persons are at risk for both respiratory and urinary tract infections. Gastroesophageal reflux is common and often leads to aspiration and anemia.

Treatment Approaches

Evolution of Attitudes to Persons with Mental Retardation

The information that has survived from ancient times on the treatment of persons with mental retardation refers primarily to those with external physical abnormalities, which might have been associated with mental retardation. In many cultures, such as in Sparta and Rome, infants with deformities were not permitted to live. Aristotle, in *Politics*, stated that there should be a law that deformed children should not be permitted to live.[3] Persons with mild mental retardation and without external deformities, however, were probably accommodated in productive tasks in primitive agriculture and industry. In those early periods, mental retardation was probably not differentiated from mental illness. The Jewish, Moslem, and early Christian traditions saw mentally retarded people as innocents who should be given care and protection. In the Middle Ages, however, they were gradually assumed to be a product of sin—that is, of the sexual union of a woman with the devil—and possessed by demons. In his writings, Martin Luther described a child with mental retardation, whom he saw as a changeling who should have been drowned.[3] Some towns cared for persons with mental retardation or mental illness in orphanages, poorhouses, or the equivalent of foster homes, such as in the town of Geel, Belgium. Many abandoned children with mental retardation were placed in hospitals where they had little chance of surviving. The modern care of persons with mental disorders, initiated at the end of the 18th century by Philipe Pinel in Paris, also affected the care of persons with mental retardation. His focus was on "moral" management (gentle and humane care, education, recreation), rather than on inducing obedience.[3] Paradoxically, in our times there are still some who focus primarily on "behavioral control" of persons with mental retardation, even by means of aversive behavioral modification. Itard, a student of Pinel, in his work with Victor, the "wild boy of Aveyron" (an abandoned, possibly autistic child), laid the foundation for the develop-

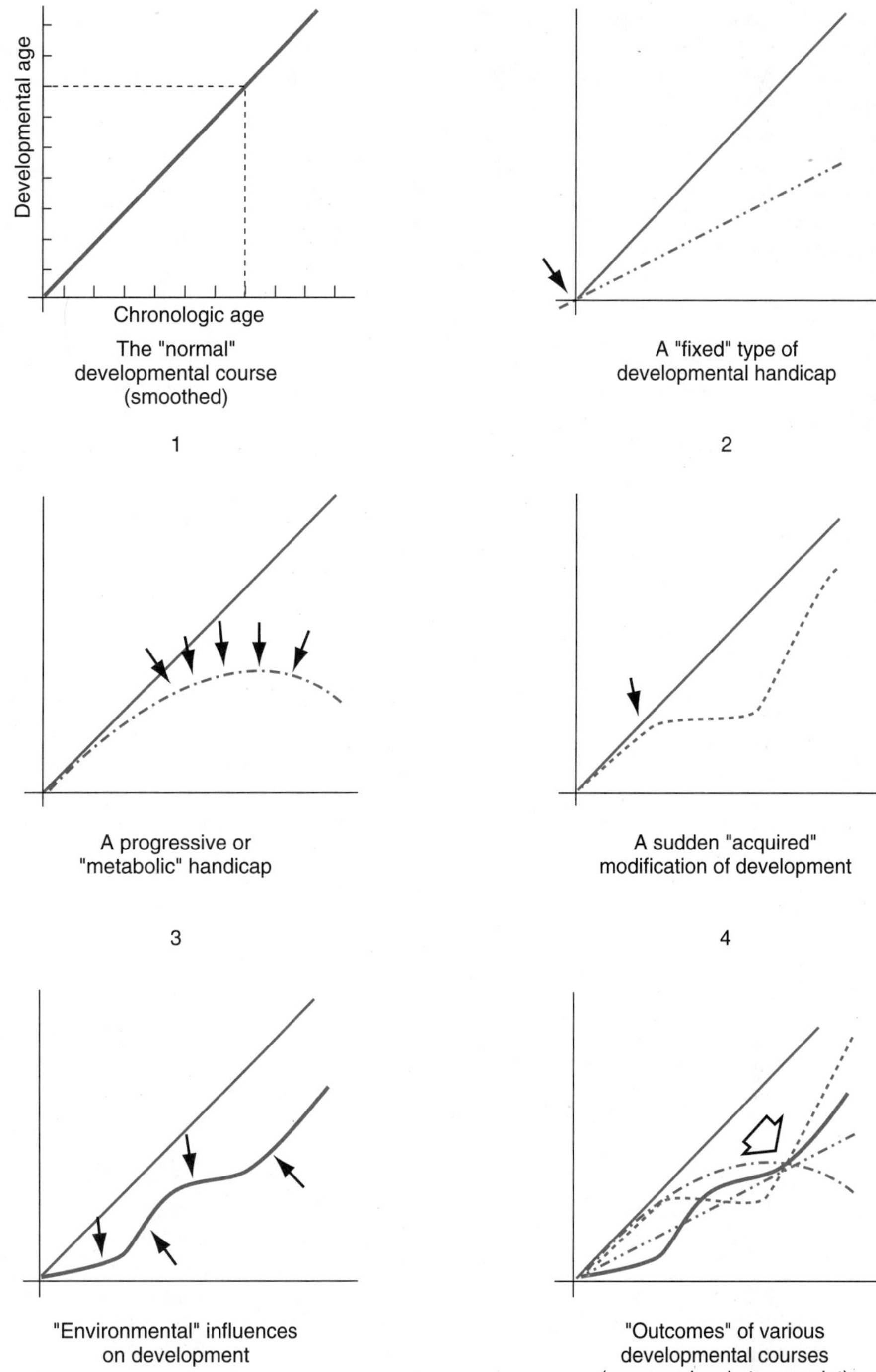

Figure 33–8 *Schematic representation of patterns of developmental disorders (arrows refer to the point of insult): 1) normal developmental course; 2) fixed, nonprogressive, type of developmental disorder; 3) metabolic type of disorder of development in which the manifestations of the underlying process (e.g., Tay-Sachs disease) occur after birth and evolve into a progressively deteriorating course; 4) acquired developmental disorder: the curve represents normal development up to a point of insult* (arrow) *to the CNS; 5) environmental disorder of development: a fluctuating course, with periods of stress* (downward arrows) *and periods of nurturance or positive intervention, or both* (upward arrows)*; 6) outcomes: the convergence* (arrow) *of the various developmental courses represents the point at which the physician becomes aware of the developmental disorder. (Adapted from Szymanski LS, Rubin LL, Tarjan G: Mental retardation. In Tasman A, Hales RE, Frances AJ [eds]: American Psychiatric Press Review of Psychiatry, Volume 8. Washington, DC: American Psychiatric Press, 1989:227.)*

ment of special education. Another of Pinel's students, Edouard Sequin, devoted his professional life to the study and treatment of mental retardation. His work formed the basis of the enlightened and educational approach to the care of persons with mental retardation and to the change of institutions from inhumane asylums to education-oriented schools.

In the colonial era, the American approach to mental retardation followed that of England. Persons with mental retardation were often lumped together with persons with mental illness and were kept in poorhouses or sometimes in hospitals or "farmed out" on public expense to the lowest bidder. Toward the middle of the century, developments in Europe started to influence the approach to mental retardation in the United States. The ideas of Sequin were the basis for the earliest school for children with mental retardation in the United States, which was established in 1847 by H. P. Wilbur in Barre, Massachusetts. In 1848, Sequin emigrated to the United States and was instrumental in the development of a number of special schools, as well as in founding (with six other physicians) the Association of the Officers of the American Institutions for Feeble Minded (currently the American Association on Mental Retardation) in 1876. Sequin viewed the mission of the residential facility as educating children with mental retardation (who could not be accommodated in schools in the community) and then returning them to their families. He advocated small institutions located in the students' communities as well as provision of services to children living with their families.[3] The first state-funded residential school was founded in Massachusetts by Samuel Gridley Howe, at first as a division of a school for the blind in 1848 and as a separate institution in 1855. Almost from the beginning, Howe was against inhumane treatment of persons with mental retardation, stating in a 1869 report to the Governor of Massachusetts: "it would be demonstrated that no idiot need be confined or restrained by force . . . ." Within the next 25 years, there were 15 public institutions.[3] At first they followed the precepts of Sequin's "moral treatment," but later they changed, reflecting the developments in medicine and in the society's perception of mental retardation. Several factors contributed to this.[31] Developments in neurology led to a more pessimistic view of mental retardation as being due to an incurable brain defect. Genealogical studies led to a mistaken belief that mental retardation was hereditary and associated with criminality and other social maladjustment. This was later reinforced with the introduction of intelligence testing, which "discovered" a high prevalence of persons with mild mental retardation (termed morons) among socially maladjusted persons (probably resulting from poverty and lack of education rather than mental retardation). Finally, with the introduction of psychoanalytic theories, psychiatrists became less interested in persons with mental retardation, who were seen as unable to benefit from dynamically oriented psychotherapy. As a result, institutions shifted from educating persons with mental retardation and protecting them from abuse to protecting the society from them. The period that followed, up to the first half of the 20th century, the "tragic interlude," witnessed the building of large institutions (although no more than 10% of persons with mental retardation were institutionalized at one time), the introduction of laws on involuntary sterilization, and segregated special education.[31]

A number of developments led to the next period, culminating in the current recognition of the rights of persons with mental retardation to services and inclusion in society. Research on the effects of attachment, and deprivation resulting from institutionalization, documented the environmental factors in the genesis of mental retardation, as well as the salutary effect of a stimulating environment and education.[32] In fact, it was a sort of a déjà vu of the work of Itard and Sequin. The U.S. Supreme Court 1954 decision in Brown v Board of Education ending racial segregation in schools, and the civil rights movement in general, sent the message that all kinds of segregation—educational and otherwise—were wrong. The work of a parents' organization (National Association for Retarded Citizens) and a variety of lawsuits led to a gradual improvement in institutions, to deinstitutionalization, and to community-based care.

The landmark lawsuits and legislation have been the following:

Wolf v Legislature of the State of Utah, 1969—all children have the right to public education regardless of the level of retardation.

Pennsylvania Association for Retarded Citizens v Commonwealth of Pennsylvania, 1971—every child can be educated; a requirement for appropriate medical and psychological evaluations was instituted.

Wyatt v Stickney, 1971 and follow-up cases—persons in institutions have a constitutional right to treatment: it set minimal standards, including staffing, medical care, and privacy; prohibited the indiscriminate use of psychotropic agents; and required the least restrictive setting.

Massachusetts Chapter 766, 1972—guarantees public education and all necessary services to all children 3 to 22 years of age; placement is according to service needs rather than diagnostic labeling, interdisciplinary core assessment with parents' participation, and educational plan specifying goals to be achieved. The parents have the right to reject the plan and appeal it.

O'Connor v Donaldson, 1975—individuals cannot be warehoused in custodial institutions.

Education for All Handicapped Children Act, PL 94-142, 1975, with later amendments known as IDEA (Individuals with Disabilities Education Act)—covers all children with disabilities from birth to age 21 years; provides the right to diagnostic,treatment, and support services for the child and the family; requires maximally feasible mainstreaming, periodic reassessments, and provision of an individualized education program.

Halderman v Pennhurst State Hospital and School, 1979 and follow-up cases—persons in institutions have a right to minimal habilitation and the least restrictive environment: it ordered closing of institutions and placement of their residents in the community. The currently active follow-up case focuses on provision of appropriate care in the community, including psychiatric care and avoidance of unnecessary use of psychotropic agents.

Many other court cases also ended with a consent decree requiring closure of the institutions as being unable to provide proper care. For instance, Michigan and New Hampshire no longer have public residential institutions.

Civil Rights of Institutionalized Persons Act (CRIPA), 1980—it gave authority to the U.S. Department of Justice to sue states to enforce constitutional rights of residents of state institutions.

Youngberg v Romeo, 1982—persons in institutions have the right to the provision of basic necessities, safety, training, habilitation, and freedom from unnecessary restraints.

Americans with Disabilities Act (ADA), 1992—prohibits discrimination in employment against persons with disabilities and requires reasonable accommodation for their special needs.

Overall Goals of Treatment of Mental Retardation

Strictly speaking, there is no specific treatment of mental retardation itself, although there might be treatments of underlying mental retardation–associated syndromes, (e.g., PKU) and of comorbid disorders (e.g., seizure disorder), if such are present. The interventions targeted at the mental retardation itself include a variety of educational, habilitative, and supportive approaches, depending on the person's individualized needs.

The current approach to the services for persons with mental retardation is based on the following principles:

- The *normalization principle*,[33] which refers to "making available to the mentally retarded patterns and conditions of everyday life that are as close as possible to the norms and patterns of the mainstream of society."
- The *right to community living,* which includes right to live with a family, preferably one's own or a substitute one if necessary (foster or adoptive).
  - No institutionalization of children, regardless of the level of retardation, and generally not of adults either. At present, some children are placed in special residential schools (usually private) for specific reasons, typically medical or behavioral needs that require specialized treatment.
  - Deinstitutionalization of adults and placement in as normal a setting as possible, for example, community residences, supervised apartments, and foster homes.
  - Education and training for all children, regardless of their disability and its degree, to a maximally possible extent in community-based programs. Mainstreaming, which refers to placement in special classes in regular schools but with participation in some activities of regular classes, rather than segregation in separate schools, has been the rule so far. The current trend is toward inclusion, which refers to full-time placement in an age-appropriate regular classroom, with the educational program being individualized according to the child's needs. Services of special educators and therapists, as necessary, are also provided in these programs.
  - Employment of adults in the community according to their abilities, ranging from sheltered workshops to the competitive job market, or occupational-recreational day programs for those with the most significant retardation.
  - Training to the maximal possible degree in the use of normal community services and facilities (shopping, banking, transportation).
  - Advocacy and appropriate protective measures, for example, against inappropriate use of pharmacological and behavioral measures as substitutes for active education and treatment.
  - Movement toward full inclusion, meaning the end of segregated services and education and provision of the specialized services in regular educational, living, and work settings.

Prevention of Mental Retardation

Primary Prevention

The goal of primary prevention is to prevent mental retardation from arising in the first place. To be effective, it should encompass medical, public health, educational, and other measures. Examples include immunizations to prevent congenital rubella, measles (encephalitis), and Rh mother-child incompatibility; measures to prevent lead poisoning and teenage pregnancies; provision of prenatal vitamin supplementation (to prevent neural tube defects); better neonatal care; and measures to prevent substance abuse in pregnancy and childhood trauma (e.g., the use of infant car seats). It is a question of personal values whether prenatal diagnosis and therapeutic abortion (e.g., if Down syndrome is found) would be called primary prevention, as childbirth rather than the disorder is prevented.

Secondary Prevention

Secondary prevention includes measures to recognize conditions that can lead to mental retardation as early as possible and to treat them to prevent retardation. Examples include the early diagnosis and treatment of PKU and other metabolic conditions and congenital hypothyroidism.

Tertiary Prevention

Tertiary prevention could be called habilitation as well[34] because it aims to attain a functional level that is as good as possible in the presence of mental retardation. It includes both biomedical and sociocultural measures, such as early intervention for disabled infants, proper education, multifaceted family support, and prevention or early treatment of medical complications that could reduce functioning (e.g., congenital cataracts and deafness in children with Down syndrome).

Prevention of Psychosocial Dysfunction

An essential part of tertiary prevention consists of preventing psychosocial dysfunction because mental disorders are an important cause of maladaptation in persons with mental retardation.[35] This category can also be subdivided. Primary prevention includes proper education and employment and opportunities to achieve in life so that the person can develop a sense of self-worth and self-esteem; training in social skills and sexuality; and provision of appropriate social supports and recreation. Secondary prevention includes early diagnosis and treatment of emerging mental disorders rather than a focus on behavioral crisis intervention only. Tertiary prevention includes good psychiatric care and habilitation as well as a proper milieu when a person has a chronic mental illness (including substance abuse) that requires continuous care. In all situations, prevention has to include measures directed both at the person and at the environment (caregivers, services, public policies).

MENTAL DISORDERS IN PERSONS WITH MENTAL RETARDATION

Persons with mental retardation have the same mental disorders as persons in the general population; thus, the discussion of definitions, etiology, pathophysiology, natural

Table 33–6 Prevalence of Psychopathology in the Mentally Retarded: Representative Epidemiological Samples*†

Study	Age (y)	Sample Characteristics	Assessment Procedure	Psychopathology: Mental Retardation Subjects	Psychopathology: Non-Mental Retardation Control Subjects
Rutter et al[38]	9–11	Entire age cohort, Isle of Wight	Parent and teacher behavioral scales; interviews; multiaxial criteria	30%–42%	6%–7%
Gillberg et al[39]	3–17	Representative 4-y birth cohort (144 Ss) from a city in Sweden	Structured parent, subject psychiatric interviews, behavioral observations: DSM-III criteria	57% of 83 mild MR 64% of 66 severe MR	None
Koller et al[40, 41]	Childhood adolescence	4-y birth cohort receiving MR services	Retrospective review of clinical information	36% school children 30% adolescents	5%
Jacobson[42]	Children and adults	Population receiving services for MR in New York state	Survey of behavioral frequency data	14% children 17% adults	None
Gath and Gumley[43]	6–17	All children with DS residing in one health region in England and matched MR comparisons	Semistructured parent and teacher interviews, behavior rating scales, and ICD-9	38% DS children 49% MR comparisons	None
Lund[44]	≥20	Cluster sample of total Danish MR population, National Registry	Adaptive and maladaptive behavior schedules; clinical interviews; DSM-III	27%	None
Iverson and Fox[45]	≥21	Random stratified sample of 165 Ss drawn from those receiving MR services in a midwestern county	Psychopathology Instrument for MR Adults (PIMRA), client or informant response; DSM-III criteria	36% total 55% mild MR 32% moderate MR 26% S-PMR	None
Gostason[46]	20–60	Random stratified sample of 122 Ss residing in a Swedish county, located in a national registry	Psychopathology rating scale; Eysenck Personality Inventory; psychiatric interviews; DSM-III criteria	33% mild MR 71% severe MR	23%

*The studies included subjects with mild to severe mental retardation.

†MR, mental retardation; DS, Down syndrome; S-PMR, severe to profound MR; Ss, subjects; ICD-9, International Classification of Diseases, 9th revision.

From Bregman JD: Current developments in the understanding of mental retardation. Part II: Psychopathology. J Am Acad Child Adolesc Psychiatry 1991; 30:861–872.

history, and so on of these disorders elsewhere in this textbook applies here as well. Therefore, this section focuses on only those aspects that are modified by the presence of mental retardation.

Epidemiology of Mental Disorders in Persons with Mental Retardation

Most, if not all, existing prevalence studies are affected by a methodological bias. The most common is biased selection of the study cohort, such as a clinic population referred because of behavior problems. Even studies that focus on unselected populations, such as persons in community-based programs, miss individuals who are not able to attend such programs (or are not accepted by them), most often because of behavior problems.

Inconsistent use of diagnostic criteria of mental disorders, particularly before the publication of the *Diagnostic and Statistical Manual of Mental Disorders,* Third Edition (DSM-III), has been common. Some large-scale studies used diagnoses reported to a state office by psychiatrists in institutions without consideration of the manner in which such diagnoses were made. Another phenomenon has been "diagnostic overshadowing"—when clinicians know that a person has mental retardation, they tend to overlook the comorbid mental disorder.[36]

The early study on an unselected population on the Isle of Wight found that the prevalence of mental disorders in children with mental retardation was several times higher than that in children without retardation.[37] The more recent population-based studies also found the prevalence was up to 70%, significantly higher than that in the general population. The prevalence has generally been higher in persons with a more severe degree of retardation. The representative studies are summarized in Table 33–6.[38–46] Virtually all types of mental disorders have been described in persons with mental retardation.

Diagnosis of Mental Disorders in Persons with Mental Retardation

Phenomenology and Variations in Presentation

There is no evidence that mental disorders seen in persons who have mental retardation are basically different from mental disorders seen in the general population. However, the clinical manifestations may be modified by the cognitive impairment; communication skills; associated sensory, motor, and other disabilities; life experiences and circumstances; and so on. The most important factor is the presence or absence of verbal language. Many diagnostic criteria are based on a person's verbal communications. For instance, it might be impossible to recognize the presence of thought disorder in a nonverbal person (similar problems are encountered with young children). The successive editions of the DSM have tried to circumvent this problem in different ways. Psychiatrists have been advised to assess the symptoms in comparison to persons at a comparable level of development (attention-deficit/hyperactivity disorder, DSM-IV[1a (p78)]). If a person cannot describe his or her own mood, observations made by others can be substituted (major depressive episode, DSM-IV[1a (p327)]). The DSM-IV also has "monosymptomatic" disorders, based on a single clinical symptom, which does not seem to be part of another mental disorder (e.g., stereotypic movement disorder). As a last resort, a not otherwise specified (NOS) category can be used. In a majority of cases, if not all, careful consideration and assessment can find an appropriate DSM-IV category that best categorizes the patient's clinical presentation.

A common concern and the reason for referral for psychiatric consultation is whether a person with mental retardation has a behavior disorder or a mental disorder (dual diagnosis). Although there is no clear definition of behavior disorder, it is usually meant to refer to a deliberate misbehavior, learned response, and attention-getting behavior. However, in the clinical presentation of every defined mental disorder, there might be elements of learned behavior—for example, caused by the responses of persons in the patient's environment. Furthermore, the concept of mental disorder in the DSM-IV does include behavioral manifestations as well as is atheoretical: the diagnosis is not made on the basis of causation unless it is clear, such as in the "due to general medical condition" category. Thus, it is preferable to avoid dichotomizing abnormal behaviors into "behavior" and "mental" disorders, but rather to try to decide which mental disorder syndrome the behavioral manifestations are part of.[47]

The term *dual diagnosis* although used frequently when mental illness and mental retardation coexist, is not helpful. For most mental health professionals, it refers to comorbidity of mental illness and substance abuse. Often it is used to classify persons, rather than their disorders, and may lead to rejection of a person so labeled from an otherwise appropriate program.[48]

Assessment

Special Issues in the Psychiatric History and Examination

The basic principles of the psychiatric diagnostic assessment of persons who have mental retardation are the same as those of persons who do not have mental retardation. What is needed is the modification of usual clinical techniques, according to the patient's discrete developmental levels in various domains, and in particular communication skills.[49]

Reasons for Referral

There are several major differences between referral to a psychiatrist of a person with mental retardation and one without. The first difference is who initiates the referral. Most persons with mental retardation do not come to the psychiatrist because they want to; they come because they are brought in by concerned caregivers (family or nonfamily). The second difference is the general nature of the presenting problem. Most frequently, it is a behavior disruptive to others or a decline in adaptive functioning. Thus, the primary reason for the referral is because the patient disturbs others, rather than because the patient is disturbed. In fact, she or he may not be disturbed at all, and the behavior might reflect appropriate adaptation to inappropriate conditions. A typical example is when a person who has mental retardation and lives in an understaffed facility discovers that the overworked staff will give attention first to persons who are disruptive rather than to those who are quiet. Thus, an individual who has depressive disorder might be neglected, whereas one who is just bored will be noticed. The third difference is what the caregiver or caregivers expect from the psychiatrist. Usually they focus on the disturbing behavior only. Frequently, the expectation is for a quick "medication review," for example, a suggestion for a drug that has not yet been tried to control only the behavior in question, regardless of the broader clinical presentation. Obviously, this approach is inappropriate because the psychiatrist, being a physician, evaluates (and treats) patients, not drugs.

The "Multi" Principle

This principle refers to the fact that persons with mental retardation usually depend on multiple providers for multiple services because of multiple needs and problems (Table 33–7). Not all needs and problems listed in Table 33–7 apply at all times to all individuals, but their relevance to the particular situation has to be carefully considered. In accordance with the principle of biopsychosocial integration, all these factors and their mutual interaction and contribution to the patient's problems and general functioning must be considered. Thus, the presenting problems must be assessed in the comprehensive context of a patient's abilities and disabilities and not as an isolated issue.[2]

Table 33–7 The Multi Principle (Persons with Mental Retardation Have Multiple Needs)

Caregivers and providers	Parents, family, teachers, attendants, counselors, supervisors, physicians
Disabilities	Cognitive, specific learning, sensory, motor, language, associated medical
Need to learn	Self-care, communication, use of community services, recreation, self-direction, social skills
Need therapies	Various medical, language, physical, occupational, vocational
Need opportunities	Work or education, or both, recreation, social, coordinated health care

Approaches to Obtaining a History

All involved caregivers should be interviewed if possible (parents, teachers, direct care workers, supervisors in workshops). Direct care staff members (e.g., from the group home and workshop supervisors) are particularly important because they can provide a firsthand description of a person's behavior. Exploring the following areas is important:

Present Illness

Reasons for Current Referral. Each of the caregivers may have different overt and hidden agendas. Some may see the patients as deliberately striving to get attention, not as mentally ill. Others might see the patients as ill and expect a magic medication that will cure the behaviors in question, without any changes in milieu, even if the patient's current program is deficient. Exploring the length of time that symptoms have been present might disclose that they have existed for a long time but that the referral has happened only now because of caregiver burnout, reduction in staffing in the facility, and so on.

Behavioral Symptoms. Concrete, longitudinal data and a factual description of events (not only opinions) should be obtained. They should be correlated with concurrent events in the person's environment and treatment interventions. Often, concrete behavioral data already exist, having been collected by behavioral psychologists at the school, workshop, or group home. Converting them into a graph is most helpful, as it permits correlation with other events and might disclose a cyclical nature of the presenting symptoms.

It is important to find out in what situations the presenting symptoms occur as well as in what situations they do not occur. For instance, it is not uncommon to find that an individual acts aggressively at the (understaffed) group home but not at the workshop, where structure and interesting tasks are offered. Obviously, a psychotropic medication is not an answer in this case.

Psychotropic Medication History. This history is essential. Unfortunately, caregivers often provide only a list of drugs, dosages, and starting and discontinuation dates, without information about the reasons they were prescribed and their effects.

General History

Nature of the Disability. Past assessments should be critically reviewed and new ones requested if needed. Many older individuals did not have access to adequate scrutiny of the cause of retardation, and even if they did, it might not reflect genetic and other advances that have occurred since the assessment was made. For instance, chromosomal analysis before the early 1980s could not have disclosed fragile X syndrome. The general adaptive behavior and the skills in various domains should be reviewed, considering strengths and deficits in all critical areas.

Past and Current Services. Educational and vocational services and the current program of behavioral management, if any, should be evaluated in terms of appropriateness, consistency, and effectiveness. Often a referral is made to the psychiatrist with the request that he or she prescribe a "chemical restraint" to "control aggression," because the "behavioral program" did not work. A detailed history might disclose, for instance, that the aggression happens only when the person is forced to engage in a workshop in table tasks, which are too difficult considering the person's poor fine motor skills and developmentally short attention span, being rewarded with tokens weekly, which is too long a period for the person with significant mental retardation to understand the relevance of the reward to behavior.

Milieu Events. One should not assume that important past events will be reported spontaneously. Systematic exploration might be required to find out about important events such as losses (e.g., siblings moving out of the house), relocations (e.g., to a group home), or sexual abuse (as suggested by behavioral changes similar to those seen in sexually abused children).

The Family. The knowledge, understanding, and reaction of family members (including siblings) to the patient's disabilities should be explored tactfully. The psychiatrist should be careful not to convey personal feelings through the questions, such as expressing condolences for their having a child with mental retardation, whereas the parents might see the care of the child as a positive challenge. In particular, the parents should not be viewed as patients, and their normal "chronic sorrow" should not be confused with pathological depression.[50] The family members' patterns of management of the patient should be explored in terms of limit setting, consistency, appropriateness of expectations to the patient's abilities, capability to advocate for services, and participation in support activities such as parents' organizations. Another important topic is the parents' ability to balance the needs of the child with mental retardation with the needs of other children.

Approaches to the Patient's Interview

The way in which the patient's interview is approached will depend on the patient's communication skills and might range from an age-appropriate verbal interview to observation only. Thus, the communication skills have to be explored first through brief, noncommittal conversation and questioning of the caregivers. If necessary, the caregivers might be used as interpreters of the patient's poorly intelligible speech or sign language. Directiveness and structure are often necessary to help the patient focus, but leading questions or suppression of spontaneous expression must be avoided. If necessary, firm and clear behavioral limits should be established at the interview's onset. Verbal and social reinforcement, as appropriate for developmental age, are helpful to let the patient know that the interviewer is appreciative of her or his abilities. The patients should be approached respectfully—if possible in a manner appropriate to the chronological age—and not as "eternal children." However, communication with them should be on the level they can understand, and their understanding should be ascertained. For instance, persons with mental retardation are afraid to be perceived as inadequate and instead of saying that they did not understand the question, they tend to agree with the interviewer's last statement. Thus, asking open-ended questions is preferable to giving a choice of answers.

Nonverbal interviewing techniques include behavioral observations, spontaneous and directed (structured) play (as developmentally and age appropriate), and other structured tasks.

Functional Analysis of Behavior

The functional analysis of behavior usually refers to systematic collection and interpretation of data on the antecedents and consequences of the behaviors of the person in question. It is important that the focus be broad, not only on immediate events but also on settings and underlying events. For instance, a person might acquire an SIB when demands are made to perform in a workshop, and the result might be that he or she is permitted to abandon the task. More extended analysis might show, however, that there was no such behavior in the past and that it has been occurring since the person was given new tasks that are too difficult.

Evaluation of Clinical Data

The clinical observations should be interpreted in light of a patient's life experiences, learning, understanding, and communication level. The global IQ or overall mental age alone is not a good guide here. In particular, the psychiatrist should

1. Differentiate between behaviors appropriate for an earlier age and those that are pathological in any age (e.g., true hallucinations).
2. Avoid over- or underdiagnosing mental disorders. It should be kept in mind that not all behaviors that disturb others are an expression of a true mental disorder: an overworked staff might promote aggressive acting out by attending to the patients only when they become aggressive. Some SIBs, such as a nonverbal person hitting herself or himself in the head, might be a result of a painful physical condition, such as an ear infection, and are in a sense a way of communicating discomfort. Conversely, one should not forget that mental retardation does not provide immunity from mental disorders (in fact, it predisposes to them), and one should not simply explain all such behaviors as attention-getting behaviors.
3. Try to make a formal Axis I and/or Axis II DSM-IV diagnosis (besides mental retardation) whenever clinically justified. The diagnostic criteria can usually be adapted to the patient's developmental level (just as one does with child patients), as delineated further on.
4. Assess the strengths, impairments, and need for supports and services in each discrete domain of the patient's functioning, as well as in the environment (community and family).
5. Obtain, if needed, evaluations and consultations with those in other disciplines—for example, language pathologists, psychologists, and neurologists.
6. Assess and understand, most importantly, the dynamic, ongoing transactional relationships among the various factors contributing to the persons's development (see Fig. 33–6).

Diagnosis of Specific Mental Disorders

Mental Disorders due to a General Medical Condition

In the DSM-IV, the term *due to a general medical condition* replaces the time-honored *organic* of previous editions. The latter was intended to be used only when both the presence of an organic factor and its etiological relationship to the mental disorder could be demonstrated. However, this category had often been used inappropriately as a "basket" diagnosis on the presumption that if the person had mental retardation, which is the result of CNS dysfunction, a coexisting mental disorder was the product of the same neuropathological condition. Such reasoning might be used, for instance, if a car accident at the age of 10 years caused brain injury that resulted in mental retardation and an emergence of personality features consistent with the particular type of neuropathological condition. It would not be be appropriate, for example, if a person had congenital mental retardation and manifested symptoms consistent with psychotic disorder at the age of 15 years. Thus, the elimination of the organic category in the DSM-IV might improve the diagnostic accuracy of mental disorders comorbid with mental retardation.

For mental disorder due to a general medical condition, the specific diagnosis of the medical disorder is coded on Axis III. The disorders that were in one section (organic mental disorders) in the DSM-III can be found in several sections in the DSM-IV. Most of them are now in the sections on categories of disorders—for example, mood disorders, anxiety disorders, and so on. If the criteria for a given disorder are met, as well as those for the disorder due to a general medical condition, the appropriate diagnosis might be, for instance, mood disorder due to . . . (the general medical condition to be specified). Three disorders due to a general medical condition are in a separate section (catatonic disorder, personality change, and mental disorder NOS). Delirium, dementia, and amnestic and other cognitive disorders are also in a separate section. All substance-related disorders are now in one section.

Similar to the DSM-III, the DSM-IV requires "the presence of mental symptoms that are judged to be the direct physiological consequence of a general medical condition."[1a] Not diagnosing "organicity" does not mean that the symptoms are not dependent on the CNS dysfunction.

Relationship of the Diagnoses of Mental Retardation and Dementia

Mental retardation can be diagnosed only if the onset is before age 18 years, whereas dementia can be (technically) diagnosed at any age. However, the diagnosis of dementia does not depend simply on the presence of a low IQ and poor adaptive skills: both a memory impairment and at least one other specified cognitive disturbance representing a decline from a previous level of functioning must be present. Because this might be difficult to determine in extremely young children, it is advised that making a diagnosis of dementia concurrent with mental retardation might not be appropriate before 4 to 6 years of age if the condition is sufficiently characterized by the diagnosis of mental retardation alone. This approach avoids an automatic double diagnosis in all cases of mental retardation from an acquired postnatal cause.

Side Effects of Medications

The side effects of medication are of importance in this population, as the use of various drugs is frequent because of associated medical, neurological, and mental disorders. Common examples include hyperactivity resulting sometimes from phenobarbital used as an anticonvulsant, depression associated with β-blockers prescribed "for aggression," and behavioral symptoms associated with withdrawal from antipsychotic agents. In the DSM-IV, these conditions might be coded as medication-induced movement disorders, other medication-induced disorder, or a substance-induced disorder under the particular category (such as mood disorders).

Disorders with Onset in Infancy, Childhood, and Adolescence

Pervasive Developmental Disorders

PDDs are often confused with mental retardation, especially when there is an impairment or lack of speech and self-stimulatory behaviors, which may also be present in significant retardation. In PDD, however, there is major impairment in interpersonal reciprocal interaction and in interpersonal communication. Conversely, persons with uncomplicated mental retardation have an ability to relate to others (according to their developmental level) and have at least some interpersonal communication skills, whether verbal or nonverbal. Mental retardation is frequently associated with these disorders: about 75% to 80% of children who have autistic disorder also have mental retardation. Thus, mental retardation and a PDD are not mutually exclusive, and the correct differential diagnostic question is whether the person has a PDD and whether it is associated with mental retardation. The DSM-IV subdivides PDD into autistic disorder, Asperger's disorder, PDD NOS, Rett's disorder, and childhood disintegrative disorder. In the last two disorders (introduced in the DSM-IV), psychomotor retardation or major skill loss is a diagnostic feature.

A detailed developmental and current history and good interviewing and observation of the patient, sometimes on several separate occasions, may be necessary to properly assess a PDD.

Attention-Deficit/Hyperactivity Disorder

Persons of any age who have mental retardation are frequently referred to a psychiatrist because of a short attention span.[51] Not attending might be situational, for example, related to the task being too difficult or too boring. In such cases, milieu changes rather than medications should be used.

In the DSM-IV, the majority of the criteria for this category are based on manifested behaviors and thus can be used even with nonverbal persons. The criteria clearly state that the symptoms must be inconsistent with the developmental level. Thus, a high level of activity and short attention span in a 6-year-old child with severe mental retardation who has learned to walk recently and busily explores the environment is not necessarily pathological.

Stereotypic Movement Disorder

This category is most frequently used with persons who have mental retardation if a stereotypic behavior is leading to significant functional impairment, if it is the focus of treatment, and if it is not better described by another diagnosis. Thus, not all self-stimulatory behaviors often seen in persons with mental retardation qualify for this diagnosis. The DSM-IV permits adding a specifier "with self-injurious behavior." SIB is one of the major reasons for psychiatric referral in this population. It is defined as repetitive behavior resulting in tissue damage that requires medical treatment and that is not better described by other diagnoses. Examples include head banging, biting oneself, hitting oneself, and picking at skin and body orifices. The prevalence is thought to be up to 3% of the persons with mental retardation but it varies, the highest prevalence being in persons with severe or profound retardation who live in institutions. Risk factors (besides severity of retardation) include blindness, PDDs, and certain mental retardation syndromes, such as Lesch-Nyhan syndrome. Current studies are investigating the possible role of endogenous opioids[52] and serotonin systems in association with compulsive behaviors.[53] However, the cause of the final clinical presentation is usually multifactorial and, besides biological factors, may include learned responses to an environmental situation and coexisting other psychopathological conditions such as depression and psychosis. Thus, a comprehensive assessment of all possible factors is needed.[54]

Schizophrenia and Other Psychotic Disorders

In the early years of psychiatry, the differentiation between mental retardation and psychosis was not clear; in particular, the self-stimulatory motor behaviors of persons with significant retardation were confused with catatonia.

The current diagnostic criteria for psychotic disorders including schizophrenia list delusions, hallucinations, and disorganized speech, the manifestation of which requires a certain degree of verbal language. However, the presence of grossly disorganized behavior coexisting with negative symptoms might be sufficient for the diagnosis of schizophrenia. Sometimes the person's behavior and affect might give a clue as to whether she or he is responding to visual or auditory hallucinations. In persons with some verbal language, evidence of hallucinations or delusions might be detected with careful interviewing and observation that avoid leading questions. For instance, one person with mild retardation when asked if he "heard voices," answered in the affirmative, later clarifying that he "was not deaf." Talking to oneself, which is seen in some persons with mental retardation, is similar to such behavior in young children who rehash the day's events or talk to an imaginary friend, but there is no evidence that they respond to actual auditory hallucinations. However, the nature of the hallucinations or delusions cannot be assessed unless the person has good language abilities; thus, diagnosis of a subtype of schizophrenia is not possible, and a more general category including psychotic disorder NOS has to be used.

The lower the patient's language abilities, the more the diagnosis has to rely on behavioral and affective manifestations. In fact, it had been suggested that an accurate diagnosis of schizophrenia may not be possible in persons with an IQ less than 50.[55] Conversely, in persons with mild mental retardation and good language capacities, the clinical presentation and diagnosis of schizophrenia are similar to those in persons without mental retardation, although the content of delusional thinking might be less sophisticated. However, one should not confuse the concreteness of thinking due to reduced cognition, with thought disorder of psychosis. Isolated, unusual beliefs have to be assessed in the context of the patient's learning, explanations received previously, and the patient's culture and cognitive ability to understand that these beliefs are unusual. Thus, the whole clinical picture, rather than single symptoms, has to be considered.[56] For instance, a child with mild to moderate mental retardation might truly believe that he hears a voice of a deceased parent admonishing him if he had been taught earlier that he might have such an experience. A good longitudinal history from caregivers who are familiar with the patient should help decide whether these features have been always present or emerged at a certain point in life and have been associated with a functional decline.

Mood Disorders

Mood disorders, depression in particular, had been rarely diagnosed in the past in persons with mental retardation because of several factors.[2] First, it had been thought that these individuals cannot become depressed because of insufficient intelligence[57] or, as viewed by some behaviorists, that their behavior problems were learned as a result of environmental deprivation (both these views denied in effect that these persons could have normal human emotions). Second, poor language capacities made the diagnosis difficult. Third, depressed persons who were disturbed but did not disturb others were often unnoticed in understaffed facilities. However, case reports on depression in persons with mental retardation had been appearing, and on review of the literature it was found that there was sufficient evidence that depression did occur often in this population.[58] The prevalence of mood disorders in persons with mental retardation and in the general population is thought to be similar.[59] The majority of the DSM-IV diagnostic criteria for major depression and for manic episodes can be well used, even if language is poorly developed: the depressed mood can be observed and reported by others, and vegetative signs and other behaviors can be observed as well. Persons with better language skills can usually report on feeling depressed, worthless, and so on. Some individuals are referred primarily because of aggressive and other disruptive behaviors.[59] A person with undiagnosed depression who is pressed to perform but lacks the means to explain how she or he feels might strike out in a manner of defending herself or himself. The nature of the behavior in manic episodes will, of course, also be affected by a person's adaptive skills and opportunities: an individual with no money or credit cards will not go on shopping sprees. There is a correlation between depressed mood and poor social skills and supports.[60] The "relocation syndrome" in persons abruptly moved to a new facility might actually be a form of depression.[2] In persons with Down syndrome, the differential diagnosis of depression will include hypothyroidism and Alzheimer-type dementia, for which these individuals are at risk. In uncomplicated depression, there is usually no evidence of loss of memory. The individual might be noncompliant and may not perform even familiar tasks, but this occurs because of lack of motivation. In dementia, a person may attempt to do a task but will not remember its details. Vegetative symptoms, depressed mood, and anhedonia will support the diagnosis of depression. The diagnosis is more difficult when depression accompanies dementia.

Anxiety Disorders

As with other mental disorders, anxiety disorders in persons with mild mental retardation and good language skills are diagnosed in essentially the same manner as in the general population. If the language skills are poor, the diagnosis is more difficult, but many DSM-IV criteria are based on observable behaviors. Generalized anxiety disorder is manifested by restlessness, reduced concentration, irritability, muscular tension, and sleep disturbance. The worrying, if not verbalized, will have to be inferred from general behavior. Posttraumatic stress disorder might often go undiagnosed in this population if the individual cannot report what had happened to him or her. The clinical presentation is similar to that seen in young children who have been abused. The DSM-IV stresses the nature of the person's response and not just the nature of the event that was experienced. Thus, a person who was nonviolently sexually exploited and had no negative response to the experience may not show all signs of posttraumatic stress disorder, even though the event constituted an abuse. Phobias have been described in this population. In fears related to certain places or individuals, the possibility of posttraumatic stress disorder (e.g., caused by abuse that the person cannot describe) has to be considered. Obsessive-compulsive disorder may be difficult to diagnose if the person does not have sufficient language to describe the persistent thoughts that cause the anxiety, which the compulsions are designed to prevent. Thus, some compulsive-appearing stereotypes seen in this population might have to be diagnosed as stereotypic movement disorder if they are the focus of treatment. Adherence to routines might be also adaptive and even encouraged by the caregivers.

Personality Disorders

Over the years, many myths have accumulated concerning the personality patterns of persons with mental retardation—that they have uniform personality features resulting from organic brain damage and that they all are aggressive, passive, dependent, and so on. Actually, these persons display a spectrum of personality traits that is as wide as that in the general population. Three factors that are generally common to persons with mental retardation and might influence their behavioral traits have been suggested: cognitive deficits (underlying, for instance, concrete thinking), neurological dysfunction (sometimes leading to a short attention span in persons with significant retardation), and environmental experiences.[2] The DSM-IV differentiates between personality traits and personality disorders. The former are "enduring patterns of perceiving, relating to, and thinking about the environment and oneself. . . ."[1a] Thus, they are part of a person's uniqueness and are not necessarily maladaptive. In contrast, personality disorders are diagnosed when the traits are maladaptive and inflexible and lead to significant distress or impairment in functioning. Usually they are diagnosed in adolescence or early adulthood, but if they are diagnosed before age 18 years, the symptoms must have been present for at least 1 year. They are assessed in the context of a person's culture, age, social background, habits, customs, and values. This is particularly relevant in the case of persons who have mental retardation and whose learning and living opportunities were unusual—for example, living in institutions or being sheltered by their families. The caregivers not infrequently reward passivity, dependence, and overcompliance. The depriving institutional environments teach the individual that disruptive behavior brings attention from the staff, even if the attention is negative. The reactions of the important persons and realization of the differences between oneself and one's peers often lead to a low self-image. The last is probably the closest to a universal personality feature of persons with mental retardation.

Various studies have described maladaptive personality features in 22% to 56% of persons with mental retardation, which have been seen as underlying the high prevalence of psychopathological conditions in this population.[59] All types of personality disorders might be seen. The diagnosis of dependent personality disorder might be difficult because dependency on others might be based on reality resulting from a lack of various skills. Avoidance traits may be seen in persons with fragile X syndrome, who also avert their gaze and are prone to anxiety. Borderline personality disorder might be seen in persons with a mild degree of retardation.

Aggression

"Aggression" is one of the most frequent reasons (if not the most frequent) for referring persons with mental retardation to a psychiatrist. On closer investigation, the actual behavior ranges from occasional swearing (verbal aggression) to serious violence. However, there is no single entity called aggression in this population that would have one explanation. It would be a gross mistake for a psychiatrist to talk about a single treatment for aggression (except for symptomatic emergency measures). Different factors must be considered in assessing the cause of aggressive behavior. It might be associated with a defined mental disorder, for example, aggression following a command hallucination, paranoid delusion, anxiety, borderline or antisocial personality, or depression. The factor of learning will reinforce aggressive behavior if it brings a desired response by the caregivers. A pathological brain condition, such as rage attacks after brain trauma or associated with temporolimbic seizure disorder, may also lead to aggression. Often, the causation follows the multi principle, and several factors are involved, all of which require evaluation and intervention.

The DSM-IV has a category of intermittent explosive disorder that can be used provided that another mental disorder has been ruled out.

Adjustment Disorders

Emotional or behavioral symptoms that are a response to a stressor, that cause distress or functional impairment, and that are not related to another Axis I disorder are categorized as adjustment disorders. It might be appropriate, for instance, when a person is precipitously moved to an unfamiliar setting, becomes confused and anxious, and exhibits maladaptive behavior. Another example might be when an adolescent with mild mental retardation is teased, called a "retard," and told that he or she will never have a girlfriend or boyfriend or live independently. In such situations, a variety of behaviors emerge, ranging from depressed mood to pseudoadolescent acting out. The condition might become chronic because the stressor never really disappears.

Overall Goals of Psychiatric Treatment of Persons with Mental Retardation

The most common mistake made by psychiatrists treating persons with mental retardation is to treat (usually with medications) single problems (usually disruptive behaviors leading to referral) and to ignore other possible problems and interventions or, at best, to assume that they are taken care of by someone else. This can be avoided by performing an adequate diagnostic assessment that follows the multi principle and considering the interaction of the various factors (see Fig. 33–6). The goal of treatment, like any other medical intervention, should not be simply to remove the offending symptom but to help the patient achieve a realistically optimal quality of life. This is not to say that the psychiatrist should be responsible for behavioral modification or vocational rehabilitation, but these approaches should be closely coordinated with specific psychiatric treatments and should be targeted toward the common therapeutic goal.

Prerequisites for a Successful Treatment Program

1. *Comprehensive diagnostic understanding.* This should follow the guidelines described earlier. The purpose is not to elucidate and treat a single diagnosis (e.g., treating depression with an antidepressant) but to understand all factors causing and perpetuating the problem, which should be eliminated, and the patient's strengths, which should be developed.
2. *Developing goals of treatment.* Both the ultimate goal and the intermediate objectives should be established. For instance, the ultimate goal might be elimination of depression and preparation for a move to semiindependent living. The intermediate goals might include amelioration of insomnia, anhedonia, and aggressive outbursts.
3. *Developing treatment priorities.* If possible, less intrusive and simpler approaches might be tried first, for example, manipulation of the milieu. If these efforts are unsuccessful, other approaches might be tried, for example, medications. Often the treatments have a synergistic effect and should be used together. For instance, stimulants might improve a person's attention and reduce impulsivity, making the patient more responsive to behavioral therapy that teaches methods of appropriately expressing refusal rather than through aggression.
4. *Monitoring treatment results.* Because multiple caregivers may be involved, it may be difficult to obtain consistent follow-up data. Using a behavioral rating scale, or even developing a simple one for a particular patient, helps measure the behaviors or symptoms and monitor progress.
5. *Avoidance of indefinite treatment.* The treatment should be result driven, that is, it should be continued as long as it can be proved, by measurable results, to be effective.
6. *Team collaboration.* All involved caregivers, including family and professionals, should be in agreement about the nature, goals, side effects, and results of the treatment. This can be achieved by open discussion and education and is especially important when psychotropic drugs are used. If some difference of opinion remains concerning which treatment should be used, the team can agree on the order in which the various approaches should be tried (usually the least intrusive ones are used first).

Pharmacotherapy

General Considerations

Pharmocotherapeutic agents, antipsychotic medications in particular, have a sad history of indiscriminate use, or rather abuse, in persons with mental retardation, especially those in institutions. They were used primarily for their side effects—to induce docility, nonspecifically, for a variety of behaviors, even if the behaviors were appropriate reactions to abnormal, understaffed, institutional, depriving environments.[61] At the height of the institutional era, more than half the persons with mental retardation living in institutions received psychotropic drugs and more than half of the drugs were antipsychotic agents.[62] As a result, there was a backlash, mostly by nonmedical professionals, that resulted in hostility to the use of any medications, even if they were clearly indicated for the treatment of a diagnosed mental disorder. Such attitudes are still often encountered, in effect denying persons with mental retardation the appropriate treatment for mental disorders they may have. Medicare regulations still refer to the use of drugs to control inappropriate behaviors rather than to treat mental illness. There is still a sort of "numbers game," with the percentage of individuals in a program who are receiving psychotropic agents being seen as an indicator of program quality (the lower, the better). With well-adjusted persons being transferred to the community, however, institutions are becoming de facto mental hospitals; thus, it is no surprise that many persons there need to be given these drugs. The issue, instead, is how many persons receiving drugs do not need them and how many not receiving drugs would benefit from them.

Research on the effectiveness of psychotropic drugs in persons with mental retardation has been affected by methodological shortcomings, such as small sample size, lack of control groups, treatment of nonspecific symptoms, lack of consistent diagnostic assessment, and possible tendency not to report negative findings.[63] Virtually no study employed control groups of persons without mental retardation but with the same mental disorder.

The use of psychotropic drugs for persons with mental retardation does not differ from that for persons without mental retardation. Therefore, because psychopharmacology is dealt with extensively elsewhere in this book, only some issues relevant to persons with mental retardation are mentioned in this section.

There is no evidence that there is a different response to psychotropic drugs in persons with and those without mental retardation, all other factors being equal.[63] Yet, most of the existing studies refer to the effectiveness of a drug in "the retarded" with a particular problem, as if it were different in the presence of retardation. What is different is the difficulty of making an accurate diagnosis and the need for several concurrent interventions.

Persons not identified as having mental retardation are usually treated with drugs for major depression, schizophrenia, and so on. Unfortunately it is still a common practice to prescribe psychotropic agents for persons with mental retardation nonspecifically "for behaviors." In one study, only 25% of persons receiving psychotropic agents had a formal psychiatric diagnosis (it is not clear how many had an adequate, comprehensive assessment rather than just a label).[64] Medically, such nonspecific treatment does not make sense; for instance, aggressive behavior might be part of the presentation of major depression, anxiety, psychosis, or even a justified anger in an otherwise mentally healthy person. Each of these situations requires a different treatment; thus, it is illogical to refer to a single treatment for aggression, but the practice survives. The practice is often encountered, especially in institutions, to deny the person habilitative programs until the "inappropriate behaviors" are eliminated through drug treatment. This practice often hides an unwillingness to commit funds to develop proper programming and ignores the fact that various treatment components act in synchrony. Obviously, the proper approach is to design a comprehensive treatment program after a comprehensive diagnostic assessment, as delineated previously. The medications might play one part in such program, although they usually are not the sole intervention.

Another unfortunate practice is to add another drug, often of the same class, when the first drug fails to reduce the undesirable behavior, without evidence that it will have a synergistic effect. Some individuals, especially those in institutions, may end up taking many drugs, without evidence that any one of them is effective. The proper approach is to institute a follow-up system as described earlier. However, it should not focus on a single behavior but on a person's global functioning. Some follow-up approaches follow the premise (without basis) that there is a linear relationship between the drug dose and the frequency of certain behavior and attempt to titrate the drug accordingly. Periodic tapering of the drug (unless clinically contraindicated) should be performed to ascertain its effectiveness.

Review of Classes of Psychotropic Drugs

Antipsychotic Agents

The use of antipsychotic drugs in persons with mental retardation is the same as that for the general population—for the treatment of psychotic symptoms, sometimes for Tourette's disorder, and as an emergency treatment of dangerous aggression. Perhaps because of the difficulty (or ignorance) of making a more specific diagnosis, antipsychotic agents have been used for the treatment of aggression, destructiveness, and SIB in persons with mental retardation. The recognition of side effects might be difficult in persons with limited language, and extended observation by trained staff may be necessary. A common mistake is to confuse akathisia with behavior problems and to make the disorder worse by increasing the dose.The tapering of antipsychotic medications should be gradual to minimize side effects from withdrawal, including behavior problems such as irritability, insomnia, and aggression.[65]

Antidepressants

Antidepressants are used primarily for the treatment of depression, as in the general population. Tricyclic antidepressants might also be effective in the treatment of attention-deficit /hyperactivity disorder, usually if stimulants and clonidine are not effective or cannot be used. Precipitation of excitement, mania, and seizure might be a problem, and careful prior diagnostic assessment and follow-up are necessary. Studies have suggested that selective serotonin reuptake inhibitors might be helpful in reducing symptoms of autistic disorder in some persons and in reducing obsessive-compulsive and self-stimulatory behaviors and SIBs (although the improvement might be short-lived) (King BH, personal communication, 1994).

Antianxiety Drugs

Antianxiety drugs, primarily benzodiazepines, are used primarily for alleviation of anxiety if it is the primary symptom or if it is associated with another mental disorder. Side effects, such as paradoxical rage reactions and serious withdrawal symptoms after chronic use, must be considered. Occasional use might be helpful in emergency situations in which extreme anxiety and associated aggression are present as well as in preparation for anxiety-inducing medical procedures. The usefulness of buspirone for the treatment of aggression has been suggested by one study.

Mood Stabilizers

Lithium carbonate has increasingly been reported as effective in bipolar disorders with mental retardation as well as in aggressive behaviors in some persons.[66]

Anticonvulsants

As in persons without mental retardation, carbamazepine and valproic acid have been effective in some studies as mood stabilizers, alone or in conjunction with lithium. They have also been beneficial in certain cases of depression. Some clinical experiences indicate that the prognosis might be better in the presence of mood lability and an abnormal electroencephalogram. As seizures are frequently associated with mental retardation, these drugs offer a parsimonious way of managing both seizures and behavioral symptoms.

Stimulants

As in persons without mental retardation, drugs such as methylphenidate, clonidine, and dextroamphetamine are effective in the treatment of attention-deficit/hyperactivity disorder. Tics are one side effect of methylphenidate: if the patient is engaging in self-stimulatory behaviors, videotaping might provide a record for later reference regarding whether additional tics have emerged. There have been some reports of behavioral improvements in certain children with autistic disorder who received fenfluramine. Because of inconsistency, side effects, and concern about long-term neurotoxicity, this drug has been not widely used.

β-Blockers

Following the earlier reports on the beneficial effects of propranolol in rage attacks associated with a definite pathological brain condition,[67] β-blockers have been tried extensively in all kinds of aggressive behavior, often with mixed or poor results. Depression might be a side effect of these agents, and because it might induce apathy, it should not be confused with improvement.

Other Agents

Naltrexone had been tried in a number of studies in cases of severe SIB. It appears that it is effective in some cases, although more research is necessary.

Psychosocial Interventions

Programmatic and Educational Approaches

The goal of these interventions is to provide a proper living and programmatic environment. For instance, certain persons easily become overstimulated, anxious, and disruptive in noisy and confused large workshops; arranging for a smaller and quieter workroom is preferable to a prescription for thioridazine. The vocational and educational program should focus on developing a person's strengths and providing an opportunity for success rather than continuous failure. In turn, this will lead to results such as an improvement in self-image. Many persons with severe mental retardation are placed in prevocational training indefinitely, for example, screwing or unscrewing nuts and bolts, although no one expects them to ever be employed on an assembly line. They often engage in a struggle with caregivers because of their noncompliance and may resort to aggression, which leads to removal for a "time out" and thus avoidance of a boring task. Creating a more suitable task—for example, one involving gross motor activity such as making rounds of the workshop to collect or deliver materials—would be more interesting and appropriate. Functional analysis of behavior is an invaluable guide to these interventions.

Psychotherapies

Individual and group psychotherapies had already been used with persons with mental retardation in the 1930s.[68] Psychotherapy in this population is not different in nature from psychotherapy in persons with average intelligence and is similar to treating children, inasmuch as in both cases the techniques and the therapist have to adapt to the developmental needs of the patient. The treatment should be driven by the patient's needs and responses and not by the therapist's theoretical orientation. Detailed techniques that can be used have been described.[69, 70] The indications are similar to those for psychotherapy in general: the presence of concerns and conflicts, especially about oneself; impairments in interpersonal skills; or other mental disturbances that may improve through psychotherapy. The prerequisites include communication skills permitting a meaningful interchange with the therapist, an ability to develop even a minimal relationship, and the availability of a trained, experienced, and unprejudiced therapist who is comfortable in working in a team setting. From applicable literature, Reiss and Benson[68] summarized the guidelines for psychotherapy in this population, which include the following:

1. Appropriate goals should be set and should be reconciled among the expectations of the caregivers, the therapist, and the patient. Common goals include improvement in self-image and impulse control, learning to express feelings in a socially appropriate manner, and understanding, in a constructive manner, one's own disabilities and strengths.
2. The verbal techniques should be adapted to the patient's language and cognitive level, and the nonverbal ones should be age appropriate.

3. Limits and directiveness should be used as needed: nondirective therapy might lead to a patient's confusion.
4. The therapist has to be active (supportive but not paternalistic), has to use herself or himself liberally as a treatment tool, and has to be able to focus on the immediate reality rather than just intellectualize. A mix of techniques, for example, cognitive psychotherapy and behavior modification, may be required.
5. As in all treatment modalities, the therapist should be involved in all aspects of the patient's program and should collaborate with other providers and with the family.

Group therapy might be particularly effective in helping patients handle issues related to the understanding of their own disability and learn social skills because of the peer support the group offers.[70] In general, therapy should be seen as a cognitive learning process, using the therapist's support and leading patients to the acquisition of understanding and necessary skills, both of concrete behaviors and of handling one's own emotions.

Behavioral Treatment

Behavioral techniques are described elsewhere in this book. There are also brief reviews of their application in persons with mental retardation.[71] Detailed functional analysis is a prerequisite. This treatment should optimally use rewards, which should be age appropriate, preferably social, and their frequency should be adapted to a person's cognitive level so that he or she can understand why they are given. Consistency is essential. Thus, if such techniques are successfully used at the school, the family or other caregivers should be trained to use them at home as well. The focus should not be on elimination of objectionable behaviors only but on teaching appropriate replacement behaviors. Aversive techniques involving active punishment (electric shocks, spraying of noxious substances into a person's face) are not used except in a few controversial settings. There is a professional consensus that these techniques should not be used at all, or only when all other techniques have failed and the patient's behavior poses severe danger to herself or himself or to others (such as intractable SIB). Even then, these techniques should be used only if proved effective and then only for a limited time.

Psychiatrist-Patient Relationship: Models of Delivery of Psychiatric Services

The psychiatric care of persons with mental retardation has often followed a path different from the care provided to the general population. A common service model has been the medication clinic, in which the psychiatrist is given little, if any, time to examine the patient and to interview the caregivers. Instead, behavioral information, which is often brief and sketchy, is presented by caregivers and focuses primarily on disruptive behaviors. The psychiatrist is expected to prescribe medications and has no voice in or knowledge of other interventions that might be used. In some cases, the psychiatrist does the actual prescribing; in others, the psychiatrist serves as a consultant to primary physicians, who may or may not follow the recommendations given. This model is obviously inadequate, even if there is another professional providing psychotherapy or behavioral therapy. It also exposes the psychiatrist to legal responsibility.[72] This model has been used in institutions especially to save on the expense of having a staff psychiatrist to provide adequate services.

The proper psychiatric care of persons with mental retardation is actually more time-consuming than the care of persons without mental retardation because of the multi factor described previously. To understand the patient's clinical presentation and provide the input necessary to all relevant aspects of treatment, the psychiatrist has to have adequate time to interview all involved caregivers, observe and interview the patient, make a home or program visit if necessary, and discuss the recommendation with all involved. Thus, the interdisciplinary team approach is necessary. It might not be realistic in all patients seen in the community, but it should be followed in all treatment-resistant cases and in residential facilities where, as a rule, there are more difficult patients.[73, 74] In all situations, psychiatrists will best use their knowledge and training in biological and behavioral aspects of medicine to help other professionals synthesize the biopsychosocial aspects of a patient's clinical presentation and treatment program.

References

1. Josephson G: Loneliness. Down Syndrome News 1992; 16:78.
1a. American Psychiatric Association: Diagnostic and Statistical Manual of Mental Disorders, Fourth Edition. Washington, DC: American Psychiatric Association, 1994.
2. Szymanski LS, Crocker AC: Mental retardation. In Kaplan HI, Sadock BJ (eds): Comprehensive Textbook of Psychiatry/V. Baltimore: Williams & Wilkins, 1989.
3. Scheerenberger RC: A History of Mental Retardation. Baltimore: Paul H Brookes Publishing, 1983.
4. Heber R: A manual on terminology and classification in mental retardation [monograph]. Am J Ment Defic 1959; 64(suppl 2).
5. American Association on Mental Retardation: Mental Retardation: Definition, Classification, and Systems of Supports. Washington, DC: American Association on Mental Retardation, 1992.
6. McLaren J, Bryson SE: Review of recent epidemiological studies of mental retardation: Prevalence, associated disorders, and etiology. Am J Ment Retard 1987; 92:243–254.
7. Taft LT, Matthews WS: Cerebral palsy. In Levine MD, Carey WB, Crocker AC (eds): Developmental-Behavioral Pediatrics, 2nd ed. Philadelphia: WB Saunders, 1992:527–533.
8. Freeman JM, Avery G, Brann AW Jr, et al: National Institutes of Health report on causes of mental retardation and cerebral palsy. From the Task Force on Joint Assessment of Prenatal and Perinatal Factors Associated with Brain Disorders. Pediatrics 1985; 76:457–458.
9. Yannet H: Diagnostic classification of patients with mental deficiency. Am J Dis Child 1945; 70:83.
10. Heber R: A manual on terminology and classification in mental retardation [monograph]. Am J Ment Defic 1959; 64(suppl 2).
11. Hayes A, Batshaw ML: Down syndrome. Pediatr Clin North Am 1993; 40:523–535.
11a. Lubs HA: A marker X chromosome. Am J Hum Genet 1969; 21:231–244.
11b. Harvey J, Judge C, Wiener S: Familial X-linked mental retardation with X chromosome abnormality. J Med Genet 1977; 14:46–50.
11c. Sutherland GR, Mulley JC, Richards RI: Fragile X syndrome: The most common cause of familial intellectual handicap. Med J Aust 1993; 158:482–485.
12. Mandel J-L, Hagerman R, Froster U, et al: Conference report. Fifth International Workshop on the Fragile X and X-Linked Mental Retardation. Am J Med Genet 1992; 43:5–27.
13. Hagberg B, Aicardi J, Dias K, et al: A progressive syndrome of autism,

dementia, ataxia, and loss of purposeful hand use in girls: Rett's syndrome: Report of 35 cases. Ann Neurol 1983; 14:471–479.
14. Armstrong DD: The neuropathology of the Rett syndrome. Brain Dev 1992; 14(suppl):S89–S98.
15. Hagberg B, Naidu S, Percy AK: Tokyo Symposium on the Rett Syndrome: Neurobiological approach—concluding remarks and epilogue. Brain Dev 1992; 14(suppl):S151–S153.
16. Percy A: Meeting report: Second International Rett Syndrome Workshop and Symposium. J Child Neurol 1993; 8:97–100.
17. Lamont LA, Dennis NR: Aetiology of mild mental retardation. Arch Dis Child 1988; 63:1032–1038.
18. Hagberg B, Hagberg G, Lewerth A, Lindberg U: Mild mental retardation in Swedish school children. II. Etiologic and pathogenetic aspects. Acta Paediatr Scand 1981; 70:445–452.
19. Bregman JD, Hodapp RM: Current developments in the understanding of mental retardation. Part I: Biological and phenomenological perspectives. J Am Acad Child Adolesc Psychiatry 1991; 30:707–719.
20. Knoll JHM, Wagstaff J, Lalande M: Cytogenetic and molecular studies in the Prader-Willi and Angelman syndromes: An overview. Am J Med Genet 1993; 46:2–6.
21. Breuning MH, Dauwerse HG, Fugazza G, et al: Rubinstein-Taybi syndrome caused by submicroscopic deletions within 16p13.3. Am J Hum Genet 1993; 52:249–254.
22. Ewart AK, Morris CA, Atkinson D, et al: Hemizygosity at the elastin locus in a developmental disorder, Williams syndrome. Nature Genet 1993; 5:11–16.
23. Graham JM: Congenital anomalies. In Levine MD, Carey WB, Crocker AC (eds): Developmental-Behavioral Pediatrics, 2nd ed. Philadelphia: WB Saunders, 1992:229–243.
24. Czeizel A, Dudas I: Prevention of the first occurrence of neural tube defects by periconceptional vitamin supplementation. N Engl J Med 1992; 327:1832–1836.
25. McQueen PC, Spence MW, Winsor EJT, et al: Causal origins of major mental handicap in the Canadian maritime provinces. Dev Med Child Neurol 1986; 28:697–707.
26. Blomquist HK, Gustavson K-H, Holmgren G: Mild mental retardation in a northern Swedish county. J Ment Defic Res 1981; 25:169–185.
27. Schmitt B, Seeger J, Kreuz W, et al: Central nervous system involvement of children with HIV infection. Dev Med Child Neurol 1991; 33:535–540.
28. Coles CD: Impact of prenatal alcohol exposure on the newborn and the child. In Woods JR, Rubin MC (eds): Clinical Obstetrics and Gynecology: Toxic Exposure in Pregnancy, Volume 2. Philadelphia: JB Lippincott, 1993; 36:255–266.
29. Huttenlocher PR: Dendritic and synaptic pathology in mental retardation. Pediatr Neurol 1991; 7:79–85.
30. Eyman RK, Grossman HJ, Chaney RH, Call TL: The life expectancy of profoundly handicapped people with mental retardation. N Engl J Med 1990; 323:584–589.
31. Donaldson JY, Menolascino FJ: Past, current and future roles of child psychiatry in mental retardation. J Am Acad Child Psychiatry 1977; 16:38–52.
32. Skeels H, Dye H: A study of the effect of differential stimulation on mentally retarded children: A follow-up report. Am J Ment Defic 1942; 46:340–350.
33. Nirje B: A Scandinavian visitor looks at U.S. institutions. In Wolfensberger W, Kugel R (eds): Changing Patterns in Residential Services for the Mentally Retarded. Washington, DC: President's Committee on Mental Retardation, 1969:51–58.
34. Rowitz L: Multiprofessional perspectives on prevention. [editorial] Ment Retard 1986; 24:1–3.
35. Szymanski LS: Prevention of psychosocial dysfunction in persons with mental retardation. Ment Retard 1987; 25:215–218.
36. Reiss A, Levitan GW, Szyszko J: Emotional disturbance and mental retardation: Diagnostic overshadowing. Am J Ment Defic 1982; 86:567–574.
37. Rutter M, Graham P, Yule W: A Neuropsychiatric Study in Childhood. London: Spastics International Medical Publications, 1970.
38. Rutter M, Graham P, Yule W: A neuropsychiatric study in childhood. In Clinics in Developmental Medicine, Volumes 35 and 36. London: Heinemann Medical Books, 1970.
39. Gillberg C, Persson E, Grufman M, Themner U: Psychiatric disorders in mildly and severely mentally retarded urban children and adolescents: Epidemiological aspects. Br J Psychiatry 1986; 149:68–74.
40. Koller H, Richardson S, Katz M, McLaren M: Behavior disturbance in childhood and the early adult years in populations who were and were not mentally retarded. J Prev Psychiatry 1982; 1:453–468.
41. Koller H, Richardson S, Katz M, McLaren M: Behavior disturbance since childhood among a 5-year birth cohort of all mentally retarded young adults in a city. Am J Ment Defic 1983; 87:386–395.
42. Jacobson J: Problem behavior and psychiatric impairment within a developmentally disabled population. I: Behavior frequency. Appl Res Ment Retard 1982; 3:121–140.
43. Gath A, Gumley D: Behaviour problems in retarded children with special reference to Down's syndrome. Br J Psychiatry 1986; 149:156–161.
44. Lund J: The presence of psychiatric morbidity in mentally retarded adults. Acta Psychiatr Scand 1985; 72:563–570.
45. Iverson JC, Fox RA: Prevalence of psychopathology among mentally retarded adults. Res Dev Disabil 1989; 10:77–83.
46. Gostason R: Psychiatric illness among the mentally retarded. A Swedish population study. Acta Psychiatr Scand 1985; 71(suppl 318):1–117.
47. Szymanski LS: Mental retardation and mental health: Concepts, aetiology and incidence. In Bouras N (ed): Mental Health in Mental Retardation: Recent Advances and Practices. Cambridge: Cambridge University Press, 1994:19–33.
48. Szymanski LS, Grossman H: Dual implications of dual diagnosis. Ment Retard 1984; 22:155–156.
49. Szymanski LS: Psychiatric diagnosis of retarded persons. In Szymanski LS, Tanguay PE (eds): Emotional Disorders of Mentally Retarded Persons. Baltimore: University Park Press, 1980:60–81.
50. Olshansky L: Chronic sorrow: A response to having a mentally defective child. Soc Casework 1962; 43:190–193.
51. Reiss S: Prevalence of dual-diagnosis in community-based day programs in the Chicago metropolitan area. Am J Ment Retard 1990; 94:578–585.
52. Sandman CA: The opiate hypothesis in autism and self injury. J Child Adolesc Psychopharmacol 1990; 1:237–248.
53. King BH: Self-injury by people with mental retardation: A compulsive behavior hypothesis. Am J Ment Retard 1993; 98:93–112.
54. Gualtieri CT: The differential diagnosis of self-injurious behavior in mentally retarded people. Psychopharmacol Bull 1989; 25:358–363.
55. Reid AH: Psychoses in adult mental defectives. II. Schizophrenic and paranoid psychoses. Br J Psychiatry 1972; 12:213–218.
56. Reiss S: Assessment of a man with dual diagnosis. Ment Retard 1992; 30:1–6.
57. Gardner WI: Occurrence of severe depressive reactions in the mentally retarded. Am J Psychiatry 1967; 124:142–144.
58. Sovner R, Hurley AD: Do the mentally retarded suffer from affective illness? Arch Gen Psychiatry 1983; 40:61–67.
59. Reiss S: Handbook of Challenging Behavior: Mental Health Aspects of Mental Retardation. Worthington, OH: IDS Publishing, 1994.
60. Reiss S, Benson BA: Psychosocial correlates of depression in mentally retarded adults: Minimal social support and stigmatization. Am J Ment Defic 1985; 89:331–337.
61. Tu JB, Smith JT: Factors associated with psychotropic medications in mental retardation facilities. Compr Psychiatry 1983; 20:289–295.
62. Lipman RS: The use of psychopharmacological agents in residential facilities for the retarded. In Menolascino FJ (ed): Psychiatric Approaches to Mental Retardation. New York: Basic Books, 1970: 387–398.
63. Bregman J: Current developments in the understanding of mental retardation, Part II: Psychopathology. J Am Acad Child Adolesc Psychiatry 1991; 30:861–672.
64. Jacobson JW: Problem behavior and psychiatric impairment within a developmentally disabled population. III: Psychotropic medication. Res Dev Disabil 1988; 9:23–38.
65. Gualtieri CT, Schroeder SR, Hicks RE, Quade D: Tardive dyskinesia in young mentally retarded individuals. Arch Gen Psychiatry 1986; 43:335–340.
66. Craft M, Ismail IA, Krishnamurti D, et al: Lithium in the treatment of aggression in mentally handicapped patients. A double-blind trial. Br J Psychiatry 1987; 150:685–689.
67. Williams DT, Mehl R, Yudodfsky S, et al: The effects of propranolol on uncontrolled rage outbursts in children and adolescents with organic brain dysfunction. J Am Acad Child Psychiatry 1982; 21:129–135.
68. Stacey CL, DeMartino MF (eds): Counseling and Psychotherapy with the Mentally Retarded. Glencoe, IL: Free Press, 1957.

69. Szymanski LS: Individual psychotherapy with retarded persons. In Szymanski LS, Tanguay PE (eds): Emotional Disorders of Mentally Retarded Persons. Baltimore: University Park Press, 1980:131–147.
70. Szymanski LS, Rosefsky QB: Group psychotherapy with retarded persons. In Szymanski LS, Tanguay PE (eds): Emotional Disorders of Mentally Retarded Persons. Baltimore: University Park Press, 1980: 174–194.
71. Jansen PE: Basic principles of behavior therapy with retarded persons. In Szymanski LS, Tanguay PE (eds): Emotional Disorders of Mentally Retarded Persons. Baltimore: University Park Press, 1980:223–240.
72. Woodward B, Duckworth KS, Gutheil TG: The pharmacotherapist-psychotherapist collaboration. Rev Psychiatry 1993; 12:631–649.
73. Szymanski LS, Eissner BA, Rosefsky QB: Mental health consultations to residential facilities for retarded person. In Szymanski LS, Tanguay PE (eds): Emotional Disorders of Mentally Retarded Persons. Baltimore: University Park Press, 1980:255–273.
74. Szymanski LS, Leaverton DR: Mental health consultations to educational programs for retarded persons. In Szymanski LS, Tanguay PE (eds): Emotional Disorders of Mentally Retarded Persons. Baltimore: University Park Press, 1980:244–253.

CHAPTER

34 Learning and Motor Skills Disorders

Larry B. Silver

For children and adolescents, school is their "workplace." Successful school performance is essential for psychological growth and development. Social competency and social skills are developed and then shaped within the family and in the school but practiced and mastered in the school. The development of self-image and self-esteem is based on successes in school. Feedback from the school concerning academic performance and social interactions influences the parents' image of their child or adolescent. Thus, if something interferes with success in school, the impact will affect the emotional, social, and family functioning of a child or adolescent.

Academic performance requires the integrated interactions of the cognitive, motor, and language functions of the brain. As detailed in the *Diagnostic and Statistical Manual of Mental Disorders,* Fourth Edition (DSM-IV), if brain dysfunction results in cognitive difficulties, it is called a learning disorder; in motor difficulties, a motor skills disorder; and in language difficulties, a language disorder. This chapter focuses on the learning disorders and motor skills disorder. Chapter 39 reviews the communication disorders, including language disorders.

Key for the mental health professional is the understanding that the underlying neurological dysfunctions that result in learning disorders and motor skills disorder have an impact on more than academic performance. These disabilities affect every aspect of the individual's life during each stage of psychosocial development.[1, 2]

Definitions

Public education laws use the term learning disabilities. DSM-IV uses the terms learning disorders and motor skills disorder. It is helpful to understand that these terms reflect the diagnostic system used but refer to the same set of difficulties.

Public school systems use the federal definition based on Public Law 94-142, Education for All Handicapped Children, and its revision, Public Law 101-476, Individuals with Disabilities Education Act. In the latter, a learning disability is defined by inclusionary and exclusionary criteria:

> Specific learning disabilities means a disorder in one or more of the basic psychological processes involved in understanding or in using language, spoken or written, which may manifest itself in an imperfect ability to listen, think, speak, read, write, spell, or to do mathematical calculations. The term includes such conditions as perceptual handicaps, brain injury, minimal brain dysfunction, dyslexia, and developmental aphasia. The term does not include children who have learning problems which are primarily the result of visual, hearing, or motor handicaps, of mental retardation, of emotional disturbance, or of environmental, cultural, or economic disadvantage.

The *Diagnostic and Statistical Manual of Mental Disorders,* Third Edition (DSM-III) was the first medical diagnostic system to refer to these problems. In this manual, the educational approach that focused on the underlying learning disabilities was not used. The focus was on the areas of academic difficulty, and academic skills disorders was the term used. The specific types of disorders reflected general areas of difficulty: developmental arithmetic disorder, developmental expressive writing disorder, and developmental reading disorder. There was no reference to motor disorders. These disorders were listed under the broad category of specific developmental disorders. This focus on developmental disorders reflected the facts that they were found in children and adolescents and that they greatly affected all

Table 34–1 Areas of Psychological Processing That Affect Learning

Area of Processing	Examples
Input	Visual or auditory perception
Integration	Sequencing, abstracting, organization
Memory	Short term, rote, long term
Output	Language, motor

aspects of development. This term did not reflect the reality that, for most persons, these disabilities will last throughout their lives. The *Diagnostic and Statistical Manual of Mental Disorders,* Third Edition, Revised (DSM-III-R) maintained the focus on specific developmental disorders and on the same three general areas of difficulty. Motor skills disorder was added.

In DSM-IV, the term academic skills disorders was changed to learning disorders. Three subtypes of learning disorders are identified: reading disorder, mathematics disorder, and disorder of written expression. Only one subtype, developmental coordination disorder, is listed under motor skills disorder.

Diagnosis

It is important to understand the criteria used in DSM-IV as well as the criteria used by school systems. In clinical practice, the need is to help the family in getting the school system to identify the child or adolescent as having a disability and to provide the necessary services. Thus, the psychiatrist must know and understand the educational criteria.

The research of the past 30 years on neurologically based learning disorders stressed not the specific skill disorder but the underlying processing problems. The psychological and educational diagnostic tests used clarify areas of learning abilities and learning disabilities covering the four phases of processing (Table 34–1). Thus, although one explores for problems with reading, mathematics, or writing, it is important in the diagnostic process also to explore for the underlying processing problems that result in these skill disorders.

DSM-IV Criteria 315.00

Reading Disorder

A. Reading achievement, as measured by individually administered standardized tests of reading accuracy or comprehension, is substantially below that expected given the person's chronological age, measured intelligence, and age-appropriate education.

B. The disturbance in criterion A significantly interferes with academic achievement or activities of daily living that require reading skills.

C. If a sensory deficit is present, the reading difficulties are in excess of those usually associated with it.

DSM-IV Criteria 315.1

Mathematics Disorder

A. Mathematical ability, as measured by individually administered standardized tests, is substantially below that expected given the person's chronological age, measured intelligence, and age-appropriate education.

B. The disturbance in criterion A significantly interferes with academic achievement or activities of daily living that require mathematical ability.

C. If a sensory deficit is present, the difficulties in mathematical ability are in excess of those usually associated with it.

DSM-IV Criteria

The criteria in DSM-IV for establishing the diagnosis of a learning disorder are as given on this page and page 638.

For each of these diagnostic categories, the instructions in DSM-IV note that if a general medical (e.g., neurological) condition or sensory deficit is present, the disorder should be coded on Axis III.

Within the motor skills disorder section of DSM-IV, there is only one subtype, developmental coordination disorder. The criteria given on page 638 establish this diagnosis.

DSM-IV Criteria 315.2

Disorder of Written Expression

A. Writing skills, as measured by individually administered standardized tests (or functional assessments of writing skills), are substantially below those expected given the person's chronological age, measured intelligence, and age-appropriate education.

B. The disturbance in criterion A significantly interferes with academic achievement or activities of daily living that require the composition of written texts (e.g., writing grammatically correct sentences and organized paragraphs).

C. If a sensory deficit is present, the difficulties in writing skills are in excess of those usually associated with it.

DSM-IV Criteria 315.9

Learning Disorder Not Otherwise Specified

A. This category is for disorders in learning that do not meet criteria for any specific learning disorder, for example, a disorder in which spelling skills are substantially below those expected given the person's chronological age, measured intelligence, and age-appropriate education.

If a general medical (e.g., neurological) condition or sensory deficit is present, the developmental coordination disorder is to be coded on Axis III.

Educational Criteria

The most recent federal guidelines for determining whether a student in a public school is eligible for special programs for learning disabilities list four criteria[3]:

1. Documented evidence indicating that general education has been attempted and found to be ineffective in meeting the student's educational needs.
2. Evidence of a disorder in one or more of the basic psychological processes required for learning. A psychological process is a set of mental operations that transform, access, or manipulate information. The disorder is relatively enduring and limits ability to perform specific academic or developmental learning tasks. It may be manifested differently at different developmental levels.
3. Evidence of academic achievement significantly below the student's level of intellectual function (a difference of 1.5 to 1.75 standard deviations between achievement and intellectual functioning is considered significant) on basic reading skills, reading comprehension, mathematical calculation, mathematical reasoning, or written expression.
4. Evidence that the learning problems are not due primarily to other handicapping conditions (i.e., impairment of visual acuity or auditory acuity, physical impairment, emotional handicap, mental retardation, cultural differences, or environmental deprivation).

DSM-IV Criteria 315.4

Developmental Coordination Disorder

A. Performance in daily activities that require motor coordination is substantially below that expected given the person's chronological age and measured intelligence. This may be manifested by marked delays in achieving motor milestones (e.g., walking, crawling, sitting), dropping things, "clumsiness," poor performance in sports, or poor handwriting.

B. The disturbance in criterion A significantly interferes with academic achievement or activities of daily living.

C. The disturbance is not due to a general medical condition (e.g., cerebral palsy, hemiplegia, or muscular dystrophy) and does not meet criteria for a pervasive developmental disorder.

D. If mental retardation is present, the motor difficulties are in excess of those usually associated with it.

The presence of a central nervous system processing deficit is essential for the diagnosis of a learning disability. A child might meet the discrepancy criteria, but without central processing deficits in functions required for learning, he or she is not considered to have a learning disability.

The question of the significant discrepancy between potential and actual achievement determines eligibility for services. Different school systems use different models for determining the extent of discrepancy.[3, 4]

Diagnosis of a Learning Disorder or Motor Skills Disorder

If a child or adolescent is experiencing academic difficulty, she or he would normally be referred to the special education professionals within the school system. However, the student with academic difficulties often presents with emotional or behavior problems and is more likely to be referred to a mental health professional. It is critical to understand this potential referral bias. This mental health professional must clarify whether the observed emotional, social, or family problems are causing the academic difficulties or whether they are a consequence of the academic difficulties and the resulting frustrations and failures experienced by the individual, the teacher, and the parents.[1, 2, 5–8]

The evaluation of a child or adolescent with academic difficulties and emotional or behavior problems includes a comprehensive assessment of the presenting emotional, behavior, social, or family problems as well as a mental status examination. The psychiatrist should obtain information from the child or adolescent, parents, teachers, and other education professionals to help clarify whether there might be a learning disorder or a motor skills disorder and whether further psychological or educational studies are needed. Descriptions by teachers, parents, and the child or adolescent being evaluated will give the psychiatrist clues that there might be one of the learning disorders or a motor skills disorder.

Children who experience problems in reading typically have difficulty in decoding the letter-sound associations involved in phonic analysis.[9] As a result, they may read in a disjointed manner, knowing a few words on sight and stumbling across other unfamiliar words. They may guess. If they have difficulty with visual tracking, they may skip words or lines. If comprehension is a problem, they report that they have to read material over and over before they understand.

Children with mathematical difficulties often display problems in attention. This is reflected in the types of errors made in computations. They may leave a problem partially completed and move on to the next. They may make impulsive mistakes, yet they are able to complete the problem correctly when this is brought to their attention. They may have difficulty shifting from one operation to the next and, as a result, add when they should subtract. They may have visual-spatial difficulties and thus misalign columns or rows and make "careless mistakes."

Children who have difficulties with writing may have a problem with handwriting. They grasp the pencil or pen differently and tightly. They write slowly, and their hand gets tired. Often, they prefer printing rather than cursive writing. Most also have problems with the language of writing. They have difficulty with spelling, often spelling phonetically. They may have difficulty with grammar, punctuation, and capitalization.[10]

Many if not most students with a learning disorder also have difficulties with memory or organization. The child or adolescent with a memory problem has difficulty following multistep directions or reads a chapter in a book but forgets what was read. Others might have sequencing problems, performing instructions out of order. In speaking or writing, the facts may come out but in the wrong sequence. Students with organizational difficulties may not be able to organize their life (notebook, locker, desk, bedroom); they forget things or lose things; they have difficulty with time planning; or they have difficulty using parts of information from a whole concept or putting parts of information into a whole concept.

Children and adolescents with a developmental coordination disorder may show evidence of gross motor or fine motor difficulties. The gross motor problems might result in difficulty with walking, running, jumping, or climbing. The fine motor problems may result in difficulty with buttoning, zipping, tying, holding a pencil or pen or crayon, arts and crafts activities, or handwriting. Both gross and fine motor difficulties may result in the individual's performing poorly in certain sports activities.

Ostrander[11] and Silver[12] suggested a set of "systems review"–type questions (Table 34–2) to be used during an interview with parents or the child or adolescent with academic difficulties suspected of having a learning disorder (learning disability) or a developmental coordination disorder. These questions focus both on the specific areas of skills and on the possible underlying processing problems.

Differential Diagnosis

The presenting problem is academic difficulty. The differential diagnostic process must clarify the reason for the academic difficulty. A "decision tree" for academic difficulties developed by Silver and Ostrander is useful for exploring all of the possible reasons for such difficulties[11] (Fig. 34–1).

Three principal areas of inquiry concerning the factors contributing to the student's learning difficulties are explored. The first involves considerations that are related to the child's or adolescent's psychiatric, medical, or psychoeducational status. The second area of inquiry is family functioning. The third area to explore involves the environmental and cultural context in which the student functions.

Evaluation of the Child or Adolescent

Difficulties in academic performance of children or adolescents can be related to a range of psychiatric, medical, or cognitive factors. To best determine the primary source of academic difficulties, the evaluation should involve a comprehensive examination of these areas. The psychiatric evaluation should clarify whether there is a psychopathological process. If one is present, it is useful first to determine whether the problems relate to a disruptive behavior disorder or to another psychiatric disorder. In particular, the disruptive behavior disorders have high comorbidity with academic difficulties. A full assessment should clarify whether a disruptive behavior disorder is causing the difficulty with academic performance or is secondary to this difficulty. Disruptive behavior disorders can result in the student's being unavailable for learning or being so disruptive as to require removal of the student from traditional learning environments. The frustration and failures caused by a learning disorder can be manifested by a disruptive behavior disorder. In some cases, the disruptive behavior disorder coexists with the learning disorder and the relation is less clear. Children and adolescents with attention-deficit/hyperactivity disorder (ADHD) have particular difficulty maintaining attention and possibly with processing information. As a result, the same variables that have an impact on their attention also have an impact on their ability to learn. In such instances, they may have a learning disorder and ADHD.

Internalizing disorders such as depression or anxiety can result in an uncharacteristic disinterest in or avoidance of school expectations. If one of the internalizing disorders is present, it is important to clarify whether it is secondary or primary to the academic difficulty. Cognitive and language deficits as well as social skills deficits are often associated with learning disorders and can contribute to a dysphoric or anxious presentation. Children with pervasive developmental disorder can be unavailable for learning or the traditional academic activities.

The medical evaluation is necessary to explore the influence of health factors on the individual's availability and ability to learn. Problems in acquiring academic content can be significantly affected by most visual or hearing deficits. Generally poor health can influence the stamina, motivation, and concentration needed to focus adequately on academic demands. Medications used for any purpose might cause sedation or other side effects that may affect the child's ability to learn. Early developmental insults can result in global or focal deficits in neurological development. Undiagnosed seizures, especially petit mal and partial complex seizures, can result in difficulties in general cognitive functioning, specific deficits in memory, and problems with attention. Orthopedic restrictions can limit an individual's ability to learn or to perform.

The evaluation of cognitive, academic, and neuropsychological functioning is critical to any assessment of learning problems. Results of this psychoeducational assessment will indicate the parameters of the individual's academic and cognitive liabilities while identifying her or his assets. In some instances, borderline cognitive develop-

Table 34–2 Screening Questions

Domain	Questions
Reading	Do you like to read?
	Can you sound out words as well as your classmates can?
	Do you know the word on sight, or not at all?
	Do you skip words or lines?
	Does it take you longer than other children to read?
	Can you remember what you read?
Mathematics	Do you know the basic facts in addition, subtraction, multiplication, and division?
	Do you often add when you should subtract or multiply?
	Do you often forget some of the steps when doing mathematics problems?
	Do you often make careless errors?
	Is your mathematics homework messy?
Writing	How is your handwriting? Can people read it?
	Can you write fast enough?
	How is your spelling? When you make spelling mistakes, can other people figure out what word you were trying to spell?
	Do you make many mistakes in capitalization, punctuation, or grammar?
Sequencing	When you speak or write, do you sometimes have difficulty getting everything in the right order or do you start in the middle, go to the beginning, then jump to the end?
	Can you name the months of the year? (let child do) Fine, now what comes after August? (Ask how he or she got the answer. Was it necessary to return to January and count up?)
	Do you have difficulty using the alphabet when using a dictionary?
	Do you have to return to *a* often to know whether the next letter is above or below the letter you are on?
Abstraction	Do you understand jokes when your friends tell them?
	Do you sometimes get confused when people seem to say something yet they tell you they meant something else?
Organization	What does your notebook look like? Is it a mess with papers in the wrong place or falling out?
	What about your desk? Your locker? Your bedroom?
	Do you have difficulty organizing your thoughts or the facts you are learning into a whole concept so that you can learn it?
	Do you find that you can read a chapter and answer the questions at the end of the chapter but that you are still not sure what the chapter is about?
Memory	Do you find that you can learn something at night and then go to school the next day and forget what you have learned?
	When talking, do you sometimes know what you want to say but halfway through you forget what you are saying? If so, do you cover up by saying things like "Oh, forget it" or "It's not important"?
Language	When the teacher is speaking in class, do you have trouble understanding or keeping up?
	Do you sometimes misunderstand people and, therefore, give the wrong answer?
	When people are talking, do you find that you have to concentrate so hard on what they say that you sometimes fall behind and have to skip quickly to what they are saying now to keep up?
	Does this sometimes cause you to get lost in class?
	Do you sometimes have trouble getting your thoughts organized when you speak?
	Do you have a problem finding the word you want to use?
Motor	Do you feel that you can run, jump, and climb as well as your friends can?
	Would you describe yourself as clumsy?
	Do you find that you often knock things over or bump into things?
	Do you have difficulty with dressing, especially with buttoning, zipping, tying? How about cutting food and eating?
	In sports do you have difficulty with throwing, hitting, and catching a ball?
	How would you describe your handwriting? Do you hold your pencil or pen differently than others? Does your hand get tired? Do you write slower than you need to in class?

From Ostrander R: Clinical observations suggesting a learning disability. Child Adolesc Psychiatr Clin North Am 1993; 2:249–263.

ment or mental retardation may be the primary explanation for learning difficulties. However, in some instances, low scores on indexes of cognitive functioning may be somewhat ambiguous and represent artificially delayed scores on cognitive measures. Developmental delays are particularly evident with a preschool child; rapid and uneven developmental changes can lead to considerable variability in findings derived by measures of intellectual functioning. If any of the clinical evaluations yield results suggestive of a learning disorder, a more involved psychoeducational assessment is needed. An appropriate psychoeducational evaluation will reveal the magnitude of the child's learning difficulties as well as the nature of the child's cognitive assets and deficits. From this understanding, appropriate interventions can be designed and special accommodations can be initiated.

Family Evaluation

A family evaluation must include an assessment of the parents and of the entire family. A judgment is made on the order in which these assessments are done. The first clinical question is whether the family is functional or dysfunctional. If the family is largely functional, there may be "normal" parenting issues that may be contributing to the child's difficulty. If there is no evidence of a psychopathological process within the family, alternative explanations should be considered that do not relate to family issues.

Normal parenting issues may be the time or energy that parents have in relating to the child's academic difficulties. Moreover, there could be family values that affect the child's educational functioning. For example, a single parent may be overwhelmed with responsibilities associated with child-rearing and, as a result, be unavailable to facilitate the child's

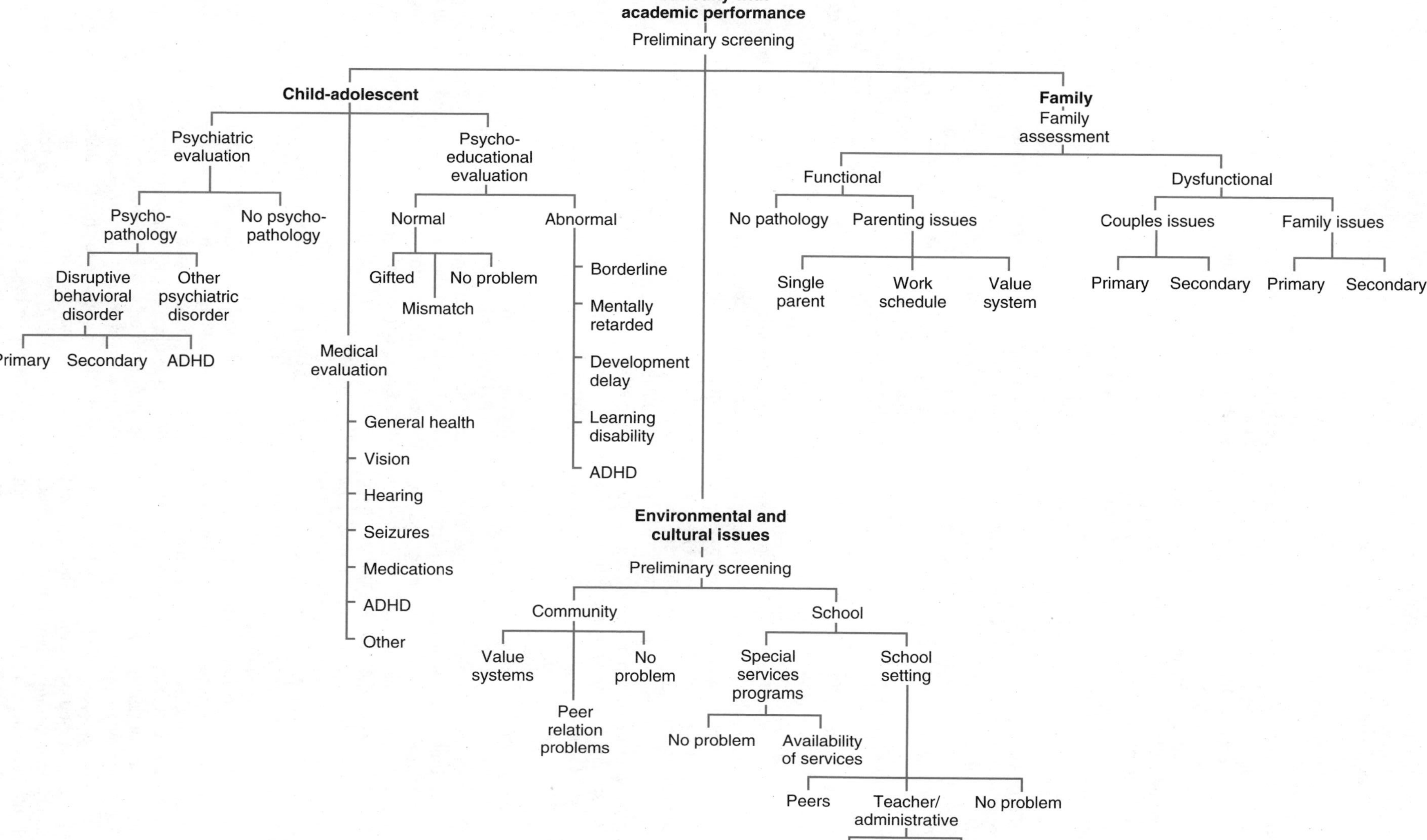

Figure 34–1 *Academic underachievement and the clinical decision-making process. ADHD, Attention-deficit/hyperactivity disorder. (From Ostrander R: Clinical observations suggesting a learning disability. Child Adolesc Psychiatr Clin North Am 1993; 2:249–263.)*

educational progress. In families in which both parents work, the demands associated with work may leave little energy for helping the child with academic challenges. The psychiatrist may also learn that education is not a family priority and that this may be in conflict with the demands and the expectations of the school.

If the family is found to be dysfunctional, the psychiatrist must assess whether the dysfunction is caused by issues involving both parents, problems with one parent, or broader family difficulties. If there is stress between the parents that results in marital difficulties, the psychiatrist should clarify whether these problems are primary or secondary to the presenting problems. That is, the marital stress may be contributing to the child's academic difficulties or may be influenced by the stress of having a child who has a learning disorder. The assessment may clarify that one parent is having psychological problems that are contributing to the couple's or family's stress. If there is family dysfunction, the psychiatrist must clarify, when possible, the difficulties that are having an impact on the family. It should be clarified whether the family dysfunction is primary or secondary to the child's academic difficulties.

Environmental and Cultural Assessment

Learning problems are attributed to cognitive deficits or behavior problems in the child or adolescent. Environmental factors involving the school or community, however, can also contribute to academic difficulties. Thus, the psychiatrist should be aware of how social, cultural, or institutional structures can influence learning. In many instances, such an awareness is developed over time and in the process of conducting a clinical practice. Data collection within this context is accomplished through formal and informal observations of the system and the cultural milieu. Through ongoing interactions with the community and the school system, a psychiatrist may develop an appreciation for the community values and the general programmatic resources provided by the school. With this understanding as a backdrop, one can conduct a more direct assessment of how specific environmental or school considerations can affect a given individual.

A child or adolescent with specific needs may be further impaired because of a limited range of services offered by the school system. For example, a child's learning disabilities may require special accommodations and services within a specific classroom; however, the school may not have allocated sufficient resources to make these accommodations available. In addition, the effectiveness of school programs can be influenced by interpersonal considerations, such as the competence and personality of the teacher or administrator. School personnel may be misinformed or uninformed about a particular psychiatric condition or have insufficient training to effectively address a particular learning difficulty. Although uncommon, more troubling influences on a child's learning can emerge when the school personnel exhibit biases or personality difficulties that affect the teacher's ability to teach. In addition to problems associated with school personnel, the degree to which the peers value academic success can either motivate or discourage a student from reaching his or her academic potential. An assessment of school-based interpersonal conflicts and alliances can provide valuable insights into their influence on learning. Whereas the school exerts a more direct influence on learning, the community influence is less direct although no less profound. For example, the value system of some communities includes high expectations for academic accomplishments, whereas other communities view academic success as largely unobtainable. Similarly, inappropriate peer pressure can either minimize or degrade the importance of academics. In more affluent communities, unusually high academic standards can place pressure on a student who has average intellectual capabilities.

Prevalence and Comorbidity

Prevalence

The true prevalence of these disorders is not known. The problem is the many case definitions used in different studies and in different settings. There remains controversy about which definition to use. The Centers for Disease Control and Prevention[13] attempted to establish the prevalence of learning disabilities. These researchers concluded that because the definition and the diagnostic criteria have not been fully standardized, consistency in the design of prevalence studies has not been maintained. Thus, accurate analyses of data over time are not possible. In the absence of good prevalence data, they concluded that between 5% and 10% was a reasonable estimate of the percentage of persons affected by learning disabilities.

In DSM-IV, prevalence figures are noted for each of the learning disorders and motor skills disorder. The prevalence of reading disorder in the United States is estimated at 4% of school-age children. It is estimated that 1% of school-age children have a mathematics disorder. No data are noted for disorder of written expression. The prevalence of developmental coordination disorder is estimated to be as high as 6% for children in the age range of 5 to 11 years.

Studies consistently note an increased prevalence of learning disabilities in boys. The ratio ranges from 3:1 to 5:1 and higher.[14–16] Studies suggest that this increased prevalence in boys may, in part, be explained by referral bias. Because they are more likely to act out, boys are more likely to be referred for study.[17] Girls appear to tolerate deficits in reading and spelling skills more easily than boys do, showing less antipathy to reading and less emotional impact.[15] Johnson and Blalock[18] found no specific cognitive differences or patterns of problems between the sexes.

Comorbidity

Individuals with a learning disorder or a motor skills disorder might have other mental disorders or a related neurological disorder. They might also have social problems.

Other Mental Disorders

It is not uncommon for children and adolescents with learning disorders or a motor skills disorder to have a diagnosable psychiatric disorder. For many, these psychological problems are secondary to the frustrations and failures experienced because these disabilities were not identified or were inadequately treated. For others, these conditions may be another reflection of a dysfunctional nervous system. The presenting behavioral or emotional issues might be the individual's characterological style for coping with a dysfunctional nervous system.

Studies of youth diagnosed as having a conduct disorder or young adults diagnosed as having a personality disorder, especially the borderline type, show that about one third have unrecognized or recognized and poorly treated learning disabilities (learning disorders).[6, 19, 20] Similar findings have been observed with adolescent boys in detention centers.[21–26]

As noted earlier, treatment approaches must be designed to address both the learning disorders or the motor skills disorder and the emotional or behavior problems. Efforts to treat the presenting emotional or psychological difficulties without efforts to treat the underlying academic problems do not usually succeed.

Social Problems

The learning disabilities that result in learning disorders or motor skills disorder may directly contribute to peer problems by interfering with success in doing activities required to interact with certain age groups (e.g., visual perception and visual-motor problems interfering with ability to quickly do such eye-hand activities as catching, hitting, or throwing a ball).

Many children and adolescents with learning disorders have difficulty learning social skills and being socially competent.[27] These individuals do not pick up such social cues as facial expressions, tone of voice, or body language and adapt their behaviors appropriately. Rourke,[28–31] using the definition of learning disabilities, identified a specific subtype of learning disabilities, called nonverbal learning disabilities, that often appear to be associated with social skills problems. The pattern of learning disabilities includes deficits in tactile perception, visual perception, complex psychomotor tasks, and accommodation to novel material as well as difficulty in simple motor skills, auditory perception, and mastery of rote material. A small subset of these students show difficulty in social and emotional functioning that includes a predisposition toward adolescent and adult depression and suicide risk.[32]

Other Psychiatric or Medical Disorders

The first neurologically based disorder recognized as frequently associated with a learning disability (learning disorder) was ADHD.[33, 34] Studies suggest that there is a continuum of disorders associated with neurological dysfunction that are often found together. Thus, when one is diagnosed, the others must be considered in the diagnostic process.

The related theme with these possibly comorbid neurologically based disorders appears to be that if something has an impact on the developing brain during pregnancy or during the critical early months of life, the effects will depend on which areas of the brain are involved and when and for how long the impact took place. This impact might be based on a familial pattern and be directed by the genetic code or might relate to subtle shifts or changes in specific amino acids at the level of the genome. In most cases, the cause or type of impact is not known.

The result is that some of the circuits or "wires" are laid down differently. We classify the presenting problems by the areas of faulty "wiring" or dysfunction. If the dysfunctional areas interfere with receiving, processing, and expressing information, the clinical problem is called a learning disability (learning disorder). If the dysfunctional areas result in difficulty receiving and expressing language, it is referred to as a language disability. If the dysfunctional areas result in difficulty with gross or fine motor activities, it is referred to as a developmental coordination disorder. If the dysfunctional areas result in hyperactivity, distractibility, or impulsivity, the clinical problem is called ADHD. Previous studies and studies in progress suggest that other disorders might be part of this continuum of brain dysfunctions. Each might reflect the brain's difficulty in modulating the many stimulant and inhibitory functions involved with cognitive, language, and motor functioning. For some, the problems relate to integrating and modulating the sensory inputs needed to coordinate body movement and motor planning activities; this clinical problem is called a sensory integrative disorder. If the dysfunctional areas relate to certain modulating tasks, the clinical picture might include motor or vocal tics, and the problem is called a chronic motor tic disorder or Tourette's disorder; or the clinical picture might include obsessive thoughts or compulsive behaviors and be called an obsessive-compulsive disorder.

The early statistical data supporting the concept of a continuum of neurological dysfunctions are growing. For individuals with learning disabilities, 20% to 25% have ADHD.[33, 34] Between 70% and 80% of individuals with ADHD have a learning disability.[33] About 60% of patients with Tourette's disorder have a learning disability.[35, 36] Further, 50% of individuals with Tourette's disorder have ADHD.[37–39] Fifty percent of patients with Tourette's disorder have obsessive-compulsive disorder.[40–42] A study in progress (L. B. Silver) attempts to correlate the frequency with which children or adolescents with a learning disability also have a language disability, ADHD, sensory integrative disorder, Tourette's disorder, or obsessive-compulsive disorder.

One set of clinical observations suggesting that these disorders are part of a continuum of neurological dysfunctions is the reaction of some children to stimulant medications. The reticular activating system, limbic system, and thalamic system constitute an interrelated system.[43] *Kindling* is the term used to describe what happens when one area of this interrelated system is modified and this alteration kindles changes farther up the system. For example, some children are prescribed a stimulant medication (methylphenidate or dextroamphetamine) and have increased anger or a rage reaction. The medication is stopped, and the behaviors stop. It is suspected that the impact of these medications on the reticular activating system kindled a reaction in the limbic system. Some children, when given the stimulant medications, show evidence of clinical depression. When the medication is stopped, the symptoms of depression stop. It is suspected that the impact of these medications on the reticular activating system kindled a reaction in the thalamic system. Still other children, when given these medications, have motor or vocal tics or obsessive-compulsive behaviors. When the medication is stopped, the behaviors disappear. It is suspected that the impact of these medications on the reticular activating system kindled a reaction in the thalamic system, setting off these modulating disorders.

Etiology

Cognitive and Language Studies

The specific constructs for understanding the probable cognitive and language bases for the specific learning disorders and motor skills disorder are discussed under each subtype in the section on treatment. The premise is that there are neurologically based processing problems that result in the disabilities.

Brain Studies

Earlier research focused on the concept of brain damage.[44, 45] Subtle central nervous system damage may result from circulatory, toxic metabolic, or other forms of insult to the fetal nervous system during a critical period of prenatal development; perinatal stresses to the brain; or stress to the nervous system during the critical early years of life (e.g., trauma, fever, inflammation). There may be a spectrum of disorders caused by prenatal, perinatal, and postnatal brain damage. Depending on location, extent of damage, time of life, and developmental stage at the time of damage, the stress might cause fetal or neonatal death, cerebral palsy, epilepsy, or mental retardation. The less severe forms might produce a variety of learning disorders.

More of the later research focused on physiological changes rather than on structural changes, that is, on the types of impacts that might affect the developing nervous system, causing areas of the brain to "wire itself" differently than expected. Galaburda and colleagues,[46, 47] doing microscopic studies of brains of individuals known to have learning disabilities, showed a consistent pattern of cortical cells that maintained an earlier developmental stage of migration and development, suggesting that something had an impact on the brain during development, halting or slowing down the normal developmental stages. Some of the factors studied as possibly contributing to the stress that results in neurological dysfunction are maternal cigarette smoking during pregnancy, convulsions during pregnancy, low fetal heart rate during the second stage of labor, lower placental weight, breech presentations, and chorionitis. Also noted is a history of maternal alcohol consumption (two to three drinks daily) during pregnancy.

Research has also focused on the genetic basis for these disorders. Several studies have shown a familial pattern in approximately 40% to 50% of children with learning disabilities.[48–50] In longitudinal studies of twins, identical pairs are more likely than fraternal pairs to be concordant for academic difficulties.[51] These studies support the possibility that this is a heterogeneous disorder.

Treatment

Treatment is directed at the underlying disabilities by use of educational interventions. Psychological interventions are also directed at any existing emotional, social, or family difficulties. In addition, social skills training may be helpful.

Educational Interventions

The goal of special educational interventions is to help children and adolescents overcome or compensate for their learning disorders or motor skills disorder so that they can succeed in school. These efforts involve remedial and compensatory approaches and use a multisensory approach that facilitates building on all areas of strength while compensating for any areas of weakness. These efforts are to be provided in as close to a regular classroom setting as possible. It is essential that the classroom teacher knows how to adapt the classroom, curriculum, and teaching style to best accommodate each student's areas of difficulty.

Educational Interventions for Reading Disorders

The process of reading involves two tasks, decoding or word recognition and reading comprehension. Decoding refers to the act of transcribing a printed word into speech. Comprehension refers to the process of interpreting the message or meaning of the text. Decoding is unique to reading and different from the recognition of words in speech; however, the linguistic skills that subserve reading comprehension are the same for both reading and listening.[52]

Reading disabilities may occur in one of three ways.[53] First, the ability to decode might be impaired but comprehension is intact. Most students with a reading disorder have a decoding problem. Second, decoding could be intact but comprehension is impaired. This relatively rare problem is the reverse of dyslexia and is called *hyperlexia.* Students can read almost any text but do not understand the text read. Third, both decoding and comprehension could be impaired. This double impairment results from a general cognitive impairment and is usually called *reading backwardness.*

Most students with a reading disorder have difficulty, sometimes extreme difficulty, acquiring the knowledge and skills essential for rapid automatic decoding. Reading comprehension, thus, is limited by weak decoding skills. Because spelling uses the same knowledge as word recognition, it is also frequently impaired.

Direct instruction in reading (and spelling and writing) is considered the essential treatment for a student with a reading disorder. These efforts are provided by a person trained to use appropriate remedial methods. These methods emphasize explicit instruction in letter-sound associations. Instruction is described as multisensory. Children see a letter and hear its name and sound; they trace the letter, saying its name and sound; and then they write the letter, repeating its name and sound. Sounds and letters are blended to form words. Reading, spelling, and writing are taught simultaneously. Instruction involves extended practice and is supplemented by speech segmentation training and study skills instructions. Parents are asked to read to their children to enhance appreciation of reading and to give the children access to knowledge normally obtained by reading.

Learning disorders, specifically reading disorders, are not cured. With appropriate interventions, children and adolescents with reading disorders learn to read and spell at a slower rate than normally developing individuals do. It is essential for these students to learn compensatory skills and for the classroom teachers to provide essential accommodations.

Educational Interventions for Mathematics Disorders

Children and adolescents with a mathematics disorder may have a wide range of symptoms, including delays in the acquisition of basic spatial and number concepts, problems learning and using number words and number facts or writing numbers correctly (and in correct alignment when doing computations), and difficulty in applying arithmetic skills when solving everyday problems.[54, 55] Because mathematics achievement is highly dependent on the quality of instruction offered students, it may be that a significant number of those students who are coded as having a learning disability by the school system do not have intrinsic mathematics disorders but have not had appropriate instruction.[56]

The understanding of the reasons for difficulty mastering mathematics is less advanced than the understanding for reading disorders. Studies clarify predictable stages through which children progress when they are learning to do arithmetic calculations.[57] Initially, the child learns informal knowledge about numbers, based on experience and strategies that develop without instruction. Relying on this informal knowledge, children devise counting procedures for solving quantitative problems. Problems often arise when children are introduced to the formal knowledge about mathematics that is presented in school. This formal knowledge depends on understanding and the correct application of complex algorithms that are not intuitively clear to the child (e.g., that our number system is based on a base-10 system). Problems may arise when children are asked early in their school years to memorize number facts. Children with delays in the development of information-processing strategies that are fundamental to memory may soon fall behind.

Treatment for a mathematics disorder involves general concerns and specific interventions. Initially, the problem of anxiety, withdrawal, defeatism, or other responses to repeated failure must be addressed.[54, 58] Much of the teaching of mathematics is based on criticism of failure. The emphasis is on getting the right answer rather than on problem solving. Because of this overfocus on getting the right answer, children may have performance anxiety or feel they are stupid in mathematics. For some, the premature pressure for speeded answers can short-circuit reasoning and foster impulsivity, resulting in the belief that mathematics has little to do with thinking. Students who have difficulty with mathematics memory may be deprived of compensatory techniques, which only adds to the problem. They are told that it is shameful to use their fingers or to mark down intermediate calculations or to use a calculator. These are considered cheating.

As noted earlier, sometimes the difficulties reflect poor teaching in mathematics. Further, mathematics learning is instruction-bound. Absenteeism, missed lessons, and inconsistency of instruction can leave gaps that result in persistent confusion. Students with learning disabilities in the areas that result in deficits in short-term memory, language, attention, or spatial perception and students with ADHD are especially susceptible to weak instruction.[59] Appropriately focused and systematic instruction in improving mathematics abilities may be all that is needed.

Specific interventions focus on the underlying difficulties. Some students have problems related to acquiring the conceptual underpinnings of the subject; some have problems related to procedural learning, recall of discrete information, and self-monitoring. Remedial efforts must take into account the student's areas of learning abilities and learning disabilities.

Educational Interventions for Disorders of Written Expression

Traditionally, little emphasis has been placed on writing in the early school grades. Much more time is spent on reading instruction. This approach is justified by the observation that receptive language skills in infants emerge before spoken words. Because infants can understand before they can speak, it has been assumed that school-age children should read before they write.[60] Until reading skills are well established, writing is usually assigned a minor role with regard to instruction. Both reading and writing require the ability to attach the correct sounds (phonemes) to the correct symbols (graphemes). Reading requires the ability to decode letters into sounds and blend these sounds into words. Writing requires outflow of the language or sounds in the brain back into graphic symbols. Thus, reading and writing problems are frequently seen together.

It is helpful to distinguish between a fine motor problem that results in difficulty with the mechanics of writing and a language-based learning disability that results in problems with the language of writing.[61] Individuals with a disorder of written expression might have a fine motor problem but always have a language-based disorder, resulting in difficulty with spelling, grammar, punctuation, capitalization, or composition.

Poor spelling might be the first indicator of a writing disorder. By third or fourth grade, additional writing problems are apparent. Children with a writing disorder exhibit grammatical and punctuation errors at the sentence level. Paragraphs are poorly organized. In later grades, taking notes is difficult. It is nearly impossible for these students to analyze a rapidly paced lecture and to write at the same time.

Treatment for a writing disorder might involve a skills approach or a holistic approach. Skills programs are often used with younger children and focus on letter-sound associations, with emphasis on reading and spelling.[62, 63] Children may be asked to listen carefully for the sounds in words and then to represent these sounds with written letters, saying each letter aloud as it is written.

The holistic approach to writing begins with the student's ideas. It involves a series of highly structured steps for narrowing ideas to one topic, writing a first draft, reading it aloud to an audience of peers, and then refining organization and language. The final step involves working on mechanics in preparation for "publishing" a draft for peers to read.

Most efforts combine these two approaches.[61] Children with a writing disorder need direct, sequential instructions in letter-sound associations and in spelling rules as well as in sentence structure and the connections between sentences and paragraphs that make text cohesive. Even with good remedial interventions, writing requires enormous effort because this disorder is not cured and must be compensated for, and this compensation must continue into adulthood. Appropriate accommodations, such as using a computer, may be needed throughout the individual's education and career.

Educational Interventions for Developmental Coordination Disorders

The approaches for helping children and adolescents with this disorder focus on academic skills, life skills, or athletic skills. That is, the focus of intervention might be on specific skills needed for school (e.g., handwriting), on dressing and other life skills (e.g., buttoning, zipping, tying, eating), or on skills needed to do better in sports (e.g., catching, hitting, throwing, running).

Occupational therapists work in all of these areas using sensory integrative approaches involving visual, visual-motor, gross motor, fine motor, proprioceptive, and vestibular stimulation and strengthening to improve functioning. Within school systems, the special education professional may work on handwriting, and the adaptive physical education teacher may work on physical education–related activities.

Psychotherapeutic Interventions

Learning disorders affect all aspects of the child's or adolescent's life. The same processing problems that interfere with reading, writing, mathematics, and language may interfere with communicating with peers and family, with success in sports and activities, and with such daily life skills as dressing oneself or cutting food.[2]

Lack of success in school can lead to a poor self-image and low self-esteem.[64–67] These individuals might feel that they have minimal control over their life and compensate by trying to be in more control.[2] Some individuals may become anxious or depressed, or a disruptive behavior disorder may develop.

Genetic and family studies show that in about 40% of children and adolescents with learning disabilities (learning disorders), there is a familial pattern.[68] Thus, from an early identification perspective, each sibling must be considered as possibly having a learning disorder. Also, there is a 40% likelihood that one of the parents may also have a learning disorder. This parent may not have known of this problem. If this is true, it will be helpful for this parent to understand. She or he may for the first time be able to understand a lifetime of difficulties or underachievement. Further, when the psychiatrist offers suggestions for this parent, the parent's areas of difficulty must be considered. Do not ask a mother to be more organized when she has been just as disorganized as her child all of her life.

The initial psychological interventions focus on educating the child or adolescent and the family about his or her difficulties.[7] The psychiatrist must help parents learn to advocate for the necessary services in school. The next level of interventions focuses on helping the family understand and work with the child or adolescent with a learning disorder.

Some children or adolescents may need specific individual, behavioral, group, or family therapy. If so, it is critical that the therapist understand the impact that the learning disorder has had on the individual and how these disabilities might affect the process of therapy.[69] As noted earlier, many students with a learning disorder have difficulties with peers and social skills problems. Social skills training might be helpful.

Education of the Individual and Family

Once the diagnosis is established, it is critical that the psychiatrist explain to the individual and to the parents what the problems are, focusing not only on the areas of learning difficulties but also on the areas of learning strengths.

Parents must understand this information so that they can develop a better understanding of their child or adolescent.[7] Mental health professionals working with these children and adolescents must understand the concept of learning disabilities (learning disorders) well enough to teach the individual and family members what the areas of disabilities and abilities are as well as the effects these disabilities have had on peer, family, and school activities.

The child or adolescent needs to begin to understand and to rethink concepts of self. Parents begin to modify their images of this child or adolescent and modify their responses and behaviors. Siblings may gain a new understanding of the problems in the family.

If the presenting behavior problems are not serious, it may be best first to provide family education and to give some time to see how this new knowledge affects the family. Concurrently, the parents are taught how to advocate for the necessary services within the school system. It may be that once the academic issues are addressed and the family begins to change, the behavior problems will diminish and no further help will be needed.

The next step is family counseling. Parents are taught how to use their knowledge of their son's or daughter's strengths and weaknesses to modify family patterns; select appropriate chores; choose appropriate activities, sports, and camps; and address stresses within the family.[7] Once taught the necessary knowledge about child or adolescent and the concepts of intervention, families can often move ahead, creatively working out their own problems.[7]

Individual Therapy

For some children and adolescents, individual behavioral therapy or psychotherapy may be indicated to help them develop new strategies for interacting with peers, parents, and teachers.

The models for this therapy are the same as for any other individual. However, knowledge of these disorders and school history help both the therapist and the individual better understand how certain problems or patterns of behaviors evolved. Because this form of therapy requires listening and talking, it is important for the therapist to know whether the individual has a disability in these areas. If so, the therapist has to develop ways of accommodating these problems if therapy is to progress. If a speech and language therapist is working with the individual, she or he might offer suggestions.

Family Therapy

The initial phases of family therapy might focus on helping the identified patient regain control over his or her behavior and helping the parents retake control of the family. A behavioral management approach is often the first intervention.

The model of family therapy used will depend on the needs of the family and the orientation of the therapist. For the child or adolescent with these disorders, it is important to keep in mind the impact of these disabilities on the individual and the family. It is also important to keep in mind the impact these disabilities might have on this individual's ability to participate in the family therapy. As with individual therapy, if the individual has difficulties with language or with other disabilities, he or she might have difficulty participating in the sessions. Accommodations will be necessary.

Social Skills Training

Children and adolescents with these disorders often have problems with peer relationships.[27, 29] There appears to be an association between poor peer relationships and a high risk for later psychological problems[70] as well as dissatisfaction and loneliness.[71] Poor childhood social skills and peer acceptance have been related to adjustment problems in adulthood.[72, 73] Thus, it is important to address these problems early.

The specific learning disabilities may be interfering with success with sports or other peer activities. In addition, many of these individuals have difficulty reading social cues or learning social skills.[27] It is not understood why these problems exist; however, they are not uncommon. Social skills training can be helpful.

Such interventions attempt to enhance social-cognitive skills and are directed at altering specific behavior patterns.[74, 75] Social-cognitive approaches are based on those cognitive processes that are related to competent, prosocial behavior. Targets of intervention are directed toward the underlying cognitive variables that are linked to positive peer acceptance.

The enhancement of social-cognitive skills typically involves three kinds of skill development: 1) accurate interpretation of social situations; 2) effective use of social behaviors in interactions with others; and 3) the evaluation of one's own performance and the ability to make adjustments, depending on the environmental context.

The first step in developing these skills typically requires the clinician to provide verbal instructions concerning the relevant skills (e.g., conversational skills). The skills are then modeled by the clinician. It is also important to discuss and emphasize positive outcomes associated with these skills. In the process, the clinician must confront and restructure thoughts that may inhibit the desired behaviors. The child is then required to rehearse the skills in simulated conditions, with the clinician providing reinforcement and corrective feedback as warranted. Generalization is stressed through homework assignments whereby skills are attempted in the natural environment and classroom.[74, 75]

Use of Medications

No medication has been found to be effective for treating the learning disorders or motor skills disorder. If the individual with these disorders also has ADHD, it is important that medication be used to minimize the hyperactivity, distractibility, or impulsivity so that the student can be available for learning.

Summary

Research on the etiology of learning disorders and motor skills disorder may not result in better treatments for individuals with such problems. However, this new knowledge should lead to prevention approaches that will decrease the numbers of individuals with such disabilities. Research on the subtypes of learning disabilities and on the underlying processes should lead to more effective models of education therapy.

Increased knowledge of brain function and brain dysfunction should clarify the continuum of neurological dysfunctions. This clarification will increase our awareness of comorbidity so that each time a child or adolescent is identified with one of the disorders, the others of the continuum will be considered as part of the diagnostic process.

Educational and academic success is critical to psychosocial growth and development as well as to the individual's role within the family. Understanding academic difficulties, the ability to diagnose learning disorders and motor skills disorder, and working collaboratively with education professionals are essential for the evaluation of children and adolescents.

Clinical Vignette 1 • Billy

Billy started first grade and did not do well. He did not master the early skills of reading and writing. The school decision was to have him repeat first grade. He did not make much more progress during his second year in first grade. Because of his age, he was promoted to second grade. He struggled through this year but fell further and further behind. When he entered third grade, he was overwhelmed. He knew that he was a year older than the other students. He was unable to do the work in class or at home and felt frustrated and stupid. Soon, he began to clown around in class and to get into fights with the other students.

Two other things happened during this third-grade year. First, his teacher became frustrated. She was trying to help him learn and he was not making progress. He was disrupting the class and preventing her from teaching the other children. The teacher handled her frustration by blaming it on the parents. She began to call them. "Billy is not completing his schoolwork." "His homework is incorrect." "He is teasing and fighting with the other children." She seemed to be saying to the parents, "Do something. Fix your kid." She did not realize that the parents were just as confused and frustrated as the teacher. Second, the parents began to disagree on parenting decisions. One felt that the best way to help Billy was to be firm and strict, and the other felt that the best way was to be understanding and permissive. They began to argue with each other and became less available to support each other.

Finally, the principal asked the parents to come to school. They were informed that Billy was not making academic progress. They were also told that the reason for his failure was that he was emotionally disturbed because of the marital conflicts. The parents were encouraged to see a mental health professional.

This psychiatrist noted that Billy had difficulty with reading, reading comprehension, handwriting, and written language. He found Billy to be frustrated with a poor self-image and low self-esteem. The parents seemed to be competent people who were also frustrated with Billy's difficulties. A full psychoeducational testing was requested. The results showed Billy to be of above-average ability but with significant learning disabilities.

Clinical Vignette 1 • • **Billy** *continued*

The psychiatrist concluded that the primary diagnosis was the learning disability. The emotional, behavioral, social, and family problems were secondary to the frustrations and failures experienced by Billy, his parents, and his teacher. By working with the family, he helped to get Billy identified as having a disability and to obtain the necessary services to help him. His behavior problems diminished and then ceased.

Clinical Vignette 2 • **Danny**

Danny was referred at age 7 years because his teacher and his parents thought he was depressed. The following is part of the process notes of the first session. The child's comments are noted; the psychiatrist's comments are in parentheses.

(Tell me about school.) I don't like to make mistakes. (Oh.) I get angry and frustrated. (What do you do?) Sometimes I feel like crying but I tough it out. (You can't cry?) The kids would think I was a baby. (What else do you feel?) I get angry with myself. I say I'm dumb or stupid or can't learn. (How do you feel when you say these things?) Bad. I'm just a jerk. (What do you do with these feelings?) I distract myself until they go away.

(Danny, why do you think you feel this way?) I don't know. (Could it have something to do with school?) I don't read or do math too good. (And the other kids . . . ?) They do it easier. (When you say that, you look upset.) Yea.

(What else happens in school?) I get scared sometimes that the teacher will be angry with me. (I see.) If she doesn't like my work she sends me back to do it again. I get mad because I did my best. (What do you do?) I distract myself and push it out of my mind. Then I do the work. (How do you push away such angry feelings?) I get busy with the work. (Don't you feel like yelling or throwing something, or . . . ?) No, that would be bad.

(You know, Danny, I get the feeling that you don't like yourself too much.) There's nothing to like. (You mean you cannot think of anything about yourself that is good?) I guess I'm alive. (As I listen to you I begin to feel very sad. I wonder if you feel the same way.) Yea.

(How do your Mommy and Daddy feel?) They love me. (Oh?) I'm their child. (And that's the reason.) I guess. (You guess?) Well, sometimes I think that Mommy wanted a girl because they don't cause as much trouble as boys. But, they may want a boy to carry on the family name. (So, you may not like yourself and now I hear you say that maybe your parents don't like you either.) Sometimes I think that.

(You know, Danny, I think the real problem is that you don't like yourself.) Yea. (And, you look so sad right now. How long have you had such feelings and thoughts?) I think they started in first grade. I couldn't do some of the work. The teacher used to make me do it again. The other kids got smiles from the teacher. I just got disappointed looks.

(What do you think was the problem in first grade?) I don't know. (You seemed to have trouble doing the school work.) Yea. (You know, I've worked with other boys and girls with problems like yours. Sometimes they worry that their problems are because they are bad and being punished or because there's something wrong with their head or maybe because they're stupid or retarded. I wonder what kind of thoughts you have.) I do think about these things. Maybe. Sometimes I think that maybe I'm retarded. (Retarded?) Yes. (That would be pretty upsetting to think that you were retarded.) Yea. (Maybe we had better find out what the problems are so that you won't have to worry about things that may not be true.) I'm just too dumb to learn anything. (I can see why you might think that way. Only, I bet you can learn. Only, maybe something is getting in the way. I'd like to find out what it is so that we can do something about it.) I can't do anything right.

Last year at the pool I hit my head a couple of times. (And, maybe that caused the problems?) Maybe that's why I'm so dumb. (I don't think that is the reason you are having trouble in school. But, then, I guess it's hard for you to believe me.) There's no hope for me.

After this session, sessions with parents, and conversations with Danny's teacher, a full psychoeducational evaluation was done. He was found to be bright but to have significant learning disabilities. He was depressed with a poor self-image and low self-esteem. However, these clinical problems were secondary to the unrecognized and untreated learning disabilities.

References

1. Silver LB: Psychological and family problems associated with learning disabilities: Assessment and intervention. J Am Acad Child Adolesc Psychiatry 1989; 28:319–325.
2. Silver LB: The secondary emotional, social, and family problems found with children and adolescents with learning disabilities. Child Adolesc Psychiatr Clin North Am 1993; 2:295–308.
3. Silver AA, Hagin RA: Disorders of Learning in Childhood. New York: John Wiley & Sons, 1992:23–42.
4. Silver AA, Hagin RA: The educational diagnostic process. Child Adolesc Psychiatr Clin North Am 1993; 2:265–281.
5. Bender WN: Secondary personality and behavioral problems in adolescents with learning disabilities. J Learn Disabil 1987; 20:280–285.
6. Hunt RD, Cohen DJ: Psychiatric aspects of learning difficulties. Pediatr Clin North Am 1984; 31:471–497.
7. Silver LB: The Misunderstood Child. A Guide for Parents of Children with Learning Disabilities, 2nd ed. New York: McGraw-Hill, 1992.
8. Valletutti P: The social and emotional problems of children with learning disabilities. Learning Disabilities 1983; 2:17–29.
9. Rourke BP, Strang JD: Subtypes of reading and arithmetical disabilities: A neuropsychological analysis. In Rutter M (ed): Developmental Neuropsychiatry. New York: Guilford Press, 1983:473–488.
10. Poplin M, Gray R, et al: A comparison of components of written expression abilities in learning disabled and non-learning dis-abled students at three grade levels. Learning Disability Q 1980; 3:46–53.
11. Ostrander R: Clinical observations suggesting a learning disability. Child Adolesc Psychiatr Clin North Am 1993; 2:249–263.
12. Silver LB: Introduction and overview to the clinical concepts of learning disabilities. Child Adolesc Psychiatr Clin North Am 1993; 2:181–192.
13. Centers for Disease Control: Assessment of the number and characteristics of persons affected by learning disabilities. In Interagency Committee on Learning Disabilities: Learning Disabilities. A Report to the U.S. Congress. Washington, DC: U.S. Department of Health and Human Services, 1987:107–123.
14. Ackerman P, Dykman R, Oglesby D: Sex and group differences in reading and attention disordered children with and without hyperkinesis. J Learn Disabil 1983; 16:407–415.
15. Finucci JM, Childs B: Are there really more dyslexic boys than girls? In Ansara A, Geshwind N, Galaburda A, et al (eds): Sex Differences in Dyslexia. Towson, MD: Orton Dyslexia Society, 1981:1–9.
16. Rutter M, Tizard J, Yule W, et al: Research report. Isle of Wight studies, 1964–1974. Psychol Med 1976; 6:313–332.
17. Berry CA, Shaywitz SE, Shaywitz BA: Girls with attention deficit disorder: A silent minority? A report on behavioral and cognitive characteristics. Pediatrics 1985; 76:801–809.
18. Johnson D, Blalock J (eds): Adults with Learning Disabilities: Clinical Studies. New York: Grune & Stratton, 1987.

19. Forness SB: Recent Concepts in Dyslexia: Implications for Diagnosis and Remediation. Virginia: ERIC Exceptional Child Education Reports, 1981.
20. Rutter M, Tizard J, Whitmore K: Education in Health and Behavior. London: Longman, 1970.
21. Berman A, Siegal A: Adaptive and learning skills in delinquent boys. J Learn Disabil 1976; 9:583–590.
22. Keilitz I, Zaremba BA, Broder PK: The link between learning disabilities and juvenile delinquency. Learning Disability Q 1979; 2:2–11.
23. Lewis D, Shanok SS, Pincus JH: Juvenile male sexual assaulters. Am J Psychiatry 1979; 136:1194–1196.
24. Lewis D, Balla D: Psychiatric correlates of severe reading disabilities in an incarcerated delinquent population. J Am Acad Child Psychiatry 1980; 19:611–622.
25. Mauser AJ: Learning disabilities and delinquent youth. Acad Ther 1974; 9:389–402.
26. Robbins DM, Beck JC, Pries R, et al: Learning disability and neuropsychological impairment in adjudicated, unincarcerated male delinquents. J Am Acad Child Psychiatry 1983; 22:40–46.
27. Hazel JS, Schumaker JB: Social skills and learning disabilities: Current issues and recommendations for future research. In Kavanagh JF, Truss TJ (eds): Learning Disabilities: Proceedings of the National Conference. Parkton, MD: York Press, 1988:293–344.
28. Rourke BP: Syndrome of nonverbal learning disabilities: The final common pathway of white-matter disease/dysfunction? Clin Neuropsychol 1987; 1:209–234.
29. Rourke BP: Socioemotional disturbances of learning disabled children. J Consult Clin Psychol 1988; 56:801–810.
30. Rourke BP: Nonverbal Learning Disabilities: The Syndrome and the Model. New York: Guilford Press, 1989.
31. Rourke BP, Fuerst DR: Learning Disabilities and Psychosocial Functioning: A Neuropsychological Perspective. New York: Guilford Press, 1991.
32. Rourke BP, Young GC, Stang JD, Russel DL: Adult outcomes of childhood central processing deficiencies. In Grand I, Adams KM (eds): Neuropsychological Assessment of Neuropsychiatric Disorders: Clinical Methods and Empirical Findings. New York: Oxford University Press, 1986:244–267.
33. Silver LB: The relationship between learning disabilities, hyperactivity, distractibility, and behavioral problems. J Am Acad Child Psychiatry 1981; 20:385–397.
34. Halperin JM, Gittelman R, Klein DF, et al: Reading-disabled hyperactive children: A distinct subgroup of attention deficit disorder with hyperactivity. J Abnorm Child Psychol 1984; 12:1–14.
35. Hagin RA, Beecher R, Pagano G, Kreeger H: Effects of Tourette syndrome on learning. In Friedhoff AJ, Chase TN (eds): Gilles de la Tourette Syndrome. New York: Raven Press, 1982.
36. Hagin RA, Kugler J: School problems associated with Tourette's syndrome. In Cohen DJ, Bruun RD, Leckman JF (eds): Tourette's Syndrome and Tic Disorders: Clinical Understanding and Treatment. New York: John Wiley & Sons, 1988.
37. Comings DE: Tourette Syndrome and Human Behavior. Durante, CA: Hope Press, 1990.
38. Comings DE, Comings BG: A controlled study of Tourette syndrome I–VII. Am J Hum Genet 1987; 41:701–866.
39. Comings DE, Comings BG: Tourette syndrome and attention deficit disorder. In Cohen DJ, Bruun RD, Leckman JF (eds): Tourette's Syndrome and Tic Disorders: Understanding and Treatment. New York: John Wiley & Sons, 1988:19–35.
40. Frankel M, Cummings JL, Robertson MM, et al: Obsessions and compulsions in Gilles de la Tourette's syndrome. Neurology 1986; 36:378–382.
41. Pauls DC, Pakstis A, Kurlan R, et al: Segregation and linkage analysis of Tourette's syndrome and related disorders. J Am Acad Child Adolesc Psychiatry 1990; 29:195–203.
42. Pitman RK, Gren RC, Jenicke MA, Mesullam MM: Clinical comparison of Tourette's disorder and obsessive-compulsive disorder. Am J Psychiatry 1987; 144:1166–1171.
43. Papez JW: A proposed mechanism of emotion. Arch Neurol Psychiatry 1937; 38:725–743.
44. Knobloch H, Pasamanick B: The syndrome of minimal cerebral damage in infancy. JAMA 1959; 70:1384–1387.
45. Towbin A: Organic causes of minimal brain dysfunction. Perinatal origin of minimal cerebral lesions. JAMA 1971; 217:1207–1209.
46. Galaburda AM, Kemper TL: Cytoarchitectonic abnormalities in developmental dyslexia: A case study. Ann Neurol 1979; 6:94–100.
47. Galaburda AM, Sherman GF, Rosen GD, et al: Developmental dyslexia: Four consecutive patients with cortical anomalies. Ann Neurol 1985; 18:222–233.
48. Silver LB: Familial patterns in children with neurologically-based learning disabilities. J Learn Disabil 1971; 4:349–358.
49. Morrison JR, Stewart MA: A family study of the hyperactive child syndrome. Biol Psychiatry 1971; 3:189–195.
50. Cantwell DP: Genetic studies of hyperactive children. In Fiere R, Rosenthal D, Brill H (eds): Genetic Research in Psychiatry. Baltimore: The Johns Hopkins University Press, 1975:273–280.
51. McCarty JJ, McCarty DJ: Learning Disabilities. Boston: Allyn & Bacon, 1969.
52. Gough PB, Tunmer WE: Decoding reading and reading disability. Remedial Spec Educ 1986; 7:6–10.
53. Shepherd MJ, Uhry JK: Reading disorder. Child Adolesc Psychiatr Clin North Am 1993; 2:193–208.
54. Fleischner JE, Garnett K: Math disorders. Child Adolesc Psychiatr Clin North Am 1993; 2:221–231.
55. Kosc L: Developmental dyscalculia. J Learn Disabil 1992; 7:165–178.
56. Carnine D: Reforming mathematics instruction: The role of curriculum materials. Behav Educ 1991; 1:37–57.
57. Ginsburg HP: Conference commentary. Presented at the Division for Learning Disabilities International Conference on Math Disabilities; 1992; Columbia University Teachers College, New York.
58. Torgeson J: The learning disabled child as an inactive learner: Educational implications. Top Learning Learning Disabilities 1982; 2:45–52.
59. Cawley JF, Miller JH: Cross-sectional comparison of the mathematical performance of children with learning disabilities: Are we on the right track toward comprehensive programming? J Learn Disabil 1989; 22:250–254.
60. Myklebust HR: Development and Disorders of Written Language, Volume I, Picture Story Language Test. Philadelphia: Grune & Stratton, 1965.
61. Uhry JK, Shepherd MJ: Writing disorder. Child Adolesc Psychiatr Clin North Am 1993; 2:209–219.
62. Cox A: Structures and Techniques: Multisensory Teaching of Basic Language Skills. Cambridge, MA: Educators Publishing Service, 1984.
63. Slingerland BH: A Multi-sensory Approach to Language Arts for Specific Language Disability Children: A Guide for Primary Teachers, Books 1–3. Cambridge, MA: Educators Publishing Service, 1971.
64. Black FW: Self-concept as related to achievement and age in learning disabled children. Child Dev 1974; 45:1137–1140.
65. Bryan T, Pearl R: Self-concept and locus of control of learning disabled children. J Clin Child Psychol 1979; 8:223–226.
66. Rogers H, Saklofske DH: Self-concepts, locus of control and performance expectations of learning disabled students. J Learn Disabil 1985; 18:244–267.
67. Shaw L, Levine MD, Belfer M: Developmental double jeopardy: A study of clumsiness and self-esteem in children with learning problems. Dev Behav Pediatr 1982; 3:191–196.
68. Johnson DJ: Review of research on specific reading, writing, and mathematics disorders. In Kavanagh JF, Truss TJ (eds): Learning Disabilities: Proceedings of the National Conference. Parkton, MD: York Press, 1988:79–163.
69. Silver LB: Psychological interventions and therapies for children and adolescents with learning disabilities. Child Adolesc Psychiatr Clin North Am 1993; 2:323–337.
70. Cowen EL, Rederson A, Babigan H, et al: Long term follow up of early detected vulnerable children. J Consult Clin Psychol 1973; 41:438–446.
71. Asher SR, Wheeler V: Children's loneliness: A comparison of rejected and neglected peer status. J Consult Clin Psychol 1985; 53:500–505.
72. Gresham FM, Elliott SN: Social skills assessment technology for LD students. Learning Disability Q 1989; 12:141–152.
73. Wiener J, Harris PJ, Shirer C: Achievement and social behavioral correlations of peer status in LD children. Learning Disability Q 1990; 13:114–126.
74. Dodge KA: Problems in social relationships. In Mash EJ, Barkley RA (eds): Treatment of Childhood Disorders. New York: Guilford Press, 1989:222–244.
75. McIntosh R, Vaughn S, Zaragaza N: A review of social interventions for students with learning disabilities. J Learn Disabil 1991; 24:451–458.

CHAPTER

35

Autistic Disorder and Other Pervasive Developmental Disorders

Bennett L. Leventhal
Martha E. Crotts
Edwin H. Cook

Autistic Disorder
Rett's Disorder
Childhood Disintegrative Disorder
Asperger's Disorder
Pervasive Developmental Disorder Not Otherwise Specified

The pervasive developmental disorders (PDDs) are a group of clinical syndromes that have two fundamental elements: developmental delays and developmental deviations. It is the presence of the deviation in combination with delays that differentiates PDDs from mental retardation and other specific developmental disorders. Thus, PDDs are not merely an arrest or delay in development but a unique set of deviant behaviors and aberrant functioning on several levels.[1] Most often, these conditions are congenital, but all certainly begin before the third year of life. The common developmental disturbances include disruptions in social interactions and communication along with presence of stereotyped behaviors, activities, and interests as well as cognitive impairment. The prototypical PDD is autistic disorder; the other PDDs, including Rett's disorder, childhood disintegrative disorder, Asperger's disorder, and PDD not otherwise specified (NOS), share certain core features with autistic disorder.

DSM-IV Criteria 299.00

Autistic Disorder

A. A total of six (or more) items from (1), (2), and (3), with at least two from (1) and one each from (2) and (3):

(1) qualitative impairment in social interaction, as manifested by at least two of the following:

(a) marked impairment in the use of multiple nonverbal behaviors such as eye-to-eye gaze, facial expression, body postures, and gestures to regulate social interaction

(b) failure to develop peer relationships appropriate to developmental level

(c) a lack of spontaneous seeking to share enjoyment, interests, or achievements with other people (e.g., by a lack of showing, bringing, or pointing out objects of interest)

(d) lack of social or emotional reciprocity

(2) qualitative impairments in communication as manifested by at least one of the following:

(a) delay in, or total lack of, the development of spoken language (not accompanied by an attempt to compensate through alternative modes of communication such as gesture or mime)

(b) in individuals with adequate speech, marked impairment in the ability to initiate or sustain a conversation with others

(c) stereotyped and repetitive use of language or idiosyncratic language

(d) lack of varied, spontaneous make-believe play or social imitative play appropriate to developmental level

(3) restricted repetitive and stereotyped patterns of behavior, interests, and activities, as manifested by at least one of the following:

(a) encompassing preoccupation with one or more stereotyped and restricted patterns of interest that is abnormal in either intensity or focus

(b) apparently inflexible adherence to specific, nonfunctional routines or rituals

(c) stereotyped and repetitive motor mannerisms (e.g., hand or finger flapping or twisting, or complex whole-body movements)

(d) persistent preoccupation with parts of objects

B. Delays or abnormal functioning in at least one of the following areas, with onset before age 3 years: (1) social interaction, (2) language as used in social communication, or (3) symbolic or imaginative play.

C. The disturbance is not better accounted for by Rett's disorder or childhood disintegrative disorder.

DSM-IV Criteria 299.80

Rett's Disorder

A. All of the following:

(1) apparently normal prenatal and perinatal development

(2) apparently normal psychomotor development through the first 5 months after birth

(3) normal head circumference at birth

B. Onset of all of the following after the period of normal development:

(1) deceleration of head growth between ages 5 and 48 months

(2) loss of previously acquired purposeful hand skills between ages 5 and 30 months with the subsequent development of stereotyped hand movements (e.g., handwringing or hand washing)

(3) loss of social engagement early in the course (although often social interaction develops later)

(4) appearance of poorly coordinated gait or trunk movements

(5) severely impaired expressive and receptive language development with severe psychomotor retardation

DSM-IV Criteria 299.10

Childhood Disintegrative Disorder

A. Apparently normal development for at least the first 2 years after birth as manifested by the presence of age-appropriate verbal and nonverbal communication, social relationships, play, and adaptive behavior.

B. Clinically significant loss of previously acquired skills (before age 10 years) in at least two of the following areas:

(1) expressive or receptive language

(2) social skills or adaptive behavior

(3) bowel or bladder control

(4) play

(5) motor skills

C. Abnormalities of functioning in at least two of the following areas:

(1) qualitative impairment in social interaction (e.g., impairment in nonverbal behaviors, failure to develop peer relationships, lack of social or emotional reciprocity)

(2) qualitative impairments in communication (e.g., delay or lack of spoken language, inability to initiate or sustain a conversation, stereotyped and repetitive use of language, lack of varied make-believe play)

(3) restricted, repetitive, and stereotyped patterns of behavior, interests, and activities, including motor stereotypies and mannerisms

DSM-IV Criteria 299.10

Childhood Disintegrative Disorder *Continued*

D. The disturbance is not better accounted for by another specific pervasive developmental disorder or by schizophrenia.

Reprinted with permission from the Diagnostic and Statistical Manual of Mental Disorders, Fourth Edition. Copyright 1994 American Psychiatric Association.

DSM-IV Criteria 299.80

Asperger's Disorder

A. Qualitative impairment in social interaction, as manifested by at least two of the following:
   (1) marked impairment in the use of multiple nonverbal behaviors such as eye-to-eye gaze, facial expression, body postures, and gestures to regulate social interaction
   (2) failure to develop peer relationships appropriate to developmental level
   (3) a lack of spontaneous seeking to share enjoyment, interests, or achievements with other people (e.g., by a lack of showing, bringing, or pointing out objects of interest to other people)
   (4) lack of social or emotional reciprocity
B. Restricted repetitive and stereotyped patterns of behavior, interests, and activities, as manifested by at least one of the following:
   (1) encompassing preoccupation with one or more stereotyped and restricted patterns of interest that is abnormal in either intensity or focus
   (2) apparently inflexible adherence to specific, nonfunctional routines or rituals
   (3) stereotyped and repetitive motor mannerisms (e.g., hand or finger flapping or twisting, or complex whole-body movements)
   (4) persistent preoccupation with parts of objects
C. The disturbance causes clinically significant impairment in social, occupational, or other important areas of functioning.
D. There is no clinically significant general delay in language (e.g., single words used by age 2 years, communicative phrases used by age 3 years).
E. There is no clinically significant delay in cognitive development or in the development of age-appropriate self-help skills, adaptive behavior (other than in social interaction), and curiosity about the environment in childhood.
F. Criteria are not met for another specific pervasive developmental disorder or schizophrenia.

Reprinted with permission from the Diagnostic and Statistical Manual of Mental Disorders, Fourth Edition. Copyright 1994 American Psychiatric Association.

DSM-IV Criteria 299.80

Pervasive Developmental Disorder Not Otherwise Specified

A. Presence of one or more of the following:
   (1) Severe and pervasive impairment in reciprocal social interaction
   (2) Severe and pervasive impairment in verbal and nonverbal communication
   (3) Presence of stereotyped behavior, interests, and activities
B. Includes "atypical" autism (criteria for autism are not met because of late age at onset, atypical symptoms, or subthreshold symptoms).
C. Criteria for the following are *not* met:
   (1) autistic disorder, Rett's disorder, childhood disintegrative disorder, Asperger's disorder
   (2) schizophrenia
   (3) schizotypal personality disorder
   (4) avoidant personality disorder

Data from American Psychiatric Association: Diagnostic and Statistical Manual of Mental Disorders, 4th ed. Washington, DC: American Psychiatric Association, 1994.

History

PDD is not a creation of the 20th century. Indeed, this clinical syndrome has been described repeatedly in folklore and clinical literature. In one of the most celebrated cases, Victor, the wild boy of Aveyron, was described by Itard[2] in 1801 as a child who was clearly without communicative and social skills as well as with some degree of mental retardation; also described was one of the first concerted treatment efforts for an individual with a PDD. Other authors have provided vivid observations of these disorders, some of which have withstood the test of time, such as Heller's[3] 1930 description of dementia infantilis (Heller's syndrome) in a group of children who, after a normal early developmental course, had severe regression with restlessness, loss of speech, and purposeless repetitive behaviors.

It is from the careful descriptions of Leo Kanner that we have the contemporary view of autism and PDD. In 1943, Kanner[4] reported the clinical picture and behavioral habits of 11 children with "fascinating peculiarities." Specifically, Kanner noted unusual language patterns, including echolalia, and pronoun reversal along with limited use of speech to communicate. Kanner's patients lacked social relatedness, seeming not to notice the feelings or presence of others, and had a persistent need for sameness in their routines and frequent repetitive activities. He labeled the syndrome early infantile autism.[5] At about the same time, Asperger[6] reported a similar developmental disorder in individuals who seemed to have more language and better cognitive functioning than most patients with autism. What he then called autistic psychopathy is now referred to as Asperger's disorder.

Kanner's original use of the term *autism* has transcended time, although not without controversy. Historically, the word autism had been associated with descriptions of schizophrenia.[7] Autism was not consistently separated from childhood schizophrenia until the mid-1970s. At that time, careful examination of childhood psychopathological conditions clarified that autistic disorder was an entity distinct from schizophrenia, with different age at onset, course, and symptom cluster.[8–11]

With the advent of the *Diagnostic and Statistical Manual of Mental Disorders,* Third Edition (DSM-III),[12] autism and the other PDDs came under the general heading of pervasive developmental disorders, which at the time included only two, infantile autism and childhood-onset PDD. However, DSM-III criteria failed to allow for changes in the developmental course of the illness and were too restrictive.[13, 14] The *Diagnostic and Statistical Manual of Mental Disorders,* Third Edition, Revised (DSM-III-R)[15] addressed some of these problems by increasing the number and detail of the criteria while also changing the name of the syndrome from infantile autism to autistic disorder and changing the name of childhood-onset PDD to PDD NOS. Broadening of diagnostic criteria meant a larger number of patients fell into the autistic disorder category even though many psychiatrists thought that some of these patients were not autistic by traditional standards and were believed to represent "false-positives."[13, 16, 17] As a result, using factor-analytical techniques and attempting to balance sensitivity and specificity, the *Diagnostic and Statistical Manual of Mental Disorders,* Fourth Edition (DSM-IV), and the *International Statistical Classification of Diseases and Related Health Problems,* 10th revision, included criteria not only for autistic disorder but also for other related PDDs.[8] The current criteria are summarized in Table 35–1.

Epidemiology

Not all childhood-onset psychiatric disorders have a well-established epidemiology. Autistic disorder is relatively rare, with prevalence rates in the range of 2 to 5 per 10,000 children. When broader definitions of autistic disorder are used, however, the prevalence rate increases to 10 to 20 per 10,000.[18] It has been suggested that the PDDs other than autistic disorder and PDD NOS are less common. Review of epidemiological studies across cultures reveals similar rates of autistic disorder and consistent phenomenology.[19]

Like most forms of childhood and adolescent psychiatric illness, autistic disorder is four times more prevalent in boys than in girls. The other PDDs seem to be similar to autistic disorder, with a greater ratio of affected boys, except in the case of Rett's disorder, which has been diagnosed only in girls.

In 1943, Kanner reported an association between high socioeconomic status and autism; however, subsequent studies have suggested that autistic disorder is seen throughout all socioeconomic levels. It is not certain whether there are differences in geographical distribution of the PDDs between urban and rural settings, even though a few studies have suggested increased rates of the PDDs in urban areas.[20, 21]

The majority of children with autistic disorder are mentally retarded. This appears to be the case in other PDDs as well. Approximately 25% to 30% of autistic children have an IQ of less than 50; 20% to 30% have an IQ of 70 of greater. Overall, intelligence levels range from profoundly retarded to above average in autistic disorder and the other PDDs.[22] A notable exception is in childhood disintegrative disorder, in which all affected children are mentally retarded.[23] In addition, follow-up studies of autistic disorder have demonstrated that mental retardation, when present, persists from the time of diagnosis onward.[24] IQs tend to be stable over time and are thought to be one of the most important predictors of outcome in autism.[25] The fundamental cognitive deficits observed consist of deficiencies in language, abstraction, sequencing, and coding operations. Relative strengths lie in visuospatial skills.[26] A small number of autistic individuals have phenomenal abilities in particular areas, such as in memory, calendar calculation, or artistic endeavors. These so-called savant talents are also seen in individuals with other developmental disorders.[27]

Etiology and Pathophysiology

At this time, the precise etiology and pathogenesis of PDDs are unknown. However, a sophisticated search for causes has led to an enormous shift in perspectives in the past two decades. Although some still argue for a so-called nurture hypothesis for causation, PDDs are among the medical disorders most influenced by nature. The most contemporary etiological theories suggest either a genetic or another early developmental disruption in the development of brain functioning with overt clinical manifestations potentially modified by social or environmental experiences.

Early biological hypotheses focused on neurotransmitter abnormalities as a cause of autistic disorder, starting with Schain and Freedman's[28] early observation of hyperserotonemia in many individuals with autism. This has been replicated numerous times,[29] proving to be one of the most enduring biological findings in psychiatry. Hyperserotonemia is most likely due to abnormalities in the function of proteins, such as the serotonin transporter and serotonin 5-HT_{2A} receptor, which are expressed in both the developing brain and platelets.[30, 31]

Because autism and the PDDs are often (~70%) associated with mental retardation, the search for etiology has included common factors. For example, individuals with fragile X syndrome are considered to have a higher prevalence rate of autism by some but not all investigators.[32, 33] Whereas fragile X syndrome may account for only a small number of cases of PDD, most children with fragile X syndrome have a PDD.[34] Other genetic disorders have been linked to autism: phenylketonuria[35] and tuberous sclerosis.[36] Behavioral characteristics and physical findings of fragile X syndrome are presented in Table 35–2. Chromosomal abnormalities associated with autistic disorder or other PDDs are listed in Table 35–3.

Table 35–1 Comparison of Domains of Diagnostic Criteria for Pervasive Developmental Disorders

	Autistic Disorder	Rett's Disorder	Childhood Disintegrative Disorder	Asperger's Disorder	Pervasive Developmental Disorder NOS
Age at onset	Delays or abnormal functioning in social interaction, language, or play by age 3 y	Apparently normal prenatal development Apparently normal motor development for first 5 mo Deceleration of head growth between ages 5 and 48 mo	Apparently normal development for at least the first 2 y Clinically significant loss of previously acquired skills before age 10 y	No clinically significant delay in language, cognitive development, or development of age-appropriate self-help skills, adaptive behavior, and curiosity about the environment in childhood	Category used in cases of pervasive impairment in social interaction, and communication, with presence of stereotyped behaviors or interests when criteria are not met for a specific disorder
Social interaction	Qualitative impairment in social interaction, as manifested by at least two of the following: • Marked impairment in the use of multiple nonverbal behaviors, e.g., eye-to-eye gaze • Failure to develop peer relationships appropriate to developmental level • Lack of spontaneous seeking to share enjoyment with other people • Lack of social or emotional reciprocity	Loss of social engagement early in the course (although often social interaction develops later)	Same as autistic disorder along with loss of social skills (previously acquired)	Same as autistic disorder	
Communication	Qualitative impairments of communication as manifested by at least one of the following: • Delay in, or total lack of, the development of spoken language • Marked impairment in initiating or sustaining a conversation with others, in individuals with adequate speech • Stereotyped and repetitive use of language or idiosyncratic language • Lack of varied, spontaneous make-believe or imitative play	Severely impaired expressive and receptive language development and severe psychomotor retardation	Same as autistic disorder along with loss of expressive or receptive language previously acquired	No clinically significant delay in language	
Behavior	Restricted, repetitive, and stereotyped patterns of behavior, as manifested by one of the following: • Preoccupation with one or more stereotyped or restricted patterns of interest • Adherence to nonfunctional routines or rituals • Stereotyped and repetitive motor mannerisms • Persistent preoccupation with parts of objects	Loss of previously acquired purposeful hand movement Appearance of poorly coordinated gait or trunk movements	Same as autistic disorder along with loss of bowel or bladder control, play, motor skills previously acquired	Same as autistic disorder	
Exclusions	Disturbance not better accounted for by Rett's disorder or childhood disintegrative disorder		Disturbance not better accounted for by another PDD or schizophrenia	Criteria are not met for another PDD or schizophrenia	

Data from American Psychiatric Association: Diagnostic and Statistical Manual of Mental Disorders, 4th ed. Washington, DC: American Psychiatric Association, 1994.

Table 35–2 Characteristics of Fragile X Syndrome

Behavioral
Mental retardation
Poor concentration
Hyperactivity
Language delay
Social discomfort manifested by anxiety, shyness, poor eye contact
Stereotypies such as hand biting or hand flapping
Physical Findings
Wide, prominent, low-set, and posteriorly rotated ears
Narrow facial structure (common after puberty)
Hypermobility of finger joints
Macroorchidism (particularly postpubertal)
Mitral valve prolapse
Prominent jaw
High-pitched speech

Twin and family studies have yielded some useful information about genetic aspects of autism. In one study, 37% of the 11 monozygotic pairs were concordant for autism, whereas none of the dizygotic pairs demonstrated concordance for the disease. Nine of the other 10 monozygotic pairs were concordant for cognitive impairment or language delay, whereas only one dizygotic pair was concordant.[37] Another study of 281 families found a striking number of nontwin siblings concordant for autism, in addition to large numbers of concordant monozygotic and dizygotic twins. A recessive gene hypothesis could not be excluded.[38] A study in the Nordic countries involving 21 pairs of twins and a set of identical triplets reported a concordance for autism of 91% in monozygotic twin pairs versus 0% in dizygotic twin pairs.[39]

Between 30% and 75% of autistic individuals have nonspecific neurological abnormalities including poor coordination, hypotonicity or hypertonicity, choreiform movements, abnormal posture and gait, tremor, and myoclonic jerking.[40] About 25% of autistic individuals have seizures by the end of adolescence or electroencephalographical abnormalities. Seizures have been highly correlated with mental retardation and may be correlated more with mental impairment than the presence of PDD or autism.[41, 42] Seizures with onset in adolescence are often generalized but usually infrequent.[43]

Table 35–3 Chromosomal Abnormalities Associated with Autistic Disorder or Other Pervasive Developmental Disorders

- Fragile X syndrome (trinucleotide expansion at Xq27.3)
- Down's syndrome (trisomy 21)
- Prader-Willi syndrome (deletion or maternal isodisomy of chromosome 15)
- Marker chromosome
- Duplication of 15q11–q13

Neurophysiological research using brain stem evoked potentials demonstrated moderate to severe delays in auditory brain stem transmission.[44] This finding has not been replicable.[45] By use of direct neuroradiological or neuropathological evidence or well-documented lesions from other cases with specific neuroanatomical or neurophysiological abnormalities, there has been a search for a lesion that underlies autism. Neuroanatomical loci for autism have been posited in the frontal, parietal, and temporal regions of the cortex and in the midbrain and cerebellum. Arguments for specific, highly localized deficits (e.g., in facial recognition or processing of gaze) have been made as well as those that propose broader deficits in information processing and cognition that have less clear implications for neurobiology. Whatever the primary deficit or deficits in autism, these deficits must affect the way in which a child acquires information and skills early in development. In addition, the hypothesized deficits must allow relative sparing of some domains (e.g., early gross motor development, sequence of development of syntax and lexical semantics, object permanence).

Magnetic resonance imaging has shown cerebellar hypoplasia in some but not all studies.[46, 47] Postmortem studies have shown abnormalities in the cerebellum,[48, 49] hippocampus, and amygdala.[48] Positron emission tomography revealed generalized hypermetabolism in one[50] but not another study.[51] Magnetic resonance spectroscopy revealed decreased levels of phosphocreatine and α-adenosine triphosphate in dorsolateral frontal cortex.[52]

Phenomenology

Although autism is heterogeneous in severity, in its relationship to intellectual delay, and in the particular symptoms manifested in any individual at a given point of time, it has consistently been the most reliably diagnosed disorder of childhood. Unusual qualities of social interaction, communication, and use of objects typical of autism are not only important to diagnosis but, along with verbal intelligence, have been found to be reliable across time and observers and to be significant predictors of psychiatric and vocational outcome.[25, 53, 54]

Kanner[4] held that autism began at or near the time of birth. Later work has revealed that the syndrome can appear from birth or after up to 30 months of apparently normal development.[55]

The central feature of these disorders is disturbance of social development, including difficulty in developing meaningful attachments and social reciprocity.[56, 57] There is clearly some variation in the clinical presentation. Some autistic children do become upset when separated from their parents by the age of 4 or 5 years. However, they still tend not to use their parents for security as often as other children do. Typically, a child with autistic disorder has abnormal patterns of eye contact and facial expression. In contrast to normal children, children with autism fail to use directed eye contact and varied facial expression to establish social contact and seem to be incapable of coordinating social cues.[58] They seem to lack empathy or the ability to perceive others' moods or responses; the child acts in a socially inappropriate manner or lacks the social responsiveness needed to succeed in social settings, leading to a failure to develop close, meaningful relationships from grade school onward. However, some autistic youth eventually develop warm, friendly relationships with family while their relationships with peers lag behind considerably.

Another area of difficulty is in the acquisition and proper use of language for communication. It is estimated that only about half of autistic children develop functional speech. This is not merely a delay in development of speech but also deviancy in speech patterns compared with normal children and children with specific language disorders. If autistic children do begin to speak, their babble is decreased in quantity and lacking in vocal experimentation.[59] When autistic children do acquire some speech, it is characteristically peculiar and missing a social aspect.[60] Some autistic children are even loquacious, although their speech tends to be repetitious and self-directed rather than aimed at maintaining a dialogue. People with autistic disorder commonly make use of stereotyped speech, including immediate and delayed echolalia, pronoun reversal, and neologisms.[61] Speech usage is idiosyncratic, may consist of concrete and poorly constructed grammar, may not be used to convey social meaning, and is often lacking in inference and imagination. The delivery of speech is frequently abnormal with atypical tone, pitch, accent, and cadence.

Individuals with autistic disorder routinely engage in unusual patterns of behavior. Most autistic people also resist or have significant difficulty with new experiences or transitions. They are often resistant to changes in their environment. They often perform stereotyped motor acts again and again, such as hand clapping or flapping, or peculiar finger movements. These movements often occur at the periphery of their vision near their own face. Some autistic children engage in self-injurious behaviors including biting or striking themselves or banging their heads. This is most likely to occur in autistic children with serious mental retardation but is also found in autistic children without mental retardation.[62] Their play only occasionally involves traditional toys and typically includes unusual preoccupations. Individuals with autistic disorder seem to have unusual sensitivity to some sensory experiences, particularly specific sounds.

Other problems in autistic disorder and other PDDs include deficits in shifting of attention and joint attention.[63, 64] Many children also have symptoms of hyperactivity and difficulty sustaining attention, but these should be distinguished from the joint attentional dysfunction found in all patients with autistic disorder. Examples of joint attention include social exchanges that include pointing, referential gaze, and gestures showing interest.

Asperger's disorder and autistic disorder, as classically described, share many common features. Asperger considered this syndrome to be a personality disorder and called it autistic psychopathy. He remarked that the children he studied began to speak at about the same time as other children did and eventually gained a full complement of language and syntax. However, he noted unusual use of pronouns, continuous repetition of certain words or phrases, and exhaustive focus of speech on particular topics. Asperger also described that the children he studied had difficulty in social reciprocity, engaged in repetitive play, and focused on certain interests excessively.[6] Thus, the predominant differentiating feature between autistic disorder and Asperger's disorder is that those with Asperger's disorder are not necessarily language delayed and do not have mental impairment.

In general, individuals with Asperger's disorder are thought to have symptoms that are a bit more mild with fewer bizarre behaviors compared with children with autistic disorder. They may be recognized as impaired at a later age, may not need as extensive school services as autistic children do, and are thought to have a better outcome than that of autistic children.[65] Some children with classic presentations of autism who later gained language skills were likened to Asperger's original descriptions, suggesting a possible continuum of developmental disorders.[66] Asperger's disorder was formally recognized as a separate PDD with the inception of DSM-IV. Much work is needed to further characterize this disorder, including information on how this disorder is to be delineated from schizoid personality disorder.[67]

Rett's disorder is a developmental disorder that preferentially strikes girls and differs substantially from autistic disorder past the toddler stage. The disorder was first described by Rett[68] in 1966 in 22 patients. Typically, the child with Rett's disorder has an uneventful prenatal and perinatal course that continues through at least the first 6 months. With onset of the disease, there is deceleration of head growth, usually between 5 months and 4 years of age. In toddlerhood, the manifestations can be similar to autistic disorder in that there is frequently impairment in language and social development along with presence of stereotyped motor movements. In particular, there is loss of acquired language; restricted interest in social contact or interactions; and the start of handwringing, clapping, or tapping in the midline of the body. The motor activity is seen together with lubrication of the hands with saliva. This type of activity begins after purposeful hand movement is lost. Serious psychomotor retardation sets in as well as receptive and expressive language impairments. Another common symptom is hyperventilation. Between the ages of 1 and 4 years, truncal apraxia and gait apraxia ensue.[69] The child with Rett's disorder may actually improve in social capabilities as time passes while progressively deteriorating in cognitive and motor function. The disorder is relatively easily differentiated from other PDDs after the child has reached the age of 4 or 5 years.[70]

Childhood disintegrative disorder and autistic disorder have some similarities in that they both involve deficits in social interaction and communication as well as repetitive behaviors. However, the symptoms of childhood disintegrative disorder appear abruptly or in the period of a few months' time after 2 years or more of normal development. There is generally no prior serious illness or insult, although a few cases have been linked to certain organic brain ailments such as measles encephalitis, leukodystrophies, or other diseases. With onset of childhood disintegrative disorder, the child loses previously mastered cognitive, language, and motor skills and regresses to such a degree that there is loss of bowel and bladder control.[23, 71] Children with childhood disintegrative disorder tend to lose abilities that would normally allow them to take care of themselves, and their motor activity contains fewer complex, repetitive behaviors than in autistic disorder. Some children with this disorder experience regression that occurs for a time and then becomes stable. Another group of children afflicted with childhood disintegrative disorder has a poorer outcome, with onset of focal neurological findings and seizures in the face of a worsening course and greater motor impairment.[72] The majority of children with this disorder deteriorate to a severe level of mental retardation; a few retain selected abilities in specific areas. Differential diagnosis of childhood disintegrative disorder requires obtaining a particularly thorough developmental history, history of course of illness, and neurological evaluation.

PDD NOS or atypical autism should be reserved for cases in which there are qualitative impairments in reciprocal social development, communication, and imaginative and flexible interests but full criteria for a specific PDD are not met. It is important in education of parents, teachers, and colleagues to be clear that PDD NOS is closely related to autistic disorder, because many families have been given diagnoses of autistic disorder and PDD NOS and have the mistaken impression that this represents strong diagnostic disagreement among diagnosticians.

Thus, autistic disorder and the other PDDs are complex clinical syndromes. It is likely there are multiple causes and perhaps even multiple additional syndromes subsumed under these diagnostic categories. However, it is clear that these are a group of syndromes that reflect substantial impairment in related areas of functioning and that these problems tend to follow a reasonably stable natural history. Furthermore, despite the variation in their syndromal presentations, these disorders are sufficiently striking and well characterized that diagnoses can be made reliably and validly, even at an early age.

Evaluation

The diagnosis of autism is carried out by gathering information about the child's historical background, behavior, and cognitive abilities (Table 35–4). Appropriate sources for this information include parents, teachers, and anyone who has regular or meaningful contact with the child. Other means of obtaining needed information are through direct observation of the child and standardized assessment. After an adequate history is obtained, a crucial step in evaluating developmental disorders lies in procuring a solid account of the developmental history. Special heed should be taken with regard to developmental phases of language, social interactions, and play.[57] Also, an investigation of any chronic illnesses or illnesses with a neurological bearing in the child should be performed, and the medical history of the family should be taken. Psychiatrists should inquire about family history of neurological disease, psychiatric disorder, developmental delay, language disorder, or learning problems.

Structured interviews are available for use in evaluating children specifically for autism, which could help psychiatrists collect and organize historical information in a reliable manner. One such instrument is the Autism Diagnostic Interview–Revised, which is a standardized, semistructured interview that can be administered to parents with autistic children.[56]

An essential piece of the comprehensive evaluation of the child is gained through direct observation of the child. Ideally, this should be done in a variety of settings to obtain an overall view of the child's behaviors and functioning under differing environmental conditions. The Autism Diagnostic Observation Schedule is recommended to structure observation for verbal children, adolescents, and adults; the PreLinguistic Autism Diagnostic Observation Schedule is recommended for diagnosis of children without sufficient verbal skills.[54, 73] A variety of other instruments are also available for evaluative purposes, including the Childhood Autism Rating Scale[74] and the Autism Behavior Checklist.[75] Another assessment instrument is the Aberrant Behavior Checklist–Community Version, which is useful for observing response to interventions.[76]

A complete physical examination, including a thorough neurological examination, is an essential component of any evaluation. Medical and dental problems that could be contributing to, or exacerbating, a child's psychiatric symptoms are important to identify and treat, if possible. Overall physical health should be assessed, and particular attention should be paid to findings that could be related to PDDs. For instance, cardiac and other congenital physical anomalies should be noted, and a skin and dysmorphology examination should be done to search for lesions consistent with genetic, metabolic, or structural disorders. All children with speech delay or articulation problems should have audiological testing, because even subtle hearing loss can affect development. Vision testing should be performed if there is any consideration of visual deficit. A high index of suspicion should be maintained for seizure disorder. There are no specific, diagnostic laboratory tests. Specialized laboratory tests are warranted only with specific indications, but these might include chromosomal analysis, amino acid studies, and electroencephalography. Although one quarter of children have nonspecific findings on structural neuroimaging scans, magnetic resonance imaging should be performed only if findings from history and physical examination suggest a potentially treatable lesion.

Chromosomal studies are indicated for children with history and physical examination findings suggestive of fragile X syndrome or other specific chromosomal abnormalities. Although genetic counseling, including chromo-

Table 35–4 **Suggested Work-up for Children and Adults with Autistic Disorder or Other Pervasive Developmental Disorders**

- History
  - Particular attention to
    - Developmental phases of language, social interactions, play
    - Family history of psychiatric and neurological disease
- Physical examination
  - Thorough physical examination including a search for
    - Neurological problems
    - Cardiac problems
    - Congenital anomalies
    - Skin lesions or abnormalities
    - Dysmorphology
- Psychological evaluation
  - Autism Diagnostic Interview–Revised
  - Autism Diagnostic Observation Schedule
  - Cognitive testing (e.g., Differential Abilities Scales)
  - Vineland Adaptive Behavior Scales
- Speech and language evaluation
- Audiological evaluation
- Visual acuity evaluation

somal analysis to exclude fragile X syndrome, is most obviously indicated for families considering a subsequent pregnancy, 25% of the boys born to maternal aunts of children with fragile X syndrome will have fragile X syndrome.

Psychological Testing

Various psychological instruments can be administered that may be invaluable in achieving a vivid, global picture of a child. Test results should never stand alone as conclusive evidence of a child's skills. The most useful measures are those that yield data about adaptive functioning, language skills, and intelligence. The Vineland Adaptive Behavior Scales[77] provide valuable information about adaptive functioning; language and communication abilities can be assessed by a number of specific measures. Intelligence tests used in this population should have a means of separating verbal from nonverbal scores because there is usually a disparity in these values in autistic people (e.g., Merrill-Palmer Scale,[78] Leiter International Performance Scale,[79] Bayley Scales of Infant Development,[80] and Differential Abilities Scales[81]).

Differential Diagnosis

Diagnosis of autistic disorder and other PDDs requires distinguishing among several disorders that consist of deviations in socialization, language, and play. One systematic approach is to examine the course of the patient from birth and, in so doing, determine whether there had ever been a period of normal development. If the child appeared to have a normal developmental phase for a period exceeding 2 years, diagnoses other than autistic disorder or another PDD should be strongly considered. Disorders to be considered in the differential diagnosis include developmental language disorder, mental retardation, acquired epileptic aphasia (Landau-Kleffner syndrome), schizophrenia, selective mutism, and psychosocial deprivation as well as other conditions listed in Table 35–5.

Table 35–5 Differential Diagnosis of Autistic Disorder and Other Pervasive Developmental Disorders

Developmental language disorder
Mental retardation
Acquired epileptic aphasia (Landau-Kleffner syndrome)
Fragile X syndrome
Schizophrenia
Selective mutism
Psychosocial deprivation
Hearing impairment
Visual impairment
Traumatic brain injury
Dementia
Metabolic disorders (inborn errors of metabolism, e.g., phenylketonuria)

Children with developmental language delay can appear to have symptoms related to autistic disorder at early ages. For example, because of their language deficits, they may seem to have communication problems and may not appear to be socially adept. However, children with language delay use relatively normal patterns of language, engage in imaginative play, and demonstrate appropriate attachment behaviors and social interactions with family and friends.[59] These children do not tend to have obsessive interests or repetitive behaviors like those seen in autistic children. They also do not respond unusually to sensory experiences as autistic children do.[82] One follow-up study comparing boys with autistic disorder versus those with severe receptive language disorder revealed that by middle childhood, about half of the boys with receptive language disorder were communicating effectively, whereas few of the boys with autistic disorder had adequate language skills.[83] This same study, however, showed that both groups continue to have some chronic social problems, as reported in another piece of work as well.[84]

Mental retardation, by itself, can be difficult to discern from autistic disorder or other PDDs in which intellectual deficits are an inherent factor. Approximately half of severely and profoundly mentally retarded children have symptoms consistent with a PDD, and it is unclear whether this is due to a high rate of PDDs in this group, an artifact of assessment, or a consequence of severe and profound mental retardation that increases risk for sensory deprivation. It is useful for planning interventions to add the secondary diagnosis of a PDD, if present. Many individuals with profound retardation have social skills expected for their mental age. For example, many of the social skills not seen in profoundly retarded individuals with autistic disorder, such as eye-to-eye gaze, are typically seen in highlighted form as early as 6 to 8 weeks of life in normally developing infants. Moderately or mildly mentally retarded individuals with qualitative impairments in social, communicative, and imaginative interests not meeting criteria for autistic disorder present another diagnostic dilemma. These individuals may fit most appropriately into the category of PDD NOS. Regardless of diagnostic category, however, autistic children and "purely" moderately retarded children should have individualized treatment plans and can often benefit from similar treatments and interventions.[85]

Acquired epileptic aphasia (Landau-Kleffner syndrome) is much more rare than autistic disorder and other PDDs. A high index of suspicion for this disorder is raised by the loss of phrase speech after the age of 30 months with electroencephalographical confirmation. Diagnosis of acquired epileptic aphasia is important because language may return after anticonvulsant or corticosteroid treatment.[86]

Schizophrenia is differentiated from autism on the basis of a number of factors. Symptoms of childhood schizophrenia consist of active phase delusions or hallucinations, lasting at least 1 month, which are rarely encountered in children with autistic disorder. Children with schizophrenia do not demonstrate the same problems with the understanding of language that children with autistic disorder do.[87] In spite of these characteristics, it is occasionally challenging to distinguish a high-functioning person with autistic disorder from a patient with schizophrenia. These situations may arise if the autistic person's thoughts and behavior are interpreted out of the context from which they come. For example, many autistic people are socially withdrawn and have deficits in self-care. Furthermore, autistic people frequently show inappropriate affect. In terms of thought processes, higher functioning autistic people tend to be ruminative and may be so obsessive as to appear illogical and thought disordered. Conversely, those who are not preoccupied with a particular interest may appear to have paucity of thought. Some autistic people do hold odd beliefs that could be mistaken for delusions.[88]

In selective mutism, the child chooses not to speak in certain situations. As in autistic disorder, the child may seem socially isolative and nonresponsive to the environment at times. A key difference between selective mutism and autistic disorder is that in selective mutism, the child's perceived social unresponsiveness is not pervasive. The selectively mute child usually is able to attach to family members, exchange conversation with them, and engage in inventive play. Some selectively mute children do have articulation problems or language delay but do not have deviations of speech such as that found in autistic children.[89]

Children with severe psychosocial deprivation can present with broad language deficiencies, stunted social development, and odd motor movements and habits.[90] However, this triad is qualitatively distinct from that seen in autistic disorder. Fortunately, many children subjected to extreme neglect, even for periods of years, can resume the developmental process at a rapid rate when they are exposed to nurturing and stimulating surroundings. Nonetheless, a child with a significant abuse or neglect history, as well as other children, should not be presumed to have autistic disorder unless a diligent assessment as described before has been completed.

Course and Natural History

As an autistic child grows older, the course of the illness may correspondingly mature and change. The portrayal of a child with autistic disorder as completely socially removed, with virtually no speech or echolalic speech, motor stereotypies, and little ability to adapt to change, is in keeping with patterns seen at a lower mental age. As a child enters the school years, the echolalic speech patterns sometimes lessen and the child begins speaking a bit more spontaneously. About 50% of autistic children who were mute in the preschool period ultimately acquire speech. Also during the school years, the child may begin to tolerate play near other children, and there can be formation of rudimentary social relations in less impaired individuals. Many bothersome preschool behaviors often later subside. Further, autistic children learn to adjust to regular demands or expectations placed on them. Peculiar interests and ritualistic behaviors, however, can and often do persist into adolescence and adulthood.

With the advent of adolescence, a small number of autistic children demonstrate significant improvement in symptoms, and this is indicative of a good outcome in the adult years. In some adolescents, however, there is considerable regression with the onset of puberty. This is reported with greater frequency in girls in some studies. From 10% to 35% undergo this regression, and if this happens, progress may not be seen again until the affected individuals are in their late 20s. Aspects of puberty such as sexual drive and menstruation are handled without much difficulty by many autistic adolescents. Some autistic individuals, however, do not understand the social implications of public masturbation or exhibitionism and engage in these behaviors. Higher functioning autistic adolescents may become aware that they differ significantly from the rest of their peers. They may even develop some interest in others and a desire to make friendships, but they lack the know-how to accomplish this. There is a tendency for autistic adolescents to become sedentary and do little if not prompted to do more. In terms of language, receptive and expressive abilities can gradually improve during the adolescent years.[43, 62, 91–94]

Follow-up studies of autistic children into adulthood show that approximately two thirds remain seriously impaired and are incapable of caring for their own needs. In fact, the majority of these individuals live in long-term institutional settings during their adult years. Between 5% and 17% of autistic adults are able to work and hold some kind of a social life in their community. In spite of social improvement in about half of autistic children for periods of years, most autistic individuals have abnormal social relationships. It is rare for an autistic adult to marry or sustain a long-term sexual relationship. Outcome in autism is overwhelmingly determined by IQ and language abilities, with IQ being the most powerful predictor. Good or fair outcomes are almost always associated with full-scale IQs of greater than 60. Along with IQ, the acquisition of useful speech by 5 years of age has been emphasized by some workers as an important predictor of positive outcome. Even in the best-case scenario in which an individual has an IQ and language abilities within a relatively normal range, there is nearly always residual social impairment that persists into adulthood.

Goals of Treatment

Initially, attempts were made to treat autism by psychoanalytic interventions.[95] There was little evidence that these treatments were of benefit, however. In the 1960s, the idea that other factors, such as IQ and language skills, played a role in terms of prognosis made it clear that treatment issues were more complex than originally thought. Behavioral treatments brought a great deal of hope for the prognosis of autism on the basis of the premise that behavior is learned. The use of behavioral methods has not had a curative effect on autism, although it has beneficial effects.[96] Unfortunately, behaviors learned by autistic children in one particular setting are not necessarily carried over to other contexts or retained well.[58]

A variety of treatments and educational interventions are thought to be most useful in treatment of individuals with autistic disorder and net the greatest gain in those who are the least mentally impaired.[97] In addition, autistic disorder is recognized as a chronic disorder with a changing course requiring long-term intervention with implementation of various treatments at any given time. In general, treatments of the other PDDs are the same as those used in autistic disorder because similar types of symptoms are targeted in these disorders. Given that there is no current cure for autistic disorder or the other PDDs, goals of treatment should encompass short-term and long-term needs of the individual and his or her family. Rutter[57] has defined goals for treatment in terms of four quintessential aims:

1. The advancement of normal development, particularly regarding cognition, language, and socialization
2. The promotion of learning and problem solving

Table 35–6 Goals for Treatment

Advancement of normal development, particularly regarding cognition, language, and socialization
Promotion of learning and problem solving
Reduction of behaviors that impede learning
Assistance of families coping with autistic disorder
Treatment of comorbid psychiatric disorders

3. The reduction of behaviors that impede the learning process
4. The assistance of families coping with autism

These goals are broad in nature; therefore, it is key to separate these goals into immediate and long-term needs. Each goal will probably require a distinct scheme of its own. It is best to treat an autistic child on an outpatient basis because institutionalization may hinder a child's ability to learn means of functioning in normal society. This can usually be accomplished, except in times of extreme stress or need, during which a child could benefit from respite care or brief hospitalization. Effective treatment often entails setting appropriate expectations for the child and adjusting the child's environment to foster success.[57] Table 35–6 summarizes the goals of treatment.

Approach to Treatment

Because the autistic individual often requires diverse treatment and services simultaneously, the imperative role of the primary physician is to be the coordinator of services. Frequent visits with the child and the child's caretakers initially allow the physician to assess the individual needs of the child while establishing a therapeutic alliance. In serving as coordinator, an effective approach often calls for the services of a number of professionals working in a multidisciplinary fashion. This group may include psychiatrists, pediatricians, psychologists, special educators, speech and language therapists, social workers, and other specialized therapists (Table 35–7).

Psychosocial Interventions

Some of the most beneficial interventions for autistic children have been achieved through the educational process. With the passage of the Education for All Handicapped Children Act of 1975 (Public Law 94-142), all handicapped children, including those with autistic disorder, were guaranteed the right to a free, appropriate public education. This right was guaranteed notwithstanding the severity or nature of the child's disability. Further, this law mandated that the education of a handicapped child must take place in the least restrictive environment while still meeting the needs of the child.

Improvement in the educational experience afforded children with autistic disorder has resulted in fewer children requiring long stays in institutional settings, as had been the case previously.[98] In fact, a study of high-functioning autistic adolescents reported improved mathematics, reading, and spelling compared with autistic children of 20 years ago. These improvements were closely associated with verbal intelligence level, which was not the case with the original sample of autistic students. This was taken to mean that autistic children are using their intellectual abilities more effectively in gaining useful academic skills.[25] However, only rare autistic children were able to perform at a level in keeping with other children their age. As a group, this was especially apparent in the area of reading comprehension. With regard to lower functioning or severely retarded autistic children, no single educational approach has been identified as superlative in improving a specific area of weakness.

A debate has been ongoing during the last several years regarding the issue of mainstreaming of handicapped children within the schools. Although there has been a move toward implementation of mainstreaming, many autistic children remain in homogeneous classrooms with children of similar needs. Currently, there are few data on the performance of autistic children within various stages of integration. It is generally believed that few autistic children will be able to function academically or behaviorally at their best if they are placed totally within a regular classroom setting with no other supports. However, there can be distinct advantages in a typical classroom for mild to moderately functioning autistic children. These include social exposure to nonautistic children and greater intellectual stimulation than is sometimes available in highly structured, special education classrooms. Whether this is truly workable seems to depend on the structure, attitude, and coping capabilities of a given program or setting.[99]

Curricula that target instruction in communication can be beneficial to the majority of children with autism. This can be done individually with even young children and can also involve teaching parents and others how to encourage communication in an autistic child. Behavioral techniques derived from operant and classical conditioning theory are used routinely by teachers and therapists working with autistic children. Reinforcing positive behaviors, failing to reinforce unwanted behaviors, and using simple techniques to replace an undesirable behavior with a more adaptive one are standard behavioral procedures. These techniques are often highly successful, except when there is severe aggression or self-injurious behaviors. More sophisticated behavioral techniques may be needed under those condi-

Table 35–7 Summary of Treatment Principles

Psychosocial Interventions
Educational
Curricula that target communication
Behavioral techniques
Structured milieu
Vocational training and placement: other specialized interventions such as speech and language therapy, physical therapy, and occupational therapy
Social skills training
Individual psychotherapy for high-functioning individuals
Medical Interventions
Cohesive physician-patient relationship
Supportive measures with families coping with autistic disorder
Behavioral treatment
Pharmacotherapy to address problem signs and symptoms

tions.[96, 100] Often, finding means of organizing a milieu that is predictable and promotes understanding and learning for the autistic child alleviates need for intensive behavior programs.[101] One research group has reported that an intensive program of behavior management begun at early ages results in significant achievements, but others have been severely critical of the methods used in this study.[102, 103]

At the other end of the spectrum, success has been achieved in placing more autistic adults in jobs and workshops in the community. How successful one is in securing a job for an autistic adult depends on the resources in the community and the ability of the adult's parents or others to advocate for her or him. Work placement and training as well as encouragement and consistent support on the job have contributed to success in the workplace for the autistic individual. Also, school curricula that stress task-oriented behaviors and teach skills in specific areas, such as in woodworking or gardening, help prepare autistic people to enter the work force and improve their marketability.[104–106]

Depending on the specific needs of the individual autistic child, a child can benefit from many different therapies or interventions. Among these are speech and language therapy, occupational therapy, and physical therapy. Some programs offer art or music therapy as a means of encouraging communication and self-expression. Brief individual psychotherapies may be helpful to those who are verbal and have a focused problem or are experiencing symptoms of anxiety or depression. Social skills groups or training may be especially beneficial for higher functioning adolescents and adults. These interventions can serve to give the individual social experience in a positive, supportive setting.[107, 108]

Physician-Patient Relationship

As with any clinical relationship, respect for the patient is the cornerstone of assessment and treatment. Many of the difficulties faced by persons with autistic disorder are related to lack of empathy, not by themselves, but by those around them. In many ways, this stems from countertransference issues toward people with culturally defined "defects."[109] It is essential that the psychiatrist keep in mind that every person, regardless of presence or absence of any diagnosis, has a human drive to be emotionally connected with others and is sensitive to her or his treatment by others. The person with autistic disorder or another PDD may have more difficulty expressing his or her interests in a consensually validated manner or may sometimes avoid relationships because of overarousal or anxiety, but this should not be mistaken for a lack of the usual drive for affiliation. In addition, one must be cognizant that drives for mastery and development of autonomy are not reduced by the presence of autistic disorder or other PDDs.

Literally all families can benefit from supportive measures from their child's physician, and some families need structured family therapy involving either their psychiatrist or another health professional skilled in this area. Helping families deal with frustration, disappointment, fear, and ambivalence with regard to their handicapped family member is tantamount to successful treatment. Other crucial steps include aiding families in arranging for special services or respite care in addition to providing behavior management techniques and emotional support. Many individuals with autistic disorder and families draw support and services through local and national organizations as well. Such agencies include the Association for Retarded Citizens, Autism Society of America, and other community support groups. Books are also available to assist families[110] and peers[111] in learning about PDDs and to assist families in adapting to having a child with autistic disorder.[112]

Pharmacotherapy

There is a paucity of an adequate number of controlled trials in all areas of pediatric psychopharmacology. There are no pharmacological agents with U.S. Food and Drug Administration–approved labeling specific for the treatment of autistic disorder or other PDDs in either children or adults. This is all the more of a problem because many of the symptoms commonly seen in autistic disorder and other PDDs (rituals, aggressive behavior, and hyperactivity) are also common in mentally retarded children and adolescents without a PDD. Some of the pharmacological strategies for the treatment of autistic disorder have been extrapolated from studies of related conditions, including attention-deficit/hyperactivity disorder and obsessive-compulsive disorder. However, before treatment is started, it is important to remember that the current state of the art is empirical treatment of target symptoms.

Before specific pharmacological agents are discussed, it must be stressed that one should not use psychopharmacological agents with the expectation that they will cure children with autistic disorder. Although this seems obvious, one should realize that many parents and teachers of children with autistic disorder expect medication to eliminate core social and cognitive dysfunction. There is no pharmacological substitute for appropriate educational, behavioral, psychotherapeutic, vocational, and recreational programming. It is essential to remember and remind parents, teachers, and others that medication should always be seen as an adjunct to these core interventions that address the core developmental challenges associated with these disorders.

Because many individuals with autistic disorder and other PDDs have impairments in language and social communication, the use of rating scales becomes an essential part of the treatment. Standard rating scales not only give the psychiatrist a framework in which to assess response to medication, but they also provide a relatively easy and straightforward way to collect standard information about the patient's functioning in a variety of settings. Although rating scales and instruments are available for several target symptoms of interest, such as attention deficit, impulsivity, and hyperactivity, the Aberrant Behavior Checklist—Community Version[76] has the advantage of asking questions appropriate for most patients with a PDD. We have found this instrument to be especially sensitive to clinical changes in the critical symptoms of hyperactivity and irritability.[113] Although rating scales cannot replace careful examination of the patient and interviews with parents and teachers, they may be graphed next to medications and dosages of medications to assist in treatment planning after several changes in the patient's clinical condition have occurred.

The use of medications to treat autistic disorder and other PDDs appears to have significant potential as an adjunct to educational, environmental, and social interventions. Regrettably, there is no diagnosis-specific treatment at

Table 35–8 Summary of Pharmacotherapy Principles

Psychosocial interventions should accompany medication treatment.
The individual's living arrangement must ensure safe, consistent administration of medications.
Maintain a high index of suspicion for comorbid disorders, and treat these appropriately.
Establish a means of monitoring effects of medications on symptoms over time.
Assess the risk/benefit ratio of starting medications and educate the patient and family about these.

present, and it will probably be some time before specific etiological or pathophysiological bases of the syndrome are known. Nonetheless, individuals with autistic disorder still have significant impairments as well as the all-too-often forgotten potential to gain skills and levels of functioning compatible with living in the community. It is a reasonable goal for psychiatrists to adopt the judicious use of psychopharmacological agents to assist in this adaptation. Of necessity, this focus on facilitating adaptation requires attention to five important principles (Table 35–8):

1. Environmental manipulations, including behavioral treatment, may be as effective as, if not more effective than, medication for symptom treatment.
2. It is essential that the living arrangement for the individual ensure safe and consistent administration and monitoring of the medication to be used.
3. Individuals with autistic disorder and other PDDs, are at as much, if not greater, risk for DSM-IV Axis I disorders. If a comorbid DSM-IV Axis I disorder is present, standard treatment for that disorder should be initiated.
4. If the medication is selected on the basis of potential effects on target symptoms, there must be an established way of specifically monitoring the response to treatment over time.
5. A careful assessment of the risk/benefit ratio must be made before initiating treatment, and to the extent possible, the patient's caretakers and the patient must understand the risks and benefits of the treatment.

Potent Serotonin Transporter Inhibitors

This class of agents includes what others describe as selective serotonin reuptake inhibitors (fluoxetine,[114] sertraline, paroxetine, and fluvoxamine[115]) as well as the less selective but potent clomipramine,[116] a tricyclic antidepressant (Table 35–9).

This group of medications is most effective when insistence on routines or rituals are present to the point of manifest anxiety or aggression in response to interruption of the routines or rituals, or after the onset of another disorder such as major depression or obsessive-compulsive disorder.[117] The common side effects associated with selective serotonin reuptake inhibitors are motor restlessness, insomnia, elation, irritability, and decreased appetite, each of which may occur alone or, more often, together. Because many of these symptoms may be present in the often cyclical natural course of autistic disorder before the medication is initiated, new symptoms, a different quality of the symptom, and occurrence of these symptoms in a new cluster are clues to side effects.[114]

Stimulants

Small but significant reductions in hyperactivity ratings may be seen in children with autistic disorder in response to stimulants such as methylphenidate,[118] dextroamphetamine, and pemoline. Stereotypies may worsen, so drug trials for the individual patient must always be assessed to determine that therapeutic effects outweigh side effects. A key distinction in assessing attentional problems of children with autistic disorder is the distinction between poor sustained attention (characteristic of children with attention-deficit/hyperactivity disorder) and poor joint attention (characteristic of children with autistic disorder). Problems in joint attention require educational and behavioral interventions or treatment of rituals with a potent serotonin transporter inhibitor. Problems in maintenance of attention of the type seen in attention-deficit/hyperactivity disorder are more likely to respond to stimulants.

Sympatholytics

The α_2-adrenergic receptor agonist clonidine reduced irritability as well as hyperactivity and impulsivity in two double-blind, placebo-controlled trials.[113, 119] However, tolerance developed several months after initiation of the treatment in each child who was treated long term.[113] Tolerance was not prevented by transdermal skin patch

Table 35–9 Psychopharmacological Approach to Presenting Symptoms in Pervasive Developmental Disorders

Rituals, Compulsions, Irritability
Potent serotonin transporter inhibitors
Selective serotonin reuptake inhibitor
Fluoxetine 5–80 mg/d in a single dose
Paroxetine 2.5–50 mg/d in one or two divided doses
Sertraline 25–200 mg/d in one or two divided doses
Fluvoxamine 25–300 mg/d in two or three divided doses
Tricyclic antidepressants
Clomipramine 25–250 mg/d in one or two divided doses
Hyperactivity, Distractibility, Impulsivity
Stimulant medications
Methylphenidate 5–60 mg/d in three to five divided doses
Dextroamphetamine 5–60 mg/d in three to five divided doses
Pemoline 37.5–112.5 mg/d in a single dose
Clonidine 0.05–0.3 mg/d in one to three divided doses or by transdermal skin patch
Naltrexone 0.5–2.0 mg/kg/d in a single dose
Aggression, Irritability
Sympatholytics
Propranolol 20–400 mg/d in three to four divided doses
Nadolol 40–400 mg/d in a single dose
Anticonvulsants
Carbamazepine to a blood level of 4–12 ng/mL
Valproate to a blood level of 50–100 ng/mL
Lithium to a serum level of 0.8–1.2 mEq/L
Neuroleptics
Naltrexone 0.5–2.0 mg/kg in a single daily dose

administration of the drug. However, tolerance may have been reduced in several cases by administering clonidine in the morning and then 6 to 8 hours later with a 16- to 18-hour interval between the last dose of one day and the first dose of the next day. If tolerance does develop, the dose should not be increased because tolerance to sedation does not occur, and sedation may lead to increased aggression due to decreased cognitive control of impulses.

β-Adrenergic receptor antagonists, such as propranolol and nadolol, have not been tested in double-blind trials in autistic disorder. However, open trials have reported the use of these medications in the treatment of aggression and impulsivity in developmental disorders,[120] including autistic disorder.[121, 122]

Neuroleptics

Typical Neuroleptics. Because they were among the first developed psychopharmacological classes, typical neuroleptics have been the most extensively studied drugs in autistic disorder. Trifluoperazine, haloperidol, and pimozide have been studied in double-blind, controlled trials lasting from 2 to 6 months. Reduction of fidgetiness, interpersonal withdrawal, speech deviance, and stereotypies has been documented in response to these treatments.[123–130] However, patients with autistic disorder are as vulnerable to potentially irreversible tardive dyskinesia as any other group is of patients.[131, 132] Owing to the often earlier age at initiation of pharmacotherapy, patients with autistic disorder treated with typical neuroleptics may be at higher risk because of the potential increased lifetime dosage of medication.

Atypical Neuroleptics. Because of the positive response of many children with autistic disorder to typical neuroleptics, similar medications with reduced risk of tardive dyskinesia must be considered. In addition, atypical neuroleptics are often effective in treating the negative symptoms of schizophrenia, which seem similar to several of the social deficits in autistic disorder. However, data are not yet available to determine whether atypical neuroleptics will be more or less effective than typical neuroleptics in autistic disorder. One reason for caution in the use of clozapine in patients with autistic disorder is the 1% risk of agranulocytosis (drug-induced neutropenia).

Anticonvulsants

Because 25% to 33% of patients with autistic disorder have seizures, the psychopharmacological management of patients with autistic disorder or other PDD must take into consideration the past or current history of epilepsy and the potential role of anticonvulsants.[42] The anticonvulsant class to be avoided, when possible, is the barbiturates (e.g., phenobarbital). Because barbiturates have been associated with hyperactivity, depression, and cognitive impairment, they should be changed to an alternative drug, depending on the seizure type.[133, 134] In addition, phenytoin (Dilantin) is sedating and causes hypertrophy of the gums and hirsutism, which may contribute to the social challenges for people with autistic disorder.

Carbamazepine and valproate may have positive psychotropic effects, particularly when cyclical irritability, insomnia, and hyperactivity are present. Several children with autistic disorder were treated with valproic acid after electroencephalographical abnormalities were found. These children had an improvement in behavioral symptoms associated with autistic disorder after valproate treatment.[135]

Naltrexone

The opiate antagonist naltrexone was suggested as a specific treatment for autistic disorder. However, double-blind trials have suggested that naltrexone has little efficacy in treating the core social and cognitive symptoms of autistic disorder.[136] Whereas the use of naltrexone as a specific treatment for autistic disorder no longer seems to be likely, it may have a role in the treatment of self-injurious behavior, although the controlled data are equivocal.[136] Controlled trials have shown a modest reduction in symptoms of hyperactivity sometimes associated with autistic disorder.[136, 137] Potential side effects include nausea and vomiting. Controlled trials in autistic disorder have not shown liver dysfunction or other physical side effects.

Naltrexone may have an adverse effect on the outcome of Rett's disorder on the basis of a relatively large, randomized, double-blind, placebo-controlled trial.[138]

Lithium

A single open trial revealed no significant improvement in symptoms in patients with autistic disorder without bipolar disorder.[139] Not surprisingly, adolescents and adults with autistic disorder are also at risk for development of bipolar disorder and are expected to respond to lithium equally well, although diagnosis of less severe or classic cases of bipolar disorder is challenging.

Anxiolytics

Benzodiazepines have not been studied systematically in children and adolescents with autistic disorder. However, their use to reduce anxiety in short-term treatment, such as before dental procedures, is similar to their use in management of anxiety in people without a PDD.

Pyridoxine and Dietary Supplements

Pyridoxine, the water-soluble essential vitamin B_6, has been used extensively as a pharmacological treatment in autistic disorder. In the doses used for autistic disorder, it is not being used as a cofactor for normally regulated enzyme function or as a vitamin; rather, it is used to modulate the function of neurotransmitter enzymes, such as tryptophan hydroxylase and tyrosine hydroxylase. Although the controlled studies of pyridoxine administered with magnesium have limitations, this is also true of all studies of interventions in autistic disorder. The role of pyridoxine, magnesium, and homeopathic treatments remains to be determined even though they enjoy considerable popularity in the community at large.

Fenfluramine

Although fenfluramine originally showed promise in the treatment of autistic disorder and associated cognitive dysfunction,[140] double-blind controlled trials did not confirm an improvement in cognitive function or a reduction in core autistic symptoms.[141, 142] However, much like naltrexone, fenfluramine may reduce hyperactivity and impulsivity commonly present in autistic disorder and other developmental disorders.[143] The potential changes in neurochemical regulation after long-term administration,[142] which *may* represent neurotoxic effects,[144] suggest that treatment with fenfluramine be recommended only after other treatments such as potent serotonin transporter inhibitors, stimulants, and sympatholytics have failed.

Conclusion

Autistic disorder and other PDDs are complex, early-onset disorders that often mark a lifelong pattern of disability. Whereas autistic disorder and the other PDDs share many symptoms with other psychiatric disorders, they remain separate and distinct conditions. Even though the precise etiology of these disorders remains elusive, a more thorough understanding of these conditions and their treatment has developed in the past two decades. Given the rapid evolution of this area of basic and clinical investigation, dramatic changes in the field are highly likely in the months and years ahead. At present, it is clear that a coordinated, multidisciplinary approach to treatment that focuses on adaptive skills and social functioning yields the best results. Similarly, a multidisciplinary approach to investigation of etiology will almost certainly lead to a broader understanding of other psychiatric conditions and provide significant insights into the broader world of behavioral neurobiology.

References

1. Rutter M: Diagnosis and definition of childhood autism. J Autism Child Schizophr 1978; 8:139–161.
2. Itard J: The Wild Boy of Aveyron [De l'Education d'un Homme Sauvage]. New York: Century, 1932.
3. Heller T: About dementia infantilis. In Howells J (ed): Modern Perspectives in International Child Psychiatry. Edinburgh: Oliver & Boyd, 1969:610–616. Originally published in 1930.
4. Kanner L: Autistic disturbances of affective contact. Nerv Child 1943; 2:217–250.
5. Kanner L: Early infantile autism. J Pediatr 1944; 25:211–217.
6. Asperger H: Die "autistischen Psychopathen" Kindesalter. Arch Psychiatr Nervenkr 1944; 117:76–136.
7. Bleuler E: Dementia Praecox or the Group of Schizophrenias. New York: International Universities Press, 1950.
8. American Psychiatric Association: Diagnostic and Statistical Manual of Mental Disorders, 4th ed. Washington, DC: American Psychiatric Association, 1994.
9. Kolvin L: Psychosis in childhood—a comparative study. In Rutter M (ed): Infantile Autism: Concepts, Characteristics, and Treatment. Edinburgh, UK: Churchill Livingstone, 1971:219–232.
10. Rutter M: Childhood schizophrenia reconsidered. J Autism Child Schizophr 1972; 2:315–337.
11. Vrono M: Schizophrenia in childhood and adolescence. Int J Ment Health 1974; 2:7–116.
12. American Psychiatric Association: Diagnostic and Statistical Manual of Mental Disorders, 3rd ed. Washington, DC: American Psychiatric Association, 1980.
13. Volkmar FR, Bregman J, Cohen DJ, et al: DSM-III and DSM-III-R diagnoses of autism. Am J Psychiatry 1988; 145:1404–1408.
14. Volkmar FR, Cohen DJ, Paul R: An evaluation of DSM-III criteria for infantile autism. J Am Acad Child Psychiatry 1986; 25:190–197.
15. American Psychiatric Association: Diagnostic and Statistical Manual of Mental Disorders, 3rd ed, revised. Washington, DC: American Psychiatric Association, 1987.
16. Factor DC, Freeman NL, Kardash A: A comparison of DSM-III and DSM-III-R criteria for autism. J Autism Dev Disord 1989; 19:637–640.
17. Hertzig ME, Snow ME, New E, et al: DSM-III and DSM-III-R diagnosis of autism and pervasive developmental disorder in nursery school children. J Am Acad Child Adolesc Psychiatry 1990; 29:123–126.
18. Bryson S, Clark B, Smith T: First report of a Canadian epidemiological study of autistic syndromes. J Child Psychol Psychiatry 1988; 29:433–445.
19. Zahner G, Pauls D: Epidemiological surveys of infantile autism. In Cohen D, Donnellan A (eds): Handbook of Autism and Pervasive Developmental Disorders. New York: John Wiley & Sons, 1987: 199–210.
20. Hoshino Y, Kumashiro H, Yashima Y, et al: The epidemiological study of autism in Fukushima-ken. Folia Psychiatr Neurol Jpn 1982; 36:115–124.
21. Steffenburg S, Gillberg C: Autism and autism-like conditions in Swedish rural and urban areas: A population study. Br J Psychiatry 1986; 149:81–87.
22. Volkmar F, Klin A, Siegel B, et al: Field trial for autistic disorder in DSM-IV. Am J Psychiatry 1994; 151:1361–1367.
23. Kurita H, Kita M, Miyake Y: A comparative study of development and symptoms among disintegrative psychosis and infantile autism with and without speech loss. J Autism Dev Disord 1992; 22:175–188.
24. Freeman BJ, Ritvo ER, Needleman R, et al: The stability of cognitive and linguistic parameters in autism: A five-year prospective study. J Am Acad Child Psychiatry 1985; 24:459–464.
25. Venter A, Lord C, Schopler E: A follow-up study of high-functioning autistic children. J Child Psychol Psychiatry 1992; 33:489–507.
26. Rutter M: Cognitive deficits in the pathogenesis of autism. J Child Psychol Psychiatry 1983; 24:513–532.
27. Frith U: Autism: Explaining the Enigma. New York: Blackwell Scientific Publications, 1989.
28. Schain RJ, Freedman DX: Studies on 5-hydroxyindole metabolism in autistic and other mentally retarded children. J Pediatr 1961; 58:315–320.
29. Anderson GM, Freedman DX, Cohen DJ, et al: Whole blood serotonin in autistic and normal subjects. J Child Psychol Psychiatry, 1987; 28:885–900.
30. Cook E, Arora R, Anderson G, et al: Platelet serotonin studies in hyperserotonemic relatives of children with autistic disorder. Life Sci 1993; 52:2005–2015.
31. Cook EH, Fletcher KE, Wainwright M, et al: Primary structure of the human platelet serotonin 5-HT_{2A} receptor: Identity with frontal cortex serotonin 5-HT_{2A} receptor. J Neurochem 1994; 63:465–469.
32. Bailey A, Bolton P, Butler L: Prevalence of the fragile X anomaly amongst autistic twins and singletons. J Child Psychol Psychiatry 1993; 34:673–688.
33. Brown W, Jenkins E, Friedman E, et al: Autism is associated with the fragile X syndrome. J Autism Dev Disord 1982; 12:303–307.
34. Reiss AL, Freund L: Fragile X syndrome, DSM-III-R, and autism. J Am Acad Child Adolesc Psychiatry 1990; 29:885–891.
35. Knoblock H, Pasamanick B: Some etiologic and prognostic factors in early infantile autism and psychosis. Pediatrics 1975; 55:182–191.
36. Smalley SL, Tanguay PE, Smith M, et al: Autism and tuberous sclerosis. J Autism Dev Disord 1992; 22:339–355.
37. Folstein S, Rutter M: Infantile autism: A genetic study of 21 twin pairs. J Child Psychol Psychiatry 1977; 18:297–321.
38. Ritvo ER, Spence MA, Freeman BJ, et al: Evidence for autosomal recessive inheritance in 46 families with multiple incidences of autism. Am J Psychiatry 1985; 142:187–192.
39. Steffenburg S, Gillberg C, Hellgren L, et al: A twin study of autism in Denmark, Finland, Iceland, Norway and Sweden. J Child Psychol Psychiatry 1989; 30:405–416.
40. Damasio AR, Maurer RG: A neurological model of childhood autism. Arch Neurol 1978; 35:777–786.
41. Deykin EY, Macmahon B: The incidence of seizures among children with autistic symptoms. Am J Psychiatry 1979; 136:1310–1312.
42. Volkmar FR, Nelson DS: Seizure disorders in autism. J Am Acad Child Adolesc Psychiatry 1990; 29:127–129.
43. Rutter M, Greenfield D, Lockyer L: A five to fifteen year follow-up study of infantile psychosis. II. Social and behavioural outcome. Br J Psychiatry 1967; 113:1183–1199.
44. Tanguay PE, Edwards RM, Buchwald J, et al: Auditory brainstem evoked responses in autistic children. Arch Gen Psychiatry 1982; 39:174–180.
45. Courchesne E, Yeung-Courchesne R, Hicks G, et al: Functioning of the brain-stem auditory pathway in non-retarded autistic individuals. Electroencephalogr Clin Neurophysiol 1985; 61:491–501.
46. Courchesne E, Yeung CR, Press GA, et al: Hypoplasia of cerebellar vermal lobules VI and VII in autism. N Engl J Med 1988; 318:1349–1354.
47. Holttum J, Minshew N, Sanders R, et al: Magnetic resonance imaging of the posterior fossa in autism. Biol Psychiatry 1992; 32:1091–1101.

48. Bauman M, Kemper T: Neuroanatomic observations of the brain in autism. In Bauman M, Kemper T (eds): The Neurobiology of Autism. Baltimore: The Johns Hopkins University Press, 1994:
49. Ritvo ER, Freeman BJ, Scheibel AB, et al: Lower Purkinje cell counts in the cerebella of four autistic subjects: Initial findings of the UCLA-NSAC autopsy research report. Am J Psychiatry 1986; 143:862–866.
50. Rumsey JM, Duara R, Grady C, et al: Brain metabolism in autism: Resting cerebral glucose utilization rates as measured with positron emission tomography. Arch Gen Psychiatry 1985; 42:448–455.
51. Herold S, Frackowiak RSJ, Le Couteur A, et al: Cerebral blood flow and metabolism of oxygen and glucose in young autistic adults. Psychol Med 1988; 18:823–831.
52. Minshew N: In vivo brain chemistry in autism: ^{31}P magnetic resonance spectroscopy studies. In Bauman M, Kemper T (eds): The Neurobiology of Autism. Baltimore: The Johns Hopkins University Press, 1994:86–101.
53. Lockyer L, Rutter M: A five- to fifteen-year follow-up study of infantile psychosis. IV. Patterns of cognitive ability. Br J Soc Clin Psychol 1970; 9:152–163.
54. Lord C, Rutter M, Goode S, et al: Autism Diagnostic Observation Schedule: A standardized observation of communicative and social behavior. J Autism Dev Disord 1989; 19:185–212.
55. Volkmar FR, Stier DM, Cohen DJ: Age of recognition of pervasive developmental disorder. Am J Psychiatry 1985; 142:1450–1452.
56. Lord C, Rutter M, Le Couteur A: Autism Diagnostic Interview—Revised: A revised version of a diagnostic interview for caregivers of individuals with possible pervasive developmental disorders. J Autism Dev Disord 1994; 24:659–685.
57. Rutter M: Infantile autism. In Shaffer D, Ehrhardt AA, Greenhill LL (eds): The Clinical Guide to Child Psychiatry. New York: Free Press, 1985:48–78.
58. Lord C: The development of peer relations in children with autism. In Morrison F, Lord C, Keating D (eds): Applied Developmental Psychology. New York: Academic Press, 1984:165–229.
59. Bartak L, Rutter M, Cox A: A comparative study of infantile autism and specific developmental receptive language disorder. I: The children. Br J Psychiatry 1975; 126:127–145.
60. Tager-Flusberg H, Anderson M: The development of contingent discourse ability in autistic children. J Child Psychol Psychiatry 1991; 32:1123–1134.
61. Volden J, Lord C: Neologisms and abnormal functional usage of language in autistic speakers. J Autism Dev Disord 1991; 21:1–22.
62. Rumsey JM, Rapoport JL, Sceery WR: Autistic children as adults: Psychiatric, social, and behavioral outcomes. J Am Acad Child Psychiatry 1985; 24:465–473.
63. Kasari C, Sigman M, Mundy P, et al: Affective sharing in the context of joint attention interactions of normal, autistic, and mentally retarded children. J Autism Dev Disord 1990; 20:87–94.
64. Mundy P, Sigman M: The theoretical implications of joint-attention deficits in autism. Dev Psychopathol 1989; 1:173–183.
65. Szatmari P, Tuff L, Finlayson MA, et al: Asperger's syndrome and autism: Neurocognitive aspects. J Am Acad Child Adolesc Psychiatry 1990; 29:130–136.
66. Wing L: Asperger's syndrome: A clinical account. Psychol Med 1981; 11:115–129.
67. Wolff S: "Schizoid" personality in childhood and adult life. Br J Psychiatry 1991; 159:615–635.
68. Rett A: On an until now unknown disease of a congenital metabolic disorder [in German]. Krankenschwester 1966; 19:121–122.
69. Hagberg B, Goutieres F, Hanefeld F, et al: Rett syndrome: Criteria for inclusion and exclusion. Brain Dev 1985; 7:372–373.
70. Olsson B, Rett A: A review of the Rett syndrome with a theory of autism. Brain Dev 1990; 12:11–15.
71. Volkmar F, Cohen D: Disintegrative disorder or "late onset" autism. J Child Psychol Psychiatry 1989; 30:717–724.
72. Corbett J, Harris R: Progressive disintegrative psychosis of childhood. J Child Psychol Psychiatry 1977; 18:211–219.
73. DiLavore P, Lord C, Rutter M: Prelinguistic Autism Diagnostic Observation Schedule (PL-ADOS). J Autism Dev Disord 1995; 25:357–379.
74. Schopler E, Reichler RJ, Renner BR: The Childhood Autism Rating Scale (CARS). Los Angeles: Western Psychological Services, 1988.
75. Krug D, Arick J, Almond P: Behavior checklist for identifying severely handicapped individuals with high levels of autistic behavior. J Child Psychol Psychiatry 1980; 21:221–229.
76. Aman M: Aberrant Behavior Checklist—Community Version. East Aurora, NY: Slosson Educational Publications, 1994.
77. Sparrow S, Balla D, Cicchetti D: Vineland Scales of Adaptive Behavior, Survey Form Manual. Circle Pines, MN: American Guidance Service, 1984.
78. Stutsman R: Merrill-Palmer Scale of Mental Tests. New York: Harcourt Brace & World, 1948.
79. Shah A, Holmes N: The use of the Leiter International Performance Scale with autistic children. J Autism Dev Disord 1985; 15:195–204.
80. Bayley N: Manual for the Bayley Scales of Infant Development. New York: Psychological Corporation, 1969.
81. Elliott C: Differential Abilities Scales. Pensacola, FL: Psychological Corporation, 1990.
82. Ornitz E, Ritvo E: The syndrome of autism: A critical review. Am J Psychiatry 1976; 133:609–621.
83. Cantwell DP, Baker L, Rutter M, et al: Infantile autism and developmental receptive dysphasia: A comparative follow-up into middle childhood. J Autism Dev Disord 1989; 19:19–31.
84. Rutter M, Mawhood L: The long-term psychosocial sequelae of specific developmental disorders of speech and language. In Rutter M, Casaer P (eds): Biological Risk Factors for Psychosocial Disorders. New York: Cambridge University Press, 1991:233–259.
85. Wing L, Gould J: Severe impairments of social interaction and associated abnormalities in children: Epidemiology and classification. J Autism Dev Disord 1979; 9:11–29.
86. Lerman P, Lerman-Sagie T, Kivity S: Effect of early corticosteroid therapy for Landau-Kleffner syndrome. Dev Med Child Neurol 1991; 33:257–260.
87. Asarnow RF, Tanguay PE, Bott L, et al: Patterns of intellectual functioning in non-retarded autistic and schizophrenic children. J Child Psychol Psychiatry 1987; 28:273–280.
88. Dykens E, Volkmar F, Glick M: Thought disorder in high functioning autistic adults. J Autism Dev Disord 1991; 21:291–302.
89. Kolvin I, Fundudis T: Elective mute children: Psychological development and background factors. J Child Psychol Psychiatry 1981; 22:219–232.
90. Hoffman-Plotkin D, Twentyman C: A multimodal assessment of behavioral and cognitive deficits in abused and neglected preschoolers. Child Dev 1984; 55:794–802.
91. Brown J: Adolescent development of children with infantile psychosis. Semin Psychiatry 1969; 1:79–89.
92. Gillberg C: Autistic children growing up: Problems during puberty and adolescence. Dev Med Child Neurol 1984; 26:125–129.
93. Kanner L, Rodriguez A, Ashenden B: How far can autistic children go in matters of social adaptation? J Autism Child Schizophr 1972; 2:9–33.
94. Lotter V: Social adjustment and placement of autistic children in Middlesex: A follow-up study. J Autism Child Schizophr 1974; 4:11–32.
95. Rank B: Adaptation of the psychoanalytic technique for the treatment of young children with atypical development. Am J Orthopsychiatry 1949; 19:130–139.
96. Carr E: The motivation of self-injurious behavior: A review of some hypotheses. Psychol Bull 1977; 84:800–816.
97. Bartak L, Rutter M: Special educational treatment of autistic children: A comparative study. 1. Design of study and characteristics of units. J Child Psychol Psychiatry 1973; 14:161–179.
98. Schopler E, Olley G: Comprehensive educational services for autistic children: The TEACCH model. In Reynolds C, Gutkin T (eds): The Handbook of School Psychology. New York: John Wiley & Sons, 1982:629–643.
99. Harris S, Handleman J, Kristoff B, et al: Changes in language development among autistic and peer children in segregated and integrated preschool settings. J Autism Dev Disord 1990; 20:23–31.
100. Gaylord-Ross R: A decision model for the treatment of aberrant behavior in applied settings. In Sailor W, Wilcox B, Brown L (eds): Methods of Instruction for Severely Handicapped Students. Baltimore: Paul H Brookes Publishing, 1980:135–158.
101. Schopler E: Towards reducing behavior problems in autistic children. In Wing L (eds): Early Childhood Autism. London: Pergamon Press, 1976:221–246.
102. Lovaas O: Behavioral treatment and normal educational and intellec-

tual functioning in young autistic children. J Consult Clin Psychol 1987; 55:3–9.
103. McEachin J, Smith T, Lovaas O: Long-term outcome for children with autism who received early intensive behavioral treatment. Am J Ment Retard 1993; 97:359–372.
104. Dunlap G, Koegel R, Johnson J, et al: Maintaining performance of autistic clients in community settings with delayed contingencies. J Appl Behav Anal 1987; 20:185–191.
105. Mesibov G: A cognitive program for teaching social behavior to verbal autistic adolescents and adults. In Schopler E, Mesibov G (eds): Social Behavior in Autism. New York: Plenum Publishing, 1986:265–280.
106. Van Bourgondien M, Schopler E: Critical issues in the residential care of people with autism. J Autism Dev Disord 1990; 20:391–400.
107. Mesibov G: Social skills training with verbal autistic adolescents and adults. J Autism Dev Disord 1984; 14:395–404.
108. Williams T: A social skills group for autistic children. J Autism Dev Disord 1989; 19:143–156.
109. Solnit A, Stark M: Mourning and the birth of a defective child. Psychoanal Study Child 1961; 16:523–537.
110. Powers M: Children with Autism: A Parent's Guide. Rockville, MD: Woodbine House, 1989.
111. Amenta C: Russell Is Extra Special: A Book About Autism for Children. New York: Brunner/Mazel, 1992.
112. Siegel B, Silverstein S: What About Me? Growing Up with a Developmentally Disabled Sibling. New York: Plenum Publishing, 1994.
113. Jaselskis CA, Cook EH, Fletcher KE, et al: Clonidine treatment of hyperactive and impulsive children with autistic disorder. J Clin Psychopharmacol 1992; 12:322–327.
114. Cook E, Rowlett R, Jaselskis C, et al: Fluoxetine treatment of patients with autism and mental retardation. J Am Acad Child Adolesc Psychiatry 1992; 31:739–745.
115. McDougle C, Naylor S, Volkmar F, et al: A double-blind placebo-controlled investigation of fluvoxamine in adults with autism. Soc Neurosci Abstr 1994; 20(pt 1):396.
116. Gordon C, State R, Nelson J, et al: A double-blind comparison of clomipramine, desipramine, and placebo in the treatment of autistic disorder. Arch Gen Psychiatry 1993; 50:441–447.
117. Ghaziuddin M, Tsai L, Ghaziuddin N: Fluoxetine in autism with depression. J Am Acad Child Adolesc Psychiatry 1991; 30:508–509.
118. Quintana H, Birmaher B, Stedge D, et al: Use of methylphenidate in the treatment of children with autistic disorder. J Autism Dev Disord 1995; 25:283–294.
119. Fankhauser MP, Karumanchi VC, German ML, et al: A double-blind, placebo-controlled study of the efficacy of transdermal clonidine in autism. J Clin Psychiatry 1992; 53:77–82.
120. Williams DT, Mehl R, Yudofsky S, et al: The effect of propranolol on uncontrolled rage outbursts in children and adolescents with organic brain dysfunction. J Am Acad Child Adolesc Psychiatry 1982; 21:129–135.
121. Ratey J, Bemporad J, Sorgi P, et al: Brief report: Open trial effects of beta-blockers on speech and social behaviors in 8 autistic adults. J Autism Dev Disord 1987; 17:439–446.
122. Ratey J, Mikkelsen E, Sorgi P, et al: Autism: The treatment of aggressive behaviors. J Clin Psychopharmacol 1987; 7:35–41.
123. Anderson LT, Campbell M, Adams P, et al: The effects of haloperidol on discrimination learning and behavioral symptoms in autistic children. J Autism Dev Disord 1989; 9:227–239.
124. Anderson LT, Campbell M, Grega DM, et al: Haloperidol in the treatment of infantile autism: Effects on learning and behavioral symptoms. Am J Psychiatry 1984; 141:1195–1202.
125. Campbell M, Anderson LT, Meier M, et al: A comparison of haloperidol and behavior therapy and their interaction in autistic children. J Am Acad Child Psychiatry 1976; 17:640–655.
126. Cohen IL, Campbell M, Posner D, et al: Behavioral effects of haloperidol in young autistic children. An objective analysis using a within subject reversal design. J Am Acad Child Psychiatry 1980; 19:665–677.
127. Ernst M, Magee HJ, Gonzalez NM, et al: Pimozide in autistic children. Psychopharmacol Bull 1992; 28:187–191.
128. Fish B, Shapiro T, Campbell M: Long-term prognosis and the response of schizophrenic children to drug therapy: A controlled study of trifluoperazine. Am J Psychiatry 1966; 123:32–39.
129. Naruse H, Nagahata M, Nakane Y, et al: A multi-center double-blind trial of pimozide (Orap), haloperidol and placebo in children with behavioral disorders, using crossover design. Acta Paedopsychiatr 1982; 48:173–184.
130. Perry R, Campbell M, Adams P, et al: Long-term efficacy of haloperidol in autistic children: Continuous versus discontinuous drug administration. J Am Acad Child Adolesc Psychiatry 1989; 28:87–92.
131. Campbell M, Adams P, Perry R, et al: Tardive and withdrawal dyskinesia in autistic children: A prospective study. Psychopharmacol Bull 1988; 24:251–255.
132. Campbell M, Locascio JJ, Choroco BA, et al: Stereotypies and tardive dyskinesia: Abnormal movements in autistic children. Psychopharmacol Bull 1990; 26:260–266.
133. Brent DA, Crumrine PK, Varma RR, et al: Phenobarbital treatment and major depressive disorder in children with epilepsy. Pediatrics 1987; 80:909–917.
134. Vining EPG, Mellits D, Dorsen MM, et al: Psychologic and behavioral effects of antiepileptic drugs in children: A double-blind comparison between phenobarbital and valproic acid. Pediatrics 1987; 80:165–174.
135. Plioplys A: Autism: Electroencephalographic abnormalities and clinical improvement with valproic acid. Arch Pediatr Adolesc Med 1994; 148:220–222.
136. Campbell M, Anderson L, Small A, et al: Naltrexone in autistic children: Behavioral symptoms and attentional learning. J Am Acad Child Adolesc Psychiatry 1993; 32:1283–1291.
137. Herman B, Asleson G, Papero P: Acute and chronic naltrexone decreases the hyperactivity of autism. Soc Neurosci Abstr 1993; 19 (pt2):1785.
138. Percy AK, Glaze DG, Schultz RJ, et al: Rett syndrome: Controlled study of an oral opiate antagonist, naltrexone. Ann Neurol 1994; 35:464–470.
139. Campbell M, Fish B, Korein J, et al: Lithium and chlorpromazine: A controlled crossover study of hyperactive severely disturbed young children. J Autism Child Schizophr 1972; 2:234–263.
140. Geller E, Ritvo ER, Freeman BJ, et al: Preliminary observations on the effect of fenfluramine on blood serotonin and symptoms in three autistic boys. N Engl J Med 1982; 307:165–169.
141. Aman MG, Kern RA: Review of fenfluramine in the treatment of the developmental disabilities. J Am Acad Child Adolesc Psychiatry 1989; 28:549–565.
142. Leventhal B, Cook E, Morford M, et al: Fenfluramine: Clinical and neurochemical effects in children with autism. J Neuropsychiatry Clin Neurosci 1993; 5:307–315.
143. Aman MG, Kern RA, Arnold LE, et al: Fenfluramine and mental retardation. J Am Acad Child Adolesc Psychiatry 1991; 30:507–508.
144. Schuster CR, Lewis M, Seiden LS: Fenfluramine: Neurotoxicity. Psychopharmacol Bull 1986; 22:148–151.

CHAPTER

36 Attention-Deficit and Disruptive Behavior Disorders

Vanshdeep Sharma
Jeffrey H. Newcorn
Kristin Matier-Sharma
Jeffrey M. Halperin

Attention-Deficit/Hyperactivity Disorder
Conduct Disorder
Oppositional Defiant Disorder

Attention-deficit/hyperactivity disorder (ADHD), conduct disorder (CD), and oppositional defiant disorder (ODD) form the attention-deficit and disruptive behavior disorders (AD-DBDs) in the *Diagnostic and Statistical Manual of Mental Disorders,* Fourth Edition (DSM-IV).[1] As a group, the AD-DBDs are the most common disorders of childhood and among the most researched areas of childhood psychopathology. Diagnostic criteria for each of the three disorders have been evolving since the advent of the *Diagnostic and Statistical Manual of Mental Disorders,* Third Edition (DSM-III),[2] although the core features have not changed substantially.

Attention-Deficit/Hyperactivity Disorder

Definition

DSM-IV Criteria

Attention-Deficit/Hyperactivity Disorder

A. Either (1) or (2):

(1) six (or more) of the following symptoms of **inattention** have persisted for at least 6 months to a degree that is maladaptive and inconsistent with developmental level:

Inattention

(a) often fails to give close attention to details or makes careless mistakes in schoolwork, work, or other activities

(b) often has difficulty sustaining attention in tasks or play activities

(c) often does not seem to listen when spoken to directly

(d) often does not follow through on instructions and fails to finish schoolwork, chores, or duties in the workplace

(e) often has difficulty organizing tasks and activities

(f) often avoids, dislikes, or is reluctant to engage in tasks that require sustained mental effort

(g) often loses things necessary for tasks or activities

(h) is often easily distracted by extraneous stimuli

(i) is often forgetful in daily activities

(2) six (or more) of the following symptoms of **hyperactivity-impulsivity** have persisted for at least 6 months to a degree that is maladaptive and inconsistent with developmental level:

Hyperactivity

(a) often fidgets with hands or feet or squirms in seat

(b) often leaves seat in classroom or in other situations in which remaining seated is expected

(c) often runs about or climbs excessively in situations in which it is inappropriate (in

DSM-IV Criteria

Attention-Deficit/Hyperactivity Disorder *Continued*

adolescents or adults, may be limited to subjective feelings of restlessness)

(d) often has difficulty playing or engaging in leisure activities quietly

(e) is often "on the go" or often acts as if "driven by a motor"

(f) often talks excessively

Impulsivity

(g) often blurts out answers before questions have been completed

(h) often has difficulty awaiting turn

(i) often interrupts or intrudes on others

A. Some hyperactive-impulsive or inattentive symptoms that caused impairment were present before age 7 years.

B. Some impairment from the symptoms is present in two or more settings (e.g., at school [or work] and at home).

C. There must be clear evidence of clinically significant impairment in social, academic, or occupational functioning.

D. The symptoms do not occur exclusively during the course of a Pervasive Developmental Disorder, Schizophrenia, or other Psychotic Disorder and are not better accounted for by another mental disorder (e.g., Mood Disorder, Anxiety Disorder, Dissociative Disorder, or a Personality Disorder).

In DSM-IV, ADHD is identified as a persistent, severe pattern of inattention or hyperactivity-impulsivity symptoms compared with other children at a comparable developmental level. Three subtypes of ADHD are identified: a predominantly hyperactive-impulsive type, a predominantly inattentive type, and a combined type. The age at onset of some of the symptoms must be before the age of 7 years. Furthermore, some symptoms causing impairment in social, academic, or occupational functioning must be evident in more than one setting.

Conduct Disorder

Definition

DSM-IV Criteria 312.8

Conduct Disorder

A. A repetitive and persistent pattern of behavior in which the basic rights of others or major age-appropriate societal norms or rules are violated, as manifested by the presence of three (or more) of the following criteria in the past 12 months, with at least one criterion present in the past 6 months:

Aggression to people and animals

(1) often bullies, threatens, or intimidates others

(2) often initiates physical fights

(3) has used a weapon that can cause serious physical harm to others

(4) has been physically cruel to people

(5) has been physically cruel to animals

(6) has stolen while confronting a victim

(7) has forced someone into sexual activity

Destruction of property

(8) has deliberately engaged in fire setting with the intention of causing serious damage

(9) has deliberately destroyed others' property

Deceitfulness or theft

(10) has broken into someone else's house, building, or car

(11) often lies to obtain goods or favors or to avoid obligations

(12) has stolen items of nontrivial value without confronting a victim

Serious violations of rules

(13) often stays out at night despite parental prohibitions, beginning before age 13 years

(14) has run away from home overnight at least twice while living in parental or parental surrogate home

(15) is often truant from school, beginning before age 13 years

B. The disturbance in behavior causes clinically significant impairment in social, academic, or occupational functioning.

C. If the individual is age 18 years or older, criteria are not met for Antisocial Personality Disorder.

The essential feature of CD is a persistent pattern of behavior in which the basic rights of others or major age-appropriate societal norms or rules are violated. At least 3 symptoms from a list of 15 must be present during the past year, with at least 1 present in the last 6 months. As with ADHD, CD problems are seen in more than one setting and cause significant impairment in functioning. CD may be diagnosed in adults as well, provided that criteria for antisocial personality disorder are not met. Subtypes of CD are determined on the basis of age at onset. The childhood-onset subtype is diagnosed in children who show at least one of the behaviors before the age of 10 years; the adolescent-onset subtype is characterized by the absence of any CD behaviors before 10 years of age.

Oppositional Defiant Disorder

Definition

DSM-IV Criteria 313.81

Oppositional Defiant Disorder

A. A pattern of negativistic, hostile, and defiant behavior lasting at least 6 months, during which four (or more) of the following are present:

(1) often loses temper

(2) often argues with adults

(3) often actively defies or refuses to comply with adults' requests or rules

(4) often deliberately annoys people

(5) often blames others for his or her mistakes or misbehavior

(6) is often touchy or easily annoyed by others

(7) is often angry and resentful

(8) is often spiteful or vindictive

Note: Consider a criterion met only if the behavior occurs more frequently than is typically observed in individuals of comparable age and developmental level.

B. The disturbance in behavior causes clinically significant impairment in social, academic, or occupational functioning.

C. The behaviors do not occur exclusively during the course of a Psychotic or Mood Disorder.

D. Criteria are not met for Conduct Disorder, and, if the individual is age 18 years or older, criteria are not met for Antisocial Personality Disorder.

The essential feature of ODD is a recurrent pattern of negativistic, defiant, and hostile behavior toward authority figures persisting for at least 6 months. The predecessor of ODD, oppositional disorder, was first described in DSM-III, but it was not grouped with either of the other two disorders. It was a diagnosis given to those children whose behavior was principally oppositional. In the *Diagnostic and Statistical Manual of Mental Disorders,* Third Edition, Revised (DSM-III-R),[3] the disorder was broadened to include minor conduct problems and was renamed ODD to better describe these children. The definition was changed only slightly in DSM-IV with the elimination of one symptom and the addition of an impairment criterion, on the basis of results from the field trials.

The rationale for grouping ADHD, CD, and ODD into the AD-DBD group is that similar areas of difficulty are present in children with these disorders. Academic difficulties, poor social skills, and overrepresentation of boys are among the shared characteristics.[4] However, this grouping also creates the impression that more is known about the causative factors and interrelationships among the three disorders than is actually the case. There has been extensive debate as to whether ADHD and ODD have discriminant validity from CD. Although there is now a consensus that ADHD and CD are separable diagnoses[5] with distinct correlates and outcome,[6] the relationship of ODD to both disorders is less clear. The DSM-III conceptualization of oppositional disorder was criticized by some investigators who thought that children with oppositional disorder did not show impairments sufficient to distinguish them from normal children[7]; others believed that oppositional disorder was simply a less severe form of CD.[8, 9] Subsequent research has indicated that ODD is at least partially distinct not only from ADHD[10] but from CD as well.[11–13] Furthermore, the impairment criterion added in DSM-IV helps to demarcate the boundary of ODD from normalcy.

Although much has been learned about the AD-DBDs in the past 15 years, including their symptomatic profiles, differential diagnosis, and patterns of comorbidity, our knowledge regarding the etiology and neurobiological basis of these conditions as well as differences in treatment efficacy as a function of ADHD subtype is incomplete and presents obstacles to accurate classification and differential diagnosis.

Epidemiology

Studies examining prevalence rates of the AD-DBDs in community samples are characterized by discrepant findings, although rates are generally high. Methodological differences, the use of different systems of classification, and differences in the definition of caseness employed by researchers make these discrepant findings difficult to interpret.[14, 15] Prevalence rates for ADHD range from 2.0%[16] to 6.3%.[17] Rates for CD have been estimated to be as low as 0.9%[18] for school-age children but as high as 8.7% in adolescents.[19] The overall prevalence of ODD varies across studies from 5.7%[20] to 9.9%.[20] In school-age children, boys have higher rates than girls for all three disorders, but only in the case of CD and in the hyperactive subtype of ADHD do these higher rates persist into adolescence.

Among the three disorders that compose the AD-DBD group, there is a high rate of comorbidity. Given the similarity of behavior problems that characterize the individual disorders, this comorbidity is hardly surprising. Data from several epidemiological studies[17, 20, 21] indicate that ODD and CD are present in 40% to 70% of children with ADHD. Conversely, among children with ODD and CD in these same studies, 40% to 60% were estimated also to have ADHD. In clinical settings, the prevalence of comorbid ODD and CD among children with ADHD is presumed to be even higher than it is in epidemiological samples, because the occurrence of these conditions together is likely to generate substantial impairment and lead to increased referrals for treatment.

Comorbidity between the AD-DBD group and other diagnostic categories is also common.[22–25] It has been estimated that 15% to 20% of children with ADHD have comorbid mood disorders,[26–29] 20% to 25% have anxiety disorders,[28–31] and 6% to 20% have learning disabilities.[32] However, when a broader definition of academic underachievement is used, the rates show a wide variability from a low of 10% to as high as 90%.[33–36] Other conditions that may occur comorbidly with the AD-DBDs include Tourette's disorder,[37–39] drug and alcohol abuse syndromes,[40–42] and mental retardation.[43, 44]

Etiology

No single cause can be identified for any of the AD-DBDs.[45, 46] The most likely reason for this is that children with AD-DBDs are a heterogeneous group. A variety of studies using neurochemical markers, family-genetic analyses, patterns of comorbidity, and family studies have begun to delineate more homogeneous groups.

Neurobiology

The principal neurotransmitter system implicated in the pathogenesis of the AD-DBD group is the catecholaminergic system, which includes the noradrenergic and dopaminergic systems. A role for the serotoninergic (5-hydroxytryptamine [5-HT]) system has more recently been elucidated. Data implicating these systems have been obtained from three lines of research: animal studies, measurement of metabolites of the three amines, and pharmacological studies. Several preclinical[47, 48] and clinical[49, 50] studies provide evidence for a role for norepinephrine in the regulation of attention and cognitive functioning (Table 36–1). Furthermore, decreased norepinephrine activity in association with low dopamine β-hydroxylase activity has also been implicated in the pathogenesis of aggressive behaviors.[51, 52] Dopamine β-hydroxylase is the enzyme responsible for the conversion of dopamine to norepinephrine, and it has been suggested that subjects with low dopamine β-hydroxylase activity may have correspondingly low norepinephrine function. Furthermore, 3-methoxy-4-hydroxyphenylglycol, the major metabolite of norepinephrine, has been measured in plasma, in urine, and in a few cases in the cerebrospinal fluid of children with AD-DBDs. Whereas findings of urinary 3-methoxy-4-hydroxyphenylglycol excretion have been inconsistent,[53–57] plasma[58] and cerebrospinal fluid[59] 3-methoxy-4-hydroxyphenylglycol concentrations have been negatively correlated with conduct problems and a measure of aggression, respectively.

The dopaminergic system has also been implicated in the regulation of attention[49, 60, 61] and response organization.[62] The role of dopamine in the regulation of activity level has long been demonstrated in preclinical studies.[63–66] Furthermore, neuroimaging studies have indicated dysfunction in the dopamine-rich striatal[67] and caudate[68] regions of the brain. However, studies measuring homovanillic acid, the major metabolite of dopamine, have been less fruitful. Only one[54] of several studies[53, 57, 69] measuring urinary excretion of homovanillic acid revealed differences between children with ADHD and normal control subjects, whereas no difference between these groups was found when cerebrospinal fluid homovanillic acid concentration was measured.[70] Finally, pharmacological studies have consistently reported that virtually all medications that are efficacious in children with ADHD affect catecholamine transmission and metabolism.[71] The most commonly used medications for ADHD, methylphenidate, dextroamphetamine, and pemoline, have primary effects on both noradrenergic and dopaminergic mechanisms.

An emerging literature indicates an association between aggressive behavior and central 5-HT function[72–75] (see Table 36–1). Numerous preclinical studies have indicated the relationship between diminished 5-HT activity and impulsive-aggressive behavior.[76] In addition, negative correlations between concentrations of 5-hydroxyindoleacetic acid, the metabolite of 5-HT, and ratings of aggression have been reported in a group of boys with AD-DBDs at the time of initial assessment[59] and at a 2-year follow-up.[77] Similarly, a reduced number of ^{3}H-imipramine binding sites, an index of presynaptic 5-HT activity, was found in children with comorbid CD and ADHD.[78, 79] Other research has focused on dynamic measures of central 5-HT function in children with AD-DBDs. One such measure is the prolactin response to a challenge dose of fenfluramine.[80] Fenfluramine is a central 5-HT releaser and reuptake inhibitor, and the prolactin response to fenfluramine assesses overall central 5-HT function. Boys with ADHD have been shown to differ in their prolactin response to fenfluramine challenge on the basis of the presence or absence of physical aggression. Aggressive boys showed an enhanced prolactin response in comparison to nonaggressive boys.[81] Although challenge studies are an emerging area of interest, it is to be noted that not all of the findings are consistent.[82]

In more recent years, techniques such as positron emission tomography and magnetic resonance imaging have shown promise in elucidating the pathophysiological mecha-

Table 36–1 Neurochemical Findings

Catecholaminergic Findings
Decreased norepinephrine activity with low dopamine β-hydroxylase activity implicated in aggressive behaviors
Plasma 3-methoxy-4-hydroxyphenylglycol concentration correlated with conduct problems
Cerebrospinal fluid 3-methoxy-4-hydroxyphenylglycol concentration correlated with a measure of aggression
Indication of dysfunction in dopamine-rich striatal and caudate regions of brain
Serotoninergic Findings
Negative correlations between cerebrospinal fluid concentration of 5-hydroxy-indoleacetic acid and ratings of aggression
Reduced number of ^{3}H-imipramine binding sites found in children with comorbid CD and ADHD
Enhanced prolactin response in aggressive boys compared with non-aggressive boys

nism of AD-DBDs, in particular that of ADHD. Positron emission tomography has shown areas of hypoperfusion in the frontal lobe and basal ganglia regions during an object-naming task[83] as well as hypoperfusion of striatal brain regions along with hyperperfusion of cerebral sensory and somatosensory areas.[67] Similarly, reduced rates of cerebral glucose metabolism have been reported in adults who met criteria for ADHD as children[84] in comparison with normal adult control subjects. Although these findings have not been replicated in adolescents, regional cerebral differences in glucose metabolism similar to those of adult patients have been reported.[85] Finally, studies using magnetic resonance imaging have reported frontal lobe abnormalities in children with ADHD compared with children with dyslexia and normal children.[86, 87]

Genetics

Evidence for genetic transmission of ADHD has come from several lines of research including family,[88–90] twin,[91, 92] and adoption[93] studies. The preponderance of evidence suggests that biological relatives of children with ADHD represent a population at risk for ADHD and supports the notion that transmission in families may be partly mediated by genetic factors. Whereas the mechanism of transmission remains unknown, segregation analyses suggest that a single gene is most likely implicated.[93, 94] However, other forms of transmission including multifactorial inheritance cannot be ruled out.[94, 95] One influential series of studies has evaluated the familial pattern of ADHD as a function of comorbidity in an attempt to define more homogeneous groups. Even though ADHD is considered to have a strong genetic component, a large number of cases cannot be explained solely by genetic factors, and it is therefore believed that children with ADHD are genetically heterogeneous.

The role of genetics in CD is less clear. It has generally been thought that there is no specific genetic substrate of aggression, with perhaps the exception of Lesch-Nyhan syndrome.[96] However, data suggest that there may be a genetic basis for some forms of aggression. Mice deficient for the gene encoding α-calcium–calmodulin–dependent kinase II show decreased fear responses and an increase in defensive aggression.[97] In addition, in a large kindred with several adult men with borderline mental retardation, a point mutation in the structural gene for monoamine oxidase A *(MAOA)* has been implicated in disturbed regulation of aggression.[98]

Environmental Factors

Family studies have revealed that a number of nongenetic familial factors also play an important role in the initiation and propagation of the behaviors characteristic of the AD-DBDs. Factors in the physical environment as well as variables intrinsic to the child, parent, and family interactions may contribute to the development and maintenance of problem behaviors. In the physical environment, overcrowding and uncomfortable living conditions have been implicated in the development of aggression.[99] Lower socioeconomic status and the absence of an intact family are psychosocial variables that appear to increase the risk.[89]

In the child, perinatal events, the child's temperament, and child neglect or abuse are contributory. Similarly, parental stress, the presence of parental psychopathological processes such as depression, and poor parental self-esteem have been implicated in the development of hyperactivity in certain children.[100] One hypothesized environmental pathway suggests that negative mood states follow from parental psychiatric illness and result in an increased perception of deviant behavior in the child. This may, in turn, lead to an increased amount of negative interactions between the parent and the child, which in a vulnerable child could result in oppositionality or conduct problems.[45]

Course and Natural History

Behaviors characteristic of the AD-DBDs are observable from the preschool years onward. As early as age 1.5 years, hyperactive behaviors such as "moves too much during sleep" have been reported, followed by the appearance of "difficulty playing quietly" and "excessive climbing/running" by age 3 years.[101] Attentional problems are usually reported after hyperactivity. However, it is likely that these problems are present early but are not reported until the child enters school, when there are increased environmental and cognitive demands placed upon him or her. Hyperactivity and attentional problems emerge gradually[102] and may overlap with the emergence of oppositional behaviors, giving the appearance of a simultaneous, rather than a sequential, onset. It is now recognized that whereas hyperactivity and, to a lesser extent, attentional problems show a gradual decline through adolescence and adulthood, a number of individuals continue to have attentional, behavioral, and emotional problems well into adolescence and adulthood.[103–106]

The presentation of oppositional behaviors shows greater variability. During the preschool years, transient oppositional behavior is common. However, when the oppositionality is of a persistent nature and lasts beyond the preschool years, the escalation to more disruptive behaviors is likely. On the basis of research data, two possible developmental trajectories have been suggested. In most oppositional children, who are usually not physically aggressive, oppositional behaviors peak around age 8 years and decline beyond that.[13, 101] In a second group of children, delinquent behaviors[107, 108] follow the onset of oppositional behaviors; early physical aggression is a key predictor of this trajectory, with physically aggressive children being more likely to progress from early oppositional behaviors to more severe and disabling conduct problems.

In general, conduct problems first appear in middle childhood. The progression of conduct problems is from rule violations, such as school attendance, to aggression toward animals and people. In males, the more serious forms of conduct problems, such as rape or mugging, generally emerge after age 13 years.[107] A different group of children show conduct problems for the first time during adolescence, without preexisting oppositional or aggressive behaviors; this group tends to have disorders that are transient and nonaggressive in nature.[107, 109–111] When conduct disorder is seen in adolescence for the first time, the problems tend to diminish by adulthood. However, if conduct disorder is present from middle childhood, there is much greater persistence of aggression through adulthood and often a history of arrests or incarceration.

Considerable data indicate that a subgroup of hyperactive children show higher rates of delinquency and substance abuse during adolescence, and this continues into adulthood.[112] Families of these children tend to be less stable, have higher divorce rates, and move more frequently. First-degree relatives have been found to have higher rates of antisocial behaviors, substance abuse, and depression.[113–115] The difficulties experienced by these adolescents and adults include poor self-esteem, difficulty in interpersonal relationships, and difficulties in holding on to jobs as well as assault and armed robbery in a minority of cases.[116] Children with childhood symptoms representing both ADHD and CD are overrepresented in this group.

Assessment

The clinical evaluation of a child with AD-DBD requires a multisource, multimethod approach.[117] In addition to the clinical interview, supplemental information may be obtained from school reports, rating scales completed by teachers and parents, psychometric data, and direct observations of the child. Several structured and semistructured interviews are available, although these tend to be used primarily in research settings. Adults are generally considered to be the best informants of disruptive behaviors, although children and adolescents may provide important data regarding internalizing symptoms and some infrequent behavior problems such as antisocial acts.[118, 119]

Rating Scales

Rating scales are among the most commonly used assessment instruments and are a useful aid for the psychiatrist. They provide a view of the child's behavior that may be different from that observed by the psychiatrist because children with AD-DBDs often do not evidence symptoms in the office. Rating scales facilitate the systematic acquisition of information about the child's behavior in different settings in a cost-effective manner. Most are standardized and provide scores that are norm referenced by age and gender. The systematic use of these instruments ensures that a complete set of specific behaviors are assessed at different points in time, enabling comparisons during the course of treatment. Teacher and parent rating scales are complementary because they yield data from different situations. Parents are knowledgeable about their child's day-to-day behavior and present information related to the child's behavior at home and her or his interaction with siblings. However, teachers are often the best source of information regarding attentional problems and disruptive behaviors, because the structured milieu of a classroom provides an appropriate setting for evaluation of cognitive function and the opportunity for behavioral comparisons with other children of the same age and grade.[120]

There is an ever growing number of rating scales, but the most commonly used are the Conners[121] and the Achenbach[122, 123] scales, which are available in parent and teacher versions and possess solid normative bases. The Conners Teacher Rating Scale–Revised is a 28-item scale that is standardized for children 3 to 17 years of age. The presence of various behaviors and their severity are rated on a 4-point scale ranging from 0 (not at all) to 3 (very much). This instrument generates three factor scores: conduct problems, hyperactivity, and inattention-passivity. It differentiates hyperactive children from normal children, clinic-referred nonhyperactive children, and learning-disabled children[124, 125] and is sensitive to medication effects.[126] The Conners Parent Rating Scale–Revised contains 48 items that are also rated on a similar 4-point scale. This scale generates five separate factors: conduct problems, learning problems, psychosomatic, impulsive-hyperactive, and anxiety. Data support the scale's ability to differentiate groups of children with ADHD from normal children as well as its sensitivity to treatment effects.

The Child Behavior Checklist is a 138-item parent report questionnaire and is useful with children aged 4 to 16 years. This instrument assesses a broad range of behavior problems and competencies and generates T scores for two broad-band factors (i.e., internalizing and externalizing). Within the internalizing domain, separate narrow-band factors labeled schizoid-anxious, depressed, uncommunicative, obsessive-compulsive, somatic complaints, social withdrawal, and immature are generated. The narrow-band externalizing factor scores assess hyperactivity, aggression, and delinquency. The Child Behavior Checklist is also available in a teacher report form,[123] which is similar to the parent form and applicable for children aged 6 to 16 years.[127]

Rating scales have several limitations, and diagnoses should not be made on the bases of these data alone. It has been consistently found that elevations on discrete scale factors do not necessarily coincide with specific psychiatric disorders.[128, 129] Furthermore, because teacher and parent ratings may be influenced by a number of informant and method biases, a child's profile may be a function of the informants used and the situation under which the child was observed.[10, 130] Finally, when the behaviors being rated are of low frequency or are episodic, rating scales can average the fluctuations characteristic of the episodic behavior[131] and thus lead to an inaccurate assessment.

Interviews

Interviews with children and their parents are an essential step in the clinical evaluation. In clinical practice, interviews usually follow a loosely structured format with a flexible approach that allows the in-depth exploration of relevant clinical information. However, this same flexibility may be the cause of poor reliability. The use of structured interviews can reduce many of the problems associated with clinical interviews. The principal advantages of structured interviews are the breadth and comprehensiveness of information gathered.[132] However, structured instruments are not necessarily well suited for clinical decision-making because they accept the parent's or teacher's determination of whether a symptom is present and do not allow clinical judgment. Semistructured interviews share some of the advantages of structured interviews, particularly in the area of the comprehensiveness of the data obtained. However, they differ from structured interviews in that the interviewer has greater flexibility in exploring areas of importance. Furthermore, the procedure for generating diagnoses is more consistent with clinical decision-making in that the interviewer determines the diagnoses on the basis of his or her clinical judgment rather than a specific diagnostic algorithm.[133] Nevertheless, both structured and semistructured interviews are lengthy and at present are used almost exclusively in research settings.

A number of structured and semistructured diagnostic interviews are currently available for use with children and include the Diagnostic Interview Schedule for Children, the Diagnostic Interview for Children and Adolescents, the Schedule for Affective Disorders and Schizophrenia for School-Age Children, the Child and Adolescent Psychiatric Assessment, the Child Assessment Schedule, and the Interview Schedule for Children. In general, findings from studies of structured interviews suggest that the reliability coefficients of interview-generated diagnoses are higher with adult than with child informants and higher for disruptive-externalizing than for internalizing disorders. Among the AD-DBDs, it has been found that CD often has better reliability and validity coefficients than ADHD.[133–135]

Psychological and Psychometric Evaluation

Psychological and cognitive test performance is generally not required to determine the presence of an AD-DBD. Yet, such evaluations may be indicated as part of a comprehensive assessment, particularly when assessment of cognitive functioning is required and is crucial for determining school placement. Information from a neuropsychological or educational evaluation can often be used to supplement the clinical evaluation by providing an understanding of the individual child's level of cognitive and attentional functioning as well as screening for suspected mental retardation or learning disabilities. These evaluations typically involve the administration of a broad-based test battery that includes measures of cognitive, linguistic, perceptual, motor, and academic functioning. These data can be extremely useful for developing a treatment plan, particularly for children with comorbid learning disabilities or specific developmental and cognitive disorders.

Other psychometric measures include computerized continuous performance tests, of which there are many varieties. In the typical format, the child monitors a series of stimuli for the presence of specified targets. The number and types of errors, as well as reaction time, typically constitute the measures of interest. Interest in creating developmentally appropriate measures of symptom domains of the AD-DBDs for preschoolers has led to the development of continuous performance tests for use in this population.[136] Although continuous performance tests have been found to differentiate children with ADHD from normal children,[137] their ability to differentiate ADHD from other clinical groups is less clear, and there is little evidence that they are able to identify individuals with enough precision to be useful as diagnostic instruments. Some authors have proposed that continuous performance tests can be used as clinical diagnostic tools,[138] but these conclusions are generally based on group differences that do not necessarily imply accurate individual classification.[128, 139] However, one report[140] suggests that when an individual makes a high number of inattention errors on the continuous performance test, the clinical diagnosis of ADHD is more likely. Continuous performance tests may be useful within the framework of a multimethod evaluation because of their unique contribution of data regarding the child's information-processing capacities during a long, dull task as well as the behavioral observations derived from this situation.

Objective measures of activity level, such as stabilometric chairs, wrist actometers, and solid-state actigraphs, have also been used in the assessment of ADHD. Although these devices provide a judgment-free assessment of activity level, their validity, as assessed by correlations with ratings of behavior, has been inconsistent. At present, it is suggested that these measures not be used to diagnose clinical syndromes.[141]

Observational Measures

Direct behavioral observation also has a role in the assessment of the AD-DBDs, but this procedure is more often performed as part of a research assessment. Various standardized methods have been used, both in a structured playroom and in a school setting. In a structured playroom setting, measures include recording the number of times a child crosses grids marked on the floor, the number of toys touched, the amount of time played with each toy, and the amount of time the child spends focused on a particular task.[142] In the school setting, typical measures include monitoring the amount of time the child spends on-task or remains in her or his seat.[143] These observational measures have consistently been found to differentiate children with ADHD from normal children, although their utility in discriminating among clinical groups is less clear.[131] Direct behavioral observations are particularly helpful in the clinical assessment of AD-DBDs in preschool children, for whom standardized diagnostic instruments and rating scales are less applicable.

Laboratory Measures

At present, no laboratory measures can serve as diagnostic tools for AD-DBDs. A study[144] of 18 families with generalized resistance to thyroid hormone found that 70% of children met criteria for ADHD and that 50% of adults met criteria for ADHD as children. However, others[145, 146] who examined children with ADHD have not found abnormalities of thyroid function. Although it has been suggested that children with AD-DBDs who have symptoms suggestive of thyroid dysfunction be evaluated for thyroid disease,[147] routine thyroid function tests are not recommended in children with ADHD because generalized resistance to thyroid hormone is an extremely rare condition.

Other Domains of Functioning

Many children with AD-DBDs have impaired social skills and consequently experience difficulties with peer relationships. Data suggest that both hyperactivity and aggression are related to peer rejection, which may occur as early as the preschool years.[102, 148] The level of hyperactivity, the age at onset of aggression, and the developmental level of the child all affect the extent of peer rejection experienced.[149] Relationships between the child and peers are sometimes assessed in research studies through peer nominations. This is done by asking children to rate other members of their class according to popularity. However, obtaining reports of peer relationships from school teachers is better suited for clinical practice. Other indicators of social impairment may include the number of times a child is suspended or expelled from school and the number of police contacts.[150] Information regarding social adjustment is crucial in treatment planning, because increased impairment in social and school function is predictive of poor outcome.

Differential Diagnoses

The relationship between ADHD and CD has been the most studied. It is now generally accepted that the two disorders can be differentiated despite the high degree of overlap, in terms of both symptom presentation and co-occurrence within individuals. ADHD can be conceptualized as a cognitive-developmental disorder, with an earlier age at onset than CD. Children with ADHD more frequently show deficits on measures of attentional and cognitive function, have increased motor activity, and have greater neurodevelopmental abnormalities.[4] In contrast, children with CD tend to be characterized by higher levels of aggression and greater familial dysfunction. A significant proportion of children present with symptoms of both ADHD and CD, and both conditions should be diagnosed when this occurs. Comorbid ADHD and CD is consistently reported to be more disabling than either disorder alone. These children retain the difficulties found in both disorders and tend to show increased levels of aggressive behaviors at an early age, which remain remarkably persistent. This is in contrast to the more typical episodic course seen in children who have CD alone.[4, 5, 111, 151] Finally, children with comorbid ADHD and CD appear to have a poorer long-term outcome than either disorder alone.

The relationship of ADHD to ODD is less well studied. However, it does appear that among children with ADHD, those who are most hyperactive-impulsive are at greatest risk for development of ODD. Nevertheless, it is possible to distinguish between the two disorders. ODD symptoms, such as "loses temper," "actively defies," and "swears," are less characteristic of children with ADHD.[10] In general, the onset of ODD symptoms peaks by age 8 years and shows a declining course thereafter. On the other hand, hyperactivity and attentional problems appear at a much earlier age[13, 102] and often persist, although the levels of inattentiveness and hyperactivity often decrease with age.

With regard to the relationship between ODD and CD, the question has been raised whether they constitute different levels of severity of a single phenomenon or should be viewed as distinct. A diagnosis of CD supersedes ODD because approximately 90% of children with CD would also meet criteria for ODD. Although the majority of children with ODD will not develop CD,[11] in some cases ODD appears to represent a developmental precursor of CD. In cases in which ODD precedes CD, the onset of CD is typically before age 10 years (childhood-onset CD). In children who have the onset of CD after the age of 10 years, symptoms of ODD and ADHD are usually not present during early childhood. It has been shown that children with ODD demonstrate lower degrees of impairment and are more socially competent compared with children with CD.[8] Furthermore, children with CD come from less advantaged families and have greater conflict with school and judicial systems compared with children with ODD. Family adversity scores in children with ODD are usually intermediate between those of children with CD and normal children.[9, 11]

Proper differential diagnosis of the AD-DBDs requires discrimination not only among ADHD, ODD, and CD but also from a wide range of other psychiatric, developmental, and medical conditions. Mood and anxiety disorders, learning disorders, mental retardation, pervasive developmental disorders, cognitive disorders, and psychotic disorders may all present with impairment of attention as well as hyperactive-impulsive behaviors. The diagnosis of ADHD in DSM-IV requires that the symptoms of inattention–cognitive disorganization and impulsivity-hyperactivity are not better accounted for by one of these conditions. In addition, a variety of medical conditions such as epilepsy, Tourette's disorder, thyroid disease, postinfectious or post-traumatic encephalopathy, and sensory impairments must be considered. Finally, many medications that are prescribed in children can mimic ADHD symptoms. Examples include anticonvulsants (e.g., phenobarbital), antihistamines, decongestants, bronchodilators (e.g., theophylline), and systemic steroids.

Treatment

Successful treatment planning in children with AD-DBDs requires consideration not only of the core symptoms but also of family and social factors and comorbidity with other disorders. Given the heterogeneity of the three disorders that make up the AD-DBDs, the wide-ranging effects of the disruptive behaviors, the high rates of comorbidity, and the presence of associated features such as learning disabilities, multimodal treatments are frequently necessary. Optimal planning for most children with ADHD should involve a combination of psychopharmacological and psychosocial treatments. A diagnosis of ODD without any comorbid condition requires behavioral interventions and not medication. Treatment of children with CD only usually entails a variety of psychosocial interventions with the possibility of augmenting treatment with one of several pharmacological agents.

Psychopharmacology

Psychopharmacological treatments of the AD-DBDs can be traced to 1937,[152] when amphetamine sulfate (Benzedrine) was successfully used to treat a heterogeneous group of behaviorally disturbed children and adolescents. The calming effect of the medication on these children as well as an increase in compliance and in academic performance was described. Subsequently, a series of studies attempted to better characterize those children who best responded to stimulant medications. Today, psychostimulants remain the medication of choice for the majority of children with ADHD, although several other medications have demonstrated efficacy and provide useful alternatives for those who are stimulant nonresponders or for whom stimulants may be contraindicated.

Stimulants

It is well established that psychostimulants are extremely effective in treating a wide range of disruptive behaviors. Nevertheless, ADHD remains the primary indication for the use of these medications. Methylphenidate, dextroamphetamine, and pemoline have been shown to be effective in treating ADHD. Of these, methylphenidate is most often prescribed and accounts for more than 90% of stimulant use in the United States.[153] The stimulants produce significant improvement in attention, motor activity, impulse control, and aggressiveness, leading to better organization of behavior and self-regulation. A number of controlled studies have also shown an improvement in academic function as well as in social interactions accompanied by a decrease in aggressiveness.

The decision to prescribe psychostimulant medication is best undertaken after a comprehensive assessment, with full consideration given to the range of pharmacological and nonpharmacological treatment options that are available. Several of the rating scales used in assessment (e.g., the Conners questionnaires) are sensitive to medication effects and can be used to monitor adequacy of dose, development of tolerance, and rebound. Before a trial with any of the stimulants, baseline data should be obtained, including a complete blood count and the child's height, weight, and blood pressure. In the case of pemoline, baseline liver function tests should be obtained as well.

The decision of which stimulant to select is best determined by considering properties intrinsic to the different medications—such as duration of activity and adverse effect profile—as well as the individual circumstances of the patient (e.g., When is peak medication level needed most? What is the individual's lifestyle?). Methylphenidate is usually the first drug tried because its adverse effect profile is somewhat more agreeable. Insomnia and appetite suppression are often present but less intense; growth retardation has been less clearly established. Short-acting methylphenidate can be given in dosing schedules of either two or three times daily; the usual starting dose is 5 mg. The dose is then increased in 5-mg increments. When a dosing schedule of three times a day is used, the third dose is usually half the morning or noon dose.[154] Dosing three times daily is particularly helpful for providing coverage during homework time and maximizing interactions with parents and peers. Doses are usually given at 4-hour intervals because the half-life is 1.5 to 2.5 hours. The upper recommended dose limit is 60 mg, although higher doses may be required in certain cases. Nonresponders to methylphenidate may respond to a different stimulant. Dextroamphetamine is often the second choice and can often be administered in a manner similar to methylphenidate.[155] Dextroamphetamine is more potent than methylphenidate, so the initial starting dose and upper dose limit are lower. The recommended dosage range is 2.5 to 40 mg. Dextroamphetamine is somewhat longer acting than methylphenidate, and therefore a dosing schedule of three times daily is less often required.

Clinical Vignette 1

George, a 17-year-old high-school senior, was referred for persistent academic underachievement and was on the verge of being asked to repeat his last year in high school. Although he seemed bright enough to do the work at school, George was often considered unmotivated. This was particularly apparent in certain classes, such as mathematics. George had been assessed several times for learning problems and had been receiving ongoing tutoring in mathematics at the time of the current assessment. However, his teachers continued to feel that George was "not working up to his potential." During the evaluation, George's parents reported that he was very fidgety until fifth grade and that his 8-year-old brother has been successfully treated with pemoline for ADHD in the past year. An empirical trial of stimulant medication was undertaken, with astonishingly good results. A program of cognitive remediation was recommended, and this combination of treatments produced sufficient improvement for George to graduate on time. He went on to college and surprised his parents by receiving a 3.5 average his first semester.

Longer acting psychostimulants may be used to minimize the on-off effects that are frequently seen with short-acting methylphenidate and dextroamphetamine. Sustained-release methylphenidate and dextroamphetamine spansules maintain their activity for 6 to 8 hours, so medication need not be administered in school. However, the clinical effects may be less robust than with short-acting preparations. More sustained effects may be achieved with pemoline, which has a half-life of 12 hours and can therefore often be given once daily. This medication may be particularly attractive to some adolescents and adults, who require sustained medication effects across a variety of situations. The clinical profiles of the three long-acting stimulants are reported to be virtually identical. The smallest pemoline dose is 18.75 mg, and the recommended upper limit is 112.5 mg/d.

Antidepressants

The noradrenergic tricyclic antidepressants, principally imipramine and desipramine, have been the most extensively studied and most often prescribed antidepressants for children with ADHD. Data supporting their efficacy have been building for the past 20 years. Usually smaller doses than those used in the treatment of depression are required, and the medication produces clinical benefit more rapidly. For desipramine, doses between 2.5 and 5 mg/kg/d have been recommended.[156] In the case of both of these medications, cardiac side effects are of concern, and premedication work-up must include at least an electrocardiogram. Tachycardia and postural hypotension are commonly seen but are not often problems. Prolongation of the PR and QT intervals may be a greater source of concern and should be reviewed with a pediatric cardiologist.

The decision to prescribe tricyclic antidepressants for children with ADHD must be made with the knowledge that several sudden deaths were reported in children taking desipramine.[157, 158] Although it has been argued that data do not support the conclusion that these agents have a high degree of cardiovascular toxicity in children,[159] proper informed consent should be obtained. Neither imipramine nor desipramine is approved by the U.S. Food and Drug Administration for the treatment of children with ADHD.

Clomipramine and fluoxetine are two serotoninergic antidepressants that have also been used in the treatment of children with ADHD. In one study, clomipramine was found to decrease scores related to aggressiveness and poor impulse control.[160] Two open studies[161, 162] have described the utility of fluoxetine in the treatment of children with ADHD with and without comorbid mood disorder. Although it is not clear how comorbidity with ODD and CD would affect this medication response, the use of selective serotoninergic reuptake inhibitors is of some interest in the comorbid group in light of findings implicating serotoninergic mechanisms in aggression.

Clinical Vignette 2

Ms. C, a 27-year-old secretary, sought professional assistance for problems focusing attention at work. She had never presented to treatment before, despite some self-reported problems with attention, because she was always able to achieve well when she dedicated herself to her work. Her grades through high school were solid, if not outstanding, and there was never any mention of a learning or attentional problem. However, she decided to seek assistance after viewing a news segment on adult ADHD. During assessment, it was learned that Ms. C experienced a bout of depression during high school and had been despondent since her father passed away the summer before. She was successfully treated with a combination of fluoxetine 20 mg daily and brief psychotherapy.

Clonidine

Clonidine has also been the subject of investigations.[163, 164] This α-adrenergic agonist, originally marketed as an antihypertensive agent, is reportedly most effective in treating symptoms of hyperactivity, impulsivity, and aggression for children with ADHD and therefore seems ideally suited for use in the group with comorbid ODD, CD, and aggression. It is also useful in treating patients with ADHD who either have diagnosed tic disorders[165] or are at increased risk for development of them, such as those children with a positive family history of tics. This is particularly important, because as many as 40% to 60% of patients with Tourette's disorder seen in psychiatric settings have ADHD,[29] and many of these individuals have significant behavior problems. Clonidine can be used alone or in combination with the stimulants, usually in doses ranging from 0.1 to 0.3 mg/d. One of its advantages is that it is relatively long acting[166] and has been successfully used to treat the initial insomnia that sometimes results from late afternoon stimulant use.[167] Clonidine is available in both tablet form and a depot skin patch preparation. The skin patch provides sustained coverage for 1 week and may be particularly useful for treating children with ADHD whose behavior is characterized by a variable pattern of extreme lability, especially in the early morning, before stimulants and oral clonidine take effect. Because clonidine is not approved by the Food and Drug Administration for use in ADHD, informed consent should clearly indicate that this is an "off-label" treatment.

Other Agents

A variety of other pharmacotherapeutic agents have been used in the treatment of aggression and episodic dyscontrol, although efficacy in children with comorbid ADHD and CD has not yet been demonstrated. Among these medications, lithium has been the best studied. Lithium has been found to be effective in well-designed studies of aggressive children[168] and impulsive-aggressive adolescent and young adult delinquents. The antiepileptic carbamazepine is another drug that has shown some efficacy for treating behavior problems characterized by aggressiveness and impulsivity. β-Adrenergic blockers such as propranolol have also been found to be useful in treating aggression but require further evaluation in children and adolescents.[169]

Neuroleptic medications, principally chlorpromazine, thioridazine, and haloperidol, have also been used in treatment of the AD-DBDs. These medications have been used for treating children with severe behavioral problems characterized by aggression and combativeness. Although these medications are approved by the U.S. Food and Drug Administration for the treatment of severe behavior problems in children, their use should be limited to those children who are refractory to all other types of pharmacological interventions.

Besides psychopharmacological interventions, electroencephalographical biofeedback therapy has been considered by some to be an alternative treatment for ADHD. However, no data support the contention that this form of therapy is efficacious in treating ADHD, either alone or in combination with other forms of treatment.

Psychosocial Interventions

A variety of psychosocial therapies have been found to be useful for treating children with AD-DBDs. These can be broadly grouped into behavioral therapy and cognitive-behavioral therapy. Because family, peer, and school interactions are important in the morbidity and maintenance of these disorders, effective psychosocial treatments target each of these areas. Whereas individual play therapy with children is a common treatment strategy used in many clinic settings and may be useful in treating comorbid symptoms, it is generally ineffective in decreasing problem behaviors of the AD-DBDs.[170]

Clinical Vignette 3

Peter, a 9-year-old boy, was referred after a psychological testing evaluation for psychotherapy for anxiety and defiant behavior. He had an IQ in excess of 130 but his schoolwork was not outstanding. He frequently called out in class and did not always complete his assignments, but he usually did well on examinations. He had few friends because of his many annoying behaviors. There were problems at home as well. Peter was intensely rivalrous with his younger brother, to the point of being aggressive, and would frequently argue with his parents. He would have tantrums if his parents tried to leave him at home with a baby sitter, so they never went out alone. After careful evaluation, it was determined that Peter suffered from ADHD as well as ODD and separation anxiety disorder. In support of this formulation, a continuous performance test revealed numerous impulsivity errors, and the Conners Teacher Rating Scale hyperactivity factor score was 2 standard deviations above the mean for Peter's age and gender. In this case, the diagnosis of ADHD was missed during the original evaluation because attention was focused on ODD and separation anxiety disorder symptoms as well as difficulties interacting with family members and peers. However, when the additional diagnosis of ADHD was made and a trial of methylphenidate undertaken, Peter showed considerable improvement in his academic performance and interactions with others. Individual psychotherapy was also recommended to treat anxiety and low self-esteem, and family counseling was recommended because of the considerable amount of family strife.

Behavioral therapy relies primarily on training parents or teachers to be the agents of change. The focus is on decreasing the frequency of problem behaviors and increasing the rate of desirable behaviors. Parent management training is one of the most common techniques and consists of group and individual sessions with parents in the clinic. The approach involves psychoeducational techniques as well as setting up behavioral programs. Consultation with classroom teachers to set up parallel behavioral programs in the school is also an important component of this treatment. Whereas some studies have demonstrated improvement in both classroom and home settings,[171, 172] others report limited gains.[173] When effective, some parent-based interventions have resulted in benefits that have generalized for periods of more than a year.[34, 115, 174] Among the limitations of this technique are the labor-intensive nature of the interventions, nongeneralizability to nontargeted behaviors, and the fact that effectiveness depends on the competence and willingness of parents and teachers to carry out the behavioral programs.[173, 175]

Another aspect of behavioral therapy is the contingency management approach, which is implemented directly with the child in the setting in which the problem behaviors occur. Although contingency management programs use appropriate reward procedures, it is generally accepted that prudent negative consequences, such as time-out and response cost, are a necessary component of treatment.[34, 45] In some situations, maintenance of appropriate behavior after withdrawal of contingencies is better for a negative consequence than for a reward.[176] Similar to behavioral therapy, contingency management approaches are extremely labor-intensive, and questions regarding their generalizability remain.

Cognitive-behavioral approaches are based on the premise that the difficulties experienced by children with AD-DBDs are a result of deficient self-control and problem-solving skills. Examples of cognitive-behavioral therapy include self-monitoring, anger control training, and self-reinforcement. Although initial studies using cognitive-behavioral therapy approaches generated promise on the basis of findings of enhanced generalization and maintenance of appropriate behaviors,[177] the initial enthusiasm has been tempered by others reporting marginal success.[178] However, some cognitive-behavioral therapy procedures, such as anger control, have shown more consistent success.[34, 179]

Despite their potential benefits, difficulties encountered with psychosocial interventions are that short-term gains are limited to the period that the programs are actually in effect. Furthermore, a substantial number of children, particularly those with the most severe presentation and with greatest psychosocial adversity, fail to show improvement. Additional problems in implementation include the unwillingness of many teachers to use behavioral programs and the fact that as many as half the parents discontinue parent training. Finally, these interventions are labor-intensive; long-term improvements have not been reported, which makes these therapies of limited value when used alone.[34, 173, 175, 178]

Impact of Comorbidity on Treatment

Despite the high prevalence of comorbidity among the AD-DBDs, only more recently has there been an attempt to systematically study the differential effects of comorbidity on treatment. The majority of studies have examined the efficacy of stimulant medications, although there are some data regarding the use of nonstimulant medications. There has been little research on the impact of comorbidity on psychosocial treatments, although enhanced efficacy from combined pharmacological and psychosocial treatments has considerable face validity.

Studies of stimulant treatment have shown that children with ADHD with and without aggression respond equally well to methylphenidate treatment in terms of ADHD symptoms.[180–182] Another study[183] indicated that children with comorbid ADHD and CD had a better stimulant response than did children with ADHD alone. Research examining whether aggression in children with ADHD can be treated with psychostimulants has mainly yielded positive findings as well.[184, 185] Finally, one study[186] found that some covert, nonaggressive symptoms (e.g., stealing) were also decreased in children with ADHD (independent of comorbidity) after treatment with methylphenidate.

A large body of research has addressed the question of whether stimulant medication improves learning and academic achievement in children with AD-DBD.[34, 187] Whereas earlier studies suggested that stimulant treatment did not lead to improvement in academic achievement,[45] later investigations[188–190] have indicated a favorable response in children with ADHD on a variety of cognitive measures in both classroom and laboratory settings. However, there has been some concern regarding the dissociation of cognitive and behavioral effects of stimulant medication. One landmark study[191] found that optimal cognitive performance was achieved at low doses (i.e., 0.3 mg/kg), whereas optimal behavioral function was achieved at high doses (i.e., 1.0 mg/kg), with an accompanying decline in cognitive function at the higher dose. Other investigators[189] have reported a linear rather than a curvilinear dose-response curve, but the study did not test high enough doses to allow any conclusion regarding the existence of a "descending limb" relative to cognitive function.

It is not yet clear whether the optimal dosage of stimulant medication required for treating children with ADHD varies as a function of comorbidity. It has been argued[187] that titrating medication to a higher dose in the presence of comorbid externalizing disorders could have a detrimental effect on learning, because generally lower doses are required to produce a change in attentional function than in behavioral function. Nevertheless, others have found that a dose as high as 0.7 mg/kg of methylphenidate leads to improvements on several cognitive measures, most notably reading.[192, 193] Still other studies have evaluated a variety of doses, with no clear pattern emerging. In some studies, low doses of methylphenidate have been used successfully to treat ADHD and aggression.[180, 181] Yet another report[182] found that 0.3 mg/kg was an effective dose of methylphenidate for children with ADHD and comorbid externalizing or internalizing disorders, but children who had ADHD and both internalizing and externalizing disorders required 0.6 mg/kg to achieve a satisfactory response. Finally, the results of these studies must be considered in light of other findings[194] suggesting little relationship between methylphenidate dose and clinical response.

In contrast to studies of children with ADHD who are aggressive, studies of stimulant response in children with ADHD with comorbid anxiety have produced somewhat inconsistent findings. Some investigations[195, 196] have shown that children with comorbid ADHD and anxiety have a poor response to stimulant medication along with a higher frequency of adverse effects[196] compared with children with ADHD who did not also have an anxiety disorder. On the other hand, others[28, 197] have found that children with ADHD and anxiety respond as well as those without comorbid anxiety when treated with an antidepressant such as Desipramine.

Conclusion

The AD-DBDs are a group of disorders that together account for the majority of referrals to child and adolescent psychiatry services. They represent a significant public health problem in terms of morbidity as well as the risk for poor outcomes in adolescence and adulthood. There has been considerable progress in more precisely elucidating the clinical presentation as well as the genetic and neurobiological bases of these disorders. One important confounding factor that has made these endeavors difficult has been the frequency and variety of comorbid conditions and the potential impact of comorbidity on natural history and treatment response. Whereas a variety of pharmacological and psychosocial interventions have been found to provide partial success, with limited short-term gains, long-term studies indicate that outcome is still poor for many children. In response to this, larger studies using multimodal treatments have been undertaken with the hope of improving the prognosis in this group of disorders.

References

1. American Psychiatric Association: Diagnostic and Statistical Manual of Mental Disorders, 4th ed. Washington, DC: American Psychiatric Association, 1994.
2. American Psychiatric Association: Diagnostic and Statistical Manual of Mental Disorders, 3rd ed. Washington, DC: American Psychiatric Association, 1980.
3. American Psychiatric Association: Diagnostic and Statistical Manual of Mental Disorders, 3rd ed, revised. Washington, DC: American Psychiatric Association, 1987.
4. Werry JS, Reeves JC, Elkind GS: Attention deficit, conduct, oppositional, and anxiety disorders in children: I. A review of research on differentiating characteristics. J Am Acad Child Adolesc Psychiatry 1987; 26:133–143.
5. Szatmari P, Boyle M, Offord DR: ADDH and conduct disorder: Degree of diagnostic overlap and differences among correlates. J Am Acad Child Adolesc Psychiatry 1989; 28:865–872.
6. Hinshaw SP: On the distinction between attentional deficits/hyperactivity and conduct problems/aggression in child psychopathology. Psychol Bull 1987; 101:443–463.
7. Rutter M, Shaffer D: DSM-III: A step forward or back in terms of the classification of child psychiatric disorders? J Am Acad Child Adolesc Psychiatry 1980; 19:371–394.
8. Rey JM, Bashir MR, Schwarz M, et al: Oppositional disorder: Fact or fiction? J Am Acad Child Adolesc Psychiatry 1988; 27:157–162.
9. Schachar R, Wachsmuth R: Oppositional disorder in children: A validation study comparing conduct disorder, oppositional disorder, and normal control children. J Child Psychol Psychiatry 1990; 31:1089–1102.
10. Waldman ID, Lilienfeld SO: Diagnostic efficiency of symptoms for oppositional defiant disorder and attention-deficit hyperactivity disorder. J Consult Clin Psychol 1991; 59:732–738.
11. Lahey BB, Loeber R, Quay HC, et al: Oppositional defiant and conduct disorders: Issues to be resolved for DSM-IV. J Am Acad Child Adolesc Psychiatry 1992; 31:539–546.
12. Loeber R: Oppositional defiant disorder and conduct disorder. Hosp Community Psychiatry 1991; 42:1099–1100.
13. Loeber R, Lahey BB, Thomas C: Diagnostic conundrum of oppositional defiant disorder and conduct disorder. J Abnorm Psychol 1991; 100:379–390.
14. Szatmari P: The epidemiology of attention-deficit hyperactivity disorders. Child Adolesc Psychiatr Clin North Am 1992; 1:361–371.
15. Bauermeister JJ, Canino G, Bird H: Epidemiology of disruptive behavior disorders. Child Adolesc Psychiatr Clin North Am 1994; 3:177–194.
16. Costello EJ, Costello AJ, Edelbrock C, et al: Psychiatric disorders in pediatric primary care. Arch Gen Psychiatry 1988; 45:1107–1116.
17. Szatmari P, Offord DR, Boyle MH: Ontario child health study: Prevalence of attention deficit disorder with hyperactivity. J Child Psychol Psychiatry 1989; 30:219–230.
18. Esser G, Schmidt MH, Woerner W: Epidemiology and course of psychiatric disorders in school-age children—results of a longitudinal study. J Child Psychol Psychiatry 1990; 32:243–263.
19. Kashani JH, Beck NC, Hoeper EW, et al: Psychiatric disorders in a community sample of adolescents. Am J Psychiatry 1987; 144:584.
20. Bird HR, Canino G, Rubio-Stipec M, et al: Estimates of the prevalence of childhood maladjustment in a community survey in Puerto Rico: The use of combined measures. Arch Gen Psychiatry 1988; 45:1120.
21. Anderson JC, Williams S, McGee R, et al: DSM-III disorders in preadolescent children: Prevalence in a large sample from the general population. Arch Gen Psychiatry 1987; 44:69.
22. Jensen JB, Burke N, Garfinkel BD: Depression and symptoms of attention deficit disorder with hyperactivity. J Am Acad Child Adolesc Psychiatry 1988; 27:742.
23. Kovacs M, Paulauskas S, Gatsonis C, Richards C: Depressive disorders in childhood. III. A longitudinal study of comorbidity with and risk for conduct disorders. J Affect Disord 1988; 15:205.
24. Livingston R, Dykman RA, Ackerman PT: The frequency and the significance of additional self-reported psychiatric diagnoses in children with attention deficit disorder. J Abnorm Child Psychol 1990; 19:465.
25. Woolston JL, Rosenthal SL, Riddle M, et al: Childhood comorbidity of anxiety/affective disorders and behavior disorder. J Am Acad Child Adolesc Psychiatry 1989; 28:707.
26. Barkley RA, Fischer M, Edelbrock C, et al: The adolescent outcome of hyperactive children diagnosed by research criteria—III. Mother-child interactions, family conflicts and maternal psychopathology. J Child Psychol Psychiatry 1991; 32:233.
27. Biederman J, Faraone SV, Keenan K, et al: Evidence of familial association between attention deficit disorder and major affective disorders. Arch Gen Psychiatry 1991; 48:633.
28. Biederman J, Faraone SV, Lapey K: Comorbidity of diagnosis in attention-deficit hyperactivity disorder. Child Adolesc Psychiatr Clin North Am 1992; 1:335–360.
29. Biederman J, Newcorn J, Sprich S: Comorbidity of attention deficit hyperactivity disorder with conduct, depressive, anxiety and other disorders. Am J Psychiatry 1991; 148:564.
30. Biederman J, Faraone SV, Keenan K, et al: Familial association between attention deficit disorder (ADD) and anxiety disorder. Am J Psychiatry 1991; 148:251.
31. Pliszka SR: Comorbidity of attention-deficit hyperactivity disorder and overanxious disorder. J Am Acad Child Adolesc Psychiatry 1992; 31:197.
32. Forness SR, Swanson JM, Cantwell DP, et al: Stimulant medication and reading performance: Follow-up on sustained dose in ADHD boys with and without conduct disorders. J Learn Disabil 1992; 25:115.
33. Cantwell DP, Baker L: Association between attention deficit–hyperactivity disorder and learning disorders. J Learn Disabil 1991; 24:88.
34. Hinshaw SP: Academic underachievement, attention deficits, and aggression: Comorbidity and implications for intervention. J Consult Clin Psychol 1992; 60:893–903.
35. McGee R, Share DL: Attention deficit disorder–hyperactivity and academic failure: Which comes first and what should be treated? J Am Acad Child Adolesc Psychiatry 1988; 27:318.
36. Semrud-Clikeman M, Biederman J, Sprich-Buckminster S, et al: Comorbidity between ADDH and learning disability: A review and

report in a clinically referred sample. J Am Acad Child Adolesc Psychiatry 1992; 31:439.
37. Pauls DL, Hurst CR, Kruger SD, et al: Gilles de la Tourette's syndrome and attention deficit disorder with hyperactivity: Evidence against a genetic relationship. Arch Gen Psychiatry 1986; 43:1177.
38. Comings DE, Comings BG: Tourette syndrome and attention deficit disorder with hyperactivity: Are they genetically related? J Am Acad Child Psychiatry 1984; 23:138.
39. Comings DE, Comings BG: A controlled study of Tourette syndrome, I: Attention deficit disorder, learning disorders, and school problems. Am J Hum Genet 1987; 41:701.
40. Wood D, Wender PH, Rheimherr FW: The prevalence of attention deficit disorder, residual type, or minimal brain dysfunction, in a population of male alcoholic patients. Am J Psychiatry 1983; 140:95.
41. Eyre SL, Rousaville BJ, Kleber HD: History of childhood hyperactivity in a clinical population of opiate addicts. J Nerv Ment Dis 1982; 170:522.
42. Alterman AI, Tarter RE, Baughman TG, et al: Differentiation of alcoholics high and low in childhood hyperactivity. Drug Alcohol Depend 1984; 15:111.
43. Hunt RD, Cohen DJ: Attentional and neurochemical components of mental retardation: New methods for an old problem. In Stark JA, Menolascino FJ, Albarelli MH, et al (eds): Mental Retardation and Mental Health: Classification, Diagnosis, Treatment Services. New York: Springer-Verlag, 1988.
44. Koller H, Richardson SA, Katz M: Behavior disturbance since childhood among a 5-year birth cohort of all mentally retarded young adults in a city. Am J Ment Defic 1983; 87:386.
45. Barkley RA: Attention-Deficit Hyperactivity Disorder: A Handbook for Diagnosis and Treatment. New York: Guilford Press, 1990.
46. Taylor EA: Childhood hyperactivity. Br J Psychiatry 1986; 149:562–573.
47. Mason ST, Fibiger HC: Noradrenalin and selective attention. Life Sci 1979; 25:1949–1956.
48. Mason ST, Iverson SD: Theories of the dorsal bundle extinction effect. Brain Res 1979; 180:107–137.
49. McCraken J: A two-part model of stimulant action on attention-deficit hyperactivity disorder in children. J Neuropsychiatry 1991; 3:201–209.
50. Halperin JM, Newcorn JH, Schwartz ST, et al: Plasma catecholamine metabolite levels in ADHD boys with and without reading disabilities. J Clin Child Psychiatry 1994; 22:219–225.
51. Rogeness GA, Hernandez JM, Macedo CA, et al: Near-zero plasma dopamine-β-hydroxylase and conduct disorder in emotionally disturbed boys. J Am Acad Child Adolesc Psychiatry 1986; 25:521.
52. Rogeness GA: Biologic findings in conduct disorder. Child Adolesc Psychiatr North Am 1994; 3:271–284.
53. Shekim WO, Javaid J, Dans JM, et al: Urinary MHPG and HVA excretion in boys with attention deficit disorder and hyperactivity treated with *d*-amphetamine. Biol Psychiatry 1983; 18:707–714.
54. Shekim WO, Sinclair E, Glaser R, et al: Norepinephrine and dopamine metabolites and educational variables in boys with attention deficit disorder and hyperactivity. J Child Neurol 1987; 2:50–56.
55. Khan AU, Dekirmenjian H: Urinary excretion of catecholamine metabolites in hyperkinetic child syndrome. Am J Psychiatry 1981; 138:108–110.
56. Rapoport JL, Mikkelsen EJ, Ebert MH, et al: Urinary catecholamine and amphetamine excretion in hyperactive and normal boys. J Nerv Ment Dis 1978; 66:731–737.
57. Shekim WO, Dekirmenjian H, Chapel JL: Urinary catecholamine metabolites in hyperactive boys treated with *d*-amphetamine. Am J Psychiatry 1977; 134:1276–1279.
58. Rogeness GA, Javors MA, Mass JW, et al: Plasma dopamine-β-hydroxylase, HVA, MHPG and conduct disorder in emotionally disturbed boys. Biol Psychiatry 1987; 22:1158–1162.
59. Kruesi MJP, Rapoport JL, Hamburger S, et al: Cerebrospinal fluid monoamine metabolites, aggression, and impulsivity in disruptive behavior disorders of children and adolescents. Arch Gen Psychiatry 1990; 47:419–426.
60. Solanto MV: Neuropharmacological basis of stimulant drug in attention deficit disorder with hyperactivity: A review and synthesis. Psychol Bull 1985; 95:387–409.
61. Levy F: The dopamine theory of attention deficit hyperactivity disorder (ADHD). Aust N Z J Psychiatry 1991; 25:277–283.
62. Oades RD: The role of noradrenaline in tuning and dopamine in switching between signals in the CNS. Neurosci Biobehav Rev 1985; 9:261–282.
63. Le Moal M, Gayley D, Cardo B: Behavioral effects of local injection of 6-hydroxydopamine in the medial ventral tegmentum in the rat; possible role of the mesolimbic dopaminergic system. Brain Res 1975; 88:190–194.
64. Shaywitz BA, Yager RD, Klopper JH: Paradoxical response to amphetamine in developing rats treated with 6-hydroxydopamine. Nature 1976; 261:153–155.
65. Shaywitz BA, Yager RD, Klopper JH: Selective brain dopamine depletion in developing rats: An experimental model of minimal brain dysfunction. Science 1976; 191:305–308.
66. Miller FE, Heffner TG, Kotake C, et al: Magnitude and duration of hyperactivity following neonatal 6-hydroxydopamine is related to the extent of brain dopamine depleted. Brain Res 1981; 229:123–132.
67. Lou HC, Henrickson L, Bruhn P, et al: Striatal dysfunction in attention deficit and hyperkinetic disorder. Arch Neurol 1989; 46:48–52.
68. Hynd GW, Hern KL, Novey ES, et al: Attention deficit hyperactivity disorder and asymmetry of the caudate nucleus. J Child Neurol 1993; 8:339–347.
69. Wender P, Epstein RS, Kopin I, et al: Urinary monoamine metabolites in children with minimal brain dysfunction. Am J Psychiatry 1971; 127:1411–1415.
70. Shetty T, Chase TN: Central monoamines and hyperactivity of childhood. Neurology 1976; 26:1000.
71. Zametkin AI, Rapoport JL: Neurobiology of attention deficit disorder with hyperactivity: Where have we come in 50 years? J Am Acad Child Adolesc Psychiatry 1987; 26:676–686.
72. Soubrie P: Reconciling the role of central serotonin neurons in human and animal behavior. Behav Brain Sci 1986; 9:319–364.
73. Brown GL, Ebert MH, Goyer PF, et al: Aggression, suicide, and serotonin: Relationships to CSF amine metabolites. Am J Psychiatry 1982; 139:741–746.
74. Linnoila M, Virkkunen M, Scheinin M, et al: Low cerebrospinal fluid 5-hydroxyindoleacetic acid concentrations differentiates impulsive from nonimpulsive aggressive behavior. Life Sci 1983; 33:2609–2614.
75. Coccaro EF, Siever LJ, Klar H, et al: Serotonergic studies of personality disorder: Correlates with behavioral aggression and impulsivity. Arch Gen Psychiatry 1989; 46:587–599.
76. Fishbein DH, Lozovsky D, Jaffe JH: Impulsivity, aggression, and neuroendocrine responses to serotonergic stimulation in substance abusers. Biol Psychiatry 1989; 25:1049–1066.
77. Kruesi MJP, Hibbs ED, Zahn TP, et al: A 2-year prospective follow-up study of children and adolescents with disruptive behavior disorders: Prediction by cerebrospinal fluid 5-hydroxyindoleacetic acid, homovanillic acid and autonomic measures? Arch Gen Psychiatry 1992; 49:429–435.
78. Stoff DM, Pollack L, Vitiello B, et al: Reduction of 3-H-imipramine binding sites on platelets of conduct disordered children. Neuropsychopharmacology 1987; 1:55–62.
79. Weizman A, Bernhout E, Weitz R, et al: Imipramine binding to platelets of children with attention deficit disorder with hyperactivity. Biol Psychiatry 1988; 23:491–496.
80. Siever LJ, Murphy DL, Slater S, et al: Plasma prolactin changes following fenfluramine in depressed patients compared to controls: An evaluation of central serotonergic responsivity in depression. Life Sci 1984; 34:1029–1039.
81. Halperin JM, Sharma V, Siever LJ, et al: Serotonergic function in aggressive and nonaggressive boys with attention-deficit hyperactivity disorder. Am J Psychiatry 1994; 151:243–248.
82. Stoff DM, Pasatiempo AP, Yeung JH, et al: Neuroendocrine responses to challenge with *dl*-fenfluramine and aggression in disruptive behavior disorders of children and adolescents. Psychiatry Res 1992; 43:263–276.
83. Lou HC, Henricksen L, Bruhn P: Focal cerebral hypoperfusion in children with dysphagia and/or attention deficit disorder. Arch Neurol 1984; 41:825–829.
84. Zametkin AJ: Cerebral glucose metabolism in adults with hyperactivity of childhood onset. N Engl J Med 1990; 323:1361–1366.
85. Zametkin AJ: Brain metabolism in teenagers with attention deficit hyperactivity disorder. Arch Gen Psychiatry 1993; 50:333–340.
86. Hynd GW, Semrud-Clikeman M, Lorys AR, et al: Corpus callosum morphology in attention deficit hyperactivity disorder: Morphologic analysis of MRI. J Learn Disabil 1991; 24:141–146.

87. Giedd JN, Castellanos FX, Casey BJ, et al: Quantitative morphology of the corpus callosum in attention deficit hyperactivity disorder. Am J Psychiatry 1994; 151:665–669.
88. Pauls DL, Shaywitz SE, Kramer PL, et al: Demonstration of vertical transmission of attention deficit disorder. Ann Neurol 1983; 14:363.
89. Biederman J, Faraone SV, Keenan K, et al: Further evidence for family-genetic risk factors in attention deficit hyperactivity disorder: Patterns of comorbidity in probands and relatives in psychiatrically and pediatrically referred samples. Arch Gen Psychiatry 1992; 49:728–738.
90. Faraone SV, Biederman J, Chen WJ, et al: Segregation analysis of attention deficit hyperactivity disorder: Evidence for single gene transmission. Psychiatr Genet 1992; 2:257–275.
91. Goodman R, Stevenson J: A twin study of hyperactivity. II: The etiological role of genes, family relationships and perinatal adversity. J Child Psychol Psychiatry 1989; 30:691–709.
92. Gilger JW, Pennington BF, DeFries JC: Twin study of the etiology of comorbidity: Attention-deficit hyperactivity disorder and dyslexia. J Am Acad Child Adolesc Psychiatry 1992; 31:343.
93. Alberts-Corush J, Firestone P, Goodman JT: Attention and impulsivity characteristics of the biological and adoptive parents of hyperactive and normal control children. Am J Orthopsychiatry 1986; 56:413–423.
94. Faraone SV, Biederman J: Genetics of attention-deficit hyperactivity disorder. Child Adolesc Psychiatr Clin North Am 1994; 3:285–301.
95. Castellanos FX, Rapoport JL: Etiology of attention-deficit hyperactivity disorder. Child Adolesc Psychiatr Clin North Am 1992; 1:373–384.
96. Palmour RM: Genetic models for the study of aggressive behavior. Prog Neuropsychopharmacol Biol Psychiatry 1983; 7:513–517.
97. Chen C, Rainnie DG, Greene RW, et al: Abnormal fear response and aggressive behavior in mutant mice deficient for α-calcium–calmodulin kinase II. Science 1994; 266:291–294.
98. Brunner HG, Nelen M, Breakefield XO, et al: Abnormal behavior associated with a point mutation in the structural gene for monoamine oxidase A. Science 1993; 262:578–580.
99. Lewis DO: Etiology of aggressive conduct disorders: Neuropsychiatric and family contributions. Child Adolesc Psychiatr Clin North Am 1994; 3:303–319.
100. Beck SJ, Young GH, Tarnowski KJ: Maternal characteristics and perceptions of pervasive and situational hyperactives and normal controls. J Am Acad Child Adolesc Psychiatry 1990; 29:558–565.
101. Loeber R, Green SM, Lahey BB, et al: Developmental sequences in the age of onset of disruptive child behaviors. J Child Family Studies 1992; 1:21–41.
102. Campbell SB: Hyperactivity in preschoolers: Correlates and prognostic implications. Clin Psychol Rev 1985; 5:405–428.
103. Weiss G, Hechtman L, Milroy T, et al: Psychiatric status of hyperactives as adults: A controlled prospective 15 year follow-up of 63 hyperactive children. J Am Acad Child Psychiatry 1985; 24:211.
104. Satterfield J, Hoppe C, Schell A: Prospective study of delinquency in 110 adolescent boys with attention deficit disorder and 89 normal adolescent boys. Am J Psychiatry 1982; 139:797–798.
105. Klein RG, Mannuzza S: Long-term outcome of hyperactive children. A review. J Am Acad Child Adolesc Psychiatry 1991; 30:383–387.
106. Lambert N, Hartsaugh C, Sassone D: Persistence of hyperactivity symptoms from childhood to adolescence and associated outcomes. Am J Orthopsychiatry 1987; 57:22–31.
107. Loeber R: Developmental and risk factors of juvenile antisocial behavior and delinquency. Clin Psychol Rev 1990; 10:1–41.
108. Loeber R, Schmaling KB: The utility of differentiating between mixed and pure forms of antisocial child behavior. J Abnorm Child Psychol 1985; 13:315–336.
109. Loeber R, Wung P, Keenan K, et al: Developmental pathways in disruptive child behavior. Dev Psychopathol 1993; 5:103–133.
110. Lucas CP: Attention deficit disorders and hyperactivity. Curr Opin Psychiatry 1992; 5:518–522.
111. Moffit TE: Juvenile delinquency and attention deficit disorder: Boys' developmental trajectories from age 3 to age 5. Child Dev 1990; 61:893–910.
112. Farrington DP: Long-term criminal outcomes of hyperactivity-impulsivity-attention deficit (HIA) and conduct problems in childhood. In Robins LN, Rutter M (eds): Straight and Devious Pathways from Childhood and Adulthood. New York: Cambridge University Press, 1990:62–81.
113. Biederman J, Munir K, Knee D: Conduct and oppositional disorder in clinically referred children with attention deficit disorder: A controlled family study. J Am Acad Child Adolesc Psychiatry 1987; 26:724.
114. Cadoret JR, Stewart MA: An adoption study of attention deficit hyperactivity/aggression and their relationship to adult antisocial personality. Compr Psychiatry 1991; 32:73–82.
115. Lahey BB, Piacentini J, McBurnett MS, et al: Psychopathology in the parents of children with conduct disorder and hyperactivity. J Am Acad Child Adolesc Psychiatry 1988; 27:163–170.
116. Hechtman L, Weiss G, Perlman T, et al: Hyperactives as young adults: Various clinical outcomes. Adolesc Psychiatry 1981; 9:295–306.
117. Gresham FM: Behavior disorder assessment: Conceptual, definitional and practical considerations. School Psychol Rev 1985; 14:495–509.
118. Barkley RA, Anastopolous AD, Guevremont DC, et al: Adolescents with ADHD: Patterns of behavioral adjustment, academic functioning and treatment utilization. J Am Acad Child Adolesc Psychiatry 1991; 30:752–761.
119. Loeber R, Green SM, Lahey BB, et al: Differences and similarities between children, mothers and teachers as informants on disruptive child behavior. J Abnorm Child Psychol 1991; 19:75–95.
120. Atkins MS, Pelham WE, Licht MH: The differential validity of teacher ratings of inattention/overactivity and aggression. J Abnorm Child Psychol 1989; 17:423–435.
121. Goyette CH, Conners CK, Ulrich RF: Normative data for Revised Conners Parent and Teacher Rating Scales. J Abnorm Child Psychol 1978; 6:221–236.
122. Achenbach TM, Edelbrock C: Manual for the Child Behavior Checklist and Revised Child Behavior Profile. Burlington, VT: Thomas Achenbach, 1983.
123. Achenbach TM, Edelbrock CS: Manual for the Teacher's Report Form and Teacher Version of the Child Behavior Profile. Burlington, VT: University of Vermont Department of Psychiatry, 1986.
124. Breen MJ, Barkley RA: Child psychopathology and parenting stress in girls and boys having attention deficit disorder with hyperactivity. J Pediatr Psychol 1988; 2:265–280.
125. Horn HF, Wagner AE, Ialongo N: Sex differences in school-aged children with pervasive attention-deficit hyperactivity disorder. J Abnorm Child Psychol 1989; 17:109–125.
126. Barkley RA, Fischer M, Newbt R, et al: Development of a multi-method clinical protocol for assessing stimulant drug responses in ADHD children. J Clin Child Psychol 1988; 17:14–24.
127. Breen MJ, Altepeter TS: Evaluating disruptive behavior disorders: Child behavior questionnaires, laboratory measurements and observations. In Breen MJ, Altepeter TS: Disruptive Behavior Disorders in Children. New York: Guilford Press, 1990:65–113.
128. Lovejoy CM, Rasmussen NH: The validity of vigilance tasks in differential diagnosis of children referred for attention and learning problems. J Abnorm Child Psychol 1990; 18:671–681.
129. Steingard R, Biederman J, Doyle A, et al: Psychiatric comorbidity in attention deficit disorder: Impact on the interpretation of Child Behavior Checklist results. J Am Acad Child Adolesc Psychiatry 1992; 31:449–454.
130. Costello EJ, Loeber R, Stouthamer-Loeber M: Pervasive and situational hyperactivity—confounding effect of informant: A research note. J Child Psychol Psychiatry 1991; 32:367–376.
131. Barkley RA: The ecological validity of laboratory and analogue assessment methods of ADHD symptoms. J Abnorm Child Psychol 1991; 19:149–178.
132. Young JG, O'Brien JD, Gutterman EM, et al: Research on the clinical interview. J Am Acad Child Adolesc Psychiatry 1987; 26:613–620.
133. Hodges K: Structured interviews for assessing children. J Child Psychol Psychiatry 1993; 34:49–68.
134. Shaffer D, Schwab-Stone M, Fisher P, et al: The Diagnostic Interview Schedule for Children–Revised (DISC-R): I. Preparation, field testing, interrater reliability, and acceptability. J Am Acad Child Adolesc Psychiatry 1993; 32:643–650.
135. Piacentini J, Shaffer D, Fisher P, et al: The Diagnostic Interview Schedule for Children–Revised Version (DISC-R): III. Concurrent criterion validity. J Am Acad Child Adolesc Psychiatry 1993; 32:658–665.
136. Harper GW, Ottinger DR: The performance of hyperactive and control preschoolers on a new computerized measure of visual vigilance: The preschool vigilance task. J Child Psychol Psychiatry 1992; 33:1365–1372.

137. Breen MJ: ADHD girls and boys: An analysis of attentional, emotional, cognitive and family variables. J Child Psychol Psychiatry 1989; 30:711–716.
138. Gordon M, Mettelman BB: The assessment of attention: I. Standardization and reliability of a behavior based measure. J Clin Psychol 1988; 44:682–690.
139. Elwood RW: Clinical discriminations and neuropsychological tests: An appeal to Bayes' theorem. Clin Neuropsychol 1993; 7:224–233.
140. Barkley RA, Grodzinski GM: Are tests of frontal lobe function useful in the diagnosis of attention deficit disorders? Clin Neuropsychol 1994; 8:121–139.
141. Halperin JM, McKay KE, Matier K, et al: Attention, response inhibition and activity level in children: Developmental neuropsychological perspectives. Adv Child Neuropsychol 1994; 2:1–54.
142. Roberts MA: A behavioral observation method for differentiating hyperactive and aggressive boys. J Abnorm Child Psychol 1990; 18:131–142.
143. Abikoff H, Gittelman R, Klein DF: Classroom observation code for hyperactive children: A replication of validity. J Consult Clin Psychol 1980; 48:555–565.
144. Hauser P, Zametkin AJ, Martinez P, et al: Attention deficit hyperactivity disorder in people with generalized resistance to thyroid hormone. N Engl J Med 1993; 328:997–1001.
145. Elia J, Gulotta C, Rose SR, et al: Thyroid function and attention-deficit hyperactivity disorder. J Am Acad Child Adolesc Psychiatry 1994; 33:169–172.
146. Spencer T, Biederman J, Wilens T, et al: Attention-deficit hyperactivity disorder (ADHD) and thyroid abnormalities. Scientific Proceedings of the Annual Meeting, Volume IX. American Academy of Child and Adolescent Psychiatry, 1993:NR-39.
147. Ciaranello RD: Attention deficit hyperactivity disorder and resistance to thyroid hormone: A new idea? N Engl J Med 1993; 328:1038–1039.
148. Milich R, Landau S: The role of social status variables in differentiating subgroups of hyperactive children. In Bloomingdale LM, Swanson JM, Klorman R (eds): Attention Deficit Disorder: Current Concepts and Emerging Trends in Attentional and Behavioral Disorders of Childhood, Volume 4. J Child Psychol Psychiatry 1991; 32:525–534.
149. Pope AW, Bierman KL, Mumma GH: Relations between hyperactive and aggressive behavior and peer relations at three elementary grade levels. J Abnorm Child Psychol 1989; 17:253–267.
150. Walker JL, Lahey BB, Russo MF, et al: Anxiety, inhibition and conduct disorder in children: I. Relations to social impairment. J Am Acad Child Adolesc Psychiatry 1991; 30:187–191.
151. Carlson GA, Rapoport MD: Diagnostic classification issues in attention-deficit hyperactivity disorder. Psychiatr Ann 1989; 19:576–583.
152. Bradley C: The behavior of children receiving Benzedrine. Am J Psychiatry 1937; 94:577–585.
153. DuPaul GJ, Barkley RA: Medication therapy. In Barkley RA (ed): Attention-Deficit Hyperactivity Disorder: A Handbook for Diagnosis and Treatment. New York: Guilford Press, 1990:573–612.
154. Greenhill LL: Pharmacotherapy: Stimulants. Child Adolesc Psychiatr Clin North Am 1992; 1:411–447.
155. Elia J: Drug treatment for hyperactive children: Therapeutic guidelines. Drugs 1993; 46:863–871.
156. Biederman J, Baldessarini RJ, Wright V, et al: A double-blind placebo controlled study of desipramine in the treatment of ADD I. Efficacy. J Am Acad Child Adolesc Psychiatry 1989; 28:777.
157. Riddle MA, Nelson JC, Kleinman CS, et al: Sudden death in children receiving Norpramin: A review of three reported cases and commentary. J Am Acad Child Adolesc Psychiatry 1991; 30:104–108.
158. Popper CW, Elliott GR: Sudden death and tricyclic antidepressants: Clinical considerations for children. J Child Adolesc Psychopharmacol 1990; 1:125–132.
159. Biederman J: Sudden death in children treated with a tricyclic antidepressant: A commentary. Biol Thera Psychiatry Newsletter 1991; 14:1.
160. Garfinkel BD, Wender PH, Sloman L, et al: Tricyclic antidepressant and methylphenidate treatment of attention deficit disorder in children. J Am Acad Child Adolesc Psychiatry 1983; 22:343–348.
161. Barrickman L, Noyes R, Kuperman S, et al: Treatment of ADHD with fluoxetine: A preliminary trial. J Am Acad Child Adolesc Psychiatry 1991; 30:762–767.
162. Gammon GD, Brown TE: Fluoxetine and methylphenidate in combination for treatment of attention deficit disorder and comorbid depressive disorder. J Child Adolesc Psychopharmacol 1993; 3:1–10.
163. Hunt RD, Minderaa RB, Cohen DJ: The therapeutic effect of clonidine in attention deficit disorder with hyperactivity: Report of a double-blind placebo-controlled crossover study. J Am Acad Child Psychiatry 1985; 24:617–629.
164. Hunt RD, Lau S, Ryu J: Alternative therapies for ADHD. In Greenhill LL, Osman BB (eds): Ritalin: Theory and Patient Management. New York: Mary Ann Liebert, 1991:75.
165. Steingard R, Biederman J, Spencer T, et al: Comparison of clonidine response in the treatment of attention-deficit hyperactivity disorder with and without comorbid tics. J Am Acad Child Adolesc Psychiatry 1993; 32:350–353.
166. Hunt RD: Treatment effects of oral and transdermal clonidine in relation to methylphenidate: An open pilot study in ADD-H. Psychopharmacol Bull 1987; 23:111–114.
167. Rubinstein S, Silver LB, Licamele WL: Clonidine for stimulant-related sleep problems. J Am Acad Child Adolesc Psychiatry 1994; 33:281–282.
168. Campbell M, Small AM, Green WH, et al: Behavioral efficacy of haloperidol and lithium carbonate. Arch Gen Psychiatry 1984; 41:650–656.
169. Campbell M, Gonzalez NM, Silva RR: The pharmacotherapy of conduct disorders and rage outbursts. Psychiatr Clin North Am 1992; 15:69–85.
170. Kazdin AE: Treatment of antisocial behavior in children: Current status and future directions. Psychol Bull 1987; 102:187–203.
171. O'Leary SG, Pelham WE: Behavior therapy and withdrawal of stimulant medication with hyperactive children. Pediatrics 1978; 61:211–217.
172. Pelham WE, Schnedler RW, Bologna N, et al: Behavioral and stimulant treatment of hyperactive children: A therapy study with methylphenidate probes in a with-in subjects design. J Appl Behav Anal 1980; 13:221–236.
173. Abikoff H, Klein RG: Attention-deficit hyperactivity and conduct disorder: Comorbidity and implications for treatment. J Consult Clin Psychol 1992; 60:681–682.
174. Schachar R, Wachsmuth R: Hyperactivity and parental psychopathology. J Child Psychol Psychiatry 1990; 31:381–392.
175. Pelham WE, Hinshaw SP: Behavioral intervention for attention-deficit hyperactivity disorder. In Turner SM, Calhoun KS, Adams HE (eds): Handbook of Clinical Behavior Therapy. New York: John Wiley & Sons, 1992:259–283.
176. Sullivan MA, O'Leary SG: Differential maintenance following reward and cost token programs with children. Behav Ther 1989; 21:139–151.
177. Kazdin AE, Bass D, Siegel T, et al: Cognitive-behavioral therapy and relationship therapy in the treatment of children referred for antisocial behavior. J Consult Clin Psychol 1989; 57:522–535.
178. Abikoff H: Cognitive training in ADHD children: Less to it than meets the eye. J Learn Disabil 1991; 24:205–209.
179. Whalen CK, Henker B: Therapies for hyperactive children: Comparisons, combinations, and compromises. J Consult Clin Psychol 1991; 59:126–137.
180. Barkley RA, McMurray MB, Edelbrock CS, et al: The response of aggressive and nonaggressive ADHD children to two doses of methylphenidate. J Am Acad Child Adolesc Psychiatry 1989; 28:873.
181. Klorman R, Brumaghim JT, Salzman LF, et al: Effects of methylphenidate on attention-deficit hyperactivity disorder with and without aggressive/noncompliant features. J Abnorm Psychol 1988; 97:413.
182. Livingston RL, Dykman RA, Ackerman PT: Psychiatric comorbidity and response to two doses of methylphenidate in children with attention deficit disorder. J Child Adolesc Psychopharmacol 1992; 2:115.
183. Taylor E, Schachar R, Thorley G, et al: Which boys respond to stimulant medication? A controlled trial of methylphenidate in boys with disruptive behavior. Psychol Med 1987; 17:121.
184. Kaplan SL, Busner J, Kupietz S, et al: Effects of methylphenidate on adolescents with aggressive conduct disorder and ADDH: A preliminary report. J Am Acad Child Adolesc Psychiatry 1990; 29:719.
185. Amery B, Minichiello MD, Brown GL: Aggression in hyperactive boys: Response to *d*-amphetamine. J Am Acad Child Adolesc Psychiatry 1984; 23:291.

186. Hinshaw SP, Heller T, McHale JP: Covert antisocial behavior in boys with attention-deficit hyperactivity disorder: External validation and effects of methylphenidate. J Consult Clin Psychol 1992; 60:274.
187. Swanson JM, Cantwell D, Lerner M, et al: Effects of stimulant medication on learning in children with ADHD. J Learning Disabilities 1991; 24:219.
188. Douglas VI, Barr RG, O'Neil ME, et al: Short-term effects of methylphenidate on the cognitive, learning and academic performance of children with attention deficit disorder in the laboratory and classroom. J Child Psychol Psychiatry 1986; 27:191.
189. Pelham WE, Bender ME, Caddell JM, et al: The dose-response effects of methylphenidate on classroom academic and social behavior in children with attention deficit disorder. Arch Gen Psychiatry 1985; 42:948.
190. Rapport MD, Stoner G, DuPaul GJ, et al: Methylphenidate in hyperactive children: Differential effects of dose on academic, learning and social behavior. J Abnorm Child Psychol 1985; 13:227.
191. Sprague RL, Sleator EK: Methylphenidate in hyperkinetic children: Differences in dose effects on learning and social behavior. Science 1977; 198:1274.
192. Richardson E, Kupietz SS, Winsberg BG, et al: Effects of methylphenidate dosage in hyperactive reading-disabled children: II. Reading achievement. J Am Acad Child Adolesc Psychiatry 1988; 27:78.
193. Kupietz SS, Winsberg BG, Richardson E: Effects of methylphenidate dosage in hyperactive reading-disabled children: I. Behavior and cognitive performance effects. J Am Acad Child Adolesc Psychiatry 1988; 27:70.
194. Rapport MD, DuPaul GL, Kelly KL: Attention-deficit hyperactivity disorder and methylphenidate: The relationship between gross body weight and drug response in children. Psychopharmacol Bull 1980; 25:285.
195. Pliszka SR: Effect of anxiety on cognition, behavior, and stimulant response in ADHD. J Am Acad Child Adolesc Psychiatry 1989; 28:882.
196. Tannock R, Schachar R: Is ADHD with comorbid overanxious disorder different from ADHD? Presented at the Annual Meeting of the American Academy of Child and Adolescent Psychiatry; October 1992.
197. Biederman J, Baldessarini RJ, Wright V, et al: A double blind placebo-controlled study of desipramine in the treatment of attention deficit disorder: III. Lack of impact of comorbidity and family history factors on clinical response. J Am Acad Child Adolesc Psychiatry 1993; 32:199.

CHAPTER

37 Feeding and Other Disorders of Infancy or Early Childhood

Irene Chatoor

Definition

In the literature, the term *feeding disorder* generally encompasses a variety of conditions ranging from problem behaviors during feeding, poor appetite, food refusal, food selectivity, food avoidance, and pica to rumination and vomiting.[1] The term feeding disorder is generally used to emphasize the dyadic nature of eating problems in infants and young children.[2]

Whereas the *Diagnostic and Statistical Manual of Mental Disorders,* Third Edition (DSM-III) did not list feeding disorder as a diagnostic category, the *Diagnostic and Statistical Manual of Mental Disorders,* Fourth Edition (DSM-IV) defines feeding disorder of infancy or early childhood as follows:

DSM-IV Criteria 307.59

Feeding Disorder of Infancy or Early Childhood

A. Feeding disturbance as manifested by persistent failure to eat adequately with significant failure to gain weight or significant loss of weight over at least 1 month.

B. The disturbance is not due to an associated gastrointestinal or other general medical condition (e.g., esophageal reflux).

C. The disturbance is not better accounted for by another mental disorder (e.g., rumination disorder) or by lack of available food.

D. The onset is before age 6 years.

This general definition of feeding disorder in DSM-IV does not take into account the heterogeneity of feeding and growth problems in infants and its implication for treatment. Some authors have used various diagnostic methods and assigned different labels to address the heterogeneity of feeding problems associated with failure to thrive.[3–5] The pediatric literature has focused primarily on failure to thrive as a diagnostic label. The term *failure to thrive* describes infants and young children who demonstrate failure in physical growth, often with delay of social and motor development. Research has used an awkward and, in many cases, not useful dichotomy, namely, the differentiation of organic from nonorganic failure to thrive. Nonorganic failure to thrive is commonly thought to reflect a failure or relative absence of adequate maternal care and warmth.[6–8] Several authors have suggested a third category of failure to thrive for patients who present with a combination of organic and nonorganic factors in the etiology of their growth disturbance.[9, 10]

Because of the diversity of feeding disorders associated with failure to thrive and the lack of a subclassification of feeding disorder as defined in DSM-IV, I proposed a classification of feeding disorders based on the definition of psychiatric disorders suggested by Wing,[11, 12] namely, that the disorder is a limited syndrome with possible links to etiological and pathophysiological factors, that the use of treatment depends on proper diagnosis, and that the diagnosis is linked to prognosis. According to these criteria, I differentiate two types of feeding disorders. The first type, developmental feeding disorders, includes three feeding disorders first described by Chatoor and colleagues[13, 14] in 1984 and 1985. These three developmental feeding disorders meet criteria for relationship disorders as defined by Anders[15]: symptoms may be expressed by one individual but reflect problems in the relationship and are expressed in relationship tasks (such as feeding the infant); the symptoms are disruptive to the daily living of one or both partners; the interactions are seen as inflexible; and the relationship has failed to progress along the expected developmental course. These three developmental feeding disorders are described by Chatoor and colleagues[14] as 1) feeding disorder of homeostasis, 2) feeding disorder of attachment, and 3) feeding disorder of separation (infantile anorexia). The second type of feeding disorder is characterized by a more acute disruption in the regulation of eating and can occur at various ages and stages of feeding development. It has been described as posttraumatic eating disorder in children[16] and posttraumatic feeding disorder in infants.[17]

Epidemiology

It is estimated that up to 35% of infants and young children have feeding problems.[18–20] These common feeding difficulties include the infant's eating "too much" or "too little," restricted food preferences, delay in self-feeding, objectionable mealtime behaviors, and bizarre food habits.[21] In a survey of 570 toddlers ranging in age from 1 to 3 years, 15% of the mothers reported that their toddlers were picky eaters. The picky eating seemed to gradually increase in the second year and peak in the third year of life.[22] Forty percent of these mothers seemed to be concerned that their toddlers were not eating enough to grow. Severe feeding problems, such as refusal to eat or vomiting, which are associated with poor weight gain, have been reported to occur in 1% to 2% of infants younger than 1 year of age.[23]

Although no studies of prevalence about the specific feeding disorders defined by Chatoor and colleagues are available, it appears that the occurrence of posttraumatic feeding disorder has been increasing because the number of infants with complex medical problems who survive is growing.

Course and Natural History

Few studies have investigated the natural history of feeding disorders. Dahl and Sundelin[24] reported that those infants who at 3 to 12 months of age were identified for refusal to eat for at least 4 weeks with no apparent medical cause had significantly more problems in eating patterns, behavior, and growth and were more susceptible to infection than the control infants at 2 years of age. At 4 years of age, 17 of the 24 children with early refusal to eat (71%) were reported by the parents as still having feeding problems.[24] A study by Marchi and Cohen,[25] who observed a sample of more than 800 children for a 10-year period from early childhood to late childhood–adolescence, found that feeding problems in young children were stable over time. This study establishes the connection between feeding problems in early childhood and eating disorders later in adolescence. They reported that gastrointestinal symptoms and picky eating during early childhood correlated with anorectic behavior during adolescence, and problem behaviors during mealtime and pica early in life were associated with bulimia nervosa during the adolescent years.

Etiology

The understanding of the etiology, the symptoms, and the treatment of specific feeding disorders in infancy has been hampered by three factors. 1) The lack of a standard classification of feeding disorders has led to a variety of descriptive labels and classifications of feeding disorders in infants and toddlers. 2) Because there is an overlap between feeding disorders and failure to thrive, these terms have been used interchangeably. However, the frequency of association has not been established. 3) Each group of investigators has addressed different aspects of feeding disorders or failure to thrive and has used different diagnostic criteria and methodologies, making these studies difficult to compare. To clarify the specificity in etiology and its implication for treatment, each feeding disorder as defined by Chatoor and colleagues is discussed separately.

Diagnosis

Several authors have addressed the multifactorial etiology of feeding disorders and the failure to thrive syndrome. Bithany and Dubowitz[26] have proposed a biopsychosocial model that incorporates the complex bidirectional interaction between an infant's characteristics and psychosocial parental factors. Woolston[27] suggested use of a multiaxial system for the diagnosis of failure to thrive. This system includes physical illness, growth failure, developmental delay, caretaker-infant interaction, observation during feeding, age at onset, and cognitive and financial disability of caretakers. Some authors have taken an interactional approach to understanding of feeding disorders and the failure to thrive syndrome.[28–30] The diagnostic assessment of feeding disorders should include assessment of the relationship of the infant and his or her primary caretakers; the infant's temperamental characteristics; the infant's medical, developmental, and feeding history; the caretakers' psychological functioning and past history; and the family's socioeconomic background, stressors, and social support system.

Treatment

Treatment begins with the first contact with the infant and her or his caregivers. The establishment of a therapeutic alliance with the caregivers is critical to any successful treatment. The diagnostic evaluation needs to identify the specific dynamics of each feeding disorder for development of a specific treatment plan. This is discussed in more detail for each feeding disorder.

FEEDING DISORDER OF HOMEOSTASIS

Definition

Defining characteristics of feeding disorder of homeostasis are presented in Table 37–1.

Epidemiology

No specific data are available. However, regulatory difficulties in newborns and young infants appear common. The most frequently used label in the pediatric literature refers to these difficulties in regulation of state and feeding as colic. However, a feeding disorder of homeostasis should be considered only in more severe cases of colic when it is associated with growth failure.

Etiology

Both infant and maternal characteristics appear to contribute to the difficulties in the regulation of feeding. The infant may have difficulties in the regulation of state from birth. He or she may be irritable or difficult to awaken for feedings. Some infants may tire quickly or become distracted during feeding and terminate feedings without taking in adequate amounts of milk to grow. Some mothers learn to compensate for these vulnerabilities of the infant by adjusting the environment and the degree of stimulation of the infant during feeding. However, other mothers become anxious, fatigued, or depressed, and consequently they inadvertently intensify feeding difficulties of their infants.

Diagnosis

Young infants who present with feeding difficulties and growth failure dating to the postnatal period need to be considered for the diagnosis of a feeding disorder of homeostasis. The evaluation should begin with obtaining a history of the mother's pregnancy and delivery and a report of the infant's history of feeding, development, and medical illnesses that might contribute to the feeding problems. In addition, the mother's functioning and her social support system need to be explored. Most important, mother and infant should be observed during feeding and during play to assess the infant's special characteristics, the infant's regulation of state and feeding behavior, and the mother's ability to read the infant's signals and to respond to them in a contingent way.

In a study of mother-infant interactions during feeding, Chatoor[31] observed that mothers and infants with feeding disorders of homeostasis showed less dyadic reciprocity compared with a control group of well-feeding mother-infant dyads.

The information from the infant's and the mother's history and the observation of the mother-infant dyad will allow determination of which factors contribute to the difficulties in the infant's regulation of feeding. Because medical problems (e.g., cardiac or pulmonary disease) may contribute to the feeding problems, their impact on the feeding relationship of mother and infant needs to be considered.

Table 37–1 Feeding Disorder of Homeostasis

This feeding disorder is characterized by difficulties in establishing regular, calm feedings and by inadequate food intake of the infant. During the first months of life, the regulation of feeding is closely tied to the mother-infant relationship. Characteristics of both the infant and the parent appear to contribute to these regulatory feeding difficulties.

Infant

- Onset of feeding difficulties between birth and 3 mo of age
- Irregular feeding pattern and poor food intake
  - Intake varies in quantity
  - Feedings vary in timing of the day and night and length of feeding
- Infant shows poor regulation of state during feeding, demonstrated by irritability, easy fatigability, or excessive sleepiness
- Lack of weight gain leading to failure to thrive

Parent

Parental anxiety, depression, psychiatric illness, or psychosocial stressors lead to the mother's inability to read the infant's cues and to facilitate calm, successful feedings.

Mother-Infant Relationship

Feedings are characterized by maternal tension and poor reciprocity between mother and infant, poor regulation of state, and inadequate food intake of the infant.

Differential Diagnosis

The following associated organic problems of the infant may contribute to but not fully explain the feeding problems:

- Prematurity, dysmaturity
- Cardiac or pulmonary disease
- Functional or structural abnormalities of the oropharynx or gastrointestinal tract (e.g., cleft palate, gastroesophageal reflux, esophageal atresia)

Course and Natural History

During the first few months of life, the foundation for the regulation of feeding, sleep, and emotions is laid. Infants with feeding problems during these early months usually trigger anxiety in their mothers and tend to have difficulties in self-regulation during the transition to self-feeding in the second year of life. The importance of the regulation of feeding for infants was highlighted by a study by Dowling,[32] who observed a group of infants with esophageal atresia requiring sham feeding during the first year of life. Those who had only gastrostomy feedings for the first months of life had severe difficulties learning how to suck, chew, and swallow and seemed to have no awareness of hunger or satiety. In addition, they demonstrated significant delays in speech and motor development combined with blunting of affect and initiative. All these developmental problems could be avoided when the mothers were instructed to hold their infants during sham feedings and have them suck from a bottle with milk that was collected from the esophageal fistula at the neck. This study points to the significance of feeding in the overall development of the infant.

Treatment

Treatment of these infants needs to be individualized. It is necessary to take maternal as well as infant factors that have interfered with feeding into consideration. Treatment can be directed toward the infant, toward the mother, and toward the mother-infant interaction. In severe cases, if the infant's growth is seriously impaired, nasogastric tube feeding might have to be used to supplement oral feedings in an infant who tires quickly. This will allow an anxious mother to relax because her infant is getting adequate nutrition to grow. A more relaxed mother can tune into her infant more readily and break the cycle of dyadic escalation of tension during feedings.

On the other hand, the intervention might have to be directed primarily toward the mother to treat her anxiety, fatigue, or depression to enable her to be more effective in dealing with her infant. In addition, most mothers can be helped by problem solving in how to facilitate a feeding environment that provides the optimal amount of stimulation for their vulnerable infants. Infants who are irritable and easily overloaded with stimulation should be fed in the quietest room of the house away from the telephone and other distractions. Videotaping the feeding and observing the tape together with the mother can heighten her awareness of the infant's reactions during feeding and enhance her ability to read the infant's cues. The therapist can then engage the mother in a dialogue on how to respond to the infant's cues most effectively. Because of the complexity of the factors that may contribute to this feeding disorder, the therapist needs to use a flexible approach addressing both partners in the feeding relationship.

Clinical Vignette 1

Jeff is a 3-month-old baby who was brought to the hospital by his 17-year-old mother and his grandmother because of feeding difficulties and lack of appropriate weight gain starting at birth. On physical examination, he appeared weak and had poor muscle tone but otherwise had no signs of physical illness. His weight was 6 lb 9 oz, which was only 4 oz above birth weight. The history revealed that Jeff's mother had had an uncomplicated pregnancy and delivery. She was a senior in high school and had missed school only a few weeks before the delivery of Jeff and 6 weeks thereafter. The mother and her three younger siblings lived with their mother. The father of the infant and the father of the mother were out of the picture. The mother and the grandmother shared taking care of Jeff. They reported that at times, Jeff would be irritable and difficult to calm for feedings. At other times, particularly in recent weeks, he would be so sleepy that it was difficult to get him awake enough to feed. Both mother and grandmother appeared distressed about Jeff's feeding difficulties.

The mother admitted that the pregnancy with Jeff was unplanned and that she broke up with Jeff's father soon after she found out that she was pregnant. She had felt anxious throughout the pregnancy because she worried about the baby's future and her own. Although she had returned to school several weeks ago, she had difficulty concentrating and had done poorly on her grades. In recent weeks, she had had difficulty sleeping at night, had felt weak during the day, had been eating poorly, and had lost some weight herself. Although she had a good relationship with her mother, she felt lonely and isolated from her peers.

Mother-infant interactions during feeding revealed a sad young mother who gently tried to awaken her lethargic infant by rubbing his hands and feet. When unsuccessful, she held his little body upright. This resulted in the infant's head dropping backward abruptly. He was startled and cried loudly. When the mother successfully calmed the infant, he went right back to sleep without drinking from the bottle. The mother looked despondent and helpless.

Diagnostic Impression

It appeared that the infant's difficulty in regulating his state, being either too irritable to calm for feedings or too lethargic to awaken for feedings, together with the mother's anxiety and inexperience had resulted in a vicious circle, leading to increasing depression in the mother and a severe feeding disorder of homeostasis in the infant.

Treatment

Because of his poor nutritional state and his lethargy, Jeff was hospitalized. For a few days, he was given nasogastric tube feedings to supplement his poor oral intake. He was assigned a primary care nurse who was experienced in feeding babies. She would take him to a quiet room on the unit for feedings and gradually increase the physical stimulation to arouse him enough to be interested in drinking from the bottle. If she moved too quickly, he would start to cry and could not be fed. After a week of increasingly successful feedings, both the mother and the grandmother were invited to observe the feedings and were later coached by the nurse to take over the feedings themselves.

At the same time, while the nurse was working with Jeff, a psychiatric resident met regularly with the mother to address her feelings of anxiety and depression. Because of the severity of her depression, the mother was prescribed an antidepressant to which she responded well. When the mother began to sleep better and Jeff became more lively and responsive, she was able to deal with him more effectively. She enjoyed the positive reinforcement by the nurse, who tutored her in how to stimulate Jeff to reach a state of calm alertness that allowed him to feed successfully.

After 3 weeks, both mother and infant had made sufficient gains to be discharged from the hospital. Back at their home, Jeff and his mother were visited weekly by a home care nurse, and the mother continued in psychotherapy and pharmacotherapy with the psychiatric resident for the next 7 months. Jeff developed into an engaging little boy who continued to be vulnerable to changes in his caretaking environment, manifested by irritability and poor feeding. His mother recovered from her depression and graduated successfully from high school.

FEEDING DISORDER OF ATTACHMENT

Definition

Defining characteristics of feeding disorder of attachment are presented in Table 37–2. This feeding disorder has been referred to in the literature as maternal deprivation,[33] deprivation dwarfism,[34] and psychosocial deprivation.[6] The growth failure and developmental delay of these infants have been considered part of a continuum of neglect and maltreatment of the child leading to insecure attachment of the infant.[35] In DSM-III, this disorder was defined as reactive attachment disorder of infancy associated with failure to thrive. However, DSM-IV has changed the definition of reactive attachment disorder to encompass only the problems in relatedness of young children.

Epidemiology

Because of the heterogeneity of diagnostic labels used by various investigators, it is difficult to assess how commonly this feeding disorder of attachment occurs. However, there appears to be a clustering of cases in the lower socioeconomic classes, as noted by Chatoor.[36]

Etiology

Much has been written about mothers whose infants fail to thrive and appear to have a disorder of attachment. They are

Table 37–2 Feeding Disorder of Attachment

This feeding disorder is characterized by a lack of engagement between mother and infant.

The mother frequently denies any feeding problem of the infant.

The infant may come to the attention of professionals because of marked growth failure or other health problems.

Infant

- Onset of growth failure between 2 and 8 mo
- The infant shows lack of age-appropriate social responsivity
  - Lack of visual engagement: hypervigilance when people are at a distance, avoidance of eye contact when approached closely
  - Lack of smiling response
  - Lack of vocal reciprocity
  - Lack of anticipatory reaching when picked up (when infant is more than 5 mo old)
  - Lack of molding and cuddling when held
- Development of infant
  - Delay in motor milestones
  - Poor muscle tone evidenced by hyperextension when picked up, surrender posture when held
  - Delayed cognitive development

Parent

Acute or chronic depression or personality disorder, drug or alcohol abuse, and high psychosocial stress appear to lead to a lack of affectionate care and lack of regular feedings of the infant.

Bottles may be propped for the infant to feed independently, or feedings may be forgotten altogether.

Mother-Infant Relationship

Feedings are characterized by a lack of mutual engagement and lack of pleasure in the relationship between mother and infant.

Differential Diagnosis

This feeding disorder needs to be differentiated from organic conditions that may lead to a lack of weight gain in the infant. However, mother and infant usually show good mutual engagement.

frequently described as suffering from character disorder, affective illness, alcohol abuse, and drug abuse.[37–40] Glaser and coworkers[41] suggested that the highest risk exists when the mother's needs take precedence over those of the infant. Fraiberg and colleagues[42] suggested that difficulties of these mothers in nurturing their infants stem from the unmet needs of the mothers during their own childhood. Drotar and Sturm[43] postulated that the manner in which traumatic or deprived childhood experiences influence the mother-infant relationship is mediated by the mother's current context of family life.

Family problems and distressed marital relationships have been reported in a number of noncontrolled and controlled studies of failure to thrive.[35, 44–47] Some authors also reported that mothers of infants with failure to thrive were more often abused by their partners or parents than were mothers of thriving infants.[35, 48] In addition, socially adverse living conditions, poverty, and unemployment are reported to be more prevalent in these families of infants with failure to thrive.[49–51]

Several authors have used the Strange Situation Procedure developed by Ainsworth and coworkers[52] to understand the attachment difficulties in the relationship of infants with failure to thrive and their mothers.[35, 53, 54] These studies reported that 45% to 93% of the infants with failure to thrive were insecurely attached, compared with significantly lower numbers of control subjects.. In addition, Benoit and associates[44] found that mothers of infants with failure to thrive were more likely than control mothers to be classified as insecurely attached to their own parents, as measured by the Adult Attachment Interview (George C, et al, unpublished data, 1985).

Taking the findings from these various studies together, the failure to thrive of these infants appears to be a critical manifestation of a failed relationship between a mother and her infant during the first year of life, when the foundation for mutual engagement and attachment is usually laid. A transgenerational pattern of insecure attachment appears to be at the root of the mother's difficulty to engage with her infant and leads to a lack of emotional and physical nurturance of the infant.

Diagnosis

Most of these infants are not brought for pediatric well-baby care but present to the emergency department because of an acute illness, when their poor nutritional state draws the attention of pediatricians. Because of their severe failure to thrive, these infants frequently require hospitalization. During the hospitalization, the psychiatric consultant is usually called in to assist in the diagnosis and treatment of the infant's growth and developmental problems. The evaluation should include an assessment of the infant's feeding, developmental, and health history, including any changes in the infant's behavior during the hospitalization. In addition, the mother's pregnancy, delivery, family situation, and social support need to be thoroughly explored. Because many of these mothers are distrustful and difficult to engage, it is advisable to perform an initial informal mental status examination of the mother to rule out severe psychiatric illness, particularly whether she suffers from depression or is abusing alcohol or drugs.

Many of these mothers are elusive and avoidant of any contact with professionals. Consequently, the observation of mother-infant interactions may have to be obtained indirectly, through the report of other professionals who admitted the infant. In a study of mother-infant interactions in infants with three types of developmental feeding disorders and matched control groups of well-feeding infants, Chatoor[31] observed that those with a feeding disorder of attachment were characterized by poor dyadic reciprocity between mother and infant and by noncontingency of the mothers to their infants' cues.

Another important part of the assessment involves the direct observation and examination of these infants. Infants with feeding disorders of attachment characteristically are weak, feed poorly, and avoid eye contact in the first few days of hospitalization. When picked up, they might scissor their legs and hold up their arms in a surrender posture to balance their heads, which seem too heavy for their little weak bodies. They usually do not cuddle like healthy well-fed infants but keep their legs drawn up or appear hypotonic like ragdolls. However, these infants appear to blossom under the tender care of a primary care nurse who engages with them during feeding and plays with them. They become increasingly responsive, begin to smile, feed hungrily, and gain weight. These striking changes in behavior of these young infants when they are fed and attended to by a nurturing caretaker are characteristic of a feeding disorder of attachment and differentiate these infants from infants with organic problems that have resulted in growth failure and developmental delays. The infants with organic failure to thrive usually respond best to their mothers and do not show the avoidance of eye contact and general withdrawal so characteristic of infants with a feeding disorder of attachment.[55, 56]

Course and Natural History

Although a number of studies have reported the follow-up of infants with nonorganic failure to thrive, the findings from these studies are difficult to compare because of an inconsistent definition of failure to thrive. In general, chronic malnutrition has been associated with cognitive and behavioral problems. Hufton and Oates[51] reported that of 21 children who had been diagnosed with nonorganic failure to thrive during infancy, at the age of 6 years, half of the children had abnormal personalities and two thirds had a delayed reading age. Two children from the original sample had died in suspicious circumstances. A similar grim outlook had been reported earlier by Elmer and associates,[57] who found that only 2 of 15 children with growth failure associated with emotional deprivation were functioning reasonably well 3 to 11 years after the initial diagnosis. Both studies reported that the children came from families with economic difficulties and high marital instability. Prospective and controlled studies confirm the developmental risk for children with an early history of nonorganic failure to thrive. Drotar and Sturm[58] compared 48 preschool children with early histories of nonorganic failure to thrive with 47 healthy children of comparable age, sex, and family demographics. The children with failure to thrive demonstrated deficits in behavioral organization, ego control, and ego resiliency and demonstrated more behavioral symptoms compared with control children. A prospective study by Black and colleagues[59] examined developmental outcome in a group of 102 low-income, inner-city children with nonorganic failure to thrive and a comparison group of 67 children with adequate growth matched for age, sex, race, and socioeconomic status. Looking at parenting styles, they found that parents of children with failure to thrive were less nurturant and more neglecting than were parents of comparison children and that children of nurturant parents consistently demonstrated better social-cognitive development across groups.

Treatment

Various treatment approaches have been proposed ranging from home-based interventions to hospitalization in severe cases. In an intervention study that compared three treatment approaches (short-term advocacy, family-centered intervention, and parent-infant intervention), Sturm and Drotar[60] found that none of the treatment methods was superior in predicting outcome. In a controlled prospective study of infants with failure to thrive by Black and coworkers,[61] infants were randomly assigned to treatment in a multidisciplinary feeding and nutrition clinic or to a home-based intervention by trained lay visitors. Children in both types of intervention improved their growth pattern; however, the mothers in the home-based intervention created a more child-focused home environment for their children with failure to thrive. Because of the complexity of the issues involved in the etiology of nonorganic failure to thrive, most psychiatrists and researchers suggest that multiple and case-specific interventions may be required. Schmitt and Mauro[62] considered an outpatient approach safe in cases of mild neglect when there is no evidence of deprivational behavior on the part of the mother, the infant is older than 12 months, and the parents have a support system and have sought medical care for previous sickness. However, these authors recommended immediate hospitalization of young infants with neglectful failure to thrive if it is associated with nonaccidental trauma; if the degree of failure to thrive is considered severe; if there is serious hygiene neglect; if the mother appears severely disturbed, abusing drugs or alcohol; if the mother lives a chaotic lifestyle and appears overwhelmed with stresses; and if the mother-infant interaction appears angry and uncaring.

During the hospitalization, a number of infant-directed interventions can be carried out while a more in-depth evaluation of the mother and the mother-infant relationship takes place. It is most important to assign a primary care nurse who can be warm and nurturing to woo the infant into a mutual relationship. Improvement of the infant's health and affective availability can then be used to engage the mother with her infant and in the treatment process. As Harris[63] pointed out, recovery from growth failure does not indicate that the parent-child relationship is adequate. The mother's ability to engage her infant and to participate in the treatment process has to be at the core of the treatment plan. Ayoub and Milner[64] reported that the degree of parental awareness and cooperation was predictive of outcome for failure to thrive.

Because these mothers frequently present with a variety of psychological and social disturbances, their problems need to be explored while nutritional, emotional, and developmental rehabilitation goes on with the infant. Many of these mothers have experienced neglect or abuse during their own childhoods, and they are distrustful and avoidant of professionals. It is important to look for and identify any positive behavior a mother shows toward her infant to use it as a building block to bolster her competence and interest in her infant. As Fraiberg and colleagues[42] pointed out, nurturance of the mother is the first critical step in the treatment to facilitate her potential to nurture her infant. Not only the mother but also the family, in its relationship to the mother-infant pair and its social and economic support, needs to be taken into consideration. As Drotar and Sturm[43] pointed out, the family can serve as a stress-buffering or stress-producing system. The hospitalization of the infant provides a critical time to assess whether the mother can be engaged in a therapeutic relationship or whether the infant needs to be placed in alternative care. In some situations of severe neglect or associated abuse, the case needs to be reported to protective services, which at times can be instrumental in mobilizing the family or in finding foster care.

Discharge from the hospital is a critical time when all services need to be in place to ensure appropriate follow-through of the treatment plan for these vulnerable infants. The treatment plan needs to be individualized for each mother-infant pair to make use of all the resources that can support their relationship. For some infants, daycare in a nurturing environment will give the mother an opportunity to pursue some of her own interests and needs and make the time with her infant more special and enjoyable. Visits by a home care nurse or regular treatment sessions in the home by a social worker, as suggested by Fraiberg and colleagues,[42] are some of the alternatives to consider because many of these mothers struggle with coming to therapy in an office setting. Because of the complexity of the problems involved in the etiology of this feeding disorder, a flexible multidisciplinary approach, coordinated by the primary therapist, is usually most effective.

Clinical Vignette 2

Sarah is a 7-month-old infant who was brought to the emergency department by her parents because of loose stools and drowsiness for the past 2 days. Physical examination revealed a moderately dehydrated and severely malnourished infant weighing only 9 lb 10 oz. The rest of her physical examination was unremarkable. She was admitted to the hospital and treated with intravenous saline solutions because of her dehydration and general weakness.

The mother reported that Sarah was her fourth child, the oldest being only 4 years old. Sarah was born full term, weighing 7 lb 2 oz. The mother's pregnancy, the birth, and the postnatal course were uneventful. The family had just recently moved to the area because the father had lost his job 5 months ago and had been promised work with a construction company in this area. The parents reported that two other children were sick with diarrhea. They left soon after Sarah was admitted to the hospital, and they did not visit her for the next 3 days. When the primary care nurse tried to contact the parents by phone, the phone was disconnected. At this point, the medical staff requested a social work consultation. After the social worker sent a telegram to the parents, they visited Sarah on the fifth day of her hospitalization in the evening, when the regular staff had left the unit. The nurse who was on call reported that both parents appeared inebriated and barely interacted with Sarah. They claimed that they could not visit during the day because of lack of transportation. The following day, the medical staff requested a psychiatric consultation and reported Sarah to protective services because of her poor hygiene on admission and the parents' unavailability to work with the staff.

Sarah's medical work-up, including a stool culture, did not reveal any organic disease. The primary care nurse described Sarah as withdrawn, avoiding eye contact, being limp, and drinking poorly from the bottle. She barely cried when she was pricked for blood tests and lay quietly in her crib when not attended to. After 7 days, the nurse had gotten Sarah to smile for the first time.

With the help of protective services, the social worker was able to set up a meeting with the mother to gain more information and to observe mother and infant during feeding and play. The mother revealed to the psychiatric consultant that she did not want to move because she knew no one in this area. She felt overwhelmed with the care of her four children and frequently propped the bottles for Sarah to feed by herself because Sarah did not seem to mind, and it saved the mother time. The mother also admitted drinking in the evening with her husband because this was the only way she could get through the evening and go to sleep. She revealed that her father used to drink heavily and beat her when she was a child and that she had sworn to herself never to touch her children. She indicated that she did not like the way her husband "roughed up" their children but denied any physical abuse toward them or herself.

Mother-infant interactions during feeding revealed a sad-looking mother who held her infant loosely on her lap. Sarah barely opened her eyes while she was suckling from the bottle. During play, the mother tried to get Sarah interested in the toys. She became animated when Sarah started to grab the rattle.

Diagnostic Impression

Sarah presented the typical behaviors of an infant with a feeding disorder of attachment. Initially, she avoided eye contact, appeared withdrawn, and fed poorly. Although she became more engaging with her special nurse, these behaviors lingered on in her interaction with her mother.

Her mother appeared well intended but overwhelmed and depressed, and she abused alcohol to numb her feelings. Her father seemed too busy in making a new start for the family to realize how ill his daughter was and how overwhelmed his wife felt.

Treatment

A multidisciplinary team consisting of the primary care nurse, the pediatric resident, the social worker, the caseworker from protective services, and the psychiatric consultant took over the treatment of this mother-infant pair. The social worker served as the mother's therapist and as the coordinator of the team. The pediatrician monitored Sarah's nutritional rehabilitation. The nurse worked with Sarah to engage her during feeding and play. The psychiatric consultant worked with mother and infant to mutually engage them in pleasurable interactions by reinforcing the mother for any response she was able to elicit from Sarah. The psychiatrist also started the mother on antidepressant medication. The caseworker arranged for the mother to be given some relief through a home helper and by placing the oldest two children in nursery school.

After a month in the hospital, Sarah had gained weight, appeared stronger, and tried to sit up. She readily smiled at her primary care nurse and engaged more easily with her mother. The mother had established a working relationship with the social worker and felt greatly relieved by the support she had received to take care of her older children. The team felt comfortable with her request to continue treatment on an outpatient basis. The mother and Sarah continued to come for weekly visits with the social worker and were seen monthly by the psychiatrist. Transportation for all visits was arranged through protective services.

This treatment regimen was maintained for the next 6 months, when Sarah's continued progress in gaining weight and reaching new developmental milestones allowed gradual phasing out of this intense therapy during the course of the next year. Even after the termination of treatment, Sarah's mother stayed in contact with the social worker and apprised her of important events in their lives.

INFANTILE ANOREXIA (FEEDING DISORDER OF SEPARATION)

Definition

In 1983, Chatoor and Egan[64a] published nine cases of food refusal leading to failure to thrive and delineated the characteristics of this feeding disorder with its onset during the developmental period of separation and individuation. They called it a separation disorder. Later, because of its similarities to anorexia nervosa, it was called infantile anorexia nervosa[65, 66] and eventually infantile anorexia.[67] Infantile anorexia most commonly begins between 9 and 18 months of age during the infant's transition to self-feeding. It is characterized by food refusal and failure to thrive of the infant in spite of intense efforts by the mother to get the infant to eat. The mother's intense efforts to feed her infant by distracting, bargaining, or forced feeding lead to increasingly provocative behaviors by the infant and result in high levels of conflict and poor reciprocity in the dyad. The toddler eats or refuses to eat in response to the interactional experiences with the mother, and the toddler's eating becomes externally instead of internally regulated (Table 37–3).

Table 37–3 Infantile Anorexia (Feeding Disorder of Separation)

This feeding disorder is characterized by food refusal of the infant and intense conflict in the mother-infant relationship over issues of autonomy, dependency, and control. The following behaviors and perceptions describe mothers and infants with this disorder.

Infant

- Onset of food refusal between age 6 mo and 3 y during the infant's transition to self-feeding
- Food refusal of the infant
  - Varies from meal to meal
  - Varies among different caretakers
  - Leads to inadequate food intake in general
- Inadequate food intake has resulted in failure to thrive
  - Weight is below the fifth percentile for age, or weight has deviated across two major percentiles in a 2- to 6-mo period
  - Weight has fallen below 90% of ideal weight for height

Parent

- Parental perception of the infant as
  - Having a poor appetite
  - Being curious and demanding of attention
  - Being difficult and stubborn during feedings, rejecting parental efforts to get infant to eat
- High parental anxiety and frustration about the infant's poor food intake expressed by at least two of the following behaviors:
  - Coaxing the infant to eat more
  - Distracting the infant with toys or games to induce the infant to eat
  - Feeding the infant around-the-clock, including at night
  - Trying different types of food if the infant does not eat
  - Forcibly feeding the infant

Mother-Infant Relationship

Mother and infant are in conflict over the infant's food intake. The infant refuses to open his or her mouth and pushes the spoon or food away while the mother coaxes, distracts, or threatens the infant to eat more.

Differential Diagnosis

Food refusal of the infant is not due to a traumatic event such as choking, gagging, insertion of feeding or endotracheal tubes, vomiting or pain due to gastroesophageal reflux, or any other medical illness.

Epidemiology

Little is known as to how frequently this feeding disorder occurs. A study by Dahl and Sundelin[23] from Sweden reported that 1% to 2% of infants younger than 1 year of age had severe feeding problems associated with refusal to eat or vomiting, resulting in poor weight gain. At 4 years, 71% of those with food refusal were reported by their parents as still having feeding problems.[24] The disorder seems to be as common among boys and girls of all racial backgrounds and clusters in the upper-middle classes.[17]

Etiology

I postulate a transactional model for the development of infantile anorexia. By this model, certain characteristics of the infant combine with certain vulnerabilities in the mother to bring out negative responses and conflict in their interactions. I hypothesize that the infant's characteristics of intense interpersonal sensitivity, poor hunger cues, and stubbornness evoke conflicts over control and limit setting in a vulnerable mother who has experienced extremes of parental discipline in the form of overcontrol or parental emotional unavailability while she was growing up. The mother's insecurity in regard to limit setting versus nurturing leads to inconsistency of her responses and fuels conflict with her infant. The mother's childhood conflicts about control frequently involved parental management of eating, resulting in the mother's difficulty not only in correctly interpreting her own signals of hunger and satiety but also in correctly reading her infant's signals.

Between 9 and 18 months, the general developmental task of separation and individuation takes on special significance in the feeding relationship. During the transition to self-feeding, mother and infant need to negotiate who is going to put the spoon in the infant's mouth; issues of autonomy versus dependency need to be worked out in the dyad. (The mother needs to figure out why the infant refuses to open her or his mouth, whether the infant wants to feed herself or himself or is satiated.) If the mother is able to read the infant's signals correctly and responds contingently, the infant will learn to differentiate physiological feelings of hunger and fullness from emotional experiences such as anger, frustration, or the wish for attention. In this case, the infant's food intake will be internally regulated through physiological cues of hunger and satiety. On the other hand, if the mother responds in a noncontingent way (offers the bottle when the infant is emotionally distressed or distracts the infant with a toy to slip more food into the infant's mouth when the infant is already satiated), the infant will learn to associate feeding with negative or positive emotional experiences. In the second case, the infant's eating will be externally controlled through the infant's emotional experiences with the caretaker, as is the case in infantile anorexia.

Diagnosis

These infants are usually referred for a psychiatric evaluation because of "nonorganic" failure to thrive. The referring pediatricians are usually impressed by the good overall development of infants with anorexia in contrast to infants with feeding disorders of attachment, who are usually developmentally delayed. In addition, mothers of anorectic infants are generally anxious because of the infants' food refusal and lack of weight gain.

The evaluation should include the infant's feeding, developmental, and health history. Although many infants are reported to have been poor feeders from birth and always more interested in looking around than focusing on the feeding, the food refusal and lack of weight gain are usually related to the transition to self-feeding and the introduction of solid food. Some infants are reported to be picky eaters and to refuse specific types of food. However, in contrast to infants with a posttraumatic feeding disorder, these infants' choices of food appear to change periodically and usually do not involve all lumpy and crunchy food.

In addition to the infant's history, the mother's perception of her infant, her family situation, her childhood background, and her own eating habits and attitude toward limit setting need to be explored. Many of these mothers have experienced their own mothers or fathers as too controlling and intrusive and have tried hard not to repeat their parents' child-rearing practices. One mother explained, "I have read so much because I wanted to be the perfect mother." These mothers usually feel anxious and ineffective because, in spite of their best efforts, their infants are failing to thrive.

Course and Natural History

At this point, no systematic data from prospective longitudinal studies are available. Anecdotal data from individual case reports suggest various outcomes. Some adults report that as children, they struggled with their mothers over eating, grew poorly, and were thin and short until midadolescence, when through encouragement of peers they increased their food intake and experienced catch-up growth. Two mothers of anorectic infants reported that when they were at the age of 6 years, their own mothers placed them in boarding schools because they were so frustrated over their children's food refusal. Although both women improved their eating pattern in the boarding schools, they remained small until they were adults, when they struggled with overeating and depression. Other mothers of infants with anorexia reported that they had been poor eaters and of low weight since infancy but never reached the degree of malnutrition of their infants. A few girls presented with classic symptoms of anorexia nervosa during late childhood and early adolescence, with a history of food refusal and poor growth dating to infancy. Although infantile anorexia has been observed in boys as frequently as in girls, only a few cases in older boys were observed. These boys presented with oppositional disorders involving many other areas of their lives as well. One adolescent boy who chose to give up his eating disorder to grow and be able to participate in sports, from which he had been excluded because of his small size, decided to fail in school to upset his mother, who was a counselor at his school.

Treatment

The psychotherapeutic intervention is based on the developmental psychopathological model of infantile anorexia as outlined in the section on etiology. The major goal of the intervention is to *facilitate internal regulation of eating* by the infant. The intervention consists of three components:

1. Assess and then explain the infant's special temperamental characteristics and developmental conflicts to the mother to help her understand the lack of expected hunger cues and the infant's struggle for control during the feeding situation.
2. Explore the mother's upbringing and the effect it has had on the parenting of her infant to help the mother understand her conflicts and difficulties in regard to limit setting.
3. Explain the concept of internal versus external regulation of eating. Help the mother to set limits and to develop mealtime routines ("food rules") that facilitate the infant's awareness of hunger, leading to internal regulation of eating, improved food intake, and growth. These food rules include
   a. Schedule meals and snacks at regular 3- to 4-hour intervals and do not allow the infant to snack or drink from the bottle or breast in between.
   b. Limit meal duration to 30 minutes.
   c. Praise the infant for self-feeding but stay emotionally neutral whether the infant eats little or a lot.
   d. Do not use distracting toys or television during feedings.
   e. Eliminate desserts or sweets as a reward but integrate them into regular meals.
   f. Put the infant in "time-out" for inappropriate behaviors during feeding (e.g., throwing the spoon or food).

These three steps in the treatment are best accomplished in three sessions lasting 2 to 3 hours each and grouped close together within a 2- to 3-week period. The intensity of this brief intervention facilitates a close therapeutic alliance between the therapist and the mother and gives the mother the opportunity to experience the support she needs to make major changes in her interactions with her infant.

This initial intensive phase of the intervention can be followed up by a telephone call and by a few visits spaced 3 and 4 weeks apart. Being aware that the mother needs to have time and space to practice the new food rules and, at the same time, of how important it is for her to have the opportunity to check in with the therapist to clarify any questions or doubts she might have is the rationale for prolonged time intervals between these sessions. Once the mother changes her rules with the infant, some infants adapt quickly and change their eating behavior quickly, whereas others can be resistant and take weeks before they seem to become aware of their hunger cues. The longer interval between appointments allows the mother the time to work with the infant on these changes without feeling pressured.

Thus far, only the mother and the infant have been taken into consideration. However, frequently the father, a childcare worker, or a relative is also involved in the infant's feeding. The intervention focuses primarily on the mother because in infantile anorexia, the mother's feeding relationship with the infant is seen as central. Nevertheless, the other relationships cannot be overlooked.

Giving the mother a choice as to whom in the family or anyone else she wants to include in the therapeutic process, and at what point she wants to do so, is part of putting the mother in control. Because many of these mothers have felt helpless as children and ineffective as parents, the empowerment of the mother is critical to the success of the treatment.

Clinical Vignette 3

John was 19 months old when he was referred for a psychiatric evaluation because of food refusal and failure to thrive. Both of his parents were professionals, but his mother had interrupted her career when John was born and stayed home to take care of him. She related that John had been a poor feeder from birth and that she was unsuccessful breast-feeding him because he seemed too busy looking around instead of sucking from the breast. After a month of poor weight gain, his mother finally gave up and switched to bottles, which seemed to improve his intake. He grew well until about 9 months of age, when his growth pattern started to decelerate. About that time, the mother remembered that John did not seem interested in feeding, refused to open his mouth when she came with the spoon, and tried to slide out of his highchair. Initially, she was able to distract him by playing games or giving him a toy to manipulate, but soon he seemed to get bored with these things, and she had to constantly come up with new distractions to keep him in his highchair. At some point she tried feeding him in the bathtub because he seemed to enjoy playing with his water toys, but this did not last long either. A few times she got so frustrated that she held him down and tried to forcibly feed him. However, he would spit everything out and start to cry when she tried to put him in his highchair afterward. The mother wondered how John could be running around all day long on the little he ate. She expressed fear of what would happen to John in the future, whether he would be a little thin boy who would be pushed around by the bigger children.

The mother revealed that she had been a poor eater when she was a child. She remembered that her father got so frustrated with her when she refused to eat that one time, he picked her up by her legs and held her upside down. She remembered struggling with her parents all through her childhood because she ate so poorly. She was a thin and short little girl until she was 14 years old, when her parents went on a trip abroad for several weeks and left her in the care of friends who were relaxed about her eating. She started to eat more, and her parents were surprised at how well she looked when they returned. She admitted that in her adult life she frequently skipped meals because she was so "busy" that she did not think about eating. She also admitted that she usually could not eat if she felt angry or anxious. She explained that her husband ate well regardless of the circumstances, and he could not understand why she and her son were such picky eaters.

In addition to the battles over eating, the mother also recalled having had a strained relationship with her father because of his drinking and his authoritarian stand toward her. With tears in her eyes, she recalled how he beat her on a number of occasions. The mother's own mother was described as kind, but the mother was so busy with the family business that she did not spend much time with her as a child. The unavailability of her own mother had weighed heavily in the mother's decision to stay home with her son.

Assessment

John was an engaging little boy who appeared comfortable with strangers as long as his mother was present. However, when his mother left the room, he became extremely distressed and took a long time to settle again even after the return of his mother. His motor development appeared excellent. He had started to walk at 10 months of age, and he climbed easily up and down the furniture.

Mother-infant interactions during feeding revealed intense conflict between mother and John. Although John had not eaten for several hours, he ate only a few bites before crying and indicating that he wanted to get out of the highchair. When his mother did not respond, he started to throw the food and feeding utensils, and his mother complied and took him out of the chair. While John ran around the room pointing to the pictures on the wall, his mother came after him, trying to slip some more food in his mouth. After a while, his mother gave up and sat in her chair looking worried and sad. John entertained himself exploring his mirror image and the furniture in the room. During the play, mother and John were able to engage in mutual pretend play. John seemed to enjoy himself. His mother, however, continued to look sad and preoccupied.

Diagnostic Impression

John and his mother appeared to have a close and affectionate relationship until it came to eating. The observation of John revealed that he was a strong-willed boy and persisted until he got his way with his mother. In addition, he appeared to be highly curious and interested in the outside world, having little awareness of his hunger.

Although the mother had experienced similar eating problems as a child and recalled eating better when her parents were away and she was not pressured to eat, she was so concerned about John's growth that she could not translate that knowledge into her dealing with John's food refusal. Instead, she engaged in the same games and battles of will with John as she had done with her parents when she was a child. The mother also revealed that even as an adult, she had difficulty regulating her eating if she experienced intense positive or negative emotions. In addition, the mother's conflicts over nurturing and control, stemming from her own childhood experiences, seemed to interfere with her ability to negotiate this developmental phase of separation and individuation with John.

Treatment

During the diagnostic evaluation, this bright and perceptive mother had started to link her own eating problems and emotional inhibition of eating with John's food refusal. She realized that her distracting and coercing John into eating had made matters worse. She wanted to be a better parent than her own parents had been to her, and she felt guilty that she had repeated some of their behavior. First, the mother needed to be reassured that she had done the best she knew and that children like John are a special challenge to any parent because of their temperamental characteristics of intense curiosity about the external world with little attention being paid to their internal signals of hunger. In addition, it was pointed out to the mother that John, like many others with this feeding disorder, is a strong-willed boy who likes to control his mother. The therapist then explained to the mother that because of the mother's anxiety about John's poor food intake, he had learned that eating or not eating was a powerful tool to assert himself. Consequently, his eating became increasingly influenced by his emotional interactions with his mother instead of by feelings of hunger. The therapist pointed out to the mother that John and his mother appeared to feel less hungry the stronger they were aroused emotionally. Therefore, eating needed to be neutralized emotionally for John to respond better to his physiological cues of hunger.

The mother decided to include her husband in the rest of the treatment sessions so he could also understand the concept of internal regulation and help her in the implementation of the food rules. The parents worked well together to tailor the food rules to John's and their individual needs. The regularity of meals posed the greatest problems to this family because of the father's irregular work hours and their wish to have family dinners together with John. The mother had some concerns in managing time-outs when John got unruly in the highchair. However, her husband helped her with the first application, and later she became more comfortable in disciplining John.

During the first few days after the introduction of the food rules, John appeared to test his mother. He would refuse to eat much during lunch and then an hour later demand the bottle. When his mother told him that he had to wait until snack time, he started crying and his mother felt bad. However, she was able to stay firm, and within a few days John got used to the new schedule and rules. Gradually, he started to eat better and sometimes he would say "tummy hungry." The parents were delighted that he started gaining weight. During a follow-up visit, they admitted that they had started to become lax with some of the rules because of houseguests and other irregularities in their lives and observed that John's eating pattern began to deteriorate quickly.

Treatment was terminated when the parents seemed to feel comfortable in understanding John's temperamental vulnerabilities and their ability to provide an environment that would foster internal regulation of eating.

Table 37–4 Posttraumatic Feeding Disorder

This feeding disorder is characterized by total food refusal of the infant or refusal to eat or swallow milk or textured food. The infant shows distress if pressured into feeding, but otherwise mother and infant may show good reciprocity.

Food Refusal by Infant

- Food refusal by infant of sudden onset
  - After an episode of choking, severe gagging, or vomiting
  - After medical illness or after medical procedures associated with pain of the oropharynx or esophagus (e.g., gastroesophageal reflux, insertion of feeding tubes or endotracheal tubes, or suctioning of the oropharynx)
- Infant appears to associate feeding with pain or distress, leading to anticipatory fear demonstrated by
  - Total food refusal (severe cases)
  - Crying and gagging and vomiting at the sight of highchair, bottle, or spoon
  - Crying, gagging, choking, or vomiting when forcibly fed
- Infant appears to associate certain types of food (milk or textured food) with pain (milder or partially treated cases), expressed by
  - Accepting spoon-fed baby food, but refusing the bottle
  - Drinking from the bottle when sleeping or asleep, but refusing the bottle when awake
  - Drinking liquids but refusing textured food
  - Accepting textured food but holding it in cheeks and spitting it out later
  - Crying, gagging, and choking when forcibly fed

Parent

- Parental anxiety and frustration secondary to food refusal by the infant, expressed by
  - Coaxing or distracting the infant with toys during feedings
  - Attempting to feed the infant day and night
  - Trying various types of food without success
  - Attempting forced feeding, leading to intensification of symptoms of anticipatory anxiety and food refusal by the infant

Mother-Infant Relationship

Mother and infant usually appear anxious and tense in anticipation of and during the feeding. The infant's food refusal may lead to intense conflict while the mother is trying to feed the infant, but otherwise mother and infant may have pleasurable interactions and usually enjoy each other during play.

Differential Diagnosis

This disorder needs to be differentiated from infantile anorexia and picky eating, which are characterized by inconsistencies in the type and texture of food the infant refuses.

POSTTRAUMATIC FEEDING DISORDER

Definition

Defining characteristics of posttraumatic feeding disorder are presented in Table 37–4. This disorder was first described by Chatoor and coworkers[16] in latency-age children as posttraumatic eating disorder. These children refused to eat any solid food after they had experienced an episode of choking. They were preoccupied with the fear of choking and dreamed about choking and dying. When approached with food, they demonstrated intense anticipatory anxiety and panic until the food was removed. Later, Chatoor[17] described this disorder in infants as posttraumatic feeding disorder. Several authors have addressed problems related to this feeding disorder under different labels, such as food refusal,[68, 69] food phobia,[5] food aversion,[70] and feeding resistance.[71]

Epidemiology

Although no studies on the prevalence of this disorder are available, it appears that the occurrence of this feeding disorder has been increasing because of the growing number of infants with complex medical problems who survive. This is reflected in a number of papers describing the symptoms and treatment of feeding disorders in infants with medical conditions.[68, 72–75]

Etiology

Although it is difficult to say what the inner experience of a young infant might be, the affective and behavioral expressions of infants provide a window to their inner life. In a study of infants diagnosed with posttraumatic feeding disorder, including also a control group of healthy eaters and a group of anorectic infants matched by age, sex, race, and socioeconomic background, Chatoor and colleagues[76] observed conflict in mother-infant interactions during feeding in both feeding-disordered groups. However, only those subjects with a posttraumatic feeding disorder demonstrated intense preoral and intraoral feeding defensiveness. They appeared distressed, cried and pushed the food away in anticipation of being fed, and kept solid food in their cheeks or spit it out if the mothers were able to place any food in their mouths. The mothers usually reported that these defensive behaviors started abruptly after the infant experienced severe vomiting, gagging, or choking or underwent invasive manipulation of the oropharynx (e.g., insertion of feeding and endotracheal tubes or vigorous suctioning).

It appears that these infants associate painful or frightening experiences with feeding and then experience intense anxiety when they are exposed to food. Interestingly, several mothers reported that not only the infants' feeding but also their sleep was greatly disrupted after the traumatic events. The infants became more fretful during the day and woke up frequently during the night, crying and appearing fearful.

Diagnosis

Some infants respond with total refusal of any type of food, liquid or solid. Their fear of food appears to override any awareness of hunger. These infants require emergency medical attention because of the danger of acute dehydration.

More commonly, the infant refuses the bottle with milk but may accept baby food because he or she experienced severe vomiting after drinking milk and appears to associate the trauma with milk. Other infants may accept the bottle with milk or juice but refuse any food offered by spoon because they gagged severely on baby food. Some infants may put baby food in their mouths but then spit out any food that has any little lumps in it. Most infants get stuck in these food refusal patterns and may lose weight or lack certain nutrients because of their limited diet.

In addition to a thorough history about the onset of the infant's food refusal and the medical and developmental history, the observation of the infant and mother during feeding is critical for understanding this feeding disorder and differentiating it from infantile anorexia and from picky eating. It is helpful to ask the mother to bring a variety of foods, including those that the infant refuses and those that she or he accepts. Infants with posttraumatic feeding disorders characteristically appear engaged and comfortable with their mothers as long as the "feared" food is out of sight. Some infants begin to show distress when they are placed in the highchair, and they struggle to get away. Others appear to eat hungrily until they are offered the feared food and the mother tries to induce the infant to eat. In less severe cases, the infant might allow the food to go into the mouth but then spit it out and show distress only when urged to swallow. This anticipatory fear of food differentiates infants with a posttraumatic feeding disorder from anorectic infants, whose food refusal appears random and related to issues of control in the relationship with the mothers. Picky eaters with sensory aversions to certain types of food might also show distress when urged to eat these foods. However, their mothers do not remember a traumatic event that seemed to trigger the food refusal behaviors, and picky eaters tend to refuse only certain types of food (e.g., green beans or carrots) but accept other vegetables and fruits of similar texture (e.g., tomatoes and apples).

Course and Natural History

Most infants seem to get locked into their food refusal patterns. The more anxiously the parents react to the infant's food refusal, the more anxious the infants appear to become, with parents and infants feeding each other's anxiety. Although no systematic longitudinal data on the course of this feeding disorder exist, individual case studies indicate that some of these infants depend for years on gastrostomy feedings to survive. Others may live on milk and puréed food until school age, when the social embarrassment of their eating behavior urges the parents to seek help. Frequently, in these long-term cases, so much tension has developed because of the child's food refusal that some parents cannot remember how it all started. In addition, as these children get older and begin to understand the reactions their food refusal elicits in their parents, their eating or not eating takes on issues of control in the parent-child relationship.

Treatment

Because of the complexity of many of these cases, a multidisciplinary team (consisting of a pediatrician or gastroenterologist, a psychiatrist or psychologist, a social worker, an occupational therapist or hearing and speech specialist, a nutritionist, and a specially trained nurse to serve as team coordinator) is best equipped to meet all the needs of these infants and their parents.

Before any psychiatric treatment can be successfully initiated, the medical and nutritional needs of these infants need to be addressed. In severe cases of total food refusal, it is important to act quickly to maintain the infant's hydration. The medical and psychiatric team members must work together to assess whether temporary nasogastric tube feedings are indicated or whether plans for a gastrostomy should be made. Unfortunately, the repeated insertion of nasogastric feeding tubes can intensify a posttraumatic feeding disorder, and infants in labile medical conditions can take months if not years to recover. In less severe cases (if the infant drinks milk but refuses all solid food or, in a reverse case, refuses the bottle but accepts baby food from the spoon), the nutritional impact of a limited diet as such needs to be assessed and plans for nutritional supplementation need to be made before the psychiatric treatment is undertaken. Otherwise, the parents will be too anxious to engage in the treatment process.

The psychiatric treatment of this feeding disorder involves a desensitization of the infant to overcome the anticipatory anxiety about eating and return to internal regulation of eating in response to hunger and satiety. It is most important to help the parents understand the dynamics of a posttraumatic feeding disorder so that they can recognize the infant's anticipatory anxiety and become active participants in the treatment. After identification of triggers of anticipatory anxiety (e.g., the sight of the highchair, the bottle, or certain types of food), a desensitization by gradual exposure can be initiated as proposed by Chatoor and colleagues,[77] or a more rapid desensitization through more intensive behavioral techniques[72] can be implemented. However, none of these treatment techniques has been systematically evaluated.

With both techniques, it is important to have a professional assess the infant's oral motor coordination because many infants who refuse to eat for extended periods fall behind in their oral motor development owing to lack of practice. Consequently, a 2-year-old may have the oral motor skills of a 1-year-old and will not be able to handle chunky food that requires chewing. The rapid introduction of table food to a child like that may lead to choking and create a setback to the desensitization process.

During the desensitization process, the infant has to be reinforced for swallowing the food. This behavioral manipulation of the infant's eating frequently leads to external regulation of eating in response to the reinforcers. Once the infant has become comfortable with eating, it is important to phase out these external reinforcers to allow the infant to regain internal regulation of eating in response to hunger and fullness. This can be a difficult transition because many infants gain control over their parents' emotions by eating or not eating. The techniques described under infantile anorexia—the implementation of food rules—can be helpful in making this transition.

In summary, the posttraumatic feeding disorder is a complex disorder that frequently requires a multidisciplinary team approach for successful intervention.

Clinical Vignette 4

Laurie was referred for a psychiatric evaluation when she was 14 months of age because she refused to eat any solid food and lived entirely on bottles. The mother reported that Laurie was a good feeder until she was 8 months old, when she choked on a Cheerio. Because Laurie had done well eating baby food, the mother wanted to introduce her to finger food, but when Laurie put the first Cheerio in her mouth, she gagged, started to cough, and turned blue. The mother turned Laurie upside down, and the Cheerio came out. Laurie cried fearfully afterward and refused to accept any more food. The next day, Laurie accepted the bottle but cried when the mother put her in the highchair, and she refused to open her mouth when the mother wanted to give her baby food. The mother tried repeatedly to feed Laurie with the spoon but noted that Laurie started crying when she saw the spoon. When the mother tried to pry open Laurie's mouth with the spoon, Laurie started gagging and vomited. After that incident, the mother gave up her efforts to feed Laurie with the spoon. She started thickening the milk to give her more calories through the bottle, hoping that eventually Laurie would accept solid food. However, each time the mother tried to reintroduce the spoon, Laurie started crying and turned away from her. The mother noted that all her coaxing, begging, and distracting of Laurie with toys had gotten her nowhere and that Laurie remained as unwilling to accept any food as she had been since she choked on the Cheerio.

Laurie was the first child of her parents, conceived after several years of infertility. Both of her parents were professionals, but her mother had stayed home since Laurie's birth. Laurie was born 2 months prematurely and had hyaline membrane disease and bronchopulmonary dysplasia, which kept her in the hospital for the first 4 months of her life. In spite of her pulmonary disease, Laurie learned to drink from the bottle a few weeks after birth and was feeding well when she was discharged from the hospital. She continued to have some respiratory difficulties and had repeated ear infections that seemed to affect her appetite temporarily. However, her overall physical development was good, and she was growing along the 10th percentiles for weight and height until the choking incident at the age of 8 months. Since then, her weight gain had slowed, and during the 2 months before she was referred, she had not grown in length. The mother also noted that since the choking incident, Laurie's sleep pattern had changed. Laurie used to sleep through the night in her own crib, but she started to wake up and cry fearfully and could not be comforted to go back to sleep. The parents started to take Laurie in their bed, and they had not been able to effect her transition back to sleep in her crib. Subsequent to her choking episode, Laurie seemed more fretful during the day. However, after she started sleeping with her parents, she returned to being cheerful. Otherwise, she had done well developmentally. She learned to walk at the age of 13 months, and she started to say a few words shortly thereafter.

Observation of mother and infant during feeding revealed that Laurie was comfortable when given the bottle. However, the moment the mother tried to put her in the highchair, she started crying and kicking to get away from her mother. When the mother managed to get Laurie strapped in the highchair, she arched her back and intensified her crying. The mother kept calm and waited for Laurie to calm herself. This took several minutes. However, the moment the mother brought out the spoon and the food, Laurie started crying again, refused to open her mouth, arched her back, and escalated in her distress until the mother took her out of the highchair. During play, the mother and her infant engaged in pleasurable interactions while Laurie was exploring the toys.

Diagnostic Impression

Laurie's food refusal seemed to be precipitated by the choking incident on a Cheerio at the age of 8 months. Since that experience, she seemed to have developed a fear of eating solid food and displayed severe anticipatory anxiety when she was placed in the highchair or when she saw the spoon or food that her mother wanted to feed her. In addition, the incident seemed to have affected her sleep and resulted in her parents' taking her into their bed. Otherwise, Laurie seemed to have a good reciprocal relationship with her mother, and the rest of her emotional and cognitive development had progressed well. Although Laurie had slowed in her physical development, the nutritional evaluation revealed no specific nutritional deficiencies. However, her oral motor development was delayed and was at the level of a 7-month-old infant.

Treatment

Laurie's symptoms were explained to the parents as a posttraumatic feeding disorder, and a three-stage treatment plan was developed.

Stage 1: Laurie had to be desensitized from her anticipatory fear of eating by being provided with pleasurable experiences of the things she associated with fear. She was to be put in the highchair without being offered any food but praised for sitting in the chair and then offered a toy to play with. Later, when comfortable with being in the highchair, she could be given her bottle to drink. The next step was to teach her to drink her milk from the cup.

Clinical Vignette 4 *continued*

Once she accomplished this, she was to be given a little bowl in which to pour the milk, and she was to use a spoon to place the thickened milk in her mouth. Gradually, the milk could then be thickened more and more for Laurie's transition to smooth baby food. During this whole process, the parents were instructed to offer praise for any effort Laurie made to self-feed and to swallow the thickened milk. Once Laurie was accomplished in eating smooth baby food, she could be offered more lumpy baby food and gradually be introduced to more chunky baby food to avoid any further choking incident.

Stage 2: Whereas initially the parents were to use a lot of praise for any of Laurie's efforts, once Laurie was at the point of feeding herself baby food, the parents were to introduce the food rules to facilitate Laurie's internal regulation of eating.

Stage 3: Once Laurie was more comfortable with eating and did not display any more anticipatory anxiety about meals, a plan for her transition back into her crib was to be developed.

The parents were comfortable with the suggestions for treatment and agreed to monthly appointments to monitor Laurie's progress and to pace the desensitization schedule. The first stage of treatment, to make Laurie feel comfortable and safe in the highchair, turned out to be the most difficult. Once Laurie started to experiment with drinking from the cup, she progressed nicely and moved through the rest of the desensitization process within 3 months. The whole treatment plan, including the return to her crib, took more than a year.

RUMINATION DISORDER

Definition

DSM-IV Criteria 307.53

Rumination Disorder

A. Repeated regurgitation and rechewing of food for a period of at least 1 month following a period of normal functioning.

B. The behavior is not due to an associated gastrointestinal or other general medical condition (e.g., esophageal reflux).

C. The behavior does not occur exclusively during the course of anorexia nervosa or bulimia nervosa. If the symptoms occur exclusively during the course of mental retardation or a pervasive developmental disorder, they are sufficiently severe to warrant independent clinical attention.

Epidemiology

Rumination disorder appears to be uncommon. It seems to occur more often in boys than in girls[78] and also in individuals with mental retardation.

Etiology

Various etiological mechanisms have been proposed. Several authors have attributed rumination to an unsatisfactory mother-infant relationship,[79–81] including lack of stimulation or neglect, and sometimes to stressful life situations of the parent. Others have considered rumination a learned behavior that is maintained by special attention and that has to be unlearned by counterconditioning.[82, 83] Herbst and associates[84] considered rumination one of the symptoms of gastroesophageal reflux. Through special radiographical techniques, they observed that the classic sucking movements of the tongue occurred after the entire esophagus was remarkably distended with refluxed barium. On the basis of their experience with two adult women with a lifetime history of rumination, Blinder and colleagues[84a] postulated that opiate receptor insensitivity or reduced endorphinergic transmission may be implicated in rumination. Chatoor and coworkers[85] proposed a biopsychosocial model by which to understand rumination. Rumination can be seen along a continuum: a patient may have gastrointestinal disease, such as hiatal hernia or reflux, and little psychiatric illness at one end of the spectrum; or the converse, a patient might have no reflux and severe psychiatric illness in the mother-infant relationship at the other end of the spectrum. Reflux or a temporary illness associated with vomiting frequently precedes the rumination. At some point, the infant seems to learn to initiate vomiting and turn it into rumination to achieve self-regulation. It appears that in circumstances in which the infant fails to elicit or loses either caring attention or tension-relieving responses from the caretaker, the infant resorts to rumination as a means of self-soothing and relief of tension. Once the infant has discovered rumination as a means of self-regulation, the rumination appears to develop into a habit that is difficult to break, like other habit disorders (e.g., head banging or hair pulling).

Diagnosis

Most frequently, infants who ruminate come to the attention of professionals because of "frequent vomiting" and weight loss. Some infants ruminate primarily during the transition to sleep when left alone, and their ruminatory activity might not be readily observed. However, these infants are frequently found in a puddle of vomitus, which should raise suspicion of rumination. Other infants can be observed to posture with the back arched, to put the thumb or whole hand into the mouth, or to suck on the tongue rhythmically to initiate the regurgitation of food. Most of the regurgitated food is initially vomited, but gradually the infant appears to learn to hold more of the food in the mouth to rechew and reswallow. "Experienced" ruminators appear to be able to bring up food through repeated tongue movements. They learn to rechew and reswallow the food without loosing any of it. Their rumination can be inferred only from the movements of their cheeks and foul oral odor because of the frequent regurgitation.

In addition to taking a thorough medical history, it is important to explore the onset of vomiting and the social context under which the symptoms developed. A medical illness or a stressor in the parents' life is frequently associated with the onset of vomiting. Some parents have noticed that the infant insists on putting her or his hand in the mouth, which makes the regurgitation worse, but most parents consider the infant's regurgitation vomiting and look for a physical explanation for the symptoms.

When exploring the stressors in the mother-infant relationship, one needs to be careful neither to alienate the mother nor to add additional stress to the relationship. It is best to observe the infant in various situations with the mother, with other caretakers, and alone in the crib during the transition into sleep. These observations will help in understanding how severe the rumination is, whether it is situational or pervasive. Some infants ruminate only when left alone or when stressed in a relationship; others appear so "addicted" to the rumination that they ruminate continuously after being fed, and they become distressed if interrupted in their ruminatory activity. In addition to assessing the rumination in the infant, the mother-infant relationship and the mother's life circumstances need to be evaluated because the mother's ability to soothe and to stimulate her infant is critical for successful intervention.

Course and Natural History

The onset of rumination is frequently in the first year of life except in individuals with developmental delays, in whom the disorder may occur during later years. Rumination has also been reported to occur in adults in association with bulimia nervosa.[86, 87] In some infants and children,[88] the disorder is believed to remit spontaneously. However, electrolyte imbalance, weight loss, dehydration, and death have been reported to result from rumination,[89] and rumination should always be taken seriously.

Treatment

Diverse theories of etiology have resulted in various proposed methods of treatment. Besides surgical interventions to prevent reflux and the early use of mechanical restraints, treatment has been primarily behavioral or psychodynamic or a combination of both.

On the basis of the assumption that rumination is a learned habit reinforced by increased attention for regurgitation, unlearning by counterconditioning has been suggested. Some authors[90–92] have used electric shock after other treatment methods had failed. A number of alternative procedures of punishment, such as aversive taste stimuli (lemon juice or hot sauce), have been developed.[89, 93] Lavigne and colleagues[82] have pointed to the difficulties of the use of aversive taste stimuli as punishment. Frequently, the infants are out of reach of the caretakers when they ruminate; consequently, the use of the lemon juice or hot sauce is inconsistent, and this delays learning. Some infants appear to become adapted to these aversive taste stimuli. These authors suggest scolding the infant by shouting no, placing the infant down, and leaving the room for 2 minutes immediately on initiation of rumination by the infant. If the infant is not ruminating on the caretaker's return, he or she is to be picked up, washed, and played with as a reward.

Whitehead and associates[94] made a distinction between two behavioral causes of rumination: 1) reward learning through increased attention for regurgitation and 2) social deprivation. Whereas punishment with time-out may be necessary for the first type, these authors consider holding the child for 10 to 15 minutes before, during, and after meals as the treatment of choice for the second type. Richmond and Eddy[95] were early proponents of a psychodynamic approach based on the assumption that rumination results from a disturbance in the mother-infant relationship. Mothers of ruminating infants were frequently found to be overwhelmed by their personal lives, which made them unavailable or tense in their relationship with their infants. Psychotherapy for the mother[96, 97] and environmental changes that produce enhanced mothering[98] have been proposed.

Before embarking on treatment, Chatoor and coworkers[85] suggested looking at each child and the child's mother individually. The diagnostic evaluation needs to determine whether the infant's rumination is situational or pervasive, whether the infant has learned to ruminate because of little stimulation and gratification from the mother, or whether the rumination serves the infant as a way of relieving tension in a stressed mother-infant relationship. After an understanding of the mother's situation has been gained, treatment is best individualized by use of a combination of psychodynamic and behavioral interventions to enhance the mother-infant relationship in general and to address the symptom of rumination in particular.

PICA

Definition

Young children with this disorder typically eat plaster, paper, paint, cloth, hair, insects, animal droppings, sand, pebbles, and dirt.

DSM-IV Criteria 307.52

A. Persistent eating of nonnutritive substances for a period of at least 1 month.

B. The eating of nonnutritive substances is inappropriate to the developmental level.

C. The eating behavior is not part of a culturally sanctioned practice.

D. If the eating behavior occurs exclusively during the course of another mental disorder (e.g., mental retardation, pervasive developmental disorder, schizophrenia), it is sufficiently severe to warrant independent clinical attention.

Epidemiology

The onset of pica is usually during the toddler age between 12 and 24 months. Because infants commonly mouth objects, it is difficult to make the diagnosis in young infants. In a survey of 12- to 36-month-old toddlers in a pediatric clinic with a population representing a broad spectrum of races and socioeconomic backgrounds, Chatoor and associates[22] reported that 22% of the mothers observed their children putting nonnutritive substances in their mouth. There was an almost linear decline of this behavior with age; 75% of 12-month-old infants were reported to put nonfood objects in their mouth, compared with an average of 15% of

2- to 3-year-old toddlers who engaged in this behavior. Most of these toddlers (88%) were good eaters, and their mothers had little concern about their growth. Estimates of the prevalence of pica among institutionalized mentally retarded individuals range from 10% to 33%.[99, 100]

The clinical profile of 108 children aged 1.5 to 10 years who practiced pica was compared with that of 50 children of the same age range without pica by Robinson and coworkers.[101] Of the patients with pica, 85% were younger than 5 years; 29% were 1.5 to 2 years of age. The male/female ratio was 1:1.4. The most common form of pica was geophagia (eating of clay, dirt, or sand). The family history for pica was positive in 41% of the patients. The authors concluded that these children with pica were more susceptible to malnutrition, anemia, diarrhea or constipation, and worm infestation. Millican and colleagues,[102] who surveyed the prevalence of pica in three groups of children aged 1 to 6 years, reported that pica occurred in 32% of an African-American low-income group and in 10% of a white middle- and upper-class population; it was highest (55%) in a group of children hospitalized for accidental poisoning. Millican and colleagues[102] observed that 63% of mothers with children with pica had pica themselves, and Gutelius and coworkers[103] reported that 87% of children with pica had either mothers or siblings with pica.

Etiology

Various theories have been proposed to explain the phenomenon of pica. Organic, psychodynamic, socioeconomic, and cultural factors have been implicated in the cause of this disorder. Some authors have suggested that inadequate dietary intake of iron and calcium leading to abnormal cravings may induce pica.[104–106] Reports that iron deficiency[107] and a low-calcium diet[108] induce pica in animals have supported this hypothesis. Other authors[109–111] have implicated psychosocial stress, maternal deprivation, parental neglect and abuse, and disorganized and impoverished family situations in the etiology of pica. In certain population groups, cultural acceptance of pica has been considered an important factor in the etiology of this disorder as well.[112–114]

Millican and colleagues[115] proposed a multifactorial etiology, whereby constitutional, developmental, familial, socioeconomic, and cultural factors interact with each other. These authors noted that the children who engaged in pica had experienced frequent separations from one or both parents followed by replacement of rapidly changing, inadequate caretakers who seemed to encourage oral gratification in response to the child's distress. They observed that these children showed a high degree of other oral activities (e.g., thumb-sucking or nail-biting). Millican and colleagues[115] interpreted the pica behavior of these young children as a distorted form of seeking gratification caused by the lack of parental availability and nurture.

Diagnosis

Because mouthing of objects is still common in toddlers between 1 and 2 years, the diagnosis of pica should be made only if the behavior is persistent and inappropriate for the child's developmental level. The diagnosis of pica should be explored in children with accidental poisoning, with lead intoxication, or with worm infestation. Young children with signs of malnutrition or iron deficiency should also be considered for the diagnosis of pica.

The assessment should include the history of the child's development in general and feeding in particular. Special attention should be given to other oral activities (e.g., thumb-sucking or nail-biting) that the child may use for self-soothing and relief of tension. In addition, the home environment and the parents' relationship with each other and with the child need to be explored to assess the parents' availability to nurture and supervise the child. Above all, mother and child should be observed during a meal and during play to gain a better understanding of their relationship and how the symptoms of pica can be understood in the context of that relationship.

If the diagnosis of pica is established, it is critical that the child undergo a thorough physical examination to rule out any of the complications associated with this disorder, such as nutritional deficiencies (especially iron deficiency), lead poisoning, intestinal infections (toxoplasmosis or intestinal parasites), or gastrointestinal bezoars.[116, 117]

Course and Natural History

In many instances, the disorder is believed to be self-limited and to remit spontaneously after a few months. However, Millican and coworkers[102] pointed to the seriousness of the developmental impact of the disorder in some children. The younger children were somewhat retarded in the use of their speech and showed conflicts about their dependency needs and aggressive feelings. Half of the adolescents evidenced some degree of depression; several had passive dependent or borderline personality disorders, engaged in other forms of disturbed oral activities (e.g., thumb-sucking, nail-biting), and abused tobacco, alcohol, or drugs. Marchi and Cohen[25] demonstrated a strong relationship between pica in childhood and symptoms of bulimia nervosa in adolescence.

Treatment

In treating pica, one must consider the various factors that appear to contribute to the development of pica as well as its complications. It is important to treat the child medically while addressing the psychosocial needs of the child and the child's family as well. The mothers need to be made aware of the dangers of pica and should be enlisted in providing a childproof environment. This might include removing lead from paint in old substandard housing units or instituting anthelmintic therapy for family pets.[116] Lourie[109] proposed a psychoeducational treatment approach that in addition to teaching the mothers the dangers of pica would also provide social support to help them become more available to their children. Other investigators have used aversive and nonaversive behavioral therapy,[99] physical restraints,[118] environmental enrichment with group or individual play,[110] and time-out and overcorrection[119] to treat this disorder.

In conclusion, a comprehensive evaluation should determine which type of treatment is best suited for the individual child and her or his family.

References

1. Benoit D: Phenomenology and treatment of failure to thrive. Child Adolesc Psychiatr Clin North Am 1993; 2:61–73.
2. Budd KS, McGraw TE, Fabisz R, et al: Psychosocial concomitant of children's feeding disorders. J Pediatr Psychol 1992; 17:91–94.

3. Woolston JL: Eating disorders in infancy and early childhood. J Am Acad Child Adolesc Psychiatry 1983; 22:114–121.
4. Sanders MR, Patel RK, Legrice B, et al: Children with persistent feeding difficulties: An observational analysis of the feeding interaction of problem and non-problem eaters. Health Psychol 1993; 12:64–74.
5. Singer L, Ambuel B, Wade S, et al: Cognitive-behavioral treatment of health-impairing food phobias in children. J Am Acad Child Adolesc Psychiatry 1992; 31:847–852.
6. Caldwell BM: The effects of psychosocial deprivation on human development in infancy. In Chess S, Thomas A (eds): Annual Progress in Child Psychiatry and Child Development. New York: Brunner/Mazel, 1971:3–22.
7. Patton RG, Gardner LI: Influence of family environment on growth: The syndrome of "maternal deprivation." Pediatrics 1962; 12:957–962.
8. Reinhart JB: Failure to thrive. In Noshpitz JD (ed): Basic Handbook of Child Psychiatry, Volume II. New York: Basic Books, 1979:593–599.
9. Homer C, Ludwig S: Categorization of etiology of failure to thrive. Am J Dis Child 1981; 135:848–851.
10. Casey PH, Bradley R, Wortham B: Social and nonsocial home environments and infants with nonorganic failure to thrive. Pediatrics 1984; 73:348–353.
11. Wing JK: International variations in psychiatric diagnosis. Triangle 1973; 12:31–36.
12. Wing JK: The concept of disease in psychiatry. J R Soc Med 1979; 72:316–321.
13. Chatoor I, Schaefer S, Dickson L, et al: Nonorganic failure to thrive: A developmental perspective. Pediatr Ann 1984; 13:829–843.
14. Chatoor I, Dickson L, Schaefer S, et al: A developmental classification of feeding disorders associated with failure to thrive: Diagnosis and treatment. In Drotar D (ed): New Directions in Failure to Thrive: Research and Clinical Practice. New York: Plenum Publishing, 1985:235–258.
15. Anders TF: Clinical syndromes, relationship disturbances and their assessment. In Sameroff AJ, Emde RN (eds): Relationship Disturbances in Early Childhood. New York: Basic Books, 1989:125–144.
16. Chatoor I, Conley C, Dickson L: Food refusal after an incident of choking: A posttraumatic eating disorder. J Am Acad Child Adolesc Psychiatry 1988; 27:105–110.
17. Chatoor I: Eating and nutritional disorders of infancy and early childhood. In Wiener J (ed): Textbook of Child and Adolescent Psychiatry. Washington, DC: American Psychiatric Press, 1991:351–361.
18. Jenkins S, Bax M, Hart H: Behavior problems in pre-school children. J Child Psychol Psychiatry 1980; 21:5–17.
19. Palmer S, Horn S: Feeding problems in children. In Palmer S, Ekvall S (eds): Pediatric Nutrition in Developmental Disorders. Springfield, IL: Charles C Thomas, 1978:107–129.
20. Richman N: A community survey of characteristics of one to two year olds with sleep disturbances. J Am Acad Child Adolesc Psychiatry 1981; 20:281–291.
21. Satter E: The feeding relationship: Problems and interventions. J Pediatr 1990; 12:115–120.
22. Chatoor I, Hamburger E, Fullard R, et al: A survey of picky eating and pica behaviors in toddlers. In Scientific Proceedings of the Annual Meeting of the American Academy of Child and Adolescent Psychiatry; October 1994; 10:50; New York, NY.
23. Dahl M, Sundelin C: Early feeding problems in an affluent society—I. Categories and clinical signs. Acta Paediatr Scand 1986; 75:370–379.
24. Dahl M, Sundelin C: Feeding problems in an affluent society. Follow-up at four years of age in children with early refusal to eat. Acta Paediatr Scand 1992; 81:575–579.
25. Marchi M, Cohen P: Early childhood eating behaviors and adolescent eating disorders. J Am Acad Child Adolesc Psychiatry 1990; 29:112–117.
26. Bithany WG, Dubowitz H: Organic concomitants of nonorganic failure to thrive: Implications for research. In Drotar D (ed): New Directions in Failure to Thrive: Implications for Research and Practice. New York: Plenum Publishing, 1985:47–68.
27. Woolston JL: Diagnostic classification: The current challenge in failure to thrive syndrome research. In Drotar D (ed): New Directions in Failure to Thrive: Implications for Research and Practice. New York: Plenum Publishing, 1985:225–235.
28. Lieberman A, Birch M: The etiology of failure to thrive: An interactional developmental approach. In Drotar D (ed): New Directions in Failure to Thrive: Research and Clinical Practice. New York: Plenum Publishing, 1985:250–277.
29. Linscheid TR, Rasnake LK: Behavioral approaches to the treatment of failure to thrive. In Drotar D (ed): New Directions in Failure to Thrive: Research and Clinical Practice. New York: Plenum Publishing, 1985:279–294.
30. Drotar D: Behavioral diagnosis in nonorganic failure to thrive: A critique and suggested approach to psychological assessment. J Dev Behav Pediatr 1989; 10:48–55.
31. Chatoor I: Diagnosis, mother-infant interaction, and treatment of three developmental feeding disorders associated with failure to thrive. Institute II: A developmental perspective on eating disorders from infancy to adulthood. Presented at the Annual Meeting of the Academy of Child and Adolescent Psychiatry; October 1991; San Francisco, CA.
32. Dowling S: Seven infants with esophageal atresia: A developmental study. Psychoanal Study Child 1977; 32:215–256.
33. Patton RG, Gardner LL: Growth Failure in Maternal Deprivation. Springfield, IL: Charles C Thomas, 1963.
34. Silver HK, Finkelstein M: Deprivation dwarfism. J Pediatr 1967; 70:317–324.
35. Crittenden PM: Non-organic failure-to-thrive: Deprivation or distortion? Infant Ment Health J 1987; 8:51–64.
36. Chatoor I: Mother-infant interactions in three developmental feeding disorders associated with failure to thrive. In Abstracts for the 60th Anniversary Meeting of the Society for Research in Child Development: March 1993: 28; New Orleans, LA.
37. Fischoff J, Witten CF, Pettit M: A psychiatric study of mothers of infants with growth failure secondary to maternal deprivation. J Pediatr 1971; 79:209–215.
38. Evans SL, Reinhart JB, Succop RA: Failure to thrive: A study of 45 children and their families. J Am Acad Child Psychiatry 1972; 11:440–457.
39. Fosson A, Wilson J: Family interactions surrounding feedings of infants with nonorganic failure to thrive. Clin Pediatr 1987; 26:518–523.
40. Polan HJ, Leon A, Kaplan MD, et al: Disturbances of affect expression in failure to thrive. J Am Acad Child Adolesc Psychiatry 1991; 30:897–903.
41. Glaser HH, Heagarty MC, Bullard DM, et al: Physical and psychological development of children with early failure to thrive. J Pediatr 1968; 73:690–698.
42. Fraiberg S, Anderson E, Shapiro U: Ghosts in the nursery. J Am Acad Child Psychiatry 1975; 14:387–421.
43. Drotar D, Sturm LA: Paternal influences in nonorganic failure to thrive: Implications for psychosocial management. Infant Ment Health J 1987; 8:37–50.
44. Benoit D, Zeanah CH, Barton ML: Maternal attachment disturbances in failure to thrive. Infant Ment Health J 1989; 10:185–202.
45. Drotar D, Eckerle D: The family environment in nonorganic failure to thrive: A controlled study. J Pediatr Psychol 1989; 14:245–257.
46. Mitchell W, Gorrell R, Greenberg R: Failure-to-thrive: A study in a primary care setting. Epidemiology and follow-up. Pediatrics 1980; 65:971–977.
47. Stewart RF: The family that fails to thrive. In Hymovich DP, Barnard MU (eds): Family Health Care. New York: McGraw-Hill, 1973:341–364.
48. Weston J, Colloton M: A legacy of violence in nonorganic failure to thrive. Child Abuse Negl 1993; 17:709–714.
49. Altemeier WA, O'Connor SM, Sherrod KB, et al: Prospective study of antecedents for nonorganic failure to thrive. J Pediatr 1985; 106:360–365.
50. Drotar D, Malone CA: Family-oriented intervention in failure to thrive. In Klaus M, Robertson MO (eds): Birth Interaction and Attachment. Skillman, NJ: Johnson & Johnson Pediatric Round Table, 1982; 6:104–112.
51. Hufton IW, Oates RK: Nonorganic failure to thrive: A long-term follow-up. Pediatrics 1977; 59:73–77.
52. Ainsworth M, Blehar M, Waters E, et al: Patterns of Attachment. Hillsdale, NJ: Lawrence Erlbaum, 1978.
53. Gordon AH, Jameson JC: Infant-mother attachment in patients with nonorganic failure to thrive syndrome. J Am Acad Child Psychiatry 1979; 18:251–259.

54. Valenzuela M: Attachment in chronically underweight young children. Child Dev 1990; 61:1984–1996.
55. Powell GF, Low J: Behavior in nonorganic failure to thrive. J Dev Behav Pediatr 1983; 4:26–33.
56. Rosenn DW, Loeb LS, Jura MB: Differentiation of organic from nonorganic failure to thrive syndrome in infancy. Pediatrics 1980; 66:698–704.
57. Elmer E, Gregg GS, Ellison P: Late results of the "failure to thrive" syndrome. Clin Pediatr 1969; 8:584–589.
58. Drotar D, Sturm L: Personality development, problem solving, and behavior problems among preschool children with early histories of nonorganic failure-to-thrive: A controlled study. Dev Behav Pediatr 1992; 13:266–273.
59. Black M, Dubowitz H, Hutcheson J, et al: A randomized clinical trial of home intervention for children with failure to thrive. Pediatrics 1995; 95:807–814.
60. Sturm L, Drotar D: Prediction of weight for height following intervention in three-year-old children with early histories of non-organic failure to thrive. Child Abuse Negl 1989; 13:19–27.
61. Black M, Hutcheson J, Dubowitz H, et al: Parenting style and developmental status among children with non-organic failure to thrive. J Pediatr Psychol 1994; 19:689–707.
62. Schmitt B, Mauro R: Nonorganic failure to thrive: An outpatient approach. Child Abuse Negl 1989; 13:235–248.
63. Harris JC: Non-organic failure to thrive syndromes. In Accardo PY (ed): Failure to Thrive in Infancy and Early Childhood. Baltimore: University Park Press, 1982:240–241.
64. Ayoub C, Milner J: Failure to thrive: Parental indicators, types, and outcomes. Child Abuse Negl 1985; 9:491–499.
64a. Chatoor I, Egan Y: Nonorganic failure to thrive and dwarfism due to food refusal: A separation disorder. J Am Acad Child Psychiatry 1983; 22:294–301.
65. Chatoor I: Infantile anorexia nervosa: A developmental disorder of separation and individuation. J Am Acad Psychoanal 1989; 17:43–64.
66. Chatoor I, Egan J, Getson P, et al: Mother-infant interactions in infantile anorexia nervosa. J Am Acad Child Adolesc Psychiatry 1988; 27:535–540.
67. Chatoor I, Kerzner B, Zorc L, et al: Two-year old twins refuse to eat: A multidisciplinary approach to diagnosis and treatment. Infant Ment Health J 1992; 13:252–268.
68. Linscheid TR, Tarnowski KJ, Rasnake LK, et al: Behavioral treatment of food refusal in a child with short-gut syndrome. J Pediatr Psychol 1987; 12:451–459.
69. Ramsay M, Zelazo P: Food refusal in failure to thrive infants: Nasogastric feeding combined with interactive behavioral treatment. J Pediatr Psychol 1988; 13:329–347.
70. Seigel L: Classical and operant procedures in the treatment of a case of food aversion in a young child. J Clin Child Psychol 1982; 11:167–172.
71. Geerstma MA, Hyams J, Pelletier J, et al: Feeding resistance after parenteral hyperalimentation. Am J Dis Child 1985; 139:255–256.
72. Benoit D: Assessment and treatment of infant feeding disorders. Presented at the 37th Annual Meeting of the American Academy of Child and Adolescent Psychiatry; October 1990; Chicago, IL.
73. Hirsig J, Baals H, Tuchsmid P, et al: Dumping syndrome following Nissen's fundoplication: A cause for refusal to feed. J Pediatr Surg 1984; 19:155–159.
74. Richard ME: Feeding the newborn with cleft lip and/or palate: The enlargement stimulate swallow rest (ESSR) method. J Pediatr Nurs 1991; 6:317–321.
75. Singer LT, Nofar JA, Benson-Szekely LT, et al: Behavioral assessment and management of food refusal in children with cystic fibrosis. J Dev Behav Pediatr 1991; 12:115–120.
76. Chatoor I, Wald M, Choy M, et al: Differential diagnosis of food refusal in infants and toddlers. In Scientific Proceedings of the Annual Meeting of the American Academy of Child and Adolescent Psychiatry, October 1994; 10:50; New York, NY.
77. Chatoor I, Kerzner B, Menvielle E, et al: A multidisciplinary team approach to complex feeding disorders in technology dependent infants. Symposium presented at the Fifth Biennial National Training Institute; 1987; Washington, DC.
78. Mayes SD, Humphrey FJ, Handford HA, et al: Rumination disorder: Differential diagnosis. J Am Acad Child Adolesc Psychiatry 1988; 27:300–302.
79. Flanagan CH: Rumination in infancy—past and present. J Am Acad Child Psychiatry 1977; 16:140–149.
80. Lourie RS: Experience with therapy of psychosomatic problems in infants. In Hoch PH, Zubin J (eds): Psychopathology of Children. New York: Grune & Stratton, 1954.
81. Sheinbein M: Treatment for the hospitalized infantile ruminator: Programmed brief social reinforcers. Clin Pediatr 1975; 14:719–724.
82. Lavigne JV, Burns WJ, Cotter PD: Rumination in infancy: Recent behavioral approaches. Int J Eating Disord 1981; 1:70–82.
83. Winton ASW, Singhi NN: Rumination in pediatric populations: A behavioral analysis. J Am Acad Child Psychiatry 1983; 22:269–275.
84. Herbst J, Friedland GW, Zboraliski FF: Hiatal hernia and rumination in infants and children. J Pediatr 1971; 78:261–265.
84a. Blinder BJ, Bain N, Simpson R: Evidence for an opioid neurotransmission mechanism in adult rumination. [letter] Am J Psychiatry 1986; 143:225.
85. Chatoor I, Dickson L, Einhorn A: Rumination: Etiology and treatment. Pediatr Ann 1984; 13:924–929.
86. Fairburn CG, Cooper PJ: Rumination in bulimia nervosa. Br Med J 1984; 288:826–827.
87. Larocca FE: Rumination in patients with eating disorders. [letter] Am J Psychiatry 1988; 145:1610.
88. Reis S: Rumination in two developmentally normal children: Case report and review of the literature. J Fam Pract 1994; 38:521–523.
89. Sajwaj JL, Agras SL: Lemon-juice therapy: The control of life-threatening rumination in a six-month-old infant. J Appl Behav Anal 1974; 7:557–563.
90. Bright GO, Whaley DL: Suppression of regurgitation and rumination with aversive agents. Mich Ment Health Res Bull 1968; 2:17–20.
91. Lang PJ, Melamed BG: Avoidance conditioning therapy of an infant with chronic ruminative vomiting. J Abnorm Psychol 1969; 74:1–8.
92. Linscheid TR, Cunningham CE: A controlled demonstration of the effectiveness of electric shock in the elimination of chronic infant rumination. J Appl Behav Anal 1977; 10:500.
93. Becker J, Turner S, Sajwaj T: Multiple behavioral effects of the use of lemon juice with a ruminating toddler-age child. Behav Modif 1978; 2:267–278.
94. Whitehead WE, Drescher VM, Movill-Corbin E, et al: Rumination syndrome in children treated by increased holding. J Pediatr Gastroenterol Nutr 1985; 4:550–556.
95. Richmond JB, Eddy E: Rumination. Pediatrics 1958; 22:49–55.
96. Menking M, Wagnitz JG: Rumination: A near fatal psychiatric disease of infancy. N Engl J Med 1969; 280:802–804.
97. Sauvage D, Leddet I, Hameury L, et al: Infantile rumination. Diagnosis and follow-up study of twenty cases. J Am Acad Child Psychiatry 1985; 24:197–203.
98. Franco K, Campbell N, Tamburrino M, et al: Rumination. The eating disorder of infancy. Child Psychiatry Hum Dev 1993; 24:91–97.
99. Danford DE, Huber AM: Pica among mentally retarded adults. Am J Ment Defic 1982; 87:141–146.
100. McAlpine C, Singhi NN: Pica in institutionalized mentally retarded persons. J Ment Defic Res 1986; 30:171–178.
101. Robinson BA, Tolan W, Golding-Beecher O: Childhood pica. Some aspects of the clinical profile in Manchester, Jamaica. West Indian Med J 1990; 39:20–26.
102. Millican FK, Lourie RS, Layman EM, et al: The prevalence of ingestion and mouthing of nonedible substances by children. Clin Proc Child Hosp DC 1962; 18:207–214.
103. Gutelius MF, Millican FK, Layman EH, et al: Children with pica: Treatment of pica with iron given intramuscularly. Pediatrics 1962; 29:1018–1023.
104. Crosby WH: Pica: A compulsion caused by iron deficiency. Br J Haematol 1976; 34:341–342.
105. Johnson NE, Tenuta K: Diets and lead blood levels of children who practice pica. Environ Res 1979; 18:369–376.
106. Singhi P, Singhi S: Pica type of "nonfood" articles eaten by Ajmer children and their significance. Indian J Pediatr 1982; 49:681–684.
107. Woods SC, Wessinger RS: Pagophasia in the albino rat. Science 1970; 169:1334–1336.
108. Jacobson JL, Snowdon CT: Increased lead ingestion in calcium deficient monkeys. Nature 1976; 162:51–52.
109. Lourie RS: Pica and lead poisoning. Am J Orthopsychiatry 1977; 41:697–699.
110. Madden NA, Russo DC, Michael FC: Environmental influences on

mouthing in children with lead intoxication. J Pediatr Psychol 1980; 5:207–216.
111. Singhi S, Singhi P, Adwani GB: Role of psychosocial stress in the case of pica. Clin Pediatr 1981; 20:783–785.
112. Danford DE: Pica and nutrition. Annu Rev Nutr 1982; 2:303–322.
113. Forsyth CJ, Benoit GM: "Rare ole dirty snacks": Some research notes on dirt eating. Deviant Behav 1989; 10:61–68.
114. Vermeer DE, Frate DA: Geophagia in rural Mississippi: Environmental and cultural contexts and nutritional implications. Am J Clin Nutr 1979; 32:2129–2135.
115. Millican FK, Dublin CC, Lourie RS: Pica. In Noshpitz JD (ed): Basic Handbook of Child Psychiatry, Volume II, Disturbances in Development. New York: Basic Books, 1979:660–666.
116. Sayetta RB: Pica: An overview. Am Fam Physician 1986; 33:181–185.
117. Glickman LT, Cypess RH, Crumrine PK, et al: *Toxocara* infection and epilepsy in children. J Pediatr 1979; 94:75–78.
118. Singhi NN, Bakker LW: Suppression of pica by overcorrection and physical restraint: A comparative analysis. J Autism Dev Disord 1984; 14:331–341.
119. Foxx RM, Martin ED: Treatment of scavenging behavior (coprophagy and pica) by overcorrection. Behav Res Ther 1975; 13:153–162.

CHAPTER

38 Tic Disorders

John T. Walkup
Mark A. Riddle

Tourette's Disorder
Chronic Motor or Vocal Tic Disorder
Transient Tic Disorder

It has been more than 100 years since Gilles de la Tourette first described the *maladie de tic* that now bears his name, Tourette's disorder. In the past 20 years, efforts to increase awareness of Tourette's disorder and the other tic disorders, improve diagnostic accuracy, decrease stigma, and stimulate research have largely been successful. The tic disorders are much less rare than previously thought. Persons with tics, especially children, are able to live active, productive lives with less overt stigma, and the research in Tourette's disorder has become a model for research in the other neuropsychiatric disorders. Current research efforts need continued support, but the next phase of the challenge is to develop a deeper understanding of the etiology and treatment of these often complex disorders. In spite of significant scientific advances, clinical understanding and treatment approaches are sometimes inadequate for the difficult clinical problems that some of these patients present to their psychiatrists.[1–3]

Various neurological and psychiatric causes for Tourette's disorder and the other tic disorders have been proposed and, at times, have competed in the medical literature. Yet the needs of patients with Tourette's disorder and the other tic disorders are not served by dichotomous approaches. Patients with tic disorders are often affected with nontic, brain-based behavioral and emotional problems that are the substance of their impairment. Modern psychiatrists are ideally suited to integrate and implement the research findings from neuroscience and psychology into modern treatment approaches. The goal of this chapter is to update and review our knowledge base and discuss approaches to the often complex treatment needs of patients with Tourette's disorder and the other tic disorders.

Phenomenology and Diagnostic Criteria

Tics

Tourette's disorder is the most notable of the tic disorders. The cardinal features of Tourette's disorder and the other tic disorders are motor and vocal tics. Motor tics are usually brief, rapid, and stereotyped movements but can also be slower, more rhythmical, or dystonic in nature. Simple motor tics are movements of individual muscle groups and include brief movements such as eye blinking, head shaking, and shoulder shrugging. Complex motor tics involve multiple muscle groups, such as a simultaneous eye deviation, head turn, and shoulder shrug. Some complex tics appear more purposeful, such as stereotyped hopping, touching, rubbing, or obscene gestures (copropraxia). Vocal tics are usually brief, staccato-like sounds but can also be words or phrases. Simple vocal tics, often caused by the forceful movement of air through the nose and mouth, include sniffing, throat clearing, grunting, or barking-type sounds. Complex vocal tics usually include words, phrases, or the repetition of one's own words or the words of others. Coprolalia, often incorrectly considered essential for the diagnosis of Tourette's disorder, is infrequent; only 2% to 6% of cases are affected.[4]

Tics most often begin in childhood, wax and wane in severity, and change in character and quality over time. Tics are exacerbated by excitement and tension and can attenuate during periods of focused, productive activity and sleep. Tics are involuntary, yet because they are briefly suppressible or can be triggered by an environmental stimulus (e.g., mimicking another person's movement, speech, or behavior), they may appear as volitional acts. If the tic is resisted, tension can develop until it is released by completion of the tic. In some individuals, tics are preceded or provoked by a thought or physical sensation referred to as a premonitory urge.[5]

Diagnostic Criteria for the Tic Disorders

There are four diagnostic categories included in the tic disorders section of the *Diagnostic and Statistical Manual of Mental Disorders,* Fourth Edition (DSM-IV)[6]: 1) Tourette's disorder; 2) chronic motor or vocal tic disorder (CT); 3) transient tic disorder; and 4) tic disorder not otherwise specified, which is a residual category for tic disorders not meeting the duration or age criteria of the other categories. In general, diagnostic decisions are based on whether both

DSM-IV Criteria 307.23

Tourette's Disorder

A. Both multiple motor and one or more vocal tics have been present at some time during the illness, although not necessarily concurrently. (A *tic* is a sudden, rapid, recurrent, nonrhythmic, stereotyped motor movement or vocalization.)

B. The tics occur many times a day (usually in bouts) nearly every day or intermittently throughout a period of more than 1 year, and during this period there was never a tic-free period of more than 3 consecutive months.

C. The disturbance causes marked distress or significant impairment in social, occupational, or other important areas of functioning.

D. The onset is before age 18 years.

E. The disturbance is not due to the direct physiological effects of a substance (e.g., stimulants) or a general medical condition (e.g., Huntington's disease or postviral encephalitis).

DSM-IV Criteria 307.21

Transient Tic Disorder

A. Single or multiple motor and/or vocal tics (i.e., sudden, rapid, recurrent, nonrhythmic, stereotyped motor movements or vocalizations).

B. The tics occur many times a day, nearly every day for at least 4 weeks, but for no longer than 12 consecutive months.

C. The disturbance causes marked distress or significant impairment in social, occupational, or other important areas of functioning.

D. The onset is before age 18 years.

E. The disturbance is not due to the direct physiological effects of a substance (e.g., stimulants) or a general medical condition (e.g., Huntington's disease or postviral encephalitis).

F. Criteria have never been met for Tourette's disorder or chronic motor or vocal tic disorder.

Specify if:

Single episode or **recurrent**

DSM-IV Criteria 307.22

Chronic Motor or Vocal Tic Disorder

A. Single or multiple motor or vocal tics (i.e., sudden, rapid, recurrent, nonrhythmic, stereotyped motor movements or vocalizations), but not both, have been present at some time during the illness.

B. The tics occur many times a day nearly every day or intermittently throughout a period of more than 1 year, and during this period there was never a tic-free period of more than 3 consecutive months.

C. The disturbance causes marked distress or significant impairment in social, occupational, or other important areas of functioning.

D. The onset is before age 18 years.

E. The disturbance is not due to the direct physiological effects of a substance (e.g., stimulants) or a general medical condition (e.g., Huntington's disease or postviral encephalitis).

F. Criteria have never been met for Tourette's disorder.

motor and phonic tics are present, duration of time affected with tics, age at onset, and lack of another medical cause for the tics. In DSM-IV, an impairment criterion was added to the diagnostic criteria.

Other diagnostic schemas have been developed for research purposes and include special diagnostic modifiers.[7] For example, tic disorders that are not witnessed by a knowledgeable observer are deemed tic disorders *by history;* the modifiers *probable* and *definite* are added as estimates of diagnostic confidence of a tic disorder diagnosis.

Epidemiology

Incidence and Prevalence

Tic disorders, especially Tourette's disorder, have historically been viewed as rare conditions. With the availability of improved epidemiological studies and more clearly defined diagnostic criteria, better estimates of the prevalence are available. Tic disorders appear to be common (1:100), whereas Tourette's disorder is less common (5:10,000) but not as rare as previously thought.[8–11] In spite of the improvement in epidemiological methods, there continue to be methodological problems that probably result in underestimates of the prevalence of all tic disorders.

The most scientifically rigorous epidemiological study to date has used a three-stage screening process to identify the lifetime occurrence of tic symptoms in all young people ages 16 to 17 years (N = 28,000) reporting for initial entry into mandatory military service in Israel.[11] Combined prevalence rates of Tourette's disorder for male and female subjects in this sample were approximately 5 per 10,000; the relative frequency of males to females was 1.67:1. Methodological problems in this study that may have led to an underestimate of the number of affected individuals included 1) subjects with mild, nonimpairing symptoms not observed during the face-to-face encounter may not have been diagnosed; 2) subjects may have been unaware of their symptoms and did not report them; 3) subjects may have attributed their tics to other causes; and 4) subjects (armed forces recruits) may have been reluctant to acknowledge the presence of symptoms because it may have had an impact on their armed forces experience.

By use of an extended direct observation in a natural setting, the prevalence rate of tics in a sample of more than 3000 students in a single school district was 10.5 and 1.3 per 1000 for male and female students, respectively.[12] There are methodological concerns about this work also, in that special education students were oversampled. However, the prevalence rate in this study more closely approximates the prevalence rates estimated by other experts.[8]

Frequently Co-occurring Symptoms or Disorders

There is considerable evidence that in clinically ascertained subjects with Tourette's disorder, there is a broad array of co-occurring clinical problems. These co-occurring problems can be more disabling than tics and are often the reason that patients seek clinical attention. The clinical range of these problems is broad and includes problems with mood, impulse control, obsessive-compulsive behaviors, anxiety, attention and learning problems, and conduct problems. In some patients, these problems reach diagnosable proportions, but in many others, they are less severe and do not fulfill diagnostic criteria. The most common co-occurring disorders are attention-deficit/hyperactivity disorder (ADHD; 50% to 60%) and obsessive-compulsive disorder (OCD; 30% to 70%). The exact relationship of these problems to Tourette's disorder is controversial and the subject of intensive research efforts.

Attention-Deficit/Hyperactivity Disorder. Upward of 50% of clinically ascertained children and adolescents with Tourette's disorder may be affected with problems of attention, concentration, activity level, or impulse control.[13, 14] In community-based epidemiological samples of subjects with Tourette's disorder, the estimated frequency of ADHD is lower (8% to 41%) than in clinic populations.[10, 11] In the epidemiological study with the lowest prevalence estimate of ADHD in Tourette's disorder (8%), subjects were 16 to 17 years of age, and the assessment of ADHD focused on current affected status (point prevalence), not lifetime diagnosis.[11] Even though the point prevalence of ADHD was more that twice that seen in the general population, factors such as the age of the sample and examination for current status probably led to an underestimate of ADHD in Tourette's disorder. The difference in ADHD prevalence estimates between clinical and epidemiological samples supports the concern that the rates of comorbidity in clinical samples overestimate the true prevalence.[15]

Increasingly, adults with Tourette's disorder are recognizing the presence and impact of ADHD symptoms in their lives and are seeking treatment. There is a paucity of available information on the methods of assessment and treatment of adults with ADHD, especially adults with Tourette's disorder and ADHD. In spite of the lack of available information to guide evaluation and treatment, it is likely that psychiatrists will be requested to respond to this new clinical challenge.

Obsessive-Compulsive Symptoms. Obsessions and compulsions are stereotyped, persistent, and intrusive thoughts and behaviors that are experienced as senseless. Because many of these thoughts and behaviors can be common, persons are considered "disordered" only when the obsessions or compulsions become severe, disabling, or time-consuming. Obsessions that are commonly seen in OCD include fears of contamination, fears of harm coming to oneself or others, scrupulosity, fear of losing control of one's impulses, counting, fear of losing things, fear of being unable to remember, or experiencing images of terrible things happening. Compulsions commonly seen in OCD include repeated or stereotyped washing and grooming rituals; repeated checking of locks, switches, or doors; and repetition of other senseless rituals.

Differences in clinical phenomenology have been noted in studies of obsessions and compulsions in patients with Tourette's disorder compared with patients with OCD (without Tourette's disorder)[16] (Table 38–1). Patients with Tourette's disorder have greater concern with physical symmetry, evenness, and exactness, which are often described as "just right" phenomena,[17] and concerns with impulse control. In contrast, patients with OCD have more frequent concerns regarding contamination and more cleaning and grooming rituals than do patients with Tourette's disorder. Also, the absolute number of independent concerns appears to be greater in patients with Tourette's disorder than in patients with OCD. Patients with OCD more often have a single concern around which their symptoms coalesce, such as contamination. In contrast, patients with Tourette's

Table 38–1 Obsessions and Compulsions Characteristic of Obsessive-Compulsive Disorder and Tourette's Disorder

	Obsessive-Compulsive Disorder	Tourette's Disorder
Obsessions	Contamination Dirt and germs Body wastes Environmental	"Just right" phenomena Symmetry Blurting out obscenity Saying the right thing Violent images Sexual thoughts Embarrassment
Compulsions	Cleaning	Touching Blinking Repeating Self-injurious behavior Hoarding Counting Ordering

Adapted from George MS, Trimble MR, Ring HA, et al: Obsessions in obsessive-compulsive disorder with and without Gilles de la Tourette's syndrome. Am J Psychiatry 1993; 150:93–97. Copyright 1993, the American Psychiatric Association. Reprinted by permission.

disorder may have multiple concerns, such as symmetry, violent or sexual images or urges, worries about losing control, or counting. Some investigators have argued that the obsessions and compulsions in Tourette's disorder are more sensory-motor in character, whereas those in OCD are more cognitive and autonomic.[18]

Relationship of the Commonly Co-occurring Symptoms and Conditions with Tourette's Disorder

There is general agreement that chronic tics are a milder form of Tourette's disorder and that OCD is an alternative expression of the Tourette's disorder genetic diathesis.[19] Research efforts to understand the relationship of Tourette's disorder to other disorders have yielded conflicting results. Some studies support a broad Tourette's disorder phenotype, whereas others identify a more circumscribed phenotype. The two major hypotheses regarding the relationship of Tourette's disorder to co-occurring disorders are presented here.

- The putative Tourette's disorder gene is responsible for Tourette's disorder, CT, OCD, and some forms of ADHD in Tourette's disorder probands and their families. Other disorders that commonly co-occur in Tourette's disorder subjects are not associated with Tourette's disorder and are not part of the Tourette's disorder phenotype. The co-occurrence of these other disorders with Tourette's disorder reflects either ascertainment bias in the sample or the development of disorders secondary to living with Tourette's disorder.

The work of Pauls and colleagues best represents this viewpoint. After their seminal work identifying the genetic relationship of Tourette's disorder to CT and OCD,[20] this research group has undertaken efforts to identify the relationship of Tourette's disorder to other disorders commonly seen in patients with Tourette's disorder. Particular controversy surrounds the relationship of ADHD with Tourette's disorder. In spite of the high frequency of co-occurrence of ADHD with Tourette's disorder, the first family study[14] that formally evaluated the association of Tourette's disorder and ADHD did not identify ADHD as an alternative manifestation of the Tourette's disorder gene. In a subsequent study, Pauls and colleagues[21] found that first-degree relatives of probands with Tourette's disorder are at increased risk for ADHD. The results were interpreted as follows. ADHD in the absence of tics is not a variant expression of the Tourette's disorder gene. If the disorders do co-occur, and ADHD develops before Tourette's disorder, then ADHD is independent of Tourette's disorder. If ADHD develops after Tourette's disorder, then it is likely that the ADHD is secondary to Tourette's disorder. This finding is supported by the increased rates of ADHD in families in which the proband had early-onset (primary and independent) ADHD compared with families in which the proband had late-onset (secondary and associated) ADHD. In the same study, speech problems, stuttering, and learning disabilities were not found to be variable expressions of the Tourette's disorder gene, and first-degree relatives do not appear to be at increased risk for the development of these disorders.

Similar methods were used in a study of the co-occurrence of phobias, generalized anxiety disorder, panic disorder, and major depressive disorder in probands with Tourette's disorder and their families.[22] The elevated rates of affective and anxiety disorders in probands and their families compared with control subjects were due primarily to the presence of these disorders in subjects affected with OCD. Rates of affective and anxiety disorders were not elevated in relatives unaffected by Tourette's disorder, CT, or OCD, suggesting that affective and anxiety disorders were not alternative expressions of the Tourette's disorder gene but were related to OCD.

- The putative Tourette's disorder gene is responsible for Tourette's disorder and the frequently associated psychiatric and behavioral problems seen in Tourette's disorder subjects.

The work of Comings and colleagues best represents this view. They posited in a series of papers[23] that a Tourette's disorder genetic factor is the underlying cause of Tourette's disorder and the comorbid conditions seen in patients with Tourette's disorder. This series of papers is based on a large sample of Tourette's disorder probands (N = 247) and their families. The subjects were evaluated by use of a combination of the family study method (i.e., direct interviews) and the family history method (i.e., single informant). The results suggest that a number of disorders including ADHD, learning disorders (LDs), obsessive-compulsive behaviors, disruptive behavior disorders, affective disorders including mania, major anxiety disorders, addictive disorders, and a variety of impulse-control problems are associated with Tourette's disorder. In this sense, Tourette's disorder is considered a spectrum disorder similar to other psychiatric disorders (e.g., affective spectrum disorders) that appear to overlap clinically or to have genetic or pathophysiological similarities.[24] These investigators further suggest that the putative Tourette's disorder gene is the major etiological factor causing the disturbances of serotonin and dopamine that underlie all these psychiatric conditions even when they are not seen in association with Tourette's disorder. Detractors describe methodological problems with this large series of studies, including lack of reliable family data (family history data, not family study data), ascertainment bias, and lack of rigorous diagnostic and severity criteria. The authors have responded to criticisms of their work by identifying logical flaws in the arguments of their detractors, especially the assumptions regarding ascertainment bias and the superiority of the family study method to the family history method for family studies.

Etiology

Genetics

Comparison of the concordance rates for Tourette's disorder in monozygotic and dizygotic twins identifies Tourette's disorder as an inherited condition. The twin studies, however, are unable to identify a particular mode of genetic transmission or to identify the breadth of the clinical phenotype. To answer these questions, other research methods are required. Segregation analyses of family study data have been used to identify the pattern of genetic transmission and alternative phenotypes of the Tourette's disorder genetic diathesis. In spite of a comprehensive body of research that identifies Tourette's disorder to be the result of an autosomal dominant single major gene, controversy remains regarding the mode of transmission and the range of phenotypic expression of Tourette's disorder. Linkage studies of Tourette's disorder have also been undertaken but to date have not been successful.

Twin Studies

Evidence from twin studies suggests an important role for both genetic and nongenetic factors in the development of Tourette's disorder. Two large twin studies[25, 26] and a follow-up study[27] showed high concordance rates in monozygotic twins for Tourette's disorder (both twins have Tourette's disorder) and for tic disorders (one twin has Tourette's disorder, the other has tics but not Tourette's disorder) (Table 38–2). In both of the studies, the concordance rate for Tourette's disorder in monozygotic twins was more than 50%. When the concordance rates were calculated for the presence of any tic disorder, they approached 100%. By comparing the concordance rates of monozygotic twins with dizygotic twins, one can separate the role of genetic factors from other environmental factors. In the one study in which such a comparison was done, the concordance rate for Tourette's disorder in monozygotic twins was significantly higher than the concordance rate in dizygotic twins,[25] further suggesting a powerful role for genetics in Tourette's disorder.

Both studies identified some differences in severity between monozygotic twins and assessed the possible role of birth weight on the differences in tic severity. Using different methods, both studies identified that the lower birth weight twin had a more severe tic disorder than the higher birth weight twin,[26, 28] providing support for the role of nongenetic factors in tic symptom severity.

Models of Inheritance

Although there have been a number of family studies of Tourette's disorder,[19, 20, 23, 29, 30] there are currently two competing models of the inheritance of Tourette's disorder presented in the literature. One of the models asserts that the Tourette's disorder gene is most likely an autosomal dominant single major gene. The other model describes a more complex pattern of inheritance, the mixed model, which includes an additive single major gene with a multifactorial background. The autosomal dominant model of Tourette's disorder best reflects the work of Pauls and colleagues, and the mixed model hypothesis best reflects the work of Comings and Comings.

Table 38–2 Concordance Rates for Tics and Tourette's Disorder in Twins*

Study		Tourette's Disorder/Tourette's Disorder	Tourette's Disorder/Tics
Price et al[25]			
MZ twins	N = 30	53% (16/30)	77% (23/30)
DZ twins	N = 13	8% (1/13)	23% (3/13)
Walkup et al†[27]			
MZ twins	N = 18	88% (16/18)	100% (18/18)
Hyde et al[26]			
MZ twins	N = 16	56% (9/16)	94% (15/16)

*MZ, Monozygotic; DZ, dizygotic.

†Follow-up study of Price and coworkers,[25] N = 30.

Table 38–3 Penetrance Estimates of the Tourette's Disorder Gene for Male and Female Subjects of Various Phenotypes

Phenotype	Males	Females
Tourette's disorder alone	45%	17%
Tourette's disorder or CT	99%	56%
Tourette's disorder, CT, or OCD	100%	71%

Adapted from Pauls DL, Leckman JF: The inheritance of Gilles de la Tourette syndrome and associated behaviors: Evidence for autosomal dominant transmission. N Engl J Med 1986; 315:993–997.

The work of Pauls and colleagues strongly suggests that Tourette's disorder is genetically transmitted by a rare autosomal dominant single major gene with variable and sex-specific penetrance; the single-gene hypothesis is particularly well supported when CT and OCD are included as alternative phenotypes of the Tourette's disorder gene. For example, on the basis of results of their family study of 27 Tourette's disorder probands and 103 first-degree relatives, they posited the following. Male subjects with the Tourette's disorder gene have a 100% chance of being affected with Tourette's disorder, CT, or OCD, with the most common presentation in male subjects (99%) being either Tourette's disorder or CT. Far fewer female subjects with the Tourette's disorder gene will experience Tourette's disorder alone (17%) or a tic disorder of any type (56%). In addition, female subjects will have OCD alone (15%) more frequently than will male subjects (1%). In this study, approximately 29% of female subjects with the putative Tourette's disorder gene will remain unaffected[20] (Table 38–3).

In contrast, Comings has asserted, on the basis of the review of more than 1800 Tourette's disorder pedigrees, that Tourette's disorder is caused by a single gene that functions in a "semidominant, semirecessive" pattern of inheritance (additive). An additive model of inheritance specifies that the number of copies of the disease gene predicts the risk for disease and, perhaps, the severity of illness.[24] Thus, an individual with only one copy of the disease allele may have mild or even no symptoms; an individual with two disease alleles is more likely to express the disease and to have a more severe course of illness.

Linkage Studies

The results of the family and twin studies and the availability for research purposes of several large kindreds with multiple affected individuals have stimulated great interest in genetic linkage studies. In an effort to find the Tourette's disorder gene, the Tourette Syndrome Association has been supporting genetics research through an international consortium of investigators for almost 15 years. Five independent sites have been evaluating a number of large kindreds and pooling their efforts to identify likely sites of the Tourette's disorder gene. These linkage studies rest on a number of assumptions: 1) the clinical phenotype includes Tourette's disorder or CT; 2) the same single gene (homogeneity) is responsible for Tourette's disorder in all the families so that genome eliminated from consideration in one family can safely be eliminated from consideration in the others; and 3) the Tourette's disorder gene is an autosomal dominant single major locus. To date, nearly the entire genome has been screened, and no marker of the Tourette's disorder gene has yet been identified.[31]

Problems with the Linkage Studies. A number of hypotheses have been offered to help explain the inability of the linkage studies to identify the Tourette's disorder gene.[32, 33]

Accurate identification of affected individuals is critical to linkage analysis. Whereas both false-positive and false-negative diagnoses have an impact on linkage studies, false-positive diagnoses have the most negative impact. False-positive diagnoses occur for two reasons: 1) the identification of a phenocopy (i.e., tics or a movement problem not caused by the Tourette's disorder gene) as a "true" case and 2) mistakes in diagnosis. In the large kindreds, the frequency of individuals with chronic tics is high compared with the frequency of individuals with Tourette's disorder. For the linkage studies to have their full statistical power, inclusion of subjects with chronic tics was necessary. It is possible that some individuals with chronic tics may have movement problems not related to the Tourette's disorder genetic diathesis, creating false-positive diagnoses and skewing the result of the linkage analysis. Pauls[32] has speculated that the presence of both chronic tics and OCD symptoms in an individual may represent tics that are part of Tourette's disorder, whereas tics in the absence of OCD symptoms may indicate an alternative etiology (phenocopy). There is also a possibility that there were errors in diagnosis. Diagnosing moderate to severe Tourette's disorder can be relatively straightforward; milder cases, or cases in which there is no evidence of tics during the interview, can be difficult. Increasingly, the standards of diagnosis for genetic studies are changing so that definite diagnoses require tics to be observed by a skilled observer and subjects must be assessed repeatedly over time.

Tourette's disorder may be heterogeneous, not homogeneous. It is possible that Tourette's disorder symptoms in one person could be caused by a gene different from that causing Tourette's disorder symptoms in another person. In the current linkage studies, homogeneity is assumed, so that sections of genome excluded in one pedigree are excluded from consideration in another pedigree. Many of the centers have gone on to examine the entire genome in individual pedigrees to address the problem created by presuming Tourette's disorder to be homogeneous.

The last concern has to do with the genetic models used in linkage analysis. The available segregation analyses based on family study data suggest that an autosomal dominant model of inheritance is most likely. If the pattern of inheritance is not strictly related to a single autosomal dominant gene, it may be more difficult to identify the Tourette's disorder gene by linkage studies of multiple large kindreds. Alternative linkage study methods for Tourette's disorder are under consideration, including the multiple, affected, sib pairs method. The sib pair methodology identifies common genome among multiple sets of affected sib pairs or other combinations of relatives such as cousins. The sib pair method is less sensitive to misdiagnoses and modeling assumptions and has been used successfully to identify the multiple genes involved in juvenile-onset diabetes.[34] Comings,[24] on the basis of his family data, suggested that linkage analysis with large kindreds will not be effective and that association studies using candidate genes are the only methods that will be effective in identifying the Tourette's disorder gene or genes.

Candidate Genes

Pursuing linkage at a specific site on the genome through the use of a candidate gene is another method for identifying the genetic locus of a given disorder. The choice of a candidate gene is often related to hypotheses regarding the candidate gene and the etiology of a given disorder. In Tourette's disorder, genes involved in the dopamine system have been perceived as ideal candidate genes because of the role of dopamine antagonist medications in tic suppression. To date, none of the attempts to link known genes controlling for dopamine to Tourette's disorder has been successful.[35]

Pathophysiology

In Tourette's disorder, the complex clinical presentation suggests several neuroanatomical sites of disease as well as neurochemical substrates. Most speculation regarding the sites of neurological dysfunction in the tic disorders have focused on the basal ganglia and their interconnections with the frontal cortex and limbic system. Abnormalities in these structures could readily cause the wide variety of motor, sensory-motor, cognitive, and affective symptoms seen in patients with Tourette's disorder. The complex phenotypic presentation seen in Tourette's disorder could also be produced by a neurochemical abnormality at various locations within this circuitry.[1]

Reports of group A β-hemolytic streptococcus–related antineuronal antibodies being associated with the development or exacerbation of tics and OCD suggest a role for infectious agents and autoimmune processes in the etiology of these complex disorders.

Anatomical and Biological Abnormalities

Neuroanatomical Abnormalities. Increasingly sophisticated imaging methods, such as volumetric magnetic resonance imaging and functional neuroimaging, have identified subtle abnormalities in the basal ganglia in Tourette's disorder and OCD. Two volumetric magnetic resonance studies identified the absence of the usual left-right asymmetry in the basal ganglia (i.e., larger left-sided basal ganglia structures in unaffected right-handed individuals), leading to speculation of hypoplasia or atrophy of the left basal ganglia in Tourette's disorder.[36, 37]

Functional neuroimaging studies, such as single-photon emission computed tomography, have identified decreased blood flow to the basal ganglia,[38] specifically the left lenticular region.[39] Positron emission tomography identified similar decrements of glucose use in the basal ganglia.[40]

Anatomical studies of postmortem brain specimens has been limited by the few brains available. In a study of a single brain specimen, a pattern of immature cell development was noted in portions of the basal ganglia.[41]

Neurochemical Abnormalities. A number of neurochemical abnormalities have been proposed in Tourette's disorder in large part on the basis of responsiveness of symptoms to specific pharmacological agents. Tic suppression with dopamine blockers such as haloperidol and α-adrenergic agonists such as clonidine have implicated the dopamine-acetylcholine and adrenergic systems, respectively. The serotonin system has been implicated because of the association of Tourette's disorder with OCD and the positive therapeutic effect of serotonin reuptake inhibitors in OCD. Reports of abnormalities in the opioid system are also intriguing. In general, the specific role of various neurochemicals and related receptors in Tourette's disorder is unclear. It is possible that they have a primary role or may be a secondary effect of another abnormality.

Dopamine. Much of the support for the role of dopaminergic overactivity in Tourette's disorder comes from studies of pharmacological agents that affect tic severity. Agents that diminish dopaminergic activity decrease tic severity in most patients with Tourette's disorder. Conversely, agents that enhance dopaminergic activity (e.g., psychostimulants) have been associated with increases in tic severity. Speculation regarding the mechanism of dopaminergic overactivity in Tourette's disorder focuses on either dopamine excess or dopamine receptor supersensitivity. There is no direct support for dopamine excess in Tourette's disorder now. However, the positive response of tics to dopamine receptor–blocking agents and early reports of low concentrations in the cerebrospinal fluid of homovanillic acid, the major dopamine metabolite, are suggestive of dopamine receptor supersensitivity.[42] Also, positron emission tomography in adults with Tourette's disorder suggests elevated D_2 receptor binding.[43] Postmortem studies of dopamine and its metabolites support neither dopamine excess nor receptor supersensitivity.[44, 45] These studies do, however, suggest that the density of the striatal presynaptic dopamine transporter may be increased. This finding could be explained by dopaminergic hyperinnervation of the striatum.[46]

Other Neurochemical Systems. There are few definitive studies on the role of other neurochemical systems in Tourette's disorder. The *serotoninergic system* has been implicated[45] on the basis of postmortem brain studies that demonstrate trends toward decreases in levels of serotonin, its precursor tryptophan, and its primary metabolite 5-hydroxyindoleacetic acid, in subcortical regions[45] in spite of normal levels in the cerebral cortex.[44] These findings, in conjunction with presumably normal serotoninergic innervation, suggest abnormalities of the metabolism of serotonin and its precursor tryptophan.[45]

The *opioid system* has a role in movement control and is localized within the basal ganglia. A preliminary postmortem brain study identified a decrease in levels of the opioid dynorphin A in striatal fibers projecting to the globus pallidus.[41] The finding of decreased dynorphin in brain tissue has not been replicated and is difficult to reconcile with a report of elevated cerebrospinal fluid dynorphin A concentrations in patients with Tourette's disorder compared with control subjects.[47] The effectiveness of opiate antagonists in the treatment of patients with Tourette's disorder is mixed; some investigators report improvement,[48] and others report few responders.[49]

Other Biological Causes. In several reports,[50, 51] the development of tics as well as obsessive-compulsive symptoms in children and adolescents has been associated with group A β-hemolytic streptococcal infection. The underlying mechanism is believed to be similar to the mechanism involved in the development of Sydenham's chorea, in which antibodies developed in the course of infection cross-react with basal ganglia tissues, resulting in the characteristic choreiform movement disorder. In the reports, patients with Tourette's disorder and OCD had an increase in antineuronal antibodies compared with control subjects. In some patients, tic or OCD symptom exacerbations occurred in concert with a rise in the streptococcus-related antineuronal antibodies. These preliminary findings link the development of a movement disorder and psychiatric symptoms to an infectious agent and autoimmune processes. It is not clear whether these cases are sporadic, in which case they represent a true alternative etiology, or are an interaction of an environmental factor and a genetic susceptibility.[51] Clearly, more research is necessary to extend these intriguing findings.

Environmental Causes of Tourette's Disorder

Whereas the evidence for a genetic etiology of Tourette's disorder is compelling, there is also evidence that environmental factors may play a role in tic symptom expression. To date, studies have not identified any specific factors that cause Tourette's disorder, yet it is increasingly clear that environmental factors have an impact on tic severity and, perhaps, even on the types of symptoms expressed. Clinical wisdom suggests that tic severity increases in response to stressful or exciting life experiences. It is also not uncommon for persons with Tourette's disorder to be able to identify a particular environmental stimulus that initiated either a bout of symptoms or a new tic symptom.

Environmental factors associated with increases in symptom severity can occur early in development, including prenatal (intrauterine) development. In a study comparing groups of Tourette's disorder subjects with severe versus mild tics, protracted vomiting by a subject's mother during her pregnancy with the subject was a risk factor for increased tic severity.[52] Because of the male preponderance of Tourette's disorder, it has been postulated that intrauterine exposure to androgenic hormones may be a factor in the development of tics and in tic severity.[53] An open-label study of flutamide, an antiandrogenic hormone, identified significant but transient tic reduction in adult men, suggesting at least a partial role for sex hormones in tic severity.[54] Family-genetic and twin studies have also been useful for identifying factors associated with tic severity. As mentioned earlier, the twin studies of Tourette's disorder identified an association between birth weight and tic severity,[26, 28] suggesting that differences in intrauterine environment may be associated with tic severity.

Although the relationship between tic severity and psychostimulants remains controversial, a comparison of tic onset in monozygotic twins discordant for stimulant exposure identified the twin treated with stimulants to have developed motor tics 6 months earlier than the twin not exposed to stimulants.[55] This study suggests that stimulant medication may precipitate an earlier onset of tics in an otherwise vulnerable individual rather than causing tics de novo.

Psychosocial Aspects of Tourette's Disorder

Psychosocial issues do not play a large etiological role in the development of the tic disorders; however, psychosocial issues do play a major role in adaptation and impairment in Tourette's disorder and are often the focus of treatment and rehabilitative efforts. Clinical work that involves the family, friends, school, and workplace is often the bedrock of treatment in a patient with Tourette's disorder. Many of the psychosocial issues in Tourette's disorder are not unique but are shared by other neuropsychiatric disorders. Chapter 21 provides a comprehensive overview of the general role of psychosocial issues in neuropsychiatric disorders. Psychosocial issues specific to Tourette's disorder are addressed in this section.

Children. For children with Tourette's disorder, the onset of symptoms occurs early in development and directly affects family life and relationships with peers and schoolmates. The diagnostic label of Tourette's disorder can be helpful for understanding the nature of a youngster's problems and can communicate the need to protect the youngster from excessive adversity. The diagnostic label can, however, be a problem. There is a tension between protecting a child with Tourette's disorder from adversity while ensuring that the child encounters and masters life's challenges. If the diagnostic label of Tourette's disorder offers too much protection, a child may run the risk of not developing a strong and complex identity adequate for the rigors of adult life. Today's children with Tourette's disorder will need to function at their highest level as adults in spite of having Tourette's disorder symptoms. Support from parents for mastering the challenges of development is key to long-term functioning of children with Tourette's disorder.

Young Adults. The transition to adulthood is difficult enough for most young people, but young adults with Tourette's disorder have a particular challenge. The transition to adulthood often occurs when an important component of their early experience and identity (i.e., Tourette's disorder) begins to show some improvement. Young adults most vulnerable during this transition are those who, as a result of their Tourette's disorder, did not develop the foundations of an adult identity as a child. These adults often face the rigors of adult life without the necessary skills to manage, but also without the presence of tic symptoms of sufficient severity to explain their impairment.

Adults. Today's adult with Tourette's disorder belongs to a different cohort than today's child with Tourette's disorder. As a result, they also have different needs. Most adults with Tourette's disorder were not diagnosed in childhood. They did not have the "protection" of the diagnosis and often experienced significant confusion, isolation, and discrimination. Some adults with Tourette's disorder have significant anger, resentment, and distrust related to their early life experiences, which can have an impact on current functioning. Many adults who appear to function well in spite of their Tourette's disorder may be doing so at an emotional cost.

Diagnosis

Clinical Presentation

Before the 1980s, only people with the most severe and clinically obvious tics were diagnosed with Tourette's disorder. The majority of these patients were adults who pursued care and were correctly diagnosed only when their tic symptoms were disabling and when classic symptoms such as coprolalia were present. Adults with milder tics generally did not pursue care and may have been stigmatized without the awareness of the cause of their movements. Children with tics were not identified at all or were identified as having other behavioral or psychiatric difficulties. Increasingly, as medical professionals and the public became more knowledgeable about tic disorders, psychiatrists began to see children at younger ages and with milder symptoms. Today, psychiatrists sometimes become involved even when the tics themselves are not obvious or even disabling. In today's clinical practice, the challenge is often not the treatment of the tics but identification of co-occurring and often more disabling psychiatric, behavioral, family, and school problems.

Which medical specialty is first consulted about a child's tic disorder is most often determined by the family's initial concern. Parents without knowledge of tic disorders may consult their pediatrician or may incorrectly pursue evaluation by an ophthalmologist for "eye movements" or an allergist for sniffing and throat clearing. If the symptoms do not get better with time or other medical treatments, parents become increasingly concerned. More than half of families who finally pursue expert consultation find out about tic disorders from news articles or television. Although the media provide information for families and guide them in the direction of help, it is not uncommon for families to be frightened by the severe symptoms and impairment in these often dramatized cases. Many parents describe as their worst fear that their child's mild tic disorder is the beginning of a permanent neuropsychiatric disorder with a deteriorating course. Other children are identified during evaluation for other problems, such as ADHD. When the diagnosis of Tourette's disorder is made as part of an evaluation for other problems, it can be particularly difficult for the family and the patient to cope with the additional and unexpected diagnosis. Clearly, at the time of the evaluation, the patient and family are often frightened and require considerable psychological support.

Some children with tics, who present directly to a neurologist or a psychiatrist for an evaluation, may have a parent who has been diagnosed with a tic disorder. In this context, children can present early in the course of their disorder, often before a clear diagnosis can be made. The parents of these children often were diagnosed with tics late in their life or experienced significant duress from their symptoms and want their child to have a better experience.

Whereas most cases of Tourette's disorder currently presenting for care are children, there are adults who seek a clinical evaluation as a result of having a child diagnosed with Tourette's disorder or learning about Tourette's disorder in the media. Often these adults have been able to function in spite of their tics. Others may have been given an incorrect diagnosis for their tic disorder or have been in treatment for co-occurring psychiatric problems without any awareness of the relationship of those problems to the tic disorder. Even though these adults have not previously been diagnosed with a tic disorder, most are aware of their tics and may have experienced the psychosocial stigma commonly associated with a tic disorder. For these adults, a new diagnosis of Tourette's disorder may be psychologically complicated. The relief provided by knowing their diagnosis may be mixed with new questions about Tourette's disorder and its potential impact on their lives.

Assessment

Tic Severity. Clinical assessment of the tic disorders begins with identification of the specific movements and sounds. It is also important to identify the severity of and impairment caused by the tics. A number of structured and semistructured instruments are available for the identification of tics and the rating of tic severity.[56] However, most of these instruments, such as the Yale Global Tic Severity Scale, are dependent on a clinical interview to collect descriptive data on the tics and resulting impairment.[57] Knowledge of the basic clinical parameters of tics and the course of illness dictates the evaluation. Questioning patients and their families about the presence of simple and complex movements in muscle groups from head to toe is a good beginning. Because vocal tics usually follow the development of motor tics, questions about the presence of simple sounds is next. Inquiring about the presence of complex vocal tics completes the tic inventory. It is helpful to elucidate other aspects of tic severity, such as the absolute number of tics; the frequency, forcefulness, and intrusiveness of the symptoms; the ability of the patient to successfully suppress the tics; and how noticeable the tics are to others. It is also important to know whether premonitory sensory or cognitive experiences are a component of specific tics because these intrusive experiences may disrupt functioning more than the tics themselves. Although the waxing and waning nature of the tics and the replacement of one tic with another do not directly affect severity, identifying the characteristic course of illness is important for diagnostic confidence.

Last, it is important to assess the impairment due to the tics themselves. Whereas tic severity is frequently correlated with overall impairment, it is not uncommon to identify patients in whom tic severity and impairment are not correlated.[58] Patients who experience more impairment than their tic symptoms apparently warrant are a particular clinical challenge. A number of clinical features of tics are associated with impairment:

- Large, disruptive, or painful motor movements
- Vocalizations that call attention to the patient
- Premonitory sensations or cognitions that intrude into consciousness
- Tics that are socially unacceptable

Associated Co-occurring Conditions. Whereas tic severity and impairment are often correlated, many patients with mild tics are most impaired by the comorbid conditions ADHD, OCD, and LDs. An adequate assessment of these conditions is part of any comprehensive evaluation. The methods of assessment of these conditions are similar to those used in patients without Tourette's disorder. The only exception is the assessment of tic-related obsessive-compulsive symptoms, for example, touching, tapping, rubbing, "evening up," repeating actions, stereotypical self-mutilation, staring, echolalia, and palilalia. Although these symptoms are often omitted from the traditional psychiatric and neurological review of symptoms, tic-related obsessions and compulsions should always be part of the routine evaluation of patients with tics, OCD, or ADHD. Similarly, an evaluation of the child's school placement, intellectual capacities, and learning strengths and weaknesses is essential.

Other Psychiatric Disorders. It is standard for any psychiatric evaluation to rule out all other psychiatric disorders. In complex cases of Tourette's disorder, the multitude of behavioral and emotional symptoms can be formulated in a number of different ways. Behavioral and emotional problems can be seen as components of the Tourette's disorder diathesis, as a reaction to having a chronic disorder, or as part of an independent psychiatric disorder that is complicating the clinical picture. Clinical formulations that oversimplify and do not consider the presence of multiple independent disorders may lead to incorrectly attributing unrelated symptoms to Tourette's disorder and may result in diagnostic imprecision and treatment failures.

It is important to identify all possible psychiatric disorders in patients with Tourette's disorder so that the hierarchy of disabling conditions can be identified and treatment initiated accordingly. Positive family history of another psychiatric disorder (e.g., major depressive disorder or panic disorder) may provide clues to the possible psychiatric disorder complicating the presentation of a patient with Tourette's disorder. For example, an older teenage boy with a long history of Tourette's disorder, ADHD, impulse-control and behavior problems, and a difficult relationship with his parents presents with increasing impulse-control problems, intrusive behavior, sexual behavior and comments, insomnia, and substance abuse. Although it would be parsimonious to consider this clinical presentation an exacerbation of Tourette's disorder, it would be clinically prudent to rule out the presence of other treatable conditions, such as a substance abuse disorder, major depressive disorder, or bipolar disorder. A positive family history of one of these disorders would provide additional support for the diagnosis.

Psychosocial Issues. Psychosocial issues can play a role in tic severity and in overall adaptation and impairment. Assessment of family, peer, and school support for the youngster (adequate protection) along with assessment for the presence of opportunities to be intellectually, physically, and socially challenged is important. The balance between protection and challenge in children is critical for long-term development. An environment that is too protective decreases opportunities for building skills. An environment that is too challenging can lead to frustration, anger, and maladaptive coping.

Physical Examination Findings. Tic assessment requires a careful evaluation of observable tic symptoms. Interestingly, the absence of tic symptoms during an evaluation, in spite of the parent's or patient's report, is not uncommon and should not necessarily lead to clinical doubt. Occasionally, an additional clinical observer may identify tics more readily than the psychiatrist conducting the evaluation. Other than the observation of tics in the interview, there are no pathognomonic physical examination findings. Patients with Tourette's disorder have been noted to have nonfocal and nonspecific subtle neurological findings ("soft" signs). If tic suppression with neuroleptic agents is considered, a more structured method of documenting the complex movements that are part of the pretreatment baseline evaluation is useful.

Laboratory Evaluation. No specific laboratory or imaging tests are helpful in making the diagnosis or assessing a patient with Tourette's disorder. Laboratory assessment is most often done as part of a routine health screen or in anticipation of medication interventions. Currently, laboratory testing for group A β-hemolytic streptococcal infections (e.g., throat culture, antistreptolysin titer, and screening for antineuronal antibodies) is experimental unless there are clinical signs and symptoms of acute infection.

Differential Diagnosis

Differential Diagnosis of Tics

Simple, rapid movements
- Myoclonus
- Chorea
- Seizures

Simple, sustained movements
- Dystonia
- Athetosis

Complex or sustained movements
- Mannerisms
- Stereotypies
- Restless legs
- Seizures

From Jankovic J: Diagnosis and classification of tics and Tourette syndrome. Adv Neurol 1992; 58:7–14.

Tics have many characteristics that differentiate them from the other movement disorders.[59] Perhaps most important to "ruling in" tics as a diagnostic possibility is the childhood history of simple motor tics in the face. Other movement disorders do not have a similar pattern of movement onset or location. There are atypical presentations of tic disorders that may resemble other movement disorders, but these would be unusual and would probably require a consultation with a movement disorders expert.

Movement disorders such as chorea and dystonia are continuous movements and can be distinguished from tics, which are intermittent. Paroxysmal dyskinesias, although episodic, are more often characterized by choreiform and dystonic movements, which are different from tics. Myoclonic movements and exaggerated startle responses are also intermittent movements but are usually large-muscle movements that occur in response to a patient-specific stimulus. Complex tics can be more difficult to differentiate from other complex movements such as mannerisms, gestures, or stereotypies. In a person with clear-cut motor tics, it may be difficult to differentiate a complex motor tic from a "camouflaged" tic, mannerism, gesture, or stereotypy. Mannerisms or gestures are often not impairing; stereotypies tend to occur exclusively in children and adults with developmental disabilities and mental retardation.[59]

It is also possible to have a tic disorder and another movement disorder. For example, tic movements can co-occur with dystonia. Similarly, it is not uncommon in tertiary referral centers to see developmentally disabled children and adults with both tics and stereotypies.

Course and Natural History

In Tourette's disorder, tic symptoms usually begin in childhood; mean age at onset is 7 years. The first tic may develop during the teenage years, but this is unusual. Motor tics of the eyes and face are the most common and earliest presenting symptoms. In many patients, the motor tics remain isolated in the face. When motor tics do progress, there is a tendency for additional tics to present sequentially from the head and face to the neck, shoulders, trunk, and extremities. Vocal tics tend to follow the development of motor tics. Complex tics of both types tend to follow the development of simple tics. Longitudinal studies suggest that tic severity is greatest in most patients during the latency and early teenage years. Most patients experience a decline in tic severity as they get older; only a small percentage of patients (10%) experience a severe or deteriorating course.[60]

The course of ADHD symptoms in persons with Tourette's disorder is similar to that in children without Tourette's disorder. ADHD symptoms usually begin earlier than the tic symptoms. Symptoms of hyperactivity attenuate before puberty, whereas problems with attention and concentration may continue into adulthood.

Obsessive-compulsive symptoms in persons with Tourette's disorder generally begin somewhat later than ADHD and tics and may actually progress differentially from tic symptoms. Tic symptoms tend to improve into adulthood; obsessive-compulsive symptoms may actually increase in severity. Long-term studies of the course of obsessive-compulsive symptoms in persons with Tourette's disorder have not been done.

Standard Approaches to Treatment

Educate the Patient and Family

The initiation of treatment can be a delicate process, given the difficulties patients and their families experience before finding appropriate care. Most families are frightened about their child's having a neuropsychiatric disorder and envision a grim prognosis. After the evaluation is completed, often in the first session, general education of the patient about the course of the tic disorder is essential (Table 38–4). Most patients and families are relieved to hear that the majority of persons with tics have consistent improvement in tic severity as they move through their teenage years and into adulthood. They are also pleased to hear that tic symptoms are not inherently impairing. In this regard, it is often helpful to cite examples of sports personalities or other public figures who

Table 38–4 Goals of Treatment

Educate the patient and family about tic disorders.
Define the co-occurring disorders.
Create a hierarchy of the clinically impairing conditions.
Treat the impairing conditions using somatic, psychological, and rehabilitative approaches.
Aid in creating a supportive yet challenging psychosocial milieu.

have identified themselves as having Tourette's disorder and are doing well both personally and professionally.

Identify Co-occurring Disorders

Once issues regarding the tics are discussed and clarified, the focus shifts to the presence of comorbid conditions. Identifying whether ADHD, LD, and OCD are present is especially important because they are often the more common impairing conditions in these children. Yet the transition to addressing the co-occurring problems is often not easy. Patients, families, and psychiatrists are usually focused on the tic symptoms. Tics are more readily apparent and relatively easy to suppress with medications, whereas the co-occurring conditions, especially if they are internalizing disorders, are easy to overlook. One of the major pitfalls of treatment of patients with Tourette's disorder is to pursue tic suppression to the exclusion of the treatment of other co-occurring conditions that are present and possibly more impairing.

It is also possible that other psychiatric disorders that are not traditionally thought to be part of the tic disorders will co-occur in patients with Tourette's disorder. Unless such complex clinical presentations are considered, patients will not receive an adequate evaluation and comprehensive treatment (Table 38–5).

Create a Hierarchy of the Clinically Impairing Conditions

Creating the hierarchy of the most impairing conditions is the next major step in treatment. Most psychiatrists, as part of their formulation, create some clinical hierarchy; yet in Tourette's disorder, with the multitude of often complex problems, it is essential that a conscious effort be made to formulate, organize, and create hierarchies for treatment.

Treat the Impairing Conditions

This section focuses on the basic strategies for tic suppression and treatment of the common co-occurring disorders. Particular emphasis is placed on the complexities of clinical treatment.

Tic Suppression: Pharmacological

The goal of pharmacological treatment is the reduction of tic severity, not necessarily the elimination of tics. Haloperidol has been used effectively to suppress motor and phonic tics for more than 30 years. Since that time, a number of other neuroleptic agents have also been identified as useful in tic suppression, including fluphenazine and pimozide. In Europe, the substituted benzamides sulpiride and tiapride and the nonneuroleptic tetrabenazine have also been shown to be useful. As new neuroleptic agents become available, clinical trials for tic suppression invariably occur. Preliminary results with risperidone have been mixed, whereas trials with clozapine are more uniformly negative.[61] The major drawback with neuroleptic agents is the frequent and significant side effects, which often preclude continued use of the medication.

There are continuing efforts to identify tic-suppressing agents with tolerable side effects. Most frequently cited in this regard are the α-adrenergic agonists clonidine and guanfacine. Both of these agents were developed as antihypertensives. These agents do not appear to be as uniformly effective in tic suppression, but they can be effective for some patients without significant side effects. Both clonidine and guanfacine also appear to be useful for some of the symptoms of ADHD, which makes these agents a reasonable first choice for those patients with both Tourette's disorder and ADHD.

Haloperidol

Haloperidol is a high-potency neuroleptic that preferentially blocks dopamine D_2 receptors. Historically, haloperidol has been the most frequently used medication for tic suppression. It is effective in a clear majority of patients, although relatively few patients are willing to tolerate the side effects to obtain the tic-suppressing benefits.

Neuroleptics are often effective at low doses, and low doses minimize side effects. For haloperidol, doses in the range of 0.5 to 2.0 mg/d are usually adequate. Starting dosages are low (0.25 to 0.5 mg/d), with small increases in dose (0.25 to 0.5 mg/d) every 5 to 7 days. Most often the medication is given at bedtime, but with low doses, some patients may require twice-a-day dosing for good tic control.

Side effects with all neuroleptics are common and are the reason that neuroleptics are not used by the majority of patients with Tourette's disorder. Side effects include those traditionally seen with neuroleptics, such as sedation, acute dystonic reactions, extrapyramidal symptoms including akathisia, weight gain, cognitive dulling, and the common anticholinergic side effects. There have also been reports of subtle, difficult to recognize side effects with neuroleptics, including clinical depression, separation anxiety, panic attacks, and school avoidance.[62]

Dosage reduction is the most prudent response to side effects, although the addition of medications such as benztropine for the extrapyramidal symptoms can be useful.

Table 38–5 Complex Clinical Presentations in Tourette's Disorder

Tics + ADHD + OCD + LD + major depressive disorder
Tics + ADHD + OCD + LD + separation anxiety disorder
Tics + ADHD + OCD + LD + panic disorder
Tics + ADHD + OCD + LD + bipolar disorder
Tics + ADHD + OCD + LD + autism–pervasive developmental disorder
Tics + ADHD + OCD + LD + substance abuse
Tics + ADHD + OCD + LD + conduct disorder
Tics + ADHD + OCD + LD + personality disorders

Dosage reduction in those children with Tourette's disorder who have been administered neuroleptics long term may be complicated by withdrawal dyskinesias and significant tic worsening or rebound. Withdrawal dyskinesias are choreoathetoid movements of the orofacial region, trunk, and extremities that appear after neuroleptic discontinuation or dosage reduction and tend to resolve in 1 to 3 months. Tic worsening even above pretreatment baseline level (i.e., rebound) can last up to 1 to 3 months after discontinuation or dosage reduction. Tardive dyskinesia, which is similar in character to withdrawal dyskinesia, most often develops during the course of treatment or is "unmasked" with dosage reductions. Rarely have cases of tardive dyskinesia been reported to occur in patients with Tourette's disorder.

Fluphenazine

Whereas fluphenazine has never undergone controlled trials, clinical experience suggests that it has somewhat fewer side effects than haloperidol. Fluphenazine has both dopamine D_1 and D_2 receptor–blocking activity, and the side effect profile is similar to that of haloperidol. Approaches to treatment are also similar, that is, treatment begins with low doses and slow upward dosage adjustments while benefits are balanced with side effects. Fluphenazine is slightly less potent than haloperidol so that starting doses are somewhat higher (0.5 to 1 mg/d), as are treatment doses (3 to 5 mg/d).

Pimozide

Pimozide is a potent and specific blocker of dopamine D_2 receptors. Its side effect profile is generally similar to that of the other neuroleptics, although it has fewer sedative and extrapyramidal side effects than haloperidol. In contrast to either haloperidol or fluphenazine, pimozide has calcium channel blocking properties that affect cardiac conduction, as evidenced by changes in the electrocardiogram. The coadministration of other medications that affect cardiac conduction, such as the tricyclic antidepressants, is generally contraindicated. Baseline and follow-up electrocardiograms are important for adequate management of patients. Beginning treatment with a dose of 1.0 mg/d is prudent, although with pimozide's long half-life, every-other-day dosing can be used to decrease the effective daily dose. Increases of up to 1 mg/d can occur every 5 to 7 days until symptoms are controlled. Most patients experience clinical benefit with few side effects with doses of 1 to 4 mg/d. Higher doses can be associated with more side effects. In a comparison of pimozide, haloperidol, and no drug in patients with Tourette's disorder and ADHD, pimozide at 1 to 4 mg/d was useful in decreasing tics and improving some aspects of cognition that are commonly impaired in ADHD.[63] The potential to have impact on both Tourette's disorder and ADHD symptoms with a single drug is a clear advantage that pimozide may have over other neuroleptics.

Sulpiride and Tiapride

Both of these agents are substituted benzamides available only in Europe. Like pimozide, they are unique in their combination of relatively specific dopamine D_2 receptor–blocking activity and the potential for reduced risk of extrapyramidal symptoms and tardive dyskinesia. Both agents have demonstrated efficacy in tic suppression.[64, 65] Efforts to initiate trials in the United States are under way.

Clonidine and Guanfacine

There is a long history of the use of the α-adrenergic agonist clonidine for suppression of tics and ADHD symptoms. Whereas controlled trials have shown that some patients benefit with symptom reduction, the overall effect of clonidine for tic suppression and ADHD is more modest than that achieved with the "gold standards" for these conditions, haloperidol and the stimulants, respectively.[66] Given clonidine's mild side effect profile, it is often the first drug used for tic suppression, especially in those children with Tourette's disorder and ADHD. Treatment is initiated at 0.025 mg/d and increased in increments of 0.025 to 0.05 mg/d every 3 to 5 days or as side effects (sedation) allow. Usual effective treatment doses are in the range of 0.1 to 0.3 mg/d and are given in divided doses (4 to 6 hours apart). Higher doses are associated with side effects, primarily sedation, and are not necessarily more effective. The onset of action is slower for tic suppression (3 to 6 weeks) than for ADHD symptoms. Side effects, in addition to sedation, include irritability, headaches, decreased salivation, and hypotension and dizziness at higher doses. Interestingly, owing to clonidine's short half-life, some patients experience mild withdrawal symptoms between doses. More severe rebound in autonomic activity and tics can occur if the medication is discontinued abruptly.[67] Some patients find that clonidine in the transdermal patch form provides a more stable clinical effect and avoids multiple doses each day. Children are usually stabilized on oral doses before they are switched to the patch. A rash at the site of the patch is a common, but manageable, complication of treatment.

Guanfacine is an α_2-adrenergic agonist that potentially offers greater benefit than clonidine because of differences in site of action, side effects, and duration of action. In nonhuman primates, guanfacine appears to bind preferentially with α_2-adrenergic receptors in prefrontal cortical regions associated with attentional and organizational functions.[68] On the basis of these animal models, it is hypothesized that guanfacine is likely to have a greater impact on attention without the significant sedation associated with the nonselective α_2-adrenergic agonist clonidine. Guanfacine's long half-life offers the advantage of twice-a-day dosing, which is more convenient than the multiple dosing required with clonidine. In an open trial of guanfacine for Tourette's disorder and ADHD symptoms, improvements in attention, hyperactivity, and tic severity were noted; side effects were minimal.[69]

Benzodiazepines

Benzodiazepines can be useful in decreasing co-morbid anxiety in patients with Tourette's disorder. In addition, clonazepam appears also to be useful in selected patients for tic reduction. Often, doses of 3 to 6 mg/d may be necessary for tic reduction. Because sedation is a significant side effect at these dosages, an extended titration phase of 3 to 6 months may be necessary. Similarly, a slow taper is required to avoid withdrawal symptoms.[70]

Tic Suppression: Nonpharmacological

Published studies of behavioral approaches to tic suppression are few but show some promise. The behavioral technique shown to be most effective is habit reversal training. For Tourette's disorder, habit reversal training is the use of a competing muscle contraction or behavioral response that opposes the tic movement. This method is usually combined with relaxation training, self-monitoring, awareness training, and positive reinforcement. In the few published studies of habit reversal training, there were marked overall reductions in tic frequency. Treatment averaged 20 training sessions during an 8- to 11-month period. Marked tic reduction was noted at 3 to 4 months. Interestingly, urges or sensations experienced before the tic movements also decreased with behavioral treatment.[71]

Psychosocial Treatments

There are no published systematic studies of psychosocial interventions for patients with Tourette's disorder. Most treatment efforts are based on a combination of traditional psychosocial interventions and clinical judgment.

Education

Perhaps the most useful psychosocial and educational intervention is to make the patient aware of the Tourette Syndrome Association, both national and local chapters. This and other self-help groups can be useful as a source of support and education for patients, families, and psychiatrists.

Therapy

Individual psychotherapy can be useful for support, development of awareness, or addressing personal and interpersonal problems more effectively. Family therapy can be useful when families have problems adjusting, functioning, and communicating. Although most families do well, some families have difficulties understanding the involuntary nature of tics and may punish their children for their tics, even after diagnosis and education. Alternatively, some families have more behavior difficulties with their children after diagnosis than before. Many parents of children with Tourette's disorder inadvertently lower general behavior expectations because of confusion about what behaviors are tics and what behaviors are not tics. Sometimes parents decrease behavior expectations for their children because of the parents' desire not to add any additional stress to the youngster's life. Also, with confusion in the field regarding the scope of problems in Tourette's disorder, some parents see all maladaptive behaviors as involuntary and do not hold their children responsible for their behaviors. For children with Tourette's disorder to do well, they need support from their family to develop effective self-control in areas not affected by Tourette's disorder so that optimal adaptation can occur.

In newly diagnosed adults, psychotherapy oriented toward adequate adjustment to the diagnosis is important but not always easy. Adult patients frequently experience a mixture of relief to finally be diagnosed and anger and resentment related to their past experiences with discrimination or inadequate medical care. Severely affected adults may also need psychotherapy to deal with the psychological and psychosocial difficulties related to having a chronic illness.

Other Psychosocial Interventions

For children, active intervention at school is essential to create a supportive yet challenging academic and social environment. Efforts to educate teachers, principals, and other students can result in increased awareness of Tourette's disorder and tolerance for the child's symptoms.

Many young adults are finding Tourette's disorder support and social groups important for interpersonal contact and continued adult development. Efforts to keep people with Tourette's disorder working are important, as are rehabilitation efforts for those who are not working. Finding housing and obtaining disability or public assistance may be necessary for the most disabled patients with Tourette's disorder.

Treatment of Co-occurring Psychiatric Disorders in Tourette's Disorder

This section focuses on the special complexities of treating the commonly co-occurring psychiatric disorders, such as ADHD, LDs, and OCD. In general, the treatment approaches in patients with Tourette's disorder are similar to approaches in patients without Tourette's disorder, but there are some differences. The details of the specific treatment approaches for ADHD, LDs, and OCD are addressed in separate chapters.

Treatment of Attention-Deficit/ Hyperactivity Disorder

Nonpharmacological Approaches

The nonpharmacological approaches to ADHD in Tourette's disorder are similar to approaches in children without Tourette's disorder. The presence both at home and at school of a structured environment, consistent behavioral management, and a generally positive, rewarding atmosphere can produce significant improvement in ADHD symptoms. Increasingly, there are specific programs for children with ADHD that go beyond basic positive programming and include more intensive and specific behavioral approaches. In spite of advances in nonpharmacological treatments, some families and psychiatrists, for a variety of reasons, find developing and implementing behavioral programs for children with ADHD difficult and do not take full advantage of the benefits of behavioral approaches.

Pharmacological Treatments

The two major difficulties in the treatment of ADHD in Tourette's disorder are the risk of side effects from the stimulants and desipramine, arguably the most potent treatment agents for ADHD, and the lack of adequate alternatives.

Stimulants

In the early 1970s, a number of reports of induction or exacerbation of tics by stimulant medications raised concerns about the role of stimulants as a cause of Tourette's disorder. At that time, the concern was that stimulants could be causing tics de novo or that increases in tic severity would endure even if stimulant medications were discontinued. Concurrent with these reports, other authors noted that tic induction or exacerbation was relatively infrequent and that the beneficial effects in some patients with Tourette's disorder outweighed any negative impact on tic severity.[72]

As a result, stimulants have been used infrequently for ADHD in Tourette's disorder. However, results of ongoing short-term double-blind, placebo-controlled trials with stimulants in Tourette's disorder are positive and support a role for stimulants in some patients with Tourette's disorder plus ADHD.[73] Increasingly, psychiatrists are cautiously, and with fully informed consent, using stimulant medication in selected children and adolescents with Tourette's disorder and ADHD. In the patient in whom tics are increased by stimulants, combined treatment with stimulants and tic-suppressing agents can be used.[73]

Desipramine

Desipramine is a tricyclic antidepressant with prominent noradrenergic activity that has been noted to improve attention and concentration in children and adolescents with ADHD and Tourette's disorder plus ADHD. Symptom improvement is often significant with lower doses than needed for depression. Side effects are generally limited. The cardiac side effects of increased heart rate and elevation in blood pressure are usually not clinically significant; however, reports of sudden death in children and adolescents[74] taking desipramine have resulted in marked reductions nationally in the use of desipramine in children and adolescents (Riddle M, personal communication, 1996).

Nortriptyline

Given the concern about the cardiac side effects of desipramine, there is increased interest in other tricyclic antidepressants like nortriptyline for ADHD. The only available report, a chart review, assessed the effect of nortriptyline in children and adolescents with Tourette's disorder plus ADHD. The majority of subjects experienced moderate to marked improvement in both ADHD and tics.[75] Although the concern regarding sudden death is less with nortriptyline than with desipramine, it is prudent to obtain baseline and follow-up electrocardiograms.

Clonidine and Guanfacine

The role of α-adrenergic agonists in Tourette's disorder and ADHD was described before in the section on tic suppression.

Deprenyl

Deprenyl is a selective monoamine oxidase B inhibitor that does not require a special tyramine-free diet. It is metabolized to isomers of amphetamine and methamphetamine. In a large open trial of children with Tourette's disorder plus ADHD, who failed other treatments for ADHD, 90% had significant improvement in their ADHD symptoms with no serious side effects. Specifically, no increases in tic severity were observed.[76]

Treatment of Obsessive-Compulsive Disorder

Nonpharmacological Approaches

The positive role of cognitive-behavioral treatments of OCD is well established in adults. Most reports of nonpharmacological treatment of OCD in children and adolescents are case studies. Only one report has a sufficient sample size and a protocol-driven, cognitive-behavioral treatment regimen to begin to establish the possible role of such treatment in children and adolescents with OCD.[77] There are no specific reports of cognitive-behavioral treatment or other nonpharmacological treatments of OCD in adults or children with Tourette's disorder. Given the success of cognitive-behavioral treatment in OCD, it is likely that patients with Tourette's disorder and OCD will also be able to benefit from cognitive-behavioral treatment.

Pharmacological Treatments

The number of agents available for the treatment of OCD in patients with and without Tourette's disorder is increasing. Currently available agents include the tricyclic antidepressant clomipramine and the specific serotonin reuptake inhibitors fluoxetine, sertraline, paroxetine, and fluvoxamine. Even though only a few of these agents have a specific indication for OCD (clomipramine and fluvoxamine), others may be effective in OCD given their serotoninergic activity. The choice of agent depends on the side effect profile, the potential drug interactions, and the psychiatrist's familiarity with the drug. See Chapter 57 for a detailed description of pharmacological treatments.

With the exception of clomipramine, all of the available agents have mild and somewhat similar side effect profiles. Despite the similarities among these medications, they are chemically different, especially in their metabolic pathway and patterns of drug interaction. The patterns of drug interaction are especially important because in children with complex presentations, multiple drugs are often used simultaneously. The reports of elevated tricyclic antidepressant levels in patients receiving tricyclic antidepressants and fluoxetine are good examples of unforeseen drug interactions with the specific serotonin reuptake inhibitors. Psychiatrists usually prescribe on the basis of their familiarity and comfort with the given medication. The increased complexity of drug interactions with the specific serotonin reuptake inhibitors requires medication choices to be based on specific characteristics of the patient and the metabolic and drug interaction profile of the medication.

Increasingly, augmentation strategies are pursued in patients with OCD and with Tourette's disorder plus OCD, when clinical symptoms remain after initial treatment. A number of strategies have been used, including augmentation with lithium, neuroleptics, buspirone, clonazepam, liothyronine sodium (T_3), and fenfluramine. Although positive outcomes of these strategies have been reported in open trials, only neuroleptic augmentation has shown benefit in controlled trials. Interestingly, controlled trials of haloperidol combined with specific serotonin reuptake inhibitors in patients with Tourette's disorder and OCD demonstrated improvement in both tic and OCD symptoms.[78]

Treatment-Refractory Cases

Strategies for approaching two types of treatment-refractory symptoms are discussed here: 1) patients who are truly treatment refractory with severe and impairing symptoms of Tourette's disorder and OCD, despite conventional and heroic treatments, and 2) patients, often children, who are clinically complex and enigmatic, and whose impairment is disproportionally greater than their tic, obsessive-compulsive, or ADHD symptoms would suggest.

Treatment-Refractory Tics

Perhaps the most important "treatment" in patients with severe incapacitating tics is a full clinical reevaluation to assess the adequacy of previous evaluations and treatment efforts. It is not uncommon for treatment-refractory patients to have had inadequate evaluations and treatment trials.

Two alternative treatment strategies are available for truly treatment-refractory tics. When a single tic or a few tics are refractory and impairing, the injection of botulinum toxin into the specific muscle group can be helpful. This strategy is most useful for painful, dystonic tics. Treatment has a long duration of action, but the effect does decrease in 2 to 4 months, and repeated injections may be necessary. Specific side effects are few other than weakness in the affected muscle. Some patients reported the loss of the premonitory sensation with their botulinum toxin treatment. For the psychiatrist, it is essential to work with an experienced neurologist.[79]

There have been reports in the literature and the media concerning the use of neurosurgical approaches for the treatment of refractory tics. To date, the optimal size and location of the surgical treatment lesions are not known. There are no well-controlled trials, although some data are available from patients with OCD and tics who were treated for OCD. In these patients, the impact on tic severity was mixed.[80] Because these approaches are particularly controversial, it is important, before considering neurosurgical approaches, to complete a detailed and exhaustive reevaluation to determine whether all other treatment options are exhausted. It is also important that patients who pursue neurosurgical approaches consider centers of clinical excellence where controlled treatment trials are ongoing. It would be optimal if the outcome of all cases treated in this manner could be available for review in the scientific literature so that conclusions based on outcome can be drawn from these complex cases.

Treatment-Refractory Obsessive-Compulsive Disorder

A similarly thorough and exhaustive reevaluation is critical for patients with Tourette's disorder plus OCD who present as treatment refractory. Diagnostic reevaluation focuses on whether other psychiatric disorders are present and disabling and whether the current hierarchy of clinical disability considers all conditions.

Pharmacological reevaluation is especially critical because there are an increasing number of new medications and potential medication combinations. Rather than repeated change from one antiobsessional agent to another, consideration can be given to augmentation strategies, because they take less time than changing agents and may offer synergistic benefits. Low-dose neuroleptic augmentation is the best first choice; controlled trials support the use of low-dose neuroleptics for augmentation of serotonin reuptake inhibitors in OCD.[78] Lithium and T_3 are proven, effective augmenters of antidepressants for depression, yet neither is proven effective in OCD. Because of the frequent overlap of OCD and major depression, lithium or T_3 augmentation may be the next best choice. Lithium or T_3 can be added to the serotonin reuptake inhibitor or to the serotonin reuptake inhibitor and neuroleptic combination. Other augmenting agents are supported only by anecdotal evidence.

Treatment-refractory or malignant OCD has been the psychiatric disorder most frequently treated with neurosurgical interventions in the modern era. Whereas it is a major treatment intervention, the surgical approaches are somewhat better defined, and the outcome in severe cases is often positive. Also, medical centers are available that specialize in the presurgical work-up and the neurosurgical procedure.[81]

Clinically Complex Patients

Clinically complex patients may be severely impaired without having severe tic or OCD symptoms. The clinically complex patient is often a diagnostic dilemma with additional diagnoses complicating the clinical picture. In addition, patients can become clinically complex when otherwise straightforward treatments are a challenge to implement.

Diagnosis

In clinically complex patients, the diagnostic challenge is not an accurate assessment of tics, ADHD, obsessive-compulsive symptoms, or LDs, although this is important. In clinically complex patients, the diagnostic goal is to identify what other conditions or factors may be present that make the current treatment approaches difficult.

From a strictly diagnostic point of view, it is the additional psychiatric conditions beyond Tourette's disorder, OCD, ADHD, and LDs that often escape clinical observation and result in diagnostic dilemmas and treatment failures (see Table 38–5).

Treatment Implementation

In clinically complex patients, particular difficulties with treatment implementation can occur. Most psychiatrists are aware of problems with treatment compliance, but clinically complex patients with Tourette's disorder present additional treatment dilemmas.

Clinical problems occur when the treating psychiatrist does not have access to critical information or is not in control of the treatment process. Traditionally, psychiatrists develop a relationship with the patient and the other major figures in the patient's life. Given the current clinical climate, a comprehensive level of involvement can be overwhelming and enormously time-consuming for the psychiatrist. Because it is increasingly difficult for the psychiatrist to be as involved as necessary, problems with poorly coordinated team efforts and the psychiatrist's lack of awareness of important clinical issues can have a negative impact on the treatment of a patient.

Psychiatrists who work with children and adolescents may wish to consider changes in their treatment approaches to these patients. Experience in tertiary care centers suggests that expanded time with the parents is a critically important and efficient approach to care. Psychiatrists who form a treatment partnership with families, respecting and addressing their concerns, educating them about Tourette's disorder, training them to evaluate and manage complex behaviors, and empowering them to be an effective advocate for their child, are providing good care. In working directly with families, the collection of important information regarding the family's and patient's functioning is direct and regular, and often small interventions can produce changes in family functioning that have a positive ripple effect throughout the life of the child. Although focusing on the family will not make all complex patients with Tourette's disorder easier to treat, less than adequate contact will certainly create barriers to clinical care.

Pharmacological Treatment Dilemmas

It is often difficult to get accurate information regarding side effects and treatment response in child patients. Parents, children, and psychiatrists, in spite of a good collaborative effort, may have different understandings of the target symptoms, side effect profile, and what constitutes a positive clinical response. This ambiguity makes any but the most robust clinical responses difficult to observe. Again, experience at tertiary referral centers suggests that the lack of a clinical response to medication in complex patients may often be related to inadequate monitoring of medicine effects and inadequate treatment trials.[82]

Clinically complex patients may not have a robust response to a single medication but may require multiple medication trials to identify which medications offer the most benefit, and in which combination. Sequential treatment trials are difficult for all involved, especially children and families, who are often looking for a single powerful intervention. Clinically complex patients, however, usually require sequential trials and combined medication regimens to experience optimal benefit. With the added complexity of treatment, there is the added risk of confusion and the need for an excellent psychiatrist-patient-family relationship. In those cases in which the relationship is not optimal, it is possible that a patient may not have the maximal clinical benefit of pharmacological interventions.

With increasing numbers of available psychotropic medications, psychiatrists become increasingly less experienced with the range of clinical effects and side effects in individual medications. In clinically complex patients, the prescription of unfamiliar medications may be necessary but may add to the risk that a trial will be discontinued prematurely because of doubt about a side effect. In addition, unusual side effects, such as the apathy or disinhibition syndromes[83, 84] seen with some patients receiving the specific serotonin reuptake inhibitors, may go unnoticed and add to clinical morbidity.

Whereas pharmacological interventions offer great promise, clinical experience suggests that excellent diagnostic skills, good relationships with the patient and family, time, and a keen eye for effects and side effects are necessary for benefits to be realized. Less intensive efforts may make patients appear more complex than necessary.

Conclusion

Tourette's disorder and the other tic disorders are model neuropsychiatric disorders with childhood onset. Many of the research efforts in the clinical and basic science of Tourette's disorder outlined in this chapter set a standard for research efforts in other childhood neuropsychiatric disorders. Future research efforts will focus on identifying the basic genetic deficit in Tourette's disorder as well as the complex prevention and rehabilitation efforts necessary to minimize morbidity and maximize long-term functioning.

References

1. Singer HS, Walkup JT: Tourette syndrome and other tic disorders: Diagnosis, pathophysiology, and treatment. Medicine (Baltimore) 1991; 70:15–32.
2. Chase TN, Friedhoff AJ, Cohen DJ: Tourette syndrome: Genetics, neurobiology and treatment. Adv Neurol 1992; 58.
3. Lombroso PJ, Scahill LD, Chappell PB, et al: Tourette's syndrome: A multigenerational, neuropsychiatric disorder. Adv Neurol 1995; 65: 305–318.
4. Robertson M: The Gilles de la Tourette syndrome: The current status. Br J Psychiatry 1989; 154:147–169.
5. Leckman JF, Walker DE, Cohen DJ: Premonitory urges in Tourette's syndrome. Am J Psychiatry 1993; 150:98–102.
6. American Psychiatric Association: Diagnostic and Statistical Manual of Mental Disorders, 4th ed. Washington, DC: American Psychiatric Association, 1994.
7. The Tourette Syndrome Classification Study Group: Definitions and classification of tic disorders. Arch Neurol 1993; 50:1013–1016.
8. Shapiro AK, Shapiro ES, Young JG, Feinberg TE: Gilles de la Tourette Syndrome, 2nd ed. New York: Raven Press, 1988.
9. Lucas AR, Beard CM, Rajput AH, Kurland LT: Tourette syndrome in Rochester, Minnesota, 1968–1979. Adv Neurol 1982; 35:267–269.
10. Caine ED, McBride MC, Chiverton P, et al: Tourette's syndrome in Monroe County school children. Neurology 1988; 38:472–475.
11. Apter A, Pauls DL, Bleich A, et al: An epidemiologic study of Gilles de la Tourette's syndrome in Israel. Arch Gen Psychiatry 1993; 50:734–738.
12. Comings DE, Himes JA, Comings BG: An epidemiological study of Tourette syndrome in a single school district. J Clin Psychiatry 1990; 51:463–469.
13. Comings DE, Comings BG: A controlled study of Tourette syndrome: I. Attention deficit disorder, learning disorders and school problems. Am J Hum Genet 1987; 41:701–741.
14. Pauls DL, Hurst CR, Kruger SD, et al: Gilles de la Tourette's syndrome and attention deficit disorder with hyperactivity: Evidence against a genetic relationship. Arch Gen Psychiatry 1986; 43:1177–1179.
15. Pauls DL, Cohen DJ, Kidd KK, Leckman JF: Tourette syndrome and neuropsychiatric disorder: Is there a genetic relationship? [letter] Am J Hum Genet 1988; 43:206–209.
16. George MS, Trimble MR, Ring HA, et al: Obsessions in obsessive-compulsive disorder with and without Gilles de la Tourette's syndrome. Am J Psychiatry 1993; 150:93–97.
17. Leckman JF, Walker DE, Goodman WK, et al: "Just right" perceptions associated with compulsive behaviors in Tourette's syndrome. Am J Psychiatry 1993; 151:675–680.
18. Miguel EC, Coffey BJ, Baer L, et al: Phenomenology of intentional repetitive behaviors in obsessive-compulsive disorder and Tourette's syndrome. J Clin Psychiatry 1993; 56: 246–255.
19. LaBuda MC, Pauls DL: Gilles de la Tourette syndrome. In Conneally PM (ed): Molecular Basis of Neurology. Boston: Blackwell Scientific Publications, 1993:199–214.
20. Pauls DL, Leckman JF: The inheritance of Gilles de la Tourette's syndrome and associated behaviors: Evidence for autosomal dominant transmission. N Engl J Med 1986; 315:993–997.
21. Pauls DL, Leckman JF, Cohen DJ: The familial relationship between Gilles de la Tourette's syndrome, attention deficit disorder, learning disabilities, and speech disorders and stuttering. J Am Acad Child Adolesc Psychiatry 1993; 32:1044–1050.
22. Pauls DL, Leckman JF, Cohen DJ: Evidence against a genetic relationship between Gilles de la Tourette's syndrome, and anxiety, depression, panic and phobic disorders. Br J Psychiatry 1994; 164:215–221.
23. Comings DE, Comings BG: A controlled study of Tourette syndrome: I–VII. Am J Hum Genet 1987; 41:701–866.
24. Comings DE: Tourette's syndrome: A behavioral spectrum disorder. Adv Neurol 1995; 65:293–303.
25. Price RA, Kidd KK, Cohen DJ, et al: A twin study of Tourette syndrome. Arch Gen Psychiatry 1985; 42:815–820.
26. Hyde TM, Aaronson BA, Randolf C: Relationship of birthweight to the phenotypic expression of Gilles de la Tourette's syndrome in monozygotic twins. Neurology 1992; 42:652–658.
27. Walkup JT, Price RA, Resnick S, et al: Non-genetic factors associated with the expression of Tourette syndrome. In Scientific Proceedings of

the Annual Meeting of the American Academy of Child and Adolescent Psychiatry; October 21–25, 1987:57; Washington, DC. Volume III.

28. Leckman JF, Price RA, Walkup JT, et al: Non-genetic factors in Gilles de la Tourette's syndrome. Arch Gen Psychiatry 1987; 44:100.
29. Eappen V, Pauls DL, Robertson MM: Evidence for autosomal dominant transmission in Tourette's syndrome—United Kingdom Cohort Study. Br J Psychiatry 1993; 162:593–596.
30. Pauls DL, Raymond CL, Leckman JL, et al: A family study of Tourette's syndrome. Am J Hum Genet 1991; 48:154–163.
31. Conneally PM, Housman D (chairs): Ninth Genetic Workshop on Tourette Syndrome sponsored by the Tourette Syndrome Association; June 17–18, 1993; Rotterdam, Netherlands.
32. Pauls DL: Issues in genetic linkage studies of Tourette syndrome: Phenotypic expression and genetic model parameters. Adv Neurol 1992; 58:151–158.
33. Wilke PJ, Ahmann PA, Hardacre J, et al: Application of microsatellite DNA polymorphisms to linkage mapping of Tourette syndrome gene(s). Adv Neurol 1992; 58:173–180.
34. Davies JL, Kawaguchi Y, Bennett ST, et al: A genome wide search for human type 1 diabetes susceptibility genes. Nature 1994; 371:130–136.
35. Heutink P, Breedveld GJ, Niermeijer MF: Progress in gene location. In Kurlan R (ed): Handbook of Tourette's Syndrome and Related Tic and Behavioral Disorders. New York: Marcel Dekker, 1993:317–335.
36. Singer HS, Reiss AL, Brown J, et al: Volumetric MRI changes in the basal ganglia of children with Tourette's syndrome. Neurology 1993; 43:950–956.
37. Peterson BS, Riddle MA, Cohen DJ, et al: Reduced basal ganglia volumes in Tourette's syndrome using 3-dimensional reconstruction techniques from magnetic resonance images. Neurology 1993; 43:941–949.
38. Hall M, Costa DC, Shields J, et al: Brain perfusion patterns with Tc^{99m}HMPAO-SPECT in patients with Gilles de la Tourette syndrome—short report. In Schmidt HAE, van der Schoot JB (eds): Nuclear Medicine: The State of the Art of Nuclear Medicine in Europe. Stuttgart: Schattauer, 1991:243–245.
39. Riddle MA, Rasmussen AR, Woods SW, Hoffer PB: SPECT imaging of cerebral blood flow in Tourette syndrome. Adv Neurol 1991; 58:207–211.
40. Stoetter B, Braun AR, Randolf C, et al: Functional neuroanatomy of Tourette syndrome: Limbic motor interactions studied with FDG PET. Adv Neurol 1992; 58:213–226.
41. Haber SN, Kowall NW, Vonsattel JP, et al: Gilles de la Tourette's syndrome: A postmortem neuropathological and immunohistochemical study. J Neurol Sci 1986; 75:225–241.
42. Singer HS, Butler IJ, Tune LE, et al: Dopaminergic dysfunction in Tourette syndrome. Ann Neurol 1982; 12:361–366.
43. Wong DF, Young LT, Pearlson GD, et al: D_2 dopamine receptors densities measured by PET are elevated in several neuropsychiatric disorders. J Nucl Med 1989; 30:731.
44. Singer HS, Hahn I-H, Krowiak E, et al: Tourette syndrome: A neurochemical analysis of postmortem cortical brain tissue. Ann Neurol 1990; 27:443–446.
45. Anderson GM, Pollak ES, Chatterjee D, et al: Postmortem analysis of subcortical monoamines and amino acids in Tourette syndrome. Adv Neurol 1992; 58:123–134.
46. Singer HS, Hahn I-H, Moran TH: Abnormalities of dopaminergic markers in postmortem striatal specimens from patients with Tourette syndrome.[abstract] Ann Neurol 1991; 28:441.
47. Leckman JF, Riddle MA, Berrettini WH, et al: Elevated CSF dynorphan A [1–8] in Tourette's syndrome. Life Sci 1988; 43:2015–2023.
48. Sandyk R: The effects of naloxone in Tourette's syndrome. Ann Neurol 1985; 18:367–368.
49. Erenberg G, Lederman RJ: Naltrexone in the treatment of Tourette's syndrome. Neurology 1989; 39(suppl 1):232–329.
50. Kiessling LS, Marcotte AC, Culpepper L: Antineuronal antibodies: Tics and obsessive compulsive symptoms. J Dev Behav Pediatr 1994; 15:421–425.
51. Swedo SE, Leonard HL, Kiessling LS: Speculations on antineuronal antibody mediated neuropsychiatric disorders of childhood. Pediatrics 1994; 93:323–326.
52. Leckman JF, Dolnansky ES, Hardin MT, et al: Perinatal factors in the expression of Tourette syndrome: An exploratory study. J Am Acad Child Adolesc Psychiatry 1990; 29:220–226.
53. Peterson BS, Leckman JF, Scahill L, et al: Steroid hormones and CNS sexual dimorphisms modulate symptom expression in Tourette's syndrome. Psychoneuroendocrinology 1992; 17:553–563.
54. Peterson BS, Leckman JF, Scahill L, et al: Steroid hormones and Tourette's syndrome: Early experience with antiandrogen therapy. J Clin Psychopharmacol 1994; 14:131–135.
55. Price RA, Leckman JF, Pauls DL, et al: Gilles de la Tourette syndrome: Tics and CNS stimulants in twins and non-twins. Neurology 1986; 36:232–237.
56. Kurlan R, McDermott MP: Rating tic severity. In Kurlan R (ed): Handbook of Tourette's Syndrome and Related Tic and Behavioral Disorders. New York: Marcel Dekker, 1993:199–220.
57. Leckman JF, Riddle MA, Hardin MT, et al: The Yale Global Tic Severity Scale: Initial testing of a clinician-rated scale of tic severity. J Am Acad Child Adolesc Psychiatry 1989; 28:566–573.
58. Singer HS, Rosenberg LA: The development of behavioral and emotional problems in Tourette syndrome. Pediatr Neurol 1989; 5:41–44.
59. Jankovic J: Diagnosis and classification of tics and Tourette syndrome. Adv Neurol 1992; 58:7–14.
60. Bruun RD, Budman CL: The natural history of Tourette syndrome. Adv Neurol 1992; 58:1–6.
61. Chappel PB, Leckman JF, Riddle MA: The pharmacologic treatment of tic disorders. Child Adolesc Psychiatr Clin North Am 1995; 4:197–216.
62. Bruun RD: Subtle and under recognized side effects of neuroleptic treatment in children with Tourette's disorder. Am J Psychiatry 1988; 145:621–624.
63. Sallee FR, Rock CM: Effects of pimozide on cognition in children with Tourette syndrome: Interaction with comorbid attention deficit hyperactivity disorder. Acta Psychiatr Scand 1994; 90:4–9.
64. Eggers CH, Rothenberger A, Berghaus U: Clinical and neurobiological findings in children suffering from tic disease following treatment with tiapride. Eur Arch Psychiatry Neurol Sci 1988; 237:223–229.
65. Robertson MM, Schnieden V, Lees AJ: Management of Gilles de la Tourette syndrome using sulpiride. Clin Neuropharmacol 1990; 3:229–235.
66. Goetz CG: Clonidine. In Kurlan R (ed): Handbook of Tourette's Syndrome and Related Tic and Behavioral Disorders. New York: Marcel Dekker, 1993:377–388.
67. Leckman JF, Ort S, Caruso KA, et al: Rebound phenomena in Tourette's syndrome after abrupt withdrawal of clonidine. Behavioral, cardiovascular, and neurochemical effects. Arch Gen Psychiatry 1986; 43:1168–1176.
68. Arnsten AFT, Cai JX, Goldman-Rakic PS: The alpha-2 adrenergic agonist, guanfacine, improves memory in aged monkeys without sedative or hypotensive side effects: Evidence for alpha-2 receptor subtypes. J Neurosci 1988; 8:4287–4298.
69. Chappell PB, Riddle MA, Scahill L, et al: Guanfacine treatment of comorbid attention deficit hyperactivity disorder and Tourette's syndrome. J Am Acad Child Adolesc Psychiatry 1995; 34:1140–1146.
70. Goetz CG: Clonidine and clonazepam. Adv Neurol 1992; 58: 245–251.
71. Azrin NH, Peterson AL: Treatment of Tourette syndrome by habit reversal: A waiting list control group comparison. Behav Ther 1990; 21:305–318.
72. Sanchez-Ramos JR, Weiner WJ: Drug induced tics. In Kurlan R (ed): Handbook of Tourette's Syndrome and Related Tic and Behavioral Disorders. New York: Marcel Dekker, 1993:183–197.
73. Gadow KD, Sverd J, Sprafkin J, et al: Efficacy of methylphenidate for attention-deficit hyperactivity disorder in children with tic disorder. Arch Gen Psychiatry 1995; 52:444–455.
74. Riddle MA, Geller B, Ryan N: Another sudden death in a child treated with desipramine. J Am Acad Child Adolesc Psychiatry 1993; 32:792–797.
75. Wilens TE, Biederman J, Geist DE, et al: Nortriptyline in the treatment of ADHD: A chart review of 58 cases. J Am Acad Child Adolesc Psychiatry 1993; 32:343–349.
76. Jankovic J: Deprenyl in attention deficit associated with Tourette's syndrome. Arch Neurol 1993; 50:286–288.
77. March J: Cognitive behavioral treatment for children and adolescents with OCD: A review and recommendations for treatment. J Am Acad Child Adolesc Psychiatry 1995; 34:7–18.
78. McDougle CJ, Goodman WK, Leckman LF, et al: Haloperidol addition in fluvoxamine refractory obsessive compulsive disorder: A double blind placebo controlled trial in patients with and without tics. Arch Gen Psychiatry 1994; 51:302–308.

79. Jankovic J: Botulinum toxin treatment of tics. In Jankovic J (ed): Therapy with Botulinum Toxin. New York: Marcel Dekker, 1994:503–509.
80. Baer L, Rauch SL, Jenike MA: Cingulotomy in a case of concomitant obsessive compulsive disorder and Tourette's syndrome. Arch Gen Psychiatry 1994; 51:73–74.
81. Mindus P, Jenike MA: Neurosurgical treatment of malignant obsessive compulsive disorder. Psychiatr Clin North Am 1992; 15:921–938.
82. Walkup JT: Clinical decision making in child and adolescent psychopharmacology. Child Adolesc Psychiatr Clin North Am 1995; 4:23–39.
83. Hoehn-Saric R, Harris GJ, Pearlson GD, et al: A fluoxetine-induced frontal lobe syndrome in an obsessive compulsive patient. J Clin Psychiatry 1992; 52:131–133.
84. Hoehn-Saric R, Lipsey JR, McLeod DR: Apathy and indifference in patients on fluoxetine and fluvoxamine. J Clin Psychopharmacol 1990; 10:343–345.

CHAPTER

39 Communication Disorders

William M. Klykylo

Expressive Language Disorder
Mixed Receptive-Expressive Language Disorder
Phonological Disorder
Stuttering
Communication Disorder Not Otherwise Specified

Definition

The disorders of communication have traditionally been insufficiently familiar to psychiatrists despite the fact that psychiatric practice is founded on communication. A knowledge of these disorders is of especially crucial importance in the care of children because they are deeply imbricated in all aspects of normal development, psychiatric illness, and the functions of daily life.

The relationship among language, cognition, and their disturbances continues to stimulate a mass of research and speculation beyond the scope of this chapter.[1] Thus, the classification of these disorders has always been controversial. Before the elaboration of the *Diagnostic and Statistical Manual of Mental Disorders,* Third Edition (DSM-III)[2] in the late 1970s, they were frequently regarded by psychiatrists as psychopathological processes manifested by a single symptom, as were elimination disorders, tics, and learning disorders. DSM-III represented an attempt to consolidate the approach of psychiatrists with that of other disciplines. It presented these disorders as specific developmental disorders grouped with academic skills disorders and resulting from the inadequate development of some specific language or speech skill. Deficits due to other demonstrable physical or neurological disorders were regarded as separate conditions.

The linkage of language and academic skills disorders, although plausible, has remained controversial, and in the *Diagnostic and Statistical Manual of Mental Disorders,* Fourth Edition (DSM-IV)[3] they are regarded as separate but often associated conditions. This section includes disorders both of speech, the oral representation of language, and of language itself. The disorders included in this section are expressive language disorder, mixed receptive-expressive language disorder, phonological disorder, stuttering, and communication disorder not otherwise specified (NOS). These disorders share many common features, as noted in Table 39–1. Selective mutism is not regarded as a disorder of communication and is included among other disorders of childhood.

Expressive Language Disorder

Expressive language disorder denotes an impairment in the development of expressive language. Its diagnosis requires the use of one or more standardized assessment measures that are individually administered. Individuals with this disorder have expressive language scores well below those obtained from measures of nonverbal intelligence and of receptive language. DSM-IV does not require any particular degree of discrepancy in scores.

The presence of a test score by itself does not define the condition; the affected individual must have clinical symptoms, which might include disturbances of vocabulary, grammar (e.g., tenses), or syntax (e.g., sentence length or complexity). The diagnosis of this condition also requires that the individual having it experience social, academic, or occupational difficulties directly related to the condition. The presence of a mixed expressive-receptive language disorder or a pervasive developmental disorder supersedes this diagnosis, and it is not made in their presence. Similarly, diagnosis may not be made in the presence of mental retardation, motor or sensory deficits, or environmental deprivation unless the expressive language difficulties experienced are beyond what would be expected for individuals with these conditions. This condition may be acquired, as from a medical condition affecting the central nervous system (CNS), or it may be developmental, in the sense of arising early in life without known origin.

Mixed Receptive-Expressive Language Disorder

The adoption of this category in DSM-IV represents the most significant change from previous classification systems,

DSM-IV Criteria 315.31

Expressive Language Disorder

A. The scores obtained from standardized individually administered measures of expressive language development are substantially below those obtained from standardized measures of both nonverbal intellectual capacity and receptive language development. The disturbance may be manifest clinically by symptoms that include having a markedly limited vocabulary, making errors in tense, or having difficulty recalling words or producing sentences with developmentally appropriate length or complexity.

B. The difficulties with expressive language interfere with academic or occupational achievement or with social communication.

C. Criteria are not met for mixed receptive-expressive language disorder or a pervasive developmental disorder.

D. If mental retardation, a speech-motor or sensory deficit, or environmental deprivation is present, the language difficulties are in excess of those usually associated with these problems.

DSM-IV Criteria 315.31

Mixed Receptive-Expressive Language Disorder

A. The scores obtained from a battery of standardized individually administered measures of both receptive and expressive language development are substantially below those obtained from standardized measures of nonverbal intellectual capacity. Symptoms include those for expressive language disorder as well as difficulty understanding words, sentences, or specific types of words, such as spatial terms.

B. The difficulties with receptive and expressive language significantly interfere with academic or occupational achievement or with social communication.

C. Criteria are not met for a pervasive developmental disorder.

D. If mental retardation, a speech-motor or sensory deficit, or environmental deprivation is present, the language difficulties are in excess of those usually associated with these problems.

Table 39–1 Features Common to All Communication Disorders

Features
Inadequate development of some aspect of communication
Absence (in developmental types) of any demonstrable causes of physical disorder, neurological disorder, global mental retardation, or severe environmental deprivation
Onset in childhood
Long duration
Clinical features resembling the functional levels of younger normal children
Impairments in adaptive functioning, especially in school
Tendency to occur in families
Predisposition toward boys
Multiple presumed etiological factors
Increased prevalence in younger age range
Diagnosis requiring a range of standardized techniques
Tendency toward certain specific associated problems, such as attention-deficit/hyperactivity disorder
Wide range of subtypes and severity

Adapted from Baker L: Specific communication disorders. In Garfinkel BD, Carlson GA, Weller EB (eds): Psychiatric Disorders in Children and Adolescents. Philadelphia: WB Saunders, 1990:257–270.

which posited the existence of receptive language disorders in a solitary form. The existence of this category reflects the clinical observation that receptive language disorders in children seldom, if ever, can occur without concurrent (and perhaps resultant) problems with expression. DSM-IV notes that this is in direct contrast with such entities as Wernicke's aphasia in adults, which affect reception alone.

Children with these conditions have significant measurable deficits in standardized individual assessments, of both receptive and expressive language, compared with their similarly assessed nonverbal intelligence. These deficiencies may occur in both verbal and sign language; interfere with social, academic, and occupational function; and, by definition in DSM-IV, do not occur in the presence of a pervasive developmental disorder. This condition may be acquired from some CNS injury, or it may be purely developmental, in which case affected individuals exhibit a persistent pattern of delayed language development. Children with this disorder may manifest any and all of the symptoms of expressive language disorder. They also have difficulty with various aspects of receptive language, including misunderstanding of individual words or whole statements and deficits in auditory processing skills (sound discrimination and association, recall, storage, and sequencing).

Phonological Disorder

This condition was formerly known as articulation or developmental articulation disorder. It is characterized by an individual's failure to use speech sounds appropriate for one's developmental level and dialect (see page 722). The affected individual may substitute one sound for another (e.g., /l/ for /r/); omit certain sounds entirely; or exhibit other errors in organization, use, or production of sounds. By definition in DSM-IV, these difficulties interfere with social, academic, or occupational function. The symptoms may occur during development without discernible cause, or they may be related to CNS, motor, or sensory dysfunction or

DSM-IV Criteria 315.39

Phonological Disorder

A. Failure to use developmentally expected speech sounds that are appropriate for age and dialect (e.g., errors in sound production, use, representation, or organization such as, but not limited to, substitutions of one sound for another [use of /t/ for target /k/ sound] or omissions of sounds such as final consonants).

B. The difficulties in speech sound production interfere with academic or occupational achievement or with social communication.

C. If mental retardation, a speech-motor or sensory deficit, or environmental deprivation is present, the speech difficulties are in excess of those usually associated with these problems.

environmental deprivation. In the last cases, the speech difficulties must be in excess of those usually associated with the particular problem for the diagnosis to be made. This condition ranges in severity from mild problems to severe disorders that render speech totally unintelligible.

Outside of DSM-IV, the term *phonology* often refers to rules governing the combination of sounds into syllables and words. In this case, a *phonological disorder* may refer to a type of disorder characterized by difficulty in generating sound combinations according to these rules.

DSM-IV Criteria 307.0

Stuttering

A. Disturbance in the normal fluency and time patterning of speech (inappropriate for the individual's age), characterized by frequent occurrences of one or more of the following:

(1) sound and syllable repetitions

(2) sound prolongations

(3) interjections

(4) broken words (e.g., pauses within a word)

(5) audible or silent blocking (filled or unfilled pauses in speech)

(6) circumlocutions (word substitutions to avoid problematic words)

(7) words produced with an excess of physical tension

(8) monosyllabic whole-word repetitions (e.g., "I-I-I-I see him")

B. The disturbance in fluency interferes with academic or occupational achievement or with social communication.

C. If a speech-motor or sensory deficit is present, the speech difficulties are in excess of those usually associated with these problems.

Stuttering

Stuttering is one of the most commonly recognized disorders of speech. Some occurrence of the symptoms of stuttering is normal in the earlier stages of development, and the condition is properly diagnosed only when the symptoms are perceived to be in excess of what is developmentally expected. Similarly, because occasional symptoms appear in the speech of nearly all persons, the diagnosis is not made unless the disturbances interfere with social, academic, or occupational function. The condition may be associated with motor or sensory deficits; when this is the case, the diagnosis is made only when symptoms exceed those expected with these problems. The characteristic symptoms of stuttering are disturbances in fluency (such as repetitions of sounds, syllables, or words; interjections; and circumlocutions) and in time patterning (sound prolongations, broken words, blocking). Cluttering, the disturbance in rate and length of speech noted in the *Diagnostic and Statistical Manual of Mental Disorders,* Third Edition, Revised (DSM-III-R), is subsumed under communication disorder NOS or expressive language disorder.

Communication Disorder Not Otherwise Specified

This category includes disorders that do not meet criteria for other specific communication disorders or do so completely. DSM-IV cites voice disorders of pitch, loudness, quality, tone, or resonance as an example.

Epidemiology (Prevalence)

Past reports of prevalence and incidence of communication disorders have been complicated by variations in setting, case finding, and diagnostic criteria. Numbers from 1% to 13% have been posited for the prevalence of language disorders and numbers as high as 32% for speech disorders.[4] In

DSM-IV Criteria 307.9

Communication Disorder Not Otherwise Specified

A. This category is for disorders in communication that do not meet criteria for any specific communication disorder; for example, a voice disorder (i.e., an abnormality of vocal pitch, loudness, quality, tone, or resonance).

the development of DSM-IV, researchers found that acquired language disorders were reported to be less common than the developmental types. Overall, between 3% and 5% of all children were suspected of having a developmental expressive language disorder. Mixed receptive-expressive language disorder is less common but may still be seen in as many as 3% of children. Speech disorders are similarly common but become less frequent with age. Phonological disorder occurs in 2% to 3% of 6- and 7-year-olds, but this prevalence falls to 0.5% by age 17 years. Stuttering occurs in approximately 1% of children 10 years old and younger, declining modestly to 0.8% in later adolescence. All of these conditions have a male to female predominance; that of stuttering is as high as 3:1. In all, the prevalence of these disturbances is comparable in magnitude to that of many other common psychiatric disorders.

Expressive Language Disorder and Mixed Receptive-Expressive Language Disorder

Phonological disorder is especially common among children with these disorders. In addition, many of these children may present at least some manifestations of learning disorders. Other conditions that are broadly considered neurodevelopmental are also noted in these children, such as motor delays, coordination disorders, and enuresis. The extent of these associations, although apparently considerable, is difficult to quantify because of methodological variations in the literature. The combination of these disorders and the stresses they create frequently lead to adjustment disorders and social withdrawal.

Cantwell and Baker[5] found that the most common psychiatric disorder among children with communication disorders overall was attention-deficit/hyperactivity disorder, representing 19% of their sample of 600 children referred for a communication evaluation. The combination of language and disruptive behavior disorders appears to be associated with greater severity of impairment in both areas. Some authors have speculated that attention-deficit/hyperactivity disorder may be concordant with an entity known as central auditory processing disorder, which refers to deficits in the processing of audible signals and can be subsumed under the DSM-IV language disorders. A total concordance is unlikely, but work[6] suggests that 50% of children with central auditory processing disorder also have attention-deficit/hyperactivity disorder. Ongoing work in neuroimaging and brain activity measurement may be expected to delineate this area more fully.

Phonological Disorder

Children with this problem may present with clearly associated causal factors, such as anatomical, neurological, or cognitive disorders, although most do not. They do have a higher prevalence of language disorders, with all their associated problems, than do normal control children. Even if free of language disorders, they are still more likely to have attention-deficit/hyperactivity disorder, although probably not as commonly as do children with language disorders. Children with phonological disorders, especially when associated with stuttering or hyperactivity, are susceptible to social discrimination and isolation, with subsequent consequences.

Stuttering

There is much less literature extant addressing the comorbidity of stuttering compared with other communication disorders. Other communication disorders are more frequently reported in those with stuttering than in normal control subjects. Stuttering is frequently accompanied by many linguistic mechanisms and social maneuvers to avoid its manifestation. Conversely, it appears more frequently and intensely in affected individuals when they experience anxieties or stress. The literature is replete with anecdotal and biographical accounts of the social and occupational discrimination, disappointment, and low self-esteem faced by persons with this condition. The negative stereotype of stutterers in society is well documented.

Etiology and Pathophysiology

Genetic Influences

Many psychiatrists believe that communication disorders tend to "run in families," but the extent to which this is true is unclear. No clear mechanisms of transmission have been elucidated, but a number of instances of family aggregation have been reported. At least one of these[7] suggested the presence of a single dominant autosomal gene. Tomblin[8] has reported increased concordance of language disorders among siblings. These reports cannot absolutely prove any genetic hypothesis; however, they are provocative. This area of inquiry is complicated not only by methodological issues but also by larger controversies over the degree to which specific features of language, such as grammar, arise from a "preprogrammed" genetic base.[9]

Pathophysiological Influences

Baker[4] and others proposed that communication disorders arise from at least three interrelated sets of factors: neurophysiological (including structural), cognitive-perceptual, and environmental (Table 39–2).

Neurophysiological Factors

The great majority of children with communication disorders give no evidence of specific CNS damage. Thus, in these children, minimal or subclinical damage has been postulated. The relative frequency of "soft" neurological signs and dominance problems in this population provokes this speculation. However, at this time, no clear neurophysiological mechanisms or disease processes can be correlated with these disorders, despite the appeal of this model to many physicians.

In a minority of children with communication disorders, a neuropathological cause is painfully apparent. Localizable brain damage may arise from trauma, infection, vascular disease, or neoplasm. Perinatal factors, such as prematurity, low birth weight, and asphyxia, have also been implicated. A number of toxic agents have been associated with communication disorders. Concerns have been raised about prenatal alcohol exposure[10] and also about the physical sequelae of abuse and neglect.[11]

Cognitive-Perceptual Factors

These hypotheses relate communication disorders to various deficits in the reception, acquisition, processing, storage, or recall of different elements of communication. Work in this

Table 39–2 Hypotheses About Influencing Factors in Communication Disorders

Types of Hypotheses	Specific Hypotheses
Neurological impairments	Specific localizable brain damage Subclinical (minimal) brain damage
Perceptual deficits	Deficits in auditory discrimination Deficits in auditory attention Deficits in auditory figure-ground Deficits in auditory memory Deficits in auditory-visual association Deficits in the processing of specific linguistic units
Cognitive deficits	Deficits in symbolic or concept development Deficits in anticipatory imagery Deficits in sorting or categorizing Deficits in hierarchical processing
Environmental factors	Inadequate parent-child interaction Socioeconomic factors (large family size, lower social class, late birth order, environmental deprivation) Medical factors (e.g., prematurity, history of recurrent otitis media)
Multifactorial etiology	Combinations of all of the above

Adapated from Baker L: Specific communication disorders. In Garfinkel BD, Carlson GA, Weller EB (eds): Psychiatric Disorders in Children and Adolescents. Philadelphia: WB Saunders, 1990:257–270.

area has largely been pursued through a multidisciplinary model addressing children with "developmental" communication disorders. Perceptual hypotheses posit that speech or language develops improperly because of a failure of input, that is, a failure of the child to perceive or process communicated information. Without proper input, proper communication cannot come about. At times, a related model of perceptual immaturity has also been proposed. This model has undeniable intuitive appeal but does not by itself explain why language development may not "catch up" despite age and maturation. Table 39–2 notes various perceptual deficits that have been implicated, including auditory discrimination, attention, memory, and visual association.

More purely cognitive hypotheses have also been proposed. Their details are beyond the scope of this chapter, but they implicate deficits in symbolization, categorizing, hierarchical processing, and related areas. The concordance between communication and learning disorders supports these hypotheses. However, not all children with communication disorders have cognitive deficits. Some authors[1] proposed that there are certain language-specific abilities; this notion is invigorated by the phenomenology of Williams' syndrome, in which affected individuals may have good language skills in the presence of mental retardation.

Environmental Factors

This category is generally taken to refer to the psychosocial environment of the child, although general medical factors such as perinatal complications or recurrent otitis media may also be included. In this way, this category may at times be overlapped with perceptual deficits; both interfere with input.

Inadequate or pathological parent-child interaction has been associated with the rate of language acquisition, although not so clearly with eventual outcome. Other socioeconomic variables, such as class, family size, income, and birth order, clearly affect the amount of verbal interaction children receive and have also been implicated. Some authors[11] have attempted to elucidate specific effects on language of child abuse, mainly in regard to syntactic form, but this is speculative at best. No definitive relationship between any psychosocial factor and the type or severity of communication disorder has been established. In the past, various psychodynamic causes have been proposed for stuttering; these have been more stigmatizing than illuminating. The association between the exacerbation of stuttering and stress is well known, however. Work in this area (as in others) has frequently confounded predisposing, triggering, and maintaining factors.[12]

Mixed Influences

Review of these influences reveals a considerable amount of overlap, with potentially complex interrelationships of causality and concurrence. Clinical observation seldom if ever suggests a unitary causality of communication disorders in real patients. Thus, these conditions in most patients are ultimately described as multifactorial. The psychiatrist should be aware that many or all of the factors cited may be present in any communication-disordered patient and may have complex effects on communication as well as other aspects of the patient's life.

Diagnosis

Phenomenology

Expressive Language Disorder

The manifestations of this condition vary with age and severity. Vocabulary, word finding, sentence length, variety of expression, and grammatical complexity may all be reduced. Most children with this disorder demonstrate a slower than expected rate of language development associated with the developmental subtype. Auxiliary words or prepositions are often omitted: "he was going to school" becomes "he going school." Word order, of essential importance in English, may be garbled. Words or phrases may be repeated. Conversation may be tangential, with sudden inappropriate changes of topic or, conversely, perseveration. Pragmatic difficulties, such as in initiating or terminating conversations, and much avoidance of conversation are also frequently seen.

These children frequently have associated learning problems because of their difficulty in responding verbally to exercises. They may have motor coordination problems and various other neurodevelopmental abnormalities documented on neurological examination, electroencephalography, or neuroimaging, although no consistent patterns are seen.

Mixed Receptive-Expressive Language Disorder

Children with this disorder may have all the problems of expressive language disorder. In addition, they do not understand all that they hear. The deficits may be mild or severe, and at times deceptively subtle, because patients may conceal them or avoid interaction. All areas and levels of language comprehension may be disturbed. Thus, the child may not understand certain words or categories of words, such as abstract quantities, or types of statements, such as conditional clauses. This may cause these children to seem not to hear or attend or to misbehave by not following commands correctly. More severely impaired children may not understand the rules of syntax or word order and thus be unable to distinguish between subjects and objects or questions and declarations. In more severe cases, disabilities may often be multiple and pervasive, affecting processing, recall, and association.

Children with this disorder may fail to understand pragmatic or social conventions of language; for example, they may fail to comprehend the verbal and nonverbal signals that accompany a change of topic or the end of a conversation. Such deficits have immense social consequences. They may even cause a child to be misidentified as having a pervasive developmental disorder. A severe language disorder is seen in Landau-Kleffner syndrome (acquired epileptic aphasia) accompanied by seizures and other CNS dysfunctions.

Phonological Disorder

This category subsumes the DSM-III-R articulation disorder and is characterized by persistent errors in the production of speech. These include omission, substitution, or distortion of sounds. Defects in the order of sounds or insertions of extraneous sounds may also be heard. The occurrence of these errors is persistent but not constant.

Baker[4] pointed out that "conditioning factors," such as the location within a word or the rate or length of a statement, may determine whether a phonological error is produced. Only some sounds are usually affected, such as the misarticulation of sibilants in lisping. Some articulation errors are expected in early childhood, especially involving sounds that are usually mastered at a later age (in English, /l/, /r/, /s/, /z/, /th/, /ch/). These errors are not regarded as pathological unless they persist and result in adverse consequences to the individual; 90% or more of children have mastered the more difficult sounds by the age of 6 to 8 years.

Stuttering

Stuttering is the communication disorder most easily recognized by both the lay public and physicians. It varies in severity among individuals. It may be more or less evident in different situations and may vary over time. It is typically most severe when the affected child is stressed or anxious and most especially when communication is expected. Children who stutter can sing or talk to themselves without difficulty. Because of its often gradual onset, children are frequently not aware of its presence at first. Over time, they may become more anxious and withdraw from conversation as the degree of social discrimination they experience increases.

Stuttering may be accompanied by various movements that may seem to either express or discharge anxiety, such as blinking, grimacing, or hyperventilation. Sometimes children who stutter may attempt to stop momentarily, by slowing down or pausing in their speech, but this is frequently unsuccessful and leads to an exacerbation. Thus, a pattern of habitual fear and avoidance emerges.

Communication Disorder Not Otherwise Specified

This category is used to describe disorders that do not fit the criteria for any of the other communication disorders. Because of the inclusiveness of this category, it is generally used to describe voice disorders only. These are disorders of pitch, intonation, volume, or resonance. Hyponasality is one example of a voice disorder, as characterized by the "adenoidal" speech that brought many children to surgery in an earlier era. Hypernasality, secondary to velopharyngeal insufficiency, may be associated with serious voice problems.

Assessment

In the Psychiatric Interview

It is essential that the psychiatrist seeing children be familiar with the expected milestones of speech and language development (see Section II). This knowledge forms the basis for effective observation in a clinical setting. The psychiatrist should ask the parents or guardians about the child's speech and language, both development and current function. Paul[13] provided a detailed outline for this, but much can be learned from even a few questions. Does the child seem to hear and understand what is being said? Does the child require visual prompts? Does the child in fact use spoken language to communicate? How long and complicated are the child's sentences? Does the child make sense to outsiders? Can she or he be clearly understood, even by strangers? Which sounds does the child find difficult? Does the child use unusual volume, pitch, or nasality? Does he or she observe the rules of conversation? Parent-child communication should also be observed.

Children must be assessed in an environment that fosters verbal communication and must be observed in a variety of interactions, because their speech and language vary so much over time in quantity and quality. For younger children, this may best be done in the context of a play situation. Rutter[14] recommended that the psychiatrist assess inner language, comprehension, production, phonation, and pragmatics. By inner language is meant symbolization, which may be observed in a younger child by the child's representational use of play materials. For example, a block could be a house or a vehicle. Comprehension is assessed through conversation and the use of developmentally appropriate questions and commands, especially with nonverbal augments or prompts. The psychiatrist should note how well a child can follow and draw inferences from a conversation. Production refers to speech—its fluency and its intelligibility. Pragmatics are those aspects of language that render it useful for social communication beyond the most concrete level. Does the child appreciate the nuances of his or her partner's conversation, for example, when they signal beginnings and endings of conversations, topic changes, or the patient's turn to talk? Pragmatic language involves nonverbal elements. Deficiencies in this area impair abstraction and may render the individual almost "robotlike." In all cases, observations should be made in as relaxed a fashion as possible, avoiding interrogation or rote exercises. If a child fails to communicate a given item, necessary help should be offered, including nonverbal prompts, so that the child has the experience of success. The sense of failure will stifle communication.

In the Classroom

In school settings, all of the phenomena seen in a clinical interview may also be pursued. Children with communication disorders often feel challenged by the demands of the classroom and may limit or withdraw from conversation entirely. Thus, the task-oriented group setting of the classroom may not produce a child's best communication. It may, however, demonstrate the practical effectiveness of the child's everyday efforts. At the same time, teachers sometimes have more individual conversations with children than even their parents do, and their experience may make them the first adults to detect communication problems. In many areas, young children receive some type of formal communication screening in school. Therefore, the teacher's input is essential in the evaluation of these children.

Developmental and Cultural Influences

The need for a psychiatrist to be aware of normal developmental expectations has been cited. In settings as geographically and culturally diverse as the English-speaking countries, special sensitivity must be exercised for the range of dialects and conversational styles encountered. English is spoken with an extraordinary range of accents, even within each dialect group. It is essential that one not pathologize a difference in intonation into a phonological disorder or of dialect into an expressive language disorder. Many American children grow up in multilingual environments and may speak with a synthesis of grammar and vocabulary, especially during their preschool years. Finally, children of minority groups who have suffered social discrimination and children who live in physically dangerous environments may necessarily be cautious and less forthcoming with language; this may be adaptive in some cases and not a disorder at all.

In general, these disorders are seen more commonly in boys than in girls. This is especially true in the case of stuttering. By contrast, no sex influences have been reported in the nondevelopmental (i.e., acquired) language disorders.

Differential Diagnosis

Expressive and Mixed Receptive-Expressive Language Disorders

These disorders are distinguished from each other by the presence or absence of receptive problems. Children with autism may have any or all of the characteristics of the language disorders. However, they have many additional problems including the use of language in a restricted and often stereotypical fashion rather than for communicative purposes. They also have difficulties with a wider range of interactions with persons and objects in their environment and exhibit a restricted range of behaviors. The language impairments of mental retardation, oral motor deficits, or environmental deprivation are not diagnosed in this category unless they are well in excess of what is expected. Language impairment due to environmental deprivation tends to improve dramatically with environmental improvement.

Sensory deficits, especially hearing impairment, may restrict language development. Any indication of potential hearing impairment, no matter how tenuous, should prompt a referral for an audiological evaluation. Obviously, hearing and language disorders can and do coexist. Some children have an acquired aphasia as a complication of general medical illness. This condition is usually temporary; only if it persists beyond the acute course of the medical illness is a language disorder diagnosed.

Phonological Disorder and Stuttering

The conditions should be distinguished from the normal dysfluencies that occur among young children. For example, misarticulation of some sounds, such as /l/, /r/, /s/, /z/, /th/, and /ch/, is common among preschoolers and resolves with age. As with the language disorders, these diagnoses are given in the case of motor or sensory deficit, mental retardation, or environmental deprivation only if the disorder is much more severe than expected in these conditions. Problems limited to voice alone are included under communication disorder NOS.

Speech and Language Assessment

A number of instruments are available for the assessment of communication (Table 39–3). Most are beyond the training of psychiatrists, whose most important contributions are interview skills and medical assessment, but a familiarity with them can help the psychiatrist develop a repertoire and knowledge of screening measures.

Because of the complex comorbidity of these disorders, they are often best assessed by an interdisciplinary team.[15] The team's activities are usually coordinated by a case manager, who is often a pediatrician or a child and adolescent psychiatrist and who usually has primary clinical responsibility in the case. The audiologist is an essential contributor to this process because, first, one must rule out a hearing disorder in any communication disorder. Children of any age, even infants, can be assessed audiologically. Psychological assessment is necessary to delineate the child's cognitive abilities and may also cast light on the child's emotional state through projective testing. Medical specialists, including pediatric neurologists and otorhinolaryngologists, as well as child and adolescent psychiatrists, should be appropriately involved. The educational specialist or liaison special educator has particular competence in developing an education prescription for the child, in assisting the family in the procedural (and at times legal) efforts required to arrange appropriate educational services, and in helping classroom teachers develop effective pedagogical approaches.

The speech and language pathologist has a graduate professional degree and should be certified by The American Speech, Language and Hearing Association. The speech and language pathologist uses a combination of interview techniques, behavioral observations, and standardized instruments to identify communication disorders as well as patterns of communication that are not pathological. The assessment of a speech and language pathologist is usually the definitive measure of the presence or absence of a communication disorder. Families may consult a speech and language pathologist directly or be referred by other professionals. The responsibility of psychiatrists and other professionals in this process is simple and straightforward:

Table 39–3 Language Tests

Test	Ages	Functions Assessed
Language Tests		
Sequenced Inventory of Communication Development (SICD)	0-4–4-0	Sound discrimination, auditory memory, receptive and expressive language
Test of Early Development (TELD)	3-0–7-11	Receptive and expressive language; oral and pointing responses
Test of Language Development (TOLD)	4-0–9-0	Auditory discrimination and memory, receptive and expressive language; oral and pointing responses
Test of Adolescent Language (TOAL)	11-0–17-5	Receptive and expressive language; oral and written responses
Clinical Evaluation of Language Function (CELF)	5-0–17-0	Screening test for auditory memory, receptive and expressive language; oral responses
Fluharty Preschool Speech and Language Screening Test	2-0–6-0	Screening test for articulation and language disorder
Tests of Specific Functions		
Peabody Picture Vocabulary Test (PPVT)	1-9–18-0	Receptive auditory vocabulary; pointing to pictures
Token Test	3-0–12-0	Receptive auditory syntax; following verbal instructions
Goldman-Fristoe-Woodcock Auditory Selective Attention Test	3-0–12-0	Auditory memory; pointing to pictures
Goldman-Fristoe-Woodcock Test of Auditory Discrimination	3-0–adult	Auditory discrimination of words; pointing to pictures
Expressive One-Word Vocabulary Test (EOWVT)	3-0–12-0	Expressive vocabulary; picture naming
Arizona Articulation Proficiency Scale	3-0–11-0	Speech articulation; picture naming

Adapted from Feinstein C, Aldershof A: Developmental disorders of learning and language. In Wiener JM (ed): Textbook of Child and Adolescent Psychiatry. Washington, DC: American Psychiatric Press, 1991.

any suspicion of a communication problem in any patient should prompt a referral to a qualified speech and language pathologist. Even when a disorder appears to be limited and benign, communication evaluation by a speech and language pathologist can disclose subtle impairments that could have profound consequences.

Course and Natural History

Expressive and Mixed Receptive-Expressive Language Disorders

Contrary to some popular beliefs, language disorders do not always spontaneously resolve, nor do children always "grow out of it." In general, the course of these disorders of the developmental type are generally recognized gradually as children grow up; the less severe cases are identified later in childhood or adolescence. Language disorders acquired secondary to other medical illnesses tend to occur more precipitously and can appear at any age.

In the case of expressive language disorder, DSM-IV reports that approximately half of affected children eventually attain normal communication skills; the remainder have persistent problems. The prognosis is worse in the case of mixed receptive-expressive language disorders, and only a minority of these children are free of some communication problems in adulthood. Even when their communication skills seem grossly normal, subtle deficits may persist. The prognosis for individuals with acquired language disorders must be assessed according to the severity of injury or medical illness as well as the premorbid state of the child in each case.

Phonological Disorder

The course of phonological disorder is much more encouraging. Milder cases may not be discovered until the child starts school. These cases often recover spontaneously, especially if the child does not encounter adverse psychosocial consequences because of her or his speech. Severe cases associated with anatomical malformations may at times require surgical intervention, and their course and outcome depend on its success. Between these two extremes are children who gradually improve, often to the point of total remission, and whose improvement may be accelerated by speech therapy.

Stuttering

Stuttering usually appears in early childhood, as early as 2 years of age and frequently about 5 years. The onset of stuttering is typically regarded as gradual, with repetition of initial consonants or first words or phrases heard in the beginning. However, a study by Yairi and colleagues[16] suggested that early stuttering often takes on a moderate to severe form and that identification of problems in this period has been affected by parents' tendency to postpone professional consultation. Children are generally not aware of this condition in themselves until it is pointed out to them by others. The disorder can wax and wane during childhood. By early adolescence, it abates in as many as 20% of cases, and 60% to 80% of individuals eventually recover totally or to a major extent. DSM-IV asserts that recovery typically occurs before age 16 years. Stuttering may persist into adulthood, often leading to adverse social and occupational consequences.

Treatment and Its Goals

Speech and language therapy typically has three major goals: the development and improvement of communication skills with concurrent remediation of deficits; the development of alternative or augmentative communication strategies, when required; and the social habilitation of the individual in regard to communication. Thus, a great range of approaches and components must be employed in treating children with communication disorders.

The speech and language pathologist plays the most direct role in treatment of these conditions. Speech and language pathologists may employ an exceedingly wide range of techniques with children. Their work, not unlike medical psychotherapy, requires both science and art. As in child psychotherapy, the participation of parents is necessary. Parent-infant work involves demonstration and modeling of language stimulation techniques. Individual therapy can usually be begun by 3 years of age, and early initiation of therapy is frequently recommended. Individual sessions can include traditional exercises along with seemingly less structured but nonetheless carefully directed verbal and play interactions. A lay observer of the session might recognize exercises of the "Peter-piper-picked-a-peck" type as therapeutic. However, the same session might also include periods of seemingly free play or undirected conversation that in fact subtly model and direct the patient in the skills of speech and language. Group therapy can also be used, especially in the development of language skills applied to a social context, but it should not be regarded as a low-budget substitute for individual treatment. In any treatment regimen, constant monitoring and regular reassessment are necessary, as is ongoing support for parents, who must reinforce the treatment at home. Similarly, regular reconsultation with other professionals from the multidisciplinary team may be required.

The treatment of stuttering has provoked special interest in recent years, particularly as its adverse consequences in adulthood have been recognized. Approaches to this problem address both the mechanics of speech and the associated attitudinal and affective patterns. Guitar[17] noted that therapists attempt to modify speech rhythm and speed, leading subjects to regularize rhythm and, as a temporary measure, prolong their speech. Thus, patients might be heard speaking in a slow, drawn out, singsong fashion. Much attention is also directed to respiration, air flow, and "gentle" onset of phonation. Drug therapy for this disorder remains at best controversial (see later). Individual and family psychotherapy may be a useful augment in reducing the stress these children encounter.

The literature on the outcome of treatment for stuttering is somewhat more complete than for the other communication disorders, because symptoms of this disorder can be readily quantified by electronic and other means. Success rates for various treatments of up to 70% have been reported, although with various follow-up periods and relapse rates.[17] Some speech and language pathologists specialize in the treatment of this disorder.[18]

The psychiatrist may have a major role in the treatment of communication disorders. These children and their families may present for psychotherapy or other treatment for disorders based on or related to communication problems. Thus, the psychiatrist may in the first place be a case finder or case manager, facilitating the evaluation and treatment of these disorders by a multidisciplinary team. The demonstrated psychiatric comorbidity of these disorders will necessitate the psychiatrist's involvement on many levels, both as a physician primarily treating a child and as a therapist, counselor, and agent of advice and support for the entire family. Psychotherapy does not directly address language disorders, although older literature has cited improvement in stuttering after family and individual treatment. The psychotherapist must, in any event, be sensitive to the manner in which communication disorders can affect or interfere with the therapeutic process. Nonverbal augments or prompts should be sensitively provided to children who need them.

The role of psychotropic medication in the management of these disorders is mainly limited to the treatment of comorbid psychiatric problems according to standard practices. From time to time, some interest in the use of drugs specifically for these conditions has arisen. In the 1960s and 1970s, some reports of haloperidol treatment for stuttering emerged. However, enthusiasm was tempered by recognition of this agent's side effects,[19] and it is seldom used for this condition today. I have received occasional reports of treatment of stuttering with tricyclic antidepressants and, more recently, selective serotonin reuptake inhibitors, which perhaps arise out of today's climate of general enthusiasm for these agents. The rationale for these treatments appears to be a hypothetical connection between stuttering and other compulsive behaviors. These accounts are provocative but do not suggest any real indication for these medications for stuttering alone.

Outcome studies of communication therapy, especially for the language disorders, have often been complicated by multiple theories of language development, diagnostic and methodological variations, lack of standardization of therapeutic techniques, and comorbidity. Thus, the literature in this area is relatively sparse and not always conclusive. Like the outcome of psychotherapy, this is a difficult area to study. Nonresponse to initial treatment may be common, requiring patience and persistence. Even when communication therapy does not lead to apparent improvements in language beyond developmental improvements, it may still facilitate the child's use of extant language for environmental control and self-control.[20]

Special Features

Comorbidity

Psychiatrists should be acutely concerned with the comorbidity of all these disorders with many psychiatric illnesses. In their seminal work, Cantwell and Baker[5] demonstrated that approximately half of the children with a speech or language disorder have some other definable Axis I clinical disorder. Similarly, among children with a psychiatric diagnosis first made, there is a remarkably increased likelihood of speech and language disorders, which often go undetected.[21] Typical are the findings of Beitchman, [22] who noted more than four times the prevalence of psychiatric illness in kindergartners with communication disorders compared with nondisordered children.

Some studies also suggest that psychiatric illness is associated with greater severity of communication problems.

For example, in Cantwell and Baker's population of 302 children with a psychiatric diagnosis as well as a speech and language disorder, the subjects were more likely to have multiple or more severe language disorders than were children with speech and language disorders who were psychiatrically well. Furthermore, language and phonological disorders are frequently concurrent in the same individuals. Unfortunately, language disorders are too often unsuspected by parents and professionals alike.

Role of Language Disorders in Psychiatric Illness. The medical and psychiatric comorbidity of these disorders has been described. At times, medical illness or injury may be clearly causative in nature; at other times, a shared origin in CNS dysfunction between communication disorders and conditions such as learning disorders can easily be proposed. The presence of communication disorders may be associated with increased severity of some conditions, most notably the disruptive behavior disorders. Can it be said that language disorders cause psychiatric disorders? The occurrence of adjustment disorders as a result of communication disorders has been cited. Cantwell and Baker,[5] in an exhaustive review, noted that language-disordered children are more likely to have a persistent, serious psychiatric illness than are children with speech disorder alone. They noted that certain features seem to predispose a child to have both academic and psychiatric disorders and that the most robust of these are language problems. Thus, whereas attributing direct causation may be too sweeping, it would appear that language disorder can be a major *component* in the genesis of some psychopathological conditions. By contrast, psychiatric illness *by itself* seems far less implicated in language disorders. The clinical consequence of all this is that psychiatrists must support and use a broad range of treatments and recognize that these disorders do not occur in an isolated context.

Academic Comorbidity and Outcome. It should come as no surprise that children with communication disorders, and especially with language disorders, are academically vulnerable. Education as we know it, especially for younger children, is largely based on language. Bashir and Scavuzzo[23] suggested that these children's vulnerability arises from the persistence of these disorders in the face of the continuing need for language in school. Moreover, even if a language disorder has been remediated, children may have failed in the meantime; it is immensely difficult for children in many schools to succeed again, once they have failed for any reason. A further complication is the comorbidity of learning disorders in these children. In all, some 50% to 75% of children with language disorders will have persistent academic problems.[24] They tend to learn less at any given time and to learn more slowly than their peers.[25] These children need ongoing comprehensive special education services and regular reevaluation of their educational needs.

Children with phonological disorder may also have persistent problems. These are generally less severe than those of language-disordered children, unless both types of disorders are present. Lewis and Fairbairn[26] reported mild but persistent problems with reading and spelling in individuals with phonological disorder, even into young adulthood. Subjects tended to improve steadily over time, however. Although most of the subjects and all of the adolescents and adults were considered normal speakers, they tended to show subtle phonological problems on specialized tests. Again, children with an associated language disorder fared less well.

Demographical and Cultural Issues in Treatment

The relationship of socioeconomic status to the occurrence of communication disorders is not altogether certain. Many studies indicate a positive correlation between communication disorders and low socioeconomic status, but other work suggests that this correlation is weak at best. The need for psychiatrists to avoid regarding variations in accent and dialect as pathological has been cited. Little empirical literature on cultural variations in communication therapy is extant. McCrary[27] and others have pointed out the need for cultural sensitivity in treatment, citing the efforts of The American Speech, Language and Hearing Association in this area.

Clinical Vignette 1 • Phonation Disorder

R.D. was as a 5-year-old girl, the only child of professional parents who had attempted for many years before R.D.'s birth to conceive a child. Her birth was received with joy and relief, and her parents admitted to having indulged her, even by their privileged standards. Her developmental history was unremarkable, except for some slight delay in toilet training compared with her age mates. She received appropriate well-child care and had no major illnesses or injuries. Her adjustment to preschool was considered appropriate when she entered at the age of 3 years, and she got along well with the other children for 2 years. She enjoyed the preschool, where individuality was accepted and encouraged. Her parents sought psychiatric evaluation for her after she reported being fearful about returning to school. When her parents questioned her, she stated that new children who had come to her school for kindergarten were teasing her. The teacher informed the parents that new students were in fact present but that no teasing had been observed.

On evaluation, a picture emerged of concerned parents who were sensitive to their child's emotional state and had sought to remedy their inexperience with children through a great deal of study and inquiry. R.D. appeared initially as a somewhat anxious child who separated from her mother with mild trepidation but soon relaxed with the psychiatrist. She was able to relate openly, gave no evidence of a major thought or affective disorder, and seemed to be of average intelligence. She exhibited a number of articulation errors, substituting /w/ for /r/ and /l/, substituting /th/ for /s/, and omitting or dropping a number of closing sounds. She stated that she was shocked at the comments of her new classmates, who were as yet unaccustomed to the uncritical atmosphere of the school, that her speech was infantile. She had never thought that her speech was unusual, nor had her parents, who believed it was normal for a child of her age. The teacher explained that she had noticed some errors in R.D.'s speech but did not wish to offend her or her parents by pointing them out.

The psychiatrist intervened by helping the child to understand that some children adopted "grown-up" speech

Clinical Vignette 1 • *continued*

later than others and that her progress could be assisted by a helping adult. He referred the family to a speech and language pathologist, whose session the parents described to the child as a "conversation party." The psychiatrist worked with the parents in joint brief focal psychotherapy, addressing issues related to the parents' sense of failure because of their child's problem and their delay in recognizing it. After 6 months, R.D.'s speech had improved and was accepted as normal by her classmates. By the age of 9 years, her speech was regarded as entirely normal by her parents and teachers and she was functioning well in all spheres. However, she continued to have subtle phonological findings as an adolescent.

Clinical Vignette 2 • **Mixed Receptive-Expressive Language Disorder**

G.B., a 6-year-old boy who lived with his parents and several siblings in an isolated area, was referred by a family physician at a rural health center who thought he might have autism. He was a child of normal appearance and good general health who exhibited no speech whatsoever. The family physician had tested his hearing and believed it was adequate; his parents agreed, because they found he had always been able to respond to a wide range of sounds, from birdcalls to thunder. They had deferred medical attention until G. was identified by the regional school as entitled to special education services. The parents were medically unsophisticated but attentive and devoted. They felt that G. was "slow" but that little could be done for him and that the family would always take care of him. They felt that they could communicate with him with gestures and reported that his older siblings were especially adept at this. The family traveled to a university diagnostic center.

Psychiatric evaluation disclosed a cheerful, interactive child who could engage in some mimetic play and was sensitive to the moods of others. On psychological evaluation, G. exhibited low-average cognitive ability on some nonverbal instruments and some receptive ability when given nonverbal prompts. Speech and language evaluation, along with family observation by all members of the diagnostic team, disclosed a severe mixed receptive-expressive language disorder for spoken language. However, G. and his siblings had developed a sign language that enabled them to communicate needs and wants as well as describe affects and comment on many activities in their home. They were referred as a group to a speech and language pathologist at their county seat. She was able to teach G. Ameslan (standard sign language), and eventually he also developed a limited oral vocabulary.

Other team members were able to document nearly average nonverbal intelligence and rule out other major psychiatric disorders. Nonetheless, G.'s school district proposed placing him in a classroom for severely mentally handicapped children. The psychiatrist was able to offer supportive psychotherapy to the parents, who had been devastated by the proposal, while the liaison special educator set about locating a class for language-disabled children in an adjacent county. G. was able to enter this class after the local school district was convinced of its educational and legal advisability. He did well there and is now in a vocational program in automobile mechanics. As a late adolescent, he still cannot speak more than 20 words and reads at a sixth-grade level, but he can follow mechanical and schematic diagrams well and relates appropriately with his classmates.

References

1. Friel-Patti S: Research in language disorders: What do we know and where are we going? Folia Phoniatr 1992; 44:126–142.
2. American Psychiatric Association: Diagnostic and Statistical Manual of Mental Disorders, 3rd ed. Washington, DC: American Psychiatric Association, 1980.
3. American Psychiatric Association: Diagnostic and Statistical Manual of Mental Disorders, 4th ed. Washington, DC: American Psychiatric Association, 1994.
4. Baker L: Specific communication disorders. In Garfinkel BD, Carlson GA, Weller EB (eds): Psychiatric Disorders in Children and Adolescents. Philadelphia: WB Saunders, 1990:257–270.
5. Cantwell DP, Baker L: Psychiatric and Developmental Disorders in Children with Communication Disorder. Washington, DC: American Psychiatric Press, 1991.
6. Riccio CA, Hynd GW, Morris MJ, et al: Comorbidity of central auditory processing disorder and attention-deficit hyperactivity disorder. J Am Acad Child Adolesc Psychiatry 1994; 33:849–857.
7. Gopnik M, Crago MB: Familial aggregation of a developmental language disorder. Cognition 1991; 39:1–50.
8. Tomblin JB: Familial concentration of developmental language impairment. J Speech Hear Disord 1989; 54:287–295.
9. Chomsky N: Language and Problems of Knowledge. Cambridge, MA: The MIT Press, 1988.
10. Abkarian GG: Communication effects of prenatal alcohol exposure. J Commun Disord 1992; 25:221–240.
11. Law J, Conway J: Effect of abuse and neglect on the development of speech and language. Dev Med Child Neurol 1992; 34:943–948.
12. Schulze H, Johannsen HS: Importance of parent-child interaction in the genesis of stuttering. Folia Phoniatr 1991; 43:133–143.
13. Paul R: Communication development and its disorders: A psycholinguistic perspective. Schizophr Bull 1982; 8:287–290.
14. Rutter M: Assessment objectives and principles. In Yule W, Rutter M (eds): Language Development and Disorders. Philadelphia: JB Lippincott, 1987:295–311.
15. McKirdy LS: Childhood language disorders. In Shaffer D, Ehrhardt AA, Greenhill L (eds): The Clinical Guide to Child Psychiatry. New York: Free Press, 1985:79–96.
16. Yairi E, Ambrose NG, Niermann R: The early months of stuttering: A developmental study. J Speech Hear Res 1993; 36:521–528.
17. Guitar B: Stammering and stuttering. In Shaffer D, Ehrhardt AA, Greenhill L (eds): The Clinical Guide to Child Psychiatry. New York: Free Press, 1985:97–109.
18. Rafuse J: Early intervention, intensive therapy can help people who stutter. Can Med Assoc J 1994; 150:754–755.
19. Andrews G, Dozsa M: Haloperidol and the treatment of stuttering. J Fluency Dis 1977; 2:217–224.
20. Goldstein H, Hockenberger EH: Significant progress in child language intervention: An 11-year retrospective. Res Dev Disabil 1991; 12:401–424.
21. Cohen NJ, Davine M, Horodezky N, et al: Unsuspected language impairment in psychiatrically disturbed children: Prevalence and language and behavioral characteristics. J Am Acad Child Adolesc Psychiatry 1993; 32:595–603.
22. Beitchman JH: Speech and language impairment and psychiatric risk: Toward a model of neurodevelopmental immaturity. Psychiatr Clin North Am 1985; 8:721–735.
23. Bashir AS, Scavuzzo A: Children with language disorders: Natural history and academic success. J Learn Disabil 1992; 25:53–65.
24. Aram DM, Hall NE: Longitudinal follow-up of children with preschool communication disorders: Treatment implications. School Psychol Rev 1989; 18:487–501.
25. Shaywitz SE: Developmental changes in learning and behavior: Results of the Connecticut longitudinal study. Presented at the Fifth Annual Conference on Learning Disorders; November 1989; Cambridge, MA.
26. Lewis BA, Fairbairn L: Residual effects of preschool phonology disorders in grade school, adolescence, and adulthood. J Speech Hear Res 1992; 35:819–831.
27. McCrary MB: Urban multicultural trauma patients. ASHA 1992; 34:37–40, 42.

CHAPTER

40 Elimination Disorders

Christopher P. Lucas
David Shaffer

Enuresis
Encopresis

Enuresis

Definition

DSM-IV Criteria 307.6

Enuresis (Not Due to a Medical Condition)

A. Repeated voiding of urine into bed or clothes (whether involuntary or intentional).

B. The behavior is clinically significant as manifested by either a frequency of twice a week for at least 3 consecutive months or the presence of clinically significant distress or impairment in social, academic (occupational), or other important areas of functioning.

C. Chronological age is at least 5 years (or equivalent developmental level).

D. The behavior is not due exclusively to the direct physiological effect of a substance (e.g., a diuretic) or a general medical condition (e.g., diabetes, spina bifida, a seizure disorder).

Specify type:

Nocturnal only: passage of urine only during nighttime sleep

Diurnal only: passage of urine during waking hours

Nocturnal and diurnal: a combination of the two subtypes above

Functional enuresis is usually defined as the intentional or involuntary passage of urine into bed or clothes in the absence of any identified physical abnormality in children older than 4 years of age (see the *Diagnostic and Statistical Manual of Mental Disorders,* Fourth Edition [DSM-IV] criteria just given). Although there is no good evidence that the condition is primarily psychogenic, it is often associated with psychiatric disorder, and enuretic children are frequently referred to mental health services for treatment.

Course and Natural History

The acquisition of urinary continence at night is the end stage of a fairly consistent developmental sequence. Bowel control during sleep marks the beginning of this process and is followed by bowel control during waking hours. Bladder control during the day occurs soon after and finally, after a variable interval, nighttime bladder control is achieved. Most children achieve this final stage by the age of 36 months. With increasing age, the likelihood of spontaneous recovery from enuresis becomes less,[1] so that, for instance, 40% of 2-year-olds with enuresis become dry in the next year and 20% of enuretic 3-year-olds become dry before age 4 years but only 6% of enuretic 4-year-olds become dry in the following year. The chronic nature of the condition is further shown in the study by Rutter and colleagues,[2] in which only 1.5% of 5-year-old bed-wetters became dry during the next 2 years.

Nocturnal enuresis is as common in boys as girls until the age of 5 years, but by age 11 years, boys outnumber girls 2:1.[1–3] Not until the age of 8 years do boys achieve the same levels of nighttime continence that are seen in girls by the age of 5 years.[4] This appears to be due to slower physiological maturation in boys. In addition, the increased incidence of secondary enuresis (occurring after an initial 1-year period of acquired continence) in boys further affects the sex ratio seen in later childhood. Daytime enuresis occurs more commonly in girls[5–7] and is associated with higher rates of psychiatric disturbance.[2]

Etiology and Pathophysiology

Identifying a cause for enuresis is not a simple task despite numerous descriptions of correlations or associations between enuresis and a wide variety of biological and psychosocial factors.

Biological factors described include a structural pathological condition or infection of the urinary tract (or both), low functional bladder capacity, abnormal antidiuretic hormone secretion, abnormal depth of sleep, genetic predisposition, and developmental delay.

Obstructive lesions of the urinary outflow tract, which can cause urinary tract infection (UTI) as well as enuresis, have been thought to be important, with a high prevalence of such abnormalities seen in enuretic children referred to urologic clinics.[8] This degree of association is not seen at less specialized pediatric centers, however, and most studies linking urinary outflow obstruction to enuresis are methodologically flawed.[9] Structural causes for enuresis should be considered the exception rather than the rule.[10]

The association between UTI and enuresis has been demonstrated in two main ways. UTI has been found to occur frequently in children, especially girls, and a large proportion (85%) of them have been shown to have nocturnal enuresis.[11]Also, in 10% of bed-wetting girls, urinalysis results show evidence of bacterial infection.[12] The consensus is that because treating the infection rarely stops the bed-wetting, UTI is probably a result rather than a cause of enuresis.[13]

The concept that children with enuresis have low functional bladder capacities has been widely promoted (Gardner A, Shaffer D, unpublished manuscript, 1994).[14] Shaffer and colleagues[15] found a functional bladder capacity one standard deviation lower than expected in 55% of a sample of enuretic children in school clinics. Although low functional capacity may predispose the child to enuresis, successful behavioral treatment does not appear to increase that capacity. It seems rather that in treated individuals, the sensation of a full (small) bladder promotes waking to pass urine so that enuresis does not occur.[16] Reduction of nocturnal secretion has been described in a small number of children with enuresis.[17, 18] This deficiency may produce excessive amounts of dilute urine during the night, overwhelming bladder capacity and causing enuresis.

It is widely believed by parents that children who have enuresis at night sleep more deeply and are especially difficult to wake. This subjective opinion was not supported by Boyd's study[19] comparing the time it took to awaken normal children and children with enuresis. Furthermore, enuresis has been shown to occur randomly with regard to stage of sleep, and any relationship is due to the amount of time spent in that stage.[20]

The evidence for some genetic predisposition is strong. Approximately 70% of children with nocturnal enuresis have a first-degree relative who also has or has had nocturnal enuresis.[21] Twin studies have shown greater monozygotic (68%) than dizygotic (36%) concordance.[22] An association between enuresis and early delays in motor, language, and social development has been noted in both prospective community samples[3, 23] and a large retrospective study of clinical subjects.[24]

Many psychosocial correlates have also been described, including delayed toilet training, low socioeconomic class, stress events, and other child psychiatric disorders. Prospective studies from New Zealand[23] and from kibbutz-raised children in Israel[24a] suggest that higher rates of enuresis are seen in children in whom toilet training is delayed until after the age of 18 months. The data on social class and enuresis are unclear. Early reports[1, 2] linked various indices of social disadvantage to increased prevalence of enuresis; however, multivariate studies[23] failed to demonstrate a relationship between primary enuresis and psychosocial disadvantage or social class, or both. Stress events seem to be more clearly associated with secondary enuresis. Reported events include the birth of a younger sibling,[25] early hospitalizations,[26] and head injury.[27]

Psychiatric disorder occurs more frequently in enuretic children than in other children. The relative frequency of disorder ranges from two to six times that in the general population and is more frequent in girls, in children who also have diurnal enuresis, and in children with secondary enuresis.[2, 3] There have been no specific types of psychiatric disorder identified in children with enuresis.[20]

There is little evidence that enuresis is a symptom of underlying disorder because psychotherapy is ineffective in reducing enuresis,[25] anxiolytic drugs have no antienuretic effect, tricyclic antidepressants exert their therapeutic effect independent of the child's mood,[28] and purely symptomatic therapies, such as the bell and pad, are equally effective in disturbed and nondisturbed children.[29]

A further explanation for the association is that enuresis, a distressing and stigmatizing affliction, may cause the psychiatric disorder. However, although some studies have shown that enuretic children who undergo treatment become happier and have greater self-esteem,[30, 31] other studies show that psychiatric symptoms do not appear to lessen in children successful with a night alarm.[15, 32]

A final possibility is that enuresis and psychiatric disorder are both the result of joint etiological factors such as low socioeconomic status, institutional care, large sibships, parental delinquency, and early and repeated disruptions of maternal care.[2, 3, 33] Shared biological factors may also be important in that delayed motor, speech, and pubertal development, already shown to be associated with enuresis, have been shown to be more frequent in disturbed enuretic children than in those without psychiatric disorder.

Diagnosis and Differential Diagnosis

The presence or absence of conditions often seen in association with enuresis, such as developmental delay, UTI, constipation, and comorbid psychiatric disorder, should be assessed and ruled out as appropriate (Fig. 40–1). Other causes of nocturnal incontinence should be excluded, for example, those leading to polyuria (diabetes mellitus, renal disease, diabetes insipidus) and, rarely, nocturnal epilepsy.

Assessment

History

Information on the frequency, periodicity, and duration of symptoms is needed to make the diagnosis and distinguish functional enuresis from sporadic seizure-associated enuresis. If there is diurnal enuresis, an additional treatment plan is required. A family history of enuresis increases the likelihood of a diagnosis of functional enuresis and may explain a later presentation for treatment. Projective identification by the affected parent may further hinder treatment. For subjects with secondary enuresis, precipitating factors should be elicited, although such efforts often represent an attempt to assign meaning after the event.

Questions that are useful in obtaining information for treatment planning include "Why is this a problem?" and "Why does this need treatment now?" because these factors may influence the choice of treatment (is a rapid effect needed?) or point to other pressures or restrictions on therapy. It is important to inquire about previous management strategies—for example, fluid restriction, night lifting, rewards, and punishments—used at home. Parents often come with the assertion that they have tried everything and that nothing has helped. Examining the reasons for failure of simple strategies is useful for ensuring that more sophisticated treatments do not befall the same fate. There is little evidence that fluid restriction is useful, although night lifting may be beneficial for the large number of children who never reach professional attention. Rewards are usually material and are given only for unreasonably high performance levels, with the delay between action and reward being too long. Physical punishment and verbal chastisements, ineffective at best, may well maintain the enuresis. Punishment is often too harsh and tends to be applied inconsistently, depending on parental mood. If specific treatments have been prescribed, either behavioral or pharmacological, it is important to discover the reasons they may have failed, for example, parental discord, noncompliance, or relapse after an initial response.

Mental Status Examination

The child's views and any misconceptions that he or she may have about the enuresis, its causes, and its treatment should be fully explored. Asking the child for three wishes may help determine whether the enuresis is a concern to the child. This may unmask marked embarrassment or guilt from behind a facade of denial about the problem and can be educational for parents who believe their children could stop wetting "if only they wanted to or tried harder." Pictures drawn by the child that describe how the child views himself or herself when enuresis is a problem and when it is not is appropriate for younger children and can graphically illustrate the misery experienced by children with enuresis.

Physical Examination

All children should have a routine physical examination, with particular emphasis placed on detection of congenital malformations, which are possibly indicative of urogenital abnormalities. A midstream specimen of urine should be examined for the presence of infection. Radiological or further medical investigation is indicated only in the presence of infected urine, enuresis with symptoms suggestive of recurrent UTI (frequency, urgency, and dysuria), or polyuria.

Treatment

Practical management for nocturnal enuresis is presented in Table 40–1.

Studies suggest that only a minority of children with enuresis are ever assessed and treated[33, 34] and that many of those who are referred do not receive adequate treatment. Many families, and clinicians, seem to accept bed-wetting as part of normal childhood.

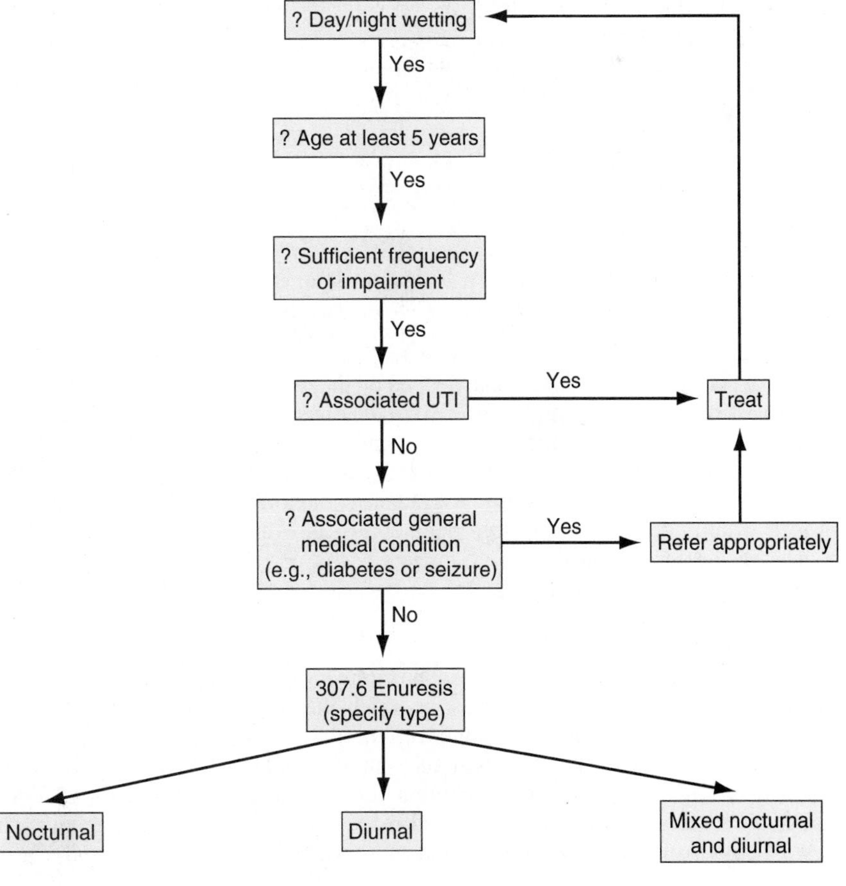

Figure 40–1 *Diagnostic decision tree for enuresis.*

Table 40–1 Practical Management of Nocturnal Enuresis

Stage	
Stage 1	**Assessment**
	Obtain history: frequency, periodicity, and duration of wetting. Why is this a problem? Why now? Mental status: views and misconceptions (parent and child). Discover reasons for previous failure or failures. Perform routine physical examination (any minor congenital abnormalities?). Midstream specimen of urine must be obtained. Radiology and further physical investigation is needed only if symptoms or evidence of urinary tract infection (dysuria and frequency or positive culture results) or polyuria.
Stage 2	**Advice**
	Education that enuresis is common and not deliberate. Aim to reduce punitive behavior. Transmit optimism: however, anticipate disappointment at no instant cure. Preview the stepwise recovery and warn of the possibility of relapse.
Stage 3	**Baseline**
	Use star chart. Focus on positive achievements (be creative). Examine the effect of simple interventions (e.g., lifting).
Stage 4	**Night Alarm**
	First-line management unless important to obtain rapid short-term effect. Demonstrate night alarm equipment in the office. Telephone follow-up within a few days of commencing therapy.
	or
	Drug Therapy
	If rapid suppression of wetting is needed (e.g., before vacation or camp, to defuse aggressive or hostile situation between child and parents and siblings). When family has *proved* incapable of using the equipment. After failure or multiple relapses. Medication of choice: DDAVP, 20–40 μg at night.

The overall goals of treatment can depend on the reason for referral. Commonly, the child is brought to the physician before some planned activity, for example, a family vacation or a trip to camp, and the need is for a rapid (e.g., pharmacological) short-term therapy. A gradual behavioral approach would not likely meet with much approval, even though it may offer a chance for a permanent cessation of wetting.

Standard Treatment

About 10% of children have a reduction in the number of wet nights after a single visit to a clinician in which the only intervention was the recording of baseline wetting frequency and simple reassurance.[35] Such reassurance should make clear that enuresis is a biological condition that is made worse by stress and that may be associated in a noncausal way with other psychiatric disorders. Younger children can be told that their problem is shared by many others of the same age. The excellent prognosis for patients who comply with therapy should be stressed. Recording the frequency of enuresis can be achieved by using a simple star chart. This is most effective if performed by the child, who records each dry night with a star. The completed chart is then shown to the parents on a daily basis, and they can provide appropriate praise and reinforcement.

Waking and Fluid Restriction. Although systematic studies have failed to show any effect of these interventions with enuretic inpatients, it may be that these strategies work for the majority of enuretic children who are not referred for treatment. If waking does appear to reduce the number of wet nights from baseline, a more systematic application may be indicated.

Surgery. Based on the premise that enuresis is causally associated with outflow tract obstruction, various surgical procedures have been advocated, for example, urethral dilatation, meatotomy, cystoplasty, and bladder neck repair.[36] This cannot be supported because in addition to the dubious concept of outflow tract obstruction per se, the surgery does not alter the urodynamics of the bladder, reported positive treatment effects are slight (no controlled studies exist), and there remains a significant potential for adverse effects (urinary incontinence, epididymitis, and aspermia).

Pharmacotherapy. Although it has been repeatedly demonstrated that temporary suppression rather than cure of enuresis is the usual outcome of drug therapy, it remains the most widely prescribed treatment in the United States.[34] Four classes of drugs have principally been employed: synthetic antidiuretic hormones, tricyclic antidepressants, stimulants, and anticholinergic agents.

Synthetic Antidiuretic Hormone. A number of randomized double-blind placebo-controlled trials have shown that the synthetic vasopeptide DDAVP (desmopressin) is effective in enuresis.[37, 38] The drug is usually administered intranasally, although oral preparations of equal efficacy have been developed (equivalent oral dose is 10 times the intranasal dose). It has been shown[39] that almost 50% of children are able to stop wetting completely with a single nightly dose of 20 to 40 μg of DDAVP given intranasally. A further 40% are afforded a significant reduction in the frequency of enuresis with this treatment. As with tricyclic antidepressants, however, when treatment is stopped, the vast majority of individuals relapse. Side effects of this medication include nasal pain and congestion, headache, nausea, and abdominal pain. Serious problems of water intoxication, hyponatremia, and seizures are rare. It is important to be aware that intranasal absorption is reduced when the patient has a cold or allergic rhinitis. The mode of action of desmopressin is unknown. It may reduce the production of nighttime urine to an amount less than the (low) functional volume of the enuretic bladder, thereby eliminating the urge to micturate. It is uncertain whether desmopressin administration is correcting a natural deficiency of vasopressin or is exerting a true pharmacological effect.

Tricyclic Antidepressants. The short-term effectiveness of imipramine and other related antidepressants has also been demonstrated via many randomized double-blind placebo-controlled trials.[35, 40, 41] Imipramine reduces the frequency of enuresis in about 85% of bed-wetters and eliminates enuresis in about 30% of these individuals. Nighttime doses of 1 to 2.5 mg/kg are usually effective,[42] and a therapeutic effect is usually evident in the first week of treatment. Relapse after withdrawal of medication is almost inevitable, so that 3 months after the cessation of tricyclic antidepressants, nearly all patients will again have enuresis at pretreatment levels.[35] Side effects are common and include dry mouth, dizziness, postural hypotension, headache, and constipation. Toxicity after accidental ingestion or overdose is a serious consideration, causing cardiac effects, including arrhythmias and conduction defects, convulsions, hallucinations, and ataxia. Concern has been expressed about the possibility of sudden death (presumably caused by arrhythmia) in children taking tricyclic drugs. The mode of action for tricyclic antidepressants is unclear. It does not appear to depend on their antidepressant properties because response is unrelated to the presence or absence of mood symptoms. One observation is that tricyclic agents seem to increase functional bladder volumes,[9] possibly resulting from noradrenergic reuptake inhibition.[40]

Stimulant Medication. Sympathomimetic stimulants such as dexamphetamine have been used to reduce the depth of sleep in children with enuresis but because, as discussed previously, there is no evidence that enuresis is related to abnormally deep sleep, their lack of effectiveness in stopping bed-wetting is no surprise.[43] Used in combination with behavioral therapy, there is some evidence that stimulants can accentuate the learning of nocturnal continence.[44]

Anticholinergic Drugs. Drugs such as propantheline, oxybutynin, and terodiline can reduce the frequency of voiding in individuals with neurogenic bladders, reduce urgency, and increase functional bladder capacity. There is no evidence, however, that these anticholinergic drugs are effective in bed-wetting, although they may have a role in diurnal enuresis.[45, 46] Side effects are frequent and include dry mouth, blurred vision, headache, nausea, and constipation.[47]

Psychosocial Treatments. The night alarm, originally developed by Pfaundler,[48] was first used in children with enuresis by Mowrer and Mowrer.[49] This system used two electrodes separated by a device (e.g., bedding) connected to an alarm. When the child wet the bed, the urine completed the electrical circuit, sounded the alarm, and the child awoke. All current night alarm systems are merely refinements on this original design. A vibrating pad beneath the pillow can be used instead of a bell or buzzer, or the electrodes can be incorporated into a single unit or can be miniaturized so that they can be attached to night (or day) clothing. With treatment, full cessation of enuresis can be expected in 80% of cases. Reported cure rates (defined as a minimum of 14 consecutive dry nights) have ranged from 50% to 100%.[50, 51]

The main problem with this form of enuretic treatment, however, is that cure is usually achieved only within the second month of treatment.[52] This factor may influence clinicians to prescribe pharmacological treatments that, although they are more immediately gratifying, do not offer any real prospect of cure. It has been suggested that adjuvant therapy with methamphetamine[44] or desmopressin[53] will reduce the amount of time before continence is achieved. Using a louder auditory stimulus[54] or using the body-worn alarm[55] may also improve the speed of treatment response. Factors associated with delayed acquisition of continence include failure of the child to wake with the alarm, maternal anxiety, and a disturbed home environment, although no influence has been seen regarding the age of the child or the initial wetting frequency.[29, 56]

A further consequence of the delayed response to a night alarm is that families fail to persist with treatment and may abandon the treatment too soon. Premature termination can occur in as many as 48% of cases[57] and is more common in families that have made little previous effort to treat the problem, in families that are negative or intolerant of bed-wetting, and in children who have other behavioral problems.[58] Aspects of treatment that may also reduce compliance with the alarm include failure to understand or follow the instructions, failure of the child to awaken, and frequent false alarms.[57] The only reported side effect of treatment with the night alarm is "buzzer ulcers" caused by the child lying in a pool of ionized urine. This problem has been eliminated with modern transistorized alarms that do not employ a continuous, relatively high voltage across the electrodes to detect enuresis.[59]

Relapse after successful treatment, if it occurs, will usually take place within the first 6 months after cessation of treatment. It is reported that approximately one third of children relapse[60]; however, no clear predictors of relapse have been identified.[61] Strategies aimed at reducing relapse rates, such as overlearning[62] or intermittent reinforcement paradigms,[63] have not been demonstrated to be of clinical value.[50]

The mode of action of the night alarm can be explained using theories of classical or operant conditioning. In classical conditioning, bladder distention or a sense of the need to pass urine becomes associated with the auditory signal, leading to the conditioned response of waking. Operant conditioning theories would view the alarm as a punishment to be avoided and may explain why individuals still become dry when the alarm is placed in the bed but is not switched on.[64] Social learning is also important because the night alarm and associated systematic recording may help the family focus on dry nights and provide contingent rewards (praise).

Table 40–2 presents various remedies for night alarm problems.

Dry Bed Technique. An elaborate collection of interventions has been designed by Azrin and colleagues[65] and includes high fluid intake, retention control training, training the child to awaken rapidly (using a nighttime alarm), and rapid reinforcement for correct daytime micturition. Without the use of a night alarm, the program produces no better effects than no treatment at all.[66] In view of the intensive effort needed by the family and adverse effects on preschool children, such as increased temper tantrums or social withdrawal,[67] the dry bed technique remains of questionable value.

Assessment and Management of Diurnal Enuresis

Daytime enuresis, although it can occur together with nighttime enuresis, has a different pattern of associations and

Table 40–2 Problem Solving for the Night Alarm *If* . . .

Bell "does not work"	Check position, connections, and batteries. If using separating sheet, check that it is porous. Check that child is not turning off equipment. Place alarm out of easy reach.
Child does not wake	Make alarm louder. Parent should wake child.
Child does not become dry	Ensure compliance. Ensure that child responds promptly. Use adjuvant DDAVP or dextroamphetamine. Ensure that child has role (e.g., change own bed-sheets) after alarm.
False alarms	Ensure that separating sheet is big enough, not soiled, and will insulate. Use thicker nightclothes.
Relapse	Repeat treatment. Consider overlearning after response to re-treatment.

responds to different methods of treatment. It is much more likely to be associated with urinary tract abnormalities, including UTI, and to be comorbid with other psychiatric disorders. As a result, a more detailed and focused medical and psychiatric evaluation is indicated. Urine should be checked repeatedly for infection, and the threshold for ordering ultrasonographical visualization of the urological system should be low. The history may make it apparent that the daytime wetting is situation specific. For example, school-based enuresis in a child who is too timid to ask to use the bathroom could be alleviated by the teacher's tactfully reminding the child to go to the bathroom at regular intervals.

Observation of children with diurnal enuresis[68] has established that they do experience an urge to pass urine before micturition but that either this urge is ignored or the warning comes too late to be of any use because of an "irritable bladder." Therefore, treatment strategies are based on establishing a pattern of toileting before the times that diurnal enuresis is likely to occur (usually between 12 noon and 5 PM) and using positive reinforcement to promote regular use of the bathroom.[69]

Portable systems that can be worn on the body and use a sensor in the underwear as well as an alarm that can be worn on the wrist have been developed. Halliday and associates[70] studied two versions of this apparatus—one in which the alarm sounding was contingent on the sensor's detecting wetness in the underwear and another in which the alarm merely went off at predetermined intervals. Interestingly, success rates (two thirds of children were cured and mostly maintained continence for a full 2-year follow-up period) showed no significant differences between the wetness alarm and the simple timed alarm. A simple therapeutic alternative, therefore, is to buy the child a digital watch with a count-down alarm timer.

Unlike nocturnal enuresis, drug treatment with tricyclic antidepressants, such as imipramine, is ineffective,[71] whereas the use of anticholinergic agents such as oxybutynin and terodiline shows a therapeutic impact on the frequency of daytime enuresis.[47, 48]

Clinical Vignette 1

John, an 8-year-old boy, was the sixth child in a sibship. He was brought by his mother for treatment of nocturnal enuresis, which was occurring on average five times a week, with no particular pattern. Two of his elder brothers had also wet the bed until the age of 10 and 13 years, respectively, as had his biological father who was no longer living with the family. The mother had become exasperated with John's wetting and had begun punishing him by forcing him to wash his bedclothes by hand every morning before school. His brothers made fun of him, and peers at school avoided him because he frequently came to school still smelling of stale urine. He was not allowed to have anything to drink after 6 PM, and a star chart was currently being used without much success. No praise was given for the two dry nights per week because his mother was convinced that this meant the enuresis was deliberate. John drew a picture describing the terror and anxiety of having a wet night. His three wishes were to stop wetting, to get a Nintendo machine of his own, and to find a real dinosaur fossil.

The initial management included an explanation of the condition, microbiological analysis of a midstream specimen of urine, and instructions on baseline recording using the star chart. Overt punishments were eliminated, although John was expected to help change his sheets, and effort was expended in trying to help his mother praise him for the dry nights he was able to achieve. After a 2-week baseline period, urinalysis results came back negative and the frequency of enuresis remained at 4 to 5 nights per week. John and his mother were instructed in the use of a night alarm and were telephoned 2 days later to check on any problems. It appeared that John was not waking with the buzzer, and they were instructed to place the alarm unit on an old cookie tin to amplify the sound. Dry nights were recorded on John's chart, with verbal praise after each one. An initial target of three dry nights per week was set, with the promise of a trip to the movies for John and the two brothers who shared a bedroom with him. This was achieved the first week, although it took a further 6 weeks before he went a full week without a wet bed. After 2 weeks of continence, the restriction on nighttime fluids was relaxed without incident. Six months later he remained dry, and school and home relationships were markedly improved.

Encopresis

Definition

DSM-IV Criteria

Encopresis

A. Repeated passage of feces into inappropriate places (e.g., clothing or floor) whether involuntary or intentional.

B. At least one such event a month for at least 3 months.

C. Chronological age is at least 4 years (or equivalent developmental level).

D. The behavior is not due exclusively to the direct physiological effect of a substance (e.g., laxatives) or a general medical condition except through a mechanism involving constipation.

Code as follows:

787.6 Encopresis, with constipation and overflow incontinence: there is evidence of constipation on physical examination or by history.

307.7 Encopresis, without constipation and overflow incontinence: there is no evidence of constipation on physical examination or by history.

Encopresis is usually defined as the intentional or involuntary passage of stool into inappropriate places in the absence of any identified physical abnormality in children older than 4 years (see DSM-IV criteria just given).

The distinction is drawn between encopresis with constipation (retention with overflow) and encopresis without constipation. Other classification schemes include making a primary-secondary distinction (based on having a 1-year period of continence) or soiling with fluid or normal feces.

Course and Natural History

Less than one third of children in the United States have completed toilet training by the age of 2 years,[72] with a mean age of 27.7 months.[73] Bowel control is usually achieved before bladder control. The age cutoff for "normality" is set at 4 years, the age at which 95% of children have acquired fecal continence.[74] As with urinary continence, girls achieve bowel control earlier than do boys.

Epidemiology

The overall prevalence of encopresis in 7- and 8-year-old children has been shown to be 1.5%, with boys (2.3%) affected more commonly than girls (0.7%). There was a steadily increasing likelihood of continence with increasing age, until by age 16 years the reported prevalence was almost zero.[75] Rutter and coworkers[76] reported a rate of 1% in 10- to 12-year-old children, with a strong (5:1) male/female ratio. Retrospective study of clinic-referred encopretic children has shown that 40% of cases are primary (true failure to gain control), with a mean age of 6.7 years, and 60% of cases are secondary, with a mean age of 8 years.[77] Eighty percent of patients were constipated, with no difference in this feature seen between primary and secondary subtypes.

Etiology and Pathophysiology

No clear single causative pathway has been established. The constipated-nonconstipated distinction does, however, generate some specificity in terms of associations that may be important etiologically. Within the first year of life, children can show a tendency toward constipation,[78] with concordance for constipation being six times more frequent in monozygotic than in dizygotic twins.[79] Fecal retention and reduced stool frequency between 12 and 24 months of age can predict later encopresis.[77] Encopretic children with constipation and overflow are found to have rectal and colonic distention, massive impaction with hard feces, and a number of specific abnormalities of anorectal physiology. These abnormalities, which may be primary or secondary to constipation, include elevated anal resting tone, decreased anorectal motility and weakness of the internal anal sphincter,[80] and dysfunction of the external anal sphincter, for example, contraction during defecation.[81, 82]

Encopresis may occur after an acute episode of constipation following illness or a change in diet.[83] In addition to the pain and discomfort caused by attempts to pass an extremely hard stool, a number of specific painful perianal conditions such as anal fissure can lead to stool withholding and later fecal soiling. Stressful events such as the birth of a sibling or attending a new school have been associated with up to 25% of cases of secondary encopresis.[77] In nonretentive encopresis, the main theories center on faulty toilet training. Stress during the training period, coercive toileting leading to anxiety and "pot phobia," and failure to learn or to have been taught the appropriate behavior[84, 85] have all been implicated. True fecal urgency, which may have a physiological or pathological basis, may also be important in a small proportion of cases.[86]

It has been asserted that primary encopresis is more common in children from lower socioeconomic class families, who received neglectful toilet training.[84] No link was found, however, between social class and encopresis in general[74, 76] or in primary encopresis specifically.[87]

Associated Features

Diagnosis and Differential Diagnosis

Although the diagnosis can rarely be confused with other less odoriferous conditions, the main efforts during the diagnostic process are to establish the presence or absence of constipation and, to a lesser extent, distinguish continuous (primary) from discontinuous (secondary) soiling (Fig. 40–2). Hersov[88] listed three types of identifiable encopresis in children: 1) it is known that the child can control defecation, but she or he chooses to defecate in inappropriate places; 2) there is true failure to gain bowel control, and the child is unaware of or unable to control soiling; and 3) soiling is due to excessively fluid feces, whether from constipation and overflow, physical disease, or anxiety. In practice, there is frequently overlap among types or progression from one to another. Unlike enuresis, fecal soiling rarely occurs at night or during sleep, and if present, is indicative of a poor prognosis.[78] Soiling due to anal masturbation has been reported, although this causes staining of the sheets rather than full stools in the bedclothes.[89]

Phenomenology

In the first group, in which bowel control has been established, the stool may be soft or normal (but different from fluid-type feces seen in overflow). Soiling due to acute

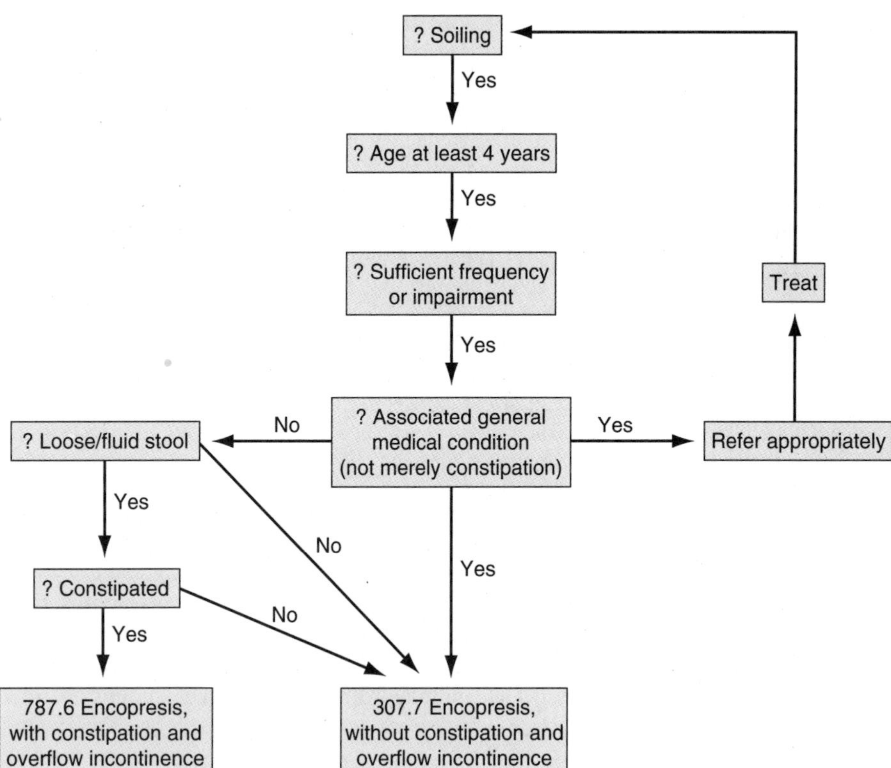

Figure 40–2 *Diagnostic decision tree for encopresis.*

stress events (e.g., the birth of a sibling, a change of school, or parental separation) is usually brief once the stress has abated, given a stable home environment and sensible management. In more severe pathological family situations, including punitive management or frank physical or sexual abuse,[90] the feces may be deposited in places designed to cause anger or irritation or there may be associated smearing of feces on furniture and walls. Other covert aggressive antisocial acts may be evident, with considerable denial by the child of the magnitude or seriousness of the problem.

In the second group, in which there is failure to learn bowel control, a nonfluid stool is deposited fairly randomly in clothes, at home, and at school. There may be conditions such as mental retardation or specific developmental delay, spina bifida, or cerebral palsy that impair the ability to recognize the need to defecate and the appropriate skills needed to defer this function until a socially appropriate time and location. In the absence of low IQ or pathological physical condition, patients have been reported as having associated enuresis, academic skills problems, and antisocial behavior. They present to pediatricians primarily and are usually younger (age 4 to 6 years) than other encopretic individuals. It is thought that this type of soiling is considerably more common in socially disadvantaged, disorganized multiproblem families[84, 85, 91] because of faulty or inconsistent training or stresses during the sensitive period of training.

In the third group, excessively fluid feces are passed, which may result from conditions that cause true diarrhea (e.g., ulcerative colitis) or, much more frequently, from constipation with overflow causing spurious diarrhea. A history of retention, either willful or in response to pain, is prominent in the early days of this form of encopresis, although later it may be less apparent because of fecal overflow. Behavior such as squatting on the heels to prevent defecation or marked anxiety about the prospect of using the toilet (although rarely amounting to true phobic avoidance) may be described.

The issue of whether a comorbid psychopathological condition is common appears to depend on where encopretic cases are sampled. Gabel and colleagues[92] found some elevation in behavioral disturbance in a pediatric sample, although it was less severe than that seen in new cases in a child psychiatric outpatient clinic. Less than 13% of encopretic children had ever been referred to a mental health specialist. Similarly, Loening-Baucke and associates[82] showed only modest elevations in Child Behavior Checklist scores and primarily in the Behavior Problem Scale. In contrast, child psychiatric studies have shown higher levels of psychopathological features, both anxiety-withdrawal and aggression.[75, 93]

Issues and Further Assessment

Having identified the presence of encopretic behavior and formed some idea of the type of encopresis (primary, secondary, or retentive, or a combination), the remaining task is to discover the presence and extent of any associated conditions, both medical and psychological. The comprehensive assessment process should include a medical evaluation, psychiatric and family interviews, and a systematic behavioral recording.

The medical evaluation comprises a history, review of systems, physical examination, and appropriate hematological and radiological tests. Although the vast majority of patients with encopresis are medically normal, a small proportion have pathological features of etiological significance. Physical causes of encopresis without retention include inflammatory bowel disease (e.g., ulcerative colitis, Crohn's disease), central nervous system disorders, sensory disorders of the anorectal region (e.g., spina bifida, cerebral palsy), or pelvic floor muscles. Organic causes of encopresis with retention include Hirschsprung's disease (aganglionosis in intermuscular and submucous plexuses of the large bowel extending proximally from the anus), neurogenic megacolon, hypothyroidism, hypercalcemia, chronic codeine or laxative usage, anorectal stenosis, and fissure.[94] It should also be remembered that these conditions rarely have their first presentation with encopresis alone.

The physical assessment should include an abdominal and rectal examination, although a plain abdominal radiograph is the most reliable way to determine the presence of fecal impaction. Anorectal manometry should be considered in the investigation of children with severe constipation and chronic soiling, especially those in whom Hirschsprung's disease is suspected.[95]

Psychiatric and family interviews should include a developmental history and a behavioral history of encopresis (antecedents, behavior, and consequences). Specific areas of stress, acute or chronic, affecting the child or family, or both, should be discovered. Associated psychopathological conditions are more commonly found in the older child, in secondary encopresis, and when soiling occurs not only in clothes. Anxiety surrounding toileting may indicate pot phobia, coercive toileting, or a history of painful defecation. A history should be obtained of the parents' previous attempts at treatment, together with previously prescribed therapy, so that reasons for previous failure can be identified and anticipated in future treatment planning.

Treatment

Practical management for encopresis is presented in Table 40–3.

Standard Treatment

The principal approach to treatment is predicated on the results of the evaluation and the clinical category assigned. This differentiates between the need to establish a regular toileting procedure in patients in whom there has been a failure to learn this social behavior and the need to address a psychiatric disorder, parent-child relationship difficulties, or other stresses in the child who exhibits loss of this previously acquired skill in association with these factors. In both cases, analysis of the soiling behavior may identify reinforcing factors important in maintaining dysfunction. Detection of significant constipation will, in addition, provide an indication for adjuvant laxative therapy.

Behavioral Treatments

Behavioral therapy is the mainstay of treatment for encopresis. In the younger child who has been toilet trained, this focuses on practical elimination skills, for example, visiting the toilet after each meal, staying there for a maximum of 15 minutes, using muscles to increase intra-abdominal pressure, and cleaning oneself adequately afterward. Parents or caretakers, or both, need to be educated in making the toilet a pleasant place to visit and should stay with the younger child, giving encouragement and praise for appropriate effort. Small children whose legs may dangle above the floor should be provided with a step against which to brace when straining. Initially, a warm bath before using the toilet may relax the anxious child and make it easier to pass stool. Systematic recording of positive toileting behavior, not necessarily being clean (depending on the level of baseline behavior), should be performed with a personal star chart. For the child with severe anxiety about sitting on the toilet, a graded exposure scheme may be indicated.

Role of the Family in Treatment

Removing the child's and family's attention from the encopresis alone and onto noticing, recording, and rewarding positive behavior often defuses tension and hostility and provides the opportunity for therapeutic improvement. Identifying and eliminating sources of secondary gain,

Table 40–3 Practical Management of Encopresis

Stage	
Stage 1	**Assessment**
	Whether primary or secondary. Is there physical cause? Presence or absence of constipation. Presence or absence of acute stress. Presence or absence of psychiatric disorder including phobic symptoms or smearing. ABC (antecedents, behavior, consequences) of encopresis including secondary gain. Discover reasons for previous failure or failures.
Stage 2	**Advice**
	Education regarding diet, constipation, and toileting. Aim to reduce punitive or coercive behavior. Transmit optimism; however, anticipate disappointment at no instant cure. Preview the stepwise recovery and warn of the possibility of relapse.
Stage 3	**Toileting**
	Baseline observation using star chart. Focus on positive achievements, e.g., toileting, rather than soiling. High-fiber diet (try bran in soup, milk shakes). Toilet after meals, 15 minutes maximum. Check that adequately rising intra-abdominal pressure is present. Graded exposure scheme if "pot phobic." *with*
	Laxatives
	Indicated if physical examination or abdominal radiograph shows fecal loading. Medication of choice: Senokot syrup (senna) up to 10 mL twice daily, lactulose syrup up to 30 mL (20 mg) twice daily. Dosage will be reduced over time; titrate with bowel frequency.
	Enemas
	Microenema (e.g., bisacodyl, 30 mL) if the bowel is excessively loaded with rock-like feces.
Stage 4	**Biofeedback**
	Consider after relapse or failure to respond to toileting or laxatives.

whereby soiling is reinforced by parental (or other individuals) actions and attention, even if negative or punitive, make positive efforts more fruitful. Some investigators advocate mild punishment techniques, such as requiring the child to clean his or her own clothes after soiling,[60] although care must be taken to prevent this from becoming too punitive. In certain settings, particularly school, attempts are made to prevent soiling by extremely frequent toileting that, although keeping the child clean, does not promote and may even hinder the acquisition of a regular bowel habit. Formal therapy, either individual or family based, is indicated in only a minority of patients with an associated psychiatric disorder, marked behavioral disturbance (e.g., smearing, other aggressive soiling), or clear remediable family or social stresses.

Physical Treatments

In patients with retention, leading to constipation and overflow, medical management is nearly always required, although it is usually with oral laxatives or microenemas alone. The use of more intrusive and invasive colonic and rectal washout or surgical disimpaction procedures is nearly always the result of the clinician's impatience rather than true clinical need.

Uncontrolled studies of combined treatment with behavioral therapy and laxatives reported marked improvement in symptoms (not cure) in approximately 70% to 80% of patients.[96, 97] Berg and colleagues[69] reported the first double-blind randomly controlled trial of the laxative Senokot (senna concentrate) and behavioral therapy, which showed no significant advantage for the laxative by 3 months. A more recent controlled randomized trial[98] comparing behavioral therapy in retentive primary encopresis, both with and without laxatives, showed that at 12-month follow-up, 51% of the combined treatment (laxative plus behavioral therapy) group had achieved remission (at least one 4-week period with no soiling episodes), compared with 36% of the behavioral therapy only group ($P = .08$). Partial remission (soiling no more than once a week) was achieved in 63% of patients with combined therapy versus 43% with behavioral therapy alone ($P = .02$). Patients receiving laxatives achieved remission significantly sooner, and the difference in the Kaplan-Meier remission curves was most striking in the first 30 weeks of follow-up ($P = .012$). When patients who were not compliant with the toileting program were removed from the analysis, however, the advantage of combined therapy was not significant. These results must also be viewed in light of Bellman's[75] findings in a follow-up study of 186 clinic patients with encopresis, which reported a 50% spontaneous remission rate at 2 years. It should also be noted that approximately 15% to 20% of patients fail to respond to or comply adequately with initial combined treatment.[78, 98]

Biofeedback Therapy

The finding that some children with treatment-resistant retentive encopresis involuntarily contract the muscles of the pelvic floor and the external anal sphincter, effectively impeding passage of stool,[99] has led to efforts to use biofeedback in this instance. Olness and associates[100] used visual feedback of internal and external sphincter pressures measured by an anal balloon in 40 children who were chronic soilers in whom conventional treatment had failed in association with emphasizing regular toileting. Normal bowel habits were acquired by 24 children (60%). It has similarly been reported that as few as six sessions of biofeedback therapy can lead to a significant reduction in symptom frequency for as many as 86% of previously treatment-resistant patients.[101]

Clinical Vignette 2

John was a 6-year-old boy, the only child of a farmer and his wife, both of whom had strong obsessional traits and were excessively fastidious and house-proud. As a 6-month-old baby, John had been prescribed senna for about 3 months around the time he began a fully solid diet. He was investigated for Hirschsprung's disease, but rectal biopsy results were negative. Toilet training was started at age 15 months because his mother was anxious to have John out of diapers by the age of 2 years. Accordingly, John was placed on the "pot" whenever he appeared to need it. This averaged 15 times a day. He would eat sitting on the pot and watch television there, and the family would not travel anywhere without this receptacle, just in case John showed any sign of needing to evacuate his bowels. When, by age 2 years, John had not established a regular toileting habit, the parents gave up and placed him back in diapers. A further brief, yet frenzied effort at training occurred at age 3 years because he would be unable to attend a local preschool program if he was not bowel trained. Not surprisingly, John was not permitted to attend. Soon after starting kindergarten, his school became exasperated with John who was soiling his clothes with almost fluid feces on a regular basis. After consulting with his mother, they assigned John a nonteaching aide who would, in a fashion similar to John's mother, be responsible for taking him to the bathroom on an increasingly frequent basis. When John continued to soil his pants, despite hourly toileting, the school urged John's parents to seek a specialist referral.

On presentation, John seemed to be a bright, if somewhat indolent, child who on the surface was not bothered by his soiling, but on further examination was upset by the fact that he had few friends and was not allowed to go swimming with his class. Physical examination showed a distended abdomen, with marked fecal impaction around the hepatic flexure of the colon. He was prescribed lactulose and senna twice daily, and a toileting program was designed. Because he was a fan of the television characters the Power Rangers, an elaborate chart embodying the important elements of this show was designed in consultation with John. Initial targets consisted of going to the bathroom for 15 minutes after each meal, with initial stars given for trying to pass anything. His mother was taught to place a hand on his abdomen to check for adequate muscular effort. Later behavioral targets became progressively more difficult. Soiling was deemphasized, and considerable effort was expended in assuaging parental anxiety that John would ever be able to pass the accumulated fecal masses. After 5 days, an enormous amount of feces was passed in the evening after a warm bath. Both John and his mother were overjoyed. This pattern was repeated over the next week, with an abdominal radiograph confirming that the colon and rectum were no longer impacted. By 6 weeks, John had established a regular thrice-daily toileting pattern, with only once-weekly accidents. Despite a high-fiber diet, efforts to reduce the laxatives completely were thwarted by recurrent retention, and the decision was made to continue with long-term fecal softeners. By 6 months, John was completely clean.

References

1. Oppel WC, Harper PA, Rider RV: Social, psychological and neurological factors associated with enuresis. Pediatrics 1968; 42:627–641.
2. Rutter ML, Yule W, Graham PJ: Enuresis and behavioral deviance: Some epidemiological considerations. In Kolvin I, MacKeith R, Meadow SR (eds): Bladder Control and Enuresis. Clinics in Developmental Medicine, Nos. 48/49. London: Heinemann/Spastics International Medical Publications, 1973:137–147.
3. Essen J, Peckham C: Nocturnal enuresis in childhood. Dev Med Child Neurol 1976; 18:577–589.
4. Verhulst FC, Van Der Lee JH, Akkerhuis GW, et al: The prevalence of nocturnal enuresis: Do DSM-III criteria need to be changed? A brief research report. J Child Psychiatry 1985; 26:989–993.
5. Blomfield JM, Douglas JWB: Bed-wetting—prevalence among children aged 4–7 years. Lancet 1956; 1:850–852.
6. Hallgren B: Enuresis I: A study with reference to the morbidity risk and symptomatology. Acta Psychiatr Neurol Scand 1956; 31:379–403.
7. Jarvelin MR, Vikevainen-Tervonen L, Moilanen I, Huttunen NP: Enuresis in seven-year-old children. Acta Paediatr Scand 1988; 77:148–153.
8. Cohen MW: Enuresis. Pediatr Clin North Am 1975; 22:545–560.
9. Shaffer D, Stephenson JD, Thomas DV: Some effects of imipramine on micturition and their relevance to their antienuretic activity. Neuropharmacology 1979; 18:33–37.
10. Sorotzkin B: Nocturnal enuresis: Current perspectives. Clin Psychol Rev 1984; 4:293–316.
11. Savage DCL, Wilson MI, Ross EM, Fee WM: Asymptomatic bacteriuria in girl entrants to Dundee primary schools. Br Med J 1969; 3:75–80.
12. Dodge WF, West EF, Bridgforth MS, Travis LB: Nocturnal enuresis in 6–10 year old children. Am J Dis Child 1970; 120:32–35.
13. Forsythe WI, Redmond A: Enuresis and spontaneous cure rate. A study of 1129 enuretics. Arch Dis Child 1974; 49:259–263.
14. Starfield SB: Functional bladder capacity in enuretic and nonenuretic children. J Pediatr 1967; 70:777–781.
15. Shaffer D, Gardner A, Hedge B: Behavior and bladder disturbance in enuretic children: A rational classification of a common disorder. Dev Med Child Neurol 1984; 26:781–792.
16. Fielding D: The response of day and night wetting children and children who wet only at night to retention control training and the enuresis alarm. Behav Res Ther 1980; 18:305–317.
17. Norgaard JP, Pederson EB, Djurhuus JC: Diurnal antidiuretic hormone levels in enuretics. J Urol 1985; 134:1029–1031.
18. Rittig S, Knudsen U, Norgaard J, et al: Abnormal diurnal rhythm of plasma vasopressin and urinary output in patients with enuresis. Am J Physiol 1989; 256:664–671.
19. Boyd MM: The depth of sleep in enuretic school children and in non-enuretic controls. J Psychosom Res 1960; 44:274–281.
20. Mikkelsen EJ, Rapoport JL: Enuresis: Psychopathology sleep stage and drug response. Urol Clin North Am 1980; 7:361–377.
21. Bakwin H. Enuresis in children. J Pediatr 1961; 58:806–819.
22. Bakwin H: Enuresis in twins. Am J Dis Child 1971; 121:222–225.
23. Fergusson DM, Horwood LJ, Shannon FT: Factors related to the age of attainment of nocturnal bladder control: An 8 year longitudinal study. Pediatrics 1986; 78:884–890.
24. Steinhausen HC, Gobel D: Enuresis in child psychiatric clinic patients. J Am Acad Child Adolesc Psychiatry 1989; 28:279–281.
24a. Kauffman M: Enuresis among kibbutz children. J Med Assoc Israel 1962; 63:251–253.
25. Werry JS, Cohrssen J: Enuresis: An etiologic and therapeutic study. J Pediatr 1965; 67:423–431.
26. Douglas JWB: Early disturbing events and later enuresis. In Kolvin I, MacKeith R, Meadow SR (eds): Bladder Control and Enuresis. Clinics in Developmental Medicine, Nos. 48/49. London: Heinemann/Spastics International Medical Publications, 1973:109–117.
27. Chadwick O: Psychological sequelae of head injury in children. Dev Med Child Neurol 1985; 27:69–79.
28. Blackwell B, Currah J: The psychopharmacology of nocturnal enuresis. In Kolvin I, MacKeith R, Meadow SR (eds): Bladder Control and Enuresis. Clinics in Developmental Medicine, Nos. 48/49. London: Heinemann/Spastics International Medical Publications, 1973:231-257.
29. Young GC, Morgan RTT: Rapidity of response to the treatment of enuresis. Dev Med Child Neurol 1973; 15:488–496.
30. Behrle FC, Elkin MT, Laybourne PC: Evaluation of a conditioning device in the treatment of nocturnal enuresis. Pediatrics 1956; 17:849–855.
31. Baker BL: Symptom treatment and symptom substitution in enuresis. J Abnorm Psychol 1969; 74:42–49.
32. Moffat MEK, Kato C, Pless IB: Improvements in self-concept after treatment of nocturnal enuresis: Randomized control trial. J Pediatr 1987; 110:647–652.
33. Miller FJW, Court SDM, Walton WS, Knox EG: Growing Up in Newcastle-upon-Tyne. London: Oxford University Press, 1960.
34. Foxman B, Valdez RB, Brook RH: Childhood enuresis: Prevalence, perceived impact and prescribed treatments. Pediatrics 1986; 77:482–487.
35. Shaffer D, Costello AJ, Hill JD: Control of enuresis with imipramine. Arch Dis Child 1968; 43:665–671.
36. Mahoney DT: Studies of enuresis. I: Incidence of obstructive lesions and pathophysiology and enuresis. J Urol 1971; 106:951–958.
37. Dimson SB: DDAVP and urine osmolality in refractory enuresis. Arch Dis Child 1986; 61:1104–1107.
38. Miller K, Klauber GT: Desmopressin acetate in children with severe primary nocturnal enuresis. Clin Ther 1990; 12:357–366.
39. Miller K, Goldberg S, Atkin B: Nocturnal enuresis: Experience with long-term use of intranasally administered desmopressin. J Pediatr 1989; 14:723–726.
40. Rapoport JL, Mikkelsen EJ, Zavardil A, et al: Childhood enuresis II: Psychopathology, tricyclic concentration in plasma, and antienuretic effect. Arch Gen Psychiatry 1980; 37:1146–1152.
41. Simeon J, Maguire J, Lawrence S: Maprotiline effects in children with enuresis and behavioral disorders. Prog Neuropsychopharmacol 1981; 5:495–498.
42. Jorgensen OS, Lober M, Christiansen J, Gram LF: Plasma concentration and clinical effect in imipramine treatment of childhood enuresis. Clin Pharmacokinet 1980; 5:386–393.
43. McConaghy N: A controlled trial of imipramine, amphetamine, pad and bell, conditioning and random awakening in the treatment of nocturnal enuresis. Med J Aust 1969; 2:237–239.
44. Young GC, Turner RK: CNS stimulant drugs and conditioning treatment of nocturnal enuresis. Behav Res Ther 1965; 3:93–101.
45. Wallace IR, Forsythe WI: The treatment of enuresis. A controlled clinical trial of propantheline, propantheline and phenobarbitone, and placebo. Br J Clin Pract 1969; 23:207–210.
46. Elmer M, Norgaard JP, Djurhuus JC, Adolfson T: Terodiline in the treatment of diurnal enuresis in children. Scand J Primary Health Care 1988; 6:119–124.
47. Baigrie RJ, Kelleher JP, Fawcett DP, Pengelly AW: Oxybutynin: Is it safe? Br J Urol 1988; 62:319–322.
48. Pfaundler M: Demonstration eines Apparates zur selbstatig Signalisieursang stattgehabter Bettnassung. Verh Ges Kinderheilk 1904; 21:219–220.
49. Mowrer OH, Mowrer WM: Enuresis: A method for its study and treatment. Am J Orthopsychiatry 1938; 8:436–459.
50. Forsythe WI, Butler RJ: Fifty years of enuretic alarms. Arch Dis Child 1989; 64:879–885.
51. Butler RJ: Establishment of working definitions in nocturnal enuresis. Arch Dis Child 1991; 66:267–271.
52. Kolvin I, Taunch J, Currah J, et al: Enuresis: A descriptive analysis and a controlled trial. Dev Med Child Neurol 1972; 14:715–726.
53. Bollard J, Nettlebeck T: A comparison of dry bed training and standard urine-alarm conditioning treatment of childhood bed-wetting. Behav Res Ther 1981; 19:215–226.
54. Finley WW, Wansley RA: Auditory intensity as a variable in the conditioning treatment of enuresis nocturna. Behav Res Ther 1977; 15:181–185.
55. Butler RJ, Forsythe WI, Robertson J: The body worn alarm in

treatment of childhood enuresis. Br J Child Psychiatry 1990; 44:237–241.
56. Dische S, Yule W, Corbett J, Hand D: Childhood nocturnal enuresis: Factors associated with outcome of treatment with an enuresis alarm. Dev Med Child Neurol 1983; 25:67–81.
57. Turner R, Young G, Rachman S: Treatment of nocturnal enuresis by conditioning techniques. Behav Res Ther 1970; 8:367–381.
58. Wagner WG, Johnson JT: Childhood nocturnal enuresis: The prediction of premature withdrawal from behavioral conditioning. J Abnorm Child Psychol 1988; 16:687–692.
59. Malem H, Knapp MS, Hiller EJ: Electronic bed-wetting alarm and toilet trainer. Br Med J 1982; 285:22.
60. Doleys DM, McWhorter MS, Williams SC, Gentry R: Encopresis: Its treatment and relation to nocturnal enuresis. Behav Ther 1977; 8:77–82.
61. Fielding D: Factors associated with drop out, relapse and failure in conditioning treatment of nocturnal enuresis. Behav Psychother 1985; 13:174–185.
62. Houts AC, Peterson JK, Liebert RM: The effect of prior imipramine treatment on the results of conditioning therapy in children with enuresis. J Pediatr Psychol 1984; 9:505–509.
63. Finley WW, Besserman RL, Clapp RK, Finley P: The effect of continuous, intermittent and placebo reinforcement on the effectiveness of the conditioning treatment for enuresis nocturna. Behav Res Ther 1973; 11:289–297.
64. Deleon G, Mandell W: A comparison of conditioning and psychotherapy in the treatment of enuresis. J Clin Psychol 1966; 22:326–330.
65. Azrin NH, Sneed TJ, Fox RM: Dry bed: A rapid method of eliminating bed-wetting (enuresis) of the retarded. Behav Res Ther 1974; 11:427–434.
66. Nettlebeck T, Langeluddecke P: Dry-bed training without an enuresis machine. Behav Res Ther 1979; 17:403–404.
67. Mattsson JL, Ollendick TH: Issues in training normal children. Behav Ther 1977; 8:549–553.
68. Fielding D, Berg I, Bell S: An observational study of posture and limb movements of children who wet by day and at night. Dev Med Child Neurol 1978; 20:453–461.
69. Berg I, Forsythe I, McGuire R: Response of bed-wetting to the enuresis alarm. Influence of psychiatric disturbance and maximum functional bladder capacity. Arch Dis Child 1982; 57:394–396.
70. Halliday S, Meadow SR, Berg I: Successful management of daytime enuresis using alarm procedures: A randomly controlled trial. Arch Dis Child 1987; 62:132–137.
71. Meadow R, Berg, I: Controlled trial of imipramine in diurnal enuresis. Arch Dis Child 1982; 57:714–716.
72. Steubens JA, Silber DL: Parental expectations vs. outcome in toilet training. Pediatrics 1974; 54:493–495.
73. Brazelton TB: A child-oriented approach to toilet training. Pediatrics 1962; 29:121–128.
74. Stein Z, Susser M: Social factors in the development of sphincter control. Dev Med Child Neurol 1967; 9:692–700.
75. Bellman M: Studies on encopresis. Acta Paediatr Scand 1966; (suppl 170):1+.
76. Rutter M, Tizard J, Whitmore K (eds): Education, Health and Behavior. London: Longman, 1970.
77. Levine MD: Children with encopresis: A descriptive analysis. Pediatrics 1975; 56:412–416.
78. Levine MD: Encopresis, its potential evaluation and alleviation. Med Clin North Am 1982; 29:315–330.
79. Bakwin H: Enuresis in twins. Am J Dis Child 1971; 121:222–225.
80. Loening-Baucke VA, Younoszai MK: Abnormal anal sphincter response in chronically constipated children. J Pediatr 1982; 100: 213–218.
81. Wald A, Chandra R, Chiponis D, Gabel S: Anorectal function and continence mechanisms in childhood encopresis. J Paediatr Gastroenterol Nutr 1986; 5:346–351.
82. Loening-Baucke VA, Cruickshank B, Savage C: Defecation dynamics and behavior profiles in encopretic children. Pediatrics 1987; 80:672–679.
83. Pettei M, Davidson M: Constipation. In Silverberg M, Daum F (eds): Textbook of Pediatric Gastroenterology. Chicago: Year Book Medical Publishers, 1988:180–188.
84. Anthony EJ: An experimental approach to the psychopathology of childhood: Encopresis. Br J Med Psychol 1957; 30:146–175.
85. Berg I, Jones KV: Functional fecal incontinence in children. Arch Dis Child 1964; 39:465–472.
86. Woodmansey AC: Emotion and the motions: An inquiry into the causes and prevention of functional disorders of defecation. Br J Med Psychol 1967; 40:207–223.
87. Olatawura M: Encopresis: A review of thirty-two cases. Acta Paediatr Scand 1973; 62:358–364.
88. Taylor E, Hersov L: Fecal soiling. In Rutter M, Taylor E, Hersov L, et al (eds): Child and Adolescent Psychiatry: Modern Approaches, 3rd ed. London: Blackwell Scientific Publications, 1994.
89. Clark AF, Taylor PF, Bhates SR: Nocturnal fecal soiling and anal masturbation. Arch Dis Child 1990; 65:1367–1368.
90. Boon F: Encopresis and sexual assault. J Am Acad Child Adolesc Psychiatry 1991; 30:479–482.
91. Easson RI: Encopresis-psychogenic soiling. Can Med Assoc J 1960; 82:624–628.
92. Gabel S, Hegedus AM, Wald A, et al: Prevalence of behavior problems and mental health utilization among encopretic children: Implications for behavioral pediatrics. J Dev Behav Pediatr 1986; 7:293–297.
93. Warson S, Caldwell M, Warinner A, et al: The dynamics of encopresis. Am J Orthopsychiatry 1954; 24:402–415.
94. Fleisher D: Diagnosis and treatment of disorders of defecation in children. Pediatr Ann 1976; 5:700–722.
95. Clayden G, Agnarsson U: Constipation in Childhood. Oxford: University Press, 1991.
96. Levine MD, Bakow H: Children with encopresis: A study of treatment outcome. Pediatrics 1976; 50:845–852.
97. Loening-Baucke VA: Elimination disorders. In Greydanus DE, Wolraich ML (eds): Behavioral Pediatrics. New York: Springer-Verlag, 1992:280–297.
98. Nolan T, Debelle G, Oberklaid F, Coffey C: Randomised trial of laxatives in treatment of childhood encopresis. Lancet 1991; 338: 523–527.
99. Loening-Baucke VA, Cruickshank BM: Abnormal defecation dynamics in chronically constipated children with encopresis. J Pediatr 1986; 108:562–566.
100. Olness K, McParland FA, Piper J: Biofeedback: A new modality in the management of children with fecal soiling. J Pediatr 1980; 96:505–509.
101. Loening-Baucke V: Biofeedback treatment for chronic constipation and encopresis in childhood: Long-term outcome. Pediatrics 1995; 96:105–110.

CHAPTER

41 Generic Substance and Polydrug Use Disorders

Thomas R. Kosten

Substance Abuse
Substance Dependence
Substance Intoxication
Substance Withdrawal

Each of the major substances of abuse is covered in a separate chapter of this section. The chapters follow the clinical orientation of this book but also provide a neurobiological background for considering these abused substances. This first chapter provides an overview of substance abuse and dependence, including its definition in the *Diagnostic and Statistical Manual of Mental Disorders,* Fourth Edition (DSM-IV); the general epidemiological features of substance abuse; its pathophysiological characteristics; and the clinical issues of diagnosis and treatment, including psychotherapy and pharmacotherapy. Many of the general principles outlined in this chapter are elaborated on in later chapters in regard to specific abused substances. Hallucinogens are discussed in the context of this chapter, except for phencyclidine. However, polydrug abuse and some relatively uncommonly abused substances (e.g., anticholinergic agents) or substances that do not clearly meet standards for abuse and dependence (e.g., steroids) are not given separate attention.

Definition

Substance Abuse and Dependence

The definitions of substance abuse and dependence are based on the dependence syndrome of Griffith Edwards.[1] Although this syndrome originally had 10 criteria, these criteria have been reduced to 7, including tolerance and withdrawal (the first 2 criteria) and a pattern of compulsive use (criteria 3 through 7) (see pages 744 and 745). The severity of dependence can be indicated by the number of criteria met (from a minimum of three to a maximum of seven) and by the first two defining criteria of this syndrome, because tolerance and withdrawal are associated with a higher risk for immediate general medical problems and a higher relapse rate. The five criteria indicating compulsive use alone may define substance dependence if at least three are present simultaneously during a 1-month period. Physiological dependence is much more likely with some drugs, such as opioids and alcohol, and is infrequent with other classes of drugs, such as hallucinogens.

This section reviews the application of the dependence syndrome to a variety of abused drugs and uses the number of dependence syndrome criteria met as a measure of severity. Treatment-seeking opioid abusers are likely to meet most of the dependence syndrome criteria, and therefore their use is at the high end of severity. Cannabis users, in contrast, are likely to meet relatively few dependence syndrome criteria, and therefore their use is of a lesser degree of severity. Individuals with alcoholism or cocaine abuse tend to demonstrate a much wider variability among treatment seekers, with the proportion of patients having relatively low levels of dependence approximately equal to those having extremely high levels of dependence. Thus, the severity of substance dependence is variable depending on the type of drug abused. This chapter also specifically refers to medications (such as anticholinergic agents, steroids, and antidepressants) and toxins (such as heavy metals, ethylene glycol, and poisons) that can produce intoxication and substance abuse but are not covered in subsequent chapters. These other substances are also unlikely to be associated with dependence. Steroid abuse is of research interest but has not been clearly identified as producing the acute reinforcement or dependence and withdrawal symptoms that characterize the abuse of other substances. Their heavy use by body builders, with the associated possible medical complications, has raised important public health issues, however.

Substance abuse is a maladaptive pattern of substance use leading to significant adverse consequences. In the areas of psychosocial, medical, or legal problems, these conse-

DSM-IV Criteria

Substance Abuse

A. A maladaptive pattern of substance use leading to clinically significant impairment or distress, as manifested by one (or more) of the following, occurring within a 12-month period:

(1) recurrent substance use resulting in a failure to fulfill major role obligations at work, school, or home (e.g., repeated absences or poor work performance related to substance use; substance-related absences, suspensions, or expulsions from school; neglect of children or household)

(2) recurrent substance use in situations in which it is physically hazardous (e.g., driving an automobile or operating a machine when imparied by substance use)

(3) recurrent substance-related legal problems (e.g., arrests for substance-related disorderly conduct)

(4) continued substance use despite having persistent or recurrent social or interpersonal problems caused or exacerbated by the effects of the substance (e.g., arguments with spouse about consequences of intoxication, physical fights)

B. The symptoms have never met the criteria for substance dependence for this class of substance.

quences must recur during a 12-month period, but tolerance, withdrawal, and compulsive use are not necessary for a substance abuse diagnosis. This diagnosis does not apply to caffeine or nicotine. Repeated intoxication contributes to this diagnosis, and two of the four DSM-IV abuse criteria overlap with the dependence criteria. The other two abuse criteria focusing on legal and interpersonal problems are not among the dependence criteria.

Substance Intoxication

Substance intoxication is a reversible substance-specific syndrome with maladaptive, behavioral, or psychological changes developing during or shortly after using the substance. It does not apply to nicotine. Recent use can be documented by a history or toxicological screening of body fluids (urine or blood). Different substances may produce similar or identical syndromes and, in polydrug users, intoxication may involve a complex mixture of disturbed perceptions, judgment, and behavior that can vary in severity and duration according to the setting in which the substances were taken. Physiological intoxication is not necessarily maladaptive and would not of itself be diagnosed. For example, caffeine-induced tachycardia with no maladaptive behavior does not meet the criteria for substance intoxication.

DSM-IV Criteria

Substance Intoxication

A. The development of a reversible substance-specific syndrome due to recent ingestion of (or exposure to) a substance. Note: Different substances may produce similar or identical syndromes.

B. Clinically significant maladaptive behavioral or psychological changes that are due to the effect of the substance on the central nervous system (e.g., belligerence, mood lability, cognitive impairment, impaired judgment, impaired social or occupational functioning) and develop during or shortly after use of the substance.

C. The symptoms are not due to a general medical condition and are not better accounted for by another mental disorder.

Substance Withdrawal

Substance withdrawal is a syndrome due to cessation of, or reduction in, heavy and prolonged substance use. It causes clinically significant impairment or distress and is usually associated with substance dependence. Most often the symptoms of withdrawal are the opposite of intoxication with that substance. The withdrawal syndrome usually lasts several days to 2 weeks.

DSM-IV Criteria

Substance Withdrawal

A. The development of a substance-specific syndrome due to the cessation of (or reduction in) substance use that has been heavy and prolonged.

B. The substance-specific syndrome causes clinically significant distress or impairment in social, occupational, or other important areas of functioning.

C. The symptoms are not due to a general medical condition and are not better accounted for by another mental disorder.

DSM-IV Criteria

Substance Dependence

A maladaptive pattern of substance use, leading to clinically significant impairment or distress, as manifested by three (or more) of the following, occurring at any time in the same 12-month period:

(1) tolerance, as defined by either of the following:

(a) a need for markedly increased amounts of the substance to achieve intoxication or desired effect

(b) markedly diminished effect with continued use of the same amount of the substance

(2) withdrawal, as manifested by either of the following:

(a) the characteristic withdrawal syndrome for the substance (refer to criteria A and B of the criteria sets for withdrawal from the specific substances)

(b) the same (or a closely related) substance is taken to relieve or avoid withdrawal symptoms

(3) the substance is often taken in larger amounts or over a longer period than was intended

(4) there is a persistent desire or unsuccessful efforts to cut down or control substance use

(5) a great deal of time is spent in activities necessary to obtain the substance (e.g., visiting multiple doctors or driving long distances), use the substance (e.g., chain-smoking), or recover from its effects

(6) important social, occupational, or recreational activities are given up or reduced because of substance use

(7) the substance use is continued despite knowledge of having a persistent or recurrent physical or psychological problem that is likely to have been caused or exacerbated by the substance (e.g., current cocaine use despite recognition of cocaine-induced depression, or continued drinking despite recognition that an ulcer was made worse by alcohol consumption)

Specify if:

With physiological dependence: evidence of tolerance or withdrawal (i.e., either item 1 or 2 is present)

Without physiological dependence: no evidence of tolerance or withdrawal (i.e., neither item 1 nor 2 is present)

Course specifiers (see text for definitions):

Early full remission

Early partial remission

Sustained full remission

Sustained partial remission

On agonist therapy

In a controlled environment

Epidemiology

Prevalence

Wide cultural variations in attitudes toward substance consumption have led to widely varying patterns of substance abuse and prevalence of substance-related disorders. Relatively high prevalence rates for the use of virtually every substance occur between the ages of 18 and 24 years, with intoxication being the initial substance-related disorder, usually beginning in the teens. Tolerance and withdrawal require a sustained period of use, and these manifestations of physical dependence for most drugs of abuse typically begin in the 20s and early 30s. Although most substance-related disorders are more common in men than in women, sex ratios can vary considerably with different drugs of abuse.

Comorbidity Patterns

In both the Epidemiological Catchment Area study and the National Comorbidity Survey, substance abuse and dependence were the most common comorbid disorders, usually appearing in combination with affective and anxiety disorders. In the National Comorbidity Survey,[2] the lifetime rate of substance abuse was 27% and the comorbid rate of depression was 19%. Furthermore, 80% of these subjects had more than one psychiatric disorder; only 20% had only one psychiatric disorder. In the Epidemiological Catchment Area study,[3] 75% of daily substance abusers had a comorbid psychiatric disorder. In studies of treatment-seeking substance abusers, the rates of other psychiatric disorders are almost uniformly higher than those in community samples, but the rates of excess comorbidity in these abusers varies with the specific abused drug. For example, in the Epidemiological Catchment Area study the lifetime rate of major depression in the community was 7%, whereas the major depression rates for substance abusers seeking treatment were 54% for opioids, 38% for alcohol, and 24% for cocaine. Rates for other disorders are compared in Table 41–1.

Etiology and Pathophysiology

The cause of substance abuse depends on a variety of biological, psychological, and social factors. Biological factors can include genetic predisposition as well as neurobiological substrates for positive and negative reinforcement by abused substances. Family genetic studies have found rates of substance abuse three to four times higher in identical twins than in dizygotic twins. Although no single biological marker or specific genetic defect has been confirmed, work has suggested that some alleles associated

Table 41–1 Lifetime Diagnoses of Substance Abusers and Community Sample

	Patients with Opioid Addiction (n = 533)	Patients with Alcoholism (n = 321)	Cocaine Abusers (n = 149)	New Haven Community (n = 3058)
Major depression	53.9	38	31.5	6.7
Bipolar disorder I (mania)	0.6	2	3.4	1.1
Schizophrenia	0.8	2	0.7	1.9
Phobia	9.6	27	11.4	7.8
Antisocial personality	25.5	41	34.9	2.1
Alcoholism	34.5	100	63.8	11.5
Drug abuse	100	43	100	5.8

with variations in the dopamine receptor may be more common in substance abusers than in individuals who are not substance abusers. Similarly, risk factor studies have found that the sons of individuals suffering from alcoholism have a general hyporesponsiveness to alcohol and sedative drugs when compared with the sons of individuals without alcoholism.

The neurobiological substrates for positive and negative reinforcement by abused substances have been examined in a wide range of animal studies. The neuronal pathways underlying positive reinforcement appear to converge on the dopaminergic pathways leading from the ventral tegmental area in the brain stem to the nucleus accumbens, which is part of the basal ganglia. Most drugs of abuse appear to act through this pathway to produce positive reinforcement and reward. Some abused drugs, such as stimulants, affect this pathway directly by increasing the amount of dopamine available to stimulate the cells in the nucleus accumbens. Other drugs, such as opioids, appear to have effects on the dopaminergic cells in the ventral tegmental area through specific μ opioid receptors and thereby indirectly affect the nucleus accumbens. Human research suggests that the nucleus accumbens itself has few μ opioids. The reinforcing effects of alcohol and benzodiazepines may be through γ-aminobutyric acid receptors. These γ-aminobutyric acid receptors also appear on the dopaminergic cells located in the ventral tegmental area. The positive reinforcing effects of hallucinogenic drugs are less clear. For example, marijuana interacts with a specific cannabinoid receptor that is primarily located in the cerebellum, and it does not appear to have a direct interaction with the dopaminergic systems in the ventral tegmental area. Other hallucinogenic drugs, such as lysergic acid diethylamide, have critical effects on serotoninergic systems, which may act on the nucleus accumbens to facilitate dopamine neurotransmission indirectly. Animal studies delineating these reinforcement pathways in the brain have shown that these systems are important for general hedonic tone and the reinforcing properties not only of abused drugs but also of pleasures derived from activities that are considered healthy alternatives to substance abuse. Thus, interventions targeted at these fundamental neuropathways might also interfere with the pleasures of normal daily living.

The negative reinforcers involved in substance dependence include the relief of withdrawal symptoms. The neurobiological systems responsible for symptoms of withdrawal are multiply determined. Two brain systems that appear to be particularly important during withdrawal are the noradrenergic system in the locus caeruleus of the brain stem and the dopaminergic system that terminates in the nucleus accumbens. The nucleus accumbens is more broadly a part of the limbic circuit, which generally is associated with mood and emotion.

The role of the locus caeruleus in drug withdrawal has been clearly delineated during opiate withdrawal. The locus caeruleus contains μ opioid receptors that inhibit locus activity when exposed to morphine. During opiate withdrawal, the locus has high levels of nerve activity, and this nerve activity appears to result from the release of chronic inhibition of the locus by morphine administration. After chronic morphine inhibition, the second-messenger system (cyclic adenosine monophosphate) hypertrophies. This hypertrophy is expressed as locus hyperactivity when morphine is removed.

After chronic administration of cocaine, opioids, or alcohol, there is an increased stimulation threshold in the nucleus accumbens so that the same level of stimulation in the nucleus produces less positive reinforcement. This might be interpreted as a type of negative reinforcement after chronic drug usage. In summary, at least two and probably more neural circuits are recruited into the negative reinforcement associated with substance dependence and thereby are important pathophysiological factors.

Psychological factors related to etiology include high rates of depressive disorders and sensation seeking, which are found in substance abusers. The association of sensation seeking with substance abuse suggests not only that drugs enhance pleasant sensations, such as a high, but also that abused drugs may provide potential control of aggressive impulses. Whether abused drugs serve as self-medication for individuals with these psychological disturbances (e.g., depression and impulsivity) has not been resolved clearly because the age at onset for major psychiatric disorders, such as depression, is older than the age at onset for substance abuse and dependence. Childhood precursors of substance abuse, including shy and aggressive behaviors, can also be precursors of later depressive disorders as well as of antisocial personality disorder, the adult expression of aggressive impulsivity.

Finally, social factors, including peer and family influences, which are not dependent on genetic inheritance, are important in leading to initial drug exposure. Kandel[4] has conducted longitudinal studies of "gateway drug" usage by adolescents. These gateway drugs are tobacco, alcohol, and marijuana. Adolescents who begin using gateway drugs in their early teens are more likely to have substance dependence in their 20s than are adolescents who begin use in their late teens. Delaying the initiation of these gateway drugs and their associated intoxication by 1 to 2 years substantially decreases the later risk of the development of substance dependence. This association between early gateway drug use and later dependence may be related to the relatively higher rates of conduct disorder and failure to complete school in those who acquire a substance-related disorder in early adolescence. Life stressors related to peers and family are also possible causative factors in substance abuse and their associated comorbid psychiatric disorders (see first clinical vignette further on).

Diagnosis

Phenomenology and Variations in Presentation

The diagnosis of substance abuse and dependence is made by eliciting an appropriate history, performing laboratory tests to confirm drug use, and observing the physiological manifestations of tolerance and withdrawal. A diagnostic decision tree is presented in Figure 41–1.

The phenomenology and variations in presentation among substance abusers are related to the wide range of substance-induced states as well as the conditions under which the patient is brought to treatment. The emergency department patient who is acutely intoxicated or suffering from a polydrug overdose can present a wide-ranging and confusing diagnostic picture. Depending on the amount of each drug ingested and the time since ingestion, the likelihood of a serious overdose can be difficult to predict. Similarly, distinguishing substance intoxication or withdrawal from an underlying psychiatric disorder or psychosis, or from chronic anxiety disorders, can involve variable presentations. In most of these cases, careful observation for a period of several hours to several days, in conjunction with urine toxicological screens, may be necessary to institute proper treatment. Many patients who use illicit "street" drugs may not know precisely what drugs they have ingested and certainly will not have a good idea of the precise amount. In addition, patients who are dependent on substances producing significant withdrawal syndromes, such as opioids and alcohol, may have a mixed picture of early intoxication and overdose followed by an evolving withdrawal syndrome; alcohol and sedative withdrawal may produce psychiatric complications (e.g., hallucinations) as well as medical complications (e.g., seizures).

The severity of withdrawal symptoms may, in part, be determined by the setting. For example, studies of opioid-dependent patients have shown that the expression of withdrawal symptoms may be substantially less when no medication treatment is available for symptom relief. As a further example of this phenomenon, individuals with opioid addiction who have been in prison without access to opioids

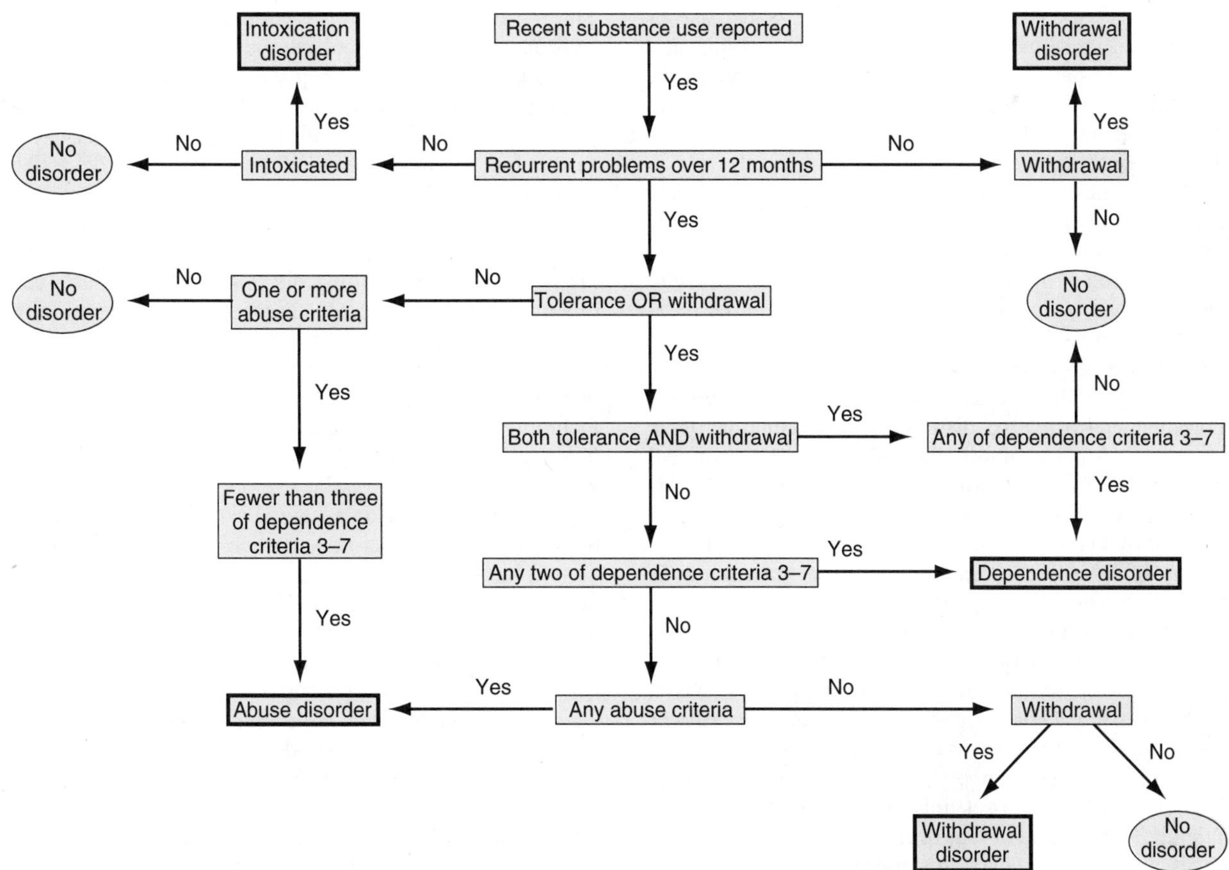

Figure 41–1 *Diagnostic decision tree for substance use disorders.*

for several years may experience precipitous opiate withdrawal when they return to the neighborhoods where they previously used heroin. This conditioned withdrawal phenomenon further supports the importance of setting in the presentation of withdrawal symptoms.

Finally, the issues of motivation for seeking treatment and a tendency to deny substance abuse can have important influences on the patient's presentation. The patient who presents for treatment because of dysphoric feelings in the context of drug dependence is likely to articulate the severity of his or her problem adequately and even exaggerate some aspects of present discomfort. In contrast, the automobile driver forced to come to a treatment program because of a driving-while-intoxicated offense is likely to minimize her or his alcohol use or any associated complications.

Assessment

Special Issues in the Psychiatric Examination

Two special issues in the psychiatric examination of substance abusers include 1) the source of information when obtaining the history of the substance abuse and 2) the management of aberrant behaviors. Information about a patient's substance abuse history can be provided not only by the patient but also by employers, family members, and school officials. When patients self-report the amount of substance abuse, there is a tendency to underreport the severity and duration of abuse, particularly if the patient is being referred to treatment by an outside source, such as the family, the employer, or the legal system. Objective verification of the exact amount of substance use is sometimes difficult, but the critical issues in arriving at a diagnosis of substance dependence does not depend on the precise amount of substance abused. Tolerance and withdrawal can be assessed independently by using tests such as the naloxone challenge and the barbiturate tolerance test. In general, estimates of the amount of drug use by significant others in the patient's life can be a good source of data on the consequences of the patient's substance abuse. Thus, the initial evaluation of a substance abuser may involve a wider range of interviews than would occur with many other types of psychiatric patients.

Behaviors important in the management of aberrant behaviors include intoxication, violence, suicide, cognitive functioning, and affective displays. The evaluation of an intoxicated substance abuser can address only a limited number of issues. These issues are primarily related to the safety of the substance abuser and other individuals who may be affected by his or her actions. Thus, a medical evaluation for signs of overdose or major cognitive impairment is critical, with consideration of detaining the patient for several hours or even days if severe complications are evident. Intoxication with sedating drugs such as alcohol can lead to significant motor and cognitive impairment, which would have an impact on a patient's capacity to drive a motor vehicle. When a patient drives a car to an evaluation and is obviously intoxicated, the psychiatrist has an obligation that the patient not get back into the driver's seat of that vehicle until the effects of that drug intoxication have worn off. This may involve contacting the police to restrain the patient from driving at least temporarily. Similar issues of police restraint can arise when an intoxicated patient becomes violent and has threatened to harm his or her employers or family members. Judgment and impulse control may be substantially affected by abused drugs, but these effects may be temporary, and a short-term preventive intervention may be sufficient to avert substantial harm to the patient or others.

Temporary suicidal behavior may be encountered in a variety of substance abusers, particularly those with alcoholism and stimulant abusers. Suicidal ideation may be intense but may clear within hours. During the evaluation session, it is important to elicit the precipitants that led the patient to seek treatment at this time and to keep the evaluation focused on specific data needed for the evaluation of substance dependence, its medical complications, and any comorbid psychiatric disorders. Many patients spend a great deal of time detailing their drug-abusing careers, but in general these stories do not provide useful material for the evaluation or for future psychotherapeutic interventions. Similarly, the evaluation should not become focused on the affective aspects of a patient's recent life because affect is frequently used as a defense to avoid discussing issues of more immediate relevance as precipitants or to act as a pretext for obtaining benzodiazepines or other antianxiety agents from the physician. Substance abusers have generally used drugs as a way of managing affect and need to develop alternative coping strategies.

Physical Examination and Laboratory Findings

The physical examination is critical for the assessment of substance abuse, particularly before pharmacotherapy is initiated. Many signs of drug withdrawal require a physical examination and cannot rely entirely on history. Because the general medical complications of substance abuse are also substantial, the most clearly ill patients must have a formal general medical evaluation. Vital signs (blood pressure, pulse, and so on) are an essential beginning, but a full examination of heart, lungs, and nervous system is minimally necessary. Transmissible infectious diseases, such as tuberculosis and venereal diseases, are common among illicit drug abusers and require screening for adequate detection. This screening protects health care personnel as well as patients. A wide variety of infectious diseases including hepatitis, endocarditis, and acquired immunodeficiency syndrome (AIDS), are also associated with intravenous drug use, and require appropriate blood studies. With alcohol abusers, a wide range of gastrointestinal complications have been described, particularly liver dysfunction.

Urine toxicological screens can be sensitive for detecting drug use within the previous 3 days for opiates and cocaine to as long as a month for cannabis. A Breathalyzer can be used for detecting alcohol use within an 8- to 12-hour period after use. Specific biological tests can also aid in the diagnosis of dependence, for example, a naloxone challenge test for assessing opioid dependence by precipitating withdrawal symptoms. Associated medical findings on physical examination include "track marks" in intravenous drug users, nasal damage in intranasal drug users, and pulmonary damage in drug smokers.

Differences in Developmental, Gender, and Cultural Presentations

From a developmental perspective, the most important impact of substance abuse and dependence is in adolescence when substance abuse not only can disrupt schooling but also can have important medical consequences because of its direct hormonal effects. For example, opioids can increase prolactin levels and at the same time decrease steroid and testosterone levels. These hormonal effects can have a direct impact on the expression of secondary sex characteristics as well as sexual behaviors during adolescence. Another critical developmental perspective is in the children of substance abusers, who may be born with a significant neonatal withdrawal syndrome from drugs such as opioids or may have behavioral and congenital abnormalities secondary to the substance abuse by their mothers—for example, fetal alcohol syndrome in the infants of mothers who are alcohol-dependent during pregnancy and the hyperactivity that has been noted in infants born to cocaine-dependent mothers.

At the other extreme of life, in the geriatric population, substance abuse might have an important iatrogenic contribution. Many chronic debilitating diseases are associated with significant pain and may be treated with opioids. Similarly, sleep disorders in the elderly are often treated with sedatives (such as benzodiazepine and barbiturates) that produce tolerance and dependence. Although most of these patients will not experience patterns of substance abuse, some patients may begin to seek out these medications from multiple physicians, so-called doctor shopping, and experience significant psychosocial impairment. Sex differences in the presentation of substance abuse problems can be related to the setting in which these problems are detected. For example, young women may come to the attention of the substance abuse treatment provider during or soon after pregnancy. When a child is born with the fetal alcohol syndrome, the mother should be identified as having a substantial problem with alcohol requiring treatment referral.

In contrast, the criminal justice system is more likely to identify male substance abusers and to insist that they get ongoing treatment as a condition of parole or probation. Some drug abuse patterns are also more common in women than in men. For example, the phenomenon of sex for crack frequently occurs in female cocaine abusers, but men infrequently obtain cocaine using this approach. Finally, although men are more likely than women to abuse drugs generally, some drugs, such as androgenic steroids, are significantly overrepresented in male drug abusers.

Cultural differences in the presentation of drug abuse can be striking. For example, the use of hallucinogens by Native Americans in religious ceremonies shows none of the abusive characteristics of adolescent hallucinogen abuse in middle-class America. Alcohol abuse can also show widely varying presentations based on the amount of alcohol that is considered culturally acceptable in various geographical settings. Thus, Asians, who are inclined to have a flushing response to alcohol, tend to use relatively small amounts. Among the French, however, the ingestion of larger amounts of alcohol is more normative and may not reflect alcohol dependence. As a further example, opioid dependence associated with chronic pain treatment in a middle-aged woman will look substantially different from opioid dependence in a 19-year-old African-American man who obtains heroin primarily from the illicit street market. In general, the cultural difference between doctor shopping for sedatives and opioids is considerably different from that associated with buying these same drugs on the illicit street market.

Differential Diagnosis

The differential diagnosis of substance-induced intoxication and withdrawal can involve a wide range of psychiatric disorders. Distinguishing substance abuse from these disorders is usually facilitated by a structured interview to elicit a wide range of psychiatric symptoms appropriately timed after the most recent substance abuse. During acute intoxication in polydrug abusers, the differential diagnosis might include psychosis, mania, organic brain syndromes, or several specific anxiety disorders. Among these anxiety disorders are generalized anxiety disorder, panic disorder, and obsessive-compulsive disorder. Distinguishing these disorders from acute intoxication with a mixture of drugs most frequently requires that the psychiatrist wait 24 to 72 hours to determine whether the symptoms persist and, therefore, whether they are independent of the drug use.

A previous history of schizophrenia, bipolar disorder, or other major psychiatric disorder that is consistent with the presenting symptoms may also be helpful in arriving at an accurate diagnosis. When patients present with psychotic or manic behavior during drug intoxication, it may be necessary to use symptomatic treatment such as a benzodiazepine or neuroleptic agent to conduct an examination. A symptomatic response to these medications should not be considered confirmation of an underlying diagnosis of psychotic disorder, however. Furthermore, some abused drugs, such as phencyclidine, may produce a sustained psychotic state that lasts longer than the usual 72 hours after acute intoxication.

Antisocial and borderline personality disorders are commonly considered in the differential diagnosis in substance-dependent patients. Many of the behavioral characteristics that contribute to these personality disorders are also common to the use of illegal and illicit drugs. In establishing these personality disorders, particularly antisocial personality, it is important to ascertain whether the behaviors are independent of the activities needed to obtain drugs. If many of the antisocial or borderline characteristics are specifically tied to the patient's abuse of drugs, these characteristics will resolve with drug abstinence and should not be considered diagnostic of a personality disorder.

The symptoms of drug withdrawal frequently overlap with those of depressive disorders, and this differential diagnosis can be particularly difficult. Furthermore, the syndrome of protracted withdrawal can include sleep and appetite disturbance as well as dysphoria that mimics dysthymic disorder and other affective disorders. Some drugs, such as opioids, appear to be minimally psychotoxic and are unlikely to produce affective syndromes. Thus, in heroin dependence, a differential diagnosis can be made several days after completing acute detoxification or while the patient is receiving agonist maintenance. With other drugs, such as stimulants and sedatives such as alcohol, depressive symptoms may be more persistent after acute detoxification, which leads to a more difficult differential diagnosis. Thus, conservatively, the psychiatrist should wait 4 to 6 weeks after acute detoxification to determine a diagnosis of affective disorder in these substance abusers. However, waiting this long is often impractical in the clinical setting in which the maintenance of any sustained abstinence may depend on relief of depressive symptoms using either medications or psychotherapy. In this regard, clinical compromises are addressed in subsequent chapters.

Course and Natural History

The natural history of substance dependence characteristically follows the course of a chronic relapsing disorder, although a large number of individuals who experiment with potentially abusable drugs in adolescence do not go on to acquire dependence. The initial phase of the natural history of experimenting with drugs has been well described in studies by Kandel,[4] who has used the concept of gateway drug use and its evolution into more serious drug dependence during adolescence and the early 20s. The later phases of dependence are characterized in the 20- to 30-year follow-up studies of individuals with alcoholism and those with opioid addiction by Vaillant.[5–7] He has documented the natural history after age 20 years, including the high mortality rates seen in substance abusers by age 40 years. Spontaneous remissions also occur in up to one third of individuals suffering from alcoholism during their early 30s.

The course of substance dependence is variable and may involve full or partial remission with six course specifiers available in the DSM-IV. For remission, none of the dependence or abuse criteria can be met for at least 1 month. Remission can then be early or sustained (12 months or longer) and partial or full. Because the first year of remission carries a particularly high risk for relapse, it has been chosen as the criterion for sustained remission. Two additional specifiers are when the patient 1) is receiving agonist therapy or 2) is in a controlled environment such as jail or a therapeutic community.

Population surveys, such as the high school senior surveys and National Institute on Drug Abuse household survey,[8] have provided repeated cross-sectional data on changing trends in substance use and its associated problems. Individuals with substance dependence also have been followed up in a variety of longitudinal treatment studies such as the Treatment Outcome Prospective Study or Drug Abuse Reporting Program.[9, 10] These survey and treatment follow-up studies provide indications of how the natural history of substance abuse changes over the course of several decades. In contrast to most medical disorders, substance abuse differs because the substances of abuse change over time as epidemics come and go and as new drugs, such as the "designer drugs," are developed. The natural history of abuse for these new substances can be unique, with patterns of sustained low-level use, such as with methylenedioxymethamphetamine, or associated social phenomena, such as parkinsonism in abusers of fentanyl-related designer drugs. Thus, the natural history of substance abuse and dependence is determined by the type of substance used and, for polydrug abusers, can be complicated by changing secular trends and epidemics lasting from months to decades.

Treatment Goals

The most common goal of any treatment is abstinence from the abused drug. Issues of "controlled use" are debated by some psychiatrists, but this is usually not a realistic goal for dependent patients. A critical, first essential treatment goal with substance abusers is often acute treatment of overdose. A psychiatrist must be aware of specific therapies, such as naloxone for opioid overdose and flumazenil for benzodiazepine or other sedative overdose. The polydrug abuser often has combined toxicity from drug interactions, such as alcohol with barbiturates or phencyclidine with cocaine. For primary substance abuse, the initial treatment involves either agonist stabilization, such as methadone maintenance, or medical detoxification when necessary because of severe withdrawal syndromes, such as may occur after alcohol or opioid dependence. After detoxification or stabilization, prevention of relapse may occur through a variety of behavioral or other psychotherapeutic approaches. Reduction in drug use without total abstinence using agonist maintenance (e.g., methadone) may be an early priority, together with the provision of essential social services for legal problems, housing, and food. After this stabilization, vocational rehabilitation and various psychotherapeutic issues may be addressed, including the management of affect, such as depression. For patients with psychosis, inpatient treatment or interventions with medication may be required before detoxification can occur.

Other treatment goals in longer term management include total abstinence and family involvement. A common treatment goal in the longer term management of patients is abstinence from all drugs while the patient advocates for controlled use of some substances. For example, alcohol use by the patient receiving methadone maintenance or the continued smoking of marijuana or even tobacco by individuals formerly suffering from alcoholism can lead to a serious conflict in treatment goals. Another goal is to change the role of family members from "enablers" or codependents with the substance abuser to treatment allies. These family members need to be engaged in treatment to work as active collaborators in the therapeutic plan for the patient. Although family treatment is commonly applied to many psychiatric disorders, it can have a particularly powerful impact with these behavioral disorders, especially in adolescent abusers.

Standard Treatments

Psychiatrist-Patient Relationship

The first issue in the psychiatrist-patient relationship is approaching the substance abuser who denies a problem with abuse. This patient must be confronted in such a way that the substance abuse problem will become accessible for treatment. This confrontation may involve an "intervention," in which a variety of the significant others and social supports of the abuser are brought together to confront the potential patient about her or his substance abuse problem. Family and employers are important contributors to such an intervention, as conceptualized by Johnson.

Once the abuse is clearly identified as a problem, a series of other issues arise, including confidentiality versus necessary disclosures, comorbid psychiatric disorders, medical evaluations, and potential for relapse. In one-to-one dealings with the patient, confidentiality must be addressed because the use of illicit drugs can be associated with a variety of illegal activities. Confidentiality must be balanced against the need to disclose enabling behaviors that can lead to a relapse of substance abuse. Psychiatric assessment is critical because of the high rates of depression and the risk of suicide in this population. A full medical assessment generally is essential because of the high rates of infectious and gastrointestinal diseases directly related to substance abuse. Medical assessment is also essential to determine whether active medical detoxification is necessary. Finally, a psychotherapeutic issue early in treatment may be distinguishing between "slips" and a full relapse. Slips are common in substance abusers, and patients must be prepared for them and not consider them failures that will inevitably lead to full relapse and dependence. Slips are more fully covered in the section on psychosocial treatments.

Pharmacotherapy

Pharmacotherapy can have several roles in substance abuse treatment, including treatment of overdose and acute intoxication (naloxone, flumazenil), detoxification or withdrawal symptom relief (benzodiazepines, clonidine), blockage of drug reinforcement (naltrexone), development of responses to the abused substance (disulfiram), treatment of psychiatric comorbidity (antidepressants), and substitution agents to produce cross-tolerance and reduce drug craving (methadone). A key role with many dependence-producing drugs is the need for detoxification, which may last from 3 days to as long as 2 weeks. Detoxification is essential if antagonist pharmacotherapies, such as naltrexone for opioid dependence, or aversive agents, such as disulfiram for alcoholism, are to be employed. Conversely, agonist maintenance treatment, such as methadone or buprenorphine for heroin dependence, does not require detoxification before beginning treatment. Using these agonists usually requires regular clinic attendance by the patient and relatively prolonged treatment of 1 to 2 years, with some patients continuing agonist therapy for up to 20 years.

A treatment decision tree is presented in Figure 41–2 and outlines potential roles for pharmacotherapy and psychotherapy. The general treatment approaches, along with their indications and side effects, are seen in Table 41–2. Medications for substance abuse and dependence can be broadly classified as those for treating withdrawal symptoms (e.g., benzodiazepines for alcohol), those for discouraging use of abused drugs by blockage (e.g.,

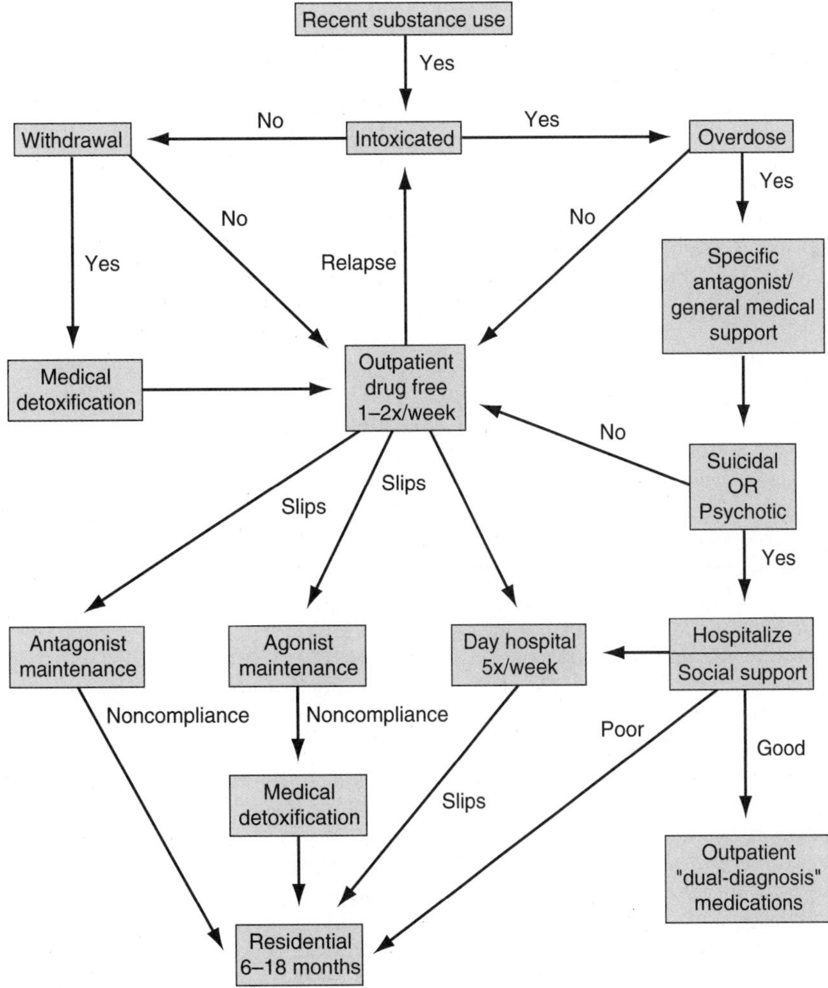

Figure 41–2 *Treatment decision tree for substance use disorders.*

Table 41–2 General Treatment Approaches: Indications and Side Effects

Treatment	Indication	Side Effects
Pharmacotherapy Detoxifications	Dependence on Alcohol Opioids Sedatives	Overmedication, if not carefully monitored Undermedication, leading to seizures
Antagonists Aversive agents Agonists	Drug-free therapy failed	Precipitated withdrawal Illness from use of abused drugs Continued dependence
Psychotherapy Self-help Outpatient Day hospital Residential	Lower level intervention failed	
Inpatient	Medical detoxification Psychotic behavior Suicidal behavior	Social cost
Urine monitoring Breath alcohol	Outpatient treatment	None

naltrexone for opioids) or aversion (e.g., disulfiram for alcohol), those for counteracting overdose (e.g., naloxone for opioids), those used for substitution of the abused drug (e.g., methadone for opioids), and those for treating comorbid psychiatric disorders (e.g., desipramine for depression). These specific medications are reviewed in later chapters. For polydrug abusers, however, the role of medications is usually limited to the need for treatment of acute overdose or detoxification.

Psychosocial Treatments

A wide range of psychosocial treatments are available in substance abuse, ranging from long-term residential treatments (6 to 8 months) to relatively low-intervention outpatient drug-free treatments with once-weekly hour-long therapy. In these outpatient treatments, professional interventions may be unavailable, and counseling is provided by nonprofessionals using group therapy. These groups may be based on extensions of self-help groups, such as Alcoholics Anonymous or Narcotics Anonymous, and use a 12-step program and the associated traditions of these fellowships.

Other treatment approaches include inpatient treatment specifically designed for detoxification and day hospital and evening programs focusing on the prevention of relapse. Behavioral treatments that have frequently been used include relapse prevention therapy as developed by Somers and Marlatt[11] and contingency contracting, in which various aversive contingencies are put in place for periods of up to 6 months to prevent a relapse to substance abuse.

Relapse prevention, a behavioral therapy for substance abusers, has articulated the distinction between slips and relapse. Slips are single, isolated episodes of substance abuse during a period of sustained abstinence. These slips can lead to relapses and dependence if the substance abuse continues. Patients are taught that slips are common and do not necessarily lead to relapses. This concept differs substantially from the Alcoholics Anonymous concept of the slippery slope, in which even a single episode of use will lead to relapse. Thus, Alcoholics Anonymous insists on complete abstinence and does not prepare its members for slips. The distinction can place the self-help groups in conflict with this cognitive-behavioral therapy. The therapies must recognize this issue and help the patient bridge this area of potential conflict. Other principles of relapse prevention therapy generally complement the self-help groups and can provide an important resource for encouraging attendance at self-help meetings.

Special Treatment Features

Psychiatric Comorbidity

Comorbid psychiatric disorders, particularly depressive and anxiety disorders, are extremely common in substance abuse, with lifetime rates approaching 50% in individuals addicted to opioids. Although the rate of major psychotic disorders among substance abusers is relatively low (3%), the rate of substance abuse in schizophrenic and manic-depressive patients may be as high as 50%.

Splitting treatment between a mental health clinic and substance abuse clinic can be a significant problem for the coordinated management of the dual diagnosis patient. A prominent problem in the management of substance abusers with comorbid psychiatric disorders is medication management within a substance abuse treatment setting, because of limited psychiatric resources. In mental health settings, the need for monitoring, using urine toxicological screens for illicit drugs and breath testing for alcohol, can pose difficult logistic and boundary problems. Integrated dual diagnosis treatments have been developed using social skills training combined with relapse prevention behavioral therapies as well as pharmacological adjuncts to standard neuroleptic agents for patients with schizophrenia.

Another special factor in treatment is the relationship between many patients and the legal system—for example, parole, probation, work release programs, or other alternatives to incarceration—because this requires the psychiatrist to report to these agencies. Contingencies must be developed with these patients to clarify the content of this reporting as well as to obtain a specific release of confidentiality so that these reporting requirements can be fulfilled.

General Medical Comorbidity

Treatment of a comorbid medical condition is essential in substance abusers because many do not seek medical care and may be seen only by the psychiatrist. The most important current comorbid disorder in substance abusers is AIDS, which is spread primarily by intravenous drug use but increasingly is also spread through sexual activity among drug abusers. Other areas of medical comorbidity include vitamin deficiencies, infectious diseases, and gastrointestinal disorders, such as cirrhosis, gastrointestinal bleeding, and peptic and duodenal ulcers. Stimulant abusers may experience cerebrovascular accidents. Also, dementing disorders need particular consideration in conjunction with alcoholism, inhalant abuse, and sedative dependence.

Demographical and Psychosocial Variables

Substance abusers are often young but seek treatment only after a delay of 5 to 10 years; the average age of patients presenting for treatment is 32 years. Because most substance abusers are young, parenting issues are critical, specifically issues of drug use during pregnancy, which can lead to "cocaine babies," fetal alcohol syndrome, and opiate withdrawal in infants. Neonatal withdrawal requires specific attention and treatments that differ from adult treatment. Geriatric substance abuse, particularly of prescribed medications, also is not well recognized and is frequently underdiagnosed. Treatment of these geriatric patients with multiple medical problems and complex medical interactions requires careful monitoring by the psychiatrist.

Treatment-Refractory Patients

A variety of escalating treatment interventions can be applied to substance abuse patients who are refractory to treatment. If initial detoxification with outpatient follow-up care is ineffective, several levels of intensified interventions can be applied, such as agonist maintenance with methadone for patients addicted to opioids, disulfiram treatment for patients with alcoholism, and perhaps antidepressants for stimulant abusers. Further interventions can include residential placement for up to 2 years to enable full psychosocial rehabilitation of refractory patients (see the second clinical vignette for an illustration of such an escalating intervention and Fig. 41–2 for a treatment decision tree detailing a series of escalating treatment levels).

Clinical Vignette 1

Vulnerability to AIDS was associated with significant posttraumatic stress disorder (PTSD) in a spouse of a patient in our methadone maintenance program. Mr. and Ms. T had both been patients in our methadone maintenance program for more than 2 years. They had stopped abusing illicit drugs since starting methadone treatment and had restabilized their lives with their two children. He had been working since starting treatment after being unemployed for several months before treatment, and they had been living in a comfortable apartment for almost 2 years. Although he had been intermittently ill during the previous year with seemingly minor infections, these illnesses did not prepare them for his hospitalization with *Pneumocystis* pneumonia followed by a diagnosis of AIDS. His health deteriorated rapidly, and he died less than 6 months after the diagnosis of AIDS. They had both refused to be tested for human immunodeficiency virus when they entered treatment, and she continued to refuse, even after his diagnosis. They had shared needles when using drugs; thus, the probability that she was also infected was high.

During the 6 weeks just before he died, she experienced some symptoms of anticipatory grief, including difficulty sleeping and loss of appetite. Psychotherapeutic treatments were instituted, and she seemed to respond well. The funeral was upsetting, but she appeared to work though the loss of her husband with a typical, several-week course of grief. Six months later, however, she began using cocaine at the urging of a friend. She was using cocaine about twice a week for 3 weeks when nightmares about her dead huband's illness recurred, and she lost interest in most activities, including caring for her children. She had classic alarm symptoms of PTSD, including being easily startled, an inability to concentrate, sleeplessness, and avoiding activities that reminded her of his illness. This last symptom was particularly problematical because it meant that she would not get any medical care and continued to refuse testing for AIDS. Because of these disturbing events and the urging of her drug treatment counselor, she stopped using cocaine, but the PTSD symptoms continued.

Treatment for her PTSD involved both psychotherapy and pharmacotherapy. The psychotherapy was focused on the trauma of the loss of her husband and her own vulnerability to AIDS. She was concerned about the impact on her children if she were to get AIDS, but this fear had led to denying the possibility of her own infection and to pulling away emotionally from her children. The psychotherapy was enhanced by pharmacological treatment with the tricyclic antidepressant imipramine. Treatment was at first attempted without this medication, but the patient could not discuss any traumatic material with the therapist. Within 2 weeks after starting the imipramine, she began sleeping and concentrating better and engaging in productive psychotherapy.

This case illustrates several points about the association of stress with substance abuse. First, substance abusers, particularly heroin addicts, can have substantial stressors in their lives, such as early deaths of spouses and vulnerability to fatal illnesses. Second, they may have problems in adjusting to these stressors, and these problems may be somewhat delayed in presentation (e.g., the PTSD was delayed for 6 months after the actual loss). Third, substance abuse (e.g., the cocaine abuse) may be an initial response to a psychological stress, even though this abuse may worsen the stress-related symptoms. Fourth, pharmacological treatments may enhance the psychotherapy needed for these stress-induced disorders. This last point suggests that PTSD may have a neurobiological substrate; this provides a rationale and target for pharmacological interventions with this stress-related disorder.

Clinical Vignette 2

A 22-year-old man with a 3-year history of cocaine abuse presented with major depressive disorder. Because he had been refractory to selective serotonin reuptake inhibitors, monoamine oxidase inhibitors, tricyclic antidepressants, and augmentation using lithium or thyroid hormone, methylphenidate was added to maintenance treatment with a tricyclic antidepressant. The psychiatrist warned the patient about the risk in prescribing methylphenidate given his past abuse of cocaine and warned that a medication change might be necessary if he experienced a cocaine-like high from the methylphenidate. Within 3 weeks, the patient called the psychiatrist telling him that he had been taking twice the daily prescribed number of pills. The psychiatrist recognized a developing addiction to methylphenidate and began to taper the schedule of methylphenidate administration. Within 3 days, the patient had exhausted a week's supply. The psychiatrist then informed the patient that outpatient detoxification had failed and recommended hospitalization.

This case illustrates how a psychiatrist is often confronted with the issue of whether to use an addictive medication to treat a primary psychiatric disorder in a patient who also has a known substance abuse problem. Other examples of this dilemma are common—a psychiatrist determines that an alcohol-abusing patient suffers from an underlying generalized anxiety disorder and that the patient's drinking may be fueled, in part, by efforts to subdue the anxiety. The patient, currently abstinent but craving alcohol, is given a trial of buspirone for anxiety, but the medication is ineffective. Should a benzodiazepine trial be initiated? Similarly, should a cocaine abuser with a certain diagnosis of residual attention deficit disorder be given a trial of methylphenidate?

Two clinical questions often arise: Is use of addictive medication flatly contraindicated in patients with any kind of substance abuse history, or is such medication prohibited only in instances of use of drugs of the same class (e.g., alcohol and benzodiazepines and methylphenidate and cocaine). In general, a psychiatrist should never rule out the use of any addictive drug if there are good symptom-based reasons for prescribing it. Nor should the psychiatrist assume that an addicting drug of one class (e.g., opiates) will be safe for an individual who abused another class, such as stimulants. However, in any situation in which a potentially addicting drug is considered for use in a remitted substance abuser, considerable caution and limit setting is warranted. Finally, inpatient management may become necessary for the evaluation and use of these risky treatment interventions.

References

1. Edwards G, Gross MM: Alcohol dependence: Provisional description of the clinical syndrome. Br Med J 1976; 1:1058–1061.
2. Kessler RC, McGonagle KA, Zhao S, et al: Lifetime and 12-month prevalence of DSM-III-R psychiatric disorders in the United States: results from the National Comorbidity Survey. Arch Gen Psychiatry 1994; 51:8–19.
3. Regier DA, Myers JK, Kramer M, et al: NIMH Epidemiologic Catchment Area Program. Arch Gen Psychiatry 1984; 41:934-941.
4. Kandel DB: Stages in adolescent involvement in drug use. Science 1975; 190:912–914.
5. Vaillant GE: What can long-term follow-up teach us about relapse and and prevention of relapse in addiction? Br J Addict 1988; 83:1147–1157.
6. Vaillant GE: Natural History of Alcoholism. Cambridge, MA: Harvard University Press, 1983.
7. Vaillant GE: A 12 year follow-up of New York narcotic addicts. II. The natural history of a chronic disease. N Engl J Med 1966; 275:1282–1288.
8. Johnson LD, O'Malley PM, Bachman JG: Drug Use, Drinking, and Smoking: National Survey Results from High School, College, and Young Adult Populations 1975–1988. Rockville, MD: National Institute on Drug Abuse, 1989.
9. Hubbard RL, Marsden ME, Rachal JV, et al: Drug Abuse Treatment: A National Study of Effectiveness. Chapel Hill, NC: University of North Carolina Press, 1989.
10. Simpson DD, Savage LJ, LLoyd MR: Follow-up evaluation of treatment of drug abuse during 1968 to 1972. Arch Gen Psychiatry 1979; 36:772–780.
11. Somers JM, Marlatt GA: Alcohol problems. In Wilson PH (ed): Principles and Practice of Relapse Prevention. New York: Guilford Press, 1992:23–42.

Bibliography

Ball JC, Meyers CP, Friedman SR: Reducing the risk of AIDS through methadone maintenance treatment. J Health Soc Behav 1988; 29:214–226.

Begleiter H, Porjesz B: Potential biological markers in individuals at high risk for developing alcoholism. Alcohol Clin Exp Res 1988; 12:488–493.

Cook CCH: The Minnesota Model in the management of drug and alcohol dependency: Miracle, method or myth? Part II. Evidence and conclusions. Br J Addict 1988; 83:735–748.

Gerstein DR, Harwood HJ (eds): Treating Drug Problems, Volume 1. Washington, DC: National Academy Press, 1990.

Goodwin DW: Is Alcoholism Hereditary? New York: Ballantine Books, 1988.

Jaffe JH: Drug addiction and drug abuse. In Gilman AG, Goodman LS, Rail T (eds): Goodman and Gilman's The Pharmacological Basis of Therapeutics, Volume 7. New York: Macmillan Publishing, 1987: 532–580.

Koob GF, Bloom FE: Cellular and molecular mechanisms of drug dependence. Science 1988; 242:715–723.

Kosten TR, Rounsaville BJ, Babor TF, et al: Substance-use disorders in DSM-III-R: Evidence for the dependence syndrome across different psychoactive substances. Br J Psychiatry 1987; 151:834–843.

Markou MA, Koob GF: Postcocaine anhedonia: An animal model of cocaine withdrawal. Neurosci Biobehav Rev 1991; 41:17–26.

McLellan AT, Luborsky L, O'Brien CP, et al: An improved evaluation instrument for substance abuse patients: The Addiction Severity Index. J Nerv Ment Dis 1980; 168:26–33.

Schuckit MA: A 10-year follow-up of sons of alcoholics: Preliminary results. Alcohol 1991; 1:147–149.

Steller JR, Stellar E: The Neurobiology of Reward and Motivation. New York: Springer-Verlag, 1985.

CHAPTER

42 Alcohol Use Disorders

Henry R. Kranzler
Thomas F. Babor
Pamela Moore

Alcohol Dependence
Alcohol Abuse

Alcohol consumption occurs along a continuum, with considerable variability in drinking patterns among individuals. There is often no sharp demarcation between "social" or "moderate" drinking and "problem" or "harmful" drinking.[1] It is clear, however, that as average alcohol consumption and frequency of intoxication increase, so does the incidence of medical and psychosocial problems.[2] The focus of this chapter is the alcohol use disorders, which according to the *Diagnostic and Statistical Manual of Mental Disorders,* Fourth Edition (DSM-IV)[3] include alcohol abuse and alcohol dependence. However, drinking may have important effects even in the absence of these diagnoses. Consequently, in this chapter, we have taken a broader approach than is traditionally employed in discussions of alcoholism.

The most visible group of people affected by alcohol problems includes those who have a syndrome of alcohol dependence and who are commonly referred to as alcoholics. In this chapter, the term alcoholic refers specifically to those individuals with alcohol dependence. A less prominent but far more numerous group consists of those persons who experience problems with their drinking but who are not seriously dependent on alcohol.[4] These individuals are variously termed alcohol abusers, problem drinkers, and incipient alcoholics. These two "worlds" of alcohol problems, one characterized by heavy drinking and the acute consequences of intoxication, the other by severe dependence and the consequences of long-term drinking, may require different approaches to diagnosis and clinical management.

Epidemiology

International Patterns of Drinking and Types of Alcohol Problems

Alcohol in beverage form is among the most widely used psychoactive drugs in the world. Alcohol consumption is highest in the European countries, North America, and Australia. Methods to produce alcohol and the psychoactive effects associated with its consumption appear to have been identified serendipitously in all cultures in which it is used, with the exception of those in the Pacific Islands and most of North America, where it was introduced by Europeans.[5]

Because of its widespread distribution and the readiness with which it is consumed in a variety of settings, people generally do not conceive of beverage alcohol as a drug. Nonetheless, its complex pharmacological actions, including a panoply of psychopharmacological effects, have led societies throughout the world to surround alcoholic beverages with a variety of rules and regulations governing their use.[5, 6] Despite these efforts at control, excessive drinking, with its adverse effects, is widespread.

Historical and epidemiological evidence may help to explain the development of different patterns of drinking that appear to be linked to types of alcoholism. These approaches provide support for the notion that patterns of drinking differ markedly between the wine-producing countries, typified by France, and the industrialized countries, such as the United States, where beer and distilled liquors are the preferred beverages.[7]

In the wine-producing Mediterranean countries (i.e., Spain, Portugal, Italy, France, and Greece), the pattern of drinking and the type of alcoholism have historically been associated with the consumption of wine as a dietary supplement as well as for its effects as a social lubricant, medicine, and stimulant for manual workers. Drinking tends to be integrated into daily activities and rituals. Wine is typically consumed in moderation by a large segment of the population, and it is used more for its social and presumed nutritional value than for its psychological effects. Drunkenness is uncommon considering the high level of daily consumption. There are few legal restrictions on the availability of alcoholic beverages. Children are introduced to alcohol gradually and naturally.

Given the high levels of alcohol consumption in the wine-producing countries, it is not surprising that they lead the world in many indicators of alcohol-related health problems. Although international statistics must be interpreted cautiously, it appears that the French, for example, rank among the highest in alcohol-related liver cirrhosis, cancer, and traffic accidents. The rate of alcohol dependence is also assumed to be extremely high in France.[8]

In contrast to the preponderance of wine drinking in the Mediterranean region, the use of distilled spirits predominates in the northern periphery of Europe. In countries such as Norway, Sweden, Finland, and Poland, there is a separation of drinking from dietary functions, the deliberate use of alcohol to produce intoxication, and the concentration of heavy drinking in a relatively small portion of the male population. As might be expected from this pattern of drinking, problems in spirits-drinking countries consist largely of alcohol-related accidents, public intoxication, and social disruption.

In the predominantly beer-drinking countries of Germany, Austria, Belgium, the United States, and the United Kingdom, per capita consumption tends to be intermediate between the wine-drinking and spirits-drinking countries. These countries are characterized by more diversified drinking customs; per capita consumption increases as a consequence of the introduction of drinking customs and beverage types from other countries.

Efforts have made it possible to estimate the prevalence of alcoholism in different cultural contexts.[9] Cross-national studies employing structured diagnostic interviews have found lifetime prevalence rates of alcohol abuse and dependence that vary from a low of 0.45% (among Chinese in Shanghai) to a high of 23% (among U.S. native Mexican-Americans).[9] These differences are not adequately explained by demographical differences in the countries studied.[10] In addition to the overall differences in lifetime prevalence rates in different countries, the prevalence of alcoholism varies considerably within countries as a function of both sex and age.[9]

Patterns of Drinking and Types of Alcohol Problems in the United States

Tables 42–1 and 42–2 show prevalence rates of abstention and light, moderate, and heavier drinking from the 1988 U.S. National Health Interview Survey, presented separately for men and women. As can be seen from the tables, only about one third of men are abstainers, whereas more than half of U.S. women do not drink alcohol. Increasing age and lower levels of education are also associated with greater rates of abstention. Similarly, black and Hispanic persons are more likely to abstain than are whites; approximately two thirds of black and Hispanic women are abstainers. Among drinkers, a sex difference is also evident; a majority of women are light drinkers, whereas among men there is greater variability in drinking level, with heavier drinking being considerably more common than it is among women. Among those who drink, age, education, and race-ethnicity are not strongly associated with the level of drinking.

The National Institute of Mental Health Epidemiological Catchment Area (ECA) survey, a study involving more than 20,000 community and institutional respondents in the United States, showed alcohol abuse and dependence to have the highest lifetime prevalence of any mental disorder.[11] That study estimated that nearly one person in seven (13.5% of the U.S. population) suffers from a *Diagnostic and Statistical Manual of Mental Disorders,* Third Edition (DSM-III)[12] alcohol use disorder at some time in his or her life.[11] Further, 8.2% to 10.4% of men and 1.0 to 1.9% of women met criteria for an alcohol use disorder during the 6 months preceding the interview.[13]

The ECA study was limited to five sites in the United States and may therefore not be representative of the entire U.S. population. A later community study, the National Health Interview Survey,[14] involved a representative sample of nearly 44,000 respondents. This study found an overall 1-year prevalence rate for the *Diagnostic and Statistical Manual of Mental Disorders,* Third Edition, Revised (DSM-III-R)[15] alcohol abuse and dependence of 8.6%. Among men, the prevalence was 13.4%; among women, it was 4.4%. The highest prevalence rates were observed among young respondents, with a gradual decline associated with increasing age. The National Comorbidity Study, based on a

Table 42–1 Prevalence of Abstinence and Drinking Levels for Men by Age, Race, and Educational Level: 1988

		Drinking Levels (%)		
Characteristics	Abstainers (%)	Light	Moderate	Heavier
Total	32	44	37	19
Age				
18–29 y	25	42	40	18
30–44 y	25	44	39	17
45–64 y	36	45	34	21
≥65 y	51	50	31	19
Race				
Black	43	45	37	18
White	30	44	37	19
Hispanic	35	48	35	17
Education				
Less than high school	46	46	33	21
High-school graduate	31	43	39	19
Greater than high school	24	44	38	18

Table 42–2 Prevalence of Abstinence and Drinking Levels for Women by Age, Race, and Educational Level: 1988

Characteristics	Abstainers (%)	Drinking Levels (%)		
		Light	**Moderate**	**Heavier**
Total	53	64	29	7
Age				
18–29 y	43	64	30	6
30–44 y	45	65	29	6
45–64 y	58	64	27	9
≥65 y	75	62	29	7
Race				
Black	67	68	26	6
White	50	64	29	7
Hispanic	66	70	25	6
Education				
Less than high school	74	66	27	8
High-school graduate	53	69	28	7
Greater than high school	40	62	30	7

national probability sample of more than 8000 respondents, included an assessment of both lifetime diagnoses and those present during the preceding 12 months. The overall lifetime prevalence of alcohol abuse and dependence in that study was 25%, nearly double that reported for the ECA study. Overall prevalence of alcohol abuse and dependence during the 12 months preceding the interview was 9.7%. Although the differences observed between these studies and the ECA are most likely related to the sampling methods, the different time frames, and the revised diagnostic criteria that were used in the later studies, they may also reflect a cohort effect, with younger cohorts showing increased rates of alcohol use disorders.

Adverse consequences of drinking include a variety of social, legal, and medical problems.[1] Overall, alcohol-related mortality in 1988 totaled 107,800 deaths, or about 5% of all deaths in the United States, putting it among the top four causes of death.[16] Of alcohol-related deaths, approximately 17% were directly attributable to alcohol, 38% resulted from diseases indirectly attributable to alcohol, and 45% were attributable to alcohol-related traumatic injury.[17] Alcohol-related mortality declined during the period 1979 to 1988. Nonetheless, age-adjusted rates remain higher for men (43.4 deaths per 100,000 population) than for women (19.4 deaths per 100,000 population) and for nonwhites (57.2 deaths per 100,000 population) than for whites (32.0 deaths per 100,000 population).[16]

Alcohol-related morbidity is manifested in virtually all organ systems.[18] The primary chronic health hazard associated with heavy drinking is cirrhosis of the liver, which in 1988 was the ninth leading cause of death in the United States.[17] Although the percentage of drivers in fatal crashes with blood alcohol levels in excess of the legal limit has declined in recent years, alcohol intoxication remains a major contributor to this and other types of accidental injury as well as to suicide and homicide.[17] Finally, heavy drinking contributes to family, work, and legal problems. In 1984, 21% of drinkers nationally acknowledged at least a minimal problem of this type, and 10% acknowledged at least a moderate problem.[19] In summary, the annual cost of heavy drinking and alcohol-related disorders in the United States (both in dollars and in suffering) is enormous. Successful efforts to reduce the burden of illness attributable to alcohol could produce substantial reductions in the social, economic, and personal costs of alcohol-related problems.

Patterns of Psychiatric Comorbidity in Individuals with an Alcohol Use Disorder

High rates of comorbid psychiatric disorders have been found in both clinical and community samples of alcohol-dependent individuals.[11, 20–24] These studies show a consistent association between alcohol abuse and dependence and a variety of other psychiatric symptoms and disorders. The ECA study, for example, revealed that 36.6% of those with a lifetime alcohol use disorder received at least one other psychiatric diagnosis, which is nearly double the rate for community respondents with no lifetime diagnosis of alcohol abuse and dependence.[11] Similarly, among individuals with one or more psychiatric disorders, 22.3% also had a lifetime alcohol use disorder, substantially greater than the overall lifetime prevalence of alcohol abuse and dependence (13.5%).[11] Women diagnosed with alcohol abuse and dependence appear to be at greater risk for a comorbid disorder; 65% of them received a comorbid psychiatric diagnosis, compared with only 44% of men with an alcohol use disorder.[24]

Foremost among the psychiatric disorders that occur more frequently in individuals with an alcohol use disorder than among those without the disorder (i.e., have an odds ratio [OR] greater than 1.0) is antisocial personality disorder (ASPD). Although ASPD is present in only 14.3% of individuals with an alcohol disorder, this translates into an OR of 21.0.[11] The fact that 73.6% of ECA respondents with ASPD also met criteria for alcohol abuse and dependence[11] suggests that there is a substantial degree of overlap between the disorders, which is in part attributable to the overlap in diagnostic criteria (e.g., antisocial behavior that is manifested as a consequence of intoxication).

Drug abuse and dependence are also common among individuals with an alcohol use disorder. In the ECA study, 21.5% of individuals with an alcohol disorder also met criteria for a drug disorder (OR = 7.1),[11] with women nearly twice as likely as men to receive the comorbid diagnosis.[24] Among individuals with a drug disorder, 47.3% also had an alcohol disorder. The association was strongest for individuals with cocaine abuse and dependence, among whom 84.8% also had an alcohol disorder (OR = 36.3). Other drug abuse and dependence diagnoses with an OR in excess of 10.0 included those involving barbiturates, opiates, amphetamines, and hallucinogens.[11]

The ECA study showed mood disorders to be present in 13.4% of those with an alcohol disorder (OR = 1.9).[11] Conversely, 21.8% of individuals with a mood disorder also had an alcohol disorder. Of the mood disorders, bipolar disorder is particularly common among individuals with an alcohol use disorder, with 5.1% having a form of the disorder. Among individuals with bipolar disorder, 43.6% have a comorbid alcohol disorder (OR = 5.1). Other mood disorders, although generally more common, show substantially lower ORs. Specifically, unipolar major depression, which is present in 16.5% of individuals with an alcohol use disorder, has an OR of only 1.3. Similarly, dysthymia, although present in 20.9% of individuals with an alcohol use disorder, has an OR of only 1.7.[11] Among individuals with an alcohol use disorder, women were about four times as likely as men to receive a diagnosis of either bipolar disorder or major depression.[24] There is also a sex differential with respect to the order of onset of diagnoses. In men, alcoholism is the antecedent diagnosis in 78% of cases of comorbidity; for women, major depression is the antecedent diagnosis in 66% of cases of comorbidity.[24]

Anxiety disorders are also highly prevalent (19.4%) among individuals with an alcohol use disorder in the ECA study.[11] However, because they are also highly prevalent in the general population, they have an OR of only 1.5. Among individuals with an anxiety disorder, 17.9% have a comorbid alcohol use disorder. Of the anxiety disorders, panic disorder appears to have the strongest association with alcoholism; 28.7% of individuals with panic disorder also have an alcohol use disorder (OR = 2.6). Obsessive-compulsive disorder is intermediate between panic disorder (OR = 2.1) and phobias (OR = 1.4).[11] Among individuals with an alcohol use disorder, women were more than three times as likely as men to have panic disorder and more than twice as likely to have phobia.[24]

Among individuals with an alcohol use disorder, the prevalence of schizophrenia is 3.8%, which is more than three times the rate of that disorder in the general population.[11] Conversely, among individuals with schizophrenia, the prevalence of a comorbid alcohol use disorder is 33.7% (OR = 3.3). Considerable attention has been focused on the substantial problems encountered in treating schizophrenic people with comorbid alcohol and drug abuse and dependence.[25]

Comorbidity influences treatment-seeking behavior. This is evidenced by the fact that 55.0% of individuals with an alcohol use disorder seeking treatment in a mental health or substance abuse setting had a comorbid nonsubstance use disorder, compared with only 24.4% of individuals with an alcohol use disorder who had not sought treatment.[11] Data from the ECA study also revealed that even after controlling for the severity of alcoholism, the number of comorbid nonsubstance diagnoses in individuals with an alcohol use disorder is significantly correlated with the frequency with which they seek treatment for psychiatric and medical problems.[24]

Given these data from the community, it is not surprising that in clinical settings, individuals with an alcohol use disorder also have a high prevalence of comorbid psychiatric disorders. Among the more common of these disorders are major depression, ASPD, drug dependence, and anxiety disorders.[21–23] However, the prevalence of comorbid disorders observed in clinical samples appears to vary as a consequence of a number of factors, including the method of assessment, the sample studied, and the recency of heavy drinking.[26, 27] Given the overlap in the diagnostic criteria for alcohol dependence and ASPD and the effects of long-term heavy drinking on mood and anxiety symptoms, care must be taken to differentiate transient, alcohol-related signs and symptoms from persistent features.[26, 27]

Powell and coworkers[22] used a structured diagnostic interview to examine the lifetime prevalence of comorbid DSM-III disorders among 565 male inpatient veterans being treated for alcohol dependence. They found that 63% of patients met criteria for a psychiatric diagnosis in addition to alcohol dependence. The most common comorbid diagnosis was depression (42% of all patients), followed by mania (20%) and ASPD (20%). Comorbid drug abuse was present in 12% of patients, with panic attacks, phobic disorder, and obsessive-compulsive disorder each diagnosed in approximately 10% of patients. A comorbid diagnosis of schizophrenia was present in 4% of patients. For those individuals with comorbid disorders, the onset of alcohol abuse and dependence occurred significantly earlier (average age of 26 years) than for those with alcohol dependence only (average age of 33 years). The onset of comorbid disorders, with the exception of depression and obsessive-compulsive disorder, occurred before the onset of alcoholism.

Hesselbrock and colleagues[21] also used a structured diagnostic interview to evaluate a group of 321 individuals with an alcohol use disorder (including 90 women) recruited from three different inpatient settings. These investigators found that 75% of men and 80% of women received one or more lifetime diagnoses in addition to alcohol abuse and dependence. For the entire group, drug abuse was the most prevalent lifetime diagnosis (45%), followed by ASPD (41%), major depression (38%), phobia (27%), obsessive-compulsive disorder (12%), panic disorder (10%), mania (4%), and schizophrenia (2%). Sex differences were also evident, with the most common comorbid diagnosis being ASPD among men (49%) and depression among women (52%). With respect to disorders other than ASPD, the onset of most comorbid disorders in women preceded the onset of alcohol abuse; among men, most comorbid disorders followed the onset of alcohol abuse.

Ross and coworkers[23] evaluated the prevalence of comorbid psychiatric disorders in a sample of 501 patients (241 women) seeking treatment at an addiction research and treatment facility. Among patients with a current alcohol use disorder (n = 370), 25% had comorbid drug abuse and dependence. Patients who received both alcohol and drug abuse and dependence diagnoses had a higher prevalence of other lifetime psychiatric diagnoses (95%) than those with only an alcohol diagnosis (78%). The most common disorder among patients with combined alcohol and drug abuse and dependence was ASPD (79%), followed by psychosexual dysfunctions (48%), major depression (36%), phobias (36%), dysthymia (23%), obsessive-compulsive disorder (18%), panic disorder (17%), pathological gambling (14%), schizophrenia (11%), and mania (3%). A similar distribution was evident among patients with no comorbid drug diagnosis, although in each case the prevalence was lower. With respect to the order of onset, alcohol abuse and dependence most commonly occurred after the onset of ASPD, schizophrenia, phobias, and panic disorder. Onset of the other comorbid disorders relative to alcohol abuse was more variable.

In summary, both community and clinical studies underscore the importance of ASPD and drug abuse and dependence as comorbid diagnoses in individuals with an alcohol use disorder. The ORs obtained for these disorders in community studies indicate that these associations are elevated not only as a function of greater treatment-seeking behavior in affected individuals but also because of commonalities in the etiology and development of alcohol abuse and dependence. Similar conclusions apply to both schizophrenia and bipolar disorder. In contrast, although anxiety disorders and depression are highly prevalent in clinical samples of alcohol-dependent individuals, their association with alcohol dependence appears largely to be due to chance, because these disorders are also highly prevalent in the general population.

Given a high rate of psychiatric comorbidity, it is axiomatic that a careful psychiatric assessment be conducted in patients being seen for alcohol treatment and that alcohol use and associated problems be evaluated in patients being seen primarily for other psychiatric conditions. Because the presence of comorbid disorders may have important implications for the development of alcoholism and its prognosis, the assessment of comorbid psychiatric illness is an essential element in the clinical evaluation. When comorbid diagnoses are present, an effort should be made to ascertain the order of onset of each disorder, because treatment and prognosis may follow from such information.[28]

Etiology and Pathophysiology

Alcoholism is a complex, multifaceted disorder that has long been recognized to run in families. There is substantial evidence from twin studies and adoption studies that a major genetic component is operative in the development of alcoholism. Nonetheless, the disorder is etiologically complex, with a variety of genetic and other vulnerability factors.[29] It has been estimated that there is a sevenfold risk of alcoholism in first-degree relatives of alcohol-dependent individuals, with male relatives of alcohol-dependent men having the greatest risk for the disorder.[30] However, that the majority of alcohol-dependent individuals do not have a first-degree relative who is alcohol dependent underscores that the risk for alcohol dependence is also determined by environmental factors, which may interact in complex ways with genetics.

Molecular Genetics

Although there is widespread agreement that a genetic factor is influential in the transmission of alcohol dependence, exactly how risk of the disorder is transmitted remains unknown. Developments in genetic research have made it possible to begin systematically to examine the molecular basis of alcohol dependence, which should provide a clearer understanding of the pathophysiology of the disorder. The search for neurochemical differences among subtypes of alcoholic individuals and between alcoholic and nonalcoholic samples has begun to generate hypotheses that can be tested by use of the rapidly developing technology of molecular genetics.

Investigations into the molecular genetics of alcoholism have largely focused on candidate genes that are not directly relevant to alcohol's neuropharmacological effects, including variant forms of the alcohol-metabolizing enzymes alcohol dehydrogenase and aldehyde dehydrogenase.[31] More recently, attention has focused on the DNA sequence that codes for the synthesis of the D_2 dopamine receptor protein. A number of studies have provided support for an increased risk of alcoholism, particularly severe alcoholism, as a function of the frequency of the minor allele of the D_2 dopamine receptor gene.[32–35] However, a substantial number of studies have failed to demonstrate such an association, and in a meta-analysis of that literature, Gelernter and associates[36] concluded that the putative association is due to sampling error and ethnic variation in allele frequencies rather than to a physiologically important association.

Other investigators have begun to examine the association between alcoholism and genes coding for proteins involved in serotoninergic neurotransmission. On the basis of evidence linking early-onset alcoholism (discussed later) with serotoninergic abnormalities, this effort would appear to be most promising in early-onset alcoholism. Nielson and colleagues[37] found an association in impulsive Finnish alcoholic individuals between cerebrospinal fluid levels of 5-hydroxyindoleacetic acid, the major metabolite of serotonin, and genotype for tryptophan hydroxylase, the enzyme that catalyzes the first step in serotonin synthesis from tryptophan. There was no association between these measures in nonimpulsive Finnish alcoholic individuals or in control subjects. Although these findings require replication, they suggest that impulsive behaviors, which have been linked to low cerebrospinal fluid levels of 5-hydroxyindoleacetic acid,[38] are genetically influenced. Subsequent investigations are likely to focus on other serotoninergic candidate genes as well as those involved in other neurotransmitter (e.g., opioidergic, glutaminergic, GABAergic) systems.

Subtypes of Alcoholism

Another approach to understanding the etiology of alcoholism is the effort to identify distinct subtypes of alcoholic individuals.[39, 40] Alcoholism has been characterized as a set of disorders called the "alcoholisms,"[41] a term that reflects its clinical and etiological heterogeneity. A variety of typological approaches have been employed in an effort to

Table 42–3 Cloninger's Alcoholism Typology

	Type 1	Type 2
Onset of problem drinking	Late onset	Early onset
Tolerance	Rapid development of behavioral tolerance	Not specified
Mood issues	Prominent guilt and anxiety about drinking	Absence of guilt and anxiety about drinking
Personality traits	High reward dependence High harm avoidance Low novelty seeking	Low reward dependence Low harm avoidance High novelty seeking

Adapted from Cloninger CR, Bohman, M, Sigvardsson S: Inheritance of alcohol abuse: Cross-fostering analysis of adopted men. Arch Gen Psychiatry 1981; 38:861–868. Copyright 1981, American Medical Association.

order the diversity of phenomena associated with alcoholism.[39, 40, 42] These include unidimensional approaches based on drinking history, drinking pattern, severity of alcohol dependence, family history of alcoholism, gender, personality style, comorbid psychiatric illness, cognitive impairment, and sociopathy.[39, 40, 42]

Efforts have sought to identify subtypes of alcoholism that differ both clinically and etiologically. The best known of these typologies of alcoholism is the "type 1–type 2" distinction, developed by Cloninger and coworkers[43] (Table 42–3) from studies of adopted sons of Swedish alcoholic people. Type 1 alcoholic individuals are characterized by the late onset of problem drinking, rapid development of behavioral tolerance to alcohol, prominent guilt and anxiety related to drinking, and infrequent fighting and arrests when drinking. Cloninger also termed this subtype milieu limited, which emphasizes the etiological role of environmental factors.

In contrast, type 2 alcoholic individuals are characterized by early onset of an inability to abstain from alcohol, frequent fighting and arrests when drinking, and the absence of guilt and anxiety concerning drinking. Cloninger postulated that transmission of alcoholism in type 2 alcoholic people was from fathers to sons, hence the term male-limited alcoholism. Differences in the two subtypes are thought to result from differences in three basic personality (i.e., temperament) traits, each of which has a unique neurochemical and genetic substrate.[44] Type 1 alcoholic individuals are characterized by high reward dependence, high harm avoidance, and low novelty seeking. In contrast, type 2 alcoholic individuals are characterized by high novelty seeking, low harm avoidance, and low reward dependence.

Cloninger[44] also hypothesized that specific neurotransmitter systems underlie personality structure. Specifically, dopamine is hypothesized to modulate novelty seeking, which is characterized by frequent exploratory behavior and intensely pleasurable responses to novel stimuli. Serotonin is hypothesized to modulate harm avoidance, which is a tendency to respond intensely to aversive stimuli and their conditioned signals. Finally, norepinephrine is hypothesized to modulate reward dependence, or the resistance to extinction of previously rewarded behavior.

Although some subsequent studies[45, 46] have failed to provide empirical support for this tridimensional personality scheme, Cloninger's typology has generated substantial research. To the degree that these or other personality dimensions are replicable and can be shown to underlie alcoholic subtypes, they should contribute substantially to an improved understanding of the etiology and development of alcoholism and to better treatment.

Babor and colleagues[47] used statistical clustering techniques to derive a dichotomous typology similar to that proposed earlier by Cloninger. The analysis identified two homogeneous subtypes that may have important implications for the etiology of alcoholism as well as for treatment outcome. Cloninger's type 1 and type A alcoholic individuals share a later onset of alcohol-related problems and the absence of antisocial characteristics. Cloninger's type 2 and type B alcoholic individuals share an early onset of alcohol-related problems and the presence of antisocial characteristics, particularly during intoxication.

Important features of the typology of Babor and colleagues include that it was derived from a clinical sample of alcoholic men and women by use of an empirical clustering technique and it has been successful in predicting outcome after alcoholism treatment, both in the original sample from which the typology was derived[47] and in an independent sample.[48] Litt and coworkers[48] found an effect of matching type A and type B alcoholic patients to different psychotherapies, suggesting that empirically derived, multivariate typological classifications may provide a useful basis for selecting treatment.

Buydens-Branchey and colleagues[49, 50] distinguished between early-onset and late-onset alcoholism in a sample of patients consecutively admitted to an inpatient rehabilitation program. Among the patients studied by Buydens-Branchey and colleagues,[50] those with early-onset alcoholism were found to have been incarcerated more frequently for violent crimes, to have made more suicide attempts, and to have been depressed more often than patients with later onset of their alcoholism. Furthermore, among the early-onset group, there was an inverse relationship between a measure of central serotoninergic activity and measures of depression and aggressivity.[50]

Diagnosis

Phenomenology and Variations in Presentation

Diagnostic criteria for alcohol use disorders in DSM-IV[3] are similar to those employed in DSM-III-R,[15] which in turn were based on the alcohol dependence syndrome of Edwards and Gross.[51] The alcohol dependence syndrome is a conception of alcoholism that includes biological elements (e.g., tolerance, withdrawal), cognitive elements (e.g., craving), and behavioral elements (e.g., impaired control).

DSM-IV Criteria 303.90

Alcohol Dependence

A maladaptive pattern of drinking as manifested by three or more of the following during a 12-month period:

(1) tolerance, that is, either:

(a) a need for markedly more alcohol to achieve intoxication

(b) markedly diminished effect despite continued consumption of the same amount of alcohol

(2) withdrawal, that is, either:

(a) two or more signs or symptoms (autonomic hyperactivity, tremor, insomnia, nausea or vomiting, transient illusions or hallucinations, psychomotor agitation, anxiety, grand mal seizures) within several hours of stopping or reducing heavy, prolonged drinking

(b) consuming alcohol or a related substance (e.g., benzodiazepines) to relieve or avoid withdrawal symptoms

(3) alcohol is often consumed in larger amounts or over a longer period than was intended

(4) there is a persistent desire to cut down or control drinking

(5) a great deal of time is spent in drinking or recovering from drinking

(6) important social, occupational, or recreational activities are given up or reduced because of drinking

(7) drinking is continued despite knowledge of having a persistent or recurrent physical or psychological problem that is likely to have been caused or exacerbated by alcohol

The DSM-IV diagnosis of alcohol dependence is given when three or more of the seven criteria are present. Because the presence of physiological dependence is associated with greater potential for acute medical problems (particularly acute alcohol withdrawal), the first criteria to be considered are tolerance and withdrawal. Other criteria reflect two other major dimensions of the alcohol dependence syndrome: 1) impaired control (i.e., alcohol is consumed in larger amounts or for a longer time than was intended; there is a persistent desire or unsuccessful efforts to cut down or control drinking; the individual continues to drink despite knowledge of a persistent or recurrent physical or psychological problem) and 2) the salience of alcohol (i.e., a great deal of time is spent drinking or recovering from its effects; important social, occupational, or recreational activities are given up or reduced because of drinking).

Once a diagnosis of alcohol dependence is given, a specification is made concerning the presence of physiological dependence. In addition, course specifiers are available. These include early remission, which is used if no criteria (full remission) or fewer than three symptoms (partial remission) of alcohol dependence are present for at least 1 month but less than 12 months. Sustained remission is used if no symptoms (full remission) or fewer than three symptoms (partial remission) of alcohol dependence are present for at least 12 months. Finally, if the individual is in a setting in which she or he has no access to alcohol, the course specifier "in a controlled environment" is used.

DSM-IV Criteria 305.00

Alcohol Abuse

A maladaptive pattern of drinking as manifested by one or more of the following during a 12-month period:

(1) recurrent drinking resulting in a failure to fulfill major role obligations at work, school, or home

(2) recurrent drinking in situations in which it is physically hazardous

(3) recurrent alcohol-related legal problems

(4) continued drinking despite having persistent or recurrent social or interpersonal problems caused or exacerbated by drinking

Note: The individual must never have met criteria for alcohol dependence.

Alcohol abuse is considered to be present only if the individual has never met criteria for alcohol dependence and he or she demonstrates a pattern of drinking that leads to clinically significant impairment or distress, as evidenced by one of the four criteria. In contrast to the criteria for alcohol dependence, which are more restrictive than those in DSM-III-R, the DSM-IV criteria for alcohol abuse are broader than was true in DSM-III-R. As with alcohol dependence, course specifiers are used to modify the diagnosis of alcohol abuse.

Assessment

Special Issues in the Psychiatric Examination and History

Although denial of alcohol-related problems is legendary among alcoholic individuals, there is substantial evidence that a valid alcohol history can be obtained, given adequate assessment procedures and the right conditions.[52, 53] A complete alcohol history should include specific questions concerning average alcohol consumption; maximal consumption per drinking occasion; frequency of heavy drinking occasions; and drinking-related social problems (e.g., objections raised by family members, friends, or people at work), legal problems (including arrests or near-arrests for driving while intoxicated), psychiatric symptoms (e.g., precipitation or exacerbation of mood or anxiety symptoms), and medical problems (e.g., alcoholic gastritis or pancreatitis).

The Alcohol Use Disorders Identification Test (AUDIT),[54] a 10-item screening instrument, may be used to organize the alcohol use history. AUDIT (Table 42–4) covers the domains of alcohol consumption, symptoms of alcohol dependence, and alcohol-related consequences. It has been shown to be sensitive and specific in discriminating alcoholic from nonalcoholic individuals and is superior to the widely used Michigan Alcoholism Screening Test[55] in identifying hazardous drinkers, that is, those heavy drinkers who have not yet experienced serious harm from their drinking.[56] A score of 8 or more on the AUDIT provides a sensitive test for the identification of hazardous drinkers.[54] For those patients in whom the AUDIT shows evidence of hazardous drinking, further inquiry is warranted, which should include assessment of the DSM-IV criteria for alcohol abuse or alcohol dependence.[3] In addition, because both prescribed and illicit drug use is common among alcoholic individuals, the interviewer should make careful inquiry about these substances as well.

It is crucial that questions concerning alcohol consumption and alcohol-related symptoms and problems be asked nonjudgmentally to enhance the likelihood of accurate reporting. Schottenfeld[57] offers a number of specific strategies and approaches to history taking in the patient with substance abuse. These include reassuring the patient that information provided will be kept confidential; beginning the interview with questions that are least likely to make the patient defensive (e.g., a review of systems or psychiatric symptoms, without relating these to alcohol use); and beginning questions with *how,* rather than with *why,* to reduce the appearance of being judgmental.

Relevant Physical Examination and Laboratory Findings

Medical illness is a common consequence of heavy drinking[1, 18] and may be present in the absence of physical dependence. Although alcoholism may show no physical or laboratory abnormalities early in its course, as it progresses, it is widely manifested throughout most organ systems. A thorough physical examination is indicated if there is evidence of medical problems in the history. The physical

Table 42–4 Alcohol Use Disorders Identification Test

1.	How often do you have a drink containing alcohol?				
	(0) Never	(1) Monthly or less	(2) Two to four times a month	(3) Two or three times a week	(4) Four or more times a week
2.*	How many drinks containing alcohol do you have on a typical day when you are drinking? [Code number of standard drinks]				
	(0) 1 or 2	(1) 3 or 4	(2) 5 or 6	(3) 7 or 8	(4) 10 or more
3.	How often do you have six or more drinks on one occasion?				
	(0) Never	(1) Less than monthly	(2) Monthly	(3) Weekly	(4) Daily or almost daily
4.	How often during the last year have you found that you were not able to stop drinking once you had started?				
	(0) Never	(1) Less than monthly	(2) Monthly	(3) Weekly	(4) Daily or almost daily
5.	How often during the last year have you failed to do what was normally expected from you because of drinking?				
	(0) Never	(1) Less than monthly	(2) Monthly	(3) Weekly	(4) Daily or almost daily
6.	How often during the last year have you needed a first drink in the morning to get yourself going after a heavy drinking session?				
	(0) Never	(1) Less than monthly	(2) Monthly	(3) Weekly	(4) Daily or almost daily
7.	How often during the last year have you had a feeling of guilt or remorse after drinking?				
	(0) Never	(1) Less than monthly	(2) Monthly	(3) Weekly	(4) Daily or almost daily
8.	How often during the last year have you been unable to remember what happened the night before because you had been drinking				
	(0) Never	(1) Less than monthly	(2) Monthly	(3) Weekly	(4) Daily or almost daily
9.	Have you or someone else been injured as a result of your drinking?				
	(0) No		(2) Yes, but not in the last year		(4) Yes, during the last year
10.	Has a relative or friend or a physician or other health care worker been concerned about your drinking or suggested you cut down?				
	(0) No		(2) Yes, but not in the last year		(4) Yes, during the last year

Record sum of individual item scores here ______________________.

*In determining the response categories, it has been assumed that one "drink" contains 10 g of alcohol.

examination provides essential information about the presence and extent of end-organ damage and should be focused on the systems most vulnerable to alcohol-related disease: the cardiovascular system, the gastrointestinal system, and the central and peripheral nervous systems.

A variety of laboratory tests, particularly those related to hepatic function (e.g., serum transaminase activity, bilirubin level, prothrombin time, and partial thromboplastin time), can be helpful in assessing the need for medical referral. Other laboratory tests (e.g., γ-glutamyltransferase activity, mean corpuscular volume of erythrocytes) can be used as objective indicators of heavy drinking[58] and, together with other physical and laboratory findings, can provide tangible evidence of the need for treatment.[59]

Elevation in γ-glutamyltransferase has been found to occur in about three fourths of alcoholics before there was clinical evidence of liver disease and is often considered to be the earliest sign of heavy alcohol consumption that is widely available clinically.[58] As with γ-glutamyltransferase, elevations of aspartate transaminase and alanine transaminase are common in other liver diseases. However, elevations in the transaminase levels are less sensitive indicators of heavy drinking; aspartate transaminase is elevated in 32% to 77% of alcoholic individuals, whereas elevations in alanine transaminase have been observed in 50% of alcoholic individuals.[58]

An elevation of mean corpuscular volume of erythrocytes, which has also been associated with folate deficiency, is more prominent in alcoholic individuals who are smokers. It often returns to normal within 2 to 4 months of abstinence.[60] Abnormalities of these indicators can be used to impress on the patient the need to reduce or discontinue drinking, although their utility is limited by their limited sensitivity to heavy drinking. Laboratory tests have also been used to monitor progress after alcoholism treatment.[61]

Carbohydrate-deficient transferrin values may be more sensitive than routine laboratory tests for the identification of heavy alcohol consumption. In one study, the carbohydrate-deficient transferrin value was found to have a sensitivity of 91% and a specificity of 100% in distinguishing alcoholic individuals from light drinkers or abstainers.[62] In that study, the values of carbohydrate-deficient transferrin correlated significantly ($r = .64$) with the amount of alcohol consumed during the preceding month. A review of subsequent studies involving approximately 2500 individuals[63] showed the test to be somewhat less sensitive (82%), although specific (97%).

In a clinical setting, where laboratory results are generally not immediately available, the alcohol breath test, which measures the amount of alcohol in expired air (providing an estimate of venous ethanol concentration), is invaluable. Although its accuracy is dependent on the patient's cooperation (which in an intoxicated patient is often a problem), the alcohol breath test can be a reliable and inexpensive method for assessing recent alcohol consumption. Venous blood levels should be obtained if dangerously high levels of intoxication are suspected, if a patient is comatose, or for medical-legal purposes. A blood alcohol level greater than 150 mg/dL in a patient showing no signs of intoxication (e.g., dysarthria, motor incoordination, gait ataxia, nystagmus, impaired attention) can be interpreted to reflect physiological tolerance (DSM-IV).[3, 58] In nontolerant individuals, a blood alcohol level in excess of 400 mg/dL can result in death, and 300 mg/dL indicates a need for emergency care.

Table 42–5 Health Problems Commonly Associated with Alcoholism

Malnutrition, muscle wasting, neuritis, vitamin deficiencies
Infectious diseases (e.g., tuberculosis)
Hepatitis, pancreatitis, gastritis
Trauma secondary to fights, accidents
Cardiovascular disease (e.g., myocardial infarction)

The psychiatrist should also be alert to other acute alcohol-related signs, including alcohol withdrawal or delirium, intoxication or withdrawal from other drugs, and the acute presentation of psychiatric symptoms. In addition, several other systemic or nonspecific health problems associated with alcoholism are listed in Table 42–5.[64]

Other laboratory evaluations that are indicated in alcoholic patients are a urine toxicology screen (to identify drug use that the patient may not recognize is a problem or which he or she denies), including opiates, cocaine, cannabis, and benzodiazepines; routine urinalysis; blood chemistry assays; hepatitis profile; complete blood count; and serological test for syphilis. For the female patient, serum testing for pregnancy should also be done.

Differences in Presentations Related to Sex, Development, and Culture

Differences in the conceptualization of alcoholism and in the willingness of individuals to endorse symptoms in response to questioning are important sources of variability in estimating the prevalence of alcoholism. Nevertheless, there appear to be substantive differences in alcoholism among different sex, age, and racial and cultural groups. Unfortunately, the high prevalence of alcoholism among young adult and middle-aged men often leads to inadequate consideration of the possibility that women and elderly individuals may drink excessively.

Women. Although women are more likely to abstain from alcohol or, if they do drink, are more likely to drink at lower levels than men, women have consistently been shown to be more sensitive to the toxic effects of alcohol.[39] In a study comparing inpatient alcoholic men and women, Parrella and Filstead[65] found that women reported having been significantly older than men when a variety of alcohol-related milestones occurred, including regular drunkenness, first awareness of the need to drink to relieve withdrawal symptoms, first attempt to stop drinking, and first realization that alcohol use was a problem. Despite drinking for fewer years at lower levels, women have levels of cognitive impairment that are comparable to men's, and alcoholic women are more susceptible than men to endocrine and neuroanatomical abnormalities.[39] The concept of "telescoping" has been used to describe the course of symptom progression observed among women who, despite beginning heavy drinking later than men, begin to experience alcohol-related problems and seek treatment sooner than men.[66]

Because alcohol is distributed in the aqueous phase, greater body fat composition among women reduces the volume of distribution. This, combined with smaller average body mass, translates into higher blood alcohol levels for women in response to a specified level of alcohol consumption.[67] In addition, less first-pass metabolism due to less gastric oxidation of ethanol among women may also contribute to the higher blood levels obtained by women after an equivalent dose of ethanol.[68] Compared with men, women with alcohol problems are also more likely to drink alone and are at greater risk for comorbid drug abuse and dependence.[69] Perhaps as a consequence of these differences, alcoholic women who seek treatment do so earlier in the course of the disorder than do men.[39]

Relevant to a discussion of drinking-related problems in women are the effects of prenatal alcohol exposure. Although a variety of adverse outcomes have been related to heavy drinking in pregnant women, the minimal amount of alcohol and the pattern of consumption necessary to produce such effects are not known. Heavy drinking in pregnant women may produce malnutrition in both the mother and the fetus as well as spontaneous abortion, preterm delivery, and intrauterine growth retardation.[70] Alcohol-related birth defects are estimated to occur in as many as 1 in 100 live births.[71] The most severe manifestation of alcohol-related birth defects, fetal alcohol syndrome, a constellation of morphological and developmental defects resulting from high-dose prenatal alcohol exposure, is estimated to occur in between 1 in 1000 and 1 in 300 live births.[71] Although diagnostic criteria for fetal alcohol syndrome are not universally agreed on, there is some agreement that the presence of prenatal or postnatal growth retardation, central nervous system involvement, and characteristic facial dysmorphology are necessary for a diagnosis of fetal alcohol syndrome.[72]

Because alcohol-related birth defects can be avoided, the evaluation of pregnant patients should routinely include questions about alcohol and other substance use. Routine screening with an instrument such as the AUDIT[54] (see Table 42–4), supplemented by questions concerning drug use, may also be useful with pregnant women, although it has not been evaluated for use in this group. Those pregnant women who are identified as heavy drinkers or drug users should be designated high risk and provided with specialized, comprehensive perinatal care, including rehabilitation and appropriate attention to related psychosocial disabilities.[71]

Adolescents. A number of features distinguish adolescents with alcohol abuse and dependence from alcoholic adults.[73] As might be expected, adolescents have comparatively short histories of heavy drinking. A corollary to this is the comparative rarity of physiological dependence on alcohol and alcohol-related medical complications among adolescents. Nonetheless, abuse of alcohol and drugs contributes in important ways to morbidity and mortality in adolescents, the leading causes of which are motor vehicle accidents, homicide, and suicide.[73]

Furthermore, adolescents are highly vulnerable to peer pressure to abuse alcohol and drugs, so that the values and behavior of the adolescent's peer group are important elements in the evaluation of alcohol use and abuse in the adolescent. The evaluation of adolescents with an alcohol use disorder must also take into account other prominent developmental issues that characterize adolescence, including the conflict inherent in asserting one's independence from the family.

A number of general diagnostic instruments have been developed specifically for use with adolescents and children. Similarly, a limited number of instruments have been developed for the assessment of substance use symptoms and disorders in adolescents. A detailed review of these instruments is available elsewhere.[73] As is generally true in dealing with adolescents, given their economic and emotional dependence, a thorough family evaluation, whenever possible, is important for understanding the adolescent's substance use and related problems.

Elderly Persons. Although heavy drinking is less prevalent in the elderly, it is nonetheless an important source of morbidity in this group. Elderly alcoholic inpatients suffer from more chronic medical problems and poorer psychosocial functioning than do the nonalcoholic elderly.[74] The increased use of prescription medications in the elderly also increases the potential for adverse pharmacokinetic interactions with alcohol. In addition, decreased cognitive functioning associated with heavy alcohol use can increase medication errors and noncompliance in this group.[75]

Because the manifestations of alcoholism in the elderly are often more subtle and nonspecific than those observed in younger individuals, alcohol abuse and dependence are often overlooked in the elderly.[75, 76] Graham[76] has suggested that self-reported alcohol consumption may be particularly unreliable in the elderly. She suggested that other sources of information, such as family and neighbors, be used to identify heavy drinkers. Ofman[75] suggested that the following areas be systematically evaluated in the elderly when heavy drinking has been identified: untreated medical illness, prescription drug abuse, psychiatric comorbidity, cognitive impairment, functional capacity, and need for social services.

Similar to the approach used with younger adults, alcoholism in the elderly has been classified by age at onset. It has been estimated that about two thirds of alcoholic elders began heavy drinking before 60 years of age, whereas the remaining third began heavy drinking after the age of 60 years.[77] Late-onset alcoholism appears to be more common among elderly women and people of higher socioeconomic status and is less frequently associated with a family history of alcoholism.[75] As might be expected, older alcoholic individuals with early-onset alcoholism also have more alcohol-related medical and psychosocial problems and are more likely to undergo alcoholism treatment.[75]

Ethnic and Racial Groups. It is difficult to generalize about ethnic and racial differences in drinking practices and alcohol-related problems. In addition to substantial differences in drinking patterns and consequences among different ethnic and racial groups, there is also considerable heterogeneity among these groups.[69]

As described earlier, black individuals are generally more likely to abstain from alcohol than are white and Hispanic, and black persons who do drink generally begin doing so at a later age. Although black individuals of all socioeconomic levels are susceptible to alcoholism, it has been most closely associated with those living in poorer urban areas. Black persons appear to enter alcoholism treatment at the same rate as do nonblack persons. Furthermore, the gender composition of black persons seeking treatment and their average educational level are comparable to those of nonblack persons.[69]

There is substantial heterogeneity among Hispanic individuals, the majority of whom in the United States are Mexican-Americans, followed in numbers by Puerto Ricans, Cubans, and Central or South Americans. As is true for many cultural elements, drinking practices vary considerably among these subgroups. In general, however, Hispanic men are somewhat more likely to abstain than are white men, whereas Hispanic women are substantially more likely to abstain than are white women. Traditionally, Hispanic men drink large quantities of alcohol episodically, often in association with social events. As they become exposed to the practice of regular drinking in the United States, total consumption increases, with a concomitant increase in risk for a variety of alcohol-related problems.[69]

Although numerically Native Americans are a small ethnic-racial group, they too are culturally diverse. Drinking practices vary widely among tribal groups, but men consistently drink more frequently and more heavily than women. A high prevalence of alcohol-related problems have been reported among a number of Native American groups. Among individuals seeking treatment for alcohol problems, Native Americans were younger and more likely to be female, unemployed, and never married.[69]

Course and Natural History

Schuckit and colleagues[78] examined the relative order of appearance of symptoms of alcohol dependence in a large series of male veterans. They found the following progression of symptoms and signs: evidence of heavy drinking during the patients' late 20s; interference with functioning in multiple areas of the patients' lives during their early 30s; loss of control, followed by an intensification of social and work-related problems and onset of medical consequences in the middle to late 30s; and severe long-term consequences by the late 30s and early 40s. This demonstration of a relatively predictable order of progression is consistent with previous studies. However, as mentioned before, women appear to experience many of these milestones at a later age than men do.[65, 66]

The study by Schuckit and coworkers[78] showed no effect of age at onset, family history of alcoholism, or comorbid psychiatric diagnoses on the order of symptom appearance. However, other features defining the course of alcoholism, particularly the response to treatment, have been shown to vary as a function of patient-related variables, including age at onset, severity of alcohol dependence, and comorbid psychiatric disorders. There is consistent evidence that early age at onset is a predictor of greater severity of alcoholism and a poorer response to treatment.[40, 47] Greater severity of alcohol dependence has also been shown to predict poorer treatment outcome.[79]

Although considered to be important in the development of alcoholism, comorbid psychiatric disorders also have prognostic significance.[80] Rounsaville and colleagues[81] found that psychiatric diagnosis at intake predicted a variety of 1-year posttreatment outcomes. Among men, the presence of a comorbid lifetime diagnosis of ASPD, major depression, or drug abuse and dependence was associated with poorer drinking outcomes. Among women, the presence of major depression predicted a better outcome on drinking-related measures, whereas those patients with ASPD or drug abuse and dependence had a poorer prognosis. Three-year posttreatment outcomes in this group of alcoholic patients also showed comorbid ASPD, major depression, and drug abuse and dependence to be associated with poorer outcomes. However, at that time, major depression was not associated with a "protective effect" for alcoholic women.[82]

Other investigators have found no difference in drinking outcomes in comparing primary alcoholic patients and alcoholic patients with a comorbid mood disorder.[28, 83, 84] However, alcoholic individuals with comorbid depression have been found to have greater psychiatric severity at follow-up than primary alcoholic patients.[83, 84] Variable findings have also been obtained concerning the prognostic significance of ASPD and drug abuse among alcoholic individuals. Both Powell and coworkers[84] and Schuckit[28] found that compared with primary alcoholic patients, alcoholic patients with either primary ASPD or a primary drug abuse diagnosis did not differ on alcoholic-related outcomes. However, in one study,[28] alcoholic individuals with these primary diagnoses reported more illicit drug use and poorer social functioning during the posttreatment period. Furthermore, Liskow and colleagues[85] found that alcoholic patients with a lifetime drug diagnosis in combination with ASPD had poorer alcohol-related outcomes.

A number of studies have shown that patients experience substantial improvement during the year after alcoholism treatment.[79] Vaillant,[86] however, found that treatment had minimal effects on long-term outcome. More long-term treatment outcome studies are needed to examine the impact of different kinds of alcoholism treatment on the course of the disorder. Additional studies are also needed to clarify both the prognostic significance of patient-related variables, including comorbid psychiatric disorders, and their interaction with different kinds of treatment.

Overall Goals of Treatment

Since the end of World War II, a wide variety of interventions have been developed to deal with alcohol-related problems.[6, 59] These interventions can be divided into three general categories: 1) secondary prevention; 2) specialized treatment programs; and 3) mutual help groups. Secondary prevention is intended to reduce alcohol-related harm and prevent alcohol dependence. It depends on screening and brief interventions. Specialized treatment is designed to treat the medical and psychiatric complications of drinking and to promote the social and psychological rehabilitation of the alcoholic person. Mutual help programs, of which Alcoholics Anonymous (AA) is a prime example, are concerned with the long-term rehabilitation of alcoholic people, many of whom require continuing care and support for many years.

When a determination has been made that an individual is drinking excessively, the nature and intensity of the intervention must be designed to address the specific treatment needs of that individual. Among heavy drinkers without evidence of alcohol-related harm, an intervention aimed at the reduction of drinking may suffice. In contrast, among alcoholic individuals, there are a variety of associated disabilities,[87] so that it is necessary to address both the exces-

Table 42–6 Goals of Alcoholism Treatment

Stabilize acute medical (including alcohol withdrawal) and psychiatric conditions, as needed.
Increase motivation for recovery.
Initiate treatment for chronic medical and psychiatric conditions, as needed.
Assist the patient in locating suitable housing (e.g., moving from a setting in which drinking is widespread), as needed.
Enlist social support for recovery (e.g., introduce to 12-step programs and, when possible, help the patient to repair damaged marital and other family relationships).
Enhance coping and relapse prevention skills (including social skills, identification and avoidance of high-risk situations).
Improve occupational functioning.
Promote maintenance of recovery through ongoing participation in structured treatment or self-help groups.

sive drinking *and* problems related to it. Consequently, alcoholism treatment is best conceived of as multimodal. Table 42–6 provides an overview of the goals of alcoholism treatment, many of which have been discussed by Schuckit.[88]

There are a number of potentially life-threatening conditions for which alcoholic individuals are at increased risk. The presence of any of the following requires immediate attention: acute alcohol withdrawal (with the potential for seizures and delirium tremens), serious medical or surgical disease (e.g., acute pancreatitis, bleeding esophageal varices), and serious psychiatric illness (e.g., psychosis, suicidal intent). In the presence of any of these emergent conditions, acute stabilization should be the first priority of treatment.

The presence of complicating medical or psychiatric conditions is an important determinant of whether rehabilitation is initiated in an inpatient or an outpatient setting. More detailed consideration of this important treatment issue is provided later. Other considerations are the alcoholic person's current living circumstances and social support network. In order for women with children to enter residential treatment, their family needs must be taken care of. Homeless people may be eager to enter residential treatment even when their medical or psychiatric condition does not warrant it.

In the alcoholic patient whose condition is stabilized or in the patient without these complicating features, the major focus should be on the establishment of a therapeutic alliance, which provides the context within which rehabilitation can occur. The presence of a trusting relationship facilitates the patient's acknowledgment of the problems associated with her or his excessive alcohol consumption and encourages open consideration of the approaches available to address the alcohol use disorder and associated disabilities. In addition to participation in structured rehabilitation, the patient should be made aware of the widespread availability of AA and the wide diversity of its membership.

Standard Approaches to Treatment

Secondary Prevention

Secondary prevention involves the early treatment of a disorder or condition to decrease the length of the illness or prevent the further development of symptoms. With respect to alcohol-related problems, secondary prevention refers to the provision of therapeutic interventions to persons who have already manifested some alcohol-related problems. These individuals may not meet criteria for an alcohol use diagnosis, or if they do, they are more likely to be diagnosed as having alcohol abuse rather than alcohol dependence.

Drinking problems are directly related to the quantity and the frequency of alcohol consumed, and they manifest themselves in terms of biological, social, and psychological consequences.[1, 2] Acute consequences tend to vary with the amount consumed per occasion; many of the medical consequences, such as liver cirrhosis, occur only with long-term alcohol use.[1] Although heavy drinking and frequent drinking are not necessarily indicative of alcoholism, they are important risk factors and can lead to health problems in the absence of alcohol dependence.

In an effort to evaluate a public health approach to the secondary prevention of alcohol-related problems, randomized studies have been conducted in more than 13 countries to evaluate the efficacy of screening technologies and low-cost intervention strategies. These studies are reviewed in detail elsewhere.[89, 90] The majority of studies show a significant difference between intervention and control conditions. However, the majority have also noted significant improvement in the control group. The trials with the largest samples[91, 92] found that approximately 40% of the patients improved in the intervention group, whereas 20% improved in the control group. Thus, an approximate doubling of spontaneous improvement may result from brief intervention. These findings suggest that brief interventions that promote reduced drinking among heavy-drinking individuals who are not severely alcohol dependent can be used in a variety of clinical settings and yield substantial clinical benefit.

Specialized Treatment

Specialized treatment refers to interventions directed at the limitation of disability or fatal complications, generally through optimal clinical management. Specialized treatment is directed primarily at the management of alcohol withdrawal, the social and psychological rehabilitation of the problem drinker, the prevention of relapse to alcohol dependence, and the management of alcohol-related medical conditions.

Specialized treatment for the management of alcohol-related problems began with the establishment of inebriate asylums in the United States and England during the late 19th century. The network of specialized residential facilities that grew up before World War I virtually ceased to exist as a result of national prohibition laws, the two world wars, and the global depression. It was only in the late 1940s that the modern approach to alcoholism treatment emerged. The treatment paradigm for the new alcoholism movement in North America was established on a professional level in the form of the Yale Plan Clinics and on the nonprofessional level in the form of AA.[93] The Yale clinics were specialized outpatient programs that experimented with a variety of medical, psychological, and social interventions considered appropriate for the complex task of rehabilitating alcohol-dependent persons. These methods included group therapy, aversive conditioning, individual psychotherapy, vocational counseling, and alcohol education as well as disulfiram therapy and other pharmacotherapies when these became available.

In addition to the expansion of residential rehabilitation programs, the management of acute alcohol intoxication and the alcohol withdrawal syndrome (commonly referred to as detoxification) was improved by the development of specialized detoxification facilities in North America and Europe.[94] These facilities expanded rapidly after widespread adoption of laws decriminalizing public intoxication.

The specialized treatment system that emerged after World War II is varied, complex, and still in the process of development. Many of its programmatic components (e.g., detoxification facilities, inpatient residential programs, outpatient clinics), and the therapeutic approaches used in these components (e.g., the 12 Steps of AA, relapse prevention), have only begun to receive systematic research attention.

Alcohol Withdrawal

The management of alcohol withdrawal represents an important initial intervention for a substantial number of alcohol-dependent patients. The objectives in treating alcohol withdrawal are the relief of discomfort, prevention or treatment of complications, and preparation for rehabilitation. Successful management of the alcohol withdrawal syndrome provides an important basis for subsequent efforts at rehabilitation.

Careful screening for concurrent medical problems is an important element in detoxification.[95] Administration of thiamine (50 to 100 mg orally or intramuscularly) and multivitamins is a low-cost, low-risk intervention for the prophylaxis and treatment of alcohol-related neurological disturbances. Good supportive care and treatment of concurrent illness, including fluid and electrolyte repletion, are essential.[95]

Social detoxification, which involves the nonpharmacological treatment of alcohol withdrawal, has been shown to be effective.[96–98] It consists of frequent reassurance, reality orientation, monitoring of vital signs, personal attention, and general nursing care.[95] Social detoxification is most appropriate for patients in mild to moderate withdrawal. The medical problems commonly associated with alcoholism[18] may substantially complicate therapy, so care must be taken to refer those patients whose condition requires medical management.

Increasingly, detoxification is being done on an ambulatory basis, which is much less costly than inpatient detoxification.[99] Inpatient detoxification is indicated for serious medical or surgical illness as well as for those individuals with a past history of adverse withdrawal reactions or with current evidence of more serious withdrawal (e.g., delirium tremens).[100]

A variety of medications have been used for the treatment of alcohol withdrawal. However, owing to their favorable side effect profile, the benzodiazepines have largely supplanted all other medications.[95] Although any benzodiazepine will suppress alcohol withdrawal symptoms, diazepam and chlordiazepoxide are often used because they are metabolized to long-acting compounds, which in effect are self-tapering. Because metabolism of these drugs is hepatic, impaired liver function may complicate their use. Oxazepam and lorazepam are not oxidized to long-acting metabolites and thus carry less risk of accumulation.

Although carbamazepine appears useful as a primary treatment of withdrawal,[101, 102] the liver dysfunction that is common in alcoholic patients may affect its metabolism, which makes careful blood level monitoring necessary. Antipsychotics are not indicated for the treatment of withdrawal except in those instances when hallucinations or severe agitation are present,[95] in which case they should be added to a benzodiazepine. In addition to their potential to produce extrapyramidal side effects, antipsychotics lower seizure threshold, which can be a particular problem during alcohol withdrawal.

Alcohol Rehabilitation

Alcohol rehabilitation, since the 19th century, has typically been provided in a residential setting lasting for periods of a month or more. Residential settings include hospital-based rehabilitation programs, freestanding units, and psychiatric units. With the growth of managed care in the 1990s, there has been a dramatic reduction in the average length of stay for residential treatment and a shift in emphasis to less costly treatment settings.

Studies comparing the relative effectiveness of inpatient and outpatient rehabilitation have generally failed to show significant differences related to the setting in which treatment is provided.[103, 104] Conclusions regarding equal effectiveness of inpatient and outpatient treatment must, however, be limited to patients who are appropriate for each type of program.[105] Many studies comparing outpatient with inpatient treatment have not controlled for the possibility that patients who choose outpatient settings are less severely alcohol dependent, less physically ill, or less psychiatrically impaired.

Inpatient treatment may be indicated when motivation is weak to continue treatment; when patients are psychotic, depressed, or suicidal; and when there are medical complications. Other factors that may also influence the choice of treatment setting include patients' social stability and the number and severity of their symptoms as well as the ability of programs to respond to individual needs.[105, 106]

Another obstacle to ambulatory treatment is the high rate of attrition usually encountered among more severely impaired alcoholic individuals treated in an outpatient setting.[107] A study by Walsh and colleagues[108] showed that workers who were randomly assigned to a 3-week inpatient alcoholism rehabilitation program had significantly better alcohol-related outcomes than did workers who were assigned to mandatory AA attendance only. Workers assigned to a third group were allowed to choose their treatment. This group had outcomes that were intermediate between the other two groups. Differences in outcome were most evident among individuals who were abusing both alcohol and cocaine.

A variety of treatments are delivered within the context of rehabilitation services. In many programs, a combination of therapeutic interventions is provided to all patients on the basis of the assumption that multiple treatments have a greater chance of meeting at least some of each patient's needs. Therapeutic approaches most often employed in both residential and outpatient programs include behavioral therapy, group therapy, family treatment, and pharmacotherapy. Controlled studies have failed to demonstrate the effectiveness of psychodynamic psychotherapy, although such treatment has been shown to be helpful in the treatment of drug abuse.[109, 110]

Behavioral Therapy

Behavioral elements most frequently employed in treatment programs are relapse prevention, social skills and assertiveness training, contingency management, deep muscle relaxation, self-control training, and cognitive restructuring.[111] Aversion therapy, based on pavlovian conditioning theory, has been virtually abandoned in the United States. Although it has been shown that the sight, smell, and taste of alcohol will acquire aversive properties if alcohol is repeatedly paired with noxious stimuli (e.g., chemically induced nausea and vomiting), the procedure is expensive and has not been shown to be superior to less heroic methods.

Behavioral therapists stress the importance of teaching new, adaptive skills to patients who engage in dysfunctional behaviors. These skills include altering conditions that precipitate and reinforce drinking as well as developing alternative ways of coping with persons, events, and feelings that serve to maintain drinking.[111] A number of studies have demonstrated the benefits of teaching social and other coping skills,[112–114] although not all studies have confirmed these findings.[115] Chaney and colleagues[116] tested a model of treatment characterized as "relapse prevention" because of its focus on identifying and coping with situations that represent high risk for heavy drinking. Patients who received skills training attended aftercare more regularly, and they had less severe (although no less frequent) relapses than did patients in control groups. These and other trials of cognitive-behavioral treatments[109] have provided the empirical basis for elaboration of a generalized relapse prevention strategy.[117]

There is also a considerable literature describing group therapy techniques in the treatment of alcoholism.[118] A study by Oei and Jackson[113] compared group therapy with individual therapy. Each of these approaches was used to provide social skills training to some patients and "traditional supportive therapy" to others. Improvement was found only among patients given social skills training. In addition, patients trained in a group setting improved more than those treated individually.

It appears that coping skills training may be most useful for subgroups of alcoholic individuals. In a prospective study, Kadden and colleagues[119] found that both psychiatric severity and sociopathy were significant predictors of treatment matching effects. Patients high on these measures relapsed at a lower rate when treated in group coping skills therapy; patients low on these measures fared better when treated with interactional group therapy.

Alcoholics Anonymous

With an estimated 87,000 groups in 150 countries, AA is by far the most widely used source of help for drinking problems in the United States and throughout the world. In addition, a number of self-help organizations have modeled themselves after AA, basing recovery from drug abuse, overeating, and other disorders on the 12 Steps of AA (Table 42–7). Unfortunately, psychiatrists often refer patients to self-help groups such as AA without adequate consideration of the patient's needs and without adequate monitoring of the patient's response, which amounts to inadequate treatment.[120] Not all people are willing to endorse the emphasis on spirituality and a disease model of alcoholism that requires lifelong abstinence as the only means to recovery, both of which are essential elements of AA. Greater familiarity with AA may help psychiatrists to identify those patients who might reasonably be expected to benefit from this approach. Psychiatrists' increased familiarity with AA, combined with their openly discussing the 12-step approach with the patient before referral and monitoring the patient's response to the meetings attended, should also increase the benefit that the patient derives from a referral to AA.

Although AA is regarded as the most useful resource for treating alcoholic people, the research literature supporting its efficacy is limited.[121] Attendance at AA tends to be correlated with long-term abstinence,[86, 122, 123] but this may be interpreted to reflect motivation for recovery; the type of motivated alcoholic individual who persists with AA might do just as well with other forms of supportive therapy. In fact, the few random assignment studies that have been conducted[108, 124–126] do not indicate that AA (or similar programs) is more effective than other types of treatment.

Personality variables do not appear to differentiate AA affiliates and nonaffiliates,[127] although there is some evidence that AA is less successful among persons with major psychiatric disorders and those of low socioeconomic status.[127, 128] The development of 12-step programs for dually diagnosed individuals may serve to enhance their

Table 42–7 The 12 Steps of Alcoholics Anonymous

1. We admitted we were powerless over alcohol—that our lives had become unmanageable.
2. Came to believe that a Power greater than ourselves could restore us to sanity.
3. Made a decision to turn our will and our lives over to the care of God *as we understood Him.*
4. Made a searching and fearless moral inventory of ourselves.
5. Admitted to God, to ourselves, and to another human being the exact nature of our wrongs.
6. Were entirely ready to have God remove all these defects of character.
7. Humbly asked Him to remove our shortcomings.
8. Made a list of all persons we had harmed, and became willing to make amends to them all.
9. Made direct amends to such people wherever possible, except when to do so would injure them or others.
10. Continued to take personal inventory and when we were wrong, promptly admitted it.
11. Sought through prayer and meditation to improve our conscious contact with God *as we understood Him,* praying only for knowledge of His will for us and the power to carry that out.
12. Having had a spiritual awakening as the result of these steps, we tried to carry this message to alcoholics, and to practice these principles in all our affairs.

appeal and efficacy among this population. Because of the widespread availability of AA and the key role it plays in providing help to alcoholic people who seek recovery, more systematic research directed at better understanding the process whereby AA exerts its beneficial effects is needed, as are methods to enhance participation in 12-step programs.

Family Treatment

The deleterious effects of alcoholism on marriages and families have been a source of interest to both psychiatrists and researchers.[129–131] Alcoholism creates major stress on the family system by threatening health, interpersonal relations, and economic functioning of family members. Although research has shown a strong association between healthy family functioning and positive outcome after alcoholism treatment,[132, 133] little systematic evaluation has been undertaken to assess the efficacy of family approaches either to reduce alcohol problems or to improve family functioning.[134]

The majority of studies have involved marital rather than family treatment. A trial of behavioral marital therapy was conducted by O'Farrell and colleagues.[129] Alcoholic individuals and their spouses were treated in aftercare for 10 weeks. At follow-up, behavioral marital therapy was found to have enhanced marital well-being more than did interactional couples therapy; a control group not receiving marital therapy showed no significant change. There was no differential improvement in drinking behavior among the three groups. Subsequently, McCrady and colleagues[135] showed behavioral marital therapy to be superior to control treatments in both the reduction of drinking and maintenance of sobriety.

In addition to specific treatment for alcoholic couples or families, self-help groups for family members of alcoholics have grown substantially.[136] Al-Anon, although not formally affiliated with AA, shares the structure and many of the tenets of the 12 Steps of AA. Al-Anon and AA meetings are often held jointly. Alateen groups, sponsored by Al-Anon for children of alcoholics, are proliferating as well.

Pharmacotherapy in Alcoholism Rehabilitation

Despite the lack of convincing evidence concerning their safety and efficacy, more than 90% of physicians in private practice reported the use of medications to treat alcoholism.[137] In general, with the exception of the central role that benzodiazepines play in the treatment of alcohol withdrawal, pharmacotherapy has not yet had a demonstrably large effect on alcoholism treatment. However, developments suggest that the use of medications may soon contribute substantially to the treatment of comorbid disorders and the prevention of relapse in alcoholic patients. A medication that reduces the risk of relapse would permit the patient to participate more effectively in psychosocial treatment, in much the same way that antidepressants are used with other therapies in the treatment of depression. A number of detailed reviews of this topic have been published.[138–142]

Aversive Drugs. Aversive drugs cause an unpleasant reaction when combined with alcohol. Disulfiram (Antabuse) is the most extensively researched aversive medication and the only one approved for use in the United States. It is given in a single daily dose of 125 to 500 mg that binds irreversibly to aldehyde dehydrogenase, permanently inactivating this enzyme. When alcohol is consumed, it is metabolized to acetaldehyde, which accumulates because of inhibition of the enzyme that metabolizes it. Elevated levels of acetaldehyde are responsible for the aversive effects associated with the disulfiram-ethanol reaction.[143]

Adverse effects from disulfiram are common. In addition to its effects on aldehyde dehydrogenase, disulfiram inhibits a variety of other enzymes. Disulfiram also reduces clearance rates of a number of medications. Common side effects of disulfiram include drowsiness, lethargy, peripheral neuropathy, hepatotoxic effects, and hypertension. The exacerbation of psychotic symptoms in schizophrenic patients and occasionally their appearance in nonschizophrenic individuals, as well as the development of depression, may be linked to inhibition of the enzyme dopamine β-hydroxylase.

Although disulfiram has been used in the treatment of alcoholism for many years, the few placebo-controlled studies that have been conducted have not shown the drug to have substantial efficacy. In a large, multicenter study conducted by the Veterans Administration, more than 600 alcoholic men were assigned randomly to groups receiving either 1 mg of disulfiram per day or a therapeutic dosage of 250 mg/d or to a control group told that they were not receiving disulfiram.[144] Results revealed a direct relationship between compliance with any of the three treatment regimens and complete abstinence. Among patients who resumed drinking, those taking a therapeutic dosage of disulfiram had significantly fewer drinking days than did patients in the other two groups. However, there was no significant difference among the three groups with respect to a variety of outcome measures, including length of time to first drink, unemployment, social stability, or number of men totally abstinent.

Many practitioners believe that by enhancing compliance with disulfiram, it is possible to increase the individual's commitment to abstinence from alcohol. However, depot formulations of the medication have not been shown to be effective, nor is such an approach approved by the U.S. Food and Drug Administration. However, a variety of approaches to enhancing compliance with disulfiram therapy have been employed.[145] These include the use of incentives, contracting with the patient and a significant other to commit themselves to the patient's taking disulfiram, providing additional information to the patient, behavioral training, and social support. Enhancement of compliance with disulfiram therapy generally requires substantial efforts[146]; consequently, use of the drug outside of a well-organized treatment program is probably unwarranted.

Given the paucity of data supporting the efficacy of disulfiram for the prevention of relapse, we do not generally endorse its use. However, if a patient requests the medication and appropriate evaluation provides no contraindication to its use, it may be beneficial. Under these circumstances, the benefit is likely to result from the positive expectations held by the patient. Whenever disulfiram is prescribed, patients should be warned carefully about its hazards, including the need to avoid over-the-counter preparations with alcohol and drugs that interact adversely with disulfiram as well as the potential for a disulfiram-ethanol reaction to result from alcohol used in food preparation.

Treatment of Comorbid Psychiatric Illness. The treatment of psychiatric comorbidity in alcoholic patients represents another approach to the treatment of alcoholism, because comorbid disorders may predispose to the development or maintenance of heavy drinking.[80] After detoxification, many alcoholic patients complain of persistent anxiety, insomnia, and general distress. This period of protracted withdrawal may last for weeks or months and may be difficult to differentiate from the emergence of diagnosable psychiatric disorders. Regardless of their cause, negative emotional states, including frustration, anger, anxiety, depression, and boredom, have been shown to contribute to relapse in a substantial proportion of alcoholic individuals.[117]

A variety of medications have been employed in an effort to improve outcomes in alcoholic patients by treating comorbid psychiatric symptoms and disorders. The use of these medications in alcoholic patients requires careful consideration of the added potential for adverse effects attributable to comorbid medical disorders and the pharmacokinetic effects of short-term and long-term alcohol consumption. With these caveats in mind, indications for the use of these medications in alcoholic patients are similar to those for nonalcoholic populations and can be arrived at only through careful psychiatric diagnosis.

In general, placebo-controlled trials of tricyclic antidepressants in depressed alcoholic patients have not provided evidence of efficacy. Research in this area, however, is characterized by substantial methodological problems.[147] Although depressive symptoms are common early in alcohol withdrawal, they frequently remit spontaneously with time.[148] For depression that persists beyond the period of acute withdrawal, a trial of an antidepressant is probably warranted.

Most studies of tricyclic antidepressants for treatment of depression in alcoholic patients have used a therapeutically inadequate dosage of the medication, with no effort made to compensate for the fact that both cigarette smoking and heavy drinking can stimulate liver enzymes that metabolize drugs. However, placebo-controlled trials of desipramine[149] and imipramine,[150] which have attempted to take these considerations into account, suggest that tricyclic antidepressants in depressed alcoholic individuals reduce depressive symptoms. Results from an open trial[151] and a placebo-controlled trial[152] of fluoxetine in small samples of depressed alcoholic patients suggest that selective serotoninergic antidepressants may also be useful in treating major depression in alcoholic patients. Preliminary evidence from these studies suggests that reduced depressive symptoms in alcoholic patients may translate into reduced drinking.[149–151]

Evaluation of the usefulness of lithium carbonate in the treatment of alcoholism has focused on its effects on both mood symptoms and drinking behavior. In two early, controlled trials,[153, 154] treatment with lithium appeared to result in a decrease in total incapacity due to drinking. Fawcett and colleagues[155] found that compliance, with either lithium or placebo, was positively associated with abstinence. In a Veterans Administration multicenter study,[156] lithium carbonate was found to be no more effective than placebo for a variety of outcomes, with both depressed and nondepressed alcoholic patients. Given the large sample size of this study, there is substantial doubt that lithium is of much utility in alcoholism treatment. Although lithium may be useful in treating alcoholic patients with bipolar disorder, no controlled trials of the medication for this indication have been reported.

A number of studies have shown chlordiazepoxide to be effective in the maintenance of alcoholic patients in long-term outpatient treatment.[157–159] However, the potential for additive central nervous system depression produced by the concurrent use of alcohol and benzodiazepines is well recognized. Furthermore, the use of benzodiazepines may itself result in tolerance and dependence and may increase depressive symptoms.[160] Although this concern may be exaggerated[161] and not all benzodiazepines may be equal in their capacity to produce dependence in alcoholic patients,[162] in general, the use of benzodiazepines in alcoholic patients is best limited to the period of detoxification.

Buspirone[163] is a nonbenzodiazepine anxiolytic that may have several advantages: it is less sedating than diazepam or clorazepate, it does not interact with alcohol to impair psychomotor skills, and its potential for abuse is small. A double-blind, placebo-controlled trial of buspirone in alcoholic patients[164] showed significantly greater retention in treatment and greater decreases in alcohol craving, anxiety, and depression scores in buspirone-treated patients. Both groups showed significant declines in drinking.

Tollefson and colleagues[165] also found that buspirone-treated subjects were less likely to discontinue treatment prematurely and had greater reductions in anxiety than did placebo-treated subjects. Although a subjective, global measure of improvement in drinking was observed for the active drug group, measures of alcohol consumption were not reported in this study. Kranzler and coworkers[166] also found that in anxious alcoholic subjects, buspirone was superior to placebo in terms of retention in treatment. Independent of whether a specific anxiety disorder was present, buspirone treatment reduced anxiety among subjects with the highest anxiety symptom scores. The active drug also delayed relapse to heavy drinking.

In contrast to these three reports, a placebo-controlled study by Malcolm and colleagues[167] of alcoholic veterans in aftercare showed no differences between buspirone- and placebo-treated patients on measures of anxiety or alcohol consumption. In comparison with the other three studies, the patients in this study were more severely alcohol dependent, and the medication was not administered in the context of a psychosocial treatment program. In summary, when combined with appropriate psychosocial treatment, buspirone appears useful in the treatment of alcoholic patients with persistent anxiety.

Antipsychotics are currently indicated only in alcoholics with a coexistent psychotic disorder or for the treatment of alcoholic hallucinosis.[95] Several placebo-controlled studies have found no advantage to the use of phenothiazines for treatment of anxiety, tension, and depression after detoxification.[141] Because of their capacity to lower seizure threshold, antipsychotics should be used with caution in alcoholic patients.

Drugs That May Directly Reduce Alcohol Consumption. A number of specific neurotransmitter systems have been implicated in the control of alcohol consumption, including endogenous opioids; catecholamines, especially dopamine; and serotonin. Although these systems appear to function interactively in their effects on drinking behavior, efforts to use medications to treat excessive drinking have increasingly focused on agents that have selective effects on specific neurotransmitter systems.

On the basis of an extensive animal literature suggesting that opioidergic neurotransmission plays a major role in the control of drinking behavior, Volpicelli and coworkers[168] examined the effects of the opioid antagonist naltrexone as an adjunct to an intensive day treatment program for veterans. Naltrexone was well tolerated and resulted in significantly less craving for alcohol, fewer drinking days, and fewer drinks per drinking day than placebo. O'Malley and colleagues[169] also found that naltrexone was well tolerated by alcohol-dependent outpatients when combined with weekly psychotherapy. These investigators found the drug to be superior to placebo with respect to the number of drinking days and the intensity of drinking.

Swift and colleagues[170] examined the effect of naltrexone on several subjective and objective measures of alcohol intoxication in nonalcoholic individuals. Compared with placebo, naltrexone augmented some of the sedative and discriminant effects of alcohol and reduced some of the positive effects of alcohol, without affecting ethanol's pharmacokinetics. On the basis of two clinical trials with naltrexone,[168, 169] the U.S. Food and Drug Administration approved the medication for use in the prevention of relapse in alcoholic patients, making it the only medication other than disulfiram approved for that indication. Another opioid antagonist, nalmefene, has also been evaluated in alcohol-dependent subjects.[171] This medication was found to be well tolerated and superior to placebo in reducing relapse. Further evaluation of the efficacy of nalmefene, including comparison of that medication with naltrexone, is warranted.

Naranjo and colleagues[172] and Gorelick[173] have reviewed the extensive experimental literature that links serotonin neurotransmission to alcohol consumption. In rodents, serotonin precursors and selective serotonin reuptake inhibitors (SSRIs) consistently decrease ethanol consumption.[172] Animal studies have also linked serotonin to aggression and readiness to ingest alcohol; human studies have linked low levels of serotonin with violent and suicidal behavior and with alcoholism.[173, 174]

In humans, the effects of SSRIs on alcohol consumption appear to be more limited and more variable than is the case with the opiate antagonists. Both short-term[175] and long-term[176] administration of zimeldine, an SSRI that was removed from clinical trials because of toxicity, has shown that it attenuates ethanol consumption. Other SSRIs that have been tested in humans to reduce alcohol consumption include citalopram,[177, 178] viqualine,[179] fluoxetine, [152, 180–182] and fluvoxamine.[183] The results from these studies have been mixed. Some studies have shown modest effects.[175–181] Other studies have shown these medications to be poorly tolerated[183] or inefficacious.[152] Gerra and associates[182] found that fluoxetine was superior to placebo in reducing the number of drinks consumed only in alcoholic individuals with a positive parental history of alcoholism. This work[182] suggests that a patient-treatment matching strategy may serve to maximize the therapeutic effects of SSRIs in alcoholic patients.

In summary, the most promising agents that directly reduce alcohol consumption are the opiate antagonists (i.e., naltrexone and nalmefene) and the SSRIs (e.g., citalopram, fluoxetine). Further research is required with naltrexone to determine the optimal dosage, duration of treatment, and concomitant psychosocial treatment strategies. Further research with nalmefene is needed to establish its efficacy in the prevention of relapse in alcoholic patients. The efficacy of the SSRIs for this indication also remains to be established. In general, trials that compare or combine medications that show initial promise for relapse prevention and that aim to match medications with a patient's characteristics are needed to determine the best strategies for pharmacotherapy in relapse prevention.

Special Features Influencing Treatment

Psychiatric Comorbidity

There is considerable evidence that links the outcome of alcoholism treatment to comorbid psychiatric illness. General measures of psychiatric illness[184] as well as the specific diagnoses of drug abuse and dependence, ASPD, and major depressive disorder have been shown to predict poorer outcomes in alcoholic patients.[81, 82] The extent to which treatment of concomitant psychiatric illness enhances alcoholism treatment outcome is unclear, although it has been advocated.[185] Early work in matching patients' characteristics to specific treatments is promising. Kadden and colleagues[119] found that alcoholic patients with greater severity of sociopathy and psychiatric illness had better outcomes when treated with cognitive-behavioral psychotherapy, compared with interactional psychotherapy. A comparable strategy has been advocated for pharmacotherapy, in which specific medications are chosen not only for patients with comorbid psychiatric disorders but also on the basis of features such as early onset of alcohol abuse and aggressivity.[142]

Demographical Features

Adolescent

Despite a paucity of controlled, age-specific treatment outcome studies of adolescents with alcohol use disorders, the need for prevention and specialized treatment for this group is clear.[73, 186] Although the extant literature indicates that some treatment is better than no treatment in substance-abusing adolescents, relapse rates are high and there is not consistent support for the superiority of any single treatment modality.[187] However, several factors have been associated with better treatment outcome: later onset of problem drinking; pretreatment attendance at school; voluntary entrance into treatment; active parental input; and availability of ancillary adolescent-specific services, including those pertaining to school, recreation, vocational needs, and contraception.[73, 186]

Brown and coworkers[187] studied precipitants of relapse in 75 substance-abusing adolescents and their parents. They found that the adolescents who relapsed after inpatient treatment did so most frequently (60%) in response to social pressures to drink or use drugs, with 33% of individuals indicating that their relapse was an attempt to cope with negative affect and 27% identifying interpersonal conflict as a precursor to relapse. Accordingly, relapse prevention techniques, including social skills training (e.g., assertiveness techniques, communication skills, strategies for controlling anger) and techniques for managing high-risk situations, may be particularly useful for adolescents.[73]

Because early and middle adolescents have not yet fully developed formal operational thinking, they may have difficulty internalizing abstract values. Treatment efforts will therefore be effective to the extent that they are less conceptualized and more goal oriented. Furthermore, the psychiatrist should consider the potential impact on treatment of other cognitive problems: learning disabilities, attention-deficit/hyperactivity disorder (either the complete syndrome or attenuated forms), and other psychiatric disorders that may previously have gone undiagnosed. Treatment of the adolescent with an alcohol use disorder also requires an appreciation of the importance of modeling, imitation, and peer pressure, which are intrinsic to identity development. The use of age-appropriate support groups (e.g., Alateen) may be particularly useful in this regard.

Geriatric

Although there are no clear data available regarding which alcoholic elders require treatment,[75] alcoholism rehabilitation in the elderly requires that consideration be given to a number of distinguishing medical and psychosocial features in this group. In addition to the high prevalence of medical problems, pharmacokinetic and pharmacodynamic variables can affect treatment outcome in elderly alcoholic patients. For example, Liskow and colleagues[188] found that the alcoholic elderly, despite having drunk less than younger patients during the month before admission, had more severe alcohol withdrawal symptoms and required a higher dosage of chlordiazepoxide. These investigators speculated that the observed differences might delay the entry of alcoholic elderly into rehabilitation.

As is true for other special populations, an important question in the treatment of elderly alcoholic patients is whether specialized treatment services improve outcome. Kofoed and coworkers[189] used a historical control group composed of elderly alcoholic patients treated in a mixed-age composition group to compare outcomes for patients treated in specialized elderly peer groups. Despite the small sample sizes, they found that patients treated in peer groups remained in treatment significantly longer and were significantly more likely to complete treatment than those treated in mixed-age groups. These investigators concluded that elder-specific treatment has differential therapeutic value.

Shifts in the demographical features of AA participants are also relevant to the elderly. Blazer[190] has observed that the current cohort of alcoholic elderly has less experience with self-help groups than do younger cohorts. Given the trend in AA toward a younger membership who are more likely to have comorbid drug abuse and dependence, the elderly can be expected to experience increased difficulty affiliating with AA. This, along with evidence suggesting an advantage for age-specific treatment in the elderly, may indicate that special efforts should be made to help the elderly alcoholic patient locate AA meetings that include a substantial proportion of older participants. This may be especially beneficial to the older alcoholic individual, who is often lonely secondary to isolation and for whom the prospect of helping others may help combat feelings of uselessness.[190]

A wide variety of treatment approaches[75] have been shown to be beneficial for the alcoholic elderly, ranging along a continuum of intensity that includes multidisciplinary inpatient treatment programs; outpatient individual therapy, group therapy, or day treatment; and outpatient recovery support groups. Despite evidence that early-onset alcoholism among the elderly shows greater severity than late-onset alcoholism, outcomes after treatment are not substantially different for these groups.[75] Treatment programs with experience in treating the alcoholic elderly are likely to be better able to coordinate rehabilitation with medical and social service providers, including case management and home visits.[75] These programs may also be best able to provide specialized peer treatment for alcoholic elders.

Gender (Including Pregnancy)

As described before, epidemiological and clinical studies have shown that alcohol use and abuse and dependence, despite being more prevalent among men, are also common among women. Nonetheless, the majority of studies related to alcohol use and its effects, including the diagnosis and treatment of alcohol use disorders, have involved men.[39, 69] Greater awareness of the impact of alcohol use on women's health and the importance of gender as a potential determinant of treatment outcome has developed. The requirement by the National Institutes of Health and the U.S. Food and Drug Administration that women and minorities be actively recruited to participate in health-related research should help to increase knowledge about alcoholism treatment outcome in these groups.

At present, however, the data available are inadequate to guide the treatment of alcoholism in women. Blume[191] pointed out that sensitivity to women's special needs and problems provides a useful general approach. She suggested that because of increased risk in women, evaluation should include special attention to the identification of physical or sexual abuse, to physical and psychiatric comorbidity, and to the presence of alcoholism and drug abuse in spouses and alcohol-related birth defects in children. To enable women with children to participate in treatment, the availability of childcare services is critical, although it must generally be arranged independent of treatment. Blume[191] also listed the following special treatment needs of women: information about the effects of substance use on the fetus, parenting skills, couples and family therapy, sober female role models, assertiveness training, and an awareness of sexism and its consequences. She also pointed out that special care must be taken to avoid creating iatrogenic drug dependence in women (e.g., through the use of benzodiazepines to treat comorbid anxiety or depressive symptoms). Whereas these are useful guidelines for treating alcoholic women, empirical research is needed to evaluate these and other issues systematically.

Ethnic and Cultural Issues and Treatment

In 1991, approximately two thirds of patients in alcoholism treatment were white, 17% were black, and 12% were Hispanic.[17] Although socioeconomic and cultural issues should be addressed in alcoholism treatment,[192] guidelines for such treatment are based largely on common sense rather than systematic outcome evaluation. Obviously, when language barriers exist, special efforts must be made to ensure adequate communication. Lex[69] suggested that treatment providers be aware of their patients' traditional patterns of drinking and how these may be influenced by acculturation, differences among groups in their perception of alcohol-related problems, the impact of sociocultural differences between patients and providers, and how prevailing social (e.g., family) relationships can affect treatment outcome.

Refractory Patients and Nonresponse to Initial Treatment

Despite competent treatment, some alcoholic patients relapse repeatedly. In fact, for many emergency department personnel, largely as a consequence of their seeing principally those patients who relapse repeatedly, the recidivist alcoholic patient has come to personify the disorder. For psychiatrists involved in the delivery of alcoholism rehabilitation services, these individuals' apparent unresponsiveness to treatment may contribute to frustration and a sense of futility. Although it is hoped that pharmacotherapy may come to play a greater role in the treatment of these individuals, it is uncertain whether this promise will be realized. Long-term residential treatment presently appears to be the only option for alcoholic patients who do not respond to more limited efforts at rehabilitation. Unfortunately, the availability of such care in many states is limited as a consequence of the effort to deinstitutionalize psychiatric patients.

Conclusion

As with other complex clinical entities, the assessment and treatment of alcoholism require recognition of the heterogeneity of drinking patterns and alcohol-related problems. The notion that it is fruitless to take a drinking history, because alcoholic individuals will not provide accurate information, is unjustified.[52] Instruments such as the AUDIT, although developed to identify heavy drinkers before they have alcohol dependence, are also useful in case finding. However, given the high prevalence of comorbid psychiatric disorders, a careful psychiatric history should also be taken in all alcoholic patients.

Comprehensive assessment provides the basis for an individualized plan of treatment. Depending on the severity of alcohol dependence, the nature of comorbid medical and psychiatric disorders, the presence of social supports, and the evidence of previous response to treatment, decisions can be made concerning the appropriate intensity and constituent elements of treatment.

Although methodologically sound research promises to provide a stronger scientific basis for the treatment of alcoholism, a number of conclusions appear warranted at this time:

1. Alcoholic individuals are heterogeneous with respect to demographical features (e.g., age, sex, and race-ethnicity), age at onset of heavy drinking, severity of alcohol dependence, and comorbid psychiatric illness.
2. The available evidence suggests that any treatment for alcoholism is better than no treatment. Although as many as two thirds of those treated demonstrate improvement, perhaps one third would have improved without treatment or with minimal intervention, suggesting that an approximate doubling in improvement results as a consequence of treatment.
3. In controlled studies, the intensity and duration of treatment have not been shown to produce pronounced differences in outcome. Similarly, medical inpatient treatment, although more costly, has generally not been found to be more effective than nonmedical residential or outpatient treatment. For patients with serious comorbid medical and psychiatric disorders, medical inpatient treatment may, nonetheless, be necessary. Some evidence indicates that continuing aftercare helps to maintain abstinence after short-term intensive rehabilitation in inpatient settings.
4. There is little evidence that any one treatment approach is superior. There is some support for certain kinds of behavioral therapy, but the effectiveness of AA and disulfiram seem to depend on the patient's characteristics and compliance. Several kinds of carefully specified and theoretically derived therapeutic approaches show promise as a basis for a new generation of ambulatory treatments. These include the relapse prevention strategies that teach the alcoholic person how to avoid high-risk relapse situations and new pharmacological agents (e.g., naltrexone) that appear to dampen the alcoholic patient's risk of relapse by reducing the reinforcement potential of alcohol. Continued improvements in treatment outcome will depend on successfully matching treatment settings and modalities to the specific needs of the individual patient.

Clinical Vignette 1

Mr. D is a 44-year-old, married service station owner who presents in the emergency department at 5 AM with a chief complaint of nausea, followed by vomiting of bright red blood. He is accompanied by his 19-year-old daughter, who succeeded in convincing her father to go to the hospital rather than to work. Mr. D had no history of hospitalizations. He denied recent medical or psychiatric problems, saying he had not been to a doctor's office for more than 15 years. Mr. D denied use of illicit or prescription drugs. Although he admitted drinking on a daily basis, he denied being alcoholic. On specific questioning, he revealed that he drank only beer, consuming in excess of 12 cans each day. During the preceding 2 years, he had been drinking only beer, but before that time, he drank vodka on a daily basis, often consuming in excess of a pint per day. He became increasingly agitated and tremulous as the interview progressed.

Family history provided by the patient's daughter revealed that both of the patient's parents were deceased. His father, who was alcoholic, had died from a myocardial infarction at age 42 years. His mother was noted to have had alcohol dependence after her husband's death; she died at age 55 years of stomach cancer. Mr. D had married at 20 years old and after 15 years of marriage was divorced owing to problems related to his drinking. There had been repeated marital conflicts for the 6 years before divorce, twice resulting in separations. The couple's only child lived with her mother but came to stay with her father when she learned that he was feeling ill.

Clinical Vignette 1 *continued*

In the emergency department, Mr. D was given nothing by mouth, and intravenous fluids were begun for hydration. Suction through a nasogastric tube produced 5 mL of dark, clotted blood. Emergency endoscopy showed inflamed, hemorrhagic gastric mucosa, with no active bleeding. There were no indications of esophageal varices, Mallory-Weiss tears, or other lesions. Before endoscopy, the patient received lorazepam 2 mg intravenously, which dramatically reduced his agitation. He was then admitted to the medical service. The next day, he agreed to be seen in consultation by a psychiatrist.

During the interview with the psychiatrist, Mr. D admitted that he had previously come to the emergency department with many of the same symptoms, although he had not previously vomited blood. Each time he had been treated with drugs that helped him calm down, and he had recovered. He acknowledged that he had been told his symptoms resulted from heavy drinking, but he denied drinking "any more than most people." Two years earlier, he had switched from vodka to beer and had limited his intake to six beers per day in an effort to avoid the gastrointestinal problems. Although he had felt some nervousness and malaise at that time, his abdominal pain and nausea gradually improved. Subsequently, his beer consumption gradually increased, and the gastrointestinal symptoms reappeared during the preceding 3 months.

The patient first consumed alcohol at the age of 14 years. He began regular drinking at age 18 years, drinking about a six-pack of beer two or three times per week after work or on weekends. At 26 years of age, he started his own business. The pressures of owning a business, combined with the freedom it permitted, led him to drink daily. As his consumption increased, he found that drinking beer at work was too conspicuous, so he began drinking vodka, which he could do surreptitiously. As his business gradually floundered, he became increasingly irritable both at work and at home. Mr. D began arguing regularly with his wife, who complained about his drinking. Eventually, his wife and daughter moved to a house in a neighboring town.

The patient denied ever having experienced a seizure but acknowledged multiple blackouts after particularly heavy drinking. In the preceding year, he had begun drinking beer early in the day to steady his hands. Toward the end of the interview, Mr. D stated that recently he had begun to think that what people had been telling him about his drinking was true. He exclaimed loudly, "I've had enough. What can I do about this? I'm willing to try anything now." On resolution of his gastric hemorrhage and alcohol withdrawal symptoms, Mr. D was referred to a partial hospitalization program for rehabilitation.

Final DSM-IV Diagnoses

Axis I: Alcohol dependence, with physiological dependence; alcohol withdrawal.

Axis II: None.

Axis III: Upper gastrointestinal bleeding (hemorrhagic gastritis); macrocytic anemia; alcoholic hepatitis.

Clinical Vignette 2

Ms. C, a 28-year-old, has been separated from her husband for 3 years. She is the mother of three children: a 2-year-old boy and 6- and 12-year-old girls. The patient has been unemployed for 6 months, her most recent job having been as a barmaid. She was referred for substance abuse treatment from court after arraignment on a charge of possession of narcotics. After 4 days in an inpatient rehabilitation program, it was noted that the patient had stopped going to group meetings and was spending most of her time alone in her room crying. She aroused particular concern in the treatment staff when she reported feeling that her life was no longer worth living. During the preceding year, the patient had twice attempted suicide by taking an overdose of pills that she bought illicitly. On both occasions, she was hospitalized briefly for observation.

When interviewed by the program psychiatrist, Ms. C complained that she missed her children too much to remain in treatment. Recently, with the help of her mother, she had been caring for her children, although the situation was being monitored by the state child welfare agency because of a charge of neglect filed by the children's paternal grandmother. Ms. C acknowledged that completion of the rehabilitation program would probably help her to retain custody of her children, but she reported that she often became sad and discouraged, especially during the evening. She described recurrent periods of depressed mood since the age of 14 years associated with initial and middle insomnia, low energy level, and poor self-esteem. She had been suffering from these symptoms for approximately 2 months before admission. She also complained of decreased appetite and concentration but denied recent weight loss, anhedonia, psychomotor agitation or retardation, or current suicidal ideation. When pressed concerning the onset of depressive symptoms, Ms. C indicated that they were generally worse during periods when she used alcohol and cocaine heavily.

A substance use history revealed that Ms. C had begun smoking cigarettes when she was 11 years old, becoming a regular smoker at 12 years old. At the time of admission, she was smoking about one pack of cigarettes daily. She also reported consuming alcohol and cannabis regularly for 13 years. She first drank alcohol at age 12 years, beginning regular drinking while in her first year in high school. Shortly thereafter, she was introduced to marijuana use, which she gradually increased to daily use of one or two joints, a practice that she continued until the time of admission. She began heavy drinking (up to 10 beers per day, three or four times per week) when she was 17 years old and a junior in high school. Since that time, her drinking gradually increased, such that during the month before admission, the patient reported drinking about a pint of spirits daily. She also reported a 5-year history of regular cocaine use, initially intranasally, but 2 years before admission, she had begun smoking the drug, and she reported smoking about $100 worth of cocaine two or three times per week during the month before admission. Although she had experimented with LSD, diazepam, and intranasal heroin, she denied regular or recent use of these drugs. She also denied intravenous drug use. One month earlier, she was found to be seronegative for human immunodeficiency virus. The patient had never before been treated for substance abuse.

The patient acknowledged having a number of alcohol- and drug-related problems, foremost among which were the legal and child custody issues. Although her husband is also a substance abuser, she felt that her substance use had contributed to their breakup, because they became verbally and at times physically abusive toward one another while intoxicated. After not drinking for a day, she often became tremulous and felt nauseated and weak. She denied any history of delirium tremens. While smoking cocaine, she had on occasion become alarmed by a painful tightness in her chest, accompanied by palpitations and by transient paranoid ideation.

Family history revealed that both of the patient's parents were alcoholic, her father having died of cirrhosis of the liver when Ms. C was 16 years old. The patient's mother was recovering, with nearly 10 years of sobriety. The patient's paternal grandfather, who had also been alcoholic, died before she was born. Ms. C is an only child. She reported that alcohol was readily available in her house when she was 12 years old and that sharing it with school friends enhanced her popularity. She did well in school until seventh grade, when she began to find school boring. Ms. C was first arrested for shoplifting when she was 14 years old. She also began to have behavior problems at school around that time and was suspended for stealing money. At the age of 16 years, Ms. C left school because of her first pregnancy. She was subsequently arrested three times, once each for shoplifting, disturbing the peace, and, immediately before admission, possession of cocaine.

Based on the history and symptoms at the time of evaluation, the psychiatrist discussed the case with the patient. Together they decided to postpone pharmacotherapy pending longitudinal evaluation of her depressive symptoms. Daily monitoring of symptoms was implemented by use of the Beck Depression Inventory.[193] In addition, cognitive-behavioral therapy for depression was initiated by the addictions counselor who had been working with Ms. C. During the subsequent week, the patient's depressive symptoms declined (the Beck Depression Inventory score decreased from 25 to 19), but she continued to have difficulty participating in the treatment program. Fluoxetine 20 mg every morning was initiated and was well tolerated during the subsequent week. After completing the 21-day inpatient program, the patient was discharged to outpatient aftercare, where medication management was continued.

Final DSM-IV Diagnoses

Axis I: Alcohol dependence, with physiological dependence; cocaine dependence; cannabis dependence; major depressive disorder.

Axis II: Antisocial personality disorder.

Axis III: None.

References

1. Babor TF, Kranzler HR, Lauerman RL: Social drinking as a health and psychosocial risk factor: Anstie's limit revisited. Recent Dev Alcohol 1987; 5:373–402.
2. Kranzler HR, Babor TF, Lauerman R: Problems associated with average alcohol consumption and frequency of intoxication in a medical population. Alcohol Clin Exp Res 1990; 14:119–126.
3. American Psychiatric Association: Diagnostic and Statistical Manual of Mental Disorders, 4th ed. Washington, DC: American Psychiatric Association, 1994.
4. Kreitman N: Alcohol consumption and the preventive paradox. Br J Addict 1986; 81:353–363.
5. Marshall M: Introduction. In Marshall M (ed): Beliefs, Behaviors, and Alcoholic Beverages: A Cross-Cultural Survey. Ann Arbor, MI: University of Michigan Press, 1979:1–11.
6. Makela K, Room R, Single E, et al (eds): Alcohol, Society, and the State, Volume I. Toronto: Addiction Research Foundation, 1981.
7. Sulkunen P: Drinking patterns and levels of consumption. An international overview. In Gibbins RJ, Israel Y, Kalant H, et al (eds): Research Advances in Alcohol and Drug Problems, Volume III. New York: John Wiley & Sons, 1976:223–281.
8. Armyr G, Elmer A, Herz U: Alcohol in the World of the 80's. Stockholm: Sober Forlags AB, 1982.
9. Helzer JE, Canino GJ: Comparative analysis of alcoholism in ten cultural regions. In Helzer JE, Canino GJ (eds): Alcoholism in North America, Europe, and Asia. New York: Oxford University Press, 1992:289–308.
10. Helzer JE, Canino GJ, Yeh EK, et al: Alcoholism—North America and Asia. Arch Gen Psychiatry 1990; 47:313–319.
11. Regier DA, Farmer ME, Rae DS, et al: Comorbidity of mental disorders with alcohol and other drug abuse: Results from the Epidemiologic Catchment Area (ECA) study. JAMA 1990; 264:2511–2518.
12. American Psychiatric Association: Diagnostic and Statistical Manual of Mental Disorders, 3rd ed. Washington, DC: American Psychiatric Association, 1980.
13. Myers JK, Weissman MM, Tischler GL, et al: Six-month prevalence of psychiatric disorders in three communities. Arch Gen Psychiatry 1984; 41:959–970.
14. Grant BF, Harford TC, Chou P, et al: Epidemiologic Bulletin No. 27: Prevalence of DSM-III-R alcohol abuse and dependence: United States, 1988. Alcohol Health Res World 1991; 15:91–96.
15. American Psychiatric Association: Diagnostic and Statistical Manual of Mental Disorders, 3rd ed. Washington, DC: American Psychiatric Association, 1987.
16. Stinson FS, DeBakey SF: Alcohol-related mortality in the United States, 1979–1988. Br J Addict 1992; 87:777–783.
17. Eighth Special Report to the U.S. Congress on Alcohol and Health. Washington, DC: U.S. Department of Health and Human Services, 1994. NIH publication 94-3699.
18. Eckardt MJ, Harford TC, Kaelber CT, et al: Health hazards associated with alcohol consumption. JAMA 1981; 246:648–666.
19. Hilton ME: The demographic distribution of drinking problems in 1984. In Clark WB, Hilton ME (eds): Alcohol in America: Drinking Practices and Problems. Albany, NY: State University of New York Press, 1991.
20. Kessler RC, McGonagle KA, Zhao S, et al: Lifetime and 12-month prevalence of DSM-III-R psychiatric disorders in the United States. Arch Gen Psychiatry 1994; 51:8–19.
21. Hesselbrock MN, Meyer RE, Keener JJ: Psychopathology in hospitalized alcoholics. Arch Gen Psychiatry 1985; 42:1050–1055.
22. Powell BJ, Penick EC, Othmer E, et al: Prevalence of additional psychiatric syndromes among male alcoholics. J Clin Psychiatry 1982; 43:404–407.
23. Ross HE, Glaser FB, Germanson T: The prevalence of psychiatric disorders in patients with alcohol and other drug problems. Arch Gen Psychiatry 1988; 45:1023–1031.
24. Helzer J, Pryzbeck T: The co-occurrence of alcoholism with other psychiatric disorders in the general population and its impact on treatment. J Stud Alcohol 1988; 49:210–224.
25. National Institute of Mental Health: Substance abuse comorbidity in schizophrenia. Schizophr Bull 1990; 16:29–123.
26. Grande TP, Wolf AW, Schubert DSP, et al: Associations among alcoholism, drug abuse, and antisocial personality disorder: A review of literature. Psychol Rep 1984; 55:455–474.
27. Kranzler HR, Liebowitz N: Depression and anxiety in substance abuse: Clinical implications. Med Clin North Am 1988; 72:867–885.
28. Schuckit MA: The clinical implications of primary diagnostic groups among alcoholics. Arch Gen Psychiatry 1985; 42:1043–1049.
29. Goldman D: Genetic transmission. Recent Dev Alcohol 1993; 11:231–248.
30. Merikangas KR: The genetic epidemiology of alcoholism. Psychol Med 1990; 20:11–22.
31. Goldman D: Molecular markers for linkage of genetic loci contributing to alcoholism. Recent Dev Alcohol 1988; 6:333–349.
32. Blum K, Noble EP, Sheridan PJ, et al: Allelic association of human dopamine D_2 receptor gene in alcoholism. JAMA 1990; 263:2055–2060.
33. Blum K, Noble EP, Sheridan PJ, et al: Association of the A1 allele of the D_2 dopamine receptor gene with severe alcoholism. Alcohol 1991; 8:409–416.
34. Comings DE, Comings BG, Muhleman D, et al: The dopamine D_2

receptor locus as a modifying gene in neuropsychiatric disorders. JAMA 1991; 266:1793–1800.
35. Parsian A, Todd R, Devor EJ, et al: Alcoholism and alleles of the human D_2 dopamine receptor locus. Arch Gen Psychiatry 1991; 48:655–663.
36. Gelernter J, Goldman D, Risch N: The A1 allele at the D2 dopamine receptor gene and alcoholism. JAMA 1993; 269:1673–1677.
37. Nielsen DA, Goldman D, Virkkunen M, et al: Suicidality and 5-hydroxyindoleacetic acid concentration associated with a tryptophan hydroxylase polymorphism. Arch Gen Psychiatry 1994; 51:34–38.
38. Asberg M, Schalling D, Traskman-Bendz L: Psychobiology of suicide, impulsivity, and related phenomena. In Meltzer HY (ed): Psychopharmacology: The Third Generation of Progress. New York: Raven Press, 1987:665–668.
39. Nixon SJ: Typologies in women. Recent Dev Alcohol 1993; 11:305–323.
40. Bohn MJ, Meyer RE: Typologies of addiction. In Galanter M, Kleber HD (eds): Textbook of Substance Abuse Treatment. Washington, DC: American Psychiatric Press, 1994:11–24.
41. Jacobson GR: The Alcoholisms: Detection, Diagnosis, and Assessment. New York: Human Sciences Press, 1976.
42. Babor TF, Lauerman RJ: Classification and forms of inebriety: Historical antecedents of alcoholic typologies. Recent Dev Alcohol 1986; 4:113–144.
43. Cloninger CR, Bohman M, Sigvardsson S: Inheritance of alcohol abuse: Cross-fostering analysis of adopted men. Arch Gen Psychiatry 1981; 38:861–868.
44. Cloninger CR: Neurogenetic adaptive mechanisms in alcoholism. Science 1987; 236:410–416.
45. Glenn SW, Nixon SJ: Applications of Cloninger's subtypes in a female alcoholic sample. Alcohol Clin Exp Res 1991; 15:851–857.
46. Schuckit MA, Irwin M, Mahler HM: Tridimensional personality questionnaire scores of sons of alcoholic and nonalcoholic fathers. Am J Psychiatry 1990; 147:481–487.
47. Babor TF, Hofmann M, Del Boca FK, et al: Types of alcoholics: I. Evidence for an empirically-derived typology based on indicators of vulnerability and severity. Arch Gen Psychiatry 1992; 8:599–608.
48. Litt MD, Babor TF, Del Boca FK, et al: Types of alcoholics: II. Application of an empirically-derived typology to treatment matching. Arch Gen Psychiatry 1992; 8:609–614.
49. Buydens-Branchey L, Branchey MH, Noumair D: Age of alcoholism onset. I. Relationship to psychopathology. Arch Gen Psychiatry 1989; 46:225–240.
50. Buydens-Branchey L, Branchey MH, Noumair D, et al: Age of alcoholism onset. II. Relationship of susceptibility to serotonin precursor availability. Arch Gen Psychiatry 1989; 46:231–236.
51. Edwards G, Gross MM: Alcohol dependence: Provisional description of a clinical syndrome. Br Med J 1976; 1:1058–1061.
52. Babor TF, Stephens RS, Marlatt GA: Verbal report methods in clinical research on alcoholism: Response bias and its minimization. J Stud Alcohol 1987; 48:410–424.
53. Hesselbrock M, Babor TF, Hesselbrock V, et al: "Never believe an alcoholic?" On the validity of self-report measures of alcohol dependence and related constructs. Int J Addict 1983; 18:593–609.
54. Saunders JB, Aasland OG, Babor TF, et al: Development of the Alcohol Use Disorders Identification Test (AUDIT): WHO collaborative project on early detection of persons with harmful alcohol consumption—II. Addiction 1993; 88:791–804.
55. Selzer ML: The Michigan Alcoholism Screening Test: The quest for a new diagnostic instrument. Am J Psychiatry 1971; 127:1653–1658.
56. Bohn MJ, Babor TF, Kranzler HR: The Alcohol Use Disorders Identification Test (AUDIT): Validation of a screening instrument for use in medical settings. J Stud Alcohol 1995; 56:423–432.
57. Schottenfeld RS: Assessment of the patient. In Galanter M, Kleber HD (eds): Textbook of Substance Abuse Treatment. Washington, DC: American Psychiatric Press, 1994:25–33.
58. Holt S, Skinner HA, Israel Y: Early identification of alcohol abuse. II. Clinical and laboratory indicators. Can Med Assoc J 1981; 124:1279–1295.
59. Babor TF, Ritson EB, Hodgson RJ: Alcohol-related problems in the primary health care setting: A review of early intervention strategies. Br J Addict 1986; 81:23–46.
60. Colman W, Herbert V: Hematologic complications of alcoholism: Overview. Semin Hematol 1980; 17:164–176.
61. Irwin M, Baird S, Smith TL, et al: Use of laboratory tests to monitor heavy drinking by alcoholic men discharged from a treatment program. Am J Psychiatry 1988; 145:595–599.
62. Stibler H, Borg S, Jousta M: Microanion exchange chromatography of carbohydrate deficient transferrin in serum in relation to alcohol consumption (Swedish patient 8400587-5). Alcohol Clin Exp Res 1986; 10:535–544.
63. Stibler H: Carbohydrate deficient transferrin in serum: A new marker of potentially harmful alcohol consumption reviewed. Clin Chem 1991; 37:2029–2037.
64. Arif A, Westermeyer J (eds): Manual of Drug and Alcohol Abuse: Guidelines for Teaching in Medical and Health Institutions. New York: Plenum Publishing, 1988.
65. Parrella DP, Filstead WJ: Definition of onset in the development of onset-based alcoholism typologies. J Stud Alcohol 1988; 49:85–92.
66. Piazza NJ, Vrbka JL, Yeager RD: Telescoping of alcoholism in women alcoholics. Int J Addict 1989; 24:19–28.
67. Goldstein DB: Pharmacokinetics of alcohol. In Mendelson JH, Mello NK (eds): Medical Diagnosis and Treatment of Alcoholism. New York: McGraw-Hill, 1992:25–54.
68. Frezza M, DiPadova C, Pozzato G, et al: The role of decreased gastric alcohol dehydrogenase activity and first-pass metabolism. N Engl J Med 1990; 322:95–99.
69. Lex BW: Alcohol problems in special populations. In Mendelson JH, Mello NK (eds): Medical Diagnosis and Treatment of Alcoholism. New York: McGraw-Hill, 1992:71–154.
70. Hannigan JH, Welch RA, Sokol RJ: Recognition of fetal alcohol syndrome and alcohol-related birth defects. In Mendelson JH, Mello NK (eds): Medical Diagnosis and Treatment of Alcoholism. New York: McGraw-Hill, 1992:639–667.
71. Finnegan LP, Kandall SR: Maternal and neonatal effects of alcohol and drugs. In Lowinson JH, Ruiz P, Millman RB (eds): Substance Abuse: A Comprehensive Textbook, 2nd ed. Baltimore: Williams & Wilkins, 1992:628–656.
72. Sokol RJ, Clarren SK: Guidelines for use of terminology describing the impact of prenatal alcohol on the offspring. Alcohol Clin Exp Res 1989; 13:597–598.
73. Kaminer Y: Adolescent Substance Abuse: A Comprehensive Guide to Theory and Practice. New York: Plenum Publishing, 1994.
74. Finlayson RE, Hurt RD, Davis LJ Jr, et al: Alcoholism in elderly persons: A study of the psychiatric and psychosocial features of 216 inpatients. Mayo Clin Proc 1988; 63:753–760.
75. Ofman D: Alcoholism and geriatric practice. In Mendelson JH, Mello NK (eds): Medical Diagnosis and Treatment of Alcoholism. New York: McGraw-Hill, 1992:501–573.
76. Graham K: Identifying and measuring alcohol abuse among the elderly: Serious problems with existing instrumentation. J Stud Alcohol 1986; 47:322–326.
77. Atkinson RM, Kofoed LL: Alcohol and drug abuse in old age: A clinical perspective. Subst Alcohol Actions Misuse 1982; 3:353–368.
78. Schuckit MA, Smith TL, Anthenelli R, et al: Clinical course of alcoholism in 636 male inpatients. Am J Psychiatry 1993; 150:786–792.
79. Lindstrom L: Managing Alcoholism: Matching Clients to Treatments. New York: Oxford University Press, 1992.
80. Meyer RE: How to understand the relationship between psychopathology and addictive disorders: Another example of the chicken and the egg. In Meyer RE (ed): Psychopathology and Addictive Disorder. New York: Guilford Press, 1986.
81. Rounsaville BJ, Dolinsky ZS, Babor TF, et al: Psychopathology as a predictor of treatment outcome in alcoholics. Arch Gen Psychiatry 1987; 44:505–513.
82. Kranzler HR, Del Boca F, Rounsaville B: Psychopathology as a predictor of outcome three years after alcoholism treatment. Alcohol Clin Exp Res 1992; 16:363.
83. O'Sullivan K, Rynne C, Miller J, et al: A follow-up study on alcoholics with and without co-existing affective disorder. Br J Psychiatry 1988; 152:813–819.
84. Powell BJ, Penick EC, Nickel EJ, et al: Outcomes of co-morbid alcoholic men: A 1-year follow-up. Alcohol Clin Exp Res 1992; 16:131–138.
85. Liskow B, Powell BJ, Nickel EJ, et al: Diagnostic subgroups of antisocial alcoholics: Outcome at 1 year. Compr Psychiatry 1990; 31:549–556.
86. Vaillant G: The Natural History of Alcoholism. Cambridge, MA: Harvard University Press, 1983.

87. Edwards G, Gross MM, Keller M, et al (eds): Alcohol Related Disabilities. Geneva: World Health Organization, 1977.
88. Schuckit MA: Goals of treatment. In Galanter M, Kleber HD (eds): Textbook of Substance Abuse Treatment. Washington, DC: American Psychiatric Press, 1994:3–10.
89. Bien TH, William R, Tonigan S: Brief interventions for alcohol problems: A review. Addiction 1993; 88:315–336.
90. Babor TF: Avoiding the horrid and beastly sin of drunkenness: Does dissuasion make a difference? J Consult Clin Psychol, 1994; 62: 1127–1140.
91. Babor TF, Grant M: Project on Identification and Management of Alcohol-Related Problems. Report on Phase I: A Randomized Clinical Trial of Brief Interventions in Primary Health Care. Geneva: World Health Organization, 1992.
92. Wallace P, Cutler S, Haines A: Randomised controlled trial of general practitioner intervention in patients with excessive alcohol consumption. BMJ 1988; 297:663–668.
93. Keller M: The old and new in the treatment of alcoholism. In Strug DL, Priyadarsini S, Hyman MM (eds): Alcohol Interventions. New York: Haworth Press, 1986:23–40.
94. DenHartog GL: A Decade of Detox: Development of Non-hospital Approaches to Alcohol Detoxification—A Review of the Literature. Substance Abuse Monograph Series. Jefferson City, MO: Division of Alcohol and Drug Abuse, 1982.
95. Naranjo CA, Sellers EM: Clinical assessment and pharmacotherapy of the alcohol withdrawal syndrome. Recent Dev Alcohol 1986; 4:265–281.
96. Naranjo CA, Sellers EM, Chater K, et al: Non-pharmacological interventions in acute alcohol withdrawal. Clin Pharmacol Ther 1983; 34:214–219.
97. Sellers EM, Naranjo CA, Harrison M, et al: Diazepam loading: Simplified treatment of alcohol withdrawal. Clin Pharmacol Ther 1983; 34:822–826.
98. Whitfield EL, Thompson G, Lamb A, et al: Detoxification of 1,024 alcoholic patients without psychoactive drugs. JAMA 1978; 293: 1409–1410.
99. Hayashida M, Alterman AL, McLellan T, et al: Comparative effectiveness and costs of inpatient and outpatient detoxification of patients with mild-to-moderate alcohol withdrawal syndrome. N Engl J Med 1989; 320:358–365.
100. Feldman DJ, Pattison EM, Sobel LC, et al: Outpatient alcohol detoxification: Initial findings on 564 patients. Am J Psychiatry 1975; 132:407–412.
101. Poutanen P: Experience with carbamazepine in the treatment of withdrawal symptoms in alcohol abusers. Br J Addict 1979; 74:201–204.
102. Malcolm R, Ballenger JC, Sturgis ET, et al: Doubleblind controlled trial comparing carbamazepine to oxazepam treatment of alcohol withdrawal. Am J Psychiatry 1989; 146:617–621.
103. Miller WR, Hester RK: Inpatient alcoholism treatment: Who benefits? Am Psychol 1986; 41:794–805.
104. Longabaugh R, McCrady B, Fink E, et al: Cost effectiveness of alcoholism treatment in partial vs. inpatient settings: Six-month outcomes. J Stud Alcohol 1983; 44:1049–1071.
105. Spicer J, Nyberg LR, McKenna TR: Apples and Oranges: A Comparison of Inpatient and Outpatient Programs. Center City, MN: Hazelden Foundation, 1981.
106. Cole SG, Lehman WE, Cole EA, et al: Inpatient vs. outpatient treatment of alcohol and drug abusers. Am J Drug Alcohol Abuse 1981; 8:329–345.
107. Seixas FA: The Missouri Alcoholism Severity Scale as a predictor of transfer from outpatient to inpatient treatment. Subst Alcohol Actions Misuse 1983; 4:423–443.
108. Walsh DC, Hingson RW, Merrigan DM, et al: A randomized trial of treatment options for alcohol-abusing workers. N Engl J Med 1991; 325:775–782.
109. Institute of Medicine: Treatment modalities: Process and outcome. In Prevention and Treatment of Alcohol Problems: Research Opportunities. Washington, DC: National Academy Press, 1989:169–213.
110. Miller WR, Hester RK: Treating the problem drinker: Modern approaches. In Miller WR (ed): The Addictive Behaviors: Treatment of Alcoholism, Drug Abuse, Gambling, Smoking, and Obesity. New York: Pergamon Press, 1980:11–141.
111. Miller PM, Mastria MA: Alternatives to Alcohol Abuse: A Social Learning Model. Champaign, Il: Research Press, 1977.
112. Ferrell WL, Galassi JP: Assertion training and human relations training in the treatment of chronic alcoholics. Int J Addict 1981; 16:959–968.
113. Oei TPS, Jackson PR: Long-term effects of group and individual social skills training with alcoholics. Addict Behav 1980; 5:129–136.
114. Oei TPS, Jackson PR: Social skills and cognitive behavioral approaches to the treatment of problem drinking. J Stud Alcohol 1982; 43:532–547.
115. Sanchez-Craig M, Walker K: Teaching coping skills to chronic alcoholics in a coeducational halfway house. 1. Assessment of programme effects. Br J Addict 1982; 77:35–50.
116. Chaney E, O'Leary M, Marlatt GA: Skill training with alcoholics. J Consult Clin Psychol 1978; 46:1092–1104.
117. Marlatt GA: Relapse prevention: Theoretical rationale and overview of the model. In Marlatt GA, Gordon JR (eds): Relapse Prevention. New York: Guilford Press, 1985:3–70.
118. Vannicelli M: Group psychotherapy with alcoholics: Special techniques. J Stud Alcohol 1982; 43:17–37.
119. Kadden RM, Cooney NL, Getter H, et al: Matching alcoholics to coping skills or interactional therapies: Posttreatment results. J Consult Clin Psychol 1989; 57:698–704.
120. Emrick CD: Alcoholics Anonymous and other 12-step groups. In Galanter M, Kleber HD (eds): Textbook of Substance Abuse Treatment. Washington, DC: American Psychiatric Press, 1994:351–358.
121. Miller WR, McCrady BS: The importance of research on Alcoholics Anonymous. In McCrady BS, Miller WR (eds): Research on Alcoholics Anonymous: Opportunities and Alternatives. New Brunswick, NJ: Rutgers Center of Alcohol Studies, 1993:3–11.
122. Polich JM, Armor DJ, Braiker HB: Patterns of alcoholism over four years. J Stud Alcohol 1980; 41:397–416.
123. Hoffman NB, Harrison PA, Belille CA: Alcoholics Anonymous after treatment: Attendance and abstinence. Int J Addict 1983; 18:311–318.
124. Ditman KS, Crawford GG, Forgy EW, et al: A controlled experiment on the use of court probation for drunk arrests. Am J Psychiatry 1967; 124:160–163.
125. Brandsma JM, Maultsby MC, Welsh RJ: The Outpatient Treatment of Alcoholism: A Review and Comparative Study. Baltimore: University Park Press, 1980.
126. Stimmel B, Cohen M, Sturiano V, et al: Is treatment of alcoholism effective in persons on methadone maintenance? Am J Psychiatry 1983; 140:862–866.
127. Ogborne AC, Glaser FB: Characteristics of affiliates of Alcoholics Anonymous: A review of the literature. J Stud Alcohol 1981; 42:661–675.
128. Snyder SH: Biological Aspects of Mental Disorder. New York: Oxford University Press, 1980.
129. O'Farrell T, Cutter HSG, Floyd FJ: Evaluating behavioral marital therapy for male alcoholics: Effects on marital adjustment and communication before and after treatment. Behav Ther 1985;16: 147–167.
130. Pattison EM, Kaufman E: Family therapy in the treatment of alcoholism. In Lansky M (ed): Family Therapy and Major Psychopathology. New York: Grune & Stratton, 1981:203–229.
131. Kaufman E: Families and family therapy in alcoholism. In Lansky M (ed): Family Approaches to Major Psychiatric Disorders. Washington, DC: American Psychiatric Press, 1985:14–44.
132. Moos RH, Finney JW, Gamble W: The process of recovery from alcoholism. II. Comparing spouses of alcoholic patients and matched community controls. J Stud Alcohol 1982; 43:888–909.
133. Moos RH, Moos BS: The process of recovery from alcoholism. III. Comparing functioning in families of alcoholics and matched control families. J Stud Alcohol 1984; 45:111–118.
134. Steinglass P: Family therapy with alcoholics: A review. In Kaufman E, Kaufmann PN (eds): Family Therapy of Drug and Alcohol Abuse. New York: Gardner, 1979:147–186.
135. McCrady BS, Noel NE, Stout RL, et al: Comparative effectiveness of three types of spouse involvement in outpatient behavioral alcoholism treatment. J Stud Alcohol 1986; 47:459–467.
136. Ablon J: Support system dynamics of Al-Anon and Alateen. In Pattison EM, Kaufman E (eds): Encyclopedic Handbook of Alcoholism. New York: Gardner, 1982.
137. Jones RW, Helrich AR: Treatment of alcoholism by physicians in private practice: A national survey. Q J Stud Alcohol 1972; 33:117–131.

138. Liskow BI, Goodwin DW: Pharmacological treatment of alcohol intoxication, withdrawal and dependence: A critical review. J Stud Alcohol 1987; 48:356–370.
139. Kranzler HR, Orrok B: The pharmacotherapy of alcoholism. In Tasman A (ed): Annual Review of Psychiatry, Volume 8. Washington, DC: American Psychiatric Press, 1989:359–379.
140. Litten RZ, Allen JP: Pharmacotherapies for alcoholism: Promising agents and clinical issues. Alcohol Clin Exp Res 1991; 15:620–633.
141. Jaffe JH, Kranzler HR, Ciraulo D: Drugs used in the treatment of alcoholism. In Mendelson JH, Mello NK (eds): Medical Diagnosis and Treatment of Alcoholism, 3rd ed. New York: McGraw-Hill, 1992: 421–461.
142. Kranzler HR, Anton RF: Implications of recent neuropsychopharmacologic research for understanding the etiology and development of alcoholism. J Consult Clin Psychol 1994; 62:1116–1126.
143. Ritchie JM: The aliphatic alcohols. In Gilman AG, Goodman LS, Rall TW, et al (eds): The Pharmacological Basis of Therapeutics, 7th ed. New York: Macmillan, 1985:372–386.
144. Fuller RK, Branchey L, Brightwell DR, et al: Disulfiram treatment of alcoholism. A Veterans Administration cooperative study. JAMA 1986; 256:1449–1455.
145. Allen JP, Litten RZ: Techniques to enhance compliance with disulfiram. Alcohol Clin Exp Res 1992; 16:1035–1041.
146. Azrin NH, Sisson RW, Meyers R, et al: Alcoholism treatment by disulfiram and community reinforcement therapy. J Behav Ther Exp Psychiatry 1982; 13:105–112.
147. Ciraulo DA, Alderson LM, Chapron DJ, et al: Imipramine disposition in alcoholics. J Clin Psychopharmacol 1982; 2:2–7.
148. Dorus W, Kennedy J, Gibbons RD, et al: Symptoms and diagnosis of depression in alcoholics. Alcohol Clin Exp Res 1987; 11:150–154.
149. Mason BJ, Kocsis JH: Desipramine treatment of alcoholism. Psychopharmacol Bull 1991; 27:155–161.
150. Nunes EV, McGrath PJ, Quitkin FM, et al: Imipramine treatment of alcoholism with comorbid depression. Am J Psychiatry 1993; 6:963–965.
151. Cornelius JR, Salloum IM, Cornelius MD, et al: Fluoxetine trial in suicidal depressed alcoholics. Psychopharmacol Bull 1993; 29:195–199.
152. Kranzler HR, Burleson JA, Korner P, et al: Fluoxetine treatment of alcoholism: A placebo-controlled trial. Am J Psychiatry 1995; 152:391–397.
153. Kline NS, Wren JC, Cooper TB, et al: Evaluation of lithium therapy in chronic and periodic alcoholism. Am J Med Sci 1974; 268:15–22.
154. Merry J, Reynolds CM, Bailey J, et al: Prophylactic treatment of alcoholism by lithium carbonate. Lancet 1976; 2:481–482.
155. Fawcett J, Clark DC, Aagesen CA, et al: A double-blind, placebo-controlled trial of lithium carbonate therapy for alcoholism. Arch Gen Psychiatry 1987; 44:248–256.
156. Dorus W, Ostrow DG, Anton R, et al: Lithium treatment of depressed and nondepressed alcoholics. JAMA 1989; 262:1646–1652.
157. Kissin B: The use of psychoactive drugs in the long-term treatment of chronic alcoholics. Ann N Y Acad Sci 1975; 52:385–395.
158. Ditman KS: Evaluation of drugs in the treatment of alcoholics. Q J Stud Alcohol 1961; 1(suppl):107–116.
159. Rosenberg CM: Drug maintenance in the outpatient treatment of chronic alcoholism. Arch Gen Psychiatry 1974; 30:373–377.
160. Schuckit M: Alcoholic patients with secondary depression. Am J Psychiatry 1983; 140:711–714.
161. Ciraulo DA, Sands BF, Shader RI: Critical review of liability for benzodiazepine abuse among alcoholics. Am J Psychiatry 1988; 145:1501–1506.
162. Jaffe JH, Ciraulo DA, Nies A, et al: Abuse potential of halazepam and diazepam in patients recently treated for acute alcohol withdrawal. Clin Pharmacol Ther 1983; 34:623–630.
163. Taylor DP, Eison M, Riblet LA, et al: Pharmacological and clinical effects of buspirone. Pharmacol Biochem Behav 1985; 23:687–694.
164. Bruno F: Buspirone in the treatment of alcoholic patients. Psychopathology 1989; 22:49–59.
165. Tollefson GD, Montague-Clouse J, Tollefson SL: Treatment of comorbid generalized anxiety in a recently detoxified alcohol population with a selective serotonergic drug (buspirone). J Clin Psychopharmacol 1992; 12:19–26.
166. Kranzler HR, Burleson JA, Del Boca FK, et al: Buspirone treatment of anxious alcoholics: A placebo-controlled trial. Arch Gen Psychiatry 1994; 51:720–731.
167. Malcolm R, Anton RF, Randall CL, et al: A placebo-controlled trial of buspirone in anxious inpatient alcoholics. Alcohol Clin Exp Res 1992; 16:1007–1013.
168. Volpicelli J, O'Brien C, Alterman A, et al: Naltrexone in the treatment of alcohol dependence. Arch Gen Psychiatry 1992; 49:867–880.
169. O'Malley SS, Jaffe AJ, Chang G, et al: Naltrexone and coping skills therapy for alcohol dependence: A controlled study. Arch Gen Psychiatry 1992; 49:894–898.
170. Swift RM, Whelihan W, Kuznetsov O, et al: Naltrexone-induced alterations in human ethanol intoxication. Am J Psychiatry 1994; 151:1463–1467.
171. Mason BJ, Ritvo EC, Morgan RO, et al: A double-blind, placebo-controlled pilot study to evaluate the efficacy and safety of oral nalmefene HCl for alcohol dependence. Alcohol Clin Exp Res 1994; 18:1162–1167.
172. Naranjo CA, Sellers EM, Lawrin MO: Modulation of ethanol intake by serotonin uptake inhibitors. J Clin Psychiatry 1986; 47(suppl): 16–22.
173. Gorelick DA: Serotonin reuptake blockers and the treatment of alcoholism. Recent Dev Alcohol 1989; 7:267–281.
174. Roy A, Linnoila M, Virkkunen M: Serotonin and alcoholism. Subst Abuse 1987; 8:21–27.
175. Amit Z, Brown Z, Sutherland A, et al: Reduction in alcohol intake in humans as a function of treatment with zimelidine: Implications for treatment. In Naranjo CA, Sellers EM (eds): Research Advances in New Psychopharmacological Treatments for Alcoholism. Amsterdam: Elsevier, 1985:189–198.
176. Naranjo CA, Sellers EM, Roach CA, et al: Zimelidine-induced variations in alcohol intake by nondepressed heavy drinkers. Clin Pharmacol Ther 1984; 35:374–381.
177. Naranjo CA, Sellers EM, Sullivan JT, et al: The serotonin uptake inhibitor citalopram attenuates ethanol intake. Clin Pharmacol Ther 1987; 41:266–274.
178. Balldin J, Berggren U, Engel J, et al: Effect of citalopram on alcohol intake in heavy drinkers. Alcohol Clin Exp Res 1994; 18:1133–1136.
179. Naranjo CA, Sullivan JT, Kadlec KE, et al: Differential effects of viqualine on alcohol intake and other consummatory behaviors. Clin Pharmacol Ther 1989; 46:301–309.
180. Gorelick DA, Paredes A: Effect of fluoxetine on alcohol consumption in male alcoholics. Alcohol Clin Exp Res 1992; 16:261–265.
181. Naranjo CA, Kadlec KE, Sanhueza P, et al: Fluoxetine differentially alters alcohol intake and other consummatory behaviors in problem drinkers. Clin Pharmacol Ther 1990; 47:490–498.
182. Gerra G, Caccavari R, Delsignore R, et al: Effects of fluoxetine and Ca-acetyl-homotaurinate on alcohol intake in familial and nonfamilial alcohol patients. Curr Ther Res 1992; 52:291–295.
183. Kranzler HR, Del Boca F, Korner P, et al: Adverse effects limit the usefulness of fluvoxamine for the treatment of alcoholism. J Subst Abuse Treat 1993; 10:283–287.
184. McLellan AT, Luborsky L, Woody GE, et al: Predicting response to alcohol and drug abuse treatments: Role of psychiatric severity. Arch Gen Psychiatry 1983; 40:620–625.
185. Pottenger M, McKernon J, Patrie LE, et al: The frequency and persistence of depressive symptoms in the alcohol abuser. J Nerv Ment Dis 1978; 166:562–570.
186. Catalano RF, Hawkins JD, Wells EA: Evaluation of the effectiveness of adolescent drug abuse treatment, assessment of risks for relapse, and promising approaches for relapse prevention. Int J Addict 1990–91; 25:1085–1140.
187. Brown SA, Vik PW, Creamer VA: Characteristics of relapse following adolescent substance abuse treatment. Addict Behav 1989; 14:291–300.
188. Liskow BI, Rinck C, Campbell J: Alcohol withdrawal in the elderly. J Stud Alcohol 1989; 50:414–421.
189. Kofoed LL, Tolson RL, Atkinson RM, et al: Treatment compliance of older alcoholics: An elder-specific approach is superior to "mainstreaming." J Stud Alcohol 1987; 48:47–51.
190. Blazer DG: Alcohol and drug problems in the elderly. In Busse EW, Blazer DG (eds): Geriatric Psychiatry. Washington, DC: American Psychiatric Press, 1989:489–511.
191. Blume SB: Alcohol and other drug problems in women. In Lowinson JH, Ruiz P, Millman RB (eds): Substance Abuse: A Comprehensive Textbook, 2nd ed. Baltimore: Williams & Wilkins, 1992:794–807.
192. Franklin JE: Alcoholism among blacks. Hosp Community Psychiatry 1989; 40:1120–1127.
193. Beck AT, Ward CH, Mendelson M, et al: An inventory for measuring depression. Arch Gen Psychiatry 1961; 4:461–471.

CHAPTER

43 Caffeine Use Disorders

Eric C. Strain
Roland R. Griffiths

Caffeine Intoxication
Caffeine Withdrawal
Caffeine Dependence
Caffeine-Induced Anxiety Disorder
Caffeine-Induced Sleep Disorder

Caffeine is the most widely consumed psychoactive substance in the world.[1] In the United States, it is estimated that more than 80% of adults consume caffeine regularly.[2] Throughout the world, caffeine use occurs in a variety of different but culturally well-integrated social contexts, such as the coffee break in the United States, teatime in the United Kingdom, and kola nut chewing in Nigeria. In the United States, for example, habitual consumption of coffee or caffeinated soda drinks with meals is extremely common and may not be readily recognized as caffeine consumption. This cultural integration of caffeine use can make the recognition of psychiatric disorders associated with caffeine use particularly difficult. However, it is important for the psychiatrist to recognize the role of caffeine as a psychoactive substance capable of producing a variety of psychiatric syndromes, despite the pervasive and well-accepted use of caffeine. In this chapter, five disorders associated with caffeine use are reviewed: caffeine intoxication, caffeine withdrawal, caffeine dependence, caffeine-induced anxiety disorder, and caffeine-induced sleep disorder.

CAFFEINE INTOXICATION

Definition

The *Diagnostic and Statistical Manual of Mental Disorders,* Fourth Edition (DSM-IV) defines caffeine intoxication as a set of symptoms that develop during or shortly after caffeine use[3] (see page 780). There may be two kinds of presentation associated with caffeine intoxication. The first presentation is associated with the *acute* ingestion of a large amount of caffeine and represents an acute drug overdose condition. The second presentation is associated with the *chronic* consumption of large amounts of caffeine and results in a more complicated presentation.

Caffeine intoxication has long been recognized as a syndrome produced by the ingestion of an excessive amount of caffeine. For example, in 1896, J. T. Rugh[4] reported the case of a traveling salesman who had nervousness, involuntary contractions in the arms and legs, a sense of impending danger, and sleep disturbance in the context of excessive coffee consumption used to maintain a highly active pace of work. Similar reports of caffeine intoxication can be found throughout the medical literature of the 1800s and early 1900s, with observations of motor unrest, insomnia, tachycardia, irritability, headache, emotional lability, anxiety, and gastrointestinal disturbances associated with the excessive use of caffeine.[5–11] Thus, caffeine intoxication represents a psychiatric disorder that has been well described for at least 100 years.

Epidemiology

Prevalence and Incidence

Despite the long history of recognition of caffeine intoxication, there is little information available about the prevalence or incidence of caffeine intoxication either in selected populations or in the general community. Four studies have examined the rate of caffeine intoxication in special populations. In a 1975 survey[12] of 220 psychiatric patients and control subjects, none of the participants had symptoms of caffeine intoxication. A 1976 survey[13] of 135 inpatients on a psychiatric unit found two cases (1.5%) of caffeine intoxication. A 1981 survey[14] of college students found 1.3% with high caffeine consumption, and these high caffeine consumers had higher levels of symptoms associated with caffeine intoxication. Finally, a 1990 survey[15] of college students found 19% reported a history of caffeine intoxication.

One study[16] examined the rate of caffeine intoxication in the general community. In a random-digit telephone survey of 166 current caffeine users in the community, 12% met the *Diagnostic and Statistical Manual of Mental Disorders,* Third Edition, Revised (DSM-III-R) criteria for caffeine intoxication in the previous year. Thus, it would

DSM-IV Criteria 305.90

Caffeine Intoxication

A. Recent consumption of caffeine, usually in excess of 250 mg (e.g., more than 2–3 cups of brewed coffee).

B. Five (or more) of the following signs, developing during, or shortly after, caffeine use:

(1) restlessness

(2) nervousness

(3) excitement

(4) insomnia

(5) flushed face

(6) diuresis

(7) gastrointestinal disturbance

(8) muscle twitching

(9) rambling flow of thought and speech

(10) tachycardia or cardiac arrhythmia

(11) periods of inexhaustibility

(12) psychomotor agitation

C. The symptoms in criterion B cause clinically significant distress or impairment in social, occupational, or other important areas of functioning.

D. The symptoms are not due to a general medical condition and are not better accounted for by another mental disorder (e.g., an anxiety disorder).

appear that the prevalence of caffeine intoxication may be between 2% and 12%. However, there clearly is a need for better characterization of both the prevalence and the incidence of caffeine intoxication, using rigorous criteria for the diagnosis, standardized assessments, and representative sampling techniques.

Comorbidity Patterns

Reports on comorbidity have often failed to distinguish chronic high caffeine consumption from a formal diagnosis of caffeine intoxication. In addition, reports on caffeine intoxication have generally failed to distinguish between a single acute episode of caffeine intoxication and a state of chronic caffeine intoxication.

Reports on caffeine intoxication typically have not found other distinct comorbid psychiatric conditions present. There have been case reports of caffeine intoxication occurring in patients with anorexia nervosa[17] and with other substance abuse disorders.[18] The symptoms of caffeine intoxication can mimic those of anxiety and mood disorders,[19] but there has been no evidence to suggest that patients with these disorders are more likely to have caffeine intoxication or that patients with caffeine intoxication are more likely to have other psychiatric disorders.

Whereas there are no clear comorbid conditions associated with caffeine intoxication (besides possibly eating disorders and other substance abuse disorders), there are comorbid conditions associated with excessive caffeine consumption (that is, habitual use of large amounts of caffeine without evidence of acute caffeine intoxication). Furlong[12] reported that higher coffee consumption was associated with the diagnosis of a personality disorder, and Winstead[13] reported that higher caffeine consumption was more likely in patients with psychotic disorders and not in patients with depressive neurotic disorders. Patients with chronic schizophrenia have been reported to eat large amounts of instant coffee,[20] and such excessive caffeine consumption may exacerbate chronic psychiatric conditions.[13, 21–24]

The relationship between caffeine consumption and anxiety disorders is considered in more detail later (in the caffeine-induced anxiety disorder section), but it is worth noting here that patients with panic disorder appear to have lower caffeine consumption[25] and that patients with panic disorder and patients with generalized anxiety disorder may be more sensitive to the effects of caffeine.[26, 27]

Excessive caffeine consumption has repeatedly been observed to be associated with smoking tobacco (nicotine dependence), and this higher consumption of caffeine in smokers may be partly due to the increased metabolism of caffeine in smokers.[28, 29] Significantly higher levels of caffeine consumption have also been noted in abstinent alcoholic individuals versus nonalcoholic individuals,[30] and usage levels of coffee, cigarettes, and alcohol have been shown to be positively related.[31, 32]

Two other psychiatric conditions are associated with the excessive consumption of caffeine. The first is delirium, which may be present in cases of extreme caffeine intoxication. For example, caffeine-induced delirium has been reported in a man who acutely consumed coffee, cola, and 800 mg of caffeine (tablets) while competing in the Iditarod dogsled race held between Anchorage and Nome, Alaska.[33] He experienced tremor, an alteration in his level of consciousness, anxiety, visual illusions and hallucinations, vertigo, and impaired memory consistent with an episode of delirium. Whereas excessive caffeine consumption may have been related to his delirium, other factors, such as fatigue and sleep deprivation, may also have contributed to his delirium. Other cases of probable caffeine-induced delirium have also been reported.[34, 35] Although DSM-IV does not officially recognize caffeine as one of the agents that can produce a substance intoxication delirium, it would seem likely that caffeine, like other psychoactive substances, could produce delirium if it is taken in sufficiently high doses.

Although it is extremely rare, another psychiatric condition that can be associated with excessive caffeine consumption is suicide. Overdose with caffeine may be fatal,[36–38] and there has been at least one report of a suicide death by caffeine overdose.[39] If there is evidence that a patient has significantly overdosed on caffeine, then it should be treated as a medical emergency requiring intensive monitoring, symptomatic treatment (e.g., for tachycardia, arrhythmias, and seizures), aspiration of the stomach, and assessment of the serum caffeine level (>100 μg/mL is generally considered toxic). Caffeine overdose has also been treated successfully with hemoperfusion.[40]

Etiology and Pathophysiology

Although caffeine intoxication is clearly related to caffeine ingestion, it is not simply the result of a person's consuming a high dose of caffeine. Rather, caffeine intoxication represents the relationship between the dose of caffeine consumed and the degree of tolerance to caffeine in that person. In addition, there may be individual differences in sensitivity to caffeine that may account for differences across people.

Tolerance represents an acquired change in responsiveness by an individual as a result of exposure to a drug, such that an increased amount of the drug is required to produce the same effect or a lesser effect is produced by the same dose of the drug. In a person who regularly consumes caffeine, tolerance may occur to the acute effects of caffeine. Thus, a sensitive person with no tolerance to caffeine might have signs and symptoms of caffeine intoxication in response to a relatively low dose of caffeine (such as 100 mg, the amount found in a typical cup of brewed coffee; Table 43–1), whereas another person with a high daily consumption of caffeine would show no evidence of intoxication with a similar dose.

Caffeine's principal mechanism of action is that of an adenosine antagonist.[41, 42] Adenosine produces a wide variety of physiological effects, including central nervous system depression, dilation of central vasculature, antidiuresis and inhibition of renin release, and inhibition of gastric secretion and respiration.[43] As an antagonist of adenosine, many of caffeine's actions can be appreciated as effects opposite to those produced by adenosine (e.g., central nervous system stimulation, decreased cerebral blood flow, increased renin release and diuresis, increased gastric secretions, and stimulation of respiration).

Caffeine also exerts effects on phosphodiesterase and intracellular calcium. With typical dietary doses of caffeine, blood levels of caffeine are believed to be too low to appreciably affect the nonadenosine mechanisms of actions, and adenosine antagonism appears to be the primary mechanism for caffeine's effects. It is not known whether these other mechanisms may mediate some of the clinical effects produced when caffeine blood levels are elevated (e.g., as may occur with caffeine intoxication).

Table 43–1 Typical Caffeine Content of Foods and Medications

Substance	Caffeine Content
Brewed coffee	100 mg/6 oz
Instant coffee	70 mg/6 oz
Decaffeinated coffee	4 mg/6 oz
Tea	40 mg/6 oz
Caffeinated soda	45 mg/12 oz
Cocoa beverage	5 mg/6 oz
Chocolate milk	4 mg/6 oz
Dark chocolate	20 mg/1 oz
Milk chocolate	6 mg/1 oz
Caffeine-containing cold remedies	25–50 mg/tablet
Caffeine-containing analgesics	25–65 mg/tablet
Stimulants	100–350 mg/tablet
Weight-loss aids	75–200 mg/tablet

Modified from American Psychiatric Association. Diagnostic and Statistical Manual of Mental Disorders, 4th ed. Washington, DC: American Psychiatric Association, 1994.

Diagnosis and Differential Diagnosis

Phenomenology and Variations in Presentation

The primary features of caffeine intoxication can be found in the diagnostic criteria from DSM-IV. There have been no studies comparing the relative contribution of the different DSM-IV criteria to the diagnosis of caffeine intoxication, although in a study of 124 general hospital patients, the most common somatic symptoms patients associated with caffeine were (in descending order of frequency) diuresis, insomnia, withdrawal headaches, diarrhea, anxiety, tachycardia, and tremulousness.[44]

In addition to the characteristics of caffeine intoxication noted in DSM-IV, there have been reports of fever,[45] irritability, tremors, sensory disturbances and tachypnea,[19] and headaches[46, 47] associated with cases of caffeine intoxication. Although a wide variety of symptoms of caffeine intoxication have been reported, the most common signs and symptoms appear to be anxiety and nervousness, insomnia, gastrointestinal disturbances, tremors, tachycardia, and psychomotor agitation.

Assessment and Differential Diagnosis

The diagnosis of caffeine intoxication is based on the history and clinical presentation of the patient, and the extent of caffeine use can be confirmed by a serum assay of the caffeine level. Recognition of the role of caffeine in the presenting syndrome ultimately diagnosed as caffeine intoxication depends on the psychiatrist's being aware of the role of caffeine in producing intoxication. In the past, caffeine use has often been overlooked in patients presenting with symptoms consistent with a caffeine use disorder.[30] However, it may be that there is presently a greater awareness of the deleterious effects of caffeine, making psychiatrists more sensitive to the inclusion of caffeine in a differential diagnosis and patients more aware of the possible role of excessive caffeine in somatic and psychological symptoms.

Several conditions should be included in the differential diagnosis of caffeine intoxication (Table 43–2). These include other substance abuse–related disorders (amphetamine or cocaine intoxication; withdrawal from sedatives, hypnotics, anxiolytics, or nicotine), other psychiatric disorders (panic disorder, generalized anxiety disorder, mania, sleep disorders), and medication-induced side effects (e.g., akathisia). Caffeine intoxication may present with a wide variety of clinical features, and the possibility of caffeine intoxication should be included in the differential diagnosis

Table 43–2 Differential Diagnosis of Caffeine Intoxication

Manic episode	Panic disorder
Amphetamine or cocaine intoxication	Generalized anxiety disorder
Sedative, hypnotic, or anxiolytic withdrawal	Medication-induced side effect (e.g., akathisia)
Nicotine withdrawal	Sleep disorders

for patients with nonspecific complaints or presentations that do not readily fit into a known diagnostic pattern.

Course and Natural History (Prognosis)

In the patient who is not tolerant to caffeine, acute caffeine ingestion producing caffeine intoxication is a time-limited condition that will rapidly resolve with cessation of caffeine use, consistent with the relatively short half-life of caffeine (3 to 6 hours).[48] In a patient who has caffeine intoxication superimposed on chronic caffeine use, abrupt termination of all caffeine use may lead to caffeine withdrawal (described in detail later). Because symptoms of caffeine withdrawal can partially overlap with symptoms of caffeine intoxication (e.g., nervousness and anxiety), the time course of symptom resolution can be expected to be protracted, lasting several days to a week or more.

Treatment

The first step in evaluating a patient with a possible diagnosis of caffeine intoxication is to obtain a careful history about all recent caffeine consumption. The possible use of beverages and medications (both prescription and over-the-counter diet aids and energy pills) should be reviewed. Some beverages (e.g., caffeine-containing soft drinks) and medications (e.g., energy pills, aids to combat sleep, or diet pills) may not be recognized as containing caffeine by the patient. The amount of caffeine acutely consumed should help clarify the diagnosis of caffeine intoxication, although it is important to determine whether the patient has been chronically consuming high doses of caffeine. If this is the case, the patient may be tolerant and therefore less likely to be experiencing caffeine intoxication.

If the patient is unable to provide an accurate history of recent caffeine consumption (e.g., because of delirium after a caffeine overdose), the patient should be emergently evaluated and medically monitored.

The primary approach to the treatment of caffeine intoxication is to teach the patient about the effects of excessive caffeine consumption. In patients who are resistant to accepting the role of caffeine in their presenting symptoms, it may be useful to suggest a trial off of caffeine as both a diagnostic and a potentially therapeutic probe. Interestingly, although caffeine is widely consumed throughout most cultures, it does not seem that people intentionally attempt to repeatedly become intoxicated with high doses of caffeine.

CAFFEINE WITHDRAWAL

Definition

As for caffeine intoxication, there is a long history of recognition that some people can also experience symptoms of caffeine withdrawal. For example, in 1893, Bridge[49] described a series of patients who had various conditions he thought were associated with the use of coffee or tea. He concluded that the cessation of coffee could be beneficial, although patients were at risk for a severe headache acutely with abrupt termination, and he recommended "reducing the rations of coffee gradually through a week or more of time."[49] This observation of headaches associated with the cessation of caffeine use has been repeatedly described and is now a well-established characteristic of caffeine withdrawal. Other features of caffeine withdrawal can include sleepiness (drowsiness, yawning), work difficulty (impaired concentration, lassitude, decreased motivation for work), irritability (decreased contentedness, well-being, and self-confidence), decreased sociability (reduced friendliness and talkativeness), influenza-like symptoms (including muscle aches and stiffness, hot or cold spells, nausea or vomiting), and blurred vision. In addition, reports of depression and anxiety may be elevated and psychomotor performance may be impaired[50, 51] (Table 43–3).

DSM-IV Research Criteria

Caffeine Withdrawal

A. Prolonged daily use of caffeine.

B. Abrupt cessation of caffeine use, or reduction in the amount of caffeine used, closely followed by headache and one (or more) of the following symptoms:

(1) marked fatigue or drowsiness

(2) marked anxiety or depression

(3) nausea or vomiting

C. The symptoms in criterion B cause clinically significant distress or impairment in social, occupational, or other important areas of functioning.

D. The symptoms are not due to the direct physiological effects of a general medical condition (e.g., migraine, viral illness) and are not better accounted for by another mental disorder.

Table 43–3 Signs and Symptoms Associated with Caffeine Withdrawal

Headache
Sleepiness, drowsiness
Impaired concentration, lassitude, work difficulty
Depression
Anxiety
Irritability
Nausea or vomiting
Muscle aches and stiffness

Although caffeine can produce a withdrawal syndrome, the Substance Use Disorders Work Group for DSM-IV had four concerns about the inclusion of caffeine withdrawal in DSM-IV: some symptoms appear to overlap (e.g., fatigue and drowsiness), more of the symptoms of caffeine withdrawal need to be well validated, caffeine withdrawal symptoms have a high prevalence in the general population, and these symptoms can have several other causes besides caffeine.[52] Thus, the diagnostic category caffeine withdrawal is included in DSM-IV as a syndrome for further study.

Epidemiology

Prevalence and Incidence

Two types of studies have examined the prevalence and incidence of caffeine withdrawal.[50, 51] In the first, caffeine withdrawal is experimentally induced; in the second, there is an epidemiological assessment of the prevalence and incidence of caffeine withdrawal in some portion of the general population, usually through the use of some form of a retrospective questionnaire. In studies of experimentally induced caffeine withdrawal, caffeine users are typically placed under conditions in which caffeine use is discontinued, and assessments determine the time course and characteristics of the caffeine withdrawal signs and symptoms produced. Numerous studies of such experimentally induced caffeine withdrawal have been conducted.[53–58] The best estimate of the incidence of caffeine withdrawal symptoms was provided in a study by Silverman and colleagues[59] in 62 normal adults with low to moderate daily caffeine consumption (an average of 235 mg of caffeine per day) who underwent a double-blind caffeine withdrawal. The study showed that 52% of participants had moderate or severe headache, 8% to 11% had symptoms associated with anxiety and depression, 8% had significantly high ratings of fatigue, and 13% used analgesics while in withdrawal. These results are similar to other studies that have found the prevalence of caffeine withdrawal to be between 35% and 49%.[60]

Although there have been many studies of experimentally induced caffeine withdrawal, there have not been a comparably large number of epidemiological assessments of caffeine withdrawal. Goldstein and Kaizer[61] assessed housewives with a retrospective questionnaire (but with no experimental manipulation) and found that about 8% to 9% of consumers of moderate and heavy amounts of coffee reported experiencing a characteristic withdrawal syndrome if they omitted drinking their morning coffee. In a telephone survey of 166 current caffeine users conducted by Hughes and coworkers,[16] 42% of these caffeine users who had stopped caffeine use for 24 hours or more reported headaches, fatigue, or drowsiness. These results are similar to those found in the Silverman study[59] of experimentally induced caffeine withdrawal. Given the large number of regular caffeine consumers (more than 80% of adults in the United States[2]), these data suggest that there may be a larger number of episodes of caffeine withdrawal than are generally recognized.

Comorbidity Patterns

It is possible to identify certain populations that may be at increased risk for development of caffeine withdrawal or caffeine withdrawal headaches, such as patients with high daily caffeine consumption[62] or patients with a history of frequent headaches.[63] However, no studies have specifically examined comorbidity in people who experience caffeine withdrawal.

Etiology and Pathophysiology

Caffeine withdrawal is the result of a decrease in the amount of caffeine consumed by an individual. Studies of caffeine withdrawal have generally focused on the complete cessation of caffeine use, although it may be possible that a relative decrease in use could also produce withdrawal symptoms.

It seems probable that caffeine withdrawal is mediated by the cessation of chronic adenosine antagonism, which is caffeine's chief pharmacological mechanism of action.[41, 42] Chronic caffeine consumption may produce a compensatory up-regulation of the adenosine system. Withdrawal may then be attributable to the functional increase in adenosine activity that occurs on termination of chronic caffeine consumption.[64–66] Adenosine produces central nervous system depression and cerebral vasodilation. Thus, acute doses of caffeine produce mild central nervous system stimulation and decreased cerebral blood flow.[67, 68] Caffeine withdrawal symptoms may be partially explained by an increase in cerebral blood flow associated with increased adenosine activity.[68, 69] The results of an electroencephalographical study that demonstrated increased alpha and beta voltage in the frontal-central cortex during caffeine withdrawal have been interpreted as being consistent with the hypothesis that caffeine withdrawal may be due to cerebral blood flow changes.[70]

Diagnosis and Differential Diagnosis

Phenomenology and Variations in Presentation

Headache. The most common feature of caffeine withdrawal is headache[50, 51] (Table 43–4). Caffeine withdrawal headache, which has also been described as a feeling of cerebral fullness, is typically a generalized throbbing headache that can be accompanied by influenza-like symptoms (such as nausea and vomiting).[50, 51] It is worsened with physical exercise and Valsalva's maneuver and is relieved with caffeine consumption. Careful double-blind studies of caffeine withdrawal have shown that headache generally occurs 12 to 24 hours after the last dose of caffeine[54, 55] (mean, 19 hours),[54] although headache onset as late as about 40 hours has been documented.[55] Caffeine withdrawal headache usually resolves within 2 to 4 days, although some subjects continue to report sporadic headaches for as long as 11 days after cessation of caffeine use.[54, 55] Although caffeine withdrawal is associated with headache, several

Table 43–4 Features of Caffeine Withdrawal Headache

Gradual onset between 12 and 40 h	Can be accompanied by influenza-like symptoms (including nausea, vomiting)
Worse with exercise or Valsalva's maneuver	Diffuse, throbbing, severe

reports have also concluded that acute caffeine or coffee consumption can produce headache.[50]

Sleepiness and Drowsiness. Sleepiness is another frequent symptom of caffeine withdrawal. Various reports have described this as increased yawning, drowsiness, or wanting to sleep.

Impaired Concentration, Lassitude, and Work Difficulty. Reports of caffeine withdrawal have also often included a component variously described as impaired concentration, work difficulty, fatigue, lassitude, weakness, or being lazy (distinct from drowsiness or sleepiness).

Anxiety or Depression. In general, reports of anxiety or depression have been less frequent than reports of sleepiness or impaired concentration. Terms that have been used to describe this attribute of caffeine withdrawal have included feelings of nervousness, jitteriness, shakiness, and restlessness.

Influenza-like Symptoms. These symptoms can encompass several of the features of caffeine withdrawal that have been noted before. People in experimentally induced caffeine withdrawal have complained of feeling as if they had influenza, that is, they had headache, fatigue, muscle aches and stiffness, hot or cold spells, nausea, and vomiting. Although relatively infrequent, nausea and vomiting with caffeine withdrawal have been reported in several studies.

Other Signs and Symptoms. Several other features of caffeine withdrawal have been noted, although they are less frequent than most of those just described. These can include impairments in psychomotor performance (usually detected only through the use of specific psychomotor tests), irritability, rhinorrhea, confusion, diaphoresis, blurred vision, and cravings for caffeine.[55]

Relationship of Headache to Other Signs and Symptoms of Caffeine Withdrawal. Although it may seem that the various symptoms of caffeine withdrawal simply represent sequelae of headache, these other symptoms of caffeine withdrawal do not always covary with the presence of headache and can occur in the absence of headache.[55, 60] This suggests that other nonheadache symptoms are distinct features of the caffeine withdrawal syndrome that can occur independently of headache in people experiencing caffeine withdrawal.

Relationship Between Caffeine Withdrawal and Dose of Caffeine. Several studies have found that either the presence of caffeine withdrawal or its severity is more likely as the daily dose of caffeine is increased,[59, 61, 62, 71] although one study[60] did not find this to be the case. It has been shown that caffeine withdrawal can occur with surprisingly low doses of caffeine—as low as 100 mg/d in one study,[55] which is the equivalent of about one cup of brewed coffee or two to three caffeinated sodas per day (see Table 43–1).

Caffeine Withdrawal in Special Populations. There has been little work on the possible unique features of caffeine withdrawal in special populations such as the elderly. However, there has been one report of eight infants with suspected caffeine withdrawal born to mothers who had heavy caffeine consumption during their pregnancies (range, 200 to 1800 mg/d).[72] Symptoms began an average of 19 hours after birth; were primarily irritability, jitteriness, and vomiting; and resolved spontaneously.

Table 43–5 Differential Diagnosis of Caffeine Withdrawal

Initiation or cessation of another medication	Other general medical conditions (e.g., migraine headache, viral illness)
Amphetamine or cocaine withdrawal	Idiopathic drug reactions

Relationship Between Caffeine Withdrawal and Postoperative Headache. Studies in patients required to abstain from caffeine in preparation for an operative procedure have shown that a history of preoperative caffeine use greater than 400 mg/d is associated with an increased risk for postoperative headache[73] and that this risk may be dose related.[71, 74] In patients with a history of caffeine consumption who consumed a caffeinated beverage on the day of a surgical procedure, the rate of postoperative headaches was lower than in those who abstained.[63]

Assessment and Differential Diagnosis

The key step in establishing a diagnosis of caffeine withdrawal is to determine the history of the person's caffeine consumption (from all dietary sources) and then establish whether there has been a change in the pattern of the person's caffeine intake. Caffeine withdrawal is probably more common than is generally recognized, and it seems that there is a tendency for people to attribute the symptoms of caffeine withdrawal to other causes besides caffeine (e.g., influenza, having a bad day). Caffeine withdrawal may be particularly common in medical settings in which patients are required to abstain from food and fluids, such as before surgical procedures and certain diagnostic tests. In addition, caffeine withdrawal may occur in settings in which the use of caffeine-containing products is restricted or banned, such as inpatient psychiatric wards. Postoperative headache has been shown to be associated with the patient's history of caffeine consumption.[63, 71, 73]

Many general medical conditions can have signs and symptoms that are similar to those found in caffeine withdrawal. Differential diagnoses could include conditions as diverse as viral illnesses; sinus conditions; other types of headaches, such as migraine and tension; other drug withdrawal states, such as amphetamine or cocaine withdrawal; and idiopathic drug reactions (Table 43–5).

Course and Natural History (Prognosis)

Caffeine withdrawal generally begins within 12 to 24 hours after discontinuation of caffeine use. The peak of caffeine withdrawal generally occurs within 24 to 48 hours, and the duration of caffeine withdrawal is generally 2 days to about 1 week. An example of the time course of caffeine withdrawal symptoms is shown in Figure 43–1. In this study, four volunteers, who initially received 100 mg/d of caffeine in capsules, were switched under double-blind conditions to placebo for a period of 12 days.[55] Symptoms (headache; feelings of lethargy, fatigue, tiredness, or sluggishness; and impaired concentration) peaked on days 1 or 2 after placebo substitution and progressively returned toward prewithdrawal levels in about a week (Fig. 43–1).

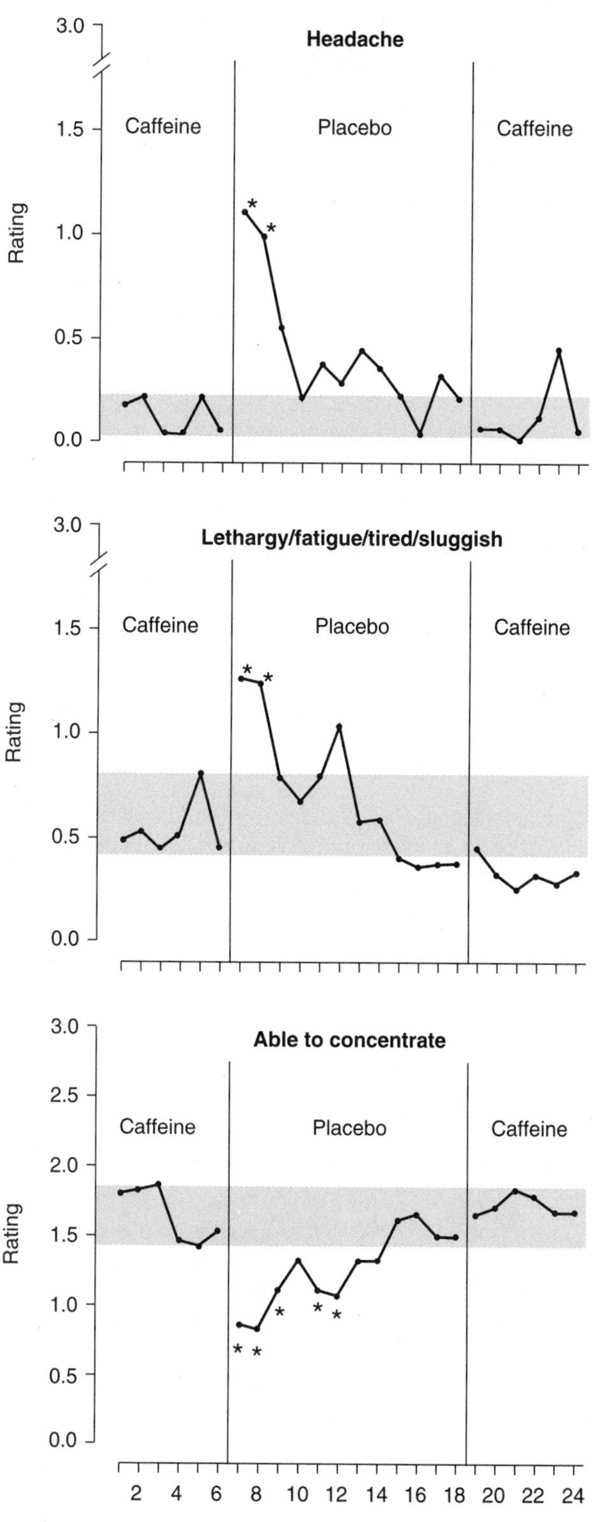

Figure 43–1 *Time course of caffeine withdrawal symptoms in four volunteers. Under double-blind conditions, subjects received capsules containing either 100 mg/d of caffeine or placebo. Assessments included subject ratings of headache; feelings of lethargy, fatigue, tiredness, or sluggishness; and ability to concentrate. Ratings ranged from 0 (not at all) to 3 (very much). Shaded areas indicate the range of means from the initial 6-day caffeine period. Asterisks indicate placebo days that are significantly different from the initial caffeine period* ($P \leq .05$). *(Data from Griffiths RR, Evans SM, Heishman SJ, et al: Low-dose caffeine physical dependence in humans. J Pharmacol Exp Ther 1990; 255:1123–1132.)*

There is considerable variability, both between people and within the same person across episodes, in the manifestations, time course, and severity of caffeine withdrawal. No studies have examined the possibility of a protracted caffeine withdrawal syndrome. Human and laboratory animal studies of caffeine withdrawal are reviewed elsewhere.[50, 51]

Treatment

There have been few studies attempting to address the treatment of caffeine withdrawal, although it has frequently been observed that the symptoms of caffeine withdrawal can be alleviated with the consumption of caffeine,[53] and this approach is probably best. There has been one report that experimentally induced caffeine withdrawal headaches responded to aspirin.[53] If the medical recommendation is made to eliminate or substantially reduce caffeine consumption, it may be useful to recommend a tapering dose schedule rather than abrupt discontinuation. Caffeine tapering (or "fading") is described in more detail in the section on caffeine dependence.

Clinical Vignette 1 • Caffeine Withdrawal

Ms. E, a 37-year-old married woman, presented with a chief complaint of episodic headaches, especially noted on weekends. Her family history was notable for alcoholism in her mother, but there was no other psychiatric illness in the family. She was a college graduate employed full-time as a clerk, had been married for 16 years, and had two healthy children. She met her husband in college and described her marriage as stable and her husband as supportive. She did not smoke tobacco, drank alcohol rarely (once every 2 to 3 months, typically one to two drinks), and did not use illicit drugs. Ms. E was not taking prescription medications, had no chronic medical illnesses, and had no past psychiatric history.

She reported that she began consuming caffeine by drinking soda as a child and regularly drank soda as she was growing up. She began drinking coffee in college and used coffee regularly when she needed to study late at night. Her current beverage of choice was coffee, which she drank without cream or sweetener, and she drank a total of five to six large mugs each day. There was a coffeepot in her office, and her first consumption of coffee was at work. She spaced her subsequent coffee use during the course of the day, with her last mug late in the afternoon at work. When she was scheduled for outpatient surgery, staff had considered canceling the procedure because of her headache after morning abstinence from caffeine. When pregnant, she had tried but had been unable to reduce her use of coffee.

She reported that she typically developed headaches in the late mornings or early afternoons and described them as diffuse, throbbing headaches that were bilateral. She had no aura, no photophobia, and no nausea or vomiting. The headaches were not clearly related to stress, and she thought they were primarily on weekends. Other symptoms associated with her headaches included feeling "dragged out," tired, and sleepy. She had tried taking aspirin and acetaminophen for the headaches and reported only partial relief with these medications. A work-up by her primary care physician revealed no disease that would account for her headaches.

Clinical Vignette 1 *continued*

On mental status examination, Ms. E was alert, appeared neatly and casually groomed, had good eye contact, and was neither psychomotor agitated nor retarded. Her speech was of normal rate and rhythm, and she had no evidence of a formal thought disorder. Her mood was good, she had a full range of expressed emotions, and she had no sleep or appetite problems. She had no evidence of delusions, hallucinations, obsessions, compulsions, or phobias and appeared to be cognitively intact and of average intelligence.

Ms. E's history of caffeine use and the nature of her headaches suggested that she might be experiencing caffeine withdrawal. On weekends, she would not drink coffee. She was counseled to try drinking a mug of coffee the next time she felt her characteristic headache, and she found this intervention produced full relief from her headache and also alleviated her feeling of lethargy. She then underwent a program of caffeine fading to decrease the overall amount of caffeine she was consuming. Once she achieved a steady level of one mug of coffee per day, she found she was able to skip a day of consuming coffee without experiencing a headache.

CAFFEINE DEPENDENCE

Definition

Before caffeine dependence by use of DSM-IV criteria is defined, it is useful to discuss the concept of dependence. In particular, it is helpful to distinguish *physical dependence* from a *clinical diagnosis of dependence.* Physical dependence is generally indicated by the presence of a withdrawal syndrome after cessation of use of the substance. A clinical diagnosis of dependence encompasses several features of pathological use of a psychoactive substance, which can include (but is not limited to) evidence of physical dependence. It is possible to exhibit physical dependence without fulfilling the criteria of a clinical dependence syndrome; the use of opioids in the treatment of cancer pain may provide an example of a patient who is physically dependent but who does not have a clinical syndrome of dependence. It is also possible to have a clinical syndrome of dependence but not be physically dependent; episodic binge alcohol use is an example of such a condition.

These distinctions between physical dependence and a clinical syndrome of dependence have often clouded discussions of caffeine dependence because there is ample evidence for a caffeine withdrawal syndrome suggesting that caffeine can produce physical dependence. However, there has been scant evidence that caffeine produces a clinical syndrome of dependence. Currently, DSM-IV uses a set of generic criteria to define a clinical syndrome of substance dependence. Notably, DSM-IV states, "A diagnosis of substance dependence can be applied to every class of substances except caffeine." This section discusses the current evidence for a caffeine dependence syndrome using the generic DSM-IV criteria.

DSM-IV Criteria

Substance Dependence

A maladaptive pattern of substance use, leading to clinically significant impairment or distress, as manifested by three (or more) of the following, occurring at any time in the same 12-month period:

(1) tolerance, as defined by either of the following:
   - (a) a need for markedly increased amounts of the substance to achieve intoxication or desired effect
   - (b) markedly diminished effect with continued use of the same amount of the substance

(2) withdrawal, as manifested by either of the following:
   - (a) the characteristic withdrawal syndrome for the substance (refer to criteria A and B of the criteria sets for withdrawal from the specific substances)
   - (b) the same (or a closely related) substance is taken to relieve or avoid withdrawal symptoms

(3) the substance is often taken in larger amounts or over a longer period than was intended

(4) there is a persistent desire or unsuccessful efforts to cut down or control substance use

(5) a great deal of time is spent in activities necessary to obtain the substance (e.g., visiting multiple doctors or driving long distances), use the substance (e.g., chain-smoking), or recover from its effects

(6) important social, occupational, or recreational activities are given up or reduced because of substance use

(7) the substance use is continued despite knowledge of having a persistent or recurrent physical or psychological problem that is likely to have been caused or exacerbated by the substance (e.g., current cocaine use despite recognition of cocaine-induced depression, or continued drinking despite recognition that an ulcer was made worse by alcohol consumption)

Epidemiology

Prevalence and Incidence

Caffeine is the most widely used psychoactive drug in the world. In the United States, it is estimated that more than 80% of adults consume caffeine on a daily basis,[2] and the average consumption among adults is approximately 211 mg/d[1]; among caffeine consumers, the average daily consumption is approximately 280 mg.[75] The average daily consumption in other countries can be considerably higher (Table 43–6).

Surprisingly, there is only one study of the prevalence of caffeine dependence based on standardized psychiatric criteria.[16] In this random telephone survey of residents of Vermont, 166 of the 202 surveyed participants reported current caffeine use. With employment of the generic DSM-III-R criteria for dependence, 27% of the 166 current caffeine users fulfilled criteria for a diagnosis of mild caffeine dependence (three or four criteria), 14% had moderate dependence (five or six criteria), and 3% had severe dependence (seven to nine criteria) in the previous year, whereas 58% did not fulfill criteria for caffeine dependence (zero to two criteria). The most commonly reported symptom of dependence was a persistent desire or one or more unsuccessful efforts to cut down or control caffeine use. Although preliminary in nature, these results suggest that there may be a large number of people who demonstrate symptoms consistent with a diagnosis of caffeine dependence based on DSM criteria, although limitations to the study (e.g., a telephone survey, a relatively small sample size) suggest that the results be viewed with caution.

Comorbidity Patterns

In a study by Strain and colleagues[76] that characterized DSM-IV diagnosed caffeine dependence in a population of 16 people initially self-identified as having problem caffeine use (the main results from this study are described in more detail later), it was found that two subjects (13%) had an additional current psychiatric diagnosis (both being anxiety disorders), and 69% had other psychiatric disorders in remission.[76] Most commonly, these other disorders were other psychoactive substance use disorders (63%), followed by mood disorders (44%), anxiety disorders (25%), or eating disorders (19%). Among the psychoactive substance use disorders, the most commonly abused substance was alcohol; 57% of the participants in the study had a past diagnosis of alcohol abuse or dependence. Five of the subjects in the study (32%) were nicotine cigarette smokers, and notably, four of these five had a history of an alcohol disorder (suggesting a clustering of caffeine dependence, smoking, and alcohol abuse or dependence). The tendency for these disorders to cluster has been previously noted,[31, 32] and the prevalence of caffeine dependence may increase as a function of the severity of the alcohol dependence.[77]

Table 43–6 Average Daily Caffeine Use in Different Countries*

Country	Average per Capita Daily Consumption (mg)
United States	211
Canada	238
Sweden	425
United Kingdom	444
World	70

*For 1981 or 1982.

Data from Gilbert RM: Caffeine consumption. In Spiller GA (ed): The Methylxanthine Beverages and Foods: Chemistry, Consumption, and Health Effects. New York: Alan R Liss, 1984:185–213.

Whereas the results of the Strain study[76] suggest high rates of comorbid conditions in people diagnosed with caffeine dependence by use of DSM-IV criteria, it should be pointed out that this study was of a small population that was self-identified as having problem caffeine use. Further studies with larger and more representative samples may demonstrate lower rates or a different pattern for the comorbid conditions found in people with caffeine dependence.

Etiology

There have been few studies examining the characteristics of caffeine dependence, and no studies have attempted to determine the etiology of caffeine dependence in subjects who fulfill specific criteria for the diagnosis. However, the *consumption* of caffeine may be influenced by several different factors, which are summarized here. Whereas these factors may help explain a predisposition to use of caffeine, it is not known whether or how they may relate to caffeine dependence.

Caffeine's Subjective Effects and Reinforcement. Several studies have shown that caffeine in low to moderate doses (20 to 200 mg) produces mild positive subjective effects of increased feelings of well-being, alertness, energy, concentration, self-confidence, motivation for work, and desire to talk to people[78, 79] and decreased feelings of being tired and sleepy.[80] However, higher doses (e.g., 800 mg) produce negative subjective effects, such as anxiety and nervousness, especially in people who have abstained from caffeine.[80–82] Caffeine has also been shown to function as a reinforcer in humans, that is, when given the choice under experimental conditions, some people consistently choose to consume caffeine rather than placebo.[60, 80, 83–86] This profile of positive subjective and reinforcing effects may help explain the wide and regular consumption of caffeine-containing substances. However, not everyone uses caffeine, and it appears that some people tend to prefer caffeine and others do not. Caffeine choosers tend to report positive subjective effects from caffeine, whereas nonchoosers report negative subjective effects,[87, 88] and people who have symptoms of caffeine withdrawal are more likely to choose to consume caffeine when given the choice.[60]

Caffeine Tolerance. Tolerance to the subjective effects of caffeine has been demonstrated to develop after 18 days in an experimental study of subjects maintained on daily caffeine.[87] Similarly, tolerance to the sleep-disrupting effects of caffeine occurs after 7 days of caffeine dosing,[89] and although acute doses of caffeine in nondependent subjects can cause mild increases in blood pressure, tolerance develops to this pressor effect within 3 days.[90, 91] Acute doses of caffeine in nondependent subjects can also produce increases in plasma epinephrine, norepinephrine, renin, and urinary catecholamines, but tolerance to these changes in humoral factors also occurs with chronic caffeine dosing.[91] Whereas tolerance has been shown for both subjective and physiological effects of caffeine, it is not clear what role the development of tolerance may have in the development of clinical dependence on caffeine.

Caffeine Withdrawal. Caffeine withdrawal, described in detail in the preceding section, is a distinct clinical syndrome characterized by signs and symptoms such as headache, sleepiness and drowsiness, impaired concentration, lassitude, work difficulty, depression, anxiety, irritability, nausea and vomiting, and muscle aches and stiffness (see Table 43–3). Caffeine consumption alleviates caffeine withdrawal symptoms,[53] and people who have symptoms of caffeine withdrawal are more likely to choose caffeine when given a choice,[60] suggesting that caffeine consumption in people with caffeine dependence may be related in part to the avoidance of caffeine withdrawal symptoms.

Genetics and Caffeine Use. Several twin studies of caffeine use have demonstrated a higher concordance rate for monozygotic versus dizygotic twins for coffee consumption, suggesting some genetic predisposition to coffee use,[92–95] and one study has reported that monozygotic twins with an affective disorder have a high concordance for reported sleep difficulties induced by caffeine.[96] However, twin studies of caffeine use have typically examined only coffee use (not all caffeine use) and have focused on caffeine use rather than caffeine dependence. Finally, it is of interest to note that there may be some genetic influence on taste sensitivity to caffeine.[97]

Increased Caffeine Use in Selected Populations. Several groups may have higher amounts of caffeine consumption than the general population.

1. Smokers: Higher amounts of caffeine are consumed by smokers,[98] and this increased consumption may reflect enhanced metabolism of caffeine in smokers.[29, 99]
2. Prisoners: In one study of prisoners, 93% were found to consume caffeine, with an average daily consumption estimated to be 805 mg.[100] Notably, this population also had high rates of smoking tobacco (79%).
3. Psychiatric patients: Surveys of psychiatric patients (typically inpatients) have found high rates of caffeine consumption. In one study, 22% consumed more than 750 mg/d[101]; in another study, the average consumption was 503 mg[102]; in a third study, 25% of patients were reported to consume five or more cups of coffee per day.[13]
4. Patients with alcoholism: There is evidence to suggest that the level of caffeine use is predictive of alcohol abuse,[32] and the prevalence of caffeine dependence increases as the severity of alcohol dependence increases,[77] although a review of the relationship between caffeine and alcohol use suggests it may be relatively weak.[31]

Other groups at risk may include substance abusers[18] and patients with anorexia nervosa.[17]

Caffeine Use, Age, Sex, and Race. There is little information about the use of caffeine as a function of age, sex, or race. One telephone survey found that older subjects used more caffeine on a daily basis.[103] Results from the Nationwide Food Consumption Survey conducted in the United States indicated that a greater percentage of whites than African-Americans consume coffee and tea, but not soft drinks (although this survey does not distinguish between caffeinated and noncaffeinated beverages).[104] This same survey indicated that there are no marked differences in rates of coffee, tea, or soft drink use for men versus women.[104]

Caffeine Use and Personality. The wide use of caffeine suggests that it is extremely unlikely that a single personality type might be associated with caffeine use. There are few systematic studies examining the possible relationship between caffeine use and particular personality types.

Summary. Whereas preliminary work suggests that there may be some factors (such as heritability) contributing to the predisposition to use caffeine, no studies have examined the possible etiological role of such factors in the development of caffeine dependence as a specific diagnosis. Caffeine dependence, like other drug dependence syndromes, in all likelihood represents the interaction of social and cultural forces, and individual histories and predispositions, operating in the context of a psychoactive substance that produces pleasant subjective effects and is reinforcing. A particular value to understanding the etiology of caffeine dependence may be the light it sheds on the understanding of drug dependence syndromes generally.

Pathophysiology

As noted in the section on caffeine withdrawal, caffeine's primary mechanism of action at typical daily doses appears to be that of an adenosine antagonist.[41, 42] However, the extent to which adenosine antagonism contributes to the caffeine dependence syndrome is not known.

Diagnosis and Differential Diagnosis

Phenomenology and Variations in Presentation

There is little information available about caffeine dependence as a distinct clinical syndrome. In the one study that characterized the features of caffeine dependence in a sample of 16 subjects using a standardized structured clinical interview, only four of the seven DSM-IV criteria were used to make the diagnosis of dependence.[76] Ninety-four percent of the subjects fulfilled criterion 2 (withdrawal), 94% fulfilled criterion 7 (use continued despite knowledge of having a persistent or recurrent physical or psychological problem that is likely to have been caused or exacerbated by the substance use), 81% fulfilled criterion 4 (persistent desire or unsuccessful efforts to cut down or control substance use), and 75% fulfilled criterion 1 (tolerance). In the telephone survey conducted by Hughes and colleagues[16] that has previously been described, and which used DSM-III-R criteria for dependence, the most commonly reported criterion in the previous year was a persistent desire or unsuccessful efforts to cut down or control substance use (reported by 51%).

Assessment and Differential Diagnosis

Caffeine dependence may be an unrecognized condition with a higher prevalence than is generally appreciated. Psychiatrists do not typically think to inquire about caffeine use and about problem use consistent with a diagnosis of caffeine dependence. However, probing for evidence of caffeine dependence may be useful, and it would be reasonable to focus on the DSM-IV criteria for dependence that are more appropriate for a substance that is widely available and generally culturally accepted. Thus, the psychiatrist should probe for evidence of tolerance, withdrawal, continued use despite a physician's recommendation that the person reduce or stop using caffeine, use despite other problems associated with caffeine, use of often larger amounts or for a longer period than intended, or persistent desires or difficulties in decreasing or discontinuing use.

Course and Natural History (Prognosis)

Although no studies have specifically examined its course and natural history, caffeine dependence appears to be a chronic relapsing disorder like other drug dependence syndromes.[105] In the Strain study[76] described before, caffeine-dependent participants reported recurrent efforts to discontinue caffeine use, with failures to discontinue use or frequent relapses.

Treatment

In a survey of physicians' practices, it was found that more than 75% of medical specialists recommended that patients reduce or eliminate caffeine for certain conditions including anxiety, insomnia, arrhythmias, palpitations and tachycardia, esophagitis or hiatal hernia, and fibrocystic disease.[106] However, stopping caffeine use can be difficult for some people. For example, in the diagnostic study of caffeine dependence,[76] subjects reported physical conditions such as acne rosacea, pregnancy, palpitations, and gastrointestinal problems that led physicians to recommend that they reduce or eliminate caffeine; all reported that they were unable to follow their physicians' recommendations.

Whereas no systematic studies have examined the treatment of people with a clearly established diagnosis of caffeine dependence, there have been case reports of the treatment of people with problem caffeine use[107–109] and one controlled study of the treatment of excessive caffeine use with caffeine tapering or fading.[110] These reports have generally described success with a combination of gradual tapering of caffeine, self-monitoring of daily caffeine use, and reinforcement for decreased use. In attempting to reduce or eliminate caffeine use, several steps may be useful (Table 43–7). During caffeine tapering, it may be useful for patients to consume extra noncaffeinated fluids, to avoid herbal preparations that contain caffeine or other psychoactive drugs, to avoid the use of anxiolytics, and to maintain a diary throughout the time they are progressively decreasing their caffeine use to monitor their progress. Abrupt cessation of caffeine should be avoided to minimize withdrawal symptoms and increase the likelihood of long-term compliance with the dietary change.

Table 43–7 A Method for Eliminating or Reducing Caffeine Use

Step 1: Use a daily diary to have the person identify all sources of caffeine in the diet, including different forms (i.e., brewed versus instant coffee) and doses, for 1 wk.

Step 2: Calculate the total milligrams of caffeine consumed on a daily basis.

Step 3: With the collaboration of the patient, generate a graded dose reduction (i.e., fading schedule) of caffeine use. Reasonable decreases would be 10% of the initial dose every few days. Allow for individualization of the caffeine fading. Rather than attempting to progressively eliminate consumption of the preferred caffeine beverage, it may be useful to suggest that the patient substitute decaffeinated for caffeinated beverages. In the case of coffee or tea, caffeine fading can be accomplished by mixing caffeinated and decaffeinated beverages and progressively increasing the proportion of decaffeinated beverage. It may be useful to have patients maintain a diary throughout the time they are progressively decreasing their caffeine use to monitor their progress.

Clinical Vignette 2 • Caffeine Dependence

Mr. S, a 32-year-old single man, presented with a chief complaint of problems controlling his caffeine use. His family history was notable for a major depressive episode in a sister and posttraumatic stress disorder in a brother who had served in Vietnam. He was a college graduate employed full-time as a nurse. He smoked a pack of cigarettes a day, drank alcohol in moderation, and occasionally used nonsteroidal antiinflammatory medication for low back pain resulting from a motor vehicle accident when he was in his early 20s. He was not taking regular prescription medications. He had taken opioids for several months after the motor vehicle accident and felt he may have been "on the verge of abusing them." However, he discontinued their use when he realized his reliance on them and had not used opioids since that time.

He tried a caffeinated beverage (coffee) at age 12 years but did not like it and did not currently drink coffee. However, he started drinking caffeinated soda regularly in nursing school when he would need to work evening or night shifts. His current consumption included seven to eight 16-oz bottles of caffeinated soda per day. He typically had his first soda within 10 to 15 minutes after arising in the morning and then spaced his consumption during the course of the day (with his last use in the evening). Physicians had recommended that he cut down or stop his caffeine use because of complaints of gastrointestinal problems and palpitations, but he had been unable to do so. His roommate had frequently objected to his caffeine use, and Mr. S had responded by decreasing the amount he drank at home and increasing the amount he drank at other locations, such as work. He had attempted to quit by abruptly terminating his soda use on several occasions but always relapsed because of headache and fatigue. He drank soda in his car and had a minor car accident once while drinking soda when driving. Mr. S also frequently drank and spilled soda in bed.

On mental status examination, Mr. S was alert, appeared neatly groomed, and sat quietly in his chair. He had good eye contact and was neither psychomotor agitated nor retarded. His speech was of normal rate and rhythm, and he had no evidence of a formal thought disorder. His mood was generally good, although he felt his roommate's concern about his soda drinking was becoming stressful, and his failed attempts to cut back on caffeine use were becoming frustrating. He had a full range of expressed emotions and had no sleep or appetite problems. He had no evidence of delusions, hallucinations, obsessions, compulsions, or phobias and appeared to be cognitively intact and of above-average intelligence.

Because of Mr. S's problems with his caffeine use, a plan was generated to attempt to decrease his caffeine use over a period of several weeks. Mr. S began by maintaining a daily diary documenting all of his caffeine consumption and then attempted to gradually taper his caffeine use by switching to decaffeinated sodas. Whereas

Clinical Vignette 2 *continued*

this was initially successful, he eventually relapsed to his previous level of caffeine use.

CAFFEINE-INDUCED ANXIETY DISORDER

Definition

In addition to the symptom of anxiety that can be a component of caffeine intoxication and caffeine withdrawal, caffeine can also produce a distinct anxiety disorder, caffeine-induced anxiety disorder.[3] The concept of a specific and separate diagnostic category for a caffeine-induced anxiety disorder is a new feature of DSM-IV, and there has been no work using this specific set of diagnostic criteria. However, there have been several studies examining the relationship between caffeine and anxiety in general, and this work is reviewed here.

Substance-induced anxiety disorders in general are distinguished by prominent anxiety symptoms that are directly related to a psychoactive substance.[3] Whereas the form of the disorder can resemble panic disorder, generalized anxiety disorder, social phobia, or obsessive-compulsive disorder, a patient with a substance-induced anxiety disorder does not need to manifest all the diagnostic criteria of one of these conditions to fulfill the diagnosis of a substance-induced anxiety disorder.

Epidemiology

Prevalence and Incidence

There are no specific data on the prevalence or incidence of caffeine-induced anxiety disorder.

Comorbidity Patterns

Several studies have examined the relationship between caffeine consumption and anxiety disorders. Interestingly, patients with anxiety disorders generally have lower levels of caffeine consumption compared with patients without an anxiety disorder,[26, 111, 112] and self-reports by patients with anxiety disorders versus control subjects show greater anxiety scores after the acute consumption of caffeine,[26, 111] suggesting that some people (such as patients with an anxiety disorder) may avoid caffeine use because of anxiety effects produced by caffeine. However, results from the National Center for Health Statistics Health and Nutrition Examination Survey found no significant association between the number of cups of coffee or tea consumed per day and the self-reported level of anxiety.[113]

Among those patients with an anxiety disorder, it appears that patients with generalized anxiety disorder[27] as well as patients with panic disorder[26, 114] may be more sensitive to the anxiogenic effects of caffeine. However, this relationship between caffeine and anxiety is complicated and may be a function of the dose of caffeine being used as a challenge in patients with an anxiety disorder. For example, panic attacks have been induced in normal control subjects challenged with sufficiently high doses of caffeine.[115]

Finally, it has also been shown that patients with high caffeine consumption have higher rates of minor tranquilizer use (benzodiazepine or meprobamate) than patients with moderate or low caffeine use.[116] It is not known whether some patients consume higher levels of caffeine to antagonize the sedative effects of minor tranquilizers, whether minor tranquilizers are prescribed in response to the anxiogenic effects produced by higher doses of caffeine,[117] or whether some underlying factor (e.g., personality) may account for the increased use of caffeine and minor tranquilizers together.

DSM-IV Criteria

Substance-Induced Anxiety Disorder

A. Prominent anxiety, panic attacks, or obsessions or compulsions predominate in the clinical picture.

B. There is evidence from the history, physical examination, or laboratory findings of either (1) or (2):

(1) the symptoms in criterion A developed during, or within 1 month of, substance intoxication or withdrawal

(2) medication use is etiologically related to the disturbance

C. The disturbance is not better accounted for by an anxiety disorder that is not substance induced. Evidence that the symptoms are better accounted for by an anxiety disorder that is not substance induced might include the following: the symptoms precede the onset of the substance use (or medication use); the symptoms persist for a substantial period of time (e.g., about a month) after the cessation of acute withdrawal or severe intoxication or are substantially in excess of what would be expected given the type or amount of the substance use or the duration of use; or there is other evidence suggesting the existence of an independent non–substance-induced anxiety disorder (e.g., a history of recurrent non–substance-related episodes).

D. The disturbance does not occur exclusively during the course of a delirium.

E. The disturbance causes clinically significant distress or impairment in social, occupational, or other important areas of functioning.

Note: This diagnosis should be made instead of a diagnosis of substance intoxication or substance withdrawal only when the anxiety symptoms are in excess of those usually associated with the intoxication or withdrawal syndrome and when the anxiety symptoms are sufficiently severe to warrant independent clinical attention.

Etiology and Pathophysiology

Caffeine-induced anxiety disorder by definition is etiologically related to caffeine. Acute doses of caffeine produce decreases in cerebral blood flow,[69] increases in cortisol,[114, 115] and changes on the electroencephalogram.[27, 118] Caffeine's primary mechanism of action appears to be that of an adenosine antagonist[41, 42] (see section on caffeine intoxication).

Diagnosis and Differential Diagnosis

The diagnosis of caffeine-induced anxiety disorder is based on evidence of an anxiety disorder etiologically related to caffeine. Uhde and coworkers[115] pointed out that excessive acute caffeine consumption mimics panic attacks; chronic caffeine consumption may mimic generalized anxiety.[119]

Other diagnostic considerations besides caffeine-induced anxiety disorder include caffeine intoxication and caffeine withdrawal, a primary anxiety disorder, and an anxiety disorder due to a general medical condition. Caffeine-induced anxiety disorder can occur in the context of caffeine intoxication or caffeine withdrawal, but the anxiety symptoms associated with the caffeine-induced anxiety disorder should be excessive relative to the anxiety seen in caffeine intoxication or caffeine withdrawal.[3] In addition to these conditions, substance-induced anxiety disorder can be produced by a variety of other psychoactive substances (e.g., cocaine).

Course and Natural History (Prognosis)

There is no known information on the course or natural history of caffeine-induced anxiety disorder.

Treatment

Although there are no studies on the treatment of caffeine-induced anxiety disorder, guidelines for treatment should generally follow those recommended for the treatment of caffeine dependence (see earlier). Thus, an initial, careful assessment of caffeine consumption should be conducted, and a program of gradual decreasing caffeine use should be instituted (see Table 43–7). Abrupt cessation of caffeine use should be avoided to minimize withdrawal symptoms and to increase the likelihood of long-term compliance with the dietary change. Given the etiological role of caffeine in caffeine-induced anxiety disorder, the prudent course of treatment would avoid the use of pharmacological agents such as benzodiazepines for the treatment of the anxiety disorder until caffeine use has been eliminated.

CAFFEINE-INDUCED SLEEP DISORDER

Definition

Psychoactive substances can produce sleep disorders distinct from the sleep disturbances associated with intoxication or withdrawal conditions produced by that substance.[3] It has long been recognized that caffeine-containing products can produce sleep disturbances, primarily in the form of insomnia. For example, Chavanne[120] wrote in 1911 that "black coffee will make some people lie awake and try to stare through the ceiling . . . ." Although caffeine primarily produces insomnia, there are case reports of hypersomnia associated with caffeine use.[121]

The primary feature of a substance-induced sleep disorder is a sleep disturbance directly related to a psychoactive substance.[3] The form of the disorder can be insomnia, hypersomnia, parasomnia, or mixed, although caffeine typically produces insomnia. In general, sleep disturbance can often be a feature of substance intoxication or withdrawal (although sleep disturbance does not typically occur with caffeine withdrawal), and caffeine-induced sleep dis-

DSM-IV Criteria

Substance-Induced Sleep Disorder

A. A prominent disturbance in sleep that is sufficiently severe to warrant independent clinical attention.

B. There is evidence from the history, physical examination, or laboratory findings of either (1) or (2):

(1) the symptoms in criterion A developed during, or within a month of, substance intoxication or withdrawal

(2) medication use is etiologically related to the sleep disturbance

C. The disturbance is not better accounted for by a sleep disorder that is not substance induced. Evidence that the symptoms are better accounted for by a sleep disorder that is not substance induced might include the following: the symptoms precede the onset of the substance use (or medication use); the symptoms persist for a substantial period of time (e.g., about a month) after the cessation of acute withdrawal or severe intoxication, or are substantially in excess of what would be expected given the type or amount of the substance used or the duration of use; or there is other evidence that suggests the existence of an independent non–substance-induced sleep disorder (e.g., a history of recurrent non–substance-related episodes).

D. The disturbance does not occur exclusively during the course of a delirium.

E. The sleep disturbance causes clinically significant distress or impairment in social, occupational, or other important areas of functioning.

Note: This diagnosis should be made instead of a diagnosis of substance intoxication or substance withdrawal only when the sleep symptoms are in excess of those usually associated with the intoxication or withdrawal syndrome and when the symptoms are sufficiently severe to warrant independent clinical attention.

order should be diagnosed in patients who are having caffeine intoxication only if the symptoms of the sleep disturbance are excessive relative to what would typically be expected.

Epidemiology

Prevalence, Incidence, and Comorbidity Patterns

There are no specific data on the prevalence, incidence, or comorbidity patterns of caffeine-induced sleep disorder.

Etiology and Pathophysiology

Caffeine-induced sleep disorder by definition is etiologically related to caffeine. Caffeine's effects on sleep can depend on a variety of factors, such as the dose of caffeine ingested, the individual's tolerance to caffeine, the time between caffeine ingestion and attempted sleep onset, and the ingestion of other psychoactive substances. In general, acute doses of caffeine in the evening produce reports of poorer sleep quality and delay the onset of sleep.[89, 122–126] For example, in a study of subjects who consumed a capsule containing either placebo or 200 mg of caffeine before their usual bedtime, average time to sleep onset was 44 minutes after placebo and 77 minutes after caffeine.[123] Interestingly, for some subjects in this study, sleep onset after caffeine ingestion was delayed up to 240 minutes.

In addition to these effects, caffeine can produce alterations in the onset of rapid eye movement sleep, the total sleep time, and the characteristics of non–rapid eye movement sleep,[89, 124–126] although these effects may depend on the dose of caffeine and individual differences in sensitivity to caffeine. The mechanism for caffeine-induced sleep disorder is not known, although caffeine's primary action appears to be that of an adenosine antagonist (as described in the section on caffeine intoxication).

Diagnosis and Differential Diagnosis

The diagnosis of a caffeine-induced sleep disorder is based on evidence of a sleep disorder etiologically related to caffeine. Other diagnostic considerations include caffeine intoxication and caffeine withdrawal, a primary sleep disorder, insomnia or hypersomnia related to another mental disorder, and a sleep disorder due to a general medical condition.[3] A caffeine-induced sleep disorder can occur in the context of caffeine intoxication or caffeine withdrawal, but the sleep symptoms associated with the caffeine-induced sleep disorder should be excessive relative to the sleep disturbance seen in caffeine intoxication or caffeine withdrawal.[3]

Course and Natural History (Prognosis)

There is little information available on the course or natural history of caffeine-induced sleep disorder. Sleep disturbances due to caffeine are more likely to occur in people who are not regular caffeine consumers.[122] In a study of caffeine use as a model of acute and chronic insomnia, subjects maintained on a high dose of caffeine (1200 mg/d) for 1 week demonstrated some adaptation to the sleep-altering effects of caffeine.[89] Thus, caffeine-induced sleep disorder may be a time-limited condition that reflects relatively acute responses to the effects of caffeine.

Treatment

There are no studies on the treatment of caffeine-induced sleep disorder. As for other conditions associated with caffeine use, such as caffeine dependence, caffeine intoxication, and caffeine-induced anxiety disorder, general guidelines for caffeine reduction can be recommended. These include an initial assessment of total caffeine consumption followed by a program of gradually decreasing caffeine use (see Table 43–7). Abrupt cessation of caffeine use should be avoided to minimize withdrawal symptoms and to increase the likelihood of long-term compliance with the dietary change. Given the etiological role of caffeine in caffeine-induced sleep disorder, the use of pharmacological agents or other interventions to improve sleep should be avoided until an adequate trial off of caffeine establishes the presence of a non–caffeine-related sleep disorder.

References

1. Gilbert RM: Caffeine consumption. In Spiller GA (ed): The Methylxanthine Beverages and Foods: Chemistry, Consumption, and Health Effects. New York: Alan R Liss, 1984:185–213.
2. Graham DM: Caffeine—its identity, dietary sources, intake and biologic effects. Nutr Rev 1978; 36:97–102.
3. American Psychiatric Association: Diagnostic and Statistical Manual of Mental Disorders, 4th ed. Washington, DC: American Psychiatric Association, 1994.
4. Rugh JT: Profound toxic effects from the drinking of large amounts of strong coffee. Med Surg Reporter 1896; 75:549–550.
5. Bram I: The truth about coffee drinking. Med Summary 1913;35: 168–173.
6. Bullard WN: The relation of tea drinking to disorders of the nervous system. Med Commun Mass Med Soc 1889; 14:71–87.
7. Cole J: On the deleterious effects produced by drinking tea and coffee in excessive quantities. Lancet 1833; 2:274–278.
8. King E: Tea and coffee intoxication. Am Med 1903; 5:182–183.
9. Love IN: Coffee, its use and abuse. JAMA 1891; 16:219–221.
10. Orendorff O: A caffeine addict with asthenopic symptoms. JAMA 1914; 62:1828–1829.
11. Powers H: The syndrome of coffee. Med J Rec 1925; 121:745–747.
12. Furlong FW: Possible psychiatric significance of excessive caffeine consumption. Can Psychiatry Assoc J 1975; 20:577–583.
13. Winstead DK: Coffee consumption among psychiatric inpatients. Am J Psychiatry 1976; 133:1447–1450.
14. Gilliland K, Andress D: Ad lib caffeine consumption, symptoms of caffeinism, and academic performance. Am J Psychiatry 1981; 138:512–514.
15. Bradley JR, Petree A: Caffeine consumption, expectancies of caffeine-enhancing performance, and caffeinism symptoms among university students. J Drug Educ 1990; 20:319–328.
16. Hughes JR, Oliveto AH, Helzer JE, et al: Indications of caffeine dependence in a population-based sample. NIDA Res Monogr 1993; 132:194.
17. Sours JA: Case reports of anorexia nervosa and caffeinism. Am J Psychiatry 1983; 140:235–236.
18. Russ NW, Sturgis ET, Malcolm RJ, et al: Abuse of caffeine in substance abusers. J Clin Psychiatry 1988; 49:457.
19. Greden JF: Anxiety or caffeinism: A diagnostic dilemma. Am J Psychiatry 1974; 131:1089–1092.
20. Benson JI, David JJ: Coffee eating in chronic schizophrenia patients. Am J Psychiatry 1986; 143:940–941.
21. DeFreitas B, Schwartz G: Effects of caffeine in chronic psychiatric patients. Am J Psychiatry 1979; 136:1337–1338.
22. Mikkelsen EJ: Caffeine and schizophrenia. J Clin Psychiatry 1978; 39:732–735.
23. Tondo L, Rudas N: The course of a seasonal bipolar disorder influenced by caffeine. J Affect Disord 1991; 22:249–251.
24. Zaslove MO, Russell RL, Ross E: Effect of caffeine intake on psychotic in-patients. Br J Psychiatry 1991; 159:565–567.
25. Lee MA, Flegel P, Greden JF, et al: Anxiogenic effects of caffeine on panic and depressed patients. Am J Psychiatry 1988; 145:632–635.
26. Boulenger JP, Uhde TW, Wolff EA, et al: Increased sensitivity to

caffeine in patients with panic disorder. Arch Gen Psychiatry 1984; 41:1067–1071.
27. Bruce M, Scott N, Shine P, et al: Anxiogenic effects of caffeine in patients with anxiety disorders. Arch Gen Psychiatry 1992; 49:867–869.
28. Brown CR, Jacob P, Wilson M, et al: Changes in rate and pattern of caffeine metabolism after cigarette abstinence. Clin Pharmacol Ther 1988; 43:488–491.
29. Parsons WD, Niems AH: Effect of smoking on caffeine clearance. Clin Pharmacol Ther 1978; 24:40–45.
30. Doucette SR, Willoughby A: Relevance of caffeine symptomatology to alcohol rehabilitation efforts. US Navy Med 1980; 10:6–13.
31. Istvan J, Matarazzo JD: Tobacco, alcohol, and caffeine use: A review of their interrelationships. Psychol Bull 1984; 95:301–326.
32. Kozlowski LT, Henningfield JE, Keenan RM, et al: Patterns of alcohol, cigarette, and caffeine and other drug use in two drug abusing populations. J Subst Abuse Treat 1993; 10:171–179.
33. Stillner V, Popkin MK, Pierce CM: Caffeine-induced delirium during prolonged competitive stress. Am J Psychiatry 1978; 135:855–856.
34. McManamy MC, Schube PG: Caffeine intoxication: Report of a case the symptoms of which amounted to a psychosis. N Engl J Med 1936; 215:616–620.
35. Shen WW, D'Souze TC: Cola-induced psychotic organic brain syndrome. Rocky Mount Med J 1979; 76:312–313.
36. Garriott JC, Simmons LM, Poklis A, et al: Five cases of fatal overdose from caffeine-containing "look-alike" drugs. J Anal Toxicol 1985; 9:141–143.
37. Mrvos RM, Reilly PE, Dean BS, et al: Massive caffeine ingestion resulting in death. Vet Hum Toxicol 1989; 31:571–572.
38. Turner JE, Cravey RH: A fatal ingestion of caffeine. Clin Toxicol 1977; 10:341–344.
39. Bryant J: Suicide by ingestion of caffeine. Arch Pathol Lab Med 1981; 105:685–686.
40. Nagesh RV, Murphey KA: Caffeine poisoning treated by hemoperfusion. Am J Kidney Dis 1988; 12:316–318.
41. Nehlig A, Daval J, Debry G: Caffeine and the central nervous system: Mechanism of action, biochemical, metabolic and psychostimulant effects. Brain Res Rev 1992; 17:139–170.
42. Snyder SH, Katims JJ, Annau Z, et al: Adenosine receptors and behavioral actions of methylxanthines. Proc Natl Acad Sci USA 1981; 78:3260–3264.
43. Barraco RA: Behavioral actions of adenosine and related substances. In Phillis JW (ed): Adenosine and Adenine Nucleotides as Regulators of Cellular Function. Boca Raton, FL: CRC Press, 1991:339–366.
44. Victor BS, Lubetsky M, Greden JF: Somatic manifestations of caffeinism. J Clin Psychiatry 1981; 42:185–188.
45. Reimann HA: Caffeinism: A cause of long-continued, low-grade fever. JAMA 1967; 202:131–132.
46. Shirlow MJ, Mathers CD: A study of caffeine consumption and symptoms: Indigestion, palpitations, tremor, headache and insomnia. Int J Epidemiol 1985; 14:239–248.
47. Stoffer SS: Coffee consumption. Arch Intern Med 1979; 139:1194–1195.
48. Balogh A, Harder S, Vollandt R, et al: Intra-individual variability of caffeine elimination in healthy subjects. Int J Clin Pharmacol 1992; 30:383–387.
49. Bridge N: Coffee-drinking as a frequent cause of disease. Trans Assoc Am Physicians 1893; 8:281–288.
50. Griffiths RR, Woodson PP: Caffeine physical dependence: A review of human and laboratory animal studies. Psychopharmacology (Berl) 1988; 94:437–451.
51. Griffiths RR, Mumford GK: Caffeine—a drug of abuse? In Bloom FE, Kupfer DJ (eds): Psychopharmacology: The Fourth Generation of Progress. New York: Raven Press, 1995:1699–1713.
52. Hughes JR: Caffeine withdrawal, dependence, and abuse. In Widiger TA, Frances AJ, Pincus HA, et al (eds): DSM-IV Sourcebook. Washington, DC: American Psychiatric Association, 1994:129–134.
53. Dreisbach RH, Pfeiffer C: Caffeine-withdrawal headache. J Lab Clin Med 1943; 28:1212–1219.
54. Griffiths RR, Bigelow GE, Liebson IA: Human coffee drinking: Reinforcing and physical dependence producing effects of caffeine. J Pharmacol Exp Ther 1986; 239:416–425.
55. Griffiths RR, Evans SM, Heishman SJ, et al: Low-dose caffeine physical dependence in humans. J Pharmacol Exp Ther 1990; 255:1123–1132.
56. Hughes JR, Higgins ST, Bickel WK, et al: Caffeine self-administration, withdrawal, and adverse effects among coffee drinkers. Arch Gen Psychiatry 1991; 48:611–617.
57. Roller L: Caffeinism: Subjective quantitative aspect of withdrawal syndrome. Med J Aust 1981; 1:146.
58. van Dusseldorp M, Katan MB: Headache caused by caffeine withdrawal among moderate coffee drinkers switched from ordinary to decaffeinated coffee: A 12 week double-blind trial. BMJ 1990; 300:1558–1559.
59. Silverman K, Evans SM, Strain EC, et al: Withdrawal syndrome after the double-blind cessation of caffeine consumption. N Engl J Med 1992; 327:1109–1114.
60. Hughes JR, Oliveto AH, Bickel WK, et al: Caffeine self-administration and withdrawal: Incidence, individual differences and interrelationships. Drug Alcohol Depend 1993; 32:239–246.
61. Goldstein A, Kaizer S: Psychotropic effects of caffeine in man. III. A questionnaire survey of coffee drinking and its effects in a group of housewives. Clin Pharmacol Ther 1969; 10:477–488.
62. Evans SM, Griffiths RR: Low-dose caffeine physical dependence in normal subjects: Dose-related effects. NIDA Res Monogr 1991; 105:446.
63. Weber JG, Ereth MH, Danielson DR: Perioperative ingestion of caffeine and postoperative headache. Mayo Clin Proc 1993; 68: 842–845.
64. Biaggioni I, Paul S, Puckett A, et al: Caffeine and theophylline as adenosine receptor antagonists in humans. J Pharmacol Exp Ther 1991; 258:588–593.
65. Green RM, Stiles GL: Chronic caffeine ingestion sensitizes the A_1 adenosine receptor–adenylate cyclase system in rat cerebral cortex. J Clin Invest 1986; 77:222–227.
66. Paul S, Kurunwune B, Biaggioni I: Caffeine withdrawal: Apparent heterologous sensitization to adenosine and prostacyclin actions in human platelets. J Pharmacol Exp Ther 1993; 267:838–843.
67. Mathew RJ, Barr DL, Weinman ML: Caffeine and cerebral blood flow. Br J Psychiatry 1983; 143:604–608.
68. Mathew RJ, Wilson WH: Caffeine consumption, withdrawal and cerebral blood flow. Headache 1985; 25:305–309.
69. Mathew RJ, Wilson WH: Substance abuse and cerebral blood flow. Am J Psychiatry 1991; 148:292–305.
70. Reeves R, Patrick G, Struve FA, et al: Quantitative changes during caffeine withdrawal. Presented at the Annual Scientific Meeting of The College on Problems of Drug Dependence; June 1994; Palm Beach, FL.
71. Galletly DC, Fennelly M, Whitwam JG: Does caffeine withdrawal contribute to postanaesthetic morbidity? Lancet 1989; 1:1335.
72. McGowan JD, Altman RE, Kanto WP: Neonatal withdrawal symptoms after chronic maternal ingestion of caffeine. South Med J 1988; 81:1092–1094.
73. Nikolajsen L, Larsen KM, Kierkegaard O: Effect of previous frequency of headache, duration of fasting and caffeine abstinence on perioperative headache. Br J Anaesth 1994; 72:295–297.
74. Fennelly M, Galletly DC, Purdie GI: Is caffeine withdrawal the mechanism of postoperative headache? Anesth Analg 1991; 72: 449–453.
75. Barone JJ, Roberts H: Human consumption of caffeine. In Dews PB (ed): Caffeine: Perspectives from Recent Research. Berlin: Springer-Verlag, 1984:59–73.
76. Strain EC, Mumford GK, Silverman K, et al: Caffeine dependence syndrome: Evidence from case histories and experimental evaluations. JAMA 1994; 272:1043–1048.
77. Hale KL, Hughes JR: The prevalence of caffeine and nicotine use and dependence among alcoholics versus non-alcoholics. Presented at the Annual Scientific Meeting of The College on Problems of Drug Dependence; June 1994; Palm Beach, FL.
78. Griffiths RR, Evans SM, Heishman SJ, et al: Low-dose caffeine discrimination in humans. J Pharmacol Exp Ther 1990; 252:970–978.
79. Silverman K, Griffiths RR: Low-dose caffeine discrimination and self-reported mood effects in normal volunteers. J Exp Anal Behav 1992; 57:91–107.
80. Griffiths RR, Woodson PP: Reinforcing effects of caffeine in humans. J Pharmacol Exp Ther 1988; 246:21–29.
81. Chait LD: Factors influencing the subjective response to caffeine. Behav Pharmacol 1992; 3:219–228.
82. Evans SM, Griffiths RR: Dose-related caffeine discrimination in

normal volunteers: Individual differences in subjective effects and self-reported cues. Behav Pharmacol 1991; 2:345–356.
83. Evans SM, Critchfield TS, Griffiths RR: Caffeine reinforcement demonstrated in a majority of moderate caffeine users. Behav Pharmacol 1994; 5:231–238.
84. Griffiths RR, Bigelow GE, Liebson IA: Reinforcing effects of caffeine in coffee and capsules. J Exp Anal Behav 1989; 52:127–140.
85. Silverman K, Mumford GK, Griffiths RR: Enhancing caffeine reinforcement by behavioral requirements following drug ingestion. Psychopharmacology (Berl) 1994; 114:424–432.
86. Hughes JR, Hunt WK, Higgins ST, et al: Effect of dose on the ability of caffeine to serve as a reinforcer in humans. Behav Pharmacol 1992; 3:211–218.
87. Evans SM, Griffiths RR: Caffeine tolerance and choice in humans. Psychopharmacology (Berl) 1992; 108:51–59.
88. Goldstein A, Kaizer S, Whitby O: Psychotropic effects of caffeine in man. IV. Quantitative and qualitative differences associated with habituation to coffee. Clin Pharmacol Ther 1969; 10:489–497.
89. Bonnet MH, Arand DL: Caffeine use as a model of acute and chronic insomnia. Sleep 1992; 15:526–536.
90. Myers MG: Effects of caffeine on blood pressure. Arch Intern Med 1988; 148:1189–1193.
91. Robertson D, Wade D, Workman R, et al: Tolerance to the humoral and hemodynamic effects of caffeine in man. J Clin Invest 1981; 67:1111–1117.
92. Gurling HMD, Grant S, Dangl J: The genetic and cultural transmission of alcohol use, alcoholism, cigarette smoking and coffee drinking: A review and an example using a log linear cultural transmission model. Br J Addict 1985; 80:269–279.
93. Partanen J, Bruun K, Markkanen T: Inheritance of Drinking Behavior: A Study of Intelligence, Personality, and Use of Alcohol in Adult Twins. Helsinki: The Finnish Foundation for Alcohol Studies, 1966.
94. Pedersen N: Twin similarity for usage of common drugs. In Gedda L, Parisi P, Nance W (eds): Twin Research 3, Part C: Epidemiological and Clinical Studies. New York: Alan R Liss, 1981:53–59.
95. Carmelli D, Swan GE, Robinette D, et al: Heritability of substance use in the NAS-NRC twin registry. Acta Genet Med Gemellol (Roma) 1990; 39:91–98.
96. Abe K: Reactions to coffee and alcohol in monozygotic twins. J Psychosom Res 1968; 12:199–203.
97. Hall MJ, Bartoshu LM, Cain WS, et al: PTC taste blindness and the taste of caffeine. Nature 1975; 253:442–443.
98. Swanson JA, Lee JW, Hopp JW: Caffeine and nicotine: A review of their joint use and possible interactive effects in tobacco withdrawal. Addict Behav 1994; 3:229–256.
99. Benowitz NL, Hall SM, Modin G: Persistent increase in caffeine concentrations in people who stop smoking. BMJ 1989; 298:1075–1076.
100. Hughes GV, Boland FJ: The effects of caffeine and nicotine consumption on mood and somatic variables in a penitentiary inmate population. Addict Behav 1992; 17:447–457.
101. Greden JF, Fontaine P, Lubetsky M, et al: Anxiety and depression associated with caffeinism among psychiatric inpatients. Am J Psychiatry 1978; 135:963–966.
102. Mayo KM, Falkowski W, Jones CAH: Caffeine: Use and effects in long-stay psychiatric patients. Br J Psychiatry 1993; 162:543–545.
103. Hughes JR, Hale KL: Starting and stopping caffeine use. Presented at the Annual Meeting of The Society of Behavioral Medicine; March 1995; San Diego, CA.
104. US Department of Agriculture, Human Nutrition Information Service: Food and Nutrient Intakes by Individuals in the United States, 1 Day, 1987–1988. Nationwide Food Consumption Survey 1987–1988, NFCS Report 87-I-1, 1993.
105. Greden JF: Caffeine and tobacco dependence. In Kaplan HI, Freedman AM, Sadock BJ (eds): Comprehensive Textbook of Psychiatry/III. Baltimore: Williams & Wilkins, 1980:1645–1652.
106. Hughes JR, Amori G, Hatsukami DK: A survey of physician advice about caffeine. J Subst Abuse 1988; 1:67–70.
107. Bernard ME, Dennehy S, Keefauver LW: Behavioral treatment of excessive coffee and tea drinking: A case study and partial replication. Behav Ther 1981; 12:543–548.
108. Foxx RM, Rubinoff A: Behavioral treatment of caffeinism: Reducing excessive coffee drinking. J Appl Behav Anal 1979; 12:335–344.
109. Hyner GC: Relaxation as principal treatment for excessive cigarette use and caffeine ingestion by a college female. Psychol Rep 1979; 45:531–534.
110. James JE, Stirling KP, Hampton BAM: Caffeine fading: Behavioral treatment of caffeine abuse. Behav Ther 1985; 16:15–27.
111. Boulenger JP, Uhde TW: Caffeine consumption and anxiety: Preliminary results of a survey comparing patients with anxiety disorders and normal controls. Psychopharmacol Bull 1982; 18:53–57.
112. Lee MA, Cameron OG, Greden JF: Anxiety and caffeine consumption in people with anxiety disorders. Psychiatry Res 1985; 15:211–217.
113. Eaton WW, McLeod J: Consumption of coffee or tea and symptoms of anxiety. Am J Public Health 1984; 74:66–68.
114. Charney DS, Heninger GR, Jatlow PI: Increased anxiogenic effects of caffeine in panic disorder. Arch Gen Psychiatry 1985; 42:233–243.
115. Uhde TW, Boulenger JP, Jimerson DC, et al: Caffeine: Relationship to human anxiety, plasma MHPG, and cortisol. Psychopharmacol Bull 1984; 20:426–430.
116. Greden JF, Proctor A, Victor B: Caffeinism associated with greater use of other psychotropic agents. Compr Psychiatry 1981; 22:565–571.
117. Roache JD, Griffiths RR: Interactions of diazepam and caffeine: Behavioral and subjective dose effects in humans. Pharmacol Biochem Behav 1987; 26:801–812.
118. Newman F, Stein MB, Trettau JR, et al: Quantitative electroencephalographic effects of caffeine in panic disorder. Psychiatry Res Neuroimaging 1992; 45:105–113.
119. Uhde TW: Caffeine provocation of panic: A focus on biological mechanisms. In Ballenger JC (ed): Neurobiology of Panic Disorder. New York: Alan R Liss, 1990:219–242.
120. Chavanne H: Coffee. J Med Soc N J 1911; 8:19–22.
121. Regestein QR: Pathologic sleepiness induced by caffeine. Am J Med 1989; 87:586–588.
122. Colton T, Gosselin RE, Smith RP: The tolerance of coffee drinkers to caffeine. Clin Pharmacol Ther 1968; 9:31–39.
123. Goldstein A: Wakefulness caused by caffeine. Naunyn Schmiedebergs Arch Pharmacol 1964; 248:269–278.
124. Karacan I, Thornby JI, Anch M, et al: Dose-related sleep disturbance induced by coffee and caffeine. Clin Pharmacol Ther 1977; 20:682–688.
125. Nicholson AN, Stone BM: Heterocyclic amphetamine derivatives and caffeine on sleep in man. Br J Clin Pharmacol 1980; 9:195–203.
126. Okuma T, Matsuoka H, Matsue Y, et al: Model insomnia by methylphenidate and caffeine and use in the evaluation of temazepam. Psychopharmacology (Berl) 1982; 76:201–208.

CHAPTER

44 Cannabis-Related Disorders

Amanda J. Gruber
Harrison G. Pope, Jr.

Definition

Cannabis-Related Disorders

As with other substances of abuse, the *Diagnostic and Statistical Manual of Mental Disorders,* Fourth Edition (DSM-IV) distinguishes a number of different cannabis-related diagnoses, which are shown in Table 44–1. These fall into two basic groups. First are disorders resulting from episodic or chronic cannabis intoxication; these include cannabis abuse and cannabis dependence. The category of cannabis dependence is further subdivided in the same manner as other types of substance dependence in DSM-IV to indicate the degree of physiological dependence, degree of remission, and presence or absence of a controlled environment. The second set of cannabis-related disorders in DSM-IV includes cannabis intoxication and psychiatric syndromes presumed to be induced by cannabis. These include cannabis intoxication delirium (i.e., a degree of disturbance beyond that normally expected with ordinary intoxication), cannabis-induced psychotic disorder (subdivided into categories of psychosis with delusions and psychosis with hallucinations), and cannabis-induced anxiety disorder (also subdivided into several types as shown in Table 44–1).

Throughout the remainder of this chapter, we discuss cannabis abuse and dependence under the general heading of cannabis use disorders; cannabis intoxication delirium, psychotic disorder, and anxiety disorder are discussed as cannabis-induced disorders. Note that cannabis intoxication, although certainly induced by cannabis, is different from other cannabis-induced disorders in the following ways: it is not, when diagnosed alone, a disorder but rather a state; it is related to the cannabis use disorders in that it is a necessary but not sufficient component of these disorders; and it is related to the other cannabis-induced disorders in that it is part of the description of these disorders—in a sense they represent states of "abnormal intoxication." In light of its close relationship to the other cannabis-related disorders, cannabis intoxication is described in detail in the diagnosis section but is not discussed separately in the other sections unless it is relevant. Before going into greater detail on these entities, however, it is necessary to provide some background information regarding cannabis botany and pharmacology.

Cannabis Botany and Pharmacology

Cannabis preparations have been widely used for their psychotropic effects since the beginning of history. The drug is prepared in different ways in different parts of the world from the flowering or fruited tops of the plant *Cannabis sativa.* Commonly, the upper leaves, tops, and stems of the plant are dried and rolled into cigarettes or smoked in a pipe, in which case the product is usually referred to as marijuana. The resin found on the leaves of the plant may be removed and dried and also smoked; this preparation is called hashish and is more commonly used in Europe and the Middle East. Finally, cannabis may be mixed with tea or food and taken orally.[1]

The principal pharmacologically active ingredient in cannabis is believed to be Δ^9- or Δ^9-*trans*-tetrahydrocannabinol (THC). The amount of THC present in cannabis preparations varies, and it is believed that illicit marijuana on the streets of the United States has increased substantially in potency, on average, in the course of the last 30 years.[2] When cannabis preparations are smoked, about 50% of the active drug is absorbed, and the effects are noticed within

Table 44-1 Cannabis-Related Disorders

	Cannabis Use Disorders
304.30	Cannabis dependence With physiological dependence Without physiological dependence Early full remission Early partial remission Sustained full remission Sustained partial remission In a controlled environment
305.20	Cannabis abuse
	Cannabis-Induced Disorders
292.89	Cannabis intoxication With perceptual disturbances
292.81	Cannabis intoxication delirium
292.11	Cannabis-induced psychotic disorder, with delusions With onset during intoxication
292.12	Cannabis-induced psychotic disorder, with hallucinations With onset during intoxication
292.89	Cannabis-induced anxiety disorder With onset during intoxication With generalized anxiety With panic attacks With obsessive-compulsive symptoms With phobic symptoms
292.9	Cannabis-related disorder not otherwise specified

minutes. The potency of the drug when it is smoked is about three times that experienced when an equivalent amount is eaten, because first-pass metabolism in the liver is avoided during the smoking process and there is an enhanced release of THC from pyrolysis of the acids. After oral intake, absorption takes up to 3 hours, and the duration of effects may last 8 to 24 hours.[3]

THC and its chemical relatives are highly lipophilic and are quickly distributed widely throughout the body. THC can cross the placenta, enter breast milk, and interact with other drugs by inducing liver enzymes and competing for plasma binding sites. It is metabolized by hydroxylation to other active metabolites that have half-lives exceeding 50 hours, such as 11-hydroxy-THC, and by conjugation to more water soluble metabolites that are excreted slowly in the bile, urine, hair, and feces. Because it is so lipophilic and stored in the body's adipose tissue, THC can be detected up to 30 days after the individual's last exposure to cannabis.[3]

Although the precise mechanism of action of THC is presently unknown, several hypotheses have been advanced. For example, there is evidence that THC may affect the serotonin system by increasing the synthesis and release of serotonin, which is thought to account for its effect on mood, its antiepileptic activity, and its ability to cause hypothermia.[3, 4] There is also some evidence that THC may have anxiolytic effects, mediated through central benzodiazepine receptors.[5] THC is also reported to produce catalepsy by dopaminergic inhibitions.[6] Anticholinergic mechanisms have been suggested to explain the impairment of memory.[7] THC has also been shown to reduce noradrenergic activity and endogenous opioids.[8] THC can potentiate the effects of alcohol, barbiturates, caffeine, and amphetamines.[4] It is possible that THC produces these effects by a third-order mechanism. A cannabinoid receptor has been described in rat brains, which when bound to cannabinoids activates a cellular second-messenger system that inhibits adenylate cyclase. Depending on the cell type, this inhibition may have many different effects. An endogenous ligand has not yet been described.[9]

Epidemiology

Cannabis Use Disorders

Cannabis is probably the most commonly used illicit substance in the world, with an estimated 200 to 300 million regular users.[3] In the United States, cannabis is generally thought to be the most widely used illicit drug, although some studies report that cocaine is competing with it on some measures of frequency of use.[3, 10] The 1992 cross-sectional household survey of alcohol and drug use estimated that 67.5 million Americans had used marijuana at least once and 8.95 million in the month before the survey.[11] Cannabis is often among the first drugs of experimentation (often in the teenage years) for all cultural groups in this country. As with most other illicit drugs, cannabis use appears more often in men, and these disorders are most common in persons between the ages of 18 and 30 years.[10]

Cannabis use is increasing in younger age groups. A report from the annual Monitoring the Future Study of high-school students contrasted consumption rates for 1992 and 1993 and indicated significant increases in marijuana use across the 8th, 10th, and 12th grades.[12] In 1993, about 13% of 8th grade students, 25% of 10th grade students, and 35% of 12th grade students had used marijuana at least once, and 5%, 11%, and 16%, respectively, used marijuana in the month before the survey. It is difficult to extrapolate from these figures to the prevalence of outright cannabis abuse or dependence.

Some index of the prevalence of current cannabis use disorders can be obtained from surveys of U.S. college students. One survey conducted at the same U.S. college in 1969, 1978, and 1989 found that 16% of college students were using marijuana once a week or more in 1969, 26% once a week or more in 1978, but only 6% in 1989.[13] These findings again suggest that only a small percentage of individuals who have tried cannabis are currently exhibiting frank cannabis abuse or dependence and, further, that the prevalence of cannabis use disorders may have declined in the past decade in the United States.

Cannabis use disorders are frequently comorbid with other substance abuse disorders.[14] Surveys of psychiatric populations[15–17] with mixed Axis I diagnoses, but not panic disorder,[18] have found a high prevalence of cannabis use. Cannabis use, abuse, and dependence are also commonly comorbid with conduct disorder in children and adolescents and with antisocial personality disorder in adults.[19, 20]

Cannabis-Induced Disorders

No formal epidemiological data exist regarding the prevalence of cannabis intoxication delirium, cannabis-induced psychotic disorder, or cannabis-induced anxiety disorder. In fact, it is not entirely certain that any of these three entities actually occurs in individuals who are free of preexisting DSM-IV Axis I disorders. For example, we were unable to find any original reports of cannabis-induced delirium in the literature except for comments about it in review articles. Whereas cannabis often causes anxiety, or even panic reactions, there is again no published study, to our knowledge, exhibiting a cohort of previously asymptomatic subjects who had a clinically significant cannabis-induced anxiety disorder. One investigator reported that there were five to seven cases of cannabis-associated anxiety reactions reported to a university health service per year and hypothesized that more occurred but were not reported. However, he noted that reassurance was all the treatment necessary, suggesting that these patients may not have met criteria for a clinically significant anxiety disorder.[21] Finally, although anecdotal reports and even case series of cannabis-induced psychotic disorder have appeared, many of these have been collected outside the United States, and most provide insufficient evidence to assess whether the subjects studied were suffering from preexisting psychotic disorders before their ingestion of cannabis.[22] Thus, the prevalence of de novo cannabis-induced psychotic disorder cannot be calculated. In one U.S. study, the investigators reviewed approximately 10,000 discharges from two psychiatric units. All cases of possible cannabis-induced mental disorders were investigated by chart review. No cases of clear-cut cannabis-induced psychotic disorder or cannabis-induced anxiety disorder were found. Thus, it appears that these disorders, at least of sufficient magnitude to prompt a psychiatric admission, are rare.[22]

Etiology and Pathophysiology

Cannabis Use Disorders

Few formal data exist regarding the mechanism by which cannabis abuse and dependence develop in individuals who experiment with the drug. However, some speculations may be advanced on the basis of studies of related issues. First, many studies have compared the attributes of nonusers or of infrequent users (i.e., those who have not had frank abuse or dependence) with characteristics of heavy users who meet criteria for dependence, and few have found any striking differences between the two groups. For example, in one investigation, the attributes of 45 college students who were heavy cannabis users (all of whom met DSM-IV criteria for cannabis dependence) were compared with 44 college students who were infrequent users (having never used the drug more than nine times within a 1-month period at any time in their lives). It was found that there were few significant differences between these groups on demographical indices, lifetime prevalence of other Axis I or Axis II disorders, scores on the Rand Mental Health Inventory, or other measures. The students with cannabis abuse or dependence differed from their infrequent-using counterparts only in that they exhibited a somewhat higher prevalence of other substance abuse disorders.[22a] These and other data suggest that there does not appear to be a particular constellation of demographical or psychopathological features that predispose a particular American adolescent more than other individuals to the development of cannabis dependence. We are unaware of any family study data that would indicate a genetic predisposition.

A hypothesis put forth by certain investigators is that some individuals with cannabis dependence may be "self-medicating" themselves for underlying psychiatric symptoms. Specifically, some patients with depression, anxiety, and negative symptoms of schizophrenia have claimed that cannabis use alleviates their symptoms.[23–26] Conversely, other investigators argue that cannabis is causing these symptoms.[27–29] We have observed this apparent self-medication phenomenon in a number of patients with underlying depressive illness or bipolar disorder. One of these cases is illustrated in clinical vignette 2 (see later). However, formal investigation of the self-medication hypothesis, to our knowledge, has not been conducted.

Although much is known about the pharmacology of cannabis and of its main active agent, THC, it is difficult to extrapolate from these pharmacological data to the mechanisms by which dependence may develop in certain individuals. It is known that THC affects many neurotransmitter systems, including the serotoninergic, dopaminergic, noradrenergic, and cholinergic systems, but it is not clear why the effects of THC are perceived as enjoyable (and presumably reinforcing) by some individuals but as dysphoric by others.

There is some evidence to suggest that as with other drugs of abuse, regular use of cannabis can produce tolerance to many of its acute physiological and psychological effects. Such tolerance may cause some individuals to increase their use to continue to experience the effect they enjoy. However, tolerance to cannabis, to the extent that it does occur, does not approach the magnitude of tolerance observed with drugs that induce frank physiological dependence, such as alcohol, barbiturates, or opioids.

Few studies have specifically looked for withdrawal symptoms from cannabis. However, it is informative that there are so many studies that have not reported any such state, which suggests that a frank withdrawal syndrome is rare. However, there are many data on animals documenting a withdrawal syndrome, and the investigators who have looked for it in heavy users forced to stop use without any taper have sometimes observed a withdrawal syndrome. The syndrome can be mildly unpleasant or cause moderate discomfort and consists of one or more of the following symptoms: restlessness, irritability, insomnia, decreased appetite, nausea, diarrhea, low-grade fever, sweats, chills, tremor, myalgia, photophobia, yawning, anergy, and depression. These symptoms are reported to begin approximately 12 hours after the last use of cannabis, reach a peak in 24 hours, and remit after 96 hours. This withdrawal state is not life threatening, like that of alcohol, or as severe as that seen with opiates. Nevertheless, avoidance of this unpleasant state may be a reason some individuals continue to use cannabis regularly.[8, 30–33]

The two clinical vignettes provided at the end of the chapter describe individuals who experienced subjective withdrawal effects (of two types) from their use of cannabis.

Cannabis-Induced Disorders

The little we understand of the mechanisms through which cannabis produces the symptoms of cannabis intoxication is discussed in the botany and pharmacology section. There are no adequate data regarding the mechanism by which cannabis intoxication delirium, cannabis-induced psychotic disorder, or cannabis-induced anxiety disorder can occur de novo in individuals without preexisting medical or psychiatric disorders. In a review of studies of patients with cannabis-induced psychotic disorder, it was found that most of the studies had not excluded individuals with a preexisting Axis I disorder, such as schizophrenia or a major mood disorder, which would render the individual vulnerable to psychotic symptoms even in the absence of cannabis use. At present, therefore, it seems possible that the majority of cannabis-induced psychotic or anxiety disorders represent exacerbations of preexisting DSM-IV Axis I psychiatric disorders in individuals who become intoxicated with the drug.[22]

Diagnosis

Cannabis-Related Disorders

To diagnose any of the cannabis-related disorders, it is important to obtain a detailed history of the individual's pattern of substance abuse (including abuse not only of cannabis but of other substances) and to attempt to substantiate this report with toxicology screening for drugs of abuse. Individuals who smoke cannabis regularly can have substantial accumulations of THC in their fat stores. Thus, for weeks after cessation of smoking, detectable levels of cannabinoids may be found in urine.[3] However, a positive response on toxicology screening for cannabinoids cannot establish any of the cannabis-related diagnoses; it is useful only as an indicator that these diagnoses should be considered.

Cannabis Dependence

This diagnosis cannot be made without obtaining a history that the cannabis use is impairing the patient's ability to function, either physically or psychologically. Areas to inquire about include the patient's performance at work, ability to carry out social and family obligations, and physical health. It is also important to find out how much of the patient's time is spent on cannabis-related activities and whether the patient has tried unsuccessfully to stop or cut down on use in the past. Many patients with this disorder will respond to offers for treatment because they realize they are unable to stop use on their own, and they notice the deleterious effect of compulsive use.[34]

Individuals with cannabis dependence frequently report spending long periods acquiring and using the drug; frequent intoxication at times when it interferes with daily activities (driving a motor vehicle or attending classes in school); and persistence of cannabis use despite psychological impairment (i.e., impaired academic function), physical impairment (i.e., bronchitis), or adverse experiences with family members or other individuals who disapprove of use. In our experience, it is uncommon to see patients with cannabis dependence in isolation because they rarely seek treatment, although as noted before, they may respond to offers for treatment if they are made aware that it is available.

This diagnosis will most often be made in patients who present with other psychiatric problems, but it is probably underdiagnosed in both psychiatric and general medical populations because it is not considered. Finally, another manner in which individuals with cannabis dependence may come to the attention of psychiatrists is when they are arrested for possession of the substance or some crime related to cannabis abuse, such as driving under the influence of the drug.

The diagnosis of cannabis dependence may suggest that the individual has been abusing the drug regularly for a long enough time to result in tolerance to many of the effects of cannabis and to experience an unpleasant withdrawal state if use is discontinued (although neither tolerance nor withdrawal is necessary for the diagnosis). The use must be compulsive, in that the individual cannot stop using the drug even if she or he perceives that it is having negative effects and wants to stop. When this diagnosis is made, it can be described further by the following specifiers: with or without physiological dependence, early full or partial remission, sustained full or partial remission, or in a controlled environment. These diagnostic distinctions must be based on the pattern of use reported by the patient.

Cannabis Abuse

The criteria for this diagnosis are similar to those for cannabis dependence. The individual's use of cannabis must have resulted in problems performing at school or work, interpersonal difficulties, unsafe behaviors such as driving a motor vehicle while intoxicated, health problems, or legal difficulties, and the individual must have continued to use cannabis despite these problems. The difference is that this diagnosis should be used when the individual's use of cannabis has not been regular, frequent, long-standing, or compulsive and the individual has not developed tolerance or the potential for a withdrawal state. As with cannabis dependence, it is a diagnosis unlikely to be made unless some other condition or circumstance brings the individual to medical attention.

Cannabis Intoxication

There are four criteria necessary to make this diagnosis. The first is that recent use of cannabis must be established. This cannot be done with toxicology screening because the result may be negative after a single episode of smoking or, alternatively, may be positive even if the individual has not used the drug for a time much longer than the period of intoxication (see pharmacology section). Thus, the recent use of cannabis must be reported by the patient or another person who witnessed the patient's use. In addition, the patient must experience symptoms of cannabis use that are described in DSM-IV as being "clinically significant maladaptive behavioral or psychological changes" and that are temporally related to the cannabis use. Third, the patient must exhibit some physical signs of cannabis use. DSM-IV requires the patient to have at least two of four signs—conjunctival injection, increased appetite, dry mouth, and tachycardia—within 2 hours of cannabis use. Fourth, symptoms cannot be accounted for by a general medical condition or another mental disorder. There is a specifier, "with perceptual disturbances," that can be used if the patient is experiencing illusions or hallucinations while not delirious and while maintaining intact reality testing.

There has been extensive research on the effects of acute cannabis intoxication. In addition to the symptoms and signs required for a DSM-IV diagnosis, many psychological and physiological effects have been reported. Awareness of these may enhance the psychiatrist's ability to recognize

DSM-IV Criteria 292.89

Cannabis Intoxication

A. Recent use of cannabis.

B. Clinically significant maladaptive behavioral or psychological changes (e.g., impaired motor coordination, euphoria, anxiety, sensation of slowed time, impaired judgment, social withdrawal) that developed during, or shortly after, cannabis use.

C. Two (or more) of the following signs, developing within 2 hours of cannabis use:

(1) conjunctival injection

(2) increased appetite

(3) dry mouth

(4) tachycardia

D. The symptoms are not due to a general medical condition and are not better accounted for by another mental disorder.

Specify if:

With perceptual disturbances

cannabis intoxication. Common physiological effects (Table 44–2) include hypertension, thirst, decreased libido, constipation, decreased intraocular pressure, irritation of the bronchial mucosa from smoking, mild bronchoconstriction followed by bronchodilation, ataxia, impaired coordination, and increased reaction time. At high doses, drowsiness, bradycardia, hypotension, peripheral vasoconstriction, hypothermia, ptosis, and pupillary constriction have been described. There is disagreement on whether cannabis produces characteristic electroencephalographical changes or alters hormone levels.[35–39]

Common psychological effects (Table 44–3) include impaired memory (especially short-term memory); perceptual and sensory distortions; disturbance in time perception; euphoria and dysphoria; restlessness; depersonalization; derealization; panic reactions; paranoid ideation; and impaired performance on a wide variety of cognitive, perceptual, and psychomotor tasks.[35–39]

Table 44–2 Common Physiological Effects of Cannabis Intoxication
Hypertension
Thirst
Decreased libido
Constipation
Decreased intraocular pressure
Irritation of bronchial mucosa from smoking
Mild bronchoconstriction followed by bronchodilation
Ataxia
Impaired coordination
Increased reaction time

Table 44–3 Common Psychological Effects of Cannabis Intoxication
Impaired memory, especially short-term memory
Perceptual and sensory distortions
Disturbance in time perception
Mood alteration
Restlessness
Depersonalization
Derealization
Panic reactions
Paranoid ideation
Impaired performance on cognitive, perceptual, and psychomotor tasks

There is considerable disagreement as to how long the residual effects of intoxication last; estimates range from a few hours to more than 6 weeks. Indeed, the question of residual effects is complicated by different investigators' definitions of the term *residual.* Some authors use the word residual to imply a "hangover" effect due to a residue of cannabis in the system. Others imply that residual effects might persist even after all cannabis has left the brain. Although the latter possibility remains largely unsupported, many studies have shown that there is at least some hangover from acute intoxication, with impairment on neuropsychological testing and on tests such as driving simulators and flight simulators persisting for 24 to a maximum of 48 hours after intoxication.[39a]

In addition, some authors report that users occasionally experience flashbacks whereby they experience symptoms of the intoxicated state long after they last used the drug. These experiences have not been formally studied. One study reports that 10% to 15% of users who did not report the use of other substances had experienced flashbacks, so they may not represent a rare phenomenon.[40–44]

Cannabis Intoxication Delirium

We have not located any original reports of this entity, although it is mentioned in various reviews. Thus, if cannabis intoxication delirium does occur in neurologically intact individuals, it is probably a rare complication. In a patient with delirium, even if recent cannabis use has been reported, a full diagnostic work-up should be performed to rule out a concomitant neurological condition.[45]

The following two substance-induced conditions are not generally diagnosed unless the symptoms are in excess of those usually associated with the intoxication or withdrawal state and are sufficiently severe to warrant independent clinical attention.

Cannabis-Induced Psychotic Disorder

There are two diagnoses allocated to this entity, one featuring delusions, the other hallucinations. The diagnosis of this disorder is readily made in individuals who have psychotic symptoms (as defined in DSM-IV) that appear immediately after ingestion of cannabis. However, a careful history is required to establish whether the individual has displayed a previous psychotic disorder before cannabis use (as is often the case in such situations) or whether the symptoms arose de novo after cannabis consumption. As mentioned earlier in the section on epidemiology, there is little evidence that cannabis-induced psychotic disorders can arise in previously asymptomatic individuals.[22]

Cannabis-Induced Anxiety Disorder

This disorder may be further described by the following specifiers: with generalized anxiety, with panic attacks, with obsessive-compulsive symptoms, and with phobic symptoms. The literature contains papers that report individuals who have anxiety, panic reactions, and paranoid ideation during the period of acute intoxication, but we are unaware of any papers that report obsessive-compulsive or phobic symptoms. As with cannabis-induced psychotic disorders, we have been unable to find clear cases of cannabis-induced anxiety disorders in individuals without a preexisting Axis I disorder.

A diagnostic decision tree is presented in Figure 44–1.

Course and Natural History

Cannabis Use Disorders

Cannabis abuse and dependence typically develop gradually, as the user proceeds from initial experimentation with the drug to progressively more frequent use. There are few data on the duration of abuse and dependence syndromes, however. Some individuals, such as college students, may exhibit a period of abuse or dependence lasting only a few weeks or months (e.g., a summer vacation), whereas other individuals may continue to use cannabis on a daily basis for many years, sometimes in conjunction with other forms of drug use.[46] For men, high career aspirations were predictive of discontinuing use.[47] Predictors of dropping out of an outpatient treatment program, and presumably continuing use, were found to be young age, financial difficulties, and psychological stress.[48]

Cannabis abuse and dependence appear to pursue a benign course in many individuals, in the sense that many studies find that individuals suffering from these disorders do not differ in ability to function in society from matched control subjects who are not users. Although some authors have described an "amotivational syndrome" associated

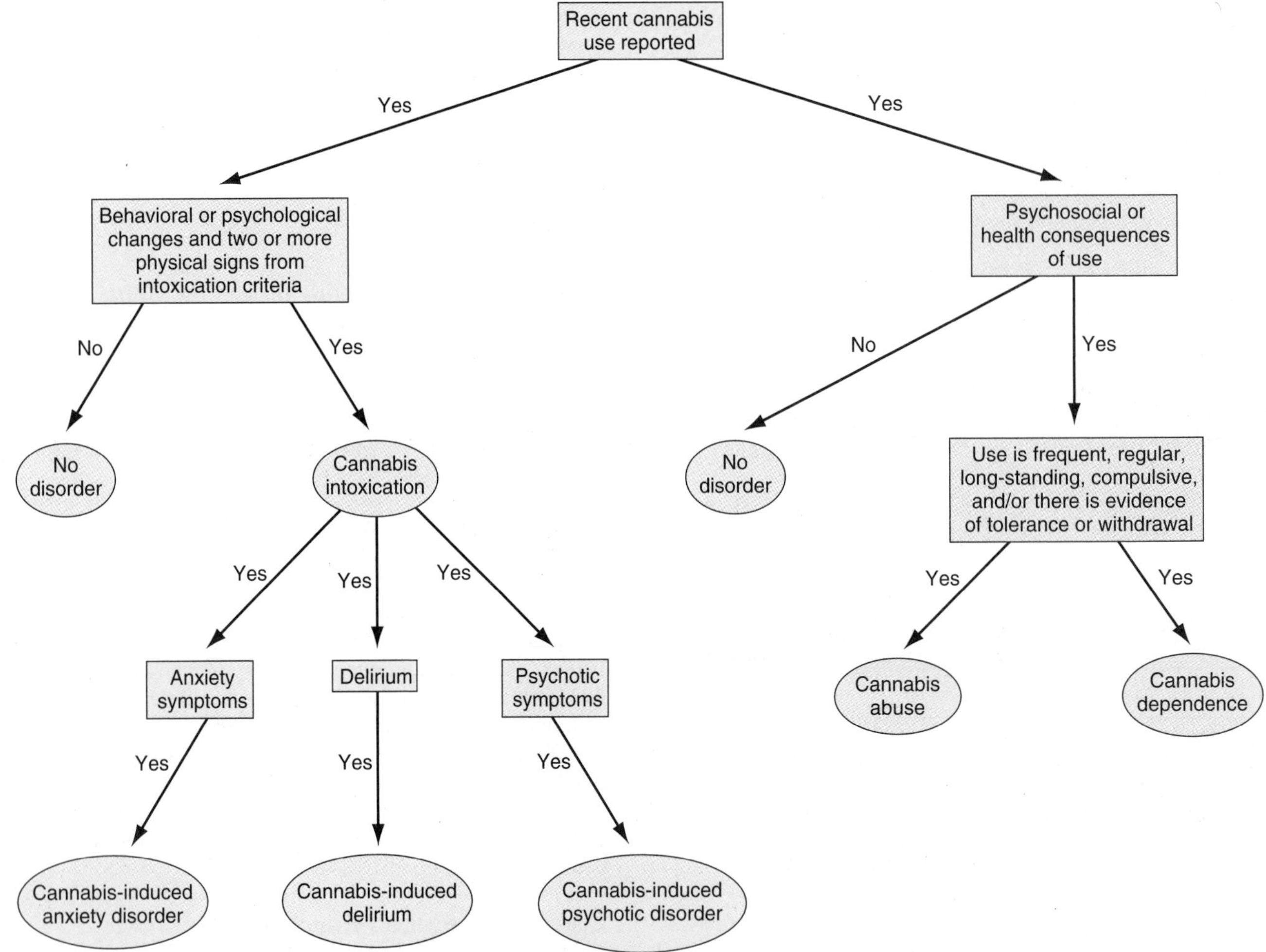

Figure 44–1 *Diagnostic decision tree for cannabis-use disorders.*

with chronic cannabis use, this has not been documented by any rigorous studies.[13, 49–61]

Cannabis-Induced Disorders

Cannabis intoxication is a self-limiting state that remits as cannabis is metabolized and eliminated from the body. If the symptoms of cannabis intoxication persist, other diagnoses should be considered. Similarly, although there are few data regarding the course of the other cannabis-induced disorders, it appears that cannabis-induced psychotic and anxiety disorders, as well as cannabis intoxication delirium, rarely persist beyond the period of acute intoxication with the drug. For example, although there have been reports of cannabis-induced psychoses persisting for days or even weeks beyond the time of acute intoxication, a review of the literature (as discussed earlier) was unable to exhibit a series of unequivocal cases in which such symptoms persisted in the absence of an underlying Axis I disorder. Therefore, symptoms of delirium, psychosis, or anxiety persisting more than 24 to 48 hours after acute cannabis intoxication suggest the possibility that another Axis I disorder, rather than cannabis itself, is responsible for the symptoms.[22]

Overall Goals of Treatment

Cannabis Use Disorders

For all cannabis-related disorders, the goal of treatment is abstinence from cannabis use. Little systematic study of treatment of cannabis abuse or dependence exists, however, because individuals with these disorders rarely independently seek treatment. Nevertheless, individuals may seek treatment if it is offered. In one investigation, a public service announcement directed at chronic marijuana users resulted in interviews of 225 people who responded. It was found that 74% reported negative consequences of their marijuana use, and 92% wanted to be treated.[34]

Most of the literature on treatment is directed at substance abuse in general and not at cannabis in particular. Fortunately, however, most of the treatment models are probably applicable to cannabis use disorders. Similarities include the treatment goal of attaining abstinence and the importance of a good psychiatrist-patient relationship. In the remainder of the section, we note the ways in which the treatment of cannabis abuse and dependence may differ from the standard substance abuse treatment model.[27]

One difference is the increased importance of toxicology screening for other drugs of abuse at the initiation of treatment. This is more important with cannabis than with other drugs of abuse because cannabis is often only one of the substances used, and specific treatment may be indicated for other substances. A second difference may occur during the process of detoxification. Unlike most other substances of abuse, cannabis continues to persist in the fat stores of the body for a long time after the last use. One author has hypothesized that slow release of cannabinoids from fatty tissue may produce the phenomenon of flashbacks, during which the user experiences phenomena like those experienced during acute intoxication, such as perceptual disturbances.[27] This persistence of cannabinoids in the body has also been suggested to cause symptoms of depression and anxiety.[27]

As discussed in the etiology and pathophysiology section, there is some evidence that heavy users of cannabis may experience a withdrawal state during detoxification. This is usually mild and requires no treatment. One author suggested the use of long-acting benzodiazepines if there are abnormal vital signs or the level of discomfort is high.[27] Because the withdrawal state is not medically dangerous, like that of alcohol, or severe, like that of opioids, most patients do not require inpatient detoxification.

For most individuals with cannabis abuse or dependence, outpatient treatment is sufficient. There are several groups of patients who tend to do better with an initial period of inpatient hospitalization: 1) patients who would not stop using as outpatients because they are in denial and require a radical form of intervention to help them acknowledge the severity of their problem; 2) patients addicted to other drugs besides cannabis, such as alcohol or opiates, who generally need an inpatient stay to monitor their detoxification; and 3) patients with comorbid medical or psychiatric problems, who may warrant inpatient treatment so that the comorbid conditions can be treated.[27]

The second stage in treatment is maintenance of abstinence. The strategies used for this are essentially the same ones used for the maintenance treatment of any substance abuser and are discussed in the next section.[27]

Cannabis-Induced Disorders

Uncomplicated cannabis intoxication rarely comes to clinical attention, and if it does, it does not require treatment other than reassurance, as it is a self-limiting condition, so it is not discussed further. Similarly, as suggested in the previous sections, symptoms of delirium, psychosis, or anxiety associated with cannabis use typically resolve promptly after the period of acute intoxication is past. No treatment is necessary other than keeping the patient safe and providing reassurance that the symptoms are caused by the drug and will stop. If the symptoms continue after more than 24 to 48 hours of abstinence from the drug, the possibility of another Axis I diagnosis must be considered. In such cases, treatment should then be directed at the primary Axis I disorder. Treatment of other Axis I disorders is covered in other chapters, so the remainder of the treatment section focuses on cannabis use disorders.

A treatment decision tree is presented in Figure 44–2.

Standard Approach to Treatment

Cannabis Use Disorders

There is no standard approach to treatment of cannabis use disorders, in that treatment of individuals with cannabis abuse or dependence in isolation is so rare that it has not been adequately studied. When patients with cannabis abuse or dependence are treated, either in isolation or jointly with other substance abuse, it is likely that they receive the same standard of care given to other substance abusers, such as alcoholic individuals or opiate addicts. The goal of treatment is abstinence from cannabis use.

For the reasons described before, few patients abusing cannabis alone require inpatient detoxification. If they do, the initial period of inpatient stay has traditionally been 21 days on the average, but it is rapidly decreasing in length.

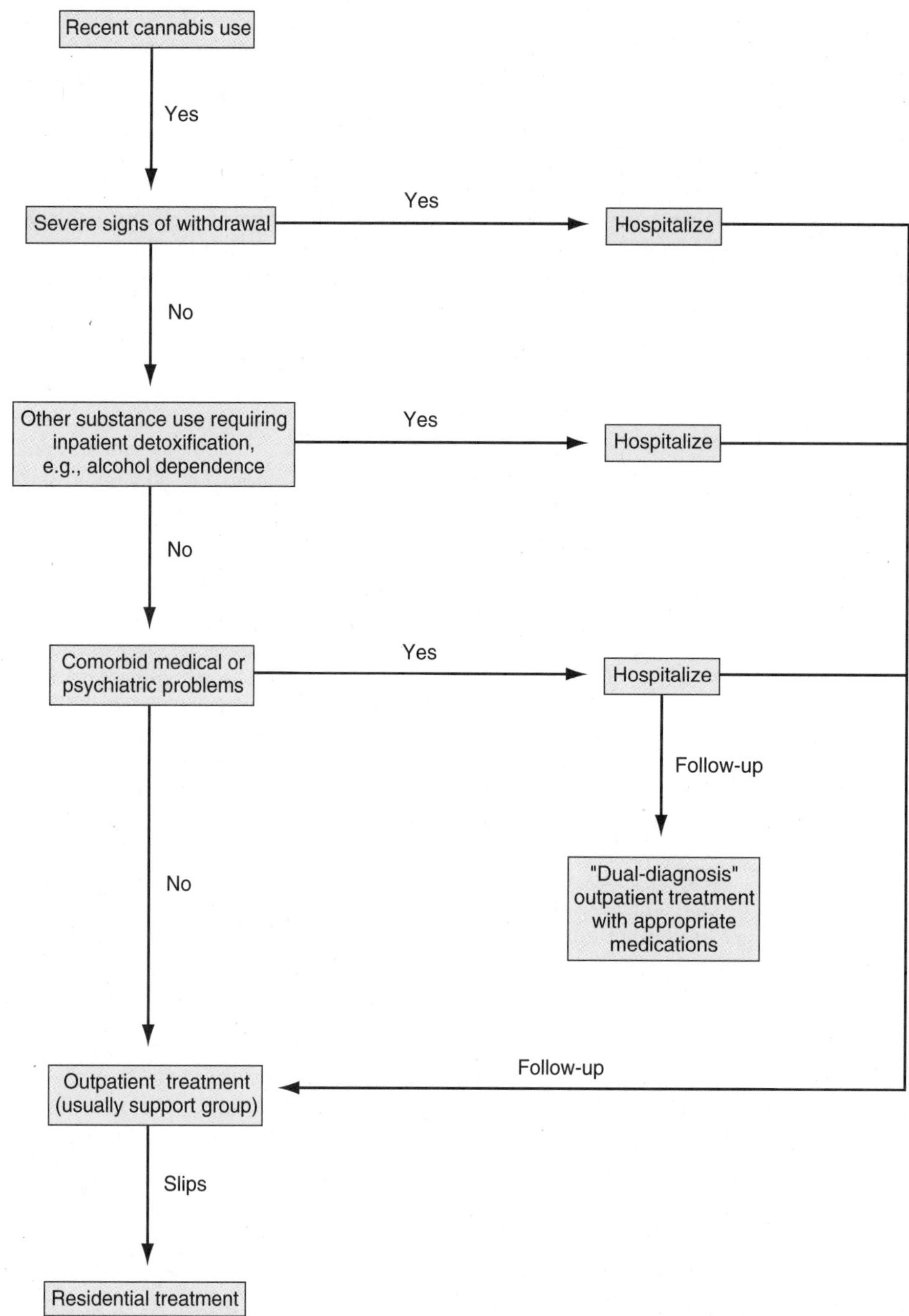

Figure 44–2 *Treatment decision tree for cannabis-use disorders.*

During this time, their detoxification is monitored; they are given medication to make them more comfortable, if necessary; and they begin to attend group therapy sessions that provide education and support. After discharge, patients continue to attend these groups on a regular basis.

Groups have been shown to be the most effective form of maintenance treatment for substance abuse; the hypothesized mechanism is that fellow group members are best able to confront each other's denial and minimization of the substance abuse problem and the rationalizations put forth by the substance abuser for continued use despite negative consequences.

Although this has not been documented by any formal studies, it appears that cannabis abuse and dependence, like most other substance use disorders, are frequently chronic. Relapses should be expected to occur, and the patient must be helped to deal with them. Patients report that the most common factor that initiates relapse is being in the company of other users. It is often useful for families and other people important in the patient's life to get involved in treatment to understand the role they play in the patient's substance abuse.[27]

Probably because there has been little research on the treatment of cannabis use disorders, some treaters have reported experimenting with different approaches. None of these approaches has been studied with use of a controlled design. There is one report of desipramine, or of tyrosine, a precursor of norepinephrine, being used to help sustain abstinence, with the rationale that cannabis has been shown to decrease noradrenergic activity and that desipramine or tyrosine would reverse this.[8] There is a report of amino acids being administered because they have been useful in treating alcoholic individuals.[62]

Another author reported using a psychoeducational approach in dual-diagnosis patients, which consisted of weekly meetings focusing on the causes of substance abuse, its consequences, principles of recovery, and relapse prevention strategies.[63] One investigator treated 22 volunteer chronic marijuana users with a combination of aversion therapy and self-management therapy and found that the subjects significantly decreased their marijuana use for 4 weeks of follow-up.[64] He later treated 47 cannabis users, 19 of whom also used alcohol, and 28 of whom also used both alcohol and cocaine, with a program of aversion therapy and narcotherapy. Of the 30 who were contacted a year afterward, 70% reported sustained abstinence. Predictors of abstinence were returning for reinforcement sessions at 30 and 90 days and the elimination of the urge to use the drugs (which was ascertained by use of narcotherapy).[65]

Special Features Influencing Treatment

Cannabis Use Disorders

The most salient feature of cannabis abuse or dependence is that it does not often occur in isolation and is often comorbid with other Axis I disorders as discussed earlier. Toxicology screening for other drugs of abuse is particularly imperative, because the most common comorbid Axis I disorders are other types of substance abuse. Depending on what other substances are abused, it may be more important to direct treatment at them, treating the cannabis abuse as a secondary condition.

Many studies have shown that cannabis abuse is common in psychiatric populations with mixed Axis I disorders. Another treatment situation frequently encountered is that of an individual with a known Axis I disorder that is being exacerbated by cannabis use. Some studies, performed with schizophrenic populations, have found that use worsens the course of the illness, whereas others have found that it does not affect the course.[65–69] It is a reasonable assumption that at least some patients with Axis I disorders (such as Mr. B in clinical vignette 2) are adversely affected by cannabis use, even if they use the drug only occasionally. In such cases, the role of cannabis as an exacerbating factor must be assessed and discussed with the patient. These patients may or may not be suitable for support groups directed primarily at substance abuse, because cannabis may represent a relatively minor portion of the patient's overall clinical picture.

Refractory Patients and Nonresponse to Initial Treatment

Cannabis Use Disorders

Probably the most common problem in managing cannabis use disorders is the high rate of relapse due to the ubiquitous availability of the drug and the large number of people who are users. Users are therefore tempted to resume use soon after a period of treatment when they find themselves in situations where they are surrounded by people using the substance. Some treaters advocate periodic random urine testing, which is an inexpensive and reliable method of monitoring abstinence, because THC remains present for such a long time and its use can be detected with infrequent testing. Some treaters do not recommend urine testing because they believe it violates the trust that is supposed to exist in the psychiatrist-patient relationship and hence renders the psychiatrist less effective.[27]

A difficult treatment situation arises when it is hypothesized that the patient is using cannabis to self-medicate a primary Axis I disorder, such as depression or an anxiety disorder. In these individuals, abstinence is difficult to achieve because the patient believes that cannabis will alleviate his or her symptoms. Relapse usually occurs repeatedly until the underlying Axis I disorder is effectively treated. Thus, in evaluating all patients with cannabis abuse or dependence, careful assessment for a comorbid Axis I disorder is essential.[23–26]

Clinical Vignette 1

Mr. A, a 21-year-old college student, first experimented with smoking marijuana in the eighth grade at the age of 13 years. Initially, he smoked marijuana once or twice a month, but by 10th grade, he was using the drug two or three times each weekend and occasionally during the week as well. By the 12th grade, he was smoking daily and would frequently be intoxicated when attending class.

On going to college, Mr. A's cannabis use increased dramatically. He and a group of several friends routinely smoked marijuana on four or five separate occasions per day, beginning promptly on awakening in the morning, smoking again midday, and smoking repeatedly from dinnertime until well after midnight. Mr. A reported that he had some tolerance to the effects of marijuana, in that he customarily smoked much more to achieve the desired effect than he recalled using in his early years in high school. It was difficult to assess whether he ever experienced symptoms of withdrawal from marijuana, because he diligently maintained an adequate supply of the drug, so that it was always available. On the rare occasions when his use of the drug was interrupted by lack of supply or by a social demand (e.g., a visit to his parents), he described a mild and nonspecific dysphoria associated with loss of access to the drug. Mr. A did not feel that he smoked marijuana in larger amounts or for a longer time than intended, because at all times he intended to smoke as frequently and regularly as possible. Several times a year, however, he resolved to cut down on his frequency of use (e.g., after doing poorly on an examination) but lost this resolve within a matter of days or even hours when his friends persuaded him to resume smoking.

Clinical Vignette 1 *continued*

Mr. A spent a good deal of time ensuring that he had an ample supply of marijuana, and he carefully anticipated "dry spells" when the supply of marijuana on the street became limited. Sometimes, he would purchase a large quantity of marijuana (several ounces), keeping about half of it for himself and selling the remainder to friends. His use of marijuana consumed several hours of his day and represented a major social ritual.

Because of Mr. A's frequent smoking of marijuana, he would frequently decline social invitations to stay at home and smoke with friends. Frequently, because of intoxication or sleep, he would miss college classes, athletic activities, or other appointments. In some instances, this posed serious problems for him; he failed two college courses during his freshman and sophomore years, causing his parents to threaten to withdraw financial support for his tuition. His parents were partially aware of his marijuana use and constantly admonished him to reduce his use or to abstain from the drug. However, even with the threat of failing college or losing his tuition money, he found that he was unable to reduce his use.

Mr. A presented to the investigators as a potential subject in a neuropsychological study that required him to be completely abstinent from cannabis for 6 months. Because of the large remuneration for this study, he resolved at last to discontinue smoking. He was monitored by the investigators with urine tests on a weekly basis to ensure that he adhered to his promise. Strongly positive urine test results (THC levels well above 50 µg/mL) persisted for more than 3 weeks after his last reported use of marijuana, although the levels declined steadily. Even 5 weeks after his last use, some detectable levels (above 10 ng/mL) were noted. At about the 3-week mark (when his level finally dropped below the 50 µg range), Mr. A reported a dramatic "waking up" of his mental faculties. He stated that his mind was "clear" in a way that it had not been in several years. During the next 6 months, in the absence of cannabis use (verified with urine testing every second week), his academic performance improved substantially. However, at the end of the 6-month period, when he concluded the neuropsychological study and received payment, he immediately scheduled a party with his friends and relapsed into smoking several times a day.

On interview with the Structured Clinical Interview for the *Diagnostic and Statistical Manual of Mental Disorders,* Third Edition, Revised (DSM-III-R), Mr. A displayed no evidence of any other Axis I or Axis II disorder besides cannabis dependence. He described some periods of heavy alcohol use and had used several other drugs (cocaine about 50 times in his lifetime, hallucinogens about 20 times, and amphetamines twice), but he had never met criteria for abuse of or dependence on another substance.

Clinical Vignette 2

Mr. B, 28 years old, was a highly successful high-school student who completed 2 years of college at a prestigious university. During his later high-school years and early college years, he used cannabis occasionally (approximately once to twice a week) but exhibited no frank abuse or dependence on the drug.

In the summer after his sophomore year in college, Mr. B experienced an episode of major depression. During this time, he began to smoke marijuana more frequently. On reflection, he recalled that his marijuana use at that time was largely motivated by the antidepressant effect that he derived from the drug. In the fall of that year, when it was time to return to college for his junior year, Mr. B developed an atypical manic episode. He spent large amounts of money, drove his parents' car across the United States following the tour of a rock band, and then misplaced the car and was unable to remember where he had left it parked. He was eventually apprehended by the police, wandering down the street in the middle of the night in a small Western town; he was returned to his home and hospitalized involuntarily.

At the time of the hospitalization, a diagnosis was made of schizoaffective disorder, bipolar type with mood-incongruent psychotic symptoms. Mr. B's history of cannabis use (which had by now escalated to several times a day for the last several months) was not specifically elicited. Mr. B was treated with lithium carbonate and fluphenazine and discharged to a partial hospitalization program.

Mr. B quickly became noncompliant with his partial hospitalization program. Within 24 hours after his discharge from the inpatient unit, he had secured a supply of marijuana and began surreptitiously smoking two to three times a day. Shortly thereafter, he discontinued his lithium and fluphenazine, left the area, and hitchhiked across the country to the West Coast.

During the course of the next 5 to 6 years, this pattern repeated itself many times. Mr. B would be hospitalized for an acute psychotic episode, typically accompanied by manic features, and would be treated with a variety of antipsychotic and antimanic medications, including neuroleptics, lithium carbonate, carbamazepine, and valproate. After discharge, he would be briefly compliant with medications and abstinent from marijuana but would quickly relapse into marijuana use, thereby leading to a new cycle of relapse and hospitalization.

After several years of this "revolving door" syndrome, it became increasingly clear to treatment personnel that Mr. B tended to develop symptoms of major depression in the wake of each psychotic episode. These symptoms were, if anything, exacerbated by his regimen of antipsychotic and antimanic agents. Although he had also received some antidepressant medications during these periods, he stated that none of these medications even approached the antidepressant efficacy of marijuana. For these reasons, as soon as the depressive symptoms began to become noticeable, he promptly resumed smoking marijuana heavily, stating that the relief from depression afforded by marijuana far outweighed the potential risk of being rehospitalized with a new psychotic episode.

During these depressive periods, Mr. B's marijuana use immediately escalated to several episodes of smoking per day, and he spent large amounts of time each day smoking the drug, maintaining an adequate supply of the drug, and recovering from its effects. Mr. B also felt that he developed some tolerance to the drug and needed to use increasing amounts of it to maintain the antidepressant effect. If he stopped using the drug, the depressive symptoms recurred quickly and frightened him; thus, he was careful to ensure that he always had an adequate supply of the drug available. Mr. B regularly experienced increasing psychotic symptoms within 2 to 4 weeks of starting to use marijuana. However, he was careful to disguise these symptoms from his treatment team, recognizing that they would lead to hospitalization or at least to an interruption of his ability to consume marijuana. Typically, he would be able to mask the psychosis for many weeks until the symptoms became so severe that his facade collapsed, and hospitalization followed quickly.

Once hospitalized, Mr. B waited for the first available time when his privileges were increased to the point that he could leave the unit and obtain more marijuana. He would then bring a supply back to the hospital, hide it in his room, and continue to smoke surreptitiously, while an inpatient, as long as a supply was accessible.

These issues were addressed in three ways. First, Mr. B was enrolled in a group directed at the issues of substance abuse and dependence. Although this group was composed primarily of abusers of other substances (especially alcohol and cocaine), who did not have a serious Axis I disorder such as that of Mr. B, he found that he had enough in common with the other group members for the group to be of value to him. Second, his psychiatrists became much more aggressive in the treatment of his depression. Currently, he is being treated with venlafaxine, 225 mg/d, in conjunction with lithium carbonate and risperidone. With the venlafaxine, he states that he experiences a greater antidepressant benefit than he has with past agents, although some residual symptoms of depression (and, hence, some temptation to resume cannabis use) still remain. Third, Mr. B is tested at random intervals (on average, once per week) for urinary THC and THC metabolites. With this regimen, he has managed to remain abstinent from cannabis for most of the last year, save for one period when he was offered some marijuana in the city, smoked it, and then almost immediately relapsed into heavy use during the next few days, followed by a brief hospitalization for a psychotic episode.

References

1. Leonard BE: Cannabis: A short review of its effects and the possible dangers of its use. Br J Addict 1969; 64:121–130.
2. Cohen S: Marijuana research: Selected recent findings. Drug Abuse Alcohol Newsletter 1986; 15:1–3.
3. Johnson BA: Psychopharmacological effects of cannabis. Br J Hosp Med 1990; 43:114–122.
4. Solomons K, Neppe VM: Cannabis—its clinical effects. S Afr Med J 1989; 76:102–104.
5. Sethi BB, Trivedi JK, Kumar P, et al: Antianxiety effect of cannabis: Involvement of central benzodiazepine receptors. Biol Psychiatry 1986; 21:3–10.
6. Gough AL, Olley JE: Delta-9-tetrahydrocannabinol and the extrapyramidal system. Psychopharmacology (Berl) 1977; 54:87–99.
7. Miller L, Branconnier R: Cannabis: Effects on memory and the cholinergic limbic system. Psychol Bull 1983; 93:441–456.
8. Tennant FS: The clinical syndrome of marijuana dependence. Psychiatr Ann 1986; 16:225–234.
9. Devane WA, Dysarz FA III, Johnson MR, et al: Determination and characterization of a cannabinoid receptor in rat brain. Mol Pharmacol 1988; 34:605–613.
10. Mueser KT, Yarnold PR, Bellak AS: Diagnostic and demographic correlates of substance abuse in schizophrenia and major affective disorder. Acta Psychiatr Scand 1992; 85:48–55.
11. National Institute on Drug Abuse: National Household Survey on Drug Abuse: Population Estimates 1992. Washington, DC: U.S. Government Printing Office, 1993. DHHS publication (SMA) 93-2053.
12. Johnston LD, O'Malley PM, Bachman JG: National Survey Results on Drug Use from the Monitoring the Future Study, 1975–1993, Volume 1, Secondary School Students. Rockville, MD: National Institutes of Health, 1994. NIH publication (SMA) 94-3809.
13. Pope HG Jr, Ionescu-Piogga M, Aizley HG, Varma DK: Drug use and lifestyle among college undergraduates in 1989: A comparison with 1969 and 1978. Am J Psychiatry 1990; 147:998–1001.
14. Miller NS, Klahr AL, Gold MS, et al: Cannabis diagnosis of patients receiving treatment for cocaine dependence. J Subst Abuse 1990; 2:107–111.
15. Brady K, Casto S, Lydiard RB, et al: Substance abuse in an inpatient psychiatric sample. Am J Drug Alcohol Abuse 1991; 17:389–397.
16. Alterman AI, Erdlen DL, LaPorte DJ, Erdlen FR: Effects of illicit drug use in an inpatient psychiatric population. Addict Behav 1982; 7:231–242.
17. Miller FT, Busch F, Tanenbaum JH: Drug abuse in schizophrenia and bipolar disorder. Am J Drug Alcohol Abuse 1989; 15:291–295.
18. Szuster RR, Pontuis EB, Campos PE: Marijuana sensitivity and panic anxiety. J Clin Psychiatry 1988; 49:427–429.
19. Weller RA, Halikas JA: Marijuana use and psychiatric illness: A follow-up study. Am J Psychiatry 1985; 142:848–850.
20. Henry B, Feehan M, McGee R, et al: The importance of conduct problems and depressive symptoms in predicting adolescent substance use. J Abnorm Child Psychol 1993; 21:469–480.
21. Pillard RC: Marijuana. N Engl J Med 1970; 283:294–303.
22. Gruber AJ, Pope HG Jr: Cannabis psychotic disorder: Does it exist? Am J Addict 1994; 3:72–83.
22a. Kouri E, Pope HG Jr, Todd D, Gruber S: Attributes of heavy versus occasional marijuana smokers in a college population. Biol Psychiatry 1995; 38:475–481.
23. Peralta V, Cuesta MJ: Influence of cannabis abuse on schizophrenic psychopathology. Acta Psychiatr Scand 1992; 85:127–130.
24. Dixon L, Haas G, Weiden PJ, et al: Drug abuse in schizophrenic patients: Clinical correlates and reasons for use. Am J Psychiatry 1991; 148:224–230.
25. Estroff TW, Gold MS: Psychiatric presentations for marijuana abuse. Psychiatr Ann 1986; 16:221–224.
26. Warner R, Taylor D, Wright J, et al: Substance use among the mentally ill: Prevalence, reasons for use, and effects on illness. Am J Orthopsychiatry 1994; 64:30–39.
27. Miller NS, Gold MS, Pottash AC: A 12-step treatment approach for marijuana *(Cannabis)* dependence. J Subst Abuse Treat 1989; 6:241–250.
28. Lex BW, Griffin ML, Mello NK, Mendelson JH: Alcohol, marijuana, and mood states in young women. Int J Addict 1989; 24:405–424.
29. Mirin SM, Shapiro LM, Meyer RE, et al: Casual versus heavy use of marijuana: A redefinition of the marijuana problem. Am J Psychiatry 1971; 127:1134–1140.
30. Jones RT, Benowitz N, Bachman J: Clinical studies of cannabis tolerance and dependence. Ann N Y Acad Sci 1976; 282:221–239.
31. Kaymakcalan S: Tolerance to and dependence on cannabis. Bull Narc 1973; 25:39–47.
32. Kaymakcalan S: The addictive potential of cannabis. Bull Narc 1981; 33:21–31.
33. Compton DR, Dewey WL, Martin BR: Cannabis dependence and tolerance production. Adv Alcohol Subst Abuse 1990; 9:129–147.
34. Roffman RK, Barnhart R: Assessing need for marijuana dependence treatment through an anonymous telephone interview. Int J Addict 1987; 22:639–651.
35. Struve FA, Straumanis JJ, Patrick G, Price L: Topographic mapping of quantitative EEG variables in chronic heavy marijuana users: Empirical findings with psychiatric patients. Clin Electroencephalogr 1989; 20:6–23.
36. Kolodny RC, Masters WH, Kolodner RM, Toro G: Depression of plasma testosterone levels after chronic intensive marijuana use. N Engl J Med 1974; 290:872–974.
37. Block RI, Farinpour R, Schlechte JA: Effects of chronic marijuana use on testosterone, luteinizing hormone, follicle stimulating hormone, prolactin and cortisol in men and women. Drug Alcohol Depend 1991; 28:121–128.
38. Braude MC, Szara SS (eds): Pharmacology of Marijuana, Volumes 1 and 2. New York: Raven Press, 1976.
39. Miller LL (ed): Marijuana: Effects on Human Behavior. New York: Academic Press, 1974.
39a. Pope HG Jr, Gruber A, Todd D: The residual neuropsychological effects of cannabis: The current status of research. Drug Alcohol Depend 1995; 38:25–34.
40. Keeler MH, Ewing JA, Rouse BA: Hallucinogenic effects of marijuana as currently used. Am J Psychiatry 1971; 128:213–216.

41. Keeler MH, Reifler CB, Liptzin MB: Spontaneous recurrence of marijuana effect. Am J Psychiatry 1968; 125:384–386.
42. Levi L, Miller NR: Visual illusions associated with previous drug abuse. J Clin Neuroophthalmol 1990; 10:103–110.
43. Annis HM, Smart RG: Adverse reactions and recurrences from marijuana use. Br J Addict 1973; 68:315–319.
44. Stanton MD, Bardoni A: Drug flashbacks: Reported frequency in a military population. Am J Psychiatry 1972; 129:751–755.
45. Halikas JA: Marijuana use and psychiatric illness. In Miller LL (ed): Marijuana: Effects on Human Behavior. New York: Academic Press, 1974:265–302.
46. Frances AK, Hales RE: Annual Review of Psychiatry, Volume 5. Washington, DC: American Psychiatric Press, 1986.
47. Hammer T, Vaglum P: Initiation, continuation or discontinuation of cannabis use in the general population. Br J Addict 1990; 85:899–909.
48. Roffman RA, Klepsch R, Wertz JS, et al: Predictors of attrition from an outpatient marijuana-dependence counseling program. Addict Behav 1993; 18:553–566.
49. Mellinger GD, Somers RH, Davidson ST, Manheimer DI: The amotivational syndrome and the college student. Ann N Y Acad Sci 1976; 282:37–55.
50. Zinberg NE, Weil AT: A comparison of marijuana users and non-users. Nature 1970; 226:119–123.
51. Simon WE, Primavera LH, Simon MG, Orndoff RD: A comparison of marijuana users and nonusers on a number of personality variables. J Consult Clin Psychol 1974; 42:917–918.
52. Lessin PJ, Thomas SA: Assessment of the chronic effect of marijuana on motivation and achievement: A preliminary report. In Braude MC, Szara S (eds): The Pharmacology of Marijuana. New York: Raven Press, 1976:681–690.
53. Kupfer DJ, Detre T, Koral J, Fajans P: A comment on the "amotivational syndrome" in marijuana smokers. Am J Psychiatry 1973; 130:1319–1321.
54. Comitas L: Cannabis and work in Jamaica: A refutation of the amotivational syndrome. Ann N Y Acad Sci 1976; 282:24–35.
55. Burdsal C, Greenberg G, Timpe R: The relationship of marijuana usage to personality and motivational factors. J Psychol 1973; 85:45–51.
56. Hochman JS, Brill NQ: Chronic marijuana use and psychosocial adaptation. Am J Psychiatry 1973; 130:132–140.
57. Campbell I: The amotivational syndrome and cannabis use with emphasis on the Canadian scene. Ann N Y Acad Sci 1976; 282:33–36.
58. Boulougouris JC, Liakos A, Stefanis C: Social traits of heavy hashish users and matched controls. Ann N Y Acad Sci 1976; 282:17–23.
59. Robins LN, Darvish HS, Murphy GE: The long-term outcome for adolescent drug users: A follow-up study of 76 users and 146 non-users. In Zubin J, Freedman AM (eds): The Psychopathology of Adolescence. New York: Grune & Stratton, 1970:159–180.
60. Mendelson JH, Kuehnle JC, Greenberg I, Mello NK: The effects of marijuana use on human operant behavior: Individual data. In Braude MC, Szara S (eds): The Pharmacology of Marijuana. New York: Raven Press, 1976:643–653.
61. Brill NQ, Christie RL: Marijuana use and psychosocial adaptation. Arch Gen Psychiatry 1974; 31:713–719.
62. Zweben JE, O'Connell K: Strategies for breaking marijuana dependence. J Psychoactive Drugs 1992; 24:165–171.
63. Nigam R, Schottenfeld R, Kosten TR: Treatment of dual diagnosis patients: A relapse prevention group approach. J Subst Abuse Treat 1992; 9:305–309.
64. Smith JW, Schmeling G, Knowles PL: A marijuana smoking cessation clinical trial utilizing THC-free marijuana, aversion therapy, and self-management counseling. J Subst Abuse Treat 1988; 5:89–98.
65. Smith JW, Frawley PJ: Treatment outcome of 600 chemically dependent patients treated in a multimodal inpatient program including aversion therapy and pentathol interview. J Subst Abuse Treat 1993; 10:359–369.
66. Negrete JC, Knapp WP, Douglas DE, Smith WB: Cannabis affects the severity of schizophrenic symptoms: Results of a clinical survey. Psychol Med 1986; 16:515–520.
67. Treffert DA: Marijuana use in schizophrenia: A clear hazard. Am J Psychiatry 1978; 135:1213–1215.
68. Cuffel BJ, Heithoff KA, Lawson W: Correlates of patterns of substance abuse among patients with schizophrenia. Hosp Community Psychiatry 1993; 44:247–251.
69. Linszen DH, Dingemans PM, Lenior ME: Cannabis abuse and the course of recent-onset schizophrenic disorder. Arch Gen Psychiatry 1994; 51:273–279.

CHAPTER

45 Cocaine Use Disorders

Elinore F. McCance

Cocaine Dependence
Cocaine Abuse
Cocaine Intoxication
Cocaine Withdrawal

Definition

Cocaine, a central nervous system stimulant produced by the coca plant, is consumed in several preparations. Cocaine hydrochloride powder is usually sniffed through the nostrils, or it may be mixed in water and injected intravenously. Cocaine hydrochloride powder is also commonly heated ("cooked up") with baking soda and water to precipitate a gel-like substance that can be smoked ("freebasing"). "Crack" cocaine is a precooked form of cocaine alkaloid that is sold on the street as small "rocks." Abundant supplies and falling prices for cocaine (1 g of cocaine can be purchased for as little as $50, "dime bags" containing about 0.1 g of cocaine cost $10, and a vial of crack [two or three small rocks] can be had for $3 to $5) have contributed greatly to the prevalence of cocaine abuse and dependence as well as other related cocaine use disorders.

Cocaine intoxication produces a state of intense euphoria that is a powerful reinforcer and can lead to the development of cocaine abuse in many individuals, although only 10% to 15% of those who try cocaine by the intranasal route of administration go on to cocaine abuse or cocaine dependence.[1] Some experience the stimulant effects of cocaine as anxiogenic; others discontinue use because of lack of easy drug availability, fear of loss of control over use, or apprehension regarding possible legal consequences of cocaine abuse. The route of administration is strongly correlated with the development of cocaine abuse and dependence, in that the intravenous and smoked routes of administration allow rapid transport of the drug to the brain, producing intense effects that are short-lived. Rapid tolerance to euphoric effects occurs, and plasma concentrations are not correlated with peak euphoria, which produces a need for frequent dosing to regain euphoric effects (binge use) and places the cocaine abuser at risk for medical and psychiatric complications of cocaine abuse.

Cocaine abuse is characterized by a maladaptive pattern of substance use demonstrated by recurrent and significant adverse consequences related to repeated drug use. Such consequences include family discord, legal and employment problems, and interpersonal problems. The person diagnosed with cocaine abuse may have significant periods during which no cocaine-related problems are experienced, but the initiation of cocaine use will herald the onset of psychosocial difficulties. Cocaine dependence is characterized by a more pervasive pattern of frequent cocaine use and a chronic cycle of psychosocial problems. In addition, medical and psychiatric symptoms associated with cocaine use may place the patient at substantial personal risk.

Whereas cocaine is not physiologically addicting, the psychological addiction is powerful and can completely dominate the life of the cocaine abuser. Binge use of cocaine may be followed by what has been described as a mild withdrawal syndrome characterized by dysphoria and anhedonia, which may resemble a depressive disorder and, in some cases, may require emergent psychiatric treatment. Some combination of these consequences of cocaine abuse is usually responsible for the identification and diagnosis of individuals with cocaine use disorders and referral to cocaine abuse treatment programs.

Epidemiology

The National Household Survey on Drug Abuse[2] conducted in 1991 found that the prevalence of lifetime cocaine use in persons 12 years of age and older was 11.5%; 3% of the population used cocaine in the past year, and 0.9% used cocaine in the past month. The highest prevalence (25.8%) of cocaine use occurred in adults aged 26 to 34 years, followed by young adults aged 18 to 25 years (17.9%). Among adults aged 18 to 25 and 26 to 34 years, the highest rates of current cocaine use occurred in the unemployed (4.9% and 5%, respectively), those with less than a high school education (3.8% and 3%, respectively), black persons (3.1% and 2.7%, respectively), and those living in the western United States (3% and 2.4%, respectively). Males aged 12 years and older were found to use cocaine at a higher rate than females aged 12 years and older (14.3% versus

9%). Furthermore, for the total population aged 12 years and older, males used cocaine at twice the rate of females in the past year and in the past month. White (11.8%), black (11.2%), and Hispanic persons (11.1%) did not differ in lifetime use of cocaine. Black and Hispanic persons were more likely to have used cocaine at twice the rate of females in both the past year ($P < .05$) and the past month ($P < .001$). The National Institute on Drug Abuse estimates that at least 2 million adults in the United States are addicted to cocaine and between 1 and 3 million people are in need of treatment for cocaine use disorders.[3]

Sex Differences in Cocaine Abuse

The prevalence of substance abuse in treatment programs and in the community has been reported to be as much as four times as high in men as in women.[4] As a result, much of our understanding of substance abuse treatment efficacy is based on predominantly male samples. However, substance abuse is the second most common psychiatric disorder in women aged 18 to 24 years.[5] The risks of cocaine and other substance abuse are significant not only for women but for their unborn children, who are at risk for neuropsychological sequelae secondary to prenatal exposure. Abuse and neglect of children are common consequences of parental addiction. There is reason to believe that women cocaine abusers differ from men in several respects, including treatment response.

Two clinical studies of treatment-seeking patients have noted several differences in epidemiological features of cocaine abuse in women compared with that in men.[6, 7] One study of 129 (95 men, 34 women) consecutive patients admitted for inpatient treatment of cocaine abuse has been reported.[6] Women cocaine abusers were significantly younger than men in age at onset of cocaine abuse and first entry to treatment. This is in contrast to studies of opioid addicts[8] and alcoholic individuals,[9] suggesting a possible premorbid characteristic that would distinguish women who become cocaine abusers from men. Men had used cocaine for a longer time than women, and whereas the amount of cocaine use did not differ, men spent more money on the drug than women did.

Women in treatment had a significantly lower overall level of social adjustment; men were more likely to be employed, to support themselves financially, and to finance their own drug habits. Women were more likely to meet diagnostic criteria for major depression; men were more likely to have a diagnosis of antisocial personality disorder. Women showed less improvement on the Hamilton Depression Rating Scale than did men, whose scores improved steadily during the course of the hospitalization. This suggests that newly abstinent women may experience greater levels of psychological distress that may persist for some time during recovery. The rapid course of addiction and slower recovery from depressive symptoms may indicate that the course after cocaine abstinence is more severe in women.

Relationship of Psychiatric Disorders to Cocaine Abuse

Epidemiological surveys have failed to identify demographical characteristics, personality traits, or features of early cocaine use that differentiate noncompulsive and heavy use.[10] The only well-documented predisposing condition related to cocaine abuse is comorbid psychiatric illness.[10] Several studies have documented the high rate of comorbid psychiatric disorders in cocaine abusers entering treatment.[11–13] These disorders include mood disorders (major depression, bipolar disorders, attention-deficit/hyperactivity disorder, anxiety disorders, and antisocial personality disorder). In general, mood disorders temporally follow the onset of cocaine abuse in patients presenting for treatment; attention-deficit/hyperactivity disorder and antisocial personality disorder precede the onset of drug abuse.[13] Finally, clinical observations of treatment-seeking cocaine abusers indicate that the amount of cocaine exposure may be the most important factor in development of cocaine abuse or dependence.[14, 15]

Course and Natural History

Cocaine produces a sense of intensified pleasure in most activities and a heightened sense of alertness and well-being. Anxiety and social inhibition are decreased. Energy, self-esteem, and self-perception of ability are increased. There is enhancement of emotion and sexual feeling.[14–16] Pleasurable experiences, although heightened, are not distorted, and hallucinations are usually absent.[15] The person engaging in low-dose cocaine use often receives positive feedback from others responding to the user's increased energy and enthusiasm. This, in combination with the euphoria experienced by the user, can be reinforcing, and cocaine use is perceived as free of any adverse consequences.

Cocaine users quickly learn that higher doses are associated with intensified and prolonged euphoria, which results in increasing use of the drug. The abuser is focused on the cocaine-induced euphoria while intoxicated and begins to compulsively pursue this state of perceived well-being. These behaviors become pivotal in the lives of cocaine abusers who continue drug abuse in the presence of increasing personal and social disaster.[14, 15]

The effects of cocaine are similar to those of amphetamine; the main difference in terms of abuse liability is in cocaine's much shorter duration of action. Whereas the plasma elimination half-life for cocaine is approximately 90 minutes, this drug produces pharmacodynamic tachyphylaxis resulting in rapidly diminishing effects in the presence of continued cocaine in the plasma. This phenomenon explains the "half-life" of cocaine-induced euphoria, which is approximately 45 minutes after intranasal use as well as characteristic binge use in which cocaine is readministered during short intervals.[15, 17] During binge use, the drug may be administered as frequently as every 10 minutes, resulting in rapid mood changes. Cocaine binges can last as long as 7 days, although the average length is 12 hours.[15]

Uncontrolled use of cocaine often begins with either increased access and resultant escalating dosages and frequency of administration or a change from intranasal use to a route of administration with more rapid onset of effects (i.e., intravenous or smoked).[10, 14, 15, 18–20] These characteristics are integral to the development of high-dose binging with cocaine. Such binges produce extreme euphoria and vivid memories. These memories are later contrasted with current dysphoria to produce intense craving, which perpetuates the binge use pattern.[14, 15] Addicts report that during binge use, thoughts are focused exclusively on the cocaine-induced effects. Normal daily needs, including sleep and nourishment, are neglected. Responsibilities to family and employer and social obligations are given up. This continues until the supply of cocaine is exhausted.

Binges are often separated by several days of abstinence; cocaine-dependent persons average one to three binges per week, which last 8 to 24 hours. Lack of an early pattern of cocaine use does not indicate a lack of impairment. This is in contrast to use patterns for opiate and alcohol dependence and is crucial to an understanding of the syndrome of cocaine dependence.[10] Although the prediction of development of cocaine use disorders is not possible on an individual basis, it is clear that those who progress to binge use of the drug will be significantly affected and constitute the majority of the treatment-seeking population.

The onset of a binge pattern of cocaine use usually results in a significant level of impairment that may be manifested by neglect of personal needs, neglect of family and job responsibilities, initiation of illegal activities necessary to support the cocaine use, and engagement in irresponsible behaviors as a result of drug intoxication or acute abstinence symptoms. One or more of these issues is the usual precipitant to seeking treatment. The cocaine abuser is likely to be ambivalent about the need for treatment, and the treatment dropout rate is high (ranging from 38% to 73%); dropout usually occurs in the early phase of treatment (during the initial evaluation process).[21, 22]

Newly abstinent cocaine abusers can be expected to experience a triphasic abstinence pattern that includes a "crash" period lasting several hours to several days; a withdrawal period characterized by minor depressive symptoms, which lasts 2 to 10 weeks; and an extinction phase, which lasts indefinitely and is characterized by intermittent drug craving that becomes more manageable with continued abstinence. These phases are described in detail later.

Like other drug and alcohol use disorders, cocaine use disorders are a group of chronic relapsing illnesses that are difficult to treat. Patients are at high risk for relapse, particularly in the first 3 months of treatment. This is because of ongoing psychosocial stressors that result from or have been exacerbated by cocaine abuse and because of the lack of a good repertoire of coping skills necessary to avoid cocaine abuse, which take time to acquire in the treatment process. Although the ability to cope with cocaine craving improves with continued abstinence, relapse to cocaine abuse or other drug and alcohol abuse will continue to be a risk indefinitely for a patient who has a history of a cocaine use disorder. This should be expected and the patient counseled during treatment about this possibility in an attempt to avoid treatment dropout. Multiple treatments may be required for patients with cocaine dependence. These may include inpatient treatment for medical or psychiatric complications of the cocaine abuse, partial hospital programs, self-help groups, psychotherapy (usually group or family therapy for patients with primary cocaine use disorders), or some combination of these treatments according to the presentation of the patient.

Etiology and Pathophysiology

Neurobiological Changes Related to Acute Cocaine Use

Cocaine has effects on multiple neurotransmitters, including release and reuptake blockade of dopamine, norepinephrine, and serotonin (5-hydroxytryptamine [5-HT]).[23] The most widely accepted explanation of cocaine-induced euphoria is that dopamine reuptake inhibition results in increased extracellular dopamine concentration in the mesolimbic and mesocortical reward pathways in the brain. Numerous studies have provided evidence for the importance of dopamine in the reinforcing properties of cocaine. Low doses of dopamine receptor antagonists, injected systemically, consistently increase cocaine self-administration in animals. This has been interpreted to be an indication of blockade of cocaine's effects.[24] In addition, 6-hydroxydopamine lesions of dopaminergic terminals in the nucleus accumbens produce extinction-like responding and a reduction in cocaine self-administration.[24] Similar lesions in other areas of the brain (frontal cortex and caudate nucleus) do not alter cocaine self-administration.[24]

In vivo brain microdialysis has also provided additional experimental data indicating that mesolimbic dopamine is associated with cocaine reward.[25] Conversely, cocaine abstinence, which is characterized by depression, irritability, and anxiety (the crash), has been hypothesized to result from dopaminergic hypoactivity. Support for this hypothesis is derived from studies of in vivo microdialysis during cocaine withdrawal.[26]

There may also be other neurochemical processes important to both the positive and the negative reinforcing properties of cocaine. Although dopamine reuptake inhibition is important to the reinforcing properties of cocaine, it cannot fully account for cocaine effects. Numerous agents that are dopamine reuptake inhibitors but are not abused by humans and are not self-administered by animals are known. These include benztropine, nomifensine, and mazindol. Similarly, other agents that are not abused by humans mimic neurochemical actions of cocaine on noradrenergic or serotoninergic systems. Therefore, none of the known singular neurochemical actions of cocaine provides a full explanation of cocaine-induced euphoria.[27]

Neurobiological Changes Related to Long-Term Cocaine Use

High-dose cocaine use for extended periods appears to result in sustained neurophysiological changes in brain systems that regulate psychological processes, specifically pleasure and hedonic responsivity.[14, 15, 28] This has been postulated to underlie a physiological addiction to cocaine with associated withdrawal phenomena that are manifested clinically as a psychological syndrome.[14, 15] Long-term cocaine administration in animals is associated with decreased intracranial electrical self-stimulation of dopaminergic brain reward areas, such as the nucleus accumbens, and an increase in the voltage required to elicit intracranial electrical self-stimulation.[14, 15] These findings imply that brain reward regions affected by cocaine may be down-regulated or less sensitive to neurotransmitter ligands. This is consistent with clinical observations of extended periods of anhedonia in

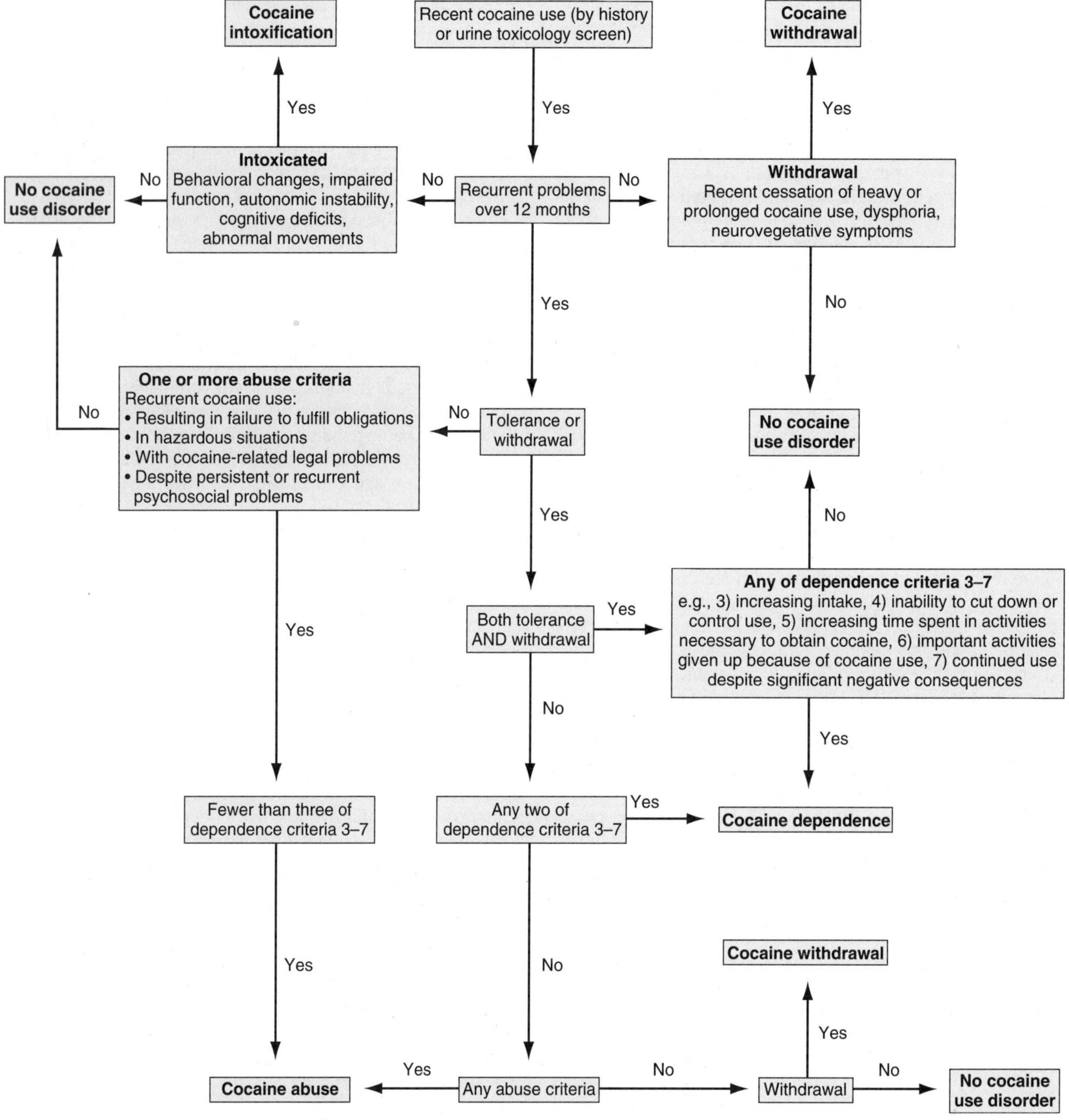

Figure 45–1 *Cocaine use disorders: diagnostic decision tree.*

cocaine abusers during abstinence and depression after cocaine use in animals.[14] Neurophysiological changes that could account for these experimental and clinical observations include findings in animal studies of dopaminergic, α-adrenergic, and β-adrenergic receptor supersensitivity induced by long-term cocaine administration, which may induce receptor alterations.[15] If dopaminergic autoreceptor supersensitivity is greater than that for postsynaptic receptors, the net effect would be decrease of dopaminergic neurotransmission. Animal studies in which cocaine is continuously administered have confirmed that such changes occur.[29, 30] However, long-term intermittent cocaine use was not associated with decreased dopaminergic transmission. Other mechanisms may play a role in regulation of cell firing and activation thresholds during long-term cocaine use, but these have yet to be elucidated.

Diagnosis of Cocaine Use Disorders

The initial evaluation period should include the collection of a complete history of all substance abuse, which is essential to accurate diagnosis and appropriate treatment. A diagnostic decision tree for cocaine use disorders is shown in Figure 45–1. The history includes the circumstances under which each drug was used, the psychoactive effects sought and obtained, the route of administration, and the frequency and amount of each drug used. Cocaine abusers frequently abuse other drugs and alcohol to enhance euphoria or to alleviate dysphoric effects associated with cocaine abuse (agitation, paranoia). A thorough history with diagnosis of other substance use disorders is important to treatment planning. Patients may need detoxification from other substances on initiation of cocaine abuse treatment. It is also important to monitor patients clinically for relapses to any substance abuse during treatment for cocaine abuse, because the use of other drugs and alcohol often leads to resumption of cocaine abuse. In addition, a thorough history of current and previous substance abuse is important so that treatment can be individualized and patients can be helped to develop coping skills that will assist them in specific situations that they identify as placing them at high risk for relapse.

A careful psychiatric history with particular attention to onset of psychiatric symptoms in relation to drug use is essential. The determination of a premorbid psychiatric illness is critical to providing appropriate treatment. For persons in whom substance abuse is an attempt to self-medicate an underlying mental illness, the introduction of psychotropic medication in conjunction with ongoing psychotherapy may terminate illicit drug use. Conversely, the evaluation of temporal onset of psychiatric symptoms may preclude erroneous use of psychotropic medication and spare the patient exposure to the potential side effects of these medications.

A complete physical examination is necessary to determine whether medical complications of substance abuse are present. Common medical problems seen in cocaine abusers include poor nutrition; vitamin deficiencies; anemia; human immunodeficiency virus infection; sexually transmitted diseases; and complications of intravenous drug use, including endocarditis, abscesses, cellulitis, and hepatitis. The evaluation should include blood studies to further define abnormalities and toxicological analysis of a urine specimen.

Cocaine Dependence

The *Diagnostic and Statistical Manual of Mental Disorders,* Fourth Edition (DSM-IV)[31] defines the essential features of

DSM-IV Criteria 304.20

Substance (Cocaine) Dependence

A maladaptive pattern of substance use, leading to clinically significant impairment or distress, as manifested by three (or more) of the following, occurring at any time in the same 12-month period:

(1) tolerance, as defined by either of the following:

(a) a need for markedly increased amounts of the substance to achieve intoxication or desired effect

(b) markedly diminished effect with continued use of the same amount of the substance

(2) withdrawal, as manifested by either of the following:

(a) the characteristic withdrawal syndrome for the substance (refer to criteria A and B of the criteria sets for withdrawal from the specific substances)

(b) the same (or a closely related) substance taken to relieve or avoid withdrawal symptoms

(3) the substance is often taken in larger amounts or over a longer period than was intended

(4) there is a persistent desire or unsuccessful efforts to cut down or control substance use

(5) a great deal of time is spent in activities necessary to obtain the substance (e.g., visiting multiple doctors or driving long distances), use the substance (e.g., chain-smoking), or recover from its effects

(6) important social, occupational, or recreational activities are given up or reduced because of substance use

(7) the substance use is continued despite knowledge of having a persistent or recurrent physical or psychological problem that is likely to have been caused or exacerbated by the substance (e.g., current cocaine use despite recognition of cocaine-induced depression, or continued drinking despite recognition that an ulcer was made worse by alcohol consumption)

Specify if:

With physiological dependence: evidence of tolerance or withdrawal (i.e., either item 1 or 2 is present)

Without physiological dependence: no evidence of tolerance or withdrawal (i.e., neither item 1 nor 2 is present)

Course specifiers

Early full remission

Early partial remission

Sustained full remission

Sustained partial remission

On agonist therapy

In a controlled environment

substance dependence as a cluster of cognitive, behavioral, and physiological symptoms indicating continued use of the substance despite significant consequences of use. There is a pattern of administration that usually results in tolerance to and compulsive self-administration of the drug and may produce a withdrawal syndrome on cessation of drug use. Cocaine dependence can develop quickly after initiation of use because of the potent euphoria produced by the drug. Furthermore, the route of administration is related to the development of cocaine dependence; intravenous and smoked routes are more highly correlated with dependence than is the intranasal route of administration.

Cocaine has a short half-life requiring frequent dosing to maintain the "high" (binge use). Persons with cocaine dependence often spend large amounts of money for the drug and may be involved in illegal activities to obtain cocaine. Binges may be separated by several days while the individual recovers or attempts to obtain more money for drug purchase. Obligations such as work and childcare may be neglected. Tolerance quickly develops, resulting in larger amounts of drug use with time. This is often associated with mental or physical complications of use including paranoia, aggressive behavior, anxiety and agitation, depression, and weight loss. Withdrawal symptoms, most prominently dysphoric mood, may be seen but are usually short-lived and clear within several days of termination of drug use.

Cocaine Abuse

Substance abuse is described by DSM-IV as a maladaptive pattern of substance use demonstrated by recurrent and significant adverse consequences related to repeated use. For example, there may be neglect of obligations to family or employer, repeated use in hazardous situations, legal problems, and recurrent social or interpersonal problems. These problems must recur within the same 12-month period. The intensity and frequency of use are less in cocaine abuse than in cocaine dependence. Episodes of abuse may occur around paydays or special occasions and may be characterized by brief periods (hours to days) of high-dose binge use followed by longer periods of abstinence or nonproblem use.

Cocaine Intoxication

The clinical effects of cocaine intoxication are characterized initially by euphoria (a high feeling) and also include agitation, anxiety, irritability or affective lability, grandiosity, impaired judgment, increased psychomotor activity, hypervigilance or paranoia, and hallucinations (visual, auditory, or tactile). Physical symptoms that accompany cocaine intoxication include hypertension, tachycardia, pupillary dilation, nausea, vomiting, tremor, diaphoresis, chest pain, arrhythmia, confusion, seizures, dyskinetic movements, dystonia, and, in severe cases, coma. These effects are more frequently seen in high-dose binge users of cocaine. Cardiovascular effects are probably a result of sympathomimetic properties of cocaine (i.e., release of norepinephrine and blockade of norepinephrine reuptake).

Cocaine Withdrawal

The principal feature of substance withdrawal is development of a substance-specific maladaptive behavioral change, which may have associated physiological and cognitive components, that results from the cessation of or reduction in heavy and prolonged substance use. The syndrome is characterized by significant distress or impairment in function, and symptoms are not better explained by a mental or physical disorder. Cocaine withdrawal develops within a few hours to a few days after stopping or reducing cocaine use that has been heavy and prolonged. The syndrome is characterized by dysphoria and two or more physiological changes including fatigue, vivid and unpleasant dreams, insomnia or hypersomnia, increased appetite, and psychomotor agitation or retardation. Anhedonia and craving for cocaine can be a part of the withdrawal syndrome. Depression and suicidal ideation are the most serious complications and require individualized assessment and treatment. The syndrome may last up to several days but generally resolves without treatment.

DSM-IV also specifies additional cocaine-induced disorders described in other diagnostic groupings with which they share phenomenology (Table 45–1). These include cocaine intoxication delirium, cocaine-induced psychotic disorder, cocaine-induced mood disorder, cocaine-induced anxiety disorder, cocaine-induced sleep disorder, and cocaine-induced sexual dysfunction. These disorders are

DSM-IV Criteria 305.60

Substance (Cocaine) Abuse

A. A maladaptive pattern of substance use leading to clinically significant impairment or distress, as manifested by one (or more) of the following, occurring within a 12-month period:

(1) recurrent substance use resulting in a failure to fulfill major role obligations at work, school, or home (e.g., repeated absences or poor work performance related to substance use; substance-related absences, suspensions, or expulsions from school; neglect of children or household)

(2) recurrent substance use in situations in which it is physically hazardous (e.g., driving an automobile or operating a machine when impaired by substance use)

(3) recurrent substance-related legal problems (e.g., arrests for substance-related disorderly conduct)

(4) continued substance use despite having persistent or recurrent social or interpersonal problems caused or exacerbated by the effects of the substance (e.g., arguments with spouse about consequences of intoxication, physical fights)

B. The symptoms have never met the criteria for substance dependence for this class of substance.

diagnosed only when symptoms are in excess of those usually associated with cocaine intoxication or cocaine withdrawal and warrant independent clinical attention. In addition, the psychiatrist should pay careful attention to the temporal relationship of the psychiatric symptoms and cocaine abuse. Symptoms of severity to warrant consideration of these diagnoses should also dissipate with continued abstinence from cocaine abuse. Symptoms that worsen after cessation of cocaine use in a period of 1 to 4 weeks should be reevaluated and other Axis I or Axis III disorders considered with modification of the treatment plan as clinically indicated.

Medical Complications of Cocaine Abuse

Cardiac toxicity is one of the leading causes of morbidity and mortality associated with cocaine use. The risk of myocardial infarct is well established in cocaine use[32–34] and is not related to dose or route of administration. The risk of cocaine-related cardiac disorders is also not restricted to those with underlying coronary artery disease.[34] However, conditions that place individuals at risk for coronary events, including hypercholesterolemia, coronary artery disease,

DSM-IV Criteria 292.89

Cocaine Intoxication

A. Recent use of cocaine.

B. Clinically significant maladaptive behavioral or psychological changes (e.g., euphoria or affective blunting; changes in sociability; hypervigilance; interpersonal sensitivity; anxiety, tension, or anger; stereotyped behaviors; impaired judgment; or impaired social or occupational functioning) that developed during, or shortly after, use of cocaine.

C. Two (or more) of the following, developing during, or shortly after, cocaine use:

(1) tachycardia or bradycardia

(2) pupillary dilation

(3) elevated or lowered blood pressure

(4) perspiration or chills

(5) nausea or vomiting

(6) evidence of weight loss

(7) psychomotor agitation or retardation

(8) muscular weakness, respiratory depression, chest pain, or cardiac arrhythmias

(9) confusion, seizures, dyskinesias, dystonias, or coma

D. The symptoms are not due to a general medical condition and are not better accounted for by another mental disorder.

Specify if:

With perceptual disturbances

Reprinted with permission from the Diagnostic and Statistical Manual of Mental Disorders, Fourth Edition. Copyright 1994 American Psychiatric Association.

DSM-IV Criteria 292.0

Cocaine Withdrawal

A. Cessation of (or reduction in) cocaine use that has been heavy and prolonged.

B. Dysphoric mood and two (or more) of the following physiological changes, developing within a few hours to several days after criterion A:

(1) fatigue

(2) vivid, unpleasant dreams

(3) insomnia or hypersomnia

(4) increased appetite

(5) psychomotor retardation or agitation

C. The symptoms in criterion B cause clinically significant distress or impairment in social, occupational, or other important areas of functioning.

D. The symptoms are not due to a general medical condition and are not better accounted for by another mental disorder.

Reprinted with permission from the Diagnostic and Statistical Manual of Mental Disorders, Fourth Edition. Copyright 1994 American Psychiatric Association.

Table 45–1 Other DSM-IV Cocaine-Induced Disorders

Code	Disorder
292.89	Cocaine intoxication *Specify if:* with perceptual disturbances
292.0	Cocaine withdrawal
292.81	Cocaine intoxication delirium
292.11	Cocaine-induced psychotic disorder, with delusions *Specify if:* with onset during intoxication
292.12	Cocaine-induced psychotic disorder, with hallucinations *Specify if:* with onset during intoxication
292.84	Cocaine-induced mood disorder *Specify if:* with onset during intoxication/with onset during withdrawal
292.89	Cocaine-induced anxiety disorder *Specify if:* with onset during intoxication/with onset during withdrawal
292.89	Cocaine-induced sexual dysfunction *Specify if:* with onset during intoxication
292.89	Cocaine-induced sleep disorder *Specify if:* with onset during intoxication/with onset during withdrawal
292.9	Cocaine-related disorder not otherwise specified

Reprinted with permission from the Diagnostic and Statistical Manual of Mental Disorders, Fourth Edition. Copyright 1994 American Psychiatric Association.

myocarditis, or variations in coronary artery anatomy, increase the risk for coronary events during cocaine use.[33–37]

Two pharmacological properties of cocaine that are pertinent to the cardiovascular system have been well documented. Cocaine increases both heart rate and blood pressure through its ability to indirectly increase sympathetic stimulation by blocking norepinephrine reuptake at adrenergic nerve endings.[32–34, 38] Cocaine also produces vasoconstriction of small vessels,[39] a characteristic that contributed to its popularity as a local anesthetic agent. These properties are thought to contribute to myocardial infarct and associated malignant arrhythmias by suddenly increasing myocardial oxygen demands with resultant ischemia.

Cocaine use may produce cardiac dysrhythmias through catecholaminergic effects that increase β-adrenergic stimulation of the myocardium.[32] Cocaine-associated arrhythmias include sinus tachycardia, ventricular premature contractions, ventricular tachycardia and fibrillation, and asystole.[32, 40, 41] Arrhythmias secondary to myocardial infarct and seizures associated with cocaine use have also been well documented.[34] β-Blockers have been used to treat cocaine-associated arrhythmias, and calcium channel blockers have been shown to be effective against cardiotoxic effects of cocaine.[33, 34, 42]

Several cases of cardiomyopathy attributed to cocaine use have been reported.[32, 43] These cases appear to be secondary to acute myocardial infarction precipitated by cocaine use, although a direct toxic effect of cocaine has not been excluded. A case of acute myocarditis in a freebase cocaine user responsive to standard treatments of prednisone and azathioprine has been reported.[34] A case of fatal dissection of the ascending aorta in a person with a history of chronic hypertension and cocaine use has also been reported.[44] A sudden increase in blood pressure after cocaine use in the presence of chronically elevated blood pressure was probably responsible for this event. Pulmonary edema may also be a fatal complication of freebase cocaine use.[45]

Cerebrovascular accidents related to cocaine use have been well documented in the medical literature.[32, 46, 47] Cerebral infarct, subarachnoid hemorrhage, intraparenchymal hemorrhage, and intraventricular hemorrhage have been observed as acute complications of cocaine use. The physiological etiology of these events appears to be related to adrenergic stimulation resulting in a sudden surge in blood pressure. Abrupt increases in blood pressure in otherwise normotensive individuals may precipitate spontaneous bleeding.[47] Additional risk would be encountered by a cocaine user with an arteriovenous malformation or cerebral artery aneurysm.

Seizures were one of the earliest known complications of cocaine abuse.[48] Cocaine produces hyperpyrexia,[49] which in combination with its effects on neurotransmitters may contribute to development of seizures. Seizures may occur as a primary effect of cocaine owing to its ability to lower the seizure threshold[50] or may be secondary to other central nervous system or cardiac events precipitated by cocaine use.[33] Whereas anticonvulsants have not been helpful in preventing cocaine-related seizures,[42] intravenous diazepam has been effective in acute management.[50]

The major medical complications of cocaine abuse are summarized in Table 45–2.

Table 45–2 Major Medical Complications Associated with Cocaine Abuse

Cardiac
Myocardial infarct
Arrhythmias
Cardiomyopathy
Pulmonary
Pneumonitis (associated with smoked cocaine)
Pulmonary edema
Central Nervous System
Hyperpyrexia
Seizure
Cerebral infarct
Subarachnoid hemorrhage
Intraparenchymal hemorrhage
Intraventricular hemorrhage
Additional Complications of Intravenous Use
Infectious diseases (human immunodeficiency virus infection, hepatitis)
Endocarditis
Cellulitis
Abscesses

Management of Cocaine Abuse and Dependence

Overview

Cocaine abuse and dependence are now the most common presenting problems in urban substance abuse treatment programs. Because the availability of cocaine has increased greatly during the past 15 years, cocaine disorders are essentially new disorders for which treatments are still evolving.

The two primary goals of cocaine treatment are 1) the initiation of abstinence through disruption of binge cycles and 2) the prevention of relapse. Treatment planning to achieve these goals must be considered in the context of the stage of the cocaine abstinence syndrome in which the patient presents. Initial assessment to determine the presenting stage is necessary to determine the level of care needed (inpatient or outpatient treatment) and other psychiatric and medical considerations important to the development of the treatment plan.

The majority of cocaine abusers are most appropriately treated in an outpatient setting. Outpatient treatment may vary by provider but generally includes multiple weekly contacts, because less frequent contact is not effective in the initiation or maintenance of abstinence.[51] These sessions consist of some combination of individual drug counseling, peer support groups, family or couples therapy, urine monitoring, education sessions, psychotherapy, and psychiatric treatment that may include pharmacotherapy for cocaine addiction or comorbid psychiatric disorders. Inpatient treatment is reserved for those who have been refractory to outpatient treatment, whose compulsive use of cocaine represents an imminent danger, who have other comorbid psychiatric disorders, who are dependent on more than one substance and require monitored detoxification, who have severe withdrawal symptoms, or who lack social supports and resources necessary to initiate successful outpatient treatment.

Cocaine Abstinence Syndrome

The cocaine abstinence syndrome[28, 52] is described as consisting of three consecutive phases: crash, withdrawal, and extinction. Each phase may be characterized in part by psychiatric symptoms, which are based on individual susceptibility and the extent of drug use.

The crash is characterized by extreme exhaustion after a binge. Initial depression, agitation, and anxiety are a common experience, followed by craving for sleep. Prolonged hypersomnolence and hyperphagia are followed by a return to normal mood, although some dysphoria may remain. Clinical management consists of observation because suicidal ideation is not uncommon. Crash symptoms resemble those of major depression, which must be excluded by observation for several days of abstinence.

Cocaine withdrawal is marked by decreased energy, lack of interest, and anhedonia. These symptoms fluctuate and are not severe enough to meet diagnostic criteria for an affective disorder. However, this subjective state experienced by the cocaine abuser and contrasted with vivid memories of cocaine-induced euphoria constitutes a strong inducement to additional cocaine use. It is during this time that relapse is most likely. Withdrawal symptoms generally diminish during 2 to 10 weeks if abstinence is maintained.

The withdrawal phase is followed by extinction, an indefinite period during which evoked craving can occur, placing the individual at increased risk for relapse. Craving is evoked by moods, people, locations, or objects associated with cocaine use (money, white powder, pipes, mirrors, or syringes) that act as cues to conditioned associations with drug use and drug-induced euphoria.[28, 52] If these conditional cues fail to initiate cocaine use, then the cues lose their potency in time and craving becomes progressively less intense until extinction of craving occurs.

Early Recovery

Patients must be helped to realize that drug use is having a significant and adverse impact on their lives. Many patients come to treatment because of family, legal, or social pressures. They are often ambivalent about the need for treatment and require education about their addiction and assistance in reviewing the consequences of cocaine use in their lives.

Initial treatment should include the encouragement of abstinence from all drug use. Patients who abuse alcohol and marijuana often do not perceive these drugs as problems. Education regarding the use of such drugs as conditioned stimuli to the use of cocaine should be emphasized.

The "disease model" of chemical dependency may be used to initiate abstinence. In this concept, emphasis is on the patient's recognizing chemical dependency as a disease that the patient needs help to control but will never cure. Comprehensive drug education should also be provided in the initial treatment phase. Frequent contacts with a drug counselor are an important part of treatment. Individual, group, and (where clinically indicated) family or marital therapy should be available. Attendance at 12-step or other self-help groups is often a useful adjunct to treatment and can be particularly helpful during the early stages of treatment when support for sobriety is essential.

The early recovery phase of treatment varies in duration from 3 to 12 months[53] and is characterized by multiple weekly contacts and participation in therapeutic modalities with the goal of initiation and maintenance of abstinence. The focus during early recovery should be on relapse prevention and development of new and adaptive coping skills, healthy relationships, and lifestyle changes that will facilitate abstinence.

Relapses are common during early recovery. Patients often feel pleased about their progress in treatment, become overly confident about their ability to control use, and test themselves. Experimentation with cocaine to prove that drug use can be controlled results in relapse, which is often associated with a significant amount of guilt. Patients should be informed about the potential for relapse from the start of the treatment process. Relapse should be reviewed with the patient in a supportive way with an emphasis on helping the patient to gain an understanding of the events leading to relapse.

Long-Term Treatment

Long-term treatment is characterized by a reduced frequency of contact (weekly group or individual therapy sessions). The focus should be on maintaining a commitment to abstinence, addressing renewed denial, and improving interpersonal skills. Participation in self-help groups should continue to be encouraged. Self-help groups based on 12-step principles encourage patients to continue to view themselves as addicts in recovery—a cognitive structuring that many recovering drug abusers find helpful in maintaining sobriety.

Psychotherapy for Cocaine Abuse

Overview

A variety of psychotherapeutic strategies for the treatment of cocaine abuse have been described,[54–58] although such treatments have not been tested in controlled trials as yet. In contrast to opiate addiction, for which psychotherapies alone are insufficient,[59, 60] there appear to be some subpopulations of cocaine abusers for whom psychotherapy alone may be adequate.[61–63] The lack of a medically dangerous withdrawal syndrome from cocaine also suggests that some cocaine abusers may respond to psychotherapy alone in an outpatient treatment setting, compared with opiate- or alcohol-dependent persons, for whom hospitalization may be required for detoxification. Another important reason for the development of psychotherapies for the treatment of cocaine abuse is that no pharmacotherapies are universally effective and psychotherapies may be useful adjuncts. Furthermore, individuals not eligible for pharmacological treatment or who do not respond to pharmacological treatment will require treatment alternatives such as psychotherapeutic interventions.

Table 45–3 Psychotherapies: The Mainstay of Cocaine Abuse Treatment

Relapse prevention therapy
Lifestyle modification
Supportive group therapy
Self-help groups (e.g., Cocaine Anonymous)
Systematic cue exposure

Psychotherapies described thus far for the treatment of cocaine abuse fall into two broad categories: 1) interpersonal or psychodynamically oriented treatments[64, 65] and 2) treatments that are behavioral or cognitive-behavioral in focus.[54, 56, 66] Psychotherapeutic approaches delivered in the context of multimodal treatment programs have been described,[67, 68] and nearly all psychiatrists emphasize the importance of self-help groups such as Cocaine Anonymous. This section describes the primary psychotherapies currently used in the treatment of cocaine abuse (Table 45–3).

Relapse Prevention Therapy

Relapse prevention therapy (RPT) is based on cognitive-behavioral principles and attempts to address the serious problem of relapse in substance use disorders through the development of self-control strategies.[69] Whereas RPT was developed as a treatment for alcohol abuse, the method is applicable to all substance use disorders in theory and has been reported to be useful in the treatment of alcohol abuse,[70, 71] smoking,[72–74] and polysubstance abuse.[75]

RPT may be especially well suited as a psychotherapeutic intervention for cocaine abusers because it encompasses several distinctive features important to treating this population. Relapse prevention is oriented toward symptom control. Although the name implies focus on the prevention of relapse, in fact this method employs several strategies intended to facilitate abstinence. The emphasis on symptom control is essential in outpatient treatment, when the cocaine abuser is likely to continue to come into contact with the drug. Relapse prevention is a flexible approach in that the therapist may select from a variety of interventions to meet the specific needs of the patient at any given point in the treatment.

Relapse prevention techniques are easily integrated into other treatment modalities. These techniques have been employed in the context of pharmacotherapy, group therapy, brief psychoeducational indoctrination groups for individuals entering drug-free treatment programs, and intervention for persons at risk for human immunodeficiency virus infection.[76] RPT is an active, directive therapy in which the therapist guides the patient through an exploration of factors associated with the maintenance of abuse, which facilitates development of skills to control substance abuse. Application of these techniques in conjunction with formulation of realistic treatment goals and anticipation of problems that may be experienced are viewed by the patient as supportive. RPT is a commonsense approach in which critical techniques may be communicated to the patient within a few weeks. This method attempts to provide the patient with a repertoire of generalizable skills that may continue to be useful after the treatment ends.

Lifestyle Modification

The maintenance of abstinence depends on the development of rewarding behavioral alternatives to cocaine use. The lives of cocaine abusers often revolve around the use of cocaine to the exclusion of all else. Cocaine abusers frequently have few friends, and social contacts may be limited to other cocaine abusers. They may be estranged from family, be unemployed or working only as a means of acquiring cocaine, have no social activities, and have legal problems related to cocaine use. Recovery is often complicated by the residual problems related to cocaine use (legal problems, financial difficulties). Patients are encouraged to identify fulfilling activities to be employed as alternatives to cocaine use. If premorbid functioning was good, patients may rediscover enjoyable activities with little difficulty. Twelve-step group attendance may be of great value in the process of lifestyle modification that will promote the maintenance of abstinence. This includes facilitating development of supportive relationships with others who can serve as positive role models. These individuals provide a resource when craving intensifies or other problems become unmanageable, which can be a trigger to relapse.

Controlled Trials of Psychotherapy for Cocaine Abuse

One randomized trial evaluating purely psychotherapeutic approaches for cocaine abuse has been reported.[77] This study assessed the efficacy of psychotherapy for cocaine abuse and contrasted two different forms of psychotherapy—RPT and interpersonal (brief psychodynamic) psychotherapy. Patients were randomly assigned to each group, and therapists were trained in each method. This 12-week study demonstrated both improved retention and an increased likelihood of 3 weeks or more of abstinence in the RPT sample. The more severe cocaine users were more likely to achieve abstinence with randomization to the RPT group; less severe cocaine users tended to improve regardless of treatment received. Cocaine abusers with depression improved with either treatment, and those with antisocial personality disorders generally did not improve in either treatment or dropped out of treatment.

Systematic Cue Exposure

One factor that may be important to relapse to drug use is that of conditioned responses produced by repeated drug administration in the presence of specific stimuli. First described by Pavlov[78] in 1927, this phenomenon has been reported for psychoactive drugs in animals and humans.[79, 80] Cocaine abusers report intense craving, arousal, and palpitations when they encounter objects, persons, or situations that remind them of their cocaine use. Such cues often result in relapse. Systematic cue exposure or extinction has been studied as an adjunct to traditional abstinence-oriented treatment programs.[81] The comprehensive treatment program in which cue exposure occurs is an inpatient unit where all relapse-producing factors are addressed. These include pharmacological, social, occupational, medical, legal, and family factors and psychiatric disorders. Whereas conditioning factors may play an important role in relapse, it is unlikely that conditioning factors would override all other factors contributing to relapse in the life of an individual patient. Thus, systematic cue exposure treatment is most effective when it is administered in a setting in which a wide range of issues important to recovery may be addressed.[82]

Pharmacotherapy for Cocaine Abuse

Pharmacotherapy for the treatment of cocaine abuse is best reserved for the patient with severe dependence who has not responded to other less intensive interventions. A variety of agents have been used for treatment of cocaine addiction, but research data supporting their use are limited, and conflicting results have been obtained in some instances. Controlled trials are lacking in this area. More work is needed to determine which subgroups of cocaine abusers are most appropriate for pharmacotherapy and what agents will provide the greatest clinical benefit and least risk to patients. Several agents with promise as pharmacotherapies for cocaine abuse have been described. Controlled studies to determine efficacy in the treatment of cocaine abuse are now ongoing.

This section reviews the various pharmacotherapies that have been used for the treatment of cocaine abuse. There are no agents approved by the U.S. Food and Drug Administration for the treatment of cocaine abuse. Therefore, careful consideration must be given to the risks and benefits of treatment with any pharmacological agent.

The development of pharmacological treatments for cocaine abuse is based on the premise that an altered neurochemical substrate underlies the chronic, high-intensity (binge) use and crash that follows binge use.[83] Clinical trials of a variety of agents that either directly or indirectly function as dopamine agonists have been undertaken for treatment of the cocaine crash. The neuroadaptation model has also served as a basis for a number of studies that have evaluated the clinical utility of more general psychotropic agents that might reverse cocaine-induced changes and possess anticraving properties, block euphoria, or decrease crash or withdrawal symptoms. The following sections review the pharmacotherapies that have been used in clinical trials for the treatment of cocaine abuse to date.

Dopaminergic Agents

Dopaminergic agents have been used to ameliorate early withdrawal symptoms associated with cocaine abstinence. The theoretical basis of this treatment is that habitual use of cocaine results in central dopamine depletion. Dopaminergic autoreceptor supersensitivity has been postulated to be the mechanism underlying dysphoria after cocaine use. This altered state of dopaminergic function (or hypofunction) may be related to drug craving and other withdrawal symptoms that lead to repeated drug use but may be corrected by use of a medication that enhances dopaminergic function.

Amantadine increases dopaminergic transmission, but whether the mechanism is dopamine release, acute effects on dopamine receptors, or dopamine reuptake blockade is unclear. Several investigators have shown that the use of amantadine at dosages of 200 to 300 mg daily reduces cocaine craving and use for several days to a month.[84, 85] Amantadine has been reported to be effective in reducing craving initially, but after 3 weeks of treatment, it was no more effective than placebo. One explanation offered for this effect is that amantadine releases dopamine into the synaptic cleft initially, but in time contributes to dopamine depletion. One controlled trial showed no difference between amantadine and placebo.[86]

Bromocriptine is a dopamine agonist with high affinity for the D_2 receptor. In a preliminary report, oral bromocriptine at 0.625 mg was reported to markedly reduce cocaine craving relative to placebo in two inpatients. This report was limited by the small sample size and lack of experimental control subjects. In addition, no information was provided as to length of abstinence from cocaine before bromocriptine treatment.[87] Bromocriptine has been reported to reduce cocaine craving and, in one report, cocaine-induced euphoria.[84] Three open trials in which bromocriptine was administered in dosages ranging from 1.25 to 2.5 mg daily yielded conflicting results regarding efficacy and have suffered from high dropout rates because of side effects.[88, 89] One double-blind trial (n = 14; 7 in each treatment group) in which bromocriptine was compared with amantadine for treatment of cocaine withdrawal symptoms showed both drugs to be effective in alleviating symptoms of withdrawal. The dose of bromocriptine used in this study ranged from 5 to 7.5 mg daily (2.5 mg, two or three times daily). Bromocriptine was poorly tolerated, with frequently reported side effects of headaches, vertigo, or syncope, and 57% of the study participants assigned to bromocriptine dropped out because of such events. One patient completed a full 10-day course of treatment with bromocriptine; five patients completed treatment with amantadine. The authors concluded that amantadine was more effective in relieving withdrawal symptoms.[84] However, the high dropout rate for the bromocriptine group made the interpretation of these results difficult, and the reported efficacy of amantadine may be misleading.

Methylphenidate has been studied for efficacy in treatment of cocaine abuse. Methylphenidate has less abuse liability than cocaine or amphetamine, a rapid onset of action, and longer duration of action than cocaine, which lends it to the model of methadone for treatment of heroin addiction. Disadvantages of methylphenidate include tolerance, abuse potential, and patients' acceptance of such a drug to treat their cocaine addiction. An open trial of methylphenidate showed it to produce a rapid decrease in cocaine use and craving. Subjects reported tolerance, diminished anticraving action in time, and a mild sense of stimulation that evoked a desire for cocaine and increased cocaine use by week 2 of the study, which resulted in discontinuation of the trial.[90] Methylphenidate was abused by antisocial cocaine abusers without childhood attention-deficit/hyperactivity disorder. There is some evidence that cocaine abusers with residual attention-deficit/hyperactivity disorder gain substantial benefit from use of methylphenidate and may become completely abstinent from cocaine use.[91]

Levodopa, a precursor of dopamine, has also been reported to have some efficacy in the acute treatment of cocaine withdrawal symptoms, with craving reduced up to 2 weeks. An open study has been reported in which subjects experiencing acute abstinence from cocaine (last cocaine use 7 to 23 hours before treatment with the study medication) were treated with a single dose of levodopa at 250 mg and carbidopa at 25 mg, which was repeated in 3 to 4 hours. Patients were interviewed after this treatment and reported improved sleep, decreased craving, and a feeling of calm relative to their previous experiences with acute cocaine abstinence. These findings await confirmation in controlled trials.

Mazindol is a dopamine reuptake inhibitor originally developed as an appetite suppressant; it has also been shown to have some efficacy in the treatment of Parkinson's disease. Tolerance has not been shown to develop, and mazindol does not induce dependence or euphoria; discontinuation of mazindol treatment has not been associated with rebound depression. These properties indicate that mazindol may be a potential pharmacotherapy for cocaine abuse. Mazindol had shown promise in an open trial, but a brief crossover study showed no significant improvement in cocaine craving or use.[92] Further controlled studies are needed to explore the potential efficacy of this agent for cocaine abuse.

Bupropion, a "second-generation" antidepressant that affects dopaminergic transmission but has little effect on noradrenergic or serotoninergic neurotransmission, has been studied as an agent for treatment of cocaine addiction. In an open pilot study, six methadone-maintained cocaine abusers participated in an 8-week outpatient study in which they received bupropion at 100 mg three times daily (the usual dose used for treatment of depression). At the 8-week follow-up, only one of the study participants was still using cocaine; at the 3-month follow-up, the four patients who achieved abstinence from cocaine during bupropion treatment remained free of cocaine use as indicated by self-report and confirmed by urinalysis.[93]

Because dopamine is thought to play a significant role in the reinforcing properties of cocaine, some have suggested that agents that block dopamine receptors, such as neuroleptics, may be useful in the treatment of cocaine abuse. Flupenthixol is a neuroleptic of the thioxanthene class approved for use in Europe as an antipsychotic and antidepressant. One open study evaluated the efficacy of flupenthixol decanoate in an outpatient population of crack smokers with poor prognoses.[94] Flupenthixol was administered in dosages of either 10 or 20 mg and was well tolerated. Cocaine craving and use decreased markedly and rapidly (within 3 days). Further controlled studies are needed to assess the efficacy of such agents.

Desipramine

The rationale for the use of the tricyclic antidepressant desipramine is the reduction of postsynaptic dopaminergic receptor sensitivity that might reverse cocaine-induced supersensitivity.[27] Rather than acting as a general antidepressant in cocaine abusers who do not have major affective disorders, desipramine may act as specific antianhedonic agent in this population. Whereas the positive aspects of desipramine for treatment of cocaine abuse include a relatively benign side effect profile, lack of abuse liability, and acceptance by patients, a significant disadvantage lies in the delayed onset of effect (approximately 2 weeks).

The first study of desipramine investigated its efficacy as an acute agent for cocaine withdrawal symptoms (10 days of treatment at a dosage of 75 mg daily), and it was found to be only minimally effective.[95] Higher dosages (200 to 250 mg daily) that were administered for longer periods (4 to 6 weeks) were more effective in initiating and maintaining longer periods of abstinence and decreased cocaine craving.[96] In these studies, desipramine was shown to be relatively free of side effects, and patients have shown good compliance after an initial dropout rate of 25% to 30% during the first 2 weeks of treatment. The initial dropout may have been the result of the delayed onset of action of desipramine. It has been postulated that the use of an acute agent such as one of the dopaminergic agonists in combination with desipramine would provide maximal clinical benefit to the cocaine-abusing patient. This hypothesis has yet to be tested clinically.

Considerations in the decision whether to treat with desipramine for cocaine abuse include adverse events associated with desipramine that may precipitate relapse in vulnerable individuals and the possibility of toxic interactions with cocaine. Desipramine has been reported to induce what has been referred to as an early tricyclic jitteriness syndrome in some patients. This syndrome has been described in cocaine abstinent patients who were having cocaine craving. Desipramine was associated with the onset of anxiety, insomnia, and stimulation reminiscent of the patients' use of cocaine. These individuals experienced severe cocaine craving and relapsed to cocaine use.[97] Furthermore, it has been reported that plasma desipramine levels greater than 200 ng/mL are associated with a greater likelihood of relapse to cocaine use, which underscores the importance of close clinical observation, including monitoring of serum desipramine concentration.

Serotoninergic Agents

The potency of cocaine as an inhibitor of 5-HT uptake actually exceeds that of dopamine by twofold to fourfold.[98] Ritz and Kuhar[98] have demonstrated that amphetamine, but not cocaine, exhibits a significant inverse relationship between drug binding to the 5-HT transporter and reinforcing effects. This has led to speculation that 5-HT may exert a dampening effect on the euphoria associated with cocaine use. This hypothesis is supported further by the findings that 5-HT synthesis or receptor blockade potentiates, but the 5-HT precursor 5-hydroxytryptophan antagonizes, cocaine-induced locomotor activity in animals. Studies have demonstrated that long-term cocaine administration results in a net decrease in 5-HT neurotransmission as a result of enhanced 5-HT autoregulatory mechanisms. This has been postulated to be a mechanism underlying the psychological consequences of chronic cocaine abuse. These findings have led to trials of medications with effects on central serotoninergic regulation for the treatment of cocaine abuse.

A small study ($n = 11$) of fluoxetine in the treatment of cocaine-abusing heroin addicts has been reported.[99] These investigators report that five of eight patients completing at least 1 week and up to 6 months of treatment with fluoxetine experienced significant decreases in cocaine craving, with reduction in cocaine use that was verified by urine toxicology screens. One study reported the open treatment of 16 methadone-maintained cocaine-dependent patients, 11 of whom were infected with human immunodeficiency virus. The mean fluoxetine dose was 45 mg daily, and the study duration was 9 weeks. Cocaine use was reduced by week 9 from baseline levels as confirmed by quantitative urine benzoylecgonine concentrations, although few subjects achieved abstinence. Fluoxetine was well tolerated in this severely medically ill sample, and there was no evidence of significant interaction with methadone. A 9-week open trial of sertraline in 11 outpatient cocaine abusers showed reduced cocaine craving and abstinence for at least 3 weeks in five subjects.[100] A 12-week pilot study of gepirone (mean dose, 16.25 mg daily) compared with placebo in 41 cocaine abusers did not provide any evidence for efficacy in the treatment of cocaine abuse.[101]

Miscellaneous Agents

Disulfiram

A study has suggested that the use of disulfiram (Antabuse) in persons with comorbid cocaine and alcohol abuse may substantially reduce cocaine use and lengthen periods of abstinence.[102] Further evidence to support the potential of disulfiram as a therapy for cocaine abuse was obtained in a study of cocaine and disulfiram administration in humans.[103] Six cocaine-dependent subjects participated in four study drug administration sessions in which they received either disulfiram 250 mg or placebo orally, 60 minutes before receiving either cocaine 2 mg/kg or placebo by nasal insufflation. There was no significant difference in cocaine high or in physiological effects during disulfiram-cocaine administration compared with administration of cocaine alone. However, subjects reported decreased craving for cocaine during disulfiram-cocaine administration, and several subjects reported significant dysphoria during disulfiram-cocaine administration. Plasma cocaine concentration during disulfiram-cocaine administration was significantly greater, and this may have contributed to the decreased craving and increased dysphoria observed in some subjects. These findings should encourage further research as to the efficacy of disulfiram in the treatment of cocaine abuse.

Buprenorphine

Intravenous cocaine abuse is a major public health problem among methadone-maintained outpatients. Opioid abusers report that the combined use of heroin or methadone with cocaine (a "speedball") is pleasant and reinforcing, whereas the use of cocaine alone has been reported by some as producing dysphoria. One potential alternative maintenance therapy for cocaine-abusing opiate addicts is the use of an agent that minimizes opioid agonism. Buprenorphine is a partial opioid antagonist. Its relatively lower opiate agonist action was postulated to have the ability to decrease the speedball interaction with cocaine, which might decrease cocaine abuse. In an open trial, 41 opioid-dependent patients self-selected for a 1-month trial of buprenorphine (mean dose, 3.2 mg daily; maximal dose, 8 mg daily) showed substantially less cocaine abuse than patients maintained with methadone (mean dose, 43 mg daily during month 1 and 54 mg daily during month 2).[104] These findings indicate the need for further investigation into the efficacy of buprenorphine for the treatment of comorbid opiate-cocaine addiction.

Carbamazepine

Carbamazepine is an anticonvulsant medication hypothesized to have potential as a therapy for cocaine abuse because of its ability to reverse cocaine-induced kindling in an animal model and to reverse the dopamine receptor supersensitivity that results from chronic cocaine use. In an open pilot study, carbamazepine appeared to have some efficacy in the treatment of cocaine abuse.[105] However, one study has reported that cocaine administration in the presence of carbamazepine was associated with significant increases in heart rate and blood pressure, suggesting possible cardiovascular toxic effects.[106] A study of carbamazepine treatment (carbamazepine plasma concentration 1 to 3 or 4 to 7 μg/mL) followed by cocaine administration in cocaine abusers reported no impact on cocaine effects in humans.[107]

Naltrexone

Naltrexone is currently being investigated as a treatment agent for cocaine abuse. One study examined the self-reported and cardiovascular effects of intravenously administered cocaine in the presence and absence of naltrexone. Five cocaine abusers were tested in a within-subjects design with doses of cocaine (0.125, 0.25, 0.50 mg/kg) after 10 days of daily administration of naltrexone (50 mg) and of placebo. Cocaine-induced increases in self-reported effects of "dollar value of cocaine" and "unpleasant" were less during naltrexone than placebo administration. Cocaine increased peak heart rate, and this was augmented by naltrexone. Cocaine-induced alterations in blood pressure did not differ across naltrexone and placebo conditions.[108] A preliminary study in which 36 patients in treatment for opiate dependence who were also cocaine abusers were administered naltrexone at 50 mg three times weekly for 1 to 6 months showed a significant reduction in cocaine abuse.[109] Participants in this treatment had five to eight times less cocaine abuse than a comparison group of opiate-dependent patients who were maintained with methadone as shown by urine toxicology screens. These results indicate that naltrexone as a pharmacotherapy should be explored in controlled clinical trials, several of which are now ongoing.

Physician-Patient Relationship

The treatment of cocaine use disorders should be undertaken by the psychiatrist in the context of a thorough understanding of the cocaine abstinence syndrome (see earlier). The psychiatrist can develop individual treatment plans for patients based on the presenting complaints and symptoms related to cocaine abuse and acute abstinence. Treatment plans include assessment for psychiatric and medical illnesses, pharmacological intervention, and RPT. A working knowledge of the cocaine abstinence syndrome is also helpful in educating patients about their disorder and helping them to understand the expected course of the disease.

The psychiatrist is generally the provider who will make decisions regarding pharmacotherapy for cocaine dependence. In making this decision, consideration of multiple factors is necessary. The psychiatrist must determine whether the patient is a candidate for pharmacotherapy on the basis of the stage of the disease and whether the patient has another psychiatric diagnosis that requires pharmacotherapy. Equally important, the psychiatrist must consider the physical status of the patient and current medication treatments as well as any potential interactions with the pharmacotherapy that is being considered to assist the patient with discontinuation of cocaine abuse. Finally, the psychiatrist must also consider the risk of relapse to cocaine use while the patient is being treated with the medication and potential adverse interactions with cocaine or other illicit drugs.

The psychiatrist must make an assessment of the therapeutic relationship before initiating pharmacological treatment for cocaine dependence. Treatment must include a plan for assessment of the effectiveness of the pharmacotherapy for the individual patient. This would include continued participation in psychotherapies for cocaine dependence as well as frequent urine toxicology screens to monitor illicit drug use; when possible, plasma concentrations of the medication used for treatment of the cocaine dependence are obtained to monitor compliance and determine optimal dosage. The following sections summarize the necessary considerations in the assessment of the decision regarding pharmacotherapy for cocaine dependence.

Whom to Treat

The first issue in whether to use pharmacotherapy for cocaine abuse is the appropriateness of the patient for such a treatment. There are three categories of patients in whom pharmacotherapy should be considered: 1) patients with other comorbid psychiatric disorders, 2) patients identified with significant general medical illnesses or medical risks from continued cocaine abuse (such as complications of intravenous drug abuse), and 3) patients in whom heavy cocaine use has resulted in neuroadaptation. This last category of patients includes those who use cocaine by a high-intensity route, such as intravenous injection or free-base smoking. Such patients use large amounts of cocaine at high frequency and experience rapid changes in brain cocaine concentration, which probably results in neurotransmitter deficits and alterations in receptor numbers. The reversal of such alterations is a rationale for pharmacotherapy for cocaine abuse.

When to Treat

Decisions regarding when to initiate and to discontinue pharmacotherapy should be based on four factors, which include 1) the phase of recovery; 2) the precipitant to treatment, including psychiatric comorbidity; 3) associated psychosocial problems; and 4) relapse potential. Those who have been refractory to nonpharmacological therapies in the past should also be considered candidates for pharmacotherapy.

Recovery from cocaine abuse may be conceptualized as evolving through a three-phase process (Table 45–4): crash, withdrawal, and extinction. The symptoms and longevity of each phase differ. During the crash, which may last several hours to 4 days, the primary symptom may be hypersomnia, for which there is no indication for medication treatment. However, some patients experience paranoia requiring emergent use of antipsychotics and benzodiazepines[110]; others may become dysphoric and suicidal, requiring hospitalization. The withdrawal phase lasts 2 to 10 weeks, and relapse potential is greatest during this time. Symptoms may resemble a depressive disorder with intense craving for cocaine[28] leading to impulsive use or significant anxiety when the cocaine abuser is exposed to settings in which cocaine was previously used. Pharmacotherapy with the goal of preventing reinitiation of cocaine use may be appropriate during this phase of treatment. During the extinction phase, which averages 3 to 12 months in duration, relapse is triggered by environmental cues resulting in cocaine craving, but the intensity of such cravings decreases in time if they are not reinforced by cocaine use. It would be unusual to initiate medication for treatment of cocaine abuse during this phase.

Relapse potential determines the duration of pharmacotherapy, which varies according to the characteristics of an individual patient's cocaine abuse, phase of recovery, progress in concomitant psychotherapy, and precipitants of treatment. The patient with psychiatric vulnerability and, to a lesser extent, the patient with medical risk may need pharmacotherapy for longer than the 1 to 3 months reported in treatment trials to date.[111] These patients may benefit from extension of medication treatment for 6 months into the extinction phase. The duration of treatment with medications initiated for symptomatic relief during the crash or withdrawal phases is related to the type of medication used. For example, use of antipsychotics for psychosis and benzodiazepines for agitation associated with cocaine abuse should be carefully evaluated during the first 1 to 2 weeks of

Table 45–4 Cocaine Abuse Recovery and Treatment

Parameter	Crash Phase	Withdrawal Phase	Extinction Phase
Duration	Several hours to 4 d	2–10 wk	3–12 mo
Treatment	Symptomatic May need hospitalization for medical or psychiatric care and assessment	RPT Self-help groups Other therapies, e.g., family, marital, individual as indicated	Continued RPT Self-help groups and additional interventions developed for individual patients
Pharmacotherapy	Benzodiazepines for agitation Antipsychotics for psychosis or agitation	**Dopaminergic agonists** Amantadine Bromocriptine **Antidepressants** Desipramine Fluoxetine Bupropion	Unusual to initiate in this phase Usual course is to taper and discontinue pharmacotherapy for cocaine abuse and monitor clinically

treatment. The risk of side effects, including tardive dyskinesia, warrants treatment that is reviewed regularly and for as brief a period as possible. Patients with psychotic symptoms extending beyond cessation of cocaine use and withdrawal should be evaluated for an underlying psychiatric disorder.

Medications that may be useful in alleviating cocaine-associated craving and anhedonia, such as amantadine, might be useful for the first several weeks of treatment and then replaced by psychotherapeutic interventions. The resolution of psychosocial and medical problems is important to institution of a plan for discontinuation of medication. Other important factors to consider include the patient's ability to stabilize in adjunctive psychotherapy, to strengthen relationships with supportive family members or non–drug-abusing friends, and to develop long-term supports through organizations such as Cocaine Anonymous. It is also important to address the use of any other substances of abuse during treatment.

Continued use of other substances often precipitates relapse to cocaine abuse. Treatment for other substance use disorders in the presence of cocaine abuse may be necessary and achieved through participation in therapeutic modalities and self-help groups specific for each substance of abuse and individual counseling tailored to the needs of the patient. RPT interventions can be generalized to problems with other substances. The decision to stop medication that has been effective should be viewed as a trial. Reinstitution of the medication, if necessary, will be more easily accomplished if a positive alliance exists between the patient and the treatment providers.

Where to Treat

Cocaine abusers require inpatient hospitalization under some circumstances. The suicidal or psychotic patient requires inpatient treatment for stabilization. Cocaine abusers who are unable to break the cycle of heavy cocaine use often benefit from inpatient treatment, which removes them from the environment in which the heavy cocaine use was occurring. Pharmacotherapy initiated during inpatient hospitalization provides an opportunity to stabilize the patient with the medication while minimizing the risk of cocaine use, which might result in an adverse interaction between the medication and cocaine.

Relapse prevention is an outpatient treatment goal. The use of medication as part of a treatment plan is a common practice in an outpatient setting. When medications are started with outpatient cocaine abusers, it is important to educate them about possible adverse interactions between the medication and cocaine. For example, tricyclic antidepressants such as desipramine block the reuptake of catecholamines, as does cocaine. Therefore, one possible result of an interaction between desipramine and cocaine is hypertension.[112] Such interactions are less likely later in treatment because long-term tricyclic antidepressant treatment decreases postsynaptic adrenergic receptor sensitivity.[113] Clearly, inpatient hospitalization provides the safest means by which to initiate pharmacotherapy for cocaine abuse. However, outpatient medication induction is frequently practiced and has not been associated with any major medical complications to date.

Common Problems in Management

Several common problems are encountered in the treatment of patients with cocaine use disorders. These include 1) relapse to cocaine use, 2) comorbid psychiatric disorders, 3) comorbid substance use disorders, 4) premature termination, and 5) treatment refractoriness.

Relapse to Cocaine Use

The psychological addiction to cocaine is powerful, and the risk for relapse to cocaine use is high during treatment. This is particularly true in outpatient treatment settings, when patients are often subject to exposure to the persons, places, and things that remind them of their cocaine use, which can induce strong craving. Patients who are recently abstinent are at high risk for relapse because they often experience the dysphoria characteristic of the cocaine withdrawal syndrome and contrast that mood state with the memory of cocaine-induced euphoria, which can be overwhelming and precipitate a new cycle of cocaine abuse. Patients early in the treatment process have not developed the coping skills that might help them to overcome drug craving and have not experienced success in remaining abstinent, which is also important in helping the patient to gain control over the cocaine craving.

Early in treatment (at 1 to 2 months), patients deliberately place themselves in a high-risk situation with the idea that they will be able to abstain from using cocaine. This usually leads to relapse and can be experienced by the patient as devastating, with a decrease in self-esteem, which can result in a decision to leave treatment.

Relapse is best addressed from the outset of the treatment process. It is important to discuss the risk of relapse for patients in cocaine treatment generally and to specifically address the concerns of individual patients regarding their relapse potential. This can form the basis for building a repertoire of coping skills for individual patients and assist them in processing a relapse in a therapeutic manner, instead of prematurely terminating treatment. For outpatients who are unable to initiate and maintain abstinence, consideration of a higher level of care (such as a partial hospital program, inpatient rehabilitation, or a long-term therapeutic community) is appropriate.

Diagnosis of Psychiatric Disorders

The diagnosis of comorbid psychiatric disorders can present a dilemma to the psychiatrist. Affective and psychotic symptoms are common during cocaine intoxication. Affective symptoms may continue for several weeks after the initiation of abstinence. In addition, relapse to cocaine or other illicit drug use is common during treatment and can exacerbate psychiatric symptoms. It can be difficult to determine whether psychiatric symptoms represent a cormorbid psychiatric disorder, an extended withdrawal syndrome, or the continuation of substance abuse. In general, affective and psychotic symptoms that occur during intoxication remit within hours to days of cessation of cocaine use and require limited use of psychotropic medication. Affective symptoms related to cocaine withdrawal may continue for weeks but generally improve in time and are not severe enough to meet criteria for a major mental disorder, such as a major depressive episode. The patient whose symptoms worsen despite treatment and in whom regular (once or twice a week randomly) urine toxicology screens reveal continued abstinence is likely to have a dual diagnosis and should receive appropriate psychiatric treatment. Patients in whom a well-documented psychiatric disorder has occurred in the absence of drug abuse should also be observed closely for the development of a comorbid psychiatric illness during treatment.

Comorbid Substance Use Disorders

Abuse of or dependence on other illicit drugs or alcohol is common in patients with cocaine use disorders. Reports have established that up to 62% to 90% of cocaine abusers are also alcohol abusers, and simultaneous use of these substances is common.[12, 13] Cocaine abusers report the comorbid use of alcohol to prolong euphoric effects and relieve the negative effects of binge cocaine use or to decrease acute abstinence symptoms. Opiates serve this purpose for some cocaine abusers, but this is less common. It is important to establish whether patients presenting for treatment abuse other substances, such as alcohol or opiates, because of the possibility of development of dependence, which often requires a medically monitored detoxification. Cannabis use is also common, although no physiological dependence develops. Patients presenting for treatment of cocaine use disorders must have a full evaluation with a urine toxicology screen to determine the extent of abuse of other drugs and alcohol. This is helpful in addressing potential risk factors for relapse and developing a plan for coping with triggers to cocaine use.

Premature Termination

Premature termination or leaving treatment is common in patients with cocaine use disorders. The most likely reason for a patient to leave treatment is relapse to cocaine use. Patients are at especially high risk for relapse in the early stages of treatment when craving is most severe and coping skills and support systems are poorly developed. Addressing this possibility from the initial contact with the patient can be helpful in that it gives the patient an understanding of what difficulties to expect in the process of abstinence initiation. In addition, discussion of the possibility of relapse and the potential for leaving treatment can also be used to help the patient develop a plan for preventing this occurrence, which will improve the chance that the patient will be successful in treatment. Processing previous treatments and reasons for failure early in treatment can also be helpful in determination of what level of care is most appropriate for the patient.

Treatment Refractoriness

The term treatment refractoriness often implies a lack of response to a therapeutic trial of a pharmacotherapy. In the case of cocaine dependence, however, there is no effective pharmacotherapy with which to treat the disorder; therefore, the term relates to a different set of occurrences in the treatment setting. Recidivism to cocaine use, treatment dropout, and multiple treatment experiences are common. Such problems are a reflection of the severity of illness and a parameter of relative treatment refractoriness. Cormorbid substance use and psychiatric disorders contribute to treatment refractoriness. Lack of accurate diagnosis and treatment contributes to relapse potential in the form of continued exposure to high-risk situations and lifestyle instability that are associated with ongoing substance abuse. Continued psychiatric symptoms, which patients attempt to relieve through cocaine use, contribute to poor treatment outcome.

Cocaine abuse does not induce a physiological dependence, although the psychological addiction is often disabling. Because there is no physiological dependence, the first treatment referral for patients with primary cocaine dependence and no other acute medical or psychiatric condition is generally to an outpatient drug abuse treatment clinic. Patients unable to initiate and maintain sobriety in an outpatient drug treatment program should be evaluated for more intensive forms of treatment. Management of these patients should include consideration of a variety of options, including pharmacotherapy (see the earlier section on pharmacotherapy for cocaine abuse) and programs that offer a graded increase in structure. For example, those who fail outpatient treatment should be considered for inpatient treatment. Such patients may require initial detoxification from another drug or alcohol or may need several days of inpatient treatment to break the cycle of cocaine use. A step-down from the inpatient level of care would include continued participation in a partial hospital program. Patients generally attend these programs 5 d/wk initially, and sessions last an average of about 4 hours. There is a gradual reduction in the number of sessions per week over time (such programs are of flexible duration, but a full program usually requires 12 weeks) and as the period of sobriety lengthens. This program can be followed with resumption of the outpatient treatment clinic level of care, which takes place fewer days per week with shorter sessions.

Patients who have failed other forms of treatment may be referred to residential programs (although the number of these programs is shrinking given the constraints on treatment that have resulted from managed care and erosion of benefits for substance abuse provided by health insurers). Residential programs vary in length and must be tailored to the needs of the patient. Such programs can be important to initiation of abstinence. These programs allow adequate time in a drug-free and supportive environment (so that the recovery process can begin) and provide sufficient time for reduction of craving for the drug and acquisition of effective relapse prevention skills.

Psychiatric Comorbidity

Treatment-seeking cocaine abusers have significant rates of psychiatric disorders.[13] Those with comorbid psychiatric disorders may use smaller doses of cocaine or less intense routes of administration (e.g., intranasal use).[28] Cocaine abuse may adversely affect the psychiatric disorder, with symptoms of psychosis or suicidal ideation occurring or worsening during the course of cocaine use. The possibility that cocaine may induce or exacerbate depression has also been suggested.[28] Patients with underlying psychotic disorders may be exquisitely sensitive to small doses of cocaine, which acutely worsens their psychiatric illness and requires pharmacological management and hospitalization.[110] Patients with comorbid psychiatric disorders complicated by substance abuse often require increased doses of psychotropic medications to control symptoms.

The diagnosis of comorbid psychiatric disorders in cocaine abusers is often challenging because the onset of many such disorders occurs in adolescence or early adulthood, the same period as for the onset of cocaine addiction. This makes determination of primary versus secondary diagnosis difficult. However, careful developmental and family histories and attention to the presence or absence of psychiatric symptoms during periods of sobriety can be helpful adjuncts and may assist in diagnostic accuracy, which is essential to providing adequate treatment.

Symptoms associated with substance use disorders, including acute intoxication and withdrawal syndromes, may be mistaken for exacerbation of the underlying psychiatric illness, resulting in misdiagnosis and inappropriate treatment. In addition, such symptoms may result in a diagnosis of a psychiatric disorder in a patient who actually suffers from a primary substance use disorder. This can result in inappropriate psychiatric treatment, which often includes psychotropic medication. This fosters denial in such patients and results in ineffective treatment of the substance use disorder. The pervasive nature of substance use disorders requires increased emphasis on substance abuse education for mental health providers, attention to substance abuse in the history taking and ongoing treatment, and urine toxicology screens and breath analysis as a routine part of treatment.

Comorbid mood disorders and residual attention-deficit/hyperactivity disorder are frequently identified in treatment-seeking cocaine abusers.[13, 14, 28, 114] Diagnostic criteria for mood disorders were met by 50% of subjects in an inpatient[13] and an outpatient[14] sample of cocaine abusers. Whereas rates for depression were similar to those seen in opiate addicts, cyclical mood disorders (bipolar disorder) occurred at much higher frequency (20% versus 1%). This suggests that such individuals may preferentially abuse cocaine over other illicit drugs.[13, 14]

Several lines of evidence point to a significant role for depression in cocaine abuse. First, the symptoms associated with the cocaine withdrawal syndrome are similar to those observed in depressive disorders. Second, it has been shown that depressive disorders were the only major psychiatric disorders that predicted cocaine use in a 2.5-year follow-up period if untreated.[115] Mood disorders have been reported to occur more frequently in first-degree relatives of cocaine abusers, compared with relatives of individuals with other types of substance use disorders.[116] The possibility that some cocaine abusers may be self-medicating a depressive disorder suggests the potential utility of antidepressants in the treatment of cocaine abuse. Antidepressant treatment may be an important means of prophylaxis for those patients with mood disorders who are known to be at risk for cocaine abuse.

Another major psychiatric disorder seen in cocaine abusers is antisocial personality disorder. Identification of this disorder is important because it is associated with poor treatment outcome in cocaine abusers. There is no clear indication for use of pharmacotherapy in patients with antisocial personality disorder. In considering pharmacotherapy, it is best to stabilize such patients for several weeks and monitor symptoms carefully to determine need for medication treatment.

Cocaine abuse is widely recognized as a significant clinical problem in patients with schizophrenia.[117, 118] Cocaine use may hasten the onset of a psychotic disorder in a vulnerable patient and may exacerbate the course of the illness by precipitating psychotic relapse[119] or by causing depression, anxiety, insomnia, agitation, or aggressiveness.[117, 120, 121] Although seemingly paradoxical, cocaine-abusing schizophrenic patients have a better prognosis than do their non–drug-abusing counterparts. Substance-abusing schizophrenic individuals have been shown to have fewer positive and negative symptoms of schizophrenia after acute treatment,[122] and those remaining in treatment tended to abstain from drug abuse and to have fewer days of hospitalization.[123, 124] These findings highlight both the detrimental influence of cocaine abuse on schizophrenia and the possibility that cocaine abuse may cause and perpetuate a disorder closely resembling schizophrenia. Specialized dual-diagnosis treatment programs that attend to both the psychiatric and substance use disorders in these patients have shown promising results and should be used when available for the treatment of these severely ill patients.[117]

Clinical Vignette 1

Mr. A, 27 years old, was admitted to an outpatient clinic for treatment of cocaine dependence. He reported intranasal use of cocaine daily for several months before seeking treatment and a 10-year history of cocaine abuse. The patient maintained abstinence during the initial weeks of treatment but complained of difficulty sitting still in groups and poor concentration. He also described a calming effect of cocaine on these chronic problems, which contributed to intensified drug craving. A psychiatric evaluation revealed a developmental history consistent with attention-deficit/hyperactivity disorder with persistence into adulthood. The history of residual symptoms was confirmed by the patient's significant other.

A trial of methylphenidate was initiated at 10 mg daily and increased to a dosage of 20 mg daily. Mr. A reported feeling calmer and better able to concentrate, with decreased cocaine craving. When methylphenidate was increased to 30 mg daily, Mr. A complained of abdominal discomfort and irritability in the evening, which reminded him of cocaine withdrawal symptoms. Although it was recommended that the dose be reduced to 20 mg daily, the patient was anxious about the occurrence of these symptoms and requested that the medication be discontinued because he feared relapse. Within several days of stopping the medication, the symptoms abated, but the attention-deficit/hyperactivity disorder symptoms returned. A trial of desipramine was initiated with titration to 150 mg daily during a 2-week period with no reported side effects. The patient reported a small improvement in concentration and decreased motor activity, but during the third week of desipramine treatment, he relapsed to cocaine use. The patient was admitted to an inpatient dual-diagnosis treatment unit for stabilization. Desipramine was reinstituted and monitored by serum concentration, which was kept in the range of 100 to 125 mg/dL with good effect. The patient continued outpatient treatment in a dual-diagnosis partial hospital program and self-help groups.

Final DSM-IV Diagnoses

Axis I: Cocaine dependence; attention-deficit/hyperactivity disorder.

Axis II: None.

Axis III: None.

Clinical Vignette 2

Mr. B is a 34-year-old divorced man with a 10-year history of freebase cocaine abuse characterized by weekly binge use of up to 6 g and alcohol use reported as two beers several times per week, but no other street drug use. He was admitted to the hospital emergency department with a chief complaint of visual hallucinations and paranoid ideation that developed during the course of several hours of binge use of cocaine. On physical examination, he was noted to be agitated with mild tachycardia and hypertension, but there were no known concurrent medical illnesses. Haloperidol at 5 mg and lorazepam at 2 mg were administered by intramuscular injection acutely for treatment of psychosis, with rapid abatement in symptoms.

The patient was transferred to a dual-diagnosis inpatient unit for further evaluation. There the resolution of visual hallucinations and paranoia occurred within 24 hours. After 2 days of hypersomnia, intermittent anxiety, and mild depressive symptoms, the patient reported that he was feeling better and began to engage in chemical dependency treatment. He was discharged to an outpatient clinic for further treatment of cocaine and alcohol abuse.

Final DSM-IV Diagnoses

Axis I: Cocaine dependence; alcohol abuse; cocaine intoxication; cocaine withdrawal.

Axis II: None.

Axis III: None.

References

1. Gawin FH: Cocaine addiction: Psychology and neurophysiology. Science 1991; 251:1580–1586.
2. National Household Survey on Drug Abuse: Main Findings 1991. Rockville, MD: Substance Abuse and Mental Health Services Administration, 1993. DHHS publication SMA 93-1980.
3. Adams EH, Kozel NJ (eds): Cocaine use in America: Introduction and overview. NIDA Res Monogr 1985; 61:35.
4. Miller JD, Cisin IH, Abelson H: The National Household Survey on Drug Abuse 1982. Washington, DC: U.S. Government Printing Office, 1983. National Institute on Drug Abuse DHHS publication ADM 82-1195.
5. Robins LN, Helzer JE, Weissman MM, et al: Lifetime prevalence of specific psychiatric disorders in three sites. Arch Gen Psychiatry 1984; 41:949–958.
6. Griffin ML, Weiss RD, Mirin SM, et al: A comparison of male and female cocaine abusers. Arch Gen Psychiatry 1989; 46:122–126.
7. Kosten TA, Gawin FH, Kosten TR, et al: Gender differences in cocaine use and treatment response. J Subst Abuse Treat 1993; 10:63–66.
8. Moise R, Reed BG, Ryan V: Issues in the treatment of heroin-addicted women: A comparison of men and women entering two types of drug abuse programs. Int J Addict 1982; 17:109–139.
9. Blume SB: Women and alcohol. JAMA 1986; 256:1476–1470.
10. Schnoll SH, Karrigan J, Kitchen SB, et al: Characteristics of cocaine abusers presenting for treatment. NIDA Res Monogr 1985; 61:171–181.
11. Kleinman PH, Miller AB, Millman RB, et al: Psychopathology among cocaine abusers entering treatment. J Nerv Ment Dis 1990; 178:442–447.
12. Weiss RD, Mirin SM, Griffin ML, et al: Psychopathology in cocaine abusers—changing trends. J Nerv Ment Dis 1988; 176:719–725.
13. Rounsaville BJ, Anton SF, Carroll KM, et al: Psychiatric diagnosis of treatment-seeking cocaine abusers. Arch Gen Psychiatry 1991; 48:43–51.
14. Gawin FH, Ellinwood EH: Cocaine dependence. Annu Rev Med 1989; 40:149–161.
15. Gawin FH, Ellinwood EH: Cocaine and other stimulants: Actions, abuse, and treatment. N Engl J Med 1988; 318:1173–1182.
16. Van Dyke C, Ungerer J, Jatlow P, et al: Intranasal cocaine: Dose relationships of psychological effects and plasma levels. Int J Psychiatry Med 1982; 12:1–13.
17. Jones RT: The pharmacology of cocaine. NIDA Res Monogr 1985; 61:182–192.
18. Siegal RK: New patterns of cocaine use: Changing doses and routes. NIDA Res Mongr 1985; 61:204–220.
19. Johnson CE: Cocaine: Pharmacology, effects, and treatment of abuse. NIDA Res Mongr 1984; 60:54–71.
20. Gawin FH, Kleber HD: Cocaine abuse in a treatment population: Patterns and diagnostic considerations. NIDA Res Monogr 1985; 61:182–192.
21. Agosti V, Nunes E, Stewart JW, et al: Patient factors related to early attrition from an outpatient cocaine research clinic: A preliminary report. Int J Addict 1991; 26:327–334.
22. Means LB, Small M, Capone DM, et al: Client demographics and outcome in outpatient cocaine treatment. Int J Addict 1989; 24:765–783.
23. Koe BK: Molecular geometry of inhibitors of the uptake of catecholamines and serotonin in synaptosomal preparations of rat brain. J Pharmacol Exp Ther 1976; 199:649–661.
24. Koob GF: Neural mechanisms of drug reinforcement. Ann N Y Acad Sci 1992; 654:171–191.
25. Fibiger HC, Phillips GA, Brown EE: The neurobiology of cocaine-induced reinforcement. Ciba Found Symp 1992; 166:96–124.
26. Weiss FY, Hurd YL, Ungerstedt MA, et al: Neurochemical correlates of cocaine and ethanol self-administration. Ann N Y Acad Sci 1992; 654:220–241.
27. Gawin FH, Kleber HD: Pharmacological treatment of cocaine abuse. Psychiatr Clin North Am 1986; 9:573–583.
28. Gawin FH, Kleber HD: Abstinence symptomatology and psychiatric diagnosis in chronic cocaine abusers. Arch Gen Psychiatry 1986; 43:107–113.
29. Dwoskin LP, Peris J, Yasuda R, et al: Repeated cocaine administration results in supersensitivity of striatal D-2 dopamine autoreceptors to pergolide. Life Sci 1988; 42:255–262.
30. Henry DJ, Greene M, White F: Electrophysiological effects of cocaine in the mesoaccumbens dopamine system: Repeated administration. J Pharmacol Exp Ther 1989; 251:833–839.
31. American Psychiatric Association: Diagnostic and Statistical Manual of Mental Disorders, 4th ed. Washington, DC: American Psychiatric Association, 1994.
32. Cregler LL, Mark H: Medical complications of cocaine abuse. N Engl J Med 1986; 315:1495–1500.
33. Gradman A: Cardiac effects of cocaine: A review. Yale J Biol Med 1988; 61:137–147.
34. Isner JM, Estes NAM, Thompson PD, et al: Acute cardiac events temporally related to cocaine abuse. N Engl J Med 1986; 315:1438–1443.
35. Koslowsky WA, Lyon AF: Cocaine and acute myocardial infarction: A probable connection. Chest 1984;85:132–133.
36. Morale R, Romanelli R, Boucek RJ: The mural left anterior descending coronary artery: Strenuous exercise and sudden death. Circulation 1980; 62:230–237.
37. Cheitlin MD: The intramural coronary artery: Another cause for sudden death with exercise. Circulation 1980; 62:238–239.
38. Webb R, Vanhoutte P: Cocaine and contractile responses of vascular smooth muscle from spontaneously hypertensive rats. Arch Int Pharmacodyn 1980; 253:241–256.
39. Van Dyke C, Barash PG, Jatlow P, et al: Cocaine: Plasma concentrations after intranasal application in man. Science 1976; 191:859–861.
40. Nanji AA, Filipenko JD: Asystole and ventricular fibrillation associated with cocaine intoxication. Chest 1984; 85:132–133.
41. Benchimol A, Bartall H, Desser KB: Accelerated ventricular rhythm and cocaine abuse. Ann Intern Med 1978; 88:519–520.
42. Nahas G, Trouve R, Demus JR, von Sitbon M: A calcium-channel blocker as antidote to the cardiac effects of cocaine intoxication. N Engl J Med 1985; 313:519–520.
43. Werner R, Lockhart J, Schwartz R: Dilated cardiomyopathy and cocaine abuse. Am J Med 1986; 81:699–701.
44. Barth CW 3d, Bray M, Roberts WC: Rupture of the ascending aorta during cocaine intoxication. Am J Cardiol 1986; 57:496.
45. Allred R, Ewer J: Fatal pulmonary edema following intravenous "freebase" cocaine use. Ann Emerg Med 1981; 10:441–442.

46. Birdy SL, Corey SM, Wrenn KD: Cocaine-related medical problems: Consecutive series of 233 patients. Am J Med 1990; 88:325–331.
47. Lichtenfield PJ, Rubin DB, Feldman RS: Subarachnoid hemorrhage precipitated by cocaine snorting. Arch Neurol 1984; 41:223–224.
48. Siegel RK: Cocaine smoking. J Psychoactive Drugs 1982; 14:271–343.
49. Roberts JR, Quattrocchi E, Howland MA: Severe hyperthermia secondary to intravenous drug abuse. Am J Emerg Med 1984; 2:373.
50. Jonsson S, O'Meara M, Young JB: Acute cocaine poisoning: Importance of treating seizures and acidosis. Am J Med 1983; 75:1061–1064.
51. Kang S-Y, Klummin PH, Woody GE, et al: Outcomes for cocaine abusers after once-a-week psychosocial therapy. Am J Psychiatry 1991; 148:630–635.
52. Gawin FH, Kleber HD: Evolving conceptualizations of cocaine dependence. Yale J Biol Med 1988; 61:123–136.
53. Millman RB: Evaluation and clinical management of cocaine abusers. J Clin Psychiatry 1988; 49(suppl): 27–33.
54. Anker AL, Crowley TJ: Use of contingency contracts in specialty clinics for cocaine abuse. NIDA Res Monogr 1982; 41:452–459.
55. Wesson DR, Smith DE: Cocaine: Treatment perspectives. NIDA Res Monogr 1985; 61:193–203.
56. O'Brien CP, Childress AR, Arndt IO, et al: Pharmacological and behavioral treatments of cocaine dependence: Controlled studies. J Clin Psychiatry 1988; 49:17–22.
57. Siegel RK: Cocaine smoking. J Psychoactive Drugs 1982; 14: 271–355.
58. Washton AM, Gold MS (eds): Cocaine: A Clinician's Handbook. New York: Guilford Press, 1987.
59. Rounsaville BJ, Kleber HD: Psychotherapy/counseling for opiate addicts: Strategies for use in different treatment settings. Int J Addict 1985; 20:869–896.
60. Woody GE, Luborsky L, McLellan AT, et al: Psychotherapy for opiate addicts: Does it help? Arch Gen Psychiatry 1983; 40:639–645.
61. Rawson RA, Obert JL, McCann MJ, et al: Cocaine treatment outcome: Cocaine use following inpatient, outpatient, and no treatment. NIDA Res Monogr 1986; 67:271–277.
62. Washton AM, Gold MS, Pottash AC: Treatment outcome in cocaine abusers. NIDA Res Monogr 1986; 67:381–384.
63. Kleber HD, Gawin FH: Cocaine abuse: A review of current and experimental treatments. NIDA Res Monogr 1984; 50:111–129.
64. Rounsaville BJ, Gawin FH, Kleber HD: Interpersonal psychotherapy adapted for ambulatory cocaine abusers. Am J Drug Alcohol Abuse 1985; 11:171–191.
65. Schiffer F: Psychotherapy of nine successfully treated cocaine abusers: Techniques and dynamics. J Subst Abuse Treat 1988; 5:131–137.
66. Carroll KM, Rounsaville BJ, Gawin FH: A comparative trial of psychotherapies for ambulatory cocaine abusers: Relapse prevention and interpersonal psychotherapy. Am J Drug Alcohol Abuse 1991; 17:229–247.
67. Washton AM: Treatment of cocaine abuse. NIDA Res Monogr 1986; 67:263–270.
68. Rawson RA, Obert JL, McCann MJ, et al: Neurobehavioral treatment for cocaine dependency. J Psychoactive Drugs 1990; 22:159–171.
69. Marlatt GA, Gordon JR (eds): Relapse Prevention: Maintenance Strategies in the Treatment of Addictive Behaviors. New York: Guilford Press, 1985.
70. Chaney EF, O'Leary MR, Marlatt GA: Skill training with problem drinkers. J Consult Clin Psychol 1978; 46:1092–1104.
71. Sanchez-Craig M, Annis HM, Bornet AR, et al: Random assignment to abstinence and controlled drinking: Evaluation of a cognitive-behavioral program for problem drinkers. J Consult Clin Psychol 1984; 52:390–403.
72. Brown RA, Lichtenstein E, McIntyre KO, et al: Effects of nicotine fading and relapse prevention in smoking cessation. J Consult Clin Psychol 1984; 52:307–308.
73. Hall SM, Rugg J, Tunstall C, et al: Preventing relapse to cigarette smoking by behavioral skills training. J Consult Clin Psychol 1984; 52:372–382.
74. Stevens VJ, Hollis JF: Preventing smoking relapse using an individually tailored skills training technique. J Consult Clin Psychol 1989; 57:420–424.
75. Hawkins JD, Catalano RF, Wells EA: Measuring effects of a skills training intervention for drug abusers. J Consult Clin Psychol 1986; 54:661–664.
76. Carroll KM, Rounsaville BJ, Keller DS: Relapse prevention strategies for the treatment of cocaine abuse. Am J Drug Alcohol Abuse 1991; 17:249–265.
77. Carroll KM, Rounsaville BJ, Gawin FH: A comparative trial of psychotherapies for ambulatory cocaine abusers: Relapse prevention and interpersonal psychotherapy. Am J Drug Alcohol Abuse 1991; 17:229–247.
78. Pavlov IP; Anrep G (ed): Conditioned Reflexes. London: Oxford University Press, 1927.
79. Grabowski J, O'Brien CP: Conditioning factors in drug dependence: An overview. In Advances in Substance Abuse: Behavioral and Biological Research. London: JAI Press, 1981.
80. O'Brien CP, Childress AR, Ehrman R: Conditioning models of drug dependence. In O'Brien CP, Jaffe J (eds): Advances in Understanding the Addictive States. New York: Raven Press, 1991:157–177.
81. O'Brien CP, Childress AR, McLellan T, et al: Integrating systematic cue exposure with standard treatment in recovering drug dependent patients. Addict Behav 1990; 15:355–365.
82. O'Brien CP, McLellan AT, Alterman A, et al: Psychotherapy for cocaine dependence. Ciba Found Symp 1992; 166:207–223.
83. Kuhar MJ, Ritz MC, Boja JW: The dopamine hypothesis of the reinforcing properties of cocaine. Trends Neurosci 1991; 14:299–302.
84. Tennant FS, Sagherian AA: Double-blind comparison of amantadine and bromocriptine for ambulatory withdrawal from cocaine dependence. Arch Intern Med 1987; 147:109–112.
85. Morgan CH, Kosten TR, Gawin FH, et al: A pilot trial of amantadine for cocaine abuse. NIDA Res Monogr 1988; 81:81–85.
86. Weddington WW, Brown BS, Haertzen CA, et al: Comparison of amantadine and desipramine combined with psychotherapy for treatment of cocaine dependence. Am J Drug Alcohol Abuse 1991; 17:137–152.
87. Dackis CA, Gold MS: Bromocriptine as a treatment of cocaine abuse. Lancet 1985; 1:1151–1152.
88. Dackis CA, Gold MS, Sweeney DR, et al: Single-dose bromocriptine reverses cocaine craving. Psychiatry Res 1987; 20:261–264.
89. Giannini AJ, Baumgartel P: Bromocriptine in cocaine withdrawal. J Clin Pharmacol 1987; 27:267–270.
90. Gawin FH, Riordan CA, Kleber HD: Methylphenidate use in non-ADD cocaine abusers—a negative study. Am J Drug Alcohol Abuse 1985; 11:193–197.
91. Khantzian EJ, Gawin F, Kleber HD, et al: Methylphenidate (Ritalin) treatment of cocaine dependence—a preliminary report. J Subst Abuse Treat 1984; 1:107–112.
92. Diakogiannis IA, Steinberg M, Kosten TR: Mazindol treatment of cocaine abuse. A double-blind investigation. NIDA Res Monogr 1990; 105:514.
93. Margolin A, Kosten T, Petrakis I, et al: Bupropion reduces cocaine abuse in methadone-maintained patients. [letter] Arch Gen Psychiatry 1991; 48:87.
94. Gawin FH, Allen D, Humblestone B: Outpatient treatment of 'crack' cocaine smoking with flupenthixol decanoate. Arch Gen Psychiatry 1989; 46:322–325.
95. Tennant FS, Rawson RA: Cocaine and amphetamine dependence treated with desipramine. NIDA Res Monogr 1982; 43:351–355.
96. Gawin FH, Kleber HD, Byck R, et al: Desipramine facilitation of initial cocaine abstinence. Arch Gen Psychiatry 1989; 46:117–121.
97. Weiss RD: Relapse to cocaine abuse after initiating desipramine treatment. JAMA 1988; 260:2545–2546.
98. Ritz MC, Kuhar MJ: Relationship between self-administration of amphetamine and monoamine receptors in brain: Comparison with cocaine. J Pharmacol Exp Ther 1989; 248:1010–1017.
99. Pollack MH, Rosenbaum JF: Fluoxetine treatment of cocaine abuse in heroin addicts. J Clin Psychiatry 1991; 52:31–33.
100. Kosten TA, Kosten TR, Gawin FH, et al: An open trial of sertraline for cocaine abuse. Am J Addict 1992; 1:349–353.
101. Jenkins SW, Warfield NA, Blaine JD, et al: A pilot trial of gepirone vs. placebo in the treatment of cocaine dependency. Psychopharmacol Bull 1992; 28:21–26.
102. Carroll K, Ziedonis D, O'Malley S, et al: Pharmacologic interventions for abusers of alcohol and cocaine: Disulfiram versus naltrexone. Am J Addict 1993; 2:77–79.
103. McCance-Katz EF, Price LH, Kosten TR, et al: Pharmacology, physiology and behavioral effects of cocaethylene in humans.

Annual Meeting of the American College of Neuropsychopharmacology; 1993; Hawaii. Abstract 237.
104. Kosten TR, Kleber HD, Morgan CH: Treatment of cocaine abuse with buprenorphine. Biol Psychiatry 1989; 26:637–639.
105. Halikas J, Kemp K, Kuhn K, et al: Carbamazepine for cocaine addiction? Lancet 1989; 1:623–624.
106. Hatsukami D, Keenan R, Halikas J, et al: Effects of carbamazepine on acute responses to smoked cocaine-base in human cocaine users. Psychopharmacology (Berl) 1991; 104:120–124.
107. Gorelick DA, Weinhold LL, Henningfield JE: Carbamazepine (CBZ) does not alter cocaine self-administration in human cocaine addicts. Annual Scientific Meeting, College on Problems of Drug Dependence; June 1993; Toronto, Canada. Abstract.
108. Kosten TR, Silverman DG, Fleming J, et al: Intravenous cocaine challenges during naltrexone maintenance: A preliminary study. Biol Psychiatry 1992; 32:543–548.
109. Kosten TR, Kleber HD, Morgan C: Role of opioid antagonists in treating intravenous cocaine abuse. Life Sci 1989; 44:887–892.
110. Castellani S, Petrie WM, Ellinwood EH: Drug-induced psychosis: Neurobiology mechanisms. In Alterman AI (ed): Substance Abuse and Psychopathology. New York: Plenum Publishing, 1985:173–210.
111. Kosten TR: Pharmacotherapy for cocaine abuse. J Nerv Ment Dis 1989; 177:379–389.
112. Fischman MW, Foltin RW, Nestadt G, et al: Effects of desipramine maintenance on cocaine self-administration by humans. J Pharmacol Exp Ther 1990; 253:760–770.
113. Charney DS, Menkes DB, Henninger GR: Receptor sensitivity and the mechanism of action of antidepressant treatment. Arch Gen Psychiatry 1981; 38:1160–1180.
114. Weiss RD, Mirin SM: Subtypes of cocaine abusers. Psychiatr Clin North Am 1986; 9:491–501.
115. Kosten TR, Rounsaville BJ, Kleber HD: Antecedents and consequences of cocaine abuse among opioid addicts: A 2.5 year follow-up. J Nerv Ment Dis 1988; 176:176–181.
116. Weiss RD, Mirin SM, Griffin ML, et al: Psychopathology in cocaine abusers—changing trends. J Nerv Ment Dis 1988; 176:719–725.
117. Roberts LJ, Shaner A, Eckman TA, et al: Effectively treating stimulant abusing schizophrenics: Mission impossible? New Dir Ment Health Serv 1992; 53:55–65.
118. Schneier FR, Siris SG: A review of psychoactive substance use and abuse in schizophrenia—patterns of choice. J Nerv Ment Dis 1987; 175:641–652.
119. Richard ML, Liskow BI, Perry PJ: Recent psychostimulant use in hospitalized schizophrenics. J Clin Psychiatry 1985; 46:79–83.
120. Alterman A, Erdlen D: Illicit substance use in hospitalized psychiatric patients: Clinical observations. J Psychiatr Treat Eval 1983; 5:377–380.
121. Yesavage J, Zarcone V: History of drug abuse and dangerous behavior in inpatient schizophrenics. J Clin Psychiatry 1983; 7:259–261.
122. Dixon L, Haas G, Weiden PJ, et al: Drug abuse in schizophrenic patients: Clinical correlates and reasons for use. Am J Psychiatry 1991; 148:224–230.
123. Hellerstein D, Meehan B: Outpatient group therapy for schizophrenic substance abusers. Am J Psychiatry 1987; 144:1337–1339.
124. Kofoed L, Kania J, Walsh T, et al: Outpatient treatment of patients with substance abuse and other co-existing psychiatric disorders. Am J Psychiatry 1986; 143:867–872.

CHAPTER

46 Phencyclidine Use Disorders

Ilana Zylberman
Joyce H. Lowinson
Stephen R. Zukin

Phencyclidine Dependence
Phencyclidine Abuse
Phencyclidine Intoxication

Phencyclidine (1-(1-phenylcyclohexyl)piperidine, PCP) was developed as a general anesthetic agent in the 1950s under the brand name Sernyl.[1–3] The drug was considered physiologically promising because of its lack of respiratory and cardiovascular depressant effects. In fact, patients under PCP anesthesia, rather than manifesting a state of relaxed sleep such as that induced by typical anesthetic agents, appeared semiconscious, with open eyes, fixed staring, flat facies, open mouth, rigid posturing, and waxy flexibility. Because of this apparent sharp dissociation from the environment without true unconsciousness, PCP and the related drug ketamine were classified as dissociative anesthetics.[4]

Approximately 50% of patients anesthetized with PCP developed behavioral syndromes including agitation and hallucinations during emergence from anesthesia.[1–3] A substantial number of subjects developed postoperative psychotic reactions, which in some cases persisted up to 10 days.[2–5] Trials of subanesthetic doses of PCP for treatment of chronic pain led to similar although less severe adverse reactions.[5] As a result, after 1965, PCP was limited to veterinary applications. Ketamine remains available for human anesthesia; side effects are less frequent and severe owing to the lower potency and shorter duration of action of ketamine compared with PCP.

Despite its well-documented aversive and disruptive behavioral effects, PCP emerged during the 1970s as a popular drug of abuse, increasing in popularity to the point that in 1979, 13% of high-school seniors had tried it.[6] Although PCP has never regained that remarkable level of popularity, it has remained a significant public health problem among certain populations and in certain geographical areas. Compared with most other drugs of abuse, PCP has more complex and potentially more harmful effects.

Epidemiology

Illicit use of phencyclidine was first noted in 1965 in Los Angeles.[7] The spread of the drug from California throughout the country was facilitated by its ease of synthesis compared with other drugs. At least six synthetic methods, some simple, are published in scientific journals.[8] Surveys of street drug samples indicated that PCP was sold under many street names (Table 46–1) and frequently combined with or misrepresented as other substances.[7, 9] During the late 1970s and early 1980s, PCP gained considerable notoriety in the popular press not only as a leading drug of abuse but as one with particularly novel and devastating effects.

According to trends in emergency department visits, deaths, initiates entering drug treatment programs, and surveys, PCP abuse increased through the 1970s, peaked in 1978 to 1979, and then declined sharply through 1981, when indicators began to show a new increase through 1984.[10] The decline in PCP use during the late 1970s and early 1980s may have resulted in part from a variety of public health and law enforcement activities, including a nationwide education campaign aimed at informing treatment programs, emergency departments health agencies, and medical examiner–coroner offices of PCP effects and treatment procedures. PCP was rescheduled from Schedule III to the much more restrictive Schedule II of the Controlled Substance Act on the basis of its limited legitimate uses and significant abuse potential. Several PCP analogues were placed in Schedule I. Required reporting of production of the precursor, piperidine, began in 1979; penalties for possession of PCP with intent to sell were increased at about the same time.[10]

In more recent years, indicators of PCP use have remained generally low; however, localized increases have been observed, in some cases associated with the use of new dosage forms (in particular, the use of "blunts," cigars filled with PCP-impregnated marijuana).[11] In the first half of 1993, the highest rates of emergency department mentions of PCP (above 4 per 100,000 population) were noted in Washington (DC), Los Angeles, New York, San Francisco, Chicago, and Philadelphia; increases were noted in 9 of 12 major cities.[11] Mortality data support the impression of significant increases in PCP use in selected cities. For example, in Philadelphia, PCP toxicology reports rose 150% between the first and second halves of 1993. African-American males accounted

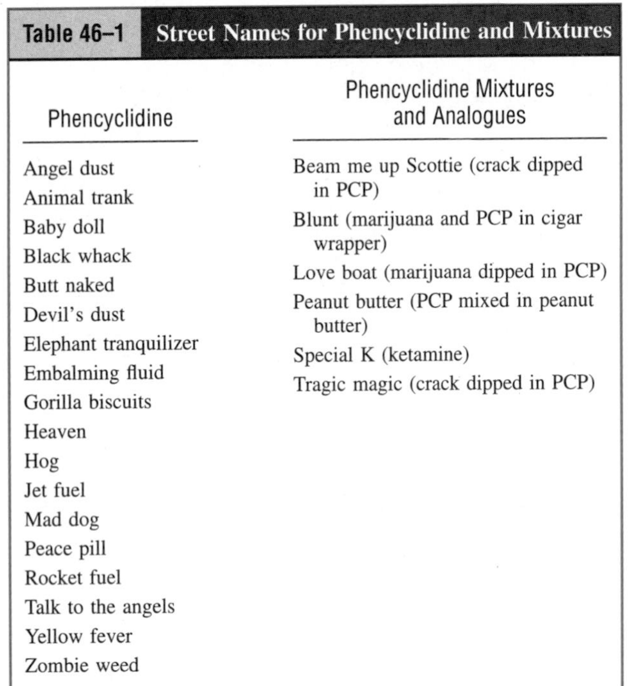

Table 46–1 Street Names for Phencyclidine and Mixtures

Phencyclidine	Phencyclidine Mixtures and Analogues
Angel dust	Beam me up Scottie (crack dipped in PCP)
Animal trank	Blunt (marijuana and PCP in cigar wrapper)
Baby doll	Love boat (marijuana dipped in PCP)
Black whack	Peanut butter (PCP mixed in peanut butter)
Butt naked	Special K (ketamine)
Devil's dust	Tragic magic (crack dipped in PCP)
Elephant tranquilizer	
Embalming fluid	
Gorilla biscuits	
Heaven	
Hog	
Jet fuel	
Mad dog	
Peace pill	
Rocket fuel	
Talk to the angels	
Yellow fever	
Zombie weed	

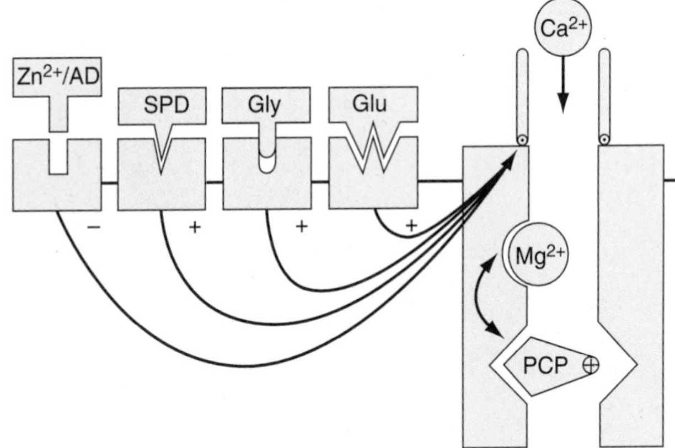

Figure 46–1 *Schematic model of* N-methyl-D-aspartate *(NMDA) receptor functioning. After magnesium blockade is relieved by membrane depolarization, the cation channel gated by the NMDA receptor can be activated by binding of* L*-glutamate and glycine. Binding of PCP within the channel blocks ion flux. There are a number of other regulatory sites external to the channel, of which two are illustrated: a site at which polyamines such as spermidine (SPD) positively modulate activation induced by* L*-glutamate (Glu) and glycine (Gly); and a site at which zinc and tricyclic antidepressants (AD) negatively modulate activation.*

for the largest proportion (47%) of those deaths, followed by white males (27%) and Hispanic males (17%).[11]

As of 1993, the highest rates of PCP use during the past year were observed among 18- to 25-year-olds, followed by 12- to 17-year-olds and 26- to 34-year-olds; rates were higher among males than females, and the highest rates of use were observed in Hispanics followed by whites and African-Americans. The highest rates were observed in the western region of the country, followed by north central and southern states. Rates were lowest in the northeast.[12] In general, PCP abusers represent 1% or less of admissions to drug treatment programs.[11]

Law enforcement data indicate that PCP availability is rising in Minnesota and New York. In Washington (DC), PCP prices are decreasing as supplies increase. PCP is sold by the fluid ounce ($250 to $450) and by the gallon ($9,000 to $12,000 in the first quarter of 1994, down from a stable $15,000 to $22,000 since 1991). An ounce of PCP-sprayed parsley, tobacco, or marijuana costs approximately $150, and a PCP cigarette costs $3 to $35.[11]

In 1983, more than 66% of PCP-related deaths reported to the Drug Abuse Warning Network involved at least one other drug. Many of the PCP-related deaths were not the result of overdose or drug interaction or reaction, but the direct result of some external event facilitated by intoxication (e.g., homicides, accidents). The various manners of death (such as drowning and being shot by police) reported are consistent with the disorientation and violent aggressive behavior that can be stimulated by PCP.[10]

Etiology and Pathophysiology

Psychotomimetic Effects

The psychotomimetic effects of PCP result from its interaction with a unique high-affinity PCP receptor, demonstrated in 1979,[13, 14] that selectively binds PCP-like drugs in rank order proportional to their behavioral potencies. By contrast, a wide variety of other drugs of abuse and neurotransmitters fail to bind to the PCP receptor at physiologically relevant concentrations.[13–17] The PCP receptor is located within the ion channel gated by the *N*-methyl-D-aspartate (NMDA) receptor complex (Fig. 46–1). When activated by binding of the major excitatory amino acid neurotransmitter of brain, L-glutamate, in the presence of the coagonist glycine, the cation channel gated by the NMDA receptor is activated, permitting influx of calcium ions. Binding of PCP-like drugs uncompetitively inhibits NMDA receptor activation by L-glutamate, thus disrupting NMDA receptor–mediated glutamatergic neurotransmission in a fashion that cannot be surmounted by increasing L-glutamate concentration. Such disruption of NMDA receptor function results in impairment of a number of mental functions including learning and memory.[18–22] In animals, exposure to PCP-type drugs has been shown to result in reversible microscopical changes, including vacuolization, in specific populations of brain neurons.[23] The applicability of these findings to humans remains to be established.

The effects of low-dose PCP administration have been extensively studied in volunteers. In normal subjects (Table 46–2), single intravenous doses of 0.05 to 0.1 mg/kg induced withdrawal, negativism, and in some cases catatonic posturing; thinking processes became concrete, idiosyncratic,

Table 46–2 Single-Dose Effects of Intravenous Phencyclidine

Withdrawal
Negativism
Catatonic posturing in some cases
Concrete, idiosyncratic, and bizarre thinking
Absence of significant physical or neurological findings

and bizarre in the absence of significant physical or neurological findings; and drug effects persisted for 4 to 6 hours.[24–29] In contrast to lysergic acid diethylamide (LSD) or amphetamine,[30, 31] PCP was noted to induce disturbances in symbolic thinking,[27, 31] perception,[27, 30] and attention[30] strikingly similar to those observed in schizophrenia. Administration of PCP to schizophrenic subjects caused exacerbation of illness-specific symptoms persisting up to several weeks,[25, 28] suggesting that schizophrenic or pre-schizophrenic individuals may be at significantly increased risk of behavioral effects from PCP abuse. At the doses used in these studies, which were equivalent to the typical 5-mg street dose,[32] serum PCP concentrations of 0.01 to 0.1 μM are attained. At such levels, the PCP receptor is the only target site that would be significantly occupied by the drug (Fig. 46–2).

Other Effects

Abusers often use PCP in higher or repeated doses leading to significantly higher serum concentrations than those associated selectively with psychotomimetic effects. In general, concentrations greater than 0.4 μM are associated with impairment of consciousness; at concentrations greater than 1.0 μM, coma, seizures, and respiratory arrest are common.[33, 34] These neurological and metabolic effects result in part from interaction of PCP with sites other than the PCP-NMDA receptor, including catecholamine and indolamine reuptake sites (see Fig. 46–2).

Pharmacokinetics

PCP is extremely lipid soluble. As a result, it can reach its brain target sites after oral, parenteral, smoked, inhaled,[35] or topical administration. Another consequence of its lipophilicity is its tendency to accumulate in lipid tissues throughout the body, including the brain.[36, 37] Flashbacks may result from mobilization of adipose stores, for example, by exercise.[36, 37]

Because of its pK_a of 8.5, PCP is largely ionized in the stomach or urinary tract. However, in the nonacidic environment of the small intestine, PCP becomes nonionized and is readily reabsorbed across the intestinal mucosa; subsequent enterohepatic recirculation may account for the fluctuating clinical course often observed.

Metabolism of PCP occurs primarily in the liver. Both PCP[38] and hydroxylated metabolites[39] are excreted in the urine. The serum half-life of PCP has been reported to vary from 4 to 72 hours.[38, 40] Its volume of distribution is 6.2 L/kg.[38]

Tolerance and Dependence

Tolerance to and dependence on PCP have not been formally investigated in humans. Clinical observations suggest that chronic PCP users are significantly less sensitive to a given dose than are casual users. In the case of ketamine, which shares the same fundamental mechanism of action as PCP, tolerance has been more formally observed in burn patients who require increased doses after a time to maintain the same level of analgesia.[41] In laboratory animals, a twofold to fourfold shift to the right in the behavioral dose-response curve for PCP is observed in most studies, with indications that tolerance develops to a much greater extent with continuous administration.[42]

Signs of severe physical withdrawal have been noted in experimental animals when PCP is withdrawn after long-term administration.[42] In monkeys, even under circumstances in which physical withdrawal symptoms are minimal, normal behaviors are disrupted for a week or more after cessation of long-term PCP administration.[43] In humans, a single study indicated that one third of 68 chronic PCP users had sought treatment to help them withdraw from PCP in the face of depressed mood, craving for the drug, and alterations in sleep and appetite that occurred when they attempted to cease drug use on their own.[44]

Diagnosis and Differential Diagnosis

Phenomenology and Variations in Presentation

Psychiatrists must be alert to the wide spectrum of effects of PCP on multiple organ systems. Because fluctuations in serum levels may occur unpredictably, a patient being treated for apparently selective psychiatric or behavioral complica-

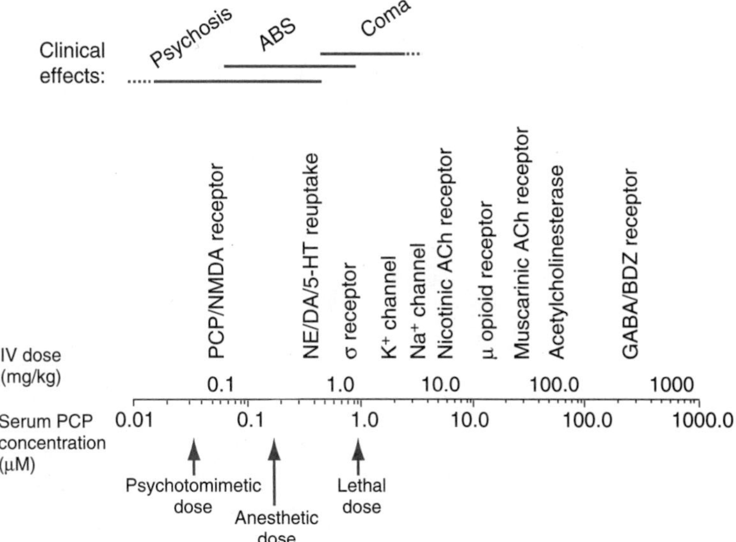

Figure 46–2 *Dose range of PCP effects. Relationship of dose of PCP and PCP affinities for brain target sites to clinical effects is illustrated. Low psychotomimetic doses of PCP act selectively at the PCP site of the NMDA receptor–channel complex. ABS, Acute brain syndrome; ACh, acetylcholine; BDZ, benzodiazepine; DA, dopamine; GABA, γ-aminobutyric acid; 5-HT, 5-hydroxytryptamine; NE, norepinephrine.*

DSM-IV Criteria 292.89

Phencyclidine Intoxication

A. Recent use of phencyclidine (or a related substance).

B. Clinically significant maladaptive behavioral changes (e.g., belligerence, assaultiveness, impulsiveness, unpredictability, psychomotor agitation, impaired judgment, or impaired social or occupational functioning) that developed during, or shortly after, phencyclidine use.

C. Within an hour (less when smoked, "snorted," or used intravenously), two (or more) of the following signs:

(1) vertical or horizontal nystagmus

(2) hypertension or tachycardia

(3) numbness or diminished responsiveness to pain

(4) ataxia

(5) dysarthria

(6) muscle rigidity

(7) seizures or coma

(8) hyperacusis

D. The symptoms are not due to a general medical condition and are not better accounted for by another mental disorder.

Specify if:

With perceptual disturbances

tions of PCP abuse may suddenly undergo radical alterations in medical status; emergency medical intervention may become necessary to avoid permanent organ damage or death. Any patient manifesting significant cardiovascular, respiratory, neurological, or metabolic derangement subsequent to PCP use should be evaluated and treated in a medical service; the psychiatrist plays a secondary role in diagnosis and treatment until physiological stability has been reached and sustained.

PCP-intoxicated patients may come to medical attention on the basis of alterations in mental status; bizarre or violent behavior; injuries sustained while intoxicated; or medical complications, such as rhabdomyolysis, hyperthermia, or seizures.[45]

Psychiatric Presentation

The presenting symptoms may be predominantly or exclusively psychiatric, without significant alterations in level of consciousness, and may closely resemble an acute schizophrenic decompensation[46] with concrete or illogical thinking, bizarre behavior, negativism, catatonic posturing, and echolalia. Subjective feelings and objective signs of "drunkenness" may or may not be present. Retrospective studies conducted during the period of widespread PCP abuse demonstrated that PCP psychosis could not reliably be distinguished from schizophrenia on the basis of presenting symptoms.[47, 48]

Studies of normal volunteers suggested that the acute psychosis induced by a single low dose of PCP usually lasts 4 to 6 hours.[49] However, in some PCP users, psychotic symptoms including hallucinations, delusions, paranoia, thought disorder, and catatonia, with intact consciousness, have been reported to persist from days to weeks after single doses.[32, 50–52] The frequency of such prolonged psychotic states after single doses has not been determined systematically. However, one study indicated that 25% of PCP-intoxicated patients required inpatient psychiatric admission.[50] PCP psychosis can occur at undetectably low serum or urinary levels of the drug.[33, 34] Sudden and impulsive violent and assaultive behaviors have been reported in PCP-intoxicated patients without previous histories of such conduct.

Nonpsychiatric Presentation

In PCP intoxication, the central nervous, cardiovascular, respiratory, and peripheral autonomic systems are affected to degrees ranging from mild to catastrophic (Table 46–3).

The level of consciousness may vary from full alertness to coma. Coma of variable duration may occur spontaneously or after an episode of bizarre or violent behavior.[52] Prolonged coma due to continued drug absorption from ruptured ingested packages of PCP has been described.[53]

Nystagmus (which may be horizontal, vertical, or rotatory) has been described in 57% of a series of 1000 patients.[35] Consequences of PCP-induced central nervous system hyperexcitability may range from mildly increased deep tendon reflexes to grand mal seizures (observed in 31 of a series of 1000 PCP-intoxicated patients) or status epilepticus.[35, 54] Seizures are usually generalized, but focal seizures or neurological deficits have been reported, probably on the basis of focal cerebral vasoconstriction.[55] Other motor signs have been observed, such as generalized rigidity, localized dystonias, facial grimacing, and athetosis.[35]

Hypertension, one of the most frequent physical findings, was described in 57% of 1000 patients evaluated, and it was found to be usually mild and self-limiting, but 4% had severe hypertension, and some remained hypertensive for days.[35] One fatal case of hypertensive crisis late in the

Table 46–3 Nonpsychiatric Findings in Phencyclidine Intoxication

Altered level of consciousness
Central nervous system changes including nystagmus, hyperreflexia, and motor abnormalities
Hypertension
Cholinergic or anticholinergic signs
Hypothermia or hyperthermia
Myoglobinuria

course of PCP intoxication has been described.[56] Tachycardia occurs in 30% of patients. PCP-induced tachypnea can progress to periodic breathing and respiratory arrest.[57] Autonomic signs seen in PCP intoxication may be cholinergic (diaphoresis, bronchospasm, miosis, salivation, bronchorrhea) or anticholinergic (mydriasis, urinary retention).[35]

Hypothermia and hyperthermia have been observed.[35] Hyperthermia may reach malignant proportions.[58]

Rhabdomyolysis frequently results from a combination of PCP-induced muscle contractions and trauma occurring in relation to injuries sustained as a result of behavioral effects. Acute renal failure can result from myoglobinuria.[59]

In children, PCP intoxication may result from ingestion of remnants of used PCP-impregnated cigarettes or from inhalation of sidestream smoke.[60–62] Young children often present with impaired consciousness, ataxia, nystagmus, staring,[60–62] or apnea.[63] Aggressive or violent behavior is unusual in this population.[45]

Assessment

Special Issues in Psychiatric Examination and History

The disruption of normal cognitive and memory function by PCP frequently renders patients unable to give an accurate history, including a history of having used PCP. Therefore, assay of urine or blood for drugs may be the only way to establish the diagnosis. PCP is frequently taken in forms in which it is mixed with other drugs, typically marijuana or cocaine, which may further complicate the diagnosis.

By disrupting sensory pathways, PCP frequently renders users hypersensitive to environmental stimuli to the extent that physical examination or psychiatric interview may cause severe agitation. If PCP intoxication is suspected, measures should be taken from the outset to minimize sensory input. The patient should be evaluated in a quiet, darkened room with the minimal necessary number of medical staff present. Assessments may need to be interrupted periodically.

Relevant Physical Examination and Laboratory Findings

Vital signs should be obtained immediately on presentation. Temperature, blood pressure, and respiratory rate are dose-dependently increased by PCP and may be of a magnitude requiring emergency medical treatment to avoid the potentially fatal complications of malignant hyperthermia, hypertensive crisis, and respiratory arrest. In all cases, monitoring of vital signs should continue at 2- to 4-hour intervals throughout treatment, because serum PCP levels may increase spontaneously as a result of mobilization of drug from lipid stores or enterohepatic recirculation.

Analgesic and behavioral changes induced by PCP not only predispose patients to physical injury but also mask these injuries, which may be found only with careful physical examination.[45]

On neurological examination, nystagmus and ataxia, although not conclusive, are strongly suggestive of PCP intoxication. Examination of deep tendon reflexes helps to establish the degree of nervous system hyperexcitability. Crossed or clonic deep tendon reflexes alert the physician to the possibility of subsequent seizures.

Because PCP is usually supplied in combination with other drugs and is often misrepresented, toxicological analysis of urine or blood is essential. However, there may be circumstances in which PCP may not be detected in urine even if it is present in the body, for example, when the urine is alkaline. On the other hand, in chronic PCP users, drug may be detected in urine up to 30 days after last use.[64] Urine should be tested for heme because of the possible complication of myoglobinuria.

Blood and urine samples should be sent for toxicological analysis. In addition, serum uric acid, creatine kinase, aspartate transaminase, and alanine transaminase elevations, common findings in PCP intoxication, were found to be associated with rhabdomyolysis in 22 of 1000 cases.[35]

Differential Diagnosis

The presence of nystagmus and hypertension with mental status changes should raise the possibility of PCP intoxication. Because of the close resemblance of both the acute and the prolonged forms of PCP psychosis to schizophrenia, and the increased sensitivity of schizophrenic patients to the psychotomimetic effects of the drug, an underlying schizophrenia spectrum disorder should be considered, particularly if paranoia or thought disorder persists beyond 4 to 6 weeks after last use of PCP. PCP psychosis may also resemble mania or other mood disorders. Therefore, in all cases, a detailed psychiatric history should be obtained. Robust response of psychotic symptoms to treatment with neuroleptics would favor a diagnosis other than simple PCP psychosis.

PCP psychosis is readily distinguishable from LSD psychosis in normal as well as in schizophrenic subjects by the lack of typical LSD effects, such as synesthesia. The cluster of psychotic symptoms, hypertension, and stereotypy may be seen in both PCP psychosis and chronic amphetamine psychosis; in such cases, accurate histories and toxicological analysis are particularly important.

In cases involving prominent PCP-induced neurological, cardiovascular, or metabolic derangement, encephalitis, head injury, postictal state, and primary metabolic disorders must be ruled out.[7] Either intoxication with or withdrawal from sedative-hypnotics may be associated with nystagmus.[45] Neuroleptic malignant syndrome should be ruled out in the differential diagnosis of PCP-induced hyperthermia and muscle rigidity.[45]

Course and Natural History

As drug levels decline, the clinical picture recedes in 5 to 21 days through periods of moderating neurological, autonomic, and metabolic impairments to a stage at which only psychiatric impairments are apparent. Once the physical symptoms and signs have cleared, the period of simple PCP psychosis may last 1 day to 6 weeks, whether or not neuroleptics are administered, during which the psychiatric symptoms and signs abate gradually and progressively. Even after complete recovery, flashbacks may occur if PCP sequestered in lipid stores is mobilized. Any underlying psychiatric disorders can be detected and evaluated only after complete resolution of the drug-induced psychosis. Although systematic studies in humans have not been carried out, clinical experience predicts a high likelihood of resumption of PCP use after recovery from PCP psychosis.

Overall Goals of Treatment

The hierarchy of treatment goals begins with detection and treatment of physical manifestations of PCP intoxication. Equally important are measures to anticipate PCP-induced impulsive, violent behaviors and provide appropriate protection for the patient and others. The patient must then be closely observed during the period of PCP-induced psychosis, which may persist for weeks after resolution of physical symptoms and signs. Finally, the possibly dramatic medical and psychiatric presentation and its resolution must not divert the attention of the psychiatrist from full assessment and treatment of the patient's drug-seeking behavior.

Standard Approach to Treatment

Physician-Patient Relationship in Psychiatric Management

In contrast to psychotic states induced by drugs such as LSD, in which "talking the patient down" may be highly effective, no such effort should be made in the case of PCP psychosis, particularly during the period of acute intoxication, because of the risk of sensory overload that can lead to dramatically increased agitation. The risk of sudden and unpredictable impulsive, violent behavior can also be increased by sensory stimulation.

Pharmacotherapy and Somatic Treatments

There is no pharmacological competitive antagonist for PCP, in contrast to opiates and benzodiazepines. Any compound competing with PCP for binding to its recognition site within the NMDA receptor–gated ion channel would also block the channel and prevent ion flux, thus exerting PCP-like effects. Oral or intramuscular benzodiazepines are recommended for agitation. Neuroleptics usually have little or no effect on acute or chronic PCP-induced psychosis or thought disorder. Because they lower the seizure threshold, neuroleptics should be used with caution. Physical restraint may be lifesaving if the patient's behavior poses an imminent threat to his or her safety or that of others; however, such restraint risks triggering or worsening rhabdomyolysis.

Because of the large volume of distribution of PCP, dialysis is ineffective as a means of clearing the drug from circulation. The "trapping" of PCP in acidic body compartments suggests either gastric gavage or urinary acidification as a measure to reduce levels of PCP in the body. However, these should be considered measures of last resort because of the possibility of electrolyte imbalance and additional nephrotoxic effects. Administration of activated charcoal has been shown to bind PCP and to diminish toxic effects of PCP in animals.[65]

Special Features Influencing Treatment

Psychiatric Comorbidity

PCP psychosis may be clinically indistinguishable from schizophrenia[25, 46] or mania.[66] It has been suggested that some patients who remain psychotic for weeks after PCP ingestion may have an underlying predisposition to schizophrenia or mania. In some series, significant percentages of patients suffering prolonged PCP-induced psychosis are subsequently hospitalized with non–drug-induced schizophrenic disorders.[46] In the case of a schizophrenic patient, responsiveness to neuroleptic treatment may resume after recovery from prolonged PCP psychosis.

General Medical Comorbidity

Patients with preexisting neurological, cardiovascular, respiratory, or renal disorders are at increased risk for complications of PCP intoxication, such as seizures, stroke, hypertensive crisis, respiratory arrest, or renal failure. Abusers of more than one drug may be at increased risk from the presence of other drugs exerting toxic effects on the same organ systems (e.g., cardiovascular effects of cocaine and amphetamine) or because of damage to specific organs secondary to infectious complications of parenteral drug use.

Clinical Vignette 1

A 22-year-old single man was brought to the emergency department by a friend who left without providing any information. The patient was severely agitated and hypervigilant, repeatedly looking over his shoulders and patrolling the examination room. Asked to explain, he said, "I'm scared. Something is after me. I can't say anything else." He was unable or unwilling to give any history. Vital signs and neurological examination findings were within normal limits. A urine sample was sent for qualitative toxicological analysis. The result, received 5 days later, was positive for PCP. His condition remained unchanged during 3 hours of observation in the emergency department. He spontaneously went to the telephone and called the friend who had brought him to the hospital but found himself unable to speak. He handed the telephone to the emergency department physician, who was able to obtain from the friend the information that the patient had smoked three PCP-impregnated marijuana cigarettes in a 12-hour period beginning 18 hours before admission. The friend stated that this had been the patient's first exposure to PCP: "He got scared and bummed out and begged me to take him to the hospital." A mental status examination revealed impaired attention and memory, with concrete interpretation of proverbs. He continued to complain of being frightened and to survey his surroundings continuously, saying, "I have to watch out or I could get hurt." He admitted to feeling in great danger from forces outside himself. He denied hallucinations. It was noted that the patient became more agitated after interviews or clinical interventions.

He was admitted to the psychiatry service, where treatment was initiated with haloperidol 2 mg three times a day, increasing to 5 mg three times daily by the third day. His mental status remained essentially unchanged from that observed in the emergency department until the end of the third week after admission, when he reported having intervals when he felt less agitated and free of his feelings of persecution. According to the staff, however, at times he was still observed looking back over his shoulder and muttering to himself. His nonpsychotic intervals gradually became more frequent. At the end of the fourth week, he began interacting with staff and visitors and participating in groups and other ward activities. At the beginning of the sixth week, mental status examination revealed no evidence of psychosis. Neuroleptic medication was discontinued without relapse. He gave a history of sporadic abuse of marijuana and cocaine during the previous 3 years. He contacted his parents, who traveled from the distant state in which they lived to participate in treatment and discharge planning. He was discharged directly to a long-term residential drug treatment program. Contacted 1 year later, he was living with his parents in the other state, participating in Narcotics Anonymous, and stated that he had been drug free since discharge from the hospital. He added, "Even if I ever use drugs again—and I hope I won't—I would never, ever use PCP."

Comment

This clinical vignette illustrates a purely psychiatric presentation of PCP psychosis, with no physical or neurological symptoms or signs 6 hours after the last dose of drug. Without the history obtained from the friend, the correct diagnosis would not have been made until the toxicology results were received. All of the patient's symptoms could have been accounted for by a non–drug-related psychiatric illness. The failure of the psychotic symptoms to respond to neuroleptic medication, and the patient's recovery by the sixth week, are typical of the prolonged PCP psychosis in an otherwise nonpsychotic individual.

Clinical Vignette 2

An 18-year-old high-school girl was transferred from the medical service to the psychiatric service 1 week after admission to the hospital. After friends had been unable to contact her for several days, the police were called and found the patient semiconscious on the floor of her apartment. While being transported to the hospital, the patient suddenly freed herself from restraints, assaulted one of the emergency medical personnel, and then lost consciousness. On presentation in the emergency department, blood pressure was noted to be 210/107 mm Hg, temperature was 104.1°F, and respiratory rate was 34 per minute. Extensive bruising was apparent on her back and lower extremities. While dehydration and electrolyte imbalances were being corrected, the patient had a grand mal seizure progressing to status epilepticus, which was treated with intravenous diazepam. Toxicological assays showed the presence of PCP in her urine; urinalysis was positive for heme.

She was admitted to the medical intensive care unit, where intensive measures to stabilize her condition were instituted. Vital and neurological signs fluctuated for the next 3 days as she slipped in and out of coma. On the fourth day, the patient regained consciousness but was delirious. She attempted to assault a nurse and was placed in four-point restraints. On transfer to the psychiatry service, temperature and blood pressure were within normal limits; deep tendon reflexes were mildly to moderately hyperactive. She was oriented to time and place, but cognitive functions were globally deficient. She refused neuroleptic medication. For the first 2 days on the service, she was mute. On the third day, she began stating repeatedly, "I was dead and I came back to life." On several occasions, staff reported that she appeared to be responding to internal stimuli, but she denied it. On the fifth day, she was able to give a history. She stated that PCP was her drug of choice and that she had used it for several years on a weekly basis. Before admission, she had obtained a new supply, in liquid form, from a source she had not previously used. She had dipped approximately 10 cigarettes in the liquid and had smoked an unknown number of them in a period of several hours. She "got high" but then "died and knew I was dead." She explained that she remembered suddenly falling to the floor and being unable to see, move, or hear for a long time. She recalled being aware of her condition and situation before being found but had no memory of events in the hospital until shortly before her transfer to the psychiatry service. She stated, "I'm a little crazy but that will clear up in another few days; it always has before. Dust [PCP] does that to a person." Mental status examination now revealed significant improvement in cognitive functioning. On the seventh day, she signed out against medical advice. During the discharge interview, she continued to maintain that she had literally died and come back to life. Three weeks after discharge, she was admitted to another hospital for treatment of PCP intoxication.

Comment

This clinical vignette illustrates the emergence of a purely psychotic picture after resolution of catastrophic medical complications of high-dose PCP intoxication. It also illustrates PCP dependence in a chronic user.

References

1. Collins VJ, Gorospe CA, Rovenstine EA: Intravenous nonbarbiturate, nonnarcotic analgesics: Preliminary studies. I. Cyclohexylamines. Anesth Analg 1960; 39:303–306.
2. Greifenstein FE, Yoskitake J, DeVault M, et al: A study of 1-aryl-cyclohexylamine for anesthesia. Anesth Analg 1958; 37:283–294.
3. Johnstone M, Evans V, Baigel S: Sernyl (CI-395) in clinical anesthesia. Br J Anaesth 1958; 31:433–439.
4. Corssen G, Domino EF: Dissociative anesthesia: Further pharmacologic studies and first clinical experience with the phencyclidine derivative CI-581. Anesth Analg 1966; 45:29–40.
5. Meyer JS, Greifenstein F, DeVault M: A new drug causing symptoms of sensory deprivation. J Nerv Ment Dis 1959; 129:54–61.
6. Johnston LD, O'Malley PM, Bachman JG: National survey results on drug use from the Monitoring the Future Study, 1975–1993, Volume I, Secondary School Students. Rockville, MD: National Institute on Drug Abuse, 1994. NIH publication 94-3809.
7. Lerner SE, Burns RS: Phencyclidine use among youth: History, epidemiology and chronic intoxication. NIDA Res Monogr 1978; 21:66–118.
8. Allen AD, Robles J, Dovenski W, et al: PCP: A review of synthetic methods for forensic clandestine investigation. Forensic Sci Int 1993; 61:85–100.
9. Siegel RK: Phencyclidine and ketamine intoxication: A study of four populations of recreational users. NIDA Res Monogr 1978; 21:119–147.
10. Crider R: Phencyclidine: Changing abuse patterns. NIDA Res Monogr 1986; 64:163–173.
11. Community Epidemiology Work Group: Epidemiologic Trends in Drug Abuse, Volume I. Rockville, MD: National Institute on Drug Abuse, 1994. NIH publication 94-3853.
12. National Household Survey on Drug Abuse: Population Estimates 1993. Rockville, MD: Substance Abuse and Mental Health Services Administration Office of Applied Studies, 1994. DHHS publication SMA 94-3017.
13. Zukin SR, Zukin RS: Specific [^{3}H]phencyclidine binding in rat central nervous system. Proc Natl Acad Sci U S A 1979; 76:5372–5376.
14. Vincent JP, Kartalovski B, Geneste P, et al: Interaction of phencyclidine ("angel dust") with a specific receptor in rat brain membranes. Proc Natl Acad Sci U S A 1979; 76:4678–4682.
15. Sircar R, Rappaport M, Nichtenhauser R, Zukin SR: The novel anticonvulsant MK-801: A potent and specific ligand of the brain phencyclidine/σ receptor. Brain Res 1987; 435:235–240.
16. Wong EHF, Knight AR, Woodruff GN: [^{3}H]MK-801 labels a site on the

N-methyl-D-aspartate receptor channel complex in rat brain membranes. J Neurochem 1988; 50:274–281.
17. Zukin SR, Fitz-Syage L, Nichtenhauser R, et al: Specific binding of [^{3}H]phencyclidine in rat central nervous tissue: Further characterization and technical considerations. Brain Res 1983; 258:277–284.
18. Handelman GE, Contreras PC, O'Donohue TL: Selective memory impairment by phencyclidine in rats. Eur J Pharmacol 1987; 140:69–73.
19. Balster RL, Chait LD: The behavioral pharmacology of phencyclidine. Clin Toxicol 1976; 9:513–528.
20. Thompson DM, Winsauer PJ, Mastropaolo J: Effects of phenyclidine, ketamine and MDMA on complex operant behavior in monkeys. Pharmacol Biochem Behav 1987; 26:401–405.
21. Butelman ER: A novel NMDA antagonist, MK-801, impairs performance in a hippocampal-dependent spatial learning task. Pharmacol Biochem Behav 1989; 34:13–16.
22. Moerschbaecher JM, Thompson DM: Differential effects of prototype opioid agonists on the acquisition of conditional discriminations in monkeys. J Pharmacol Exp Ther 1983; 226:738–748.
23. Olney JW, Labruyere J, Price MT: Pathological changes induced in cerebrocortical neurons by phencyclidine and related drugs. Science 1989; 244:1360–1362.
24. Bakker CB, Amini FB: Observations on the psychotomimetic effects of Sernyl. Compr Psychiatry 1961; 2:269–280.
25. Luby ED, Cohen BD, Rosenbaum F, et al: Study of a new schizophrenomimetic drug, Sernyl. Arch Neurol Psychiatry 1959; 81:363–369.
26. Ban AT, Lohrenz JJ, Lehmann HE: Observations on the action of Sernyl—a new psychotropic drug. Can Psychiatr Assoc J 1961; 6:150–156.
27. Davies BM, Beech HR: The effect of 1-arylcyclohexylamine (Sernyl) on twelve normal volunteers. J Ment Sci 1960; 106:912–924.
28. Domino EF, Luby E: Abnormal mental states induced by phencyclidine as a model of schizophrenia. In Domino EF (ed): PCP (Phencyclidine): Historical and Current Perspectives. Ann Arbor, MI: NPP Books, 1981.
29. Rodin EA, Luby ED, Meyer JS: Electroencephalographic findings associated with Sernyl infusion. Electroencephalogr Clin Neurophysiol 1959; 11:796–798.
30. Rosenbaum G, Cohen BD, Luby ED, et al: Comparisons of Sernyl with other drugs. Arch Gen Psychiatry 1959; 1:651–656.
31. Cohen BD, Rosenbaum G, Luby ED, Gottlieb JS: Comparison of phencyclidine hydrochloride (Sernyl) with other drugs. Arch Gen Psychiatry 1961; 6:79–85.
32. Burns RS, Lerner SE: Perspectives: Acute phencyclidine intoxication. Clin Toxicol 1976; 9:477–501.
33. Walberg CB, McCarron MM, Schulze BW: Quantitation of phencyclidine in serum by enzyme immunoassay: Results in 405 patients. J Anal Toxicol 1983; 7:106–110.
34. Pearce DS: Detection and quantitation of phencyclidine in blood by use of [2H5]phencyclidine and select ion monitoring applied to non-fatal cases of phencyclidine intoxication. Clin Chem 1976; 22:1623–1626.
35. McCarron MM, Schulze BW, Thompson GA, et al: Acute phencyclidine intoxication: Incidence of clinical findings in 1,000 cases. Ann Emerg Med 1981; 10:237–242.
36. James SH, Schnoll SH: Phencyclidine: Tissue distribution in the rat. Clin Toxicol 1976; 9:573–582.
37. Misra AL, Pontani RB, Bartolemeo J: Persistence of phencyclidine (PCP) and metabolites in brain and adipose tissue and implications for long-lasting behavioral effects. Res Commun Chem Pathol Pharmacol 1979; 24:3431–3445.
38. Cook CD, Brine DR, Jeffcoat AR: Phencyclidine disposition after intravenous and oral doses. Clin Pharmacol Ther 1982; 31:625–634.
39. Wong LK, Biemann K: Metabolites of phencyclidine. Clin Toxicol 1976; 9:583–591.
40. Done AK, Aronow R, Miceli JN: Pharmacokinetic observations in the treatment of phencyclidine poisoning: A preliminary report. In Rumack BH, Temple AR (eds): Management of the Poisoned Patient. Princeton, NJ: Science Press, 1977: 79–95.
41. Carroll ME: PCP: The dangerous angel. In Snyder SH (ed): The Encyclopedia of Psychoactive Drugs. New York: Chelsea House, 1985:41. Updated 1992.
42. Balster RL: Clinical implications of behavioral pharmacology research on phencyclidine. NIDA Res Monogr 1986; 64:148–162.
43. Slifer BL, Balster RL, Woolverton WL: Behavioral dependence produced by continuous phencyclidine infusion in rhesus monkeys. J Pharmacol Exp Ther 1984; 230:339–406.
44. Tennant FS Jr, Rawson RA, McCann M: Withdrawal from chronic phencyclidine dependence with desipramine. Am J Psychiatry 1981; 138:845–847.
45. Baldridge BE, Bessen HA: Phencyclidine. Emerg Med Clin North Am 1990; 8:541–550.
46. Luisada PV: The phencyclidine psychosis: Phenomenology and treatment. NIDA Res Monogr 1978; 21:241–253.
47. Erard R, Luisada PV, Peele R: The PCP psychosis: Prolonged intoxication or drug-precipitated functional illness? J Psychedelic Drugs 1980; 12:235–245.
48. Yesavage JA, Freeman AM III: Acute phencyclidine (PCP) intoxication: Psychopathology and prognosis. J Clin Psychiatry 1978; 44:664–665.
49. Javitt DC, Zukin SR: Recent advances in the phencyclidine model of schizophrenia. Am J Psychiatry 1991; 148:1301–1308.
50. Allen RM, Young SJ: Phencyclidine-induced psychosis. Am J Psychiatry 1978; 135:1081–1084.
51. Rainey JM, Crowder MK: Prolonged psychosis attributed to phencyclidine: Report of three cases. Am J Psychiatry 1975; 132:1076–1078.
52. McCarron MM, Schulze BW, Thompson GA, et al: Acute phencyclidine intoxication: Clinical patterns, complications, and treatment. Ann Emerg Med 1981; 10:290–297.
53. Jackson JE: Phencyclidine pharmacokinetics after a massive overdose. Ann Intern Med 1989; 111:613–615.
54. Kessler GF, Demers LM, Berlin C: Phencyclidine and fatal status epilepticus. [letter] N Engl J Med 1974; 291:979.
55. Crosley CJ, Binet EF: Cerebrovascular complications in phencyclidine intoxication. J Pediatr 1979; 94:316–318.
56. Eastman JW, Cohen SN: Hypertensive crisis and death associated with phencyclidine poisoning. N Engl J Med 1975; 231:1270–1271.
57. Hurlbut KM: Drug-induced psychosis. Emerg Med Clin North Am 1991; 9:31–53.
58. Thompson TN: Malignant hyperthermia from PCP. [letter] J Clin Psychiatry 1979; 40:327.
59. Patel R, Connor G: A review of thirty cases of rhabdomyolysis-associated acute renal failure among phencyclidine users. Clin Toxicol 1986; 23:547–556.
60. Karp HN, Kaufman ND, Anand SK: Phencyclidine poisoning in young children. J Pediatr 1980; 97:1006–1009.
61. Schwartz RH, Einhorn A: PCP intoxication in seven young children. Pediatr Emerg Care 1986; 2:238–241.
62. Welch MJ, Correa GA: PCP intoxication in young children and infants. Clin Pediatr 1980; 19:510–514.
63. Burns RS, Lerner SE, Corrado R: Phencyclidine—states of acute intoxication and fatalities. West J Med 1975; 123:345–349.
64. Simpson JM, Khajawallam AM, Alatorre E: Urinary phencyclidine excretion in chronic abusers. J Toxicol Clin Toxicol 1982-83; 19:1051–1059.
65. Picchioni AL, Consroe PF: Activated charcoal—a phencyclidine antidote, or hog in dogs. [letter] N Engl J Med 1979; 300:202.
66. Slavney PR, Rich GB, Pearlson GD, et al: Phencyclidine abuse and symptomatic mania. Biol Psychiatry 1977; 12:697–700.

CHAPTER

47 Inhalant-Related Disorders

Charles W. Sharp
Neil Rosenberg

The term *inhalant abuse* is used to describe a variety of drug-using behaviors that cannot be classified by their pharmacology or toxicology but are grouped based on their primary mode of administration. Although other substances are inhaled (e.g., tobacco, marijuana with or without phencyclidine, and even heroin or crack), this is not the primary route of administration; therefore, they do not fall into this classification. Several subcategories of inhalants can be established based on chemical classes of products and primary abuse groups as follows: 1) industrial or household cleaning and paint-type solvents including paint thinners or solvents, degreasers or dry cleaner solvents, solvents in glues, art or office supply solvents such as correction fluids, and solvents in magic markers; 2) gases used in household or commercial products, such as butane in lighters, fluorocarbons in electronic (personal computer, office equipment) cleaners or refrigerant gases, and the aerosol refillers; 3) household aerosol sprays such as paint, hair, and fabric protector sprays; 4) medical anesthetic gases, such as ether, chloroform, halothane, and nitrous oxide; and 5) aliphatic nitrites. Nitrous oxide is also available in whipped cream dispensers (e.g., whippets) and for octane boosters in car racing and used outside the medical theater by nonprofessionals. Most of the foregoing compounds affect the central nervous system directly, whereas nitrites act on cardiovascular smooth muscle rather than as anesthetic agents in the central nervous system. The nitrites are also used primarily as sexual enhancers rather than as mood alterants. Therefore, discussion of inhalant abuse herein deals primarily with substances other than nitrites. One item worthy of note: the exclusion of anesthetics in the *Diagnostic and Statistical Manual of Mental Disorders*, Fourth Edition (DSM-IV), is not medically correct, as almost all of the inhalants act as typical anesthetics and some, particularly the anesthetics nitrous oxide and trichloroethylene (TCE), are abused by the primary inhalant abuser discussed herein. Thus, the following discussion includes the abuse of anesthetics in general but does not focus on this aspect of the problem.

Substances Inhaled

Volatile substances (or inhalants) are ubiquitous. The practice of inhalation to produce euphoria can be traced to the ancient Greeks.[1] At the turn of the 19th century, Humphry Davy in England, experimenting with the newly discovered gas nitrous oxide, discovered its mind-altering effects.[2] Ether and, later, chloroform parties occurred frequently; some even suggested that ether might be used to treat addiction. These substances are still used today.[3, 4] The 20th century brought the use of gasoline and along with it many other volatile mixtures including many solvents, cleaners, aerosols, degreasers, and glues. Table 47–1 enumerates the solvents (frequently noted on the labels) of the corresponding popular products currently used for recreational purposes. Despite the widespread availability and inhalation of these substances, it was not until the 1950s that reporters[5] and judicial action focused nationwide attention on "glue sniffing." The term is still widely used today to describe most of these substances. It is important to keep in mind that there are many different chemicals in these different products, all of which have different physiological effects and different toxicities as well as different chemical properties. Sometimes the substances are listed; however, many times the container lacks sufficient detail to identify the potential toxin(s).

An analysis of questionnaires regarding the inhalation of various products (Table 47–2) indicated that gasoline and glue were popular.[6, 7] Glue may be popular to the initiate because of the name glue sniffing often associated with this practice. Also frequently mentioned are spray paints, nitrous oxide, correction fluids, and butane-type gases. A more detailed questionnaire[8] ranked correction fluids at the top, with glue, gasoline, and spray paint being the next most

Table 47–1 Chemicals Commonly Found in Inhalants

Inhalant	Chemicals
Adhesives	
Airplane glue	Toluene, ethyl acetate
Other glues	Hexane, toluene, methyl chloride, acetone, methyl ethyl ketone, methyl butyl ketone
Special cements	Trichloroethylene, tetrachloroethylene
Aerosols	
Paint sprays	Butane, propane, fluorocarbons, toluene, hydrocarbons
Hair sprays	Butane, propane, chlorofluorocarbons (CFCs)
Deodorants, air fresheners	Butane, propane, CFCs
Analgesic spray	CFCs
Asthma spray	CFCs
Fabric spray	Butane, trichloroethane
Personal computer cleaners	Dimethyl ether, hydrofluorocarbons
Anesthetics	
Gaseous	Nitrous oxide
Liquid	Halothane, enflurane
Local	Ethyl chloride
Cleaning Agents	
Dry cleaners	Tetrachloroethylene, trichloroethane
Spot removers	Xylene, petroleum distillates, chlorohydrocarbons
Degreasers	Tetrachloroethylene, trichloroethane, trichloroethylene
Solvents and Gases	
Nail polish remover	Acetone, ethyl acetate, toluene
Paint remover	Toluene, methylene chloride, methanol, acetone, ethyl acetate
Paint thinnners	Petroleum distillates, esters, acetone
Correction fluids and thinners	Trichloroethylene, trichloroethane
Fuel gas	Butane, isopropane
Cigar or cigarette lighter fluid	Butane, isopropane
Fire extinguisher propellant	Bromochlorodifluoromethane
Food Products	
Whipped cream aerosols	Nitrous oxide
Whippets	Nitrous oxide
Room Odorizers	
Poppers, fluids (Rush, Locker Room)	Isoamyl, isobutyl, isopropyl, or butyl-nitrite (now illegal) or cyclohexyl

frequently mentioned. The fluorocarbons seem to be used less, possibly because they are now less readily available. However, outbreaks of theft of air conditioner fluids (by breaking the conduit lines) and numerous deaths attributed to the inhalation abuse of these fluorocarbons indicate otherwise.[9] Many aerosols now use low-molecular-weight hydrocarbons as the propellant instead of fluorocarbons. The fad of inhaling butane lighter and other cooking gases, as well as isobutane-propane propellants of aerosol products, in the United States and in England[10–15] demonstrates that this replacement of one toxin with something else often does not solve the potential for inhalation abuse. The availability of the pure gas in pressurized containers (lighter replenishers) nullifies the need to separate these gases from other substances in aerosols. Even medications are susceptible to misuse, as some individuals have inhaled, beyond the point of medication, the fluorocarbons in their asthma inhalers.[16, 17] This is one of the few marketable uses of Freon-type fluorocarbons in products available for public consumption.

In an effort to determine the basis of choosing one solvent over another, Evans and Raistrick[13, 14] summarized the "sniffer's" perceptions when they sniffed two different substances, butane gas or toluene. Moods, thoughts, hallucinations (except tactile), and colors appeared similar with either compound. However, time passed slowly with butane and more rapidly with toluene. This one study would indicate that butane may be an acceptable substitute for some of the most widely used substances, products containing toluene, and may be used for some time to come. The use of butane may be a basis for an increased number of deaths.

Not only are various commercial household products used for pleasure, so are many anesthetics, mostly by medical personnel.[18–21] That these substances are abused by middle-class professionals not only demonstrates the diversity of the groups that abuse inhalants but also focuses on the basic nature of the physical properties of most of these volatile agents. Almost all solvents produce anesthesia if sufficient amounts are inhaled. However, the decreased ability of an agent to produce anesthesia may or may not correlate with an increased abuse of a substance and needs further exploration.

The disorder described in this chapter is classified under inhalant-related disorders in DSM-IV and subdivided into two groups: inhalant use disorders and inhalant-induced disorders.

Inhalant Use Disorders

304.60 Inhalant Dependence

Dependence on inhalants is primarily psychological, with a less dramatic associated physical dependence occurring in some heavy users. Physical tolerance of some solvents has been documented by animal studies only under unusual conditions.[22] The urgent need to continue use of inhalants has been reported among individuals with heavy use, although the nature of this phenomenon is unknown. A mild withdrawal syndrome occurs in 10 to 24 hours after cessation of use and lasts for several days. Symptoms include general disorientation, sleep disturbances, headaches, muscle spasms, irritability, nausea, and fleeting illusions. However, this is not a documented or characteristic withdrawal syndrome that is useful in a clinical setting. The need to continue is undeniably strong in many individuals; unique treatments other than the drug therapy and/or psychotherapy used for other drug dependence need to be developed.

305.90 Inhalant Abuse

Abuse of inhalants may lead to harm to individuals (e.g., accidents involving automobiles, falling from buildings when in an impaired or intoxicated state [illusionary feel-

Table 47–2 Inhalant Use (Percent), 1993 Data*

	Age 12–17 Years (n = 6978)		Age 18–25 Years (n = 5531)		Age 26–36 Years (n = 8342)	
Solvent or Gas	Life	30 Day	Life	30 Day	Life	30 Day
Gasoline	1.6	(0.5)	1.5	(0.2)	1.6	–
Spray paint	1.0	0.2	0.8	–	0.6	–
Glue	1.9	0.3	1.3	0.2	1.1	–
Correction fluids	0.7	0.1	0.5	–	0.3	–
Nitrous oxide	0.7	0.1	4.7	0.5	3.7	0.2
Aerosol sprays	1.0	0.2	0.3	0.1	0.6	–
Thinners	0.5	0.1	0.5	–	0.5	–
Butanes	0.6	0.1	0.7	–	0.1	–
Nitrites	0.1	–	2.7	0.3	4.4	0.1

*Total interviewed = 26,489. Parentheses indicate that the number is not statistically valid; –, sample too small.

Data from Substance Abuse and Mental Health Services Administration: National Household Survey on Drug Abuse: Population Estimates 1993. (Special unpublished analysis.) Washington, DC: U.S. Government Printing Office, 1994. DHHS publication (SMA) 94-3017.

ings], or self-inflicted harm, such as attempted or successful suicide). Frozen lips caused by rapidly expanding gases[23] or serious burns[24] may also occur. Chronic inhalant use is often associated with familial conflict and school problems.

Inhalant-Induced Disorders

The primary disorder is inhalant intoxication, which is characterized by the presence of clinically significant maladaptive behavioral or psychological changes (e.g., belligerence, assaultiveness, apathy, impaired judgment, impaired social or occupational functioning) that develop during the intentional short-term, high-dose exposure to volatile inhalants (diagnostic criteria A and B in DSM-IV). The maladaptive changes occurring after intentional and nonintentional exposure include disinhibition, excitedness, lightheadedness, visual disturbances (blurred vision, nystagmus), incoordination, dysarthria, an unsteady gait, and euphoria. Higher doses of inhalants may lead to depressed reflexes, stupor, coma, and death, sometimes caused by cardiac arrhythmia. Lethargy, generalized muscle weakness, and headaches may occur some hours later, depending on the dose.

Epidemiology

Prevalence

Inhalant abuse is a worldwide problem. Countries are increasingly evaluating the abuse of solvents.[11, 25, 26] The pattern of inhalant abuse is exemplified by two national

DSM-IV Criteria 292.89

Inhalant Intoxication

A. Recent intentional use or short-term, high-dose exposure to volatile inhalants (excluding anesthetic gases and short-acting vasodilators).

B. Clinically significant maladaptive behavioral or psychological changes (e.g., belligerence, assaultiveness, apathy, impaired judgment, impaired social or occupational functioning) that developed during, or shortly after, use of or exposure to volatile inhalants.

C. Two (or more) of the following signs, developing during, or shortly after, inhalant use or exposure:

(1) dizziness

(2) nystagmus

(3) incoordination

(4) slurred speech

(5) unsteady gait

(6) lethargy

(7) depressed reflexes

(8) psychomotor retardation

(9) tremor

(10) generalized muscle weakness

(11) blurred vision or diplopia

(12) stupor or coma

(13) euphoria

D. The symptoms are not due to a general medical condition and are not better accounted for by another mental disorder.

Table 47–3 Inhalant Use (Percent), 1994 Data

	High School*			Household†		
	8th Grade (n = 17,708)	10th Grade (n = 16,080)	12th Grade (n = 15,929)	Age 12–17 Years (n = 21,773)	Age 18–25 Years (n = 28,027)	Age 26–36 Years (n = 36,588)
Lifetime	19.9	18.0	17.7	7.0	10.0	11.1
Annual	11.7	9.1	7.7	4.0	3.0	0.9
30-day	5.6	3.6	2.7	1.6	0.8	0.4
Daily	0.2	0.1	0.1			

*From Johnston LD, O'Malley PM, Bachman JG: National Survey Results on Drug Use from the Monitoring the Future Study, 1975–1994. Washington, DC: U.S. Government Printing Office, 1995. NIH publication 95-4026.

†From Substance Abuse and Mental Health Services Administration: National Household Survey on Drug Abuse: Population Estimates 1994. Washington, DC: U.S. Government Printing Office, 1995. DHHS publication (SMA) 95-3063.

studies in the United States, the annual Monitoring the Future (previously known as High School Senior)[27] and National Household surveys, and also by state surveys such as the New York[28] and Texas[8, 29] surveys. Also, a survey of the drug abuse problem in difficult populations (e.g., those in group homes, halfway houses, psychiatric and correctional institutions) was published as the Washington, DC Metropolitan Area Drug Study: 1991.[29a]

Current estimates of sniffing volatile substances to "get high" rank inhalants high in the "ever use" category of substance abuse, especially for the younger population. Some surveys of teenage use showed that one in five had tried an inhalant and that up to 3% (600,000 persons) of the U.S. population had done so in the past month.[6, 7, 28] As many as 20,000 to 40,000 youth got high on inhalants several times a month. Some of the highest rates were noted for eighth-graders[30] (Table 47–3). This rate exceeded that for marijuana use in 1993. The rate of marijuana use increased in 1994 relative to that of inhalants. The prevalence of inhalant use is nearly double that of cocaine use in these younger groups. Adults also inhale; they seem more selective in the products they use and probably are fewer in number, as many teenagers do not continue to indulge.

Sociocultural Factors

The practice of "sniffing," "snorting," "huffing," "bagging," or inhaling to get high describes various forms of inhalation.[31] These terms variously describe the inhalation of volatile substances from 1) filled balloons, 2) bags, and 3) soaked rags and/or sprayed directly into oral orifices. Abusers can be identified by various telltale clues, such as organic odors on the breath or clothes, stains on the clothes or around the mouth, empty spray paint or solvent containers, and other unusual paraphernalia. These clues may enable one to identify a serious problem of solvent abuse before it causes serious health problems or death.

Most volatile substances are widely available and are inhaled to provide a quick high, often to make users forget their problems and relieve boredom. Solvent abusers, more than other drug users, are poor, come from broken homes, and do poorly in school.[32, 33] There are also many other types of inhalant abusers (e.g., medical personnel,[34–36] homosexuals, college students) who inhale one or another of these solvents to get high or feel good.

There is an interesting correlation between alcohol and solvents. Some time ago, degreaser's flush (so described because of a flushing of the face) was observed when occupational workers left their degreasing vats and drank alcohol after leaving work.[37, 38] Also, heavy drinking has been associated with occupational toluene exposure.[39] Both humans and rats have been noted to be thirsty when exposed to toluene and alcohol.[40, 41] Whether either substance may accentuate the use of the other is unknown; an attempt to study the acute effects of low levels of alcohol and toluene in human volunteers failed to produce any interaction by their behavioral measures.

Psychiatric Disturbances in Organic Solvent Abuse

There is little evidence that inhalant abuse either coexists with other mental disorders or is predelictive of any such altered state. Psychiatric disorders related to solvent abuse were reviewed[42]; it was concluded that psychiatric morbidity is "highest in those referred to psychiatric hospitals and lowest in clinics dealing exclusively with VS [volatile substance (solvent)] abuse." There have been few studies of comorbidity in psychiatric hospital populations and almost no studies in other populations. In an analysis of dual diagnoses, drug abuse was stated to coexist with depression and anxiety disorders[43]; however, neither this study nor another on dual diagnoses of drug abuse disorders and mental disorders[44] identified an inhalant abuse disorder in its subjects. The reason may be that the latter populations are seldom identified or characterized because of lack of recognition of this area of drug abuse and are not available in treatment for study.

On the other hand, there is little doubt that personality disorders of an antisocial type are common in solvent abusers. A study of older drug users[45] observed that most of the patients had antisocial personality disorders. Most were admitted for their drug dependence, with a prominent use of solvents (for 5 to 13 years); they also used marijuana, alcohol, stimulants, and other drugs. The interpretation was that an age-dependent progression of antisocial behavior occurred for those previously self-selecting solvent use.

In another study of psychiatric emergency room admittants,[46] "inhalant users differed significantly from matched other drug users in that they displayed significantly more self-directed destructive behavior, as well as some degree of recent suicidal and homicidal behavior." Cognitive measures of these groups supported the antisocial and self-destructive nature of inhalant abusers.[32] Another study of psychiatric subjects, not identifying any group as being inhalant abusers,[47] did not associate any mental disorder with the use of inhalants. Although 9% of this group used inhalants as well as other drugs, there may not have been a sufficient number of subjects to identify any disorder. Overall, there is accepted knowledge that long-term solvent abusers are among the most difficult to work with based on antisocial traits; also, it is likely that inhalants prevent their continued growth and development.[33, 48]

Only in one study on the follow-up of inhalant abusers[49] has a personality disorder been associated with inhalant abuse. Twenty-two subjects were selected at random from an unknown number of patients in a 5-year period. Many were considered on admission to have a personality deviation but were subsequently diagnosed as substance abusers. Subjects primarily inhaled a toluene-based glue on a daily basis for 2 years or more. Paranoid psychosis was diagnosed for 19 of the subjects; 3 had temporal lobe epilepsy. Family alcoholism, crime, and other negative lifestyles were present, but no family history of hospitalization for severe mental illnesses was found.

Other reports of single cases associated psychiatric-related illnesses with exposure to a variety of solvents.[50–54] The symptoms ranged from mild tremors and disorientation, anxiety, and impaired attention and memory to hallucinations[53, 55–57] and "schizophreniform psychosis."[50]

One study looked into whether the use of drugs was related to attention-deficit/hyperactivity disorder or depression[58] and could be used to predict the onset of these disorders. For boys, but not girls, once-a-year use of either marijuana or "glue" at age 15 years was predicted at age 11 for those who had both disorders. However, this infrequent use (once a year) is not what one would consider that of a drug user; these subjects might be better classified as drug experimenters.

Reports of suicides in the inhalant population[59] raise the question of an association of mental disorders with inhalant exposure, which bears further investigation. This situation may be related to the earlier studies[32] identifying self-aggressive tendencies in inhalant abusers.

Studies defining comorbidity of any mental disorder with inhalant abuse remain difficult, partly because solvent abusers (maintaining a high level of inebriation for a sustained period) are mostly inaccessible, limited in number, and heterogeneous, and, in those accessed, it is difficult to study only inhalant abuse effects (dissociated from other drug effects) in a polydrug abuse group. Clinical evaluations are also compromised by the residual solvents (in fatty tissue), which alter psychometric measures.

Toxicology of Inhalant Abuse

The majority of inhalant abusers never reach a hospital or outpatient facility. Although many do not need medical attention for their inhalant habit, of those who do, many often die before reaching the hospital as a result of asphyxia, cardiac arrhythmia, or related overdose effects after inhaling fluorocarbons, low-molecular-weight hydrocarbon gases (butane, propane), nitrous oxide, or other solvents during either the first or a subsequent episode.[10, 11, 15, 60–64] Death may occur after inhalation of toluene-containing substances as a result of metabolic acidosis or related kidney failure if left untreated. Death may also occur accidentally when the subject is intoxicated.[59, 65] Although it is not common, anesthetics abused by medical personnel or others have also been indicated as a cause of death; death related to nitrous oxide use is often due to asphyxia.[66–68] In most cases, inhalation does not lead to death. Some of the more common acute syndromes of the intoxicated state are listed in Table 47–4.

Table 47–4 Symptoms Related to Solvent Abuse (Not All for Gases and Nitrites)

Moderate Intoxication
Dizziness
Headache
Lethargy
Disorientation, incoherence
Ataxia, gait (uncoordinated movement)
Odoriferous, foul breath (solvent vapors)
Strong Intoxication
Blurred Vision
Belligerence
Nausea, vomiting
Irritability
Delirium
Slurred speech
Severe (Rare)
Seizures
Violent actions

Clinical Manifestations After Chronic Inhalant Abuse

Chronic high-level exposure to organic solvents occurs in the inhalant abuse setting at levels several thousand times higher than in the occupational setting and results in numerous irreversible disease states. Some toxicities have been validated through animal studies; others have been only tentatively correlated with certain substances. Table 47–5 describes several well-characterized disorders and identifies the solvent when corroborated by animal studies. Some substances have been strongly correlated with a disorder through numerous case studies as the toxin most likely to produce those syndromes. The following discussion briefly describes these conditions and the important associated symptoms. Neurological disorders, those most important to the topic at hand, are discussed first.

Neurological Sequelae of Chronic Inhalant Abuse

The nervous system may be affected at many levels by organic solvents as well as other neurotoxic substances. Because of their nonfocal presentation, neurotoxic disorders may be confused with metabolic, degenerative, nutritional,

Table 47–5 Diseases Observed in Humans After Chronic Inhalant Abuse

Condition	Syndrome	Substance	Animal Studies*
Slowly Reversible and/or Irreversible Syndromes			
Encephalopathy	Cognitive dysfunction	"Toluene,"† other solvents	—
Cerebellar syndrome	Limb dysmetria	"Toluene"	Rat
	Dysarthria		—
Sensorineural otic	High-frequency hearing loss	TCE, toluene	Rat, mouse
Sensorineural			
Optic nerve	Visual loss	"Toluene"	—
Oculomotor	Oculomotor disturbances (nystagmus)	Xylene, TCE	Rabbits
Myeloneuropathy	Sensory loss	Nitrous oxide	Rat, mouse
	Spasticity		
Axonal neuropathy	Distal sensory loss, limb weakness	Hexane, methyl butyl ketone	Rat, monkey
Cardiotoxicity	Arrhythmia	Chlorofluorocarbons, butanes, propanes	Mouse, rat, dog
Leukemia	Myelocytic	Benzene	Rat, mouse
Mostly Reversible Syndromes			
Trigeminal neuropathy	Numbness, paresthesia	TCE and/or dichloroacetylene	Rat
Renal acidosis	Metabolic acidosis	"Toluene"	Rat
	Hypokalemia		—
Carboxyhemoglobin	Hypoxia	Methylene chloride, tobacco	Human, rat
Methemoglobinemia	Syncope, blue	Nitrites, organic	Rat
Neonatal syndrome	Retarded growth, development	"Toluene"	Rat
Hepatotoxicity	Fatty vacuoles, plasma liver enzymes	Chlorohydrocarbons	Rat
Immunomodulatory	Loss of immune cell function	Nitrites, organic	Rat

*Symptoms observed in animal studies with these solvents.

†Quotation marks around substance indicates uncertainty about this solvent (alone) producing these symptoms.

or demyelinating diseases.[69] This is illustrated in the setting of chronic toluene abuse, which clinically may resemble the multifocal demyelinating disease multiple sclerosis in the findings on neurological examination.[70–72] In addition, neurotoxic syndromes rarely have specific identifying features on diagnostic tests such as computed tomography, magnetic resonance imaging (MRI), or nerve conduction studies.[69] As a result, subjects who are mildly intoxicated may be difficult to diagnose. Chronic inhalant abuse, on the other hand, produces a specific MRI picture with a combination of diffuse white matter changes and low signal intensity in the basal ganglia and thalamus.[73–75]

Many organic solvents produce nonspecific effects (e.g., encephalopathy) after exposure to extremely high concentrations; a few produce relatively specific neurological syndromes. Two neurotoxic syndromes, a peripheral neuropathy and an ototoxicity, are well correlated with organic solvents. Less commonly, a cerebellar ataxia syndrome or a myopathy may occur alone or in combination with any of these clinical syndromes.

Central Nervous System Involvement (Encephalopathy)

Grabski[76] first reported a case of persistent neurological consequences of chronic inhalation of toluene-containing solvents; this was further described by Knox and Nelson in 1966.[77] Other types of severe neurotoxicity were subsequently described, including cognitive dysfunction[70–72, 78] and cerebellar ataxia.[54, 70, 72, 79–81] This encephalopathy was characterized using computed tomography[72, 82] and, more extensively, MRI.[75, 77, 83–88] The most common syndrome is that of multifocal central nervous system involvement[71, 72, 75, 80, 83, 84, 87–89]; in only one study was abstinence documented before clinical evaluation.[71] Microencephalopathy is now emerging as a possible embryopathic syndrome in infants of women exposed to "solvent (toluene-based)."[90, 91]

Most reports emphasized the cerebellar and cognitive dysfunction, with most cases showing combined impairment of cerebral and cerebellar functions as well as pyramidal changes. Neurological abnormalities varied from mild cognitive impairment to severe dementia, associated with elemental neurological signs such as cerebellar ataxia, corticospinal tract dysfunction, oculomotor abnormalities, tremor, deafness, and hyposmia. Cognitive dysfunction was the most disabling and frequent feature of chronic toluene toxicity and may be the earliest sign of permanent damage. Dementia, when present, was typically associated with cerebellar ataxia and other signs.[71]

Rosenberg and colleagues[83] utilized MRI to study the brains of chronic abusers of toluene-containing substances and interpreted the encephalopathy as a diffuse central nervous system white matter change with the following abnormalities: 1) diffuse cerebral, cerebellar, and brain stem atrophy; 2) loss of differentiation of the gray and white matter throughout the central nervous system; and 3) increased periventricular white matter signal intensity on T2-weighted images.[84] These MRI measures seemed to correlate with the extent of exposure and the impairment of the individual's capabilities as measured on several neuropsychological tests.[84] Others[75, 88] corroborated these findings.

MRI results[74] may suggest a possible mechanism for the abnormalities in the basal ganglia and thalamus. The MRI analyses of eight chronic toluene abusers revealed diffuse white matter changes and marked hypointensity in the basal ganglia and thalamus, all seen on T2-weighted images (Fig. 47–1). Thus, the hypointensity of the basal ganglia and thalamus on T2-weighted magnetic resonance images of brains of chronic toluene abusers may be related to partitioning of toluene into the lipid membranes in these areas.

Pathology

Few detailed pathological studies have been done.[73, 86, 92] The predominant feature in these studies is that of a leukoencephalopathy. A study of three cases[86] (one of which was previously reported by Rosenberg and colleagues[73]) found pathological changes similar to those in adrenoleukodystrophy, a rare hereditary disorder affecting the white matter. Gross pathological study revealed a patchy loss of myelin (Fig. 47–2). The overall pathological study revealed a demyelinating process grossly manifest as brain atrophy, including macrophages containing unusual cytoplasmic bodies with an increase of long-chain fatty acids similar to that seen in adrenoleukodystrophy.[86] These findings suggest that toluene is a white matter toxin. A lipid analysis of this tissue revealed an increase in long-chain fatty acids in the white matter, also similar to findings in adrenoleukodystrophy, suggesting similar mechanisms of demyelination in both disorders.

Although the evidence is not conclusive that toluene is the primary substance responsible for these anomalies, animal studies have defined a toluene-induced motor

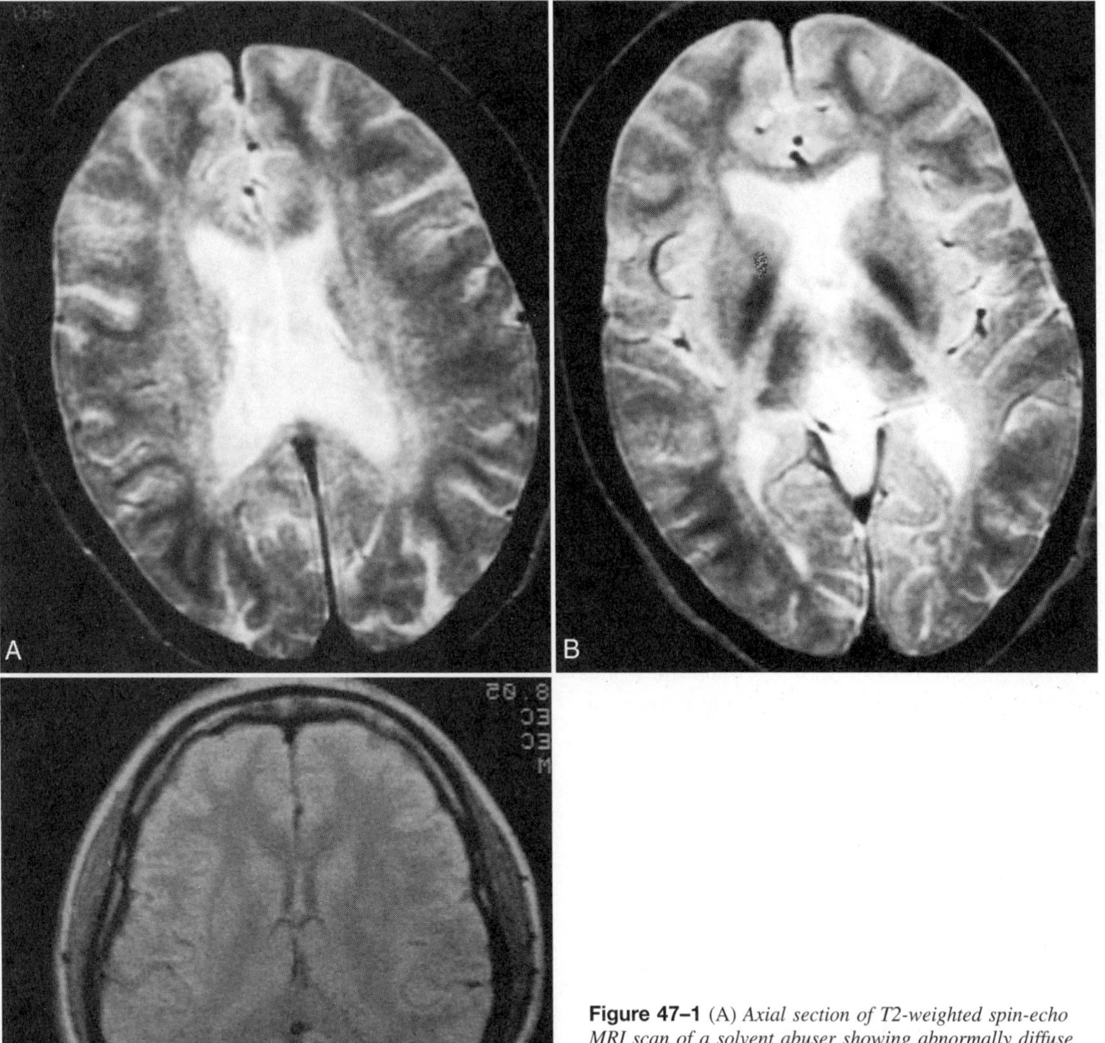

Figure 47–1 (A) *Axial section of T2-weighted spin-echo MRI scan of a solvent abuser showing abnormally diffuse white matter changes and loss of gray-white differentiation.* (B) *Lower axial section of T2-weighted spin-echo MRI scan of a solvent abuser showing decreased signal intensity in the thalamus and global pallidus bilaterally, in addition to diffuse increased signal intensity in white matter.* (C) *Axial section of T2-weighted spin-echo MRI scan comparable to that of a normal subject. These are similar to those in studies reported by Rosenberg and colleagues.*[73]

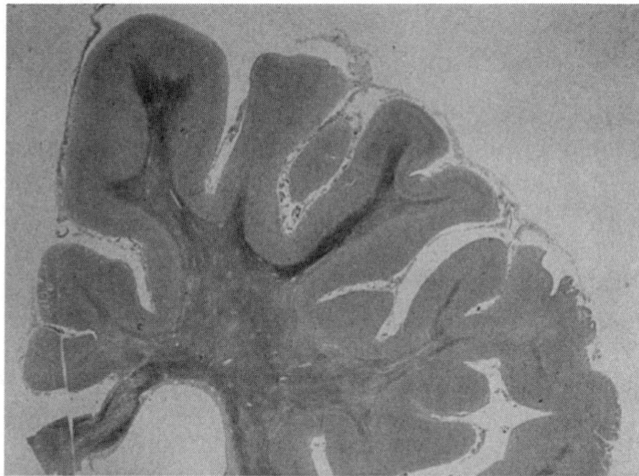
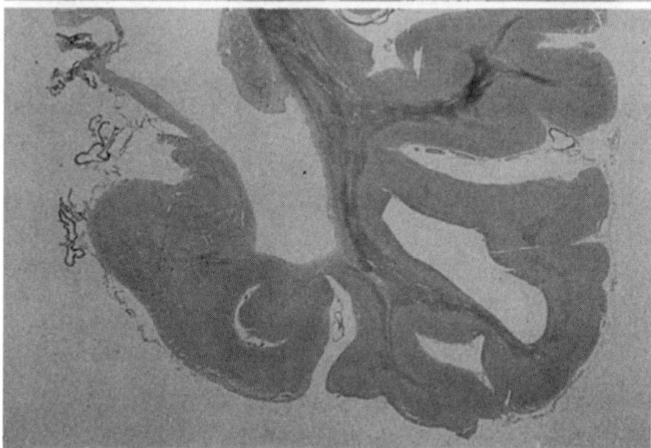

Figure 47–2 *Patchy loss of myelin in central, convolutional, and callosal white matter. (Luxol fast blue–periodic acid–Schiff stain.) (From Kornfeld M, Moser AB, Moser HW, et al: Solvent vapor abuse leukoencephalopathy. Comparison to adrenoleukodystrophy. J Neuropathol Exp Neurol 1994; 53:389–398.)*

syndrome that is characterized by a widened landing foot splay and a short and widened gait that may be related to the cerebellar syndrome in humans.[93] This is produced by either toluene or TCE. Other animal studies have noted increased levels of glial cell marker proteins after toluene exposure,[94] which may or may not be related to the white matter changes. High levels of hippuric acid or cresols[95] in the urine would be indicative of toluene exposure, and urine trichloroacetate would be useful in diagnosing exposure to trichlorinated hydrocarbons. Other analytical measures may be worth exploring in more rigorous research studies.[96, 97]

Central Nervous System Involvement Possibly Related to Lead

Toxicities similar to those already noted may be caused by tetraethyllead (or its metabolite triethyllead) after prolonged or extensive inhalation of gasoline.[57, 98–106] It is less clear whether unleaded gasoline, which contains some of the previously described solvents, produces similar encephalopathies. In cases in which high lead levels are observed, hallucinations and disorientation, dysarthria, chorea, and convulsions have been reported (Table 47–6). The symptoms have also included moderate to severe ataxia, insomnia, anorexia, slowed peripheral nerve conduction, limb tremors, dysmetria, and sometimes limb paralysis. In most cases the electroencephalogram is normal, but in severe states an abnormal to severely depressed cortical electroencephalogram is observed. Because many of these symptoms in the early stages of the disease can be reversed by chelation therapy with ethylenediaminetetraacetic acid, dimercaprol (BAL), or penicillamine, it is important to check the serum lead levels in any chronic inhalant abuser.

Ototoxicity

Sensorineural hearing loss[107] is one of the more commonly occurring clinical neurotoxic syndromes related to inhalant abuse, along with a related equilibrium disorder.[108] Neural conduction, most readily diagnosed by brain stem auditory evoked responses, was abnormal in several case studies.[70, 83, 89, 109–111] These studies suggest that brain stem auditory evoked responses would detect early central nervous system injury related to toluene or other solvent inhalation at a time when the neurological examination and MRI scans are normal. Brain stem auditory evoked responses may be a sensitive screening test for monitoring individuals at risk from toluene exposure and for early detection of central nervous system injury. However, although specific in revealing abnormalities characteristic of central nervous system involvement in chronic inhalant abuse, brain stem auditory evoked responses revealed abnormalities in less than 10% of a chronic inhalant abuse population (Rosenberg NL, unpublished).

The hearing loss was originally classified as one of high frequency (it probably still is for humans). It is now more clearly delineated as a midfrequency hearing loss in the range between 8 and 16 kHz for animals; few changes occur at frequencies above 20 kHz in rats exposed to solvents.[112, 113]

As with the *n*-hexane–produced peripheral neuropathy, there exists an animal model for the study of the target organ neurotoxicity. Pryor's laboratory was the first to demonstrate persistent irreversible high-frequency hearing loss by cued behavioral responses, auditory brain stem evoked responses, and related pathological conditions in animals. This neuropathy can be produced in days after high exposures to specific solvents and is considered to originate with the destruction of cochlear cells, which contributes to a central conduction pathology, as observed in the human studies noted earlier.[114–116] Many others have reproduced and extended these findings on toluene and TCE; similar analogues, benzene and trichloroethane, do not produce these changes.

Table 47–6 Mostly Irreversible Syndromes Caused by Chronic Inhalant Use Observed in Humans

Condition	Syndrome	Substance
Encephalopathy	Cognitive dysfunction, possible delirium, possible seizures	Lead (gasoline)
Cerebellar syndrome	Limb dysmetria, dysarthria, truncal ataxia, tremors	Lead (gasoline)
Sensorineural (optic)	Nystagmus	Lead (gasoline)
Peripheral nerves	Possible slower nerve conduction	

Table 47–7 Auditory Response After Exposure to Different Solvents

Solvent	Hearing Loss
Benzene	No
Toluene	Yes
Ethylbenzene	Yes
n-Propylbenzene	Yes
Isopropylbenzene (cumene)	No
Methoxybenzene	Yes
1,4-Dimethylbenzene (*p*-xylene)	Yes
1,2-Dimethylbenzene (*o*-xylene)	No
1,3-Dimethylbenzene (*m*-xylene)	No
Styrene	Yes
Monochlorobenzene	Yes
Carbon disulfide	Yes
Dichloromethane	No
Trichloroethane	No
TCE	Yes
Tetrachloroethylene	No
Acetone	No
Methyl ethyl ketone	No
Ethyl alcohol	No
n-Hexane	No

Because of the quantitative animal model available, Pryor's group has conducted a structure-activity study of many solvents in an effort to define the basic moiety responsible.[117] Table 47–7 lists the different compounds and their activities. The common feature of the most hazardous compounds is the presence of unsaturation in the chemical structure, not dissimilar to that occurring in fatty acids. That is, the less saturated the chemical structure, the more toxic it is. Further work needs to be done to clarify the chemical and molecular basis of this toxicity. Niklasson and colleagues[118] also analyzed the effects of some of these compounds on the vestibular function and correlated the changes with nystagmus.

Knowledge from other animal studies should assist in the delineation of many of these parameters. For example, hexane augments toluene toxicities,[119] presumably through a reduction in the metabolism of toluene, which slows the elimination of toluene, the probable toxin. The reverse was found for the production of hexane neuropathies, as hexane metabolites, not hexane, are the toxins. Related studies of genetic differences in different inbred mice populations demonstrated in C57, but not CBA mice, an age-related hearing loss[120] that may indicate different rates of metabolism or other differences.

Other Cranial Nerve Involvement

A study of four subjects[121] supported earlier observations of pendular nystagmus and related eye movement disorders in sniffers of various solvents. Oculomotor dysfunction and tremor were seen only in severely affected individuals.[71] Optical neuropathy[55, 73, 81, 110, 122, 123] and oculomotor dysfunction[70, 121] have been observed after exposure to toluene-containing substances, pupillary damage after exposure to TCE,[124] and optical neuritis after methyl ethyl ketone exposure.[125] Hollo and Varga[126] suggested that visual function measures may be useful in detecting early toxic effects in solvent abusers. All of these neuropathies can be identified with specific cranial nerves (Table 47–8).

These changes have yet to be specifically correlated with these or other chemicals.[127] Optic damage needs to be corroborated through animal studies. A study after TCE exposure in rabbits for 12 weeks measured a decreased amplitude of visual evoked responses; the responses slowly returned to normal 6 weeks after exposure.[128]

Hexane is not usually considered a central nervous system toxin; however, some clinical studies have indicated that *n*-hexane affects the central nervous system. Also, experimental animal studies have shown that *n*-hexane causes axonal degeneration in the central nervous system.[129–131] Clinically, cranial neuropathy, spasticity, and autonomic dysfunction occasionally occur.[132] Of all these possible actions, animal studies have demonstrated only the optical-toxic effects of 2,5-hexanedione, a toxic metabolite of hexane, in rats.[133] Until these issues are further clarified through human and animal studies, *n*-hexane should be primarily considered a peripheral nervous system toxin.

Anosmia is an often described syndrome of inhalant abuse. It would be expected that solvents would diminish the olfactory responses; however, it has seldom been studied. Mergler and Beauvais[134] found that olfactory perception was reduced after 7 hours of exposure to toluene and returned to normal a couple of hours after cessation of exposure. Anosmia or hyposmia was detected on clinical examination utilizing simple bedside measures in chronic inhalant abusers.[71]

Trigeminal Neuropathy

One neurological manifestation associated with TCE intoxication is a slowly reversible trigeminal neuropathy.[135, 136] Cranial neuropathies were noted after general anesthesia with TCE more than 40 years ago. Individuals developed paresthesia around the lips, which then spread to involve the entire trigeminal distribution bilaterally. Motor weakness also occasionally occurred. Resolution of the trigeminal neuropathy occurs slowly, which is thought to indicate segmental or nuclear trigeminal involvement.

There has been a long-term controversy about whether or not unmetabolized TCE causes trigeminal neuralgia or the neurotoxicity is due to dichloroacetylene, an environmental breakdown product of TCE.[137, 138] The incidence in humans can be disputed; however, animal studies do demonstrate the production of trigeminal neuralgia by TCE, as well as dichloroacetylene.[139] There are no reports of trigeminal

Table 47–8 Cranial Nerve Abnormalities Noted in Inhalant Abuse

Cranial Nerve	Dysfunction
I	Hyposmia, anosmia
II	Optic neuropathy
III, IV, VI	Oculomotor disorders: nystagmus, opsoclonus, ocular dysmetria
VIII	Sensorineural hearing loss

neuropathy noted for solvent abusers despite common inhalation of this solvent from different products.[53]

Myeloneuropathy

Nitrous oxide is not an organic solvent; however, it is widely abused by adolescents,[68, 140] adults,[68] and professional personnel.[34, 141, 142] Nitrous oxide is a common anesthetic widely used in dentistry; it is also used as a propellant for whipped cream. High levels of nitrous oxide exposure produce a myeloneuropathy with both central and peripheral components, even in the presence of adequate oxygen.[143] The symptoms include numbness and weakness in the limbs, loss of dexterity, sensory loss, and loss of balance. The early neurological features indicate sensorimotor polyneuropathy; however, with persistent abuse, a myelopathy with severe spasticity may develop. There is also a combined degeneration of the posterior and lateral columns of the cord resembling that in vitamin B_{12} deficiency.[143] Studies focusing on the mechanism of this action indicate that cobalamins (vitamin B_{12}) are inactivated by nitrous oxide, primarily at the level of the enzyme methionine synthase, which needs vitamin B_{12} to function.[144] This enzyme is important in maintenance of the myelin sheath.[145] Flippo and Holder[145] noted that paresthesia and other neuropathic symptoms resulting from spinal cord degeneration were produced after prolonged anesthesia in vitamin B_{12}–deficient patients. Administration of vitamin B_{12} (or folinic acid) dramatically aids recovery of these surgical patients and may assist recovery in solvent abusers,[142] especially once the myelopathy appears. The use of methionine should also be considered.[146]

In regard to dependence on nitrous oxide, studies of mice selectively bred for alcohol dependence showed a cross-dependence on nitrous oxide.[147] They also observed handling-induced convulsions shortly after cessation of nitrous oxide, which could be prevented by either alcohol or nitrous oxide. This might indicate a physical dependence on nitrous oxide that needs to be dealt with in treatment of this drug abuse state.

Peripheral Neuropathy

Two organic solvents were identified as neurotoxins after an investigation of peripheral neuropathies in an industrial setting when methyl isobutyl ketone was replaced by methyl butyl ketone (MBK).[148] Cases of *n*-hexane polyneuropathy have been reported both after occupational exposure[149–151] and after deliberate inhalation of vapors from products containing *n*-hexane, such as glues,[152–160] gasoline,[161, 162] and naphtha.[163] Both *n*-hexane and MBK[164] are metabolized to the same neurotoxin, 2,5-hexanedione, and produce a peripheral neuropathy. 2,5-Hexanedione is responsible for most, if not all, of the neurotoxic effects of exposure to *n*-hexane or MBK.[165, 166] Methyl ethyl ketone alone produces neither clinical nor pathological evidence of a peripheral neuropathy in experimental animals[165]; however, it acts synergistically with MBK or *n*-hexane in experimental animals and probably in humans.[132, 167, 168] This potentiation of toxicity of one compound (MBK or *n*-hexane) by an otherwise nontoxic compound (methyl ethyl ketone) underscores the difficulty in sorting out toxic effects of individual solvents contained in a mixture.

Clinically and pathologically, the neuropathy occurring with *n*-hexane or MBK is that of a distal axonopathy.[129] The clinical syndrome is an initially painless sensorimotor polyneuropathy, which begins after chronic exposure; weight loss may be an early symptom. Sensory and motor disturbances are noted initially in the hands and feet, and sensory loss involves primarily small fiber sensation (i.e., light touch, pin prick, temperature) with relative sparing of large fiber sensation (i.e., position and vibration). Electrophysiological studies reveal an axonal polyneuropathy and pathologically multifocal axonal degeneration, multiple axonal swellings, and neurofilamentous accumulation at paranodal areas.[169] Overlying the axonal swellings, thinning of the myelin sheath occurs. These findings are typical of a distal axonopathy or dying-back neuropathy described in relation to other toxic and metabolic causes of peripheral neuropathy.

Prognosis for recovery correlates directly with the intensity and duration of the toxic exposure. Residual neuropathy is seen only in the most severely affected individuals, some of whom still continue to inhale despite warnings of further debilitation.

Non–Nervous System Toxicity of Inhalant Abuse

Most of the known adverse clinical effects of inhalant abuse relate to the nervous tissue. There are, however, other significant adverse effects on other organ systems, including the kidney, liver, lung, heart, and hemopoietic systems.

Renal Toxicity

Some time ago, Gabow and others[80, 170, 171] described the effects of toluene-containing substances on the kidneys, which often result in hospitalization of inhalant abusers. Young people present most often; however, young adults also present with renal disease after sniffing glue, spray paint, and other solvent products.[88, 172–183]

This dysfunction, which may rapidly reappear in individuals who return to their habit after release from the hospital, is characterized by hyperchloremic metabolic acidosis, hypokalemia, hypocalcemia, and other electrolyte imbalances. Solvents usually cause a unique distal-type tubular acidosis, but proximal tubules are also affected (the distal tubule is responsible for the known electrolyte and metabolic imbalance; the proximal type is responsible for the wasting of amino acids and other proteins). These subjects often have associated gastrointestinal involvement, including nausea, vomiting, and severe abdominal cramps. Severe rhabdomyolysis may render some subjects nearly paralyzed. Other renal disorders related to solvents were reviewed by Lauwerys and colleagues,[184] and cases of glomerulonephritis in commercial settings (painters, degreasers) were described by Daniell and coworkers.[185] An unusual, possibly high-risk, category of individuals (diabetic) who might present with both acetone and solvent breaths in an unconscious state at the emergency department are of concern.[186] In addition, an interstitial nephritis leading to renal failure has been reported by Taverner and associates.[187]

On the basis of these reports, renal dysfunction appears to be one of the most common toxic effects noted for solvent abusers. Although this renal damage is usually reversible, other organs, particularly brain, are the target of repetitive acidosis and any depletion of important amino acids. This may be the basis for some of the observed neurological deficits.[188]

Of all the solvents, toluene is most often correlated with this disease; however, other solvents, including chlorinated hydrocarbons, are frequently the basis for renal disease in these populations. Further animal studies are necessary to clarify specific solvent toxicities similar to those associated with nephrotic changes after exposure to halogenated hydrocarbons[189, 190] and petroleum hydrocarbons.[191]

Pregnancy. Clinicians especially need to be alert for pregnant women who abuse these solvents. Not only do they present to the clinic with renal tubular acidosis, but the fetuses are also affected.[183, 192, 193] This condition places the mother at risk for hypokalemia and associated cardiac dysrhythmias and rhabdomyolysis.[183] Preterm labor therapy (β-mimetics and intravenous fluids) exacerbated the maternal and fetal problems. Fatty livers may also be observed in these subjects.[194] Treatment for their metabolic imbalance needs immediate attention.

Treatment. For pregnant as well as other patients, electrolyte repletion usually restores the kidney function and eliminates the muscle spasms, even in the more severely affected patients, in a few days. Correction of salt and electrolyte imbalance, including potassium, calcium, magnesium, phosphate, and bicarbonate,[174, 183] is important and may be considered in the treatment of solvent abusers for muscle fatigue even in the absence of more severe kidney disorders. Caution about the use of bicarbonate early in the treatment of these subjects has been discussed by Lavoie and coworkers.[195]

Hepatotoxicity

Chlorohydrocarbons (e.g., TCE, chloroform, carbon tetrachloride, halothane) have been noted to be hepatotoxic.[3, 77, 196–204] In animals, acetone and more complex ketones potentiate this halocarbon hepatotoxicity.[205] Thus, the potential for hepatotoxicity in these individuals may be greater than expected.

Inhalation of correction fluids,[206] which contain TCE and trichloroethanes and tetrachloroethanes [207] increases the likelihood of observing more of these toxicities in inhalant abusers. Methylene chloride may be hepatotoxic at high levels[208] and is a solvent likely to be present in substances used by inhalant abusers. Also, a user of butanes, who also added carburetor cleaner to his repertoire, presented with "fatal fulminant hepatic failure"[209]; this raises the possibility that there are other hepatotoxicities that go undetected in inhalant users.

Pulmonary Toxicity

Solvents do irritate the lungs; however, few pulmonary problems have been reported.[210] In two studies, mild pulmonary hypertension, acute respiratory distress, increased airway resistance and residual volume, and restricted ventilation were noted. Increased airway resistance or residual volume may be more clearly noted after an exercise challenge.[211, 212] An increase in respiratory (viral) illness, often noted in clinical reports, may be related to solvent exposure. In Australia,[213] aspiration pneumonia was noted as a major cause of death in aboriginal sniffers. In sniffers in the United States, aspiration pneumonia has not been a major cause of death. How to generalize the impact of dual exposure to solvent and infection is uncertain, but animal studies have measured decreased pulmonary bactericidal activity after exposure to solvents (e.g., dichloroethylene).[214] Animal studies have also measured pulmonary fibrosis in mice after solvent (TCE)[215] exposure.

Any change may be slow in onset but most likely is enhanced by the other substances volatilized along with the solvent (e.g., polystyrenes, tars), utilized by the subject (tobacco and marijuana), or related to other conditions.[216] Because of the potential for cause and augmentation by other substances, the amount of smoking should always be considered in any treatment of these individuals.

Cardiotoxicity

One of the most common causes of solvent abuse–induced deaths is cardiac arrhythmia, especially ventricular fibrillation and cardiac arrest.[217–223] In 1970, Bass[61] reported deaths related to fluorocarbons; subsequently, fluorocarbons were demonstrated to cause arrhythmias in animals.[224] Since then, most fluorocarbon propellants have been replaced by butanes and propane. However, similar arrhythmias were observed after the abuse of the same aerosols, lighter (gas) fluids, and cooking gases.[15, 225, 226] Chenoweth[227] has shown that butane, hexane, heptanes, gasoline, some anesthetics, and toluene also produce these arrhythmias. Although less common, glue sniffing exposure[218, 228, 229] and TCE-containing stain removers[220, 230] have been linked to arrhythmias, myocarditis, and cardiac arrest. Organic nitrites have also been reported to produce bradycardia.[231]

When arrhythmias are observed, antiarrhythmic therapy should be used.[217] Recovery from cardiopulmonary arrest is not common; however, a successful resuscitation from fluorocarbon overexposure is of interest.[232] Cardiopulmonary resuscitation (mouth to mouth) followed by electrodefibrillation within 7 minutes was the primary aspect of the emergency treatment. Exercise and epinephrine exacerbate these cardiotoxicities, and efforts to minimize these situations should therefore be instituted. Anesthesia should not be induced in patients shortly after intoxication, and one should probably avoid the use of halogenated hydrocarbons in other circumstances in which heavy solvent exposure is suspected.

Hematopoietic Toxicity

Of great concern are the incidences of neoplasm in solvent abusers. A common solvent, benzene, has long been identified as causing aplastic anemia and acute myelocytic leukemia.[233, 234] Benzene is present in thinners, varnish removers and other solvents, and gasoline, which may lead to various neoplasms.[184, 228] Based on the release of the nitrite ion in blood after the administration of organic nitrites, the ability to produce nitrosamines has fueled the speculation that nitrites are carcinogenic.[235–238] Yet, in contrast to sodium nitrite, organic nitrites produce methemoglobin instantly in vitro[239] and may therefore not be around long enough to produce nitrosamines. Thus, the rapid oxidation of organic nitrites by hemoglobin and the fact that detectable levels of organic nitrites in blood are noted only briefly after administration[240] question this hypothesis. Although mutagenicity appears possible under special conditions, carcinogenicity is far from proved.

Also of concern are the hematological changes caused by various solvents, most of which are reversible because of the regenerative nature of red blood cells. Carbon monoxide, at high levels, produces cerebral hypoxia, which may subsequently have permanent neurological sequelae; it also produces carboxyhemoglobin. This occurs with exposure to a common solvent, methylene chloride,[241] as well as to cigarette smoke. The acute elevation of carboxyhemoglobin after exposure to methylene chloride has been studied in controlled experiments in humans.[242–244] The elevation is a result of the metabolism of the solvent methylene chloride to carbon monoxide,[245–248] and therefore the hypoxic effect of carbon monoxide as well as its narcotic actions must be taken into account in considering the actions of methylene chloride. The levels of carboxyhemoglobin may become sufficiently high to cause brain damage[249] or death.[250]

One group of substances, the organic nitrites, produce a different hematological change, the formation of methemoglobin and hemolytic anemia.[251, 252] This group of substances includes the volatile liquid amyl, butyl, isopropyl, and possibly cyclohexyl organic nitrites. During the late 19th and early 20th centuries amyl nitrite was used in clinical practice as a vasodilator to treat angina pectoris. Although this use of the drug is uncommon today, it may be used for diagnostic purposes in echocardiographic examinations[231] and for cyanide poisoning.[239] These drugs are not the typical solvents previously described; however, they are often included in the inhalant abuse category. As with nitrous oxide, different individuals (predominantly homosexuals) are the primary abusers of these volatile nitrites, which cause sphincter dilation and penile engorgement. Use by others for nonsexual purposes is unclear. A study could not correlate changes in regional blood flow with any psychological measures or somatic changes[253]; also, isoamyl nitrite did not substitute for barbiturates as a reinforcing agent as does toluene and other solvents.[254] These studies do not offer any explanation for why individuals become dependent on nitrites. However, the finding by Mathew and colleagues[253] that nitrites reduce anger, fatigue, and depression may offer a clue.

The nitrites are not usually considered toxic during inhalation because of syncope (fainting). However, Guss and coworkers[255] noted a dangerously high 37% methemoglobin level in a normal subject who had used isobutyl nitrite. Methemoglobinemia is the major identified toxicity of organic nitrites and is the cause of several deaths.[256] However, there is a specific treatment for nitrite overdose. The high and slowly reversible reduction of methemoglobin can be aided by the use of methylene blue.[257]

Organic nitrites have also been reported to alter immune function as measured by direct lymphocytic actions[258] or in whole-animal studies.[259] These effects are of special concern in the development of acquired immunodeficiency syndrome; Haverkos and associates[260] reviewed the possible link between the development of Kaposi's sarcoma and high amyl or butyl nitrite use. Seage and colleagues,[261] however, proposed that the link is with and related to enhancement of the accessibility of the human immunodeficiency virus.

Early studies did not show major effects of organic nitrites on isolated immune or bacterial cells[262, 263]; however, studies by Soderberg's group[258] showed that isobutyl nitrite inhalation resulted in disruption of T-dependent immune mechanisms, including the induction of antibodies and cytotoxic T cells and of macrophage tumoricidal activity. This loss of immunity depended on habitual exposure and lasted for up to 5 to 7 days after exposures were terminated. The inhalant apparently produces this immunotoxicity by altering accessory cell functions, probably macrophage functions.

Neonatal Syndrome

Reports continue to provide evidence of problems in newborns of mothers who chronically abuse solvents,[183, 192, 264–266] including abnormal growth similar to that in the fetal alcohol syndrome. The mothers inhaled paint "reducer" (thinner?) and paint sprays and some drank various quantities of alcohol. Thus, toluene may augment the fetal alcohol syndrome when alcohol is also consumed. It is also worth noting that the mothers of the infants in Hersh's[266] study showed ataxia, mild tremors, and slurred speech, and the mothers in the other studies presented with severe renal tubular acidosis. Newborns of these women showed growth retardation and some dysmorphic features including microcephaly and also distal acidosis and aminoaciduria.[183, 193] Some of these abnormalities were observed in rodents exposed to toluene[264]; however, the extent and severity of the effects are unclear. An interesting in vitro exposure of rat embryos to toluene produced no malformations but did produce growth and developmental retardation.[267] Embryonic death may result from high doses of these solvents. Developmental effects are typified by an ataxic syndrome identified in young rats exposed to high levels of toluene throughout pregnancy (Pryor GT, personal communication).

Nitrous oxide has been shown to produce some "major visceral and minor skeletal (fetal) abnormalities."[268] Surprisingly, these abnormalities are protected against by halothane but not by folinic acid. Also, animal studies demonstrated fetal toxicities of the liver caused by carbon tetrachloride[269] and malformations by chloroform.[270] With so little knowledge and yet with all the potential dangers, it is important that pregnant women not be exposed to high concentrations of solvents. It is encouraging to know that a critical prospective study of workers exposed to low levels of solvent showed no more abnormalities than in the carefully matched control subjects.[271] This does not, however, diminish the need for pregnant women to avoid exposure to most solvents, especially at the high levels incurred through deliberate abuse.

Treatment

Individuals need different treatments based on the severity of their dependence and any medical complications. Primary care should address the medical issues identified earlier as well as other medical concerns before dealing with the dependence on solvents and other drugs. During this period, sedatives, other depressants, neuroleptics, and other forms of pharmacotherapy are not useful in the treatment of inhalant abusers and should be avoided in most cases as they are likely to exacerbate the depressed state. Once it is determined that the individual is detoxified, that is, has low levels of solvent or other depressant drug, then therapy with other drugs, such as antianxiety drugs, may be useful. The determination of detoxification, even in the absence of drug (solvent) administration, is not well defined or systematic. It may take several days for the major "reversible" intoxication state to be reduced to a level at which coherent cognition can occur. The use of various psychological assessment tools can assist not only in evaluating the intoxication but also in following the progress of the treatment. Little can be done during this period other than to facilitate improvement of the basic health of these individuals, provide supportive care, and build the individual's self-esteem.

There is no accepted treatment approach for inhalant abuse. It should also be emphasized that there are various categories of solvent abusers, from those who may use only one substance (e.g., only nitrous oxide or butanes) to heavy users of a variety of solvents and gases. Many drug treatment facilities refuse treatment of the inhalant abuser, because many feel that inhalant abusers are resistant to treatment[272] or that there is no standard or accepted treatment. One facility that focuses solely on the comprehensive treatment of inhalant abusers, the International Institute for Inhalant Abuse, based in Colorado, uses a three-phase model that allows longer periods of treatment. Longer periods of treatment are needed to be able to address the complex psychosocial, economic, and biophysical issues of the inhalant abuser. When brain injury, primarily in the form of cognitive dysfunction, is present, the rate of progression in the treatment process is even slower. As few treatment approaches with solvent abusers have been evaluated, none on a broad scale, all treatments should consider several important parameters including the following:

- Culture
- Family structure
- Living environment
- Peer interactions
- Individual's ability to learn and adapt
- Establishment of self-image
- Individual attitudes and behavioral characteristics
- Building basic life skills
- Social bonding

Some of these issues may be dealt with only through treating these individuals separately, especially in the early periods of treatment.

The inhalant abuser typically does not respond to usual drug rehabilitation treatment modalities. Several factors may be involved, particularly for the chronic abuser, who may have significant psychosocial problems. Treatment becomes slower and progressively more difficult when the severity of brain injury worsens as abuse progresses through transient social use (experimenting in groups) to chronic use in isolation. For these and other reasons, longer therapies are necessary than are utilized in most drug treatment facilities. Also, neurological impairment, the breadth of which still needs to be established, may be a major complication slowing the progress of rehabilitation. This is not as significant a problem with other forms of drug abuse.

Drug screening would be useful in monitoring inhalant abusers. Routine urine screening for hippuric acid (the major metabolite of toluene metabolism) performed two or three times weekly can detect the high level of exposure to toluene commonly seen in inhalant abusers. As alcohol is a common secondary drug of abuse among inhalant abusers, alcohol abuse should be monitored and considered in the approach to treatment.

Clinical Vignette

A 15-year-old Native American boy was brought to the emergency department by the police after being arrested for vandalism and stealing. He was found with about a dozen butane cigarette lighters and some whippet canisters that he had stolen. When taken into custody, he was staggering and appeared confused. At the emergency department, he had a "gasoline-like" smell on his breath and was disoriented to time. On a brief neurological examination, he had nystagmus and cerebellar ataxia (wide-based gait, poor finger-to-nose pointing). A urine toxicology test for hippuric acid was positive. Because of his neurological findings an MRI scan was obtained. The scan showed multifocal white matter hypodensities consistent with demyelinating axonal degeneration. He was admitted to the hospital for observation and released 3 days later after a medical history could be obtained from him. He had run away from his home reservation a year earlier and had been abusing alcohol and a wide range of inhalants including butane, nitrous oxide, and toluene (glue sniffing) on an almost daily basis. The diagnosis was inhalant use disorder, dependence.

Courtesy of Thomas R. Kosten

References

1. Carroll E: Notes on the epidemiology of inhalants. NIDA Res Monogr 1977; 15:14–24.
2. Bergman NA: Humphry Davy's contribution to the introduction of anesthesia: A new perspective. Perspect Biol Med 1991; 34:534–541.
3. Hutchens KS, Kung M: "Experimentation" with chloroform. Am J Med 1985; 78:715–718.
4. Kringsholm B: Sniffing-associated deaths in Denmark. Forensic Sci Int 1980; 15:215–225.
5. Kerner K: Current topics in inhalant abuse. NIDA Res Monogr 1988; 85:8–29.
6. Substance Abuse and Mental Health Services Administration: National Household Survey on Drug Abuse: Population Estimates 1993. (Special unpublished analysis.) Washington, DC: U.S. Government Printing Office, 1994. DHHS publication (SMA) 94-3017.
7. Substance Abuse and Mental Health Services Administration: National Household Survey on Drug Abuse: Population Estimates 1994. Washington, DC: U.S. Government Printing Office, 1995. DHHS publication (SMA) 95-3063.
8. Fredlund EV, Spence RT, Maxwell JC, Kavinsky JA: Substance Use Among Texas Department of Corrections Inmates, 1988. Austin, TX: Texas Commission on Alcohol and Drug Abuse, February 1990.
9. Litovitz TL, Clark LR, Soloway RA: 1993 annual report of the American Association of Poison Control Centers Toxic Exposure Surveillance System. Am J Emerg Med 1994; 12:546–584.
10. Wright SP, Pottier ACW, Taylor JC, et al: Trends in Deaths Associated with Abuse of Volatile Substances, 1971–1993. Report 8. London: St. George's Hospital Medical School, 1995.
11. Ramsey J, Anderson HR, Bloor K, Flanagan RJ: An introduction to the practice, prevalence and chemical toxicology of volatile substance abuse. Hum Toxicol 1989; 8:261–269.
12. Mathew B, Kapp E, Jones TR: Commercial butane abuse, a disturbing case. Br J Addict 1989; 84:563–564.
13. Evans AC, Raistrick D: Patterns of use and related harm with toluene-based adhesives and butane gas. Br J Psychiatry 1987; 150:773–776.

14. Evans AC, Raistrick D: Phenomenology of intoxication with toluene-based adhesives and butane gas. Br J Psychiatry 1987; 150:769–773.
15. Siegel E, Wason S: Sudden death caused by inhalation of butane and propane. [letter] N Engl J Med 1990; 323:1638.
16. O'Callaghan C, Milner AD: Aerosol treatment abuse. Arch Dis Child 1988; 63:70.
17. Thompson PJ, Dhillon P, Cole P: Addiction to aerosol treatment: The asthmatic alternative to glue sniffing. Br Med J [Clin Res] 1983; 287:1515–1516.
18. Jacob B, Heller C, Daldrup T, et al: Fatal accidental enflurane intoxication. J Forensic Sci 1989; 34:1408–1412.
19. Krause JG, McCarthy WB: Sudden death by inhalation of cyclopropane. J Forensic Sci 1989; 34:1011–1012.
20. Nordin C, Rosenqvist M, Hollstedt C: Sniffing of ethyl chloride—an uncommon form of abuse with serious mental and neurological symptoms. Int J Addict 1988; 23:623–627.
21. Yamashita M, Matsuki A, Oyama T: Illicit use of modern volatile anaesthetics. Can Anaesth Soc J 1984; 31:76–79.
22. Evans EB, Balster RL: Inhaled 1,1,1-trichloroethane–produced physical dependence in mice: Effects of drugs and vapors on withdrawal. J Pharmacol Exp Ther 1993; 264:726–733.
23. Wheeler MG, Rozycki AA, Smith RP: Recreational propane inhalation in an adolescent male. J Toxicol Clin Toxicol 1992; 30:135–139.
24. Scerri GV, Regan PJ, Ratcliffe RJ, Roberts AH: Burns following cigarette lighter fluid abuse. Burns 1992; 18:329–331.
25. Smart RG: Inhalant use and abuse in Canada. NIDA Res Monogr 1988; 85:121–139.
26. Kozel N, Sloboda Z, de la Rosa M: Epidemiology of Inhalant Abuse: An International Perspective. NIDA Res Monogr. Washington, DC: U.S. Government Printing Office, 1995; 148 NIH publication 95–3831.
27. Johnston LD, O'Malley PM, Bachman JG: National Survey Results on Drug Use from the Monitoring the Future Study, 1975–1994. Washington, DC: U.S. Government Printing Office, 1995. NIH publication 95–4026.
28. Johnson BD, Frank B, Marel R, et al: Statewide Household Survey of Substance Abuse, 1986. Illicit Substance Use Among Adults in New York State's Transient Population. New York, 1988.
29. Fredlund EV, Spence RT, Maxwell JC, Kavinsky JA: Substance Use Among Texas Department of Corrections Inmates. Austin, TX: Texas Commission on Alcohol and Drug Abuse, 1988.
29a. Prevalence of Drug Use in the DC Metropolitan Area Household and Nonhousehold Populations: 1991. National Institute on Drug Abuse, National Institutes of Health Technical Report 8, 1994.
30. Edwards RW: Drug use among 8th grade students is increasing. Int J Drug Addict 1993; 28:1621–1623.
31. Sharp CW, Spence R, Beauvais F (eds): A Volatile Research Agenda on Inhalant Abuse. NIDA Res Monogr. Washington, DC: U.S. Government Printing Office, 1992:1–10. DHHS publication 129 (ADM) 93–3475.
32. Korman M, Matthews RW, Lovitt R: Neuropsychological effects of abuse of inhalants. Percept Mot Skills 1981; 53:547–553.
33. Oetting ER, Webb J: Psychosocial characteristics and their links with inhalants, a research agenda. In Sharp CW, Spence R, Beauvais F (eds): A Volatile Research Agenda on Inhalant Abuse. NIDA Res Monogr. Washington, DC: U.S. Government Printing Office, 1992: 59–98. DHHS publication 129 (ADM) 93–3475.
34. Jastak JT: Nitrous oxide and its abuse. J Am Dent Assoc 1991; 122:48–52.
35. Spencer JD, Raasch FO, Trefny FA: Halothane abuse in hospital personnel. JAMA 1976; 235:1034–1035.
36. England A, Jones RM: Inhaled anaesthetic agents: From halothane to the present day. Br J Hosp Med 1992; 48:254–257.
37. Pardys S, Brotman M: Trichloroethylene and alcohol: A straight flush. [letter] JAMA 1974; 229:521–522.
38. Stewart RD, Hake CL, Peterson JE: "Degreasers' flush," dermal response to trichloroethylene and ethanol. Arch Environ Health 1974; 29:1–5.
39. Antti-Poika M, Juntunen J, Matikainen E, et al: Occupational exposure to toluene: Neurotoxic effects with special emphasis on drinking habits. Int Arch Occup Environ Health 1985; 56:31–40.
40. Kira S, Ogata M, Ebara Y, et al: A case of thinner sniffing: Relationship between neuropsychological symptoms and urinary findings after inhalation of toluene and methanol. Ind Health 1988; 26:81–85.
41. Pryor GT, Howd RA, Uyeno ET, Thurber AB: Interactions between toluene and alcohol. Pharmacol Biochem Behav 1985; 23:401–410.
42. Ron MA: Volatile substance abuse: A review of possible long-term neurological, intellectual and psychiatric sequalae. Br J Psychiatry 1986; 148:235–246.
43. Anthenelli RM, Schuckit MA: Affective and anxiety disorders and alcohol and drug dependence: Diagnosis and treatment. J Addict Dis 1993; 12:73–87.
44. Ries RK: The dually diagnosed patient with psychotic symptoms. J Addict Dis 1993; 12:103–122.
45. Dinwiddie SH, Zorumski CF, Rubin EH: Psychiatric correlates of chronic solvent abuse. J Clin Psychiatry 1987; 48:334–337.
46. Korman M, Semler I, Trimboli F: A psychiatric emergency room study of 162 inhalant users. Addict Behav 1980; 5:143–147.
47. Fernandez-Pol B, Bluestone H, Mizruchi MS: Inner-city substance abuse patterns: A study of psychiatric inpatients. Am J Drug Alcohol Abuse 1988; 14:41–50.
48. Oetting ER, Edwards RW, Beauvais F: Social and psychological factors underlying inhalant abuse. NIDA Res Monogr 1988; 85:172–203.
49. Byrne A, Kirby B, Zibin T, Ensminger S: Psychiatric and neurological effects of chronic solvent abuser: A case report. J Clin Psychiatry 1991; 36:735–738.
50. Goldbloom D, Chouinard G: Schizophreniform psychosis associated with chronic industrial toluene exposure: Case report. J Clin Psychiatry 1985; 46:350–351.
51. Katzelnick DJ, Davar G, Scanlon JP: Reversibility of psychiatric symptoms in a chronic solvent abuser: A case report. J Neuropsychiatry Clin Neurosci 1991; 3:319–321.
52. Roberts FP, Lucas EG, Marsden CD, Trauer T: Near-pure xylene causing reversible neuropsychiatric disturbance. [letter] Lancet 1988; 2:273.
53. Levy AB: Delirium induced by inhalation of typewriter correction fluid. Psychosomatics 1986; 27:665–666.
54. Malm G, Lying-Tunell U: Cerebellar dysfunction related to toluene sniffing. Acta Neurol Scand 1980; 62:188–190.
55. Channer KS, Stanley S: Persistent visual hallucination secondary to chronic solvent encephalopathy: Case report and review of the literature. J Neurol Neurosurg Psychiatry 1983; 46:83–86.
56. Chadwick OF, Anderson HR: Neuropsychological consequences of volatile substance abuse: A review. Hum Toxicol 1989; 8:307–312.
57. Goldings AS, Stewart RM: Organic lead encephalopathy: Behavioral change and movement disorder following gasoline inhalation. J Clin Psychiatry 1982; 43:70–72.
58. Henry B, Feehan M, McGee R, et al: The importance of conduct problems and depressive symptoms in predicting adolescent substance use. J Abnorm Child Psychol 1993; 21:469–480.
59. Garriott J: Death among inhalant abusers. In Sharp CW, Spence R, Beauvais F (eds): A Volatile Research Agenda on Inhalant Abuse. NIDA Res Monogr. Washington, DC: U.S. Government Printing Office, 1992:181–192. DHHS publication (ADM) 93–3480.
60. Al-Alousi LM: Pathology of volatile substance abuse: A case report and a literature review. Med Sci Law 1989; 29:189–208.
61. Bass M: Sudden sniffing death. JAMA 1970; 212: 2075–2079.
62. Fitzgerald RL, Fishel CE, Bush LL: Fatality due to recreational use of chlorodifluoromethane and chloropentafluoroethane. J Forensic Sci 1993; 38:477–483.
63. Groppi A, Polettini A, Lunetta P, et al: A fatal case of trichlorofluoromethane (Freon 11) poisoning. Tissue distribution study by gas chromatography–mass spectrometry. J Forensic Sci 1994; 39:871–876.
64. Wason S, Gibler WB, Hassan M: Ventricular tachycardia associated with non-Freon aerosol propellants. JAMA 1986; 256:78–80.
65. Clark MA, Jones JW, Robinson JJ, Lord JT: Multiple deaths resulting from shipboard exposure to trichlorotrifluoroethane. J Forensic Sci 1985; 30:1256–1259.
66. Fraunfelder FT: Nitrous oxide warning. Am J Ophthalmol 1988; 105:688.
67. Suruda AJ, McGlothlin JD: Fatal abuse of nitrous oxide in the workplace. J Occup Med 1990; 32:682–684.
68. Wagner SA, Clark MA, Wesche DL, et al: Asphyxial deaths from the recreational use of nitrous oxide. J Forensic Sci 1992; 37:1008–1015.
69. Schaumburg HH, Spencer PS: Recognizing neurotoxic disease. Neurology 1987; 37:276–278.
70. Lazar RB, Ho SU, Melen O, Daghestani AN: Multifocal central

nervous system damage caused by toluene abuse. Neurology 1983; 33:1337–1340.

71. Hormes JT, Filley CM, Rosenberg NL: Neurologic sequelae of chronic solvent vapor abuse. Neurology 1986; 36:698–702.
72. Fornazzari L, Wilkinson DA, Kapur BM, Carlen PL: Cerebellar, cortical and functional impairment in toluene abusers. Acta Neurol Scand 1983; 67:319–329.
73. Rosenberg NL, Kleinschmidt-DeMasters BK, Davis KA, et al: Toluene abuse causes diffuse central nervous system white matter changes. Ann Neurol 1988; 23:611–614.
74. Unger E, Alexander A, Fritz T, et al: Toluene abuse: Physical basis for hypointensity of the basal ganglia on T2-weighted MR images. Radiology 1994; 193:473–476.
75. Caldmeyer KS, Pascuzzi RM, Moran CC, Smith RR: Tolune abuse causing reduced MR signal intensity in the brain. AJR 1993; 161:1259–1261.
76. Grabski DA: Toluene sniffing producing cerebellar degeneration. Am J Psychiatry 1961; 118:461–462.
77. Knox JW, Nelson JR: Permanent encephalopathy from toluene inhalation. N Engl J Med 1966; 275:1494–1496.
78. King MD: Neurological sequelae of toluene abuse. Hum Toxicol 1982; 1:281–287. 1982.
79. Boor JW, Hurtig HI: Persistent cerebellar ataxia after exposure to toluene. Ann Neurol 1977; 2:440–442.
80. Streicher HZ, Gabow PA, Moss AH, et al: Syndromes of toluene sniffing in adults. Ann Intern Med 1981; 94:758–762.
81. Takeuchi Y, Hisanaga N, Ono Y, et al: Cerebellar dysfunction caused by sniffing of toluene-containing thinner. Ind Health 1981; 19:163–169.
82. Schikler KN, Seitz K, Rice JF, Strader T: Solvent abuse associated cortical atrophy. J Adolesc Health Care 1982; 3:37–39.
83. Rosenberg NL, Spitz MC, Filley CM, et al: Central nervous system effects of chronic toluene abuse—clinical, brainstem evoked response and magnetic resonance imaging studies. Neurotoxicol Teratol 1988; 10:489–495.
84. Filley CM, Heaton RK, Rosenberg NL: White matter dementia in chronic toluene abuse. Neurology 1990; 40:532–534.
85. Ikeda M, Tsukagoshi H: Encephalopathy due to toluene sniffing. Report of a case with magnetic resonance imaging. Eur Neurol 1990; 30:347–349.
86. Kornfeld M, Moser AB, Moser HW, et al: Solvent vapor abuse leukoencephalopathy. Comparison to adrenoleukodystrophy. J Neuropathol Exp Neurol 1994; 53:389–398.
87. Poungvarin N: Multifocal brain damage due to lacquer sniffing: The first case report of Thailand. J Med Assoc Thai 1991; 74:296–300.
88. Xiong L, Matthes JD, Li J, Jinkins JR: MR imaging of spray heads: Toluene abuse via aerosol paint inhalation. AJNR 1993; 14:1195–1199.
89. Metrick SA, Brenner RP: Abnormal brainstem auditory evoked potentials in chronic paint sniffers. Ann Neurol 1982; 12:553–556.
90. Arnold GL, Kirby RS, Langendoerfer S, Wilkins-Haug L: Toluene embryopathy: Clinical delineation and developmental follow-up. Pediatrics 1994; 93:216–220.
91. Pearson MA, Hoyme HE, Seaver LH, Rimsza ME: Toluene embryopathy: Delineation of the phenotype and comparison with fetal alcohol syndrome. Pediatrics 1994; 93:211–215.
92. Escobar A, Aruffo C: Chronic thinner intoxication: Clinocopathologic report of a human case. J Neurol Neurosurg Psychiatry 1980; 43:986–994.
93. Pryor GT: A toluene-induced motor syndrome in rats resembling that seen in some solvent abusers. Neurotoxicol Teratol 1991; 13:387–400.
94. Huang J, Asaeda N, Takeuchi Y, et al: Dose dependent effects of chronic exposure to toluene on neuronal and glial cell marker proteins in the central nervous system of rats. Br J Ind Med 1992; 49:282–286.
95. Meulenbelt J, de Groot G, Savelkoul TJ: Two cases of acute toluene intoxication. Br J Ind Med 1990; 47:417–420.
96. Takahashi S, Kagawa M, Shiwaku K, Matsubara K: Determination of S-benzyl-*N*-acetyl-L-cysteine by gas chromatography/mass spectrometry as a new marker of toluene exposure. J Anal Toxicol 1994; 18:78–80.
97. Selden A, Hultberg B, Ulander A, Ahlborg G Jr: Trichloroethylene exposure in vapour degreasing and the urinary excretion of *N*-acetyl-beta-D-glucosaminidase. Arch Toxicol 1993; 67:224–226.
98. Coodin FJ, Dawes C, Dean GW, et al: Riposte to "Environmental lead and young children." Can Med Assoc J 1980; 123:469–471.
99. Eastwell HD: Elevated lead levels in petrol "sniffers." Med J Aust 1985; 143:563–564.
100. Goodheart RS, Dunne JW: Petrol sniffer's encephalopathy. A study of 25 patients. Med J Aust 1994; 160:178–181.
101. Reese E, Kimbrough RD: Acute toxicity of gasoline and some additives. Environ Health Perspect 1993; 101(suppl 6):115–131.
102. Remington G, Hoffman BF: Gas sniffing as a form of substance abuse. Can J Psychiatry 1984; 29:31–35.
103. Robinson RO: Tetraethyl lead poisoning from gasoline sniffing. JAMA 1978; 240:1373–1374.
104. Seshia SS, Rajani KR, Boeckx RL, Chow PN: The neurological manifestations of chronic inhalation of leaded gasoline. Dev Med Child Neurol 1978; 20:323–334.
105. Valpey R, Sumi SM, Copass MK, Goble GJ: Acute and chronic progressive encephalopathy due to gasoline sniffing. Neurology 1978; 28:507–510.
106. Prockop LD, Karampelas D: Encephalopathy secondary to abusive gasoline inhalation. J Fla Med Assoc 1981; 68:823–824.
107. Rybak LP: Hearing: The effects of chemicals. Otolaryngol Head Neck Surg 1992; 106:677–686.
108. Sasa M, Igarashi S, Miyazaki T, et al: Equilibrium disorders with diffuse brain atrophy in long-term toluene sniffing. Arch Otorhinolaryngol 1978; 221:163–169.
109. Biscaldi GP, Mingardi M, Pollini G, et al: Acute toluene poisoning. Electroneurophysiological and vestibular investigations. Toxicol Eur Res 1981; 3:271–273.
110. Ehyai A, Freemon FR: Progressive optic neuropathy and sensorineural hearing loss due to chronic glue sniffing. J Neurol Neurosurg Psychiatry 1983; 46: 349–351.
111. Morrow LA, Steinhauer SR, Hodgson MJ: Delay in P300 latency in patients with organic solvent exposure. Arch Neurol 1992; 49:315–320.
112. Crofton KM, Zhao X: Mid-frequency hearing loss in rats following inhalation exposure to trichloroethylene: Evidence from reflex modification audiometry. Neurotoxicol Teratol 1993; 15:413–423.
113. Jaspers RM, Muijser H, Lammers JH, Kulig BM: Mid-frequency hearing loss and reduction of acoustic startle responding in rats following trichloroethylene exposure. Neurotoxicol Teratol 1993; 15:407–412.
114. Pryor GT, Dickinson J, Howd RA, Rebert CS: Transient cognitive deficits and high-frequency hearing loss in weanling rats exposed to toluene. Neurobehav Toxicol Teratol 1983; 5:53–57.
115. Rebert CS, Sorenson SS, Howd RA, Pryor GT: Toluene-induced hearing loss in rats evidenced by the brainstem auditory-evoked response. Neurobehav Toxicol Teratol 1983; 5:59–62.
116. Rebert CS, Day VL, Matteucci MJ, Pryor GT: Sensory-evoked potentials in rats chronically exposed to trichloroethylene: Predominant auditory dysfunction. Neurotoxicol Teratol 1991; 13:83–90.
117. Pryor GT: Solvent-induced neurotoxicity: Effects and mechanisms. In Chang LW, Dyer RS (eds): Handbook of Toxicology. New York: Marcel Dekker, 1995.
118. Niklasson M, Tham R, Larsby B, Eriksson B: Effects of toluene, styrene, trichloroethylene, and trichloroethane on the vestibulo- and opto-oculo motor system in rats. Neurotoxicol Teratol 1993; 15:327–334.
119. Nylen P, Hagman M, Johnson AC: Function of the auditory and visual systems, and of peripheral nerve, in rats after long-term combined exposure to *n*-hexane and methylated benzene derivatives. I. Toluene. Pharmacol Toxicol 1994; 74:116–123.
120. Li HS, Johnson AC, Borg E, Hoglund G: Auditory degeneration after exposure to toluene in two genotypes of mice. Arch Toxicol 1992; 66:382–386.
121. Maas EF, Ashe J, Spiegel P, et al: Acquired pendular nystagmus in toluene addiction. Neurology 1991; 41:282–285.
122. Keane JR: Toluene optic neuropathy. Ann Neurol 1978; 4:390.
123. Takeuchi Y: Visual disorders due to organic solvent poisoning. Jpn J Ind Health 1988; 30:236–247.
124. Feldman RG, White RF, Currie JN, et al: Long-term follow-up after single toxic exposure to trichloroethylene. Am J Ind Med 1985; 8:119–126.
125. Berg EF: Retrobulbar neuritis. Ann Ophthalmol 1971; 3:1351–1353.
126. Hollo G, Varga M: Toluene and visual loss. [letter; comment] Neurology 1992; 42:266. Comment on: Neurology 1991; 41:282–285.
127. Odkvist LM, Larsby B, Fredrickson JMF, et al: Vestibular and

oculomotor disturbances caused by industrial solvents. J Otolaryngol 1980; 9:57–58.
128. Blain L, Lachapelle P, Molotchnikoff S: Evoked potentials are modified by long term exposure to trichloroethylene. Neurotoxicology 1992; 13:203–206.
129. Schaumburg HH, Spencer PS: Degeneration in central and peripheral nervous systems produced by pure *n*-hexane: An experimental study. Brain 1976; 99:183–192.
130. Bruhn P, Arlien-Soborg P, Gyldensted C, Christensen EL: Prognosis in chronic toxic encephalopathy. Acta Neurol Scand 1981; 64:259–272.
131. Frontali N, Amantini MC, Spagnolo A, et al: Experimental neurotoxicity and urinary metabolites of the C5–C7 aliphatic hydrocarbons used as glue solvents in shoe manufacture. Clin Toxicol 1981; 18:1357–1367.
132. Altenkirch H, Wagner HM, Stoltenburg-Didinger G, Steppat R: Potentiation of hexacarbon-neurotoxicity by methyl-ethyl-ketone (MEK) and other substances: Clinical and experimental aspects. Neurobehav Toxicol Teratol 1982; 4:623–627.
133. Backstrom B, Collins VP: The effects of 2,5-hexanedione on rods and cones of the retina of albino rats. Neurotoxicology 1992; 13:199–202.
134. Mergler D, Beauvais B: Olfactory threshold shift following controlled 7-hour exposure to toluene and/or xylene. Neurotoxicology 1992; 13:211–215.
135. Feldman RG, Niles C, Proctor SP, Jabre J: Blink reflex measurement of effects of trichloroethylene exposure on the trigeminal nerve. Muscle Nerve 1992; 15:490–495.
136. Ruijten MW, Verberk MM, Salle HJ: Nerve function in workers with long term exposure to trichloroethene. Br J Ind Med 1991; 48:87–92.
137. Laureno R: Trichloroethylene does not cause trigeminal neuropathy. [letter] Muscle Nerve 1993; 16:217.
138. Lash TL, Green LC: Blink reflex measurement of effects of trichloroethylene exposure on the trigeminal nerve. Muscle Nerve 1993; 16:217–219.
139. Barret L, Torch S, Leray CL, et al: Morphometric and biochemical studies in trigeminal nerve of rat after trichloroethylene or dichloroacetylene oral administration. Neurotoxicology 1992; 13:601–614.
140. Schwartz RH, Calihan M: Nitrous oxide: A potentially lethal euphoriant inhalant. Am Family Pract 1984; 30:171–172.
141. Gillman MA: Nitrous oxide abuse in perspective. Clin Neuropharmacol 1992; 15:297–306.
142. Vishnubhakat SM, Beresford HR: Reversible myeloneuropathy of nitrous oxide abuse: Serial electrophysiological studies. Muscle Nerve 1991; 14:22–26.
143. Layzer RB: Myeloneuropathy after prolonged exposure to nitrous oxide. Lancet 1978; 2:1227–1230.
144. Nunn JF: Clinical aspects of the interaction between nitrous oxide and vitamin B_{12}. Br J Anaesth 1987; 59:3–13.
145. Flippo TS, Holder WD Jr: Neurologic degeneration associated with nitrous oxide anesthesia in patients with vitamin B_{12} deficiency. Arch Surg 1993; 128:1391–1395.
146. Fujinaga M, Baden JM: Methionine prevents nitrous oxide–induced teratogenicity in rat embryos grown in culture. Anesthesiology 1994; 81:184–189.
147. Belknap JK, Laursen SE, Crabbe JC: Ethanol and nitrous oxide produce withdrawal-induced convulsions by similar mechanisms in mice. Life Sci 1987; 41:2033–2040.
148. Allen N, Mendell JR, Billmaier DJ, et al: Toxic polyneuropathy due to methyl *n*-butyl ketone: An industrial outbreak. Arch Neurol 1975; 32:209–218.
149. Herskowitz A, Ishii N, Schaumburg H: N-hexane neuropathy: A syndrome occurring as a result of industrial exposure. N Engl J Med 1971; 285:82–85.
150. Mallov JS: MBK neuropathy among spray painters. JAMA 1976; 235:1455–1457.
151. Mendell JR, Saida K, Ganansia MF, et al: Toxic polyneuropathy produced by methyl *n*-butyl ketone. Science 1974; 185:787–789.
152. Dittmer DK, Jhamandas JH, Johnson ES: Glue-sniffing neuropathies. Can Fam Physician 1993; 39:1965–1971.
153. Gonzalez EG, Downey JA: Polyneuropathy in a glue sniffer. Arch Phys Med Rehab 1972; 53:333–337.
154. Goto I, Matsumura M, Inove N, et al: Toxic polyneuropathy due to glue sniffing. J Neurol Neurosurg Psychiatry 1974; 37:848–853.
155. King PJL, Morris JGL, Pollard JD: Glue sniffing neuropathy. Aust N Z J Med 1985; 15:293–299.
156. Means ED, Prockop LD, Hooper GS: Pathology of lacquer thinner induced neuropathy. Ann Clin Lab Sci 1976; 6:240–250.
157. Korobkin R, Asbury AK, Sumner AJ, Nielsen SL: Glue-sniffing neuropathy. Arch Neurol 1975; 32:158–162.
158. Oh SJ, Kim JM: Giant axonal swelling in "huffer's" neuropathy. Arch Neurol 1976; 33:583–586.
159. Takeuchi Y: *n*-Hexane polyneuropathy in Japan: A review of *n*-hexane poisoning and its preventive measures. Environ Res 1993; 62:76–80.
160. Towfighi J, Gonatas NK, Pleasure D, et al: Glue sniffer's neuropathy. Neurology 1976; 26:238–243.
161. Gallassi R, Montagna P, Pazzaglia P, et al: Peripheral neuropathy due to gasoline sniffing—a case report. Eur Neurol 1980; 19:419–421.
162. Hall DMB, Ramsey J, Schwartz MS, Dookun D: Neuropathy in a petrol sniffer. Arch Dis Child 1986; 61:900–901.
163. Tenenbein M, deGroot W, Rajani KR: Peripheral neuropathy following intentional inhalation of naphtha fumes. Can Med Assoc J 1984; 131:1077–1079.
164. Menkes JH: Toxic polyneuropathy due to methyl *n*-butyl ketone. [letter] Arch Neurol 1976; 33:309.
165. Spencer PS, Schaumburg HH, Sabri MI, Veronesi B: The enlarging view of hexacarbon neurotoxicity. Crit Rev Toxicol 1980; 7:279–357.
166. Graham DG, Anthony DC, Boekelheide K: In vitro and in vivo studies of the molecular pathogenesis of *n*-hexane neuropathy. Neurobehav Toxicol Teratol 1982; 4:629–634.
167. Altenkirch H, Stoltenburg G, Wagner HM: Experimental studies on hydrocarbon neuropathies induced by methyl-ethyl-ketone. J Neurol 1978; 219:159–170.
168. Saida K, Mendell JR, Weiss HS: Peripheral nerve changes induced by methyl *n*-butyl ketone and potentiated by methyl ethyl ketone. J Neuropathol Exp Neurol 1976; 35:207–225.
169. Spencer PS, Schaumburg HH, Raleigh RL, Terhaar CJ: Nervous system degeneration produced by the industrial solvent methyl *n*-butyl ketone. Arch Neurol 1975; 32:219–222.
170. Will AM, McLaren EH: Reversible renal damage due to glue sniffing. Br Med J 1981; 283:525–526.
171. Bennett RH, Forman HR: Hypokalemic periodic paralysis in chronic toluene exposure. Arch Neurol 1980; 37:673.
172. Batlle DC, Sabatini S, Kurtzman NA: On the mechanism of toluene-induced renal tubular acidosis. Nephron 1988; 49:210–218.
173. Carlisle EJ, Donnelly SM, Vasuvattakul S, et al: Glue-sniffing and distal renal tubular acidosis: Sticking to the facts. J Am Soc Nephrol 1991; 1:1019–1027.
174. Davidman M, Schmitz P: Renal tubular acidosis. A pathophysiologic approach. Hosp Pract (Off Ed) 1988; 23:77–81, 84–88, 93–96.
175. Gupta RK, van der Meulen J, Johny DV: Oliguric acute renal failure due to glue-sniffing. Case report. Scand J Urol Nephrol 1991; 25:247–250.
176. Jone CM, Wu AH: An unusual case of toluene-induced metabolic acidosis. Clin Chem 1988; 34:2596–2599.
177. Kaneko T, Koizumi T, Takezaki T, Sato A: Urinary calculi associated with solvent abuse. J Urol 1992; 147:1365–1366.
178. Marjot R, McLeod AA: Chronic non-neurological toxicity from volatile substance abuse. Hum Toxicol 1989; 8:301–306.
179. Miller L, Pateras V, Friederici H, Engel G: Acute tubular necrosis after inhalation exposure to methylene chloride. Report of a case. Arch Intern Med 1985; 145:145–146.
180. Mizutani T, Oohashi N, Naito H: Myoglobinemia and renal failure in toluene poisoning: A case report. Vet Hum Toxicol 1989; 31:448–450.
181. Nelson NA, Robins TG, Port FK: Solvent nephrotoxicity in humans and experimental animals. Am J Nephrol 1990; 10:10–20.
182. Patel R, Benjamin J Jr: Renal disease associated with toluene inhalation. Clin Toxicol 1986; 24:213–223.
183. Wilkins-Haug L, Gabow PA: Toluene abuse during pregnancy: Obstetric complications and perinatal outcomes. Obstet Gynecol 1991; 77:504–509.
184. Lauwerys R, Bernard A, Viau C, Buchet JP: Kidney disorders and hematotoxicity from organic solvent exposure. Scand J Work Environ Health 1985; 11(suppl 1):83–90.
185. Daniell WE, Couser WG, Rosenstock L: Occupational solvent exposure and glomerulonephritis. JAMA 1988; 259:2280–2283.
186. Brown JH, Hadden DR, Hadden DS: Solvent abuse, toluene acidosis and diabetic ketoacidosis. Arch Emerg Med 1991; 8:65–67.
187. Taverner D, Harrison DJ, Bell GM: Acute renal failure due to interstitial nephritis induced by 'glue-sniffing' with subsequent recovery. Scott Med J 1988; 33:246–247.

188. Yamamoto S, Mori NYH, Miyata M, Kanai K: Neurogenic bladder caused by toluene abuse. Acta Urol Jpn 1992; 38:459–462.
189. Lock EA: Mechanism of nephrotoxic action due to organohalogenated compounds. Toxicol Lett 1989; 46:93–106.
190. Kimbrough RD, Mitchell FL, Houk VN: Trichloroethylene: An update. J Toxicol Environ Health 1985; 15:369–383.
191. Short BG, Burnett VL, Cox MG, et al: Site-specific renal cytotoxicity and cell proliferation in male rats exposed to petroleum hydrocarbons. Lab Invest 1987; 57:564–577.
192. Goodwin TM: Toluene abuse and renal tubular acidosis in pregnancy. Obstet Gynecol 1988; 71:715–718.
193. Lindemann R: Congenital renal tubular dysfunction associated with maternal sniffing of organic solvents. Acta Paediatr Scand 1991; 80:882–884.
194. Paraf F, Lewis J, Jothy S: Acute fatty liver of pregnancy after exposure to toluene. A case report. J Clin Gastroenterol 1993; 17:163–165.
195. Lavoie FW, Dolan MC, Danzl DF, Barber RL: Recurrent resuscitation and 'no code' orders in a 27-year-old spray paint abuser [clinical conference]. Ann Emerg Med 1987; 16:1266–1273.
196. Baerg RD, Kimberg DV: Centrilobular hepatic necrosis and acute renal failure in "solvent sniffers." Ann Intern Med 1970; 73:713–720.
197. Benjamin SB, Goodman ZD, Ishak KG, et al: The morphologic spectrum of halothane-induced hepatic injury: Analysis of 77 cases. Hepatology 1985; 5:1163–1171.
198. Clearfield HR: Hepatorenal toxicity from sniffing spot-remover (trichloroethylene). Dig Dis 1970; 15:851–856.
199. Farrell G, Prendergast D, Murray M: Halothane hepatitis. Detection of a constitutional susceptibility factor. N Engl J Med 1985; 313:1310–1314.
200. Hakim A, Jain AK, Jain R: Chloroform ingestion causing toxic hepatitis. J Assoc Physicians India 1992; 40:477.
201. Hodgson MJ, Heyl AT, Van Thiel DH: Liver disease associated with exposure to 1,1,1-trichloroethane. Arch Intern Med 1989; 149:1793–1798.
202. Litt IF, Cohen MI: Danger . . . vapor harmful: Spot-remover sniffing. N Engl J Med 1969; 281:543–544.
203. Mizutani K, Shinomiya K, Shinomiya T: Hepatotoxicity of dichloromethane. Forensic Sci Int 1988; 38:113–128.
204. Stewart A, Witts LJ: Chronic carbon tetrachloride intoxication. 1944 [classical article]. Br J Ind Med 1993; 50:8–18.
205. Plaa GL: Experimental evaluation of haloalkanes and liver injury. Fundam Appl Toxicol 1988; 10:563–570.
206. Greer JE: Adolescent abuse of typewriter correction fluid. South Med J 1984; 77:297–298.
207. Ong CN, Koh D, Foo SC, et al: Volatile organic solvents in correction fluids: Identification and potential hazards. Bull Environ Contam Toxicol 1993; 50:787–793.
208. Cordes DH, Brown WD, Quinn KM: Chemically induced hepatitis after inhaling organic solvents. West J Med 1988; 148:458–460.
209. McIntyre AS, Long RG: Fatal fulminant hepatic failure in a 'solvent abuser.' Postgrad Med J 1992; 68:29–30.
210. Devathasan G, Low D, Teoh PC: Complications of chronic glue (toluene) abuse in adolescents. Aust N Z J Med 1984; 14:39–43.
211. Reyes de la Rocha S, Brown MA, Fortenberry JD: Pulmonary function abnormalities in intentional spray paint inhalation. Chest 1987; 92:100–104.
212. Schikler KN, Lane EE, Seitz K, Collins WM: Solvent abuse associated pulmonary abnormalities. Adv Alcohol Subst Abuse 1984; 3:75–81.
213. Currie B, Burrow J, Fisher D, et al: Petrol sniffer's encephalopathy. Med J Aust 1994; 160:800–801.
214. Sherwood RL, O'Shea W, Thomas PT, et al: Effects of inhalation of ethylene dichloride on pulmonary defenses of mice and rats. Toxicol Appl Pharmacol 1987; 91:491–496.
215. Forkert PG, Forkert L: Trichloroethylene induces pulmonary fibrosis in mice. Can J Physiol Pharmacol 1994; 72:205–210.
216. Cartwright TR, Brown ED, Brashear RE: Pulmonary infiltrates following butane 'fire-breathing.' Arch Intern Med 1983; 143:2007–2008.
217. McLeod AA, Marjot R, Monaghan MJ, et al: Chronic cardiac toxicity after inhalation of 1,1,1-trichloroethane. Br Med J [Clin Res] 1987; 294:727–729.
218. Cunningham SR, Dalzell GWN, McGirr P, Khan MM: Myocardial infarction and primary ventricular fibrillation after glue sniffing. Br Med J [Clin Res] 1987; 294:739–740.
219. Boon NA: Solvent abuse and the heart. [editorial] Br Med J [Clin Res] 1987; 294:722.
220. Wright MF, Strobl DJ: 1,1,1-Trichloroethane cardiac toxicity: Report of a case. J Am Osteopath Assoc 1984; 84:285–288.
221. Ong TK, Rustage KJ, Harrison KM, Brook IM: Solvent abuse. An anaesthetic management problem. Br Dent J 164:150–151.
222. King GS, Smialek JE, Troutman WG: Sudden death in adolescents resulting from the inhalation of typewriter correction fluid. JAMA 1985; 253:1604–1606.
223. Zakhari S, Salem H: Cardiac toxicology of solvents. In Baskin SI (ed): Principles of Cardiac Toxicology. Boca Raton, FL: CRC Press, 1991:465–501.
224. Taylor GJ, Harris W: Cardiac toxicity of aerosol propellants. JAMA 1970; 214: 81–85.
225. Bass M: Abuse of inhalation anesthetics. [letter] JAMA 1984; 251:604.
226. Roberts MJD, McIvor RA, Adgey AAJ: Asystole following butane gas inhalation. Br J Hosp Med 1990; 44:294.
227. Chenoweth MB: Abuse of inhalation anesthetic drugs. NIDA Res Monogr 1977; 15:102–111.
228. Knight AT, Pawsey CG, Aroney RS, et al: Upholsterers' glue associated with myocarditis, hepatitis, acute renal failure and lymphoma. Med J Aust 1991; 154:360–362.
229. Wernisch M, Paya K, Palasser A: Cardiovascular arrest after inhalation of leather glue. Wien Med Wochenschr 1991; 141:71–74.
230. Hantson P, Vandenplas O, Dive A, Mahieu P: Trichloroethylene and cardiac toxicity: Report of two consecutive cases. Acta Clin Belg 1990; 45:34–37.
231. Rosoff MH, Cohen MV: Profound bradycardia after amyl nitrite in patients with a tendency to vasovagal episodes. Br Heart J 1986; 55:97–100.
232. Brilliant LC, Grillo A: Successful resuscitation from cardiopulmonary arrest following deliberate inhalation of Freon refrigerant gas. Del Med J 1993; 65:375–378.
233. Austin H, Delzell E, Cole P: Benzene and leukemia. A review of the literature and a risk assessment. Am J Epidemiol 1988; 127:419–439.
234. Yardley-Jones A, Anderson D, Parke DV: The toxicity of benzene and its metabolism and molecular pathology in human risk assessment. Br J Ind Med 1991; 48:437–444.
235. Dunkel VC, Rogers-Back AM, Lawlor TE, et al: Mutagenicity of some alkyl nitrites used as recreational drugs. Environ Mol Mutagen 1989; 14:115–122.
236. Osterloh J, Goldfield D: Butyl nitrite transformation in vitro, chemical nitrosation reactions, and mutagenesis. J Anal Toxicol 1984; 8:164–169.
237. Mirvish SS, Haverkos HW: Butyl nitrite in the induction of Kaposi's sarcoma in AIDS. [letter] N Engl J Med 1987; 317:1603.
238. Yamamoto M, Ishiwata H, Yamada T, et al: Studies in the guinea-pig stomach on the formation of *N*-nitrosomethylurea, from methylurea and sodium nitrite, and its disappearance. Food Chem Toxicol 1987; 25:663–668.
239. Klimmek R, Krettek C, Werner HW: Ferrihaemoglobin formation by amyl nitrite and sodium nitrite in different species in vivo and in vitro. Arch Toxicol 1988; 62:152–160.
240. Osterloh JD, Goldfield D: Uptake of inhaled *n*-butyl nitrite and in vivo transformation in rats. J Pharm Sci 1985; 74:780–782.
241. Horowitz BZ: Carboxyhemoglobinemia caused by inhalation of methylene chloride. Am J Emerg Med 1986; 4:48–51.
242. Stewart RD, Fisher TN, Hosko MJ, et al: Experimental human exposure to methylene chloride. Arch Environ Health 1972; 25:342–348.
243. Gamberale F, Annwall G, Hultengren M: Exposure to methylene chloride. II. Psychological functions. Scand J Work Environ Health 1975; 1:95–103.
244. Winneke G: The neurotoxicity of dichloromethane. Neurobehav Toxicol Teratol 1981; 3:391–395.
245. Stewart RD, Fisher TN: Carboxyhemoglobin elevation after exposure to dichloromethane. Science 1972; 176:295–296.
246. Kubic VL, Andres MW, Engel RR, et al: Metabolism of dihalomethanes to carbon monoxide. I. In vivo studies. Drug Metab Dispos 1974; 2:53–57.
247. Ratney RS, Wegman DH, Elkins HB: In vivo conversion of methylene chloride to carbon monoxide. Arch Environ Health 1974; 28:223–226.
248. Astrand I, Ovrum P, Carlsson A: Exposure to methylene chloride. I. Its concentration in alveolar air and blood during rest and exercise and its metabolism. Scand J Work Environ Health 1975; 1:78–94.

249. Barrowcliff DF, Knell AJ: Cerebral damage due to endogenous chronic carbon monoxide poisoning caused by exposure to methylene chloride. J Soc Occup Med 1979; 29:12–14.
250. Manno M, Chirillo R, Daniotti G, et al: Carboxyhaemoglobin and fatal methylene chloride poisoning. [letter] Lancet 1989; 2:274.
251. Wason S, Detsky AS, Platt OS, Lovejoy FH Jr: Isobutyl nitrite toxicity by ingestion. Ann Intern Med 1980; 92:637–638.
252. Brandes JC, Bufill JA, Pisciotta AV: Amyl nitrite–induced hemolytic anemia. Am J Med 1989; 86:252–254.
253. Mathew RJ, Wilson WH, Tant SR: Regional cerebral blood flow changes associated with amyl nitrite inhalation. Br J Addict 1989; 84:293–299.
254. Rees DC, Knisely JS, Balster RL, et al: Pentobarbital-like discriminative stimulus properties of halothane, 1,1,1-trichloroethane, isoamyl nitrite, flurothyl and oxazepam in mice. J Pharmacol Exp Ther 1987; 241:507–515.
255. Guss DA, Normann SA, Manoguerra AS: Clinically significant methemoglobinemia from inhalation of isobutyl nitrite. Am J Emerg Med 1985; 3:46–47.
256. Wood RW, Cox C: Acute oral toxicity of butyl nitrite. J Appl Toxicol 1981; 1:30–31.
257. Smith M, Stair T, Rolnick MA: Butyl nitrite and a suicide attempt. Ann Intern Med 1980; 5:719–720.
258. Soderberg LSF, Barnett JB: Inhalation exposure to isobutyl nitrite inhibits macrophage tumoricidal activity and modulates inducible nitric oxide. J Leukoc Biol 1995; 57:135–140.
259. Gaworski CL, Aranyi C, Hall A 3d, et al: Prechronic inhalation toxicity studies of isobutyl nitrite. Fundam Appl Toxicol 1992; 19:169–175.
260. Haverkos HW, Kopstein AN, Wilson H, Drotman P: Nitrite inhalants: History, epidemiology and possible links to AIDS. Environ Health Perspect 1994; 102:858–861.
261. Seage GR 3d, Mayer KH, Horsburgh CR Jr, et al: The relation between nitrite inhalants, unprotected receptive anal intercourse, and the risk of human immunodeficiency virus infection. Am J Epidemiol 1992; 135:1–11.
262. Lewis DM, Lynch DW: Toxicity of inhaled isobutyl nitrite in BALB/c mice: Systemic and immunotoxic studies. NIDA Res Monogr 1988; 83:50–58.
263. Jacobs RF, Marmer DJ, Steele RW, Hogue TR: Cellular immunotoxicity of amyl nitrite. J Toxicol Clin Toxicol 1983; 20:421–449.
264. Donald JM, Hooper K, Hopenhayn-Rich C: Reproductive and developmental toxicity of toluene: A review. Environ Health Perspect 1991; 94:237–244.
265. Hersh JH, Podruch PE, Rogers G, Weisskopf B: Toluene embryopathy. J Pediatr 1985; 106:922–927.
266. Hersh JH: Toluene embryopathy: Two new cases. J Med Genet 1989; 26:333–337.
267. Brown-Woodman PD, Webster WS, Picker K, Ritchie HE: Embryotoxicity of xylene and toluene: An in vitro study. Ind Health 1991; 29:139–152.
268. Mazze RI, Fujinaga M, Baden JM: Halothane prevents nitrous oxide teratogenicity in Sprague-Dawley rats; folinic acid does not. Teratology 1988; 38:121–127.
269. Cagen SZ, Klaassen CD: Hepatoxicity of carbon tetrachloride in developing rats. Toxicol Appl Pharmacol 1979; 50:347–354.
270. Murray FJ, Schwetz BA, McBride JG, Staples RE: Toxicity of inhaled chloroform in pregnant mice and their offspring. Toxicol Appl Pharmacol 1979; 50:515–522.
271. Eskenazi B, Gaylord L, Bracken MB, Brown D: In utero exposure to organic solvents and human neurodevelopment. Dev Med Child Neurol 1988; 30:492–501.
272. Jumper-Thurman P, Beauvais F: Treatment of volatile solvent abusers. In Sharp CW, Spence R, Beauvais F (eds): A Volatile Research Agenda on Inhalant Abuse. NIDA Res Monogr. Washington, DC: U.S. Government Printing Office, 1992:203–213. DHHS publication (ADM) 93–3480.

CHAPTER

48

Nicotine Use Disorder

Susan J. Fiester

Nicotine Dependence

Definition

Dependence on nicotine was first included as a substance use disorder in the *Diagnostic and Statistical Manual of Mental Disorders,* Third Edition (DSM-III).[1] A specifier is used to designate the presence or absence of physiological dependence, depending on whether item 1 or 2 is present or whether both are absent. Further specifiers can be used for the course, for example, early full remission or sustained partial remission.

A tobacco withdrawal syndrome occurring after abstinence was also first classified as a disorder in DSM-III.[1] The current *Diagnostic and Statistical Manual of Mental Disor-*

DSM-IV Criteria 305.10

Nicotine Dependence

A pattern of nicotine use, leading to clinically significant impairment or distress, as manifested by at least three of seven criteria occurring at some time during a 12-month period:

(1) tolerance

(a) absence of nausea, dizziness, and other characteristic symptoms of nicotine despite using substantial amounts or

(b) a diminished effect with continued use of the same amount of nicotine

(2) withdrawal

(a) presence of a characteristic withdrawal syndrome (see nicotine withdrawal) or

(b) the use of the substance or related substances to relieve or avoid withdrawal symptoms, for example, smoking a cigarette immediately upon waking in the morning after a night of abstinence or immediately smoking a cigarette after disembarking from a long plane flight in order to relieve withdrawal symptoms

(3) use of nicotine in larger amounts or over a longer period than was intended, for example, using up a package of cigarettes faster than originally intended

(4) persistent desire or unsuccessful efforts to cut down or control nicotine use, for example, most smokers desire to stop smoking but numerous attempts are often required before successful cessation is achieved.

(5) a great deal of time spent in activities necessary to obtain the substance, in use of the substance, or in recovery from its effects, for example, chain smokers who spend a good deal of the day in smoking activity or smokers with work-site smoking restrictions who interrupt their work repeatedly for cigarette "breaks"

(6) important social occupational, or recreational activities given up or reduced because of substance use, for example, some smokers may have had to change jobs because of an inability to accommodate their smoking to workplace restrictions, although this would be uncommon

(7) continued use despite having a persistent or recurrent physical or psychological problem that is likely to have been caused or exacerbated by nicotine use, for example, continued smoking after the occurrence of a myocardial infarction or in the face of marital conflict related to the person's smoking

ders, Fourth Edition (DSM-IV), nicotine withdrawal syndrome describes a characteristic set of symptoms that develops after the abrupt cessation or a reduction in the use of nicotine products after at least several weeks of daily use and is accompanied by four of the following signs and symptoms: 1) dysphoria or depressed mood; 2) insomnia; 3) irritability, frustration, or anger; 4) anxiety; 5) difficulty concentrating; 6) restlessness or impatience; 7) decreased heart rate; and 8) increased appetite or weight gain.[2] The withdrawal symptoms must also cause clinically significant distress or impairment in social, occupational, or other important areas of functioning and must not be secondary to a general medical condition or be accounted for by another mental disorder.

Other symptoms may be associated with nicotine withdrawal, including craving for nicotine, which is a factor thought to be significant in relapse; a desire for sweets; and impaired performance on tasks requiring vigilance. To some extent, the degree of physiological dependence predicts the severity of the withdrawal syndrome and the difficulty that the individual will experience stopping smoking. The Fagerstrom Tolerance Questionnaire is an instrument that was developed to assess the degree of physical dependence on nicotine[3] (see section on evaluation and assessment). In addition to frank symptoms, other objective biological and physiological changes are associated with nicotine withdrawal, for example, generalized slowing of electroencephalographic activity, decreases in catecholamine and cortisol levels, changes in rapid eye movement, impairment on neuropsychological testing, and decreased metabolic rate.

Epidemiology

Nicotine addiction from cigarette smoking and smokeless tobacco use is the most prevalent form of chemical dependence in the United States.[3] Cigarette smoking is the primary preventable cause of morbidity and mortality in the United States, with an estimated 434,000 premature deaths occurring each year from smoking-related illnesses and 50,000 additional deaths occurring in nonsmokers from exposure to environmental tobacco smoke.[4, 5] Smoking is the cause of 90% of all lung cancers and 80% to 90% of all chronic obstructive pulmonary disease and is associated with a two times greater risk of death from stroke and coronary heart disease.[4] Smoking is also associated with an increased incidence of cancer at a number of other sites, including the larynx, oral cavity, esophagus, cervix, bladder, pancreas, and kidney and is associated with complications of pregnancy and negative effects on the fetus, including low birth weight.[4] Smoking has also been shown to have detrimental effects on nonsmokers exposed to tobacco smoke, particularly children.[4] Smoking causes 10 times the morbidity and mortality of all other substances of abuse combined and results in a total of $22 billion in direct medical costs for treating smoking-related illness and an estimated $43 billion in lost productivity per year.[6] The prevalence of smoking is increasing in most developing countries, whereas it is decreasing in most industrialized countries. In the United States, there has been increasing societal pressures for individuals to stop smoking; however, despite an increase in the proportion of smokers quitting, 25% of the U.S. population continues to smoke, with a lifetime prevalence of nicotine dependence of 20%.[4] Only 45% of the population has never smoked.

The prevalence of cigarette smoking is higher at lower socioeconomic levels. Slightly more males than females smoke, although more males than females are successful in stopping smoking. There is evidence that the consumption of cigarettes per smoker is increasing, leaving a more hard core group of smokers. There has also been a recent increase in the rate of smoking among adolescents, particularly in the number of teenage girls smoking. This is particularly alarming as smokers start smoking at an early age, with more than 60% of smokers beginning by age 14 years, and nearly all by age 18 years.

Comorbidity

Nicotine dependence and smoking are more common in individuals with comorbid psychiatric disorders than in the general population.[7, 8] Fifty-five percent to 90% of individuals with psychiatric disorders smoke versus approximately 25% of the general population. The prevalence of smoking is especially high in persons with schizophrenia, those with affective disorders, and individuals with alcoholism or other substance use disorders. The data are weaker for an association between anxiety disorders and smoking. Between 75% and 92% of persons with schizophrenia smoke.[8] The odds ratio for "ever smoked" is 4.7 in persons suffering from alcoholism, 2.4 for individuals with major depressive disorder, 1.8 for persons with agoraphobia, 1.6 for individuals with dysthymia, and 1.6 for patients with panic disorder.[8] Conversely, there is also evidence that affective, anxiety, and substance use disorders may be more common in individuals who smoke than in those who do not or in those who have never smoked.[8] Finally, there is evidence that up to 75% of smokers with a history of major depressive disorder acquire depressed mood during the first week of withdrawal versus only 30% of smokers with no depressive history and that the withdrawal syndrome may be more severe in smokers with a history of depression.[9] The presence of depressive symptoms during withdrawal is also associated with failed cessation attempts.[10, 11] Self-reported depressive symptoms during adolescence also predict later frequency and duration of smoking.[12] Several studies suggest a genetic predisposition to both nicotine dependence and co-occurring depression[13, 14] (see section on special considerations in treatment).

Etiology and Pathophysiology

Nicotine is the primary psychoactive agent in tobacco smoke and smokeless tobacco and has powerful addictive properties.[15] As an indication of the addictive potential of this substance, one third to one half of all children and adolescents who smoke one cigarette progress to become habitual users. Nicotine is considered by some to be a "gateway drug" to the use of other substances and is the first substance used by a large majority of alcohol and substance abusers.[16] Nicotine is readily absorbed in the lung from tobacco smoke or through the mucous membranes with smokeless tobacco. Nicotine enters the blood stream and is available to the brain within 7 to 9 seconds (shorter than with intravenous administration). Its peak effect occurs within 1 minute, and effects are present after a single puff of smoke. With a half-life of approximately 2 hours, the level of nicotine in the blood stream gradually accumulates during the day, dropping but persisting overnight.

Nicotine has a multitude of effects. It acts in two primary areas of the brain—the mesolimbic dopaminergic system, which is related to the euphoriant effects of the drug, and the locus caeruleus, which mediates stress reactions and vigilance and relates to the higher mental and cognitive functions. Centrally, there are specific nicotine receptor sites (the nicotinic cholinergic receptors) throughout the central nervous system in the hypothalamus, hippocampus, thalamus, midbrain, brain stem, and cerebral cortex. In addition, nicotine affects nearly all aspects of the endocrine-neuroendocrine system, including the catecholamine, serotonin, corticosteroid, and pituitary hormones. Its endocrine effects are mediated via the hypothalamic-pituitary axis and the adrenal medullary cortex. Centrally it causes release of acetylcholine, norepinephrine, serotonin, dopamine, vasopressin, growth hormone, corticotropin, cortisol, prolactin, and β-endorphins.

Nicotine has stimulant and depressive effects on both the central and the peripheral nervous systems. It also affects the cardiovascular system (increased heart rate and blood pressure), gastrointestinal system, and skeletal motor system. Nicotine alters brain energy metabolism and stimulates the peripheral cholinergic nervous system (sympathetic and parasympathetic). Through this variety of central and peripheral actions, nicotine improves mood and decreases anxiety, decreases distress in response to stressful stimuli, and decreases aggression; improves overall cognitive function and performance (improves reaction time, concentration, vigilance, and stimulus-processing capacity); and decreases the appetite for simple carbohydrates, decreases stress-induced eating, and increases resting metabolic rate.

Nicotine is a highly addictive substance that causes physical and psychological dependence that is similar to that of opiates and other substances of abuse.[4, 17, 18] It is highly reinforcing, leading to compulsive use.[19] Effects are related to dose, and tolerance to its actions develop rapidly, resulting in increased intake. Smokers adjust smoking behavior to regulate and maintain the level of nicotine in the blood stream. A withdrawal syndrome develops in response to reduced intake or total abstinence and involves both physiological and psychological symptoms.[15] Withdrawal symptoms overlap with those of alcohol and other substances of abuse.[20] In addition to the physiologically addictive aspects of nicotine, smoking is highly conditioned to cues in the environment.

Course and Natural History

Cessation attempts result in high relapse rates, with the relapse curve for smoking cessation paralleling that for opiates: 65% of those who stop smoking relapse in 3 months and another 10% relapse in 3 to 6 months.[21] The relapse rate is 80% by 1 year. Even after 1 to 2 years, 15% of those remaining abstinent relapse. Relapse can occur even after a long time, with a third of former smokers who are abstinent at 1 year eventually relapsing 5 to 10 years after cessation. Thus, nicotine dependence can be thought of as a chronic relapsing illness with a course of intermittent episodes alternating with periods of remission for most smokers.

Less than 25% of the individuals who have quit smoking are successful on their first attempt. Repeated failures are common before successful abstinence, with the average smoker attempting cessation two or three times before success. Prior attempts at quitting do not predict future failure, that is, there is no relationship between prior attempts at quitting and future success.

Table 48–1 Factors Predicting Success in Smoking Cessation
Reactivity (heart rate) to smoking-related cues
Smoking habits of family and friends
Support from spouses, partners, family members, friends
Deficits in social skills and assertiveness
Severity of withdrawal symptoms
Ability to cope with effects occurring in response to cues or triggers

Withdrawal symptoms are most severe within the first 1 to 3 days of abstinence, often continue for 3 to 4 weeks, and in some persons last for up to 6 months or longer.[11] Current depressive symptoms and a history of depression are predictors of relapse. Weight gain may also contribute to relapse, particularly in women. In contrast, several factors have been found to predict success at smoking cessation[22] (Table 48–1). Predictors include individual factors, manifestations of the addiction such as severity of withdrawal, and social and environmental circumstances.

Treatment of nicotine addiction with resultant abstinence can result in highly beneficial health effects.[23] Short-term effects (within a month) include a significant reduction in respiratory symptoms and respiratory infections such as influenza, pneumonia, and bronchitis. Excess risk of death from coronary heart disease is reduced after 1 year and continues to decline over time. In patients with coronary heart disease, smoking cessation decreases the risk of recurrent myocardial infarction and cardiovascular death by 50%. The mortality rate from all causes returns to that of a person who has never smoked by 10 to 15 years of abstinence. Pulmonary function can also return to normal if chronic obstructive changes have not already occurred at the time of cessation.

Evaluation and Assessment

Before formal intervention is undertaken to assist the patient with smoking cessation, it is important to perform a comprehensive evaluation to determine the physiological, psychological, and behavioral factors that are most significant in the initiation and maintenance of the smoking and nicotine addiction. Comprehensive evaluation of the patient should involve an assessment of the pattern of smoking (timing, location, circumstances) and the degree of nicotine dependence, including the number of cigarettes smoked per day, the nicotine yield of the brand of cigarettes, and the number of pack years (number of packs smoked per day multiplied by the number of years smoked). The degree of dependence can be assessed with the Fagerstrom Tolerance Questionnaire, which predicts the severity of withdrawal.[3] It assesses factors such as smoking soon after awakening, smoking when ill, difficulty refraining from smoking, the degree to which the first cigarette of the day is the most difficult to give up, and smoking more in the morning than in the afternoon. In addition, urinary, blood, or saliva cotinine levels can be obtained to assess the amount of nicotine ingested (cotinine is a primary metabolite of nicotine), although these tests are costly and results often are not obtained quickly enough to be clinically useful. Tests for carbon monoxide levels, which are less costly and can be obtained in a few minutes, can also be used to assess nicotine intake or monitor for relapse. Carbon monoxide levels also predict the severity of nicotine withdrawal. This is important because a high degree of nicotine dependence may be an indicator for using a nicotine replacement strategy.

A history of prior cessation attempts should include the nature of prior treatments, length of abstinence, timing of relapse, and factors specifically related to relapse (e.g., environmental or interpersonal triggers). A history of specific withdrawal symptoms and their severity and duration is critical, as is an assessment of the smoker's social and environmental contexts, for example, whether other household members smoke and available family and social supports.

An assessment should be made of the person's reasons for quitting and his or her motivation and commitment. The individual's stage of readiness for stopping smoking is also important, that is, whether the person is not yet seriously considering stopping smoking (precontemplation), is seriously considering stopping (contemplation), has begun to think about the necessary steps to stop smoking (preparation), or is actually attempting to stop smoking (action).[24] Knowledge about smoking and nicotine dependence is also important to assess because deficits in knowledge and information can have a deleterious effect on smoking cessation attempts.

Assessment of the psychiatric history is also essential. Numerous studies have shown the significance of depression in relation to smoking. Studies have shown increased prevalence rates of cigarette smoking in patients with a variety of psychiatric disorders, such as major depressive disorder, schizophrenia, and alcohol and substance abuse (see section on comorbidity). The presence of these comorbid disorders may also make successful smoking cessation less likely (see section on special features influencing treatment).

Assessing the patient for a history of current alcohol or other substance use is also important, as the prevalence of smoking in persons with alcoholism as well as in other substance abusers is much higher than that in the general population. It may also be more difficult for individuals with current or prior substance use and abuse or dependence to stop smoking, as there is evidence that persons with alcoholism and other substance abusers start smoking earlier and are more physiologically dependent on nicotine as assessed by several factors.[25] In addition, the use of alcohol or other substances may be intimately linked to smoking cigarettes and can serve as a strong trigger for craving and ultimate relapse.

A careful medical history should also be obtained. The presence of significant tobacco-related medical illness can serve as crucial leverage to help motivate the individual to attempt cessation. Current medications and medical conditions may also be important considerations in determining the approach to cessation, especially with regard to pharmacotherapy. The individual should be assessed for pulmonary symptoms and signs (cough), and if there is a long history of significant nicotine use, pulmonary function tests should be considered. The presence of significant cardiovascular disease, especially a history of recent myocardial infarction, is especially relevant to planning psychopharmacological interventions. If the individual is taking psychotropic drugs, plasma levels may need to be evaluated because smoking accelerates the metabolism of a number of drugs, and cessation can increase blood levels of medications, including antidepressants and antipsychotic agents.[26, 27] This can result in significant changes in clinical status or the occurrence of side effects or adverse effects.[26]

Overall Approach to Treatment

The general approach to the treatment of nicotine dependence must be viewed as having three primary components: physiological, psychological, and behavioral. The physiological dependence has already been described and parallels the characteristics of other physiologically addicting substances (compulsive use, dose-related effects, rapid tolerance leading to increased intake, and the presence of a withdrawal syndrome). Psychological dependence involves the reasons a person smokes, for example, to regulate affect, to improve mood and sense of well-being, to satisfy craving; and to provide stimulation and relaxation.[27] The behavioral component involves environmental and social cues that become associated with smoking cigarettes, for example, drinking coffee or alcohol, talking on the telephone, taking a work break, or smoking at parties or social functions. The direct beneficial effects of nicotine on, for example, mood become highly positively reinforcements, as do the associated behaviors or activities, which can act as powerful triggers for relapse during attempts at cessation.

The importance of each of these factors in initiating and maintaining smoking can vary considerably in different individuals. As a result, smoking cessation interventions should be tailored to the individual and his or her particular circumstances. This may be one reason why "one size fits all" generic treatment interventions have had such a low success rate. It must also be kept in mind that nicotine dependence is as complex in its components and determinants as other addictions and that more comprehensive multicomponent treatments may be required for the achievement of successful abstinence.

Treatment

It is apparent from prevalence data that many smokers have successfully attempted smoking cessation on their own.[28] Seventy-five percent to 80% of smokers report a desire to stop smoking, with 35% attempting to stop each year. Most of these individuals relapse relatively quickly, however, and the overall rate of smoking cessation in the general population is only 3% to 4% per year. Despite this, 50% of regular smokers are eventually able to quit smoking. More than 90% of smokers quit without the assistance of professionals or formal programs. The advantage of quitting without professional intervention is the decreased expense and time commitment. The primary unassisted method of smoking cessation is precipitous cessation (cold turkey), which is used by more than 80% of smokers. Some smokers attempt to limit intake, taper the number of cigarettes smoked, or switch to a reduced tar or nicotine brand. Special filters and holders are also available to decrease the amount of smoke that is available from a cigarette. These methods are usually unsuccessful because smokers have been shown to alter smoking behavior by increasing the frequency and volume or duration of the inhalation to ensure maintenance of adequate blood levels of nicotine to prevent withdrawal symptoms.[29, 30] Some smokers use nonprescription pills that are analogues of nicotine, such as lobeline, to help manage or prevent withdrawal symptoms. These agents have not been shown to be effective in controlled studies.[31]

Only about 10% of those who attempt cessation are ultimately successful. Even smokers with major health conditions, such as chronic obstructive pulmonary disease or cardiovascular disease, often have a difficult time attaining and maintaining abstinence. Numerous psychological and pharmacological treatments have been developed to assist with smoking cessation. Psychosocial approaches include a wide variety of interventions such as nicotine fading, aversive techniques, and cognitive and/or behavioral therapies. A wide variety of pharmacotherapeutic treatments have also been developed to assist with withdrawal and maintenance of abstinence, including nicotine replacement therapy and nonspecific therapies to mitigate withdrawal symptoms.

Psychosocial intervention alone, pharmacotherapy alone, or combined approaches may be used. Given patients' preferences and current concerns with cost-effectiveness, less costly single-modality interventions are often used initially, whereas more costly multimodal interventions are often reserved for persons in whom cessation attempts have failed. Whether failure with unaided or minimal intervention attempts may have a negative effect on future cessation attempts is not known; however, some research suggests that with each repeated cessation attempt, the person gains additional knowledge and experience that may contribute to success in future cessation attempts.

Algorithms for smoking cessation involving stepped care have been developed.[32] For smokers not yet ready to quit, use of interventions to increase motivation and presentation of information about treatments to assist with cessation are appropriate. Discussing reasons for the person to consider quitting—for example, health consequences for that specific individual—and the factors that may have prevented an attempt is important. Written materials and brief advice from the physician are methods of providing such information and increasing motivation. Preparation for quitting may include self-monitoring or keeping a diary of smoking behavior, planning rewards for successful abstinence, and making a list of reasons for and potential benefits of quitting. Sources of social support should also be identified.

When a smoker is ready for a cessation attempt, a "quit date" should be selected. After cessation, close monitoring should occur during the early period of abstinence. Before the quit date, the person should be encouraged to explore and organize social support for the self-attempt. Plans to minimize cues associated with smoking (e.g., avoiding circumstances likely to contribute to relapse) are important, as is considering alternative coping behaviors for situations with a higher potential for relapse. A telephone or face-to-face follow-up during the first few days after cessation is critical because this is the time that withdrawal symptoms are most severe, with 65% of patients relapsing by 1 week. A follow-up face-to-face meeting within 1 to 2 weeks allows a discussion of problems that have occurred (e.g., difficulties managing craving) and serves as an opportunity to provide reinforcement for ongoing abstinence. Even after the early period of abstinence, periodic telephone or face-to-face contacts can provide continued encouragement to maintain abstinence, allow problems with maintaining abstinence to be addressed, and give feedback regarding the ongoing health benefits of abstinence from cigarettes.

If an initial attempt at cessation with information and brief advice from the physician has been unsuccessful, pharmacotherapy may be used unless contraindications are present or unless the person has had few or no significant withdrawal symptoms. The two most common approaches are nicotine replacement (transdermal patch or nicotine polacrilex gum) and clonidine (oral or transdermal patch). If a cessation attempt with pharmacotherapy is unsuccessful, group behavioral therapy should be added. This is often available through organizations such as the American Cancer Society or the American Heart Association or through local hospitals that provide health prevention and public education programs. If pharmacotherapy is unacceptable or contraindicated, behavioral therapy alone should be provided. Failure with pharmacotherapy or behavioral therapy alone suggests the need for more detailed in-depth assessment and more intensive, multimodal interventions, which are described in the section on repeated relapse.

Pharmacological Intervention

The numerous parallels between nicotine addiction and other addictions—such as the presence of a withdrawal syndrome and the use of pharmacotherapy for replacement and/or managing withdrawal—have formed the basis for the development of a variety of pharmacotherapeutic interventions for treating nicotine dependence.

Four different approaches with different foci have been used for the pharmacological treatment of nicotine addiction (Table 48–2). Of the four pharmacotherapeutic interventions, nicotine replacement is most widely used. Nicotine replacement is also indicated in the presence of a high degree of physiological dependence. The intent is to substitute a safer, medically prescribed substance for nicotine and then to taper the substance in a manner that prevents or minimizes withdrawal. This approach is similar to the use of benzodiazepines to treat alcohol withdrawal syndrome or methadone substitution and taper in the treatment of heroin addiction. The substituted nicotine initially prevents significant withdrawal symptoms that may lead to relapse during the early period of smoking cessation. The substituted nicotine is then gradually tapered and discontinued. Replacement produces a lower overall plasma level of nicotine than that experienced with smoking. Replacement not only avoids the strongly reinforcing peaks in plasma level but also prevents the emergence of withdrawal symptoms by maintaining the nicotine plasma level above a threshold.

Table 48–2 Approaches to the Pharmacological Treatment of Nicotine Addiction
Nicotine replacement or substitution (agonist administration)
Blockade therapy (antagonist administration)
Nonspecific attenuation therapy
Deterrent therapy

The earliest nicotine substitute, approved in 1984, was nicotine polacrilex gum, which slowly releases nicotine from an ion exchange resin. The nicotine is absorbed through the buccal mucous membranes. Placebo-controlled studies of nicotine gum treatment in smoking cessation clinics show a doubling of abstinence rates[33] with the 4-mg dose possibly providing a better outcome than the 2-mg dose for persons who are highly nicotine dependent.[34] Nicotine gum is more effective when used in conjunction with some type of psychosocial intervention, particularly behavioral therapy. Used with only brief advice in general medical practice, it increases abstinence by only about 30%.[33] Outcome is more positive when a definite schedule for gum use is prescribed—for example, one piece of gum per hour while awake—than when used on an as-needed basis.[35, 36] Some studies suggest that it is also more effective when used for a longer period, for example, greater than 3 months.[35] Tapering may be necessary after 4 to 6 months of use, especially for individuals using higher total daily doses of gum. Nicotine gum may be especially appropriate for individuals who identify oral stimulation as an important aspect or function of their smoking.

Nicotine polacrilex gum is contraindicated in patients with tempormandibular joint problems, dental problems, and dentures as well as in patients who have recently experienced a myocardial infarction. Nicotine gum requires a highly motivated patient and a good deal of time in instructing the patient in proper use of the gum. Many individuals find the gum difficult to learn to use properly. It may not be used in temporal proximity to ingestion of acidic substances such as coffee, soda, or orange juice because the acidic environment in the mouth interferes with its release and absorption. Specifics of the proper use of nicotine gum are provided by Schneider.[37] Side effects and adverse effects include sore mouth and tongue, mouth ulcers, hiccups, jaw ache, gastrointestinal symptoms (flatulence, indigestion, nausea), anorexia, and palpitations. Nicotine substitution continues to expose the cardiovascular system to the effects of nicotine and has pharmacodynamic interactions with other medications, for example, theophylline, propranolol, imipramine, and caffeine. In addition, some individuals may become dependent on the nicotine gum, with approximately 6% to 9% of those using gum to assist with cessation still using gum at 1 year.[38]

A more recently developed form of nicotine replacement therapy is the transdermal delivery system (transdermal nicotine patch). The transdermal patch provides continual sustained release of nicotine, which is absorbed through the skin. This form of nicotine replacement more than doubles the 1-year cessation rate.[39] There appears to be a dose-response relationship, with the patients receiving higher doses attaining higher cessation rates. However, in contrast to the use of nicotine gum, in which a high level of nicotine dependence predicts better response, smokers with low nicotine dependence and those with high nicotine dependence have equally good outcomes with the use of the transdermal nicotine patch. In fact, one study showed that the use of a double dose of transdermal nicotine provided a better outcome in highly nicotine-dependent smokers.

The transdermal patch has several advantages when compared with nicotine gum. It is more effective than gum when combined with brief advice from the physician. It is also more reliable in decreasing nicotine craving, possibly as a result of the higher, more constant level of nicotine maintained. It also completely eliminates the conditioning of repeated nicotine use, which remains present with the use of nicotine gum. Compliance rates are higher because it involves once-daily dosing. It can also be used more discreetly and can be used despite dental or temporomandibular joint problems. Specifics on the proper use of transdermal nicotine are provided by Gourley.[40]

Transdermal nicotine is well tolerated, although about 25% of patients have significant local skin irritation or erythema, and 10% discontinue the patch because of intolerable side effects. Other side effects include sleep problems with the 24-hour patches. There may be less reliable dosing secondary to a highly variable rate of absorption. Toxicity has occurred with serious consequences in a few cases in which smokers have continued heavy cigarette smoking while using the transdermal nicotine patch. However, transdermal nicotine may cause less activation of blood coagulation and have less impact on the sympathetic nervous system than nicotine polacrilex gum; therefore, it may be preferable in the presence of cardiac disease.[41, 42] One study found that it could be safely used in patients with stable coronary artery disease.[43] Both forms of nicotine replacement appear to delay rather than reduce weight gain after cessation.[44]

Both nicotine polacrilex gum and transdermal nicotine are effective when used alone without psychosocial intervention, although cessation rates are improved with the addition of even brief advice and are doubled with the addition of behavioral therapy. The use of either form of nicotine replacement has not been associated with an increased relapse rate after cessation when compared with placebo.[45] Some experts suggest using nicotine gum concurrently with transdermal nicotine on an as-needed basis to cover emergent withdrawal symptoms or craving not controlled by replacement from the transdermal patch, whereas others suggest simply increasing the dose of the transdermal patch or using gum initially and then switching to the patch.[40, 46] Combining transdermal nicotine and nicotine gum increases the potential for significant side effects.

Several other forms of nicotine replacement are being developed, including a nicotine aerosol provided through an inhaler (smokeless cigarette) and a nicotine nasal spray. Nicotine from the nasal spray is rapidly absorbed and produces a higher nicotine blood level than does transdermal nicotine or gum. A major concern about the nasal spray is the potential for abuse because it replicates smoking's repeated administration of nicotine, resulting in reinforcing peaks in the plasma level of the drug. In support of this concern are two studies that found that a significant proportion of patients remaining abstinent after 1 year were still using the spray.[47] In addition, some individuals report a "euphoria" from the use of the spray. Use of the inhaler or spray might be reserved as a second-level treatment for persons who fail at attempts with other forms of nicotine replacement (gum, patch). Alternatively, it might be used as a transitional form of nicotine replacement before the use of nicotine gum or transdermal nicotine.

The nicotine inhaler provides nicotine through a cartridge that must be "puffed." Absorption is primarily through the oropharyngeal mucosa. Although the blood level of nicotine is lower than with other forms of nicotine replacement, the inhaler has been shown to be effective, with a 1-year cessation rate of 15%.[48] Side effects of the inhaler and spray include local irritation, obviousness of use, and the need for multiple dosing. Finally, nicotine tablets for buccal absorption are being developed; however, neither these nor the inhaler or spray is currently available in the United States. One other substance, lobeline, which is a weak partial nicotine receptor agonist, has not been shown to be effective.

The second pharmacological approach to treating nicotine addiction involves blockade therapy or antagonist administration. An agent is administered that blocks the reinforcing properties of nicotine in the same way that naltrexone blocks opiate effects. The advantage of this approach over nicotine replacement is that it does not provide the continued reinforcing effects of nicotine and does not continue exposing the person to the potentially damaging effects of nicotine. Several agents have been used, but mecamylamine, which has central and peripheral blockade effects, is the only agent that has been shown to be effective to date. Although it initially increases smoking behavior because it decreases the effective level of nicotine available from smoking, overall it mitigates the reinforcing properties of nicotine.

Mecamylamine has significant side effects secondary to ganglionic blockade, including orthostatic hypotension and possible serious adverse effects such as ileus and urinary retention. Acceptability is low, especially in heavy smokers, because it requires the patient to relinquish the reinforcing effects of nicotine and potentially experience increased withdrawal symptoms. It has been used primarily to assist with withdrawal and may be most appropriate for light smokers when significant withdrawal is not anticipated or in smokers whose medical problems preclude continuation of nicotine, especially those with cardiovascular disease or peripheral vascular disease. Antagonists may be more useful after the initial period of withdrawal to assist with continued abstinence in the same way that naltrexone is used to help maintain abstinence in treating heroin dependence. One study found the combined use of mecamylamine and nicotine replacement to be more effective than nicotine replacement alone.

The third pharmacological approach involves nonspecific attenuation therapy. In this approach, a pharmacological agent is used to mitigate abstinence symptoms in a manner similar to the use of clonidine to reduce withdrawal symptoms in opioid dependence. The agent most commonly used has been clonidine in both oral and transdermal forms. Clonidine is an antihypertensive drug with central sympatholytic activity. Despite this activity, it is unclear why clonidine is effective, as there is no evidence of increased sympathetic activity in nicotine withdrawal. Meta-analysis shows that the odds ratio for successful cessation with clonidine alone versus placebo is 1.7 (no behavioral therapy); it is 4.2 with the addition of behavioral therapy.[49] Studies have shown clonidine to be particularly effective in decreasing craving, irritation, and restlessness.[50] Clonidine appears to be more effective in women than in men and may be less effective in patients with a history of major depressive disorder.[50, 51]

Clonidine is advantageous in that its use allows the discontinuation of nicotine administration. This may be preferable for some individuals who are philosophically opposed to nicotine replacement or for whom continued nicotine administration is contraindicated. Potential side effects and adverse effects include sedation, dry mouth, and hypotension. The clonidine patch provides a steady-state blood level with decreased side effects and increased compliance when compared with oral administration. Oral clonidine may be used together with transdermal clonidine to cover emergent withdrawal symptoms, but blood pressure must be carefully monitored to ensure that hypotension does not occur. Smaller doses are indicated in the outpatient setting because of the risk of hypotension. β-Blockers, such as metoprolol, oxprenolol, and propranolol, have been studied because of their potential for decreasing anxiety; however, to date they have not been found effective in improving abstinence rates.[31]

Buspirone, a nonsedative, nonaddictive, nonbenzodiazepine antianxiety agent, has been shown to decrease craving, anxiety, and fatigue during withdrawal from nicotine. Although in some studies it failed to reduce withdrawal symptoms, in other studies it significantly increased the cessation rate.[31] It has few side effects—in particular it does not cause weight gain; however, therapeutic effects may not occur for 2 to 3 weeks after initiation of therapy. Thus, buspirone administration may need to start before an attempt at smoking cessation, with the dosage titrated upward for several weeks. One current study is investigating the utility of transdermal nicotine replacement combined with buspirone. Equivocal results have been found for the use of sedative-hypnotic agents and anxiolytic agents such as alprazolam, meprobamate, and diazepam in the treatment of nicotine addiction.[39] Studies of naloxone and naltrexone have also shown equivocal results.[31]

Antidepressants have been used in an attempt to attenuate withdrawal symptoms, to treat or prevent emergent depressive symptoms or episodes in the early phase of cessation, and to prevent relapse of depressive episodes in patients with a history of depression. Antidepressants may provide significant benefits in special populations of patients with current or prior major depressive disorder or dysthymic disorder or with current depressive symptoms when these factors predict a poor outcome. Given that negative affect has been shown to be the most common antecedent of a smoking relapse, this approach appears promising.[52] If antidepressants are used, pretreatment is necessary because the benefit of the medication may not be apparent for 1 to 3 weeks.

Studies of specific antidepressants showed that doxepin decreased craving and cigarette use and increases abstinence.[53] Imipramine was found to be effective in a small group of patients with a history of major depressive disorder.[54] Administration of nortriptyline and fluoxetine resulted in smoking cessation in nearly all subjects without recurrence of depression.[55] However, side effects of the tricyclic antidepressants include increased appetite, weight gain, and sedation. Bupropion, a novel antidepressant with dopaminergic activity, was also shown to be effective in increasing the cessation rate in persons who are not depressed (28% versus 4% at 12 weeks).[56] It was well tolerated and did not produce weight gain. Tryptophan has also shown positive results.[57] Use of selective serotonin reuptake inhibitors could avoid the side effect of weight gain if these drugs are found to be effective. Studies of zimeldine and citalopram (selective serotonin reuptake inhibitors not approved for use in the United States), which are used to treat persons suffering from alcoholism, showed no effects on smoking.[58]

Stimulants have been studied because of their potential to improve vigilance and possibly reduce withdrawal symptoms, some of which are similar to symptoms of attention-deficit/hyperactivity disorder. Hughes' review of these studies suggested equivocal results.[31] Because increased appetite and weight gain commonly occur with cessation of smoking, trials of anorectic drugs such as fenfluramine and phenylpropanolamine have been carried out.[59, 60] Both drugs have been effective in reducing weight gain after cessation of smoking and improving abstinence rates. One further nonspecific pharmacotherapeutic approach has been the use of agents (citric acid or other aerosols) to induce sensory effects similar to those of smoking such as a "throat scratch." This approach decreased craving but resulted in no increase in abstinence rates. Finally, Hughes[31] reviewed several other approaches such as alkalinization of the urine with sodium bicarbonate, the use of glucose and corticotropin, and the use of anticholinergic agents. Few controlled trials have been carried out, although results in uncontrolled studies for some approaches are promising.

The fourth pharmacological approach to treating nicotine dependence and withdrawal is deterrent therapy or use of a drug to produce an aversive effect if nicotine is used, similar to the use of disulfiram with alcohol dependence. The primary drug used has been silver acetate in a gum or lozenge preparation. If a cigarette is smoked, sulfite salts are produced when silver acetate contacts the sulfides in tobacco smoke, producing an unpleasant taste. Unfortunately, there is not an acceptable preparation, as the existing gum has a short duration of action.

Combined or serial pharmacotherapeutic approaches may also be beneficial, especially in more difficult to treat cases of nicotine addiction. Examples of such combinations include the following:

- Nicotine replacement (gum and/or transdermal) combined with clonidine to cover any emergent withdrawal symptoms[4] (no controlled studies of this approach to date)
- Pretreatment with an antidepressant followed by the use of nicotine replacement to cover acute withdrawal symptoms
- Pretreatment with an antidepressant, with clonidine added for acute withdrawal symptoms

The issue of whether longer term pharmacotherapy is beneficial in improving cessation rates remains unresolved. There may be some smokers who are unable to stop smoking without ongoing nicotine replacement, similar to individuals dependent on heroin who must be maintained on methadone. Although long-term use of nicotine patches and nicotine polacrilex gum has not been approved, successful maintenance in smokers who have chronic relapses would significantly reduce a number of the serious health risks associated with smoking, although it would continue to expose individuals to the effects of nicotine.

Ongoing maintenance antidepressant treatment for a time may also be necessary for some individuals with a history of serious depressive illness or for those who have had significant depressive symptoms emerge on cessation that do not improve with time.

Table 48–3 Psychosocial Interventions for the Treatment of Nicotine Addiction

Self-help
Brief advice from the physician
Nicotine fading
Aversive techniques
Cognitive-behavioral therapies
Social support
Hypnosis
Acupuncture

Psychosocial Treatments

An incredible variety of psychosocial interventions has been developed to assist with the cessation of smoking. A number of the more commonly used psychosocial treatments are reviewed in Table 48–3. Psychosocial interventions, particularly behavioral therapy, have been shown to increase abstinence rates significantly.[45] However, only 7% of smokers attempting to quit smoking are willing to participate in behavioral therapy.[45] In addition, it is more expensive than pharmacotherapy and more labor-intensive.

Self-help

Some geographical areas have Smokers Anonymous groups that are structured similarly to the Alcoholics Anonymous or Narcotics Anonymous groups. The Smokers Anonymous groups are based on the 12-step approach to recovery from addictions. No formal controlled studies of the benefits of this intervention have been carried out. In addition, self-help written materials can play an important role in educating patients about the negative health effects of nicotine, the benefits of quitting, and the nature of the addiction.

Brief or Minimal Physician-Delivered Interventions (Physicians' Advice)

Even a brief face-to-face intervention by a physician in getting a patient to quit smoking can increase the likelihood of cessation 2- to 10-fold.[61] Physicians can inquire about a patient's smoking status, urge the patient to stop smoking, and spend a brief time counseling the patient about how to stop. Multiple follow-up interventions, even telephone contacts by nonphysician staff, can further improve the cessation rate. Resources are available to assist physicians in providing effective antismoking interventions, which can even be used by those not highly skilled in counseling. Physicians' advice appears to be most successful with patients having a serious medical problem or specific medical reason for quitting (e.g., pregnancy or congestive heart disease). In addition, because an estimated 70% of smokers in the United States visit their physicians at least once a year, an important opportunity exists for providing this type of smoking cessation intervention.

Nicotine Fading

Nicotine fading involves switching to a brand of cigarettes with lower nicotine and gradually reducing the number of cigarettes smoked on a schedule over time, usually several weeks. After successful reduction to a significantly lower level of nicotine, smoking is discontinued. Self-monitoring is usually involved in this process.

Aversive Techniques

The most commonly used aversive techniques are rapid smoking and smoke holding. Rapid smoking involves inhaling cigarette smoke every 6 seconds until the smoker becomes ill. Several repetitions over several sessions are usually planned. Smoke holding involves holding smoke in the mouth and continuing to breathe. Both techniques have been found effective and safe even in patients with medical complications from smoking. A limiting factor in the use of these techniques is acceptability by the patient.

Cognitive-Behavioral Therapy

Self-monitoring involves the identification of affective, cognitive, and environmental cues that trigger smoking behavior. Contingency contracting involves developing rewards for not smoking or punishment for smoking, or both, in which the patient participates in the development of the reward-punishment scheme. As an example, a patient might give an amount of money to a friend or person overseeing the treatment. The money would be returned only if the patient successfully stopped smoking for a prescribed period; otherwise, the money would be forfeited.

Stimulus control strategies involve removing or altering cues that have been strongly associated with smoking, for example, avoiding certain situations that are likely to increase craving or trigger smoking. Cue extinction involves repeated exposure of the individual to cues or triggers associated with smoking. Eventually the cue or trigger is no longer associated with smoking. Coping skills training involves the development of skills to manage situations without resorting to smoking. Cognitive approaches involve specific techniques such as reframing or restricting thoughts related to smoking or replacing thoughts about smoking with thoughts of another content. Use of techniques such as assertiveness training can contribute to improved coping.

Relapse prevention training involves the development of problem-solving skills to assist the person in coping with situations or emotions that might be likely to precipitate relapse as well as the development of alternative behaviors appropriate for high-risk situations. Individuals learn to manage an abstinence violation ("slip" or "lapse") in a way that prevents a relapse to smoking. Discussing ways of managing withdrawal symptoms, such as sleep disturbance and irritability, can also be useful, and if performed in a group setting can allow individuals to learn from others struggling with cessation. Stress management and relaxation training are often also used as adjunctive interventions. These interventions can be provided individually or in a group setting. Problems with the group format include a generally low compliance rate, lack of availability of groups in all geographical areas or at a given point in time, and patient preference not to participate in a group intervention. Problems with the individual format include higher cost and the need for a larger number of counselors per population. One controlled trial found that a cognitive intervention focused on enhancing the regulation of affect produced a better outcome in smokers with a history of major depressive disorder suggesting some potential benefit of providing more expensive, time-intensive interventions to specific populations of patients.[62]

Social Support

Despite the fact that there has been little controlled research examining whether psychosocial intervention with spouses and significant others or families can increase abstinence rates, overall social support for individuals who are attempting to stop smoking appears to improve the outcome. Others in the smoker's immediate family or social circle can be involved in their treatment through education about appropriate supportive behaviors.

Hypnosis

Studies suggest that hypnosis has little more than a weak positive effect on outcome in smoking cessation.[63, 64] In addition, not all people are hypnotically suggestive; therefore, the technique may have limited applicability, availability, and acceptability.

Acupuncture

A meta-analysis of studies on the effect of acupuncture shows no evidence of efficacy on the outcome of smoking cessation.[65] Positive effects likely represent a placebo effect related to the patient's expectations.

Combined Psychosocial and Psychopharmacological Therapies

A review by Hughes,[45] who performed a meta-analysis of existing studies of combined psychosocial and pharmacological treatments for smoking cessation, found that the addition of nicotine gum to psychosocial therapies resulted in a 60% to 80% increase in abstinence, whereas addition of transdermal nicotine produced a 40% to 80% increase in abstinence. Addition of psychosocial therapies to nicotine replacement (gum or transdermal) resulted in a 60% to 80% increase in abstinence with nicotine gum and an odds ratio of 3.1 for transdermal nicotine. Studies of combined nicotine gum and psychosocial treatment showed additive, possibly synergistic positive, effects. No combined studies with transdermal nicotine have been carried out.

The odds ratio for successful cessation with clonidine alone versus placebo is 1.7. Adding clonidine to a behavioral therapy regimen resulted in an odds ratio of 4.2 when compared with placebo. No studies have examined the effect of adding psychosocial therapy to clonidine. One study combined psychosocial and psychopharmacological therapy using tranquilizers, placebo, and no drug conditions crossed with group, individual, and no contact psychosocial conditions. This study found that psychosocial intervention was effective, tranquilizers were not, and the combination produced no increased benefit.[66] In regard to which modalities of psychosocial therapy are more effective, a traditional psychotherapy group plus nicotine gum in one study

Table 48–4 Effectiveness of Smoking Cessation Interventions

Intervention	Rate
No professional or formal intervention	5%
Physicians' advice	10%
Nicotine polacrilex	15%
Transdermal nicotine	20%
Behavioral therapy	30%
Transdermal nicotine or nicotine polacrilex plus behavioral therapy	35%

From Hughes JR: Behavioral support programs for smoking cessation. Mod Med 1994; 62:22–27.

produced a better outcome than did a didactic group (28% versus 17%).[67]

A summary of overall cessation rates was compiled by Hughes[68]; it demonstrated that these rates are highest for combined psychosocial and psychopharmacological interventions, although transdermal nicotine alone and behavioral therapy alone resulted in substantial success in smoking cessation (Table 48–4). Essentially, nicotine replacement therapy, particularly transdermal nicotine, doubles the long-term abstinence rate, whereas behavioral therapy doubles the effectiveness of transdermal nicotine.[45]

Problems in Management: Repeated Relapse

Although generally effective treatments have been developed for smoking cessation, there are few research data to support the selection of specific treatments or modalities for specific patients with nicotine dependence or to determine the timing and duration of interventions. Questions regarding treatment specificity become even more complicated when treating smokers who have had multiple unsuccessful attempts at cessation with repeated relapse, those who have been totally unable to stop smoking, or those who are able to maintain abstinence for only brief periods. Treatment algorithms applied to the general population of smokers may have little relevance to the smoker who suffers chronic relapses. Given the lack of data regarding treatment specificity, the key to planning interventions with smokers who have had repeated relapses is a comprehensive reevaluation to determine the unique set of factors related to repeated relapse in a given individual. This analysis can serve as the basis for the development of an individualized comprehensive treatment program.

In approaching evaluation and treatment planning, it is important not to view the smoker as a "failure" but rather to understand how failure to adequately understand the illness of nicotine dependence as it presents in the particular patient has resulted in ineffective treatment with a poor outcome. Although it might seem obvious that treatment in smokers who have had repeated relapses would require more intensive interventions or multiple-component interventions, or both, this assumes that prior single interventions were adequate in intensity and properly provided and that there was adequate compliance so that the person received an adequate "dose" of treatment. If these standards have not been met, treating with a previously used single therapy and ensuring the adequacy of all aspects of the treatment may be appropriate. For example, a patient may have relapsed despite being treated with nicotine polacrilex gum because an intermittent dosing schedule was prescribed or because of improper use of the gum, both of which resulted in an inadequate overall dose of nicotine replacement followed by withdrawal symptoms and relapse. Such a patient might be treated with transdermal nicotine to improve compliance and ensure a stable plasma level of nicotine to prevent withdrawal symptoms. Alternatively, the dose of nicotine the patient was prescribed may have been too high, leading to adverse effects, discontinuation of the transdermal patch, and subsequent relapse. Providing a lower dose that is tolerated may lead to successful cessation with a single previously used treatment. An inappropriate single treatment may also have been provided, as in the case of a male patient treated with clonidine for the management of withdrawal symptoms when research data show that clonidine is effective primarily in women. A single treatment may have been inappropriate in that it was focused on an area that is not critical, whereas an area critical to the maintenance of abstinence has been overlooked. A patient without a high degree of physiological dependence on nicotine may have been treated with nicotine replacement while the fact that her husband is a heavy smoker was not addressed. A future cessation attempt might be preceded by conjoint sessions with the spouse to motivate him to also stop smoking, to educate him about the psychological effects of smoking and the behavioral changes that may accompany cessation, and to enlist his aid in providing a more supportive environment for cessation (e.g., not smoking at home or in the presence of the patient).

Even with multiple interventions, an important aspect of relapse may have been overlooked. For example, both nicotine replacement and group therapy may have been provided to a woman who then made a conscious decision to start smoking again to lose the weight gained during the cessation attempt. In this case, educating the woman about the effects of nicotine on metabolism and providing an individual cognitive intervention to assist her in reframing and accepting the weight gain as a return to a normal weight that was abnormally lowered by nicotine might make a critical difference in the success of the cessation attempt. Planning to address weight loss at a future time after abstinence has been solidly established is an example of how serial treatment interventions might be used successfully. Alternative modalities might also be appropriate. For example, a group behavioral therapy might have been prescribed for a person who was so anxious and uncomfortable in the presence of others that he or she avoided attending many of the sessions and was unable to participate even when present. Providing individual sessions in which key elements of the behavioral therapy are presented and discussed might lead to more successful cessation.

The degree of aggressiveness in treating smokers who have repeated relapses will, in part, depend on the immediacy and seriousness of the consequences of continued smoking. For example, a pregnant woman endangering the health of a developing fetus is a situation that requires immediate intervention. Likewise a man with severe cardiac or vascular disease in whom continued smoking poses a serious threat to health or life may require immediate aggressive multimodal interventions.

The skills, knowledge, and experience of a specialist may be required in complex cases in which more intensive or aggressive individualized treatment is indicated or when more complex psychosocial interventions such as relapse prevention are tailored to the individual. Smokers who suffer repeated relapses may require more frequent monitoring as well as coordination of multiple services or interventions that can involve considerable expenditure of clinical time. This is especially true for persons with serious medical or psychiatric problems or for pregnant women who require careful coordination of treatment through active collaboration with medical caretakers. The person providing or overseeing treatment for smokers who have chronic relapses must accept the reality of an ongoing long-term relationship that may be demanding of her or his time and attention as well as clinical acumen if appropriate support and monitoring are to be available during the process of smoking cessation and abstinence.

With regard to reassessing specifics of treatment, it is important to determine if prior pharmacotherapy has been used. If nicotine replacement has not been used previously, if there are no contraindications to its use, and if it is acceptable to the smoker, it should be included as an element of a future treatment plan. As noted previously, assessing whether prior pharmacotherapy has been adequate in its focus, dose, and duration is also important. Some smokers who have had repeated relapses may require multiple pharmacological agents, a longer duration of treatment, long-term maintenance with nicotine replacement, or a combination of these modalities.

When pharmacotherapy has been assessed as adequate, the addition of group behavioral therapy should be considered, as data show a significant benefit in improving cessation rates when behavioral therapy is added to pharmacotherapy.[45] A history of depressive episodes or current depressive symptoms may have been overlooked. In such a case, or when significant depressive symptoms have emerged during the acute withdrawal period, pretreatment with antidepressant medication added to the prior treatment regimen may result in successful cessation.

In reevaluating the psychosocial area, it is important to determine if prior psychosocial interventions (e.g., group behavioral therapy) have been provided. Group behavioral therapy most often includes components with several foci: providing information and education about nicotine dependence; developing and improving coping skills, especially those related to situations in which relapse is likely; presenting basic aspects of the 12-step program; and providing emotional support during withdrawal and early abstinence. If prior group therapy has not been used or does not appear to have been adequate, referral to an appropriate group may be indicated. Whether more dynamically oriented group therapy is beneficial has not been investigated in a controlled fashion.

The benefit of individual therapy has not been formally studied; however, if adequate group behavioral therapy has previously been provided, and there does not appear to be a deficit in knowledge, an individual behavioral approach focusing on specific aspects of relapse may be useful. Some individuals may have idiosyncratic factors related to relapse that can be adequately addressed only in individual psychotherapy. The person may also have more of an opportunity in individual psychotherapy to discuss the difficulties of cessation, grieve the loss of the smoking and its role in his or her life, express anger, and discuss stresses in life that may have contributed to relapse. Finally, individuals who find participation in a group therapy format unacceptable may be candidates for individual psychotherapy.

The family and home environment should also be reassessed to determine if the smoker is receiving adequate support from the spouse, significant other, family, and general social circle. Conjoint marital or family sessions may be beneficial to educate family members about smoking cessation and the psychological, physiological, and behavioral changes that can occur with cessation. The family can also be counseled about what types of behaviors can undermine rather than support the smoking cessation effort. Family members can also assist and support the smoker in complying with treatment, for example, attending group meetings or encouraging the patient to call the physician, rather than discontinuing treatment, if adverse effects result from pharmacotherapy. The presence of one or more active smokers in the household may also need to be addressed before successful smoking cessation can occur, as this factor predicts relapse.

Alterations in various aspects of the smoker's lifestyle may be required to ensure successful cessation and ongoing abstinence. The person may need to change ingrained daily behavioral patterns such as socializing and smoking during the morning work break with coworkers or avoiding other common situations that are likely to precipitate relapse. Alterations in diet and the addition of an exercise regimen may also be helpful, although there are no controlled studies to support this.

Finally, ongoing monitoring and feedback regarding improvement in medical conditions related to cigarette smoking and nicotine use may be helpful in maintaining a high level of motivation for continued abstinence, particularly in smokers with more serious medical conditions.

Some smokers may not be able to achieve successful abstinence with outpatient treatment despite intensive multiple interventions. Inpatient treatment represents a drastic intervention that should be reserved for the most treatment-resistant patients who have been completely unsuccessful at cessation despite repeated attempts and despite treatment with a variety of interventions. Inpatient treatment can provide the most intensive and aggressive program of treatment interventions coupled with close monitoring and prevention of access to nicotine. It requires a commitment of both time and money, however, as almost no insurance policies reimburse for such treatment. Follow-up data from the few programs in existence suggest that it may be effective for some highly treatment-resistant smokers.[69, 70]

Special Considerations in Treatment: Psychiatric Comorbidity

The prevalence of smoking in psychiatric patients has been found to be much higher than in the general population.[7] Psychiatric patients are generally also much less likely to be able to successfully stop smoking.[71] The strongest association of smoking is with schizophrenia.[8] Several reasons for this powerful association have been postulated, including the effect of nicotine in decreasing drug-induced side effects and in increasing dopamine in the frontal and prefrontal areas, which could positively influence negative symptoms or improve prefrontal cognitive function.[8, 72]

Both epidemiological studies and studies of clinical populations have found a strong association between smoking and depression.[8] There is a higher lifetime prevalence of major depressive disorder in smokers than in nonsmokers.[7, 73, 74] Furthermore, persons with a history of depression or those who are currently experiencing a major depressive disorder have a higher prevalence of cigarette smoking than do patients with no history of major depressive disorder.[7, 73] Finally, smokers with a history of major depressive disorder experience a much greater frequency of this disorder and increased severity of depressive symptoms occurring during cessation.[75, 76]

The presence of depression is also associated with an increased risk of relapse and difficulty maintaining abstinence. Depressed smokers are less likely to succeed in maintaining abstinence from nicotine for any time; abstinence after 9 years was nearly two times greater for former smokers without a history of major depressive disorder.[74] The relationship between depression and nicotine dependence and smoking is of special concern for women smokers, as the incidence of major depressive disorder is much higher in women, and the association of depression with smoking is stronger in women.[8] Because depression may cause relapse or prevent attempts at cessation, treatment with antidepressants has been suggested as a way of improving outcome.

An 80% to 90% rate of smoking has also been found in persons with active alcoholism.[77, 78] Some data suggest that smokers with alcoholism may be more behaviorally, but not physically, dependent on nicotine than are other smokers.[25] In addition, it appears that successful smoking cessation in persons with active alcoholism is much less likely than in individuals recovering from alcoholism; the cessation rate in these latter individuals is similar to that in the general population of smokers. Nicotine replacement may be especially beneficial in assisting persons recovering from alcoholism to stop smoking, and adding behavioral therapy may address the social and other skills deficits that are present in persons suffering from alcoholism and that may contribute to relapse.[25] Although programs that treat alcoholism and other drug addictions are often reluctant to address nicotine dependance, there are no experimental studies showing that smoking cessation increases the relapse rate in persons suffering from alcoholism. In fact, successful smoking cessation has been shown in several studies to be associated with successful recovery from alcoholism.[25] Finally, smoking cessation may confound the assessment of withdrawal symptoms in alcohol cessation. Studies also show higher rates of cigarette smoking in drug abusers,[79] specifically in cocaine abusers.[80]

The association of smoking with anxiety disorders is not as strong as it is with depressive disorders, nor does it appear that the presence of comorbid anxiety disorders negatively influences smoking cessation. However, there is some increased prevalence of smoking in persons with agoraphobia and those with mild panic disorder.[8]

Clinical Vignette 1

A 32-year-old married man, Mr. N, consulted his internist and stated that he wished to stop smoking but had been unable to do so on numerous prior attempts. During the last 2 years, he had twice tried to quit cold turkey and was able to abstain from smoking for only 2 days before starting again. During these periods of abstinence, he experienced severe nicotine withdrawal symptoms, including irritability, insomnia, restlessness, and trouble concentrating that interfered with his ability to perform his job. He reported that he started smoking again when his wife threatened to put him out of the house because she was so upset about his behavior and when he found himself making extensive errors in his paperwork at the office.

Mr. N was provided with literature about smoking and nicotine dependence, particularly about nicotine withdrawal. He was asked to read these materials with his wife. Because he smoked two packs of cigarettes per day and scored high on the Fagerstrom Tolerance Questionnaire, and because prior relapse appeared to be primarily the result of withdrawal symptoms, nicotine replacement was thought to be the treatment of choice. Because he frequently drank coffee during the day, the transdermal nicotine patch was chosen as the preferred route of administration.

He was prescribed the transdermal nicotine patch in the highest dose and instructed in its use, its potential risks and benefits, and its potential side effects and adverse effects. He was told to select a quit date, notify the physician of this date, apply the patch, and stop smoking. He was instructed to call the physician 2 days after he stopped smoking and weekly thereafter for the first month for the purpose of monitoring and changing the dose of the patch when appropriate and for encouragement and feedback on how his cessation attempt was progressing.

After stopping smoking, Mr. N experienced minimal withdrawal symptoms and was supported in his cessation effort by his wife. His work performance did not suffer significantly. The dose of the transdermal patch was reduced from 21 mg during the first month to 14 mg during the second month and finally to 7 mg during the third month. Because he was apprehensive about discontinuing the 7-mg patch, he met with his physician to discuss his fears about relapse and ways of coping with certain situations he thought might be difficult. The patch was continued for an additional month, and after its discontinuation, Mr. N was able to maintain successful abstinence. One year later, he called his physician after having relapsed. Because he had been smoking less than a pack of cigarettes per day for only 2 weeks, he was placed on the lowest dose patch for only 2 weeks, after which the patch was discontinued. He discussed with his physician the situation in which the relapse had occurred and developed an alternative for handling such a situation in the future. He was able to again successfully stop smoking and remained abstinent.

Clinical Vignette 2

A 50-year-old divorced woman had been smoking one to two packs of cigarettes per day for more than 30 years. She reported only one prior attempt to quit, which resulted in significant depressive symptoms that resolved after she returned to smoking. However, the symptoms had been so disabling that she never again seriously considered another cessation attempt. She reported a period of significant depressive symptoms of several months' duration after her divorce 2 years previously, with some lingering symptoms that met the criteria for dysthymic disorder. She had not previously received treatment for her depressive symptoms. She lived alone and had a limited social support system.

A selective serotonin reuptake inhibitor antidepressant was prescribed, and after approximately 1 month there was significant improvement in her depressive symptoms. During this time she had been provided with educational materials about smoking and smoking cessation and 2 weeks before had begun to attend an 8-week-long behaviorally oriented group for smoking cessation at the local community hospital clinic. After choosing a quit date, she was prescribed nicotine gum and instructed in its use. She used approximately 10 to 15 pieces of the 2-mg dose per day. She successfully completed the smoking cessation group and continued both nicotine gum and her antidepressant medication for the next 4 months with monthly monitoring. At that time, she gradually tapered and discontinued the nicotine gum during a period of 2 months. She continued her antidepressant medication with monthly monitoring for the next 3 months. At that time, she was free of depressive symptoms, had become more socially active, and had remained abstinent from cigarettes. The antidepressant was discontinued, and she remained free of depression and was abstinent from nicotine 2 years later.

References

1. American Psychiatric Association: Diagnostic and Statistical Manual of Mental Disorders, 3rd ed. Washington, DC: American Psychiatric Association, 1980.
2. American Psychiatric Association: Diagnostic and Statistical Manual of Mental Disorders, 4th ed. Washington, DC: American Psychiatric Association, 1994.
3. Fagerstrom K-O: Measuring the degree of physical dependence to tobacco smoking with reference to individualization of treatment. Addict Behav 1978; 3:235–241.
4. The Health Consequences of Smoking: Nicotine Addiction: A Report of the U.S. Surgeon General. Rockville, MD: Office on Smoking and Health, Public Health Service; 1988. DHHS publication CDC 88-8406.
5. Smoking-Attributable Mortality and Years of Potential Life Lost—United States, 1988. Atlanta: Centers for Disease Control; 1991. DHHS publication CDC 91-8017.
6. Smoking Tobacco and Health. A Fact Book. Washington, DC: U.S. Department of Health and Human Services; revised October 1989. DHHS publication CDC 87-8397.
7. Hughes JR, Hatkusami DK, Mitchell JE, et al: Prevalence of smoking among psychiatric outpatients. Am J Psychiatry 1986; 143:993–997.
8. Glassman AH: Cigarette smoking: Implications for psychiatric illness. Am J Psychiatry 1993; 150:546–553.
9. Covey LS, Glassman AH, Stetner F: Depression and depressive symptoms in smoking cessation. Compr Psychiatry 1990; 31:350–354.
10. West RJ, Hajek P, Belcher M: Severity of withdrawal symptoms as a predictor of outcome of an attempt to quit smoking. Psychol Med 1989; 19:981–985.
11. Hughes JR: Tobacco withdrawal in self-quitters. J Consult Clin Psychol 1992; 60:689–697.
12. Kandel DB, Davies M: Adult sequelae of adolescent depressive symptoms. Arch Gen Psychiatry 1986; 43:255–262.
13. Carmelli D, Swan GE, Robinette D, et al: Heritability of substance use in the NAS-NRC twin registry. Acta Genet Med Gemellol (Roma) 1990; 39:91–98.
14. Kendler KS, Neale MC, MacClean CJ, et al: Smoking and major depression. Arch Gen Psychiatry 1993; 50:36–43.
15. Benowitz NL: Pharmacological aspects of cigarette smoking and nicotine addiction. N Engl J Med 1988; 319:1318–1330.
16. Henningfield JE, Clayton R, Pollin W: Involvement of tobacco in alcoholism and illicit drug use. Br J Addict 1990; 85:279–292.
17. Henningfield JE: Pharmacologic basis and treatment of cigarette smoking. J Clin Psychiatry 1984; 45:24–34.
18. Jarvik ME, Henningfield JE: Pharmacologic treatment of tobacco dependence. Pharmacol Biochem Behav 1988; 30:279–294.
19. Henningfield JE, Goldberg SR: Control of behavior by intravenous nicotine injections in human subjects. Pharmacol Biochem Behav 1983; 19:989–992.
20. Hughes JR, Higgins ST, Bickel WK: Nicotine withdrawal versus other drug withdrawal syndromes: Similarities and dissimilarities. Addiction 1994; 89:1461–1470.
21. Hunt WA, Barnett LW, Branch LG: Relapse rates in addiction process. J Clin Psychol 1971; 27:455–461.
22. Kabat GC, Wynder EL: Determinants of quitting smoking. Am J Public Health 1987; 77:1301–1305.
23. The Health Benefits of Smoking Cessation: A Report of the Surgeon General. Washington, DC: U.S. Department of Health and Human Services, 1990.
24. Prochaska JO: Stages and process of self-change of smoking: Toward an integrative model of change. J Consult Clin Psychol 1983; 51:390–395.
25. Hughes JR: Treatment of smoking cessation in smokers with past alcohol/drug problems. J Subst Abuse Treat 1993; 10:181–187.
26. Lee EW, D'Alonzo GE: Cigarette smoking, nicotine addiction and its pharmacologic treatment. Arch Intern Med 1993; 153:34–48.
27. Goldstein MG, Niaura R, Abrams DB: Pharmacological and behavioral treatment of nicotine dependence: Nicotine as a drug of abuse. In Stoudemire A, Fogel BS (eds): Medical Psychiatric Practice. Washington, DC: American Psychiatric Press, 1991.
28. Fiore MC, Novonty TE, Pierce JP, et al: Methods used to quit smoking in the United States. Do cessation programs help? JAMA 1990; 263:2760–2765.
29. Moss RA, Prue DM: Research on nicotine regulation. Behav Ther 1982; 13:31–46.
30. Russell MAH: Nicotine intake and its regulation by smokers. In Martin WR, VanLoon GR, Iwamoto ET, et al (eds): Tobacco, Smoking and Nicotine: A Neurobiological Approach. New York: Plenum Publishing, 1987:25.
31. Hughes JR: Non-nicotine pharmacotherapies for smoking cessation. J Drug Dev 1994; 6:197–203.
32. Hughes JR: An algorithm for smoking cessation. Arch Fam Med 1994; 3:280–285.
33. Lam WL, Sze PC, Sacks HS, Chalmer TC: Meta-analysis of randomized controlled trials of nicotine chewing gum. Lancet 1987; 2:27–29.
34. Tonnesen P, Fryd V, Hansen M, et al: Two and four mg nicotine chewing gum and group counseling in smoking cessation: An open, randomized controlled trial with a 22 month follow-up. Addict Behav 1988; 13:17–27.
35. Fagerstrom KO, Melen B: Nicotine chewing gum in smoking cessation: Efficacy, nicotine dependence, therapy duration, clinical recommendations. In Grabowski J, Hall SM (eds): Pharmacological Adjuncts in Smoking Cessation. Bethesda, MD: National Institute on Drug Abuse, 1985; 53:102–109.
36. Goldstein MG, Niaura R, Follick MJ, Abrams DB: Effects of behavioral skills training and schedule of nicotine gum administration on smoking cessation. Am J Psychiatry 1989; 146:56–60.
37. Schneider N: How to Use Nicotine Gum and Other Strategies to Quit Smoking. New York: Pocket Books, 1988.
38. Hajek P, Jackson P, Belcher M: Long-term use of nicotine chewing gum. JAMA 1988; 260:1593–1596.
39. Hughes JR: Pharmacotherapy of nicotine dependence. In Schuster CR, Gust SW, Kuhar MJ (eds): Pharmacological Aspects of Drug Dependence: Towards an Integrative Neurobehavioral Approach. Handbook of Experimental Pharmacology. Forchheim, Germany: Springer-Verlag, 1994.
40. Gourley S: The pros and cons of transdermal nicotine therapy. Med J Aust 1994; 160:152–159.
41. Rennard S, Daughton D, Fortmann S, et al: Transdermal nicotine enhances smoking cessation in coronary artery disease patients. [abstract] Chest 1991; 100:55.
42. Benowitz NL, Fitzgerald GA, Wilson M, Xhang Q: Nicotine effects on

eicosanoid formation and hemostatic function: Comparison of transdermal nicotine and cigarette smoking. J Am Coll Cardiol 1993; 22:1159–1167.
43. Anonymous: Nicotine replacement therapy for patients with coronary artery disease. Working Group for the Study of Transdermal Nicotine in Patients with Coronary Artery Disease. Arch Intern Med 1994; 154:989–995.
44. Gross J, Stitzer ML, Maldonado J: Nicotine replacement: Effects of post-cessation weight gain. J Consult Clin Psychol 1989; 57:87–92.
45. Hughes JR: Combining behavioral therapy and pharmacotherapy for smoking cessation: An update. In Oken LS, Blaine JD, Boren JJ (eds): Integrating Behavior Therapies with Medication in the Treatment of Drug Dependence. NIDA Res Monogr. Washington, DC: U.S. Government Printing Office, 1995:92–109.
46. Fagerstrom KO, Schneider NG, Lunell E: Effectiveness of nicotine patch and nicotine gum in individual versus combined treatments for tobacco withdrawal symptoms. Psychopharmacology (Berl) 1993; 11:271–277.
47. Sutherland G, Stapleton JA, Russell MAH, et al: Randomised controlled trial of nasal nicotine spray in smoking cessation. Lancet 1992; 340:324–329.
48. Tonneson P, Norregaard J, Mikkelsen K, et al: A double blind trial of a nicotine inhaler for smoking cessation. JAMA 1993; 269:1268–1271.
49. Glassman AH, Stetner F, Walsh Raizman PS, et al: Heavy smokers, smoking cessation and clonidine: Results of a double-blind, randomized trial. JAMA 1988; 259:2863–2866.
50. Glassman AH, Jackson WK, Walsh BT, Roose SP: Cigarette craving, smoking withdrawal and clonidine. Science 1985; 226:864–866.
51. Covey LS, Glassman AH: A meta-analysis of double-blind placebo-controlled trials of clonidine for smoking cessation. Br J Addict 1991; 86:991–998.
52. Shiffman S: Relapse following smoking cessation: A situational analysis. J Consult Clin Psychol 1982; 50:71–86.
53. Edwards NB, Murphy JK, Downs AD, et al: Doxepin as an adjunct to smoking cessation: A double-blind pilot study. Am J Psychiatry 1989; 146:373–376.
54. Jacobs MA, Spilken AZ, Norman MM, et al: Interaction of personality and treatment conditions associated with success in a smoking control program. Psychosom Med 1971; 33:545–556.
55. Humfleet G, Hall S, Reus V, et al: The efficacy of nortryptyline as an adjunct to psychological treatment for smokers with and without depressive histories. In Adler M (ed): Problems of Drug Dependence 1995. NIDA Res Monogr. Washington, DC: U.S. Government Printing Office, in press.
56. Ferry LH, Robbins AS, Scariati PD, et al: Circulation 1992; 86:I–671.
57. West RJ, Hack S: Effect of cigarettes on memory search and subjective ratings. Pharmacol Biochem Behav 1991; 38:281–286.
58. Sellers EM, Naranjo CA, Kadlec K: Do serotonin uptake inhibitors decrease smoking? Observations in a group of heavy drinkers. J Clin Psychopharmacol 1987; 7:417–420.
59. Spring B, Wurtman J, Gleason R, et al: Weight gain and withdrawal symptoms after smoking cessation: A preventive intervention using *d*-fenfluramine. Health Psychol 1991; 10:216–223.
60. Klesges RC, Klesges LM, Myers AW, et al: The effects of phenylpropanolamine on dietary intake, physical activity and body weight after smoking cessation. Clin Pharmacol Ther 1990; 47:747–754.
61. American Cancer Society/National Cancer Institute: Quit for Good: A Practitioners' Stop-Smoking Guide. Bethesda, MD: National Institutes of Health, 1989. Publication 89-1825.
62. Hall SM, Munoz R, Reus V: Depression and smoking treatment: A clinical trial of an affect regulation treatment. NIDA Res Monogr 1992; 119:326.
63. Schwartz JL: Review and Evaluation of Smoking Cessation Methods: The U.S. and Canada, 1978–1985. Bethesda, MD: National Institutes of Health, 1987. NCI publication 87-2940.
64. Schwartz J: Methods for smoking cessation. Clin Chest Med: Smoking cessation 1991; 12:737–753.
65. Ter Riet G, Kleijnen J, Knipschild P: A meta-analysis of studies into the effects of acupuncture on addiction. Br J Gen Pract 1990; 40:379–382.
66. Schwartz JL, Dubitsky M: One-year follow-up results of a smoking cessation program. Can J Public Health 1968; 59:161–165.
67. Hajek P, Belcher M, Stapleton J: Enhancing the impact of groups: An evaluation of two group formats for smokers. Br J Clin Psychol 1985; 24:289–294.
68. Hughes JR: Behavioral support programs for smoking cessation. Mod Med 1994; 62:22–27.
69. Hurt RD, Lowell CD, Offord KP, et al: Inpatient treatment of severe nicotine dependence. Mayo Clin Proc 1992; 67:823–828.
70. Docherty JP: Residential treatment. In Cocores JA (ed): The Clinical Management of Nicotine Dependence. New York: Springer-Verlag, 1991:266–279.
71. Hughes JR: Possible effects of smoke-free inpatient units on psychiatric diagnosis and treatment. J Clin Psychiatry 1993; 54:109–114.
72. Hughes JR, McHugh P: Nicotine and neuropsychiatric disorders: Schizophrenia. In Clarke P, Quik M, Thureau K, Adloleper F (eds): Effects of Nicotine on Biological Systems II. Advances in Pharmacological Sciences. Basel: Birkhauser Verlag, 1995:301–305.
73. Glassman AH, Helzer JE, Covey LS, et al: Smoking, smoking cessation and major depression. JAMA 1990; 264:1546–1549.
74. Anda RF, Williamson DF, Escobedo LG, et al: Depression and the dynamics of smoking: A national perspective. JAMA 1990; 264:1541–1545.
75. Glassman AH, Covey L, Stetner F: Smoking cessation and major depression. In Proceedings of the 28th Annual Meeting of the American College of Neuropsychopharmacology, 1989; Nashville, TN.
76. Hall SM, Munoz R, Reus V: Smoking cessation, depression and dysphoria. NIDA Res Monogr 1991; 105:312–313.
77. Bobo JK: Nicotine dependence and alcoholism epidemiology and treatment. J Psychoactive Drugs 1989; 21:323–329.
78. Istvan J, Matarazzo JD: Tobacco, alcohol and caffeine use: A review of their interrelationships. Psychol Bull 1984; 95:301–326.
79. Burling TA, Ziff DC: Tobacco smoking: A comparison between alcohol and drug abuse inpatients. Addict Behav 1988; 13:185–190.
80. Budney AJ, Higgins ST, Hughes JR, Bickel WK: Nicotine and caffeine use in cocaine-dependent individuals. J Subst Abuse 1993; 5:117–130.

CHAPTER

49 Opioid-Related Disorders

George E. Woody
Laura F. McNicholas

Definition

The term *opioids* describes a class of substances that act on opioid receptors. Numerous opioid receptors have been identified, but the physiological and pharmacological responses in humans are best understood for the μ and κ receptors. The μ receptor, for which morphine is a prototypical agonist, appears to be the one most closely related to opioid analgesic and euphorigenic effects. Opioids can be naturally occurring substances such as morphine, semisynthetics such as heroin, and synthetics with morphine-like effects such as meperidine. These drugs are prescribed as analgesics, anesthetics, antidiarrheals, and cough suppressants. In addition to morphine, heroin, and meperidine, the opioids include codeine, hydromorphone, methadone, oxycodone, and fentanyl, among others. Drugs such as buprenorphine, a partial agonist at the μ receptor, and pentazocine, an agonist-antagonist, are also included in this class because their physiological and behavioral effects are mediated through opioid receptors. Some of the most commonly abused opioids are listed in Table 49–1.

As with other substances, there are two general categories of opioid-related disorders: opioid use disorders and opioid-induced disorders. Opioid use disorders include opioid dependence and opioid abuse. Opioid dependence has two sets of specifiers, the first set being with physiological dependence (i.e., tolerance or withdrawal, or both) or without physiological dependence. The second set of specifiers consists of course specifiers: early full remission, early partial remission, sustained full remission, sustained partial remission, on agonist therapy, and in a controlled environment. As of this writing, the agonist therapy category is used only in the treatment of opioid dependence and not in the treatment of other opioid-related disorders or substance dependencies.

Opioid-induced disorders include opioid intoxication, opioid withdrawal, opioid intoxication delirium, opioid intoxication psychotic disorders, opioid intoxication mood disorders, opioid intoxication sexual dysfunctions, opioid intoxication sleep disorder, and opioid withdrawal sleep disorder. Only the first two opioid-induced disorders are discussed in this chapter.

The defining features, according to the *Diagnostic and Statistical Manual of Mental Disorders,* Fourth Edition (DSM-IV), of opioid dependence, abuse, intoxication, and withdrawal are similar to those for other substances.[1] Essentially, opioid dependence is a cluster of cognitive, behavioral, and physiological symptoms indicating that the affected person is using high doses of opioids in a compulsive manner and that there is loss of control over use. Cocaine, hallucinogens, solvents, and other substances do not always produce withdrawal symptoms, but opioid dependence is almost always accompanied by significant tolerance and withdrawal.

Opioid abuse consists of intermittent use of one or more opioids in the absence of compulsive use and significant tolerance or withdrawal, or both, but resulting in recurrent social, legal, or personal problems or in use that is physically hazardous. Opioid intoxication involves clinically significant maladaptive behaviors or psychological changes that are associated with acute opioid drug effects. Opioid withdrawal is a syndrome associated with abrupt cessation or reduction of opioid use in persons who have been taking opioids in sufficient quantities and amounts to have developed neuroadaptation to their μ or κ, or both, agonist effects. Opioid withdrawal symptoms are generally opposite those of intoxication, as is described later.

Epidemiology

Prevalence and Incidence

Heroin is the most commonly used drug of the opioid class. The 1991 National Household Survey on Drug Abuse

Table 49–1 Opioids*

Drug	Active Metabolite	Route of Administration	Relative Potency	Medical Use	Plasma Half-Life (Hours)	Duration of Action (Hours)
Morphine		IM	1.00	Analgesia	2	4.0–6.0
Heroin	Morphine	IM	1.0–2.0	None	0.5	3.0–5.0
Codeine		PO	0.05	Analgesia, antitussive	2.0–4.0	4.0–6.0
Fentanyl		IM	40.0–100.0	Analgesia	3.0–4.0	1.0–2.0
Hydromorphone		IM	13.00	Analgesia	2.0–3.0	4.0–6.0
Oxycodone		PO	0.5–1.0	Analgesia		4.0–6.0
Methadone		PO	0.50	Analgesia, opioid substitution	15.0–40.0	18.0–30.0
l-α-Acetyl-methadol (LAAM)		PO	0.40	Opioid substitution	14.0–104.0†	48.0–80.0
	Nor-LAAM				13.0–130.0†	
	Dinor-LAAM				97.0–430.0†	
Buprenorphine		SL	N/A (partial agonist)	Analgesia (opioid substitution, investigational)	6.0–12.0	4.0–6.0 (for analgesia) 12.0–48.0‡

*IM, intramuscular; PO, by mouth; SL, sublingual; N/A, not applicable.

†At steady state.

‡Appears to be dose dependent.

obtained information on nonmedical use of analgesics and heroin separately.[2] Of the population sampled, 6.1% had ever used analgesics; 2.5% had used them in the last year; and 0.7% had used them in the last month. The survey also showed that 1.3% had used heroin in their lifetime and 0.2% had used it in the last year (use in the last month was not reported). It is unclear what proportion of the users met criteria for dependence or abuse because diagnoses were not part of the survey.

The Epidemiological Catchment Area Study, completed in 1985 and using *Diagnostic and Statistical Manual of Mental Disorders,* Third Edition (DSM-III) criteria, found that 0.7% of the target population had ever met criteria for opioid dependence or abuse.[3] Among those who had ever met criteria, 18% reported use in the last month and 42% reported having had a problem with opioids in the last year. This study, and other similar epidemiological surveys, may underestimate the true prevalence of opioid use disorders, as they do not often include persons in prisons or those who are homeless. More recent estimates indicate that there may be as many as 2 million opioid addicts in the United States, although exact figures are difficult to obtain.

Minority group members who live in economically deprived areas have been overrepresented among persons with opioid dependence in the United States since the 1920s. However, in the late 1800s and early 1900s, opioid dependence was seen more often among white middle-class persons, often in rural areas. Currently, most of the cases of heroin dependence are found in large metropolitan areas, and almost half of the nation's heroin addicts are estimated to be in the northeastern United States, where ready access to opioid drugs appears to be a significant risk factor. The purity and availability of heroin for sale to addicts "on the street" have increased markedly during the last several years. This increase in purity and quantity is probably a significant contributor to the increase in opioid-related emergency department visits and in applications for methadone treatment that has occurred.[4] In addition to urban populations, medical personnel who have ready access to opioids are also at increased risk for opioid abuse and dependence.

Comorbidity Patterns

Abuse of other substances such as cocaine or alcohol or a history of drug-related crimes such as possession or distribution of drugs, forgery, burglary, robbery, larceny, or receiving stolen goods, or both, is commonly associated with opioid dependence. However, this picture is not typically seen in health care professionals and others who have easy, legitimate access to controlled substances. In these cases, problems with state licensing boards, hospital credentialing panels, and other administrative agencies are found. Divorce, unemployment, and irregular employment are often seen in opioid-dependent persons from all socioeconomic levels.

For many people, the effect of taking an opioid for the first time is dysphoric rather than euphoric, and nausea and vomiting may result. Chronic opioid users experience mood swings ranging from sedation and euphoria when intoxicated to anxiety and dysphoria when experiencing withdrawal. Opioid users also have an increased prevalence of psychiatric and medical disorders, especially infectious diseases, as is described in more detail later.

Etiology and Pathophysiology

Opioid-related disorders, as in the case of other substance-related disorders, are thought to arise from a variety of social, psychological, and biological factors, many of which interact to produce a "case." Among the factors identified as especially important are incidence of opioid use within the individual's immediate social environment and peer group; availability of opioids; having a history of childhood conduct disorder or adult antisocial personality disorder; and a family history of a substance use disorder. The families of persons with opioid dependence are likely to have higher levels of psychopathology, especially an increased incidence of alcohol and drug use disorders, and antisocial personality disorder.[5] These findings may argue for a genetic susceptibility to substance use disorders. However, more exact information regarding the nature or location of potential genetic factors is not available at this time, nor is information on the influence of psychological and environmental factors on the expression of a presumed genetic predisposition.

The exact mechanism or mix of factors that produce opioid dependence or abuse is unknown, as are the factors that contribute to the chronic, relapsing pattern that is typically seen in these patients. Studies by Dole[6] and Kreek[7] suggest that persons who have used opioids regularly for extended periods (years) experience physiological alterations as a consequence of chronic use that are permanent and that contribute to an inability to achieve periods of sustained remission. The exact nature of these physiological alterations has not yet been identified. Studies by Wikler[8] and O'Brien and colleagues[9] have demonstrated the existence of conditioned drug responses that can persist for years and that may contribute to relapse in formerly dependent individuals.

DSM-IV Criteria 292.89

Opioid Intoxication

A. Recent use of an opioid.

B. Clinically significant maladaptive behavioral or psychological changes (e.g., initial euphoria followed by apathy, dysphoria, psychomotor agitation or retardation, impaired judgment, or impaired social or occupational functioning) that developed during, or shortly after, opioid use.

C. Pupillary constriction (or pupillary dilation due to anoxia from severe overdose) and one (or more) of the following signs, developing during, or shortly after, opioid use:

(1) drowsiness or coma

(2) slurred speech

(3) impairment in attention or memory

D. The symptoms are not due to a general medical condition and are not better accounted for by another mental disorder.

Diagnosis and Differential Diagnosis

Phenomenology and Variations in Presentation

Heroin is usually taken by injection, although it can be smoked, inhaled through the nose (snorted), or taken orally. Smoking and snorting are commonly seen only when pure heroin is available and are currently on the rise in the northeastern United States; tar heroin is commonly smoked in the Pacific Northwest. Hydromorphone (Dilaudid), morphine, and meperidine (Demerol) are usually injected, although they can be taken orally; fentanyl is always injected. Codeine and other analgesics made for oral ingestion (such as Percodan and Percocet) are usually taken orally. All of these drugs can cause intoxication, withdrawal, dependence, and abuse.

In addition to being treated in programs specifically designed for substance use disorders, patients with opioid-related disorders are seen throughout the medical treatment system, including private practices, emergency departments, and consultation and liaison settings. Physicians practicing in penal institutions see large numbers of persons with opioid use disorders, as these disorders are associated with high levels of criminal activity. Accidents and injuries due to violence that is associated with buying or selling drugs are common, and patients with opioid-related disorders are frequently seen on trauma and surgical services. In some areas, violence accounts for more opioid-related deaths than overdose or human immunodeficiency virus (HIV) infection.

Intoxication

Intoxication is characterized by maladaptive and clinically significant behavioral changes developing within minutes to a few hours after opioid use. Symptoms include an initial euphoria sometimes followed by dysphoria or apathy. Psychomotor retardation or agitation, impaired judgment, and impaired social or occupational functioning are commonly seen during intoxication.

Intoxication is accompanied by pupillary constriction unless there has been a severe overdose with consequent anoxia and pupillary dilation. Persons with intoxication are often drowsy (described as being "on the nod") or even obtunded, have slurred speech and impaired memory, and demonstrate inattention to the environment to the point of ignoring potentially harmful events. Dryness of secretions in the mouth and nose, slowing of gastrointestinal activity, and constipation are associated with both acute and chronic opioid use. Visual acuity may be impaired as a result of pupillary constriction. The magnitude of the behavioral and physiological changes resulting from opioid use depends on the dose as well as on the individual characteristics of the user, such as rate of absorption, chronicity of use, and tolerance. Symptoms of opioid intoxication usually last for several hours but are dependent on the half-life of the particular opioid ingested. Severe intoxication after an opioid overdose can lead to coma, respiratory depression, pupillary dilation, unconsciousness, and death.

Withdrawal

Withdrawal is a clinically significant, maladaptive behavioral and physiological syndrome associated with cessation

DSM-IV Criteria 292.0

Opioid Withdrawal

A. Either of the following:

(1) cessation of (or reduction in) opioid use that has been heavy and prolonged (several weeks or longer)

(2) administration of an opioid antagonist after a period of opioid use

B. Three (or more) of the following, developing within minutes to several days after criterion A:

(1) dysphoric mood

(2) nausea or vomiting

(3) muscle aches

(4) lacrimation or rhinorrhea

(5) pupillary dilation, piloerection, or sweating

(6) diarrhea

(7) yawning

(8) fever

(9) insomnia

C. The symptoms in criterion B cause clinically significant distress or impairment in social, occupational, or other important areas of functioning.

D. The symptoms are not due to a general medical condition and are not better accounted for by another mental disorder.

or reduction of opioid use that has been heavy and prolonged (see DSM-IV Criteria box). It can also be precipitated by use of an opioid antagonist such as naloxone or naltrexone.

Patients in opioid withdrawal typically demonstrate signs and symptoms that are opposite to the acute agonist effects. The first of these symptoms are subjective and consist of complaints of anxiety, restlessness, and an "achy feeling" that is often located in the back and legs. These symptoms are accompanied by a wish to obtain opioids (sometimes called craving) and drug-seeking behavior, along with irritability and increased sensitivity to pain. In addition, patients typically demonstrate three or more of the following: dysphoric or depressed mood; nausea or vomiting; diarrhea; muscle aches; lacrimation or rhinorrhea; increased sweating; yawning; fever; insomnia; pupillary dilation; fever; and piloerection. Piloerection and withdrawal-related fever are rarely seen in clinical settings (other than prison), as they are signs of advanced withdrawal in persons with a significant degree of physiological dependence; opioid-dependent persons with habits of that magnitude usually manage to obtain drugs before withdrawal becomes so far advanced.

For short-acting drugs such as heroin, withdrawal symptoms occur within 6 to 24 hours after the last dose in most dependent persons, peak within 1 to 3 days, and gradually subside during a period of 5 to 7 days. Symptoms may take 2 to 4 days to emerge in the case of longer acting drugs such as methadone and *l*-α-acetylmethadol (LAAM). Less acute withdrawal symptoms are sometimes present and can last for weeks to months. These more persistent symptoms can include anxiety, dysphoria, anhedonia, insomnia, and drug craving.

Dependence

Dependence is diagnosed by the signs and symptoms associated with compulsive, prolonged self-administration of opioid drugs that are used for no legitimate medical purpose or, if a medical condition exists that requires opioid treatment, are used in doses that greatly exceed the amount needed for pain relief. Persons with opioid dependence typically demonstrate continued use despite adverse physical, behavioral, and psychological consequences. Almost all persons meeting criteria for opioid dependence have significant levels of tolerance and will experience withdrawal on abrupt discontinuation of opioid drugs. Persons with opioid dependence tend to develop such regular patterns of compulsive drug use that daily activities are typically planned around obtaining and administering the drug.

Opioids are usually purchased on the illicit market, but they can also be obtained by forging prescriptions, faking or exaggerating medical problems, or receiving simultaneous prescriptions from several physicians. Physicians and other health care professionals who are dependent often obtain opioids by writing prescriptions or by diverting opioids that have been prescribed for their own patients.

Abuse

Abuse is a maladaptive pattern of intermittent use of opioids in hazardous situations (e.g., driving under the influence, being intoxicated while using heavy machinery or working in dangerous places) or periodic use resulting in adverse social, legal, or interpersonal problems. All of these signs and symptoms can also be seen in persons who are dependent; abuse is characterized by less regular use than dependence (i.e., compulsive use not present) and by the absence of significant tolerance or withdrawal. As with other substance use disorders, abuse and dependence are hierarchical, and thus persons diagnosed as having opioid abuse must never have met criteria for opioid dependence.

Assessment

Special Issues in the Psychiatric Examination and History

A nonjudgmental and supportive yet firm approach to these patients is especially important. They typically have engaged in antisocial or other forms of problematic behavior. They are often embarrassed or afraid to describe the extent of their behavior and have extremely low self-esteem. At the same time, they are prone to be impulsive and manipulative and to act out when frustrated. Communicating a feeling of nonjudgmental support in the context of setting limits, along with a clear and informed effort to provide appropriate help, encourages optimal therapeutic opportunities. This approach allows the patient to describe his or her current situation fully while beginning to help restore a sense of self-esteem and well-being.

DSM-IV Criteria 304.00

Substance (Opioid) Dependence

A maladaptive pattern of opioid use, leading to clinically significant impairment or distress, as manifested by three (or more) of the following, occurring at any time in the same 12-month period:

(1) tolerance, as defined by either of the following:

(a) a need for markedly increased amounts of opioids to achieve intoxication or desired effect

(b) markedly diminished effect with continued use of the same amount of opioid

(2) withdrawal, as manifested by either of the following:

(a) the characteristic withdrawal syndrome for opioids (refer to criteria A and B of the criteria set for opioid withdrawal)

(b) an opioid is taken to relieve or avoid withdrawal symptoms

(3) opioids are often taken in larger amounts or over a longer period than was intended

(4) there is a persistent desire or unsuccessful efforts to cut down or control opioid use

(5) a great deal of time is spent in activities necessary to obtain opioids (e.g., visiting multiple doctors or driving long distances), use opioids (e.g., chain-smoking), or recover from their effects

(6) important social, occupational, or recreational activities are given up or reduced because of opioid use

(7) opioid use is continued despite knowledge of having a persistent or recurrent physical or psychological problem that is likely to have been caused or exacerbated by opioids

Specify if:

With physiological dependence: evidence of tolerance or withdrawal (i.e., either item 1 or 2 is present)

Without physiological dependence: no evidence of tolerance or withdrawal (i.e., neither item 1 nor 2 is present)

DSM-IV Criteria 305.50

Substance (Opioid) Abuse

A. A maladaptive pattern of opioid use leading to clinically significant impairment or distress, as manifested by one (or more) of the following, occurring within a 12-month period:

(1) recurrent opioid use resulting in a failure to fulfill major role obligations at work, school, or home (e.g., repeated absences or poor work performance related to opioid use; opioid-related absences, suspensions, or expulsions from school; neglect of children or household)

(2) recurrent opioid use in situations in which it is physically hazardous (e.g., driving an automobile or operating a machine when impaired by opioid use)

(3) recurrent opioid-related legal problems

(4) continued opioid use despite having persistent or recurrent social or interpersonal problems caused or exacerbated by the effects of the opioids (e.g., arguments with spouse about consequences of intoxication, physical fights)

B. The symptoms have never met the criteria for opioid dependence.

Relevant Physical Examination and Laboratory Findings

Physical Examination. Sclerosed veins (tracks) and puncture marks on the lower portions of the upper extremities are common in intravenous drug users. When these veins become unusable or otherwise unavailable, persons usually switch to veins in the legs, neck, or groin. Veins sometimes become so badly sclerosed that peripheral edema develops. When intravenous access is no longer possible, persons often inject directly into their subcutaneous tissue (skin-popping), resulting in cellulitis, abscesses, and circular-appearing scars from healed skin lesions. Tetanus is a relatively rare but extremely serious consequence of injecting into the subcutaneous tissues. Infections including bacterial endocarditis, hepatitis B and C, and HIV infection, also occur in other organ systems.

Persons who snort heroin or other opioids often develop irritation of the nasal mucosa. Difficulties in sexual function are common, as are a variety of sexually transmitted diseases. Men often experience premature ejaculation associated with opioid withdrawal and impotence during intoxication or chronic use. Women commonly have disturbances of reproductive function and irregular menses.

Laboratory Findings. During dependence, routine urine toxicology tests are often positive for opioid drugs. Urine tests remain positive for most opioids for 12 to 36 hours. Methadone and LAAM, because they are longer acting drugs, can be identified for several days. Fentanyl is not detected by standard urine tests but can be identified by more specialized procedures. Testing for fentanyl is not necessary in most programs but needs to be performed for assessment and treatment of health care professionals such as anesthesiologists who have access to this drug. Concomitant laboratory evidence of other abusable substances, such as cocaine, marijuana, alcohol, amphetamines, and benzodiazepines, is common.

Hepatitis screening tests are often positive, either for hepatitis B antigen (signifying active infection) or for hepatitis B or C antibody, or both (signifying past infection). Mild to moderate elevations of liver function tests are common, usually as a result of resolving hepatitis, of toxic injury to the liver due to contaminants that have been mixed with the injected opioid, or of concomitant use of other hepatotoxic drugs such as alcohol. Low platelet count, anemia or neutropenia, and positive HIV tests or low $CD4^+$ cell counts are often signs of HIV infection that has been acquired via injection drug use or by unprotected sexual activity that may be related to a substance use disorder.

Subtle changes in cortisol secretion patterns and body temperature regulation have been observed for up to 6 months after opioid detoxification.[10] These biological alterations have been attributed to prolonged withdrawal, as described earlier.

Developmental and Sex Differences

Opioid use disorders can occur at any age, including adolescence and the geriatric years, but most affected persons are between 20 and 45 years old. Neonates whose mothers are addicted can experience opioid withdrawal, as is discussed later. Rarely, young children are affected, with some cases of heroin dependence having been reported in persons who are 8 to 10 years of age. Men are more commonly affected, with the male/female ratio typically thought to be 3:1 or 4:1.

Differential Diagnosis

Individuals who are dependent on street opioids are usually easy to diagnose because of the physical signs of intravenous use, drug-seeking behavior, reports from independent observers, lack of medical justification for opioid use, urine test results, and signs and symptoms of intoxication or withdrawal.

The signs and symptoms of opioid withdrawal are fairly specific, especially lacrimation and rhinorrhea, which are not associated with withdrawal from any other abusable substances. Other psychoactive substances with sedative properties, such as alcohol, hypnotics, and anxiolytics, can cause a clinical picture that resembles opioid intoxication. A diagnosis can usually be made by the absence of pupillary constriction or by the response to a naloxone challenge. In some cases, intoxication is due to opioids along with alcohol or other sedatives. In these cases, the naloxone challenge does not reverse all of the sedative drug effects.

Opioid addicts often present with psychiatric signs and symptoms such as depression or anxiety syndromes. Such subjective distress often serves to motivate the patient to seek treatment and thus can be therapeutically useful. These symptoms can be the result of opioid intoxication or withdrawal, or they might result from the pharmacological effects of other substances that are also being abused, such as cocaine, alcohol, or benzodiazepines. They may also represent independent, non–substance-induced psychiatric disorders that require long-term treatment. The correct attribution of psychiatric symptoms that are seen in the context of opioid dependence and abuse follows the principles that are outlined in the substance-related section and other relevant parts of DSM-IV.

Opioids are much less likely to produce psychopathology than are most other drugs of abuse, and in some instances they reduce psychiatric symptoms. In these cases, symptoms emerge not during opioid use but after it is discontinued. Examples of this phenomenon have been observed by physicians in methadone maintenance programs, who occasionally see an exacerbation of symptoms of schizophrenia in patients with schizophrenia who are detoxifying from methadone.

Although most cases of opioid-related disorders can be diagnosed fairly easily for the reasons already stated, some clinical situations present diagnostic problems. One situation is that in which a person successfully conceals his or her opioid dependence for years, continuing drug use until it is revealed as a result of severe medical or social complications. Other patients can present different kinds of diagnostic challenges. Among these challenges are persons who fabricate or exaggerate the signs and symptoms of a painful illness (such as kidney stones, migraine headache, or back pain) to obtain opioids. Because pain is subjective and difficult to measure, and because some of these individuals can be skillful and deceptive, diagnosis can be difficult and time-consuming. Drugs that are obtained in such deceptions may be used by the individual in the service of her or his dependence or abuse or may be sold on the illicit drug market for profit. These individuals cause problems not only for physicians but also for patients with legitimate disorders who need opioids for pain relief. Patients who have real problems that should be treated promptly with opioids are sometimes denied treatment or given inadequate amounts of opioid analgesics owing to uncertainty or disbelief about the legitimacy of their complaints. Patients with cancer, kidney stones, or other painful conditions have sometimes suffered considerably from this type of "reverse discrimination."

Clinical Vignette 1

A 43-year-old man was referred for evaluation and treatment of pain by the medical director of his health maintenance organization. He had been receiving Percodan on a regular basis (four per day) for the last 2 years from an internist for chronic pain secondary to kidney problems. Before his referral, he had been in and out of emergency departments for 6 years for treatment of renal pain. He had been prescribed narcotics on numerous occasions, and his health plan had been billed for his care. As a result, the health plan had limited treatment to only his internist and had refused to pay for any care unless it was approved in advance.

Review of his medical records revealed that he had had a thorough work-up for kidney disease on several occasions and that he had an arteriovenous malformation with periodic bleeding and clot formation; he had also passed kidney stones on at least two occasions. Cystoscopy done previously showed evidence of traumatic lesions in the wall of the bladder that were secondary to instrumentation.

The social and occupational history showed that he had worked at two hospitals and on one occasion had impersonated a psychologist. During previous employment he had improperly used a company vehicle. When his supervisor attempted to have him fired, he turned the proceedings around and almost had the supervisor fired for failing to follow proper administrative procedures. Currently, he was working as an administrative aide for the city courts and was in a hurry to "get his prescription filled" so that he could return to work. He described some of the problems that he had experienced in attempting to obtain "proper treatment" from the health plan and expressed annoyance that he had been referred to the drug program for evaluation. He was concerned about confidentiality and felt that people he knew might see him entering the program and think that he had a drug problem. During the initial interview, he described his contacts in government, implying that he would not hesitate to complain if his treatment was inadequate or unsatisfactory.

On examination, he was well dressed, in no acute distress, and superficially friendly. There were no signs of anxiety, depression, loose associations, or homicidal or suicidal ideas. His mood was in a normal range and his affect was appropriate, although it seemed as if he could become angered easily if frustrated or provoked. There were no overt signs or symptoms of opioid withdrawal or intoxication. After examination and on the basis of the history, it was decided to give him a trial of methadone for pain, and a dose of 20 mg was administered. During the next hour the patient was observed to become sleepy, with his speech slurred and rambling; his respiratory and heart rates were mildly depressed, and his pupils were constricted, all symptoms of opioid intoxication. Later, the patient admitted that he had not been using the Percodan; in fact, he had sold it for "extra spending money."

Course and Natural History

Opioid dependence can begin at any age, but problems associated with opioid use are most commonly first observed in the late teens or early 20s. Once dependence occurs it is usually continuous for many years, even though periods of abstinence are frequent. Recurrence is common even after many years of forced abstinence, such as occurs during incarceration. Increasing age appears to be associated with a decrease in prevalence. This tendency for dependence to remit generally begins after age 40 years and has been called "maturing out." However, many persons have remained opioid dependent for 50 years or longer. Thus, although spontaneous remission can and does occur, most cases of opioid dependence follow a chronic, relapsing course.

One exception to this typical picture was observed in armed services personnel who became opioid dependent while serving in Vietnam. On return to the United States, less than 10% relapsed, although they experienced an increased rate of other substance use disorders such as dependence on alcohol and stimulants.[11]

Overall Goals of Treatment

Treatment for intoxication usually takes place in an emergency department, although it may also occur in the physician's office; withdrawal is usually seen in many settings, including emergency departments and treatment programs. The goal is to relieve the acute symptoms and engage the patient in long-term, specialized treatment for the substance use disorder. Most patients seeking longer term treatment have dependence, and thus the following discussion focuses on treatments for opioid dependence.

All treatments for opioid dependence usually take place in three phases: acute, rehabilitation, and supportive. These phases extend for varying lengths of time depending on the response to treatment, the patient's involvement and motivation, his or her social situation, and the resources available.

Acute Phase. The acute phase begins at the time the patient seeks treatment and extends for several days, weeks, or even months. During this period, the patient is usually in great distress, having opioid withdrawal symptoms and elevated levels of anxiety and depression. She or he may also have acute medical, family, social, employment, or legal problems.

The goal of the acute phase is twofold: 1) to assess accurately the nature and severity of the substance use disorder or disorders and 2) to develop a short-term plan to relieve the immediate distress and engage the patient in treatment. A longer term program is usually necessary to reduce or eliminate opioid dependence and its associated problems. The acute phase is typically done in an inpatient detoxification unit in preparation for entry into a rehabilitation program or in an outpatient methadone treatment program if maintenance is the best option. Progress is assessed by successful detoxification or by stabilization by use of methadone, as demonstrated by the absence of withdrawal symptoms and of illicit opioids in urine. Most persons with opioid dependence opt for methadone maintenance, although a smaller but significant number seek inpatient, drug-free rehabilitation in either a short-term residential program or a therapeutic community. A smaller number undergo detoxification and are treated with naltrexone.

Rehabilitation Phase. The goals of this phase are to solidify the progress made in the acute phase and to help the patient achieve a more extended period of sobriety from opioids and other drugs. The use of other substances such as alcohol, cocaine, or marijuana is common among persons with opioid dependence, and these problems are addressed along with the opioid dependence during the rehabilitation phase. Appropriate treatment strategies should be developed for other problems that are associated with the dependence. In some cases, these problems may have been transitory and resolved at the time of acute treatment; in others, they are persistent, and long-term treatment is indicated. In every case, the treatment program should aim to carry through with the addiction-focused treatment that has been started and to address other problems as they are identified. During all phases of treatment, staff should observe the patient for the development or emergence of new problems that were not identified during the initial assessment.

If treatment is taking place in an inpatient drug-free unit, the rehabilitation phase can be intensive and may include group and individual therapy, participation in self-help groups, and educational sessions about the causes and consequences of opioid dependence and other substance use disorders. If done in an outpatient methadone program, the treatment typically requires that the patient attend clinic daily and participate in counseling or group therapy, or both, at least weekly. In either setting, problems that are associated with the substance use disorder should be identified and systematically addressed. This phase typically lasts about a month if the patient is in an inpatient program or outpatient day hospital, may last from 2 to 6 months in a less intensive outpatient program, but may extend for 12 to 18 months in a therapeutic community. Agonist substitution therapy with methadone or LAAM is, by design, aimed to be long term and can last for extended periods, with some patients being successfully maintained for 10 years or more.

Supportive Phase. Entrance into this phase occurs only when the patient has made good progress in rehabilitation. The supportive phase begins when the substance use disorder has been in remission for a period of months or longer or when control over unprescribed opioid use has been established with the use of agonist therapy. Associated problems will also have been addressed and be under good control. This phase aims to consolidate the gains made in earlier phases and to extend them if possible.

The supportive phase almost always takes place in an outpatient setting. During this phase, there is usually a gradual shift of responsibility for maintaining abstinence and other aspects of rehabilitation away from formal treatment and toward the patient. In many cases, this is seen by a reduction in treatment, with therapy sessions being reduced from weekly or more to biweekly or even monthly. As in earlier phases, the patient is encouraged to develop a sustained involvement in self-help groups such as Narcotics Anonymous, Methadone Anonymous, or Double-Trouble.

Standard Approaches to Treatment

Physician-Patient Relationship

A positive physician-patient relationship facilitates treatment of patients with any psychiatric condition, including opioid-related disorders. It is important for the therapist to communicate a sense of support along with the importance of structure and setting reasonable limits on inappropriate behavior. The basis for this relationship is begun on the first visit by spending the necessary time to understand the nature and extent of the patient's addiction-related problems. At the same time, it is important to let the patient know what is expected and what will not be tolerated and to make certain that the patient understands that her or his active participation in treatment is essential to provide the best chance for recovery.

Two problematic countertransference situations can arise. One is when the therapist is overly supportive. This situation is often seen when the therapist does not set reasonable limits or encourage the patient to take responsibility for rehabilitation. The other situation is when the therapist reacts with frustration, anger, or disrespect for the patient's problems. Each of these countertransference problems is more apt to occur with patients who have high levels of psychopathology or who engage in manipulative or antisocial behavior. It is "normal" to become sympathetic, angry, or frustrated at times when dealing with these patients, and to be without these and other feelings would be less than human. On the other hand, it is important to be aware of the feelings as they arise so as to prevent or reduce the chances that they will intrude and disrupt the objective, consistent, helping relationship that is an important aspect of a healthy physician-patient relationship.

One approach that many therapists find helpful in dealing with these patients is to see the behavioral problems associated with opioid dependence as part of the problem and as things to be worked on in therapy. At the same time, it is important to be willing and able to suspend patients from treatment for engaging in behaviors that, for example, 1) threaten other patients or staff, such as making direct or covert threats, carrying weapons, selling drugs, or engaging in overtly aggressive behavior; or 2) threaten the integrity of the clinic milieu, such as submitting an altered urine sample, diverting methadone, or bringing illicit substances into the clinic.

Pharmacotherapy

Intoxication

Acute intoxication can easily be reversed by administering naloxone (Narcan) subcutaneously or intravenously. Because naloxone is a short-acting drug, effective for only 30 to 60 minutes, it is important to observe the patient after the naloxone dose wears off to make certain that he or she does not again exhibit signs and symptoms of an overdose. Such observation is especially important in the case of an overdose with methadone or any other long-acting opioid. It is necessary to administer naloxone for a prolonged time, and in these cases, an intravenous drip can be utilized until the opioid has been metabolized and its effects are no longer life threatening.

It is usually difficult to determine the dose of naloxone that will reverse respiratory depression and other life-threatening signs of overdose without also precipitating opioid withdrawal in the case of patients who are dependent on opioids. Although treatment with 0.4 to 0.8 mg of naloxone, intravenously or subcutaneously, should reverse most opioid overdoses, patients with opioid dependence could have severe precipitated withdrawal from such doses. If a patient is suspected of being dependent, it is safer to begin a slow intravenous push administration of 0.1 to 0.2 mg of naloxone and monitor the patient's respiratory status and level of consciousness; it is not necessary or desirable for the patient to have signs and symptoms of withdrawal. If the patient needs continuous naloxone administration while the opioid is being metabolized and excreted, the dose should be titrated, by adjusting the rate of the intravenous infusion, so that the patient's respiratory and cardiovascular status is stable.

Withdrawal

Withdrawal can be treated simply by administering an opioid, such as methadone, at the lowest effective dose that maintains the patient's level of dependence. Methadone (20 to 30 mg), administered orally, usually stops the signs and symptoms of withdrawal, but this dose may not be sufficient to suppress withdrawal for 24 hours. In an inpatient setting, this presents no problem, as the patient may receive a second dose from 2 to 16 hours after the first, depending on when the withdrawal symptoms are observed.

If the patient is being treated in an outpatient setting, it is usually not possible to adjust the dosing schedule as easily. If higher doses are required, which they often are in cases of high levels of physiological dependence, they should be administered only if signs and symptoms of withdrawal persist for 1.5 hours or more after the first opioid dose. The patient should not be given more than 30 mg in a single dose unless the current level of physiological dependence is clearly documented. U.S. Food and Drug Administration requirements do not permit administering more than 30 mg in a single dose on the first day of methadone treatment or more than 40 mg in divided doses on the first day of treatment. After the first day, when the initial level of tolerance is better known, the dose is less heavily regulated and the physician has more leeway to use her or his best judgment about the most appropriate dose. Generally, doses are not increased more rapidly than 10 to 15 mg/d.

The patient's estimation of the amount of opioid needed to suppress withdrawal should be tempered by the knowledge that persons using opioids regularly exaggerate their level of physiological dependence, usually from fear that the physician will not prescribe enough methadone. These patient reports must be very carefully assessed. Cases have been documented in which physicians took the patient's word at face value, prescribed high doses of methadone (50 to 80 mg) without having objective evidence on the patient's level of tolerance, and caused a serious overdose requiring naloxone reversal. It is always safest to give a lower dose (20 to 30 mg) and then to check the patient again at a later time, after the methadone has had an opportunity to work. If withdrawal symptoms persist, another 10 to 20 mg can be given. The process can be repeated until the patient is stable.

Detoxification

Detoxification is the first step for patients who enter a drug-free rehabilitation program. Unlike detoxification from alcohol and other substance use disorders in which outpatient treatment is often effective, detoxification from opioids is usually not successful unless done in an inpatient setting. Exceptions are patients who have been stably maintained with methadone for extended periods and who slowly reduce their dose over months or even years. As with all substance use disorders, detoxification that is not followed by meaningful involvement in therapy, self-help groups, or a combination of both is almost never successful.

Detoxification, except in a methadone-maintained outpatient setting, is most easily accomplished by using oral doses of methadone, given three to four times a day, and slowly decreasing the dose over 5 to 7 days depending on the dose needed initially to suppress withdrawal symptoms. Patients are usually started with 20 to 40 mg/d, given in divided doses; when the dose that is required to suppress withdrawal symptoms for 24 hours is determined, it is then lowered by 5 to 10 mg/d until it reaches zero. Optimally, one should be able to observe the patient for 1 to 2 days after the methadone has been discontinued to make certain that he or she is stable enough to enter rehabilitation; however, this is not always possible.

An alternative to using opioids for detoxification is the use of adrenergic agonists. Clonidine, an α-adrenergic agonist with inhibitory action primarily at the locus caeruleus, has been used to depress the overactivity of the sympathetic nervous system that is seen in patients who are withdrawing from opioids.[12, 13] It was found to be effective (80% to 90% success rate) among inpatient populations in decreasing the signs and symptoms of opioid withdrawal. As with other pharmacotherapies, outpatient detoxification with clonidine has not been as successful as inpatient treatment. Problems identified in clonidine detoxification include hypotension, lethargy, insomnia, dizziness, and oversedation. All of these problems are more easily managed in a hospital rather than in an outpatient setting.

Patients who are opioid dependent are often dependent on other drugs as well, commonly benzodiazepines, alcohol, and cocaine. Detoxification from these substances can be done along with opioid detoxification. Cocaine dependence does not usually require pharmacotherapy for detoxification; however, patients should be observed for the development of acute depression that can be associated with the crash. Alcohol and benzodiazepines often require pharmacotherapy, usually with a drug such as chlordiazepoxide, a long-acting benzodiazepine. Oxazepam, a short-acting benzodiazepine with a simple metabolic pathway and a low abuse liability, or phenobarbital is also commonly used. Patients who are dependent on alprazolam are probably best detoxified with phenobarbital, as it appears to work better than do other benzodiazepines, which do not fully suppress all the withdrawal symptoms of alprazolam.[13a]

Opioid Substitution Therapy

Methadone maintenance has been the mainstay of pharmacotherapy for opioid dependence since its introduction by Dole and Nyswander.[14, 15] Since the 1970s, LAAM, a long-acting congener of methadone, has been used experimentally for maintenance treatment. LAAM was approved by the U.S. Food and Drug Administration for maintenance therapy and is now available for general use in opioid treatment programs. More recently, buprenorphine has been studied in clinical trials as a maintenance therapy in opioid-dependent patients; it is currently in experimental stages and shows considerable promise as an alternative to methadone maintenance.

Methadone is an orally effective, long-acting agonist at the μ opioid receptor, and maintenance therapy with methadone is designed to support patients with opioid dependence for months or years while the patient engages in counseling and other therapy to change his or her lifestyle. Experience with methadone has shown it to be both safe and effective. Although patients in methadone maintenance show physiological signs of opioid tolerance, side effects are minimal and the patient's general health and nutritional status improve. Further, investigators have shown that criminal behavior decreases in as many as 85% of patients and employment among maintenance patients typically ranges from 40% to 80%.

Methadone maintenance programs are licensed and regulated by the U.S. Food and Drug Administration and the Drug Enforcement Administration. For a person to be eligible for methadone maintenance, she or he must be at least 18 years of age, must be physiologically dependent on heroin or other opioids, and must have been dependent on opioids for at least 1 year. Care must be taken to screen out the occasional applicant who has been using opioids for brief periods or who has no past or current history of opioid dependence with physiological features. This screening can be done in a variety of ways, including observing the patient during a 12- to 24-hour period for the signs and symptoms of opioid withdrawal; administering a naloxone challenge test; or gathering information from independent observers such as family, probation officers, or staff in other treatment programs. Urine drug tests are also important, although they are not diagnostic of dependence.

Each clinic sets its own rules within the guidelines set by state and federal agencies. Many clinics are open only 6 days a week, thus giving all patients at least one take-home dose of methadone weekly; others are open 7 days a week and require a patient to earn any take-home privileges by compliance with the clinic rules and abstinence from abusable substances (including alcohol). All clinics must obtain urine toxicological test results on patients, but the frequency varies from two or three times a week to once a month. Despite evidence that patients taking higher (>60 mg/d) doses of methadone are more successful in maintaining drug-free urine,[16] some clinics and states have set upper limits on the dose of methadone. Some clinics have limits of 30 or 40 mg, doses that are clearly too low for many patients. Dosage should be prescribed on an individual basis in such a way that patients have little chance of achieving an opioid effect from illicit drugs.

Psychosocial Treatments

Drug Counseling and Psychotherapy

Psychosocial interventions are used in all treatments for substance-related disorders. The most extensive use of psychosocial treatments occurs in drug-free rehabilitation programs, in which a combination of education about drug effects and addiction, motivational enhancement, family therapy, individual and group counseling, and participation in self-help groups is included, often on a daily basis. Patients who successfully complete rehabilitation are usually followed up in a less intensive setting, with psychosocial therapies continuing on a weekly or biweekly basis. The focus of these therapies in this later phase of treatment is to sustain the gains that have been made, follow-up on problems identified earlier, prevent relapse, and identify new problems that may arise and that need further intervention.

All methadone maintenance clinics must provide counseling for patients, but the amount required is up to the clinic's discretion. Data are available indicating that psychosocial treatments are necessary to maximize the efficacy of methadone maintenance and that increased levels of psychosocial treatments significantly enhance the efficacy of methadone treatment.[17]

Most psychosocial treatments are provided by bachelor's- or master's-level therapists with training and experience in treating persons with substance use disorders. A few studies have shown that doctoral-level persons, such as psychiatrists or clinical psychologists who are trained to deliver cognitive, supportive-expressive, or other psychotherapies, are more effective for patients who have high levels of psychiatric symptoms.[18, 19] For these "dually diagnosed" patients, psychotherapy is often combined with pharmacotherapies that are appropriate for their coexisting psychiatric disorders.

Therapeutic Communities

In addition to entering 21- to 28-day intensive rehabilitation programs, some persons with opioid dependence enter therapeutic communities. These are long-term (≥12 months) residential programs that emphasize personal responsibility, honesty, and community involvement. Many persons entering these programs are under legal pressure as a consequence of drug-related crimes or are otherwise highly motivated to participate in treatment and become drug free. Therapeutic communities may be especially useful for persons who have not responded to other, less intensive modalities or those with long histories of antisocial behavior. Although these programs can be highly effective among patients who remain in treatment,[20] many opioid-dependent patients are unable to tolerate their rules and structure and drop out of treatment early.

In addition to the benefits that they deliver to persons who remain in treatment, therapeutic communities serve another important function. Many graduates of these programs do extremely well over long periods even though they have extensive histories of severe opioid dependence and its associated problems. These persons can serve as excellent role models for other patients and often become successful therapists in therapeutic communities or other treatment programs.

Special Features Influencing Treatment

As in other types of substance-related disorders, many patients with opioid dependence and abuse are ambivalent about stopping drug use. This ambivalence is often reflected in poor motivation to enter and remain in treatment. It is important that staff are aware of this ambivalence and make all reasonable efforts to resolve it in favor of treatment participation and cessation of drug use. Avoiding unnecessary delays in entering treatment, having a hopeful and nonjudgmental attitude, performing a comprehensive evaluation, and developing a treatment plan that is responsive to the patient's needs all help get the patient engaged and involved in treatment.

Patients often lack the motivation or are unable, for a variety of practical reasons, to enter long-term treatment programs such as therapeutic communities. This reluctance is often not a problem if methadone maintenance is available. However, it can become an issue in the case of persons who have not responded to methadone treatment. These patients have typically been treated with methadone maintenance on repeated occasions in different programs and have demonstrated continuing high levels of opioid and other unprescribed drug use. In such cases, strong encouragement to enter a therapeutic community or other long-term residential program is usually indicated; however, the patient's reluctance to follow through can present a difficult clinical situation for which there often is no good solution.

Psychiatric Comorbidity

Antisocial personality disorder is much more common in persons with opioid dependence than in the general population. Diagnostic studies of persons with opioid dependence have typically found rates of antisocial personality disorder ranging from 20% to 50%, compared with less than 5% in the general population.[21] Posttraumatic stress disorder is also seen with increased frequency among persons with opioid use disorders, as is the case in other types of substance use disorders.

Opioid-dependent persons are especially at risk for the development of depressive symptoms and for episodes of mild to moderate depression that meet symptomatic and duration criteria for major depressive disorder. These syndromes may represent either organic mood disorders or independent depressive illnesses. Brief periods of depression are especially common during chronic intoxication or withdrawal or in association with psychosocial stressors that are related to the dependence. Insomnia is common, especially during withdrawal. Delirium or brief, psychosis-like symptoms are occasionally seen during opioid intoxication.

Although opioids can produce psychopathology, they are much less psychotoxic than most other drugs of abuse. Unlike other drugs that produce dependence (with the exception of nicotine), opioids generally reduce rather than initiate or magnify psychiatric symptoms. Opioids have antianxiety and weak antipsychotic effects. Patients maintained with methadone, even at high doses and for long periods, have not been observed to develop new psychiatric disorders. This situation is quite unlike that seen in persons who use high doses of alcohol or other sedatives for long periods, who often develop serious depression, or in those using high doses of stimulants such as cocaine or amphetamines, which often produce psychosis-like symptoms.

General Medical Comorbidity

HIV infection and acquired immunodeficiency syndrome have become some of the most common medical complications of intravenous drug use. The incidence of HIV infection is rising markedly among intravenous drug users, of whom opioid-dependent individuals constitute a large proportion. HIV infection rates have been reported to be as high as 60% among persons dependent on heroin in some areas of the United States.[22] Because of the long incubation period before the development of acquired immunodeficiency syndrome, it is expected that future years will see marked increases in morbidity and mortality associated with HIV infection. Sharing of injecting equipment, including needles, "cookers," and cotton, and engaging in high-risk sexual behaviors are the main pathways to infection. Sexual transmission is a more common route of HIV transmission for women than men because HIV is spread more readily from men to women than from women to men. Women who are intravenous drug users and who also engage in prostitution or other forms of high-risk sexual behavior are at extremely high risk for HIV infection. Cocaine use has also been found to be a significant risk factor across all drug-using populations, including those with opioid dependence.[23, 24]

Opioid dependence is associated with a high death rate, with approximately 10 deaths per 1000 patients per year. Deaths among opioid-dependent persons most often result from overdose, accidents, or injuries. In addition, potentially fatal medical complications include cellulitis, hepatitis, tuberculosis, and endocarditis. All of these are more common in persons with HIV infection. The cocaine and alcohol dependence that is often seen among opioid-dependent persons contributes to this medical morbidity via cirrhosis, cardiomyopathy, myocardial infarction, and cardiac arrhythmias.

Tuberculosis has become a particularly serious problem, especially among persons who use drugs intravenously. In most cases, infection with the tubercle bacillus is asymptomatic and evident only by the presence of a positive tuberculin skin test. However, many cases of active tuberculosis have been found, especially among those who are infected with HIV. These individuals often have a newly acquired infection but also are likely to experience reactivation of a prior infection owing to their impaired immune function.

HIV infection has also been seen in about one third of infants born to HIV-positive mothers, many of whom are intravenous drug users or the partners of intravenous drug users. In addition, physiological dependence on opioids is seen in about half the infants born to women who are opioid dependent.[25] This can produce a severe withdrawal syndrome requiring medical treatment. HIV infection in the neonate occurs by passive transfer of the virus during gestation, labor, or delivery or in the postpartum period, often by nursing. Evidence has shown that treatment of HIV-positive pregnant women with zidovudine significantly reduces the incidence of HIV infection in the neonate.[26] In some African countries, thorough washing of infants born to HIV-infected mothers immediately after delivery is currently being tested in an effort to reduce the incidence of neonatal HIV infection. Low birth weight, seen in children of opioid-dependent mothers, is usually not marked and is generally not associated with serious adverse consequences.

Demographical Features

Childhood and Adolescence

Opioid dependence is rare in childhood. Opioid use often begins in adolescence, with the onset of dependence in the late teens or early 20s. The number of persons who try opioid drugs and do not develop abuse or dependence is unknown but probably significant. Persons who develop an opioid use disorder typically progress from use to abuse or dependence over a period of years, such that they do not meet criteria for a diagnosis until they have been using the drug for several years. As is the case with alcohol and other substances, a few persons have an extremely rapid onset of dependence and meet criteria within a year of their first use of opioid drugs.

Geriatric Age Group

Most persons in the geriatric age group who have an opioid-related disorder had the onset of the disorder at an earlier age, and it has simply continued with the typical remissions and exacerbations. Occasionally, persons develop opioid abuse or dependence for the first time during their geriatric years. Few data are available on the extent of this problem, but it is relatively small compared with the much larger number of persons who develop these disorders in their late teens or early 20s.

Ethnic and Cultural Issues in Treatment

Many persons with opioid use disorders are African-American or Hispanic. These individuals often have life experiences that are different from those of many physicians and other health care professionals. Among these experiences are discrimination and prejudice, which can create interpersonal sensitivities that are not found among members of other ethnic groups. It is extremely important for treatment providers to appreciate the extent of these problems and sensitivities and to avoid even the appearance of prejudice or favoritism based on membership in an ethnic group.

As a result of these ethnic sensitivities, transference reactions with themes of lack of respect or prejudice are often seen. These themes usually originate from genuine perceptions of prejudice or discrimination. Occasionally, however, they are used in manipulative attempts to obtain favors from programs. It is important for treatment providers to maintain a therapeutic environment and a professional staff that can appropriately diagnose and address these concerns when they are expressed.

Refractory Patients or Nonresponse to Initial Treatment

In judging response to treatment, it is important to be clear about the standards that are used in judging success. Many patients with opioid dependence have been using opioids for 10 to 20 years or more and have a large number of social, legal, employment, medical, and psychiatric problems. Significant improvement in one or more of these areas is often a meaningful and socially productive goal of treatment, even though "cure" is not achieved.

Unfortunately, many policymakers (and even some treatment providers) apply an acute disease model in assessing outcome. They expect a cure, often defined as total abstinence and full social functioning after rehabilitation. In this model, treatment is judged a failure when anything short of an ideal outcome occurs. Use of this acute care model is inappropriate. Substance-related disorders, particularly dependence, are almost always chronic, relapsing conditions with high levels of associated social, medical, and psychiatric problems. Assessing outcome in terms of improvement compared with baseline levels of functioning, and in ways that capture the many areas of adjustment that are usually disturbed, is the most realistic and accurate approach. Similar approaches are taken in assessing outcome for other chronic disorders, such as schizophrenia, rheumatoid arthritis, asthma, and hypertension.

Meaningful improvement in one or more of the important target areas is a valid measure of progress in treating substance-related disorders, as in other chronic conditions. Treatment retention, meaningful reduction in drug use, ability to sustain remission, and improvement in addiction-related problems are typical indicators that can be used to assess outcome. Such indicators also allow for assessment based on degrees of improvement rather than on an all-or-none (i.e., abstinent-nonabstinent) phenomenon. In the case of drug-free programs such as therapeutic communities, studies have shown that improvement in drug use and addiction-related problems can occur even among patients who drop out of treatment early, with 1 month being the cutoff point at which meaningful benefits typically begin to occur.[20] Use of opioid drugs is highly correlated with relapse to dependence in drug-free treatments; thus, sustained abstinence is an important and necessary goal.

In the case of methadone maintenance, meaningful reduction in opioid and nonopioid use is often observed, even though total abstinence may not occur. Unlike drug-free therapies, in which drug use is usually associated with relapse, patients using methadone maintenance are more likely to be able to use opioids sporadically without a full relapse to uncontrolled dependence. Thus, reductions in drug use and crime, even though they fall short of total abstinence, and improvement in employment and other areas of adjustment can be particularly meaningful indicators of progress in opioid substitution therapy. Studies have shown significant associations between sustained involvement in methadone treatment and reduced rates of HIV infection. These reductions in HIV infection were achieved without achieving zero risk among the methadone patients; there were simply much lower levels of risk among those in methadone maintenance than among those who were not in treatment.[27]

As in other substance use disorders, persons with opioid use disorders usually respond to treatment only after one or more false starts. In any type of treatment, whether drug-free or agonist substitution therapy, the fact that a person does not respond well on the first or second try, or responds briefly and then relapses, is not a cause for alarm. In fact, nonresponse or partial response to initial treatment attempts is the norm. It is important, however, that the staff realize that simply taking a step toward relieving the problem by asking for help is a positive act and that this effort on the part of the patient is acknowledged and encouraged to continue. Patience and sustained efforts for an extended period are important. Some of the most difficult patients will, over a period of years, achieve an excellent response to methadone maintenance or will achieve a sustained, drug-free remission. Such cases require the involvement of the patient in the treatment process, combined with help from the treatment staff. Thus, maintaining an optimistic attitude, believing that any patient can "make it," and not becoming discouraged are important elements of treatment.

Several areas need to be examined when patients are responding only partially or not responding at all. The first area and one of the most important is to determine if there are psychiatric, family, social, or medical problems that are not being addressed. If so, appropriate interventions can often be developed, with a resulting improvement in outcome. A second area is the therapist-patient relationship. The ability to form a positive, helping relationship with treatment providers has been shown to be associated with a positive outcome.[28] Occasionally, switching the patient from one therapist to another has a positive effect; however, this strategy should be used selectively, as it could encourage projection and avoidance of personal responsibility. A third area is treatment setting and length of stay. In some cases, a more extended length of stay in a residential program or halfway house is necessary because of the severity of the dependence or its associated problems, or both.

In the case of persons receiving methadone or LAAM who continue to abuse opioids, cocaine, alcohol, or benzodiazepines, admission for brief inpatient stabilization while substitution therapy is continued may be helpful. Increasing the methadone or LAAM dose to higher levels often works in cases of continuing opioid use. Methadone doses in the range of 80 to 120 mg/d, originally proposed by Dole and Nyswander,[14] are sometimes necessary to achieve a significant reduction in opioid self-administration. Increasing the amount of counseling, occasionally to a daily basis, until the drug use stops sometimes works. In the case of persons who abuse or are dependent on alcohol, liberal use of Breathalyzer testing combined with a requirement that the Breathalyzer register zero before the patient receives the daily methadone or LAAM dose usually helps. Some patients respond to detoxification followed by disulfiram therapy. Contingencies such as providing take-home doses in response to extended periods of drug-free urine test results and requiring that the patient be engaged in work or school as a condition for dispensing take-home medication are also effective motivators.

Clinical Vignette 2

A 42-year-old man presents for treatment of opioid dependence; this is his sixth episode of methadone maintenance. The patient has a long history of alcoholism that has interfered with treatment in the past, and he has begun using cocaine regularly. Historically, the patient has done fairly well with methadone as far as illicit opioid use is concerned, but his clinic attendance and ability to comply with clinic rules, especially regarding take-home doses, have been severely compromised by his alcohol use. In the past, the patient would remain in treatment for about a year, then become angry over his inability to obtain take-home doses (because of ongoing positive Breathalyzer readings), and drop out of treatment; relapse to opioid use always immediately followed. During previous treatment episodes, the patient had frequently been offered inpatient detoxification for his alcoholism but always refused because 1) "alcohol was not his problem, heroin was the problem" and 2) he could not take time off work (as a stockperson in a liquor store). When the patient presented for treatment this time, he had severe social stressors; he was unemployed (secondary to his alcohol problems) and living with his parents, who were threatening to put him out because of his drug use.

The patient was told that this time methadone would not be offered unless he first entered the hospital. After some discussion, he agreed that as part of his treatment plan he would first enter the hospital for 21 to 28 days of treatment including alcohol detoxification and stabilization on methadone; he would then be discharged to maintenance therapy. This approach worked. After inpatient discharge, the patient kept regular counseling appointments, continued to attend self-help meetings to which he had been introduced while on the inpatient unit, *requested* daily Breathalyzer testing, and turned down an offer to return to his job in the liquor store. During the past 3 years, his liver function tests have returned to normal levels, he has been stable with use of 65 mg/d of methadone, with urine tests negative for opioids, although occasionally his urine is positive for cocaine. He has been able to comply fully with a treatment regimen for a back injury sustained 2 years ago and is currently enrolled in school.

Another, more powerful form of treatment is to require certain behaviors contingent on remaining in treatment, or a treatment contract. This intervention is most easily used in substitution therapy programs, in which the patient is given the option of stopping unprescribed drug use, keeping counseling appointments, and looking for a job as conditions of remaining in the program. Such an intervention can work; however, it is important to make certain that it is used selectively. If applied too early, it can force premature suspension of a person who might respond to continued therapy; if applied in anger, it can make the patient worse and probably reduce future chances for effective rehabilitation. It is best reserved for patients who have not responded to treatment despite being in the program for months or even years (in other words, long enough to have had a good chance to have made progress), whose associated problems have been thoroughly evaluated and addressed, whose dose of methadone is sufficiently high to attenuate the effects of self-administered opioids and who are making little or no effort to help themselves. Dually diagnosed and HIV-positive patients require special consideration, and interventions such as treatment contracts should be used with unusually great caution in these individuals.

In difficult cases, a single intervention is often not enough; rather, a series of coordinated efforts is necessary. For example, the patient's dose of methadone is increased while he or she is in an inpatient unit in the context of detoxification from several substances, followed by requiring a contract mandating increased counseling and attendance at self-help groups after the patient returns to the outpatient program.

References

1. Substance related disorders. In Diagnostic and Statistical Manual of Mental Disorders, 4th ed. Washington, DC: American Psychiatric Association, 1994:175–272.
2. National Household Survey on Drug Abuse; Population Estimates 1991 Revised. Washington, DC: U.S. Department of Health and Human Services, Public Health Service, Alcohol, Drug Abuse, and Mental Health Administration, 1991. DHHS publication (ADM)92-1887.
3. Robins LN, Regier DA: Psychiatric Disorders in America: The Epidemiologic Catchment Area Study. New York: Free Press, 1991: 116–154.
4. Thirteen heroin deaths spark wide police investigation. New York Times, August 31, 1994:1.
5. Rounsaville BJ, Kosten TR, Weissman MM, et al: Psychiatric disorders in relatives of probands with opiate addiction. Arch Gen Psychiatry 1991; 48:33–42.
6. Dole VP: Biochemistry of addiction. Ann Rev Biochem 1970; 39:821–840.
7. Kreek MJ: Tolerance and dependence: Implications for the pharmacological treatment of addiction. In Harris LS (ed): Problems of Drug Dependence, 1986. Proceedings of the 48th Annual Scientific Meeting of the Committee on Problems of Drug Dependence. Rockville, MD: U.S. Department of Health and Human Services, 1987:77–86. DHHS publication (ADM)87-1508.
8. Wikler A: Opioid Dependence: Mechanisms and Treatment. New York: Plenum Publishing, 1980.
9. O'Brien CP, Testa T, O'Brien TJ, et al: Conditioned narcotic withdrawal in humans. Science 1977; 195:1000–1002.

10. Martin WR, Jasinski DR: Physiological parameters of morphine dependence in man—tolerance, early abstinence, protracted abstinence. J Psychiatr Res 1969; 7:9–17.
11. Robins LN, Helzer JE, Davis DH: Narcotic use in Southeast Asia and afterward. Arch Gen Psychiatry 1975; 32:955–961.
12. Gold MS, Redmond DE, Kleber HD: Clonidine blocks acute opiate withdrawal symptoms. Lancet 1978; 2:599–602.
13. Gold MS, Pottach AC, Sweeney DR, Kleber HD: Opiate withdrawal using clonidine. JAMA 1980; 243:343–346.
13a. Ravi NV, Maany I, Burke WM, et al: Detoxification with phenobarbital of alprazolam-dependent polysubstance abusers. J Subst Abuse Treat 1990; 7:55–58.
14. Dole VP, Nyswander ME: A medical treatment for diacetylmorphine (heroin) addiction. JAMA 1965; 193:646–650.
15. Dole VP, Nyswander M: Successful treatment of 750 criminal addicts. JAMA 1968; 206:2708–2710.
16. Ball JC, Ross, A: The Effectiveness of Methadone Maintenance Treatment. New York: Springer-Verlag, 1991.
17. McLellan AT, Arndt IO, Metzger DS, et al: The effects of psychosocial services on substance abuse treatment. JAMA 1993; 269:1953–1959.
18. Woody GE, McLellan AT, Luborsky L, et al: Psychiatric severity as a predictor of benefits from psychotherapy: The Penn-VA study. Am J Psychiatry 1984; 141:1172–1177.
19. Woody GE, McLellan AT, Luborsky L, et al: Sociopathy and psychotherapy outcome. Arch Gen Psychiatry 1985; 42:1081–1086.
20. De Leon G, Skodol A, Rosenthal MS: Phoenix House. Changes in psychopathological signs of resident drug addicts. Arch Gen Psychiatry 1973; 28:131–135.
21. Rounsaville BJ, Weissman MM, Wilber CH: The heterogeneity of psychiatric diagnosis in treated opiate addicts. Arch Gen Psychiatry 1982; 39:161–166.
22. DesJarlais DC, Friedman SR, Novice DM, et al: HIV 1 infection among intravenous drug users in Manhattan, New York City 1977 to 1987. JAMA 1989; 261:1008–1012.
23. Chiasson MA, Stoneburner RL, Hildebrandt D, et al: Heterosexual transmission of HIV-1 associated with the use of smokable freebase cocaine (crack). AIDS 1991; 5:1121–1126.
24. Larrat EP, Zierler S: Entangled epidemics: Cocaine use and HIV disease. J Psychoactive Drugs 1993; 25:207–221.
25. Finnegan LP, Wapner RJ: Narcotic addiction in pregnancy. In Neibyl JR (ed): Drug Abuse in Pregnancy. Philadelphia: Lea & Febiger, 1987:203–222.
26. Connor EM, Sperling RS, Gelber R, et al: Reduction of maternal-infant transmission of human immunodeficiency virus type 1 with zidovudine treatment. N Engl J Med 1994; 331:1173–1180.
27. Metzger DS, Woody GE, McLellan AT, et al: HIV conversion among in and out-of-treatment intravenous drug users in Philadelphia. J Acquir Immune Defic Syndr 1993; 6:1049–1056.
28. Luborsky L, McLellan AT, Woody GE, et al: Therapist success and its determinants. Arch Gen Psychiatry 1985; 42:602–611.

CHAPTER

50 Sedative, Hypnotic, or Anxiolytic Use Disorders

Donald R. Wesson
Walter Ling
David E. Smith

Sedative, Hypnotic, or Anxiolytic Use Disorders

Sedative, Hypnotic, or Anxiolytic Intoxication

Sedative-hypnotics and anxiolytics include prescription sleeping medications and most medications used for the treatment of anxiety. Pharmacologically, alcohol is appropriately included among sedative-hypnotics; however, it is generally considered separately, as it is in this book.

The medications usually included in the category of sedative-hypnotics are listed in Table 50–1. The sedative-hypnotics include a chemically diverse group of medications. Although buspirone is marketed for the treatment of anxiety, its pharmacological profile is sufficiently different that it is not usually included among the sedative-hypnotics. Antidepressant medications may also have antianxiety properties, and their sedative effects are often used to assist in sleep induction; however, they are usually excluded from the sedative-hypnotic classification.

Sedative-hypnotics are among the most commonly prescribed medications. They are also often misused and abused and can produce severe, life-threatening dependence. With the exception of the benzodiazepines and zolpidem, overdose with sedative-hypnotics can be lethal. The benzodiazepines are rarely lethal if taken alone; in combination with alcohol, however, they too can be lethal.

When the benzodiazepines were introduced into clinical medicine in the early 1960s, their safety in the overdose situation led physicians to believe that they were without harmful effects. Over time, there was recognition that the benzodiazepines could produce severe physiological dependence and could be drugs of abuse. Nonetheless, their medical utility in treatment of disabling anxiety, episodic sleep disturbances, and seizures has made them indispensable to medical practice.

Considerations of sedative-hypnotic use disorders should reflect a sensible balance between their medical utility and adverse events arising from medical treatment and their use as intoxicants or as self-medication of symptoms resulting from abuse of other drugs. This chapter, which focuses on disorders defined in the *Diagnostic and Statistical Manual of Mental Disorders,* Fourth Edition (DSM-IV) as resulting from sedative-hypnotic use, is weighted toward adverse consequences.

In common use, concepts of drug abuse, misuse, and addiction are deeply rooted in social values and attitudes and have been encoded into laws. For example, moderate use of alcohol is widely sanctioned for adults, but public intoxication or driving with an alcohol blood level above 0.8 to 1 mg/dL is generally considered alcohol abuse. Prescription medications are not sanctioned as intoxicants.

The term *misuse* is commonly applied to prescription sedative-hypnotics, but the DSM-IV does not provide specific criteria for misuse as it does for abuse and dependence. When medications are taken in higher doses or more frequently than prescribed, or by someone other than the person for whom the medication was prescribed, or for reasons other than what would normally be considered medical use, the behavior is generally considered misuse of the medication.

DSM-IV[1] defines abuse and dependence in terms of behavioral and physiological consequences to the person taking the medication. The criteria for abuse and dependence apply as uniformly as possible across classes of drugs, and the criteria do not distinguish the source of the medication or the intended purpose for which it was taken. Further, when most people, including physicians, speak of drug dependence, they are referring to physical dependence. DSM-IV uses the term dependence to denote a more severe form of substance use disorder than abuse, and it uses the specifier "with or without physiological dependence" to indicate whether the patient has significant physical dependence. Physiological dependence is not required for a DSM-IV diagnosis of drug dependence. A diagnosis of substance dependence is made only when a patient has dysfunctional behaviors that are a *result* of the drug use.

The qualification that the dysfunctional behavior be the result of drug use is extremely important but, in a practical sense, is often difficult to establish with certainty. In considering the diagnosis of sedative-hypnotic dependence

Table 50–1 Medications Usually Included in the Category of Sedative-Hypnotics

Generic Name	Trade Names	Common Therapeutic Use	Therapeutic Dose Range (mg/d)
Barbiturates			
Amobarbital	Amytal	Sedative	50–150
Butabarbital	Butisol	Sedative	45–120
Butalbital	Fiorinal, Sedapap	Sedative/ analgesic	100–300
Pentobarbital	Nembutal	Hypnotic	50–100
Secobarbital	Seconal	Hypnotic	50–100
Benzodiazepines			
Alprazolam	Xanax	Antianxiety	0.75–6
Chlordiazepoxide	Librium	Antianxiety	15–100
Clonazepam	Klonopin	Anticonvulsant	0.5–4
Clorazepate	Tranxene	Antianxiety	15–60
Diazepam	Valium	Antianxiety	5–40
Estazolam	ProSom	Hypnotic	1–2
Flunitrazepam	Rohypnol*	Hypnotic	1–2
Flurazepam	Dalmane	Hypnotic	15–30
Halazepam	Paxipam	Antianxiety	60–160
Lorazepam	Ativan	Antianxiety	1–16
Midazolam	Versed	Anesthesia	—
Oxazepam	Serax	Antianxiety	10–120
Prazepam	Centrax	Antianxiety	20–60
Quazepam	Doral	Hypnotic	15
Temazepam	Restoril	Hypnotic	7.5–30
Triazolam	Halcion	Hypnotic	0.125–0.5
Others			
Chloral hydrate	Noctec, Somnos	Hypnotic	250–1000
Ethchlorvynol	Placidyl	Hypnotic	200–1000
Glutethimide	Doriden	Hypnotic	250–500
Meprobamate	Miltown, Equanil, Equagesic	Antianxiety	1200–1600
Methyprylon	Noludar	Hypnotic	200–400
Zolpidem	Ambien	Hypnotic	5–10

*Rohypnol is not marketed in the United States.

among patients who are being treated for an anxiety disorder, it is not always possible to ascertain with certainty whether the behavioral dysfunction is produced by the underlying psychiatric disorder or by the drug use. Different attribution is often the basis of disagreement among psychiatrists, patients, and patients' families. A patient whose panic attacks are ameliorated by a medication may exhibit what may be interpreted as drug-seeking behavior if access to the medication is threatened.

The terms *anxiolytic* and *minor tranquilizer* are also frequently sources of confusion. In classic pharmacology, sedative-hypnotics are drugs or medications that produce a dose-related depression of consciousness. Drug classes are formed by combining drugs or medications that have similar pharmacological profiles, often studied in animals. This classification has less meaning for psychiatrists, who are usually interested in anxiolytic medications that can reduce anxiety without producing unwanted sedation.

Epidemiology

Most people do not find the subjective effects of sedative-hypnotics pleasant or appealing beyond their therapeutic effects (e.g., relief of anxiety or facilitation of sleep). Many addicts, on the other hand, have a subjectively different response to sedative-hypnotics and like the subjective effects of sedative-hypnotics.[2] The qualitative difference in subjective response to medications by addicts is extremely important in understanding why medication treatments that are efficacious for nonaddicts cannot be used in the same way for addicts.

Patterns of Abuse

Some sedative-hypnotics, such as the short-acting barbiturates, are primary drugs of abuse—that is, they are injected for the rush or are taken orally to produce a state of disinhibition similar to that achieved with alcohol.

Barbiturates

During the late 1960s and early 1970s, the short-acting barbiturates secobarbital and pentobarbital were common drugs of abuse. Addicts dissolved the tablets or the contents of capsules in water and injected the solution. The desired effect was the rush, a dreamy, floaty feeling lasting a few minutes after the injection. After the rush, the addict is intoxicated. The intoxication is not qualitatively different than that produced by oral ingestion of a short-acting barbiturate.

Injection of a barbiturate is associated with the usual infectious risk of injecting street drugs, but the barbiturates are particularly pernicious if inadvertently injected into an artery or if the solution is injected or leaked from a vein or artery into tissue surrounding the vessel. Barbiturates are irritating to tissue, and the affected tissue becomes hard and abscessed. In addition, barbiturate solution injected into an artery produces intense vasoconstriction and blockage of the arterioles, resulting in gangrene of areas supplied by the artery.

Methaqualone

Methaqualone (Quaalude) was removed from the U.S. market in 1984 because of its abuse. Subsequently, it has continued to be sold on the street-drug black market. Some tablets sold on the black market as Quaalude contain methaqualone, apparently diverted from countries where methaqualone is still available; others contain diazepam, phenobarbital, or another sedative-hypnotic.

Benzodiazepines

Most sedative-hypnotics are not primary drugs of abuse. Benzodiazepines, for example, are often used or misused by addicts to self-medicate opiate withdrawal, to intensify the central nervous system effects of methadone, or to ameliorate the adverse effects of cocaine or methamphetamine. Unlike most drugs of abuse, which are manufactured in clandestine laboratories and distributed through the street-drug black market, the sedative-hypnotics are manufactured by pharmaceutical companies. Sedative-hypnotics that are used and abused by addicts are obtained from the black market, where they have been diverted from medical channels, or are obtained from physicians and pharmacies under treatment subterfuge.

Rohypnol

Most benzodiazepines abused in the United States are domestically manufactured. An exception is flunitrazepam (Rohypnol, Narcozep), a potent benzodiazepine hypnotic not marketed in the United States but widely available by prescription in many other countries in 1- or 2-mg dosage forms. In cities in Mexico along the U.S. border, "patients" may purchase prescriptions in a physician's office and then obtain at a Mexican pharmacy a 90-day supply of medication that can be brought into the United States. The medications most often obtained are flunitrazepam, diazepam, and alprazolam. The medications are often sold on the U.S. drug black market. In addition to being available by small-scale prescription diversion, flunitrazepam is smuggled into the United States along the border with Mexico and is smuggled from Colombia into Miami.

Flunitrazepam has many street names, including rophies, ropies, roopies, roofies, ruffes, rofinol, loops, and wheels.[3] Tablets of Rohypnol have the name of the manufacturer, Roche, engraved on them and a number indicating the milligram strength (either 1 or 2). Drug abusers usually prefer the 2-mg tablets, which are often called "Roche dos" or just "Roche" (usually pronounced "row-shay").[4] Reports from other countries suggest that flunitrazepam has considerable appeal among heroin addicts.[5, 6]

Zolpidem

Zolpidem (Ambien) is an imidazopyridine hypnotic, chemically unrelated to the benzodiazepines; however, it binds to a subunit of the same γ-aminobutyric acid–benzodiazepine (GABA-BZ) complex as the benzodiazepines,[7, 8] and its sedative effects are reversed by the benzodiazepine antagonist flumazenil. Zolpidem has been extensively used in Europe for several years. Relatively few cases of abuse have been reported. Case reports from Italy suggested that some patients increase the dosage many times that prescribed and that zolpidem produces a withdrawal syndrome similar to that of other sedative-hypnotics.[9] The case histories illustrated significant tolerance to zolpidem and the rapid production of withdrawal symptoms that might be expected from a potent, short-acting sedative-hypnotic.

Zolpidem is rapidly absorbed and has a short half-life (2.2 hours). Its sedative effects are additive with alcohol. Like triazolam, zolpidem decreases brain metabolism of glucose.[10]

Some investigators have suggested that zolpidem does not produce tolerance or physical dependence.[11] Mice were administered zolpidem or midazolam (both 30 mg/kg) by gastric intubation for 10 days. Animals treated with midazolam, but not zolpidem, showed tolerance to the drug's sedative effects and a lowered seizure threshold after the drug was stopped. Further, the benzodiazepine antagonist flumazenil precipitated withdrawal in the midazolam-treated animals but not in those treated with zolpidem.

Studies of baboons suggested that zolpidem is reinforcing and that it produces tolerance and physical dependence.[12] In a free-choice paradigm, baboons consistently self-administered zolpidem intravenously at higher rates than either the vehicle solution alone or the triazolam. After 2 weeks of zolpidem self-administration, substitution of the vehicle solution alone resulted in suppression of food-pellet intake, which the investigators interpreted as zolpidem withdrawal. Baboons trained to discriminate oral doses of either phenobarbital (10 mg/kg) or lorazepam (1.8 mg/kg) from placebo responded to zolpidem as though it were an active drug more than 80% of the time. In another experiment, animals developed tolerance to zolpidem-induced ataxia and sedation during 7 days of drug administration. The investigators concluded that the rates of self-administration of zolpidem were similar to those of pentobarbital and higher than those maintained by 11 benzodiazepines that they had studied.

The package insert for Ambien is typically noncommittal on the subject of dependence and withdrawal: "The U.S. clinical trial experience from zolpidem does not reveal any clear evidence for withdrawal syndrome," and, later, "available data cannot provide a reliable estimate of the incidence, if any, of dependency, or the relationship of any dependency to dose and duration of treatment."[13]

Efficacy trials of sedative-hypnotics do not typically reveal much about dependence and withdrawal because dosage is carefully controlled and people with a history of alcohol or other sedative-hypnotic misuse or dependence are usually excluded from participating. Only after the marketing of medications do patients with a history of drug abuse or misuse get access to the drug.

Psychotic Reactions

A report from Belgium described two cases of transient psychosis after the first dose of 10 mg of zolpidem.[14] Neither patient had a history of drug abuse or misuse, and neither was using alcohol at the time. Both patients experienced a transient psychosis with visual hallucinations beginning 20 to 30 minutes after 10 mg of zolpidem. Both patients previously used benzodiazepines without difficulty and both were amnestic for the psychotic episode.

A report from Spain described a 20-year-old woman with severe anorexia who became terrified by visual hallucinations and illusions 20 minutes after taking a 10-mg dose of zolpidem.[15] She had full recall of the psychotic episode. A week later, she took a 5-mg dose of zolpidem and experienced a similar episode of reduced intensity. A week later, she took 2.5 mg and again experienced visual distortions.

Acute Intoxication

The acute toxicity of sedative-hypnotics consists of slurred speech, incoordination, ataxia, sustained nystagmus, impaired judgment, and mood lability. In large amounts, sedative-hypnotics produce progressive respiratory depression and coma. The amount of respiratory depression produced by the benzodiazepines is much less than that produced by the barbiturates and other sedative-hypnotics.

Consistent with its general approach, the DSM-IV diagnosis of intoxication requires "clinically significant maladaptive behavioral or psychological changes" developing after drug use in addition to the signs and symptoms of acute toxicity. The DSM-IV criteria for intoxication are summarized here.

DSM-IV Criteria 292.89

Sedative, Hypnotic, or Anxiolytic Intoxication

A. Recent use of a sedative, hypnotic, or anxiolytic.

B. Clinically significant maladaptive behavioral or psychological changes (e.g., inappropriate sexual or aggressive behavior, mood lability, impaired judgment, impaired social or occupational functioning) that developed during, or shortly after, sedative, hypnotic, or anxiolytic use.

C. One (or more) of the following signs, developing during, or shortly after, sedative, hypnotic, or anxiolytic use:

(1) slurred speech

(2) incoordination

(3) unsteady gait

(4) nystagmus

(5) impairment in attention or memory

(6) stupor or coma

D. The symptoms are not due to a general medical condition and are not better accounted for by another mental disorder.

Dependence

Barbiturates can produce tolerance and physiological dependence. Physiological dependence can be induced within several days with continuous infusion of anesthetic doses. Patients who are taking barbiturates daily for a month or more above the upper therapeutic range listed in Table 50–1 should be presumed to be physically dependent and in need of medically managed detoxification.

The withdrawal syndrome from short-acting sedative-hypnotics is similar to that from alcohol. Signs and symptoms of sedative-hypnotic withdrawal include anxiety, tremors, nightmares, insomnia, anorexia, nausea, vomiting, postural hypotension, seizures, delirium, and hyperpyrexia. The syndrome is qualitatively similar for all sedative-hypnotics; however, the time course of symptoms depends on the particular drug. With short-acting sedative-hypnotics (e.g., pentobarbital, secobarbital, meprobamate, oxazepam, alprazolam, and triazolam), withdrawal symptoms typically begin 12 to 24 hours after the last dose and peak in intensity between 24 and 72 hours. (Symptoms may develop more slowly in patients with liver disease or in the elderly because of decreased drug metabolism.) With long-acting drugs (e.g., phenobarbital, diazepam, and chlordiazepoxide), withdrawal symptoms peak on the fifth to eighth day.

During untreated sedative-hypnotic withdrawal, the electroencephalogram may show paroxysmal bursts of high-voltage, slow-frequency activity that precede the development of seizures. The withdrawal delirium may include confusion and visual and auditory hallucinations. The delirium generally follows a period of insomnia. Some patients may have only delirium, others only seizures, and some may have both delirium and convulsions.

As is described in the later section on benzodiazepines, benzodiazepines may also produce a severe, protracted withdrawal syndrome, and withdrawal symptoms may be produced in some patients after cessation of long-term therapeutic dosing.

Iatrogenic Dependence

Patients treated for months to years with benzodiazepines and other sedative-hypnotics may become physically dependent on sedative-hypnotics. The possibility of physical dependence should be discussed with the patient and, in some cases, the patient's family. The distinction between physical dependence as a process of neuroadaptation and physical dependence as a consequence of a substance abuse disorder should be explained in detail. Patients need to be advised against abruptly stopping the medication.

Etiology and Pathophysiology

Sedative-Hypnotics and GABA Receptors

Many neurons in the central nervous system have receptors for the neurotransmitter GABA. Stimulation of $GABA_A$ is generally inhibitory; however, under conditions of intense activation, dendritic $GABA_A$ receptors excite rather than inhibit neurons.[16] Benzodiazepines attach to a receptor complex that has an allosteric relation to $GABA_A$ receptors. Benzodiazepine receptors have multiple subunits, and occupancy of the benzodiazepine receptor with an agonist potentiates the effect of $GABA_A$ in modulating chloride ionophores. The molecular pharmacology of the receptor is exceedingly complex. Chronic exposure to benzodiazepines may uncouple the benzodiazepine receptor from the $GABA_A$ receptor.[17, 18] The uncoupling has important ramifications for long-term treatment with benzodiazepines and benzodiazepine dependence.[19] There is evidence in animals that benzodiazepine receptor density is increased by stress and corticosterone and that the effects are affected by sex hormones.[20] Alcohol causes enhancement of benzodiazepine binding in the cortex.[21]

Genetic Factors

There is considerable evidence that the propensity to develop alcohol dependence has a genetic component. Preclinical studies suggested that the encephalographic response to benzodiazepines is different in alcohol-preferring rats.[22] In sons of alcoholics, diazepam produces significantly less effects on eye movement tasks that are reliable and quantitative measures of benzodiazepine effects but produces significantly greater pleasurable effects.[23] The differential response of sons of alcoholics may reflect altered functional sensitivity of the central GABA-benzodiazepine receptor system.

Benzodiazepines produce a dose-related decrease in brain metabolism of glucose. Compared with nonalcoholic control subjects, recently detoxified alcoholic subjects show comparable responses to lorazepam in the occipital and cerebellar glucose metabolism but significantly less decrease in glucose metabolism in the thalamus, basal ganglia, and orbitofrontal cortex.[24]

Diagnosis and Differential Diagnosis

The diagnosis of sedative-hypnotic abuse and dependence is based primarily on drug use history and the DSM-IV criteria of continuing behavior dysfunction as a result of the drug abuse. With a dependence disorder developing from prescribed use, the practical difficulty is determining when the dysfunction is a result of the drug use rather than the disorder for which the medication was prescribed.

A patient who has found that a medication is effective at reducing distressing symptoms may display behavior that can be viewed as drug seeking if the patient's access to the medication is challenged.

Phenomenology and Variations in Presentations

Physical Dependence in Non–Drug-Dependent Medical Patients

Long-term use of benzodiazepines can result in physical dependence in non–drug-dependent medical patients. Withdrawal symptoms or return of symptoms suppressed by the benzodiazepines may make discontinuation difficult. In a study of benzodiazepine discontinuation, patients who had received long-term benzodiazepine therapy were gradually tapered off their benzodiazepine. Thirty-two percent of long half-life and 42% of short half-life benzodiazepine-treated patients were unable to achieve abstinence.[24a]

Some patients who are physically dependent on or unable to discontinue a medication do not necessarily have a substance abuse disorder. Physical dependence results from neuroadaptive changes from long-term exposure to a medication. Inability to discontinue the medication may simply mean that patients are unwilling to tolerate the severity of postwithdrawal symptoms that develop. In the absence of dysfunction produced by the medication, the decision to continue taking it may be appropriate medication maintenance. Patients who do not have a substance abuse disorder take medications in the quantity prescribed. They follow their physicians' recommendations, and they do not abuse other drugs.

Presentation in Drug-Abusing Patients

Abusers of alcohol and other drugs rarely present for primary treatment of sedative-hypnotic dependency. From the drug-abusing patient's point of view, sedative-hypnotic use is an effort to self-medicate anxiety or insomnia, which is often the result of alcohol or stimulant abuse. Despite their assertion that the medication is being taken for symptom relief, they often take the medication in larger than physician-prescribed doses, combine the medication with intoxicating amounts of alcohol or other drugs, and purchase quantities of medications from street sources. They may also use the medication as an intoxicant when other drugs are not available.

Cultural and Minority Issues in Assessment and Treatment

There are marked class and ethnic differences in beliefs and values about the use of intoxicants and medications. The dominant culture in the United States prohibits the use of any intoxicant other than alcohol and places limits on tolerated behaviors while intoxicated (e.g., public intoxication, driving an automobile while intoxicated). Many groups within the United States have a much broader acceptance of other drugs, particularly marijuana, and prescription medications as intoxicants or intoxicant extenders (e.g., flunitrazepam and alcohol combination).

Many youths see the distinction between medication, sanctioned only for treatment of disease under the prescription of a physician, and recreational drugs as arbitrary and pharmacologically irrational. For some, medications such as methaqualone simply extend the number of available intoxicants.

A strength of the drug abuse and dependence criteria of DSM-IV is that the criteria are behaviors that most people would agree are dysfunctional.

Assessment

Drug Use History

The patient's drug use history is usually the first source of information that is used in assessing sedative-hypnotic abuse or dependence. If the sedative-hypnotics were being used for treatment of insomnia or anxiety, the history is often best obtained as part of the history of the disorder and its response to treatment. A detailed use of all sedative-hypnotics, including alcohol, should be elicited from the patient. When framed in terms of the presenting disorder, patients are generally more candid about their drug use and their relationship with past treating physicians.

For many reasons, patients may minimize or exaggerate their drug use and not accurately report the behavioral consequences of their use. High doses of benzodiazepines, or therapeutic doses of benzodiazepines in combination with alcohol, may disrupt memory. Patients are likely to attribute impairment of function to the underlying disorder rather than to the medication use. Observations of patients' behavior by family members can be valuable information. Whenever possible, medical and pharmacy records should be obtained to help piece together as accurate a picture of drug use as possible. Pharmacy records may be helpful in establishing and verifying patients' drug use history, and urine testing can be useful in verifying recent drug use history.

Patients who are obtaining some or all of their medication from street sources may not know what they have been taking, as deception in the street-drug marketplace is common. For example, tablets sold as methaqualone have been found to contain phenobarbital or diazepam.

Physical Findings

Sustained horizontal nystagmus is a reliable indicator of sedative-hypnotic intoxication. Onset of tremor, abnormal sweating, and blood pressure or pulse increase may be produced by sedative-hypnotic withdrawal.

Laboratory Tests

Urine toxicology can be useful in monitoring patients' use of drugs and in confirming a history of drug or medication use. Laboratory markers can be useful in assessing alcohol use.

Course and Natural History

Once a DSM-IV diagnosis of sedative-hypnotic dependence is established, it is unlikely that a patient will be able to return to controlled, therapeutic use of abusable sedative-hypnotics. All sedative-hypnotics, including alcohol, are cross-tolerant, and physical dependence and tolerance are quickly reestablished if a patient resumes use of sedative-hypnotics.

If after sedative-hypnotic withdrawal the patient has another primarily psychiatric disorder, such as generalized anxiety disorder, panic attacks, or insomnia, treatment strategies other than sedative-hypnotics should be used, if at all possible. Definitive diagnosis of a psychiatric disorder during early abstinence is often not possible because protracted withdrawal symptoms may mimic anxiety disorders, and disruption of sleep architecture for days to months after drug withdrawal is extremely common.

If the sedative-hypnotic dependence has developed secondary to stimulant or alcohol use, primary treatment of the chemical dependence should be a priority. Often the symptom that was driving the sedative-hypnotic use disappears after the patient is drug abstinent.

Treatment

Physician-Patient Relationship

Treatment of sedative-hypnotic dependence that has developed from treatment of an underlying psychiatric disorder is almost always a lengthy undertaking. The first phase of treatment is to establish the drug use and, to the extent possible, the underlying psychiatric diagnoses and to establish a therapeutic alliance with the patient. The art of treatment is knowing when the therapeutic alliance is sufficiently established to institute drug withdrawal and knowing when outpatient treatment is not progressing adequately.

In the era of managed health care, it can be difficult, if not impossible, to get medical payors to agree to inpatient treatment of "low-dose" dependence. Although patients may experience intensely disturbing symptoms and may not be able to tolerate symptoms and comply with medication regimens, not everyone accepts low-dose dependence as a valid syndrome, and medical reviewers may attribute symptoms arising during withdrawal as mismanagement of symptom reemergence.

Detoxification

Three general strategies are used for withdrawing patients from sedative-hypnotics, including benzodiazepines. The first is to use decreasing doses of the agent of dependence. The second is to substitute phenobarbital or some other long-acting barbiturate for the addicting agent and gradually withdraw the substitute medication.[25–28] The third, used for patients with a dependence on both alcohol and a benzodiazepine, is to substitute a long-acting benzodiazepine, such as chlordiazepoxide, and taper it during 1 to 2 weeks.

Detoxification Strategies for Sedative-Hypnotics

1. Use decreasing doses of the agent of dependence.
2. Substitute phenobarbital or other long-acting barbiturate and gradually withdraw.
3. Substitute a long-acting benzodiazepine and taper during 1 to 2 weeks.

The pharmacological rationale for phenobarbital substitution is that phenobarbital is long acting and little change in blood levels of phenobarbital occurs between doses. This allows the safe use of a progressively smaller daily dose. Phenobarbital is safer than the shorter acting barbiturates; lethal doses of phenobarbital are many times higher than toxic doses, and the signs of toxicity (e.g., sustained nystagmus, slurred speech, and ataxia) are easy to observe. Finally, phenobarbital intoxication usually does not produce disinhibition, so most patients view it as a medication, not as a drug of abuse.

The withdrawal strategy selected depends on the particular benzodiazepine, the involvement of other drugs of dependence, and the clinical setting in which the detoxification program takes place.

The gradual reduction of the benzodiazepine of dependence is used primarily in medical settings for dependence arising from treatment of an underlying condition. The patient must be cooperative, must be able to adhere to dosing regimens, and must not be abusing alcohol or other drugs.

Substitution of phenobarbital can also be used to withdraw patients who have lost control of their benzodiazepine use or who are polydrug dependent. Phenobarbital substitution has the broadest use for all sedative-hypnotic drug dependencies and is widely used in drug treatment programs.

Stabilization Phase

The patient's history of drug use during the month before treatment is used to compute the stabilization dose of phenobarbital. Although many addicts exaggerate the number of pills they are taking, the patient's history is the best guide to initiating pharmacotherapy for withdrawal. Patients who have overstated the amount of drug that they have taken will become intoxicated during the first day or two of treatment. Intoxication is easily managed by omitting one or more doses of phenobarbital and recalculating the daily dose.

To compute the initial starting dose of phenobarbital, the patient's average daily use of each sedative-hypnotic is computed. Then, the daily dose of each drug is multiplied by the phenobarbital conversion constant, shown in Tables 50–2 and 50–3. The phenobarbital withdrawal equivalents for each drug are then added together. The maximal phenobarbital dose is 500 mg/d. The patient's average daily sedative-hypnotic dose is converted to the phenobarbital withdrawal equivalent using a conversion value such as that shown in Table 50–2. The daily amount is divided into three doses.

Table 50–2 Phenobarbital Withdrawal Equivalents of Nonbenzodiazepines

Generic Name	Trade Name	Dose Equal to 30 mg of Phenobarbital for Withdrawal* (mg)	Phenobarbital Conversion Constant
Barbiturates			
Amobarbital	Amytal	100	0.33
Butabarbital	Butisol	100	0.33
Butalbital†	Fiorinal	100	0.33
Pentobarbital	Nembutal	100	0.33
Secobarbital	Seconal	100	0.33
Others			
Chloral hydrate	Noctec, Somnos	500	0.06
Ethchlorvynol	Placidyl	500	0.06
Glutethimide	Doriden	250	0.12
Meprobamate	Miltown	1200	0.025
Methyprylon	Noludar	200	0.15
Zolpidem	Ambien	5	6

*Phenobarbital withdrawal conversion equivalence is not the same as therapeutic dose equivalency.

†Butalbital is in combination with opiate or nonopiate analgesics.

Before receiving each dose of phenobarbital, the patient is checked for signs of phenobarbital toxicity: sustained nystagmus, slurred speech, or ataxia. Of these, sustained nystagmus is the most reliable. If nystagmus is present, the scheduled dose of phenobarbital is withheld. If all three signs are present, the next two doses of phenobarbital are withheld, and the daily dosage of phenobarbital for the next day is halved.

Table 50–3 Phenobarbital Withdrawal Equivalents of Benzodiazepines

Generic Name	Trade Name	Dose Equal to 30 mg of Phenobarbital for Withdrawal* (mg)	Phenobarbital Conversion Constant
Alprazolam	Xanax	1	30
Chlordiazepoxide	Librium	25	1.2
Clonazepam	Klonopin	2	15
Clorazepate	Tranxene	7.5	4
Diazepam	Valium	10	3
Estazolam	ProSom	1	30
Flurazepam	Dalmane	15	2
Halazepam	Paxipam	40	0.75
Lorazepam	Ativan	2	15
Oxazepam	Serax	10	3
Prazepam	Centrax	10	3
Quazepam	Doral	15	2
Temazepam	Restoril	15	2
Triazolam	Halcion	0.25	120

*Phenobarbital withdrawal conversion equivalence is not the same as therapeutic dose equivalency.

Signs of Phenobarbital Toxicity

- Sustained nystagmus
- Slurred speech
- Ataxia

If the patient is in acute withdrawal and has had, or is in danger of having, withdrawal seizures, the initial dose of phenobarbital is administered by intramuscular injection. If nystagmus and other signs of intoxication develop after 1 to 2 hours after the intramuscular dose, the patient is in no immediate danger from barbiturate withdrawal. Patients are maintained with the initial dosing schedule of phenobarbital for 2 days. If the patient has neither signs of withdrawal nor phenobarbital toxicity (slurred speech, nystagmus, unsteady gait), phenobarbital withdrawal is begun.

Withdrawal Phase

Unless the patient develops signs and symptoms of phenobarbital toxicity or sedative-hypnotic withdrawal, phenobarbital is decreased by 30 mg/d. Should signs of phenobarbital toxicity develop during withdrawal, the daily phenobarbital dose is decreased by 50% and the 30 mg/d withdrawal is continued from the reduced phenobarbital dose. Should the patient have objective signs of sedative-hypnotic withdrawal, the daily dose is increased by 50% and the patient is restabilized before continuing the withdrawal.

Psychosocial Treatment

Psychotherapy

Psychotherapy in treatment of drug dependence has been much maligned; two reasons for this deserve consideration. First, some psychotherapists treat drug dependence as a symptom of an underlying disorder and use a self-medication model of drug abuse that assumes that the drug abuse will cease if the underlying causes are understood. Second, during the early recovery of patients from drug dependence, some therapists mobilize strong affect, memories, or emotions that their patients are unable to tolerate and, consequently, they relapse to drug abuse.

The self-medication model, even if accurate in a particular case, is not a good one because once drug abuse or dependence becomes established the drug use takes on a life of its own regardless of the underlying reason for initiation. Rarely is treatment with insight-oriented psychotherapy successful in stopping the drug use. During early recovery, most patients are coping with subtle withdrawal symptoms, repairing relationships, and learning to function without reliance on psychoactive drugs. Patients with underlying psychiatric disorders may have the additional burden of emergence of symptoms that had been ameliorated by their drug use. Psychotherapy during early recovery should be supportive and focused on coping with current life difficulties. Psychotherapists should remain vigilant for symptoms of panic attacks, generalized anxiety, depression, or sleep disturbances that interfere with current function and should initiate appropriate psychopharmacological or somatic treatments when appropriate. Studies of benzodiazepine discontinuation have noted that some patients report recurrences of clinical symptoms after discontinuation.[29, 30]

Psychotherapy can, however, have an important role in motivating a patient for primary treatment of drug dependency. Therapists can help break down patients' denial of their drug dependence by helping them see how drug use is interfering with relationships and undermining their ability to function. In some instances, it is desirable to continue the psychotherapeutic relationship while the patient is undergoing treatment for chemical dependence. With drug abusers, it is often desirable to separate the medication management from psychotherapy to prevent the psychotherapy from becoming bogged down in discussions of medications and medication side effects.

Twelve-Step Recovery

Alcoholics Anonymous, Narcotics Anonymous, and Cocaine Anonymous groups are important treatment adjuncts for many people recovering from alcohol and other forms of drug dependence. Although many groups are becoming more tolerant of appropriate use of pharmacotherapies, many individuals who attend 12-step recovery meetings are adamantly opposed to any form of psychotropic medication use and counsel fellow members to stop their use. Strong opposition to medications is usually based on their own, or friends', bad experience with medications. Some individuals recover without medications and believe that recovery is of better quality if not supported by a pharmacological crutch.

Patients with underlying psychiatric disorders and the need for treatment with psychopharmacotherapeutic medications often require ongoing support from their psychotherapist if they must have medication.

Additional Treatment Considerations

Psychiatric Comorbidity

Most patients who are being prescribed long-term benzodiazepine therapy have underlying major depressive disorder, panic disorder, or generalized anxiety disorder. The clinical dilemma is deciding which patients are receiving appropriate maintenance therapy for a chronic psychiatric condition. Physical dependence on benzodiazepines may be acceptable if the patient's disabling anxiety symptoms are ameliorated. The reason for the patient's request for benzodiazepine withdrawal from long-term, stable dosing should be carefully explored. Valid reasons to discontinue benzodiazepine treatment include 1) breakthrough of symptoms that were previously well controlled; 2) impairment of memory or other neurocognitive functions; and 3) abuse of alcohol, cocaine, or other medications.

Patients with severe underlying psychiatric disorders may have unrealistic hopes of becoming medication free. Often the origin of request for benzodiazepine withdrawal comes from concerned friends or relatives. Patients' "problems" may be reframed as the use of "addictive medications" or "dependence" rather than the underlying psychopathology. As a practical matter, a trial of medication discontinuation may be undertaken with the understanding that return to a benzodiazepine or use of an antidepressant or other medications may be appropriate.

Treatment of Refractory Patients

Drug Abusers

Many abusers of alcohol or other drugs have symptoms that would reasonably indicate treatment with benzodiazepines or other sedatives if they were not drug abusers. Treating drug abusers with benzodiazepines or other sedatives while they are still abusing drugs is generally not helpful, however. Such patients are at high risk of misusing or abusing the medications, and the medication may enable them to continue abuse of their primary drug. Drug abusers who are symptomatic because of drug toxicity need hospitalization and detoxification. In patients with drug dependence disorders, abstinence from all abusable medications is the preferred treatment goal, particularly during the first 6 months of abstinence.

In patients who do not have a drug dependence disorder, return to benzodiazepine use after detoxification may have a different implication than among patients with a drug dependence disorder. The term *relapse,* which is clearly pejorative, could reasonably be applied to patients who self-administer a benzodiazepine when benzodiazepine abstinence is the agreed on goal of treatment. However, the term relapse should not be applied to patients without a substance abuse disorder who return to prescribed benzodiazepine use because emerging symptoms are not otherwise manageable.

Underlying Psychiatric Conditions

Numerous studies have documented a high prevalence of psychopathological conditions among alcohol and drug abusers. Although the abuse of drugs can induce a psychopathological condition, and there is considerable uncertainty as to the extent to which drug abuse itself contributes to estimates of psychopathology, it is clinically apparent that some drug abusers have severe underlying psychopathological conditions that must be treated if patients are to remain abstinent and functional.

BENZODIAZEPINES

For treatment of anxiety and insomnia, the benzodiazepines have largely supplanted the older sedative-hypnotics. The benzodiazepines have a major advantage over the older compounds. In an overdose, the older sedative-hypnotics are lethal at 10 to 15 times the usual therapeutic doses. Benzodiazepines, if taken alone, have a therapeutic ratio exceeding 100. In combination with alcohol or other drugs, the benzodiazepines may contribute to the lethality, but death from a benzodiazepine overdose is rare. Some atavistic uses of the older compounds remain, driven primarily by economic considerations and misguided attempts to reduce abuse of benzodiazepines by addicts and perceived overprescription of benzodiazepines by physicians.

Abuse Potential

Most people do not like the subjective effects of benzodiazepines, especially in high doses. Even among drug addicts, the benzodiazepines alone are not common intoxicants. They are, however, widely used by drug addicts to self-medicate opiate withdrawal and to alleviate the side effects of cocaine and amphetamines. Patients receiving methadone maintenance use benzodiazepines to boost (enhance) the effects of methadone. Some alcoholic patients use benzodiazepines either in combination with alcohol or as a second-choice intoxicant if alcohol is unavailable. Fat-soluble benzodiazepines that enter the central nervous system quickly are usually the benzodiazepines preferred by addicts.

Addicts whose urine is being monitored for benzodiazepines prefer benzodiazepines with high milligram potency, such as alprazolam or clonazepam. These benzodiazepines are excreted in urine in such small amounts that they are often not detected in drug screens, particularly with thin-layer chromatography.

High-Dose Benzodiazepine Withdrawal Syndrome

Studies of humans have established that large doses of chlordiazepoxide[31] and diazepam,[32] taken for 1 month or more, produce a withdrawal syndrome that is clinically similar to the withdrawal syndrome produced by high doses of barbiturates.[33] Other benzodiazepines have not been studied under such precise conditions, but numerous case reports leave no doubt that they also produce a similar withdrawal syndrome when taken in excess of the upper therapeutic range.

Treatment of High-Dose Benzodiazepine Dependence

For high-dose benzodiazepine dependence, the pharmacological treatment strategy is the same as that for barbiturates. The phenobarbital conversion equivalents are shown in Table 50–3. The dose conversions computed using Table 50–3 prevent the emergence of severe withdrawal of the classic sedative-hypnotic type. As discussed next, some patients who take high doses of benzodiazepines, or even therapeutic doses for months to years, may have prolonged withdrawal symptoms. The phenobarbital dosage conversions computed using Table 50–3 are not adequate to control symptoms.

Low-Dose Benzodiazepine Withdrawal Syndromes

Many people who have taken benzodiazepines in therapeutic doses for months to years can abruptly discontinue the drug without developing withdrawal symptoms. The symptoms for which the benzodiazepine was being taken often return. The return of symptoms is called *symptom reemergence* (or recrudescence). Patients' symptoms of anxiety, insomnia, or muscle tension abate during benzodiazepine treatment. When the benzodiazepine is stopped, symptoms return to the same level as before benzodiazepine therapy. The reason for making a distinction between symptom rebound and symptom recurrence is that symptom recurrence suggests that the original symptoms have not been adequately treated, whereas symptom rebound suggests a transient withdrawal syndrome. But other patients, taking similar amounts of a benzodiazepine, develop symptoms ranging from mild to severe when the benzodiazepine is stopped or when the dosage is substantially reduced. Characteristically, patients tolerate a gradual tapering of the benzodiazepine until they are at 10% to 20% of their peak dose. Further reduction in benzodiazepine dose causes patients to become increasingly symptomatic. In addiction medicine literature, the low-dose benzodiazepine withdrawal syndrome may be called therapeutic dose withdrawal, normal dose withdrawal, or benzodiazepine discontinuation syndrome.

Many patients experience a transient increase in symptoms for 1 to 2 weeks after benzodiazepine withdrawal. The symptoms are an intensified return of the symptoms for which the benzodiazepine was prescribed. The transient form of symptom intensification is called *symptom rebound.* The term comes from sleep research in which rebound insomnia is commonly observed after sedative-hypnotic use. Symptom rebound lasts a few days to weeks after discontinuation.[34] Symptom rebound is the most common withdrawal consequence of prolonged benzodiazepine use.

A few patients experience a severe, protracted withdrawal syndrome that includes symptoms (e.g., paresthesia and psychosis) that were not present before. This withdrawal syndrome has generated much of the concern about the long-term safety of the benzodiazepines.

Protracted Benzodiazepine Withdrawal Syndrome

Protracted benzodiazepine withdrawal may consist of relatively mild withdrawal symptoms such as anxiety, mood instability, and sleep disturbance analogous to the protracted withdrawal syndrome described for alcohol and other drugs[35] (described in DSM-IV[1(p265)]). In some patients, the protracted withdrawal syndrome from benzodiazepines can be severe and disabling and last many months.

There is considerable controversy surrounding even the existence of this syndrome, which evolves primarily from the addiction medicine literature. Many symptoms are nonspecific and often mimic an obsessive-compulsive disorder with psychotic features. As a practical matter, it is often difficult in the clinical setting to separate symptom reemergence from protracted withdrawal. New symptoms, such as increased sensitivity to sound, light, and touch and paresthesia, are particularly suggestive of low-dose withdrawal.

The protracted benzodiazepine withdrawal has no pathognomonic signs or symptoms, and the broad range of nonspecific symptoms produced by the protracted benzodiazepine withdrawal syndrome could also be the result of agitated depression, generalized anxiety disorder, panic disorder, partial complex seizures, and schizophrenia. The time course of symptom resolution is the primary differentiating feature between symptoms generated by withdrawal and symptom reemergence. Symptoms from withdrawal gradually subside with continued abstinence, whereas symptom reemergence and symptom sensitization do not.

The waxing and waning of symptom intensity are characteristic of the low-dose protracted benzodiazepine withdrawal syndrome. Patients are sometimes asymptomatic for several days, and then, without apparent reason, they become acutely anxious. Often there are concomitant physiological signs (e.g., dilated pupils, increased resting heart rate, and increased blood pressure). The intense waxing and waning of symptoms are important in distinguishing low-dose withdrawal symptoms from symptom reemergence.

Risk Factors for Low-Dose Benzodiazepine Withdrawal

Some drugs or medications may facilitate neuroadaptation by increasing the affinity of benzodiazepines for their receptors. Phenobarbital, for example, increases the affinity of diazepam to benzodiazepine receptors,[36, 37] and prior treatment with phenobarbital has been found to increase the intensity of chlordiazepoxide (45 mg/d) withdrawal symptoms.[38] Patients at increased risk for development of the low-dose withdrawal syndrome are those with a family or personal history of alcoholism, those who use alcohol daily, and those who concomitantly use other sedatives. Case-control studies suggest that patients with a history of addiction, particularly to other sedative-hypnotics, are at high risk for low-dose benzodiazepine dependence. The short-acting, high-milligram-potency benzodiazepines appear to produce a more intense low-dose withdrawal syndrome.[39]

Treatment of Protracted Benzodiazepine Withdrawal

Phenobarbital conversions based on Table 50–3 are not adequate to suppress symptoms. For example, someone discontinuing 20 mg of diazepam would have a computed phenobarbital conversion of 60 mg. In managing low-dose withdrawal, an approach is to begin with about 200 mg/d of phenobarbital and then taper the phenobarbital, slowly as tolerated. If palpitations or other symptoms of autonomic hyperactivity are bothersome, β-adrenergic blockers, such as propranolol,[40] or α_2-adrenergic agonists, such as clonidine, may be useful adjuncts. Reports on the use of clonidine to reduce benzodiazepine withdrawal severity have yielded mixed results. Clinical case reports have suggested its usefulness,[41, 42] although a three-patient controlled study did not confirm its effectiveness.[43] Intermittent treatment with β-adrenergic blockers is preferred, as chronic treatment may produce alterations in β-adrenergic receptor sensitivity.[44]

Clinical Vignette 1

A 33-year-old woman was referred by her internist for treatment of alcohol dependence after an overdose of alprazolam (Xanax) and alcohol. The patient had ingested about 30 tablets of alprazolam (2 mg) and a bottle of wine after an argument with her husband. The patient and her husband were in the process of an acrimonious separation, and, during the 3 months before her hospitalization, the patient had increased her alcohol consumption to 1.5 bottles of wine each night. The patient stated that she had wanted to die and that she had heard that the combination of alprazolam and alcohol was lethal. She had not previously made a suicide attempt; however, she was under the ongoing care of a psychiatrist because of panic attacks. A previous psychiatrist had started the patient with alprazolam about 6 years before the overdose. Before she had started alprazolam, the panic attacks had become disabling. While she was taking 4 mg/d of alprazolam, the panic attacks became infrequent, and when they occurred were much attenuated. She had resumed employment as a travel agent. Her usual alcohol consumption consisted of one or, at the most, two glasses of wine with the evening meal. Until the overdose, she took alprazolam exactly as prescribed, 2 mg twice a day at the same time each day. Her psychiatrist verified that her refills were consistent with her history. The patient was frightened by having overdosed and acknowledged that her alcohol use was excessive and that she needed treatment; however, she did not want to discontinue alprazolam because she feared return of the panic attacks.

Discussion

This patient presents a challenging clinical situation, often referred to in the chemical dependence treatment field as dual diagnosis: a major psychiatric disorder and chemical dependence. Alcohol and drug treatment programs generally want patients to discontinue all psychoactive medications when they enter treatment. Chemical dependence treatment staff often observe that alcohol-abusing patients increase their use of prescription medication when they stop drinking.

Because the patient's panic attacks had been disabling, and because the alcohol abuse seemed a response to an acute situational stress, the patient began outpatient (4 nights/wk) chemical dependence treatment, she and her husband began couples therapy, and the patient increased the frequency of visits with her psychiatrist. With the increased support, the patient completed the separation from her husband, remained abstinent from alcohol, and remained on a carefully monitored dose of alprazolam.

Clinical Vignette 2

A 45-year-old man entered inpatient treatment for alcohol dependence. He lived alone and acknowledged drinking up to a fifth of vodka every day. He made many attempts to stop drinking; however, each time, within 24 hours, he became tremulous, sweaty, and nauseous. During the past 10 years, he had had three inpatient detoxifications from alcohol, each followed by a year or more of abstinence. After treatment, he attended three to five Alcoholics Anonymous meetings per week. When asked about medication use, he said that he had been taking lorazepam (Ativan), but it did not help so he stopped it. He denied use of other medications. He denied ever having had a withdrawal seizure.

After admission to the hospital, the patient was treated with chlordiazepoxide (Librium), 25 to 50 mg every hour as needed, for alcohol withdrawal signs and symptoms. For the first 24 hours, he received 250 mg of chlordiazepoxide. He appeared comfortable and, on the second hospital day, participated in group therapy. While sitting in group therapy, he suddenly stood up, fell forward, and had a grand mal seizure lasting about 2 minutes. Subsequently, he revealed that he had been taking 6 to 12 mg/d of lorazepam up to the day before admission.

Discussion

For a variety of reasons, patients may not reveal all their use of prescription medications or street drugs when they enter an alcohol or drug abuse treatment program. In some instances, patients may want to "protect" the prescribing physician or keep open the option of having access to medications that they believe would not be sanctioned by physicians working in an alcohol or drug treatment program. The psychotropic medication history is often best obtained as part of the general medical history, in which the patient is asked about any recent treatment of medical problems. Patients are often put at ease by overt assurances of confidentiality and by an explanation of why the drug use history is needed. Indirect questions may be productive—for example, "If we had tested your urine yesterday for all drugs and medications that you had taken during the 3 days just before you came in, what would the tests have shown?" This kind of questioning often provokes patients to ask about if, or how long, a particular drug or medication they are taking can be detected.

References

1. Diagnostic and Statistical Manual of Mental Disorders, 4th ed. Washington, DC: American Psychiatric Association, 1994.
2. Griffiths RR, Roache JD: Abuse liability of benzodiazepines: A review of human studies evaluating subjective and/or reinforcing effects. In Smith DE, Wesson DR (eds): The Benzodiazepines: Current Standards for Medical Practice. Hingham, MA: MTP Press, 1985:209–225.
3. Baker G: Metro: Downtown. New Times, July 12–20, 1993, page 7.
4. Dade Drug Fax Information for Action, February 28, 1994; 1:1.
5. San L, Tato J, Torrens M, et al: Flunitrazepam consumption among heroin addicts admitted for in-patient detoxification. Drug Alcohol Depend 1993; 32:281–286.
6. Bond A, Seijas D, Dawling S, Ladner M: Systemic absorption and abuse liability of snorted flunitrazepam. Addiction 1994; 89:821–830.
7. Byrnes JJ, Greenblatt DJ, Miller LG: Benzodiazepine receptor binding of nonbenzodiazepines *in vivo:* Alpidem, zolpidem and zopiclone. Brain Res Bull 1992; 29:905–908.
8. Langer SA, Arbilla S, Scatton B, et al: Receptors involved in the mechanism of action of zolpidem. In Sauvanet JP, Langer SZ, Morselli PL (eds): Imidazopyridines in Sleep Disorders. New York: Raven Press, 1988:55–70.
9. Cavallaro R, Regazzetti MG, Covelli G, Smeraldi E: Tolerance and withdrawal with zolpidem. Lancet 1993; 342:374–375.
10. Piercey MF, Hoffmann WE, Cooper M: The hypnotics triazolam and zolpidem have identical metabolic effects throughout the brain: Implications for benzodiazepine receptor subtypes. Brain Res 1991; 554:244–252.
11. Perrault G, Morel E, Sanger DJ, Zivkovic B: Lack of tolerance and physical dependence upon repeated treatment with the novel hypnotic zolpidem. J Pharmacol Exp Ther 1992; 263:298–303.
12. Griffiths RR, Sannerud CA, Ator NA, Brady JV: Zolpidem behavioral pharmacology in baboons: Self-injection, discrimination, tolerance and withdrawal. J Pharmacol Exp Ther 1992; 260:1199–1208.
13. Physicians' Desk Reference. Montvale, NJ: Medical Economics, 1994:2191.
14. Ansseau M, Pitchot W, Hansenne M, Moreno AG: Psychotic reactions to zolpidem. Lancet 1992; 339:809.
15. Iruela LM, Ibañez-Rojo V, Baca E: Zolpidem-induced macropsia in anoretic woman. Lancet 1993; 342:443–444.
16. Staley KJ, Soldo BL, Proctor WR: Ionic mechanisms of neuronal excitation by inhibitory $GABA_A$ receptors. Science 1995; 269:977–981.
17. Wong G, Lyon T, Skotnick P: Chronic exposure to benzodiazepine receptor ligands uncouples the gamma-aminobutyric acid type A receptor in WSS-1 cells. Mol Pharmacol 1994; 46:1056–1062.
18. Klein RL, Whiting PJ, Harris RA: Benzodiazepine treatment causes uncoupling of recombinant GABA-A receptors expressed in stably transfected cells. J Neurochem 1994; 63:2349–2352.
19. Ladner M: Biological processes in benzodiazepine dependence. Addiction 1994; 89:1413–1418.
20. Wilson MA, Biscardi R: Sex differences in GABA/benzodiazepine receptor changes and corticosterone release after acute stress in rats. Exp Brain Res 1994; 101:297–306.
21. Negro M, Chinchetru MA, Fernandez-Lopez A, Calvo P: Effect of chronic ethanol treatment on the gamma-aminobutyric acid mediated enhancement of [^{3}H]flunitrazepam binding in rat cortex and hippocampus. J Neurochem 1992; 58:1916–1922.
22. Robledo P, Lumeng L, Li TK, Ehlers CL: Effects of MK 801 and diazepam on the EEG of P and NP rats. Alcohol Clin Exp Res 1994; 18:363–368.
23. Cowley DS, Roy-Byrne PP, Radant A, et al: Eye movement effects of diazepam in sons of alcoholic fathers and male control subjects. Alcohol Clin Exp Res 1994; 18:324–332.
24. Volkow ND, Wang GJ, Hitzemann R, et al: Decreased cerebral response to inhibitory neurotransmission in alcoholics. Am J Psychiatry 1993; 150:417–422.

24a. Schweizer E, Rickels K, Case WG, Greenblatt DJ: Long-term therapeutic use of benzodiazepines. II. Effects of gradual taper. Arch Gen Psychiatry 1990; 47:908–915.

25. Smith DE, Wesson DR: A new method for treatment of barbiturate dependence. JAMA 1970; 213:294–295.
26. Smith DE, Wesson DR: A phenobarbital technique for withdrawal of barbiturate abuse. Arch Gen Psychiatry 1971; 24:56–60.
27. Smith DE, Wesson DR: Benzodiazepine dependency syndromes. J Psychoactive Drugs 1983; 15:85–95.
28. Smith DE, Wesson DR: Benzodiazepine dependency syndromes. In Smith DE, Wesson DR (eds): The Benzodiazepines: Current Standards for Medical Practice. Hingham, MA: MTP Press, 1985:235–248.
29. Rickels K, Schweizer E, Case WG, Greenblatt DJ: Long-term therapeutic use of benzodiazepines. I. Effect of abrupt discontinuation. Arch Gen Psychiatry 1990; 47:899–907.
30. Schweizer E, Rickels K, Case WG, Greenblatt DJ: Carbamazepine treatment in patients discontinuing long-term benzodiazepine therapy: Effects on withdrawal severity and outcome. Arch Gen Psychiatry 1991; 48:448–452.
31. Hollister LE, Motzenbecker FP, Degan RO: Withdrawal reactions from chlordiazepoxide (Librium). Psychopharmacology 1961; 2:63–68.
32. Hollister LE, Bennett JL, Kimbell I, et al: Diazepam in newly admitted schizophrenics. Dis Nerv Syst 1963; 24:746–750.
33. Isbell H: Addiction to barbiturates and the barbiturate abstinence syndrome. Ann Intern Med 1950; 33:108–120.
34. American Psychiatric Association Task Force on Benzodiazepine Dependency: Benzodiazepine Dependence, Toxicity, and Abuse. Washington, DC: American Psychiatric Association, 1990.
35. Geller A: Protracted abstinence. In Miller N (ed): Comprehensive Handbook of Drug and Alcohol Addiction. New York: Marcel Dekker, 1991:905–913.
36. Skolnick P, Concada V, Barker JL, et al: Pentobarbital: Dual action to increase brain benzodiazepine receptor affinity. Science 1981; 211: 1448–1450.
37. Olsen RW, Leeb-Lundberg F. Convulsant and anti-convulsant drug binding sites related to GABA-regulated chloride ion channels. In Costa E, DiChiara G, Gessa GL (eds): GABA and Benzodiazepine Receptors. New York: Raven Press, 1981:93–102.
38. Covi L, Lipman RS, Pattison JH, et al: Length of treatment with anxiolytic sedatives and response to their sudden withdrawal. Acta Psychiatr Scand 1973; 49:51–64.
39. Rickels K, Schweizer E, Case WG, Greenblatt DJ: Long-term therapeutic use of benzodiazepines. I. Effects of abrupt discontinuation. Arch Gen Psychiatry 1990; 47:899–907.
40. Tyrer P, Rutherford D, Huggett T: Benzodiazepine withdrawal symptoms and propranolol. Lancet 1981; 1:520–522.
41. Vinogradov S, Reiss AL, Csernansky JG: Clonidine therapy in withdrawal from high-dose alprazolam treatment. Am J Psychiatry 1986; 143:1590–1592.
42. Kreharan MS, Crammer JL: Clonidine in benzodiazepine withdrawal. Lancet 1985; 1:1325–1326.
43. Goodman WK, Charney DS, Price LH, et al: Ineffectiveness of clonidine in the treatment of the benzodiazepine withdrawal syndrome: Report of three cases. Am J Psychiatry 1986; 143:900–903.
44. Glaubiger G, Lefkowitz RJ: Elevated beta-adrenergic receptor number after chronic propranolol treatment. Biochem Biophys Res Commun 1977; 78:720–725.

CHAPTER

51 Dementia, Delirium, and Other Cognitive Disorders

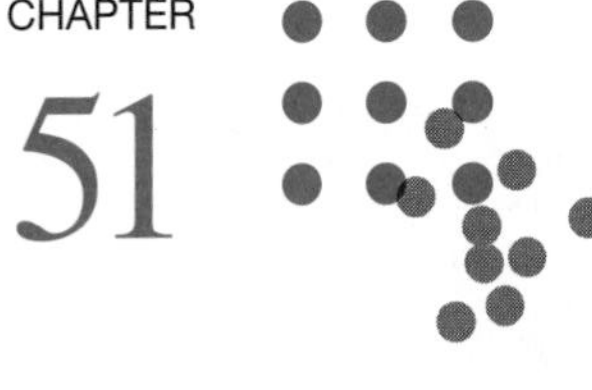

Robert L. Frierson

Mental Disorders due to a General Medical Condition
- Psychotic Disorder
- Anxiety Disorder
- Mood Disorder
- Sexual Dysfunction
- Sleep Disorder
- Catatonic Disorder
- Personality Change

Dementia
- Dementia of the Alzheimer Type
- Dementia due to Pick's Disease
- Dementia due to Parkinson's Disease
- Dementia due to Huntington's Disease
- Vascular Dementia
- Dementia due to HIV Disease
- Dementia due to Head Trauma
- Substance-Induced Persisting Dementia
- Dementia due to Other General Medical Conditions
- Dementia due to Multiple Etiologies

Delirium
- Delirium due to a General Medical Condition
- Substance Intoxication Delirium
- Substance Withdrawal Delirium

Amnestic Disorders
- Amnestic Disorder due to a General Medical Condition
- Substance-Induced Persisting Amnestic Disorder

This chapter reviews dementia, delirium, amnestic and other cognitive disorders and the mental disorders due to a general medical condition. Traditionally, these conditions have been classified as organic brain disorders to distinguish them from such diseases as schizophrenia, mania, and major depressive disorder, the so-called functional disorders. With the publication of the fourth edition of the *Diagnostic and Statistical Manual of Mental Disorders* (DSM-IV), the distinction between functional and organic disorders was eliminated. Significant research into the neurobiological aspects of psychiatric disorders and the utilization of sophisticated neurodiagnostic tests such as positron emission tomographic scanning in schizophrenics led to the inescapable conclusion that every psychiatric condition has a biological component. Thus the term functional became obsolete and even misleading.

The conditions formerly called organic are classified in DSM-IV into three groupings: 1) delirium, dementia, and amnestic and other cognitive disorders; 2) mental disorders due to a general medical condition; and 3) substance-related disorders.[1] Delirium, dementia, and amnestic disorders are classified as cognitive because they feature impairment in such parameters as memory, language, or attention as a cardinal symptom. Each of these three major cognitive disorders is subdivided into categories that ascribe the etiology of the disorder to a general medical condition, the persisting effects of a substance, or multiple etiologies. A "not otherwise specified" category is included for each disorder.[1]

In the case of delirium, the primary disturbance is in the level of consciousness with associated impairments in orientation, memory, judgment, and attention. Dementia features cognitive deficits in memory, language, and intellect. The amnestic disorder is characterized by impairment in memory in the absence of clouded consciousness or other noteworthy cognitive dysfunction. In general, the cognitive disorders should represent a decline from a previous higher level of function, of either acute (delirium) or insidious (dementia) onset, and should interfere with the patient's social or occupational functioning.[1]

Mental Disorders due to a General Medical Condition

Disorders in this category represent a significant change from the nomenclature and organizational structure of the third edition of the *Diagnostic and Statistical Manual of Mental Disorders* (DSM-III). These disorders were previously termed organic, as in organic delusional disorder or organic mood disorder, without regard to the specific etiology (e.g., specific general medical condition or substance). In DSM-IV the term organic was removed and these mental disorders related to a general medical condition are now included with other disorders exhibiting the same primary symptom. For example, mood disorder due to a general medical condition is now included in the mood disorders section of DSM-IV. This classification is designed to encourage the psychiatrist to consider a mental disorder due to a general medical condition in the differential diagnosis of all psychiatric presentations.[1]

In most instances, there are no infallible criteria for determining whether a particular medical condition is etiologically related to an observed mental disorder. Factors that may help in establishing this association include 1) a temporal relationship between the onset, worsening, or remission of the general medical condition and that of the mental disturbance; 2) a past history of the same mental disorder during an episode of the medical condition; 3) documentation in the scientific literature of a similar mental reaction to the medical condition; and 4) the presence of features that are not typical of the primary mental disorder. In many instances, there is a significant delay between the correction of the medical condition and resolution of the mental symptoms produced by it. This is especially true for elderly patients and those with previously compromised brain function. Some such medical conditions may involve structural changes in the brain (e.g., significant head injury) and are irreversible.

Diagnostic Categories

Psychotic Disorder due to a General Medical Condition

Psychotic disorder due to a general medical condition features prominent delusions and/or hallucinations that are believed to be due to the direct physiological effects of a general medical condition. The medical history, physical examination, or laboratory findings should provide evidence that the psychotic features are the result of the condition, and the psychosis should not be attributable to another mental disorder. To meet the criteria for psychotic disorder due to a general medical condition, the hallucinations or delusions must not be observed only during the course of a delirious episode.

The nature of the hallucinations can give some indication of the inciting condition. For example, certain types of olfactory hallucinations are common in temporal lobe epilepsy.[1, 2]

Many medical conditions can produce psychosis. Rosenbaum reported that 83% of institutionalized Huntington's patients exhibited delusions.[2] Alzheimer's disease is frequently accompanied by psychosis. Approximately 50% of patients with Alzheimer's disease exhibit delusions during the course of their disease.[2] Persecutory beliefs are commonly seen, and Capgras' syndrome and phantom border syndrome have also been reported.[2] Temporal lobe epilepsy is accompanied by a schizophrenia-like illness in between 7% and 23% of patients.[2] The average period between onset of the epilepsy and the beginning of the psychosis is 14 years, although some patients become psychotic within a few months of the first seizure.[2] Thyroid disease, cerebral neoplasms, adrenal dysfunction, and systemic lupus erythematosus are among the more common disorders associated with psychosis. The differential diagnosis is between psychotic features associated with delirium, dementia (Alzheimer's or vascular), substance-induced psychotic disorder, a primary psychotic disorder, and an affective disorder with psychosis. In many instances, pharmacological management of the psychosis is necessary regardless of etiology.

Anxiety Disorder due to a General Medical Condition

In anxiety disorder due to a general medical condition, the anxiety must be due to the direct effects of a medical disturbance and can take the form of panic attacks, obsessions, or compulsions. The symptoms must not be attributable to delirium or some other condition such as adjustment disorder with anxiety. The anxious state should also be of significant severity to impair social or occupational functioning. Many medical conditions can produce anxiety. These include such endocrinological conditions as hyperthyroidism, pheochromocytoma, and Cushing's disease; insulinoma and other causes of hypoglycemia; carcinoid syndrome; acute intermittent porphyria; and certain cardiovascular conditions. Substance-induced anxiety must be excluded before the diagnosis of anxiety due to a general medical condition is made. There may be significant lag time between correction of the medical condition and resolution of the anxiety.

Mood Disorder due to a General Medical Condition

In mood disorder due to a general medical condition, a persistent and prominent mood disturbance is found to be due to the effects of a general medical condition. The mood can be depressed, either moderately so or resembling a major depressive disorder, present with features of mania, or be of mixed type. Medical conditions that can produce mood disturbances include cerebrovascular accidents (CVAs), degenerative disorders, multiple sclerosis, adrenal dysfunction, thyroid disease, acquired immunodeficiency syndrome (AIDS), syphilis, and carcinoma of the pancreas. Mood disorders due to a general medical condition must be differentiated from delirium, substance-induced mood disorder, bereavement, and such primary psychiatric disorders as bipolar disorder, major depressive disorder, and adjustment disorder with depressed mood.

Sexual Dysfunction due to a General Medical Condition

In sexual dysfunction due to a general medical condition, a clinically significant dysfunction is believed to be related to the medical ailment. The sexual difficulty can include a variety of disorders such as dyspareunia, changes in libido, erectile dysfunction, and orgasmic disorders. The abnormality must be severe enough to cause significant distress or difficulties in interpersonal relationships. This category of sexual dysfunction has several subtypes:

1. Female hypoactive sexual desire disorder
2. Male hypoactive sexual desire disorder
3. Male erectile disorder
4. Female dyspareunia
5. Male dyspareunia
6. Other female sexual dysfunction
7. Other male sexual dysfunction

Medical conditions that may produce sexual dysfunction due to a general medical condition include diabetes mellitus, spinal cord abnormalities, endocrinological disorders, and various genitourinary conditions.[1]

Sleep Disorder due to a General Medical Condition

In sleep disorder due to a general medical condition, the essential feature is a significant disturbance in sleep due to a general medical condition. The subtypes of the sleep disturbance are 1) insomnia type, 2) hypersomnia type, 3) parasomnia type, and 4) mixed. The parasomnia type implies the presence of abnormal behavior or physiological events that occur in conjunction with sleep. Examples include nightmare disorder, sleep terror disorder, and sleepwalking disorder.

Medical conditions that can produce a sleep disorder include degenerative disorders such as Parkinson's and Huntington's diseases, endocrine conditions, infectious states (especially viral encephalitis), and the rare Kleine-Levin syndrome. Sleep disorders due to a general medical condition must be differentiated from expected disruptions in sleep such as hypnagogic and hypnopompic phenomena, primary sleep disorders, substance abuse–related sleep disorders, and sleep disorders related to a primary mental disorder such as major depressive disorder.

Catatonic Disorder due to a General Medical Condition

In catatonic disorder due to a general medical condition, the catatonic state is considered to be secondary to a medical disorder. Catatonia is characterized by one or more of the following: absent or excessive motor activity, negativism, mutism, unusual movements, and mimicking the words (echolalia) or actions (echopraxia) of the examiner. Negativism is the motiveless resistance to all attempts to be moved or to all verbal instructions, and mutism entails voicelessness without evidence of structural abnormalities.

DSM-IV Criteria 293.89

Catatonic Disorder due to . . . [Indicate the General Medical Condition]

A. The presence of catatonia as manifested by motoric immobility, excessive motor activity (that is apparently purposeless and not influenced by external stimuli), extreme negativism or mutism, peculiarities of voluntary movement, or echolalia or echopraxia.

B. There is evidence from the history, physical examination, or laboratory findings that the disturbance is the direct physiological consequence of a general medical condition.

C. The disturbance is not better accounted for by another mental disorder (e.g., a manic episode).

D. The disturbance does not occur exclusively during the course of a delirium.

Coding note: Include the name of the general medical condition on Axis I, e.g., 293.89, catatonic disorder due to hepatic encephalopathy; also code the general medical condition on Axis III.

The excess motor activity in catatonia is generally purposeless, without regard to external stimuli. Immobility can involve waxy flexibility (catalepsy) or stupor. Such individuals may maintain a certain posture for hours, regardless of how bizarre or uncomfortable the position appears.

Diagnosis. To employ the diagnosis of catatonia due to a general medical condition, there must be some evidence that the catatonia is the result of a medical disorder. Such evidence may come from the laboratory findings, physical examination, or the medical history. The diagnosis is not made if the catatonia is secondary to another mental disorder such as schizophrenia, mania, or major depression. Schizophrenia, catatonic type, involves such abnormalities of thought as delusions and hallucinations without a causative medical condition. Delirious states often involve motor abnormalities including catatonia and are produced by various medical conditions; thus the diagnosis of catatonia due to a general medical condition should not be made if catatonia occurs exclusively during the course of a delirium. Movement disorders induced by medications or drugs of abuse can also produce catatonia.

Many medical conditions can produce catatonia. Various disorders of the brain (tumors, trauma, infection, inflammation, and vascular conditions) and such metabolic conditions as hypercalcemia, hepatic encephalopathy, and diabetic ketoacidosis may lead to catatonic states. Physiological consequences of catatonia such as contractures and decubitus can occur.

Personality Change due to a General Medical Condition

In personality change due to a general medical condition, there exists a persistent disturbance in personality that is determined to be the direct consequence of a general medical disorder. This personality disturbance should represent a change from a previously established personality structure or, in the case of a child, a significant deviation from normal development. As in other mental disorders due to a medical condition, the personality disturbance should produce significant distress or impair social or occupational functioning.

Representative features of the personality change include lability of affect, impulsivity, poor judgment, loss of social inhibitions, apathy, aggressiveness, and paranoia. Family members often describe the affected individual as "not himself."[1] The particular manifestation of the personality disturbance is often related to the area of the brain affected. The frontal lobes are involved in the engagement of attention, the inhibition of inappropriate behavior, and the initiation and planning of complex behaviors. Thus, a disorder affecting this area may result in loss of inhibition regarding aggressive and sexual behavior; lack of interaction with the environment; and subsequent apathy, indifference, and withdrawal. Conditions that affect the temporal lobes (typically epileptic foci) may produce such features as elation, rage, verbosity, hyperreligiosity, and a strong sense of morality that may evolve into self-righteousness. In contrast to the sexual acting out of patients with frontal lobe involvement, those with temporal lobe processes often exhibit hyposexuality.

DSM-IV Criteria 310.1

Personality Change due to . . . [Indicate the General Medical Condition]

A. A persistent personality disturbance that represents a change from the individual's previous characteristic personality pattern. (In children, the disturbance involves a marked deviation from normal development or a significant change in the child's usual behavior patterns lasting at least 1 year.)

B. There is evidence from the history, physical examination, or laboratory findings that the disturbance is the direct physiological consequence of a general medical condition.

C. The disturbance is not better accounted for by another mental disorder (including other mental disorders due to a general medical condition).

D. The disturbance does not occur exclusively during the course of a delirium and does not meet criteria for a dementia.

E. The disturbance causes clinically significant distress or impairment in social, occupational, or other important areas of functioning.

Specify type:

Labile type: if the predominant feature is affective lability

Disinhibited type: if the predominant feature is poor impulse control as evidenced by sexual indiscretions, etc.

Aggressive type: if the predominant feature is aggressive behavior

Apathetic type: if the predominant feature is marked apathy and indifference

Paranoid type: if the predominant feature is suspiciousness or paranoid ideation.

Other type: if the predominant feature is not one of the above, e.g., personality change associated with a seizure disorder

Combined type: if more than one feature predominates in the clinical picture

Unspecified type

Coding note: Include the name of the general medical condition on Axis I, e.g., 310.1, personality change due to temporal lobe epilepsy; also code the general medical condition on Axis III.

Personality change due to a general medical condition can be classified into several subtypes. If the primary feature is affective lability, as in some CVAs the disorder is of labile type. Disinhibited type, often seen after significant head trauma, may involve such sexual behavior as exhibitionism or public masturbation. Aggressive-type personality change may occur in epileptic patients and in the early stages of Huntington's disease with frontal lobe involvement.

Apathetic type can occur in any condition that primarily affects the frontal lobes. Paranoid type also occurs frequently in seizure disorders, especially those generated from the temporal lobe.

A variety of medical conditions can produce alterations in personality. Head trauma, cerebrovascular disease, epilepsy, and central nervous system neoplasms are the most common causes. Other conditions including Huntington's disease, systemic lupus erythematosus, multiple sclerosis, human immunodeficiency virus (HIV) spectrum illness, and endocrine disorders have also been implicated.

Diagnosis. Personality change due to a general medical condition must be differentiated from dementia. Occasionally a patient with such a personality change subsequently-develops other cognitive disturbances commonly associated with dementia. The diagnosis should then be upgraded to dementia. Personality change due to a general medical condition should not be diagnosed if the change occurs only during a delirium and does not persist on resolution of the delirious state. Personality change may occur in other disorders such as schizophrenia, panic disorder, and delusional disorders.

In personality disorders (coded on Axis II), the personality disturbance does not represent a change from a previously established personality pattern. Although some personality changes due to a general medical condition begin in childhood and may be lifelong, in general personality disorders are more persistent than medically related personality changes. Except in instances in which structural damage occurs, personality changes resulting from a medical condition are theoretically reversible if the condition is corrected. Personality disorders have no such association with a medical disorder.

Medical Conditions Associated with Mental Disorders

Endocrine Disorders

Hyperfunction and hypofunction of the thyroid gland have been associated with a variety of psychiatric symptoms. Hyperthyroidism features anxiety, confusion, and agitated depression. Hypothyroidism, in its most severe form, so-called myxedema madness, can involve paranoid delusions, delirium, mania, and hallucinations.

Hyperparathyroidism produces hypercalcemia with resultant delirium, apathy, and personality changes. Cognitive impairment occurs in a minority of patients. Hypocalcemia can also result in personality changes and delirium.

Hypofunction of the adrenal glands, as in chronic adrenocortical insufficiency (Addison's disease), can produce apathy, irritability, and depression. Rarely, confusion and depression may result. Adrenocortical hyperplasia (Cushing's disease) can produce depression, amnesia, agitation, and even suicide. Sheehan's syndrome, a condition seen in postpartum women, involves hemorrhage into the pituitary gland and can present with agitation, mania, psychosis, or depression.

Infectious Disorders

Infectious diseases can produce a variety of mental symptoms. Rabies encephalitis can produce agitation, restlessness, and phobia, and herpes simplex encephalitis may cause olfactory and gustatory hallucinations, changes in personality, and psychotic behavior. Herpes has a predilection for the frontal and temporal lobes. Neurosyphilis, Creutzfeldt-Jakob disease, subacute sclerosing panencephalitis, infections with HIV, and kuru can produce mental impairment as well. These conditions are discussed in more detail in the section on the dementias.

Metabolic Disorders

Metabolic encephalopathies are serious conditions that often feature anxiety, disorientation, and memory loss. Hepatic, uremic, and hypoglycemic encephalopathies are common complications of disease states. Acute intermittent porphyria is a disorder of heme synthesis with resultant porphyrin excess. Polyneuropathy, psychosis, and colicky abdominal pain occur. It is an inherited disorder (autosomal dominant) that may also feature anxiety and depression. Barbiturates may precipitate an attack of acute porphyria.

Neurological Conditions

Many patients with epilepsy exhibit mental disorders including psychosis, depression, and changes in personality. Multiple sclerosis is a demyelinating disorder that occurs in young adults. Women and persons living in cold, temperate climates may be more at risk. Cognitive changes occur in about 50% of sufferers, and behavioral abnormalities include personality changes, depression, and euphoric mood that some have described as hypomanic. Multiple sclerosis sufferers are at significant risk for suicide.

Dementia, Delirium, and Other Cognitive Disorders

Dementia

Dementia is defined in DSM-IV as a series of disorders characterized by the development of multiple cognitive deficits (including memory impairment) that are due to the direct physiological effects of a general medical condition, the persisting effects of a substance, or multiple etiologies (e.g., the combined effects of a metabolic and a degenerative disorder).[1] The disorders constituting the dementias share a common symptom presentation and are identified and classified on the basis of etiology. The cognitive deficits exhibited in these disorders must be of significant severity to interfere with either occupational functioning or the individual's usual social activities or relationships. In addition, the observed deficits must represent a decline from a higher level of function and not be the consequence of a delirium. A delirium can be superimposed on a dementia, however, and both can be diagnosed if the dementia is observed when the delirium is not in evidence. Dementia typically is chronic and occurs in the presence of a clear sensorium. If clouding of consciousness occurs, the diagnosis of delirium should be

Table 51–1 DSM-IV Classification of Dementia

Dementia of the Alzheimer type
Early onset versus late onset
Uncomplicated
With delirium
With delusions
With depressed mood
Vascular dementia
Uncomplicated
With delirium
With delusions
With depressed mood
Dementia due to head trauma
Dementia due to Parkinson's disease
Dementia due to HIV disease
Dementia due to Huntington's disease
Dementia due to Pick's disease
Dementia due to Creutzfeldt-Jakob disease
Dementia due to other general medical conditions (e.g., neurosyphilis, normal-pressure hydrocephalus)
Substance-induced persisting dementia
Dementia due to multiple etiologies
Dementia not otherwise specified

considered. The DSM-IV classification of dementia is reviewed in Table 51–1.

Epidemiology

The prevalence of dementias is not precisely known. Estimates vary depending on the age range of the population studied and whether the individuals sampled were in the general community, acute care facilities, or long-term nursing institutions. A review of 47 surveys of dementia conducted between 1945 and 1985 indicated that dementia increased exponentially, doubling every 5 years up to age 95 years, and that this condition was equally distributed among men and women, with Alzheimer's dementia (AD) much more common in women.[3] A National Institute of Mental Health Multisite Epidemiological Catchment Area study revealed a 6-month prevalence rate for mild dementia of 11.5% to 18.4% for persons older than 65 years living in the community.[4] The rate for severe dementia among these community dwellers was 6%. The rate for severe dementia was higher for the institutionalized elderly. Fifteen percent of the elderly in retirement communities, 30% of nursing home residents, and 54% of the elderly in state hospitals were severely demented.[5]

Studies suggest that the fastest growing segment of the U.S. population consists of persons older than the age of 85 years, 15% of whom are demented.[6] Half of the U.S. population currently lives to the age of 75 years and one quarter live to the age of 85.[7] A study of 2000 consecutive admissions to a general medical hospital revealed that 9% were demented and, of those, 41% were also delirious on admission.[8] The cost of providing care for demented patients exceeds $100 billion annually (about 10% of all health care expenditures) and the average cost to families in 1990 was $18,000 a year.[7]

Clinical Features

Essential to the diagnosis of dementia is the presence of cognitive deficits that include memory impairment and at least one of the following abnormalities of cognition: aphasia, agnosia, apraxia, or a disturbance in executive function.[1]

Memory function is divided into three compartments that can easily be evaluated during a Mental Status Examination. These are immediate recall (primary memory), recent (secondary) memory, and remote (tertiary) memory. Primary memory is characterized by a limited capacity, rapid accessibility, and a duration of seconds to minutes.[9] The anatomic site of destruction of primary memory is the reticular activating system, and the principal activity of the primary memory is the registration of new information. Primary memory is generally tested by asking the individual to repeat immediately a series of numbers in the order given. Because primary memory testing measures such parameters as attention, concentration, and ability to follow instructions, the results are often abnormal for the demented patient. This loss of ability to register new information accounts in part for the confusion and frustration the demented patient feels when confronted with unexpected changes in daily routine.

Secondary memory has a much larger capacity than primary memory, a duration of minutes to years, and relatively slow accessibility. The anatomic site of dysfunction for secondary memory is the limbic system, and individuals with a lesion in this area may have little difficulty repeating digits immediately but show rapid decay of these new memories. In minutes, the patient with limbic involvement may be totally unable to recall the digits or even remember that a test has been administered.[9] Thus, secondary memory represents the retention and recall of information that has been previously registered by primary memory. Clinically, secondary memory is tested by having the individual repeat three objects after having been distracted (usually by the examiner's continuation of the Mental Status Examination) for 3 to 5 minutes. Like primary memory, secondary recall is often impaired in dementia. However, because a secondary memory deficit involves preservation of memory registration, the demented patient may successfully use various schemes and clues to remember the three objects. Often if the examiner gives the demented patient a clue (such as "one of the objects you missed was a color"), the patient correctly identifies the object. Giving clues to the demented patient with a primary memory loss is pointless, because the memories were never registered. Wernicke-Korsakoff syndrome is an example of a condition in which primary memory may be intact while secondary recall is impaired.

Tertiary (remote) memory has a capacity that is probably unlimited, and such memories are often permanently retained. Access to tertiary memories is rapid, and the anatomical dysfunction in tertiary memory loss is in the association cortex.[9] In the early stages of dementia, tertiary memory is generally intact. It is tested by instructing the individual to remember personal information or past material. The personal significance of the information often influences the patient's ability to remember it. For example, a woman who worked for many years as a seamstress might remember many details related to that occupation but could not recall the names of past presidents or three large cities in the United States. Thus, a patient's inability to remember highly significant past material is an ominous finding. Collateral data from informants is essential in the proper assessment of memory function. In summary, primary and secondary memories are most likely to be impaired in dementia, with tertiary memory often spared until late in the course of the disease.

In addition to defects in memory, patients with dementia often exhibit impairments in language, recognition, object naming, and motor skills. Aphasia is an abnormality of language that often occurs in vascular dementias involving the dominant hemisphere. Because this hemisphere controls verbal, written, and sign language, these patients may have significant problems interacting with people in their environment. Patients with dementia and aphasia may exhibit paucity of speech, poor articulation, and a telegraphic pattern of speech (nonfluent, Broca's aphasia). This form of aphasia generally involves the middle cerebral artery with resultant paresis of the right arm and lower face.[6] Despite faulty communication skills, patients with dementia with nonfluent aphasia have normal comprehension and awareness of their language impairment. As a result, such patients often present with significant depression, anxiety, and frustration.

By contrast, patients with dementia with fluent (Wernicke's) aphasia may be quite verbose and articulate but much of the language is nonsensical and rife with such paraphasias as neologisms and clang (rhyming) associations. Whereas nonfluent aphasias are usually associated with discrete lesions, fluent aphasia can result from such diffuse conditions as dementia of the Alzheimer type. More commonly, fluent aphasias occur in conjunction with vascular dementia secondary to temporal or parietal lobe CVA. Because the demented patients with fluent aphasia have impaired comprehension, they may seem apathetic and unconcerned with their language deficits, if they are in fact aware of them at all. They do not generally display the emotional distress of patients with dementia and nonfluent aphasia (Table 51–2).

Patients with dementia may also lose their ability to recognize. Agnosia is a feature of a dominant hemisphere lesion and involves altered perception in which, despite normal sensations, intellect, and language, the patient cannot recognize objects. This is in contrast to aphasia in which the patient with dementia may not be able to name objects but can recognize them.[7] The type of agnosia depends on the area of the sensory cortex that is involved. Some demented patients with severe visual agnosia cannot name objects presented, match them to samples, or point to objects named by the examiner. Other patients may present with auditory agnosia and be unable to localize or distinguish such sounds as the ringing of a telephone. A minority of demented patients may exhibit astereognosis, inability to identify an object by palpation.

Demented patients may also lose their ability to carry out selected motor activities despite intact motor abilities, sensory function, and comprehension of the assigned task. Affected patients cannot perform such activities as brushing their teeth, chewing food, or waving goodbye when asked to do so.[10]

The two most common forms of apraxia in demented patients are ideational and gait apraxia. Ideational apraxia is the inability to perform motor activities that require sequential steps and results from a lesion involving both frontal lobes or the complete cerebrum. Gait apraxia, often seen in such conditions as normal-pressure hydrocephalus, is the inability to perform various motions of ambulation. It also results from conditions that diffusely affect the cerebrum.

Table 51–2 Classification of Aphasias

Type	Language	Comprehension	Motor
Wernicke's (receptive)	Impaired Fluent Articulate Paraphasias	Impaired	Normal
Broca's (expressive)	Nonfluent Sparse Telegraphic Inarticulate	Intact	Right hemiparesis
Global	Nonfluent Mute	Impaired	Variable right hemiplegia

Impairment of executive function is the inability to think abstractly, plan, initiate, and end complex behavior. On Mental Status Examination, patients with dementia display problems coping with new tasks. Such activities as subtracting serial sevens may be impaired.

Obviously, aphasia, agnosia, apraxia, and impairment of executive function can seriously impede the demented patients' ability to interact with their environments. An appropriate Mental Status Examination of the patient with suspected dementia should include screening for the presence of these abnormalities.

Associated Features and Behavior

In addition to the diagnostic features already mentioned, patients with dementia display other identifying features that often prove problematic. Poor insight and poor judgment are common in dementia and often cause patients to engage in potentially dangerous activities or make unrealistic and grandiose plans for the future. Visual-spatial functioning may be impaired, and if patients have the ability to construct a plan and carry it out, suicide attempts can occur. More common is unintentional self-harm resulting from carelessness, undue familiarity with strangers, and disregard for the accepted rules of conduct.

Emotional lability, as seen in pseudobulbar palsy after cerebral injury, can be particularly frustrating for caregivers, as are occasional psychotic features such as delusions and hallucinations. Changes in their environment and daily routine can be particularly distressing for demented patients, and their frustration can be manifested by violent behavior.

Course

The course of a particular dementia is influenced by its etiology. Although historically the dementias have been considered progressive and irreversible, there is, in fact, significant variation in the course of individual dementias. The disorder can be progressive, static, or remitting.[1] In addition to the etiology, factors that influence the course of the dementia include 1) the time span between the onset and the initiation of prescribed treatment, 2) the degree of reversibility of the particular dementia, 3) the presence of comorbid psychiatric disorders, and 4) the level of psychosocial support.

The previous distinction between treatable and untreatable dementias has been replaced by the concepts of reversible, irreversible, and arrestable dementias. Most reversible cases of dementia are associated with shorter duration of symptoms, mild cognitive impairment, and superimposed delirium. Specifically, the dementias caused by drugs, depression, and metabolic disorders are most likely to be reversible. Other conditions, such as normal-pressure hydrocephalus, subdural hematomas, and tertiary syphilis, are more commonly merely reversible. Although potentially reversible dementias should be aggressively investigated, in reality only 8% of dementias are partially reversible and about 3% fully reversible.[11]

Differential Diagnosis

Memory impairment occurs in a variety of conditions including delirium, amnestic disorders, and depression.[1] In delirium, the onset of altered memory is acute and the pattern typically fluctuates (waxing and waning) with increased proclivity for confusion during the night. Delirium is more likely to feature autonomic hyperactivity and alterations in level of consciousness. In some cases a dementia can have a superimposed delirium (Fig. 51–1).

Patients with major depression often complain of lapses in memory and judgment, poor concentration, and seemingly diminished intellectual capacity. Often these symptoms are mistakenly diagnosed as dementia, especially in elderly populations. A thorough medical history and Mental Status Examination focusing on such symptoms as hopelessness, crying episodes, and unrealistic guilt in conjunction with a family history can be diagnostically beneficial. The term *pseudodementia* has been used to denote cognitive impairment secondary to a functional psychiatric disorder, most commonly depression.[12] In comparison with demented patients, those with depressive pseudodementia exhibit better insight regarding their cognitive dysfunction, are more likely to give "I don't know" answers, and may exhibit neurovegetative signs of depression. Pharmacological treatment of the depression should improve the cognitive dysfunction as well. Because of the rapid onset of their antidepressant action, the use of psychostimulants (methylphenidate, dextroamphetamine) to differentiate between dementia and pseudodementia has been advocated by some authors.[13] Some authors have proposed abandonment of the term pseudodementia, suggesting that most patients so diagnosed have both genuine dementia and a superimposed affective disorder (Fig. 51–2).

An amnestic disorder also presents with a significant memory deficit but without the other associated features such as aphasia, agnosia, and apraxia. If cognitive impairment occurs only in the context of drug use, substance intoxication or substance withdrawal is the appropriate diagnosis. Although mental retardation implies below average intellect and subsequent impairment in other areas of function, the onset is before 18 years of age and abnormalities of memory do not always occur. Mental retardation must be considered in the differential diagnosis of dementias of childhood and adolescence along with such disorders as Wilson's disease (hepatolenticular degeneration), lead intoxication, subacute sclerosing panencephalitis, HIV spec-

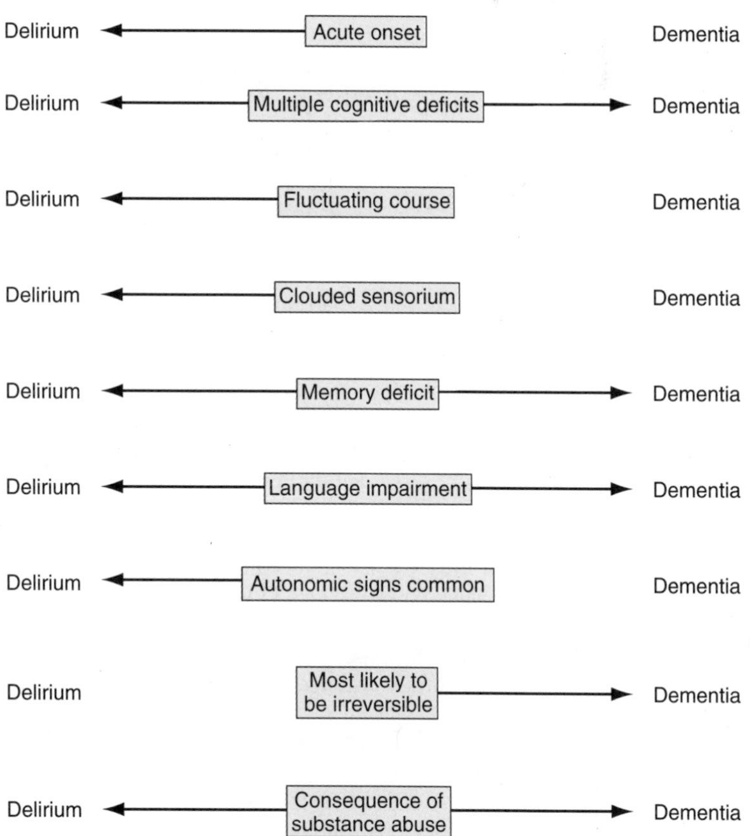

Figure 51–1 *Differentiation of delirium and dementia.*

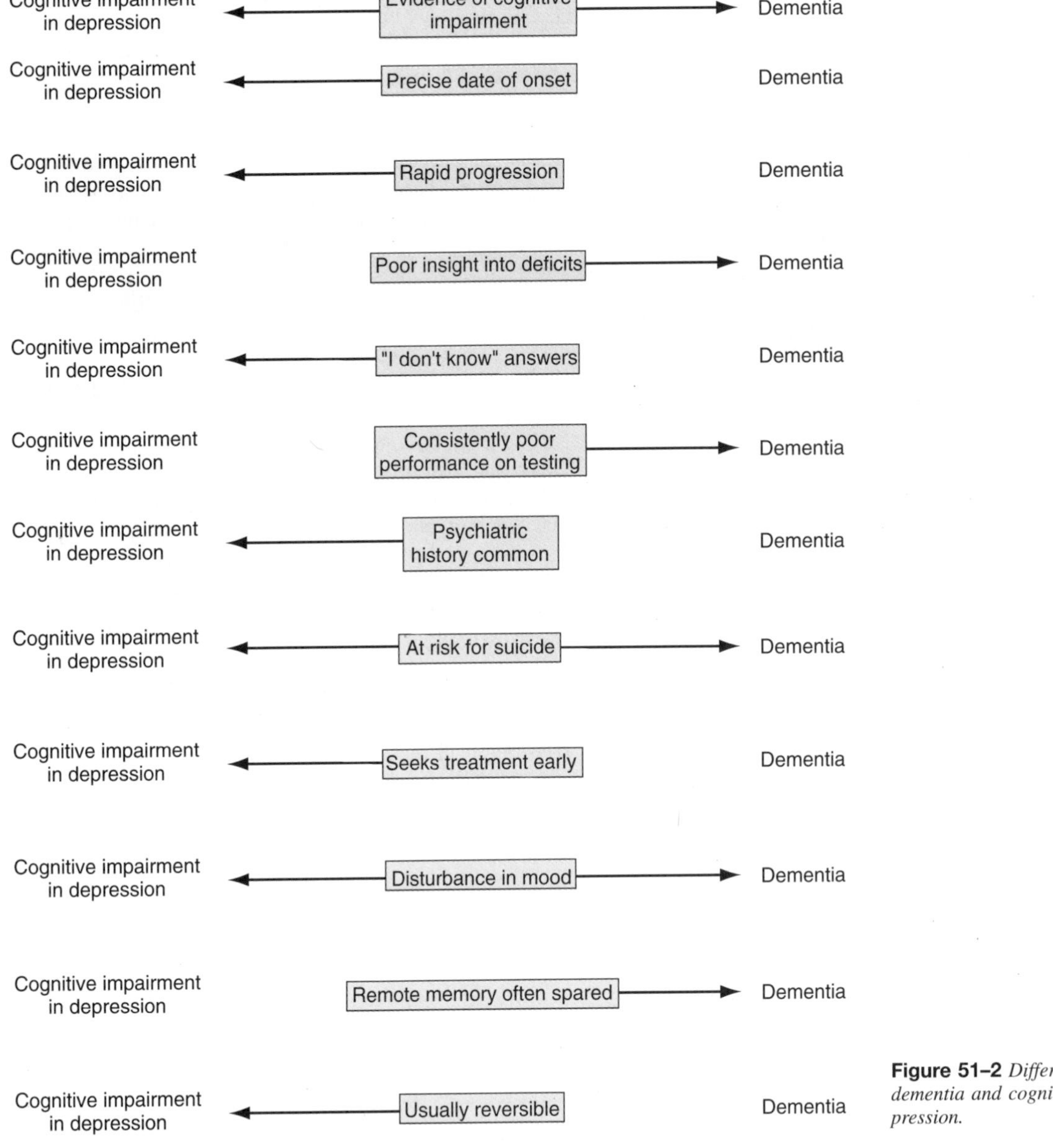

Figure 51–2 *Differential diagnosis of dementia and cognitive impairment in depression.*

trum disorders, and substance abuse, particularly abuse of inhalants.

Patients with schizophrenia may also exhibit a variety of cognitive abnormalities, but this condition also has an early onset, a distinctive constellation of symptoms, and does not result from a medical condition or the persisting effects of a substance. Factitious disorder must be distinguished from dementia. Unlike dementia, this condition presents with inconsistent symptoms that, although similar in some respects, are not totally consistent with those of a dementia. Dementia must also be distinguished from benign senescence (normal aging). Only when such changes exceed the level of altered function to be expected for the patient's age is the diagnosis of dementia warranted.[1]

Physical and Neurological Examinations in Dementia

The physical examination may offer clues to the etiology of the dementia; however, in the elderly, one must be aware of the normal changes associated with aging and differentiate them from signs of dementia. Often the specific physical examination findings indicate the area of the central nervous system affected by the etiological process. Parietal lobe dysfunction is suggested by such symptoms as astereognosis, constructional apraxia, anosognosia, and problems with two-point discrimination.[10] The dominant hemisphere parietal lobe is also involved in Gerstmann's syndrome, which includes agraphia, acalculia, finger agnosia, and right-left confusion.

Reflex changes such as hyperactive deep tendon reflexes, Babinski's reflex, and hyperactive jaw jerk are indicative of cerebral injury. However, primitive reflexes such as the palmomental reflex, which occurs in 60% of normal elderly people, and the snout reflex seen in a third of elderly patients are not diagnostically reliable for dementia.[14]

Ocular findings such as nystagmus (as in brain stem lesions), ophthalmoplegia (Wernicke-Korsakoff syndrome), anisocoria, papilledema (hypertensive encephalopathy), cortical blindness (Anton's syndrome), visual field losses (CVA hemianopia), Kayser-Fleischer rings (Wilson's disease), and Argyll Robertson pupils (syphilis, diabetic retinopathy) can offer valuable clues to the etiology of the cognitive deficit.[15]

Movement disorders including tremors (Parkinson's disease, drug intoxication, cerebellar dysfunction, Wilson's disease), chorea (Huntington's disease, other basal ganglia lesions), myoclonus (subacute sclerosing panencephalitis, Creutzfeldt-Jakob disease, Alzheimer's disease, anoxia), and asterixis (hepatic disease, uremia, hypoxia, carbon dioxide retention) should be noted.

Gait disturbances, principally apraxia (normal-pressure hydrocephalus, inhalant abuse, cerebellar dysfunction) and peripheral neuropathy (Korsakoff's syndrome, neurosyphilis, heavy metal intoxication, solvent abuse, isoniazid or phenytoin toxicity, vitamin deficiencies, and HIV spectrum illnesses), are also common in dementia. Extrapyramidal symptoms in the absence of antipsychotics may indicate substance abuse, especially phencyclidine abuse, or basal ganglia disease. Although the many and varied physical findings of dementia are too numerous to mention here, it should be obvious that the physical examination is an invaluable tool in the assessment of dementia (Table 51–3).

Mental Status Examination

The findings on the Mental Status Examination vary depending on the etiology of the dementia. Some common abnormalities have been discussed previously (see earlier section on clinical features). In general, symptoms seen on the Mental Status Examination, whatever the etiology, are related to the location and extent of brain injury, individual adaptation to the dysfunction, premorbid coping skills and psychopathology, and concurrent medical illness.[3]

Disturbance of memory, especially primary and secondary memory, is the most significant abnormality. Confabulation may be present as the patient attempts to minimize the memory impairment. Disorientation and altered levels of consciousness may occur but are generally not seen in the early stages of dementia uncomplicated by delirium. Affect may be affected as in the masked facies of Parkinson's disease and the expansive affect and labile mood of pseudobulbar palsy after cerebral injury. The affect of patients with hepatic encephalopathy is often described as blunted and apathetic. Lack of inhibition leading to such behavior as exposing oneself is common, and some conditions such as tertiary syphilis and untoward effects of some medication can precipitate mania. The Mental Status Examination, in conjunction with a complete medical history from the patient and informants and an adequate physical examination, is essential in the evaluation and differential diagnosis of dementia (Table 51–4).

Table 51–3 Physical Signs Associated with Dementia or Delirium

Physical Sign	Condition
Myoclonus	Creutzfeldt-Jakob disease Subacute sclerosing panencephalitis Postanoxia Alzheimer's disease (10%) AIDS dementia Uremia Penicillin intoxication Meperidine toxicity
Asterixis	Hepatic encephalopathy Uremia Hypoxia Carbon dioxide retention
Chorea	Huntington's disease Wilson's disease Hypocalcemia Hypothyroidism Hepatic encephalopathy Oral contraceptives Systemic lupus erythematosus Carbon monoxide poisoning Toxoplasmosis Pertussis, diphtheria
Peripheral neuropathy	Wernicke-Korsakoff syndrome Neurosyphilis Heavy metal intoxication Organic solvent exposure Vitamin B_{12} deficiency Medications: isoniazid, phenytoin

Table 51–4 Evaluation of Dementia

Medical history and physical examination
Family interview
Routine laboratory
- Chemistry (SMA 20)
- Urinalysis
- Hematology (complete blood count)

Other routine tests
- Chest radiography
- Electrocardiography

Specialized laboratory
- Thyroid functions
- VDRL (fluorescent treponemal antibody screen if indicated)
- Drug screen
- Vitamin B_{12} and folate levels
- Cerebrospinal fluid analysis (if indicated)
- HIV testing (if indicated)

Other studies
- Computed tomography or magnetic resonance imaging
- Electroencephalography

Degenerative Causes of Dementia

Dementia of the Alzheimer Type. ***Historical Perspective.*** In 1906 Alois Alzheimer reported a case of presenile dementia in a 51-year-old woman who displayed progressive memory loss and disorientation. His presentation was published in *Allgemeine Zeitschrift für Psychiatrie und Psychisch-Gerichtliche Medizin* in 1907. His closing paragraph described the condition that was later to bear his name and serves as an eloquent call for continued research.[9]

> In summary, we are apparently confronted with a distinctive disease process. An increasing number of unusual diseases have been discovered during the past few years. These observations show that we should not be satisfied to take a clinically unclear case and, by making great efforts, fit it into one of the known disease categories. Undoubtedly, there are many more psychiatric dis-

> eases than are included in our textbooks. Often a subsequent histological examination would show the peculiarity of the case. Then gradually we would be able to separate individual diseases clinically from the large classes of diseases in our textbooks and define their clinical characteristics more precisely.[16]

Two years earlier, Alzheimer had written of miliary plaque formations that often appeared in the brains of patients with senile dementia.[17] He and his coworkers subsequently described neurofibrillary changes and granulovacuolar degeneration in senile and presenile dementia.[17] Almost 90 years later, Alzheimer's disease is the most common form of dementia and remains a major focus of scientific investigation.

Epidemiology. Alzheimer's disease is the most common cause of dementia, accounting for 55% to 65% of all cases.[12] There were fewer than 3 million cases in 1980, but the Census Bureau predicted that there will be more than 10 million American citizens with Alzheimer's disease by the year 2050.[18] Prevalence of the disease doubles with every 5 years between the ages of 65 and 85 years.[19] Onset of symptoms occurs after the age of 40 years in 96% of cases and between the ages of 45 and 65 years in 80% of patients.[20] Some authors separate Alzheimer's disease into senile and presenile forms, but the two disorders represent the same pathological process.[7] Significantly, however, early-onset Alzheimer's disease is associated with a more rapid course than later onset disease.[21]

Alzheimer's disease affects women three times as often as men, for unknown reasons.[22] Furthermore, at least one study suggests that dementia, including Alzheimer's, is more common in black than in white American women.[23] Comparison of population studies in diverse countries shows strikingly similar prevalence rates.[19]

Longitudinal studies have revealed the importance of family history as a risk factor; however, no consistent genetic pattern has been established. Nonetheless, the incidence of progressive dementias including Alzheimer's in first-degree relatives older than 90 years approaches 50%.[12] For Alzheimer's alone, the probability of developing dementia if a first-degree relative (parent or sibling) is afflicted is four times that of the general population, and if two or more first-degree relatives have the disease the risk is increased eightfold compared with a normal sample of U.S. citizens.[19] Forty-three percent of monozygotic twins are concordant for the disorder, compared with only 8% of dizygotic twins.[7]

In addition to age, gender, and family history, the presence of Down's syndrome, a history of head trauma, and a low level of education have been proposed as risk factors. Most studies concur that individuals with trisomy 21 develop the features of AD by age 35 years; however, studies looking at the possibility that families with a member who has AD are more likely to produce offspring with Down's syndrome have had inconclusive results.[24] Significant head injury, as either a single incident or a chronic occurrence as in sports injuries, increases the risk of developing Alzheimer's by a factor of 2.[19] An uneducated person older than 75 years is about twice as likely to develop dementia as one who has 8 years or more of schooling.[19] Risk factors found in some but not all studies include myocardial ischemia in the elderly, birth to a mother older than age 40 years, and exposure to aluminum.[19] For a more detailed examination of risk factors in AD, please see *Alzheimer's Disease,* edited by Terry and colleagues.[25]

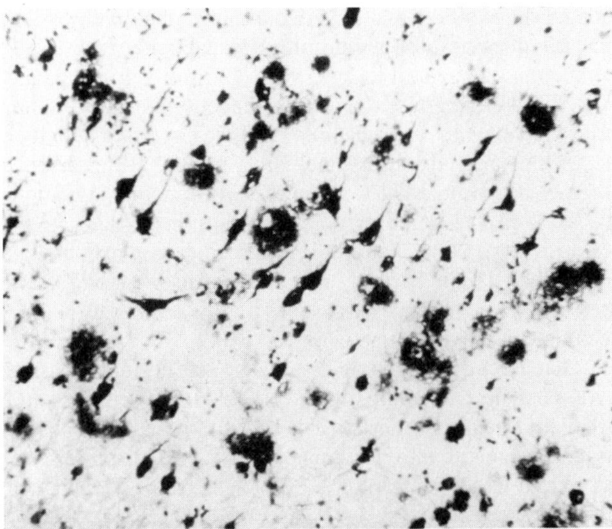

Figure 51–3 *Numerous neuritic plaques and neurofibrillary tangles in a patient with Alzheimer's disease. (Courtesy of Joseph Parker, MD, Duke University Medical Center, Durham, NC.)*

Pathology. The etiology and pathogenesis of Alzheimer's disease are unknown. Multiple agents and pathways are likely involved in this disorder.[26] Many hypotheses have been proposed regarding the cause and progression of Alzheimer's disease including genetic factors, slow or unconventional viruses, defective membrane metabolism, endogenous toxins, autoimmune disorders, and neurotoxicity of such trace elements as aluminum and mercury.[26]

The brains of patients with Alzheimer's disease contain many senile plaques, neurofibrillary tangles, and Hirano's bodies[7] (Figs. 51–3 and 51–4). There is degeneration of nerve cells, but the significant atrophy seen on neurodiag-

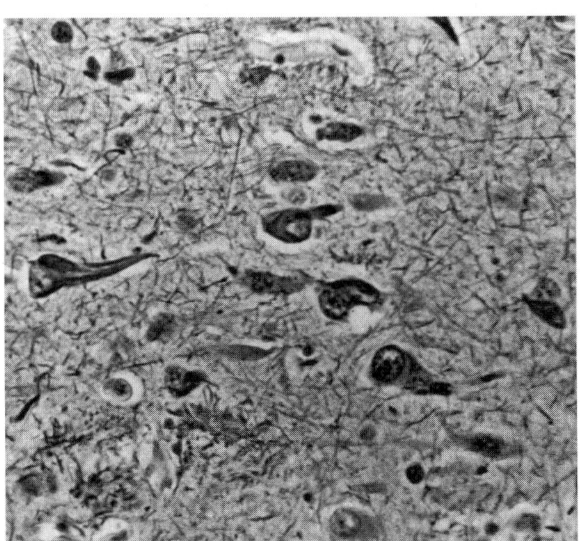

Figure 51–4 *Intraneuronal neurofibrillary tangles with neuritic plaques in a patient with Alzheimer's disease. (Courtesy of Joseph Parker, MD, Duke University Medical Center, Durham, NC.)*

nostic examination may be more the result of shrinkage of neurons and loss of dendritic spines than of actual neuronal loss.[27] The atrophy is most apparent in the associational cortex areas, and early on the primary motor and sensory areas are relatively spared (Figs. 51–5 and 51–6). Significant degenerative changes in neurons are seen in the hippocampus, locus caeruleus, and nucleus basalis of Mynert.[7] With advancing disease, these changes, in effect, separate the hippocampus from the remainder of the brain. Initially, the parietal and temporal regions are most affected by plaques and tangles, accounting for the memory impairment and parietal lobe–associated syndromes (some apraxias, hemi-attention, anosognosia, Gerstmann's syndrome) occasionally associated with Alzheimer's disease. Neurofibrillary tangles do not correlate with the severity of the dementia; however, the concentration of neuritic plaques is directly associated with the severity of the disease.[10]

Neurochemically, the brains of patients with Alzheimer's disease exhibit significant cholinergic abnormalities.[11] There is a profound decrease in acetylcholine (ACh) in almost all patients, as well as decreased immunological activity of somatostatin- and corticotropin-releasing factors.[11] The enzyme required for ACh synthesis, choline acetyltransferase, is also greatly reduced. Other studies suggest involvement of noradrenergic and serotoninergic systems in later onset disease and diminished γ-aminobutyric acid (GABA).[11] Specifically, the noradrenergic deficiencies seen in younger patients may be connected to changes in the locus caeruleus, and abnormalities of serotonin to effects on the raphe nuclei.[12] The serotoninergic neurons of the raphe nuclei in patients with Alzheimer's disease contain 6 to 39 times as many neurofibrillary tangles as those of age-appropriate control subjects, and noradrenergic neurons from the locus caeruleus of patients with Alzheimer's disease show neuronal loss of 40% to 80%.[12] Unfortunately, despite these observed neurochemical abnormalities, neurotransmitter-related treatment with cholinergic and GABAergic agents has proved largely unsuccessful.

Although the involvement of cholinergic transmission along the hippocampus and nucleus basalis is essential to the ability to learn new information, it seems that many of the symptoms of Alzheimer's disease are not explainable solely on the basis of cholinergic abnormalities. Thus, investigators have examined a number of other potential etiological or contributory agents.

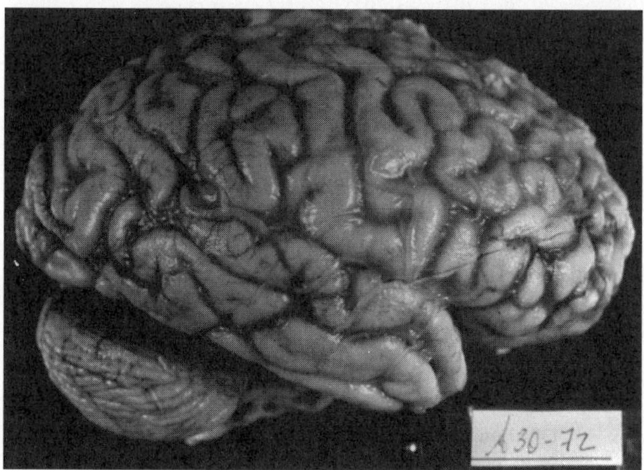

Figure 51–5 *Gross specimen showing prominent frontal lobe atrophy in a patient with Alzheimer's disease. (Courtesy of Joseph Parker, MD, Duke University Medical Center, Durham, NC.)*

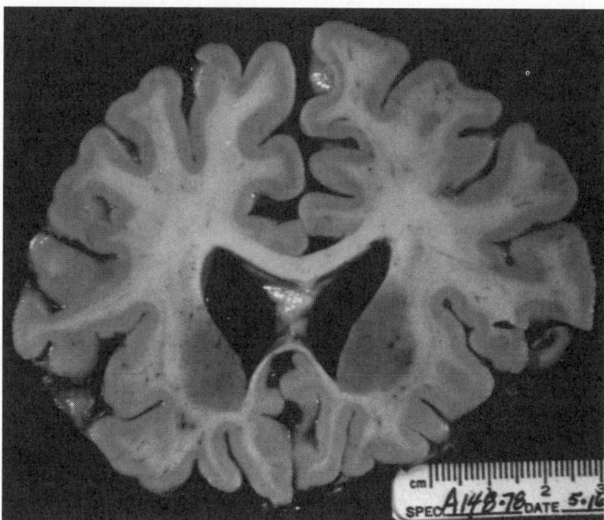

Figure 51–6 *Cortical and white matter atrophy. (Courtesy of Joseph Parker, MD, Duke University Medical Center, Durham, NC.)*

Some researchers have investigated the role of β-amyloid protein in Alzheimer's disease, and some assert that this material, a significant component of all plaques, is a major contributor to the neurodegenerative changes in the disease as both an initiater and a promoter of the disease.[28] Supporting this assertion are genetic studies of families with inheritable forms of presenile dementia, which show that disease occurrence is linked to mutations involving β-amyloid–related systems.[29] This hypothesis targets the protein found in senile plaques; other investigators have focused on the neurofibrillary tangles and the identification of a major component of its helical filament, the tau protein.[29, 30] Specifically, these researchers analyzed the possibility that modification of tau protein, predominantly by phosphorylation, is an important feature of AD.[31–33]

Aluminum, the third most common element in the universe, is absorbed from the gastrointestinal tract, lungs, nasal passage, and skin.[25, 34, 35] In 1897 Dollken[36] first demonstrated that aluminum injected in rabbits produced degeneration of neurons. In 1937 Scherp and Church[37] reported various neurological abnormalities including nystagmus, ataxia, and death in rabbits 10 to 18 days after a single injection of aluminum. In 1965 Klatzo and associates[38] discovered neurofibrillary tangles in rabbits receiving intracerebral injections of aluminum. Crapper and Dalton[39] reported increased aluminum in the brain of patients with Alzheimer's disease, with about a quarter of such samples showing concentrations three standard deviations above the control values. Other studies of bulk brain aluminum in patients with Alzheimer's disease have shown no such elevation.[26] The current consensus appears to be that although aluminum and other elements such as iron and mercury might accelerate neuronal degeneration in AD, these elements are not primary etiological agents.

The role of genetic factors in the development of AD has received increased attention as the role of the apolipoprotein E4 allele as a major genetic susceptibility risk factor has been confirmed by numerous studies.[40] In 1993 Corder and colleagues[41] studied 234 members of 42 families with late-onset AD. Of 95 affected members, 80% had the E4 allele, compared with 26% in the general population.[41] Furthermore, in these families, 91% of those homozygous for E4 had developed Alzheimer's disease by 80 years of age, evidence that the APOE *e4* allele is causing these familial cases.[41] In a study of 176 autopsy specimens of confirmed AD, Schmechel and coworkers in 1993 found that 65% of patients carried at least one apolipoprotein E *e4* gene.[40] Examination of all such studies indicates that between 25% and 40% of AD cases can be attributable to this marker, making its presence one of the most common risk factors yet discovered for AD.[40, 41]

Finally, several studies suggest that changes in membrane function, metabolism, and morphology are involved in the pathology of AD. Nonetheless, the basic molecular defect responsible for AD dementia has not been defined.[42]

The neuropathology of Alzheimer's disease should be compared with the normal neuropathic effects of aging. These include the following:

1. The leptomeninges become more fibrotic and are more adherent to the brain surface with increased opacity.
2. The ventricles show slight to moderate enlargement that increases with the passage of time.
3. The distance between the dura and the brain is increased.
4. Sulci widen and gyri become narrower.
5. The number of neurons decreases slightly.
6. The weight of the brain decreases in the fourth and fifth decades, with significant decrease by the age of 80 years.
7. Neurofibrillary tangles and senile plaques occur in virtually every elderly individual by the 10th decade of life.[7]

Laboratory and Radiological Findings. The role of laboratory determinations in the evaluation for AD is to exclude other causes of dementia, especially those that may prove reversible or arrestable. Before death, AD is largely a diagnosis of exclusion. Throughout the course of this disorder, laboratory values are essentially normal. Some nonspecific changes may occur, but electroencephalography and lumbar puncture are not diagnostic. As the disease progresses, computed tomography (CT) and magnetic resonance imaging (MRI) may show atrophy in the cerebral cortex and hydrocephalus ex vacuo (Fig. 51–7). MRI may show nonspecific alteration of white matter (leukoariosis), and eventually the electroencephalogram (EEG) shows diffuse background slowing.

Pneumoencephalography has demonstrated enlarged ventricles and widening of cortical sulci in Alzheimer's disease, and positron emission tomography in the later stages shows decreased cerebral oxygen and glucose metabolism in the frontal lobes. At present, in the work-up of a patient with a slowly progressive dementia, a good family history and physical examination and laboratory and radiographic tests to rule out other causes of dementia are the most effective tools in the diagnosis of Alzheimer's disease.

Clinical Features. The course and clinical features of AD parallel those discussed for dementia in general. Typically, the early course of AD is difficult to ascertain because the patient is usually an unreliable informant, and the early signs may be so subtle as to go unnoticed even by the patient's closest associates.[9] These early features include impaired memory, difficulty with problem solving, preoccupation with long past events, decreased spontaneity, and an inability to respond to the environment with the patient's usual speed and accuracy.[9] Patients may forget names, misplace household items, or forget what they were about to do. Often the individuals have insight into these memory deficits and occasionally convey their concerns to family members. Such responses as "You're just getting older," and "I do that sometimes myself" are common from those so informed, and as a result the patient becomes depressed, which can further affect cognitive functioning. Anomia, or difficulty with word finding, is common in this middle stage of Alzheimer's disease. Eventually the patient develops schemes, word associations, and excuses ("I never was very good in math") to assist in retention and cover up deficits. The patient may also employ family members as a surrogate memory.[9]

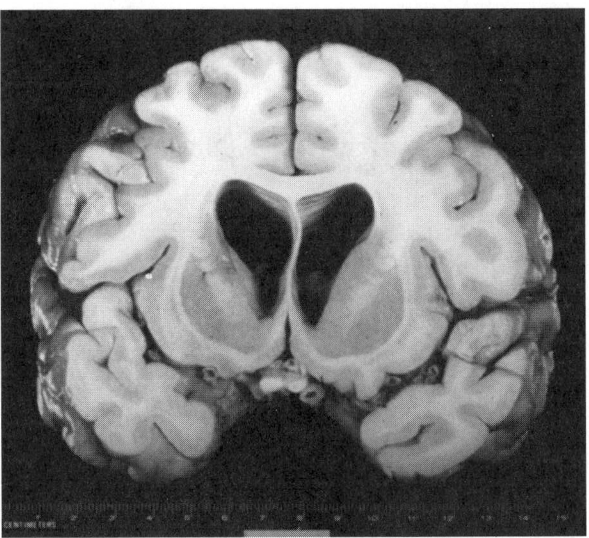

Figure 51–7 *Hydrocephalos ex vacuo in a patient with Alzheimer's disease. (Courtesy of Joseph Parker, MD, Duke University Medical Center, Durham, NC.)*

Because memory loss is usually most obvious for newly acquired material, the patient tries to avoid unfamiliar activities. Typically, the patient is seen by the physician when confusion, aggression, wandering, or some other socially undesirable behavior ensues. At that time, disorders of perception and language may appear. The patient often turns to a spouse to answer questions posed during the history taking. By this time the affected individual has lost insight into his or her dementia and abandons attempts to compensate for memory loss.[9] Finally, in the late stage of Alzheimer's disease, physical and cognitive effects are marked. Disorders of gait, extremity paresis and paralysis, seizures, peripheral neuropathy, extrapyramidal signs, and urinary incontinence are seen, and the patient is often no longer ambulatory. The aimless wandering of the middle stage has been replaced by a mute, bedridden state and decorticate posture. Myoclonus oc-

DSM-IV Criteria

Dementia of the Alzheimer Type

A. The development of multiple cognitive deficits manifested by both

(1) memory impairment (impaired ability to learn new information or to recall previously learned information)

(2) one (or more) of the following cognitive disturbances:

(a) aphasia (language disturbance)

(b) apraxia (impaired ability to carry out motor activities despite intact motor function)

(c) agnosia (failure to recognize or identify objects despite intact sensory function)

(d) disturbance in executive functioning (i.e., planning, organizing, sequencing, abstracting)

B. The cognitive deficits in criteria A1 and A2 each cause significant impairment in social or occupational functioning and represent a significant decline from a previous level of functioning.

C. The course is characterized by gradual onset and continuing cognitive decline.

D. The cognitive deficits in criteria A1 and A2 are not due to any of the following:

(1) other central nervous system conditions that cause progressive deficits in memory and cognition (e.g., cerebrovascular disease, Parkinson's disease, Huntington's disease, subdural hematoma, normal-pressure hydrocephalus, brain tumor)

(2) systemic conditions that are known to cause dementia (e.g., hypothyroidism, vitamin B_{12} or folic acid deficiency, niacin deficiency, hypercalcemia, neurosyphilis, HIV infection)

(3) substance-induced conditions

E. The deficits do not occur exclusively during the course of a delirium.

F. The disturbance is not better accounted for by another Axis I disorder (e.g., major depressive disorder, schizophrenia).

Code based on type of onset and predominant features:

With early onset: if onset is at age 65 years or below

290.11 With delirium: if delirium is superimposed on the dementia

290.12 With delusions: if delusions are the predominant feature

290.13 With depressed mood: if depressed mood (including presentations that meet full symptom criteria for a major depressive episode) is the predominant feature. A separate diagnosis of mood disorder due to a general medical condition is not given.

290.10 Uncomplicated: if none of the above predominates in the current clinical presentation

With late onset: if onset is after age 65 years

290.3 With delirium: if delirium is superimposed on the dementia

290.20 With delusions: if delusions are the predominant feature

290.21 With depressed mood: if depressed mood (including presentations that meet full symptom criteria for a major depressive episode) is the predominant feature. A separate diagnosis of mood disorder due to a general medical condition is not given.

290.0 Uncomplicated: if none of the above predominates in the current clinical presentation

Specify if:

With behavioral disturbance

Coding note: Also code 331.0 Alzheimer's disease on Axis III.

casionally occurs. Significantly, affective disturbances remain a distinct possibility throughout the course of the illness. AD progresses at a slow pace for 8 to 10 years to a state of complete helplessness.

Treatment. The two principles of management in AD are to treat what is treatable without aggravating existing symptoms and to support caregivers, who are also victims of this disease. Despite the significant decrease in ACh and choline acetyltransferase in Alzheimer's disease, treatments based on the cholinergic hypothesis have been unsuccessful.[10] With the goal of increasing the central nervous system concentrations of ACh, precursors of ACh including choline and lecithin have been tried, as well as centrally acting anticholinesterases such as physostigmine and tetrahydroacridine, with the hope of decreasing ACh metabolism.[11] ACh agonists such as areocholine, oxotremorine, and bethanechol have been investigated and release of ACh has been stimulated from cerebral neurons by using piracetam (a cyclic relative of GABA) and nafronyl oxalate (Praxilene).[11] These pharmacological interventions have yielded inconsistent results and been largely ineffective.

Because vasopressin levels are slightly decreased in the hippocampus of patients with Alzheimer's disease and somatostatin is adversely affected as well, attempts were made to replace these agents with little effect. In the belief that improving blood flow might be of benefit, such agents as the metabolic enhancer and vasodilator ergoloid mesylates (Hydergine) (an ergot alkaloid) were tried. Hydergine did seem to have some benefit; however, these effects may have been related to its mild antidepressant action.[11, 43] Onset of action of any beneficial effects of Hydergine was quite long.

Corticotropin release is promoted by corticotropin-releasing factor, which is decreased in patients with AD, but clinical trials with corticotropin were disappointing.[44, 45] Animal studies suggested that the opioid antagonist naloxone (Narcan) increases memory performance; however, trials with this agent and the oral, long-acting antagonist naltrexone (Trexan) were unproductive.[46–48]

Despite lackluster effects of physostigmine, a second cholinesterase inhibitor has shown promise.[49] Tetrahydroaminoacridine (tacrine) produced significant cognitive improvement in 16 of 17 patients with AD in an early study.[50] Subsequent studies have been less impressive, but significant improvement in a number of scales measuring cognitive performance illustrated the benefit of this agent for some patients. Side effects, particularly hepatic and cholinergic, were noted; however, in 1993 the U.S. Food and Drug Administration approved tacrine for the treatment of AD.[46]

Other unsuccessful drug trials included the use of the monoamine oxidase B inhibitor L-deprenyl, thiamine, and nicotine.[51–53]

Whereas much attention has been focused on research aimed at understanding and altering the pathogenesis of AD, less work has been done regarding appropriate pharmacological agents for the varied psychological manifestations of the disease. Depression is often associated with AD. If antidepressant medication is to be used, low doses (about one third to one half of the usual initial dose) are advised, and only agents with minimal anticholinergic activity should be employed. Appropriate choices would be the newer selective serotonin reuptake inhibitors such as paroxetine (Paxil), fluoxetine (Prozac), and sertraline (Zoloft). Trazodone (Desyrel) has occasionally been employed because of its sedative properties. If tricyclic antidepressants are used, the secondary amines (desipramine, nortriptyline) are recommended over the tertiary ones (amitriptyline, doxepin). Careful attention to the possible side effects of these agents, particularly orthostatic hypotension, lowering of the seizure threshold, urine retention, and interference with the acquisition of new knowledge, is suggested.

Anxiety and psychosis, particularly paranoid delusions, are common in AD. Benzodiazepines inhibit new memory and should be avoided if possible. Antipsychotic medications with high anticholinergic potential (thioridazine, chlorpromazine) may also affect memory, so their use must be weighed against the beneficial sedation they might produce. Haloperidol has less anticholinergic activity but may aggravate some AD symptoms such as extrapyramidal signs. Newer agents such as risperidone and clozapine might be of benefit for amelioration of psychotic symptoms. In summary, the psychopharmacological management is designed to ameliorate cognitive deficits if possible; control agitated, psychotic, and dangerous behavior; and treat any underlying psychiatric disorder (e.g., major depression) that might be comorbid with the dementia.

The appropriate management of AD entails more than psychopharmacological intervention. Other elements of the treatment plan should be environmental manipulation and support for the family.

In the attempt to maintain patients with Alzheimer's disease in their homes for as long as possible, some adjustment of their environment is important. Written daily reminders can be helpful in the performance of daily activities. Prominent clocks, calendars, and windows are important, and an effort should be made to minimize changes in the patient's daily activities. Repeated demonstrations of how to lock doors and windows and operate appliances are helpful, and arranging for rapid dialing of essential telephone numbers can be important. Maintaining adequate hydration, nutrition, exercise, and cleanliness is essential.

The family of the patient with Alzheimer's disease is also a victim of the disease. Family members must watch the gradual deterioration of the patient and accept that a significant part of their own lives must be devoted to the care of the individual. Difficult decisions about institutionalization and termination of life support are distinct possibilities, and the patients often turn their anger and paranoia toward the caregiver. Education is a valuable treatment tool for families. Information about the disease and peer support are available through Alzheimer's associations, and many such agencies provide family members with a companion for the patient to allow the family some time away. Many studies suggest that the primary reason for institutionalization of these patients is the tremendous burden of care they pose for their families. Aimless wandering seems to be a particularly disturbing behavior. Unfortunately, the unfamiliar surroundings of a nursing home often increase the patient's level of confusion and anxiety.

For these reasons, family members are at risk for depression, anxiety syndromes, insomnia, and a variety of other psychological manifestations. Should these occur, they should be promptly treated. The National Alzheimer's Education and Referral Service can be accessed by calling 1-800-621-0379.

Dementia due to Pick's Disease. Pick's disease is a rare form of progressive dementia clinically indistinguishable from Alzheimer's disease. It is about one fifth as common as AD.[53] Pick's disease occurs in middle adult life and has a duration that varies from 2 to 15 years. It has a strong familial tendency, but a definite genetic pattern has not been established.[11] ACh levels are reduced.

The pathology of Pick's disease involves prominent changes (e.g., sclerosis, atrophy) in the frontal and temporal lobes (Fig. 51–8). The parietal and occipital lobes are spared. Alzheimer himself noted the argentophilic (staining silver) intraneuronal inclusion Pick's bodies.

The clinical features of Pick's disease are quite similar to those of Alzheimer's disease, and as neither condition is curable, an elaborate differential diagnosis is unnecessary. Because of parietal sparing, such features as apraxia and agnosia are less common in Pick's disease, and visual-spatial ability, often impaired in Alzheimer's disease, is preserved.[11] Given the prominent changes in the frontal lobe, disinhibited

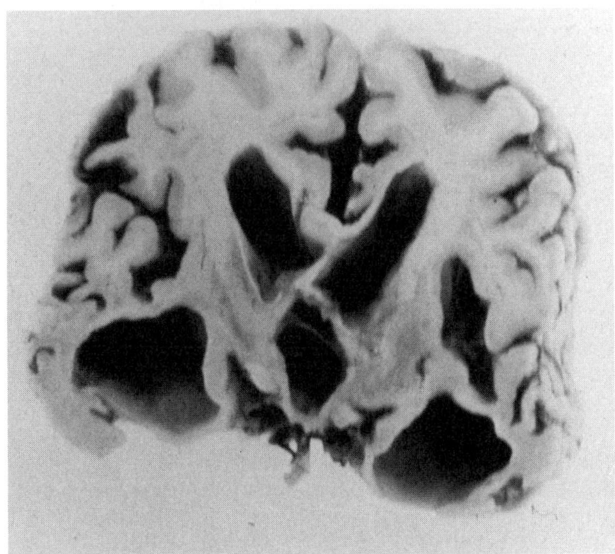

Figure 51–8 *Severe lobar sclerosis and atrophy in a patient with Pick's disease. (Courtesy of Joseph Parker, MD, Duke University Medical Center, Durham, NC.)*

behavior, loss of social constraints, and lack of concern about appearance and matters of personal hygiene occur relatively early in Pick's disease. Such speech disorders as echolalia and logorrhea are common, and patients with Pick's disease are more likely to develop Klüver-Bucy syndrome (orality, hyperphagia, hypersexuality, placidity) indicative of damage to the temporal lobes.[54] Significant memory impairment may occur relatively late in the course, and eventually the patient becomes listless, mute, and ultimately decerebrate and comatose. The treatment of Pick's disease is symptomatic.

Dementia due to Parkinson's Disease. James Parkinson did not consider cognitive deficits to be a feature of the disease that now bears his name.[7] In fact, although dementia rarely occurs as an initial symptom of Parkinson's disease, it is found in nearly 40% of patients older than 70 years of age.[55] The disease results from loss of dopamine production in the basal ganglia and can be idiopathic, postencephalitic, or drug induced. Usually the patient is 50 years of age or older, and unlike Alzheimer's and Pick's dementias, this disease occurs slightly more often in men.[7] Dementia most commonly occurs in cases of Parkinson's disease in which the decline has been rapid and response to anticholinergics has been poor.

The pathology of Parkinson's disease involves depigmentation of the so-called pigmented nuclei of the brain (locus caeruleus, substantia nigra). These nuclei then contain eosinophilic Lewy's bodies. As in Alzheimer's disease, the cerebral cortex of many of these patients contains many senile plaques and neurofibrillary tangles, loss of neurons, and decreased concentrations of choline acetyltransferase.[55]

The clinical features of Parkinson's disease are well described, with the cardinal triad being tremor, rigidity, and bradykinesia. Associated symptoms include a festinating gait, micrographia, and an expressionless facial countenance. The treatment involves the use of anticholinergic and dopaminergic agents.

Dementia due to Huntington's Disease. Dementia is also a characteristic of Huntington's disease, an autosomal dominant inheritable condition localized to chromosome 4. Unfortunately, this condition does not become apparent until age 35 to 45 years, usually after childbearing has occurred. Fifty percent of offspring are affected. There is also a juvenile form of the disease. Huntington's disease affects about 4 in 100,000 people, making it a significant cause of dementia in middle-aged adults.[55]

The pathology of Huntington's disease involves selective destruction in the caudate and putamen.[55] In the caudate nuclei, GABA concentrations are reduced to 50% of normal.[55] The frontal lobes of the cerebral cortex are also involved, but GABA and choline acetyltransferase concentrations are normal.

The most noticeable clinical feature of Huntington's disease is the movement disorder, which involves both choreiform movements (frequent movements that cause a jerking motion of the body) and athetosis (slow writhing movements). In the juvenile form of Huntington's disease, which represents about 3% of all cases, the chorea is replaced by dystonia, akinesia, and rigidity, and the course of the disease is more rapid than in the adult form.[55] In the early stages of the disease, the chorea is not as noticeable and may be disguised by the patient by making the movements seem purposeful.

The dementia typically begins 1 year before or 1 year after the chorea and, unlike patients with other dementias, patients with Huntington's disease are often well aware of their deteriorating mentation. This may be a factor in the high rates of suicide and alcoholism associated with this condition. Although attempts have been made to increase ACh and GABA concentrations in these patients, such pharmacological interventions have been unsuccessful, and the dementia is untreatable. Genetic counseling is indicated.

Vascular Dementia. Vascular dementia usually results from multiple CVAs or one significant CVA. It is generally considered the second most common cause of dementia after Alzheimer's disease, accounting for about 10% of all cases.[11, 12] Men are twice as likely as women to be diagnosed with this condition.[54] Vascular dementia is characterized by a stepwise progression of cognitive deterioration with accompanying lateralizing signs (see page 908). It is always associated with evidence of systemic hypertension and usually involves renal and cardiac abnormalities. Risk factors for the development of a vascular dementia include those generally associated with obstructive coronary artery disease, including obesity, hypercholesterolemia, smoking, hypertension, stress, and lack of exercise. The actual incidence of vascular dementia has decreased somewhat with better standards of care, improved diagnostic techniques, and lifestyle changes.

Clinical Features. Vascular dementia is characterized by the early appearance of lateralizing signs. Spasticity, hemiparesis, ataxia, and pseudobulbar palsy are common. Pseudobulbar palsy is associated with injury to the frontal lobes and results in impairment of the corticobulbar tracts. It is characterized by extreme emotional lability, abnormal speech cadence, dysphagia, hyperactive jaw jerk, deep tendon reflexes, and Babinski's reflex.

CT, MRI, and gross specimens show cerebral atrophy and infarctions, with the radiological procedures showing

DSM-IV Criteria 290.4x

Vascular Dementia

A. The development of multiple cognitive deficits manifested by both

(1) memory impairment (impaired ability to learn new information or to recall previously learned information)

(2) one (or more) of the following cognitive disturbances:

(a) aphasia (language disturbance)

(b) apraxia (impaired ability to carry out motor activities despite intact motor function)

(c) agnosia (failure to recognize or identify objects despite intact sensory function)

(d) disturbance in executive functioning (i.e., planning, organizing, sequencing, abstracting)

B. The cognitive deficits in criteria A1 and A2 each cause significant impairment in social or occupational functioning and represent a significant decline from a previous level of functioning.

C. Focal neurological signs and symptoms (e.g., exaggeration of deep tendon reflexes, extensor-plantar response, pseudobulbar palsy, gait abnormalities, weakness of an extremity) or laboratory evidence indicative of cerebrovascular disease (e.g., multiple infarctions involving cortex and underlying white matter) that are judged to be etiologically related to the disturbance.

D. The deficits do not occur exclusively during the course of a delirium.

Code based on predominant features:

290.41 With delirium: if delirium is superimposed on the dementia

290.42 With delusions: if delusions are the predominant feature

390.43 With depressed mood: if depressed mood (including presentations that meet full symptom criteria for a major depressive episode) is the predominant feature. A separate diagnosis of mood disorder due to a general medical condition is not given.

209.40 Uncomplicated: if none of the above predominates in the current clinical presentation

Specify if:

With behavioral disturbance

Coding note: Also code cerebrovascular condition on Axis III.

multiple lucencies and the gross specimens revealing distinct white matter lesions[11, 56] (Figs. 51–9, 51–10, and 51–11). The EEG is abnormal but nonspecific, and positron emission tomography reveals hypometabolic areas.[11] Vascular dementia is differentiated from AD on the basis of its mode of progression, early appearance of neurological signs, and radiographical evidence of cerebral ischemia.

Treatment. Primary prevention and secondary prevention are important in the treatment of cerebrovascular disorders. Lifestyle changes are effective in arresting the progress of the disease; however, no known pharmacological treatment can reverse the effects of a completed stroke.[12] Such interventions as anticoagulants for frequent transient ischemic attacks after a hemorrhagic lesion is excluded, aspirin for decreasing platelet aggregation, and surgical removal of obstructing plaques probably do not reverse the mental state.[12]

Depression occurs in 50% to 60% of patients with CVAs and responds to traditional antidepressants. Amitriptyline, in less than antidepressant doses, improves both CVA depression and pseudobulbar palsy. Physical rehabilitation is essential and often results in an improvement in mood and outlook.

Infectious Causes of Dementia

Subacute Sclerosing Panencephalitis. Subacute sclerosing panencephalitis is an infectious cause of dementia that usually appears in childhood. The average age at onset is 10 years, and most patients are male and live in rural areas.[11, 57] It is diagnosed on the basis of periodic complexes on the EEG and an elevated measles titer in the cerebrospinal fluid (CSF). The CT scan shows cerebral atrophy and dilated ventricles.

It has been postulated that a mutant measles virus is the infectious agent, based on the high CSF measles antibody titer and the fact that the disease is virtually nonexistent in children who have been vaccinated for measles.[57] Affected patients show an insidious onset of impairment of cognition usually preceded by behavioral problems.

Creutzfeldt-Jakob Disease. Dating from original descriptions by Creutzfeldt in 1920 and Jakob in 1921, this disease has received intense scientific scrutiny.[9] The primary features of Creutzfeldt-Jakob disease are dementia, basal ganglia and cerebellar dysfunction, myoclonus, upper motor neuron lesions, and rapid progression to stupor, coma, and death in a matter of months. The disease generally affects people 65 years of age or older, with a duration of 1 month

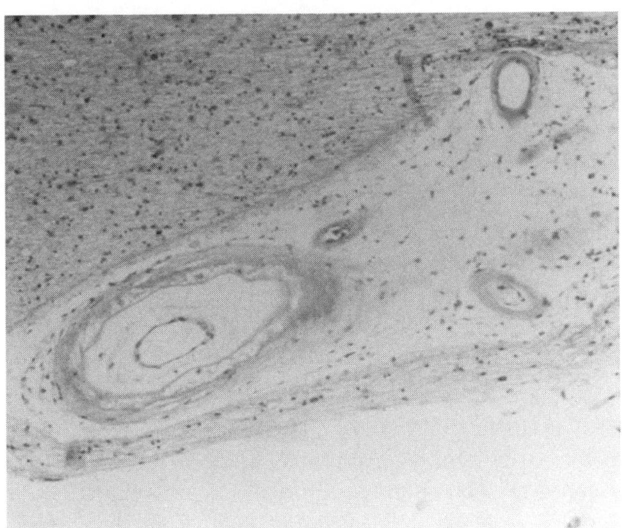

Figure 51–9 *Arteriosclerotic vessels in cerebral ischemia. (Courtesy of Joseph Parker, MD, Duke University Medical Center, Durham, NC.)*

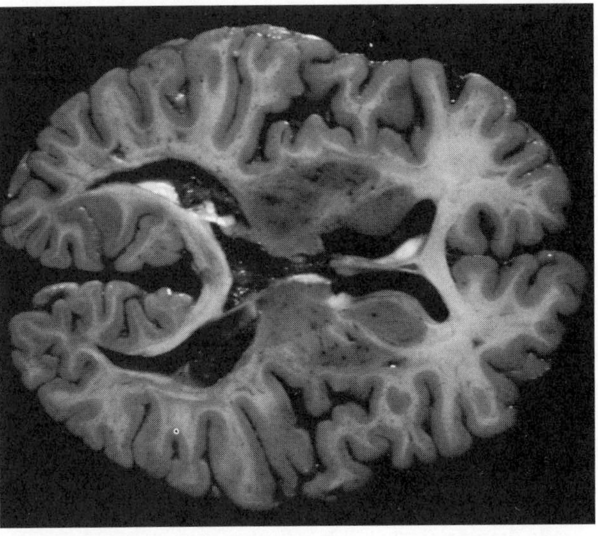

Figure 51–11 *Multiple lucencies in basal nuclei with reduced white matter in vascular dementia. (Courtesy of Joseph Parker, MD, Duke University Medical Center, Durham, NC.)*

to 6 years and an average life span after disease onset of 15 months.[9]

The clinical and pathological features of Creutzfeldt-Jakob have been produced experimentally by injecting animals with brain tissue from affected adults. It has unknowingly been transferred to humans by organ transplantation, cerebral electrodes, and pituitary growth hormone.[58, 59] These incidents, although tragic, illustrated the infectious nature of this condition, and the agent of transmission is believed to be a prion-containing protein (not DNA or RNA). These prions have been detected in the cerebral cortex of autopsy specimens of both patients with Creutzfeldt-Jakob disease and victims of kuru, a fatal disease transmitted by cannibalism.[54, 60] Slow viruses have also been implicated as infectious agents in kuru.

The memory loss in Creutzfeldt-Jakob disease involves all phases of memory, with recent (secondary) memory the most impaired. Personality changes, immature behavior, and paranoia are early signs, and virtually every aspect of brain functioning can be involved. Motor disorders including rigidity, incoordination, paresis, and ataxia usually follow.

As with subacute sclerosing panencephalitis, the EEG in Creutzfeldt-Jakob disease shows periodic complexes and biopsy specimens reveal a characteristic spongiform encephalopathy and occasional amyloid plaques[11] (Fig. 51–12).

Acquired Immunodeficiency Syndrome. AIDS was first described in the United States in 1979. Two years later, the Centers for Disease Control and Prevention announced the

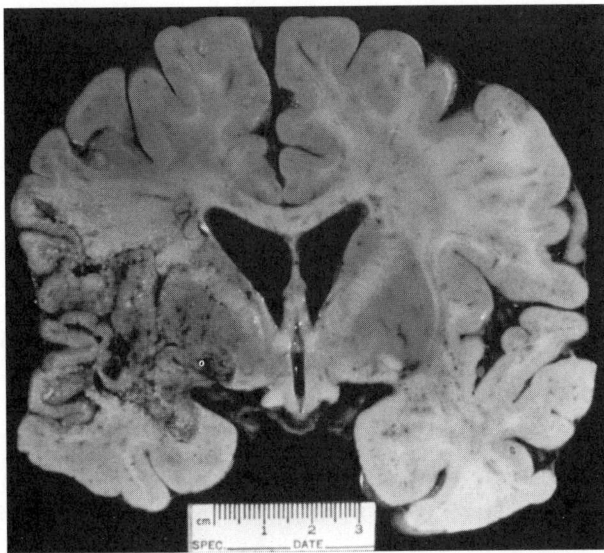

Figure 51–10 *Subacute left frontotemporal infarction. (Courtesy of Joseph Parker, MD, Duke University Medical Center, Durham, NC.)*

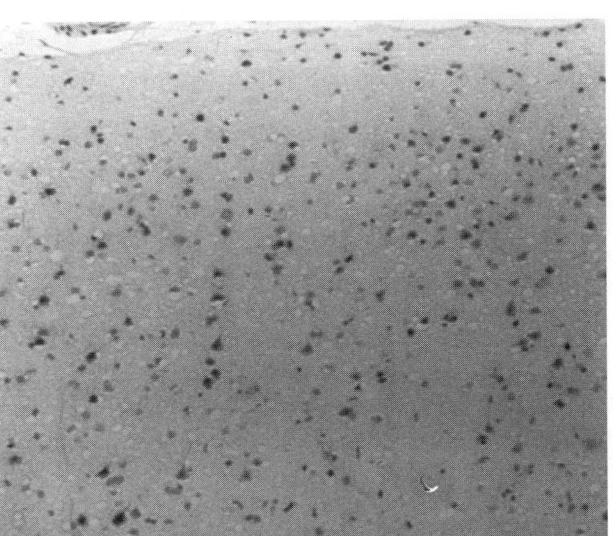

Figure 51–12 *Spongiform encephalopathy in a patient with Creutzfeldt-Jakob disease. (Courtesy of Joseph Parker, MD, Duke University Medical Center, Durham, NC.)*

unexplained occurrence of *Pneumocystis carinii* pneumonia and Kaposi's sarcoma in previously healthy homosexual men.[60] Since then, the number of AIDS cases has risen exponentially, and by November 1994 more than 185,000 Americans had died of this condition.

In the truest sense, AIDS is not a disease but an increased susceptibility to a variety of diseases caused by loss of immunocompetence. It may result from infection with HIV, a retrovirus that attaches to the CD4 molecule on the surface of the T4 (thymus-derived) lymphocyte. Then, using reverse transcriptase, the virus reverses the usual sequence of genetic information and becomes integrated into the host cell's DNA.[11] The ultimate result is destruction of the T4 cell, replication of the virus, a defect in cell-mediated immunity, and the development of various opportunistic infections and neoplasms.

The epidemiology of HIV spectrum disease has changed significantly in the 16 years since its identification. Initially, homosexual and bisexual men with multiple partners were, according to the Centers for Disease Control and Prevention, the highest risk group. Intravenous drug abusers and recipients of tainted blood products were soon added to high-risk groups. In the 1990s the number of new infections among homosexual men decreased significantly and rates for women, intravenous drug abusers who share contaminated needles, and infants born to infected mothers increased significantly. Intravenous drug abusers, regardless of sexual orientation, represent the fastest growing population of the newly infected people. Conversely, instances of transmission by blood products have decreased since the development of laboratory testing for HIV antibodies. The Centers for Disease Control and Prevention has now established a reactive HIV antibody screen, presence of an opportunistic condition, and a $CD4^+$ cell count of 200 or less (normal being 1000 to 1500) as criteria for the diagnosis of AIDS.

AIDS is now best considered as part of the spectrum of HIV infection.[61] There are four stages of infection.

Stage 1: Acute infection: Most infected persons remember no signs or symptoms at the time of the initial infection. The acute syndrome follows infection by 4 to 6 weeks and is characterized by fevers, rigors, muscle aches, maculopapular rash, diarrhea, and abdominal cramps. These symptoms, often mistaken for those of influenza, resolve spontaneously after 2 to 3 weeks.

Stage 2: Asymptomatic carrier: This stage follows the acute infection. The patient is without symptoms for a variable amount of time. The mean symptom-free period has increased significantly since the disease was first identified and is now about 10 years. Most of the estimated 2 million infected Americans are at this stage. Even though these individuals are asymptomatic, they are carriers of the disease and can infect others.

Stage 3: Generalized adenopathy: In older terminology, this stage was referred to as the AIDS-related complex. It is characterized by palpable lymph nodes that persist for longer than 3 months. These nodes must be outside the inguinal area and due to no other condition except HIV.

Stage 4: Other diseases:

1. Constitutional symptoms such as lingering fever, wasting syndromes, and intractable diarrhea.
2. Secondary infections including *P. carinii* pneumonia, cytomegalovirus retinitis, parasitic colitis, and oral and esophageal thrush.
3. Secondary neoplasms such as Kaposi's sarcoma and B-cell lymphomas.
4. Neurological diseases (AIDS dementia complex).

Thus, the diagnosis of AIDS is made when an infected individual develops either a $CD4^+$ cell count of less than 200 or a certain condition listed in stage 4.[61]

Dementia due to HIV Disease. Initially, the behavioral abnormalities observed in HIV-positive patients were attributed to the emotional reaction to the disease. Subsequent investigations demonstrated that neurological complications occur in 40% to 45% of patients with AIDS, and in about 10% of cases neurological signs are the first feature of the disease.[7, 62] The neurological signs present in AIDS are believed to be related to both the direct effects of the virus on cells (such as macrophages) that enter the central nervous system and the neurological conditions that opportunistically affect these patients. Ho and colleagues[63] reported that 90% of the brains of AIDS patients examined showed neuropathological abnormalities. AIDS dementia must be considered in the differential diagnosis of dementia in older patients, because about 10% of AIDS patients are older than 50 years of age.[7, 64]

Patients with AIDS dementia present with impairments of cognitive, behavioral, and motor systems. The cognitive disorders include memory impairment, confusion, and poor concentration. Behavioral features include apathy, reclusivity, anhedonia, depression, delusions, and hallucinations. Motor symptoms include incoordination, lower extremity paresis, unsteadiness, and difficulty with fine motor movements like handwriting and buttoning clothes.[7, 11] As the disease progresses, parkinsonism and myoclonus develop.

Lateralizing signs such as tremors, focal seizures, abnormal reflexes, and hemiparesis can result. The protozoan *Toxoplasma gondii* commonly infects the central nervous system and can be diagnosed by CT or by increased toxoplasmosis antibody titers.[11] Discrete cerebral lesions are also produced by fungi such as *Candida* and *Aspergillus, Mycobacterium tuberculosis,* and viruses such as cytomegalovirus and papovavirus. Papovavirus causes progressive multifocal leukoencephalopathy.[11] Tertiary syphilis has increased significantly since the advent of AIDS, and neoplasms such as lymphomas, metastatic Kaposi's sarcoma, and gliomas are also causes of AIDS dementia.

Many confounding factors can increase cognitive dysfunction in AIDS, including a high incidence of drug and alcohol abuse; medications such as histamine H_2 receptor antagonists (cimetidine), corticosteroids, narcotics, and antiviral drugs (e.g., zidovudine [formerly azidothymidine, AZT]) that increase confusion; and coexistent depression (Table 51–5).

The CT scan shows cerebral atrophy and MRI reveals nonspecific white matter abnormalities.[11] Neoplasms and lesions such as in toxoplasmosis are also visible. Lumbar puncture reveals a pleocytosis and elevated protein levels, and autopsy demonstrates an atrophic brain with demyelination, multinuclear giant cells, and gliosis of the cerebral cortex.[11]

Table 51–5 Neuropsychiatric Effects of AIDS-Related Drugs

Drug	Use	Effect
Ketoconazole (Nizoral)	Antifungal	Severe depression Suicidality (rare)
Foscarnet	Cytomegalovirus retinitis Herpes	Depression Confusion
Ganciclovir	Cytomegalovirus retinitis	Anxiety Psychosis
Bactrim	*Pneumocystis* pneumonia	Hallucinations Depression Apathy
Pentamidine	*Pneumocystis* pneumonia	Delirium Hallucinations
Interferon alfa	Cancer	Depression
Rifampin	Tuberculosis	Delirium Behavioral changes
Isoniazid	Tuberculosis	Memory disturbance Psychosis
Dronabinol (Marinol)	Appetite stimulant Wasting syndrome Nausea	Depression Anxiety Psychosis Euphoria
Zalcitabine (DDC)	Antiviral	Psychosis Amnesia Confusion Depersonalization Depression Mania Suicidality Mood swings
Didanosine	Antiviral	Anxiety
Zidovudine (AZT)	Antiviral	Confusion, mania Depression, anxiety

Treatment. The increase in life span of patients affected by HIV is directly related to improvements in treating the opportunistic conditions that occur. Aerosol pentamidine as prophylaxis for *P. carinii* pneumonia and ganciclovir for cytomegalovirus retinitis are examples of effective intervention. The use of antiviral agents has generated some controversy. Zidovudine, the first antiviral treatment for AIDS approved by the U.S. Food and Drug Administration, increased or stabilized $CD4^+$ cell concentrations in early studies. Later investigations revealed that zidovudine has a narrow window of effectiveness and may not be appropriate immediately after such exposure as a needle stick. Side effects of zidovudine include blood dyscrasias, peripheral neuropathy, seizures, lymphomas, confusion, anxiety, mania, and a Wernicke-Korsakoff type of picture.[11]

Studies suggest that administration of zidovudine to HIV-positive patients during pregnancy, intravenously during delivery, and to the neonate for 6 weeks after birth can decrease the percentage of infants who seroconvert from 30% to as low as 10%. However, results of studies of the effectiveness of zidovudine in children already HIV-positive have been disappointing.

Subsequent antiviral agents such as dideoxyinosine and dideoxycytidine (DDC) have been associated with painful neuropathy and pancreatic disorders. DDC in particular can produce serious neuropsychiatric complications. Combined therapy with two antiviral agents may be more effective than single-drug therapy.

The treatment of neuropsychiatric disorders in AIDS involves utilizing agents that are least likely to interfere with other medications prescribed or to exacerbate the symptoms of the disease. AIDS-related depression has responded well to the selective serotonin reuptake inhibitor antidepressants and to psychostimulants. The selective serotonin reuptake inhibitors, particularly fluoxetine, may inhibit the cytochrome P-450 enzyme system and retard the metabolism of agents such as antiarrhythmics, benzodiazepines, and anticonvulsants that AIDS patients may be taking. Careful attention to drug-drug interactions and monitoring of blood levels of affected medications are recommended. Among the psychostimulants, methylphenidate is preferred to dextroamphetamine because of the latter's tendency to produce dyskinesias. Anticholinergic agents can increase confusion; however, low-dose tricyclic antidepressants are often used for their sedative, appetite stimulant, and analgesic properties. The secondary amine tricyclic antidepressants (nortriptyline, desipramine) may be less anticholinergic, but most tricyclic agents can produce some degree of bone marrow suppression. Lithium carbonate, which produces a leukocytosis, may be of benefit in recurrent unipolar and treatment-resistant depression.

In summary, AIDS dementia is best treated by identifying the associated medical condition, instituting appropriate therapy, and managing behavior in the interim.

Neurosyphilis. During the late 19th century, neurosyphilis was responsible for a significant number of admissions to psychiatric hospitals.[11] The condition had decreased in incidence after the causative agent *(Treponema pallidum)* was identified and penicillin treatment became readily available. The rise of AIDS in the 1980s and 1990s has led to an increase in the number of diagnosed cases of neurosyphilis.[11] Infection with *T. pallidum* is generally divided into four stages.[65]

Primary syphilis occurs 3 to 6 weeks after contact with the organism. The symptoms include a chancre at the site and regional lymphadenopathy. Affected persons are infectious.

Secondary syphilis begins 6 to 8 weeks after the primary stage. It is manifested by a maculopapular rash over the trunk, and especially over the soles of the feet and palms. The person is constitutionally ill with fever and adenopathy. Occasionally, secondary syphilis is asymptomatic in the last few weeks.

Latent syphilis presents with a normal examination and seropositivity. If patients with latent syphilis continue to have a normal CSF profile 2 years after diagnosis, they are at low risk for neurosyphilis.

Late syphilis consists of ongoing inflammatory disease most likely in the aorta or nervous system (neurosyphilis), the latter occurring in about 10% of patients. The neurosyphilis of the late stage can consist of 1) asymptomatic neurosyphilis, 2) meningovascular syphilis, and 3) parenchymal neurosyphilis. The parenchymal neurosyphilis consists of general paresis, which occurs about 20 years after infection and includes cognitive impairment, myoclonus, dysarthria, personality changes, irritability, psychosis, grandiosity, and mania.[65] Untreated general paresis leaves the patient a helpless invalid. The second form of parenchymal neurosyphilis is tabes dorsalis with onset 25 to 30 years after initial infection. Tabes features loss of position and vibratory sense, areflexia in lower extremities, chronic pain, ataxia, and incontinence.[65]

The original screening test for syphilis is the Venereal Disease Research Laboratory (VDRL) test. This test has a significant false-positive rate, especially in the elderly and in patients with addictions and autoimmune disorders.[11] The VDRL test may revert to negative after a number of years, and 20% to 30% of patients in the stage of late syphilis have a negative (nonreactive) VDRL result. A more specific test is the fluorescent treponemal antibody screen, which is positive 95% of the time in neurosyphilis. The false-positive rate for the fluorescent treponemal antibody screen is extremely low, and reversion to a nonreactive state is unlikely. In addition to a positive VDRL result, the CSF in patients with neurosyphilis generally shows pleocytosis.

Dementia secondary to neurosyphilis produces various physical findings in advanced cases. These may include dysarthria, Babinski's reflex, tremor, Argyll Robertson pupils, myelitis, and optic atrophy. Although notorious, delusions of grandeur in neurosyphilis are rare. A reactive CSF VDRL result or a positive serum fluorescent treponemal antibody result in a patient with neurological symptoms who cannot document treatment should be treated with appropriate antibiotic therapy. Penicillin often improves cognitive deficits and corrects CSF abnormalities, but complete recovery is rare.

Dementia due to Head Trauma

Head trauma is the leading cause of brain injury for children and young adults.[7] It is estimated that more than 7 million head injuries and 500, 000 related hospital admissions occur in the United States annually.[7, 66] Traumatic head injuries result in concussions, contusions, or open head injuries, and the physical examination often reveals such features as blood behind the tympanic membranes (Battle's sign), infraorbital ecchymosis, and pupillary abnormalities.[7] The psychiatric manifestations of an acute brain injury are generally classified as a delirium or amnestic disorder; however, head trauma–induced delirious states often merge into a chronic dementia. Episodes of repeated head trauma, as in dementia pugilistica (punchdrunk syndrome), can lead to permanent changes in cognition and thus are appropriately classified as demented states. The punchdrunk syndrome is seen in aging boxers and includes dysarthric speech, emotional lability, slowed thought, and impulsivity.[7, 11, 67, 68]

A single head injury may result in a postconcussional syndrome with resultant memory impairment, alterations in mood and personality, hyperacusis, headaches, easy fatigability, anxiety, belligerent behavior, and dizziness. Alcohol abuse, postural hypotension, and gait disturbances are often associated with head injuries that result in dementia.

Substance-Induced Persisting Dementia

In instances in which the features of dementia result from central nervous system effects of a medication, toxin, or drug of abuse (including alcohol), the diagnosis of dementia due to the persisting effects of a substance should be made.[1] The most common dementias in this category are those associated with alcohol abuse, accounting for about 10% of all dementias.[12] The diagnosis of alcohol abuse dementia requires that the cognitive changes persist after the cessation of alcohol use and are not the result of changes in mentation associated with early abstinence, amnestic episodes (blackouts), or Wernicke-Korsakoff syndrome. In addition to various nutritional deficiencies and the toxic effects of alcohol itself, alcohol abusers are more prone to develop dementia as a result of head trauma and chronic hepatic encephalopathy.

Epidemiology of Alcohol-Induced Dementia. Chronic alcohol abuse is the third leading cause of dementia. It affects a higher proportion of women than men, and alcohol-

DSM-IV Criteria

Substance-Induced Persisting Dementia

A. The development of multiple cognitive deficits manifested by both
   (1) memory impairment (impaired ability to learn new information or to recall previously learned information)
   (2) one (or more) of the following cognitive disturbances:
      (a) aphasia (language disturbance)
      (b) apraxia (impaired ability to carry out motor activities despite intact motor function)
      (c) agnosia (failure to recognize or identify objects despite intact sensory function)
      (d) disturbance in executive functioning (i.e., planning, organizing, sequencing, abstracting)

B. The cognitive deficits in criteria A1 and A2 each cause significant impairment in social or occupational functioning and represent a significant decline from a previous level of functioning.

C. The deficits do not occur exclusively during the course of a delirium and persist beyond the usual duration of substance intoxication or withdrawal.

D. There is evidence from the history, physical examination, or laboratory findings that the deficits are etiologically related to the persisting effects of substance use (e.g., a drug of abuse, a medication).

Code: [specific substance]–induced persisting dementia:

(291.2 alcohol; 292.82 inhalant; 292.82 sedative, hypnotic, or anxiolytic; 292.82 other [or unknown] substance)

induced dementia is a relatively late occurrence, generally following 15 to 20 years of heavy drinking.[12] Dementia is more common in individuals with alcoholism who are malnourished. The CT scan shows cortical atrophy and ventricular dilatation after about 10 years with neuronal loss, pigmentary degeneration, and glial proliferation.[12] The frontal lobes are the most affected, followed by parietal and temporal areas.[12] The amount of deterioration is related to age, number of episodes of heavy drinking, and total amount of alcohol consumed over time.

Clinical Features. Alcohol-induced dementia secondary to the toxic effects of alcohol develops insidiously and often presents initially with changes in personality. Increasing memory loss, worsening cognitive processing, and concrete thinking follow. The dementia may be affected by periodic superimposed delirious states including those caused by recurrent use of alcohol and cross-sensitive drugs, respiratory disease related to smoking, central nervous system hemorrhage secondary to trauma, chronic hypoxia related to recurrent seizure activity, folic acid deficiency, and higher rates of some neoplasms among those with alcoholism (Table 51–6).

Treatment. The presence of dementia makes the treatment of alcoholism more difficult. Most treatment programs depend on education about substance abuse, working the 12 steps, some degree of sociability, and such relatively abstract concepts as secondary gratification and a higher power. Such treatment programs are often reluctant to engage in the painstaking repetition that patients with alcohol-induced dementia often require. These patients may become frustrated in peer support groups such as Alcoholics Anonymous. Despite these obstacles, patients with alcoholism who complete a treatment program and remain sober do have some improvement in their mental state. There is an initial improvement that peaks at 3 to 4 weeks, followed by a slow but steady improvement detected at 6 to 8 months. In general, the presence of a cognitive deficit (dementia) dictates an alcohol treatment program that is behavior based, concrete, structured, supportive, and repetitive.

Other Substances. Many other agents can produce dementia as a result of their persisting effects. Exposure to such heavy metals as mercury and bromide, chronic contact with various insecticides, and use of various classes of drugs of abuse may produce dementia. In particular, the abuse of organic solvents (inhalants) has been associated with neurological changes.[69–73] The inhalants are generally classified as anesthetics (halothane, chloroform, ether, nitrous oxide), solvents (gasoline, paint thinners, antifreeze, kerosene, carbon tetrachloride), aerosols (insecticides, deodorants, hair sprays), and nitrites (amyl nitrite). The solvent category is particularly toxic to the brain. In addition, acute anoxia may result from the common practice of inhaling a substance with a plastic bag around the head. Such neurological findings as peripheral neuropathy, paresis, paresthesias, areflexia, seizures, signs of cerebellar damage, and Babinski's sign are common. Although the cerebellum is often involved, any area of the cerebral cortex may be affected[72] (Table 51–7).

Table 51–6 Central Nervous System Sequelae of Alcohol Abuse

- Blackouts
- Dementia
- Marchiafava-Bignami disease
- Wernicke-Korsakoff syndrome
- Hepatic encephalopathy
- Delirium tremens
- Withdrawal seizures
- Episodic dyscontrol (pathological intoxication)
- Alcoholic hallucinosis
- Head injury

Table 51–7 Neurological Effects of Selected Inhalants

Agent	Use	Effect
n-Hexane	Organic solvent	Peripheral neuropathy
Methyl butyl ketone	Paint thinner	Polyneuropathy
Toluene	Paint thinner	Cognitive dysfunction Cerebellar ataxia Optic neuropathy Sensorineural hearing loss Dementia
Trichloroethylene	Metal degreasing Extracting oils	Trigeminal neuropathy
Methylene chloride	Paint stripping Aerosol propellant	Carbon monoxide poisoning Hypoxic encephalopathy
1,1,1-Trichloroethane	Solvent Industrial degreasing	Cerebral hypoxia

Dementia due to Other General Medical Conditions

Normal-Pressure Hydrocephalus. Normal-pressure hydrocephalus is generally considered the fifth leading cause of dementia after Alzheimer's, vascular, alcohol-related, and AIDS dementias. Long considered reversible but often merely arrestible, normal-pressure hydrocephalus is a syndrome consisting of dementia, urinary incontinence, and gait apraxia.[11, 74, 75] It results from subarachnoid hemorrhage, meningitis, or trauma that impedes CSF absorption.[11]

Unlike other dementias, the dementia caused by normal-pressure hydrocephalus has physical effects that often overshadow the mental effects.[9] Psychomotor retardation, marked gait disturbances, and, in severe cases, complete incontinence of urine occur.[9] A cisternogram is often helpful in the diagnosis, and CT and MRI show ventricular dilatation without cerebral atrophy. CSF analysis reveals a normal opening pressure, and glucose and protein determinations are within the normal range.

The hydrocephalus can be relieved by insertion of a shunt into the lateral ventricle to drain CSF into the chest or abdominal cavity, where it is absorbed. Clinical improvement with shunting approaches 50%, with a neurosurgical complication rate of 13% to 25%.[11, 77] Infection remains the most common complication.

DSM-IV Criteria

Dementia due to Other General Medical Conditions

A. The development of multiple cognitive deficits manifested by both

(1) memory impairment (impaired ability to learn new information or to recall previously learned information)

(2) one (or more) of the following cognitive disturbances:

(a) aphasia (language disturbance)

(b) apraxia (impaired ability to carry out motor activities despite intact motor function)

(c) agnosia (failure to recognize or identify objects despite intact sensory function)

(d) disturbance in executive functioning (i.e., planning, organizing, sequencing, abstracting)

B. The cognitive deficits in criteria A1 and A2 each cause significant impairment in social or occupational functioning and represent a significant decline from a previous level of functioning.

C. There is evidence from the history, physical examination, or laboratory findings that the disturbance is the direct physiological consequence of one of the general medical conditions listed below.

D. The deficits do not occur exclusively during the course of a delirium.

294.9 Dementia due to HIV Disease

Coding note: Also code 043.1 HIV infection affecting central nervous system on Axis III.

294.1 Dementia due to Head Trauma

Coding note: Also code 854.00 head injury on Axis III.

294.1 Dementia due to Parkinson's Disease

Coding note: Also code 332.0 Parkinson's disease on Axis III.

294.1 Dementia due to Huntington's Disease

Coding note: Also code 333.4 Huntington's disease on Axis III.

290.10 Dementia due to Pick's Disease

Coding note: Also code 331.1 Pick's disease on Axis III.

290.10 Dementia due to Creutzfeldt-Jakob Disease

Coding note: Also code 046.1 Creutzfeldt-Jakob disease on Axis III.

294.1 Dementia due to . . . [Indicate the General Medical Condition Not Listed Above]
For example, normal-pressure hydrocephalus, hypothyroidism, brain tumor, vitamin B_{12} deficiency, intracranial radiation

Coding note: Also code the general medical condition on Axis III.

Wilson's Disease. Hepatolenticular degeneration (Wilson's disease) is an inherited autosomal recessive condition associated with dementia, hepatic dysfunction, and a movement disorder. Localized to chromosome 13, this disorder features copper deposits in the liver, brain, and cornea.[11, 78, 79] Symptoms begin in adolescence to the early 20s and cases are often seen in younger children.[7, 80] Wilson's disease should be considered along with Huntington's disease, AIDS dementia, substance abuse dementia, head trauma, and subacute sclerosing panencephalitis in the differential diagnosis of dementia that presents in adolescence and early adulthood. Personality, mood, and thought disorders are common, and physical findings include a wing-beating tremor, rigidity, akinesia, dystonia, and the pathognomonic Kayser-Fleischer ring around the cornea.[11, 81] Wilson's disease can mimic other conditions including Huntington's disease, Parkinson's disease, atypical psychosis, and neuroleptic-induced dystonia.[7] Slit-lamp ocular examination, abnormal liver function tests, and markedly decreased serum ceruloplasmin levels are diagnostic. Chelating agents such as penicillamine, if administered early, can reverse central nervous system and nonneurological findings in about 50% of cases.[7, 11]

Other Medical Conditions. In addition to the conditions mentioned previously, other medical illnesses can be associated with dementia. These include endocrine disorders (hypothyroidism, hypoparathyroidism), chronic metabolic conditions (hypocalcemia, hypoglycemia), nutritional deficiencies (thiamine, niacin, vitamin B_{12}), structural lesions (brain tumors, subdural hematomas), and multiple sclerosis.[82–84]

Dementia due to Multiple Etiologies

Dementia may have more than one cause in a particular patient. Certain types of dementia tend to occur together, including alcohol-induced persisting dementia and dementia caused by head trauma, vascular dementia and dementia of the Alzheimer type, and alcohol abuse dementia and a

DSM-IV Criteria

Dementia due to Multiple Etiologies

A. The development of multiple cognitive deficits manifested by both

(1) memory impairment (impaired ability to learn new information or to recall previously learned information)

(2) one (or more) of the following cognitive disturbances:

(3) aphasia (language disturbance)

(4) apraxia (impaired ability to carry out motor activities despite intact motor function)

(5) agnosia (failure to recognize or identify objects despite intact sensory function)

(6) disturbance in executive functioning (i.e., planning, organizing, sequencing, abstracting)

B. The cognitive deficits in criteria A1 and A2 each cause significant impairment in social or occupational functioning and represent a significant decline from a previous level of functioning.

C. There is evidence from the history, physical examination, or laboratory findings that the disturbance has more than one etiology (e.g., head trauma plus chronic alcohol use, dementia of the Alzheimer's type with the subsequent development of vascular dementia).

D. The deficits do not occur exclusively during the course of a delirium.

Coding note: Use multiple codes based on specific dementias and specific etiologies, e.g., 290.0 dementia of the Alzheimer's type, with late onset, uncomplicated; 290.40 vascular dementia, uncomplicated.

Table 51–8 Causes of Dementia

Causes of Dementia
Vascular
Multiinfarct
CVA
Binswanger's disease
Degenerative
Alzheimer's disease
Pick's disease
Huntington's disease
Parkinson's disease
Toxic
Medications
Alcohol
Poisons
Inhalants
Heavy metals
Infectious
HIV spectrum illness
Neurosyphilis
Creutzfeldt-Jakob disease
Kuru
Subacute sclerosing panencephalitis
Metabolic
Chronic hypoglycemia
Electrolyte imbalances
Vitamin deficiencies
Endocrine
Thyroid abnormalities
Parathyroid abnormalities
Trauma
Single head injury
Dementia pugilistica
Neoplastic
Primary brain tumor
Metastatic brain tumor

nutritional dementia. For the purpose of DSM-IV diagnosis, all conditions contributing to the dementia should be diagnosed.

Treatment of Dementia

Most of the treatment strategies for dementia have been discussed previously (see treatment of dementia of the Alzheimer type). In summary, the management of dementia involves 1) identification and, if possible, correction of the underlying cause; 2) environmental manipulation to reorient the patient; 3) intervention with the family by means of education, peer support, providing access to community organizations, discussing powers of attorney, living wills, and institutionalization if appropriate, and arranging therapy if indicated; and 4) pharmacological management of psychiatric symptoms and behavior. Low-dose antipsychotics with minimal anticholinergic potential and occasionally short-acting benzodiazepines (e.g., lorazepam) are the drugs of choice. Because depression occasionally accompanies dementia, pharmacotherapy with antidepressants of low anticholinergic and hypotensive potential is often indicated. For patients with dementia secondary to drug or alcohol abuse, appropriate referral for rehabilitation is essential.

Tables 51–8, 51–9, and 51–10 summarize the causes of dementia.

Delirium

Delirium (acute confusional state, toxic metabolic encephalopathy) is the behavioral response to widespread distur-

Table 51–9 Causes of Dementia in Adolescence

Causes of Dementia in Adolescence
Huntington's disease (juvenile type)
Hepatolenticular degeneration (Wilson's disease)
Subacute sclerosing panencephalitis
AIDS
Substance abuse (especially inhalants)
Head trauma

Table 51–10 Causes of Dementia in Children

Causes
Head injury (including child abuse)
Subacute sclerosing panencephalitis
AIDS

bances in cerebral metabolism.[3, 85–89] The term *delirium* is derived from the Latin for "off the track," and some have labeled the condition reversible madness.[86, 89, 90] Like dementia, delirium is not a disease but a syndrome with many possible causes that result in a similar constellation of symptoms. DSM-IV describes five categories of delirium based on etiology (Table 51–11).

Historical Perspective

Delirium was reported as early as Hippocrates' time by Celsus in the first century AD.[12] In 1813 Sutton described the syndrome of delirium tremens and its relationship to alcoholism and Wernicke described the condition that bears his name.[12] Lipowski[85–87, 89] proposed a concept of delirium that would include a variety of behavioral syndromes, some global, others focal, and others that would mimic the common functional disorders.[12]

Epidemiology

The overall prevalence of delirium in the community is low, but delirium is common in hospitalized patients. Lipowski[86] reported studies of elderly patients and suggested that about 40% of them admitted to general medical wards showed signs of delirium at some point during the hospitalization. Because of the increasing numbers of elderly in this country and the influence of life-extending technology, the population of hospitalized elderly is rising; so is the prevalence of delirium. The intensive care unit, geriatric psychiatry ward, emergency department, alcohol treatment units, and oncology wards have particularly high rates of delirium.[12] Massie and colleagues[91] reported that 85% of terminally ill patients studied met criteria for delirium, as did 100% of postcardiotomy patients in a study by Theobald.[92] Overall, it is estimated that 10% of hospitalized patients are delirious at any particular point in time.[12]

Predisposing factors in the development of delirium include old age, young age (children), previous brain damage, prior episodes of delirium, malnutrition, sensory impairment (especially vision), and alcohol dependence. In general, the mortality and morbidity of any serious disease are doubled if delirium ensues.[12] The risk of dying is greatest in the first 2 years after the illness, with a higher risk of death from heart disease and cancer in women and from pneumonia in men.[93] Overall, the 3-month mortality rate for persons who have an episode of delirium is about 28%, and the 1-year mortality rate for such patients may be as high as 50%.[54]

Table 51–11 DSM-IV Classification of Delirium

Classification
Delirium due to a general medical condition (indicate the condition)
Substance intoxication delirium
Substance withdrawal delirium
Delirium due to multiple etiologies (indicate the etiologies)
Delirium not otherwise specified

Pathophysiology

ACh is the primary neurotransmitter believed to be involved in delirium, and the primary neuroanatomical site involved is the reticular formation.[12] Thus, one of the frequent causes of delirium is the use of drugs with high anticholinergic potential. As the principal site of regulation of arousal and attention, the reticular formation and its neuroanatomical connections play a major role in the symptoms of delirium. The major pathway involved in delirium is the dorsal tegmental pathway projecting from the mesencephalic reticular formation to the tectum and the thalamus.[54]

Clinical Features

According to DSM-IV, the primary feature of delirium is a diminished clarity of awareness of the environment.[1] Symptoms of delirium are characteristically global, of acute

DSM-IV Criteria 293.0

Delirium due to . . . [Indicate the General Medical Condition]

A. Disturbance of consciousness (i.e., reduced clarity of awareness of the environment) with reduced ability to focus, sustain, or shift attention.

B. A change in cognition (such as memory deficit, disorientation, language disturbance) or the development of a perceptual disturbance that is not better accounted for by a preexisting, established, or evolving dementia.

C. The disturbance develops over a short period of time (usually hours to days) and tends to fluctuate during the course of the day.

D. There is evidence from the history, physical examination, or laboratory findings that the disturbance is caused by the direct physiological consequences of a general medical condition.

Coding note: If delirium is superimposed on a preexisting dementia of the Alzheimer's type or vascular dementia, indicate the delirium by coding the appropriate subtype of the dementia, e.g., 290.3 dementia of the Alzheimer's type, with late onset, with delirium.

Coding note: Include the name of the general medical condition on Axis I, e.g., 293.0 delirium due to hepatic encephalopathy; also code the general medical condition on Axis III.

onset, fluctuating, and of relatively brief duration. In most cases of delirium, an often overlooked prodrome of altered sleep patterns, unexplained fatigue, fluctuating mood, sleep phobia, restlessness, anxiety, and nightmares occurs. A review of nursing notes for the days before the recognized onset of delirium often illustrates early warning signs of the condition.

Several investigators have divided the clinical features of delirium into abnormalities of 1) arousal, 2) language and cognition, 3) perception, 4) orientation, 5) mood, 6) sleep and wakefulness, and 7) neurological functioning.[54]

The state of arousal in delirious patients may be increased or decreased. Some patients exhibit marked restlessness, heightened startle, hypervigilance, and increased alertness. This pattern is often seen in states of withdrawal from depressive substances (e.g., alcohol) or intoxication by stimulants (phencyclidine, amphetamine, lysergic acid diethylamide). Patients with increased arousal often have such concomitant autonomic signs as pallor, sweating, tachycardia, mydriasis, hyperthermia, piloerection, and gastrointestinal distress. These patients often require sedation with neuroleptics or benzodiazepines. Hypoactive arousal states such as those occasionally seen in hepatic encephalopathy and hypercapnia are often initially perceived as depressed or demented states. The clinical course of delirium in any particular patient may include both increased and decreased arousal states. Many such individuals display daytime sedation with nocturnal agitation and behavioral problems (sundowning).

Perceptual abnormalities in delirium represent an inability to discriminate sensory stimuli and to integrate current perceptions with past experiences.[85–92] Consequently, patients tend to personalize events, conversations, and so forth that do not directly pertain to them, become obsessed with irrelevant stimuli, and misinterpret objects in their environment.[85–90] The misinterpretations generally take the form of auditory and visual illusions. Patients with auditory illusions, for example, might hear the sound of leaves rustling and perceive it as someone whispering about them. Paranoia and sleep phobia may result. Typical visual illusions are that intravenous tubing is a snake or worm crawling into the skin or that a respirator is a truck or farm vehicle about to collide with the patient. The former auditory illusion may lead to tactile hallucinations, but the most common hallucinations in delirium are visual and auditory.

Orientation is often abnormal in delirium. Disorientation in particular seems to follow a fluctuating course, with patients unable to answer questions about orientation in the morning, yet fully oriented by the afternoon. Orientation to time, place, person, and situation should be evaluated in the delirious patient. Generally, orientation to time is the sphere most likely impaired, with orientation to person usually preserved. Orientation to significant people (parents, children) should also be tested. Disorientation to self is rare and indicates significant impairment. The examiner should always reorient patients who do not perform well on this parameter of the Mental Status Examination, and serial testing of orientation on subsequent days is important.

Language and Cognition. Patients with delirium frequently have abnormal production and comprehension of speech. Nonsensical rambling and incoherent speech may occur. Other patients may be completely mute. Memory may be impaired, especially primary and secondary memory. Remote memory may be preserved, although the patient may have difficulty distinguishing the present from the distant past.[54]

Mood. Patients with delirium are susceptible to rapid fluctuations in mood. Unprovoked anger and rage reactions occasionally occur and may lead to attacks on hospital staff. Fear is a common emotion and may lead to increased vigilance and an unwillingness to sleep because of increased vulnerability during somnolence. Apathy, such as that seen in hepatic encephalopathy, depression, use of certain medications (e.g., sulfamethoxazole [Bactrim]), and frontal lobe syndromes, is common, as is euphoria secondary to medications (e.g., corticosteroids, DDC, zidovudine) and drugs of abuse (phencyclidine, inhalants).

Neurological Symptoms

Neurological symptoms often occur in delirium. These include dysphasia as seen after a CVA, tremor, asterixis (hepatic encephalopathy, hypoxia, uremia), poor coordination, gait apraxia, frontal release signs (grasp, suck), choreiform movements, seizures, Babinski's sign, and dysarthria. Focal neurological signs occur less frequently.

Sleep-Wakefulness Disturbances

Sleeping patterns of delirious patients are usually abnormal. During the day they can be hypersomnolent, often falling asleep in midsentence, whereas at night they are combative and restless. Sleep is generally fragmented, and vivid nightmares are common. Some patients may become hypervigilant and develop a sleep phobia because of concern that something untoward may occur while they sleep.

Causes of Delirium

The cause of delirium may lie in intracranial processes, extracranial ones, or a combination of the two. The most common etiological factors are as follows.[94]

Infection Induced. Infection is a common cause of delirium in hospitalized patients. The usual abnormalities in hematology, serology, and vital signs are noted except in persons (elderly, chronic alcohol abusers, chemotherapy patients, those with HIV spectrum disease) who may not be able to mount the typical response. Bacteremia, septicemia (especially that caused by gram-negative bacteria), pneumonia, encephalitis, and meningitis are common offenders. The elderly are particularly susceptible to delirium secondary to urinary tract infections.

Metabolic and Endocrine Disturbances. Metabolic causes of delirium include hypoglycemia, electrolyte disturbances, and vitamin deficiency states. The most common endocrine causes are hyperfunction and hypofunction of the thyroid, adrenal, pancreas, pituitary, and parathyroid.

Metabolic causes may involve consequences of diseases of particular organs, such as hepatic encephalopathy resulting from liver disease, uremic encephalopathy and postdialysis delirium resulting from kidney dysfunction, and carbon dioxide narcosis and hypoxia resulting from lung disease. The metabolic disturbance or endocrinopathy must be known to induce changes in mental status and must be confirmed by laboratory determinations or physical examination, and the temporal course of the confusion should coincide with the disturbance.[94] In some individuals, particularly the elderly, brain injured, and demented, there may be a significant lag time between correction of metabolic parameters and improvement in mental state.

Low-Perfusion States. Any condition that decreases effective cerebral perfusion can cause delirium. Common offenders are hypovolemia, congestive heart failure and other causes of decreased stroke volume such as arrhythmias, and anemia, which decreases oxygen binding. Maintenance of fluid balance and strict measuring of intake and output are essential in delirious states.

Intracranial Causes. Intracranial causes of delirium include head trauma, especially involving loss of consciousness, postconcussive states, and hemorrhage; brain infections; neoplasms; and such vascular abnormalities as CVAs, subarachnoid hemorrhage, transient ischemic attacks, and hypertensive encephalopathy.

Postoperative States. Postoperative causes of delirium may include infection, atelectasis, postpump confusion, lingering effects of anesthesia, thrombotic and embolic phenomena, and adverse reactions to postoperative analgesia. General surgery in an elderly patient has been reported to be followed by delirium in 10% to 14% of cases and may reach 50% after surgery for hip fracture.[86]

Sensory and Environmental Changes. Many clinicians underestimate the disorienting potential of an unfamiliar environment. The elderly are especially prone to develop environment-related confusion in the hospital. Individuals with preexisting dementia, who may have learned to compensate for cognitive deficits at home, often become delirious once hospitalized. In addition, the nature of the intensive care unit often lends itself to periods of high sensory stimulation (as during a "code") or low sensory input, as occurs at night.[95] Often, patients use such external events as dispensing medication, mealtimes, presence of housekeeping staff, and physicians' rounds to mark the passage of time. These parameters are often absent at night, leading to increased rates of confusion during nighttime hours.[96] Often, manipulating the patient's environment (see section on treatment) or removing the patient from the intensive care unit can be therapeutic.

Substance Intoxication Delirium. The list of medications that can produce the delirious state is extensive (Table 51–12). The more common ones include such antihypertensives as methyldopa and reserpine, histamine (H_2) receptor antagonists (cimetidine), corticosteroids, antidepressants, narcotics (especially opioid) and nonsteroidal analgesics, lithium carbonate, digitalis, baclofen (Lioresal), anticonvulsants, antiarrhythmics, colchicine, bronchodilators, benzodiazepines, sedative-hypnotics, and anticholinergics. Of the narcotic analgesics, meperidine can produce an agitated delirium with tremors, seizures, and myoclonus.[3, 97] These features are attributed to its active metabolite normeperidine, which has potent stimulant and anticholinergic properties and accumulates with repeated intravenous dosing.[3, 97] In general, adverse effects of narcotics are more common in those who have never received such agents before (the narcotically naive) or who have a history of a similar response to narcotics.

Lithium-induced delirium occurs at blood levels greater than 1.5 mEq/L and is associated with early features of lethargy, stuttering, and muscle fasciculations.[54] The delirium may take as long as 2 weeks to resolve even after lithium has been discontinued, and other neurological signs such as stupor and seizures commonly occur. Maintenance of fluid and electrolyte balance is essential in lithium-induced delirium. Facilitation of excretion with such agents as

DSM-IV Criteria

Substance Intoxication Delirium

A. Disturbance of consciousness (i.e., reduced clarity of awareness of the environment) with reduced ability to focus, sustain, or shift attention.

B. A change in cognition (such as memory deficit, disorientation, language disturbance) or the development of a perceptual disturbance that is not better accounted for by a preexisting, established, or evolving dementia.

C. The disturbance develops over a short period of time (usually hours to days) and tends to fluctuate during the course of the day.

D. There is evidence from the history, physical examination, or laboratory findings of either (1) or (2):

(1) the symptoms in criteria A and B developed during substance intoxication

(2) medication use is etiologically related to the disturbance

Note: This diagnosis should be made instead of a diagnosis of substance intoxication only when the cognitive symptoms are in excess of those usually associated with the intoxication syndrome and when the symptoms are sufficiently severe to warrant independent clinical attention.

Note: The diagnosis should be recorded as substance-induced delirium if related to medication use.

Code: [specific substance] intoxication delirium:

(291.0 alcohol; 292.81 amphetamine [or amphetamine-like substance]; 292.81 cannabis; 292.81 cocaine; 292.81 hallucinogen; 292.81 inhalant; 292.81 opioid; 292.81 phencyclidine [or phencyclidine-like substance]; 292.81 sedative, hypnotic, or anxiolytic; 292.81 other [or unknown] substance [e.g., cimetidine, digitalis, benztropine])

Table 51–12 Selected Drugs Associated with Delirium

Antihypertensives	Indomethacin
Amphotericin B	Ketamine
Antispasmodics	Levodopa
Antituberculous agents	Lidocaine
Baclofen	Lithium
Barbiturates	Meperidine
Cimetidine	Morphine
Corticosteroids	Procainamide
Colchicine	Pentamidine
Contrast media	Tricyclic antidepressants
Digitalis	Zalcitabine (DDC)
Ephedrine	Zidovudine (AZT)

aminophylline and acetazolamide helps, but hemodialysis is often required.[54]

Principles to remember in cases of drug-induced delirium include the facts that 1) blood levels of possibly offending agents are helpful and should be obtained, but many persons can become delirious at therapeutic levels of the drug, 2) drug-induced delirium may be the result of drug interactions and polypharmacy and not the result of a single agent, 3) over-the-counter medications and preparations (e.g., agents containing caffeine or phenylpropanolamine) should also be considered, and 4) delirium can be caused by the combination of drugs of abuse and prescribed medications (e.g., cocaine and dopaminergic antidepressants).

The list of drugs of abuse that can produce delirium is extensive. Some such agents have enjoyed a resurgence after years of declining usage. These include lysergic acid diethylamide, psilocybin (hallucinogenic mushrooms), heroin, and amphetamines. Other agents include barbiturates, cannabis (especially dependent on setting, experience of the user, and whether it is laced with phencyclidine ["superweed"] or heroin), jimsonweed (highly anticholinergic), and mescaline. In cases in which intravenous use of drugs is suspected, HIV spectrum illness must be ruled out as an etiological agent for delirium.

The physical examination of a patient with suspected illicit drug–induced delirium may reveal sclerosed veins, "pop" scars caused by subcutaneous injection of agents, pale and atrophic nasal mucosa resulting from intranasal use of cocaine, injected conjunctiva, and pupillary changes. Toxicological screens are helpful but may not be available on an emergency basis.

Substance Withdrawal Delirium. Alcohol and certain sedating drugs can produce a withdrawal delirium when their use is abruptly discontinued or significantly reduced. Withdrawal delirium requires a history of use of a potentially addicting agent for a sufficient amount of time to produce dependence. It is associated with such typical physical findings as abnormal vital signs, pupillary changes, tremor, diaphoresis, nausea and vomiting, and diarrhea. Patients generally complain of abdominal and leg cramps, insomnia, nightmares, chills, hallucinations (especially visual), and a general feeling of "wanting to jump out of my skin."

Some varieties of drug withdrawal, although uncomfortable, are not life threatening (e.g., opioid withdrawal). Others such as alcohol withdrawal delirium are potentially fatal. Withdrawal delirium is much more common in hospitalized patients than in patients living in the community. The incidence of delirium tremens, for example, is 1% of all those with alcoholism but 5% of hospitalized alcohol abusers. Improvement of the delirium occurs when the offending agent is reintroduced or a cross-sensitive drug (e.g., a benzodiazepine for alcohol withdrawal) is employed. The causes of delirium are summarized in Table 51–13.

Diagnosis

Appropriate work-up of delirious patients includes a complete physical, mental status, and neurological examination.

History taking from the patient, any available family, previous physicians, the old chart, and the patient's current nurse is essential. Previous delirious states, etiologies identified in the past, and interventions that proved effective should be elucidated. The appropriate evaluation of the delirious patient is reviewed in Figure 51–13.

Differential Diagnosis. Delirium must be differentiated from dementia, because the two conditions may have

DSM-IV Criteria

Substance Withdrawal Delirium

A. Disturbance of consciousness (i.e., reduced clarity of awareness of the environment) with reduced ability to focus, sustain, or shift attention.

B. A change in cognition (such as memory deficit, disorientation, language disturbance) or the development of a perceptual disturbance that is not better accounted for by a preexisting, established, or evolving dementia.

C. The disturbance develops over a short period of time (usually hours to days) and tends to fluctuate during the course of the day.

D. There is evidence from the history, physical examination, or laboratory findings that the symptoms in criteria A and B developed during, or shortly after, a withdrawal syndrome.

Note: This diagnosis should be made instead of a diagnosis of substance withdrawal only when the cognitive symptoms are in excess of those usually associated with the withdrawal syndrome and when the symptoms are sufficiently severe to warrant independent clinical attention.

Code: [specific substance] withdrawal delirium:

(291.0 alcohol; 292.81 sedative, hypnotic, or anxiolytic; 292.81 other [or unknown] substance)

Table 51–13 Causes of Delirium

Causes of Delirium
Medication effect or interaction
Substance intoxication or withdrawal
Infection
Head injury
Metabolic disarray
Acid-base imbalance
Dehydration
Malnutrition
Electrolyte imbalance
Blood glucose abnormality
Carbon dioxide narcosis
Uremic encephalopathy
Hepatic encephalopathy
Cerebrovascular insufficiency
Congestive heart failure
Hypovolemia
Arrhythmias
Severe anemia
Transient ischemia
Acute CVA
Endocrine dysfunction
Postoperative states
Postcardiotomy delirium
Environmental factors
Intensive care unit psychosis
Sleep deprivation

different prognoses.[89, 98] In contrast to the changes in dementia, those in delirium have an acute onset.[85] The symptoms in dementia tend to be relatively stable over time, whereas clinical features of delirium display wide fluctuation with periods of relative lucidity. Clouding of consciousness is common in delirium, but demented patients are usually alert. Attention and orientation are more commonly disturbed in delirium, although the latter can become impaired in advanced dementia. Perception abnormalities, alterations in the sleep-wakefulness cycle, and abnormalities of speech are more common in delirium. Most important, a delirium is more likely to be reversible than is a dementia.

Delirium and dementia can occur simultaneously; in fact, the presence of dementia is a risk factor for delirium. Some studies suggest that about 30% of hospitalized patients with dementia have a superimposed delirium.

Delirium must often be differentiated from psychotic states related to such conditions as schizophrenia or mania and factitious disorders with psychological symptoms. Generally, the psychotic features of schizophrenia are more constant and better organized than are those in delirium, and patients with schizophrenia seldom have the clouding of consciousness seen in delirium. The "psychosis" of patients with factitious disorder is inconsistent, and these persons do not exhibit many of the associated features of delirium. Apathetic and lethargic patients with delirium may occasionally resemble depressed individuals, but tests such as the

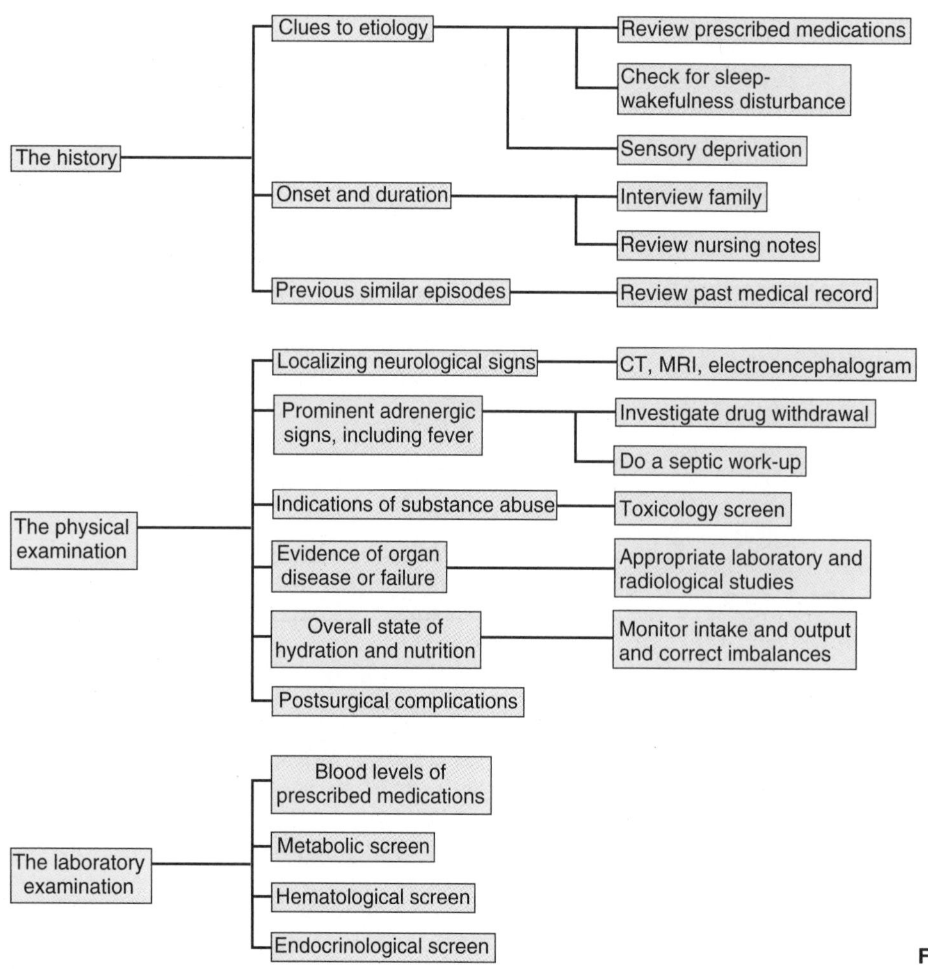

Figure 51–13 *Evaluation of delirium.*

EEG distinguish between the two. The EEG demonstrates diffuse slowing in most delirious states, except for the low-amplitude, fast activity EEG pattern seen in alcohol withdrawal.[85, 99–101] The EEG in a functional depression or psychosis is normal.

Management

Once delirium has been diagnosed, the etiological agent must be identified and treated. For the elderly, the first step generally involves discontinuing or reducing the dosage of potentially offending medications. Some delirious states can be reversed with medication, as in the case of physostigmine administration for anticholinergic delirium. However, most responses are not as immediate, and attention must be directed toward protecting the patient from unintentional self-harm, managing agitated and psychotic behavior, and manipulating the environment to minimize additional impairment. Supportive therapy should include fluid and electrolyte maintenance and provision of adequate nutrition. Reorienting the patient is essential and is best accomplished in a well-lit room with a window, clock, and visible wall calendar. Familiar objects from home such as a stuffed animal, favorite blanket, or photographs are helpful. Patients who respond incorrectly to questions of orientation should be provided with the correct answers, and because these individuals often see many consultants, physicians should introduce themselves and state their purpose for coming at every visit. Physicians must take into account that impairments of vision and hearing can produce confusional states, and the provision of appropriate prosthetic devices may be beneficial. Around-the-clock accompaniment by hospital-provided "sitters" or family members may be required.

Despite these conservative interventions, the delirious patient often requires pharmacological intervention. The liaison psychiatrist is the most appropriate person to recommend such treatment. The drug of choice for the agitated, delirious patient is haloperidol (Haldol).[102] It is particularly beneficial when given by the intravenous route, and some authors have reported using dosages as high as 260 mg/d without adverse effect.[102–107] Extrapyramidal symptoms may be less common with haloperidol administered intravenously as opposed to orally and intramuscularly.[108] In general, doses in the range of 0.5 to 5.0 mg intravenously are used, with the frequency of administration depending on a variety of factors including the patient's age. Lorazepam (Ativan) has also proved effective in doses of 0.5 to 2.0 mg intravenously. Some authors have suggested that haloperidol and lorazepam act synergistically when given in combination to the agitated delirious patient.[106] If the delirium is secondary to drug or alcohol withdrawal, benzodiazepines or clonidine should be used. For patients who are mildly agitated or amenable to taking medications by mouth, oral haloperidol or lorazepam is appropriate. Longer acting benzodiazepines should be avoided in patients with hepatic or pulmonary disease. Antipsychotics with high anticholinergic potential and depot preparations of neuroleptics should be avoided (Table 51–14).

Table 51–14 Managing the Delirious Patient
Identify and correct the underlying cause.
Protect the patient from unintentional self-harm.
Stabilize the level of sensory input.
Reorient patient as often as possible.
Employ objects from the patient's home environment.
Provide supportive therapy (fever control, hydration).
Streamline medications.
Correct sleep deprivation.
Manage behavior with appropriate pharmacotherapy.
Address postdelirium guilt and shame for behavior that occurred during confusion.

Outcome of Delirium

After elimination of the cause of the delirium, the symptoms gradually recede during 3 to 7 days. Some symptoms in certain populations may take weeks to resolve. The age of the patient and the period of time the patient was delirious affect the symptom resolution time.[54] In general, the patient has a spotty memory for events that occurred during delirium. These remembrances are reinforced by comments from the staff ("You're not as confused today") or the presence of a sitter or use of wrist restraints. Patients should be reassured that they were not responsible for their behavior while delirious and that no one hates or resents them for the behavior they may have exhibited. As mentioned earlier, delirious patients have an increased risk of mortality in the next year. Patients with underlying dementia show residual cognitive impairment after resolution of delirium, and it has been suggested that a delirium may merge into a dementia.[54]

Amnestic Disorders

The amnestic disorders are characterized by a disturbance in memory related to the direct effects of a general medical condition or the persisting effects of a substance.[1] The impairment should interfere with social and occupational functioning and represent a significant decline from the previous level of functioning. The amnestic disorders are differentiated on the basis of the etiology of the memory loss. These disorders should not be diagnosed if the memory deficit is a feature of a dissociative disorder, is associated with dementia, or occurs in the presence of clouded sensorium, as in delirium (Table 51–15).

Epidemiology

The exact prevalence and incidence of the amnestic disorders are unknown.[54] Memory disturbances related to specific conditions such as alcohol abuse and head trauma have been studied, and these appear to be the two most common causes of amnestic disorders. Kaplan and coworkers[54] reported that in the hospital setting the incidence of

Table 51–15 DSM-IV Classification of Amnestic Disorders
Amnestic disorder due to a general medical condition (indicate the condition)
Substance-induced persisting amnestic disorder
Amnestic disorder not otherwise specified

DSM-IV Criteria 294.0

Amnestic Disorder due to . . . [Indicate the General Medical Condition]

A. The development of memory impairment as manifested by impairment in the ability to learn new information or the inability to recall previously learned information.

B. The memory disturbance causes significant impairment in social or occupational functioning and represents a significant decline from a previous level of functioning.

C. The memory disturbance does not occur exclusively during the course of a delirium or a dementia.

D. There is evidence from the history, physical examination, or laboratory findings that the disturbance is the direct physiological consequence of a general medical condition (including physical trauma).

Specify if:

Transient: if memory impairment lasts for 1 month or less

Chronic: if memory impairment lasts for more than 1 month

Coding note: Include the name of the general medical condition on Axis I, e.g., 294.0 amnestic disorder due to head trauma; also code the general medical condition on Axis III.

alcohol-induced amnestic disorders is decreasing while that of amnestic disorders secondary to head trauma is on the rise.[12] This may be related to rigorous efforts by hospital personnel to decrease the incidence of iatrogenic amnestic disorder by giving thiamine before glucose is administered.

Etiology

Amnesia results from generally bilateral damage to the areas of the brain involved in memory. The areas and structures so involved include the dorsomedial and midline thalamic nuclei, such temporal lobe–associated structures as the hippocampus, amygdala, and mamillary bodies.[12, 54] The left hemisphere may be more important than the right in the occurrence of memory disorders. Frontal lobe involvement may be responsible for such commonly seen symptoms as apathy and confabulation.[12, 54]

The specific causes of amnestic disorders include 1) systemic medical conditions such as thiamine deficiency; 2) brain conditions, including seizures, cerebral neoplasms, head injury, hypoxia, carbon monoxide poisoning, surgical ablation of temporal lobes, electroconvulsive therapy, and multiple sclerosis; 3) altered blood flow in the vertebral vascular system, as in transient global amnesia; and 4) effects of a substance (drug or alcohol use and exposure to toxins).[54, 110–112]

Conditions that affect the temporal lobes such as herpes infection and Klüver-Bucy syndrome can produce amnesia. Among drugs that can cause amnestic disorders, triazolam (Halcion) has received the most attention, but all benzodiazepines can produce memory impairment, with the dose utilized being the determining factor[113] (Table 51–16).

Clinical Features

Patients with amnestic disorder have impaired ability to learn new information (anterograde amnesia) or cannot remember material previously learned (retrograde amnesia). Memory for the event that produced the deficit (e.g., a head injury in a motor vehicle accident) may also be impaired.[54, 114]

Remote recall (tertiary memory) is generally good, so patients may be able to relate accurately incidents that occurred during childhood but not remember what they had for breakfast. As illustrated by such conditions as thiamine amnestic syndrome, immediate memory is often preserved. In some instances, disorientation to time and place may occur, but disorientation to person is unusual.

The onset of the amnesia is determined by the precipitant and may be acute as in head injury or insidious as in poor nutritional states.[53] DSM-IV characterizes short-duration amnestic disorder as lasting less than 1 month

DSM-IV Criteria

Substance-Induced Persisting Amnestic Disorder

A. The development of memory impairment as manifested by impairment in the ability to learn new information or the inability to recall previously learned information.

B. The memory disturbance causes significant impairment in social or occupational functioning and represents a significant decline from a previous level of functioning.

C. The memory disturbance does not occur exclusively during the course of a delirium or a dementia and persists beyond the usual duration of substance intoxication or withdrawal.

D. There is evidence from the history, physical examination, or laboratory findings that the memory disturbance is etiologically related to the persisting effects of substance use (e.g., a drug of abuse, a medication).

Code: [specific substance]–induced persisting amnestic disorder:
(291.1 alcohol; 292.83 sedative, hypnotic, or anxiolytic; 292.83 other [or unknown] substance)

Table 51–16 Causes of Amnestic Disorders

Herpes simplex encephalopathy
Substance-induced (alcohol) blackouts
Wernicke-Korsakoff syndrome
Multiple sclerosis
Klüver-Bucy syndrome
Electroconvulsive therapy
Seizures
Head trauma
Carbon monoxide poisoning
Metabolic
Hypoxia
Hypoglycemia
Medications
Triazolam
Barbiturates (thiopental sodium)
Diltiazem (Cardizem)
Zalcitabine (DDC)
Cerebrovascular disorders

and long-duration disorder lasting 1 month or longer. Often individuals lack insight into the memory deficit and vehemently insist that their inaccurate responses on a Mental Status Examination are correct.

Selected Amnestic Disorders

Blackouts. Blackouts are periods of amnesia for events that occur during heavy drinking.[115] Typically, a person awakens the morning after consumption and does not remember what happened the night before. Unlike delirium tremens, which is related to chronicity of alcohol abuse, blackouts are more a measure of the amount of alcohol consumed at any one time. Thus, blackouts are common in binge pattern drinkers and may occur the first time a person ingests a large amount of alcohol. Blackouts are generally transient phenomena but may persist for weeks or months after cessation of drinking. They may be produced by agents with cross-sensitivity to alcohol, such as benzodiazepines. Blackouts should not be confused with alcohol-induced dementia, which presents with cortical atrophy on CT scans, associated features of dementia, and a usually irreversible course.

Korsakoff's Syndrome. Korsakoff's syndrome is an amnestic disorder caused by thiamine deficiency. Although generally associated with alcohol abuse, it can occur in other malnourished states such as marasmus, gastric carcinoma, and HIV spectrum disease.[116, 117] This syndrome is usually associated with Wernicke's encephalopathy, which involves ophthalmoplegia, ataxia, and confusion. Korsakoff's syndrome is often associated with a neuropathy and occurs in about 85% of untreated patients with Wernicke's disease.[54] Complete recovery from Korsakoff's syndrome is rare.

Head Injury. Head injuries can produce a wide variety of neurological and psychiatric disorders, even in the absence of radiological evidence of structural damage. Delirium, dementia, mood disturbances, behavioral disinhibition, alterations of personality, and amnestic disorders may result.[54] Amnesia in head injury is for events preceding the incident and the incident itself, leading some physicians to consider these patients as having factitious disorders or being malingerers. The eventual duration of the amnesia is related to the degree of memory recovery that occurs in the first few days after the injury.[54, 114, 118] Amnesia after head injury has become a popular plot device in novels and motion pictures, many of which depictions have erroneously suggested that a second blow to the head is curative.

Differential Diagnosis

Amnestic disorders must be differentiated from the less disruptive changes in memory that occur in normal aging, the memory impairment that is accompanied by other cognitive deficits in dementia, the amnesia that might occur with clouded consciousness in delirium, the stress-induced impairment in recall seen in dissociative disorders, and the inconsistent amnestic deficits caused by factitious disorder.

Treatment

As in delirium and dementia, the primary goal in the amnestic disorders is to discover and treat the underlying cause. Because some of these conditions are associated with serious psychological states (e.g., suicide attempts by hanging, carbon monoxide poisoning, deliberate motor vehicle accidents, self-inflicted gunshot wounds to the head, and chronic alcohol abuse), some form of psychiatric involvement is often necessary. In the hospital, continuous reorientation by means of verbal redirection, clocks, and calendars can allay the patient's fears. Supportive individual psychotherapy and family counseling are beneficial.

Clinical Vignette 1

A 75-year-old woman presented to the emergency room with complaints of memory loss and inability to "think straight." For the past month, she and her family had noted a marked change in her mental state that "seemed to happen overnight." She would forget the names of her grandchildren and showed little interest in activities she had previously enjoyed. Apparently, she had been hospitalized twice in the past for depression but had never exhibited cognitive impairments. On the Mental Status Examination, she exhibited marked psychomotor retardation and a blunted affect. She was oriented only to person and all three spheres of memory were significantly impaired. In fact, she responded to most questions with a shrug of her shoulders and the comment "I don't know." As the interview continued she became more frustrated with her inability to perform, and asked the physician to "stop asking all these questions." She was hospitalized and a complete work-up was initiated.

The evaluation for dementia revealed negative results of drug and heavy metal screening, the absence of any potentially offending medications, normal CT and MRI scans, and a normal EEG. Chemistry assays, hematology, thyroid functions, vitamin studies, serological tests for syphilis, chest radiography, and urinalysis were normal. Psychological testing revealed inconsistent cognitive deficits.

A psychiatric consultation was obtained, and it was recommended that a trial of psychostimulants be undertaken to rule out the possibility of depression as the cause of her cognitive impairment. The following day she received methylphenidate, 2.5 mg at 7:00 AM and 2.5 mg at noon before lunch. She tolerated the medication well, and her dose was increased to 7.5 mg on the second day. By the

Clinical Vignette 1 *continued*

third day, she demonstrated improvement in her affect, concentration, and attention span, and in subsequent days her cognition improved significantly. Eventually, she had a complete recovery and the methylphenidate was discontinued after 2 months without relapse.

This case illustrates the difficulty in distinguishing dementia from cognitive impairment in depression. Features suggestive of depression included the relatively rapid onset, the patient's insight into the cognitive deficits, presence of some vegetative signs of depression, absence of an identified medical condition judged to be responsible, pervasive yet inconsistent cognitive deficits, a past history of treatment for depression, and a positive response to a psychostimulant trial. The psychostimulant was chosen because the onset of action is faster than that of the other antidepressant agents. The principal problems encountered in treating a patient such as this are the tendency of physicians to underdiagnose depression in the elderly and the hesitancy of many caregivers to use psychostimulants for the treatment of depression.

Clinical Vignette 2

A 33-year-old man was referred to the emergency department because of a change in his mental status. According to the family, he had become markedly agitated, paranoid, and, at times, belligerent. In addition, they reported nausea and vomiting for the past 36 hours. Because he appeared by clinical examination and laboratory testing (urinalysis, complete blood count) to be dehydrated, the patient was admitted to the medicine service. A psychiatric consultation was requested on the third hospital day.

On psychiatric evaluation, the patient gave a history of being HIV-positive for 3 years as a result of intravenous drug use. He denied using drugs or alcohol for the past year. Since being diagnosed HIV-positive, he had taken zidovudine and Bactrim daily. This patient also had a history of bipolar disorder that had been stabilized with lithium carbonate. During the interview, the patient was disoriented in all spheres except person. He thought he was at home in his kitchen. He had poor primary and secondary memory and tended to talk about distant events as if they were occurring at the present time. He felt that someone was torturing his daughter and had even wandered down to the basement of the hospital looking for her. There were visual and auditory hallucinations, and physical examination revealed a tremor accentuated with intention, reflex abnormalities, ataxia, and mild aphasia. His therapist and family reported that they had "never seen him like this," even during past exacerbations of his bipolar disorder.

Laboratory studies showed no signs of acute infection, a CD4$^+$ cell count of 10, a low therapeutic lithium level, and a negative drug screen. Complete blood count and urinalysis values had reverted to normal after hydration. Chest radiography was unremarkable, and CT and MRI scans showed only mild atrophy. Zidovudine, Bactrim, and lithium had been discontinued at the time of admission.

The patient was started on haloperidol with some improvement in his psychotic features, but his overall cognitive state continued to deteriorate. The diagnosis was AIDS dementia and nursing home placement was required.

This complicated case illustrates the difficulty in determining the specific diagnostic category for an observed cognitive impairment. Dementia related to HIV disease, acute mania, persisting effects of a substance, delirium, and cognitive impairment (delirium, dementia, mood disturbance) secondary to medication (see Table 51–12) were all considered. Based on his past history, laboratory examination, HIV-positive status, markedly reduced CD4$^+$ cell count, and associated physical findings, the patient was diagnosed as having AIDS dementia. This can be a difficult diagnosis to make, because in many cases CT and MRI scans are unremarkable.

References

1. First M (ed): Diagnostic and Statistical Manual of Mental Disorders, 4th ed. Washington, DC: American Psychiatric Association, 1994: 123–174.
2. Cummings JL: Organic psychosis. Psychosomatics 1988; 29:16–26.
3. Slaby AE, Erle SR: Dementia and delirium. In Stoudemire A (ed): Psychiatric Care of the Medical Patient. New York: Oxford University Press, 1993:415–455.
4. Kallmann MH: Mental status assessment in the elderly. Prim Care 1989; 16:329–347.
5. Cummings JL, Benson DF: Dementia: A Clinical Approach. Boston: Butterworth, 1983.
6. Henderson AS: Epidemiology of dementia disorders. Adv Neurol 1990; 51:15–25.
7. Berg R, Franzen M, Wedding D: Neurological disorders. In Screening for Brain Impairment, 2nd ed. New York: Springer Publishing, 1994.
8. Erkinjuntii T, Wikstrom J, Paolo J, et al: Evaluation of 2000 consecutive admissions. Arch Intern Med 1986; 146:1923–1926.
9. Karp H: Dementia in adults. In Baker AB, Baker LH (eds): Clinical Neurology, Volume 3. New York: Harper & Row, 1984:1–32.
10. Kaufman D: Aphasia and related disorders. In Clinical Neurology for Psychiatrists. Philadelphia: WB Saunders, 1990:146–171.
11. Kaufman D: Dementia. In Clinical Neurology for Psychiatrists. Philadelphia: WB Saunders, 1990:107–146.
12. Korvath T, Siever L, Mohs R, Davis K: Organic mental syndromes and disorders. In Kaplan H, Sadock B (eds): Comprehensive Textbook of Psychiatry V, Volume I. Baltimore: Williams & Wilkins, 1989:599–642.
13. Frierson RL, Wey JJ, Tabler JB: Psychostimulants for depression in the medically ill. Am Fam Physician 1991; 43:163–170.
14. Wolfson LI, Katzman R: The neurological consultation at age 80. In Katzman R, Terry RD (eds): Neurology of Aging. Philadelphia: FA Davis, 1983:221–244.
15. Victor M, Adams RD: Common disturbances of vision, ocular movement, and hearing. In Wintrobe MM, Thron GW, Adams RD (eds): Harrison's Principles of Internal Medicine, Volume 1, 7th ed. New York: McGraw-Hill, 1974:100–110.
16. Wilkins RH, Brody IA: Neurological classics. XX: Alzheimer's disease. Arch Neurol 1969; 21:109–115.
17. Bick KL: Early story of Alzheimer's disease. In Terry RD, Katzman R, Bick KL (eds): Alzheimer's Disease. New York: Raven Press, 1994.
18. Evans DA: Estimated prevalence of Alzheimer's disease in the United States. Milbank Q 1990; 68:276–289.
19. Katzman R, Kawas C: Epidemiology of dementia and Alzheimer's disease. In Terry RD, Katzman R, Bick KL (eds): Alzheimer's Disease. New York: Raven Press, 1994:105–123.
20. Lechtenberg R: The Psychiatrist's Guide to Diseases of the Nervous System. New York: John Wiley & Sons, 1982.
21. Lezak MD: Neuropsychological Assessment, 2nd ed. New York: Oxford University Press, 1983.
22. Bachman DL, Wolf PA, Linn R, et al: Prevalence of dementia of probable presenile dementia of the Alzheimer type in the Farmingham study. Neurology 1992; 42:115–119.

23. Heyman A, Fillenbaum G, Prosnitz B, et al: Estimated prevalence of dementia among elderly black and white community residents. Arch Neurol 1991; 48:594–599.
24. Burger PC, Vogel FS: The development of the pathologic changes of Alzheimer's disease and senile dementia in patients with Down's syndrome. Am J Pathol 1973; 73:457–476.
25. Terry RD, Katzman R, Bick KL (eds): Alzheimer's Disease. New York: Raven Press, 1994:65–74.
26. Markesbery WR, Ehmann WD: Brain trace elements in Alzheimer's disease. In Terry RD, Katzman R, Bick KL (eds): Alzheimer's Disease. New York: Raven Press, 1994.
27. Wolf JK: Practical Clinical Neurology. Garden City, NY: Medical Examination Publishing, 1980.
28. Cotman CW, Pike CJ: Beta amyloid and its contributions to neurodegeneration in Alzheimer's disease. In Terry RD, Katzman R, Bick KL (eds): Alzheimer's Disease. New York: Raven Press, 1994:305–317.
29. Kidd M: Paired helical filaments in electron microscopy of Alzheimer's disease. Nature 1963; 197:192–193.
30. Wisniewski HM, Narang HK, Terry RD: Neurofibrillary tangles of paired helical filaments. J Neurol Sci 1976; 27:173–181.
31. Delacourte A, Defossez A: Alzheimer's disease: Tau proteins, the promoting factors of microtubule assembly are major components of paired helical filaments. J Neurosci 1986;76:173–186.
32. Grundke-Igbal I, Igbal K, Quinlan M, et al: Microtubule-associated protein tau: A component of paired helical filaments. J Biol Chem 1986; 261:6084–6089.
33. Nukina N, Ihara Y: One of the antigenic determinants of paired helical filaments is related to tau protein. J Biochem (Tokyo) 1986; 99:1541–1544.
34. Ganrot PO: Metabolism and possible health effects of aluminum. Environ Health Perspect 1986; 65:363–441.
35. Perl DP, Good PF: Uptake of aluminum in central nervous system along nasal-olfactory pathways. Lancet 1987; 1:1028.
36. Dollken V: Ueber die Wirkung des Aluminums mit besonderer Berucksichtigung der durch das Aluminum verursachten Lasionem in zentral Nervensystem. Arch Exp Pathol Pharmakol 1897; 40:98–120.
37. Scherp HW, Church CF: Neurotoxin action of aluminum salts. Proc Soc Exp Biol Med 1937; 36:851–853.
38. Klatzo I, Wisniewski N, Streicher E: Experimental production of neurofibrillary degeneration. I. Light microscopic observation. J Neuropathol Exp Neurol 1965; 24:187–199.
39. Crapper DR, Dalton AJ: Alterations in short term retention, conditioned avoidance response, acquisition and motivation following aluminum-induced neurofibrillary degeneration. Physiol Behav 1972; 10:925–933.
40. Katzman R: Apolipoprotein E4 as the major genetic susceptibility factor for Alzheimer's disease. In Terry RD, Katzman R, Bick KL (eds): Alzheimer's Disease. New York: Raven Press, 1994:455–457.
41. Corder EH, Saunder AM, Strittmatten WJ, et al: Gene dose of apolipoprotein E type 4 allele and the risk of Alzheimer's disease in late onset families. Science 1993; 261:921–923.
42. Pettegrew JW, McClure RJ, Kanfer JN: The role of membranes and energetics in Alzheimer's disease. In Terry RD, Katzman R, Bick KL (eds): Alzheimer's Disease. New York: Raven Press, 1994:369–387.
43. Jenike MA, Albert MS, Heller H, et al: Combination therapy with lecithin and ergoloid mesylates for Alzheimer's disease. J Clin Psychiatry 1986; 47:249–251.
44. Ferris SH, Sathananthan G, Gershon S, et al: Cognitive effect of ACTH 4–10 in the elderly. Neuropeptides 1976; 5:73–78.
45. Soininen H, Koskinen T, Helkala E-L, et al: Treatment of Alzheimer's disease with a synthetic ACTH 4–9 analog. Neurology 1985; 35:1348–1351.
46. Thal L: Clinical trials in Alzheimer's disease. In Terry RD, Ketzman R, Bick KL (eds): Alzheimer's Disease. New York: Raven Press, 1994:431–445.
47. Henderson VW, Roberts E, Wimer C, et al: Multicenter trial of naloxone in Alzheimer's disease. Ann Neurol 1989; 25:404–406.
48. Hyman BT, Eslinger PJ, Damasio A: Effect of naltrexone in senile dementia of the Alzheimer type. J Neurol Neurosurg Psychiatry 1985; 48:1169–1171.
49. Mohs RC, Davis BM, Johns CA, et al: Oral physostigmine in treatment of patients with Alzheimer's disease. Am J Psychiatry 1985; 142:28–33.
50. Summers WK, Majorski LV, Marsh GM, et al: Oral tetrahydroaminoacridine in long term treatment of senile dementia, Alzheimer type. N Engl J Med 1986; 315:1241–1245.
51. Tariot P, Cohn R, Sunderland T, et al: L-Deprenyl in Alzheimer's disease. Arch Gen Psychiatry 1987; 44:427–433.
52. Blass J, Gleason P, Brush DPD, Thaler H: Thiamine and Alzheimer's disease. Arch Neurol 1988; 45:833–835.
53. Nolan K, Black R, Langberg J, Blass J: A trial of thiamine in Alzheimer disease. Arch Neurol 1991; 48:81–83.
54. Kaplan H, Sadock B, Grebb J: Kaplan and Sadock's Synopsis of Psychiatry, 7th ed. Baltimore: Williams & Wilkins, 1994.
55. Kaufman DM: Involuntary movement disorders. In Clinical Neurology for Psychiatrists, 3rd ed. Philadelphia: WB Saunders, 1990:358–410.
56. Hershey LA, Modic MT, Greenough PG, Jaffe DF: Magnetic resonance imaging in vascular dementia. Neurology 1987; 37:29–36.
57. Zilber N, Rannon L, Alter M, et al: Measles, measles vaccination, and risk of subacute sclerosing panencephalitis (SSPE). Neurology 1983; 33:1558–1564.
58. Marzewski DJ, Towfighi J, Harrington MG, et al: Creutzfeldt-Jakob disease following pituitary-derived human growth hormone therapy: A new American case. Neurology 1988; 38:1131–1133.
59. Rappaport EB, Graham DJ: Pituitary growth hormone from human cadavers: Neurologic disease in 10 recipients. Neurology 1987; 37:1211–1213.
60. Prusiner SB: Prions and neurodegenerative diseases. N Engl J Med 1987; 317:1571.
61. Wilson JD, Braunwald E, Isselbacher KJ, et al: Acquired immune deficiency syndrome (AIDS). In Wilson JD, Braunwald E, Isselbacher KJ, et al (eds): Harrison's Principles of Internal Medicine, Companion Handbook, 12th ed. New York: McGraw-Hill, 1991:474–477.
62. Pajeau AK, Roman G: HIV encephalopathy and dementia. Psychiatr Clin North Am 1992; 15:455–466.
63. Ho D, Bredesen DE, Vinters HV, Daar ES: AIDS dementia complex. Ann Intern Med 1989; 2:400–409.
64. Scharnhorst S: AIDS dementia complex in the elderly: Diagnosis and management. Nurse Pract 1992; 17:41–43.
65. Summergrad P, Rauch S, Neal RR: Human immunodeficiency virus and other infectious disorders affecting the central nervous system. In Stoudemire A, Fogel BS (eds): Psychiatric Care of the Medical Patient. New York: Oxford University Press, 1993.
66. Bond MR: Neurobehavioral sequelae of closed head injury. In Adams G, Adams KM (eds): Neuropsychological Assessment of Neuropsychiatric Disorders. New York: Oxford University Press, 1986.
67. Jordan BD: Neurologic aspects of boxing. Arch Neurol 1987; 44:453–459.
68. Mawdsley C, Fergusen FR: Neurologic disease in boxers. Lancet 1963; 2:795–801.
69. Annau Z: The neurobehavioral toxicity of trichloroethylene. Neurobehav Toxicol Teratol 1981; 3:417–424.
70. Byrne A, Kirby B: The neurotoxicity of inhaled toluene. [letter] Can J Psychiatry 1990; 35:282.
71. Errebo-Knudson EO, Olsen F: Organic solvents and presenile dementia (the painter's syndrome): A critical review of the Danish literature. Sci Total Environ 1986; 48:45–67.
72. Grabski DA: Toluene sniffing producing cerebellar degeneration. Am J Psychiatry 1961; 118:461–462.
73. Knox JW, Nelson JR: Permanent encephalopathy from toluene inhalation. N Engl J Med 1966; 275:1494–1496.
74. Fisher CM: Hydrocephalus as a cause of gait disturbance in the elderly. Neurology 1982; 32:1358–1363.
75. Benson DF, LeMay M, Patten DH, et al: Diagnosis of normal pressure hydrocephalus. N Engl J Med 1970; 283:609–615.
76. Foltz EL, Ward AA Jr: Communicating hydrocephalus from subarachnoid bleeding. J Neurosurg 1956; 13:546–566.
77. Black PM: Idiopathic normal-pressure hydrocephalus: Result of shunting in 62 patients. J Neurosurg 1980; 52:371–377.
78. Chung YS, Ravi SD, Borge GF: Psychosis in Wilson's disease. Psychosomatics 1986; 27:65–66.
79. Cartwright GE: Diagnosis of treatable Wilson's disease. N Engl J Med 1978; 298:1347–1350.
80. Saito T: Presenting symptoms and natural history of Wilson's disease. Eur J Pediatr 1987; 146:261–265.
81. Starosta-Rubinstein S, Young AB, Kluin K, et al: Clinical assessment

of 31 patients with Wilson's disease. Arch Neurol 1987; 44:365–370.

82. Mortell EJ: Idiopathic hypoparathyroidism with mental deterioration: Effect of treatment on intellectual function. J Clin Endocrinol 1946; 6:266–271.
83. Peterson P: Psychiatric disorders in primary hyperparathyroidism. J Clin Endocrinol 1968; 28:1491–1496.
84. Plum F, Posner JB, Hain RF: Delayed neurological deterioration after anoxia. Arch Intern Med 1962; 110:18–25.
85. Lipowski ZJ: Delirium (acute confusional states). JAMA 1987; 258:1789–1792.
86. Lipowski ZJ: Delirium in the elderly patient. N Engl J Med 1989; 320: 578–582.
87. Lipowski ZJ: Delirium: Acute Confusional States. New York: Oxford University Press, 1990.
88. Engel GL, Roman J: Delirium: A syndrome of cerebral insufficiency. J Chronic Dis 1959; 9:260–277.
89. Lipowski ZJ: Transient cognitive disorders (delirium, acute confusional states) in the elderly. Am J Psychiatry 1983; 140:1426–1436.
90. Tobias CR, Turms DM, Lippmann SB: Psychiatric disorders in the elderly: Psychopharmacologic management. Postgrad Med 1988; 83:313–319.
91. Massie M, Holland J, Glass E: Delirium in terminally ill cancer patients. Am J Psychiatry 1983; 140:1048–1050.
92. Theobald D: Delirium: Definition, evaluation, and management in the critically ill patient. Indiana Med 1987; 80:526–528.
93. Black DW, Wanack G, Winokur G: The Iowa record linkage study II: Excess mortality among patients with organic mental disorders. Arch Gen Psychiatry 1985; 42:78–81.
94. Francis J, Martin D, Kapoor W: A prospective study of delirium in hospitalized elderly. JAMA 1990; 263:1097–1101.
95. Lipowski ZJ: Sensory and information inputs overload: Behavioral effects. Comp Psychiatry 1975; 16:199–221.
96. Cameron DE: Studies in senile nocturnal delirium. Psychiatr Q 1941; 15:47–53.
97. Eisendrath SJ, Goldman B, Douglas J, et al: Meperidine-induced delirium. Am J Psychiatry 1987; 144:1062–1065.
98. Lipowski ZJ: Differentiating delirium from dementia in the elderly. Clin Gerontol 1982; 1:3–10.
99. Obrecht R, Okhomina FOA, Scott DF: Value of EEG in acute confusional states. J Neurol Neurosurg Psychiatry 1979; 42: 75–77.
100. Pro JD, Wells CE: The use of the electroencephalogram in the diagnosis of delirium. Dis Nerv Syst 1977; 38:804–808.
101. Brenner RP: The electroencephalogram in altered states of consciousness. Neurol Clin 1985; 3:615–631.
102. Gelfand SB, Indelicato J, Benjamin J: Using intravenous Haldol to control delirium. Hosp Community Psychiatry 1992; 43:215.
103. Steinhart MJ: The use of haloperidol in geriatric patients with organic mental disorder. Curr Ther Res 1983; 33:132–143.
104. Adams F: Emergency intravenous sedation of delirious medically ill patients. J Clin Psychol 1988; 48(suppl):22–27.
105. Tesar GE, Murray GB, Cassen NH: Use of intravenous Haldol in the treatment of agitated cardiac patients. J Clin Psychopharmacol 1985; 5:344–347.
106. Fernandez F, Holmes VF, Adams F, Kavanaugh JJ: Treatment of severe, refractory agitation with a haloperidol drip. J Clin Psychol 1988; 49:239–241.
107. Carter JG: Intravenous haloperidol in the treatment of acute psychosis. Am J Psychiatry 1986; 143:1316–1317.
108. Menza MA, Murray GB, Holmes VF, et al: Decreased extrapyramidal symptoms with intravenous Haldol. J Clin Psychol 1987; 48:278–280.
109. Weddington WW: The mortality of delirium: An underappreciated problem? Psychosomatics 1982; 23:1232–1235.
110. Hodges JR, Warlow CP: The aetiology of transient global amnesia: A case-control study of 114 cases with prospective follow-up. Brain 1990; 113:639–657.
111. Melo TP, Ferro JM, Ferro H: Transient global amnesia: A case control study. Brain 1992; 115:261–270.
112. Fisher CM, Adams RD: Transient global amnesia. Acta Neurol Scand 1964; 39:605–608.
113. Kirk T, Roache JD, Griffiths RR: Dose-response evaluation of the amnestic effects of triazolam and pentobarbital in normal subjects. J Clin Psychopharmacol 1990; 10:160–167.
114. Garquonine PG: Learning in post traumatic amnesia following extremely severe closed head injury. Brain Inj 1991; 5:169–174.
115. Tarter RE, Schneider DU: Blackouts: Relationship with memory capacity and alcoholism history. Arch Gen Psychiatry 1976; 33:1492–1495.
116. Reulen JB, Girard DE, Cooney TG: Wernicke's encephalopathy. N Engl J Med 1985; 312:1035–1039.
117. Victor M: The Wernicke-Korsakoff Syndrome, 2nd ed. Philadelphia: FA Davis, 1987.
118. Saneda DL, Corrigan JD: Predicting clearing of posttraumatic amnesia following closed head injury. Brain Inj 1992; 6:167–170.

Index

Note: Page numbers in *italics* indicate illustrations; those followed by t indicate tables.

D

J

K

N

Q

R

S

ISBN 0-7216-5256-5 VOL. I